THE TAXATION
OF
COMPANIES

2008

THE TAXATION OF COMPANIES

2008

Michael Feeney

Published by
Tottel Publishing Ltd
Maxwelton House
41–43 Boltro Road
Haywards Heath
West Sussex
RH16 1BJ

Tottel Publishing Ltd
Fitzwilliam Business Centre
26 Upper Pembroke Street
Dublin 2

ISBN 978 1 84766 107 4
© Tottel Publishing Ltd 2008
Published annually by LexisNexis Butterworths from 1998 to 2004
Published annually by Tottel Publishing Ltd since 2005

British Library Cataloguing-in-Publication Data
A catalogue record for this book is available from the British Library

Typeset by Marlex Editorial Services Ltd., Dublin, Ireland
Printed in the UK by CPI William Clowes
Beccles NR34 7TL

Foreword

This (twelfth) edition of *The Taxation of Companies* is again mainly concerned with the inclusion of important changes affecting the company tax system introduced by the latest Finance Act, FA 2008, as well as those resulting from case law development, Revenue practice, new or revised tax treaties and the many changes that inevitably suggest themselves over the course of a further year.

For companies, the most important change brought about by the Finance Act is the new tax regime for certain foreign dividends. Other important changes include the relaxation of the close company surcharge regime in relation to dividends paid within a group of Irish resident companies, the introduction of the Profit Resource Rent Tax for certain petroleum leases, accelerated capital allowances for expenditure by trading companies on certain energy-efficient equipment, the relaxation of the preliminary tax rules for small and start-up companies and for companies during the initial years following a change to IFRS or equivalent Irish GAAP for gains and losses from financial instruments, an improved research and development tax credit regime incorporating a rolling base year, and the treatment of certain pre-sale dividends as additional consideration for capital gains tax purposes,

To secure that foreign sourced dividends will not be subject to a rate of taxation higher than that applying to domestic sourced dividends, and in the wake of the *FII GLO* decision, foreign dividends received on or after 1 January 2007 from underlying trading profits sourced from an EU country or a country with which Ireland has a double tax treaty are taxable at the 12.5% rate. The full amount of the foreign dividend is chargeable at the 12.5% rate when certain conditions are met, even though part of the dividend may not be paid out of trading profits.

In relation to the legislation providing for onshore pooling (as described in **14.214**), the availability of the 12.5% corporation tax rate on certain foreign dividends means that there are now two pools of credits available, those at the 12.5% rate and those at 25%. Excess credits arising on dividends taxed at the 12.5% rate will be available for offset only against tax on other dividends taxed at that rate. Excess credits at the higher rate can be used against dividend income at either rate. Excess credits may be carried forward to later periods for use against tax on dividends taxed at 12.5% in those years or for use against dividends taxable at the 25% rate.

The availability of the 12.5% tax rate for foreign dividends has a number of corporation tax consequences, some of a quite technical nature. Trading losses and charges, including such losses and charges surrendered by way of group relief, may now be offset against such dividends and their use is no longer confined to reducing trading income. That in turn has the further effect that, since these losses and charges are available to reduce "profits of more than one description", they are not taken into account in determining "profits brought into charge to corporation tax" and "total income brought into charge to corporation tax" (see **2.602** and **2.603**). A further technical change involving the meaning of "total income" for the purposes of the manufacturing relief formula has also been necessary (see for example **7.202.3**). Finally, and as a further consequence, a company may now, for double tax relief purposes, elect to allocate trading losses and charges against such of its profits "as it thinks fit" (see in particular **14.208**).

Michael Feeney

April 2008

Contents

Chapter 4 Losses, Collection of Tax at Source and Charges on Income

Chapter 10 Close Companies

Chapter 12 Special Types of Companies

Chapter 15 Self-Assessment and Administration

Contents

Chapter 1

Introduction & Outline

1.1 INTRODUCTION

The system under which companies are currently subject to tax in Ireland is based on legislation introduced in the Corporation Tax Act 1976 (CTA 1976) and in the Finance Acts of 1976 and subsequent years which added to or amended that Act, and which is now contained in the Taxes Consolidation Act 1997 (TCA 1997). The company tax system is also substantially based on the Income Tax Acts and the Capital Gains Tax Acts insofar as principles and rules in those acts are applied for the purpose of computing income and chargeable gains of companies; the relevant legislation is now also contained in TCA 1997.

In practice, a typical computation of the taxable trading profit of a company would be based on income tax rules insofar as these rules help to determine what constitutes taxable income, how income under the various sources is to be calculated, and what expenses can be deducted for tax purposes. The rules for computing taxable income under the various cases of Schedule D and those governing the calculation and availability of capital allowances contained in the Income Tax Acts apply equally to companies and other taxpayers. Similarly, the computational and other rules for calculating capital gains as contained in the Capital Gains Tax Acts are used for the purposes of computing "chargeable gains" of companies as they are for computing capital gains of any other taxpayers.

1.2 HISTORICAL PERSPECTIVE

The commencement date for corporation tax was 6 April 1976 but many companies came within the charge to the tax at an earlier date. The profits of companies which had sources of income prior to 6 April 1976 could have been within the charge as far back as 1 April 1974. Furthermore, certain transactions taking place on or after 27 November 1975, the date on which the Corporation Tax Bill was introduced, were within the ambit of particular corporation tax provisions, obviously for anti-avoidance reasons. Prior to the introduction of corporation tax, companies were liable to income tax, corporation profits tax and (for a brief period, ie in respect of disposals on or after 6 April 1974) capital gains tax. Transitional rules dealt with the changeover from that regime to the corporation tax system and these were concerned with such matters as relief for income tax and corporation profits tax losses forward, the adaptation of the system of capital allowances, and the bases on which the various classes of income, including taxed income, and capital gains were first brought within the corporation tax charge.

In relation to the taxation of income, the position of companies just prior to the introduction of corporation tax was that they were liable, along with the general body of taxpayers, to income tax at the standard rate of 35% and to a special company tax, known as corporation profits tax (CPT), at 23%. A peculiar feature of this dual system of taxing companies was that the test for taxing worldwide income in the case of income tax was company residence while CPT was charged on the worldwide income of Irish incorporated companies. (At that time, the place of incorporation had no effect on the tax residence of a company.) A non-resident company was subject to income tax on Irish source income while CPT was charged, in the cases of companies incorporated outside Ireland, on any profits arising from the carrying on in Ireland of a trade or business or any undertaking of a similar character insofar as those profits arose in Ireland.

Companies subject to income tax and CPT paid tax at an effective rate of about 50%. The amount of CPT payable was allowable as a deduction in computing profits subject to income tax. Thus, the effective income tax rate was 26.95% (35% x 77%) which, together with the 23% CPT rate, gave a combined rate of 49.95%. The standard rate of corporation tax at its commencement was 50% so that, on the changeover to that tax, companies experienced a marginal increase in their effective tax rate.

The idea of a single company tax made sense when compared to the previous dual tax system what with the need for two computations, two tax returns, two assessments and two sets of rules for computing profits. A company resident but not incorporated in Ireland paid income tax on all its profits but not necessarily CPT. Irish incorporated but non-resident companies were, broadly, subject to CPT only. Income tax assessments were by reference to income tax years while CPT assessments were made for accounting periods. The different rules for computing profits meant that certain expenses allowable for income tax purposes were not deductible for CPT. Deductions for capital allowances differed as the amount computed for income tax purposes required to be apportioned to the relevant accounting period for CPT purposes.

The possible form of a new system of company taxation was discussed in two White Papers published the early 1960s. The question was considered in some detail in a third White Paper, Company Taxation in Ireland, published in 1972. That publication considered the three main forms of company taxation in operation in economically developed countries, generally referred to as (a) the two-rate system, (b) the separate system and (c) the imputation system. Fundamental to the evaluation of these systems was a recognition of the phenomenon of "economic double taxation" which arose through the taxation of the profits of companies and of the dividends paid by them.

The quest for the ideal balance as between taxing companies in respect of their profits and their shareholders in respect of the dividends they receive from those companies exercised many minds at that time and is still today an occasional topic for consideration; indeed, it has even been suggested that companies should pay no tax on their profits, leaving all taxation to be levied at the personal level as and when those profits are extracted in the form of dividends. (At the other end of the spectrum, a somewhat crude concept of equity is exemplified in the occasional call for companies to be taxed at the same rates as individuals!)

1.3 CORPORATE TAX SYSTEMS

Full economic double taxation would occur where a company is subjected to taxation on its profits whether distributed or not and where the shareholders are then taxed on any dividends received from the company without any allowance or credit in respect of the company tax paid on the profits from which the dividends were derived. The impact of this double taxation could be mitigated either by applying a lower rate of tax to profits which are distributed, or by reducing the amount of income tax payable on dividends received by giving a credit for part of the company tax paid on the profits out of which those dividends were received.

The separate system is the one which produces full economic double taxation and, if introduced, would mean having to set a company tax rate intended to result in a required yield to the exchequer from the combined amounts of company and personal taxation. The lower the amount of profits distributed the higher would the company tax rate need to be, and vice versa. This in turn would require having to anticipate the overall pattern of dividend distributions by companies.

Economic double taxation is alleviated in the two-rate system by imposing a lower rate of company tax on profits which are distributed. The dividends are subjected to personal tax in the hands of individual recipients of the dividends but the reduced rate of corporation tax on the profits from which those dividends are derived means that full economic double taxation does not occur. Relief is given at the company level. In consequence, dividends paid to other domestic companies would attract tax in the hands of the recipient company except possibly where paid to a parent company with a view to being paid onwards to the ultimate shareholders. Withholding tax would normally be deducted from dividends paid and accounted for to the Revenue, and would be available as a credit against the shareholder's tax liability on the dividend or for repayment to the shareholder.

The German two-tier corporate tax system dates from the immediate post-war period and the very large differential between the rates of company tax which formerly applied to distributed and undistributed profits was intended to ensure large payouts in the form of dividends so that companies would then be forced to go to the capital markets to finance the expansion which was critical at a time when the economy was being rebuilt. This result did not ensue, however, because owners of companies still preferred to accumulate profits and to avoid the additional tax burden that followed from the fact that the company and personal taxes combined were greater than the higher rate company tax. Under German tax reform measures, a uniform rate of 25% replaced the split-rate system incorporating the 40% and 30% rates. The effect of this reform was to reduce the aggregate tax rate (including the trade tax) on business income of German companies to about 40%. Further tax reform planned for 2008 includes a reduction in the federal tax rate and the discontinuance of the deduction of the trade tax in calculating taxable profits, resulting in a reduction of the overall corporate tax rate from about 40% to less than 30%.

The separate and the two-rate systems allow for a greater amount of profits to be distributed than is the case under the imputation system, since both involve lower rates of company tax where larger amounts of profits are distributed. Under the imputation system, the full burden of taxation is borne by the company. In this sense, it came closest to the system already in existence in Ireland prior to the introduction of corporation tax and, as is will be seen, involved little if any change as regards the effects on companies and their shareholders. A system which imposed the full measure of tax at the company level would also ensure that maximum value would be derived from incentive tax reliefs, such as free depreciation and export sales relief, which were a significant feature of the Irish tax system in the early 1970s and for some time afterwards.

The opposing biases of the separate and the two-rate systems, one in favour of retentions and self-financing and the other favouring distributions, left the middle ground to the imputation system which was neutral in not positively encouraging the retention of profits while not acting as an incentive to make distributions either. The desire for a neutral policy in this respect recognised the importance of allowing companies to accumulate savings to finance further expansion and shareholders to build up funds to invest in new share issues. CTA 1976 introduced a company tax system which operated as an imputation system up to 5 April 1999.

The imputation system

An imputation system makes no distinction between distributed and undistributed profits and charges all company profits at the same rate of corporation tax. Shareholders are entitled to a credit for a part of the corporation tax relating to the profits out of which the dividends were paid and this credit is offset against the income liability on the dividends or, where no liability arises, is paid to the shareholders. Thus, relief from full economic double taxation is given at shareholder level. Withholding tax is not appropriate as dividends will have been paid out of profits which have borne corporation tax at the full rate. In fact, as a part of the company tax is "imputed" to the shareholder, a tax credit representing that imputed tax attaches to each dividend and the shareholder is treated as having received a "gross" dividend of the amount of the cash dividend received plus the amount of the related tax credit. The imputation system effectively came to an end on 5 April 1999 with the abolition of tax credits (and the introduction of dividend withholding tax) after that date.

The tax regime introduced by CTA 1976 was, as mentioned above, an imputation system. As already suggested, there was no real economic impact on either companies or their shareholders resulting from the changeover to the new system in 1976. This can be illustrated by comparing the position of a dividend paid out of profits of £1,000 both before and after the introduction of the imputation system:

Example 1.3.1

	"Old" system	Imputation system
	£	£
Profits	1,000	1,000
CPT @ 23%	230	
	770	
Income tax @ 35%	270	
CT @ 50%		500
After tax	500	500

Assuming a full dividend distribution, a dividend voucher would contain the following:

	"Old" system	Imputation system
	£	£
Gross dividend	770	
Income tax	270	
Tax credit		270
Net dividend	500	
Dividend		500

At the commencement of corporation tax, the standard tax credit was fixed at 35/65ths of the amount of the cash dividend, or 35% of the aggregate of the dividend and related tax credit. This of course equated with income tax at 35% of a similar gross dividend under the old system. The effect was the same for the shareholder although in theory there was a difference. Under the old system, a company paid income tax and its distributed profits were treated as the profits of its shareholders. Consequently, the income tax paid by the company on its distributed profits was treated as paid on behalf of the shareholders. The income tax shown on the dividend voucher in Example **1.2.1** is the income tax paid by the company and it as also treated as paid by the shareholder. Where the full profits were not distributed, as would normally be the case, the income tax shown on each shareholder's dividend voucher would have been a proportionate part of the income tax paid by the company in respect of its distributed profits.

The most obvious difference in the form of the dividend voucher is the absence, under the corporation tax system, of any reference to a "gross" dividend. Whereas income tax was formerly charged on a gross dividend, it is now payable in respect of the combined dividend and tax credit. Inevitably, however, the convenience afforded by the simple and easily understood "gross dividend" meant that that phrase continued to be used widely throughout the life of the imputation system.

Under imputation, the underlying concept was different to that inherent in the system it replaced. This was inevitably the case as companies paid only corporation tax on their profits and the (individual) shareholders paid income tax in respect of their dividends. A shareholder could not therefore be entitled to a credit for any income tax paid by the company which could be regarded as having been paid on his behalf. Instead, the shareholder was entitled to a credit for part of the corporation tax paid by the company. Initially, that credit equated with the credit that would have been available for income tax had the old system continued. The tax effect on the shareholder remained the same therefore on the changeover from the old system to the corporation tax system. As the corporation tax rate was altered from time to time, the part of the corporation tax available for credit to shareholders, the "imputed" credit, was correspondingly adjusted.

It will be seen that the effective rate of CPT just prior to the introduction of corporation tax was 15%. Because the CPT paid was deductible as an expense in computing profits liable to income tax at 35%, its effective rate was 65% x 23% = 15% (approximately). This pure corporation tax element (which was not imputed to shareholders) always remained at 15%. Consequently, it was always possible to anticipate the tax credit rate corresponding to any newly announced corporation tax rate. For example, with a 36% corporation tax rate, the imputed part was 36% - 15% ie 21%. In the tax credit fraction, the imputed rate figure became the numerator and the denominator was 100 less the numerator. Thus, the fraction in this case is 21/79ths. That principle, however, ceased to apply with effect from 3 December 1997 when the tax credit rate was reduced to 11/89ths as the commencement of the process of phasing out the tax credit altogether (see **1.5** below).

The White Paper of 1972 recognised that the then existing system of company taxation was in effect an imputation system in that full economic double taxation of dividends was avoided by means of the availability of a credit for tax paid by the dividend paying company. A drastic change in the system was best avoided and it was considered best to rationalise the existing dual tax system into a single company tax without altering the rates or incidence of tax. Thus the first corporation tax rate was 50% of which 35% was imputed to shareholders in respect of dividends. The separation of company and personal taxation was therefore achieved with no economic impact on either the company or the shareholder.

Although the White Paper considered the possibility of imposing a minimum level of corporation tax where a dividend was paid, in the form of an advance payment equivalent to the tax credit, surprisingly no such provision was included in CTA 1976. This led to situations in which it was possible to benefit from a tax credit, and to claim payment of a tax credit, where no corporation tax had been paid by the dividend paying company. Thus, tax which had not been paid could be "imputed". This shortcoming was not rectified until 1983 with the introduction of the advance corporation tax legislation. Tax credits and advance corporation tax were abolished after 5 April 1999 thus bringing the imputation system to an end on that date.

1.4 MEANING OF "COMPANY"

Only companies are subject to corporation tax. *Company* is defined in TCA 1997, s 4(1) as "any body corporate [including] a trustee savings bank within the meaning of the Trustee Savings Banks Act 1989", but not including the Health Service Executive, a grouping within the meaning of TCA 1997, s 1014(1) (a European Economic Interest Grouping (EEIG)), a vocational educational committee established under the Vocational Education Act 1930, a committee of agriculture established under the Agriculture Act 1931, a local authority within the meaning of the Local Government Act 1941 s 2(2), or a body established under the Local Government Services (Corporate Bodies) Act 1971.

A body corporate is, broadly, any body of persons having an identity conferred on it by law and separate from the identities of the members comprising it. All companies established under the Companies Acts, with or without limited liability, whether limited by share capital or by guarantee, are clearly included. Also included are societies registered under the Industrial and Provident Societies Acts, such as cooperative societies, friendly societies, and companies established by statute or incorporated by charter, whether in Ireland or abroad, such as Bord na Móna, Aer Lingus Group plc, the Electricity Supply Board, Radio Telefís Éireann and Shannon Free Airport Development Company Ltd.

Examples of bodies not having identities separate from those of their members and therefore not companies are private clubs, sporting clubs, unregistered friendly societies, partnerships and other similar associations.

1.5 PRINCIPAL FEATURES OF CORPORATION TAX

Corporation tax is charged, generally, on the total or worldwide profits of Irish resident companies. "Profits" for this purpose means income from all sources with the addition of chargeable gains. Companies not resident in Ireland but carrying on a trade in Ireland through or from a branch or agency are subject to corporation tax in respect of the trading profits arising from that branch or agency and in respect of chargeable gains from the disposals of certain Irish based assets, principally land and buildings situated in Ireland and Irish based assets used for the purposes of the trade carried on through the branch or agency. As a rule, corporation tax is not charged on dividends and other distributions received from Irish resident companies.

A company's income is computed under income tax rules and income from the different sources is computed in accordance with the rules of the appropriate Cases of Schedule D. The amount of chargeable gains is computed under capital gains tax rules and, depending on the respective capital gains and corporation tax rates, is included in profits subject to corporation tax at an adjusted amount. Exceptionally, gains from disposals of development land and from unquoted shares deriving the greater part of their value from development land do not form part of a company's profits for corporation tax purposes. In respect of such gains, a company is subject to capital gains tax rather than corporation tax.

A corporation tax return may include certain income tax elements. Income which has been received under deduction of income tax, such as patent royalties, yearly interest and other annual payments, is included in profits but a deduction for the income tax suffered is allowed against the corporation tax payable; alternatively the tax is repaid to the extent that it exceeds the liability to corporation tax. Payments which a company is obliged to make under deduction of standard rate income tax are required to be included in its corporation tax return and the tax accounted for to the Revenue at the same time as the company's corporation tax is due for payment.

Companies are liable to corporation tax by reference to accounting periods and not at all for years of assessment which are relevant only for income tax and capital gains tax purposes. An accounting period is generally the period for which a company makes up its accounts but, since an accounting period may not exceed twelve months, there are rules for determining accounting periods in cases where a period of account exceeds twelve months. Rules also fix the commencement and final dates of accounting periods in certain circumstances such as when a company comes within the charge to corporation tax for the first time, or acquires a source of income, or begins or ceases to trade.

The rate of corporation tax is fixed for a financial year (the calendar year) and, where the rate is altered, it will be necessary for a company whose accounting period does not coincide with the financial year to apportion its profits, on a time basis, to each financial year. The appropriate rate of corporation tax is then applied to each part of the accounting period.

The standard corporation tax rate was reduced to 40% from 1 April 1991 and to 38% from 1 April 1995. This was the beginning of the programme for reducing company tax rates annually with the target rate of 12.5% being installed from 1 January 2003. Reduced corporation tax rates (30%, 28%, 25%) operated during the period 1 April 1996 to 31 December 1999 after which date the standard rate had dropped to 24%. A 12.5% rate was introduced from 1 January 2000 for trading income that did not exceed certain levels. "Passive" income (investment and rental income) and certain categories of trading income are taxable from 1 January 2001 at a fixed 25% rate.

Corporation tax legislation provides for incentive reliefs which are available only to companies. Since the 1950s, companies which exported goods which they had manufactured in Ireland were entitled to claim full exemption from tax on the resulting profits for a period of fifteen years and relief on a tapering basis for a further five years. Dividends paid out of profits benefiting from the relief were exempted from income tax. The relief was terminated on 5 April 1990. The relief as it extended to dividends was phased out later. Companies based in the Shannon free airport zone were eligible for complete exemption from corporation tax in respect of qualifying transactions which covered the export sales of goods produced, manufactured or processed within the airport, the repair or maintenance of aircraft within the airport and other activities which were considered to contribute to the use or development of the airport. Dividends paid out of exempted profits were exempted from income tax. As with export sales relief, the Shannon incentive came to an end on 5 April 1990 and the dividend exemption was later phased out.

For manufacturing companies, a relief from corporation tax came into effect on 1 January 1980. Manufacturing relief essentially replaced export sales relief and the Shannon exemption. Companies which were not already benefiting from either export sales relief or the Shannon relief by 1 January 1980 were, generally, prevented from doing so from that date. Manufacturing relief differs from its two predecessors in a number of ways. A company's eligibility for the relief depends entirely on the extent to which its profits are derived from the manufacture of goods, or from the deemed manufacture of goods, in Ireland and not at all on whether the claimant company has exported its product. The relief is not an exemption but a reduction in tax which results in an effective corporation tax rate of 10% on the profits from manufacturing.

Dividends paid out of manufacturing profits do not carry through any relief to the shareholders. In fact, up to 5 April 1999, shareholders were penalised in that a dividend from manufacturing profits carried a credit of one-eighteenth only of the amount of the dividend, so that the incidence of personal taxation on these dividends was greater than was the case with dividends from non-manufacturing profits. The position up to 1989 was even more severe for shareholders in manufacturing companies as dividends from these companies were deemed to have been paid primarily out of manufacturing profits and only out of other profits where the manufacturing profits had been used up.

A dividend or other distribution paid by an Irish company is chargeable to income tax under Schedule F. Under the imputation system, individual shareholders were entitled (for dividends received up to 5 April 1999) to a tax credit in respect of such dividends. The credit was available for set off against the resulting tax liability or, where appropriate, for payment to the shareholder. Distributions are not normally taken into account for the purposes of corporation tax and liability under Schedule F is essentially confined to resident individuals. A distribution made by an Irish resident company is referred to as "franked investment income", being income which has already been charged to corporation tax.

Dividends and other distributions paid by Irish resident companies, on or before 5 April 1999, resulted in certain cases in a liability to advance corporation tax (ACT) on the part of the dividend paying company. Where the tax credit attaching to a dividend paid in an accounting period exceeded the aggregate of tax credits on dividends received in the same period, an ACT liability equivalent to the amount of the excess tax credit resulted. ACT paid was creditable against the general or "mainstream" corporation tax liability of the period in which the related dividend was paid. ACT which could not be utilised against mainstream corporation tax ("surplus" ACT) could be deducted from the mainstream corporation tax of subsequent accounting periods or against the corporation tax liability of previous periods ending not more than twelve months before the period in which the surplus arose. Surplus ACT could also be surrendered for offset against the corporation tax liability of a fellow group member for the period in which the surplus arose.

The legislative provisions dealing with ACT were deleted by FA 2003 which, however, introduced a provision enabling companies having surplus ACT carried forward from earlier years to continue to offset such surplus ACT against their corporation tax in future accounting periods.

Special corporation tax rules apply to close companies. The legislation dealing with the meaning of "close company" is complex but a close company in most cases is one which is under the control of five or fewer persons or which is under the control of its directors. Most Irish companies are close companies as the concept applies to most private companies and to some public companies. Close companies are subject to tax impositions not applicable to other companies. Benefits provided by close companies to their shareholders or other "participators", or to their "associates", and which are not otherwise subject to tax, are treated as distributions. Excessive interest paid to certain directors of close companies or to their associates is also subject to distribution treatment; the amount above a prescribed limit is treated as a distribution. A close company which makes a loan to a participator or an associate of a participator may be obliged to pay a temporary tax equivalent to standard rate tax on the grossed up amount of the loan. Close companies which have not distributed investment or rental income within a certain time are subject to a 20% surcharge on the after tax amount of such income. Close service or professional companies are liable to a 20% surcharge on their after tax undistributed investment and rental income and to a 15% surcharge on half of their after tax undistributed service or professional income.

A trading loss may be carried forward, without time limit, for relief against profits from the same trade in future accounting periods. A trading loss may (subject to restrictions on the use of trading losses applying from 6 March 2001 - see below) be offset against profits of any description of the same accounting period, and provided the company was then carrying on the trade, against profits of any description of immediately preceding accounting periods ending within a period equal in length to the period in which the loss was incurred. A loss which may be offset against profits of an earlier period is confined to so much of that loss as cannot be utilised against profits of a later accounting period.

A manufacturing loss (ie, a loss arising from activities carried on by a company in respect of which, if a profit had resulted from those activities, the company would be eligible for the 10% corporation tax rate) could not, prior to 1 January 2003, be offset against any profits other than manufacturing profits but, from that date, may be set against any trading profits. A manufacturing loss may be offset against trading profits of the same accounting period and, if the company was then carrying on the trade in respect of which the loss arose, against trading profits of immediately preceding accounting periods ending within a period equal in length to the period in which the loss was incurred. A manufacturing loss may be carried forward against profits of the trade in succeeding periods.

A trading loss (whether from manufacturing or other activities) incurred by a company in an accounting period ending on or after 6 March 2001 may not be offset against profits of that accounting period other than trading profits. From that date, however, trading losses may be used on a value basis to relieve corporation tax payable on non-trading profits.

The corporation tax group relief provisions recognise the economic relationship existing between members of a group of companies by allowing trading losses and certain other deficiencies of a group member to be offset against the taxable profits of another group member or members. A group comprises a parent company and all its 75% subsidiaries, all companies being resident in a "relevant Member State" (an EU Member State or an EEA State with which Ireland has a tax treaty). A loss incurred by a company for an accounting period may only be offset against a fellow group member's taxable profits of the same period. Such losses may, however, be set against trading profits only but may be used on a value basis to relieve tax in respect of non-trading profits.

Capital losses may not be surrendered by a group member and may only be used to shelter chargeable gains of that member for the current period or for subsequent accounting periods. Irish resident members of a capital gains tax group (including in certain cases Irish branches of non-Irish relevant Member State companies) may, however, transfer assets between them without incurring liability to corporation tax in respect chargeable gains; any gains are deferred until such time as the relevant assets are disposed of outside the group. A capital gains tax group comprises a parent company and all its 75% subsidiaries with the addition of any 75% subsidiaries of those subsidiaries, all companies being resident in a relevant Member State. Where a group member which had acquired an asset from another group member subsequently leaves the group, it becomes liable to corporation tax in respect of the chargeable gain which had been deferred at the time of the acquisition of that asset.

Where a trade is transferred between companies under common ownership (75% at least) any trading losses existing at the time of the transfer are acquired by the transferee company. Assets of the trade which had attracted capital allowances are treated as acquired by the transferee company at tax written down values for capital allowances purposes. Under legislation which adopted the "Mergers Directive", similar treatment applies where the 75% common ownership requirement is not satisfied if the transfer consideration consists entirely of the issue of securities to the transferring company. Other legislation implementing the Mergers Directive provides for capital gains tax group treatment where the member companies concerned are not both Irish resident.

Irish resident companies which derive profits from trading transactions carried on outside Ireland, and non-resident companies deriving profits from trades exercised in Ireland, will normally be subject to taxation in two countries. Such double taxation will usually be relieved by the operation of a tax treaty whereby the tax suffered in respect of the foreign earnings is allowed against the home country tax liability on the same profits. Dividends paid by Irish resident companies to foreign shareholders are subject to dividend withholding tax (DWT), with certain exemptions applying where paid to residents of EU or tax treaty countries. Dividends received from abroad by Irish resident companies are in most cases received net of withholding taxes. Credit for these taxes is available in accordance with the terms of tax treaties. Depending on the extent of the shareholding held, many of the tax treaties to which Ireland is a party provide for credit in respect of tax paid by the dividend paying company. The "underlying" tax creditable is proportionate to the amount of the dividend paid out of the distributable profits of the paying company.

Under unilateral provisions of Irish domestic tax legislation, credit is available for foreign tax, consisting of withholding taxes and taxes paid on the profits of the dividend paying company, in respect of certain dividends received from companies resident in countries with which Ireland does not have a tax treaty. Relief is also available for third country taxes of such companies and, where a foreign company has itself received a dividend from a third company, for taxes of such a third company including withholding taxes on the dividend. The company claiming the credit may be an Irish resident company or a non-Irish relevant Member State company where the dividend forms part of the profits of that company's Irish branch or agency.

1.6 CORPORATION TAX RATES

1.6.1 Introduction

Recognising that, in order to sustain continued growth in terms of inward investment and indigenous industry, it was necessary to retain the attraction of a low corporation rate together with the more traditional incentives, government has repeatedly expressed its commitment to the continuation of the standard 12.5% rate of corporation tax for the foreseeable future. Apart from manufacturing trades and other businesses eligible for the 10% corporation tax rate, the services sector, as an increasingly important creator of employment, can look forward to enjoying the benefits of a low corporation tax rate.

1.6.2 12.5% and 25% corporation tax rates

A 12.5% corporation tax rate came into force on 1 January 2003. This rate was reached by a gradual reduction in the standard company rate, a process which essentially commenced on 1 January 1998 and which can be summarised as follows:

	First £50,000 %	First £100,000 %	Standard rate %
From 1.4.97 to 31.12.97	28		36
From 1.1.98 to 31.12.98	25		32
From 1.1.99 to 31.12.99		25	28
From 1.1.00 to 31.12.00	–	–	24
From 1.1.01 to 31.12.01	–	–	20
From 1.1.02 to 31.12.02	–	–	16
From 1.1.03	–	–	12.5

The 12.5 % corporation tax rate applies to trading profits only. From 1 January 2000, a 25% corporation tax rate applies to certain, mainly "passive", income of companies, ie income chargeable to tax under Cases III (interest, dividends, discounts, foreign income), Case IV (royalties and other miscellaneous income) and Case V (rental income) of Schedule D. Other income chargeable at the 25% rate is income from working minerals, petroleum activities and dealing in or developing land other than construction operations. Any income which qualifies or would qualify (were it not for the fact that the trade in question did not commence in time to qualify) for the 10% corporation tax rate is not chargeable at the 25% rate.

1.6.3 10% corporation tax rate

In a press release on 22 July 1998, the government announced that it had reached agreement with the European Commission on the phasing out of the 10% corporation tax rate. The main features of the announcement are as follows.

For manufacturing trades approved for grant assistance by the industrial development agency (the Industrial Development Authority in Ireland, Shannon Free Airport Development Company, Údarás na Gaeltachta, the Industrial Development Agency, Ireland, Forbairt, Forfás, Enterprise Ireland) on or before 31 July 1998, or other manufacturing trades which were being carried on before 23 July 1998, entitlement to the 10% rate continues up to 31 December 2010. For all other manufacturing trades, the 10% corporation tax rate ceased to apply after 31 December 2002.

IFSC licensed operations approved on or before 31 July 1998 are eligible for the 10% corporation tax rate up to 31 December 2005. Those approved after 31 July 1998 qualified for the 10% rate up to 31 December 2002 and are taxable thereafter at the 12.5% rate.

Licensed Shannon operations approved on or before 31 May 1998 are eligible for the 10% corporation tax rate up to 31 December 2005. Those approved after 31 May 1998 qualified for the 10% rate up to 31 December 2002 and are taxable thereafter at the 12.5% rate.

Cut-off for IFSC and Shannon operations

The deadline for approval of new IFSC and Shannon projects was 31 December 1999. Any project established in either of these locations after that date is subject to the standard corporation tax rate.

Certain companies, such as captive insurance and reinsurance companies, captive finance companies, agency fund management companies and securitisation vehicles, may be regarded as extensions of existing IFSC operations (ie, of the manager) and may be approved after 31 December 1999.

Chapter 2

Interpretation

2.1 Introduction

Although the definitions and meanings of key words and phrases occurring in legislation dealing with the taxation of companies are included in the appropriate chapters and sections of this book, it is considered useful to include a short chapter dealing with the most important and most frequently encountered of these. What follows is based mainly on Taxes Consolidation Act 1997 (TCA 1997), ss 1, 2 and 4 (interpretation). This section commences with explanations as to what is denoted by "the Corporation Tax Acts" and "the Tax Acts"; these are covered below, as are the meanings of "the Income Tax Acts" and "the Capital Gains Tax Acts".

TCA 1997 ss 2 and 4 define key words and expressions such as "company", "franked investment income", "ordinary share capital" and "within the charge to", the procedure in some of these cases being to refer to definitions elsewhere. Also dealt with in TCA 1997 is the meaning of "control", which is defined both in TCA 1997, s 11 and TCA 1997, s 432. The separate definitions are relevant for different purposes of tax legislation and the more important of the relevant provisions to which the respective definitions apply are identified below.

The circumstances in which a person is treated as being "connected with" another person are set out in TCA 1997, s 10. Again, these are dealt with below; examples illustrating the meanings of "control" and "connected with", as well as the relevance of "control" in relation to the latter, are included in **2.302** and **2.401.4**.

Although they are included in the appropriate places (eg, in connection with the provisions on group relief and capital gains tax group treatment), the definitions of the various kinds of subsidiary and share capital are included again in this chapter for convenience as are the rules for ascertaining the amounts of share capital held in a company through other companies.

Finally, the phrases "profits brought into charge", "total income brought into charge", "profits on which corporation tax falls finally to be borne" and "charged with tax under Schedule D" are explained in **2.602-605** below and references to the main corporation tax provisions to which they apply are given.

2.2 ENACTMENTS

With effect from 6 April 1967, the Income Tax Act 1967 consolidated all previous income tax legislation in the Income Tax Act 1918 and in subsequent Finance Acts and which was still in force up to that date. No further consolidation was effected up to the Taxes Consolidation Act 1997 (TCA 1997). In the meantime, legislation dealing with corporation tax in the Corporation Tax Act 1976 and subsequent Finance Acts, and capital gains tax in the Capital Gains Tax Act 1975 in the Capital Gains Tax (Amendment) Act 1978 and in subsequent Finance Acts, has been enacted. Most of the legislation contained in these enactments and remaining in force are now included in TCA 1997. (Provisions in those enactments which, though still in force, are now obsolete and no longer necessary, have not been carried into TCA 1997.)

The designations "the Corporation Tax Acts", "the Tax Acts", "the Income Tax Acts", and "the Capital Gains Tax Acts", which collectively comprise all of the income tax, corporation tax and capital gains tax legislation in force up to the enactment of the Taxes Consolidated Act 1997, are explained below.

The Corporation Tax Acts

The Corporation Tax Acts means the enactments relating to corporation tax in TCA 1997 and in any other enactment, together with the Income Tax Acts in so far as those Acts apply for the purposes of corporation tax (TCA 1997, s 1(2)).

Except where the context otherwise requires, in the Tax Acts, and in any enactment passed after TCA 1997 which by any express provision is to be construed as one with those Acts, *tax*, where neither income tax nor corporation tax is specified, means either of those taxes (TCA 1997, s 2(2)). This is without prejudice to the provisions of TCA 1997, s 76 (see **3.102.2**) which apply income tax law for certain purposes of corporation tax, so that the employment of *income tax* rather than *tax* in any provision of the Income Tax Acts does not conclusively indicate that that provision is not applied to corporation tax by that section (TCA 1997, s 2(3)).

The Tax Acts

The Tax Acts means the Income Tax Acts (as defined) and the Corporation Tax Acts (as defined) (TCA 1997, s 1(2)).

The Income Tax Acts

The Income Tax Acts means the enactments relating to income tax in TCA 1997 and in any other enactment (TCA 1997, s 1(2)).

The Capital Gains Tax Acts

The Capital Gains Tax Acts means the enactments relating to capital gains tax in TCA 1997 and in any other enactment (TCA 1997, s 1(2)).

Stamp Duties Consolidation Act 1999

All of the stamp duty, including capital duty, legislation previously contained in the Stamp Duties Management Act 1891, and subsequent Finance Acts was re-codified in 1999 and is now contained in the Stamp Duties Consolidation Act 1999 (SDCA 1999).

2.3 CONNECTED PERSONS

2.301 General

2.302 Companies

2.301 General

2.301.1 Introduction

For the purposes of the Tax Acts and the Capital Gains Tax Acts, unless the context otherwise requires, any question as to whether a person is connected to another person is to be determined in accordance with TCA 1997, s 10(3)-(8). Any provision that one person is connected to another person is to be taken as meaning that they are connected to one another (TCA 1997, s 10(2)). Clearly therefore, if Amon Glass is connected to Windows Ltd, Windows Ltd is connected to Amon Glass.

The fact that Amon Glass is connected to Windows Ltd (and Windows Ltd to Amon Glass) does not, however, mean that if Amon Glass is connected also to Robert Pane (and Robert Pane is connected to Amon Glass) that Windows Ltd is also connected to Robert Pane (or that Robert Pane is connected to Windows Ltd). It is of course possible that Robert Pane is connected to Windows Ltd but that would have to be the result of a separate test not involving Amon Glass.

2.301.2 Individuals

A person is connected with an individual if that person is:

(a) the individual's husband or wife;

(b) a relative (see below) of the individual;

(c) a relative of the individual's husband or wife;

(d) the husband or wife of a relative of the individual; or

(e) the husband or wife of a relative of the individual's husband or wife (TCA 1997, s 10(3)).

A *relative* of an individual means a brother, sister, ancestor or lineal descendant of that individual. For the purposes of the Capital Gains Tax Acts, a "relative" also means an uncle, aunt, niece or nephew. An individual may also be connected with other persons under other provisions of TCA 1997, s 10 as dealt with below.

2.301.3 Partners

Except in relation to acquisitions or disposals of partnership assets pursuant to *bona fide* commercial arrangements, a person is connected to:

(a) any person with whom he is in partnership; and

(b) the husband, wife or a relative of any individual with whom he is in partnership (TCA 1997, s 10(5)).

If a company or a trustee of a settlement is a partner in a partnership, that company or trustee (as trustee) is similarly connected with any other partner or with the husband, wife or a relative of any individual who is a partner in the partnership.

2.301.4   Trustees

A person in his capacity as trustee of a settlement is connected to:

(a)   any individual who in relation to the settlement is a settlor;

(b)   any person (whether an individual, company or trustee of another settlement) who is connected with an individual who in relation to the settlement is a settlor; and

(c)   a body corporate which is deemed to be connected with that settlement, and a body corporate is so deemed in any accounting period or year of assessment if, at any time in that period or year, it is a close company (see **10.103**) (or is not a close company only because it is not resident in the State) and the participators then include the trustees of, or a beneficiary under, the settlement (TCA 1997, s 10(4)).

A *settlement* is defined as including any disposition, trust, covenant, agreement or arrangement, and any transfer of money or other property or of any right to money or other property. A *settlor* in relation to a settlement means any person by whom the settlement was made, and a person is deemed to have made a settlement if the person has made or entered into the settlement directly or indirectly and, and in particular, if the person has provided or undertaken to provide funds directly or indirectly for the purpose of the settlement, or has made with any person a reciprocal arrangement for that other person to make or enter into the settlement (TCA 1997, s 10(1)).

2.302   Companies

2.302.1   General

A company is connected to another person (whether an individual, a company, or a trustee of a settlement) if that other person has control of it or if that other person and persons connected with that other person together have control of it (TCA 1997, s 10(7)). *Company* has the same meaning as in TCA 1997, s 4(1) (see **1.3**). For the meaning of "control", see **2.401** below.

> **Example 2.302.1.1**
>
> J Foley is connected with Daly Ltd, and Daly Ltd is connected with J Foley, if J Foley and his brother R Foley have between them sufficient of the voting shares in Daly Ltd to give them control of the company (see meaning of "control" below). In this event, Daly Ltd is also connected with R Foley since he and a person connected with him (his brother, J Foley) together have control of Daly Ltd.
>
> If Daly Ltd controls a second company, Curley Ltd, not only are Daly Ltd and Curley Ltd connected with each other, but J Foley and R Foley are each also connected with Curley Ltd, as they together can control its affairs through their control of Daly Ltd.

An interesting point arises as to whether a company is connected to a person (eg, a spouse) connected with the controlling shareholder of the company. The company is not connected to any person connected with the controlling shareholder unless that other person at least has some shares, voting power or other means of control in the company. For example, if Mr T Murphy and Ms s Murphy (brother and sister) own 75% of the total share capital and voting power in Murphy Ltd and all the other shares are held by unconnected persons, Mr T Murphy's wife, who holds no shares or other interest in the company, is not connected to Murphy Ltd. However, if Mrs Murphy held even one share, she would then be connected with Murphy Ltd as she and persons connected to her would have control of the company.

2.302.2 Companies under common control

As well as being connected to each other under TCA 1997, s 10(7), two companies are also connected with each other:

(a) if the same person has control (see **2.401**) of both companies;

(b) if a person has control of one company and persons connected with him, or that person and persons connected with him, have control of the other company (TCA 1997, s 10(6)(a)); or

(c) if a group of two or more persons has control of each company, and each group either consists of the same persons or could be regarded as consisting of the same persons by treating (in one or more cases) a member of either group as replaced by a person with whom he is connected (TCA 1997, s 10(6)(b)).

Example 2.302.2.1

W Flint controls Steel Ltd and the trustees of a settlement of which W Flint is the settlor control Whitehill Ltd. Steel Ltd and Whitehill Ltd are therefore connected to each other (under (b) above).

Example 2.302.2.2

Holland Ltd is controlled by Ms Warren and Ms Howell and Midland Ltd is controlled by Ms Warren and Northridge Ltd, each person concerned holding 50% of the shares in the respective companies. Ms Howell controls Northridge Ltd. Holland Ltd and Midland Ltd are therefore connected with each other. In this case, the two groups of shareholders would consist of the same persons if Northridge Ltd were replaced in the second group by Ms Howell (or if Ms Howell were replaced in the first group by Northridge Ltd). Holland Ltd and Midland Ltd are connected to each other under (c) above.

In relation to a case involving the control of two companies by two or more persons and as to whether those companies are connected, it may be possible to read TCA 1997, s 432(3) (see **2.401.1**) so as to apply that provision by reference to the smallest group of persons that have control of the two companies concerned or, alternatively, so as to take into account any larger aggregation of interests in the companies. In a simple case in which the shareholding/voting interests in a company are held as to, say, 80% and 20% respectively by A and B, it must be correct that the company is controlled simply by A rather than by a group comprising A and B; in this case, the 20% interest of B is of no significance as regards any real question concerning control. The position is less straightforward in a case where no one person has control but the overriding principle is the same and it is suggested that the better view, and the one more consistent with a commonsense and practical application of the connected company provisions, is to look at the control position by reference to the smallest group of persons having control.

Example 2.302.2.3

The ordinary share capital of Meridian Ltd is held as to 25% each by Albert, Beverly, Cynthia and Dan. Albert owns 49%, with Beverly, Cynthia and Dan each owning 2%, of the ordinary share capital of Waverly Ltd. As to whether Meridian Ltd and Waverly Ltd are connected companies will depend on how control of these companies is to be viewed.

If it is correct, for the purposes of the connected companies rules, that Meridian Ltd is controlled not just by any three of its shareholders but also by four of them, the companies are connected. This is because, clearly, the group of four also controls Waverly Ltd.

Waverly Ltd is also controlled by Albert and any one of the other three shareholders. This is the smallest group that has control of Waverly Ltd and on this basis the companies are not connected since that group of two does not control Meridian Ltd. It is suggested that applying the control test in this way reflects the better view of the matter.

If Albert owned 40%, and Beverly and Cynthia each owned 6%, of Waverly Ltd, the two companies would be connected. The smallest group with control of Waverly Ltd would now comprise these three shareholders and this group also has control of Meridian Ltd.

2.302.3   Persons acting together to control company

Any two or more persons acting together to secure or exercise control of, or to acquire a holding in, a company are treated in relation to that company as connected to one another and with any person acting on the direction of any of them to secure or exercise control of the company (TCA 1997, s 10(8)). For the meaning of "control", see **2.401**.

There is a particular difficulty in interpreting the meaning of "acting together" in the context of the connected person rules. In practice, the outcome of this question in any case will depend on the particular circumstances of the case and on whether or not there is evidence of the fact that the shareholders are in fact acting in concert to secure control. In *Steele v EVC International NV* [1996] STC 785 it was relevant, in connection with a claim to credit relief, to decide whether the shareholders in a company owned as to 50% each by an Italian company and members of a UK group were acting together. It was found on the evidence that the company's shareholders were "acting together to secure or exercise control" of the company (see also **8.310.2**).

Unlike the other rules of TCA 1997, s 10, for a person to be connected with another person by virtue of TCA 1997, s 10(8) requires that the persons concerned should actually act together to control the company. If two or more persons satisfy that requirement, they are regarded as being connected with each other but only in relation to the company in question.

Example 2.302.3.1

Mr Kirby and Mr Norman, two otherwise unconnected persons, hold respectively 30% and 25% of the issued share capital of Winona Ltd. The remaining 45% of the shares are held by Mr Malpas, the managing director of Winona Ltd, who is not connected to either Mr Kirby or Mr Norman.

Mr Kirby and Mr Norman are unhappy with the manner in which Mr Malpas is running the company and agree that they will consistently act together to outvote Mr Malpas and thereby secure that the business of Winona Ltd will be conducted in a more beneficial way than heretofore. This agreement is put into practice and Mr Kirby and Mr Norman are treated as connected persons in relation to Winona Ltd.

As a result of the agreement carried out by Mr Kirby and Mr Norman, it follows that Mr Kirby is also connected to Winona Ltd as he and Mr Norman (now connected to him) together have control of the company. Similarly, Mr Norman is also connected to Winona Ltd.

Mr Kirby and Mr Norman have similar holdings in another company, Malvern Ltd, but do not act together to control its affairs. Their connection with each other in relation to Winona Ltd does not result in them being connected to each other in relation to Malvern Ltd.

See also Example **2.401.4.7**.

2.4 CONTROL

2.401 TCA 1997, s 432
2.402 TCA 1997, s 11

2.401 TCA 1997, s 432

2.401.1 Meaning of "control"

There are two definitions of "control" in the Corporation Tax Acts. TCA 1997, s 432 defines "control" for the purposes of the legislation on close companies but that definition is used for other purposes of corporation tax, not least in relation to the "connected persons" provisions of TCA 1997, s 10. "Control" is also defined in TCA 1997, s 11 (see **2.402**).

TCA 1997, s 432 sets out the circumstances in which a person has, or persons have, control of a company for various purposes of the Tax Acts and the Capital Gains Tax Acts, including for the purposes of determining whether a person is connected to another person (see **2.3** above).

A person has *control* of a company if such person exercises, or is able to exercise, or is entitled to acquire, control, direct or indirect (see **2.401.5** below regarding direct or indirect control), over the company's affairs. In particular, and without prejudice to the foregoing, a person has control of a company if he possesses or is entitled to acquire:

(a)   the greater part of the share capital or issued share capital of the company;

(b)   the greater part of the voting power in the company;

(c)   such part of the company's issued share capital as would, on a full distribution of the company's income among the participators (see below), but ignoring for this purpose any entitlement of a loan creditor, entitle him to receive the greater part of the amount so distributed; or

(d)   such rights as would entitle him to receive the greater part of the company's assets available for distribution among the participators, eg on a winding up (TCA 1997, s 432(2)).

Where two or more persons together satisfy any of the conditions for control, they are to be taken to have control of the company (TCA 1997, s 432(3)). This provision is relevant for the purposes of the definition of "close company" in TCA 1997, s 430 (see **10.103**) where it is seen that close company status is determined by reference to the control exercised by persons taken together. Another example of its relevance is TCA 1997, s 627 (capital gains tax exit charge – see **9.106**) where the meaning of "foreign company" depends on the level of control exercised over the company by one or more persons resident in a "relevant territory" (ie countries with which the government has concluded a double tax treaty).

Another important instance of the relevance of TCA 1997, s 432(3) is in relation to TCA 1997, s 10(6)(b) in determining whether companies are connected to one another and (see Example **2.302.2.3**). In this case a question arises as to whether it is correct to view control by two or more persons by reference to the minimum level of interests held in the company which confer control or by reference to any aggregation of such interests held. As suggested in **2.302.2**, the former would seem to be the better view.

Being "entitled to" denotes a present entitlement to acquire something at a future date or a future entitlement to acquire something (TCA 1997, s 432(4)).

Note that the specific forms of control listed above are without prejudice to the general meaning of control. In *IRC v BW Noble Ltd* 12 TC 911, it was held that to have control it is not necessary to be able to carry a special resolution; a 50% shareholder with a casting vote at general meetings of the company had control of that company. In *British American Tobacco Co Ltd v IRC* 29 TC 49, approving the judgment in the *Noble* case, it was held that a bare majority of votes in general meetings of a company was sufficient to confer a controlling interest in that company notwithstanding that this was insufficient to secure the passing of a special resolution or a resolution requiring a special majority.

There does not seem to be a basis for regarding as an instance of indirect control over a company the position of a shareholder with a minority of voting control in a second company which controls the first-mentioned company (see also **2.401.5** below).

2.401.2   Participators

A *participator* in relation to a company (see more detailed treatment in **10.102**) is any person having a share or interest in the capital or income of the company and also includes:

(a)   any person who possesses or is entitled to acquire share capital or voting rights in the company;

(b)   any loan creditor of the company;

(c)   any person who possesses, or is entitled to acquire, a right to receive or participate in distributions (ignoring any amounts treated as distributions under close company rules only) of the company or any amounts payable (in cash or in kind) to loan creditors by way of a premium on redemption; and

(d)   any person entitled to secure that the income or assets (whether present or future) of the company will be applied directly or indirectly for his benefit (TCA 1997, s 433(1).

2.401.3   Associates

The relevance of identifying "associates" is particularly important in relation to the question of control as interests of associates are attributed to the persons with whom they are associated for that purpose (see **2.401.4** below). An *associate* in relation to any participator (or any other person – see more detailed discussion in **10.102**) is:

(a)   any relative of the participator (ie, spouse, ancestor, lineal descendant, brother or sister – not including the spouse of a relative or the relative of a spouse);

(b)   the trustee or trustees of a settlement (including any disposition, trust, covenant, agreement, or arrangement, and any transfer of money or other property or of any right to money or other property) of which the participator or any relative of his (living or dead) is or was the settlor;

(c)   where the participator has an interest in any shares or obligations of the company which are subject to any trust or are part of the estate of a deceased person, any other person interested therein; or

(d)   any partner (which could include a company) of the participator (TCA 1997, s 433(3)).

A *settlor* for the purposes of paragraph (b) above means any person by whom the settlement was made or entered into and in particular includes any person who provided or undertook to provide funds for the settlement or who has made reciprocal arrangements with another person for that other person to make or enter into the settlement. It was held in *IRC v Buchanan* 37 TC 365 that a trust created by a will is not a disposition, and therefore not a settlement. It followed that a testator of a will is not a settlor.

2.401.4 Attribution

For the purposes of TCA 1997, s 432(2), (3) above, there is to be attributed to any person any rights or powers of a nominee for him, ie any rights or powers which another person possesses on his behalf or may be required to exercise on his direction or behalf (TCA 1997, s 432(5)).

Also for the purposes of TCA 1997, s 432(2), (3) there is to be attributed to any person all the rights and powers of:

(a) any company of which he has control;

(b) any company of which he and his associates have control;

(c) any two or more companies of which he has control;

(d) any two or more companies of which he and his associates have control;

(e) any associate of his; or

(f) any two or more associates of his (TCA 1997, s 432(6)).

The rights and powers of a company or associate that may be attributed to a person in accordance with (a)–(f) above include those attributed to that company or associate by virtue of TCA 1997, s 432(5), ie the rights and powers of any nominee for the company or associate. The rights and powers of a company or associate attributable to a person in accordance with (a)–(f) do not, however, include any rights or powers attributed to an associate by virtue of TCA 1997, s 432(6) itself. In other words, there is no double attribution. Thus, for example, an interest in company A, attributed to an associate of a participator in company A by virtue of that associate's control of another company having an interest in company A, is not then in turn attributed to the participator (see examples below).

Such rights and powers attributed under TCA s 432(6) are to be attributed so as to result in the company being treated as under the control of five or fewer participators if it can be so treated. (In this connection, see also **10.102** in relation to "control" and the meaning of "close company".)

The somewhat complex attribution rules described above are illustrated in the following examples which are concerned with the level of control held by Mr Marx in relation to Harp Ltd.

Example 2.401.4.1

Mr Marx owns 55% of the share capital in Woolsack Ltd and 15% of the share capital in Harp Ltd. Woolsack Ltd owns 30% of the share capital in Harp Ltd.

As Woolsack Ltd is controlled by Mr Marx, its 30% interest in Harp Ltd is attributed to him. Accordingly, Mr Marx's interest in Harp Ltd is 45% (15% + 30%).

No part of Mr Marx's interest in Harp Ltd is attributed to Woolsack Ltd.

Example 2.401.4.2

Mr Marx owns 45% and Ms Engels, his sister, owns 20% of the share capital in Woolsack Ltd. Mr Marx owns 20% and Woolsack Ltd owns 30% of the share capital in Harp Ltd.

Mr Marx and his associate, Ms Engels, have control of Woolsack Ltd (65%). Accordingly, the 30% interest which Woolsack Ltd has in Harp Ltd is attributed to Mr Marx. Mr Marx's interest in Harp Ltd is therefore 50% (20% + 30%).

Ms Engels' 30% interest in Harp Ltd through Woolsack Ltd is not further attributed to Mr Marx.

Example 2.401.4.3

Mr Marx owns 45% and Ms Engels, his sister, owns 20% of the share capital in Woolsack Ltd. Mr Marx owns 20% of the share capital in Harp Ltd. Mr Marx owns 25% and Ms Engels owns 35% of the share capital in Waco Ltd. Woolsack Ltd owns 30% and Waco Ltd owns 20% of the share capital in Harp Ltd.

Mr Marx and his associate, Ms Engels, have control of both Woolsack Ltd (65%) and Waco Ltd (60%). Accordingly, the 30% and 20% interests respectively held by Woolsack Ltd and Waco Ltd in Harp Ltd are attributed to Mr Marx. Mr Marx's interest in Harp Ltd is therefore 70% (20% + 30% + 20%).

Ms Engels' interests in Harp Ltd, 30% through Woolsack Ltd and 20% through Waco Ltd, are not further attributed to Mr Marx.

Example 2.401.4.4

Mr Marx owns 20% and Ms Engels, his sister, owns 15% of the share capital in Harp Ltd. Mr Bismarck, who is a business partner of Mr Marx, owns 25% of the share capital in Harp Ltd.

The 15% and 25% interests held by Ms Engels and Mr Bismarck in Harp Ltd are attributed to Mr Marx and his interest in Harp Ltd is therefore 60% (20% + 15% + 25%).

Example 2.401.4.5

Mr Marx owns 20% and 60% of the share capital in Harp Ltd and Woolsack Ltd respectively. Mr O'Quinn holds 15% of the share capital in Harp Ltd as nominee for Ms Engels, Mr Marx's sister. Mr O'Quinn also holds 13% of the share capital in Harp Ltd as nominee for Woolsack Ltd. Ms Engels holds 55% of the voting power in Waco Ltd and Waco Ltd owns 8% of the share capital in Harp Ltd.

Mr O'Quinn's 15% and 13% interests in Harp Ltd are attributed to Ms Engels and Woolsack Ltd respectively and therefore to Mr Marx. Mr Marx's interest in Harp Ltd is therefore 48% (20% + 15% + 13%).

Ms Engels, through her control of Waco Ltd, has attributed to her the share capital of 8% in Harp Ltd. That 8% interest is, however, not further attributed to Mr Marx (because it is only attributed to his associate by virtue of TCA 1997, s 432(6)).

The wide definition of control can result in a concept of overlapping control in the sense that control of a company may be held simultaneously and independently by different people or groups of people. For example, three individuals owning between them 55% of the issued share capital of a company would control that company but so would, say, three other individuals who between them own sufficient shares to give them majority voting control over the company. Furthermore, any shares held by one shareholder and attributed to another will be counted at least twice. This factor can have a significant influence where it is required to ascertain whether a certain category or a certain number of shareholders have control of a company.

Example 2.401.4.6

The issued share capital of Maplewood Ltd is held as follows:

	A shares	B shares (voting)	Total
C Reynolds	2,700	165	2,865
M Jackson	660	240	900
R Thomas	1,350	75	1,425
V Thomas (R Thomas' wife)	750	75	825
L Johnson (V Thomas' brother)	750	75	825
Resine Ltd (controlled by C Reynolds)	1,500	75	1,575
	7,710	705	8,415

Some of the above shareholders are taken together as one person. The shares of Resine Ltd are attributed to C Reynolds giving him a total of 4,440 shares. The shares of Resine Ltd are, however, included again in their own right.

R Thomas and V Thomas are associates of one another which gives R Thomas a combined holding of 2,250 shares. V Thomas is an associate of both R Thomas and L Johnson which gives her a combined total of 3,075 (1,425 + 825 + 825). V Thomas' shares are also attributed to her associate L Johnson, to bring his total to 1,650 (825 + 825). This gives the following position:

C Reynolds	4,440
M Jackson	900
Resine Ltd	1,575
R Thomas	2,250
V Thomas	3,075
L Johnson	1,650
	13,890

As a result of the attribution rules, a total of 13,890 shares are attributed to the shareholders although the total number of shares in issue is only 8,415. C Reynolds controls Maplewood Ltd on his own, since he is deemed to have 52.76% of the issued share capital. The position relating to voting power is as follows.

	Held	Held + Attributed
C Reynolds	165	240
M Jackson	240	240
Resine Ltd	75	75
R Thomas	75	150
V Thomas	75	225
L Johnson	75	150
	705	1,080

A total of 1,080 voting shares are deemed to be held by the shareholders although only 705 such shares are actually held. No one person has control of the company on this basis. If it is required to know if M Jackson and L Johnson have control between them (for example, because they are not resident in a relevant territory – see **11.116.6**), it is seen that they have control on the basis of possessing 55.32% of the voting control in the company.

The following example illustrates the operation of the control rules as they would be applied in ascertaining whether certain persons are connected to each other.

Example 2.401.4.7

The issued share capital of Kermit Ltd consists of 40,000 A ordinary shares of €1 each and 40,000 B ordinary shares of €1 each. The A shares carry one vote per share and the B shares are non-voting. Otherwise, the two classes of share capital rank pari passu in all respects. The shares are held as follows:

	Total	A Ord	B Ord
Ms L Vegas	24,000	12,000	12,000
Mr W Vegas (her husband)	4,000	Nil	4,000
Trustees of settlement (settlor, Ms T Pavel – Mr Vegas' sister)	8,000	4,000	4,000
Tularosa Investments Ltd (controlled by Ms & Mr Vegas)	6,000	Nil	6,000
	42,000	16,000	26,000
Other shareholders (not connected with Ms L Vegas)	38,000	24,000	14,000
	80,000	40,000	40,000

There are no loan creditors (within the meaning of TCA 1997, s 433(6)). The beneficiaries of the settlement have no interest in either Kermit Ltd or Tularosa Investments Ltd.

Ms L Vegas and persons connected with her (the three other shareholders named above) have the right to more than 50% of the profits available for distribution by way of dividend (as well as of the net assets in a winding up) due to their holding of 42,000 out of the 80,000 A and B shares. This is regardless of the fact that they do not have sufficient voting power to ensure that the affairs of the company are conducted in accordance with their wishes.

In view of the control exercised by Ms L Vegas, she is connected with Kermit Ltd. Mr W Vegas is similarly treated as controlling Kermit Ltd and therefore also as connected with that company. The trustees of the settlement are connected with both Ms and Mr Vegas – Mr Vegas is a relative (brother) of the settlor and Ms Vegas is also connected with her (wife of her relative) so that each of them is connected with the trustees.

Assuming that Ms Pavel has no shares or other interest in Tularosa Investments Ltd, she is not connected with that company. The trustees of the settlement cannot, therefore, be connected with Tularosa Investments Ltd under TCA 1997, s 10(4) (see **2.301.4** above). Assuming that the trustees do not hold any shares in Tularosa Investments Ltd, they are not connected with it under TCA 1997, s 10(7) either (see **2.302.1** above).

The combined holdings in Kermit Ltd of Tularosa Investments Ltd and of persons connected with that company (Ms Vegas and Mr Vegas) amount to 12,000 A (voting) and 22,000 B (non-voting) shares. This is insufficient to give Tularosa Investments Ltd and persons connected with it control of Kermit Ltd under any of the tests for control in TCA 1997, s 432. Kermit Ltd and Tularosa Investments Ltd are not, therefore, connected persons.

The trustees of the settlement and persons connected with them (again Ms Vegas and Mr Vegas) hold 16,000 A (voting) shares and 20,000 B shares in Kermit Ltd (out of the total of 80,000 shares); the settlor does not hold any shares in Kermit Ltd. Consequently, the trustees do not control Kermit Ltd and are not, therefore, connected to it.

2.401.5 Associate companies

A company is associated to another company at any time if, at that time or at any time within one year previously, one of the two companies has control of the other company or both companies are under the control of the same person or persons (TCA 1997, s 432(1)).

The question of associated companies arises in a number of contexts, for example, in relation to certain close company matters (see **10.204** and **10.301–303**), the corporation tax rate (see **3.101.2–3** and **3.101.5**) and IFRS, **3.305.4**).

2.401.6 Direct or indirect control

The specific forms of control listed in **2.401.1** above are without prejudice to the general meaning of control. The general definition of control in TCA 1997, s 432(2) refers both to direct and indirect control over the company's affairs. The reference to "control" there is to control at the level of general meetings of shareholders since it is that control that confers on its holder the power to make the ultimate decisions as to the business of the company and in that sense to control its affairs (*Steele v EVC International NV* [1996] STC 785).

There does not seem to be a basis for regarding as an instance of indirect control over a company the position of a shareholder with a minority of voting control in a second company which controls the first-mentioned company. Thus, if P and Q own shares carrying 25% and 75% respectively of the voting control in A Ltd and A Ltd has 100% control of B Ltd, P does not thereby have 25% control of B Ltd. This is because P does not have control at the level of general meetings of the shareholders of B Ltd. Q, however, does have such control and is, in any event, regarded as having control of B Ltd since all the rights and powers of A Ltd, a company controlled by Q, are to be attributed (by virtue of TCA 1997, s 432(6)(a) – see **2.401.4**) to Q.

Example 2.401.6.1

The equity and voting control interests in Sitka Ltd are as represented below. A Flynn and G Cross are Irish resident individuals. Details regarding beneficial interests and other matters relating to the M Mann Trust are unclear. Spruce Ltd holds the entire equity and voting control in Sitka Ltd.

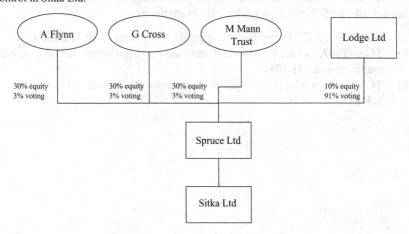

It is necessary for tax purposes to determine whether Sitka Ltd is controlled by the two Irish resident individuals. Clearly, Sitka Ltd is controlled by Spruce Ltd. As well as being controlled by Lodge Ltd on the basis of voting control, Spruce Ltd is also controlled by the two individuals since between them they hold more than 50% of the ordinary shares in the company. Does it then follow that the two individuals have control of Sitka Ltd?

Since Spruce Ltd can exercise control over the affairs of Sitka Ltd, it controls that company (in accordance with the general meaning of "control"). In view of the extent of its voting control in Spruce Ltd, Lodge Ltd controls Spruce Ltd since, again, it can exercise control over its affairs. Lodge Ltd therefore also (indirectly) controls Sitka Ltd since it can exercise control over the affairs of the company (Spruce Ltd) which in turn can exercise control over the affairs of Sitka Ltd. In other words, Lodge Ltd has control of Sitka Ltd at the level of general meetings of that company.

While the two individuals are regarded as having control of Spruce Ltd, on the basis of their combined equity holdings (one of the particular meanings of "control"), they do not have control of Sitka Ltd. This is because they do not exercise control over the affairs of Spruce Ltd and therefore cannot exercise control over the affairs of Sitka Ltd. In other words, they do not have control over Sitka Ltd at the level of general meetings of that company.

The above conclusion is on the assumption that A Flynn and G Cross are not associates of one other. If they were such associates (by virtue of, say, being partners in the same partnership), all the rights and powers of Spruce Ltd, a company of which they together have control, would be attributed to each of them in accordance with TCA 1997, s 432(6). Accordingly, the ability of Spruce Ltd to exercise control over the affairs of Sitka Ltd would be attributed to each of them so that each (and also obviously both together) would then be regarded as having control of Sitka Ltd.

2.402   TCA 1997, s 11

TCA 1997, s 11 also defines "control". The definition in this case is "for the purposes of, and subject to, the provisions of the Corporation Tax Acts which apply this section". *Control*, in relation to a company, means the power of a person to secure, by means of the holding of shares or the possession of voting power in or in relation to that or any other company, or by virtue of any powers conferred by the articles of association or other document regulating that or any other company, that the affairs of the first-mentioned company are conducted in accordance with the wishes of that person and, in relation to a partnership, means the right to a share of more than one-half of the assets, or of more than one-half of the income, of the partnership.

This definition of "control" is applied, for example, by:

(a)   TCA 1997, s 173 (company acquiring its own shares – see **11.306.7**);

(b)   TCA 1997, s 130(5) (distributions: assets transferred between company members – see **11.108**);

(c)   TCA 1997, s 424(1) (groups: arrangements for transfer of company – see **8.310**).

2.5 SUBSIDIARIES

2.501 Introduction
2.502 51% subsidiary
2.503 75% subsidiaries
2.504 90% subsidiaries
2.505 Determination of amount of capital held in company through other companies

2.501   Introduction

Throughout the legislation dealing with the taxation of companies there are, not surprisingly, many references to subsidiaries. These references reflect some of the different degrees of ownership of subsidiary companies and corporation tax legislation provides definitions of three types of subsidiary: 51% subsidiary, 75% subsidiary and 90% subsidiary. The most frequently encountered of these is the 75% subsidiary, not least because of its relevance for the purposes of group relief and group capital gains tax treatment. The definitions of the three kinds of subsidiary are contained in TCA 1997, s 9.

TCA 1997, s 176 (purchase of unquoted shares by issuing company or its subsidiary – see **11.304**) makes certain provisions in relation to a payment made by a company which is a subsidiary, within the meaning of CA 1963 s 155, of another company on the acquisition of shares of that other company. Under CA 1963 s 155, a company is deemed to be a *subsidiary* of another company if:

(a)   that other company:

  (i)   is a member of it and controls the composition of its board of directors; or

  (ii)   holds more than half in nominal value of its equity share capital; or

  (iii)   holds more than half in nominal value of its shares carrying voting rights (other than voting rights which arise only in specified circumstances); or

(b)   the first-mentioned company is a subsidiary of any company which is that other company's subsidiary.

In relation to (a)(i) above, CA 1963, s 31, defines *member*. The subscribers of the memorandum of a company are deemed to have agreed to become members of the company and, on its registration, are to be entered as members in its register of members. Every other person who agrees to become a member of a company and whose name is entered in its register of members is a member of the company (see **11.105.8**).

The definitions of the various subsidiaries in TCA 1997, s 9 are as follows:

2.502   51% subsidiary

A company is a *51% subsidiary* of another company if and so long as more than 50% of its ordinary share capital is owned directly or indirectly by that other company (TCA 1997, s 9(1)(a)). Ownership for this purpose means beneficial ownership. A 51% holding of the ordinary share capital is not necessary as long as the share capital held exceeds 50%, for example 50.001%.

51% subsidiaries are relevant, *inter alia*, in the context of:

(a)   group payments (see **8.201**);

(b)   the meaning of an unquoted company in TCA 1997, s 173(4), for the purposes of TCA 1997, s 176 (purchase of unquoted shares by issuing company or its subsidiary – see **11.305**);

(c)   TCA 1997, s 130(4) and (5) (see **11.108**);

(d)   non-application of dividend withholding tax to dividends paid by 51% subsidiary (TCA 1997, s 172B(8) – see **11.116.4**).

2.503 75% subsidiaries

A company is a *75% subsidiary* of another company if and so long as not less than 75% of its ordinary share capital is owned directly or indirectly by that other company (TCA 1997, s 9(1)(b)). Ownership for this purpose means beneficial ownership.

The 75% parent-subsidiary relationship is the most important relationship, not only for group relief purposes, but for the purposes of many other provisions of the Tax Acts, for example:

(a)   corporation tax groups (TCA 1997, s 411(1) (see **8.103**);

(b)   capital gains tax groups (TCA 1997 ss 616-626 – see **9.202.1**);

(c)   company reconstructions without change of ownership (TCA 1997, s 400 – see **4.109**).

2.504 90% subsidiaries

A company is a *90% subsidiary* of another company if and so long as not less than 90% of its ordinary share capital is directly owned by that other company.

An important difference in the definition of a 90% subsidiary, as compared with that for a 51% subsidiary or a 75% subsidiary, is that only direct holdings are recognised.

The meaning of "90% subsidiary" is relevant for the purposes of the group relief provisions as they relate to a consortium (TCA 1997, s 411(3) – see **8.102** and **8.303**).

2.505 Determination of amount of capital held in company through other companies

For the purposes of the definitions of "51% subsidiary" and "75% subsidiary", both direct and indirect holdings of ordinary share capital are taken into account. A company (A) may have an indirect holding of ordinary share capital in another company (E) through intermediary companies (say, B, C and D). Essentially, the percentage of ordinary share capital indirectly held by A in E is arrived at by multiplying the percentage of ordinary share capital held by A in B by the percentage held by B in C by the percentage held by C in D by the percentage held by D in E. There may be indirect holdings through more than one intermediary company or chain of intermediary companies. Thus, company A may hold further ordinary share capital in company E through companies G and H. The indirect holding through that chain of intermediaries is arrived at in the same way as for the chain comprising companies B, C and D. The total holding by company A in company E is the aggregate of the indirect holdings through the two chains of intermediaries. Any ordinary share capital held directly by company A in company E is also aggregated with the indirect holdings.

References to ownership are to be construed as references to beneficial ownership (TCA 1997, s 9(3)).

The amount of ordinary share capital of one company owned by a second company through another company or companies is to be determined in accordance with the rules in TCA 1997, s 9(5) to (10). The rules are as follows.

1. Where, in the case of a number of companies, the first company directly owns ordinary share capital of the second and the second directly owns ordinary share capital of the third, the first company is deemed to own ordinary share capital of the third through the second. If the third directly owns ordinary share capital of a fourth, the first is deemed to own ordinary share capital of the fourth through the second and the third, and the second is deemed to own ordinary share capital of the fourth through the third, and so on.

2. (a) Any number of companies of which the first company directly owns ordinary share capital of the next and the next directly owns ordinary share capital of the next again, and so on, are referred to as a series. If there are more than three such companies in the series, any three or more of them also comprise a series;

    (b) in any series—

        (i) the company which owns ordinary share capital of another through the remainder is referred to as the first owner;

        (ii) that other company the ordinary share capital of which is so owned is referred to as the last owned company;

        (iii) the remainder, if one only, is referred to as an intermediary and, if more than one, are referred to as a chain of intermediaries;

    (c) a company in a series which directly owns ordinary share capital of another company in the series is referred to as an owner;

    (d) any two companies in a series of which one owns ordinary share capital of the other directly, and not through one or more of the other companies in the series, are referred to as being directly related to one another.

3. Where every owner in a series owns the whole of the ordinary share capital of the company to which it is directly related, the first owner is deemed to own through the intermediary or chain of intermediaries the whole of the ordinary share capital of the last owned company.

4. Where one of the owners in a series owns a fraction of the ordinary share capital of the company to which it is directly related, and every other owner in the series owns the whole of the ordinary share capital of the company to which it is directly related, the first owner is deemed to own that fraction of the ordinary share capital of the last owned company through the intermediary or chain of intermediaries.

5. Where—

    (a) each of two or more of the owners in a series owns a fraction, and every other owner in the series owns the whole, of the ordinary share capital of the company to which it is directly related, or

    (b) every owner in a series owns a fraction of the ordinary share capital of the company to which it is directly related, the first owner is deemed to own through the intermediary or chain of intermediaries such fraction of the ordinary share capital of the last owned company as results from the multiplication of those fractions.

6.   Where the first owner in any series owns a fraction of the ordinary share capital of the last owned company in that series through the intermediary or chain of intermediaries in that series, and also owns another fraction or other fractions of the ordinary share capital of the last owned company, either—

(a)   directly, or

(b)   through an intermediary or intermediaries which is not a member or are not members of that series, or

(c)   through a chain or chains of intermediaries of which one or some or all is not a member or are not members of that series, or

(d)   in a case where the series consists of more than three companies, through an intermediary or intermediaries which is a member or are members or the series, or through a chain or chains of intermediaries consisting of some but not all of the companies of which the chain of intermediaries in the series consists,

then, for the purpose of ascertaining the amount of the ordinary share capital of the last owned company owned by the first owner, all those fractions are to be aggregated and first owner is deemed to own the sum of those fractions.

2.6 DEFINITIONS

2.601 Various definitions
2.602 "Profits brought into charge"
2.603 "Total income brought into charge"
2.604 "Profits on which corporation tax falls finally to be borne"
2.605 "Charged with tax under Schedule D"
2.606 "Securities"

2.601 Various definitions

Various definitions relevant for the purposes of the Tax Acts (except where otherwise provided or the context otherwise requires) are provided in TCA 1997 ss 2(1) and 4(1).

Accounting date: the date to which a company makes up its accounts (see also **3.105**).

Period of account: the period for which a company makes up its accounts.

Branch or agency: any factorship, agency, receivership, branch or management.

Chargeable asset: see **9.102.5**.

Chargeable gains: has the meaning as in the Capital Gains Tax Acts (ie every gain accruing on or after 6 April 1974, except so far as otherwise expressly provided by CGTA), but does not include gains accruing on disposals which were made before 6 April 1976 (see **9.102.5**).

Charges on income: has the meaning given by TCA 1997, s 243(1) (see **4.402**).

Close company: has the meaning given by TCA 1997 ss 430 and 431 (see **10.103**).

Company: see **1.3**.

Distribution: has the meaning given by TCA 1997 Part 6 Chapter 2 (see **11.101-108**) and ss 436 (see **10.202**) and 437 (see **10.203**).

The financial year: followed by a reference to the year 1996 or any other year means the year beginning on 1 January of such year (see **3.101**).

Franked investment income: income of a company resident in the State which consists of a distribution made by another company resident in the State. The amount of the franked investment income is the amount or value of the distribution (TCA 1997, s 156(1)).

Franked payment: the sum of the amount or value of a distribution made by a company resident in the State. References to any accounting or other period in which a franked payment is made are references to the period in which the distribution is made (TCA 1997, s 156(2)).

Group relief: has the meaning assigned to it by TCA 1997, s 411 (see **8.302.1**).

Income: is not defined for corporation tax purposes generally (but see **3.102.2**).

Interest: means both annual or yearly interest and interest other than annual or yearly interest (see **4.305**).

Ordinary share capital: in relation to a company means all the issued share capital (by whatever name called) of the company, other than capital the holders whereof have a right to a dividend at a fixed rate, but have no other right to share in the profits of the company (see also **8.103.2**).

Preference dividend: means a dividend payable on a preferred share or preferred stock at a fixed rate per cent or, where a dividend is payable on a preferred share or preferred stock partly at a fixed rate per cent and partly at a variable rate, such part of that dividend as is payable at a fixed rate per cent.

Profits: means income and chargeable gains: "income" is not defined for corporation tax purposes generally (see **3.102.1**).

Standard rate per cent: for a year of assessment, means 26 where the standard rate for that year is 26% and similarly as regards any reference to the standard rate per cent for a year of assessment for which the standard rate is other than 26% (TCA 1997, s 4(1)). Currently, the standard rate is 20%.

Within the charge to: a source of income is "within the charge to" corporation tax or income tax if that tax is chargeable on the income arising from it, or would be so chargeable if there were any such income, and references to a person, or to income, being within the charge to tax, is to be similarly construed.

2.602   "Profits brought into charge"

References in the Corporation Tax Acts to *profits brought into charge to corporation tax* are references to the amounts of those profits chargeable to corporation tax before any deduction therefrom for charges on income, expenses of management or other amounts which can be deducted from, or set against, or treated as reducing, profits of more than one description (TCA 1997, s 4(4)(a)).

Those profits are the sum of the company's income from all sources with the addition of any chargeable gains for the period but before deducting any amount which would reduce profits of more than one description, such as charges on income, management expenses under TCA 1997, s 83, a loss under TCA 1997, s 396(2), excess capital allowances under TCA 1997, s 308(4), or group relief under TCA 1997, s 420. For accounting periods ending on or after 31 January 2007, trading losses, excess trading charges and group relief for trading losses and charges are deductible against certain Case III income (foreign dividends taxable at 12.5% rate – see **3.101.5**) and are accordingly amounts which can be deducted from or set off against or treated as reducing profits of more than one description.

Thus, for example, charges on income paid in an accounting period are allowed as a deduction under TCA 1997, s 243(2) against a company's profits brought into charge to corporation tax for the period (see **4.404**).

2.603   "Total income brought into charge"

References in the Corporation Tax Acts to *total income brought into charge to corporation tax* are references to the amount, calculated before any such deduction therefrom for charges on income, expenses of management or other amounts which can be deducted from, or set against, or treated as reducing, profits of more than one description, of the total income from all sources included in any profit brought into charge to corporation tax (TCA 1997, s 4(4)(b)).

TCA 1997, s 448(5B) modifies "total income brought into charge to corporation tax" by providing that, for the purposes of the manufacturing relief formula, it is to be reduced by any amounts allowed under TCA 1997, s 243A, 396A or 420A, as well as an amount equal to so much of the profits of the period in question as are charged to tax in accordance with TCA 1997, s 21A (the higher rate of corporation tax – see **3.101.4**) This adjustment to what normally constitutes total income brought into charge to corporation tax is to prevent a distortion that would otherwise occur in arriving at the amount of manufacturing relief.

TCA 1997, s 448(2)(b) provides that corporation tax referable to income from the sale of goods (ie, the tax which is reduced by the relief) is an amount which bears to the "relevant corporation tax" the same proportion as the income from the sale of those goods bears to "the total income brought into charge to corporation tax". The formula emerging from this provision ensures that manufacturing relief does not apply to income other than manufacturing income.

2.604   "Profits on which corporation tax falls finally to be borne"

References in the Corporation Tax Acts to *an amount of profits on which corporation tax falls finally to be borne* are references to the amount of those profits after making all deductions and giving all reliefs that for the purposes of corporation tax are made or given from or against those profits, including deductions and reliefs which under any provision are treated as reducing them for those purposes (TCA 1997, s 4(4)(c)).

For example, "I" in TCA 1997, s 22(7) (reduced rate of corporation tax) means "the amount of the company's profits for the accounting period on which corporation tax falls finally to be borne exclusive of the part of the profits attributed to chargeable gains" (see **7.202.6**).

2.605   "Charged with tax under Schedule D"

In the case of income of Irish residents, "charged with tax under Schedule D" refers to any income, wherever arising (apart from income charged to tax under Schedules C, E or F). For non-residents, references to payments "charged with tax under Schedule D" are essentially references to Irish source income and which, accordingly, is income within the scope of Irish taxation. Most payments encountered in practice will accordingly fall within the description "charged with tax under Schedule D" (see **4.303.1**).

2.606   "Securities"

There is nowhere in the Tax Acts a complete or exhaustive definition of "securities". Definitions typically take the form of "securities includes ...". Thus, in TCA 1997, s 135(8) (see **11.101** and **11.106**) it is provided that "securities" includes securities not creating or evidencing a charge on assets. TCA 1997, s 748 (see **4.109.5** and **4.303.8**) provides that "securities" includes "stocks and shares" while in TCA 1997, s 812 (see **3.208.5**) "securities" includes "stocks and shares of all descriptions". These provisions seem to suggest that the word "securities" as normally understood would involve some form of document creating or evidencing a charge on assets and that it would not include stocks and shares. It would be useful therefore to have some insight into the meaning of "securities" as it is generally to be understood. Some assistance on this matter may be derived from the case of *Williams v Singer* 7 TC 419 through the following extracts from the judgments of Viscount Cave and Lord Shaw of Dunfermline. First, Viscount Cave:

> My Lords, the normal meaning of the word "securities" is not open to doubt. The word denotes a debt or claim, the payment of which is in some way secured. The security would generally consist of a right to resort to some fund or property for payment; but I am not prepared to say that other forms of security (such as a personal guarantee) are excluded. In each case, however, where the word is used in its normal sense, some form of secured liability is postulated. No doubt the meaning of the word may be enlarged by an interpretation clause contained in a statute, as by the interpretation clauses in the Conveyancing and Law of Property Act, 1881, the Settled Land Act, 1882, the Trustee Act, 1893, and the Finance Act, 1916; or the context may show, as in certain cases relating to the construction of wills, (*In re Rayner* LR [1904] 1 Ch 176; *In re Grant & Eason LR* [1905] 1 Ch 336), that the word is used to denote, in addition to securities in the ordinary sense, other investments such as stocks or shares. But, in the absence of any such aid to interpretation, I think it clear that the word "securities" must be construed in the sense above defined, and accordingly does not include shares or stock in a company. In the present case there is no interpretation clause, and there appears to me to be no context which affects the ordinary meaning of the word "securities".

Second, Lord Shaw of Dunfermline:

> The word "securities" has no legal signification which necessarily attaches to it on all occasions of the use of the term. It is an ordinary English word used in a variety of collocations: and it is to be interpreted without the embarrassment of a legal definition and simply according to the best conclusion one can make as to the real meaning of the term as it is employed in, say, a testament, an agreement, or a taxing or other statute as the case may be. The attempt to transfer legal definitions derived from one collocation to another leads to confusion and sometimes to a defeat of true intention. Of these two things, accordingly, "foreign possessions" and "foreign securities", which of the two terms fits the case of the shares in the Singer Company of New Jersey? A security means a security upon something. Securities, in the present instance, being in contrast with, or separation from, possessions, cannot be taken as the same word would be taken if applied, for instance, to the lodging by a customer of securities with his bank; in which case the term would naturally apply to the scrip which he hands over the counter. Securities in the Fourth Case of Schedule D appear to me to mean securities upon something as contrasted with the possession of something. The term involves the idea of the relation of creditor with debtor, the creditor having a security over property, concern, assets, goods or other things, which are, so to speak, put in pledge by the debtor and form the security for the fulfilment of his obligation to the creditor. This is not the position of Mr. Singer's title. He is a shareholder. The relation between him and his fellow shareholders is not that of creditor with debtor but of partner or joint adventurer with the other shareholders. His relation with the company is that of part owner of the concern. The property which he so holds falls, in my opinion, accordingly, as a matter of construction, under the term "possessions" and not under the term "securities". The remarks of Mr Justice Wright in *Bartholomay Brewing Company v Wyatt*, and of Lord Justice Moulton in *Gramophone Ltd v Stanley* may, as was argued, have been obiter, but I am humbly of opinion that they were entirely sound.

2.7 INTERPRETATION ACT 2005

2.701 Introduction

The Interpretation Act 2005 ("the 2005 Act") came into operation on 1 January 2006. Previous interpretation legislation (the Interpretation Act 1889, the Interpretation Act 1923, the Interpretation Act 1937 and the Interpretation (Amendment) Act 1993) was repealed by Section 3 of the 2005 Act. In the 2005 Act, a reference to *Act* means—

(a) an Act of the Oireachtas, and

(b) a statute which was in force in Saorstát Éireann immediately before the date of the coming into operation of the Constitution and which continued in force by virtue of Article 50 of the Constitution (Interpretation Act 2005, s 2(1)).

2.702 Construing ambiguous or obscure provisions

The Interpretation Act 2005 ("the 2005 Act") came into operation on 1 January 2006. Previous interpretation legislation (the Interpretation Act 1889, the Interpretation Act 1923, the Interpretation Act 1937 and the Interpretation (Amendment) Act 1993) was repealed by Section 3 of the 2005 Act. In the 2005 Act, a reference to *Act* means—

(a) an Act of the Oireachtas, and

(b) a statute which was in force in Saorstát Éireann immediately before the date of the coming into operation of the Constitution and which continued in force by virtue of Article 50 of the Constitution (Interpretation Act 2005, s 2(1)).

Of particular relevance to taxation statutes is section 5 which deals with construing ambiguous or obscure provisions etc. The section reads as follows:

(1) In construing a provision of any Act (other than a provision that relates to the imposition of a penal or other sanction)—

    (a) that is obscure or ambiguous, or

    (b) that on a literal interpretation would be absurd or would fail to reflect the plain intention of—

        (i) in the case of an Act to which paragraph (a) of the definition of "Act" in section 2(1) relates, the Oireachtas, or

        (ii) in the case of an Act to which paragraph (b) of that definition relates, the parliament concerned,

the provision shall be given a construction that reflects the plain intention of the Oireachtas or parliament concerned, as the case may be, where that intention can be ascertained from the Act as a whole.

(2) In construing a provision of a statutory instrument (other than a provision that relates to the imposition of a penal or other sanction)—

    (a)   that is obscure or ambiguous, or

    (b)   that on a literal interpretation would be absurd or would fail to reflect the plain intention of the instrument as a whole in the context of the enactment (including the Act) under which it was made,

the provision shall be given a construction that reflects the plain intention of the maker of the instrument where that intention can be ascertained from the instrument as a whole in the context of that enactment.

2.703   General rules of construction

The rules of construction are contained in s 18 of the 2005 Act:

The following provisions apply to the construction of an enactment:

    (a)   *Singular and plural:* A word importing the singular shall be read as also importing the plural, and a word importing the plural shall be read as also importing the singular;

    (b)   *Gender:*

        (i)   A word importing the masculine gender shall be read as also importing the feminine gender;

        (ii)   In an Act passed on or after 22 December 1993, and in a statutory instrument made after that date, a word importing the feminine gender shall be read as also importing the masculine gender;

    (c)   *Person:* "Person" shall be read as importing a body corporate (whether a corporation aggregate or a corporation sole) and an unincorporated body of persons, as well as an individual, and the subsequent use of any pronoun in place of a further use of "person" shall be read accordingly;

    (d)   *Adopted child:* A reference, however expressed, to a child of a person shall be read as including—

        (i)   in an Act passed after the passing of the Adoption Act 1976 a reference to a child adopted by the person under the Adoption Acts 1952 to 1998 and every other enactment which is to be construed together with any of those Acts, or

        (ii)   in an Act passed on or after 14 January 1988 (the commencement of section 3 of the Status of Children Act 1987), a child to whom subparagraph (i) relates or a child adopted outside the State whose adoption is recognised by virtue of the law for the time being in force in the State;

    (e)   *Distance:* A word or expression relating to the distance between two points and every reference to the distance from or to a point shall be read as relating or referring to such distance measured in a straight line on a horizontal plane;

    (f)   *Series description:* Where a consecutive series is described by reference to the first and last in the series, the description shall be read as including the first and the last in the series;

    (g)   *Marginal and shoulder notes, etc:* Subject to section 7, none of the following shall be taken to be part of the enactment or be construed or judicially noticed in relation to the construction or interpretation of the enactment:

(i)   a marginal note placed at the side, or a shoulder note placed at the beginning, of a section or other provision to indicate the subject, contents or effect of the section or provision,

(ii)   a heading or cross-line placed in or at the head of or at the beginning of a Part, Chapter, section, or other provision or group of sections or provisions to indicate the subject, contents or effect of the Part, Chapter, section, provision or group;

(h)   *Periods of time:* Where a period of time is expressed to begin on or be reckoned from a particular day, that day shall be deemed to be included in the period and, where a period of time is expressed to end on or be reckoned to a particular day, that day shall be deemed to be included in the period;

(i)   *Time:* Where time is expressed by reference to a specified hour or to a time before or after a specified hour, that time shall be determined by reference to the Standard Time (Amendment) Act 1971;

(j)   *Offences by corporations:* A reference to a person in relation to an offence (whether punishable on indictment or on summary conviction) shall be read as including a reference to a body corporate.

2.704   Commencement of legislative provisions

Section 16 of the 2005 Act provides as follows:

(1) Subject to subsection (2), every provision of an Act comes into operation on the date of its passing.

(2) Where an Act or a provision of an Act is expressed to come into operation on a particular day (whether the day is before or after the date of the passing of the Act and whether the day is named in the Act or is to be fixed or ascertained in a particular manner), the Act or provision comes into operation at the end of the day before the particular day.

(3) Subject to subsection (4), every provision of a statutory instrument comes into operation at the end of the day before the day on which the statutory instrument is made.

(4) Where a statutory instrument or a provision of a statutory instrument is expressed to come into operation on a particular day (whether the day is before or after the date of the making of the statutory instrument and whether the day is named in the instrument or is to be fixed or ascertained in a particular manner), the statutory instrument or provision comes into operation at the end of the day before the particular day. corporate.

2.705   Construction of statutory instruments

A word or expression used in a statutory instrument has the same meaning in the statutory instrument as it has in the enactment under which the instrument is made (Interpretation Act 2005 s 19).

2.706   Interpretation provisions

Section 20 of the 2005 Act provides as follows:

(1) Where an enactment contains a definition or other interpretation provision, the provision shall be read as being applicable except in so far as the contrary intention appears in—

(a)   the enactment itself, or

(b)   the Act under which the enactment is made.

(2) Where an enactment defines or otherwise interprets a word or expression, other parts of speech and grammatical forms of the word or expression have a corresponding meaning.

Section 21 of the 2005 Act deals with the interpretation of words and expressions contained in the *Schedule* to the Act (see below) as follows:

(1) In an enactment, a word or expression to which a particular meaning, construction or effect is assigned in Part 1 of the Schedule has the meaning, construction or effect so assigned to it.

(2) In an enactment which comes into operation after the commencement of this Act, a word or expression to which a particular meaning, construction or effect is assigned in Part 2 of the Schedule has the meaning, construction or effect so assigned to it.

2.707   Other provisions

A provision of the 2005 Act applies to an enactment except in so far as the contrary intention appears in the 2005 Act, in the enactment itself or, where relevant, in the Act under which the enactment is made. The provisions of the 2005 Act relating to other Acts also apply to the 2005 Act unless the contrary intention appears in the 2005 Act (Interpretation Act 2005, s 4).

In construing a provision of any Act or statutory instrument, a court may make allowances for any changes in the law, social conditions, technology, the meaning of words used in that Act or statutory instrument and other relevant matters, which have occurred since the date of the passing of that Act or the making of that statutory instrument, but only in so far as its text, purpose and context permit (Interpretation Act 2005, s 6).

The date of the passing of an Act of the Oireachtas is the date of the day on which the Bill for the Act is signed by the President (Interpretation Act 2005, s 15(1)).

2.708   Schedule to the 2005 Act

The Schedule to the 2005 Act, dealing with the interpretation of particular words and expressions, is as follows:

PART 1

"affidavit", in the case of a person for the time being allowed by law to declare instead of swearing, includes declaration;

"British statute" means an Act of the Parliament of the former United Kingdom of Great Britain and Ireland;

"Circuit Court" means the Circuit Court as established and for the time being maintained by law;

"commencement", when used in relation to an enactment, means the time at which the enactment comes into operation;

"Constitution" means the Constitution of Ireland enacted by the people on 1 July 1937, as amended;

"Dáil Éireann" means the House of the Oireachtas to which that name is given by section 1 of Article 15 of the Constitution;

"District Court" means the District Court as established and for the time being maintained by law;

"financial year", in relation to an exchequer financial year, means the period which is coextensive with a calendar year;

"Government" means the Government mentioned in Article 28 of the Constitution;

"Great Britain" does not include the Channel Islands or the Isle of Man;

"High Court" means the High Court as established and for the time being maintained by law pursuant to Article 34 of the Constitution;

"land" includes tenements, hereditaments, houses and buildings, land covered by water and any estate, right or interest in or over land;

"local financial year" means a period which is coextensive with a calendar year;

"midnight" means, in relation to a particular day, the point of time at which the day ends;

"Minister of the Government" means a member of the Government having charge of a Department of State;

"month" means a calendar month;

"oath", in the case of a person for the time being allowed by law to affirm or declare instead of swearing, includes affirmation or declaration;

"Oireachtas" means the National Parliament provided for by Article 15 of the Constitution;

"ordnance map" means a map made under the powers conferred by the Survey (Ireland) Acts 1825 to 1870;

"President" means the President of Ireland or any Commission, or other body or authority, for the time being lawfully exercising the powers and performing the duties of the President;

"pre-union Irish statute" means an Act passed by a Parliament sitting in Ireland at any time before the coming into force on 1 January 1801 of the Act entitled "An Act for the Union of Great Britain and Ireland";

"rateable valuation" means the valuation under the Valuation Act 2001 of the property concerned;

"rules of court" means rules made by the authority for the time being having power to make rules regulating the practice and procedure of the court concerned;

"Saorstát Éireann statute" means an Act of the Oireachtas of Saorstát Éireann;

"Seanad Éireann" means the House of the Oireachtas to which that name is given by section 1 of Article 15 of the Constitution;

"statutory declaration" means a declaration made under the Statutory Declarations Act 1938;

"Supreme Court" means the Supreme Court as established and for the time being maintained by law pursuant to Article 34 of the Constitution;

"swear", in the case of a person for the time being allowed by law to affirm or declare instead of swearing, includes affirm and declare;

"week" means the period between midnight on any Saturday and midnight on the following Saturday;

"week-day" means a day which is not a Sunday;

"writing" includes printing, typewriting, lithography, photography, and other modes of representing or reproducing words in visible form and any information kept in a non-legible form, whether stored electronically or otherwise, which is capable by any means of being reproduced in a legible form;

"year", when used without qualification, means a period of 12 months beginning on the 1st day of January in any year.

PART 2

"Companies Acts" means the Companies Acts 1963 to 2001 and every other enactment which is to be read together with any of those Acts;

"full age", in relation to a person, means the time when the person attains the age of 18 years or sooner marries, or any time after either event;

"functions" includes powers and duties, and references to the performance of functions include, with respect to powers and duties, references to the exercise of the powers and the carrying out of the duties;

"Member State" means, where the context so admits, a Member State of the European Communities or of the European Union;

"Minister of State" means a person appointed under section 1 of the Ministers and Secretaries (Amendment) (No. 2) Act 1977 to be a Minister of State;

"public holiday" means a public holiday determined in accordance with the Organisation of Working Time Act 1997;

"Social Welfare Acts" means the Social Welfare (Consolidation) Act 1993 and every other enactment which is to be read together with that Act;

"working day" means a day which is not a Saturday, Sunday or public holiday.

Chapter 3

Charge to Corporation Tax

3.1 INTRODUCTION

3.101 Charge and rates of corporation tax
3.102 Profits, income and chargeable gains
3.103 Trading
3.104 Capital allowances and related charges
3.105 Accounting periods
3.106 Residence of companies
3.107 Non-resident companies

3.101   Charge and rates of corporation tax

3.101.1

Taxes Consolidation Act 1997 (TCA 1997), s 26(1) provides that, "subject to any exceptions provided for by this Act", a company shall be chargeable to corporation tax on all its profits wherever arising. As will be seen, there are specific exemptions and exclusions which remove profits from the charge to corporation tax, for example, income of the Voluntary Health Insurance Board, profits from exempted Shannon operations, and distributions from Irish resident companies. Furthermore, non-resident companies are not subject to corporation tax in respect of their worldwide income.

Companies are liable to corporation tax in respect only of profits beneficially arising to them. Thus, profits accruing for the benefit of a company under any trust are taxable as are profits arising to a company under a partnership in circumstances where they would be taxable if they had arisen to it directly. A company is chargeable to corporation tax on profits arising on the winding up of the company. On the other hand, a company is not chargeable in respect of profits accruing to it in a fiduciary or representative capacity except in respect of any beneficial interest it has in those profits.

Corporation tax is charged on the profits of companies for financial years. The first financial year within the charge was the financial year 1974 which was the period 1 April 1974 to 31 December 1974. Otherwise the financial year means the calendar year. Assessments to corporation tax are, however, made by reference to accounting periods and the profits arising in an accounting period are, where necessary, apportioned between the financial years in which the accounting period falls. The rate of corporation tax for the financial years 1974 1975 and 1976 was 50% and was 45% for the next five financial years 1977 to 1981. Thereafter, changes in the corporation tax rate took effect on 1 April rather than on 1 January so that the rate was sometimes fixed for parts of financial years. In those cases, where appropriate, parts of calendar years were deemed to be financial years. From 1 January 1998, however, changes in corporation tax rates again take effect from 1 January.

The corporation tax rates to date are as follows:

Financial years within	Rate	Legislation	Lower rate
1 April 1974 to 31 December 1976	50%	CTA 1976 s 1	40%
1 January 1977 to 31 December 1981	45%	FA 1977 s 15(1)	35%
1 January 1982 to 31 March 1988	50%	FA 1982 s 26(1)	40%
1 April 1988 to 31 March 1989	47%	FA 1988 s 33(1)	40%

Financial years within	Rate	Legislation	Lower rate
1 April 1989 to 31 March 1991	43%	FA 1988 s 33(1)	N/A
1 April 1991 to 31 March 1995	40%	FA 1990 s 37(1)	N/A
1 April 1995 to 31 March 1996	38%	FA 1995 s 54(1)	
		TCA 1997, s 21	N/A
			Reduced rate
1 April 1996 to 31 March 1997	38%	TCA 1997 ss 21(1), 22(1)	30%
1 April 1997 to 31 December 1997	36%	TCA 1997 ss 21(1), 22(1)	28%
1 January 1998 to 31 December 1998	32%	TCA 1997 ss 21(1), 22(1)	25%
1 January 1999 to 31 December 1999	28%	TCA 1997 ss 21(1), 22(1)	25%
			Higher rate
1 January 2000 to 31 December 2000	24%	TCA 1997 ss 21(1), 21A(3)	25%
1 January 2001 to 31 December 2001	20%	TCA 1997 ss 21(1), 21A(3)	25%
1 January 2002 to 31 December 2002	16%	TCA 1997 ss 21(1), 21A(3)	25%
1 January 2003 onwards	12.5%	TCA 1997 ss 21(1), 21A(3)	25%

3.101.2 Lower rate of corporation tax

Up to 31 March 1989, companies with annual profits (ie, including chargeable gains) not exceeding £25,000 (€31,750) could claim to have their *income* (to exclude chargeable gains) taxed at a lower rate of corporation tax. The lower rate was 40% for all periods except that it was 35% at the time when the standard rate was 45%. Where profits exceeded £25,000 (the "lower relevant maximum amount"), but did not exceed £35,000 (€44,450) (the "upper relevant maximum amount), a claim could be made for relief from tax the effect of which was to give an effective tax rate between the lower rate and the standard rate; the rate moved nearer to the standard rate the closer the profit figure was to the upper relevant maximum amount.

Both the lower and the upper relevant maximum amounts were apportioned on a time basis for any accounting period which was shorter than twelve months. They were also divided by one plus the number of associated companies of the claimant company. A company was treated as another company's associated company at any time if at that time one of the two had control of the other, or both were under the control of the same person or persons (CTA 1976 s 28(4)). "Control" was as defined in what is now TCA 1997, s 432 (see **2.401**). For this purpose, any company which had not carried on any trade or business at any time in the accounting period or, if an associated company for part only of the accounting period, which had not carried on any trade or business for that part of the accounting period, was disregarded. For the purpose of determining the number of associated companies, a company which was an associated company for part only of an accounting period was counted, and two or more companies which were associated companies for different parts of an accounting period were also counted.

3.101.3 Reduced rate of corporation tax

A reduced corporation tax rate of 30% was introduced with effect from 1 April 1996 for the first £50,000 (€63,500) of income (CTA 1976 s 28A, now TCA 1997, s 22). The operation of this reduced rate, which applied for accounting periods or part accounting periods up to 31 December 1999, was fundamentally different from that applying to the CTA 1976 s 28 version as it applied to all companies regardless of the amount of income or profits. The £50,000 amount was time apportioned for any accounting period of a company which is shorter than twelve months and was divided by one plus the number of associated companies of that company. The associated companies rule avoided a weakness contained in the older CTA 1976 s 28 regime in that only those associated companies which had income within the charge to corporation tax were counted. This avoided the often difficult task of trying to identify what companies in an international group were associated companies for Irish tax purposes. The reduced rate is discussed in detail in the 2001-02 and prior editions of this book.

3.101.4 Higher rate of corporation tax

With effect from 1 January 2000, a 25% corporation tax rate applies to profits of companies in so far as those profits consist of income chargeable to corporation tax under Case III, IV or V of Schedule D or of income of an excepted trade (TCA 1997, s 21A(3)). This is, however, subject to TCA 1997, s 21A(4) which provides that the higher rate does not apply to the profits of a company to the extent that they consist of income from the sale of goods. For this purpose, income from the sale of goods means the income that would be "the income from the sale of those goods", as defined in TCA 1997, s 448(3), for the purposes of a claim under TCA 1997, s 448(2) (see **7.202.3**) if the company in question had sufficient profits and made a manufacturing relief claim (TCA 1997, s 21A(4A)).

TCA 1997, s 21A is also subject to TCA 1997, s 21B which provides for the taxation of foreign dividends at the 12.5% rate (see **3.101.5**).

The categories and descriptions of income chargeable to tax under Cases III, IV and V are described in **3.207-209**. See also **3.102.2** in relation to foreign trades.

Excepted trades

An *excepted trade* is a trade consisting only of trading operations or activities which are excepted operations (TCA 1997, s 21A(1)). If a trade consists partly of excepted operations and partly of other operations or activities, each part is treated as a separate trade for the purposes of TCA 1997, s 21A. A proportion of the total amount receivable from sales made and services rendered, and of the expenses incurred, in the course of the trade is to be apportioned to each part on a just and reasonable basis (TCA 1997, s 21A(2)). The part of the trade consisting only of excepted operations on this basis is also treated as an excepted trade.

Excepted operations means any one or more of the following operations or activities—

    (a)   dealing in or developing land, other than such part of that operation or activity as consists of—

        (i)   construction operations (as listed under Construction in **7.204.6**, with the exception of (f)), or

  (ii) dealing by a company in land which, in relation to the company, is
     qualifying land,
 (b) working minerals; and
 (c) petroleum activities.

The exclusion of (f) from *Construction*, referred to in (a)(i) above, means that excepted operations include operations which form an integral part of, or are preparatory to, or are for rendering complete, the drilling for or extraction of minerals, oil, natural gas or the exploration or exploitation of natural resources.

Dealing in or developing land is to be construed in accordance with TCA Part 22 Chapter 1 (ss 639-647 – see **13.3**). In this connection, TCA 1997, s 639(1) defines *development*, in relation to any land, as:

 (a) the construction, demolition, extension, alteration or reconstruction of any
   building on the land; or
 (b) the carrying out of any engineering or other operation in, on, over or under the
   land to adapt it for materially altered use;

and *developing* and *developed* are to be construed accordingly.

Construction operations in TCA 1997, s 21A has the same meaning as in the legislation dealing with payments to subcontractors (see **7.204.6**) and includes the operations listed in (a) above (with the exception of reconstruction) so that where any of these activities is involved it will not be regarded as "dealing in or developing land" for the purposes of the higher corporation tax rate. Furthermore, since "construction operations" also include operations that are preparatory to other construction operations, they would include the activities listed in (b) where these are carried out by a company for the purposes of enabling it to carry out construction operations as listed in (a). Thus, where a company's trade consists of or includes "construction operations", that trade, or the part of the trade that includes the construction operations, will not be regarded as "dealing in or developing land".

Qualifying land is essentially fully developed land. It is defined in TCA 1997, s 21A(1), in relation to a company, as land which is disposed of at any time by the company, being land:

 (a) on which a building or structure had been constructed by or for the company
   before that time; and
 (b) which had been developed by or for the company to such an extent that it could
   reasonably be expected at that time that no further development (within the
   meaning of TCA 1997, s 639(1) – see definition above) of the land would be
   carried out in the period of 20 years beginning at that time (other than a
   development which is not material and which is intended to facilitate the
   occupation of, and the use or enjoyment of, the building or structure for the
   purposes for which it was constructed).

A development of land on which a building or buildings had been constructed is not *material* for the purposes mentioned in (b) if it consists of one or both of the following:

 (i) an exempt development; and
 (ii) a development, not being an exempt development, if the total floor area of the
   building or buildings on the land after such development is not greater than

120% of the total floor area of the building or buildings on the land calculated without regard to that development.

An *exempt development* is a development within Class 1 of Part 1 of the Second Schedule to the Local Government Planning and Development Regulations 1994 (SI 86/ 1994), which complies with the conditions and limitations specified in column 2 of that Part which relate to that Class.

Working, in relation to minerals, includes digging, searching for, mining, getting, raising, taking, carrying away and treating minerals and the sale or other disposal of minerals. *Minerals* means all substances (other than the agricultural surface of the ground and other than turf or peat) in, on or under land, whether obtainable by underground or by surface working, and includes all mines, whether or not they are already opened or in work, and also includes the cubic space occupied or formerly occupied by minerals. (See also **13.4** regarding mining activities.)

Petroleum activities means any one or more of the following activities:

(a)   petroleum exploration activities;
(b)   petroleum extraction activities; or
(c)   the acquisition, enjoyment or exploitation of petroleum rights.

Petroleum exploration activities means activities carried on in searching for deposits of petroleum, in testing or appraising such deposits or in winning access to such deposits for the purposes of such searching, testing or appraising.

Petroleum extraction activities means activities carried on in:

(a)   winning petroleum from any land (including foreshore and land covered by water) including searching in that land and winning access to such petroleum;
(b)   transporting as far as dry land (land not permanently covered by water) petroleum so won from a place not on dry land; or
(c)   effecting the initial treatment and storage of petroleum so won from any land.

Petroleum rights means rights to petroleum to be extracted or to interest in, or to the benefit of, petroleum.

Petroleum has the same meaning as in s 2(1) of the Petroleum and Other Minerals Development Act 1960 (see **13.502**).

See also **13.503** in relation to the corporation tax rate for profits from petroleum activities.

25% rate of corporation tax

TCA 1997, s 21A(3)(a) provides that, subject to TCA 1997, ss 21A(4) and 21B, corporation tax is to be charged on the profits of companies in so far as those profits consist of income chargeable to corporation tax under Case III, IV or V of Schedule D or of income of an excepted trade, at the rate of 25% for the financial year 2000 and subsequent financial years.

For the above purposes, the profits of a company for an accounting period are to be treated as consisting of income of an excepted trade for the accounting period after deducting from the amount of that income the amount of charges on income paid in the accounting period wholly and exclusively for the purposes of that trade (TCA 1997, s 21A(3)(b)). The trade charges to be deducted from the income of an excepted trade are those charges which actually relate to that trade. In this respect, the approach to trade charges is different to that relating to "manufacturing" charges which are arrived at by apportioning the total amount of trade charges by reference to the amount of turnover from the sale of manufactured goods (see **4.405**).

TCA 1997, s 21A makes no specific provision regarding the treatment of charges other than charges relating to an excepted trade. As regards trade charges, these will be deducted in any event from trading income.

The statutory position regarding the treatment of other (ie, non-trade) charges on income, as well as losses and group relief, is unclear. In relation to periods up to 5 March 2001, Revenue practice is to allocate such charges, as well as losses and group relief, on a proportionate basis (but see further below regarding apportionment) although they will accept computations in which those charges etc are deductible primarily against income taxable at the 25% rate. See, for instance, Example **4.405.1** and, similarly, in relation to TCA 1997 ss 396(2) and 420, Examples **8.306.1.1** and **8.306.1.2**. For periods from 6 March 2001, a similar practice obtains in relation to non-trade charges and losses in respect of which TCA 1997, s 396(2) or s 420 is still relevant (ie, excepted trade losses).

Profits taxable at higher rate in certain cases

As mentioned above, there is no provision in TCA 1997, s 21A for the deduction of charges on income (apart from charges relating to an excepted trade) from income chargeable at the 25% rate. Similarly, in a case in which a deduction for group relief under TCA 1997, s 420 or a trading loss under TCA 1997, s 396(2) is to be made, or indeed where any deduction from profits of more than one description is to be made, TCA 1997, s 21A does not indicate whether such deduction is to be taken into account in ascertaining what amount of profits "consist of" income chargeable under Case III etc. Logically, one might expect that for this purpose taxable profits should be apportioned in the ratio of Case III etc income over total income. The Revenue Commissioners consider that apportionment should be applied but, as stated above, they will accept computations in which charges etc are deducted primarily against income taxable at the higher rate.

If apportionment were to be applied, there could be difficulties as regards the precise method to be adopted in certain cases.

Example 3.101.4.1

Price Ltd has the following results for its latest accounting period:

	€
Case I	100,000
Case III	40,000
	140,000
Interest treated as a charge on income	70,000
Profits subject to corporation tax	70,000

Using apportionment, the position is straightforward and corporation tax would be as follws:

€70,000 x 100/140 = €50,000 @ 12.5%	6,250
€70,000 x 40/140 = €20,000 @ 25%	5,000
Corporation tax	11,250

In a case where there is manufacturing income qualifying for the 10% corporation tax rate, it is necessary to have regard to TCA 1997, s 21A(4) which provides that s 21A is not to apply to the extent that profits consist of income from the sale of goods (see also *Profits to which TCA 1997, s 21A does not apply* below). The words "to the extent that those profits consist of" may be contrasted with "in so far as those profits consist of" in TCA 1997, s 21A(3). Thus, it might be that TCA 1997, s 21A(4) means that s 21A does not apply to profits up to the amount of income from the sale of goods, and without any apportionment of such income) whereas TCA 1997, s 21A(3) means that the 25% corporation tax rate applies to Case III etc income in so far as the profits of the company concerned are accounted for by such income (which could involve apportionment). On the other hand, it is possible that the contrasting wording employed in TCA 1997, s 21A(3) and (4) is purely fortuitous and is without any significance.

Example 3.101.4.2

The facts are the same as in Example **3.101.4.1** except that the Case I profits are entirely derived from manufacturing activities qualifying for the 10% corporation tax rate.

On an apportionment basis, corporation tax might be as follows:

	€
Profits subject to corporation tax	70,000
€70,000 x 100/140 = €50,000 @ 10% (effective)	5,000
€70,000 x 40/140 = €20,000 @ 25%	5,000
Corporation tax	10,000

However, TCA 1997, s 21A(4) provides that s 21A does not apply to the profits of a company *to the extent* that those profits consist of income from the sale of goods. It is at least arguable that the words "to the extent that" mean that income from the sale of goods must be excluded from taxable profits before applying the 25% corporation tax rate. Income from the sale of goods is €100,000. On that basis, no part of the profits of €70,000 would be subject to the higher rate.

See, however, earlier remarks under *25% rate of corporation tax* above in relation to Revenue practice.

Profits to which TCA 1997, s 21A *does not apply*

Certain profits of a company are outside the scope TCA 1997, s 21A altogether. TCA 1997, s 21A(4) provides that the section does not apply to the profits of a company for any accounting period:

(a) to the extent that those profits consist of income from the sale of goods (manufacturing income) (TCA 1997, s 21A(4)(a)); and

(b) to the extent that those profits consist of income which arises in the course of any of the following trades—

   (i) non-life insurance,

   (ii) reinsurance, and

   (iii) life business, in so far as the income is attributable to shareholders of the company (TCA 1997, s 21A(4)(b)).

Effect on manufacturing relief formula

To prevent distortion in the calculation of manufacturing relief which would otherwise occur if the amount of "relevant corporation tax" included corporation tax calculated at the higher rate as well as at the standard rate, TCA 1997, s 448(5A) provides that relevant corporation tax is not to include any corporation tax calculated at the higher rate. Accordingly, the "relevant corporation tax" of a company for an accounting period is reduced in any such case by an amount determined by the formula:

$$\frac{R}{100} \times S$$

where –

R is the rate specified in TCA 1997, s 21A(3) (ie, the higher rate of corporation tax) in relation to the accounting period; and

S is an amount equal to so much of the profits of the company for the accounting period as are charged to tax in accordance with TCA 1997, s 21A.

Again, to prevent distortion in the manufacturing relief formula, it follows that the amount of total income in the denominator must also be reduced by the amount of the company's income which is chargeable at the higher rate for the accounting period. (See also **7.202.2** and **7.202.3**.)

Example 3.101.4.3

The profits of Clinton Ltd for its current accounting priod consist of the following:

	€
Manufacturing profits	70,000
Non-manufacturing profits	150,000
Case III	200,000
Charges on income (non-trade)	300,000
Corporation tax computation:	
Case I	220,000
Case III	200,000
	420,000
Charges on income (non-trade)	300,000
Profits chargeable	120,000
Corporation tax:	
€50,000[2] @ 25%	12,500
€70,000[1] @ 10% (effective)	7,000
Payable	19,500

Notes:

[1] Manufacturing income is €70,000. The higher rate does not apply to the profits of a company to the extent that those profits consist of manufacturing income (TCA 1997, s 21A(4)).

[2] TCA 1997, s 21A(3) provides that corporation tax is to be charged at the higher rate on the profits of a company in so far as those profits consist of income chargeable under Case III, Case IV etc. This provision, however, is subject to TCA

1997, s 21A(4) (see note 1) so that any manufacturing income is taken out of the chargeable profits before ascertaining what profits are chargeable at the higher rate. In so far as the remaining chargeable profits consist of Case III income, they are taxable at the higher rate.

Example 3.101.4.4

The position is as in Example **3.101.4.3** except that manufacturing and non-manufacturing profits are €150,000 and €70,000 respectively. The corporation tax computation is as follows:

	€
Case I	220,000
Case III	200,000
	420,000
Charges on income (non-trade)	300,000
Profits chargeable	120,000
Corporation tax @ 10% (effective)[1]	12,000

Notes:

[1]   Manufacturing income is €150,000. The higher rate does not apply to the profits of a company to the extent that those profits consist of manufacturing income (TCA 1997, s 21A(4)).

3.101.5   Taxation of foreign dividends

Introduction

Domestic sourced dividends are exempt from corporation tax but the underlying profits will have suffered corporation tax at 12.5% where the profits are generated from trading activities. To be compatible with EU law in the light of the *FII GLO* decision (see **3.205**), foreign sourced dividends should not be subject to a rate of taxation higher than that applying to domestic sourced dividends. Foreign dividends received on or after 1 January 2007 from underlying trading profits sourced from an EU country or a country with which Ireland has a double tax treaty are taxable at the 12.5% rate. The full amount of the foreign dividend is chargeable at the 12.5% rate when certain conditions are met, even though part of the dividend may not be paid out of trading profits. The conditions are–

(a)   that 75% or more of the dividend paying foreign company's profits are trading profits from that company or lower tier companies resident in the EU or in a country with which Ireland has a double tax treaty; and

(b)   that the aggregate value of the trading assets used by the dividend receiving company and all of its subsidiaries is at least 75% of the aggregate value of all of those companies' assets.

If these conditions are satisfied, an apportionment of the dividend received as between the 12.5% and 25% rates of tax is not required; the full dividend is taxable at the 12.5% rate.

In taxing foreign sourced dividends, credit is available for any foreign withholding taxes suffered and for underlying taxes on profits out of which the dividend is paid (see **14.201-210**).

In accordance with legislation providing for onshore pooling (see **14.214**), where foreign dividends have suffered foreign tax in excess of the Irish rate, excess foreign tax credits in respect of these dividends may be offset against Irish tax on dividends which have suffered foreign tax at a rate lower than the Irish rate. The availability of the 12.5% corporation tax rate on certain foreign dividends means that there are two pools of credits available, those at the 12.5% rate and those at 25%. Excess credits arising on dividends taxed at the 12.5% rate will be available for offset only against tax on other dividends taxed at that rate. Excess credits at the higher rate can be used against dividend income at either rate. Excess credits may be carried forward to later periods for use against tax on dividends taxed at 12.5% in those years or for use against dividends taxable at the 25% rate (where the excess credits arise on similarly taxed dividends).

Additionally, portfolio corporate investors receiving dividends from a company resident in an EU Member State or a country with which Ireland has a double tax treaty will be taxed on those dividends at the 12.5% rate. A portfolio investor in a company is an investor with a holding of not more than 5% (and not more than 5% of the voting rights) in the dividend paying company. The dividend is deemed to have been paid out of the trading profits of the payee company.

Foreign dividends taxable at 12.5% rate

Subject to satisfying certain conditions, a company may claim to have certain dividends received by it from a company resident in a relevant territory subject to corporation tax at the 12.5% rate and not at the higher rate provided for by TCA 1997, s 21A. As respects any accounting period, the claim is to be included with the company's corporation tax return for that period (TCA 1997, s 21B(5), (6)). TCA 1997, s 21B applies as respects an accounting period of a company where the company receives a dividend chargeable under Case III of Schedule D from another company (ie, a foreign dividend) and the dividend is paid by the other company out of trading profits of that company (TCA 1997, s 21B(3)).

A *relevant territory* is a Member State of the EU or a territory with which Ireland has a tax treaty.

Where, however, the income of a company (the "first-mentioned company") which is chargeable to tax under Case III of Schedule D for an accounting period includes a dividend paid to it by another company, resident in a relevant territory, and the first-mentioned company—

(a)   does not own, directly or indirectly, either alone or together with a person who is connected (within the meaning of TCA 1997, s 10 - see **2.302**) with it, more than 5% of the share capital of the other company, and

(b)   does not hold more than 5% of the voting rights in the other company,

the dividend is treated for the purposes of TCA 1997, s 21B(3) as a dividend paid by the other company out of trading profits of that company (TCA 1997, s 21B(4)). Accordingly, companies that are portfolio investors are taxable at the 12.5% rate in respect of dividends from companies resident in a relevant territory.

For the above purposes, *trading profits*, in relation to a company for an accounting period, means the aggregate of so much of the profits of the company for that period as are, on a just and reasonable basis, attributable to—

(i) the carrying on by the company of a trade, and

(ii) the amount of dividends received by the company which are treated as trading profits by virtue of TCA 1997, s 21B (see below),

but does not include amounts attributable to profits, or to dividends received by a company which are paid out of profits, of an excepted trade (within the meaning of TCA 1997, s 21A – see **3.101.4** above).

So much of a dividend received by a company (the "first-mentioned company") which is paid by another company out of trading profits of that company is treated as trading profits of the first-mentioned company. Where the profits of the other company out of which the dividend was paid to the first-mentioned company consist of a dividend out of the trading profits of a third company, that dividend is also treated as trading profits out of which the dividend received by the first-mentioned company has been paid, and so on indefinitely (TCA 1997, s 21B(1)(b)(ii)).

References to a company by which a dividend is paid apply only to a company that throughout the period out of the profits of which the dividend was paid was, by virtue of the law of a relevant territory, resident for the purposes of tax in such a relevant territory, and for this purpose *tax*, in relation to a relevant territory, means any tax imposed in the relevant territory which corresponds to corporation tax in the State (TCA 1997, s 21B(1)(b)(i)). Accordingly, the dividend paying company at any level must be tax resident in a relevant territory.

In relation to a company for any accounting period, *profits* means—

(a) where the profit and loss account, or income statement, of the company for that period is required to be laid before the annual general meeting of the company, the amount of profits, after taxation, as shown in that profit and loss account, or that income statement, and

(b) in any other case, the amount of profits, after taxation, as shown in the profit and loss account, or income statement, of the company which is prepared in accordance with an accounting framework that, in the territory in which the company is incorporated, is generally accepted as presenting a fair view of the profit for that period.

The period out of the profits of which a dividend is paid by a company is—

(i) if the dividend is paid by the company for a specified period, that period,

(ii) if the dividend is not paid for a specified period but is paid out of specified profits, the period in which those profits arise, or

(iii) if the dividend is paid by the company neither for a specified period nor out of specified profits, the last period for which accounts of the company were made up and which ended before the dividend became payable (TCA 1997, s 21B(1)(b)(iii)).

Where, however, the total dividend exceeds the profits available for distribution for a period identified in accordance with above procedure, so much of the dividend as is equal to the excess is regarded as paid out of profits of the preceding period (other than profits of that period treated as previously distributed), and that period is then treated as a period identified in accordance with the same procedure for the purposes of any further application of this rule (TCA 1997, s 21B(1)(b)(iv)).

For the purposes of TCA 1997, s 21B—

(a) subject to (b), the proportion of a dividend paid by a company for a period that is to be regarded as paid out of trading profits is the same proportion as the amount of trading profits of the company for that period bears to the total profits of the company for the period, and

(b) a dividend received by a company (the "receiving company") within the charge to corporation tax in the State which is paid by a company (the "paying company") out of the profits of a period is treated as paid out of trading profits of the paying company

for that period if—

(i) not less than 75% of the total profits of the paying company for the period are trading profits, and

(ii) the value, at the end of the accounting period in which the dividend is received, of assets (other than specified assets) used by the receiving company, and each company of which the receiving company is the parent company (within the meaning of TCA 1997, s 626B – **9.213.2**), during that period for the purposes of the carrying on by those companies of a trade or trades is not less than 75% of the value at the end of that period of the assets (other than specified assets) of those companies, and for this purpose an asset shall be treated as a *specified asset* if it consists of—

(I) shares of one of those companies held by another of those companies, or

(II) loans made by one of those companies to another of those companies (TCA 1997, s 21B(2)).

In other words, the full amount of a foreign dividend received by a company will be chargeable at the 12.5% rate, and no apportionment is required, where certain conditions are met, notwithstanding that a part of the dividend may not be paid out of trading profits. The conditions are—

(a) that 75% or more of the dividend-paying company's profits are trading profits, either trading profits of that company or dividends received by it out of trading profits of lower tier companies that are resident in relevant territories, and.

(b) that on a consolidated basis an asset condition must be satisfied by the dividend receiving company and all of its subsidiaries: the aggregate value of the trading assets of those companies must not be less than 75% of the aggregate value of all of their assets.

3.101.6   12.5% rate of corporation tax for certain income

Introduction

With effect from 1 January 2000, a 12.5% rate of corporation tax applies to the trading income (other than trading income taxable at the effective 10% corporation tax rate or at the 25% corporation tax rate) of a company where that income does not exceed a prescribed annual threshold amount. Where the annual trading income exceeds that threshold amount but is less than a prescribed higher threshold amount, marginal relief applies. Where the length of an accounting period of a company is less than twelve months, the threshold amounts are proportionately reduced. Similarly, where a company has one or more associated companies, these amounts are reduced by one plus the number of associated companies.

For the financial years 2001 and 2002, profits from qualifying shipping activities are subject to corporation tax at the rate of 12.5%.

The 12.5% corporation tax rate applies to trading income generally from 1 January 2003. (See the 2003 edition of this book for a more detailed treatment and examples illustrating the operation of the 12.5% rate in the above circumstances.)

3.101.7 20% rate of corporation tax

A special effective 20% rate of corporation tax applies to the trading income of a company from dealing in residential development land, and to certain capital gains on disposals of such land which are treated as income for tax purposes. Income from dealing in residential development land is, on a claim to that effect, taxed at 20%.

Trading income from dealing in residential development land

Where in an accounting period a company carries on an excepted trade the operations or activities of which consist of or include dealing in land which, at the time at which it is disposed of by the company, is residential development land, the corporation tax payable by the company for the accounting period, in so far as it is referable to trading income from dealing in residential development land, is to be reduced by one-fifth (TCA 1997, s 644B(2)(a)). Thus, the 25% corporation rate which would otherwise apply is effectively reduced to 20%.

TCA 1997, s 644B applies in relation to accounting periods ending on or after 1 January 2000. In this connection, where an accounting period of a company begins before 1 January 2000 and ends on or after that day, it is to be divided into two parts, one beginning on the day on which the accounting period begins and ending on 31 December 1999 and the other beginning on 1 January 2000 and ending on the day on which the accounting period ends, and both parts are to be treated as separate accounting periods of the company (TCA 1997, s 644B(2)(b)).

Residential development land is defined in TCA 1997, s 644A(1) as land:

(a)   disposed of to:

   (i)   a housing authority (within the meaning of s 23 of the Housing (Miscellaneous Provisions) Act 1992),

   (ii)   the National Building Agency Limited (being the company referred to in s 1 of the National Building Agency Limited Act, 1963), or

   (iii) a body standing approved of for the purposes of s 6 of the Housing (Miscellaneous Provisions) Act 1992,

   which land is specified in a certificate in writing given by a housing authority or the National Building Agency Limited, as appropriate, as land being required for the purposes of the Housing Acts, 1966 to 1998,

(b) in respect of which permission for residential development has been granted under s 26 of the Local Government (Planning and Development) Acts 1963 to 1999, and such permission has not ceased to exist; or

(c) which is, in accordance with a development objective (as indicated in the development plan of the planning authority concerned), for use solely or primarily for residential purposes.

Residential development includes any development which is ancillary to the development and which is necessary for the proper planning and development of the area in question.

TCA 1997, s 644B provides for the effective 20% corporation tax rate by way of a relief from tax chargeable at the 25% rate. The relief is one-fifth of the corporation tax payable for the accounting period in question in so far as that tax is referable to trading income from dealing in residential development land. For that purpose, the corporation tax *referable to trading income from dealing in residential development land* is a proportion of the corporation tax referable to income from an excepted trade. That proportion is the amount receivable by the company concerned from the disposal in the accounting period in the course of the excepted trade of residential development land, exclusive of so much of that amount as is attributable to construction operations within the meaning of TCA 1997, s 21A (see **3.101.4** which refers to the list of operations under *Construction* in **7.204.6**, with the exception (f)), over the total amount receivable by the company in the period, exclusive of so much of that amount as is attributable to construction operations within the meaning of TCA 1997, s 21A, in the course of the excepted trade. In relation to the denominator in the fraction suggested here, it would seem that since the amount receivable by a company in the course of an excepted trade would not include anything attributable to construction operations, there would be nothing to exclude by way of an amount "attributable to construction operations within the meaning of TCA 1997, s 21A".

The *corporation tax referable to income from an excepted trade* is in turn a proportion of the corporation tax charged in accordance with TCA 1997, s 21A (ie, at the 25% rate) for the period in question, the proportion being the amount of the company's profits treated as consisting of income from the excepted trade over the total amount of the profits of the company for the period charged at 25%.

The relief can accordingly be represented by the following formula, where RDL denotes residential development land and CO refers to construction operations:

$$1/5 \times CT \text{ charged @ } 25\% \times \frac{\text{income from excepted trade}}{\text{total profits charged @ } 25\%} \times \frac{\text{receipts from disposals of RDL} \quad CO \text{ receipts}}{\text{total receipts in course of excepted trade}}$$

Example 3.101.7.1

The following information is relevant to Cashel Ltd for its latest accounting period:

	€
Profit from dealing in development land (as adjusted for tax)	1,200,000
– including profits from construction operations (apportioned on just and reasonable basis)	300,000
Turnover from transactions of dealing in development land	3,500,000

– including turnover from disposals of land to the National Building
Agency   2,000,000
Interest income   150,000

Some construction work had been carried out on the land disposed of to the National
Building Agency Ltd and, of the turnover amount of €2,000,000, €700,000 is attributable to
construction operations.

Corporation tax computation

	€	€
Case I		1,200,000
Case III		150,000
		1,350,000
Corporation tax:		
€300,000 @ 12.5%	37,500	
€1,050,000 @ 25%	262,500	300,000
TCA 1997, s 644B relief		20,893
Tax payable		279,107

TCA 1997, s 644B relief

$$1/5 \times €262,500 \times \frac{900,000}{1,050,000} \times \frac{(2,000,000-700,000)}{2,800,000^1} = €20,893$$

Notes:

[1]   The turnover from disposals in the course of the excepted trade is €2,800,000
(€3,500,000 less the amount attributable to construction operations and therefore
attributable to the part of the trade not treated as an excepted trade).

Capital gains on certain disposals of residential development land

The effective 20% corporation tax rate also applies to capital gains on certain disposals
of residential development land which are treated as income for tax purposes. Where the
income of a company which is chargeable under Case IV of Schedule D by virtue of
TCA 1997, s 643 (see **13.309**) consists of or includes an amount in respect of a gain
obtained from disposing of land which, at the time of its disposal, is residential
development land, the corporation tax payable by the company for the accounting period
in question, in so far as it is referable to that gain, is reduced by one-fifth (TCA 1997,
s 644B(3)(a)).

For this purpose, the corporation tax *referable to a gain from disposing of residential
development land* is a proportion of the corporation tax referable to a gain from the
disposal of land which is treated by virtue of TCA 1997, s 643 as income chargeable
under Case IV of Schedule D. That proportion is so much of the amount of the gain so
treated as income chargeable under Case IV (the "specified amount") as is attributable
to the disposal of residential development land (exclusive of any part of the gain as is
referable to construction operations, within the meaning of TCA 1997, s 644A – see
below) carried out by the company over the specified amount.

The corporation tax referable to a gain from disposing of land which is treated by
virtue of TCA 1997, s 643 as income chargeable under Case IV of Schedule D is in turn
a proportion of the corporation tax charged in accordance with TCA 1997, s 21A (ie, at

the 25% rate) for the period in question, the proportion being the amount of the company's profits consisting of income chargeable under Case IV of Schedule D by virtue of TCA 1997, s 643 over the total amount of the profits of the company for the period charged at 25%.

The relief can accordingly be represented by the following formula, where RDL denotes residential development land and CO refers to any part of the gain as is referable to construction operations:

$$1/5 \times CT \text{ charged} @ 25\% \times \frac{\text{income chargeable Case IV}}{\text{total profits charged} @ 25\%} \times \frac{\text{gain attributable to RDL disposals}}{\text{amount of gain chargeable Case IV}} \quad \frac{CO}{}$$

Construction operations, as defined in TCA 1997, s 644A in relation to residential development land, means operations of any of the descriptions referred to in the definition of "construction operations" in TCA 1997, s 530(1) (see under *Construction* in **7.204.6**) other than such operations as consist of –

(a)   the demolition or dismantling of any building or structure on the land;

(b)   the construction or demolition of any works forming part of the land, being roadworks, water mains, wells, sewers or installations for the purposes of land drainage; or

(c)   any other operations which are preparatory to residential development on the land other than the laying of foundations for such development.

3.102   Profits, income and chargeable gains

3.102.1   Profits

For corporation tax purposes, *profits* means "income and chargeable gains", and *chargeable gain* has the same meaning as it has in the Capital Gains Tax Acts. The word "profits" will often refer to what is, for corporation tax purposes, income. The most obvious example is trading profits. Technically, these profits are part of "income" for corporation tax purposes. "Profits" refers to a company's total income from all sources as well as its chargeable gains. Obviously, a company may have only income for an accounting period so that its total income constitutes its profits for that period. If its income comprises only trading income, that income is also its profits. Conversely, if only chargeable gains arise, those gains will comprise the profits of the company. The Tax Acts sometimes refer to "gains" when in fact what is involved is an item which is part of income. Thus, the charge to tax under Case V of Schedule D is in respect of "profits or gains" from rents (TCA 1997, s 75(1). The reference to "gains" in these contexts has nothing to do with chargeable gains.

3.102.2   Income

Income is not defined for corporation tax purposes generally. Income is computed in accordance with income tax principles. TCA 1997, s 76(1) states:

> Except as otherwise provided by the Tax Acts, the amount of any income shall for the purposes of corporation tax be computed in accordance with income tax principles, all questions as to the amounts which are or are not to be taken into account as income, or in computing income, or charged to tax as a person's income, or as to the time when any such

amount is to be treated as arising, being determined in accordance with income tax law and practice as if accounting periods were years of assessment.

In this context, "income tax law" in relation to any accounting period means the law as it applies to the charge of income tax on individuals for the year of assessment in which the period ends. Accordingly, for corporation tax purposes, income is to be computed under the Schedules and Cases which apply for income tax purposes and in accordance with the provisions applicable to those Schedules and Cases. The amount, or amounts if there is more than one source, computed for income together with any amounts to be included in respect of chargeable gains are aggregated to arrive at "total profits".

In computing income from any source, but subject to any enactment authorising such a deduction, no deduction is to be made for:

(a) dividends or other distributions (TCA 1997, s 76(5)(a));

(b) any yearly interest, annuity or other annual payment (TCA 1997, s 76(5)(b));

(c) payments mentioned in TCA 1997, s 104 (see *Mining and other rents* in **4.301**), being—

    (i) any rent (including a toll, duty, royalty or annual or periodic payment in the nature of rent, whether payable in money or money's worth) payable in respect of any premises or easements which are used, occupied or enjoyed in connection with any of the concerns the profits or gains of which are taxable under Case I(b) of Schedule D (quarries, mines, ironworks, gasworks, canals, waterworks, docks, tolls, railways, bridges, ferries and other concerns of a similar nature), and

    (ii) any yearly interest, annuity or other annual payment reserved in respect of, or charged on, or issuing out of, any premises, not being a rent or payment in respect of an easement,

(d) payments mentioned in TCA 1997, s 237(2) ie any royalty or other sum paid in respect of the user of a patent wholly out of profits or gains brought into charge to tax, but not including any sum which is, or but for any exemption from tax would be, chargeable to tax under Case V of Schedule D.

TCA 1997, s 77(3) overrides the prohibition of a deduction for yearly interest in computing trading income. The prohibition in TCA 1997, s 76(5) is stated to be subject "to section 77 and to any enactment applied by this section which expressly authorises such a deduction". In computing income chargeable under Case V of Schedule D, TCA 1997, s 97(2)(e) and (f) authorises a deduction for interest on borrowed money employed in the purchase, improvement or repair of the premises from which the rent assessable under Case V arises. Neither TCA 1997, s 76 nor TCA 1997, s 77 refers specifically to this enactment by way of overriding the prohibition of a deduction for yearly interest. TCA 1997, s 75 is the main provision applicable to Case V of Schedule D and since TCA 1997, s 76(3) provides that income is to be computed under the Schedules and Cases applying to income tax, and in accordance with the provisions applicable thereto, it can be taken that the express authorisation in TCA 1997, s 97(2)(e) is applied by TCA 1997, s 76.

TCA 1997, s 76(6) provides, "without prejudice to the generality of subsection (1)" (quoted above), that any provision of the Income Tax Acts, or of any other statute, conferring an exemption from income tax, or providing for the disregarding of a loss, or providing for a person to be charged to income tax in respect of any amount (whether expressed to be income or not and whether an actual amount or not), are, except as otherwise provided, to have effect for corporation tax purposes. Thus the income tax provisions dealing with such matters as stallion and greyhound fee exemption (effective up to 31 July 2008 – see TCA 1997 ss 231 and 233), patent income exemption (TCA 1997, s 234(2)), charitable exemption (TCA 1997, s 208), the disallowance for Case I or II purposes of any loss not connected with a trade or profession (TCA 1997, s 81(2)(e)), the disallowance of losses for Case V purposes in cases of favoured lettings (TCA 1997, s 75(4)), and deemed income from certain "cum div" sales of government securities (TCA 1997, s 815), apply also for corporation tax purposes.

Nothing in TCA 1997, s 71 (foreign securities and possessions), however, is to be applied by TCA 1997, s 76 for the purposes of corporation tax purposes. TCA 1997, s 18(1) lists the kinds of income which come within the charge to tax under the various Cases of Schedule D. Those within Case III include the types of income described as "pure income profit" (see *Annual payments* in **4.301**), eg interest, annuities and other annual payments, as well as all discounts, interest from public revenue securities, interest paid without deduction of tax in respect of government securities, and income from foreign securities. In relation to the last mentioned category, TCA 1997, s 71 contains certain provisions dealing with the amount to be included in the charge under Case III but these, as mentioned above, have no application to companies.

Where the income to be included for Case III purposes comprises profits from a foreign trade, the trading income is computed in accordance with the rules applicable to Case I. While most categories of Case III income are "pure income profit" and are therefore taxable on the amount receivable without any deductions, the position is obviously different with a foreign trade which is, technically, a Case III source but in other respects is no different from a trade assessable under Case I. It makes sense therefore that the income from a foreign trade should be computed in the same way as for a Case I trade.

A foreign trade is one which is carried on wholly outside the State. In *Colquhoun v Brooks* 2 TC 490 Lord Macnaghten stated that "there are other provisions which it is not necessary to go through which seem to show that the "first case" (Case I), though clearly applying to a trade carried on partly abroad and partly in Great Britain, was not intended to apply to a trade carried on exclusively abroad". Thus, a company carrying on a trade in Ireland but also through branches in one or more foreign jurisdictions is taxable under Case I on all of its trading profits. Applying the decision in *The San Paulo (Brazilian) Railway Company Ltd v Carter* 3 TC 407, a trade cannot be said to be wholly carried on abroad if it is under the control and management of persons resident in Ireland even if those persons are acting through agents and managers resident abroad. In this connection it was observed by Lord Parker in *The Egyptian Hotels Ltd v Mitchell* 6 TC 542 that "where the brain which controls the operation from which the profits and gains arise is in this country, the trade or business is, at any rate partly, carried on in this country".

Where a company, through its board of directors, exercises a general oversight of a trade carried on abroad, even though the trade is otherwise carried on by locally based managers, that trade would probably be regarded as one which is assessable under Case I (*Ogilvie v Kitton* 5 TC 338). On the other hand, where the board in Ireland takes no part in the actual management or running of the trading operations of a trade carried on abroad, that trade would normally be considered to be a foreign trade. It will be seen that that position would be quite rare.

As to whether a trade is assessable under Case I or Case III may not appear to be very significant since the rules for computing income are the same in each case. However, a company carrying on a Case III trade is treated less favourably where a loss is incurred as such a loss may only be utilised to relieve profits of the same trade in subsequent accounting periods (see **4.105**). In addition, with effect from 1 January 2000, profits from a foreign trade taxable under Case III are subject to the higher (25%) rate of corporation tax (see **3.101.4**).

Enactments which apply, by virtue of TCA 1997, s 76 or otherwise, both to income tax and corporation tax are not affected in their operation by reason of the fact that they are distinct taxes and, so far as is consistent with any provisions relating to corporation tax, those enactments apply as if the two taxes were one tax. In particular, any matter in a case involving two individuals which is relevant to both of them in relation to income tax will in a similar case involving an individual and a company be relevant to the individual in relation to income tax and to the company in relation to corporation tax. Thus, for example, TCA 1997, s 89 provides, *inter alia*, that where trading stock is sold on the discontinuance of a trade to a person carrying on a trade in the State and who is entitled to a deduction against trading profits in respect of the cost of that stock, the value of the trading stock is to be taken to be the amount received on its sale. If the seller is an individual and the buyer a company, the selling price will be brought into the computation of trading profits for income tax purposes in the case of the seller and as a deduction in computing trading profits for corporation tax purposes in the case of the buyer.

TCA 1997, s 77 qualifies the effect of TCA 1997, s 76 in applying income tax law for corporation tax purposes. In relation to a company beginning or ceasing to carry on a trade, or a company beginning or ceasing to be within the charge to corporation tax in respect of a trade, TCA 1997, s 77(2)(a) provides that the company's income is to be computed as if the trade had then commenced or, as the case may be, ceased, whether or not in fact the trade had then commenced or ceased. Accordingly, if a company commences or ceases to carry on a trade which was previously or, as the case may be, will be carried on by some other person, the company's income is to be computed as if the trade had at that point commenced or, as the case may be, ceased. Thus, for example, TCA 1997, s 89, which provides for the valuing of trading stock belonging to a trade on its discontinuance, would apply, by reason of TCA 1997, s 77(2), on the transfer of the trade to another person as if the trade itself had ceased. Again, the provisions dealing with balancing allowances and charges do not operate by reason only of a person ceasing to carry on a trade but may operate on the occasion of the permanent cessation of the trade itself. Accordingly, where a company ceases to carry on a trade which is taken over by another person, the balancing allowances and charges provisions will have effect is if the trade had ceased.

The effect of TCA 1997, s 77(2) is similar to that of TCA 1997, s 69(1), (2) which treat a trade or profession as having commenced or as having been permanently discontinued where there is a change in the persons engaged in carrying it on. The scope of TCA 1997, s 77(2) is somewhat wider as it also deals with the circumstances of a company coming within and ceasing to be within the charge to corporation tax.

The operation of TCA 1997, s 77(2) is subject to any income tax provision which is applied for corporation tax purposes and which provides that a trade is not to be treated as permanently discontinued. TCA 1997, s 303(3) would seem to be an example of such a provision. TCA 1997, s 303 provides that on the permanent discontinuance of a trade in respect of which capital expenditure on dredging has been incurred, a balancing allowance equal to the unallowed capital expenditure on dredging is to be made to the person last carrying on the trade (see **5.603**). TCA 1997, s 303(3) provides that for the purposes of that section a trade is not to be treated as discontinued (as it would be by virtue of TCA 1997, s 69(1)) on a change in the persons engaged in carrying it on.

Where a company has income from foreign securities and possessions, that income is treated as reduced by any sum paid "in respect of income tax in the place where the income has arisen" (TCA 1997, s 77(6)). The wording of this provision is taken from TCA 1997, s 71(1)(b) but the full wording of the income tax provision is inappropriate to the position of companies. The reference to "income tax" here must be to any tax on income. The expression "income tax" is not defined for corporation tax purposes generally. There is a reference to "income tax" in TCA 1997, s 2(3) but this is not a definition of the term. The reduction of foreign source income by reference to foreign tax is made only where such a deduction cannot be made under, and is not forbidden by, any provision of the Income Tax Acts as applied by CTA 1976. So, for example, a deduction is not available where the company could have claimed a credit for foreign tax under the provisions of a double tax treaty. It is specifically provided in TCA 1997 Sch 24 paragraph 7(3) that a deduction for foreign tax is to be made to the extent that a credit for that tax cannot be given.

The charge to tax under Case III of Schedule D in respect of income from foreign securities and possessions is extended to non-resident companies to the extent that those companies are chargeable to tax in respect of income of those descriptions. A non-resident company carrying on a trade through an Irish branch or agency would be subject to corporation tax in respect of income from any foreign securities or possessions which are used by, or held by or for, that branch or agency (TCA 1997, s 25(2)). Any such income is liable to corporation tax as income chargeable under Case III of Schedule D but without prejudice to any income tax provision specifically exempting a non-resident from income tax on any particular description of income, for example, TCA 1997, s 43 which exempts non-residents from income tax in respect of interest from government securities, or TCA 1997, s 49 which exempts non-residents from income tax on interest from certain semi-State and public bodies.

CTA 1976 Second Schedule Part I applied and adapted certain income tax provisions for corporation tax purposes. Its provisions amended provisions of the Income Tax Acts insofar as this was necessary to adapt income tax legislation for corporation tax purposes.

Most of the paragraphs of CTA 1976 Second Schedule Part I make amendments to the Income Acts to incorporate appropriate references to tax credits, distributions, Schedule F, the Corporation Tax Act 1976, the income of a company, accounting periods, chargeable periods, and to definitions of such items as ordinary share capital, material interest, control, connected companies, associate, company, distribution, emoluments and participators. Other paragraphs provide that certain income tax provisions are to apply for corporation tax purposes as they apply for income tax purposes, that references to income tax are to have effect as if they were or included references to corporation tax, that references to a year of assessment are to be read as references to an accounting period, and that references to the Income Tax Acts are to taken as references to the Corporation Tax Acts.

The meaning of "income" so far as provided for in corporation tax legislation has been dealt with in the foregoing paragraphs. The computation of income from a trade (or profession) is governed by long standing rules evolved from case law and accounting principles. Other rules, prohibiting deductions in computing income, are contained in income tax legislation. All of these rules apply for the purposes of computing trading income of any person and are accordingly relevant to companies as well as to any other person carrying on a trade. These rules are outlined in **3.2** below.

3.102.3   Chargeable gains

For corporation tax purposes "profits" means income and chargeable gains and "chargeable gain" has the same meaning as in the Capital Gains Tax Acts. Taxpayers other than companies are liable to capital gains tax in respect of chargeable gains while companies are liable to corporation tax in respect of these gains. TCA 1997, s 21(3) provides that a company "shall not be chargeable to capital gains tax in respect of gains accruing to it so that it is chargeable in respect of them to corporation tax" (ie, is not to be chargeable to capital gains tax in respect of the gains if it is chargeable to corporation tax in respect of them). There is one exception to this. "Chargeable gain" does not include any chargeable gain accruing on "relevant disposals" ie disposals of "development land" within the meaning of TCA 1997, s 648. In respect of any such disposal, a company is within the charge to capital gains tax rather than corporation tax.

It is provided in TCA 1997, s 649(1) that "a company shall not be chargeable to corporation tax in respect of chargeable gains accruing to it on relevant disposals". Accordingly, such gains are not regarded as profits of the company for the purposes of corporation tax but are instead chargeable to capital gains tax. The position of a company in respect of development land gains is the same as for taxpayers generally and the capital gains tax provisions regarding the computation of chargeable gains on disposals of development land, the tax returns required, and the time for payment of the resulting tax, apply to a company as they apply to any other person (see **9.101** regarding the charge to corporation tax on capital gains).

In arriving at the amount of a chargeable gain accruing to a company, the computation is carried out in accordance with the rules contained in the Capital Gains Tax Acts for the purpose of computing chargeable gains for all taxpayers. TCA 1997, s 78(5) provides that, except as otherwise provided by the Corporation Tax Acts, chargeable gains and allowable losses are to be computed for corporation tax purposes in accordance with the principles applying for capital gains tax and that all questions as to the amounts which are or are not to be taken into account as chargeable gains or as allowable losses, or in computing gains or losses, which are to be charged to tax as a person's gain, and all questions as to the time when any such amount is to be treated as accruing being determined in accordance with the provisions relating to capital gains tax as if accounting periods were years of assessment.

Any reference to income tax or to the Income Tax Acts in enactments relating to capital gains tax is, in the case of a company, to be construed as a reference to corporation tax or to the Corporation Tax Acts (subject to certain exceptions – see **9.101**).

The computation of chargeable gains for corporation tax purposes is provided for in TCA 1997, s 78. That section provides that, for a company with chargeable gains, the amount of capital gains tax in respect of those gains is calculated as if the company were liable to capital gains tax and as if accounting periods were years of assessment. TCA 1997, s 31 provides that capital gains tax is to be charged on the total amount of chargeable gains accruing in the year of assessment after deducting any allowable losses accruing in that year and, so far as not already allowed in any previous year, allowable losses accruing in any previous year of assessment, but not for any year prior to 1974/75. For companies, the reference to allowable losses is to be read as referring to "relevant allowable losses", which means any allowable losses accruing to a company in an accounting period and any allowable losses accruing to the company while it was within the charge to corporation tax and so far as not allowed as a deduction from chargeable gains accruing in any previous accounting period.

While chargeable gains of a company are computed for the accounting periods in which the gains arose, the year of assessment in which any gain arises must be taken into account. Except at a time when the rates of capital gains tax and corporation tax are the same, it is necessary to ascertain the amount of capital gains tax which would have been payable by the company had that tax applied in order to compute the amount of the chargeable gain to be included in profits. The capital gains tax amount is arrived at by applying the capital gains tax rate in force for the year of assessment in which the chargeable gain arose. Furthermore, it is necessary to identify the years of assessment in which the gain arose and in which the asset disposed of was acquired for the purpose of applying the appropriate multiplier in calculating the indexed cost.

Having ascertained the amount of capital gains tax which *would* be payable (if capital gains tax applied), the amount to be included in the profits of the company for the accounting period as chargeable gains is the amount which if charged at the standard rate of corporation tax would produce an amount equal to the amount of capital gains tax.

The application by TCA 1997, s 78 of capital gains tax rules for corporation tax purposes is not affected in its operation by reason of the fact that capital gains tax and corporation tax are distinct taxes. Capital gains tax rules, so far as consistent with any enactments relating to corporation tax, apply as if the two taxes were one tax. In particular, any matter in a case involving two individuals which is relevant to both of them in relation to capital gains tax will in a similar case involving an individual and a company be relevant to the individual in relation to income tax and to the company in relation to corporation tax. For example, in the case of an acquisition of an asset by a company from an individual who is connected with the company, for the purposes of corporation tax on chargeable gains the acquisition will be deemed to be for a consideration equal to the market value of the asset, while for the purposes of capital gains tax the disposal will also be deemed to be for a consideration equal to that market value.

CTA 1976 Second Schedule Part II applied and adapted capital gains tax provisions for corporation tax purposes in the same way as CTA 1976 Second Schedule Part I did in relation to income tax provisions. Its paragraphs implemented the changes necessary to adapt capital gains tax legislation for corporation tax purposes. The general application of capital gains tax provisions for the purpose of computing chargeable gains is contained in TCA 1997, s 78.

CTA 1976 Second Schedule Part II also provided that certain capital gains tax provisions are to apply for corporation tax purposes as they apply for capital gains tax purposes. It also amended CGTA Sch 1 paragraph 3(3)(a) (now TCA 1997, s 552(3)(a)) which provides for the allowability in certain circumstances of interest charged to capital by a company. The effect of this provision is that the sums allowable under TCA 1997, s 552(1) for the purposes of computing a chargeable gain or allowable loss include, in the case of a company, the amount of interest charged to capital other than the amount of such interest which has been taken into account for the purposes of relief under the Income Tax Acts or could have been so taken into account but for an insufficiency of income, profits or gains (see **9.101**). TCA 1997, s 552(3)(a) is relevant for the purposes of capital gains tax on disposals by companies of development land; as regards corporation tax on chargeable gains, there is a corresponding provision in TCA 1997, s 553 (see **9.102.17**).

3.103   Trading

3.103.1   Introduction

For many reasons, it is often important to know whether or not a company is carrying on a trade. Where a trade is not being carried on, the ability to deduct expenses for tax purposes is relatively limited. There is wider scope for claiming deductions in respect of such items as wages and salaries, interest, foreign exchange losses, professional fees and capital allowances in connection with a trade.

The scope for using losses and charges on income is widest where incurred in trading operations (subject to the restrictions pertaining to manufacturing trades). For the purposes of manufacturing relief for International Financial Services Centre operations, it will always be essential that the operations be seen to amount to the carrying on of a trade. The question as to whether a partnership exists may turn on whether a trade is being carried on.

Trade is defined in TCA 1997, s 3(1) as including "every trade, manufacture, adventure or concern in the nature of trade". This does not help greatly as Lord Denning in *Griffith v JP Harrison (Watford) Ltd* 40 TC 281 would agree where he said that a trade and an adventure in the nature of trade are things which are well enough understood in most situations but which most people would be hard pressed to define.

As normally understood, trading means the carrying on of business or the engaging in activities on a regular or habitual basis and normally with a view to realising a profit. The manufacture and sale of goods and the buying and selling of goods will invariably constitute the carrying on of a trade. The provision of services for reward in the form of fees or commission will also amount to the carrying on of a trade unless the activity is regarded as a profession.

Activities may however be carried on, even resulting in profits or losses, which fall short of being regarded as a trade and which will therefore not be charged to tax under Case I of Schedule D. The gains or losses may be capital in nature and therefore subject to capital gains tax treatment. Non capital profits or gains may be considered to arise from an activity which does not amount to a trade, in which case they are likely to be assessable under Case IV of Schedule D.

In certain circumstances, investment income may be regarded as arising from the carrying on of a trade (see **3.207.2**).

In the case of IFSC companies, activities from dealing in certain "securitised" assets are treated as trading activities. Similar activities engaged in by companies other than IFSC companies are treated as annual profits or gains taxable under Case III but those profits or gains are computed in accordance with the provisions applicable to Case I (TCA 1997, s 110(2)(b) – see **7.206.11**).

3.103.2   The "badges of trade"

Not surprisingly, the question of what constitutes a trade has been examined by the courts over the years. In the UK in 1995, the Royal Commission on the Taxation of Profits and Income identified "badges of trade", factors which case law up to then had suggested would have an important bearing on the question whether a trade or an adventure in the nature of trade was in question. These were as follows:

Subject matter realised: was the item which was the subject of the transaction or transactions a type of object, product, commodity etc which is normally the subject of a trading transaction as distinct from one more usually acquired as an investment?

Length of period of ownership: in that trading involving the sale of goods normally means holding the goods for a relatively short time, are the items in question sold shortly after their acquisition or are they held for a longer period as would normally be the case with an investment?

Frequency and number of transactions: in that trading normally involves habitual activity, are the transactions numerous and carried out regularly?

Supplementary work on or in connection with the property realised: has the person making the sale or sales carried on any work on the goods sold, whether as full processing or as repairs or otherwise making the goods more readily saleable? Has he in an organised or commercial way taken steps to find buyers, to advertise the goods etc?

Circumstances giving rise to the realisation of the property: were there any special circumstances dictating or requiring the sale which might negate the concept of trading? For example, in the case of property which might otherwise be held as an investment, was a sale after a short period of ownership occasioned by, say, a decision to emigrate on an outbreak of civil disturbance?

Motive: was the object of the transaction or transactions to deal in the property sold as distinct from holding it as an investment?

Obviously, the badges of trade cannot produce conclusive answers in every situation. Common sense will play a large part in most cases. The badges provide guidelines as to how the question as to whether a trade exists may be best approached. Some of the badges may not be relevant in a particular case. The indications provided by one badge may appear to contradict those given by another. Taking the indications given by all of the badges together will often be indicative of the presence or otherwise of a trade.

3.103.3   Dealing or investment

The courts have considered many cases in which the question was whether a particular activity involved dealing (trading) or the mere holding of investments. The holding of investments over a period of years during which income is derived from those investments is unlikely to constitute dealing. Profits or losses arising from the realisation of the investments are likely to be capital profits or losses, subject to capital gains tax treatment. An important consideration is whether the transactions in question are part of "an operation of business in carrying out a scheme for profit making" (*Californian*

Copper Syndicate v Harris 5 TC 159). In the case of *Lewis Emanuel & Son Ltd v White* 42 TC 369, a fruit and vegetable importing company was held also to be carrying on a trade of dealing in securities. The fact that the taxpayer was a company was influential in the decision; a company is more likely to possess a commercial organisation and the apparatus of a profit making concern.

As to whether a trade is being carried on is a mixed question of fact and law; it is a matter of law as to what "trade" means but the answer in any particular case will depend on the facts of that case. In *Edwards v Bairstow and Harrison* 36 TC 207 two individuals, a director of a leather manufacturing company and an employee of a spinning firm, purchased a cotton spinning plant intending to dispose of it quickly at a profit. Although hoping to dispose of the plant in one lot, they were forced to dispose of it in five separate lots over a fifteen month period. Despite the finding of the Appeal Commissioners that the transaction was not an adventure in the nature of trade, and the decisions in the High Court and Court of Appeal that the finding of fact by the Commissioners could not be upset, the House of Lords held that on the evidence before the Commissioners and the legal meaning of "trade", the only reasonable conclusion was that the transaction was an adventure in the nature of trade.

3.103.4   Single transaction

It is often considered that a single transaction cannot amount to the existence of a trade; one of the badges of trade is the frequency and number of transactions, and a trade normally involves habitual activity. No single factor is, however, likely to be conclusive in any case. In most cases, a single transaction will not amount to a trade but this is not always true as was seen in the *Edwards v Bairstow and Harrison* case. In *Wisdom v Chamberlain* 45 TC 103, the entertainer Norman Wisdom realised a profit of £48,000 on the purchase and sale of silver within one year. The Chancery Division held that as the silver had been purchased, using borrowed money, as a hedge against a devaluation of sterling, the transaction was not a trading one. The Court of Appeal reached the opposite conclusion holding that, even though the purchase of the silver was a hedge, it was effected with the intention of making a profit which indicated clearly that the transaction was an adventure in the nature of trade.

3.103.5   Profit motive

One of the badges of trade is the presence of a profit motive but, again, the absence of a profit motive does not necessarily lead to the conclusion that a trade is not being carried on. In *IRC v The Incorporated Council of Law Reporting* 2 TC 105, it was held that it is not necessary to the carrying on of a trade that the people carrying it on should desire or wish to make a profit, although it will almost always be the case that a trade will involve the idea of a profit.

A person cannot be engaged in the carrying on of a trade or an adventure in the nature of trade unless in a reasonable sense he is conducting business on commercial principles (*British Legion, Peterhead Branch v IRC* 35 TC 509). If conducting business on commercial principles, it does not matter from what motive the person is acting or to what purpose the profits made are devoted.

In *IRC v Old Bushmills Distillery Co Ltd* 12 TC 1148, the selling off of stocks of whiskey over a period after the liquidator had ceased to trade was held not to be trading. The selling off of the stocks was the only practical way of realising the assets.

3.103.6 Case I

Trading profits are charged to tax under Case I of Schedule D. TCA 1997, s 18(2), (3) provide for the charge to tax under the various Cases of Schedule D and, as respects Case I, charges tax in respect of:

(a)   any trade;

(b)   profits or gains arising out of any lands, tenements and hereditaments in the case of any of the following concerns:

   (i)   quarries of stone, slate, limestone or chalk, or quarries or pits of sand, gravel or clay;

   (ii)   mines of coal, tin, lead, copper, pyrites, iron and other mines;

   (iii) ironworks, gasworks, salt springs or works, alum mines or works, waterworks or streams of water, canals, inland navigations, docks, drains, tolls, railways and other ways, bridges, ferries and other concerns of the like nature having profits from or arising out of any lands, tenements or hereditaments.

3.103.7 Illegal trades

The Irish courts have found that the profits of a wholly illegal trade or business cannot be assessed to tax. In *Hayes v Duggan* 1 ITR 195, which involved the promotion of lotteries, an illegal activity, it was held that the profits from a lawful trade some of which were derived from illegal methods were assessable but that the profits from a wholly illegal transaction or trade were not assessable. This conclusion followed in *Collins v Mulvey* 2 ITR 291 where the business in question was the setting up of automatic slot machines, an activity which constituted a criminal offence under the law. The decision was, however, rejected in the UK case *Mann v Nash* 16 TC 523 where it was held that the fact that a trade was illegal did not prevent it from being assessed to tax.

The effect of *Hayes v Duggan* and *Collins v Mulvey* was neutralised by TCA 1997, s 58 which provides that the profits of any trade consisting of or involving illegal activities may be assessed under Case IV of Schedule D.

3.103.8 Expenditure involving crime

By way of response to an OECD recommendation to prohibit a tax deduction in respect of illegal payments made to a foreign official, TCA 1997, s 83A denies a tax deduction in computing the amount of any income chargeable to tax under Schedule D for any payment the making of which constitutes a criminal offence or, in the case of a payment made outside the State, where the payment, if made in the State, would constitute a criminal offence. The prohibition applies to companies as respects accounting periods ending on or after 31 January 2008.

In computing any income chargeable to tax under Schedule D, no deduction may be made for any expenditure incurred—

(a)   in making a payment the making of which constitutes the commission of a criminal offence, or

(b) in making a payment outside of the State where the making of a corresponding payment in the State would constitute a criminal offence (TCA 1997, s 83A(1)).

No such expenditure may be included in computing any expenses of management (see **12.603.3** and **12.703**) in respect of which relief may be given under the Tax Acts (TCA 1997, s 83A(2)).

3.104 Capital allowances and related charges

In computing trading profits for tax purposes, or other income such as income from letting property, no deduction may be made in respect of capital expenditure, whether in respect of the cost of capital assets purchased or by way of depreciation. Instead, deductions in the form of capital allowances as prescribed by the Tax Acts may be made. There are two broad categories of assets in respect of which capital allowances may be claimed, plant and machinery (including equipment, fixtures and fittings) and industrial buildings.

The rules pertaining to capital allowances and related charges (balancing charges) are contained in TCA 1997 Part 9 (ss 268-321). TCA 1997, s 321(2)-(7) are interpretational provisions relating to that Part and to certain other capital allowances provisions of TCA 1997. The subject of capital allowances is dealt with in more detail in Chapter **5**.

TCA 1997, s 307(2)(a) provides that capital allowances and balancing charges which fall to be made for any accounting period in taxing a trade are to be given effect by treating any such allowance or charge as a trading expense or trading receipt in that period. Accordingly, the concept of excess capital allowances does not feature in corporation tax. Where capital allowances for an accounting period exceed the tax adjusted profits against which they are to be deducted as a trading expense, the excess is treated as a trading loss for that period. In that respect, capital allowances are, generally, treated no differently to any other deductible expense; an exception would be the case of "specified capital allowances" in the case of a leasing trade (TCA 1997, s 403).

TCA 1997, s 307(1) provides that in computing a company's profits for any accounting period, "there shall be made" all such deductions and additions as are required to give effect to the provisions of the Tax Acts which relate to allowances (including investment allowances) and charges in respect of capital expenditure. As is explained in **5.101**, the reference to "shall be made" is not mandatory in relation to allowances but is merely directive in that it requires the relevant allowances to be made on due claim by the company concerned.

3.105 Accounting periods

TCA 1997, s 27(1) provides that, "except as otherwise provided by the Corporation Tax Acts, corporation tax shall be assessed and charged for any accounting period of a company on the full amount of the profits arising in the period (whether or not received in or remitted to the State) without any other deduction than is authorised by this Act". The reference to "except as otherwise provided by this Act" is to allow for situations in which corporation tax is not charged on a company's full profits, for example, in the case of a charitable company or a credit union, or where only the profits of an Irish branch or agency of a non-resident company are chargeable profits for corporation tax purposes.

Assessments to corporation tax are made by reference to accounting periods and profits arising in an accounting period are, where necessary, apportioned between the financial years in which the accounting period falls.

In practice, an accounting period of a company will usually be the period for which it makes up its accounts. For obvious reasons, that cannot be the position in all cases. The corporation tax system would become inoperable if it were possible for a company to delay making returns and paying tax merely by extending indefinitely the period for which accounts were made up. Consequently, corporation tax legislation does not permit accounting periods of more than twelve months. It is also necessary to have other rules fixing the starting and ending dates of accounting periods so as to prevent manipulation of accounting periods which could result in profits being taxed at an incorrect rate, or losses being allowed in unintended ways. These rules are contained in TCA 1997, s 27(2). An accounting period of a company begins whenever:

(a) the company, not then being within the charge to corporation tax, comes within it whether by reason of the coming into force of any provision of the Corporation Tax Acts, or by the company becoming resident in the State or acquiring a source of income, or otherwise; or

(b) an accounting period of the company ends without the company then ceasing to be within the charge to corporation tax.

If a chargeable gain or allowable loss accrues to a company at a time which is not otherwise within an accounting period of the company, an accounting period begins at that time and the chargeable gain or allowable loss is regarded as accruing in that accounting period. If the company has unused allowable capital gains tax losses which accrued before 6 April 1976 (ie, for the years 1974/75 or 1975/76), they may be allowed for corporation tax purposes as if they accrued to the company while within the charge to corporation tax (TCA 1997 Sch 32 paragraph 19).

An accounting period of a company ends on the first occurrence of any of the following:

(a) the expiration of twelve months from the beginning of the accounting period;

(b) an accounting date of the company (see below);

(c) the end of any period for which a company does not make up accounts;

(d) the company beginning or ceasing to trade;

(e) the company beginning or ceasing to be within the charge to corporation tax in respect of a trade carried on by it or (if there is more than one trade) in respect of all the trades carried on by it;

(f) the company beginning or ceasing to be resident in the State;

(g) the company ceasing to be within the charge to corporation tax.

An "accounting date" of a company is the date to which the company makes up its accounts (TCA 1997, s 4(1)). The expression "makes up its accounts" refers to the accounts on which the auditors have formally reported in accordance with the Companies Acts and which are laid before the company in general meeting. Interim or management accounts for the information of the directors, even if audited, are not accounts which have been "made up" (*Jenkins Productions Ltd v CIR* 29 TC 142).

TCA 1997, s 27 provides some further guidelines for particular situations.

In the unusual circumstances in which a company carrying on more than one trade makes up accounts for those trades to different dates, without having a general accounting date, the Revenue Commissioners have discretion to determine which of the accounting dates is to be treated as the end of the accounting period.

As regards (d) above, it will occasionally be the case that a company carrying on a trade will begin to carry on another trade. That should not be the occasion of the end of an accounting period; beginning to trade is not the same as beginning to carry on a trade. Likewise, ceasing to carry on one of a number of trades will not trigger the end of an accounting period.

The situations envisaged in (e) above would include a non-resident company that is within the charge to tax by virtue of its carrying on one or more trades in Ireland. Where the company is carrying on more than one trade, an accounting period will end where it ceases to carry on all of the trades, but not where it ceases to carry on one of its trades or to carry on only some of them. It would seem that the reference to "beginning" to be within the charge to corporation tax in respect of a trade or "of all the trades carried on by it" is inappropriate in the case of a non-resident company. Since the company would not previously have been within the charge to corporation tax, that event would trigger the commencement, but not the end, of an accounting period.

The commencement of the winding up of a company is the end of an accounting period of the company and the beginning of a new one. Thereafter, an accounting period ends only on the expiration of twelve months from its beginning or on the completion of the winding up. The winding up of a company for this purpose is deemed to commence on the passing by the company of a resolution for its winding up or on the presentation of a winding up petition if no such resolution has previously been passed and a winding up order is made on the petition. A winding up also commences "on the doing of any other act for a like purpose" in the case of a winding up otherwise than under the Companies Act 1963 (TCA 1997, s 27(7)).

There may still be circumstances in which the beginning or end of an accounting period is uncertain. An inspector may be uncertain because of the absence of returns or other information. In those cases, the inspector may make an assessment for such period, which must not exceed twelve months, "as appears to him or her appropriate" (TCA 1997, s 27(8)). That period will then be treated for all purposes as an accounting period of the company unless subsequent events show that some other period should be the accounting period. This might happen as a result of the inspector becoming aware of further information which makes it appropriate to revise the accounting period, or as a result of the company on appeal against an assessment in respect of some other matter discloses the true accounting periods. In the latter case, the assessment which has been made is to have effect as an assessment or assessments for the true accounting period or periods. Other assessments may then be made for any such periods as would have been made at the time when the appealed assessment was made.

The foregoing rules do not clearly assist in identifying an accounting period of a company which has no source of income and no function but to receive and pay dividends. For such a company, typically a holding company, it might be necessary to know in what accounting period it received certain dividends, for example, in order to calculate the amount of an exempt distribution. The company may never come within the charge to corporation tax and, if so, it could not have an accounting period beginning by reason of another accounting period ending since no other such period could have begun.

A resident company which is not otherwise within the charge to corporation tax is, however, deemed by TCA 1997, s 27(4) to come within it at the time when it "commences to carry on business". It could therefore perhaps be regarded as coming within the charge to corporation tax on the basis that its function as a holding company constitutes the carrying on of a "business". Although the company is not actually brought within the charge to corporation tax by being a holding company, it could be deemed by TCA 1997, s 27(4) as coming within the charge on its commencing to carry on the "business" of a holding company. The concept of a company carrying on the "business" of a pure holding company would be consistent with, say, the reference in TCA 1997, s 247(2)(a)(ii) to a company whose *business* consists wholly or mainly or the holding of stocks, shares or securities. Accordingly, an accounting period of a pure holding company may begin on the date when it commences to act as a holding company, probably when it acquires its first subsidiary company or companies.

Apportionment

As noted above, profits arising in an accounting period are, where necessary, apportioned between the financial years in which the accounting period falls. This is provided for in TCA 1997, s 26(3). The question of apportioning profits will also arise in cases where a single period of account is split into two or more accounting periods. In either case, the apportionment will be carried out on a time basis. TCA 1997, s 4(6) provides that, except where otherwise provided by the Corporation Tax Acts, any apportionment to different periods is to be made on a time basis according to the respective lengths of those periods. One instance of "except where otherwise provided" might be TCA 1997, s 107(2) but, as will be seen below, the basis provided for in that subsection also, in effect, requires apportionment on a time basis according to the respective lengths of the periods in question.

As regards any profits or gains chargeable under Case I, II or IV of Schedule D, TCA 1997, s 107(1) provides that where it is necessary, to determine the profits or gains or losses of any period, to divide and apportion to specific periods the profits or gains or losses for any period for which accounts have been made up, or to aggregate any such profits or gains or losses or any apportioned parts of such profits or gains or losses, it is lawful to make such division and apportionment or aggregation (TCA 1997, s 107(1)). Any apportionment is then made in proportion to the number of months or fractions of months in the respective periods (TCA 1997, s 107(2)).

It is to be noted that TCA 1997, s 107, providing for apportionment on a time basis and which would be relevant for apportioning profits of a long period of account to accounting periods, does not extend to profits chargeable under Case III or Case V or to chargeable gains. (For chargeable gains, see **9.101**.) For profits assessable under Case III or Case V, it would seldom if ever be necessary to resort to apportionment to determine the respective amounts to be included in accounting periods or financial years. TCA 1997, s 26(3), however, which deals with apportionment to financial years for corporation tax purposes, provides for apportionment of profits generally.

It will also be noted that for the purposes of both TCA 1997, ss 26(3) and 107(1), apportionment is to apply only where it is "necessary". Where, for example, it is possible to ascertain the profits of two or more accounting periods by reference to the company's business records, which is likely to be the case where only a small number of transactions are involved, apportionment will not be necessary (*Marshall Hus & Partners Ltd v Bolton* [1981] STC 18).

The general corporation tax basis for apportionment on a time basis is TCA 1997, s 4(6) mentioned above. This provision would appear to apply regardless of what is included in the total profits of a company. Thus, where the company has Case III income for a period of account in excess of 12 months, it would be appropriate to time apportion the amount received in the period of account to the accounting periods concerned, rather than to allocate the amounts received in each accounting period. A similar approach would apply in respect of chargeable gains.

3.106 Residence of companies

3.106.1 Significance of a company tax residence

Residence is a material factor for companies in determining tax liability and for the purpose of applying many provisions of tax legislation. The most important consequence for most companies of being resident in the State is that they are subject to corporation tax in respect of their worldwide profits and not merely in respect of Irish source profits. Tax residence for companies is also of importance for other reasons, including the following:

  (a)   distributions from Irish resident companies are subject to income tax under Schedule F;
  (b)   distributions from Irish resident companies are not, generally, subject to corporation tax nor are such distributions taken into account in computing income for corporation tax;
  (c)   only Irish resident companies may claim patent income exemption;
  (d)   residence is the primary requirement for tax treaty benefits;
  (e)   only a resident company can be a close company.

3.106.2 Meaning of tax residence for companies

Central management and control: case law

Subject to TCA 1997, s 23A, which, with effect from 11 February 1999, generally treats companies incorporated in the State as resident in the State (see below), there is no statutory definition of "residence" for companies apart from that in TCA 1997, s 234 which applies for the purposes of patent income exemption. That section provides that a company is to be regarded as a resident of the State if it is managed and controlled in the State. As will be seen, that definition accords with the meaning of residence as laid down in case law.

The earliest case that dealt with the question of company tax residence is *Calcutta Jute Mills Co Ltd v Nicholson* 1 TC 83 which established that residence is a concept appropriate to a company and that it is located where a company's centre of control is. The same decision was reached in *Cesena Sulphur Co Ltd v Nicholson* 1 TC 88.

The most important case is *de Beers Consolidated Mines v Howe* 5 TC 198 in which it was found that a company's residence is where its real business is carried on and that that was where the central management and control actually abides. The "central management and control" test was endorsed in *Bullock v Unit Construction Co Ltd* 38

TC 712. That case is of importance in emphasising the point that central management and control is a question of fact and that central management and control is not necessarily located where it appears to be located, for example, where the board of directors holds its meetings.

The exercise of management and control does not necessarily require any minimum level of active involvement in the affairs of a company and can often be exercised tacitly.

The concept of central management and control is directed at the highest level of control of the business of a company and is not in itself determined by reference to the place where the main operations of the business are found. In *Union Corporation Ltd v IRC* 34 TC 269, a company incorporated and having its registered office in South Africa carried out its business operations partly in South Africa and partly in London. Most of the company's staff and some of the directors lived in South Africa. The South African directors had power of attorney which empowered them in wide terms to manage and control the company's business in South Africa. The majority of the directors, however, resided in London and they exercised ultimate control over the company's activities and general policy. It was found that "the supremacy" rested with the board in London and the company was held to be resident in the UK.

Management and control is entirely one of fact and the factors that together are decisive one case may not be conclusive in another case. The place where the directors of the company meet is usually indicative of where central management and control is exercised and consequently where the company is resident. This is because central management and control is in most cases actually exercised through the medium of directors' meetings.

The place where the directors meet is not, however, necessarily conclusive of where management and control is exercised. Where *de facto* management and control is found to be effected otherwise than through the medium of directors' meetings, it will be necessary to look to other tests. It may sometimes happen that the board of directors, although apparently exercising management and control by way of conducting board meetings and passing resolutions, are doing no more than carrying out the instructions of, and implementing policy formulated by, others. If the functions of the board are usurped by a parent company board in a different country (the issue in the *Unit Construction* case), management and control and therefore residence will be located in that other country.

It need not be assumed, however, where the board of directors of a company takes account of the wishes of its parent company board in another country, or takes advice or directions from that board, that it cannot be seen as exercising management and control. It would probably be quite unusual and unreasonable to expect a subsidiary company board to act totally independently of and without regard to the wishes and policies of its parent company. Shareholder control is a fact of life and cannot be ignored by the directors. The fact that the directors of a company may be appointed and removed by the parent company does not of itself indicate that they cannot carry out their proper function as directors and exercise real management and control.

That parent company management and control need not so easily be conceded is illustrated by the decision in *Untelrab Ltd v McGregor (and related appeals)* 1996 SSCD 1. The directors of two Channel Islands incorporated subsidiaries of Unigate plc resided in Bermuda and the Channel Islands respectively, and held board meetings and took operational decisions in those jurisdictions. The subsidiaries took advice from the parent company in London but no major decisions were taken from there. Many major decisions of the subsidiaries' directors were, however, made on the basis of "instructions" received from London. Resolutions were drafted in London and the subsidiary boards appeared to do what they were told to do. The Special Commissioners pointed out that it is customary for a parent company to operate through the boards of its subsidiary companies and that it would be exceptional for a parent to usurp control from its subsidiaries. Doing what it is told to do does not mean that a subsidiary board cannot exercise real management and control as long as it exercises discretion in coming to its decisions and would refuse to carry out any improper or unwise transactions. Although complaisant to the will of its parent company, each subsidiary did actually undertake its own decisions and was resident where the board meetings took place.

The result in the *Untelrab* case was a Special Commissioners' decision but was accepted by the Inland Revenue and was not taken further. The case involved a public company at parent level. As to whether a similar result would have emerged in a private or family company situation, where the policy making function would be likely to be much more concentrated, cannot be taken for granted.

Endorsement for the *Untelrab* decision comes by way of the Chancery Division judgment in *Wood & anor v Holden* [2005] STC 789 where, again, a distinction was made between cases in which a local board of directors has regard to the wishes of its parent company directors but would not have acted on those wishes if they were unlawful or wrong, and where a local board simply carries out the wishes or instructions of its parent company without any consideration or other input. In this connection, the reputation and standing of the local directors is likely to be a relevant factor. Also of value from this judgment is the observation that, where a company incorporated in a jurisdiction other than that of its parent holds infrequent and short board meetings there because it has little or no activity (such as is often the case with, say, a pure holding company), that is not an indication that central management and control is likely to be situated in the jurisdiction of the parent company. If little activity is called for, the fact that there is little activity is not significant and what is relevant is where that little activity takes place. The decision of the Chancery Division was upheld in the High Court and the Court of Appeal.

The case of *Egyptian Delta Land & Investment Co Ltd v Todd* 14 TC 138 concerned a company incorporated and with registered offices in England which derived its income from property in Egypt. The directors and shareholders of the company had their meetings in Egypt, dividends were declared in Egypt and the share registers were kept there. The filing of statutory returns, the keeping of the register of members and directors and related matters took place in England. On the basis that Egypt was the place where the directors exercised their control, the House of Lords held that that was where the company resided.

As residence is dependent on where management and control is exercised, and since that is a question of fact, it is quite possible for a company to be resident in two jurisdictions. That would be true where central management and control is divided, a very rare situation but one which occurred in *The Swedish Central Railway Co Ltd v Thompson* 9 TC 342. Furthermore, since residence may now also be determined by reference to the place of incorporation (see below), a company can also for that reason be resident in more than one jurisdiction.

Management and control of a company's business, in all but the simplest cases, goes beyond the day to day carrying out of that company's normal business transactions. Management and control is directed at the highest level of control and involves such matters as the formulation of company policy, how the company deals with such matters as financing and capital structure, where it invests surplus funds, whether it should acquire other businesses or dispose of some of its businesses, whether it should penetrate new markets and whether it should be involved with new products and services. The question of management and control will embrace these factors insofar as they are present in any case.

Questions to be addressed in connection with the determination of company tax residence in any case might include the following:

(a)   Who are the present directors, distinguishing the chairman, and where do they, or a majority of them, reside?

(b)   Where are the directors' meetings held?

(c)   Where are the questions of important company policy determined?

(d)   Where are major contracts negotiated or agreements concluded?

(e)   Where are the company seal, minute books, share register and other books of the company kept?

(f)   Where are accounts made up?

(g)   Where are the accounts audited?

(h)   Where are the bank accounts of the company kept?

(i)   Have the directors delegated any of their powers?

(j)   Where are the shareholders' meetings, general and extraordinary, held?

(k)   Where is the company's head office located?

It will be readily apparent that some of the questions listed above carry greater weight than others. Of itself, the place where a company's bank accounts are kept is unlikely to be significant, whereas the place at which the questions of important company policy are decided is likely to be crucial. In the end, the residence of a company will be decided when all relevant factors taken together are taken into account.

Place of incorporation: statutory position

TCA 1997, s 23A was enacted to bring certain Irish registered, but hitherto non-Irish resident, companies within the ambit of the corporation tax system by deeming them to be tax resident in Ireland. A company which is incorporated in the State is, generally, treated as resident in the State for tax purposes.

This position does not apply where the company in question or a related company carries on a trade in the State and either the company is ultimately controlled by persons resident in the EU or in a tax treaty country or the company or a related company is a quoted company. Furthermore, a company which is regarded by virtue of a tax treaty as resident in a territory other than the State and not resident in the State is treated for the purposes of TCA 1997, s 23A also as being not resident in the State.

TCA 1997, s 23A applies from 11 February 1999 to companies incorporated on or after that date and, as respects companies which were incorporated before 11 February 1999, with effect from 1 October 1999.

Subject to TCA 1997, s 23A(3) and (4), a company which is incorporated in the State is to be regarded for the purposes of the Tax Acts and the Capital Gains Tax Acts as resident in the State (TCA 1997, s 23A(2)). A company incorporated in the State will not be so regarded, however, if it is a "relevant company" and it either carries on a trade in the State or it is "related to" a company which carries on a trade in the State (TCA 1997, s 23A(3)). A company which is regarded, for the purposes of a tax treaty to which Ireland is a party, as resident in a territory other than the State and not resident in the State is to be treated as not resident in the State (TCA 1997, s 23A(4)). With regard to TCA 1997, s 23A(4), most tax treaties to which Ireland is a party provide a "tie-breaker" clause within the Residence article whereby the residence of a company is to be treated as situated where its "place of effective management" (see below) is situated.

A *relevant company* is a company:

(i)   which is under the control, directly or indirectly, of a person or persons—

    (I)   who is or are resident for tax purposes, by virtue of the law of any relevant territory, in a relevant territory or territories; and

    (II)   who is or are not under the control, directly or indirectly, of a person who is, or persons who are, not so resident; or

(ii)   which is, or is related to, a company the principal class of the shares of which is substantially and regularly traded on one or more than one recognised stock exchange in a relevant territory or territories.

A *relevant territory* is a Member State of the European Union or, not being such a Member State, a territory with which Ireland has a tax treaty. Tax in (i)(I) above means tax imposed in the relevant territory or territories and which corresponds to income tax or corporation tax.

A company is treated as *related to* another company if one company is a 50% subsidiary of the other company or both companies are 50% subsidiaries of a third company. A company is a *50% subsidiary* of another company if and so long as not less than 50% of its ordinary share capital is owned directly or indirectly by that other company. TCA 1997, s 23A(1)(b)(i)(II) in fact defines "50% subsidiary" by applying the definition of "75% subsidiary" in TCA 1997, s 9 (see **2.503**) and by substituting "50%" for the references to "75%" in that definition. This enables the definition of "50% subsidiary" to be subject to the detailed rules for determining the amount of capital held in a company through other companies (see **2.505**).

For the purposes of the definition of "50% subsidiary", the equity entitlement provisions of TCA 1997 ss 412-418 (see **8.304**) are to apply but with references to "50%" being substituted for references to "75%" where appropriate, and as if TCA 1997, s 411(1)(c) were deleted ((ie, ignoring requirements relating to EU residence and to shares held as "trading stock" – see **8.302.2-302.3**)).

In the definition of "relevant company" above, control is to be construed in accordance with TCA 1997, s 432(2)-(6) as if in TCA 1997, s 432(6) (see **2.401.4**) "five or fewer participators" were substituted by:

(a)   as regards "control" in (i)(I), "persons who, by virtue of the law of any relevant territory ... are resident for the purposes of tax in a relevant territory or relevant territories" (see Example 3.106.2.3 below); and

(b)   as regards "control" in (i)(II), "persons not resident for the purposes of tax in a relevant territory ..." (TCA 1997, s 23A(1)(b)(ii)).

Example 3.106.2.1

Ebbing Ltd is incorporated in Ireland but is managed and controlled in Guernsey and is wholly owned by Thurston Ltd, a UK company whose shareholders are all resident in the UK.

Ebbing Ltd is a relevant company as it is under the control of a person who is tax resident in a relevant territory, the UK, and because that person, Thurston Ltd, is not under the control of a person or persons not resident in a relevant territory.

Ebbing Ltd will not be regarded as tax resident in Ireland by virtue of TCA 1997, s 23A if it, or a company to which it is related, carries on a trade in Ireland.

The relevance of the meaning of "control" (i)(II) above is illustrated in the following example.

Example 3.106.2.2

Ebbing Ltd is incorporated in Ireland but is managed and controlled in Guernsey and is wholly owned by Thurston Ltd, a UK company wholly owned by an Indian company whose shareholders are all resident in India.

Ebbing Ltd is not a relevant company because, although it is under the control of a person who is tax resident in a relevant territory, that person, Thurston Ltd, is under the control of persons not resident in a relevant territory.

The wide meaning of "control" as defined in TCA 1997, s 432 can have unexpected consequences, as is seen in the following example.

Example 3.106.2.3

Tinsley Ltd, a company incorporated in Ireland but managed and controlled in the Isle of Man, is owned as follows:

	%
Alex Tolstoy	13
Tanya Tolstoy	13
Olivia Stroessner	13
George Stroessner	13
6 unrelated individuals owning 8% each	48
	100

Alex and Tanya Tolstoy are resident in Belarus and Olivia and George Stroessner are resident in Paraguay. Ownership refers to both equity holdings and voting rights. Tinsley Ltd has a small branch in Dublin through which sales are made to a few Irish customers.

Sean Tolstoy, a son of Alex and Tanya Tolstoy, has been residing in Russia for a number of years. Lorraine Stroessner, a daughter of Olivia and George Stroessner, has been residing in Finland for a number of years. Neither Sean Tolstoy nor Lorraine Stroessner has any interest in or connection with Tinsley Ltd.

In accordance with TCA 1997, s 432(6), the shareholdings of Alex and Tanya Tolstoy are attributed to Sean Tolstoy (an associate of each) so that he is deemed to own 26% of Tinsley Ltd. Similarly, the shareholdings of Olivia and George Stroessner are attributed to Lorraine Stroessner so that she is also deemed to own 26% of the company.

TCA 1997, s 432(6) (as applied by TCA 1997, s 23A(1)(b)(ii)) provides that such attributions are to be made under the subsection as will result in the company being treated as under the control of persons tax resident in a relevant territory if it can be so treated. The company can be so treated by virtue of TCA 1997, s 432(3) which provides that, where two or more persons satisfy any of the conditions for control, they are to be taken to have control of the company. Accordingly, Sean Tolstoy and Lorraine Stroessner, who are residents of relevant territories but who have no connection with the company, are treated as having control of Tinsley Ltd and the company is therefore a relevant company. Since it is also carrying on a trade in Ireland, it is not regarded by virtue of TCA 1997, s 23A as being tax resident in Ireland.

Place of effective management

As seen above in relation to TCA 1997, s 23A(4), most tax treaties include in their article on Residence a "tie-breaker" clause whereby the residence of a company is to be treated as situated where its "place of effective management" is. According to the Commentary on the OECD Model Treaty, the place of a company's effective management is the place where key management and commercial decisions necessary for the conduct of its business are in substance made. It will normally be the place where the most senior persons or group of persons (eg, a board of directors) make their decisions, the place where the actions to be taken by the company as a whole are determined. No definitive rule can be given, however, and all relevant facts and circumstances must be examined to determine the place of effective management. A company may have more than one place of effective management but it can have only one such place at any one time.

The question inevitably arises as to what is the difference between the place of effective management (relevant to the tie-breaker question) and the place of central management and control (the basis for tax residence), and indeed as to whether there is such a real difference. The question must remain unresolved in view of the differences of opinion on the subject and difficulties of determining the place of effective management (discussed briefly below). The meaning attributed by the OECD Model Treaty Commentary, with its emphasis on key management decisions and the place where the most senior persons make their decisions, make it difficult indeed to envisage different locations being identified for these two kinds of management. Nevertheless, "effective management" is still considered by some (eg, the Inland Revenue in the UK) as denoting something less than central management and control. Developments in information and communication technology have exacerbated the difficulties in determining where the place of effective management of a company is located. For example, management decisions could be agreed on during virtual meetings that cannot be identified to a particular location. This aspect was examined as part of the OECD work on e-commerce and in February 2001 the OECD Technical Advisory Group on Monitoring the Application of Existing Treaty Norms for the Taxation of Business Profits (TAG) released for comments its discussion draft entitled "The impact of the Communications Revolution on the Application of "Place of Effective Management" as a Tie Breaker Rule". The TAG subsequently examined the comments received on that draft and concluded that they supported the alternative options of providing clarification of the place of effective management concept as a tie-breaker rule and developing a hierarchy of different approaches that would constitute a new tie-breaker rule.

In May 2003, the TAG released a further discussion draft entitled "Place of effective management concept: suggestions for a changes to the OECD Model Convention" and recommended that the OECD Working Party No 1 on Tax Conventions and Related Questions examine the various alternative proposals discussed in that draft in light of the comments to be received with a view to deciding whether and how the Convention should be amended. These proposals are being examined by the working party.

The meaning of "place of effective management" (POEM) was considered by the Special Commissioners in the UK in *Trevor Smallwood Trust v HMRC* [2008] UK SPC SPC00669 (19 February 2008). The Commissioners pointed out that the two concepts, central management and control (CMC) and POEM served entirely different purposes, the former determining whether or not a company is resident in the UK and the latter being a tie-breaker in resolving cases of dual residence by determining in which of two states it is to be found. CMC is essentially a one-country test whose purpose is not to decide where residence is situated but whether or not it is situated in the UK, even though courts do sometimes express their decisions in terms of a company being resident in a particular foreign jurisdiction. POEM, unlike CMC, is concerned with what happens in both states since its purpose is to resolve the question of residence where this cannot be achieved applying domestic law.

The Commissioners expressed the view that "effective" in this context should be understood in the sense of the French *effective* (*siège de direction effective*), which connotes "real". The Special Commissioner in *Wensleydale's Settlement Trustees v IRC* [1996] STC (SCD) 241 was quoted with approval:

> I emphasise the adjective "effective". In my opinion it is not sufficient that some sort of management was carried on in the Republic of Ireland such as operating a bank account in the name of the trustees. "Effective" implies realistic, positive management.

Having reviewed various authorities, the OECD Commentary and the proposed TAG changes thereto, the Commissioners concluded as follows:

> Accordingly, there is nothing in this additional material that changes our initial view that, having regard to the ordinary meaning of the words in their context and in the light of their object and purpose, we should approach the issue of POEM as considering in which state the real top level management (or the realistic, positive management) … is found.

As to whether POEM and CMC are the same, the conclusion must be that they are not. The distinction, however, is largely attributable to the fact that the two concepts serve entirely different purposes: the function of POEM, in contrast with CMC, is to determine, for the purposes of the tax treaty in question, in which of the two states a company is to be regarded as tax resident if the domestic laws of those states would otherwise point to different places of residence. Despite the word "central", it is apparently not impossible to find CMC in two countries. A company may have more than one place of management but can have only one place of *effective* management at any one time. If one of the two states determines residence by reference to CMC, it seems inevitable that POEM will be in that country. If, however, CMC is the test applied in both countries and, exceptionally, different conclusions are reached on that basis, it will be necessary to determine in which country POEM is situated.

Mergers Directive

Council Directive No 2005/19/EC amended the 1990 EU Mergers Directive in a number of respects (see **9.301**). One of these amendments makes provision for a tax neutral regime for the transfer of the registered office of a European Company or a European Co-operative Society between Member States.

The legal form of the European Company, or *Societas Europaea* ("SE"), was created by the European Council on the 8 October 2001. It became subject to Community law in all EU Member States on 8 October 2004. According to the EU, the *objective* of the Statute for a European company is "to create a European company with its own legislative framework. This will allow companies incorporated in different Member States to merge or form a holding company or joint subsidiary, while avoiding the legal and practical constraints arising from the existence of fifteen different legal systems".

In June 2003, the Council of the European Union reached political agreement on the draft regulation on the European Cooperative Society, or *Societas Cooperativa Europaea* ("SCE") and the accompanying draft Directive on worker involvement. The intention of the regulation is to provide cooperatives with the same opportunities for European-level operation as provided by the European Company Statute (ECS) for private limited companies.

An SE or an SCE whose registered office is in Ireland is, subject to TCA 1997, s 23A, regarded for the purposes of the Tax Acts or the Capital Gains Tax Acts as tax resident in Ireland (TCA 1997, s 23B(1)). Being "subject to TCA 1997, s 23A, an SE or an SCE with a registered office in Ireland may nevertheless be regarded as tax resident in another jurisdiction be reason of TCA 1997, s 23A(3) or (4), as explained above.

An SE which transfers its registered office out of Ireland in accordance with Article 8 of Council Regulation (EC) No 2157/2001 on the Statute for a European Company (SE), and an SCE which transfers its registered office out of Ireland in accordance with Article 7 of Council Regulation (EC) No 1435/2003 on the Statute for a European Cooperative Society (SCE) is not to be treated as ceasing to be tax resident in Ireland by reason only of that transfer (TCA 1997, s 23B(2)).

3.107   Non-resident companies

3.107.1   Chargeable profits and geographical scope

A company not resident in the State is not subject to corporation tax unless it carries on a trade in the State through a branch or agency. This is provided for in TCA 1997, s 25 which then goes on to state that where a non-resident company does in fact carry on a trade through an Irish branch or agency it will be chargeable to corporation tax on all its chargeable profits wherever arising. At first glance this provision seems curious as one might expect corporation tax in that situation to be confined to profits arising in Ireland and not profits "wherever arising". The key to this is the reference to "chargeable profits". This is defined, in relation to a non-resident company carrying on a trade through an Irish branch or agency, as:

(a)   any trading income arising directly or indirectly through or from the branch or agency;

(b)   any income from property or rights used by, or held by or for, the branch or agency (excluding distributions received from Irish resident companies); and

(c)   such chargeable gains as would but for the Corporation Tax Acts be subject to capital gains tax in the case of a non-resident company,

but such chargeable profits do not include chargeable gains accruing to a company on the disposal of assets which, at or before the time the chargeable gains accrued, were not used in or for the purposes of the trade and were not used or held or acquired for the purposes of the branch or agency (TCA 1997, s 25(2)). (TCA 1997, s 25 is presumably now, in practice at any rate, subject to TCA 1997, s 1035A – see under *Independent agents acting for non-resident financial trading companies* in **3.107.2** below.)

Thus, for example, the trading profits of a non-resident company which are subject to corporation tax are those which arise through or from its Irish based branch or agency wherever they arise; the Irish branch may have profits arising to it both from within Ireland and from abroad.

The meaning of "income from property or rights used by, or held by or for, the branch or agency" was considered in *Murphy v Dataproducts (Dublin) Ltd* (29 January 1988) HC. The company was incorporated in the State but its residence (management and control) was moved to the Netherlands on 19 July 1979. While the company continued to carry on its manufacturing business through its Dublin branch, it opened a bank account in Switzerland into which surplus profits of the Dublin branch were lodged. No tax was payable on the trading profits because of export sales relief. The Swiss bank account was managed for investment purposes by the Dutch company in accordance with decisions made by its US parent. Some of the moneys in the Swiss bank account were returned to the Dublin branch to meet an unexpected operational shortfall but the management in Dublin had no control over the moneys or their investment or their disposal.

The appeal was concerned with the question as to whether the interest earned on the moneys deposited in the Swiss bank account were subject to corporation tax under TCA 1997, s 25(2)(a) as being income from property "used by" the Dublin branch or "held by" or "held for" that branch. It was held in the High Court that these moneys were not "used by" the Irish branch but were used by the *company* which controlled the bank account and whose decision it was to transfer some of the moneys to the Dublin branch. The moneys withdrawn were "used by" the company *for* the Irish branch, but not "used by" the branch. Moneys returned for the use of the Irish branch became moneys "held by or for" that branch and any income earned in Ireland on *those* moneys was liable to corporation tax. Neither were the moneys held in the Swiss bank account "held by" the Dublin branch or "held for" that branch. They were "held by the *Swiss* branch for" the *company*. The decision is useful in illustrating how TCA 1997, s 25(2)(a) is capable of being applied with something approaching mathematical precision.

Where a non-resident company receives a payment from which income tax has been deducted, and that payment is part of, or is taken into account in computing, the company's income chargeable to corporation tax, that income tax is to be set off against any corporation tax assessable on that income for the accounting period in which the payment is taken into account (TCA 1997, s 25(3)). The income tax will be repayable to the company when the assessment for the period is finally determined and where it is established that a repayment is due, for example where the company has losses sufficient to cover the payments which have borne income tax. Where the company's corporation tax liability for the period is less than the amount of the income tax deducted from payments received, the excess income tax will be repayable.

A non-resident company not carrying on a trade through a branch or agency (or permanent establishment, as the case may be) in the State is nevertheless liable to income tax in respect of income arising from sources in the State. For example, liability to income tax would arise to such a company that has interest income from a bank deposit with an Irish based bank. Similarly, rental income derived from Irish based property owned by a non-resident company would be liable to income tax under Case V of Schedule D. In the case of Irish source interest income, however, where the company is resident in a country in respect of which a tax treaty with Ireland is in force, the usual position is that the interest will be exempt from Irish tax under the appropriate tax treaty article.

The chargeable gains subject to corporation tax are any gains which, if the company (being a company carrying on a trade in the State through a branch or agency) were not subject to corporation tax, would be subject to capital gains tax. Those gains, described in TCA 1997, s 29(3), are chargeable gains on the disposal of:

(a) land and buildings in the State;

(b) minerals (as defined in the Minerals Development Act 1940 s 3 – see below) in the State or any rights, interests or other assets in relation to mining or minerals or the searching for minerals;

(c) assets situated in the State which, at or before the disposal, were used for the purposes of a trade carried on in the State through a branch or agency or which were used or held or acquired for use by or for the purposes of the branch or agency; or

(d) exploration or exploitation rights in a designated area;

(e) unquoted shares deriving their value or the greater part of their value directly or indirectly from assets of the kind described in (a), (b) or (d) above; and

(f) assets situated outside the State of an overseas life assurance company (within the meaning of TCA 1997, s 706(1) – see **12.603.11**), being assets that were held in connection with the life business (within the meaning of TCA 1997, s 706(1)) carried on by the company, which at or before the time the chargeable gains accrued were used or held by or for the purposes of that company's branch or agency in the State.

Regarding (b) above, *minerals* is defined in the Minerals Development Act 1940 s 3 as "all substances (other than the agricultural surface of the ground and other than turf of peat) in, on or under land, whether obtainable by underground or by surface working, and includes all mines, whether or not they are already opened or in work, and also includes the cubic space occupied or formerly occupied by minerals."

In (c) above, assets which were used in connection with a trade carried on in the State through a branch or agency include assets which had ceased to be so used at the time of disposal.

The kinds of disposals the chargeable gains on which can be subject to corporation tax in the case of a non-resident company have been listed in (a) to (e) above. These include disposals of exploration or exploitation rights in a designated area. "Exploration or exploitation rights" is as defined in TCA 1997, s 13(1) and means rights to assets produced by exploration or exploitation activities or to interests in or to the benefit of such assets. Exploration or exploitation activities are activities carried on in connection with the exploration or exploitation of so much of the sea-bed and sub-soil and their natural resources as are situated in the State or in a designated area. A *designated area* is an area designated by order under the Continental Shelf Act 1968 s 2.

References in the Tax Acts to "the State" are to the Republic of Ireland, its islands and its territorial seas. The law governing the extent of the territorial seas is partly derived from international law and practice. The Maritime Jurisdiction Act 1959 provides that the territorial seas extend to the three-mile limit. The rights of coastal states in regard to the exploitation of the sea and sea-bed well beyond territorial waters is dependent on such concepts as the "economic zone" and the "continental shelf". The Geneva Convention on the Continental Shelf defines the "continental shelf" as extending to the point where exploitation of the natural resources is admitted by the depth of superjacent waters. The "economic zone" would extend no further than two hundred miles from the coastline. The right to natural resources in designated areas of the continental shelf is vested, in the case of Ireland, in the Minister for Transport, Energy and Communications under the Continental Shelf Act 1969.

The geographical scope of income tax, capital gains tax and corporation tax in relation to exploration or exploitation activities and rights was extended by TCA 1997, s 13 (as applied by TCA 1997, s 23 for corporation tax). Profits or gains from exploration or exploitation activities carried on in a designated area are treated as profits or gains from activities in the State and profits or gains from exploration or exploitation rights are treated as profits or gains from property in the State.

In the case of a non-resident, profits or gains arising from exploration or exploitation activities carried on in the State or in a designated area, or from exploration or exploitation rights, are treated for tax purposes as profits or gains of a trade carried on by that person in the State through a branch or agency. To summarise:

(a) TCA 1997, s 13 treats the designated areas as part of the State for corporation tax purposes;

(b) TCA 1997, s 25 subjects to corporation tax the trading income arising from a branch or agency, and income from property or rights used by, or held by or for, the branch or agency, in the case of a non-resident company carrying on a trade in the State through a branch or agency;

(c) TCA 1997, s 13 treats profits or gains arising to a non-resident company from exploration or exploitation activities carried on in the State or in a designated area, or from exploration or exploitation rights, as profits or gains of a trade carried on by that company in the State through a branch or agency: this brings such profits or gains within the scope of TCA 1997, s 25;

(d) TCA 1997, s 13 treats the designated areas as part of the State for capital gains tax purposes;

(e) TCA 1997, s 25(2)(b) subjects to corporation tax the chargeable gains of a non-resident company which would be subject to capital gains tax were it not for the fact that the company is subject to corporation tax;

(f) TCA 1997, s 29(6) treats gains of a non-resident company on the disposal of exploration or exploitation rights in a designated area as gains on the disposal of assets situated in the State: this brings such gains within the scope of TCA 1997, s 25.

A gain on the disposal of unquoted shares is subject to capital gains tax in the case of a person not ordinarily resident in the State where the shares derive the greater part of their value from:

(a) land or buildings in the State;

(b) minerals in the State or any rights, interests or other assets in relation to mining or minerals or the searching for minerals;

(c) exploration or exploitation rights in a designated area.

For a non-resident company carrying on a trade in the State through a branch or agency, such gains are accordingly chargeable to corporation tax (TCA 1997, s 25(2)(b)). TCA 1997, s 29(1) effectively provides that a disposal of shares *"deriving* their value or the greater part of their value" from the above mentioned kinds of assets (for convenience, referred to here as "specified assets") is subject to capital gains tax in the hands of a non- resident. This can only mean that the shares are so chargeable where they derive their value or the greater part of their value at the time of disposal. It would be nonsensical to include shares within this charge on the basis that their value or the greater part of their value can be accounted for by the ownership of Irish based property in the past. Thus, a company whose main asset was Irish based property might dispose of that property and reinvest the proceeds in quoted shares. If shares in the company owned by a non- resident are later disposed of, no part of the value of those shares would be derived from the property at the time of sale.

The fact that the shares derived their value from the property at some time prior to the disposal, even where the value of the shares at the disposal date is indirectly attributable to an appreciation in the value of the property formerly held, does not mean that the shares derive their value from that property at the time they are disposed of. Once the property is disposed of, the shares are no longer "deriving their value" from that property but from the assets now held.

The legislation gives no guidance as to how the extent to which shares derive their value from specified assets is to be measured. In certain situations no difficulty will be encountered.

Example 3.107.1.1

Samara Ltd, a non-resident company not carrying on a trade in Ireland, disposes of its 100% interest in Tara Ltd, an Irish resident unquoted company, to an unrelated party for €1.5m. At the date of sale, Tara Ltd owned a freehold property in Dublin valued at €700,000 and owned no other "specified assets". Clearly, the shares sold did not derive the greater part of their value from the Irish based property. Samara Ltd is therefore not subject to corporation tax in respect of any gain arising on the disposal of the shares.

The position illustrated in this example is simpler and more straightforward than would be encountered in most situations in practice. The link between the value of a company and the property owned by it would not usually be as evident. Company indebtedness is one of the factors which will normally have to be taken into account so that the question as to whether the value of the company is mainly derived from property held will not be a simple one of taking the value of that property as a percentage of the value of the company as a whole.

Example 3.107.1.2

The position is as in Example **3.107.1.1** except that the Dublin property is worth €1m at the time the shares were sold by Samara Ltd. There is a debt of €300,000 charged on the property.

Since the property is encumbered by the €300,000 debt, it must be that it accounts for only €700,000 of the value of Tara Ltd at the time the shares are sold; the property could not be realised without first discharging the debt so that it cannot be correct to attribute €1m of the value of the company to the property.

The conclusion reached in the above example cannot, however, be established with certainty from the legislation, which offers no guidance on the matter. In the absence of such guidance, it might be thought that the correct approach would be to attribute any debt to the assets to which that debt relates (because the debt was incurred in connection with the acquisition of those assets or is charged on them) and to allocate any other debt proportionately between all of the assets. It is understood that the approach of the Revenue Commissioners is to ignore the indebtedness and simply to compare the gross value of the specified assets with the value of the shares in the company. If the former amount represents more than half of the latter amount, the shares are regarded as deriving the greater part of their value from the specified assets. The question as to how shares in a company derive their value is not so straightforward and will depend on a number of circumstances, such as the nature of the trade or business of the company and the use made of its assets. The value is derived from a number of factors and not just by reference to assets owned. In ascertaining whether or not shares in a company derive the greater part of their value from land in Ireland, it can hardly be correct procedure simply to decide the matter on the basis that the value of that land is more than 50% of the value of the shares.

The approach to valuing a company will differ significantly depending on whether the company is a trading or a non-trading company. For a trading company, the significant factor is the trade itself that will be valued by reference to its earnings record and its potential for future earnings. The company's tangible assets may be taken into account in the valuation exercise but would not be the decisive factor. The valuation of a non-trading company would be by reference to its underlying assets but even here there are no rules or procedures that would assist in deciding the extent to which particular assets account for the value of the shares in the company.

Since TCA 1997, s 29(1) operates by reference to the underlying specified assets of certain quoted shares, there may be an implication that an assets basis of valuation is appropriate, and this would make some sense, although, as already stated, the section does not make this clear. Assuming the assets basis is to be used, the valuation issue should be approached in a realistic and not artificial way. It would be quite artificial, however, to attempt to value a company by reference to its assets alone and without regard to its liabilities. It is basic company law that a company is a legal entity distinct from its shareholders who have no proprietary interest in the assets of that company (*Salomon v Salomon & Co* [1897] AC 22). A company whose only asset is land would derive all of its value from that land but, if the land is mortgaged to its full value, the shareholders would be entitled to nothing. The shares would only have value on the basis of what would be received by the shareholders on a winding up.

Where a particular asset of a company is encumbered by debt, and perhaps also where any company indebtedness is directly attributable to that asset, it would seem correct on an assets basis valuation to take that indebtedness into account in evaluating the extent to which the asset accounts for the value of the shares in the company. Where indebtedness does not relate to any particular assets, an apportionment of that indebtedness over all of the assets might be reasonable; alternatively, the indebtedness might be ignored altogether. In the latter case, the gross value of the specified assets might represent more than half of the value of the shares in the company whereas in the former case, by apportioning debt rateably, the net value of the specified assets might represent less than half of the share value.

Territorial scope

A number of UK court decisions have addressed the question as to whether there is an implied territorial limit to certain kinds of tax provisions. The general principle that a such a tax provision, though expressed in general terms, must be limited (territorially) in some way is echoed in the observation of the Earl of Halsbury in *Cook v Charles A Vogeler Co* [1901] AC 102 that "English legislation is primarily territorial", and similarly in *Ex parte Blain* (1879) 12 Ch D 522 where James LJ said that "if a foreigner remains abroad, if he has never come into this country at all, it seems to me impossible to imagine that the English legislature could have ever intended to make such a man subject to particular English legislation.

The same principle was applied in *Colquhoun v Brooks* 2 TC 493 where Lord Herschell said that "The Income Tax Acts, however, themselves impose a territorial limit, either that from which the taxable income is derived must be situate in the United Kingdom or the person whose income is to be taxed must be resident there".

In *Clarke v Oceanic Contractors Inc* [1983] STC 35, the House of Lords, in a majority decision, held that a territorial limitation was to be implied into the PAYE collection mechanism. In that case, what was considered was not so much the territorial limits of the taxing powers of the UK parliament as such but the extent to which administrative obligations can be imposed on persons outside the UK. Such obligations could only be imposed on persons sufficiently established in the UK to enable the obligation to be enforced against them. The intention of the legislation was not to impose unenforceable obligations.

The case of *Agassi v Robinson* [2006] STC 1056 concerned an assessment made in respect of payments received by a company that did not have a presence in the UK from another such company arising from marketing services resulting from the ability of a well-known tennis player to attract publicity. The taxpayer company sought to rely on the reasoning in *Oceanic Contractors* and judgment in the High Court had been in favour of the Inland Revenue. The view of the High Court was that the focus of the legislation was on non-residents and it would be surprising if it could not extend to payments between offshore persons. The UK Court of Appeal, however, reversed the decision of the High Court and allowed the taxpayer's appeal.

In the opinion of the Court of Appeal, the reach of the territorial principle was that, unless the contrary was expressly enacted or plainly implied, UK legislation was applicable only to British subjects or by foreigners who, by coming to the UK, had made themselves subject to British jurisdiction. The territorial principle was a principle of considerable strength and was inherent in any act of Parliament and there would need to be good reason for excluding it. It applied not only to legislation imposing a charge to tax, the primary tax charge, but also to legislation imposing a duty to collect or account for tax. The difficulty of enforcing a liability to collect tax against a person outside the UK was a strong reason for not disregarding the territorial principle.

Although conceding that the territorial principle was relevant, the House of Lords, in a four to one majority decision, held that the territorial limitation could not be carried through to the primary tax charge: it could not have been the intention of Parliament to provide that a tax liability could be avoided simply be ensuring that all payments were made by foreign entities. However, one has to question the logic of reasoning which recognises that certain withholding provisions have been enacted because the primary taxpayer has no connection with the UK, so that the tax cannot be collected from that person, but assumes that it makes sense to pursue some other person from whom, equally, it may not be possible to recover that tax.

3.107.2 Trading

A company not resident in the State is subject to corporation tax if it carries on a trade in the State through a branch or agency and, if it does so, it will be chargeable to corporation tax on all its chargeable profits wherever arising (but see below under *Independent agents acting for non-resident financial trading companies*). Those profits (the "chargeable profits") are any trading income arising directly or indirectly through or from the branch or agency and any income from property or rights used by, or held by or for, the branch or agency.

TCA 1997, s 1034 provides that a non-resident person is to be assessable and chargeable to income tax (including corporation tax – see below) in the name of any trustee, guardian, or committee of such person, or of any factor, agent, receiver, branch or manager, whether such factor, agent, receiver, branch or manager has the receipt of the profits or gains or not. Thus, the fact that an agent, factor etc does not actually receive the profits of the non-resident will not prevent him being assessable on behalf of that non-resident. TCA 1997, s 1035 goes on to provide that a non-resident person is to be assessable and chargeable to income tax in respect of any profits or gains arising, whether directly or indirectly, through or from any factorship, agency, receivership, branch or management, and is to be so assessable and chargeable in the name of the factor, agent, receiver, branch or manager. Thus, any assessment to be made is limited to the profits or gains realised by the factorship, agency etc through which the non-resident exercises the trade in Ireland.

The provisions of TCA 1997 ss 1034 and 1035 relating to the assessment and charge of income tax on persons not resident in the State, in so far as they are applicable to tax chargeable on a company, apply with any necessary modifications in relation to corporation tax chargeable on companies not resident in the State (TCA 1997, s 1040).

Although in the majority of cases, there will be little difficulty in deciding whether or not a non-resident company is trading in Ireland through a branch or agency, the question nevertheless poses difficulties in many situations where the activities carried on in Ireland are not the same as those carried on by the company as a whole. For example, a non-resident manufacturing company selling goods to customers in Ireland may not carry out any manufacturing in Ireland but may have Irish based employees or agents who initiate and maintain contact with customers. The company may have premises, whether owned or rented, at which its goods are stocked and from where they are dispatched to customers. The premises may include offices that are used by the employees or agents to deal with telephone enquiries and at which correspondence with the head office and with customers and potential customers is handled. Depending on all of the circumstances of the case, the company may or may not be regarded as carrying on a trade in Ireland.

A "branch or agency" is defined for corporation tax purposes as any factorship, agency, receivership, branch or management (TCA 1997, s 4(1)). In cases where the company is resident in a country with which Ireland has a tax treaty, liability to corporation tax will, in effect, depend on whether or not the company carries on a trade in Ireland through a permanent establishment. The meaning of "permanent establishment" depends on the definition of the term in the relevant tax treaty. For the present, it is fair to say that its meaning is similar to that of "branch or agency" and, indeed, the definitions in all of the treaties include references to "branch" and "agency".

Branch or agency: case law background

Assuming a non-resident company has a branch or agency in Ireland, it is necessary to establish whether or not the company is carrying on a trade in Ireland through that branch or agency. It is this question that has had to be decided in the many UK cases on the subject. Essentially, the question has come down to whether the non-resident company was trading *in* or was trading *with* the UK, the host country. If merely trading *with* the host country there is no liability to corporation tax in that country and the question therefore is whether or not the operations and activities of the company in the host country are sufficient to lead to the conclusion that it must be regarded as carrying on a trade *in* that country.

On the basis of the relevant UK case law, which is persuasive authority in Ireland, a significant factor leading to the conclusion that a non-resident company is trading in Ireland is the presence of an employee or agent or other representative in Ireland who has and exercises authority to conclude contracts with customers in the name of and on behalf of the company.

In a number of early UK decisions involving foreign wine merchants, non-resident enterprises were held to be carrying on trading activities in the UK. In *Tischler v Apthorpe* 2 TC 89, *Pommery & Greno v Apthorpe* 2 TC 182, and *Werle & Co v Colquhoun* 2 TC 402, the decisive factor was that wine was sold through agents in the UK. In all cases, the UK based agents concluded contracts for the sale of wine on behalf of their principals. In *Watson v Sandie & Hull* 3 TC 611, a UK commission agent who sold goods of his US principal in his own name and who collected the sale proceeds was held to be trading in the UK.

In two further cases, *Thomas Turner (Leicester) Ltd v Rickman* 4 TC 25, and *Wilcock v Pinto* 9 TC 111, the basic facts were similar in that while the principal's authority was required in relation to the conclusion of sales contracts, the contracts were in fact concluded in the UK. In *Gavazzi v Mace* 10 TC 698, it was found that a UK agent acting on behalf of a non-resident principal was an authorised person for the purposes of concluding contracts with UK customers.

What was common to all of the above cases was the fact that contracts were concluded in the UK in the name of the foreign principal. Thus, the common factor can be fairly easily identified and is seen to be absent in the following cases where non-residents were held not to be trading in the UK. In *Grainger v Gough* 3 TC 311, an English based agent obtained orders from customers in England and transmitted them to his principal in France for execution. It was a fact that the agent did not conclude contracts on behalf of the principal who was accordingly held not to be trading in the UK.

Interestingly, at the earlier Divisional Court stage of this case, Escher MR considered that the fact that sales of champagne to English customers were a daily occurrence, that an English based agent was appointed for the purpose of obtaining orders from English customers which were transmitted to France, and that the merchant was in the business of selling champagne and getting money for it in England, were factors which collectively pointed to trading in the UK. He was of opinion that the English sales of champagne had become a business by reason of the magnitude of the operation.

This view was overturned in the House of Lords where Lord Herschell observed that the factor which had been the principal test in earlier cases was the habitual making of contracts in England, a factor which had been overlooked by Escher MR. Thus, even where the activities of an agent acting in one country on behalf of a principal in another country are very extensive and varied, they are unlikely to result in the principal being regarded as carrying on a trade in the first mentioned country as long as the agent does not habitually enter into contracts on behalf of the principal. The source of the test appears to be *Erichsen v Last* 1 TC 351 where it was found that trading occurred "whenever profitable contracts are habitually made in England, by or for foreigners, with persons in England".

In *MacLaine & Co v Eccott* 10 TC 481, the importance of the place where contracts are concluded was emphasised, as is illustrated in the following passage from the judgment of Viscount Cave LC:

> The question whether a trade is exercised in the UK is a question of fact, and it is undesirable to attempt to lay down any exhaustive test of what constitutes such an exercise of trade; but I think it must now be taken as established that in the case of a merchant's business, the primary object of which is to sell goods at a profit, the trade is (speaking generally) exercised or carried on ... at the place where the contracts are made. No doubt reference has sometimes been made to the place where payment is made for the goods sold or to the place where the goods are delivered, and it may be that in certain circumstances these are material considerations; but the most important, and indeed the crucial, question is where are the contracts of sale made?

In the case of *FL Smidth & Co v Greenwood* 8 TC 193, an English employee at his London office discussed requirements of UK purchasers and reported to his principal in Denmark. All contracts were negotiated from, and were made in, Denmark. The Danish principal was held not to be trading in the UK. In the course of his judgment, Atkin LJ said that although operations of importance took place in the UK in that orders were solicited there and the adaptation of the goods bought for the buyer's business was supervised there, there was no evidence to support the view that the operations from which the profits in substance arose took place other than in Denmark.

Independent agents acting for non-resident financial trading companies

TCA 1997, s 18(1) provides that tax under Schedule D is to be charged in respect of the annual profits or gains arising to a person not resident in the State from, inter alia, any trade or profession exercised in the State. TCA 1997, s 1035 provides, inter alia, that a non-resident person is assessable and chargeable to income tax (and in the case of a company, by virtue of TCA 1997, s 1040, to corporation tax) in respect of profits or gains arising, directly or indirectly, through or from any agency (implicitly an agency in the State) and is so assessable in the name of the agent. This potential charge to tax on non-residents carrying on a financial trade in the State through an agent is removed in certain circumstances. TCA 1997, s 1035A(3) provides that, notwithstanding TCA 1997, s 18(1), a non-resident person is not to be assessable and chargeable to income tax (including corporation tax by virtue of TCA 1997, s 1040 – see above) in respect of any profits or gains arising or accruing for a chargeable period to the non-resident person from a financial trade exercised in the State solely through an authorised agent who, throughout the chargeable period is independent in relation to the non-resident person.

The effect of TCA 1997, s 1035A is to place persons resident in non-treaty countries on the same footing as those in treaty countries where the relevant treaty secures that an agent of independent status acting for such non-resident person in the ordinary course of business is not to constitute a permanent establishment of that person.

A *financial trade* is a trade exercised in the State by a non-resident person through an authorised agent under and within the terms of the authorised agent's authorisation.

An *authorised agent* is:

(a) a person acting as an investment business firm, or an authorised member firm –

　(i) under the authorisation given by the Central Bank of Ireland under section 10(1) of the Investment Intermediaries Act 1995 or, as the case may be section 18 of the Stock Exchange Act 1995, and not subsequently revoked; or

　(ii) under an authorisation, which corresponds to either of the authorisations referred to in (i), given by a competent authority in another Member State for the purpose of Council Directive 93/22/EEC of 10 May 1993 (OJ No L141, of 11.6.1993, p27) as amended or extended from time to time, and not subsequently revoked; or

(b) a credit institution duly authorised by virtue of Directive No 2000/12/EC or 20 March 2000 (OJ No L126, of 26.5.2000, p1) which provides investment business services and in so doing does not exceed the terms of its authorisation and that authorisation has not been revoked (TCA 1997, s 1035A(1)).

The terms *investment business firm*, *investment business services* and *competent authority* have the meanings assigned to them by section 2 of the Investment Intermediaries Act 1995.

The term *authorised member firm* has the meaning assigned to it by section 3 of the Stock Exchange Act 1995.

An authorised agent through whom a non-resident person exercises a financial trade in the State is independent in relation to that person for any chargeable period throughout which:

(i) the agent does not otherwise act on behalf of the non-resident person;

(ii) the agent, when acting on behalf of the non-resident person, does so in an independent capacity and in the ordinary course of the agent's business;

(iii) the requirements referred to below in relation to the financial trade are satisfied (TCA 1997, s 1035A(2)(a)).

An authorised agent will not be regarded as acting in an independent capacity when acting on behalf of a non-resident person unless, having regard to its legal, financial and commercial characteristics, the relationship between them is the same as that between persons carrying on independent businesses that deal with each other at arm's length (TCA 1997, s 1035A(2)(b)).

The requirements referred to in (iii) above are that:

(a) the aggregate of the amount of the profits or gains of the trade, to which the authorised agent and persons who are both resident in the State and connected with (see **2.3**) the agent have a beneficial entitlement, does not exceed 20% of the amount of the profits or gains of the trade; or

(b) the Revenue Commissioners are satisfied that it is the intention of the authorised agent that the aggregate of the amount of the profits or gains of the trade, to which the agent and persons who are resident in the State and connected with the agent, have beneficial entitlement does not exceed 20% of the amount of the profits or gains of the trade and that the reasons for the failure to fulfil that intention at that time are of a temporary nature (TCA 1997, s 1035A(4)).

References to an amount of profits or gains of a trade exercised in the State by a non-resident person to which another person has a beneficial entitlement are to the amount of profits or gains of the trade to which the other person has, or may acquire, a beneficial entitlement by virtue of:

(i) an interest of the other person (whether or not an interest giving a right to an immediate payment of a share of the profits or gains of the trade) in property in which the whole or any part of the profits or gains of the trade are represented; or

(ii) any interest of the other person in, or other rights in relation to, the non-resident person (TCA 1997, s 1035A(2)(c)).

TCA 1997, s 25 provides that a non-resident company carrying on a trade in the State through an agency is chargeable to corporation tax on all its chargeable profits. Technically, this provision does not appear to be limited in its application by TCA 1997, s 1035A, which has effect in relation to TCA 1997, s 18 only. In practice, it is assumed that TCA 1997, s 25 would not take precedence in a case in which TCA 1997, s 1035A applies.

Permanent establishment: fixed place of business

In tax treaty cases, liability to corporation tax in Ireland in the case of a non-resident will depend on whether or not the company carries on a trade in Ireland through a permanent establishment. The "business profits" article of a treaty will typically provide that a non-Irish resident company will be taxable only in its home country unless it carries on business in Ireland through a permanent establishment situated in Ireland, in which case its profits attributable to that permanent establishment may be taxed in Ireland. Since, under domestic Irish tax legislation, a non-resident company can only be within the charge to corporation tax if it carries on a trade in Ireland through a branch or agency (which comes to much the same thing as a permanent establishment), the profits of such a company will be subject to corporation tax only where they arise from a trade (and not necessarily a "business") carried on by it through a permanent establishment in Ireland.

As already mentioned, the meaning of "permanent establishment" is to be derived from the definition of the term in the relevant treaty. In the OECD Model Convention, *permanent establishment* means a fixed place of business through which the business of an enterprise (the non-resident company) is wholly or partly carried on. The term specifically includes a branch, place of management, office, factory, workshop and a mine, oil or gas well, quarry or other place of extraction of natural resources. Not included are:

(a)   the use of facilities solely for the purpose of storage, display or delivery of goods or merchandise belonging to the enterprise;

(b)   the maintenance of a stock of goods or merchandise belonging to the enterprise solely for the purpose of storage, display or delivery, or for processing by another enterprise;

(c)   the maintenance of a fixed place of business solely for the purpose of purchasing goods or merchandise or of collecting information, for the enterprise;

(d)   the maintenance of a fixed place of business solely for the purpose of carrying on, for the enterprise, any other activity of a preparatory or auxiliary character;

(e)   the maintenance of a fixed place of business solely for any combination of the previously mentioned activities provided the overall activity of that place remains of a preparatory or auxiliary character.

The meaning of "permanent establishment", in its physical aspect, is therefore very widely defined. It can include any fixed place of business, including a customer's premises or part thereof, or an amount of space put at the disposal of the enterprise. A fixed place of business will not be a permanent establishment unless it is one through which the business of the enterprise is wholly or partly carried on. In effect, the carrying on of a business through a fixed place is part of the definition of a permanent establishment.

A non-resident company not carrying on any trade, but which is carrying on a "business" through a fixed place of business in Ireland, will not, as mentioned above, be subject to corporation tax in Ireland. The company will, however, have a permanent establishment ("a fixed place of business through which the business of the enterprise is wholly or partly carried on") in Ireland. This may have certain tax implications for the company. For example, if Irish source interest arises to the permanent establishment, the company will not be able to benefit from a tax treaty for the purpose of avoiding the deduction of Irish withholding tax from the interest; interest articles in tax treaties typically deny benefits where the company has a permanent establishment (PE) in Ireland with which the debt-claim from which the interest arises is effectively connected.

The Canadian case *The Queen v Dudney* A-707-98 is of particular interest as respects the meaning of a fixed place of business, or "fixed base". The Canadian Federal Court of Appeal found that Mr Dudney, a US resident contractor, was not subject to Canadian tax on income earned in Canada under a personal services contract as he had no "fixed base" in Canada. Dudney, who worked for a consulting firm that entered into a master services agreement with a third party, carried out his duties at that party's Canadian premises. Most of these duties, which involved training and mentoring, were performed at the offices of the people being trained or mentored. A space available to Dudney, the use of which was strictly limited to activities related to the services agreement, was not often used by him.

The Court expressed the view that Dudney did not acquire a fixed place of business wherever his services were provided and agreed, by analogy, that a Canadian lawyer does not acquire a fixed place of business in the office of a client in the US merely by attending to the client's affairs there, even if the client insists on the lawyer's personal presence. The fact that Dudney's contract subsisted for a period of more than a year was irrelevant. The duration of the contract would be relevant only if there was in fact a place of business whereas Dudney did not in fact have a place of business.

Permanent establishment: agents

Article 5(5) of the Model Convention deals with dependent agents. Where a dependent agent of an enterprise (a non-resident company) has, and habitually exercises, in Ireland an authority to conclude contracts in the name of the enterprise, that enterprise is deemed to have a PE in Ireland in respect of any activities which that agent undertakes for the enterprise, unless the activities in question are limited to those mentioned in Article 5(4) (see (a) to (e) above in relation to *fixed place of business*).

To constitute a PE, the agent must be dependent on the enterprise he represents. The agent must not have independent status of the kind referred to in Article 5(6), for example, of the kind normally associated with brokers or general commission agents. An agent who is bound to follow instructions relating to the business is dependent on the enterprise. As to whether an agent is dependent or independent of the enterprise would be determined by reference to his obligations in relation to that enterprise. An agent may be materially dependent on the enterprise if he is bound to follow its instructions although that fact alone would not give rise to a PE; a broker, general commission agent or other commercial agent would also be materially dependent on the enterprise but would also be in business on his own account and therefore personally independent of the enterprise. A dependent agent for the purposes of Article 5(5) is one who is materially but also *personally* dependent on the enterprise in that his obligation to follow the instructions of the enterprise is not confined to specific transactions but is comprehensive in nature. Thus, for example, an employee who is bound to an enterprise by virtue of a contract of employment is subject to an obligation to make his services comprehensively available to that enterprise and is both materially and personally dependent on the enterprise.

To amount to a PE, an agent must have authority to conclude contracts in the name of the enterprise he represents. As to whether or not an agent has such authority is a question of fact to be decided on in the light of the particular economic situation. Where an Irish based agent has authority to negotiate all elements of a contract in a way that is binding on the enterprise, the agent is regarded as exercising his authority in the State, even if formal signature of the contract is made by some other person outside the State. The authority could be restricted to specific lines of business within the enterprise's overall business activities. In that event, the profits attributable to the PE would be restricted to profits arising from business contracted by the agent. Direct transactions by the enterprise would be disregarded for the purposes of determining profits attributable to the PE.

To constitute a PE, an agent must habitually exercise in the State an authority to conclude contracts in the name of the enterprise. There must be a certain degree of permanence pertaining to the agent's activities in the State. Accordingly, an agent would not constitute a PE on the basis of the conclusion of a single contract. The authority to conclude contracts should be exercised repeatedly and not merely occasionally. The frequency with which an agent concludes contracts should be considered in the light of what is normal in the actual line of business concerned. An important factor here is whether the activities performed by the agent were from the outset devised for a lengthy period or merely as a temporary expedient. It is not necessary that the continuous activity be exercised throughout by the same person. It is sufficient for the post of dependent agent to have been established.

If a PE is found to exist on the basis of Article 5(1)-(4), it will not matter whether the persons whose activities are carried on through the PE are independent or not, or whether or not they have authority to conclude contracts. Thus, an enterprise will have a PE if it has the use of a fixed place of business through which its agent is carrying on activities on its behalf even if he has no authority to conclude contracts. The fact that such an agent performs some activities on behalf of the enterprise from his home (eg, by telephone) would not of itself give rise to a PE, other than in the unlikely event that the home was at the disposal of the enterprise for the purposes of its business.

An independent agent will only avoid being a PE of an enterprise to the extent that he is acting in the ordinary course of his business. As to what would amount to acting in the ordinary course of business in any case will depend on what is normal for the particular line of business concerned. It has been held (relative to the treaty between Germany and the Netherlands) in the case of a general agent operating in the transport insurance business that his outwardly unrestricted authority to conclude insurance contracts was consistent with acting in the normal course of business for the line of business concerned. As to how an agent of one enterprise arranges his business relations with other principals is not in itself decisive as such arrangements may depend on factors and occurrences outside the control of the enterprise.

Where an independent agent, on behalf of an enterprise, carries on activities outside the normal course of his business, that fact will not necessarily result in the agent being a PE of that enterprise. Those activities would not, for example, result in a PE of the enterprise where the agent did not also have an authority, in law or in fact, to conclude contracts covering such activities, or if the activities were merely of a preparatory or auxiliary character within the meaning of Article 5(4).

A question that has arisen from time to time is whether a subsidiary of a foreign parent company can constitute a PE of the parent. The outcome of two decisions of the French court in 2003 is that a subsidiary can indeed constitute such a PE although in both instances the finding was that there was in fact no PE. The reasons for the decisions in these cases are of some interest. The case of *Société Interhome AG* involved the French subsidiary of a Swiss company whose business was the fulfilling of mandates with owners of vacation homes located in various European countries to rent those homes to third parties. Its subsidiaries, including its French subsidiary, took care of the maintenance of the houses, signed the rental contracts and supervised the execution of the rental agreements in return for a commission-based remuneration. In its decision of 20 June 2003, the French Supreme Court held that, although the subsidiary was a dependent agent of its parent, it was not able to bind the parent in commercial relationships relating the parent's activities; the delegation of authority for entering into rental agreements with tenants and supervising those agreements was not related to the parent's activity. Accordingly the subsidiary did not constitute a PE of its Swiss parent.

In the case of *Société Intercontainer*, a French company in the containers and railway materials business was also a commission agent for its Belgian parent company. It had received delegated powers from its parent to provide services to French clients and to solicit potential new clients for the parent. In its decision of 26 November 2003, the French administrative Court found that, although the subsidiary had the power to conclude contracts on behalf of its parent, it could be regarded as having independent status; this was because the parent did not exercise detailed control over the organisation and staff of the subsidiary, the subsidiary remained responsible for the accuracy of the various elements of the offers proposed to clients and bore the related costs of these offers, it had not been established or even claimed that the subsidiary was exercising its activity solely or mainly for the account of the parent, and it had not been established that the commercial relationship between the parties was ruled by conditions other than ones resulting from the free interaction of supply and demand.

The above cases confirm that, in order for a subsidiary to constitute a PE of its foreign parent company, two conditions must apply: it must be a dependent agent and it must have the authority to bind its parent. The conditions are cumulative and if one of them is not satisfied there is no PE. This, however, is no more than is stated above in relation to article 5(5) of the Model Convention regarding the position of dependent agents.

Core v auxiliary activities

An important distinction in this regard is that to be made between what are sometimes termed "core" activities and those referred to as "auxiliary" activities. Auxiliary activities are excluded by Article 5 of the OECD Model Convention from the meaning of PE. Activities which would be regarded as giving rise to a PE would be those carried on by a dependent agent having and habitually exercising authority to conclude contracts in the name of the enterprise as well as those carried on through a fixed place of business, including such items as a place of management, a branch or an office. Activities in this latter category may be referred to as "core" activities.

Core activities would evidently include manufacturing and selling. It is more difficult to be definitive about such activities as pre-sales (or pre-contract) activities. Mere advertising would be accepted as a preparatory or auxiliary activity. Solicitation of orders could, arguably, be regarded as a core activity (though not before the point at which the first customer is signed up) even where the related sales orders would be subject to approval by the head office abroad. The test in any such case is where do the profits of the foreign enterprise in substance arise. The negotiation of contracts, even where finalised by the head office abroad, would be a core activity. It may not always be clear as to where the dividing line should be drawn between mere contact activities, which would not normally suggest a PE, and soliciting activities, which might well result in a PE (but see further below on this).

In a Danish administrative decision, it was found that the function of an office set up by a German company which was staffed, inter alia, with sales persons who prospected for sales in Denmark, was performing work which was more than of an auxiliary nature and that the office therefore constituted a PE. This was despite the fact that any sales orders generated were subject to approval by the head office in Germany. It may well be the case that a PE will exist even where no negotiating activities are carried on through a fixed place of business. The overriding principle here is that a preparatory or auxiliary activity is one which is so remote from the actual realisation of profits that it is difficult to allocate any profit to the fixed place of business in question by reason of those activities. Soliciting for business could arguably be viewed as an important ingredient in the realisation of profits and therefore as a core activity. On the other hand, Atkin LJ in *Smidth v Greenwood* 8 TC 193 said that although soliciting for orders in the UK was an operation of importance, it was merely ancillary to the exercise of the company's trade abroad.

In a German case (*Betriebs-Berater Bundesfinanzhof* – decision of 30 November 1996), a Dutch company owning a pipeline which ran through Germany was held to have a PE there. The company had no fixed place of business and no employees in Germany and the mechanism operating the pipeline was situated in the Netherlands. The decision suggests that it is possible to have a PE without any human presence. Indeed, it would appear that the likes of vending machines and other automated devices, as well as fully automated pumping stations and similar facilities may very well be PEs where the enterprise in question is engaged in business beyond the mere installation of these devices. Representatives of the German Finance Ministry have stated that the pipeline decision is not of relevance for telecommunications servers. (See also under *Electronic Commerce* below.) It would appear to be of some significance, however, that the definition of a PE in domestic German tax legislation, where a PE need only serve the enterprise in question, is broader than that in the Netherlands-Germany treaty definition.

The OECD Model Convention view is that a pipeline should not constitute a PE if its functions are preparatory or auxiliary to the specific enterprise.

Business connection test

Where an enterprise of one country performs business activities in a second country and maintains a fixed place of business there, it will not necessarily have a PE in that country. For this purpose it is necessary that there is a specific connection between the business activity and the fixed place of business. This condition is referred to as the "business connection test". A question which then sometimes arises is whether this test is met when an auxiliary activity conducted through a fixed place of business serves a core activity performed outside it. For example, the activities carried on by an Italian company through its Irish office may be accepted as being merely preparatory or auxiliary activities, but a representative of the company may be involved in a core activity, eg negotiation, elsewhere in Ireland but not through a fixed place of business.

The question then would be whether the existence of these two aspects satisfies the business connection test so that the negotiating activities would be seen as being conducted through a fixed place of business. In short, the question would be whether the fixed place of business has an "attraction effect" on the core business activity performed outside it. The conclusion, reflecting the OECD view of the matter, is that there would not be such an attraction effect and that there would not be a PE even, it appears, where the auxiliary activities supported that core business. The authorities in some countries would not take this view but it is likely that the Irish tax authorities would follow the OECD approach.

What profits are taxable?

Where the activities carried on through a PE comprise both core and auxiliary activities, it will be necessary to ascertain what profits are the taxable profits of that PE. There is no clear answer to this question except to refer to the standard "business profits" article of tax treaties which states that the profits to be taxed are so much of them as is attributable to the PE. It would seem to be necessary therefore to decide whether profits are being derived from the auxiliary activities. If the auxiliary activities and the core activities are interconnected, with the auxiliary activities supporting the core activities, it would be difficult to resist the argument that profits derived from both categories of activities should be included. Where the two categories of activity are not so connected and are quite independently carried on, it is arguable that the auxiliary activities are not of themselves profit generating or at least, as already stated above, that they are sufficiently remote from the realisation of profits of the enterprise that it would be difficult to allocate any profit to them.

If both core and auxiliary activities are carried on through an Irish based fixed place of business, it should be possible to confine any profit attribution to the core activities provided these are separate from, and are not in any way dependent on, the auxiliary activities. If such a connection does exist, it may then be necessary to attribute some profit not only to the core activities but to the auxiliary activities as well. In that case, the question as to precisely what profits should be attributed to the PE is likely to be a complex matter. In arriving at the proper allocation of profits, due weight should be given to the relative importance of the Irish based activities as compared with the overall activities of the non-resident company in relation to the business concerned.

Where it is established that an enterprise of a treaty country has a permanent establishment in the other country, it is necessary to determine what are the profits on which the PE is liable to tax. The simplistic answer would be the profits arising from the trade or business carried on through that PE.

The view of the authorities in some jurisdictions is that once a foreign enterprise has set up a permanent establishment within their territory, it has brought itself within their fiscal jurisdiction to such an extent that all profits that the enterprise derives from that territory, whether from the PE or otherwise, can properly be subjected to tax there. This view does not find favour in the Commentary on the Model Convention, the preferred view being that the fiscal authorities should look at the separate sources of profit that the enterprise derives from their country and should apply the PE test to each. Many treaties provide that where an enterprise carries on business through a PE, "the profits of the enterprise may be taxed in the other State but only so much of them as is attributable to that permanent establishment".

The question as to how profits should be allocated to a PE is extremely complex and is subject to widely differing views. The typical "business profits" article in tax treaties provides that "there shall be attributed to such permanent establishment the profits which would have accrued to it if it were a separate enterprise engaged in the same or similar activities under the same or similar conditions and carrying on business as an independent enterprise". There are two basic approaches to the separate enterprise theory, which can be described as the functional approach and the territorial approach. The territorial approach treats a PE as in effect a fictitious separate legal entity to which income and expenses are allocated as if it were a separate company. It is likely that the Irish, as well as the UK, tax authorities would tend to favour the territorial approach which at least has the appearance of following the "separate enterprise" fiction. There is a danger that that fiction might sometimes be applied in too literal a fashion with results that would go beyond what is reasonable.

The functional approach would attribute profits to each part of an enterprise. Where a PE participates in a transaction, a commission or other remuneration should be allocated accordingly. The basis of the approach would therefore be that each part of an enterprise operating internationally should be remunerated for its function within that enterprise. All internal performances would be remunerated in accordance with their usefulness to the enterprise as a whole. The functional approach goes to the heart of the matter by giving due weight to the place in which the key functions (control, risk etc) are performed.

Electronic commerce

Members of the OECD Committee on Fiscal Affairs reached a consensus on how to apply one of the conditions that, under tax treaties, determine the right of a country to tax profits from electronic commerce. The Committee had been mandated to clarify how the definition of "permanent establishment" in the Model Convention applies in the context of electronic commerce, particularly in relation to the use of web-sites and servers. This matter is discussed in **14.109.1**.

3.107.3 Revenue criteria and guidelines on PE (permanent establishment)

In Issue 26 of Tax Briefing, the Revenue Commissioners published an article headed "Criteria & Guidelines on Permanent Establishment". The following are some excerpts from this article which reflects features of the Commentary on the PE article from the OECD Model Convention.

Criteria to determine if a PE exists

Whether or not a PE exists is a question of fact. Each case must be considered on its own facts. Below are guidelines for determining whether a PE exists, ie whether there is "a fixed place of business in the State in which the business of the enterprise is wholly or partly carried on".

There must be a place of business

A place, though normally a particular portion of space, is to be read in the context of it being used to define "establishment". The term "place of business", therefore, means all the tangible assets used for carrying on the business. It covers any premises, facilities or installations used for carrying on the business whether or not they are used exclusively for that purpose. Thus, a place of business may exist where no premises are available or required for carrying on the business of the enterprise and it simply has a certain amount of space at its disposal.

The place of business may be situated in the business facilities of another enterprise. It may be owned or rented by or be otherwise at the disposal of the business.

The place must be fixed

(a)   The place of business must be established at a certain place. In this regard it is necessary that a link exists between the place of business and a specific geographic point.

(b)   For equipment to constitute a PE, it must remain on a particular site but does not have to be fixed to the soil on which it stands. Where roads are being built, canals constructed etc and the activities performed at each particular spot are part of a single project, the project is regarded as a PE.

(c)   The place of business must have a certain degree of permanency. Mere business relations with enterprises or other customers in the contracting State do not give the requisite degree of permanency. Similarly, a place of business which is of a purely temporary nature cannot constitute a PE, eg a once-off stall at a trade exhibition. A place of business which is not of a purely temporary nature can be a PE even if it exists in practice only for a very short period of time because of:

- the special nature of the activity (eg, a building site), or
- as a consequence of special circumstances (eg, death of the taxpayer, investment failure), its premature liquidation.

The business must be wholly or partly carried on in the fixed place of business.

For a place of business to constitute a PE, the enterprise using it must carry on its business wholly or partly in it. The activity need not be of a productive character. Interruptions of operations encountered in the normal course of the business of an enterprise do not affect the permanence test, provided the business activities are resumed at the same place.

Operations must be carried out on a regular basis. For example, a space in a market place could be a PE provided it is occupied regularly over a period.

Agents

Article 5(4) of the Ireland/UK Convention deals with dependent agents. A dependent agent of a UK enterprise who has and habitually exercises in the State an authority to conclude contracts in the name of the enterprise constitutes a PE here.

Dependent

The agent must be dependent on the enterprise he/she represents. He/she must not have independent status of the kind referred to in Article 5(6) (eg brokers, general commission agents). An agent who is bound to follow instructions relating to the business is dependent on the enterprise. Employees of an enterprise are always dependent agents.

An agent must have power to bind the enterprise.

Authority to conclude contracts

The dependent agent must have authority to conclude contracts in the name of the enterprise he/she represents. Whether or not an agent has such authority is a question of fact and is normally decided against the background of the economic situation. If there are valid reasons for the enterprise to reserve its right to conclude contracts itself (eg, where major contracts are involved) the agent may be considered not to have an authority to conclude contracts. If the agent has authority to negotiate all elements of a contract in a way that is binding on the enterprise, the agent is regarded as exercising his/her authority in the State, even if formal signature of the contract is made by some other person outside the State. The authority could be restricted to specific lines of business within the enterprise's overall business activities. If this is the case, the profits attributable to the PE would be restricted to profits arising from business contracted by the agent. Direct transactions by the enterprise would be disregarded for the purposes of determining profits attributable to the PE.

Habitual exercise

The agent must habitually exercise in the State his/her authority to conclude contracts in the name of the enterprise. There must be a certain degree of permanence. An agent would not constitute a PE on the basis of the conclusion of a single contract. The frequency with which an agent concludes contracts will amount to habitual exercise if it corresponds with what is normal in the line of business concerned. In cases of doubt, the continuity of the agent's exercise of authority should be measured by application of the same criteria as those applied under the general PE concept laid down in Article 5(1). It is not necessary that the continuous activity be exercised throughout by the same person. It is sufficient for the post of dependent agent to have been established.

Residence

It is not necessary that the agent must be resident in the State. It is considered that where the foreign enterprise is a sole trader or partnership, the sole trader or any of the partners would be an agent for this purpose. Thus, a Northern Ireland subcontractor who habitually concludes contracts in the State in the name of the enterprise constitutes a PE of the UK enterprise.

Construction industry – existence of a PE

Under Article 8 of the Ireland/UK Convention, the profits of a UK based enterprise are taxable in the State only if the enterprise carries on business here through a PE situated here. While all the general principles outlined earlier apply to the construction industry, particular difficulties arise in determining whether a PE is in existence in construction cases. This is especially so where the question to be determined is whether, in a particular case, a building site constitutes a PE.

Given the high number of Northern Ireland based enterprises who carry out construction work in the State, Article 5 of the Ireland/UK Convention is regularly invoked to establish the existence or otherwise of the PE in the State. Article 5(3) of the OECD Model Convention provides:

> a building site or construction or installation project constitutes a permanent establishment only if it lasts more than 12 months.

Unlike the OECD Model Convention, the Ireland/UK Convention makes no reference to building sites. [*Author's note:* In fact, article 5(2)(h) of the treaty provides that "permanent establishment" is to include especially "a building site or construction or installation project which lasts for more than six months" (SI 1998/494).]

Revenue view is that, as the Ireland/UK Convention does not specify a period of time before which a building site cannot be a PE, every building site which is a fixed place of business of the enterprise is wholly or partly carried on, is a PE.

In this context:

   (a)   The place of business is the building itself;

   (b)   The place of business is at a fixed location – the site; and

   (c)   The work is wholly or partly carried on in the building site.

A building site is generally regarded as having the requisite degree of permanency as regards a contractor, if the contractor is present on the site for two or more months. However, a building site is regarded as a PE if in existence for a shorter period, where:

   (a)   a contractor brings a significant amount of plant, machinery or equipment onto it; or

   (b)   the contract is a significant one.

In general, Revenue would regard any contract valued at €635,000 or more as constituting a PE.

Revenue also take the view that in the case of road building, the building site is any point along the roadway or proposed roadway where machinery may be left at night.

Meat industry – existence of a PE

Where a contractor provides services in a meat factory, the factory premises can constitute a PE where the requirements mentioned above under the heading "Criteria to determine if a PE exists" are satisfied.

Mutual agreement procedure

Where a person has a PE in the State, he/she is taxable here on the profits attributable to the PE. Under the Ireland/UK Convention, a UK resident with a PE in the State is entitled to credit in the UK for tax paid in the State in respect of profits attributable to the PE. If the UK Inland Revenue rule that the person does not have a PE in this State, credit for Irish tax will not be allowed against the person's UK tax liability. In this event, the person should request a review under Article 24 of the Convention (ie, mutual agreement). Under the terms of Article 24, the two authorities will arrive at a mutual determination regarding the existence of a PE in the State. The request for such a review should be made to the Revenue authority of the state in which the person is resident.

3.107.4 Government and other public loans: computation of losses

Interest on, and profits or gains on the disposal of, securities issued by the government, local authorities and certain semi-state bodies are exempted from tax where the securities are beneficially owned by persons not ordinarily resident in the State (TCA 1997 Part 4 Ch 2 (ss 60-64)). A non-resident company carrying on a trade in the State benefits from this exemption. However, in the case of a non-resident company carrying on a financial trade, such as banking or insurance, interest on, and profits derived on disposals of, such securities are treated as trading receipts of the trade (TCA 1997, s 398).

The securities affected are those dealt with in TCA 1997, s 43 (securities issued by the Minister for Finance), TCA 1997, s 37 (securities of Dublin Airport Authority, Radio Telefís Éireann, Bord Gáis Éireann, Córas Iompar Éireann and Bord na Móna), TCA 1997, s 50 (securities of local authorities issued outside the State), TCA 1997 Sch 32 paragraph 1(1) (stock of local authorities, under section 87 Local Government Act 1946), TCA 1997, s 38 (State-guaranteed securities), TCA 1997, s 39 (securities of certain European bodies – the European Community, the European Coal and Steel Community, the European Atomic Energy Committee and the European Investment Bank – issued in the State), TCA 1997, s 40 (securities of International Bank for Reconstruction and Development), and TCA 1997, s 41 (stock or other securities of a body designated under section 4(1) of the Securitisation (Proceeds of Certain Mortgages) Act 1995).

The removal of the exemption of tax applies where any of the above mentioned securities was acquired by a non-resident company after 29 January 1992, in the case of securities within TCA 1997, s 43, or after 15 May 1992 in other cases, and is held by or for a branch or agency through which it carries on a trade in the State, and if the interest on, or other profits or gains from, the security would be taxable under Case I or IV of Schedule D, or under Case III in accordance with TCA 1997, s 726 (overseas life assurance companies – see **12.603.8**), were it not for the exemption from tax. The exemption from tax is not to apply in such cases so that the branch or agency will be liable to corporation tax under Case I or IV, or TCA 1997, s 726, in respect of the interest or gains.

In ascertaining whether and to what extent a non-resident financial institution or assurance company has incurred a loss in a trade carried on in the State through a branch or agency, income and gains from any of the above-mentioned securities issued on or before 29 January 1992 or 15 May 1992, as the case may be, (which are still exempt) must be included as trading receipts as if the tax exemption did not apply. Thus, a loss brought forward from an accounting period ended on or before 29 January 1992 or 15 May 1992, as the case may be, to a period ended after 29 January 1992 or 15 May 1992, as the case may be, must be reduced by income and gains from the exempt securities. In computing a trading loss for an accounting period ended after 29 January 1992 or 15 May 1992, as the case may be, income and gains from the exempt securities must, again, be taken into account as if they were not exempt.

3.107.5   Exemption in respect of certain interest

Interest received from Shannon/IFSC companies and specified collective investment undertakings

TCA 1997, s 198(1)(c) provides for an exemption from income tax in the case of a company not resident in the State in respect of interest paid by:

(a)   a company in the course of carrying on licensed Shannon operations within the meaning of TCA 1997, s 445 (see **7.205.16**);

(b)   a company in the course of carrying on licensed financial services operations within the meaning of TCA 1997, s 446 (see **7.205.17**); or

(c)   a specified collective investment undertaking within the meaning of TCA 1997, s 734 (see **12.805.2**) (TCA 1997, s 198(1)(c)(i)).

The exemption provided is without prejudice to any charge under the Corporation Tax Acts on the profits of a non-resident company. Thus, the possibility of a corporation tax charge on a non-resident company where it operates an Irish branch or agency is preserved.

Interest received from relevant persons

A company which is not resident in the State and which is regarded as being a resident of a relevant territory is not chargeable to income tax in respect of interest paid by a relevant person in the ordinary course of a trade or business carried on by the relevant person (TCA 1997, s 198(1)(c)(ii)).

A *relevant person* means a company or a collective investment undertaking as defined in TCA 1997, s 246 (see **4.305** under *Relevant interest*).

A company is regarded as being a resident of a relevant territory if:

(a)   where the relevant territory is a territory with the government of which arrangements have been made, the company is regarded as being a resident of that territory under those arrangements; and

(b)   in any other case, the company is by virtue of the law of the relevant territory resident for the purposes of tax in that territory.

Relevant territory means a Member State of the European Communities other than the State or, not being such a Member State, a territory with the government of which arrangements have been made (ie, with which Ireland has a tax treaty). *Tax*, in relation to a relevant territory, means any tax imposed in that territory which corresponds to corporation tax in the State.

Interest on quoted Eurobonds

A person who is not resident in the State and who is regarded as being a resident of a relevant territory (see above) is not chargeable to income tax in respect of interest paid by a company where the interest is interest to which TCA 1997, s 64(2) applies (interest on quoted Eurobonds – see **4.305**) or interest paid in respect of an asset covered security within the meaning of s 3 of the Asset Covered Securities Act 2001 (TCA 1997, s 198(1)(c)(iii)).

Interest paid on a relevant security

There is an exemption from income tax in the case of a company not resident in the State, or a person not ordinarily resident in the State, for interest paid in respect of a "relevant security", ie a security issued by a company in the course of carrying on relevant trading operations within the meaning of TCA 1997, s 445 or 446 (Shannon or IFSC operations) on terms which oblige it to redeem the security within 15 years after the date of issue (see also **7.205.16**) (TCA 1997, s 198(2)), Accordingly, the exemption may apply only in respect of securities issued on or before 31 December 2005.

Interest paid by securitisation vehicles

A person who is not resident in the State and who is regarded as being a resident of a relevant territory (see above) is not chargeable to income tax in respect of interest paid, on or after 6 February 2003, by a qualifying company within the meaning of TCA 1997, s 110 (securitisation of assets – see **7.206.11**) and provided the interest is paid out of the assets of the qualifying company (TCA 1997, s 198(1)(c)(iv)). The exemption from income tax applies as respects any asset:

(a)   acquired or, as a result of an arrangement with another person, held or managed, by a qualifying company; or

(b)   in relation to which a qualifying company has entered into a legally enforceable arrangement with another person;

on or after 6 February 2003 (TCA 1997, s 198(4)).

As regards interest on loan capital falling within the exemptions relating to Shannon/IFSC companies or relevant securities as described above, the Revenue will accept that any discount realised thereon will be treated in the same way as interest on the loan capital provided:

(a)   the investor is not resident in Ireland;

(b)   the investor is not chargeable in the name of a person (including a trustee) or in the name of an agent or branch in Ireland having the management or control of the discount; and

(c)   the investor is not liable to corporation tax on income from an Irish branch or agency or to income tax on the profits of a trade carried on in Ireland to which the discount is attributable.

For all other cases in which discount is realised by a non-Irish investor, there is a technical liability to Irish tax.

3.107.6   Other matters

Distributions received from Irish resident companies

For the treatment of distributions received by a non-resident company from a company resident in the State, see **11.110**.

Payments by non-resident companies

See **4.303.5**.

3.2   COMPUTATION OF CORPORATION TAX

3.201   Computation of income: basic principles

3.201.1   Introduction

Rules affecting the computation of income for corporation tax purposes were dealt with in **3.102.2** above. It is appropriate to refer here to the principles governing the computation of trading income as provided for in income tax legislation and as evolved from case law. TCA 1997, s 81(2) (general rule as to deductions) provides that in computing the amount of the profits or gains to be charged to tax under Case I or II of Schedule D, no sum may be deducted in respect of:

(a)   any disbursement of expenses, not being money wholly and exclusively laid out or expended for the purposes of the trade or profession;

(b)   any disbursement of expenses for domestic or private purposes;

(c)   the rent of any dwelling house or domestic offices, except where used for the purposes of the trade or profession and then only as determined by the inspector and, generally, so as not to exceed two thirds of the rent *bona fide* paid for the dwelling house or offices;

(d)   any sum expended for repairs of premises occupied, or for the supply, repairs or alterations of any implements, utensils, or articles employed for the purposes of the trade or profession, beyond the sum actually expended for those purposes;

(e)   any loss not connected with or arising out of the trade or profession;

(f)   any capital withdrawn from, or any sum employed or intended to be employed as capital in, the trade or profession;

(g)   any capital employed in improvements of premises occupied for the purposes of the trade or profession;

(h)   any interest which might have been paid (notional interest) if interest had been chargeable on any of the foregoing sums;

(i)   any debts, other than debts proved to the satisfaction of the inspector to be bad and doubtful debts to the extent that they are respectively estimated to be bad – the value of any debts due from a debtor who is bankrupt or insolvent is the amount reasonably expected to be received on those debts;

(j)   any average loss beyond the actual amount of loss after adjustment;

(k)   any sum recoverable under an insurance or contract of indemnity;

(l)   any annuity or other annual payment (other than interest) payable out of the profits or gains;

(m)   any royalty or other sum paid in respect of the user of a patent.

The reasoning behind most of these rules is readily apparent. It is evident that domestic or private expenditure should not be an allowable trading expense and that expenditure on the rent of a dwelling house should only be allowable to the extent that the house is used for the purposes of the trade. Similarly, any expenditure which is reimbursed under an insurance policy is not effectively borne and is not therefore allowable. Deductions made in respect of debts are subject to the requirement that they are proved to be bad "to the satisfaction of the inspector" or that their recovery is doubtful, and to the extent only that they are "respectively estimated" to be bad. Provisions made in respect of debts must therefore be specific; no allowance may be made for a general provision in respect of doubtful debts.

Probably the most important rules are those providing for the restriction of expenditure to that incurred wholly and exclusively for trading purposes and for the disallowance of capital expenditure. These two restrictions are the subject of a vast amount of case law concerned with allowable expenditure for tax purposes. It is worthwhile therefore to refer to some of the more important cases dealing with each of these aspects.

3.201.2   "Wholly and exclusively"

If expenditure is incurred partly for trading purposes and partly for other purposes, as will often be the case, it is not allowable. In practice, it is advisable in such cases to charge only the business element, estimated as fairly as possible, in the accounts of the trade. In that way, the full amount charged should be accepted as having been wholly and exclusively expended for the purposes of the trade. While it is necessary that allowable expenditure should be wholly and exclusively incurred for the purposes of the trade, there is no requirement that the expenditure must benefit only the person who incurred it. In *Usher's Wiltshire Brewery Ltd v Bruce* 6 TC 399, it was held that the fact that expenditure by a brewery in connection with its tied houses benefited the publicans who carried on their businesses there, as well as the brewery itself, did not prevent that expenditure being deductible from the profits from the brewing business.

In the case of *Copeman v William Flood and Sons Ltd* 24 TC 53, remuneration paid to a son and daughter whose father controlled the company was held to be partly disallowable to the extent that it was not paid out wholly and exclusively for the purposes of the company's trade. The allowable portion was confined to the amount considered to be commensurate with the duties performed and the responsibilities assumed.

Expenditure for the purpose of preserving a company's business from the threat of nationalisation was held to be deductible as it was accepted that the sole reason for the expenditure was to maintain the existence of the trade (*Morgan v Tate and Lyle* 35 TC 367).

Compensation paid to a customer injured by a falling chimney at the taxpayer's licensed premises was disallowed (*Strong and Co of Romsey Ltd v Woodifield* 5 TC 215).

The expenditure was incurred by the taxpayer in its capacity as householder and not in the course of its trade.

In *Godden v A Wilson's Stores (Holdings) Ltd* 40 TC 161, a payment made to terminate a service agreement on the occasion of the discontinuance of a company's business was found not to have been expended for the purpose of enabling the company to earn its profits. The expenditure related to the termination of the business. The fact that it arose out of, or was connected with, the trade being discontinued was not sufficient to satisfy the requirement that it should be for the purposes of the trade.

A lump sum paid to a director who had been appointed for life, in order to secure his retirement, was held to be allowable on the ground that his retirement was in the interests of the trade (*Mitchell v Noble* 11 TC 372).

The cost of a barrister's clothing was held not to be expenditure incurred wholly and exclusively for the purposes of her profession (*Mallalieu v Drummond* [1981] STC 391). While it was accepted that the particular items of clothing in question were specifically acquired for the purpose of court appearances, it was held nevertheless that another purpose of having those items was the personal one associated with any other acquisition of clothing.

Legal and professional costs incurred by persons carrying on a trade are sometimes disallowed as not being incurred wholly and exclusively for the purposes of that trade. In *Allen v Farquharson Brothers and Co* 17 TC 59, the costs of employing solicitors and counsel in connection with an appeal against income tax assessments were held to be disallowable. Legal costs and accountancy fees incurred in connection with an appeal in which the appellants were held to be entitled to a deduction for certain remuneration of an estate manager were disallowed (*Smith's Potato Estates Ltd v Bolland* 30 TC 267). The expenses in these cases were considered not to have been incurred to enable the taxpayers to earn profits from their trades.

In *Vodafone v Shaw* [1997] STC 734, the activities of a UK mobile telephone network operation were split between three companies for the purpose of meeting regulatory requirements. The appellant, the group parent company, paid a substantial sum to terminate an onerous technical service agreement. The Appeal Commissioners had found that the group was regarded by its directors as a single functional trading entity in relation to the service agreement so that the purpose of the termination payment was to benefit the group as a whole and not the appellant company itself, the trading entity. Accordingly, the payment was not deductible as a trading expense. The Court of Appeal found as a fact that the intention of the directors was to benefit the trading entity and they gave no conscious thought to the position of individual companies so it followed that they did not consciously set out to benefit any particular one of them. Their intention therefore was exclusively to serve the purposes of the appellant company's trade and the payment to cancel the onerous agreement was therefore expenditure incurred wholly and exclusively for the purposes of that company's trade.

Salary paid by a company to an employee seconded to work for a French subsidiary to help rescue it from its financial difficulties was held to be deductible (*Robinson v Scott Bader & Co* [1981] STC 436). It was found that the sole purpose of the secondment was to protect the taxpayer's own commercial interests in France. The decision was based on a finding of fact but the circumstances are probably exceptional.

A question sometimes arises as to whether a company providing finance to other companies, particularly associated companies, is carrying on a trade so that a deduction may be claimed in respect of losses arising in respect of advances made. In *Stone & Temple Ltd v Waters* [1995] STC 1, a company which was a member of a group provided finance to a fellow group member carrying on a restaurant business. Its claim that the advances made were deductible as trading expenses was rejected. It was held that the advances were not made in the course of any trade of banking or money lending and that the company was not carrying on any trade.

In *Garforth v Tankard Carpets Ltd* [1980] STC 251, a company, TC, failed in its claim for a deduction in respect of payments it had made to an associated company, TP, pursuant to security it had given for the liability of TP under a guarantee and security given by TP for bank loans to TP's parent company JLT. JLT handled TC's products and provided it with raw materials and administrative services. The payments by TC were found to be part of an arrangement in the interest of all three companies and on that basis could not have been wholly and exclusively incurred for the purposes of TC's trade.

In *Sycamore plc v Fir, Maple Ltd v Fir* 1997 SSCD 1 (Sp C 104) a company, S, which supplied goods to a subsidiary company, E, also made an interest free loan to that company. E ceased trading owing money to s for goods supplied. s took over part of E's trading stock and credited its value to the inter-company loan account and also paid some of E's creditors. s claimed deductions for the debt owed to it by E in respect of goods supplied and the amount paid to its creditors. The amount was allowed in part. The Special Commissioner held that the value of the stock originally supplied and subsequently recovered should have been credited to the trade account rather than to the loan account but that the balance of the trading debt written off was an allowable deduction. The amount written off in respect of E's creditors was wholly and exclusively for trading purposes. *Garforth v Tankard Carpets* was distinguished.

Interest on money borrowed to replace capital in any form formerly employed in a trade, profession or other business, where the capital was, within the five year period preceding the date of replacement, withdrawn from such use for use otherwise than in connection with a trade, profession or other business, is regarded as not being interest wholly and exclusively laid out or expended for the purposes of a trade, profession or other business (TCA 1997, s 254). This provision is directed at attempts to divert business assets to personal use and would appear to have little if any relevance for companies.

Interest payable on a loan which had been drawn down immediately following the redemption by a company of its preference shares was held to be deductible as a trading expense (*MacAonghusa v Ringmahon Company* SC 29 May 2001). The inspector of taxes had argued that the purpose of taking out the loan was to repay capital and that the interest expense was not wholly and exclusively incurred for trading purposes. TCA 1997, s 254 (see above) was not in question. The taxpayer argued that while the loan was used to redeem the preference shares, the ongoing interest was laid out to retain the benefit of the borrowing and therefore to enable the company to carry on its trade. While the loan was undoubtedly for the redemption of shares, the ongoing interest was in quite a different position as the related borrowing became merged with the ordinary ongoing liabilities of the company in its trading.

The basis of the Supreme Court decision essentially was that the deductibility of the interest should depend on whether or not it was paid wholly and exclusively for trading purposes in the period in which it was paid. The court accepted that the position that arose here was no different in principle to what would have been the case if the company had at all times financed its business by bank borrowings. The governing principle, exemplified in the Canadian case *Trans-Prairie Pipelines Limited v Minister of National Revenue* 70 DTC 6351, was that interest on borrowings should be deductible for periods in which the borrowings were employed in the trade and not that it should be deductible for the life of the loan as long as its first use was in the trade. (See also **3.202.4.**) It must follow from the Supreme Court decision that interest on borrowings to enable a trading company to pay, for example, dividends or tax should also be deductible as a trading expense, assuming the ongoing borrowings are not being employed for non-trading purposes. Indeed, in the *Trans-Prairie* case, reference was made to other Canadian cases in which interest on borrowings to pay dividends was held to be deductible for tax purposes.

The *Ringmahon* judgment confirms that the test for deductibility of interest is the use to which the related borrowings are put when the interest is paid. In this connection, a question may arise concerning the correctness of deducting the entire amount of interest paid in an accounting period where there are both trade and non-trade assets on the balance sheet. If the amount of the borrowings exceeds the net trading assets, it will be difficult to claim that all of those borrowings are being used for trading purposes. In other cases, there may be a question as to whether borrowings should be apportioned between the trade and non-trade assets with a consequential disallowance of part of the related interest. There is little if any evidence of interest being disallowed in such circumstances, perhaps due to uncertainty regarding the correct method that should be employed for the purpose. The UK Special Commissioners' decision in *Dixon v HMRC* [2006] STC (SCD) may be of some interest here, resulting as it did in the Commissioners making an allocation of interest as between business and non-business use in a manner that would seem to be at odds with the thinking behind the approach advocated in *Ringmahon*.

3.201.3   Capital v revenue expenditure

Even where expenditure can be shown to have been incurred wholly and exclusively for the purposes of a trade, it may nevertheless be disallowed if it is capital expenditure. TCA 1997, s 81(2)(f) provides that, in computing profits or gains chargeable to tax under Case I or II of Schedule D, no sum is to be deducted in respect of "any capital withdrawn from, or any sum employed or intended to be employed as capital in, the trade". An example of capital expenditure for this purpose is depreciation on fixed assets (*Re Addie & Sons* 1 TC 1). (See also **3.204.9** regarding income v capital receipts.)

One of the tests developed by case law for distinguishing between capital and revenue makes a distinction between fixed and circulating capital. Fixed capital of a company is the permanent capital of its business, capital which it retains or is renewed only at long intervals in the form of assets that either generate income without the need for further action by the company (eg, shares held by an investment company) or are employed to produce income (eg, premises, plant and machinery). Circulating capital is intended to produce profits by parting with it, by turning it over in the course of the business cycle, eg debtors, stocks and work in progress. Generally, receipts or expenditure relating to fixed capital will be capital in nature and will be excluded from the computation of income or loss while receipts and expenses relating to circulating capital will be included.

Clearly, the above distinction will be more obviously understood in relation to the assets side of the balance sheet. Although it is also relevant to the characterisation of liabilities, it is not as clear that liabilities can be distinguished in terms of fixed and circulating "capital". Furthermore, as a test, its usefulness has been questioned as it was, for example, by Jenkins LJ in *Reynolds and Gibson v Crompton* 33 TC 288 where he suggested that "circulating capital" was no more than an expression used to denote capital expended in the course of a trade with a view to the disposal at a profit of the assets produced or acquired by means of such expenditure and represented at different stages by cash, assets into which the cash has been converted, and debts owing from customers to whom those assets have been sold. Applying the test "begs the question" as expenditure on assets may be characterised as circulating capital only if the acquisition of those assets is itself an operation of the trade.

In *Van den Berghs Ltd v Clark* 19 TC 390 (see further below), Lord Macmillan also found the differentiation between fixed and circulating capital not to be very helpful as a criterion for distinguishing capital from revenue expenditure.

The preferred ("enduring benefit") test for making the distinction between capital and revenue expenditure was that enunciated in *Atherton v British Insulated and Helsby Cables Ltd* 10 TC 155 where Viscount Cave said:

> When an expenditure is made, not only once and for all, but with a view to bringing into existence an asset or an advantage for the enduring benefit of a trade, I think there is very good reason (in the absence of special circumstances leading to an opposite conclusion) for treating such expenditure as properly attributable not to revenue but to capital.

There are echoes of this in the Australian case *Sun Newspapers Ltd v Federal Taxation Comrs* (1938) 61 CLR 337 where Dixon J said:

> There are I think three matters to be considered (a) the character of the advantage sought, and in this matter its lasting qualities may play a part, (b) the manner in which it is to be used, relied upon or enjoyed, and in this and under the former head recurrence may play its part and (c) the means adopted to obtain it, that is, by providing periodical reward or outlay to cover its use or enjoyment for periods commensurate with the payment or by making final provision or payments so as to secure future use or enjoyment.

The enduring benefit test of Viscount Cave, notwithstanding its own enduring character, should not be applied so as to push its usefulness beyond its natural limitations. The case in question concerned the creation by a company of an asset in the form of a pension fund which was to last for the remaining life of the company. Attempts to apply the test in an overly rigid or simplistic manner are likely to lead to questionable conclusions. The test is not appropriate for dealing with situations relating to long term trading arrangements (as, for example, was explained by Lord Reid in *Strick v Regent Oil* – see below). The test does not take account of the fact that various types of what are undoubtedly capital expenditure may not result in any net benefit or advantage, for example the cost of moving from one business premises to another. Neither does the test take account of expenditure incurred to get rid of a disadvantage such as an onerous contract or liability. Thus a payment to remove an employee will be a revenue expense (as in *Mitchell v Noble* 11 TC 372 – see also **3.201.2**) but payments to remove other kinds of burdens are likely to be capital in nature.

A difficulty of applying the enduring benefit test is the uncertainty regarding the extent to which the advantage or asset is "enduring". The purchase of an asset will endure but temporary licensing will not. But will expenditure incurred on hire purchase endure? In *Taxation Comrs v Nchanga Consolidated Copper Mines Ltd* [1964] AC 948, Lord Radcliffe said that it would be a misuse of the authority of the *Atherton* decision to say that to secure a benefit for a business is *prima facie* to incur capital expenditure except where the benefit is so transitory as not to endure at all.

There are important cases which deal with the question of expenditure being incurred for the purpose of obtaining the release from an onerous contract or liability. The decisions in these cases have largely turned on the matter in respect of which the release was being sought. In *Anglo-Persian Oil Co v Dale* 16 TC 253, a lump sum payment made to cancel an agency contract was held to be an allowable deduction. The company had appointed another company to act as its agent in "Persia and the East" and the payment was made to secure the termination of the agency agreement as the company decided that its affairs in the East could best be managed by its own organisation. Although it is reasonable to suppose that the cancellation of such an agency agreement was likely to have long term consequences, in that the business of the company could be run to better advantage in the future, this did not mean that the payment was capital expenditure. It was found that the payment did not create any enduring advantage or benefit for the company's trade; the cancellation of the agreement "merely effected a change in its business methods and internal organisation, leaving its fixed capital untouched".

The above decision contrasts with that in *Countess Warwick Steamship Co Ltd v Ogg* 8 TC 652 where payments made in connection with the cancellation of a contract for the construction of a ship were held to be capital in nature and therefore not deductible. As the subject matter of the compensation payment was itself a capital asset, it followed that the payment for its cancellation was capital expenditure. A similar conclusion was reached in the case of *Mallett v Staveley Coal and Iron Co Ltd* 13 TC 772 which concerned the payment of a lump sum for the surrender by a company of leases of certain coal seams with several years to run. The payment was held to be capital expenditure as it was made to get rid of capital assets. In *Whitehead v Tubbs (Elastics) Ltd* [1984] STC 1, a payment for the release from an onerous debenture was held to constitute capital expenditure. It was found that the payment enabled the company to trade more profitably and that it secured for it enduring advantages of a capital nature. In *Van den Berghs Ltd v Clark* 19 TC 390, which can be distinguished from the *Anglo-Persian* case above, damages paid by a company for breach of joint venture agreements were held to relate to a capital asset as the contract related to the whole structure of the company's profit-making apparatus.

Not surprisingly, there have been many cases dealing with expenditure on premises and in which the decision to be made was whether the expenditure in question was in respect of mere repairs, which would be regarded as revenue expenditure, or was for the replacement of an asset. The cost of replacing a chimney which was a separate structure was held to be capital expenditure (*O'Grady v Bullcroft Main Collieries Ltd* 17 TC 93) whereas expenditure on replacing a chimney which was part of a factory building, including the cost of removing the old one, was found to be revenue expenditure (*Samuel Jones and Co (Devondale) Ltd v IRC* 32 TC 513). Expenditure on extensive repairs carried out under the terms of a covenant in a lease was held to be capital expenditure (*Jackson v Laskers Home Furnishers Ltd* 37 TC 69). Expenditure on the demolition of an old spectator stand at a football ground and its replacement by a modern stand was found to be capital expenditure. A claim that the replacement represented repairs, on the basis that the stand was part of a larger premises, was rejected. An alternative claim for capital allowances in respect of expenditure on the stand as "plant" was also rejected; the stand was the place within which, and not by means of which, spectators watched matches (*Brown v Burnley Football and Athletic Club Co Ltd* [1980] STC 424).

In an Irish case, *Curtin v M Ltd* 1960 IR 97, a claim that part of the expenditure on rebuilding premises should be considered as expenditure on repairs was rejected. It was held that the work carried out resulted in new premises and the expenditure was therefore capital expenditure. In another Irish case, *Martin Fitzgerald v CIR* 1 ITC 100, the cost of fitting out temporary premises pending the rebuilding of other premises destroyed by fire was held to be capital expenditure. In yet another Irish case, *Vale v Martin Mahony and Bros Ltd* 2 ITC 331, the cost of installing sanitary facilities at the direction of the public health authority was held to be capital expenditure.

The distinction between capital and revenue expenditure in other areas was the subject of a number of Irish cases. The cost of replacing fixtures and plant with specifications different from those being replaced but which did not contain any element of improvement was held to be revenue expenditure (*Hodgkins v Plunder and Pollack (Ireland) Ltd* 3 ITC 135). The expense of removing the top-soil of a quarry was held to be revenue expenditure (*Milverton Quarries Ltd v Revenue Commissioners* 3 ITC 279). Lump sum payments and increased grants made by a main distributor to a petrol retailer to secure the exclusive sales of the distributor's products by the retailer were held to be revenue expenditure (*Dolan v AB Company Ltd* (15 March 1968, unreported) SC). About 75% of the agreements were for periods of five years or less though a small number were for periods of up to 20 years. The majority judgment in the Supreme Court relied on the decision in *Bolam v Regent Oil Co Ltd* 37 TC 56 in which sums paid to obtain exclusivity agreements for periods of up to six years were held to be revenue in nature. Instalment payments made for the supply for ten years of technical information and an exclusive licence in Ireland in any patents held by the payee were held to be capital expenditure (*S Ltd v O'Sullivan* (28 February 1972, unreported), HC).

In *Strick v Regent Oil Co Ltd* 43 TC 1, a petrol marketing company paid a lump sum under an exclusivity agreement to a retailer as a premium for the grant of a lease of his business premises. The premises were subsequently subleased back to the retailer who covenanted to sell only the company's products under the terms of the sublease. The premiums were held to be capital in nature as the company had acquired an interest in land which interest enabled it to grant a sublease with a valuable covenant in its favour. The House of Lords indicated that a single payment for a lease for no more than three years might be revenue in nature since over such a short period the overall result is fair. They indicated that a lump sum paid for an agreement for a period of 20 years or more exhibited the "once and for all" nature of capital expenditure.

Referring to the enduring benefit test, it was pointed out by Lord Reid that Viscount Cave was dealing with a case where the payment was made literally once and for all and where the asset or advantage was to last as long as the company lasted. There was nothing to indicate that what Viscount Case had in mind would include a case in which the asset or advantage would last for a short period of years after which further outlay would be required to secure a corresponding asset or advantage. It was suggested that Viscount Cave intended to link "enduring" with "once and for all" and that he had in mind a single payment for an advantage that would last for an indefinite time rather than an advantage of limited duration.

Finally, distinguishing the decision in *Bolam v Regent Oil* (see above), Lord Reid noted that the longest ties in that case were for five or six years, that a business cannot be managed on a day to day basis and that there must be arrangements for future supplies and sales so that it is not unreasonable to look five or six years ahead (as happens with the familiar "five-year plan"). Such arrangements are reasonably regarded as an ordinary incident of marketing and the associated cost a part of the ordinary running expenses of the business. If the payment will need to be repeated after five years, it can be regarded as a recurring payment and there is no serious distortion of the profit and loss account for that period if payment is made by way of a lump sum instead of being spread over that period.

In *Vallambrosa Rubber Co v Farmer* 5 TC 529, Lord Dunedin said that capital expenditure is something that is going to be spent once and for all and income expenditure is a thing that is going to recur every year. In *Ounsworth v Vickers Ltd* 6 TC 671, Rowlatt J drew a distinction between revenue and capital expenditure as one between expenditure that was to meet a continuous demand and expenditure made once and for all. In *Taxation Comrs v Nchanga Consolidated Copper Mines Ltd* [1964] AC 948, Lord Radcliffe referred to a demarcation between the cost of creating, acquiring or enlarging the permanent structure of which the income is to be the produce or fruit and the cost of earning that income itself or performing the income earning operations.

The deductibility of legal and professional expenses usually requires some consideration as these costs are frequently incurred in connection with the acquisition of capital assets or are otherwise for capital purposes. Legal and other professional expenses incurred in connection with the acquisition of a property, including a lease, or in relation to the purchase of shares in a company, would constitute capital expenditure following the principles emerging from the relevant case law. Fees paid or expenses incurred in obtaining, for the purposes of a trade, the registration of a trade mark or the renewal of registration of a trade mark are allowable in computing the profits or gains of the trade. Fees in connection with the obtaining of registration of a trade mark would normally be capital in nature but their allowability is specifically provided for in TCA 1997, s 86.

Legal fees in connection with debt collection or for the purpose of dealing with product liability claims or expenses incurred for the purpose of maintaining or defending existing rights would normally be revenue in nature and therefore deductible in computing profits or gains of a trade for tax purposes. Legal expenses incurred for the purpose of protecting a company's title to land and buildings used for its trade were held to be deductible for tax purposes (*Southern v Borax Consolidated Ltd* 23 TC 597).

There is no rule whereby the treatment of expenditure on the part of the payer determines its character for tax purposes in the hands of the recipient. It is not unusual to encounter an item of expenditure that is revenue expenditure of the payer but a capital receipt of the recipient, and vice versa.

3.202 Computation of income: other legislative provisions

3.202.1 Pre-trading expenditure

Pre-trading expenses which are wholly and exclusively laid out for the purposes of the trade in the three years prior to its commencement are treated as incurred at the time the trade is set up and are therefore deductible in calculating trading income of that trade once it commences (TCA 1997, s 82). Charges on income (see **4.404**) paid wholly and exclusively for the purposes of the trade prior to commencement of trading are similarly treated as paid at the time the trade is set up. The expenses covered by TCA 1997, s 82 are expenses and charges not otherwise allowable or deductible for trading purposes but which would have been so deductible had they been incurred after the trade was set up and commenced.

Expenses treated by TCA 1997, s 82 as incurred at the time a trade is set up are not so treated for the purposes of TCA 1997, s 396(2) or 420 (TCA 1997, s 82(3)). They cannot therefore form part of a loss which may be set against total profits under TCA 1997, s 396(2) or 420 (see **4.101** and **8.305**). Expenses allowable by virtue of TCA 1997, s 82 may not be allowed under any other provision of the Tax Acts.

TCA 1997, s 82(3) does not include any reference to TCA 1997, s 396A, 396B, 420A or 420B. Currently, the references to TCA 1997 ss 396(2) and 420 are of little effect since trading losses (other than exceptionally) cannot be set against total profits.

3.202.2 Business entertainment

Apart from TCA 1997, s 81(2), there are particular legislative provisions which restrict the allowability of certain kinds of expenditure for the purpose of computing income of a trade or profession. TCA 1997, s 840 prohibits the deduction of business entertainment expenses in computing profits or gains chargeable to tax under Schedule D. The prohibition also applies for the purpose of computing expenses of management for which a deduction may be claimed under TCA 1997, s 83 (see **12.703**). Also disallowed is any expenditure incurred in providing anything incidental to entertainment. "Business entertainment" means entertainment (including the provision of accommodation, food and drink or any other form of hospitality in any circumstances whatsoever) provided directly or indirectly by a person in connection with a trade (including a business, profession or employment) carried on by that person but not including anything provided by him for *bona fide* members of his staff unless its provision for them is incidental to its provision also for others.

The prohibition of a deduction applies also where the entertainment is provided by any member of the person's staff or by any person providing or performing any service for the first mentioned person where the entertainment is provided in the course of, or is incidental to, the provision or performance of the service.

There is an equivalent restriction of capital allowances in respect of any asset used or provided for use wholly or partly for the purpose of providing business entertainment or for providing anything incidental thereto. The restriction applies to the extent that the asset is used in providing the entertainment.

Expenditure on the provision of a gift is disallowed in the same way as expenditure on business entertainment. Typical examples would be bottles of spirits at Christmas or free goods from stock. Probably not included would be items such as inexpensive pens, calendars and other objects containing the donating firm's logo.

3.202.3 Motor vehicles

Cars purchased or leased before 1 July 2008

There are restrictions both as regards capital allowances and hiring expenses in the cases of "expensive" cars (as there were in relation to running expenses for accounting periods ending before 1 January 2002). These are contained in TCA 1997, Part 11 which is now largely replaced by the provisions of Part 11C (see below). Writing down allowances may only be claimed in respect of the full cost of passenger motor cars costing no more than a ceiling amount, the *specified amount*; otherwise, allowances may only be claimed on an assumed cost equivalent to the specified amount (see **5.212**). The cost to be taken into account for the purposes of this provision is the "relevant cost", which is the actual cost where the vehicle is purchased by the person providing it and, where the vehicle is not so purchased, the retail price at the time it was first provided for use by that person. The cars affected are those constructed or adapted for the carriage of passengers, other than vehicles of a type not commonly used as private vehicles and unsuitable to be so used. Lorries, vans and trucks are not affected but the restriction applies to estate cars and station wagons.

Expenditure on the hiring (not including hire purchase) or leasing of a passenger car is restricted in the proportion which the specified amount bears to the relevant cost of the car at the time it was made. The relevant cost for this purpose is the retail price at the time the car is provided for use and, as a rule of thumb, that price is generally taken to be the list price less 10%. The specified amount which applies is the one in force at the time the expenditure is incurred. In other words, the lease expenditure incurred in any accounting period will be restricted by reference to the specified amount or amounts in force for that period. Where the specified amount changes during the accounting period, the old and new specified amounts are applied to the respective amounts of expenditure incurred up to and from the date of change.

The restrictions on capital allowances and hiring of passenger vehicles apply to expenditure incurred on the provision or hiring on or after 16 May 1973 or, where the expenditure was incurred under a contract entered into before 16 May 1973, to expenditure incurred later than twelve months after that day. The initial specified amount was £2,500 (€3,174.35) and this amount has been amended in subsequent Finance Acts; the specified amount has been increased with effect from the dates set out below and the increased amount in each case refers to expenditure incurred on or after the date in question or, in the case of leasing expenditure incurred before 23 January 1997 where the expenditure was incurred under a contract entered into before the date in question, to expenditure incurred within twelve months after that date. The increased specified amount in each case applies in respect of expenditure incurred in the period shown in the following table:

Expenditure Incurred	Specified Amount €	Legislation
A/Ps ending on or after 1/1/07	24,000	TCA 1997, s 373(2)(p)
A/Ps ending on or after 1/1/06	23,000	TCA 1997, s 373(2)(o)
A/Ps ending on or after 1/1/02	22,000	TCA 1997, s 373(2)(n)
A/Ps ending on or after 1/1/01	21,585.55	TCA 1997, s 373(2)(m)

Expenditure Incurred	Specified Amount	Legislation
	€	
1/12/99 – last A/P ending before 1/1/01 (new cars)	20,950.68	TCA 1997, s 373(2)(l)
2/12/98 – 30/11/99 (new cars)	20,315.81	TCA 1997, s 373(2)(k)
3/12/97 – 1/12/98 (new cars)	19,680.94	TCA 1997, s 373(2)(j)
23/1/97 – 2/12/97 (new cars)	19,046.07	TCA 1997, s 373(2)(i)
9/2/95 – 22/1/97 (new cars)	17,776.33	TCA 1997, s 373(2)(h)
27/1/94 – 8/2/95	16,506.60	TCA 1997, s 373(2)(g)
30/1/92 – 26/1/94	12,697.38	TCA 1997, s 373(2)(f)
26/1/89 – 29/1/92	8,888.17	TCA 1997, s 373(2)(e)
28/1/88 – 25/1/89	7,618.43	TCA 1997, s 373(2)(d)
6/4/86 – 27/1/88	5,078.95	TCA 1997, s 373(2)(c)
29/1/76 – 5/4/86	4,444.08	TCA 1997, s 373(2)(b)
16/5/73 – 28/1/76	3,174.35	TCA 1997, s 373(2)(a)

The cost of a car in excess of the specified amount is to be disregarded in computing any renewal allowance (see **5.108**) in respect of the car. Where this restriction applies, the allowance is computed as if the cost of the car were the specified amount. Where, however, the car is in turn replaced (whether the car then bought costs more or less than the specified amount) the renewals allowance on that occasion is to be computed on the basis that its sale proceeds or trade-in price is scaled down in the proportion which the specified amount bears to its cost. A proportionately smaller amount of proceeds is therefore deducted from the cost of the replacement car in arriving at the renewal allowance. (See **5.213** regarding capital allowances restrictions by reference to emissions-based limits.) TCA 1997, s 375 provides that for the purposes of the renewals basis computation—

(a) an amount equal to the specified amount of the renewals expenditure is included in the Case I computation; and

(b) the reduction from the cost of the new car in respect of the sale proceeds of the replaced car is limited to the proportion of those proceeds that the specified amount bears to the original cost of that car.

TCA 1997, s 377 imposes a restriction on the amount which may be claimed in respect of the hire (the lease rent or other cost of hiring, other than hire purchase) of cars in computing trade profits. If the original retail price of the car exceeds the specified amount, the deduction for car hire, if otherwise allowable, is to be reduced in the proportion which the specified amount bears to that price. The restriction is complementary to TCA 1997, s 374 (see **5.212.1**) which provides that capital allowances in respect of capital expenditure in purchasing a private motor car are given only up to the same specified amount.

The reference to the original retail price (the "retail price" at the time a vehicle was "first made") suggests that the retail price of the leased vehicle at the time it was new should be taken, whether or not the car was new at the time the lease was entered into. In practice, the retail price of a leased car is usually taken for these purposes as being 90%

of its list price (for a retail sale), as published by the main distributor in the country for the type of car in question (based on the 10% discount normally available where a new car is purchased for cash).

Where, in the case of a motor vehicle costing in excess of the specified amount, a hire-purchase agreement is prematurely terminated without the hire-purchaser becoming the owner, the payments made on foot of the agreement are treated as ordinary hire payments and are restricted accordingly under TCA 1997, s 377. Additionally, hire-purchase instalments as between capital and "interest" (the revenue element) are apportioned and the revenue element is allowed as a deduction (TCA 1997, s 378).

In the case of a motor car acquired by hire purchase, the position is generally straightforward where the trader completes the agreement by paying all the instalments and duly becomes the owner of the car. Capital allowances are given from the outset (subject to the specified amount restriction), normally by reference to the cash price in the agreement.

On the other hand, if the trader pays some of the instalments but does not complete the agreement thereby never becoming the owner, TCA 1997, s 378(2) treats all the instalments and any other amounts paid under the agreement as if they had been lease rental payments. Accordingly, the capital allowances given are withdrawn retrospectively. The Case I computation is revised by allowing as a deduction the actual hire purchase instalments paid (restricted by reference to the specified limit) as if each instalment (capital and interest elements) had been a lease rent under a leasing agreement (TCA 1997, s 378(3)). The deduction previously allowed for the hire purchase interest is added back in the revised computation for each period of account affected.

Where a trading company which had hired (otherwise than by way of hire-purchase) a car costing in excess of the specified amount subsequently becomes its owner, so much of the company's total expenditure on both hire and acquisition as does not exceed the retail price of the car when it was made is treated as capital expenditure on the acquisition of the car and the company's capital allowances are restricted to what they would have been had it purchased the car for that amount in the first place. Only the excess of the total expenditure over the retail price is treated as a charge for hire and this excess is apportioned rateably over the hire period with a consequential adjustment of the deductions for hire already allowed (TCA 1997, s 379).

The restrictions provided for by TCA ss 374, 375, 378(2), (3) and 379 do not apply where a vehicle is provided wholly or mainly for the purpose of the carriage of members of the public in the ordinary course of trade (TCA 1997, s 380(1)). Nor do they apply in relation to a vehicle provided by a company that is a manufacturer of a vehicle, or of parts or accessories for such a vehicle, if that company shows that the vehicle was provided solely for the purpose of testing the vehicle or parts or accessories for such vehicle (TCA 1997, s 380(2)).

Emissions-based restriction on deduction for hire of cars

TCA 1997, Part 11C provides for the deductibility of expenditure incurred on, and related matters concerning, the leasing of cars in various emissions categories. Part 11C is to a large extent a restatement of Part 11, modified to take account of the emissions-based restrictions. The scheme, which links the availability of capital allowances and leasing expenses to the carbon emission levels of cars, applies in respect of cars leased on or after 1 July 2008. The provisions cater for three broad categories of business car: those whose carbon dioxide emissions do not exceed 155g/km, those whose emissions are between 156 and 190g/km and those whose emissions are above 190g/km.

Part 11C applies to a vehicle which is a mechanically propelled road vehicle constructed or adapted for the carriage of passengers (subsequently referred to here as a "restricted vehicle"), other than a vehicle of a type not commonly used as a private vehicle and unsuitable to be so used. Excluded from the provisions of TCA 1997, Part 11C are vehicles acquired for short term hire (taxis etc) and vehicles acquired for testing.

The restriction on deductible expenses does not apply where a vehicle is provided wholly or mainly for the purpose of the carriage of members of the public in the ordinary course of trade (TCA 1997, s 380P(1)). Nor does it apply in relation to a vehicle provided by a company that is a manufacturer of a vehicle, or of parts or accessories for such a vehicle, if that company shows that the vehicle was provided solely for the purpose of testing the vehicle or parts or accessories for such vehicle; but, if during the period of five years beginning with the time when the vehicle was provided, the company puts it, to any substantial extent, to a use which does not serve that purpose only, the restriction will be deemed to apply in relation to the vehicle (TCA 1997, s 380P(2)).

The carbon dioxide emissions (the CO_2 emissions "confirmed by reference to the relevant EC type approval certificate or EC certificate of conformity" – TCA 1997, s 380K) referable to any vehicle in the categories A to G are as set out in the following Table.

TABLE

Vehicle category	CO_2 Emissions (CO_2g/km)
A	0g/km up to and including 120g/km
B	More than 120g/km up to and including 140g/km
C	More than 140g/km up to and including 155g/km
D	More than 155g/km up to and including 170g/km
E	More than 170g/km up to and including 190g/km
F	More than 190g/km up to and including 225g/km
G	More than 225g/km

Where the Revenue Commissioners are not satisfied of the level of CO_2 emissions relating to a vehicle by reference to any document other than either of the above-mentioned certificates, or where no document has been provided, the vehicle will be treated as if it were a vehicle in Category G.

For the above purposes, *CO_2 emissions* means the level of carbon dioxide (CO_2) emissions for a vehicle measured in accordance with the provisions of Council Directive 80/1268/EEC of 16 December 1980 (OJ No L 375 of 31 December 1980, p36) (as amended) and listed in Annex VIII of Council Directive 70/156/EEC of 6 February 19702 (OJ No L 42 of 23 February 1970, p1) (as amended) and contained in the relevant EC type approval certificate or EC certificate of conformity or any other appropriate documentation which confirms compliance with any measures taken to give effect in the State to any act of the European Communities relating to the approximation of the laws of Member States in respect of type approval for the type of vehicle concerned.

The limits on deductible expenses are provided for in TCA 1997, s 380M (see above regarding TCA 1997, s 377 in relation to cars leased before 1 July 2008). For the purposes of the section, *specified amount*, in relation to expenditure incurred on the hiring of a vehicle, means €24,000, where the expenditure was incurred by a company in an accounting period ending on or after 1 January 2007. The restriction is complementary to TCA 1997, s 380L (see **5.213**) which provides that capital allowances in respect of capital expenditure in purchasing a private motor car are given only up to the same specified amount.

Where apart from TCA 1997, s 380M the amount of any expenditure on the hiring (otherwise than by means of hire-purchase) of a vehicle to which this Part applies would be allowed to be deducted or taken into account as mentioned in TCA 1997, s 375 (limit on renewals allowance for cars - see above), the amount of that expenditure will—

(a) in the case of a vehicle in Category A, B or C, be increased or reduced, as the case may be, in the proportion which the specified amount bears to the retail price of the vehicle at the time it was made,

(b) in the case of a vehicle in category D or E where the retail price of the vehicle at the time it was made was—

    (i) less than or equal to the specified amount, be reduced by 50%, and

    (ii) greater than the specified amount, be reduced in the proportion which 50% of the specified amount bears to that price, and

(c) in the case of a vehicle in category F or G, be nil (TCA s 380M).

TCA 1997, s 380N (see above regarding TCA 1997, s 378 in relation to cars leased before 1 July 2008) deals with the case in which a hire purchase agreement ends without the potential purchaser becoming the owner of the vehicle. A re-categorisation of payments previously made into leasing payments, suitably apportioned, is then made.

Where a company, having incurred capital expenditure on the provision of a restricted vehicle under a contract providing that it will or may become the owner of the vehicle on the performance of the contract, ceases to be entitled to the benefit of the contract without becoming the owner of the vehicle, that expenditure will, in so far as it relates to the vehicle, be disregarded for capital allowances purposes and in determining what amount (if any) is allowable as provided for in TCA 1997, s 375 (see above) (TCA 1997, s 380N(2)). In any such case, all payments made under the contract are treated for tax purposes (including in particular for the purposes of TCA 1997, s 380M) as expenditure incurred on the hiring of the vehicle otherwise than by means of hire-purchase (TCA 1997, s 380N(3)).

Where the person providing the vehicle takes it under a hire-purchase contract, then, in apportioning the payments under the contract between capital expenditure incurred on the provision of the vehicle and other expenditure, so much of those payments are to be treated as such capital expenditure as is equal to the price which would be chargeable, at the time the contract is entered into, to the person providing the vehicle if that person were acquiring it on a sale outright (TCA 1997, s 380N(4)).

TCA 1997, s 380O (see above regarding TCA 1997, s 379 in relation to cars leased before 1 July 2008) provides for circumstances where the lessee or hirer of a vehicle becomes the owner. An aggregation of all payments is made before being apportioned into capital and leasing payments.

Where, having hired (otherwise than by means of hire purchase) a restricted vehicle, a company subsequently becomes the owner of the vehicle, then, for the purposes of the Tax Acts (and in particular sections 380L (capital allowances - see **5.213.3**) and 380M)—

(a)   so much of the aggregate of the payments for the hire of the vehicle and of any payment for the acquisition of the vehicle as does not exceed the retail price of the vehicle at the time it was made is treated as capital expenditure incurred on the provision of the vehicle, and as having been incurred when the hiring began, and

(b)   the payments treated as expenditure on the hiring of the vehicle will be rateably reduced so as to amount in the aggregate to the balance (TCA 1997, s 380O).

In other words, where the company which had hired a car costing in excess of the specified amount subsequently becomes its owner, so much of its total expenditure on both hire and acquisition as does not exceed the retail price of the car is treated as capital expenditure on the acquisition of the car and the company's capital allowances are restricted to what they would have been had it purchased the car for that amount in the first place. Only the excess of the total expenditure over the retail price is treated as a charge for hire and this excess is apportioned rateably over the hire period with a consequential adjustment of the deductions for hire already allowed.

3.202.4 Interest

Interest paid by companies, whether "short" or yearly interest, is deductible in computing trading or professional income as long as the borrowings in respect of which the interest is paid are undertaken wholly and exclusively for the purposes of the trade or profession. It is also necessary that the interest should not be regarded as being a capital expense. The decision in *European Investment Trust Co Ltd v Jackson* 18 TC 1 was that interest on borrowings that were employed or intended to be employed as capital in the company's trade of selling motor cars on hire purchase was not deductible as a trading expense. The issued share capital of the company was small and its business was financed mainly by borrowings from its parent company. Further advances were made as each hire purchase transaction was entered into. These borrowings did not therefore represent the company's day-to-day trading requirements but were the financial base from which it was able to carry on its trade. A company that was "thinly capitalised" fell to have its interest expense disallowed for tax purposes. A similar conclusion emerged from *Ward v Anglo American Oil Co Ltd* 19 TC 94.

TCA 1997, s 81(2)(f) provides that, in computing profits or gains chargeable to tax under Case I or II of Schedule D, no sum is to deducted in respect of "any capital withdrawn from, or any sum employed or intended to be employed as capital in, the trade". The effect of the above decisions in the UK was removed by legislation in which the provision corresponding to TCA 1997, s 81(2)(f) concludes with the words: "but so that this paragraph shall not be treated as disallowing the deduction of any interest". In practice, the Revenue Commissioners do not seek to disallow interest in circumstances similar to those arising in the *European Investment Trust* case and interest which satisfies the "wholly and exclusively" test will be deductible as a trading expense whether or not the related borrowings can be regarded as on capital account. It seems to be widely accepted that interest for the use of money is of an inherently revenue nature, somewhat analogously with the case of rent payable for the use of premises. In *Beauchamp v F W Woolworth plc* [1988] STC 714 (see also **3.405**), Nourse J in the Court of Appeal expressed the view that the *European Investment Trust* decision was incorrect.

In the strange case of *Wharf Properties Ltd v CIR* [1997] STC 351, it was held that interest on capital borrowings was itself capital in nature, following the dictum of Upjohn J in *Chancery Lane Safe Deposit & Offices v IRC* 43 TC 83, that "the cost of hiring money to rebuild a house is just as much a capital cost as the cost of hiring labour to do the rebuilding". Thus the basis for the capital v revenue distinction in relation to borrowings would be the use to which the borrowings are put in the relevant period. The Privy Council sought to distinguish its decision from those in other cases on the somewhat puzzling ground that these were concerned with the question as to whether or not particular borrowings represented a capital or revenue *receipt*. The decision implies that the deductibility or otherwise of interest could alter over time, depending on changes in circumstances (see also regarding the *Ringmahon* case below).

The judgment in *Brosnan v Mutual Enterprises Limited* 5 ITR 138 (which was concerned with the treatment of exchange losses on borrowings – see **3.405**) suggests that the Irish courts would attach particular importance to the question whether the borrowings in question are *a means of fluctuating and temporary accommodation (rather than to the term of the borrowing)*. The Revenue Commissioners have, however, stated that there are dicta in the High Court indicating that the judge would have attached significance to the fact that the borrowings in question were incurred to acquire a capital asset. It is difficult to know what weight, if any, should be attached to such dicta. Interestingly, in the Supreme Court case *MacAonghusa v Ringmahon Company* (29 May 2001, unreported) SC (see **3.201.2** above), Geoghegan J quoted with approval from a submission from Counsel for the taxpayer in which it was stated that the essence of interest is that it must be looked at in each year, that the taxation treatment is not necessarily coloured by the fact that the principal was used for a capital purpose, and that "indeed it is not so coloured at all because if one builds a factory on borrowings, which is clearly a capital expenditure and the borrowings would not be an allowable deduction, nonetheless the interest is an allowable deduction as has been agreed with the Revenue".

Interest which is treated as a "distribution (**10.203** and **11.106**) may not, however, be deducted as a trading expense (TCA 1997, s 76(5)(a)). Accordingly, interest which, *inter alia*, is paid in respect of borrowings from a non-resident parent or fellow subsidiary company is, as a rule, not deductible and it is this, rather than thin capitalisation, which tends to be the basis for disallowance of interest paid by companies which are heavily dependent on foreign parent company funding.

Interest paid by a company on borrowings employed in the purchase, repair or improvement of premises from which it derives rents is, subject to exceptions in the case of certain residential property – see **3.209.3**), allowable as a deduction in computing the amount of profits or gains chargeable to tax under Case V of Schedule D (TCA 1997, s 97(2)(e), (f)). No such deduction may, however, be made for any period prior to the date on which the premises are first occupied by a lessee for the purposes of a trade or undertaking or for use as a residence (TCA 1997, s 105).

Interest which does not qualify as a trading expense or which is not deductible in computing profits or gains chargeable to tax under Case V of Schedule D, may only be deductible for tax purposes as a charge on income, and for this purpose the interest must qualify for relief under TCA 1997, s 247 (see **4.403**).

3.202.5 Pension contributions

Any sum paid by a company as an employer by way of contribution under an "exempt approved scheme" within the meaning of TCA 1997, s 774 is deductible, for the purposes of Case I or II of Schedule D, as an expense incurred in the year in which the sum is paid. TCA 1997, s 775 confirms, as respects accounting periods ending after 21 April 1997, that the deduction is available in respect of sums *paid* into an approved scheme and not for provisions or accruals in respect of such payments. Furthermore, in relation to payments made after 21 April 1997, no deduction may be allowed in respect of sums paid into a scheme to the extent that provisions in excess of contributions actually paid have already been allowed for tax purposes. Although TCA 1997, s 774(6)(b) provides that the deduction to be made for any accounting period is to be in respect of sums paid in that period, it would appear that there may be cases in which deductions have been made in respect amounts provided.

Schemes will be approved for this purpose, and for the purpose of other benefits (exemption from income tax and capital gains tax in respect of the investment income and capital gains of the scheme, tax relief for employee contributions, and exemption from employee income tax in respect of employer contributions), on meeting certain conditions regarding the nature and purpose of the scheme, and as respects the benefits provided under the scheme, as set out in TCA 1997, s 772. The benefits extended to approved schemes are intended to encourage both employers and employees to set aside sums during the course of the employees' working years to provide for their retirement. It is an important part of national policy that as many employees as possible have made arrangements to provide for an adequate level of income for their retirement, and it is to be expected therefore that only schemes with terms and benefit conditions consistent with that policy should benefit. The conditions relating to an approved scheme are as follows:

(a) the scheme is *bona fide* established for the sole purpose of providing relevant benefits in respect of service as an employee, being benefits payable to, or to the widow, children or dependants or personal representatives of, the employee;

(b) the scheme is recognised by the employer and employees to whom it relates and that all employees eligible for membership have received written particulars of all essential features of the scheme relevant to them;

(c) there is a person resident in the State who is responsible for discharging all duties imposed by TCA 1997 Part 30 Ch 1;

(d) the employer is a contributor to the scheme;

(e) the scheme is established in connection with some trade (including a profession) or undertaking (including the management of rents from property or an investment company) carried on in the State by a person resident in the State;

(f) no repayment may be made in respect of any employee's contributions under the scheme, either during the subsistence of the scheme or later.

The conditions regarding benefits are as follows:

(a)   the maximum benefit for an employee on retirement at a specified age, not earlier than 60 and not later than 70, or on earlier retirement through incapacity, is a pension not exceeding one-sixtieth of final remuneration (ie the average annual remuneration for the final three years of service) for each year of service, up to a maximum of 40 years;

(b)   any pension payable to a widow of an employee who dies before retirement is a pension payable on his death which may not exceed two-thirds of the maximum pension to which that employee would have been entitled had he continued to serve in the employment until his normal retirement date at a rate of remuneration equal to his final remuneration;

(c)   any lump sums provided for the widow, children, dependants or personal representatives of an employee who dies before retirement must not exceed, in the aggregate, four times the employee's final remuneration;

(d)   any benefit for a widow of an employee payable on his death after retirement must be a pension in an amount not exceeding two-thirds of any pension or pensions payable to the employee;

(e)   any pensions for the children or dependants of an employee who dies before retirement or on his death after retirement may not exceed, in the aggregate, one-half of the pension mentioned in (b) or (d) above, as the case may be;

(f)   subject to TCA 1997, s 772(3A) (see below), the only lump sum which an employee may take, if so permitted under the rules of the scheme, is a sum, by way of commuting his pension, not exceeding three-eightieths of final remuneration for each year of service up to a maximum of 40;

(g)   no benefits other than those described above are payable under the scheme.

As respects schemes approved on or after 6 April 1999, certain pensioners may, on retirement, opt to have the value of their pension fund transferred to themselves or to an approved retirement fund subject to a specified amount being transferred to an approved minimum retirement fund (AMRF) (TCA 1997, s 772(3A)). Alternatively, pensioners may opt to have the specified amount invested in a retirement annuity payable to them immediately. The amount which must be transferred to an AMRF or used to purchase an annuity is the lesser of €63,500 and the value of the pension fund, net of the normal tax-free lump sum referred to in (f) above.

The Revenue Commissioners may, if they think fit, approve a scheme notwithstanding that it does not satisfy one or more of the prescribed conditions, in particular:

(a)   a scheme which provides the maximum benefits even though the employee has less than 40 years' service,

(b)   a scheme under which benefits are payable on early retirement within 10 years before the specified age or on earlier incapacity,

(c)   a scheme which permits a repayment of employees' contributions, with interest, in certain contingencies, or

(d)   a scheme which relates to a trade or undertaking carried out only partly in the State and by a non-resident person.

Schemes which fail to satisfy the prescribed conditions in other ways may also be approved. In exercising their discretionary powers as described above, the Revenue Commissioners may attach to the approval such conditions as they think proper to attach. The discretionary powers normally exercised by the Revenue Commissioners fall within guidelines and practices which are set out in the Revenue brochure *Occupational Pension Schemes: Notes on Approval under the* Finance Act 1972.

Contributions made by an employer company under an exempt approved scheme are deductible as a trading expense in the period in which they are paid (TCA 1997, s 774(6)(b)). The deduction is allowed only to the extent that the contributions relate to employees in the trade or profession in respect of which the company is assessable to corporation tax under Case I or II of Schedule D. The expenses of management of an investment company for an accounting period are increased by the amount of pension scheme contributions allowable to the company under TCA 1997, s 774(6)(b). This is provided for in TCA 1997, s 772(3) and the treatment also applies to insurance companies; TCA 1997, s 707(1) provides that TCA 1997, s 772 is, subject to certain modifications, to apply for the purposes of computing the profits of a company carrying on life business.

A sum not paid by an employer by way of an ordinary annual contribution is treated, as the Revenue Commissioners direct, either as an expense incurred in the period in which the sum is paid or as an expense to be spread over such period of years as the Commissioners think proper (TCA 1997, s 774(7)(b)). With effect from 7 February 2003, however, the setting back of contributions against income of earlier years is confined to contributions deducted from a lump sum payable on retirement to provide for dependants' benefits or contributions made on retirement in connection with a previous repayment of contributions or of benefits previously provided to the member of a scheme (such as a marriage gratuity), where the contributor had previously left a scheme.

The term "ordinary annual contribution" is not defined in tax legislation but in accordance with regulations developed by the tax authorities over the years is understood to refer to an amount calculated on the basis of an actuarial report to be necessary to fund the amount of the maximum allowable benefit under the pension scheme or an annual contribution of a fixed amount or calculated on some definite basis by reference to the earnings, contributions or numbers of the members of the pension fund. Special contributions, being contributions in addition to the ordinary annual contributions made by the employer, are often paid into a pension scheme whether to fund past service not already funded or to increase the existing level of benefits. There would also seem to be a requirement that ordinary annual contributions should reflect a commitment to, or an expectation of, a regular pattern of payments calculated on a consistent basis. Payments not exhibiting a basis for calculation or limited by reference to ability to pay may result in such payments being treated as special contributions.

For the year 2003 and subsequent years, non-ordinary annual contributions paid for a tax year between the end of that year and the filing date for the tax return are allowed for the tax year, subject to limits, where a claim is made by the return filing date for the year. Contributions that cannot be allowed either in the preceding year or in the year of payment may be carried forward and allowed in following years, subject to the age-based limits for those years.

Special contributions will usually be allowed in full in the period of payment where the aggregate of all special contributions made in that period does not exceed the higher of €6,350 and the aggregate of all ordinary annual contributions made in the period. If the limit is exceeded, the period over which the special contributions are to be spread is arrived at by dividing the amount of those contributions by the aggregate of the ordinary annual contributions (or €6,350 if higher) payable in the period in question. The maximum period over which the special contributions are spread is five years. Fractions of over a half are rounded up and other fractions are rounded down, except that if the fraction is between 1 and 2, the period of spread is two years.

Where contributions are made by an employer to a pension scheme which is not an exempt approved scheme, the contributions will also be deductible as a trading expense on general principles, ie if they are incurred wholly and exclusively for the purposes of the employer's trade. The allowability of such contributions made by a company might be questioned where the employees in respect of whom the contributions have been made are interested to a substantial extent in the share capital of the company. In those circumstances, it might be difficult to demonstrate that the contributions are made wholly and exclusively for the purposes of the company's trade. Normally, however, the contributions should be deductible and, in this respect, the position of an unapproved scheme would be no different to that of an exempt approved scheme.

Should special contributions to an unapproved pension scheme be made by a company for any period, however, there could be difficulty in establishing that they are an expense incurred wholly and exclusively for the purposes of its trade. TCA 1997, s 774 provides for the deduction of contributions by reference to the period of payment. That would not be the basis for deduction where the scheme is unapproved; the expense allowable for any period in those cases would be the amount which relates to that period. This might raise questions as to when, if at all, a deduction should be given for special contributions made.

A payment made to commute a pension payable to a former employee was held to be a deductible revenue expense (*Hancock v General Reversionary and Investment Company Ltd* 7 TC 358). As the pension which would have continued to be payable without the commutation would have been a revenue item, the payment intended to relieve the company of that liability was itself a revenue payment.

On the repayment to an employee during his lifetime of any contributions previously made by him to an exempt approved scheme, a charge to tax arises under Case IV of Schedule D (TCA 1997, s 780). No tax is charged where the employee exercises his employment outside the State. Tax is charged at a flat rate of 25% on the full amount of the contribution repaid.

A charge to tax also arises in respect of any payment to an employer out of funds held for the purposes of an exempt approved scheme related to a trade carried on by the employer. The payment is taken into account in computing income of the trade for the accounting period (in the case of a company) in which it becomes due for payment (TCA 1997, s 782).

Where the employer carries on an undertaking other than a trade (or profession), the charge to tax is made under Case IV of Schedule D (TCA 1997, s 782(1)(b)).

3.202.6   Redundancy payments

A lump sum, within the meaning of the Redundancy Payments Act 1967, paid by an employer to one or more employees in respect of an employment wholly in a trade or profession carried on by the employer is allowable as a deduction in computing the profits or gains of the trade or profession for the purposes of Case I or II of Schedule D (TCA 1997, s 109(2)). Likewise, a lump sum paid by an employer in respect of an employment wholly in a business carried on by the employer, where expenses of management are allowable under TCA 1997, s 109(3) (investment companies) or TCA 1997, s 707 (life companies), is treated as expenses of management eligible for relief for the purposes of the appropriate section. Where a lump sum has been allowed under TCA 1997, s 109, the amount of the rebate (within the meaning of the Redundancy Payments Act 1967) recoverable is treated as a trading receipt of the trade or profession. In the case of an investment company or a life company, the amount of any such rebate is deducted from the amount of the lump sum allowable as expenses of management under TCA 1997, s 109.

Where a lump sum is paid after the discontinuance of a trade or profession, the net amount deductible is regarded as having been paid on the last day on which the trade or profession was carried on. Where paid after the discontinuance of a business carried on by an investment company or life company, the net amount allowable is treated as if it were expenses of management incurred on the last day on which the business was carried on.

Where all or part of a lump sum is paid by the Minister for Labour under section 32 of the Redundancy Payments Act 1967, the employer is treated as having made that payment to the extent that the employer has reimbursed the Minister.

The allowance for redundancy payments on the statutory basis outlined above is made where an allowance cannot otherwise be made. Redundancy payments will be deductible in the case of a trade or profession where they are incurred wholly and exclusively for the purposes of that trade or profession. In the case of a continuing trade or profession, redundancy payments made to employees in respect of the termination of their employment will normally qualify on that basis as a deduction in computing the profits or gains of the trade or profession. In *Smith v Incorporated Council of Law Reporting* 6 TC 477, a gratuity paid voluntarily to a retiring employee was held to be deductible on the ground that the expectation of such a payment attracted other employees and might also induce them to accept smaller salaries than they would otherwise have been prepared to accept. Where the trade or profession ceases at or about the time the redundancy payments are made, any non-statutory redundancy payments are unlikely to be deductible as it will probably not be possible to show that they have been incurred wholly and exclusively for the purposes of the trade or profession in those circumstances.

Relevant to the question of deductibility of redundancy payments is the distinction between capital and revenue. Thus, a sum set aside to provide income to be used for invalid employees (*Rowntree Ltd v Curtis* 8 TC 678), a lump sum paid to form the nucleus of an unapproved pension fund (*British Insulated & Helsby Cables v Atherton* 10 TC 155) and a sum paid for insurance against pensions to former servants (*Morgan Crucible Co Ltd v IRC* 17 TC 311) have all been held to be non-deductible capital payments. On the other hand, annual payments to a trust fund established by a company to purchase shares in the company for the benefit, inter alia, of employees (*Heather v P-E Consulting Group Ltd* 48 TC 293), contributions by a company to a trust fund established for the benefit of older employees (*Jeffs v Ringtons Ltd* 58 TC 680), a payment to commute an annual pension already granted to an employee (*Hancock v General Reversionary and Investment Company* 7 TC 358 – see also **3.202.5** above) and a payment made to commute an annual liability for insurance premiums (*Green v*

Cravens Railway Carriage & Wagon Co Ltd 32 TC 359) have been held to be deductible revenue payments.

The deciding factor in these cases is the benefit derived from the payment made. If the benefit is in substance a capital asset the payment will be a capital payment whereas, if it is simply the discharge of what would otherwise be future revenue liabilities, the payment will be a revenue one. The essential distinction, in the *Morgan Crucible*, *P-E Consulting*, *Ringtons* and *Hancock* cases, was between insuring for a lump sum against liability to pay a pension (capital) and commuting a pension for a lump sum (revenue).

Where a lump sum is paid by an employer in respect of an employment wholly in maintaining or managing premises the related expenses of which are deductible under TCA 1997, s 97, the excess of the lump sum over any amount of rebate recoverable is treated, if not otherwise so treated under that section, as a payment made by the employer in respect of the maintenance or management of the premises. If the payment was made after the latest time that it could be taken into account under TCA 1997, s 97, it is treated as having been made at that time.

3.202.7 Charges on income

Payments which are charges on income, within the meaning of TCA 1997, s 243(1), may not be deducted in computing income from any source for corporation purposes. Instead, charges are deducted from the total profits of the company for the period in which they are paid. Where there are excess charges for any period, the amount of such charges, to the extent that they have been wholly and exclusively incurred for the purposes of the company's trade, are treated as a loss or part of a loss for the purposes TCA 1997, s 396 and are accordingly deductible as trading expenses of the trade for subsequent periods. The treatment of charges on income is dealt with fully in **4.4**.

3.202.8 Payments for know-how

A person carrying on a trade may be entitled to a deduction as a trading expenses for expenditure incurred on acquiring technical information, known as know-how, for use in the trade. The deduction will be available provided the expenditure is incurred wholly and exclusively for the purposes of the trade and provided it is not capital expenditure. Many payments for know-how would, however, constitute capital expenditure and would not be deductible as a trading expense for that reason. TCA 1997, s 768 caters for this situation by providing for the deduction as a trading expense of payments for know- how where such payments would not otherwise be deductible.

Where a person incurs expenditure on know-how for use in a trade carried on by him or, having incurred expenditure on know-how, sets up and commences a trade in which the know-how is used, such part of that expenditure as would not otherwise be allowed is to be treated as expenses in computing the profits or gains of the trade for the purposes of Case I of Schedule D. Where the expenditure is incurred before the commencement of the trade, it is treated as incurred at the time of commencement.

The amount to be allowed as a deduction in respect of expenditure incurred by a person on know-how is limited to the amount incurred wholly and exclusively on the acquisition of know-how for bona fide commercial reasons and which was not incurred as part of a scheme or arrangement the main purpose or one of the main purposes of which is the avoidance of tax (TCA 1997, s 768(3A)).

Where a person acquires a trade or part of a trade, including know-how used in that trade or part trade, or where that know-how is acquired by another person connected with (within the meaning of TCA 1997, s 10 - see **2.3**) that person, the expenditure incurred on the acquisition of the know-how may not be deducted as an expense under TCA 1997, s 768. The expenditure would not be deductible on general principles either on the basis that it would be capital expenditure. Neither will relief be given under TCA 1997, s 768 where the buyer of the know-how is a body of persons over whom the seller has control or the seller is a body of persons over whom the buyer has control, or both the buyer and the seller are bodies of persons under the control of some other person.

A body of persons could be either a company or a partnership. *Control* for the above purposes is as defined in TCA 1997, s 312(1); in relation to a company it means the power of a person to secure, by means of the holding of shares or the possession of voting power in or in relation to that or any other company, or by virtue of any powers conferred by the articles of association or other document regulating that or any other company, that the affairs of the first mentioned company are conducted in accordance with the wishes of that person. This definition contrasts with the definition of "control" in TCA 1997, s 432 (see **2.401**) which is more specific as to the ways in which a person may be regarded as having or exercising control over a company's affairs.

Know-how is defined in TCA 1997, s 768(1) as industrial information and techniques likely to assist in the manufacture or processing of goods or materials, or in the carrying out of any agricultural, forestry, fishing, mining or other extractive operations.

The Revenue Commissioners may, in relation to a claim by a company, or any other person, that expenditure on know-how is allowed to be deducted—

(a) consult with any person (an *expert*) who in their opinion may be of assistance in ascertaining the extent to which such expenditure is incurred on know-how, and

(b) notwithstanding any obligation as to secrecy or other restriction on the disclosure of information imposed by, or under, the Tax Acts or any other statute or otherwise, but other than in the circumstances referred to below, disclose any detail in the company's claim which they consider necessary for such consultation (TCA 1997, s 768(5)(a)).

Before disclosing information to any expert, the Revenue Commissioners are required to make known to the company—

(i)   the identity of the expert whom they intend to consult, and

(ii) the information they intend to disclose to the expert (TCA 1997, s 768(5)(b)(i)).

Where the company shows to the satisfaction of the Revenue Commissioners (or on appeal to the Appeal Commissioners) that disclosure of such information to that expert could prejudice its trade, the Revenue Commissioners may not make such disclosure (TCA 1997, s 768(5)(b)(ii)).

3.202.9 Patents and trade marks

Fees paid or expenses incurred in obtaining, for the purposes of a trade, the grant of a patent or an extension of the term of a patent are, notwithstanding anything in TCA 1997, s 81(2)(m) (disallowing as a trading expense any royalty or other sum paid in respect of the user of a patent), deductible as an expense of the trade (TCA 1997, s 758).

The allowance here is for expenses incurred in connection with the obtaining of a patent or the extension of the term of a patent and not for the cost of the patent itself. What is allowable therefore are such expenses as legal fees and fees paid to a patent agent and other expenses incurred in connection with the granting or extension of patent rights.

A similar allowance is available in relation to trade marks. Fees paid or expenses incurred in obtaining, for the purposes of a trade, the registration of a trade mark or the renewal of registration of a trade mark, are, notwithstanding anything in TCA 1997, s 81(2)(f) (disallowing capital expenditure), deductible as expenses of the trade (TCA 1997, s 86).

3.202.10 Scientific research

A person carrying on a trade is entitled to deduct:

(a)   the full amount of non-capital expenditure incurred by it on scientific research;

(b)   any sum paid to an approved body carrying on scientific research to enable that body to undertake scientific research relating to the trade; or

(c)   any sum paid to an Irish university to enable that university to undertake scientific research relating to the trade.

as an expense in computing the profits or gains of that trade (TCA 1997, s 764). Expenditure incurred or sums paid on or after 6 April 1968 by a person carrying on a trade will be deductible on the above basis notwithstanding that the scientific research is not related to any trade being carried on by that person.

Allowances for capital expenditure on scientific research are also provided for in TCA 1997, s 765. The relief is by way of spreading the amount of the expenditure over five years but, for expenditure incurred on or after 6 April 1965, the full amount expended may be written off in the period in which the expenditure was incurred or, where the expenditure was incurred before the trade commenced, in the period in which the trade commenced.

The provisions of TCA 1997 ss 764-765 are dealt with more fully in **5.601**.

3.202.11 Value of trading stock at discontinuance of trade

TCA 1997, s 89 provides that where trading stock is sold or transferred for valuable consideration on the discontinuance of a trade to a person carrying on or intending to carry on a trade in the State and who is entitled to a deduction against trading profits in respect of the cost of that stock, the value of the trading stock is to be taken to be:

(a)   where the person to whom the stock is sold or transferred is not connected (see below) with the seller, the amount realised on the sale or, as the case may be, the amount which is the value of the consideration given for the transfer; and

(b)   where those persons are connected, what would have been the price received had the sale or transfer been a transaction between independent persons dealing at arm's length (TCA 1997, s 89(2)(a)).

Where the trading stock is sold or transferred on the discontinuance of a trade but not in the circumstances described in the previous paragraph, its value is to be taken as the amount which it would have realised if sold in the open market on the discontinuance (TCA 1997, s 89(2)(b)).

Trading stock means property of any description, whether real or personal, which is either:

(i) property such as is sold in the ordinary course of the trade in relation to which the expression is used or would be so sold if it were mature or if its manufacture, preparation, or construction were complete; or

(ii) materials such as are used in the manufacture, preparation, or construction of property such as is sold in the ordinary course of that trade (TCA 1997, s 89(1)(a)).

For the purposes of TCA 1997, s 89, *trading stock*, in relation to a trade, includes any services, articles or materials which, if the trade were a profession, would be treated as work in progress of the profession for tax purposes (TCA 1997, s 89(1)(b)(i)).

In the case of a transfer of stock in the circumstances described in (b) above but where the arm's length price is more than the "acquisition value" (essentially, the book value – see below) of the stock and is also more than the price received for it, and subject to a joint election by both parties, the value of the stock sold is to be taken to be an amount equal to the greater of its acquisition value and the price received for it (TCA 1997, s 89(4)).

"Acquisition value" means the amount which would, in computing the taxable profits of the discontinued trade, have been deductible as representing the purchase price of the stock if it had been sold immediately before the discontinuance of the trade in the circumstances described in (b) above and on the assumption that the period for which those profits were to be computed began immediately before the sale (TCA 1997, s 89(5)).

For the purposes of TCA 1997, s 89, two persons are connected with each other if:

(a) they are connected with each other within the meaning of TCA 1997, s 10 (see **2.3**);

(b) one of them is a partnership and the other has a right to a share in the partnership;

(c) one of them is a body corporate and the other has control (within the meaning of TCA 1997, s 11 – see **2.402**) over that body;

(d) both of them are partnerships and some other person has a right to a share in each of them; or

(e) both of them are bodies corporate or one of them is a partnership and the other is a body corporate and, in either case, some other person has control over both of them (TCA 1997, s 89(1)(b)(ii)).

3.202.12 Premiums for leases

TCA 1997, s 102 provides for a deduction in charging to tax the profits or gains of a trade or profession carried on by lessees in certain circumstances. The circumstances arise where an amount has become chargeable to tax under TCA 1997 ss 98, 99 or 100 in relation to any premises, or would have become so chargeable but for TCA 1997, s 103(3) or but for any exemption from tax, and the premises are wholly or partly occupied for the purposes of a trade or profession by the person entitled to the lease, estate or interest in respect of which the amount chargeable arose. The circumstances in which a charge to tax under the above-mentioned sections arises are summarised in the following paragraphs.

TCA 1997, s 98 applies where the payment of a premium is required under a lease the duration of which does not exceed fifty years, or under the terms subject to which that lease is granted. The lessor is treated as becoming entitled, when the lease is granted, to an amount of rent (apart from any actual rent receivable) equal to the amount of the premium less one-fiftieth of that amount for each complete period of twelve months, other than the first, comprised in the term of the lease. In certain circumstances, a lease is deemed to have required the payment of a premium. For example, a sum payable by the lessee in lieu of any rent or as consideration for the surrender of the lease, or a sum other than rent payable as consideration for the variation or waiver of any of the terms of the lease, is treated as a premium (see **3.209.2**).

Where a sum in lieu of rent is paid, the term of the lease is treated as including only the period in respect of which that sum was paid, ie the period for which a lesser rent or no rent is payable. In the case of a sum paid in lieu of rent or a sum paid for the cancellation of a lease, the taxable amount in respect of the deemed premium is treated as becoming due when the sum in question becomes payable by the lessee. The value of any work (not including work the cost of which would be a deductible expense to the lessor if he were required to undertake it) carried out by a lessee on premises under an obligation imposed by the terms under which a lease is granted is also deemed to be a premium.

TCA 1997, s 99 creates a charge under Case IV on any profit or gain realised on the assignment of a lease, for a period not exceeding fifty years, which was granted at undervalue. A lease is regarded as granted at undervalue if no premium, or a premium of an amount which is less than the arm's length premium for the lease, was received in respect of the grant (see **3.208.6**).

TCA 1997, s 100 imposes a charge to tax under Case IV on a person who sells an estate or interest in land where the terms of the sale entitle the vendor, or a person connected with him, either to a reconveyance of the interest sold at some future time, or to the grant of a lease directly or indirectly out of the interest sold (not including a lease commencing within one month of the sale). Where a reconveyance is provided for, the Case IV charge is on the excess of the sale consideration for the interest sold over the price at which it is to be reconveyed. Where the earliest date on which the reconveyance can take place is at least two years after the sale, the chargeable amount is the excess referred to less one-fiftieth thereof for each complete year, other than the first, in the period between the sale and that date. Where the grant of a lease is provided for, other than where the lease begins to run within one month after the sale, the grant is deemed to be a reconveyance for a sum equal to the amount of the premium (if any) for the lease and the value at the date of sale of the right to receive a conveyance of the reversion immediately after the lease begins to run (see **3.208.6**).

The person occupying the premises in any of the above situations, whether or not the original lessee, is treated as having paid, in addition to any rent actually paid, rent in respect of the premises of an amount equal to a proportionate part of the amount chargeable on the person who granted the lease. The proportion in this case is the length of the period during which the premises are occupied for the purposes of the trade or profession over the length of the relevant period, and the rent is to be taken as accruing from day to day. In relation to this latter point, where the chargeable amount arises in respect of the surrender of a lease, it is suggested, although the point is not fully clear, that the deduction is available for the period in which the surrender takes place: TCA 1997 s 98(3)(b) provides that the taxable amount is treated as becoming due when the sum in question becomes payable by the lessee so that the corresponding deduction to the lessee should also be for that period. For any accounting period for which a deduction is due to a company occupying premises for the purposes of its trade or profession therefore, the deemed rent paid is calculated as a proportion of the amount chargeable on the lessor as represented by the ratio of the length of that period to the length of the relevant period. The "relevant period" is:

(a) where the lessor is chargeable under TCA 1997, s 98, the full duration of the lease;

(b) where the lessor is chargeable under TCA 1997, s 99, the period of the lease remaining at the date of the assignment;

(c) where the lessor is chargeable under TCA 1997, s 100, the period commencing at the date of the sale and ending on the date fixed for the reconveyance or the grant of the lease, or, if no such date is fixed, the earliest date on which the reconveyance or grant could take place in accordance with terms of the sale.

In practice, a person entitled to a deduction in accordance with TCA 1997, s 102 will not always easily be aware of the entitlement to that deduction. As the deduction due is tied to the amount in respect of which the lessor has been charged to tax, a lessee of premises used in the carrying on of a trade or profession has no direct means of ascertaining what allowances may be due. It is in the interests of a person taking over a lease to obtain full particulars of any circumstances in which the lessor has been charged to tax under TCA 1997, s 98, 99 or 100.

A similar deduction is given by TCA 1997, s 103 for the purposes of computing income assessable under Case V of Schedule D. TCA 1997, s 97(2) authorises a deduction for any rent paid by the person chargeable under Case V of Schedule D and for this purpose the deemed rent is calculated by reference to the amount chargeable on the lessor under TCA 1997, s 98, 99 or 100 is treated as rent paid, in addition to any rent actually paid (see **3.209.2**).

3.202.13 Restrictive covenants

Any sum or valuable consideration given by a person carrying on a trade or profession which is chargeable to tax under TCA 1997, s 127(2) (charge under Schedule E or Case III of Schedule D in respect of payments received for restrictive covenants) on an individual holding an office or employment may be deducted as an expense in computing for the purposes of Schedule D the profits or gains of that person's trade or profession (TCA 1997, s 127(4)). In the case of a company, the deduction is made for the accounting period in which the payment is made or the valuable consideration given.

Where a sum paid or valuable consideration given by an investment company (within the meaning of TCA 1997, s 83 – see **12.702**), or a company to which TCA 1997, s 83 applies by virtue of TCA 1997, s 707 (expenses of management of assurance companies – see **12.603.3**), is chargeable to tax in accordance with TCA 1997, s 127(2), the sum paid or the value of consideration given is treated for the purposes of TCA 1997, s 83 as an expense of management for the accounting period in which the sum is paid or valuable consideration is given (TCA 1997, s 127(5)).

3.202.14 Removal expenses

Arising out of the decision in *Granite Supply Association v Kitton* 5 TC 168, expenses of moving from one business premises to another are not allowable deductions in computing the profits of a trade or profession. The Revenue Commissioners are, however, generally prepared to allow the expenses of moving trading stock where the trade in question is continuing. Expenses in moving plant and machinery are not covered by this practice and are probably therefore not allowable as trading expenses. Any such expenses may be added to the cost of the plant and machinery for the purposes of computing capital allowances.

3.202.15 Relief for the long-term unemployed

As an incentive for the long-term unemployed to take up employment and for employers to employ such individuals, TCA 1997, s 88A provides respectively for an additional personal allowance to employees concerned and for a double deduction to their employers in computing trading profits.

A long-term unemployed individual, or "qualifying individual", is an individual who has been unemployed for at least 12 months and who is in receipt of either an unemployment payment (unemployment benefit or unemployment assistance) or the one-parent family allowance from the Department of Social, Community and Family Affairs. Time spent on certain activities, programmes or courses for the unemployed may in certain circumstances be taken into account for the purposes of calculating the 12 month period of unemployment.

A double deduction may be claimed in computing the profits of the trade or profession of the employer in respect of the emoluments paid to a qualifying individual in the first 36 months of a qualifying employment and for the employer's PRSI contribution in respect of those emoluments. The double deduction is provided for in TCA 1997, s 88A(2) and the subsection applies where, in the computation of the amount of the profits or gains of a trade or profession for a chargeable period, an employer is otherwise entitled to a deduction for (i) emoluments payable to a qualifying individual in respect of a qualifying employment and (ii) employer's contributions to the Social Insurance Fund payable in respect of those emoluments under the Social Welfare Acts. In any such case, the employer will be entitled in that computation to an additional deduction equal to the amount of the first-mentioned deduction as respect the qualifying employment.

The additional deduction may not be claimed in respect of a chargeable period or part of such period which is outside the three year qualifying period in relation to the qualifying employment. Neither may such additional deduction be claimed where the employer, or the qualifying individual, is benefiting or has benefited under an employment scheme, whether statutory or otherwise. An "employment scheme" for this purpose means a scheme or programme which provides for the payment in respect of an employment to an employer or employee of a grant, subsidy or other such payment and which is funded directly or indirectly by the State or by any board established by statute or by any public or local authority.

3.202.16 Appropriations to and from stock-in-trade

Where in an accounting period trading stock is disposed of otherwise than in the course of trade, it is necessary to credit an appropriate amount in the computation of the profits of the trade for tax purposes for that period. The UK case *Sharkey v Wernher* 36 TC 275 established that the amount to be so credited should be the market value at the time. This decision was applied in *Petrotim Securities Ltd v Ayres* 41 TC 389 in relation to a disposal of shares at gross under-value as part of a tax avoidance scheme. *Petrotim Securities* was in turn applied in *Ridge Securities Ltd v CIR* 44 TC 373 which involved the purchase by a share-dealing company of War Loan from an associated company (in fact, the taxpayer company in the *Petrotim Securities* case) and where it was held that the transaction was not a trading transaction and that the acquisition price should be market value and not, as was much lower, the actual purchase price.

The UK Revenue consider that the effect of *Sharkey v Wernher* is that where a trader takes goods from trading stock for personal use, or disposes of goods otherwise than in the course of trade, the amount to be credited for tax purposes in relation to the transaction is the market value of the goods; this treatment does not apply, however, to services rendered to a trader personally or to expenditure incurred on the construction of a fixed asset for use in a trade.

The principle in *Sharkey v Wernher* is not relevant to purchases and sales in the course of trading, even where not at arm's length (unless the price involved is such as to suggest that the transaction is not a trading transaction). Thus, in *Craddock v Zevo Finance* 27 TC 267, where a property-dealing company acquired property at a substantial overvalue from its associated company, the Revenue failed in its claim to substitute market value for the actual purchase price. Thus, generally, the Revenue cannot rewrite the terms of a genuine bargain for tax purposes. Not surprisingly, neither can a taxpayer so that, in *Jacgilden (Weston Hall) v Castle* 45 TC 685, a property-dealing company which acquired property at a substantial undervalue from its controlling shareholder failed in its contention to substitute market value for the actual price paid in the transaction.

The decision in *Sharkey v Wernher* is inconsistent with that in *Dublin Corporation v McAdam* 2 TC 387 in which it was held that "no man ...can trade with himself: he cannot ... make in what is its true sense of meaning, taxable profits by dealing with himself". In practice, *Sharkey v Wernher* is not followed in Ireland and the approach of the Revenue Commissioners is to bring the amount of the trading stock into the tax computation at cost. In particular, this is exemplified in relation to the trade of bloodstock breeding in Ireland (see **13.107.4**) where transfers from the stud farm to racing (as well as transfers from racing to stud) are to be taken at cost.

Appropriations to trading stock of assets previously held otherwise than for trading are, also based on *Sharkey v Wernher*, generally treated in the UK as involving a disposal and reacquisition at market value. The general practice in Ireland is, again, to treat such appropriations as taking place at cost. TCA 1997, s 618(1) (see **9.205.3**), however, seems to assume that a transfer by a non-trader to a trader within a capital gains group would normally take place at market value.

3.202.17 Restriction of employee benefit contributions

TCA 1997, s 81A contains measures affecting deferred compensation schemes that seek to align the timing of allowable deductions for employers in respect of contributions to employee benefit schemes with the time the benefit from those contributions is received by the employees. Amounts allowable in accordance with legislation dealing with employee profit sharing schemes, employee share ownership trusts, savings-related share option schemes, approved share option schemes, approved pension arrangements and certain accident benefit schemes are not affected.

TCA 1997, s 81A will be relevant in a number of circumstances, for example where, by reason of the establishment of an employee benefit trust (EBT), cash is paid to, or shares are transferred to, employees where there is a timing difference between the payment to the employee benefit scheme by the employer and the receipt of the payment or shares by the employee. Where, for example, an Irish employer company incurs expense by way of making a cash payment to an EBT for the purposes of enabling that body to acquire shares in the employer company's parent company, the ensuing corporation tax deduction is to be made by reference to the period or periods in which the employees become taxable on the resulting benefits, ie the period or periods in which they receive shares from the EBT.

An *employee benefit scheme* is a trust, scheme or other arrangement for the benefit of persons who are employees of an employer. An *accident benefit scheme* is an employee benefit scheme under which benefits may be provided only by reason of a person's disablement, or death, caused by an accident occurring during the person's service as an employee of the employer (TCA 1997, s 81A(1)(a)).

An *employee benefit contribution* is made if, as a result of any act or omission—

(i)   any assets are held, or may be used, under an employee benefit scheme, or
(ii)   there is an increase in the total value of assets that are so held or may be so used (or a reduction in any liabilities under an employee benefit scheme) (TCA 1997, s 81A(1)(b)(i)).

A reference to a person's *employee* includes a reference to the holder of an office under that person.

TCA 1997, s 81A does not apply in relation to any deduction that is allowable:

(a)   in respect of anything given as consideration for goods or services provided in the course of a trade or profession;
(b)   in respect of contributions under an accident benefit scheme;
(c)   under TCA 1997 Part 17 (profit sharing schemes, employee share ownership trusts, approved stock option schemes); or
(d)   under TCA 1997 Part 30 (occupational pension schemes, retirement annuities, purchased life annuities and certain pensions) (TCA 1997, s 81A(7)).

TCA 1997, s 81A, subject to subsection (7), applies where—

(a)   a calculation is made of the amount of a person's profits or gains to be charged to tax under Case I of II of Schedule D for a chargeable period (accounting period or year of assessment) beginning on or after 3 February 2005; and
(b)   a deduction would otherwise be allowed for tax purposes for that period in respect of employee benefit contributions made, or to be made, by that person (the "employer") (TCA 1997, s 81A(2)).

A deduction for employee benefit contributions may be allowed only to the extent that, during the chargeable period in question or within nine months from the end of that period:

(i)   qualifying benefits are provided out of the contributions; or

(ii)   qualifying expenses are paid out of the contributions (TCA 1997, s 81A(3)(a)).

For the above purposes, *qualifying benefits* are provided where there is a payment of money or a transfer of assets, otherwise than by way of a loan, and the recipient or a person other than the recipient is or would, if resident, ordinarily resident and domiciled in the State, be chargeable to income tax in respect of the provision of such benefits (TCA 1997, s 81A(1)(b)(ii)).

In relation to a scheme manager and an employee benefit scheme, *qualifying expenses* does not include expenses that, if incurred by the employer, would not be allowed as a deduction in calculating the profits or gains of the employer to be charged to tax under Case I or II of Schedule D but otherwise includes any expenses of a scheme manager (apart from the provision of benefits to employees of the employer) incurred in the operation of the employee benefit scheme (TCA 1997, s 81A(1)(a)).

A *scheme manager* is a person who administers an employee benefit scheme or any person to whom an employer pays money or transfers an asset and such person is entitled or required, under the provisions of an employee benefit scheme, to retain or use the money or asset for or in connection with the provision of benefits to employees of the employer.

Any qualifying benefits provided or qualifying expenses paid by a scheme manager after the receipt by that party of employee benefit contributions is to be regarded, for the purposes of TCA 1997, s 81A(3)(a), as provided or paid out of those contributions up to the total amount of the contributions as reduced by the amount of any benefits or expenses previously provided or paid as referred to in that paragraph. For that purpose, no account is to be taken of any other amount received or paid by the scheme manager (TCA 1997, s 81A(3)(b)).

Any amount disallowed under TCA 1997, s 81A(3) will be allowed as a deduction for a subsequent chargeable period to the extent that qualifying benefits are provided out of the employee benefit contributions in question before the end of that period (TCA 1997, s 81A(4)(a)). For this purpose, any qualifying benefits provided by a scheme manager after the receipt by that party of employee benefit contributions is to be regarded as being provided out of those contributions up to the total amount of the contributions as reduced by the amount of any benefits or expenses previously provided or paid as referred to in TCA 1997, s 81A(3)(a) or (4)(a). For that purpose, no account is to be taken of any other amount received or paid by the scheme manager (TCA 1997, s 81A(4)(b)).

Where the provision of a qualifying benefit takes the form of the transfer of an asset, the amount provided is to be taken to be the total of—

(i)   the amount, if any, expended on the asset by a scheme manager or, where the asset consists of new shares in a company connected with (within the meaning of TCA 1997, s 10 – see **2.302**) the employer, or rights in respect of such shares, issued by the connected company, the market value of those shares or rights, at the time of the transfer; and

(ii)   where the asset was transferred to a scheme manager by the employer, the amount of the deduction that would be allowed (to the employer) as referred to in TCA 1997, s 81A(2) (see above) (TCA 1997, s 81A(5)).

Thus, the amount provided might consist of the market value of shares issued by the parent company of the employer company which value has been cross-charged to the employer. Again, it might consist of the amount incurred by the employer company in acquiring shares in its parent company which shares are transferred to an EBT.

Where the amount so calculated is greater than the amount in respect of which an employee is chargeable to income tax in respect of the transfer (the "second-mentioned amount"), the deduction to be allowed in accordance with TCA 1997, s 81A(3) or (4) may not exceed the second-mentioned amount (TCA 1997, s 81A(5)(c)). If the amount that is subject to income tax in the hands of the employee is less than the cost to the employer, the deduction available to the employer is reduced for corporation tax purposes. This would be the case where, say, the value of shares passing to employees has fallen relative to their value when the employer company incurred expense in connection with their provision. In such circumstances, the employee will be taxable by reference to the lower amount. If the employer company has incurred expense equal to the original value of the shares, the tax deduction available to it is restricted to the amount on which the employee is taxable. Thus, the employer is entitled to a deduction when and to the extent that the employees are taxable in respect of the benefit. (See also **3.305.5** under *Share-based consideration*.)

If the calculation referred to in TCA 1997, s 81A(2) is made before the end of the nine-month period mentioned in TCA 1997, s 81A(3) —

(a)   the nine-month period is, for the purposes of making the calculation, to be taken to be the period ending at the time the calculation is made; and

(b)   after the end of the nine-month period the calculation is, if necessary, to be adjusted to take account of any benefits provided, expenses paid or contributions made within that period but after the time of the calculation (TCA 1997, s 81A(6)).

3.203   Deductions and allowances

3.203.1   General

The Tax Acts contain provisions for deductions and allowances in respect of payments and donations which are not, or which are not obviously, trade related. Some of the relevant provisions apply specifically to companies while others apply both to companies and to other taxpayers.

In the cases of most of the items concerned, companies may claim relief for payments made as expenses in computing trading profits. In certain cases, relief is by way of deduction as expenses of management. In one case, relief is by way of credit, against tax payable by the company concerned, in respect of the market value of the item donated.

3.203.2   Profit sharing schemes

Provisions in TCA 1997 Part 17 Ch 1 (ss 509-518) enable a company to establish an approved profit sharing scheme (APPS) under which shares in the company or in a connected company may, subject to conditions, be appropriated tax free to eligible employees. The purpose of the legislation is to facilitate the acquisition of shares by employees in the company or group in which they are employed but in accordance with the form of a scheme approved by the Revenue Commissioners. Tax benefits obtained may be withdrawn, in whole or in part, where the trustees dispose of any of a participant's shares at any time before the *release date* (the day ending three years after the day on which the shares were appropriated to the participant).

Subject to satisfying certain conditions, however, a participant in an APPS need not hold scheme shares for the three year period. The three year requirement is waived in the case of an appropriation of shares made on or after 11 March 1998, which shares have been transferred to the trustees of an APPS by the trustees of a Revenue approved ESOT (see **3.203.3** below). The conditions to be satisfied are that—

(a) immediately prior to the transfer of the shares from the ESOT to the APPS, the shares had been held in the ESOT for a period of at least three years;

(b) the participant was a beneficiary under the ESOT at all times during the three year period ending on the date of appropriation of the shares (TCA 1997, s 511A(2)).

Where the shares were held for less than three years in an ESOT, the three year requirement in relation to the APSS is reduced proportionately.

Where the above conditions are met, the period of retention (see below) ends on, and the release date becomes, the day following the day on which the shares were appropriated to the participant (TCA 1997, s 511A(1)).

The profit sharing scheme must be set up under a trust deed which provides for the administration of the scheme by trustees resident in the State. The shares which are the subject of the scheme are first acquired by the trustees and are paid for by funds provided to them by the company, or in the case of a group scheme, by a participating company. The shares may be shares which are newly issued by the company concerned or by a connected company, as will most often be the case, or existing shares of the company or of a connected company. The scheme shares must remain in the hands of the trustees for a period of two years (*the period of retention*) from the date they are appropriated to the participating employees in accordance with their respective entitlements under the terms of the scheme. During that period, the shares may not be assigned, charged or otherwise disposed of. The maximum "initial market value" (normally the market value of the shares at the date of appropriation) of shares appropriated to any one employee in any tax year is €12,700 or, subject to certain conditions (ie, in respect of shares which previously had been held in an ESOT as security for borrowings by the ESOT and where the shares had been held in the ESOT for a minimum period of 10 years), €38,100.

Shares which result in the above limit being breached are referred to as "excess shares" while shares appropriated to an ineligible individual are "unauthorised shares". Where there is an appropriation of excess or unauthorised shares, the individual concerned is charged at a later date to income tax under Schedule E on the full market value of those excess or unauthorised shares (TCA 1997, s 515(4)-(7)).

Scheme shares must form part of the ordinary share capital of the company concerned or of a connected company and must be either shares of a class quoted on a recognised stock exchange, or shares in a company which is not under the control of any other company, or shares in a company which is under the control of a company whose shares are quoted on a recognised stock exchange and which is not a close company or which would not be a close company if resident in the State. The shares must be fully paid up, not redeemable, and not subject to any restrictions which do not apply to all shares of the same class.

Part-time employees must be entitled to participate in an approved profit sharing scheme on the same basis as full-time employees.

In respect of a profit sharing scheme approved on or after 11 March 1998, the Revenue Commissioners must be satisfied that there are no features of the scheme which would act as a disincentive to employees or former employees of the company to participate in the scheme and, where the company concerned is a member of a group of companies, that the scheme does not have the effect of conferring benefits wholly or mainly on the directors of companies in the group or on those employees of group companies who are in receipt of higher or the highest levels of remuneration (TCA 1997 Sch 11 paragraph 4(1A)). A "group of companies" means a company and any other companies of which it has control (within the meaning of TCA 1997, s 432 – see **2.401**).

Any sum expended in an accounting period by the company which has established the profit sharing scheme, or by a participating company, in making payments to the trustees of an approved scheme are deductible in computing, for the purposes of Schedule D, the profits or gains of a trade carried on by that company (TCA 1997, s 517). The costs of establishing the scheme are also to be allowed as a deduction for corporation tax purposes. If the company is an investment company for the purposes of TCA 1997, s 83 or a life company in respect of which TCA 1997, s 83 is applied by TCA 1997, s 707 (deduction in respect of expenses of management), the sum expended is to be included in the sums expended as management expenses for that period. The deduction is given where either—

(a) the sum paid is applied by the trustees within the specified period in acquiring shares for appropriation to individuals who are eligible to participate in the scheme by virtue of being employees or directors of the paying company; or

(b) the sum paid is necessary to meet the reasonable expenses of the trustees in administering the scheme.

The "specified period" referred to above is the period of nine months beginning on the day following the period of account in which the sum is charged as an expense of the company which incurred it, or such longer period as the Revenue Commissioners by notice in writing allow.

A deduction in respect of sums expended in an accounting period may not exceed the company's trading income for that period or, in the case of an investment company or life company, the income for that accounting period after taking into account any other sums which are deductible as expenses of management under TCA 1997, s 83. Accordingly, scheme payments for which relief cannot be taken in the period of payment may not be carried forward or carried back and will therefore go unrelieved.

"Trading income" in the case of a trading company means the income from the trade computed for the purposes of Case I of Schedule D before any deduction in respect of profit sharing scheme payments, after any set-off or reduction of income in respect of losses by virtue of TCA 1997, s 396 or s 397, after any deduction or addition by virtue TCA 1997, s 307 or 308 (capital allowances and balancing charges), and after any deduction by virtue of TCA 1997, s 666 (stock relief). Furthermore, the deduction may not exceed such sum as is, in the opinion of the Revenue Commissioners, reasonable, having regard to—

(a) the number of employees or directors of the company making the payment who have agreed to participate in the scheme;

(b) the services rendered by them to the company;

(c) the levels of their remuneration;

(d) the length or their service; or

(e) any similar factors.

3.203.3 Employee share ownership trusts

TCA 1997, s 519 contains measures which provide tax reliefs in respect of certain employee share ownership trusts (ESOTs). The trusts in question are ESOTs which have been approved by the Revenue Commissioners in accordance with the provisions of TCA 1997 Sch 12 and which approval has not been withdrawn. The reliefs are as follows:

(a) a company may claim a deduction for corporation tax purposes in respect of—

  (i) the costs of setting up an approved ESOT, and

  (ii) contributions to the trustees of an approved ESOT where the company, or a company which it controls, has employees who are beneficiaries under the ESOT and where the contributions are expended by the trustees during a period, referred to as the "expenditure period", on one more "qualifying purposes",

(b) dividends received before 11 March 1998 by trustees of an approved ESOT in respect of securities held by them are not liable to the surcharge under TCA 1997, s 805 in respect of undistributed income; dividends received on or after 11 March 1998 are not chargeable to income tax at all if, and to the extent that, the dividend income is expended within the expenditure period (see below) by the trustees for one or more of the qualifying purposes (see below); and

(c) transfers of securities by the trustees of an approved ESOT to trustees of an approved profit sharing scheme (see **3.203.2**) are exempt from capital gains tax in respect of any chargeable gains arising.

TCA 1997, s 519(2) provides for the relief for a company which expends a sum in establishing an approved trust or in making a payment by way of contribution to the trustees of a trust which at the time of the payment is an approved trust. In the case where a contribution is made, the company or a company which it then controls must have employees who are eligible to benefit under the terms of the trust and, before the expiry of the expenditure period, the sum contributed must be expended by the trustees for one or more of the qualifying purposes. Sums expended by the trustees are taken to have been expended in the order in which the sums are received by them, irrespective of the number of companies making payments.

The *expenditure period* is the period of 9 months beginning with the day following the end of the accounting period in which the sum is expended by the company, or such longer period as the Revenue Commissioners may allow by notice given to the company. TCA 1997, s 432 (see **2.401**) applies for the purpose of determining whether one company is controlled by another.

A *qualifying purpose* is any of the following:

(a) the acquisition of shares in the company which established the trust;

(b)   the repayment of sums borrowed;

(c)   the payment of interest on sums borrowed;

(d)   the payment of any sum to a person who is a beneficiary under the terms of the trust deed;

(e)   the payment of any sum or the transfer of securities to the personal representatives of a deceased beneficiary under the terms of a trust deed;

(f)   the meeting of expenses.

Where a company expends a sum as described above in any accounting period, the sum is deductible in computing, for the purposes of Schedule D, the profits or gains for that period of a trade carried on by the company. Alternatively, if the company is an investment company (see **12.702**), or a life assurance company entitled to deduct management expenses in accordance with TCA 1997, s 707 (see **12.603.3**), the sum expended may be deducted as an expense of management in accordance with TCA 1997, s 83(2) in computing the profits of the company for that period.

In the case of a sum expended in establishing a trust, if the trust is established more than 9 months after the end of the accounting period in which the sum is expended, it will be treated as expended in the accounting period in which the trust is established.

Where the Revenue Commissioners, in accordance with TCA 1997 Sch 12, withdraw approval of an ESOT as a qualifying ESOT, TCA 1997, s 519 has no further effect as and from the date the withdrawal has effect as regards any sum expended by a company in making a payment to the trust.

The conditions for approval of an ESOT are set out in TCA 1997 Sch 12 and are summarised as follows:

(a)   the ESOT must be established by a company (the "founding company") which may not be controlled by another company;

(b)   in respect of an ESOT approved on or after 11 March 1998, the Revenue Commissioners must be satisfied, where the founding company is a member of a group of companies, that the scheme does not have the effect of conferring benefits wholly or mainly on the directors of companies in the group or on those employees of group companies who are in receipt of higher or the highest levels of remuneration (TCA 1997 Sch 12 paragraph 2(2)): a "group of companies" means a company and any other companies of which it has control (within the meaning of TCA 1997, s 432 – see **2.401**);

(c)   the forms of trustees provided for are: majority employee representation, paritarian trust with equal company/ employee representation, or a single corporate trustee with equal company/ employee representation on the board of directors;

(d)   all employees and full-time directors of a company within the founding company's group (ie, the founding company or a company controlled by the founding company where the ESOT concerned is expressed to extend to that company) who have been such for a qualifying period of not more than three years must be eligible to be beneficiaries under the ESOT;

(e)   former employees and directors may, within 18 months of their departure, be included;

(f)   former employees and directors may, within 15 years of their departure and subject to certain conditions, be included;

(g) employees and directors cannot be beneficiaries of the trust if they have, or had within the previous twelve months, a material interest (ie, more than 5% of the ordinary share capital) in the company;

(h) the functions of the trustees must be to acquire shares in the founding company (either out of contributions from the company or borrowings) for distribution to beneficiaries;

(i) shares must be transferred to beneficiaries by the trustees within 20 years of their acquisition by the trustees;

(j) sums of money received by the trustees, such as sums received from the founding company, or dividends received, must be expended, normally within nine months, for one or more qualifying purposes; and

(k) shares or sums, or both, must be offered to all beneficiaries of the ESOT and the transfers must be made at the same time and be made on similar terms.

3.203.4 Savings-related share option schemes: approved share option schemes

Savings-related share option schemes

TCA 1997 Part 17 Chapter 3 (ss 519A-519C) and Schedules 12A and 12B contain provisions for save as you earn (SAYE) share schemes. A SAYE share scheme incorporates two features: an approved savings-related share option scheme and a certified contractual savings scheme. The purpose of the latter is to fund the purchase of shares allocated to employees under an approved savings-related share option scheme.

A company which establishes a savings-related share option scheme is entitled to a deduction for corporation tax purposes in respect of the costs of establishing that scheme. A savings-related share option scheme is a scheme approved by the Revenue Commissioners in accordance with TCA 1997 Sch 12A and which approval has not been withdrawn. Where an individual obtains a right to acquire shares in his employing company in accordance with a savings-related share option scheme, or in a group company in accordance with a group scheme, no tax will be chargeable in respect of the receipt or exercise of that right except in certain circumstances where the option is exercised within three years of it being obtained.

The company which establishes a savings-related share option scheme is referred to as the "grantor" in relation to that scheme and, where the grantor has control of another company or companies, the scheme may extend to all or any of those companies. A scheme in those circumstances is a group scheme.

The Minister for Finance may, in accordance with provisions contained in TCA 1997 Sch 12B, specify the requirements in relation to the operation of the certified contractual savings scheme. These requirements will determine the classes of person who may enter savings contracts under the scheme, the level of contribution to be made and the sum to be paid or repaid to individuals participating in the scheme.

TCA 1997, s 519B provides for the relief for corporation tax purposes to a company which incurs costs in establishing a savings-related share option scheme. The section applies to a sum expended on or after 6 April 1999 by a company in establishing a savings-related share option scheme of which the Revenue Commissioners approve in accordance with the provisions of TCA 1997 Sch 12A and under which no employee or director obtains rights before such approval is given (TCA 1997, s 519B(1)). That sum is to be included—

  (a)   in the sums to be deducted in computing for the purposes of Schedule D the profits or gains of a trade carried on by the company; or

  (b)   if the company is an investment company which is entitled to a deduction for management expenses (see **12.702–704**) or a life assurance company in respect of which management expenses are allowable by virtue of TCA 1997, s 707 (see **12.603.3**), as part of the sums to be deducted under TCA 1997, s 83(2) as expenses of management in computing the profits of the company for corporation tax purposes (TCA 1997, s 519B(2)).

Where the Revenue approval is given later than nine months from the day following the end of the accounting period in which the sum is expended, the sum is treated as expended in the accounting period in which the approval is given and not in the accounting period in which the sum is expended (TCA 1997, s 519B(3)).

The conditions to be complied with in order to obtain approval for a savings-related share option scheme are set out in TCA 1997 Sch 12A. These conditions govern the type of company, eligibility, type of shares, exercise of rights, acquisition of shares, and their share price. Some of the more important conditions are as follows:

  (a)   all employees and full-time directors of the company establishing the scheme, or of a group company, who have been such for a qualifying period of not more than three years must be eligible to participate in the scheme on similar terms (so that they must be eligible to obtain and exercise rights to acquire shares);

  (b)   employees and directors cannot be participants if they have or had, within the previous 12 months, a material interest (ie, more than 15% of the ordinary share capital) in a close company (see **10.103**) which is either the company whose shares are to be acquired by the exercise of rights obtained under the scheme, or which has control of the company whose shares are to be acquired by such exercise or is a member of a consortium which owns that company;

  (c)   in relation to the type of shares which are to be the subject of the scheme, the shares must form part of the ordinary share capital of—

     (i)   the company which established the scheme,

     (ii) a company which has control of the company which established the scheme, or

     (iii) a company which is a company, or which has control of a company, which—

        (I)   is a member of a consortium (see below) owning either the company which established the scheme or a company which has control of that company, and

        (II) beneficially owns not less than 15% of the ordinary share capital of the company so owned,

    and must be—

     (i)   of a class quoted on a recognised stock exchange,

     (ii) shares in a company not under the control of another company, or

     (iii)   shares in a company which is under the control of a company whose shares are quoted on a recognised stock exchange;

(d)   subject to certain exceptions (including death, cessation of employment by reason of injury, disability, redundancy or reaching pensionable age), rights must not be capable of being exercised later than six months after the bonus date of the certified contractual savings scheme (the date on which repayments under the scheme are due);

(e)   monthly contributions to the certified contractual savings scheme must be sufficient to secure, as nearly as possible, repayment of an amount equal to the amount required to pay for as many shares as the individual has the right to acquire;

(f)   the maximum monthly savings allowable under a certified contractual savings scheme is €320 with a minimum amount not exceeding €12 (which amounts may be varied by the Minister for Finance);

(g)   shares acquired under an approved savings-related share option scheme may only be paid for out of the proceeds of a certified contractual savings scheme;

(h)   the price at which shares may be acquired must be settled at the date the option is granted and may be at a discount of up to 25% of the market value at that time.

For the purposes of (c)(iii)(I) above, a company is a member of a consortium that owns another company if it is one of not more than five companies which between them beneficially own not less than 75% of the other company's ordinary share capital and each of which beneficially owns not less than 5% of that capital (TCA 1997 Sch 12A paragraph 1(3)).

References to control in relation to a company are to be construed in accordance with TCA 1997, s 432 (see **2.401**).

In a case where a company uses a dedicated trust or a subsidiary company as part of an SAYE scheme to hold scheme shares, such trust or subsidiary will not be liable to capital gains tax in respect of any disposal of those shares to employees under the terms of the scheme. Accordingly, the capital gains tax base cost of the shares to the employees will be the price actually paid by them for those shares. No deduction for corporation tax purposes will be available to the company in respect of any expenses incurred by it in arranging for the acquisition of the shares by the trust or subsidiary.

TCA 1997, s 519A(3A) provides that where, in exercising a right in accordance with the provisions of an approved SAYE scheme, an individual acquires scheme shares from a relevant body, neither a chargeable gain nor an allowable loss will accrue to the relevant body on the disposal of the scheme shares. The individual will, notwithstanding the market value rule in TCA 1997, s 547(1)(a) (see **9.102.14**), be deemed for capital gains tax purposes to have acquired the scheme shares for a consideration equal to the amount paid for their acquisition.

A *relevant body* is a trust or a company which exists for the purpose of acquiring and holding scheme shares.

Any sum expended by the company which established the approved SAYE scheme, either directly or indirectly, to enable a relevant body to acquire scheme shares is not to be included—

(a) in the sums to be deducted in computing for the purposes of Schedule D the profits or gains of a trade carried on by the company; or

(b) if the company is an investment company within the meaning of TCA 1997, s 83 (see **12.7**) or a company in the case of which that section applies by virtue of 707 (management expenses of life assurance companies – see **12.603.3**), in the sums to be deducted under TCA 1997, s 83(2) as management expenses in computing the profits of the company for corporation tax purposes (TCA 1997, s 519B(2A)).

Approved share option schemes

TCA 1997, s 519D provides for tax relief in respect of share options granted to employees under schemes approved by the Revenue Commissioners. Under an approved scheme, employees are not chargeable to income tax on the exercise of the option but are instead subject to capital gains tax on the full gain (ie, the difference between the amount paid for the shares and the amount received) on a disposal of the shares. A requirement of the scheme is that there must be a minimum period of three years between the date of the grant of the option and the date of any subsequent sale of the shares. To qualify for Revenue approval, schemes must be open to all employees and must provide that all employees be eligible to participate in the scheme on similar terms. Any service requirement for eligibility may not exceed three years.

Under the similar terms rule, options may be granted by reference to remuneration, length of service or other similar factors. The fact that new employees will receive options in their first year of employment at a different date or a different price from the generality of employees, or that employees will not receive options in the run up to retirement, will not breach these rules.

The scheme must not contain features which would discourage qualifying employees from participating or have the effect of conferring benefits wholly or mainly on directors or higher paid employees of the company. It may, however, contain a "key employee" element where options may be granted without the similar terms conditions. In any such case, no more than 30% of the total number of shares over which rights are granted under the scheme in any year may be used in the key employee element. Employees may not participate in both elements within the same year.

Shares used in the scheme must form part of the company's ordinary share capital and, in general, must not be subject to restrictions that do not apply to other shares of the same class.

Similarly to savings-related share option schemes, there is a prohibition on the deduction of sums expended, either directly or indirectly, to enable a relevant body to acquire scheme shares. Any sum expended by the company which has established an approved share option scheme, either directly or indirectly, to enable a relevant body to acquire scheme shares is not to be included—

(a) in the sums to be deducted in computing for the purposes of Schedule D the profits or gains of a trade carried on by the company; or

(b) if the company is an investment company within the meaning of TCA 1997, s 83 (see **12.7**) or a company in the case of which that section applies by virtue of 707 (management expenses of life assurance companies – see **12.603.3**), in the sums to be deducted under TCA 1997, s 83(2) as management expenses in computing the profits of the company for corporation tax purposes (TCA 1997, s 519D(6)).

This prohibition on the deduction of sums expended by a company to enable a relevant body to acquire approved scheme shares is surprising in one respect at least. The inference to be drawn from TCA 1997, s 81A (see **3.202.17**) is that payments of this kind to a third party (which must include a "relevant body") are indeed deductible except that the deduction may have to be deferred. It would then appear that the effect of TCA 1997, s 519D(6) is that such payments are not deductible if made in respect of an approved scheme but not if made in respect of an unapproved scheme. If this is correct, it can hardly have been what was intended by the legislation.

3.203.5 Donations of heritage items

TCA 1997, s 1003 provides relief for certain gifts to approved bodies by treating the value of the gift as a credit against tax. An *approved body* for this purpose means:

(a)   the National Archives;

(b)   the National Gallery of Ireland;

(c)   the National Library of Ireland;

(d)   the National Museum of Ireland;

(e)   the Crawford Art Gallery Cork Limited;

(f)   the Irish Museum of Modern Art; or

(g)   in relation to the offer of a gift of a particular item or collection of items, any other body owned or funded by the State or by any public or local authority as may be approved by the Minister for Arts, Heritage, Gaeltacht and the Islands for the purposes of TCA 1997, s 1003.

A gift which qualifies for relief (a "relevant gift") is a gift of a heritage item to an approved body made on or after 2 June 1995 for which the donor receives no consideration whatsoever directly or indirectly from the approved body or otherwise. A *heritage item* is any kind of cultural item including:

(a)   any archaeological item, archive, book, estate record, manuscript and painting; and

(b)   any collection of cultural items and any collection thereof in their setting

which on application to the selection committee (which is comprised mainly of directors of the above-mentioned approved bodies) is determined by it, after consideration of evidence in relation to the matter and after seeking and considering the opinion of the approved body to which the gift is to be made and the Heritage Council, the Arts Council or other appropriate body, to be an item or collection of items which is an outstanding example of the type of item involved, pre- eminent in its class, whose export from the State would constitute a diminution of the accumulated cultural heritage of Ireland, and which is suitable for acquisition by the approved body.

On receipt of a relevant gift, the designated officer of the approved body will give a certificate to the donor (and a copy to the Revenue Commissioners) in a form prescribed by the Revenue Commissioners certifying the receipt of the gift and the transfer of the ownership of the heritage item which is the subject of the gift to the approved body. On submission of the certificate to the Revenue Commissioners, the person who has made the gift is treated as having made on the date of that submission a payment on account of tax of an amount equal to the market value of the relevant gift on the date on which the heritage item was submitted for determination by the selection committee.

Tax in respect of which a payment on account is deemed to be made means income tax, corporation tax, capital gains tax, gift tax or inheritance tax, as the case may be. The deemed payment on account will, in the case of a company which has made a relevant gift, be offset first against any arrears of tax (including any interest and penalties) for the accounting period in which the relevant gift is made, then against any current liability to corporation tax for that period, and then against any future liability to corporation tax as nominated by the company. No refund of tax may be made as a result of the making of a relevant gift and no interest will be payable in respect of any overpayment of tax arising from the offset of a deemed payment on account resulting from the making of a relevant gift.

The selection committee may not make any determination where the market value of any item or collection of items at the valuation date—

(a) is less than €150,000 (but in the case of a collection of items, at least one item must have a minimum value of €50,000 – except that the selection committee may make a determination in respect of an item or collection of items consisting wholly of archival material or manuscripts in which case the minimum valuation threshold will not apply); or

(b) exceeds an amount (not to be less than €150,000) which, when added to the market value of any other heritage items donated by the same person in the same calendar year, exceeds €6m.

An item or collection of items will cease to be a heritage item where it is sold or disposed of otherwise than to an approved body, or where the owner notifies the selection committee in writing that it is not intended to make a gift thereof to an approved body, or the gift is not made to an approved body within the calendar year following the year in which the determination is made by the selection committee.

The Revenue Commissioners are required for the year 1995 and each subsequent calendar year to compile a list of the names, descriptions and values of the heritage items in respect of which relief was given and, notwithstanding any obligation as to secrecy imposed on them by the Acts (ie the Tax Acts (other than TCA 1997 Part 6 Ch 8, Part 18 Ch 2 and Part 42 Ch 4), the Capital Gains Tax Acts, the Capital Acquisitions Tax Act 1976 and the enactments amending or extending that Act, and any instruments made thereunder) or by the Official Secrets Act 1963, to include the list in their annual report to the Minister for Finance.

Payment of tax by means of donation to Irish heritage trust

TCA 1997, s 1003A provides for a scheme of tax relief for heritage property donated to an Irish heritage trust (the "Trust"). The relief applies to a person, including a company, making a gift of heritage property to the Trust. It takes the form of a payment on account of an amount equal to the value of the property against the donor's tax liabilities, including liability to corporation tax and capital gains tax. For the purposes of the relief, *heritage property* means a building or a garden which, on application in writing to the Minister for the Environment, Heritage and Local Government by a person who owns the building or garden, is determined by the Minister to be a building which is:

(i)   an outstanding example of the type of building or garden involved;

(ii)   pre-eminent in its class;

(iii)   intrinsically of significant scientific, historical, horticultural, national, architectural or aesthetic interest; and

(iv)   suitable for acquisition by the Trust;

and for this purpose a building includes—

(I)   any associated outbuilding, yard or land where the land is occupied or enjoyed with the building as part of its garden or designated landscape and contributes to the appreciation of the building in its setting, and

(II)   the contents of the building (furnishings historically associated with the building and in respect of which the Minister is satisfied that they are important in establishing the historic or aesthetic context of the building).

A determination by the Minister will only be made in respect of a property which, at the date an application is made for a determination (the *valuation date*), has a market value, as determined by the Revenue Commissioners, not exceeding an amount equal to €6m - M, where M is an amount (which may be nil) equal to the market value at the valuation date of the heritage property (if any) or aggregate of the market values at the respective valuation dates of all the heritage properties (if any) in respect of which a determination, or determinations, has been made in any one calendar year and not revoked in that year.

3.203.6   Relief for expenditure on significant buildings and gardens

Notwithstanding any limitation in TCA 1997, s 865(4) on the time within which a claim for repayment is required to be made (see **15.204.2**), TCA 1997, s 482 provides for relief to any person who has incurred "qualifying expenditure" in respect of "an approved building" which is either owned or occupied by him. Relief is given by treating the full amount of the qualifying expenditure as if it were an amount of a loss from a trade sustained in the chargeable period (accounting period in the case of a company) in which the expenditure was incurred. It is not necessary that the person claiming the relief is in fact carrying on a trade.

In respect of expenditure incurred in an accounting period beginning on or after 23 May 1994, relief will only be allowed to a company if details of the dates and times when the building is open to the public are provided to the National Tourism Development Authority on or before 1 November in the accounting period for which the claim is made. This condition must also be fulfilled in each of the accounting periods comprising whichever is the shortest of the following periods:

(a)   the period consisting of the accounting periods since 23 May 1994;

(b)   the period consisting of the accounting periods since a determination by the Revenue Commissioners under TCA 1997, s 482(5)(a)(ii) was made (see below under *Approved Building*) in relation to the building;

(c)   the period consisting of the accounting periods since the approved building was purchased or occupied by the company; or

(d)   the period consisting of the five accounting periods immediately preceding the accounting period for which the claim is made.

It is a condition for obtaining relief that the above information is provided to the National Tourism Development Authority on the understanding that it may be published for the promotion of tourism.

Relief under TCA 1997, s 482 may not be given for any accounting period before that in which an application is made by the company to the Revenue Commissioners under TCA 1997, s 482(5)(a) for a determination under that subparagraph.

A company obtaining relief under TCA 1997, s 482 is treated as having incurred a loss in a trade separate from any trade actually carried on by the company. Accordingly, the provisions of TCA 1997, s 396 (see **4.101**) will apply for the purposes of giving relief in respect of that deemed loss. The company will therefore be entitled to set the deemed loss against its total profits for the accounting period in which the expenditure is incurred (TCA 1997, s 482(2)). A claim under TCA 1997, s 482(2) is unaffected by the provisions of TCA ss 396A and 420A (see **4.103** and **8.306.2**) (TCA 1997, s 482(11)).

Qualifying expenditure to the extent that it cannot be set against a company's income for the accounting period in which it is incurred may be carried forward as far as required to the following two accounting periods (TCA 1997, s 482(3)). Thus, a company, or group, that has substantial taxable profits during the three periods commencing with the period of the expenditure will be at an advantage as compared with a company or group whose profits for those periods are insufficient to absorb the amount of the qualifying expenditure. It will also be seen that the benefit of the relief could be adversely affected where any of the three accounting periods is a short period.

A deemed loss in the accounting period in which the qualifying expenditure is incurred cannot be set against profits of any preceding period since the notional trade cannot have been carried on in that earlier period (see **4.101** – *Set off of losses against profits*).

Approved garden

In respect of "relevant expenditure" (see below) incurred on or after 6 April 1993, the relief provided for by TCA 1997, s 482 applies, with any necessary modifications, in relation to an approved garden as it applies in relation to qualifying expenditure incurred in respect of an approved building (TCA 1997, s 482(9)). An *approved garden* is a garden (other than a garden being land occupied or enjoyed with an approved building as part of its garden or grounds of an ornamental nature) which, on application to the Minister for Arts, Heritage, Gaeltacht and the Islands and the Revenue Commissioners by the person who owns or occupies the garden, is determined:

(a)   by the Minister to be a garden which is intrinsically of significant horticultural, scientific, historical, architectural or aesthetic interest; and

(b)   by the Revenue Commissioners to be a garden to which reasonable access is afforded to the public.

Approved building

Relief may be claimed in respect of a building which is owned or occupied by the person claiming the relief. The building must be one which, following an application by that person, is determined by the Minister for Arts, Heritage, Gaeltacht and the Islands to be a building which is intrinsically of significant scientific, historical, architectural or aesthetic interest, and by the Revenue Commissioners to be a building either:

(a)   to which reasonable access is afforded to the public; or

(b)   which is in use as a tourist accommodation facility (see below) for at least 6 months in any calendar year ("the required period") including not less than 4 months in the period commencing on 1 May and ending on 30 September in any such year (TCA 1997, s 482(5)(a)).

For the purpose of satisfying the condition regarding reasonable access to the public, the following further conditions must be satisfied:

(i)   the access to the public must be to the whole or a substantial part of the building at the same time;

(ii)   subject to temporary closure necessary for the purposes of the repair, maintenance or restoration of the building, access to the public must be afforded for not less than 60 days in any year, and—

    (I)   such period must include, as respects determinations made by the Revenue Commissioners in accordance with (a) or (b) above–

        (A)   before the passing of Finance Act 2000, not less than 40 days, and

        (B)   on or after the passing of Finance Act 2000, not less than 40 days of which not less than 10 are weekend days (ie, a Saturday or a Sunday),

    during the period from 1 May to 30 September, and

    (II)   in respect of each such period, on each such day access is afforded in a reasonable manner and at reasonable times for a period, or periods in the aggregate, of not less than 4 hours;

(iii)   the price, if any, paid by the public in return for that access is in the opinion of the Revenue Commissioners reasonable in amount and does not operate to preclude the public from seeking access to the building; and

(iv)   the Revenue Commissioners are satisfied that—

    (I)   details relating to that access are publicised or drawn to the attention of the public by way of advertisement, leaflet, press notice or similar means annually,

    (II)   a notice containing the details of the dates and times at which access is afforded to the public—

        (A)   is displayed on the days on which such access is so afforded and in a conspicuous location at or near the place where the public can gain entrance to the building concerned, and

        (B)   is so displayed so as to be easily visible and legible by the public, and

    (III)   conditions, if any, in regard to that access are such that they would not act as a disincentive to the public from seeking such access.

Although the Revenue Commissioners may, before the passing of Finance Act 2000, have made a determination in accordance with (a) or (b) above that a building is a building to which reasonable access is afforded to the public, relief in relation to qualifying expenditure incurred in an accounting period of a company beginning on or after 1 January 1995 in respect of a building may not be given unless the company which owns or occupies the building satisfies the Revenue Commissioners on or before 1 November in that period that it is a building to which reasonable access is afforded to the public having regard to –

(a) (ii)(I)(A) above, where the qualifying expenditure is incurred in an accounting period beginning before 1 October 2000; and

(b) (ii)(I)(B) above, where the qualifying expenditure is incurred in an accounting period beginning on or after 1 October 2000 (TCA 1997, s 482(8)).

A *tourist accommodation facility* means an accommodation facility registered in the register of guest houses maintained and kept by the National Tourism Development Authority under Part III of the Tourist Traffic Act 1939, or listed in the list published or caused to be published by that Authority under section 9 of the Tourist Traffic Act 1957.

Qualifying expenditure

In relation to an approved building, "qualifying expenditure" means expenditure incurred by the person who owns or occupies the approved building on one or more of the following:

(a) the repair, maintenance or restoration of the approved building or the maintenance or restoration of any land occupied or enjoyed with the approved building as part of its garden or grounds or an ornamental nature; and

(b) to the extent that the aggregate expenditure in a chargeable period does not exceed €6,350—

(i) the repair, maintenance or restoration of an approved object in the approved building,

(ii) the installation, maintenance or replacement of a security alarm system in the approved building, and

(iii) public liability insurance for the approved building.

For the purpose of determining whether and to what extent qualifying expenditure incurred on or after 12 February 1998 in relation to an approved building is or is not incurred in a chargeable period, only so much qualifying expenditure as is properly attributable to work actually carried out during the period is treated as having been incurred in that period.

Relevant expenditure

In relation to an approved garden, "relevant expenditure" means:

(a) in the case of expenditure incurred in a chargeable period, being the year 1997-98 and any subsequent year of assessment, or an accounting period of a company beginning on or after 6 April 1997, expenditure incurred by the person who owns or occupies the approved garden on one or more of the following:

(i) the maintenance or restoration of the approved garden, and

(ii) to the extent that the aggregate expenditure in a chargeable period does not exceed €6,350—

> (I) the repair, maintenance or restoration of an approved object in the approved garden,
>
> (I) the installation, maintenance or replacement of a security alarm system in the approved garden, and
>
> (III) public liability insurance for the approved garden, and

(b) in the case of expenditure incurred in a chargeable period earlier than that referred to in (a) above, expenditure incurred by the person who owned or occupied the approved garden on the maintenance or restoration of the garden (TCA 1997, s 482(1)(a)).

Withdrawal of relief

Relief under TCA 1997, s 482 may be withdrawn in certain circumstances. Where, as a result of any alteration made to a building or any deterioration of the building, the Minister for Arts, Heritage, Gaeltacht and the Islands considers that the building is no longer one that is intrinsically of significant scientific, historical, architectural or aesthetic interest, he may by notice in writing to the owner or occupier revoke his previous determination. The revocation has effect from the date the Minister considers that the building ceased to be a building coming within the above description. No expenditure incurred on the building after that date may qualify for relief.

If reasonable access to the building ceases to be afforded to the public, the Revenue Commissioners may, by notice in writing to the owner or occupier, revoke their previous determination. The revocation has effect from the date on which the Commissioners consider that such access ceased.

If the building ceases to be used as a tourist accommodation facility for the period of at least six months in any calendar year, the Revenue Commissioners may revoke, by notice in writing, their previous determination with effect from the date on which the building ceased to be so used. Any expenditure incurred after the effective date of the revocation will not qualify for relief. Any relief given in respect of qualifying expenditure incurred on the building in the five years immediately preceding the effective date will be withdrawn.

TCA 1997, s 482(5)(e) permits a switch of use of an approved building. Where the building was previously approved on the basis that reasonable access is afforded to the public, the building may be switched to use as a tourist accommodation facility. Likewise, where the building has been approved on the basis of being a tourist accommodation facility, it may be switched to use as a building in respect of which reasonable access is provided to the public. In either case, a new determination will be made by the Revenue Commissioners which will be effective from the date of the original determination.

Claims

A claim for relief under TCA 1997, s 482 must be in a form prescribed by the Revenue Commissioners and should be accompanied by such statements in writing as regards the qualifying expenditure, including any statements by persons to whom payments were made, as may be indicated in the prescribed form. Any claim for set-off of a deemed loss against the profits of a company will be subject to the two year time limit prescribed by TCA 1997, s 396(9) in relation to trading losses.

3.203.7   Investment in renewable energy generation

Introduction

Companies are entitled to relief for investment in certain renewable energy projects. Eligibility extends to those companies which are successful in the Third Alternative Energy Requirement Competition (AER III – 1997) initiated by the Minister for Public Enterprise. The relief took effect from 18 March 1999 (the date specified by the Minister for Finance – SI 65/1999) and ends on 31 December 2011.

The relief takes the form of a deduction from the profits of a company in respect of an investment in new shares in a company setting up a renewable energy project. Qualifying projects for this purpose are those in the solar, wind, hydro and biomass technology categories, having been individually approved by the Minister for Public Enterprise through the issue of a certificate.

The maximum amount of relief is the lesser of 50% of all capital expenditure, excluding expenditure on land and net of grants, on a single project, and €9.525m. Investment by any one company or group of companies in more than one energy renewal project is capped at €12.7m per annum.

Relief will be withdrawn in cases where shares are held for less than five years.

Qualifying energy project

A *qualifying energy project* is a renewable energy project in respect of which the Minister for Public Enterprise has given a certificate. The Minister may, on an application to him by a qualifying company, give a certificate stating, in relation to a renewable energy project to be undertaken by the company, that the project is a qualifying energy project (TCA 1997, s 486B(2)(a)). The application must be in such form and must contain such information as the Minister may direct. The certificate will be subject to such conditions as the Minister may consider proper and specifies in the certificate (TCA 1997, s 486B(2)(b)).

A *renewable energy project* means a renewal energy project (including a project successful in the Third Alternative Energy Requirement Competition (AER III – 1997) initiated by the Minister for Public Enterprise (TCA 1997, s 486B(1)) in one or more of the following categories of technology:

  (a)   solar power;
  (b)   windpower;
  (c)   hydropower; and
  (d)   biomass.

The Minister may amend or revoke any condition (including an amended condition) specified in a certificate and is required to give to the qualifying company concerned notice in writing of the amendment or revocation (TCA 1997, s 486B(2)(c)). Failure by a company to comply with any of the conditions specified in a certificate will constitute the failure of an event to happen by reason of which relief is to be withdrawn (see under *Claims* below). The Minister may then, by notice in writing served by registered post on the company, revoke the certificate (TCA 1997, s 486B(2)(e)).

The relief

Relief under TCA 1997, s 486B is available to a company which makes a relevant investment. A *relevant investment* means a sum of money which is:

(a) paid in the qualifying period by a company on its own behalf to a qualifying company in respect of new ordinary shares in the qualifying company and is paid by the company directly to the qualifying company;

(b) paid by the company for the purposes of enabling the qualifying company to undertake a qualifying energy project; and

(c) used for those purposes by the qualifying company within two years of the receipt of that sum,

but does not include a sum of money paid to the qualifying company on terms which provide that it will be repaid.

A *qualifying company* is a company which is incorporated and solely resident in the State and which exists solely for the purposes of undertaking a qualifying energy project. The *qualifying period* means the period commencing on the commencement date, 18 March 1999, and ending on 31 December 2011.

New ordinary shares means new ordinary shares forming part of the ordinary share capital of a qualifying company which, throughout the period of five years commencing on the date such shares are issued, carry no present or future preferential right to dividends, or to a company's assets on its winding up, and no present or future preferential right to be redeemed.

Where in any accounting period a company makes a relevant investment, it will be entitled on making a claim to that effect to a deduction of an amount equal to the relevant investment (a *relevant deduction*) from its total profits for that period (TCA 1997, s 486B(3)). Where the amount of the relevant deduction exceeds the company's profits for the period, the excess amount is to be carried forward to the succeeding accounting period and then treated as a relevant investment made in that period. If the amount carried forward to the subsequent period exceeds the profits of that period, the excess can again be carried forward to the next succeeding period and so on until the relevant deduction has been fully allowed. There is no provision whereby an excess relevant deduction may be carried back to a previous period or surrendered under the group relief provisions.

Where a company is entitled, or would on a claim be entitled, to relief under TCA 1997, s 486B in respect of any sum or any part of a sum, as a relevant deduction from its total profits for an accounting period, it will not be entitled to any other relief for that sum or part sum under any other provision of the Tax Acts or the Capital Gains Tax Acts (TCA 1997, s 486B(14)(a)).

Where a company has made a relevant investment by means of a subscription for new ordinary shares of a qualifying company and none of those shares is disposed of by the company within five years of their acquisition by that company, the sums allowable as deductions from the consideration received in the capital gains tax computation on the disposal of those shares (see **9.102.3**) is to be determined without regard to any relief under TCA 1997, s 486B which the company has obtained, or would be entitled to obtain if it had made a claim. Where, however, those sums exceed the consideration received, they are to be reduced by the lesser of:

(i)   the amount of the relevant deduction allowed to the company under TCA 1997, s 486B in respect of the subscription for those shares; and

(ii)   the amount of the excess (TCA 1997, s 486B(14)(b)).

Limits on relief

Where in any period of twelve months ending on the day before an anniversary of the commencement date, the amount or aggregate amount of the relevant investments made, or treated as made, by a company or by the company and all companies which at any time in that period are connected with the company (see **2.302**), exceeds €12.7m, no relief may be given in respect of the excess. Where in any such case there is more than one relevant investment, the relief is to be allocated to each relevant investment. The allocation is to be carried out by the inspector or, on appeal, the Appeal Commissioners by making such apportionment of the available relief as is just and reasonable. Where necessary, each company is to be given relief proportionate to the amount of the relevant investment or the aggregate amount of the relevant investments made by it in the period (TCA 1997, s 486B(4)).

While, for the duration of the qualifying period, the aggregate of deductible relevant investments cannot exceed €63.5m (€12.7m for each of the five twelve-month periods ending on the day preceding an anniversary of the commencement date), it is possible for a company or group of companies to obtain relief of up to €25.4 for a single accounting period.

TCA 1997, s 486B(5) provides for a maximum amount of relief in respect of a single project. Relief may not be given in respect of a relevant investment made at any time in a qualifying company if, at that time, the aggregate of the amounts of that relevant investment and all other relevant investments made in the qualifying company at or before that time exceeds the lesser of:

(a)   50% of the relevant cost of the project; or

(b)   €9.525m.

For the above purposes, *relevant cost* in relation to a qualifying energy project means the amount of the capital expenditure incurred or to be incurred by the qualifying company for the purposes of undertaking the qualifying energy project reduced by an amount equal to such part of that expenditure as is attributable to the acquisition of, or of rights in or over, land, and by such part of the expenditure as has been or is to be met directly or indirectly by the State or by any person other than the qualifying company.

Claims

A claim to relief may be allowed at any time after the time when payment is made of a sum in respect of which relief is claimed. Relief will then be allowed in respect of the payment of the sum to a qualifying company if:

(i)   that payment, if it is used, within two years of its being paid, by the qualifying company for the purposes of a qualifying energy project, will be a relevant investment; and

(ii)   all the conditions specified in TCA 1997, s 486B for the giving of the relief are or will be satisfied.

Any claim for relief in respect of a relevant investment in a company will not be allowed unless it is accompanied by a certificate issued by the company in such form as the

Revenue Commissioners may direct and certifying that the conditions for relief, in so far as they apply to the company and the qualifying energy project, are or will be satisfied in relation to that relevant investment (TCA 1997, s 486B(7)). Before issuing the certificate, the qualifying company must furnish the authorised officer (the officer authorised in writing by the Revenue Commissioners for the purposes of TCA 1997, s 486B) with:

(a) a statement to the effect that it satisfies or will satisfy the conditions for the relief in so far as they apply in relation to the company and the qualifying energy project;

(b) a copy of the certificate, including a copy of any notice given by the Minister for Public Enterprise specifying the amendment or revocation of a condition specified in that certificate in respect of the qualifying energy project (see under *Qualifying energy project* above); and

(c) such other information as the Revenue Commissioners may reasonably require (TCA 1997, s 486B(8)).

A certificate may not be issued by a company as above without the authority of the authorised officer or in relation to a relevant investment in respect of which relief may not be given by virtue of the 50%/ €9.525m limit (see *Limits on relief* above).

A company will not be entitled to relief in respect of a relevant investment unless the relevant investment:

(a) has been made for *bona fide* commercial reasons and not as part of a scheme or arrangement the main purpose or one of the main purposes of which is the avoidance of tax;

(b) has been or will be used for the purposes of undertaking a qualifying energy project; and

(c) is made at the risk of the company and neither the company nor any person who is connected with the company (**2.302**) is entitled to receive any payment in money or money's worth or other benefit directly or indirectly borne by or attributable to the qualifying company, apart from a payment made on an arm's length basis for goods or services supplied or a payment out of the proceeds of exploiting the qualifying energy project to which the company is entitled under the terms subject to which the relevant investment is made (TCA 1997, s 486B(12)).

Withdrawal of relief

Relief will be withdrawn if, by reason of the happening of any subsequent event including the revocation by the Minister for Public Enterprise of the certificate given to the company (see above) or the failure of an event to happen which at the time the relief was given was expected to happen, the company making the claim was not entitled to the relief allowed.

Where a company has made a relevant investment by means of a subscription for new ordinary shares of a qualifying company and any of those shares are disposed of at any time within five years after the time when the payment in respect of which relief is claimed has been made, a claim to relief under TCA 1997, s 486B may not be allowed in respect of the amount subscribed for those shares. Any such relief already given will then be withdrawn.

3.203.8   Donations to approved bodies etc

Introduction

TCA 1997, s 848A provides for a scheme of relief for donations to certain qualifying bodies, including approved bodies providing education in the arts, the Scientific and Technical Education Investment Fund, bodies that promote the Universal Declaration of Human Rights, certain bodies approved for research, authorised charities, and educational institutions or bodies in the State. In the cases of corporate donations, the company in question may claim a deduction for the donation to the approved body as if it were a trading expense. The minimum qualifying donation in any year to any one approved body is €250.

The relief

Relief is available to a company that proves to the satisfaction of the Revenue Commissioners that it has made a relevant donation. A *relevant donation* made by a company is a donation which satisfies certain conditions and takes the form of a payment, or the donation as the case may be, made in an accounting period by the company (the "donor") of either or both (i) a sum or sums of money, and (ii) designated securities valued at their market value at the time the donation is made, amounting to, in aggregate, at least €250 to an approved body. If the accounting period in which the donation is made is less than 12 months, the minimum amount is proportionately reduced. An *"approved body"* is a body specified in Part 1 of Schedule 26A (see below).

Designated securities for the above purposes are shares (including stock) and debentures of a class quoted on a recognised stock exchange.

The conditions which have to be satisfied for the purposes of TCA 1997, s 848A, in relation to a donation made by a company, are as follows:

(a)   the donation is not subject to a condition as to repayment;

(b)   neither the donor nor any person connected with (see **2.302**) the donor receives a benefit in consequence of making the donation, either directly or indirectly;

(c)   the donation is not conditional on or associated with, or part of an arrangement involving, the acquisition of property by the approved body, otherwise than by way of gift, from the donor or a person connected with the donor; and

(d)   subject to TCA 1997, s 848A(4), the donation—

(i)   would not be deductible in computing the profits or gains of a trade or profession for the purposes of corporation tax, and

(ii)   would not be an expense of management (see **12.703**) deductible in computing the total profits of a company (TCA 1997, s 848A(3)).

Where a company makes a relevant donation in an accounting period and claims relief from tax by reference to that donation, the amount of the donation is treated for corporation tax purposes as a deductible trading expense of a trade carried on by the company in, or an expense of management deductible in computing the total profits of the company for, that accounting period (TCA 1997, s 848A(4)). The claim should be made with the company's corporation tax return required to be delivered in accordance with TCA 1997, s 951 (see **15.104**) (TCA 1997, s 848A(5)).

Approved bodies

The bodies approved for the purposes of TCA 1997, s 848A, as listed in TCA 1997 Sch 26A, are as follows:

(i) a body approved for education in the arts in accordance with Part 2 (see below);

(ii) a body approved as an eligible charity in accordance with Part 3 (see below);

(iii) an institution of higher education within the meaning of section 1 of the Higher Education Authority Act 1971, or any body established for the sole purpose of raising funds for such an institution;

(iv) an institution in receipt of public funding which provides courses to which a scheme approved by the Minister for Education and Science under the Local Authorities (Higher Education Grants) Acts 1968 to 1992, applies or any body established in the State for the sole purpose of raising funds for such an institution;

(v) an institution of higher education which provides courses which are validated by the Higher Education Training and Awards Council under the provisions of the Qualifications (Education and Training) Act 1999;

(vi) an institution or other body which provides primary education up to the end of the sixth standard, based on a programme prescribed or approved by the Minister for Education and Science;

(vii) an institution or other body which provides post-primary education up to the level of either or both the Junior Certificate and the Leaving Certificate based on a programme prescribed or approved by the Minister for Education and Science;

(viii) a body to which TCA 1997, s 209 applies being a body for the promotion of the observance of the Universal Declaration of Human Rights or the implementation of the European Convention for the protection of Human Rights and Fundamental Freedoms or both the promotion of the observance of that Declaration and the implementation of that Convention;

(ix) the company incorporated under the Companies Acts 1963 to 2001, on 30 January 2003, as US-Ireland Alliance Limited.

Approval of a body for education in the arts – TCA 1997 Sch 26A, Part 2

An *approved body* for the purposes of TCA 1997 Sch 26A, Part 2, means any body or institution which may be approved of by the Minister for Finance and which:

(a) provides any course one of the conditions of entry to which is related to the results of the Leaving Certificate Examination, a matriculation examination of a recognised university in the State or an equivalent examination held outside the State; or

(b) (i) is established on a permanent basis solely for the advancement of one or more approved subjects,

(ii) contributes to the advancement of that subject or those subjects on a national or regional basis, and

(iii) is prohibited by its constitution from distributing to its members any of its assets or profits.

For the above purposes, *approved subject* means:

(a) the practice of architecture;

(b) the practice of art and design;

(c) the practice of music and musical composition;

(d) the practice of theatre arts;

(e) the practice of film arts; or

(f) any other subject approved of for the purpose of TCA 1997 Sch 26A, Part 2, by the Minister for Finance.

The Minister for Finance may, by notice in writing given to the body or institution, as the case may be, withdraw the approval of any body or institution for the purposes of TCA 1997 Sch 26A, Part 2, and the body or institution will cease to be an approved body from the day after the date of a notice which is to be published as soon as possible in Iris Oifigiúil.

Where any body to which TCA 1997 Sch 26A, Part 2, relates has been approved or is the holder of an authorisation under any enactment and that approval or authorisation has not been withdrawn on the day before the coming into operation of TCA 1997, s 848A, such body is to be deemed to be an approved body for the purposes of that section (TCA 1997, s 848A(14)).

Approval of body as an eligible charity – TCA 1997 Sch 26A, Part 3

An *eligible charity* means any body in the State that is the holder of an authorisation that is in force. Subject to conditions, the Revenue Commissioners may, on application to them by a body in the State, and on the furnishing of the body to them of such information as the Commissioners may reasonably require, issue to the body a document ("*an authorisation*") stating that the body is an eligible charity for the purposes of TCA 1997 Sch 26A, Part 3. The authorisation may only be issued where the Commissioners are satisfied that:

(a) the body is a body of persons or a trust established for charitable purposes only;

(b) the income of the body is applied for charitable purposes only;

(c) before the date of making application for relief, the body has been granted exemption from tax for the purposes of TCA s 207 (see **12.1002**) for a period of at least two years;

(d) the body provides such other information to the Revenue Commissioners as they may require for the purposes of giving the authorisation; and

(e) the body complies with such conditions, if any, as the Minister for Social, Community and Family Affairs may, from time to time, specify for the purposes of TCA 1997 Sch 26A, Part 3.

The eligible charity is required to publish information reasonably required by the Minister for Finance, including audited accounts of the charity consisting of an income and expenditure account or a profit and loss account for its most recent accounting period, and a balance sheet as at the last day of that period.

An authorisation has effect for a period, not exceeding five years, as determined by the Revenue Commissioners and specified in the authorisation. Where the Commissioners are satisfied that an eligible charity has ceased to comply with the above described conditions, including the requirements relating to published information, they may, by notice in writing served by registered post on the charity, withdraw the authorisation of the charity with effect from such date, subsequent to the date of the notice, as is specified therein.

Where any body to which TCA 1997 Sch 26A, Part 3, relates has been approved or is the holder of an authorisation under any enactment and that approval or authorisation has not been withdrawn on the day before the coming into operation of TCA 1997, s 848A, such body is to be deemed to be an approved body for the purposes of that section (TCA 1997, s 848A(14)).

Capital gains tax

Where relief is claimed under TCA 1997, s 848A in respect of a donation of quoted securities to a charity, capital gains tax relief under TCA 1997, s 611 (see **12.1003**) will not be available.

3.203.9 Donations to certain sports bodies

Introduction

TCA 1997, s 847A provides, with effect from 1 May 2002, for tax relief in respect of donations to certain sports bodies for the funding of capital projects. Eligibility for relief requires the approval of the Minister for Tourism, Sport and Recreation. The estimated aggregate cost of the project in question must not exceed €40m and the sports body must hold a certificate from the Revenue Commissioners to the effect that the body is, in the opinion of the Commissioners, a body of persons to which TCA 1997, s 235 applies (ie, its income is exempt from tax being a body established for and existing for the sole purpose of promoting athletic or amateur games or sports). In addition, the body must hold a valid tax clearance certificate.

The minimum qualifying donation by a company in an accounting period is €250, proportionately reduced where the length of the accounting period is less than twelve months.

Definitions

TCA 1997, s 847A(1) contains the definitions relevant to the operation of the scheme of tax relief.

Acts means the Tax Acts, the Capital Gains Tax Acts (see **2.2**), and the Value-Added Tax Act 1972 and the enactments amending or extending that Act, and any instrument made thereunder.

An *approved sports body* is a body in possession of:

(a) a certificate from the Revenue Commissioners stating that in their opinion the body is a body of persons to which TCA 1997, s 235 applies (a body established and existing for the sole purpose of promoting athletic or amateur games or sports etc – see **3.213.17**); and

(b) a valid tax clearance certificate,

but does not include a body to whom the Revenue Commissioners have given a notice under TCA 1997, s 235(1).

An *approved project* is a project in respect of which the Minister has given a certificate under TCA 1997, s 847A(4) (see below), which certificate has not been revoked under that subsection. The Revenue Commissioners may consult with the Minister in relation to any question arising as to whether a project is an approved project (TCA 1997, s 847A(15)).

Minister means the Minister for Tourism, Sport and Recreation.

A *project*, in relation to an approved sports body, means one or more of the following:

(a) the purchase, construction or refurbishment of a building or structure, or part of a building or structure, to be used for sporting or recreation activities provided by the approved sports body;

(b) the purchase of land to be used by the approved sports body in the provision of sporting or recreation facilities;

(c) the purchase of permanently based equipment (excluding personal equipment) for use by the approved sports body in the provision of sporting or recreation facilities;

(d) the improvement of the playing pitches, surfaces or facilities of the approved sports body; and

(e) the repayment of, or the payment of interest on, money borrowed by the approved sports body on or after 1 May 2002 for any of the purposes mentioned in (a) to (d) above.

A *relevant donation* is a donation which satisfies the requirements of TCA 1997, s 847A(5) (see below) and takes the form of the payment by a person (the "donor") of a sum or sums of money amounting to at least €250 to an approved sports body which, in the case of a company, is made in an accounting period. The Revenue Commissioners may consult with the Minister in relation to any question arising as to whether a donation is a relevant donation (TCA 1997, s 847A(15)).

A *relevant accounting period*, in relation to a relevant donation made by a company, is the accounting period in which that donation is made by the company.

Tax clearance certificate

Where a body which is in compliance with the obligations imposed on it by the Acts in relation to:

(a) the payment or remittance of any taxes, interest or penalties required to be paid or remitted under the Acts to the Revenue Commissioners; and

(b) the delivery of any returns required to be made under the Acts,

applies to the Collector-General in that behalf, the Collector-General will issue to the body a certificate (a *tax clearance certificate*) for the purposes of TCA 1997, s 847A stating that the body is in compliance with those obligations (TCA 1997, s 847A(3)(a)).

Certification of approved project

The Minister, on the making of an application by an approved sports body in advance of the undertaking by that body of a project, may give a certificate to that body stating that the project to be undertaken by it may be treated as an approved project for the purposes of TCA 1997, s 847A. The Minister may, by notice in writing given to the body, revoke the certificate and the project will cease to be an approved project as respects any donations made to the body after the date of the Minister's notice.

The Minister may not give a certificate to any body in respect of a project if the aggregate cost of the project is, or is estimated to be, in excess of €40m (TCA 1997, s 847A(4)).

Requirements for relevant donation

The requirements for a relevant donation made by a company to an approved sports body are that:

(a) it is made to the approved sports body for the sole purpose of funding an approved project;

(b) it is or will be applied by the approved sports body for that purpose;

(c) apart from TCA 1997, s 847A, it is neither deductible in computing for tax purposes the profits or gains of a trade or profession nor an expense of management deductible in computing the total profits of a company;

(d) it is not a relevant donation to which TCA 1997, s 848A (donations to approved bodies etc – see **3.203.8**) applies;

(e) it is not subject to a condition as to repayment;

(f) neither the donor nor any person connected with (see **2.3**) the donor receives, directly or indirectly, a benefit in consequence of making the donation, including, in particular, a right to membership of the approved sports body or a right to use the facilities of that body;

(g) it is not conditional on or associated with, or part of an arrangement involving, the acquisition of property by the approved sports body, otherwise than by way of gift, from the donor or a person connected with the donor (TCA 1997, s 847A(5)).

The relief

Where a company makes a relevant donation, other than a donation denied relief by reason of the €40m ceiling on aggregate donations received (see below), the amount of the donation is treated for corporation tax purposes as:

(a) a deductible trading expense of a trade carried on by the company in the relevant accounting period; or

(b) an expense of management deductible in computing the total profits of the company for the relevant accounting period (TCA 1997, s 847A(7)).

A claim for relief by a company should be made with the corporation tax return required to be made for the relevant accounting period (TCA 1997, s 847A(8)).

€40m ceiling on aggregate of donations received

No relief may be given in respect of a relevant donation made at any time to an approved sports body in respect of an approved project if, at that time, the aggregate of the amounts of that relevant donation and all other relevant donations made to the approved sports body in respect of the approved project at or before that time exceeds €40m (TCA 1997, s 847A(18)).

Obligations of approved sports body

An approved sports body is required, on the acceptance of a relevant donation, to give to the person making it a receipt:

(a)   containing a statement that—

    (i)   it is a receipt for the purposes of TCA 1997, s 847A,

    (ii)   the body is an approved sports body for the purposes of TCA 1997, s 847A,

    (iii)   the donation in respect of which the receipt is given is a relevant donation for the purposes of TCA 1997, s 847A, and

    (iv)   the project in respect of which the relevant donation has been made is an approved project,

(b)   showing—

    (i)   the name and address of the person making the relevant donation,

    (ii)   the amount of the relevant donation in both figures and words,

    (iii)   the date the relevant donation was made,

    (iv)   the full name of the approved sports body,

    (v)   the date on which the receipt was issued, and

    (vi)   particulars of the approved project in respect of which the relevant donation has been made, and

(c)   signed by a duly authorised official of the approved sports body (TCA 1997, s 847A(16)).

A receipt is not required to be given where the relevant donation will be denied relief by reason of the €40m ceiling (see above) applicable to the aggregate of donations received (TCA 1997, s 847A(17)).

Every approved sports body, when required to do so by notice in writing from the Minister, must, within the time limited by the notice prepare and deliver to the Minister a return containing particulars of the aggregate amount of relevant donations received by the body in respect of each approved project (TCA 1997, s 847A(14)).

Where relief under TCA 1997, s 847A has been given in respect of a relevant donation and:

(a)   the donation has not been used by the sports body concerned for the purpose of undertaking the approved project concerned; or

(b)   the relief is otherwise found not to have been due,

relief under TCA 1997, s 235(2) (see **3.213.17**) will not apply to the amount of that relevant donation (TCA 1997, s 847A(19)).

3.203.10 Expenses relating to superannuation schemes

A company may be entitled to a deduction for tax purposes for certain payments made in connection with a superannuation scheme. This entitlement arises where a superannuation scheme is established in connection with a trade or undertaking carried on by the company or where such an established scheme is altered, and the company makes a payment in respect of expenses (including a payment in respect of professional fees, but not including a payment by means of a contribution towards the cost of providing the benefits payable under the scheme) in connection with such establishment or alteration. If the scheme, or altered scheme, is approved by the Revenue Commissioners under TCA 772 (see **3.202.5**), the amount of the payment will be allowable as a deduction in the computation of the profits or gains of the trade or undertaking as an expense incurred when the payment is made (TCA 1997, s 84).

3.204 Grants and other receipts

3.204.1 Grants

The following payments are disregarded for all purposes of the Tax Acts:

(a) an employment grant under section 3 or 4 (as amended by the Shannon Free Airport Development Company Limited (Amendment) Act 1983) of the Shannon Free Airport Development Company Limited (Amendment) Act 1970 (TCA 1997, s 225(1));

(b) an employment grant under section 25 of the Industrial Development Act 1986 (TCA 1997, s 225(1));

(c) an employment grant under section 12 of the Industrial Development Act 1993 (TCA 1997, s 225(1));

(d) employment grants or recruitment subsidies made to an employer in respect of a person employed by such employer under

(i) the Back to Work Allowance Scheme administered by the Minister for Social, Community and Family Affairs,

(ii) any scheme which may be established by the Minister for Enterprise, Trade and Employment for the purposes of promoting the employment of individuals who have been unemployed for three years or more and which is to be administered by An Foras Áiseanna Saothair,

(iii) paragraph 13 of Annex B to an operating agreement between the Minister for Enterprise, Trade and Employment and a County Enterprise Board, being a board specified in the Schedule to the Industrial Development Act 1995,

(iv) the Employment Support Scheme administered by the National Rehabilitation Board,

(v) the Pilot Programme for the Employment of People with Disabilities, administered by the Rehab Group,

(vi) the European Union Leader II Community Initiative 1994 to 1999, administered in accordance with operating rules determined by the Minister for Agriculture and Food,

(vii) the European Union Operational Programme for Local Urban and Rural Development administered by Area Development Management Limited,

(viii) the Special European Union Programme for Peace and Reconciliation in Northern Ireland and the Border Counties or Ireland, approved by the EU,

(ix) the Joint Northern Ireland/ Ireland INTERREG Programme 1994 to 1999, approved by the EU, or

(x) any initiatives of the International Fund for Ireland designed by the International Fund for Ireland (Designation and Immunities) Order 1986 (SI 1986/394) as an organisation to which Part VIII of the Diplomatic Relations and Immunities Act 1967, applies (TCA 1997, s 226);

(e) a grant made on or after 1 April 1993 under section 10(5)(a) of the Údarás na Gaeltachta Act 1979 (under the scheme known as "Deontais Fhostaíochta ó Údarás na Gaeltachta do Thionscnaimh Sheirbhíse Idir-Náisiúnta" or the scheme known as "Deontais Fhostaíochta Ó Údarás na Gaeltachta do Thionscail Bheaga Dhéantúsaíochta") or section 21(5)(a) (as amended by the Industrial Development (Amendment) Act 1991) of the Industrial Development Act 1986 (under the scheme known as "Scheme Governing the Making of Employment Grants to Small Industrial Undertakings) (TCA 1997, s 223).

With the exception of (c), each of the above exemptions applies whether the payment was made before or after the enactment of the legislation concerned.

Other grants will normally be made to finance the purchase of fixed assets and will therefore be capital in nature. For capital allowances purposes, the cost of qualifying assets will be restricted by the amount of grant receivable (see **5.208.2**).

3.204.2 National Co-operative Farm Relief Services Ltd

National Co-operative Farm Relief Services Ltd ("the National Co-operative") was established in 1980 to provide farm relief services. TCA 1997, s 221 provides that any grant made under the agreement dated 4 July 1991, and amendments made thereto, between the Minister for Agriculture and Food and the National Co-operative for the provision of financial support for farm relief services are to be disregarded for all purposes of the Corporation Tax Acts.

The transfer of moneys under the same agreement by the National Co-operative to a member co-operative is also ignored for all purposes of the Corporation Tax Acts. A member co-operative means a society engaged in the provision of farm relief services which has been admitted to membership of the National Co-operative. A society in this context means a society registered under the Industrial and Provident Societies Acts 1893 to 1978.

3.204.3 Patent income

A person who is a resident of the State and not resident elsewhere may claim to have certain patent income exempted (treated as "disregarded income") for all purposes of the Income Tax Acts (TCA 1997, s 234). Such income is also disregarded for corporation tax purposes by virtue of TCA 1997, s 76(6). In the case of a company, "a resident of the State" means a company which is managed and controlled in the State. The income which is disregarded is *income from a qualifying patent*, meaning any royalty or other sum paid in respect of the use of the invention to which the qualifying patent relates. (The legislation refers to "the *user* of the invention" but this can be taken, for all practical purposes, to refer to the use of the invention.) "Other sum" includes any sum paid for the grant of a licence to exercise rights under the patent. Thus, a capital sum received in respect of the grant of a licence to use an invention which is the subject of a qualifying patent is not taxable under TCA 1997, s 757 whereas the receipt of a sum for the outright sale of any patent rights would be so taxable (see also **13.605**).

A *qualifying patent* is a patent in respect of which the work leading to the invention which is the subject of the patent was carried out in the State. The work would include research, planning, processing, experimenting, testing, devising, designing and developing. The exemption applies in respect of income received for the use of an invention in respect of which a patent application has been made even where the patent has not yet been granted. If, however, the patent application proves to be unsuccessful, any exemption previously availed of is withdrawn and any necessary additional assessments will be made to recover the tax in question.

From 6 April 1995, patent income arising to individuals may not be disregarded other than in the case of an individual who carried out, alone or with others, the research, planning, processing, experimenting, testing, devising, designing, development or other similar activity leading to the invention which is the subject of the qualifying patent.

To prevent the unintended use of patent income exemption, the definition of *income from a qualifying patent* has been amended on a number of occasions. Where a royalty or other sum, paid on or after 23 April 1996, exceeds the amount which would have been paid if the payer and the payee were independent persons acting at arm's length, the excess amount does not qualify as income from a qualifying patent.

The reference to independent persons acting at arm's length means that it will be necessary, in any case in which there are unusual or special circumstances, to ensure that the royalty or other sum does not exceed the amount which would be payable between persons acting wholly independently. To be free of this requirement, it is not enough that the parties to the royalty or licence agreement arc not "connected"; any unusual, special or particular circumstances which take the transaction out of the norm will make it necessary to ensure that the royalty or other sum is not excessive. Although there will be rare exceptions, the fact that the sum payable is excessive will usually itself be indicative that the transaction is not at arm's length. In practice, to ensure that all income from a qualifying patent will be exempted for tax purposes, professional advice should be sought as to what level of royalty or other income may be taken in respect of the use of the patent

For companies, the meaning of *income from a qualifying patent* is restricted, with effect from 11 April 1994, to sums paid:

(a)　for the purposes of activities which are regarded as the manufacture of goods for the purposes of manufacturing relief (the 10% corporation tax rate), with the exception of international financial services operations and operations, apart from the maintenance or repair of aircraft, which qualify for the 10% corporation tax rate by virtue of being Shannon operations;

(b)　for the purposes of activities which would fall within (a) if they were carried out in the State; or

(c)　by a person who is not connected (within the meaning of TCA 1997, s 10 – see **2.3**) with the recipient of the royalty or other sum, and who has not entered into any arrangement for the purpose, or mainly for the purpose, of avoiding being "connected with" that person.

The meaning of "disregarded income" is further restricted where the person paying the royalty or other sum is connected with the person who is beneficially entitled to that sum. Income from a qualifying patent which is received by a company from a company with which it is connected is not disregarded income; such income is referred to as "specified income". In that case, the amount of the distribution or distributions made, on or after 28 March 1996, out of the specified income in any accounting period which will be treated as made out of disregarded income may not exceed the amount of the aggregate expenditure incurred by it, and by fellow group members, on research and development activities in that period and in the two previous accounting periods.

The amount of the expenditure on research and development activities means non-capital expenditure incurred by a company and comprising:

(a)   such part of the emoluments paid to its employees engaged in carrying out research and development activities related to the company's trade as are paid to them for the purposes of those activities;

(b)   expenditure on materials or goods used solely by it in carrying out research and development activities related to its trade; and

(c)   any amount paid to another person (unconnected with the company) to carry out research and development activities related to the company's trade.

Research and development activities means systematic, investigative or experimental activities which are carried on wholly or mainly in the State (ie where not less than 75% of the total amount expended in the course of such activities is expended in the State), which involve innovation or technical risk, and are carried on for the purpose:

(a)   of acquiring new knowledge with a view to that knowledge having a specific commercial application; or

(b)   creating new or improved materials, products, devices, processes or services,

as well as other activities carried on wholly or mainly in the State for a purpose directly related to the carrying on of the above-mentioned activities.

Specifically excluded are activities carried on by way of market research, market testing, market development, sale promotion or consumer surveys, quality control, the making of cosmetic modifications or stylistic changes to products, processes or production methods, management studies or efficiency surveys, and research in social sciences, arts or humanities.

For the purposes of ascertaining what companies are members of the same group, the meaning of *group* is the same as for the purposes of group relief (see **8.103**) except that there is no requirement that any company should be Irish resident. In addition, two companies are members of a group if both are wholly or mainly under the control of the same individual or individuals, that is, where at least 75% of the ordinary share capital of each company is owned directly or indirectly by the same individual or individuals. TCA 1997 ss 412-418 contain anti-avoidance provisions which counter attempts to create artificial groups (see **8.304**). The additional tests for a group relationship as prescribed by these sections, the "profit distribution test" and the "asset distribution test", are applicable here also. In cases where companies are under the control of the same individual or individuals, they apply as if references to "parent company" were references to an individual or individuals.

The purpose of the patent income exemption is to encourage and reward effort leading to worthwhile inventions and the development of genuinely new products. The legislative provisions restricting the availability of patent income exemption are intended to confine the benefits of the exemption to those situations. This accounts for the requirement, where the parties are connected, that the amount of exempt dividends paid by a patent company should be related back to expenditure on research and development. As an alternative to meeting that requirement, the company in receipt of the royalties may apply in writing to the Revenue Commissioners for a determination to the effect that they are satisfied that the invention which is patented involved radical innovation and that it was patented for *bona fide* commercial reasons and not mainly to avoid liability to tax.

An EU Green Paper published at the end of 1995 defined "radical innovation" as "completely new and qualitatively different". Where an invention has resulted in a completely new product or process, there would be little doubt but that radical innovation has been involved. There is less certainty where the result of an invention is a modest improvement in an existing product or process. Where a product is involved, it is likely that a small but real improvement would qualify as radical innovation but the position relating to a small improvement to a process remains doubtful. It is most unlikely that an incremental change to an existing product or process would be regarded as radical innovation. For the purpose of making their determination, the Revenue will consider any evidence submitted to them and may consult with any person who may be of assistance to them in the matter. The Revenue Commissioners' determination may be appealed to the Appeal Commissioners and all of the provisions relating to appeals against income tax assessments, the rehearing of appeals, and the stating of a case for the opinion of the High Court on a point of law (see **15.209**), will apply in the case of such an appeal and with any necessary modifications.

A dividend or other distribution made by a company out of disregarded patent income is itself treated as not being income for income tax purposes and, where received by a company in respect of eligible shares, is treated as disregarded income for corporation tax purposes (TCA 1997, s 141). *Eligible shares* are shares which are fully paid up, which carry no preferential right to dividends or assets on a winding up and no preferential right to be redeemed, and which are not the subject of any treatment different from the treatment applying to all shares of the same class.

Where the income out of which the distribution is made consists partly of exempted income and partly of other income, the distribution is treated as two distributions, one being from exempted income and the other being from income which is not exempted. The legislation does not, however, prescribe a method for apportioning the distribution for this purpose. In fact, TCA 1997, s 141(9) seems to provide that a distribution for any accounting period must be treated as coming out of the non-exempted income of that period first and, where that income is insufficient, out of other non-exempted income of the most recent accounting period. It is unlikely that this is the intention of the legislation and the position which is likely to be agreed by the Revenue Commissioners is that a distribution out of mixed income should be apportioned in the ratio of exempted and non-exempted income.

From 6 April 1994, distributions out of disregarded income are no longer treated as disregarded income for income tax purposes except where received by:

(a) an individual who carried out, alone or with others, the research, testing or other work which led to the invention which is the subject of the patent in respect of which the disregarded income arose; or

(b) an individual in receipt of a distribution in respect of eligible shares.

See also **13.607**.

3.204.4 Nomination income

Certain income from stallions is exempted from tax (TCA 1997, s 231 – see **13.107.6**). The exemption applies to stallion service or "nomination" income arising up to 31 July 2008. The income exempted is:

(a)   income arising to the owner of a stallion standing in Ireland ("ordinarily kept on land in the State") from the service by the stallion of mares within the State;

(b)   income arising to the owner of a share or shares in a stallion standing in Ireland from the service by the stallion of mares within the State;

(c)   income arising to the owner of a share or shares in a stallion standing outside Ireland from the service by the stallion of mares within the State where the share owner carries on a trade of bloodstock breeding in the State and where the share ownership was acquired and is held primarily to service mares owned or partly owned by the share owner in the course of that trade;

(d)   income arising to a shareowner as described in (b) or (c) from the sale of rights to stallion services (sales of "nominations").

A distribution out of exempt nomination or stallion fee income is treated as not being income for income tax purposes and, where received by a company, as exempt profits of the company (TCA 1997, s 140(3)). Where the income out of which a distribution is made consists partly of exempted income and partly of other income, the distribution is treated as two distributions, one being from exempted income and the other being from income which is not exempted. The legislation does not, however, prescribe a method for apportioning the distribution for this purpose. In fact, TCA 1997, s 140(7) seems to provide that a distribution for any accounting period must be treated as coming out of the non-exempted income of that period first and, where that income is insufficient, out of other non-exempted income of the most recent accounting period. It is unlikely that this is the intention of the legislation and it is understood that a distribution out of mixed income may be treated as coming first out of exempted income.

By virtue of TCA 1997, s 233(2), stud greyhound fees are also exempt from tax. The exemption applies in respect of profits or gains arising to companies up to, but not after, 31 July 2008. In respect of accounting periods commencing on or after 1 January 2004, the exempt profits arising to a company in respect of its activities from greyhound stud services are required to be included in the company's annual return of income. Where a notice under TCA 1997, s 951(6) (exclusion from obligation in relation to making of a tax return – see **15.104.3**) has been issued to any person to whom greyhound stud services income has arisen, that person is treated as if such a notice had not been issued. The obligations relating to the keeping records (TCA 1997, s 886 – see **15.204**) apply as if the exempt profits were taxable profits (TCA 1997, s 233(3)). For the above purposes, profits and losses are to be computed in accordance with the Tax Acts as if the exemption from tax were not available (TCA 1997, s 231(4)).

3.204.5 Woodlands

Profits or gains arising from the occupation of woodlands managed on a commercial basis and with a view to realising profits are exempt from taxation (TCA 1997, s 232(2)). In respect of accounting periods commencing on or after 1 January 2004, however, the exempt profits arising to a company in respect of its activities from the occupation of woodlands are required to be included in the company's annual return of income (TCA 1997, s 232(2)). Where a notice under TCA 1997, s 951(6) (exclusion from obligation in relation to making of a tax return – see **15.104.3**) has been issued to any person to whom exempt income from the management of woodlands has arisen, that person is treated as if such a notice had not been issued. The obligations relating to the keeping records (TCA 1997, s 886 – see **15.204**) apply as if the exempt profits were taxable profits (TCA 1997, s 232(3)). For the above purposes, profits and losses are to be computed in accordance with the Tax Acts as if the exemption from tax were not available (TCA 1997, s 232(4)). For the above purposes, *woodlands* means woodlands in the State. The occupation of any land denotes having the use of that land (TCA 1997, s 232(1)).

In *Jaggers v Ellis* 1996 SpC 98, the Special Commissioner in the UK held that the term "woodlands" implies the production of timber with the result that a plantation of Christmas trees was not woodlands and no exemption was due in respect of profits from the sales of the trees. "Timber" typically means wood suitable for use in buildings or for carpentry and on that basis it was correct that timber was unlikely to be produced from a Christmas tree plantation. Nevertheless, the decision in this case is surprising as it is difficult to see a clear justification for the limitation put on the term "woodlands" by the Special Commissioner. There was apparently expert evidence to the effect that the land occupied by the taxpayer was not woodlands. However, the normal dictionary meaning of "woodlands" is land covered with wood (meaning trees) and the term is not limited to any kind of trees or trees grown for any particular purpose. It seems unlikely that an Irish court would deny exemption in a case involving the occupation of a Christmas tree plantation managed on a commercial basis.

The fact that occupation is a condition of the exemption means that not all profits derived from woodlands are necessarily exempt from taxation. An owner of woodlands might receive income from granting a right to some other person to fell trees on the lands and to remove and sell the timber. It might be difficult for the owner in that case to show that the income received has arisen from the *use* of the land. Nor is it certain that the person given the right to fell and take away the timber would be entitled to exemption as such activity might fall short of "the occupation of woodlands managed on a commercial basis". In *Russell v Hird* [1983] STC 541, it was held that the decision as to who is the occupier of land at a particular time is a question of fact. In that case, it was found that two individuals who entered into an arrangement involving the felling and sale of timber on land belonging to a third person conducted the operation in such an active way as to be seen to be the paramount occupiers of the land. It is most unlikely that this decision, where the facts were somewhat special, would mean that, say, a timber merchant who typically enters land to fell timber and to remove it for sale would be entitled to woodlands exemption.

Where the landowner is the person who derives the profits from the sale of the timber, the exemption will be available whether the trees are sold as standing timber or as felled and cut up, even using a sawmill. What is necessary for the exemption to apply is that the profits of the landowner are derived from the management of the woodlands on a commercial basis, whether the owner has planted the trees or has acquired previously planted woodlands. While the use of a sawmill to cut up timber for the purpose of making it more saleable will not of itself operate to deny tax exemption, it is important that the operations of the mill do not involve further processing so as to render the activity a trade assessable under Case I of Schedule D.

In *Christie v Davies* 26 TC 398, it was held that profits earned by a landowner who had set up a sawmill were not assessable as trading profits (being covered instead by the Schedule B assessment on the land: the corresponding result in Ireland would be exemption). The sawmill was well equipped with machinery, some of which would not normally be found in a sawmill, and the work carried out there involved the use of the cut timber to produce fences, gates and other products. The judgment in this case was criticised in the later decision in *IRC v Williamson Bros* 31 TC 370 which concerned the purchase by a firm of timber merchants and sawmillers of woodlands from which timber was cut and sold off in a rough state. It was held that the profits from this activity arose from the occupation of woodlands and were therefore covered by the Schedule B assessment. The work done on the felled timber was far less than that carried out in the *Christie v Davies* case but the same decision was reached.

Perhaps more helpful is the decision in *Collins v Fraser* 46 TC 143 which would suggest that exemption applies in respect of profits up to the point that the timber becomes part of the stock in trade of a separate trade, the point at which the normal exploitation of the woodlands ceases. Again, the case concerned the use of a sawmill for converting round timber sourced from woodlands occupied by the appellant. The round timber was converted into planks and then into thin boards some of which were sold and some of which were used to produce boxes and crates for sale. It was held that the profits from the activity up to and including the production of planks were covered by the Schedule B assessment and that the profits from the conversion into boards, boxes and crates were assessable as trading profits.

A distribution out of exempt profits from the occupation of woodlands managed on a commercial basis is treated as not being income for income tax purposes and, where received by a company, as exempt profits of the company (TCA 1997, s 140(3)). Where the income out of which a distribution is made consists partly of exempted income and partly of other income, the distribution is treated as two distributions, one being from exempted income and the other being from income which is not exempted. The legislation does not, however, prescribe a method for apportioning the distribution for this purpose. In fact, TCA 1997, s 140(7) seems to provide that a distribution for any accounting period must be treated as coming out of the non-exempted income of that period first and, where that income is insufficient, out of other non-exempted income of the most recent accounting period. It is unlikely that this is the intention of the legislation and the position which is likely to be agreed by the Revenue Commissioners is that a distribution out of mixed income should be apportioned in the ratio of exempted and non-exempted income.

3.204.6   Exemption for certain securities

Any security which the Minister for Finance has power to issue for the purposes of raising any money or loan may be issued with a condition that any interest arising is not to be liable to corporation tax as long as the security is held continuously from the date of issue in the beneficial ownership of a qualifying company to which the security is issued (TCA 1997, s 44(2)). For this purpose, a *qualifying company* is a company:

    (a)   (i)   which is solely resident in Ireland,

(ii)   whose business consists wholly or mainly of the carrying on of a relevant trade or trades, or the holding of stocks, shares or securities of a company which exists wholly or mainly for the purpose of the carrying on of a relevant trade or trades, and

(iii)   of which not less than 90% of its issued share capital is held by a foreign company or companies, or by a person or persons directly or indirectly controlled by a foreign company or companies, or

(b)   which is a foreign company carrying on a relevant trade through a branch or agency in the State.

A *relevant trade* is a trade carried on wholly or mainly in the State, but does not include a trade consisting wholly or mainly of:

(a)   banking within the meaning of the Central Bank Act, 1971;

(b)   assurance business within the meaning of section 3 of the Insurance Act 1936;

(c)   selling goods by retail; or

(d)   dealing in securities,

but goods are deemed not to be sold by retail if they are sold to—

(i)   a person who carries on a trade of selling goods of the class to which the goods so sold to such person belong,

(ii)   a person who uses goods of that class for the purposes of a trade carried on by such person, or

(iii)   a person, other than an individual, who used goods of that class for the purposes of an undertaking carried on by such person.

A *foreign company* is a company which is:

(a)   not resident in the State; and

(b)   under the control of a person or persons resident in a relevant territory (a territory with which Ireland has a tax treaty).

For the purposes of (b), *control* is to be construed in accordance with TCA 1997, s 432(2)-(6) (see **10.102**) except that "persons resident in a relevant territory" is to be read for "five or fewer participators".

Exemption in respect of certain other securities

The excess of the amount received on the redemption of a unit of certain securities over the amount paid for the unit on its issue is exempt from tax (except where the excess is taken into account in computing the profits of a trade). The securities to which this exemption applies are as follows:

(a)   non-interest-bearing securities issued by the Minister for Finance under section 4 of the Central Fund Act 1965 (TCA 1997, s 45(1));

(b)   securities created and issued by the Minister for Finance under the Central Fund (Permanent Provisions) Act 1965, or any other powers to that effect (TCA 1997, s 48);

(c)   securities created and issued by the Minister for Finance under the Central Fund (Permanent Provisions) Act 1965, known as Investment Bonds;

(d) any stock, debenture, debenture stock, certificate of charge, or other security which is issued with the approval of the Minister for Finance given under any Act of the Oireachtas and in respect of which the payment of interest and repayment of capital is guaranteed by the Minister under that Act, but excluding securities to which section 4 of the Central Fund Act 1965, TCA 1997, s 45(1), or TCA 1997, s 46 applies (TCA 1997, s 48).

The above provisions do not apply to issues of securities within the meaning of TCA 1997, s 48(4), ie non-interest bearing securities issued by the Minister for Finance at a discount, including Exchequer Bills and Exchequer Notes, Agricultural Commodities Intervention Bills issued by the Minister for Agriculture, and assets which are strips of securities within the meaning of FA 1970 s 54(10) (see **3.207.3**).

Where, however, the owner of any such security (ie the person who would be entitled on a redemption of the security to the proceeds of that redemption) sells or otherwise disposes of the security or receives on its redemption an amount greater than the amount paid by him for the security on its issue or otherwise, any profit, gain or excess arising is exempt from tax where the owner is not ordinarily resident in the State.

3.204.7   Taxation of reverse premiums

A reverse premium (broadly, a payment made in return for the recipient agreeing to enter into a lease or tenancy) is treated by TCA 1997, s 98A as a receipt of a revenue nature (TCA 1997, s 98A(2)). (Under general principles, a reverse premium would normally be treated as being of a capital nature.) It is assessable as rent unless it is assessable as a receipt of a trade or profession or is deductible from the amount treated as expenses of management of a life assurance company which is not charged to tax under Case I of Schedule D.

A reverse premium is charged to tax in the first relevant chargeable period where two or more of the persons who enter into the transaction or arrangements are connected and the terms of the arrangements are not what would be expected if those persons were dealing at arm's length. Where an assurance company is involved, the reverse premium reduces the expenses of management for the period in which the premium is received. Otherwise, a reverse premium is chargeable in accordance with the established principles of commercial accounting.

A *reverse premium* is defined as a payment or other benefit received by a person by way of inducement in connection with a relevant transaction being entered into by that person or by a person connected with that person. A *relevant transaction* is a transaction under which a person is granted an estate or interest in, or a right over, land (TCA 1997, s 98A(1)(a)). It follows from the reference to "an estate or interest" that a sale of a freehold is not a relevant transaction.

A typical example of a reverse premium is a cash payment to cover or reduce the tenant's cost of fitting out the premises to be leased. Since a reverse premium extends to "other benefits" and is therefore not confined to cash payments, it would also include the supply and installation by a landlord of fixtures and fittings required by the tenant, or payments to third parties on behalf of the tenant (at least to the extent that such provision or payment is not part of the lease itself). The provision in a lease agreement for a rent free, or reduced rent, period of occupation would not be a reverse premium since it would be part of the lease itself and could not therefore be an inducement to enter into the lease.

The amount or value of a reverse premium is, subject to TCA 1997, s 98A(4) and (6), treated as if it were an amount of rent (TCA 1997, s 98A(3)). Where a relevant transaction is entered into by a person receiving a reverse premium and is entered into for the purposes of a trade or profession carried on or to be carried on by that person, the amount or value of the premium is to be taken into account in computing the profits or gains of that trade or profession under Case I or II of Schedule D, as the case may be, as if it were a receipt of that trade or profession (TCA 1997, s 98A(4)).

Where:

(a)   two or more of the persons who enter into relevant arrangements are connected with each other; and

(b)   the terms of those arrangements are not such as would reasonably have been expected if those persons had been dealing at arm's length,

the whole of the amount or value of the reverse premium is, subject to TCA 1997, s 98A(3), (4) (see above), treated as accruing in the first relevant chargeable period (TCA 1997, s 98A(5)).

For the above purposes, *relevant arrangements* means a relevant transaction and any arrangements entered into in connection with it, whether before, at the same time or after it. The *first relevant chargeable period* means:

(a)   the chargeable period (accounting period or year of assessment) in which a relevant transaction is entered into; or

(b)   if a relevant transaction is entered into—

(i)   by a person receiving a reverse premium, and

(ii)   for the purposes of a trade or profession which that person is about to carry on,

the chargeable period in which the person commences to carry on the trade or profession (TCA 1997, s 98A(1)(a)).

Persons are connected with each other if they are connected within the meaning of TCA 1997, s 10 (see **2.3**) at any time during the chargeable period or periods when the relevant arrangements are entered into.

Where a reverse premium is received by an assurance company carrying on life business (within the meaning of TCA 1997, s 706 – see **12.601**) in respect of which it is chargeable to tax otherwise than in accordance with the rules applicable to Case I of Schedule D (see **12.603**), the amount or value of the reverse premium is deducted from the amount treated as the company's expenses of management for the accounting period in which the premium is received (TCA 1997, s 98A(6)).

TCA 1997, s 98A does not apply to a payment or benefit:

(a)   received by an individual in connection with a relevant transaction and the transaction relates to the grant of an estate or interest in, or a right in or over premises occupied or to be occupied by him as his only or main residence;

(b)   to the extent that it is consideration for the transfer of an estate or interest in land which constitutes the sale in a sale and lease-back arrangement where the terms of that arrangement at the time the arrangement is entered into are on bona fide commercial terms; or

(c) to the extent that, apart from TCA 1997, s 98A, it is taken into account in computing the profits or gains of a trade or profession under Case I or II of Schedule D, as the case may be, as a receipt of that trade or profession (TCA 1997, s 98A(7)).

A *sale and lease-back arrangement* is an arrangement under which a person disposes of the full estate or interest held by him in land to another person and the terms subject to which the disposal is made provide for the grant of a lease of an interest in or right in or over the land concerned to him by that other person (TCA 1997, s 98A(1)(a)).

When does the charge to tax arise?

As regards the period or periods for which a reverse premium is taxable, the position relating to arrangements involving connected persons dealing at other than arm's length, and reverse premiums received by certain life assurance companies, has been described above. The general position is that a reverse premium will be chargeable in accordance with the established principles of commercial accounting. In accordance with UITF (Urgent Issues Task Force) 28, a reverse premium received should be spread, on a straight-line basis, over the term of the lease or, if shorter, the period ending on the date of the first rent review that would adjust the rent to the prevailing market rate.

SSAP 21, although it does not deal with incentives for leases, requires lessees to charge operating lease rentals on a straight-line basis over the term of the lease, even if the payments are not made on that basis, unless another systematic and rational basis is more appropriate.

3.204.8 Release of debts previously set off

Where a liability which has been incurred in respect of the purchase of goods or materials, for services rendered or otherwise as a trading or professional expense, has been deducted in computing taxable profits for any accounting period, and the liability is subsequently released in whole or in part during the continuance of the trade or profession, the amount released must be included as a trading receipt in the period in which the release is effected (TCA 1997, s 87(1)). In *British Mexican Petroleum Co Ltd v Jackson* 16 TC 570, it was held, in relation to a trader in financial difficulty who had obtained a release from a liability to one of its creditors, that this did not justify reopening the accounts for the year in which the liability was incurred. Furthermore, on the facts of the case, the release did not constitute a trading receipt, being more in the nature of an additional contribution of capital. By virtue of TCA 1997, s 87(1), a release in those circumstances would give rise to a taxable receipt.

Note that TCA 1997, s 87 applies where a trading debt has been "released" and not, say, where it has merely been written off or simply not pursued. It can be argued that the section only applies in the case of a formal release of a trading debt and not where, for example, the creditor merely writes off the debt, fails to invoice or demand payment, or fails to present a cheque for payment. Thus, the release, to come within TCA 1997, s 87, must involve a contractual arrangement. There would not be a release merely because, say, the debtor is bankrupt or in liquidation. That a proper release should be formal derives from the fact that a mere write-off or failure to pursue by the creditor does not "release" the debtor from his obligation to pay.

3.204.9 Other receipts: income v capital

The treatment of various kinds of receipts for taxation purposes has been the subject of numerous decisions in case law. As with payments made (see **3.201.3**), it can, despite the large volume of case law on the subject, frequently be impossible to decide with certainty whether a payment received is of an income or of a capital nature. As Lord Reid in *Strick v Regent Oil Co Ltd* 43 TC 1 observed, it is a question which must be answered in light of all the circumstances which it is reasonable to take into account, and the weight which must be given to a particular circumstance in a particular case must depend rather on common sense than on a strict application of any single legal principle. Many tax practitioners will readily identify with Templeman J in *Tucker v Granada Motorway Services Limited* 53 TC 92 where he said in relation to this question:

> The forensic field of conflict involved … is an intellectual minefield in which the principles are elusive…analogies are treacherous…precedents appear to be vague signposts pointing in different directions…and the direction-finder is said to be "judicial common sense"…the practice of judicial common sense is difficult in Revenue cases.

A fireclay goods manufacturing company received compensation from a railway company for not working fireclay under or near a railway line. The land continued to be held by the company and the House of Lords held that the compensation was effectively for the loss of a capital asset which had become sterilised (*Glenboig Union Fireclay Co Ltd v IRC* 12 TC 427).

The greater part of the trading stock of a company of timber merchants was destroyed by fire. The full amount of the resulting proceeds of an insurance policy was held to be a trading receipt (*Green v Gliksten and Son Ltd* 14 TC 364). Insurance proceeds received in respect of the loss of, or damage to, fixed assets would, by contrast, be treated as a capital receipt. A company insured against loss of profits consequent on fire and the premiums were allowed as a deduction for tax purposes. Moneys received following a fire which destroyed the company's premises were held to be taxable as income (*R v British Columbia Fir and Cedar Lumber Co Ltd PC* [1932] ATC 441). A company insured against accidents to its employees and the premiums were allowed for tax purposes. Proceeds received (part of which were applied to defray funeral expenses) following the accidental death of an employee were held to be taxable (*Gray and Co Ltd v Murphy* 23 TC 225).

A lump sum received by a company for agreeing to cancel a contract to build two ships was held to be a taxable receipt of the company's trade (*Short Brothers v C IR* 12 TC 955). In *Blackburn v Close Brothers Ltd* 39 TC 164, a payment received by a company for rescinding a contract for secretarial services was held to be of a revenue nature and assessable as trading income.

In *Van den Berghs Ltd v Clark* 19 TC 390, damages paid by a company for breach of a joint venture agreement was held to relate to a capital asset as the contract related to the whole structure of the company's profit-making apparatus. In the same case, an amount received by the company for the cancellation of its future rights under joint venture agreements, which constituted a capital asset of the company, was held to be a capital receipt. On the other hand, in *Kellsall Parsons & Co v IRC* 21 TC 708, compensation for the loss of an agency agreement was held to be in the nature of income as it did not result in the substantial stultification of the taxpayer's business.

In making the necessary distinction between income and capital receipts, the objective will invariably be to identify the matter in respect of which the receipt arises. If a capital asset is identified, the receipt will tend to be capital also, and vice versa. The case of *CIR v John Lewis Properties plc* [2003] STC 117 is useful in this regard for five indicia of a capital payment identified by Lord Justice Dyson and it is worth quoting in full from this part of the judgment:

> I would identify the following factors in a case such as the present as being relevant to the question whether a payment is capital or income. I emphasise "such as the present" because the guidance derived from cases dealing with one situation may have little application to a wholly different situation. The first factor is duration. If what is disposed of is long-lasting, it is more likely to be a capital asset than if it is something which is evanescent. The cases show that an asset which has an enduring or long-lasting quality is likely to be regarded as a capital asset, and payment received for its acquisition a capital receipt. The converse may not, however, be true. As Lord Wilberforce pointed out in *Strick* (page 353F), if on a consideration of the nature of the asset in the context of the trade in question, it is seen to be appropriate to classify it as fixed rather than as circulating capital, "the brevity of its life is an irrelevant circumstance". Context is, therefore, all important. But in the context of the disposal of the right to receive income for a lump sum, the period over which the income is receivable is relevant to the proper classification of the payment for tax purposes. The majority of their Lordships in *Strick* considered that, if a premium had been paid for a tie in respect of a period of 21 years, but without the grant of a lease, the payment would have been capital.

> Secondly, the value of the asset assigned is also a relevant factor: see, for example, per Lord Upjohn in *Strick*, at page 345G–346C.

> Thirdly, the fact that the payment causes a diminution in the value of the assignor's interest is material. In my view, there is nothing in the authorities to indicate that, unless there has been a permanent impairment of the value of the property, the payment cannot be capital. It is true that in some of the cases, the fact that the value of the property was permanently diminished was regarded as pointing decisively towards the conclusion that the payment was capital. Examples of these are the cases grouped together by Arden LJ as illustrative of what she terms "the realisation principle". Examples are *Glenboig Union Fireclay Co Ltd v IRC* 1922 SC (HL) 112 , *Trustees of Earl of Haig v IRC* 1939 SC 676, *Nethersole v Withers* (1948) 28 TC 501 and *McLure (Inspector of Taxes) v Petre* [1988] 1 WLR 1386. But these authorities do not support the corollary that, absent a permanent diminution in the value of the property, the payment cannot be capital. Indeed, in *Nethersole* Lord Greene MR made the very point at page 510:

>> "One might perhaps have expected that where a piece of property, be it copyright or anything else, is turned to account in a way which leaves in the owner what we may call the reversion in the property, so that upon the expiration of the rights conferred, whether they are to endure for a short or a long period, the property comes back to the owner intact, the sum paid as consideration for the grant of the rights, whether consisting of a lump sum or of periodical or royalty payments, should be regarded as of a revenue nature."

> He continued at page 511:

>> "A principle on some such lines as these would not, we think, be out of accord with the popular idea of the distinction between capital and income. But it is not, we think, open to this Court to adopt it as in itself affording a sufficient test…"

The fact that the diminution is not permanent is not fatal to the classification of the payment as capital. Clearly, if the diminution is permanent, that will suggest strongly that the payment is capital. But the converse is not true. Otherwise, it is difficult to see how the receipt of a premium for the grant of a lease at a nominal rent can ever be capital, because the grant of such a lease diminishes the value of the landlord's reversion, but only for the duration of the lease. And yet it is plain that the premium for the grant of such a lease for even a short period is capital: see *Strick*. I should add that, in my view, the question whether there has been a diminution of the value of the assignor's interest should be judged at the date of the assignment. At that date, there has been a diminution in its value: if the assignor were to sell his reversion at that date, he would receive less than if he had not disposed of the right to receive the income from the asset for a period of time.

I would, therefore, hold that the fact that the disposal of the asset has caused the value of the assignor's interest to be diminished is a relevant factor. It seems to me that the amount by which the value of the reversionary interest is diminished is also of some materiality. This should reflect the duration of the asset that has been assigned (my first relevant factor) and its value (my second relevant factor), so that it is likely that the longer the period and the greater the value of the asset, the greater will be the diminution in the value of the reversionary interest. The greater the diminution in the value of the reversionary interest, the more likely it is that the payment should properly be classified as capital.

The fourth relevant factor is whether the payment is of a single lump sum. If a payment is one of a series of recurring payments made at frequent intervals, it is likely to be income in the hands of the payee. On the other hand, a single lump sum for the once and for all disposal of a particular asset is more likely to be a capital payment. In *Strick*, Lord Reid pointed out (page 316G) that ever since the *Vallombrosa* case [1910] SC 519, "recurrence as against a payment once and for all has been accepted as one of the criteria in a question of capital or income". See also per Lord Morris at page 333B-334A. In some contexts, the fact that payments are recurrent does not tell one anything about whether they are of a capital or revenue nature. For example, in the context of trade, some capital assets only last a very short time and have to be replaced regularly. But a transaction such as a rent factoring agreement with which this appeal is concerned does not involve assets of that kind, any more than did the transactions examined in *Strick*. Mr Goldberg submits that the possibility of recurrence of payments does not, of itself, make a receipt income: there must be more than the mere possibility of recurrence, and in the context of the realisation of an asset, there must also be the existence of a trade relating to the asset: the possibility of recurrence is not relevant to a disposal of a capital asset by a non-trader. I agree that the possibility of recurrence of payments does not, of itself, make a receipt income. It is no more than a relevant factor. But I do not agree that the possibility of recurrence is irrelevant except in relation to the disposal of an asset in the context of trade. It seems to me that the observations of Lord Reid in *Strick* about the relevance of recurring payments were not intended to be restricted to the context of trade, but were quite general in their application.

Fifthly, if the disposal of the asset is accompanied by a trandsfer of risk in relation to it, that tends to suggest that the sum paid for the asset is capital: see per Lord Hoffmann in *MacNiven (Inspector of Taxes) v Westmoreland Investments Ltd* [2001] 2 WLR 377 at paragraph 54.

3.205 Distributions received

TCA 1997, s 129 provides as follows:

Except as otherwise provided by the Corporation Tax Acts, corporation tax shall not be chargeable on dividends and other distributions of a company resident in the State, nor shall any such dividends or distributions be taken into account in computing income for corporation tax.

"Distribution" is defined in TCA 1997, s 130 (see **11.101**) and the term includes any dividend paid by a company, including a capital dividend. Distributions from Irish resident companies are referred to as *franked investment income* (TCA 1997, s 156). Since they will have been paid out of profits which have been subjected to corporation tax (or will have resulted in the payment of advance corporation tax – see **11.2**), no corporation tax is payable by the recipient of such distributions: they are "franked" for this purpose. Nor are they taken into account in computing income for corporation tax purposes.

TCA 1997, s 20 imposes a charge to income tax under Schedule F in respect of dividends and other distributions of Irish resident companies. A company is not, generally, subject to tax on any distribution from an Irish resident company. For years of assessment after 1975/76, the charge of income tax does not apply to the income of an Irish resident company nor, in the case of a non-resident company, to its income within the charge to corporation tax (chargeable profits of a non-resident company carrying on a trade in Ireland through a branch or agency). Irish resident companies are subject to corporation tax only and the Schedule F charge does not apply to them.

With effect from 6 April 1999, certain non-residents are exempted from Irish income tax in respect of distributions made to them by Irish resident companies (see **11.110**). The exemption applies to those non-residents who are exempted from dividend withholding tax (see **11.121.6**). Up to 5 April 1999, there was an effective exemption from income tax for all non-resident shareholders in respect of distributions made by Irish resident companies.

TCA 1997, s 129 applies "except as otherwise provided by the Corporation Tax Acts". Thus, for example, in computing income from pension business, franked investment income is taken into account as part of the profits of a life assurance company notwithstanding its exclusion by TCA 1997, s 129 from the charge to corporation tax (TCA 1997, s 717(4)).

Another exception is TCA 1997, s 138(3) which provides, "notwithstanding any provision of the Tax Acts", for dividends in respect of certain preference shares, to be chargeable to corporation tax under Case IV of Schedule D. This measure was introduced in conjunction with CTA 1976 s 84A (now TCA 1997 ss 133 and 134 – see **11.107**) with the intention of precluding banks and other lenders from using preference shares as a means of providing tax efficient financing. In this context, "shares" includes stock. The shares affected do not include preference shares:

(a)   which are quoted on a stock exchange in the State;

(b)   which are not so quoted but which carry rights in respect of dividends and capital which are comparable with such rights attaching to fixed-dividend shares quoted on a stock exchange in the State; or

(c)   which are non-transferable shares issued by a company, in the course of carrying on qualifying Shannon operations (within the meaning of TCA 1997, s 445) or international financial services operations (within the meaning of TCA 1997, s 446), to a company none of the shares of which is beneficially owned, directly or indirectly, by an Irish resident and which is not chargeable to corporation tax in respect of its profits.

Distributions received from non-resident companies

Dividends received from non-resident companies, being income from foreign possessions, are taxable under Case III of Schedule D. A dividend from a foreign-incorporated company which is tax resident in Ireland (by virtue of being centrally managed and controlled in Ireland) is not so taxable and, in the hands of a company, is not chargeable to corporation tax (TCA 1997, s 129). By the same token, a dividend from an Irish incorporated company that is not tax resident in Ireland is taxable under Case III. The fact that the company which pays a dividend is incorporated in a foreign country does not mean that that dividend constitutes foreign source income. In *Bradbury v English Sewing Cotton Co Ltd* 8 TC 481, it was held that a company incorporated in the state of New Jersey in the US but which was tax resident in the UK was a UK source of income rather than a foreign possession.

As regards distributions other than dividends, TCA Part 6 Chapter 2 (ss 130-135) (see **11.101-108**) and ss 436-437 (see **10.202-203**) provide for an extended meaning of distributions for the purposes of the Corporation Tax Acts. Although the term "distribution" as used for the purposes of the Corporation Tax Acts would appear to be relevant only for the purposes of the treatment of such distributions made by Irish resident companies, the meaning of "distribution" in TCA Part 6 Chapter 2 is not stated to be confined to distributions from Irish resident companies. Thus, for example, a payment of interest falling within TCA 1997, s 130 made by an Irish branch of a non-resident company would be treated as a distribution and would not be allowable as a deduction in computing the profits of the branch for corporation tax purposes.

The status for Irish tax purposes of amounts, other than dividends, payable by foreign companies and which fall within any of the descriptions of "distribution" in TCA 1997, s 130 is, however, not clear in all cases. In most instances, there will not be any particular difficulty in deciding whether or not a distribution received from a foreign company is an income distribution and as such liable to tax under Case III. Payments made by way of a return of capital or as some other form of return of capital will not be taxable as income, nor would a return of a shareholder's capital in the course of a winding up of a foreign company be so taxable (other than in the case of a company carrying on a trade of dealing in investments).

In deciding whether or not a distribution received from a non-resident company is income in the hands of a company within the charge to corporation tax in Ireland, the relevant question to be decided is whether the capital of the shareholder company in the foreign company remains intact after the distribution is made. Where it is, it will almost invariably be the case that the distribution is received as income from a foreign possession regardless of how the payment is described in the books of the foreign company. The case of *IRC v Trustees of Joseph Reid deceased* 30 TC 431 was concerned with the treatment for UK purposes of a "capital" dividend paid out of capital profits of a South African company. It was held that, as the capital in the distributing company remained intact, the dividend was income from a foreign possession.

As to whether a payment made by a non-resident company is to be regarded as income or as a return of capital for the purposes of Irish tax will depend on the nature of the payment according to the general or company law of the country in which the paying company is incorporated. In *Rae v Lazard Investment Co Ltd* 41 TC 1, a company incorporated in the state of Maryland in the US transferred part of its business to another

US company in exchange for shares in that other company. The first company then distributed the shares acquired in the other company to its shareholders. It was held that a UK company which was a shareholder in the first company did not receive its distribution as income notwithstanding that it continued to hold the same number of shares in the first company as it held before the distribution. This was because, under the law of the state of Maryland, the distribution was made as a "distribution on partial liquidation". The distribution was accordingly impressed with the quality of a return of capital and was capital for all purposes. In determining whether a distribution from a non-resident company should be characterised for Irish tax purposes as income or as a return of capital, the question to be addressed is whether or not, having regard to local law, the corpus of the asset is left intact after the distribution. If it is, the distribution will be an income receipt; otherwise it will be a capital receipt.

In *Courtaulds Investments Ltd v Fleming* 46 TC 111, a distribution made by an Italian company out of its share premium reserve was held to be a return of capital. Under Italian law, the distributing company was required to allocate a certain percentage of its net annual profits to a legal reserve until it reached 20% of its share capital. The reserve had at all times to be treated under Italian law in the same way as if it were paid up capital of a company so that distributions out of that reserve were impressed with the quality of capital.

Based on the principles emerging from the above established UK cases, which can be expected to be applicable for Irish tax purposes also, where it is established that a distribution is a return of capital (as determined by the law of the relevant foreign country), the distribution should not be taxable as income from a foreign possession and, conversely, where it cannot be so established, it will fall to be treated as income taxable under Case III of Schedule D.

On the other hand, it is felt that a strict application of those principles in all cases would not be justified. Consider the case of an Irish company in receipt of a payment for the buy-back of its shares in a UK company. By virtue of TCA 1997, s 130, the amount received would, generally, be a distribution if it were received from an Irish company. There is similar treatment under equivalent UK provisions. The tax treatment in Ireland of such a distribution from a UK resident company to an Irish company cannot, however, be determined by the tax provisions of either country. Under UK company law provisions, the payment would come within the meaning of "distribution" (as it would under equivalent Irish company law provisions). Thus, following the decisions in the above-mentioned UK cases, it is sometimes considered that such payments must be treated as distributions for Irish tax purposes.

This analysis of the matter must, however, be questionable. A payment received in respect of a buy-back of shares is, fundamentally, no different to any other payment received in respect of the disposal of an asset. Reliance in this context on a company law definition of "distribution" (which is for the particular purposes of restricting the profits out of which distributions may be made) seems misconceived. Furthermore, it is relevant to note that the decisions in the two cases mentioned above were to the effect that the payments in question were capital in nature. The inverse is not necessarily true; it does not seem to be correct to deduce from this that any payment that cannot be categorised as capital for company law purposes must *ipso facto* be regarded as income. Nor does it seem to be correct to conclude that a payment falling within a broad definition of "distribution" set out in company law for a particular purpose must be regarded as being of an income nature under the general law of the country concerned.

EU law principles

Dividends from Irish resident companies are not subject to corporation tax but dividends from overseas companies are taxable subject to credit relief depending on circumstances. This difference in treatment has been the subject of litigation before the European Court of Justice, most significantly in *FII Group Litigation v CIR* (FII GLO) (C-446/04).

The ECJ considered the conflicting interests of UK corporate taxpayers and the Exchequer in the context of the freedom of establishment (Article 43 of the EC Treaty) and the free movement of capital (Article 56). These conflicting interests arose in the context of the tax treatment of dividend income in the hands of UK corporate taxpayers but specifically as regards the extent that there is a difference between the UK tax treatment of foreign-source dividend income and domestic-source dividend income.

The FII GLO (Group Litigation Order) was made by the UK High Court in 2003 and a number of questions were referred for determination to the ECJ in 2004. The case was heard by the ECJ in November 2005 and in April 2006 the Advocate-General delivered his preliminary opinion to the Court. The ECJ delivered its judgment on 12 December 2006.

The UK approach to the taxation of dividend income is similar to that in Ireland: double taxation is reduced or avoided by use of an exemption system for domestic-source dividends and a credit system for cross border dividends. The taxpayers in *FII GLO* contended that that system, exempting only domestic-source dividend income, was in breach of the EC Treaty, arguing that it had the effect of treating UK corporate taxpayers receiving foreign source income on terms less favourable than UK companies receiving domestic-source income. The former category, whether their foreign investments constituted holdings or less than 10% (portfolio) or 10% or more (non-portfolio), were taxed on their dividend income whereas the latter group were not, giving rise to an unjustified restriction on the freedom of establishment and the free movement of capital.

The Court restated the principle that, although direct taxation falls within the competence of Member States, they must nevertheless exercise that competence consistently with community law. Accordingly, whatever approach is adopted, the freedoms guaranteed by the treaty preclude a Member State from treating foreign-source dividends less favourably than domestic-source dividends, unless such different treatment relates to situations which are not objectively comparable or is justified by overriding reasons in the general interest.

The Court concluded that the UK was not prohibited from operating an exemption system for domestic-source dividends together with a credit/imputation system for foreign-source dividends. To be compatible with community law, however, the foreign-source dividends should not be subject to UK taxation at a rate higher than the rate applying to domestic-source dividends. The UK is obliged to prevent foreign-source dividends, whether from portfolio or from non-portfolio holdings, from being liable to a series of tax charges by ensuring that the amount of tax paid by the non-resident dividend paying company is offset against the amount of tax for which the recipient company is liable (up to the limit of that amount).

For companies with less than 10% voting control, the Court unequivocally concluded that the UK provisions were in breach of the Treaty. It was not acceptable for domestic source dividends to be exempt from corporation tax when foreign-source dividends were subject to that tax and entitled to relief only as regards any withholding charged on those dividends.

In relation to non-portfolio holdings, the Court held that the EC Treaty is not breached in circumstances where the domestic tax rate applied to foreign-source dividends is not higher than the rate applied to domestic-source dividends, and the tax credit is at least equal to the amount of tax paid in the source State.

Foreign dividends received on or after 31 January 2008

Domestic sourced dividends are exempt from corporation tax but the underlying profits will have suffered corporation tax at 12.5% where the profits are generated from trading activities. To be compatible with EU law in the light of the *FII GLO* decision, foreign sourced dividends should not be subject to a rate of taxation higher than that applying to domestic sourced dividends. Foreign dividends received on or after 31 January 2008 from underlying trading profits sourced from an EU country or a country with which Ireland has a double tax treaty are taxable at the 12.5% rate. The full amount of the foreign dividend is chargeable at the 12.5% rate when certain conditions are met, even though part of the dividend may not be paid out of trading profits. See **3.101.5** for detailed treatment of this measure.

3.206 Income tax on payments made or received

No payment made by a resident company is to be treated for income tax purposes as paid out of profits or gains brought into charge to income tax (TCA 1997, s 24(1)). No payment made by a resident company will accordingly come within the provisions of TCA 1997, s 237. Payments such as yearly interest, annuities and other annual payments, and patent royalties ("relevant payments") are governed by the provisions of TCA 1997, s 238 and TCA 1997, s 239 (see **4.302** and **4.303**). Any right or obligation under the Income Tax Acts to deduct income tax from any payment is not affected by the fact that the recipient is a company not chargeable to income tax in respect of the payment.

Relevant payment means:

(a) any payment made on or after 6 April 1976 from income tax is deductible and to which the provisions of TCA 1997, s 238(3)-(5) apply; and

(b) any amount which under TCA 1997, s 438 is deemed to be an annual payment.

The payments from which income tax is deductible and to which the provisions of TCA 1997, s 238(3) to (5) apply have been described in **4.303**, **4.304** and **4.305**. Certain loans made by close companies to participators or their associates which are deemed by TCA 1997, s 438 to be annual payments (see **10.204**) are also relevant payments.

Companies are required for each accounting period to make a return of relevant payments made in that period and of the income tax for which they are accountable in respect of those payments. Where a return is required for any accounting period, it must be made within nine months from the end of that period TCA 1997, s 239(4). That return is now part of the corporation tax return which a company is required make in accordance with TCA 1997, s 884. (TCA 1997, s 239(4) does not, however, provide that a return should be made not later than the 21st of the month in which the period of nine months ends.) Relevant payments are among the items which a company is required to include in its corporation tax return (TCA 1997, s 884(2)(d) and (e)).

For the purposes of the charge, assessment, collection and recovery from the company of the income tax due, and of any interest and penalties thereon, in respect of relevant payments made in any accounting period, that income tax is treated as corporation tax payable by the company for that period (TCA 1997, s 239(11)(a)). The corporation tax return is required to be made within nine months of the end of the accounting period (but in any event not later than the 21st of the month in which that period of nine month ends) (TCA 1997 ss 950(1) and 951(1)). No provision of TCA 1997, s 239 may prejudice the powers of the Revenue to recover tax by means of an assessment or otherwise.

Tax in respect of relevant payments made in any accounting period is due at the same time as the preliminary tax for that period is due. The tax is due without the making of an assessment, as is the case with preliminary tax, but an assessment may be made if the tax is not paid on time. Estimated assessments may be made by an inspector where a relevant payment has not been included in a return or where the inspector is not satisfied with a return. For the purposes of interest on unpaid tax, the tax assessed is treated as payable at the time it would have been payable if a correct return had been made.

A company could make a relevant payment on a date which does not fall within an accounting period. That would be the case where, for example, a company has not to date come within the charge to corporation tax but has borrowed money on which it has paid yearly interest from which tax is deductible under TCA 1997, s 246. The payment in that case must be returned, and the tax paid, within six months of the date the payment was made. Any assessment made in those circumstances is treated as for the year of assessment in which the relevant payment was made. The income tax in that case is not treated as corporation tax by virtue of TCA 1997, s 239(11)(a).

Where a company has received income from which tax has been deducted at source in an accounting period in which it has made any relevant payments, the tax on income received may be set against the tax due on the relevant payments. The claim for offset should be included in the return of relevant payments. Where the income tax on relevant payments has been paid before the claim is allowed, the excess amount will be repaid to the company (TCA 1997, s 239(7)). Any such entitlement to repayment of income tax is not affected by the fact that the income tax paid is treated as corporation tax in accordance with TCA 1997, s 239(11)(a). Proceedings for collection of tax, including proceedings by way of distraint, may not be commenced in relation to tax which is the subject of a claim for offset but this does not affect the date when the tax is due. A claim for offset may not stop proceedings already begun. Where any offset has been made, the tax offset is treated as tax paid or repaid as the case may be. Tax which has been set against tax on relevant payments may not, evidently, be repaid or credited under TCA 1997, s 24(2).

Where an Irish resident company receives a payment from which income tax has been deducted, that income tax is to be set off against any corporation tax assessable on the company for the accounting period in which the payment is received (TCA 1997, s 24(2)). Where the company is wholly exempt from corporation tax, it will be entitled to repayment of the income tax. Otherwise, the income tax will be repayable to the company when the assessment for the period is finally determined and it is established that a repayment is due. This will be the case, for example, where the company has losses sufficient to cover the payments which have borne income tax, in which case the full income tax will be repayable. Where the company's corporation tax liability for the period is less than the amount of the income tax deducted from payments received, the excess income tax will be repayable.

Similar provision is made in TCA 1997, s 25(3) in respect of non resident companies which are liable to corporation tax (see **3.107.1**).

3.207 Case III

3.207.1 Introduction

As noted in **3.102.2**, TCA 1997, s 76(1) provides that the amount of any income for corporation tax purposes is to be computed in accordance with income tax principles, and that all questions as to the amounts which are or are not to be taken into account as income, or in computing income, are to be determined in accordance with income tax law and practice as if accounting periods were years of assessment. For the purposes of ascertaining liability to tax, income or profits chargeable under Case III are deemed to issue from a single source (TCA 1997, s 70(1)).

Income tax law in relation to any accounting period means the law as it applies to the charge of income tax on individuals for the year of assessment in which the period ends. Accordingly, for corporation tax purposes, income is to be computed under the Schedules and Cases which apply for income tax purposes and in accordance with the provisions applicable to those Schedules and Cases. It is appropriate, therefore, to outline the rules and principles governing the Cases of Schedule D apart from Case I; Case III is dealt with first and this is followed by Cases IV and V.

3.207.2 Income charged

The charge to tax under Case III of Schedule D is provided for in TCA 1997, s 18(2). Tax under Case III is charged on the following types of income:

(a) interest of money, whether yearly or otherwise, or any annuity, or other annual payment, whether such payment is payable within or outside the State, either as a charge on any property of the person paying the same by virtue of any deed or will or otherwise, or as a reservation out of it, or as a personal debt or obligation by virtue of any contract, or whether the same is received and payable half-yearly or at any shorter or more distant periods but not including any payment chargeable under Case V of Schedule D;

(b) all discounts;

(c) profits on securities bearing interest payable out of the public revenue other than such as are charged under Schedule C;

(d) interest on any securities issued or deemed within the meaning of TCA 1997, s 36 to be issued, under the authority of the Minister for Finance, in cases where such interest is paid without deduction of tax;

(e) income arising from securities outside the State except such income as is charged under Schedule C;

(f) income arising from possessions outside the State.

(g) profits or gains arising from activities from dealing in certain "securitised" assets engaged in by companies other than IFSC companies.

Where some other provision of the Income Tax Acts requires tax to be charged under one of the other Cases of Schedule D, however, the income in question may be charged under another such Case (TCA 1997, s 18(3). Thus, while interest and discounts are normally chargeable under Case III, such income received by a bank in the ordinary course of its trade of banking is included as trading receipts in calculating its profits taxable under Case I. Similarly, deposit interest received from banks, buildings societies and certain other deposit takers carrying on business in the State is, in general, taxable under Schedule D Case IV and not under Case III (see **3.208.3**).

Interest, annuities and annual payments

Tax is charged under heading (a) of Case III on any interest of money, whether yearly or otherwise, and any annuity or other annual payment, whether such payment is payable out of it, or as a personal debt or obligation by virtue of any contract. The meaning of "annual payment" has already been discussed in **4.301** where it was seen that only payments which are "pure income profit" in the hands of the recipient are annual payments. (It was also seen there that in certain cases patent royalties could be annual payments. Such royalties would therefore be assessable under Case III, even where not received from abroad.) The fact that a payment is receivable half yearly or at any shorter or longer intervals does not prevent it from being an annual payment chargeable under Case III, but any rent or other payment taxable under Schedule D Case V is specifically excluded.

Interest paid or credited on any "relevant deposit" with a bank, building society, trustee savings bank, the Post Office Savings Bank and certain other deposit takers is payable subject to deduction of income tax at source and is taxable under Case IV (TCA 1997, s 261(c)(i)).

In *Re Euro Hotel (Belgravia) Ltd* 1975 STC 682, it was held that "interest of money" normally required the existence of a sum by reference to which the payment said to be interest was to be ascertained and that there cannot be interest of money unless there is the requisite "money" for the payment to be said to be "interest of". A payment for the delay in performing obligations other than the payment of a sum of money is not a payment of "interest". Furthermore, the sum of money must be a sum that is due to the person entitled to the interest. In his judgment in this case, Megarry J quoted some authorities on the meaning of "interest", including:

(a) money paid for the use of money lent (the principal), or for forbearance of a debt, according to a fixed ratio (rate per cent) – *Shorter Oxford English Dictionary* (3rd edn);

(b) compensation for a delay in payment – Farwell J in *Bond v Barrow Haematite Steel Co* (a company law case); and

(c) payment by time for the use of money – Rowlatt J in *Bennett v Ogston* 15 TC 374.

Interest was described in *Schulze v Bensted* 7 TC 30 as recompense measured by time for the use of money. In *Riches v Westminster Bank Ltd* 28 TC 159, Lord Wright said that the essence of interest is that it is a payment which becomes due because the creditor has not had his money at the due date. Interest may therefore be seen as the profit which the creditor might have made if he had the use of the money or the loss he has suffered because he did not have that use. Statutory interest on damages was held to be interest even though there was no enforceable debt during the time it was deemed to have accrued: the amount of the damages constituted an identifiable amount which could be regarded as principal.

In general, interest of money arises in any case where money is paid by one person (the debtor) to compensate another person (the creditor) for the fact that the debtor has for some time had the use of money due to the creditor, whether as the result of a deposit or loan or by reason of a delay in the debtor's paying to the creditor a sum of money owed. It was held in *The Norseman* [1957] 2 All ER 660 that interest awarded by the Admiralty Court on damages for collision, and included in the total award of damages, is interest of money.

In *Bennett v Ogston* it was held, in relation to money being repaid by instalments, that so much of the instalments collected as did not represent repayment of capital was interest of money. In *Re Euro Hotel (Belgravia) Ltd* on the other hand (see above), payments made due to a delay in fulfilling other obligations, and not for the delay in making a payment of money, were held not to be payments of interest although calculated at an annual rate per cent by reference to a sum of money. In *Chevron Petroleum UK Ltd and others v BP Development Ltd and others* [1981] STC 689, a sum described as interest charged on a net shortfall under a cost sharing agreement was held to be interest even though it was not known in advance which of the parties would incur the interest. A sum which by its nature is interest of money retains that nature even if wrapped up with some other sum where the whole amount is paid in the form of a single indivisible sum.

A question on which there is surprisingly little clear guidance is when is bank deposit interest assessable to tax. The governing principle for income taxable under Case III is that it arises, and is therefore taxable, only when it enures for the benefit of the recipient. Despite the famous dictum of Mr Justice Rowlatt (*Leigh v CIR* 11 TC 590) to the effect that receivability without receipt is nothing, it has often been stated that in the case of interest which arises *de die in diem*, such as bank deposit interest, the depositor is entitled to such interest at the end of each day, whether or not it has already been credited to the account by the bank, and that the interest is effectively received on that basis. This would appear to be borne out by the fact that a depositor may uplift his deposit at any time so that any interest accrued at that point may be obtained.

On the other hand, in *Girvan v Orange Personal Communications Services Ltd* [1998] STC 567, it was held that bank interest could not be assessed until such time as it was credited by the bank. The case in question concerned an arrangement in which the crediting of interest on a bank deposit was deferred until a specified future date or earlier closing of deposit accounts. The mere fact that the taxpayer could have asked for payment of interest did not mean that it was income; the interest in question must in fact be received before it is liable to tax. Thus, it would seem that the fact that interest on deposit accrues from day to day and can be received at the end of each day is not sufficient to render it taxable; it would apparently be necessary (in the case of any interest not yet credited) for the depositor actually to close the account in order for any accrued interest to arise.

Underpinning the above and other UK court decisions is the general rule that income is taxed on a receipts basis unless the Taxes Acts direct otherwise. Due to the relevance of accounting principles, the accruals basis necessarily applies for the purposes of Case I and II but there is no obvious authority for its application to other cases (although it might be possible to infer that income taxable under Case V is taxable on the accruals basis since there is provision there for relief in respect of amounts not received).

Thus, in *Grey v Tiley* 16 TC 414, it was held that the general rule applicable to Case IV income is that it arises when it is received rather than when it falls due. In *Dewar v CIR* 19 TC 561, it was held that as the taxpayer had not received any interest, it could not be included in his income. These decisions were approved in *Whitworth Park Coal v IRC* 38 TC 531. In this case, Viscount Simonds acknowledged the difficulty of ascertaining the meaning of the words "income arising" (which are relevant for both Case III and Case IV purposes). He went on to suggest that the word "arising" is not the most important word here, pointing out that "no income can arise before there is any income, and as soon as there is income the income has arisen". Accordingly, the crucial word is "income", a word that he thought cannot be defined.

Explaining that for a trader account must be taken of trading debts that have not yet been received, Viscount Simonds said that it would give a false picture of the trader's position to put the cost of goods or rendering services into his accounts without putting anything against that until the price has been paid. It is different where there is no trade or profession and where no profit and loss account is made up. Sums (such as interest or other pure income profit) paid to a person are his income and it would be a great hardship to such a person to require him to pay tax on sums owing to him but of which he cannot yet obtain payment. There is nothing here corresponding to a trader writing off bad debts in a subsequent year. Traders are often required to pay tax on things not yet received and which may never be received but there is no reported case of a non-trader in this position; in fact there are cases, including *Grey v Tiley*, in which the opposite effect has resulted.

Viscount Simonds went on to say that whereas traders pay tax on the balance of profits or gains and bring money owed to them into account in striking that balance, ordinary individuals are not assessable and do not pay tax until they get the money because until then it is not part of their income. (It is not apparent that this principle would need to be modified where the recipient is a company rather than an "ordinary individual". The taxpayer was in any event a company and Viscount Simonds' view was that it could not have been assessed and required to pay tax on amounts that accrued during years before those amounts were paid, even if the exact amount which had accrued could have been determined.) Even if it were possible to spread income back over years when it became due and payable, there is nothing on which to base an inference that income, once it has been received, can be regarded as having arisen not only before it was received but even before it was payable and while it was merely accruing.

Dunmore v McGowan [1978] STC 217 was concerned with the question as to when a taxpayer received interest in respect of a bank deposit account. Commenting on the above passage from Viscount Simonds, Stamp J asked what was meant by the word "get" and suggested that to say that individuals do not pay tax until they *get* the money is to some extent to beg the question since it was necessary to read the whole of the *Whitworth Park* judgment to know precisely what is meant by the word "get". He also warned against pressing the "receivability without receipt is nothing" doctrine too far. It was held that the interest was received, or "got", when it was credited to the deposit account. It was received even though it might not have been paid to the taxpayer until a later date. Thus the relevant question is when does the income enure for the benefit of the taxpayer. Once the deposit interest is credited, it enures for the depositor's benefit in the sense that it may reduce his liabilities or increase his estate.

There is therefore a considerable body of support in case law for the conclusion that income assessable under Case III or Case IV is taxable on a receipts basis. Or, perhaps it would be more accurate to say that such income is not taxable before it is received (see below). Central to the reasoning behind this conclusion is that such income is not income at all unless and until received, which is very close to Mr Justice Rowlatt's "receivability without receipt is nothing".

As to how the underlying principle is to be applied to the more unusual situation in which there is a receipt of income before it is accrued is less clear. "Receivability without receipt" does not directly address this question; accordingly, if there has already been a receipt, it might still be argued that the correct basis of assessment is by reference to the year or period in which the income in question is accrued or earned. In this type of situation, however, it could hardly be argued, once the income has been received, that no income has arisen "before there is any income". In his judgment, Viscount Simonds nowhere says that the receipts basis rather than the accruals basis is the correct basis of assessment; rather that the company should not be taxed on amounts accrued but which had not been paid when the assessment was made. But note above the general rule that income is taxed on a receipts basis unless the Taxes Acts indicate otherwise (which they do not except in relation to Cases I and II). In any event, TCA 1997, s 817B, as discussed below, provides a statutory basis for the taxation of interest on a receipts basis where that interest is received before it is accrued.

In the *Whitworth Park* case, Lord Keith of Avonholm concluded that the payments received by the company were income of the year in which they were received, which was reasonable in that case since the income had not been received at the time it was accrued. He also made reference to the St Lucia case (*St Lucia Usines and Estates Co Ltd v Colonial Treasurer of St Lucia* [1924] AC 508) in which "income arising or accruing" was in point and in which it was held that no income arose or accrued until receipt. Again, in *Girvan v Orange Personal Communications Services Ltd*, the conclusion was that bank deposit interest could not be assessed until such time as it was credited by the bank. But none of this is authority for a general proposition that the receipts basis rather than the accruals basis is the correct basis of assessment.

Thus, as regards income assessable under Case III or Case IV, while there is a considerable body of case law to support the conclusion that such income does not arise until it is received, that is, before it is received, that is not to say that the receipts basis as such must prevail over the accruals basis, so that there is no basis for the view that income prepaid is properly assessable as it is received rather than when it is accrued.

An anti-avoidance provision, effective for interest received on or after 29 February 2000, secures that interest in certain circumstances is taxable in the period in which it is received and not, as would otherwise be the case, on an accruals basis. TCA 1997, s 817B provides, as regards a company, that where in relation to an accounting period (the "earlier chargeable period") the company receives interest in the period, so much of the amount of interest:

(a)   as would otherwise not be taken into account in computing the company's income chargeable to tax under Schedule D for the earlier chargeable period; and

(b) would be so taken into account for a subsequent accounting period or periods,

is to be taken into account in computing the company's income so chargeable for the earlier chargeable period and not for the subsequent accounting period or periods.

This provision ensures that no tax advantage will arise where interest which is to accrue over a number of years is paid in the first of those years with the intention that, while the payer might be entitled to a tax deduction for the full amount immediately, the recipient would only be taxable over the period for which the interest accrues.

In certain circumstances, interest or other investment income may be taxed under Case I of Schedule D rather than under Case III. Such income may be regarded as part of a company's trading income. Thus, for example, it was seen in relation to insurance companies (see **12.605.2**) that investment income may be taxed under Case I or under some other Case of Schedule D, and that the inspector of taxes has the option of choosing which Case is to be applied. The basis for this is the decision in *Liverpool & London & Globe Insurance Co v Bennett* 6 TC 327. The normal practice of the Irish Revenue is to compute income under the rules of Case III, IV or V as appropriate but to assess the income in question under Case I. As to whether investment income will in any case be included as a Case I receipt or be assessed under Case III will depend entirely on the circumstances. In *Nuclear Electric v Bradley* [1996] STC 405, investment income used to fund future potential liabilities to individuals other than customers was held not to be trading income.

The judgment in the *Nuclear Electric* case provides a useful summary of precedent case law on the question as to when investment income amounts to a trading receipt of the taxpayer. In this connection, Lord Jauncey contrasted the position of insurance companies and banks part of whose business is the making and holding of investments to meet current liabilities with businesses of which the making and holding of investments form no part (as was found to be the case in *Nuclear Electric*). It was acknowledged that in between these two ends there will fall other types of businesses whose position is not so clear.

Lord Jauncey referred to the case of *Bank Line Ltd v IRC* [1974] STC 342 where Lord Cameron pointed out that although receipts from investments may be derived from a replacement fund comprising sums set aside out of profits of trading in previous years and which facilitates the continued carrying on of the taxpayer's trade, there is a material difference between such investments and the investment of funds which are or can be at call to meet current demands of a trading activity. In order that receipts from investments can constitute trading income, the nature of the trade in question must be such that the making and holding of investments at interest is an integral part of that trade. In the case of an insurance or bank business, that test is easily satisfied as the investments of such concerns are made not merely for the sake of investment but for the sake of having a fund readily available to meet liabilities of the business if these are needed. As noted by Buckley LJ in the *Bank Line* case, the funds of an insurance company are necessarily at risk of claims by policyholders immediately the policies are effected.

Although satisfied that the funds invested in the *Nuclear Electric* case, being very large and intended to be invested for a long period, were clearly not employed in the company's business, Lord Jauncey did not wish this conclusion to be taken as suggesting that sums held by a trader in an interest-bearing account to meet current or short-term trading liabilities should be similarly considered. Despite the emphasis on the making and holding of investments at interest as being an integral part of a trade, therefore, it is nevertheless entirely possible for a company whose trade does not meet that test to include in its trading profits for tax purposes interest earned from an account used to meet current or short-term liabilities of that trade.

Discounts

Tax is charged, under heading (b) of Case III, on all discounts. The charge applies to profits on discount transactions other than those carried out in the course of a trade (which are taxable under Case I) and those that can properly be regarded as capital in nature. Despite the reference to "all discounts" therefore, not all discounts are included for Case III purposes. Discounts typically arise in relation to instruments such as bills of exchange, promissory notes, exchequer bills etc. A profit on a discount transaction may be realised either by holding the bill to maturity or by selling it before maturity at a price in excess of that paid for it. In *Brown v National Provident Institution* 8 TC 57, it was held that the whole of the difference between the amount paid for a treasury bill and the amount received on its sale and maturity was a profit on a discount and was taxable under Case III.

Discounts are undoubtedly related to interest. The Oxford English Dictionary defines "discount" as "the deduction made from the amount of a bill of exchange or promissory note, by one who gives value for it before it is due, this deduction being calculated at a defined rate per cent for the time the document has to run; practically the interest charged by a banker or bill-discounter for advancing the value of a bill before it is due".

Nevertheless, discount and interest are not the same. In *Thompson v Giles* (1824), Holroyd J stated that "in the interest account interest upon the amount is charged upon each bill until it is actually paid; but when a bill is discounted the interest to be deducted is calculated up to the time when it becomes due and for no longer period". The distinction was reinforced by the decision in *Willingale v International Commercial Bank Ltd* [1978] STC 75. It was pointed out there that, unlike interest, discount is not earned nor does it accrue from day to day. Discount does not accrue by reference to time but is merely payable in full on maturity. It would make no sense for a bank to lend money at interest none of which is payable until the principal is repayable. The fact that the profit and loss account of a company which discounts or purchases bills of exchange is credited with "accrued discount" does not alter this conclusion. What is happening here is that the company is merely anticipating a profit that has not yet been realised. What goes into the profit and loss account is a fractional part of what it is hoped the profit will ultimately be although, typically, due to a number of factors, that profit is not really ascertainable until the bill is sold or reaches maturity.

The difference between income and capital, as far as discounts are concerned, was considered in *Lomax v Peter Dixon & Son Ltd* 25 TC 353. An English company advanced £319,600 to a Finnish company which issued £340,000 in notes of £500 at a discount of 6% in respect of the sum owing. Interest on the notes was payable at 1% above the lowest discount rate of the Bank of Finland during each year. The notes were to be paid off at a premium of 20% if the amount of the Finnish company's profits was sufficient for the purpose. Between 1933, when the notes were issued, and 1940 the notes were duly paid off at a premium. The Court of Appeal held that the discount and premium on the notes were capital payments and therefore not chargeable to income tax. In short, where in addition to issuing notes at a discount, interest is specifically provided for, the discount is not income. Note that premiums, provided they are not disguised as interest, are not interest. Genuine premiums paid to reflect credit risk, or to preserve the real value of the loan principal after inflation, and paid in addition to a full interest coupon, are not interest.

On the other hand, discount arising where a bill of exchange or a treasury bill has been discounted and where the bill is short-dated and carries no interest, would be assessable on the recipient as income. In *Davies v Premier Investment Co Ltd* 27 TC 27, a premium paid by a company on the redemption of six year registered convertible notes issued at par and carrying no interest was held to be interest of money within Case III. The fact that no commercial rate of interest was charged was the important difference as compared with *Lomax v Peter Dixon* so that, on a proper construction of the matter, the premium received by the company was in the nature of interest to compensate the company for being deprived of the use of its money over the six-year period.

The discount at which exchequer bills are issued is of a type envisaged by the charge under Case III as this discount constitutes income. TCA 1997, s 45(1) exempts discounts relating to exchequer bills and other non-interest bearing securities issued by the Minister for Finance under Central Fund (Permanent Provisions) Act 1965 s 4. The exemption does not apply if the discount is received in the course of a trade, eg banking. The exemption applies to the excess of the amount received on the redemption of a unit of the non-interest bearing security over the amount paid for the unit on its issue. No exemption is available in respect of a profit realised by selling the exchequer bill before its maturity or as a result of purchasing the bill after its issue even if held until its maturity.

A similar exemption was provided by TCA 1997, s 48 in respect of the premium on the redemption of securities issued by the Minister for Finance under the Central Fund (Permanent Provisions) Act 1965. It also exempted from tax the premium on the redemption of any stock, debenture or other security, which is issued with the approval of the Minister for Finance under any Act of the Oireachtas and in respect of which the payment of interest and the repayment of capital is guaranteed by the Minister for Finance. The exemptions in TCA 1997, s 45(1) and TCA 1997, s 48 are disapplied by TCA 1997, s 45(2) insofar as they relate to the discounts on the issue of either Exchequer Bills issued by the Minister for Finance or Agricultural Commodities Intervention Bills issued by the Minister for Agriculture and Food. Accordingly, any discount on the issue of bills under either of these headings is now taxable as income under Case III.

TCA 1997, s 45(2) does not affect the discount on the issue of government securities where the payment of the interest and repayment of capital is guaranteed by the Minister for Finance. The discount (if any) on the issue of any such securities remains exempt from tax, except in the case where it has to be included as a trading receipt in taxing the profits of a trade (eg, in the case of bank or dealer in securities).

Interest unpaid and accrued, and added to or capitalised as loan principal for accounting or banking purposes, remains interest (*IRC v Oswald* 26 TC 435). The interest was regarded as paid only when actually discharged. The *Oswald* case was also concerned with the question of payments from a mixed capital and interest fund. The amount of the fund available for payment was less than the full amount of principal and interest due and it was held that only the amount in excess of the principal amount was interest. This followed the centuries old Clayton's case in which it was held that the parties are free to decide how much of any mixed fund payment consists of interest; in the absence of any clear agreement, it was appropriate next to look at how the payment was dealt with in the recipient's books, then to ascertain how it was dealt with by the payer and, finally, to apply the last in first out (LIFO) principle.

Strips of securities

TCA 1997, s 55 deals with the taxation aspects of the stripping of Irish gilts and other securities, whether Irish or foreign. Under the legislation, the tax costs of the separate elements of a stripped security are identified. Essentially, the original cost of the total security is split between its different parts on the basis of the relative market values at the date of the strip. The strip elements can be reassembled for tax purposes as a security comprised of separate and independent parts on the same valuation basis. This matter is dealt with in more detail in **3.207.3** below.

Interest on government securities

Tax is charged under heading (c) of Case III on interest payable out of the public revenue on securities other than interest charged under Schedule C. Tax is charged under heading (d) on any securities issued or deemed by TCA 1997, s 36 to be issued under the authority of the Minister for Finance, where such interest is paid without deduction of tax, in effect, all interest on Irish government national loans and on loan stocks and similar securities issued by such bodies as Dublin Airport Authority, the Electricity Supply Board, Bord na Móna, Radio Telefís Éireann, Bord Gáis Éireann and Córas Iompair Éireann.

Interest on the government and other securities taxable under these headings is normally payable half yearly on dates which vary with the security concerned. While the underlying price of each security may fluctuate with interest rates and other market conditions, the normal tendency is for the price to stabilise as interest accrues over each half yearly period up to the "ex div" date. Each security normally goes "ex div" about five weeks before the date on which the half yearly interest is payable. Accordingly, if the security is sold after this date, it is the vendor and not the purchaser who is entitled to the next interest payment. Conversely, if the security is sold "cum div", no part of the accrued interest is payable to the vendor although the price received on sale is inflated to reflect the accrued interest element.

Prior to 25 January 1984, the vendor of a security sold "cum div" was not taxable on the interest element accrued in his sale price, while the purchaser was assessable under Schedule D Case III on the full amount of the next interest payment even if he had acquired the security at a price including the accrued interest element just before the "ex div" date. These principles were established clearly, in the case of a vendor, in an early case, *Wigmore v Thomas Summerson & Son Ltd* 9 TC 577 and the principle was confirmed, in the case of a purchaser, in a more recent case, *Schaffer v Cattermole* [1979] STC 670.

TCA 1997, s 815 alters the vendor's position in respect of the accrued interest element on a "cum div" sale or transfer by taxing the accrued interest amount, but only where he had held the security for less than two years. For the charge to tax which may arise under Case IV on the vendor (or transferor), see **3.208.7**.

Foreign source income

Tax is charged under heading (e) of Case III on income arising from foreign securities (if not taxed under Schedule C), while heading (f) charges tax on income from foreign possessions. (Some interesting comments on the meaning of "securities" and "possessions" are made by Lord Shaw of Dunfermline in *Williams v Singer* 7 TC 419 – see **2.605**). The distinction between the two words was also referred to in *Lord Manton's Trustees v Steele* 3 TC 549 where Rowlatt J said that it is a question of the difference between someone who had a claim on a debtor and a person who merely had a right to receive profits on property. The two headings tax all forms of income from foreign sources, notwithstanding that such income is of a type which would, if it arose within the State, be taxable under a different Case or Schedule. The only exceptions are Schedule C income and any foreign dividends from which the paying agent (normally a bank in the State) has deducted income tax under Schedule D.

Although foreign source income is assessed under Case III, the main computational rules of the Schedule or Case under which any particular type of income would be chargeable if arising from an Irish source are, for the most part, applied. On the other hand, in applying the Case III basis of assessment rules (see below), all foreign income irrespective of its nature is treated as Case III income (except if received after deduction of Irish income tax by a paying agent etc). (See also **3.102.2** re foreign trades).

Securitisation

In the case of IFSC companies, activities from dealing in certain "securitised" assets are treated as trading activities. Similar activities engaged in by companies other than IFSC companies are treated as annual profits or gains taxable under Case III but those profits or gains are computed in accordance with the provisions applicable to Case I (TCA 1997, s 110(2)(b) – see **7.206.11**).

3.207.3 Strips of securities

Strips of an interest bearing security are created when the right to receive each interest payment and the right to the redemption of capital can be traded separately. A strip market involves the trading of both the right to interest (coupons) and principal in respect of issued bonds as separate securities. For example, in the case of a 20-year interest bearing bond, individual yearly interest coupons, or a range of such coupons, could be "stripped" and traded separately from the principal. By creating separate securities from interest and principal, an issuer can meet the requirements of investors with varying investment time horizons. Thus, a 20-year bond could effectively be split and issued as a five year interest strip to an investor requiring a medium term investment with the remainder to, say, a pension fund for whom a longer term investment is more appropriate. This flexibility considerably enhances the liquidity of Irish gilt and other bond issues.

Stripped securities work on the basis that each stripped element is separate from the original security. In a strip market, investors will want to be able to reassemble the separate elements of a security in accordance with their investment objectives and for this purpose may purchase coupons from other securities with amounts and payment dates which match those for strips already held.

TCA 1997, s 55 provides taxation measures for dealing with the stripping of Irish gilts and other securities, whether Irish or foreign. One such measure identifies the tax cost of the separate elements of a stripped security. Essentially, the original cost of the total security is split between its different parts on the basis of the relative market values at the date of the strip. The strip elements can be reassembled for tax purposes as a security comprised of separate and independent parts on the same valuation basis.

Authority for stripping of Irish gilts

FA 1970 s 54 permits Irish government domestic currency bonds to be stripped. Under FA 1970 s 54(10), the Minister for Finance may nominate any securities issued under subsection (1) (see below) of that section as securities under which each obligation to make a payment, whether of principal or of interest, may be separated and each such separated obligation, referred to as "strips", are deemed to constitute securities for the purposes of the section. Securities so created may be used to constitute securities fungible with the securities from which the strips were derived.

FA 1970, s 54(1) provides that for the purpose of raising money for the Exchequer, the Minister may create and issue securities bearing interest at such rate as he thinks fit or no interest and subject to such conditions as to repayment, redemption or any other matter as he thinks fit.

Creation and acquisition of strips

TCA 1997, s 55(2) deals with the creation by a person of a strip of a unit of a security. At the time of the strip, the unit of the security is deemed to have been sold for an amount equal to its then market value and the person is then deemed to have acquired each strip for a proportion of the "opening value" (see definition below) of the unit, based on the market value of each strip at that time as a proportion of the aggregate market value of each of the strips of the unit.

The profit earned by the investor in respect of each strip is taxable as income. Each strip is deemed to be a non-interest bearing security any profits or gains on the disposal of which is chargeable to tax under Case III of Schedule D (unless charged under Case I, eg for a dealer in securities). Capital gains tax treatment does not apply in respect of the principal element of a stripped security, as would have been the case in the absence of TCA 1997, s 55, and the capital gains tax exemption for gains on disposals of gilts does not apply as respects the principal element of a stripped gilt.

Where a person, other than a financial institution or a securities trader, acquires a strip of an Irish gilt otherwise than in accordance with TCA 1997, s 55(2) (ie otherwise than by way of creating a strip), the strip is treated as costing an amount equal to the lower of the price paid and a proportion of the nominal value of the unit of the security. The proportion of the nominal value of the unit is the amount which bears the same proportion to the nominal value of that unit as the market value of the strip at the time of issue of the security *would have* borne to the aggregate of the market value at that time of each of the strips of the unit if the strip had been created at the time of issue of the security.

Definitions

For the above purposes, the *nominal value* in relation to a unit of a security means:

(a) where the interest on the unit of the security is expressed to be payable by reference to a given value, that value; and

(b) in any other case, the amount which was paid for the unit of the security on its issue.

The *opening value* in relation to a unit of a security from which strips of the unit have been created by a person means:

(a) in the case of a person carrying on a trade consisting wholly or partly of dealing in securities of which the unit is an asset in respect of which any profits or gains are chargeable to tax under Case I of Schedule D, an amount equal to the market value of the unit of the security at the time the strips were created; and

(b) in any other case, an amount equal to the lesser of—

(i) the market value of the unit at the time the strips were created, and

(ii) the nominal value of the unit.

Securities includes:

(a) assets which are not chargeable assets for the purposes of capital gains tax by virtue of TCA 1997, s 607 (government and other securities); and

(b) stocks, bonds and obligations of any government, municipal corporation, company or other body corporate whether creating or evidencing a charge on assets or not.

Strip in relation to a unit of a security means an obligation of the person who issued the security to make a payment, whether of interest or of principal, which has been separated from other obligations of that person to make payments in respect of the unit of the security.

Reassembly of strips into a unit

The reconstitution of a unit of a security from a series of strips is treated as a disposal of the strips and an acquisition of the unit. The strips are treated as deep discount securities the profits or gains on the disposal or redemption of which are assessable as income.

TCA 1997, s 55(4) provides that on the reconstitution by a person of strips of a unit of a security into a unit of the security:

(a) each of the strips is deemed to have been sold at that time by the person for an amount equal to the market value at that time; and

(b) the person is deemed to have acquired at that time the unit of the security for an amount equal to the aggregate of the market value at that time of each of the strips.

Mark to market

Investors in strips of securities, including gilts, are taxable in respect of the annual growth in value of the stripped security. TCA 1997, s 55(5) provides that strips are deemed to have been sold and immediately reacquired at their market value each year. A company which holds a strip on the "relevant day" (the last day of its accounting period) is deemed to have on that day disposed of and immediately reacquired the strip at the market value of the strip on that day. In any such case, the amount to be included in the profits or gains chargeable to tax under Case III of Schedule D for the accounting period concerned is the aggregate of the amounts of any profits or gains arising on the deemed disposals in the period less the aggregate of the amounts of any losses arising on such deemed disposals in the period. Also deducted are any losses arising on deemed disposals in any previous accounting period to the extent not allowed against profits or gains of previous accounting periods.

Non-residents

To enable non-resident investors to continue to invest in gilt issues in a tax-free manner, assets which are strips are included in the meaning of "securities" in TCA 1997, s 48(4)(c) so that where the owner of any such security sells or otherwise disposes of the security or receives on its redemption an amount greater than the amount paid by him for the security on its issue or otherwise, any profit, gain or excess arising is exempt from tax where the owner is not ordinarily resident in the State (see also **3.204.6**). The exemption does not apply in respect of corporation tax chargeable on the income of an Irish branch or agency of a non-resident company.

3.207.4   Computation of income

TCA 1997, s 70(2), (3) provides that the profits or income chargeable under Case III are to be taxed on the full amount arising without any deduction. Schedule D Case III income is by its nature generally receivable as pure income profit so that expenses are not normally incurred in earning it and the absence of any deduction in computing the amount assessable is to be expected. Any expenses incurred in acquiring an investment or other source of Case III income are regarded as capital expenditure so that no deduction may be made. An investment company the income of which typically includes Case III income may deduct its expenses of management from total profits for corporation tax purposes (see **12.703**).

As regards Case III income arising from sources within the State, no capital allowances or other reliefs for capital expenditure are available. Any loss that may be incurred on the disposal of an investment or other source of Case III income is a capital loss which is completely disregarded in taxing income. Relief for any such loss may, however, be available against chargeable capital gains in accordance with capital gains tax rules.

Different considerations arise in connection with certain types of income from foreign sources, ie profits or gains in respect of which there cannot be a profit without taking into account expenses incurred in earning those profits or gains. That position clearly applies to trades and professions exercised wholly abroad so as to be taxable as foreign possessions and rental income derived from foreign based real property. In general, the deductions and allowances made in taxing the foreign income are those that would be made if the type of income in question had arisen from a source within the State.

Trades (or professions) falling within the Case III charge, because exercised wholly abroad, are very rare (see **3.102.2**). Most trades carried on abroad by Irish resident companies are taxable under Case I, typically as a branch of the overall trade. A trade taxable under Case III is most likely to be encountered in the context of an Irish company carrying on a trade as a partner in a foreign partnership. In this connection, TCA 1997, s 77(5) provides that the income from a trade the profits of which are chargeable under Case III is to be computed in accordance with the provisions applicable to Case I.

3.208   Case IV

3.208.1   Income charged

Tax under Case IV of Schedule D is charged under TCA 1997, s 18(2) on any annual profits or gains not falling under any other Case of Schedule D and not charged by any other Schedule. In addition, Schedule D Case IV applies to charge to tax other types of gains which are not income but which have been brought within the charge to tax as deemed income. The "income" charged to tax under Case IV may, therefore, be considered under two main headings, namely (a) income not otherwise charged to tax, and (b) gains charged by special provisions.

Case IV has for many years been viewed as the "sweeper" Case intended to bring within the charge to tax as income all annual profits or gains not specifically brought within any of the other Cases or Schedules. It does not necessarily follow that every profit or gain not otherwise chargeable as income will be brought within Case IV. In *Leeming v Jones* 15 TC 333, Lord Dunedin in the House of Lords stated that Case VI (UK equivalent of Case IV) "necessarily refers to the words of Schedule D", that is, it must be a Case concerned with annual profits and gains, and he referred to the limitations of the words "profits and gains" as pointed out by Lord Blackburn many years previously in *Attorney General v Black* 1 TC 52 where he said that profits and gains in Case VI must mean profits and gains "ejusdem generis" with the profits and gains specified in the preceding five Cases.

So that a profit or gain is taxable under the main Case IV charging rule of TCA 1997, s 18(2), ie as distinct from any of the special provisions which bring gains within the charge as deemed income, it must be capable of being regarded as "annual" and it must be of the nature of income and not of capital. It has become accepted that while the word "annual" may mean something that recurs every year, that is only one of its meanings and its meaning is not limited to that meaning. In *Martin v Lowry* 11 TC 297, "annual" was said to mean "in the current year, occurring in the year of assessment". In *Ryall v Hoare* 8 TC 521 Rowlatt J, in a well-known passage in page 526 said the following:

> It is inveterate now that the letting of a furnished house for a few weeks in one year will attract income tax, under this Case, upon the profit made by the letting.... Now, recognising that position, it seems to me that "annual" here can only mean "in any year", and that the phrase "annual profits or gains" means profits or gains in any year as the succession of the years comes round.

While the income from the letting of a furnished house is now taxable under Schedule D Case V, this reference to a short letting of a furnished house illustrates the point that it is possible for a casual profit or gain realised over a very short period to be "annual" so as to be taxable under Case IV. The essential test is whether the gain is of an income as distinct from a capital nature. In other words, to be taxable under Case IV, the gain in question must be of a type analogous to, or "ejusdem generis" with, the types of profits or gains mentioned in the other Cases of Schedule D. The circumstances in which a profit or gain may be taxed under Schedule D Case IV can be further explained by reviewing a few of the tax cases on the subject.

In *Leeming v Jones* 15 TC 333, the taxpayer was one of a syndicate of four who secured an option to purchase a rubber estate; the object of the syndicate was the promotion of a company to which the estate should be sold at a profit. The General Commissioners had found as a fact that there was no trade or adventure in the nature of a trade. Based on that finding, the House of Lords held that the profit was not of an income nature, but was a profit arising from an accretion in value of the asset and the realisation of that enhanced value. The gain was not, therefore, taxable under Schedule D Case VI (Case IV in Ireland).

Leeming v Jones involved an isolated transaction where property was acquired and resold within two months. The question as to whether a profit from an isolated transaction can be taxed under Case I as arising from an adventure in the nature of a trade has been discussed in **3.103.4**. It appears to be firmly established in case law that a profit on an isolated transaction consisting of the purchase and resale of any property, when not undertaken in the course of a trade, can only be taxed under Schedule D Case I if the transaction is an adventure in the nature of a trade. If, as was held as a fact by the Commissioners in *Leeming v Jones* there is no trade or adventure in the nature of a trade, the profit cannot be assessed under Schedule D Case IV. Lawrence LJ, whose reasoning was later approved by Lord Dunedin in the House of Lords, could not see how an isolated transaction consisting of the purchase and resale of property, if it was not an adventure in the nature of a trade, could be a transaction "ejusdem generis" with such an adventure.

It is necessary to distinguish what may be an isolated transaction involving the rendering of services from one involving the purchase and resale of an item of property. While the latter cannot be taxed unless falling within Case I, there have been a number of decisions where a profit from a one-off service transaction has been held taxable under Case VI (Case IV in Ireland). In *Ryall v Hoare* (see above), a director of a company was held to be taxable under Case VI on a commission received for personally guaranteeing the company overdraft, although this was a once only transaction. Similarly, an isolated commission received by a company director from a syndicate for underwriting shares in a new company being floated was held to be taxable under Case VI (*Lyons v Cowcher* 10 TC 438). The commission in each case was considered to be within the concept of annual profits or gains or "something which is in the nature of interest or fruit, as opposed to principal or tree". Rowlatt J (again in *Ryall v Hoare)* used those words and distinguished such income from:

> the well known case of a casual profit made upon an isolated buying and selling of some article; that is a capital accretion, and unless it is merged with other similar transactions in the carrying on of a trade, and the trade is taxed, no tax is exigible in respect of a transaction of that kind.

In *Cooper v Stubbs* 10 TC 29, the point at issue concerned two individuals who had undertaken on their own account over a period of years a series of speculations by way of buying and selling cotton futures, not with a view to receiving or delivering cotton, but with a view to gaining a profit on the balance. The Special Commissioners found as a fact that there was no trade carried on. They further held that the dealings were gambling transactions and that the profits were not annual profits assessable under Case VI. It was held by the Court of Appeal that the finding of the Commissioners that the transactions in question did not constitute the carrying on of a trade was entirely one of fact with which the court could not interfere, but that the profits arising from the transactions were annual profits or gains taxable under Case VI. (Readers of this case might well wonder why the activity under consideration did not amount to a trade. Rowlatt J, in the High Court, held that the Commissioners had reached the wrong conclusion on this point but the judges in the Court of Appeal felt unable to overturn the Commissioners' finding of fact.)

In his judgment in the Court of Appeal, Atkin LJ considered the transactions entered into by Mr Stubbs to be real transactions and not mere bets, although they may have been of a speculative nature. The contracts entered into gave rise to real contractual rights which could be enforced by either party to the contracts. Relating this to the main charging words of Schedule D, which refers to annual profits or gains arising from any kind of property whatsoever, these contractual rights were property and the gains derived from them were, in the circumstances of the case, annual profits or gains taxable under Case VI.

The question as to whether sums paid by publishers of newspapers for news or stories of public interest to persons not otherwise taxable as writers were taxable under Case VI arose in a number of cases. In *Trustees of Earl Haig v CIR* 22 TC 725, the trustees of the late Earl Haig were paid certain sums by a publisher for authorising his war diaries to be used for a biography of the Field Marshal. The biography was written by Mr Duff Cooper who had full use of the material in the diaries (subject to certain restrictions). The diaries remained the property of the trustees. The Special Commissioners had found as a fact that the trustees, in turning the diaries to account, had not carried on any trade or adventure. It was held that the sums received by the trustees were capital payments in return for a partial realisation of an asset and were not assessable under Case VI.

By contrast, in *Hobbs v Hussey* 24 TC 153, sums paid by *The People* for the serial rights of a once infamous individual, William C Hobbs, for his life story, were held to be taxable under Case VI. The articles were compiled from the appellant's dictation, but he was not otherwise involved in any literary newspaper work. He contended that the transaction was an isolated sale of property, namely, the copyright in the series of articles, and that the payments received were capital in his hands. It was held that the true nature of the transaction was the performance of services by the appellant, the sale of the copyright in the articles being subsidiary to those services, and that the payments received were annual profits or gains. The case of *Earl Haig's Trustees* was distinguished.

Similarly, in *Housden v Marshall* 38 TC 233, an amount paid to a well known jockey for his reminiscences of his life and experiences on the turf was held to be taxable under Case VI. The fact that the jockey, Bryan Marshall, performed some services in the matter by making his reminiscences available and by providing photographs and other material was held to be sufficient to make the matter one of a reward for services. Important features of the *Earl Haig's Trustees* case, where the war diaries were very valuable and the subject of copyright, were not present in Mr Marshall's case.

Considerations similar to those described above arose in *Alloway v Phillips* [1980] STC 490, but it was necessary to consider the additional question as to whether there were profits or gains arising from property in the UK, as the recipient was a non-resident. The taxpayer was the wife of a Mr Wilson who was convicted and sentenced to imprisonment in the "great train robbery" case. He escaped from prison to Canada where the taxpayer joined him. While she was in Canada a reporter from an English newspaper visited her there to get information for writing articles about her for publication in the newspaper. Based on a contract which provided, inter alia, for the newspaper company to have the sole and exclusive world rights to publish her story, and on covenants by the taxpayer restricting her from providing material relating to the matter to other persons, sums were paid by the newspaper to an intermediary in London for the taxpayer.

It was accepted that the sums were earned in a tax year when the taxpayer was not resident in the UK. Consequently, for tax to be charged on her under Case VI, there had to be income from property in the UK. It was argued that the taxpayer had derived her profits from the services that she had rendered in Canada and that the contract was only machinery for collecting the reward for her services. This argument was rejected and it was held that she was taxable on the sums paid by the newspaper company. In his judgment in the Court of Appeal, Lord Denning MR said:

> This case comes under Case VI of Schedule D. It seems to be clear that this wife had property in the United Kingdom. She had a chose in action here. She had a right to receive from the News of the World the sum of £39,000. That was situate in England. Dicey and Morris on the Conflict of Laws says: 'Choses in action generally are situate in the country where they are properly recoverable or can be enforced'. It seems to me that she had her chose of action in this country worth an actual gain of £39,000.

Among other types of income which do not fall under any Case or Schedule and which are, therefore, assessable under Case IV are income from leasing machinery or plant (other than as a trade - see **5.3**), copyright royalties (when not received as trading receipts of a profession) and income from patents (see **13.602**).

3.208.2 Other gains chargeable under Case IV

Apart from annual profits or gains taxable under Case IV because they do not fall under any other Case or Schedule, there are a number of gains or transactions which are regarded by special provisions in the Tax Acts as giving rise to income chargeable to income tax or corporation tax under Case IV. The provisions of relevance to companies are listed below.

Special provisions charging tax under Case IV	*Reference*
General:	
Partnership profits not allocated to any partner	**13.701.4**
Capital sums for sale of patent rights	**13.605-6**
Capital sums for sale of scheduled mineral assets	**13.410**
Rent, royalties etc received from mining, quarrying etc concerns	**13.413**
Premiums for grant or surrender of lease, payments in lieu of rent or for variation or waiver of terms of lease, where received other than by lessor	**3.208.6**
Refunds of employees' and non-trading employers' contributions from approved pension schemes	**3.202.5**
Charge to tax on holders of units in collective investment undertakings	**12.805.3**
Charge to tax on holders of units in investment undertakings	**12.806.9**
Charge to tax on interest subject to DIRT (TCA 1997, s 261(c)(i))	**3.208.3**

Anti-avoidance:

Special provisions charging tax under Case IV	*Reference*
Gains on certificates of deposit and assignable deposits	**3.208.5**
Shares issued in lieu of dividends	**3.208.5**
Sale or transfer of right to untaxed interest without sale or transfer of securities	**3.208.5**
Government securities etc sold "cum div"	**3.208.7**
Transactions associated with loans or credit	**3.208.8**
Offshore income gains	**3.210.3**
Assignment of lease granted at undervalue	**3.208.6**
Charge on sale of land with right to reconveyance	**3.208.6**
Dividends received in respect of certain preference shares	**3.205**
Gains of capital nature from land or property deriving value from land	**13.309.4**

Certain balancing charges:	
Machinery or plant leased otherwise than in course of trade of leasing	**5.301.1**
Industrial buildings sold while temporarily out of use after cessation of trade	**5.409.1**
Patent rights where not taxable under Schedule D Case I	**13.602**
Interest in industrial building subject to a lease immediately before disposal (dock undertakings)	**5.505.2**

Recovery of excess reliefs etc:	
Excess double taxation relief	**3.208.10**
Tax under deducted on annual payments etc due to change in tax rate	**3.208.10**
Gains from illegal or unknown sources	**3.208.9**
Excess group relief	**8.315.1**

3.208.3 Deposit interest retention tax

TCA 1997 Part 8 Ch 4 (ss 256-267) requires banks, building societies and other "relevant deposit takers" to deduct, and pay over to the Collector-General, the appropriate tax when paying or crediting interest on "relevant deposits". The appropriate tax is a sum representing income tax to be deducted at the standard rate in force at the time the interest is paid or credited or, in the case of interest on a deposit in a "special savings account", at the rate of 15%.

TCA 1997, s 261 contains the rules for the taxation of the recipient of deposit interest subject to deduction of retention tax (referred to as "relevant interest"). A company chargeable to corporation tax, which has made the required declaration to the relevant deposit taker, will not suffer retention tax on interest paid or credited on any deposit made on or after the operative date 1 January 1993. However, for any deposit made before that date, it will continue to receive the interest net of the retention tax and, if it fails to make the required declaration, the same will apply to interest on deposits on or after the operative date 1 January 1993. In any case, all the company's deposit interest remains income chargeable to corporation tax, but any retention tax suffered is set off against the company's liability to corporation tax and, if the retention tax exceeds the corporation tax, the excess retention tax is repayable to the company (TCA 1997, s 261(b) and TCA 1997, s 24(2)).

Any interest received from a building society in respect of shares in that society is treated as interest income in the hands of any recipient and not as a distribution of the society or as franked investment income in the hands of any company resident in the State (TCA 1997, s 261(a)). This is to ensure that the deposit interest retention tax rules apply and that the income is taxable under Schedule D Case IV and not under Schedule F.

3.208.4 Leasing of machinery or plant

The profits or gains from the leasing of machinery or plant are taxable under Case IV if the leasing activity is not carried out in the course of a trade of leasing. The question as to whether or not a person exercises a trade of leasing has to be determined on the facts in each particular case. Clearly, if there is a full leasing business, it is taxable under Case I. Since leasing is effectively another form of providing finance, a bank or other financial concern which leases machinery or plant in conjunction with its other business is usually taxable under Case I, and not Case IV, on its leasing profits. However, a manufacturing or other type of business which happens to lease machinery which it does not at the time require for its own trade is not normally regarded as trading in leasing and would probably be taxable under Case IV, rather than under Case I, on its leasing profits. On the other hand, a manufacturing company which sells and leases the goods it produces is more likely to be taxable under Case I (*Gloucester Railway Carriage & Wagon Co Ltd v IRC* 12 TC 720).

The method of computing taxable profits of a company assessable under Case IV in respect of the leasing of machinery or plant (or indeed any other goods) is similar to what it would be if the company were carrying on a trade of leasing assessable under Case I. The Case IV leasing profit is normally the excess of the lease rents receivable in the relevant accounting period over any expenses of a revenue nature incurred in that period wholly and exclusively in earning the leasing income. In practice, it may well be that most of the expenses of repairs, servicing etc of the leased machinery will be made the responsibility of the lessee so that the lessor company may not have many expenses to deduct. However, if it does incur expenses on repairs or other items, it would be entitled to deduct those expenses in computing the Case IV leasing profit.

Clearly, no expenditure of a capital nature may be deducted in the computation and the Case IV leasing profit, or loss, is arrived at before deducting capital allowances, if any, in respect of capital expenditure incurred in acquiring, constructing or producing the leased machinery. The capital allowances available to a company leasing machinery or plant (provided that the burden of wear and tear falls on it) and the manner in which they are given, have been discussed in **5.301**. As explained there, capital allowances are made to a lessor of machinery or plant taxable under Case IV by way of discharge or repayment of tax and the capital allowances are given primarily against the income or profits derived from the leasing activity. Any balancing charges resulting from the sale of the leased machinery or from any other event giving rise to a balancing charge are taxable as additional income under Case IV.

Should the deductible expenses incurred for the purpose of the Case IV leasing activity exceed the lease rents in any accounting period, because, say, a lessor company incurs substantial repair costs in a period for which it cannot fully lease the machinery or plant, the resulting loss from the leasing activity may be set off against any other profits or gains from any Case IV activities in the same period. The leasing loss may not, however, be set off against any other income from non-Case IV sources, but is carried forward for set off against any Case IV income of the next period, and so on.

3.208.5 Anti-avoidance

Many tax-avoidance schemes seek to convert what would otherwise be income into a gain of a capital nature. The taxation of these gains is effected by bringing them within the charge to tax under Case IV. Measures dealing with some of these such schemes are outlined below.

1. Certificates of Deposit: Unlike an ordinary bank deposit held by a company in respect of which interest accrues to it on a day by day basis, thus enabling it to receive the interest by withdrawing the deposit, interest on certificates of deposit or assignable deposits is normally only payable on reaching the maturity date. By selling a certificate or assignable deposit before the maturity date for a capital sum reflecting the accrued interest, the company could derive a capital profit which was not chargeable to tax.

TCA 1997, s 814 provides that any gain arising from the disposal of a certificate of deposit or an assignable deposit is deemed to be an annual profit or gain chargeable under Case IV unless it is otherwise taxable as income on the person making that disposal. An example of such a gain being taxable otherwise is a gain from a certificate of deposit or assignable deposit realised by a bank or other company dealing in deposits which is taxable on the gains under Case I.

For the purposes of TCA 1997, s 814, a *certificate of deposit* is defined as "a document relating to money, in any currency, which has been deposited with the issuer or some other person, being a document which recognises an obligation to pay a stated amount to bearer or to order, with or without interest, and being a document by the delivery of which, with or without endorsement, the right to receive that stated amount, with or without interest, is transferable. An *assignable deposit* is defined as "a deposit of money, in any currency, which has been deposited with any person whether it is to be repaid with or without interest and which at the direction of the depositor, may be assigned with or without interest to another person.

2. Shares Issued in Lieu of Cash Dividends: Where a person receives shares of an Irish resident unquoted company as a result of the exercise of an option to acquire them in lieu of a dividend or other distribution of profits by the company, TCA 1997, s 816 taxes the shares received as income under Case IV. The income charged is an amount equal to the sum which the person, say a company, would have received if it had taken the distribution in cash. The Case IV income is the actual amount of the cash that would have been payable.

TCA 1997, s 816(1) defines *share* as including stock and any other interest in the company concerned. Accordingly, the charge to tax applies whether the option is to take shares, stock or any other interest (eg, an unsecured loan stock) in the company. TCA 1997, s 816 does not, however, apply to tax a bonus or other issue of shares if the recipient company has no option to take a cash distribution instead. A person is regarded as having an option to receive either cash or shares not only when he is required to choose one or the other, but also where he is offered the one subject to a right, however expressed, to choose the other instead. A person's abandonment of, or failure to exercise, any right to take shares in lieu of a dividend (or vice versa) is treated as if it were the exercise of an option.

TCA 1997, s 816 applies in similar circumstances to tax a person resident in the State if he receives shares, stock or any other interest in a non-resident company in lieu of a cash dividend. In this event, the assessment is again made on an amount equal to the cash distribution which could have been taken, but it is made under Schedule D Case III and not under Case IV.

As respects shares issued on or after 3 December 1997, TCA 1997, s 816 also applies to quoted companies. Where the company is a non-resident company, the treatment is the same as in the case of an unquoted company. Accordingly, an amount equal to the amount which would have been received by a person by way of cash distribution is deemed to be income received from the company and is treated as income of that person from securities and possessions outside the State and assessable to tax under Case III.

Where the quoted company is resident in the State, the amount in question is treated as a distribution made by the company and as a distribution received by the person to whom the shares were issued (see also **11.1**).

A *quoted company* is defined as a company whose shares, or any class of whose shares:

(a)   are listed in the official list of the Irish Stock Exchange or on any other stock exchange; or

(b)   are quoted on the Developing Companies Market, or the Exploration Securities Market, of the Irish Stock Exchange or on any similar or corresponding market of any other stock exchange.

For capital gains purposes, where TCA 1997, s 816 applies as respects an issue of shares, the cash which the shareholder might have received instead of the shares is treated as consideration given for those shares (see **9.402.3**). Accordingly, it is treated by virtue of TCA 1997, s 584(4) as enhancement expenditure on the original shares held and will be indexed by reference to the multiplier appropriate to the year of assessment in which the expenditure is deemed to be incurred, ie in which the additional shares are issued.

3. Transfer of Right to Receive Interest: A charge to tax arises under TCA 1997, s 812 on the owner of any securities in respect of any particular interest payable on those securities if he sells or transfers the right to receive that particular interest, but does not sell or transfer the securities themselves. For the purposes of TCA 1997, s 812, securities includes stocks and shares of all descriptions, ie it includes government, local authority etc loan stocks, shares in companies and any other stocks and shares, whether issued in the State or anywhere else in the world. For the purposes of TCA 1997, s 812, interest includes dividends, annuities and shares of annuities, as well as interest on any securities, stocks and shares.

Where there is such a sale or transfer of any interest on securities which are not themselves sold or transferred, the interest is deemed for all purposes of the Income Tax Acts to be the income of the owner of the securities (except where the owner is not the beneficial owner of the securities, being, for example, a trustee of a settlement where some other person, say a life tenant, is beneficially entitled to the income arising from the said securities; the interest the right to which has been sold would then be treated as the income of the beneficiary).

The interest the right to which has been sold or transferred by a company is deemed to be the income of the company for the accounting period in which the right to receive the particular interest is sold or transferred. Thus, the income from the securities could be taxable on the company in an accounting period different to that in which the income is actually payable. For example, if on 31 December 2005, a company sold its right to receive the next two half yearly payments of interest on €30,000 10% Exchequer Stock 2010 without selling the security, it would be assessable for the year ended 31 December 2005 on the €3,000 interest due to be paid in the year ending 31 December 2006.

The assessment under TCA 1997, s 812 on the owner of the securities is made under Case IV if the securities are of such a character that the interest payable may be paid without deduction of income tax. However, if the person assessable shows that the proceeds of sale or other realisation of the right to receive the income on the securities has been charged to tax under Schedule C (public revenue dividends) or, if foreign interest or dividends under Schedule D (Part 4 Ch 2 – foreign dividends collected by Irish banks and others ("encashment tax")), he is entitled to credit for any tax which he has borne. Where the income in question is Schedule F income, eg a dividend from a resident company, the assessment on the owner is made under that Schedule as if it were his own income.

3.208.6 Premiums for leases and related payments

A charge to tax under Case V arises where the payment of a premium is required under a lease, or under the terms subject to which the lease is granted, and where the duration of the lease does not exceed fifty years. In addition, a sum payable by a lessee in lieu of any rent or as consideration for the surrender of the lease, or a sum other than rent payable as consideration for the variation or waiver of any of the terms of the lease, is treated as a premium (TCA 1997, s 98 – see **3.209.2**).

1. Premiums and other payments to person other than lessor:

Where a premium or other payment mentioned above is due to a person other than the lessor (being a person connected with the lessor in the case of a payment for the variation or waiver of any of the terms of the lease), the payment is treated as an annual profit or gain of that other person and is chargeable to tax under Case IV (TCA 1997, s 98(5)). The provisions of TCA 1997, s 10 (see **2.3**) are relevant for the purpose of ascertaining whether a person is connected with another person.

The amount taxable under Case IV is the amount which would have been taxable on the lessor under Case V if the payment had been made to that lessor. Accordingly, the taxable amount is the fraction $(51 - n)/50$ (see **3.209.2**) as applied to the premium or other sum arising under TCA 1997, s 98(1), (3) or (4) as appropriate.

2. Assignment of lease granted at undervalue:

TCA 1997, s 99 creates a charge under Case IV on any profit or gain realised on the assignment of a lease, for a period not exceeding fifty years, which was granted at undervalue. A lease is regarded as granted at undervalue if no premium, or a premium of an amount which is less than the arm's length premium for the lease, was received in respect of the grant.

The charge under TCA 1997, s 99 applies to a proportion of the excess of the consideration received for the assignment over the premium, if any, for which the lease was granted, in so far as it is not greater than a proportion of the "amount forgone" (ie the additional premium that would have been required had the lease been granted on the basis of an arm's length transaction). If no premium became payable on the grant of the lease, the amount forgone is taken as the full premium which would have been charged in the case of an arm's length transaction.

The proportion of the excess consideration or, if lower, of the amount forgone, is determined by applying the fraction $(51 - n)/50$ used in arriving at the amount of the taxable premium under TCA 1997, s 98 (see **3.209.2**). The taxable amount arises in the period in which the assignment takes place.

Example 3.208.6.1

On 1 April 2005, Ms McDermott granted a 35 year lease of a property to Horizon Ltd, a company which she controls, for an annual rent of €4,400 and a premium of €56,000. On 1 September 2007, Horizon Ltd sold the lease to Mitchell Ltd, an unconnected company, for €200,000. In connection with its corporation tax return for the year ended 31 December 2007, Horizon Ltd agreed with the inspector of taxes that the terms of the lease are such as would, in an arm's length transaction, have commanded a premium of €170,000 on the original grant.

Ms McDermott is charged under TCA 1997, s 98 on an additional rent of €17,920 (ie, €56,000 x (51 - 35)/50), treated as receivable on 1 April 2005, by reference to the actual premium of €56,000 received. As the lease had been granted at undervalue, the assignor, Horizon Ltd, is charged under Case IV for the year ended 31 December 2007 on an amount of €36,480, computed as follows:

	€
Consideration for assignment of lease	200,000
Less: actual premium paid	56,000
Excess consideration (A)	144,000
Amount forgone:	
Arm's length premium	170,000
Less: actual premium paid	56,000
Amount forgone (B)	114,000
Taxable amount:	
	36,480

$$€114,000 \text{ (lower of A and B)} \times \frac{(51 - 35)}{50} =$$

TCA 1997, s 99 also applies to an assignment of a lease, which has been previously assigned, for a consideration which exceeds the consideration for which it was last assigned. The assignor in that case is charged to tax under Case IV in the way indicated below, but the taxable amount may be reduced, by virtue of TCA 1997, s 103(3). The amount chargeable in respect of the second assignment, before any reduction, is calculated as follows:

(a) the excess consideration received for the current assignment over the cost of acquiring the lease is ascertained (c); –

(b) a revised amount forgone is calculated by deducting from the original amount forgone (ie at the date of grant of the lease) the excess consideration on the first assignment (d);

(c)   the amount chargeable is arrived at by applying the TCA 1997, s 98 formula
      $((51-n)/50)$ to the lower of C and D.

The same procedure is followed where the second assignee sells the lease to a third assignee, and so on. The procedure is repeated for any further assignment until the point where the amount forgone is reduced to nil, when TCA 1997, s 99 has no further effect. The reduction provided for in TCA 1997, s 103(3) is dealt with below (see *4. Successive taxable events*). In the above example, since the excess consideration is greater than the amount forgone, no charge under Case IV would arise on any further assignment since the revised amount forgone (d) would be nil.

A company which sells or assigns a leasehold interest in property in the course of a trade of dealing in or developing land will normally bring the full sale proceeds into its accounts as a trading receipt and will therefore include those proceeds in the computation of trading profits assessable under Case I. Where the company is liable under TCA 1997, s 99 on the assignment of the same leasehold granted at undervalue, the amount assessed under Case IV is deducted from the trading receipt in arriving at the Case I profits figure (TCA 1997, s 99(2)).

3. Sale of land with right to reconveyance or lease:

TCA 1997, s 100(1) imposes a charge to tax under Case IV on a person who sells an estate or interest in land where the terms of the sale entitle the vendor, or a person connected with him, either to a reconveyance of the interest sold at some future time, or to the grant of a lease directly or indirectly out of the interest sold (not including a lease commencing within one month of the sale).

Where a reconveyance is provided for, the Case IV charge arises on the excess of the sale consideration for the interest sold over the price at which it is to be reconveyed. Where the earliest date on which the reconveyance can take place is at least two years after the sale, the chargeable amount is the excess referred to less one-fiftieth thereof for each complete year, other than the first, in the period between the sale and that date.

Where the grant of a lease is provided for, other than where the lease begins to run within one month after the sale, the grant is deemed to be a reconveyance for a sum equal to the amount of the premium (if any) for the lease and the value at the date of sale of the right to receive a conveyance of the reversion immediately after the lease begins to run.

The purpose of the provision is counter attempts to realise a tax free gain by selling an interest in property at a certain price and by reacquiring it later at a lower price, or by obtaining the use of the property again by means of a lease on favourable terms.

In the case of a sale with a right to a reconveyance, if the earliest date on which the reconveyance can take place is at least two years after the sale, the taxable amount is determined in accordance with the following formula:

$$\text{Taxable amount} = E \times \frac{(50-n)}{50}$$

where—

E =   the excess of the sale price over the reconveyance price, and

n =   the number of complete years comprised in the period between the sale and the
      earliest reconveyance date.

Example 3.208.6.2

On 1 June 2007, Wenger Ltd assigns a 35 year leasehold interest in a commercial property for the sum of €180,000 on terms which require the purchaser, Fergus Ltd, on receipt of six months' notice in writing, to reconvey the leasehold to Grahame Ltd, a company connected with Wenger Ltd, for a consideration of €120,000 at any time between four and six years after the assignment.

Assuming Wenger Ltd makes up accounts to 31 December each year, it is liable to corporation tax under Case IV for the year ended 31 December 2007 on an amount of €56,400 computed as follows:

	€
Consideration for assignment	180,000
Reconveyance price	120,000
Excess	60,000

$$\text{Taxable amount} = €60,000 \times \frac{(51-4)}{50} = \quad 56,400$$

Where, under the terms of the sale, there is no fixed reconveyance date and the reconveyance price varies with the date, the lowest possible price under the agreement for sale is used in the calculation of the taxable amount (TCA 1997, s 100(2)(a)). Where there is no fixed reconveyance date so that tax is initially calculated without the formula reduction, tax may subsequently be recalculated by taking the actual reconveyance date as if it were the date fixed by the terms of the sale. In the formula therefore, "n" will be the complete number of years (if more than one) and the reconveyance price is taken as the price payable on the date of sale. On a claim for that purpose within six years from the date of the reconveyance, the tax overpaid is to be repaid (TCA 1997, s 100(2)(b)).

Example 3.208.6.3

The position is as in Example **3.208.6.2** but the assignment provides for a reconveyance price of €108,000 if the reconveyance takes place between four and five years after the date of sale, and for a price €128,000 if it takes place between five and six years after the sale. Fergus Ltd reconveys the property to Grahame Ltd on 18 August 2012, ie over five years from the date of the assignment on 1 June 2007. The relevant Case IV computations for the year ended 31 December 2007 are as follows:

Initial computation

	€
Consideration for assignment	180,000
Lowest reconveyance price	108,000
Excess	72,000
Earliest reconveyance date (1/6/11) – 4 years	

$$\text{Taxable amount} = €72,000 \times \frac{(51-4)}{50} = \quad 67,680$$

Revised computation

	€
Consideration for assignment	180,000
Reconveyance price	128,000
Excess	52,000

Actual reconveyance date (18/8/12): n = 5

$$\text{Taxable amount} = €52,000 \times \frac{(51 - 5)}{50} = \underline{\underline{47,840}}$$

Where the terms of the sale of an interest in land provide for the grant of a lease, directly or indirectly, out of that interest, TCA 1997, s 100(3) provides that the amount taxable under Case IV is to be calculated in accordance with TCA 1997, s 100(1) and (2) but as if the grant were a reconveyance of the interest at a price equal to the aggregate of the premium, if any, for the lease and the value at the sale date of the right to receive a conveyance of the reversion (the interest superior to the lease) immediately after the lease begins to run. This provision does not apply if the lease is granted, and begins to run, within one month after the sale; this allows for a genuine sale and leaseback, without a Case IV tax penalty (but without prejudice to any capital gains tax liability), where the leaseback is completed within one month.

TCA 1997, s 100(4) provides that for the purpose of computing the profits or gains of a trade of dealing in land, any trading receipt falling within the Case IV charge by virtue of TCA 1997, s 100 is to be treated as reduced by the amount assessable under Case IV. Where tax is reduced on a claim under TCA 1997, s 100(2)(b) (see above), the trading receipt is retrospectively reduced by the lower Case IV taxable amount.

Example 3.208.6.4

The position is as in Example **3.208.6.3** except that Wenger Ltd sells the 35 year leasehold interest in the course of a trade of property dealing. The amount to be brought into the Case I computation for the year ended 31 December 2007 in respect of the sale as follows:

	€
Sale proceeds	180,000
Amount initially taxable under Case IV	67,680
	112,320

Assuming Wenger Ltd makes its TCA 1997 100(2)(b) claim within the prescribed six year time limit, the Case I profit figure is increased as follows:

	€
Initial Case IV amount	67,680
Revised Case IV amount	47,840
Increase in Case I profit	19,840

4. Successive taxable events:

Any of the events giving rise to a charge to tax under Case IV, by virtue of TCA 1997 ss 98(5), 99 and 100, may be followed by a later event involving the same premises and giving rise to a Case IV charge under the same provisions. Where the later event occurs in relation to a lease granted out of, or a sale, assignment or other disposition of, the lease, estate or interest by reference to which the prior taxable event arose, TCA 1997, s 103(3) applies to reduce the amount which would otherwise be chargeable under Case IV in respect of the later event. The reduction is the excess, if any, of the amount chargeable on the later event over the appropriate fraction of the amount chargeable in respect of the prior event.

The appropriate fraction is L/P where L is the duration of the relevant period in respect of the later chargeable amount and P is the duration of the relevant period in respect of the prior chargeable amount. For the purposes of TCA 1997, s 99, the relevant period is the part of the duration of the lease remaining at the date of the assignment giving rise to the Case IV charge. For TCA 1997, s 100, it is the period beginning on the date of the sale giving rise to the Case IV charge and ending on the date fixed by the sale agreement as the date for the reconveyance or the grant of the lease or, if that date is not fixed, on the earliest date at which the reconveyance or grant could be made.

Example 3.208.6.5

On 1 July 2006, Hedwig Ltd granted a 21 lease of premises to its associated company Ulrika Ltd for an annual rent of €3,500 and a premium of €42,000. Hedwig Ltd is accordingly taxable under Case V on an additional deemed rent as follows:

$$€42,000 \times \frac{51-21}{50} = €25,200$$

On 1 April 2007, Ulrika Ltd assigns the 21 year lease to Roland Ltd for a consideration of €130,000. The company later agrees with the inspector of taxes that the lease would have commanded a premium of €105,000 had it been granted on arm's length terms on 1 July 2006. As the lease was therefore granted at an undervalue, Ulrika Ltd is taxable under Case IV on the assignment by virtue of TCA 1999 s 99. For its accounting year ended 30 December 2007, the amount is calculated as follows:

	€
Consideration for assignment	130,000
Less: premium paid	42,000
Excess consideration	88,000
Amount forgone – arm's length premium	105,000
Less: premium paid	42,000
Amount forgone	63,000
Taxable amount (before TCA 1997, s 103(3)) €63,000 x (51 – 21)/50	37,800

The TCA 1997, s 103(3) reduction is calculated as follows:

	€
Relevant period (L) – 1/4/07 to 30/6/27 (20.25 years)	
Relevant period (P) – 1/7/06 to 30/6/27 (21 years)	
Taxable amount:	
Later chargeable amount	37,800
Less: fraction of prior chargeable amount €25,200 x 20.25/21	24,300
Case IV amount	13,500

3.208.7 Bond washing

The term "bond washing" refers to the realisation of gains tax free by acquiring government securities, usually shortly after the last "ex div" date, and selling them "cum div" shortly before the next "ex div" date. This device was used particularly in buying and selling short dated securities where there were unlikely to be significant movements in the underlying capital price so that a gain approximating to the accrued interest element in the sale price almost always arose. Since such capital gains on the sale of all Irish government securities are exempted from capital gains tax, the gain realised was also tax free.

TCA 1997, s 815, which has effect for all sales or transfers of securities made after 25 January 1984, counters this form of anti-avoidance. "*Securities*" for this purpose is defined in TCA 1997, s 815(1) as excluding shares (within the meaning of the Companies Act 1963) of a company (also within the meaning of the Companies Act 1963) or similar body, but as including:

(a) securities issued under the authority of the Minister for Finance;

(b) stocks issued by any local authority or harbour authority mentioned in the First Schedule to the Harbour Act 1946;

(c) land bonds issued under the Land Purchase Acts;

(d) debentures, debenture stock, certificates of charge or other forms of security issued by the Electricity Supply Board, Bord Gáis Éireann, Radio Telefís Éireann, Córas Iompair Éireann, Bord na Móna or Dublin Airport Authority;

(e) securities issued by the Housing Finance Agency under section 10 of the Housing Finance Agency Act 1981;

(f) securities issued by a body designated under section 4(1) of the Securitisation (Proceeds of Certain Mortgages) Act 1995;

(g) securities issued in the State, with the approval of the Minister for Finance, by the European Community, the European Coal and Steel Community, the International Bank for Reconstruction and Development, the European Atomic Energy Community or the European Investment Bank;

(h) securities issued by An Post and guaranteed by the Minister for Finance;

(i) futures contracts, being unconditional contracts for the acquisition or disposal of any of the instruments referred to above and which require delivery of the instrument in respect of which the contracts are made;

(j) stocks, bonds and obligations of any government, municipal corporation, company or other body corporate whether or not creating or evidencing a charge on assets.

A company which is the owner of a security and which sells or transfers that security so that interest becomes payable to another person in respect of it is liable, by virtue of TCA 1997, s 815(2), to tax under Case IV. The charge does not apply to a company in the following situations:

(a) where the security has been held by the same company for a continuous period of at least two years immediately before the later of the date of the contract for the sale or transfer and the date of the payment of the consideration for the sale;

(b) if the company carries on a trade consisting wholly or partly of dealing in securities chargeable to corporation tax under Case I; or

(c) if the security is one the interest on which is treated as a distribution for the purposes of the Corporation Tax Acts (see **11.106**) (TCA 1997, s 815(3)).

A company which has sold or transferred any security (for the purposes of TCA 1997, s 815) is treated by TCA 1997, s 815(2) as if it had received an amount of interest accruing on a day to day basis over the period from the date it acquired the security to the date of the contract for the sale or transfer or, if a longer period results, to the date of the payment of the consideration for the sale. The interest for this period is the "accrued interest". The rate of interest used in computing this accrued interest is the rate of interest actually payable on the security in question.

The company is charged to corporation tax under Case IV on the excess of the "accrued interest" over the interest, if any, actually received on the security during its period of ownership. The interest actually received is also taxable on the company under the ordinary rules. For example, if the interest in question is interest on a government security which is not taxed at source, the actual interest is taxed under Case III.

If the period of ownership over which accrued interest is to be taken into account falls within two or three accounting periods, Case IV assessments are made for each period straddled by the period of ownership.

Example 3.208.7.1

On 15 April 2007, Stockwell Ltd purchased €25,000 (nominal) of a government security carrying a 12% interest coupon, with interest payable half yearly on 15 January and 15 July. On 15 July 2007, the company received its half yearly interest of €1,500 but entered into a contract to sell the entire holding on 1 December 2007 just before the stock went "ex div". The consideration for the sale is paid on 15 December 2007.

Stockwell Ltd is taxable for the year ended 31 December 2007 under Case III in respect of the €1,500 interest received on 15 July 20077.

As the result of its sale of the security is that the interest due on 15 January 2008 is receivable by some other person, the purchaser, TCA 1997, s 815(2) applies so that the company is assessable under Case IV for the year ended 31 December 2007 on the following amount:

Period of ownership (or accrual):

Date security acquired by Stockwell Ltd – 15 April 2007

Date of contract for sale – 1 December 2007

Date of payment for sale – 15 December 2007

	€
Interest accrued from 15 April 2007 to 15 December 2007	
€25,000 x 12% pa x 245/365	2,014
Less: amount of interest taxed Case III (received 15 July 2007)	1,500
Taxable Case IV	514

Example 3.208.7.2

The position is as in Example **3.208.7.1** except that Stockwell Ltd did not purchase the government stock until, say, 9 June 2007 by which time it had gone "ex div". It will not therefore receive any interest on the holding prior to the "cum div" sale on 1 December 2007. The position will then be as follows:

	€
Interest accrued from 9 June 2007 to 15 December 2007:	
€25,000 x 12% pa x 190/365	1,562
Less: amount of interest taxed Case III	Nil
Taxable Case IV	1,562

Where the owner of a security causes or authorises that security to be sold or transferred, TCA 1997, s 815(2)(a) also charges tax under Case IV. TCA 1997, s 815(2)(c) is an anti-avoidance rule which deals with the case in which, under the terms of a sale or transfer or any associated agreement, arrangement, understanding, promise or undertaking, the owner of the security agrees to buy back or reacquire the security. It also covers the case where the owner acquires an option, which is subsequently exercised, to buy back the security. In any such case, the charge on the said owner is based on the interest deemed to accrue up to the next interest date after the date of the sale or transfer.

Securities acquired at different times

A company may sell or transfer part only of a holding of a security which it has acquired by means of two or more separate acquisitions at different times. Unless the sale or transfer occurs two years or more after the date of the later or latest acquisition, the part sold must be matched with the appropriate acquisition. This is necessary to determine whether any part of the amount sold is derived from an acquisition made two years or more before the date of the sale or transfer (so that no charge arises in respect of that part included in the sale or transfer). It is also necessary to determine the beginning of the period of ownership over which interest is deemed to accrue for the purposes of the computation of the amount to be charged in respect of the part sold or transferred.

Undertakings for collective investments in transferable securities

Undertakings for collective investments in transferable securities (UCITSs) were not, prior to FA 1993, liable either to income tax or capital gains tax (apart from withholding tax on interest paid or retained by the undertaking). However, the investor was fully accountable for the tax arising on the income and for the capital gains tax arising on the disposal.

FA 1993 s 17 (now TCA 1997, s 738) introduced a new regime for the taxation of a UCITS whereby an undertaking which is a company is liable to corporation tax for any accounting period, in respect of income and chargeable gains, at a rate equal to the standard rate of income tax for the year of assessment in which the accounting period falls. Where the accounting period falls into two tax years for which there are different standard rates of tax, the rate of corporation tax is a composite of the two standard income tax rates arrived at by time apportioning the accounting period between the parts falling into the two tax years. As the undertaking is taxed as described above, the investor has no further liability either in respect of the income or the chargeable gains.

TCA 1997, s 815(3)(c) excludes UCITSs and unit trusts from the bond washing provisions of TCA 1997, s 815. This is because the changes introduced in FA 1993 ensure that tax is charged at the standard rate on both income and chargeable gains, thereby rendering the bond washing provisions unnecessary. TCA 1997, s 815(3)(c) relieves the burden of calculating TCA 1997, s 815 interest and also simplifies the accounting for and administration of government gilt gains and interest (see also **12.805**).

3.208.8 Transactions associated with loans

Prior to FA 1974, it was possible to claim unrestricted relief for interest paid to a bank. A claim for any such interest paid could be made under ITA 1967 s 496 (repealed with effect from 6 April 1997). The ability to claim relief in respect of interest paid was significantly curtailed by FA 1974 Chapter III and by provisions in subsequent Finance Acts. As a result, apart from interest incurred wholly and exclusively for the purposes of a trade, and interest incurred on borrowings for the purchase, improvement or repair of premises from which rents taxable under Case V are derived (see **3.209**), a company may only obtain relief for interest as a charge on income where the interest is in respect of borrowings used to invest in or to lend to companies in the circumstances provided for in TCA 1997, s 247 (see **4.403**). So that the provisions which restrict interest relief are not circumvented, TCA 1997, s 813 charges to tax under Case IV certain sums arising from transactions connected with loans or the giving of credit. The provisions of TCA 1997, s 813 apply in relation to transactions effected:

(a) with reference to the lending of money or the giving of credit;
(b) with reference to the varying of the terms on which money is lent or credit is given; or
(c) with a view to enabling or facilitating any arrangements concerning the lending of money or the giving of credit.

The transaction may be one between the lender or creditor and the borrower or debtor, or between either of them and a person connected with the other or between a person connected with one and a person connected with the other.

TCA 1997, s 813(3) treats the payment of any annuity or other annual payment which is not interest, being a payment chargeable to tax under Schedule D, as if it were a payment of annual interest. Without the provision, it would be possible for a lender to advance money in consideration for the borrower's contracting to pay him an annuity or other annual payment not covered by the interest restrictions. Any such annuity or annual payment is treated as interest so that the payer obtains no greater tax relief than would have been available if interest had been paid.

TCA 1997, s 815(4), (5) and (6) deal with three different types of transaction which, in the absence of these provisions, would enable a company to reduce its total taxable income. The effect of these provisions on the three kinds of transaction in question is illustrated in the examples below. In these examples, Crocker Ltd requires the use of €24,000 for a non-trading purpose for a period of 18 months commencing on 1 November 2000. Interest on the borrowings does not qualify for relief for tax purposes. In the absence of TCA 1997, s 813, the company might have proceeded in the ways indicated in the examples which also show how the advantage sought by the company in each case would be denied.

Example 3.208.8.1

Crocker Ltd agrees to sell to a prospective lender, Yreka Ltd, an Irish government loan stock for the sum of €24,000. The loan stock produces annual interest of €2,880 payable on 15 January and 15 July each year. Yreka Ltd also agrees to sell back the government stock to Crocker Ltd for €24,900 on 1 May 2007. Crocker Ltd makes up accounts each year to 31 December.

Without TCA 1997, s 813, Crocker Ltd would have had the use of €24,000 and would have reduced its taxable income attributable to it in the year ended 31 December 2006 by €2,880 and in the year ended 31 December 2007 by €1,440, ie by government stock interest payments due on 15 January 2006 15 July 2006 and 15 January 2007.

However, tax is charged by TCA 1997, s 813(4) under Case IV on Crocker Ltd for each of the two accounting periods on an amount equal to the income arising from the government stock until the stock is repurchased. Accordingly, Crocker Ltd is taxed under Case IV on a sum of €2,880 for the year ended 31 December 2006 and on €1,440 for the year ended 31 December 2007.

The operation of TCA 1997, s 813(4) is without prejudice to the tax position of Yreka Ltd which will therefore be subject to tax on the three interest payments received by it.

TCA 1997, s 813(4) would also apply if, instead of agreeing to sell back the government stock, Yreka Ltd grants an option to Crocker Ltd to buy or otherwise acquire either the government stock or some other asset where Crocker Ltd exercises that option.

The anti-avoidance measure operates whether the buy back or option agreement is part of the original sale agreement or is the subject of a collateral agreement, and whether the original conveyance of the asset is by simple transfer or gift rather than by way of an actual sale.

Example 3.208.8.2

The position is as in Example **3.208.1** except that rather than contracting to sell its government stock, Crocker Ltd agrees, in consideration for an advance of €24,000 from Yreka Ltd, to assign to that company its right to receive the interest on the government stock as long as the advance remains outstanding. Crocker Ltd repays the advance on 1 May 2007 and Yreka Ltd receives the half yearly interest payments of €1,440 made on 15 January 2006, 15 July 2006 and 15 January 2007.

Tax under Case IV is charged on Crocker Ltd for each of the years ended 31 December 2006 and 31 December 2007 on a sum equal to the loan stock interest assigned to Yreka Ltd. As in Example **3.208.8.1**, Crocker Ltd is assessable on €2,880 and €1,440 respectively for the two periods.

The operation of TCA 1997, s 813(5) is without prejudice to the tax position of Yreka Ltd which will therefore be subject to tax on the three interest payments received by it.

TCA 1997, s 813(5) would apply in the same way if the transaction had provided for Crocker Ltd to surrender or otherwise waive or forego income arising from property without selling or transferring that property.

Example 3.208.8.3

The position is as in Example **3.208.2** except that Eureka Ltd, a company connected with Yreka Ltd, has issued loan stock of €24,000 to Crocker Ltd and Crocker Ltd now agrees to waive annual interest of €2,880 on this loan stock in consideration for an advance of €24,000 from Yreka Ltd, interest free. The intention of the waiver is to cancel taxable income of Crocker Ltd and thereby compensate it for its inability to obtain a tax deduction for the interest that would otherwise have been payable on the advance from Yreka Ltd.

Tax under Case IV is charged on Crocker Ltd on an amount of €2,880 for each year for which the arrangement is in operation.

If the income assigned, surrendered, waived or forgone is income payable subject to deduction of income tax, TCA 1997, s 813(7) provides that the "borrower" is taxable by virtue of TCA 1997, s 813(5) on the gross amount of the income. The provision applies where the transaction is effected between the "borrower" and a person connected with the "lender" or vice versa, or is effected between persons connected with the "borrower" and the "lender". In any such case the "borrower", as the person who receives the advance, is the person taxable on the income.

Example 3.208.8.4

The position is as in Example **3.208.8.1** except that Crocker Ltd is about to purchase the film rights to a novel in which Yreka Ltd holds the copyright. On 1 November 2005, Crocker Ltd contracts to purchase the film rights for €24,000. Yreka Ltd agrees to allow the debt to remain outstanding until 1 May 2007 in consideration for Crocker Ltd agreeing that the first €2,880 of copyright royalties each year will continue to be payable to Yreka Ltd until the purchase price is paid. If the total royalties receivable fall short of €2,880 for any year, Yreka Ltd is entitled to recoup the arrears due to it out of future royalties.

By virtue of TCA 1997, s 813(6), Crocker Ltd is treated for the purposes of TCA 1997, s 813(5) as if it had surrendered a right to income of an amount equal to the royalties foregone under the agreement to defer the payment of the purchase price of €24,000. The company is therefore taxed under Case IV in each relevant accounting period on a sum equal to the royalties forgone in that period. Again, TCA 1997, s 813(7) provides that the amount taxable is the gross royalties forgone.

Example 3.208.8.5

The position is as in Example **3.208.8.4** but Crocker Ltd does not in fact pay the outstanding purchase price of €24,000 until 1 November 2007. No royalties arose for the period 1 November 2005 to 31 December 2005, royalties receivable for the year ended 31 December 2007 amounted to €2,460 and in the period 1 January 2007 to 1 November 2007 amounted to €3,300.

The Case IV assessments on Crocker Ltd arising out of TCA 1997, s 813(6) for the relevant accounting periods are as follows:

	€
Y/e 31/12/05:	
Royalties forgone 1/11/05 to 31/12/05	Nil
Y/e 31/12/06:	
Royalties forgone	2,460
Y/e 31/12/07:	
Royalties forgone in period 1/1/07 to 1/11/07	
€2,880 x 304/365	2,399
Deficit for y/e 31/12/06 (€2,880 – €2,460)	420
Deficit for y/e 31/12/05 €2,880 x 61/365*	481
Assessable	3,300

*   arrears that would have been recouped in last period if no credit agreement.

In applying the provisions of TCA 1997, s 813, TCA 1997, s 10 applies for the purpose of determining whether a person is connected with another person (see **2.3**).

3.208.9   Gains from illegal or unknown sources

Prior to FA 1983, the profits or gains from a trade or business that was wholly illegal could not be taxed. TCA 1997, s 58 (formerly FA 1983 s 19) enables an inspector of taxes to assess under Case IV any profits or gains notwithstanding that at the time the assessment is made:

(a)   the source from which the profits or gains arose was not known to the inspector;

(b)   the profits or gains were not known to the inspector to have arisen wholly or partly from a lawful source of activity; or

(c)   the profits or gains arose, and were known to the inspector to have arisen, from an unlawful source or activity.

Any profits or gains charged under this section are to be described in the assessment as "miscellaneous income". An assessment so made cannot be discharged by the Appeal Commissioners or by any court by reason only of the fact that the income should have been described in some other way.

3.208.10 Recovery of excess reliefs

Certain excess tax reliefs may be recovered by means of assessments under Case IV. A Case IV assessment may also be made to recover tax underdeducted on annual payments due to a change in the rate of income tax. Provisions relevant to companies are as follows:

1. Excess double taxation relief: The principles applying for giving relief for foreign tax by way of credit against Irish tax and for computing the amount of the foreign income that is brought into the final corporation tax computation are discussed in **14.2**. In the event of excess relief being given, because of failure to tax the full grossed up amount of the foreign income (see **14.202**) or because of an incorrect calculation of the credit for foreign tax, any necessary additional assessment to tax may be made under Case IV to rectify the position (TCA 1997 Sch 24 paragraph 11).

2. Increase in rate of tax: The standard rate of income tax is altered from time to time so that the amount of income tax which is required to be deducted at source from certain interest, dividends or other annual payments will change. In the event that tax has not been deducted at an increased rate (for example, because tax has been withheld in a tax year before the legislation providing for an increase in the standard rate has been passed), an assessment may be made under Case IV on the person entitled to the payment to charge the tax underdeducted. Any agent entrusted with the payment of any interest or other payment affected by this provision is required, if so requested, to furnish the Revenue Commissioners with a list detailing the payments in question and the names and addresses of the persons to whom they were made (TCA 1997, s 1087(1)).

TCA 1997, s 1087(1) applies to any public revenue dividends and interest taxable under Schedule C, to foreign dividends collected by a bank or other paying agent in the State required to deduct income tax under Schedule D, and to annuities and other annual payments and to patent royalties from which income tax is deductible under TCA 1997, s 238 (see **4.303**). The provision does not apply to annuities and other annual payments paid wholly out of income chargeable to tax since, in any such case, the payer is not obliged to deduct income tax (TCA 1997, s 237 – see **4.302**); TCA 1997, s 1087(1) refers to income tax which "is required to be deducted". TCA 1997, s 1087(3) provides that the section has no application to "distributions" from companies as defined in TCA 1997 Part 6 Ch 2 (see **11.101**), but it does apply to interest from which a paying company is required by TCA 1997, s 246 to deduct income tax (see **4.305**).

Where a person paying an annuity or other annual payment from which there is either an entitlement (TCA 1997, s 237) or an obligation (TCA 1997, s 238) to deduct income tax does not deduct tax at the time of payment, he is not, generally, entitled to recover the tax out of a later payment. An exception to this rule is the case of a payment made in a tax year before the passing of a Finance Act increasing the rate of income tax to be deducted for that year. In that event, TCA 1997, s 1087(2) provides that the person who made the payment from which income tax was deducted at the old rate is entitled to make up any deficiency in the amount deducted from the next payment made after the passing of the Act. Further, if there is no later payment from which the income tax underdeducted can be recouped, the income tax underdeducted may be recovered as a debt from the payee.

3.208.11 Basis of assessment and Case IV losses

Unlike the position for Cases I, II and V of Schedule D, there are no specific rules regarding the method of computing the amount of the income taxable under Case IV other than the requirement that the full amount of the profits or gains arising in the tax year (not relevant for companies) is to be computed. However, as the concept of an annual profit or gain implies an excess of receipts over any expenses incurred in earning those receipts, it may in principle be taken that expenses of a revenue nature incurred directly for that purpose should be deductible. In practice, it is likely that an inspector will apply some form of "wholly and exclusively incurred" test, although this does not have any statutory basis for Schedule D Case IV. Expenditure of a capital nature is clearly not deductible. Further, no deduction may be claimed in computing any Case IV income for any business entertainment expenses (TCA 1997, s 840).

It was held in *Grey v Tiley* 16 TC 414 that profits or gains within Schedule D Case VI (Case IV in Ireland) arise when they are received, or at least not before they are received. See also discussion in **3.207.2** regarding *Whitworth Park Coal v IRC* 38 TC 531.

Relief for losses

If in any accounting period, a company sustains a loss in a transaction of a type which, if it had been profitable, would have been taxable under Case IV, it may claim under TCA 1997, s 399 to have that loss set off against any other profits or gains on which it is assessed under Case IV for the same period (see also **4.106**). If and to the extent that the other Case IV income for that period is insufficient to absorb the loss, the unused loss is carried forward for set off against Case IV income in the next or any subsequent accounting period. If carried forward, a Case IV loss must be set off to the maximum extent possible from the first available Case IV income and so on until fully absorbed. There are no provisions whereby a Case IV loss may be set off against any other type of income or profits, whether in the same or in any other accounting period (but see **5.302** regarding excess capital allowances for leased machinery).

3.209   Case V

3.209.1   Introduction

Case V of Schedule D deals with the taxation of rents and other receipts from leases (as well as subleases) of land, buildings and similar premises and from rights in or over lands. The charge to tax under Case V is generally made on the net profit rents arising, ie gross rents receivable less revenue expenditure on the maintenance and upkeep of the property and interest on borrowings for the purchase, repair or improvement of the premises from which the rents arise. The scope for deducting expenses for Case V purposes is narrow, particularly as compared with the position for Case I, and only expenses specifically authorised by the relevant legislation may be deducted.

Where a person receives a premium on the granting of a lease, the rent receivable in respect of the letting in question will usually be lower than would otherwise be the case. Accordingly, premiums on leases are taxable as if they were additional rental income.

Capital expenditure incurred on lands, buildings and other premises from which rental income is derived is generally not deductible in arriving at the net profit rent for tax purposes. However, industrial building allowances may be claimed in respect of capital expenditure on industrial buildings which are leased (see **5.5**). Furthermore, relief is allowed in respect of capital expenditure incurred on the construction of residential accommodation for letting in certain designated areas (see **6.104**, **6.205**, **6.307** and **6.407**). Capital allowances are available in respect of the cost of construction of multi-storey car-parks, and the allowances may be claimed by a lessor against Case V income from the letting of these car-parks (see **5.605** and **6.203.3**). Lessors of commercial buildings situated in designated urban renewal areas may claim capital allowances in respect of the capital expenditure incurred on those buildings (see **6.102** and **6.203**).

3.209.2 Income charged

Certain profits or gains from real property are taxed by TCA 1997, s Part 4 Ch 8 (ss 96-106) under Case V. These profits or gains are those arising from:

  (a)   any rent in respect of any premises; and

  (b)   any receipts in respect of any easement.

Rents or other receipts from premises or easements used in connection with certain mines, quarries ironworks, gasworks, canals and other works are, however, taxable under Case I rather than under Case V (see **4.301**).

An *easement*" is defined in TCA 1997, s 96 as including "any right, privilege or benefit in, over or derived from premises". *Premises* is also defined in that section and means "any lands, tenements or hereditaments in the State". *Rent* is stated in TCA 1997, s 96 as including:

  (i)   any rent charge, fee farm rent and any payment in the nature of rent, notwithstanding that the payment may relate partly to premises and partly to goods or services, and

  (ii)   any payment made by the lessee to defray the cost of work of maintenance of or repairs to the premises, not being work required by the lease to be carried out by the lessee.

Lease includes an agreement for lease and any tenancy, but does not include a mortgage. The meanings of *lessor* and *lessee* derive from "lease".

Where a company pays a capital sum to another person in return for the transfer of a right to receive rent, any income arising to the company as a result of that transfer is chargeable to tax under Case V (TCA 1997, s 106A(3)). This will not apply, however, where the consideration received by the company is a capital sum within the meaning of TCA 1997, s 110 (securitisation of assets – see **7.206.11**) acquired by a qualifying company in the course of its business and the asset was acquired from a person other than an individual (TCA 1997, s 106A is an anti-avoidance provision enacted to counter schemes involving the transfer by individuals of taxable rental income to a company.)

Rental income arises where a person owning an interest in land, whether a freehold interest or a leasehold interest (whether derived from the freehold interest or from any superior leasehold interest), grants to another person a right under a lease, sublease or tenancy, to use the land or any buildings on the land. A formal lease or tenancy agreement is not essential to create a liability under Case V. The above definition of "rent" suggests that it would include an expense incurred by a tenant which, under the terms of the lease or tenancy, is the responsibility of the landlord. Where the payment by the tenant includes an amount for goods or services such as heating, cleaning, caretaking, which the landlord has agreed to provide under the terms of the lease or tenancy, that payment is also part of the rent receipts for the purposes of the Case V computation.

Receipts from easements arise where a person owning an interest in land gives to another person, for consideration in money or money's worth, any right to use the land or any part of the land in circumstances which do not amount to a lease or tenancy. Examples would be receipts from the grant of hunting, shooting or fishing rights in or over land, or a payment received for permitting a sign or advertisement hoarding to be placed or sited on land.

Premiums and deemed premiums for leases: general

Income chargeable under Case V includes a proportion of any premium required on the granting of the lease where the duration of the lease does not exceed fifty years. The appropriate proportion of the premium is usually included in the Case V computation as an additional payment of rent received in the period in which the lease is granted.

A charge to tax under Case V arises where the payment of a premium is required under a lease, or under the terms subject to which the lease is granted, and where the duration of the lease does not exceed fifty years (TCA 1997, s 98). The lessor is treated as becoming entitled, when the lease is granted, to an amount of rent (apart from any actual rent receivable) equal to the amount of the premium less 2% of that amount for each complete period of twelve months, other than the first such period, comprised in the term of the lease.

In certain circumstances, a lease is deemed to have required the payment of a premium. For example, a sum payable by the lessee in lieu of any rent or as consideration for the surrender of the lease (TCA 1997, s 98(3)), or a sum other than rent payable as consideration for the variation or waiver of any of the terms of the lease (TCA 1997, s 98(4)), is treated as a premium.

Where a sum in lieu of rent is paid, the term of the lease is treated as including only the period in respect of which that sum was paid, ie the period for which a lesser rent or no rent is payable. In the case of a sum paid in lieu of rent or a sum paid for the cancellation of a lease, the taxable amount in respect of the deemed premium is treated as becoming due when the sum in question becomes payable by the lessee. The value of any work (not including work the cost of which would be a deductible expense to the lessor if he were required to undertake it) carried out by a lessee on premises under an obligation imposed by the terms under which a lease is granted is also deemed to be a premium (TCA 1997, s 98(2)).

Where a premium or other payment mentioned above is due to a person other than the lessor, the payment may be treated as an annual profit or gain of that other person (and not as rent) and is chargeable to tax under Case IV (and not Case V) of Schedule D (see **3.208.6** in relation to this and other Case IV charges under TCA 1997 ss 99 and 100).

Where a premium or deemed premium is treated as rent, the amount to be included as additional rent is, as stated above, an amount equal to the premium reduced by 2% of the premium for each complete period of twelve months, not including the first such period, comprised in the term of the lease. If, however, the duration of the lease is less than two complete years, the full premium is included. The taxable amount can therefore be represented by the following formula:

$$\text{Taxable amount} = P - P \times \frac{(n-1)}{50}$$

where—

P = the amount of the premium; and

n = the number of complete years comprised in the term of the lease.

The same result follows from the following more convenient formula which is the one most often used in practice:

$$\text{Taxable amount} = P \times \frac{(51-n)}{50}$$

Example 3.209.2.1

On 1 January 2007, Sackville Ltd, which has been in receipt of rental income for a number of years, grants a lease of premises for 21 years and nine months to O'Connell Ltd in consideration of an annual rent of €6,000, subject to five-yearly reviews, and a premium of €30,000. The net rental income, assuming deductible expenses of €2,250, in the case of Sackville Ltd for its year ended 31 December 2007 is as follows:

	€	€
Rent receivable		6,000
Deemed additional rent:		
Premium	30,000	
Reduced by €30,000 $\times \frac{(21-1)}{50}$	12,000	
		18,000
		24,000
Less: deductible expenses		2,250
Assessable Case V amount		21,750

In practice, the following more concise computation is used:

	€
Rent receivable	6,000
Deemed additional rent:	
€30,000 $\times \frac{(51-21)}{50} =$	18,000
	24,000
Less: deductible expenses	2,250
Assessable Case V amount	21,750

As mentioned above, the value of any work carried out by a lessee on premises under an obligation imposed by the terms under which a lease is granted is also deemed to be a premium, except for work the cost of which would be a deductible expense to the lessor if he were required to undertake it. The deemed premium in that case is equal to the amount by which the lessor's interest, immediately after the commencement of the lease, falls short of what it would have been had the work been carried out. The assumed enhancement in value is usually taken as the capitalised value of the increase in rent which could have been expected had the lessor carried out the work.

Example 3.209.2.2
Parnell Ltd grants a 21 year lease of a property, which it holds under a long lease, to Mr Healy on 1 June 2007 for an annual rent of €7,200 and a premium of €35,000. Under the terms of the lease, Mr Healy is obliged to carry out specific refurbishment work on the property at a cost of €17,000. If the work were to be carried out by Parnell Ltd, it is estimated that the property could command an additional annual rent of €3,000. Based on a capitalisation factor of 7, the interest of Parnell Ltd in the property on 1 June 2007 would have been greater by €21,000. The additional premium deemed by TCA 1997, s 98(2) to have been required under the lease is therefore €21,000.
Parnell Ltd makes up annual accounts to 31 December and its Case V computation for the year ended 31 December 2007 is as follows:

	€
Rent receivable €7,200 x 7/12	4,200
Deemed additional rent:	
$€35,000 \times \dfrac{(51-21)}{50} =$	21,000
Deemed additional rent re deemed premium:	
$€21,000 \times \dfrac{(51-21)}{50} =$	12,600
Assessable Case V amount (before any expenses)	37,800

A sum payable by a lessee in lieu of the whole or any part of the rent or as consideration for the surrender of the lease is treated as a premium (TCA 1997, s 98(3)). The deemed premium is an amount equal to the sum payable and is taxable for the period in which the sum is payable. Where the sum is payable in lieu of the whole or part of the rent, the taxable amount is computed on the assumption that the term of the lease is limited to the period for which no rent, or the reduced rent, is payable. Accordingly, in the formula for calculating the amount of the deemed premium, "n" means the number of complete years included in that period.

Example 3.209.2.3
The position is as in Example **3.209.2.1** but the terms under which the lease is granted provide that the lessee, O'Connell Ltd, is to pay Sackville Ltd a lump sum of €18,000 on 1 January 2007 in consideration for the company agreeing to a reduced annual rent of €1,500 for the period 1 January 2007 to 31 December 2011.

As well as the additional rent of €18,000 already deemed to arise, a further amount of deemed rent must be included, by reference to the date on which the €18,000 is payable, computed as follows:

€

$$€18,000 \times \frac{(51-5)}{50} = \qquad\qquad 16,560$$

A sum payable by the lessee, other than rent, as consideration for the variation or waiver of any of the terms of the lease is treated as a premium (TCA 1997, s 98(4)). The additional rent is deemed to be received on the date on which the agreement for the variation or waiver is entered into and the taxable amount is computed on the assumption that in the formula for calculating the amount of the deemed premium, "n" means the number of complete years included in the period for which the variation or waiver has effect.

Example 3.209.2.4

Usher Ltd occupies premises under a 35 year lease granted on 1 July 1988 under which it pays an annual rent of €10,000. On 1 November 2007 the company enters into an agreement with Aston Ltd, the current lessor, under which, in consideration for a lump sum of €12,500, Aston Ltd will accept a reduced annual rent of €6,000 for the six years commencing on 1 January 2008.

The amount of additional rent deemed to be received by Aston Ltd on 1 November 2007 is computed as follows:

€

$$€12,500 \times \frac{(51-6)}{50} = \qquad\qquad 11,250$$

Premiums and deemed premiums: successive taxable events

Any of the events giving rise to a charge to tax under Case IV, by virtue of TCA 1997, s 98(1), (2) or (4), may be followed by a later event involving the same premises and giving rise to a Case V charge under the same provisions. Where the later event occurs in relation to a lease granted out of, or a sale, assignment or other disposition of, the lease, estate or interest by reference to which the prior taxable event arose, TCA 1997, s 103(3) applies to reduce the amount which would otherwise be chargeable under Case V in respect of the later event. The reduction is the excess, if any, of the amount chargeable on the later event over the appropriate fraction of the amount chargeable in respect of the prior event. The appropriate fraction is L/P where L is the duration of the relevant period in respect of the later chargeable amount and P is the duration of the relevant period in respect of the prior chargeable amount. For the purposes of TCA 1997, s 98, the relevant period is the full duration of the lease.

Example 3.209.2.5

The position is as in Example **3.209.2.1** where Sackville Ltd granted a 21 years and nine months lease of premises to O'Connell Ltd on 1 January 2007 at a premium of €30,000. On 1 April 2007, O'Connell Ltd, which made up annual accounts to 30 September, grants a 10 year sublease to Mr Earls at an annual rent and a premium of €12,000. The amount treated by TCA 1997, s 98(1) as additional rent to be included in the Case V computation of O'Connell Ltd for the year ended 30 September 2007 is as follows:

Later chargeable amount re sublease:

€

$$€12,000 \times \frac{(51-10)}{50} = \qquad\qquad 9,840$$

Prior chargeable amount re lease:

$$€30,000 \times \frac{(51-21)}{50} = \qquad\qquad 18,000$$

Relevant period (L) – duration of sublease	10.00
Relevant period (P) – duration of lease	21.75
Later chargeable amount	9,840
Less: prior chargeable amount €18,000 x 10/21.75	8,276
Additional rent chargeable under Case V	1,564

Case V: deductions for premiums and deemed premiums

A person who derives rental income from premises in which he is the holder of the lease, estate or interest in respect of which an amount was chargeable to tax under TCA 1997, s 98, 99 or 100 is entitled by virtue of TCA 1997, s 103(2) to a deduction, as a deduction under TCA 1997, s 97(2), in computing the surplus or deficiency in respect of the rent. The deduction is available during any part of the "relevant period" in which the lessee is entitled to the lease, estate or interest in question.

For the purposes of TCA 1997, s 98, the "relevant period" is the period treated in that section as being the duration of the lease. For TCA 1997, s 99, it is the part of the duration of the lease remaining at the date of the assignment giving rise to the Case IV charge. For TCA 1997, s 100, it is the period beginning on the date of the sale giving rise to the Case IV charge and ending on the date fixed by the sale agreement as the date for the reconveyance or the grant of the lease or, if that date is not fixed, on the earliest date at which the reconveyance or grant could be made.

For example, if a company sells a 35 year leasehold interest to a second company for €150,000 with a right to reconveyance for €100,000 in four years' time, the company will be liable under TCA 1997, s 100 on 47/50ths of €50,000 (see Example **3.208.6.2**). If the second company is in receipt of rental income from the premises subject to the lease for the four years, it will be entitled to a deduction of €47,000 at €11,750 for each of those years.

If there are two events each giving rise to a charge under TCA 1997, s 98, 99 or 100 on the first company, the later chargeable amount will have been reduced by the appropriate fraction of the prior chargeable amount (see Example **3.209.2.5** above). The deduction in the second company's Case V computation will then be as follows:

(a) where the later chargeable amount is greater than the appropriate fraction of the prior chargeable amount, the TCA 1997, s 103(2) deduction is for the prior chargeable amount only (spread over the relevant period);

(b) where the appropriate fraction of the prior chargeable amount is greater than the later chargeable amount, the later chargeable amount, spread over the relevant period, is fully deductible, and in addition there is a deduction for a reduced prior chargeable amount (also spread over the relevant period), by reference to the formula PCA x (F – LCA)/F where

PCA = the prior chargeable amount,

F = the appropriate fraction of PCA, and

LCA = the later chargeable amount.

The effect of the above is that the Case V deduction can never exceed the prior chargeable amount (a) and, where the relevant period for the later event is shorter than that for the prior event, the total deduction will be less than the prior chargeable amount.

Taxation of reverse premiums

A reverse premium is treated by TCA 1997, s 98A as a receipt of a revenue nature (TCA 1997, s 98A(2)). It is assessable as rent unless it is assessable as a receipt of a trade or profession or is deductible from the amount treated as expenses of management of a life assurance company which is not charged to tax under Case I of Schedule D. A reverse premium is charged to tax in the first relevant chargeable period where two or more of the persons who enter into the transaction or arrangements are connected and the terms of the arrangements are not what would be expected if those persons were dealing at arm's length. Where an assurance company is involved, the reverse premium reduces the expenses of management for the period in which the premium is received. Otherwise, a reverse premium is chargeable in accordance with the established principles of commercial accounting.

A *reverse premium* is defined as a payment or other benefit received by a person by way of inducement in connection with a relevant transaction being entered into by that person or by a person connected with that person. A *relevant transaction* is a transaction under which a person is granted an estate or interest in, or a right over, land (TCA 1997, s 98A(1)(a)).

The amount or value of a reverse premium is, subject to TCA 1997, s 98A(4) and (6), treated as if it were an amount of rent (TCA 1997, s 98A(3)). Where a relevant transaction is entered into by a person receiving a reverse premium and is entered into for the purposes of a trade or profession carried on or to be carried on by that person, the amount or value of the premium is to be taken into account in computing the profits or gains of that trade or profession under Case I or II of Schedule D, as the case may be, as if it were a receipt of that trade or profession (TCA 1997, s 98A(4)).

Where—

(a) two or more of the persons who enter into relevant arrangements are connected with each other; and

(b) the terms of those arrangements are not such as would reasonably have been expected if those persons had been dealing at arm's length,

the whole of the amount or value of the reverse premium is, subject to TCA 1997, s 98A(3), (4) (see above), treated as accruing in the first relevant chargeable period (TCA 1997, s 98A(5)).

For the above purposes, *relevant arrangements* means a relevant transaction and any arrangements entered into in connection with it, whether before, at the same time or after it. The *first relevant chargeable period* means—

(a) the chargeable period (accounting period or year of assessment) in which a relevant transaction is entered into, or

(b) if a relevant transaction is entered into—

 (i) by a person receiving a reverse premium, and

 (ii) for the purposes of a trade or profession which that person is about to carry on,

the chargeable period in which the person commences to carry on the trade or profession (TCA 1997, s 98A(1)(a)).

Persons are connected with each other if they are connected within the meaning of TCA 1997, s 10 (see **2.3**) at any time during the chargeable period or periods when the relevant arrangements are entered into.

Where a reverse premium is received by an assurance company carrying on life business (within the meaning of TCA 1997, s 706 – see **12.601**) in respect of which it is chargeable to tax otherwise than in accordance with the rules applicable to Case I of Schedule D (see **12.603**), the amount or value of the reverse premium is deducted from the amount treated as the company's expenses of management for the accounting period in which the premium is received (TCA 1997, s 98A(6)).

TCA 1997, s 98A does not apply to a payment or benefit—

(a) received by an individual in connection with a relevant transaction and the transaction relates to the grant of an estate or interest in, or a right in or over premises occupied or to be occupied by him as his only or main residence;

(b) to the extent that it is consideration for the transfer of an estate or interest in land which constitutes the sale in a sale and lease-back arrangement where the terms of that arrangement at the time the arrangement is entered into are on bona fide commercial terms; or

(c) to the extent that, apart from TCA 1997, s 98A, it is taken into account in computing the profits or gains of a trade or profession under Case I or II of Schedule D, as the case may be, as a receipt of that trade or profession (TCA 1997, s 98A(7)).

A *sale and lease-back arrangement* is an arrangement under which a person disposes of the full estate or interest held by him in land to another person and the terms subject to which the disposal is made provide for the grant of a lease of an interest in or right in or over the land concerned to him by that other person (TCA 1997, s 98A(1)(a)).

3.209.3 Computation

The computation of the net profit rent under Case V commences with the calculation of the surplus or deficiency for each separate rent and the total receipts from easements. The total Case V income arising to a company in an accounting period is the aggregate of the surpluses reduced by the aggregate of the deficiencies (TCA 1997, s 97(1)), but ignoring any surplus or deficiency in respect of excluded lettings (TCA 1997, s 75(4) – see below). See also **3.209.4** regarding deduction for certain expenditure on refurbishment.

For each lease or tenancy agreement, the computation for any accounting period involves the deduction, from the rent receivable for the period, of the outgoings in respect of that rent in so far as they are authorised by TCA 1997, s 97(2) and by any other relevant provisions of the Income Tax Acts. The amount of any premium for the grant of the lease, which is taxable under TCA 1997, s 98 (see above), is taken into account in arriving at the surplus or deficiency for the rent in question.

The amount of rent to be included for any accounting period is the amount receivable for that period, whether received or not. If, however, it can be shown that the whole or part of the rent is irrecoverable on the default of the tenant, or as a result of it being waived by the lessor without consideration and to avoid hardship, the amount not recovered is excluded from the Case V computation (TCA 1997, s 101). Any tax overpaid by reason of the prior inclusion of the amount not recovered will be repaid following an appropriate amendment to the assessment and, where any amount which has been excluded is later recovered, the additional tax due will become payable following the appropriate amended assessment.

The deductible expenses to which a lessor company is entitled, as provided for by TCA 1997, s 97(2), are as follows:

(a)   any rent payable by it in respect of the premises or portion thereof;

(b)   any sums borne by it in accordance with the conditions of the lease, in the case of a rent under lease and, in any other case (easements), as an expense of the transaction under which the rent or other payment is received (eg, rates);

(c)   the cost to the company of any services rendered or goods provided by it, otherwise than by way of maintenance or repairs, for which it receives no separate consideration, where it is legally bound, in the case of a rent under lease, to provide them and, in any other case (easements), being an expense, not of a capital nature, of the transaction under which the rent or other payment is received;

(d)   the cost of maintenance, repairs, insurance and management of the premises borne by the company, other than expenses of a capital nature;

(e)   interest on borrowed money employed in the purchase, improvement or repair of the premises.

TCA 1997, s 97(3) requires that any expenses deductible by a company under TCA 1997, s 97(2) must be such as would be deductible in computing the profits of a trade for the purposes of Case I as if the receipt of the rent were the carrying on of a trade during the currency of the relevant lease or during the period for which the company was entitled to the rent. This requirement applies separately to each lease or tenancy agreement. Accordingly:

(a)   the expense must be incurred wholly and exclusively for the purposes of earning the rent;

(b)   expenses incurred before the commencement of, or after the termination of, the relevant lease or tenancy are not deductible;

(c)   any business entertainment expenses incurred are not deductible;

(d)   excess motor leasing and running expenses are disallowable;

(e)   management expenses may include contributions to an exempt approved pension scheme in relation to employees engaged in the maintenance, management or other transactions relating to the leased property.

An appropriate apportionment is to be made of any expenses or other payments attributable partly to the leased premises and partly to other premises (TCA 1997, s 97(4)). No deduction may be made in respect of any expense which is otherwise deductible in computing the income of the company for tax purposes (TCA 1997, s 97(5)), for example, salaries and wages of employees engaged both in the management of the rented premises and in a trade carried on by the company in respect of which the company is entitled to a deduction for Case I purposes.

Expenses incurred by a company after the termination of a lease but before the grant of a new lease of the same premises are deemed to have been incurred during the currency of the first lease, subject to three conditions (TCA 1997, s 97(3)(b)) as follows:

(a)   the expenses would otherwise be deductible under TCA 1997, s 97(2);

(b)   the company which was the lessor immediately before the termination of the lease was not in occupation of any part of the premises during the period after the termination, but was entitled to possession of the premises; and

(c)   at the end of the period following the termination, the premises have become subject to another lease granted by the company.

In relation to the deduction for expenses of management authorised by TCA 1997, s 97(2)(d), it was held in *Stephen Court Ltd v Browne* 5 ITR 680 that an auctioneer's letting fee and a solicitor's costs incurred in connection with the negotiation of leases were properly deductible under TCA 1997, s 97(2)(d) as expenses of management of the premises in respect of which the leases were granted. In response to the argument that the expenses in question were capital in nature, Mr Justice McWilliam expressed the opinion that the capital of the appellant company was the premises concerned and not the lease and that the company's business was both the letting of premises and the collection of rents; it was incorrect to view the capital of the company as a form of landlord's interest divorced from the ownership of the premises so that the business to be managed would be confined to the collection of rents.

In practice, although not strictly part of the cost of management of a premises, mortgage protection policy premiums paid are treated as allowable deductions in computing rental income for Case V purposes.

There is no restriction on the amount of interest deductible under TCA 1997, s 97(2)(e) provided the conditions for allowability are satisfied. Only interest paid during the period for which the premises are leased is deductible, including any period for which the premises are temporarily vacant after the termination of a lease – see the three conditions in relation to TCA 1997, s 97(3)(b) above.

TCA 1997, s 105 provides that no deduction may be made in respect of interest paid on borrowed money or rent payable for any period prior to the date on which the premises concerned are first occupied by a lessee for a trade or undertaking or for use as a residence. The purpose of this restriction is to prevent a deduction being obtained where a lease is commenced in contrived circumstances, where, say, the tenant is not in a position to occupy the premises until a later date and accordingly pays a nominal rent in the meantime.

TCA 1997, s 109(4) provides that an employer's lump sum redundancy payment under section 46 of the Redundancy Payments Act 1967 may be deducted as an expense of maintaining or managing leased premises provided the payment is made in respect of an employment involved wholly in maintaining or managing leased premises producing rents taxable under Case V. The allowance is confined to the statutory lump sum payable.

A Case V loss for a company arises where the aggregate of the rent deficiencies arising in any accounting period exceeds the aggregate of the surpluses for the same period. Surpluses or deficiencies from excluded lettings (see below) are not taken into account.

A Case V loss for any accounting period may be set off against Case V income of previous accounting periods for a period equal in length to the period of the loss, and any remaining loss may then be set against Case V income of any subsequent accounting period (TCA 1997, s 399(2)).

An allowance (ie, a capital allowance) which falls to be made to a company for any accounting period and which is given "by way of discharge or repayment of tax" (eg, a writing down allowance available against income from the letting of machinery or plant (TCA 1997, s 298(1)), or in charging its income under Case V, and is to be available primarily against the specified class of income, is to be deducted as far as possible against income of that class. Where the allowance is not fully used in that way because of an insufficiency of income, it may under TCA 1997, s 308(4) be allowed against profits of any description of the same accounting period and (if the company was then within the charge to tax) of preceding accounting periods for a period equal in length to the period in which the allowance arose.

Capital allowances may be claimed in respect of certain capital expenditure incurred on the purchase of fixtures and fittings for furnished rented residential accommodation. Normal wear and tear allowances are allowable against rental income.

The provisions of TCA 1997, s 284 (wear and tear allowances) apply to the letting of any premises the profits or gains from which are chargeable under Case V of Schedule D as they apply in relation to trades (TCA 1997, s 284(6)). The purpose of this provision is to enable capital allowances to be claimed in respect of capital expenditure incurred on fixtures and fittings for furnished rented residential accommodation. TCA 1997, s 284(7) provides that s 284(6) is to apply in respect of capital expenditure incurred on the provision of machinery or plant other than motor vehicles where—

(a)   the expenditure is incurred wholly and exclusively in respect of a house which is used solely as a dwelling which is or is to be let as a furnished house; and

(b)   the house is provided for renting or letting on *bona fide* commercial terms in the open market.

TCA 1997, s 284(6) and (7) is the statutory basis for a former practice under which a lessor of private residential accommodation could claim allowances in respect of fixtures and fittings, including such items as furniture, kitchens and bathroom suites, against the income from the letting of those premises. Technically, a lessor of private residential accommodation could not have claimed capital allowances by virtue of TCA 1997, s 298(1) (allowances to lessors) as the lessee would not have been carrying on a trade (see **5.301.1**).TCA 1997, s 300(4) provides that any wear and tear allowance made under or by virtue of TCA 1997, s 284(6) is to be made in charging the relevant person's income under Case V of Schedule D. Thus, capital allowances for expenditure incurred on fixtures and fittings in rented residential accommodation may be set against rental income. (See also **5.105.1**.)

Where capital allowances arise to a company for any accounting period by virtue of TCA 1997, s 284(6), any loss or deficiency incurred for that period, to the extent attributable to those capital allowances, may not be set against other profits of the company under TCA 1997, s 396(2) or 308(4) (see **4.101** and **5.416.3**). Any excess capital allowances may accordingly only be carried forward and set against profits from the letting of the house in subsequent periods.

The deficiency which may be offset against profits of a preceding period is confined to so much of that deficiency as cannot be utilised against profits of a later accounting period. In other words, a deficiency which is the subject of a TCA 1997, s 308(4) claim must be used first against the total profits of the period in which the deficiency arose and then against the profits of the preceding period or periods.

For the purpose of offsetting a deficiency against the profits of the preceding period or periods, profits are apportioned on a time basis; where an accounting period falls partly before the immediately preceding period or periods equal in length to the period of the Case V deficiency, only a proportionate part of the profits of that accounting period may be relieved.

Any allowance still not fully utilised may then under TCA 1997, s 308(3) be carried forward to succeeding accounting periods and set against income of the specified class for those periods.

3.209.4 Excluded lettings

Where a company receives a rent under a lease which is insufficient, taking one year with another, to meet its costs of fulfilling its obligations under the lease and its expenses of maintenance, repairs, insurance and management of the leased premises, that letting must be left out of account for the purposes of computing income assessable under Case V (TCA 1997, s 75(4)). In applying this provision, since it is required to take "one year with another", the fact that a surplus arises in one accounting period of a company will not of itself result in the letting ceasing to be an excluded letting; evidently, neither does the fact that a deficiency arises for a letting in one period of itself bring the letting within the scope of TCA 1997, s 75(4). If a deficiency arises for a letting as a result of expenses other than those mentioned above, eg interest on qualifying borrowings, the letting will not be an excluded one for that reason.

For the purpose of determining whether there is sufficient income from a letting to meet the lessor's obligations as detailed above, an appropriate sum in respect of any premium payable under the lease must be included with the rent, where the duration of the lease does not exceed fifty years. There is no definition of "appropriate sum" for this purpose. It does not mean the full amount of the premium but would appear to mean a proportionate amount arrived at, in the case of a company, by reference to the length of the accounting period in question as a fraction of the length of the lease period.

3.209.5 Apportionments on sale of premises

TCA 1997, s 106 caters for the situation in which rented premises are sold and it is necessary to apportion receipts and outgoings between the vendor and the purchaser. The effect of the section is to provide for the same apportionment for tax purposes as is provided for under the terms of the sale.

TCA 1997, s 106(1), (2) deal with the case in which a receipt, such as a rent due, or an expense, such as rates, for a period straddling the date of completion of the sale, may be due for payment after the contract date but before completion. In that situation the vendor would normally receive the rent or pay the expense and would then account to the purchaser for the proportion attributable to the period after the date of completion, the net adjustment arising being deducted from or added to the payment made by the purchaser for the acquisition of the premises.

The part of any rent due for payment in the period from the date of the contract to the date of completion that is apportioned to the purchaser is treated, for Case V purposes, as received by the vendor on behalf of the purchaser immediately after completion of the sale. The treatment of expenses is dealt with similarly.

Where the rent or expense for a period straddling the completion date becomes due for payment on a date before the date of the sale contract, the same apportionment is made. The purchaser in that case is again deemed to have received, immediately after the completion date, any such rent collected by the vendor apportioned by reference to the time after the completion date. The same treatment applies to any corresponding expense paid by the vendor.

TCA 1997, s 106(3) deals with the situation which arises where a rent receipt or an expense for a period straddling the completion date is due for payment after that date (ie, rents or expenses in arrear). For Case V purposes, the proportion of any such rent due to the vendor is treated as having been received by him immediately before completion and there is a corresponding treatment in respect of any expense.

3.210 Offshore income gains

3.210.1 Introduction

An *offshore fund* may consist of:

(a) a company resident outside the State (overseas company);
(b) a unit trust scheme the trustees of which are not resident in the State; or
(c) any other arrangements taking effect under foreign law and under which rights in the nature of co-ownership are created (TCA 1997, s 743(1)).

Prior to the enactment of FA 1990 Part I Ch VII (now TCA 1997 Part 27 Ch 2 (ss 740-747)), it was possible to avoid liability to income tax by allowing an investment in an offshore fund to "roll up", that is, to accumulate over a period of years as profits were reinvested. The investment would eventually be realised at which point the profit element included would be a capital gain. This was advantageous for the investor as capital gains tax treatment was more favourable than income tax treatment (or corporation tax on income treatment in the case of a company). Payment of tax was deferred until the investment was realised and capital gains tax indexation was available. For an individual investor, a further benefit was the availability or the annual capital gains tax exemption.

While many offshore funds make income distributions, generally an offshore fund is a fund designed to roll up income with the result that, when an investor disposes of his holding, he receives a sum equivalent or approximately equivalent to his initial capital investment plus the income rolled up on that investment.

By way of background, the type of arrangement that prompted the introduction of the offshore funds legislation was an investment promoted by financial institutions and referred to as offshore roll-up funds. Such funds would have been formed abroad, often in low tax jurisdictions, and investors would have been invited to subscribe for preference shares, usually redeemable at any time at the option of the investor. The redemption price was linked directly to the value of the company's underlying assets.

Normally, these assets were gilt-edged stock the income from which was reinvested in further such stock. Higher rate taxpayers with substantial investment income were thus afforded a means of converting income taxable at the marginal income tax rate into capital gain.

TCA 1997, s 745 provides that a gain accruing from the disposal of a material interest in a non-qualifying offshore fund is subject to tax as income rather than as a capital gain. A non-qualifying offshore fund is, briefly, a fund which accumulates or "rolls up" its profits in that it does not distribute them from year to year to its investors. A chargeable gain arising on the disposal, on or after 12 February 1998, of a material interest in an offshore fund which is not a non-qualifying offshore fund is subject to capital gains tax at a rate of 40% (see **3.210.8**).

Income or gains arising from foreign entities that are transparent, such as partnerships, do not generally give rise to a charge under the offshore funds legislation. Irish investors are taxable on their shares of the income or gains accruing to such entities as they arise and it would not, accordingly, be appropriate to apply the offshore fund provisions in those circumstances.

3.210.2   Material interest in offshore fund

A material interest in an offshore fund is an interest in respect of which, at the date of acquisition of that interest, it could be reasonably expected that at some time within seven years from the time of acquisition of the interest, the holder of the interest would be able to realise the value of the interest. Essentially, it is an interest that can be realised as a share of the market value of the underlying assets of the overseas company (or assets subject to the unit trust scheme or arrangements). If the interest held is not a material interest, the investor concerned cannot be charged to tax in accordance with the offshore funds legislation. In the absence of at least one material interest, an overseas vehicle cannot be an offshore fund at all. Thus, for example, holdings of shares in a quoted UK resident public company would not normally be material interests as it is most unlikely that the value of such shares would be expected to vary consistently with the asset value of the company.

Where shares in an overseas company are listed on a stock exchange, it is possible that the quoted price would at certain times correspond to underlying net asset value. This, however, will not of itself make the shares a material interest in an offshore fund. The shares would be considered a material interest only if, at the time they were acquired, the investor had a reasonable expectation of a future sale at or near net asset value. If, on the other hand, the shares have historically been habitually traded at or near net asset value, an investor is likely to have acquired a material interest.

The determining factor in relation to whether or not there is a material interest is the investor's prospect of realising or not realising the interest in question. If, at the time the interest was acquired, it could reasonably be expected that the value of the interest could be realised within seven years, the interest is a material interest. The seven-year period test is intended to exclude venture capital funds that normally have a life of just under ten years. The test of the investor's expectation is an objective one in that it is not sufficient for the investor to argue that he personally did not expect to realise his interest within seven years.

TCA 1997, s 743(2) provides that the interest of a person in an offshore fund is a *material interest* if, at the time it was acquired, it could reasonably be expected that the value of the interest could be realised, whether by transfer, surrender or in any other manner, within seven years beginning at the time of the acquisition. A person is deemed to be able to realise the value of an interest if he can realise an amount, in money or in the form of assets to the value of that amount, which is reasonably approximate to the proportion of the underlying assets of the offshore fund represented by his interest (TCA 1997, s 743(3)).

If an interest in an offshore fund is at any time worth substantially more on the open market than the value of the portion of the underlying assets represented by that interest, the ability to realise such market value is not to be regarded as an ability to realise an amount equivalent to the value of the underlying assets (TCA 1997, s 743(4)). It appears that it is intended, inter alia, that an investment in a company with substantial goodwill resulting, say, from the way in which the underlying, usually portfolio, investments are managed (as distinct from a company that is a mere investment holding vehicle), should not be viewed as an offshore fund. As was seen above, a condition of being an offshore fund is that the investor can realise an amount which is reasonably approximate to the proportion of the underlying assets of the offshore fund represented by his interest so that if the amount realisable is substantially less than the proportion of the underlying assets because, for example, some of those assets cannot easily be realised, the fund will, again, not be viewed as an offshore fund.

The following items are not material interests in an offshore fund:

(a) a normal commercial loan from a bank (TCA 1997, s 743(5)(a));

(b) a right arising under an insurance policy (TCA 1997, s 743(5)(b));

(c) a shareholding in an overseas company if—

  (i)   the shares are held by a company and such holding is necessary or desirable for the maintenance and development of the trade of that company or a company associate with it,

  (ii) the shares entitle the holder to at least 10% of the total voting rights in the company and at least 10% of the assets of the company in the event of its being wound up after all debts and liabilities have been paid,

  (iii) not more than ten persons (participators) hold shares in the overseas company and all the shares in that company confer both voting rights and a right to participate in the assets on a winding up, and

  (iv) at the time of its acquisition of the shares the company had a reasonable expectation that it could realise the value of its interest within seven years by reason only of the existence of either or both—

    (I) an arrangement whereby it could, within the seven year period, realise the value of the shares by requiring the other participators to purchase them, and

    (II) provisions of either an agreement between the participators or the constitution of the overseas company under which the company will be wound up within a period that is, or is reasonably expected to be, shorter than the seven year period (TCA 1997, s 743(6));

(d) an interest in an overseas company in respect of which the holder has the right to have the company wound up and, in the event of the winding up, would be entitled, by virtue of that interest and any other interest then held in the same capacity, to more than 50% of the assets remaining after paying all liabilities and debts (TCA 1997, s 743(8)).

With regard to (c) above, this exception to the meaning of "material interest" is to ensure that interests in joint trading ventures, carried on through the medium of a foreign company, are not brought within the offshore funds charge to tax. Situations that might otherwise be affected are buy-out agreements between participants in a trading venture, and short-term overseas trading operations. In either case, it could be argued that the investors had a reasonable expectation of realising the value of their interests within seven years. To prevent such interest from being chargeable, it is provided that shares in an overseas company do not constitute a material interest if the conditions listed in (c) are satisfied.

The market value rules in TCA 1997, s 548 are to apply in computing the value of a material interest in an offshore fund (TCA 1997, s 743(9)). The interest is valued at the price which the units might reasonably be expected to realise on a sale in the open market. Where there are separate published buying and selling prices for the units, however, the market value of an interest is the buying price (being the lower price) as published on the relevant date.

3.210.3 Disposal of material interest in non-qualifying offshore funds

Non-qualifying offshore funds

Unless an offshore fund is certified by the Revenue Commissioners as being a "distributing fund", it will be a non-qualifying offshore fund. A *distributing fund* for any "account period" (see below) is a fund which distributes to its unit holders (whether holders of material interests or otherwise) at least 85% of the income of the fund for the period. The Revenue Commissioners must also certify that the total distribution is not less than 85% of the "Irish equivalent profits" for the period, that is, the amount on which corporation tax would be chargeable. The distribution must be made within 6 months of the end of the account period and must be made in such form that, if received by a resident person other than in the course of a trade or profession, it would be taxed under Case III of Schedule D. A fund may not be certified as a distributing fund for an account period if at any time during the period:

(a) more than 5% of the value of the assets of the fund consists of interests in other offshore funds (TCA 1997, s 744(3)(a));

(b) more than 10% of the value of the assets of the fund consists of interests in a single company (TCA 1997, s 744(3)(b)). The interest must be valued on the most recent occasion on which the fund acquired an interest in the company for consideration in money or money's worth. For this purpose, an interest acquired as a result of a share exchange transaction involving a company reorganisation or merger is to be disregarded so as not to affect qualification, provided no net consideration has been given. Similarly, there is to be disregarded an interest in a company carrying on a banking business in the State or elsewhere and which provides current or deposit account facilities in any currency, where the interest consists of a current or deposit account provided in the normal course of the company's banking business;

(c)   the assets of the fund include a shareholding of more than 10% of the issued share capital of any company or of any class of that share capital (TCA 1997, s 744(3)(c)); or

(d)   there is more than one class of material interest in the offshore fund and they do not all receive proper distribution benefits (TCA 1997, s 744(3)(d)). For this purpose there is to be disregarded any interests in an offshore fund which are held solely by managers of the assets of the fund, which carry no right or expectation to participate in any of the profits of the fund, and on a winding up or redemption no right to receive anything other than the return of the price paid for the interests (TCA 1997, s 744(6)).

In relation to (d) above, the classes of material interest in an offshore fund, where there is more than one such class of interest, do not receive proper distribution benefits unless, if each class were in a separate offshore fund, each such fund could be certified as distributing more than 85% of its income.

Without the provisions of (a) to (d) above, it would be possible for a fund to reinvest its investors' money in a second fund which would then accumulate the income accruing on that money. Since the first fund would have no income to distribute, it could then claim to have satisfied the distribution requirement.

TCA 1997 Sch 19 Part 2 modifies the above conditions in the cases of:

(1)   reinvestment in another fund which distributes at least 85% of its income: where, in relation to assets of the fund (the "primary fund") which consist of or include interests in another offshore fund which could be certified as a distributing fund, the primary fund could not be certified as a distributing fund by reason only of not complying with conditions (a), (b) or (c) in the requirements for certification as a distributing fund (see above), the interests in that other fund are to be left out of account;

(2)   investment in a trading company: the 10% limit on investments in a single company is increased to 20% and the 10% limit applying to the issued share capital of any company or of any class of that share capital is increased to 50%;

(3)   investment in a wholly owned subsidiary: for the purposes of conditions (a) to (c) in the requirements for certification as a distributing fund, the percentage of receipts, expenditure, assets and liabilities of the subsidiary corresponding to the percentage of share capital owned by the offshore fund is regarded as receipts, expenditure, assets and liabilities of the fund, and the interest of the fund in the subsidiary and any distributions or other payments made between the fund and the subsidiary are left out of account;

(4)   investment in a company providing management and administrative services: condition (c) in the requirements for certification (the 10% limit applying to the issued share capital of any company or of any class of that share capital) does not apply to so much of the assets of an offshore fund as consists of issued share capital of a company which is a wholly owned subsidiary of the fund or a subsidiary management company of the fund;

(5)   *de minimis* holdings in companies: for the purposes of condition (c) in the requirements for certification, holdings not exceeding a certain percentage are ignored. That percentage is 5% of the aggregate of "excess holdings" and interests in other offshore funds which are not qualifying funds. An excess

holding is any holding exceeding the 10% limit for the purposes of condition (c) above.

In (4) above, a wholly owned subsidiary is a company whose business consists wholly of dealing in material interests in the offshore fund for the purposes of and in connection with the management and administration of the business of the fund, and which is not entitled to any distribution in respect of any material interest held by it. A subsidiary management company is a company carrying on no business other than the provision of services of holding property occupied or used in connection with the management or administration of the fund and the provision of administrative, management and advisory services to the fund, either for the fund alone or for the fund and for any other offshore fund which has an interest in the company, and whose remuneration for the services has been determined on an arm's length basis.

The circumstances in which an *account period* may begin and end are set out in TCA 1997, s 744(8)-(10). An account period begins on 6 April 1990 or, if later, when the offshore fund begins to carry on its activities, as well as immediately following the end of any previous account period. An account period ends at the earliest of:

(a)   12 months after the beginning of the account period;

(b)   the accounting date of the offshore fund; and

(c)   the date of cessation of the fund's activities.

An account period of a non-resident company ends when the company becomes resident in the State.

Disposal of material interest

The anti-avoidance provisions of the offshore funds legislation apply for any chargeable period (year of assessment or accounting period) in the case of a disposal of units in a non-qualifying offshore fund, ie one which has not for that period satisfied the distribution test as set out in TCA 1997 Sch 19 Part 1. The provisions also apply to the disposal of assets in an Irish resident company or unit trust scheme where, before 1 January 1991, the company or scheme was non-resident and the assets constituted a material interest in the fund.

An asset is disposed of for the purposes of the offshore funds legislation if it would be regarded as disposed of under the provisions of the Capital Gains Tax Acts, but subject to certain modifications to prevent the avoidance of a charge to income tax under the offshore funds provisions (TCA 1997, s 741(2)). For example, share for share transactions in the context of company reconstructions and amalgamations are not normally regarded as disposals for capital gains tax purposes (TCA 1997, s 586 and 587 – see **9.404** and **9.405**). That treatment does not, however, apply for the purposes of the offshore funds legislation where the acquiring company, being a distributing fund, issues shares or debentures in exchange for shares or debentures of another company ("the acquired company") which is or was at the material time a non-qualifying offshore fund (TCA 1997, s 741(5)). The exchange is regarded as being a disposal of interests in the acquired company at market value at the time of the exchange (TCA 1997, s 741(6)). The same treatment applies to any arrangement where persons are treated as exchanging shares or debentures or other securities in a non-qualifying offshore fund for assets which do not constitute interests in such a fund.

Material time in relation to a material interest means any time on or after 6 April 1990, where the asset was acquired on or before that date, and otherwise the earliest date on which any relevant consideration was given for the acquisition of the asset. *Relevant consideration* means consideration which would be taken into account under normal capital gains tax rules in computing the amount of a gain or loss.

Charge to corporation tax

An offshore income gain is charged to tax under Case IV of Schedule D as income arising to the person making the disposal (TCA 1997, s 745(1)). The income is regarded as arising at the time of the disposal and, in the case of a company, is treated as profits or gains arising in the accounting period in which the disposal takes place. TCA 1997 ss 25(2)(b), 29 and 30 (see **9.102.2**) apply to corporation tax in respect of offshore income gains as they apply to chargeable gains (TCA 1997, s 745(2)). Irish resident companies are taxable in respect of all offshore income gains while non-resident companies are taxable in respect of such gains where the underlying assets consist of:

(a)   land (including buildings) in the State;

(b)   minerals (as defined in the Minerals Development Act 1940 s 3 – see **3.107.1**) in the State or any rights, interests or other assets in relation to mining or minerals or the searching for minerals;

(c)   assets which, at or before the time when the chargeable gains accrued, were used in or for the purposes of a trade carried on by him in the State through a branch or agency, or which at or before that time were used or held or acquired for use by or for the purposes of the branch or agency;

(d)   exploration or exploitation rights in a designated area;

(e)   unquoted shares deriving their value or the greater part of their value directly or indirectly from such assets as are described in (a), (b) or (d) above.

In relation to (c) above, all trading assets, wherever situated, are included whereas for the purposes of TCA 1997, s 29 as it relates to chargeable gains, only such assets as are situated in the State are included (see **9.102.2**).

A charity is exempt from tax in respect of offshore income gains provided the gains are applied for charitable purposes only (TCA 1997, s 745(5)). A charity is any body established "for charitable purposes only" (see **12.1002**). Where a property which represents, directly or indirectly, an offshore income gain held on charitable trusts ceases to be so held, the trustees are treated as if they had disposed of and immediately reacquired the property at market value and any gain accruing is treated as not accruing to a charity. This provision affects a charity which has been tax exempt and which later engages in non-charitable activities and applies its accumulated income or gains for those purposes.

Where a disposal made by a company relates to settled property, as defined in TCA 1997, s 5(1) (any property held in trust, other than property held by a nominee or bare trustee, but not including any property held by a trustee or assignee in bankruptcy or under a deed of arrangement), and the general administration of the trust is ordinarily carried on outside the State and the trustees or a majority of them are resident and ordinarily resident outside the State, no charge to corporation tax will be made in respect of the offshore income gain arising (TCA 1997, s 745(6)).

A chargeable gain arising to a non-resident closely controlled company, and not chargeable to capital gains tax by virtue of TCA 1997, s 29 (see above), may be proportionately attributed by TCA 1997, s 590 to any Irish resident participators in the company (see **9.102.22** and **9.408**). TCA 1997 ss 579 and 579A-579F contain similar provisions in relation to gains arising to non-resident trusts with Irish resident beneficiaries and capital payments received by such beneficiaries from offshore trusts (but see below in connection with the amendment, by FA 2002, of TCA 1997, s 579A). These provisions are applied by TCA 1997, s 746(1), (2) to offshore income gains. Thus, tax will not be avoided by Irish resident participators or beneficiaries where it is arranged that an offshore income gain arises to a non-resident company or trust.

TCA 1997, s 597A, as introduced by FA 1999, imposed a capital gains tax charge on a beneficiary who received a capital payment from the trust in so far as that payment could be matched with a gain made by the trust. As, however, the operation of both TCA ss 579 and 579A could in certain circumstances result in gains in excess of those realised by the trust being liable to tax, TCA 1997, s 579 was effectively repealed by FA 2002.

Accordingly, following FA 2002, TCA 1997, s 579 (non-resident trusts) does not apply as respects chargeable gains accruing after 5 April 1999 to trustees of a settlement to which TCA 1997, s 579A applies. That section applies to a settlement for any year of assessment, beginning on or after 6 April 1999, during which the trustees are at no time resident or ordinarily resident in the State, and:

(a)   the settlor does not have an interest in the settlement at any time in that year of assessment; or

(b)   the settlor does have an interest in the settlement but—

    (i)   was not domiciled in the State, and

    (ii)   was neither resident nor ordinarily resident in the State,

in that year of assessment, or when the settlor made the settlement (TCA 1997, s 579A(2)).

Where, for the year of assessment 2002 or any subsequent year, chargeable gains are treated as accruing to a beneficiary under a settlement by virtue of TCA 1997, s 579, such chargeable gains will, notwithstanding that section, be treated as accruing to the settlor in relation to the settlement and not to any other person, if the settlor is resident or ordinarily resident in the State, whether or not the settlor is the beneficiary (TCA 1997, s 579A(2)(f)).

Computation of offshore income gain

Where a person makes a *material disposal* (a disposal of a material interest in a non-qualifying offshore fund), it is necessary first to calculate the *unindexed gain* (or "Part 1 gain") being the chargeable gain, ignoring any relief in respect of indexation ("the indexation allowance") in accordance with TCA 1997, s 556 (TCA 1997 Sch 20 Part 1). No relief is allowed under TCA 1997, s 600 (transfer of business to a company) in calculating the amount of the unindexed gain. Where the computation results in a loss, the disposal is treated as giving rise to neither a gain nor a loss.

Where the interest was acquired or is treated (see below) as acquired before 6 April 1990, the computation is carried out by reference to a deemed cost, without indexation, equal to the market value of the interest at 6 April 1990. The gain resulting from this disposal is referred to as *the gain since the 6th day of April 1990*.

Where the interest was acquired on or after 6 April 1990 in circumstances in which the previous owner was treated as realising neither a gain nor a loss (apart from a case in which a no gain/ no loss result was applied by the indexation rules – TCA 1997, s 556(4)), the purchaser is treated as having acquired the interest at the same time as that previous owner. This treatment is repeated through any number of previous acquisitions in similar circumstances until the first acquisition before 6 April 1990 or, as the case may be, until an acquisition on a material disposal on or after that date is reached. If the gain arising since 6 April 1990 (based on the deemed acquisition of the interest at market value on that date) is less than the unindexed gain on the disposal, the offshore income gain is treated as being an amount equal to the gain since 6 April 1990.

Where a disposal involves an equalisation element (see below), the "Part 1 gain" is the amount which would be the offshore income gain on that disposal if it were a material disposal calculated in accordance with that Part (TCA 1997 Sch 20 paragraph 8(1)).

For the purposes only of determining the amount of any Part I gain on a disposal involving an equalisation element, there is to be treated as a disposal any event which is normally regarded as taking place at no gain/no loss by virtue of certain enactments (TCA 1997 Sch 20 paragraph 8(2)). These enactments are TCA 1997, s 584(3) (reorganisation or reduction of a company's share capital), TCA 1997, s 733 (reorganisation of units in a unit trust scheme) and TCA 1997, s 585 (conversion of securities).

If a disposal involving an equalisation element is one in respect of which the person making the disposal is treated by any enactment (apart from a case in which a no gain/ no loss result was applied by the indexation rules – TCA 1997, s 556(4)) as realising neither a gain nor a loss, that enactment is not to apply for the purposes of determining the Part I gain, if any, on the disposal (TCA 1997 Sch 20(3)).

The amount of the offshore income gain arising on a material disposal is the amount of the unindexed gain on that disposal (Part 1 gain). Where, however, "the gain since the 6th day of April 1990" is less than "the unindexed gain" on the disposal, the offshore income gain is an amount equal to the former amount.

3.210.4 Disposal involving an equalisation element

Where a disposal is made by an offshore fund which is operating equalisation arrangements, it is treated as giving rise to an offshore income gain of an amount equal to the "equalisation element" relevant to the asset disposed of.

Where equalisation arrangements are in operation, part of the price paid by an investor for an interest in the fund is in respect of the right to receive the income element which has accrued in the period from the last distribution date to the acquisition date. On the next distribution date, the investor will receive a distribution equal to that made to all other participants in the fund; in effect, that distribution will include a part refund ("equalisation element") of the amount paid by the investor to acquire his interest. That element is not treated for tax purposes as an income receipt.

When the interest of the investor is ultimately redeemed by the fund, the interest disposed of will include the income element accruing from the last distribution date to the date of disposal. (That element is a part of the next distribution; the price paid by a new investor acquiring the interest of the first investor will include an amount for the right to receive the pre-acquisition part of the next distribution, in the same way as the purchase price paid by the first investor included such an amount – see above.) As this equalisation element is received as part of the disposal proceeds, it would normally be treated as part of a capital receipt. The offshore funds legislation, however, treats the equalisation element as income chargeable to tax under Case IV of Schedule D. The legislation applies only to the equalisation element at the time of *disposal*.

The income element purchased by an investor in an offshore fund is credited to an equalisation account. On the occasion of the next distribution, an equivalent sum is debited to the equalisation account. As already noted, this element is not treated as income of the investor for tax purposes; it is instead deducted from the capital gains tax cost base as a return of capital.

TCA 1997, s 742(1) provides that an offshore fund is regarded as operating *equalisation arrangements* if, and at a time when, arrangements are in existence which have the result that where:

(a)　a person acquires by way of initial purchase a material interest in the fund at some time *during* a period relevant to the arrangements; and

(b)　the fund makes a distribution for a period which begins *before* the date of the acquisition of that interest,

the amount of the distribution paid to the person, if he still retains the material interest, will include a payment of capital which is debited to an account ("the equalisation account") maintained under the arrangements and which is determined by reference to the income which *had* accrued to the fund at the date of his acquisition.

An acquisition by way of initial purchase in a fund is an acquisition by way of subscription for, or allotment of, new shares, units or other interests issued or created by the fund, or an acquisition by way of direct purchase from the persons concerned with the management of the fund (*the managers of the fund*) where the sale by them is made in their capacity as managers of the fund.

The equalisation element is the amount which would be credited to the fund's equalisation account in respect of accrued income if, on the date of the disposal, the asset disposed of were acquired by another person by way of initial purchase (TCA 1997 Sch 20 paragraph 6(2)). When an interest in an offshore fund is redeemed, the same interest will not in practice be acquired at the same time by another person. The "accrued income" is therefore reckoned on the assumption that another investor immediately subscribes for the same interest by way of subscription for, or allotment of, new shares, units or other interests issued or created by the fund, or by way of acquisition from the managers of the fund. In that case, the accrued income element would be credited to the equalisation account. The above amount may, however, fall to be reduced in the following circumstances.

Where the person disposing of the interest had purchased it after the beginning of the period by reference to which the accrued income is calculated, the equalisation element may be reduced by the following amount:

(a)　where the interest was acquired on or after 6 April 1990, the amount which at the acquisition date was credited to the equalisation account in respect of accrued income or, in the case of an acquisition by way of additional purchase, the amount which would have been credited if the acquisition had been an initial purchase; and

(b) in any other case, the amount which would have been credited to that account in respect of accrued income if that acquisition had been an acquisition by way of initial purchase on 6 April 1990 (TCA 1997 Sch 20 paragraph 6(4)).

Where the period by reference to which the accrued income is calculated began before 6 April 1990 and ended after that date, and the interest was acquired by the person making the disposal at or before the beginning of that period, the equalisation element is reduced by the amount which would have been credited to the equalisation account in respect of accrued income as if the acquisition had been an initial purchase on 6 April 1990 (TCA 1997 Sch 20 paragraph 6(5)).

To the extent that the accrued income amount represents profits from dealing in commodities (tangible assets dealt with on a commodity exchange in any part of the world other than currency, securities, debts or other assets of a financial nature), 50% of the accrued income is left out of account in determining the equalisation element (TCA 1997 Sch 20 paragraph 6(6)).

If a disposal involving an equalisation element does not result in an unindexed gain ("Part 1 gain"), no offshore income gain arises. If the offshore income gain on a disposal involving an equalisation element would otherwise exceed the Part I gain on that disposal, the offshore income gain is to be reduced to an amount equal to the Part I gain (TCA 1997 Sch 20 paragraph 7).

As mentioned above (see *Computation of offshore income gain* in **3.210.3** above), where a disposal involves an equalisation element, the "Part 1 gain" is the amount which would be the offshore income gain on that disposal if it were a material disposal calculated in accordance with Part 1. Transactions treated for capital gains tax purposes as taking place at no gain/ no loss (TCA 1997, s 584(3) – reorganisation or reduction of a company's share capital, TCA 1997, s 733 – reorganisation of units in a unit trust scheme, or TCA 1997, s 585 – conversion of securities) are treated as disposals for this purpose (TCA 1997, s 742(5), (6)).

3.210.5 Qualifying offshore funds

A distributing fund may be referred to as a qualifying offshore fund (in contrast to a non-qualifying offshore fund). It is a fund which:

(a) is certified by the Revenue Commissioners as a "distributing" fund in that it has satisfied the "distribution test", requiring "a full distribution policy", provided for in TCA 1997 Sch 19 Part 1; and

(b) satisfies the following conditions of TCA 1997, s 744(3), namely that—

 (i) not more than 5% of the fund's total assets in value may consist of interests in other offshore funds,

 (ii) not more than 10% of the fund's total assets in value may consist of interests in a single company,

 (iii) not more than 10% of the issued share capital, or of any class of the share capital, of a single company may be included in the fund's assets, and

 (iv) if there is more than one class of material interest in the offshore fund, they all receive proper distribution benefits.

These conditions are dealt with in more detail under the heading of **3.210.3** above. The distribution test is applied in respect of an "account period". The circumstances in which an account period may begin and end are set out in TCA 1997, s 744(8)-(10). An account period begins on 6 April 1990 or, if later, when the offshore fund begins to carry on its activities, as well as immediately following the end of any previous account period. An account period ends at the earliest of:

(a)   12 months after the beginning of the account period;

(b)   the accounting date of the offshore fund; and

(c)   the date of cessation of the fund's activities.

An account period of a non-resident company ends when the company becomes resident in the State.

The distribution test

An offshore fund is regarded by TCA 1997 Sch 19 paragraph 1(1) as pursuing "a full distribution policy" with respect to an account period if a distribution is made for that period and the distribution:

(a)   represents at least 85% of the income of the fund for the period;

(b)   is not less than 85% of the fund's Irish equivalent profits for the period;

(c)   is made in such form that if any sum forming part of it were received by an Irish resident (otherwise than as trading income) it would be taxable under Case III of Schedule D; and

(d)   is made during or within six months of the end of the account period.

An offshore fund which has no income, and no Irish equivalent profits, for an account period is regarded as pursuing a full distribution policy. Where a fund does not make up accounts for an account period, it is regarded as not pursuing a full distribution policy.

TCA 1997 Sch 19 paragraph 1(4) deals with situations in which an accounting period contains two or more account periods by providing that:

(i)   the income shown in the accounts of the fund must be apportioned on a time basis between those account periods; and

(ii)   a distribution made for a period which includes two or more account periods must be apportioned between those periods on a time basis.

Where a distribution is made out of specified income, but not for a specified period, it must be attributed to the account period in which it actually arose. Accordingly, the distribution will be regarded as made for the account period in which it arose. If the distribution is made neither out of specified income nor for a specified period, it is treated as made for the last account period before the distribution is made.

If the distribution for an accounting period exceeds the income for that period and it was made for a period which included two or more account periods, so that it would be apportioned between the two account periods on a time basis, the excess amount must be reapportioned, as may be just and reasonable, to any another account period (or if there is more than one such period, between those periods) which falls wholly or partly within the accounting period for which the distribution was made. The excess amount is then treated as an additional distribution, or series of distributions, for preceding account periods in respect of which the distributions or aggregate distributions, as the case may be, would otherwise be less than the income of the period. The excess is to be applied to later periods before earlier ones until it is used up (TCA 1997 Sch 19 paragraph 1(5)).

Offshore funds which are restricted by the law of any foreign territory, by reason of an excess of losses over profits, as regards the making of distributions for a period which is or includes an account period, are permitted a deduction, in determining the amount of their income for the period, for any amount which cannot be distributed by reason of the restriction (TCA 1997 Sch 19 paragraph 1(6)).

Where an offshore fund operating equalisation arrangements is treated as making a distribution (see *Distribution test: disposals involving equalisation element* below), the distribution is treated as complying with condition (c) above (TCA 1997 Sch 19 paragraph 2). For the purposes of the 85% of income and 85% of Irish equivalent profits tests (conditions (a) and (b)), distributions made by offshore funds operating equalisation arrangements to the managers of the fund, in their capacity as managers, are ignored.

Distribution test: Irish equivalent profits

Irish equivalent profits of an offshore fund for an account period is defined in TCA 1997 Sch 19 paragraph 5(2) as the total profits of the fund (excluding chargeable gains), after allowing for any deductions available against those profits (see below), on which corporation tax would be chargeable on the assumption that:

(a) the fund is an Irish resident company in the period;

(b) the account period is an accounting period of the company;

(c) any dividends or other distributions receivable by the company from Irish resident companies and which would normally be left out of account in computing income for corporation tax purposes would nevertheless be brought into account in that computation as if they were dividends or distributions of a non-resident company.

It is specifically provided that interest referred to in TCA 1997, s 43, 49, 50 or 63 on Irish government, local authority etc securities, which has been received without deduction of tax is to be included in Irish equivalent profits (TCA 1997 Sch 19 paragraph 5(5)).

The deductions available against profits include:

(i) a deduction equal to any amount which is allowed as a deduction in determining the fund's income by reason of being prevented by the law of a foreign territory from distributing that amount (see above under *The distribution test*);

(ii) any amount of Irish income tax paid by way of withholding tax or otherwise (but not including any tax credit to which the fund is entitled) in respect of the income of the account period in question, provided the tax has not been repaid to the fund; and

(iii) a deduction in respect of foreign tax which was taken into account in calculating the income of the fund for the account period in question, but which because it is referable to capital rather than income, is not taken into account by virtue of TCA 1997, s 71(1) or TCA 1997, s 77(6) where the income was not remitted to the State.

Distribution test: disposals involving equalisation element

Although the offshore funds legislation applies to disposals of material interests in non-qualifying funds, it applies also to disposals of material interests in qualifying offshore funds which operate equalisation arrangements. A disposal of this kind is treated as giving rise to an offshore income gain of an amount equal to the "equalisation element" relevant to the asset disposed of.

Where an offshore fund operating equalisation arrangements is treated as making a distribution, the distribution is treated as complying with condition (c) above (TCA 1997 Sch 19 paragraph 2). This treatment applies to disposals in the following circumstances:

(a)   the disposal is of a material interest in the fund;

(b)   the disposal is one to which—

    (i)   the offshore funds legislation applies, whether or not by a qualifying offshore fund operating equalisation arrangements or otherwise, or

    (ii)   the offshore funds legislation would apply generally if a reorganisation or reduction of a company's share capital within TCA 1997, s 584(3), a reorganisation of units in a unit trust scheme within TCA 1997, s 733, or a conversion of securities within TCA 1997, s 585, constituted a disposal,

(c)   the disposal is not one in respect of which, during the period relevant to the equalisation arrangements and before the disposal, the income of the offshore fund (other than an offshore fund which is a non-resident company) is Case III income or is income in the nature of Case III income (see below); and

(d)   the disposal is one which is to the fund itself or to the managers of the fund in their capacity as such.

Income which is in the nature of Case III income, for the purposes of (c) above, is income of such a nature that if it arose:

(i)   to companies resident in the State or to individuals resident and domiciled in the State in respect of holdings of interests in the fund—

    (I)   would be chargeable to tax under Case III of Schedule D, or

    (II)   would be chargeable to tax under Case III on the assumption that any of that income deriving from assets within the State had derived from assets outside the State, and

(ii)   if it arose to the holders of interests which are not such companies or individuals, would be chargeable under Case III as above if they were resident or, in the case of individuals, domiciled, resident and ordinarily resident, in the State.

The amount representing "income accrued to the date of the disposal" in TCA 1997 Sch 19 paragraph 2(1) is the amount which would be credited to the equalisation account of the offshore fund in respect of accrued income if, on the date of disposal, the material interest disposed of were acquired by another person by way of initial purchase (TCA 1997 Sch 19 paragraph 2(3)). This provision is necessary as, when an interest in an offshore fund is redeemed, the same interest will not in practice be acquired at the same time by another person. The "accrued income" is therefore reckoned on the assumption that another investor immediately subscribes for the same interest by way of subscription for, or allotment of, new shares, units or other interests issued or created by the fund, or by way of acquisition from the managers of the fund. In that case, the accrued income element would be credited to the equalisation account.

Where an interest in an offshore fund which was acquired by way of initial purchase is disposed of as above, the amount which would represent income accrued up to the date of the disposal must be reduced by the amount which on that acquisition was credited to the equalisation account of the fund as accrued income. If, in the period during which the accrued income is calculated, there has been more than one material interest acquisition by way of initial purchase, the deduction to be made is the amount credited to the equalisation account on the last such acquisition before the disposal in question (TCA 1997 Sch 19 paragraph 2(4)).

A distribution treated as having been made by an offshore fund in the circumstances of TCA 1997 Sch 19 paragraph 2, as described above, is treated for those purposes as:

(a) chargeable to tax under Case III of Schedule D (if received by an Irish resident person otherwise than as trading income);

(b) paid out of the fund's income for the account period in which the disposal occurs; and

(c) paid immediately before the disposal to the person who was then the holder of the interest disposed of (TCA 1997 Sch 19 paragraph 2(5)).

For the purposes of the 85% of income and 85% of Irish equivalent profits tests, distributions made by offshore funds operating equalisation arrangements to the managers of the fund, in their capacity as managers, are ignored (TCA 1997 Sch 19 paragraph 2(6)).

Distribution test: income taxable under Case III

TCA 1997 Sch 19 paragraph 3 refers to the income of an offshore fund (other than an offshore fund which is a non-resident company) which is Case III income or is income in the nature of Case III income (see below). If sums forming part of such income do not actually form part of a distribution complying with conditions (c) and (d) in the distribution test (see above), they will be deemed to have satisfied those conditions and to have been made out of the income of which they form part and as having been paid to the holders of the interests to which they are referable.

Income which is in the nature of Case III income for the above purpose is income of such a nature that if it arose:

(a) to companies resident in the State or to individuals resident and domiciled in the State in respect of holdings of interests in the fund—

(i) would be chargeable to tax under Case III of Schedule D, or

(ii) would be chargeable to tax under Case III on the assumption that any of that income deriving from assets within the State had derived from assets outside the State, and

(b) if it arose to the holders of interests which are not such companies or individuals, would be chargeable under Case III as above if they were resident or, in the case of individuals, domiciled, resident and ordinarily resident, in the State.

Distribution test: commodity income

Where an offshore fund derives profits for any account period from dealing in commodities (tangible assets dealt with on a commodity exchange in any part of the world other than currency, securities, debts or other assets of a financial nature), 50% of those profits are left out of account in determining the fund's income and Irish equivalent profits for the period, for the purposes of (a) and (b) in the distribution test respectively (85% of income and of Irish equivalent profits) and for the purposes of ascertaining the Irish equivalent profits. *Dealing* includes dealing by way of futures contracts and traded options (TCA 1997 Sch 19 paragraph 4).

An offshore fund which has income from dealing in commodities and other income for an account period may, for the purposes of the 85% tests in (a) and (b), apportion its expenditure between profits from dealing in commodities and other income in such a manner as is just and reasonable. In determining how much, if any, by way of management expenses under TCA 1997, s 83 is deductible in arriving at the amount of the Irish equivalent profits, the part of the business of the fund which does not consist of dealing in commodities is to be treated as a business carried on by a separate company.

In the case of a disposal by an offshore fund which operates equalisation arrangements and where any amount which was or could have been credited to the equalisation account in respect of accrued income represents profits from dealing in commodities, a deduction of one-half of that accrued income is also made in determining the part of the disposal consideration representing income accrued to the date of disposal.

Offshore income gains: equalisation element

Although the offshore funds legislation applies to disposals of material interests in non-qualifying funds, it also applies to a disposal of a material interest in a qualifying offshore fund which operates "equalisation arrangements". Where a disposal of this kind takes place, it is treated as giving rise to an offshore income gain of an amount equal to the "equalisation element" relevant to the asset disposed of. The equalisation element, as noted above, is the amount which would be credited to the fund's equalisation account in respect of accrued income if, on the date of the disposal, the asset disposed of were acquired by another person by way of initial purchase.

Where a qualifying offshore fund operates equalisation arrangements, the charge to tax under Case IV applies to the equalisation element included in any disposal of a material interest in that fund (TCA 1997 Sch 20 paragraph 6(1)). The charge does not apply in cases where the disposal proceeds fall to be taken into account as a trading receipt. The charge to tax in the case of qualifying offshore funds is without prejudice to the Case IV liability applying to non-qualifying offshore funds.

3.210.6 Switching

The switching of investments between different offshore funds and between different sub-funds of an offshore umbrella fund can in many cases be effected without liability to tax under Case IV. The position can be summarised as follows:

Offshore fund	Switches between sub-funds	Switches between funds
Unit-linked fund		
(no offshore income gain – TCA 1997, s 743(5))	Not taxable	Not taxable
Other non-corporate funds	Taxable	Taxable
Corporate funds (TCA 1997 ss 583, 585-587, 733)		
Distributor funds (no offshore income gain)	Not taxable	Not taxable
Distributor funds (equalisation element)	Not taxable[1]	Taxable[1]
Non-distributable funds	Not taxable[3]	Taxable[2]

Notes:

[1]   TCA 1997, s 742(6): Relief for switches between sub-funds on basis of TCA 1997, s 585 (conversion of securities). No relief for inter-fund switches.

[2]   TCA 1997, s 741(5), (6): No relief for inter-fund switches.

[3]   TCA 1997, s 741(5), (6): Relief available for disposals within TCA 1997, s 585.

3.210.7   Deduction of offshore income gains in determining capital gains

To prevent a double charge to tax, the amount of the offshore income gain is deducted from the consideration for the capital gains tax disposal in circumstances where a disposal resulting in an offshore income gain also gives rise to a capital gain (TCA 1997, s 747(3)). For the purposes of offshore income gains, this provision replaces a similar provision in TCA 1997, s 551 (exclusion from consideration for disposals of sums chargeable to income tax). In the case of a part disposal, however, no deduction is made in respect of an offshore income gain (TCA 1997, s 747(4)).

TCA 1997, s 747 makes other provisions for the avoidance of double taxation in cases of disposals in respect of which there is no chargeable gain at the time of disposal, where the chargeable gain is deferred under certain provisions in TCA 1997 ss 583, 585-587, 600 and 733.

TCA 1997, s 600 deals with the situation in which a person other than a company transfers a business as a going concern to a company wholly or partly in exchange for shares issued to that person by the company. In that case, the chargeable gain arising on the disposal of the chargeable assets being transferred is apportioned, on the basis of market value, between the value of the shares issued and the value of any other consideration (cash, loan account or other assets). The part of the gain apportioned to the other consideration is subject to capital gains tax in the normal way while the part apportioned to the value of the shares is not assessed but is instead deducted from the allowable cost for the purpose of calculating a gain or loss on the ultimate disposal of the shares. Capital gains tax on that part of the gain is therefore deferred.

Where a disposal of a material interest in a non-qualifying offshore fund forms part of a transfer to which TCA 1997, s 600 applies and part of the consideration is in a form other than shares, a proportionate part of that gain cannot be deferred. In that case, the value of the consideration received by the transferor in exchange for the business is reduced by deducting, from the consideration other than in the form of shares, an amount equal to the offshore income gain (TCA 1997, s 747(5)).

In computing the amount of an offshore income gain, the deferral relief provided by TCA 1997, s 586 (company amalgamations by exchange of shares – see **9.404**) does not apply in the case of a disposal of a material interest in a non-qualifying offshore fund; instead there is a deemed disposal at market value (see *Disposal of material interest* in **3.210.3** above). In any such case, an amount equal to the offshore income gain is treated as consideration given for the new holding, to be deducted in calculating the gain or loss on a subsequent disposal of that holding (TCA 1997, s 747(6)).

As mentioned above under the heading *Computation of offshore income gain* in **3.210.3**, a disposal involving an equalisation element and which is treated for capital gains tax purposes as taking place at no gain/ no loss (TCA 1997, s 584(3) – reorganisation or reduction of a company's share capital, TCA 1997, s 733 – reorganisation of units in a unit trust scheme, or TCA 1997, s 585 – conversion of securities) is treated as a disposal for the purpose of computing a "Part 1 gain" (TCA 1997, s 742(5), (6)). In that case also, an amount equal to the offshore income gain is treated as consideration given for the new holding, to be deducted in calculating the gain or loss on a subsequent disposal of that holding (TCA 1997, s 747(6)).

Where there is a disposal (otherwise than to the offshore fund in question, or to the managers of the fund in their capacity as such) of an interest in an offshore fund which operates equalisation arrangements (so that a tax charge has been made in respect of the equalisation element included in the disposal proceeds) and a distribution referable to the asset disposed of is subsequently made to the person who made the disposal, or to a person connected with him (see **2.3**), the amount of the distribution is to be reduced by an amount equal to the offshore income gain. If that amount exceeds the amount of the first distribution, the balance is to be set against any subsequent distribution until that balance is used up (TCA 1997, s 747(7)).

3.210.8 Capital gains tax rate

A chargeable gain arising on the disposal, on or after 12 February 1998, of a material interest in an offshore fund which is not a non-qualifying offshore fund, or of an interest in certain resident companies and unit trust schemes, is subject to capital gains tax at a rate of 40%.

TCA 1997, s 747A(4) provides that, notwithstanding TCA 1997, s 28(3) (capital gains tax rate), the rate of capital gains tax in respect of capital gains accruing to a person on the disposal of an asset to which TCA 1997, s 747A applies is to be 40%. TCA 1997, s 747A applies to a disposal on or after 12 February 1998 by a person of an asset if at the time of the disposal:

(a) the asset constitutes a material interest in an offshore fund which is not and was not at any material time a non-qualifying offshore fund; or

(b) the asset constitutes an interest in a company resident in the State or in a unit trust scheme the trustees of which are at that time resident in the State, and at a material time on or after 1 January 1991 the company or unit trust scheme was an offshore fund other than a non-qualifying offshore fund and the asset constituted a material interest in that fund (TCA 1997, s 747A(2)).

The provisions of TCA 1997, s 741(2)-(9) apply for the purposes of TCA 1997, s 747A as if references there to a non-qualifying offshore fund were references to an offshore fund. For the provisions of these subsections, see *Disposal of material interest* in **13.210.3** above.

3.210.9   Returns of material interest in offshore funds

As respects a material interest in an offshore fund, TCA 1997, s 895 (returns in relation to foreign accounts – see **15.104.5**) is to apply, with any necessary modifications, where it would not otherwise apply to:

(a)   every person carrying on in the State a trade or business in the ordinary course of the operations of which such person acts as an intermediary in, or in connection with, the acquisition of such an interest in the same manner as it applies to every intermediary within the meaning of TCA 1997, s 895(1); and

(b)   to a person resident or ordinarily resident in the State who acquires such an interest, in the same manner as it applies to a person resident in the State opening an account, in which a deposit which he beneficially owns is held, at a location outside the State,

as if in TCA 1997, s 895:

(i)   references to a deposit were references to any payment made by a person resident or ordinarily resident in the State in acquiring a material interest in an offshore fund;

(ii)   references to a foreign account were references to such an interest;

(iii)   references, however expressed, to the opening of a foreign account were references to the acquisition of such an interest; and

(iv)   references to a relevant person were references to an offshore fund.

For the above purposes, *offshore fund* has the meaning assigned to it in TCA 1997, s 743(1) (see above) except that a relevant UCITS within the meaning of TCA 1997, s 893(1) (see **12.809**) is not to be regarded as an offshore fund (TCA 1997, s 896(1)).

3.210.10 Certain offshore funds: taxation and returns

With effect from 1 January 2001, a new system of taxing persons who hold an interest in certain offshore funds came into force (TCA 1997, Part 27 Chapter 4). Whereas previously the gain on disposal of such an interest could be liable to capital gains tax at the rate of 40% (TCA 1997, s 747A(4) – see **3.210.8**) or to income tax in the case of an individual, a new rate of 23% applies in respect of persons other than companies; the 25% corporation tax rate applies in the case of companies. In the cases of interests in offshore funds not covered by the new system, the 40% capital gains rate continues to apply. The 2001 regime was introduced to match a similar regime introduced in 2000 for collective funds in Ireland (as dealt with in **12.806**).

The offshore funds to which the new system applies are those based in an EU Member State other than Ireland, a Member State of the EEA, or a member of the OECD and with which Ireland has a tax treaty.

Irish residents acquiring an interest in offshore funds to which the new regime applies are deemed to be chargeable persons for self-assessment purposes and are required to include details of the acquisition in their tax returns. Profits from the investment in these funds are taxed at the 23% rate of tax (20% in the case of an income payment) or, in the case of a company, at 25%. (The 23% rate is also the exit tax rate applying to investment in domestic collective funds – see **12.806.8**.) The 23% rate or, in the case of companies, the 25% rate, only applies where details of the payment from the offshore fund are included in a tax return made on time by the person; otherwise, the 40% capital gains rate or, as the case may be, tax on income at the appropriate rate, applies.

Definitions

TCA 1997, s 747B contains a number of definitions. A *deemed disposal* is a disposal of the type provided for in TCA 1997, s 747E(6) (see below under *Disposal of an interest in an offshore fund*).

Offshore fund has the meaning assigned to it in TCA 1997, s 743(1) (see **3.210.1**). TCA 1997 Part 27 Chapter 4 applies to an offshore fund which:

(a)   being a company, the company is resident in;

(b)   being a unit trust scheme, the trustees of the unit trust scheme are resident in; or

(c)   being any arrangements referred to in TCA 1997, s 743(1) (any arrangements not within (a) or (b) taking effect under foreign law and under which rights in the nature of co-ownership are created - see **3.210.1**), those arrangements take effect by virtue of the law of,

an offshore state (TCA 1997, s 747B(2)).

An *offshore state* is a state other than the State which is:

(i)   a Member State of the European Communities;

(ii)   a state which is an EEA state; or

(iii) a state which is a member of the OECD, the government of which has entered into a tax treaty with Ireland.

OECD means the organisation known as the Organisation for Economic Co-operation and Development.

EEA state means a state, other than the State, which is a Contracting party to the EEA Agreement. *EEA Agreement* means the Agreement on the European Economic Area signed at Oporto on 2 May 1992, as adjusted by the Protocol signed at Brussels on 17 March 1993.

TCA 1997 Part 27, Chapter 4 does not, however, apply to an offshore fund other than an offshore fund which—

(a)   (i)   is an undertaking for collective investment formed under the law of an offshore state,

       (ii)   is similar in all material respects to an investment limited partnership (within the meaning of the Investment Limited Partnership Act 1994 – see **12.802.1** and **12.802.5**), and

(iii) holds a certificate authorising it to act as such an undertaking, being a certificate issued by the authorities of that state under laws providing for the proper and orderly regulation of such undertakings,

(b) is a fund which is authorised by or under any measures duly taken by a Member State for the purposes of giving effect to—

    (i) Council Directive 85/611/EEC on the coordination of laws, regulations and administrative provisions relating to undertakings for collective investment in transferable securities (UCITS), or

    (ii) any amendment to that Directive,

(c) (i) is a company formed under the law of an offshore state,

    (ii) is similar in all material respects to an authorised investment company (within the meaning of Part XIII of the Companies Act 1990 - see **12.801**, **12.802.4**),

    (iii) holds an authorisation issued by the authorities of that state under laws providing for the proper and orderly regulation of such companies and that authorisation has not ceased to have effect, and

    (iv) is an investment company—

        (I) which raises capital by promoting the sale of its shares to the public, or

        (II) each of the shareholders of which is an investor which, if the company were an authorised investment company within the meaning of Part XIII of the Companies Act 1990 would be a collective investor (see **12.802.4**) within the meaning of section 739B, or

(d) (i) is a unit trust scheme, the trustees of which are not resident in the State,

    (ii) is similar in all material respects to an authorised unit trust scheme (within the meaning of the Unit Trusts Act 1990 - see **12.802.2**),

    (iii) holds an authorisation issued by the authorities of that offshore state under laws providing for the proper and orderly regulation of such schemes and that authorisation has not ceased to have effect, and

    (iv) provides facilities for the participation by the public, as beneficiaries under the trust, in profits or income arising from the acquisition, holding, management or disposal of securities or any other property whatsoever (TCA 1997, s 747B(2A)).

This provision is a modification of the tax treatment of certain offshore funds created under legislation of EU and EEA Member States and certain OECD countries. The general rules applying to offshore funds, and which ensure that income from such funds is appropriately taxed, are contained in TCA 1997, Part 27. However, special rules, comparable to those applying to collective funds in the State, apply in relation to offshore funds in EU and EEA Member States and certain OECD countries. These involve payments from the fund to an individual being taxed at 23% where they are included in the individual's tax return, or otherwise at the individual's marginal tax rate.

The effect of the modification is that these special rules will apply only to an offshore fund that is similar in all material respects to domestic "gross roll up" funds, therefore in practice being confined to four categories of offshore fund, ie an investment limited partnership, a UCITS, an investment company or a unit trust scheme. Offshore funds that are denied the special treatment provided for by Chapter 4 by reason only of this exclusion are, from 20 February 2007, no longer subject to the offshore funds legislation in any respect so that their income and gains are taxable in accordance with general taxation principles similarly to the position applying to Irish entities outside the scope of the domestic "gross roll up" regime. Capital gains are subject to capital gains tax at the 20% rather than the 40% rate.

Without prejudice to the meaning, in TCA 1997, s 743 (see **3.210.1**), of "offshore fund" for the purposes of TCA 1997, Part 27 Chapter 4, where by reason of the above-described exclusion that Chapter does not apply to an offshore fund (ie, the fund is denied the special treatment provided for by Chapter 4 because not included as one of the entities listed in (a) to (d) above), TCA 1997, Chapter 2 and s 747A (see **3.210.8**) will not apply in respect of that fund (TCA 1997, s 747AA). Accordingly, neither the offshore fund provisions generally nor the 40% capital gains tax rate will apply. The entities in question are unregulated companies and co-ownership arrangements and partnerships in an EU Member State, an EEA state, or a member of the OECD with which Ireland has a double taxation agreement.

TCA 1997, ss 747B(2A) and 747AA apply in respect of income arising and gains accruing on or after 20 February 2007 but certain "grandfathering" provisions apply to material interests in certain offshore funds (unless they would have been deemed to be personal portfolio investment undertakings) held on that date.

Material interest is to be construed in accordance with TCA 1997, s 743 (see **3.210.1**).

A *relevant event* in relation to an offshore fund is the ending of a relevant period, where *relevant period* means a period of eight years beginning with the acquisition of a material interest in the fund and each subsequent period of eight years beginning immediately after the preceding relevant period.

A *relevant payment is* any payment, including a distribution, made to a person in respect of a material interest in an offshore fund where such payments are made annually or at more frequent intervals, other than a payment made in consideration of the disposal of an interest in an offshore fund.

Payment in respect of offshore funds

With effect on and from 1 January 2001, a person, other than a company, who has a material interest in an offshore fund and who receives a payment from the offshore fund is subject to tax as follows. If the income represented by the payment is correctly included in a return of income made on time, the income is taxable:

(i) where the payment is a relevant payment—

(I) in the case of an offshore fund which is a personal portfolio investment undertaking (see **12.806.8**), at the rate determined by the formula: (S + 23) per cent – where s is the standard rate per cent for the year of assessment in which the payment is made, and

(II) in any other case, the standard rate per cent; and

(ii)   where the payment is not a relevant payment and is not made in consideration of the disposal of an interest in the offshore fund—

    (I)   in the case of an offshore fund which is a personal portfolio investment undertaking, at the rate determined by the formula: $(S + 23)$ per cent – where s is the standard rate per cent for the year of assessment in which the payment is made, and

(II)   in any other case, at a rate determined by the formula: $(S + 3)$ per cent – where s is the standard rate per cent (TCA 1997, s 747D(a)(i)).

If the income represented by the payment is not correctly included in a return of income made on time, it is taxable—

(a)   in the case of an offshore fund which is a personal portfolio investment undertaking, at the rate determined by the formula: $(H + 20)$ per cent – where H is the rate per cent determined in relation to the person by TCA 1997, s 15 (the marginal rate of income tax applying) for the year of assessment in which the payment is made, and

(b)   in any other case, at a rate determined by TCA 1997, s 15 (TCA 1997, s 747D(a)(ii)).

In the case of a company with an interest in an offshore fund and which receives a payment from that fund, and where the payment is not taken into account as a receipt of a trade carried on by the company, the income represented by the payment is chargeable to tax under Case III of Schedule D (TCA 1997, s 747D(b)). Accordingly, the rate at which the income is taxed is 25% (see **3.101.4**). The above exception refers to an investor which is a company carrying on a financial trade where the investment is part of its "trading stock". That company will be taxable on any payment arising from its investment at the corporation tax rate appropriate to trading profits (and not at the 25% rate applicable to income taxable under Case III of Schedule D).

Disposal of an interest in an offshore fund

With effect on and from 1 January 2001, where a person having a material interest in an offshore fund disposes of an interest in the fund and the disposal results in a gain computed as described below, and except where the gain is taken into account in computing the profits or gains of a trade carried on by a company, the gain is treated as an amount of income chargeable to tax under Case IV of Schedule D, and—

(a)   where the person is a company, notwithstanding TCA 1997, s 21A(3) (25% corporation tax rate – see **3.101.4**), the rate of corporation tax to be charged on that income is the rate determined by the formula: $(S + 3)$ per cent – where s is the standard rate per cent for the year of assessment in which the disposal is made, and

(b)   where the person is not a company and has correctly included details of the disposal in a return made, the rate of income tax to be charged on that income is, notwithstanding TCA 1997, s 15 (the marginal rate of income tax), the rate determined—

    (i)   in the case of an offshore fund which is a personal portfolio investment undertaking (see **12.806.8**), by the formula: $(S + 20)$ per cent – where s is the standard rate per cent for the year of assessment in which the disposal is made, and

(ii) in any other case, by the formula: $(S + 3)$ per cent – where s is the standard rate per cent (TCA 1997, s 747E(1)).

The above exception refers to an investor which is a company carrying on a financial trade where the investment is part of its "trading stock". That company will be taxable on any gain arising from its investment at the corporation tax rate appropriate to trading profits.

The amount of the gain accruing on a disposal of an interest in an offshore fund is the amount that would be computed for capital gains tax purposes but without regard to TCA 1997, s 556(2) (indexation – see **9.102.3**) (TCA 1997, s 747E(2)). Where, however, a capital gains computation would result in a loss, and notwithstanding TCA 1997 ss 538 and 546 (assets lost or destroyed; negligible value; allowable losses – see **9.102.3**), a gain on the disposal of a foreign life policy is to be treated as nil and for the purposes of the Tax Acts and the Capital Gains Tax Acts no loss will be treated as accruing on the disposal (TCA 1997, s 747E(3)(a)).

The concept of a "deemed disposal" of a material interest in an offshore fund is explained in TCA 1997, s 747E(6). It is a disposal which is deemed to have been made when there is a relevant event (the ending of an eight-year period). Where there is such a deemed disposal, the owner of the material interest is deemed to have disposed of the whole of the material interest immediately before the time of that event and immediately to have reacquired it at its market value at that time.

Where, in respect of a material interest in an offshore fund:

(i) a gain on a disposal is treated as nil in accordance with TCA 1997, s 747E(3)(a);

(ii) that disposal is *not* a deemed disposal; and

(iii) a person was chargeable to tax in respect of an earlier deemed disposal of a material interest in the fund,

then the provisions of TCA 1997, s 865 (repayment of tax – see **15.204.2**), apart from subsection (4) (time within which a repayment claim may be made), are to apply and the inspector of taxes may make such repayment or set-off as is necessary to secure that the aggregate of tax payable in respect of the material interest does not exceed the tax that would have been payable if TCA 1997, s 747E(6) had not been enacted (TCA 1997, s 747E(3)(b)). Accordingly, where the computation discloses a loss, the overall tax payable in respect of the material interest is not to exceed the amount that would be payable on the assumption that there had not been a deemed disposal and reacquisition of that interest at market value at the time of the earlier event mentioned in (iii) above.

The above-described position relates to relevant events occurring on or after the date of the passing of FA 2006 in respect of a material interest in an offshore fund acquired on or after 1 January 2001.

Where, as a result of a disposal by a company, an amount of income is chargeable to tax under Case IV of Schedule D, that amount may not be reduced by a claim made by the company under TCA 1997, s 396 (see **4.101**), 396B (see **4.103**) or 399 (see **4.106**) (TCA 1997, s 747E(4)).

Scheme of reconstruction or amalgamation

Where an offshore fund is reconstructed or amalgamated, the cancellation of the original units will not result in a liability to tax and the cost of the new units is taken to be the cost of the old units. For this purpose, *scheme of reconstruction or amalgamation* means an arrangement under which each person having a material interest in an offshore fund (the "old interest") receives in place of that old interest a material interest in another offshore fund (the "new interest") in respect of or in proportion to, or as nearly as may be in proportion to, the value of the old interest and as a result of which the value of that old interest becomes negligible (TCA 1997, s 747F(1)).

Where, in connection with a scheme of reconstruction or amalgamation, a person disposes of an old interest and receives in place of that old interest a new interest, the disposal of the old interest will not give rise to a gain but the new interest will be treated for the purposes of TCA 1997, s 747E(2) (the amount to be computed for capital gains tax purposes – see above) as acquired at the same time and at the same cost as the old interest (TCA 1997, s 747F(2)).Returns on acquisition of foreign life policy

A person acquiring a material interest in an offshore fund in any chargeable period (a year of assessment or, in the case of a company, an accounting period – see **15.102.3**) is deemed to be a chargeable person for that period for the purposes of TCA 1997 ss 951 (obligation to make a return – see **15.104**) and 1084 (surcharge for late returns – see **15.103.5**). The return of income to be delivered for that period should include the following particulars:

(a) the name and address of the offshore fund;

(b) a description, including the cost to the person, of the material interest acquired; and

(c) the name and address of the person through whom the material interest was acquired (TCA 1997, s 747C).

3.211 Exchange of shares held as "trading stock"

3.211.1 Introduction

In a case where shares in a company are held as "trading stock" of a trader, any exchange of shares which occurs as part of a merger or reconstruction will not give rise to a tax charge at that time. This treatment is similar to that obtaining for capital gains tax purposes by virtue of TCA 1997 ss 584-587 (see **9.402-9.405**). Thus, an exchange of shares is treated as involving no disposal of shares and the new holding is equated with the original shares so that the charge to tax is deferred until such time as the new holding is disposed of. In the event of consideration other than shares being received for the original shares, a charge to tax arises at the time of the exchange in relation to that consideration.

3.211.2 Exchange of shares

TCA 1997, s 751A is concerned with transactions involving a disposal of shares (referred to as "original shares") in exchange for other shares (referred to as a "new holding"). A *new holding*, in relation to any original shares of a company, means the shares in and debentures of the company which as a result of the reorganisation or reduction of capital represent the original shares (including such, if any, of the original shares as remain). *Original shares* means shares held before and concerned in the reorganisation or reduction of capital (TCA 1997, s 584(1)). TCA 1997, s 751A applies in certain cases involving original shares:

(a)   to which a person carrying on a business consisting wholly or partly of dealing in securities is beneficially entitled; and

(b)   which are such that a profit on their sale would form part of the trading profits of that business (TCA 1997, s 751A(2)).

Specifically, TCA 1997, s 751A applies to any transaction, being a disposal of original shares which, if those shares were other than shares mentioned in TCA 1997, s 751A(2) (ie, not held as "trading stock" of a share dealer), would result in the disposal not being treated as a disposal by virtue of TCA 1997 ss 584–587 (see **9.402-9.405**).

3.211.3   Deferral of charge to tax

For the purposes of any computation of trading profits chargeable to tax under Case I of Schedule D, a transaction to which TCA 1997, s 751A applies (as described in **3.211.2** above) is treated as not involving any disposal of the original shares. The new holding is treated as the same asset as the original shares (TCA 1997, s 751A(4)).

     If the person disposing of the original shares receives or becomes entitled to receive any consideration in addition to the new holding, only a proportion of the original shares is treated as not having been disposed of at that time. That proportion is the proportion which the market value of the new holding at the time of the transaction bears to the aggregate of that value and the market value at that time (or, if it is cash, the cash amount) of that additional consideration (TCA 1997, s 751A(5)).

     The above-described treatment applies in a similar way in relation to any computation made for the purposes of TCA 1997, s 707(4) (restriction of relief for management expenses of a life assurance company – see **12.603.3**) where the original shares held by the company concerned and the new holding are treated as the same asset by virtue of any of TCA 1997 ss 584-587.

3.212   Stock lending/Sale and Repo transactions

3.212.1   Introduction

Stock lending and repo transactions involve the temporary transfer of stock or securities from one party to another with a simultaneous commitment to reverse the transaction at some point in the future. There is a difference between a stock loan and a repo transaction in that in the case of a repo contract there is an agreed return date whereas in a stock loan contract there is no pre-agreed return date. What follows below is based on a Revenue Statement of Practice first issued in 1999 and updated in 2001.

     From a tax viewpoint, there are two important aspects to stock lending and repo transactions:

Transfer of title

A key feature of these transactions is that there is a transfer of legal title which is later reversed on completion. If the taxation treatment of these transactions were to reflect their legal form, a charge to capital gains tax or income/corporation tax might arise. The substance of the transactions, however, is essentially one of lending.

Income receipts/payments

Where stock is on loan the borrower is normally entitled to any dividend/interest payments made since, as seen above, a transfer of legal title takes place so that the stock is held in the borrower's name. However, the borrower will normally be required to reimburse the lender for any dividend payments. The compensating payment which thereby arises is termed a "manufactured payment".

The effect of the reimbursement transaction is that the lender is put in the same position as if he had not loaned the stock and had received the real dividend, and the borrower as if he had not borrowed the stock and so received no dividend.

In stock lending transactions the profit earned by the lender will either be reflected in a small margin between the selling and repurchase price or in the form of a side fee paid by the borrower, depending on the particular circumstances.

3.212.2   Revenue approach

Arrangements have been agreed by the Revenue Commissioners to recognise the substance of these transactions, to tax only the accounting profit earned and, in general, to leave both the borrower and lender in the same position as if no stock loan had taken place. In particular these arrangements mean that:

(a)   a stock loan or a repo will not be regarded as a disposal/acquisition for tax purposes. Similarly, the subsequent return of the stock by the borrower will not be regarded as an acquisition/disposal. If the loan and return take place at different prices, any profit earned will be treated as a fee received by the lender and taxable in full;

(b)   manufactured payments will normally be taxable in the hands of the recipient. However, manufactured payments will be treated as exempt from tax when received by a lender for whom the corresponding real dividend would have been an exempt receipt or would not have given rise to Irish tax if it had been received by the lender, for example—

(i)   the receipt of manufactured payments by tax exempt funds such as charities, pension funds or the pension fund business of a life assurance company,

(ii)   the receipt of manufactured dividends in respect of Irish equities by an Irish resident company for whom the real dividends would have ranked as franked investment income, or

(iii)   the receipt of manufactured payments in respect of overseas securities by Irish taxable lenders for whom the real dividends on such securities would have attracted a nil Irish tax liability by virtue of an entitlement to a credit against Irish tax for foreign underlying tax. This situation will apply only where the combined rate of foreign underlying tax and withholding tax would have exceeded the Irish tax rate if the lender had received the real dividend. If the manufactured payment on such dividends exceeds the real dividend received (net of foreign withholding tax, but before Irish encashment tax), the excess will be taxable in full;

(c)   stock lending fees received by tax exempt funds will be regarded as exempt for tax purposes provided the income from the stock loaned would also have been exempt from tax;

(d)   manufactured payments will normally be deductible by borrowers against the real dividends or interest in computing the borrower's liability to Irish tax. In the relevant tax computation, the amount of the manufactured payment must be deducted directly from the related real dividends or interest and should not be deducted from any other income (see below). No deduction will be given for the manufactured payment where the real dividend or interest—

    (i)   is exempt from tax either because the income is franked investment income or because the borrower is an exempt fund, or

    (ii)   does not give rise to Irish tax in the hands of the borrower by virtue of an entitlement to credit relief for foreign underlying tax,

(e)   by way of exception to (d) above, where an Irish taxable borrower borrows overseas securities from an Irish taxable lender, the borrower may choose, in order to maximise the benefit of any available credit relief for foreign withholding tax on the real dividend or interest, to treat the manufactured payment as if it was a charge on income and so deduct it form total profits rather than directly from the real dividend or interest. This facility will not apply where credit relief is also available for underlying tax in respect of the real dividend or interest;

(f)   rebates of interest on cash collateral will be deductible against the interest arising on such cash collateral;

(g)   transfers of stock which take place under a stock loan or repo transaction to which these arrangements apply will be treated as exempt from Irish stamp duties;

(h)   manufactured payments are accepted as not being "relevant distributions" for the purposes of dividend withholding tax.

In (d) above it is seen that, in a corporation tax computation involving a manufactured payment, the amount of the payment must be deducted directly from the related real dividends or interest. This requirement relates to the foreign tax rules in TCA 1997 Sch 24 paragraphs (3) and (4) (see **14.202** and **14.212**) and is to ensure that the manufactured payment is deducted from the real dividend rather than being apportioned with other expenses over all income. An IFSC company relying on the Revenue practice will accordingly have to apply direct attribution rather than the statutory apportionment rule in TCA 1997 Sch 24 paragraph (3).

3.212.3 Conditions and restrictions

The arrangements outlined above will apply subject to the following conditions and restrictions:

(a)   The arrangements will apply to lending and borrowing institutions whether trading or non-trading which are within the scope of Irish tax and which are companies, building societies, pension funds, charities or collective investment funds.

There is no requirement that both parties to the stock lending or repo transaction be within the scope of Irish tax. The arrangements will not apply to individuals or partnerships.

(b) Subject to the two exceptions outlined below, the arrangement will apply to—

(i) all interest-bearing, discounted and premium-bearing securities.

(ii) equities quoted on recognised stock exchanges.

The first exception to the above concerns Irish equities that are lent across dividend payment dates. In relation to stock lending/sale and repurchase transactions involving Irish equities, the arrangements will not apply unless the lender, if he had received the real dividend and had filed any required declarations or claims, would have been eligible for exemption from he dividend withholding tax provisions under domestic law or the terms of a tax treaty.

The second exception relates to Irish corporate bonds which are lend across coupon dates. The arrangements will not apply to stock lending/sale and repurchase transactions involving Irish corporate bonds, except in either of the following circumstances—

(i) where the lender of the bonds is eligible for exemption from the interest withholding tax provisions under domestic law or the terms of a tax treaty or,

(ii) where both parties to the transaction are subject to the interest withholding tax provisions.

This condition also applies where collateral provided by a borrower includes Irish securities; in such cases the Revenue practice applies to the provision of collateral over a dividend date only where the borrower is exempt from Irish dividend/interest withholding tax.

(c) Stocks/securities may be denominated in any currency.

(d) Statutory audited accounts of the relevant institutions, insofar as these transactions are concerned, must recognise the substance rather than the form of the activities. In this regard the accounts must be unqualified. The Revenue Commissioners will apply the tax treatment in line with the accounting treatment. Deviations from this will not be allowed. (This condition does not apply to a counterparty who is outside the scope of Irish tax.)

(e) Any party to a stock lending/sale and repurchase transaction who avails of the terms of these arrangements is required to keep a record of any such transactions. (This condition does not apply to a counterparty who is outside the scope of Irish tax.)

(f) It has been decided to limit these arrangements to transactions extending for periods of 6 months or less.

(g) These arrangements will be effective for stock lending/sale and repurchase transactions which take place on or after 6 April 1999.

These arrangements will be kept under review. The Revenue Commissioners reserve the right to withdraw any or all of these arrangements in the event of their being used for tax avoidance purposes. In particular, the Revenue Commissioners are aware that exempt vehicles, such as pension funds, could be utilised to secure tax benefits that would otherwise not be available. If this happens, these arrangements will be withdrawn and the strict technical position applied.

Any unusual situations not dealt with above will be examined by the Revenue Commissioners on a case by case basis.

3.213   Exemptions from tax

3.213.1   Bodies exempt from corporation tax

Profits arising to any of the following bodies are exempt, by virtue of TCA 1997, s 220, from corporation tax:

1. A company authorised by virtue of a licence granted by the Minister for Finance under the National Lottery Act 1986;
2. The Dublin Docklands Development Authority;
3. An Bord Pinsean – The Pensions Board;
4. The Irish Horseracing Authority;
5. The company incorporated on 1 December 1994 as Irish Thoroughbred Marketing Limited;
6. The company incorporated on 1 December 1994 as Tote Ireland Limited;
7. The Commission for Electricity Regulation.

3.213.2   Certain income of Housing Finance Agency plc

Notwithstanding any provision of the Corporation Tax Acts, income arising to the Housing Finance Agency plc:

(a) from the business of making loans and advances under section 5 of the Housing Finance Agency Act, 1981, which income would otherwise have been chargeable to corporation tax under Case I of Schedule D; and
(b) which income would otherwise have been chargeable to corporation tax under Case III of Schedule D,

is exempt from corporation tax (TCA 1997, s 218).

3.213.3   Income of body designated under Irish Takeover Panel Act 1997

Notwithstanding any provision of the Corporation Tax Acts, income arising in any accounting period ending after 30 April 1997 to the body designated by the Minister for Enterprise, Trade and Employment under s 3 of the Irish Takeover Panel Act 1997 is exempt from corporation tax (TCA 1997, s 219).

3.213.4   Income of credit unions

Income arising to a credit union which is:

(a) registered as such under the Credit Union Act 1997; or
(b) deemed to be so registered by virtue of section 5(3) of that Act,

is, with effect from the date of the registration or deemed registration of the credit union, exempt from corporation tax (TCA 1997, s 219A).

3.213.5   Income of Investor Compensation Company Ltd

Notwithstanding any provision of the Corporation Tax Acts, profits arising in any accounting period ending on or after 10 September 1998 to the company known as The Investor Compensation Company Limited, incorporated on 10 September 1998, are exempt from corporation tax (TCA 1997, s 219B).

3.213.6   National Co-operative Farm Relief Services Ltd

The following payments are disregarded for all purposes of the Corporation Tax Acts (see also **3.204.2**):

(a)   a grant made under Article 3.1 of the first agreement by the Minister for Agriculture and Food to the National Co-operative (the society (being a society registered under the Industrial and Provident Societies Acts 1893 to 1978)) registered on 13 August 1980 as National Co-operative Farm Relief Services Limited);

(b)   a transfer of moneys under Article 3.6 of the first agreement (the agreement in writing dated 4 July 1991 between the Minister for Agriculture, Food and Forestry and the National Co-operative for the provision of financial support for farm relief services, together with every amendment of the agreement in accordance with Article 9.1 of that agreement) by the National Co-operative to a member co-operative;

(c)   a payment made under Article 3.1(a) of the second agreement (the agreement in writing dated 16 May 1995 between the Minister for Agriculture, Food and Forestry and the National Co-operative for the provision of financial support for the development of agricultural services, together with every amendment of the agreement in accordance with Article 9.1 of that agreement) by the Minister for Agriculture and Food to the National Co-operative; and

(d)   a transmission of moneys under Article 3.4 in respect of payments under Article 3.1(a) of the second agreement by for Agriculture and Food to the National Co-operative to a member co-operative (ie, a society engaged in the provision of farm relief services which has been admitted to membership of the National Co-operative) (TCA 1997, s 221).

3.213.7   Small enterprise grants

A grant to which TCA 1997, s 223 applies is to be disregarded for the purposes of the Tax Acts. That section applies to a grant made under section 10(5)(a) of the Údarás na Gaeltachta Act, 1979, or section 21(5)(a) (as amended by the Industrial Development (Amendment) Act, 1991) of the Industrial Development Act, 1986, being an employment grant—

(a)   in the case of s 10(5)(a) of the Údarás na Gaeltachta Act 1979, under the scheme known as "Deontais Fhostaíochta Údarás na Gaeltachta do Thionscnaimh Sheirbhíse Idir-Náisiúnta" or the scheme know as "Deontais Fhostaíochta ó Údarás na Gaeltachta do Thionscail Bheaga Dhéantúsaíochta"; or

(b)   in the case of s 21(5)(a) of the Industrial Development Act1986 (as so amended), under the scheme know as "Scheme Governing the Making of Employment Grants to Small Industrial Undertakings".

3.213.8   Grants to medium and large industrial undertakings

A grant to which TCA 1997, s 224 applies is to be disregarded for the purposes of the Tax Acts. That section applies to a grant made under section 10(5)(a) of the Údarás na Gaeltachta Act, 1979, or section 21(5)(a) (as amended by the Industrial Development (Amendment) Act, 1991) of the Industrial Development Act, 1986, being an employment grant:

(a)   in the case of section 10(5)(a) of the Údarás na Gaeltachta Act, 1979, under the scheme known as "Deontais Fhostaíochta ó Údarás na Gaeltachta do Ghnóthais Mhóra/Mheánmhéide Thionsclaíocha"; or

(b)   in the case of section 21(5)(a) of the Industrial Development Act, 1986 (as so amended), under the scheme known as "Scheme Governing the Making of Employment Grants to Medium/Large Industrial Undertakings".

3.213.9   Employment grants

A grant to which TCA 1997, s 225 applies is to be disregarded for the purposes of the Tax Acts. That section applies to an employment grant made under:

(a)   section 3 or 4 (as amended by the Shannon Free Airport Development Company Limited (Amendment) Act, 1983) of the Shannon Free Airport Development Company Limited (Amendment) Act 1970;

(b)   section 25 of the Industrial Development Act 1986; or

(c)   section 12 of the Industrial Development Act 1993.

3.213.10   Certain employment grants and recruitment subsidies

An employment grant or recruitment subsidy to which TCA 1997, s 226 applies is to be disregarded for the purposes of the Tax Acts. That section applies to an employment grant or recruitment subsidy made to an employer in respect of a person employed by such employer under:

(a)   the Back to Work Allowance Scheme, being a scheme established on the 1st day of October, 1993, and administered by the Minister for Social, Community and Family Affairs;

(b)   any scheme which may be established by the Minister for Enterprise, Trade and Employment with the approval of the Minister for Finance for the purposes of promoting the employment of individuals who have been unemployed for 3 years or more and which is to be administered by An Foras Áiseanna Saothair;

(c)   paragraph 13 of Annex B to an operating agreement between the Minister for Enterprise, Trade and Employment and a County Enterprise Board, being a board specified in the Schedule to the Industrial Development Act 1995;

(d)   as respects grants or subsidies paid on or after the 6th day of April, 1997, the Employment Support Scheme, being a scheme established on the 1st day of January, 1993, and administered by the National Rehabilitation Board;

(e)   as respects grants or subsidies paid on or after the 6th day of April, 1997, the Pilot Programme for the Employment of People with Disabilities, being a programme administered by a company incorporated on the 7th day of March, 1995, as The Rehab Group;

(f)   the European Union Leader II Community Initiative 1994 to 1999, and which is administered in accordance with operating rules determined by the Minister for Agriculture and Food;

(g)   the European Union Operational Programme for Local Urban and Rural Development which is to be administered by the company incorporated under the Companies Acts 1963 to 1990, on the 14th day of October, 1992, as Area Development Management Limited;

(h)   the Special European Union Programme for Peace and Reconciliation in Northern Ireland and the Border Counties of Ireland which was approved by the European Commission on the 28th day of July 1995;

(i)   the Joint Northern Ireland/Ireland INTERREG Programme 1994 to 1999, which was approved by the European Commission on the 27th day of February 1995; or

(j)   any initiative of the International Fund for Ireland, which was designated by the International Fund for Ireland (Designation and Immunities) Order, 1986 (SI 394/1986), as an organisation to which Part VIII of the Diplomatic Relations and Immunities Act 1967, applies.

3.213.11 Certain income of specified non-commercial state-sponsored bodies

Income arising to a non-commercial state-sponsored body (a body specified in TCA 1997 Schedule 4 – see below):

(a)   which but for TCA 1997, s 227 would have been chargeable to tax under Case III, IV or V of Schedule D; and

(b)   from the date such body was incorporated under the Companies Acts, 1963 to 1990, or was established by or under any enactment,

is disregarded for the purposes of the Tax Acts.

However, a non-commercial state-sponsored body:

(i)   which has paid income tax or corporation tax shall not be entitled to repayment of that tax; and

(ii)   shall not be treated as—

(I)   a company within the charge to corporation tax in respect of interest for the purposes of paragraph (f) of the definition of "relevant deposit" in section 256 (Interest payments by certain deposit takers – Deposit Interest Retention Tax (DIRT)), or

(II)   a person to whom section 267 (Repayment of DIRT in certain cases) applies.

The non-commercial state-sponsored bodies listed in TCA 1997 Schedule 4 are as follows:

Agency for Personal Service Overseas;

Beaumont Hospital Board;
Blood Transfusion Service Board;
Board for Employment of the Blind;
An Bord Altranais;
An Bord Bia – The Irish Food Board;
The National Tourism Development Authority;
An Bord Glas;
An Bord Iascaigh Mhara;
Bord na Gaeilge;
Bord na Leabhar Gaeilge;
Bord na Radharcmhastóirí;
An Bord Pleanála;
Bord Scoláireachtaí Comalairte;
An Bord Tráchtála – The Irish Trade Board;
An Bord Uchtála;
Building Regulations Advisory Body;
The Central Fisheries Board;
The Courts Service;
CERT Limited;
The Chester Beatty Library;
An Chomhairle Ealaíon;
An Chomhairle Leabharlanna;
An Chomhairle Oidhreachta – The Heritage Council;
Coiste An Asgard;
Combat Poverty Agency;
Comhairle na Nimheanna;
The Health Service Executive;
Commission for Communications Regulation;
Cork Hospitals Board;
A County Enterprise Board;
Criminal Injuries Compensation Tribunal;
Dental Council;
Drug Treatment Centre Board;
Dublin Dental Hospital Board;
Dublin Institute for Advanced Studies;
Eastern Regional Fisheries Board;
Economic and Social Research Institute;
Employment Equality Agency;
Environmental Protection Agency – An Ghníomhaireacht um Chaomhnú Comhshaoil;
Eolas – The Irish Science and Technology Agency;
Federated Dublin Voluntary Hospitals;
Fire Services Council;
An Foras Áiseanna Saothair;
Forbairt;
Forfás;
The Foyle Fisheries Commission;

Garda Síochána Appeal Board;
Garda Síochána Complaints Board;
Health Research Board – An Bord Taighde Sláinte;
Higher Education Authority;
Hospitals Trust Board;
The Independent Radio and Television Commission – An Coimisiún um Raidio agus Teilifís Neamhspleách;
The Industrial Development Agency (Ireland);
The Industrial Development Authority;
Institiúid Teangeolaíochta Éireann;
Institute of Public Administration;
The Irish Auditing and Accounting Supervisory Authority;
The Irish Film Board;
The Irish Medicines Board;
The Labour Relations Commission;
Law Reform Commission;
The Legal Aid Board;
Leopardstown Park Hospital Board;
Local Government Computer Services Board – An Bord Seirbhísí Ríomhaire Rialtais Áitiúil;
Local Government Staff Negotiations Board – An Bord Comhchaibidlí Foirne Rialtais Áitiúil;
The Marine Institute;
Medical Bureau of Road Safety – An Lia-Bhiúró um Shábháilteacht ar Bhóithre;
The Medical Council;
The National Authority for Occupational Safety and Health – An tÚdarás Náisiúnta um Shábháilteachta agus Sláinte Ceirde;
National Cancer Registry;
The National Concert Hall Company Limited – An Ceoláras Náisiúnta;
National Council for Educational Awards;
National Council for the Elderly;
The National Economic and Social Council;
The National Economic and Social Forum;
National Health Council;
The National Milk Agency;
National Heritage Council – Comhairle na hOidhreachta Náisiúnta;
National Rehabilitation Board;
The National Roads Authority – An tÚdarás um Bóithre Náisiúnta;
National Safety Council – Comhairle Sábháilteacht Náisiúnta;
National Social Services Board;
The Northern Regional Fisheries Board;
The North Western Regional Fisheries Board;
Office of the Data Protection Commissioner;
The Pensions Board;
The Personal Injuries Assessment Board;
Postgraduate Medical and Dental Board;

The Radiological Protection Institute of Ireland;
The Refugee Agency;
Rent Tribunal;
Royal Hospital Kilmainham Company;
Saint James's Hospital Board;
Saint Luke's and St Anne's Hospital Board;
Salmon Research Agency of Ireland Incorporated;
Shannon Free Airport Development Company Limited;
The Shannon Regional Fisheries Board;
The Southern Regional Fisheries Board;
The South Western Regional Fisheries Board;
Tallaght Hospital Board;
Teagasc;
Temple Bar Renewal Limited;
Údarás na Gaeltachta.

3.213.12 Income of designated bodies under the Securitisation (Proceeds of Certain Mortgages) Act 1995

Income arising to a body designated under section 4(1) of the Securitisation (Proceeds of Certain Mortgages) Act 1995, is exempt from income tax and corporation tax.

3.213.13 Harbour authorities and port companies

Relevant profits or gains of a relevant body which is a harbour authority are exempt from tax under Schedule D (TCA 1997, s 229). A *relevant body* is:

(i)   a harbour authority within the meaning of the Harbours Act 1946,
(ii)   a company established pursuant to section 7 of the Harbours Act 1996, or
(iii) any other company which controls a harbour and carries on a trade which consists wholly or partly of the provision in that harbour of such facilities and accommodation for vessels, goods and passengers as are ordinarily provided by harbour authorities specified in paragraph (i), and companies specified in paragraph (ii) which control harbours, situate within the State, in those harbours.

Relevant profits or gains means so much of the profits or gains of a relevant body controlling a harbour situate within the State as arise from the provision in that harbour of such facilities and accommodation for vessels, goods and passengers as are ordinarily provided by:

(a)   harbour authorities specified in (i) above; and
(b)   companies specified in (ii) above,

of the definition of "relevant body", which control harbours, situate within the State, in those harbours.

3.213.14 National Treasury Management Agency

Profits arising to the National Treasury Management Agency in any accounting period are exempt from corporation tax (TCA 1997, s 230(1)). Any income, annuity or other annual payment paid by the National Treasury Management Agency is to be paid without deduction of income tax (TCA 1997, s 230(2)).

3.213.15 National Pensions Reserve Fund Commission

Profits arising to the National Pensions Reserve Fund Commission are exempt from corporation tax (TCA 1997, s 230A).

3.213.16 National Development Finance Agency

Profits arising to the National Development Finance Agency in any accounting period are exempt from corporation tax (TCA 1997, s 230AB(1)). Any income, annuity or other annual payment paid by the National Development Finance Agency is to be paid without deduction of income tax (TCA 1997, s 230AB(2)).

3.213.17 Income of athletic or other sporting bodies

Exemption from corporation tax is available in respect of so much of the income of any approved body of persons as is shown to the satisfaction of the Revenue Commissioners to be income which has been or will be applied to the sole purpose of promoting athletic or amateur games or sports (TCA 1997, s 235(2)).

For this purpose *approved body of persons* means any body of persons established for and existing for the sole purpose of promoting athletic or amateur games or sports and any company that, as respects any accounting period ending before 6 April 1984, was granted exemption from corporation tax under ITA 1967 s 349, as applied for corporation tax by TCA 1997, s 76(6) (TCA 1997, s 235(1)).

Exemption will be denied to any body or persons concerning which the Revenue Commissioners, following such consultation, as may seem necessary, with such body as in their opinion may be of assistance to them, give a notice in writing stating that they are satisfied that the body was not established for the sole purpose of promoting athletic or amateur games or sports, or that it no longer exists for such purposes or commences to exist wholly or partly for the purpose of securing a tax advantage.

Where relief under TCA 1997, s 847A has been given in respect of a relevant donation (donations to approved sports bodies – see **3.203.9**) and:

(a)   the donation has not been used by the sports body concerned for the purpose of undertaking the approved project concerned; or

(b)   the relief is otherwise found not to have been due,

relief under TCA 1997, s 235(2) will not apply to the amount of that relevant donation (TCA 1997, s 847A(19)).

3.214   Deduction for interest: anti-avoidance

Interest payable is deductible as a trading expense subject to the general test applying to most trading expenses, ie that it is incurred wholly and exclusively for the purposes of the trade. In practice, interest will not be disallowed where it is payable in respect of borrowings used for capital purposes, eg to purchase a business premises or to acquire plant, machinery, equipment etc, as long as the borrowings are used for the purposes of the trade. Certain interest, although incurred wholly and exclusively for trading purposes, may be disallowed where it is treated as a distribution (see **10.202**, **10.203**, **11.106**).

TCA 1997, s 817C is an anti-avoidance measure that restricts the amount of interest deductible as a trading expense in an accounting period. It is directed at arrangements under which a trading company claims a deduction for the amount of (accrued) interest where:

  (a)   the interest is payable, directly or indirectly, to a connected person (see **2.302**) (being interest which, if paid, would be chargeable to tax under Schedule D (see **2.605**));

  (b)   the interest would otherwise be allowable in computing the trading income of the company; and

  (c)   (i)   if the connected person is chargeable to tax in respect of the interest, the interest does not fall to be taken into account in computing the trading income of a trade carried on by that person, or

         (ii)   in any other case, if the connected person were resident in the State the interest would not fall to be taken into account in computing the trading income of a trade carried on by that person (TCA 1997, s 817C(2)).

Regarding (a) above, only interest chargeable to tax under Schedule D is taken into account. Thus, for example, the anti-avoidance provision would not apply to interest paid to a UK lender by the UK branch of an Irish resident company (and assuming the lender is not within the charge to Irish tax). There would be no question of the Irish company being obliged to withhold tax on payment of the interest in this case.

Category (c)(i) essentially refers to interest paid to Irish residents and to Irish source interest paid to foreign (mostly corporate) recipients who are not resident in a "relevant territory" (an EU or tax treaty country) (since these two groups are "chargeable to tax in respect of the interest") where the interest does not constitute a trading receipt, but excepting the case of a foreign corporate recipient not ultimately controlled by Irish residents (see below).

Category (c)(ii) covers situations other than those in (c)(i) (so that it refers to (mainly corporate) recipients resident in a relevant territory who, by virtue of TCA 1997, s 198(1)(c) (see **3.107.5**), are not chargeable to tax in respect of the interest). Accordingly, it refers to Irish source interest paid to (mainly corporate) foreign recipients who, by virtue of being resident in a relevant territory, are not taxable in respect of that interest (but excepting the case of a company not ultimately controlled by Irish residents – see below), but where (if the recipients were Irish resident) the interest would not be taken into account as a trading receipt.

TCA 1997, s 817C will not apply where the connected person to whom the interest is payable is a company which:

  (a)   is not resident in Ireland; and

  (b)   is not under the control, whether directly or indirectly, of a person who is, or persons who are, resident in Ireland, and for this purpose—

         (i)   *control* is to be construed in accordance with TCA 1997, s 432(2)-(6) (see **2.401**) as if in subsection (6) "persons resident in the State" were substituted for "five or fewer participators", and

(ii) a company will not be treated as under the control whether directly or indirectly, of a person or persons if that person or those persons are, in turn, under the control of another person or other persons (TCA 1997, s 817C(2A)).

Thus, the interest restriction provided for by TCA 1997, s 817C does not apply where the company receiving the interest is not resident in Ireland and is not under the ultimate (as confirmed by (b)(ii) above) control of Irish residents.

Relevant case law indicates that interest is taxable under Case III of Schedule D on a receipts basis, or at least that it is not taxable before receipt (see **3.207.2**), and it would accordingly be relatively easy to arrange for the payment of interest between connected persons so that it becomes taxable at a time that is much later than that in which it is deductible for tax purposes.

Where a company has a liability to a connected person (the "relevant liability") and the interest receivable by the connected person in respect of that liability is not, or would not be, taxable as a trading receipt (as explained in (c) above), the amount of the interest that would otherwise be deductible for tax purposes for an accounting period is restricted by TCA 1997, s 817C(3). The interest deductible by a company for an accounting period may not exceed an amount equal to the excess of –

(A) the aggregate of the amounts of interest on the relevant liability that are chargeable on the connected person, or that would be so chargeable but for the provisions of TCA 1997, s 198 (exemption for certain interest – see **3.107.5**) or by reason of the provisions of a tax treaty, for all chargeable periods the basis periods for which end on or before the last day of the accounting period; over

(B) the aggregate of the amounts of interest on the relevant liability that have been allowed or relieved in computing trading income for tax purposes for all earlier accounting periods.

For the above purposes, *chargeable period*, if the recipient of the interest is a company, means an accounting period and, where the recipient is not a company, a year of assessment while *basis period* means the period on the profits or gains of which income tax is finally computed for the purposes of Schedule D.

Example 3.214.1

Aston Ltd, a trading company, has an outstanding loan from Cole Ltd, a company with which it is connected. The loan is used by Aston Ltd entirely for trading purposes. The following amounts of interest on the borrowings have been charged in the accounts of Aston Ltd and paid to Cole Ltd:

	Aston Ltd	*Cole Ltd*
	y/e 31 Dec	*y/e 30 Sept*
	€	€
2004	10,000	4,000
2005	14,000	6,000
2006	12,000	18,000

Cole Ltd has been taxed for each of its accounting periods by reference to the above amounts of interest received. In accordance with TCA 1997, s 817C(3), the amount of interest deductible to Aston Ltd for the year ended 31 December 2006 is as follows:

	€
Cole Ltd – aggregate of interest taxable to 2006	28,000
Aston Ltd – aggregate allowed to 2005	24,000
Therefore amount allowable 2006	4,000

Thus, by 31 December 2006, the total amount both deductible and allowable is €28,000.

The amount of interest restricted for an accounting period in accordance with TCA 1997, s 817C(3) is treated as payable for the following period (TCA 1997, s 817C(4)).

Example 3.214.2

The position is as in Example **3.214.3** and in the subsequent year to 31 December 2007 the interest payable by Aston Ltd to Cole Ltd is €13,000 but the interest paid to Cole Ltd is €20,000. An amount of €8,000, being the amount disallowed in the previous period, is also treated as payable by Aston Ltd and accordingly the total amount treated as payable for the year ending 31 December 2007 is €21,000. The amount deductible, however, is €20,000 (4,000 + 6,000 + 18,000 + 20,000 – 10,000 – 14,000 – 4,000).

TCA 1997, s 817C applies as respects any accounting period ending on or after 6 February 2003. Thus, for the first accounting period affected, there will be a recapture of the entire amount by which interest payable to date on the relevant liability exceeds the amount of interest actually paid. For each subsequent period, the amount of interest allowable to the paying company will normally (ie, apart from cases where there is a change of accounting period) be the same as the amount taxable to the recipient (as is seen in the above example).

In attempting to circumvent TCA 1997, s 817C, a trading company might borrow from an unconnected person while a connected person would lend an equivalent amount to the unconnected person. For various accounting periods, the trading company would pay interest to the third party in amounts considerably less than the amounts accrued while the third party would pay equivalent amounts of interest to the connected person. TCA 1997, s 817C(5), however, cancels out the benefit of this kind of arrangement by treating the interest payable by the trading company as being payable to the connected person so that TCA 1997, s 817C will apply.

3.3 ACCOUNTING PRINCIPLES

3.301 Introduction
3.302 Valuation of stocks and work in progress
3.303 Leasing of plant and machinery
3.304 FRS 12
3.305 International Financial Reporting Standards (IFRS)

3.301 Introduction

Profits and losses of a trade or profession are, subject to statutory provisions, computed in accordance with the correct rules of commercial accounting (*Heather v P-E Consulting Group Limited* 48 TC 293). In *Willingale v International Commercial Bank Ltd* [1978] STC 75, it was held that the inclusion in tax computations of profits earned on discounted bills only when realised, either on sale or maturity, was correct even though, for accounting purposes, the profits had been correctly spread over the life of the bill. Here there was a divergence between what was correct for accountancy purposes and what was a cardinal principle of income tax law, namely, that a profit is not to be taxed until realised.

In *Odeon Associated Theatres Ltd v Jones* 48 TC 257, the taxpayer company, which operated a large number of cinemas, effected repairs to a number of cinemas which, due to wartime restrictions, were in need of repair and decoration. The state of disrepair of the cinemas did not affect their purchase price nor did it restrict their use for public showing. The repairs were effected over a period of time. In the light of the decision in *Law Shipping Co Ltd v CIR* 12 TC 621, the Revenue sought to disallow the proportion of the cost referable to the years before the cinemas were acquired, as being expenditure of a capital nature. The Court of Appeal found that the whole of the expenditure was allowable and distinguished the *Law Shipping* decision; the cinemas, unlike the asset in the *Law Shipping* case, remained usable despite their state of disrepair. In *Whimster & Co v CIR* 12 TC 813, the taxpayer, a company operating ships on time charter to it, claimed to deduct the excess of future hire payable on charters then unexpired over the amounts which would have been payable had the charters been at current rates (rates having fallen due to a depression in the shipping industry). The claim was refused.

In one of the principal Irish cases dealing with the influence of accountancy practice, *Cronin v Cork and County Property Co Ltd* 3 ITR 198, the majority shareholder granted a 34 year lease of a property to the company subject to an annual rent of £2,500. A few weeks later, the company sold its interest in the property to the shareholder's wife, the minority shareholder, for £100 and the company was then put into voluntary liquidation. The company claimed a deduction in respect of the capitalised value of the lease from the majority shareholder. Under TCA 1997, s 641 (see **13.306.4**), the formula produced a value of £25,000 and, as compared with a market value of £100 for the leasehold interest at the date of assignment, the company incurred a loss following its liquidation. The question for decision in the case was whether, in the light of TCA 1997, s 641, the computation of profits of persons dealing in or developing land should conform with the ordinary principles of commercial accounting. In the Supreme Court, Griffin J, referring to the *Odeon Theatres* and *Whimster* decisions, held that the treatment adopted by the taxpayer was not in accordance with commercial accounting practice and refused the company's claim. All that was necessary was to look at the amount expended on the acquisition of the interest in the land and the amount received for its disposal.

In *PJ Carroll and Co Ltd v OCulacháin* [1988] IR 705 it was held that historical cost accounting, as opposed to current cost accounting, was the correct method to be used for determining trading profits even though current cost accounting was based on SSAP 16. On the other hand, the Court of Appeal in the UK ruled that, in the absence of specific statutory provisions, the proper basis for determining profits for tax purposes was that provided for by the ordinary principles of commercial accountancy (*Gallagher v Jones* [1993] STC 537). The Court of Appeal's decision is based on an acceptance of SSAP 21 (Accounting for leases and hire purchase contracts). In the leading judgment in that case, Sir Thomas Bingham MR said: "I find it hard to understand how any judge-made rule could override the application of a generally accepted rule of commercial accountancy which ... was not shown to be inconsistent with the true facts or otherwise inapt to determine the true profits or losses of the business".

In *Murnaghan Brothers Ltd v Ó Maoldomhnaigh* 4 ITR 304, the High Court decided that the appellant company was entitled to stock relief for an accounting period arising out of a contract to acquire land despite a condition that possession should be retained by the vendors until some time in the following period. The inclusion of the full purchase price of the land in the accounts for the period in question was accepted as being in accordance with correct principles of accounting.

The approach to the relevance of accounting principles for taxation purposes in Ireland, as seen from case law (as, for example, in the *PJ Carroll* case above), is that trading income should be computed in accordance with *correct* accounting principles. This contrasts with the current UK statutory position which is that trading income is to be computed in accordance with generally accepted accounting practice (GAAP), subject to any adjustment required or authorised by law; prior to 2002, the statutory position in the UK was that trading profits were to be computed on an accounting basis which gives a true and fair view.

The only statutory reference in Irish tax legislation to accounting practice is that in TCA 1997, s 80A (re short-term leases of plant and machinery in which there is a brief definition of "normal accounting practice" – see **3.303.7**). Judicial comments from the *P-E Consulting Group* case, mentioned above, include the observation that the courts are not bound by the evidence of accountants and that it is up to the judge to decide whether a witness's evidence exemplifies "sound accountancy principles". "Sound" and "correct" would seem to mean the same thing but it is far from clear as to what "normal" denotes in this context and as to whether it might extend to GAAP.

The method of computing trading profits for the purposes of income and corporation tax has been settled for many years. As enunciated by Sir John Pennycuick V-C in the *Odeon Associated Theatres* case referred to above: "For the purposes of Case I or II of Schedule D the profits of a trade, profession or vocation must be computed on an accounting basis which gives a true and fair view, subject to any adjustment required or authorised by law in computing profits for those purposes." Although the requirement that the accounting basis in question must give a true and fair view involves the application of a legal standard, the courts are guided as to its content by the expert opinions of accountants as to what the best current accounting practice requires. The experts will in turn be guided by authoritative statements of accounting practice issued or adopted by the Accounting Standards Board.

The conjoint appeal cases of *Small v Mars UK Limited; HMRC v William Grant & Sons Distilleries Ltd* [2007] UKHL 15 (March 2007) were concerned with the treatment of depreciation that had been transferred to stock. There were, obviously, differences in the underlying facts relating to the two cases, as well as in the accounting treatment adopted by the two companies, but from a taxation standpoint the essential principle involved was the same. It is worth looking at these cases in some detail, not least for the discussion on relevant tax and accounting principles as set out in the leading judgment of Lord Hoffmann.

The dispute concerned the computation of the trading profits of Mars UK Ltd (*Mars*), a confectionery and pet food manufacturer, and William Grant & Sons Distillers Ltd (*Grant*), a producer of Scotch whisky. In each case, in accordance with current accounting standards, certain deductions had been made for the depreciation of fixed assets. UK legislation equivalent to TCA 1997, s 81(2)(f) denies a deduction for "any sum employed or intended to be employed as capital in...the trade". Although the language is by no means clear, this has always been taken as prohibiting a deduction for the depreciation of capital assets (*Re Addie & Sons* 1 TC 1 – see **3.201.3**). The question was to identify which sums had been so deducted.

To find the answer, it was necessary to examine the methodology employed by *Mars* and *Grant* in making their computations. This followed the relevant accounting standards. First, Statement of Standard Accounting Practice ("SSAP") 12, which was in force in 1996 when the Mars accounts were drawn up, states in paragraph 16 of SSAP 12: "The accounting treatment in the profit and loss account should be consistent with that used in the balance sheet. Hence, the depreciation charge in the profit and loss account for the period should be based on the carrying amount of the asset in the balance sheet, whether historical cost or revalued amount. The whole of the depreciation charge should be reflected in the profit and loss account."

In 1999, SSAP 12 was replaced by FRS 15 (Tangible fixed assets) in which paragraph 77 clarified and refined the requirements of paragraph 16 of SSAP 12 as follows: "The depreciable amount of a tangible fixed asset should be allocated on a systematic basis over its useful economic life. ... The depreciation charge for each period should be recognised as an expense in the profit and loss account unless it is permitted to be included in the carrying amount of another asset."

The combined effect of these standards is that the depreciation deducted in the profit and loss account for a given period should correspond with the depreciation shown in the balance sheet as having occurred over that period - "unless it is permitted to be included in the carrying amount of another asset". What is meant by this exception is best explained by reference to note 1 to SSAP 9 (Stocks and long-term contracts): "The determination of profit for an accounting year requires the matching of costs with related revenues. The cost of unsold or unconsumed stocks will have been incurred in the expectation of future revenue, and when this will not arise until a later year it is appropriate to carry forward this cost to be matched with the revenue when it arises; the applicable concept is the matching of cost and revenue in the year in which the revenue arises rather than in the year in which the cost is incurred."

This fundamental principle is given effect by taking the revenue which has arisen in the relevant year and deducting from it only those costs which are attributable to those sales. These costs may have been incurred in the year in question, or they may have been incurred in earlier years and carried forward, in accordance with the general principle, to be matched with the related sales when they occur. The costs of stocks which remain unsold at the year end are not deducted for the purpose of computing the profit in that year but are carried forward to be matched against the revenue from their sale in future years.

SSAP 9, paragraph 17, states that the cost of stocks includes not only the cost of purchasing the materials but also the "costs of conversion" which include costs "specifically attributable to units of production" such as direct labour and expenses and also "production overheads" which are incurred "in respect of materials, labour or services for production, based on the normal level of activity, taking one year with another". Paragraph 20 specifically provides that such overheads should include the depreciation of assets "which relate to production".

From SSAP 9 it can therefore be seen that where, in relation to the general requirement of paragraph 77 of FRS 15 that depreciation shown in the balance sheet should be deducted in the profit and loss account for the related period, an exception is made for a case in which depreciation is "permitted to be included in the carrying amount of another asset", this is intended to include the carrying forward of an appropriate part of the depreciation as part of the cost of stocks, to be deducted as and when the stocks are sold in a future year.

Both *Mars* and *Grant* prepared their accounts in accordance with the above standards. They divided the depreciation which occurred during the year or was carried in the opening stock figure into two parts, being the depreciation in fixed assets which related to the production of goods sold during the year or in assets which were not used for production at all ("A") and the depreciation in fixed assets which related to production of unsold stocks ("B"). The companies deducted A from the current year's revenue and carried forward B as part of the cost of unsold stocks.

In the case of *Grant*, cost of sales did not include B and an accounts note stated that operating profit was stated "after charging depreciation". The amount for total depreciation (A + B) was given but the amount for depreciation "included within stock" (B) was deducted from this total. The *Mars* accounts were less explicit in this regard and an accounts note stated that profit on ordinary activities before taxation was stated after charging "depreciation on tangible fixed assets" and then gave a figure for A and B together but a further note stated that B had been "included in the stock valuation". There was no dispute that the cost of sales figure in the profit and loss account included A but not B. On the foregoing admitted facts, Lord Hoffmann thought that it was plain and obvious that, as only A had been deducted, the TCA 1997, s 81(2)(f) equivalent statue did not require B to be added back.

The UK Revenue, however, submitted that whatever the methodology described by the accounting standards, the companies must be deemed to have deducted both A and B and then added a sum equal to B back into profits *in some other character* which does not affect the deduction in respect of depreciation. Acknowledging that the effect on the profit computation was the same as if B had not been deducted, their position was that that was only because the value of B and the sum added back happened to be the same. The basis for this was that a deduction of anything less than the entire depreciation in the year would be contrary either to some fundamental principle of accounting or to the requirements of the Companies Act 1985.

Lord Hoffmann noted the view that treating depreciation carried in stock as a cost excluded from the current year's computation and held back for a future year's computation is a category mistake; stock is an asset which has a value and cannot be a cost. But that appeared to him to confuse the role of stock in a balance sheet with its role in a profit and loss account. The balance sheet is a statement of assets and liabilities on a given date and in that statement stock is indeed one of the assets. The profit and loss account, on the other hand, is concerned with revenue and costs and in that context the figure for stock represents a cost which SSAP 9 requires to be kept out of the computation of profit for the year but recorded to be carried over into the computation for a future year.

In this connection, the Revenue pointed out that when the value of the stock in the balance sheet and the costs held over in the profit and loss account happened to coincide, as when stock is valued at cost, the conceptual differences are concealed but the situation will be different where the value of the stock falls below cost. Then it must be entered in the balance sheet at realisable value and a corresponding adjustment made to the profit and loss account so that the figure representing stock in the profit and loss computation cannot simply be regarded as a cost. It is something entirely different.

Lord Hoffmann saw no difficulty with accommodating this situation if one keeps in mind that the profit and loss account is concerned with revenue and expenses. A fall in the value of stock to below cost, although it involves no immediate outgoing or loss of income, is something which the principle of prudence requires should be treated as an expense and reflected in a deduction from that year's profit. There is no conceptual problem about recognising such a write-down as an immediate expense but carrying the cost of stock forward to be a future expense.

Reference was made to various company law provisions including the requirement that, in the case of a fixed asset with a limited useful economic life, the amount of its purchase price or production cost, less in appropriate cases its estimated residual value, is to be reduced by provisions for depreciation calculated to write off that amount systematically over the period of the asset's useful economic life. In Lord Hoffmann's opinion, there was nothing in any of these provisions which would prevent depreciation (or any other cost) being deducted in a subsequent year if that is calculated to give a true and fair view of the profits.

Referring to a requirement that cost of sales should take into account depreciation, he noted that this said nothing about how it should be taken into account. Likewise, in respect of the requirement that the balance sheet value of an asset should be systematically reduced, he noted that it said nothing about when that reduction should be taken into the computation of profit. Obviously any reduction in the balance sheet value for depreciation must at some time be reflected in a profit and loss account deduction, but there is nothing to say that the respective entries must coincide. This is not surprising in the light of the overriding requirement of company law that the accounts should give a true and fair view.

The Special Commissioners heard and allowed the appeals of both *Mars* and *Grant* against assessments which added back that part of the year's depreciation (described above as "B"). The Revenue then appealed successfully against the *Mars* decision to Lightman J in the Chancery Division and against the *Grant* decision to the Court of Session (in Scotland). Both *Mars* and *Grant* appealed to the House of Lords; in the case of *Mars*, directly from Lightman J. For the reasons I have given, Lord Hoffmann concluded that the Chancery Division and the majority in the Court of Session were wrong to hold that B should have been added back and agreed with the dissenting opinion of Lord Reed in the Court of Session. Both appeals were accordingly allowed and the decisions of the Special Commissioners restored.

In *Johnston v Britannia Airways* [1994] STC 763, the precedence of accounting principles is again emphasised. In that case, the taxpayer company was obliged to have a major overhaul of its 737 engines carried out every 17,000 hours. It sought, under the accruals method, to take a deduction in a current accounting period in respect of the future costs of the overhaul. In the High Court in the UK, Knox J found that the accounting principles employed by the company were no different to the ordinary principles applied by experienced accountants in dealing with the costs of major engine overhauls. In considering whether there was anything in statute or case law which would disallow the provisions made by the company, Knox J referred to *Owen v Southern Railway of Peru Ltd* 36 TC 602 which approved the general principle that it was proper for a taxpayer to charge against receipts each year an accurately discounted assessment of its future discounted liabilities. (In that case, it was held that the taxpayer company's calculation of its liability for future leaving payments to employees was not sufficiently accurate to justify the deduction claimed.)

The impact of FRS 12 would appear to be that the provision made by the company in the *Britannia Airways* case was not justified (see **3.304**).

The case of *Herbert Smith v Honour* [1999] STC 173 involved a firm which had occupied a number of business premises (the old premises) and which transferred its business to new premises. It made a provision in its accounts for the excess of the rents it would be liable to pay in the future in respect of the old premises over the rents it would be able to charge in respect of them. The Revenue disallowed the provision for the excess rentals on the basis that the accounts anticipated a liability which it was not entitled to do in ascertaining its profits for tax purposes. The Chancery Division allowed the provision applying the overriding rule that income tax is to be charged on the full amount of the profits or gains of the year of assessment.

A central question which was considered in this case was whether there is a rule of tax law against the anticipation of liabilities. It was found that there is no such rule and that a rule which prohibited the anticipation of liabilities would be inconsistent with resort to generally accepted principles of commercial accounting in many cases since it would have the effect of disallowing provisions made in accordance with the concept of prudence. Those accounting principles themselves operated to preclude illegitimate anticipation and the relevance of accounts prepared in according with those principles was not subject to a general exception which would prohibit a deduction for sums by way of provision in accordance with the prudence concept. It would seem that one of the implications of FRS 12 (see **3.304**) is that the decision in the *Herbert Smith* case will not be overturned.

Accounting principles with specific application to particular types of businesses will in general be followed for taxation purposes. Where accounts have been drawn up correctly, it is not correct for taxation purposes to make any adjustment to the results disclosed by reference to knowledge gained later. Thus, estimates reasonably made and used in accounts should not be corrected using hindsight (*Symons v Weeks* [1983] STC 195).

The accounting principle whereby closing stock in trade is brought into the accounts at the lower of cost and net realisable value is followed for tax purposes. An exception is the case of investments dealt in by a financial institution. In *AB Ltd v MacGiolla Riogh* 3

ITC 301, it was held that the mere writing down of book values to accord with market values was not an allowable procedure for tax purposes in such cases. The rationale for this decision is that investments have the ability to generate income in the form of interest, dividends etc and as such cannot be considered to be trading stock. (See also **3.305.3** regarding the acceptance in certain cases of the "mark to market" basis for recognising unrealised gains and losses on investments.)

3.302 Valuation of stocks and work in progress

3.302.1 General

The value to be placed on the opening and closing trading stock of a business is an essential part of arriving at the true measure of the profits of that business. *Trading stock* for this purpose includes work in progress. SSAP 9 defines *stocks and work in progress* as goods or other assets purchased for resale, consumable stores, raw materials and components purchased for incorporation into products for sale, products and services in intermediate stages of completion, and finished goods.

Any method of computing the value of stocks and work in progress which is recognised by the accountancy profession is an acceptable method of valuation for taxation purposes provided the method is consistently applied and does not conflict with taxing statutes as interpreted in case law. An acceptable basis is referred to by the Revenue as a "valid basis". By contrast, a "non-valid basis" is one which does not accord with the standard of acceptability of a valid basis, and includes a valuation which, although in form made on a recognised basis, pays insufficient regard to the facts.

The valuation basis set out in SSAP 9, which, as with other SSAPs, applies only to incorporated bodies, is regarded as a valid basis. The Standard distinguishes between long term contract work in progress and other stocks and work in progress. The amount at which stocks and work in progress, other than long term contract work in progress, should be stated in financial statements is the total of the lower of cost and net realisable value of the separate items of stock and work in progress or of groups of similar items. Long term contract work in progress should be brought into financial statements at cost plus any attributable profit, less any foreseeable losses and progress payments received and receivable. Where, however, an anticipated loss on an individual contract exceeds the cost incurred to date less progress payments received and receivable, the excess should be shown separately as a provision.

Cost is defined in SSAP 9 as expenditure which has been incurred in the normal course of business in bringing the product or service to its present location and condition and it should include, in addition to the cost of purchase, such costs of conversion as are appropriate to that location and condition. *Cost of purchase* includes import duties, transport and handling costs and any other directly attributable costs less trade discounts, rebates and subsidies. The cost of conversion comprises the costs which are specifically attributable to units of production, ie direct labour, direct expenses and subcontracted work, production overheads, and any other overheads attributable to bringing the product or service to its present location and condition. Production overheads are those overheads incurred in respect of materials, labour or services for production, based on the normal level of activity, taking one year with another.

Net realisable value is the actual or estimated selling price, net of trade discounts but before settlement discounts, less all further costs to completion and all costs to be incurred in marketing, selling and distributing.

A long term contract is one entered into for the manufacture or building of a single substantial entity or the provision of a service where the time taken to manufacture, build or provide is such that a substantial proportion of the contract work will extend for a period exceeding one year. Attributable profit is that part of the total profit currently estimated to arise over the duration of the contract (after allowing for likely increases in costs so far as not recoverable under the terms of the contract) which fairly reflects the profit attributable to that part of the work performed at the accounting date. Foreseeable losses are those losses which are currently estimated to arise over the duration of the contract (after allowing for increases in costs so far as not recoverable under the terms of the contract).

Most of the normal accounting methods of arriving at cost are accepted for tax purposes, including the first-in first-out (FIFO) method, standard cost and average cost. Stock valuation methods which are not acceptable for tax purposes are LIFO and "base stock". The base stock method was found to be an unacceptable basis of valuation for tax purposes in the case of *Patrick v Broadstone Mills Limited* 35 TC 44. Although it was an acceptable basis for accounting in the industry in question, it was found not to be acceptable for tax purposes as base stock does not relate to the actual cost of goods on hand at the beginning and end of the accounting period.

It is permissible to apply the lower of cost and net realisable value principle to individual stock items; it is not necessary to take the lower of cost and net realisable value in relation to the stocks as a whole (*CIR v Cock, Russell & Company Limited* 29 TC 397).

The case of *Duple Motor Bodies Limited v Ostime* 39 TC 537 was concerned with the question as to whether, in the case of a manufacturing company, it was permissible to value work in progress on the basis of direct cost only (materials and labour) or whether indirect costs (a proportion of indirect factory and office expenses) should also be taken into account (the "on-cost" method). It was found that either method was in accordance with accepted accounting principles and that the direct cost method, which was the approach adopted by the company, could not be shown to be inconsistent with income tax rules.

3.302.2   Long term contracts

The Revenue Commissioners published a Memorandum in April 1975 in response to a request from the accountancy bodies for clarification of the tax implications of the publication of SSAP 9. In relation to long term contracts, the Memorandum states that where it is anticipated that the contract as a whole will result in a loss, a proportion of the overall loss may, for tax purposes, usually be taken into account year by year during the remaining period of the contract provided that all contracts, whether profitable or not, are dealt with on the same basis. The proportion of the overall loss may be calculated either by reference to time (normally up to the due completion date of a contract) or to expenditure incurred.

Where the work on the long term contract has been substantially completed and it is therefore possible to assess the financial outcome with reasonable certainty, it will normally be permissible to take account at that point of any likely increases in costs to the extent that they are not recoverable under the terms of the contract, for example, foreseeable further expenditure representing obligations arising out of the contract up to the time of final delivery, and a reasonable provision to allow expenditure under any guarantee or warranties included in the contract.

The Memorandum states that it is not permissible for tax purposes to take account of expenditure which has not been incurred and that a provision for an expected future loss on the contract as a whole will not be allowable for tax purposes to the extent that it is in excess of the amount of the foreseeable loss. In Tax Briefing Issue 41 however, following the publication of FRS 12 (see **3.304**), the Revenue confirmed that a provision for a loss on a contract, made in accordance with paragraph 9 of Part 1 of SSAP 9, is no longer precluded on the basis that the provision takes account of expenditure which has not yet been incurred.

3.302.3 Professions

In the cases of professional firms, particularly larger firms, it is normal accounting practice to credit the cost of accrued professional staff time on unbilled work in the accounts as work in progress at the end of each period. Where a professional assignment or project extends over a long period, such costs are carried forward at the end of the period to be written off in the following period.

Since the aim of this practice is to carry forward costs, only the time costs of employees should, in strictness, be included and not that of, say, the owner or partners of a firm. However, it is common practice to include the cost of partners' time also in the calculation of work in progress. Provided a reasonable method of computing work in progress is adopted and is applied consistently, the tax treatment will follow the accounting treatment.

The rationale for including work in progress in the accounts of manufacturing concerns does not, however, exist in the cases of professional firms. In the former case, factory work in progress can be evaluated objectively whereas, in the cases of professional firms, no comparable asset has been created. For this reason, the exclusion of work in progress in the accounts of professional firms can be justified. Where an intangible service is being provided, and in particular where, as is often the case, the firm does not have a legal right to receive income before a project is completed, work in progress can justifiably be excluded altogether.

As noted earlier, SSAP 9 requires the inclusion of work in progress, but it does not apply to the preparation of accounts for professions. The Standard explains that the determination of profit for an accounting year requires the matching of costs with related revenues and this is the basis for the inclusion of work in progress where relevant. Where revenue will not arise until a later period, it is appropriate to carry forward the cost to be matched with the revenue when it arises. The Revenue are also concerned to ensure that the basis on which profits are accounted for for tax purposes should take account of the need to match costs with the related income. Applied to work in progress of professional firms, this would have the effect of deferring a deduction for the cost of work in progress until such time as the work is billed.

3.302.4 Preparation of accounts for tax purposes – Revenue Statement of Practice

The view of the Revenue Commissioners is that the "earnings basis" is the strictly correct basis for preparing accounts for tax purposes. The earnings basis for computing the profits or gains of a trade or profession for any period is defined in TCA 1997, s 91(5)(a) as the basis in accordance with which "all credits and liabilities accruing during that period as a consequence of the carrying on of the trade or profession are brought into account in computing those profits or gains for tax purposes, and not otherwise". This basis is acceptable in all circumstances.

Accounts prepared on other bases have been accepted for tax purposes in the cases of individuals and partnerships carrying on professions. The Revenue Statement of Practice SP-IT/2/92 sets out the basis on which accounts of professional firms may be drawn up for tax purposes. The basis does not apply to an individual carrying on a profession as a barrister due to the particular arrangements applying to the payment of fees in that profession. The Statement of Practice was occasioned by Revenue concern as to the basis on which certain accounts had been prepared; it was considered that these accounts had been prepared on bases which did not provide an orderly and consistent framework for determining profits and that, in particular, the matching of costs with related income could fall significantly out of line.

The Statement of Practice notes that all companies as well as individuals and partnerships carrying on trades (other than certain farmers) are required to prepare accounts on the earnings basis. That basis would in all cases take both debtors and creditors into account and work in progress would also be included where normal accountancy principles would require that it be taken into account. It has already been argued here that it is not always necessary to bring in work in progress and that its omission would not be in conflict with acceptable accountancy practice, for certain businesses at least.

It has been long standing practice for the Revenue Commissioners to accept, in the case of an individual or partnership carrying on a profession, accounts prepared on a basis other than the earnings basis. This basis is referred to as the "conventional basis". It includes the cash basis and would in fact refer to anything less than a full earnings basis.

In the case of "commencement" situations involving professions, the Revenue will insist that the accounts for the first three years from the date of commencement must be prepared on an earnings basis. "Commencement" includes the case in which an individual who succeeds to a profession which had been carried on by another individual or by a partnership is deemed to have commenced the carrying on of a profession, as well as the case in which a "relevant period" commences in the case of a partnership profession.

After the end of the three year commencement period, a professional firm may change over from an earnings basis to an acceptable conventional basis. Such change must, however, be complete. This means that the conventional basis must be applied without taking into account the fact that some amounts which will be taken into account after the change will already have been credited in the previous period under the earnings basis.

Other than in commencement situations as described in the previous paragraph, where it has been the practice in the case of an individual or partnership to prepare accounts on the conventional basis, the Revenue Commissioners will continue to accept accounts prepared on that basis subject to the following conditions:

(a)   there will be no material difference between the amount of profits computed on the conventional basis and the amount that would have been arrived at on a full earnings basis;

(b)   bills for services rendered or work done are issued at regular and frequent intervals; and

(c)   the accounts include a note containing precise details of the basis used.

To be acceptable for tax purposes, a conventional basis should normally include debtors and creditors. Work in progress need only be included where its exclusion would materially affect the profit figure. Provisions for specific doubtful debts made in accordance with accepted accountancy principles are allowable for tax purposes. In the view of the Revenue Commissioners, a provision consisting of a proportion of long standing small debts is a specific provision for tax purposes, provided the amount can be justified by reference to previous experience in that practice.

The Statement of Practice outlines the approach to be adopted by the Revenue Commissioners in relation to firms which, in good faith, have submitted accounts on an unacceptable basis. Where a firm changes to an acceptable basis, whether an earnings basis or an acceptable conventional basis, for the purposes of preparing accounts forming the basis for the tax year 1992/93 (or 1993/94 where the 1992/93 accounts were finalised at the date of the Statement of Practice) the Revenue will not normally seek to reopen prior years.

A further transitional measure dealt with in the Statement of Practice relates to the charge to tax under TCA 1997, s 94 in respect of the value of work in progress where there has been a change from a conventional basis to the earnings basis, or a change of conventional basis, in the case of a profession. Tax is charged under Case IV of Schedule D on the value of any work in progress debited at the time of change and allowed as a deduction insofar as there has been no corresponding credit brought into account for tax purposes. The Statement of Practice permits the taxable amount to be spread evenly over the years of assessment up to and including the year 1997/98. The first year for which this treatment will apply will normally be 1992/93, or 1993/94 where the 1992/93 accounts were finalised before the date of the Statement.

Where the deferral treatment is in operation and an individual ceases to carry on a profession so that there are remaining deferred amounts which have not yet been assessed to tax, the Revenue will, on receipt of a claim, treat such deferred amounts as post-cessation receipts chargeable to tax under the provisions of TCA 1997, s 91 for the years of assessment in which these would have been assessed if the cessation had not taken place. Where no such claim is made, the amounts in question must be brought into charge to tax in the final year of assessment. A cessation in this context includes a deemed cessation where a profession which was carried on by an individual is succeeded to by another individual or a partnership, or a deemed cessation in the case of a partner leaving a partnership.

3.302.5 Change in basis of valuation

In the Memorandum published with SSAP 9 in April 1975, the Revenue Commissioners gave their view as to the tax treatment of changes in the basis for valuing stocks and work in progress. The treatment will differ depending on whether the change is from one valid basis to another valid basis or is a change from a non-valid basis to a valid basis. The Memorandum refers to "stocks" which is to be understood to include manufacturing work in progress but not professional work in progress.

There should be a good reason for any change in an existing valid basis. Thus a change could be justified on the grounds that the new basis is preferable because it will give a fairer presentation of the results and of the financial position of the business. Another example justifying a change in basis would be that of a company taken over by another company or group and consequently adapting its basis to conform with that of the acquiring group or company.

On a change from one valid basis to another valid basis, the basis used for the closing stock for the year of change should also be applied to the opening stock for that year. The valuations for previous periods will not normally be revised, whether the change is to a higher or a lower level.

On a change from a non-valid basis to a valid basis, the new basis is to be applied to both the opening and closing values of the year of change. In addition, past liabilities will be reviewed but, provided there is no question of fraud, wilful default or neglect, the Revenue will not normally seek to recover tax for past years on an amount greater than that involved in the uplift of the opening valuation for the period in which the new basis is first adopted.

In the Indian case, *Bombay Commissioner of Income Tax v Ahmedabad New Cotton Mills Company Limited* 46 TLR 68, the issue concerned an improper stock valuation where both opening and closing stocks had been undervalued. It was held that the real profits of the year could not be ascertained by raising the value of closing stock to the proper amount while not taking into account a similar revision of the opening stock figure. The principle underlying this decision is that the profit for the period in question is to be measured and that this could not be properly done without arriving at the opening and closing stock values on the same basis.

In *Pearce v Woodall-Duckham* [1978] STC 372, a company was engaged in design and construction work under long term contracts and, until the end of 1968, work in progress on contracts was brought into the accounts at the end of each year at prime cost, the profit on the contracts being brought into account only on the expiry of the contract maintenance period. The company changed its policy in 1969, adopting an accrued profit basis whereby, for contracts where more than 25% of the anticipated final prime cost had been incurred, work in progress was valued on the basis of the proportion of estimated profit attributable to the work done. Work in progress at the beginning of 1969 was revalued on the new basis resulting in an uplift of some £580,000 over the closing valuation for 1968 made under the old basis. While the sum was brought into the accounts for 1969 and described as "surplus" arising from the change in accounting basis, the company claimed that it was not chargeable to corporation tax as it was not a trading profit and that, even it were a trading profit, it was attributable to a year or years prior to 1969. In the Court of Appeal it was held that the sum of £580,000 was a trading profit taxable in 1969. The inclusion of the surplus was considered to be a genuine economic writing up of the work in progress and therefore a part of the profit arising for 1969.

The effect of the decision in *Woodall-Duckham* is that there should be neither a tax free uplift nor a double charge to tax as a result of a change in the basis of valuation of work in progress; it is not correct that the opening and closing figures in the year of change must be on the same basis.

The position as confirmed by the *Woodall-Duckham* judgment can be illustrated in the following simple example.

Example 3.302.5.1

Assume that following a change in the basis on which work in progress was valued, the closing value is calculated at €400,000. The closing value for the immediately preceding year was €200,000 but, on the new basis, the opening value is restated at €350,000, an uplift of €150,000. Sales for the year of change are €1m. The profit and loss account is as follows:

	€000		€000
Sales			1,000
Opening WIP	350		
Closing WIP	400		50
Profit			1,050

The uplift of €150,000 in the opening value is regarded as a profit attributable to the year of change resulting in an overall taxable profit of €1,200,000. The converse position also applies in that the taxable profit falls to be reduced where the value of opening work in progress on the revised basis is less than the value computed under the old basis.

In simple terms, the argument against the *Woodall-Duckham* decision would be that by including opening and closing work in progress valued on different bases, the resulting taxable profit for the year of change will include profits for more (or less, as the case may be) than one year. The Court of Appeal judges would say otherwise. In this connection Orr LJ compared the position here with that obtaining in the case of a write down of the value of trading stock or the write off of bad debts. If in a given year a trader decides that the value of his trading stock or the value of a trading debt owed to him is valueless or is reduced in value, he would write down the stock or write off the bad debt, and the decision to do so would take effect for tax purposes in the year in which it is taken although the value of the stock or debt may have been reducing in value in previous years. The position should be the same, in principle, where a trader writes up the value of work in progress by attributing to it a fair share of the final gross margin.

The policy adopted by the company was to bring in work in progress at the end of each year at prime cost, any profit on contracts not being brought into account until the expiry of the contract maintenance period. That policy was changed in 1969 to an accrued profit basis. In the case of a contract whose performance, in terms of work in progress, runs for more than one year, the new policy was to attribute to work done a percentage of the total gross margin which the company would eventually be entitled to receive as part of the contract price, but subject to certain safeguards, for example the non-inclusion of any element of gross margin until more than 25% of the anticipated final prime cost had been incurred. Orr LJ found that the element of gross margin which the new basis required to be brought into account could not be attributed to any year prior to 1969 just as no part of a bad debt could be attributed to a year earlier than that in which it was recognised as bad.

The change in policy resulted in a situation in which there would, for the year of change, be work in progress valued on the lower basis at the beginning of the year and which, at the end of the year, when it would have crossed the 25% threshold, would be valued on the higher basis. In the opinion of Stamp LJ the resulting uplift in value clearly represented an item falling to be brought into account on the receipts side of the trading account in ascertaining the trading profits during the year of change. If that was not the case, the difference would never become subject to taxation. Dealing with the objection that, for the purposes of computing trading profits like must be compared with like, he pointed out that in relation to a contract which had crossed the 25% threshold during the year, we are not comparing like with like but are ascertaining the value at the beginning of the year on one basis and the value at the end of the year on a different basis.

Stamp LJ further observed that he could see no justification for not adopting the same approach in relation to contracts which already at the end of 1968 had crossed the 25% threshold. The effect of any other approach would be to ignore the element of profit recognised by the revaluation of work in progress. This observation makes it clear that the principle emerging from the *Woodall-Duckham* decision was not dependent on the fact that some contracts had passed the 25% threshold but on the more basic premise that the value of work in progress had been written up as a result of a change in policy. In bringing in the value of work in progress at the beginning and the end of the year of change, Stamp LJ noted that we are not comparing like with like but that that must always be the case when for good commercial reasons, and without infringing any principle of income tax law, including the rule that we must not anticipate a profit, the value of trading stock or work in progress falls to be written up or written down.

Counsel for the company had submitted that the uplift following the change in policy represented a previously unrecognised trading profit of earlier years which should not therefore be included in the 1969 results. Stamp LJ disposed of this point by pointing out that the uplift is merely one of the items brought into the accounts for the purposes of determining profit so that its inclusion in one year would not infringe the principle that tax for any financial year should be charged on profits arising in that year.

TCA 1997, s 95A(2) makes provision for cases to which TCA 1997, s 94(3) (which deals with professions only) does not apply in which there has been a change in the basis for valuing work in progress in computing the taxable profits of a trade or profession and where the amount of the work in progress at the time of the change is allowed as a deduction for the period following the period of the change. To the extent that there is an increase in the value of the work-in-progress for the period of the change, that increase is taxable as part of the profits of the trade or profession. The increase referred to is the excess of the value of the work in progress at the time of change in the basis of valuation over the counterbalancing credit taken into account for tax purposes for the period preceding the period of change.

TCA 1997, s 95A(3) provides for relief in cases where the increase is the result of the application of "UITF Abstract 40" which relates to the basis of valuation of work-in-progress in the case of contracts to provide services. While any such increase is chargeable to tax, the charge is spread over five years instead of being imposed in the year of change. In the case of a trade or profession that is permanently discontinued within the five year period, tax will be chargeable for the period of discontinuance on the fraction of the increase so as to ensure that the full increase is accounted for for tax purposes.

UITF Abstract 40 refers to the guidance issued on 10 March 2005 by the Urgent Issues Task Force of the Accounting Standards Board on Application Note G of Financial Reporting Standard 5. *Accounting Standards Board* means the body known as the Accounting Standards Board established under the articles of association of The Accounting Standards Board Limited (a UK company limited by guarantee) (TCA 1997, s 95A(1)).

3.303   Leasing of plant and machinery

3.303.1   General

Before considering the tax implications of leasing plant and machinery for the purposes of a trade, it may be useful to summarise briefly the nature and accounting treatment of both finance and operational leasing, as well as hire purchase. A finance lease is, basically, a lease under which the present value of the lease payments is greater than 90% of the value of the asset being leased at the inception of the lease. An operating lease is a lease other than a finance lease.

In the accounts of a company leasing plant or machinery under a finance lease, the assets are recognised in the balance sheet. The balance sheet will also show the liability to pay future instalments while the interest element of the lease payments is brought to the profits and loss account. The assets are depreciated over the term of the lease or over their useful life.

Assets leased under an operational lease are not recognised in the balance sheet of the company concerned. Instead, the total lease payments are brought to the profit and loss account.

For tax purposes, no distinction is made between finance and operational leases; the full amount of the periodic lease payments is deductible in arriving at the amount of the company's taxable trading profits. No capital allowances may be claimed in respect of the leased assets (other than in the fairly exceptional case where the "burden of wear and tear" is borne by the lessee company – see **5.304**). The tax treatment reflects the legal rather than the economic effect of the lease agreement and, for an operational lease, follows the accounting treatment.

A hire purchase agreement is similar to a lease but with the important legal difference that the hirer will or may become the owner of the asset in question on performance of the contract. The accounting treatment of assets acquired under hire purchase is the same as for a finance lease.

The tax treatment of a hire purchase transaction also follows the legal effect of the contract. Capital allowances may be claimed in respect of the capital element of the periodical hire purchase payments while the interest element is tax deductible as a revenue expense. TCA 1997, s 284(2)(a) provides that the wear and tear allowance for machinery or plant for a chargeable period is an amount equal to 20% of the *actual cost* of the machinery or plant so that the usual result is a write off of that cost over five years (see **5.203.3**). Although, for the purposes of TCA 1997, s 284, the day on which any expenditure is incurred is the day on which the sum in question becomes payable (TCA 1997, s 316(2)), the wear and tear allowance due for any accounting period in respect of plant or machinery being acquired under hire purchase is based on the actual cost of the assets regardless of what amount of expenditure was incurred on them by way of instalments payable in that period.

Some areas of difficulty arising in respect of the tax treatment of leased plant and machinery have been dealt with in Press Releases issued by the Revenue Commissioners in late 1996 and 1997. These address problems associated with rebates of rental, trade-in allowances or upfront payments, and early termination payments. The contents of these statements are summarised below and the examples used are taken directly from that source.

3.303.2   Rental rebates

Where a finance lease is written on the basis that the lessor will recover his full capital investment together with funding costs and profit by the end of the primary period of the lease (a "full pay-out" lease), the tax position will be quite straightforward if the asset has no commercial value at the end of that period. This, however, is seldom the case in practice and if, as is usually the position, the asset has some residual value at that point, the lessee will have acquired some "equity" in the asset equal to that value (see *Littlewoods Mail Order Stores Ltd v McGregor* 45 TC 519). Accordingly, most leasing agreements contain a provision to the effect that on a sale of the asset at the end of the primary period the lessee will be entitled to a rebate of rentals equivalent to the sale proceeds less a small final payment by way of handling charge. In effect, this recognises that the lease payments up to the end of the primary period were merely "provisional" amounts which are now adjusted by way of rebate. The rebate is clearly a revenue receipt.

The appropriate tax treatment, following the Revenue view, is that the rebated amount should be included as a taxable receipt in the period in which it becomes payable to the lessee. In certain cases, particularly with assets tending to have a high residual value at the end of the primary lease period, this approach may produce significant distortion in the tax treatment with a high tax liability for the accounting period in which the primary period ends following earlier periods of relatively modest liability.

Under a Revenue approved arrangement involving LADCo ("Leased Asset Disposal Company"), a lessee may acquire ownership of an asset previously leased and which has first been disposed of to LADCo at open market value. The arrangement followed discussions between the Revenue and Irish Finance Houses Association, under whose auspices LADCo was set up, arising from Revenue concerns regarding certain practices which were perceived to facilitate a loss in VAT revenue. The disposal to LADCo also ensures the avoidance of a possible hire purchase tax trap that would otherwise present problems were the asset to be sold directly to the lessee (see **3.303.4**).

Under the arrangement, the lessor invoices LADCo for the sale to it of the leased asset. LADCo in turn sells the asset to the lessee and issues the appropriate invoice. The lessor issues a credit note to the lessee in respect of the rebate of rentals.

Example 3.303.2.1

	€
Market value of asset at end of lease (ie, cost to lessee)	5,000
Net final payment due by lessee to finance company (lessor)	500

The lessee should include the market value of the asset as a trading receipt for the period in which the transaction takes place and claim capital allowances by reference to the cost of the asset, ie €5,000. The lessee is entitled to a deduction for the final payment to the finance company, ie the net amount on which the lessee is taxable is €4,500.

	€
Final payment made by lessee (balance owing on lease)	500
Rebate of rentals, ie market value of asset	5,000
Net amount to be included in calculating trading profits	4,500

Where a rebate of rentals arises in respect of motor vehicle leasing charges which have been restricted under TCA 1997, s 377 (see **3.202.3**), only the proportion of the rebate corresponding to the proportion of lease rentals which has been allowed will be taxable.

Under TCA 1997, s 379, where a person who has leased a motor vehicle to which TCA 1997, s 377 applies subsequently becomes the owner of the vehicle, the tax treatment as a leased asset up to that point falls to be revised. The arrangement has technically become one for hire purchase and the revision has retrospective effect to the commencement of the lease. Leasing charges paid plus the amount paid to acquire the vehicle are aggregated and the person is treated as having acquired the vehicle at its retail price when it was manufactured with the balance of the expenditure being treated as hiring charges which are spread over the period of hiring.

Where TCA 1997, s 379 applies, the treatment regarding lease termination described above will not apply. In the case of a finance lease, however, a person may opt to have the lease termination dealt with in accordance with that treatment, in which case TCA 1997, s 379 will not apply.

3.303.3 Trade-in allowances

At the end of the primary lease period, a lessee company may wish to trade in the existing leased asset, acquired through the LADCo mechanism, for a new leased asset. Effectively the market value of the asset being traded in is a rebate of rentals already paid. Alternatively, the company may make an upfront payment of an amount equivalent to the amount of the rebate of rentals received. For commercial and security reasons, as well as for capital allowances purposes, a lessor is unlikely to agree to write the new lease on the basis of a net cost which would reflect the trade-in/ upfront amount. The lease will therefore be written on the basis of the full gross cost of the new asset with the trade-in amount being treated as an advance rental.

The Revenue view of the taxation consequences of this arrangement is that the lessee may write off the trade-in/ upfront payment over the period during which it is expected that the asset will be leased, generally the primary period of the new lease. In cash flow terms, this result is less than satisfactory for the lessee since, although the trade-in/ upfront payment is matched by the amount of the rebate of rentals received, the tax treatment differs in that the former amount is taxed immediately while the latter payment is spread over a number of years.

The position that would apply if the decision in the UK case *Gallagher/Threlfall v Jones* [1993] STC 537 were followed in Ireland is even more unfavourable to the lessee. That case concerned a sole trader who had entered into a finance lease arrangement for the acquisition of a boat for his boat hire business where an upfront payment and 17 equal monthly instalments were payable within the primary period two years. The inspector refused to allow the upfront payment for the first period for which accounts of the business were made up, contending that it should be allowed over the primary period of the lease.

The Court of Appeal went a considerable step further, based on evidence of an expert accounting witness as to the significance of SSAP 2 (Disclosure of accounting policies) and SSAP 21 (Accounting for leases and hire purchase contracts), by holding that the lessee's entitlement to an allowance in respect of the upfront payment should be even smaller than the inspector was prepared to allow. The apparent basis for the smaller allowance was the perception that the useful life of the boat was considerably longer than two years. The Court of Appeal did not accept that the allowance should be based on the legal obligation of the lessee to make payments in accordance with the lease agreement.

The Irish Revenue view on upfront payments is based on SSAPs 2 which provides for the matching of revenues with associated costs. The Irish Revenue point out that a judgment will have to be made as to the expected period over which an asset will be leased and that where it is reasonably certain at the inception of the lease that the lessee will exercise the option to lease the asset beyond the primary period, the payment should be written off over the period during which it is expected that the asset will be leased; otherwise, the payments may be written off over the primary period. As to whether either interpretation, UK or Irish, is technically correct is difficult to say. The traditional view in such matters is to apply "the ordinary principles of commercial accounting" unless those principles are to be set aside by some statutory provision of tax law. One such principle is the accruals concept (SSAP 2) which provides for the matching of revenues and associated costs. This is taken to mean that:

(a) ordinary recurring payments under a finance lease should be written off on a straight line basis over the period during which it is expected that the asset will be leased; and

(b) initial lease rentals under the lease or upfront payments made by the lessee represent a payment in advance of lease rentals and are allowed over the period during which it is expected that the asset will be leased.

A problem which impacts on this question and on certain other tax issues is the apparent failure to balance a number of sometimes conflicting accounting principles. The accruals concept may not always guarantee the same result when due account is taken of the need to have regard to the principles of income recognition and matching.

The following example, as with the other examples, is taken from one of the Revenue statements.

Example 3.303.3.1

	€
Leased asset cost	25,000
Upfront payment paid by lessee to supplier	10,000
Total payable to finance company including finance charges	20,000

Payable under finance lease:
Upfront payment of €10,000 plus €5,000 per annum over 4 years (primary period).
The lessee is allowed the annual amounts payable under the new finance lease plus €2,500 per annum in respect of the upfront payment:

	€
Payable under finance lease	5,000
Upfront payment spread	2,500
Total allowed to lessee/ charged on lessor	7,500

Note:
In practice, lessees frequently seek to deduct the upfront payment in the year in which the lease is taken out, ie, in the above example they claim €15,000 for the year (ie, upfront payment of €10,000 and first annual payment of €5,000) and €5,000 for each subsequent year. This is incorrect.

The following example considers the position of a trade-in of an asset which has been leased for a new leased asset.

Example 3.303.3.2

A leased asset is traded in for €5,000 against a replacement asset which is leased for a primary period of 4 years at €7,000 per annum. At the time of the trade-in the leasing company is owed €500 on the leased asset. The lessee should include the amount realised on trade in (€5,000) as a trading receipt and claim a deduction for this amount over the primary leasing period. The net amount to be claimed by the lessee in year 1 of the new lease is:

	€
Rebate of rentals (net) (i)	4,500
Leasing charge for new asset	7,000
Upfront payment (trade-in €5,000 x 25%)	1,250
Allowable (ii)	8,250
Net amount allowable year 1 (ii) – (i)	3,750

3.303.4   Early termination payments

A lessee will sometimes wish to terminate a lease before the end of the primary lease period. This will usually involve the making of a payment to the lessor amounting at least to the net present value of the outstanding instalments of lease rental over the primary period. Since a payment of this kind would be made to terminate a lease and thereby avoid further payments of a revenue nature, it might be considered to be tax deductible as a trading expense, based on the decision in *Anglo-Persian Oil Ltd v Dale* 16 TC 253. On the other hand, in *Tucker v Granada Motorway Services Ltd* [1979] STC 393, it was held that a payment in consideration for varying the terms of an onerous lease was capital in nature. What emerges from that case is that a payment is likely to be regarded as capital in nature if it relates to the cancellation of an identifiable asset (such as a lease: there was no such identifiable asset in the *Anglo-Persian* case).

There may also be a basis for distinguishing between a case in which a payment is made simply to get rid of an onerous lease or other asset and one in which, under the terms of the lease itself (which would be more typical of leases of plant and machinery than of leases of real property), there is provision for early termination based on the lease rentals outstanding.

The principle that emerges from the *Granada Motorway* decision would appear to be that a lump sum payment is not tax deductible where it represents a charge imposed on the lessee as consideration for early release from his lease obligation, but might be tax deductible otherwise.

The Irish Revenue have expressed the view that where an early termination results from a genuine change in the lessee's intentions, no attempt will be made to re-characterise the lease agreement as a hire purchase transaction.

3.303.5 Defeasance payments

In many cases, a lessee will enter into a defeasance arrangement with a third party to provide that, in consideration of an upfront payment, the third party agrees to make the rental payments under the lease. Although the view of the Revenue Commissioners regarding these upfront payments is that they are capital in nature, they are prepared to allow them as expenses provided the amounts involved are written off over the life of the lease.

3.303.6 Leasing and hire purchase

A hire purchase transaction involves the hire of an asset where the hirer will *or may* acquire ownership of the asset. This contrasts with a leasing transaction where ownership of the asset does not pass to the lessee and where the lessee's interest is confined to the right to use the assets on lease.

Arising out of the Consumer Credit Act 1995, finance companies have been much more willing to enter into hire purchase transactions than was previously the case. Under earlier legislation in the form of the Hire Purchase Acts 1946 to 1980, the owner of the asset on hire purchase was unable, without obtaining a court order, to recover the asset from the hirer where not less than one-third of the hire purchase price had been paid whereas the hirer could terminate the agreement at any stage. As these provisions applied to non-consumers (persons acting in the course of a trade, business or profession), they were repealed by the Consumer Credit Act 1995.

A hire purchase agreement is defined in the Hire Purchase Acts 1946 to 1980 as "an agreement for the bailment of goods under which the bailee *may* buy the goods or under which the property in the goods will *or may* pass to the bailee ...". In a hire purchase transaction, the full cost of the asset concerned is paid for by the hirer together with a finance charge over a period of time on the understanding that the hirer will acquire ownership of the asset after the final payment.

For tax purposes where, as is normally the position, the hirer has the option to acquire the asset at the end of the hire period, it has been held that the rentals are comprised of both revenue and capital elements (*Darngavil Coal Co Ltd v Francis* 7 TC 1). The revenue element represents payment for the hire of the asset and is deductible as a trading expense where the asset is used for the purposes of the hirer's trade or profession.

The capital element represents the purchase price of the option to acquire the asset. Although there are no specific tax provisions dealing with capital allowances involving hire purchase transactions, it has been accepted in practice that the hirer is entitled to the related capital allowances. There is implicit support for this approach in TCA 1997, s 299(2) (allowances to lessees – see **5.303**).

On the other hand, it would not be correct to assume that the mere existence of a purchase option would be sufficient to entitle a hirer to capital allowances in respect of the related assets. Thus, where the option price more or less equates to the market value of the asset at the time of exercise, the implication must be that the hire purchase rentals should be seen as representing payment for hire only.

A lease agreement which provides that the lessee may acquire the leased asset at the end of the lease term, or at the end of the primary lease period, for a nominal sum or for an amount which is clearly below the market value of the asset at that time, is, technically, a hire purchase agreement. The lessor will not in that event be entitled to capital allowances in respect of the expenditure on the asset. Instead, the lessee may claim capital allowances by reference to the capital element of the hire purchase rentals. Where the lessee may acquire the asset at the end of the leasing period, but at its market value at that time, it would seem, as indicated above, that the lessee would not have incurred capital expenditure up to that point and would therefore not be entitled to capital allowances by reference to any part of the hire purchase rentals.

On the other hand, the lessor may also be denied capital allowances if the agreement could be considered to be a hire purchase agreement. As a hire purchase agreement (see definition above) is an agreement under which the hirer *may* buy the goods or under which the property in the goods will *or may* pass to the hirer, an agreement that includes such a feature or an agreement entered into on such an understanding may well amount to a hire purchase agreement.

3.303.7 Short-term leases of plant and machinery

Introduction

Under normal rules relating to the taxation of lessors of plant and machinery, income is computed by treating gross lease payments as income and allowing a deduction for capital allowances in respect of the expenditure on the leased assets. This approach results in a difficulty for many lessors in that allowances are given over a period much greater in length than the period during which lease payments are received. To remove the tax consequences of this timing mismatch, TCA 1997, s 80A provides an alternative mechanism for taxing lessors of short-life assets.

Lessors of short-life assets may, for tax purposes, account for those assets in accordance with accounting rules. This will result in the "interest" element of the lease payments being charged to tax but without a deduction for capital allowances.

The definition of "relevant short-term lease" is complex and for this purpose it is necessary to understand the meaning of certain terms:

Asset means machinery or plant.

In relation to a leased asset, *fair value* means an amount equal to the consideration expected to be paid for the asset at the inception of the lease on a sale negotiated at arm's length, less any grants receivable.

Inception of the lease means the date on which the leased asset is brought into use by the lessee, or the date on which the lease payments under the lease first accrue, whichever is the earlier.

Lease payments means the lease payments over the term of the lease to be paid to the lessor in relation to the leased asset, including any residual amount payable to the lessor at or after the end of the lease term and which is guaranteed by the lessee, or by a person connected with the lessee (within the meaning of TCA 1997, s 10 – see **2.3**), or under the terms of any scheme or arrangement between the lessee and any other person.

In relation to machinery or plant provided for leasing, *lessor* and *lessee* mean respectively the person to whom the machinery or plant is or is to be leased and the person providing the machinery or plant for leasing, and the terms include respectively the successors in title of a lessee or a lessor (TCA 1997, s 403(1)).

Normal accounting practice means normal accounting practice in relation to the accounts of companies incorporated in the State.

In relation to an asset, *predictable useful life* means the useful life of the asset estimated at the inception of the lease, having regard to the purpose for which it was acquired and on the assumption:

(a) that its life will end when it ceases to be useful for the purpose for which it was acquired; and

(b) that it will be used in the normal manner and to the normal extent throughout its life.

Relevant period means the period:

(a) beginning at the inception of the lease; and

(b) ending at the earliest time at which the aggregate of the lease payments payable up to that time, discounted to their present value at the inception of the lease, equals 90% or more of the fair value of the leased asset, and, for this purpose, the lease payments are discounted at the rate which, when applied at the inception of the lease to the amount of the lease payments, produces discounted present values the aggregate of which equals the amount of the fair value of the leased asset at the inception of the lease.

In relation to a company, *relevant short-term asset* means an asset:

(a) the predictable useful life of which does not exceed 8 years; and

(b) the expenditure on which is incurred by the company during the accounting period relating to the claim to follow accounting practice in relation to the lease income.

A *relevant short-term lease* is a lease:

(a) of a relevant short-term asset; and

(b) the relevant period in relation to which does not exceed 8 years.

Claim to apply accounting practice

Where a company makes an appropriate claim, the amount to be included in its trading income in respect of all relevant short-term leases is the amount of income from such leases computed in accordance with normal accounting practice (TCA 1997, s 80A(2)(a)). In that event, the company will not, in respect of expenditure incurred on assets that are the subject of relevant short-term leases, be entitled to any allowance under TCA 1997, s 670 (mine development allowance – see **13.402**), Part 29 (allowances for capital expenditure on patent rights (see **13.603**), scientific and research (see **5.601**), research and development (see **7.403**)), or any other provision relating to the making of allowances in accordance with TCA 1997 Part 9 (capital allowances – see **5.2**) (TCA 1997, s 80A(2)(b)).

Where the foregoing treatment applies, the income from relevant short-term leases will be treated for the purposes of TCA 1997, s 403 (ring-fencing of leasing trades – see **5.305**) as if it were not income from a trade of leasing (TCA 1997, s 80A(2)(c)).

A claim for the above-described treatment, which may be made in respect of an accounting period ending on or after 4 February 2004, is to be made by the time the relevant corporation tax return for the period falls to be made. The claim will apply as respects expenditure incurred on or after the commencement date of the accounting period (TCA 1997, s 80A(3)).

Many companies making an election under TCA 1997, s 80A will, for some years at least, have both a ring-fenced and a non-ring-fenced leasing trade for tax purposes. It will not be possible to use any excess capital allowances arising from the ring-fenced trade against income from the non-ring-fenced trade.

3.304   FRS 12

3.304.1 Introduction

Financial Reporting Standard 12 Provisions, Contingent Liabilities and Contingent Assets (FRS 12), which sets out the principles of accounting for provisions, contingent liabilities and contingent assets, was issued by the Accounting Standards Board in September 1998. Its provisions are mandatory for accounting periods ending on or after 23 March 1999. The objective of FRS 12 is to ensure that appropriate recognition criteria and measurement bases are applied to provisions, contingent liabilities and contingent assets and that sufficient information is disclosed in the notes to the financial statements to enable users to understand their nature, timing and amount.

3.304.2   Main provisions of FRS 12

FRS 12 sets down the circumstances in which a business must make a provision and when it may not make a provision. A provision is defined as a "liability of uncertain timing or amount". Provisions can be distinguished from other liabilities such as trade creditors and accruals because there is uncertainty about the timing or amount of the future expenditure required in settlement. By contrast, trade creditors are liabilities to pay for goods or services that have been received or supplied and that have been invoiced or formally agreed with the supplier.

FRS 12 is not concerned with provisions that relate to the carrying value of assets, such as bad debt provisions and stock provisions.

FRS 12 applies to all financial statements that are intended to give a true and fair view in accounting provisions, contingent liabilities and contingent assets, except:

(a)   those resulting from financial instruments that are carried at fair value;

(b)   those resulting from executory contracts, except where the contract is onerous;

(c)   those arising in insurance entities from contracts with policy-holders; and

(d) those covered by more specific requirements in another FRS or a SSAP, eg long-term contracts, deferred tax, non-onerous leases, pension costs.

A provision should be recognised when:

(a) an entity has a present obligation (legal or constructive) as a result of a past event;

(b) it is probable that a transfer of economic benefits will be required to settle the obligation; and

(c) a reliable estimate can be made of the amount of the obligation.

If these conditions are not met, no provision should be recognised.

An obligation may be either legal or constructive. A legal obligation is one that derives from a contract, from legislation or from any other operation of law. A constructive obligation is one that derives from an entity's actions where, by an established pattern of past practice, published policies or a sufficiently specific current statement, the entity has indicated to other parties that it will accept certain responsibilities and, as a result, the entity has created a valid expectation on the part of those other parties that it will discharge those responsibilities.

In most cases it will be clear as to whether a present obligation exists. Where, exceptionally, this is not so, a past event is deemed to give rise to a present obligation if, taking account of all available evidence, it is more likely than not that a present obligation exists at the balance sheet date. In rare circumstances, for example in a lawsuit, it may be disputed whether certain events have occurred or whether those events result in a present obligation. To determine whether a present obligation exists at the balance sheet date, account should be taken of all available evidence, including, for example, the opinion of experts. The evidence considered should include any additional evidence provided by events occurring after the balance sheet date.

A past event that leads to a present obligation is referred to as an obligating event. There will be an obligating event only where there is no realistic alternative to settling the obligation created by the event. That in turn will be the case where settlement can be enforced by law or, in the case of a constructive obligation, where the event creates valid expectations in other parties that the obligation will be discharged. The only obligations recognised in an entity's balance sheet are those that exist at the balance sheet date. Where an entity can avoid future expenditure by its future actions, for example by changing its method of operation, it has no present liability for that future expenditure and no provision will be recognised.

To be recognised for the purposes of FRS 12, an obligation must not only be a present obligation but there must also be the probability of a transfer of economic benefits to settle that obligation. A transfer of economic benefits or other event is regarded as probable if the event is more likely than not to occur, ie the probability that the event will occur is greater than the probability that it will not. Where there are a number of similar obligations (eg, product warranties or similar contracts), the probability that a transfer will be required in settlement is determined by considering the class of obligations as a whole.

The use of estimates is an essential part of the preparation of financial statements and does not undermine their reliability. This will be especially true of provisions which by their nature are more uncertain than most other balance sheet items. Other than in extremely rare cases, an entity will be able to determine a range of possible outcomes and can therefore make an estimate of the obligation that is sufficiently reliable to use in recognising a provision. Where no reliable estimate can be made, a liability exists that cannot be recognised and that liability should be disclosed as a contingent liability.

Provisions previously considered appropriate, for example because of the prudence principle, will no longer be permitted. Furthermore, where there is a change of accounting policy resulting from the adoption of FRS 12, it will be necessary not only to make the appropriate entries in the profit and loss account but also to adjust the balance sheet so that the effect of FRS 12 is fully reflected (FRS 3). A provision previously made but which is no longer justified must therefore now be reversed and reported as a prior year adjustment.

3.304.3 Taxation implications of FRS 12

The Tax Acts, apart from TCA 1997, s 81(2)(i) (deduction in respect of doubtful debts), do not contain any specific rules dealing with the tax treatment of provisions. The Revenue approach, up to FRS 12, has been to treat a provision made in connection with a trade as deductible if it did not seek to anticipate a loss, the expenditure in respect of which it was made would be allowable (eg, it was not capital expenditure), it was made in accordance with correct principles of commercial accounting, it could be estimated with reasonable accuracy, and it was made correctly to ascertain the full profits of the trade for tax purposes.

The Revenue approach to the tax treatment of provisions following FRS 12 is set out in Tax Briefing Issue 41 and the relevant text is reproduced in **3.304.5** below. The Revenue accept that there is no rule of tax law which prohibits a provision for future losses where such provision is required in accordance with a system of commercial accounting which correctly ascertains the full profits of a trader for tax purposes. A provision made in accordance with generally accepted accounting practice, including one made in accordance with FRS 12, is made in accordance with such a system.

As was seen in **3.301**, the outcome of a number of recent tax cases in the UK has been to place an increased emphasis on the precedence of accounting principles. In the February 1999 edition of Tax Bulletin, Issue 39, the Inland Revenue in the UK have highlighted the importance of accounting principles where they state that "accounting standards will be relevant for tax when it comes to deciding in which periods revenue receipts and expenses fall, unless there is a specific tax rule which provides to the contrary". While it is not certain that the decisions in these cases will be followed by the Irish courts, the Revenue Commissioners, in Issue 41 of Tax Briefing, have indicated (see **3.304.5**) that their view of the tax treatment of provisions in the light of FRS 12 takes account of these decisions.

Probably the most important outcome of FRS 12 is the need to review certain provisions previously made in accounts. Thus, provisions made in accordance with the prudence principle but which can no longer be considered to be appropriate may have to be reversed in the accounts for a current period. A provision will only be justified where there is an obligating event, that is, where there is no realistic alternative to settling the obligation created by the event. In many cases where a provision has been made in accordance with the prudence principle it will not be possible to contend that there is no realistic alternative to incurring the relevant expenditure forming the basis for the provision.

In the *Britannia Airways* case (see **3.301** above), the taxpayer could, instead of overhauling the 737 engines, have sold off the aircraft so that there was a realistic alternative to overhauling. Although there was a legal obligation on the company to overhaul its aircraft every three years, that did not make the cost of overhaul a liability as no obligation existed independently of the company's future actions. There was therefore no present obligation on the part of the company so that, in terms of FRS 12, no provision for future expenditure was justified.

The situation encountered in *Britannia Airways* is dealt with in Example 11B in Appendix III to FRS 12. It is stated there that instead of recognising a provision for future refurbishment costs, the depreciation of the aircraft would take account of the future incidence of maintenance costs, ie an amount equivalent to the expected maintenance costs would be depreciated over three years. Accordingly, a deduction for tax purposes would be due in respect of this deferred revenue expenditure as it is amortised in the profit and loss account. In this connection, the fact that expenditure has been capitalised in the accounts of a company does not necessarily mean that it is capital expenditure; the better view would appear to be that, regardless of the accounting treatment, expenditure will be capital or otherwise depending on the application of the appropriate tax principles.

As regards the question of the timing of expenditure for tax purposes, it will generally be the case that the tax treatment will follow the accounts treatment. Thus, FRS 12 is likely to have a significant impact on the timing of certain deductions for tax purposes.

As mentioned in **3.304.2** above, where there is a change of accounting policy resulting from the application of FRS 12, a provision made in an earlier accounting period but which is no longer justified will require to be reversed currently and reported as a prior year adjustment. Where the provision had been allowed for tax purposes in the earlier period, the profits for the current period should be increased by the reduction in the provision. (See Example 1 from Issue 41 of Tax Briefing in **3.304.5** below.)

3.304.4 FRS 12 – Summary

General

(a) Financial Reporting Standard 12, "Provisions, Contingent Liabilities and Contingent Assets", sets out the principles of accounting for provisions, contingent liabilities and contingent assets. Its objective is to ensure that appropriate recognition criteria and measurement bases are applied to provisions, contingent liabilities and contingent assets and that sufficient information is disclosed in the notes to the financial statements to enable users to understand their nature, timing and amount.

Definitions

(b) In the FRS a provision is a liability that is of uncertain timing or amount, to be settled by the transfer of economic benefits. A contingent liability is either (i) a possible obligation arising from past events whose existence will be confirmed only by the occurrence of one or more uncertain future events not wholly within the entity's control; or (ii) a present obligation that arises from past events but is not recognised because it is not probable that a transfer of economic benefits will be required to settle the obligation or because the amount of the obligation cannot be measured with sufficient reliability. A contingent asset is a possible asset arising from past events whose existence will be confirmed only by the occurrence of one or more uncertain future events not wholly within the entity's control.

Scope

(c) The FRS applies to all financial statements that are intended to give a true and fair view in accounting for provisions, contingent liabilities and contingent assets except:

- those resulting from financial instruments that are carried at fair value,

- those resulting from executory contracts, except where the contract is onerous,

- those arising in insurance entitles from contracts with policy-holders,

- those covered by more specific requirements in another FRS or a SSAP.

Recognition

Provisions

(d) A provision should be recognised when an entity has a present obligation (legal or constructive) as a result of a past event, it is probable that a transfer of economic benefits will be required to settle the obligation, and a reliable estimate can be made of the amount of the obligation. Unless these conditions are met, no provision should be recognised.

Present obligation

(e) Where it is not clear whether a present obligation exists, a past event is deemed to give rise to a present obligation if, taking account of all available evidence, it is more likely than not that a present obligation exists at the balance sheet date.

Past event

(f) For an event to be an obligating event, it is necessary that the entity has no realistic alternative to settling the obligation created by the event. This will be the case only where the settlement of the obligation can be enforced by law or, in the case of a constructive obligation, the event (which may be an action of the entity) creates valid expectations in other parties that the entity will discharge the obligation. The only liabilities recognised in an entity's balance sheet are those that exist at the balance sheet date. Where an entity can avoid future expenditure by its future actions, for example by changing its method of operation, it has no present liability for that future expenditure and no provision is recognised.

(g) An event that does not immediately give rise to an obligation may do so at a later date, because of changes in the law or because an act (for example, a sufficiently specific public statement) by the entity gives rise to a constructive obligation. Where details of a proposed new law have yet to be finalised, an obligation arises only when the legislation is virtually certain to be enacted as drafted.

Probable transfer of economic benefits

(h)   For a liability to qualify for recognition there must be not only a present obligation but also the probability of a transfer of economic benefits to settle that obligation. A transfer of economic benefits in settlement of an obligation is regarded as probable if the outflow is more likely than not to occur. Where there are a number of similar obligations (eg product warranties or similar contracts) the probability that a transfer will be required in settlement is determined by considering the class of obligations as a whole.

Reliable estimate of the obligation

(i)   An entity will normally be able to determine a range of possible outcomes and can therefore make an estimate of the obligation that is sufficiently reliable to use in recognising a provision. In the extremely rare case where no reliable estimate can be made, a liability exists that cannot be recognised. That liability is therefore disclosed as a contingent liability.

Contingent liabilities

(j)   An entity should not recognise a contingent liability.

Contingent assets

(k)   An entity should not recognise a contingent asset.

Measurement

Best estimate

(l)   The amount recognised as a provision should be the best estimate of the expenditure required to settle the present obligation at the balance sheet date. The provision is measured before tax, as the tax consequences of the provision, and changes in it, are dealt with under SSAP 15 'Accounting for deferred tax'.

Risks and uncertainties

(m)   The risks and uncertainties that inevitably surround many events and circumstances should be taken into account in reaching the best estimate of the amount of the provision. Care is needed to avoid duplicating adjustments for risk and uncertainty with consequent overstatement of a provision.

Present value

(n)   Where the effect of the time value of money is material, the amount of a provision should be the present value of the expenditures expected to be required to settle the obligation. The discount rate (or rates) should be a pre-tax rate (or rates) that reflect(s) current market assessments of the time value of money and the risks specific to the liability. The discount rate(s) should not reflect risks for which future cash flow estimates have been adjusted.

Future events

(o)   Future events that may affect the amount required to settle the entity's obligation should be reflected in the amount of a provision where there is sufficient objective evidence that they will occur. The effect of possible new legislation is taken into consideration in measuring an existing obligation when sufficient objective evidence exists that the legislation is virtually certain to be enacted.

Expected disposal of assets

(p) Gains from the expected disposal of assets should not be taken into account in measuring a provision. Instead such gains are assessed for recognition under the principles of asset recognition, which include the requirements in FRS 11 'Impairment of Fixed Assets and Goodwill'.

Reimbursements

(q) Where some or all of the expenditure required to settle a provision is expected to be reimbursed by another party, the reimbursement should be recognised only when it is virtually certain that reimbursement will be received if the entity settles the obligation. The reimbursement should be treated as a separate asset. The amount recognised for the reimbursement should not exceed that of the provision. In the profit and loss account, the expense relating to a provision may be presented net of the amount recognised for a reimbursement.

Changes in provisions

(r) Provisions should be reviewed at each balance sheet date and adjusted to reflect the current best estimate. If it is no longer probable that a transfer of economic benefits will be required to settle the obligation, the provision should be reversed.

(s) Where discounting is used, the size of a provision will change in each period to reflect the passage of time. This change is recognised as interest expense and disclosed separately from other interest on the face of the profit and loss account.

Use of provisions

(t) A provision should be used only for expenditures for which the provision was originally recognised.

Disclosure

(u) For each class of provision, an entity should disclose:

  – the carrying amount at the beginning and end of the period,

  – additional provisions made in the period, including increases to existing provisions,

  – amounts used (ie, incurred and charged against the provision),

  – amounts reversed unused,

  – the change in the discounted amount arising from the passage of time and the effect of any change.

Comparative information need not be disclosed for these items. In addition the entity should give:

  (i) a brief description of the nature of the obligation, and the expected timing of any resulting outflows of economic benefits:

  (ii) an indication of the uncertainties about the amount or timing of those outflows; and

  (iii) the amount of any reimbursement, and of any asset that has been recognised for that expected reimbursement.

(v) Unless the possibility of any transfer in settlement is remote, for each class of contingent liability at the e balance sheet date a brief description of the nature of the contingent liability should be disclosed and, where practicable, an estimate of its financial effect and an indication of the uncertainties relating to the amount or timing of any outflow. The entity should also disclose the possibility of any reimbursement.

(w) Where an inflow of economic benefits is probable, the entity should give a brief description of the nature of the contingent assets at the balance sheet date and, where practicable, an estimate of their financial effect.

(x) In extremely rare cases, disclosure of some or all of the information required can be expected to prejudice seriously the position of the entity in a dispute with other parties on the subject matter of the provision, contingent liability or contingent asset. In such cases the information need not be disclosed; but the general nature of the dispute should be disclosed, together with the fact that, and reason why, the information has not been disclosed.

3.304.5 FRS 12 – Revenue approach to provisions

The following is reproduced (with slight modifications) from the Revenue publication Tax Briefing Issue 41 dealing with accounting rules and taxation in the light of the publication of FRS 12.

General rule as regards provisions

Apart from TCA 1997, s 81(2)(i) which deals with the allowance for doubtful debts, the Tax Acts are silent as regards the question of provisions. Accordingly, the allowability of a provision will depend on whether the provision is necessary in ascertaining the full profits for tax purposes.

 Revenue has up to now treated a provision as allowable for tax purposes if:

  – the provision did not seek to anticipate a loss i.e. the provision did not refer to expenditure which had not been incurred [see paragraph 12 of the Revenue Commissioners' memorandum (April 1975) to the Accountancy Bodies on SSAP 9 – the text of paragraph 12 is set out at the end of this article];

  – the expenditure in respect of which the provision was made would be an allowable deduction in computing profits for tax purposes – for example, the expenditure would not be capital expenditure;

  – it is made in accordance with the correct principles of commercial accounting;

  – it can be estimated with a reasonable degree of accuracy;

  – it is made to correctly ascertain the full profits for tax purposes, being the receipts during the year and the expenditure laid out to earn those receipts.

New Revenue approach to provisions

In the light of a number of recent UK court decisions, Revenue is prepared to accept that there is no longer any rule of tax law which prohibits a provision for future losses, where such a provision is required in accordance with a system of commercial accounting which correctly ascertains the full profits for tax purposes of the trader. Revenue accepts that a provision made in accordance with generally accepted accounting practice [GAAP], including a provision made in accordance with FRS 12, is made in accordance with such a system. Revenue also accepts that a provision for a loss on a contract, made in accordance with paragraph 9 of Part 1 of SSAP 9, is no longer precluded on the basis that the provision takes account of expenditure that has not yet been incurred. The other requirements governing the allowability of a provision, which are listed above, continue to apply.

Where there is a doubt as to whether a provision is allowable for tax purposes, taxpayers should avail of the expression of doubt facility in TCA 1997, s 955(4).

An examination of the facts supporting provisions is a normal part of Revenue's audit programmes.

Prior year adjustments arising from FRS 12

FRS 12 introduces a more stringent test as regards the making of provisions in accounts. Where provisions have been made in previous years, an accounting adjustment may be required to the first accounts for periods ended on or after 23 March 1999. FRS 12 states that any such adjustment should be made by restating the comparative figures for the preceding year and adjusting the opening balance of the reserves for the cumulative effect.

The treatment, for tax purposes, of such an accounting adjustment will depend on whether the provision was allowed for tax purposes for the period in which it was made. If the provision was allowed for tax purposes for the period in which it was made, the accounting adjustment should be included in the profits for tax purposes of the period in which the change in accounting policy took place.

Example 3.304.5.1

A provision of €200k was made for the accounting period ended 31 March 2000. The provision was allowed for tax purposes for that period. In the period ended 31 March 2003 the provision is reduced to €120k, in accordance with FRS 12. The reduction of €80k appears as an adjustment to the comparative figures for the period ended 31 March 2002 in the 2003 accounts and an increase in the opening reserves for the year ended 31 March 2003 of that amount. In calculating the profits for tax purposes for the period ended 31 March 2003, the profits should be increased by the reduction in the provision, ie the increase in the reserves.

If the provision was not allowed for tax purposes for the period in which it was made (because, for example, it was not capable of estimation with a reasonable degree of accuracy), an appropriate tax adjustment would have been made for the period in which the provision was made. In these circumstances, the provision as adjusted under FRS 12 will be allowable for tax purposes, provided it does not breach any of the rules listed above. Assuming it is allowable, it may be claimed for the period in which the change of accounting policy takes place.

Example 3.304.5.2

A provision of €100k was made in the accounting period ended 31 March 2001. In calculating the profits for tax purposes, the provision had been added back. In accordance with FRS 12, the provision is reduced to €40k in the year ended 31 March 2002. The reduction in the provision appears as a restatement of the comparative figures for the year ended 31 March 2001 in the 2002 accounts and an increase in the reserves for the year ended

31 March 2002 of €60k (ie, write back of excess provision). Assuming there is no tax rule precluding a deduction for the provision, the provision revised in accordance with FRS 12 may be claimed for the period ended 31 March 2002 (€40k).

Provisions disallowed for tax purposes in the past

Where a provision was previously disallowed on the basis that it anticipated a loss, the earlier year will not be re-opened. The return of income for these periods, which would have taken account of such an adjustment, would have been prepared in accordance with the practice generally prevailing at the time. The provision, calculated in accordance with FRS 12, may be claimed in the first open accounting period ending on or after 23 March 1999.

Provisions which should have been disallowed for tax purposes in the past

Where a provision had been claimed for tax purposes for accounting periods ending before 23 March 1999 and allowed under the self-assessment system, Inspectors will not now seek to disallow the provision on the grounds that the provision anticipates a loss. Where provisions which are not allowable for some other reason [e.g. because they are capital in nature] had been claimed for tax purposes in the period in which they were made, taxpayers should contact their local Inspector to agree the adjustment due for the earlier period together with any interest and penalties which may arise.

[References to the period in which a provision was made include a reference to basis periods for years of assessment.]

3.305 International Financial Reporting Standards (IFRS)

3.305.1 Introduction and outline

For any period of account (a period for which a company makes up its accounts) commencing on or after 1 January 2005, all EU companies listed on a stock exchange are required to prepare their consolidated financial statements for the group in accordance with a common set of accounting standards referred to as International Financial Reporting Standards (IFRS), or International Accounting Standards (IAS), in place of Irish generally accepted accounting practice (Irish GAAP). As Irish GAAP is undergoing a process of change as it converges with IFRS, however, issues arising from the introduction of IFRS are of relevance to companies generally.

FA 2005 s 48 (introducing TCA 1997 ss 76A, 76B and 76C and Sch 17A, and amending TCA 1997 ss 4 (definitions), 81 (general rule for deductions), 110 (securitisation), 321 (making of allowances and charges), 766 (credit for research and development)) provides for the tax implications of the move by companies to IFRS. While IFRS is required in the case of the consolidated accounts of a group of companies, accounts of companies individually may be prepared in accordance with either IFRS or Irish GAAP. The financial reporting framework must be the same for the individual accounts of the parent company of a group and the individual accounts of the subsidiary companies unless there are good reasons for not following this group consistency requirement. Once a company transfers to IFRS it must continue to use that method of accounting other than in exceptional circumstances.

As has traditionally been the case, the computation of taxable profits commences with the profit as disclosed in the accounts of the company. (Consolidated accounts are irrelevant for tax purposes.) If a company chooses to prepare its accounts under IFRS, those accounts will again be the starting point for the computation of profits. Taxable trading income is to be computed in accordance with IFRS and provides also for transitional rules to be applied in respect of the changeover from Irish GAAP to IFRS. The section provides for specific treatment in the cases of certain items, principally the following:

Where unrealised gains on financial assets and liabilities based on movements in their fair value are taken into account in calculating profits and losses of a company, they will also be taken into account in calculating taxable income.

In the event that a company within a group prepares its accounts in accordance with Irish GAAP while another group member uses IFRS, any transactions between those companies must be accounted for, for tax purposes, by both companies on the basis of Irish GAAP if a tax advantage would otherwise result.

There are provisions for certain changes concerning the rules for deductibility of expenses for tax purposes:

- share-based consideration given by a company is generally disallowable for tax purposes except that share-based payments allowable prior to the change over to IFRS, for example, a payment made by a company to another company in respect of the issue by the latter company of shares to the first-mentioned company's employees, continue to be allowable;

- interest payable by a company, and expenditure by a company on research and development, continue to be allowable for tax purposes even though under IFRS the interest or expenditure may be included for accounts purposes in the value of an asset.

Special provision is made for securitisation entities (to which TCA 1997, s 110 applies) to ensure the continuation of the tax neutral treatment of those entities notwithstanding the change to preparing accounts using IFRS.

Labour costs included in the cost of an asset qualifying for capital allowances are to be included in the cost of the asset for capital allowances.

Expenditure on research and development continues to qualify for credit for R&D expenditure notwithstanding that under IFRS it may be included in the cost of an asset for accounting purposes. Interest may not be taken into account in calculating expenditure on R&D for the purposes of the credit.

There are transitional measures designed to avoid double counting for tax purposes, or the falling out of the tax system, of income or expenses on the change over to IFRS. Similar transitional rules apply in respect of the move to IFRS in the case of the taxation of unrealised gains on financial instruments. The profits, losses and expenses that would otherwise fall out of the system are to be taxed or allowed as appropriate over a five-year period. A transitional measure relating to bad debt provisions is intended to ensure that the deductibility for tax purposes of any bad debts incurred by a company is not affected by reason of the change over to IFRS.

The transitional measures apply also in relation to any gradual move to IFRS as well as where an Irish GAAP standard is converging with IFRS. As to whether the transitional arrangements will apply in the latter case will depend on the matters covered by the standard concerned. Transitional provisions may apply in respect of the convergence of separate Irish GAAP standards in periods different to those for their corresponding IFRS standards if the convergences are in different periods and the matters covered by each are relevant to those provisions.

Against the background of the publication of Financial Reporting Standards within Irish GAAP as part of a process of convergence between Irish GAAP and IFRS, there are rules relating to cases in which the trading profits or losses of a company for an accounting period are computed in accordance with relevant accounting standards but where for preceding periods they have been computed in accordance with standards other than relevant accounting standards. *Relevant accounting standards* for this purpose are IFRS or Irish GAAP based on published standards equivalent to IFRS (see **3.305.6** below).

Taxable income is to be increased by amounts receivable which, as a result of the change in accounting rules, would otherwise not be taken into account for tax purposes either before or after the change to IFRS; correspondingly, taxable income is to be reduced by amounts receivable which, as a result of the change in accounting rules, would otherwise be taken into account twice for tax purposes, once before the change over and once afterwards. Similar adjustments are prescribed in respect of expenses. The resulting adjustment is to be taxed or allowed over a period of five years.

Any accounting adjustment to bad debt provisions has traditionally only been followed for tax purposes where it relates to specific provisions. Under IFRS, the method for calculating provisions for bad debts is more specific than was previously the case. Adjustments that are properly calculated in accordance with relevant accounting standards are to be deductible for tax purposes. No adjustment to taxable profits is to be made in respect of the restatement of the doubtful debts provision at the point of transition to IFRS. If, however, the level at any time of the provision for doubtful debts falls below its level at the point of transition, an adjustment is to be made to taxable profits at that time to ensure that there is no loss of deductibility for actual bad debts incurred.

An adjustment is to be made at the point of transition to IFRS in the case of financial instruments. For example, a company that was taxable before the move to IFRS on the basis of realised gains on financial instruments will become taxable following the move to IFRS on increases and decreases in the fair value of such instruments in accordance with IFRS. On the change over to IFRS, movements in the fair value of such instruments from the value at the point of moving are to be taken into account for tax purposes. Without any such adjustment, the difference between the cost of an instrument acquired before the move and its value at the point of the move would fall out of account for tax purposes. Such difference is taken into account for tax purposes but is spread over a five-year period.

A loss on the disposal of such an instrument, where within a short period there is a purchase and sale of an instrument of the same class, in the six months before the move to IFRS is to be spread over five years. Where a financial instrument was taxed before the move to IFRS on the basis of movements in value but under IFRS falls to be taxed on a realisation basis, the cost of the instrument for tax purposes is to be taken to be its value at the point of the move to IFRS.

The treatment which follows, including that in **3.305.5** and **3.305.7-10**, incorporates certain material and examples based on the Guidance Note on Section 48 of the Finance Act published by the Revenue Commissioners in January 2006 and on further guidance material issued by the Revenue in February 2008.

3.305.2 Computation of profits or gains: accounting standards

Profits and gains of a trade or profession carried on by a company are to be computed for the purposes of Case I or II of Schedule D in accordance with generally accepted accounting practice, subject to any adjustment required or authorised by law in computing such profits or gains for those purposes (TCA 1997, s 76A(1)).

The reference to "law" above must be to the Tax Acts, statutory instruments and any directly applicable EU law as well as to case law, whether Irish, UK, EU or otherwise, since the question of adjustments to be made in computing taxable income is influenced significantly by decisions of case law. Examples of adjustment required would be the disallowance of capital expenditure or entertainment expenditure charged in the accounts, the deduction of capital allowances etc.

As to whether an item of expenditure is capital or revenue will not necessarily be determined by the related accounting treatment. While influential, the accounting treatment will not be followed in this respect where it is at variance with tax principles.

TCA 1997 Schedule 17A (transitional measures – see **3.305.6**) is to apply to a company as respects any matter related to the computation of income of the company where as respects that matter:

(a) for an accounting period, profits or gains of a trade or profession carried on by the company are computed in accordance with relevant accounting standards (RAS – briefly, IAS or Irish GAAP stated to embody IAS – see **3.305.6** below); and

(b) for preceding accounting periods, profits or gains of a trade or profession carried on by the company are computed in accordance with standards other than RAS (TCA 1997, s 76A(2)).

Thus, the transitional measures relate to situations in which companies make a piecemeal transition to IFRS. This would be the case where, for example, Irish GAAP moves gradually towards IFRS. As to whether or not the transitional arrangements apply to the convergence of an Irish GAAP standard to IFRS will depend on the matters in question. Transitional provisions could apply to the convergence of separate Irish GAAP standards in different periods to their respective IFRS standards if the convergences are in different periods and the matters covered by each are relevant to the transitional provisions.

Generally accepted accounting practice

For the above purposes, *generally accepted accounting practice* means:

(a) in relation to the affairs of a company or other entity that prepares accounts in accordance with international accounting standards (IAS accounts), generally accepted accounting practice with respect to such accounts; and

(b) in any other case, Irish generally accepted accounting practice (Irish GAAP) (TCA 1997, s 4(1)).

Accordingly, the profit or loss on which tax computations are to be based are, where IFRS is applied, the net income or loss in accordance with the Income Statement and, where Irish GAAP is applied, the net profit or loss as disclosed by the profit and loss account. In the case of IFRS, amounts reflected in the Statement of Changes in Equity are not included in profits for tax purposes until such amounts are included in the Income Statement.

In the unlikely event that any realised gain or loss in respect of a trading item is not reflected in the Income Statement for the period in question, it should be included for tax purposes for that period to the extent that it has not already been so included for tax purposes by reference to movements in fair value or arising out of transitional adjustments. If any profit or loss so taken into account is brought into the Income Statement at a later stage, an adjustment will of course be required so as not to have it taken into account twice for tax purposes.

International accounting standards (IAS)

In (a) above, *international accounting standards* (IAS) means the international accounting standards, within the meaning of Regulation (EC) No 1606/2002 of the European Parliament and the Council of 19 July 2002 on the application of international accounting standards (*the Regulation*).

Where the European Commission in accordance with the Regulation adopts an IAS with modifications, then as regards matters covered by that standard:

(i)   generally accepted accounting practice with respect to IAS accounts will be regarded as permitting the use of the standard either with or without the modifications; and

(ii)   accounts prepared on either basis will be regarded as prepared in accordance with IAS (TCA 1997, s 4(7))).

Irish generally accepted accounting practice (Irish GAAP)

In (b) above, *Irish generally accepted accounting practice* means generally accepted accounting practice with respect to accounts (other than IAS accounts) of companies incorporated or formed under the laws of the State, being accounts that are intended to give a true and fair view.

Case III and Case IV

Trading income chargeable to tax under Case III is to be computed in accordance with Case I rules as is the case also with income chargeable under Case IV where such income is to be computed in accordance with Case I rules (see **3.2081**), and to securitisation vehicles in accordance with TCA 1997, s 110 (see **3.305.5** below).

Leasing

In the case of leasing transactions, lessors continue to be taxable on lease payments received subject to capital allowances in respect of the leased assets while the treatment of lessees also remains unchanged (see **3.303**). TCA 1997, s 80A, which provides for exceptional treatment for certain short-term leases (see **3.303.7**), also continues to apply.

Notwithstanding TCA 1997, s 76A and subject to TCA 1997, s 80A, the income of a lessor company from a finance lease in the course of a trade of leasing is not the amount of income from the lease computed in accordance with generally accepted accounting practice. Such finance lease income is to be computed, subject to the provisions of the Corporation Tax Acts apart from TCA 1997, s 76A, by treating:

(a) lease payments receivable in respect of the lease as trading receipts of the trade; and

(b) any disbursements or expenses laid out or expended for the purposes of earning those lease payments as trading expenses of the trade (TCA 1997, s 76D(2)).

In addition, of course, a deduction would also be available for capital allowances in respect of the cost of the leased assets.

A *finance lease* is a lease which, under generally accepted accounting practice, falls to be treated as a finance lease (TCA 1997, s 76D(1)). For accounting purposes, a lease of an asset is treated as a finance lease if it is one which transfers substantially all the risks and rewards of ownership of the asset from the lessor to the lessee. A finance lease, sometimes referred to as a capital lease, is accounted for as a loan from the lessor to the lessee to fund the lessee's acquisition of the asset. A finance lease effectively allows the lessee to finance the purchase of the asset even where, in strictness, the lessee never acquires the asset. A finance lease will, typically, give the lessee control over the asset for a large proportion of its useful life, providing the lessee with the benefits and risks of ownership.

The amount regarded as a loan appears as an asset in the balance sheet of the lessor and rental receipts are treated partly as repayment of that loan and partly as interest on it. Conversely, the lessee treats the deemed loan as a liability and records a similar amount as the value of the leased asset on the other side of the balance sheet. Again, rental payments are split into interest and repayments of principal while the asset is depreciated in the same way as other assets which the lessee legally owns. (A lease which is not a finance lease is classed as an operating lease. Operating lease rentals paid by the lessee or, as the case may be, received by the lessor, are simply taken to the profit and loss account as the expense or income accrues – which is not necessarily when rentals are paid or received.)

Where, in relation to a finance lease of machinery and plant—

(a) the wear and tear allowances fall to be made to the lessee and not to the lessor, and

(b) where the lessee is within the charge to tax in the State, it has been demonstrated that the lessee will only claim a deduction, in computing income within the charge to tax, in respect of the interest element of lease payments,

Revenue will accept that the lessor's taxable income from the lease is the income from the lease computed in accordance with accounting practice.

Deferred consideration

Under IAS 18, the difference between the fair value of deferred consideration and its nominal amount may be recognised as interest or other operating income. Where the consideration is itself a trading receipt, any such income will also be recognised as a trading receipt for tax purposes when it is included in profit or loss. Where the cost of an asset is deferred, it is the actual expenditure on the asset that is to be taken into account in computing the amount of any capital allowances that may be due. Notional interest would not be relevant for capital allowances purposes.

Example 3.305.2.1

An item of plant is sold at the beginning of an accounting period on terms such that it will not actually be paid for in cash until the end of the following period. The accounting and tax position of the seller and the buyer is as follows:

		Accounts	*Tax*
		€	€
Seller			
Period 1	Discounted value of sale	160,000	160,000
	Imputed interest	20,000	20,000
		180,000	180,000
Period 2	Imputed interest	20,000	20,000
Purchaser			
Period 1	Balance sheet	160,000	
	Income statement	20,000	
Period 2	Income statement	20,000	

For capital allowances purposes, the allowable cost, in period 1, is €200,000

Where, under IFRS, a net present value of decommissioning or restoration costs associated with an asset is included as part of the cost of that asset, it is the actual expenditure on the asset that will qualify for capital allowances. Any amount for expected decommissioning or restoration costs should be ignored, as should any subsequent unwind of the value of those costs.

3.305.3   Unrealised gains and losses in certain cases

Unrealised gains on financial assets and liabilities, based on movements in their fair value, that are taken into account in calculating profits and losses of a company are also to be taken into account in calculating taxable income.

A profit or gain from a financial asset or a financial liability of a company which, in accordance with relevant accounting standards (RAS – briefly, IAS or Irish GAAP stated to embody IAS – see **3.305.6** below), is:

(a)   calculated on the basis of fair values of the asset or the liability in an accounting period; and

(b)   included in the profit or loss of the company for the accounting period,

is to be taken into account on that basis in computing profits or gains of the company for that period for the purposes of Case I or II of Schedule D (TCA 1997, s 76B(2)).

Fair value is relevant only to IFRS or Irish GAAP standards stated to embody IFRS and that are based on fair values. The reference in (a) above is to fair "values": a comparison of two values within the accounting period concerned is envisaged and the profit or gain or loss will be by reference to the movement in the fair value of the asset or liability in the period.

Thus, the realisation basis for the taxation of gains and losses on financial assets and liabilities continues to apply to companies that remain on Irish GAAP until convergence with IFRS.

As regards (a), the profit or gain (or loss) will be the movement in the fair value of the asset or liability in the accounting period; as regards (b), that profit or gain (or loss), computed by reference to the movement in fair values, is included for accounting purposes in the company's Income Statement or profit and loss account.

Where movements in fair values of financial assets or liabilities in an accounting period are included for accounting purposes in the profit or loss of a company for that period, it is on that basis that income (and losses) from those assets and liabilities will be brought into the tax computation. An amount will be regarded as included in profit and loss for this purpose if:

(a)   where IFRS is used, the amount is reflected in the Income Statement;

(b)   where Irish GAAP is used, the amount is reflected in the profit and loss account.

The above-described treatment applies only to financial assets and liabilities that are trading assets for tax purposes and not to assets and liabilities in general.

The so called "mark to market" basis, which would allow unrealised gains and losses to be brought into the computation of trading profits, has for some time been accepted concessionally in relation to certain financial services companies in order to avoid administrative difficulties that would otherwise result if the realisation basis were to be insisted on. It would appear, for trading companies applying RAS, that market to market treatment now has a statutory basis. This also raises questions as to the extent to which the decision in *AB Ltd v MacGiolla Riogh* 3 ITC 301 (see **3.301**) must continue to be followed.

For the above purposes, *financial asset*, *financial liability* and *fair value* have the meanings assigned to them by international accounting standards (TCA 1997, s 76B(1)(a)). In IAS 39, *fair value* is described as the amount for which an asset could be exchanged, or a liability settled, between knowledgeable, willing parties in an arm's length transaction. The concept of fair value is also used in Irish GAAP standards, for example in FRS 26. Its meaning is, however, developed in various places within the IAS beyond that simple description depending on the particular transaction under discussion. Market value as understood for tax purposes, which is relevant for the purposes of TCA 1997 Sch 17A (see **3.305.6** below under *Financial instruments*), although similar to, cannot be equated with, fair value.

In IAS No 32, *financial asset* is any asset that is:

(a)   cash;

(b)   an equity instrument of another entity;

(c)   a contractual right:

  (i)   to receive cash or another financial asset from another entity, or

  (ii)   to exchange financial assets or financial liabilities with another entity under conditions that are potentially favourable to the entity; or

(d)   a contract that will or may be settled in the entity's own equity instruments and is:

    (i)   a non-derivative for which the entity is or may be obliged to receive a variable number of the entity's own equity instruments, or

    (ii)   a derivative that will or may be settled other than by the exchange of a fixed amount of cash or another financial asset for a fixed number of the entity's own equity instruments. For this purpose, the entity's own equity instruments do not include instruments that are themselves contracts for the future receipt or delivery of the entity's own equity instruments.

A *financial liability* is any liability that is:

  (a)   a contractual obligation:

    (i)   to deliver cash or another financial asset from another entity, or

    (ii)   to exchange financial assets or financial liabilities with another entity under conditions that are potentially unfavourable to the entity; or

  (b)   a contract that will or may be settled in the entity's own equity instruments and is:

    (i)   a non-derivative for which the entity is or may be obliged to deliver a variable number of the entity's own equity instruments, or

    (ii)   a derivative that will or may be settled other than by the exchange of a fixed amount of cash or another financial asset for a fixed number of the entity's own equity instruments. For this purpose, the entity's own equity instruments do not include instruments that are themselves contracts for the future receipt or delivery of the entity's own equity instruments.

A *derivative* is described in IAS No 39 as a financial instrument or other contract within the scope of that Standard with all three of the following characteristics:

  (a)   its value changes in response to the change in a specified interest rate, financial instrument price, commodity price, foreign exchange rate, index of prices or rates, credit rating or credit index, or other variable (sometimes called the "underlying");

  (b)   it requires no initial net investment or an initial investment that is smaller than would be required for other types of contracts that would be expected to have a similar response to changes in market factors; and

  (c)   it is settled at a future date.

A *financial instrument* is any contract that gives rise to a financial asset of one entity and a financial liability or equity instrument of another entity.

References to *profits or gains* include references to losses. The amount of a loss incurred in a trade or profession in an accounting period is to be computed in the same way as profits or gains from the trade or profession in that period would have been computed (TCA 1997, s 76B(1)(b)). (See also **3.305.6** below regarding transitional measures affecting financial assets and liabilities.)

The foregoing concepts are of relevance only to companies that have moved to IFRS or where Irish GAAP standards stated to embody IFRS apply.

3.305.4   Different accounting policies within a group

Outline

In general, all members of a group will be required to move to IFRS at the same time. However, the IFRS accounting regulations (European Communities (International Financial Reporting Standards & Miscellaneous Amendments) Regulations 2005 (SI 116 of 2005)) provide that the requirement for all companies within a group to use the same financial reporting framework will not apply if there are good reasons for not doing so and those reasons are disclosed in the financial statements of the parent company. In such a situation, TCA 1997, s 76C provides for a single framework for computing profits for tax purposes in the case of transactions between two associated companies, one of which uses IFRS and the other of which uses Irish GAAP. The rules only apply if a tax advantage would otherwise result from the use of different standards.

A claim to group relief by one company in respect of a loss incurred by another company would not itself be regarded as a transaction between the companies notwithstanding that a payment for the group relief may be made. However, where transactions between two members of a group are accounted for on different bases by them, a tax advantage could arise by virtue of a group relief claim.

TCA 1997, s 76C applies regardless as to whether or not there is an avoidance motive. In considering the application of this provision, regard should be had to whether, in the overall context, a net tax advantage arises: determining the amount of a tax advantage arising involves taking account of disadvantages arising from the use of different accounting standards.

Anti-avoidance

If a tax advantage would otherwise result in a case where a company within a group prepares its accounts in accordance with Irish GAAP while another group member uses IFRS, any transactions between those companies must be accounted for, for tax purposes, by both companies on the basis of Irish GAAP.

In this connection, *tax advantage* means:

(a)   a reduction, avoidance or deferral of any charge or assessment to tax, including any potential or prospective charge or assessment; or

(b)   a refund of or a payment of an amount of tax, or an increase in an amount of tax refundable or otherwise payable to a person, including any potential or prospective amount so refundable or payable (TCA 1997, s 76C(1)).

For the purposes of computing profits or gains of a company preparing accounts in accordance with IAS from a transaction between, or a series of transactions involving, the company and another company with which it is associated and which prepares accounts in accordance with Irish GAAP, and a tax advantage would otherwise accrue to the company as a result of using IAS rather than GAAP, the Corporation Tax Acts are to apply as if the company prepared its accounts in accordance with Irish GAAP (TCA 1997, s 76C(2)). Specifically, this provision applies where—

(a)   one of the associated companies (within the meaning of TCA 1997, s 432(1) – see **2.401.5**) is within the charge to tax under Case I or Case II and prepares its accounts under IFRS (IAS);

(b) the other company, also within the Case I or II charge, prepares its accounts under Irish GAAP;

(c) there is a transaction between, or a series of transactions involving, those companies; and

(d) a tax advantage would otherwise accrue to the company that prepares its accounts under IFRS as compared with what the outcome would have been had its accounts been prepared using Irish GAAP.

A series of transactions in relation to two companies will not avoid being a series of transactions merely because:

(i) there is no transaction in the series to which both of the companies are parties;

(ii) that parties to any arrangement in pursuance of which the transactions in the series are entered into do not include one or both of those companies;

(iii) there are one or more transactions in the series to which neither of the companies is a party (TCA 1997, s 76C(1)(b)).

3.305.5 Rules for deductibility of expenses for tax purposes

Share-based consideration

Share-based consideration given by a company either for goods or services or to its employees or directors is disallowable for tax purposes, whether the shares are shares in the company itself or in a connected company. Certain expenses which had always been tax deductible, however, remain deductible, including payments made by a company to another company to issue shares to the first company's employees or for the purchase of shares by a company for its employees.

No sum may be deducted in respect of any consideration given for goods and services, or consideration given to an employee or director of a company, which consists, directly or indirectly, of shares in the company, or a connected company (within the meaning of TCA 1997, s 10 - see **2.302**), or a right to receive such shares, except to the extent:

(a) of the amount of the expenditure incurred by the company on the acquisition of the shares at a price that does not exceed the price that would have been payable if the shares were acquired by way of a bargain made at arm's length (TCA 1997, s 81(2)(n)(i)),

(b) where the shares are shares in a connected company, of any payment by the company to the connected company for the issue or transfer by that company of the shares, being a payment that does not exceed the amount that would have been payable in a transaction between independent persons acting at arm's length (TCA 1997, s 81(2)(n)(ii)), or

(c) of other expenditure incurred or, as the case may be, payment made to the connected company by the company in connection with the right to receive such shares which is incurred or, as the case may be, made for bona fide commercial purposes and does not form part of any scheme or arrangement of which the main purpose or one of the main purposes is the avoidance of liability to income tax, corporation tax or capital gains tax (TCA 1997, s 81(2)(n)(iii)).

TCA s 81(2)(n) was introduced in the context of the transition to IFRS and the requirement for a company that issues shares to employees to recognise the related cost in its profit and loss account. The background to this position is that under Irish GAAP generally, where no expenditure is incurred, no amount would appear in the company's profit and loss account in respect of such shares and shares or share options given to an employee or director would not qualify as a deductible expense of the company concerned. Under IFRS, an amount is to be shown in respect of such shares as an expense of the company.

The reference in TCA 1997, s 81(2)(n)(ii) to "any payment made by the company" is taken to mean that, in computing income for Case I purposes, a deduction for any such payment will not be due for any accounting period prior to that in which the payment is made; that a deduction will not be due on an accruals basis. Provided that all other conditions regarding deductibility are met, the Revenue accept that a deduction may be taken for the accounting period in which the payment is made. (It is questionable, however, that the reference implies a "paid" basis for any allowable deduction. Rather, in respect of shares given to an employee or director, the apparent intention is to restrict the deductible amount to the payments made to the connected company - whenever such payments might be made. On the other hand it might, admittedly, be difficult in practice to claim the correct deduction in an accounting period earlier than that in which the payments are made.)

In certain cases, notwithstanding that part of a payment made by a company may not be charged as an expense in its Income Statement, the Revenue will in practice accept that a deduction should be made for the payment provided—

(a) no other deduction is claimed directly or indirectly in respect of the share-based remuneration concerned,

(b) the amount of the payment does not exceed an amount that would have been paid in a similar transaction between independent persons acting at arm's length, and

(c) the payment does not form part of any scheme or arrangement of which the main purpose or one of the main purposes is the avoidance of liability to income tax, corporation tax or capital gains tax.

Arising from the above, cross charges from foreign parent companies to their Irish subsidiaries continue to be deductible for tax purposes as long as they are on arm's length terms. Amounts spent in purchasing shares on arm's length terms are also deductible. Accordingly, a prohibition on deduction will apply only in cases where employees of a company are issued with shares in the company itself. Where a company purchases shares in itself on the market for the purpose of making them available to employees, a deduction should be available. Although TCA 1997, s 184 (see **11.310** regarding the re-issue of treasury shares treated as an issue of new shares) might suggest otherwise, it is considered that a deduction would nevertheless be available. A buy back of shares, off market, should be subject to the same treatment. Although the expenditure might have the appearance of capital expenditure, if the buy back is for the purpose of making the shares available to employees (probably an unusual scenario), a deduction would seem to be justified.

Example 3.305.5.1

Employees of a quoted company are given options to acquire shares in the company for €20 per share, being the market value of the shares at that time. The vesting period is 5 years. At the end of the 5 years, the company issues shares to the employees.

Assumed accounting treatment

The fair value of the option, assumed to be €10, is recognised as an expense in the income statement over the vesting period at €2 per year.

Tax treatment

As no expenditure has been incurred by the company in providing the shares, no deduction is available in respect of the share options or the issue of shares.

Example 3.305.5.2

Employees of a quoted company are given options to acquire shares in the company for €20 per share, being the market value of the shares at that time. The vesting period is 5 years. At the end of the 5 years, the company buys the shares in the market for €60 per share and sells them to the employees for €20 per share.

Assumed accounting treatment

As in Example **3.305.5.1**

Tax treatment

As no expenditure has been incurred in acquiring the shares prior to the end of the vesting period, amounts expensed each year before that time are disallowed. When the company incurs the expenditure on acquiring the shares, a deduction will be due. The deduction will be €40 (ie, the difference between the expenditure of €60 and the €20 received from the employee in each case).

Example 3.305.5.3

Employees of a subsidiary of a quoted company are given options to acquire shares in the quoted company for €20 per share, being the market value of the shares at that time. The vesting period is 5 years. At the end of the 5 years, the subsidiary buys the shares in the market for €60 per share and sells them to the employees for €20 per share.

Assumed accounting treatment

As in Example **3.305.5.1**

Tax treatment

As no expenditure has been incurred in acquiring the shares prior to the end of the vesting period, amounts expensed each year before that time are disallowed. When the subsidiary incurs the expenditure on acquiring the shares, a deduction will be due. The deduction will be €40 (ie, the difference between the expenditure of €60 and the €20 received from the employee in each case).

Example 3.305.5.4

The facts are as in Example **3.305.5.3** except that the subsidiary company acquires the shares directly from the quoted company on their issue for a payment equal to their market value.

The tax treatment would be as in Example **3.305.5.3**. There would be no tax implications for the parent company as the issue of the shares would simply add to its share capital.

Where a trust is used to hold shares for subsequent transmission to employees, the question of deductibility would be determined by reference to TCA 1997, s 81A (see **3.202.17**).

Where the consideration given by a company for the acquisition of a business consists of shares in the company, the consideration will not be regarded for the purposes of TCA 1997, s 81A as being given for goods or services. In a case involving the transfer of goods that constitute trading stock of both the transferor and the transferee in return for shares in the transferee company, a deduction for the value of the stock transferred will not be denied if it can be shown that the value of the stock is taken into account in computing trading income of the transferor.

Interest capitalised and expenditure on R&D

TCA 1997, s 81(3) (introduced by FA 2005) preserves the pre-existing position relating to the tax deductibility of interest and of expenditure on research and development. It specifically provides that interest payable, and expenditure on research and development incurred, by a company will not be denied a deduction in calculating taxable trading income by reason only that under IFRS it is included for accounting purposes in the cost of an asset. Under IFRS, such costs may have to be included in the cost of an asset rather than being treated as an expense so that they would not appear in the accounts as an expense in earning profits. TCA 1997, s 81(3) ensures that these costs continue to be deductible for tax purposes. Where expenditure on research and development is amortised, the deduction for tax purposes in respect of that expenditure will be made in accordance with the amortisation.

TCA 1997, s 81(3)(a) provides that, in respect of a company:

(i)   interest payable by the company; and

(ii) expenditure on research and development incurred by the company,

will not be prevented from being an allowable deduction for tax purposes in computing profits or gains for the purposes of Cases I or II of Schedule D by reason only that for accounting purposes they are brought into account in determining the value of an asset.

In the above connection, however, an amount will not be regarded as deductible in computing taxable profits or gains of a company to the extent that a deduction has been made in respect of that amount in computing such profits or gains for a previous accounting period, or the company has benefited from a tax relief under any provision in respect of that amount for a previous accounting period (TCA 1997, s 81(3)(b)).

The application of the above-described rule ensures that a double deduction will not be available, for example in a case where under IFRS an amount is included as part of the cost of an asset but where a deduction had already been given for tax purposes for that amount in an earlier accounting period. In such a case, the later deduction would not be made.

The accounting treatment of an item of expenditure will not automatically convert revenue expenditure into capital expenditure, or vice versa, for tax purposes. The fact that expenditure is charged to fixed assets may lend support to an argument that the expenditure is capital expenditure for tax purposes. However, if on tax principles the expenditure is of a revenue nature, charging it to capital does not make it capital expenditure for tax purposes.

Where expenditure which is revenue in nature and deductible for tax purposes is spread over the accounts of more than one year in accordance with relevant accounting standards, the tax deduction will also be spread in accordance with the accounting treatment.

Securitisation

The tax neutral treatment of securitisation entities is preserved under IFRS. Such entities may continue to compute their taxable income and profits based on Irish GAAP as it applied in 2004 thereby enabling them to preserve their tax neutrality.

TCA 1997, s 76A (computation of profits and gains: accounting standards – see **3.305.2** above) is to have effect in relation to a qualifying company (within the meaning of TCA 1997, s 110 (securitisation of assets) – see **7.206.11**) but on the basis that *generally accepted accounting practice* means Irish generally accepted accounting practice as it applied for a period of account ending on 31 December 2004. A qualifying company may, for any accounting period, elect that TCA 1997, s 76A is not to apply as respects that period or any subsequent accounting period. Such election is irrevocable (TCA 1997, s 110(6)). Thus, a qualifying company can, for tax purposes, continue to use accounts prepared on the basis of Irish GAAP as it applied for a period of account ending on 31 December 2004 or make an irrevocable election to change over to IFRS for any period of account beginning on or after 1 January 2005.

Labour costs capitalised

Labour costs included in the cost of an asset qualifying for capital allowances are included in the cost of the asset for capital allowances. For the purposes of TCA 1997 Part 9 (relief of capital expenditure), TCA 1997, s 321(2A) provides that, subject to TCA 1997, s 316 (references to capital expenditure – see **5.102**), references to expenditure in relation to an asset:

(a)   include expenditure on labour costs, including emoluments paid to employees of a company; and

(b)   do not include interest payable,

which for accounting purposes is taken into account by the company in determining the value of the asset.

Royalties as charges on income

In the case of patent royalty payments that are revenue in nature, they will not be prevented from being regarded as charges on income solely because they are included in the cost of an asset in accordance with IFRS (see **4.402**).

Credit for expenditure on research and development

Expenditure on research and development (R&D) continues to qualify for credit for R&D expenditure notwithstanding that under IFRS it may be included in the cost of an asset for accounting purposes. Interest may not be taken into account in calculating expenditure on R&D for the purposes of the credit. The definition of *expenditure on research and development* accordingly means (see also **7.402**) expenditure, other than expenditure on a building or structure, incurred by the company in the carrying on by it of research and development activities in a relevant Member State, being expenditure:

(a)   which is allowable for tax purposes in Ireland as a deduction in computing trading income otherwise than by virtue of TCA 1997, s 307 (allowances for capital expenditure in taxing a trade), *or would be so allowable but for the fact that for accounting purposes it is brought into account in determining the value of an intangible asset,* or is relieved by TCA 1997 Part 8 (as a charge on income);

(b)   on machinery or plant which qualifies for capital allowances under TCA 1997 Part 9 or Part 29 Chapter 2 (allowances for capital expenditure on scientific and research); or

(c)   which qualifies for an allowance under TCA 1997, s 764 (scientific research allowances).

In the definition of "expenditure on research and development" in TCA 1997, s 766, certain types of expenditure are excluded. One of these is any amount of interest notwithstanding that such interest is brought into account by the company in determining the value of an asset.

3.305.6   Transitional measures

TCA 1997 Schedule 17A contains transitional measures to apply where a company's taxable profits begin to be calculated using IFRS (including converged Irish GAAP standards). The transitional arrangements apply to each new standard as regards matters covered by the standard. Schedule 17A is designed to avoid double counting for tax purposes, or the falling out of the tax system, of income or expenses on the change over to IFRS. A transitional measure relating to bad debt provisions is designed to ensure that the deductibility for tax purposes of any bad debts incurred by a company is not affected by reason of the change over to IFRS; where a debt is written off against a provision that has not been deducted for tax purposes, the write-off will be deductible. Transitional rules also apply in respect of the move to IFRS in the case of the taxation of unrealised gains on financial instruments. The profits, losses and expenses that would otherwise fall out of the system are to be taxed or allowed as appropriate over a five-year period.

TCA 1997 Schedule 17A applies to a company as respects any matter related to the computation of company's income where as respects that matter:

(a)   for an accounting period, profits or gains of a trade or profession carried on by the company are computed in accordance with relevant accounting standards (RAS); and

(b)   for preceding accounting periods, profits or gains of a trade or profession carried on by the company are computed in accordance with standards other than RAS.

Relevant accounting standards (RAS)

In TCA 1997 Schedule 17A, *relevant accounting standards* means:

(a)   international accounting standards (IAS); or

(b)   as regards the matters covered by those published standards, Irish generally accepted accounting practice (GAAP) which is based on published standards—

(i)   which are stated so as to embody, in whole or in part, IAS; and

(ii)   the application of which would produce results that are substantially the same as those produced by the application of IAS (TCA 1997 Sch 17A paragraph 1).

The reference in (b) above reflects the move towards a convergence of Irish GAAP and IAS. For all practical purposes, references here to the change over to IFRS and to RAS may be taken to mean the same thing. The changeover date will be clear in cases where the move is from Irish GAAP to IAS. Since RAS comprehends both IAS and converged Irish GAAP, the changeover date may not be so clear where converged Irish GAAP is concerned. The change over is likely to be a gradual or step process in many cases leaving open the possibility that there may be a number of changeover dates, and over more than one accounting period, involved.

Amounts receivable and deductible: transitional

Taxable income is to be increased by amounts receivable which, as a result of the change in accounting rules, would otherwise not be taken into account for tax purposes either before or after the change to IFRS (RAS). Correspondingly, taxable income is to be reduced by amounts receivable which, as a result of the change in accounting rules, would otherwise be taken into account twice for tax purposes, once before the change over and once afterwards. Similar adjustments are prescribed in respect of expenses. The resulting adjustment is to be taxed or allowed over a period of five years.

Taxable amount exceeding deductible amount

An amount equal to the excess of the "taxable amount" over the "deductible amount" is treated as a trading receipt for the first accounting period in respect of which profits or gains of the company for the purposes of Case I or II of Schedule D are computed in accordance with RAS (TCA 1997 Sch 17A paragraph 2(2)(a)). Separate arrangements apply for bad debts and financial instruments (see below).

In relation to a company, *taxable amount* means the aggregate of the amounts of:

(a) so much of an amount receivable by the company, being an amount receivable that would have been taken into account as a trading receipt in computing the profits or gains of the company for Case I or II purposes if the amount had accrued in an accounting period for which such profits or gains were computed in accordance with RAS, as is not so taken into account—

    (i) for an accounting period for which such profits or gains of the company are computed in accordance with RAS; or

    (ii) for an accounting period ending before the first accounting period in respect of which such profits or gains are so computed, and

(b) so much of an expense incurred by the company that is deductible in computing the profits or gains of the company for Case I or II purposes for an accounting period for which such profits or gains are computed in accordance with RAS as was deducted in computing such profits or gains for any accounting period ending before the first accounting period of the company in respect of which such profits or gains were so computed.

Briefly, a taxable amount is any amount receivable that did not accrue in a period for which RAS is used but which has not been taken into account for tax purposes for any such period or for any period before RAS was first used, as well as any expense deductible under RAS but which has been deducted for any period before RAS was first used. Such taxable amounts are treated as trading receipts of the first accounting period in which RAS is used to prevent them from falling out of the tax system or, in the case of expenses, to ensure that they are not doubly allowed.

In relation to a company, *deductible amount* means the aggregate of the amounts of:

(a) so much of any amounts receivable by the company which falls to be taken into account as a trading receipt in computing profits or gains of the company for an accounting period for Case I or II purposes in accordance with RAS as was also taken into account as a trading receipt in computing such profits or gains of the company for any accounting period ending before the first accounting period in respect of which such profits or gains of the company were so computed; and

(b) so much of an expense incurred by the company, being an expense that would have been deductible in computing profits or gain of the company for Case I or II purposes if the expense had been incurred in an accounting period for which such profits or gains were computed in accordance with RAS, as—

    (i) was not deducted in computing the profits or gains of the company for Case I or II purposes for an accounting period ending before the first accounting period in respect of which such profits or gains of the company are computed in accordance with RAS, and

    (ii) is not deductible in computing the profits or gains of the company for Case I or II purposes for any accounting period for which such profits or gains are so computed.

Briefly, a deductible amount is any amount receivable that falls to be taken into account as a trading receipt for a period for which RAS is used but which has also been so taken into account for any period before RAS was first used, as well as any expense that was not incurred in a period for which RAS is used but was not taken into account for tax purposes for any period before RAS was first used or for any period for which RAS is used. Such deductible amounts are netted against trading receipts of the first accounting period in which RAS is used to ensure that they are not doubly taxed or, in the case of expenses, to ensure that they do not fail to be allowed once.

An amount ("relevant amount") treated as a trading receipt of an accounting period ("relevant accounting period") in the above circumstances will not, however, be taken into account for that period. Instead, a part of the relevant amount will be so taken into account for each accounting period falling wholly or partly into the period of five years beginning at the commencement of the relevant accounting period. That part will be such amount as bears to the relevant amount the same proportion as the length of the accounting period, or, as the case may be, the part of the accounting period falling into the period of five years, bears to five years (TCA 1997 Sch 17A paragraph 2(2)(b)).

Where any accounting period in which such an adjustment is to be made is the last accounting period in which a company carried on a trade or profession, the part of the relevant amount to be taken into account for that period will be the part required to ensure that the whole of that amount is accounted for (TCA 1997 Sch 17A paragraph 2(2)(c)).

Deductible amount exceeding taxable amount:

Should the deductible amount exceed the taxable amount, that excess will be treated as a deductible trading expense of the company's trade carried on by it for the first accounting period in respect of which profits or gains for Case I or II purposes of the company are computed in accordance with RAS (TCA 1997 Sch 17A paragraph

2(3)(a)). (Separate transitional arrangements apply for bad debts and financial instruments – see below.)

Any such amount ("relevant amount") so treated as a deductible trading expense for an accounting period ("relevant accounting period") will, however, not be taken into account for that period. Instead, a part of the relevant amount will be so taken into account for each accounting period falling wholly or partly into the period of five years beginning at the commencement of the relevant accounting period. That part will be such amount as bears to the relevant amount the same proportion as the length of the accounting period, or, as the case may be, the part of the accounting period falling into the period of five years, bears to five years (TCA 1997 Sch 17A paragraph 2(3)(b)).

Where any accounting period in which such an adjustment is to be made is the last accounting period in which a company carried on a trade or profession, the part of the relevant amount to be taken into account for that period will be the part required to ensure that the whole of that amount is accounted for (TCA 1997 Sch 17A paragraph 2(3)(c)).

Example 3.305.6.1

Under a three-year contract entered into in early 2004, Therapeutics Ltd is entitled to an up-front commission of €120,000 and, in accordance with Irish GAAP, accounts for the full €120,000 as revenue for that year. The company moves to IFRS at the end of 2004. Under IFRS, the €120,000 is to be spread over the three-year period of the contract. For 2005 and for 2006, therefore, €40,000 is included as revenue in the company's P&L account. Since €120,000 has been recognised in the 2004 accounts, there has clearly been a double counting of some of the revenue under the contract.

Transitional adjustments are accordingly made in tax computations so that the €40,000 for 2005 is deducted in tax computations over a five year period, and likewise the amount of €40,000 taxable for the year 2006. The result can be summarised as follows:

	Irish GAAP	IFRS	IFRS	IFRS	IFRS	IFRS	Total
	2004	2005	2006	2007	2008	2009	
	€	€	€	€	€	€	€
Revenue	120,000	40,000	40,000				200,000
Adjust re 2005		(8,000)	(8,000)	(8,000)	(8,000)	(8,000)	(40,000)
Adjust re 2006		(8,000)	(8,000)	(8,000)	(8,000)	(8,000)	(40,000)
Case I profits	120,000	24,000	24,000	(16,000)	(16,000)	(16,000)	120,000

Note that the adjustment relating to the 2006 deductible amount, as well as that relating the 2005 deductible amount, is first made for the year 2005, the first accounting period of the company for which its profits or gains are computed in accordance with RAS.

Bad debts: transitional

The interaction between tax law and accounting practice is such that provisions for doubtful debts comprise specific provisions (which relate to estimations of specific debts) and general provisions. Any adjustment to such provisions is not taken into account for tax purposes to the extent that it relates to general provisions. Under RAS, the method for calculating a provision for doubtful debts is more specific than was the case before RAS applied and adjustments to such provisions which are properly calculated in accordance with RAS are treated as deductible for tax purposes.

Under IFRS (RAS) therefore, in contrast with the previous regime where the method for deducting bad debts provisions was to follow the accounting adjustment only where it related to specific provisions, adjustments that are properly calculated in accordance with RAS are to be deductible for tax purposes. No adjustment to taxable profits is to be made in respect of the restatement of the doubtful debts provision at the point of transition to RAS. If, however, the level at any time of the provision for doubtful debts falls below its level at the point of the transition, an adjustment is to be made to taxable profits at that time to ensure that there will be no loss of deductibility for actual bad debts incurred.

TCA 1997 Sch 17A paragraph 3 provides that where, as respects any period of account for which a company makes up its accounts in accordance with RAS, the amount of the opening bad debts provision exceeds the higher of:

(a) the current bad debts provision (the closing provision for the period); and

(b) the specific bad debts provision (the closing provision before moving to RAS),

the excess, reduced by any amount treated under the paragraph as a trading expense for any earlier period of account or, if there is more than one such amount, by the aggregate of such amounts, is to be treated as a trading expense of the company's trade for the period of account (TCA 1997 Sch 17A paragraph 3(3)).

In relation to a company, *opening bad debts provision* means so much of the aggregate value of debts at the beginning of the first relevant period of account of the company as represents the extent to which they are estimated to be impaired in accordance with RAS.

In relation to a company, *first relevant period of account* means the first period of account in respect of which the company prepares its accounts in accordance with RAS.

In relation to a period of account of a company, *current bad debts provision* means so much of the aggregate value of debts at the end of the period of account as represents the extent to which they are estimated to be impaired in accordance with RAS.

In relation to a company, *specific bad debts provision* means the aggregate of the amounts of doubtful debts which are respectively estimated to be bad at the end of the period of account immediately preceding the first relevant period of account of the company.

Bad debts provisions in accordance with RAS will be allowed on an ongoing basis so that in effect all provisions will be treated as specific for tax purposes. In the period of change over to IFRS, some general provisions will accordingly be re-classified for tax purposes as specific provisions but no tax deduction will be available for such re-classified amounts. A tax deduction will, however, subsequently become available for the amount re-classified if and to the extent that the bad debt provision falls below its level at the point of change over to RAS.

Example 3.305.6.2

The following are bad debt provision details and the appropriate tax treatment on a change over to RAS.

	Balance sheet	P&L account	Tax adjustment	Taxable
	€	€	€	€
Specific provision 31.12.04 (Irish GAAP)	10,000	–		–

Prior year adjustment	3,000	–	–	
Opening provision 1.1.05 (RAS)	13,000			
Closing provision 31.12.05 (RAS)	11,000	2,000	(2,000)	Nil
Closing provision 31.12.06	8,000	3,000	(1,000)	2,000
			(3,000)	

At the end of 2005, the opening bad debts provision of €13,000 exceeds the current bad debts provision of €11,000 (which is higher than the specific bad debts provision of €10,000) by €2,000 so that that amount is deducted for tax purposes for the year 2005. At the end of 2006, the opening bad debts provision exceeds the specific bad debts provision of €10,000 (which is now higher than the current bad debts provision) by €3,000 so that that amount, less the adjustment of €2,000 made for 2005, is deducted for tax purposes for 2006.

Example 3.305.6.3

	Period 1	Period 2	Period 3	Period 4	Period 5
	€	€	€	€	€
(a) Current bad debts provision	80,000	90,000	60,000	55,000	40,000
(b) Specific bad debts provision	50,000	50,000	50,000	50,000	50,000
Higher of (a) and (b)	80,000	90,000	60,000	55,000	50,000
Opening bad debts provision	70,000	70,000	70,000	70,000	70,000
Treated as trading expense	n/a	n/a	[1] 10,000	[2] 5,000	[3] 5,000

(1)   €70,000 – 60,000
(2)   €70,000 – 55,000 – 10,000
(3)   €70,000 – 50,000 – 15,000

A debt that may be taken into account for the above purposes may not be taken into account for the purposes of TCA 1997 Sch 17A paragraph 4 (financial instruments – see below).

Financial instruments: transitional

Prior to the move to IFRS (RAS), gains and losses in respect of financial instruments were generally computed for tax purposes on a realised basis. A *financial instrument* is any contract that gives rise to a financial asset of one entity and a financial liability or equity instrument of another entity (see **3.305.3** above regarding *financial asset* and *financial liability*). Under RAS, gains and losses are accounted for on the basis of movements in the fair values of such instruments in accordance with the Income Statement.

Thus, for example, if a financial instrument was purchased for €100,000 and sold for €140,000, the gain of €40,000 was, prior to RAS, included in taxable income at the time of sale. Under RAS, gains and losses on such instruments are accounted for on the basis of the movement in the fair values of such instruments in accordance with the Income Statement – and that basis will apply also for tax purposes in accordance with TCA 1997, s 76B(2). For example, if the instrument was purchased in period 1 for €100,000, increased in value to €110,000 by the end of that period, decreased in value to €95,000 by the end of period 2 and was sold in period 3 for €140,000, the taxable amounts are as follows:

	€	€
Period 1	gain 10,000	(110,000 – 100,000)
Period 2	loss 15,000	(95,000 – 110,000)
Period 3	gain 45,000	(140,000 – 95,000)

An adjustment is to be made at the point of transition to IFRS in the case of financial instruments. For example, a company that was taxable before the move to IFRS on the basis of realised gains on financial instruments will become taxable following the move to IFRS by reference to increases and decreases in the fair value of such instruments in accordance with IFRS. Such changes give rise to potential for double counting or for amounts to be left out of account altogether in computing taxable profits or losses. The legislation identifies the amounts of any such gains and losses and ensures that they will be taken into account for tax purposes at the point of transition but so that the amounts in question will be spread forward over a five-year period.

Where, prior to the transition to IFRS, the trading income of a company in respect of any financial assets or liabilities was computed for tax purposes on a mark to market basis and, after the transition, is computed on the basis of fair values, a substantial change in the computation of that income is unlikely.

So that certain amounts (comprising the "taxable amount" – see below), where they are profits or gains, do not fall out of the tax system or, where they consist of losses, are not allowed twice, such amounts are treated as trading receipts of the first accounting period commencing after the changeover day. To ensure that certain amounts (comprising the "deductible amount" – see below), where they are losses, are deducted for tax purposes or, where they consist of profits or gains, are not taxed twice, such amounts are netted against the taxable amount of the first accounting period commencing after the changeover day. If the deductible amount exceeds the taxable amount, the excess is treated as a deductible trading expense of the first accounting period. The taxable amount or deductible amount is spread over five years or over a shorter period where the trade in question comes to an end within the five year period. (See further below regarding these rules.)

In relation to a company, *changeover day* means the last day of the accounting period immediately preceding the first accounting period of the company in respect of which its profits or gains are computed in accordance with RAS which are, or include, RAS in relation to profits or gains or losses on financial assets and financial liabilities (TCA 1997 Sch 17A paragraph 4(1)).

In relation to a company, *taxable amount* means the aggregate of the amounts of:

(a)   profits or gains accruing on or before the changeover day on a financial asset or financial liability of the company, being profits or gains that had not been realised on or before that day and which would have been taken into account in computing the company's profits or gains for Case I or II purposes if they had accrued in an accounting period commencing after the changeover day, as would otherwise not be so taken into account for any accounting period of the company; and

(b)   any loss, accruing and not realised in a period or periods (the "first-mentioned period or periods") ending on or before the changeover day on a financial asset or financial liability of the company, which falls to be taken into account in computing the company's profits or gains for Case I or II purposes for an accounting period or periods commencing before the changeover day as would otherwise be taken into account twice in computing those profits or gains by virtue of a profit, gain or loss, accruing in a period that includes the first-mentioned period or periods, being taken into account in computing the company's profits or gains for Case I or II purposes for an accounting period commencing after the changeover day (TCA 1997 Sch 17A paragraph 4(1)).

Briefly, a taxable amount is any amount of profits or gains on a financial asset or liability that does not accrue in any period for which RAS is used but which has not been taken into account for tax purposes for any period before RAS was first used, as well as any loss on a financial asset or liability that is deductible under RAS but which has also been deducted for any period before RAS was first used. Thus, it can be either an unrealised gain that might fall out of the tax system or an unrealised loss that might be taken into account twice for tax purposes. Such taxable amounts are treated as trading receipts of the first accounting period in which RAS is used to prevent them, where they are profits or gains, from falling out of the tax system or, where they are losses, to ensure that they are not doubly allowed.

In relation to a company, *deductible amount* means the aggregate of the amounts of:

(a)   any loss on a financial asset or financial liability of the company accruing on or before the changeover day, being a loss that had not been realised on or before that day and which would have been taken into account in computing the company's profits or gains for Case I or II purposes if it had accrued in an accounting period commencing after the changeover day, as would otherwise not be so taken into account for any accounting period of the company; and

(b)   profits or gains on a financial asset or financial liability, accruing and not realised in a period or periods (the "first-mentioned period or periods") ending on or before the changeover day on a financial asset or financial liability of the company, which fall to be taken into account in computing the company's profits or gains for Case I or II purposes for an accounting period or periods commencing before the changeover day as would otherwise be taken into account twice in computing those profits or gains by virtue of a profit, gain or loss, accruing in a period that includes the first-mentioned period or periods, being taken into account in computing the company's profits or gains for Case I or II purposes for an accounting period commencing after the changeover day (TCA 1997 Sch 17A paragraph 4(1)).

In other words, a deductible amount is any loss on a financial asset or liability that was not incurred in a period for which RAS is used but was not taken into account for tax purposes for any period before RAS was first used or for any period for which RAS is used, as well as any amount of profits or gains on a financial asset or liability that falls to be taken into account as a trading receipt for a period for which RAS is used but which has also been so taken into account for any period before RAS was first used. Thus, it can be an unrealised loss that might not be counted at all for tax purposes or an unrealised gain that might be counted twice for tax purposes. Such deductible amounts are netted against taxable amounts of the first accounting period in which RAS is used to ensure that, as regards losses, they do not fail to be allowed once or, in the case of profits or gains, that they are not doubly taxed.

Where, prior to the move by a company to RAS, its trading income as regards particular financial assets and liabilities was computed for tax purposes on a "mark to market" basis rather than the general realised basis, and after the move that income is computed on the basis of fair values, it is unlikely that there will have been a substantial change in the computation of taxable income. Nonetheless, there may be instances where "fair value" under RAS will not equate to market value as used previously. Where this gives rise to a prior year adjustment on the move to RAS, any such adjustment will be dealt with under the transitional measures.

Instances of taxable amounts and deductible amounts in the context of a move from a realised to an unrealised basis as well as in the context of a move from an unrealised to a realised basis are as follows:

1. Realised basis to unrealised basis: taxable amount

	€
Cost of financial instrument during 2004	100,000
Fair value December 2004	130,000
Instrument sold in 2005	150,000

Prior to RAS, the company was taxed on a realised basis. As nothing was realised, the increase in value of €30,000 did not crystallise for tax purposes.

Under RAS the company is taxed on movements in the fair value reflected in the Income Statement. Fair value has increased in 2005 so that the company becomes taxable on €20,000. Thus, overall, it is taxed only on €20,000 even though it made a gain of €50,000. The "taxable amount" is €30,000, the amount that would otherwise not have been counted at all for tax purposes.

2. Unrealised basis to realised basis: taxable amount

Paragraph (b) of the definition of "taxable amount" deals with an unusual situation in which a company has been taxed on an unrealised basis ("mark to market") before the move to RAS and on an effective realised basis after the move to RAS (because the assets concerned are categorised under RAS as "available for sale" assets and accordingly, and subject to impairment, any gain or loss will generally be posted directly to equity and recycled to the Income Statement on realisation).

	€
Cost of financial instrument during 2004	100,000
Fair value December 2004	80,000
Instrument sold in 2005	90,000

Prior to RAS, the company was taxed on a "mark to market" basis and would have obtained a deduction for the loss of €20,000 in 2004.

Under RAS, the company is taxed on an effective "realised basis" in accordance with the accounting treatment and will be entitled to relief for the loss of €10,000 (€100,000 – €90,000) reflected in the Income Statement. Thus, overall, it would obtain a deduction of €30,000 (€20,000 in 2004 and €10,000 in 2005) even though it actually made a loss of only €10,000.

The "taxable amount" is €20,000, the amount that would be doubly relieved.

3. Realised basis to unrealised basis: deductible amount

Paragraph (a) of the definition of "deductible amount" deals with the more usual situation in which a company will have been taxed on a realised basis prior to RAS when it moves to an effective unrealised basis in accordance with the fair value movement reflected in the Income Statement.

	€
Cost of financial instrument during 2004	100,000
Fair value December 2004	80,000
Instrument sold in 2005	110,000

Prior to RAS, the company was taxed on a realised basis. As nothing was realised, the loss of €20,000 does not crystallise for tax purposes.

Following the move to RAS, the company is taxed on movements in fair value reflected in the Income Statement. Fair value has increased from €80,000 to €110,000 in 2005 so the company becomes taxable on €30,000. Thus, overall, it would fall to be taxed on €30,000 even though it only made a gain of €10,000 (€110,000 – €100,000). This is because the fair value loss in 2004, being unrealised, had been disregarded.

The "deductible amount" is €20,000.

4. Unrealised basis to realised basis: deductible amount

Paragraph (b) of the definition of "taxable amount" deals with an unusual situation in which a company has been effectively taxed on an unrealised basis ("mark to market") before the move to RAS and under RAS on an effective "realised basis" (because the assets concerned are categorised under RAS "available for sale" assets and accordingly, and subject to impairment, any gain of loss will generally be recycled to the Income Statement on realisation.)

	€
Cost of financial instrument during 2004	100,000
Fair value December 2004	130,000
Instrument sold in 2005	150,000

Prior to RAS, the company was taxed, on a "mark to market" basis, on the increase in value of €30,000 in 2004.

Following the move to RAS, the company is taxed on an effective realised basis in accordance with its profit as reflected in the Income Statement so that, when the asset is sold in 2005, the taxable amount is €50,000 (€150,000 – €100,000). Thus, overall, it would be taxed on €80,000 (€30,000 in 2004 and €50,000 in 2005) even though its gain was €50,000 only.

The "deductible amount" is what would have been the doubly taxed amount of €30,000.

There are rules in TCA 1997 Sch 17A paragraph 4 setting out the appropriate tax treatment where (1) the taxable amount exceeds the deductible amount and (2) where the deductible amount exceeds the taxable amount.

(1) Taxable amount exceeds deductible amount:

An amount equal to the excess of the taxable amount in relation to a company over the deductible amount is treated as a trading receipt for the first accounting period of the company commencing after the changeover day (TCA 1997 Sch 17A paragraph 4(2)(a)).

An mount ("relevant amount") treated as a trading receipt of an accounting period ("relevant accounting period") in the above circumstances is not, however, taken into account for that period. Instead, a part of the relevant amount will be taken into account for each accounting period falling wholly or partly into the period of five years beginning at the commencement of the relevant accounting period. That part will be such amount as bears to the relevant amount the same proportion as the length of the accounting period, or, as the case may be, the part of the accounting period falling into the period of five years, bears to five years (TCA 1997 Sch 17A paragraph 4(2)(b)).

Where any accounting period in which such an adjustment is to be made is the last accounting period in which a company carried on a trade or profession, the part of the relevant amount to be taken into account for that period will be the part required to ensure that the whole of that amount is accounted for (TCA 1997 Sch 17A paragraph 4(2)(c)).

(2) Deductible amount exceeds taxable amount:

Should the deductible amount exceed the taxable amount, the excess will be treated as a deductible trading expense of the company's trade carried on by it for the first accounting period of the company commencing after the changeover day (TCA 1997 Sch 17A paragraph 4(3)(a)).

Any such amount ("relevant amount") so treated as a deductible trading expense for an accounting period ("relevant accounting period") will, however, not be taken into account for that period. Instead, a part of the relevant amount will be taken into account for each accounting period falling wholly or partly into the period of five years beginning at the commencement of the relevant accounting period. That part will be such amount as bears to the relevant amount the same proportion as the length of the accounting period, or, as the case may be, the part of the accounting period falling into the period of five years, bears to five years (TCA 1997 Sch 17A paragraph 4(3)(b)).

Example 3.305.6.4

During the year 2004, Second Active Ltd acquires a gilt for €10,000. Under Irish GAAP, the gilt is brought into the balance sheet at 31 December 2004 at its cost although its fair value at that date is €12,000, and the taxation treatment of the gilt is on a realisation basis so that no profit or loss is recognised for the year. In accordance with IFRS, the gilt is included at its fair value of €14,000 in the balance sheet at 31 December 2005 and, in accordance with the corresponding taxation treatment, a taxable gain of €2,000 is recognised for the year 2005. The unrealised gain of €2,000, the excess of fair value over cost at the change over to IFRS at the end of 2004, is also recognised for taxation purposes but is taxed as to €400 for 2005 and as to €400 for each of the subsequent years up to and including 2009.

Where any accounting period in which such an adjustment is to be made is the last accounting period in which a company carried on a trade or profession, the part of the relevant amount to be taken into account for that period will be the part required to ensure that the whole of that amount is accounted for (TCA 1997 Sch 17A paragraph 4(3)(c)).

Anti-avoidance: spreading of certain losses

Outline

TCA 1997 Sch 17A paragraph 4 also contains an anti-avoidance measure directed at companies wishing to circumvent the spreading of losses under the foregoing provisions by realising losses on financial assets and liabilities before the move to RAS. Although the measure is not conditional on the presence of a tax avoidance motive, it is understood that in practice it will not be applied in the cases of financial assets and liabilities the taxable profit on which has been calculated on a mark to market basis prior to the move to RAS as this treatment is unlikely to give rise to a significant advantage.

The measure applies to losses incurred by a company on the disposal, in the course of a trade or profession, of financial assets and liabilities which the company replaces with similar instruments within a period of four weeks before, or four weeks after, the disposal. Disposals affected are those that take place within a period of six months before the first accounting period of the company for which its accounts are prepared using RAS in relation to financial assets and liabilities. Disposals before 1 January 2005, however, are not affected.

The losses affected are not fully deductible in the accounting period in which they arise. Instead, one-fifth of the loss is deductible in that accounting period and one-fifth in each of the following four periods. Where any accounting period for which such an amount is deductible is the last accounting period in which the company carried on a trade or profession, any remaining balance of the loss is deductible in that period.

Legislation

A loss to which the anti-avoidance measure applies is a loss incurred by a company on the disposal at any *relevant time* (a time after 1 January 2005 which is in a period of six months ending on the changeover day) of any financial asset or financial liability where, within a period beginning four weeks before and ending four weeks after that disposal, the company acquired a financial asset or financial liability of the same class providing substantially the same access to economic benefits and exposure to risk as would have been provided by the reacquisition of the asset or liability disposed of (TCA 1997 Sch 17A paragraph 4(4)).

Where a company has incurred a loss to which the anti-avoidance measure applies ("relevant loss"), the loss that would otherwise be taken into account in computing profits or losses or gains for tax purposes for an accounting period ("relevant accounting period") is not to be taken into account but instead a part of the relevant loss will be taken into account for each accounting period falling wholly or partly into the period of five years beginning at the commencement of the relevant accounting period. That part will be such amount as bears to the relevant loss the same proportion as the length of the accounting period, or, as the case may be, the part of the accounting period falling into the period of five years, bears to five years (TCA 1997 Sch 17A paragraph 4(5)(a)).

Where any accounting period in which such an adjustment is to be made is the last accounting period in which a company carried on a trade or profession, the part of the relevant loss to be taken into account for that period will be the part required to ensure that the whole of that amount is accounted for (TCA 1997 Sch 17A paragraph 4(5)(b)).

Thus, a loss on disposal of a financial instrument in circumstances where, within a short period before or after the disposal, there has been both a purchase and a sale of an instrument of the same class, in the six months before the move to IFRS, will be spread over five years.

The Revenue will not require the application of TCA 1997 Sch 17A paragraph 4(5) unless there is a sale and re-purchase resulting in a realised loss that would have been spread if the asset had been retained until after the move to IFRS.

Preliminary tax

In relation to the due date for payment of corporation tax (TCA 1997, s 958 – see **15.103.2–3**), the requirement to pay preliminary tax for an accounting period within that period is relaxed as regards the first, second and third accounting periods of a company for which profits or gains of the company are computed for tax purposes in accordance with relevant accounting standards which are, or include, relevant accounting standards in relation to profits or gains or losses on financial assets or liabilities. TCA 1997, s 958 is to have effect as if the minimum payment required did not take into account profits or gains or losses accruing, and not realised, in the accounting period on financial assets or financial liabilities as are attributable to changes in value of those assets or liabilities in the part of the period that is after the end of the month immediately preceding the month in which the preliminary tax or, as the case may be, the first instalment of preliminary tax, for the period is payable (see **15.103.3**).

3.305.7 Hedge accounting

Companies may seek to protect themselves against movements in the value of financial assets and liabilities, resulting, say, from interest rate or exchange rate movements, through the use of appropriate hedging instruments intended to match movements in the fair value of hedged assets and liabilities with corresponding opposite movements in the value of the hedging instruments. Such hedging instruments may consist of derivative contracts, such as swaps or options, or non-derivative financial assets and liabilities intended to hedge risks.

Without hedge accounting, there would be a distortion in the results reflected in the Income Statement if hedging instruments were to be fair valued through profit and loss but movements in the hedged items were not so reflected. The outcome would be a timing mismatch as between the recognition of the movements in the respective values of the hedged assets and liabilities and the hedging instruments.

Where the strict conditions for hedge accounting are met, gains and losses on hedging instruments and the corresponding losses and gains on the hedged items will be recognised in the same Income Statement. Matching under hedge accounting will also have effect for tax purposes.

In the case of cash flow hedging, as movements in the fair value of the hedging instrument are not reflected in profit and loss in the Income Statement until the relevant cash flow arises, TCA 1997, s 76B does not require them to be included in computing income for Case I or II purposes.

With fair value hedging, however, the hedging instrument *is* fair valued through profit and loss. In the case of a "fair value" hedged item that would not otherwise be fair valued through profit and loss in the Income Statement, hedge accounting requires that an appropriate part of the fair value movement is to be reflected in profit and loss in the Income Statement so as to remove volatility from the Income Statement. The part of fair value movement of the hedged asset that is reflected in the Income Statement should also be included in computing Case I or II income for tax purposes.

Where hedge accounting is not applicable, derivatives will be fair valued through the Income Statement and the accounting treatment of non-derivative currency hedging financial assets and liabilities will follow their treatment in IAS 39 (depending on their classification). This may result in some cases in "hedging" gains and losses not being recognised at the same time as the losses and gains on the hedged items, or in one being recognised in the Income Statement and the other in equity.

TCA 1997, s 79 provides for both foreign currency exchange differences on long-term borrowings and the matching exchange differences on hedging contracts to be brought into the computation of a trading company's profits for tax purposes on the basis of the appropriate accounting treatment. This treatment applies to accounts prepared under IFRS. The reference in the section to "profit and loss account" may be taken to include a reference to the Income Statement where IFRS applies.

3.305.8 Foreign currency issues

Under IAS 21, a company may present its financial statements in any currency. If a company's presentation currency differs from its functional currency, its results and financial position are translated into the presentation currency in accordance with IAS 21. Companies are permitted to calculate taxable profits and losses in terms of their functional currency. The resulting profit or loss is then expressed in euro by reference to the average exchange rate for the accounting period in question.

The use, for tax purposes, of financial statements in the presentation currency should disregard any exchange differences arising on translation from the functional currency to the presentation currency. Profits and losses for tax computation purposes should be directly equivalent (by reference to the relevant exchange rate) to the profits and losses derived from the functional currency accounts.

3.305.9 Double taxation relief

An Irish company trading in a foreign territory through a branch or agency will usually be subject to tax in both jurisdictions on the resulting profits. In general, such double taxation will be relieved by reducing the Irish tax on the doubly taxed income by the foreign tax on that income.

In certain cases, the rules for calculating income will differ as between countries. For example, Ireland effectively taxes income from "available for sale" financial assets on a realised basis whereas other countries may tax such income by reference to movements in the fair value of the assets and therefore at an earlier time. In such circumstances, double tax relief may be denied since there will be no doubly-taxed income. Furthermore, when the income is subsequently recognised for tax purposes in Ireland, there will be no foreign tax to be offset against the Irish tax on that income.

Where, due to a mismatch of this kind in relation to income arising from financial assets and liabilities, it appears likely that there would otherwise be an overall loss of credit for foreign tax in relation to foreign branch income, the income will continue to be taxed in Ireland under normal Irish tax principles but any foreign tax payable in respect of the same income, irrespective of when it is payable, may be included in the Irish foreign tax credit computation. This Revenue practice applies in cases where the doubly taxed income is income that is recognised in the foreign jurisdiction earlier than when it is recognised for Irish tax purposes. The practice does not refer to the converse situation in which Ireland recognises the income at an earlier stage but does not rule out the possibility of an equivalent practice for that situation also.

The objective of this approach is to ensure that where foreign tax can be identified as relating to the same income as that on which Irish tax is payable, the foreign tax may be credited against the Irish tax when the income is recognised in Ireland for tax purposes although the foreign tax may be payable in respect of the income at a different time. This practice must be applied consistently from year to year and may not result in foreign tax being credited more than once against Irish tax, or in credit being given for foreign tax that is not ultimately payable (without repayment or set-off) in the foreign jurisdiction (due, for example, to the existence of losses).

3.4 FOREIGN CURRENCY ISSUES

3.401 Introduction

In recent decades, the transaction of business in foreign currencies has become an established fact of commercial life. The translation of income, expenses, assets and liabilities expressed in one currency into another currency can have a significant impact on the financial statements of companies as can the effect of hedging transactions entered into to protect against adverse movements in currency exchange rates. Companies which will be concerned with this subject are those whose purchases or sales are to a significant extent conducted in foreign currencies and those which conduct their business or part of their business through foreign branches.

The tax issues which arise for companies in connection with foreign currency exposure fall mainly into two areas, those related to trading transactions and those related to borrowing. These matters are considered in the following sections as are foreign currency aspects of capital allowances and losses and certain foreign exchange issues relevant to capital gains tax.

Before dealing with the taxation treatment of foreign exchange transactions, it is appropriate to refer to the accounting treatment of foreign currency transactions

3.402 Accounting treatment

A currency exchange difference (currency exchange profit or loss) will usually arise where foreign currency denominated amounts are translated or converted into euro. If a company purchases goods from abroad in, say US dollars, the transaction will be entered in the company's books at the time of the purchase in euro, arrived at by translating the dollar amount into euro at the rate of exchange between the two currencies at the date of the transaction. When payment is made for the goods, the euro equivalent of the dollar payment is likely to be different to that entered in the company's books at the time of purchase as the relationship between the two currencies will probably have changed in the meantime. The difference in the euro amount will be a realised exchange gain or loss and will be credited or debited accordingly to the company's profits and loss account.

If the purchase transaction has not been settled at the company's year end, the dollar amount will be translated into euro at the year end rate of exchange and the gain or loss will again be brought to the profit and loss account as an unrealised exchange difference. In the following period, when the purchase price is paid, the difference between the euro equivalent of the dollar amount paid and its equivalent at the previous balance sheet date will result in another exchange profits or loss. This realised difference is debited or credited to the profit and loss account of that accounting period.

Foreign currency denominated assets and liabilities, for example shares acquired for Sterling, or borrowings drawn down in US dollars, will also be revalued at the year end and included in the balance sheet at their adjusted euro values. The resulting differences between the opening and closing euro values are again brought to the profit and loss account for the period.

The accounting standard SSAP 20, issued by the Accounting Standards Committee of the Consultative Committee of the Accounting Bodies of the UK and the Republic of Ireland, deals with the subject of foreign currency translation with a view to establishing best accounting practice in relation to the treatment of foreign currency transactions.

"Local currency" is defined as the currency of the primary economic environment in which a company operates and generates its net cash flows. "Monetary items" (or monetary assets and liabilities) are money held and amounts payable and receivable in money, for example, cash, bank balances, debtors, creditors, and money payable and receivable. Non-monetary items, by contrast, would include fixed assets, stock in trade, investments, intangible assets (eg goodwill, licences, trade marks, patents), prepayments and prepaid expenses. Short term monetary items are those which fall due within one year of the balance sheet date while other monetary items are regarded as long term.

The main principles governing the accounting treatment of exchange differences as set out in SSAP 20 are as follows:

(a) Foreign currency denominated purchases and sales and other profits and loss items should be translated into euro at the rate in force on the day the transaction is entered into.

(b) Monetary assets and liabilities denominated in foreign currencies should be translated into euro at balance sheet date at the spot exchange rate, ie the rate of exchange for spot transactions, at that date (referred to as the closing rate).

(c) Exchange gains and losses relating to settled transactions and unsettled short term monetary items should be reported as part of the profit or loss in respect of ordinary activities for the period (unless they relate to extraordinary items).

(d) Exchange gains and losses on long term monetary items should generally be recognised in the profit and loss account.

Where a transaction is to be settled at a contracted rate of exchange, the rate of exchange specified in the contract may be used as the translation rate. This rate may also be used where a trading transaction is covered or hedged by a matching forward contract. There may also be matching forward contracts relating to balance sheet items, eg a forward purchase of a foreign currency to hedge a loan taken out in that currency. The rate of exchange specified in the contract may be used in those cases also.

3.403   Trading transactions

Certain foreign exchange profits and losses are recognised as being part of the overall profit or loss of a trade for the period in which they arise. Thus, in the case of goods purchased from abroad for foreign currency, the euro equivalent of the foreign currency amount stated on the purchase invoice may be different at the date of payment from what it was when the transaction was originally booked. If it is greater, an exchange loss will result; if less, there will be an exchange profit. The exchange loss or profit in this case is treated as a trading transaction and will be included in arriving at the final profit or loss for tax purposes.

Where the trading profits are subject to tax at less than the full corporation tax rate, for example because of the availability of the 10% corporation tax rate, any exchange profit arising which is a trading transaction will effectively be taxed at the rate applicable to the trading profits as a whole.

In strictness, it is necessary to distinguish between realised and unrealised exchange gains and losses and to recognise only the former in computing tax profits or losses on the basis of the long held principle that neither profits nor losses should be anticipated. An unrealised profit or loss results from the translation of monetary assets and liabilities at balance sheet date where the rate differs from that ruling at the date the items were first recorded.

Looking again at the case of the importer, it will sometimes be the case that the accounting year end will fall after the purchase invoice has been raised but before the goods are paid for. By that date there may be exchange differences resulting from currency movements between the invoice date and balance sheet date. Gains or losses resulting from these movements will be unrealised.

It is correct accounting procedure to recognise unrealised exchange gains and losses as part of the trading results for the period in which they arise. Exchange differences resulting from balance sheet translation of foreign currency denominated trade creditors and debtors are now accepted as the recognition of actual gains or losses for tax purposes, bringing modern day tax practice into line with the accounting approach on this question.

Some guidance in the matter of how foreign exchange gains and losses are to be treated for tax purposes, in particular whether such gains and losses are part of trading profits, can be obtained from a number of decided cases. A firm of fur importing agents placed a deposit on furs at the time they were received. The proceeds of sale, less commission and a deposit, were remitted to the principal at year end. A devaluation in sterling resulted in the deposits showing a profit. It was held that the profit was part of the trading profits of the agents and therefore assessable as such (*Landes Brothers v Simpson* 19 TC 62).

A similar decision was reached in *Imperial Tobacco Co of Great Britain and Ireland v Kelly* 25 TC 292. Wartime restrictions led to the sale of surplus dollars which had been accumulated for the purchase of tobacco leaf. The profit realised on the sale was held to be assessable as part of the company's trading income. It was found that the dollars had not lost the revenue character which attached to them when they were originally purchased.

By contrast, a gain resulting from the holding of Chinese dollar deposits abroad during the course of an agency was held to be a capital gain (*Davies v The Shell Company of China Ltd* 32 TC 133). The company required its Chinese agents to deposit with it sums in Chinese dollars to secure any sums due to it by the agents. The deposits were converted into sterling until the agencies were eventually terminated, at which time the agents were repaid in Chinese currency. During the period the money was on deposit, the Chinese dollar had depreciated against sterling so that a gain arose on the purchase of the dollars to pay the agents. The effect of the conversion of the Chinese deposits into sterling and the subsequent repurchase of Chinese dollars at a lower rate was in the nature of an appreciation of a capital asset, not forming part of the assets employed as circulating capital in the trade. The deposits received were loans rather than trading receipts.

The case of *Pattison v Marine Midland Ltd* [1984] STC 10 is interesting in that it is concerned with the question of fixed capital borrowing and with the concepts of matching and "tax fragmentation". In 1971, Marine Midland, a company engaged in borrowing and lending money in dollars and other non-UK currencies, issued a ten year subordinated loan stock to raise $15m, the proceeds of which were used to make dollar advances to its customers. For the most part the company matched its borrowings and advances in each foreign currency. In 1976 the loan stock was redeemed by means of $15m drawn from its dollar funds being the proceeds of dollar advances repaid by customers. In the meantime, the appreciation of the dollar against sterling meant that the $15m at the date of redemption was worth £2.5m more than it was worth at the date of issue.

The UK Revenue position was that the company had made a taxable profit of £2.5m from its trading activities but that the equivalent loss on the loan stock was on fixed capital account and was therefore not deductible in calculating the taxable profit. This approach illustrates the phenomenon of "tax fragmentation", the situation whereby the two components of a matched position, though cancelling each other out in the commercial world, must be looked at differently for tax purposes. Fortunately in this case the company won its case in the House of Lords where it was held that in fact no exchange profit or loss had arisen in the first place. The view was that since the company had not converted any part of the $15m raised into sterling, there was no profit or loss for tax purposes resulting from exchange rate movements.

It is to be noted that the decision was concerned with foreign currency transactions of a trading company and is in no way a guide or authority on transactions coming within the capital gains tax code. In an Irish context, see below regarding TCA 1997, s 79B.

Matching foreign currency assets with certain foreign currency share capital

A company may elect to have gains or losses, whether arising on disposals or on a mark to market basis, arising on matched foreign currency liabilities included as part of its trading income. Where in relation to an accounting period or a company, a foreign currency asset has been matched by the company with a relevant foreign currency liability, any gain or loss, whether realised or unrealised, on the relevant foreign currency liability is taken into account in computing the company's trading income (TCA 1997, s 79B(3)). The matching election is available to a company with a non-euro functional currency where it has made loans or has issued redeemable share capital in another currency, including the euro. (In addition, unrealised gains or losses included in a company's profit and loss account as a result of the "fair valuing" or "marking to market" (see **3.305.3**) of assets on an annual basis may be matched with the corresponding loss or gain on the relevant foreign currency liability.)

A *foreign currency asset*, in relation to a company, is an asset of the company the consideration for the acquisition of which consists solely of an amount denominated in a currency other than the functional currency (within the meaning of TCA 1997, s 402 – see **3.407**) of the company and any gain on the disposal of which would be taken into account in computing income of the company chargeable to tax under Case I of Schedule D.

A *relevant foreign currency liability*, in relation to a company, is a liability (not being a relevant monetary item within the meaning of TCA 1997, s 79 – see **3.406**) which arises from a sum subscribed for paid-up redeemable share capital denominated in a currency other than the functional currency of the company.

A company may, by giving notice in writing to the inspector of taxes, specify that a foreign currency asset denominated in a currency other than the functional currency of the company is to be matched with a corresponding relevant foreign currency liability denominated in that currency as is specified by the company. Such notice is to be given within three weeks after the acquisition by the company of the foreign currency asset (TCA 1997, s 79B(2)). Where in relation to an accounting period of a company, a foreign currency asset has been matched with a relevant foreign currency liability, any gain or loss, realised or unrealised, on the relevant foreign currency liability is to be taken into account in computing the company's trading income (TCA 1997, s 79B(3)).

IFSC companies may elect, before 15 December 2006, to match all foreign currency assets held on 2 February 2006 (the date of publication of Finance Bill 2006) with an equivalent amount of redeemable share capital denominated in the same currency.

The Revenue are prepared to permit a company, whether IFSC or otherwise, to make, on or before 15 December 2006, an election to match of all its relevant currency assets acquired on or after 1 January 2006 and held on 1 December 2006 with an equivalent amount of redeemable share capital denominated in the same currency. Any such election must be made in respect of all assets held so that it is not possible to select particular assets for this treatment. Otherwise (ie, in respect of assets acquired after 1 December 2006), matching treatment may be elected for, within the prescribed time limit, in respect of particular assets. Where this would give rise to an administrative burden, Revenue are prepared to accept an election covering all future acquisitions of assets. The relevant election will remain in place until formally withdrawn from which time asset by asset elections must be made.

Revenue are prepared to agree, in the case of short term assets which are rolled over a number of times before disposal, to allow an election to be made with three weeks from the date on which the asset is first acquired. Thus, it is not necessary to re-elect each time the asset is rolled over where the financial terms remain unaltered.

The amount of a company's gain or loss on the discharge of a relevant foreign currency liability is the amount that would be the gain accruing to, or as the case may be the loss incurred by, the company on the disposal of an asset acquired by it at the time the liability was incurred and disposed of at the time at which the liability was discharged if:

(i)   the amount given by the company to discharge the liability was the amount given by it as consideration for the acquisition of the asset (TCA 1997, s 79B(1)(b)(iii)(I)); and

(ii) the amount of the liability incurred by the company was the consideration received by it on the disposal of the asset (TCA 1997, s 79B(1)(b)(iii)(II)).

Example 3.403.1

Eros Ltd issues 500,000 redeemable shares of $1 each at a time when the exchange rate is $1.1:€1. Later, when the shares are redeemed, the exchange rate is $1.2:€1.

There is a gain on the discharge of the foreign currency liability as follows:

	€
Consideration received: amount of liability incurred	454,545

Consideration given: amount given to discharge liability	416,667
Gain on discharge of liability	37,878

Where a company disposes of a relevant foreign currency asset that has been matched with a corresponding relevant foreign currency liability but the company does not discharge the liability at that time, the company is deemed to discharge the liability, and to incur a new liability equal to the amount of the liability, at that time (TCA 1997, s 79B(1)(b)(i)).

If a relevant foreign currency asset has been matched by a company with a corresponding relevant foreign currency liability incurred by it before the time it acquired the asset, the company is deemed to discharge the foreign currency liability, and to incur a new liability equal to the amount of the liability, at that time (TCA 1997, s 79B(1)(b)(ii)). Thus, the "consideration" received on the eventual disposal (or deemed disposal) of the liability will be its euro equivalent at the time the foreign currency asset was acquired.

Example 3.403.2

Oakland Ltd, a company whose business consists of the lending of funds to its customers at interest, has outstanding receivables of $4m from US dollar advances to customers made at a time when the exchange rate was $1:€1.08. It has also issued redeemable share capital of $5m. It applies to treat the receivables as matched by a corresponding amount of $4m of its redeemable capital. Oakland Ltd later calls in the dollar receivables and exchanges the proceeds for euro, at which time the exchange rate is $1:€1.1. No share capital is redeemed at that time.

Oakland Ltd is deemed, at the time the trade receivables were advanced, to have discharged $4m of its foreign currency liability (the redeemable shares) and to have incurred a new such liability of $4m at that time. Accordingly, the consideration deemed to be received (at 1.08) is €4,320,000 (TCA 1997, s 79B(1)(b)(iii)(II)).

At the time the receivables are repaid, Oakland Ltd is deemed to have discharged the corresponding $4m of its foreign currency liability. Accordingly, the consideration deemed to be given (at 1.1) is €4.4m (TCA 1997, s 79B(1)(b)(iii)(I)).

The corporation tax computation is as follows:

	€	€
Consideration for the disposal ($4m @ 1.1)		4,400,000
Loss on discharge of liability:		
Consideration received	4,320,000	
Consideration given	4,400,000	
Currency loss on liability	80,000	
Cost of receivables ($4m @ 1.08)		4,320,000
Currency gain on disposal of receivables		80,000

What emerges from TCA 1997, s 79B would seem to be at odds with the decision in *Marine Midland*. If that decision were to be applied, and had the company in the above example used the dollar proceeds to redeem the share capital, the exchange gain on the receivables, although the receivables constitute a foreign currency asset, would not have been treated as a trading receipt as there would have been no conversion of dollars.

One point on which the legislation is not clear is how matching is to be applied in a case where the amount of the relevant foreign currency liability is less than the amount of the corresponding foreign currency asset. The logical approach would be to apply the liability proportionately to the asset.

Example 3.403.3

Abbot Ltd, a company whose business consists of the lending of funds to its customers at interest, has an outstanding trade receivable of $3m from a time at which the exchange rate was $1:€1.05. Its issued redeemable share capital includes dollar denominated share capital of $2m. It now applies to treat the trade receivable as matched by a corresponding amount of redeemable share capital. Abbot Ltd later recovers 50% of the receivable, for $1.5m, at which time the exchange rate is $1:€0.95. The borrowings are also discharged at that time.

Abbot Ltd is deemed, at the time the trade receivable was advanced, to have discharged its foreign currency liability (the redeemable share capital) of $2m and at the same time to have incurred a new such liability of $2m. Accordingly, the consideration deemed to be received on the discharge of 50% of the liability (at €1.05) is €1,050,000 (TCA 1997, s 79B(1)(b)(iii)(II)).

At the time 50% of the receivable was paid, Abbot Ltd is deemed to have discharged a corresponding $1m (50%) of its foreign currency liability. Accordingly, the consideration deemed to be given (at 0.95) is €0.95m (TCA 1997, s 79B(1)(b)(iii)(I)).

The corporation tax computation is as follows:

	€	€
Consideration for the disposal ($1.5m @ 0.95)		1,425,000
Gain on discharge of liability:		
Consideration received	1,050,000	
Consideration given	950,000	
Currency gain on liability	100,000	
Cost ($1.5 @ 1.05)		1,575,500
Currency loss on disposal of receivable		150,000

Since only two-thirds of the receivable has been matched in this instance, only that proportion of the loss arising is matched by a gain on the liability.

3.404   Foreign branches

The accounting standard on "Foreign Currency Translation" (SSAP 20) prescribes two methods for accounting for the trading results, assets and liabilities of foreign branches, the "closing rate" or "net investment" method and the "temporal method".

The principle behind the closing rate method is that the head office has an investment in the foreign branch all of which is at risk due to exchange rate fluctuations. On this view, the branch generally operates independently as a separate business with its own funding in the foreign jurisdiction and its operations are not normally dependent on the reporting currency of the investing company. The underlying assumption is that the branch will normally be financed, at least partly, by borrowings in its local currency.

The closing rate method involves the preparation of the branch accounts in the appropriate foreign currency and their subsequent translation into euro for inclusion in the overall company accounts. All amounts in the year end balance sheet for the branch are translated into euro at the rate of exchange ruling on the balance sheet date, ie the closing rate. The profit and loss account figures may be translated at the closing rate or at the average rate for the accounting period provided that the method adopted is applied consistently from year to year.

Exchange differences will arise where, as will usually be the case, the closing rate differs from the corresponding closing rate for the previous period: there will be an exchange difference for the opening net assets by reference to the difference between the opening and the closing rates. Where the profit and loss account items are translated at the average rate, there will be a further difference since all of the items in the balance sheet are translated at the closing rate. SSAP 20 requires that these differences be recorded as movements on reserves, and not in the profit and loss account. For tax purposes, accordingly, these differences will not be brought into the computation of the profit or loss for the period.

For tax purposes, no exchange differences on individual transactions will need to be taken into account since the profit and loss account as a whole will have been translated into euro. An exception would be differences arising from transactions involving foreign currencies other than the currency of the country in which the branch is operating. Any such differences will have been translated into euro in the same way as any other branch receipts and expenses and the differences will be treated for tax purposes in the same way as any other exchange differences. Differences arising from trading transactions, eg from the translation or conversion of trade creditors or debtors, will be part of the trading profit or loss (apart from differences brought to reserves in the circumstances outlined above). The tax treatment of differences related to borrowings will depend on the nature of the borrowings and, for accounting periods commencing on or after 1 January 1995, on the effect of TCA 1997, s 79, as discussed in **3.406** below.

The temporal method is the appropriate method where a foreign branch is not operated as a separate business, where it is more in the nature of an extension of the company's trade. Under this method, purchases, sales, expenses, receipts from debtors, payments to creditors and other profit and loss items are converted to euro at the relevant exchange rates ruling at the date of each transaction. Exchange differences will arise on settlement of amounts due to and from the branch, on the use of foreign currency bank balances to pay for branch outgoings and on the year end translation of foreign currency liabilities and monetary assets of the branch into euro. The effect is that the figures for the transactions of the branch are integrated into the overall company financial statements in the same way as those for the company as a whole.

Under the temporal method, it follows that exchange differences arising from foreign branch transactions and from the year end translation of foreign currency liabilities and monetary assets are dealt with in the same way for tax purposes as if they related to transactions and year end translations of the company as a whole. Differences arising from trading transactions are included as part of the trading profit or loss. The tax treatment of differences related to borrowings will depend on the nature of the borrowings and, for accounting periods commencing on or after 1 January 1995, may be determined by TCA 1997, s 79, as discussed in the next section.

Where tax is paid by an Irish resident company in respect of its foreign branch profits, the tax will, if a tax treaty is in force, be available as a credit against the Irish corporation tax in respect of the same profits. Where there is no treaty, the tax will be deductible in arriving at the amount of the branch profits liable to corporation tax in Ireland. The credit or deduction for foreign tax should be translated into euro at the exchange rate ruling at the date the tax was paid. In practice, the foreign tax should in any event have been translated at that rate where the temporal method has been used since expenses will have been translated at the relevant transaction rates. Where the closing method of accounting has been used, it may be permissible, particularly where a deduction is to be made for the foreign tax, to translate the foreign tax into euro at the rate used to translate the branch results for tax purposes for the period in question, ie the average rate of exchange for the period.

3.405   Foreign currency borrowing: case law background

Where foreign currency is borrowed to hedge a trading debt, any resulting exchange profit or loss will be within the ambit of the trade and will therefore form part of the trading profit or loss for tax purposes. In effect a hedging gain will offset the exchange loss on the underlying trading transaction, while a hedging loss will be matched by an exchange gain on the trading transaction. Where a company is liable to corporation tax at less than the full rate it can be assumed that a hedging gain will be taxed at the effective rate of tax on the trading profits.

Exchange gains and losses on the repayment of longer term foreign currency borrowings may be treated as capital in nature. The question whether a profit or loss resulting from the repayment of a foreign currency loan should be taken into account in computing trading profits or losses depends on whether the loan is properly to be regarded as on "fixed or circulating capital account".

In making the appropriate distinction the traditional approach, based on the decision in *European Investment Trust Co Ltd v Jackson* 18 TC 1, was to seek to establish what part the borrowing plays in the capital structure of the business, whether on the one hand it effectively adds to the capital base of the business, and is therefore employed as capital in that business, or is, on the other hand, for a short or indefinite period, providing temporary financial accommodation. Alternatively, a distinction might be made by reference to the use to which the borrowings are put, for example whether on the one hand they are on the security of, or are for the purchase of, fixed assets, or on the other hand are for the purpose of financing a particular trading transaction, such as the purchase of stock, or for general trading purposes and repayable out of profits generated from trading.

In the case of *Beauchamp v F W Woolworth plc* [1988] STC 714, [1989] STC 570, where the company sought a deduction for substantial exchange losses on the repayment of two US dollar loans taken out for a term of about five years, the High Court in the UK held that it is the nature of the loan which is the decisive factor and that the use to which the moneys borrowed are put is relevant only where there would still be some doubt after applying the primary test. On that basis the loans were held to have been on fixed capital account and the exchange losses were disallowed. In July 1988 the Court of Appeal reversed this decision and found that the purpose for which the loans were taken out outweighed the terms on which they were made and that the losses should be allowed.

The Revenue were eventually successful in the House of Lords where Lord Templeman held that where a company borrows money for five years it has obtained an asset or advantage which endures for that term; a loan of that nature increases the capital of the borrower. A loan can be of a revenue nature only where "it is part of the ordinary day to day incidence of carrying on the business" and this cannot be the case "unless the loan is temporary and fluctuating and is incurred in meeting the ordinary running expenses of the business". Lord Templeman instanced the current account as the most common form of provision for the payment of trading expenses and the receipt of trading revenues and described "income borrowing" as "a thing that is going to recur every year". Thus it would seem that loans extending for a period of more than twelve months would be regarded as being on fixed capital account.

Exchange gains and losses on the repayment of fixed capital borrowings are disregarded for the purposes of computing taxable profits. It was clarified in the Woolworth case that this treatment derives from general principles and not from the statutory prohibition (Irish equivalent TCA 1997, s 81(2)(f)) of deductions for "any capital withdrawn from or any sum employed or intended to be employed as capital in the trade".

Such gains and losses are also not recognised for capital gains tax purposes since they relate to liabilities whereas the capital gains tax code is concerned with disposals of assets.

In Ireland the Woolworth case is, of course, not binding but is of persuasive authority. In practice, the Irish Revenue authorities would have regard to Woolworth but would not automatically decide the matter by reference to whether or not the borrowing is to extend beyond one year. The term of the borrowing would be the primary test following Woolworth, but other factors, such as the role of the borrowings in the capital structure of the business and (to a lesser extent) the purpose and actual use made of the borrowed funds, would also be influential.

The case of *Brosnan v Mutual Enterprises Limited* 5 ITR 138 (Supreme Court, 1997) would suggest that the courts in Ireland would not rigidly apply the *Woolworth* principle and would attach particular importance to the question whether the borrowings in question are *a means of fluctuating and temporary accommodation*. This is a question of fact to be determined by all of the relevant circumstances in each case.

Mutual Enterprises Limited borrowed Stg£280,000 to finance the purchase of premises costing IR£300,000 in which it carried on its trade of licensed victualler and restaurateur. The loan was expressly made and was approved for that purpose. It was repayable on demand but terms were provided for repayment in stages over five years. The loan was converted from time to time into various European currencies with the result that exchange losses of about IR£70,000 were incurred. The company claimed the losses in computing its trading profits/ losses for corporation tax purposes.

In the High Court ([1995] 2 ILRM 304) the judge, while hinting that the fact that the borrowings were clearly for the purpose of acquiring a capital asset would indicate capital borrowing, did not consider that no reasonable judge could have concluded that the loan was a means of fluctuating and temporary accommodation. It was suggested that the Circuit Court judge might have attached less weight to the purpose of the borrowings in this case than he did to the fact that the borrowings were repayable on demand. The decision of the High Court was confirmed by the Supreme Court.

3.406 Foreign currency borrowing: statutory position

TCA 1997, s 79 brings foreign exchange gains and losses arising in respect of any *relevant monetary item* (ie, money held or payable by a company for the purposes of its trade) into the computation of trading income for corporation tax purposes (TCA 1997, s 79(2)). That treatment will apply where the gain or loss results directly from a change in a currency exchange rate and provided the profit or loss is properly credited or debited to the company's profit and loss account. In this connection, SSAP 20 provides that exchange gains and losses should be brought into the profit and loss account regardless of whether or not they are realised or unrealised.

It will be noted that a "relevant monetary item" does not include money receivable. As regards "money held", this obviously refers to foreign currency and the question arises as to whether it includes money held in a bank account and not just cash physically held. The Revenue view is that it does not include foreign currency deposited with a bank (although a bank account may be a relevant contract – see below). It would seem that creditors (but not debtors) would be relevant monetary items.

One result of TCA 1997, s 79 is that it does not matter whether exchange gains and losses are realised or unrealised or whether the related trade borrowings are deemed to be of a revenue or of a capital nature.

The above-described treatment will also apply to a hedging contract (*relevant contract*), that is, a contract entered into by a company for the purposes of eliminating or reducing the risk of loss being incurred due to a change in the value of a relevant monetary item and where the change in value results directly from a change in a rate of exchange. A good example of a relevant contract is a currency swap. A bank deposit account may also be a relevant contract, for example, a foreign currency deposit account used to hedge foreign currency borrowing. (It should be noted, however, that where a foreign currency deposit is accepted as hedging a relevant monetary item, that will not prejudice the character of the income arising from the deposit.)

The position prior to the enactment of TCA 1997, s 79 in 1994 (then CTA 1976 1976, s 12A) was that a gain or loss arising to a company in respect of a hedging contract or in respect of foreign currency held by a company for the purposes of a trade would have been subject to capital gains tax treatment (although, in the case of foreign currency held for trading purposes, any such gain or loss would have been cancelled by a corresponding loss or gain on trading account). It is now specifically provided, in relation to these items, that any gain or loss resulting directly from a change in a rate of exchange is not to be a chargeable gain or allowable loss (TCA 1997, s 79(3)).

Many companies whose functional currency is other than the euro will hedge their corporation tax liability, typically by contracting for the forward purchase of euro to meet that liability. In the absence of special provisions, any gain arising out of such a contract would be a chargeable gain subject to corporation tax. A contract to hedge a tax liability is not a "relevant contract" as it does not relate to a monetary item: "monetary item" covers money payable for the purposes of a company's trade, but that description would not extend to money due in respect of a tax liability.

A gain or loss resulting from a "relevant tax contract" is not a chargeable gain or allowable loss. A *relevant tax contract* is a contract entered into by a company to eliminate or reduce the risk of loss due to a change in the euro value of money payable to satisfy a liability to corporation tax, that change being a direct result of a change in the exchange rate between the company's functional currency and the euro. The gain or loss not treated as a chargeable gain is, in the case of a gain, so much of that gain as does not exceed the loss that would have been incurred in the absence of the contract and, in the case of a loss, so much of that loss as does not exceed the gain that would have arisen in the absence of the contract.

Change in currency of the State on 1 January 1999

Gains or losses arising to a trading company on 1 January 1999 as a result of the replacement of the currency of a Member State of the European Union (EU) by the euro were treated for tax purposes in the same way as exchange gains and losses on foreign currency transactions were treated for the purposes of TCA 1997s 79 generally. Broadly, therefore, the tax treatment of such gains or losses followed the accounting treatment.

TCA 1997, s 79(1)(c) provided that, for the purposes of TCA 1997, s 79, a gain or loss arising to a company which resulted directly from a change in a rate of exchange was to include a gain or loss which resulted directly from an event which substituted for the currency of an EU Member State another currency of that State, ie the euro, where the euro, as a result of the event, became the functional currency of that company. For this purpose, *functional currency* is as defined in TCA 1997, s 402 (see **3.407** below) and means the currency of the primary economic environment in which a company operates or, in the case of a non-resident company operating in Ireland through a branch, the currency of the primary economic environment in which the company carries on its trading activities in Ireland. The currency of the primary economic environment was determined by reference to the currency in which revenue and expenses were primarily generated and by reference to the currency in which the company, or branch, primarily borrowed and loaned. If a company prepared its profit and loss account in euro for any period, the functional currency of the company for that period would be the euro.

TCA 1997, s 79(1)(c) was enacted to cater for the fact that on 1 January 1999 the currencies of various EU Member States would change over to the euro. Thus, for example, a company within the charge to corporation tax in Ireland and whose functional currency was the Deutschmark (DM) might, for its first accounting period ending on or after 1 January 1999, have included in its profit and loss account a gain or loss resulting from, say, the conversion of a debtor item in Italian lire into euros (which would have been converted directly from lire into euros and not into DMs and then into euros). Thus, in accordance with TCA 1997, s 79(2), the resulting profit or loss would be brought into the computation of trading income for corporation tax purposes.

Since, as stated above, TCA 1997, s 79(1)(c) applied only where the event which substituted the euro for the currency of an EU Member State also resulted in the euro becoming the functional currency of the company in question, it had no application where the functional currency of the company did not change. Thus, for example, where the functional currency of a company prior to 1 January 1999 was the US dollar and continues to be the US dollar from that date, TCA 1997, s 79(1)(c) has no effect.

3.407 Capital allowances and losses

(a) Capital allowances

The amount on which assets purchased in a foreign currency may be claimed for capital allowances purposes is the euro equivalent of the foreign currency cost at the date the expenditure is incurred.

On the other hand, where foreign currency is acquired to purchase fixed assets and there is not a significant delay in purchasing the assets, the allowable cost would be the euro cost of acquiring the currency.

Where foreign currency is borrowed to finance the purchase of qualifying assets, any additional cost resulting from an appreciation of the foreign currency at the date of repayment does not qualify for relief. This follows the decision in *Ben-Odeco Ltd v Powlson* [1978] STC 460.

TCA 1997, s 402 is concerned with the calculation of capital allowances and loss relief of trading companies which have a functional currency other than euro.

Functional currency is defined as the currency of the primary economic environment in which a company operates or, in the case of a non-resident company operating in Ireland through a branch, the currency of the primary economic environment in which the company carries on its trading activities in Ireland. The currency of the primary economic environment will be determined by reference to the currency in which revenue and expenses are primarily generated and by reference to the currency in which the company, or branch, primarily borrows and lends. If a company prepares its profit and loss account in euro for any period, the functional currency of the company for that period will be the euro. *Profit and loss account* means the account of the company, or, in the case of a non-resident company carrying on a trade in the State through a branch or agency, the account of the business carried on through or from that branch or agency, which in the opinion of the company's auditor appointed under section 160 of the Companies Act 1963, presents a true and fair view of the profit and loss of the company or, as the case may be, of the business.

Under the treatment provided for in TCA 1997, s 402(2)(a), which applies in respect of capital expenditure incurred by a company on or after 1 January 1994, capital allowances and balancing charges are computed in terms of the company's functional currency and are treated as trading expenses and receipts in computing trading income or losses expressed in that functional currency.

Example 3.407.1

The functional currency of Hallart Ltd is the US dollar. For the two years ended 31 December 2006 and 2007 the euro/ US dollar exchange rates were 1:1.277 and 1:1.327 respectively. The computation of trading profits for corporation tax purposes for each of the two years would be on the following lines:

Year ended 31 December 2006	$
Tax adjusted profits (before capital allowances)	200,000
Capital allowances	20,000
	180,000
	€
euro equivalent @ €1:$ 1.277	141,000

Year ended 31 December 2007	$
Tax adjusted profits	250,000
Capital allowances	20,000
	230,000
	€
euro equivalent @ €1: $ 1.327	196,000

Capital allowances	$
Expenditure y/e 31/12/07	100,000
WDA @ 20%	20,000

	80,000
WDA y/e 31/12/07	20,000
WDV	60,000

TCA 1997, s 402(2)(b) provides a method for dealing with the situation in which the functional currency of a company changes. Briefly, the effect of this method is that total capital allowances available cannot exceed the amount of capital expenditure expressed in the new functional currency at the exchange rate pertaining at the time the expenditure was incurred.

Where a company has incurred expenditure, or has claimed capital allowances, in terms of a particular currency and its functional currency for a subsequent period is a currency other than that currency, that expenditure and those allowances should be expressed in terms of the new functional currency by reference to a rate of exchange for the two currencies for the date on which the expenditure was incurred. This will ensure that the total capital allowances in respect of the company's expenditure will equal the capital expenditure as expressed in terms of the new functional currency. The rate of exchange to be used for this purpose is a *representative rate of exchange* which means an exchange rate for the two currencies in question, being the midmarket rate at the close of business recorded by the Central Bank of Ireland, or by a similar institution in another jurisdiction, for the two currencies.

Example 3.407.2

The position is as in Example **3.407.1** except that the functional currency of Hallart Ltd for the year ended 31 December 2007 is the pound sterling (£). A representative rate of exchange for the US dollar and the pound sterling at the date the capital expenditure was incurred is 1:0.54. The capital allowances position is as follows:

Capital allowances y/e 31 December 2006	$
Expenditure	100,000
WDA y/e 31/12/06	20,000
WDV 1/1/07	80,000

Capital allowances restated in pounds sterling	£
Expenditure $100,000 @ 0.54 =	54,000
WDA y/e 31/12/06 =	10,800
WDV 1/1/07	43,200
WDA y/e 31/12/07	10,800
WDV 1/1/08	32,400

The capital allowances figure for the year ended 31 December 2006 is left undisturbed as far as the computation for that period is concerned. The expenditure and capital allowances are restated in pounds sterling, however, to facilitate the calculation of capital allowances in pounds sterling for the year ended 31 December 2007.

Capital allowances: change-over to euro

Economic and Monetary Union (EMU) commenced on 1 January 1999 when the euro became the currency of euro-participating Member States (see **3.409**). A change in functional currency occasioned solely by the introduction of the euro is not treated as a change in functional currency for the purposes of TCA 1997, s 402 (TCA 1997, s 402(1)(d)). Accordingly, tax written down values for capital allowances purposes at 1 January 1999 in a currency of a participating Member State are simply converted to euro at 1 January 1999 at the fixed rate of exchange between that currency and the euro (see **3.409.3** re fixed rate of exchange at 1 January 1999).

A change-over to the euro as the functional currency is not treated as a change in the functional currency of the company concerned requiring a re-statement of the amount of capital expenditure incurred or capital allowances referable thereto at the representative exchange rate for those currencies at the date the expenditure was incurred (TCA 1997, s 402(1)(d)). Instead, capital allowances subsequent to the change-over are based on the amount of the capital expenditure in the original currency translated into euro at the change-over date. In effect, the original capital expenditure, capital allowances claimed and tax written down value are all translated directly into euro at the same rate. From that point, capital allowances are computed in euro.

Where, on or after 1 January 1999, a company changes its functional currency from a non-participating currency to the euro, capital expenditure incurred before that date, or allowances computed by reference to that expenditure, will be expressed in terms of Irish pounds by reference to the exchange rate pertaining at the date the expenditure was incurred. The resulting amounts are then converted to euro using the fixed rate of exchange between the Irish pound and the euro.

See 2001-2002 edition of this book for a more detailed treatment of this topic.

(b) Losses

In the case of company whose functional currency is other than the euro, the amount of any trading loss, including a terminal loss, which is to be set off by a company against income or profits of any accounting period will be computed in terms of the company's functional currency. The amount will then be expressed in euro by reference to the rate of exchange used to arrive at the amount of the company's trading income for the period in terms of euro – in practice, the average rate for the period.

Example 3.407.3

The functional currency of Ronne Ltd is the US dollar. It incurred a tax loss of $300,000 for the year ended 31 December 2005 and made taxable profits of $200,000 and $250,000 for the years ending 31 December 2006 and 31 December 2007 respectively. The average euro/US dollar exchange rates for the later two years were 1:1.275 and 1:1.328 respectively. The treatment of the losses is as follows:

		$
Year ended 31 December 2005		
Tax adjusted loss		300,000

		€
Year ended 31 December 2006		
Taxable profit	$200,000 @ 1.275 =	255,000
Loss forward	$300,000	
Set-off	$200,000 @ 1.275 =	255,000
Loss forward	$100,000	

Year ended 31 December 2007		€
Taxable profit	$250,000 @ 1.328 =	332,000
Less: loss forward	$100,000 @ 1.328 =	132,800
Taxable		199,200

As for capital allowances, the legislation caters for the situation in which there is a change in the currency in which a company operates. A method is provided for computing the amount which is to be set off against the trading profits of a company for an accounting period in respect of a loss which was computed in a currency other than the functional currency of that period. The loss, or any set-off referable to that loss, should be expressed in terms of the new functional currency by reference to an average rate of exchange (the "average of representative rates of exchange") for the two currencies for the period in which the loss arose (TCA 1997, s 402(3)(b)).

Example 3.407.4

The position is the same as in Example **3.407.3** except that the functional currency of Ronne Ltd for the year ended 31 December 2007 is the pound sterling (£) and its profit for that year is £130,000. Rates of exchange are:

$/ £ – average of representative rates of exchange		
Year ended 31 December 2005		1:0.570
€/£ – average rate of exchange		
Year ended 31 December 2007		1:0.674

		$
Year ended 31 December 2005		
Tax adjusted loss		300,000
Year ended 31 December 2006		
Tax adjusted profit		200,000
Set-off		200,000
		Nil

Year ended 31 December 2007
As the functional currency of Ronne Ltd is now the pound sterling, it is necessary to restate the loss for year ended 31 December 2005, and the set-off of part of that loss for the year ended 31 December 2006, in pound sterling terms using a representative rate of exchange for the first of those years, the year in which the loss arose:

		£
Loss y/e 31 December 2005	$300,000 @ 0.570 =	171,000
Set-off y/e 31 December 2007	$200,000 @ 0.570 =	114,000
Loss forward		56,000

	£	€
Profit y/e 31 December 2007	130,000 @ 0.674 =	193,000
Loss forward	56,000 @ 0.674 =	83,000
Taxable		110,000

A change in functional currency will not give rise to any revision of the calculation of capital allowances or losses for earlier periods. The amount of the loss incurred and the amount of set-off of any part of that loss are restated to ascertain the amount available in the current period in terms of the new functional currency.

Losses: change-over to euro

As is the case with capital allowances (see above), a change in functional currency occasioned solely by the introduction of the euro is not treated as a change in functional currency for the purposes of TCA 1997, s 402 (TCA 1997, s 402(1)(d)). Accordingly, any tax loss forward at 1 January 1999 in a currency of a participating Member State is simply converted to euro at 1 January 1999 at the fixed rate of exchange between that currency and the euro (see **3.409.3** re fixed rate of exchange at 1 January 1999).

A change-over to the euro is not treated as a change in the functional currency of the company concerned for the purpose of re-stating the amount of any loss or set-off referable to that loss. Accordingly, the loss, or any set-off referable to that loss, will not be expressed in terms of the euro by reference to an average rate of exchange (the "average of representative rates of exchange") for the old currency and the euro for the period in which the loss arose.

Instead, on a change-over from the old currency to the euro, and whether or not a loss incurred by a company, or any set-off referable thereto, has been computed in terms of a currency other than the old currency, the loss, or any set-off referable to that loss, is to be expressed in terms of the euro by reference to the fixed conversion rate between the old currency and the euro at 1 January 1999 (see **3.409.3**).

Where, on or after 1 January 1999, a company changes its functional currency from a non-participating currency to the euro, any tax loss, and any set-off referable thereto, that arose before that date is expressed in terms of Irish pounds by reference to the average rate of exchange (the "average of representative rates of exchange) for the two currencies for the period in which the loss arose. The resulting amount is then converted to euro using the fixed rate of exchange between the Irish pound and the euro.

See 2001-2002 edition of this book for a more detailed treatment of this topic.

3.408 Capital gains tax

Capital gains tax (for companies, corporation tax on "chargeable gains") is a tax on the disposal of assets. In contrast with income tax, which has developed rules over a long period based largely on accounting and commercial practice (as well as commonsense), the capital gains tax code is a set of precise, and sometimes artificial, rules with results that may often be surprising. This is particularly true in the area of foreign exchange transactions where "tax fragmentation" is all too frequently a feature.

TCA 1997, s 532 provides that any currency, other than Irish currency (the euro), is an asset for the purposes of the tax (see **9.102.5**). Consequently, each time there is a disposal of a foreign currency a capital gains tax computation is required. Since, for capital gains tax purposes, any amount subject to income tax is to be deducted from the consideration received, however, transactions on revenue account are not affected. Examples of capital gains tax currency disposals are the repayment of a foreign currency loan, the application of the proceeds of a foreign currency loan to purchase goods or fixed assets, and the exchange of a foreign currency for another currency.

In each case the capital gain, or loss, is computed by reference to the euro equivalent of the currency at the date of disposal over euro equivalent of the currency at the date of its acquisition. It is not permissible, following the rule in *Bentley v Pike* [1981] STC

360, to compute the gain or loss in the foreign currency and then to convert the result into euro. The practical consequences of this rule may sometimes be surprising.

The outcome of *Whittles v Uniholdings Ltd (No 3)* [1996] STC 914 is an example of tax fragmentation. A company borrowed US dollars to finance an investment, at the same time entering into a forward contract to purchase sufficient dollars to repay the loan. During the 10 month period of the loan, the pound sterling depreciated substantially against the dollar. It was held in the Court of Appeal that the loan and the forward contract had to be considered separately so that the company was denied a capital gains tax loss in respect of the loan while being liable in respect of its gain on the disposal of its rights under the forward contract (see also **9.102.17**).

Although a debt is an asset, the general rule is that in the hands of the original lender it is not an asset for capital gains tax purposes (TCA 1997, s 541). That this should not be seen as some form of draftsman's benevolence is readily apparent when one realises that a gain is seldom realised on the disposal of a debt, whereas of course a loss may well arise. A debt denominated in a foreign currency is more likely to produce a gain (or loss) on disposal but is still subject to the general rule.

An exception to the TCA 1997, s 541 rule on debts is a credit balance in a bank account denominated in a foreign currency. The implications of this for certain capital gains tax computations are likely to be unwelcome. It is necessary each time the bank account balance is increased to calculate the euro equivalent of the amount added to establish the capital gains tax cost. This involves translating any interest into euro at the date the interest is credited. Similarly, any withdrawal from a foreign currency bank account is a disposal for capital gains tax purposes, the amount withdrawn being converted to euro at the date of withdrawal. The base cost is then the euro cost of the amount withdrawn calculated on a first in first out basis.

While the practice of the UK Revenue is to disregard transfers between bank accounts denominated in the same foreign currency, the Irish Revenue insist on treating each such transfer as a disposal for capital gains tax purposes. This will not of course be a problem in the case of any transaction not subject to capital gains tax, such as would be the case with foreign currency bank accounts operated for trading purposes.

On 1 January 1999, certain bank accounts formerly denominated in foreign currencies will have been re-denominated in terms of the euro which is also, from that date, Irish currency. In any such case, an exchange gain or loss which would arise on the disposal of the debt (ie, the account) on 31 December 1998 is deemed to arise on that date (TCA 1997, s 541A(1)). Any gain so arising, however, will not be liable to capital gains tax until such time as the debt is disposed of, ie the account is uplifted (TCA 1997, s 541A(2)). The withdrawal of part of the funds in the account would be a disposal of part of the debt and capital gains tax, as appropriate, would be payable accordingly. The satisfaction of the debt or part of the debt is treated as a disposal of the debt or of that part at the time when the debt or that part is satisfied (TCA 1997, s 541(3)).

Another exception to the TCA 1997, s 541 rule is a "debt on a security". The disposal of a debt denominated in a foreign currency which is a "debt on a security" may therefore give rise to a chargeable gain or loss. *Security* is defined as including "any loan stock or similar security whether of any government or of any public or local authority or of any company and whether secured or unsecured" but excluding government and other securities which are not chargeable assets. Further light was thrown on this matter in the case of *Ramsay (WT) Ltd v CIR* [1981] STC 174 where it was confirmed that, to be a debt on a security, a debt need not be constituted or evidenced by a document; it would seem that the term would relate to a debt having the characteristics of "marketability" and therefore of a loan stock or debenture.

TCA 1997, s 541(7) provides that certain issues of debentures in relation to company reorganisations and issues of debentures under the Mergers Directive legislation are to be treated for capital gains tax purposes as being debts on a security (see **9.102.11**).

3.409   Economic and Monetary Union

3.409.1 Introduction

On 1 January 1999, the commencement date for Economic and Monetary Union (EMU), the euro became the currency of participating Member States. On that date, national currencies of the Member States ceased to exist in their own right. Those currencies continued as legal tender but only as expressions of the euro. Euro notes and coins became available on 1 January 2002.

3.409.2 Change-over to euro

Businesses had the option to change over to the euro at any time during the transitional period so that different businesses were enabled to make the change at different times during that period. In this regard, the Revenue operated a procedure to accommodate the change-over process to suit the needs of the business sector. This topic is dealt with in previous editions of this book.

3.409.3 Fixed conversion rate

The conversion rate between the Irish pound and the euro was fixed irrevocably on 1 January 1999. Once a company decided to change its operating currency from the Irish pound (or other functional currency) to the euro, accounts and tax computations were prepared in euro. It was necessary for all amounts carried or brought forward at the point of the change to be converted into euro at the fixed rate of exchange. Where the change-over was from Irish pounds, as was the case in the vast majority of situations, the fixed rate to be used was the above-mentioned fixed exchange rate between the Irish pound and the euro at 1 January 1999. Where a company's functional currency at the date of change- over was other than the Irish pound, the conversion rate to be used was the fixed rate between that currency and the euro.

In certain cases, a company's functional currency will be a currency other than a currency of an EU Member State, eg the US dollar. As at 1 January 1999, and assuming the company did not change its functional currency, the reporting position of the company for tax purposes from 1 January did not change significantly.

Chapter 4

Losses, Collection of Tax at Source and Charges on Income

4.1 LOSSES

4.101   Trading losses

For corporation tax purposes, a trading loss is computed in the same way as a trading profit. The corporation tax computation starts with the profit or loss as disclosed by the accounts, disallowable items such as depreciation, expenditure of a capital nature, general provisions, balancing charges, entertainment and excess motor expenses, are added back, and other items such as investment and rental income, grants, previously disallowed provisions written back and capital allowances, are deducted. This procedure will result in an "adjusted" profit or loss for tax purposes. Where a loss arises, no distinction is made between the part of the loss which is attributable to capital allowances (if any) and the remaining part of the loss (see **5.105.2**).

Carry forward of losses

A trading loss may be carried forward, without time limit, for relief against profits from the same trade of future accounting periods (Taxes Consolidation Act 1997 (TCA 1997), s 396(1)). Relief for offset of a loss carried forward from a previous accounting period is by way of claim but there is no statutory time limit for making such a claim. Under the self-assessment system, however, a loss forward would need to be claimed in the corporation tax return for the first period for which it can be utilised. If this is not done, an assessment made in accordance with the return cannot be amended to incorporate the loss forward.

A loss forward must be claimed against the first available profits of the same trade. TCA 1997, s 396(1) provides that where a claim is made to set a trading loss incurred in an accounting period against the profits of a later period, those profits are treated as reduced by the amount of the loss or by so much of that loss as cannot, on that claim or on a claim (if made) under TCA 1997, s 396(2), 396A(3) or 396B(2) (see **4.103**), be relieved against income or profits of an earlier period. Where a loss forward is not claimed for an accounting period for which it could have been claimed, the loss cannot then be claimed against trading profits of a later period; the amount of a loss forward which can be claimed for any accounting period is limited to the amount which could not have been claimed against income or profits of an earlier accounting period.

Example 4.101.1

The tax adjusted results of Apex Ltd for the three years to 31 December 2007 are as follows:

Year ended		€
31 December 2005	loss	1,000,000
31 December 2006	profit	800,000
31 December 2007	profit	1,200,000

Apex Ltd is a manufacturing company but for the year ended 31 December 2007 it was, exceptionally, because of fire damage to its premises, obliged to buy in almost all of the goods which it sold during that period. Anticipating that its corporation tax liability for the year ended 31 December 2007 would reflect very little manufacturing relief, the company did not claim any loss forward in its corporation tax return for the year ended 31 December 2006. In its corporation tax return for the year ended 31 December 2007, the loss forward of €1,000,000 was claimed against the profits of €1,200,000. The claim is disallowed, however, on the basis that €800,000 of the loss forward could have been offset against the trading income of the year ended 31 December 2006. The deduction in respect of loss forward for the year ended 31 December 2007 is restricted to €200,000.

Likewise, any claim for loss forward will be restricted to the extent that the loss has been offset against income or profits of an earlier accounting period on foot of a claim under TCA 1997, s 396(2), 396A(3) or s 396B(2).

Since a loss forward may only be offset against the profits of the same trade, it will be relevant to consider whether the trade being carried on at the time the loss is being claimed is the same trade in which the loss was incurred in the first place. As to whether a company is or is not carrying on the same trade at different times is a question of fact. In *Bolands Ltd v Davis* 1 ITC 91, a flour milling and bread baking company closed down its two mills after incurring losses. About half of the flour it milled had been used to supply the bakeries. After about eight months the mills were re-opened, mainly to supply the bakeries. It was held that the same trade had been carried on throughout. In another case, a company of contractors closed its premises and for more than five years had no plant or works although its directors tried unsuccessfully to obtain new contracts throughout the period of the closure. Following a change of shareholders and a fresh injection of capital, the company acquired new plant and a number of profitable contracts were obtained. It was held that the company's trade had continued throughout.

In *Gordon & Blair Ltd v CIR* 40 TC 358, a brewing company ceased brewing but continued to sell beer which was supplied to its specification by another company. It was held that the company had ceased one trade, the trade of brewing, and commenced another trade, the trade of selling beer.

A loss incurred in a trade in an accounting period is to be computed for the purposes of TCA 1997, s 396 in the same way as trading income from the trade in that period would have been computed (TCA 1997, s 396(5)).

Trading income for the purposes of TCA 1997, s 396 means, in relation to any trade, the income which falls or would fall to be included in respect of the trade in the total profits of the company. TCA 1997, s 396(6) deals with the case in which in an accounting period a company incurs a loss in a trade in respect of which it is within the charge to corporation tax under Case I or III of Schedule D, and in a later period to which the loss or any part of it is carried forward under TCA 1997, s 396(1) relief in respect of that loss or part loss cannot be given, or cannot fully be given, due to an insufficiency of trading income. In that case, any interest or dividends on investments which would fall to be taken into account as trading receipts in computing that income, except for the fact that they have been subject to tax under other provisions, are to be treated for the purposes of TCA 1997, s 396(1) as if they were trading income of the trade.

TCA 1997, s 396(6) accordingly deals with the case of a company such as a financial concern which receives interest and dividends (other than dividends from Irish resident companies). While, in strictness, these items are in the nature of trading receipts in the hands of such a company, they may in practice have been subject to taxation treatment appropriate to income other than trading income. For example, untaxed interest from Irish government securities or dividends from foreign companies may have been charged to tax under Case III of Schedule D. In any such case, a loss from the trade of the company would be set off not only against the trading profits charged to tax under Case I but also against the investment income charged under Case III.

Dividends from Irish resident companies are not within the charge to corporation tax (TCA 1997, s 129 – see **3.205**) and any loss of a financial concern will not be available for carry forward against such dividends. Relief may, however, be available in such circumstances under TCA 1997, s 158 (see **4.202**).

TCA 1997, s 396(7) provides that where charges on income (see **4.402** and **4.404**) paid by a company in an accounting period exceed the amount of profits against which they are deductible, the excess amount of the charges or, if the amount is smaller, the payments included in the charges which were made wholly and exclusively for the purposes of the company's trade ("trade charges"), are treated as trading expenses for the purpose of computing a loss which may be carried forward under TCA 1997, s 396(1) and set off against trading income of subsequent periods.

Example 4.101.2

Axel Ltd made a taxable profit of €60,000 in the year to 31 December 2006 and incurred a trading loss of €400,000 in the period to 30 June 2007 when it also paid charges of €600,000 consisting of patent royalties of €500,000 and interest of €10,000 qualifying as a charge on income.

Loss relief is available as follows:

Period ended 30 June 2007	€	€
Trading loss		400,000
Excess charges:		
royalties carried forward		500,000
interest unrelieved		100,000

Year ended 31 December 2006		€
Trading profit		600,000
Less: trading loss carried back under TCA 1997, s 396(2)	400,000	
Restricted (€60,000/2)		300,000
Taxable		300,000
Loss carried forward		100,000

Add: excess charges (trade charges)	500,000
Total carried forward to y/e 30 June 2006	600,000

For the purposes of TCA 1997, s 396, references to a company carrying on a trade refer to the company carrying it on so as to be within the charge to corporation tax in respect of it (TCA 1997, s 396(8)).

Set off of losses against profits

Under TCA 1997, s 396(2), a trading loss may be offset:

(a)   against profits of any description (before charges) of the same accounting period; and

(b)   provided the company was then carrying on the trade, against profits of any description (before charges) of immediately preceding accounting periods ending within a period equal in length to the period in which the loss was incurred.

In view of the restrictions on the use of "relevant trading losses" effective from 6 March 2001 (see **4.103**), TCA 1997, s 396(2) is now largely redundant, being relevant only in relation to excepted trades.

A loss which may be offset against profits of an earlier period is confined to so much of that loss as cannot be utilised against profits of a later accounting period. In other words, a loss which is the subject of a TCA 1997, s 396(2) claim must be used firstly against the total profits of the period in which the loss arose, as in (a) above, and then against the profits of the preceding period or periods, as in (b) above. For the purposes of (b), profits are apportioned on a time basis; where an accounting period falls partly before the immediately preceding period or periods equal in length to the period of the loss, only a proportionate part of the profits of that accounting period may be relieved.

Example 4.101.3

Post Ltd, a company carrying on a trade of working minerals (an excepted trade), made a trading profit of €140,000 for the year ended 31 December 2006 and a loss of €170,000 in the same trade for the nine months ended 30 September 2007. The company had a chargeable gain of €20,000 (as adjusted for corporation tax) for the period ended 30 September 2007. A claim for relief under TCA 1997, s 396(2) is made in respect of the loss. Firstly, the chargeable gain of €20,000 is covered by part of the loss, leaving a balance of €150,000 available against the profits of the preceding period.

The profits of the year ended 31 December 2006 which may be relieved may not exceed the part of those profits proportionate to the part of the period falling within the nine months immediately preceding the period of the loss. Therefore only €105,000 (9/12 x €140,000) may be covered by the loss from the period ended 30 September 2007. The balance of the loss, €45,000, is carried forward.

Example 4.101.4

Ante Ltd, a company carrying on a trade of land dealing (an excepted trade), had profits and losses as follows:

	€
Nine months ended 30 June 2006	
Profits (including chargeable gain €20,000)	60,000
Six months ended 31 December 2006	
Profits	90,000

Year ended 31 December 2007

Trading loss   200,000

A claim for relief under TCA 1997, s 396(2) is made in respect of the loss.

The loss may be set off against total profits of the two periods ending 31 December 2006 and 30 June 2006 as both periods end within the twelve months immediately preceding the year ended 31 December 2007. As three ninths of the period ended 30 June 2006 falls before the twelve month period, however, only six ninths of the total profits may be relieved. Relief will therefore be as follows:

	€
Nine months ended 30 June 2006	
Profits	60,000
TCA 1997s 396(2)	40,000
Taxable	20,000
Six months ended 31 December 2006	
Profits	90,000
TCA 1997, s 396(2)	90,000
Taxable	Nil
Year ended 31 December 2007	
Loss	200,000
TCA 1997, s 396(2)	130,000
Loss forward	70,000

A company may not make a claim under TCA 1997, s 396(2) to set part of a loss against profits; the subsection provides that the company may make a claim requiring that "the loss" be set off. If, however, a part of the loss is being surrendered by way of group relief (and it is possible to make a group relief claim for less than the full amount available – see **8.315.1**), it must follow that a TCA 1997, s 396(2) claim may then be made for the balance of that loss.

A claim for relief under TCA 1997, s 396(2) must be made within two years of the end of the accounting period in which the loss occurred (TCA 1997, s 396(9)). In a UK case, *R v IRC, ex parte Unilever plc and related application* [1996] STC 681, it was held that where the Revenue had accepted informal claims for loss relief over a period of 20 years, it would be unfair and an abuse of power to insist on a formal claim being made within the time limit.

Relief under TCA 1997, s 396(2) is not allowed where a loss has been incurred in a farming or market gardening trade which is not being carried on on a commercial basis and with a view to the realisation of profit (TCA 1997, s 663). Since, however, a trade of farming is a relevant trade, it would in any event not be possible to make a claim under TCA 1997, s 396(2) in respect of a farming loss. A loss incurred in a trade falling within Case III of Schedule D (see **4.105**) may not be offset under TCA 1997, s 396(2).

4.102   Ring-fencing of losses

Certain provisions restrict the use of losses or losses attributable to capital allowances to particular classes of income. Under these provisions, where the full amount of the loss or capital allowances available for any period cannot be utilised in full, they may be allowed only against the same class of income for subsequent periods. No other kinds of profits may be relieved by those losses or capital allowances and their use is accordingly "ring-fenced". The most significant provisions which provide for the ring-fencing are the following:

(a)   capital allowances in respect of leased machinery or plant: allowances are confined to income from the leasing activity, whether assessable as trading income under Case I of Schedule D or under Case IV of Schedule D (TCA 1997, s 403 – see **5.305.6** and **5.305.7**));

(b)   capital allowances of a limited partner: allowances are confined to the share of income from the partnership trade (TCA 1997, s 1013 – see **13.703**));

(c)   losses and capital allowances in respect of a qualifying ship used in a qualifying shipping trade: allowances are confined to income from qualifying shipping activities or income from the letting on charter of a qualifying ship (TCA 1997, s 407(4)(a) – see **5.105.4**, **5.213** and **5.305**);

(d)   writing down allowances and initial allowances (but not balancing allowances) in respect of holiday cottages: allowances confined to income from trade under Case I of Schedule D or income from leasing under Case V of Schedule D (TCA 1997, s 405 – see **5.416.5**);

(e)   capital allowances (Seaside Resort Areas: writing down allowances, initial allowances and balancing allowances) in respect of registered holiday apartments and other self-catering accommodation: allowances confined to income from trade under Case I of Schedule D or income from leasing under Case V of Schedule D (TCA 1997, s 355 – see 2001-2002 or earlier editions of this book).

A loss incurred by a company carrying on a trade of leasing, to the extent that it is attributable to specified capital allowances (TCA 1997, s 403 – see **5.305**), may not be set off against the total profits of the company under TCA 1997, s 396(2) nor may it be surrendered by way of group relief. In view of the treatment of "relevant trading losses" for accounting periods ending on or after 6 March 2001 (see **4.103** and **8.306.2**), such a loss cannot be set against total profits anyway.

4.103   Treatment of "relevant trading losses"

Manufacturing losses (for periods up to 31 December 2002)

Up to 31 December 2002, a manufacturing loss ("a loss from the sale of goods", ie a loss arising from activities carried on by a company in respect of which, if a profit had resulted from those activities, the company would be eligible for the 10% corporation tax rate – see **7.203.1**) could not be offset against profits taxable at the standard corporation tax rate. A manufacturing loss arising in a "relevant accounting period" (see **7.201.2**) could be offset against manufacturing profits (income from the sale of goods) of the same accounting period and, if the company was then carrying on the trade in respect of which the loss arose, against manufacturing profits of immediately preceding accounting periods ending within a period equal in length to the period in which the loss was incurred. A manufacturing loss could be carried forward against profits of the trade (whether manufacturing or not) in succeeding periods.

For accounting periods ending after 31 December 2002, the treatment of manufacturing losses is governed by the provisions relating to relevant trading losses (see under *Relevant trading losses* below).

(For a more detailed treatment of the position up to 31 December 2002, see the 2002 edition of this book.)

In calculating *income from the sale of goods* for manufacturing relief purposes, a deduction is made for any amount for which relief has been claimed in respect of a trading loss to the extent that it has been allowed against the company's "income for the relevant accounting period from the sale of those goods" (TCA 1997, s 448(3)(b) - see **7.202.3**). A loss from the sale of goods does not include any amount mentioned in TCA 1997, s 407(4)(b), ie a loss in a qualifying shipping trade, since such losses are ring-fenced (see **5.213**).

Relevant trading losses

A trading loss (other than a loss arising in an excepted trade) incurred by a company in an accounting period may not be offset against profits of that accounting period other than income taxable at the 10% or the standard corporation tax rates.

For the purposes of this restriction, the following definitions are relevant.

Relevant trading loss, in relation to a company's accounting period, means a loss incurred by the company in the accounting period in a trade carried on by the company, other than:

(a)   so much of the loss as is a loss incurred in an excepted trade within the meaning of TCA 1997, s 21A (see **3.101.4**); and

(b)   any amount which is or would, if TCA 1997, s 403(8) had not been enacted, be the relevant amount of the loss (see **5.305.6** for the meaning of *the relevant amount of the loss* in the context of the ring-fencing of leasing capital allowances) for the purposes of TCA 1997, s 403(4).

The purpose of (b) is to ensure that the restriction on the use of certain leasing losses cannot be circumvented by reason of a definition of "relevant trading loss" that would include such losses. If the leasing losses were such relevant trading losses, they could be used to shelter any "relevant trading income", and not just income from a leasing trade, in accordance with TCA 1997, s 396A. The reference to TCA 1997, s 403(8) is to secure that leasing losses from operations in Shannon or the IFSC, which are exempted from the leasing restriction, are nevertheless not to be regarded as relevant trading losses.

Relevant trading income, in relation to an accounting period of a company, means the trading income of the company for that period (excluding any income taxable under Case III of Schedule D) other than so much of that income as is income of an excepted trade within the meaning of TCA 1997, s 21A (TCA 1997, s 396A(1) and s 243A(1)).

Notwithstanding TCA 1997, s 396(2) (which allows for the deduction of trading losses against total profits – see **4.101**), the amount of a trading loss incurred by a company in an accounting period is deemed, for the purposes of that subsection, to be reduced by the amount of a relevant trading loss incurred by it in that period (TCA 1997, s 396A(2)).

Where a company incurs such a relevant trading loss in an accounting period, the company may claim to set that loss against its:

(a)   income specified in TCA 1997, s 21A(4)(b) (certain life, non-life and reinsurance trades – see **3.101.4**);

(b)   relevant trading income; and

(c)   income excluded from TCA 1997, s 21A(3) by virtue of TCA 1997, s 21B (foreign dividends eligible for 12.5% corporation tax rate - see **3.101.5**),

of that accounting period and, provided the company was then carrying on the trade, of preceding accounting periods ending within a period equal in length to the period in which the relevant trading loss was incurred (TCA 1997, s 396A(3)).

The income (to the extent that it includes income described in (a) or (b) above) of such preceding periods is reduced by the amount of the relevant trading loss or by so much of that loss as cannot be relieved against income of a later accounting period. Thus, a relevant trading loss must first be used to reduce income of the period in which the loss is incurred (if there is, unusually, any such income as described in (a) or (b) above in that period) before being set against any such income of preceding periods.

There is no requirement to take into account any claim under TCA 1997, s 396B in respect of tax payable for the period of the loss before setting off a relevant trading loss against income of preceding periods. In fact, any possible claim under TCA 1997, s 396A must be taken into account before claiming relief under TCA 1997, s 396B (see under *Relief on value basis for relevant trading losses* below).

There is no provision (similar to that for group relief – see **8.306.2**) whereby relief under TCA 1997, s 396A(3) is to be denied to Case III losses or losses incurred in a farming trade where such losses are excluded from TCA 1997, s 396(2). At least as regards farming, however, this is not necessarily an oversight as, since farming is a relevant trade, a farming loss cannot be set against non-trading profits. By the same token, a farming loss cannot in any event be used for the purposes of TCA 1997, s 396(2).

A claim for relief must be made within two years from the end of the accounting period in which the loss is incurred (TCA 1997, s 396A(5)).

For the purposes of giving relief for any preceding accounting periods, the income specified in TCA 1997, s 21A(4)(b) or the relevant trading income is apportioned on a time basis; where an accounting period falls partly before the immediately preceding period or periods equal in length to the period of the loss, only a proportionate part of the income specified in TCA 1997, s 21A(4)(b) or the relevant trading income of that accounting period may be relieved (TCA 1997, s 396A(4)).

A claim under TCA 1997, s 482(2) (relief for expenditure on significant buildings and gardens – see **3.203.6**) is unaffected by TCA 1997, s 396A (TCA 1997, s 482(11)).

The relevant trading income against which a relevant trading loss may be deducted by a company for any accounting period is the company's relevant trading income for that period, effectively the company's trading income which is taxable at either the 10% or the standard corporation tax rate.

Example 4.103.1

Forza Ltd had the following results for its latest relevant accounting period:

	€
Sales of goods	750,000
Sales of merchandise (not manufactured by company	250,000
Trading income (loss)	(100,000)
Case III	300,000

Computation:

		€	
Case III			300,000
Corporation tax @ 25%			75,000
Relief on value basis (see below):		€	
– manufacturing loss €75,000 @ 10%		7,500	
– trading loss, balance €25,000 @ 12.5%		3,125	10,625
Payable			64,375

The loss of €100,000 may be utilised under:

(a) TCA 1997, s 396A(3) against trading profits of immediately preceding accounting periods;

(b) TCA 1997, s 396(1) – carry forward of loss against trading profits (whether manufacturing or not) of succeeding accounting periods;

(c) TCA 1997, s 420A – group relief against trading profits;

(d) TCA 1997, s 396B – relief on a value basis against tax on the investment income – see below; or

(e) TCA 1997, s 420B – group relief on value basis (see **8.306.3**).

Relief on value basis for relevant trading losses

Excess trading losses incurred by a company may be used, on a value basis, to reduce the amount of that company's corporation tax. The tax which may be so reduced, referred to as the *relevant corporation tax*, is the company's corporation tax otherwise payable for the accounting period in question, after any reduction by virtue of TCA 1997, s 243B (similar relief on value basis for trade charges – see **4.405**) but before any reduction by virtue of TCA 1997, s 420B (similar relief on value basis for group relief – see **8.306.3**) and also before taking into account any tax payable by virtue of TCA 1997, s 239 (annual payments – see **4.306**), 241 (certain payments by non-resident companies – see **4.303.5**), 440 (surcharge on undistributed investment and estate income – see **10.302**) or 441 (surcharge on undistributed income of service companies – see **10.303**) and, in the case of a company carrying on life business, any corporation tax which would be attributable to policyholders' profits (see **12.603.6**).

The "excess" loss in respect of which relief may be claimed by a company for an accounting period is the excess of the relevant trading loss for that period over the aggregate of the amounts that could, if a timely claim for such set off had been made by the company, have been set off in respect of the loss against income of the company for that period and for the preceding period, in accordance with TCA 1997, s 396A(3) (mainly relevant trading income (including any manufacturing income) – also income of certain life, non-life and reinsurance trades – see **3.101.4**) (TCA 1997, s 396B(2)).

For the purposes of TCA 1997, s 396B, *relevant trading loss* has the same meaning as for TCA 1997, s 396A (see above) (TCA 1997, s 396B(1)).

Where a claim for relief in respect of an excess relevant trading loss is made for any accounting period, the relevant corporation tax for the period of the claim and, if the company was then carrying on the trade, for preceding accounting periods (see below), is reduced:

(a)   in so far as the excess consists of a loss from the sale of goods, by an amount equal to 10% of that loss; and

(b)   in so far as the excess consists of a non-manufacturing loss, by an amount equal to that loss multiplied by the standard rate of corporation tax for the accounting period (TCA 1997, s 396B(3)).

The amount for a *loss from the sale of goods* (manufacturing loss) is arrived at by apportioning the total amount of loss arising by reference to the amount of the turnover from the sale of "goods" over the amount of turnover from the sale of "goods and merchandise", ie after applying the turnover apportionment method used to calculate manufacturing income (TCA 1997, s 448(1)(b)). Where the trading loss includes any amount that is not referable to sales of goods and merchandise (eg, services income), that amount must be excluded from the amount of the trading loss before applying the turnover apportionment. A loss from the sale of goods does not include any amount mentioned in TCA 1997, s 407(4)(b), ie a loss in a qualifying shipping trade, since such losses are ring-fenced (see **5.213**).

A claim for relief must be made within two years from the end of the accounting period in which the loss is incurred (TCA 1997, s 396B(6)).

For the purposes of giving relief for any preceding accounting periods, the reduction in tax may have to be apportioned on a time basis; where an accounting period falls partly before the immediately preceding period or periods equal in length to the period in which the excess arises, the reduction in tax may not exceed a proportionate part of the relevant corporation tax for that accounting period (TCA 1997, s 396B(4)).

The amount of any loss available for the purposes of TCA 1997, s 396(1) (loss forward) is treated as reduced by an amount calculated to produce the same result as if the "excess" loss used for the purposes of the credit claim had been set against taxable income. Accordingly, that "amount" is the aggregate of (i) 10 times the amount in (a) above and (ii) the amount in (b) above grossed up at the standard rate of corporation tax applicable (TCA 1997, s 396B(5)). Effectively, that aggregate is the amount of the excess loss used for the purposes of the claim for credit under TCA 1997, s 396B(3).

The amount which is treated as reducing a loss forward for the purposes of TCA 1997, s 396(1) is, however, treated as increased where, for the accounting period in question, a "relevant amount" is deductible from, or may be treated as reducing, profits of more than one description. A *relevant amount* is an amount (other than any amount incurred for trading purposes) of charges on income, expenses of management or other amount deductible from, or which may be treated as reducing, profits or more than one description (not being an allowance to which effect is given under TCA 1997, s 308(4) – capital allowances in excess of Case V income – see **5.105.3**). The amount is re-calculated upwards on the basis that no deduction had been made in respect of the relevant amount. This provision ensures that the result of the TCA 1997, s 396B claim is the same as if a loss equal to the excess had been used to displace any relevant amount (TCA 1997, s 396B(5)(c)).

As regards the meaning of "relevant amount" above, it would seem that as well as excluding amounts deductible by virtue of TCA 1997, s 308(4), there should be a similar exclusion for amounts deductible by reason of TCA 1997, s 420.

Example 4.103.2

The following are the results of Dauphin Ltd for the year ended 31 March 2008:

			€	€
Trading loss	– non-manufacturing		44,000	
	– manufacturing		11,000	55,000
Trade charges	– non-manufacturing		4,000	
	– manufacturing		1,000	5,000
Non-trade charges				13,000
Case III income				30,000
Trading income year to 31 March 2007	– non-manufacturing		8,000	
	– manufacturing		2,000	10,000
TCA 1997, s 243B(2) excess:			€	€
Relevant trading charges				5,000
– allowed TCA 1997, s 243A				—
Excess				5,000
TCA 1997, s 396B(2) excess:				
Relevant trading loss				55,000
– allowed TCA 1997, s 396A(3)				10,000
Excess				45,000
Corporation tax computation:				
Case III				30,000
Deduct non-trade charges				13,000
				17,000
Corporation tax @ 25%				4,250
TCA 1997, s 243B(3) relief:				
€1,000 @ 10%			100	
€4,000 @ 12.5%			500	600
Relevant corporation tax for TCA 1997, s 396B [2]				3,650
TCA 1997, s 396B(3) relief:				
€29,200 @ 12.5%				3,650
Payable				—

TCA 1997, s 396(1):

Trading charges net of TCA 1997, s 243B (5,000 - 5,000)	Nil
Trading loss net of TCA 1997 ss 396A/396B (55,000 - 10,000 - 29,200)	15,800
Balance of TCA 1997, s 396(1) loss (subject to TCA 1997, s 396B(5)(c))	15,800

TCA 1997, s 396B(5)(c):

The "amount" of €29,200 giving rise to the relief under TCA 1997, s 396B(3) is increased to what it would have been had the non-trade charges not been deductible[1]	45,000
Revised loss net of TCA 1997, s 396A(3)/396B(3) (55,000 - 10,000 - 45,000)	Nil
Therefore final TCA 1997, s 396(1) loss forward	Nil

Notes:

(1)   If the non-trade charges had not been deductible, Case III would have been €30,000 resulting in corporation tax of €7,500. The TCA 1997, s 396B(3) relief would then have been €9,000 @ 10% + €36,000 @ 12.5% = €5,400. Thus, the revised "amount" is €45,000.

(2)   The "relevant corporation tax" against which credits may be claimed is: TCA 1997, s 243B, corporation tax before any other credits; TCA 1997, s 396B, corporation tax after any TCA 1997, s 243B credits; TCA 1997, s 420B, corporation tax after any TCA 1997, s 243B or 396B credits.

4.104   Terminal losses

Where a trade carried on by a company ceases, terminal loss relief may be claimed by the company in respect of trading losses incurred, and charges paid wholly and exclusively for the purposes of the trade, in the last twelve months prior to the cessation (TCA 1997, s 397). Relief for terminal loss is available against profits arising from the same trade in the three years preceding the last twelve months of trading but *after* all other available loss reliefs are claimed.

Example 4.104.1

Yield Ltd incurred a loss of €120,000 in its final period of trading, six months to 30 November 2007. Results for the preceding four years were:

Year to 31 May:	€
2007	(50,000)
2006	80,000
2005	50,000
2004	40,000

(a) TCA 1997, s 396A(3) relief must be claimed first:

	€
Loss year to 31/5/07	(50,000)
TCA 1997, s 396(2) claim re year to 31/5/06	80,000
Profit (balance) y/e 31/5/06	30,000

(b) Terminal loss

	€
6 months to 30/11/07	120,000
6 months to 31/5/07	Nil
Terminal loss	120,000

(c) TCA 1997, s 397 relief

	€
(i) 6 months to 30/11/06 (balance)	Nil
(ii) Year to 31/5/06	30,000
(iii) Year to 31/5/05	50,000
(iv) 6 months to 31/5/04 (€40,000 x 6/12)	20,000
	100,000
Terminal loss	(120,000)
Unrelieved	(20,000)

If a terminal loss consists of or includes a manufacturing loss (see **4.103**), there is no restriction as regards the trading profits against which it may be offset under TCA 1997, s 397; it can be set against either manufacturing or non-manufacturing profits of the three preceding years (but after any other available claim, including the setting off of the loss against any available manufacturing profits).

TCA 1997, s 397(3) applies the provisions of TCA 1997, s 396(5) to (8) (see **4.101** above) for terminal loss relief purposes. Accordingly, for terminal loss purposes:

(a)　a loss is to be computed in the same way as profits;

(b)　terminal loss relief is available against interest and dividends (other than dividends from an Irish resident company) of a financial trading concern;

(c)　charges on income in excess of profits and which have been paid for the purposes of the trade may, up to the amount of the excess, be treated as creating a loss qualifying for terminal loss relief (see Example **4.104.2** below); and

(d)　terminal loss relief is available only to a company which is within the charge to corporation tax at all material times.

Furthermore, TCA 1997, s 397(3) provides that terminal loss relief may not operate to displace relief under TCA 1997, s 243 or 243A for charges on income paid wholly and exclusively for the purposes of the trade (see Example **4.104.2**).

Example 4.104.2

Endgame Ltd carried on an excepted trade (for the purposes of TCA 1997, s 21A – see **3.101.4**) up to 31 March 2008 when the trade ceased. Its results for the last five accounting periods of trading are as follows:

	y/e 30/6/04	y/e 30/6/05	y/e 30/6/06	y/e 30/6/07	p/e 31/3/08
	€000	€000	€000	€000	€000
Case I	140	180	130	79	(440)
Case III	35	35	35	35	20
Chargeable gains (adjusted)	15	75	40	30	–
Trade charges paid	45	50	80	80	55
Non-trade charges paid	15	15	15	12	15

The taxable profits for the above periods after claiming terminal loss relief are as follows:

	y/e 30/6/04 €000	y/e 30/6/05 €000	y/e 30/6/06 €000	y/e 30/6/07 €000	p/e 31/3/08 €000
Case I	140	180	130	79	Nil
Case III	35	35	35	35	20
Chargeable gains	15	75	40	30	-
Profits	190	290	205	144	20
TCA 1997, s 396(2) relief[1]				108	20
	190	290	205	36	Nil
Terminal loss[2]	35	180	125	12	
	155	110	80	24	
Trade charges	(45)	(50)	(80)	(24)	
Non-trade charges	(15)	(15)			
Taxable	95	5	Nil	Nil	

Notes:

1   The TCA 1997, s 396(2) loss must be offset before claiming terminal loss relief (TCA 1997, s 397(1)(b)). As the loss arose for a nine-month period, the profits of the year ended 30 June 2007 against which it may be set off must be restricted to 9/12ths.

2   Terminal loss is computed as follows:

	€	€
Loss for final period	440	
Utilised TCA 1997 s396(2)	128	312
Trade charges		55
		367
Loss for period 1/4/07 – 30/6/07	Nil	
Excess charges[3]	14	14
Terminal loss		381

3   For the year ended 30 June 2007, the excess of charges paid over profits is €92,000 - €36,000 = €56,000 (which excess is not greater than the amount of the trade charges of €80,000).

In accordance with TCA 1997, s 396(7), these excess charges are treated as if they were trading expenses of the trade. These deemed trading expenses are time apportioned to the period 1 April 2007 to 30 June 2007, ie €56,000 x 3/12ths = €14,000.

TCA 1997, s 397(3) provides that TCA 1997, s 396(7) is to apply for terminal loss relief purposes. The amount of €14,000 is therefore treated as additional trading expenses incurred in the final twelve months of the trade and is accordingly included as part of the terminal loss.

4   For the year ended 30 June 2007, terminal loss relief of €12,000 is claimed. Terminal loss relief cannot operate to displace relief for trade charges (TCA 1997, s 397(3)) but may displace non-trade charges. Before allowing terminal loss relief for

this period, the profits of €36,000 were covered by charges of €36,000 but the non-trade charges are now displaced by terminal loss relief.

As to how the charges of €36,000 are to be treated as consisting respectively of trade and non-trade charges, however, is not clear from the legislation. Since the excess charges treated as trading expenses for any period cannot exceed the amount of trade charges paid in that period, the entire excess could in effect be regarded as comprising trade charges only. For the year ended 30 June 2007, that would leave a balance of trade charges €24,000 (€80,000 - €56,000) and all of the non-trade charges of €12,000 to cover the profits of €36,000. An amount of €12,000 relating to non- charges displaced could then be covered by terminal loss relief.

In this connection, as terminal loss relief may only be claimed against trading profits, it is necessary to identify the amount of trading profits included in the profits of €36,000 (profits as reduced by the TCA 1997, s 396(2) loss). Again, the relevant legislation does not deal with this point. A reasonable approach would be to treat the profit figure of €36,000 as made up proportionately of trading profits, Case III income and chargeable gains. Accordingly, the amount included for trading profits would be €36,000 x 79/144 = €19,750 which would permit an offset of €12,000 by way of terminal loss relief. However, the precise statutory position relating to this aspect is not clear.

[5] For the year ended 30 June 2006, trade charges are €80,000. Terminal loss relief may not operate to displace relief for trade charges so that the terminal loss relief for this period is restricted to €125,000 leaving profits of €80,000 to be covered by trade charges.

[6] For the year ended 30 June 2005, since the trade charges do not exceed the profits other than trading income (Case III and chargeable gains), the full amount of the trading income can be covered by terminal loss.

[7] For the year ended 30 June 2004, the maximum amount of trading income against which terminal loss may be set is 3/12ths since the three year set off period extends back to 1 April 2004 only. The terminal loss relief is therefore €140,000 x 3/12 = €35,000.

[8] The unused terminal loss is €381,000 – (€12,000 + €125,000 + €180,000 + €35,000) = €29,000. Unused trade charges, from the year ended 30 June 2007, are €80,000 – (€24,000 + €14,000) = €42,000. Unused non-trade charges are €15,000 + €12,000 + €15,000 = €42,000.

4.105   Case III losses

In respect of trades the profits of which are assessable under Case III (see **3.102.2** and **3.207.4**), relief under TCA 1997, s 396(2) is not available. Losses arising from such a trade may therefore only be carried forward against future profits from the same trade. Terminal loss relief may, however, be claimed in the same way as for a Case I trade.

A Case III trade is one which is carried on abroad. It does not denote a trade carried on through a foreign branch (the profits of which are taxed under Case I as part of the overall trade) but a trade which is effectively controlled from abroad (albeit belonging to an Irish resident – a fairly unusual situation).

4.106   Case IV losses

Profits taxable under Case IV of Sch. D include profits of transactions or activities which do not amount to a trade (see **3.208.1**). Where in any accounting period a company incurs a loss in a transaction or activity in respect of which it is within the charge to tax under Case IV, the loss may be set against the income from similar transactions for the same or any subsequent accounting period (TCA 1997, s 399(1)). The loss is to be set off firstly against any Case IV profits of the accounting period in which the loss was incurred and then against Case IV profits of subsequent periods, beginning with the earliest of those periods.

TCA 1997, s 814 includes in profits assessable under Case IV any gains arising from the disposal or exercise of a right to receive money stated in a certificate of deposit or of a right to receive money arising from an assignable deposit. Where a company sustains a loss in a transaction of this kind, the loss may be set off against other Case IV profits and also against any interest arising on the money the right to which has been disposed of.

See **5.105.3**, **5.416.4** and **5.505.2** for treatment of Case IV capital allowances.

4.107   Case V and other deficiencies

A Case V loss (aggregate of deficiencies in excess of aggregate of surpluses computed in accordance with TCA 1997, s 97(1) – taxation of rents under short leases (see **3.209**)) for any accounting period may be set off against Case V income of previous accounting periods for a period equal in length to the period of the loss, and any remaining loss may then be set against Case V income of any subsequent accounting period (TCA 1997, s 399(2)).

An allowance (ie a capital allowance) which falls to be made to a company for any accounting period and which is given "by discharge or repayment of tax" (eg a writing down allowance available against income from the letting of machinery or plant (TCA 1997 ss 298(1) and 278(3), (4)), or in charging its income under Case V, and is to be available primarily against the specified class of income, is to be deducted as far as possible against income of that class. Where the allowance is not fully used in that way because of an insufficiency of income, it may under TCA 1997, s 308(4) be allowed against profits of any description of the same accounting period and (if the company was then within the charge to tax) of preceding accounting periods for a period equal in length to the period in which the allowance arose.

The deficiency which may be offset against profits of a preceding period is confined to so much of that deficiency as cannot be utilised against profits of a later accounting period. In other words, a deficiency which is the subject of a TCA 1997, s 308(4) claim must be used first against the total profits of the period in which the deficiency arose and then against the profits of the preceding period or periods.

For the purpose of offsetting a deficiency against the profits of the preceding period or periods, profits are apportioned on a time basis; where an accounting period falls partly before the immediately preceding period or periods equal in length to the period of the Case V deficiency, only a proportionate part of the profits of that accounting period may be relieved.

Any allowance still not fully utilised may then under TCA 1997, s 308(3) be carried forward to succeeding accounting periods and set against income of the specified class for those periods.

See **5.416.3** and **5.505.1** for treatment of Case V capital allowances.

4.108 Late submission of returns: restriction of relief

Where a company fails to deliver a return of income for any accounting period within nine months of the end of that period, any claim to relief under TCA 1997, s 308(4), s 396(2), 396A(3) or s 399(2) is restricted so that the amount by which the profits of the company are reduced is 50% (75% if the return is not more than two months late) of the amount by which they would otherwise have been reduced, subject to a maximum restriction of €158,715 (€31,740 if the return is not more than two months late) (TCA 1997, s 1085).

Similarly, TCA 1997, s 1085(2)(ba) provides that where a company fails to deliver a return of income for an accounting period on or before the specified return date, the total amount of the relevant trading loss that may be set off by virtue of TCA 1997, s 396B(2) for the period is to be treated as reduced by 50% (25% if the return is not more than two months late), subject to a maximum restriction of €158,715 (€31,740 if the return is not more than two months late).

In a case where a company that fails to deliver a timely return of income is claiming relief under TCA 1997, s 396B, it would seem that there is no requirement to restrict any amount of profits for the purposes of TCA 1997, s 1085; relief in this case is by way of a reduction in tax only.

4.109 Company reconstructions without change of ownership

4.109.1 Introduction

The transfer of a trade from one company to another is the occasion of a discontinuance of that trade. It would seem, as a fact, that a trade can exist apart from the person or persons who may be carrying it on at any time and that it is possible for a trade to be transferred from one company to another without the trade being discontinued. TCA 1997, s 77(2), however, provides that where a company begins or ceases to carry on a trade, its income is to be computed as if that were the commencement or, as the case may be, discontinuance of the trade, whether or not the trade is in fact commenced or discontinued. The statutory position, therefore, is that a transfer of a trade results in the discontinuance of that trade at the time the transfer takes place. As will be seen below, TCA 1997, s 400 (company reconstructions without change of ownership) is an exception to this result.

Where a trade is discontinued or treated as discontinued, the tax implications generally are that:

(a) balancing allowances or balancing charges arise in respect of fixed assets which were used in the trade and which have attracted capital allowances;

(b) any trading losses may not be carried forward;

(c) trading stock is treated as disposed of, where it is sold to an unconnected person who is about to carry on a trade in the State, at the price paid for it, and generally in any other case at its open market price (TCA 1997, s 89 – see **3.102.2**).

Generally, and apart from TCA 1997, s 400, there is no statutory guidance as to what is the effect for tax purposes of a transfer of part of a trade from one company to another or a merging of trading activities into an existing trade of a transferee company. In the case of the transferor company, an important question will be whether the part of the activities remaining after a part of its trade is transferred is a continuation of the trade, or whether the change resulting from the transfer is such that the remaining activities constitute a new trade. As regards the transferee company, relevant considerations will be whether the merged activities and the trade into which they have been merged constitute two trades, a single new trade (which would mean that the transferee's former trade has been discontinued), or a single continuing trade.

Transferor company

The status of the trading activities which remained following the transfer of part of a trade was considered in *Rolls-Royce Motors Ltd v Bamford* [1976] STC 162. The company's trade was initially comprised solely of the manufacture and sale of motor cars but the trade later included the manufacture and sale of aero-engines and engines for light aircraft. Following the appointment of a receiver in 1971, the aero-engine business, which then accounted for about 80% of the company's business, was transferred to a state-owned company. The question which then arose was whether the remaining activities (manufacture of cars and light-aircraft engines) were a continuation of the company's trade or a new trade.

It was held that the difference in the scale of the activities carried on before and after the transfer of the aero-engine business was so significant as to mean that there had been a discontinuance of the company's trade at the time of that transfer. In the course of his judgment, Walton J observed that if there is substantially a complete division of a company's trade into separate parts, notwithstanding that the trade of the same general nature is carried on afterwards by each of the two now separate entities, it would appear that neither of them is carrying on the same trade as the composite whole formerly carried on.

Although the fact that the activities transferred in the *Rolls-Royce* case comprised about 80% of the company's trade up to that time was conclusive of a discontinuance of the trade, it was also the case that the transferred activities were different to those which were retained. This prompts the question whether the result would have been the same had the company been carrying on a single type of activity and then transferred a part of the trade consisting of about 80% of those activities (or 50%, or even 30%, of those activities). The answer, again based on the judgment of Walton J, would appear to be that if there is a sudden and dramatic change in the activities of a trade brought about by the loss of activities on a considerable scale, there has been a discontinuance of that trade. It will of course be entirely be a question of fact and degree as to what will constitute such a dramatic change in any particular case.

Transferee company

Where a transferee company merges certain trading activities into its existing trade, that may result in the commencement of a new single trade where the merged and the pre-existing activities of the company are of a similar scale (*George Humphries & Co v Cook* 19 TC 191). It is more likely, where the scale of the merged activities is significantly smaller, that a single continuing trade is being carried on by the transferee company.

TCA 1997, s 400: outline

Where a company transfers a trade or part of a trade to another company and the companies are in common ownership to the extent of not less than 75%, the discontinuance by the former company is disregarded for the purposes of provisions dealing with losses and capital allowances and charges. As will be seen later, this provision applies to the transfer of a part of a trade and to the transfer of activities which of themselves are not sufficient to amount to a trade.

Ownership for the purposes of TCA 1997, s 400 is determined by reference to the ultimate shareholdings in the transferor and transferee companies. The section will therefore apply in cases of transfers of trades between group members but will also have effect in non-group situations where there is substantial identity in the ownership, direct or indirect, of the ordinary share capital of the two companies.

TCA 1997, s 400 applies only to the trade or trade activities which are transferred to the transferee company. Where there is a transfer of some of the trading activities of a company and the circumstances are that the remaining activities are insufficient to avoid a discontinuance of the trade, any losses attributable to those remaining activities may not be carried forward. The losses could be preserved by arranging for the remaining activities to be transferred simultaneously to another company under 75% common ownership so as to trigger TCA 1997, s 400.

If the effect of the merging of trading activities with an existing trade of a transferee company is that a new trade has been created, TCA 1997, s 400 will, again, not apply; for this purpose it would be necessary that the transferee company carries on the merged activities as part of its trade. Tax losses attributable to the merged activities could be preserved by arranging for the transfer of the merged and the pre-existing activities of the transferee company to another company under 75% common ownership; again, this would bring the transfer within the ambit of TCA 1997, s 400.

4.109.2 Transfer of trade

TCA 1997, s 400(5) has effect where one company ("the predecessor") ceases to carry on a trade and another company ("the successor") begins to carry it on, and:

(a)   on or at any time within two years after that event the trade or an interest of at least a three-fourths share in it belongs to the same persons as the trade or such an interest belonged to at some time within a year before that event; and

(b)   the trade is not, within the period taken for the comparison under (a), carried on otherwise than by a company which is within the charge to tax in respect of it.

The times at which the 75% identity of ownership of the trade should be established so that TCA 1997, s 400 will apply are *any time* within two years after the transfer of the trade and *some time* within a year before that event. Clearly, therefore, there is no question of the 75% identity of ownership having to be present throughout the three year period implied above, or indeed throughout any period. It would be sufficient, for the purposes of TCA 1997, s 400, for the 75% identity of ownership requirement to be established on one day only within two years after the transfer of trade and on one day only within one year before that event, and the ownership of the company could be otherwise at any time before or after each of these days.

In (b) above, the reference to the period taken for the comparison under (a) does not refer to the full three year period implied there. It should be read in the context of the other references to "at any time within" and "at some time within". Accordingly, the period taken for the comparison would be the period between the latest time at which the conditions in (a) are satisfied in relation to the predecessor company and the earliest time at which those conditions are satisfied in relation to the successor company. The reference is not of great significance, however, as the period indicated is relevant only where the trade is carried on otherwise than by a company within the charge to tax in respect of it.

From the above it will be seen that the 75% identity of ownership condition may not be fulfilled at or around the time a trade is transferred between two companies. Thus, the condition might only be fulfilled at a point which is, say, twenty-three months after the time the trade was transferred. In any such case, there will be a need to make appropriate revisions to the computations of one or both companies concerned. For example, a balancing charge made on the predecessor company would be cancelled or a loss forward would fall to be allowed to the successor company. In this connection, TCA 1997, s 400(14) provides that any relief to be given "by means of discharge or repayment of tax" is to be given on the making of a claim.

TCA 1997, s 400(5) refers only to a cessation of a trade and to another company beginning to carry on that trade, and does not contain any reference to a part of a trade. TCA 1997, s 400(11) makes it clear, however, that TCA 1997, s 400 is concerned also with the case in which a company ceases to carry on part of a trade (TCA 1997, s 400(11), second limb) and where another company begins to carry on "the activities of that part" as its trade or part of its trade. Furthermore, it would appear that the section covers the situation in which the trading activities transferred (and which together with the activities of the transferee company with which they are merged constitute a trade) do not of themselves amount to a trade (*Falmer Jeans v Rodin* [1990] STC 270). Accordingly, the situations covered by TCA 1997, s 400 are:

1. predecessor ceases to trade and successor takes over that trade as its whole trade;
2. predecessor ceases to trade and successor merges that trade with its own trade;
3. predecessor transfers part of its trade:
    (i)   where the activities of that part are sufficient of themselves to amount to a trade; or
    (ii) where the activities of that part are not of themselves sufficient to amount to a trade,
    and successor takes over that part as its whole trade;
4. predecessor transfers part of its trade:
    (i)   where the activities of that part are sufficient of themselves to amount to a trade; or
    (ii) where the activities of that part are not of themselves sufficient to amount to a trade,
    and successor merges that part with its own trade.

In *Laycock v Freeman Hardy & Willis Ltd* 22 TC 288, a company selling shoes retail was denied relief for losses of shoe manufacturing trades carried on by two of its subsidiaries after acquiring the assets and those companies and commencing to manufacture the shoes itself. It was held that the company had not succeeded to the trades of the subsidiaries as those trades consisted of the manufacture of shoes and their sale (to the parent) wholesale whereas after the change the sales of the manufactured shoes was by retail. The decision is distinguished from that in *Briton Ferry Steel Co Ltd v Barry* 23 TC 414 which concerned a parent company in the business of producing steel bars which it supplied to subsidiaries which used them for manufacturing tin plate. The parent took over the assets of the subsidiaries and commenced to manufacture the tin plate itself. It was held to have succeeded to the trades of the subsidiaries since their trades, the sale of tin plate, continued.

4.109.3 Trading losses

Where TCA 1997, s 400 applies, the successor will be entitled to relief under TCA 1997, s 396(1) (loss forward) for any amount for which the predecessor would have been entitled to claim relief if it had continued to carry on the trade, in the same way as if the loss had been sustained by the successor itself. This treatment is subject to any claim that the predecessor might have made under TCA 1997, s 396(2) in respect of the loss. The predecessor will not be entitled to any relief under TCA 1997, s 397 (terminal loss) except as provided by TCA 1997, s 400(9) (see below).

It will be helpful to consider the treatment of tax losses incurred by the predecessor company by reference to the different possibilities catered for by TCA 1997, s 400.

(1) Transfer of whole trade: successor carries on that trade as its whole trade

In this case, no complication arises and the successor will be entitled to set all of the losses unused at the date of the transfer of trade against its own trading profits. Clearly, there are no implications for the predecessor.

(2) Transfer of whole trade: successor merges that trade with its own trade

The losses attaching to the trade transferred may be offset against the profits of the successor's trade but only against the profits attributable to the trade transferred. This follows from the first limb of TCA 1997, s 400(11) which effectively provides that the part of the trade represented by the trade taken over from the predecessor is to be treated as a separate trade insofar as this is necessary to give effect to TCA 1997, s 400. Incidentally, the first limb is stated to be "for the purposes of this subsection". This makes no sense and presumably the reference was intended to be (as it is in the case of the second limb) to "for the purposes of this section".

For example, assume that the profits of a successor company for an accounting period are €100,000 and that these include €40,000 attributable to the part of the trade represented by a trade acquired from a predecessor company. If at the commencement of that period there are €75,000 of unused losses from the trade taken over from the predecessor, only €40,000 of those losses may be used for the current period; it is assumed for this purpose that €40,000 of the profits arose from a separate trade of the successor (although for all other purposes there is no separate trade). The intention of this provision clearly is to ensure that losses cannot be utilised to an extent greater than would have been the case if there had been no transfer of trade.

TCA 1997, s 400(12) provides that for the purpose of treating a successor's trade as comprising two separate trades, any necessary apportionment is to be made of receipts or expenses. TCA 1997, s 400(13) provides for the determination by the Appeal Commissioners of any question concerning an apportionment under TCA 1997, s 400(12) where it appears that the amount to be apportioned is material as respects the related tax liability.

TCA 1997, s 400 does not prescribe any method for apportioning profits. In practice, the apportionment required may be quite straightforward, for example where the trade taken over continues to be run as a separate department or branch. Where the trade taken over is fully integrated into the successor's trade so that subsequently it becomes difficult or impossible to identify that trade as a separate part of the enlarged trade, it would appear that there will be no option but to estimate, as far as this is possible, what the profits of the enlarged trade attributable to the acquired trade would be for any accounting period. There is no generally applicable procedure which may be prescribed for the purposes of this exercise and it will be entirely a matter of arriving at the fairest apportionment possible having regard to the facts and circumstances of the particular case.

One obvious basis for apportionment in certain cases is by turnover. This might be a suitable basis where the turnover related to the trade acquired is easily identifiable, eg where the trade taken over comprises one or more retail outlets. Depending on circumstances, it may be possible to carry out a more accurate or scientific apportionment where the company and departmental records permit. It would be necessary to adopt a different approach in the case of a vertical integration, eg where manufacturing and retailing are combined into a single trade (and assuming of course that the combined activity is accepted as a single trade). It would be necessary there to ascertain the profits from manufacturing on the basis of hypothetical sales to the retailing side of the business, perhaps based on sales of the former manufacturing trade or based on sales of a comparable business.

In a fully integrated business, there may be no separate identifiable characteristics which would assist in identifying profits of a trade taken over. This might be the case because there is no longer any physical differentiation between the trade taken over and the trade into which it has been merged, for example where the nature of the trade acquired is identical with that into which it has been merged, where staff and other resources of the trade acquired are brought together under one roof, and where it becomes difficult to identify separate customers of the former separate trades. The only approach to be taken is to identify the profits of the deemed separate trades in as reasonable a manner as possible.

(3) Transfer of part of trade: successor carries on that trade as its whole trade

The successor will be entitled to set all of the unused losses of the part of the trade transferred against its own trading profits. It will be necessary to apportion the losses at the date of the transfer as between the part of the trade transferred and the remaining part; TCA 1997, s 400(11), second limb, effectively provides that the part of the trade transferred is to be treated as having been carried on by the predecessor as a separate trade insofar as this is necessary to give effect to TCA 1997, s 400. TCA 1997, s 400(12) provides that, for the purpose of treating a predecessor's trade as comprising two separate trades, any necessary apportionment is to be made of receipts or expenses. TCA 1997, s 400(13) provides for the determination by the Appeal Commissioners of any question concerning an apportionment under TCA 1997, s 400(12) where it appears that the amount to be apportioned is material as respects the related tax liability.

As already noted above, where there is a transfer of some of the trading activities of the predecessor and the circumstances are that the remaining activities are insufficient to avoid a discontinuance of the trade, any losses attributable to those remaining activities may not be carried forward. The losses could be preserved in that case by arranging at the time of the transfer for the remaining activities also to be transferred, to another company under 75% common ownership, so as to trigger TCA 1997, s 400.

(4) Transfer of part of trade: successor merges that part with its own trade

The tax consequences here are in effect a combination of (2) and (3). Apportionments will be required of the tax loss being carried forward to the successor's trade and of subsequent profits of the successor until such time as the available losses are used up.

4.109.4 Capital allowances

Where a company ceases to carry on a trade, its income is to be computed as if that were the discontinuance of the trade (TCA 1997, s 77(2) – see **4.109.1**). The permanent discontinuance of a trade carried on by a company, where machinery or plant has not previously ceased to belong to the company, is one of the events which triggers a balancing allowance or charge where that machinery or plant has attracted capital allowances (see **5.207**). A disposal of the machinery or plant is also such an event. Where TCA 1997, s 400 applies, the discontinuance and the disposal are disregarded for the purposes of balancing allowances and charges. In addition, the successor qualifies for any writing down allowances to which the predecessor would otherwise have been entitled.

TCA 1997, s 400(6) provides that the trade is not to be treated as permanently discontinued nor a new trade as set up and commenced for the purpose of the allowances and charges provided for by TCA 1997, s 307 (capital allowances and related charges), but:

(a)   there is to be made to or on the successor in accordance with TCA 1997, s 307 all such allowances and charges as would, if the predecessor had continued to carry on the trade, have fallen to be made to or on it; and

(b)   the amount of any such allowance or charge is to be computed as if:

(i)   the successor had been carrying on the trade since the predecessor had begun to do so; and

(ii)   as if everything done to or by the predecessor had been done to or by the successor (but

so that no sale or transfer which on the transfer of the trade is made to the successor by the predecessor of any assets in use for the purpose of the trade may be treated as giving rise to any such allowance or charge).

In short therefore, the effect of TCA 1997, s 400(6) is that on a transfer of its trade no balancing allowance or charge is made to or on the predecessor and that the assets being transferred pass to the successor at their tax written down values. The fact that everything done to or by the predecessor is deemed to have been done to or by the successor is not to have the effect that any sale or transfer made by the predecessor to the successor on the transfer of the trade gives rise to any balancing allowance or charge.

If the transfer of trade occurs during, rather than at the end of, the accounting periods of the two companies, the question arises as to how capital allowances are to be computed for the final accounting period of the predecessor and the initial accounting period of the successor. The stated purpose of TCA 1997, s 400(6) would be realised if writing down allowances were calculated first for the full twelve month period and then apportioned between the predecessor and the successor by reference to the respective lengths of the period up to and after the transfer of the trade, and such an approach appears to be in accordance with accepted practice.

The two companies will not, of course, always make up accounts to the same date. Where different accounting year ends apply, it will still be possible to compute writing down allowances so as to give effect to TCA 1997, s 400(6). Assume, for example, that the trade is transferred on 1 July 2004, that the predecessor makes up accounts to 31 December 2004 but that the successor makes up accounts to 31 March 2005. Writing down allowances would be calculated initially for twelve months and apportioned as to 50% each to the two companies. Based on the tax written down value after this calculation, writing down allowances for a further three months would then be calculated and the resulting amount added to the 50% amount already computed to give the aggregate allowance due to the successor for the period ending 31 March 2005. This would give the same allowance as would have resulted had the predecessor continued to carry on the trade but assuming a change of accounting date to 31 March.

A strict reading of TCA 1997, s 400(6) would seem to support the view that the allowances for the 12-month period go entirely to the successor. As to what is the correct position regarding balancing allowances and charges in a case where assets transferred are disposed of by the successor before the end of its first accounting period after the transfer is not clear. Perhaps the allowance or charge would be apportioned in the same way as writing down allowances, as described above, but again a strict reading seems to suggest that these are matters for the successor only.

4.109.5 Securities held as trading stock

Certain securities (including stocks and shares) held as trading stock are to be treated as if they had been sold by the predecessor to the successor at market value for the purposes of TCA 1997, s 748 (purchase and sale of securities – "bond washing"). This ensures that the bond washing provisions will apply to the predecessor and the successor on the basis that the successor acquired the securities from the predecessor at market value.

TCA 1997, s 749 and Sch 21 operate to disallow the element of accrued interest in the original purchase price of the securities sold and apply where the securities in question are held for a period not exceeding six months. The formula for the calculation of the disallowed interest element (the "appropriate proportion of the interest") is:

$$\text{interest} \times \frac{\text{length of period 1}}{\text{length of period 2}}$$

where—

Period 1 = the number of days beginning with the earliest date on which the securities could have been quoted *ex div* in respect of the last interest paid before the interest included in the purchase price began to accrue (in short, the last *ex div* date before purchase), and ending with the day before the company purchased the securities, and

Period 2 = the number of days beginning with the first date referred to in the definition of period 1, and ending with the day before the earliest date on which the securities could have been quoted *ex div* in respect of the interest received by the company in the following period (in short, the day before the first *ex div* date for the interest in the following period).

TCA 1997, s 749 does not apply to overseas securities purchased on a short-term basis by a dealer in the ordinary course of that dealer's trade subject to the following conditions –

(i) that the interest paid on all overseas securities to which TCA 1997 Part 28 Chapter 1 (see below) applies is brought into account as a trading receipt in computing the dealer's profits or gain or losses for the accounting period; and

(ii) where credit against tax in accordance with a double tax treaty or under any unilateral credit relief or other provision would otherwise be due, that the dealer elects in writing, by the specified return date (see **15.104.1**) for the period in question, that the credit is not to be allowed (TCA 1997, s 749(2A)).

Where an election in accordance with (ii) above has been made:

(a) credit against tax in respect of the interest is not to be allowed by virtue of TCA 1997 Part 14 (s 449 – see **14.4**) or Part 35 (ss 826-835 and Schedule 24 – see **14.2**);

(b) the election is to be included in the dealer's tax return required under TCA 1997, s 951 (see **15.104**) for the accounting period; and

(c) the election is to have effect only for the accounting period for which it is made (TCA 1997, s 749)2B)).

For the above purpose, *overseas securities* means securities issued:

(i) by a government of a territory outside the State;

(ii) by a foreign local authority, foreign local government or foreign public authority; or

(iii) by any other body of persons not resident in the State.

A *foreign local authority* is an authority corresponding in substance to a local authority for the purposes of the Local Government Act 2001, which is established outside the State and whose functions are carried on primarily outside the State.

A *foreign local government* is any local or regional government in any jurisdiction outside the State.

A *foreign public authority* is an authority, corresponding in substance to a public authority for the purposes of the Local Government Act 2001, which is established outside the State and whose functions are carried on primarily outside the State.

Neither does TCA 1997, s 749 apply for a chargeable period if the securities, not being chargeable assets for capital gains tax purposes by virtue of TCA 1997, s 607 (see **9.102.15**), are securities purchased by the dealer in the ordinary course of the trade of dealing in securities and the interest payable in respect of all such securities to which TCA 1997 Part 28 Chapter 1 (see below) applies is brought into account in computing the profits or gains arising from, or losses sustained in, the trade for that period (TCA 1997, s 749(2C)).

TCA 1997 Part 28 Chapter 1 (ss 748-751B) applies in the case of a purchase by a person (the "first buyer") of any securities and their subsequent sale where the result is that interest becoming payable in respect of the securities is receivable by the first buyer but does not apply in a case where:

(a)   the time between the purchase by the first buyer and that buyer's taking steps to dispose of the securities exceeds six months; or

(b)   that time exceeds one month and in the opinion of the Revenue Commissioners the purchase and sale were each effected at the current market price and the sale was not effected in pursuance of an agreement or arrangement made before or at the time of purchase (TCA 1997, s 748(3)).

4.109.6   Terminal loss available to predecessor

If the successor ceases to carry on the trade within four years of succeeding to it and its trading income is insufficient to absorb the full amount of the terminal loss available under TCA 1997, s 397, the unused balance of that loss may be availed of by the predecessor against its income from the trade (TCA 1997, s 400(9)). The balance is to be given to the predecessor as if it had incurred the loss, including any amount treated as a loss under TCA 1997, s 397(3) (see **4.104** above). If the successor ceases to carry on the trade within *one* year of succeeding to it, relief may be given to the predecessor under TCA 1997, s 397 in respect of any loss incurred by it, or in respect of any amount treated as such a loss under TCA 1997, s 397(3). In this way, the predecessor will obtain relief for its own loss incurred within twelve months before trading finally ceases, as well as for the successor's loss as provided for above.

4.109.7   Further transfers of trade within period for comparison

It may happen, during "the period taken for the comparison" (under (a) in *Transfer of trade* above, ie the period between the latest time at which the conditions in (a) are satisfied in relation to the predecessor company and the earliest time at which those conditions are satisfied in relation to the successor company), that after the transfer of trade there is a further such transfer. TCA 1997, s 400(10) provides that where the successor ceases to carry on the trade and a third company begins to carry it on, no relief is to be given to the predecessor by virtue of TCA 1997, s 400(9) by reference to that event. In other words, once the trade is transferred on to a third company, the provisions in TCA 1997, s 400(9) allowing the predecessor company to benefit from the terminal loss provisions as described above will not apply. Otherwise, however, TCA 1997, s 400(6) to (9) (trading losses, capital allowances and terminal losses available to predecessor – see above) will apply both in relation to the first and the second transfer.

There is no requirement that the trade, once it passes to the third company, should be owned by substantially (three-fourths at least) the same persons before and after that transfer as there was in respect of the first transfer. In relation to the first transfer, any reference to "successor" includes a reference to the successor at either event (ie the second company and the third company), and in relation to the second transfer any reference to "predecessor" includes a reference to the predecessor at either event (ie the first company and the second company). Available losses and capital allowances of both predecessors will therefore carry through for the benefit of the third company notwithstanding that that company has no ownership connection with the first or second company. TCA 1997, s 400(10) does not apply where the common ownership condition is satisfied in relation to the second transfer. Where that is the case, TCA 1997, s 400 will apply to each transfer without regard to TCA 1997, s 400(10). TCA 1997, s 400(10) will apply to a third or subsequent transfer of the trade as it applies to the second transfer.

Example 4.109.7.1

Havalos Ltd, a 75% subsidiary of Sherwood Ltd for some years, transfers its trade to Wayside Ltd on 1 April 1997. On 1 August 1997, Wayside Ltd transfers the trade to Markham Ltd. Wayside Ltd becomes a 75% subsidiary of Sherwood Ltd on 1 February 1998.

Markham Ltd, the "third company", is entitled to unused losses of the trade (previously carried on by Havalos Ltd and subsequently by Wayside Ltd) and to capital allowances based on the tax written down values of assets of the trade qualifying for capital allowances, in the same way as Wayside Ltd had been entitled in relation to the trade carried on by Havalos Ltd. This follows from TCA 1997, s 400(10) although Markham Ltd may be totally unrelated to any of the other companies.

The same position would apply if Markham Ltd, rather than Wayside Ltd, had become a 75% subsidiary of Sherwood Ltd.

4.109.8   Ownership of trade

For the purposes of TCA 1997, s 400, a trade carried on by two or more persons is treated as belonging to them in the shares in which they are entitled to the profits of the trade. A trade or interest in a trade belonging to any person as trustee (otherwise than for charitable or public purposes) is treated as belonging to the persons for the time being entitled to the income under the trust. In *Pritchard v MH Builders Ltd* 45 TC 360, it was held that a company in liquidation held its trade upon trust but that no one was entitled to the income of the trust.

A trade or interest in a trade belonging to a company engaged in carrying it on may be regarded as belonging to:

(a)   the holders of the ordinary share capital of the company, and in proportion to the amount of their holdings of that capital; or

(b)   where the company is a subsidiary company, its parent company or the holders of the ordinary share capital of the parent company, and in proportion to the amount of their holdings of that capital.

For the above purpose, any ordinary share capital owned by a company may be regarded as owned by a person or body of persons having the power to secure, by means of the holding of shares or by the possession of voting power in or in relation to the company, or by virtue of any power conferred by the articles of association or other document regulating any company, that the affairs of the company owning the share capital in question are conducted in accordance with his or their wishes (TCA 1997, s 400(2)).

References to ownership for the above purpose are to beneficial ownership. A company is deemed to be a subsidiary of another company if and so long as not less than

75% of its ordinary share capital is owned by that other company, whether directly or through another company or other companies, or partly directly and partly through another company or other companies. The amount of ordinary share capital of one company owned by a second company through another company or other companies, or partly directly and partly through another company or other companies, is to be determined in accordance with TCA 1997, s 9(5) to (10) (see **2.505**). Where a company is a subsidiary of another company, that other company is to be considered as its parent company unless both are subsidiaries of a third company.

In determining for the purposes of TCA 1997, s 400 whether or to what extent a trade belongs at different times to the same persons, persons who are relatives of one another and the persons from time to time entitled to the income under any trust are respectively to be treated as a single person. For this purpose, *relative* means husband, wife, ancestor, lineal descendant, brother or sister.

Example 4.109.8.1

Ajusco Ltd carries on both a manufacturing trade and a retail trade. The company's ordinary share capital is held in the following percentages:

	%
Patrick Lee	30
Sarah Lee (Patrick Lee's wife)	30
Roberta Lee (Patrick Lee's sister)	20
Joseph Lee (Roberta Lee's husband)	12
David Lee (Roberta & Joseph Lee's son)	8
	100

Patrick and Roberta Lee agree to split the company so that the manufacturing business will be owned by Patrick and his wife and the retailing business by Roberta and her family. Accordingly, the manufacturing business is to be transferred to Mixquic Ltd and the retailing business to Xalpa Ltd, the respective shareholdings in which are to be as follows:

Mixquic Ltd		*Xalpa Ltd*	
Patrick Lee	50%	Roberta Lee	50%
Sarah Lee	50%	Joseph Lee	30%
		David Lee	20%

Transfer of Trade to Mixquic Ltd:
Patrick's shareholdings can be aggregated with those of his relatives (Sarah and Roberta) so that he is treated as owning 80% (30% + 30% + 20%) of Ajusco Ltd and 100% of Mixquic Ltd. The ownership requirement of TCA 1997, s 400 is therefore satisfied.

Transfer to Trade to Xalpa Ltd:
Roberta's shareholdings can be aggregated with those of her relatives (Patrick, Joseph and David) so that she is treated as owning 70% (20% + 12% + 8% + 30%) of Ajusco Ltd and 100% of Xalpa Ltd. On that basis, the TCA 1997, s 400 ownership requirement is not satisfied.

Contract for sale

As already noted above, ownership for the purposes of TCA 1997, s 400 means beneficial ownership. It was held in *Sainsbury plc v O'Connor* [1991] STC 318 that the grant of a call option did not result in the loss of beneficial ownership as long as the registered owner of the shares retained all of the normal benefits associated with share ownership (especially the right to receive dividends) during the period of the option. By the same token, the grant of a right of pre-emption does not impair beneficial ownership. Similarly, beneficial ownership will not be affected where there is a shareholders' agreement providing for a restriction on the right to sell shares.

Where shares are subject to an unconditional contract for sale, the vendor ceases to be the beneficial owner of them from the date of that contract. In the case of an unconditional contract, the position will depend on the particular rights of the vendor during the interim period.

In *Wood Preservation v Prior* 45 TC 112, the owner of certain shares entered into a contract of sale for the shares conditional on the consent of a third party. While the consent was being sought, the owner agreed not to procure the declaration of any dividends in respect of the shares. It was held that the owner ceased to be the beneficial owner of the shares from the date of the contract notwithstanding the fact that the purchaser could not be regarded as having become the beneficial owner at that time.

Some limit to the significance of this decision is indicated in the *Sainsbury* judgment where it was suggested that the decision had relevance only where the rights of the vendor are frozen during the period from the commencement of the agreement to the time it becomes unconditional. Normally, where the vendor continues to be entitled to dividends while the contract is conditional, beneficial ownership of the shares will not be lost (see **8.302.4**).

Effect of liquidation

When a company commences to be wound up, it ceases to be the beneficial owner of its assets (*Pritchard v MH Builders (Wilmslow) Ltd* 45 TC 360). The assets are then held on trusts under which the beneficial interest in them is in abeyance. Accordingly, if a transfer of trade is to be made by a company which has gone into liquidation, it is necessary that the transfer takes place within one year of the commencement of the winding up; otherwise, since the trade would have belonged to no one for the year prior to the transfer, TCA 1997, s 400 would not apply. A similar issue can arise in relation to the two year period after the transfer of trade where a company in liquidation transfers its trade to a subsidiary.

Example 4.109.8.2

Waterside Ltd is put into liquidation on 1 March 2000 and on 14 April 2000 its trade is transferred to Lakeview Ltd, a wholly owned subsidiary company. On completion of the liquidation, the shares in Lakeview Ltd are transferred to the shareholders of Waterside Ltd (who remain the same throughout the liquidation period). This transfer takes place on 19 May 2002.

Although the Lakeview shares end up in the ownership of the persons who (indirectly) owned them before the transfer of the trade, the ownership condition of TCA 1997, s 400 is not satisfied. This is because, during the two year period immediately following the transfer of trade, the shares in that company were not in the beneficial ownership of anyone.

4.109.9 Loss buying

As is explained in **4.110** below, anti-avoidance provisions in TCA 1997, s 401 apply in the case of a change in ownership of a tax loss company. Where a TCA 1997, s 400 transfer of trade occurs and there is also a change in the ownership of one of the companies involved, it will be necessary to have regard to the provisions of TCA 1997, s 401, in particular TCA 1997, s 401(4). This aspect is discussed in **4.110**.

4.109.10 The Mergers Directive

TCA 1997 Part 21 (ss 630-638) implements Council Directive No. 90/434/ EEC (the "Mergers Directive") the purpose of which is to remove barriers (mainly by deferring capital gains tax which would otherwise accrue) to mergers, divisions, transfers of assets and exchanges of shares between companies from different Member States. The legislation extends the benefits of the Directive, which apply to transactions between companies from two Member States, to transactions between companies which are Irish resident. TCA 1997, s 631 contains measures which are very similar in their effect to those in TCA 1997, s 400, the difference being that the former will have application in situations not covered by TCA 1997, s 400. Where the situation is covered by TCA 1997, s 400, that provision is to apply rather than the provisions in TCA 1997, s 631 (see also **9.302**).

TCA 1997, s 631 provides certain reliefs in respect of the transfer by a company of the whole or a part of a trade carried on by it in the State to another company where the transfer consideration consists entirely of the issue of securities (the *new assets*) to the transferring company. A company which transfers part of a trade to another company is treated as having carried on that part of its trade as a separate trade. "*Securities*" means shares and debentures while *shares* includes stock. The consequences of the transfer, as provided for in TCA 1997, s 631(2), are as follows:

(1) No balancing allowance or balancing charge will arise under TCA 1997, s 307 or s 308 as a result of the disposal of the assets by the transferring company.

(2) The acquiring company takes over the assets transferred at their tax written down values. All allowances and charges in respect of those assets are made to or on the acquiring company on the same basis as if the transferring company had continued to carry on the trade and had continued to use the assets for the purposes of the trade and as if the acquiring company had been carrying on the trade since the transferring company began to do so and as if everything done to or by the transferring company had been done to or by the receiving company.

As regards (1) and (2) above, TCA 1997, s 631(2) will not apply in any case where, as respects the assets transferred, TCA 1997, s 400 applies. For example, if the trade transferred is substantially owned (to the extent of 75% at least) by the same person or persons before and after the transfer, TCA 1997, s 400 will apply instead of TCA 1997, s 631(2). The tax consequences are, however, the same.

The above provisions of TCA 1997, s 631(2) will not apply if, immediately after the time of the transfer, the assets transferred in the course of the transfer are not used for the purposes of a trade carried on by the acquiring company in the State.

Neither will TCA 1997, s 631(2) apply if the transferring company and the acquiring company jointly elect, by notice in writing to the inspector, that the provisions of the section should not apply. The notice is to be made by the time by which the transferring company's corporation tax return for the accounting period in which the transfer takes place falls to be made.

Example 4.109.10.1

Weston Ltd and Union Ltd are unrelated companies. Under a merger agreed between the boards of the two companies, Weston Ltd transfers its trade carried on in Ireland to Union Ltd in return for an issue of new ordinary shares in Union Ltd giving it a 35% equity interest in Union Ltd.

As regards the fixed assets transferred with the trade in respect of which Weston Ltd had obtained capital allowances, the transfer does not give rise to any balancing allowance or charge by reason of the disposal of those assets. Union Ltd is entitled to claim capital allowances on the assets transferred based on the tax written down values as at the time of the transfer.

TCA 1997, s 400 does not apply to the transfer as there is not a 75% identity of ownership of the trade before and after its transfer. Unlike TCA 1997, s 400, there is no provision for the carry forward of any trading losses which might have been available to Weston Ltd up to the time of the transfer of the trade to Union Ltd.

The intention of TCA 1997, s 631(2) is to put the acquiring company in the same position as the transferor company as regards the assets transferred. To this end, the subsection provides that allowances and charges are to be made on the acquiring company as if everything done to or by the transferring company had been done to or by the receiving company. Tax provisions of this kind inevitably throw up difficulties as regards the extent to which they are to be applied. For example, if the transferring company had earlier acquired any of the assets from an associated company in circumstances to which TCA 1997, s 312(5) applied (see **5.103**), this will have had some effect on the amount of any balancing charge to be made on the company in respect of the assets. A similar position might apply in respect of an earlier acquisition of assets by the transferring company to which TCA 1997, s 400 applied. Taken strictly, it would seem that the effect of any such provision would be carried through for the acquiring company in a case to which TCA 1997, s 631(2) applies.

4.110 Change of ownership – disallowance of trading losses

4.110.1 Disallowance of trading losses

TCA 1997, s 401 disallows the carry-forward of trading losses under TCA 1997, s 396 (and income tax and corporation profits tax losses under TCA 1997 Sch 32 paras 16 and 18 respectively) if:

(a) within a period of three years, there is both a change in the ownership of a company and (either earlier or later in that period, or at the same time) a major change in the nature or conduct of the trade carried on by the company; or

(b) at any time after the scale of the activities of the trade carried on by a company has become small or negligible, and before there is any considerable revival of the trade, a change in the ownership of the company occurs.

TCA 1997, s 401(2) provides that relief may not be given by setting a loss incurred by the company concerned in an accounting period beginning before the change of ownership against any income or other profits of an accounting period ending after the change or ownership.

Change of ownership for the purposes of TCA 1997, s 401 is considered by reference to the beneficial holdings of the company's ordinary share capital, a change taking place where more than 50% of the ordinary share capital changes hands (see detailed treatment below). Ordinary share capital is defined in TCA 1997, s 2(1) as "all the issued share capital (by whatever name called) of the company other than capital the holders whereof have a right to a dividend at a fixed rate, but have no other right to share in the profits of the company".

A major change in the nature or conduct of a trade includes:

(a)   a major change in the type of property dealt in, or services or facilities provided, in the trade; or

(b)   a major change in customers, outlets or markets of the trade

and such a major change will be regarded as occurring even if the change is the result of a gradual process which began outside the three year period.

In *Willis v Peeters Picture Frames Ltd* [1983] STC 453, it was found that a company which had sold its products direct to customers, mainly wholesalers, and which later did this through distribution companies had not effected a major change in the conduct of its trade. The decision in *Purchase v Tesco Stores Ltd* [1984] STC 304 suggests that a "major" change is one which is something more than significant but which is less than fundamental. In that case, which involved a claim to stock relief, as a result of discontinuing the issue of trading stamps and reducing prices, a company achieved a substantial increase in turnover. It was held that a major change in the company's trade had occurred.

While the *Tesco Stores* decision is readily understandable in the context of stock relief, its relevance for the purposes of TCA 1997, s 401 is doubtful. It does not seem correct that an increase in turnover, even a substantial one, is a proper basis for concluding that there has been a major change in the nature or conduct of a trade; the intention of TCA 1997, s 401 is to counter schemes involving transfer pricing manipulation between related companies. Furthermore, there are indications in the *Peeters Pictures Frames* case that a major change in the nature or conduct of a trade refers, or refers primarily, to qualitative rather than to quantitative changes.

In another stock relief case, a company which carried on a business of minting coins and medallions from precious metals purchased its principal supplier's entire stock of gold and then purchased gold directly from wholesalers. This led to a substantial increase in stock levels. It was held that there had been a major change in the conduct of the company's trade (*Pobjoy Mint Ltd v Lane* [1984] STC 327). In *Cronin v Lunham Brothers Ltd* HC 1985, it was found that the cessation by a company of the slaughtering of pigs and the manufacture of meat products, and the resumption of these activities some sixteen months later, had not amounted to a major change in the company's trade, although the company was used as a distribution centre during the sixteen month period.

Where TCA 1997, s 401 has effect, no relief is given under TCA 1997, s 396 by way of setting a loss incurred by the company in an accounting period beginning *before* the change of ownership against any income or other profits of an accounting period ending *after* the change or ownership (TCA 1997, s 401(2)). For this purpose, in relation to the accounting period in which the change of ownership takes place, the part ending with the change of ownership and the part after the change are treated as two separate accounting periods and the profits or losses of the accounting period are to be apportioned to the two parts. This apportionment is carried out on a time basis according to the respective lengths of the two parts. If, however, it appears that that method would work unreasonably or unjustly, such other method is to be used as appears just and reasonable (TCA 1997, s 401(3)).

In relation to any relief available under TCA 1997, s 400 (company reconstructions without change of ownership – see **4.109.3**), the restriction of losses under TCA 1997, s 401(2) applies as if any loss sustained by a predecessor company had been sustained by a successor company and as if the references to a trade included references to the trade as carried on by a predecessor company (TCA 1997, s 401(4)). Thus, if within a three year period there is a major change in the trade of a predecessor company, a transfer of that trade to a successor company, and a change in ownership of the successor company, TCA 1997, s 401(2) will operate to deny the use of those losses to the successor company beyond the time of the change in ownership (as well as any losses incurred by the successor company itself prior to the change in ownership). The major change in the predecessor's trade is attributed to the successor.

If, on the other hand, there is within a three year period a change of ownership of a predecessor company followed by a transfer of its trade to a successor company, and there is a subsequent major change in the nature or conduct of the trade, TCA 1997, s 401 will have no effect. This is because there has been no change in the ownership of the successor company; the earlier change in the ownership of the predecessor company is not relevant.

Where TCA 1997, s 401 is triggered by events or circumstances occurring at a time after a change of ownership (which will be not more than three years after that change), an assessment may be made giving effect to the section at any time up to four years from that time, or the latest of those times (TCA 1997, s 401(6)).

The fact that TCA 1997, s 401(2) affects only the company whose ownership has changed gives rise to interesting possibilities in a case where there is a change in ownership of a loss making company. The new owners will be concerned to turn the company around as quickly as possible and to generate profits which will be sheltered by the losses available. It will be essential to achieve this result without bringing about a major change in the nature or conduct of the trade within three years. If, however, the trade is transferred to another company within the same group before any such major change is effected, TCA 1997, s 401(2) cannot apply to deny the use of the losses to the successor company as there will have been no change in ownership of that company.

Losses restricted by virtue of TCA 1997, s 401(2) may include capital allowances (since for corporation tax purposes capital allowances are treated as deductions in computing profits or losses of a company). Where a balancing charge would arise by reference to an event occurring after a change in ownership of a company and it is attributable to allowances forming part of a loss which has been restricted by the operation of TCA 1997, s 401(2), those allowances are to be disregarded for that purpose (TCA 1997, s 401(5)). This will have the effect of reducing or eliminating the balancing charge that would otherwise be made since the amount of a balancing charge may not exceed the aggregate of allowances obtained in respect of the asset concerned.

For the purposes of the foregoing provision, it is to be assumed that the capital allowances arising in the period before the change in ownership of the company have been set against profits or gains of the company before any losses not attributable to those allowances have been so utilised. Any capital allowances which are thereby deemed to have been set off against profits or gains will therefore not be disregarded for the purposes of calculating any balancing charge.

4.110.2 Change in ownership

General

The detailed rules for determining when a change in ownership of a company takes place are contained in TCA 1997 Sch 9. There is a change in the ownership of a company if:

(a) a single person acquires more than 50% of the ordinary share capital of the company;

(b) two or more persons each acquire a holding of 5% or more of the ordinary share capital of the company and those holdings together amount to more than 50% of that ordinary share capital; or

(c) two or more persons each acquire a holding of the ordinary share capital of the company and the holdings together amount to more than 50% of that ordinary share capital, but disregarding a holding of less than 5% unless it is in addition to an existing holding and the two holdings together amount to 5% of more of the ordinary share capital of the company.

With regard to (a) above, if a single person initially owns 50% of the ordinary share capital of a company (having subscribed for those shares on their issue) and later, even within three years, acquires a further 3%, that person has not acquired more than 50% of the share capital; only 3% has been "acquired". The wording in (c) above underlines the distinction to be made between acquired and existing holdings. In this instance only 3% of the share capital has changed hands.

To ascertain whether there has been a change in ownership of a company, shareholdings at any two points in time within a three year period may be compared, ignoring any intervening acquisitions or disposals of shares. Generally, there is a change in ownership if at the second point more than half of the ordinary share capital has changed hands since the first point. For this purpose, shares acquired on a death or by unsolicited gift are disregarded as is a holding of less than 5% unless it is in addition to an existing holding and the two holdings together amount to 5% or more. Acquisitions by, and holdings of, persons who are connected with one another (within the meaning of TCA 1997, s 10 – see **2.3**) are aggregated as if they were acquisitions by, and holdings of, one and the same person.

Example 4.110.2.1

The ordinary share capital of Bellemont Ltd is owned on 12 December 2007 as to 99% by John Keaton and as to 1% by David Cleary. On the following day, 13 December 2007, the percentage shareholdings are 49% to John Keaton and 51% to David Cleary. Thus, 50% of the ordinary share capital has changed hands but there has been no change in ownership for the purposes of TCA 1997, s 401 since more than half of the ordinary share capital has not changed hands.

On 17 December 2007 Jane Carroll (who is not connected with either of the two existing shareholders) acquires 2% of the ordinary share capital of the company from John Keaton so that the percentage shareholdings are now 51% to David Cleary, 47% to John Keaton and 2% to Jane Carroll. At this point there has still not been a change of ownership as, although 52% of the ordinary share capital of Bellemont Ltd has passed from John Keaton to the other parties, the holding of Jane Carroll, being less than 5%, is disregarded.

On 20 December 2007, Jane Carroll acquires a further 3% of the ordinary share capital of Bellemont Ltd from John Keaton. At this point there has been a change of ownership:

ownership of 55% of the ordinary share capital has passed from John Keaton to other parties each now holding at least 5%.

Comparisons of shareholdings in a company at two points in time may be made in terms of percentage holdings of the company's total ordinary share capital at the respective times. A person whose percentage holding is greater at the second point is treated as having acquired a percentage holding equal to the increase. This approach will facilitate the necessary comparisons in cases where there has been an issue of shares or any other reorganisation of share capital.

Where, due to extraordinary rights or powers held by a person, whether or not a member of the company, ownership of ordinary share capital may not be an appropriate test of whether there has been a major change in the persons for whose benefit the losses or capital allowances may ultimately enure, holdings of all kinds of share capital, including preference shares, or any particular category of share capital, or voting rights or any other special kind of power, may be taken into account instead of ordinary share capital in considering whether there has been a change in ownership of the company.

Where loss relief has been restricted in accordance with TCA 1997, s 401 due to a change in ownership of a company, no transaction or circumstance before the time of the change may be taken into account in determining whether there is any subsequent change in ownership.

Groups of companies

A change in ownership of a company is disregarded if:

(a)   immediately before the change the company is the 75% subsidiary of another company; and

(b)   although there has been a change in the direct ownership of the company, it continues after the change to be a 75% subsidiary of the other company.

If there has been a change in the ownership of a company which itself has a 75% subsidiary, whether owned directly or indirectly, TCA 1997, s 401 applies as if there had also been a change in the ownership of that subsidiary unless the change in ownership of the first-mentioned company is to be disregarded in the circumstances described in the previous paragraph.

Time of change in ownership

Where an acquisition of ordinary share capital, or of other property or rights, taken into account in determining whether there has been a change in ownership of a company is the result of a contract of sale or option or other contract, or the acquisition was made by a person holding such a contract, the time when the change in ownership takes place is to be determined as if the acquisition had been made when the contract was made with the holder or when the benefit of it was assigned to him. Accordingly, in the case of a person exercising an option to purchase shares, he is to be regarded as having purchased them when he acquired the option.

Provisions regarding ownership

A company is deemed to be a 75% subsidiary of another company if and so long as not less than 75% of its ordinary share capital is owned by that other company, whether directly or through another company or companies, or partly directly and partly through another company or companies. References to ownership are to beneficial ownership. The amount of ordinary share capital of one company owned by a second company through another company or companies is to be determined in accordance with the rules in TCA 1997, s 9(5) to (10) (see **2.505**).

4.2 SET OFF OF LOSSES AGAINST FRANKED INVESTMENT INCOME

In the case of franked investment income (distributions of Irish resident companies) received prior to 6 April 1999, it was possible for a company to set off certain losses against such income for the purpose of claiming payment of the related tax credits.

Where income of a company included a tax credit, certain losses could be offset against franked investment income so that payment of any attaching tax credit could be claimed. A claim could be made to offset the following against franked investment income:

(a)   trading losses;

(b)   charges on income;

(c)   certain capital allowances under.

Where a claim was made, any offset had to be made in the first instance against any profits normally chargeable to corporation tax and then against franked investment income (*treated* as chargeable to corporation tax).

Relief could claimed for the current accounting period and, for the purposes of a set-off of a trading loss or an excess of capital allowances over rental income, and provided the company was then carrying on the trade, or was within the charge to tax, as the case may be, against franked investment income of the immediately preceding accounting period or periods ending within a period equal in length to the period in which the loss was incurred. Where an accounting period fell partly before the immediately preceding period or periods equal in length to the period of the loss or deficiency, only a proportionate part of the chargeable profits, if any, of that accounting period could be relieved.

Where losses or other deficiencies had been used for the purposes of a claim and a company required, at a later date, to utilise them more beneficially against taxable profits, it could make a claim for this purpose, but the tax credits previously claimed would then be recovered from the company by a Case IV assessment

The above relief was extended to include trading losses brought forward and terminal trading losses *but* only for financial concerns for whom franked investment income would be taxed as a Case 1 receipt were it not for the fact that franked investment income is exempt from corporation tax. The relief applied in the case of franked investment income in respect of which the financial concern was entitled to a tax credit, ie where the distributions in question are made before 6 April 1999.

4.3 COLLECTION OF TAX AT SOURCE

4.301 Deduction of tax at source: introduction
4.302 TCA 1997, s 237
4.303 TCA 1997, s 238
4.304 Payments to non-residents
4.305 Yearly interest
4.306 TCA 1997, s 239: relevant payments
4.307 Interest and Royalties Directive
4.308 Interest and Royalties: Switzerland

4.301 Deduction of tax at source: introduction

Collection of tax at source is an established and widespread means of enforcing and facilitating tax compliance. This feature of tax legislation involves the collection of tax at the point of payment and therefore obliges the payer, and not the person who receives or is beneficially entitled to the income, to account for tax. Except in the case of payments made to unregistered subcontractors, where the rate is 35%, deduction at source is at the standard rate of tax in force at the time of payment.

There are many provisions which oblige payers of income to withhold tax at the point of payment. This chapter is primarily concerned with those provisions which have particular application to companies or which need to be understood in relation to the discussion on charges on income which is dealt with later in this chapter.

TCA 1997 ss 237 and 238 have long been fundamental to the whole question of deduction of tax at source. Although TCA 1997, s 237 is not of relevance to companies, it seems appropriate to include some discussion of its provisions here by way of background. Both sections deal with annual payments, patent royalties and certain mining and other rents and it will be helpful to examine these items at the outset.

Annual payments

"Annual payment" is a key concept in tax law and its meaning is derived from case law. As the phrase would suggest, it was once taken to mean a payment which recurs annually but it soon became obvious that it was necessary to develop the concept further. Its meaning is clearly implied, by explaining what it is not, in the following excerpt from the judgment of Scrutton LJ in *Earl Howe v IRC* 7 TC 289:

> It is not all payments made every year from which income tax can be deducted. For instance, if a man agrees to pay a motor garage £500 a year for five years for the hire and upkeep of a car, no one suggests that the person paying can deduct income tax from each yearly payment. So if he contracted with a butcher for an annual sum to supply all his meat for a year, the annual instalment would not be subject to tax as a whole in the hands of the payee, but only that part of it which was profits.

The meaning of "annual payment" as "pure income profit" was developed in *Re Hanbury* 38 TC 588 in which Greene MR stated:

> There are two classes of annual payments which fall to be considered for income tax purposes. There is, first of all, that class of annual payment which the Acts regard and treat as being pure income profit of the recipient undiminished by any deduction. Payments of interest, payments of annuities ... are payments which are regarded as part of the income of the recipient, and the payer is entitled in estimating his total income to treat those payments

as payments which go out of his income altogether. The class of annual payment which falls within that category is quite a limited one. In the other class there stand a number of payments, nonetheless annual, the very quality and nature of which make it impossible to treat them as part of the pure income profit of the recipient, the proper way of treating them being to treat them as an element to be taken into account in discovering what the profits of the recipient are.

In *Rank Xerox v Lane* 1978 STC 449, it was stated in the Court of Appeal that:

> Where the position of the payee is such that his absolute entitlement to receive payments is wholly independent of any outgoings or expenses to which he may be liable we can see no reason in principle why the payments should not be "pure income profit" and therefore an "annual payment".

Pure income profit therefore denotes income of the kind that does not require the incurring of expense. Thus, amounts received by a shopkeeper in respect of the sale of goods could not be pure income profit as the sales receipts are clearly only ingredients in the profits of the shopkeeping business as a whole, and it is necessary to take into account various kinds of expenses before the profit can be identified. On the other hand, interest earned on a deposit account, an annuity received under a deed of covenant, or an amount received by way of alimony are instances of pure income profit as the full amount received is profit.

An annual payment must also be one which arises by virtue of a binding legal obligation. The mere payment on a regular basis, say an annual gift of €1,000, would not in itself constitute an annual payment; such a payment would be a mere application of income rather than one which could be said to "go out of" the income of the payer. The concept of going out of the payer's income in this sense is what makes the payment a "charge on income" and thus something that is deducted in estimating "total income". A payment by way of a covenanted annuity, or an alimony payment, would be a charge on the income of the payer and an annual payment as the payer is obliged to make the payments provided for under deed of covenant or court settlement.

Annual payments do not include any payments of a capital nature as these would not constitute "pure income profit". Thus, payments which are instalments of a capital sum are not annual payments. In *Vestey v IRC* 40 TC 112 it was held that the income element of payments made annually and which had both capital and income elements was an annual payment.

Although the payment of a capital sum by instalments does not give rise to annual payments, payments in return for the acquisition of a capital asset may be income in nature. There is a distinction to be made between a stream of income payments and instalments of a capital sum received as the price of the asset. In *Delage v Nugget Polish Co* [1905] LT 682, it was held that payments received in return for granting rights to a secret process were income in nature. The payments in question were based on a percentage of the payer's gross receipts over a period.

To summarise, an annual payment is one which is capable of recurring annually, is payable under a binding legal obligation and which constitutes pure income profit in the hands of the recipient. The intervals at which the payments are to be made, eg weekly, monthly, do not affect the character of the payments as annual payments as long as they are capable of continuing beyond a year.

Patent royalties

TCA 1997 ss 237 and 238 refer to any royalty, or other sum, which is "paid in respect of the user of a patent". To ascertain whether a royalty or other sum is brought within these sections, therefore, it is necessary to know whether there is a patent in respect of which the sum is paid. The payments in question are those which are being paid by reason of the payer using or being entitled to use an invention, process, formula, information or other result of the patent. The word "user" in this context denotes the right to enjoy. There are other kinds of royalty which are not covered by TCA 1997 ss 237 and 238, such as copyright royalties and many other kinds of royalty or other payments made for rights or access to formulae, secret processes, or technical know-how, as their use or exploitation is not derived from a patent and is not incidental to any rights protected by patent (*Paterson Engineering Co Ltd v Duff* 25 TC 43).

As with other kinds of payments covered by TCA 1997 ss 237 and 238, only royalties which are in the nature of income are within the section. In the case of *IRC v British Salmson Aero Engines Ltd* 22 TC 29, a lump sum payment made for an exclusive right to use a patent but which was payable in three instalments was held to be a capital payment. (At the same time, other payments paid yearly, without any provision for or reference to the payment of a lump sum, were held to be income payments.) In the case of *Constantinesco v Rex* 11 TC 730, a lump sum payment made by the Royal Commission on Awards to Inventors in respect of its use of a patent, for a number of years previously, was held to be in respect of the user of a patent and to be of an income nature.

TCA 1997, ss 237 and 238 apply to patent royalties but in neither section is there any reference to whether or not such royalties should, or would, be annual payments. The sections apply irrespective of whether or not the royalties may be annual payments under general principles. Accordingly it must be correct that the sections could apply to patent royalties in some cases by virtue of their being annual payments. (It would also follow that certain patent royalies are properly assessable under Case III of Schedule D (as noted in **3.207.2**), even where not received from abroad.)

Mining and other rents

By virtue of TCA 1997, s 104(2), TCA 1997 ss 237 and 238 also apply to certain mining and other rents and royalties by treating these payments as if they were royalties paid in respect of the user of a patent. The payments in question are:

(a)   any rent payable in respect of any premises or easements which are used, occupied or enjoyed in connection with any of the concerns the profits or gains of which are taxable under Case I(b) of Schedule D (quarries, mines, ironworks, gasworks, canals, waterworks, docks, tolls, railways, bridges, ferries and other concerns of a similar nature – see **3.103.6**); and

(b)   any yearly interest, annuity or other annual payment reserved in respect of or charged on or issuing out of any premises, not being a rent or payment in respect of an easement.

Any rent of the type mentioned in (a) above and which is rendered by the supply of produce of any of the concerns liable to tax under Case 1(b) of Schedule D is not, however, treated as if it were a royalty paid in respect of the user of a patent and is not subject to TCA 1997, s 237 or s 238.

An *easement* is defined in TCA 1997, s 96(1) as including "any right, privilege or benefit in, over or derived from premises". *Premises* is also defined in that section and means "any lands, tenements or hereditaments in the State". TCA 1997, s 96(1) provides that *rent* includes:

(i) any rent charge, fee farm rent and any payment in the nature of rent, notwithstanding that the payment may relate partly to premises and partly to goods or services; and

(ii) any payment made by the lessee to defray the cost of work of maintenance of or repairs to the premises, not being work required by the lease to be carried out by the lessee".

4.302   TCA 1997, s 237

TCA 1997, s 237(1), (2) reads as follows:

(1) Where any annuity or any other annual payment apart from yearly interest of money (whether payable in or outside the State ... whether payable half- yearly or at any shorter or more distant periods), is payable wholly out of profits or gains brought into charge to income tax—

(a) the whole of those profits or gains shall be assessed and charged with income tax on the person liable to the annuity or annual payment, without distinguishing the same,

(b) the person liable to make such payment, whether out of the profits or gains charged with tax or out of any annual payment liable to deduction, or from which a deduction has been made, shall be entitled on making such payment to deduct and retain out of such payment a sum representing the amount of the income tax on such payment at the standard rate of income tax for the year in which the amount payable becomes due,

(c) the person to whom such payment is made shall allow such deduction on the receipt of the residue of such payment, and

(d) the person making such deduction shall be acquitted and discharged of so much money as is represented by the deduction as if that sum had been actually paid.

(2) Where any royalty or other sum is paid in respect of the user of a patent wholly out of profits or gains brought into charge to income tax, the person paying the royalty or other sum shall be entitled on making the payment to deduct and retain out of the payment a sum representing the amount of income tax on the payment at the standard rate of income tax for the year in which the royalty or other sum payable becomes due".

Brought into charge to income tax

The payments dealt with by TCA 1997, s 237 are not stated (as payments within TCA 1997, s 238 are – see **4.303**) to be "charged with tax under Schedule D" (see **2.605**). Nevertheless it is considered that the section must be confined to such payments.

To be within TCA 1997, s 237 a payment must have been made "wholly out of profits or gains brought into charge to income tax". Any payment made other than out of income which is chargeable to income tax is not included. Accordingly, payments made out of tax exempt income do not come within the section. Neither do any payments made by Irish resident companies since they are liable to corporation tax and not income tax; no payment made by a resident company is to be treated for income tax purposes as paid out of profits or gains brought into charge to income tax (TCA 1997, s 24(1) – see also **3.206**). The "profits or gains brought into charge to income tax" refers to the income of a taxpayer on which income tax is payable. In the case of an individual it would typically be the total income (net of charges on income) after personal allowances and reliefs. If, however, that amount is less than the amount of the charges on income, allowances will be restricted so as to "retain in charge" an amount of taxable income equal to the amount of the charges on income (TCA 1997, s 459(1)).

In *Allchin v Corporation of South Shields* 25 TC 445, it was held that profits brought into charge to tax for any year are the profits assessable for that year and in respect of which tax is payable. In the case of *Trinidad Petroleum Development Co Ltd v IRC* 21 TC 1, a trading loss brought forward from an earlier year was held to be deductible in arriving at the amount of profits brought into charge to tax for the purposes of ascertaining what income was available to cover annual payments made in the current year.

Where a payment falls within TCA 1997, s 237(1) by reason of being payable wholly out of profits or gains brought into charge to income tax, the subsection provides that the whole of those profits or gains are to be assessed and charged to tax on the person making the payment. Although, as a "charge on income", the payment would normally be deducted in arriving at "total income" of the payer, it is included in the income of the payer for the purposes of charging tax. That part of the income is, however, charged to tax at the standard rate only (TCA 1997, s 16(2)).

Example 4.302.1

The following information relates to an accounting period of an individual trader:

	€	€
Gross profit		60,000
Covenanted annuity	3,000	
Overheads	18,000	21,000
Net profit		39,000
Tax computation:		
Net profit		39,000
Disallow annuity (TCA 1997, s 81(2)(l))		3,000
Case I		42,000
Personal allowances		12,000
Taxable		30,000
@ appropriate rate(s)		27,000
@ standard rate		3,000
		30,000

The amount of profits brought into charge to income tax is €30,000. As the annuity is paid wholly out of this amount, it comes within TCA 1997, s 237. On payment of the annuity, the taxpayer may deduct tax at the standard rate in force for the year in which payment was due.

TCA 1997, s 243 provides for the deduction of charges on income in arriving at total profits and is accordingly the basis on which charges "go out of" the total profits of companies just as charges on income go out of the total income of persons liable to income tax. TCA 1997, s 243 is concerned with those payments which are paid out of a company's profits "brought into charge to corporation tax" and the treatment of annual payments and other charges on income of companies is governed by corporation tax provisions and, to some extent, by TCA 1997, s 238, but not at all by TCA 1997, s 237.

4.303   TCA 1997, s 238

4.303.1   General

TCA 1997, s 238(1), (2) reads as follows:

(1) On payment of any annuity or other annual payment (apart from yearly interest of money) charged with tax under Schedule D, or of any royalty or other sum paid in respect of the user of a patent, not payable or not wholly payable out of profits or gains brought into charge, the person by or through whom (regarding "by or through whom", see **4.305**) any such payment is made shall deduct out of such payment a sum representing the amount of the income tax on such payment at the standard rate of tax in force at the time of the payment.

(2) Where any such payment is made by or through any person, that person shall forthwith deliver to the Revenue Commissioners an account of the payment, or of so much of the payment as is not made out of profits or gains brought into charge, and of the income tax deducted out of the payment or out of that part of the payment, and the inspector shall assess and charge the payment of which an account is so delivered on that person.

TCA 1997, s 238(4), (5) of the section provide for the making of an assessment by the inspector where there is default in delivering an account as required by TCA 1997, s 238(3) or where that account is not satisfactory, and for the application of the provisions of the Income Tax Acts relating to chargeable persons, appeals, collection and recovery of income tax, and the rehearing of appeals, to apply also to the charge, assessment, collection and recovery of income tax under TCA 1997, s 238.

TCA 1997 ss 237 and 238 differ in a number of important ways. The deduction of tax by the payer is permissive in TCA 1997, s 237, but mandatory in TCA 1997, s 238. Tax under deducted in respect of an annual payment for TCA 1997, s 238 purposes is not recoverable from future instalments of the annual payment (*Tenbry Investments Ltd v Peugeot Motor Co Ltd* [1992] STC 79). Payments which do not fall within TCA 1997, s 237 because not wholly payable out of profits brought into charge to income tax are within the scope of TCA 1997, s 238 and the sections are complementary in this respect. Payments made out of tax exempt income would be within the scope of TCA 1997, s 238.

TCA 1997, s 238 is concerned with payments "charged with tax under Schedule D" (see **2.605**). Irish resident persons are subject to tax under Schedule D in respect of their worldwide income, as are non-resident persons in respect of their Irish source income. Most payments encountered in practice will accordingly fall within the description "charged with tax under Schedule D". As the income of companies is to be computed for corporation tax purposes under the Schedules and Cases applying for purposes of income tax, payments (other than interest) charged to corporation tax are within the ambit of TCA 1997, s 238.

The meaning of "brought into charge to income tax" has already been considered, in **4.302** above, in relation to TCA 1997, s 237. TCA 1997, s 238 deals with payments not payable or not wholly payable out of profits "brought into charge", meaning brought into charge to income tax. (Since a company within the charge to corporation tax is not within the charge to income tax, the section applies to annual payments etc made by such a company. See also **3.206** in relation to TCA 1997, s 24(1).) Where the amount of taxable income for a year is less than the amount of charges paid for that year, the section will apply to the part of the charges not so covered by the taxable income. Adapting Example **4.302.1**, this can be illustrated as follows:

Example 4.303.1.1

The following information relates to an accounting period of an individual trader:

	€	€
Gross profit		10,000
Covenanted annuity paid	6,000	
Overheads	8,000	14,000
Net loss		4,000

Tax computation:	
Net loss	4,000
Disallow annuity (TCA 1997, s 81(2)(l))	6,000
Case I	2,000

Taxable	
- TCA 1997, s 237 @ standard rate	2,000
- TCA 1997, s 238 @ standard rate	4,000
	6,000

The amount of profits brought into charge to tax is €2,000 – personal allowances are restricted to retain €2,000 in charge, the amount in respect of which the taxpayer *is entitled to* deduct tax (459(1)). €4,000 of the annuity is not paid out of profits brought into charge and the taxpayer *is obliged to* deduct tax from this amount.

Charges on income paid out of capital are within the scope of TCA 1997, s 238 as they are not paid out of profits or gains brought into charge to income tax. Where paid out of a mixed fund of capital and income, charges are assumed to have been paid in priority out of income and only out of capital to the extent that the they are not covered by income. This principle emerges from the judgment in *Central London Railway Co Ltd v IRC* 20 TC 102 but the facts in that case were such that no assumption needed to be made as the company had charged the payments in question to capital and that was where they properly belonged. They were therefore not paid out of profits brought into charge to income tax and the then equivalent of TCA 1997, s 238 applied to them. That decision was followed in *Chancery Lane Safe Deposit & Offices Co Ltd v IRC* 43 TC 83. See also *Fitzleet Estates v Cherry* 51 TC 708.

Payments other than those described in TCA 1997, s 238 are brought within its provisions and are therefore subject to the withholding tax regime and the regulatory provisions of TCA 1997, s 238(4), (5). It may be useful to list these kinds of payments here.

4.303.2 Rents paid abroad

TCA 1997, s 1041 applies the provisions of TCA 1997, s 238 to certain payments made, whether in Ireland or elsewhere, directly (ie not through an agent, trustee or other representative) to a person whose usual place of abode is outside Ireland. The payments are those which arise in respect of rents chargeable to tax under Case V of Schedule D, or in respect of profits or gains chargeable to tax under Case IV of Schedule D which arise under the terms of a lease but to a person other than the lessor, or which otherwise arise out of a disposition or contract such that if they arose to the person who made the disposition or contract would be chargeable under Case V. The recipient of the rent or other payment in cases covered here may, exceptionally, be Irish resident but may nevertheless have his usual place of abode outside Ireland.

Apart from situations covered in TCA 1997, s 1041, the provisions of TCA 1997, s 238 do not apply to any rents or other sums falling due for payment on or after 6 April 1969 where the person beneficially entitled to them is chargeable to tax under Case V of Schedule D, or would be so chargeable but for any exemption from tax.

4.303.3 Patent rights

TCA 1997, s 757 brings into charge to tax under Case IV of Schedule D a capital sum comprising or included in the net proceeds of the sale by a resident person of any patent rights. Where the sale is by a non-resident person and the patent rights relate to an Irish patent, TCA 1997, s 238 applies to the capital sum as if it were an annual payment not brought into charge to income tax.

4.303.4 Scheduled mineral assets

TCA 1997, s 683 brings within the charge to tax under Case IV of Schedule D a capital sum comprising or included in the net proceeds of sale by a resident person of any scheduled mineral asset. Where the sale is by a non-resident person TCA 1997, s 238 applies to the capital sum as if it were an annual payment not brought into charge to income tax.

4.303.5 Payments by non-resident companies

For accounting periods ending on or after 1 April 1990, a non-resident company which is within the charge to corporation tax, and which is required by TCA 1997, s 238(3) to deliver an account to the Revenue Commissioners, is also required to make a return to the inspector of payments made by the company from which income tax is required to be deducted in accordance with TCA 1997, s 238(2), and of the tax deducted from those payments. The income tax returned is treated for the purposes of the charge, collection and recovery of that tax as if it were corporation tax chargeable for the period for which the return is required (TCA 1997, s 241).

4.303.6 Land dealing

TCA 1997, s 643 imposes a charge to tax under Case IV of Schedule D in respect of capital gains arising from the disposal of certain land (land acquired with a view to sale, land held as trading stock, land developed by a company – see **13.309**). Where any consideration or other amount thus chargeable under Case IV arises to a non-resident person, TCA 1997, s 238 may apply to any payment forming part of that amount as if the payment were an annual payment charged with tax under Schedule D (TCA 1997, s 644).

4.303.7 Mining and other rents

TCA 1997, s 104 provides that TCA 1997 ss 237 and 238 also apply to certain mining and other rents and royalties by treating these payments as if they were royalties paid in respect of the user of a patent (see also **4.301** above).

4.303.8 Bond washing

Anti-avoidance provisions in TCA 1997 ss 748-751 apply to certain "bond washing" transactions involving purchases and ex dividend sales of securities (including stocks and shares). The right of a seller of securities to receive interest on the securities sold gives rise to benefits in various situations and the anti-avoidance measures are designed to counteract these benefits, eg by excluding the interest from the seller's income against which a trading loss is being set off. Where a purchaser of securities is a company which carries on a trade other than of dealing in securities, and any annual payment payable by the company is to any extent payable out of the interest, TCA 1997, s 238 applies to that annual payment.

4.303.9 Dividend stripping

Other anti-avoidance rules in TCA 1997 ss 752-753 are aimed at certain dividend stripping transactions of persons carrying on a trade of dealing in shares or other investments or who are exempt from tax. The section applies to a share dealing company acquiring 10% or more of the issued share capital of a company of a certain class (essentially shares other than preference shares) and which, within ten years of the acquisition, receives dividends or other distributions on those shares. In so far as it is paid out of pre-acquisition profits, any such dividend or distribution received is treated as a trading receipt. The section also applies, for example, in the case of a tax exempt person purchasing shares, extracting dividends from the profits accumulated prior to the purchase, and then (prior to 6 April 1999) claiming payment of the tax credit attaching to the dividend. TCA 1997, s 752(4) prevents this in certain cases by setting aside the tax exemption. It also provides, where the exempted person makes an annual payment out of the distribution in respect of which the exemption was wholly or partly set aside, that the annual payment is to be treated as a payment falling within TCA 1997, s 238 (see **4.303**), ie as not payable out of taxed profits.

TCA 1997, s 237 has no effect in relation to companies but charges, apart from "interest of money", paid by companies are governed by the provisions of TCA 1997, s 238. The regulatory type provisions contained in TCA 1997, s 238(3)-(5) have effect subject to the provisions of TCA 1997, s 239 which deal more comprehensively with such matters as returns, assessment, collection and repayments in relation to companies.

The withholding provisions governing interest of money are contained in TCA 1997, s 246 and these are dealt with in **4.305** below.

4.304   Payments to non-residents

It has been seen that TCA 1997, s 237 allows for the deduction of tax from annual payments and other charges while TCA 1997, s 238 imposes an obligation to withhold tax in these cases. As seen in **4.301** above, TCA 1997, s 238 applies to payments "charged with tax under Schedule D". Accordingly, the payments in question are those in respect of which the recipient is subject to tax under Schedule D, ie Irish residents, or where the payments are Irish source payments. As to what determines where the source of a payment is is by no means clear and the question is a difficult one, as will appear from the discussion which follows.

Where the recipient of an annual payment or other charge is a non-resident, a conflict which can result is exemplified by the case of *Keiner v Keiner* 34 TC 346. The case involved payments made by a UK resident to his former wife in accordance with a deed executed under the law of New Jersey in the US. Mr Keiner sought to deduct tax under the then UK equivalent of TCA 1997, s 237 but it was held that his former wife's right to receive the payments gross under New Jersey law overrode his entitlement to do so. Had the equivalent of TCA 1997, s 238 been in question, the dilemma for Mr Keiner would have been even greater.

In *IRC v Broome's Executors* 19 TC 667, interest was paid abroad by the executors of an individual who had been resident in both the UK and Kenya and who had borrowed money from a resident of Kenya secured by an equitable mortgage of land in that country as well as shares in a UK registered company. Tax would be deductible from the interest payments if they were "charged with tax under Schedule D". While it was accepted that tax was not so deductible during the lifetime of the borrower, he having been resident in Kenya where the money was borrowed and the security given (so that the *situs* was not then in the UK), it was held that tax was deductible from payments made by the executors, who were UK resident, "out of a source arising in" the UK (eg, payments remitted from a London bank account, thereby pointing to the relevance of the resources available to the executors to discharge their obligations in relation to the loan).

There are many cases dealing with the location of debts. The location of a simple contract debt (a debt arising from a contract, whether verbal or written, which is not of record or under seal) is the place where the debtor resides, where he can be sued (*Attorney General v Bouwens* (1838) 4 M&W 171; *English, Scottish and Australian Bank Ltd v IRC* [1932] AC 238, HL). Similarly, in *New York Life Insurance Co Ltd v Public Trustee* [1924] 2 Ch 101, CA, it was held that a simple contract debt was situated in the country in which the debtor resides; if there is more than one country of residence, the terms of the contract may serve to localise the debt. A debt under a letter of credit has been found to be situated where it is in fact payable against documents (*Power Curber International Ltd v National Bank of Kuwait* [1981] 2 All ER 607).

The fact that a company which pays a dividend is incorporated in a foreign country does not mean that that dividend constitutes foreign source income. In *Bradbury v English Sewing Cotton Co Ltd* 8 TC 481, it was held, in a majority judgment, that a company incorporated in the state of New Jersey in the US but which was tax resident in the UK (so that its worldwide income was subject to tax in the UK) was a UK source of income rather than a foreign possession. Shares in a company have been held to be locally situated where the head office of the company is (*re Ewing* [1881] 6PD, at page 6). Dividends are a division of the company's profits, which arise where the company's seat and directing power are.

A company's tax residence would not, however, necessarily be of such importance in determining the source of interest; dividends are paid out of the overall profits of a company, which may not be the case with interest - which may be linked to a part only of the company's business. Where interest on an unsecured loan is not so linked, however, the tax residence of the company paying it is likely to be relevant in determining the source of that interest.

The above approach would be consistent with the view, from the *Broome's Executors* case, that regard should be had to the resources out of which payment of interest can be enforced. Different considerations would apply in the case of a loan taken out for the purposes of a trade carried on by a non-resident company through branch in Ireland. In that case, it would seem that the debtor is to be found in Ireland; the tax presence of such a company in Ireland, together with its obligation to register for company law purposes as having a place of business in Ireland, thereby facilitating enforcement of the debt in Ireland, would point to an Irish source of the interest payable.

The decision in *Keiner v Keiner* may be of limited relevance in relation to the question of the source of interest since it was concerned with the question of the rights of the parties to the arrangement in question. *Westminster Bank Executor and Trustee Co (Channel Islands) Ltd v National Bank of Greece NA* 46 TC 472 (for convenience, often referred to as the *Greek Bank* case) reinforced the view that an annual payment by an Irish resident company to a foreign resident and made from a non-Irish source is outside the scope of TCA 1997, s 238 or, in the case of interest, s 246: not being within the scope of Irish taxation, it is not charged to tax under Schedule D.

The case concerned bonds issued by a bank in Greece and guaranteed by another Greek bank and which became unenforceable in Greece with no interest being paid. Neither bank was resident, and neither carried on business, in the UK. The guarantor was succeeded by another bank which did carry on business in the UK and which was held to be liable to pay the interest on the bonds. It deducted tax from the interest payments on the basis that they were annual payments charged with tax under Case III of Schedule D. Case III in the UK dealt with UK source income and it was argued that the source of the payments was the UK as payment could only be enforced in the UK. It was held, however, that the *situs* of the original debt was not the UK. The following are extracts from the leading judgment of Lord Hailsham in the House of Lords:

> I have come to the conclusion that the source of the obligation in question was situated outside the United Kingdom. This obligation was by a principal debtor which was a foreign corporation. That obligation was guaranteed by another foreign corporation which, as was conceded before us, had at no time any place of business within the United Kingdom. It was secured by lands and public revenues in Greece. Payment by the principal debtor of principal or interest to residents outside Greece was to be made in sterling and whether at the office of Hambros Bank or Erlangers Limited or (at the option of the holder) at the National Bank of Greece in Athens, Greece, by cheque on London ... In my view, the bond itself is a foreign document, and the obligations to pay principal and interest to which the bond gives rise were obligations whose source is to be found in this document.

In conclusion Lord Hailsham stated:

> In the instant case both the principal debtor and the original guarantor were wholly resident abroad, and the source from which the income was contemplated to be paid was certainly intended to be remitted from abroad and was partly secured by property situated abroad.

The conclusion was that the bonds were not a UK source of income because the principal debtor and the original guarantor were foreign resident, the moneys from which the interest payments were to be made were to be remitted from abroad, and the debt was partly secured on property situated abroad. The House of Lords placed no importance on the fact that the bonds could only be enforced in the UK and in this respect the decision would seem to have lessened the significance of *Keiner v Keiner.* *Although the issue was left open in that case, the judgment suggests that* the source of the payments was seen to be in the US by reason of the obligation being governed by New Jersey law (consistently with the outcome in *Bingham v IRC* 36 TC 254 - see below – which involved a similar issue).

The *Greek Bank* case is regarded by the UK Revenue as a leading one on the question of source, with particular relevance for branch borrowings. For a withholding obligation to apply, the interest in question must have a UK source. As to what is properly to be regarded as the source of interest payments is itself a complex matter but the question will usually depend on whether the source of the obligation to pay the interest (the loan document or contract) is situated in the UK. Generally, an obligation to pay interest will be situated in the place where the primary obligation to pay it is performed. Irish tax legislation (as also appears to be the case with UK legislation) does not provide any guidance on the question of the source. In the view of the UK Revenue (developed in the aftermath of the *Greek Bank* case), the most important factors in relation to the source of interest payments are:

(a)   the residence of the debtor (being the place where the debt is to be enforced – considered by the UK Revenue to be a key factor in the light of the *Kwok Chi Leung* case mentioned below);

(b)   the source from which interest is in fact paid;

(c)   the place where the interest is paid; and

(d)   the nature and location of the security for the debt.

A key indicator of the location of the source of interest, therefore, is the place where payment can effectively be enforced. Thus, in the case of a secured debt, the question of the security and where it can be enforced would be an important factor. In the case of an unsecured obligation, it would be appropriate to look to the location where the indebtedness can be effectively enforced against the debtor. The place where payment of the interest is to be made does not seem to be of any particular significance in this context.

While the identity of the guarantor was a factor in the *Greek Bank* case, it is unlikely that what would otherwise be foreign source interest would be regarded as Irish source by reason only that the borrowing is guaranteed by an Irish company. That factor alone would be insufficient to enable the withholding obligation to be enforced and other factors such as the existence of other security, the funds out of which the interest payments would be made, and the identity of the issuer would be more likely to determine the matter.

As a general rule for resolving conflicts of law , *choses in action* are situated in the country in which they are properly recoverable and can be enforced. In the case of a debt, the rights of recovery and enforcement will normally be where the debtor resides, hence the relevance of the place of residence of the debtor. In *Alloway v Phillips* [1980] STC 490 (see also **3.208.1**), the right to receive a lump sum from a newspaper in London (a *chose in action*), even though under a contract for services rendered outside the UK, was held to represent a UK source, the sum accordingly being taxable under Case VI (Case IV in Ireland) of Schedule D.

The concept of residence for conflict of laws purposes does not necessarily coincide with the meaning of residence for tax purposes. Thus, for example, a company is regarded as resident for the former purposes where it is incorporated and/or where it does business. If the company is resident in two or more places, the place in which the primary obligation must be performed is decisive (as, for example, in the *Kwok Chi Leung* case – see below).

The question of the location of loan stock issued under seal in the UK by a UK incorporated public company was considered in an Irish case, *Murtagh v Samuel Rusk* [2005] IEHC 316, VI ITR 817. The instrument giving rise to the issue of the loan stock was drawn up and executed in the UK following a board resolution passed there and the instrument was governed by and was to be construed in accordance with English law. The loan stock and related instruments had, however, been physically removed to the Isle of Man where they were held until the relevant maturity dates. The loan stock, being under seal, was a specialty debt and, in the absence of any register, the debt was held to be where the loan notes happened to be. A specialty debt is an obligation under seal securing a debt or a debt due under statute, or a contract or obligation expressed in a deed. Following *Commissioners of Stamps v Hope* [1891] AC 476, the locality of a specialty debt is the place where the instrument happens to be. The following passage from Dicey and Morris, *The Conflict of Laws* (12th edn, 1993 Vol 2), is illuminating: "For taxation purposes, a debt due on a deed or other specialty is situate in the country where the deed itself is situate from time to time and not in a country where the debtor resides".

A security represented by a document of title the property in which passes by delivery (a bearer security) has been held for UK inheritance tax purposes to be located in the place where that document is found at the material time (*Attorney General v Bouwens* (1838) 4 M&W 171; *Winans v Attorney General* [1910] AC 27).

As indicated above, as to whether or not the source of an annual payment (apart from interest) is foreign seems to depend primarily on where the right to the payment can be enforced. In *Chamney v Lewis* 17 TC 318, a UK resident entitled to an annuity under a deed of separation executed in India was held to be in receipt of income from a foreign possession. A similar conclusion was reached in *IRC v Anderström* 13 TC 482 which involved a UK resident entitled to alimony under a Swedish court order. In *Forbes v Dundon* 2 ITR 491, based on these cases, Kenny J in the High Court concluded that:

> ... a legal right to which a person resident in this country is entitled and which is situate outside Ireland and which may be enforced by legal proceedings in a country outside Ireland is either "a security" or "a possession" for the purpose of Income Tax Acts and income which comes from such a right is either "income arising from securities in a place out of Ireland" or "income arising from possessions in a place out of Ireland".

He accordingly concluded that the UK State Retirement Pension was a foreign source, since the taxpayer:

> has a legal right by proceedings before the minister or the tribunal established under the Act to payment of the retirement pension and that the High Court in England has power to review the decisions of the minister or of the tribunals.

In the above UK cases, the payer was resident abroad but it was the character of the obligation, rather than the residence of the payer, which seems to have been decisive. Again, in *Bingham v IRC* 36 TC 254, concerning a UK resident making annual payments to a non-resident, it was held that the foreign court order under which the payments were made was a foreign source and the payments, being received by a non-resident, were accordingly outside the scope of UK taxation.

In *Stokes v Bennett* 34 TC 337, annual payments under a UK court order, payable by a non-UK resident, were held to be subject to withholding at source under the equivalent of TCA 1997, s 238. The payments had a UK source, ie the court order, and the residence of the payer was not relevant.

While the source of a payment will usually be situated in the country whose laws are stated to apply to the contract in question, this may be subject to exceptions. Thus, following the decision in *IRC v Broome's Executors* (see above), payments out of the Irish estate of a deceased person, even though the governing contract might have been executed abroad, would have an Irish source.

The case of *Kwok Chi Leung Karl v Comr of Estate Duty* [1988] STC 728 was concerned with the question of a debt due from a company registered in Liberia where it also had its address for service and where the sum represented by the debt was recoverable. Management and control of the company was in Hong Kong. The debt was expressed to be payable in Liberia and, applying *New York Life Insurance* (see above), it was held to be situated there, that being its place of "residence" for the purpose and where, under the contract creating the debt, the primary obligation to pay was expressed to be performed. What was decided in this case is where the debt was located but that is not necessarily a basis for fixing the source of any interest payable on the debt. The *Greek Bank* decision may accordingly have placed excessive reliance on this judgment in holding that the residence of the debtor is the most important factor whereas there are strong grounds for pointing to the situs of the funds from which payment is made as being the key factor.

An obvious question that arises in relation to interest paid to a non-resident is whether all interest paid by an Irish resident has an Irish source. What would be the position where, say, interest is paid to a UK lender by the UK branch of an Irish resident company? The fact that a payer of interest abroad is Irish resident cannot of itself mean that the source of the interest is in Ireland, that the interest must be "charged with tax under Schedule D". Conversely, interest paid by a non-Irish resident on an Irish loan (for example, secured on Irish land) to an Irish branch of a non-resident company (or indeed to any other recipient) may have an Irish source.

In the case of patent royalties (albeit not referred to as "charged with tax under Schedule D") paid to a non-resident, it would seem correct that TCA 1997, s 238 should apply to them only where they are within the scope of Irish taxation (but see below regarding the territorial principle). The withholding mechanism can hardly be intended to apply to income which is outside the scope of Irish taxation. Following the above-described principles, it would seem that a foreign patent is a non-Irish source and that the resulting royalties, where paid to a non-resident, would normally fall outside the scope of the section. In *International Combustion v IRC* 16 TC 532 (see further below), it was held that the source of royalties paid under a US patent in respect of its use by a licensee in its manufacturing trade was the UK trade itself. It may be noted that a European patent, in so far as it designates the State, grants the same rights and remedies under Irish law as an Irish patent; see Patents Act 1992, s 119(1)(a).

In *International Combustion*, a French firm had acquired from the US owner of patent rights the sole right to manufacture and sell machinery in the eastern hemisphere. The appellant, a UK company, was appointed agent for the French firm for the manufacture and sale of the machinery in the parts of the British Empire within the eastern hemisphere. Payments due by the appellant to the French firm under the agency arrangement were in fact made directly to the US owner and in amounts equal to the amounts due by the French firm to the US owner. It was held that the payments arose from property in the UK. The appellant had claimed that the source of the payments was in France since that was where the agency agreement had been made. (That the patent was a US patent was not in issue.)

The source of the payments had been found by the Special Commissioners to be the right to manufacture in the UK and accordingly the income arose from property in the UK. Rowlatt J in the High Court essentially agreed, holding that the income arose from an agency of the appellant company in the UK. He emphasised that his decision was made precisely on the facts of the case and acknowledged that difficult questions were likely to arise in other cases "not very far removed from this".

That TCA 1997, s 238 should only be applicable to royalties within the scope of Irish taxation is based on a general legal presumption to the effect that Irish legislation does not have extra-territorial effect (_Hamilton v Hamilton_ [1982] IR 446). In this connection see **3.107.1** regarding _Clarke v Oceanic Contractors Inc_ [1983] STC 35 and _Agassi v Robinson_ [2006] STC 1056. Although the House of Lords in the latter case acknowledged the relevance of the territorial principle, it declined to carry this through to the primary tax charge but it would seem that the principle remains undisturbed as regards obligations to collect or account for tax.

Where the Irish trading branch of a non-resident company holds a foreign patent, royalties arising from those patents will form part of the company's trading profits chargeable under Schedule D so that, arguably, the royalties will be within the scope of Irish taxation and TCA 1997, s 238 will apply to them. In practice, however, it may well be that the view that only royalties paid under Irish patents come within TCA 1997, s 238 would prevail. It is also arguable, however, where a non-resident company receives royalties in respect of an Irish patent which it holds as part of its foreign trade, that such royalties fall outside the scope of Irish taxation. This is on the basis that the royalties are merely elements in the profits of a trade exercised outside Ireland by a non-resident (and are thus outside the scope of Irish taxation - see _Carson v Cheyney's Executors_ 38 TC 240).

Exemption from withholding on interest and royalties – EC Directive

See **4.307**.

4.305   Yearly interest

FA 1974 s 50(1) (now repealed) removed "interest of money" from the ambit of what is now TCA 1997 ss 237 and 238 as regards interest in respect of any period beginning on or after 10 January 1974.

The withholding tax provision for interest is now in TCA 1997, s 246(2) and applies only to "yearly interest charged with tax under Schedule D". The provision does not apply to "short" interest and it is relevant therefore to understand the distinction between yearly and short interest. Short loans were described in _Goslings & Sharpe v Blake_ 2 TC 450 as "loans made for a period short of one year, loans which are not intended to be continued, and are not continued, for a longer period". Interest in respect of damages is yearly if calculated for a period of a year or more (*CIR v Barlow* 21 TC 354). The characteristics of yearly interest were described in *CIR v Duncan Hay* 8 TC 686. Yearly interest is interest in respect of a loan:

(a)　which is not a short loan, ie a loan which may not run for a period of a year or more;

(b)　which has a degree of permanence;

(c)　which is in the nature of an investment (but see below);

(d)　which is not repayable on demand (but, again, see below); and

(e)　which has a "tract of future time".

In general, yearly interest is taken to be interest on a loan which runs or is capable of running for a period of a year or more. The intentions of the parties may also be influential in this respect. In *Cairns v MacDiarmid* 56 TC 556, the point was made that interest on a loan was yearly interest notwithstanding that the loan was repayable after a short period, or even on demand, if it was made with the intention that it would remain outstanding and would bear interest from year to year. In the same case it was also observed that the word "investment" (see (b) in relation to *Duncan Hay* above) may be misleading as it is possible to have a very short-term investment, such as an overnight deposit, that would not involve any annual interest.

Interest arising in the case of a loan with no period specified is yearly interest, even where in practice the period may be significantly less than a year. Credit card interest is regarded by the Revenue Commissioners (in contrast with the view of the UK Inland Revenue) as yearly interest. The Commissioners regard certain default interest as not being yearly on the basis that amounts outstanding in default of *bona fide* contractual obligations are by their nature repayable immediately. In fact, such amounts should not be outstanding at all and would therefore fall short of being loans in the strict sense and are clearly not in the nature of an investment and do not have a measure of permanence or a tract of future time.

That it was immaterial (to the question whether interest is yearly interest) that the related debt should be repayable on demand was further affirmed in *Mink & Others v Inspector of Taxes* [1999] STC(SCD) 17. In that case it was also confirmed that the labelling of debts as "short term banking loans" was not determinative of the status of the loans and that what was critical in deciding whether interest is yearly interest is the intention of the parties at the time the loan is made that the debt should subsist beyond a period of one year.

The question whether interest is yearly interest also arose in the case of *Minsham Properties v Price* [1990] STC 718. Although the borrowing in question was repayable on demand, had replaced an overdraft, and was expected to be repaid when the company sold its trading stock so that it would not be long outstanding, and no security was taken, the interest was nevertheless found to be yearly interest. In reaching this conclusion, it was noted that the company would not have been able to repay the debt if demanded without some refinancing since it had no cash readily available, that the company had been provided, by its parent, with something akin to long term or permanent finance which the overdraft did not provide, that the loan supported or protected the company, and that it was essentially a long term commitment by the parent company in much the same way as an investment in the shares in the company.

The additional tests provided in the *Duncan Hay* case would make it impossible to convert a long-term loan into a short loan merely by advancing the repayment date and rolling the loan forward. A series of short-term loans would, generally, be treated as a single loan. Interest on a loan which was repayable after exactly one year was held to be annual interest (*Ward v Anglo American Oil Company Limited* 19 TC 94).

Interest calculated at a yearly rate is not necessarily yearly interest. Mortgage interest, even where the loan was repayable on demand in certain circumstances, was held in *Corinthian Securities Ltd v Cato* 46 TC 93 to be yearly interest.

The withholding obligation provided for in TCA 1997, s 246 applies where yearly interest "charged with tax under Schedule D" (see **2.605**) is paid:

(a)   by a company (defined as "any body corporate") otherwise than when paid in a fiduciary or representative capacity to a person whose usual place of abode is in the State; or

(b)   by any person to another person whose usual place of abode is outside the State.

Thus, the section applies to companies regardless of the place of abode of the recipient whereas it applies to other persons only when making payments of yearly interest to persons whose usual place of abode is outside Ireland. There is, since 10 January 1974, no *entitlement* as such to deduct tax from any interest payments. There is only an *obligation* to deduct tax in the case of yearly interest and this obligation applies in the way described above.

In the cases of payments coming within TCA 1997, s 246, the person by or through whom the payment is made must deduct tax at the standard rate in force at the time of payment. The TCA 1997, s 238(2) requirement to withhold tax at standard rate is therefore carried into TCA 1997, s 246. Furthermore, the regulatory provisions of TCA 1997, s 238(3)-(5) apply to payments coming within TCA 1997, s 246 as they apply to payments within TCA 1997, s 238(2).

The obligation to deduct tax is on the person "by or through whom" the interest is paid and not, if different, on the person who bears the interest. This is the position even where a direct payment by the borrower might be exempted from the obligation to withhold (see below). A typical case in which this situation arises is that of a solicitor paying or receiving interest on behalf of a client. In *Rye & Eyre v IRC* 19 TC 164, Lord Atkin said the words covered those who pay as principals and those who pay as agents. In *Aeolian Co Ltd v IRC 20 TC 547*, a guarantor company which paid certain dividend amounts under the terms of the guarantee was obliged to account for withholding tax on the payments. The withholding obligation cannot be avoided by arranging for the borrower to pay yearly interest through a third party conduit.

As TCA 1997, s 246 applies to interest only, there is no question of it applying to other payments which, while akin to or related to interest, are nevertheless not interest, for example, discounts, interest guarantee payments and interest swap payments. Withholding may, however, apply separately in cases of payments that are "annual payments" (see **4.303.1**).

Interest that may be paid without deduction of tax

The obligation to deduct tax in accordance with TCA 1997, s 246(2) does not apply to certain categories of interest and these are:

(a)   interest paid in the State on an advance from a bank (including a building society – see below) carrying on a *bona fide* banking business in the State;

(b)   interest paid by a bank (including a building society – see below) carrying on a *bona fide* banking business in the State in the ordinary course of such business;

(c)   interest paid in the State by a company to another company, being a company to which TCA 1997, s 246(5)(a) applies (a company carrying on a trade which includes the lending of money – see below) and as long as that other company remains such a company;

(d)   interest paid in the State to an investment undertaking within the meaning of TCA 1997, s 739B (see **12.806.3**);

(e)   interest paid to a person whose usual place of abode is outside the State by a company in the course of carrying on international financial services activities in the Custom House Docks Area or by Shannon based companies entitled to the 10% corporation tax rate or by a specified collective investment undertaking within the meaning of TCA 1997, s 734 (see **12.805.2** and below);

(f)   interest paid, on or after 6 February 2003, in the State to a qualifying company within the meaning of TCA 1997, s 110 (securitisation of assets – see **7.206.11**);

(g)   interest paid, on or after 6 February 2003, by a qualifying company (within the meaning of TCA 1997, s 110) to a person who, by virtue of the law of a relevant territory (a Member State of the EC other than Ireland or a country with which Ireland has a tax treaty), is resident for tax purposes in that territory (see below under *Relevant interest* in relation to the position of US companies, including LLCs), except, in a case where the person is a company, where such interest is paid to the company in connection with a trade or business carried on in the State by the company through a branch or agency;

(h)   interest paid by a company which has been authorised by the Revenue Commissioners to pay interest without deduction of income tax (such authorisations given only exceptionally due to the range of alternative exemptions currently available);

(i)   interest paid on securities in respect of which the Minister for Finance has authorised that payment be made without deduction of tax, ie government loan interest (TCA 1997, s 36 – see **3.207.2**);

(j)   interest paid to an Irish resident by an industrial and provident society;

(k)   interest treated under TCA 1997, s 437 as a distribution (excessive interest to certain directors and their associates (see **10.203**));

(l)   interest, other than interest in (a) to (k) above, paid by a relevant person in the ordinary course of a trade or business carried on by that person to a company which, by virtue of the law of a relevant territory, is resident for the purposes of tax (ie, any tax imposed in such territory which corresponds to income tax or corporation tax in the State) in the relevant territory, except where the interest is paid to that company in connection with a trade or business which is carried on in the State by that company through a branch or agency (see *Relevant interest* below) (TCA 1997, s 246(3)(h));

(m)   interest on quoted Eurobonds, subject to conditions (TCA 1997, s 64 – see below);

(n)   interest paid between certain group members (see **8.202**);

413

(o) relevant interest (ie, interest in respect of a relevant deposit and from which DIRT is deductible in accordance with TCA 1997, s 256 (TCA 1997, s 257(3));

(p) payments made in respect of a wholesale debt instrument, subject to conditions (see below); and

(q) interest which in accordance with TCA 1997, s 267I(1) may be paid without deduction of tax (see **4.307.3** re Interest and Royalties Directive – *Withholding not to apply*).

The withholding obligation does not apply to interest "paid in the State" to a bank carrying on a *bona fide* banking business in the State (see (a) above). The exemption would apply in the case of interest paid to the Irish branch of a foreign bank as long as the loan transaction in question was a branch transaction and the servicing account (which would usually be identified in the governing agreement) into which the interest is to be paid is located in Ireland.

Interest paid to a bank would be regarded as exempt from withholding where the bank did not provide the original advance but took an assignment of the original loan, or part of the loan, from a foreign institutional lender.

Interest paid to a foreign branch of an Irish bank would not be considered as paid in the State. In *Maude v IRC* 23 TC 63, interest on money borrowed from a Channel Islands branch of a UK bank was "payable in the United Kingdom" as the loan contract did not exclude the right of the borrower to pay the interest at the UK head office of the bank. The equivalent Irish legislation, however, requires that the interest is "paid" in the State.

For the above purposes, a "bank" includes a building society within the meaning of TCA 1997, s 256(1), ie a building society within the meaning of the Building Societies Acts 1989, or a society established in accordance with the law of any other Member State of the European Communities which corresponds to that Act.

Interest paid to an Irish branch of a non-resident company would in practice be accepted as paid to a person whose usual place of abode is in the State where the company is liable to corporation tax in respect of its profits arising through or from that branch (or "permanent establishment").

The purpose of (c) above is to extend the exemption from the withholding tax requirement already available to banks and building societies to other financial services companies that make loans in the ordinary course of business. TCA 1997, s 246(5)(a) applies to a company –

(a) which advances money in the ordinary course of a trade which includes the lending of money,

(b) in whose hands any interest payable in respect of money so advanced is taken into account in computing the trading income of the company, and

(c) which:

   (i)   has notified in writing the appropriate inspector to whom the company makes the return referred to in TCA 1997, s 951 (see **15.104.1-2**) that it meets the requirements in (a) and (b); and

   (ii) has notified the paying company in writing that it is a company which meets those requirements and that it has made the notification referred to in (i), and has provided that company with its tax reference number.

A company that is no longer a company to which (a) applies is required, when it ceases to be such a company, immediately to notify in writing the appropriate inspector and the paying company (TCA 1997, s 246(5)(b)).

For the purposes of (c) above, the exemption from the obligation to deduct withholding tax applies in the case of interest paid in respect of a "relevant security" where paid by an IFSC or Shannon company. A relevant security means a security issued by a company in the course of carrying on relevant trading operations within the meaning of TCA 1997, s 445 or 446 on terms which oblige it to redeem the security within 15 years after the date of issue. The exemption from withholding tax applies without regard to the fact that the IFSC or Shannon company will no longer be carrying on relevant trading operations after 31 December 2002 or, as the case may be, 31 December 2005, and may accordingly apply in respect of interest payable after those dates.

In order to ascertain whether interest can be paid gross to a particular bank, it may be necessary to know whether the bank is one carrying on a *bona fide* banking business in the State. The difficulty that can be encountered in this situation is illustrated in the UK case *Hafton Properties Ltd v McHugh* [1987] STC 16 where it was held that interest should have been paid under deduction of tax as the bank in question, an Isle of Man bank, was found not to be carrying on a *bona fide* banking business in the UK. In Ireland, a list of banks accepted as carrying on a *bona fide* banking business in the State is maintained by the Revenue Commissioners. The list includes the main commercial banks which deal with the public generally, and the trustee savings banks. Concerns engaged in wholesale banking business only are unlikely to be accepted as carrying on a *bona fide* banking business.

Companies may be authorised by the Revenue Commissioners to pay interest gross and a list of these companies, mainly financial institutions, is also maintained. Inclusion on the list is by agreement with the Revenue and the authorisation permits the payment as well as the receipt by the company included to be made without deduction of tax. In practice, a company paying interest may require evidence of the authorisation before any payment is made.

Any income, annuity or other annual payment paid by the National Treasury Management Agency is to be paid without deduction of income tax (TCA 1997, s 230(2)) (See **3.213.14**). Any income, annuity or other annual payment paid by the National Development Finance Agency is to be paid without deduction of income tax (TCA 1997, s 230AB(2)) (See **3.213.16**).

Interest treated as a distribution under TCA 1997, s 437 does not require deduction of tax on payment (see (j) above). In fact this will be true of any payment treated by the Corporation Tax Acts as a distribution. Distributions of companies resident in the State are, generally, chargeable to income tax under Schedule F (TCA 1997, s 20(1)) and as such are not chargeable under any other provision of the Income Tax Acts (TCA 1997, s 20(2)) whereas TCA 1997, s 246 applies only to yearly interest charged with tax under Schedule D. While income of a resident company (or of a non-resident company subject to corporation tax in respect of that income), including a distribution received from an Irish resident company, is not chargeable to income tax (TCA 1997, s 21(2)), and where it is such a distribution is therefore not within the Schedule F charge, such distribution is not subject to corporation tax either (TCA 1997, s 129) and is for that reason not charged with tax under Schedule D. Again, therefore, the withholding requirement of TCA 1997, s 246 does not apply.

With effect from 6 April 1999, certain non-residents are exempted from Irish income tax in respect of distributions made to them by Irish resident companies. The exemption applies to those non-residents who are exempted from dividend withholding tax (see **11.116.6**). Up to 5 April 1999, there was an effective exemption from income tax for all non-resident shareholders in respect of distributions made by Irish resident companies. Accordingly, if the recipient is a non-resident company (not within the charge to corporation tax), the distribution is either exempt from Irish income tax or is subject to dividend withholding tax. Again, TCA 1997, s 246 will not apply. Under TCA 1997, s 130(2)(d)(iv), interest paid by a company to a non-resident associated company (75% equity relationship) is (subject to TCA 1997 ss 130(2B) and 452 – see **11.106**) treated as a distribution. Such interest is not subject to the withholding tax requirement of TCA 1997, s 246 as it is not charged with tax under Schedule D. (See discussion in **11.106** regarding this matter in the light of the decision in *Asahi Synthetic Fibres (Ireland) Ltd v Murphy* 3 ITR 246.)

Relevant interest

In relation to interest paid in the circumstances described in (1) in the above list of persons to whom interest may be paid gross (referred to in TCA 1997, s 891A(1) as "relevant interest" – see also below), *relevant person* means a company or an investment undertaking. *Investment undertaking* means –

(a) a unit trust mentioned in TCA 1997, s 731(5)(a) (a unit trust in respect of all of the issued units in which are assets such that any gain accruing on the disposal of them by the unit holder would be wholly exempt from capital gains tax, so that gains accruing to the unit trust itself are not chargeable gains – see also **12.805.4** and **12.806.3**);

(b) a special investment scheme within the meaning of TCA 1997, s 737 (see **12.805.4**);

(c) an investment undertaking within the meaning of TCA 1997, s 739B (see **12.806.3**); or

(d) a common contractual fund within the meaning of TCA 1997, s 739I(a) (see **12.810.2**).

A *relevant territory* means a Member State of the European Communities other than Ireland or a territory, other than such a Member State, with which Ireland has a tax treaty.

The requirement that the recipient should be tax resident in a relevant territory will not be met in certain cases, probably most notably by US companies since the concept of tax residence is not recognised under US tax law. The Revenue will accept that exemption from withholding is available in the case of a company incorporated in the US and taxable there on its worldwide income. Furthermore, a US limited liability company (LLC) is normally a transparent entity for US tax purposes and is therefore not regarded as tax resident in the US. The Revenue are prepared to look through an LLC and to determine the question of exemption from withholding by reference to the circumstances of the ultimate beneficial recipient(s) of the interest, provided business is conducted through the LLC for market and not for tax avoidance reasons. A similar position applies for the purposes of (g) above – interest paid by a securitisation vehicle to an LLC.

Every relevant person who pays relevant interest in a chargeable period is obliged to prepare and deliver to the appropriate inspector (see **15.104.2**) on or before the specified return date for the chargeable period (see **15.104.1**) a return of all relevant interest so paid stating in the case of each person to whom that interest was paid—

- (i)　the name and address of the person;
- (ii)　the amount of relevant interest paid to the person in the chargeable period; and
- (iii)　the territory in which the person is resident for tax purposes (TCA 1997, s 891A(2)).

TCA 1997 ss 1052 and 1054 (see **15.104.4** and **15.204**) are to apply to a failure by a relevant person to deliver a return of relevant interest as they apply to a failure to deliver a return referred to in TCA 1997, s 1052 (TCA 1997, s 891A(2)(c)).

Interest on quoted Eurobonds

The requirement to withhold tax on payment of interest does not apply to interest on quoted Eurobonds:

- (a)　where the person by or through whom the payment is made is not in the State (ie, where the interest is paid by a non-Irish based paying agent); or
- (b)　the payment is made by or through a person in the State (an Irish based paying agent), and:
  - (i)　the quoted Eurobond is held in a recognised clearing system; or
  - (ii)　the person who is the beneficial owner of the quoted Eurobond and who is beneficially entitled to the interest is not resident in the State and has made an appropriate declaration to that effect to the person by or through whom the interest is paid (TCA 1997, s 64(2)).

A *quoted Eurobond* means a security which:

- (a)　is issued by a company;
- (b)　is quoted on a recognised stock exchange; and
- (c)　carries a right to interest.

Recognised clearing system, referred to above, means the following clearing systems:

- (i)　Bank One NA, Depository and Clearing Centre;
- (ii)　Central Moneymarkets Office;
- (iii)　Clearstream Banking SA;
- (iv)　Clearstream Banking AG;
- (v)　CREST;
- (vi)　Depository Trust Company of New York;
- (vii)　Euroclear;
- (viii)　Monte Titoli SPA;
- (ix)　Netherlands Centraal Instituut voor Giraal Effectenverkeer BV;
- (x)　National Securities Clearing System;
- (xi)　Sicovam SA;
- (xii)　SIS Sega Intersettle AG; and

(xiii)   any other system for clearing securities which is for the time being designated, for the purposes of TCA 1997, s 246A or any other provision of the Tax Acts or the Capital Gains Tax Acts which applies that section, by order of the Revenue Commissioners as a recognised clearing system (TCA 1997, s 246A(2)(a)).

For the above purposes, the Revenue Commissioners may by order designate one or more than one system for clearing securities as a "recognised clearing system" (TCA 1997, s 246A(2)(b)). That order may contain such transitional and other supplemental provisions as appear to the Revenue Commissioners to be necessary or expedient and may be varied or revoked by a subsequent order (TCA 1997, s 246A(2)(c)).

Relevant foreign securities means any such stocks, funds, shares or securities as give rise to dividends to which TCA 1997 Part 4 Ch 2 (ss 60–64 – foreign dividends and paying agents etc) applies, or any such securities as give rise to foreign public revenue dividends, within the meaning of TCA 1997, s 32 (dividends payable out of any public revenue).

Wholesale debt instruments

Subject to conditions, payments made in respect of a wholesale debt instrument of an approved denomination may be made without deduction of tax as required by TCA 1997, s 246(2) (TCA 1997, s 246A(3)).

A *wholesale debt instrument* is a certificate of deposit or commercial paper, as appropriate.

A *certificate of deposit* is an instrument, either in physical or electronic form, relating to money in any currency which has been deposited with the issuer or some other person, being an instrument:

(a)   issued by a financial institution;

(b)   which recognises an obligation to pay a stated amount to bearer or to order, with or without interest; and

(c)   (i)   in the case of instruments held in physical form, by the delivery of which, with or without endorsement, the right to receive the stated amount is transferable; or

       (ii)   in the case of instruments held in electronic form, in respect of which the right to receive the stated amount is transferable.

Commercial paper means a debt instrument, either in physical or electronic form, relating to money in any currency, which:

(a)   is issued by—

       (i)   a financial institution (see below); or

       (ii)   a company that is not a financial institution;

(b)   recognises an obligation to pay a stated amount;

(c)   carries a right to interest or is issued at a discount or at a premium; and

(d)   matures within two years.

A *financial institution* is:

(i)   a person who holds or has held a licence under s 9 of the Central Bank Act 1971,

(ii)   a person referred to in s 7(4) of the Central Bank Act 1971, or

(iii) a credit institution (within the meaning of the European Communities (Licensing and Supervision of Credit Institutions) Regulations, 1992 (SI 395/1992)) which has been authorised by the Central Bank of Ireland to carry on the business of a credit institution in accordance with the provisions of the supervisory enactments (within the meaning of those Regulations) (TCA 1997, s 906A(1)).

An *approved denomination*, in relation to a wholesale debt instrument, is a denomination of not less than:

(a)   in the case of an instrument denominated in euro, €500,000;

(b)   in the case of an instrument denominated in United States Dollars, $500,000;

(c)   in the case of an instrument denominated in a currency other than euro or United States Dollars, the equivalent in that other currency of €500,000.

For the purposes of (c) above, the equivalent of an amount of euro in another currency is to determined by reference to the rate of exchange, in the case of instruments issued under a programme, at the time the programme under which the instrument is to be issued is first publicized and, in the case of all other instruments, on the date of issue of the instrument.

In the case of a payment made in respect of a wholesale debt instrument, if the person by or through whom the payment is made is not resident in the State and the payment is not made by or through a branch or agency through which a non-resident company carries on a trade or business in the State, and:

(i)   the wholesale debt instrument is held in a recognised clearing system (see below); and

(ii) the wholesale debt instrument is of an approved denomination.

TCA 1997, s 246(2) will not apply to that payment. Neither will the wholesale debt instrument be treated as a relevant deposit for the purposes of the legislation dealing with deposit interest retention tax (DIRT) (TCA 1997, s 246A(3)).

Likewise, in the case of a payment made in respect of a wholesale debt instrument, if the person by or through whom the payment is made is resident in the State or the payment is made either by or through a branch or agency through which a non-resident company carries on a trade or business in the State, and:

(a)   the wholesale debt instrument is held in a recognised clearing system and is of an approved denomination;

(b)   the person who is beneficially entitled to the interest is a resident of the State and has provided his tax reference number to the "relevant person" (the person by or through whom the payment in respect of the wholesale debt instrument is made); or

(c)   the person who is the beneficial owner of the wholesale debt instrument and who is beneficially entitled to the interest is not resident in the State and has made an appropriate declaration (see below).

TCA 1997, s 246(2) will not, subject to TCA 1997, s 246A(4) or (5), apply to that payment. (Neither will the wholesale debt instrument be treated as a relevant deposit for the purposes of the legislation dealing with deposit interest retention tax (DIRT).)

Recognised clearing system, referred to above, means the following clearing systems:

(i)	Bank One NA, Depository and Clearing Centre;
(ii)	Central Moneymarkets Office;
(iii)	Clearstream Banking SA;
(iv)	Clearstream Banking AG;
(v)	CREST;
(vi)	Depository Trust Company of New York;
(vii)	Euroclear;
(viii)	Monte Titoli SPA;
(ix)	Netherlands Centraal Instituut voor Giraal Effectenverkeer BV;
(x)	National Securities Clearing System;
(xi)	Sicovam SA;
(xii)	SIS Sega Intersettle AG; and
(xiii)	any other system for clearing securities which is for the time being designated, for the purposes of TCA 1997, s 246A or any other provision of the Tax Acts or the Capital Gains Tax Acts which applies that section, by order of the Revenue Commissioners as a recognised clearing system (TCA 1997, s 246A(2)(a)).

The Revenue Commissioners may, for the above purposes, by order designate one or more than one system for clearing securities as a "recognised clearing system" (TCA 1997, s 246A(2)(b)). That order may contain such transitional and other supplemental provisions as appear to the Revenue Commissioners to be necessary or expedient and may be varied or revoked by a subsequent order (TCA 1997, s 246A(2)(c)).

A relevant person (see above) is subject to a number of fiduciary obligations as regards payments made in respect of a wholesale debt instrument in cases included in (a) or (b) above (wholesale debt instrument held in a recognised clearing system, or the person who is beneficially entitled to the interest is a resident of the State etc). The relevant person, on being so required by written notice from a Revenue officer in relation to any person named in the notice, is required to deliver an account in writing of the amount of any payment made in respect of a wholesale debt instrument to that person together with details of the person's name and address and tax reference number if such details have not otherwise been furnished (TCA 1997, s 246A(4)(b)).

The declaration referred to in (c) above is a declaration in writing to a relevant person which:

(a)   is made by a person ("the declarer") to whom any payment in respect of which the declaration is made is payable by the relevant person, and is signed by the declarer;

(b)   is made in such form as may be prescribed or authorised by the Revenue Commissioners;

(c)   declares that at the time the declaration is made the person who is beneficially entitled to the interest is not resident in the State;

(d)   contains as respect the person mentioned in paragraph (c) –

    (i)   the name of the person;

    (ii)   the address of that person's principal place of residence; and

    (iii)   the name of the country in which that person is resident at the time the declaration is made;

(e) contains an undertaking by the declarer that, if the person referred to in (c) above becomes resident in the State, the declarer shall notify the relevant person accordingly; and

(f) contains such other information as the Revenue Commissioners may reasonably require (TCA 1997, s 246A(5)).

A relevant person is required to keep and retain for the longer of:

(i) a period of six years after the declaration is made; and

(ii) a period which ends not earlier than three years after the latest date on which any payment in respect of which the declaration was made is paid,

all declarations of the kind mentioned above that have been made in respect of any payment made by the relevant person.

In addition, on being required by notice given in writing by a Revenue officer, the relevant person is required to make such declarations available to that officer within the time specified in the notice (TCA 1997, s 246A(7)).

Exemption from withholding on interest and royalties – EC Directive

See **4.307**.

4.306   TCA 1997, s 239: relevant payments

The administrative type provisions of TCA 1997, s 238(3)-(5) have effect subject to the provisions of TCA 1997, s 239 which regulate the time and manner in which Irish resident companies are to account for and pay income tax in respect of "relevant payments" and are to be repaid income tax in respect of payments received by them. The section also deals with such matters as returns, assessment, collection and repayment in relation to relevant payments. *Relevant payment* means:

(a) any payment made on or after 6 April 1976 from which income tax is deductible and to which the provisions of TCA 1997, s 238(3)-(5) apply; and

(b) any amount which under TCA 1997, s 438 is deemed to be an annual payment.

The payments from which income tax is deductible and to which the provisions of TCA 1997, s 238(3)-(5) apply have been described in **4.303**, **4.304** and **4.305**. Certain loans made by close companies to participators or their associates which are deemed by TCA 1997, s 438 to be annual payments (see **10.204**) are also relevant payments. Payments ("relevant amounts") from which a life assurance company carrying on foreign life assurance business is required to deduct and account for income tax at standard rate are treated as annual payments and as relevant payments for the purposes of TCA 1997, s 239 (TCA 1997, s 710(3)(b) – see **12.603.6**).

Companies are required for each accounting period to make a return of relevant payments made in that period and of the income tax for which they are accountable in respect of those payments. Where a return is required for any accounting period, it must be made within nine months from the end of that period TCA 1997, s 239(4). That return is now part of the corporation tax return which a company is required make in accordance with TCA 1997, s 884. With a view to streamlining the form-filling, assessment and payment procedures associated with relevant payments for accounting periods ending on or after 1 April 1990, these payments are now among the items which a company is required to include in its corporation tax return (TCA 1997, s 884(2)(d), (e). For the purposes of the charge, assessment, collection and recovery from the company of the income tax due, and of any interest and penalties thereon, in respect of relevant payments made in any accounting period, that income tax is treated as corporation tax payable by the company for that period (TCA 1997, s 239(11)(a)). The corporation tax return is required to be made within nine months of the end of the accounting period (but in any event not later than the 21st of the month in which that period of nine month ends) (TCA 1997 ss 950(1) and 951(1)). No provision of TCA 1997, s 239 may prejudice the powers of the Revenue to recover tax by means of an assessment or otherwise.

Tax in respect of relevant payments made in any accounting period is due at the same time as the preliminary tax for that period is due. The tax is due without the making of an assessment, as is the case with preliminary tax, but an assessment may be made if the tax is not paid on time. Estimated assessments may be made by an inspector where a relevant payment has not been included in a return or where the inspector is not satisfied with a return. For the purposes of interest on unpaid tax, the tax assessed is treated as payable at the time it would have been payable if a correct return had been made.

It is quite possible for a company to make a relevant payment on a date which does not fall within an accounting period. That would be the case where, for example, a company has not to date come within the charge to corporation tax but has borrowed money on which it has paid yearly interest from which tax is deductible under TCA 1997, s 246. The payment in that case must be returned, and the tax paid, within six months of the date the payment was made. Any assessment made in those circumstances is treated as for the year of assessment in which the relevant payment was made. The income tax in that case is not treated as corporation tax by virtue of TCA 1997, s 239(11)(a).

Where a company has received income from which tax has been deducted at source in an accounting period in which it has made any relevant payments, the tax on income received may be set against the tax due on the relevant payments. The claim for offset should be included in the return of relevant payments. Where the income tax on relevant payments has been paid before the claim is allowed, the excess amount will be repaid to the company (TCA 1997, s 239(7). Any such entitlement to repayment of income tax is not affected by the fact that the income tax paid is treated as corporation tax in accordance with TCA 1997, s 239(11)(a). Proceedings for collection of tax, including proceedings by way of distraint, may not be commenced in relation to tax which is the subject of a claim for offset but this does not affect the date when the tax is due. A claim for offset may not stop proceedings already begun. Where any offset has been made, the tax offset is treated as tax paid or repaid as the case may be. Tax which has been set against tax on relevant payments may not, evidently, be repaid or credited under TCA 1997, s 24(2).

4.307 Interest and Royalties Directive

4.307.1 Introduction

TCA 1997 Part 8 Chapter 6 (ss 267G-267I) gives effect to Council Directive No 2003/49/EC, providing for a common system of taxation applicable to interest and royalty payments made between associated companies of different Member States. Interest and royalties to which this legislation applies are exempt from corporation tax and income tax. Accordingly, payments of royalties and interest are exempt from the withholding provisions that would otherwise apply. These provisions are, as respects royalties, TCA 1997, s 238 (see **4.304**) and, as respects interest, TCA 1997, s 246(2) (see **4.305**) and TCA 1997, s 257 (DIRT). In any case in which tax is nevertheless deducted at source, the recipient company in question (which will be tax resident in a Member State other than Ireland) will be entitled to a refund of the tax deducted.

Provision is also made for credit against corporation tax in respect of any withholding tax charged on interest or royalties by Greece or Portugal and any withholding tax charged on royalties by Spain.

TCA 1997 Part 8 Chapter 6 applies in respect of payments of interest and royalties made on or after 1 January 2004.

4.307.2 Definitions

TCA 1997, s 267G contains a number of definitions, including the following.

Member State

Member State means a Member State of the European Communities.

Directive

Directive means Council Directive 2003/49/EC of 3 June 2003 (OJ No L 157, 26.6.2003, p 49) as amended.

Company

For the purposes of TCA 1997 Part 8 Chapter 6, *company* means a company of a Member State, and *company of a Member State* has the meaning assigned to it by Article 3(a) of the Directive. In Article 3(a), "company of a Member State" means any company—

(i)   taking one of the forms listed in the Annex to the Directive (see below); and

(ii) which in accordance with the tax laws of a Member State is considered to be resident in that Member State and is not, within the meaning of a double taxation convention on income concluded with a third state, considered to be resident for tax purposes outside the Community; and

(iii) which is subject to one of the following taxes without being exempt, or to a tax which is identical or substantially similar and which is imposed after the date of entry into force of the Directive in addition to, or in place of, those existing taxes:

Austria	Körperschaftsteuer
Belgium	impôt des sociétés/ vennootschapsbelasting
Denmark	Selskabsskat
Finland	yhteisöjen tulovero/inkomstskatten för samfund
France	impôt sur les sociétés
Germany	Körperschaftsteuer
Greece	phoros eisodematos nomikon prosopon
Ireland	corporation tax
Italy	imposta sul reddito delle persone giuridiche

Luxembourg	impôt sur le revenue des collectivités
Netherlands	Vennootschapsbelasting
Portugal	imposto sobre o rendimento das pessoas colectivas
Spain	impuesto sobre sociedados
Sweden	statlig inkomstskatt
UK	corporation tax

The forms of company listed in the Annex to the Directive are:

Austria	Aktiengesellschaft, Gesellschaft mit beschränkter Haftung (GmbH),
Belgium	société anonyme/naamloze vennootschap, société en commandite par actions/commanditaire vennootschap op aandelen, société privé à responsabilité limitée/besloten vennootschap met beperkte aansprakelijkheid, and those public law bodies that operate under private law
Denmark	aktieselskab, anpartsselskab
Finland	osakeyhtiö/aktiebolag, osuuskunta/andelslag, säästöpankki/sparbank, vakuutusyhtiö/försäkringsbolag
France	société anonyme, société en commandite par actions, société à responsabilité limitée, and industrial and commercial public establishments and undertakings
Germany	Aktiengesellschaft, Kommanditgesellschaft auf Aktien, Gesellschaft mit beschränkter Haftung (GmbH), bergrechtliche Gewerkschaft
Greece	anonymi etairia
Ireland	public companies limited by shares or by guarantee, private companies limited by shares or by guarantee, bodies registered under the Industrial and Provident Societies Acts, building societies registered under the Building Societies Acts
Italy	società per azioni, società in accomandita per azioni, società a responsabilità limitata, and private entities carrying on industrial and commercial activities
Luxembourg	société anonyme, société en commandite par actions, société à responsabilité limitée
Netherlands	naamloze vennootschap, besloten vennootschap met beperkte aansprakelijkheid
Portugal	commercial companies or civil law companies having a commercial form, cooperatives and public undertakings incorporated in accordance with Portuguese law
Spain	sociedad anónima, sociedad comanditaria por acciones, sociedad de responsabilidad limitada, public law bodies which operate under private law
Sweden	aktiebolag, försäkringsaktiebolag
UK	companies incorporated under the law of the United Kingdom

Interest

Interest means income from debt-claims of every kind, whether or not secured by mortgage and whether or not carrying a right to participate in the debtor's profits and, in particular, income from securities and income from bonds or debentures, including premiums and prizes attaching to such securities, bonds or debentures, but does not include penalty charges for late payment.

Royalties

Royalties means payments of any kind as consideration for:

    (a)   the use of, or the right to use—

        (i)   any copyright of literary, artistic or scientific work, including cinematograph films and software,

        (ii)   any patent, trade mark, design or model, plan, secret formula or process,

    (b)   information concerning industrial, commercial or scientific experience;

    (c)   the use of, or the right to use, industrial, commercial or scientific equipment.

Tax

In relation to a Member State other than the State, *tax* means any tax imposed in that Member State which is specified in Article 3(a)(iii) of the Directive (see list under *Company* above).

Associated companies

A company is treated as an *associated company* of another company during an uninterrupted period of at least 2 years throughout which:

    (a)   one of them directly controls not less than 25% of the voting power of the other company; or

    (b)   in respect of those companies, a third company directly controls not less than 25% of the voting power of each of them.

4.307.3 Exemption from tax

A company tax resident in a Member State other than Ireland is not chargeable to corporation tax or income tax in respect of interest or royalties to which TCA 1997, s 267H applies, except where the interest is, or as the case may be the royalties are, paid to the company in connection with a trade which is carried on in the State by that company through a permanent establishment (PE) (TCA 1997, s 267I(2)). TCA 1997, s 267H applies to the following payments of interest and royalties between associated companies:

    (a)   interest or royalties paid by an Irish resident company to a company resident in a Member State other than Ireland;

    (b)   interest or royalties paid by an Irish resident company to a PE situated in a Member State ("first Member State") other than Ireland, being a PE of a company resident in a Member State other than Ireland through which it carries on a business in the first Member State;

    (c)   interest or royalties paid by an Irish PE of a non-resident company to a company resident in a Member State other than Ireland;

    (d)   interest or royalties paid by an Irish PE of a non-resident company to a PE situated in a Member State ("first Member State") other than Ireland, being a

PE of a company resident in a Member State other than Ireland through which it carries on a business in the first Member State (TCA 1997, s 267H(1)).

For the above purposes, the recipient must be the beneficial owner or, in the case of a PE, must be treated as the beneficial owner, of the interest or royalties. A PE of a company in a Member State is treated as being the beneficial owner of interest or royalties if:

(i)   the debt-claim, right or asset in respect of which the interest arises, or as the case may be the royalties arise, consists of property or rights used by, or held by or for, the PE; and

(ii) the interest or royalties are taken into account in computing income of the PE which is subject to one of the taxes specified in Article 1.5(b) (see below) or Article 3(a)(iii) (see list under *Company* above) of the Directive.

The taxes specified in Article 1.5(b) (which also includes those specified in Article 3(a)(iii) – see above) are, in the case of Belgium, the impôt des non-résidents/belasting der niet-verblijfhouders and, in the case of Spain, the Impuesto sobre la Renta de no Residentes, as well as a tax that is identical or substantially similar and which is imposed after the date of entry into force of the Directive in addition to, or in place of, those existing taxes.

Relief is not available in the case of:

(a)   interest or royalties paid –

   (i)   to a company where the debt-claim, right or asset in respect of which the payment is made consists of property or rights used by, or held by or for, a PE of the company through which the company carries on a trade –

    (I)   in the State, or

    (II) in a territory which is not a Member State, or

  (ii) by a company for the purposes of a business carried on by it through a PE in a territory which is not a Member State,

(b)   interest on a debt-claim in respect of which there is no provision for repayment of the principal amount or where the repayment is due more than 50 years after the creation of the debt; or

(c)   so much of any royalties paid as exceeds the amount which would have been agreed by the payer and the beneficial owner of the royalties if they were independent persons acting at arm's length (TCA 1997, s 267H(2)).

As regards (a)(ii) above, withholding may not apply in any event. The source of the payment will often be other than in Ireland (see **4.304**), for example, where interest is paid by a foreign branch in respect of borrowings drawn down by and used for the purposes of the branch business; as such, the payment would not be "charged with tax under Schedule D".

Withholding not to apply

Where TCA 1997, s 238 (see **4.304**), 246(2) (see **4.305**) or 257 (DIRT) would otherwise apply, they are not to apply in respect of interest or royalties to which TCA 1997, s 267H applies (TCA 1997, s 267I(1)). Thus no withholding is required under these provisions.

Credit relief

TCA 1997, s 267J provides that where interest or royalties are received by an Irish resident company from an associated company, credit will be allowed for:

(a) any withholding tax charged on the interest or royalties by Greece or Portugal; and

(b) any withholding tax charged on the royalties by Spain,

pursuant to the derogations provided for in the Directive against corporation tax in respect of the interest or royalties to the extent that credit for such withholding tax would not otherwise be allowed. (See also **14.10.**)

Greece and Portugal are exempted under the Directive from the obligation to exempt interest and royalties from tax until the date of application referred to in Article 17(2) and (3) of Council Directive 2003/48/EC of 3 June 2003 - 1 January 2005 but subject to conditions. During a transitional period of eight years commencing with that date, the maximum permissible withholding rate is 10% for the first four years and, for the remaining four years, 5%.

Spain is exempted from the obligation to exempt royalty payments from tax until the date of application referred to in Article 17(2) and (3) of Council Directive 2003/48/EC of 3 June 2003 - 1 January 2005 but subject to conditions. During a transitional period of six years commencing with that date, the maximum permissible withholding rate is 10%.

The above-mentioned transitional periods may be extended.

Anti-avoidance

TCA 1997 ss 267G-267J will not apply to interest or royalties unless it can be shown that the payment of the interest or royalties was made for bona fide commercial reasons and does not form part of any arrangement or scheme of which the main purpose or one of the main purposes is avoidance of liability to income tax, corporation tax or capital gains tax (TCA 1997, s 267K(1).

Company ceasing to satisfy requirements for exemption

Where a company which:

(a) is entitled to receive a payment of interest or royalties from any person; and

(b) had received from that person a payment of interest or royalties which was exempt for tax in accordance with the Directive;

ceases to fulfill the requirements for exemption specified in the Directive, the company is obliged without delay to inform that person that it has so ceased (TCA 1997, s 267K(2)).

4.308   Interest and Royalties: Switzerland

4.308.1   Introduction

Provisions equivalent to those in the Interest and Royalties Directive ("the Directive") are extended to Swiss companies as part of an agreement between the EU and Switzerland providing for measures in Switzerland equivalent to the EU Directive on the Taxation of Savings. TCA 1997, s 267L accordingly provides for the necessary exemption from Irish tax in respect of interest and royalty payments to Swiss companies.

4.308.2   Exemption from tax

TCA 1997, s 267L provides for exemptions from tax (corporation tax and income tax) and withholding tax in respect of certain payments of interest and royalties made to or for the benefit of Swiss resident companies and Swiss permanent establishments of EU resident companies. The exemption will not apply in the case of a payment to a Swiss company in connection with a trade carried on by the company in Ireland through a permanent establishment. The exemption is given effect by extending the provisions of TCA 1997 ss 267G–267I (see **4.307.2** and **4.307.3**) to payments to which s 267L applies.

TCA 1997, s 267L applies to a payment, being interest or royalties, made to or for the benefit of:

(a)   a company which—

    (i)   is the beneficial owner of the interest or royalties, as the case may be;

    (ii)   is, by virtue of the law of Switzerland, resident for the purposes of tax in Switzerland; and

    (iii)   is not treated, by virtue of any tax treaty between Switzerland and another country, as resident in any country that is not—

        (I)   a Member State of the European Communities; or

        (II)   Switzerland; or

(b)   a permanent establishment situated in Switzerland through which a company carries on business in Switzerland, being a permanent establishment that would, in accordance with the Directive, be treated as the beneficial owner of the interest or royalties (TCA 1997, s 267L(1)).

TCA 1997 ss 267G–267I are to have effect in relation to payments within TCA 1997, s 267L as if:

(a)   a reference in those sections to a Member State of the European Communities included a reference to Switzerland;

(b)   a reference in those sections to a company of a Member State included a company (including a company that takes one of the forms specified in Article 15 of the Agreement attached to the Council Decision (2004/911/EC) of 2 June 2004 on the signing and conclusion of the Agreement between the EC and the Swiss Confederation providing for measures equivalent to those in Council Directive 2003/48/EC of 3 June 2003 on taxation of savings income in the form of interest payments and the accompanying Memorandum of Understanding – OJ No L385, 29.12.2004, p 28) resident for the purposes of tax in Switzerland; and

(c)   a reference in those sections to tax included any tax imposed in Switzerland that corresponds to income tax or corporation tax in Ireland (TCA 1997, s 267L(2).

As can be seen from **4.307.3**, TCA 1997, s 267G is concerned with interpretation of relevant words and phrases, s 267H with the types of entity to which the payments of interest and royalties apply, and s 267I with exemption from tax and withholding tax.

TCA 1997, s 267K (see *Company ceasing to satisfy requirements for exemption* in **4.307.3**) applies in relation to TCA 1997, s 267L as it applies in relation to ss 267G–267I.

4.4 CHARGES ON INCOME

4.401   Charges on income: introduction
4.402   Meaning of "charges on income"
4.403   Interest as a charge on income
4.404   Deduction for charges on income
4.405   Treatment of "relevant trading charges"

4.401   Charges on income: introduction

Corporation tax legislation provides for the deduction of charges on income against the total profits of companies. This deduction is provided for by TCA 1997, s 243 which is accordingly the basis on which charges "go out of" the total profits of companies just as charges on income go out of the total income of persons liable to income tax. TCA 1997, s 243 is concerned with those payments which are paid out of a company's profits "brought into charge to corporation tax". Accordingly, charges on income do not include any payments which are deductible in computing income from any source (see also *Brought into charge to income tax* in **4.302**). In computing the trading profits of a company for any accounting period in which it has incurred charges on income, the amount debited in the profit and loss account is added back and the amount paid in the period is deducted from the total profits.

Furthermore, since charges on income are deductible only where they have been paid out of profits brought into charge to corporation tax, any payments treated as paid out of capital in the books of the company concerned will not be deductible under TCA 1997, s 243 (see **4.303.1** above).

4.402   Meaning of "charges on income"

The items which constitute charges on income are to a large extent those with which TCA 1997 ss 237 and 238 are concerned and which were accordingly described in some detail in **4.301**. The definition of "charges on income" in TCA 1997, s 243 specifically includes the kinds of payments listed in TCA 1997, s 237 and in TCA 1997, s 104. Charges on income comprise of:

(a)   yearly interest (see **4.305**);

(b)   annuities and other annual payments (see *Annual payments* in **4.301**);

(c)   payments mentioned in TCA 1997, s 104 (see *Mining and other rents* in **4.301** and **4.303.7**), being—

    (i)   any rent (including a toll, duty, royalty or annual or periodic payment in the nature of rent, whether payable in money or money's worth) payable in respect of any premises or easements which are used, occupied or enjoyed in connection with any of the concerns the profits or gains of which are taxable under Case I(b) of Schedule D (quarries, mines, ironworks, gasworks, canals, waterworks, docks, tolls, railways, bridges, ferries and other concerns of a similar nature), and

    (ii)   any yearly interest, annuity or other annual payment reserved in respect of or charged on or issuing out of any premises, not being a rent or payment in respect of an easement;

(d)   payments mentioned in TCA 1997, s 237(2) (see below);

(e)   any other (ie, short) interest payable on an advance from a bank carrying on a *bona fide* banking business in a Member State of the European Communities or from a person who in the opinion of the Revenue Commissioners is:

    (i)   *bona fide* carrying on a business as a member of a stock exchange in a Member State of the European Communities; or

    (ii)   *bona fide* carrying on the business of a discount house in a Member State of the European Communities.

As regards (d) above, TCA 1997, s 237(2) commences as follows: "Where any royalty or other sum is paid in respect of the user of a patent wholly out of profits or gains brought into charge to income tax ...". As already explained in **4.302**, payments made by Irish resident companies are not paid out of profits or gains brought into charge to income tax; the treatment of annual payments and other charges on income of companies is governed principally by corporation tax provisions and not at all by TCA 1997, s 237. So what are the payments "mentioned in" TCA 1997, s 237(2)? Do they comprise "any royalty or other sum .. paid in respect of the user of a patent" or the extended "any royalty or other sum .. paid in respect of the user of a patent wholly out of profits or gains brought into charge to income tax"? If the latter, patent royalties paid by a company would not fall within the definition of charges on income.

For the purposes of (e) above, *bank* means:

(a)   a person who is the holder of a licence granted under section 9 of the Central Bank Act 1971; or

(b)   a person who holds a licence or other similar authorisation under the law of any other Member State of the EC which corresponds to a licence granted under section 9,

and includes a building society within the meaning of TCA 1997, s 256(1), ie a building society within the meaning of the Building Societies Act, 1989, or a society established in accordance with the law of any other Member State of the European Communities which corresponds to that Act.

It is interesting to note in the pre-Consolidation legislation that CTA 1976 s 10(3)(a) (now TCA 1997, s 243(4)(a)), when referring to the payments mentioned in ITA 1967 s 433(2) (now TCA 1997, s 237(2)) refers to them as "yearly interest, etc, *payable wholly out of taxed profits*" so that there is a clear indication here that the extended description of those payments was meant to apply (but apparently without adverting to the fact that this would prevent patent royalties from being charges on income). In the equivalent UK provision, from which TCA 1997, s 237 has been copied, the reference to "wholly out of profits or gains brought into charge to income tax" is separated from the description of the payments themselves so that it is not necessary to take that phrase into account at all in relation to the meaning of charges on income. To secure the inclusion of patent royalties in the definition of charges on income, the wording of TCA 1997, s 237(2) would need to have been on the lines of: "Where any royalty or other sum *paid* in respect of the user of a patent *is paid* wholly out of profits or gains ..." In that way, it would have been clear that the payments "mentioned in" that subsection were simply "any royalty or other sum paid in respect of the user of a patent".

No payment mentioned in (a) to (d) above made by a company to a non-resident person will be treated as a charge on income unless:

(a)   the paying company, in accordance with the provisions of TCA 1997, s 238, or TCA 1997, s 238 as applied by TCA 1997, s 246 (yearly interest), deducts income tax for which it accounts under TCA 1997, s 238 and s 239 or, as the case may be, under TCA 1997, s 238 and 241 (payments made by non-resident companies – see **4.304**);

(b)   the payment is made out of income brought into charge to tax under Case III of Schedule D and which arises from foreign securities and possessions (TCA 1997, s 243(5)); or

(c)   in respect of accounting periods ending on or after 3 February 2005, the payment is one to which TCA 1997, s 238 or 246(2) do not apply by virtue of TCA 1997, s 267I (see below).

In the case of (a) above, the requirement to deduct tax is waived where:

(i)   the paying company is authorised by the Revenue Commissioners to pay gross, eg where such authorisation is given by virtue of the terms of a double tax treaty providing that interest paid to a non-resident is exempt from Irish tax;

(ii)   the interest is interest referred to in TCA 1997, s 246(3)(a), (b) or (h) (see **4.305** – (a), (b) and (h) in list of recipients to whom interest may be paid without deduction of tax); or

(iii)   the interest is interest to which TCA 1997, s 64(2) applies, ie interest on quoted Eurobonds (see **4.305**).

Regarding (c) above, TCA 1997, s 267I (see **4.307.3**) provides that where the withholding provisions of TCA 1997, s 238 (see **4.303**), 246(2) (see **4.305**) or 257 (DIRT) would otherwise apply to a payment of interest or royalties to which the Interest and Royalties Directive applies, they will not apply to that payment. Thus, for the purposes of TCA 1997, s 243, and for accounting periods ending on or after 3 February 2005, payments exempted from withholding tax under the Directive will not be denied a deduction as a charge on income on that account.

The following payments are not treated as charges on income:

(a)   in the case of any royalty or other sum in respect of the user of a patent, where the payment is in respect of capital expenditure and, in any other case, where the payment is charged to capital (TCA 1997, s 243(6)(a));

(b)   any payment which is not ultimately borne by the paying company (TCA 1997, s 243(6)(a));

(c)   any payment which is not made under a liability incurred for a valuable and sufficient consideration (TCA 1997, s 243(6)(b));

(d)   in the case of a non-resident company, any payment not incurred wholly and exclusively for the purposes of a trade carried on by it in the State through a branch or agency (TCA 1997, s 243(6)(b));

(e)   dividends or other distributions (TCA 1997, s 243(1));

(f)   any payment which is deductible in computing profits or any description of profits, eg interest as a business expense for Case I or Case II purposes (TCA 1997, s 81(2)(a)), interest as a deduction in computing rental income (TCA 1997, s 97(2)(e)) or foreign rental income (TCA 1997, s 71(4)), or any annual interest, annuity or annual payment paid to a non-resident person out of income from foreign securities and possessions (TCA 1997, s 71(1)(c)) (TCA 1997, s 243(1)).

As regards (a) above, in the case of patent royalty payments that are revenue in nature, they will not be prevented from being regarded as charges on income solely because they are included in the cost of an asset in accordance with IFRS (see **3.305.5**).

In relation to (b), if a payment of interest has been guaranteed, it would seem that any payment by the guarantor is a payment of interest (see *Westminster Bank Executor and Trustee Co (Channel Islands) Ltd v National Bank of Greece* 46 TC 472 (**4.304** above) and *Hendy v Hadley* [1980] STC 292). If the guarantor, being a company, is subsequently reimbursed, the payment would not have been ultimately borne by it and would not constitute a charge on income.

The requirement in (c) that the payment must be made under a liability incurred for a valuable and sufficient consideration does not apply to certain covenanted payments as detailed above. In *Ball v National and Grindlays Bank Ltd* 47 TC 287, payments made under covenant to a non-charitable trust to provide for the education of employees' children were held to have been provided for insufficient consideration. The consideration in the form of the business advantage secured by the covenant (employee goodwill) was manifestly inadequate to be seen as representing a fair equivalent of the liability incurred.

The meaning of charges on income for the purposes of TCA 1997, s 243 is subject "to any other express exceptions". The exceptions would include the following which, however, are no longer relevant:

(a) charges on income payable out of income consisting of exempted trading operations for the purposes of CTA 1976 Part V (exempted Shannon trading operations – no longer relevant) (CTA 1976 s 77);

(b) interest on money borrowed by non-resident financial concerns for the purchase of tax-free securities (TCA 1997, s 846(2)(b)).

4.403   Interest as a charge on income

4.403.1   Introduction

TCA 1997, s 243(7) prohibits the treatment of interest as a charge on income unless the interest is in respect of a loan to a company to defray money applied for a purpose mentioned in TCA 1997, s 247(2) and the conditions specified in TCA 1997, s 247(3) are satisfied. Apart from business interest, interest allowable in computing Case V profits and annual interest allowable in computing certain Case III income, a company may only obtain relief in respect of interest which is a charge on income.

It is relevant to note that interest which satisfies the conditions of TCA 1997, s 247 will not be a charge on income unless it also comes within the definition of "charges on income" as defined in **4.402** above. Accordingly, interest which is not yearly interest, and which is not interest of the kind described in (*e*) of that definition (interest paid to a bank carrying on a *bona fide* banking business etc), will not be a charge on income even if it falls within TCA 1997, s 247.

TCA 1997, s 247(5) provides that interest eligible for relief under TCA 1997, s 247 is to be deducted from or set off against the income (not being income referred to in TCA 1997, s 25(2)(a)) of the borrower for the year of assessment in which the interest is paid.

This provision relates to years of assessment and will be of relevance only to non-resident companies not within the charge to corporation tax. Relief for interest qualifying under TCA 1997, s 247 will thus be available for offset against the Irish source income of non-resident companies which do not carry on a trade through a branch or agency in Ireland or, where they carry on such a trade, which have Irish source income which is not effectively connected with that branch or agency.

Thus, for example, a non-resident company which has borrowed money to invest in an Irish company would be entitled (subject to satisfying the conditions for relief in TCA 1997, s 247) to claim interest on those borrowings against its income in the form of dividends from the Irish company. The reference to TCA 1997, s 25(2)(a) above is to trading income arising through or from an Irish branch or agency or from property or rights used by, or held by or for, the branch or agency. Relief for interest is not available against such income by virtue of TCA 1997, s 247(5) but may well be available as a charge on income by virtue of TCA 1997, s 243(6)(b) (see **4.402** – item (d) in list of payments not treated as charges on income).

Where relief is given under TCA 1997, s 247 in respect of interest on a loan, no relief or deduction under any other provision of the Tax Acts may be given or allowed in respect of interest on the loan (TCA 1997, s 247(6)). This measure to ensure the prevention of a double deduction for interest is probably unnecessary; it is difficult to envisage circumstances in which interest relieved by virtue of TCA 1997, s 247(5) could be relieved under any other provision of the Tax Acts.

Interest relief is subject to anti-avoidance measures directed at certain related-party borrowing (see **4.403.5** below).

Interest swap payments

Interest swap payments, though related to the underlying interest, are not interest so accordingly do not qualify for relief under TCA 1997, s 247. Nevertheless, in certain circumstances, the Revenue may be prepared to agree that interest swap payments can be treated as increasing the underlying interest paid for the purposes of relief under TCA 1997, s 247. Interest swap receipts in similar circumstances would be treated as reducing the underlying interest payments so that relief would be available for interest net of such swap receipts.

4.403.2   Qualifying loans

A qualifying loan for the purposes of TCA 1997, s 247(2) is a loan to a company to defray money applied:

(a)   in acquiring any part of the share capital of:

    (i)   company which exists wholly or mainly for the purpose of carrying on a trade or trades;

    (ii)   a company whose income consists wholly or mainly of profits or gains chargeable to tax under Case V of Schedule D;

    (iii)   a company whose business consists wholly or mainly of the holding of stocks, shares or securities of a company described in (i) or (ii), or

(b)   in lending to a company referred to in (a) money which is used wholly and exclusively for the purposes of a trade or business of the company or of a connected company, or

(c) in paying off another loan in respect of which the conditions necessary for relief under TCA 1997, s 247(2) were satisfied. In practice, the Revenue accept that a holding company of another holding company may be treated as a company within TCA 1997, s 247(2)(a)(iii) (see (iii) above).

A company is connected with another company if it is one of the companies described in (a)(i), (ii) or (iii) above and if it is connected for the purposes of TCA 1997, s 10, but except for the purposes of TCA 1997, s 247(4A) (anti-avoidance in respect of certain related-party borrowing – see **4.403.5**). A company is connected with another company for the purposes of TCA 1997, s 10

(i) if the same person has control of both, or a person has control of one and persons connected with him, or he and persons connected with him, have control of the other, or

(ii) if a group of two persons has control of each company, and the groups either consist of the same persons or could be regarded as consisting of the same persons by treating (in one or more cases) a member of either group as replaced by a person with whom he is connected (TCA 1997, s 247(1)(b)).

This matter is examined in more detail in **2.305–306** and the meaning of "control" is as provided for in TCA 1997, s 432 and is considered in **2.401**.

A loan is not a qualifying loan unless it is made in connection with the application of the borrowed money for one or more of the purposes permitted by TCA 1997, s 247(2) and is made either at the time of, or within a reasonable time of, that application (TCA 1997, s 247(4). Any application of the proceeds of a loan for a non-qualifying purpose before being applied for a qualifying purpose will operate to deny relief. To ensure entitlement to relief, documentation relating to the loan should specify the purpose, which of course should be a qualifying purpose, for which the loan is being made and the proceeds should then be applied for that purpose and for no other purpose.

One of the purposes for which a qualifying loan may be taken up is to pay off another loan which itself satisfied the conditions for relief under TCA 1997, s 247(2). Specifically, the replaced loan should be one in respect of which relief could have been obtained had it not been paid off (and, if it was an interest free loan, where interest relief could have been obtained if it had been interest bearing). This further qualifying purpose allows for a qualifying replacement loan to be replaced itself, since the first replacement loan will have fulfilled the conditions for relief under TCA 1997, s 247(2).

The requirement regarding the purpose of the borrowing need only be fulfilled at the time the loan is advanced. For example, if the investee company (referred to as "the company concerned") is a holding company at the time the investor company defrays the borrowed money, but ceases to be so while the investor company ("the borrower") continues to pay interest, the loan will continue to be a qualifying loan.

It is possible to have a qualifying loan where the borrower has been formed or acquired to carry on a trade but where no trade has yet been carried on at the time the borrowed money has been defrayed; the relevant condition is that the company "*exists wholly or mainly to carry on a trade or trades*. As to what would be the position in that case where the borrower never in fact commences to carry on any trade, the legislation is unclear. To satisfy the trading condition in the first place, it would be necessary to be able to demonstrate by some objective means that a trade is about to be carried on. In that case, failure to commence any trading operations would be quite exceptional. In practice it is difficult to envisage a case in which an borrower would not recover money which had been invested or onlent once it is clear that the intended trade will not materialise.

A more likely possibility would be the failure of a borrower to which borrowed money had been onlent to continue to use that money wholly and exclusively for the purposes of its trade. Certainly it is necessary that the money onlent should initially be so used. It would seem that the correct view is that the money should continue to be used wholly and exclusively for trading purposes for as long as the borrower requires to obtain interest relief. While the status of the borrower is a matter for consideration only at the time at which it defrays the money it has borrowed, the requirement that the proceeds onlent must be "money which *is used* wholly and exclusively for trading purposes would seem to preclude any other use for that money at any time.

In a case where the company concerned is a pure holding company, it is necessary that money onlent to it be used wholly and exclusively for the purposes of its *business*; the question of using the money in connection with a trade does not arise here. As to what business use would qualify in this context is not fully clear. Since the business of a pure holding company might consist of no more than acquiring and holding stocks, shares and securities of trading or rental companies, it could only use money borrowed to acquire such investments. The company concerned, the holding company, would itself qualify for interest relief, subject to satisfying the conditions of TCA 1997, s 247(3), but the borrower would qualify only if the further onlending by the holding company could be shown to be for the purposes of its business. (For a discussion on the meaning of "business", see **13.304**). It would seem that that use of the moneys onlent to the company concerned would indeed be a qualifying use given the nature of its business as a holding company. Furthermore, if the trading or rental companies to which the moneys had been further onlent are "connected" companies of the holding company, the condition regarding use would be fulfilled in any event.

The question of what constitutes the use of money wholly and exclusively for the purposes of the trade or business of the company concerned will not normally give rise to difficulty. It would seem that the requirement can be interpreted broadly and that it would be satisfied as long as the moneys onlent are used in any way in connection with the investee company's trade or business. The reference to "business" here may give some additional comfort in this respect.

Example 4.403.2.1

Allegro Ltd borrowed €1,000,000 from its parent company some years ago and used the proceeds mainly to purchase fixed assets for its trade and to some extent to fund working capital requirements. Interest on this borrowing has been allowed as a deduction against trading income. In accordance with long standing practice, the fact that most of the borrowing has been used to purchase capital assets has not resulted in any of the related interest being treated as capital expenditure.

Following a group reorganisation, Allegro Ltd has become a subsidiary of a new holding company, Presto Ltd, whose function is to act as "banker" for the group. Accordingly, Presto Ltd borrows €1,000,000 and lends the proceeds to Allegro Ltd. Allegro Ltd repays the original €1,000,000 loan.

The question that arises is whether the use of the moneys onlent by Presto Ltd to Allegro Ltd to enable it to repay its original borrowing is the use of those moneys wholly and exclusively for the purposes of the trade or business of Allegro Ltd. It would seem that that would be the case. The use of the money advanced by Presto Ltd to repay Allegro Ltd's original borrowing, the proceeds of which had been used for trading purposes, would itself be the use of moneys for a trading purpose. The position is no different from the use of moneys borrowed to repay trade creditors; in both cases moneys are being used to satisfy indebtedness which has arisen solely in a trading context.

In *Macniven v Westmoreland Investments Ltd* [2001] STC 237, accrued interest was paid by a property-holding company out of the proceeds of an interest-free loan. The interest-free loan, which was made by the pension scheme whose trustees indirectly owned the company, was made partly to secure the orderly winding down of the company and partly to facilitate the payment of the accrued interest so as to qualify the interest as a charge on income. The company was held to be an investment company for UK tax purposes although it was being wound down. The payments of interest, which had been made wholly out of money borrowed for the purpose, were held to be payments of interest for the purposes of the legislation dealing with deductions for charges on income (see also **4.403.5** below).

Where the money borrowed is used to acquire share capital of the company concerned, there are no requirements relating to the use to which the moneys subscribed are to be employed by that company.

4.403.3 Conditions for relief

The conditions specified in TCA 1997, s 247(3) to be satisfied by the borrower are that:

(a) when the interest is paid, the borrower has a material interest in the company concerned or in a company connected with that company;

(b) for the period from the application of the proceeds of the loan until the interest is paid, at least one director of the borrower was also a director of the company concerned or of a company connected with that company; and

(c) the borrower did not in the period mentioned in (b) recover any capital from the company concerned or from a company connected with that company.

A *material interest* in relation to a company means the beneficial ownership of, or the ability to control, directly or through the medium of a connected company or connected companies or by any other indirect means, more than 5% of the ordinary share capital of the company.

Unlike the conditions relating to a qualifying loan, which need to be satisfied only at the time the proceeds of the loan are defrayed, the above conditions for interest relief must continue to be satisfied for as long as relief is required.

Example 4.403.3.1

Andante Ltd lent €100,000 some years ago to Lento Ltd, a trading company in which it held 5% of the ordinary share capital. The money advanced was used at all times for the purposes of Lento's trade. One of Andante's directors is also a director of Lento Ltd. Andante Ltd recently acquired a further 0.5% of Lento's share capital so that it now has a material interest in that company. At the same time, Andante Ltd has become obliged to pay off the €100,000 loan and to find replacement borrowings from another source. It does this and wishes to claim interest relief under TCA 1997, s 247 on the basis that it now fulfils the material interest condition for relief.

The new loan is not used to defray money applied in lending to Lento Ltd; it has replaced a loan which was used to advance money to Lento Ltd for the purposes of that company's trade and which therefore fulfilled the conditions of TCA 1997, s 247(2), ie the replaced loan was a qualifying loan. Interest relief was not available, however, because Andante Ltd did not have a material interest in Lento Ltd at the time the interest on the loan was paid.

At the time the loan was replaced, however, the material interest condition was fulfilled so that relief could have been obtained in respect of that loan had it not been paid off. The replacement loan is therefore a qualifying loan. It remains to decide whether Andante Ltd can now obtain interest relief in respect of the new loan.

Assuming that there has been no recovery of capital from Lento Ltd, interest relief may be claimed as Andante Ltd will have a material interest in Lento Ltd at the time interest is paid and there will be at least one director on the board of both companies throughout the period from the application of the proceeds of the loan to the time interest is paid.

The inclusion of connected companies with the company concerned allows for relief for interest on a more flexible basis than would otherwise be the case. The condition regarding use of funds onlent may be fulfilled either by the company concerned or by its connected company. The material interest condition for relief to the borrower allows for a material interest in the company concerned or in a company connected with that company. The requirement for a common director can be met by ensuring that at least one director of the borrower is also a director of the company concerned or of a company connected with that company.

4.403.4 Recovery of capital

The third condition for relief is that the borrower should not have recovered, or be deemed to have recovered, any capital from the company concerned or from a company connected with that company during the period from the application of the proceeds of the loan until the interest was paid or, in certain circumstances, within the period beginning two years before the date the loan proceeds were invested (TCA 1997, s 247(3)(c)). It is inevitable that some such rule should operate here as otherwise the essential purpose of TCA 1997, s 247 would be frustrated. For example, a company could obtain a loan, onlend the proceeds to a company in which it has a material interest and then withdraw an equivalent amount of money from that company, or from another company that is connected with that company. The money withdrawn could be used for a non-business purpose. Interest relief would be claimed on its borrowings which had been onlent. The rules relating to recovery of capital are contained in TCA 1997, s 249.

If, in the case of a qualifying loan, at any time after the application of the proceeds of the loan the borrower recovers any amount of capital from the company concerned or from a company connected with that company, or is deemed to have recovered any amount of capital from the company concerned, and does not use the amount recovered, or an amount equal to the amount deemed to have been recovered, to repay the loan, the borrower will be treated as if it had at that time repaid out of the loan an amount equal to the amount of capital recovered. From that point, the interest in respect of which relief may be claimed will be reduced by an amount equal to interest on the amount of capital recovered or deemed to be recovered (TCA 1997, s 249(1)(a)(iii)). Where part only of a loan fulfils the relief conditions in TCA 1997, s 247, the reduction is to be made in priority from interest relating to the qualifying part of the loan (TCA 1997, s 249(1)(b)).

Where relief is claimed for interest on a substituted loan (see (c) in **4.403.2**), the rules relating to recovery of capital apply as if both the substituted and the replacement loans were one loan (TCA 1997, s 249(3)). Accordingly, where interest relief on a replaced loan would have been restricted following a recovery of capital, that restriction applies to interest on the replacement loan.

Specified loan

As is seen below, the recovery of capital rules are modified in certain circumstances where the repayment of a loan is of a "specified loan" (essentially a loan for trading purposes). A *specified loan*, in relation to a company, is:

(i)   any loan or advance made to the company before 6 February 2003 (other than a loan referred to in (ii)); or

(ii)   any loan or advance in respect of which any interest paid is deductible, or, if interest were charged would be deductible, or, if the company were within the charge to Irish tax, would be deductible –

     (I)   in computing the company's profits or gains for the purpose of Case I of Schedule D; or

     (II)   in computing the company's profits or gains for the purpose of Case V of Schedule D (TCA 1997, s 249(1)(a)(i)).

Recovery of capital

A borrower is treated as having recovered an amount of capital from the company concerned or from a connected company if:

(a)   it receives consideration of that amount or value for the sale of any part of the ordinary share capital of the company concerned or of a connected company, or receives consideration of that amount or value by way of repayment of any part of that share capital;

(b)   the company concerned or a connected company repays that amount of a loan or advance from the borrower; or

(c)   the borrower receives consideration of that amount or value for assigning any debt due to it from the company concerned or from a connected company (TCA 1997, s 249(2)(a)).

Recovery of capital in the relevant period

In relation to a loan to which TCA 1997, s 247 applies, a recovery of capital in the relevant period can result in a restriction or denial of interest relief. The *relevant period* means the period beginning two years before, and ending on, the date of application of the proceeds of the loan.

    Where at any time in the relevant period in relation to a loan to which TCA 1997, s 247 applies, the borrower recovered any amount of capital from the company concerned, except in the case of a repayment of a specified loan, the borrower will be treated as having, immediately after the application of the loans proceeds, repaid out of the loan an amount equal to the amount of the capital recovered. Interest in respect of which relief may be claimed will then be reduced by an amount equal to interest on the amount of capital so recovered, The recovery of capital will, however, not be taken in account to the extent that the amount recovered was applied by the borrower—

(i)   in acquiring share capital or in lending in accordance with TCA 1997, s 247(2(a) or (b) (see (a) and (b) under **4.403.2** above); or

(ii)   before the application of the loan proceeds, in repaying any other loan to which TCA 1997, s 247 applies (TCA 1997, s 249(1)(a)(ii)).

The borrower will not, for the above purposes, be treated as having repaid an amount out of a loan to the extent of any amount of capital recovered that has previously been treated as being a repayment of a loan. Thus, a recovery of capital within the two year relevant period that has already had the effect of restricting or denying interest relief on another TCA 1997, s 247 loan will not be taken into account again.

Deemed recovery of capital

The borrower may be deemed to have recovered capital from the company concerned. Where the company concerned is a company to which TCA 1997, s 247(2)(a)(ii) applies (ie, a company whose business consists wholly or mainly of the holding of stocks, shares or securities of trading companies or rental companies – see **4.403.2** above – but see further below about this), the borrower is deemed to have recovered from the company concerned an amount equal to the amount of any capital recovered by that company from another company where more than 50% of the ordinary share capital of that other company is directly owned by the company concerned, but only to the extent that the amount is not applied by the company concerned:

(i)   in repaying any loan or part of a loan made to it by the borrower (since that constitutes a recovery of capital by the borrower in any event);

(ii)   in the redemption, repayment of purchase of any of its ordinary share capital acquired by the borrower (again, since that constitutes a recovery of capital by the borrower in any event);

(iii)   in acquiring share capital or in lending in accordance with TCA 1997, s 247(2(a) or (b) (see (a) and (b) under **4.403.2** above); or

(iv)   in repaying a loan to which TCA 1997, s 247 applies (TCA 1997, s 249(2)(aa)(i)).

In this connection, there are rules relating to the recovery of capital by the company concerned similar to those relating to the borrower. The company concerned is treated as having recovered an amount of capital from another company if:

(a)   it receives consideration of that amount or value for the sale of any part of the ordinary share capital of the other company, or receives consideration of that amount or value by way of repayment of any part of that share capital;

(b)   the other company repays that amount of a loan or advance from the company concerned, other than a repayment in respect of a specified loan; or

(c)   the company concerned receives consideration of that amount or value for assigning any debt due to it from the other company (TCA 1997, s 249(2)(aa)(ii)).

It may happen that more than one borrower has made a loan to, or has acquired share capital of, the company concerned. In that event, the amount deemed to have been recovered in accordance with the above rules is to be apportioned between the borrowers in proportion to the aggregate amount of any loan made and any money applied by each borrower in acquiring that share capital. If the borrowers agree between them to such other apportionment of the amount as they may consider appropriate, and jointly so specify in writing to the inspector, the amount deemed to have been so recovered will be apportioned accordingly (TCA 1997, s 249(2)(aa)(iii)).

As seen above, TCA 1997, s 249(2)(aa)(i) refers to a company concerned to which TCA 1997, s 247(2)(a)(ii) applies. Since that subparagraph applies only in a case where the borrower has applied the money borrowed in acquiring ordinary share capital of the company concerned, it can be argued that TCA 1997, s 249(2)(aa)(i) does not apply in a case where the borrower has used the money borrowed to make a loan. Clearly, however, this narrower interpretation is not intended as can be seen from TCA 1997, s 249(2)(aa)(iii) above which envisages a borrowing company either making a loan or applying money in acquiring share capital.

It will be seen that the recovery of any amount which is used to reduce the borrower's loan has no effect on subsequent relief for interest paid. Interest payments from that time will of course be lower by reason of the reduction in the amount of the loan, but full relief will be available for the reduced interest payable. Clearly, where any amount recovered is used to repay other (non-qualifying) borrowings, relief in respect of subsequent interest payments will be restricted.

The repayment by the company concerned or a connected company of an amount of a loan or advance from the borrower is a recovery of capital whether or not the repayment relates to the qualifying loan or to some other loan.

In the case of a sale of share capital or the assignment of a debt otherwise than by way of a bargain made at arm's length, the sale or assignment is deemed to be for consideration of an amount equal to the market value of the share capital or debt in question (TCA 1997, s 249(2)(b)).

Where a loan is a qualifying loan by reason of having replaced another qualifying loan (TCA 1997, s 247(2)(c)), the recovery of capital rules apply as if both the original loan and the loan which replaced it were one loan. Accordingly, any recovery of capital after the application of the proceeds of the original loan is taken into account for the purposes of restricting relief, and any restriction of relief that applied to the original loan will also apply to the replacement loan.

In practice, where a recovery of capital has been made, the calculation of interest qualifying for relief should be relatively straightforward. For the accounting period in the which the recovery is made, the full amount of interest paid in respect of the loan is first identified, and from that amount is deducted an amount of interest relating to the amount of capital recovered. This procedure will be followed for each subsequent period in which interest on the loan is paid.

Example 4.403.4.1

Some years ago, Mercury Ltd borrowed €100,000 which it used to subscribe €80,000 for 10% of the ordinary share capital in Apollo Ltd. €15,000 was lent to Apollo Ltd for working capital purposes in connection with its trade, and the balance of €5,000 was lent to Mars Ltd, a connected company of Apollo Ltd, in connection with its business of renting property. One director of Mercury Ltd has at all relevant times also been on the board of Apollo Ltd.

At the beginning of its current accounting period, Mercury Ltd sold 50% of its shares in Apollo Ltd, then worth €70,000, to Quicksilver Ltd, a connected company, for €50,000 which it used to pay off part of the €100,000 loan. At the same time, the €15,000 loan to Apollo Ltd was assigned to a third party for full value while Mars Ltd repaid its €5,000 loan. These amounts were used to purchase quoted shares.

Interest on the full €100,000 loan qualified for relief under TCA 1997, s 247 up to the beginning of the current accounting period. For the current accounting period, the amount of interest qualifying for relief, assuming a rate of 10% applied, is as follows:

	€	€
€50,000 @ 10% =		5,000
Less:		
(i) shares sold (deemed to be at market value)	70,000	
– used to reduce loan	50,000	
	20,000	
(ii) debt assigned	15,000	
(iii) Mars Ltd loan repaid	5,000	
Capital recovered not used to reduce loan	40,000	
€40,000 @ 10% =		4,000
Interest relief		1,000

4.403.5 Anti-avoidance

TCA 1997, s 817A

TCA 1997, s 817A provides for a disallowance of interest payments made on or after 29 February 2000 and which arise out of a tax avoidance scheme. One type of scheme at which the provision is directed involves the drawing down of a loan for a number of years with the related interest being paid in advance for the full term of the loan. A scheme of this kind was possible because interest allowed as a charge on income for an accounting period is allowed on the basis of the interest paid, rather than accrued, in the period so that relief could be claimed currently for an amount which largely related to future periods. Such schemes can also be in a form which secures that the economic position of the borrower is restored to what it was shortly after the commencement of the scheme. The case of *Cairns v MacDiarmid* [1983] STC 178 was concerned with such a scheme where an interest deduction was denied but on the basis of the general anti-avoidance doctrine enunciated (but not followed in Ireland) in *Ramsay (WT) Ltd v CIR* [1981] STC 174.

TCA 1997, s 817A(1) provides that relief may not be given for interest paid where a scheme has been effected or arrangements have been made such that the sole or main benefit expected to accrue to the borrower from the transaction under which the interest is paid is a reduction in liability to tax. In the case of a payment which would give rise to a claim to group relief in respect of excess interest as a charge on income, the question as to what benefit might be expected to accrue from the scheme is to be determined by reference to the positions of both the claimant and surrendering companies taken together (TCA 1997, s 817A(2)).

TCA 1997, s 817A is copied from ICTA 1988 s 787 in the UK and in this context it is interesting to note the view of the UK Inland Revenue as to the circumstances in which the anti-avoidance measure is likely to be invoked. At the time of the introduction of ICTA 1988 s 787, undertakings were given by Ministers to the effect that the Revenue would not seek to use the legislation to deny relief in cases of genuine commercial arrangements designed to minimise the burden of tax. An important distinction was drawn between tax planning involving a judiciously arranged borrowing scheme and an out and out avoidance scheme. The Inland Revenue indicated that the section would not therefore easily be invoked.

In *Macniven v Westmoreland Investments Ltd* [2001] STC 237, accrued interest was paid by a property-holding company out of the proceeds of an interest-free loan. The interest-free loan, which was from the pension scheme whose trustees indirectly owned the company, was made partly to secure the orderly winding down of the company and partly to facilitate the payment of the accrued interest so as to qualify the interest as a charge on income. In the Court of Appeal, reversing the Chancery Division and restoring the decision of the Special Commissioners, the payments of interest, which had been made wholly out of money borrowed for the purpose, were held to be payments of interest for the purposes of the legislation dealing with deductions for charges on income. This decision was confirmed in the House of Lords where it was held that the interest payments were unquestionably genuine payments and that there was no justification for giving the word "payment" any meaning other than the satisfaction of an obligation to pay. It was found that the interest was not paid pursuant to a tax avoidance motive as it had arisen under original loans taken out for genuine and bona fide reasons.

The Court considered ICTA 1988 s 787 and decided that the interest payments did not come within the terms of that section. In his judgment, Peter Gibson LJ rejected the Revenue contention that the transaction under which the interest was paid was that which made it possible for the interest to be paid (ie, the interest-free loan) and that the main benefit to the company was its anticipated liability to shelter profits from tax. The preferred view was that the transaction under which the interest was paid was the loan agreement. ICTA 1988 s 787 in its natural construction does not require an examination of the circumstances surrounding each payment of interest. Reference was made to the Ministerial statement made at the time of introduction of the section to the effect that the intention of the measure was to prevent tax avoidance by what purported to be payments of interest in advance on large artificial borrowings. Reference was also made to a statement by the Financial Secretary to the Treasury pointing out that the purpose of the legislation was to remove the eligibility for tax relief for interest paid under a scheme where the sole or main benefit that might be expected to accrue from the *loan transaction* would be the obtaining of such relief.

The judgment in the *Macniven* case is also notable for its emphasis on the distinction to be made between unacceptable tax avoidance and acceptable tax mitigation. Tax mitigation involves the taxpayer taking advantage of a fiscally attractive option afforded to him by the tax legislation and the genuine suffering of the economic consequences intended to be suffered in taking this course. It would be wrong as a matter of statutory construction to deny to the parties concerned the consequences of the exercise of their right to adopt whatever course was more advantageous to them to crystallise a genuine tax loss, even if there was a tax purpose influencing their choice. The company in this case had a genuine accrued interest liability under genuine loans and the fact that it borrowed from the trustees the money used to pay the interest did not mean that the payment of interest was not as genuine as the loan.

Excess charges on income may be surrendered within a group of companies (see **8.305.5**). Thus it is possible in a group situation to convert interest deductible at a low rate of tax, as in the case of a manufacturing company, into a standard rate deduction where borrowing is undertaken by a group finance company. Borrowings of the finance company could be onlent to the manufacturing company at a low rate of interest or even interest-free. The resulting unused interest deduction would then be surrendered as excess charges on income to a group company taxable at the standard rate of corporation tax thereby converting the tax value of the interest deduction from 10% to standard rate (or, in a more likely future scenario, from 12.5% to 25%). Although likely to be undertaken so that the benefit accruing is a reduction of a tax liability, a borrowing arrangement of this nature is unlikely to fall foul of TCA 1997, s 817A if the rationale underlying the *Macniven* decision is not to be disturbed.

Related-party borrowing

Outline

TCA 1997, s 247(4A) is an anti-avoidance measure that follows an EU trend of expanding the scope of thin capitalisation provisions to prevent erosion of the tax base, although no broadly-based thin capitalisation provisions are included in the Irish legislation. Interest relief is denied in the case of related-party (under common control as to more than 50%) borrowing used to finance the acquisition of a related entity. The target of this anti-avoidance measure is "internal debt" transactions in which a new holding company is geared with related-party borrowing for the purpose of acquiring an existing operating entity. The effect of such avoidance is the introduction of interest expense which erodes the Irish tax base. TCA 1997, s 247(4A) has effect in respect of borrowings made on or after 2 February 2006.

The effect of the anti-avoidance measure is to deny interest relief for related-party borrowing (or third party borrowing financed back-to-back from a related-party) used to:

(a) acquire equity in a company where either that company or the company from which the equity is acquired is a related company; or

(b) make a loan to a holding company which that company uses to acquire capital of a company where either that company or the company from which the capital is acquired is a related company.

Certain borrowing transactions remain unaffected by TCA 1997, s 247(4A). Relief is unaffected where third party borrowing is used to acquire a company, whether related or not, and interest on related-party borrowing continues to qualify for relief where the borrowed funds are used to finance the acquisition of a hitherto unrelated entity. Relief is also unaffected where the related-party borrowing is used to onlend money to a related trading company for use in its trade, or to replace a related-party borrowing that took place before 2 February 2006, or is a qualifying third party borrowing that took place at any time.

The anti-avoidance measure is subject to a number of exclusions which take account of the fact that many related-party borrowings do not have a tax avoidance or base erosion purpose. Interest relief is not denied in the case of related-party borrowing used to finance an acquisition by subscription of newly issued shares and which meets two tests. Firstly, the purpose of the transaction must be the provision of equity to increase the capital of a trade or business; secondly, the objective of the transaction must not include the provision of funds to the original lender (or to a related party of that lender) to achieve the indirect repayment of the loan, for example through a "round-trip" cash transaction.

To the extent that related-party borrowing (after 2 February 2006) is used for an investment that generates equivalent foreign interest or dividend income (both of which are subject to tax in Ireland) or Irish interest income that is not itself tax deductible in the hands of the investing company or any related company, a corresponding amount of interest payable remains deductible.

Denial of relief

Interest relief is denied in the case of a loan to an investing company to defray money applied:

(i)   an acquiring any part of the ordinary share capital of, or

(ii)   in lending to a company money which is used directly or indirectly to acquire any part of the capital (which would include shares other than ordinary shares but is unlikely to be intended to include securities, eg loan stock) of,

a company, where the acquisition is from the company or another company being in either case a company which, at the time the capital is acquired or immediately after that time, was connected with the investing company and if the loan is made to the investing company by a person who is connected with that company (TCA 1997, s 247(4A)(a)).

The reference in (ii) above to an "indirect" use of money onlent must include any case in which the capital of a company is acquired as a result of the money being onlent. It would appear that for this purpose there is no limit to the number of companies through which the onlent funds might pass before the acquisition is made as long as it is the case that the acquisition is the outcome of the investing company onlending the moneys it has borrowed.

Where, as part of or in connection with a scheme or arrangement for the making of a loan to the investing company by a person (the "first-mentioned person") who is not connected with the investing company, another person who is connected with the investing company directly or indirectly makes a loan to, or a deposit with, or otherwise provides funds to, the first-mentioned person or to a person who is connected with the first-mentioned person, the loan made to the investing company is treated as being a loan made to the investing company by a person with whom it is connected (TCA 1997, s 247(4A)(b)).

Transactions not affected: use of funds for trade or business

Relief will not be denied in accordance with TCA 1997, s 247(4A)(a) above in the case of interest on a related-party loan (the "original loan") made to a company to finance a share subscription, ie where:

(a)   the original loan is used to defray money applied—

  (i)   in acquiring ordinary share capital of another company on the issue of the share capital by the other company, or

  (ii)   in lending to a company money which is used directly or indirectly for the purposes of acquiring ordinary share capital of another company on the issue of the share capital by the other company, and

(b)   the purpose of the transaction is to provide equity to increase the aggregate of the capital available to the other company for use by it wholly and exclusively in its trade or business and not to provide funds to the original lender, or related party of that lender, to bring about the indirect repayment of the loan, specifically where the transaction is not a part of any arrangement or understanding entered into in connection the original loan the purpose, or one of the purposes, of which is to provide moneys, directly or indirectly—

(i)   to the person (referred to in (ii) below as the "original lender") who made the original loan so as to achieve in that way, directly or indirectly, the effective repayment of the original loan or the greater part of it, or

(ii) to another person who is connected with the original lender so as to achieve in that way a provision of moneys that is, notwithstanding that the moneys are being provided (as part of the arrangement or understanding) to a person other than the original lender, equivalent to the achievement directly or indirectly of the effective repayment, referred to in (i) above, of the original loan or the greater part of it,

at a time before interest ceased to be payable by the investing company in respect of the original loan or such greater part of it (TCA 1997, s 247(4A)(c)).

Example 4.403.5.1

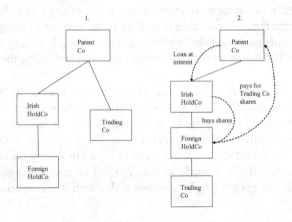

Irish HoldCo has borrowed from its parent company to acquire newly issued ordinary shares in Foreign HoldCo. Foreign HoldCo issues the shares for the purposes of increasing its capital for use by it wholly and exclusively for the purposes of its business as a holding company (in this case to facilitate its acquisition of Trading Co). By virtue of TCA 1997, s 247(4A)(c), however, Irish Holdco will be unable to claim a deduction for interest on the loan from Parent Co since the share issue is part of an arrangement or understanding one of the purposes of which is to provide moneys to Parent Co, the original lender.

Share capital issued to facilitate the repayment of a loan to the original lender will not always or necessarily prevent the investing company from obtaining relief. Thus, share capital will not be treated as issued by a company as part of an arrangement or understanding as envisaged in (b) above solely because it is used directly or indirectly in paying off to the original lender, or to a person connected with that lender, a loan, advance or debt (the "other loan")) other than the original loan where:

(a)   the other loan was used wholly and exclusively for the purposes of a trade or business of the company and not as part of any arrangement or understanding entered into in connection with the other loan the purpose or one of the purposes of which was to provide moneys, directly or indirectly—

   (i)   to a person (the "original lender") who made, or directly or indirectly funded, the other loan and thereby to achieve directly or indirectly the effective repayment of the other loan or the greater part of it, or

   (ii)   to another person who is connected with the original lender and thereby to achieve a provision of moneys that is, notwithstanding that the moneys are being provided (as part of the arrangement or understanding) to a person other than the original lender, equivalent to the achievement directly or indirectly of the effective repayment, referred to in (i), of the other loan or the greater part of it,

   at a time before interest ceased to be payable by the company in respect of the other loan or such greater part of it, and

(b)   interest on the other loan, if it had been made on or after 2 February 2006, would have been deductible in computing profits, or any description of profits, for the purposes of corporation tax—

   (i)   if the other loan had not been paid off, and

   (ii)   on the assumption, if the other loan was free of interest, that it carried interest (TCA 1997, s 247(4A)(h)).

Thus, it is permissible to use the proceeds of the share capital issue to pay off to the original lender, or to a connected person, another loan which was used wholly and exclusively for the purposes of a trade or business of the company issuing the shares but provided that other loan was not used as part of an arrangement or understanding intended to achieve its effective repayment or, where the other loan was made to a connected person, provided it was not used as part of an arrangement or understanding intended to achieve an outcome equivalent to its effective repayment to the original lender, and provided also that the other loan would satisfy the conditions for relief in force for loans made on or after 2 February 2006.

Relevant income exclusion

TCA 1997, s 247(4A)(e) provides that, to the extent that related-party borrowing is used for an investment as a result of which the interest on which relief is claimed is matched by foreign interest or dividend income (both being subject to tax in Ireland) or Irish interest income that is not itself tax deductible by the investing company or any company connected with it, a corresponding amount of interest payable will be allowable. (See more detailed treatment below.) In this connection, TCA 1997, s 247(4A)(d) describes that matching income (referred to as *relevant income*).

TCA 1997, s 247(4A)(d) provides that where the use, whether direct use by the investing company or subsequent indirect use through another company as investee or borrower or through a sequence of companies acting, in turn, as investees or borrowers, of a loan (the "original loan") received by the investing company involves lending or the acquisition of shares so that such use results in:

(i)   interest (which is not deductible in computing income or profits for corporation tax purposes by the investing company or any company connected with that company) being received in, or being receivable in respect of, an accounting period, so as to be income, or an amount credited in computing income, chargeable to corporation tax for that period; or

(ii) dividends or other distributions chargeable to corporation tax being received in an accounting period,

and the interest in (i) is, or the dividends or distributions in (ii) are, income of the investing company or of a connected company, being income that would not have arisen but for the direct use or indirect use of the original loan, that income is regarded as *relevant income*.

In a case in which, say, interest in (i) is not itself taxable income for Irish tax purposes but is taken into account in computing income, it is that "gross" interest (and not the net amount after an appropriate allocation of expenses) that constitutes relevant income.

As regards (ii) above, is the amount of any dividend to be taken into account the "cash" amount received or the dividend as "grossed up" for the purposes of double tax relief? Although the position is not clear, a reasonable approach might be to include the grossed up amount of the dividend except in a case where grossing up does not apply because credit relief is not available or, exceptionally, is not being claimed, in which case the actual amount of the dividend received would be included.

In certain circumstances (as envisaged by TCA 1997, s 247(4A)(f) - see below), interest that is not deductible may, for the purposes of (i) above, be deemed to be deductible interest thereby restricting the amount of interest payable that may be regarded as matched by relevant income.

The matching income treatment mentioned above is dealt with in TCA 1997, s 247(4A)(e). If relief for interest ("relevant interest") paid by the investing company in an accounting period (the "relevant accounting period") in respect of the original loan would otherwise be denied relief by virtue of TCA 1997, s 247(4A)(a), relief will nevertheless not be denied in respect of so much of the relevant interest as does not exceed the relevant income of the investing company for the relevant accounting period.

Where:

(a)   the relevant interest *does* exceed the relevant income of the investing company (giving rise to a *relevant excess*) for the relevant accounting period;

(b)   relief could not otherwise be claimed for corporation tax purposes in respect of the relevant interest to the extent of the relevant excess;

(c)   the investing company and a company connected with it (the "electing company") jointly elect and notify the inspector of taxes of that election in such form as the Revenue Commissioners may require; and

(d)   the aggregate value of relevant interest that may be deducted by virtue of the election, by one or more companies other than the investing company, does not exceed the relevant excess,

an amount of relevant interest equal to the relevant excess may be deducted from the total profits, reduced by any other relief from corporation tax, of the electing company, for the accounting period (the "second-mentioned period") for which the relevant income of the electing company is chargeable to corporation tax, as does not exceed the lesser of:

(i)　the amount of the relevant income of the electing company for the second-mentioned period which may be apportioned on a time basis to the relevant accounting period (by reference to the proportion which the length of the period common to the relevant accounting period and the second-mentioned accounting period bears to the length of the second-mentioned accounting period); and

(ii)　the amount by which the apportioned part of that relevant income of the electing company exceeds the aggregate of any amounts; being—

(I)　the amounts of any relief, which is referable to the second-mentioned accounting period, surrendered at any time by the electing company under TCA 1997 Part 12 Chapter 5 (corporation tax group relief provisions - see **8.3**), or

(II)　the amounts, not referred to in (I), of any losses which could have been, but were not, set off under TCA 1997, s 396(2) (see **4.101**) against profits of the second-mentioned accounting period.

Example 4.403.5.2

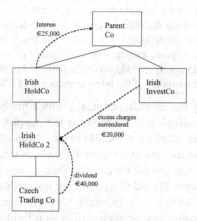

In the above structure, a parent company loan to Irish HoldCo was used to acquire the share capital of Irish HoldCo 2 which in turn used the proceeds to acquire Czech Trading Co. Relevant income of Irish HoldCo, the electing company, is €40,000 and the relevant excess is €25,000. Irish HoldCo 2 has also claimed group relief of €20,000 from Irish InvestCo. All relevant companies have identical accounting periods.

The amount of the total profits of Irish HoldCo 2 against which the relevant excess may be deducted is €20,000. Accordingly, no relief is available in respect of the balance of the relevant excess, €5,000.

Example 4.403.5.3

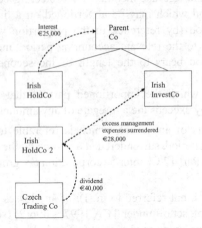

The position is the same as for Example **4.403.5.2** except that Irish HoldCo 2 has not claimed any group relief but instead has surrendered excess management expenses of €28,000 to Irish InvestCo for the relevant accounting period.

The total profits against which the relevant excess may be deducted are €40,000 but the relevant interest which may be deducted is limited to the lesser of (i) the relevant income and (ii) the excess of the relevant income over the amount of relief surrendered by Irish HoldCo 2 by way of group relief, ie €40,000 - €28,000 = €12,000. Accordingly, no relief is available in respect of the balance of the relevant excess, €13,000.

Relief for interest paid by the investing company which has been allowed by virtue of the "relevant income" exclusion is deemed for the purposes of TCA 1997 Sch 24 paragraph 4(5) (double tax relief - see **14.208**) to have been allocated by "the company concerned" to its relevant income by reference to which the relief was allowed. The foreign tax in respect of that relevant income is then disregarded for the purposes of TCA 1997 Sch 24 paragraphs 9E and 9F (pooling of tax credits: dividends - see **14.214**: interest - see **14.215**) (TCA 1997, s 247(4A)(e)). This reference is to a company's option to allocate charges on income against such profits as it thinks fit. In this instance, the interest deductible under TCA 1997, s 247 is to be allocated against the relevant income described above. If the relevant income is foreign income subject to credit relief, this mandatory allocation will operate to dilute that relief. Where the company concerned is not the investing company itself, any credit relief it is claiming in respect of relevant income will be restricted even though the relevant interest in question will be interest paid by the investing company.

Example 4.403.5.4

The following details are relevant to Power Investments Ltd for its latest accounting period:

	€
Interest received from Italian debtor	2,400
Italian withholding tax @ 10%	240
TCA s 247 interest paid by fellow group member	2,000
Corporation tax computation	
Income	2,400
TCA s 247 interest allocated	2,000

"Irish measure" of foreign income	400
Foreign tax rate (240/400) 60%	
Net foreign income (400 - 240)	160
Gross up @ 25% (lower rate)	213
Credit (213-160)	53
Excess credit (240-53)	187
Revised income (2,400-187)	2,213
Corporation tax @ 25%	553
Less: credit	53
Net tax payable	500
Without TCA 1997, s 247(4A)(e), the position would be:	
Income	2,400
Corporation tax @ 25%	600
Less: credit	240
Net tax payable	360

Example 4.403.5.5

The following details are relevant to Boyne Ltd for its latest accounting period:

	€
Interest received from Italian debtor	2,400
Italian withholding tax @ 10%	240
Trading expenses	1,600
TCA s 247 interest paid by fellow group member	2,000

Corporation tax computation

Trading profit	800
TCA s 247 interest allocated (max)	800
Therefore credit	Nil
Excess credit	240
Revised income (800-240)	560
Corporation tax @ 25%	70
Without TCA 1997, s 247(4A)(e), the position would be:	
Trading profit	800
Net foreign income (800-240)	560
Gross up @ 12.5%	640
Corporation tax @ 12.5%	80
Less: credit	80
Net payable	Nil

Example 4.403.5.6

The position is the same as in Example **4.403.5.4** except that group relief is claimed from the fellow group member in respect of excess charges (the TCA s 247 interest).

€

Corporation tax computation

Income	2,400
Less: group relief	2,000
"Irish measure" of foreign income	400
Net foreign income (400 - 240)	160
Gross up @ 25%	213
Corporation tax @ 25%	53
Less: credit	53
Net tax payable	Nil

In this case, the position is the same with or without TCA 1997, s 247(4A)(e).

A company's "relevant income" may be increased or reduced by an amount of profit or gain, or loss, as the case may be, directly related to that income or to the source of that income (eg, the loan in respect of which interest income arises) being an amount arising:

(a) by virtue of a change in a rate of exchange within the meaning of TCA 1997, s 79 (foreign currency: computation of income and chargeable gains – see **3.406**); or

(b) from any contract (hedging contract) entered into by the company for the purpose of eliminating or reducing the risk of loss being incurred by it due to a change in a rate of exchange (within the meaning of TCA 1997, s 79) or in a rate of interest (TCA 1997, s 247(4A)(g)).

Where, as part of or in connection with any scheme or arrangement for the making of a loan to any company (the "borrower") which is connected with the investing company, by a person (the "first-mentioned person") who is not connected with the investing company, another person who is connected with the investing company directly or indirectly makes a loan to, a deposit with, or otherwise provides funds to, the first-mentioned person or to a person who is connected with that person, interest payable by the first-mentioned person to the other person in respect of the loan, deposit or other funds is treated for the purposes of TCA 1997, s 247(4A)(d)(i) (interest not tax deductible by the investing company or a connected company - see above) as interest that *is* deductible in computing income or profits for corporation tax purposes by the investing company or a company connected with it (so that interest to that extent is not matched by relevant income and is accordingly not deductible to the investing company) (TCA 1997, s 247(4A)(f)).

Example 4.403.5.7

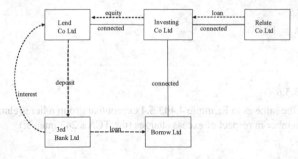

Investing Co Ltd has borrowed from Relate Co Ltd, a connected company, with a view to onlending the proceeds to Borrow Ltd, with which it is also connected. By virtue of TCA 1997, s 247(4A)(a) it will be unable to claim a deduction for interest on the loan from Relate Co Ltd. The above structure is accordingly set up with a view to taking advantage of the exception provided for by TCA 1997, s 247(4A)(d), (e). Investing Co Ltd uses the loan proceeds to capitalise a subsidiary, Lend Co Ltd. By a special arrangement with 3rd Bank Ltd, a third party bank, Lend Co Ltd puts the proceeds of the share issue on deposit with that bank, which in turn lends an equivalent amount to Borrow Ltd.

The result of this arrangement is that Lend Co Ltd receives "relevant income", in an amount equivalent (or nearly equivalent) to the interest payable by Investing Co Ltd, and which consists of interest that is not tax deductible to Investing Co Ltd or to any person connected with Investing Co Ltd. Since, however, the arrangement involves the making of a loan to Borrow Ltd (connected with Investing Co Ltd) and another person, Lend Co Ltd (also connected with Investing Co Ltd), makes a deposit with 3rd Bank Ltd (unconnected), interest payable by the bank to Lend Co Ltd is deemed to be interest that is tax deductible to Investing Co Ltd or its connected company, thereby taking the arrangement out of the exception provided for by TCA 1997, s 247(4A)(d), (e). The interest payable by Investing Co to Relate Co Ltd is therefore denied relief under TCA 1997, s 247.

4.404 Deduction for charges on income

Charges on income paid by a company in any accounting period are deducted from the total profits of the company for that period. In the corporation tax computation, any amount debited in the company's accounts in respect of charges on income is added back. The amount actually paid in respect of charges, which may be different from the amount debited in the accounts, is allowed against the company's total profits as reduced by any other relief from corporation tax other than group relief in accordance with TCA 1997, s 420 (TCA 1997, s 243(2)).

For this purpose, any short interest payable in the State to a bank which is carrying on a *bona fide* banking business in the State, or to a person *bona fide* carrying on a stock exchange or discount house business in the State, is treated as paid on its being debited to the paying company's account in the books of the lender (TCA 1997, s 243(4)). It would seem from the decision in *MacArthur v Greycoat Estates Mayfair Ltd* [1996] STC 1 that yearly interest would also be treated as paid for this purpose when it is debited to the paying company's account.

Interest paid by cheque is regarded as paid when the cheque is received by the payee (*Parkside Leasing v Smith* [1985] STC 63). It would appear that it is not regarded as having been received by the payee, however, until the cheque is cleared (although this conclusion may not be totally free from doubt). Where interest is added to the amount of the principal debt in the books of the payee, it is not paid until the debt is discharged (*Minsham Properties v Price* [1990] STC 718).

The deduction for charges on income is in respect of those charges in so far as paid out of the company's chargeable profits, the "profits brought into charge to corporation tax". Charges are "paid out of" profits if they are not deductible in computing those profits for tax purposes. No deduction may be made for any period in which there are no chargeable profits to cover the charges paid. A part of the amount in respect of charges paid in an accounting period may be deducted to the extent that there are chargeable profits available for the period.

The "profits brought into charge to corporation tax" are the profits chargeable to corporation tax before any deduction from those profits in respect of charges on income, expenses of management, or other amounts which can be deducted from or set against or treated as reducing profits of more than one description (TCA 1997, s 4(4)(a) – see also **2.602**). Trading losses, trading charges and group relief claimed in accordance with TCA 1997, ss 396A(3), 243A(3) and 420A(3) respectively are set off against trading profits (relevant trading income) and, following FA 2008, also against foreign dividends taxable at the 12.5% rate (see **3.101.5**). As such, these reliefs are now amounts deductible against profits of more than one description.

Charges paid by a company, within the meaning of TCA 1997, s 243 (but not within TCA 1997, s 243A since these are deductible in computing trading profits), for any period are deductible from the total profits of the company for that period reduced by any other relief from corporation tax (eg, trading loss, trading charges, group relief in respect of a trading loss or excess trading charges, terminal loss (subject to TCA 1997, s 397(3) - see 4.104), but before any losses surrendered to it by another company by way of group relief in accordance with TCA 1997, s 420.

Example 4.404.1

Crown Ltd had the following results for the year ended 31 December 2006:

	€	€
Case I profits		65,000
Excess capital allowances from rental property		25,000
Annuities paid		7,000
Group relief available (trading loss)		30,000
Computation:		
Profits before reliefs		65,000
Allow:		
excess capital allowances	25,000	
group relief	30,000	
charges on income	7,000	62,000
Taxable		3,000

The "profits brought into charge to corporation tax" are €35,000, ie Case I profits less TCA 1997, s 420A loss surrendered by way of group relief (a loss not available against profits of more than one description). The charges on income are paid out of those profits. The profits against which the charges are allowed as deductions are €10,000, ie the total profits reduced by reliefs apart from any TCA 1997, s 420 group relief (TCA 1997, s 243(2)).

Example 4.404.2

Crown Ltd had the following results for the year ended 31 December 2006:

	€	€
Case I trading profits		65,000
Excess capital allowances from rental property		25,000

Annuities paid		37,000
Group relief available (trading loss)		30,000
Computation:		
Profits before reliefs		65,000
Allow:		
excess capital allowances	25,000	
group relief	30,000	
charges on income	10,000	65,000
Taxable		Nil

The "profits brought into charge to corporation tax" are €35,000, ie Case I profits less group relief €30,000 under TCA 1997, s 420A. The amount of charges on income paid out of those profits cannot exceed €35,000. The profits against which the charges are allowable, however, are €10,000 only, as in the previous example, so that out of the total charges of €37,000 only €10,000 is deductible.

Example 4.404.3

The position is the same as in Example **4.404.2** except that the accounting period in question is the year ended 30 September 2008:

	€	€
Case I profits		65,000
Excess capital allowances from rental property		25,000
Annuities paid		37,000
Group relief available (trading loss)		30,000
Computation:		
Profits before reliefs		65,000
Allow:		
excess capital allowances	25,000	
group relief (maximum)	30,000	
charges on income	10,000	65,000
Taxable		Nil

The "profits brought into charge to corporation tax" are €65,000, ie Case I profits *before* group relief €30,000 under TCA 1997, s 420A - since such group relief is now allowable against profits of more than one description (see also **3.101.5** and **4.103**). The amount of charges on income paid out of those profits is €37,000. The profits against which the charges are allowable, however, are €10,000 only, as in the previous example, so that out of the charges of €37,000 paid out of profits charged to corporation tax only €10,000 is deductible.

TCA 1997, s 396(7) caters for the situation in which charges on income paid by a company exceed the amount of profits against which they are deductible. The excess amount of the charges or, if the amount is smaller, the payments included in the charges which were made wholly and exclusively for the purposes of the company's trade, are treated as trading expenses for the purpose of computing a loss which may be carried forward under TCA 1997, s 396(1) and set off against trading income of subsequent periods or in computing the amount of a terminal loss for the purposes of relief under TCA 1997, s 397.

Example 4.404.2

The treatment of excess charges on income paid by Quasar Ltd and Pulsar Ltd for the same accounting period differs by reason of the amount of the profits brought into charge in each case:

	Quasar Ltd		Pulsar Ltd	
	€	€	€	€
Profits		31,500		1,500
Patent royalties	28,000		28,000	
Interest as a charge	6,100	34,100	6,100	34,100
Chargeable profits		Nil		Nil
(a) excess charges		2,600		32,600
(b) business charges paid		28,000		28,000
Carried forward under TCA 1997, s 396(1)		2,600		28,000

Pre-trading charges

Charges on income paid by a company wholly and exclusively for the purposes of a trade, but paid before the time the trade is set up and commenced, are treated, to the extent not otherwise deducted from total profits of the company, as paid at the time the trade is set up and commenced (TCA 1997, s 243(3)). Thus, if the charges have already been deducted for any period before trading commences, say against investment income or chargeable gains, they will not then be treated as paid on the date the trade commenced. Since "relevant trading charges" may not, by virtue of TCA 1997, s 243A(2) (see **4.405**), be deducted against total profits, however, it would seem that the only trading charges that might have been deducted from total profits prior to the commencement of trading would be charges incurred for the purposes of an excepted trade (see **3.101.4** regarding TCA 1997, s 21A).

Such relevant trading charges could, however, already have been used on a value basis (see **4.405**) to relieve tax paid on non-trading income or chargeable gains. TCA 1997, s 243(3)(c) provides that an allowance or deduction may not be made under any provision of the Tax Acts, other than TCA 1997, s 243(3), for any expenditure or payment treated as incurred on the day a trade is set up and commenced. Although it is not entirely clear, this may (retrospectively) deny relief on a value basis in the above circumstances.

4.405   Treatment of "relevant trading charges"

Restriction of manufacturing charges (for periods up to 31 December 2002)

For accounting periods ending on or before 31 December 2002, relief for "charges on income paid for the purpose of the sale of goods" (referred to here as "manufacturing charges") by a company in a relevant accounting period (see **7.201.2**) were not, for corporation tax purposes, allowed as deductions against the relevant trading income (see below) other than manufacturing income included in that relevant trading income, of a company for the relevant accounting period. Such charges were allowed as deductions against the company's income from the sale of goods for the accounting period, but as reduced by any manufacturing losses available. Excess manufacturing charges could be carried forward and set against trading profits (whether or not from manufacturing) of later periods in accordance with TCA 1997, s 396(1). For accounting periods ending after 31 December 2002, the treatment of manufacturing charges is governed by the provisions relating to relevant trading charges (see under *Restriction of relevant trading charges* below).

In computing manufacturing income for any accounting period, a deduction is made for any trading charges paid in that period to the extent that they have been allowed against the company's "income for the relevant accounting period from the sale of those goods" (TCA 1997, s 448(3)(b) - see **7.202.3**).

Restriction of relevant trading charges

Charges on income paid by a company for the purposes of its trade in an accounting period may not be offset against the total profits of that accounting period but may be deducted against the company's relevant trading income as well as against foreign dividends taxable at the 12.5% corporation tax rate.

For the purposes of this restriction, the following definitions are relevant.

Relevant trading charges on income, in relation to a company's accounting period, means the charges on income paid by the company in the accounting period wholly and exclusively for the purposes of a trade carried on by the company, other than so much of those charges as are charges on income paid for the purposes of an excepted trade within the meaning of TCA 1997, s 21A (see **3.101.4**).

Relevant trading income, in relation to an accounting period of a company, means the trading income of the company for that period (excluding any income taxable under Case III of Schedule D) other than so much of that income as is income of an excepted trade within the meaning of TCA 1997, s 21A.

Notwithstanding TCA 1997, s 243 (which allows for the deduction of charges on income against total profits – see **4.404**), relevant trading charges on income paid by a company in an accounting period may not be deducted against the total profits of the company for that period (TCA 1997, s 243A(2)). Where a company pays such relevant trading charges on income in an accounting period and those charges would otherwise be allowed as deductions against total profits for that period, they are to be allowed instead as deductions against –

(a)   income specified in TCA 1997, s 21A(4)(b) (certain life, non-life and reinsurance trades – see **3.101.4**);

(b)   relevant trading income, and

(c)   income excluded from TCA 1997, s 21A(3) by virtue of TCA 1997, s 21B (foreign dividends eligible for 12.5% corporation tax rate - see **3.101.5**),

of the company for the accounting period but as reduced by any amount set off against that income under TCA 1997, s 396A (TCA 1997, s 243A(3)).

The income against which relevant trading charges may be deducted by a company for any accounting period is the company's relevant trading income for that period, effectively the company's trading income which is taxable at either the 10% or the 12.5% corporation tax rates, or the income mentioned in (a) and (c) above. Where, however, the company makes a claim under TCA 1997, s 396A for the period in respect of a relevant trading loss (a loss in a trade, profits from which would have been taxable at the 10% or the standard corporation tax rate – see **4.103**), the relevant trading charges are deductible only against the income in question net of that relevant trading loss.

Example 4.405.1

The following are the results of Mann Ltd for its latest accounting period (ending after 17 February 2008):

	€	€
Sales of goods		7,500,000
Sales of merchandise (not manufactured by company)		2,500,000
Trading income		600,000
Case III		500,000
Charges		
- patent royalties	800,000	
- interest (TCA 1997, s 247)	200,000	1,000,000
TCA 1997, s 396A(3) loss from following period		150,000

Computation:

		€
Trading income		600,000
Loss relief TCA 1997, s 396A(3)	150,000	
Charges (relevant trading charges, as restricted)	450,000	
		600,000
Case I		Nil
Case III		500,000
Total income		500,000
Charges (TCA 1997, s 247)		200,000
		300,000

Corporation tax:		
Case III (net of TCA 1997, s 247) €300,000 @ 25%		75,000
Excess manufacturing charges €262,500 @ 10%[1]	26,250	
Excess trade charges, balance €87,500 @ 12.5%[1]	10,938	37,188
		37,812

Manufacturing income:

	€
Relevant sum (trading income after turnover apportionment)	450,000
Less TCA 1997, s 448(3)(b) amounts: [2]	
- trading loss and charges €600,000	450,000
Manufacturing income	Nil

Excess charges:

	€
Royalties paid for purposes of trade	800,000
Maximum allowable	450,000
Excess[1]	350,000

As income from the sale of goods (manufacturing income) is nil, there is no manufacturing relief.

Notes:

1   See below re TCA 1997, s 243B under *Relief on value basis for relevant trading charges.*

2   See **7.202.3** regarding the effect of trading losses and charges on the calculation of manufacturing income. The relevant sum is 75% of the Case I profit. On a proportionate basis, the aggregate of the trading loss and trading charges allowable against this sum is €600,000 x 75% = €450,000.

Example 4.405.2

Spring Ltd had the following results for its latest accounting period (ending after 17 February 2008):

	€
Sales of goods	8,000,000
Sales of merchandise	2,000,000
Charges - patent royalties	1,000,000
Trading income	3,000,000

Computation:

Trading income	3,000,000
Charges (relevant trading charges)	1,000,000
Case I	2,000,000
Corporation tax @ 12.5%	250,000

Manufacturing relief:

$$\frac{(4/5 \times 3,000,000) - 800,000}{2,000,000} \times €250,000 \times 1/5 = \underline{40,000}$$

Net corporation tax	210,000

Trading charges against manufacturing income	€
€1,000,000 x 80% =	800,000

Relief on value basis for relevant trading charges

Excess trading charges paid by a company may be used, on a value basis, to reduce the amount of that company's corporation tax. The tax which may be so reduced, the *relevant corporation tax*, is the company's corporation tax otherwise payable for the accounting period in question, before any reduction by virtue of TCA 1997, s 396B or 420B (similar reliefs on value basis for trading losses (see **4.103**) and group relief (see **8.306.3**)) and also before taking into account any tax payable by virtue of TCA 1997, s 239 (annual payments see **4.306**), 241 (certain payments by non-resident companies – see **4.303.5**), 440 (surcharge on undistributed estate and investment income – see **10.302**) or 441 (surcharge on undistributed income of service companies - see **10.303**).

The "excess" in respect of which relief may be claimed by a company for an accounting period is the excess of the relevant trading charges for that period over the aggregate of the amounts allowed as deductions against the income of the company for that period in accordance with TCA 1997, s 243A (relevant trading income, including any manufacturing income) (TCA 1997, s 243B(2)). Note that trading charges are automatically allowed as deductions by virtue of TCA 1997, s 243A, and not by virtue of a claim under that provision, so that they will always have been used before any relief under TCA 1997, s 243B can arise.

Where a claim for relief in respect of an excess of relevant trading charges is made for any accounting period, the relevant corporation tax for that period is reduced–

(a)   in so far as the excess consists of charges on income paid for the purpose of the sale of goods, by an amount equal to 10% of those charges; and

(b)   in so far as the excess consists of non-manufacturing charges, by an amount equal to those charges multiplied by the standard rate of corporation tax for the accounting period (TCA 1997, s 243B(3)).

The amount for *charges on income paid for the purpose of the sale of goods* (manufacturing charges) in any period is arrived at by apportioning the total amount of charges on income paid wholly and exclusively for the purposes of the trade (trade charges) in that period by reference to the amount of turnover from the sale of "goods" over the amount of turnover from the sale of "goods and merchandise", ie on the same basis as manufacturing income is computed where there are sales of both manufactured and non-manufactured goods (TCA 1997, s 243B(1)). Where the trading income of a company includes income other than income from sales of goods and merchandise (eg, services income), any trade charges referable to such income should be excluded from the amount of the trade charges that are to be apportioned on the turnover basis.

The amount of any relevant trading charges available for the purposes of the Tax Acts (for example, TCA 1997, s 396(7) which treats such charges as trade expenses in computing a loss forward for the purposes of TCA 1997, s 396(1)) is treated as reduced by an amount calculated to produce the same result as if the "excess" charges used for the purposes of the credit claim had been set against taxable income. Accordingly, that "amount" is the aggregate of (i) 10 times the amount in (a) above and (ii) the amount in (b) above grossed up at the standard rate of corporation tax applicable (TCA 1997, s 243B(4)). Effectively, that aggregate is the amount of the excess trade charges used for the purposes of the claim for credit under TCA 1997, s 243B(3).

Example 4.405.3

The following are the results of McAlester Ltd for its latest relevant accounting period:

	€	€
Trading income – non-manufacturing	32,000	
– manufacturing	8,000	40,000
Trade charges – non-manufacturing	48,000	
– manufacturing	12,000	60,000
Non-trade charges		13,000
Case III income		20,000

TCA 1997, s 243B(2) excess:

Relevant trading charges	60,000
– allowed TCA 1997, s 243A	40,000
Excess	20,000

Corporation tax computation:

Case III	20,000
Deduct non-trade charges	13,000
	7,000
Corporation tax @ 25% ("relevant corporation tax")	1,750
TCA 1997, s 243B(3) relief:	
€14,000 @ 12.5%	1,750
Payable	–

TCA 1997, s 243B(4):

Total relevant trading charges	60,000
Profits against which charges deducted TCA 1997, s 243A	40,000
	20,000
Used TCA 1997, s 243B	14,000
Balance treated as TCA 1997, s 396(1) loss (TCA 1997, s 396(7))	6,000

Chapter 5

Capital Allowances

5.1 PRINCIPLES

5.101 Introduction
5.102 Capital expenditure
5.103 Control and main benefit sales
5.104 Sale, insurance, salvage or compensation moneys
5.105 Manner of making allowances and charges
5.106 Accelerated capital allowances
5.107 Effect of succession to trade etc
5.108 Renewals basis

5.101   Introduction

In computing trading or professional income, no deduction may, generally, be made in respect of capital expenditure (TCA 1997, s 81(2)(f)). Similarly, in computing other income for tax purposes, such as income from letting property, no deduction may be made in respect of capital expenditure, whether in respect of the cost of capital assets purchased or by way of depreciation. Instead, the Tax Acts provide for deductions in the form of capital allowances. There are two broad categories of assets in respect of which capital allowances may be claimed, machinery or plant (including equipment, fixtures and fittings) and industrial buildings.

Capital allowances and balancing charges which fall to be made for any accounting period in taxing a trade are to be given effect by treating them as trading expenses or trading receipts in that period (TCA 1997, s 307(2)(a)). For corporation tax purposes, there is accordingly no such concept as excess capital allowances. Where capital allowances for an accounting period exceed the tax adjusted profits against which they are to be deducted as a trading expense, the excess is treated as a trading loss for that period. In that respect, capital allowances are, generally, treated no differently to any other deductible expense; an exception would be the case of "specified capital allowances" in the case of a leasing trade (TCA 1997, s 403 – see **5.305**).

TCA 1997, s 307(1) provides that in computing a company's profits for any accounting period, "there shall be made" all such deductions and additions as are required to give effect to the provisions of the Tax Acts which relate to allowances (including investment allowances) and charges in respect of capital expenditure. The reference to "shall be made" is not mandatory in relation to allowances but is merely directive in that it requires the relevant allowances to be made on due claim by the company concerned (*Elliss v BP Northern Ireland Refinery Ltd; Elliss v BP Tyne Tanker Co Ltd* [1987] STC 52).

The scheme of capital allowances provided for in tax legislation permits the write-off of a taxpayer's expenditure on qualifying assets over a period. For many years, machinery or plant was written off over its life on a reducing balance basis, except that where it was disposed of or ceased to be used, an adjustment by way of balancing allowance or balancing charge was made to ensure that the aggregate allowances given equated to the cost of the asset less any proceeds received on disposal. A balancing allowance is given for the amount by which the unallowed expenditure (the "tax written down value") on the asset exceeds the disposal proceeds. Conversely, a balancing charge is made for the amount by which the disposal proceeds exceed the tax written down value. A balancing charge is effectively additional income of the period in which the relevant disposal takes place.

Since 1992, machinery or plant is written off on a straight-line basis, at a rate of 15% per annum for six years and 10% for the final year from 1 April 1992 to 31 December 2000, for expenditure incurred on or after 1 January 2001 and up to 3 December 2002 at 20% per annum for five years, and from 4 December 2002 at 12.5% per annum over eight years. This treatment was originally provided for (by FA 1992 s 26 – now repealed) in respect of machinery or plant (other than vehicles suitable for the conveyance by road of persons or goods or the haulage by road of other vehicles, for which the rate was 20% per annum on a reducing balance basis) provided for use on or after 1 April 1992. For chargeable periods ending on or after 6 April 1996, and in respect of expenditure incurred before 1 January 2001, the 15% straight-line regime applies to all machinery or plant (other than motor vehicles for which the 20% per annum reducing balance basis continued) whenever provided while, for expenditure incurred from 1 January 2001 to 3 December 2002, allowances are calculated at 20% per annum, and for expenditure incurred on or after 4 December 2002 at 12.5% per annum, for all machinery or plant including motor vehicles (except taxis and cars for short-term hire).Capital allowances are also given in respect of industrial buildings and structures. These have always been calculated on a straight-line basis, at 2% per annum up to 15 January 1975 and at 4% per annum after that date, except that for hotels, which are treated as industrial buildings, the rate was 10% per annum up to 26 January 1994, 15% per annum from 27 January 1994 to 3 December 2002, and 4% per annum after that date. A farm buildings allowance of 15% per annum was available up to 26 January 1994 after which date the rate became 15% per annum, on a straight-line basis.

Expenditure on new machinery or plant, industrial buildings and farm buildings was eligible for accelerated allowances, or free depreciation but, except in the International Financial Services Centre and for certain financial services operations in the Shannon Customs Free Airport, this incentive came to an end on 31 January 1992. The free depreciation regime commenced for machinery or plant on 1 April 1971 and continued up to 31 March 1988. During that period, a writing down allowance could be taken for any amount from basic rates up to 100% of the expenditure on assets provided. A similar position applied for industrial buildings from 2 February 1978 up to 31 March 1988. For the period 1 April 1988 to 31 March 1992, the maximum write off for machinery or plant and industrial buildings was 75% up to 31 March 1989, 50% up to 31 March 1991, and 25% up to 31 March 1992. For farm buildings, accelerated allowances at up to 30% were available for the period 6 April 1980 to 31 March 1989, at up to 50% for the two years to 31 March 1991, and at up to 25% for the year ended 31 March 1992.

An initial allowance of 20%, based on expenditure incurred, was introduced for new machinery or plant on 6 April 1956. The rate was increased to 40% from 14 December 1961, to 50% from 1 April 1967, to 60% from 1 April 1968 and, in line with the free depreciation regime for writing down allowances, to 100% from 1 April 1971. The phasing out of initial allowances, with reducing rates of 75%, 50% and 25%, followed the pattern for writing allowances and no initial allowances applied after 31 March 1992.

Initial allowances for industrial buildings commenced in respect of expenditure incurred on or after 30 September 1956. The allowance was originally set at 10% of the expenditure incurred and the rate was increased to 20% from 14 December 1961 with a further increase to 50% from 16 January 1975. The initial allowance rate was reduced to 25% from 1 April 1991 and the allowance came to an end on 31 March 1992. The 100% initial allowance was retained for the International Financial Services Centre and for certain financial services operations in the Shannon Customs Free Airport. For hotels, the rate of initial allowance was 10% up to 31 March 1992. For farm buildings a 20% initial allowance was in operation for the period 6 April 1974 to 5 April 1980.

The main capital allowances are the writing down allowances in respect of machinery or plant and industrial buildings and structures, as outlined above. Other kinds of allowances for capital expenditure are those relating to scientific research, dredging, patent rights, mining exploration and development and urban renewal buildings.

Capital allowances legislation applies both to income tax and to corporation tax. Prior to the enactment of the Corporation Tax Act 1976 (CTA 1976), all of the legislation was contained in the Income Tax Act 1967. CTA 1976 s 21 applied and adapted income tax provisions for corporation tax purposes but the rules relating to basis periods are of no application to companies (CTA 1976 s 21(2)). CTA 1976 Schedule 1 introduced amendments mainly to make capital allowances provisions relevant to both taxes. One such measure was to relate capital allowances to accounting periods rather than to income tax years, for corporation tax purposes. CTA 1976 Schedule 1 para 1(2) (now TCA 1997, s 321(2)) defines certain phrases which have different meanings depending on whether they are used for income tax or for corporation tax purposes. These are:

(a)   *chargeable period*: either an accounting period of a company or a year of assessment;

(b)   *chargeable period or its basis period*: either the basis period for a year of assessment or the accounting period of a company;

(c)   *chargeable period related to expenditure*: the year of assessment in the basis period for which the expenditure is incurred or the accounting period of a company in which the expenditure is incurred;

(d)   *chargeable period related to a sale or other event*: the year of assessment in the basis period for which the sale or other event takes place or the accounting period in which the sale or other event occurs.

Example 5.101.1

In the year ended 31 December 2007, Canon Ltd ceased altogether to use a computer system in respect of which capital allowances had been claimed. The chargeable period related to the "event" (the computer system ceasing to be used) is the year ended 31 December 2007. TCA 1997, s 288 provides for a balancing allowance or charge to be made for the chargeable period related to the event, ie, for the year ended 31 December 2007.

5.102   Capital expenditure

The availability of capital allowances depends in all cases on capital expenditure being incurred. TCA 1997, s 316(1) clarifies the meaning of "capital expenditure" and "capital sums" for the purposes of writing down allowances in respect of industrial buildings, patents and dredging and in relation to other matters affecting capital allowances. "Capital expenditure" and "capital sums" excludes any expenditure or sum which is allowed to be deducted in computing trading or professional profits for tax purposes. The distinction between capital and non-capital expenditure is discussed in **3.201.3**. Any capital expenditure debited in the profit and loss account of a company is added back in the computation of trading profits and may then qualify for capital allowances depending on whether or not the expenditure falls into one of the qualifying categories.

Capital allowances are, generally, calculated by reference to the cost incurred by a company in acquiring an asset, or in constructing a building or structure, or in developing or otherwise providing an asset for use in the trade or other activity the profits from which are subject to corporation tax.

Where two or more assets are purchased or sold in one transaction, there must be a just apportionment of the total consideration in arriving at the cost or sale proceeds of each asset on which capital allowances may be claimed or balancing allowance or balancing charge computed. All assets or other property acquired or disposed of in one bargain are deemed to have been purchased or sold together. The total purchase or sale price must be justly apportioned even where the parties to the transaction have agreed or purport to have agreed separate prices for the separate items.

Where an asset is acquired in exchange for other property, the capital expenditure incurred on its acquisition is deemed to be for an amount equal to the value of the property given in exchange for it. Where the exchange involves more than one asset, the same rule applies subject to any necessary apportionment between the assets.

The amount of any expenditure for capital allowances purposes is net of any grant receivable in respect of that expenditure. The capital expenditure in question is regarded as not having been incurred in so far is it has been met, directly or indirectly, by the State or by any board established by statute or by any public or local authority. This treatment is provided for in various sections in the Tax Acts including TCA 1997 ss 763(5) (scientific research), 670(2) (mine development allowance), 317(2) (industrial buildings allowance, dredging), 317(2) and 762(1) (patents), 658(13) (farm buildings allowance) and 317(3) (machinery or plant writing down and initial allowances).

VAT included in the purchase price of assets must be excluded from the expenditure incurred on those assets for capital allowances purposes where the purchaser is entitled to an input credit or refund in respect of the VAT. Where there is no entitlement to a VAT credit or refund, VAT is part of the cost on which capital allowances may be claimed, for example VAT on private motor vehicles in most cases.

If the purchase of an asset is financed by a non-recourse loan (so that the lender has recourse only to the asset itself and any income generated from that asset), that does not alter the fact that the borrower has incurred the capital expenditure on that asset (see *Airspace Investments Ltd v Moore* 5 ITR 3). It was held in *Stokes v Costain Property Investments Ltd* [1984] STC 204 that land development expenditure financed by a loan which was to be repaid on the satisfactory completion of the development agreement had been incurred by the developer and that the expenditure should not be regarded as having been met by a third party.

Transfer of business to a company

It will frequently be the case that a sole trader (or partnership) incorporates a business so that the business is transferred as a going concern to a company in return for an issue of shares in the company. This will usually involve a transfer of assets on which capital allowances are available. For this purpose, a part or proportion of the shares issued by the company should be regarded as expenditure incurred by it in acquiring those assets. From the standpoint of the sole trader, the transfer of the assets would be treated as a "sale", the disposal value again being a proportionate part of the shares issued.

The foregoing approach is supported by the decision in *Osborne v Steel Barrel Co Ltd* 24 TC 293 which was concerned with the question of the cost of stock-in-trade to a company that had acquired an undertaking from an individual in return for cash and an issue of shares. When shares are allotted credited as fully paid, the primary liability is satisfied by a consideration other than cash passing from the allottee. When the company agrees to credit the shares as fully paid, it gives up what it would otherwise have had, ie the right to call for payment of the par value in cash. The question to be decided in any such case is what amount of cash is represented by the issue of the fully paid shares: that amount would be a sum of cash equal to the par value of the shares.

5.103 Control and main benefit sales

5.103.1 Introduction

Anti-avoidance measures in TCA 1997, s 312 are designed to prevent advantage being taken of sales at artificial prices, particularly in situations involving common control. The principal effect of the section is to substitute market value for the actual price at which the relevant assets are sold.

5.103.2 Control sales

Where the actual selling price of an asset is not the same as that which the asset would have fetched if sold in the open market, TCA 1997, s 312(3) provides that the open market price is to be substituted for the purpose of calculating capital allowances or balancing allowances or charges, as regards both the buyer and the seller, where:

(a) the buyer is a body of persons over whom the seller has control; or

(b) the seller is a body of persons over whom the buyer has control; or

(c) both the buyer and the seller are bodies of persons and some other person has control over both of them.

A body of persons includes a company as well as other entities, such as a partnership or a society. A person is regarded as having control over a company if he has power, whether derived from the holding of shares, voting power or powers conferred by the articles of association or other document regulating the company, to secure that the affairs of the company are conducted in accordance with his wishes.

The market value rule does not apply where on a sale of machinery or plant the open market price at the time of sale is greater than the amount which would be taken, for the purpose of calculating any balancing charge to be made on the seller, to be the original expenditure incurred by the seller on that machinery or plant. In that case, instead of deeming the machinery or plant to have been sold at open market value, it is treated for TCA 1997, s 312(3) purposes as having been sold at an amount equal to the amount taken as the seller's original purchase price (TCA 1997, s 312(4)). Normally, that is the actual price paid by the seller. In certain cases, however, the price at which the seller is treated as having purchased the machinery or plant would not be the actual price paid by him, for example, where the acquisition was deemed to be at market value because of the application of TCA 1997, s 312 at the time of that acquisition, or where the deemed expenditure incurred is the price less the amount of grant receivable in respect of the machinery or plant.

The exception in TCA 1997, s 312(4) does not apply where machinery or plant (and not any other kind of asset) which was never used was sold by a person in the course of a business consisting of or including the manufacture or supply of machinery or plant of that class. In that case, where a control situation exists, the open market price is used whether or not that price is greater than the seller's acquisition cost.

In a control situation, the buyer and the seller of any assets qualifying for capital allowances may jointly elect under TCA 1997, s 312(5) to substitute the tax written down value at the date of sale for the open market price of the asset provided that amount is less than the open market price. This election is not available where either of the parties is not resident in the State at the date of sale and where an allowance or charge, as the case may be, would not be made to or on that party as a result of the sale. The election could be made, for example, where the seller is non-resident but is within the charge to corporation tax in respect of a trade carried on in the State through a branch or agency so that a balancing allowance or balancing charge would be made in relation to that trade.

The expression "tax written down value" in relation to an election under TCA 1997, s 312(5) means:

(a) in the case of an industrial building or structure, the "residue of expenditure" (see **5.409**) immediately before the sale;

(b) in the case of machinery or plant, the amount of expenditure still unallowed immediately before the sale (see **5.207.2**);

(c) in the case of patent rights, the amount of capital expenditure on acquiring the rights still unallowed immediately before the sale (see **13.604.2**).

The TCA 1997, s 312(5) election must be made jointly. No time limit is prescribed but, in practice, this would need to be done when filing the self assessment return. The joint election should ideally accompany the earliest return being made by one of the parties to the election.

Example 5.103.2.1

Jasmine Ltd, which made up its accounts to 31 December each year, purchased equipment for €24,000 on 17 December 2005. It claimed a wear and tear allowance of €3,000 at 12.5% for each of the three years ended 31 December 2005, 2006 and 2007; the tax written down value at 31 December 2007 was €15,000. On 1 February 2008 the equipment was sold for €18,000 to another company under the same control. The open market price of the equipment at that date was €28,000.

For the purposes of TCA 1997, s 312(3), Jasmine Ltd is deemed to have sold the equipment for €24,000, its original acquisition cost, since the open market price at the date of sale is greater than this amount. The resulting balancing charge is therefore €9,000, the aggregate of the allowances claimed. The buyer is also deemed to have acquired the equipment for €24,000.

Jasmine Ltd and the buyer could make a joint election under TCA 1997, s 312(5) to use the tax written down value of €15,000 as the selling/acquisition price for the purposes of their respective capital allowances computations. Where both parties are companies under 100% common control, the election would usually be made; otherwise, the fact that one party avoids a balancing charge at the expense of the other, or is denied a balancing allowance to the advantage of the other, would probably mean that the election should not be made.

Assets which have attracted capital allowances may be transferred between companies under common control in the context of a transfer of a trade or part of a trade. The position here may be governed by TCA 1997, s 400 (company reconstructions without change of ownership). The related consequences are discussed in **4.109.4**.

5.103.3 Main benefit sales

As well as dealing with common control transactions, TCA 1997, s 312 applies open market value treatment in cases where it appears, in relation to a sale of property or in respect of transactions which include a sale of property, that the sole or main benefit that might accrue to one or more of the parties involved is the obtaining of a capital allowance. In this respect, the section is directed at arrangements which are designed to result in an amount of capital allowances which is greater than would normally be available (see *Barclays Mercantile Industrial v Melluish* [1990] STC 314).

The provisions of TCA 1997, s 312(4), (5) apply to these arrangements in the same way as they apply in common control situations. Consequently, if the actual selling price of an asset is different from the open market price of the asset, the open market price will be substituted for the price paid. The relevant balancing allowance or charge in the case of the seller will be calculated accordingly and the open market price will be the basis for capital allowances claims of the buyer.

The election to substitute tax written down value for open market value, which can be made in a common control situation, is not available where TCA 1997, s 312 applies to main benefit sales. The one exception to the application of the market value rule in these cases is that provided for in TCA 1997, s 312(4); as in common control situations, open market price will not be applied to machinery or plant where it would exceed the seller's cost or deemed cost.

5.104 Sale, insurance, salvage or compensation moneys

Certain events, such as the sale, destruction or loss of an asset for which capital allowances have been obtained, or the complete cessation of use of a building or structure, give rise to a balancing allowance or balancing charge. In calculating the allowance or charge, the tax written down value (see **5.207.2**) of the asset is compared with the sale, insurance, salvage or compensation moneys arising in respect of the asset. TCA 1997, s 318 defines "sale, insurance, salvage or compensation moneys". It means:

(a) where the event is the sale of any property, including the sale of a right to use or otherwise deal in machinery or plant consisting of computer software, the net proceeds of sale;

(b) where the event is the demolition or destruction of any property, the net amount received for what is left of the property, plus any insurance moneys received in respect of the demolition or destruction, and any other compensation received by way of a capital sum;

(c) where the event is the permanent loss of any machinery or plant, except in consequence of its demolition or destruction, any insurance moneys received in respect of the loss and any other compensation received by way of a capital sum;

(d) where the event is that a building or structure ceases altogether to be used, any compensation received by way of a capital sum; and

(e) where the event is a cessation referred to in TCA 1997, s 274(2A)(b) (relevant facility ceasing to be such – see **5.409.1**), the aggregate of—

(i)   the residue off expenditure (within the meaning of TCA 1997, s 277 – see **5.409.2**) incurred on the construction or refurbishment of the building or structure immediately before that event, and

(ii) the industrial building allowances made in respect of the capital expenditure incurred on the construction or refurbishment of the building or structure.

The references to the "net proceeds or sale" and the "net amount received" in (a) and (b) would imply that deductions in respect of such items as advertising expenses, salvage expenses and auctioneer's fees may be made from any amount received.

The time of any sale is the time of completion or the time when possession is given, whichever is the earlier.

Where two or more assets are sold in one transaction, there must be a just apportionment of the total consideration received in arriving at the sale proceeds of each asset on which a balancing allowance or balancing charge is computed. All assets or other property disposed of in one bargain are deemed to have been sold together. The total sale price must be justly apportioned even where the parties to the transaction have agreed or purport to have agreed separate prices for the separate items.

Where an asset is disposed of in exchange for other property, the value of the property received in exchange is taken as the net sale proceeds. Where the exchange involves more than one asset, the same rule applies subject to any necessary apportionment between the assets.

VAT included in the sale proceeds for any assets must be excluded from the amount brought into the computation of balancing allowance or balancing charge.

Computer software

Where TCA 1997, s 288(3A) applies (ie, where a right to use machinery or plant consisting of computer software is granted by a company to another person while the company retains an interest in that machinery or plant – see **5.207.2**), the "sale, insurance, salvage or compensation moneys" means the consideration in money or moneys worth received by the company for the grant of the right (TCA 1997, s 318(aa)).

5.105   Manner of making allowances and charges

5.105.1   General

Capital allowances may be made to a company in any of the following ways:

(a)   in taxing the company's trade;

(b)   in charging the company's income under Case V of Schedule D;

(c)   by means of discharge or repayment of tax.

Capital allowances are given in taxing a trade where the relevant capital expenditure was incurred for the purposes of that trade and if the assets concerned are held or used in the trade. Thus, wear and tear allowances in respect of machinery or plant may be claimed under TCA 1997, s 284 by a company carrying on a trade in any accounting period where the company has incurred capital expenditure on the provision of that machinery or plant for the purposes of the trade, provided that machinery or plant belongs to the company and is in use for the purposes of the trade at the end of the accounting period.

The section provides that the allowance is to be made "in taxing the trade". Balancing allowances and balancing charges in respect of machinery or plant are to be made to a person "in taxing such person's trade" (TCA 1997, s 300). Again, an annual allowance or balancing allowance or charge arising in respect of a person's interest in, or on a person's disposal of, an industrial building is to be made to or on the person "in taxing such person's trade" (TCA 1997, s 278(1)).

In the case of a company, an allowance given in taxing a trade is given effect by treating the allowance as a trading expense of the trade while a charge made in taxing the trade is treated as a trading receipt of the trade.

In the case of a lessor entitled to writing down allowances or balancing allowances in respect of industrial buildings in the State, capital allowances are given in charging the letting income under Case V of Schedule D or in the rare cases (eg, the letting of a building for use in a dock undertaking) where the letting income is charged under Case IV of Schedule D. The allowances in these cases are to be given primarily against the income chargeable under Case V or Case IV as the case may be, including any income chargeable under these Cases in the form of a balancing charge; balancing charges are made in taxing the letting income. A similar position applies in the case of lessors of other buildings or structures which are treated in the same way as industrial buildings (buildings in the Custom House Docks Area and other designated areas) by virtue of FA 1986 s 42 (as saved by TCA 1997 Sch 32 para 11).

Capital allowances are given by means of discharge or repayment of tax where for example they relate to assets used in connection with the earning of income assessable under Case IV of Schedule D. Balancing charges arising in the same situations are chargeable under Case IV of Schedule D. The income of a lessor from the leasing of machinery or plant, other than in the case of a trade of leasing machinery or plant, is assessable under Case IV of Schedule D. TCA 1997, s 298(1) provides for writing down allowances to a lessor of machinery or plant, where the burden of wear and tear thereof falls directly on that lessor, on the same terms as would apply if the machinery or plant were in use for the purposes of a trade carried on by the lessor. The income from this activity falls within Case IV of Schedule D, being "annual profits or gains not within any other Case of Schedule D" (TCA 1997, s 18(2)). A balancing charge arising to the lessor is made as if the machinery or plant were in use for the purposes of a trade carried on by the lessor (TCA 1997, s 298(2)). Writing down allowances, initial allowances and balancing allowances made to the lessor are to be made "by means of discharge or repayment of tax" and are available primarily against income from the letting of machinery or plant (TCA 1997, s 300(2)). Any balancing charge is made under Case IV of Schedule D (TCA 1997, s 300(3)).

Writing-down allowances for capital expenditure on the purchase of transmission capacity rights, made in accordance with TCA 1997, s 769D(2), are to be made by means of discharge or repayment of tax (see **5.608.5**).

"By means of discharge or repayment of tax" is one of the seemingly arcane concepts found in various parts of the Tax Acts the precise meaning of which may appear difficult to explain. In fact its meaning can be taken quite literally but there is little or no practical difference in the way in which allowances are given by means of discharge or repayment of tax as compared, say, with the making of allowances in taxing a trade. The concept of giving capital allowances by means of discharge or repayment denotes the discharge or cancellation of the relevant Case IV assessment, or of part of the assessment, by reference to the quantum of the capital allowances in question, or, where tax in respect of an assessment has already been paid, the repayment of some or all of the tax paid as a result of deducting the capital allowances. ("Discharge or repayment" is not, however, confined to Case IV situations – see for example, **4.109.2** regarding TCA 1997, s 400(14).) In practice, especially since the introduction of self assessment, capital allowances will have been claimed in the relevant Case IV return and the resulting assessment will give effect to the allowances as it would in the case of allowances claimed under Case I or Case V of Schedule D.

TCA 1997, s 300(4) provides that any wear and tear allowance made under or by virtue of TCA 1997, s 284(6) (see **3.209.3**) is to be made in charging the relevant person's income under Case V of Schedule D. Thus, capital allowances for expenditure incurred on fixtures and fittings in rented residential accommodation may be set against rental income and this provision, introduced by FA 2000 with effect from 6 April 2000, puts on a statutory basis a practice which had been in operation for many years. (See also **5.105.3**.)

No specific provision is made for the manner in which capital allowances in the form of industrial building allowances are to be made to a lessor where the buildings are situated outside the State. The related income is taxable under Case III of Schedule D and, in practice, allowances have been given in the same way as if the income had been assessable under Case V of Schedule D. Since 23 April 1996, with some exceptions to cater for transitional situations, expenditure on the construction of an industrial building situated outside the State is not treated as expenditure on an industrial building for the purposes of capital allowances.

5.105.2 Allowances and charges in taxing a trade

Capital allowances for any accounting period of a company are in the first instance set off against the income of the relevant class for that period. Where the capital allowances exceed the income of that class for the period in question, the excess may be used against other income but the rules dealing with this aspect vary depending on the manner in which the capital allowances concerned are made.

As regards allowances made in taxing a trade carried on by a company, they are treated as allowances made in computing trading income (TCA 1997, s 321(4)) and are given effect by treating them as a trading expense and therefore deducted in arriving at the amount of the company's profit or loss for the purposes of Case I of Schedule D, while balancing charges made in taxing a trade are treated as receipts of the trade (TCA 1997, s 307(2)(a)). As a consequence of this treatment, any excess capital allowances in an accounting period will create or augment a trading loss for that period which is treated for all purposes of corporation tax in the same way as any other kind of trading loss; except in the case of "specified capital allowances" in a leasing trade and other ring fencing provisions (see *Ring fencing of allowances* below), no distinction is made for any corporation tax purpose between losses created by capital allowances and other losses, nor between the part of a trading loss attributable to capital allowances and the remaining part of that loss.

For the purposes of carrying forward an unused trading loss (TCA 1997, s 396(1), or the set-off of such loss against profits of the company, or the use of such losses to relieve tax payable thereon, in the same or preceding accounting periods (TCA 1997 ss 396(2) (see **4.101**), 396A(3) and s 396B(3)) (see **4.103**) any capital allowances giving rise to or included in the loss are, again, not distinguished.

Example 5.105.2.1

The following information is relevant in the case of Tableware Ltd, a company carrying on a retail distribution business:

	y/e 30/9/06	p/e 31/3/07	y/e 31/3/08
	€	€	€
Trading profit (loss) before capital allowances	30,000	45,000	(60,000)
Capital allowances	25,000	27,000	45,000
Balancing charge	3,000	8,000	15,000
Deposit interest	4,000	4,000	5,000
Rents (net of allowable deductions)	22,000	23,000	25,000
Chargeable gains (adjusted)	10,000	Nil	40,000

The corporation tax computations are as follows:

	€	€	€
Case I – trading profits	30,000	45,000	Nil
Balancing charge	3,000	8,000	Nil
	33,000	53,000	Nil
Capital allowances	25,000	27,000	Nil
Case I	8,000	26,000	Nil
Case III	4,000	4,000	5,000
Case V	22,000	23,000	25,000
Income	34,000	53,000	30,000
Chargeable gains	10,000	Nil	40,000
Profits	44,000	53,000	70,000

The trading loss for year ended 31 March 2008 is as follows:

	€
Adjusted loss	60,000
Balancing charge	15,000
	45,000
Capital allowances	45,000
Trading loss	90,000

Tableware Ltd makes a claim under TCA 1997, s 396A(3) to offset this loss against its relevant trading income of accounting periods ending within the 12 months immediately preceding that period, ie the nine months ended 31 March 2007 and the year ended 30 September 2006. Losses must be set off as far as possible against profits of a later period before those of an earlier period. Since the period ended 30 September 2006 falls partly before the 12 month period immediately preceding the year ended 31 March 2008, only the part of the profits of that period falling within the 12 month period, arrived at by way of time appoitionment, may be relieved. The loss of €150,000 is set off as follows:

	y/e 30/9/06	p/e 31/3/07	y/e 31/3/08
	€	€	€
Case I (relevant trading income)	8,000	26,000	Nil
	4,000	26,000	Nil
Trading income subject to corporation tax	4,000	Nil	Nil

For the year ended 30 September 2006, only 6/12ths of the trading income may be covered by the loss; the 12 month period in respect of which the loss is available is the period 1 April 2006 to 31 March 2007. Of the total loss of €90,000, €30,000 has been utilised under TCA 1997, s 396A(3). The balance of €60,000 is available for the purposes of relief under TCA 1997, s 396B(3) (see **4.103**). Thus, corporation tax on profits of €70,000 for the year to 31 March 2007 is €17,500 and relief on a value basis against this amount is €60,000 at 12.5% = €7,500, balance payable €10,000.

5.105.3   Allowances made under Case V and by means of discharge or repayment

TCA 1997, s 308(1) deals with capital allowances made in charging the income of a company under Case V of Schedule D as well as allowances which are to be given by means of discharge or repayment, and which are available primarily against a specified class of income. The capital allowances for any accounting period are to be given in the first instance against the income from the specified class for that period. Balancing charges are treated as income of the same class as that against which the corresponding allowances are made (TCA 1997, s 308(2)).

Where capital allowances to be made in charging income under Case V of Schedule D or by means of discharge or repayment of tax are not fully utilised because of an insufficiency of income of the class of income against which they are primarily to be deducted, the unused amount:

(a)   is carried forward, unless utilised in accordance with (b), to the next accounting period provided the company remains within the charge to tax (TCA 1997, s 308(3));

(b)   may be offset against profits of any description (before charges) of the same accounting period and, provided the company was then within the charge to tax, against profits of any description (before charges) of immediately preceding accounting periods ending within a period equal in length to the period in which the allowances arose (TCA 1997, s 308(4)).

The excess capital allowances which may be offset against profits of a preceding period are confined to so much of those allowances as cannot be utilised against profits of a later accounting period. Excess capital allowances which are the subject of a TCA 1997, s 308(4) claim must first be used against the total profits of the period in which the excess arose and then against the profits of the preceding period or periods. For the purpose of setting excess capital allowances against profits of preceding accounting periods, profits are apportioned on a time basis; where an accounting period falls partly before the immediately preceding period or periods equal in length to the period of the excess capital allowances, only a proportionate part of the profits of that accounting period may be relieved.

A company may have both a loss available for relief under TCA 1997, s 396(2) or s 396A(3) and excess capital allowances available for relief under TCA 1997, s 308(4). Where the excess capital allowances are to be carried back to a period part of which falls before the period mentioned in (b) above, the amount of the profits of that period which may be reduced by those allowances may not, together with the amount of the trading loss carried back under TCA 1997, s 396(2) or s 396A(3), as the case may be, exceed the part of the profits proportionate to the part of the period falling within the period mentioned in (b) (TCA 1997, s 308(5)).

Example 5.105.3.1

Ammonex Ltd had taxable profits of €84,000 for the year ended 31 March 2007 and an allowable loss of €50,000 for the nine months ended 31 December 2007. In the period ended 31 December 2007 it had rental income of €60,000 against which industrial building allowances of €90,000 were available. The company claims relief under TCA 1997 ss 396A(3) and 308(4).

The accounting period for which Ammonex Ltd had a profit ends within the nine months immediately preceding the nine months ended 31 December 2007 and the loss of €50,000 and excess capital allowances of €30,000 may therefore be offset against the profits of that period. The profits of the year ended 31 March 2007 are relieved first by the loss under TCA 1997, s 396A(3). This reduces the profits to €34,000. The TCA 1997, s 308(4) claim is then made in respect of this amount. As part of the accounting period falls before the nine month period, however, the maximum reduction which can be made to profits of that period is 9/12ths of €84,000, or €63,000. A reduction of €50,000 has already been made under TCA 1997, s 396A(3) leaving a balance of €13,000 to be reduced by the TCA 1997, s 308(4) claim. The unused capital allowances of €17,000 are carried forward.

Capital allowances in respect of plant & machinery etc

The capital allowances referred to above and which may be made in charging the income of a company under Case V of Schedule D or by means of discharge or repayment are industrial building allowances available to a lessor of industrial buildings. With effect from 6 April 2000, TCA 1997, s 300(4) provides that any wear and tear allowance made under or by virtue of TCA 1997, s 284(6) (see **3.209.3**) is to be made in charging the relevant person's income under Case V of Schedule D. Thus, capital allowances for expenditure incurred on fixtures and fittings in rented residential accommodation may be set against rental income and this provision, introduced by FA 2000 with effect from 6 April 2000, puts on a statutory basis a practice which had been in operation for many years.

TCA 1997, s 406 provides for certain restrictions on the use of capital allowances for fixtures and fittings for furnished residential accommodation. TCA 1997, s 284(6) and (7) provide the basis for the availability of capital allowances against income from the letting of rented residential accommodation. The allowances which are available by virtue of TCA 1997, s 284(7) are allowances in respect of capital expenditure on the provision of machinery or plant (including furniture, fixtures and fittings) other than vehicles suitable for the conveyance by road of persons or goods or the haulage by road of other vehicles, where such expenditure is incurred wholly and exclusively in respect of a house used solely as a dwelling which is or is to be let as a furnished house and where the house is provided for renting or letting on *bona fide* commercial terms in the open market). TCA 1997, s 406 provides that where a company incurs capital expenditure of the type referred to in TCA 1997, s 284(7), the following provisions are not to apply to the relevant capital allowances:

(a) TCA 1997, s 308(4) – set off against a company's total profits of excess capital allowances given by means of discharge or repayment of tax or capital allowances in excess of income charged under Case V of Schedule D – see **4.107**); or

(b) TCA 1997, s 420(2) – set off, by way of group relief, against a company's total profits of excess capital allowances given by way of discharge or repayment of tax or capital allowances in excess of income charged under Case V of Schedule D.

5.105.4 Ring fencing of allowances

Certain capital allowances, those which are made in charging income assessable under Case V of Schedule D and those which are given by means of discharge or repayment of tax, are to be allowed primarily against a specified class of income and, where there is an insufficiency of income of that class, may be allowed against other profits. There are, however, provisions which confine the use of capital allowances to particular classes of income. Under these provisions, where the full amount of capital allowances available for any period cannot be utilised in full, they may be allowed against the same class of income for subsequent periods. No other kinds of profits may be relieved by those capital allowances and the use of the allowances are therefore "ring-fenced". Accordingly, neither TCA 1997, s 396(2) nor TCA 1997, s 308(4) may apply or have effect in relation to any loss to the extent attributable to these capital allowances. The most significant provisions which provide for the ring-fencing of capital allowances are the following:

(a) capital allowances in respect of leased machinery or plant (see **5.305**): allowances are confined to income from the leasing activity, whether assessable as trading income under Case I of Schedule D or under Case IV of Schedule D (TCA 1997, s 403);

(b) capital allowances of a limited partner: allowances are confined to the share of income from the partnership trade (TCA 1997, s 1013 – see **13.703**);

(c) capital allowances ("specified capital allowances" – see **5.213**) in respect of a qualifying ship used in a qualifying shipping trade: allowances are confined to

  (i) income from a qualifying shipping trade, and

  (ii) income from the letting on charter of a qualifying ship other than letting on charter which is a qualifying shipping activity (ie, other than letting on charter where the operation of the ship and crew remain under the direction and control of the letting company – already included in (i)) (TCA 1997, s 407(4));

(d) writing down allowances and initial allowances (but not balancing allowances) in respect of holiday cottages: allowances confined to income from trade under Case I or income from leasing under Case V (see **5.416.5**);

(e) writing down allowances and initial allowances (but not balancing allowances) in respect of registered holiday apartments and other self-catering accommodation: allowances confined to income from trade under Case I or income from leasing under Case V (see **6.402.2**).

5.106 Accelerated capital allowances

5.106.1 Introduction

For many years, during most of the 1970s and 1980s, various forms of accelerated capital allowances were available so that instead of writing down the cost of machinery or plant or industrial buildings at normal rates, taxpayers could write off larger amounts of the expenditure in the period in which the assets were purchased or provided for use, or in subsequent periods where appropriate. Accelerated capital allowances consisted of initial allowances at rates of up to 100% of expenditure, or "free depreciation" at any rate from the basic rate for the asset in question up to 100% of expenditure at the option of the taxpayer.

Accelerated allowances were available in respect of new ("unused and not secondhand") machinery or plant (with the exception of motor vehicles), industrial buildings and farm buildings up to 31 January 1992, but continue to be available after that date in certain circumstances, eg, for activities carried on in the International Financial Services Centre and in the Shannon Customs-Free Airport. During the free depreciation regime, which was in operation from 1 April 1971 to 31 March 1988, writing down allowances could be taken for any amount from basic rates up to 100% of the expenditure on assets provided. A similar position applied for industrial buildings from 2 February 1978 up to 31 March 1988.

5.106.2 Phasing out of accelerated capital allowances

After 31 March 1988, accelerated capital allowances began to be phased out. The position is summarised as follows.

Expenditure incurred	*Maximum rate*
1 April 1988 – 31 March 1989	75%
1 April 1989 – 31 March 1991	50%
1 April 1991 – 31 March 1992	25%
From 1 April 1992	Nil

An initial allowance of 20% of the expenditure incurred on new machinery or plant was provided for from 6 April 1956. The rate was increased to 40% from 14 December 1961, to 50% from 1 April 1967, to 60% from 1 April 1968 and, in line with the free depreciation regime for writing down allowances, to 100% from 1 April 1971. The phasing out of initial allowances, with reducing rates of 75%, 50% and 25%, followed the pattern for writing allowances and no initial allowances were available for expenditure incurred after 31 March 1992.

An initial allowance in respect of capital expenditure incurred on or after 30 September 1956 on the construction of an industrial building or structure was provided for, initially at 10% (TCA 1997, s 278(1)). The rate of initial allowance was increased to 20% from 14 December 1961 and was further increased to 50% from 16 January 1975. In line with the phasing out of accelerated capital allowances, the rate of initial allowance for industrial buildings was reduced to 25% from 1 April 1991 and the allowance came to an end on 31 March 1992.

The phasing out of accelerated capital allowances is by reference to the various dates on which expenditure was incurred, as described above. This permits a taxpayer to continue to claim free depreciation after the final cut-off date, 1 April 1992, in respect of capital expenditure incurred before that date, where less than the maximum allowable percentage of expenditure incurred has been written off. Where less than the full amount of free depreciation available has been claimed in any period, any balance of free depreciation may be claimed in a subsequent period. TCA 1997, s 285(3) prohibits any free depreciation claims for chargeable periods ending on or after 6 April 1999. This will oblige taxpayers to take up the balance of any free depreciation available in the meantime as otherwise the full entitlement to accelerated capital allowances will not have been obtained. This cut-off measure applies also to free depreciation available for machinery or plant in the designated areas as provided for in TCA 1997, s 285. In no case, however, does the cut-off affect claims covered by TCA 1997, s 271(3)(a), 273(5)(a), 283(4)(a) or 285(5)(a) (International Financial Services Centre).

5.106.3 Continuation of accelerated capital allowances

The full free deprecation allowance and the 100% initial allowance were retained for the International Financial Services Centre, for certain financial services operations in the Shannon Customs-Free Airport and in certain other circumstances (see **5.204.3** and **5.205.5**). For hotels, the rate of initial allowance was 10% up to 31 March 1992. For farm buildings a 20% initial allowance was in operation for the period 6 April 1974 to 5 April 1980.

5.107 Effect of succession to trade etc

Where a person succeeds to a trade or profession and the original trade or profession is treated as discontinued, any property belonging to the discontinued trade which is taken over by the successor without being sold is treated for capital allowances purposes as having been sold to the successor at the time of the succession for the price it would have fetched in an open market sale. The normal consequences of a sale follow, that is, a balancing allowance or balancing charge to or on the predecessor and writing-off allowances to the successor (TCA 1997, s 313(1)).

The foregoing treatment applies in the case of a continuing partnership trade or profession. By virtue of TCA 1997, s 1009 (partnerships involving companies – see **8.312**), a trade or profession carried on in partnership is treated as continuing so long as there are at least two partners in the partnership and on each change in the composition of the partnership there is at least one common partner before and after the change. In any such circumstances, the introduction of a new partner or the retirement of an existing partner does not result in the discontinuance of the partnership trade or profession.

In the case of a continuing partnership trade or profession, capital allowances and balancing charges are to be made to or on the persons carrying on the partnership on the assumption that the trade or profession had at all times been carried on by one and the same person; changes in the composition of the partnership are ignored. The amount of any allowance or charge to be made at any time to or on the persons then carrying on the partnership trade or profession is to be computed as if those persons had at all times been carrying on that trade or profession and as if everything done by their predecessors in that trade or profession had been done by them. This treatment is subject to TCA 1997, s 1010 (capital allowances and balancing charges in partnership cases – see **13.702**) which contains rules for the apportionment of allowances and charges among persons in a partnership (TCA 1997, 313(2)).

5.108   Renewals basis

A renewals basis is generally available as an alternative to capital allowances. In computing profits, a deduction may be made for the cost of a replacement item less the proceeds of sale, trade-in price, or scrap value of the replaced item. If the replacement item is an improvement on the replaced item, however, the deduction will be restricted to the cost of replacing a like item.

In *Caledonian Railway Company v Banks* 1 TC 487, a railway company was allowed to deduct its expenditure on renewals of plant in computing its profits. The company had claimed statutory wear and tear allowances additionally but this was rejected since it could not be entitled to a deduction for deterioration twice over.

The fact that expenditure on the replacement of a large number of knives and lasts installed in complicated machinery has been held to be capital expenditure, notwithstanding that their average life was only three years (*Hinton v Maden & Ireland Ltd* 38 TC 391 – see **5.202.1**), the cost of renewals of trade implements, utensils etc is allowed as a deduction under TCA 1997, s 81(2)(d).

5.2 MACHINERY OR PLANT

5.201   Capital allowances available

5.202   Meaning of "machinery or plant"

5.203   Wear and tear allowances

5.204   Free depreciation

5.205   Initial allowances

5.206   Notional wear and tear allowances

5.207   Balancing allowances and balancing charges

5.208   Capital grants

5.209   Roll over of balancing charges

5.210   Successive balancing adjustments

5.211   Plant used partly for non-trading purposes

5.212   Restriction of capital allowances on private motor vehicles

5.213   Emissions-based restriction of capital allowances for cars

5.214   Qualifying shipping trades: ring fencing

5.201   Capital allowances available

Capital allowances may be claimed in respect of capital expenditure on machinery or plant provided for use in a trade (or profession) carried on or exercised by a company which has incurred the expenditure. Subject to certain conditions, capital allowances may also be claimed by a company which incurs capital expenditure on machinery or plant which is leased for use by another person (see **5.301**); a lessee of machinery or plant may, in certain circumstances, be entitled to claim capital allowances in respect of the items leased (see **5.303**).

A balancing allowance is given on the occurrence of certain events, including a sale, relating to machinery or plant where the taxpayer's net capital expenditure, after taking account of any sale or disposal proceeds, has not been fully relieved by way of capital allowances. On the other hand, where the capital allowances obtained up to the point of sale or other event exceed net capital expenditure, a balancing charge is made to claw back the excess allowances (see **5.207**).

Under TCA 1997, s 765, a company carrying on a trade may claim an allowance in respect of capital expenditure on scientific research, including expenditure on machinery or plant (see **5.601**).

Free depreciation for capital expenditure on machinery or plant provided for use after 31 March 1992 and initial allowances in respect of capital expenditure incurred after that date are no longer available, except in the types of cases dealt with in **5.204.3**.

Generally, therefore, only annual wear and tear allowances, balancing allowances and balancing charges are now relevant. Free depreciation in respect of machinery or plant provided for use in a trade or profession before 1 April 1992 may still be claimed where the related capital expenditure has not been fully been written off, but subject to TCA 1997, s 285(3) which prohibits any claim to free depreciation for accounting periods ending on or after 6 April 1999.

5.202 Meaning of "machinery or plant"

5.202.1 General

The words "machinery" and "plant" have been the subject of a considerable amount of litigation and judicial interpretation. While the meaning of "machinery" is reasonably clear, the word "plant" has given rise to some difficulty and has been the subject of a number of tax cases. The term "plant and machinery", rather than "machinery or plant", is heard more often and accordingly in practice means the same thing. The term "machinery or plant" may, however, be more logical in the sense that the difference between the two words tends to be blurred and a particular item, if it is not clearly covered by one, is likely to be covered by the other. The term "machinery or plant" also covers, in practice, a range of items often grouped under the words "furniture, fixtures and fittings".

The classic definition of "plant" comes from the case of *Yarmouth v France* [1887] 19 QBD 647 in which Lindley LJ said that "plant", in its ordinary sense, "includes whatever apparatus is used by a businessman for carrying on his business – not his stock in trade which he buys or makes for sale; but all goods and chattels, fixed or moveable, live or dead, which he keeps for permanent employment in his business". The definition of plant is therefore very wide; it includes manufacturing machinery, office machinery and equipment, fixtures and fittings, desks, filing cabinets, computers, commercial and private motor vehicles and such other "apparatus" which may be used in the character of plant for the purpose of the business in question.

That definition was used as a general test of the meaning of the word "plant" by the House of Lords in *Hinton v Maden & Ireland* 38 TC 391. The subject of the appeal in that case was a large number of knives and lasts, with lives of from one to five years, which were installed in complicated machinery used in manufacturing. They were held to be part of the machinery or plant. The Crown had taken the view that the expenditure on the knives and lasts was on revenue account but the fact that the average life of the items was only three years did not prevent them from being capital expenditure and from being plant in the circumstances of the case. On the other hand, expenditure on wallpaper patterns with a life of less than two years was held to constitute revenue expenditure (*Rose v Campbell* 44 TC 500).

5.202.2 Plant v premises

A distinction is drawn between premises *within* which a trade is carried on and plant *with* which it is carried on. The function of premises is to provide a setting, shelter, or the context or framework for the carrying on of a trade whereas plant is something which is itself used in the trade. Movable prefabricated buildings used by a school as a laboratory and a gymnasium were held not to be plant (*St John's School v Ward* [1974] STC 7). Likewise, in *Thomas v Reynolds* [1987] STC 135, an inflatable cover for a tennis court was held not to be plant.

In *Benson v Yard Arm Club* [1979] STC 266, it was held that a hulk used as a floating restaurant was a structure within which the restaurant business was carried on and not apparatus used in the carrying on of the trade.

5.202.3   Premises as plant

The fact that an asset is premises does not exclude it from being plant also. In *IRC v Barclay Curle & Co Ltd* 45 TC 221, the full amount of expenditure incurred in providing a dry dock for the purpose of a trade of ship builders and repairers was held to be in respect of plant. The expenditure included preliminary excavation costing £187,000, concrete work in constructing the dock amounting to £500,000, and ancillary plant costing £243,000. The fact that the dry dock was a structure did not prevent its being treated as plant when it fulfilled the function of plant in the trade in question. The important distinction is between a structure which is *merely* the setting in which the trade is carried on and a structure which constitutes the apparatus with which it is carried on.

The *Barclay Curle* decision was applied in *Schofield v R & H Hall Ltd* [1975] STC 353 where grain silos were held to be plant, as being in the nature of a tool in relation to the company's trade and as being more than a general setting for the trade. The company used the silos in its business of importing grain for sale to manufacturers and millers. Each silo was essentially a large concrete structure into which were built concrete bins and a small structure containing plant and machinery consisting of gantries, conveyor belts, mobile chutes and other items. The silos were found to play a part in the process of reception, distribution and discharge of grain. The Crown's contention that the company carried on the trade of storage and that the silos were grain stores forming part of the setting was rejected. The court in this case referred to the judgment in *Margrett v Lowestoft Water & Gas Co Ltd* 19 TC 488 where the function of a water tower was described as "the harnessing of the natural element of gravity to perform a trade function".

In *Dixon v Fitch's Garage Ltd* [1975] STC 480, a canopy constructed over the pumps of a petrol filling station to provide shelter while the process of delivering fuel was carried on was held not to be plant. It was found that as the canopy did not help to supply the petrol, but only helped to make the customers and staff more comfortable, it was only part of the setting.

The opposite conclusion was reached in the Irish case *Ó Culacháin v McMullan Brothers* 4 ITR 284 where the facts were very similar. It was held in this case that a petrol station canopy qualifies as plant under TCA 1997, s 284 as it has an integral function in promoting sales and has a functional role in advertising the presence of the station and attracting customers. The decision is interesting as an example of the importance of how a case is presented. Here, as compared to the *Fitch's Garage* case, the functional nature and role of the canopy were emphasised to good effect.

In *Cooke v Beach Station Caravans Ltd* [1974] STC 402, it was held that the total expenditure of a caravan park proprietor on excavating and lining two swimming pools and installing heating, filtration and a purifying system was expenditure on plant. The pools were held to be part of the apparatus used by the business of a caravan park operator. Megarry J in his judgment noted that "nobody could suggest that the principal function of the pool was merely to protect the occupants from the elements". On the other hand, in *Gray v Seymour's Garden Centre (Horticulture)* [1995] STC 706, a specialised glasshouse used in a garden centre business was held to constitute no more than a purpose built structure and not to be plant; it had a roof which was used to control ventilation but had no integrated heating system.

The decision in *Seymour's Garden Centre* was applied in the case of an electricity company which claimed capital allowances in respect of its expenditure on an underground substation. It was held that the structure of the substation functioned as a premises from which the company's trade was carried on and not as apparatus with which it was carried on. It was accepted that certain components of the substation were plant (*Bradley v London Electricity plc* [1996] STC 1054).

In *Ó Srianáin v Lakeview Ltd* 3 ITR 219, it was held that a deep pit poultry house and equipment was plant in the trade of egg producing on the basis that the poultry house provided an "environment designed for the benefit of the hens to assist in the purpose of increasing the egg production". The judgment in this case is interesting not least for its review of previous, mainly UK, cases concerning the meaning of "plant".

In *O'Grady v Roscommon Racecourse Committee* 4 ITR 425, it was held that improvements to a racecourse stand (excluding work on two bars) was expenditure on plant. The decision here contrasted with that in *Brown v Burnley Football & Athletic Club Ltd* [1980] STC 424 in which a concrete stand at a football ground was held not to constitute plant (although the seating contained within the stand did qualify as plant).

5.202.4   Part of premises v separate asset

Where an asset is attached to premises, it will be necessary to consider whether it forms part of those premises or whether it is a separate asset. In *IRC v Scottish & Newcastle Breweries Ltd* [1982] STC 296, the company, which operated hotels and licensed premises, incurred capital expenditure on electric light fittings, decor and murals for its hotels and licensed premises. It was found that the company's trade included the provision of accommodation in a context which included atmosphere, judged in the light of the market which the particular premises were intended to serve. It was held that the light fittings, decor and murals were of such a design and so laid out that they fell to be regarded as apparatus serving a functional purpose in the company's trade and that they were, therefore, plant. The context of the situation in which the question arises is critical, as underlined by Lord Cameron, who pointed out that the question is a practical one and that the answer is "conditioned not only by reference to the nature of a trade but to the particular operations and methods of the taxpayer in the pursuance of his particular business".

In *Dunnes Stores (Oakville) Ltd v Cronin* 4 ITR 68, the *Scottish & Newcastle Breweries* case was distinguished where it was held that a supermarket supplying groceries and drapery was not in the business of supplying ambience so that a demountable suspended ceiling did not qualify as plant.

In *Wimpey International Ltd v Warland* [1989] STC 273, it was held that items such as external fascia boards, wall panels, mirrors, fixed internal dividing screens, units of decorative brickwork fixed to walls by steel ties, colourful ceiling rails, and built-in storage units and dispensers used in a restaurant premises were not part of the premises, but that floor tiles, fixed floor coverings, wall tiles, shop fronts, suspended ceilings, raised floors and stairways formed part of the premises.

A company trading as wholesale merchants erected, in a single-storey warehouse, a storage platform made of chipboard on a steel grid supported by pillars and bolted to the ground. The platform covered most of the warehouse area. Additional lighting was installed beneath the platform. In the Chancery Division, it was accepted that the platform was a movable temporary structure and was not part of the premises but that the lighting was part of the premises (*Hunt v Henry Quick Ltd* [1992] STC 633). A similar conclusion was reached in *King v Bridisco Ltd* [1992] STC 633.

In *J Lyons & Co Ltd v Attorney General* [1944] 1 All ER 159, it was held that electric lamps, their sockets and connecting cords were not plant, but were part of the general setting in which the business was carried on.

In *Jarrold v John Good & Sons Ltd* 40 TC 681, it was held that something which forms part of the setting of a trade may nevertheless be plant if it is more a part of the apparatus than part of the setting. While the word "plant" does not normally cover the permanent structure of a building in which a business is carried on, in the particular circumstances of this case it was held that movable office partitioning was plant.

5.202.5 Intellectual property

A barrister's collection of law books was held to be plant, being chattels kept for use in carrying on the barrister's profession (*Breathnach v McCann* 3 ITR 113). In *McVeigh v Sanderson* 45 TC 273, wallpaper designs were held not to constitute plant but the cost of printing blocks incorporating and reflecting the value of the designs did qualify as plant. It would seem that expenditure on the acquisition of intellectual property rights, although related to plant, would not itself qualify as plant.

5.202.6 Case law

The outcome of considerable litigation concerning the meaning of "plant" is that the word has acquired a very specialised meaning for tax purposes. It was acknowledged in *Cole Brothers Ltd v Phillips* [1982] STC 307 that "plant" is used in a highly artificial and "judge-made" sense while in *Attwood v Andruff Car Wash* [1996] STC 110 it was admitted that the concept of plant has lost touch with any ordinary dictionary meaning of the word as it now extends to such diverse objects as a swimming pool and barrister's books.

Lord Cameron, in the *Scottish & Newcastle Breweries* case, expressed the opinion that there can be no standard pattern of permissible plant in respect of each industry, trade or profession covered by the relevant legislation. In light of the general principle accepted by the courts since *Yarmouth v France*, the question must be resolved by reference to the particular circumstances of the case under review. "I see no reason in principle," he added, "why, in the case of a taxpayer engaged in this service industry, he should not be entitled to claim that what has been provided to embellish the surroundings provided by him in his premises should be held to be as much "plant" of his business as the beds or chairs or carpets with which he had furnished his bedrooms or lounges".

5.202.7 Computer software

Generally, the established method of acquiring computer software is such that it does not constitute an outright purchase of that software; the related expenditure is incurred to licence the software which does not therefore "belong" to the person acquiring it. To cater for this situation, it is provided in TCA 1997, s 291(1) that where a person carrying on a trade incurs capital expenditure in acquiring a right to use or otherwise deal with computer software for the purposes of the trade, the right, and the software itself, is treated as machinery or plant for the purposes of the provisions dealing with capital allowances including, in particular, wear and tear allowances, initial allowances and balancing allowances and charges.

The right to use or otherwise deal with computer software would include rights to duplicate or further develop computer programs.

In the more unusual situation in which a person carrying on a trade incurs capital expenditure in making an outright purchase of computer software for purposes of the trade, so that the software belongs to that person, any such computer software that would not otherwise constitute machinery or plant (eg, software in non-physical form) is deemed to be machinery or plant for the purposes of the provisions dealing with capital allowances.

5.203   Wear and tear allowances

5.203.1   General

A company carrying on a trade is entitled by virtue of TCA 1997, s 284(1) to an annual allowance, normally referred to as a wear and tear allowance, in respect of capital expenditure incurred by it in providing machinery or plant for the purposes of the trade.

A company leasing machinery or plant (apart from any case in which the company is carrying on a *trade* of leasing) is entitled under TCA 1997, s 298(1) to the same wear and tear allowances as a person carrying on a trade, provided it bears the burden of the wear and tear (see **5.301**). If a company carrying on a trade is a lessee of machinery or plant on terms which provide that the burden of wear and tear of the machinery or plant falls directly on it (as opposed to the lessor), the annual wear and tear allowance in respect of the machinery or plant may be claimed by that company (see **5.303**).

5.203.2   Conditions for wear and tear allowance

A company carrying on a trade in any "chargeable period" (ie, an accounting period in the case of a company) is entitled to a wear and tear allowance for that period in respect of any item of machinery or plant if the conditions for the allowance are met. These conditions are as follows:

(a)   the company has incurred capital expenditure in providing the machinery or plant for the purposes of the trade;

(b)   the machinery or plant was in use for those purposes at the end of the accounting period;

(c)   the machinery or plant belongs to the company at the end of the accounting period; and

(d)   the machinery or plant, while used for the purposes of the trade, is wholly and exclusively so used (TCA 1997, s 284(1)).

Condition (c) is likely to give rise to difficulties in cases of plant within a building or on land and which in law is regarded as "fixtures". A fixture is broadly an object placed on land or in buildings with a view to enhancing them on a long term basis. A test which is commonly applied in deciding whether the object in question is a fixture is the extent of the damage which would be caused in removing it from the land or building to which it is attached. In *Maye v Revenue Commissioners* 3 ITR 332 (where the question of fixtures was relevant for VAT purposes), it was held that a television aerial was a fixture by reason of the firmness of its attachment to a building and the fact that it was designed to enhance the use of the building as a dwelling.

In *Stokes v Costain Property Investments Ltd* [1984] STC 204, it was held that a lift installed by a tenant became landlord's fixtures and did not therefore belong to the tenant. The tenant was not entitled to capital allowances in respect of the lift therefore, nor was the landlord since he had not incurred the relevant capital expenditure.

In *Melluish v BMI* [1995] STC 964, equipment leased to local authorities became fixtures on the land owned by the authorities. Although the lease agreement provided that the equipment was to be returned to the taxpayer on the termination of the lease and that it should continue to be movable property owned by the taxpayer, it was held that it constituted fixtures owned by the local authorities. The terms agreed by the parties could not alter the legal effect of what had occurred which was that the plant belongs to the person if he is in law or in equity the absolute owner of it.

Condition (d) applies in respect of machinery or plant provided for use for the purposes of a trade after 31 March 1990. In effect, plant is regarded as "provided for use" for a trade on a date if its first use in the trade occurs on that date.

The purpose of condition (d) is to prevent any wear and tear allowance being given for an item of machinery or plant where the business use and non-business use occur at the same time. The phrase "while used for the purposes of the trade" allows an item of plant to be used partly for business purposes and partly for non-business purposes without removing the entitlement to wear and tear provided the business and non-business uses occur at different times (even in the same day). For example, where a motor car is used for business journeys and non-business journeys, wear and tear allowances will continue to be given, but will be restricted to the business use proportion of the total use.

Condition (d) was introduced following a Circuit Court decision to the effect that an accountant's suit qualified for capital allowances as "plant". The fact that the accountant wore the suit to be properly dressed for his business at the same time as he wore it for his own personal need to be clothed did not disqualify the suit because, prior to the amendment, there was no requirement that it had to be wholly and exclusively used for his profession. In the case of a company, simultaneous business and non-business use is not easily envisaged.

5.203.3 Amount of wear and tear allowance

FA 1992 s 26 introduced a fundamental change in the method of calculating the wear and tear allowance for machinery or plant (other than vehicles suitable for the conveyance by road of persons or goods or the haulage by road of other vehicles – referred to here as "excepted vehicles"). The 1992 rule, effected by way of substituting a new subsection (1) (now TCA 1997, s 284(1), (2)) and deleting the original subsections (7) and (8) of ITA 1967 s 241, applied in the case of any item of machinery or plant (other than an excepted vehicle) which was first used in the trade or profession after 31 March 1992. For expenditure incurred on or after 1 January 2001, the treatment of excepted vehicles, apart from taxis and cars used for short-term hire, was brought into line with that relating to machinery or plant generally – see (b) below.

For accounting periods ended before 6 April 1996, ITA 1967 s 241(1), (7) and (8) remained in force in their pre-FA 1992 form for the purposes of wear and tear allowances for excepted vehicles and continued to apply in that form for all items of machinery or plant which were first used in the trade or profession before 1 April 1992. ITA 1967 s 241(7) and (8) were repealed by FA 1996 with effect from 6 April 1996. TCA 1997, s 284(1), (2) apply as respects accounting periods ended after 5 April 1996. TCA 1997, s (2)(a)(ii) effectively replaces ITA 1967 s 241(7) and (8), which had continued to be relevant for excepted vehicles, by providing for the continuation (for expenditure up to 31 December 2000) of the 20% reducing balance wear and tear allowance for excepted vehicles.

To provide a uniform method of claiming capital allowances for all machinery or plant (apart from excepted vehicles), ITA 1967 s 241(1A) (now obsolete) provided that, for accounting periods ended after 5 April 1996, the straight-line basis applies to machinery or plant provided before 1 April 1992 also. For this purpose, the starting point is the tax written value at the end of the last accounting period ending before 6 April 1996.

In certain circumstances (see **5.103**) a company is deemed to have purchased plant for a price equal to its open market value at the time of purchase or, subject to joint election, for a price equal to its tax written down value at that time. In any such case, the wear and tear allowance is calculated by reference to the deemed purchase price and not by reference to the actual cost of the purchase.

Where a capital grant or other subsidy is obtained or obtainable directly or indirectly from the State, or any statutory board or any public authority, in respect of a company's capital expenditure on machinery or plant, the relevant wear and tear allowances are based on the net capital expenditure after deducting such grant or subsidy (TCA 1997, s 317(3)).

(a) Plant provided from 1 April 1992 to 31 December 2000

TCA 1997, s 284(2)(a)(i) provides that the wear and tear allowance for machinery or plant, other than for excepted vehicles (see below), for a chargeable period in which the four conditions described above are met is an amount equal to 15% of the actual cost of the machinery or plant, including in that actual cost any expenditure in the nature of capital expenditure on the machinery or plant by way of renewal, improvement or reinstatement. This straight-line method of writing down the cost of machinery or plant normally results in that cost being fully written off over seven years.

In contrast to the position which obtained in respect of machinery or plant provided before 1 April 1992, there is no distinction made between machinery or plant which is new and unused at the time it is provided for use and other machinery or plant. Similarly, no distinction is made between different types of machinery or plant (other than excepted vehicles) which suffer varying degrees of wear and tear. In all cases, the 15% straight-line method is applied.

For the purposes of TCA 1997, s 284, the day on which any expenditure is incurred is the day on which the sum in question becomes payable (TCA 1997, s 316(2)). On the change over in 1992 to the 15% straight-line method of writing off capital expenditure on machinery or plant, no definition of "expenditure incurred" was provided. That definition was added by way of inserting what is now TCA 1997, s 316(2). It would appear, however, that the date on which capital expenditure is regarded as incurred for the purposes of TCA 1997, s 284 is not particularly significant. To be entitled to capital allowances for any accounting period, it is necessary only that the person claiming the allowance "has incurred capital expenditure" on the provision of the machinery or plant;

it is not necessary that the full amount of the expenditure has been incurred in that period. Thus, traders acquiring machinery or plant on hire purchase terms will be entitled to claim wear and tear allowances by reference to the full cost of the assets even though they will only have incurred capital expenditure on the amount of the instalments paid to date.

The position as outlined in the previous paragraphs is subject to three qualifications. Firstly, TCA 1997, s 284(4) limits the amount of the wear and tear allowance which may be given for any accounting period so that it cannot exceed the actual cost of the machinery or plant to the company claiming the allowance, as reduced by the aggregate of all wear and tear allowances and any initial allowance (if relevant) obtained for previous accounting periods in respect of the same expenditure. Actual cost, for this purpose, includes, in addition to the acquisition cost, any expenditure of a capital nature in respect of the machinery or plant by way of renewal, improvement or reinstatement.

In certain cases, a company carrying on a trade may not actually obtain, in respect of machinery or plant, a wear and tear allowance, or may obtain an allowance which is less than a normal wear and tear allowance, for one or more accounting periods. In any such case, TCA 1997, s 287 deems a normal wear and tear allowance to have been given for each such accounting period. This matter is dealt with in more detail in **5.206**.

The second qualification is to the effect that the amount of the wear and tear allowance for any accounting period must be proportionately reduced where the length of the period is less than one year (TCA 1997, s 284(2)(b)). The amount of the allowance is the appropriate fraction of twelve months (where the numerator is the number of months, including any fraction of a month if necessary, comprised in the accounting period) applied to 15% of the capital expenditure involved. The resulting amount may not exceed the balance of the capital expenditure as reduced by previous capital allowances obtained. The appropriate treatment is illustrated in the following simple example.

The third qualification is contained in TCA 1997, s 283(6) and is to the effect that, if an initial allowance is obtained for any accounting period in respect of any item of machinery or plant, no wear and tear allowance may be given for the related capital expenditure for the same period. TCA 1997, s 283(6) also prevents the increased wear and tear (free depreciation) allowance being obtained in respect of the capital expenditure for any accounting period subsequent to that for which the initial allowance is given.

This rule will be relevant where capital expenditure on new machinery or plant is incurred before 1 April 1992, but where the first use of the plant in the trade or profession does not take place until after 31 March 1992. In that case, if a 25% initial allowance is claimed in respect of capital expenditure incurred in, say, the accounting period 1 April 1991 to 31 March 1992, no wear and tear allowance may be made for that period.

TCA 1997, s 283(6) also prevents a wear and tear allowance for the same chargeable period, and denies any increased wear and tear allowance for any later period, where a 50% initial allowance is obtained in respect of the capital expenditure on machinery or plant. A 100% initial allowance was available in respect of capital expenditure on machinery or plant up to 31 March 1988 after which date the rate of the allowance commenced to be scaled down. For the period 1 April 1988 to 31 March 1989, when a 75% initial allowance was available, it was possible also to claim an annual wear and tear allowance in the same period for which this initial allowance was obtained. After 31 March 1989, a wear and tear allowance could not be claimed for any period in which an initial allowance was obtained.

TCA 1997, s 284(8) provides for wear and tear allowances to Dublin Airport Authority in respect of machinery or plant. Dublin Airport Authority will be deemed to have incurred on the "vesting day" (see **5.401.4**) capital expenditure on the provision of machinery or plant which is vested in it on that day. For this purpose, the cost of the machinery or plant will be arrived at by deducting from its original cost an amount equal to the amount of any wear and tear allowances that would have been made since the machinery or plant had been provided had a claim for those allowances been made and allowed.

TCA 1997, s 284(2)(a)(ii) provides for wear and tear allowances in respect of excepted vehicles, ie, vehicles suitable for the conveyance by road of persons or goods or the haulage by road of other vehicles. These vehicles include all private motor cars, motor cycles, vans, lorries, trucks, taxis, buses, coaches, breakdown trucks and tractors. Plant such as forklift trucks which can only be used for moving goods for short distances, for example within a factory area, are not excepted vehicles and, if first used in the relevant trade or profession after 31 March 1992, attract wear and tear allowances under the 15% straight-line regime.

The wear and tear allowances available to a company which incurs capital expenditure on the provision of an excepted vehicle are provided for in TCA 1997, s 284(2)(a)(ii). The allowance for any accounting period is 20% of the value of the vehicle at the commencement of the accounting period, such value to be taken to be the actual cost to the company of the vehicle reduced by the total of any allowances made to the company under TCA 1997, s 284 for previous accounting periods in respect of the vehicle. Wear and tear allowances are to be computed for each successive accounting period, therefore, by writing down the capital expenditure on the excepted vehicle on a reducing balance basis. This is achieved by applying the 20% rate of wear and tear to the "tax written down value" of the vehicle at the beginning of the accounting period. (For motor vehicles purchased after 31 December 2000, allowances are computed on the straight-line basis – see below.)

At the taxpayer's option, and for accounting periods ending on or after 1 January 2002, the tax written down value of expenditure incurred prior to 1 January 2001 on machinery or plant may be "pooled" so that it may be written off at 20% per annum on a straight-line basis. Where for any accounting period ending on or after 1 January 2002 a wear and tear allowance would be due in accordance with the legislation relating to expenditure incurred before 1 January 2001 (20% reducing balance for motor vehicles and 15% straight-line for other machinery or plant), a company may elect that the wear and tear allowance for that period and any subsequent period in respect of each and every item of the machinery or plant concerned is, subject to TCA 1997, s 284(4), to be an amount equal to:

(a)   where the allowance would otherwise be 15%, 20% of the amount of the capital expenditure incurred on the provision of that machinery or plant which remains unallowed at the commencement of the period; and

(b)   where the allowance would otherwise be 20% on the reducing balance basis (ie, for motor vehicles), 20% of the amount of the capital expenditure incurred on the provision of that machinery or plant which remains unallowed at the commencement of the period (TCA 1997, s 284(2)(ab)).

An election as above is irrevocable and is required to be made, in the case of a company, in its corporation tax return (see **15.104**) for which a wear and tear allowance is to be made in accordance with TCA 1997, s 284(2)(ab) (TCA 1997, s 284(2)(ac)).

For the purposes of the wear and tear computation, a vehicle is deemed to have the tax written down value, as described above, at the beginning of the accounting period, whether the vehicle was in use at the beginning of that period or was provided for use at some time during the period.

(b) Expenditure incurred on machinery and plant from 1 January 2001 to 3 December 2002

TCA 1997, s 284(2)(aa) provides that the wear and tear allowance for machinery or plant for a chargeable period in which the four conditions described in **5.203.2** are met is an amount equal to 20% of the actual cost of the machinery or plant, including in that actual cost any expenditure in the nature of capital expenditure on the machinery or plant by way of renewal, improvement or reinstatement. This straight-line method of writing down the cost of machinery or plant will result in that cost being fully written off over five years.

At the taxpayer's option, and for accounting periods ending on or after 1 January 2002, the tax written down value of expenditure incurred prior to 1 January 2001 on machinery or plant may be "pooled" so that it may be written off at 20% per annum on a straight-line basis. Where, for any accounting period ending on or after 1 January 2002, a wear and tear allowance would be due in accordance with the legislation relating to expenditure incurred before 1 January 2001 (20% reducing balance for motor vehicles and 15% straight-line for other machinery or plant), a company may elect that the wear and tear allowance for that period and any subsequent period in respect of each and every item of the machinery or plant concerned is, subject to TCA 1997, s 284(4), to be an amount equal to:

(a) where the allowance would otherwise be 15%, 20% of the amount of the capital expenditure incurred on the provision of that machinery or plant which remains unallowed at the commencement of the period; and

(b) where the allowance would otherwise be 20% on the reducing balance basis (ie, for motor vehicles), 20% of the amount of the capital expenditure incurred on the provision of that machinery or plant which remains unallowed at the commencement of the period (TCA 1997, s 284(2)(ab)).

An election as above is irrevocable and is required to be made, in the case of a company, in its corporation tax return (see **15.104**) for which a wear and tear allowance is to be made in accordance with TCA 1997, s 284(2)(ab) (TCA 1997, s 284(2)(ac)).

For the purposes of the wear and tear computation, a vehicle is deemed to have the tax written down value, as described above, at the beginning of the accounting period, whether the vehicle was in use at the beginning of that period or was provided for use at some time during the period.

(c) Expenditure incurred on machinery and plant from 4 December 2002

TCA 1997, s 284(2)(ad) provides that the wear and tear allowance for machinery or plant for a chargeable period in which the four conditions described in **5.203.2** are met is an amount equal to 12.5% of the actual cost of the machinery or plant, including in that actual cost any expenditure in the nature of capital expenditure on the machinery or plant by way of renewal, improvement or reinstatement. This straight-line method of writing down the cost of machinery or plant will result in that cost being fully written off over eight years.

TCA 1997, s 284(2)(ad) does not apply in the case of:

(i) machinery or plant to which TCA 1997, s 284(3A) relates (accelerated allowances for certain sea fishing boats – see **5.204.5**);

(ii) machinery or plant consisting of a car within the meaning of TCA 1997, s 286 (taxis and cars for short-term hire – see (d) below); or

(iii) machinery of plant provided under the terms of a binding contract evidenced in writing before 4 December 2002 and in respect of the provision of which capital expenditure is incurred on or before 31 December 2003.

For the purposes of TCA 1997, s 284, the day on which any expenditure is incurred is the day on which the sum in question becomes payable (TCA 1997, s 316(2)). The date on which capital expenditure is regarded as incurred for the purposes of TCA 1997, s 284 is, however, not particularly significant. To be entitled to capital allowances for any accounting period, it is necessary only that the person claiming the allowance "has incurred capital expenditure" on the provision of the machinery or plant; it is not necessary that the full amount of the expenditure has been incurred in that period. Thus, traders acquiring machinery or plant on hire purchase terms will be entitled to claim wear and tear allowances by reference to the full cost of the assets even though they will only have incurred capital expenditure on the amount of the instalments paid to date.

The position as outlined in the previous paragraphs is subject to three qualifications. Firstly, TCA 1997, s 284(4) limits the amount of the wear and tear allowance which may be given for any accounting period so that it cannot exceed the actual cost of the machinery or plant to the company claiming the allowance, as reduced by the aggregate of all wear and tear allowances and any initial allowance (if relevant) obtained for previous accounting periods in respect of the same expenditure. Actual cost, for this purpose, includes, in addition to the acquisition cost, any expenditure of a capital nature in respect of the machinery or plant by way of renewal, improvement or reinstatement.

In certain cases, a company carrying on a trade may not actually obtain, in respect of machinery or plant, a wear and tear allowance, or may obtain an allowance which is less than a normal wear and tear allowance, for one or more accounting periods. In any such case, TCA 1997, s 287 deems a normal wear and tear allowance to have been given for each such accounting period. This matter is dealt with in more detail in **5.206**.

The second qualification is to the effect that the amount of the wear and tear allowance for any accounting period must be proportionately reduced where the length of the period is less than one year (TCA 1997, s 284(2)(b)). The amount of the allowance is the appropriate fraction of twelve months (where the numerator is the number of months, including any fraction of a month if necessary, comprised in the accounting period) applied to 12.5% of the capital expenditure involved. The resulting amount may not exceed the balance of the capital expenditure as reduced by previous capital allowances obtained. The appropriate treatment is illustrated in the following simple example.

Example 5.203.3.1

Vintage Products Ltd incurs capital expenditure of €40,000 on 10 April 2003, in its year ended 31 December 2003, on the purchase and installation of new manufacturing machinery. The machinery is first used in the company's trade on 20 April 2003. The company makes up its next account to 31 March 2004 and subsequently maintains that year end accounting date. Wear and tear allowances for all relevant periods are as follows:

	€
Year ended 31/12/03:	
W & T €40,000 x 12.5%	5,000
Period 1/1/04 – 31/3/04:	
W & T €40,000 x 12.5% x 3/12	1,250
Years ended 31/3/05 to 31/3/10:	
W & T €40,000 x 12.5% x 6	30,000
Year ended 31/3/11:	
W & T (max)	3,750
	40,000

The third qualification is contained in TCA 1997, s 283(6) and is to the effect that, if an initial allowance is obtained for any accounting period in respect of any item of machinery or plant, no wear and tear allowance may be given for the related capital expenditure for the same period. TCA 1997, s 283(6) also prevents the increased wear and tear (free depreciation) allowance being obtained in respect of the capital expenditure for any accounting period subsequent to that for which the initial allowance is given.

This rule will be relevant where capital expenditure on new machinery or plant is incurred before 1 April 1992, but where the first use of the plant in the trade or profession does not take place until after 31 March 1992. In that case, if a 25% initial allowance is claimed in respect of capital expenditure incurred in, say, the accounting period 1 April 1991 to 31 March 1992, no wear and tear allowance may be made for that period.

TCA 1997, s 283(6) also prevents a wear and tear allowance for the same chargeable period, and denies any increased wear and tear allowance for any later period, where a 50% initial allowance is obtained in respect of the capital expenditure on machinery or plant. A 100% initial allowance was available in respect of capital expenditure on machinery or plant up to 31 March 1988 after which date the rate of the allowance commenced to be scaled down. For the period 1 April 1988 to 31 March 1989, when a 75% initial allowance was available, it was possible also to claim an annual wear and tear allowance in the same period for which this initial allowance was obtained. After 31 March 1989, a wear and tear allowance could not be claimed for any period in which an initial allowance was obtained.

TCA 1997, s 284(8) provides for wear and tear allowances to Dublin Airport Authority in respect of machinery or plant. Dublin Airport Authority will be deemed to have incurred on the vesting day (see **5.401.4**) capital expenditure on the provision of machinery or plant which is vested in it on that day. For this purpose, the cost of the machinery or plant will be arrived at by deducting from its original cost an amount equal to the amount of any wear and tear allowances that would have been made since the machinery or plant had been provided had a claim for those allowances been made and allowed.

(d) Taxis and cars for short-term hire

TCA 1997, s 286 provides that the rate of the wear and tear allowance for taxis and cars used for short-term hire to the public is 40%, but only for vehicles used for qualifying purposes within the section. For any other vehicles, the rate is 12.5% (on the straight-line basis for expenditure incurred on or after 4 December 2002).

The rate of 40% applies in respect of the capital expenditure on any cars used for a qualifying purpose and is only available for capital allowances given in taxing a trade that consists of, or includes, the use of the cars for qualifying purposes. It is not therefore available to a lessor who leases the car to the person carrying on the trade.

The 40% rate is calculated on the reducing balance method applicable for motor vehicles (see above). For a company chargeable to corporation tax, the first chargeable period for which the 40% applied was its first accounting period ending after 5 April 1987.

A car is used for "qualifying purposes" if it is used, in the ordinary course of a trade, for the purposes of:

(a) short-term hire (as defined below) to members of the public; or

(b) the carriage of members of the public while the car is a licensed public hire vehicle fitted with a taximeter in pursuance of the Road Traffic (Public Service Vehicles) Regulations 1963 (SI 191/1963).

A car is regarded as used for qualifying purposes if a minimum of 75% of its total use is use for qualifying purposes. This test has regard to the periods of time in which the car is used or is available for use. In determining whether the test is met, the periods of time during which the car is actually used for a qualifying purpose is measured as a percentage of the total periods of time when the car is either used or is available for use for any purpose. Any period in which the car is off the road for repairs, servicing, etc may be disregarded. Mileage is not relevant.

The test is applied separately for each accounting period of a company in determining whether the 40% or the 20% rate is to be used. The 75% qualifying use test is deemed to be satisfied for any accounting period if:

(a) the car is in use, or is available for use, in that period for qualifying purposes for no less than 50% of the total time; and

(b) the 75% use test is met either for the immediately preceding or the immediately succeeding accounting period.

Short-term hire is defined, in relation to any car, as the hire of the car under a hire-drive agreement (within the meaning of section 3 of the Road Traffic Act 1961) for a continuous period not exceeding eight weeks.

For the qualifying use test to be met in respect of any car used for short-term hire, 75% or more of the total use of the car during the relevant accounting period must be used under hire-drive agreements for periods of short-term hire. Any period for which the car is hired for a continuous period exceeding eight weeks, or any period for which it is in use for any other purpose, is counted as a period of non-qualifying use.

For the purpose of the qualifying use test, if one period of hire of a car to a person (the hirer) by a car hire company is followed within seven days by a further period of hire to the same hirer by the same company (whether or not the same car is hired), the two periods of hire are aggregated. If the aggregated period exceeds eight weeks, neither of the two periods counts as a period of short-term hire. For this purpose, the hire of a car within seven days to a person connected with the hirer is treated as being to the hirer, and the hire of a car within seven days by a person connected with the company is treated as hire by the company. Any question as to whether or not a person is connected with another person is to be determined in accordance with TCA 1997, s 10(3)-(8) (see **2.3**)).

(e) Plant (other than excepted vehicles) provided before 1 April 1992

The position regarding wear and tear allowances in respect of machinery or plant provided before 1 April 1992 was, briefly, as follows. ITA 1967 s 241(1), (7) and (8), in their pre-FA 1992 s 26 form, provided for the rate and method of calculating wear and tear allowances for all machinery or plant provided for use in a trade before 1 April 1992. Where the machinery or plant was first used in a trade before that date, these subsections continued to apply for all subsequent wear and tear allowances in respect of the same machinery or plant used in that trade for accounting periods ending before 6 April 1996. For subsequent accounting periods, the procedure is governed by TCA 1997, s 284 in its present form (see (a) and (b) above).

In contrast with the straight-line method, wear and tear allowances for accounting periods ended before 6 April 1996 in respect of machinery or plant provided before 1 April 1992 were computed for each successive accounting period on the "reducing balance" method. This involved applying the appropriate rate of allowance (10%, 12.5% or 25%) to the tax written down value of each category of machinery or plant at the beginning of the accounting period for which the allowance is to be given.

The computation was therefore a product of two factors, the tax written down value at the beginning of the accounting period and the appropriate rate of wear and tear.

The rate of wear and tear provided for under the pre-FA 1992 regime was a sum equal to five-fourths of the amount considered by the Appeal Commissioners to be just and reasonable as representing the diminished value by reason of the wear and tear of the machinery or plant during the accounting period in question. However, for machinery or plant (other than the excepted vehicles and ships) which, at the time it was provided for use in the trade or profession, was new (ie, unused and not second-hand), FA 1968 s 4 substituted a different rate of wear and tear (the "actual rate") for the rate which would otherwise apply under ITA 1967 s 241(1).

The actual rate of wear and tear required by FA 1968 s 4 to be applied for such new machinery or plant varied by reference to the "basic rate" of wear and tear for the type of plant concerned. In this context, the "basic rate of wear and tear " referred to the rate needed to give the amount which the Appeal Commissioners would consider just and reasonable to measure the diminished value by reason of wear and tear. The basic rate was the rate before applying the five-fourths multiple mentioned in ITA 1967 s 241(1).

FA 1968 s 4 (now repealed) provided for three wear and tear categories where the actual rate is determined as follows:

Basic rate	*Actual rate*
Not more than 8.75%	10%
Over 8.75% but less than 15%	12.5%
15% or more	25%

As already mentioned, in order to provide a uniform method of claiming capital allowances for all machinery or plant (apart from excepted vehicles), ITA 1967 s 241(1A) provided that, for accounting periods ended after 5 April 1996, the straight-line basis applies to machinery or plant provided before 1 April 1992 also. For this purpose, the starting point is the tax written value at the end of the last accounting period ending before 6 April 1996.

5.204   Free depreciation

5.204.1   General

With some exceptions, increased wear and tear, or free depreciation, allowances have ceased to be available for any machinery or plant first provided for use for the purposes of a trade on or after 1 April 1992. However, as there are certain exceptions (eg, machinery or plant provided for a trade carried on in the International Financial Services Centre and for certain financial services operations in the Shannon Customs Free Airport), and as the free depreciation rules continue to apply from that date for machinery or plant first used before that date, it remains appropriate to consider this incentive.

Where still relevant, TCA 1997, s 285 provides that a person carrying on a trade is entitled to claim an increased wear and tear allowance in respect of the cost of new machinery or plant (other than motor vehicles) provided for use in any area other than a designated area for the purposes of that trade. The section permits the same increased wear and tear allowance to be claimed in respect of new machinery or plant (other than motor vehicles) provided for use in a designated area (basically an underdeveloped area of the State).

The increased wear and tear allowance is generally referred to as a "free depreciation" allowance; a company entitled to the allowance is free, subject to certain limits, to specify the amount by which it wishes to increase the normal wear and tear allowance for the accounting period in question. It may not, however, specify an allowance lower than the normal wear and tear allowance.

A company carrying on a trade is entitled to claim a free depreciation allowance in respect of the capital expenditure on any item of machinery or plant for an accounting period where all of the following conditions are met:

(a)   the machinery plant is "qualifying machinery or plant" provided for the trade;

(b)   the capital expenditure in providing the machinery or plant was incurred by the company;

(c)   the machinery or plant was in use for the purposes of the trade at the end of the relevant accounting period;

(d) the machinery or plant belongs to the company at the end of the accounting period;

(e) the machinery or plant, while used for the purposes of the trade, is wholly and exclusively so used (TCA 1997, s 284(2));

(f) the capital expenditure has not already been fully written down by wear and tear (including increased wear and tear) allowances obtained for any previous accounting period (TCA 1997, s 284(4)); and

(g) the machinery or plant was either provided for the trade before 1 April 1992 or is within one of the exceptions provided for in TCA 1997, s 271, 273, 283 or 285 (see **5.204.3** below).

A lessor of qualifying machinery or plant who bears the burden of the wear and tear is also entitled to claim a free depreciation allowance if the corresponding conditions are met (see **5.301**). A lessee of machinery or plant, although entitled by TCA 1997, s 299(1) to a normal wear and tear allowance in the case where the burden of wear and tear falls directly on him, is not normally entitled to the free depreciation allowance (but see **5.303** for exception).

To consist of "qualifying machinery or plant" on which a free depreciation allowance may be claimed, machinery or plant must be new, ie, unused and not second-hand, at the time it was first provided for use in the relevant trade. In the case of leased plant, it must have been new when it was first leased. No free depreciation may be claimed on any excepted vehicle (ie, one suitable for the conveyance by road of persons or goods or for the haulage by road of other vehicles). Plant such as forklift trucks which can only be used for moving goods within short distances, eg, within a factory area, is accepted as qualifying for free depreciation.

For qualifying machinery or plant provided for use before 1 April 1988, free depreciation of up to 100% of the capital expenditure is available. For machinery or plant provided for use between 1 April 1988 and 31 March 1992, other than in certain excepted cases, the maximum free depreciation was progressively reduced from 75% to 25% of the amount of the expenditure. For machinery or plant provided after 31 March 1992, free depreciation is only available in the excepted cases (see below).

The free depreciation allowance in respect of the capital expenditure on any item of qualifying machinery or plant may, to the extent available, be claimed in full for the first relevant accounting period in relation to that item. Alternatively, the claimant company is entitled to spread the available free depreciation on any item of plant over two or more accounting periods, which may or may not include the first accounting period (provided that the conditions for a free depreciation allowance continue to be met in each accounting period for which the allowance is claimed).

For a company, the first relevant accounting period is the period in which the machinery or plant is provided for use. As with the normal wear and tear allowance (see **5.203.2**), "provided for use" is taken as meaning "first used".

The qualifying expenditure for which a free depreciation claim may be made is the same capital expenditure as that on which the normal wear and tear allowances are given. If any grant or similar subsidy has been received towards the capital expenditure in providing any machinery or plant, the general rule is that only the net capital cost after deducting the grant may be written down by free depreciation allowances (TCA 1997, s 317(3)). The treatment of grants, as well as details of certain exceptions to the requirement to deduct them from the cost of machinery or plant, is discussed in **5.208**.

A claim to free depreciation is treated as an increased wear and tear allowance under the rules of TCA 1997, s 284. Any other references in the Tax Acts to an allowance under TCA 1997, s 284 are taken as including a reference to a wear and tear allowance as increased by a claim for free depreciation. If a claim is made for such an increased wear and tear allowance for any item of machinery or plant for any accounting period, no claim for an initial allowance may be made for the same item for the same period or for any later period (TCA 1997, s 285(8)).

5.204.2 Phasing out of free depreciation

In general, no free depreciation allowance may be claimed in respect of any item of machinery or plant which is provided for first use in a trade after 31 March 1992 (TCA 1997, s 285(3)(a)). There are certain exceptions to this general rule (see below). This complete withdrawal of the free depreciation allowance, other than in the excepted cases, took effect after the end of the period 1 April 1988 to 31 March 1992 during which the maximum amount which could be claimed as free depreciation, in one or more accounting periods, was progressively reduced from the 100% rate.

The phasing out of free depreciation allowances for machinery or plant, other than for the excepted cases, is summarised as follows:

Date provided for use	Maximum free depreciation
1 April 1988 to 31 March 1989	75%
1 April 1989 to 31 March 1991	50%
1 April 1991 to 31 March 1992	25%
On or after 1 April 1992	none

5.204.3 Exceptions to phasing out

(a) 100% free depreciation

A company can, by virtue of TCA 1997, s 285(4), (5), continue to claim free depreciation up to a maximum of 100% of the capital expenditure on qualifying machinery or plant (whether in one or more accounting periods) in any of the following circumstances:

(i) where the machinery or plant is provided for use for "relevant trading operations" (TCA 1997, s 445) carried on in the Shannon Customs-Free Airport;

(ii) where machinery or plant is provided for use for "relevant trading operations" (TCA 1997, s 446) carried on in the Dublin International Financial Services Centre;

(iii) where the machinery or plant is provided under a binding contract entered into before 28 January 1988 (whether or not grant-aided), subject to the expenditure being incurred before 31 December 1995;

(iv) where the machinery or plant is provided for the purposes of a project approved by one of the three industrial development agencies (the Industrial Development Authority, the Shannon Free Airport Development Company Limited or Údarás na Gaeltachta) on or before 31 December 1988, subject to the expenditure being incurred before 31 December 1995 (or before 31 December 1996 where the project was approved in the period 1 January 1986 and 31 December 1988);

(v) where the machinery or plant is provided before 1 April 1991 for the purposes of a trade or part of a trade of hotel-keeping which is carried on in a building or structure for which there was a binding contract entered into in the period from 28 January 1988 to 31 May 1988.

Exception (iii) could, prior to FA 1995, have been invoked in respect of machinery or plant purchased at any time, even several years later, in any case where the related binding contract had been completed before 28 January 1988. However, TCA 1997, s 285(5) imposes a 31 December 1995 deadline by which date the related expenditure had to be incurred to preserve the entitlement to the 100% free depreciation incentive.

For the purpose of exception (iv), it is the approval of the project by the relevant industrial development agency which must be given by 31 December 1988. Prior to FA 1995 there was no time deadline within which the machinery or plant had to be provided for use in a trade. FA 1995 s 26 (now TCA 1997, s 285(5)), however, imposed a 31 December 1995 deadline; alternatively, if the project was approved in the period 1 January 1986 to 31 December 1988, the deadline was 31 December 1996.

Furthermore, the 100% free depreciation deduction is only available for machinery or plant acquired for the purposes of the particular *project* which received the approval from the relevant industrial development agency. For this purpose, a project submitted for approval is normally in the form of a business plan from an industrial undertaking applying for grant assistance. The business plan usually gives details of the machinery or plant and any other fixed assets needed to implement the project.

In any case where free depreciation is claimed in respect of any item of machinery or plant provided for use after 31 March 1988, it is necessary to establish that the item in question has been acquired for the approved project within the terms of the business plan submitted. Additional plant acquired some years later for the same trade or undertaking, if not specified, or at least envisaged, within the original plan, is unlikely to come within exception (iv). In this connection, it will probably be relevant to have regard to what was actually set out in the business plan on the basis of which the project was approved.

For the purpose of exception (v), the machinery or plant must be provided before 1 April 1991, but the date of the expenditure is not relevant; it is the binding contract for the hotel (or similar building or structure) which must be entered into within the dates stated and not the contract for the plant.

(b) 50% Free depreciation

A company can, by virtue of TCA 1997, s 285(6), (7), continue to claim free depreciation up to a maximum of 50% of the capital expenditure on qualifying machinery or plant (whether in one or more accounting periods) in any of the following circumstances:

(a) where the machinery or plant is provided for the purpose of a project approved for grant assistance by the Industrial Development Authority, the Shannon Free-Airport Development Company Limited or Údarás na Gaeltachta in the period 1 January 1989 to 31 December 1990, subject to the expenditure being incurred:

    (i)   before 31 December 1997, or

    (ii)   before 30 June 1998 if its provision is solely for use in an industrial building or structure referred to in TCA 1997 ss 271(3)(c) and 273(7)(a)(i) and such expenditure would have been incurred before 31 December 1997 were it not for the initiation of legal proceedings which were the subject of an order of the High Court made before 1 January 1998; or

    (iii)   before 31 December 2002 if the project is approved for TCA 1997, s 130 ("section 84") loan financing and is specified in the list referred to in TCA 1997, s 133(8)(c)(iv)); (TCA 1997, s 283(3)(b), (5)),

  (b)   where machinery or plant is provided for the purposes of a trade or part of a trade of hotel-keeping carried on in a building or structure which is to be registered in a register kept by the National Tourism Development Authority under the Tourist Traffic Acts, 1939 to 1995, but only if a binding contract has been entered into before 31 December 1990 for the provision of the building or structure, subject the expenditure being incurred before 31 December 1995.

The 50% free depreciation deduction available under the above two exceptions is not conditional on the time by which the machinery or plant is first used. The applicable deadlines relate to the time the relevant expenditure was incurred. It is also clear that the plant for which the allowance is sought must be within the terms of the business plan submitted (see remarks relating to exception (iv) for the continued 100% free depreciation). For exception (b), it is the date of the binding contract for the building or structure (and not that for the plant) which is relevant. If the project has been approved by the relevant date (exception (a)) or if the contract for the building has been entered into before the relevant date (exception (b)), the 50% free depreciation deduction may be claimed as long as the expenditure is incurred before 31 December 1995.

To avail of exception (b), a further condition must be met: the building or structure for the trade of hotel-keeping must actually be registered within six months after the date of the completion thereof in the the National Tourism Development Authority register. Should the 50% or any lower free depreciation allowance be made where the necessary registration did not take place within the required six months period, the excess of the free depreciation allowances given over the normal wear and tear allowances will be withdrawn and any additional assessment required to correct the overallowance may be made.

5.204.4   Free depreciation in different periods

The date on which any item of qualifying machinery or plant is provided for first use in a company's trade is important since, in most cases, it determines whether any free depreciation allowance at all can be claimed. Where free depreciation can be so claimed, the date on which the machinery or plant was provided for first use also fixes the maximum free depreciation deduction which may be made in respect of the relevant capital expenditure over the entire life of the machinery or plant in the trade concerned. The position may be considered by reference to the different periods in which machinery or plant is provided for first use as follows:

(a) Provided for use after 31 March 1992

As a general rule, free depreciation is not available in respect of any machinery or plant provided on or after 1 April 1992. However, free depreciation allowances of up to 100% of the expenditure may be claimed in any of the excepted cases within TCA 1997, s 285(5) and free depreciation allowances of up to 50% in any of the cases within TCA 1997, s 285(7), as described above. In any such case, the maximum free depreciation, 100% or 50% as the case may be, may be claimed for the first accounting period. Alternatively, a company may take the available free depreciation allowances in one or more such accounting periods as it wishes (assuming the conditions for the allowance are met in relation to the accounting period for which the claim is made).

For machinery or plant first used in a trade after 31 March 1992, the normal wear and tear allowance for each accounting period is 20% (15% for expenditure incurred before 1 January 2001) of the capital expenditure on the straight-line basis, except when the amount of the allowance is reduced proportionately in the case where the length of the accounting period is shorter than 12 months (see **5.203.3**). Accordingly, the amount claimed as free depreciation for any accounting period must be an amount in excess of 15% (or the appropriate proportion of 15%) of the qualifying expenditure

Accordingly, in any of the excepted cases, a company has the option of claiming either a free depreciation allowance or an initial allowance for each item of machinery or plant, but not both.

However, it may claim free depreciation on one item and an initial allowance on another item, whether or not the allowances fall into the same accounting period. Since the free depreciation and initial allowances, where available, are given at the same rate, in most cases it may not matter which type of accelerated allowance is claimed, but several points should be noted.

Firstly, since free depreciation is given by reference to the date on which machinery or plant is provided for use, while initial allowances are given by reference to the date the qualifying expenditure is incurred, it is possible for the two dates to fall in different accounting periods. Where this happens, a claim for initial allowance may result in the allowance being obtained for an accounting period earlier than would be the case if free depreciation had been claimed (where the date the expenditure is incurred is in an earlier accounting period than that in which the plant is first used). The converse may also be true but is more unlikely.

Secondly, if free depreciation is claimed, the taxpayer has the option of spreading the allowance over two or more accounting periods, whereas an initial allowance must always be claimed in full for the accounting period in which the capital expenditure is incurred. While any capital allowances in excess of the taxable profits of one accounting period can be carried forward as a loss for set off against taxable profits of a later period, it may well be advantageous for a company to have a lower taxable profit (after capital allowances) for one accounting period, but not a nil profit, and to have greater capital allowances in the next accounting period. In short, free depreciation offers greater flexibility than the initial allowance.

(b) Provided for use from 1 April 1991 to 31 March 1991

For machinery or plant provided for use after 31 March 1991 but not later than 31 March 1992, free depreciation up to a maximum of 25% of the qualifying expenditure may be claimed. However, free depreciation is available up to 100% of the qualifying expenditure on any item of plant which is within any of the exceptions in TCA 1997, s 285(5), or up to a maximum of 50% of the expenditure for machinery or plant within any of the exceptions in TCA 1997, s 285(7) (see **5.204.3** above). In any of these cases, the maximum free depreciation available to a company could be claimed either for the first accounting period in which the machinery or plant is first used or in such one or more accounting periods decided on by the company (so long as the conditions for a free depreciation allowance continue to be met).

The restrictions which prevent a free depreciation allowance being obtained for any accounting period where an initial allowance has been claimed in respect of the same item of machinery or plant, and which deny an initial allowance where free depreciation has been claimed, operated in the same way as for machinery or plant provided for use after 31 March 1992 (see above).

A normal wear and tear allowance remains available for any accounting period for which a free depreciation allowance is not obtained, and provided no initial allowance was claimed. In applying the 25% limit, when the aggregate of all allowances which have been taken as free depreciation in respect of the same item of machinery or plant reaches 25% of capital expenditure, only normal wear and tear allowances may be claimed thereafter. Any wear and tear allowances obtained at the normal rate only are not aggregated for this purpose.

Where the 25% aggregate amount of free depreciation has not yet been claimed, any balance should be taken at latest in the last accounting period ending before 6 April 1999 as TCA 1997, s 285(3)(b) prohibits any claim to free depreciation, other than in the excepted cases (see above), for accounting periods ending on or after that date.

(c) Provided for use from 1 April 1989 to 31 March 1991

For machinery or plant provided for use after 31 March 1989 but not later than 31 March 1991, free depreciation up to a maximum of 50% of the qualifying expenditure may be written off. However, free depreciation of up to 100% of the qualifying expenditure was available in respect of machinery or plant within any of the exceptions in TCA 1997, s 285(5) (see **5.204.3** above). In any of these cases, the maximum free depreciation available to a company could be claimed either for the first accounting period in which the machinery or plant is first used or in such one or more accounting periods decided on by the company (so long as the conditions for a free depreciation allowance continue to be met).

The restrictions which prevent a free depreciation allowance being obtained for any accounting period where an initial allowance has been claimed in respect of the same item of machinery or plant, and which deny an initial allowance where free depreciation has been claimed, operated in the same way as for machinery or plant provided for use after 31 March 1992 (see above).

A normal wear and tear allowance remains available for any accounting period for which a free depreciation allowance is not obtained, and provided no initial allowance was claimed. In applying the 50% limit, when the aggregate of all allowances which have been taken as free depreciation in respect of the same item of machinery or plant reaches 50% of capital expenditure, only normal wear and tear allowances may be claimed thereafter. Any wear and tear allowances obtained at the normal rate only are not aggregated for this purpose.

Where the 50% aggregate amount of free depreciation has not yet been claimed, any balance should be taken at latest in the last accounting period ending before 6 April 1999 as TCA 1997, s 285(3)(b) prohibits any claim to free depreciation, other than in the excepted cases (see above), for accounting periods ending on or after that date.

(d) Provided for use from 1 April 1988 to 31 March 1989

For machinery or plant provided for use after 31 March 1988 but not later than 31 March 1989, free depreciation up to a maximum of 75% of the qualifying expenditure may be written off. However, free depreciation could be taken at up to 100% of the qualifying expenditure on any item of plant which is within any of the exceptions in TCA 1997, s 285(5) (see **5.204.3** above). In any of these cases, the maximum free depreciation available to a company could be claimed either for the first accounting period in which the machinery or plant is first used or in such one or more accounting periods decided on by the company (so long as the conditions for a free depreciation allowance continue to be met).

The restrictions which prevent a free depreciation allowance being obtained for any accounting period where an initial allowance has been claimed in respect of the same item of machinery or plant, and which deny an initial allowance where free depreciation has been claimed, operated in the same way as for machinery or plant provided for use after 31 March 1992 (see above).

A normal wear and tear allowance continued to be available for any accounting period for which a free depreciation allowance is not obtained. It was, however, possible to claim a normal wear and tear allowance for the same accounting period for which a 75% initial allowance was obtained. In applying the 75% free depreciation limit, when the aggregate of all allowances which have been taken as free depreciation in respect of the same item of machinery or plant reaches 75% of capital expenditure, only normal wear and tear allowances may be claimed thereafter. Any wear and tear allowances obtained at the normal rate only are not aggregated for this purpose.

Where the 75% aggregate amount of free depreciation has not yet been claimed, any balance should be taken at latest in the last accounting period ending before 6 April 1999 as TCA 1997, s 285(3)(b) prohibits any claim to free depreciation, other than in the excepted cases (see above), for chargeable periods ending on or after that date.

(e) Provided for use before 1 April 1988

For qualifying expenditure on machinery or plant provided for use before 1 April 1988, the free depreciation election permitted a company to take an allowance, in excess of a normal allowance, of up to 100% of the expenditure as an increased wear and tear allowance for the accounting period in which the machinery or plant was first provided for use. Alternatively, the company could take the normal wear and tear allowance without making any free depreciation election. If less than a 100% allowance was taken in the first accounting period, the company could claim either an increased or a normal wear and tear allowance for the following or any later period until the balance of the expenditure is fully written off.

Where the full amount of free depreciation has not yet been claimed, any balance should be taken at latest in the last accounting period ending before 6 April 1999 as TCA 1997, s 285(3)(b) prohibits any claim to free depreciation, other than in the excepted cases (see above), for accounting periods ending on or after that date.

5.204.5   Accelerated allowances for certain sea fishing boats

A scheme of capital allowances for whitefish fishing boats, which applies for a six year period commencing on 4 September 1998 (the day appointed by order by the Minister for Finance – SI 132/1998), provides for a first year allowance of 50% of the expenditure incurred and a write off of the balance at 15% for six years and 10% for the final year.

The fishing boats (referred to here as qualifying fishing boats) in respect of which the scheme applies are sea fishing boats registered in the Register of Fishing Boats and in respect of which capital expenditure is incurred in the period of six years commencing on the appointed day, being expenditure certified by Bord Iascaigh Mhara as capital expenditure incurred for the purpose of fleet renewal in the polyvalent and beam trawl segments of the fishing fleet. The "appointed day" is defined as such day as the Minister for Finance may, by order, appoint.

Subject to TCA 1997, s 284(3A)(ba) (see below), TCA 1997, s 284(3A)(b) provides for wear and tear allowances to be made to any person in respect of a qualifying fishing boat during a writing-down period of 8 years beginning with the first chargeable period (accounting period in the case of a company) at the end of which the boat belongs to that person and is in use for the purposes of that person's trade. The allowance is an amount equal to:

(a) for the first year of the 8 year writing-down period, 50% of the actual cost of the boat, including any expenditure in the nature of capital expenditure on the boat by means of renewal, improvement or reinstatement;

(b) for each of the next 6 years of the writing-down period, 15% of the balance of the actual cost after deducting any allowance made in accordance with (a); and

(c) for the final year of the writing-down period, 10% of the balance of the actual cost after deducting any allowance made in accordance with (a).

Where a chargeable period is a period of less than a year in length, the wear and tear allowance for that period is reduced proportionately; it may not exceed the portion of the amount specified in (a), (b) or (c) above (whichever is appropriate) as bears to that amount the same proportion as the length of the chargeable period bears to a period of one year.

In respect of capital expenditure incurred on or after 30 March 2001, wear and tear allowances to be made to a company in respect of qualifying sea fishing boats are to be made during a writing-down period of 6 years beginning with the first accounting period at the end of which the fishing boats belongs to the company and are in use for the purposes of the company's trade, and will be an amount equal to:

(i) for the first writing-down period, 50% of the actual cost of the fishing boats, including in that cost any expenditure in the nature of capital expenditure on those boats by means of renewal, improvement or reinstatement; and

(ii) as respects the next 5 years of the writing down period, 20% of the balance of that actual cost after the deduction of any allowance made in accordance with (i) (TCA 1997, s 284(3A)(ba)).

The provisions of TCA 1997, s 403(4), (5) dealing with the ring-fencing of capital allowances for expenditure incurred by a company in respect of leased machinery or plant (see **5.305**) do not apply in the case of expenditure on qualifying fishing boats (TCA 1997, s 403(5A)(b)(ii)).

5.204.6   Accelerated allowances for certain energy-efficient equipment

Outline

The capital allowances legislation in TCA 1997, Part 9 Chapter 2 includes a scheme of accelerated capital allowances in respect of expenditure by companies on certain energy-efficient equipment bought for the purposes of the trade. The scheme, which will run for a trial period of three years, applies to new equipment in designated classes of technology. Equipment eligible under the scheme is included in a list established by the Minister for Communications, Energy and Natural Resources (with the approval of the Minister for Finance) and maintained by the Sustainable Energy Authority of Ireland.

The main features of the new scheme are as follows:

Capital allowances of 100% are available in the first year in which the expenditure is incurred on the equipment covered by the scheme. To qualify for these allowances, the equipment must meet certain energy-efficiency criteria and be specified on a list of approved products. Listed energy-efficient equipment falls into one of three classes of technology and expenditure must be above a certain minimum amount to qualify for the increased allowance.

The technology classes (and minimum expenditure amounts) are: motors and drives (€1,000), lighting (€3,000) and building energy management systems (€5,000). The list is established, and is subject to amendment, by order of the Minister for Communications, Energy and Natural Resources. Sustainable Energy Ireland (SEI) will be responsible for maintaining the list.

The scheme, which is to run to 31 December 2010, is confined to new energy-efficient equipment purchased by companies, and does not apply to equipment that is leased, let or hired.

The new scheme is subject to clearance by the European Commission from a State aid perspective and will come into operation by way of commencement order to be made by the Minister for Finance following such clearance.

Accelerated capital allowances

Where for any chargeable period a wear and tear allowance is to be made under TCA 1997, s 284 to a company which has incurred capital expenditure on the provision of energy-efficient equipment for the purposes of a trade carried on by it, TCA 1997, s 284(2) applies as if the reference in TCA 1997, s 284(2)(ad) (see under *Expenditure incurred on machinery or plant from 4 December 2002 in* **5.203.3**) to 12.5% were a reference to 100% (TCA 1997, s 285A(2)).

For this purpose, *energy-efficient equipment* means equipment, named on and complying with the criteria stated on the specified list, provided for the purposes of a trade and which at the time it is so provided is unused and not second-hand. The *specified list* is the list of energy-efficient equipment which—

(a)   complies with TCA 1997, s 285A(3) and (4), and

(b)   is maintained for the purposes of this section by Sustainable Energy Ireland – The Sustainable Energy Authority of Ireland

The specified list may contain only such equipment that—

(a)   is in a class of technology specified in column (1) of the Table in TCA 1997, Schedule 4A (see below), and

(b)   is of a description for that class of technology specified in column (2) of the Table (TCA 1997, s 285A(3)).

The Minister for Communications, Energy and Natural Resources, after consultation with and the approval of the Minister for Finance—

(a)   will by order make the specified list—

    (i)   stating the energy efficiency criteria to be met for, and

    (ii)   naming the eligible products in,

    each class of technology specified in column (1) of the Table, and

(b)   may by order amend the specified list—

    (i)   stating energy efficiency criteria to be met for, or

    (ii)   naming eligible products in,

    any class of technology specified in column (1) of the Table (TCA 1997, s 285A(4)).

Accelerated allowances in accordance with TCA 1997, s 285A may not be made—

(a)   to any person other than a company,

(b)   where the energy-efficient equipment is leased, let or hired to any person,

(c)   in respect of expenditure incurred in a chargeable period on the provision of energy-efficient equipment in relation to a class of technology where the amount of that expenditure is less than the minimum amount specified in column (3) of the Table in relation to that class of technology,

(d)   in respect of expenditure incurred on the provision of equipment where that expenditure is not incurred in the *relevant period*, ie the period from 31 January 2008 to 31 December 2010 (TCA 1997, s 285A(5), (6), (7)(a)).

Where expenditure on equipment is incurred on or after 31 January 2008 but before the first order is made under TCA 1997, s 285A(4), and that equipment would have qualified as energy-efficient equipment had such an order been made at the time the expenditure was incurred, TCA 1997, s 285A will apply as if the order had been made at that time (TCA 1997, s 285A(7)(b)).

Where TCA 1997, s 285A applies to capital expenditure incurred by a company on the provision of energy-efficient equipment and that equipment would not otherwise be treated as machinery or plant, that equipment is to be treated as machinery or plant for capital allowances purposes (TCA 1997, s 285A(8)).

TABLE

Class of technology (1)	Description (2)	Minimum amount (€) (3)
Motors and drives	*Motor:* An asynchronous electric motor with a power rating of 1.1kW or greater, either standalone or as part of other equipment, meeting a specified efficiency standard.	€1,000
	Variable speed drive: A drive that is specifically designed to drive an AC induction motor in a manner that rotates the motor's drive shaft at a variable speed dictated by an external signal.	
Lighting	Lighting units, comprising fittings, lamps, and associated control gear, that meet specified efficiency criteria, or lighting control systems designed to improve the efficiency of lighting units. Includes occupancy sensors and high efficiency signs.	€3,000
Building energy management systems	Computer-based systems, designed primarily to monitor and control building energy use with the aim of optimising energy efficiency and meeting specified efficiency standards.	€5,000

5.205   Initial allowances

5.205.1   General

Initial allowances have ceased to be available generally for expenditure incurred on machinery or plant on or after 1 April 1992. As with free depreciation, however, there are certain exceptions and it is therefore still appropriate to consider the question of initial allowances.

Where still relevant, TCA 1997, s 283 provides that a person carrying on a trade is entitled to claim an initial allowance in respect of capital expenditure incurred on new machinery or plant (other than excepted motor vehicles – see condition (d) below) for the purposes of a trade. TCA 1997, s 301(2) extends the provisions of TCA 1997, s 283 to give initial allowances in corresponding circumstances for new machinery or plant (other than the excepted motor vehicles) provided for the purposes of a profession.

A lessor of machinery or plant who bears the burden of the wear and tear is also entitled to an initial allowance, where available, in respect of qualifying capital expenditure incurred in providing the leased plant (TCA 1997, s 298(1) – see **5.301**). A company using machinery or plant which it has leased for the purposes of its trade may claim an initial allowance in respect of the qualifying expenditure on the machinery or plant where it bears the burden of the wear and tear of that machinery or plant (TCA 1997, s 299(1) – see **5.303**).

A company carrying on a trade is entitled to an initial allowance in respect of the capital expenditure on any item of machinery or plant for an accounting period where all of the following conditions are met:

(a)   the machinery or plant on which the capital expenditure is incurred must be new, ie, it must be unused and not second-hand (except that for this purpose any ship, even if it has been used or is second-hand, is deemed to be new);

(b)   the capital expenditure must have been incurred by the company claiming the initial allowance (except where the initial allowance is claimed by a lessee who bears the burden of wear and tear and who is thereby entitled to the allowance under TCA 1997, s 299(1));

(c)   the machinery or plant, while used for the purposes of the trade, must be wholly and exclusively so used – for expenditure incurred after 31 March 1990;

(d)   the machinery or plant must not be an excepted vehicle (ie, a motor vehicle which is suitable for the conveyance by road of persons or goods or for the haulage by road of other vehicles);

(e)   no free depreciation allowance has been obtained in respect of the same item of machinery or plant for the same or any earlier accounting period; and

(f)   the capital expenditure must have been incurred before 1 April 1992 or must be within one of the exceptions of TCA 1997, s 283(4) or TCA 1997, s 283(5) (see *Exceptions* below).

Condition (d) excludes from the allowance all private motor cars, lorries, tractors, delivery vans, buses and other commercial vehicles, but does not exclude plant such as forklift trucks which can only be used for moving goods short distances.

The capital expenditure on which the initial allowances are based is, as the general rule, the net capital expenditure after deducting any grants or other subsidies which are obtained directly or indirectly from the State, any statutory board or any public authority (TCA 1997, s 317). The treatment of grants, as well as details of certain exceptions to the requirement to deduct them from the cost of machinery or plant, is discussed in **5.208**.

The initial allowance, where available, may be claimed on the qualifying expenditure as an alternative to claiming free depreciation. No initial allowance is available for any accounting period in respect of any item of machinery or plant for which free depreciation has been claimed for the same or any earlier accounting period (TCA 1997, s 285(8)).

Initial allowances are given for the chargeable period related to the expenditure. In the case of a company, this refers to the accounting period in which the expenditure is incurred.

TCA 1997, s 283(7) imposes a limit to the amount of the initial allowance which may be obtained for capital expenditure on machinery or plant for any accounting period. The initial allowance for an accounting period may not exceed the amount which, when added to the aggregate amount of any wear and tear and initial allowances obtained in respect of the same machinery or plant for the same or for previous accounting periods, would result in the total allowances exceeding the actual cost of the plant.

5.205.2 Date expenditure incurred

For initial allowance purposes, the date on which the capital expenditure on the machinery or plant is incurred is the date on which the sum in question becomes payable (TCA 1997, s 316(2)). The date on which a sum due in respect of capital expenditure becomes payable is normally the agreed date for payment specified in the agreement between the seller and the purchaser, whether or not the actual payment is made by this date. If no date for payment is specified, there may be a presumption in the case of a sale on credit that the amount is due one month from the date of invoice, although in practice the date of the invoice is frequently taken as the due date. Initial allowances on plant acquired by hire purchase are given on the capital element of the total instalments due for payment in each relevant accounting period.

The phasing out process for initial allowances, involving a reduction from 100% to zero over the period 31 March 1988 to 1 April 1992, is similar to that for free depreciation, as discussed in **5.204.3**. The circumstances in which the 100% and 50% initial allowances are still available, by virtue of TCA 1997, s 283(3)(a) and TCA 1997, s 283(3)(b) respectively, are the same as those for free depreciation (see **5.205.5** below).

As an exception to the general rule that expenditure is incurred on the date it becomes payable, TCA 1997, s 316(3) provides that any capital expenditure incurred before the commencement of a trade is treated as incurred on the date on which the trade commenced.

5.205.3 Initial allowance and free depreciation

The position regarding the interaction of initial allowances and free depreciation is the same as was discussed in **5.204.4**. The position is as follows:

(1) if a free depreciation allowance is made for any accounting period in respect of any item of machinery or plant, no initial allowance may be made in relation to that item for the same or any later period (TCA 1997, s 285(8));

(2) if a 50% initial allowance is made for any accounting period in respect of capital expenditure on any item of machinery or plant within any of the exceptions in TCA 1997, s 283(5), no free depreciation allowance may be made in respect of that item for the same or any subsequent accounting period (TCA 1997, s 283(6)).

There are, however, two situations in which an initial allowance may be obtained where no free depreciation allowance is available. Firstly, an initial allowance, but no free depreciation allowance, is available for the capital expenditure in acquiring a second-hand ship (the only exception to the unused and not second-hand condition). Secondly, a company which has acquired machinery or plant on lease, in respect of which it bears the burden of wear and tear, and which is thereby entitled to a wear and tear allowance under TCA 1997, s 299(1), is also entitled to the initial allowance in all cases where that allowance is available, but is not entitled to any free depreciation allowance unless the contract of letting provides that it shall, or may, become the owner of the plant when the contract is performed (see **5.303**).

5.205.4 Phasing out of initial allowances

The rates of initial allowance which applied from the date of their introduction in 1956 up to 31 March 1988 are as follows:

Expenditure incurred	Rate
6 April 1956 to 31 December 1961	20%
14 December 1961 to 31 March 1967	40%
1 April 1967 to 31 March 1968	50%

1 April 1968 to 31 March 1971	60%
1 April 1971 to 31 March 1988	100%

In general, initial allowances for machinery or plant have ceased to be available for capital expenditure incurred after 31 March 1992 (ITA 1967 s 251(3)). There are certain exceptions to this general rule (see below). The phasing out process for the initial allowance (apart from the excepted cases) is summarised in the following table:

Expenditure incurred	*Rate*
1 April 1988 to 31 March 1989	75%
1 April 1989 to 31 March 1991	50%
1 April 1991 to 31 March 1992	25%
On or after 1 April 1992	Zero

5.205.5 Exceptions to phasing out

(a) 100% initial allowance

After 31 March 1988 companies continued, by virtue of FA 1988 s 51/TCA 1997, s 283(3)(a), (4), to be entitled to claim a 100% initial allowance, irrespective of the date of the expenditure on the qualifying machinery or plant, in any of the following circumstances:

(a)　where the machinery or plant is provided:

　　(i)　before 23 April 1996 for use for the purposes of trading operations, or

　　(ii)　on or after 23 April 1996, by a company for use for the purposes of trading operations carried on by the company,

　　which are "relevant trading operations" within the meaning of TCA 1997, s 445, carried on in the Shannon Customs Free Airport (TCA 1997, s 283(4)(a));

(b)　where the machinery or plant is provided:

　　(i)　before 23 April 1996 for use for the purposes of trading operations, or

　　(ii)　on or after 23 April 1996, by a company for use for the purposes of trading operations carried on by the company,

　　which are "relevant trading operations" within the meaning of TCA 1997, s 446, carried on in the Dublin International Financial Services Centre (TCA 1997, s 283(4)(a));

(c)　where the machinery or plant was provided under a binding contract entered into before 28 January 1988 (whether or not grant-aided), subject to the expenditure being incurred before 31 December 1995 (FA 1988 s 51(1)(c));

(d)　where the machinery or plant was provided for the purposes of a project approved by one of the three industrial development agencies (the Industrial Development Authority, the Shannon Free Airport Company Limited or Údarás na Gaeltachta) on or before 31 December 1988, subject to the expenditure being incurred before 31 December 1995 (FA 1988 s 51(1)(cc));

(e)　where the machinery or plant was provided for the purposes of a project approved by one of the three industrial development agencies in the period 1

January 1986 to 31 December 1988, subject to the expenditure being incurred before 31 December 1996 (TCA 1997, s 283(4)(b));

(f) where the machinery or plant was provided before 1 April 1991 for the purposes of a trade or part of a trade of hotel-keeping carried on in a building or structure in respect of which there was a binding contract entered into in the period from 28 January 1988 to 31 May 1988 (FA 1988 s 51(1)(d)).

Exception (c) could, prior to FA 1995, have been invoked in respect of machinery or plant for which the expenditure was incurred at any time, even several years later, in any case where the related binding contract had been completed before 28 January 1988. However, FA 1988 s 51(1)(c) imposed a 31 December 1995 deadline before which date the related expenditure had to be incurred to preserve the entitlement to the 100% free depreciation incentive.

For the purpose of exception (d), it is the approval of the project by the relevant industrial development agency which must be given by 31 December 1988. Prior to FA 1995 there was no time limit within which the machinery or plant had to be provided for use in a trade. FA 1988 s 51(1)(cc), however, imposed a 31 December 1995 deadline; alternatively (exception (e), if the project was approved in the period 1 January 1986 to 31 December 1988, the deadline was 31 December 1996.

Furthermore, the 100% initial allowance is only available for machinery or plant acquired for the purposes of the particular *project* which received the approval from the relevant industrial development agency. For this purpose, a project submitted for approval is normally in the form of a business plan from an industrial undertaking applying for grant assistance. The business plan usually gives details of the machinery or plant and any other fixed assets needed to implement the project.

In any case where an initial allowance is claimed in respect of expenditure incurred after 31 March 1988 in respect of machinery or plant, it is necessary to establish that the item in question has been acquired for the approved project within the terms of the business plan submitted. Additional plant acquired some years later for the same trade or undertaking, if not specified, or at least envisaged, within the original plan, is unlikely to come within exceptions (d) or (e). In this connection, it will probably be relevant to have regard to what was actually set out in the business plan on the basis of which the project was approved.

For the purpose of exception (f), the machinery or plant must be provided before 1 April 1991, but the date of the expenditure is not relevant; it is the binding contract for the hotel (or similar building or structure) which must be entered into within the dates stated and not the contract for the plant.

If the binding contract is for only a part of a building or structure (eg, a contract for an extension to an existing hotel building), it would appear that this exception may only apply where the machinery or plant is provided for use in the part of the building or structure the subject of the contract (eg, in the extension).

(b) 50% Initial allowance

After 31 March 1989, companies continued to be entitled to claim a 50% initial allowance in respect of capital expenditure incurred on qualifying machinery or plant in any of the following circumstances:

(a)   where the machinery or plant is provided for the purpose of a project approved for grant assistance by an industrial development agency (the Industrial Development Authority, the Shannon Free-Airport Company Limited or Údarás na Gaeltachta) in the period 1 January 1989 to 31 December 1990, subject to the expenditure being incurred:

(i)   before 31 December 1997, or

(ii)   before 30 June 1998 if its provision is solely for use in an industrial building or structure referred to in TCA 1997 ss 271(3)(c) and 273(7)(a)(i) and such expenditure would have been incurred before 31 December 1997 were it not for the initiation of legal proceedings which were the subject of an order of the High Court made before 1 January 1998; or

(iii)   before 31 December 2002 if the project is approved for TCA 1997, s 130 ("section 84") loan financing and is specified in the list referred to in TCA 1997, s 133(8)(c)(iv)); (TCA 1997, s 283(3)(b), (5)),

(b)   where machinery or plant is provided for the purposes of a trade or part of a trade of hotel-keeping carried on in a building or structure which is to be registered in a register kept by the National Tourism Development Authority under the Tourist Traffic Acts, 1939 to 1987, but only if a binding contract has been entered into before 31 December 1990 for the provision of the building or structure, subject the expenditure being incurred before 31 December 1995 (FA 1990 s 81(1)(c)).

The 50% initial allowance available under the above two exceptions is not conditional on the time by which the machinery or plant is first used. Prior to FA 1995 there was no requirement as to the time within which the expenditure had to be incurred; however, FA 1990 s 81(1)(c)/TCA 1997, s 283(5) imposed the deadlines mentioned in the above exceptions. It is also clear that the plant for which the allowance is sought must be within the terms of the business plan submitted (see remarks relating to exception (d) and (e) for the continued 100% initial allowance).

For exception (ii), it is the date of the binding contract for the building of structure (not that for the plant) which is relevant. If the project has been approved by the relevant date (exception (i)) or if the contract for the building has been entered into before the relevant date (exception (ii)), the 50% initial allowance may be claimed as long as the expenditure is incurred before 31 December 1995.

To avail of exception (ii), a further condition must be met: the building or structure for the trade of hotel-keeping must actually be registered within six months after the date of the completion thereof in the the National Tourism Development Authority register. Should the 50% initial allowance have been availed of where the necessary registration did not take place within the required six months period, the excess of the allowance over the amount of the normal wear and tear allowances will be withdrawn and any additional assessment required to correct the excess allowance may be made.

5.205.6 Initial allowance in different periods

(a) Expenditure incurred after 31 March 1992

As a general rule, no initial allowances are available in respect of capital expenditure incurred in respect of machinery or plant on or after 1 April 1992. However, a 100% initial allowance may be claimed in any of the excepted cases within FA 1988 s 51(1)(c), (cc)/TCA 1997, s 283(4) and a 50% allowance in any of the cases within FA 1990 s 81(1)(c)/ TCA 1997, s 283(5) (see *Exceptions* above).

If the 100% initial allowance is taken for an accounting period by reference to capital expenditure incurred in that period, clearly no wear and tear allowance or free depreciation may be obtained for the same or any later accounting period. Since the cost will have been fully written off, TCA 1997, s 284(4) prevents any further allowance (while the plant continues to be used in the same trade).

If a 50% initial allowance is taken in any of the excepted cases within FA 1990 s 81(1)(c)/TCA 1997, s 283(5) for any accounting period in respect of capital expenditure incurred in that period, TCA 1997, s 283(6) operates to prevent either the normal wear and tear allowance or any free depreciation allowance being given for the same accounting period. However, the normal wear and tear allowance (but not a free depreciation allowance) is available for each subsequent accounting period until the capital expenditure is fully written off by the initial allowance and the subsequent wear and tear allowances.

For capital expenditure incurred after 31 March 1992 which still qualifies for the 50% initial allowance due to FA 1990 s 81(2)/ TCA 1997, s 283(3)(b), the normal straight-line 15% (20% if expenditure incurred on or after 1 January 2001) wear and tear allowance is available (except where the machinery or plant was provided for first use in the trade before 1 April 1992 when the reducing balance method applies). If the 50% initial allowance is taken in that case, the effect is to write off as capital allowances 50% of the expenditure in the first accounting period, 15% in each of the next three accounting periods (or possibly 20% in the next two periods), and the balance of 5% in the fifth accounting period (or possibly 10% in the fourth accounting period, as appropriate).

(b) Expenditure incurred from 1 April 1991 to 31 March 1992

For capital expenditure incurred on machinery or plant after 31 March 1991 but not later than 31 March 1992, a 25% initial allowance was available (ITA 1967 s 251(4)(b)). However, a 100% initial allowance could have been taken in respect of capital expenditure within any of the exceptions in FA 1988 s 51, and a 50% initial allowance was available for capital expenditure within any of the exceptions in FA 1990 s 81 (see **5.205.5** above).

If the 25% or 50% initial allowance was obtained for any accounting period in respect of the capital expenditure incurred between 1 April 1991 and 31 March 1992, TCA 1997, s 283(6) provides two further rules. Firstly, no wear and tear (or free depreciation) allowance could be taken in respect of the same item of machinery or plant for the same accounting period. Secondly, no free depreciation allowance is available in respect of that machinery or plant for any subsequent accounting period. The normal wear and tear allowance, on the reducing balance basis, was of course available for the next accounting period (based on the amount of the capital expenditure as reduced by the

25% or 50% initial allowance obtained for the accounting period in which the expenditure was incurred).

(c) Expenditure incurred from 1 April 1989 to 31 March 1991

For expenditure incurred in respect of machinery or plant after 31 March 1989 but not later than 31 March 1991, a 50% initial allowance could be claimed (ITA 1967 s 251(4)(b)(ii)). However, a 100% initial allowance was available in respect of capital expenditure incurred in respect of machinery or plant within any of the exceptions in FA 1988 s 51 (see **5.205.5** above). Where the 100% initial allowance was obtained due to any of these exceptions, no wear and tear allowance was available as the capital expenditure would have been fully allowed by way of initial allowance (ITA 1967 s 241(6)/ TCA 1997, s 284(4)).

If the 50% initial allowance was obtained for any accounting period in respect of capital expenditure incurred during the period 1 April 1989 to 31 March 1991, the two further rules in respect of capital expenditure incurred in the year ended 31 March 1992 (see (b) above) are relevant here also (TCA 1997, s 283(6)) so that no wear and tear or free depreciation allowance could be claimed for the same accounting period and only a normal wear and tear allowance may be claimed for any subsequent period.

(d) Expenditure incurred from 1 April 1988 to 31 March 1989

For capital expenditure incurred in respect of machinery or plant after 31 March 1988 but not later than 31 March 1989, a 75% initial allowance was available (ITA 1967 s 251(4)(b)(i)). However, a 100% initial allowance was available in respect of qualifying expenditure on machinery or plant within any of the exceptions of FA 1988 s 51 (see **5.205.5** above). Where the 100% initial allowance was obtained in any of these excepted cases, no wear and tear allowance was available as the capital expenditure would have been fully written off (ITA 1967 s 241(6)/ TCA 1997, s 284(4)).

If the 75% initial allowance was obtained in respect of capital expenditure on any item of machinery or plant incurred during the period 1 April 1988 to 31 March 1989, TCA 1997, s 283(6) provides that no free depreciation allowance may be taken in respect of that item. However, TCA 1997, s 283(6) does not prevent a normal wear and tear allowance being obtained for the same accounting period in which the 75% initial allowance was taken.

(e) Expenditure incurred before 1 April 1988

For capital expenditure on new machinery or plant incurred in the period from 1 April 1971 to 31 March 1988, a company could claim a 100% initial allowance (ITA 1967 s 251(4)(d)). This resulted in the full amount of the expenditure being allowed in the accounting period in which the expenditure was incurred. Accordingly, no wear and tear or free depreciation allowance is available for any other accounting period (TCA 1997, s 284(4)).

5.206 Notional wear and tear allowances

If in any accounting period in which machinery or plant has been used by a company, whether or not for its trade, either no wear and tear allowance or an allowance which is less than the normal wear and tear allowance has been taken by the company in respect of that machinery or plant, TCA 1997, s 287 requires that for the purposes of TCA 1997, s 284(3), (4) (see **5.203.3**), a normal wear and tear allowance is deemed to have been taken in respect of the machinery or plant for the period in question.

For the purposes of TCA 1997, s 284(4) (total capital allowances not to exceed cost), TCA 1997, s 287 effectively reduces the cost of the machinery or plant in question by a "notional wear and tear allowance" (ie, one which reduces the tax written down value but which does not result in a reduction of taxable profits) for each relevant accounting period in addition to any actual wear and tear allowance given for that period. The amount of the notional allowance is an amount equal to the excess of the "normal wear and tear allowance" for the relevant accounting period over the amount of the wear and tear allowance, if any, actually taken for that period.

For the purposes of TCA 1997, s 287, *normal wear and tear allowance* for an accounting period is defined as the wear and tear allowance (excluding any free depreciation element) which would have been made for that period if all of the following conditions, as set out in TCA 1997, s 287(3), had been fulfilled in relation to the period:

(a) the trade had been carried on by the company in question ever since the date it acquired the machinery or plant;

(b) the full amount of the profits or gains from the trade had been chargeable to tax since that date;

(c) the trade had at no time consisted wholly or partly of Shannon exempted trading operations;

(d) the machinery or plant had been used by the company solely for the purposes of the trade ever since that date;

(e) a proper claim had been duly made by the company for a wear and tear allowance in respect of the machinery or plant for every relevant accounting period; and

(f) there was no question of any sum being payable to the company, directly or indirectly, in respect of, or taking account of, the wear and tear of the machinery or plant.

The normal wear and tear allowance for any accounting period is therefore arrived at on the assumption that a full wear and tear allowance had actually been obtained for each relevant accounting period since the company had acquired the machinery or plant, whether or not that was actually the case. The different circumstances in which a company might not receive a normal wear and tear allowance for an accounting period are suggested in the above assumptions (a) to (f).

For example, a company which had purchased an item of plant for use in its trade might use that item for some non-trading purpose during an accounting period. If this happens for, say eight months out of a twelve month accounting period, the wear and tear allowance actually given to the company for that period would be restricted to 4/12ths of the normal wear and tear allowance.

Again, a company which carried on exempted trading operations in the Shannon Airport area might use certain machinery or plant in one or more accounting periods for the purpose of those operations. Since the profits were fully exempted from corporation tax (CTA 1976 s 71 – see **6.103**), the company would have received no wear and tear allowance at all in respect of the machinery or plant in question for the period or periods involved. The Shannon exemption expired on 5 April 1990 but a notional wear and tear allowance might still require to be made in respect of machinery or plant used in an exempted trade before 6 April 1990 and used in the same trade after that date when the trade is no longer exempted.

It is appropriate to consider TCA 1997, s 287 separately for (a) machinery or plant (other than motor vehicles purchased before 1 January 2001) provided on or after 1 April 1992 and (b) all machinery or plant (including motor vehicles) provided before 1 April 1992, and motor vehicles purchased from 1 April 1992 to 31 December 2000.

(a) Machinery or plant (other than motor vehicles purchased before 1 January 2001) provided on or after 1 April 1992

For machinery or plant provided for the purposes of a trade on or after 1 April 1992, the fact that TCA 1997, s 287 may require a notional allowance to be deducted for one accounting period has no effect on the amount of the actual wear and tear allowance to be made for any later accounting period except where, by virtue of TCA 1997, s 284(4), an allowance must be denied or restricted where the total of allowances, including notional allowances, would otherwise exceed the cost of the machinery or plant in question. The calculation of wear and tear allowances for any later period will normally continue to be made at 12.5% (20% for expenditure incurred from 1 January 2001 to 3 January 2002 and 15% for expenditure incurred before 1 January 2001) of the cost of the machinery or plant.

For machinery or plant (other than motor vehicles purchased before 1 January 2001) first used in a trade after 31 March 1992, TCA 1997, s 287 has effect in the latest accounting period for which a wear and tear allowance may be made and in the accounting period in which a balancing event (event giving rise to a balancing allowance or charge) occurs.

Example 5.206.1

On 31 March 2003, Jarrold & Sons Ltd purchased new computer equipment for €12,000 for use in its research and development trade. The equipment is put into use in the year ending 31 December 2003 and a wear and tear allowance is accordingly claimed for each of the first two accounting periods.

During the year ended 31 December 2005, the company earned an exceptionally large part of its profits from royalty income disregarded for tax purposes under TCA 1997, s 234 and decided not to claim any wear and tear allowance for that period. For all subsequent periods, wear and tear allowances were claimed.

The capital cost of the computer equipment is written down for tax purposes as follows:

	€
Cost of equipment	12,000
Years ended 31/12/03 and 31/12/04:	
W & T €12,000 x 12.5% x 2	3,000
WDV 1/1/05	9,000
Year ended 31/12/05:	
Notional W & T €12,000 x 12.5%	1,500
WDV 1/1/06	7,500
Years ended 31/12/06 to 31/12/10:	
W & T €12,000 x 12.5% x 5	7,500
WDV 31/12/10	Nil

(b) Machinery or plant provided before 1 April 1992, and motor vehicles purchased before 1 January 2001

In the case of machinery or plant (other than motor vehicles) provided before 1 April 1992, ITA 1967 s 241(1A) provided that the amount of capital expenditure incurred, on which the 15% wear and tear allowance is to be calculated, was to be deemed to be that expenditure as reduced by the total amount of any wear and tear and initial allowances made for any chargeable period ending on or before 5 April 1996. ITA 1967 s 241(1A) was not carried into TCA 1997, nor is there a reference to ITA 1967 s 241(1A)(a) (as there is in FA 1970 s 14), the subsection being no longer relevant for periods ending after 5 April 1992.

For machinery or plant provided before 1 April 1992, and for all motor vehicles purchased before 1 January 2001, the FA 1970 s 14/ TCA 1997, s 287 requirement for a notional allowance to be deducted for one accounting period affects the amount of the actual wear and tear allowance to be made for any later accounting period (as allowances were calculated on the reducing balance basis). It may also have the effect that an allowance in a later period will be denied or restricted where the total of allowances, including notional allowances, would otherwise exceed the cost of the machinery or plant in question. Where the section operates, a notional allowance must be deducted, in addition to any actual allowance, in arriving at the tax written down value for the purposes of the wear and tear computation for the next accounting period.

5.207 Balancing allowances and balancing charges

5.207.1 General

A balancing allowance or charge (referred to hereafter as a "balancing adjustment") arises under TCA 1997, s 288(1) on the occasion of any of the following events (referred to hereafter as "balancing events"), in respect of machinery or plant for which any capital allowance has been obtained by a company carrying on a trade:

(a)   the sale of the machinery or plant or other event whereby the machinery or plant ceases to belong to the company;

(b)   the machinery or plant permanently ceasing to be used for the trade, while continuing to belong to the company;

(c)   the permanent discontinuance of the trade where the machinery or plant has not previously ceased to belong to the company;

(d)   the grant by the company to another person of a right to use or deal with machinery or plant consisting of computer software (see **5.202.7**) where the monetary consideration for the grant constitutes a capital sum (or would constitute a capital sum if there were consideration in money);

(e)   the occurring of any event treated as being equivalent to the permanent discontinuance of the trade, eg, a change in the ownership of the trade or the company ceasing to be within the charge to corporation tax, treated by TCA 1997, s 77(2)(a) as the permanent discontinuance of the trade (TCA 1997, s 320(5)).

TCA 1997, s 298(2) applies the rules relating to balancing allowances and balancing charges in corresponding circumstances to a lessor of machinery or plant let on such terms that the burden of wear and tear falls directly on that lessor (see **5.301**).

The purpose of a balancing adjustment is to ensure that the total capital allowances given in respect of any item of machinery or plant over its entire period of use for the trade equate with the trader's net capital expenditure (after crediting the sale proceeds or any other residual value required to be taken into account for tax purposes). In the case of a trading company, a balancing adjustment is made in the corporation tax computation for the accounting period in which the sale or other balancing event occurs. A balancing allowance arising in respect of the sale of machinery or plant in an accounting period is given as a trading expense of the trade for that period, in the same way as any other capital allowance, and a balancing charge arising in similar circumstances is treated as a trading receipt of the trade.

With effect from 1 January 2002, a balancing charge in respect of machinery or plant being disposed of may not be made where the amount of the sale, insurance, salvage or compensation moneys received for the machinery or plant is less than €2,000, other than in the case of a sale or other disposal to a connected person (see **2.3**) (TCA 1997, s 288(3B)).

The calculation of the balancing adjustment for each item of machinery or plant concerned is made by comparing the "sale, insurance, salvage or compensation moneys" with the "amount still unallowed" of the capital expenditure on the provision of the machinery or plant for the trade.

In a straightforward case, the amount still unallowed is the same as the tax written down value of the item of plant concerned at the commencement of the accounting period in which the sale or other balancing event occurs, ie, it is the original capital expenditure in providing the machinery or plant for the trade less the sum of the wear and tear, free depreciation and initial allowances previously obtained. The net sale proceeds are normally compared with this tax written down value. Where the net sale proceeds are less than the tax written down value, a balancing allowance is made; conversely, if the net sale proceeds exceed the tax written down value, a balancing charge arises.

A grant may be paid under the scheme for compensation in respect of the decommissioning of fishing vessels implemented by the Minister for the Marine and Natural Resources pursuant to European Council Regulation No 3699/93. Any balancing charge arising as the result of the receipt of such a grant may be spread in equal instalments over three chargeable periods, instead of being levied in full for the chargeable period in which the grant is received (TCA 1997, s 288(6)).

In accordance with the scheme for compensation in respect of the decommissioning of fishing vessels implemented by the Minister for Agriculture, Fisheries and Food in accordance with Council Regulation (EC) No 1198/2006 of 27 July 2006 (OJ No L233, 15 August 2006, p1) concerning compensation for decommissioning of fishing vessels, if a balancing charge arises as a result of this compensation, the charge will be spread over five years, commencing in the year in which the compensation is paid (TCA 1997, s 288(6A)).

A balancing adjustment must be calculated separately for each item of machinery or plant ceasing to be used in the trade during a particular accounting period.

Example 5.207.1.1

In the year to 31 December 2007, Zevon Printers Ltd sells a printing machine and a computer, which it had used in its trade, for €56,000 and €6,000 respectively. A van is crashed and written off during the same period and the company receives €24,000 by way of insurance proceeds for the loss. Based on the tax written down values at 1 January 2007, as shown below, the balancing adjustments for the year ended 31 December 2007 are computed as follows:

	Printing machine	Van	Computer
	€	€	€
WDV 1/1/07	68,000	21,200	2,800
Less: sale/insurance proceeds	56,000	24,000	6,000
Balancing allowance	12,000		
Balancing charges		2,800	3,200

5.207.2   Meaning of "amount still unallowed"

In relation to any expenditure incurred by a company on the provision of machinery or plant, TCA 1997, s 292 defines the *amount still unallowed* as the amount of that expenditure less the sum of the following allowances previously made in respect of the expenditure:

(a)   any initial allowance made to the company which incurred the expenditure;

(b)   all wear and tear allowances, including any free depreciation allowances;

(c)   any wear and tear allowances deemed by TCA 1997, s 296 or s 297 to have been made (see **5.206**);

(d)   any scientific research allowance (see **5.601**); and

(e)   any previous balancing allowances.

For the purposes of determining the amount still unallowed, any part of the expenditure on providing the plant that is met directly or indirectly by the State, by any board established by statute, or by any public or local authority, is disregarded (TCA 1997, s 317(2)). In other words, a capital grant received from any governmental agency, eg, the Industrial Development Authority, any statutory board, public authority etc must be deducted from the "gross" capital cost of the plant.

Computer software

In a case in which a balancing event described in (d) in **5.207.1** above occurs (grant to another person of right to use or deal with machinery or plant consisting of computer software), and following that event the company which granted the right retains an interest in the machinery or plant, then:

(a)   the amount of the capital expenditure "still unallowed" at that time, and which is to be taken into account in calculating the balancing allowance or balancing charge, is such portion of the unallowed expenditure relating to the machinery or plant as the sale, insurance, salvage or compensation moneys bear to the aggregate of those moneys and the market value of the machinery or plant which remains undisposed of, and the balance of the unallowed expenditure is to be attributed to the machinery or plant which remains undisposed of; and

(b)   the amount of capital expenditure incurred on the machinery of plant in question is treated as reduced by such portion of that expenditure as the sale, insurance, salvage or compensation moneys bear to the aggregate of those moneys and the market value of the machinery or plant which remains undisposed of (TCA 1997, s 288(3A)).

Thus, for the purposes of calculating a balancing allowance or balancing charge in a case where a right to use machinery or plant consisting of computer software is granted by a company to another person for consideration, while the company retains an interest in that machinery or plant, the tax written down value of that machinery or plant can be represented by the following formula:

$$\text{WDV of P \& M at time of grant} \times \frac{\text{consideration received}}{\text{consideration received} + \text{MV of remaining P \& M}}$$

Similarly, the reduced cost of the machinery or plant following the event can be represented by the formula:

$$\text{Cost of P \& M - cost of P \& M} \times \frac{\text{consideration received}}{\text{consideration received} + \text{MV of remaining P \& M}}$$

5.207.3 Maximum balancing charge

TCA 1997, s 288(4)(b) provides that the amount of any balancing charge in respect of any item of machinery or plant may not exceed the aggregate of the capital allowances previously given to the company which incurred the expenditure and in whose trade the plant has been used. In applying this limit, only capital allowances actually given to the company which has carried on the trade are taken into account. Any wear and tear allowances deemed to have been made (as in (c) above) are ignored; the purpose of a balancing charge is to claw back any excess of capital allowances actually given over the company's net capital expenditure, after crediting sales proceeds or other residual value.

Example 5.207.3.1

Audio Sales Ltd purchases an item of equipment on 17 May 2006 costing €12,200. The company claims only normal wear and tear allowances for the years ended 31 December 2006 and 31 December 2007. Having incurred related advertising costs of €360, it sells the equipment for €13,000 on 11 January 2008. The computation of the balancing adjustment is as follows:

	Equipment
	12.5%
	€
Cost of equipment	12,200
W & T y/e 31/12/06	1,525
	10,675
W & T y/e 31/12/07	1,525
WDV 1/1/08	9,150
Net sale proceeds (after advertising costs)	12,640
Surplus on sale	3,490
Balancing charge: limited to allowances obtained €1,525 x 2	3,050

There are exceptions to the rule that a balancing charge may not exceed the aggregate of capital allowances actually given to a company disposing of machinery or plant. The rule does not apply in any case in which the company disposes of plant or machinery in respect of which capital allowances had been claimed by a previous owner and where the company and that owner had jointly elected to the effect that the machinery or plant was to be treated as having been transferred at its tax written down value at the time of sale. In any such case, the maximum balancing charge will effectively be the aggregate of the capital allowances actually obtained by the two parties. The cases in which the maximum balancing charge is affected in this way are as follows:

(a) where the company disposing of the machinery or plant had acquired it by way of gift or at less than market value and an election under TCA 1997, s 289(6) had been made – see below);

(b) where an election had been made under TCA 1997, s 312(5) in respect of a transfer of machinery or plant between two companies under common control (see **5.103.2**).

Example 5.207.3.2

Minerva Ltd, an Irish resident company, purchased new equipment for the purposes of its trade on 1 March 2003 at a cost of €30,000.

Minerva Ltd disposes of the equipment on 4 November 2007 by way of a sale to its fellow subsidiary company Asgard Ltd, also Irish resident, for €10,000. The open market value of the equipment on the date of sale was €18,000.

Minerva Ltd and Asgard Ltd are under common control so that TCA 1997, s 312 must be applied to determine the transaction price for capital allowances purposes for both companies (see **5.103.2**). The tax written down value of the equipment for the purposes of the sale to Asgard Ltd is arrived at as follows:

	€
Purchase price	30,000
Capital allowances obtained:	
W & T ys/e 31/12/03 to 31/12/06 (€30,000 x 12.5% x 4)	15,000
WDV at 1/1/07 (and on 4/11/07)	15,000

TCA 1997, s 312(3) requires the disposal as having taken place at the market value €18,000 but TCA 1997, s 312(5) permits the companies to substitute a price equal to the seller's tax written down value of €15,000. The companies jointly make an election to this effect. Accordingly, no balancing charge is made on Minerva Ltd. In addition, the deemed capital expenditure incurred by Asgard Ltd is the tax written down value of €15,000.

Asgard Ltd, which makes up accounts each year to 31 October, uses the equipment in its trade from 4 November 2007 to 3 December 2010 when it sells it for €15,500. The capital allowances position for Asgard Ltd in relation to the equipment acquired from Minerva Ltd is as follows:

	€
Year ended 31 October 2008:	
Deemed cost of acquisition (TCA 1997, s 312(5) election)	15,000
W & T €12,000 x 12.5%	1,875
WDV 1/11/08	13,125
Year ended 31 October 2009:	
W & T	1,875
WDV 1/11/09	11,250

Year ended 31 October 2010:

W & T	1,875
WDV 1/11/10	9,375

Year ended 31 October 2011:

Disposal on 3/12/10 for	15,500
Excess proceeds	6,125
Maximum balancing charge: (€15,000 + €1,875 x 3)[1]	20,625
Therefore balancing charge	6,125

Notes:

[1]   Although the excess sale proceeds over tax written down value, €6,125, is greater than the amount of the capital allowances obtained by Asgard Ltd, the balancing charge is nevertheless €6,125 since the aggregate of the capital allowances obtained by both parties is greater than this amount (TCA 1997, s 312(5)).

Computer software

Where TCA 1997, s 288(3A) applies (ie, where a right to use machinery or plant consisting of computer software is granted by a company to another person while the company retains an interest in that machinery or plant – see **5.207.2**), the amount of the allowances previously given, and which represents the maximum balancing charge which may be made, is to be apportioned so that—

(a)   such portion of those allowances as the sale, insurance, salvage or compensation moneys bear to the aggregate of those moneys and the market value of the machinery or plant which remains undisposed of is to be attributed to the grant of the right to use or otherwise deal with the machinery or plant; and

(b)   the balance of those allowances is to be attributed to the machinery or plant which remains undisposed of (TCA 1997, s 288(4)(c)).

5.207.4   Cessation of trade, gifts etc

The events giving rise to a balancing adjustment are not confined to sales and other circumstances in which sale, insurance, salvage or compensation moneys are received. There are other cases in which an event is treated as a sale of the machinery or plant at its open market value at the date in question. The market value rule is also applied in certain circumstances even where there is a sale or other disposal of the machinery or plant.

Cessation of trade

When there is a permanent discontinuance of a trade, any plant remaining unsold at the date of discontinuance must be valued in one of two ways for the purposes of the computation of the resulting balancing allowance or charge. Firstly, if at or about the time the trade ceases, the machinery or plant is sold for an amount which is not less than its open market price, the amount of the net proceeds of the sale is taken as the sale, insurance, salvage or compensation moneys. Alternatively, if at that time the machinery or plant is destroyed or permanently lost, any insurance or other compensation moneys actually received in respect of the plant, with the addition of any net proceeds for the remaining property, is taken as the sale, insurance etc moneys (TCA 1997, s 289(2)).

The effect of this rule generally is to enable the actual net sale proceeds to be used in a case where the plant is sold off within a reasonable time after the cessation of trade as part of the normal process of realising the assets. For this purpose, there is no specific time limit within which the sale must be made. If it is evident that reasonable attempts are being made to realise the plant as soon as possible after the cessation of the trade, the net proceeds ultimately realised are likely to be accepted for the balancing adjustment computation even if it takes up to, say, six months or a year to complete the realisation.

Secondly, if after the permanent discontinuance of the trade the machinery or plant continues to belong to the person who had carried on the trade, and unless the case is one falling within the first rule above, the open market price of the machinery or plant at the date of the cessation of trade is taken as being the sale, insurance, salvage or compensation moneys for the purpose of the balancing adjustment computation (TCA 1997, s 289(3)(a)(i)). In practice it may be difficult to estimate what is the open market price of many types of second-hand plant, unless there is an active second-hand market for them (as there is in the case of motor cars). Consequently, it is not unusual for the taxpayer and the inspector to agree to take the open market price as being equal to the tax written down value of the plant, thus settling the matter without giving rise to a balancing allowance or charge.

Surprisingly, there is no clear legislative guidance as to how balancing charges arising after a trade has ceased are to be taxed. It would seem that the only tax head for such charges is Case IV of Schedule D in which case they would be taxable at the 25% corporation tax rate. Furthermore, any losses unused at the date trade has ceased would not be available to cover such balancing charges although Revenue would, in practice, probably agree to the set off of losses forward against the balancing charges (see **5.409.1** in relation to industrial buildings balancing charges). There is a clear case for a legislative amendment that would ensure that balancing charges arising in the context of a trade should not be taxed at the 25% rate.

Gifts and sales at less than market price

In the event of any gift of machinery or plant (unusual for a company), whether during the continuance of the trade or on its cessation, the balancing adjustment computation is made as if the plant had been sold at its open market price at the date of the gift; similarly, open market price is substituted for the actual sale consideration if the machinery or plant is sold at less than its open market price (TCA 1997, s 289(3)). TCA 1997, s 289(3) does not affect a sale of machinery or plant to which the non-arm's length transaction rules of TCA 1997, s 312 apply; that section relates to sales of plant between companies under common control and contains its own market price rule which applies whether the sale is at less than or more than that price (see **5.103**). By contrast, TCA 1997, s 289(3) does not substitute the open market price for an actual sale consideration that is higher than the open market price.

The open market price rule of TCA 1997, s 289(3) does not apply where plant is given away or sold at less than its market price to an employee or to a director of a company in circumstances where the recipient is chargeable to income tax under the Schedule E benefit in kind rules. In that event, the actual sale proceeds, if any, are used to calculate the employer's balancing allowance or charge (TCA 1997, s 289(4)). To the extent that any price paid by the employee or director falls short of the open market price, a Schedule E assessment would probably be raised in respect of the shortfall.

In certain cases, the person receiving machinery or plant given away or sold at less than market price may be acquiring it for use in a trade or other activity. In that case, the recipient is deemed to have purchased it at its open market price at the date of the gift or sale (TCA 1997, s 289(5)) so that all subsequent wear and tear allowances and any balancing adjustments are computed by reference to that price, except where an election under TCA 1997, s 289(6) has effect.

Subject to TCA 1997, s 289(6A) (an anti-avoidance provision – see below), TCA 1997, s 289(6) permits a company which gives away or sells machinery or plant at less than market value, and the person receiving it for use in a trade or other activity, to make an election to substitute for the open market price the amount of the expenditure on providing the machinery or plant still unallowed to the company immediately before the gift or sale, but only where that amount is lower than the open market price. Where an election is made by the parties jointly in writing to the inspector, the consequences are as follows:

(a)   in the balancing adjustment computation for the company (the vendor or donor) the amount still unallowed is taken as the sale consideration so that no balancing allowance or balancing charge arises; and

(b)   subsequent wear and tear allowances, and any later balancing allowance, of the person acquiring the machinery or plant are based on a deemed acquisition cost equal to the amount still unallowed to the company; but

(c)   if a balancing charge results from a later sale or other balancing event affecting the person acquiring the machinery or plant, the upper limit to that charge is the aggregate of the capital allowances actually made to both the company and that person during the successive periods of use in their respective trades.

TCA 1997, s 289(6) applies only where the donor or seller is connected with the recipient or purchaser (see **2.302**). Furthermore, it does not apply in any case where the donor or seller is not a company and the recipient or purchaser is a company (TCA 1997, s 289(6A)). This provision is intended to counter tax avoidance schemes designed to avoid a balancing charge following the disposal of machinery or plant or to pass on a balancing charge from an individual to a company.

The election under TCA 1997, s 289(6) requires the amount still unallowed as defined by TCA 1997, s 292 (see above) to be used and not, if different, the tax written down value as computed for wear and tear purposes (see **5.203.3**).

Example 5.207.4.1

Yard Arm Ltd purchased a truck for €38,000 on 17 April 2004 and used it for the purposes of its trade throughout its accounting years ended 31 December 2004 and 31 December 2005. For the full year ended 31 December 2005, the company lent the truck to Benson Ltd, a company wholly owned by Jim Benson, the managing director and controlling shareholder of Yard Arm Ltd, which has been carrying on a trade on its own account for some time. The accounts of Benson Ltd are also made up each year to 31 December.

Yard Arm Ltd sells the truck to Benson Ltd on 1 January 2007 for €16,000 when its open market price is €25,000. Unless the TCA 1997, s 289(6) election is made, TCA 1997, s 289(3) requires the open market price of €25,000 to be taken for the capital allowances computations of both parties, as the actual sale price is lower. The position is then as follows:

	€	€
Yard Arm Ltd		
Cost price		38,000
W & T y/e 31/12/04	4,750	
W & T y/e 31/12/05	4,750	9,500
		28,500
Notional W & T y/e 31/12/06		4,750
Amount still unallowed 31/12/06		23,750
Deemed sale price (open market price 1/1/07)		25,000
Balancing charge y/e 31/12/07		1,250
Benson Ltd		
Cost of acquisition (open market price)		25,000
W & T y/e 31/12/07 €25,000 x 12.5%		3,125
WDV 31/12/06		21,875

If Benson Ltd later sells the truck, its balancing adjustment computation will be carried out by reference to the deemed capital expenditure €25,000 as written down by the capital allowances for the year ended 31/12/07 and any later periods.

Example 5.207.4.2

The position is as in Example **5.207.4.1** except that Yard Arm Ltd and Benson Ltd jointly elect under TCA 1997, s 289(6) to substitute the amount still unallowed to Yard Arm Ltd immediately before the sale, €23,750, for the open market price. This results in the following position:

	€
Yard Arm Ltd	
Amount still unallowed	23,750
Deemed selling price – amount still unallowed	23,750
Balancing adjustment y/e 31/12/07	Nil

	€
Benson Ltd	
Deemed cost of acquisition	23,750
W & T y/e 31/12/07	2,969
WDV 31/12/07	20,781

If Benson Ltd later sells the truck on 19 August 2008 for €34,000, its balancing adjustment is as follows:

	€	€
WDV 1/1/08		20,781
Sale proceeds		34,000
Surplus on sale		13,219

Balancing charge limited to actual W & T allowances:

Yard Arm Ltd (before sale to Benson Ltd)	9,500	
Benson Ltd	2,969	12,469
Therefore balancing charge		12,469

5.207.5 Notional allowances

In certain circumstances, for the purposes of computing a balancing allowance or charge for an accounting period, TCA 1997, s 296(1) deems a wear and tear allowance to have been made for one or more *previous* accounting periods. The deemed or "notional" wear and tear allowance does not result in any reduction in profits (or increase in a loss) but reduces the amount still unallowed (the tax written down value) to be used in the computation of the balancing allowance or balancing charge on the ultimate sale of the machinery or plant in question. The provisions of TCA 1997, s 296 also apply, in the same circumstances, in the case of a balancing event other than a sale.

The circumstances in which a notional writing down of capital expenditure is made are set out in TCA 1997, s 296(2). The notional allowance is made for each previous accounting period of a company to which the machinery or plant belonged, and which incurred the related expenditure, where any of the following circumstances existed in that period:

(a) the machinery or plant was not used by the company for the purposes of its trade during the accounting period;

(b) the trade was not carried on by the company during the accounting period;

(c) the trade was carried on in such circumstances during the accounting period that, otherwise than by virtue of the Shannon exemption provisions of CTA 1976, Part V, the full amount of the profits was not liable to be charged to tax; or

(d) the tax payable for the accounting period was reduced by reason of the export sales relief provisions of CTA 1976, Part IV.

If any of these circumstances is present in the accounting period, the company will not obtain a normal wear and tear allowance for that period. The requirement to deduct the notional allowance when calculating the balancing adjustment is to ensure that the expenditure is written down to the extent it would have been if the machinery or plant had been used for the trade throughout the company's period of ownership and as if the profits of the trade had been fully subject to tax.

The notional allowance to be written off for any accounting period to which TCA 1997, s 296 applies is the excess of the "normal" wear and tear allowance for the accounting period over the wear and tear allowance, if any, actually given for that period. The phrase "normal wear and tear allowance" does not appear in TCA 1997, s 296 but the notional write down prescribed by the section is in the same terms as the definition of "normal wear and tear allowance" in TCA 1997, s 287 (see **5.206** above). Accordingly, TCA 1997, s 296(1) effectively identifies a normal wear and tear allowance for any previous accounting period as such wear and tear allowance or greater wear and tear allowance, if any, in respect of machinery or plant as would have been given to a company for that accounting period if all of the conditions, as set out below, had been fulfilled (whether or not they had in fact been fulfilled) in that period:

(a) the trade had been carried on by the company ever since the date on which it acquired the machinery or plant now the subject of the balancing adjustment;

(b) the company had carried on the trade since that date in circumstances under which its profits were fully chargeable to tax;

(c) the machinery or plant had been used by the company solely for the purposes of the trade ever since that date;

(d) the company had made a proper claim for a wear and tear allowance in respect of the machinery or plant for each relevant accounting period; and

(e) the trade had at no time consisted wholly or partly of Shannon exempted trading operations.

Generally, the notional allowances to be deducted in arriving at the amount of the capital expenditure still unallowed for the purposes of the balancing adjustment computation will be the same as those required by TCA 1997, s 287 in corresponding circumstances for the wear and tear computations for the accounting periods over the period of use (see **5.206**).

TCA 1997, s 296(5) provides that nothing in the section is to affect the rule in TCA 1997, s 288(4)(b) which limits any balancing charge so that it can never exceed the aggregate of the capital allowances actually received in respect of the machinery or plant in question during the period of its use in the trade. In any case where there is an excess of sale or other disposal proceeds over tax written down value (after all actual and notional allowances have been deducted), that surplus must be compared with the total of the actual allowances obtained (ie, excluding the notional allowances). The balancing charge must therefore be restricted to recapture only the actual allowances.

Example 5.207.5.1

Harland & Co Ltd has carried on a trade for several years, making up accounts annually to 31 December. It purchased new equipment costing €24,000, which is put into use in the trade on 13 November 2003 and obtains a normal wear and tear allowance of €3,000 for each of the years ended 31 December 2005 and 31 December 2006.

Harland & Co Ltd lends the equipment to a charitable organisation for the period 1 January 2007 to 31 August 2008 and on its return puts it to use in its trade again. The company sells the equipment on 20 January 2009 for €20,000. No capital allowances are obtained by the company in respect of the equipment for the year ended 31 December 2007 and for the following year it obtains one third of the normal wear and tear allowance.

The balancing adjustment computation for the sale in the year ended 31 December 2009 is as follows:

	€	€
Cost		24,000
W & T y/e 31/12/05		3,000
WDV 31/12/05		21,000
W & T y/e 31/12/06		3,000
WDV 31/12/06		18,000
Notional W & T y/e 31/12/07[1]		3,000
WDV 31/12/07		15,000

Notional W & T y/e 31/12/08 (2/3)[2]	2,000	
W & T y/e 31/12/08 (1/3)[3]	1,000	3,000
WDV 31/12/08		12,000
Sale proceeds		20,000
Surplus on sale		8,000

Actual allowances obtained:

W & T y/e 31/12/05	3,000	
W & T y/e 31/12/06	3,000	
W & T y/e 31/12/07	1,000	7,000
Therefore balancing charge		7,000

Notes:

[1] Since no actual wear and tear allowance is obtained for the year ended 31 December 2007, TCA 1997, s 296 requires a notional allowance for the full period to be deducted.

[2] The notional allowance deducted for the year ended 31 December 2008 is the difference between a normal wear and tear allowance for that period, €3,000, and the actual allowance of €1,000.

[3] The actual allowance is only 1/3rd of the normal allowance to take account of the fact that the equipment was not in use for the company's trade for eight months of the accounting period. In this case, the notional allowance is the same under both TCA 1997, s 287 and TCA 1997, s 296.

The notional allowance for an accounting period as prescribed by TCA 1997, s 296 for the purposes of a balancing adjustment may, in certain cases, differ from the notional allowance provided for in TCA 1997, s 287. TCA 1997, s 296 does not require the deduction of a notional allowance in respect of an earlier accounting period for which a company has been exempted from corporation tax due to the Shannon exemption provided for in CTA 1976 Part V. TCA 1997, s 287, however, requires the deduction of a notional allowance, in respect of any accounting period in which the machinery or plant was used where the Shannon exemption applied, for the purpose of calculating wear and tear allowances for subsequent periods.

A notional allowance must also be deducted in another type of situation in arriving at the amount unallowed in respect of the cost of machinery or plant for the purposes of a balancing adjustment. TCA 1997, s 297 requires such a deduction in any case where:

(a) any sums have been paid, or are payable, directly or indirectly to the company concerned in respect of, or which take account of, the wear and tear of the machinery or plant due to its use for the purposes of the trade; and

(b) those sums do not fall to be taken into account as the income of the company or in computing the profits of the trade carried on by it.

In any such case, the amount of the expenditure unallowed immediately before the sale or other event is reduced by a notional allowance equal to the total of the sums received by the company towards the wear and tear of the plant (less any part of those sums taken into account as income). The effect of the adjustment is to decrease or eliminate a balancing allowance or to create or increase a balancing charge. The amount of any such balancing charge may not, however, exceed the aggregate of the capital allowances actually obtained by the company during its period of use of the plant (TCA 1997, s 297(2)).

5.208 Capital grants

5.208.1 Background

Prior to FA 1986, the treatment of grants in respect of the capital expenditure on machinery and plant for wear and tear, free depreciation and initial allowances purposes differed from that for grants for the purposes of industrial buildings allowances. For machinery or plant, the capital allowances during the period of use of the plant in the trade were based on the gross cost, before deducting the grant, but subject to a requirement that the grant was to be taken into account at the time of calculating the balancing allowance or balancing charge on the disposal of the plant or other balancing event.

For capital expenditure incurred on or after 29 January 1986 on machinery or plant in respect of which a grant is receivable from the State or any statutory board or any public or local authority, FA 1986 s 52(1)(a) (now TCA 1997, s 317(3)(a)) provided that capital allowances were to be calculated on the basis of the net of grant expenditure. FA 1986 s 52(1)(b)/TCA 1997, s 317(3)(b), however, permitted allowances to be claimed on the gross expenditure in certain transitional cases. TCA 1997, s 317(4) provides for a further exception by allowing capital allowances to be claimed in respect of the gross expenditure incurred on certain machinery or plant used by a company carrying on a food processing trade.

TCA 1997, s 317(3)(a)(i)(II), (ii) provides that any grant or contribution made directly or indirectly by the State *or by any other person* on or after 6 May 1993 towards the cost of machinery or plant must be deducted from that cost for capital allowances purposes.

TCA 1997, s 317(3)(a) does not apply in the case of capital expenditure grant-aided under the terms of an agreement finally approved on or before 29 January 1986 by a Department of State, any board established by statute or any public authority, or under the terms of an agreement which was the subject of negotiations in progress on 29 January 1986 with any of the above bodies and which was finally approved by such body not later than 31 December 1986.

In *Cyril Lord Carpets v Schofield* 42 TC 637, capital expenditure which had been incurred and which was subsequently reimbursed by way of grant was held to have been met directly or indirectly by the person providing the grant.

5.208.2 Net expenditure treatment

In general, capital allowances in respect of expenditure incurred by a person on machinery or plant are calculated by reference to the capital expenditure incurred on or after 6 May 1993 as reduced by the amount met directly or indirectly by the State, by any board established by statute, by any public or local authority or by any other party other than the first mentioned person. The general rule applies in all cases of grant-aided capital expenditure on machinery or plant other than the excepted cases mentioned below.

5.208.3 Exceptions

Prior to FA 1986, all the capital allowances apart from balancing allowance and charge were calculated by reference to the gross expenditure before deducting any grants. This treatment applied in all cases in which the capital expenditure on the plant was incurred before 29 January 1986, but ceased to be applicable for grant-aided expenditure incurred after 28 January 1986, other than in certain excepted cases. The gross expenditure treatment still applies in any of the following circumstances:

(a) where the capital expenditure is incurred by a company in providing "qualifying machinery or plant" for the purposes of a food processing trade carried on by it in the State (TCA 1997, s 317(4));

(b) where the grant-aided expenditure is incurred by any person before 29 January 1986;

(c) where the grant is payable under the terms of an agreement which was finally approved not later than 29 January 1986 by a Department of State, any body established by statute, or any public or local authority (TCA 1997, s 317(3)(b)(i)); and

(d) where the grant is payable under the terms of an agreement which was the subject of negotiations in progress on 29 January 1986 with, and which was finally approved on or before 31 December 1986 by, any such Department, statutory body or authority (TCA 1997, s 317(3)(b)(ii)).

For the purposes of exception (a), *qualifying machinery or plant* is defined as machinery or plant used solely in the course of a process of manufacture whereby processed food (as defined below) is produced. Machinery or plant which is used otherwise than in the course of such a manufacturing process is not qualifying machinery or plant. To qualify for the gross cost treatment, the company claiming the allowances must be the company carrying on the food processing trade and the company must have incurred the relevant capital expenditure itself. Machinery or plant which is leased by the food processing company is expressly excluded, irrespective of whether the lessor or the lessee is the person entitled to the capital allowances. The case provided for in TCA 1997, s 299(1), where a lessee who bears the burden of wear and tear is deemed to be the person who incurred the capital expenditure, is specifically excluded.

A *food processing trade* is defined as a trade which consists of or includes the manufacture of processed food. The trade may, therefore, include other activities, but if the grant-aided machinery or plant is used even partly for any such other activities, it does not qualify for the gross cost treatment.

Processed food is defined as goods, manufactured within the State in the course of a trade by a company, which:

(a) are intended for human consumption as a food;

(b) have been manufactured by a process involving the use of machinery or plant; and

(c) as a result of the process differ substantially in form and value from the materials to which the process has been applied.

In addition, the process by which the goods are produced must not consist primarily of:

(i) the acceleration, retardation, alteration or application of a natural process; or

(ii) the application of methods of preservation, pasteurisation or any similar treatment.

The gross expenditure treatment for food processing trades of companies continues to be relevant without regard to the date on which the expenditure on the qualifying machinery or plant is incurred. This exception was provided for in TCA 1997, s 317(4) and applies to food processing trades with retrospective effect to 29 January 1986.

5.208.4 Gross expenditure treatment

(a) Allowances during period of use

The position here is straightforward. Normal wear and tear allowances and any free depreciation or initial allowance are calculated under the normal rules ignoring the grant.

Example 5.208.4.1

Midland Foods Ltd carries on a meat processing trade and makes up accounts to 31 December each year. For the purposes of a project involving an extension to its factory premises, the company incurs the following grant-aided capital expenditure on new plant to be used solely in the meat processing activity:

Expenditure incurred	Gross cost	Grant
	€	€
1. 21 August 2003	35,000	10,500
2. 18 September 2003	60,000	12,000

Since the plant is qualifying plant used by a company in a food processing trade, capital allowances (other than a balancing allowance or charge) are based on the gross cost. The capital allowances computations for the two years ended 31 December 2003 and 31 December 2004 are as follows:

	Item 1	Item 2
	€	€
Year ended 31 December 2003:		
Gross cost of plant	35,000	60,000
W & T @ 12.5%	4,375	7,500
WDV 31/12/03	30,625	52,500
Year ended 31 December 2004:		
W & T @ 12.5%	4,375	7,500
WDV 31/12/04	26,250	45,000

(b) Balancing allowances and charges

As explained in **5.207**, on the disposal of any machinery or plant in respect of which any capital allowances have been obtained, a balancing allowance or charge is made by reference to the difference between the "sale, insurance, salvage or compensation moneys" and the "amount still unallowed" in respect of the capital expenditure incurred in providing the plant. In this case, it is only at the time of the sale or other balancing event that the amount of any grant is taken into account when applying the gross expenditure treatment.

In all cases, the amount of the grant is deducted in arriving at the "amount still unallowed" which is compared with the sale or other value in respect of the particular item of machinery or plant. Since during the period of use of the plant in the trade, capital allowances computations have been carried out by reference to gross expenditure, the full amount of the grant is now deducted in arriving at the final tax written down value which is to be compared with the sale or other value for the purpose of calculating the balancing adjustment.

Example 5.208.4.2

The position is the same as in Example **5.208.4.1** with the additional information that plant item 2 (gross cost €60,000, grant €12,000) is sold on 11 February 2005 for €35,000. It is therefore necessary to determine what balancing allowance or balancing charge is to be made for the year ended 31 December 2005.

Since the capital allowances on this plant have been based on the company's gross cost of €60,000, the balancing adjustment computation now requires the grant to be deducted in arriving at the amount of expenditure still unallowed in respect of this item. The computation is as follows:

	€
WDV 1/1/05	48,125
Less: grant not previously deducted	12,000
Final WDV (date of sale)	36,125
Net sale proceeds	35,000
Balancing allowance y/e 31/12/05	1,125

5.208.5 Capital allowances in excess of net expenditure

Where capital allowances in respect of machinery or plant for which a grant has been received have been based on the gross cost of that machinery or plant during the period of use for the trade, it may happen that the aggregate of the capital allowances obtained over this period exceeds the amount of the net capital expenditure (after deducting the grant). That will be the case where the tax written down value of the machinery or plant at the point of sale is less than the amount of the grant.

TCA 1997, s 288(5)(a) provides that the excess, if any, of the aggregate of all initial allowances and wear and tear allowances, including any free depreciation, made over the net cost of the plant after deducting the grant is to be brought into the balancing adjustment computation as if it were additional sale proceeds.

Example 5.208.5.1

Again, the position is as in Example **5.208.4.1** except that plant item 1 (gross cost of €35,000 in 2003, grant of €10,500) is sold on 21 March 2010 (in the accounting period ended 31 December 2010) for €4,000.

The company's capital allowances computation in respect of this item of plant for the five years ended 31 December 2005 to 31 December 2009 is as follows:

	€
Year ended 31 December 2005:	
WDV 1/1/05 (per Example **5.208.4.1**)	26,250
W & T €35,000 x 12.5% x 5	21,875
WDV 31/12/09	4,375

Less: grant not previously deducted (part only)[1]		4,375
Amount still unallowed at date of sale		Nil

		€
TCA 1997, s 288(5)(a) applies as follows:		
Total W & T allowances received €4,375 x 7		30,625
Original expenditure net of grant		24,500
Excess of allowances over net expenditure ("excess allowances")		6,125

The final balancing adjustment computation is now as follows:

		€
Actual sales proceeds		4,000
Additional "proceeds" (TCA 1997, s 288(5)) – excess allowances as above		6,125
Balancing charge[2]		10,125

Notes:

[1]   Although the capital grant was €10,500, the amount deducted in arriving at the unallowed amount at the time of the balancing event is limited to the tax written down value at that time – the deduction of the grant cannot produce a negative figure.

[2]   The effect of the balancing charge of €10,125 is to leave Midland Foods Ltd with aggregate net capital allowances of €20,500 (€30,625 during the period of use less the €10,125 clawed back) in respect of the item of plant. This reconciles with the company's net capital outlay after taking credit for the actual sales proceeds, as follows:

	€	€
Gross cost incurred		35,000
Less: met by grant	10,500	
Actual sale proceeds	4,000	14,500
Net capital outlay		20,500

5.209   Roll over of balancing charges

A company which has incurred a balancing charge on the disposal of machinery or plant may elect to "roll over" the charge where the machinery or plant is replaced (TCA 1997, s 290). That election may also be made where a balancing charge occurs as the result of the giving away of the machinery or plant or its withdrawal from use in the trade, again where the machinery or plant is replaced. The replacement item of machinery or plant, which may be new or second-hand, need not be identical with that replaced, but should normally perform a broadly similar function. In practice, there is generally little difficulty in determining when there is a replacement.

The roll over election must be made by notice in writing to the inspector, but the inclusion in the relevant tax return of a reference to the fact that the balancing charge is being rolled over is normally accepted as being sufficient notice. There is no specific time limit for making the election, but it should be made before the assessment for the period in question becomes final and conclusive. It is not essential that the machinery or plant be replaced in the same accounting period as that in which the sale or other event occurs. The election may be made even if the replacement plant is provided a number of months later in a different accounting period.

The effect of the rollover election varies depending on whether the capital expenditure (net of any government or other grant) on providing the replacement item is greater or less than the amount of the balancing charge. If the net capital expenditure on the replacement item exceeds the balancing charge that would otherwise be made, no balancing charge is made; if the balancing charge exceeds the net capital expenditure on replacement, the balancing charge is reduced to the amount of the excess. Thus, it is possible to have a complete or a partial roll over. For the effect of a roll over election in the case of private motor vehicles costing more than the "relevant capital limit" see **5.212.5**.

In the case of a complete roll over, the amount of the balancing charge that would otherwise be made is deducted from the cost of the replacement item on which any subsequent initial allowance, free depreciation or wear and tear allowances are calculated. Further, when a balancing adjustment has to be made in respect of a later sale or other event in connection with the replacement item, the amount of the expenditure still unallowed on that item prior to the sale or other event must be reduced by an amount equal to the balancing charge rolled over on the previous sale. This deduction is referred to as a "deemed initial allowance".

In the event of a partial roll over of a balancing charge on the sale or other event of any item of machinery or plant, no initial allowance, free depreciation, wear and tear allowance or balancing allowance may be claimed in respect of the cost of that replacement item. Further, on the occasion of a subsequent balancing event affecting the replacement item, the amount of the expenditure still unallowed is reduced by a deemed initial allowance of an amount equal to the capital expenditure on the replacement item net of any government or other grant. This always has the effect of producing a nil amount still unallowed for the balancing adjustment computation.

In the event that the replacement item of machinery or plant is itself replaced at a later date, any new balancing charge may be the subject of a new roll over election against the cost of the new item. This process may be continued indefinitely as long as machinery or plant is replaced. A roll over election is not, however, always the best option. For example, where a balancing charge arises for an accounting period in which a company has sustained a trading loss, or where the amount of its total income is low, it may be preferable to accept the balancing charge in that period so as to be in a position to claim higher capital allowances on the replacement item in later periods when the amount of total income is greater.

5.210 Successive balancing adjustments

In certain situations, a company could be subject to balancing adjustments at different times in respect of the same item of machinery or plant. For example, successive balancing adjustments would arise where any item of machinery or plant ceases permanently to be used in a trade but continues to belong to the company (the first event) and where, at a later date, either the item is sold or given away while the trade continues or is permanently discontinued (the second event). Successive balancing adjustments would also be required if the item of machinery or plant is first withdrawn from one trade and then used by the same company in another trade and subsequently becomes subject to a balancing allowance or balancing charge, for example, on a later sale in respect of the second trade.

TCA 1997, s 288(5)(b) provides that the computation of the balancing adjustment in respect of the machinery or plant for the second event is to take account of the balancing adjustment already made in respect of the first event. The second computation is made by applying the ordinary rules to the company's original capital expenditure, grants (if any) received, and the total capital allowances made or deemed to have been made to it over the entire period of its ownership. Any balancing allowance given in respect of the first event should be deducted in arriving at the amount of the expenditure still unallowed at the time of the second event, whereas any balancing charge made on the first event should be taken as increasing the amount still unallowed.

5.211   Plant used partly for non-trading purposes

Where a company uses an item of machinery or plant only partly for the purposes of its trade during any accounting period, a part of the capital allowances otherwise available for that period must be disallowed. On the eventual sale of (or other event concerning) that item, it is necessary for the purposes of the balancing adjustment computation to take account of all the relevant circumstances, in particular the extent to which the item was used for non-trading purposes (TCA 1997, s 294). The balancing allowance or charge is then given or made on such an amount "as may be just and reasonable".

5.212   Restriction of capital allowances on private motor vehicles

5.212.1   General

Capital allowances in respect of motor vehicles have always been confined to annual wear and tear allowances; there has never been any question of an incentive allowance such as an initial allowance of a free depreciation allowance being available in respect of motor vehicles. On the other hand, the wear and tear allowances available in respect of certain vehicles have, following FA 1973, been "capped" by reference to their cost price. The earliest ceiling amount (the *specified amount*), prescribed by FA 1973 s 25 (now TCA 1997 ss 373 and 374), was €3,174.35 and this has been adjusted upwards by various Finance Acts.

For cars purchased on or after 1 July 2008, see **5.213** regarding capital allowances restrictions by reference to emissions-based limits.

The capital allowances restriction applies to all private motor vehicles within the definition in TCA 1997, s 373(1), that is, mechanically propelled road vehicles constructed or adapted for the carriage of passengers, other than vehicles of a type not commonly used as a private vehicle and unsuitable to be so used. For convenience, these vehicles can be referred to here as "private motor vehicles". The capital allowances restrictions do not apply to any vehicle which is provided or hired, wholly or mainly for the purpose of hire to, or for the carriage of, members of the public in the ordinary course of trade (TCA 1997, s 380(1)). The motor vehicles subject to the restriction are the same as those affected by the motor running expenses restriction (see **3.202.3**).

It follows from the definition of TCA 1997, s 373(1) that there is no restriction of capital allowances for lorries and other commercial vehicles which are not constructed or adapted for the carriage of passengers, nor for vehicles provided or leased wholly or mainly for the purpose of hire to members of the public or for the purpose of the carriage of members of the public (eg, taxis, buses).

Where the capital expenditure incurred in providing a private motor vehicle for a trade exceeds the specified amount in operation at the time the expenditure is incurred (which, for accounting periods ending on or after 1 January 2001, means the specified amount in operation for that period), all capital allowances over the entire period of use of that vehicle are restricted by reference to that limit. The fact that the specified amount may subsequently be increased for expenditure incurred at a later date does not alter the specified amount for the vehicles provided before that date.

The restriction in TCA 1997, s 374 applies for the purposes of wear and tear allowances under TCA 1997, s 284 and for any balancing allowance under TCA 1997, s 288. In the event of a balancing charge on a sale or other balancing event, the amount of the charge is restricted in a similar way.

TCA 1997 ss 373(2)(p) and 374 restrict to €24,000 the expenditure on which capital allowances may be claimed in respect of any private motor vehicle where the capital expenditure on providing the vehicle was incurred in an accounting period ending on or after 1 January 2006. This limit applies whether the car is purchased new or secondhand and regardless of when the car was first registered in the State.

The position which obtained for accounting periods ending before 1 January 2001 can be illustrated by reference to the conditions relating to the limit of €20,950.68. TCA 1997 ss 373(2)(l) and 374 restrict to €20,950.68 the expenditure on which capital allowances may be claimed in respect of any private motor vehicle where the capital expenditure on providing the vehicle was incurred on or after 1 December 1999. The specified amount immediately prior to that date was €20,315.81. The specified amount of €20,950.68 applies only in respect of a vehicle which, on or after 1 December 1999, is one which is not a used or secondhand vehicle and which is first registered in the State under FA 1992 s 131 (registration system incorporating vehicle registration tax) without having previously been registered elsewhere under a similar system. Unless the above conditions are fulfilled, the specified amount will be less than €20,950.68 – see table below. If expenditure is incurred on or after 1 December 1999 in respect of a car which is a used or a secondhand vehicle (even if first registered on or after that date in the State under FA 1992 s 131 without having been registered elsewhere), the specified amount is €16,506.60.

To summarise, where capital expenditure on the provision of a private motor vehicle was incurred on or after 1 December 1999, but in an accounting period ending before 1 January 2001, the specified amount for that vehicle is €20,950.68 provided the car is one which, on or after 1 December 1999, was:

(a) not a used or secondhand vehicle; and

(b) first registered in the State under FA 1992 s 131 without having been registered elsewhere.

Unless both of the above conditions were fulfilled, the specified amount for capital allowances purposes would have been less than €20,950.68, the actual amount applicable being dependent on the circumstances.

The specified amount provision for capital allowances on private motor vehicles corresponds to a similar provision in TCA 1997, s 377, which, in the case of a leased or hired car, restricts the deduction for the lease rental payments or other costs of hiring.

There are, accordingly, equivalent restrictions which apply whether a private motor vehicle is provided for a company's trade by way of purchase or by way of leasing. In addition, there is a corresponding restriction which applies in respect of any trading deduction for the cost of replacing private motor vehicles where a taxpayer uses the renewals basis (see **5.108, 3.202.3**).

For accounting periods ending before 1 January 2001, the specified amount at any time depended on the date the expenditure was incurred. In relation to expenditure incurred up to 22 January 1997, if such expenditure was incurred within 12 months after the day on which an increased specified amount took effect and under a contract entered into before that day, the specified amount applicable was the one that applied for the period prior to the increase. Accordingly, this provision affected specified amounts up to and including the €17,776.33 amount. For the purposes of the specified amounts up to and including the €16,506.60 amount, there is no requirement that a vehicle should be unused and not secondhand. For the specified amounts up to and including the €12,697.38 amount, there is no requirement regarding first registration.

The following table sets out the specified amounts (using euro amounts to two decimal places, as provided for in TCA 1997, s 373(2)) which apply for expenditure incurred on private motor vehicles:

Expenditure Incurred	Specified Amount	Legislation
	€	
A/Ps ending on or after 1/1/06	23,000	TCA 1997, s 373(2)(o)
A/Ps ending on or after 1/1/02	22,000	TCA 1997, s 373(2)(n)
A/Ps ending on or after 1/1/01	21,585.55	TCA 1997, s 373(2)(m)
1/12/99 – last A/P ending before 1/1/01 (new cars)	20,950.68	TCA 1997, s 373(2)(l)
2/12/98 – 30/11/99 (new cars)	20,315.81	TCA 1997, s 373(2)(k)
3/12/97 – 1/12/98 (new cars)	19,680.94	TCA 1997, s 373(2)(j)
23/1/97 – 2/12/97 (new cars)	19,046.07	TCA 1997, s 373(2)(i)
9/2/95 – 22/1/97 (new cars)	17,776.33	TCA 1997, s 373(2)(h)
27/1/94 – 8/2/95	16,506.60	TCA 1997, s 373(2)(g)
30/1/92 – 26/1/94	12,697.38	TCA 1997, s 373(2)(f)
26/1/89 – 29/1/92	8,888.17	TCA 1997, s 373(2)(e)
28/1/88 – 25/1/89	7,618.43	TCA 1997, s 373(2)(d)
6/4/86 – 27/1/88	5,078.95	TCA 1997, s 373(2)(c)
29/1/76 – 5/4/86	4,444.08	TCA 1997, s 373(2)(b)
16/5/73 – 28/1/76	3,174.35	TCA 1997, s 373(2)(a)

FA 2003 made no provision to increase the specified amount from €22,000.

5.212.2 Wear and tear allowances

The wear and tear allowances for motor vehicles used in a trade are calculated under the ordinary rules for calculating capital allowances except that the allowances are based on the amount up to the specified amount as prescribed by TCA 1997, s 373(2). For second- hand motor vehicles the limit is €12,697.60 for expenditure after 29 January 1992. For any car the cost of which is less than the specified amount, unrestricted wear and tear allowances are given by reference to the actual capital expenditure incurred.

Earlier specified amounts are relevant where it is necessary to have regard to the original cost of the car for the purposes of calculating balancing allowances or charges.

5.212.3 Balancing allowances and balancing charges

In the case of the sale or other event involving a motor vehicle which has been subjected to restricted capital allowances in accordance with TCA 1997, s 374, the computation of the balancing allowance or balancing charge requires only a proportion of the sale, salvage, insurance or other compensation moneys to be taken into account. The proportion of these moneys taken into account is in the ratio that the specified amount bears to the original capital expenditure incurred in providing the vehicle for the trade. The specified amount for this purpose is the limit actually applicable to the original acquisition (and not the limit current at the time of the balancing event).

For example, in the case of a private vehicle purchased for use in a trade in July 2001 for €23,000, and sold for €13,000 in March 2004, the amount to be brought into the balancing adjustment computation in respect of the sale proceeds is an amount calculated by multiplying the actual sale proceeds of €13,000 by the specified amount of €17,000 and dividing the result by the original capital expenditure of €23,000.

5.212.4 Acquisition at market value etc

In certain cases, the open market price (or vendor's tax written down value) is required to be substituted for the actual acquisition cost to a company carrying on a trade. This feature has been discussed in relation to machinery and plant generally at **5.103** and **5.207.4**. Where either of the situations covered by (a) and (b) below is relevant to the acquisition, whether by purchase or gift, of a motor car the original capital expenditure on which exceeded the relevant capital limit in force at the time it was incurred by a prior owner, an adjustment is necessary to arrive at the opening "cost" figure for the new owner's capital allowance computations. The situations in which a market value, or tax written down value, adjustment is required are as follows:

(a)   the car is acquired in a transaction covered by TCA 1997, s 312, ie, a transaction the sole or main benefit of which is the obtaining of capital allowances, or a transaction between two companies under common control (see **5.103**); or

(b)   the prior owner gave or sold the car at less than its market value to the company acquiring it for use in its trade (see **5.207.4**).

Where in either of these situations it would otherwise be necessary for the company acquiring the car to base its capital allowances on the open market price at the date of acquisition, it is deemed instead to have acquired the car for an amount equal to the open market price multiplied by the amount of the relevant capital limit and divided by the prior owner's cost of acquisition. Where the situation is governed by an TCA 1997, s 289(6) or s 312(5) joint election (substitution for the open market price of a lower tax written down value), the new owner's capital allowances are based on an amount arrived at by assuming (a) that the prior owner had acquired the car for an amount equal to the relevant capital limit and (b) that this deemed cost had been written down by normal capital allowances during the previous owner's period of ownership.

Where it is eventually required of the acquiring company to calculate a balancing allowance or balancing charge on a motor vehicle acquired in any of these circumstances, only the proportion of the sale proceeds or other value receivable by it as is represented by the ratio of the relevant capital limit to the prior owner's acquisition cost is taken into account. Where successive transactions not involving a normal sale (ie, one not coming within (a) or (b) above) occur, it is the acquisition cost of the owner before the first such transaction that is applied in arriving at each successive new owner's capital allowances. Once a normal sale intervenes, the capital expenditure incurred by previous owners ceases to be relevant.

Example 5.212.4.1

On 3 January 2003, Albacore Ltd purchased a motor car costing €44,000 for the use of its managing director. On 15 June 2006, the company sold the car to W Baker Ltd, its fellow subsidiary company, for €13,000 when its market value was €24,000. Albacore Ltd had obtained wear and tear allowances based on the specified amount of €22,000, resulting in a tax written down value of €13,750 at the end of its accounting year to 31 December 2005. Since the companies are under common control, and assuming that an election under TCA 1997, s 312(5) is not made, W Baker Ltd must bring the car into its capital allowance computations at an assumed cost of €11,774, arrived at as follows:

$$\text{Market value } €24,000 \times 22,000/44,000 = €12,000$$

W Baker Ltd uses the car for the purposes of its trade for the remainder of the year ended 31 December 2006, but the car is damaged in an accident during the year ended 31 December 2007 and is sold for €4,000, with no insurance compensation being receivable. The capital allowances computations for W Baker Ltd for the years ended 31 December 2006 and 31 December 2007 are as follows:

	€
Deemed acquisition cost as above	12,000
W & T y/e 31/12/06	1,500
WDV 31/12/06	10,500
Sale proceeds: €4,000 x 22,000/44,000	2,000
Balancing allowance 31/12/07	8,500

5.212.5   Balancing charge on replacement of car

As explained in **5.209**, a company replacing an item of machinery or plant may elect under TCA 1997, s 290 to roll over any balancing charge arising on the sale of that item. Where the replaced item is a private motor vehicle, the roll over rules are applied as if the capital expenditure on the new car was limited to the specified amount.

Example 5.212.5.1

Oakville Ltd, a manufacturing company making up accounts to 31 December each year, purchased a new car on 16 August 2006 at a cost of €25,000 for use in its trade. For the year ended 31 December 2006, the company obtained a wear and tear allowance in respect of the car, restricted by reference to the specified amount of €22,000. On 9 October 2007, the company purchased a new car costing €28,000 and traded in the original car for €23,000.

The capital allowances computations for the cars for the years ended 31 December 2006 and 31 December 2007 are as follows:

	€
Cost of first car	25,000
Cost for capital allowances	22,000
W & T y/e 31/12/06	2,750
WDV 31/12/06	19,250
Sale proceeds: €23,000 x 22,000/25,000	20,240
Balancing charge (if no roll over election) y/e 31/12/07	990

For the next few years, Oakville Ltd elects under TCA 1997, s 290 to roll over the balancing charge. Since the expenditure of €28,000 on the replacement car, as limited to €22,000 for capital allowances purposes, exceeds the amount of the balancing charge, there is a complete roll over. The capital allowances computation for the year ended 31 December 2007 is as follows:

	€
Tax cost of replacement car:	22,000
Less: balancing charge rolled over	990
Net expenditure for capital allowances	21,010
W & T y/e 31/12/07	2,626
WDV 31/12/07	18,384

5.213 Emissions-based restriction of capital allowances for cars

5.213.1 Introduction

A revised scheme of capital allowances for passenger motor vehicles, linking the availability of capital allowances and leasing expenses to the carbon emission levels of vehicles, applies in respect of cars purchased on or after 1 July 2008. The relevant legislation provides for three broad categories of business car: those whose carbon dioxide emissions do not exceed 155g/km, those whose emissions are between 156 and190g/km and those whose emissions are above 190g/km. Any balancing allowances or balancing charges arising on a subsequent disposal of vehicles are computed on a proportional basis thereby ensuring that the appropriate amount of relief is given. (See also **3.202.3** regarding motor vehicle hire expenses, hire purchase etc.)

5.213.2 Vehicles subject to restriction

TCA 1997, Part 11C and not Part 11 applies to a vehicle which is a mechanically propelled road vehicle constructed or adapted for the carriage of passengers (subsequently referred to here as a "restricted vehicle"), other than a vehicle of a type not commonly used as a private vehicle and unsuitable to be so used. Excluded from the provisions of TCA 1997, Part 11C are vehicles acquired for short term hire (taxis etc) and vehicles acquired for testing.

The restriction on capital allowances does not apply where a vehicle is provided wholly or mainly for the purpose of the carriage of members of the public in the ordinary course of trade (TCA 1997, s 380P(1)). Nor does it apply in relation to a vehicle provided by a company that is a manufacturer of a vehicle, or of parts or accessories for such a vehicle, if that company shows that the vehicle was provided solely for the purpose of testing the vehicle or parts or accessories for such vehicle; but, if during the period of five years beginning with the time when the vehicle was provided, the company puts it, to any substantial extent, to a use which does not serve that purpose only, the restriction will be deemed to apply in relation to the vehicle (TCA 1997, s 380P(2)).

The carbon dioxide emissions (the CO_2 emissions "confirmed by reference to the relevant EC type approval certificate or EC certificate of conformity" – TCA 1997, s 380K) referable to any vehicle in the categories A to G are as set out in the following Table.

TABLE

Vehicle category	CO_2 Emissions (CO_2g/km)
A	0g/km up to and including 120g/km
B	More than 120g/km up to and including 140g/km
C	More than 140g/km up to and including 155g/km
D	More than 155g/km up to and including 170g/km
E	More than 170g/km up to and including 190g/km
F	More than 190g/km up to and including 225g/km
G	More than 225g/km

Where the Revenue Commissioners are not satisfied of the level of CO_2 emissions relating to a vehicle by reference to any document other than either of the above-mentioned certificates, or where no document has been provided, the vehicle will be treated as if it were a vehicle in Category G.

For the above purposes, *CO_2 emissions* means the level of carbon dioxide (CO_2) emissions for a vehicle measured in accordance with the provisions of Council Directive 80/1268/EEC of 16 December 1980 (OJ No L 375 of 31 December 1980, p36) (as amended) and listed in Annex VIII of Council Directive 70/156/EEC of 6 February 19702 (OJ No L 42 of 23 February 1970, p1) (as amended) and contained in the relevant EC type approval certificate or EC certificate of conformity or any other appropriate documentation which confirms compliance with any measures taken to give effect in the State to any act of the European Communities relating to the approximation of the laws of Member States in respect of type approval for the type of vehicle concerned.

5.213.3 Emissions-based limits

TCA 1997, s 380L provides for modified levels of capital allowances which apply to cars in different emissions categories and for a proportionate balancing allowance or charge in the event that the vehicle is subsequently disposed of. For the purposes of the section, *specified amount*, in relation to expenditure incurred on the provision of a vehicle, means €24,000, where the expenditure was incurred by a company in an accounting period ending on or after 1 January 2007.

In relation to a restricted vehicle, where an allowance which would otherwise be made under TCA 1997, s 284 is to be increased or reduced under TCA 1997, s 380L, any reference in the Tax Acts to an allowance made under TCA 1997, s 284 is to be construed as a reference to that allowance as so increased or reduced (TCA 1997, s 380L(1)). The allowances under TCA 1997, s 284 to be taken into account in computing the amount of expenditure still unallowed at any time (eg, to compute a balancing allowance or charge) are to be determined by reference to the allowances computed in accordance with TCA 1997, s 380L, and the expenditure incurred on the provision of the vehicle to be taken into account for capital allowances purposes is to be determined accordingly (TCA 1997, s 380L(1)).

TCA 1997, s 284 applies as if, for the purposes of that section, the actual cost of the vehicle were taken to be—

(a)   in the case of a vehicle in category A, B or C, an amount equal to the specified amount,

(b)   in the case of a vehicle in category D or E, where the retail price of the vehicle at the time it was made was—

    (i)   less than or equal to the specified amount, 50% of that price, and

    (ii)   greater than the specified amount, 50% of the specified amount, and

(c)   in the case of a vehicle in category F or G, nil (TCA 1997, s 380L(3)).

Where expenditure has been incurred on the provision of a restricted vehicle, any balancing allowance or balancing charge is to be computed, in a case where there are sale, insurance, salvage or compensation moneys, as if the amount of those moneys (or, where in consequence of any provision of the Taxes Acts, other than Part 11 or TCA 1997, s 380L, some other amount is to be treated as the amount of those moneys, that other amount) were—

(a)   in the case of a vehicle in category A, B or C, increased or reduced, as the case may be, in the proportion which the specified amount bears to the actual amount of that expenditure,

(b)   in the case of a vehicle in category D or E where the expenditure incurred was—

    (i)   less than or equal to the specified amount, reduced by 50%, and

    (ii)   greater than the specified amount, reduced in the proportion which 50% of the specified amount bears to that actual amount of that expenditure, and

(c)   in the case of a vehicle in category F or G, nil (TCA 1997, s 380L(4)).

Where expenditure is incurred on the provision of a restricted vehicle—

(a)   the person providing the vehicle (the "prior owner") sells the vehicle or gives it away so that TCA 1997, s 289(5), or that subsection as applied by TCA 1997, s 289(6), applies (see under *Gifts and sales at less than market value* in **5.207.4**) in relation to the purchaser or donee,

(b)   the prior owner sells the vehicle and the sale is a sale to which TCA 1997, s 312 (control and main benefit sales – see **5.103**) applies, or

(c)   in consequence of a succession to the trade or profession of the prior owner, TCA 1997, s 313(1) (succession to trade etc – see **5.107**) applies, then, in relation to the purchaser, donee or successor, the price which the vehicle would have fetched if sold in the open market or the expenditure incurred by the prior owner on the provision of the vehicle is treated for the purposes of TCA 1997, s 289, 312 or 313(1), as the case may be, as—

(i) in the case of a vehicle in Category A, B or C, an amount equal to the specified amount,

(ii) in the case of a vehicle in Category D or E where the retail price of the vehicle at the time it was made was—

    (I) less than or equal to the specified amount, 50% of that price, and

    (II) greater than the specified amount, 50% of the specified amount, and

(iii) in the case of a vehicle in Category F or G, nil,

and, in the application of TCA 1997, s 380L(4) to the purchaser, donee or successor, references to the expenditure incurred on the provision of the vehicle shall be construed as references to the expenditure so incurred by the prior owner (TCA 1997, s 380L(5)(a)).

Where the foregoing treatment has applied, and no sale or gift of the vehicle has since occurred other than one to which either TCA 1997, s 289 or 312 applies, then, in relation to all persons concerned, the like consequences as those above will ensue as respects a gift, sale or succession within (a) to (c) above which occurs on any subsequent occasion as would ensue if the person who in relation to that sale, gift or succession is the prior owner had incurred expenditure on the provision of the vehicle of an amount equal to the expenditure so incurred by the person who was the prior owner on the first-mentioned occasion (TCA 1997, s 380L(5)(b)).

In the application of TCA 1997, s 290 ("roll over" of balancing charge - see **5.209**) to a case where the vehicle is the new machinery referred to in that section, the expenditure is to be disregarded in so far as it exceeds—

(a) in the case of a vehicle in Category A, B or C, the specified amount,

(b) in the case of a vehicle in Category D or E, where the retail price of the vehicle at the time it was made was—

    (i) less than or equal to the specified amount, 50% of that price, and

    (ii) greater than the specified amount, 50% of the specified amount, and

(c) in the case of a vehicle in Category F or G, nil,

but without prejudice to the application of TCA 1997, s380L(1)-(5) to the vehicle.

Expenditure may not be regarded for the purposes of TCA 1997, Part 11C as having been incurred by a person in so far as the expenditure has been or is to be met directly or indirectly by the State or by any person other than the first-mentioned person (TCA 1997, s 380L(7)).

5.214 Qualifying shipping trades: ring fencing

TCA 1997, s 407(4) provides for the "ring fencing" of capital allowances in respect of qualifying ships with the result that the allowances are not available to a company to offset any of its profits chargeable to corporation tax other than income of a qualifying shipping trade and certain ship chartering income. The terms *qualifying ship, qualifying shipping trade* and *qualifying shipping activities* are defined in **7.205.6** in connection with the availability of manufacturing relief for qualifying shipping activities. The ring fencing provision restricts the use of the "specified capital allowances" (capital allowances relating to a qualifying ship used in a qualifying shipping trade – see below), which may be allowed only:

(a) in computing the income from a qualifying shipping trade; or

(b) in computing or charging to tax any income from the letting on charter of the qualifying ship to which the specified capital allowances refer (other than letting on charter which is a qualifying shipping activity) (TCA 1997, s 407(4)(a)).

The foregoing is reinforced by the further provision to the effect that the specified capital allowances are not allowable in computing any other income or profits of a company or in taxing any other trade of the company or in charging any other income to corporation tax.

A loss, including a loss created by, or which includes, specified capital allowances, incurred in the relevant period in a qualifying shipping trade may not be set off:

(i) under TCA 1997, s 396(2) against any profits except to the extent of any income included in those profits which is income from a qualifying shipping trade; or

(ii) against total profits of another company under the group relief provisions (TCA 1997, s 420(1)) except to the extent of any income included in those profits which is income from a qualifying shipping trade (TCA 1997, s 407(4)(b)).

In view of the restrictions on the use of "relevant trading losses" (see **4.103** and **8.306.2**), a claim under TCA 1997, s 396(2) or 420(1) would be ineffective anyway since these provisions are of relevance only in respect of "excepted trades" (which would not include a qualifying shipping trade). On the other hand, since any losses arising would be relevant trading losses, there is nothing in TCA 1997, s 407 to prevent claims being made under TCA 1997, s 396A, 396B, 420A or 420B.

As regards (a) above, the specified capital allowances in question would be deducted as an expense in computing the Case I income of a company's qualifying shipping trade. A company owning a qualifying ship may let that ship on charter otherwise than for use in qualifying shipping activities (a "dry lease"). In any such case, in accordance with (b) above, a leasing company may set the specified capital allowances against leasing income which, because the ship is chartered on a "dry lease" basis, is not income from a qualifying shipping activity. The use of the specified capital allowances in respect of a particular qualifying ship is restricted to the above-described income from the chartering of that ship. The *specified capital allowances*, which are subject to the restrictions in TCA 1997, s 407(4)(a), are capital allowances in respect of:

(1) expenditure incurred by any person in the relevant period in providing a qualifying ship for use in, or intended to be used in, a qualifying shipping trade; or

(2) the diminished value by reason of wear and tear during the relevant period of a qualifying ship in use for the purposes of a qualifying shipping trade.

In relation to (1), it seems that it is possible to have specified capital allowances in a case where a qualifying ship is chartered on dry lease (not a qualifying shipping trade) as long as the ship in question is also in use in a qualifying shipping trade (or is intended for such use).

The *relevant period* is the period from 1 January 1987 to 31 December 2010. A *qualifying shipping trade* is a trade carried on by a company consisting solely of certain qualifying shipping activities involving, primarily, the use of an Irish registered ship at least 51% owned by an Irish resident person, or persons, in transporting passengers and/or cargo by sea. The "wet leasing" of a qualifying ship by a company, ie, where the ship is operated by, and its crew remains under the direction and control of, the company, is also a qualifying shipping activity.

The definition of "specified capital allowances" is such as to confine the allowances subject to the ring fence restriction to the capital allowances in respect of a qualifying ship used or intended to be used in a qualifying shipping trade. The restrictions do not apply to limit the uses otherwise available for capital allowances on other ships. The ring-fenced capital allowances include initial allowances, free depreciation and the annual wear and tear allowances in respect of capital expenditure incurred after 31 December 1986 on the qualifying ship. They also include, where capital expenditure is incurred before 1 January 1987, the annual wear and tear allowances (and any free depreciation) claimed in respect of the use of the qualifying ship after 31 December 1986.

The activity described in (b) above (ie, the letting on charter of a qualifying ship in the course of a trade other than a letting which is a qualifying shipping activity – a "dry lease") is deemed, by TCA 1997, s 407(4)(c), to be a trade of leasing for the purposes of TCA 1997, s 403 and to be a separate trade for those purposes (see **5.305**). This is despite the provision in TCA 1997, s 403(1)(c) to the effect that leasing does not include the letting on charter of a ship in the course of a trade of operating ships carried on by a company.

Where, however, a binding contract in writing for the acquisition or construction of a ship was concluded on or after 1 July 1996, TCA 1997, s 407(4)(c) will not apply, subject to conditions (TCA 1997, s 407(5)). Such letting on charter will not be subject to the ring-fencing treatment of leasing trades provided for by TCA 1997, s 403 where the terms of the lease comply with the provisions of clauses (I) and (II) of TCA 1997, s 404(1)(b)(i) (so that the lease is not a "balloon lease" – see **5.306**) and where the lessee produces a "relevant certificate" to the Revenue Commissioners. A *relevant certificate* is a certificate issued by the Minister for the Marine and Natural Resources, with the consent of the Minister for Finance, certifying, on the basis of a business plan and any other information supplied by the lessee, that the Minister is satisfied that the lease in question:

(a) will result in the upgrading and enhancement of the lessee's fleet leading to improved efficiency and the maintenance of competitiveness;

(b) (i) has the potential to create a reasonable level of additional sustainable employment and other socio-economic benefits in the State, or

(ii) will assist in maintaining or promoting the lessee's trade in the carrying on of a qualifying shipping activity, and the maintenance of a reasonable level of additional sustainable employment and other socio-economic benefits in the State, and

(c) will result in the leasing of a ship which complies with current environmental and safety standards (TCA 1997, s 407(1)).

The Minister must, before issuing the certificate, be satisfied that the lease is for *bona fide* commercial purposes and is not part of a scheme or arrangement the main purpose, or one of the main purposes, of which is the avoidance of tax (TCA 1997, s 407(2)).

The removal of the TCA 1997, s 403 ring-fencing provision, subject to conditions as described above, is intended to result in a less restrictive ring-fencing regime for the activities dealt with in TCA 1997, s 407(4)(a)(ii), ie, the letting on charter of a qualifying ship other than letting on charter which is a qualifying shipping activity (a "dry lease" letting); whereas TCA 1997, s 403 would restrict the use of the specified capital allowances to income from the ship (the leasing of which is deemed to be a separate trade of leasing), the effect of the removal of this ring-fencing provision is intended to permit the specified capital allowances in the case of an activity within TCA 1997, s 407(4)(a)(ii) to be set against leasing income whether arising in the course of a qualifying shipping trade or from the dry lease chartering of the qualifying ship.

5.3 LEASED MACHINERY OR PLANT

5.301   Capital allowances for lessors
5.302   Relief for lessors' unused capital allowances
5.303   Capital allowances for lessees
5.304   Burden of wear and tear
5.305   Lessors' capital allowances restricted
5.306   "Balloon" leasing

5.301   Capital allowances for lessors

5.301.1   General

A company may claim capital allowances in respect of machinery or plant owned by it and which is leased to another person, provided the "the burden of the wear and tear" of the machinery or plant falls directly on it (TCA 1997, s 298(1)). Similarly, the balancing allowance and balancing charge provisions apply in the case of a company which has leased machinery or plant in respect of which it has obtained capital allowances and which has been disposed of or which has ceased to be leased by it (TCA 1997, s 298(2)). The question as to when the lessor is regarded as bearing the burden of the wear and tear of plant is discussed in **5.304**.

A company which leases machinery or plant in respect of which it bears the burden of wear and tear, may claim wear and tear allowances in respect of the capital expenditure on that machinery or plant as if during the period of the letting, the plant was in use for the purposes of a trade carried on by it. If the expenditure qualifies, the company may also claim appropriate free depreciation or initial allowances. The legislative provisions dealing with capital allowances in relation to a person carrying on a trade are therefore applied to a lessor of plant. Thus, if a balancing charge arises to a company disposing of plant which it had leased to another person, it is entitled under TCA 1997, s 290 to roll over that charge in the event that the plant is replaced by new plant which is leased (see **5.209**).

It is not necessary for a company leasing machinery or plant to be carrying on a trade of leasing in order to be entitled to capital allowances. If in fact the company does carry on a trade consisting of or including the leasing of machinery or plant, it will be entitled to the capital allowances and will be subject to any balancing charges arising in the ordinary way in taxing the profits of that trade. This position applies not only to a specialist machinery or plant leasing trade (including vehicle leasing), but also to banks and similar financial institutions that include plant leasing as part of their trades.

Where a company leases machinery or plant otherwise than in the course of a trade, the income derived from the leasing is taxable under Schedule D Case IV. To obtain the relevant capital allowances, a non-trading lessor must make a claim to that effect within 24 months of the end of each relevant accounting period (TCA 1997, s 298(1)). In *Macsaga Investment Co Ltd v Lupton* 44 TC 659, it was held that capital allowances applied only to plant and machinery used in a trade. Accordingly, if the lessor's leasing activity is not in the course of a trade, it would be necessary, for the lessor to be entitled to capital allowances, that the plant and machinery be used in the course of the lessee's trade.

Wear and tear allowances, including free depreciation, and any balancing allowances are given to the non-trading leasing company by way of discharge or repayment of tax and are available primarily against its income from the letting of machinery or plant as assessable under Schedule D Case IV. Any balancing charges made on the company are made under Schedule D Case IV (TCA 1997, s 300(3)). Thus, the company's capital allowances for an accounting period must first be deducted from the leasing income assessable for that period to the extent that the income equals or exceeds the capital allowances claimed. In practice, where the capital allowances calculations are included as part of the relevant Case IV computation in the tax return, that will be accepted as the making of a proper claim.

Capital allowances which fall to be made to a company for any accounting period and which are given "by discharge or repayment of tax" (eg, a writing down allowance available against income from the letting of machinery or plant (TCA 1997, s 298(1)), and are to be available primarily against the specified class of income, are to be deducted as far as possible against income of that class. Where the allowances are not fully used in that way because of an insufficiency of income, they may under TCA 1997, s 308(4) be allowed against profits of any description of the same accounting period and (if the company was then within the charge to tax) of preceding accounting periods for a period equal in length to the period in which the allowance arose. TCA 1997, s 403, however, restricts the manner in which a company may use excess capital allowances on machinery or plant leased by it by way of set off against its total profits (see **5.302** and **5.305**).

The deficiency which may be offset against profits of a preceding period is confined to so much of that deficiency as cannot be utilised against profits of a later period. In other words, a deficiency which is the subject of a TCA 1997, s 308(4) claim must be used first against the total profits of the period in which the deficiency arose and then against the profits of the preceding period or periods.

For the purpose of offsetting a deficiency against the profits of the preceding period or periods, profits are apportioned on a time basis; where an accounting period falls partly before the immediately preceding period or periods equal in length to the period of the Case V deficiency, only a proportionate part of the profits of that accounting period may be relieved. Any allowance still not fully utilised may then under TCA 1997, s 308(3) be carried forward to succeeding accounting periods and set against income of the specified class for those periods.

5.301.2 Accelerated capital allowances

With certain exceptions (see **5.204.3** and **5.205.5**), accelerated capital allowances (free depreciation and initial allowances) ceased to be available in respect of machinery or plant provided, or capital expenditure incurred, as the case may be, by a leasing company after 31 March 1992.

A company leasing machinery or plant is entitled to the same initial allowances and increased wear and tear allowances (free depreciation) under the same circumstances and subject to the same conditions as a company entitled to those allowances in respect of its own trade. Accordingly, the leasing company which incurs the capital expenditure on new machinery or plant to be leased to a person carrying on a trade or profession is entitled to claim an initial allowance under TCA 1997, s 283(2) for the accounting period in which the expenditure was incurred. Similarly, a leasing company which has incurred capital expenditure on new machinery or plant in respect of which it bears the burden of the wear and tear is entitled under TCA 1997, s 285 to have its wear and tear allowance under TCA 1997, s 284 increased by the amount specified by it, provided the machinery or plant continues to be leased out at the end of the relevant accounting period.

It follows that the restrictions on accelerated capital allowances contained in ITA 1967 s 251(4) (initial allowances) and TCA 1997, s 285(2)(b), (3) (free depreciation) apply in a corresponding way to any leased machinery or plant for which these allowances are available. The lessor's initial allowance for the leased plant was reduced (from 100%) to 75% where the capital expenditure was incurred in the period from 1 April 1988 to 31 March 1989, and reduced to 50% for expenditure incurred after 31 March 1989. Similarly, for leased machinery or plant first provided as new for letting from 1 April 1988 to 31 March 1989, the maximum increased wear and tear allowance which could be claimed was restricted to 75% (and to 50% for plant first provided for letting after 31 March 1989). The exceptions provided for in TCA 1997 ss 283(4)(a) and 295(5)(a) (eg, plant provided for use in the International Financial Services Centre), which allow 100% accelerated capital allowances to continue to be claimed, apply in the same way for leased plant (see **5.204.3** and **5.205.5**).

For capital expenditure on new machinery or plant incurred after 31 March 1988 and before 1 April 1989, a leasing company which bore the burden of wear and tear of the machinery or plant leased was entitled to the benefit of both the 75% initial allowance and the normal wear and tear allowance for the accounting period in which the expenditure was incurred. If any initial allowance was given in respect of that expenditure, no free depreciation allowance could be obtained thereon either for the first period or for any subsequent period (TCA 1997, s 283(6)(b)).

However, for capital expenditure incurred after 31 March 1989, TCA 1997, s 283(7)(a) prevents any wear and tear allowance being given for the first accounting period if the initial allowance is claimed for that period in respect of the same expenditure. No free depreciation allowance may be obtained for any subsequent period in respect of the same expenditure (see **5.204.4–5.205.6**).

5.302   Relief for lessors' unused capital allowances

TCA 1997, s 403 restricts the manner in which a company may use excess capital allowances on machinery or plant leased by it by way of set off against its total profits. Restrictions apply whether the machinery or plant is leased by a company in the course of a trade of leasing or by a company chargeable to tax under Schedule D Case IV in respect of its leasing income. The position which obtained prior to TCA 1997, s 403 continues to have effect for certain grant-aided leased plant and for expenditure on leased plant incurred before 25 January 1984.

Subject to certain exceptions, TCA 1997, s 403 prevents a company which leases machinery or plant in the course of *any* trade from setting off capital allowances on the leased plant (other than certain excepted capital allowances) against any profits other than trading income derived from the leasing of the plant. For machinery or plant acquired for leasing in the period 25 January 1984 to 12 May 1986, capital allowances in respect of any grant-aided expenditure are excepted capital allowances and remain eligible for set off against total profits under the rules applying to capital expenditure incurred prior to 25 January 1984. For machinery or plant acquired for leasing after 12

May 1986, this exceptional treatment applies only where the machinery or plant is leased for use in a "specified" trade. This matter is discussed in detail in **5.305**.

TCA 1997, s 403 prevents a non-trading leasing company of machinery or plant from setting off its capital allowances on machinery or plant provided for leasing against any profits other than profits comprising plant leasing income. However, a non-trading lessor company remains entitled to include any excepted capital allowances in a claim for set off against its total profits. For machinery or plant provided for leasing from 25 January 1984 to 12 May 1986, capital allowances in respect of any grant-aided expenditure are excepted capital allowances and continue to benefit from the treatment applying to expenditure incurred before 25 January 1984. For machinery or plant provided for leasing after 12 May 1986 (other than certain films), the excepted capital allowances treatment is not available at all to the non-trading lessor, except in cases dealt with in certain transitional provisions. Again, the current rules (including the transitional reliefs) are dealt with more fully in **5.305**.

Both a trading and non-trading leasing company remain entitled to carry forward, for use in any subsequent accounting period, any capital allowances on leased plant to the extent that the allowances cannot be fully used against the plant leasing income for the chargeable period to which they relate. The right to carry forward any unused wear and tear allowances, free depreciation, initial allowances or balancing allowances in respect of the leased plant is an automatic one and does not require a specific claim within any time limit.

The manner in which a company carrying on a leasing trade utilises the related capital allowances brought forward is the same as that for any other capital allowances of a trade but with the restriction that the capital allowances brought forward (other than any excepted capital allowances) can only be set off against the leasing trade income for the following periods. Any excepted capital allowances brought forward may be set off against *any* income of the trade for following periods.

In the case of a non-trading leasing company, any capital allowances brought forward are added to the corresponding leased plant allowances for the following period and must be set off against the next available Case IV leasing income. To the extent that the leasing income for the next accounting period is insufficient to absorb the amount brought forward, the unused balance is carried forward without time limit to successive accounting periods until fully absorbed by subsequent Case IV leasing income.

TCA 1997, s 404 places further restrictions on the set-off of capital allowances on certain leases of plant and machinery where the lease was entered into on or after 23 December 1993. The section provides that the capital allowances may only be set off against income from that particular lease, as distinct from the income from all other leases as was previously the case.

TCA 1997, s 404 is aimed at leases, referred to as "balloon leases" (see **5.306**), where there is a fluctuation in the repayments so that most of the repayments are not made until the end of the primary period of the lease. It applies only to leases of plant and machinery and does not affect hotels, industrial buildings, or urban renewal allowances. Neither does it apply to leasing operations carried out in the IFSC or the Shannon Customs Free Airport. The rules are relaxed in the case of agricultural machinery to allow for seasonal factors which may influence the repayments.

5.303   Capital allowances for lessees

A company which is a lessee of machinery or plant for use in its own trade, but which does not incur the related capital expenditure, may be entitled to capital allowances. This will be the case where the two following conditions are met:

(a)   the machinery or plant is let to the company on terms of its being bound to maintain and deliver it over in good condition at the end of the lease; and

(b)   the burden of the wear and tear of the machinery or plant will in fact fall directly on the company (TCA 1997, s 299(1)).

A lessee company is not, however, entitled to claim free depreciation allowances unless the contract of letting provides that it shall, or may, become the owner of the plant when the contract is performed. If the plant is leased under such a contract and free depreciation is claimed, but the company does not in fact become the owner of the plant on completion of the contract, any free depreciation allowances (to the extent that they are in excess of the ordinary wear and tear allowances) are withdrawn and any necessary additional assessments or adjustments of assessments are made (TCA 1997, s 299(2)).

The capital allowances to which a lessee company is entitled are made in respect of the capital expenditure incurred by the lessor in providing the machinery or plant. The capital expenditure is deemed to have been incurred by the company and the plant is deemed to belong to it. The capital allowances are made to the company in taxing the profits of its trade. A balancing allowance or charge is made to or on the company if (a) it ceases to lease the plant or (b) it ceases permanently to use the plant in its trade or (c) it ceases permanently to carry on the trade.

In calculating any balancing allowance or balancing charge for a lessee company which has obtained capital allowances, it is only the sale, insurance, salvage or compensation moneys received by it that are taken into account. Any sale or other proceeds received in respect of the sale of the plant by the lessor are not relevant. In fact, a sale by the lessor may not necessarily involve the end of the lessee's period of use in its trade as it may continue to lease the machinery or plant from the new owner.

A somewhat unusual result can occur in the case of a trading company which leases a building which includes plant, such as lifts or heating installations, under a lease which binds the company to maintain such plant as forms part of the building and to deliver it over in good condition at the end of the lease. In effect, the company is required to bear the burden of wear and tear in respect of that plant. If in such a case a company which has obtained capital allowances on the plant sells its interest in the lease of the building, part of the proceeds of sale must be allocated to the plant and included in the calculation of the company's balancing allowance or charge.

Difficult considerations will arise where a lessee company which has qualified for capital allowances under TCA 1997, s 299(1) assigns the lease to another party. The question of the company's entitlement to relevant capital allowances may need to be reviewed having regard to the new position in which it may no longer be clear that the burden of the wear and tear of the machinery or plant has fallen on the company. Since the company will not have disposed of the machinery or plant (although it will no longer be deemed to own it), it may not be clear that a balancing adjustment is due. The position of the assignee is also unclear. It is arguable that the assignee is entitled to capital allowances by reference to the original cost price of the machinery or plant, being the person to whom the machinery or plant is let, provided of course that the conditions of TCA 1997, s 299(1) are again fulfilled.

For the tax treatment of lessees of plant and machinery who do not qualify for capital allowances, see **3.303**.

5.304 Burden of wear and tear

In any case in which capital allowances are to be claimed in respect of leased machinery or plant, it is important to determine whether the lessor or the lessee bears the burden of wear and tear; the capital allowances on any item of plant cannot be obtained by both lessor and lessee. For the lessor to be entitled to the allowances, the conditions of TCA 1997, s 298(1) must apply, ie, the plant must be "let upon such terms that the burden of the wear and tear thereof falls directly on the lessor". On the other hand, a lessee company may only claim capital allowances under TCA 1997, s 299(1) if in fact it directly bears the wear and tear of the plant and if it is bound to hand over the plant in good condition at the end of the lease.

The exact meaning of the phrase "the burden of wear and tear" in this context is often quite difficult to apply in practice and it may not always be clear as to whether it applies to the lessor or the lessee. This question was raised in *Lupton v Cadogan Gardens Developments Ltd* 47 TC 1. A hotel premises containing lifts, boilers and other machinery and plant was leased by the company for 90 years from September 1960. The lease contained covenants by the lessees to maintain the premises, including the plant, and to keep them in good and substantial repair and to deliver them up so maintained and repaired at the end of the lease, and as often as necessary to replace worn out plant with other items of similar quality. It was accepted that all the items of plant were likely to require replacing once or more during the full term of the lease. Both lessors and lessees claimed the capital allowances.

It was held in the Court of Appeal that the burden of wear and tear fell on the lessees. The lease was still in its earlier years and there was no doubt that the plant in question would have worn out and disappeared before the end of the lease and would, under its terms, require to be replaced by the lessees at their expense. The fact that the lessees would be allowed deduct the whole cost of replacing the items of plant in calculating their trading profits was not considered to be relevant.

The concept of the burden of wear and tear was subject to judicial comment in *Macsaga Investment Co Ltd v Lupton* 44 TC 659 where the company in that case, the lessors, had contended that the words meant something quite different from a mere obligation to maintain and keep the plant in good repair. They claimed the words meant depreciation in value in so far as it could not be made good by proper and adequate expenditure on maintenance and repair. Lord Denning MR considered that wear and tear meant depreciation and that the burden fell on the company, but Salmon LJ took the view that the burden of the wear and tear fell on the tenant who covenanted to maintain the plant and deliver it over in good condition at the end of the lease. In fact, this case was decided on the grounds that a lessor is not entitled to capital allowances, even if he bears the burden of wear and tear, where the lessee does not use the asset for his own trade. The lessee in this case was the Minister of Works who did not carry on any trade, profession, office or employment.

In *MacCarthaigh v Daly* 3 ITR 253, the phrase "wear and tear" was described by O'Hanlon J as "that sort of wearing out of articles due to use which is not capable of being avoided by ordinary processes of maintenance and repair and which will eventually necessitate a replacement or abandonment of the plant and machinery".

In view of the doubt which remains as to where the burden of wear and tear falls, particular care is required of a lessor of plant as regards the wording of the lease agreement if the entitlement to capital allowances is to be assured. This will be particularly true in the case of an agreement containing a clause requiring the lessee to maintain the plant in good repair. In such a case, it is usual to add the words "fair wear and tear excepted" at the end of such a clause. A lessor company would normally be regarded as satisfying the wear and tear test if the obligation to replace the plant falls on it or, if it is intended that the plant will simply wear out during the lease and not need replacing, if that company is the person which actually bears the capital loss as the plant wears out. The fact that the lease agreement may require the lessee to keep the plant insured during the period of the letting does not, of itself, place the onus of replacement on the lessee.

The fact that the lease agreement contains a covenant by the lessee to maintain the plant and deliver it over in good condition at the end of the lease may not be sufficient to entitle a lessee company to the capital allowances. It must also be in a position to show that the burden of wear and tear actually does or will fall on it. This additional requirement was prescribed following the decision in *Union Coal Storage Co Ltd v Simpson* 22 TC 547. In that case, it was held that the lessee who met the first condition was entitled to the allowances although the lessor (a non-resident person not liable to tax) had in fact undertaken the financial burden of replacing the worn out plant. That ruling could not now be given in favour of a lessee in view of the two conditions in TCA 1997, s 299(1).

5.305   Lessors' capital allowances restricted

5.305.1   General

A loss incurred by a company from the leasing of machinery or plant, to the extent that it is attributable to "specified capital allowances", may not be set off against the total profits of the company under TCA 1997, s 396(2) or 308(4) nor may it be surrendered by means of group relief (in accordance with TCA 1997, s 420, 420A or 420B). TCA 1997, s 403 provides that specified capital allowances available to a lessor of machinery or plant may only be used to reduce or offset the income arising from the leasing activity, whether that income is taxable under Schedule D Case I as the profits of a trade of leasing, under Case IV if no trade is involved, or under Case III if the leasing activity is carried on outside the State. (See, however **5.305.8** below in connection with the relaxation of this restriction in certain cases.)

To the extent that the specified capital allowances create or increase a trading loss for which relief may be claimed under any of the loss relief provisions mentioned above, the relevant part of that loss is only available to reduce or offset any income from plant leasing, but not any other income or profits. In view of the restrictions on the use of "relevant trading losses" (see **4.103** and **8.306.2**), however, a claim under TCA 1997, s 396(2) or 420(1) would be of no avail in any event since these provisions are of relevance only in respect of "excepted trades" (which would not include a trade of leasing).

TCA 1997, s 403 does not prevent a lessor company from claiming the full capital allowances to which it is entitled but it restricts the use of the specified capital allowances to the income from the leasing activity. It does not affect the carry forward of a loss created or increased by specified capital allowances. Capital allowances which are not specified capital allowances (referred to here as the "excepted capital allowances") continue to be available to create or increase a loss which may be offset against a company's trading income whether from leasing or otherwise but not, in view of the restrictions relating to relevant trading losses, against profits generally.

For the purposes of TCA 1997, s 403, the letting of any item of machinery or plant on hire, as well as the letting on charter of a ship or aircraft which has been provided for such letting, is regarded as the leasing of machinery or plant (TCA 1997, s 403(1)(b)). Not included as the leasing of machinery or plant, however, is the letting of a ship (other than a "qualifying ship" in certain circumstances – see below) on charter in the course of the carrying on by a company of a trade of operating ships where the letting would fall to be regarded as part of the activities of that trade.

The ring-fencing provisions of TCA 1997, s 403 do not apply in the case of a qualifying fishing boat in respect of which accelerated capital allowances may be claimed under TCA 1997, s 284(3A) (see **5.204.5**).

5.305.2 Trade of leasing

A *trade of leasing* is a trade consisting wholly of the leasing of machinery or plant or a part of another trade treated as a separate trade of leasing. Banking is a typical example of a trade part of which consists of the leasing of machinery or plant. If a company leases any machinery or plant in the course of a trade which does not consist wholly of such leasing, that trade is to be treated as two separate trades (TCA 1997, s 403(2)).

A consequence of separate trade treatment is that the profit or loss of the deemed separate trades must be identified. The capital allowances for the machinery or plant provided for the separate trade of leasing (other than any excepted capital allowances) may then only be offset against the leasing profits. In splitting the overall trading profit or loss between the two deemed trades, suitable apportionments must be made of any receipts or expenses not solely or directly related to either the leasing or non-leasing activities.

Ships – letting on charter

As mentioned in **5.305.1** above, the letting of any item of machinery or plant on hire, as well as the letting on charter of a ship or aircraft which has been provided for such letting, is regarded as the leasing of machinery or plant. The letting of a ship on charter (other than the letting on charter of a *qualifying* ship in the course of a trade other than a qualifying shipping trade – see below), where the letting is in the course of a trade of operating ships, is not treated as the leasing of machinery or plant (TCA 1997, s 403(1)(c)). TCA 1997, s 403 does not apply to such lettings, therefore, so that it is possible to use the capital allowances for a ship let on charter to reduce or offset the profits of the whole trade of operating ships (including the chartering income). TCA 1997, s 407(4)(c) (see **5.213**) provides that, notwithstanding TCA 1997, s 403(1)(c), the letting on charter of a qualifying ship other than a letting on charter which is a qualifying shipping activity is to be regarded as a trade of leasing and to be a separate trade (separate from any other trade including any other leasing trade) for the purposes of

TCA 1997, s 403. For the definitions of "qualifying ship" and "qualifying shipping trade", see **7.205.6.**

Where, however, a binding contract in writing for the acquisition or construction of a ship was concluded on or after 1 July 1996, this provision affecting the letting on charter of a qualifying ship (apart from a letting on charter which is a qualifying shipping activity – see below re "wet lease") will not apply, subject to conditions (TCA 1997, s 407(5)). Such letting on charter will not be subject to the TCA 1997, s 403 ring-fencing treatment of leasing trades where the terms of the lease comply with the provisions of clauses (I) and (II) of TCA 1997, s 404(1)(b)(i) (see **5.306** – definition of "relevant lease") and where the lessee produces a "relevant certificate" to the Revenue Commissioners ((TCA 1997, s 407(5)). A *relevant certificate* is a certificate issued by the Minister for the Marine, with the consent of the Minister for Finance, certifying, on the basis of a business plan and any other information supplied by the lessee, that the Minister is satisfied that the lease in question:

(a) will result in the upgrading and enhancement of the lessee's fleet leading to improved efficiency and the maintenance of competitiveness;

(b) has the potential to create a reasonable level of additional sustainable employment and other socio-economic benefits in the State, or will assist in maintaining or promoting the lessee's trade in the carrying on of a qualifying shipping activity, and the maintenance of a reasonable level of additional sustainable employment and other socio-economic benefits in the State; and

(c) will result in the leasing of a ship which complies with current environmental and safety standards (TCA 1997, s 407(1)).

The Minister must, before issuing the certificate, be satisfied that the lease is for *bona fide* commercial purposes and is not part of a scheme or arrangement the main purpose, or one of the main purposes, of which is the avoidance of tax.

Reference is made above to a "wet lease". With this kind of lease, also sometimes referred to as a "non-demise" charter, the lessor provides the ship, crew, fuel, provisions etc and is responsible for the direction and control of the ship and crew throughout the period of the charter. It contrasts with a "dry lease" or "bare-boat" charter where the lessor provides the ship only and the lessee is responsible for the provision of the crew and the direction and control of the vessel and crew.

In summary:

(i) for the purposes of TCA 1997, s 403, as a general rule, the letting on charter of a ship in the course of a trade of operating ships is not regarded as the leasing of machinery or plant;

(ii) by way of exception to (i), but subject to (iii) below, the letting on charter of a *qualifying* ship where the letting is a "dry lease" (a letting on charter that is not a qualifying shipping activity) is subject to the ring fencing rules of TCA 1997, s 403;

(iii) notwithstanding (ii), the letting on charter, by way of a dry lease, of a qualifying ship acquired on or after 1 July 1996 is, subject to conditions, excluded from (ii) and is accordingly governed by the less restrictive ring-fencing provisions of TCA 1997, s 407.

Capital allowances in respect of expenditure on a qualifying ship in the case of (ii), therefore, can only be used to reduce or offset the part of the income of the whole trade which arises from the letting on charter of that ship.

Another type of trade affected is the trade of leasing films, whether for showing in cinemas, on television or otherwise. In such a trade, it is the film itself which is treated as the machinery or plant on which capital allowances are given by reference to the cost of making the film (if leased by the film making company) or its cost of purchase (if acquired for leasing by another person). For films provided for leasing from 25 January 1984 to 12 May 1986, the rules for excepted capital allowances apply in the same way as for other leased machinery or plant, but TCA 1997, s 403 now excepts only certain films from its restrictions (see below).

5.305.3 The specified capital allowances

"The specified capital allowances" are defined as capital allowances in respect of:

(a) expenditure incurred on machinery or plant provided for leasing in the course of a trade of leasing; or

(b) the diminished value of such machinery or plant by reason of wear and tear,

but excluding the excepted capital allowances in respect of machinery or plant to which TCA 1997, s 403(7), (8) and (9) apply – as detailed below.

Capital allowances (whether wear and tear, initial allowances, free depreciation or balancing allowances) in respect of machinery or plant provided for leasing in the course of a trade of leasing, are specified capital allowances unless one of the exceptions applies. In this connection, the words "provided for leasing" in relation to any period should be read as meaning that the machinery or plant is available for leasing in that period in the course of the lessor's trade; it is not necessary that the plant is first provided for leasing in that period.

The position governing machinery or plant provided for leasing is subject to the qualification that further restrictions, provided for in TCA 1997, s 404, may apply in respect of certain leases ("balloon" leases) of plant and machinery entered into on or after 23 December 1993 where the value of the asset concerned is more than €63,500. These further restrictions are described in **5.306**.

5.305.4 The excepted capital allowances

In relation to machinery or plant provided for leasing, *lessor* and *lessee* mean respectively the person to whom the machinery or plant is or is to be leased and the person providing the machinery or plant for leasing, and the terms include respectively the successors in title of a lessee or a lessor (TCA 1997, s 403(1)).The excepted capital allowances (which may be the subject of a claim for set-off against the lessor's non-leasing trading income), are those in respect of:

(a) machinery or plant (other than a film), *but only if* all of the following conditions are met:

(i) the terms of the lease include an undertaking by the lessee that, during a period ("the relevant period") which is not less than three years and which commences on the day the machinery or plant is first brought into use by the lessee, the machinery or plant so provided will—

(I) where it is so provided before 4 March 1998, be used by the lessee for the purposes only of a "specified trade" (see **5.305.5** below) carried on in the State by the lessee, and

(II) where it is so provided on or after 4 March 1998, be used by the lessee for the purposes only of a specified trade carried on in the State by the lessee and that it will not be used for the purposes of any other trade, or business or activity other than the lessor's trade,

(ii) the machinery or plant is in fact used for the specified trade for that three year period, and

(iii) the machinery or plant is provided for leasing to a lessee who is not connected with the lessor (TCA 1997, s 403(9)(b));

(b) a film (not being either or both a film negative and its associated soundtrack, or a film tape or a film disc – hence the leasing of a master film negative is subject to the ring fence) provided for leasing which is a film made wholly or partly in the State, but only if the cost of making the film is met directly or indirectly, wholly or partly, by the Irish Film Board under the authority given to it by the Irish Film Board Act 1980 s 6 or 7 (TCA 1997, s 403(7)); and

(c) machinery or plant provided for leasing, whenever the expenditure was incurred, in the course of the carrying on by the lessor of trading operations qualifying for the 10% corporation tax rate in Shannon Airport (TCA 1997, s 445) or in the International Financial Services Centre (TCA 1997, s 446), and in respect of which no initial allowance or allowance by way of free depreciation has been, or will be, made (TCA 1997, s 403(8)).

Condition (a)(i)(II) above, which applies from 4 March 1998, is aimed at schemes involving the leasing of machinery or plant by a lessor (typically a financial institution subject to corporation tax at the standard rate) where the machinery or plant would be on-leased by a Shannon company to a non-resident lessee for use outside the State. It was possible to avoid the ring-fencing provisions in such cases on the basis that the lessee was using the machinery or plant for the purposes of a specified trade (even though it was also being used by the non-resident lessee). For machinery or plant provided on or after 4 March 1998, that is no longer possible as it is now required that the machinery plant is not also used for the purposes of any other trade, business or activity. Where, however, the lessor is an IFSC or a Shannon company carrying on a specified trade, this condition does not apply.

5.305.5 The specified trades

TCA 1997, s 403(9)(a)(i) describes the kinds of trade which, if carried on by a lessee or a lessor of machinery or plant, entitle a lessor company to the "excepted capital allowances" treatment (see **5.305.4** above) in respect of its capital allowances on the leased items. To satisfy the conditions as to the specified trade for which the leased machinery or plant is used, the trade carried on by the lessee or lessor must, throughout the relevant three year period, consist wholly or mainly of:

(a) the manufacture of goods; or

(b) any other activity which would, if the lessee or lessor were to claim manufacturing relief under TCA 1997 Part 14 (ss 442-457), be regarded as the manufacture of goods.

The types of activities which are deemed to be the manufacture of goods within TCA 1997 Part 14, so as to be eligible for the 10% corporation tax rate, are described **7.205**. Some of these activities became eligible for the 10% rate of corporation tax with effect from various dates in the year 1987. A qualifying shipping trade is specifically excluded from the definition of "specified trade" for the purposes of TCA 1997, s 403 (TCA 1997, s 407(6)). No capital allowances available to a lessor of a ship or any other machinery or plant leased to a person carrying on a shipping trade, therefore, are excepted capital allowances.

A lessee's trade is regarded as consisting wholly or mainly of any of the activities listed in (a) and (b) above where not less than 75% of the total amount receivable by the lessee from all sales made or services rendered in the course of the trade in the relevant three year period is from sales made or services rendered in the course of that particular activity (TCA 1997, s 403(9)(a)(ii)).

The "connected persons" rules of TCA 1997, s 10 (see **2.3**) are applied to determine whether or not the lessee is connected with the lessor.

In any case where it appears to the inspector or, on appeal, to the Appeal Commissioners that the lessee's undertaking regarding the use of the leased plant has not been fulfilled, any relief obtained by a lessor company, from the inclusion of capital allowances in respect of the plant in question in any loss offset against any non-leasing income, will be withdrawn. For this purpose, any necessary assessments may be made on the lessor.

Example 5.305.5.1

Samsun Ltd, a leasing company, incurred capital expenditure in providing machinery and plant for leasing in the course of its trade. The company's capital allowances for the accounting period in question, in respect of machinery or plant provided for leasing, are as follows:

	General plant	*Motor vehicles*
	€	€
For use by lessees in trades within TCA 1997 Part 14	62,000	32,400
For use by lessees in other trades	75,300	29,800

In addition to the above capital allowances, Samsun Ltd claims capital allowances totalling €58,900 for the accounting period in respect of office equipment and motor vehicles for use in its trade but not for leasing. The company's capital allowances for the period are analysed between specified capital allowances (subject to the TCA 1997, s 403 restrictions) and other capital allowances as follows:

	Specified capital allowances	*Other capital allowances*
	€	€
Not provided for leasing		58,900
Specified trades		94,400
Other trades	105,100	
	105,100	153,300

Notes:

1   It is assumed that none of the lessees is connected with Samsun Ltd and that all the lessees give and honour the required undertakings to use the leased plant for their specified trades for the whole of their respective three year periods.

5.305.6   Trading lessors

As a practical matter, it is necessary for a company carrying on a trade of leasing machinery or plant to have separate capital allowances computations for machinery or plant attracting the specified capital allowances and other machinery or plant. The non-specified capital allowances comprise both the excepted capital allowances on machinery or plant provided for leasing and the capital allowances on any other machinery or plant used for the trade other than for leasing, eg, office equipment used by the lessor.

A company was (in respect of accounting periods ending before 6 March 2001 – thereafter only in the case of an excepted trade, which however would not include a trade of leasing) normally entitled under TCA 1997, s 396(2) to set off a trading loss incurred in an accounting period against its total profits for the same period, and for the immediately preceding period or periods equal in length to the period of the loss. In view of the current definitions of "relevant trading loss" in TCA 1997 ss 396A and 420A(1) (which are identical and apply also for ss 396B(1) and 420B), a loss in a leasing trade, not being a relevant trading loss, cannot be set off against relevant trading income generally.

Relevant trading loss, in relation to a company's accounting period, means a loss incurred by the company in the accounting period in a trade carried on by the company, other than:

(a)   so much of the loss as is a loss incurred in an excepted trade within the meaning of TCA 1997, s 21A (see **3.101.4**); and

(b)   any amount which is or would, if TCA 1997, s 403(8) had not been enacted, be the relevant amount of the loss (see below) for the purposes of TCA 1997, s 403(4) (TCA 1997 ss 396A(1) and 420A(1)).

The purpose of (b), which is effective in respect of loss claims made on or after 3 February 2005, is to ensure that the restriction on the use of certain leasing losses cannot be circumvented by reason of a definition of "relevant trading loss" that would include such losses. If the leasing losses were such relevant trading losses, they could be used to shelter any "relevant trading income", and not just income from a leasing trade, in accordance with TCA 1997, s 396A. The reference to TCA 1997, s 403(8) is to secure that leasing losses from operations in Shannon or the IFSC, which are exempted from the leasing restriction, are nevertheless not to be regarded as relevant trading losses.

If required, a company may include capital allowances in respect of machinery or plant used in its trade in arriving at the loss available for set off (see **4.101**); any capital allowances attributable to the trade are deducted as an expense in computing the trading profit or loss. Alternatively, if the company is a member of a group of companies it may, under the group relief provisions, surrender a trading loss that it has incurred in an accounting period to another company for set off against that company's total profits but, for accounting periods ending on or after 6 March 2001, only where the loss arises in an excepted trade (see **8.305**), as well as any Case IV deficiency attributable to specified capital allowances in a non-trading leasing activity (see below).

In the case of a trade of leasing, TCA 1997, s 403(4)(a) provides that, to the extent that a trading loss is created or increased by any specified capital allowances, the "relevant amount of the loss" (see below) is restricted. The relevant amount of the loss will not be available:

(i) for relief under TCA 1997, s 396(2) (ie, for set off against any profits of the company) other than profits consisting of income from the leasing trade; or

(ii) to be surrendered by way of group relief except, as respects accounting periods ending on or after 3 February 2005, to the extent that it could be set off under TCA 1997, s 420A against income of a trade of leasing carried on by the claimant company but ignoring "(b)" in the definition of "relevant trading loss" above.

Accordingly, the relevant amount of the loss may be set against income from the leasing trade or against income from a leasing trade of a fellow group member (on the assumption that the leasing trade loss can be treated as a relevant trading loss). It will be seen that, for accounting periods ending on or after 3 February 2005, the leasing ring-fence provisions are relaxed so as to permit leasing trade losses of a company to be offset against leasing trade income of another company within the same group. (See also *FA 2005 changes: summary* below for a more detailed treatment of this somewhat convoluted change.)

This treatment applies to trades assessable under Case I of Schedule D and there is a corresponding treatment where leasing income is assessable under Case IV of Schedule D, where a trade is not being carried on (see below).

A company carrying on a leasing trade will not necessarily have all of the loss incurred by it in an accounting period restricted to its trade of leasing; the restriction applies only to the relevant amount of the loss. *The relevant amount of the loss* is:

(a) the full amount of the loss from the trade of leasing (ie, after excluding any part of the total Case I loss attributable to any non-leasing activities carried on by the company in the course of its trade) or; if it is less

(b) an amount equal to—

(i) where only specified capital allowances are included, the amount of the specified capital allowances, or

(ii) where there are both specified capital allowances and other capital allowances, the lower of

(I) the specified capital allowances, and

(II) the excess of the loss from the trade of leasing over the other capital allowances relevant to that trade.

In the event that the full amount of the loss from the trade of leasing does not exceed the total of the other capital allowances for the accounting period, there is no restriction under TCA 1997, s 403(4). For this purpose, the other capital allowances include both the excepted capital allowances on the machinery or plant provided for leasing and any other capital allowances for other machinery etc (eg, office equipment used by the lessor).

Example 5.305.6.1

	Copper Ltd €	Zinc Ltd €	Lead Ltd €	Iron Ltd €
Profit (loss)	100,000	(100,000)	100,000	140,000
Other capital allowances			(60,000)	(60,000)
Specified capital allowances				
	(120,000)	(120,000)	(120,000)	(120,000)
	(20,000)	(220,000)	(80,000)	(40,000)
Relevant amount of loss	(20,000)	(120,000)	(20,000)	Nil

The objective of the rules for computing the relevant amount of the loss (the amount of loss which may be offset only against income from the trade of leasing) is to confine the relevant amount of the loss to the amount of the loss which is attributable to specified capital allowances. In the case of Copper Ltd, the relevant amount of the loss is the loss itself, which is less than the amount of the specified capital allowances. In the case of Zinc Ltd, the loss is €220,000 but the specified capital allowances are only €120,000 so that that is amount of the relevant amount of the loss.

Lead Ltd has both specified capital allowances and other capital allowances, and the relevant amount of the loss is the amount by which the loss exceeds the other capital allowances; in that way, the relevant amount of the loss is confined to the amount of the loss which is attributable to specified capital allowances. Iron Ltd also has both specified capital allowances and other capital allowances. In this case, however, the amount of the loss is less than the specified capital allowances; as long as the loss does not exceed the specified capital allowances, the relevant amount of the loss is nil.

There is no corresponding restriction affecting capital allowances that are not specified capital allowances. Any other such capital allowances remain fully available for inclusion in a claim under TCA 1997, s 396(2) (but in theory only since a claim under that provision can be made only in the case of an excepted trade – see above). TCA 1997, s 403 in no way affects the right of a company to set off a trading loss, before capital allowances, against income from a non-leasing trade.

FA 2005 changes: summary

Prior to FA 2005, a loss in a leasing trade was a relevant trading loss; hence it could have been used to offset relevant trading income in accordance with TCA 1997, s 396A, thereby circumventing the ring-fence provisions, which do not contain a reference to that section. (It could not, however, have been used in this way for the purposes of TCA 1997, s 420A since the leasing ring-fence provisions extended simply to "group relief" claims.) FA 2005 corrected this weakness in the legislation by adding "(b)" in the definition of "relevant trading loss" in TCA 1997 ss 396A(1) and 420A(1); accordingly, for the purposes of the ring-fence provisions, a leasing loss is not to be regarded as a relevant trading loss and therefore cannot be used for the purposes of a claim under TCA 1997, s 396A.

Since, however, FA 2005 is also intended to permit leasing trade losses of a company to be offset against leasing trade income of a fellow group company, it is necessary for that purpose to disregard "(b)" in the definition of "relevant trading loss"; hence, such losses revert to being relevant trading losses for that purpose. TCA 1997, s 403(4)(a)(ii) accordingly provides that the ring-fence provisions applying to group relief are not to apply to the extent that the leasing loss could, by ignoring "(b)" in the definition of "relevant trading loss", be set off under TCA 1997, s 420A against income of a trade of leasing carried on by the claimant company.

Standard capital allowances (ie, excluding initial allowances and free depreciation) of a leasing trade in the IFSC/Shannon are not specified capital allowances for the purposes of the ring-fence provisions. Prior to FA 2005, a loss attributable to such capital allowances was a relevant trading loss and could therefore have been used for a claim under TCA 1997, s 396A, 396B, 420A or 420B (but not under TCA 1997, s 396(2) or 420). As with other leasing losses, these losses are no longer relevant trading losses. Thus, TCA 1997, s 403(4)(a)(ii) also applies to these losses so as to permit group relief claims in the same way as for other leasing losses.

It would seem, however, that the qualification is unnecessary in the case of the IFSC/Shannon. Since an IFSC/Shannon leasing loss is no longer a relevant trading loss, it follows that the loss may be used for group relief purposes in accordance with TCA 1997, s 420. (Perhaps fortuitously, this also avoids the difficulty whereby, because the losses are no longer relevant trading losses, they could not now be used for a claim under TCA 1997, s 396B or 420B.) A TCA 1997, s 420 claim, unlike a TCA 1997, s 420A claim, allows the loss to be used against total profits. A claim for offset against total profits can also be made under TCA 1997, s 396(2). All of the above is, however, subject to the licensing regime whereby certificates issued to IFSC/Shannon companies include an undertaking which effectively prevents such leasing trade losses from being used other than against profits from the leasing trade.

5.305.7 Non-trading lessors

The entitlement of a company to set off, against its total profits, any excess capital allowances (other than initial allowances) in respect of machinery or plant leased in circumstances in which the leasing income is taxable under Case IV has been discussed in **5.302**. TCA 1997, s 403(5) provides that the capital allowances set off against total profits in any such case must exclude capital allowances in respect of expenditure incurred on the provision of the leased machinery or plant, but with certain exceptions. As for a trading lessor, all capital allowances in respect of the leased machinery or plant, including the excepted capital allowances, are available for set-off against the leasing income of the accounting period to which they apply and, where not fully used against that income, for carry forward against the leasing income of the following or any subsequent accounting period. To the extent that they are not fully utilised in the current accounting period, only excepted capital allowances may, in accordance with TCA 1997, s 308(4), be set off against total profits of the same accounting period or of the immediately preceding period or periods equal in length to the current period. Excepted capital allowances only may also, in accordance with TCA 1997, s 420(2), be surrendered under the group relief provisions.

The position of a non-trading lessor differs from that of a trading lessor in that the excepted capital allowances of the former do not include capital allowances in respect of machinery or plant to which TCA 1997, s 403(8) (ie, leasing in the course of the carrying on by the lessor of trading operations in Shannon Airport or in the International Financial Services Centre) or TCA 1997, s 403(9)(b) (ie, where the terms of the lease include an undertaking by the lessee that the machinery or plant will be used only for the purposes of a "specified trade" for a period of at least three years and the machinery or plant is in fact so used) apply. Non-trading lessors' unrestricted capital allowances are limited to those in respect of machinery or plant to which TCA 1997, s 403(7) applies.

Accordingly, the only capital allowances in respect of machinery or plant provided for leasing which may be included in a claim under TCA 1997, s 308(4) are capital allowances in respect of a film made wholly or partly in the State, but only if the cost of making the film has been or is to be met directly or indirectly, wholly or partly, by the Irish Film Board (irrespective of when the expenditure on making the film is incurred) (TCA 1997, s 403(7)).

5.305.8   Relaxation of ring fence for certain companies

The ring fence treatment is relaxed in certain circumstances. So as not to have an unduly adverse impact on companies that carry on a trade consisting primarily of leasing, losses and capital allowances for accounting periods ending on or after 1 January 2006 may be offset against a wider range of income than was the position for previous periods. The relaxed treatment applies to a company whose activities (or the activities of a group of which the company is a member) consist wholly or mainly of the leasing of plant or machinery and where not less than 90% of the activities of the company consists of one or more of: the leasing of plant and machinery, the provision of loans to fund the purchase of plant or machinery of the type that it leases, or the provision of leasing expertise in relation to such plant or machinery. Such companies are entitled to set losses and capital allowances from leasing against income from such activities. This measure, provided for in TCA 1997, s 403(1)(d), is described in more detail as follows.

Where, in relation to a company:

(a)   the activities—

     (i)   of the company, or

     (ii)   of the company and all companies of which it is a 75% subsidiary (see **2.503**) *and* all companies which are its 75% subsidiaries, or

     (iii)   of the company and all companies (being companies which are resident for the purposes of tax ("tax" meaning any tax imposed in the territory which corresponds to corporation tax in the State) in the same territory in which the company is so resident) of which it is a 75% subsidiary (see **2.503**) *or* all companies which are its 75% subsidiaries,

     consist wholly or mainly of the leasing of machinery or plant, and

(b)   not less than 90% of the activities of the company consist of one or more of the following:

     (i)   the leasing of machinery or plant;

     (ii)   the provision of finance and guarantees to fund the purchase of machinery or plant of a type which is similar to the type of machinery or plant leased by the companies referred to in (a) above;

     (iii)   the provision of leasing expertise in connection with machinery or plant of a type which is similar to the type of machinery or plant leased by the companies referred to in (a) above;

     (iv)   the disposal of machinery of plant acquired by the company in the course of its leasing trade;

(v) activities which are ancillary to the activities referred to in (i) to (iv) above:

then, subject to TCA 1997, s 80A(2)(c) (since income from short-term leases is computed following accounting principles – see **3.303.7** – such income is excluded here), income from the company's trade of leasing is to be treated as including—

(A) income from the activities referred to in (b), and

(B) chargeable gains on the disposal of machinery or plant acquired by the company in the course of its leasing trade, the amount of such gain being computed without regard to any adjustment made under TCA 1997, s 556(2) (indexation relief – see **9.102.3**).

Thus, regarding (a) above, the "wholly or mainly" condition may be met by the leasing company itself, or by the group of which it is a member, or by the group of companies that are resident in the same territory as the company itself and of which it is a member. The fact that "and" appears in (a)(ii) whereas "or" is used in (a)(iii) above does not appear to have any significance.

5.306 "Balloon" leasing

5.306.1 Introduction

The set-off of capital allowances against certain income from the leasing of machinery or plant is restricted by TCA 1997, s 404. This provision ring-fences capital allowances arising in the case of any such lease of machinery or plant by restricting their set-off to income from that lease.

The restriction applies in the case of a "relevant lease" (often referred to as a "balloon" lease) entered into on or after 23 December 1993, ie a lease that does not have a broadly even spread of payments over its term. Capital allowances in respect of the assets subject to the relevant lease may be set off against the income from that lease and not against any other income, including any other leasing income.

A relevant lease is a lease under whose terms there is a fluctuation in the lease payments such that most of the amount payable is not paid until close to the end of the primary period of the lease. The primary period is, basically, the period during which the lessor's expenditure on the assets leased is recovered. The restriction on use of capital allowances to the income from the lease does not apply where the lease payments in the primary period of the lease are payable on a broadly even basis (by satisfying conditions (I) and (II) in the definition of "relevant lease" (see below)).

5.306.2 Relevant lease

The definition of "relevant lease" is complex. It is necessary first to understand the meaning of certain terms:

Chargeable period: in the case of a company, an accounting period;

Fair value: the consideration which would be payable for the leased asset at the inception of the lease on a sale negotiated at arm's length, less any grants receivable;

Inception of the lease: the date on which the leased asset is brought into use by the lessee, or the date on which the lease payments first accrue, whichever is the earlier;

Lease payments: the lease payments payable over the term of the lease including any residual amount payable to the lessor at or after the end of the lease term and which is guaranteed by the lessee, or by a person connected with the lessee (within the meaning of TCA 1997, s 10 – see **2.3**), or under the terms of any scheme or arrangement between the lessee and any other person;

Predictable useful life: the useful life of an asset, estimated at the inception of the lease, having regard to the purpose for which it was acquired and on the assumption that its life will end when it ceases to be useful for the purpose for which it was acquired and that it is going to be used in the normal manner and to the normal extent throughout its life;

Relevant lease payment: the amount of any lease payment provided for under the terms of the lease or, where the lease provides for the amount of any lease payment to be determined by reference to the European Interbank Offered Rate (EURIBOR) and a record of which is kept by the Central Bank, or a similar rate, the amount calculated by reference to that rate on the assumption that the rate at the inception of the lease is the rate at the time of the payment. The relevant lease payments are, therefore, the lease payments provided under the lease whether stated in terms of the actual amounts payable or in terms of amounts to be arrived at by reference to EURIBOR or a similar rate. In the latter case, the amounts are notional amounts determined in any case by applying EURIBOR or a similar rate *at the date of the inception of the lease* instead of at the date on which the lease payment is made;

Relevant period: the period beginning at the inception of the lease and ending at the earliest time at which the aggregate of relevant lease payments payable up to that time, discounted to their present value at the inception of the lease, equals 90% or more of the fair value of the leased asset or, if earlier, at the end of the predictable useful life of the asset. Relevant lease payments are discounted for the above purpose at the rate which, when applied at the inception of the lease to the amount of the relevant lease payments, produces discounted present values the aggregate of which equals the fair value of the leased asset at the inception of the lease. If the result of the above calculation is a period of more than 7 years, the calculation is to be re-done using a percentage of 95% instead of 90%;

Relevant lease payments related to a chargeable period: the relevant lease payments under the lease or the amounts which are treated as the relevant lease payments and which, if they were the actual amounts payable under the lease, would fall to be taken into account in computing the income of the lessor for that chargeable period or its basis period or any earlier such period. The lease payments under the lease (see definition of "relevant lease payment" above) are the lease payments provided under the lease whether stated as amounts payable or as arrived at by reference to EURIBOR or a similar rate. Amounts which "are treated" as the relevant lease payments are notional amounts for the purposes of this definition and are the amounts determined by applying EURIBOR or a similar rate *at the date of the inception of the lease* instead of at the date on which the lease payment is made.

Where an accounting period of a company (a "chargeable period") straddles the beginning or the end of a relevant period, it is divided into two parts which are treated as separate accounting periods so that the part falling into the relevant period is treated as an accounting period within the relevant period.

TCA 1997, s 404(1)(b)(i) provides that a lease of an asset is a *relevant lease* unless:

(I)   for *any* chargeable period (accounting period in the case of a company) of the lessor falling wholly or partly into the relevant period, the aggregate of relevant lease payments related to that period and to any earlier periods is not less than an amount calculated by the formula:

$$W \times P \times \frac{90 + (10 \times W)}{100}$$

where—

  P   is the aggregate of the amounts of relevant lease payments payable by the lessee in relation to the leased asset in the relevant period, and

  W   is an amount determined by the formula:

$$\frac{E}{R}$$

  where—

  E   is the length of the part of the relevant period which has expired at the end of the chargeable period, and

  R   is the length of the relevant period, and

(II) except for any inconsequential amount of relevant lease payments, the excess of the total relevant lease payments under the lease over the aggregate relevant lease payments in the relevant period is payable to the lessor, or would be so payable if the relevant lease payments were the actual amounts payable under the lease, within a period the duration of which does not exceed:

  (a)   where the relevant period exceeds seven years and it is necessary to recalculate the length of the period by substituting 95% for 90%, one-ninth of the duration of the relevant period, and

  (b)   where it is not so necessary, one-seventh of the duration of the relevant period,

  or one year, whichever is the greater, and which commences immediately after the end of the relevant period.

What the formula in (I) above is intended to produce is a target amount of relevant lease payments against which the cumulative lease payments to date are compared. If the cumulative lease payments fall short of the target amount, the lease is a relevant lease. If the target amount is matched or exceeded, the second test, as set out in (II) above, is then applied. The formula in the first test will produce a figure which will fall between 90% and 100% of the aggregate of the relevant lease payments in the relevant period. The percentage will move evenly between 90% and 100% as the relevant period expires. For example, if at the end of a particular accounting period one half of the relevant period has expired, the formula will result in a figure which is 95% of the aggregate relevant lease payments in the relevant period. Where the cumulative lease payments at that point do not match that figure, the lease is a relevant lease (subject to some exceptions as explained later). Otherwise, the second test is applied.

The second test requires that the excess of the total relevant lease payments under the lease over the aggregate of the relevant lease payments in the relevant period is payable to the lessor within a prescribed period (see below); otherwise (subject to some exceptions) the lease is a relevant lease. Where the relevant lease payments are not actual payments (see definition of "relevant lease payment" above), the test is applied as if those payments were actual payments. Relevant lease payments of an inconsequential amount paid after the prescribed period are ignored. An amount of relevant lease payments not exceeding 5% of the fair value of the leased asset, or €2,540, whichever is the lesser, is regarded as inconsequential. The amount which may be ignored is to be estimated at the inception of the lease and is the discounted value at the end of the prescribed period of the payments in question. The payments are discounted at the rate specified in the definition of "relevant period" (TCA 1997, s 404(1)(b)(iii)).

The duration of the prescribed period depends on whether or not in the definition of "relevant period" it is necessary to apply the 90% rate to the fair value of the leased asset. The prescribed period is the period of one year commencing immediately after the relevant period or, if greater:

(a)   one-seventh of the duration of the relevant period where the 90% rate is applied to the fair value of the leased asset in the definition of "relevant lease"; and

(b)   one-ninth of the duration of the relevant period where the 95% rate is applied to the fair value of the leased asset in that definition.

Agricultural machinery

The meaning of "relevant lease" in the case of a lease of agricultural machinery is modified by substituting for the amount of relevant lease payments for an accounting period, one-half of that amount together with one-half of the amount of relevant lease payments for a period equal in length to that period and ending immediately before the commencement of that period (TCA 1997, s 404(4)). As compared with other leases of machinery or plant, therefore, a lease involving agricultural machinery will not as easily fall to be treated as a relevant lease. This is to allow for the effect of seasonal factors on the timing of lease payments.

5.306.3   Ring-fencing

Subject to TCA 1997, s 404(2A), the leasing of an asset under a relevant lease is treated as a separate trade of leasing (a "specified leasing trade") distinct from all other activities, including other leasing activities, of the lessor (TCA 1997, s 404(2)(a)). TCA 1997 ss 308(4) (allowances made under Case V and by way of discharge or repayment – see **5.105.3**) and 420(2) (group relief in respect of excess capital allowances – see **8.305.3**) will not apply in relation to capital allowances in respect of expenditure incurred on the provision of an asset or on account of the wear and tear of an asset that is provided by a person for leasing under a relevant lease (TCA 1997, s 404(2)(b)).

The ring-fencing treatment provided for by TCA 1997, s 403 (see **5.305** above) applies to a specified leasing trade. A company leasing machinery or plant in the course of a trade may only set off a trading loss attributable to specified capital allowances against its income from that trade. This treatment applies to trades assessable under Case I of Schedule D. Similar treatment applies where leasing income is assessable under Case IV of Schedule D, where a trade is not being carried on, and for group relief purposes (see **8.305**), so that any trading loss or Case IV deficiency attributable to specified capital allowances may not be surrendered by way of group relief.

As with TCA 1997, s 403, the restrictive treatment applies only in relation to "the relevant amount of the loss". Where all of the company's capital allowances are specified capital allowances, the relevant amount of the loss is the lesser of the amount of the loss incurred and the amount of the specified capital allowances. Where there are both specified capital allowances and other capital allowances, the relevant amount of the loss is the amount of the loss incurred or, if less, the lesser of the amount of the specified capital allowances and the amount by which the loss exceeds the amount of the other capital allowances. If the loss does not exceed the other capital allowances, the relevant amount of the loss is nil (see Example **5.305.6.1**).

Example 5.306.3.1

Tobruck Ltd, a leasing company, makes up its accounts to 31 December each year. The company incurs expenditure of €3m on an asset for leasing and shortly afterwards, on 1 July 2004, enters into an agreement with a customer for the lease of the asset for a period of 5 years. The terms of the lease include an annual lease payment of €200,000 for four years commencing on 1 July 2004 and a payment of €4m on 1 July 2008. It is also agreed that a company connected with the lessee will purchase the asset at the end of the lease term (on or around 1 July 2009) for €600,000, which is its anticipated residual value at that time. The predictable useful life of the asset is 8 years.

Capital allowances at 12.5% per annum are claimed by Tobruck Ltd in respect of the leased asset, ie, €375,000 for each year ended 31 December.

The commencement of the relevant period is 1 July 2004. 90% of the fair value of the asset is €2.7m. To calculate the amount of relevant lease payments with a discounted value of at least €2.7m on 1 July 2004, the rate to be used is the rate which, when applied to the amount of the relevant lease payments totalling €5.4m, produces an aggregate value equal to €3m, the fair value of the leased asset at the inception of the lease. That rate is 17.5529%. On 1 July 2008 relevant lease payments total €4,800,000 and their discounted value as at 1 July 2004, using the rate of 17.5529%, is €2,732,709, which is more than 90% of the fair value of the leased asset. The relevant period is therefore the period commencing on 1 July 2004 and ending on 1 July 2008.

The accounting periods of Tobruck Ltd which fall wholly or partly within the relevant period are the years ended 31 December 2004 to 31 December 2008 inclusive but the first and the final of those periods is each divided into separate accounting periods; the first accounting period within the relevant period is therefore the period 1 July 2004 to 31 December 2004 and the final accounting period within the relevant period is 1 January 2005 to 1 July 2008.

The next step is to ascertain whether the lease is a relevant lease. Applying the formula in the definition of "relevant lease" to, say, the year ended 31 December 2006, the target amount is as follows:

$$2.5/4 \times €4,800,00 \times \frac{90 + (90 \times 2.5/4)}{100} = €2,887,500$$

The relevant lease payments for the year ended 31 December 2006 and for the two previous accounting periods amount to €500,000. This aggregate, clearly, is not greater than €2,887,500. It will be found that a similar result will follow for the other accounting periods within the relevant period. The lease is therefore a relevant lease.

The lease is a separate trade distinct from the general leasing trade of Tobruck Ltd. The capital allowances of €375,000 can only be utilised against the income from the relevant lease. The income from this source is €200,000 for each period less attributable expenses, say, €50,000, net €150,000. Accordingly, capital allowances of €150,000 may be used in each of the four accounting periods ending within the relevant period leaving a balance of

€900,000 (€225,000 x 4) to be carried forward to the year ended 31 December 2008 when they can be set off against the substantial leasing income for that period. (See also Example **5.306.4.1** below.)

Example 5.306.3.2

Tripoli Ltd, a leasing company, makes up its accounts to 31 December each year. On 31 December 2004, the company enters into a lease agreement for the lease of an asset purchased for €3m on the same date. The lease period is 8 years and the terms of the lease include an annual lease payment of €540,000 for seven years commencing on 31 December 2004 and a payment of €650,000 on 31 December 2011. It is also agreed that immediately after the expiration of the lease, on 1 January 2013, a company connected with the lessee will purchase the asset for €50,000, which is the anticipated residual value of the asset at that time. The predictable useful life of the asset is 10 years.

Capital allowances at 12.5% per annum are claimed by Tripoli Ltd in respect of the leased asset, ie €375,000 for eight years ended 31 December 2004 to 31 December 2011.

The commencement of the relevant period is 31 December 2004. 90% of the fair value of the asset is €2.7m. To calculate the amount of relevant lease payments with a discounted value of at least €2.7m on 31 December 2004, the rate to be used is the rate which, when applied to the amount of the relevant lease payments totalling €4.48m, produces an aggregate value equal to €3m, the fair value of the leased asset at the inception of the lease. That rate is 12.9209%. On 31 December 2010 relevant lease payments total €3,780,000 and their discounted value at 31 December 2004 is €2,703,440 which is greater than 90% of the fair value of the leased asset. The relevant period is therefore the period commencing on 31 December 2004 and ending on 31 December 2010.

The next step is to ascertain whether the lease is a relevant lease. The accounting periods of Tripoli Ltd which fall wholly or partly within the relevant period are the years ended 31 December 2004 to 31 December 2010 inclusive. Applying the formula in the definition of "relevant lease" to, say, the year ended 31 December 2009, the target amount is as follows:

$$5/6 \times €3,780,000 \times \frac{90 + (10 \times 5/6)}{100} = €3,097,500$$

The relevant lease payments for the year ended 31 December 2009 and for the five previous years amount to €3,240,000. This aggregate is greater than €3,097,500. It will be found that a similar result will follow for the other accounting periods within the relevant period. The lease is therefore not a relevant lease on this count. The second test is now applied.

The total relevant lease payments under the lease are €4.48m. The prescribed period is one year, being greater than one-seventh of the duration of the relevant period (six years). That period ends on 31 December 2011. The only relevant lease payment due after that period is the €50,000 payable by the company acquiring the asset (on 1 January 2013) and it is included as it is not inconsequential, being greater than the lesser of €2,540 and 5% of the fair value of the leased asset. The excess of the total relevant lease payments, €4,480,000, over the aggregate of the relevant lease payments in the relevant period, €3,780,000, is €700,000. The prescribed period is the year ended 31 December 2011 and the relevant lease payments due to Tripoli Ltd in that period are €650,000. As this amount is less than €700,000, the lease is a relevant lease.

Since the lease is a "relevant long-term lease", being the lease of an asset the predictable useful life of which exceeds eight years (see below re modification of ring-fence treatment), losses and capital allowances may be set off against the company's income from the lease but also against its income from any other long-term leases and against any other income from activities related to leasing, or against such income of a connected company. The capital allowances of €375,000 could in the first instance be set against the income from the relevant lease. The income from this source is €440,000 for each period less attributable expenses, say, €150,000, net €290,000. Accordingly, capital allowances of €290,000 would be set against that income but the remaining allowances of €85,000 would be available to be set against any other long-term leasing income and any income from lease-related activities of the company.

Modification of ring-fence treatment for certain long-term leases

The ring-fence treatment is modified in the case of a long-term lease so that losses and capital allowances on the assets concerned may be set off against income from other long-term leases: the deemed separate trade includes not only the letting of the asset under the long-term lease concerned but also the letting of any other asset under a long-term lease. Furthermore, in the case of a company whose trading income consists wholly or mainly (ie, more than 50%) of leasing and which satisfies the relevant 90% activities test (see **5.305.8** above), the losses and capital allowances may be set off against its income from leasing and activities related to leasing or against such income of a connected company.

The relaxation applies to a *relevant long-term lease*, which means a lease of an asset the predictable useful life of which exceeds eight years. The meaning of *predictable useful life* in relation to an asset is the same as for TCA 1997, s 80A (short term leases of plant and machinery – see **3.303.7**); accordingly, it refers to the useful life of the asset estimated at the inception of the lease, having regard to the purpose for which it was acquired and on the assumption:

(a) that its life will end when it ceases to be useful for the purpose for which it was acquired; and

(b) that it will be used in the normal manner and to the normal extent throughout its life.

TCA 1997, s 404(2A)(b), by way of relaxing the ring-fence treatment, provides that where:

(i) in the course of a trade an asset is provided by a person for leasing under a relevant lease; and

(ii) the lease is a relevant long-term lease,

then, the ring-fence treatment in TCA 1997, s 404 is to apply as if:

(I) in TCA 1997, s 404(2)(a) (see above), the separate trade treatment were to be applied in respect of the letting of an asset under a relevant lease together with the letting of any other asset under a relevant long-term lease, and

(II) the treatment provided for by TCA 1997, s 403(4)(a) (see **5.305.6**), to the effect that a trading loss created or increased by specified capital allowances is restricted, were modified.

The effect of the "modified" TCA 1997, s 403(4)(a) for the above purposes is that, in the case of a trade of leasing, to the extent that a trading loss is created or increased by any specified capital allowances, the "relevant amount of the loss" is restricted and that amount of the loss will not be available:

(i) for relief under TCA 1997, s 396(2) except to the extent that it can be set off under that provision against—

(I) the company's income from the trade of leasing (which appears to be intended to refer only to the income from the relevant long-term lease concerned, even though the ring-fenced specified leasing trade includes all relevant long-term leases),

(II)   in the case of a company referred to in TCA 1997, s 403(1)(d) (a company carrying on a business the activities of which, or the activities of which and of certain 75% related companies, consist wholly or mainly of leasing machinery or plant, and which satisfies the relevant 90% activities test – see **5.305.8** above), income specified in TCA 1997, s 403(1)(d)(ii)(V)(A) and (B) (ie, leasing income and income from certain leasing-related activities as well as chargeable gains on the disposal of machinery or plant acquired by a company in the course of its leasing trade – as referred to in (A) and (B) in **5.305.8** above), or

(III)   income from the leasing by the company of any other asset under a relevant long-term lease, or

(ii)   to be surrendered by way of group relief except to the extent that it—

(I)   could be set off under TCA 1997, s 420A (group relief for relevant trading losses – see **8.306.2**) against income of a trade of leasing carried on by the claimant company if "(b)" in the definition of "relevant trading loss" (see below) were to be ignored, or

(II)   where the surrendering company and the claimant company are companies referred to in TCA 1997, s 403(1)(d) (see (i)(II) above), can be set off—

(A) under TCA 1997, s 420A against income specified in TCA 1997, s 403(1)(d)(ii)(V)(A) and (B) (see (i)(II) above), or

(B) under TCA 1997, s 420A against income from the leasing by the company of any other asset under a relevant long-term lease.

Regarding the reference in (ii)(I)) above to ignoring "(b)" in the definition of "relevant trading loss", the background is as follows. Prior to FA 2005, a loss in a leasing trade was a relevant trading loss; hence it could have been used to offset relevant trading income in accordance with TCA 1997, s 396A, thereby circumventing the ring-fence provisions, which do not contain a reference to that section. FA 2005 therefore added "(b)" in the definition of "relevant trading loss" in TCA 1997 ss 396A(1) and 420A(1); the effect of this is that, for the purposes of the ring-fence provisions, a leasing loss is not to be regarded as a relevant trading loss and therefore cannot be used for the purposes of a claim under TCA 1997, s 396A.

Since, however, the intention of TCA 1997, s 404(2A) is to permit a long-term leasing trade loss of a company to be offset against leasing and other qualifying income of a fellow group company, it is necessary for that purpose to disregard "(b)" in the definition of "relevant trading loss"; hence, such losses revert to being relevant trading losses for that purpose. TCA 1997, s 404(2A)(b) accordingly provides that the ring-fence provisions applying to group relief are not to apply to the extent that the leasing loss could, by ignoring "(b)" in the definition of "relevant trading loss", be set off under TCA 1997, s 420A against leasing and other qualifying income of the claimant company.

5.306.4 Relevant lease: exceptions

Notwithstanding the meaning of "relevant lease" as already described, a lease in respect of which the relevant period exceeds 10 years is not a relevant lease if the following conditions are fulfilled:

(a) the leased asset is provided for the purposes of a project, specified in the list referred to in TCA 1997, s 133(8)(c)(iv), which has been approved for grant aid by the Industrial Development Authority, the Shannon Free Airport Development Company Ltd or Údarás na Gaeltachta (see **11.107.2**);

(b) the leased asset is provided for the purposes of a project approved for grant assistance by one of the above bodies on or before 31 December 1990 and not for the purposes of trading operations within TCA 1997, s 445 (Shannon) or s 446 (International Financial Services Centre);

(c) the aggregate relevant lease payments for any accounting period falling within the three year period beginning at the inception of the lease (the "first period") is not less than the amount calculated by the following formula:

$$V \times \frac{D}{100} \times \frac{80}{100} \times \frac{M}{12}$$

where—

D is the six-month EURIBOR, a record of which is maintained by the Central Bank of Ireland,

M is the number of months in the accounting period, and

V is the fair value of the asset at the inception of the lease;

(d) as respects any accounting period falling wholly or partly within the period (the "second period") commencing immediately after the first period and ending at the end of the relevant period, the aggregate relevant lease payments for the period and for any earlier period falling wholly or partly within the second period is not less than an amount calculated by the formula:

$$\frac{E}{R} \times P$$

where—

E is the length of the part of the second period which has expired at the end of the chargeable period,

P is the aggregate of relevant lease payments payable by the lessee for the second period, and

R is the length of the second period; and

(e) except for any inconsequential amount of relevant lease payments, the excess of the total relevant lease payments under the lease over the aggregate relevant lease payments in the relevant period is payable to the lessor, or would be so payable if the relevant lease payments were the actual amounts payable under the lease, within a period of one year after the end of the relevant period (TCA 1997, s 404(1)(b)(ii)).

Where a chargeable period of a company (an accounting period) straddles the beginning or the end of the first period or the second period, it is divided into two parts which are treated as separate accounting periods, and the part falling into the first or the second period, as the case may be, is treated as an accounting period within that period (TCA 1997, s 404(1)(b)(iv)).

Where a lease with relevant payments denominated in a foreign currency ("relevant currency") is a relevant lease but would not be a relevant lease if TCA 1997, s 404(1)(b)(i), (iii) (see **5.306.2** above), (ii) and (iv) (see above) were applied by reference to the value of those relevant lease payments in the relevant currency, the lease will not be treated as a relevant lease (TCA 1997, s 404(1)(b)(v)). Thus, a foreign currency denominated lease that does not meet the requirements to have the lease payments spread evenly by reason only of exchange rate movements will not be ring-fenced.

A lease of an asset will not be a relevant lease if it is a lease of an asset with a useful life of not more than eight years and the lease period does not exceed five years, the cumulative amount of lease payments up to the end of any accounting period (apart from the first accounting period relevant to the lease) equates with annual payments of approximately one-eighth of the original value of the asset, and capital allowances in respect of the asset are calculated by reference to the amount of use of the asset in the period concerned. TCA 1997, s 404(6)(a) provides that a lease of an asset is not a relevant lease if a binding contract in writing for the letting of the asset was concluded before 23 December 1993, or:

(a) the relevant period does not exceed five years;

(b) the predictable useful life of the asset does not exceed eight years;

(c) the lease provides for lease payments to be made at annual or more frequent regular intervals throughout the relevant period such that, in relation to any chargeable period ("current chargeable period") falling wholly or partly into the relevant period (other than the earliest such chargeable period), the aggregate of the amounts of lease payments payable under the lease before the end of the current chargeable period is not less than an amount determined by the formula—

$$\frac{V \times T}{2920}$$

where—

V   is an amount equal to the fair value of the asset at the inception of the lease, and

T   is the number of days in the period commencing at the inception of the lease and ending at the end of the current chargeable period, and

(d) the lessor has made an election in relation to the lease for the treatment referred to below.

The test in (c) is that the lease payments to be made by a company for any accounting period falling wholly or partly within the relevant period (excluding the first such accounting period) must be such that the total amount of lease payments scheduled to be paid by the end of that accounting period is not less than the proportion of the fair value of the leased asset represented by the part of the lease period that has elapsed at the end of the accounting period over a period of eight years.

The treatment referred to in (d) above is that, where the machinery or plant used in a chargeable period is not used throughout that period, the amount of the wear and tear allowance for the period is to be reduced proportionately by reference to the part of the period of use over the full length of the chargeable period (TCA 1997, s 404(6)(b)).

Example 5.306.4.1

The facts are as in Example **5.306.3.1**. The relevant period does not exceed five years and the predictable useful life of the leased asset does not exceed eight years. It remains to ascertain whether the lease avoids being a relevant lease by reference to the test in (c) above, ie whether the total of lease payments to be paid by 31 December 2006 is not less than the proportion of the fair value of the leased asset represented by the part of the lease period that has elapsed by that date over a period of 2,920 days.

The aggregate amount of lease payments due by 31 December 2006 is €500,000. The fair value of the asset is €3m and the number of days from the inception of the lease on 1 July 2004 to 31 December 2006 is 914. The relevant proportion of the fair value of the asset is accordingly €3m x 914/2,920 = €939. As this is greater than €500,000, the lease remains a relevant lease.

5.306.5   Alteration or termination of lease

Subject to TCA 1997, s 404(4A) (see below), an alteration, at any time after 11 April 1994, to the terms of a lease of an asset entered into before that day can result in a lease which had not been treated as a relevant lease being treated as being such a lease from its inception (TCA 1997, s 404(4)). In consequence, relief previously given under TCA 1997, s 308 (capital allowances in excess of Case IV income), 396 (offset of trading losses against total profits) or s 420 (group relief) will be withdrawn. Relief may also be withdrawn in the case of an agreement to terminate a lease coupled with a new agreement to lease the asset, whether made by the same lessor and lessee, by the lessor and a person connected with (within the meaning of TCA 1997, s 10 – see **2.3**) the lessee, by the lessee and a person connected with the lessor, or by person connected with the lessor and a person connected with the lessee.

An alteration or termination which may lead to the withdrawal of relief is one occurring after 11 April 1994 whereby the aggregate of lease payments payable (or which would be payable if the relevant lease payments were the actual payments made) after any time exceeds the aggregate of the relevant lease payments which would have been payable after that time if the alteration or termination had not taken place. Not affected by this provision is any alteration or termination effected for *bona fide* commercial reasons. Effect is given to any withdrawal of relief for the chargeable period in which the alteration or termination takes place. The lessor is obliged to include details of the alteration or termination giving rise to the withdrawal of relief in the corporation tax return for that period.

Any amount of relief withdrawn is treated as income arising in the chargeable period in which the alteration or termination occurs. Furthermore, the amount of relief withdrawn (the "relevant amount") is to be increased by an amount determined by the formula:

$$A \times \frac{R}{100} \times M$$

where—

A   is the relevant amount;

M   is the number of days in the period beginning with the date on which tax for the chargeable period for which the relief was originally given was due, and ending on the date on which tax for the period for which the relief was withdrawn is due; and

R   is 0.0273% for each day or part of a day.

TCA 1997, s 404(4A) provides that the alteration of certain leases, entered into prior to 2 February 2006, that were not subject to ring-fence treatment will not result in those leases being so subject provided the alteration does not involve a delay of more than 20 years in any payment under the lease. Furthermore, the alteration will not affect the tax treatment of a defeasance payment under the lease unless it involves a reduction in a payment which is not a payment calculated by reference to interest rates.

Where the terms of a lease entered into before 2 February 2006, being a lease which would apart from TCA 1997, s 404(1)(b)(ii) or (6)(a) (see **5.306.4** above) have been a relevant lease, are altered after that day, then:

(i)   the lease will not be treated as a relevant lease by virtue of that alteration, and

(ii)   unless the alteration involves a reduction in the value of any payment (or a part of a payment) under the lease, not being a payment (or a part of a payment) the amount of which is computed under the lease by reference to any rate of interest, the alteration will be disregarded as respects the treatment for tax purposes of any defeasance payment made in connection with the lease (TCA 1997, s 404(4A)(a)).

The above relaxation will not, however, apply as respects a lease if any amount payable under the lease is, by virtue of the alteration in its terms, to be paid more than 20 years after the time at which it would otherwise have been payable (TCA 1997, s 404(4A)(b)).

5.306.6   Anti-avoidance

An anti-avoidance measure ensures that a lease of an asset on or after 11 April 1994 by a lessor to a person who previously owned that asset will be treated as a relevant lease except where:

(a)   the asset is new and unused; or

(b)   the lease would not be a relevant lease if, in the definition of "relevant lease", "W x P" were substituted for the formula:

$$W \times P \times \frac{90 + (10 \times W)}{100}$$

and the provision in TCA 1997, s 404(1)(b)(ii) excluding certain leases for which the relevant period exceeds 10 years were ignored (TCA 1997, s 404(5)).

The above reference to a lessor leasing an asset to a person who previously owned that asset includes references to a person connected with the lessor leasing the asset to that person or to a person connected with that person.

5.4 INDUSTRIAL BUILDINGS AND STRUCTURES

5.401   Qualifying buildings

5.401.1   Industrial building or structure

A company is entitled to capital allowances in respect of capital expenditure incurred on the construction of a building or structure which is to be an industrial building or structure occupied for the purposes of a trade carried on by it or by a qualifying lessee. An *industrial building or structure* (referred to here as an industrial building) is defined in TCA 1997, s 268(1) as a building or structure in use for the purposes of:

(a)   a trade carried on in a mill, factory or other similar premises, including a trade carried on in a laboratory the sole or main function of which is the analysis of minerals, including oil and natural gas, in connection with the exploration for, or the extraction of, such minerals;

(b)   a dock undertaking;

(c)   growing fruit, vegetables or other produce in the course of a trade of market gardening within the meaning of TCA 1997, s 654;

(d)   the trade of hotel-keeping;

(e)   the intensive production of cattle, sheep, poultry or eggs in the course of a trade other than the trade of farming;

(f)   a trade consisting of the operation or management of an airport and which is an airport runway or an airport apron used solely or mainly by aircraft carrying passengers or cargo for hire or reward;

(g)   a trade consisting of the operation or management of a nursing home within the meaning of section 2 of the Health (Nursing Homes) Act 1990, being a nursing home registered under section 4 of that Act;

(h)   a trade consisting of the operation or management of an airport, other than a building or structure referred to in (f) above;

(i)   a trade consisting of the operation or management of a convalescent home for the provision of medical and nursing care for persons recovering from treatment in a hospital, being a hospital that provides treatment for acutely ill patients, and in respect of which convalescent home the Health Service Executive is satisfied that the convalescent home satisfies the requirements of sections 4 and 6 of the Health (Nursing Homes) Act 1990, and any regulations made under section 6 of that Act as if it were a nursing home within the meaning of section 2 of that Act;

(j)   a trade which consists of the operation or management of a qualifying hospital;

(k)   for the purpose of a trade which consists of the operation or management of a qualifying sports injuries clinic;

(l)   for the purposes of a trade consisting of the operation or management of a qualifying mental health centre; or

(m)   for the purposes of a trade consisting of the operation or management of a qualifying specialist palliative care unit.

Dock undertaking

In (b) above, *dock* means any harbour, wharf, pier or jetty or other works in or at which vessels can ship or unship merchandise or passengers and *dock undertaking* is to be construed accordingly. In *Patrick Monahan (Drogheda) Ltd v O'Connell* 3 ITR 661, following *Baytrust Holdings Ltd v IRC* [1971] 1 WLR 133 (a stamp duty case), it was held that "undertaking" denoted the business or enterprise undertaken by a trader. The taxpayer's business, which was that of a shipping agent, stevedore, customs clearance agent and coal importer, was held to be a dock undertaking.

Hotel-keeping

In relation to (d) above, a building or structure in use for the purposes of the trade of hotel-keeping includes a building or structure in use as a holiday camp registered in the register of holiday camps kept under the Tourist Traffic Acts 1939 to 2003 or, in respect of expenditure incurred on its construction up to 3 December 2002 (or up to 31 December 2006 on its construction or refurbishment in certain circumstances, or up to 31 July 2008 in certain other circumstances), in use as a holiday cottage if registered in any register of holiday cottages established by the National Tourism Development Authority (TCA 1997, s 268(3), (13).

See **5.404** regarding the restriction by TCA 1997, s 270(4)-(7) of qualifying expenditure for buildings used for the trade of hotel-keeping, registered holiday camps and holiday cottages. In the case of expenditure incurred in the period 1 January 2007 to 31 December 2007, only 75% of expenditure incurred is treated as incurred, and in the case of expenditure incurred in the period 1 January 2008 to 31 July 2008, only 50% of expenditure incurred is treated as incurred.

A holiday cottage in respect of which expenditure on its construction or refurbishment is incurred up to 31 December 2006 (rather than 31 December 2002) qualifies as an industrial building if:

(i)   (I)   a planning application (not being an application for outline permission within the meaning of section 36 of the Planning and Development Act 2000), in so far as planning permission is required, in respect of the holiday cottage is made in accordance with the Planning and Development Regulations 2001 to 2002,

(II)   an acknowledgment of the application, confirming that it was received on or before 31 December 2004, is issued by the planning authority in accordance with article 26(2) of the Planning and Development Regulations 2001 (SI No 600 of 2001), and

(III)   the application is not an invalid application in respect of which a notice is issued by the planning authority in accordance with article 26(5) of those regulations,

(ii) (I)   a planning application, in so far as planning permission was required, in respect of the holiday cottage was made in accordance with the Local Government (Planning and Development) Regulations 1994 (SI No 86 of 1994), not being an application for outline permission within the meaning of article 3 of those regulations),

(II)   an acknowledgment of the application, confirming that it was received on or before 10 March 2002, is issued by the planning authority in accordance with article 29(2)(a) of the regulations mentioned in (I), and

(III)   the application is not an invalid application in respect of which a notice is issued by the planning authority in accordance with article 29(2)(b)(i) of those regulations, or

(iii) where the construction or refurbishment work on the holiday cottage represented by that expenditure is exempted development for the purposes of the Planning and Development Act 2000 by virtue of Part 2 of the Planning and Development Regulations 2001 (SI 600/2001) and—

(I)   a detailed plan in relation to the development work is prepared,

(II)   a binding contract in writing, under which the expenditure on the development is incurred, is in existence, and

(III)   work to the value of 5% of the development costs is carried out,

not later than 31 December 2004 (TCA 1997, s 268(13)(b)).

A holiday cottage in respect of which expenditure on its construction or refurbishment is incurred up to 31 July 2008 (rather than 31 December 2002) qualifies as an industrial building if:

(i)   the conditions relating to planning applications in (i), (ii) or (iii) above, as the case may be, have been satisfied,

(ii) (I)   subject to TCA 1997, s 270(7)(a) and (b) (see **5.404**), the person constructing or refurbishing the holiday cottage has, on or before 31 December 2006, carried out work to the value of not less than 15% of the actual construction or refurbishment costs of the cottage,

(I)   that person or, where the holiday cottage is sold by that person, the person who is claiming a deduction in relation to the expenditure can show that the condition in (I) was satisfied,

(iii) a binding contract in writing, under which the expenditure on the construction or refurbishment of the holiday cottage is incurred, was in existence on or before 31 July 2006, and

(iv)   such other conditions, as may be specified in regulations made by the Minister for Finance, have been satisfied, such conditions to be limited to those necessary to ensure compliance with the laws of the European Communities governing State aid or with a decision of the Commission of the European Communities regarding compatibility with the common market having regard to Article 87 of the European Communities Treaty (TCA 1997, s 268(13)(c)).

For the purposes of determining whether and to what extent capital expenditure incurred on the construction (within the meaning of TCA 1997, s 270(2) – see **5.404**) of:

(a)   a building or structure in use for the purposes of the trade of hotel keeping; or

(b)   a building of structure deemed to be a building or structure in use for such purposes by virtue of TCA 1997, s 268(3) (holiday camp or holiday cottage – see **5.401.1**),

is incurred or not incurred before 31 July 2008, only such amount of that capital expenditure as is properly attributable to work on the construction or refurbishment of the building or structure actually carried out on or before 31 July 2008 will be treated as having been incurred on or before that date (TCA 1997, s 316(2A)).

A building or structure in use for the purposes of a trade of hotel-keeping will not be regarded as an industrial building or structure as respects capital expenditure incurred on or after 3 February 2005 unless it is registered in the appropriate register of hotels. TCA 1997, s 268(14) provides that a building or structure in use for the purposes of the trade of hotel-keeping (but not including one *deemed* to be such a building or structure) may not, as respects capital expenditure incurred on or after 3 February 2005 on its construction (within the meaning of TCA 1997, s 270: expenditure on construction to be construed as including expenditure on refurbishment – see **5.404**), be treated as an industrial building or structure unless it is registered in the register of hotels kept under the Tourist Traffic Acts 1939 to 2003.

As respects capital expenditure incurred on or before 31 July 2006 on the construction or refurbishment of a building or structure in use for the purposes of the trade of hotel-keeping, this provision does not apply unless:

(a)   (i)   a planning application (not being an application for outline planning permission within the meaning of section 36 of the Planning and Development Act 2000), in so far as planning permission was required, in respect of the construction or refurbishment work on the building or structure represented by that expenditure, was made in accordance with the Planning and Development Regulations 2001 to 2004,

        (ii)   an acknowledgment of the application, confirming that the application was received on or before 31 December 2004, was issued by the planning authority in accordance with article 26(2) of the Planning and Development Regulations 2001 (SI 600/2001), and

        (iii)   the application was not an invalid application in respect of which a notice was issued by the planning authority in accordance with article 26(5) of those regulations,

(b)   (i)   a planning application, in so far as planning permission was required, in respect of the construction or refurbishment work on the building or structure represented by that expenditure, was made in accordance with the Local Government (Planning and Development) Regulations 1994 (SI 86/1994), not being an application for outline permission within the meaning of article 3 of those regulations,

(ii) an acknowledgment of the application, confirming that the application was received on or before 10 March 2002, was issued by the planning authority in accordance with article 29(2)(a) of the Planning and Development Regulations 2001 (SI No 600 of 2001), and

(iii) the application was not an invalid application in respect of which a notice was issued by the planning authority in accordance with article 29(2)(b)(i) of those regulations,

(c) where the construction or refurbishment work on the building or structure represented by that expenditure is exempted development for the purposes of the Planning and Development Act 2000 by virtue of Part 2 of the Planning and Development Regulations 2001 (SI No 600 of 2001) and—

(i) a detailed plan in relation to the development work was prepared,

(ii) a binding contract in writing, under which the expenditure on the development is incurred, was in existence, and

(iii) work to the value of 5% of the development costs was carried out,

not later than 31 December 2004, or

(d) (i) the construction or refurbishment of the building or structure is a development in respect off which an application for a certificate under section 25(7)(a)(ii) of the Dublin Docklands Development Authority Act 1997 was made to the Authority (within the meaning of that Act),

(ii) an acknowledgment of the application, confirming that the application was received on or before 31 December 2004, was received by that Authority, and

(iii) the application was not an invalid application (TCA 1997, s 268(15)).

As respects capital expenditure incurred on or after 3 February 2005, a guest house or holiday hostel registered in the appropriate register is deemed to be a building or structure in use for the purposes of the trade of hotel-keeping and qualifies for capital allowances accordingly. This provision does not affect any guest house or holiday hostel that may have already qualified for allowances under TCA 1997, s 268. TCA 1997, s 268(2C) provides that a building or structure (other than one that is in use for the purposes of the trade of hotel-keeping) which is in use as:

(a) a guest house and is registered in the register of guest houses kept under the Tourist Traffic Acts 1939 to 2003, or

(b) a holiday hostel and is registered in the register of holiday hostels kept under the Tourist Traffic Acts 1939 to 2003,

is, as respects capital expenditure incurred on or after 3 February 2005 on its construction (within the meaning of TCA 1997, s 270: expenditure on construction to be construed as including expenditure on refurbishment – see **5.404**), to be deemed to be a building or structure in use for the purposes of the trade of hotel-keeping.

TCA 1997, s 268(2D) provides that a building or structure which is comprised in, and is in use as part of, premises which are registered in the register of caravan sites and camping sites kept under the Tourist Traffic Acts 1939 to 2003 are, as respects capital expenditure incurred on or after 1 January 2008 on its construction (within the meaning of section TCA 1997, s 270 - see **5.404**), to be deemed to be a building or structure in use for the purposes of the trade of hotel-keeping.

Accordingly, such buildings and structures are included in the scheme of industrial building annual writing down allowances at 4% of qualifying expenditure that is currently available in relation to expenditure incurred on the construction and refurbishment of hotels, holiday camps, guesthouses and holiday hostels which are registered in the appropriate register maintained by Fáilte Ireland.

For capital expenditure incurred on or after 20 March 2001, a building or structure in use for the purposes of the trade of hotel-keeping is not treated as an industrial building or structure where any part of that expenditure has been or is to be met, directly or indirectly, by grant assistance or any other assistance which is granted by or through the State, any board established by statute, any public or local authority or any other agency of the State (TCA 1997, s 268(11)). Whereas, for the purposes of industrial building allowances generally, capital expenditure is reduced by the amount of any grant assistance (see **5.404**), any grant received for a hotel building means that no industrial building allowances may be claimed in respect of that building.

For capital expenditure incurred on the construction or refurbishment of a building or structure where the construction or refurbishment commenced on or after 6 April 2001 (being capital expenditure in respect of which a writing-down allowance in excess of 4% for an accounting period would otherwise be available under TCA 1997, s 272), a building or structure in use for the purposes of the trade of hotel-keeping is not treated as an industrial building or structure unless, on making an application by the person who incurred the expenditure, the National Tourism Development Authority gives a certificate in writing to that person, in relation to that expenditure, stating:

(a) that it has received a declaration from that person as to whether or not that person is—

    (i) a small or medium-sized enterprise within the meaning of Annex 1 to Commission Regulation (EC) No 70/2001 of 12 January 2001 (OJ No L10 of 13 January 2001, p 33) on the application of Articles 87 and 88 of the European Communities Treaty to State aid to small and medium-sized enterprises, or

    (ii) a micro, small or medium-sized enterprise within the meaning of the Annex to Commission Recommendation of 6 May 2003 concerning the definition of micro, small and medium-sized enterprises,

(b) that the expenditure concerned falls within the meaning of "initial investment" contained in point 4.4 of the "Guidelines on National Regional Aid" (OJ No C 74, 10.3.1998, p 9) prepared by the Commission of the European Communities;

(c) that, in the case of expenditure incurred on or after 1 January 2003 on the construction or refurbishment of a building or structure provided for the purposes of a project that is subject to the notification requirements of the "Multisectoral framework on regional aid for large investment projects" (OJ No C 107, 7.4.1998, p7) prepared by the Commission of the European

Communities, or the "Multisectoral framework on regional aid for large investment projects" (OJ No C 70, 19.3.2002, p8) prepared by the Commission of the European Communities, as the case may be, approval of the potential capital allowances involved has been received from that Commission by the Minister for Finance, or by such other Minister of the Government, agency or body as may be nominated for that purposes by the Minister for Finance; and

(d) that such person has undertaken to furnish to the Minister for Finance, or to such other Government Minister, agency or body as may be nominated for that purpose by the Minister for Finance, upon request in writing by the Minister concerned or that agency or body, such further information as may be necessary to enable compliance with the reporting requirements of—

   (i) the Regulation referred to in (a) above or the Multisectoral framework referred to in (c) above,

   (ii) "Community guidelines on State aid for rescuing and restructuring firms in difficulty (OJ No C 288, 9.10.1999, p2) prepared by the Commission of the European Communities, or

   (iii) any other European Communities Regulation or Directive under the European Communities Treaty governing the granting of State aid in specific sectors (TCA 1997, s 268(12)).

Regarding (a) above, this refers to the EU Commission's "Community guidelines on State aid for rescuing and restructuring firms in difficulty" and its definition of micro, small and medium-sized enterprises. In relation to the latter, applicants for Fáilte Ireland certification are required to operate a self-assessment procedure.

According to guidance notes published by the National Tourism Development Authority, the information sought in the case of a company must, generally, be provided to the National Tourism Development Authority by the company's auditors.

Where the National Tourism Development Authority certificate declares that the enterprise is not a small or medium sized enterprise (SME), as defined, the National Tourism Development Authority will pass a copy of that certificate to the Department of Finance. The Department of Finance will incorporate this into its periodic notification of State Aids to the European Commission.

The National Tourism Development Authority or its agents may seek to audit the information provided, on a sample basis. The National Tourism Development Authority's certificate will be valid for a period of two years after its issue date.

The guidance notes also contain a definition of small and medium-sized enterprises, and related definitions, the Form of Auditors' Certificate to the National Tourism Development Authority, with schedule of relevant information attached, Form of Undertaking to the National Tourism Development Authority from Applicant Enterprise, and the Form of the National Tourism Development Authority certification. The notes may be downloaded from www.bftrade.travel.ie.

Market gardening

As regards (c), TCA 1997, s 655(3) provides that market gardening is to be treated as a trade; TCA 1997, s 654 describes market gardening as the occupation of land in the State as a nursery or garden for the sale of the produce of that land (but excluding the occupation of land used for the growth of hops).

Buildings for recreation or welfare of workers

Any building or structure provided by a company carrying on any of the trades or undertakings listed in (a) to (h) above is treated as an industrial building or structure if it is provided for the recreation or welfare of workers employed in the trade or undertaking in question, and if used for that purpose (eg, a canteen).

5.401.2   Mill, factory or other similar premises

A trade carried on in a "mill, factory or other similar premises" normally requires the trade to be one which consists of or includes the manufacture of goods, but the phrase "for the purposes of" permits the inclusion of buildings not used in the manufacturing process itself and which are ancillary to that process, such as a warehouse used by a manufacturer for storing raw materials and finished goods related to the manufacturing trade. This does not, of course, permit a non-manufacturer who constructs a warehouse for use in a warehousing or distributive trade to claim industrial building allowances.

On the other hand, an Irish sales branch of a foreign manufacturing company could claim industrial buildings allowances in respect of expenditure it incurs on the construction of a warehouse used to store goods manufactured by the company abroad and sold in Ireland through the branch; since the company's trade is one of manufacturing, and the warehouse is used for the purposes of that trade (albeit that no manufacturing is carried on by the Irish branch), the warehouse is an industrial building.

In *Ellerker v Union Cold Storage Co Ltd* 22 TC 195, cold stores for meat were held to be premises similar to mills as they were equipped with machinery for the purpose of subjecting the meat and other commodities to an artificial temperature. The words "mill" and "factory" were described as follows:

> I take it that a factory is a building used for the purpose of manufacture of goods equipped with machinery and that the word is generally understood in that sense. It is a building where goods are made. The meaning of the word "mill" is also, I think, plain enough. A mill is a building where goods are subjected to treatment or processing of some sort and machinery is used for that purpose.

In *IRC v Leith Harbour and Dock Commons* 24 TC 118, grain elevators were held to be similar to mills. Following the *Barclay Curle* and *R & H Hall* decisions (see **5.202.3**), the cold stores and grain elevators in the above cases could also probably be regarded as plant.

In *Vibroplant Ltd v Holland* [1982] STC 164, a building used for the servicing and repair of plant was held not to be a factory or other similar premises as it was not used to make goods. In *Girobank v Clarke* [1996] STC 540, a building which housed high speed machinery for processing documents was found not to be a premises similar to a mill; to be similar to a mill, the processes carried on there would need to involve the use of machinery "to alter the physical nature of the materials to which they are applied and with a view to that alteration making that material more suitable for, or to add to its value for, commercial use as merchandise or wares".

In *O'Connell v Waterford Glass Ltd* (14 April 1983) HC, TL 122, a factory complex, including a building designed as an administrative centre, the main part of which played a key role in the manufacturing operations, was held to be a single industrial unit. It would not, however, seem to be necessary for a premises in which the manufacturing process is not carried out to be part of the factory building itself. As long as a building is in use for the purposes of a trade carried on in a mill, factory or similar premises, eg, a warehouse, it will constitute an industrial building. In a modern context, if a manufacturing process is controlled and regulated by a computer installation housed in a premises separate from, and even remote from, the manufacturing premises, the premises in which it is housed should qualify as an industrial building.

Certain types of buildings do not qualify for industrial building allowances, even if used for the purposes of a manufacturing or other qualifying trade (see **5.401.6–7**).

5.401.3 Laboratories for mineral analysis

In respect of capital expenditure incurred on or after 25 January 1984, the meaning of "mill, factory or other similar premises" is to be taken as including a laboratory used solely or mainly for the analysis of minerals in connection with the exploration for, or the extraction of, such minerals. As well as including oil and natural gas, the term "mineral" can be taken to include any other types of minerals such as lead, zinc, coal, silver, copper etc.

The requirement that the laboratory for mineral analysis be used in connection with the exploration for or the extraction of minerals does not necessarily require that the person claiming the allowances is the person carrying out the exploration or extraction activity. A company using a laboratory for the provision of a mineral analysis service for other persons carrying on a mineral exploration or extraction activity is entitled to claim industrial building allowances in respect of capital expenditure incurred on the construction of the laboratory.

5.401.4 Airport buildings and structures

With effect from 24 April 1992, an "industrial building or structure" includes a building or structure in use for the purposes of a trade consisting of the operation or management of an airport, and which is an airport runway or an airport apron used solely or mainly by aircraft carrying passengers or cargo for hire or reward (TCA 1997, s 268(1)(f)). TCA 1997, s 268(1)(h) (inserted by FA 1998) extends the availability of industrial building allowances to capital expenditure on other buildings associated with the management and operation of an airport, for example, terminal buildings. The allowances available are in the form of an annual writing-down allowance of 4% per annum.

TCA 1997, s 268(1)(h) applies to Dublin Airport Authority plc as well as other airport operators. "Dublin Airport Authority" (DAA) means the Dublin Airport Authority, public limited company, and includes—

(a) where a day has been appointed under section 5 of the State Airports Act 2004 in respect of the Cork Airport Authority plc, that company, and

(b) where a day has been appointed under the said section 5 in respect of the Shannon Airport Authority plc, that company (TCA 1997, s 268(10)).

Under the State Airports Act, which came into effect in October 2004, DAA assumed responsibility for all the assets, liabilities and contracts of the former Aer Rianta.

Qualifying expenditure in the case of DAA is expenditure incurred on or after the vesting day. The *vesting day* is the day appointed by order under section 9(6) of the State Airports Act 2004 in respect of DAA and such other day or days as may be appointed by order or orders under section 5 of the State Airports Act 2004 in respect of the Cork Airport Authority plc, and the Shannon Airport Authority plc. In the case of other airport operators, the commencement date for qualifying expenditure is 27 March 1998, the date of the passing of FA 1998 (TCA 1997, s 268(9)(e)).

In addition, for airport buildings or structures (other than airport runways and aprons) already in existence on the commencement date, available industrial building allowances are based on a residual amount being the original cost of construction less an amount represented by the writing down allowances that would have been made had the buildings qualified as industrial buildings or structures before the commencement date (TCA 1997, s 272(3A)).

Airport runways and aprons were, as mentioned above, eligible since 1992 for industrial building allowances. Where such structures were already in existence and were vested in DAA on the "vesting day", expenditure is deemed to have been incurred by DAA on that day and in an amount equal to the amount of the capital expenditure originally incurred on construction less an amount represented by the writing down allowances that would have been made in respect of that capital expenditure for the period up to the day before the vesting day had a claim for those allowances been made and allowed (TCA 1997, s 272(3B)).

Provision is also made in TCA 1997, s 284(8) for wear and tear allowances to DAA in respect of machinery or plant. DAA will be deemed to have incurred on the vesting day capital expenditure on the provision of machinery or plant which was vested in it on that day. For this purpose, the cost of the machinery or plant is arrived at by deducting from its original cost an amount equal to the amount of any wear and tear allowances that would have been made since the machinery or plant had been provided had a claim for those allowances been made and allowed.

5.401.5 Private nursing homes

TCA 1997 268(1)(g) provides that an industrial building or structure includes a building or structure in use for the purposes of a trade consisting of the operation or management of a nursing home (including a building or structure in use as a qualifying residential unit – see below). Capital allowances are available in respect of capital expenditure on the construction, extension or refurbishment of buildings used as private registered nursing homes as well as for expenditure on the conversion of an existing building into such a nursing home. To qualify for capital allowances, a nursing home must be registered under s 4 of the Health (Nursing Homes) Act 1990 ("registered nursing home").

Capital allowances are available in respect of expenditure incurred on or after 3 December 1997 and are in the form of an industrial building annual allowance of 15% per annum for six years and 10% for the seventh year. The allowances are available in respect of buildings in use for the purposes of a trade consisting of the operation or management of a nursing home. Allowances will be clawed back where the building ceases to be a qualifying building within ten years.

No balancing charge may be made to claw back allowances claimed in the case of a sale of the building or other event which occurs more than ten years after the building is used.

Notwithstanding the seven-year write-off period for capital allowances, the tax life (during which allowances may be transferred to a purchaser) for buildings first used (or first used after refurbishment) on or after 1 February 2007 is 15 years. TCA 1997, s 272(4)(f) provides, subject to TCA 1997, s 272(4)(fa) (regarding qualifying residential units - see below), in relation to a building or structure that is to be regarded as an industrial building or structure as being a qualifying nursing home, that the tax life of that building or structure is:

(a) seven years from the time the building or structure was first used;

(b) as respects a building or structure that is first used on or after 1 February 2007, 15 years beginning with the time it was first used; or

(c) where capital expenditure on the refurbishment of the building or structure is incurred and, subsequent to the incurring of that expenditure, it is first used on or after 1 February 2007, 15 years from the time it was first used subsequent to the incurring of that expenditure (see also **5.406**).

No balancing allowance or charge may be made by reason of an event occurring more than (i) where the building or structure was first used before 1 February 2007, 10 years after it was first used, or (ii) where the building or structure was first used on or after 1 February 2007, 15 years after it was first used, or (iii) where capital expenditure on the refurbishment of the building or structure is incurred and, subsequent to the incurring of that expenditure, the building or structure is first used on or after 1 February 2007, 15 years after it was first used subsequent to incurring that expenditure (TCA 1997, s 274(1)(b)(iia)). (See below in relation to qualifying residential units.)

Qualifying residential units

As respects capital expenditure incurred in the period from 25 March 2002 to 30 April 2010, a house in use as a qualifying residential unit is deemed to be a building or structure in use for the purposes of a trade consisting of the operation or management of a registered nursing home. This provision does not, however, apply in respect of expenditure incurred on the construction of a qualifying residential unit where any part of the expenditure has been or is to be met, directly or indirectly, by grant assistance or any other assistance granted by or through the State, any board established by statute, any public or local authority or any other agency of the State (TCA 1997, s 268(3B), (3C)).

A house is not a qualifying residential unit unless

(a) the following information has been provided to the Health Service Executive, by the person who is entitled to the relevant interest in relation to the capital expenditure incurred on the construction or refurbishment of the house, for onward transmission to the Minister for Health and Children and the Minister for Finance:

(i) the amount of the capital expenditure actually incurred on the construction or refurbishment of the house;

(ii) the number and nature of the investors that are investing in the house;

(iii) the amount to be invested by each investor; and

(iv) the nature of the structures which are being put in place to facilitate the investment in the house,

together with such other information as may be specified by the Minister for Finance, in consultation with the Minister for Health and Children, as being of assistance in evaluating the costs, including but not limited to exchequer costs, and the benefits arising from the operation of tax relief for qualifying residential units,

(b)   the Health Service Executive, in consultation with the Minister for Health and Children, gives a certificate in writing after the house is first leased or, where capital expenditure is incurred on the refurbishment of a house, first leased subsequent to the incurring of that expenditure, stating that it is satisfied that

    (i)   the house and the development in which it is comprised complies with all the conditions in TCA 1997, s 268(3A) (see below), and

    (ii)   the information required in accordance with (a) above has been provided, and

(c)   an annual report in writing is provided, by the person who is entitled to the relevant interest in relation to the capital expenditure incurred on the construction or refurbishment of the house, to the Health Service Executive, for onward transmission to the Minister for Health and Children and the Minister for Finance, by the end of each year in the twenty year period referred to in TCA 1997, s 272(4)(fa) (see below), which

    (i)   confirms whether the house and the development in which it is comprised continue to comply with all the conditions in TCA 1997, s 268(3A) (see below), and

    (ii)   provides details of the level of occupation of the house for the previous year including the age of and, as the case may be, the nature of the infirmity of the occupants (TCA 1997, s 268(3E)).

See **5.404** regarding the restriction by TCA 1997, s 270(4)-(6) of qualifying expenditure on qualifying residential units. In the case of expenditure incurred in the period 1 January 2007 to 31 December 2007, only 75% of expenditure incurred is treated as incurred, and in the case of expenditure incurred in the period 1 January 2008 to 31 July 2008, only 50% of expenditure incurred is treated as incurred.

A *qualifying residential unit* means a house (including any building or part of a building used or suitable for use as a dwelling and any out office, yard, garden or other land appurtenant to or usually enjoyed with that building or part building) which:

(a)   is constructed on the site of, or on a site which is immediately adjacent to the site of, a registered nursing home;

(b)   is—

    (i)   a single storey house, or

    (ii)   a house that is comprised in a building of one or more storeys in relation to which a fire safety certificate under Part III of the Building Control Regulations 1997 (SI No 496 of 1997) (as amended from time to time) is required and, prior to the commencement of the construction works on the building, is granted by the building control authority (within the meaning of section 2 of the Building Control Act 1990, as amended by the Local Government (Dublin) Act 1993 and the Local Government Act 2001) in whose functional area the building is situated, where—

        (I)   the house is, or (as the case may be) the house and the building in which it is comprised are, designated and constructed to meet the needs of persons with disabilities, including in particular the needs or persons who are confined to wheelchairs, and

    (II)   the house consists of one or two bedrooms, a kitchen, a living room, bath or shower facilities, toilet facilities and a nurse call system linked to the registered nursing home,

(c) is comprised in a development of not less than 10 qualifying residential units where—

    (i)   that development also includes a day-care centre,

    (ii)   those units are operated or managed by the registered nursing home and an on-site caretaker is provided,

    (iii)   back-up medical, including nursing care, is provided by the registered nursing home to the occupants of those units when required by those occupants,

    (iv)   except where the relevant interest in relation to capital expenditure incurred on the construction or refurbishment of all qualifying residential units in a development is held by a company, not less than 20% of those units are made available for renting to persons who are eligible for a rent subsidy from the Health Service Executive, subject to service requirements to be specified by the Health Service Executive in advance and to the condition that nothing in this requirement may require that the Health Service Executive take up all or any of the units so made available, and

    (v)   except where the relevant interest in relation to capital expenditure incurred on the construction or refurbishment of all qualifying residential units in a development is held by a company, the rent to be charged in respect of any such unit made available in accordance with (iv) is not more than 90% of the rent which would be charged if that unit were rented to a person who is not in receipt of a subsidy referred to in (iv), and

(d) (i) is leased to a person and, as the case may be, the spouse of that person—

    (I)   who is, or are, not connected (within the meaning of TCA 1997, s 10 - see **2.3**) with the lessor,

    (II)   who has or have been selected as the occupant or occupants of the house by the registered nursing home, and

    (III)   either the person or the spouse of that person has been certified by a person who is registered in the General Register of Medical Practitioners, as requiring such accommodation by reason of old age or infirmity, or

is leased to the registered nursing home on condition that it will be subsequently leased to a person or persons referred to in (i) and which is subsequently used for no purpose other than use by such person or persons (TCA 1997, s 268(3A)).

Where TCA 1997, s 270(8) applies (see below) in relation to a qualifying residential unit (within the meaning of TCA 1997, s 268(3A)), the tax life of that building or structure is

(i)   20 years beginning with the time when the unit was first used, or

(ii)   where capital expenditure on the refurbishment of the unit is incurred, 20 years beginning with the time when the unit was first used subsequent to the incurring of that expenditure (TCA 1997, s 272(4)(fa)).

As explained in **5.404** in relation, inter alia, to a qualifying residential unit, the amount of capital expenditure incurred up to 31 July 2008 on the construction or refurbishment of that unit which qualifies for industrial buildings allowances is restricted. The amount of such expenditure treated as incurred for the purposes of the making of capital allowances or the charging of any balancing charges is to be reduced—

(a)   in the case of expenditure incurred in the period from 25 March 2007 to 31 December 2007, to 75%, and

(b)   in the case of expenditure incurred in the period 1 January 2008 to 31 July 2008, to 50%,

of the amount which would otherwise be so treated (TCA 1997, s 270(5)).

Where, however, capital expenditure is incurred on or after 1 May 2007 under a contract or agreement entered into on or after that date for the construction, refurbishment or development of a qualifying residential unit, the above reference to capital expenditure incurred up to 31 July 2008 is to be taken as a reference to capital expenditure incurred up to 30 April 2010. The amount of expenditure treated as incurred for the purposes of the making of capital allowances or the charging of any balancing charges is to be reduced, instead of as in (a) and (b) above, as follows:

(a)   in the case of expenditure incurred by a company in the period 1 May 2007 to 30 April 2010, to 75%, and

(b)   in the case of expenditure incurred by a person other than a company in the period from 1 May 2007 to 30 April 2010, to 50%,

of the amount which would otherwise be so treated (TCA 1997, s 270(8)).

For the purposes of determining, in relation to a claim for capital allowances, whether and to what extent capital expenditure incurred on the construction or refurbishment of a building or structure referred to in TCA 1997, s 270(4)(a), (b), (c), (d), (e), (f), (g), (h) or (i) (see above – restriction of amount of qualifying expenditure) is or is not incurred in:

(a) (i)   where TCA 1997, s 270(4)(i) applies (qualifying residential unit – see above), the period from 1 January 2006 to 24 March 2007, and

     (ii)   in any other case, the period 1 January 2006 to 31 December 2006,

(b) (i)   where TCA 1997, s 270(4)(i) applies (qualifying residential unit), the period from 25 March 2007 to 31 December 2007, and

     (ii)   in any other case, the period 1 January 2007 to 31 December 2007,

(c)   the period 1 January 2008 to 31 July 2008, or

(d)   where TCA 1997, s 270(8) applies in relation to a qualifying residential unit (see **5.401.5**), the period 1 May 2007 to 30 April 2010,

Where TCA 1997, s 270(8) applies in relation to a qualifying residential unit, only the amount of the expenditure as is properly attributable to work on the construction or refurbishment of the unit actually carried out in such a period is (notwithstanding the general rule regarding the time any capital expenditure is to be treated as incurred) to be treated as having been incurred in the period (TCA 1997, s 316(2B) (see also **5.404**)).

Where TCA 1997, s 270(8) applies in relation to a qualifying residential unit, no balancing allowance or charge may be made by reason of an event occurring more than (i) 20 years after the unit was first used, or (ii) where capital expenditure on the refurbishment of the unit is incurred, 20 years after it was first used subsequent to incurring that expenditure (TCA 1997, s 274(1)(b)(iib))

5.401.6 Private convalescent homes

Private convalescent homes, as envisaged in TCA 1997, s 268, are to be used as an alternative to hospital care for patients recovering from acute hospital treatment. TCA 1997, s 268(1)(i) provides that an industrial building or structure includes a building or structure in use for the purposes of a trade consisting of the operation or management of a convalescent home for the provision of medical and nursing care for persons recovering from treatment in a hospital. The hospital in question must be a hospital that provides treatment for acutely ill patients. The convalescent home must be one in respect of which the health board in whose functional area the convalescent home is situated is satisfied that the convalescent home satisfies the requirements of ss 4 and 6 of the Health (Nursing Homes) Act 1990, and any regulations made under s 6 of that Act as if it were a nursing home within the meaning of s 2 of that Act. Effectively, TCA 1997, s 268(1)(i) treats a convalescent home as if it were a nursing home and the regulatory provisions of the Health (Nursing Homes) Act 1990, apply to convalescent homes as they apply to nursing homes.

Allowances are available for expenditure incurred on or after 2 December 1998 on the construction, extension and refurbishment of a convalescent facility and on the conversion of an existing building into such a facility.

Notwithstanding the seven-year write-off period for capital allowances, the tax life (during which allowances may be transferred to a purchaser) for buildings first used (or first used after refurbishment) on or after 1 February 2007 is 15 years. TCA 1997, s 272(4)(f) provides, in relation to a building or structure that is to be regarded as an industrial building or structure as being a private convalescent home, that the tax life of that building or structure is:

(a)   seven years from the time the building or structure was first used;

(b)   as respects a building or structure that is first used on or after 1 February 2007, 15 years beginning with the time it was first used; or

(c)   where capital expenditure on the refurbishment of the building or structure is incurred and, subsequent to the incurring of that expenditure, it is first used on or after 1 February 2007, 15 years from the time it was first used subsequent to the incurring of that expenditure.

No balancing allowance or charge may be made by reason of an event occurring more than (i) where the building or structure was first used before 1 February 2007, 10 years after it was first used, or (ii) where the building or structure was first used on or after 1 February 2007, 15 years after it was first used, or (iii) where capital expenditure on the refurbishment of the building or structure is incurred and, subsequent to the incurring of that expenditure, the building or structure is first used on or after 1 February 2007, 15 years after it was first used subsequent to incurring that expenditure (TCA 1997, s 274(1)(b)(iia)).

5.401.7 Qualifying hospitals

Industrial building writing down allowances may be claimed over a seven-year period in respect of capital expenditure on the provision of acute private hospital facilities. Qualifying expenditure is expenditure incurred on or after a date appointed by order of the Minister for Finance.

Writing down allowances are available in respect of buildings or structures in use for the purposes of a trade consisting of the operation or management of a qualifying hospital.

Notwithstanding the seven-year write-off period for capital allowances, the tax life (during which allowances may be transferred to a purchaser) for buildings first used (or first used after refurbishment) on or after 1 February 2007 is 15 years. TCA 1997, s 272(4)(ga) provides, in relation to a building or structure that is to be regarded as an industrial building or structure as being a qualifying hospital, that the tax life of that building or structure is:

(a) seven years from the time the building or structure was first used;

(b) as respects a building or structure that is first used on or after 1 February 2007, 15 years beginning with the time it was first used; or

(c) where capital expenditure on the refurbishment of the building or structure is incurred and, subsequent to the incurring of that expenditure, it is first used on or after 1 February 2007, 15 years from the time it was first used subsequent to the incurring of that expenditure.

No balancing allowance or charge may be made by reason of an event occurring more than (i) where the building or structure was first used before 1 February 2007, 10 years after it was first used, or (ii) where the building or structure was first used on or after 1 February 2007, 15 years after it was first used, or (iii) where capital expenditure on the refurbishment of the building or structure is incurred and, subsequent to the incurring of that expenditure, the building or structure is first used on or after 1 February 2007, 15 years after it was first used subsequent to incurring that expenditure (TCA 1997, s 274(1)(b)(via)).

Qualifying hospital means a hospital which:

(a) is a private hospital (within the meaning of the Health Insurance Act 1994 (Minimum Benefits) Regulations 1996 (SI 1996/83));

(b) has the capacity to provide and normally provides medical and surgical services to persons every day of the year;

(c) has the capacity to provide out-patient services and accommodation on an overnight basis of not less than 70 in-patient beds or day-case and out-patient medical and surgical services and accommodation for such services of not less than 40 beds;

(d) contains an operating theatre or theatres and related on-site diagnostic and therapeutic facilities;

(e) contains facilities to provide not less than five of the following services: accident and emergency, cardiology and vascular, eye, ear, nose and throat, gastroenterology, geriatrics, haematology, maternity, medical, neurology, oncology, orthopaedic, respiratory, rheumatology, paediatric, and mental health services (within the meaning of the Mental Health Act 2001);

(f) in the case of a building or structure which—

(i) is first used on or after 1 February 2007, or

(ii) where capital expenditure on the refurbishment of the building or structure is incurred, is, subsequent to the incurring of that expenditure, first used on or after 1 February 2007,

provides to the Health Service Executive relevant data, for onward transmission to the Minister for Health and Children and the Minister for Finance, in relation to—

(I) the amount of the capital expenditure actually incurred on the construction or refurbishment of the building or structure,

(II) the number and nature of the investors that are investing in the building or structure,

(III) the amount to be invested by each investor, and

(IV) the nature of the structures which are being put in place to facilitate the investment in the building or structure,

together with such other information as may be specified by the Minister for Finance, in consultation with the Minister for Health and Children, as being of assistance in evaluating the costs, including but not limited to exchequer costs, and the benefits arising from the operation of tax relief under TCA 1997, Part 9 for qualifying hospitals;

(g) undertakes to the Health Service Executive—

(i) to make available annually, for the treatment of persons who have been awaiting in-patient or out-patient hospital services as public patients, not less than 20% of its capacity, subject to service requirements to be specified by the Health Service Executive in advance and to the proviso that this stipulation will not require the Health Service Executive to take up all or any part of the capacity made available to it by the hospital, and

(ii) in relation to the fees to be charged in respect of the treatment afforded to any such person, that such fees will not be more than 90% of the fees that would be charged in respect of similar treatment afforded to a person who has private medical insurance, and

(h) in respect of which the Health Service Executive, in consultation with the Minister for Health and Children and with the consent of the Minister for Finance, gives, during the period of—

(i) 10 years beginning with the time when the building or structure was first used, or

(ii) as respects a building or structure which is first used on or after 1 February 2007, 15 years beginning with the time the building or structure was first used, or

(iii) where capital expenditure on the refurbishment of a building or structure is incurred and, subsequently is first used on or after 1 February 2007, 15 years beginning with the time the building or structure was first used subsequent to the incurring of that expenditure,

stating that it is satisfied that the hospital complies with the conditions mentioned in (a)-(g) above;

and includes any part of the hospital which consists of rooms used exclusively for the assessment or treatment of patients but does not include any part of the hospital which consists of consultants' rooms or offices (TCA 1997, s 268(2A)).

Expenditure incurred on the construction of a building or structure in use for the purposes of a trade of operating or managing a qualifying hospital will not qualify for industrial building allowances where the relevant interest in relation to the expenditure is held by—

(a) a company;

(b) the trustees of a trust;

(c) an individual who is involved in the operation or management of the qualifying hospital concerned either as an employee or director or in any other capacity; or

(d) a property developer (within the meaning of TCA 1997, s 843A – a person carrying on a trade consisting wholly or mainly of the construction or refurbishment of buildings or structures with a view to their sale) or a person connected with (see **2.3**) such property developer, where either of those persons incurred the capital expenditure on the construction of that building or structure, or such expenditure was incurred by any other person connected with the property developer.

In any such case, the building or structure will not, as regards a claim for an industrial building allowance by any such person (and not as regards a claim by other investors in the same building or structure), be regarded as an industrial building or structure irrespective of whether the relevant interest is held by any of the above persons in a sole or joint capacity or jointly or in partnership with another person or persons (TCA 1997, s 268(1A)).

5.401.8   Sports injuries clinics

Industrial building allowances may be claimed in respect of expenditure incurred on the construction or refurbishment of buildings used as private sports injuries clinics. The sole or main business of the clinic must be the diagnosis, alleviation and treatment of sports-related injuries. The clinic must provide day-patient, in-patient and out-patient medical and surgical services and in-patient accommodation of at least 20 beds, and must contain an operating theatre or theatres and on-site diagnostic and therapeutic facilities. Not less than 20% of the capacity of the clinic must be available for public patients and it must provide a discount of at least 10% to the State in respect of the fees charged in respect of the treatment of public patients.

Qualifying expenditure is capital expenditure incurred in the period 15 May 2002 to 31 December 2006 or, where TCA 1997, s 268(16) applies, to 31 July 2008 (TCA 1997, s 268(9)(h)). TCA 1997, s 268(16) applies where:

(a) the person constructing or refurbishing the clinic has, on or before 31 December 2006, carried out work to the value of not less than 15% of the actual construction or refurbishment costs of the clinic; and

(b) that person or, where the clinic is sold by that person, the person who is claiming a deduction in relation to the expenditure can show that the condition in (a) was satisfied.

See **5.404** regarding the restriction by TCA 1997, s 270(4)-(6) of qualifying expenditure for buildings used for the trade of managing a sports-injury clinic. In the case of expenditure incurred in the period 1 January 2007 to 31 December 2007, only 75% of expenditure incurred is treated as incurred, and in the case of expenditure incurred in the period 1 January 2008 to 31 July 2008, only 50% of expenditure incurred is treated as incurred.

Annual allowances available in respect of qualifying expenditure are at a rate of 15% for the first six years with the balance of 10% being available in the seventh year. Any annual allowances given are subject to a balancing charge if the clinic is sold within 10 years. To comply with European Commission rules on EU State aid, a clinic will not qualify for allowances where the relevant interest

A qualifying sports injury clinic is a medical clinic:

(a) which does not (other than by virtue of (e) below), provide health care services to a person pursuant to his entitlements under Chapter II or Part IV of the Health Act 1970;

(b) in which the sole of main business carried on is the provision, by or under the control of medical or surgical specialists, of health care consisting of the diagnosis, alleviation and treatment of physical injuries sustained by persons in participating, or in training for participation, in athletic games or sports;

(c) which has the capacity to provide day-patient, in-patient and out-patient medical and surgical services and in-patient accommodation of at least 20 beds;

(d) which contains an operating theatre or theatres and related on-site diagnostic and therapeutic facilities;

(e) which undertakes to the Health Service Executive—

(i) to make available annually, for the treatment of persons who have been awaiting day-patient, in-patient or out-patient hospital services as public patients, not less than 20% of its capacity, subject to service requirements to be specified by the Health Service Executive in advance and to the condition that nothing in this requirement may require the Health Service Executive to take up all or any part of the capacity made available to the health board by the medical clinic, and

(ii) in relation to the fees to be charged in respect of the treatment afforded to any such person, that they are not more than 90% of the fees that would be charged for similar treatment afforded to a person who has private medical insurance, and

(f) in respect of which the Health Service Executive, in consultation with the Minister for Health and Children and with the consent of the Minister for Finance, gives, during the period of 10 years beginning with the time the building or structure was first used, an annual certificate in writing stating that it is satisfied that the medical clinic complies with the conditions mentioned in (a) to (e) above; and

includes any part of the clinic that consists of rooms used exclusively for the assessment or treatment of patients but does not include any part of the clinic consisting of consultants' rooms or offices (TCA 1997, s 268(2B)).

Expenditure incurred on the construction of a building or structure in use for the purposes of a trade of operating or managing a qualifying sports injuries clinic will not qualify for industrial building allowances where the relevant interest in relation to the expenditure is held by:

(a)   a company;

(b)   the trustees of a trust;

(c)   an individual who is involved in the operation or management of the qualifying sports injuries clinic concerned either as an employee or director or in any other capacity; or

(d)   a property developer (a person carrying on a trade consisting wholly or mainly of the construction or refurbishment of buildings or structures with a view to their sale), where either such property developer or a person connected with (see **2.3**) such property developer incurred the capital expenditure on the construction of that building or structure.

In any such case, the building or structure will not be regarded, as regards a claim for an industrial building allowance by any such person (and not as regards a claim by other investors in the same building or structure), as an industrial building or structure irrespective of whether the relevant interest is held by any of the above persons in a sole or joint capacity or jointly or in partnership with another person or persons (TCA 1997, s 268(1B)).

5.401.9   Qualifying mental health centres

Industrial building allowances on lines similar to those for qualifying hospitals are available also in respect of expenditure incurred on or after 27 January 2007 on the construction or refurbishment of qualifying mental health centres. Qualifying expenditure for this purpose is expenditure on a "centre", as defined. The Health Executive Authority must certify on an annual basis for 15 years from first use that the centre is an approved centre. The centre must also have a minimum of 20 in-patient beds.

A *qualifying mental health centre* is a centre (within the meaning of section 62 of the Mental Health Act 2001) which:

(a)   is an approved centre for the purposes of the Mental Health Act 2001;

(b)   has the capacity to provide day-patient and out-patient services and accommodation on an overnight basis of not less than 20 in-patient beds;

(c)   provides to the Health Service Executive relevant data, for onward transmission to the Minister for Health and Children and the Minister for Finance, in relation to—

(i)   the amount of the capital expenditure actually incurred on the construction or refurbishment of the centre,

(ii) the number and nature of the investors that are investing in the centre,

(iii) the amount to be invested by each investor, and

(iv) the nature of the structures which are being put in place to facilitate the investment in the centre,

together with such other information as may be specified by the Minister for Finance, in consultation with the Minister for Health and Children, as being of assistance in evaluating the costs, including but not limited to exchequer costs, and the benefits arising from the operation of tax relief under capital allowances legislation for qualifying mental health centres,

(d) undertakes to the Health Service Executive—

(i) to make available annually, for the treatment of persons who have been awaiting day-patient, in-patient or out-patient services as public patients, not less than 20% of its capacity, subject to service requirements to be specified by the Health Service Executive in advance and to the proviso that nothing may require the Health Service Executive to take up all or any part of the capacity made available to it by the centre, and

(ii) that fees to be charged in respect of the treatment afforded to any such person may not be more than 90% of what would be charged for similar treatment afforded to a person who has private medical insurance, and

(e) in respect of which the Health Service Executive, in consultation with the Minister for Health and Children and with the consent of the Minister for Finance, gives an annual certificate in writing during the period of—

(i) 15 years beginning with the time the centre was first used, or

(ii) where capital expenditure on the refurbishment of the centre is incurred, 15 years beginning with the time the centre was first used subsequent to the incurring that expenditure,

stating that it is satisfied that the centre complies with the conditions in (a)-(d) above, and—

(I) subject to (II), includes any part of the centre which consists of rooms used exclusively for the assessment or treatment of patients, but

(II) does not include any part of the centre which consists of consultants' rooms or offices (TCA s 268(1C)).

Where the relevant interest (see **5.403**) in relation to capital expenditure incurred on the construction of a building or structure in use as a qualifying mental health centre is held by:

(a) a company;

(b) the trustees of a trust;

(c) an individual who is involved in the operation or management of the centre concerned either as an employee or director or in any other capacity; or

(d) a property developer (within the meaning of TCA 1997, s 843A – a person carrying on a trade consisting wholly or mainly of the construction or refurbishment of buildings or structures with a view to their sale), or a person connected with (see **2.3**) such property developer, where either of those persons incurred the capital expenditure on the construction of that building or structure, or such expenditure was incurred by any other person connected with the property developer,

then, that building or structure may not, as regards a claim for capital allowances, be regarded as an industrial building or structure irrespective of whether that relevant interest is held by the person referred to in (a)-(d) above in a sole capacity or jointly or in partnership with another person or persons (TCA 1997, s 268(1D)).

Notwithstanding the seven-year write-off period for capital allowances, the tax life of a qualifying building (during which allowances may be transferred to a purchaser) is 15 years from the time it is first used or, where capital expenditure is incurred on its refurbishment, 15 years after it was first used subsequent to the incurring of that expenditure (TCA 1997, s 272(4)(i)).

No balancing allowance or charge may be made in respect of a qualifying building or structure by reason of an event occurring more than 15 years after the building was first used or, where capital expenditure on its refurbishment is incurred, 15 years after the building or structure is first used subsequent to incurring that expenditure (TCA 1997, s 274(1)(b)(viii)).

5.401.10 Qualifying specialist palliative care units

Industrial building allowances on lines similar to those for qualifying private hospitals and qualifying mental health centres are available in respect of expenditure incurred, on or after the date of coming into operation of FA 2008 s 25, on the construction or refurbishment of a qualifying specialist palliative care unit. The allowances apply to expenditure on units providing day patient, out-patient and overnight palliative care. Entitlement to allowances is subject to certain conditions including conditions regarding the treatment of public patients. The annual writing down allowance is 15% of the qualifying expenditure. FA 2008 s 25 comes into operation on such day or days as the Minister for Finance may by order or orders appoint and different days may be appointed for different purposes or different provisions.

For expenditure to qualify, the development of a facility must have prior approval from the Health Service Executive (HSE), with the consent of the Minister for Health and Children, as being in line with national development plans and needs assessments for palliative care facilities. A qualifying facility must also have a minimum of twenty in-patient palliative care beds. The HSE must certify, on an annual basis for fifteen years from the time of first use, that the facility has satisfied the terms and conditions in the legislation. A claw-back of the allowances will apply if a facility is sold or ceases to be used for the purposes of palliative care during this period.

Where the relevant interest in relation to capital expenditure incurred on the construction of a building or structure in use for the purposes of a trade consisting of the operation or management of a qualifying specialist palliative care unit (see (m) in **5.401.1**) is held by—

(a) a company,

(b) the trustees of a trust,

(c) an individual who is involved in the operation or management of the unit concerned either as an employee or director or in any other capacity, or

(d) a property developer (within the meaning of TCA 1997, s 843A – see **5.607.4**) or a person who is connected with the property developer, in the case where either of such persons incurred the capital expenditure on the construction of that building or structure, or such expenditure was incurred by any other person connected with (see **2.3**) the property developer,

that building or structure will not, as regards a claim for any industrial building allowance by any such person, be regarded as an industrial building or structure irrespective of whether that relevant interest is held by the person referred to in paragraph (a), (b), (c) or (d), as the case may be, in a sole capacity or jointly or in partnership with another person or persons (TCA 1997, s 268(1E)).

A *qualifying specialist palliative care unit* is a building or structure—

(a) which is a hospital, hospice (within the meaning of section 47 (as amended by section 16 of the Public Health (Tobacco)(Amendment) Act 2004) of the Public Health (Tobacco) Act 2002) or similar facility which has palliative care as its main activity,

(b) which, before entering into a legal commitment for its design, commissioning, construction or refurbishment, is approved by the Health Service Executive, with the consent of the Minister for Health and Children, as being in accordance with national development plans or national needs assessments for palliative care facilities,

(c) which has the capacity to provide

    (i) day-patient and out-patient palliative care services, and

    (ii) palliative care accommodation on an overnight basis of not less than 20 in-patient beds,

(d) in respect of which relevant data is provided to the Health Service Executive, for onward transmission to the Minister for Health and Children and the Minister for Finance, in relation to

    (i) the amount of the capital expenditure actually incurred on the construction or refurbishment of the unit,

    (ii) the amount, if any, of such expenditure which has been or is to be met directly or indirectly by the State or by any other person by way of grant or other financial assistance,

    (iii) the number and nature of the investors that are investing in the unit,

    (iv) the amount to be invested by each investor, and

    (v) the nature of the structures which are being put in place to facilitate the investment in the unit, together with such other information as may be specified by the Minister for Finance, in consultation with the Minister for Health and Children, as being of assistance in evaluating the costs, including but not limited to exchequer costs, and the benefits arising from the operation of tax relief by way of industrial building allowances for qualifying specialist palliative care units,

(e) in relation to which an undertaking is given to the Health Service Executive—

    (i) to make available annually, for the palliative care of persons who have been awaiting day-patient, in-patient or out-patient palliative care services as public patients, not less than 20% of its capacity, subject to service requirements to be specified by the Health Service Executive in advance and to the proviso that the Health Service Executive is not thereby required to take up all or any part of the capacity made available to the Health Service Executive by the unit, and

    (ii)   in relation to the fees to be charged in respect of the palliative care afforded to any such person, that such fees may not be more than 90% of the fees which would be charged in respect of similar palliative care afforded to a person who has private medical insurance, and

(f)   in respect of which the Health Service Executive, in consultation with the Minister for Health and Children and with the consent of the Minister for Finance, gives an annual certificate in writing during the period of

    (i)   15 years beginning with the time when the unit was first used, or

    (ii)   where capital expenditure on the refurbishment of the unit is incurred, 15 years beginning with the time when the unit was first used subsequent to the incurring of that expenditure, stating that it is satisfied that the unit complies with the conditions mentioned in paragraphs (a) to (e) (TCA 1997, s 268(2BA)).

In the above definition, *palliative care* means the active total care of patients who suffer from illnesses or diseases which are active, progressive and advanced in nature and which are no longer curable by means of the administration of existing or available medical treatments.

A qualifying specialist palliative care unit includes any part of the unit which consists of rooms used exclusively for the assessment, treatment or care of patients. It does not, however, include any part of the unit which consists of consultants' rooms or offices, or any part of the unit in which a majority of the persons being maintained are being treated for acute illnesses (TCA 1997, s 268(2BB)).

5.401.11 Buildings situated abroad

In respect of expenditure incurred prior to 23 April 1996, a building did not have to be situated in Ireland in order to qualify as an industrial building. Industrial building allowances could be claimed in respect of capital expenditure on buildings or structures in use for a qualifying trade carried on wholly or partly in another country. For example, capital expenditure incurred by an Irish resident manufacturing company on the construction of a warehouse in Northern Ireland for the purpose of storing goods prior to their sale qualified for the allowances.

Expenditure incurred by a company on or after 23 April 1996, on the construction of, or on the acquisition of the "relevant interest" (see **5.403**) in, a building or structure which is not situated in the State is treated as not being expenditure on an industrial building or structure unless:

(a)   the company had entered into a binding contract in writing for the acquisition of the site for the building or structure or had entered into an agreement in writing in relation to an option to acquire the site on or before 23 April 1996; and

(b)   the company had entered into a binding contract in writing for the construction of the building or structure on or before 1 July 1996; and

(c)   the construction of the building or structure had commenced on or before 1 July 1996 and had been completed before 30 September 1998; and

(d)   the building or structure is to be constructed or is being constructed and will be used for the purposes of a trade the profits or gains from which are taxable in the State (TCA 1997, s 268(5)).

5.401.12 Non-qualifying buildings

Certain types of building are specifically disqualified from being industrial buildings or structures. Even if used for the purposes of a qualifying trade or undertaking, no allowances may be claimed for any building or structure in use as:

(a)   a dwelling house (except in the case of a qualifying holiday cottage referred to in TCA 1997, s 268(3) (see **5.401.1**) or a qualifying residential unit referred to in TCA 1997, s 268(3A) (see **5.401.5**));

(b)   a retail shop;

(c)   a showroom; or

(d)   an office;

or for any purpose ancillary to the purposes of any of those kinds of buildings or structures. A retail shop includes any premises of a similar character where retail trade or business, including repair work, is carried on (TCA 1997, s 268(7)(a)). In *Dolton Bournes & Dolton Ltd v Osmond* [1955] 1 WLR 62, it was held that premises to which only trade customers, and not the general public, had access was not a retail shop.

In *Sarsfield v Dixons Group plc* and related appeals, it was held in the Court of Appeal (9 July 1998) that a warehouse in use for a purpose ancillary to the purposes of a retail shop did not qualify for industrial building allowances. The warehouse had been used, prior to May 1981, as a storage and distribution depot for goods prior to their delivery to retail shops and did not qualify for industrial building allowances. After May 1981, the business concerned was transferred to another group company which carried on the business of a transport undertaking (a qualifying purpose for UK industrial building allowances) but at the same time for the purpose of receiving, storing and delivering goods purchased by other group companies for sale from their retail shops. The Chancery Division [1997] STC 283) had held that the warehouse was not excluded from the meaning of an industrial building even if used for a purpose ancillary to the use of retail shops. The Court of Appeal, however, held that the warehouse was so excluded even where, as in this case, it was used in the carrying on of a separate independent undertaking.

As regards (d), the meaning of "office" was considered in the Scottish case *IRC v Lambhill Ironworks Ltd* 31 TC 393. In that case, the part of a building containing the drawing office of a company carrying on business as structural steel engineers was held to be an industrial building or structure, and was not disqualified on the grounds of being an office. On the facts of the case, the Court of Session concluded that the drawing office was much more ancillary to the purposes of the industrial buildings in which the assembly and erecting operations were carried on than it was to the purposes of the managerial office. In practice, drawing offices and similar office type facilities directly related or ancillary to the main qualifying industrial activity are accepted as being industrial buildings. Where part of a building or structure qualifies as an industrial building and another part does not so qualify, the whole of that building or structure will nevertheless qualify if the cost of construction of the non-qualifying part does not exceed 10% of the total capital expenditure incurred on the construction of the whole building (TCA 1997, s 268(8)). For example, if the cost of construction of a factory building, including offices and showrooms, is €1.3m, the full amount of the expenditure will qualify for industrial building allowances if the cost of the offices and showrooms does not exceed €130,000. If the cost of the offices and showrooms was, say, €150,000, industrial building allowances would be available in respect of €1,150,000, the amount attributable to the qualifying part only.

For the purposes of the 10% test, if a company has incurred expenditure on more than one building, it is necessary to look at each building separately. For example, if a factory comprises two or more buildings, and if offices and showrooms are constructed separately from the factory units, industrial building allowances will not be available in respect of the separate non-qualifying parts whether or not their cost is less than 10% of the entire buildings cost.

In *Abbott Laboratories Ltd v Carmody* 44 TC 569, the company incurred expenditure on the construction of a factory for the manufacture of pharmaceutical products. The factory comprised four blocks, one being an administrative block, and the blocks were connected by roads. All the blocks were served by a common heating system by means of interconnecting pipes. The administrative block, with which the case was concerned, was physically connected to the pharmaceutical block by a covered passageway.

The Special Commissioners held that the relevant legislation was not intended to apply to an extensive factory site to enable it to be treated as one unit for capital allowances purposes. The High Court disagreed and sent the case back to the Commissioners for reconsideration on the footing that the layout of the buildings was not in law incapable of being an industrial building or structure. The Commissioners again ruled that the administrative block did not qualify under the 10% test as it was not sufficiently physically integrated with the other structural units within the layout. The various units were considered to be separate entities although sharing common facilities. This decision was then approved by the High Court. It is thought likely that this decision would be followed in similar circumstances in Ireland.

A practical point which occasionally arises in relation to the 10% test concerns the correct approach to be taken where the cumulative expenditure on offices and other non-qualifying parts of an industrial building alternately fall below and above the 10% level. TCA 1997, s 268 does not, in relation to the 10% test, provide clear guidance on this point. The only workable interpretation of this aspect of the legislation is to consider the matter separately for each accounting period in which the position arises.

For example, if at the end of its accounting year to 31 December 2001 a company had incurred a total of €90,000 in respect of offices comprised in a factory building the total cost of which is €950,000, the entire expenditure qualifies for industrial building allowances in that accounting period. Assuming the rate of annual allowance for the entire expenditure is 4%, the annual allowance for the year ended 31 December 2001 is €38,000. In the following year to 31 December 2002, the company incurs €120,000 on the building, €20,000 in respect of offices. The expenditure on the offices now totals €110,000 out of a total of €1,070,000, ie, 10.28% so that the expenditure on the offices does not qualify. This means that of the expenditure of €120,000 for the year ended 31 December 2002, an annual allowance of 4% is available in respect of expenditure of €100,000, ie, €4,000. There would be no question of disallowing the cumulative office expenditure of €110,000 leading to a revamping of industrial building allowances claims for all relevant previous periods.

References in the industrial building allowances legislation to a building or structure are to be construed as including references to a part of a building or structure, except where the reference is comprised in a reference to the whole of a building or structure (TCA 1997, s 320(2)). Capital expenditure on the construction of part of a building qualifies for industrial building allowances if the whole building, or the part on which the expenditure is incurred, is an industrial building within the definition in TCA 1997, s 268(1). Thus, capital expenditure on altering or extending an existing building will itself qualify for industrial building allowances. Furthermore, expenditure on the same building incurred at different times is treated separately for the purposes of the allowances and a separate writing off life applies to each such item of expenditure (see **5.402**).

5.401.13 Anti-avoidance: room ownership schemes

TCA 1997, s 409 denies capital allowances in cases where persons, usually in a partnership, invest in a hotel under an arrangement whereby their investment is eventually transmuted into a self-contained room or suite; while the investment would initially be part of a hotel, it may ultimately (when the partnership comes to an end) be privately used or rented.

TCA 1997, s 409(4) provides that no initial or annual industrial building allowance will be made in respect of a hotel investment by a hotel partnership where, in connection with any such investment, there exists a room ownership scheme. A *room ownership scheme* exists where, at the time a hotel investment is made by a hotel partnership, there is an agreement, arrangement, understanding, promise or undertaking (whether express or implied and whether or not enforceable or intended to be enforceable by legal proceedings), under or by virtue of which any member of the partnership, or a person connected (within the meaning of TCA 1997, s 10 – see **2.3**) with that member, may:

(a)   acquire on preferential terms an interest in; or

(b)   retain for use other than for the purposes of the trade of hotel-keeping;

any room or rooms in, or any particular part of, the building or structure which is the subject of the hotel investment.

A hotel investment made by one or more than one member of a hotel partnership is deemed to be made by the hotel partnership. A *hotel investment* means capital expenditure incurred either on the construction of, or the acquisition of a relevant interest in, a building or structure which falls to be regarded as an industrial building or structure within the meaning of TCA 1997, s 268(1)(d), other than a building or structure in use as a holiday camp or as a holiday cottage.

A *hotel partnership* includes any syndicate, group or pool of persons, whether or not a partnership, through or by means of which a hotel investment is made. A *member*, in relation to a hotel partnership, includes every person who participates in that partnership or who has contributed capital, directly or indirectly, to that partnership.

Preferential terms referred to above means terms under which an interest is acquired for a consideration which, at the time of the acquisition, is or may be other than its market value. *Market value* means the price which the interest might reasonably be expected to fetch on a sale in the open market. The acquisition of the interest at less than market value would have been facilitated by the availability of capital allowances.

5.402   General scheme of industrial building allowances

Qualifying expenditure on an industrial building or structure is written off for tax purposes over a specified period, the length of which depends on the type of building or structure involved and the date on which the expenditure is incurred. There are two types of allowance available: an initial allowance called "industrial building allowance" (IBA) and an industrial building annual allowance (IBAA), referred to as a writing down allowance; TCA 1997, s 321(6)(a) provides that the term "writing down allowance", as regards any reference which is partly to a year of assessment before 1976/77, includes an annual allowance. In addition, increased writing down allowances (free depreciation) may be claimed for qualifying expenditure on certain industrial buildings except, in the case of expenditure incurred after 31 March 1988, where an initial allowance has been made in respect of the same expenditure (see **5.407.3**).

An industrial building initial allowance may be claimed by a company which incurs qualifying expenditure on the construction of the building or structure in the circumstances outlined in **5.405**. The company which incurred the expenditure on the building is also entitled to the annual writing down allowances, and to claim any increased allowances that may be available, if it continues to hold the "relevant interest" in relation to that expenditure. Writing down allowances are made to a company for an accounting period where it holds the relevant interest in relation to the expenditure at the end of that period. No writing down allowance is, however, given in respect of expenditure incurred after 31 March 1989 for a year of assessment or accounting period if an initial allowance is made for the same period.

The "relevant interest" is the particular interest (eg, freehold, leasehold etc) which the person who incurred the expenditure held in the building or structure in question at the time that expenditure was incurred (see also **5.403**).

Annual writing down allowances for industrial buildings are made on a straight-line basis, ie, at the rate which would write off the qualifying expenditure evenly over a specified writing down period, assuming no initial allowances or free depreciation are claimed. The writing down period for the construction expenditure on any building begins on the date the building is first used for any purpose and ends 10, 25 or 50 years later, depending on the kind of building or structure involved and the date of the expenditure (see **5.414**). For example, capital expenditure incurred in 1984 on a factory building first put into use on 1 March 1997 attracts a writing down allowance of 4% which writes off one twenty-fifth of the expenditure each year over a period of 25 years from 1 March 1997 to 28 February 2022. For an accounting period of less than one year, the fraction used is proportionately reduced.

In general, an initial allowance is made to the person who actually incurred the expenditure on construction, while writing down allowances and any balancing allowances or charges are related to that expenditure. However, where any building or structure is sold by a person who has incurred expenditure on its construction before the building has been used for any purpose, the construction expenditure incurred before the sale is deemed to have been incurred by the person purchasing the relevant interest in the building (see **5.408**).

In the event of a sale of the relevant interest in an industrial building (or on the happening of certain other events) before the end of its specified writing down period, a balancing allowance is made for any unrelieved capital expenditure (after crediting any sale etc proceeds) or a balancing charge is made if the sale or other proceeds exceed the unrelieved expenditure (see **5.409**). No balancing charge can be made for any sale or other event occurring after the end of the writing down period of any industrial building.

A person who purchases the relevant interest in a building or structure during its writing down period becomes entitled to claim writing down allowances for the remainder of that period, provided the building or structure continues to qualify as an industrial building or structure. However, the rate of the writing down allowance and the amount of the expenditure to which it is applied will be revised, as explained in **5.410.2**.

Capital expenditure on the construction of an industrial building may be incurred in one or more accounting periods. Alternatively, further capital expenditure for which industrial building allowances are available may be incurred on the alteration, improvement, or extension of an existing industrial building, or may be incurred on another type of building for the purposes of converting it for use in a qualifying trade. In any such case, TCA 1997, s 320(2) requires the rules relating to the industrial building initial allowances to be applied by construing any reference to a building or structure as if it included a reference to a part of any building or structure. Similarly, TCA 1997, s 320(2) permits the writing down allowances and balancing allowances or charges to be computed separately for expenditure on different parts of the same building.

It follows that initial and writing down allowances will, where necessary, have to be computed separately for qualifying expenditure incurred in different accounting periods, even where that expenditure relates to the same building or structure. The rules relating to the writing down period for industrial buildings in each qualifying trade category are applied separately to the qualifying expenditure incurred in each accounting period. In the event that different rates of allowances (and writing down periods) apply, depending on whether the expenditure has been incurred before or after a given date, the computations must be made and the industrial buildings records kept accordingly.

For the calculation of any balancing allowance or charge on a sale or other event involving an industrial building the expenditure on which has been incurred at different dates, see **5.412**.

Since the definition of an industrial building has regard to the use to which the building or structure is being put at any relevant time, it is possible for a building that has qualified for capital allowances to cease to be used as an industrial building. In any such event, no writing down allowances are given for any such periods of "non-industrial" use, nor may a balancing allowance be obtained or a balancing charge be made on a sale or other balancing adjustment event occurring after the building has so ceased to be used. While no initial allowance can be claimed unless the building is used for a qualifying trade or undertaking when it is first put into use, writing down allowances may be obtained at a later date if the building becomes an industrial building by being used for a qualifying trade.

The industrial building allowances, and any balancing allowance or charge arising on a sale or other event, are also available, subject to certain conditions, to a company which leases a qualifying building. The increased writing down allowance is not, however, available to the lessor of the industrial buildings; free depreciation is available only to a company which incurs the qualifying expenditure on a building that is to be occupied for its own trade. For the treatment of capital allowances, and balancing allowances and charges, for lessors of industrial buildings, see **5.5**.

5.403 Meaning of "relevant interest"

A company which incurs capital expenditure on a building may hold the freehold interest in the land on which the building is constructed or may hold some form of leasehold interest in the land. It may hold the leasehold interest that was created directly out of the freehold (the head lease) or it may be entitled to an inferior lease or sublease granted out of a superior leasehold interest which may or may not be the head lease. The company may be the occupier of the land (including any buildings on the land) or it may hold its particular interest subject to a lease or sublease granted to another party who either occupies the land or holds that sublease subject to an inferior sublease. In short, it is possible for the land to be occupied by the freeholder or there may be a chain of leases and subleases between the freeholder and the person occupying the land.

The entitlement to the industrial building writing down allowances and balancing allowances, and the liability to any balancing charge, in respect of any capital expenditure always follows the person holding the relevant interest in relation to that expenditure, whether or not that relevant interest has changed hands since the expenditure was incurred. The meaning of the term "relevant interest" is therefore obviously of some importance. While it refers to a particular interest in a building (and in the land), it is expressed as being "in relation to" expenditure on the building.

TCA 1997, s 269(1) defines the *relevant interest*, in relation to any expenditure incurred on the construction of a building or structure, as the interest in that building or structure to which the person who incurred the expenditure was entitled when he incurred it. The definition applies whether or not the building in question is being constructed for use in a type of trade or undertaking qualifying for industrial building allowances. Even if a building is used for other purposes for some years after its construction, the person holding the relevant interest in relation to any qualifying construction expenditure is entitled to the industrial building writing down allowances in any later year (within the writing down period for the expenditure) if the building is subsequently used for a qualifying trade or undertaking.

Example 5.403.1

In the year 2002, Monarch Ltd incurred capital expenditure of €670,000 on the construction of a building on land in which interests at that time were held as follows:

Holder of interest	Interest
Albion Ltd	Freehold
Liffey Ltd	subject to 999 years lease (head lease)
Monarch Ltd	subject to 99 year sublease

The relevant interest in relation to the €670,000 expenditure is the 99 year sublease held by Monarch Ltd in 2002. Monarch Ltd assigns this sublease to McPherson Ltd in 2005 and McPherson Ltd thereby becomes the holder of the relevant interest and is entitled to the industrial building writing down allowances from that year onwards as long as the building is used for a qualifying trade or undertaking.

In relation to the meaning of the "relevant interest", TCA 1997, s 269(2), (3) also provide that:

(a)   the relevant interest in relation to any expenditure does not cease to be the relevant interest where a lease or other inferior interest is created out of it;

(b)   if a person is entitled to two or more interests in a building or structure at the time he incurs the construction expenditure, the relevant interest is the interest that is reversionary on all the other interests; and

(c)   where the relevant interest is a leasehold interest, and it is extinguished

>   (i)   by surrender, or

>   (ii)   through the acquisition, by the person entitled to the relevant interest, of the interest which is reversionary on that interest,

the interest into which that leasehold interest merges thereupon becomes the relevant interest.

Example 5.403.2

The facts are as in Example **5.403.1** but in 2008 McPherson Ltd creates a further sublease for 35 years in favour of Schofield Ltd so that the 99 year lease of McPherson Ltd becomes subject to this 35 year sublease. Schofield Ltd uses the building as a factory in its manufacturing trade but in 2009 incurs further capital expenditure €230,000 on alterations and improvements to the building.

The creation of the 35 year sublease in favour of Schofield Ltd does not cause the 99 year lease of McPherson Ltd to cease to be the relevant interest in relation to the year 2002 expenditure of €670,000 so that McPherson Ltd continues to be entitled to the writing down allowances in respect of that expenditure (so long as it holds the 99 year lease). These allowances are given against the Schedule D Case V income of McPherson Ltd from the sublease to Schofield Ltd (see **5.505**).

The relevant interest in relation to the expenditure of €230,000 incurred in 2009 is the 35 year sublease that was held by Schofield Ltd at the time it incurred that expenditure. That company is therefore the person entitled to the industrial building allowances on the expenditure of €230,000 (but not on the €670,000) so long as it retains this interest in the land and buildings, assuming the buildings continue to be used for a qualifying purpose.

Example 5.403.3

The facts are as in Example **5.403.2** except that in the year 2008 the 35 year sublease is granted to Liffey Ltd (instead of to Schofield Ltd). Liffey Ltd incurs the capital expenditure of €230,000 in 2009 in altering the building for use in its manufacturing trade. The interests in the building are now held as follows:

Holder of interest	*Interest*
Albion Ltd	freehold, subject to
Liffey Ltd	999 year head lease, subject to
McPherson Ltd	99 year sublease, subject to
Liffey Ltd	35 year sublease

Since Liffey Ltd holds both the 999 year head lease and the 35 year sublease when it incurs the expenditure of €230,000 in 2009, the relevant interest in relation to that expenditure is the 999 year head lease, ie, the interest that is reversionary on (ie, superior to) the interests below it in the chain. This does not affect the relevant interest in relation to the year 2002 expenditure of €670,000 so that McPherson Ltd as the holder of the 99 year sublease remains the person entitled to the writing down allowances on this expenditure so long as Liffey Ltd (or any subsequent holder of the 35 year sublease) continues to use the building for a qualifying purpose.

Example 5.403.4

The facts are as in Example **5.403.3** but in the year 2011 McPherson Ltd surrenders its 99 year sublease to Liffey Ltd for a suitable consideration so that it and the 35 year sublease are both extinguished by being merged into the 999 year head lease held by Liffey Ltd.

Liffey Ltd is now the person holding the relevant interest in relation to the year 2002 expenditure of €670,000 which had previously attached to the 99 year sublease. It therefore becomes entitled to the writing down allowances on this expenditure as well as to the allowances on the year 2009 expenditure of €230,000.

5.404 Qualifying expenditure

Industrial building initial, writing down and balancing allowances are all made by reference to the capital expenditure incurred on the construction of an industrial building (as defined in **5.401.1**). In order to qualify for the allowances, the expenditure must be on the construction of the building; any expenditure incurred on the acquisition of, or of rights in or over, any land is specifically excluded and does not qualify (TCA 1997, s 270(2)(a)). However, it is accepted that the cost of work done on the site by way of levelling, cutting or otherwise preparing the land for the construction of the building is part of the cost of that construction. Capital expenditure on constructing factory roads, walls, protective mounds, fencing etc within a factory site is also qualifying expenditure.

Expenditure incurred on the construction of a building or structure includes expenditure on the refurbishment of the building or structure (TCA 1997, s 270(2)). *Refurbishment* means any work of construction, reconstruction, repair or renewal, including the provision of water, sewerage or heating facilities carried out in the course of repair or restoration, or maintenance in the nature of repair or restoration, of a building or structure.

Other types of expenditure which must be excluded from the industrial building allowance computation are expenditure on the provision of machinery or plant, or on any asset treated as machinery or plant, and any expenditure on which a scientific research or a mine development allowance may be claimed (TCA 1997, s 270(2)(b), (c)). On the other hand, any capital expenditure incurred on preparing, cutting, tunnelling or levelling land in preparing that land to be a site for the installation of machinery or plant is treated as expenditure on a building or structure (TCA 1997, s 268(4)). The expenditure will therefore qualify for industrial building allowances if the machinery or plant is used for one of the qualifying purposes described in **5.401.1**. No industrial building allowances may, however, be claimed on any expenditure that is deductible in computing Case I trading income, eg, expenses of a revenue nature in repairing a building (TCA 1997, s 316(1)(a)).

The capital expenditure on which industrial building allowances are computed excludes any part of the expenditure that has been, or is to be, met directly or indirectly by the State, by any board established by statute or by any public or local authority or, since 6 May 1993, by any person other than the person who incurred the expenditure in question (TCA 1997, s 317(2)). Accordingly, any capital grants received or receivable from such bodies as the Industrial Development Authority, Shannon Free-Airport Development Co Ltd, Údarás na Gaeltachta, the National Tourism Development Authority, as well as from public and local authorities, or any third party, must be deducted so that only the capital expenditure net of amounts so deducted qualifies for allowances. (See also **5.401.1** in relation to effect of grant assistance for hotel buildings.)

Restriction of amount of qualifying expenditure for certain categories

For certain categories of buildings or structures, the amount of capital expenditure on the construction or refurbishment which qualifies for industrial buildings allowances is restricted. The buildings or structures affected, listed in TCA 1997, s 270(4)(a)-(i), are as follows:

(a)   a building or structure in use for the purpose of the trade of hotel-keeping or which, by virtue of TCA 1997, s 268(3) is deemed to be in use for that purpose (registered holiday camp or holiday cottage (TCA 1997, s 268(1)(d) – see **5.401.1**);

(b)   a building or structure in use for the purposes of a trade consisting of the management of a sport-injury clinic (TCA 1997, s 268(1)(k) – see **5.401.8**);

(c)   a multi-storey car park (TCA 1997, s 344 – see **5.605**);

(d)   an industrial building within a qualifying area for the purposes of the 1998 Scheme (TCA 1997, s 372C – see **6.102**) or a commercial premises within that area (TCA 1997, s 372D – see **6.103**);

(e)   an industrial building within a qualifying area for the purposes of the Rural Areas Scheme (TCA 1997, s 372M – see **6.202**) or a commercial premises within that area (TCA 1997, s 372N – see **6.203**);

(f)   a qualifying park and ride facility (TCA 1997, s 372U – see **6.401** and **6.402**) or a qualifying commercial premises on the site of a park and ride facility (TCA 1997, s 372W – see **6.403**);

(g)   an industrial building within the site of a qualifying area for the purposes of the Town Renewal Scheme (TCA 1997, s 372AC – see **6.302**) or a commercial premises within that area (TCA 1997, s 372AD – see **6.303**);

(h)   a qualifying building used for third level education (TCA 1997, s 843 – see **5.606**); and

(i)   a qualifying residential unit treated as a building or structure used in a trade of operating or managing a registered nursing home (TCA 1997, s 268(3A) – see **5.401.5**).

Subject to TCA 1997, s 270(6) and (7) (see below) (and to TCA 1997, s 270(8) in the case of a qualifying residential unit - see **5.401.5**), the amount of capital expenditure or, as the case may be, qualifying expenditure on the construction or refurbishment of a building or structure in any of the above categories, treated as incurred for the purposes of the making of capital allowances or the charging of any balancing charges, is to be reduced:

(a)   in the case of expenditure incurred in—

(i)   where TCA 1997, s 270(4)(i) applies (see (i) above), the period from 25 March 2007 to 31 December 2007, and

(ii)   in any other case, the period 1 January 2007 to 31 December 2007,

to 75%, and

(b)   in the case of expenditure incurred in the period 1 January 2008 to 31 July 2008, to 50%,

of the amount which would otherwise be so treated (TCA 1997, s 270(5)).

TCA 1997, s 270(7) provides for certification by the relevant local authority where transitional relief for expenditure incurred after 31 December 2006 is sought in the cases of certain projects. The reliefs affected are those in respect of hotels, holiday camps and holiday cottages, the 1998 urban renewal scheme (except in relation to premises fronting on to a qualifying street – see **6.101.3**), the rural renewal scheme and the town renewal scheme. The relevant local authority is required to certify that it is satisfied that the 15% condition relating to construction (or construction and refurbishment in certain cases) has been met by 31 December 2006, the amount of capital expenditure incurred on construction or refurbishment incurred by 31 December 2006, and the projected amount of the balance of the capital expenditure to be incurred on construction or refurbishment.

TCA 1997, s 270(7) applies to a building or structure to which TCA 1997, s 270(4)(a), (d) (other than a qualifying premises which fronts on to a qualifying street within the meaning of TCA 1997, s 372A), (e) or (g) applies (ie, the categories mentioned in the preceding paragraph) and in relation to which building or structure it must be shown that the condition in:

(i)   in the case of a hotel, holiday camp or holiday cottage—

    (I)   TCA 1997, s 268(13)(c)(ii)(I) (see **5.401.1** – to the effect that work to the value of not less 15% of the actual construction or refurbishment costs of a holiday cottage was carried out on or before 31 December 2006), or

    (II)   as the case may be, 272(9)(b)(i) (see **5.406**) and 274(1B)(b)(i) (see **5.409.1**) (in both cases, that work to the value of not less than 15% of the actual construction or refurbishment costs of the building or structure was carried out on or before 31 December 2006),

(ii)   in the case of the 1998 urban renewal scheme, TCA 1997, s 372A(3)(a) (see **6.101.1** – to the effect that work to the value of not less 15% of the actual construction or refurbishment costs of the building or structure, or part of the building or structure, was carried out on or before 31 December 2006),

(iii)   in the case of the rural renewal scheme, TCA 1997, s 372L(3)(a) (see **6.201.1** – to the effect that work to the value of not less 15% of the actual construction or refurbishment costs of the building or structure was carried out on or before 31 December 2006), or

(iv)   in the case of the town renewal scheme, TCA 1997, s 372AA(3)(a) (see **6.301.1** – to the effect that work to the value of not less 15% of the actual construction or refurbishment costs of the building or structure was carried out on or before 31 December 2006),

was satisfied before 31 December 2006 (TCA 1997, s 270(7)(a)).

The above conditions will be regarded as satisfied only:

(a)   where (ii) applies, the relevant local authority (within the meaning of TCA 1997, s 372A – see **6.101.2**), and

(b)   in any other case, the local authority (within the meaning of the Local Government Act 2001)

in whose administrative area the building or structure is situated gives a certificate in writing on or before 30 March 2007 to the person constructing or refurbishing the building or structure stating:

(i) that it is satisfied that work to the value of not less than 15% of the actual construction or refurbishment costs of the building or structure involved was carried out on or before 31 December 2006;

(ii) the actual amount of the capital expenditure incurred on the construction or refurbishment of the building or structure by 31 December 2006; and

(iii) the projected amount of the balance of the capital expenditure (other than that referred to in (ii)), which is to be incurred on the construction or refurbishment of the building or structure (TCA 1997, s 270(7)(b)).

An application for a certificate must be made on or before 31 January 2007 by the person who is constructing or refurbishing the building or structure. In considering whether to give a certificate, the local authority is to have regard to guidelines in relation to the giving of such certificates issued by the Department of the Environment, Heritage and Local Government.

Where TCA 1997, s 270(7) applies, the amount of capital expenditure referred to in TCA 1997, s 270(4) (see above) which is to be treated as incurred in the period 1 January 2007 to 31 July 2008 for the purposes of making allowances and charges may not exceed the amount certified by the local authority in relation to the building or structure (TCA 1997, s 270(7)(c)).

The provisions of TCA 1997, s 270(7) are to apply in priority to the application of the provisions of TCA 1997, s 270(5), (6) (see above) and where they apply to reduce the amount of capital expenditure to be treated as incurred in the period 1 January 2007 to 31 July 2008, such reduction is to be made in relation to expenditure incurred in the period 1 January 2008 to 31 July 2008 in priority to the period 1 January 2007 to 31 December 2007 (TCA 1997, s 270(7)(d)).

The above-described treatment (ie, as provided for by TCA 1997, s 270(4), (5) and, as the case may be, (7)) is modified in a case where TCA 1997, s 279 (buildings purchased unused – see **5.408**) applies. In relation to the above categories of buildings, that section applies as if—

(a) in TCA 1997, s 279(1) the definition of the "net price paid" (see **5.408.4**) were an amount represented by the formula:

$$B \times \frac{C}{D + E}$$

where—

B is the amount paid by the purchaser of the relevant interest in the building or structure;

C is the amount of the expenditure actually incurred on the construction of the building or structure as reduced in accordance with TCA 1997, s 270(5) and, as the case may be, (7) (as above);

D is the amount of the expenditure actually incurred on the construction of the building or structure; and

E is the amount of any expenditure actually incurred but disallowed by virtue of TCA 1997, s 270(2) (expenditure on the acquisition of rights in or over land etc – see above);

(b) TCA s 279(2)(b) (see **5.408.2**) were to be read so as to mean that the person who buys the relevant interest is deemed to have incurred expenditure on the construction of the building or structure equal to the lesser of—

   (i) that expenditure reduced in accordance with TCA 1997, s 270(5) and, as the case may be, (7) (as above), and

   (ii) the net price paid (as defined in TCA 1997, s 279(1) but as applied by the formula in (a) above) by that person for that interest, and

(c) TCA 1997, s 279(3) (see **5.408.3**) were to be read so as to mean that the purchaser is deemed to have incurred capital expenditure on the construction of the building or structure of an amount equal to the amount in (ii) above (and not by reference to the lesser of the amounts in (i) and (ii) above) (TCA 1997, s 270(6)).

Date expenditure incurred

Expenditure is treated as incurred when the amount in question becomes payable (TCA 1997, s 316(2)), but any expenditure incurred by a person about to carry on a trade is treated as being incurred on the day trading commences (TCA 1997, s 316(3)). This rule is subject to TCA s 316(2A) and (2B).

For the purposes only of determining, in relation to a claim for capital allowances for industrial buildings, whether and to what extent capital expenditure incurred on the construction or a building or structure in use for the purposes of the trade of hotel-keeping or deemed to be in use for such a purpose (registered holiday camp or holiday cottage is or is not incurred on or before 31 July 2008, only such an amount of that expenditure as is properly attributable to work done on the construction or refurbishment of the building or structure actually carried out on or before 31 July 2008 is (notwithstanding the general rule regarding the time any capital expenditure is to be treated as incurred) to be treated as having been incurred on or before that time (TCA 1997, s 316(2A)). This provision is relevant in relation to hotels and holiday camps (rate of writing down allowances – see **5.406**) and in relation to holiday cottages (extension of qualifying expenditure date to 31 July 2008 in certain circumstances – see **5.401.1**).

For the purposes of determining, in relation to a claim for capital allowances, whether and to what extent capital expenditure incurred on the construction or refurbishment of a building or structure referred to in TCA 1997, s 270(4)(a), (b), (c), (d), (e), (f), (g), (h) or (i) (see above – restriction of amount of qualifying expenditure) is or is not incurred in:

(a) (i) where TCA 1997, s 270(4)(i) applies (qualifying residential unit – see above), the period from 1 January 2006 to 24 March 2007, and

   (ii) in any other case, the period 1 January 2006 to 31 December 2006,

(b) (i) where TCA 1997, s 270(4)(i) applies (qualifying residential unit), the period from 25 March 2007 to 31 December 2007, and

   (ii) in any other case, the period 1 January 2007 to 31 December 2007,

(c) the period 1 January 2008 to 31 July 2008, or

(d) where TCA 1997, s 270(8) applies in relation to a qualifying residential unit (see **5.401.5**), the period 1 May 2007 to 30 April 2010,

only the amount of that expenditure as is properly attributable to work on the construction or refurbishment of the building or structure actually carried out in such a period is (notwithstanding the general rule regarding the time any capital expenditure is to be treated as incurred) to be treated as having been incurred in the period (TCA 1997, s 316(2B)).

Commencement dates for categories of expenditure

Capital allowances for industrial buildings were first introduced by the Finance (Miscellaneous Provisions) Act 1956 (now consolidated in TCA 1997). No industrial building allowances have at any time been available for any capital expenditure incurred before 30 September 1956. Since industrial building allowances were only granted with effect from later dates for certain of the trade categories now qualifying for allowances, the question of writing down allowances and balancing allowances or charges only arises for buildings in these categories where the relevant expenditure has been incurred on or after the commencement date for allowances in the trade concerned. The earliest expenditure dates for the relevant trade categories are as follows:

Trade category	*No allowances on expenditure before:*
Mill, factory or similar premises	30 September 1956
Laboratory for mineral analysis	25 January 1984
Dock undertaking	6 April 1959
Market gardening	7 April 1964
Hotel keeping:	
general	30 September 1956
holiday camps	6 April 1960
holiday cottages	1 July 1968
guest house or holiday hostel	3 February 2005
caravan and camping sites	1 January 2008
Intensive production of livestock, poultry, eggs	6 April 1971
Buildings for recreation etc of employees (all above trades)	6 April 1969
Multi-storey car parks (see **5.605**)	29 January 1981
Airport buildings and structures (see **5.401.4**):	
airport runways and aprons	24 April 1992
other airport buildings and structures	27 March 1998
Nursing home	3 December 1997
Private convalescent home (see **5.401.6**)	2 December 1998
Qualifying hospitals (see **5.401.7**)	15 May 2002
Qualifying mental health centre (see **5.401.9**)	23 January 2007
Qualifying specialist palliative care unit (see **5.401.10**)	Date(s) of Ministerial order(s)

5.405 Initial allowances

5.405.1 General

In general, the initial allowance of 50% ceased to be available for capital expenditure on industrial buildings or structures incurred after 31 March 1991. There are certain exceptions provided by TCA 1997, s 273(6), (7)(a) (see **5.405.4**). For capital expenditure incurred from 1 April 1991 to 31 March 1992, an initial allowance of 25% was available (also subject to exceptions provided by TCA 1997, s 273(6), (7)(a)).

A company which incurs capital expenditure on the construction of a building or structure is entitled under TCA 1997, s 271 to an industrial building allowance where certain conditions are met as follows:

(a) the building is to be an industrial building for use in a trade or undertaking carried on either:

   (i)   by the person incurring the expenditure, or

   (ii)   by a qualifying lessee (TCA 1997, s 271(2)), and

(b) the building is in fact an industrial building, ie, one used in a qualifying trade, when it first comes to be used (TCA 1997, s 271(6)).

Apart from the case of a person purchasing a new building before it has been used for any purpose (see **5.408**), no initial allowance may be claimed by a company which does not itself incur the expenditure on the construction of the building. However, a company incurring capital expenditure on altering, improving or extending an existing building is entitled to the initial allowance on that expenditure if the two conditions are met in relation to that expenditure at the time it is incurred. It is essential that the building is not used for a non-qualifying purpose, even on a temporary basis, before being used for the purposes for a qualifying trade, as this will disqualify the expenditure from entitlement to the initial allowance.

Apart from the case where an industrial building is first used in its own trade by the company incurring the expenditure, the initial allowance may also be claimed by a lessor incurring qualifying expenditure if the building is first occupied by a qualifying lessee for the purposes of a qualifying trade carried on by that lessee. For this purpose, a qualifying lessee is described in TCA 1997, s 271(2)(b) as a lessee occupying the industrial building under:

(a) a lease to which the relevant interest in the building is reversionary (a "relevant lease"); or

(b) a lease to which a relevant lease mentioned in (a) is reversionary, but only if the relevant lease is a lease granted to the Industrial Development Authority (IDA), Shannon Free-Airport Co Ltd (SFADCO) or Údarás na Gaeltachta (ÚnaG).

In order for a lessor company to be entitled to an industrial building initial allowance in respect of any qualifying construction expenditure, the lease held by the person who carries on the particular qualifying trade (eg, manufacturing, market gardening) must be a lease as described in (a) or (b) above. No initial allowance is made to a lessor unless the lessee in question in fact uses the building for the purposes of a qualifying trade from the commencement of his tenancy (or if later, from the date on which the building is first used for any purpose after its construction). In the event that the building is first used, even if only temporarily, by a person other than a qualifying lessee before its use by him, the lessor company is not entitled to the initial allowance.

The question as to when a particular lease is a lease to which the relevant interest is reversionary gives rise to some difficulty. It is necessary to consider the matter in relation to the particular lessor company which is seeking to obtain the initial allowance for the construction expenditure incurred by it (or, if it has purchased the building before its first use for any purpose, for the expenditure deemed to have been incurred – see **5.408**). If the lessor's interest in the building at the time it incurred the expenditure was the freehold interest, and if the lessee carrying on the qualifying trade holds the head lease, or only lease, granted out of the freehold, the lessee's interest is the lease to which the relevant interest (in this case, the freehold) is reversionary. The same applies if a company incurring the expenditure is the person holding the head lease and the lessee carrying on the qualifying trade has a sublease granted directly out of the head lease.

Where a company incurring the capital expenditure (the superior lessor) holds its interest in the building (the relevant interest in relation to that expenditure) subject to a lease granted to another person (the main lessee) and the main lessee holds his interest subject to a sublease held by the person carrying on the qualifying trade (the sublessee), the position is more difficult. Although it may be argued that the superior lessor's interest is reversionary on both of the inferior leasehold interests, it does appear that TCA 1997, s 271(2) was intended to deny the superior lessor the initial allowance in this situation, other than where the main lessee is either the IDA, SFADCO or ÚnaG. The legislation therefore operates on the basis that it is only the main lessee's interest (and not that of the sublessee) that is the lease to which the superior lessor's relevant interest is reversionary.

Accordingly, to secure entitlement to the industrial building allowances, a prospective lessor company which incurs construction expenditure should either grant the lease directly to the person carrying on the qualifying trade (or who is about to do so) or grant a lease directly to the IDA, SFADCO or ÚnaG on the understanding that the body in question will grant a sublease directly to the qualifying trader.

An initial allowance is made to a company carrying on a trade for the accounting period in which the expenditure is incurred.

5.405.2 Date expenditure incurred

Expenditure is treated as incurred when the amount in question becomes payable (TCA 1997, s 316(2)), but any expenditure incurred by a person about to carry on a trade is treated as being incurred on the day trading commences (TCA 1997, s 316(3)). For expenditure incurred before the commencement of a trade, therefore, an initial allowance is made for the accounting period in which the trade commences.

5.405.3 Rates of allowance

The rates of initial allowance for qualifying industrial buildings expenditure in the respective trade categories, and the dates from which allowances at those rates have applied, are as follows:

Trade category	Expenditure incurred	Initial allowance
Mill, factory or similar premises, and dock undertaking	16/1/75 – 31/3/91	50%
	1/4/91 – 31/3/92	25%
	1/4/92 onwards	Nil
Multi-storey car parks	29/1/81 – 31/3/91	50%
	1/4/91 – 31/3/92	25%
	1/4/92 onwards	Nil

Laboratories for mineral analysis	25/1/84 – 31/3/91	50%
	1/4/91 – 31/3/92	25%
	1/4/92 onwards	Nil
Market gardening, and intensive production of livestock, poultry, eggs	6/4/74 – 31/3/92	20%
	1/4/92 onwards	Nil
Hotel keeping (including holiday camps and holiday cottages)	30/9/56 – 31/3/92	10%
	1/4/92 onwards	Nil

For capital expenditure incurred in the period 1 April 1988 to 31 March 1989 in respect of certain categories of assets (mill, factory or similar premises, laboratory for mineral analysis, dock undertaking), a company claiming free depreciation could either claim:

(a) a 50% initial allowance together with an annual allowance of 4% for the accounting period in which the expenditure was incurred; or

(b) provided that the building or other asset was in use for the company's trade at the end of the accounting period, an increased annual allowance of up to 75% of the expenditure for that period.

Before 1 April 1988 it was possible to claim a 50% initial allowance (for the above categories of industrial buildings) for the period in which the expenditure was incurred and an increased annual allowance (free depreciation) in subsequent periods in respect of the same expenditure. ITA 1967 s 254(7) (as introduced by FA 1988 s 44 – later amended by FA 1989 s 14, as discussed below) provided that where an industrial building initial allowance was made in respect of expenditure incurred on or after 1 April 1988, a claim under FA 1978 s 25 to increase an annual allowance under ITA 1967 s 264 could not be made in respect of the same expenditure.

In the case of capital expenditure incurred on or after 1 April 1989, TCA 1997, s 271(5) (previously ITA 1967 s 254(7) as amended by FA 1989 s 14) generally provides that where an industrial building initial allowance is made for any chargeable period:

(a) no annual allowance (whether basic or accelerated) may be given under TCA 1997, s 274 for the same chargeable period in respect of the same expenditure; and

(b) no increased annual allowance may be made in respect of the expenditure for any subsequent chargeable period.

This restriction has effect not only in relation to expenditure attracting the 50% initial allowance rate (mill, factory etc, laboratory for mineral analysis, dock undertaking) but also in relation to the other categories of expenditure for which lower rates of initial allowance apply. In the case of buildings used for market gardening (20% initial allowance), intensive production of cattle (20%), hotels not in the National Tourism Development Authority register (10%) which do not carry any free depreciation election, the rule still applies to deny any annual allowance for the accounting period in which the initial allowance is claimed. Similarly, for multi-storey car parks which attract a 50% initial allowance but no free depreciation, the 4% annual allowance only commences to run in the second accounting period if the initial allowance is claimed in the first period.

The provisions which prevent a claim in respect of the same expenditure for either an initial allowance and a writing down allowance for the same period, or a claim for both an initial allowance and free depreciation, do not apply in the case of excepted expenditure within TCA 1997, s 271(3)(a) as described below (TCA 1997, s 271(4)(a)).

5.405.4   Excepted expenditure

Initial allowances are not generally available for capital expenditure incurred on or after 1 April 1992 in respect of an industrial building or structure (ITA 1967 s 254(2B)); initial allowances for expenditure on or after 1 April 1991 on the category covering mills, factories etc, laboratories for mineral analysis and dock undertakings were reduced from 50% to 25% (ITA 1967 s 254(2A)(aa)). TCA 1997, s 271(4)(a) provides for the continuance of the initial allowance, however, in the cases of:

(a)   an industrial building or structure provided before 23 April 1996 for use for the purpose of trading operations, or provided on or after 23 April 1996 by a company for use for the purposes of trading operations carried on by the company, which are "relevant trading operations" carried out by companies in either the Shannon Customs-Free Airport (TCA 1997, s 445) or in the Dublin International Financial Services Centre (TCA 1997, s 446), but excluding an industrial building or structure provided by a lessor to a lessee other than in the course of the carrying on by the lessor of those relevant trading operations (TCA 1997, s 271(3)(a));

(b)   an industrial building provided for the purposes of a project approved by an industrial development agency (IDA, SFADCO, ÚnaG) before 1 January 1989, subject to the expenditure being incurred before 31 December 1995 (or 31 December 1996 as respects an industrial building or structure provided for the purposes of a project approved by an industrial development agency in the period 1 January 1986 to 31 December 1988 (TCA 1997, s 271(3)(b)); and

(c)   an industrial building or structure provided for the purposes of a project approved for grant assistance by an industrial development agency in the period 1 January 1989 to 31 December 1990 subject to the expenditure on the provision of the building being incurred:

    (i)   before 31 December 1997, or

    (ii)   before 30 June 1998 if such expenditure would have been incurred before 31 December 1997 were it not for the initiation of legal proceedings which were the subject of an order of the High Court made before 1 January 1998, or

    (iii)   before 31 December 2002 if the project is approved for TCA 1997, s 130 ("section 84") loan financing and is specified in the list referred to in TCA 1997, s 133(8)(c)(iv)) (TCA 1997, s 271(3)(c)).

For expenditure falling within TCA 1997, s 268(1)(a) and (b) (mills, factories etc, laboratories for mineral analysis and dock undertakings) the rate of initial allowance is 50%; in the case of an industrial building or structure within (a) above, however, the initial allowance applies only in respect of expenditure which is incurred before 25

January 1999. As can be seen in the case of a building or structure within (b), the latest date for incurring expenditure for initial allowance purposes is 30 December 1996 while for the purposes of (c) the latest date is 31 December 2002.

For expenditure falling within TCA 1997, s 268(1)(c) and (e) (market gardening, intensive production of cattle, sheep etc) the rate is 20%. In any other case, the rate is 10%.

5.406   Writing down allowances

An industrial building writing down or annual allowance is made for any accounting period to a company which holds the relevant interest in the building or structure at the end of that period, provided that the building or structure was then in use for the purposes of a qualifying trade or undertaking (TCA 1997, s 272(2)). The writing down allowance follows the relevant interest in the building and may therefore be claimed by a company that has acquired the relevant interest either directly from the person who incurred the expenditure originally, or from any intermediate purchaser, as well as by a company which incurred the expenditure if it continues to hold the relevant interest.

Clearly, no writing down allowance is available after the end of the specified writing down period nor after the qualifying capital expenditure has been fully written off by previous initial allowances and/or writing down allowances. Further, if the building has ceased, other than temporarily, to be used as an industrial building, no writing down allowances may be claimed, but, should it come to be used again for the purposes of a qualifying trade, the right to claim the annual allowances is revived provided that the writing down period has not expired.

A building which ceases temporarily to be used and which, immediately before the period of temporary disuse, was an industrial building, is deemed to continue to be an industrial building while in temporary disuse (TCA 1997, s 280(1)). The writing down allowances will therefore continue to be made during this period. There is no precise definition of what constitutes "temporary" in this context, but it is thought that a period of temporary disuse could extend for several years if there is a reasonable likelihood that the premises will be used again.

Where a building is deemed to continue to be an industrial building by virtue of TCA 1997, s 280(1) and, if on the last occasion that the building was in use as an industrial building:

(a)   it was in use for the purposes of a trade which has since been permanently discontinued; or

(b)   the relevant interest in the building was subject to a lease which has since come to an end,

any writing down allowances or balancing allowances falling to be made to any person in respect of the building during any period for which the temporary disuse continues after either of the events in (a) and (b) is to be made by way of discharge or repayment of tax. Similarly, any balancing charge falling to be made during that period is to be made under Case IV of Schedule D (TCA 1997, s 280(2)).

In some cases, the person who originally incurred the capital expenditure on the construction of a building might have been prevented from claiming any industrial building initial allowance because the conditions for that allowance were not met at the time. This does not prevent a claim for writing down allowances by the person holding the relevant interest in relation to that expenditure if the conditions for writing down allowances are met at a later date. However, no writing down allowances are available in respect of capital expenditure incurred before 30 September 1956 (nor, for some of the trade categories, for expenditure incurred before later qualifying dates – see **5.404**). In the case of a building which was not used in a qualifying trade originally, but which later comes to be used for such a trade, the industrial building annual allowance may be claimed by the person holding the relevant interest in relation to any construction expenditure incurred, from the earliest qualifying date for the trade in question (see Example **5.406.1** below).

Although writing down or annual allowances apply to expenditure incurred on or after 30 September 1956, they were only available from the tax year 1960/61. The first period for which a company could have claimed an annual allowance in respect of an industrial building or structure was the tax year 1960/61, provided it was entitled to the relevant interest in the building or structure at the end of the basis period for that tax year (normally the year ending in the year 1959/60).

The rates of annual writing down allowance for each of the qualifying trade categories, in respect of capital expenditure incurred on or after the dates shown below, and the corresponding writing down periods, are as follows:

Trade category	Expenditure from	Annual allowance	Writing down period
Mill, factory, dock undertaking or similar premises	16 Jan 1975	4%[1]	25 years
Laboratory for mineral analysis	25 Jan 1984	4%[1]	25 years
Market gardening	7 Apr 1964	10%	10 years
Holiday cottages	1 Jan 1960 (to 3 Dec 2002[3])	10%[2]	10 years
Guest houses or holiday hostels	3 February 2005	4%	25 years
Hotels and holiday camps	1 Jan 1960 to 26 Jan 1994	10%[2]	10 years
	27 Jan 1994 to 3 Dec 2002[4]	15%[2]	6 years
		+ 10%	7th year
	4 Dec 2002	4%	25 years
Caravan and camping sites	1 Jan 2008	4%	25 years
Intensive production of cattle etc	6 Apr 1971	10%	10 years
Multi-storey car-parks	29 Jan 1981	4%	25 years
Urban renewal buildings	23 Oct 1985	4%[1]	25 years
Airport buildings and structures:			
runways and aprons	24 Apr 1992	4%	25 years
other buildings and structures[5]	27 March 1998	4%	25 years
Private nursing homes[6]	3 Dec 1997	15%	6 years
		+ 10%	7th year
Private convalescent homes	2 Dec 1998	15%	6 years
		+ 10%	7th year
Qualifying hospitals[7]	15 May 2002	15%	6 years
		+ 10%	7th year

Qualifying mental health centres[8]	23 January 2007	15%	6 years
		+ 10%	7th year
Qualifying specialist palliative care units[8]	Date(s) of Ministerial order(s)	15%	6 years
		+ 10%	7th year

Notes:

[1] For expenditure incurred prior to 16 January 1975, the rate was 2%.

[2] For expenditure incurred on hotels prior to 1 January 1960, the rate was 2%.

[3] Subject to transitional arrangements whereby allowances available for expenditure up to 31 December 2004 on certain conditions.

[4] Subject to transitional arrangements whereby 7 year write-off continues to be available in respect of construction or refurbishment expenditure up to 31 July 2006 and subject to further transitional arrangements whereby 7 year write-off continues to be available in respect of construction or refurbishment expenditure up to 31 July 2008.

[5] Expenditure on existing buildings of DAA deemed to be incurred on vesting day (see **5.401.4**).

[6] For qualifying residential units in respect of which capital expenditure was incurred on or after 1 May 2007, the tax life is 20 years (see **5.401.5**).

[7] Notwithstanding the seven-year write-off period, the tax life of a building or structure first used on or after 1 February 2007 is 15 years from the time it was first used or, where capital expenditure on the refurbishment of the building or structure is incurred and, subsequent to incurring that expenditure, the building or structure is first used on or after 1 February 2007, 15 years from the time it was first used after the incurring of that expenditure. (For a building or structure first used before 1 February 2007, the tax life is seven years from the time it was first used.)

[8] Notwithstanding the seven-year write-off period, the tax life is 15 years from the time the building or structure is first used or, where capital expenditure on the refurbishment of the building or structure is incurred, 15 years from the time it was first used after the incurring of that expenditure.

The normal annual allowance of 4% and the writing down life of 25 years in respect of mills, dock undertakings and airport buildings and structures (and generally for hotels in respect of expenditure incurred on or after 4 December 2002) are respectively provided for in TCA 1997, s 272(3)(a)(ii), (e), (g) and TCA 1997, s 272(4)(a)(ii), (e). For private nursing homes and convalescent homes, the annual allowance of 15% and seven year writing down period are respectively provided for in TCA 1997, s 272(3)(f) and (4)(f) (see also **5.401.5**). The current regime for multi- storey car parks is dealt with in **5.605**.

The above rates of writing down allowance are on the basis of an accounting period of 12 months. For any accounting period of shorter duration, the rate of allowance must be reduced in the proportion that the number of months in the accounting period bears to 12 months (TCA 1997, s 321(7)).

Annual writing down allowances were first available for the tax year 1960/61 by reference to expenditure incurred on or after 30 September 1956. The rate then was 2% and the rate was increased to 4% for expenditure incurred on or after 16 January 1975. For hotels, holiday camps and holiday cottages, the rate was increased from 2% to 10% from 1 January 1960 but reverted to 4% for capital expenditure on construction incurred on or after 4 December 2002 (or for expenditure on construction or refurbishment incurred after 31 July 2006 in certain cases, or for expenditure on construction or refurbishment incurred after 31 July 2008 in certain other cases – see below).

Expenditure on the construction on or after 4 December 2002 (or on the construction or refurbishment after 31 December 2006 in certain cases) of holiday cottages ceased altogether to qualify for allowances – see **5.401.1**).

Expenditure incurred up to 31 December 2006 on the construction or refurbishment of a hotel (including holiday camp) continues to qualify for writing down allowances at 15% per annum (for six years, plus 10% in year seven) if—

(a) (i) a planning application (not being an application for outline permission within the meaning of section 36 of the Planning and Development Act 2000), in so far as planning permission is required, in respect of the building or structure is made in accordance with the Planning and Development Regulations 2001 to 2002,

(ii) an acknowledgment of the application, confirming that it was received on or before 31 December 2004, is issued by the planning authority in accordance with article 26(2) of the Planning and Development Regulations 2001 (SI No 600 of 2001), and

(iii) the application is not an invalid application in respect of which a notice is issued by the planning authority in accordance with article 26(5) of those regulations,

(b) (i) a planning application, in so far as planning permission was required, in respect of the building or structure was made in accordance with the Local Government (Planning and Development) Regulations 1994 (SI No 86 of 1994), not being an application for outline permission within the meaning of article 3 of those regulations,

(ii) an acknowledgment of the application, confirming that it was received on or before 10 March 2002, is issued by the planning authority in accordance with article 29(2)(a) of the regulations mentioned in (i), and

(iii) the application is not an invalid application in respect of which a notice is issued by the planning authority in accordance with article 29(2)(b)(i) of those regulations,

(c) where the construction or refurbishment work on the building or structure represented by that expenditure is exempted development for the purposes of the Planning and Development Act 2000 by virtue of section 4 of that Act or by virtue of Part 2 of the Planning and Development Regulations 2001 (SI No 600 of 2001) and—

(i) a detailed plan in relation to the development work is prepared,

(ii) a binding contract in writing, under which the expenditure on the development is incurred, is in existence, and

(iii) work to the value of 5% of the development costs is carried out,

not later than 31 December 2004, or

(d) (i) the construction or refurbishment of the building or structure is a development in respect of which an application for a certificate under section 25(7)(a)(ii) or the Dublin Docklands Development Act 1997 is made to the Authority (within the meaning of that Act),

(ii)   an acknowledgment of the application, confirming that it was received on or before 31 December 2004, is issued by that Authority, and

(iii)   the application is not an invalid application (TCA 1997, s 272(8)).

Expenditure incurred up to 31 July 2008 on the construction or refurbishment of a hotel (including holiday camp) continues to qualify for writing down allowances at 15% per annum (for six years, plus 10% in year seven) if—

(a)   the relevant conditions in (a), (b), (c) or (d) above, as the case may be, relating to planning applications, have been satisfied,

(b)   (i)   subject to TCA 1997, s 270(7)(a) and (b) (see **5.404**), the person constructing or refurbishing the building or structure has, on or before 31 December 2006, carried out work to the value of not less than 15% of the actual construction or refurbishment costs of the building or structure,

(ii)   that person or, where the building or structure is sold by that person, the person who is claiming a deduction in relation to the expenditure can show that the condition in (i) was satisfied,

(c)   a binding contract in writing, under which the expenditure on the construction or refurbishment of the building or structure is incurred, was in existence on or before 31 July 2006, and

(d)   such other conditions, as may be specified in regulations made by the Minister for Finance, have been satisfied, such conditions to be limited to those necessary to ensure compliance with the laws of the European Communities governing State aid or with a decision of the Commission of the European Communities regarding compatibility with the common market having regard to Article 87 of the European Communities Treaty (TCA 1997, s 272(9).

For the purposes of determining whether and to what extent capital expenditure incurred on the construction (within the meaning of TCA 1997, s 270(2) – see **5.404**) of:

(a)   a building or structure in use for the purposes of the trade of hotel keeping, or

(b)   a building of structure deemed to be a building or structure in use for such purposes by virtue of TCA 1997, s 268(3) (holiday camp or holiday cottage – see **5.401.1**),

is incurred or not incurred before 31 July 2008, only such amount of that capital expenditure as is properly attributable to work on the construction or refurbishment of the building or structure actually carried out on or before 31 July 2008 will be treated as having been incurred on or before that date (TCA 1997, s 316(2A)).

Where a writing down allowance has been made to a company in respect of capital expenditure incurred on the construction of a building or structure used for the purposes of the trade of hotel-keeping, and at the end of the accounting period for which the allowance has been made the building is not in use for those purposes, then:

(a)   the building will not be treated as ceasing to be an industrial building if, on ceasing to be used for the hotel trade, it is converted to use for the purposes of a trade consisting of the operation or management of a nursing home (as described above); and

(b)   for the accounting period in question and any subsequent accounting period, the building or structure will be treated as if it were in use for the purposes of a hotel trade if it is in use for the purposes of the nursing home at the end of that period (TCA 1997, s 272(7)).

For industrial building allowances purposes therefore, the company may continue to claim writing down allowances in respect of the building or structure as if the hotel trade had continued.

TCA 1997, s 271(5)(a) provides that where an industrial building allowance is made for any chargeable period in respect of capital expenditure incurred on the construction of a building or structure to which TCA 1997, s 271(3)(c) applies ((c) in **5.405.4** above), an annual writing down allowance cannot be made for the same period in respect of the same expenditure. The annual allowance (but not any increased annual allowance) is available for later accounting periods in the ordinary way. For a fuller discussion of these points, see **5.405.3**.

Example 5.406.1

Folkston Ltd, a company that makes up accounts to 31 December each year, incurred expenditure of €1,260,000 on 13 January 1984 in respect of the construction of a new warehouse. The building commenced to be used on 11 August 1984 for the purposes of the company's trade of warehousing. On 1 January 2007, the company commenced manufacturing operations and began to use the warehouse for the purposes of that trade. Accordingly, it became entitled to claim industrial building writing down allowances (but not the initial allowance or increased writing down allowance) as follows:

	€
Construction expenditure 13/1/84	1,260,000
IBAA y/e 31/12/07 (first period eligible)	50,400
IBAA y/e 31/12/08	50,400

Note:

For the period of non-industrial use, 11 August 1984 to 31 December 2006, notional writing down allowances must be written off the expenditure of €1,260,000 (see **5.411**).

Refurbishment expenditure

For expenditure incurred up to 5 April 1991, industrial building annual allowances under TCA 1997, s 272 have been available only in the case of construction expenditure incurred (or deemed to be incurred, where a new building is bought unused). In other words, the allowance generally applied only to new buildings. TCA 1997, s 276 broadens the scope of the 4% writing down allowance so that, for expenditure incurred on or after 6 April 1991, that allowance may be claimed in respect of general refurbishment of an existing building or structure.

Refurbishment means any work of construction, reconstruction, repair or renewal, including the provision of water, sewerage or heating facilities carried out in the course of repair or restoration, or maintenance in the nature of repair or restoration, of a building or structure.

The annual allowance is now available in respect of works of repair or renewal, the laying on of water supply, the installation of central heating, the provision of sewerage facilities, provided these works are carried out as part of general restoration or repair work on a building or structure.

Refurbishment expenditure of this nature is also relevant in the case of repairs and other work carried out on buildings under the 1994 Urban Renewal regime (see **6.3**), the seaside resort scheme (**6.4**) and the multi-storey car-park scheme (**5.605**).

Example 5.406.2

Maclenny Ltd has carried on a manufacturing trade since 1 July 2002 and has always made up its accounts to 31 December. The company is registered for VAT. It initially rented its manufacturing premises on a short lease and on the expiry of that lease purchased the freehold of the factory building for €240,000. The factory building was originally constructed in 1986 and all the industrial building allowances in respect of the related cost had been claimed by the previous owner.

The company obtained a quotation in September 2006 for the refurbishment of the entire premises as follows:

	€	€
Rewiring		8,000
Roof repairs		14,600
New floors		11,000
Painting		2,800
Plastering		4,200
Dry rot treatment		6,400
Canteen refurbishment		2,600
		49,600[1]
VAT x 13.5%		6,696
		56,296
New carpets[2]	6,000	
VAT x 21%	1,260	7,260
Total		63,556

Assuming that the company incurs the expenditure on or before 31 December 2006, it will be entitled to industrial building annual allowances as follows:

Accounting period	Allowance
	€
y/e 31 December 2006 (year 1 of 25)[3]	1,984
y/e 31 December 2007 (year 2 of 25)	1,984
y/e 31 December 2030 (year 25 of 25)	1,984

Notes:

[1] Under TCA 1997, s 319, allowances are calculated on the VAT-exclusive amount.

[2] The expenditure on carpets does not qualify for allowances as it is not capital expenditure on the refurbishment of the building.

[3] The annual writing down allowance is €49,600 x 4% = €1,984.

In the event that the industrial building is sold before the end of the full 25 year writing down period, the residue of the allowance becomes available to the purchaser, to be written off over the remaining part of the writing down period (TCA 1997, s 272(4) as applied by TCA 1997, s 276).

Example 5.406.3

The facts are as in Example **5.406.2** except that on 31 March 2010 Maclenny Ltd sells the refurbished factory premises to Jensen Ltd which uses it in its manufacturing trade. Maclenny Ltd has claimed writing down allowances for the years ended 31 December 2006, 2007, 2008 and 2009, ie €1,984 x 4 = €7,936. The balance of the writing down allowances available to Jensen Ltd is 21 x €1,984 = €41,664.

When the 25 year writing down period has expired, no balancing allowances or charges may be made on the occasion of the sale of the building (TCA 1997, s 274(1)(b)(i)(II)).

5.407 Increased writing down allowances

5.407.1 Free depreciation: general

In general, increased writing down allowances, and free depreciation, have ceased to be available for industrial buildings or structures where the capital expenditure has been incurred after 31 March 1992. For capital expenditure incurred from 1 April 1988 to 31 March 1992, the maximum allowance available by way of free depreciation over the writing down period of an industrial building was reduced in stages from 100% in the way described in **5.407.3** below.

TCA 1997, s 273 enables a company to claim an increased writing down allowance for capital expenditure incurred by it after 1 February 1978 on the construction of a building or structure which was to be occupied by it for the purposes of any of the following activities:

(a)   a trade carried on in a mill, factory or other similar premises;

(b)   a dock undertaking;

(c)   a trade of hotel keeping; or

(d)   a trade carried on in a laboratory for mineral analysis (for expenditure incurred after 24 January 1984).

The right to claim free depreciation is not available in respect of buildings in use for market gardening trades or for the intensive production of cattle, sheep, poultry or eggs. In the case of a trade of hotel keeping, free depreciation is available only if the expenditure on which it was claimed was incurred on the construction of premises registered in a register kept by the National Tourism Development Authority under the Tourist Traffic Acts 1939 to 1995; premises used as a holiday camp or holiday cottages are eligible for free depreciation if so registered. The entitlement to the normal writing down allowance in respect of market gardening and other relevant buildings is not altered by their non-eligibility for the increased allowance election.

TCA 1997, s 273 permits a company holding the relevant interest in the qualifying industrial building at the end of any accounting period to elect to have its normal writing down allowance on the qualifying expenditure increased by such an additional amount as it may specify. It may make this election for one or more accounting periods during the writing down period of the building until the qualifying capital expenditure has been fully written off but subject to certain restrictions where the qualifying expenditure is incurred after 31 March 1988 (see below). It is also necessary that the building is in use for a qualifying trade or undertaking at the end of the relevant period. Where the full amount of free depreciation has not yet been claimed, any balance should be taken at latest in the last accounting period ending before 6 April 1999 as TCA 1997, s 273(3)(b) prohibits any claim to free depreciation, other than in the *Excepted cases* (see **5.407.3** below), for accounting periods ending on or after 6 April 1999.

A lessor of an industrial building, irrespective of the trade category for which the building is used, is not entitled to claim any increased writing down allowance since TCA 1997, s 273 requires the expenditure to have been incurred by the person actually using the building for the qualifying trade. For the same reason, a person who did not incur the qualifying expenditure, but who subsequently acquired the relevant interest in the building, and who may have become entitled to claim the normal writing down allowances in respect of the building, is not entitled to the increased writing down allowance.

5.407.2 Expenditure before 1 April 1988

For capital expenditure incurred before 1 April 1988 on a qualifying industrial building, a company may for any accounting period claim an increased writing down allowance to write off up to 100% of the expenditure not previously allowed (TCA 1997, s 273). This is subject to TCA 1997, s 273(3)(b) which prohibits any claim to free depreciation, other than in the *Excepted cases* (see **5.407.3** below), for accounting periods ending on or after 6 April 1999.

A company's entitlement to an annual writing down allowance for any accounting period is subject to the conditions that at the end of that period the relevant interest in the building or structure is held by the company and that the building or structure is an industrial building. On that basis, a claim to write off 100% of the expenditure in the first available period may be made. In addition, the company may claim an increased writing down allowance in respect of expenditure incurred prior to 1 April 1988 in any accounting period after an industrial building initial allowance has been obtained for the same expenditure regardless of whether the claim is for an accounting period ending before, on or after 31 March 1988.

5.407.3 Phasing out of accelerated capital allowances

TCA 1997, s 273(2)(b) limits the total amount which may be claimed as increased writing down allowances for qualifying capital expenditure incurred after 31 March 1988 on industrial buildings (but subject to the exceptions in TCA 1997, s 273(5) – see **5.106.3** and *Excepted cases* below). For capital expenditure incurred in the period from 1 April 1988 to 31 March 1989, the maximum amount of increased writing down allowances (subject to exceptions described below) which may be claimed over the writing down period for the buildings, whether in one or more accounting periods, may not exceed 75% of the qualifying expenditure.

For capital expenditure incurred in the period 1 April 1989 to 31 March 1991, the maximum amount of increased writing down allowances available is 50% of the expenditure, whether in one or more accounting periods. For capital expenditure incurred in the period from 1 April 1991 to 31 March 1992 the maximum increased writing down allowance is 25% of the expenditure (TCA 1997, s 273(2)(b)). Capital expenditure incurred on or after 1 April 1992 does not qualify for increased writing down allowance (TCA 1997, s 273(3)). In applying the 75%, 50% and 25% limits, the full amount of any writing down allowance, including the increase (and not merely the increase itself), is taken into account, but any normal allowance obtained for any accounting period is disregarded. For example (and using euro equivalent amounts), if an increased allowance of €20,000 is claimed in respect of qualifying capital expenditure of €400,000 incurred in the year ended 31 December 1991 and if a normal writing down allowance of €16,000 (4%) is claimed in the year ended 31 December 1992, the maximum writing down allowance available for the year ended 31 December 1993 is €80,000 (25% of €400,000 less free depreciation of €20,000 already claimed and disregarding the normal allowance of €16,000).

TCA 1997, s 271(5) provides that no increased writing down allowance may be claimed under TCA 1997, s 273 in respect of any capital expenditure incurred if an industrial building initial allowance has been made in respect of the same expenditure (ie, in relation to a building or structure to which TCA 1997, s 271(3)(c) relates – see **5.405.4** in (c)). A company entitled to industrial building allowances for any accounting period must therefore decide, before the relevant assessment for that period becomes final and conclusive, whether or not to claim an initial allowance under TCA 1997, s 271 (where that allowance is still available) for that period. If the assessment incorporating the initial allowance is finalised, only normal writing down allowances may be claimed for subsequent accounting periods on the same expenditure.

For qualifying capital expenditure incurred after 31 March 1989 but before 1 April 1991, it normally made no difference whether a company claimed a 50% initial allowance or a 50% increased annual allowance for the accounting period in which the expenditure was incurred. However, if the building or structure on which the expenditure was incurred during the relevant accounting period was not in use for the qualifying trade at the end of that period, a claim could have been made for the 50% initial allowance by reference to the date of the expenditure, whereas the first annual allowance (whether normal or increased) would only have been available for the next accounting period when the industrial building was in use.

For qualifying capital expenditure incurred in the period from 1 April 1988 to 31 March 1989, increased annual allowances of up to 75% were available, as compared with initial allowances of only 50%. Thus, where a choice was available, it would normally have been more beneficial to claim an increased annual allowance instead of an initial allowance in respect of that expenditure.

In respect of expenditure incurred in the period from 1 April 1988 to 31 March 1992, a company may claim free depreciation for an accounting period subsequent to 31 March 1992 as long as it continues to hold the relevant interest in the building or structure and the building or structure is still in use for a qualifying purpose. No free depreciation claim, however, may be made in respect of such expenditure for any accounting period ending on or after 6 April 1999 (TCA 1997, s 273(3)(b)).

TCA 1997, s 271(5)(b), which prevents a claim for both an initial allowance and free depreciation in respect of the same expenditure, does not apply in the cases within TCA 1997, s 271(3)(a), (b) (see **5.405.4**) but does apply to such expenditure within TCA 1997, s 271(3)(c).

Excepted cases

TCA 1997, s 273(4) provides that TCA 1997, s 273(2)(b) and (3) do not apply, so that free depreciation claims which permit up to 100% of the cost of an industrial building or structure may continue to be made in the cases of:

(a) an industrial building or structure provided before 23 April 1996 for use for the purpose of trading operations, or provided on or after 23 April 1996 by a company for use for the purposes of trading operations carried on by the company, which are "relevant trading operations" carried out by companies in either the Shannon Customs Free-Airport (TCA 1997, s 445) or in the Dublin International Financial Services Centre (TCA 1997, s 446), but excluding an industrial building or structure provided by a lessor to a lessee other than in the course of the carrying on by the lessor of those relevant trading operations (TCA 1997, s 271(5)(a));

(b) an industrial building or structure the expenditure on the provision of which was incurred under a binding contract entered into on or before 27 January 1988, subject to the expenditure being incurred before 31 December 1995 (TCA 1997, s 271(5)(b)); and

(c) an industrial building provided for the purposes of a project approved by an industrial development agency (the Industrial Development Authority, Shannon Free Airport Development Co Ltd, Údarás na Gaeltachta) on or before 31 December 1988, subject to the expenditure being incurred before 31 December 1995 (or 31 December 1996 as respects an industrial building or structure provided for the purposes of a project approved by an industrial development agency in the period 1 January 1986 to 31 December 1988 (TCA 1997, s 271(3)(b)).

TCA 1997, s 273(6), (7) provide for a maximum free depreciation rate of 50% of qualifying expenditure incurred on or after 1 April 1989 in the cases of:

(a) an industrial building or structure provided for the purposes of a project approved for grant assistance by an industrial development agency in the period 1 January 1989 to 31 December 1990 subject to the expenditure on the provision of the building being incurred:

    (i) before 31 December 1997, or

    (ii) before 30 June 1998 if such expenditure would have been incurred before 31 December 1997 were it not for the initiation of legal proceedings which were the subject of an order of the High Court made before 1 January 1998, or

    (iii) before 31 December 2002 if the project is approved for TCA 1997, s 130 ("section 84") loan financing and is specified in the list referred to in TCA 1997, s 133(8)(c)(iv)), and

(b) a building or structure which is to be an industrial building or structure within the meaning of TCA 1997, s 268(1)(d) (ie, for the purposes of the trade of hotel- keeping) where the expenditure was incurred before 31 December 1995, provided a binding contract for the provision of the building or structure was entered into before 31 December 1990, and provided the building or structure is registered within 6 months after the date of the completion of that building or structure in a register kept by the National Tourism Development Authority under the Tourist Traffic Acts 1939 to 1995.

5.408 Buildings purchased unused

5.408.1 General

An industrial building initial allowance is made under TCA 1997, s 271 to a company which incurs the capital expenditure on the construction of a building or structure which is to be used for a qualifying trade. TCA 1997 ss 272 and 274 provide respectively for annual allowances and balancing allowances (or charges) on the same construction expenditure to be made in the case of a company which owns the interest which the person who incurred the construction expenditure had at the time it was incurred. TCA 1997, s 277 contains rules relating to the writing off of the construction expenditure.

TCA 1997, s 279 adapts these rules to deal with the case where the relevant interest in any building or structure is sold after expenditure has been incurred on the construction of the building, but before the building is first used for any purpose. This situation may arise where the construction expenditure is incurred by a speculative builder or other person carrying on a trade of constructing buildings for sale. It would also arise where, say, a company which constructs a building intends to use it for its own trade or for leasing, but which for whatever reason sells its relevant interest before the building is used for any purpose. The section also applies if the relevant interest is sold when the building is only partly constructed, eg, when a speculative builder goes out of business.

See also **5.404** regarding restricted qualifying expenditure for certain categories of buildings and structures.

Where TCA 1997, s 279 applies, it requires any industrial building initial allowance, writing down allowance and balancing allowance or charge to be based on a deemed cost of construction instead of the actual expenditure incurred by the person selling the relevant interest. It gives effect to this by applying the provisions of TCA 1997 ss 271, 272, 274 and 277 on the following assumptions:

(a) the person who purchased the relevant interest in the unused building (or, if there is more than one sale of the relevant interest before the first use of the building, the latest purchaser before the building is used) is deemed to be the person who incurred the construction expenditure;

(b) the person in question is treated as if he had incurred expenditure on the construction of the building of an amount determined in one of two ways (instead of the actual expenditure on the construction – see below); and

(c) the construction expenditure is deemed to have been incurred on the date on which the purchase price becomes payable (and not when the construction actually took place).

The construction expenditure deemed to have been incurred by the purchaser depends on whether the actual expenditure before the sale was incurred by a person carrying on a trade which consists, wholly or partly, in the construction of buildings with a view to their sale, eg, a builder, or by a person not carrying on such a trade. The different rules for determining the deemed cost of construction, by reference to which all subsequent industrial building allowances are given, are discussed separately below for buildings constructed other than in the course of a building trade and for buildings constructed by builders.

Arising out of the restrictions on accelerated capital allowances provided for by ITA 1967 s 254(2A), (2B) and FA 1978 s 25(2), (2A) (now TCA 1997, s 273(2)(b), (3)(a)) (see **5.106**), the date on which the purchase price for the sale of the relevant interest becomes payable is of particular significance. The fact that the actual construction expenditure before the sale may have been incurred before 1 April 1988 will not entitle the purchaser of the relevant interest to the 100% increased annual allowances if the purchase price became payable on or after that date. If the purchase price is payable on or after 1 April 1988, the accelerated capital allowances for all chargeable periods are restricted, in the aggregate, to a maximum of 75% (or 50%, or 25% as the case may be) of the deemed construction expenditure, the exact percentage being dependent on the date the price is payable (see **5.407.3**).

5.408.2   Construction other than by a builder

Where the construction expenditure has been incurred by a person, not being a person carrying on a building trade, the person purchasing the relevant interest in the building from him is deemed to have incurred construction expenditure equal to the lower of the actual construction expenditure incurred before the sale of the relevant interest and "the net price paid" (see definition in **5.408.4** below) by the purchaser for the relevant interest (TCA 1997, s 279(2)(b)). If there is more than one sale of the relevant interest before the first use of the building (or within one year after the building commences to be used), industrial building allowances are based on the lower of the expenditure actually incurred on the construction of the building and the net price paid on the *last* sale before the building is used (or on the last sale within one year after the building commences to be used).

Example 5.408.2.1

Zoltan Ltd, a company carrying on a wholesaling and warehousing trade, owns a freehold site and employs a building contractor to construct a new building for use in its trade. The building is completed in February 2007 at a construction cost to Zoltan Ltd of €840,000. However, before the building can be used, the business of Zoltan Ltd collapses. On 7 August 2007, Zoltan Ltd sells the freehold interest to William Penney for €750,000 payable on 12 September 2007. On 13 January 2008, Penney grants a 35 year lease in the still unused building to Zhivago Ltd which immediately starts to use the building for its manufacturing trade.

The consequences of these transactions are as follows:

(1)   William Penney, as the purchaser of the freehold interest (the relevant interest) in the building, is deemed to have incurred construction expenditure of €750,000 (ie, its purchase price (assumed in this case to be equal to the "net price paid"), as this is lower than the actual cost to Zoltan Ltd for the construction of the building);

(2)   as long as the building continues to be used for a manufacturing trade, Penney (or any subsequent holder of the freehold interest) is entitled to writing down allowances at the rate of 4% until the deemed construction expenditure of €750,000 is fully written off.

TCA 1997, s 270(6) (restriction of amount of qualifying expenditure for certain building categories – see **5.404**) modifies the above-described treatment in cases where the qualifying expenditure is to be restricted. In any such case, TCA s 279(2)(b) is to be read so as to mean that the person who buys the relevant interest is deemed to have incurred expenditure on the construction of the building or structure equal to the lesser of—

(i) that expenditure as reduced in accordance with TCA 1997, s 270(5) (as explained in **5.404**); and

(ii) the "net price paid" (but as defined by the modified formula prescribed by TCA 1997, s 270(6) – see **5.408.4**) by that person for that interest.

5.408.3 Construction by builder

Where expenditure has been incurred by a builder on the construction of a building or structure and, before the building or structure is used (or within one year after it commences to be used – see below), the relevant interest is sold by the builder to a company, being the first person to use the building, the company is deemed to have incurred capital expenditure on the construction of the building of an amount equal to the net price (see definition in **5.408.4** below) paid by it to the builder for the relevant interest in the building (and not by reference to the builder's cost if that is less) (TCA 1997, s 279(3)(a)). It would be inequitable to restrict the deemed cost in this case to the expenditure incurred by the builder as this would not include the amount of the builder's profit. The actual construction cost to the builder is therefore disregarded and ceases to have any relevance for all purposes of industrial building allowances and balancing charges. In other words, any initial allowances, writing down allowances or subsequent balancing adjustments are based on the builder's sale price including his profit, if any, but excluding any stamp duty, legal or other costs of acquisition.

Example 5.408.3.1

Thomas Horne, a builder, erects a building at a cost of €500,000 on a site the freehold interest in which he had acquired many years ago at no cost. The building is suitable for use either as a factory or as a warehouse. The construction was completed on 29 March 2007.

On 4 November 2007, Horne sold his freehold interest (the relevant interest) for €600,000 to Crown Ltd, a manufacturing company, the full consideration being payable on that date. The building was not used in any way until the purchaser acquired possession for the purposes of its manufacturing trade which commenced on 30 March 2008. Crown Ltd makes up accounts to 31 December each year. The consequences of the above transactions are as follows:

(a) Thomas Horne is not entitled to any industrial building allowances in respect of his construction expenditure of €500,000;

(b) Crown Ltd is treated as the person who incurred the construction expenditure. The construction expenditure is deemed to be the €600,000 paid to Thomas Horne (and the actual construction expenditure incurred by Horne is disregarded completely);

(c) the deemed construction expenditure of €600,000 is treated by TCA 1997, s 279 as having been incurred on 4 November 2007, the date on which the purchase price was payable by Crown Ltd (and not when the construction took place) but, as this is before the commencement of the trade, TCA 1997, s 316(3) treats the expenditure as being incurred on the first day of trading, ie, on 30 March 2008;

(d) Crown Ltd is entitled to industrial building annual allowances of €600,000 x 4% = €24,000.

Where there is more than one sale of the relevant interest in a building constructed by a builder before the building is first used (or within one year after it commences to be used), the last purchaser concerned is deemed to have incurred, on the date when his purchase price becomes payable, construction expenditure equal to the lower of (a) the purchase price that was paid on the sale by the builder and (b) the net price paid by the last purchaser before the building is first used (TCA 1997, s 279(3)(b)). In other words, the figure by reference to which industrial building allowances are made is the price paid to the builder or, if lower, the net price paid by the last purchaser of the relevant interest before the building is first used.

Example 5.408.3.2

The facts are as in Example **5.408.3.1** except that Thomas Horne sold the freehold interest in the building to Robert Coyne on 6 October 2007 for a net price of €560,000. Coyne had intended to lease the building to Crown Ltd, but that company then offered to purchase the freehold interest for €640,000. Coyne accepted the offer and the building was sold to Crown Ltd for €640,000, payable on 21 February 2008. Crown Ltd commenced trading on 4 April 2008. This results in the following consequences:

(a) neither Horne nor Coyne is entitled to any industrial building allowances;

(b) Crown Ltd is deemed to have incurred capital expenditure on the construction of the building on 21 February 2008 and is entitled to industrial building allowances on deemed expenditure of €560,000, ie on Horne's sale price, as this is lower than the €640,000 paid on the last sale before the first use of the building; but

(c) due to the fact that the manufacturing trade of Crown Ltd, for which the building is to be used, does not commence until 4 April 2008, TCA 1997, s 316(3) treats the "construction" expenditure of €560,000 as having been incurred on 4 April 2008 (instead of on 21 January 2008).

TCA 1997, s 270(6) (restriction of amount of qualifying expenditure for certain building categories – see **5.404**) modifies the above-described treatment in cases where the qualifying expenditure is to be restricted. In any such case TCA 1997, s 279(3) is to be read so as to mean that the purchaser is deemed to have incurred capital expenditure on the construction of the building or structure of an amount equal to that expenditure as reduced in accordance with TCA 1997, s 270(5) (as explained in **5.404**) (and not by reference to the lesser of that amount and the "net price paid").

5.408.4 Treatment of land cost

The cost of acquiring land or of acquiring the relevant interest in the land must be excluded in arriving at the expenditure qualifying for industrial building allowances (see **5.404**). Prior to the enactment of TCA 1997, s 279(1), which took effect from 6 April 1990, there was no requirement in the case of a building purchased unused from a builder to exclude the builder's cost relating to the land element (see Example **5.408.3.1**). The industrial building allowance was therefore based on the net price paid to the builder without any deduction for the builder's cost of acquiring the relevant interest in the land on which he had constructed the building. This resulted from the wording of TCA 1997, s 279, which referred to the net price paid for the "relevant interest" in the building. That interest, as defined by TCA 1997, s 269 (see **5.403**) clearly envisages an interest, whether freehold or leasehold, which can only exist in relation to land (including any buildings on that land).

   Where a building had been purchased unused from a non builder who had constructed it before selling the relevant interest, it was necessary to exclude the land cost element from the cost of construction so that the amount qualifying for industrial building allowances could not exceed the actual construction expenditure. However, where the net price paid for the relevant interest in the building is less than the actual construction expenditure, any capital allowances on or after the building came into use as an industrial building would have been computed by reference to the net price without any deduction for the cost of land element.

TCA 1997, s 279(1) provides that industrial building allowances in respect of industrial buildings purchased unused are to be computed by reference to the net price paid as restricted by the land element cost. The "the net price paid" (see Example **5.408.5.1** below) is in accordance with the formula:

$$ B \times \frac{C}{C+D} $$

where—

B   is the amount paid by a person on the purchase of the relevant interest in the building or structure;

C   is the amount of the expenditure actually incurred on the construction of the building or structure;

D   is the amount of any expenditure actually incurred which is expenditure for the purposes of TCA 1997, s 270(2)(a),(b) or (c) – expenditure on the acquisition of, or of rights in or over, any land, on the provision of machinery or plant or on any asset treated as machinery or plant, and in respect of which an allowance is available under TCA 1997, s 765(1) (capital expenditure on scientific research) or TCA 1997, s 670 (mine development allowance).

The definition of "the net price paid" is modified by TCA 1997, s 270(6) (restriction of amount of qualifying expenditure for certain building categories – see **5.404**) applies. In relation to those categories of buildings, the net price paid is the product of the following formula:

$$ B \times \frac{C}{D+E} $$

where—

B   is the amount paid by the purchaser of the relevant interest in the building or structure;

C   is the amount of the expenditure actually incurred on the construction of the building or structure as reduced in accordance with TCA 1997, s 270(5) (see **5.404**);

D   is the amount of the expenditure actually incurred on the construction of the building or structure; and

E   is the amount of any expenditure actually incurred but disallowed by virtue of TCA 1997, s 270(2) (expenditure on the acquisition of rights in or over land etc – see **5.404**).

5.408.5   Building bought within one year of first use

TCA 1997, s 279(2) permits an industrial building initial allowance or an industrial building annual allowance to be claimed where the building is bought within one year after it is first used. For either of these allowances to be available, it is a condition that no other person has claimed any industrial building allowance in respect of the same building.

Example 5.408.5.1

On 3 February 2006, Redcliff Ltd, a building company, purchased a derelict site for €212,000. It built a 60 room hotel on the site in the period March to October 2006 at a cost of €1,280,000. The hotel premises were fitted out in December 2006 and the hotel was ready for use on 1 January 2007.

Redcliff Ltd had always intended to sell the hotel on completion, but the proposed purchaser, Camacho Ltd, was unable to complete the purchase.

On 10 February 2007, Redcliff Ltd took steps to run the hotel itself, recruiting staff for the purpose, until such time as another purchaser could be found. On 9 July 2007, a purchaser, Medeiros Ltd, was found and the hotel was sold to that company for €2,080,000. Medeiros Ltd immediately commenced to trade as hotelier from the building.

Medeiros Ltd, which had been a dormant company prior to the purchase, prepares its first accounts for the period ended 31 December 2007. The "net price paid" by it is computed in accordance with TCA 1997, s 279(1) as follows:

$$€2.08m \times \frac{1,280,000}{1,280,000 + 212,000} = €1,784,450$$

The industrial building annual allowance is €1,784,450 x 15% = €267,668.[1]

Note:

[1]   As Medeiros Ltd purchased the building within one year of its first being used, and since no other person, including Redcliff Ltd, has claimed an industrial building allowance in relation to the building, Medeiros Ltd is entitled under TCA 1997, s 279(2) to claim the allowance.

5.409   Balancing allowances and charges

5.409.1   Balancing adjustments: general

In the circumstances set out in TCA 1997, s 274(1)(a), a balancing allowance or balancing charge (referred to in either case as a balancing adjustment) is made to or on a company. The circumstances are as follows:

(a)   capital expenditure has been incurred, on or after 30 September 1956, on the construction of a building or structure;

(b)   any industrial building allowance, initial or writing-down, has been made for any one or more accounting periods; and

(c)   any of the following events (balancing events) occurs:

  (i)   the relevant interest in the building or structure is sold,

  (ii)   the relevant interest, if it is a leasehold interest, comes to an end otherwise than as the result of the acquisition by the person entitled to that interest of the interest which is reversionary on it (ie, the immediately superior interest),

  (iii)   the building or structure is demolished or destroyed or, without being demolished or destroyed, ceases altogether to be used, or

  (iv)   consideration (other than rent or an amount treated or, as respects consideration received on or after 26 March 1997, partly treated, as rent under TCA 1997, s 98) is received by the person entitled to the relevant interest in respect of an interest which is subject to the relevant interest.

TCA 1997, s 277(7) states that where consideration of the type referred to in (c)(iv) above is received and a balancing allowance arises, the amount by which the residue of the expenditure before the balancing event exceeds the amount of that consideration is to be written off (but see **5.409.2** below).

TCA 1997, s 311(3) provides for two other balancing events – an exchange of the relevant interest and, if it is a leasehold interest, the surrender of the relevant interest for valuable consideration. In either case, the value of the consideration given by the other party for the exchange or surrender is taken as being the net sale proceeds for the purposes of computing the balancing adjustment.

The inclusion of (c)(iv) above as a balancing event is primarily an anti-avoidance measure (TCA 1997, s 274(1)(a)(iv)). It is intended to deal with the case where the owner of the relevant interest in the industrial building creates a new interest in the building which is marginally inferior to the relevant interest (for example, the creation of a lease for 999 years out of a freehold) and, as consideration, receives a sum which is not taxable as income and not brought into account in computing taxable income (see Example **5.409.2.2**). The reference to "partly treated" is necessary to secure that a balancing *allowance* is not obtained in the case of a lease (not a long lease, ie, not exceeding fifty years) of a building or structure which provides for the payment of a very small premium. Since under the tax rules relating to rent only part of the premium is treated as rent (see **3.209.2**), it could be contended, in the absence of a reference to "partly treated", that the remaining part is consideration other than rent and that a balancing allowance could therefore be claimed.

In respect of consideration of the type referred to in (c)(iv) and which is received on or after 5 March 2001, no balancing allowance may be made – see further in relation to this point in **5.409.2** below.

For any of the balancing events, described in (c)(i)-(iv) above, occurring before 6 April 1990, a balancing adjustment was required only if the event occurred at a time when the building or structure was an industrial building or structure. This position was unsatisfactory because it enabled the person owning the relevant interest to avoid a balancing charge by changing the use of the building from an industrial to a non-industrial use, even for a short period, before disposing of the relevant interest. The former reference to "while the building or structure is an industrial building or structure" was accordingly deleted (by FA 1990 s 78) from TCA 1997, s 274(1)(a).

What is now TCA 1997, s 274(1)(a)(iii) had been amended by FA 1994 s 22 to provide that a balancing event would occur when the holder of the relevant interest ceases to use the building as an industrial building. The purpose of this amendment was to enable balancing allowances and charges to be computed without long delays in situations where there might have been difficulty in determining whether or not a building had ceased altogether to be used. That amendment, however, gave rise to a further difficulty in that a lessor of an industrial building could suffer a balancing charge where a tenant changed the use to which the building was put. The FA 1994 s 22 amendment was therefore cancelled, with retrospective effect, by FA 1995 s 24 so that the balancing event in what is now TCA 1997, s 274(1)(a)(iii) again became: "the building or structure ... ceases altogether to be used".

No balancing allowance or charge can arise on a sale or other event occurring after the end of the writing down period of the expenditure in question (see table in **5.406**) (TCA 1997, s 274(1)(b)(i)(II)). For example, in the case of a factory building the qualifying expenditure on which was incurred after 15 January 1975, no balancing adjustment is required by reason of any event occurring more than 25 years after the date the building was first put into use for any purpose. Furthermore, the cessation of a qualifying trade is not an event requiring a balancing adjustment, provided the owner does not dispose of the relevant interest and so long as the building continues to be used for some purpose.

For hotels, holiday camps and holiday cottages, the rate for annual writing down allowances was increased from 2% to 10% from 1 January 1960 but reverted to 4% for capital expenditure on construction incurred on or after 4 December 2002 (or for expenditure on construction or refurbishment incurred after 31 July 2006 in certain cases or, after 31 July 2008 in certain other cases – see **5.406**). Expenditure incurred up to 31 December 2006 or, in certain cases up to 31 July 2008, on the construction or refurbishment of a hotel (including a holiday camp, but not a holiday cottage, guest house or holiday hostel) continues to qualify for writing down allowances at 15% per annum (for six years, plus 10% in year seven) on a transitional basis, as explained in **5.406**.

Correspondingly, for expenditure incurred on or after 4 December 2002 on a building or structure which is a hotel or holiday camp, the period beyond which a balancing allowance or charge may not be made is 25 years after the building or structure was first used (TCA 1997, s 274(1)(b)(iii)(III)). However, the 7 year period continues to apply in relation to such capital expenditure incurred on or before 31 December 2006 (and in certain other cases, on or before 31 July 2008 (see further below) if:

(a) (i) a planning application (not being an application for outline permission within the meaning of section 36 of the Planning and Development Act 2000), in so far as planning permission is required, in respect of the building or structure is made in accordance with the Planning and Development Regulations 2001 to 2002,

(ii) an acknowledgment of the application, confirming that it was received on or before 31 December 2004, is issued by the planning authority in accordance with article 26(2) of the Planning and Development Regulations 2001 (SI No 600 of 2001), and

(iii) the application is not an invalid application in respect of which a notice is issued by the planning authority in accordance with article 26(5) of those regulations,

(b) (i) a planning application, in so far as planning permission was required, in respect of the building or structure was made in accordance with the Local Government (Planning and Development) Regulations 1994 (SI No 86 of 1994), not being an application for outline permission within the meaning of article 3 of those regulations,

(ii) an acknowledgment of the application, confirming that it was received on or before 10 March 2002, is issued by the planning authority in accordance with article 29(2)(a) of the regulations mentioned in (i), and

    (iii)   the application is not an invalid application in respect of which a notice was issued by the planning authority in accordance with article 29(2)(b)(i) of those regulations, or

(c)   where the construction or refurbishment work on the building or structure represented by that expenditure is exempted development for the purposes of the Planning and Development Act 2000 by virtue of section 4 of that Act or by virtue of Part 2 of the Planning and Development Regulations 2001 (SI 600/2001) and—

    (i)   a detailed plan in relation to the development work is prepared,

    (ii)   a binding contract in writing, under which the expenditure on the development is incurred, is in existence, and

    (iii)   work to the value of 5% of the development costs is carried out,

not later than 31 December 2004, or

(d)   (i)   the construction or refurbishment of the building or structure is a development in respect of which an application for a certificate under section 25(7)(a)(ii) of the Dublin Docklands Development Act 1997 is made to the Authority (within the meaning of that Act),

    (ii)   an acknowledgment of the application, confirming that it was received on or before 31 December 2004, is issued by that Authority, and

    (iii)   the application is not an invalid application (TCA 1997, s 274(1A)).

The seven year writing-down period continues to apply in relation to capital expenditure incurred on or before 31 July 2008 on a building or structure which is a hotel or holiday camp if:

(a)   the relevant conditions in (a), (b), (c) or (d) above, as the case may be, relating to planning applications, have been satisfied;

(b)   (i)   subject to TCA 1997, s 270(7)(a) and (b) (see **5.404**), the person constructing or refurbishing the building or structure has, on or before 31 December 2006, carried out work to the value of not less than 15% of the actual construction or refurbishment costs of the building or stucture,

    (ii)   that person or, where the building or structure is sold by that person, the person who is claiming a deduction in relation to the expenditure can show that the condition in (i) was satisfied,

(c)   a binding contract in writing, under which the expenditure on the construction or refurbishment of the building or structure is incurred, was in existence on or before 31 July 2006; and

(d)   such other conditions, as may be specified in regulations made by the Minister for Finance, have been satisfied, such conditions to be limited to those necessary to ensure compliance with the laws of the European Communities governing State aid or with a decision of the Commission of the European Communities regarding compatibility with the common market having regard to Article 87 of the European Communities Treaty (TCA 1997, s 274(1B).

For the purposes of determining whether and to what extent capital expenditure incurred on the construction (within the meaning of TCA 1997, s 270(2) – see **5.404**) of:

(a)   a building or structure in use for the purposes of the trade of hotel keeping; or

(b)   a building of structure deemed to be a building or structure in use for such purposes by virtue of TCA 1997, s 268(3) (holiday camp or holiday cottage – see **5.401.1**),

is incurred or not incurred before 31 July 2006, only such amount of that capital expenditure as is properly attributable to work on the construction or refurbishment of the building or structure actually carried out on or before 31 July 2006 will be treated as having been incurred on or before that date (TCA 1997, s 316(2A)).

A balancing allowance is given to, or any balancing charge is made on, the person entitled to the relevant interest in the building immediately before the sale or other event. For a company, the balancing adjustment is made for the accounting period in which the sale or other event occurs.

There is no clear legislative guidance as to how balancing charges arising after a trade has ceased are to be taxed. It would seem that the only tax head for such charges is Case IV of Schedule D in which case they would be taxable at the 25% corporation tax rate. Furthermore, any losses unused at the date trade has ceased would not be available to cover such balancing charges although, in practice, Revenue have been prepared to agree to the set off of losses forward against balancing charges in such circumstances. There is surely a persuasive case for a legislative amendment that would ensure that balancing charges arising in the context of a trade should not be taxed at the 25% rate.

As seen in **5.406**, a building which ceases temporarily to be used and which, immediately before the period of temporary disuse, was an industrial building, is deemed to continue to be an industrial building while in temporary disuse (TCA 1997, s 280(1)). The writing down allowances will therefore continue to be made during this period. In any such case, if on the last occasion that the building was in use as an industrial building:

(a)   it was in use for the purposes of a trade which has since been permanently discontinued; or

(b)   the relevant interest in the building was subject to a lease which has since come to an end,

any writing down allowances or balancing allowances falling to be made to any person in respect of the building during any period for which the temporary disuse continues after either of the events in (a) and (b) is to be made by way of discharge or repayment of tax. Similarly, any balancing charge falling to be made during that period is to be made under Case IV of Schedule D (TCA 1997, s 280(2)).

Example 5.409.1.2

Maxfly Ltd has been entitled to industrial building allowances for some years in respect of its expenditure on a factory building used in its manufacturing trade. The company ceased to use the building on 31 December 2006 at which time the cessation of use was expected to be temporary so that the building is treated as continuing to be an industrial building and allowances continue to be available. The company's trade, however, ceased on 30 June 2007 and the building is sold on 30 September 2007.

A balancing charge arises based on the sale proceeds received by Maxfly Ltd. At this point, the company is not carrying on a trade. The balancing charge is made under Case IV of Schedule D.

Relevant facilities: change of use

A balancing charge is imposed in the cases of certain buildings and structures, referred to as relevant facilities, which cease, within the holding period for balancing charge purposes, to be the type of building or structure for which industrial building allowances were originally given. The charge arises in cases where the buildings or structures were first used, or were first used after refurbishment, on or after 1 January 2006.

Buildings affected are registered nursing homes, qualifying residential units, convalescent homes, qualifying private hospitals, qualifying mental health centres, qualifying specialist palliative care units and certain childcare facilities. In calculation a balancing charge, an amount of money is deemed to have been received where the building or structure ceases to be a relevant facility. Where, however, a building or structure ceases to be one type of relevant facility and, within a period of six months, becomes another type of such facility, the charge will not apply.

A *relevant facility* is a building or structure which:

(a)   is in use for the purposes of a trade consisting of the operation of a private nursing home (see **5.401.5**);

(b)   is in use as a qualifying residential unit which, by virtue of TCA 1997, s 268(3B) is deemed to be a building or structure referred to in (a) (see **5.401.5**);

(c)   is in use for the purposes of a trade consisting of the operation or management of a convalescent home (see **5.401.6**);

(d)   is in use for the purposes of a trade consisting of the operation or management of a qualifying hospital (see **5.401.7**);

(e)   is in use for the purposes of a trade consisting of the operation or management of qualifying mental health centre (see **5.401.9**);

(f)   is in use for the purposes of a trade consisting of the operation or management of a qualifying specialist palliative care unit (see **5.401.10**); or

(g)   is a qualifying premises in use for the purposes of providing a pre-school service or pre-school service and day-care or other services to cater for children other than pre-school children (see **5.607**) (TCA 1997, s 274(2A)(a)).

Where:

(i)   a building or structure is a relevant facility as described within (a)-(g) above;

(ii)   an industrial building allowance has been given in respect of capital expenditure on the construction or refurbishment of the building or structure;

(iii)   the building or structure ceases to be a relevant facility,

then, subject to TCA 1997, s 274(2A)(c) (see below), that cessation is treated as an event giving rise to a balancing charge to be made on the person entitled to the relevant interest (see **5.403**) in the building or structure concerned immediately before that event occurs for the accounting period in which the event occurs (TCA 1997, s 274(2A)(b)).

An event triggering a balancing charge will not arise if, within six months of ceasing to be a relevant facility, the building or structure concerned is again a relevant facility within any of the descriptions in (a)-(g) above (other than the description by reference to which it was previously a relevant facility) (TCA 1997, s 274(2A)(c)).

TCA 1997, s 274(2A) applies in relation to a building or structure which is first used on or after 1 January 2006 or, where capital expenditure on the refurbishment of the building or structure is incurred is, subsequent to the incurring of that expenditure, first used on or after 1 January 2006.

See **5.104** regarding sale, insurance, salvage or compensation moneys for the purpose of calculating balancing charges.

5.409.2 Computation of balancing adjustment

The calculation of the balancing allowance or balancing charge is made by comparing the "sale, insurance, salvage or compensation moneys" (or consideration of the type referred to in TCA 1997, s 274(1)(a)(iv) – see below), if any, with the "residue of the expenditure" immediately before the sale or other event. Where the "sale, insurance, salvage or compensation moneys" are less than the residue, a balancing allowance is made; conversely, if greater, a balancing charge arises (TCA 1997, s 274(3), (4)).

However, the amount of any balancing charge cannot exceed the aggregate of the industrial building allowances actually made to the person concerned in respect of the related capital expenditure (TCA 1997, s 274(8)).

The meaning of "sale, insurance, salvage or compensation moneys", as defined in TCA 1997, s 318, has been explained in **5.104**. As indicated there, in the normal case of the sale of an industrial building, it is the net proceeds of the sale that are taken. For the special rules which require the open market price of the relevant interest in the building to be used instead, see **5.103** (non-arm's length transactions).

With regard to "consideration of the type referred to in TCA 1997, s 274(1)(a)(iv) (item c(iv) in the list of balancing events in **5.409.1** above), TCA 1997, s 274(3), by way of an anti-avoidance measure, provides that there is to be no balancing allowance in the case of consideration of this type which is received on or after 5 March 2001. TCA 1997, s 274(4), which provides for balancing charges, is unchanged in this respect.

The sale of the relevant interest in a building may involve the sale of an asset the capital expenditure on which only partly qualified for industrial building allowances. For example, no such allowances could have been given in respect of the cost of acquiring the land on which subsequent expenditure in constructing the buildings was incurred. Similarly, construction expenditure incurred before 30 September 1956 (or a later starting date for certain of the qualifying trade categories) was not eligible for the allowances. In any such case, the sale proceeds or any other sale, insurance, salvage or compensation moneys must be apportioned on a "just" basis to exclude from the balancing adjustment computation any part attributable to assets representing expenditure for which no industrial building allowances could be claimed (TCA 1997, s 282(2)).

TCA 1997, s 277 prescribes the method for determining the "residue of expenditure" in respect of any capital expenditure incurred on the construction of any building or structure In the more usual case where there is a sale of, or other balancing event affecting, an industrial building which has not been the subject of any previous sale or other relevant event, the residue of the expenditure is determined as follows:

> the qualifying expenditure on the building (as reduced by any government etc grants),
>
> *less*
>
> any initial allowances previously obtained,

less

all writing down allowances previously obtained (including any increased allowances claimed),

less

any notional allowances required to be deducted (see **5.411**).

Where a building or structure ceases altogether to be used, the outcome of this balancing event, since it does not involve the receipt of any proceeds, must be a balancing allowance equal to the residue of expenditure. A subsequent sale of the building or structure will trigger another balancing event. While it would be expected that this must result in a balancing charge equal to the proceeds on sale (proceeds less nil residue), it would appear that the residue in this case will continue to be what it was at the time of the first balancing event. While TCA 1997, s 277(5) provides that a write-off is to be made from the residue where a balancing allowance is made, this applies only to a balancing allowance arising "on the occasion of a sale".

As noted in **5.409.1** above relation to the balancing event described in (c)(iv) (consideration other than rent received on creation of a long lease), the amount by which the residue of the expenditure before that balancing event exceeds the amount of that consideration is to be written off (TCA 1997, s 277(7)). As also seen above, however, there can be no balancing allowance in the case of consideration of this type received on or after 5 March 2001.

The times at which the various allowances are regarded as being written off are set out in TCA 1997, s 277, as follows:

(a)   any initial allowance is written off at the time when the building (or the relevant part of the building) is first used;

(b)   the writing down allowance (including any increased allowances) for any accounting period is written off at the end of that period;

(c)   if the balancing event also occurs on the last day of the accounting period, the writing down allowance for that period is deducted first before the balancing adjustment is calculated; and

(d)   any notional allowance required to be deducted in respect of a period of non-qualifying use is written off at the particular time when it is necessary to determine the residue of the expenditure.

Example 5.409.2.1

Murray Growers Ltd commenced trading as market gardeners on 1 March 2005 and incurred capital expenditure on the construction of industrial buildings for use in its trade as follows:

Period	*Expenditure*
	€
1/10/04 – 28/2/05	66,000
1/3/05 – 31/12/05	64,000
1/1/06 – 31/12/06	90,000
	220,000

This expenditure was incurred in respect of three buildings which were brought into use as follows:

Building	Expenditure	Date
	€	
A	76,000	1/3/05
B	54,000	15/2/06
C	90,000	20/12/06

The following information is also relevant:

(a) In January 2003, Murray Growers Ltd had acquired a 21 year lease of the land on which the buildings were constructed at a cost of €31,000 (not included in the expenditure on which capital allowances were calculated);

(b) On 12 January 2008, the company sold the 21 year lease in the buildings (including the land) for €250,000, but continued its market gardening trade elsewhere.

Capital allowances in the form of writing down allowances obtained in respect of the total construction expenditure of €220,000 for the accounting periods ended 31 December 2005, 2006 and 2007 are as follows:

	€
Period 1/3/05 – 31/12/05:	
€76,000 x 10%	7,600
Year ended 31/12/06:	
€220,000 x 10%	22,000
Year ended 31/12/07:	
€220,000 x 10%	22,000
	51,600

The sale of the relevant interest for €250,000 in the year ended 31 December 2008 results in the following balancing adjustment:

	€	€
Construction expenditure		220,000
Less: capital allowances obtained (as above)	51,600	
Notional allowances for non-industrial use	Nil	
		51,600
		168,400
Sale proceeds	250,000	
Less: proportion allocated to land[1]	30,876	
		219,124
Surplus attributable to buildings		50,724
Capital allowances obtained		51,600
Therefore balancing charge		50,724

Note:

[1] To exclude the land element, Murray Growers Ltd agrees with the inspector of taxes that the sale proceeds should be apportioned in the ratio which the original cost of the lease bears to the combined costs of the lease and the construction of the buildings:

$$\text{€250,000} \times \frac{31,000}{31,000 + 220,000} = \text{€30,876}$$

Example 5.409.2.2

In 2002, W Stephens & Co Ltd incurred €640,000 on the construction of a factory building on a site in which it held a 999 year lease. The company leased the factory to Ellis Ltd, a manufacturing company, on a 21 year lease from 1 November 2003. The company makes up accounts to 31 December each year and the residue of the expenditure at 31 December 2006 is calculated as follows:

	€
Construction cost	640,000
Less: capital allowances to date:	
Annual allowances €640,000 x 4% x 4	102,400
Residue of expenditure 31/12/06	537,600

On 10 January 2007, W Stephens & Co Ltd creates a 99 year lease (to which the 21 year lease is subject) of the factory building in favour of George & Co Ltd for a premium of €600,000. As the premium is not treated as rent under TCA 1997, s 98, being a lease for more than 50 years (see **3.202.13**), TCA 1997, s 274(1)(a)(iv) (see balancing event (c)(v) above) applies and a balancing charge on W Stephens & Co Ltd arises as follows:

	€
Residue of expenditure 31/12/06	537,600
Less: amount received for grant of inferior interest	600,000
Balancing charge year ended 31/12/07	62,400

5.410 Capital allowances after sale of building

5.410.1 Introduction

A company which purchases the relevant interest in a building or structure the capital expenditure on the construction of which was incurred after 29 September 1956 (or after a later starting date for certain trade categories) is entitled to the industrial building writing down allowances if the building is used by it (or by a lessee) in one of the qualifying trade categories. It does not matter that the building may not have been used immediately prior to the purchase for a qualifying industrial purpose, or if there had never been any such prior use. It is the type of use to which the building is put at any relevant time following the company's acquisition of the relevant interest that is relevant in determining whether or not it is entitled to any writing down allowance for any accounting period. However, the approach to the computation of the writing down allowances after the purchase varies depending on whether or not the building was in use as an industrial building at the time the relevant interest was sold to it.

5.410.2 Sale of building: industrial building allowances previously given

Where the relevant interest in a building or structure is sold while it is an industrial building or structure (ie, while it is in use for a qualifying trade or undertaking), the residue of the expenditure immediately before the sale is treated as reduced by any balancing allowance made to, or as increased by any balancing charge made on, the vendor (TCA 1997, s 277(5), (6)). The purchaser of the relevant interest is then entitled, so long as the building continues to be an industrial building, to writing down allowances based on the residue of the expenditure, as so adjusted. The rate of writing down allowance after the sale is, however, different to what it has been up to that point. The new rate is the rate which is necessary to write off the residue of the expenditure on a straight-line basis evenly over the rest of the writing down period of the expenditure (TCA 1997, s 272(4)). For example, if a building with a 25 year writing down period commencing from its first use on 1 September 1996 is sold, while an industrial building, on 1 September 2002, the subsequent writing down allowances are made at the rate of one nineteenth of the adjusted residue of the expenditure for each 12 month accounting period from 1 September 2002 to 31 August 2021.

In the case of a qualifying hospital (see **5.401.7**), buildings and structures first used (or first used after refurbishment) on or after 1 February 2007 have a tax life (during which allowances may be transferred to a purchaser) of 15 years (previously seven years) (TCA 1997, s 272(4)(ga)).

Where the purchase price for the building or structure is less than the residue of the expenditure, the residue is treated as being the amount of that purchase price; in other words, writing down allowances to the purchaser are calculated by reference to the purchase price (TCA 1997, s 272(5)).

In the event of any subsequent sale of the relevant interest in the building while it is an industrial building during the writing down period, the residue of the expenditure must again be decreased or increased, as appropriate, by the balancing allowance or charge on that sale and a new rate of writing down allowance struck for the balance of the writing down life remaining at the time of that sale.

The writing down period of the construction expenditure on a building never changes irrespective of the number of times the relevant interest may change hands. Further, even if the original owner of the relevant interest has obtained capital allowances totalling 100% of the construction expenditure before selling it, the adjustment of the residue of the expenditure by the amount of a balancing charge made on the seller has the effect of reinstating capital expenditure for purposes of writing down allowances after the sale.

Example 5.410.2.1

Atlas Ltd, a manufacturing company since 1995, makes up accounts to 31 December each year. In the year ended 31 December 1999, it incurred capital expenditure of €900,000 on the construction of a new factory building on land the freehold interest in which it had acquired previously for €130,000. The building was first used in its trade on 1 January 2000. Atlas Ltd used the building in its manufacturing trade throughout the period 1 January 2000 to 30 June 2007, when it sold the entire freehold interest (the relevant interest) for €930,000 to Hyde Ltd, another manufacturing company. Atlas Ltd had claimed the maximum industrial building allowances to which it was entitled during its period of ownership of the building. The respective positions of the two companies following the sale of the building are as follows:

Atlas Ltd

Atlas Ltd had obtained the following capital allowances in respect of the total construction expenditure of €900,000 for the years ended 31 December 2000 to 31 December 2006:

€900,000 x 4% x 7 =   €252,000

The balancing charge computation for the year ended 31 December 2007 is as follows:

	€	€
Construction cost		900,000
Less: total industrial building allowances (as above)		252,000
Residue of expenditure		648,000
Sales proceeds	930,000	
Less: proportion allocated to land cost, say	117,379	812,621

$$€930,000 \times \frac{130,000}{900,000 + 130,000}$$

Surplus on sale allocated to buildings		164,621
(less than allowances obtained €252,000)		
Therefore balancing charge		164,621

Note:

> The first writing down allowance was not available until the year ended 31 December 2000 as the newly constructed building was not put into use for the purposes of the qualifying trade until that period.

Hyde Ltd

Hyde Ltd, already trading as a manufacturer, makes up its accounts 31 March each year. It puts the newly acquired factory into use in its trade on 1 August 2007. It is entitled to claim the industrial building writing down allowance for its year ended 31 March 2008 and for each subsequent accounting period so long as the building is in use for its manufacturing trade.

The writing down allowance for each 12-month accounting period during which the building remains an industrial building is determined as follows:

	€
Residue of expenditure (prior to sale)	648,000
Add: balancing charge made on Atlas Ltd	164,621
Residue of expenditure (after sale)	812,621

Length of remainder of writing down period:
30 June 2007 to 31 December 2024 (ie, 17 years 6 months (17.5 years))
Therefore annual allowance for each 12 month period
€812,621 x 1/17.5   46,435

Where the relevant interest which is sold relates to a building in respect of which industrial building allowances were given, the sale being at a time when the building was not an industrial building (ignoring any periods of temporary disuse following immediately on a period of qualifying use), different considerations are relevant. As normally happens, a balancing adjustment is made on the vendor in accordance with TCA 1997, s 274(1). It is again necessary to calculate the residue by reference to any balancing adjustments on the sale (TCA 1997, s 277(6), (7)). This calculation is, however, relevant only in so far as the purchaser of the building cannot subsequently claim writing down allowances in excess of the amount of the residue following sale (TCA 1997, s 272(6)).

The writing down allowance to which the purchaser is entitled is the amount arrived at by applying the writing down rate applicable to the category of use (eg, 4% for a mill, factory or similar premises) to the original construction expenditure incurred (TCA 1997, s 272(2)). Exceptionally in this situation, it would appear that writing down allowances may be claimed after the expiry of the writing down life of the building. This is because the amendment by FA 1990 s 78 of TCA 1997, s 274(1) (then ITA 1967 s 265(1)), permitting a balancing adjustment to be made on the sale or other event relating to the building at a time when it was not an industrial building, was not accompanied by a corresponding amendment to TCA 1997, s 272(4) (then ITA 1967 s 264(3)) affecting the purchaser.

5.410.3 Sale of building: no industrial building allowances previously given

If a building which had not been an industrial building, at the time it is acquired by a company, subsequently commences to be an industrial building (by being used for the purposes of a qualifying industrial trade by the company as the holder of the relevant interest in relation to the original construction expenditure), that company becomes entitled to claim industrial building writing down allowances under the ordinary rules. On the acquisition of the building, there is no change in the rate of allowance applicable for the trade category in question, since TCA 1997, s 272(4) (as discussed in **5.410.2** above) only applies where there is a sale at a time when the building is in use as an industrial building.

Accordingly, the acquiring company now carrying on a qualifying trade is entitled to writing down allowances on the original cost of construction incurred by the previous owner or, if the previous owner had purchased the building unused, on the cost of construction deemed to have been incurred by him under TCA 1997, s 279 (see **5.408**). The rate of writing down allowances for the acquiring company is determined for the particular qualifying trade category by reference to the date or dates on which the original construction expenditure was incurred (or deemed to have been incurred). The writing down period of the building similarly remains fixed for the relevant trade category by reference to the date of its first use for any purpose by the previous owner, or by any earlier owner.

If and when the acquiring company sells the relevant interest in the building during its writing down period, the residue of the expenditure is determined as the original construction expenditure less all previous industrial building allowances made to the company and to any previous owner while it was an industrial building, and less the appropriate notional allowances for all periods of non-industrial use since the building was first used for any purpose by any owner of the relevant interest.

Example 5.410.3.1

Usher Ltd, a speculative building company, constructs a building on a freehold site which it owns. The building is completed at a cost to the company of €210,000 on 31 May 1997. It sells the freehold interest in the building for €235,000 on 1 July 1997 to Eden Ltd, which puts the building into use for the purposes of its distribution business on 1 August 1997.

On 1 August 2006, having used the building for the distribution business only, Eden Ltd sells the freehold interest for €500,000 to Aston Ltd, which immediately puts the building into use for the purposes of its manufacturing trade. The consequences of these transactions are as follows:

(a) Eden Ltd is deemed to have incurred construction expenditure of €235,000 (the price paid to the builder – see **5.408.3**) on the building on 1 July 1997, but is not entitled to any initial or writing down allowances for this expenditure as the building was not an industrial building;

(b) on putting the building into use for the purposes of a qualifying trade, Aston Ltd becomes entitled to writing down allowances from 1 August 2006, but based on the deemed construction expenditure of €235,000 incurred by Eden Ltd;

(c) assuming a continued qualifying use from 1 August 2006, an annual allowance of €9,400 (4% x €235,000) is available for the remainder of the 25 year writing down period, ie, up to 31 July 2022 (from the date of first use of the building); and

(d) for the purposes of computing a balancing allowance or charge in the event of a further sale of the relevant interest in the building on or before 31 July 2022, the expenditure of €235,000 would be written down by the amount of the actual allowances claimed but also by the notional allowances for the 9 years of non-qualifying use up to 1 August 2006, ie, €235,000 x 4% x 9 = €84,600.

5.411 Deduction of notional allowances

Under TCA 1997, s 277(4), a notional writing down allowance (ie, one which is not an actual allowance and which has no effect on the computation of profit or loss) is made in arriving at the residue of the expenditure if, for any period or periods after the date on which the building or structure is first used for any purpose, the building was not in use for the purposes of a qualifying trade or undertaking. The notional allowance must be written off the expenditure where it is necessary to determine the amount of the residue. Normally, this will be at the time of a sale of the relevant interest in the building, or on the occurrence of one of the other events requiring a balancing allowance or charge to be computed.

The amount to be written off in any relevant case is arrived at by computing the notional writing down allowances at the appropriate rate or rates for accounting periods of a total length equal to the period or periods during which the building or structure was not in use as an industrial building or structure. If there has been no sale or other balancing event since the date of first use for any purpose, the rate of the notional allowance is the normal writing down allowance rate for the trade category concerned appropriate to the date of the expenditure. If, on the other hand, the building or structure was previously sold while an industrial building, any notional allowance required for a period subsequent to such previous sale is made at the same annual rate as that determined under TCA 1997, s 272(4) (see **5.410.2**).

Where a balancing allowance or charge arises in the case of a building, while it is an industrial building, and where there has been any period of non-industrial use since the first use of the building (or since any prior sale as an industrial building), TCA 1997, s 274(5)(b) provides that the balancing allowance or charge is to be reduced to allow for the fact that writing down allowances were not available for the period of non-industrial use. Where this happens, the balancing allowance or charge that would otherwise apply is first computed by comparing the residue of the expenditure (after actual and notional allowances) with the sale, insurance, salvage or compensation moneys. This "provisional" allowance or charge is then adjusted to arrive at the final balancing allowance (BA) or balancing charge (BC), as follows:

$$\text{Final BA/BC} = \frac{\text{industrial use period}}{\text{relevant period}} \times \text{provisional BA/BC}$$

As usual, any balancing charge may not exceed the amount of the actual allowances made. For the above calculation, it is necessary to determine the length of the relevant period and of the industrial use period (defined below).

If the building or structure was an industrial building or structure at the end of the basis period for any tax year prior to the year 1960/61 (so that no annual allowance would have been claimed for that year – 1960/61 was the first year for annual allowances), it is necessary to write off an amount of 2% in respect of each such year. If the building is subsequently sold when in use as an industrial building, any balancing allowance or charge on such sale is reduced by TCA 1997, s 274(5)(b) in the same way as for a sale after a period which included a period or periods of non-industrial use.

Relevant period

The relevant period is the period beginning when the building was first used for any purpose and ending on whichever of the following days is appropriate:

(a) if the event giving rise to the balancing allowance or charge occurs on the last day of the accounting period (for a company), that day; or

(b) otherwise, the last day of the immediately preceding accounting period.

However, if there was any previous sale of the building when it was in use as an industrial building, the relevant period in relation to the current sale begins on the day immediately following the date of that prior sale or, where there has been more than one such sale, the last such sale (and not on the date of first use of the building).

Industrial use period

The industrial use period, in the case of a company, is the expression used here to denote the period of time equal in length to the total length of all the accounting periods (or basis periods for years of assessment prior to 1976/77) for which an industrial building writing down allowance was given (but excluding the whole or any part of any period not falling within the relevant period).

Where, however, for any accounting period within the writing down period for the building, the construction expenditure in question has previously been written down to nil, so that no writing down allowance is made for the period, that accounting period remains part of the industrial use period (TCA 1997, s 274(5)(c)).

Example 5.411.1

On 17 November 1988, Strahan Ltd incurred €280,000 on the construction of a warehouse which it brought into use on 1 January 1989 for the purposes of its distribution business. On 1 July 2000, the company commenced a new manufacturing business for which the warehouse is used. Industrial building writing down allowances at 4% of the original cost of construction are claimed for the company's accounting year ended 31 December 2000 and following accounting periods.

The warehouse is sold for €500,000 (excluding proportion allocated to land) on 31 March 2007. The resulting balancing adjustment is computed as follows:

	€
Construction cost	280,000
Less: industrial building annual allowances for	
7 years ended 31/12/00 to 31/12/06	
€280,000 x 4% x 7	78,400
	201,600
Less: notional allowances for period of non-industrial use	
€280,000 x 4% x 11.5[1]	128,800
Residue of expenditure before sale	72,800
Sale proceeds (excluding land)	500,000
Surplus on sale (31/3/07)	427,200
Provisional balancing charge y/e 31/12/07	427,200

Relevant period:

1/1/89 (date of first use) to 31/12/06[2] = 18 years

Industrial use period (within relevant period):

1/7/00 to 31/12/06 = 6.5 years

Balancing charge y/e 31/12/07:

€427,200 x 6.5/18 =	154,267

Limited by TCA 1997, s 274(8) to actual allowances	78,400

Notes:

[1] The period of non-industrial use is the 11 years and 6 months from 1 January 1989 to 30 June 2000.

[2] As the sale took place on 31 March 2007, which is not the last day of the accounting period ending 31 December 2007, the relevant period ends on 31 December 2006.

5.412   Sale of building constructed at different dates

An industrial building may have been constructed in more than one accounting period so that the related construction expenditure may have been incurred at different stages in its writing down period. Again, some of the expenditure may have been incurred before the commencement date for industrial building allowances in the trade concerned. If such a building is sold as one unit while still an industrial building, it may be necessary to apportion the sale consideration for the whole building between the parts of the building representing the different expenditures so as to exclude from the balancing adjustment computation the appropriate proportion of the sale proceeds attributable to any construction expenditure not subject to a balancing allowance or charge.

The requirement of TCA 1997, s 282(2) to apportion the sale consideration on a "just" basis where part of the expenditure did not qualify for industrial building allowances has been discussed in the context of the land cost element in **5.409**. This provision is also applicable if part of the expenditure had been incurred before industrial building allowances were available for the particular trade category, but where a balancing adjustment falls to be made in respect of later construction expenditure which did qualify. The question as to what is a just apportionment of the sale proceeds must depend on the facts of the particular case.

For example, if a factory building had been constructed as one unit over a period that fell partly before and partly on or after 30 September 1956 so that only the expenditure on or after that date qualified for industrial building allowances, the apportionment of the proceeds of a sale in, say, 1995 might appropriately be made by reference to the respective construction costs incurred before, and on or after, 30 September 1956. On the other hand, a different basis of apportionment might be required on the sale of a factory building constructed originally in 1953, for which there were no capital allowances, but which had been extended by qualifying expenditure in, say, 1984.

While no question of any balancing allowance or charge has to be considered if there is a sale or other relevant event after the end of the writing down life of all the construction expenditure on an industrial building, an apportionment of the sale or other moneys is required if one part of the construction expenditure has reached the end of its writing clown life, but another part has not.

Example 5.412.1

Merrion Park Ltd incurred €570,000 on the construction of a hotel building which it first put into use in its hotel trade on 1 January 1993. During its year ended 31 December 2000, the company built an extension to the hotel at a further cost of €250,000. The extension was first used for the company's hotel trade on 1 July 2000. On 29 September 2007, the entire hotel building was destroyed by fire and eventually insurance proceeds of €420,000 were received in full settlement of the company's insurance claim.

Since the writing down period for the original expenditure of €570,000 had expired on 31 December 2002, 10 years after the original building was first used, it is necessary to limit the balancing adjustment by reference to the expenditure of €250,000. It is considered that an apportionment of the insurance proceeds by reference to historical cost would not be reasonable due to the effect of inflation in the period 1993 to 2000.

The company obtained a professional opinion to the effect that had the entire building, including the extension, been constructed in 2000, the total cost would have come to €1,300,000. On this basis, the balancing adjustment computation would be as follows:

	€
Construction cost of extension	250,000
Less: industrial building allowances obtained:	
IBAA years ended 31/12/00 – 31/12/06	
€25,000 x 7	175,000
Residue of expenditure (31/12/06)	75,000
Insurance proceeds – proportion attributable to extension:	
€420,000 x 250,000/1,300,000	80,769
Balancing charge y/e 31/12/07 (extension only)	5,769

5.413 Anti-avoidance: balancing allowances

TCA 1997, s 275 prevents the avoidance of tax which would result from the obtaining by a "relevant person" of a balancing allowance through certain arrangements involving the sale of the relevant interest in an industrial building where that interest is subject to an inferior interest. An *inferior interest* is defined as any interest in or right over the building or structure in question, whether granted by the relevant person or by someone else.

TCA 1997, s 275 applies in the following circumstances:

(a) the relevant interest in a building or structure is sold subject to an inferior interest;

(b) as a result of the sale, an industrial building balancing allowance would, but for TCA 1997, s 275, be made to or for the benefit of the relevant person (the person entitled to the relevant interest immediately before the sale); and

(c) either:

    (i) the relevant person, the purchaser of the relevant interest and the grantee of the inferior interest, or any two of them, are connected with each other within the meaning of TCA 1997, s 10 – see **2.3**, or

    (ii) it appears with respect to the sale or the grant of the inferior interest, or with respect to transactions including the sale or grant, that the sole or main benefit expected to accrue to the parties or any of them was the obtaining of an industrial building writing down or balancing allowance.

Where all three circumstances apply, TCA 1997, s 275(3) provides that the net sales proceeds, for the purposes of any balancing allowance computation in respect of the sale of the relevant interest in the building, is to be either:

(a) the actual net proceeds of sale plus an amount equal to any premium receivable by the relevant person for the grant of the inferior interest (in a case where a commercial rent is payable by the grantee of the inferior interest); or

(b) the amount of any premium receivable by the relevant person for the granting of the inferior lease, plus an amount equal to what the sales proceeds would have been if a commercial rent (having regard to any premium actually payable) had been payable (in a case where no rent or no commercial rent is payable).

This "notional" net sales proceeds figure may not, however, exceed the amount necessary to secure that no balancing allowance will be made. It cannot create a balancing charge in a case where no balancing charge would result in the absence of these rules. If in any case the result of TCA 1997, s 275 is to reduce or cancel entirely the normal balancing allowance in respect of any capital expenditure, the normal balancing allowance must still be deducted for the purposes of arriving at the residue of that expenditure immediately after the sale (TCA 1997, s 275(4)).

A *commercial rent* is such rent as might reasonably be expected to be received having regard to the premium payable for the grant of the interest if the transaction had been at arm's length. For the purposes of (a) and (b) above, *premium* is defined as including any capital consideration except so much of any sum as corresponds to any amount of rent or profits falling to be computed by reference to that sum under TCA 1997, s 98 (see **3.202.13**). In other words, any premium or other sum payable in respect of the granting of a lease, to the extent that it is taxable as rent by TCA 1997, s 98, is not to be treated as a premium in applying the provisions of TCA 1997, s 275(3). However, any part of the premium that is not so taxable under the rules of TCA 1997, s 98 must be taken into account in arriving at the amount of the net sale proceeds as described above.

5.414   Rates and writing down periods

The current rates of industrial building initial and writing down allowances, and the dates of the expenditure for which they are given, have been summarised respectively in **5.405.3** and **5.406**. Since it may still be relevant for balancing allowances and balancing charges purposes to consider capital expenditure incurred on earlier dates, the table below summarises the rates of allowances and writing down periods that have applied since industrial building allowances were introduced. Except where indicated in the notes below, the period beyond which a balancing allowance or charge may not be made is the same as the writing down period.

Date of expenditure	Rate of allowance		Writing down period
	Initial	*Annual*	
Mill, factory or similar premises:			
30/9/56 – 13/12/61[6]	10%	2%	50 years
14/12/61 – 15/1/75	20%	2%	50 years
16/1/75 – 31/3/91	50%	4%	25 years
1/4/91 – 31/3/92	25%	4%	25 years
1/4/92 -	Nil	4%	25 years
Dock undertaking:			
6/4/59 – 13/12/61[6]	10%	2%	50 years
14/12/61 – 15/1/75	20%	2%	50 years
16/1/75 – 31/3/91	50%	4%	25 years
1/4/91 – 31/3/92	25%	4%	25 years
1/4/92 -	Nil	4%	25 years
Market gardening:			
7/4/64 – 5/4/65[8]	10%	-	10 years
6/4/65 – 5/4/74	10%	10%	10 years
6/4/74 – 31/3/92	20%	10%	10 years
1/4/92 -	Nil	10%	10 years
Holiday cottages:			
30/9/56 – 31/12/59[6]	10%	2%	50 years
1/1/60 – 31/3/92	10%	10%	10 years
1/4/92 – 3/12/02[9]	Nil	10%	10 years
Guest houses or holiday hostels:			
3/2/05 -	Nil	4%	25 years
Hotels and holiday camps:			
30/9/56 – 31/12/59[6, 7]	10%	2%	50 years
1/1/60 – 31/3/92	10%	10%	10 years
1/4/92 – 26/1/94	Nil	10%	10 years
27/1/94 – 3/12/02	Nil	15%	6 years
		+ 10%	7th year[2]
4/12/02 -	Nil	4%	25 years

Date of expenditure	Rate of allowance		Writing down period
	Initial	*Annual*	
Caravan and camping sites			
1/1/08 -	Nil	4%	25 years
Intensive production of cattle etc:			
6/4/71 – 5/4/74	–	10%	10 years
6/4/74 – 31/3/91	20%	10%	10 years
1/4/91 – 31/3/92	20%	10%	10 years
1/4/92 -	Nil	10%	10 years
Multi-storey car-parks:			
29/1/81 – 31/3/91	50%	4%	25 years
1/4/91 – 31/3/92	25%	4%	25 years
1/4/92 -	Nil	4%	25 years
Laboratories for mineral analysis:			
25/1/84 – 31/3/91[1]	50%	4%	25 years
1/4/91 – 31/3/92	25%	4%	25 years
1/4/92 -	Nil	4%	25 years
Airport runways and aprons:			
24/4/92 -	Nil	4%	25 years[3]
Airport buildings and structures			
vesting day – 1/1/99	Nil	4%	25 years[4]
Private nursing homes[11]			
3/12/97	Nil	15%	6 years
		+ 10%	7th year[5]
Private convalescent homes	Nil	15%	6 years
		+ 10%	7th year[5]
Qualifying hospitals	Nil	15%	6 years
		+ 10%	7th year[5]
Qualifying mental health centres	Nil	15%	6 years
		+ 10%	7th year[10]
Qualifying specialist palliative care units	Nil	15%	6 years
		+ 10%	7th year[10]

Notes:

[1] For the right to elect for an increased writing down allowance, in respect of expenditure incurred after 1 February 1978 (or in the case of a laboratory for mineral analysis – 24 January 1984), see **5.407**.

[2] No balancing allowance or charge may be made by reason of an event occurring more than 7 years after the building or structure was first used.

[3] No balancing allowance or charge may be made by reason of an event occurring more than 10 years after the building or structure was first used or, in the case of a building or structure in existence on the vesting day and vested in Air Rianta, more than 10 years after the vesting day.

⁴   No balancing allowance or charge may be made by reason of an event occurring more than 10 years after the building or structure was first used or, in the case of a building or structure already in existence on the vesting day and vested in Dublin Airport Authority, more than 10 years after the vesting day or, in the case of a building or structure already in existence on 27 March 1998 in any other case, more than 10 years after that date.

⁵   No balancing allowance or charge may be made by reason of an event occurring more than (i) where the building or structure was first used before 1 February 2007, 10 years after it was first used, or (ii) where the building or structure was first used on or after 1 February 2007, 15 years after it was first used, or (iii) where capital expenditure on its refurbishment is incurred and subsequently the building or structure is first used on or after 1 February 2007, 15 years after it was first used subsequent to the incurring of that expenditure.

⁶   No annual allowance was available for any year prior to 1960/61.

⁷   Holiday camps are treated as hotels. No allowance, initial or annual, for any year prior to 1960/61.

⁸   Expenditure from 7 April 1964 qualifies. No allowance, initial or annual, for any year prior to 1965/66.

⁹   Subject to transitional arrangements whereby allowances available for expenditure up to 31 December 2004 on certain conditions.

¹⁰   No balancing allowance or charge may be made by reason of an event occurring more than 15 years after it was first used or, where capital expenditure on its refurbishment is incurred, 15 years after it was first used subsequent to the incurring of that expenditure.

¹¹   For qualifying residential units in respect of which capital expenditure was incurred on or after 1 May 2007, no balancing allowance or charge may be made by reason of an event occurring more than 20 years after the unit was first used or, where capital expenditure on its refurbishment is incurred, 20 years after it was first used subsequent to the incurring of that expenditure (see **5.401.5**).

5.415   Special provisions for leases

TCA 1997, s 281 provides for the availability of writing down allowances in certain circumstances involving the deemed continuation of a lease, and for the inclusion of certain sums arising on the termination of a lease in the computation of balancing allowances or charges. A company holding a leasehold interest in land (including buildings) may have incurred capital expenditure in constructing a building on the land, or in extending an existing building, or it may have purchased or otherwise acquired a leasehold interest that is the relevant interest in relation to such capital expenditure. In either event, under normal rules, the company is entitled to writing down allowances so long as it retains that interest and the buildings are in use for a qualifying trade or undertaking. If the leasehold interest comes to an end, it is necessary to compute a balancing allowance or charge by comparing the residue of the expenditure related to the leasehold interest with any sale, insurance, salvage or compensation moneys received (see **5.409**).

TCA 1997, s 281 contains three rules relating to the termination of a leasehold interest and which modify the normal treatment outlined above. These rules are as follows:

(a) If a company which is the lessee of a building, with the permission of the lessor, remains in possession after the termination of the lease, but without the granting of a new lease to it, the original lease is deemed to continue so long as the lessee actually remains in possession. Consequently, the lessee continues to be entitled to writing down allowances on any qualifying expenditure incurred by it, or by any previous holder of the leasehold interest. Furthermore, no question of a balancing allowance or charge arises so long as the lessee continues to remain in possession with the consent of the lessor.

(b) Where, on the termination of a lease, a new lease is granted to a lessee company, either due to its being entitled by statute to a new lease or in pursuance of an option available to it under the terms of the first lease, the second lease is treated as if it were a continuation of the first lease. In other words, there is no question of a balancing allowance or charge arising and the lessee continues to be entitled to the writing down allowances.

(c) Where, on the termination of a lease, the lessor pays any sum to the lessee in respect of a building or structure comprised in the lease, the lease is treated as if it had come to an end by reason of its surrender in consideration of the payment received. This means that the sum paid to the lessee must be brought into account in the sale or other moneys brought into the computation of any balancing allowance or charge in respect of any capital expenditure attaching to the leasehold interest. This situation could arise, for example, where the lessee agrees for a consideration to surrender its leasehold interest before its proper termination date or where it receives some payment from the lessor at the end of a lease period, say in consideration for not exercising a legal right or an available option for a renewal or the granting of a new lease.

5.416   How industrial buildings allowances are made

5.416.1 Introduction

The rules governing the manner in which capital allowances are given and balancing charges made have been discussed generally in **5.105**. For industrial building allowances purposes, there are specific provisions dealing with the manner in which allowances are given and balancing charges are made (including allowances and charges relating to other buildings or structures treated as industrial buildings or structures, eg, commercial buildings in urban renewal areas).

The rules vary depending on whether the person entitled to the allowances in respect of the relevant building or structure ("the premises") is the person who uses the premises for the purposes of a trade carried on by him, or is a lessor deriving rental or other income taxable under Schedule D Case V from the premises, or is a lessor deriving rental or other income from the premises taxable otherwise than under Case V.

5.416.2 Premises used for trade of person entitled to allowances

Where the premises are used by a company entitled to the capital allowances in respect of the capital expenditure for the purpose of a trade carried on by it, the industrial building initial and writing down allowance, and any balancing allowance or balancing charge on a disposal or other event giving rise thereto, are made to or on that company in taxing its trade (TCA 1997, s 278(1)). In the case of a company, an allowance given in taxing a trade is given effect by treating the allowance as a trading expense of the trade while a charge made in taxing the trade is treated as a trading receipt of the trade (see **5.105.2**).

Normally, a building or structure only qualifies for the industrial building allowances if it is in use for the purposes of a trade (see **5.401.1**). However, as already indicated, a building or structure (other than an industrial building) which is situated in a designated urban renewal area (including the Dublin Custom House Docks area) is treated as if it were an industrial building. A company using a building or structure in any of these areas for the purpose of its trade is entitled to the industrial building allowances, and is subject to a balancing charge where relevant, in taxing its trade.

The effect of granting of an industrial building allowance in taxing the profits of a trade is to require the allowance to be deducted from the taxable profit as computed under Schedule D Case I (or possibly Case II) for the relevant accounting period. Conversely, any balancing charge is added to the taxable profits of the trade.

Where industrial building allowances given in taxing the profits of a trade for any accounting period exceed the taxable profits for that period, the excess constitutes a trading loss which may be carried forward against future profits from the same trade. Alternatively, the loss may be set off against the total profits of the company for the same accounting period and, if the company was then carrying on the trade, against the total profits of immediately preceding accounting periods equal in length to the period in which the loss arose (TCA 1997, s 396(2) – see **4.101**). The loss may also be surrendered under the group relief provisions (TCA 1997, s 411 – see **8.3**).

5.416.3 Allowances for lessors chargeable under Schedule D Case V

Where a company which is entitled to an industrial building initial or writing down allowance or a balancing allowance, or which is subject to a balancing charge, in respect of any premises is a lessor chargeable to tax under Schedule D Case V, the allowance or charge is made to or on it in charging its income under that Case (TCA 1997, s 278(1)).

The industrial building initial or writing down allowance and any balancing allowance is available to the Case V lessor company "primarily against" its income chargeable to corporation tax under Case V or any balancing charge under that Case (TCA 1997, s 278(6)).

Accordingly, the total of the industrial building writing down, balancing and initial allowances due to a lessor company taxable under Case V for any accounting period is deducted from or set off against its income chargeable to corporation tax under Case V (and against any balancing charges within that Case) for the same period (TCA 1997, s 308(1), (2)). To the extent that the total of all the industrial building allowances for any accounting period exceeds the sum of the lessor's Case V income and balancing charges for that period, the excess is carried forward under TCA 1997, s 308(3) for set off against the Case V income and balancing charges for the next accounting period (and so on for succeeding periods until fully used up).

A company taxable under Case V as a lessor may, alternatively, offset any industrial building allowances which cannot be offset against the Case V income and balancing charges in the period for which the allowances arise against the total profits for that period; such excess allowances may also, if the company was then within the charge to tax, be offset against total profits of the immediately preceding accounting periods equal in length to the period in which the excess arose (TCA 1997, s 308(4)).

The rules regarding the manner of giving industrial building allowances to a Case V lessor are discussed further and illustrated in **5.505.1**.

5.416.4 Allowances for lessors chargeable under Schedule D Case IV

Where a company which is entitled to an industrial building initial or writing down allowance, or balancing allowance, in respect of any premises is a lessor chargeable to tax otherwise than under Case V, the allowance is given by way of discharge or repayment of tax (TCA 1997, s 278(2), (3), (4)).

Apart from the case of rental or other income from the leasing of premises situated outside the State which is taxable under Case III as the income from a foreign possession, any income from the leasing of premises which is not within Case V is chargeable to tax under Case IV (although there are very few instances of this). Where income is so chargeable, any industrial building allowances in respect of the premises are available primarily against income chargeable under Case IV and/or any balancing charge within that Case (TCA 1997, s 278(6)) and are to be given "by way of discharge or repayment of tax" (see **4.107**).

The provisions of TCA 1997, s 308(4), as discussed above in relation to Case V lessors, are applicable in a corresponding way where any of the industrial building allowances are to be given by way of discharge or repayment of tax. In this connection the available income is all income chargeable under Case IV ("income of the specified class"), which includes many types of miscellaneous income. Any Case IV industrial building allowances are available to be set off against the total of the income taxable within that Case (and not only against the income from premises).

To the extent that any industrial building allowances within Case IV for any accounting period (ie, given by way of discharge or repayment of tax) exceed the total income and any balancing charges taxable under that Case, a company has the same choices as for Case V industrial building allowances, that is, to carry forward the excess industrial building allowances to succeeding accounting periods for offset against income of the same class, to offset the excess allowances against the total profits for the period in which the excess arises and, if the company was then within the charge to tax, against total profits of the immediately preceding accounting periods equal in length to the period in which the excess arose (TCA 1997, s 308(4)).

5.416.5 Registered holiday cottages: limitation on set-off against other income

Industrial building writing down and initial allowances may be restricted where they relate to expenditure incurred on the acquisition or construction of a building or structure which is, or is to be, a building or structure in use as a holiday cottage, as defined in TCA 1997, s 268(3) (see **5.401.1**). Subject to TCA 1997, s 405(3) (see below) TCA 1997, s 405(1) restricts the use of these capital allowances. The holiday cottages referred to in TCA 1997, s 268(3) are those included in a register of holiday cottages established by the National Tourism Development Authority under the provisions of any Act of the Oireachtas passed after 29 July 1969.

The effect of the restriction is that the writing down allowances and any initial allowance for capital expenditure incurred on registered holiday cottages may not be used for any of the following purposes:

(a) to create or increase a trading loss to be set off against the total profits of a company by virtue of a claim under TCA 1997, s 396(2) – see **4.101**);

(b) to be set off against a company's total profits by virtue of a claim under TCA 1997, s 308(4) – capital allowances given by way of discharge or repayment of tax or capital allowances in excess of Case V income – see **4.107**); or

(c) in respect of expenditure incurred on or after 6 April 2000, to be set off against a company's total profits by virtue of a claim under TCA 1997, s 420(2) – group relief in respect of excess capital allowances given by way of discharge or repayment of tax or in charging income under Case V of Schedule D.

Accordingly, the industrial building writing down allowance and any initial allowance in respect of a company's capital expenditure on holiday cottages within TCA 1997, s 405 may only be set off against the company's Case I income or balancing charges (if the holiday cottages are in use for its own trade) or against its Case IV or V income or balancing charges (where the company is entitled to the allowances as a lessor of the holiday cottages). The allowances may be so set off against the Case I, Case IV or Case V income either in the accounting period to which they relate or in a subsequent accounting period by way of carry forward of unused allowances.

TCA 1997, s 405 makes no reference to balancing allowances so that there is no restriction on the use of any balancing allowance which may arise on the disposal of the holiday cottages (or other event requiring a balancing adjustment) and any such balancing allowances continue to be available for set off against total profits.

As seen above, the ring-fencing treatment of capital allowances applies only to the National Tourism Development Authority registered holiday cottages. The obligation to register holiday cottages with the National Tourism Development Authority applies only to group schemes, which would involve the letting or operation of 8 or more cottages (not including any unit used for management or administration purposes). That being the case, Case I rather than Case V treatment is likely to be appropriate in these cases.

The restriction provided for in TCA 1997, s 405 does not apply to a building or structure which is in use as a holiday cottage and comprised in premises first registered on or after 6 April 2001 in a register of approved holiday cottages established by the National Tourism Development Authority under Part III of the Tourist Traffic Act 1939, where, prior to such premises becoming to registered:

(a) the building or structure was a qualifying premises within the meaning of TCA 1997, s 353 (capital allowances for non-industrial buildings in Seaside Resort Areas – see 2001-2002 or earlier editions of this book), by virtue of being in use for the purposes of the operation of a tourist accommodation facility specified in a list published under s 9 of the Tourist Traffic Act 1957; and

(b) the provisions of TCA 1997, s 355(4) (Seaside Resort Areas: limitation on set-off against other income – see 2001-2002 or earlier editions of this book) did not apply to expenditure incurred on the acquisition, construction or refurbishment of that building or structure, by virtue of the provisions of TCA 1997, s 355(5) (TCA 1997, s 405(3)).

5.416.6 Limited partnerships

Capital allowances made by way of discharge or repayment of tax to which a limited partner is entitled by virtue of its participation in a trade and which, to the extent that they exceed the income of the class to which they relate, may normally be set off against total profits in accordance with TCA 1997, s 308(4). TCA 1997, s 1013(2)(b) restricts the extent to which a partner company may avail of TCA 1997, s 308(4) by confining the excess capital allowances to the company's share of profits arising from the partnership trade (see **13.703**).

5.416.7 Property investment schemes

TCA 1997, s 408 counteracts the use of industrial building allowances through certain property investment schemes. The section restricts the manner in which capital allowances may be set off against income other than income arising from the interest held in the particular building or structure. The restriction applies to schemes or arrangements which provide facilities for the public, or a section of the public, to share income or gains arising from the acquisition, holding or disposal of an interest in a building or structure.

A *property investment scheme* means any scheme or arrangement to provide facilities, whether promoted by public advertisement or otherwise, for the public or a section of the public to share, either directly or indirectly, whether as beneficiaries under a trust or by any other means, in income or gains arising or deriving from the acquisition, holding or disposal of, or of an interest in, a building or structure or a part thereof. It does not include a scheme or arrangement in respect of which the Revenue Commissioners or, on appeal, the Appeal Commissioners, based on information provided to them, are of the opinion that:

(a)   the manner in which the persons share in the income or gains; and

(b)   the number of persons who so share,

are in accordance with a practice which commonly prevailed in the State during the period of 5 years ending immediately before 30 January 1991 for the sharing of such income or gains by persons resident in the State so that the persons concerned qualified for relief, as regards companies, under TCA 1997, s 308(4).

Where a company holds an interest in or deriving from a building or structure pursuant to a property investment scheme (a "specified interest"), TCA 1997, s 308(4) is not to have any effect as respects an allowance under TCA 1997, s 271 (industrial building allowance) or TCA 1997, s 272 (industrial building annual allowance) which falls to be made to the company by reason of the holding of that interest. The effect of this restriction is that no part of the capital allowances arising may be used by the company against any of its profits apart from the income from the building or structure held under the property investment scheme.

The restriction does not apply to a scheme or arrangement which, in the opinion of the Revenue Commissioners (which is subject to appeal to the Appeal Commissioners), is in accordance with a practice for the sharing of income or gains which commonly prevailed in the State in the 5 years up to 30 January 1991 where the participants qualified for relief by way of set-off of the capital allowances against income or profits other than income from the building or structure in question.

In practice, it is understood that schemes involving up to 13 investors may be approved by the Revenue Commissioners.

5.5 LEASED INDUSTRIAL BUILDINGS

5.501 Introduction
5.502 Initial allowance
5.503 Writing down allowances
5.504 Balancing allowances and charges
5.505 Manner of granting allowances to lessors
5.506 Foreign leased industrial buildings

5.501 Introduction

A company in receipt of rental income from an industrial building or structure is entitled to the same capital allowances as a company which uses industrial buildings for a trade, provided it meets the conditions under which the various allowances are available to a lessor. As an exception, a lessor is not entitled to claim the increased writing down allowance (free depreciation) provided for by TCA 1997, s 273 (see **5.407.1**)

The meaning of the term "industrial building or structure", as it appears in TCA 1997, s 268, has been explained in **5.401.1** – ie, a building or structure in use for the purposes of certain specified types of trade, for example, manufacturing, market gardening, or hotel keeping. The entitlement of a lessor to capital allowances against Schedule D Case V income is limited to capital expenditure on industrial buildings which are, at the relevant time, in use by the lessee for one of the types of qualifying trade. Writing down allowances may, however, continue to be claimed during a period of temporary disuse immediately following use in a qualifying trade (see **5.503**), while a balancing allowance or charge may similarly arise in a period of temporary disuse (see **5.504**)

A non-resident company with Case V rental income from leasing an industrial building in the State is normally chargeable to income tax (and not corporation tax) so that it is given industrial building allowances by reference to years of assessment. A non-resident company subject to corporation tax in respect of Case V income from an industrial building held in the course of, or as part of the property of, a trade carried on through a branch or agency in the State is, however, entitled to industrial building allowances by reference to accounting periods.

The industrial building allowances to which a lessor company is entitled, provided it meets the necessary conditions in any case, are summarised as follows:

(a)   initial allowance: in respect of qualifying capital expenditure (**5.404**) incurred by the company itself, if the conditions set out in **5.502** are met;

(b)   writing down, or annual, allowance: in respect of qualifying capital expenditure, whether or not incurred by the company itself, if it holds the relevant interest in relation to that expenditure at the relevant time (**5.503**); and

(c)   balancing allowance: in respect of unallowed qualifying expenditure, if any, on sale of, or on the happening of certain other events relating to, the relevant interest (**5.504**).

The rates of the initial and writing down allowances vary depending on the trade category of the industrial buildings concerned and the date on which the qualifying capital expenditure was incurred. The rates of initial allowance are those set out in **5.405.3**, while those for the writing down allowances are as given in **5.406** (except that the references there to the election for the increased writing down allowance are not relevant to a lessor of industrial buildings). For the lessor's liability to a balancing charge on the sale of an industrial building, see **5.504**

5.502 Initial allowance

With some exceptions, initial allowances ceased to be available for expenditure incurred on or after 31 March 1992. The following is an outline the position that applied up to that date. For further details on capital allowances available in respect of industrial buildings see **5.401-5.416**.

An industrial building initial allowance may be claimed by a company which is the lessor of an industrial building or structure, and which has incurred capital expenditure on its construction, where the following conditions are met:

(a)   the building or structure is occupied by a qualifying lessee for the purposes of a trade carried on by that lessee;

(b)   the building is occupied by the qualifying lessee as an industrial building at the time of the commencement of the tenancy; and

(c)   the building, or the part of the building, on which the capital expenditure has been incurred has not been used for any purpose before the qualifying tenancy commences (TCA 1997, s 271(2)).

The lessor company's entitlement to the initial allowance is therefore primarily dependent on the type of trade carried on by the qualifying lessee at the time the lease or tenancy commences to run (assuming that this is after the lessor constructed the building). In the case of capital expenditure incurred by the company on extending or altering an existing building already occupied by a qualifying lessee, it is the type of trade carried on by the lessee at the time the expenditure is incurred that is relevant. If at that time the lessee's trade (for which he occupies the building) is a qualifying trade (eg, manufacturing, dock undertaking, market gardening, hotel keeping or the intensive production of cattle, sheep, poultry, eggs), the lessor may claim the industrial building allowance.

The term qualifying lessee as used here has been explained in **5.405.1**. As suggested there, on a strict interpretation of the legislation the lessor is entitled to an industrial building initial allowance in respect of any qualifying construction expenditure only if, at the time he incurs that expenditure, he holds the interest in the premises that is immediately superior to the leasehold interest held by (or about to be granted to) the lessee carrying on or about to carry on a qualifying trade. For example, if the lessor constructs a building on land which he holds on a 35 year lease, the lessee is a qualifying lessee only if his tenancy is a sublease granted directly out of the 35 year leasehold interest. This strict and rather narrow interpretation of the relevant legislation may be open to challenge as it might be argued that the superior lessor's interest is reversionary on all the leasehold interests that are inferior to it, but so far that position has not been established.

TCA 1997, s 271 also entitles a lessor to the initial allowance in respect of capital expenditure incurred on a building which is leased to one of the industrial development agencies and which is then sublet by that agency to a person carrying on a qualifying trade. The lessor company may claim an initial allowance in any such case where it has leased the building (for subletting to the trader) to:

(a) the Industrial Development Authority;

(b) the Shannon Free Airport Development Co Ltd; or

(c) Údarás na Gaeltachta.

It is not essential that the qualifying lease exists at the time the expenditure is incurred. The company incurring the expenditure may claim the initial allowance if it subsequently grants a qualifying lease, but only where the building is not used for any purpose between the date the expenditure was incurred and the commencement of the qualifying tenancy. On the other hand, even if the building is leased for a qualifying *purpose*, but it is not *in fact* used as an industrial building when it first comes to be used, the lessor company loses its entitlement to the initial allowance; if any allowance has already been granted, it must be withdrawn and any necessary additional assessments made (TCA 1997, s 271(6)).

The initial allowance is given to a lessor for the "appropriate chargeable period" (TCA 1997, s 271(2)). The appropriate chargeable period in the case of a lessor company means (TCA 1997, s 271(1)) the later of:

(a) the accounting period in which the expenditure is incurred; or

(b) the accounting period in which the relevant tenancy (the tenancy to which the relevant interest is reversionary) commences.

In a case where the lessee carrying on the qualifying trade occupies the building under a lease from one of the industrial development agencies (see above), the relevant tenancy is the tenancy which the industrial development agency in question holds under its lease from the lessor so that it is the date on which that tenancy commences which is relevant for the purposes of (b) above. In a case where the lessee occupies the building under a lease directly from the lessor (ie, under the lease to which the relevant interest in the building is reversionary), the lessee's tenancy under that lease is the relevant tenancy.

For a lessor company chargeable to corporation tax, the initial allowance is given for the accounting period in which the expenditure is incurred, provided the relevant tenancy has commenced before the end of that period. If the relevant tenancy does not commence until some time in a later accounting period, the lessor does not obtain the initial allowance until that later period.

It is possible, in one case, for a lessor company to claim the industrial building allowance although it will not have incurred the expenditure on the construction of the building. This is where, before a building has been first used for any purpose after its construction, the lessor has purchased the relevant interest in the building from the person who constructed it or, alternatively, from an intermediate purchaser who acquired it from the other person. In such a case, the provisions of TCA 1997, s 279 deem the lessor company to have incurred the construction expenditure.

The provisions of TCA 1997, s 279 are applied to a company which is the lessor as they are to a company which itself is carrying on the qualifying trade. The amount of capital expenditure which the company is deemed to have incurred, by reference to which its initial allowances are calculated, may vary depending on whether the building was constructed by a person constructing buildings in the course of a building trade, or by a non-builder (see **5.408**).

The initial allowance is significantly more important to a company as the lessor of an industrial building than it is for a company which is entitled to the allowance in respect of an industrial building constructed by it for use in its own trade. This is because the industrial building free depreciation option under TCA 1997, s 273 which the latter may take (for certain types of industrial buildings) is not available to the lessor (see **5.407.1**). Accordingly, if a lessor company wishes to obtain accelerated capital allowances in respect of its qualifying expenditure, the only option is to claim the initial allowance.

The rate of initial allowance for a lessor of an industrial building is the same as that available to the person carrying on a trade. For a building used in a trade carried on in a mill, factory or similar premises, an initial allowance equal to 50% of the qualifying expenditure is given (if the expenditure was incurred before 1 April 1991). For the rates of initial allowance in respect of industrial buildings used for the other types of qualifying trades, see **5.405.3**.

Example 5.502.1

On 30 June 1990, Reno Ltd purchased the freehold interest[1] in a new building which had recently been constructed by Benteen Ltd, a speculative building company. The cost of construction to Benteen Ltd (in equivalent euro terms) was €320,000 and Reno Ltd paid €425,000 for the purchase of the freehold. Reno Ltd makes up accounts annually to 31 March. Between the date of purchase and 19 February 1991, it incurred further expenditure of €44,000 on carrying out improvements to the building.

On 19 February 1991, Reno Ltd granted a 21 year lease to Rosebud Ltd,[2] a newly incorporated company about to commence a manufacturing business. That company's tenancy began on 1 April 1991 and its trade commenced on 1 June 1991. The building was entirely unused in the period from the completion of construction to 1 April 1991 when Rosebud Ltd occupied it for the purposes of setting up its manufacturing trade.

Since the building was purchased unused from a speculative builder, TCA 1997, s 279 treats Reno Ltd as if it had incurred capital expenditure of €425,000 (ie, the net purchase price paid) on the construction of the building. It is deemed by TCA 1997, s 279 to have incurred capital expenditure of €425,000 on 30 June 1990,[3] and it has actually incurred further expenditure of €44,000 in the year ended 31 March 1991. However, since the qualifying lessee's tenancy did not commence until 1 April 1991, it obtains an initial allowance for the year ended 31 March 1992 as follows:

	€
Capital expenditure:	
On purchase of building unused	425,000
Incurred directly	44,000
	469,000
Industrial building initial allowance y/e 31/3/92:	
€469,000 x 25%	117,250

Notes:

1. The freehold interest held by Benteen Ltd, the company which incurred the actual construction expenditure at the time of that expenditure, is the "relevant interest" (TCA 1997, s 269 – see **5.403**).

2. Rosebud Ltd is a qualifying lessee from the time it starts to use the building for its manufacturing trade.

3. The date on which the relevant interest is purchased from the builder is the date on which the purchaser's "construction" expenditure is deemed to be incurred (TCA 1997, s 279).

5.503 Writing down allowances

An industrial building writing down allowance is made to a company which is the lessor of a building for each accounting period at the end of which the following conditions are met:

(a) the building is an industrial building or structure, ie, one in use for a qualifying trade; and

(b) the lessor's interest in the building is the relevant interest in relation to the capital expenditure in respect of which the allowance is claimed (TCA 1997, s 272(2)).

No writing down allowance may be claimed for any capital expenditure incurred before 30 September 1956, or in respect of any capital expenditure (whenever incurred) after the end of the specified writing down period for that expenditure (see **5.402**).

It is not necessary for the expenditure to have been eligible for an initial allowance when it was incurred, nor does it matter whether the company which incurred the expenditure did so at the time in the capacity of trader, lessor or otherwise. Once the company holds the relevant interest related to the construction expenditure at the end of a particular accounting period, it is entitled to the writing down allowance for that period, if the building is occupied at that time by *any* lessee carrying on a qualifying trade.

For the purposes of the writing down allowance, the relevant interest held by the lessor in the building does not have to be the interest immediately superior to the leasehold interest held by the person for the time being occupying the building for the qualifying trade. This contrasts with the normal rule governing the lessor's entitlement to the initial allowance. For example, assume that A Ltd, which makes up accounts to 31 December each year, incurred expenditure of €250,000 on the construction of a building in 2000 on land in which it had held the freehold, and granted a lease of the building to B Ltd, which in turn granted a sublease to C Ltd. If the building is in use for the purposes of the manufacturing trade of C Ltd on 31 December 2001, A Ltd is entitled to claim the 4% writing down allowance for the year ended 31 December 2001. Since the freehold interest is the relevant interest in relation to the expenditure of €250,000, the fact that A Ltd now derives its rent from the sublessor (B Ltd) does not prevent it obtaining the annual allowance.

A company which is a lessor holding the relevant interest in a building which ceases temporarily to be an industrial building, either because the lessee ceases to carry on a qualifying trade or because the lease comes to an end, remains entitled to the writing down allowance during a period of temporary disuse *immediately* following use as an industrial building (TCA 1997, s 280(1)). Even if the eventual new use is not as an industrial building, the company continues to be entitled to the writing down allowance if it holds the relevant interest at the end of the accounting period while the temporary disuse continues. However, if a new non-qualifying use begins, it ceases to be able to claim the writing down allowance (unless and until the building is used again for a qualifying trade).

The rate of writing down allowance made to a lessor is the same as that to which a person carrying on a trade would be entitled, and is therefore dependent on the type of qualifying trade being carried on by the lessee and on the date on which the qualifying expenditure was incurred (see **5.406**). For example, if the expenditure was incurred after

15 January 1975 on a building in use for a trade carried on in a mill, factory or similar premises, the writing down allowance is 4% for each relevant accounting period.

The allowance is based on the actual construction expenditure incurred, unless varied by the rules of TCA 1997, s 279 for buildings purchased unused (see **5.408**) or, if the relevant interest in a building changes hands while it is an industrial building, on the residue of the expenditure (as adjusted) at that time (see **5.410.2**). In the latter case, the lessor's subsequent writing down allowances are at the rate necessary to write off the residue of the expenditure evenly over the rest of the writing down period for the relevant construction expenditure.

Although the increased writing down allowance (free depreciation) election of TCA 1997, s 273 is not normally available to the lessor of industrial buildings, there is one possible exception. This relates to the case in which a current lessor company had incurred the qualifying capital expenditure after 1 February 1978 on a building which was first used in its own qualifying trade, but where the company subsequently ceased to trade and leased the building for use by the lessee in a qualifying trade. In such a case, the lessor retains the right to elect for the increased writing down allowance unless, and until, the relevant expenditure has been completely written off.

Capital expenditure after 31 March 1989

TCA 1997, s 271(5) denies any company, being a lessor of an industrial building, an annual allowance for the same accounting period as that for which it obtains an initial allowance in respect of the same expenditure. This applies where the capital expenditure in question is incurred after 31 March 1989. For qualifying expenditure incurred on or before that date, the previous rules allowed the lessor both an initial allowance and the ordinary annual allowance for the relevant year of assessment or accounting period.

Example 5.503.1

The facts are as in Example **5.502.1** where, on 19 February 1991, Reno Ltd has leased to Rosebud Ltd the building in respect of which it was treated as incurring the capital expenditure totalling €469,000. Assume that Rosebud Ltd assigns its 21 year lease to Fetterman Ltd on 26 February 2000 and that Fetterman Ltd immediately occupies the building for the purpose of its wholesaling trade. Reno Ltd continues as the lessor.

In addition to the initial allowance of €117,250 obtained for the year ended 31 March 1992, Reno Ltd is entitled to the following writing down allowances for the relevant accounting periods:

	€
Year ended 31/3/91:[1]	
No writing down allowance	Nil
Years ended 31/3/92 – 31/3/99:[2]	
€469,000 x 4% x 8	150,080
Year ended 31/3/00:	
No writing down allowance[3]	Nil

Notes:

[1]   The building was not in use as an industrial building on the last day of the year ended 31 March 1991: the tenant's lease did not commence until 1 April 1991.

2   The building was in use as an industrial building on the last day of each period, but the assignment of the lease by Rosebud Ltd does not require any balancing allowance or charge as Reno Ltd did not dispose of the relevant interest (see **5.504**).

3   No writing down allowance is made for the year ended 31 March 2000 as the building ceased to be used as an industrial building before 31 March 2000, the last day of that accounting period.

5.504   Balancing allowances and charges

A lessor company which has obtained an initial allowance or writing down allowance in respect of any capital expenditure on a building or structure is entitled to a balancing allowance, or is subject to a balancing charge, under TCA 1997, s 274(1) on the occasion of any of the following events where it holds the relevant interest immediately before the event in question:

(a)   it sells the relevant interest in the building;

(b)   the building is demolished or destroyed or, without being demolished or destroyed, ceases altogether to be used; or

(c)   the relevant interest, being a leasehold interest, comes to an end (except where it ends by reason of the lessor's acquiring the immediately superior interest).

No balancing adjustment is required as a result of any event occurring after the end of the specified writing down period of the expenditure in question.

A sale or other disposal by the lessee of his leasehold interest in an industrial building does not itself require any balancing adjustment to be made in the case of the lessor. If the assignee of that leasehold interest (the new lessee) does not continue to use the building as an industrial building, however, no further writing down allowances may be claimed by the lessor but no balancing allowance or charge is triggered. It is only if the building ceases altogether to be used that the balancing adjustment is made.

The calculation of balancing allowances and charges in respect of an industrial building, based on the difference between the amount of the sale, insurance, salvage or compensation moneys and the residue of the expenditure immediately before the sale or other relevant event, has been fully explained in **5.409.2** and does not need to be further considered here.

5.505   Manner of granting allowances to lessors

5.505.1   Case V

A lessor company obtains capital allowances on industrial buildings (initial, writing down and balancing allowances), and is subject to balancing charges, in charging its income under Schedule D Case V (TCA 1997, s 278(1)). The allowances are available primarily against the company's income taxable under Case V or against any balancing charges under that Case (TCA 1997, s 278(6)). In practice, a company's balancing charges for any accounting period are usually deducted first from its Case V capital allowances (including any balancing allowances) for the same period, but any excess of balancing charges over allowances is assessable under Case V as if it were additional rental income for the period.

Industrial building allowances are deducted from the total of the lessor's Case V income for the accounting period in question, ie, from the excess of the aggregate of the company's rent surpluses over deficiencies as assessable to tax for that period. The fact that part of the total Case V income is made up of surpluses (less any deficiencies) mainly from rents from premises other than industrial buildings does not restrict the deduction of the industrial building allowances. These allowances are given if there is an overall net surplus in the Case V computation, even if there is a net deficiency of rental income from the industrial buildings.

Where a lessor company is entitled to an industrial building initial or writing down allowance, or a balancing allowance, or is subject to a balancing charge, in respect of any premises the income from which is chargeable to tax under Case V, the allowance or charge is made to or on that company in charging its income under that Case (TCA 1997, s 278(1)).

An industrial building writing down initial or allowance and any balancing allowance is available to a Case V lessor company "primarily against" its income chargeable to corporation tax under Case V or any balancing charge under that Case (TCA 1997, s 278(6)).

Accordingly, the total of the industrial building writing down, balancing and initial allowances due to a lessor company taxable under Case V for any accounting period is deducted from or set off against its income chargeable to corporation tax under Case V (and against any balancing charges within that Case) for the same period (TCA 1997, s 308(1), (2)). To the extent that the total of all the industrial building allowances for any accounting period exceeds the sum of the company's Case V income and balancing charges for that period, the excess is carried forward for set off against the Case V income and balancing charges for the next accounting period, and so on for succeeding periods until fully used up (TCA 1997, s 308(3)).

A company taxable under Case V as a lessor may, alternatively, offset any industrial building allowances which cannot be offset against the Case V income and balancing charges in the period for which the allowances arise against the total profits for that period; such excess allowances may also, if the company was then within the charge to tax, be offset against total profits of the immediately preceding accounting periods equal in length to the period in which the excess arose (TCA 1997, s 308(4)).

Example 5.505.1.1

WA Anderson Ltd constructed glasshouses costing €150,000 in the period from October 2005 to 31 March 2006. The glasshouses were leased, under a 15 year lease commencing on 1 July 2006, to O'Quinn Producers Ltd for use in its trade of market gardening. O'Quinn Producers Ltd is responsible for all outgoings in respect of the leased premises, and pays €10,000 per annum by way of rent. O'Quinn Producers Ltd also paid a premium of €40,000 for the grant of the lease.

In addition to its income from this lease, WA Anderson Ltd is in receipt of Case V income from other lettings, one of which is the lease of a warehouse which cost €220,000 to construct in 1995 and is currently in use for the purposes of a manufacturing business carried on by the lessee. On 26 March 2007, WA Anderson Ltd paid a building contractor €280,000 as the agreed contract price for having constructed an extension to this warehouse which is immediately available to the lessee, but the rent payable is not revised until 1 April 2011. WA Anderson Ltd incurred interest charges in respect of various loans used to finance the costs of acquiring and constructing properties for leasing, the interest on which is deductible as a Case V expense under TCA 1997, s 97(2)(e).

WA Anderson Ltd makes up accounts to 31 December each year. The Case V computations for the years ended 31 December 2006 and 2007 are as follows:

	Glasshouses	*Warehouse*	*Other lettings*
	€	€	€
Year ended 31 December 2006:			
Rents receivable	5,000	23,000	42,000
Premium on lease (1/7/06)[1]	28,800		
	33,800	23,000	42,000
Expenses etc (TCA 1997, s 97(2)):			
Interest on loans	6,600	9,500	3,700
Other allowable expenses		8,600	5,400
	6,600	18,100	9,100
Surplus for year (before capital allowances)	27,200	4,900	32,900
Year ended 31 December 2007:			
Rents receivable	10,000	23,000	17,000
Expenses etc:			
Interest on loans	6,900	10,200	3,500
Other allowable expenses		2,400	3,900
	6,900	12,600	7,400
Surplus for year	3,100	10,400	9,600

The industrial building allowances for the years ended 31 December 2006 and 2007 are dealt with as follows in the Case V computations:

	y/e 31/12/06	*y/e 31/12/07*
	€	€
Surpluses for year:		
Glasshouses	27,200	3,100
Warehouse	4,900	10,400
Other lettings	32,900	9,600
Total Case V income	65,000	23,100
Industrial building allowances:		
Glasshouses		
WDA (10% of €150,000)	15,000	15,000
Warehouse (1995) – WDA (4% of €220,000)	8,800	8,800
Warehouse (26/3/07) – WDA (4% of €280,000)		11,200
	23,800	35,000

Net Case V income (after capital allowances)	41,200	Nil
Excess capital allowances		11,900

Note:

[1]   The amount taxable under TCA 1997, s 98(1) as additional rent in respect of the premium of €40,000 payable on 1/7/06 on the granting of the 15 year lease to the glasshouses is:

$$€40,000 \times (51\text{-}15)/50 = €28,800$$

5.505.2   Case IV

Where a lessor company entitled to an industrial building initial or writing down allowance, or balancing allowance, in respect of any premises is chargeable to tax otherwise than under Case V, the allowance is given by way of discharge or repayment of tax (TCA 1997, s 278(2)-(4)).

Apart from the case of rental or other income from the leasing of premises situated outside the State which is taxable under Case III as the income from a foreign possession, any income from the leasing of premises which is not within Case V is chargeable to tax under Case IV. TCA 1997, s 278(1) provides for the industrial building initial allowance to be made by way of discharge or repayment of tax if the qualifying expenditure is in respect of a building that is the subject of a lease, but then provides that this is not the case where the income of the leased building is chargeable under Case V. TCA 1997, s 278(3), (4) contains similar provisions regarding the industrial building writing down and balancing allowances if the relevant interest in the building is subject to a lease at the relevant time but, again, not where any Case V income is concerned.

Assessments under Case IV for lessors are fairly rare (but see below) and, where income is so chargeable, any industrial building allowances in respect of the premises are available primarily against income chargeable under Case IV and/or any balancing charge within that Case (TCA 1997, s 278(5), (6)) and are to be given "by way of discharge or repayment of tax" (see **4.107**).

TCA 1997, s 104 charges tax under Case IV on rents, royalties and certain other payments received in respect of premises or easements used, occupied or enjoyed in connection with any of the types of concern listed in Case I(b) (TCA 1997, s 18(2)). The concerns in question are those which derive profits or gains arising out of lands, tenements and hereditaments which are taxable under Case I(b) in respect of any of the activities described in that Case, including quarries of stone, slate, limestone or chalk, or quarries or pits of sand gravel or clay, mines of coal, tin, lead, copper pyrites, iron and other mines, ironworks, gasworks, waterworks, docks, canals, inland navigations, docks, drains or levels, fishings, rights or markets or fairs, tolls, railways and other ways, bridges, ferries and other concerns of a like nature having profits from or arising out of any lands, tenements or hereditaments.

These rents and other receipts are included in the types of payment which are subject to deduction of income tax at source (see **4.301**). They comprise the only exception to the normal rule that all rents and receipts from easements from lands, tenements and hereditaments in the State are taxable under Case V. The charge to tax under Case IV in respect of these mining and other rents is therefore relevant where the owner of the lands or other premises in question derives a rent, royalty or any yearly interest, annuity, or other annual payment for allowing the lands to be used for mining, quarrying, inland waterways, docks or any of the other concerns listed above.

The preceding paragraphs outline the types of leasing income chargeable to tax under Case IV but they do not explain the circumstances in which an industrial building subject to a lease gives rise to rental income that is not taxable under Case V. Although rental income from industrial buildings situated outside the State constitute income taxable under Case III, it is unlikely that that is the intended exception to the Case V designation; in any event, such buildings no longer qualify as industrial buildings (see **5.506**).

The likely exception is buildings let for use in a dock undertaking. In such a case, the lessor derives rent that is taxable under Case IV by virtue of TCA 1997, s 104 (see above) whereas none of the other types of concern giving rise to rents and other receipts chargeable under Case IV is a qualifying trade for the purposes of the definition of an industrial building.

Accordingly, if the let premises in use for the dock undertaking entitle a company which is the lessor to industrial building allowances, it is entitled to those allowances primarily against its rental income in respect of the building let to the dock undertaking.

Although chargeable under Case IV, a company in receipt of these mining or other rents normally receives them as taxed income and they are dealt with as such in its corporation tax computations. Any rent in respect of the premises or easements in question that is paid in kind, ie, in produce of the concern in question (eg, in limestone quarries) is taxed under Case IV on its market value as it is outside the scope of the rules for deduction of tax at source.

The provisions of TCA 1997, s 308(4), as discussed above in relation to Case V lessors, are applicable in a corresponding way where any of the industrial building allowances are to be given by way of discharge or repayment of tax. In this connection the available income is all income chargeable under Case IV ("income of the specified class"), which includes many types of miscellaneous income. Any Case IV industrial building allowances are available to be set off against the total of the income taxable within that Case (and not only against the income from premises).

To the extent that any industrial building allowances within Case IV for any accounting period (ie, given by way of discharge or repayment of tax) exceed the total income and any balancing charges taxable under that Case, a company has the same choices as for Case V industrial building allowances, that is, to carry forward the excess industrial building allowances to succeeding accounting periods for offset against income of the same class, to offset the excess allowances against the total profits for the period in which the excess arises and, if the company was then within the charge to tax, against total profits of the immediately preceding accounting periods equal in length to the period in which the excess arose (TCA 1997, s 308(4)).

In the event that a balancing charge arises in respect of a disposal of the lessor's relevant interest in the leased building, that balancing charge is taxable under Case IV (TCA 1997, s 278(5)).

5.506 Foreign leased industrial buildings

An Irish resident company which receives rents from immovable property situated abroad is subject to tax in respect of its the net income from those rents under Schedule

D Case III (rather than under Case V). Where the foreign rental income is derived from an industrial building, being a building occupied for the purposes of a qualifying trade, the company was, up to 1996, entitled to industrial building initial, writing down and balancing allowances, and subject to the same balancing charges, as if the industrial building were situated in the State.

Prior to FA 1996, a building did not have to be situated in Ireland to qualify as an industrial building. A company could claim industrial building allowances in respect of capital expenditure on buildings or structures in use for a qualifying trade carried on wholly or partly in another country. Thus, capital expenditure incurred by an Irish resident manufacturing company on the construction of a UK based warehouse for the purpose of storing goods prior to their sale qualified for the allowances.

Expenditure incurred by a company on or after 23 April 1996, on the construction of, or on the acquisition of the "relevant interest" (see **5.403**) in, a building or structure which is not situated in the State is treated as not being expenditure on an industrial building or structure unless:

(a) the company had entered into a binding contract in writing for the acquisition of the site for the building or structure or had entered into an agreement in writing in relation to an option to acquire the site on or before 23 April 1996; and

(b) the company had entered into a binding contract in writing for the construction of the building or structure on or before 1 July 1996; and

(c) the construction of the building or structure had commenced on or before 1 July 1996 and had been completed before 31 December 1997; and

(d) the building or structure is to be constructed or is being constructed and will be used for the purposes of a trade the profits or gains from which are taxable in the State (TCA 1997, s 268(5)).

In general, prior to FA 1996, the definition of an industrial building or structure in TCA 1997, s 268, ie, one in use for a qualifying trade (eg, manufacture, hotel keeping etc) applied without reference to whether or not the building was situated in the State or abroad. However, market gardening buildings and holiday cottages situated abroad did not qualify in any event for any industrial building allowances as the relevant definition of market gardening buildings refers only to cases where the trade is carried on in the State, while only holiday cottages registered by the National Tourism Development Authority qualify for allowances. In the case of buildings in use for a manufacturing trade or for the trade of hotel keeping, there was no requirement up to 22 April 1996 that the trade should be one carried on in the State.

5.6 MISCELLANEOUS CAPITAL ALLOWANCES

5.601 Scientific research allowances
5.602 Pre-commencement training
5.603 Dredging expenditure allowances
5.604 Trade effluents expenditure
5.605 Multi-storey car-parks
5.606 Buildings used for third level education
5.607 Buildings used for certain childcare purposes
5.608 Transmission capacity rights
5.609 Milk quotas

5.601 Scientific research allowances

A trading company which incurs capital expenditure on scientific research is entitled to a capital allowance equal to 100% of that expenditure. The allowance is made in taxing the profits of the company's trade for the accounting period in which the expenditure is incurred (TCA 1997, s 765(1)).

Scientific research is defined as meaning any activities in the fields of natural or applied science for the extension of knowledge. The scientific research allowance does not, however, apply to any expenditure incurred in the acquisition of rights in, or arising out of, scientific research. For example, scientific research may lead to an invention which is patented but no allowance is given for purchasing or acquiring rights in a patent. A company is entitled to the scientific research allowance in respect of capital expenditure on any scientific research, even if not related to its own trade (TCA 1997, s 765(2)).

In *Texaco (Ireland) Ltd v Murphy* 4 ITR 91, in was held that exploring for oil constituted "scientific research" but this did not extend to the subsequent drilling for oil. Exploration was carried out for the purpose of the extension of knowledge.

A trading company which incurs capital expenditure on scientific research before it sets up and commences its trade is entitled to the allowance for the accounting period in which its trade commences, but only where the research is related to its trade. No allowance is given for capital expenditure on scientific research incurred before the commencement of a trade if the research is not related to the trade.

The capital expenditure on which the scientific research allowance is given may be incurred on the production of an asset (scientific data or blueprints, processes, formulae etc) or on items purchased, eg, machinery or plant, to be used in the trade for the research in question ("an asset representing capital expenditure on scientific research"). If any such asset ceases for any reason to be used for the research relating to the trade of a company which incurred the expenditure, the company must include as a trading receipt in its Schedule D Case I computation the lower of (a) the value of the asset immediately before it ceases to be used for the scientific research and (b) the scientific research allowance previously obtained for the expenditure on the asset (TCA 1997, s 765(3)(a)).

Capital expenditure on scientific research that is met directly or indirectly out of moneys provided by the State, or by any person other than the person claiming the scientific research allowance, must be excluded and cannot be the subject of any allowance (TCA 1997, s 763(5)). Furthermore, the same expenditure cannot give rise to an allowance in relation to more than one trade (TCA 1997, s 763(6)). Where the expenditure is represented wholly or partly by assets, no wear and tear or other form of capital allowance can be obtained for the expenditure, except for a possible wear and tear allowance after any such asset ceases to be used for scientific research (TCA 1997, s 765(4)).

In the case of an asset representing capital expenditure on scientific research, being machinery or plant, if that asset ceases to be used for the research, but is used for other purposes in the trade of the person who incurred the expenditure, a wear and tear allowance may be claimed under the ordinary capital allowances rules. The cost of the plant on which this wear and tear allowance is based is the actual cost of the plant as reduced by the net scientific research allowance previously obtained in respect of this plant. In other words, the reduction from the actual capital cost equals the scientific research allowance made originally less the amount credited as a trading receipt at the time the plant ceased to be used for the research (TCA 1997, s 765(3)(b)).

Example 5.601.1

Colson Ltd, a manufacturing company, incurred capital expenditure of €45,000 on scientific research in its accounting year ended 31 December 2005. The expenditure included €17,000 on items of plant to be used wholly for the purposes of the research. Capital grants of 17.5% were received towards the cost of the expenditure.

On 30 September 2007, an item of plant which had cost €7,000 (before grant aid) was withdrawn from the scientific research use and transferred to normal production. The value of this item was agreed to be €4,800 on the date of its withdrawal. The consequences are as follows:

	€
Year ended 31 December 2005:	
Scientific research allowance	
€37,125 (€45,000 – grant of €7,875) x 100%	37,125
Year ended 31 December 2007:	
Trading receipt – machine withdrawn:	
Lower of value of asset 30/9/05, €4,800, and	
scientific research allowance obtained €5,775 (€7,000 – grant €1,225)	4,800

Colson Ltd is entitled to claim wear and tear allowances on the machine withdrawn from scientific research use with effect from its accounting year ended 31 December 2007 on a deemed capital cost of €6,025, but as reduced by notional wear and tear allowances as follows:

	€	€
Actual cost (before grant)		7,000
Less: scientific research allowance in 2005	5,775	
Add: allowance withdrawn as trading receipt 2007	4,800	
		975
Deemed cost in 2005		6,025
Less: notional wear and tear allowances (see **5.206**)		
y/e 31/12/05 – €6,025 x 15%	904	

y/e 31/12/06 – €6,025 x 15%	<u>904</u>
	<u>1,808</u>
WDV 31/12/06	4,217
W & T y/e 31/12/07 €6,025 x 15 %	<u>904</u>

5.602   Pre-commencement training

A company about to carry on a trade in the production for sale of manufactured goods is entitled to writing down allowances for expenditure incurred before the date of commencement of trade on the recruitment and training of workers or staff for employment in the trade. The staff training writing down allowances are available only for expenditure which, if it had been incurred after the commencement of trade, would have been deductible as an expense under the rules of Schedule D Case I. In other words, the expenditure must have been incurred wholly and exclusively for the purposes of the intended trade (TCA 1997, s 769).

It is a further condition for obtaining the deduction that the expenditure on the recruitment and training must have been in respect of persons all or a majority of whom are Irish citizens, but there is no requirement that the trainees should have been resident in the State before their recruitment. Any expenditure that is met directly or indirectly by the State, by any board established by statute or by any public or local authority, eg, by Industrial Development Authority training grants, or by any person other than the taxpayer since 6 May 1993, must be excluded and is not eligible for the writing down allowances.

These allowances are regarded as capital allowances and the rules applicable to capital allowances generally apply to them. The writing down allowances are given for a writing down period of three years beginning on the date the trade actually commences. Expenditure is treated as being incurred on the date on which the sum in question becomes payable; consequently, if this date is on or after the first day of trading, the expenses are deductible in the ordinary way in the Case I computation and no writing down allowances are made.

Example 5.602.1

Grant Ltd commences a manufacturing business on 1 September 2004 but before doing so it incurs expenditure of €11,600 on the recruitment and training of workers between 1 March 2004 and 31 August 2004. Further expenditure of €4,900 is spent on recruitment and training of additional workers from 1 September 2004 to 31 December 2004. All the workers are Irish citizens.

The later expenditure of €4,900 is deductible as a trade expense in the company's Case I computation for its first accounting period to 31 December 2004. The writing down allowances given in respect of the pre-commencement training etc expenditure of €11,600 are as follows:

	€
1 September 2004 to 31 December 2004:	
€11,600 x 4/36	1,289
Year ended 31 December 2005:	
€11,600 x 12/36	3,867
Year ended 31 December 2006:	
€11,600 x 12/36	3,867

Year ended 31 December 2007:
€11,600 x 8/36   2,577

5.603   Dredging expenditure allowances

A company carrying on a qualified trade, and which incurs capital expenditure on dredging, may be entitled to capital allowances in respect of the expenditure. A qualifying trade for the purpose of these allowances provided for by TCA 1997, s 303 is defined in TCA 1997, s 302(1) as one which either (a) consists of the maintenance or improvement of the navigation of a harbour, estuary or waterway, or (b) is any of those types of trade or undertaking in respect of which there is an entitlement to industrial building allowances under TCA 1997, s 268(1) (see **5.401.1**). "Dredging" is limited to things done in the interests of navigation but, subject to that, includes the removal of anything forming part of or projecting from the bed of the sea or of any inland water. The allowances are also available for capital expenditure on the widening of an inland waterway in the interests of navigation under the same rules as apply to dredging (TCA 1997, s 301(1)).

Capital allowances for dredging expenditure are made to a company carrying on a trade falling within (a) above where the expenditure is incurred for the purposes of that trade. In the case of trades falling within (b), the dredging allowances may only be claimed if the capital expenditure on dredging is for the benefit of vessels coming to, leaving or using any dock or other premises occupied by the company for the purposes of its trade. It would appear therefore that a company carrying on a trade within (b) must occupy a dock, warehouse or other premises directly adjoining a harbour, estuary, canal or inland waterway. The allowances could be claimed, for example, by a dock undertaking or by a manufacturing company which has premises situated beside the sea or waterway that has been dredged.

A company which contributes a capital sum to expenditure on dredging incurred by another person is treated as incurring the capital expenditure on that dredging equal to the amount of the contribution and is accordingly entitled to the dredging allowances on that amount. Any allowances to which the other person is otherwise entitled are reduced by the amount of the contribution (TCA 1997, s 303(7)).

No dredging expenditure allowance may be made if an industrial building initial allowance or an industrial building writing down allowance may be claimed for the expenditure (TCA 1997, s 303(8)). The dredging allowance may, however, be claimed where qualifying dredging expenditure is incurred before the relevant trade is commenced but with a view to the carrying on of the trade (TCA 1997, s 303(6)).

Where capital expenditure on dredging is incurred partly for the purposes of a qualifying trade and partly for other purposes, the expenditure is to be apportioned in a manner that is just and fair between the qualifying trade and the other purposes. In a case where part only of a trade or undertaking is a qualifying trade, the part which qualifies and the other part are to be treated as if they were separate trades (TCA 1997 ss 303(5) and 302(1)).

The capital allowances given for qualifying dredging expenditure are:

(a)   an initial allowance equal to 10% of the expenditure;

(b)   writing down allowances during a writing down period of 50 years; and

(c)   a balance allowance given on the permanent discontinuance of the trade (TCA 1997, s 303(1)).

In the case of a company chargeable to corporation tax, the initial allowance is given for, and the 50 year writing down period begins with, the accounting period in which the expenditure is incurred, except where this accounting period precedes the commencement of the relevant trade. In that event, the allowances start with the first accounting period in which the company both carries on the trade and occupies the dock or other premises in connection with which the expenditure was incurred (TCA 1997, s 302(2)).

A company which incurs the relevant capital expenditure is entitled to a balancing allowance on the permanent discontinuance of its trade if the expenditure in question has not already been fully written down by initial allowances and writing down allowances obtained for previous accounting periods and for the accounting period in which the trade or undertaking ceases. The balancing allowance is in an amount equal to the amount of the expenditure less the allowances made in respect of it for the period of discontinuance and for any previous periods (TCA 1997, s 303(2)). For this purpose, and as an exception to the deemed cessation rule in TCA 1997, s 77(2), a trade is not treated as discontinued, and no balancing allowance is made, by reason of a change in the persons carrying on the trade (TCA 1997, s 303(3)).

The dredging capital allowances are not made to a company in respect of any capital expenditure to the extent that that expenditure has been met directly or indirectly by the State, by any board established by statute or by any public or local authority or by any person other than the company in question (TCA 1997, s 317(2)).

5.604   Trade effluents expenditure

A company carrying on a trade or about to commence a trade is entitled to capital allowances in respect of capital sums contributed by it to a local authority towards the cost of certain capital expenditure of an approved trade effluents scheme and, in respect of capital expenditure incurred on or after 15 February 2001, for the purposes of funding new water supply infrastructure. An *approved scheme* is defined as a scheme undertaken by a local authority with the approval of the Minister for the Environment and Local Government for the treatment of trade effluents. Trade effluents are defined as liquid or other matter discharged into public sewers from premises occupied for the purposes of a trade.

Local authority means the council of a county or the corporation of a county or other borough or the council of an urban district.

The company obtains the allowances if the contributions are used by the local authority to provide an asset which is to be used for the purposes of the approved scheme. It is entitled to claim the same capital allowances as if the contribution to the scheme were expenditure by it on the provision of a similar asset for its trade. Depending on the nature of the asset, the company is entitled to a wear and tear allowance for machinery or plant or, alternatively, industrial building writing down allowances for buildings, on the amount of its capital contribution (TCA 1997, s 310(2)).

A trade effluent scheme may be provided by a local authority to deal with the trade effluents to be discharged from a particular company's factory premises or the scheme may service a number of such premises, eg, in an industrial estate. Each company involved is entitled to the allowance on its particular contributions to assets provided by the local authority for the scheme. Where a company has made a capital contribution for such a purpose, and if it subsequently transfers the whole of its trade, the person taking over the trade is entitled to any wear and tear or industrial building writing down allowances after the transfer as the transferor would have had if it continued the trade. If only part of the trade is transferred, this provision applies only to so much of the allowances as is properly referable to the part of the trade transferred.

Example 5.604.1

Rio Tinto Ltd, a company about to commence a manufacturing trade, makes a capital contribution of €90,000 to its local County Council as a contribution towards the cost of an approved trade effluents scheme. The expenditure is allocated as to €36,000 towards the cost of buildings to be used for the scheme and the balance of €54,000 for new machinery and plant.

The company commenced trading on 1 January 2007 and makes up accounts to 31 December in that year. It is entitled to capital allowances for the year ended 31 December 2007 as follows:

	€
Industrial building:	
IBAA €36,000 x 4%	1,440
Machinery and plant:	
W & T €54,000 x 12.5%	6,750

The company may also be entitled to capital allowances in respect of a capital sum contributed to capital expenditure incurred by a local authority on the provision of an asset to be used for the purposes of the supply of water under an agreement in writing between the company and the local authority.

As with trade effluent expenditure, and depending on the nature of the asset, the company is entitled to a wear and tear allowance for machinery or plant or, alternatively, industrial building writing down allowances for buildings, on the amount of its capital contribution (TCA 1997, s 310(2)).

In relation to both trade effluent and water supply expenditure, where a company is entitled to a wear and tear allowance for any accounting period under TCA 1997, s 284, that section is to operate as if the reference to 12.5% of the cost of machinery or plant etc were a reference to 12.5% of the capital sum contributed in the accounting period (TCA 1997, s 310(2A)).

5.605   Multi-storey car-parks

TCA 1997 Sch 32 para 9 provides for capital allowances in respect of capital expenditure incurred from 29 January 1981 to 31 March 1991 on the construction of multi-storey car-parks. After that date, no allowances have been available under that provision in respect of multi-storey car-parks. Allowances for multi-storey car-parks are available within the Custom House Docks, Temple Bar and 1994 urban renewal schemes (see 2001-2002 and prior editions of this book).

Qualifying expenditure is capital expenditure incurred in the period 15 May 2002 to 31 December 2006 or, where TCA 1997, s 268(16) applies, to 31 July 2008 (TCA 1997, s 268(9)(h)). TCA 1997, s 268(16) applies where:

(a) the person constructing or refurbishing the clinic has, on or before 31 December 2006, carried out work to the value of not less than 15% of the actual construction or refurbishment costs of the clinic; and

(b) that person or, where the clinic is sold by that person, the person who is claiming a deduction in relation to the expenditure can show that the condition in (a) was satisfied.

See **5.404** regarding the restriction by TCA 1997, s 270(4)-(6) of qualifying expenditure on multi-storey car parks. In the case of expenditure incurred in the period 1 January 2007 to 31 December 2007, only 75% of expenditure incurred is treated as incurred, and in the case of expenditure incurred in the period 1 January 2008 to 31 July 2008, only 50% of expenditure incurred is treated as incurred.

Under a scheme which runs from 1 July 1995 to 30 June 1998 (or to 30 June 1999 in certain cases – see below), TCA 1997, s 344 provides for capital allowances for capital expenditure on multi-storey car-parks. It effectively extends the reliefs available to car-parks in areas designated under the 1994 Urban Renewal Scheme to car-parks outside those areas.

The *qualifying period* for capital allowances in respect of multi-storey car-parks, as provided for in TCA 1997, s 344(1), is the period 1 July 1995 to 30 June 1998 but, in certain circumstances, the termination date is 30 September 1999, in certain other cases, 31 December 2006 or 31 July 2008. The 30 September 1999 deadline applies where the relevant local authority gave a certificate in writing on or before 30 September 1998 to the person constructing or refurbishing the qualifying multi-storey car-park stating that it was satisfied that not less than 15% of the total cost of the car-park and its site had been incurred before 1 July 1998. In considering whether to give such a certificate, the local authority must have regard only to guidelines in relation to the giving of such certificates issued by the Department of the Environment and Local Government for the purposes of the definition of "qualifying period".

The 31 December 2006 deadline applies where 15% of the cost of the building is incurred by 30 September 2003 but this extension does not apply in respect of buildings in the Cork and Dublin Corporation jurisdictions. The definition of "qualifying period" in TCA 1997, s 344(1) provides that the normal deadline of 30 June 1998 is extended to 31 July 2006 where, in relation to the construction or refurbishment of the qualifying multi-storey car-park concerned (not being such a car-park any part of the site of which is within either of the county boroughs of Cork or Dublin), the relevant local authority gave a certificate in writing on or before 31 December 2003, to the person constructing or refurbishing the car-park stating that it was satisfied that not less than 15% of the total cost of the car-park and its site had been incurred on or before 30 September 2003. In considering whether to give such a certificate, the local authority must have regard only to guidelines in relation to the giving of such certificates issued by the Department of the Environment and Local Government for the purposes of the definition of "qualifying period".

The 31 July 2008 deadline applies where, in relation to the construction or refurbishment of the qualifying multi-storey car park, the relevant local authority has issued the certificate referred to in above on or before 31 December 2003, and :

(a) the person constructing or refurbishing the qualifying multi-storey car park has, on or before 31 December 2006, carried out work to the value of not less than

15% of the actual construction or refurbishment costs of the multi-storey car park; and

(b)   that person or, where the qualifying multi-storey car park is sold by that person, the person who is claiming a deduction in relation to the expenditure can show that the condition in (a) was satisfied.

See **5.404** regarding the restriction by TCA 1997, s 270(4)-(6) of qualifying expenditure on multi-storey car parks. In the case of expenditure incurred in the period 1 January 2007 to 31 December 2007, only 75% of expenditure incurred is treated as incurred, and in the case of expenditure incurred in the period 1 January 2008 to 31 July 2008, only 50% of expenditure incurred is treated as incurred.

A *multi-storey car-park* is defined as a building or structure consisting of two or more storeys wholly in use to provide parking space for mechanically propelled vehicles for members of the public generally. The car-park must not give any preference to any particular class of person and the parking facility must be provided upon payment of an appropriate charge. There is also a certification process which must be completed whereby the relevant local authority must certify that the car-park has been developed in accordance with criteria laid down by the Minister for the Environment and Local Government. In this context, the *relevant local authority* is:

(a)   the corporation of a county or other borough or, where appropriate, the urban district council; or

(b)   in respect of an administrative county, the council of the county concerned,

in whose functional area the multi-storey car park is situated.

Both new construction expenditure and refurbishment expenditure may qualify for the capital allowances. However, where the expenditure is refurbishment expenditure, the amount incurred must equal at least 20% of market value of the car-park immediately before the expenditure is incurred; otherwise none of the refurbishment expenditure actually incurred will qualify for capital allowances under TCA 1997, s 344 (but may instead qualify if the property is situated in the Custom House Docks Area or in an area designated under the 1994 Urban Renewal Scheme – see 2001-2002 and prior editions). Where by virtue of TCA 1997, s 344(2) an allowance is given under TCA 1997 Part 9 Ch 1 (industrial building allowances) in respect of capital expenditure incurred on the construction or refurbishment of a qualifying multi-storey car-park, no allowance may be given in respect of that expenditure under the said Chapter 1 by virtue of any other provision of the Tax Acts (TCA 1997, s 344(8)).

A company incurring qualifying expenditure may claim either the industrial building initial allowance or, if it is a car-park operator, free depreciation. The rates of allowances available are set in the first instance at 50% initial allowance and 4% annual writing down allowance with the option to claim free depreciation up to 100% (TCA 1997, s 344(4)(a), (b)). However, the allowances actually made are then restricted to one- half of the amount which would otherwise be available (TCA 1997, s 344(6)). In effect, this means that the effective rates of allowances are 25% initial allowance and 2% writing down allowance with free depreciation up to 50%. The maximum allowances which may be claimed cannot, in the aggregate, exceed 50% of the amount of qualifying expenditure. Thus, a company claiming the full amount of free depreciation available to it as an owner operator will obtain allowances on 50% of the expenditure incurred; a lessor will effectively receive initial allowances of 25% of the expenditure incurred and annual writing down allowances of 2% thereafter until the aggregate amount claimed amounts to 50% of the expenditure incurred. The industrial building allowances rules relating to the making of balancing allowances or charges are applicable as discussed in **5.409** with two exceptions.

Firstly, whatever balancing allowance or charge is calculated is reduced to one-half of the amount so calculated, just as the capital allowances made will have been reduced by one-half (TCA 1997, s 344(6)(b). The amount of any balancing charge is subject to the overall limit as set out in TCA 1997, s 274(8) so that it cannot exceed the aggregate of the allowances actually given.

Secondly, no balancing charge may be made if the event which would otherwise give rise to the charge occurs more than 13 years after the car-park was first used or, in a case where TCA 1997, s 276 applies, more than 13 years after the expenditure was incurred. While a balancing charge cannot arise after this time, however, a balancing allowance may still arise at any time up to 25 years after first use or the date on which the expenditure was incurred. This is because TCA 1997, s 344(5) does not reduce the specified writing down period of the property. Since the car-park is treated as an industrial building, as defined by TCA 1997, s 268(1)(a), it has a writing down period of 25 years by virtue of TCA 1997, s 272(4)(a); TCA 1997, s 344 specifically qualifies the period of time within which a balancing charge may arise but it does not alter the actual writing down period of the building. By the same token, a purchaser of the car-park after year 13 may qualify for capital allowances from the date of purchase to the end of the property's 25 year writing down period if, under the normal rules used to calculate the residue before sale (as discussed in **5.410.2**), a residue before sale exists by reason of the qualifying expenditure not having been entirely written down prior to the end of year 13. Of course, whatever allowances the new owner would be entitled to under the normal rules of TCA 1997, s 272(4) will be reduced by one-half by virtue of the operation of TCA 1997, s 344(6)(a).

Example 5.605.1

Metro Car Parks Ltd constructed and opened a new car park in Waterford during its accounting year ended 31 December 2000 at a cost of €280,000. Assuming the company will claim only basic rate writing down allowances in the 13 years up to 31 December 2012 and that in January 2013 it sells the car-park to All-right Parking Ltd for €120,000, the balancing allowance due to Metro Car Parks Ltd and the allowances due to All-right Parking Ltd are calculated as follows:

	€
Qualifying cost	280,000
Allowances claimed by Metro Car Parks Ltd	
€280,000 x 4% x 13 x 50% = €72,800	145,600
Residue before sale	134,400
Sale price	120,000
	14,400

The balancing allowance to Metro Car Parks Ltd will be €7,200 (€14,400 x 50%).

All-right Parking Ltd will be entitled to allowances based on its purchase price over the remainder of the writing down period for the car-park, ie, an annual writing down allowance of €5,000 for 12 years (€120,000/12 = €10,000 x 50% = €5,000).

The aggregate allowances claimed by both Metro Car Parks Ltd and All-right Parking Ltd over the 25 year writing down period for the car-park (including the balancing allowance made to Metro Car Parks Ltd) will be €140,000 (€72,800 + €7,200 + €60,000).

In line with the extension of the termination date for entering into qualifying leases for the purposes of the double rent allowance, capital allowances in respect of expenditure on related multi-storey car-parks are increased from the maximum of 50% of expenditure to 100% of expenditure, with effect from 1 August 1998. In the case of multi-storey car-parks, a qualifying lease for the purposes of the double rent allowance is one entered into within the qualifying period or within one year of the end of such period, ie, by 31 July 1998. Capital allowances in respect of such car-parks is accordingly increased from 50% to 100% of the capital expenditure incurred from 1 August 1998. In certain cases (where 15% of the total cost of the project is incurred before 1 July 1998), the final date for entering into a qualifying lease will be 30 June 1999. In those cases, maximum capital allowances remain at 50% of expenditure.

The increase in capital allowances to 100% of expenditure is provided for in TCA 1997, s 344(6A). The 50% restriction on capital allowances as provided for in TCA 1997, s 344(6) is to apply and have effect as respects capital expenditure on the construction or refurbishment of a qualifying multi-storey car-park, which is incurred after 31 July 1998, only if a qualifying lease, within the meaning of TCA 1997, s 345 (basically a lease in respect of a qualifying premises granted in the qualifying period, or within one year from the end of that period, on bona fide commercial terms to an unconnected lessee, and subject to certain restrictions relating to "enterprise areas" – see 2001-2002 or earlier editions of this book), is granted in respect of the qualifying multi-storey car-park in respect of which that expenditure is incurred.

5.606　Buildings used for third level education

5.606.1　Introduction

TCA 1997, s 843 provides for industrial building allowances in respect of capital expenditure incurred by approved institutions on the construction of qualifying premises. The buildings in respect of which allowances may be made are buildings which are not industrial buildings or structures within the meaning of TCA 1997, s 268 and which are in use for the purposes of third level education or associated sporting or leisure activities provided by an approved institution and are let to such an institution. Allowances relate both to construction expenditure and to expenditure on the provision of machinery or plant.

See **5.404** regarding the restriction by TCA 1997, s 270(4)-(6) of qualifying expenditure for buildings used for third level education. In the case of expenditure incurred in the period 1 January 2007 to 31 December 2007, only 75% of expenditure incurred is treated as incurred, and in the case of expenditure incurred in the period 1 January 2008 to 31 July 2008, only 50% of expenditure incurred is treated as incurred. Allowances will be available only where the approved institution has raised at least 50% of the cost of the total expenditure before the commencement of construction.

Capital allowances consist of an industrial building annual allowance of 15% of the expenditure incurred over seven years. No balancing charge may be made in respect of a qualifying premises as a result of any event occurring more than seven years after the premises were first used.

Qualifying period

TCA 1997, s 843 defines the *qualifying period* as the period beginning on 1 July 1997 and ending on 31 December 2006 or, where TCA 1997, s 843(1A) applies, ending on 31 July 2008. Accordingly it applies to qualifying expenditure incurred only during that period.

TCA 1997, s 843(1A) applies in relation to the construction of a qualifying premises where:

(a) the person constructing the qualifying premises has, on or before 31 December 2006, carried out work to the value of not less than 15% of the actual construction costs of the premises; and

(b) that person or, where the qualifying premises is sold by that person, the person who is claiming a deduction in relation to the expenditure can show that the condition in (a) was satisfied.

5.606.2 Approved institution

An approved institution means:

(a) an institution of higher education within the meaning of section 1 of the Higher Education Authority Act 1971; or

(b) an institution in the State in receipt of public funding which provides courses to which a scheme approved by the Minister for Education and Science under the Local Authorities (Higher Education Grants) Acts 1968 to 1992, applies; or

(c) any body engaged in the provision of third level health and social services education or training which is approved by the Minister for Health and Children for the purposes of TCA 1997, s 843 and is in receipt of public funding in respect of the provision of such education and training.

5.606.3 Qualifying expenditure

Qualifying expenditure means, subject to TCA 1997, s 843(8) (see below), capital expenditure incurred on:

(a) the construction of a qualifying premises; or

(b) the provision of machinery or plant

which—

(i) in the case of an institution referred to in (a) or (b) of the definition of "approved institution" (see above in **5.606.2**), is , following the receipt of the advice of An tÚdarás, approved for that purpose by the Minister for Education and Science with the consent of the Minister for Finance, and

(ii) in the case of a body referred to in (c) of the definition of "approved institution", is approved for that purpose by the Minister for Health and Children with the consent of the Minister for Finance.

Whereas the capital allowances provided for TCA 1997, s 843 are primarily directed at buildings used by third level educational institutions, qualifying expenditure for this purpose refers equally to machinery or plant. The capital allowances available are the same for both buildings and machinery or plant.

For the purposes of entitlement to capital allowances, expenditure must be approved by the Minister for Education and Science on the advice of An tÚdarás. *An tÚdarás* means the Body established by section 2 of the Higher Education Authority Act 1971.

No capital allowance may be made in respect of qualifying expenditure on a qualifying premises unless, before the commencement of construction of the premises, or, in the case of the construction of a qualifying premises to be used for the purposes of certain sporting or leisure activities (see below), before 1 July 2001, the Minister for Finance certifies that:

(a) an approved institution has procured or otherwise secured a sum of money, none of which has been met directly or indirectly by the State, which sum is at least 50% of the qualifying expenditure to be incurred on the premises; and

(b) such sum is to be used solely by the approved institution for the following purposes:

  (i)   paying interest on money borrowed for the purpose of funding the construction of the premises,

  (ii) paying rent on the premises during such times as it is the subject of a letting on such terms as are referred to in the above definition of "qualifying premises", and

  (iii) purchasing the premises following the termination of the letting referred to in (ii) (TCA 1997, s 843(4)).

The qualifying premises to be used for certain sporting or leisure activities referred to above are qualifying premises which consist of a building or structure which is to be used for the purposes of sporting or leisure activities associated with third level education provided by an approved institution where, in relation to that premises, an application for certification under TCA 1997, s 843(4) was made, and the construction of that premises commenced prior to 15 February 2001.

A certificate may not be given by the Minister for the above purposes unless an application for certification was made before 1 January 2005 (TCA 1997, s 843(7)).

Notwithstanding the approval required from the Minister for Education and Science and the consent required from the Minister for Finance in relation to the case described in (i) of the definition of "qualifying expenditure" above, and the above-mentioned certificate required from the Minister for Finance in so far as that expenditure is concerned, the approval mechanism may be delegated to An tÚdarás on the basis of criteria to be agreed between the Ministers concerned. This facility follows the decision to provide for the funding of certain projects by the Research and Development Fund as announced by the Minister for Education and Science in November 1998.

Accordingly it is provided in TCA 1997, s 843(8) that the Minister for Education and Science and the Minister for Finance may, either generally in the case of institutions referred to in (a) or (b) of the definition of "approved institution" (see above) or in respect of capital expenditure to be incurred on any particular type of qualifying premises to be used by any such institution, and subject to such conditions, if any, which they may see fit to impose, agree to delegate and may so delegate in writing to An tÚdarás the above-mentioned powers and duties relating to approval, consent and certification. Where the Ministers so delegate, then, as respects the matters so delegated—

(i)   the definition of "qualifying expenditure", in relation to the case described in
(i) of that definition above, is to apply on the basis that the expenditure is to be
approved by An tÚdarás; and

(ii) as if the above references to the Minister for Finance, regarding certification,
were references to An tÚdarás.

5.606.4   Qualifying premises

Qualifying premises means a building or structure which:

(a)   apart from TCA 1997, s 843 is not an industrial building or structure within the
meaning of TCA 1997, s 268 (see **5.401.1**); and

(b)   (i)   is in use for the purposes of third level education or associated sporting or
leisure activities provided by an approved institution; or

(ii)   is let to an approved institution,

but does not include any part of a building or structure in use as, or as part of, a dwelling
house.

5.606.5   Allowances

TCA 1997, s 843 provides in general that all of the provisions in the Tax Acts relating to
the making of allowances or charges in respect of capital expenditure which is incurred
by a company on the construction of an industrial building or structure are,
notwithstanding anything to the contrary therein, to apply in relation to qualifying
expenditure on a qualifying premises:

(a)   as if the qualifying premises were a building or structure in respect of which an
allowance falls to be made for the purposes of corporation tax under TCA 1997
Part 9 Ch 1 by reason of its use for a purpose specified in TCA 1997,
s 268(1)(a) (ie, a mill, factory or other similar premises – see **5.401.1**); and

(b)   where any activity carried on by the company in the qualifying premises is not
a trade, as if it were a trade.

In general, the entitlement to an industrial building initial allowance arises under TCA
1997, s 268(1) where a person has incurred capital expenditure on the construction of a
building or structure which is to be an industrial building or structure occupied for the
purposes of a trade by the person who incurs the capital expenditure or by a lessee who
occupies the property under a relevant lease (ie, a lease to which the relevant interest, as
defined in TCA 1997, s 269, is reversionary). For expenditure incurred on or after 1
April 1992, however, industrial building initial allowances are not generally available,
and are not available for the purposes of TCA 1997, s 843.

The entitlement of a company to an industrial building annual allowance arises under
TCA 1997, s 272(2) where, at the end of an accounting period, the company is entitled
to the relevant interest in the building and the building is in use as an industrial building.
An allowance may be given under TCA 1997, s 843(2) in relation to any qualifying
expenditure on a qualifying premises only in so far as the expenditure is incurred in the
qualifying period (TCA 1997, s 843(2A)).

The *qualifying period* is the period commencing on 1 July 1997 and ending on 31
July 2006.

For the purposes of the capital allowances available by virtue of TCA 1997, s 843 in respect of qualifying buildings, it is necessary that all of the conditions for obtaining the allowances as set out in TCA 1997 Part 9 Ch 1 as well as those in TCA 1997, s 843 are satisfied.

TCA 1997, s 843(3) provides for an annual writing down allowance of 15% of the amount of the qualifying expenditure incurred in the qualifying period on the qualifying premises. In no case, however, may the allowance made for any accounting period exceed the residue of the expenditure at the end of the immediately preceding accounting period (TCA 1997, s 272(6)). Accordingly, the qualifying expenditure will normally be written off over seven accounting periods at 15% for each of the first six periods and at 10% for the seventh period.

For the purposes of determining whether and to what extent capital expenditure incurred on the construction of a qualifying premises is incurred or not incurred in the qualifying period, only such amount of that capital expenditure as is properly attributable to work on the construction or refurbishment of the premises actually carried out during the qualifying period will be treated as having been incurred in that period (TCA 1997, s 843(9)).

5.606.6 Balancing allowances and charges

TCA 1997, s 274 (as applied by TCA 1997, s 843) requires a balancing allowance or balancing charge to be computed if, in relation to a qualifying premises in respect of which any capital allowances have been obtained, any of the following events occurs:

(a) the relevant interest in the building is sold;

(b) the relevant interest in the building is exchanged (TCA 1997, s 311(3));

(c) the building is demolished or destroyed;

(d) the building ceases altogether to be used;

(e) the relevant interest, if it is a leasehold interest, either

    (i) comes to an end, otherwise than on the person entitled to it acquiring the reversionary interest, or

    (ii) is surrendered for valuable consideration (TCA 1997, s 311(3)).

Where a building or structure is held for a period of at least 7 years, no balancing charge may be made by reason of any of the balancing events specified in TCA 1997, s 274(1) (TCA 1997, s 843(5)). The writing down life of the industrial building is also 7 years. A purchaser of the property may be entitled to capital allowances where the purchase takes place not more than 7 years after the premises was first used. The cessation of a qualifying trade is not an event requiring a balancing adjustment, provided the owner does not dispose of the relevant interest and so long as the building continues to be used for some purpose.

The rules for calculating the amount of the balancing adjustment are the same as those for industrial buildings as discussed in **5.409.2**. The provisions outlined in **5.411** (deduction of notional allowances), **5.412** (sale of building constructed at different dates) and **5.413** (anti-avoidance: balancing allowances) must also be applied where relevant.

5.607 Buildings used for certain childcare purposes

5.607.1 Introduction

Capital allowances may be claimed in respect of capital expenditure incurred on childcare facilities which meet certain standards for such facilities as provided for under the Childcare Act, 1991. The allowances consist of an annual allowance of 15% for six years and an allowance of 10% for the seventh year for capital expenditure on a building or part of a building used as a childcare facility.

Where the building ceases to be used as a childcare facility within ten years of its first being used as such, allowances will be clawed back by way of a balancing charge.

5.607.2 Qualifying expenditure

Qualifying expenditure means capital expenditure incurred on the construction, conversion or refurbishment of a qualifying premises.

5.607.3 Qualifying premises

Qualifying premises means a building or structure which:

(a)　is not otherwise an industrial building or structure within the meaning of TCA 1997, s 268 (see **5.401.1**); and

(b)　is in use for the purposes of providing:

(i)　a pre-school service, or

(ii)　a pre-school service and a day-care or other service to cater for children other than pre-school children,

and in respect of which it can be shown (to the extent that it is being used for the purposes of providing a pre-school service) that the requirements of Regulation 10 or 11(1), as appropriate, of the Child Care (Pre-School Services) (No 2) Regulations 2006 (SI No 604 of 2006), have been complied with,

but does not include any part of a building or structure in use as or as part of a dwelling house (TCA 1997, s 843A(1)).

Pre-school child and *pre-school service* have the meanings respectively assigned to them by s 49 of the Child Care Act 1991.

5.607.4 Allowances

TCA 1997, s 843A(2) provides in general that all of the provisions in the Tax Acts relating to the making of allowances or charges in respect of capital expenditure which is incurred by a company on the construction or refurbishment of an industrial building or structure are, notwithstanding anything to the contrary therein, to apply in relation to qualifying expenditure on a qualifying premises:

(a)　as if the qualifying premises were a building or structure in respect of which an allowance falls to be made for the purposes of corporation tax under TCA 1997 Part 9 Ch 1 by reason of its use for a purpose specified in TCA 1997, s 268(1)(a) (ie, a mill, factory or other similar premises – see **5.401.1**); and

(b)　where any activity carried on by the company in the qualifying premises is not a trade, as if it were a trade.

In general, the entitlement to an industrial building initial allowance arises under TCA 1997, s 268(1) where a person has incurred capital expenditure on the construction of a building or structure which is to be an industrial building or structure occupied for the purposes of a trade by the person who incurs the capital expenditure or by a lessee who occupies the property under a relevant lease (ie, a lease to which the relevant interest, as defined in TCA 1997, s 269, is reversionary). For expenditure incurred on or after 1 April 1992, however, industrial building initial allowances are not generally available, and are not available for the purposes of TCA 1997, s 843A.

The entitlement of a company to an industrial building annual allowance arises under TCA 1997, s 272(2) where, at the end of an accounting period, the company is entitled to the relevant interest in the building and the building is in use as an industrial building.

For the purposes of the capital allowances available by virtue of TCA 1997, s 843A in respect of qualifying buildings, it is necessary that all of the conditions for obtaining the allowances as set out in TCA 1997 Part 9 Ch 1 as well as those in TCA 1997, s 843A are satisfied.

In respect of expenditure incurred on or after 1 December 1999, TCA 1997, s 843A(3) provides for an annual writing down allowance of 15% of the amount of the qualifying expenditure on the qualifying premises. In no case, however, may the allowance made for any accounting period exceed the residue of the expenditure at the end of the immediately preceding accounting period (TCA 1997, s 272(6)). Accordingly, the qualifying expenditure will normally be written off over seven accounting periods at 15% for each of the first six periods and at 10% for the seventh period.

Notwithstanding the seven-year write-off period for capital allowances, the tax life (during which allowances may be transferred to a purchaser) for a qualifying premises first used (or first used after refurbishment) on or after 1 February 2007 is 15 years. TCA 1997, s 843A(3)(c) provides, in relation to a qualifying premises, that the tax life of that premises is:

(a)   as respects a qualifying premises that is first used on or after 1 February 2007, 15 years beginning with the time it was first used; or

(b)   where qualifying expenditure on the refurbishment or conversion of the premises is incurred and, subsequent to the incurring of that expenditure, is first used on or after 1 February 2007, 15 years from the time it was first used subsequent to the incurring of that expenditure.

No balancing allowance or charge may be made by reason of an event occurring more than (i) where the qualifying premises was first used on or after 1 February 2007, 15 years after it was first used, or (ii) where qualifying expenditure on the refurbishment or conversion of the premises is incurred and, subsequent to the incurring of that expenditure, the premises is first used on or after 1 February 2007, 15 years after it was first used subsequent to incurring that expenditure (TCA 1997, s 843A(4A)).

Accelerated capital allowances

In respect of expenditure incurred on or after 1 December 1999, capital allowances of 100% of expenditure are available both to owners of childcare facilities and to investors who wish to invest by way of leasing arrangements. The relevant provision comes into operation on such day as the Minister for Finance may by order appoint.

TCA 1997, s 843A(3A) provides that for the purposes of the application by TCA 1997, s 843A(2) of TCA 1997 ss 271 and 273 (industrial building allowances and accelerated writing-down allowances) in relation to qualifying expenditure incurred on or after 1 December 1999 on a qualifying premises:

(a)   TCA 1997, s 271 is to apply as if various references (not relevant for the purposes of TCA 1997, s 843A) were deleted and as if TCA 1997, s 271(4) (rates of industrial building allowances) were substituted by a provision to the effect that the allowance is to be of an amount equal to 100% of the qualifying capital expenditure; and

(b)   TCA 1997, s 273 is to apply as if various references and provisions (eg, TCA 1997, s 273(2)(b) and (3)-(7) (phasing out of free depreciation)) were deleted. Accordingly TCA 1997, s 843A(3A) secures that a 100% free depreciation allowance is available in respect of qualifying capital expenditure incurred in respect of a qualifying premises.

Property developers

Capital allowances may not be claimed under TCA 1997, s 843A(3) or (3A) in respect of qualifying expenditure incurred on a qualifying premises on or after 1 January 2008—

(a)   where a property developer or a person connected with (within the meaning of TCA 1997, s 10 – see **2.3**) the property developer is entitled to the relevant interest (see **5.403**) in that qualifying expenditure, and

(b)   either of the persons in (a) incurred the qualifying expenditure on that qualifying premises, or such expenditure was incurred by any other person connected with the property developer (TCA 1997, s 843A(5)).

A *property developer* for this purpose is a person carrying on a trade which consists wholly or mainly of the construction or refurbishment of buildings or structures with a view to their sale.

The above restriction came into operation on 21 June 2000, the day appointed by order of the Minister for Finance for that purpose. In the explanatory memorandum to FA 2000 it is stated that, following consultations with the European Commission, a property developer will not be able to avail of *any* capital allowances for expenditure on the construction, refurbishment or extension of a childcare premises as this constitutes a State Aid.

It would seem, however, that there is nothing to prevent a property developer from claiming normal industrial building writing-down allowances by virtue of TCA 1997, s 843A(2); the prohibition relates only to subsections (3) and (3A) of TCA 1997, s 843A. It will be recalled that subsection (2) provides that all of the provisions in the Tax Acts relating to the making of allowances or charges in respect of capital expenditure which is incurred on the construction or refurbishment of an industrial building or structure are to apply in relation to qualifying expenditure on a qualifying premises under TCA 1997, s 843A.

5.607.5 Balancing allowances and charges

TCA 1997, s 274 (as applied by TCA 1997, s 843A) requires a balancing allowance or balancing charge to be computed if, in relation to a qualifying premises in respect of which any capital allowances have been obtained, any of the following events occurs:

(a) the relevant interest in the building is sold;

(b) the relevant interest in the building is exchanged (TCA 1997, s 311(3));

(c) the building is demolished or destroyed;

(d) the building ceases altogether to be used;

(e) the relevant interest, if it is a leasehold interest, either

    (i) comes to an end, otherwise than on the person entitled to it acquiring the reversionary interest, or

    (ii) is surrendered for valuable consideration (TCA 1997, s 311(3)).

Where a building or structure is held for a period of at least 10 years, no balancing charge may be made by reason of any of the balancing events specified in TCA 1997, s 274(1) (TCA 1997, s 843A(4)). The ten year period runs from the date the qualifying premises was first used or, where allowances have been received in respect of refurbishment expenditure, from the date the qualifying expenditure on refurbishment was incurred. The writing down life of the industrial building is also 7 years. A purchaser of the property may be entitled to capital allowances where the purchase takes place not more than 7 years after the premises was first used. The cessation of a qualifying trade is not an event requiring a balancing adjustment, provided the owner does not dispose of the relevant interest and so long as the building continues to be used for some purpose.

The rules for calculating the amount of the balancing adjustment are the same as those for industrial buildings as discussed in **5.409.2**. The provisions outlined in **5.411** (deduction of notional allowances), **5.412** (sale of building constructed at different dates) and **5.413** (anti-avoidance: balancing allowances) must also be applied where relevant.

5.608 Transmission capacity rights

5.608.1 Introduction

Although prior to the enactment of FA 2000 capital allowances had been available to companies operating in the telecommunications industry in respect of investments in the physical infrastructure, such as cabling and other equipment, there was no provision for allowances for expenditure on long-term rights to use advanced communications infrastructure, or what are commonly referred to as indefeasible rights of use (IRUs). TCA 1997 Part 29 Chapter 4 (ss 769A-769F), introduced by FA 2000 s 64, provides for the availability of capital allowances in respect of qualifying expenditure incurred on the purchase of "capacity rights", being long-term rights to use wired, radio or optical transmission paths for the transfer of data and information. These rights typically cover periods of 10 to 25 years. References to the purchase of capacity rights include references to the acquisition of a licence in respect of capacity rights.

An IRU confers on the holder a right to transmit voice, data or information over cable (optical or wired), satellite or other radio systems, or between two points over a "geographically diverse path", so that the identification of the particular cable system is not in itself critical to the meaning of an IRU. The provisions of the legislation on transmission capacity rights are widely drawn and would cover IRUs as described above and would cover IRUs whether or not located in Ireland.

Capital allowances are available to a company which incurs qualifying expenditure on the purchase of capacity rights on or after 1 April 2000 although the legislation only comes into operation on the date of the passing of Finance Act 2003.

A company that incurs qualifying expenditure on capacity rights is entitled to a writing down allowance against its trading profits or against income receivable by it in respect of the exploitation of the rights. The writing down period is a period of seven years, or the rights period, whichever is longer. There are provisions for the clawback of allowances claimed where the proceeds on a subsequent sale of rights exceed the tax written down value of the rights. Correspondingly, additional allowances will be given where subsequent sale proceeds are less than tax written down value, or where the rights expire. Where there is a disposal of a part of the capacity rights, any disposal proceeds will reduce the allowable cost, and therefore allowances, for the period of disposal and for subsequent periods.

A sale of a part of capacity rights includes the grant of a licence in respect of the capacity rights in question. If a licence granted by a company entitled to any capacity rights is a licence to exercise those rights to the exclusion of the grantor and all other persons for the whole of the remainder of the term of the rights, the grantor is treated as selling the whole of the rights.

5.608.2   Definitions and related matters

Capacity rights means the right to used wired, radio or optical transmission paths for the transfer of voice, data or information.

A *writing-down period* is:

(a)   a period of seven years; or

(b)   where the capacity rights are purchased for a specified period exceeding seven years, the number of years for which the capacity rights are purchased,

commencing with the beginning of the accounting period related to the expenditure (TCA 1997, s 769B(2)(a)).

Accounting period related to the expenditure is not defined but presumably it means the accounting period in which the expenditure in question is incurred. (See **5.101** as regards TCA 1997, s 321(2) and *chargeable period related to expenditure*.)

Qualifying expenditure means capital expenditure incurred on the purchase of capacity rights, but not including expenditure incurred on or after 6 February 2003 consisting of a licence fee or other payment made to the Commission for Communications Regulation in respect of a licence or permission granted by that Commission on or after that date under:

(a)   the Wireless Telegraphy Acts 1926 to 1988; or

(b)   the Postal and Telecommunications Services Act 1983.

A reference to the sale of part of capacity rights includes a reference to the grant of a licence in respect of the capacity rights in question. A reference to the purchase of capacity rights includes a reference to the acquisition of a licence in respect of capacity rights. If a licence granted by a company entitled to any capacity rights is a licence to exercise those rights to the exclusion of the company and all other persons throughout the remainder of the term for which the rights subsist, the company is to be treated as thereby selling those rights (TCA 1997, s 769A(2)).

Although clearly the legislation dealing with capacity rights applies to companies only, it includes important references to chargeable periods and related concepts. In this connection, TCA 1997, s 321(2) explains certain relevant phrases (see **5.101**) as follows:

(a)   *chargeable period*: either an accounting period of a company or a year of assessment;

(b)   *chargeable period or its basis period*: either the basis period for a year of assessment or the accounting period of a company;

(c)   *chargeable period related to expenditure*: the year of assessment in the basis period for which the expenditure is incurred or the accounting period of a company in which the expenditure is incurred;

(d)   *chargeable period related to a sale or other event*: the year of assessment in the basis period for which the sale or other event takes place or the accounting period in which the sale or other event occurs.

For the most part, it is likely in practice that a reference to a chargeable period will be to an accounting period, that a reference to a chargeable period related to expenditure will be to the accounting period in which the expenditure is incurred, that a reference to a chargeable period related to a sale or other event will be to the accounting period in which the sale or other event occurred, and that a reference to a chargeable period or its basis period will be to an accounting period.

The relevance of years of assessment and basis periods derives from the possibility that certain non-resident companies not carrying on a trade in Ireland through a branch or agency/ permanent establishment will be in receipt of income from Irish source capacity rights and will accordingly be subject to income tax in Ireland. Assessments made on such companies would of course be for years of assessment.

5.608.3   Writing-down allowances

Where, on or after 1 April 2000, a company incurs qualifying expenditure on the purchase of capacity rights, it will be entitled to a writing-down allowance in respect of that expenditure during the writing-down period. The writing-down allowance is determined by the formula:

$$A \times \frac{B}{C}$$

where:

A   is the amount of the qualifying expenditure incurred on the purchase of the capacity rights;

B   is the length of the part of the chargeable period falling within the writing-down period; and

C   is the length of the writing-down period (TCA 1997, s 769B(2)(b)).

In other words, the amount of the writing-down allowance is the fraction of the qualifying expenditure incurred represented by the length of the chargeable period (or, as the case may be, the length of the part of that period falling within the writing-down period) for which the allowance is being made over the length of the writing-down period. Since the writing-down period commences with the beginning of an *accounting* period, it may happen that a chargeable period that is a year of assessment does not all fall within the writing-down period.

TCA 1997, s 769B(3) contains an anti-avoidance measure to prevent an allowance being artificially created in connection with a sale of capacity rights within a group of companies where the allowance would not otherwise be available. Where a company (the "buyer") incurs qualifying expenditure on the purchase from another company (the "seller") of capacity rights, no allowance will be made to the buyer in respect of that expenditure if both companies are companies within a group of companies, unless an allowance had been made to the seller (or would have been made to the seller if it had not sold those rights) in respect of the capital expenditure it incurred on the purchase of those rights.

A *group of companies* consists of a company and any other companies of which it has control or with which it is associated. A company is associated with another company where it could reasonably be considered that:

(a)   any person or any group of persons or groups of persons having a reasonable commonality of identity has or have, as the case may be, or had the means or power, either directly or indirectly, to determine the trading operations carried on or to be carried on by both companies; or

(b)   both companies are under the control of any person or any group of persons or groups of persons having a reasonable commonality of identity.

Control is as defined in TCA 1997, s 432 (see **2.401**).

Any expenditure incurred by a company for the purposes of a trade that it is about to carry on is treated as if the expenditure had been incurred by the company on the first day on which it carries on the trade. This rule will, however, not apply if, before the date on which the trade has commenced, the company has sold all the capacity rights (TCA 1997, s 769B(2)(c)).

No writing-down allowance may be made to a company in respect of any expenditure unless the allowance is to be made to it in taxing its trade or unless any income receivable by the company in respect of the rights would be liable to tax (TCA 1997, s 769B(1)). Thus, capital allowances made to a company in respect of expenditure on capacity rights will normally be made in computing the company's trading income for corporation tax purposes (see **5.105.2**). Alternatively, a company, perhaps a non-resident company, may derive income from its ownership of capacity rights in circumstances where the company is not carrying on a trade. The income so derived may accordingly be taxed under Case IV of Schedule D in which case the writing-down allowances will be set against that income by means of "discharge or repayment of tax" (see **5.608.5** below and also **5.105.1**).

5.608.4   Effect of lapse of capacity rights

TCA 1997, s 769C deals with a number of scenarios in which there is a lapse of capacity rights, whether by reason of those rights coming to an end without being renewed or by reason of the rights being wholly or partly sold. The tax consequences of the events in question are as follows.

Discontinuance of writing-down allowances

Where a company incurs qualifying expenditure on the purchase of capacity rights and any of the following events occurs within the writing-down period:

(a) the rights come to an end without provision being made for their subsequent renewal;

(b) the rights cease altogether to be exercised;

(c) the company sells all the rights or so much of them as it still owns;

(d) the company sells part of the rights and the amount of the net proceeds of the sale (in so far as they consist of capital sums) is not less than the amount of the qualifying expenditure remaining unallowed;

no writing-down allowance may be made to the company for the chargeable period related to the event or for any subsequent chargeable period (TCA 1997, s 769C(1)).

Example 5.608.4.1

In its year ended 31 December 2006, Flagstaff Ltd incurs qualifying expenditure of €30m on the acquisition, for a period of 8 years, of capacity rights for use in its trade. On 1 January 2008 the company sells off part of the rights for a sum of €25m.

The writing-down period in relation to the rights purchased is the period of 8 years from 1 January 2006 to 31 December 2013. The writing-down allowance for each of the years ended 31 December 2006 and 31 December 2007 is €30m x 12/96 = €3.75m. The amount of the expenditure remaining unallowed at the date of sale is €22.5m. The amount of the net proceeds of sale is not less than this amount.

Flagstaff Ltd is not entitled to claim any writing-down allowances in respect of its expenditure on capacity rights for the year ended 31 December 2008 or for any subsequent period.

See also Example **5.608.4.4** below in relation to the balancing charge arising.

Lapse of rights or outright sale where proceeds less than unallowed expenditure

Where a company incurs qualifying expenditure on the purchase of capacity rights and any of the following events occurs within the writing-down period:

(a) the rights come to an end without provision being made for their subsequent renewal;

(b) the rights cease altogether to be exercised;

(c) the company sells all the rights or so much of them as it still owns and the amount of the net proceeds of the sale (in so far as they consist of capital sums) is less than the amount of the qualifying expenditure remaining unallowed;

a "balancing allowance" is to be made to the company equal to:

(i) in the case of (a) or (b), the amount of the qualifying expenditure remaining unallowed; and

(ii) in the case of (c), the amount of the qualifying expenditure remaining unallowed less the net proceeds of the sale (TCA 1997, s 769C(2)).

Example 5.608.4.2

The position is as in Example **5.608.4.1** except that on 1 January 2008 Flagstaff Ltd sells all of its capacity rights for €20m. As before, the amount of the expenditure remaining unallowed at the date of sale is €22.5m. The amount of the net proceeds of sale is less than this amount.

Flagstaff Ltd is entitled to a balancing allowance of €22.5m – €20m = €2.5m.

Example 5.608.4.3

The position is as in Example **5.608.4.1** except that on 1 January 2008 Flagstaff Ltd ceases altogether to use the capacity rights. The amount of the expenditure remaining unallowed at the date the company ceases to use the rights is €22.5m.

Flagstaff Ltd is entitled to a balancing allowance of €22.5m.

Sale of all or part of rights for proceeds in excess of unallowed expenditure

Where a company which has incurred qualifying expenditure on the purchase of capacity rights sells all or any part of those rights and the amount of the net proceeds of the sale (in so far as they consist of capital sums) exceeds the amount of the capital expenditure remaining unallowed, if any, a "balancing charge" is to be made on the company for the chargeable period related to the sale on an amount equal to:

(a) the excess; or

(b) where the amount of the qualifying expenditure remaining unallowed is Nil, the amount of net proceeds of the sale (TCA 1997, s 769C(3)).

Example 5.608.4.4

The position is as in Example **5.608.4.1**. It was seen in that example that Flagstaff Ltd ceased to be entitled to any further writing-down allowances after the year ended 31 December 2007.

In addition, a balancing charge is made on Flagstaff Ltd in an amount of €25m – €22.5m = €2.5m.

Sale of part of rights for proceeds not in excess of unallowed expenditure

Where a company which has incurred qualifying expenditure on the purchase of capacity rights sells a part of those rights and TCA 1997, s 769C(3) does not apply (ie, where the amount of the sale proceeds does not exceed the amount of the qualifying expenditure remaining unallowed), the amount of any writing-down allowance to be made in respect of that expenditure for the chargeable period related to the sale or for any subsequent chargeable period is to be an amount determined by:

(a) subtracting the amount of the net proceeds of the sale (in so far as they consist of capital sums) from the amount of the qualifying expenditure remaining unallowed at the time of the sale; and

(b) dividing the result by the number of complete years of the writing-down period which remained at the beginning of the chargeable period related to the sale,

and so on for any subsequent sales (TCA 1997, s 769C(4)).

Example 5.608.4.5

The position is as in Example **5.608.4.1** except that on 1 January 2008 Flagstaff Ltd sells the part of its capacity rights for €18m. As before, the amount of the expenditure remaining unallowed at the date of sale is €22.5m. The amount of the net proceeds of sale is less than this amount.

The number of complete years of the writing-down period remaining on 1 January 2008 is 6. For the year ended 31 December 2008 and subsequent periods within the writing-down period, Flagstaff Ltd is entitled to a writing-down allowance, in respect of its expenditure on capacity rights, of (€22.5m – €18m)/6 = €0.75m.

The amount of the qualifying expenditure remaining unallowed

The "amount of the qualifying expenditure remaining unallowed" in all of the above situations is the amount of the qualifying expenditure less the amount of any writing-down allowances made in respect of that expenditure for chargeable periods before the chargeable period related to the event in question and less also the amount of the net proceeds of any previous sale, by the company which incurred the expenditure, of any part of the rights acquired by the expenditure in so far as those proceeds consist of capital sums (TCA 1997, s 769C(5)).

The second deduction mentioned above takes account of a case in which a company had previously disposed of a part of its capacity rights for a capital sum in circumstances where no balancing allowance or charge had been made.

Example 5.608.4.6

The position is as in Example **5.608.4.5** where on 1 January 2008 Flagstaff Ltd had sold a part of its capacity rights for €18m. These proceeds were less than €22.5m, the amount of the expenditure remaining unallowed at the date of that sale. For the year ended 31 December 2008 and subsequent periods, Flagstaff Ltd was entitled to a writing-down allowance of €0.75m.

Assume that on 1 January 2010 Flagstaff Ltd sold a further part of the capacity rights for €4m.

The amount of the qualifying expenditure remaining unallowed on 1 January 2010 is as follows:

	€m	€m
Cost of capacity rights		30
Less:		
Writing-down allowances for 2 years to 31.12.07 (3.75 x 2)	7.5	
Writing-down allowances for 2 years to 31.12.08 (0.75 x 2)	1.5	9
		21
Proceeds of previous sale		18
Expenditure remaining unallowed		3
Proceeds of second sale		4
Balancing charge (TCA 1997, s 769C(3))		1

A balancing allowance may not be made in respect of any expenditure unless a writing-down allowance has been made in respect of that expenditure, or unless such an allowance could have been made in respect of that expenditure but for the happening of the event giving rise to the balancing allowance (TCA 1997, s 769C(6)(a)). Accordingly, a balancing allowance may be made in a situation in which, say, a company sells all of its capacity rights in the same accounting period in which it bought those rights. Assuming the proceeds of sale are less than the amount of the qualifying expenditure incurred by the company in acquiring the rights, the amount of the balancing allowance will be the amount of the expenditure incurred less the sale proceeds.

The total amount on which a balancing charge is made in respect of any expenditure may not exceed the total writing-down allowances actually made in respect of that expenditure less, if a balancing charge has previously been made in respect of that expenditure, the amount on which that charge was made (TCA 1997, s 769C(6)(b)).

5.608.5   Manner of making allowances and charges

An allowance or charge made in connection with qualifying expenditure incurred on the purchase of capacity rights is to be made to or on a company in taxing the company's trade if:

(a)   the company is carrying on a trade the profits or gains of which are, or (if there were any such profits) would be, chargeable to corporation tax for the chargeable period for which the allowance or charge is made; and

(b)   at any time in the chargeable period or its basis period the capacity rights in question, or other rights out of which they were granted, were used for the purposes of that trade (TCA 1997, s 769D(1)).

Otherwise, an allowance in connection with qualifying expenditure incurred on the purchase of capacity rights is to be made by means of discharge or repayment of tax and is to be available against income from capacity rights. Correspondingly, any charge made is to be made under Case IV of Schedule D (TCA 1997, s 769D(2)).

Although the legislation providing for capital allowances in respect of expenditure on capacity rights is contained in TCA 1997 Part 29 Chapter 4, TCA 1997 Part 9 Chapter 4 is to apply as if the legislation were contained in that chapter. Accordingly, Part 9 Chapter 4 will be relevant in relation to such matters as the manner of making allowances and charges, the treatment of grants, control and "main benefit" sales, and the time at which expenditure is incurred (see **5.1** generally). Any reference in the Tax Acts to any capital allowance to be given by way of discharge or repayment of tax and to be available or available primarily against a specified class of income is to include a reference to any capital allowance given in accordance with TCA 1997, s 769D(2) (TCA 1997, s 769E(1)).

In TCA 1997 Part 9 Chapter 4 (as applied by virtue of TCA 1997, s 769E(1) to capacity rights), the reference in TCA 1997, s 312(5)(a)(i) to the sum mentioned in paragraph (b) of that subsection is, in the case of capacity rights, to be construed as a reference to the amount of the qualifying expenditure on the acquisition of the capacity rights remaining unallowed, computed in accordance with TCA 1997, s 769C (TCA 1997, s 769E(2)). In TCA 1997, s 312(5)(b), the reference is to the amount of the expenditure "still unallowed" (the tax written down value – see **5.103.3**) but the amount of the qualifying expenditure remaining unallowed as defined in TCA 1997, s 769C (see **5.608.4** and Example **5.608.4.6** above) has a meaning somewhat different to that in TCA 1997, s 312(5).

5.609   Milk quotas

See **13.204**.

Chapter 6

Urban and Other Renewal Incentives

6.1 URBAN RENEWAL INCENTIVES: 1998 SCHEME

6.101   Introduction
6.102   Construction or refurbishment of industrial buildings
6.103   Construction or refurbishment of commercial premises

6.101   Introduction

6.101.1   The 1998 urban renewal scheme

The scheme operates as follows:

(a)   a process of designation, based on Integrated Area Plans produced by local authorities, focuses on the physical and socio-economic renewal of areas;

(b)   the authorities recommend areas for designation to an advisory panel of the Department of the Environment and Local Government which will in turn make recommendations to the Minister of that Department;

(c)   the Minister for Finance will make orders applying one or more tax incentives, as provided for in Taxes Consolidation Act 1997 (TCA 1997) Part 10 Ch 7, for the areas designated by the Minister for the Environment and Local Government;

(d)   the incentives provided for may vary in mix for different areas; unlike urban renewal legislation to date, there will accordingly be no blanket entitlement to all of the reliefs for any particular qualifying area;

(e)   there is provision to discriminate as between specific types of commercial developments for tax incentive purposes.

The 1998 scheme, generally, ran from 1 August 1998 to 31 December 2002.

In respect of a separate qualifying period which ran from 6 April 2001 to 31 December 2004, the scheme was extended to cover qualifying streets to provide certain incentives under the Living over the Shop Scheme. The purpose of the scheme was to provide residential accommodation in the vacant spaces over commercial premises in the five cities of Cork, Dublin, Galway, Limerick and Waterford. The reliefs were to be applied to specific lengths of streetscape to be recommended by the Minister for the Environment and Local Government following recommendation by the relevant local authority concerned and approval by a special panel of experts. The incentives were available in respect of buildings fronting on to qualifying streets and which existed on 13 September 2000 or which were replacement buildings where it was necessary to demolish the original building following a demolition order or for structural reasons.

An incentive relief for lessors of residential premises is provided for in TCA 1997 Part 10, Chapter 11 (ss 372AK-372AT) and this is dealt with in **6.5**.

6.101.2   Definitions

Qualifying period

TCA 1997, s 372A(1) defines the *qualifying period* as:

(a)   subject to TCA 1997, s 372B and in relation to a qualifying area (see **6.101.3** below), the period from 1 August 1998 to—

(i)   31 December 2002, or

(ii) where TCA 1997, s 372A(1A) applies, 31 December 2006, or

(iii) where TCA 1997, s 372A(1A) and (3) apply, 31 July 2008; and

(b) subject to TCA 1997, s 372BA and in relation to a qualifying street (see **6.101.3** below), the period from 6 April 2001 to—

(i) 31 December 2004, or

(ii) where TCA 1997, s 372(1B) applies, 31 December 2006, or

(iii) where TCA 1997, s 372A(1B) and (3) apply, 31 July 2008.

TCA 1997, s 372A(1A) applies where the relevant local authority gives a certificate in writing on or before 30 September 2003 to the person constructing or refurbishing a building or structure, or part of a building or structure, the site of which is wholly within a qualifying area, stating that it is satisfied that not less than 15% of the total cost of constructing or refurbishing the building or structure, or the part of the building or structure, and the acquisition of the site thereof had been incurred on or before 30 June 2003, provided the application for such certificate is received by the authority on or before 31 July 2003.

TCA 1997, s 372A(1B) applies in relation to a qualifying street, as respects capital expenditure incurred on the construction or refurbishment of a building or structure if:

(a) (i) a planning application (not being an application for outline permission within the meaning of section 36 of the Planning and Development Act 2000), in so far as planning permission is required, in respect of the construction or refurbishment work on the building or structure represented by that expenditure, is made in accordance with the Planning and Development Regulations 2001 to 2003,

(ii) an acknowledgment of the application, confirming that it was received on or before 31 December 2004, is issued by the planning authority in accordance with Article 26(2) of the Planning and Development Regulations 2001 (SI 600/ 2001), and

(iii) the application is not an invalid application in respect of which a notice is issued by the planning authority in accordance with article 26(5) of those regulations,

(b) (i) a planning application, in so far as planning permission was required, in respect of the construction or refurbishment work on the building or structure represented by that expenditure, was made in accordance with the Local Government (Planning and Development) Regulations 1994 (SI 86/1994), not being an application for outline permission within the meaning of article 3 of those regulations,

(ii) an acknowledgment of the application, confirming that it was received on or before 10 March 2002, was issued by the planning authority in accordance with article 29(2)(a) of the regulations mentioned in (i), and

(iii) the application is not an invalid application in respect of which a notice is issued by the planning authority in accordance with article 29(2)(b)(i) of those regulations, or

(c) where the construction or refurbishment work on the building or structure represented by that expenditure is exempted development for the purposes of the Planning and Development Act 2000 by virtue of section 4 of that Act or by virtue of Part 2 of the Planning and Development Regulations 2001 (SI 600/2001) and—

(i)   a detailed plan in relation to the development work is prepared,

(ii)   a binding contract in writing, under which the expenditure on the development is incurred, is in existence, and

(iii)   work to the value of 5% of the development costs is carried out,

not later than 31 December 2004.

Subject to TCA 1997, s 270(7)(a) and (b) (see **5.404**), TCA 1997, s 372A(3) applies in relation to the construction or refurbishment of a building or structure or part of a building or structure which fronts on to a qualifying street or the site of which is wholly within a qualifying where:

(a)   the person constructing or refurbishing the building or structure or part of the building or structure has, on or before 31 December 2006, carried out work to the value of not less than 15% of the actual construction or refurbishment costs of the building or structure or part of the building or structure, and

(b)   that person or, where the building or structure or part of the building or structure is sold by that person, the person who is claiming a deduction in relation to the expenditure can show that the condition in (a) was satisfied, and

(c)   in the case of a building or structure or part of a building or structure the site of which is wholly within a qualifying area where—

(i)   a binding contract in writing, under which the expenditure on the construction or refurbishment of the building or structure or part of the building or structure is incurred, was in existence on or before 31 July 2006, and

(ii)   such other conditions, as may be specified in regulations made by the Minister for Finance, have been satisfied, such conditions to be limited to those necessary to ensure compliance with the laws of the European Communities governing State aid or with a decision of the Commission of the European Communities regarding compatibility with the common market having regard to Article 87 of the European Communities Treaty.

See **5.404** regarding the restriction by TCA 1997, s 270(4)–(7) of qualifying expenditure on buildings and structures in qualifying areas. In the case of expenditure incurred in the period 1 January 2007 to 31 December 2007, only 75% of expenditure incurred is treated as incurred, and in the case of expenditure incurred in the period 1 January 2008 to 31 July 2008, only 50% of expenditure incurred is treated as incurred.

Refurbishment

Refurbishment, in relation to a building or structure, and except for the purposes of TCA 1997, s 372H (rented residential accommodation: deduction for refurbishment expenditure), means any work of construction, reconstruction, repair or renewal, including the provision or improvement of water, sewerage or heating facilities, carried out in the course of the repair or restoration, or maintenance in the nature of repair or restoration, of the building or structure.

Replacement building

Replacement building, in relation to a building or structure which fronts on to a qualifying street, means a building or structure or part of a building or structure which is constructed to replace an existing building, where:

(a)   a notice under section 3(1) or an order under section 3(5) of the Local Government (Sanitary Services) Act 1964, which required the demolition of the existing building or part of that building, was given or made on or after 13 September 2000 and before 31 March 2001, and the replacement building is consistent with the character and size of the existing building; or

(b)   the demolition of the existing building (being a single storey building) was required for structural reasons in order to facilitate the construction of an additional storey or additional storeys to the building which was or were necessary for the restoration or enhancement of the streetscape.

Existing building

Existing building means a building or structure which fronts on to a qualifying street and which existed on 13 September 2000.

Façade

A *façade*, in relation to a building or structure or part of a building or structure, is the exterior wall of the building or structure, or of the part of the building or structure, as the case may be, which fronts on to a street.

Street

Street includes part of a street and the whole or part of any road, square, quay or lane.

Relevant local authority

Relevant local authority means:

(a)   in relation to a qualifying area—

    (i)   the county council or the city council or the borough council or, where appropriate, the town council, within the meaning of the Local Government Act, 2001, in whose functional area the area is situated, or

    (ii)   the authorised company (within the meaning of section 3(1) of the Urban Renewal Act 1998) which prepared the integrated area plan (within the meaning of that section) in respect of the area, and

(b)   in relation to a qualifying street, in respect of the cities of Cork, Dublin, Galway, Limerick or Waterford, the city council of the city in whose functional area the street is situated.

Market value

In relation to a building, structure or house, *market value* means the price which the unencumbered fee simple of the building, structure or house would fetch if sold in the open market in such manner and subject to such conditions as might reasonably be calculated to obtain for the vendor the best price for the building, structure or house, less the part of that price which would be attributable to the acquisition of, or rights in or over, the land on which the building, structure or house is constructed.

Qualifying area

A *qualifying area* is an area or areas specified as a qualifying area under TCA 1997, s 372B (see **6.101.3** below).

Qualifying street

A *qualifying street* is a street specified as a qualifying street under TCA 1997, s 372BA (see **6.101.3** below).

6.101.3 Ministerial order

Qualifying areas

The Minister for Finance may designate by order (see below under *Statutory instruments*) certain areas to be qualifying areas for one or more of the reliefs provided for under the 1998 scheme. The order may discriminate between various categories of commercial development as regards the reliefs. Orders will prescribe in relation to such areas the period in which the scheme is to operate.

It is provided in TCA 1997, s 372B(1) that the Minister for Finance may, on the recommendation of the Minister for the Environment and Local Government (such recommendation to take into consideration an Integrated Area Plan submitted by a local authority, or by a company established by a local authority, to that Minister in respect of an area identified by it), by order direct that:

(a) the area or areas described (being wholly located within the boundaries of the area to which the Integrated Area Plan relates) in the order is or are to be a qualifying area for the purposes of one or more provisions of TCA 1997 Part 10 Ch 7;

(b) where such an area or areas is or are to be a qualifying area for the purposes of TCA 1997, s 372D (capital allowances for certain commercial premises)—

   (i) one or more of the categories of building or structure mentioned below will or will not be a qualifying premises within the meaning of that section and

   (ii) that area or those areas will be a qualifying area for the purposes of either or both the construction of, and the refurbishment of, a qualifying premises within the meaning of that section (TCA 1997, s 372B(1)(b));

(c) where such an area or areas is or are to be a qualifying area for the purposes of TCA 1997, s 372AP (see **6.504.2**), that section is to apply in relation to that area or those areas in so far as the section relates to one or more of the following:

   (i) expenditure incurred on the construction of a house,

   (ii) conversion expenditure incurred in relation to a house, and

   (iii) refurbishment expenditure incurred in relation to a house;

(d) as respects any such area described in the order, the definition of "qualifying period" in TCA 1997 ss 372A (see above) is to be construed as a reference to such period as will be specified in the order in relation to that area; but no such period specified in the order may commence before 1 August 1998 or end after—

    (i)   31 December 2002, or

    (ii)   where TCA 1997, s 372A(1A) applies (see **6.101.2**), 31 December 2006 or

    (iii) where TCA 1997, s 372A(1A) and (3) apply, 31 July 2008;

(e)   as respects any such area so described in the order, the definition of "qualifying period" in TCA 1997, s 372AL (see **6.502**) is to be construed as a reference to such period as will be specified in the order in relation to that area; but no such period specified in the order may commence before 1 August 1998 or end after—

    (i)   31 December 2002, or

    (ii)   where TCA 1997, s 372AL(2) applies, 31 December 2006 or,

    (iii) where TCA 1997, s 372AL(2) and (3) apply, 31 July 2008 .

TCA 1997, s 372AL(2) applies where the relevant local authority gives a certificate in writing on or before September 2003 to the person constructing, converting or refurbishing a building or part of a building, the site of which is wholly within a qualifying urban area, stating that it is satisfied that not less than 15% of the total cost of constructing, converting or refurbishing the building or part of the building and the acquisition of the site thereof had been incurred on or before 30 June 2003, provided the application for such certificate is received by the authority on or before 31 July 2003. In considering whether to give a certificate, the relevant local authority must have regard only to guidelines issued by the Department of the Environment and Local Government in relation to the giving of such certificates.

    TCA 1997, s 372AL(3) applies in relation to the construction, conversion or refurbishment of a building or part of a building which fronts on to a qualifying street or the site of which is wholly within a tax incentive area where:

(a)   the person constructing, converting or refurbishing the building or part of the building has, on or before 31 December 2006, carried out work to the value of not less than 15% of the actual construction, conversion or refurbishment costs of the building or part of the building, and

(b)   that person or, where the building or part of the building is sold by that person, the person who is claiming a deduction in relation to the expenditure can show that the condition in (a) was satisfied.

Section 9 of the Urban Renewal Act 1986, provides that the Minister, having considered an integrated area plan submitted to him under section 7 of that Act and any recommendations referred to in section 8 of the Act which are contained in or have accompanied the plan, may recommend to the Minister for Finance that he make, with respect to the matters concerned, an order in accordance with (a), (b) or (c) above.

    Consequently, the Minister may direct that a particular area is a qualifying area for, say, a period of one year only so that the dates 1 August 1998 and 31 December 2002 or 31 July 2006, as the case may be, merely provide the parameters within which the Minister has discretion to designate any particular area. It would seem to be the case, where no period is specified in an order in relation to an area, that that area is in fact designated for the full period (or at least from the date of the announcement of the designation until 31 December 2002 or, as the case may be, 31 July 2006).

The categories of building or structure referred to in (b) above are:

(a)   buildings or structures consisting of office accommodation;

(b)   multi-storey car-parks;

(c)   any other buildings or structures in respect of which not more than 10% of the capital expenditure incurred in the qualifying period on their construction or refurbishment relates to the construction or refurbishment of office accommodation;

(d)   the façade of a building or structure or part of a building or structure referred to in (a) above;

(e)   the façade of a building or structure or part of a building or structure referred to in (c) above (TCA 1997, s 372B(2)).

Every order made by the Minister is to be laid before Dáil Éireann as soon as possible after it is made. The order may be annulled as a result of the passing of a resolution by the Dáil to that effect within 21 days. In that event, any action taken by any person in the period between the issue of the order and its annulment will be treated as if it were taken under a valid order (TCA 1997, s 372B(3)).

Notwithstanding an order under TCA 1997, s 372B(1), the granting of relief under TCA 1997 Part 10 Chapters 7 and 11 is to be subject to such other requirements as may be specified in or under the Act referred to in TCA 1997, s 372A(2). In that subsection, it is provided that TCA 1997 Part 10 Chapters 7 and 11 are to apply if the Oireachtas passes an Act which refers to those Chapters and provides for the renewal of certain urban areas and the submission of plans ("Integrated Area Plans") to the Minister for the Environment and Local Government which have been drawn up by local authorities, or companies established by local authorities, in respect of an area or areas identified by such an authority or company on the basis of criteria prepared by that Minister, including physical and socio- economic renewal of such area or areas (TCA 1997, s 372A(2)).

As indicated above, a designation order may specifically include or exclude multi-storey car-parks, office development or mixed development (buildings or structures where not more than 10% of the capital expenditure incurred on their construction or refurbishment relates to the construction or refurbishment of office accommodation, ie where even a small amount of office space is involved). Accordingly, not only will there be a targeting of areas deemed to be in need of renewal but the type of development considered to be most appropriate for any such area will be specified for that area. Commercial development other than office development and actual industrial buildings will be permitted without restriction.

TCA 1997, s 372K (see **6.101.6** below) details certain restrictions relating to the availability of reliefs under the 1998 scheme. These restrictions arise out of EU approval of the scheme and it has been seen that the availability of the double rent allowance has been ruled out so that no orders will in fact be made in relation to that allowance.

Qualifying streets

The Minister for Finance may designate by order certain streets to be qualifying streets for one or more of the reliefs provided for under the 1998 scheme.

It is provided in TCA 1997, s 372BA(1) that the Minister for Finance may, on the recommendation of the Minister for the Environment and Local Government (such recommendation to take into consideration proposals submitted by a local authority to that Minister in respect of a street identified by it), by order direct that:

(a) the street described (being a street situated in the functional area of the relevant local authority) in the order is to be a qualifying street for the purposes of one or more provisions of TCA 1997 Part 10 Chapters 7 or 11;

(b) where such a street is to be a qualifying street for the purposes of TCA 1997, s 372D (capital allowances for certain commercial premises), the categories of building or structure mentioned below will not be a qualifying premises within the meaning of that section (TCA 1997, s 372BA(1)(b));

(c) where such a street is to be a qualifying street for the purposes of TCA 1997, s 372AP (see **6.504.2**), that section is to apply in relation to that street in so far as the section relates to one or more of the following:

    (i) expenditure incurred on the construction of a house,

    (ii) conversion expenditure incurred in relation to a house, and

    (iii) refurbishment expenditure incurred in relation to a house; and

(d) as respects any such street so described in the order and in so far as the provisions dealing with the 1998 Scheme is concerned, the definition of "qualifying period" in TCA 1997, s 372A (see **6.101.2**) is to be construed as a reference to such period as is to be specified in the order in relation to that street; but no such period specified in the order may commence before 6 April 2001 or end after—

    (i) 31 December 2004, or

    (ii) where TCA 1997, s 372A(1B) (see **6.101.2** above) applies, 31 December 2006, or

    (iii) where TCA 1997, s 372A(1B) and (3) apply, 31 July 2008; and

(e) as respects any such street so described in the order and in so far as TCA 1997 Part 10 Chapter 11 (relief for lessors of rented residential accommodation – see **6.502**) is concerned, the definition of "qualifying period" in TCA 1997, s 372AL (see above) is to be construed as a reference to such period as is to be specified in the order in relation to that street; but no such period specified in the order may commence before 6 April 2001 or end after—

    (i) 31 December 2004, or

    (ii) where TCA 1997, s 372AL(1A) applies (see **6.502**), 31 December 2006, or

    (iii) where TCA 1997, s 372AL(1A) and (3) (see above) apply, 31 July 2008.

The categories of building or structure referred to in (b) above are buildings or structures:

(a) other than those in use for the purposes of the retailing of goods or the provision of services only within the State;

(b) in use as offices; and

(c) in use for the provision of mail order or financial services.

Thus, and to conform with EU State Aids rules, the relief in respect of commercial property is confined to premises used essentially for the retailing or supply of local goods and services.

Every order made by the Minister is to be laid before Dáil Éireann as soon as possible after it is made. The order may be annulled as a result of the passing of a resolution by the Dáil to that effect within 21 days. In that event, any action taken by any person in the period between the issue of the order and its annulment will be treated as if it were taken under a valid order (TCA 1997, s 372BA(3)).

Notwithstanding an order under TCA 1997, s 372BA(1), no relief from corporation tax may be given in respect of the construction, refurbishment or conversion of a building, structure or house which fronts on to a qualifying street unless the local authority has certified in writing that such construction, refurbishment or conversion is consistent with the aims, objectives and criteria for the Living over the Shop Scheme, as outlined in a circular of the Department of the Environment and Local Government entitled "Living Over The Shop Scheme", reference numbered UR 43A and dated 13 September 2000, or in any further circular of that Department amending paragraph 6 of the first-mentioned circular for the purposes of increasing the aggregate length of street allowable, to the manager of the relevant local authority concerned (TCA 1997, s 372BA(4)).

Statutory instruments

Statutory instruments dealing with the locations in which the urban renewal scheme applies have been published. These contain the necessary Ministerial order in each case as well as the designation of the particular qualifying area or qualifying project. The following is a list of these instruments:

Location	*Reference*
Athlone	SI 2002/222
Athy	SI 2002/223
Balbriggan	SI 2002/224
Ballina	SI 2002/225
Blanchardstown	SI 2002/226
Buncrana	SI 2002/227
Carlow	SI 2002/228
Clondalkin	SI 2002/229
Cobh	SI 2002/230
Cork – City Docks Area	SI 2002/231
Dun Laoghaire	SI 2002/232
Dundalk	SI 2002/233
Kildare	SI 2002/234
Kilkenny	SI 2002/235
Longford	SI 2002/236
Mallow	SI 2002/237
Monaghan	SI 2002/238
Mullingar	SI 2002/239
Passage West/Glenbrook	SI 2002/240

Location	Reference
Portlaoise	SI 2002/241
Shannon	SI 2002/242
Sligo	SI 2002/243
Thurles	SI 2002/244
Tuam	SI 2002/245
Tullamore	SI 2002/246

6.101.4   Prevention of double relief

Where any relief under TCA 1997 Part 10 Ch 7 is given in relation to capital expenditure or other expenditure incurred on, or rent payable in respect of, any building, structure or premises, relief may not be given in respect of that expenditure or rent, as the case may be, under any other provision of the Tax Acts (TCA 1997, s 372K(3)).

6.101.5   Non-application of relief in certain cases

Property developers

Capital allowances may not be claimed under TCA 1997, s 372C (accelerated allowances in respect of industrial buildings etc) or s 372D (certain commercial premises) by a property developer in respect of expenditure incurred on the construction or refurbishment of a building or structure or a qualifying premises. This prohibition applies—

(a)   where the property developer is entitled to the relevant interest (see **5.403**) in relation to the expenditure concerned; and

(b)   either the property developer or a person connected with (see **2.3**) the property developer incurred the expenditure on the construction or refurbishment of the qualifying building concerned (TCA 1997, s 372K(1)(a)).

A *property developer* for this purpose is a person carrying on a trade which consists wholly or mainly of the construction or refurbishment of buildings or structures with a view to their sale.

Grant-assisted expenditure

TCA 1997 ss 372C (**6.102**) and s 372D (**6.103**) do not apply In respect of expenditure incurred on or after 6 April 2001 on the construction or refurbishment of a building or structure or a qualifying premises the site of which is wholly within a qualifying area where any part of the expenditure has been met, directly or indirectly, by grant assistance or any other assistance which is granted by or through the State, any board established by statute, any public or local authority or any other agency of the State (TCA 1997, s 372K(1)(aa)).

Restrictions for certain sectors and industries and large investment projects

TCA 1997, s 372K(1)(b) restricts the availability of capital allowances for buildings in use in certain sectors and industries or which are provided for the purposes of certain large investment projects. These restrictions are in line with EU approval of the 1998 scheme. This approval ruled out the availability of the double rent allowance with the result that orders designating areas for the purposes of the scheme will make no provision for that allowance.

Capital allowances may not be claimed under TCA 1997, s 372C (accelerated allowances in respect of industrial buildings etc) or s 372D (certain commercial premises):

(a) in respect of expenditure incurred on the construction or refurbishment of a building or structure or a qualifying premises which is in use for the purposes of a trade, or any activity treated as a trade, carried on by the person who is entitled to the relevant interest, within the meaning of TCA 1997, s 269 (see **5.403**), in relation to that expenditure and such trade or activity is carried on wholly or mainly—

    (i) in the sector of agriculture, including the production, processing and marketing of agricultural products,

    (ii) in the coal industry, fishing industry or motor vehicle industry, or

    (iii) in the transport, steel, shipbuilding, synthetic fibres or financial services sectors (TCA 1997, s 372K(1)(b)), or

(b) in respect of expenditure incurred on or after 1 January 2003 on the construction or refurbishment of any building or structure or qualifying premises provided for the purposes of a project that is subject to the notification requirements of—

    (i) the "Multisectoral framework on regional aid for large investment projects" (OJ No C 107, 7.4.1998, p7) prepared by the Commission of the European Communities, or

    (ii) the "Multisectoral framework on regional aid for large investment projects" (OJ No C 70, 19.2.2002, p8) prepared by the Commission of the European Communities,

    as the case may be, unless approval of the potential capital allowances involved has been received from that Commission by the Minister for Finance, or by such other Minister of the Government, agency or body as may be nominated for that purpose by the Minister for Finance (TCA 1997, s 372K(1)(c)).

Apportionment

A part of a building or structure situated in a qualifying area may qualify for allowances under the 1998 scheme and apportionment of expenditure on a floor area basis is provided for this purpose where a building straddles the boundary or a qualifying area.

For the purposes of TCA 1997 ss 372C (accelerated capital allowances for industrial buildings) and 372D (commercial buildings), where the site of any part of a building or structure is situate outside the boundary of a qualifying area and where expenditure incurred or treated as having been incurred in the qualifying period is attributable to the building or structure in general, such an amount of that expenditure is to be deemed to be attributable to the part which is situate outside the boundary as bears to the whole of that expenditure the same proportion as the floor area of the part situate outside the boundary of the qualifying area bears to the total floor area of the building or structure (TCA 1997, s 372K(2)).

6.102   Construction or refurbishment of industrial buildings

6.102.1   Accelerated capital allowances for industrial buildings

TCA 1997, s 372C provides for accelerated capital allowances in respect of expenditure incurred in the qualifying period on the construction or refurbishment of an industrial building or structure or part of an industrial building or structure the site of which is wholly within a qualifying area.

See **5.404** regarding the restriction by TCA 1997, s 270(4)-(6) of qualifying expenditure on industrial buildings in qualifying areas. In the case of expenditure incurred in the period 1 January 2007 to 31 December 2007, only 75% of expenditure incurred is treated as incurred, and in the case of expenditure incurred in the period 1 January 2008 to 31 July 2008, only 50% of expenditure incurred is treated as incurred.

An industrial building is "a mill, factory or other similar premises" (TCA 1997, s 268(1)(a)). Factories and manufacturing plants will therefore be qualifying premises in a qualifying area under TCA 1997 Part 10 Ch 7. TCA 1997, s 372C applies to an industrial building or structure which is used for a purpose specified in TCA 1997, s 268(1)(a). Accordingly, accelerated capital allowances are available only in respect of construction or refurbishment expenditure carried out in respect of a mill, factory or other similar premises. Thus, for example, hotels do not qualify for allowances.

In general, the entitlement to an industrial building initial allowance arises under TCA 1997, s 271(2) where a person has incurred capital expenditure on the construction of a building or structure which is to be an industrial building or structure occupied for the purposes of a trade by the person who incurs the capital expenditure or by a lessee who occupies the property under a relevant lease (ie, a lease to which the relevant interest, as defined in TCA 1997, s 269, is reversionary). In the case of a company which is an owner-occupier, an initial allowance can be claimed in the accounting period in which the expenditure was incurred. In the case of a lessor company, the initial allowance may be claimed in the accounting period in which the tenancy commences. Where capital expenditure is incurred by a company prior to the commencement of trading, the expenditure is treated as if it were incurred on the day on which the company commences to trade (TCA 1997, s 316(3)).

The entitlement to an industrial building annual allowance arises under TCA 1997, s 272(2) where, at the end of an accounting period, a company is entitled to a relevant interest in the building and the building is in use as an industrial building.

For the purposes of the following discussion on the capital allowances available on industrial buildings under TCA 1997 Part 10 Ch 7, it is assumed that all of the conditions for obtaining the allowances as set out in TCA 1997 Part 9 Ch 1 as well as those in TCA 1997 Part 10 Ch 7 have been satisfied.

6.102.2   Allowances

Where a building which is an industrial building as defined in TCA 1997, s 268(1)(a) is newly *constructed or refurbished*, and the building lies wholly within a qualifying area, the following allowances are available:

owner-occupier:

- industrial building initial allowance 50% plus industrial building annual allowance 4%; or

– free depreciation 50% plus industrial building annual allowance 4%;

lessor:

– industrial building initial allowance 50% plus industrial building annual allowance 4%.

In the case of refurbishment expenditure, however, accelerated allowances may by claimed on the amount of expenditure incurred only if the total amount of the expenditure so incurred is not less than an amount which is equal to 10% of the market value of the building or structure immediately before that expenditure was incurred (TCA 1997, s 372C(4)). Otherwise, basic rate allowances only will be available in respect of refurbishment expenditure.

In determining whether and to what extent capital expenditure incurred on the construction or refurbishment of a qualifying premises is or is not incurred in the qualifying period, only such an amount of that capital expenditure as is properly attributable to work on the construction or refurbishment of the premises actually carried out during the qualifying period may be treated as having been incurred in that period (TCA 1997, s 372C(6)).

Grant-assisted expenditure

TCA 1997, s 372C does not apply In respect of expenditure incurred on or after 6 April 2001 on the construction or refurbishment of a building or structure the site of which is wholly within a qualifying area where any part of the expenditure has been met, directly or indirectly, by grant assistance from the State of from any other person (TCA 1997, s 372K(1)(aa)).

6.102.3 Balancing allowances and charges

TCA 1997, s 274 provides that a balancing allowance or balancing charge is to be computed if, in relation to a qualifying premises in respect of which any capital allowances have been obtained, any of the following events occurs:

(a)   the relevant interest in the building is sold;

(b)   the relevant interest in the building is exchanged (TCA 1997, s 311(3));

(c)   the building is demolished or destroyed;

(d)   the building ceases altogether to be used;

(e)   the relevant interest, if it is a leasehold interest, either:

    (i)   comes to an end, otherwise than on the person entitled to it acquiring the reversionary interest, or

    (ii)   is surrendered for valuable consideration (TCA 1997, s 311(3)).

Where the industrial building or structure is held for a period of at least 13 years, no balancing charge may be made (TCA 1997, s 372C(5)). The writing down life of the industrial building is nevertheless 25 years. Accordingly, while a balancing charge may not arise later than 13 years after the building is first used or, where TCA 1997, s 276 applies (refurbishment expenditure – see **5.407.5**), later than 13 years after the expenditure was incurred, a balancing allowance may still be made at any time up to 25 years after the building is first used, or, as the case may be, the refurbishment expenditure is incurred. Similarly, a purchaser of the property may still be entitled to capital allowances even where the purchase takes place more than 13 years after first use/expenditure incurred. Furthermore, the cessation of a qualifying trade is not an event requiring a balancing adjustment, provided the owner does not dispose of the relevant interest and so long as the building continues to be used for some purpose. The rules of TCA 1997, s 272(4) (new rate of allowance to write off residue of expenditure evenly over the rest of the writing down period of the expenditure – see **5.410**) continue to apply to industrial buildings in the designated areas.

6.102.4   TCA 1997, s 372C in detail

The allowances as detailed above arise under TCA 1997, s 372C(2), (3). These provisions refer to the underlying legislation of TCA 1997, s 271 (initial allowance) and TCA 1997, s 273 (free depreciation).

TCA 1997, s 372C(2) provides, subject to—

(a)   TCA 1997, s 372C(4) (minimum refurbishment expenditure incurred to be not less than 10% of market value of building or structure – see **6.102.2** above),

(b)   TCA s 270(4)-(7) (only 75% of expenditure incurred in the period 1 January 2007 to 31 December 2007 is treated as incurred and only 50% of expenditure incurred in the period 1 January 2008 to 31 July 2008 is treated as incurred; local authority certified cap on expenditure treated as incurred – see **5.404**), and

(c)   TCA 1997, s 316(2B) (only the amount of expenditure as is properly attributable to work actually carried out in a period may be treated as having been incurred in that period – see **5.404**),

that TCA 1997, s 271 is to have effect in relation to qualifying capital expenditure as if various references (not appropriate for the purposes of TCA 1997, s 372C) were deleted and as if TCA 1997, s 271(4) (rates of industrial building allowances) were substituted by a provision to the effect that the allowance is to be of an amount equal to 50% of the qualifying capital expenditure. TCA 1997, s 372C(2) accordingly secures that the 50% initial allowance rate will be available in respect of qualifying expenditure incurred in the qualifying period (see **6.101.2**) on buildings or structures in the qualifying areas.

TCA 1997, s 372C(3) similarly provides, subject again to TCA 1997 ss 372C(4), 270(4)-(6) and 316(2B), that TCA 1997, s 273 is to have effect in relation to qualifying capital expenditure as if various references and provisions not appropriate for the purposes of TCA 1997, s 372C (eg, TCA 1997, s 273(3)-(7)) were deleted and as if TCA 1997, s 273(2)(b) (phasing out of free depreciation) were substituted by a provision to the effect that any allowance in respect of qualifying expenditure made under TCA 1997, s 272 and increased under TCA 1997, s 273(2)(a), whether claimed for one or more chargeable periods, may not in the aggregate exceed 50% of that qualifying expenditure. Accordingly TCA 1997, s 372C(3) secures that the 50% free depreciation rate is available for the purposes of the section.

The allowances available for industrial buildings consist of an initial allowance of 50% or (for owner-occupiers) free depreciation of 50%, and an annual allowance of 4%. It is not possible to obtain allowances of 50% + 4% in one period. TCA 1997, s 271(5) provides that where an initial allowance has been made under TCA 1997, s 271 for any period, no annual allowance under TCA 1997, s 272 may be made for the same period nor may free depreciation be claimed in any subsequent period in respect of the same expenditure. TCA 1997, s 273(8) provides that where, for any chargeable period, a writing down allowance under TCA 1997, s 272 in respect of qualifying expenditure is increased under TCA 1997, s 273, no initial allowance under TCA 1997, s 271 may be made in respect of that expenditure for that or any subsequent chargeable period.

6.103　Construction or refurbishment of commercial premises

6.103.1　Capital allowances for commercial premises

TCA 1997, s 372D provides for capital allowances in respect of expenditure in respect of construction or refurbishment incurred on a commercial property in a qualifying area.

See **5.404** regarding the restriction by TCA 1997, s 270(4)-(6) of qualifying expenditure on commercial buildings in qualifying areas. In the case of expenditure incurred in the period 1 January 2007 to 31 December 2007, only 75% of expenditure incurred is treated as incurred, and in the case of expenditure incurred in the period 1 January 2008 to 31 July 2008, only 50% of expenditure incurred is treated as incurred.

For the purposes of capital allowances available under the 1998 urban renewal scheme in respect of commercial premises, TCA 1997, s 372D(1) defines *qualifying premises* as a building or structure or part of a building or structure the site of which is wholly within a qualifying area or which fronts on to a qualifying street and which must not already be an industrial building or structure as defined in TCA 1997, s 268. Thus, for example, hotels do not qualify for the allowances available under TCA 1997, s 372D; mills, factories and other similar premises qualify for allowances under TCA 1997, s 372C (see above).

To qualify for capital allowances, the commercial property must either be in use for the purposes of a trade or profession, or, regardless of whether or not it is so used, is let on *bona fide* commercial terms for such consideration as might be expected to be paid in respect of a letting negotiated on an arm's length basis.

Specifically excluded from the definition of qualifying premises is any part of a building which is in use as a dwelling house. There is no exclusion, in the definition of qualifying premises in TCA 1997, s 372D, of any building or part of a building in use as an office.

Where part of a building or structure is, and part is not, a qualifying premises, the building or structure and every part of it is treated as a qualifying premises if the capital expenditure incurred in the qualifying period on the construction or refurbishment of the non-qualifying part is not more than 10% of the total capital expenditure which has been incurred in that period on the construction or refurbishment of the building or structure (TCA 1997, s 268(8)).

6.103.2　Basis for capital allowances

TCA 1997, s 372D(2) provides the basis for capital allowances in respect of capital expenditure incurred on the construction or refurbishment of a qualifying premises. That subsection provides that all of the provisions of the Tax Acts (other than TCA 1997, s 372C – see **6.102** above in relation to industrial buildings) relating to the making of allowances and charges in respect of the construction or refurbishment of an industrial building are to apply to construction or refurbishment expenditure on qualifying premises as defined in TCA 1997, s 372D(1).

The qualifying premises is treated as if, at all times at which it is a qualifying building, it were an industrial building as defined in TCA 1997, s 268(1)(a) (ie, a mill, factory or other similar premises) in respect of which an allowance may be made under TCA 1997, s 271 (initial allowance) or s 272 (annual allowance). Where the property is let, any activity carried on in the property which is not a trade is treated as if it were a trade.

Allowances may not be given by virtue of TCA 1997, s 372D(2) in respect of any capital expenditure on the refurbishment of qualifying premises unless the total amount of capital expenditure so incurred is not less than an amount equal to 10% of the market value of the qualifying premises immediately before that expenditure is incurred (TCA 1997, s 372D(3)). Whereas failure to satisfy the 10% refurbishment expenditure test in TCA 1997, s 372C operates to deny accelerated capital allowances in respect of industrial buildings and structures in a qualifying area, failure to satisfy the test for TCA 1997, s 372D purposes results in a denial of any capital allowances in respect of commercial premises in a qualifying area.

In the case of a qualifying premises which fronts on to a designated street (a premises which is a qualifying premises by reason of fronting on to a qualifying street), allowances will be given by virtue of TCA 1997, s 372D(2) in respect of any capital expenditure in the qualifying period on the construction or refurbishment of the premises only if:

(a)   the qualifying premises are comprised in the ground floor of an existing building or a replacement building; and

(b)   apart from the capital expenditure incurred in the qualifying period on the construction or refurbishment of the premises, expenditure is incurred on the upper floor or floors of the existing building or the replacement building, as the case may be, which is eligible expenditure within the meaning of TCA 1997 Part 10 Chapter 11 (reliefs for lessors of rented residential accommodation – see **6.504.6**) (being eligible expenditure on necessary construction – see below), or conversion expenditure or refurbishment expenditure within the meaning of that Chapter,

and in respect of which a deduction has been given, or would on due claim being made be given, under TCA 1997, s 372AP (TCA 1997, s 372D(3A)(a)).

For the purposes of (b)(i) and (iv) above, *necessary construction*, in relation to an existing building, means one or more of the following:

(a)   construction of an extension to the building which does not exceed 30% of the floor area of the building immediately before expenditure on the construction, conversion or refurbishment of the building was incurred, where such extension is necessary for the purposes of facilitating access to, or providing essential facilities in, one or more qualifying premises within the meaning TCA 1997, s 372F or 372I (see above);

(b)   construction of an additional storey or additional storeys to the building which was or were necessary for the restoration or enhancement of the streetscape; or

(c)   construction of a replacement building (TCA 1997, s 372A(1)).

Allowances will nevertheless not be given by virtue of TCA 1997, s 372D(2) in respect of any capital expenditure incurred in the qualifying period on the construction or refurbishment of the qualifying premises as exceeds the amount of the deduction, or the aggregate amount of the deductions, which has been given, or which would on due claim being made would be given, under TCA 1997, s 372AP in respect of the eligible expenditure mentioned above (TCA 1997, s 372D(3A)(b)).

Allowances may be given in respect of capital expenditure incurred on the construction or refurbishment of a qualifying premises only in so far as that expenditure is incurred in the qualifying period (TCA 1997, s 372D(2)(b)). In determining whether and to what extent capital expenditure incurred on the construction or refurbishment of a qualifying premises is or is not incurred in the qualifying period, only such an amount of that capital expenditure as is properly attributable to work on the construction or refurbishment of the premises actually carried out during the qualifying period may be treated as having been incurred in that period (TCA 1997, s 372D(7)).

6.103.3 Allowances

Where expenditure is incurred on the *construction or refurbishment* of a qualifying premises which is a building situated wholly within a designated area, all of the provisions of the Tax Acts (except TCA 1997, s 372C) apply to the expenditure incurred as if it were expenditure on which capital allowances would be available under TCA 1997 ss 271 and 272, so that industrial building initial allowances, industrial building annual allowances and free depreciation are available in respect of the expenditure as if the property were a mill, factory or other similar premises. To qualify for the allowances the expenditure must, as already noted above, be incurred in the qualifying period (see **6.101.2** and **6.101.3**) and the work in respect of which the expenditure has been incurred must actually be carried out within that period.

The capital allowances available by virtue of TCA 1997, s 372D (and by virtue of the one-half restriction referred to in TCA 1997, s 372D(6) – see below) are as follows:

owner-occupier:

   – industrial building initial allowance 50% plus industrial building annual allowance 4% for the balance so as to write off 100% of qualifying expenditure; or
   – free depreciation 50%;

lessor:

   – industrial building initial allowance 25% plus industrial building annual allowance 4% for the balance so as to write off 100% of qualifying expenditure.

In the case of refurbishment expenditure, allowances may by claimed on the amount of expenditure incurred only if the total amount of the expenditure so incurred is not less than an amount which is equal to 10% of the market value of the building or structure immediately before that expenditure was incurred. Otherwise, no allowances will be available in respect of refurbishment expenditure.

Grant-assisted expenditure

TCA 1997, s 372D does not apply In respect of expenditure incurred on or after 6 April 2001 on the construction or refurbishment of a qualifying premises the site of which is wholly within a qualifying area where any part of the expenditure has been met, directly or indirectly, by grant assistance or any other assistance which is granted by or through the State, any board established by statute, any public or local authority or any other agency of the State (TCA 1997, s 372K(1)(aa)).

6.103.4 Balancing charges

TCA 1997, s 372D(5) provides that no balancing charge may be made where the qualifying premises is held for a period of at least 13 years. The writing down life of the building is nevertheless 25 years. Accordingly, while a balancing charge may not arise later than 13 years after the building is first used or, where TCA 1997, s 276 applies (see **5.407.5**), later than 13 years after the expenditure was incurred, a balancing allowance may still be made at any time up to 25 years after the building is first used, or, as the case may be, the refurbishment expenditure is incurred. Similarly, a purchaser of the property may still be entitled to capital allowances even when the purchase takes place more than 13 years after first use/expenditure incurred.

6.103.5 TCA 1997, s 372D in detail

The allowances as detailed above arise under TCA 1997, s 372D(4). This provision refers to the underlying legislation of TCA 1997, s 271 (initial allowance) and TCA 1997, s 273 (free depreciation).

TCA 1997, s 372D(2)(a) provides, subject to:

(a)   TCA 1997, s 372D(2)(b) and (5) (see below), and (3) (refurbishment expenditure incurred to be not less than 10% of market value of building or structure – see **6.103.2** above),

(b)   TCA s 270(4)-(7) (only 75% of expenditure incurred in the period 1 January 2007 to 31 December 2007 is treated as incurred and only 50% of expenditure incurred in the period 1 January 2008 to 31 July 2008 is treated as incurred; local authority certified cap on expenditure treated as incurred – see **5.404**), and

(c)   TCA 1997, s 316(2B) (only the amount of expenditure as is properly attributable to work actually carried out in a period may be treated as having been incurred in that period – see **5.404**),

that all of the provisions of the Tax Acts (other than TCA 1997, s 372C – see **6.102** above in relation to industrial buildings) relating to the making of allowances and charges in respect of the construction or refurbishment of an industrial building are to apply:

(i)   as if a qualifying premises were at all times at which it is a qualifying premises a building or structure in respect of which an allowance is to be made under the provisions relating to the making of industrial building allowances; and

(ii)   where any activity carried on in the qualifying premises or, in a case where the façade of a building or structure or part of a building or structure is a qualifying premises, carried on in that building or structure or the part of that building or structure, is not a trade, as if it were a trade.

An allowance may be given in respect of capital expenditure only in so far as that expenditure is incurred in the qualifying period (TCA 1997, s 372D(2)(b)).

TCA 1997, s 372D(4)(a) provides that TCA 1997, s 271 is to have effect in relation to qualifying capital expenditure incurred in the qualifying period on the construction or refurbishment of a qualifying premises as if various references (not relevant for the purposes of TCA 1997, s 372D) were deleted and as if TCA 1997, s 271(4) (rates of industrial building allowances) were substituted by a provision to the effect that the allowance is to be of an amount equal to 50% of the qualifying capital expenditure. TCA 1997, s 372D(4)(a) accordingly secures that the rate of initial allowance in respect of expenditure on qualifying premises in a qualifying area in respect of expenditure incurred in the qualifying period will be 50%.

TCA 1997, s 372D(4)(b) similarly provides that TCA 1997, s 273 is to have effect in relation to qualifying capital expenditure as if TCA 1997, s 273(3)-(7) (not appropriate for the purposes of TCA 1997, s 372D) were deleted and that TCA 1997, s 273(2)(b) (phasing out of free depreciation) were replaced by a provision to the effect that free depreciation in respect of any qualifying expenditure, whether claimed for one chargeable period or more than one such period, is not to exceed 50% in the aggregate of the amount of that expenditure. Accordingly TCA 1997, s 372D(4)(b) provides for the availability of free depreciation of up to 50% in respect of expenditure in the qualifying period.

TCA 1997, s 271(5) provides that where an initial allowance has been made under TCA 1997, s 271 for any chargeable period, no annual allowance under TCA 1997, s 272 may be made for the same period nor may free depreciation be claimed in any subsequent period in respect of the same expenditure. TCA 1997, s 273(8) provides that where, for any chargeable period, a writing down allowance under TCA 1997, s 272 in respect of qualifying expenditure is increased under TCA 1997, s 273, no initial allowance under TCA 1997, s 271 may be made in respect of that expenditure for that or any subsequent chargeable period.

For the purposes of determining, in relation to a claim under TCA 1997, s 271 or 273 as applied by TCA 1997, s 372D, whether and to what extent capital expenditure incurred on the construction or refurbishment of an industrial building or structure is or is not incurred in the qualifying period, only such amount of that capital expenditure as is properly attributable to work carried out during the qualifying period may be treated as having been incurred in that period (TCA 1997, s 372D(7)).

6.2 RURAL AREAS SCHEME

6.201   Introduction
6.202   Construction or refurbishment of industrial buildings
6.203   Construction or refurbishment of commercial premises

6.201   Introduction

6.201.1   Rural areas scheme

TCA 1997 Part 10 Ch 8 provides for a scheme of incentives to encourage rural renewal and improvement. The scheme is a pilot renewal initiative intended to invigorate certain areas of rural Ireland on lines similar to those obtaining in the renewal schemes already in operation mainly for urban areas. The rural renewal scheme is targeted on a pilot basis at parts of the upper Shannon region and covers counties Leitrim and Longford and certain areas in counties Cavan, Roscommon and Sligo on a District Electoral Division basis.

The tax incentives relating to rented residential accommodation apply for the period 1 June 1998 to 31 December 2002. The incentives providing for capital allowances and for double rent allowance cannot commence until formal EU Commission approval is obtained. On receipt of such approval, the scheme will commence on the date of a commencement order to be made by the Minister for Finance and will run to 31 December 2002.

An incentive relief for lessors of residential premises is provided for in TCA 1997 Part 10, Chapter 11 (ss 372AK-372AT) and this is dealt with in **6.5**.

6.201.2   Definitions

Qualifying period

TCA 1997, s 372L(1) defines the *qualifying period* as, for the purposes of TCA 1997 ss 372M, 372N and 372O (capital allowances for industrial buildings and commercial premises), the period commencing on 1 July 1999 and ending on:

   (i)   31 December 2004; or
  (ii)   where TCA 1997, s 372L(2) applies, 31 December 2006; or
 (iii)   where TCA 1997, s 372L(2) and (3) apply, 31 July 2008.

TCA 1997, s 372L(2) applies, as respects capital expenditure incurred on the construction or refurbishment of a building or structure, if:

  (a)   (i)   a planning application (not being an application for outline permission within the meaning of section 36 of the Planning and Development Act 2000), in so far as planning permission is required, in respect of the construction or refurbishment work on the building or structure represented by that expenditure, is made in accordance with the Planning and Development Regulations 2001 to 2003,

       (ii)   an acknowledgment of the application, confirming that it was received on or before 31 December 2004, is issued by the planning authority in accordance with article 26(2) of the Planning and Development Regulations 2001 (SI 600/2001), and

(iii)   the application is not an invalid application in respect of which a notice is issued by the planning authority in accordance with article 26(5) of those regulations,

(b)   (i)   a planning application, in so far as planning permission was required, in respect of the construction or refurbishment work on the building or structure represented by that expenditure, was made in accordance with the Local Government (Planning and Development) Regulations 1994 (SI 86/1994), not being an application for outline permission within the meaning of article 3 of those regulations,

(ii)   an acknowledgment of the application, confirming that it was received on or before 10 March 2002, was issued by the planning authority in accordance with article 29(2)(a) of the regulations mentioned in (i), and

(iii)   the application was not an invalid application in respect of which a notice is issued by the planning authority in accordance with article 29(2)(b)(i) of those regulations, or

(c)   where the construction or refurbishment work on the building or structure represented by that expenditure is exempted development for the purposes of the Planning and Development Act 2000 by virtue of section 4 of that Act or by virtue of Part 2 of the Planning and Development Regulations 2001 (SI 600/2001) and—

(i)   a detailed plan in relation to the development work is prepared,

(ii)   a binding contract in writing, under which the expenditure on the development is incurred, is in existence, and

(iii)   work to the value of 5% of the development costs is carried out,

not later than 31 December 2004.

Subject to TCA 1997, s 270(7)(a) and (b) (see **5.404**), TCA 1997, s 372L(3) applies in relation to the construction or refurbishment of a building or structure or part of a building or structure the site of which is wholly within a qualifying area where—

(a)   the person constructing or refurbishing the building or structure has, on or before 31 December 2006, carried out work to the value of not less than 15% of the actual construction or refurbishment costs of the building or structure,

(b)   that person or, where the building or structure is sold by that person, the person who is claiming a deduction in relation to the expenditure can show that the condition in (a) was satisfied,

(c)   a binding contract in writing, under which the expenditure on the construction or refurbishment of the building or structure is incurred, was in existence on or before 31 July 2006, and

(d)   such other conditions, as may be specified in regulations made by the Minister for Finance, have been satisfied, such conditions to be limited to those necessary to ensure compliance with the laws of the European Communities governing State aid or with a decision of the Commission of the European Communities regarding compatibility with the common market having regard to Article 87 of the European Communities Treaty.

See **5.404** regarding the restriction by TCA 1997, s 270(4)-(7) of qualifying expenditure on buildings and structures in qualifying areas. In the case of expenditure incurred in the period 1 January 2007 to 31 December 2007, only 75% of expenditure incurred is treated as incurred, and in the case of expenditure incurred in the period 1 January 2008 to 31 July 2008, only 50% of expenditure incurred is treated as incurred.

Refurbishment

Refurbishment, in relation to a building or structure means any work of construction, reconstruction, repair or renewal, including the provision or improvement of water, sewerage or heating facilities, carried out in the course of the repair or restoration, or maintenance in the nature of repair or restoration, of the building or structure.

Market value

In relation to a building, structure or house, *market value* means the price which the unencumbered fee simple of the building, structure or house would fetch if sold in the open market in such manner and subject to such conditions as might reasonably be calculated to obtain for the vendor the best price for the building, structure or house, less the part of that price which would be attributable to the acquisition of, or rights in or over, the land on which the building, structure or house is constructed.

6.201.3   Qualifying rural area

A qualifying rural area is any area described in TCA 1997 Sch 8A. These are as follows:

Cavan

The District Electoral Divisions of Arvagh, Springfield, Killeshandra, Milltown, Carrafin, Grilly, Kilconny, Belturbet Urban, Ardue, Carn, Bilberry, Diamond, Doogary, Lissanover, Ballymagauran, Ballyconnell, Bawnboy, Templeport, Benbrack, Pedara Vohers, Tircahan, Swanlinbar, Kinawley, Derrynananta, Dunmakeever, Dowra, Derrylahan, Tuam, Killinagh, Eskey, Teebane, Scrabby, Loughdawan, Bruce Hall, Drumcarban, Corr, Crossdoney and Killykeen.

Leitrim

The administrative county of Leitrim.

Longford

The administrative county of Longford.

Roscommon

The District Electoral Divisions of Ballintober, Castleteheen, Carrowduff, Kilbride North, Lissonuffy, Killavackan, Termonbarry, Roosky, Kilglass North, Kilglass South, Bumlin, Cloonfinlough, Killukin (in Roscommon Rural District), Strokestown, Annaghmore, Tulsk, Coolougher, Ballinlough, Kiltullagh, Cloonfower, Artagh South, Artagh North, Ballaghaderreen, Edmondstown, Loughglinn, Buckill, Fairymount, Castlereagh, Frenchpark, Bellangare, Castleplunket, Baslick, Breedoge, Altagowlan, Lough Allen, Ballyfarnan, Keadue, Aghafin, Ballyformoyle, Crossna, Kilbryan, Boyle Rural, Boyle Urban, Tivannagh, Rushfield, Tumna North, Tumna South, Killukin (in Boyle No 1 Rural District), Oakport, Rockingham, Danesfort, Cloonteem, Kilmore, Elia, Ballygarden, Aughrim East, Aughrim West, Creeve (in Boyle No 1 Rural District),

Creeve (in Roscommon Rural District), Elphin, Rossmore, Cloonyquinn, Ogulla, Mantua, Lisgarve, Kilcacumsy, Kilcolagh, Estersnow, Croghan, Killummod, Cregga, Cloonygormican, Kilbride South, Kilgefin, Cloontuskert, Drumdaff and Kilteevan.

Sligo

The District Electoral Divisions of Ballintogher East, Ballynakill, Lisconny, Drumfin, Ballymote, Cloonoghill, Leitrim, Tobercurry, Kilturra, Cuilmore, Kilfree, Coolavin, Killaraght, Templevanny, Aghanagh, Kilmactranny, Ballynashee, Shancough, Drumcolumb, Riverstown, Lakeview, Bricklieve, Drumrat, Toomour, Kilshalvy, Killadoon, Streamstown, Cartron, Coolaney, Owenmore, Temple, Annagh, Carrickbannagher, Collooney and Ballintogher West.

6.201.4 Prevention of double relief

Where any relief under TCA 1997 Part 10 Ch 8 is given in relation to capital expenditure or other expenditure incurred on, or rent payable in respect of, any building, structure or premises, relief may not be given in respect of that expenditure or rent, as the case may be, under any other provision of the Tax Acts (TCA 1997, s 372T(2)).

6.201.5 Non-application of relief in certain cases

Property developers

Capital allowances may not be claimed under TCA 1997, s 372M (accelerated allowances in respect of industrial buildings etc) or s 372N (certain commercial premises) by a property developer in respect of expenditure incurred on the construction or refurbishment of a building or structure or a qualifying premises. This prohibition applies:

(a)   where the property developer is entitled to the relevant interest (see **5.403**) in relation to the expenditure concerned; and

(b)   either the property developer or a person connected with (see **2.3**) the property developer incurred the expenditure on the construction or refurbishment of the qualifying building concerned (TCA 1997, s 372T(1)(a)).

A *property developer* for this purpose is a person carrying on a trade which consists wholly or mainly of the construction or refurbishment of buildings or structures with a view to their sale.

Grant-assisted expenditure

Capital allowances may not be claimed under TCA 1997, s 372M (accelerated allowances in respect of industrial buildings etc) or s 372N (certain commercial premises) in respect of expenditure incurred on or after 6 April 2001 on the construction or refurbishment of a building or structure or a qualifying premises where any part of that expenditure has been met, directly or indirectly, by grant assistance or any other assistance which is granted by or through the State, any board established by statute, any public or local authority or any other agency of the State (TCA 1997, s 372T(1)(aa)).

Restrictions in relation to certain sectors and industries and large investment projects

TCA 1997, s 372T(1)(b) restricts the availability of capital allowances for buildings in use in the agricultural sector and in certain other sectors and industries. These restrictions are in line with EU approval of the rural renewal scheme. This approval ruled out the availability of the double rent allowance with the result that orders designating areas for the purposes of the scheme will make no provision for that allowance.

Capital allowances may not be claimed under TCA 1997, s 372M (accelerated allowances in respect of industrial buildings etc) or s 372N (certain commercial premises)—

(a) in respect of expenditure incurred on or after 1 January 2003 on the construction or refurbishment of any building or structure or qualifying premises provided for the purposes of a project that is subject to the notification requirements of—

    (i) the "Multisectoral framework on regional aid for large investment projects" (OJ No C 107, 7.4.1998, p 7) prepared by the Commission of the European Communities, or

    (ii) the "Multisectoral framework on regional aid for large investment projects" (OJ No C 70, 19.2.2002, p 8) prepared by the Commission of the European Communities,

as the case may be, unless approval of the potential capital allowances involved has been received from that Commission by the Minister for Finance, or by such other Minister of the Government, agency or body as may be nominated for that purpose by the Minister for Finance (TCA 1997, s 372T(1)(ab)),

(b) in respect of expenditure incurred on the construction or refurbishment of a building or structure or a qualifying premises which is in use for the purposes of a trade, or any activity treated as a trade, carried on by the person who is entitled to the relevant interest, within the meaning of TCA 1997, s 269 (see **5.403**), in relation to that expenditure and such trade or activity is carried on wholly or mainly—

    (i) in the sector of agriculture, including the production, processing and marketing of agricultural products,

    (ii) in the coal industry, fishing industry or motor vehicle industry,

    (iii) in the transport, steel, shipbuilding, synthetic fibres or financial services sectors (TCA 1997, s 372T(1)(b)), or

(c) in relation to any building or structure or qualifying premises which is in use for the purposes of a trade, or any activity treated as a trade, where the number of individuals employed or engaged in the carrying on of the trade or activity amounts to or exceeds 250 (TCA 1997, s 372T(1)(c)).

6.202 Construction or refurbishment of industrial buildings

6.202.1 Accelerated capital allowances for industrial buildings

TCA 1997, s 372M provides for accelerated capital allowances in respect of expenditure incurred in the qualifying period on the construction or refurbishment of an industrial building or structure in a qualifying area.

See **5.404** regarding the restriction by TCA 1997, s 270(4)-(7) of qualifying expenditure on industrial buildings in a qualifying rural area. In the case of expenditure incurred in the period 1 January 2007 to 31 December 2007, only 75% of expenditure incurred is treated as incurred, and in the case of expenditure incurred in the period 1 January 2008 to 31 July 2008, only 50% of expenditure incurred is treated as incurred.

An industrial building is "a mill, factory or other similar premises" (TCA 1997, s 268(1)(a)). Factories and manufacturing plants will therefore be qualifying premises in a qualifying rural area under TCA 1997 Part 10 Ch 8. TCA 1997, s 372M applies to an industrial building or structure which is used for a purpose specified in TCA 1997, s 268(1)(a) or (b). Accordingly, accelerated capital allowances are available only in respect of construction or refurbishment expenditure carried out in respect of a mill, factory or other similar premises. Thus, for example, hotels do not qualify for allowances.

TCA 1997, s 268(1)(b) refers to buildings or structures in use for the purposes of a dock undertaking. The inclusion of this reference permits the granting of allowances for expenditure on facilities such as piers and jetties.

In general, the entitlement to an industrial building initial allowance arises under TCA 1997, s 271(2) where a person has incurred capital expenditure on the construction of a building or structure which is to be an industrial building or structure occupied for the purposes of a trade by the person who incurs the capital expenditure or by a lessee who occupies the property under a relevant lease (ie, a lease to which the relevant interest, as defined in TCA 1997, s 269, is reversionary). In the case of a company which is an owner-occupier, an initial allowance can be claimed in the accounting period in which the expenditure was incurred. In the case of a lessor company, the initial allowance may be claimed in the accounting period in which the tenancy commences. Where capital expenditure is incurred by a company prior to the commencement of trading, the expenditure is treated as if it were incurred on the day on which the company commences to trade (TCA 1997, s 316(3)).

The entitlement to an industrial building annual allowance arises under TCA 1997, s 272(2) where, at the end of an accounting period, a company is entitled to a relevant interest in the building and the building is in use as an industrial building.

TCA 1997 372M will not apply in relation to any building or structure in use for the purposes of a trade where the number of individuals employed or engaged in the carrying on of the trade amounts to 250 or more (TCA 1997, s 372T(1)).

For the purposes of the following discussion on the capital allowances available on industrial buildings under TCA 1997 Part 10 Ch 8, it is assumed that all of the conditions for obtaining the allowances as set out in TCA 1997 Part 9 Ch 1 as well as those in TCA 1997 Part 10 Ch 8 have been satisfied.

6.202.2 Allowances

Where a building which is an industrial building as defined in TCA 1997, s 268(1)(a) is newly *constructed or refurbished*, and the building lies wholly within a qualifying rural area, the following allowances are available:

owner-occupier:

- industrial building initial allowance 50% plus industrial building annual allowance 4%; or
- free depreciation 50% plus industrial building annual allowance 4%;

lessor:

– industrial building initial allowance 50% plus industrial building annual allowance 4%.

In the case of refurbishment expenditure, however, accelerated allowances may by claimed on the amount of expenditure incurred only if the total amount of the expenditure so incurred is not less than an amount which is equal to 10% of the market value of the building or structure immediately before that expenditure was incurred (TCA 1997, s 372M(4)). Otherwise, basic rate allowances only will be available in respect of refurbishment expenditure.

In determining whether and to what extent capital expenditure incurred on the construction or refurbishment of a qualifying premises is or is not incurred in the qualifying period, only such an amount of that capital expenditure as is properly attributable to work on the construction or refurbishment of the premises actually carried out during the qualifying period may be treated as having been incurred in that period (TCA 1997, s 372M(6)).

6.202.3 Balancing allowances and charges

TCA 1997, s 274 provides that a balancing allowance or balancing charge is to be computed if, in relation to a qualifying premises in respect of which any capital allowances have been obtained, any of the following events occurs:

(a) the relevant interest in the building is sold;

(b) the relevant interest in the building is exchanged (TCA 1997, s 311(3));

(c) the building is demolished or destroyed;

(d) the building ceases altogether to be used;

(e) the relevant interest, if it is a leasehold interest, either:

(i) comes to an end, otherwise than on the person entitled to it acquiring the reversionary interest, or

(ii) is surrendered for valuable consideration (TCA 1997, s 311(3)).

Where the industrial building or structure is held for a period of at least 13 years, no balancing charge may be made (TCA 1997, s 372M(5)). The writing down life of the industrial building is nevertheless 25 years. Accordingly, while a balancing charge may not arise later than 13 years after the building is first used or, where TCA 1997, s 276 applies (see **5.407.5**), later than 13 years after the expenditure was incurred, a balancing allowance may still be made at any time up to 25 years after the building is first used, or, as the case may be, the refurbishment expenditure is incurred. Similarly, a purchaser of the property may still be entitled to capital allowances even where the purchase takes place more than 13 years after first use/expenditure incurred. Furthermore, the cessation of a qualifying trade is not an event requiring a balancing adjustment, provided the owner does not dispose of the relevant interest and so long as the building continues to be used for some purpose. The rules of TCA 1997, s 272(4) (new rate of allowance to write off residue of expenditure evenly over the rest of the writing down period of the expenditure – see **5.410**) continue to apply to industrial buildings in the designated areas.

6.202.4 TCA 1997, s 372M in detail

The allowances as detailed above arise under TCA 1997, s 372M(2), (3). These provisions refer to the underlying legislation of TCA 1997, s 271 (initial allowance) and TCA 1997, s 273 (free depreciation).

TCA 1997, s 372M(2) provides, subject to:

(a) TCA 1997, s 372M(4) (minimum refurbishment expenditure incurred to be not less than 10% of market value of building or structure – see **6.202.2** above),

(b) TCA 1997, s 270(4)-(7) (only 75% of expenditure incurred in the period 1 January 2007 to 31 December 2007 is treated as incurred and only 50% of expenditure incurred in the period 1 January 2008 to 31 July 2008 is treated as incurred; local authority certified cap on expenditure treated as incurred – see **5.404**), and

(c) TCA 1997, s 316(2B) (only the amount of expenditure as is properly attributable to work actually carried out in a period may be treated as having been incurred in that period – see **5.404**),

that TCA 1997, s 271 is to have effect in relation to qualifying capital expenditure as if various references (not relevant for the purposes of TCA 1997, s 372M) were deleted and as if TCA 1997, s 271(4) (rates of industrial building allowances) were substituted by a provision to the effect that the allowance is to be of an amount equal to 50% of the qualifying capital expenditure. TCA 1997, s 372M(2) accordingly secures that the 50% initial allowance rate will be available in respect of qualifying expenditure incurred in the qualifying period (see **6.201.2**) on buildings or structures in the qualifying areas.

TCA 1997, s 372M(3) similarly provides, subject again to TCA 1997 ss 372C(4), 270(4)-(6) and 316(2B), that TCA 1997, s 273 is to have effect in relation to qualifying capital expenditure as if various references and provisions not relevant for the purposes of TCA 1997, s 372M (eg, TCA 1997, s 273(3)-(7)) were deleted and as if TCA 1997, s 273(2)(b) (phasing out of free depreciation) were substituted by a provision to the effect that any allowance in respect of qualifying expenditure made under TCA 1997, s 272 and increased under TCA 1997, s 273(2)(a), whether claimed for one or more chargeable periods, may not in the aggregate exceed 50% of that qualifying expenditure. Accordingly TCA 1997, s 372M(3) secures that the 50% free depreciation rate is available for the purposes of the section.

The allowances available for industrial buildings consist of an initial allowance of 50% or (for owner-occupiers) free depreciation of 50%, and an annual allowance of 4%. It is not possible to obtain allowances of 50% + 4% in one period. TCA 1997, s 271(5) provides that where an initial allowance has been made under TCA 1997, s 271 for any period, no annual allowance under TCA 1997, s 272 may be made for the same period nor may free depreciation be claimed in any subsequent period in respect of the same expenditure. TCA 1997, s 273(8) provides that where, for any chargeable period, a writing down allowance under TCA 1997, s 272 in respect of qualifying expenditure is increased under TCA 1997, s 273, no initial allowance under TCA 1997, s 271 may be made in respect of that expenditure for that or any subsequent chargeable period.

6.203   Construction or refurbishment of commercial premises

6.203.1   Capital allowances for commercial buildings and structures

TCA 1997, s 372N provides for capital allowances in respect of expenditure in respect of construction or refurbishment incurred on a commercial property in a qualifying rural area.

See **5.404** regarding the restriction by TCA 1997, s 270(4)-(7) of qualifying expenditure on commercial premises in a qualifying rural area. In the case of expenditure incurred in the period 1 January 2007 to 31 December 2007, only 75% of expenditure incurred is treated as incurred, and in the case of expenditure incurred in the period 1 January 2008 to 31 July 2008, only 50% of expenditure incurred is treated as incurred.

For the purposes of capital allowances available under the qualifying rural areas scheme in respect of commercial premises, TCA 1997, s 372N(1) defines *qualifying premises* as a building or structure the site of which is wholly within a qualifying rural area and which must not already be an industrial building or structure as defined in TCA 1997, s 268. Thus, for example, hotels do not qualify for the allowances available under TCA 1997, s 372N; mills, factories and other similar premises qualify for allowances under TCA 1997, s 372M (see above).

To qualify for capital allowances, the commercial property must either be in use for the purposes of a trade or profession or for the purposes of an approved scheme (see below) or, regardless of whether or not it is so used, is let on *bona fide* commercial terms for such consideration as might be expected to be paid in respect of a letting negotiated on an arm's length basis.

An *approved scheme* is a scheme undertaken with the approval of a local authority which has as its object, or amongst its objects, the provision of sewerage facilities, water supplies or roads for public purposes.

Specifically excluded from the definition of qualifying premises is any part of a building which is in use as a dwelling house. There is no exclusion, in the definition of qualifying premises in TCA 1997, s 372N, of any building or part of a building in use as an office.

Where part of a building or structure is, and part is not, a qualifying premises, the building or structure and every part of it is treated as a qualifying premises if the capital expenditure incurred in the qualifying period on the construction or refurbishment of the non-qualifying part is not more than 10% of the total capital expenditure which has been incurred in that period on the construction or refurbishment of the building or structure (TCA 1997, s 268(8)).

6.203.2   Basis for capital allowances

TCA 1997, s 372N(2) provides the basis for capital allowances in respect of capital expenditure incurred on the construction or refurbishment of a qualifying premises. That subsection provides that all of the provisions of the Tax Acts (other than TCA 1997, s 372M – see **6.202** above in relation to industrial buildings) relating to the making of allowances and charges in respect of the construction or refurbishment of an industrial building are to apply to construction or refurbishment expenditure on qualifying premises as defined in TCA 1997, s 372N(1).

The qualifying premises is treated as if it were an industrial building as defined in TCA 1997, s 268(1)(a) (ie a mill, factory or other similar premises) in respect of which an allowance may be made under TCA 1997, s 271 (initial allowance) or 272 (annual allowance). Where the property is let, any activity carried on in the property which is not a trade is treated as if it were a trade.

Allowances may not be given by virtue of TCA 1997, s 372N(2) in respect of any capital expenditure on the refurbishment of qualifying premises unless the total amount of capital expenditure so incurred is not less than an amount equal to 10% of the market value of the qualifying premises immediately before that expenditure is incurred (TCA 1997, s 372N(3)). Whereas failure to satisfy the 10% refurbishment expenditure test in TCA 1997, s 372M operates to deny accelerated capital allowances in respect of industrial buildings and structures in a qualifying area, failure to satisfy the test for TCA 1997, s 372N purposes results in a denial of any capital allowances in respect of commercial premises in a qualifying area.

Allowances may be given in respect of capital expenditure incurred on the construction or refurbishment of a qualifying premises only in so far as that expenditure is incurred in the qualifying period (TCA 1997, s 372N(2)(b)). In determining whether and to what extent capital expenditure incurred on the construction or refurbishment of a qualifying premises is or is not incurred in the qualifying period, only such an amount of that capital expenditure as is properly attributable to work on the construction or refurbishment of the premises actually carried out during the qualifying period may be treated as having been incurred in that period (TCA 1997, s 372N(7)).

TCA 1997 372N will not apply in relation to any building or structure in use for the purposes of a trade, or any activity treated as a trade, where the number of individuals employed or engaged in the carrying on of the trade or activity amounts to 250 or more (TCA 1997, s 372T(1)(b)).

6.203.3 Allowances

Where expenditure is incurred on the *construction or refurbishment* of a qualifying premises which is a building situated wholly within a qualifying rural area, all of the provisions of the Tax Acts (except TCA 1997, s 372M) apply to the expenditure incurred as if it were expenditure on which capital allowances would be available under TCA 1997 ss 271 and 272, so that industrial building initial allowances, industrial building annual allowances and free depreciation are available in respect of the expenditure as if the property were a mill, factory or other similar premises. To qualify for the allowances the expenditure must, as already noted above, be incurred in the qualifying period (see **6.201.2**) and the work in respect of which the expenditure has been incurred must actually be carried out within that period.

The capital allowances available by virtue of TCA 1997, s 372N (and by virtue of the one-half restriction referred to in TCA 1997, s 372N(6) – see below) are as follows:

owner-occupier:

- industrial building initial allowance 50% plus industrial building annual allowance 4% for the balance so as to write off 100% of qualifying expenditure; or
- free depreciation 50%;

lessor:

- industrial building initial allowance 50% plus industrial building annual allowance 4% for the balance so as to write off 100% of qualifying expenditure.

In the case of refurbishment expenditure, allowances may by claimed on the amount of expenditure incurred only if the total amount of the expenditure so incurred is not less than an amount which is equal to 10% of the market value of the building or structure immediately before that expenditure was incurred. Otherwise, no allowances will be available in respect of refurbishment expenditure.

6.203.4   Balancing charges

TCA 1997, s 372N(5) provides that no balancing charge may be made where the qualifying premises is held for a period of at least 13 years. The writing down life of the building is nevertheless 25 years. Accordingly, while a balancing charge may not arise later than 13 years after the building is first used or, where TCA 1997, s 276 applies (see **5.407.5**), later than 13 years after the expenditure was incurred, a balancing allowance may still be made at any time up to 25 years after the building is first used, or, as the case may be, the refurbishment expenditure is incurred. Similarly, a purchaser of the property may still be entitled to capital allowances even when the purchase takes place more than 13 years after first use/expenditure incurred.

6.203.5   TCA 1997, s 372N in detail

The allowances as detailed above arise under TCA 1997, s 372N(4). This provision refers to the underlying legislation of TCA 1997, s 271 (initial allowance) and TCA 1997, s 273 (free depreciation).

TCA 1997, s 372N(2)(a) provides that TCA 1997, s 271 is to have effect in relation to qualifying capital expenditure incurred in the qualifying period on the construction or refurbishment of a qualifying premises as if various references (not relevant for the purposes of TCA 1997, s 372N) were deleted and as if TCA 1997, s 271(4) (rates of industrial building allowances) were substituted by a provision to the effect that the allowance is to be of an amount equal to 50% of the qualifying capital expenditure. TCA 1997, s 372N(4)(a) accordingly secures that the rate of initial allowance in respect of expenditure on qualifying premises in a qualifying area in respect of expenditure incurred in the qualifying period will be 50%.

TCA 1997, s 372N(2)(a) provides, subject to:

(a)   TCA 1997, s 372N(2)(b) (allowances only where expenditure incurred in qualifying period – see **6.203.2** above), (3) (minimum refurbishment expenditure incurred to be not less than 10% of market value of building or structure – see **6.203.2** above), (4) (see above) and (5) (see below),

(b)   TCA s 270(4)-(7) (only 75% of expenditure incurred in the period 1 January 2007 to 31 December 2007 is treated as incurred and only 50% of expenditure incurred in the period 1 January 2008 to 31 July 2008 is treated as incurred; local authority certified cap on expenditure treated as incurred – see **5.404**), and

(c) TCA 1997, s 316(2B) (only the amount of expenditure as is properly attributable to work actually carried out in a period may be treated as having been incurred in that period – see **5.404**),

that all of the provisions of the Tax Acts (other than TCA 1997, s 372M – see **6.202** above in relation to industrial buildings) relating to the making of allowances and charges in respect of the construction or refurbishment of an industrial building are to apply—

(i) as if a qualifying premises were at all times at which it is a qualifying premises a building or structure in respect of which an allowance is to be made under the provisions relating to the making of industrial building allowances; and

(ii) where any activity carried on in the qualifying premises is not a trade, as if it were a trade.

TCA 1997, s 372N(4)(b) similarly provides that TCA 1997, s 273 is to have effect in relation to qualifying capital expenditure as if TCA 1997, s 273(3)-(7) (not appropriate for the purposes of TCA 1997, s 372N) were deleted and that TCA 1997, s 273(2)(b) (phasing out of free depreciation) were replaced by a provision to the effect that free depreciation in respect of any qualifying expenditure, whether claimed for one chargeable period or more than one such period, is not to exceed 50% in the aggregate of the amount of that expenditure. Accordingly TCA 1997, s 372N(4)(b) provides for the availability of free depreciation of up to 50% in respect of expenditure in the qualifying period.

TCA 1997, s 271(5) provides that where an initial allowance has been made under TCA 1997, s 271 for any chargeable period, no annual allowance under TCA 1997, s 272 may be made for the same period nor may free depreciation be claimed in any subsequent period in respect of the same expenditure. TCA 1997, s 273(8) provides that where, for any chargeable period, a writing down allowance under TCA 1997, s 272 in respect of qualifying expenditure is increased under TCA 1997, s 273, no initial allowance under TCA 1997, s 271 may be made in respect of that expenditure for that or any subsequent chargeable period.

For the purposes of determining, in relation to a claim under TCA 1997, s 271 or 273 as applied by TCA 1997, s 372N, whether and to what extent capital expenditure incurred on the construction or refurbishment of an industrial building or structure is or is not incurred in the qualifying period, only such amount of that capital expenditure as is properly attributable to work carried out during the qualifying period may be treated as having been incurred in that period (TCA 1997, s 372N(7)).

6.3 URBAN RENEWAL INCENTIVES: TOWN RENEWAL SCHEME

6.301   Introduction
6.302   Construction or refurbishment of industrial buildings
6.303   Construction or refurbishment of commercial premises

6.301   Introduction

6.301.1   Town renewal scheme

TCA 1997 Part 10 Ch 10 (inserted by FA 2000) provides for a new scheme of tax reliefs to foster town renewal and improvement. The scheme operates as follows:

    (a)   the scheme provides for a process of applying incentives to qualifying areas based on Town Renewal Plans prepared by County Councils. These plans are designed to restore or improve the built fabric of Irish towns, to promote sensitive infill and to revitalise the centres of small towns;

    (b)   County Councils will recommend areas in which tax incentives are to be applied to a Department of the Environment and Local Government Expert Advisory Panel which will, in turn, make recommendations to the Minister of that Department;

    (c)   the Minister for Finance will make orders applying one or more tax incentives, as provided for in TCA 1997 Part 10 Ch 10, to qualifying areas recommended by the Minister for the Environment and Local Government;

    (d)   a similar range of tax reliefs is available under the scheme as is available under the 1998 Urban Renewal Scheme;

    (e)   under the Urban and Rural renewal schemes, EU approval was conditional on the exclusion of the business incentives in certain specified cases. Accordingly, under those schemes, the benefits of capital allowances cannot accrue to property developers nor can capital allowances apply where any premises is to be used in the agricultural sector, the coal, fishing or motor vehicle industries, the transport, steel, shipbuilding, synthetic fibres or financial service industries or where the premises is used in very large projects. Similar provision is made in the case of the town renewal scheme.

The town renewal scheme ran from 1 April 2000 to 31 December 2003.

An incentive relief for lessors of residential premises is provided for in TCA 1997 Part 10, Chapter 11 (ss 372AK-372AT) and this is dealt with in **6.5**.

6.301.2   Definitions

Qualifying period

TCA 1997, s 372AA(1) defines *qualifying period* as, subject to TCA 1997, s 372AB (see **6.301.3** below), the period commencing on 6 April 2001 and ending on:

    (a)   31 December 2004; or
    (b)   where TCA 1997, s 372AA(1A) applies, 31 December 2006; or
    (c)   where TCA 1997, s 372AA(1A) and (3) apply, 31 July 2008.

TCA 1997, s 372AA(1A) applies, as respects capital expenditure incurred on the construction or refurbishment of a building or structure, if—

(a) (i) a planning application (not being an application for outline permission within the meaning of section 36 of the Planning and Development Act 2000), in so far as planning permission is required, in respect of the construction or refurbishment work on the building or structure represented by that expenditure, is made in accordance with the Planning and Development Regulations 2001 to 2003,

(ii) an acknowledgment of the application, confirming that it was received on or before 31 December 2004, is issued by the planning authority in accordance with article 26(2) of the Planning and Development Regulations 2001 (SI 600/2001), and

(iii) the application is not an invalid application in respect of which a notice is issued by the planning authority in accordance with article 26(5) of those regulations,

(b) (i) a planning application, in so far as planning permission was required, in respect of the construction or refurbishment work on the building or structure represented by that expenditure, was made in accordance with the Local Government (Planning and Development) Regulations 1994 (SI 86/1994), not being an application for outline permission within the meaning of article 3 of those regulations,

(ii) an acknowledgment of the application, confirming that it was received on or before 10 March 2002, was issued by the planning authority in accordance with article 29(2)(a) of the regulations mentioned in (i), and

(iii) the application was not an invalid application in respect of which a notice is issued by the planning authority in accordance with article 29(2)(b)(i) of those regulations, or

(c) where the construction or refurbishment work on the building or structure represented by that expenditure is exempted development for the purposes of the Planning and Development Act 2000 by virtue of section 4 of that Act or by virtue of Part 2 of the Planning and Development Regulations 2001 (SI 600/2001) and—

(i) a detailed plan in relation to the development work is prepared,

(ii) a binding contract in writing, under which the expenditure on the development is incurred, is in existence, and

(iii) work to the value of 5% of the development costs is carried out,

not later than 31 December 2004.

Subject to TCA 1997, s 270(7)(a) and (b) (see **5.404**), TCA 1997, s 372AA(3) applies in relation to the construction or refurbishment of a building or structure or part of a building or structure the site of which is wholly within a qualifying area where:

(a) the person constructing or refurbishing the building or structure or part of a building or structure has, on or before 31 December 2006, carried out work to the value of not less than 15% of the actual construction or refurbishment costs of the building or structure or part of the building or structure,

(b) that person or, where the building or structure or part of the building or structure is sold by that person, the person who is claiming a deduction in relation to the expenditure incurred can show that the condition in (a) was satisfied, and

(c)   a binding contract in writing, under which the expenditure on the construction or refurbishment of the building or structure or part of the building or structure is incurred, was in existence on or before 31 July 2006, and

(d)   such other conditions, as may be specified in regulations made by the Minister for Finance, have been satisfied, such conditions to be limited to those necessary to ensure compliance with the laws of the European Communities governing State aid or with a decision of the Commission of the European Communities regarding compatibility with the common market having regard to Article 87 of the European Communities Treaty.

See **5.404** regarding the restriction by TCA 1997, s 270(4)-(7) of qualifying expenditure on buildings and structures in qualifying areas. In the case of expenditure incurred in the period 1 January 2007 to 31 December 2007, only 75% of expenditure incurred is treated as incurred, and in the case of expenditure incurred in the period 1 January 2008 to 31 July 2008, only 50% of expenditure incurred is treated as incurred.

Refurbishment

In relation to a building or structure, *refurbishment* means any work of construction, reconstruction, repair or renewal, including the provision or improvement of water, sewerage or heating facilities, carried out in the course of the repair or restoration, or maintenance in the nature of repair or restoration, of the building or structure.

Street

Street includes part of a street and the whole or part of any road, square, quay or lane.

Market value

In relation to a building, structure or house, *market value* means the price which the unencumbered fee simple of the building, structure or house would fetch if sold in the open market in such manner and subject to such conditions as might reasonably be calculated to obtain for the vendor the best price for the building, structure or house, less the part of that price which would be attributable to the acquisition of, or rights in or over, the land on which the building, structure or house is constructed.

Qualifying area

A *qualifying area* is an area or areas specified as a qualifying area under TCA 1997, s 372AB (see **6.301.3** below).

Façade

In relation to a building or structure, part of a building or structure, or a house, *façade* means the exterior wall of the building or structure, of the part of the building or structure, or of the house, as the case may be, which fronts on to a street.

6.301.3   Ministerial order

It is provided in TCA 1997, s 372AB(1) that the Minister for Finance may, on the recommendation of the Minister for the Environment and Local Government (such recommendation to take into consideration a Town Renewal Plan submitted by a local authority to that Minister in respect of an area identified by it), by order direct that:

(a)   the area or areas described (being wholly located within the boundaries of the area to which the Town Renewal Plan relates) in the order is or are to be a qualifying area for the purposes of one or more provisions of TCA 1997 Part 10 Chapter 10 or Chapter 11 (tax incentive areas – see **6.502**) (TCA 1997, s 372AB(1)(a));

(b)   where such an area or areas is or are to be a qualifying area—

    (i)   for the purposes of TCA 1997, s 372AC (accelerated capital allowances for certain industrial buildings and structures – see **6.302**), that area or those areas is or are to be a qualifying area or areas for the purposes of one or more of the following—

        (I)   the construction,

        (II)   the refurbishment, and

        (III)   the refurbishment of the façade,

    of a building or structure to which that section applies,

    (ii)   for the purposes of TCA 1997, s 372AD (capital allowances for certain commercial premises – see **6.303**)—

        (I)   one or more of the categories of building or structure mentioned below will or will not be a qualifying premises within the meaning of that section, and

        (II)   that area or those areas is or are to a qualifying area or areas for the purposes or either or both the construction or, an the refurbishment of, a qualifying premises within the meaning of that section (TCA 1997, s 372AB(1)(b)),

(c)   where such an area or areas is or are to be a qualifying area for the purposes of TCA 1997, s 372AP (tax incentive area – see **6.502**), that section is to apply in relation to that area or those areas in so far as the section relates to one or more of the following:

    (i)   expenditure incurred on the construction of a house,

    (ii)   conversion expenditure incurred in relation to a house,

    (iii)   refurbishment expenditure incurred in relation to a house, and

    (iv)   refurbishment expenditure incurred in relation to the façade of a house (TCA 1997, s 372AB(1)(ba)), and

(d)   as respects any such area described in the order, the definition of "qualifying period" in TCA 1997 ss 372AA (see above) and 372AL(1) (see **6.502**) is to be construed as a reference to such period as will be specified in the order in relation to that area; but no such period specified in the order may commence before—

    (i)   in the case of TCA 1997 ss 372AC and 372AD, 6 April 2001, and

    (ii)   in the case of any provision of TCA 1997 Part 10, Chapter 11 (see **6.5**), 1 April 2000,

    or end after 31 December 2004 or—

(I) in the case of TCA 1997 ss 372AC (accelerated allowances in respect of construction or refurbishment of industrial buildings and structures – see **6.302.1** below) and 372AD (allowances in respect of construction or refurbishment of commercial premises – see **6.303.1** below)—

    (A) where TCA 1997, s 372AA(1A) applies (see **6.301.2** above), end after 31 July 2006, or

    (B) where TCA 1997, s 372AA(1A) and (3) (see **6.301.2**) apply, end after 31 July 2008, and

(II) in the case of any provision of TCA 1997 Part 10 Chapter 11 (relief for lessors of rented residential accommodation)—

    (A) where TCA 1997, s 372AL(1A) applies (see **6.502**), end after 31 December 2006, or

    (B) where TCA 1997, s 372AL(1A) and (3) (see **6.502**) apply, end after 31 July 2008 (TCA 1997, s 372AB(1)(c)).

The categories of building or structure referred to in (b)(ii)(I) above are:

(a) buildings or structures in use as offices;

(b) any other buildings or structures and in respect of which not more than 10% of the capital expenditure incurred in the qualifying period on their construction or refurbishment relates to the construction or refurbishment of buildings or structures in use as offices;

(c) the façade of a building or structure or part of a building or structure referred to in (a); and

(d) the façade of a building or structure or part of a building or structure referred to in (b) (TCA 1997, s 372AB(2)).

Every order made by the Minister for Finance is to be laid before Dáil Éireann as soon as possible after it is made. The order may be annulled as a result of the passing of a resolution by the Dáil to that effect within 21 days. In that event, any action taken by any person in the period between the issue of the order and its annulment will be treated as if it were taken under a valid order (TCA 1997, s 372AB(3)).

Notwithstanding an order under TCA 1997, s 372AB(1), the granting of relief under TCA 1997 Part 10 Chapter 10 or Chapter 11 (see **6.5**) is to be subject to such other requirements as may be specified in or under the Act referred to in TCA 1997, s 372AA(2). In that subsection, it is provided that TCA 1997 Part 10 Chapters 10 and 11 are to apply if the Oireachtas passes an Act (see below) which refers to those Chapters and provides for the renewal of certain urban areas and the submission of plans ("Town Renewal Plans") to the Minister for the Environment and Local Government which have been drawn up by county councils (being county councils as referred to in such Act) in respect of an area or areas identified by such an authority on the basis of criteria prepared by that Minister, including physical and socio-economic renewal of such area or areas (TCA 1997, s 372AA(2)). The Act referred to above is now the Urban Renewal Act 1998.

As indicated above, a designation order may specifically include or exclude multi-storey car-parks, office development or mixed development (buildings or structures where not more than 10% of the capital expenditure incurred on their construction or refurbishment relates to the construction or refurbishment of office accommodation, ie where even a small amount of office space is involved). Accordingly, not only will there be a targeting of areas deemed to be in need of renewal but the type of development considered to be most appropriate for any such area will be specified for that area. Commercial development other than office development and actual industrial buildings will be permitted without restriction.

TCA 1997, s 372AJ (see **6.301.6** below) details certain restrictions relating to the availability of reliefs under the town renewal scheme. These restrictions arise out of EU approval of the scheme.

6.301.4   Prevention of double relief

Where any relief under TCA 1997 Part 10 Ch 10 is given in relation to capital expenditure or other expenditure incurred on, or rent payable in respect of, any building, structure or premises, relief may not be given in respect of that expenditure or rent, as the case may be, under any other provision of the Tax Acts (TCA 1997, s 372AJ(3)).

6.301.5   Non-application of relief in certain cases

Property developers

Capital allowances may not be claimed under TCA 1997, s 372AC (accelerated allowances in respect of industrial buildings etc) or s 372AD (certain commercial premises) by a property developer in respect of expenditure incurred on the construction or refurbishment of a building or structure or a qualifying premises. This prohibition applies:

(a)   where the property developer is entitled to the relevant interest (see **5.403**) in relation to the expenditure concerned; and

(b)   either the property developer or a person connected with (see **2.3**) the property developer incurred the expenditure on the construction or refurbishment of the qualifying building concerned (TCA 1997, s 372AJ(1)(a)).

A *property developer* for this purpose is a person carrying on a trade which consists wholly or mainly of the construction or refurbishment of buildings or structures with a view to their sale.

Grant-assisted expenditure

Capital allowances may not be claimed under TCA 1997, s 372AC (accelerated allowances in respect of industrial buildings etc) or s 372AD (certain commercial premises) in the case of expenditure incurred on or after 6 April 2001 on the construction or refurbishment of a building or structure or a qualifying premises where any part of that expenditure has been or is to be met, directly or indirectly, by grant assistance or any other assistance which is granted by or through the State, any board established by statute, any public or local authority or any other agency of the State (TCA 1997, s 372AJ(1)(aa)).

Restriction of allowances to small or medium-sized enterprises

Capital allowances may not be claimed under TCA 1997, s 372AC (accelerated allowances in respect of industrial buildings etc) or s 372AD (certain commercial premises) in the case of expenditure incurred on or after 6 April 2001 on the construction or refurbishment of a building or structure or a qualifying premises unless the relevant interest, within the meaning of TCA 1997, s 269 (see **5.403**), in such expenditure is held by a small or medium-sized enterprise within the meaning of Annex 1 to Commission Regulation (EC) No 70/2001 of 12 January 2001 (OJ No L10 of 13 January 2001, p 33), or, as the case may be, by a micro, small or medium-sized enterprise within the meaning of the Annex to Commission Recommendation of 6 May 2003 concerning the definition of micro, small or medium-sized enterprises (TCA 1997, s 372AJ(1)(ab)). The inclusion of the last-mentioned group of entities above follows the EU Commission's "Community guidelines on State aid for rescuing and restructuring firms in difficulty", for the purpose of EU State Aid rules, and its definition of micro, small and medium-sized enterprises.

Restrictions for certain sectors and industries and large investment projects

There are restrictions on the availability of capital allowances for buildings in use in certain sectors and industries or which are provided for the purposes of certain large investment projects. These restrictions are in line with EU approval of the town renewal scheme.

Capital allowances may not be claimed under TCA 1997, s 372AC (accelerated allowances in respect of industrial buildings etc) or s 372AD (certain commercial premises):

(a) in respect of expenditure incurred on the construction or refurbishment of a building or structure or a qualifying premises which is in use for the purposes of a trade, or any activity treated as a trade, carried on by the person who is entitled to the relevant interest, within the meaning of TCA 1997, s 269 (see **5.403**), in relation to that expenditure and such trade or activity is carried on wholly or mainly—

    (i) in the sector of agriculture, including the production, processing and marketing of agricultural products,

    (ii) in the coal industry, fishing industry or motor vehicle industry, or

    (iii) in the transport, steel, shipbuilding, synthetic fibres or financial services sectors (TCA 1997, s 372AJ(1)(b)), or

(b) in respect of expenditure incurred on or after 1 January 2003 on the construction or refurbishment of any building or structure or qualifying premises provided for the purposes of a project that is subject to the notification requirements of—

    (i) the "Multisectoral framework on regional aid for large investment projects" (OJ No C 107, 7.4.1998, p 7) prepared by the Commission of the European Communities, or

    (ii) the "Multisectoral framework on regional aid for large investment projects" (OJ No C 70, 19.2.2002, p 8) prepared by the Commission of the European Communities, as the case may be, unless approval of the potential capital allowances involved has been received from that Commission by the Minister for Finance, or by such other Minister of the Government, agency or body as may be nominated for that purpose by the Minister for Finance (TCA 1997, s 372AJ(1)(c)).

Apportionment

A part of a building or structure situated in a qualifying area may qualify for allowances under the town renewal scheme and apportionment of expenditure on a floor area basis is provided for this purpose where a building straddles the boundary or a qualifying area.

For the purposes of TCA 1997 ss 372AC (accelerated capital allowances for industrial buildings) and 372AD (capital allowances for commercial buildings), where the site of any part of a building or structure is situate outside the boundary of a qualifying area and where expenditure incurred or treated as having been incurred in the qualifying period is attributable to the building or structure in general, such an amount of that expenditure is to be deemed to be attributable to the part which is situate outside the boundary as bears to the whole of that expenditure the same proportion as the floor area of the part situate outside the boundary of the qualifying area bears to the total floor area of the building or structure (TCA 1997, s 372AJ(2)).

6.302   Construction or refurbishment of industrial buildings

6.302.1   Accelerated capital allowances for industrial buildings

TCA 1997, s 372AC provides for accelerated capital allowances in respect of expenditure incurred in the qualifying period on the construction or refurbishment of an industrial building or structure or part of an industrial building or structure the site of which is wholly within a qualifying area.

See **5.404** regarding the restriction by TCA 1997, s 270(4)-(7) of qualifying expenditure on industrial buildings in a qualifying area. In the case of expenditure incurred in the period 1 January 2007 to 31 December 2007, only 75% of expenditure incurred is treated as incurred, and in the case of expenditure incurred in the period 1 January 2008 to 31 July 2008, only 50% of expenditure incurred is treated as incurred.

An industrial building is "a mill, factory or other similar premises" (TCA 1997, s 268(1)(a)). Factories and manufacturing plants will therefore be qualifying premises in a qualifying area under TCA 1997 Part 10 Ch 10. TCA 1997, s 372AC applies to an industrial building or structure which is used for a purpose specified in TCA 1997, s 268(1)(a). Accordingly, accelerated capital allowances are available only in respect of construction or refurbishment expenditure carried out in respect of a mill, factory or other similar premises. Thus, for example, hotels do not qualify for allowances.

In general, the entitlement to an industrial building initial allowance arises under TCA 1997, s 271(2) where a person has incurred capital expenditure on the construction of a building or structure which is to be an industrial building or structure occupied for the purposes of a trade by the person who incurs the capital expenditure or by a lessee who occupies the property under a relevant lease (ie, a lease to which the relevant interest, as defined in TCA 1997, s 269, is reversionary). In the case of a company which is an owner-occupier, an initial allowance can be claimed in the accounting period in which the expenditure was incurred. In the case of a lessor company, the initial allowance may be claimed in the accounting period in which the tenancy commences.

Where capital expenditure is incurred by a company prior to the commencement of trading, the expenditure is treated as if it were incurred on the day on which the company commences to trade (TCA 1997, s 316(3)).

The entitlement to an industrial building annual allowance arises under TCA 1997, s 272(2) where, at the end of an accounting period, a company is entitled to a relevant interest in the building and the building is in use as an industrial building.

For the purposes of the following discussion on the capital allowances available on industrial buildings under TCA 1997 Part 10 Ch 10, it is assumed that all of the conditions for obtaining the allowances as set out in TCA 1997 Part 9 Ch 1 as well as those in TCA 1997 Part 10 Ch 10 have been satisfied.

6.302.2 Allowances

Where a building which is an industrial building as defined in TCA 1997, s 268(1)(a) is newly *constructed or refurbished*, and the building lies wholly within a qualifying area, the following allowances are available:

owner-occupier:

– industrial building initial allowance 50% plus industrial building annual allowance 4%; or
– free depreciation 50% plus industrial building annual allowance 4%;

lessor:

– industrial building initial allowance 50% plus industrial building annual allowance 4%.

In determining whether and to what extent capital expenditure incurred on the construction or refurbishment of a qualifying premises is or is not incurred in the qualifying period, only such an amount of that capital expenditure as is properly attributable to work on the construction or refurbishment of the premises actually carried out during the qualifying period may be treated as having been incurred in that period (TCA 1997, s 372AC(5)).

6.302.3 Balancing allowances and charges

TCA 1997, s 274 provides that a balancing allowance or balancing charge is to be computed if, in relation to a qualifying premises in respect of which any capital allowances have been obtained, any of the following events occurs:

(a) the relevant interest in the building is sold;
(b) the relevant interest in the building is exchanged (TCA 1997, s 311(3));
(c) the building is demolished or destroyed;
(d) the building ceases altogether to be used;
(e) the relevant interest, if it is a leasehold interest, either:

(i) comes to an end, otherwise than on the person entitled to it acquiring the reversionary interest, or

(ii) is surrendered for valuable consideration (TCA 1997, s 311(3)).

Where the industrial building or structure is held for a period of at least 13 years, no balancing charge may be made (TCA 1997, s 372AC(4)). The writing down life of the industrial building is nevertheless 25 years. Accordingly, while a balancing charge may not arise later than 13 years after the building is first used or, where TCA 1997, s 276 applies (refurbishment expenditure – see **5.407.5**), later than 13 years after the expenditure was incurred, a balancing allowance may still be made at any time up to 25 years after the building is first used, or, as the case may be, the refurbishment expenditure is incurred. Similarly, a purchaser of the property may still be entitled to capital allowances even where the purchase takes place more than 13 years after first use/expenditure incurred. Furthermore, the cessation of a qualifying trade is not an event requiring a balancing adjustment, provided the owner does not dispose of the relevant interest and so long as the building continues to be used for some purpose. The rules of TCA 1997, s 272(4) (new rate of allowance to write off residue of expenditure evenly over the rest of the writing down period of the expenditure – see **5.410**) continue to apply to industrial buildings in the designated areas.

6.302.4   TCA 1997, s 372AC in detail

The allowances as detailed above arise under TCA 1997, s 372AC(2), (3). These provisions refer to the underlying legislation of TCA 1997, s 271 (initial allowance) and TCA 1997, s 273 (free depreciation).

TCA 1997, s 372AC(2) provides, subject to:

(a)   TCA 1997, s 372AJ (non-application of reliefs in certain cases – see **6.301.5** above),

(b)   TCA s 270(4)-(7) (only 75% of expenditure incurred in the period 1 January 2007 to 31 December 2007 is treated as incurred and only 50% of expenditure incurred in the period 1 January 2008 to 31 July 2008 is treated as incurred; local authority certified cap on expenditure treated as incurred – see **5.404**), and

(c)   TCA 1997, s 316(2B) (only the amount of expenditure as is properly attributable to work actually carried out in a period may be treated as having been incurred in that period – see **5.404**),

that TCA 1997, s 271 is to have effect in relation to qualifying capital expenditure as if various references (not appropriate for the purposes of TCA 1997, s 372AC) were deleted and as if TCA 1997, s 271(4) (rates of industrial building allowances) were substituted by a provision to the effect that the allowance is to be of an amount equal to 50% of the qualifying capital expenditure. TCA 1997, s 372AC(2) accordingly secures that the 50% initial allowance rate will be available in respect of qualifying expenditure incurred in the qualifying period (see **6.301.2**) on buildings or structures in the qualifying areas.

TCA 1997, s 372AC(3) similarly provides, again subject to:

(a)   TCA 1997, s 372AJ;

(b)   TCA s 270(4)-(6); and

(c)   TCA 1997, s 316(2B),

that TCA 1997, s 273 is to have effect in relation to qualifying capital expenditure as if various references and provisions not appropriate for the purposes of TCA 1997, s 372C (eg, TCA 1997, s 273(3)-(7)) were deleted and as if TCA 1997, s 273(2)(b) (phasing out of free depreciation) were substituted by a provision to the effect that any allowance in respect of qualifying expenditure made under TCA 1997, s 272 and increased under

TCA 1997, s 273(2)(a), whether claimed for one or more chargeable periods, may not in the aggregate exceed 50% of that qualifying expenditure. Accordingly TCA 1997, s 372AC(3) secures that the 50% free depreciation rate is available for the purposes of the section.

The allowances available for industrial buildings consist of an initial allowance of 50% or (for owner-occupiers) free depreciation of 50%, and an annual allowance of 4%. It is not possible to obtain allowances of 50% + 4% in one period. TCA 1997, s 271(5) provides that where an initial allowance has been made under TCA 1997, s 271 for any period, no annual allowance under TCA 1997, s 272 may be made for the same period nor may free depreciation be claimed in any subsequent period in respect of the same expenditure. TCA 1997, s 273(8) provides that where, for any chargeable period, a writing down allowance under TCA 1997, s 272 in respect of qualifying expenditure is increased under TCA 1997, s 273, no initial allowance under TCA 1997, s 271 may be made in respect of that expenditure for that or any subsequent chargeable period.

6.303   Construction or refurbishment of commercial premises

6.303.1   Capital allowances for commercial premises

TCA 1997, s 372AD provides for capital allowances in respect of expenditure in respect of construction or refurbishment incurred on a commercial property in a qualifying area.

See **5.404** regarding the restriction by TCA 1997, s 270(4)-(7) of qualifying expenditure on commercial premises in a qualifying area. In the case of expenditure incurred in the period 1 January 2007 to 31 December 2007, only 75% of expenditure incurred is treated as incurred, and in the case of expenditure incurred in the period 1 January 2008 to 31 July 2008, only 50% of expenditure incurred is treated as incurred.

For the purposes of capital allowances available under the town renewal scheme in respect of commercial premises, TCA 1997, s 372AD(1) defines *qualifying premises* as a building or structure or part of a building or structure the site of which is wholly within a qualifying area and which must not already be an industrial building or structure as defined in TCA 1997, s 268. Thus, for example, hotels do not qualify for the allowances available under TCA 1997, s 372AD; mills, factories and other similar premises qualify for allowances under TCA 1997, s 372AC (see above).

To qualify for capital allowances, the commercial property must either be in use for the purposes of a trade or profession, or, regardless of whether or not it is so used, is let on *bona fide* commercial terms for such consideration as might be expected to be paid in respect of a letting negotiated on an arms length basis.

Specifically excluded from the definition of qualifying premises is any part of a building which is in use as a dwelling house. There is no exclusion, in the definition of qualifying premises in TCA 1997, s 372AD, of any building or part of a building in use as an office.

Where part of a building or structure is, and part is not, a qualifying premises, the building or structure and every part of it is treated as a qualifying premises if the capital expenditure incurred in the qualifying period on the construction or refurbishment of the non-qualifying part is not more than 10% of the total capital expenditure which has been incurred in that period on the construction or refurbishment of the building or structure (TCA 1997, s 268(8)).

6.303.2   Basis for capital allowances

TCA 1997, s 372AD(2) provides the basis for capital allowances in respect of capital expenditure incurred on the construction or refurbishment of a qualifying premises. That subsection provides that all of the provisions of the Tax Acts (other than TCA 1997, s 372AC – see **6.302** above in relation to industrial buildings) relating to the making of allowances and charges in respect of the construction or refurbishment of an industrial building are to apply to construction or refurbishment expenditure on qualifying premises as defined in TCA 1997, s 372AD(1).

The qualifying premises is treated as if, at all times at which it is a qualifying building, it were an industrial building as defined in TCA 1997, s 268(1)(a) (ie, a mill, factory or other similar premises) in respect of which an allowance may be made under TCA 1997, s 271 (initial allowance) or s 272 (annual allowance). Where the property is let, any activity carried on in the property which is not a trade is treated as if it were a trade (TCA 1997, s 372AD(2)).

Allowances may be given in respect of capital expenditure incurred on the construction or refurbishment of a qualifying premises only in so far as that expenditure is incurred in the qualifying period (TCA 1997, s 372AD(2)(b)). In determining whether and to what extent capital expenditure incurred on the construction or refurbishment of a qualifying premises is or is not incurred in the qualifying period, only such an amount of that capital expenditure as is properly attributable to work on the construction or refurbishment of the premises actually carried out during the qualifying period may be treated as having been incurred in that period (TCA 1997, s 372AD(5)).

6.303.3   Allowances

Where expenditure is incurred on the *construction or refurbishment* of a qualifying premises which is a building situated wholly within a designated area, all of the provisions of the Tax Acts (except TCA 1997, s 372AC) apply to the expenditure incurred as if it were expenditure on which capital allowances would be available under TCA 1997 ss 271 and 272, so that industrial building initial allowances, industrial building annual allowances and free depreciation are available in respect of the expenditure as if the property were a mill, factory or other similar premises. To qualify for the allowances the expenditure must, as already noted above, be incurred in the qualifying period (see **6.301.2** and **6.301.3**) and the work in respect of which the expenditure has been incurred must actually be carried out within that period.

The capital allowances available by virtue of TCA 1997, s 372AD are as follows:

owner-occupier:

- – industrial building initial allowance 50% plus industrial building annual allowance 4% for the balance so as to write off 100% of qualifying expenditure; or
- – free depreciation 50%;

lessor:

- – industrial building initial allowance 50% plus industrial building annual allowance 4% for the balance so as to write off 100% of qualifying expenditure.

6.303.4   Balancing charges

TCA 1997, s 372AD(4) provides that no balancing charge may be made where the qualifying premises is held for a period of at least 13 years. The writing down life of the building is nevertheless 25 years. Accordingly, while a balancing charge may not arise later than 13 years after the building is first used or, where TCA 1997, s 276 applies (see **5.407.5**), later than 13 years after the expenditure was incurred, a balancing allowance may still be made at any time up to 25 years after the building is first used, or, as the case may be, the refurbishment expenditure is incurred. Similarly, a purchaser of the property may still be entitled to capital allowances even when the purchase takes place more than 13 years after first use/expenditure incurred.

6.303.5   TCA 1997, s 372AD in detail

The allowances as detailed above arise under TCA 1997, s 372AD(3). This provision refers to the underlying legislative provisions of TCA 1997, s 271 (initial allowance) and TCA 1997, s 273 (free depreciation).

TCA 1997, s 372AD(2)(a) provides, subject to:

(a)   TCA 1997, s 372AD(2)(b) (requirement that expenditure be incurred in qualifying period – see **6.303.2** above), (3) (see below) and (4) (balancing charges – see **6.303.4** above), and 372AJ (non-application of reliefs in certain cases – see **6.301.5**);

(b)   TCA s 270(4)-(7) (only 75% of expenditure incurred in the period 1 January 2007 to 31 December 2007 is treated as incurred and only 50% of expenditure incurred in the period 1 January 2008 to 31 July 2008 is treated as incurred; local authority certified cap on expenditure treated as incurred – see **5.404**); and

(c)   TCA 1997, s 316(2B) (only the amount of expenditure as is properly attributable to work actually carried out in a period may be treated as having been incurred in that period – see **5.404**);

that all of the provisions of the Tax Acts (other than TCA 1997, s 372AC – see **6.302** above in relation to industrial buildings) relating to the making of allowances and charges in respect of the construction or refurbishment of an industrial building are to apply:

(i)   as if a qualifying premises were at all times at which it is a qualifying premises a building or structure in respect of which an allowance is to be made under the provisions relating to the making of industrial building allowances; and

(ii)   where any activity carried on in the qualifying premises, or, in a case where the façade of a building or structure or part of a building or structure is a qualifying premises, carried on in that building or structure or part of that building or structure, is not a trade, as if it were a trade.

TCA 1997, s 372AD(3)(a) provides that TCA 1997, s 271 is to have effect in relation to qualifying capital expenditure incurred in the qualifying period on the construction or refurbishment of a qualifying premises as if various references (not relevant for the purposes of TCA 1997, s 372AD) were deleted and as if TCA 1997, s 271(4) (rates of industrial building allowances) were substituted by a provision to the effect that the allowance is to be of an amount equal to 50% of the qualifying capital expenditure. TCA 1997, s 372AD(3)(a) accordingly secures that the rate of initial allowance in respect of expenditure on qualifying premises in a qualifying area in respect of expenditure incurred in the qualifying period will be 50%.

TCA 1997, s 372AD(3)(b) similarly provides that TCA 1997, s 273 is to have effect in relation to qualifying capital expenditure as if TCA 1997, s 273(3)-(7) (not appropriate for the purposes of TCA 1997, s 372AD) were deleted and that TCA 1997, s 273(2)(b) (phasing out of free depreciation) were replaced by a provision to the effect that free depreciation in respect of any qualifying expenditure, whether claimed for one chargeable period or more than one such period, is not to exceed 50% in the aggregate of the amount of that expenditure. Accordingly TCA 1997, s 372AD(4)(b) provides for the availability of free depreciation of up to 50% in respect of expenditure in the qualifying period.

TCA 1997, s 271(5) provides that where an initial allowance has been made under TCA 1997, s 271 for any chargeable period, no annual allowance under TCA 1997, s 272 may be made for the same period nor may free depreciation be claimed in any subsequent period in respect of the same expenditure. TCA 1997, s 273(8) provides that where, for any chargeable period, a writing down allowance under TCA 1997, s 272 in respect of qualifying expenditure is increased under TCA 1997, s 273, no initial allowance under TCA 1997, s 271 may be made in respect of that expenditure for that or any subsequent chargeable period.

For the purposes of determining, in relation to a claim under TCA 1997, s 271 or 273 as applied by TCA 1997, s 372AD, whether and to what extent capital expenditure incurred on the construction or refurbishment of an industrial building or structure is or is not incurred in the qualifying period, only such amount of that capital expenditure as is properly attributable to work carried out during the qualifying period may be treated as having been incurred in that period (TCA 1997, s 372AD(5)).

6.4 PARK AND RIDE FACILITIES AND RELATED DEVELOPMENTS

6.401 Introduction
6.402 Construction or refurbishment of certain park and ride facilities
6.501 Introduction

6.401 Introduction

6.401.1 Outline

TCA 1997 Part 10 Chapter 9 (ss 372U-372Z) contains measures aimed at encouraging the establishment of park and ride facilities in the larger urban areas. Accelerated capital allowances up to 100% of expenditure are provided for in respect of expenditure on the construction or refurbishment of these facilities. Relief is also given for expenditure on the construction or refurbishment of certain commercial premises located at park and ride facilities.

Allowances are available for expenditure on commercial and residential developments only to the extent that the total expenditure does not exceed 50% of total allowable expenditure at a park and ride facility. Similarly, allowances may be claimed in respect of expenditure on residential accommodation up to a maximum of 25% of total allowable expenditure at the park and ride facility.

The scheme ran for a period of three years from 1 July 1999 to 30 June 2002.

An incentive relief for lessors of residential premises is provided for in TCA 1997 Part 10, Chapter 11 (ss 372AK-372AT) and this is dealt with in **6.5**.

6.401.2 Definitions

Qualifying period

TCA 1997, s 372U(1) defines the *qualifying period* as the period commencing on 1 July 1999 and ending on:

(i)   31 December 2004, or

(ii)   where TCA 1997, s 372U(1A) applies, 31 December 2006; or

(iii)   where TCA 1997, s 372(1A) and (3) apply, 31 July 2008.

TCA 1997, s 372U(1A) applies, as respects capital expenditure incurred on the construction or refurbishment of a building or structure, if:

(a) (i)   a planning application (not being an application for outline permission within the meaning of section 36 of the Planning and Development Act 2000), in so far as planning permission is required, in respect of the construction or refurbishment work on the building or structure represented by that expenditure, is made in accordance with the Planning and Development Regulations 2001 to 2003,

    (ii)   an acknowledgment of the application, confirming that it was received on or before 31 December 2004, is issued by the planning authority in accordance with article 26(2) of the Planning and Development Regulations 2001 (SI 600/2001), and

(iii) the application is not an invalid application in respect of which a notice is issued by the planning authority in accordance with article 26(5) of those regulations,

(b) (i)a planning application, in so far as planning permission was required, in respect of the construction or refurbishment work on the building or structure represented by that expenditure, was made in accordance with the Local Government (Planning and Development) Regulations 1994 (SI 86/1994), not being an application for outline permission within the meaning of article 3 of those regulations,

(ii) an acknowledgment of the application, confirming that it was received on or before 10 March 2002, was issued by the planning authority in accordance with article 29(2)(a) of the regulations mentioned in (i), and

(iii) the application was not an invalid application in respect of which a notice is issued by the planning authority in accordance with article 29(2)(b)(i) of those regulations, or

(c) where the construction or refurbishment work on the building or structure represented by that expenditure is exempted development for the purposes of the Planning and Development Act 2000 by virtue of section 4 of that Act or by virtue of Part 2 of the Planning and Development Regulations 2001 (SI 600/2001) and—

(i) a detailed plan in relation to the development work is prepared,

(ii) a binding contract in writing, under which the expenditure on the development is incurred, is in existence, and

(iii) work to the value of 5% of the development costs is carried out,

not later than 31 December 2004.

TCA 1997, s 372U(3) applies in relation to the construction or refurbishment of a building or structure which is a qualifying park and ride facility or a qualifying premises where:

(a) the person constructing or refurbishing the building or structure has, on or before 31 December 2006, carried out work to the value of not less than 15% of the actual construction or refurbishment costs of the building or structure, and

(b) that person or, where the building or structure is sold by that person, the person who is claiming a deduction in relation to the expenditure can show that the condition in (a) was satisfied.

Guidelines

Guidelines means guidelines in relation to:

(a) the location, development and operation of park and ride facilities;

(b) the development of commercial activities located at qualifying park and ride facilities; and

(c) the development of certain residential accommodation located at certain qualifying park and ride facilities, issued by the Minister for the Environment and Local Government following consultation with the Minister for Public Enterprise and with the consent of the Minister for Finance (TCA 1997, s 372U(1)).

Guidelines may include provisions relating to all or any one or more of the following:

(a) the criteria for determining the suitability of a site as a location for a park and ride facility;

(b) the conditions to apply in relation to the provision of transport services to and from a park and ride facility, including provision for a formal agreement between a transport service provider and a park and ride facility operator where these functions are discharged by separate persons;

(c) the hours of operation of a park and ride facility and the level and structure of charges to be borne by members of the public in respect of parking and the use of transport services to or from a park and ride facility;

(d) the minimum number of vehicle parking spaces to be provided in a park and ride facility;

(e) the proportion of parking space, if any, in a park and ride facility which may, subject to any necessary conditions, be allocated for purposes connected with any commercial or residential development at a park and ride facility;

(f) the requirements to apply in relation to the development and operation of commercial activities, if any, at a park and ride facility, including requirements necessary to ensure that those activities do not have an adverse effect on the development and operation of the park and ride facility;

(g) the requirements to apply in relation to the provision of residential accommodation, if any, at a park and ride facility, including requirements necessary to ensure that such accommodation does not have an adverse effect on the development and operation of the park and ride facility (TCA 1997, s 372U(2)).

Park and ride facilities

A *qualifying park and ride facility* is a park and ride facility in respect of which the relevant local authority, in consultation with such other agencies as may be specified in the guidelines, gives a certificate in writing to the person constructing or refurbishing such a facility stating that it is satisfied that the facility complies with the criteria and requirements laid down in the guidelines.

Park and ride facility means:

(a) a building or structure served by a bus or train service, in use for the purpose of providing, for members of the public generally, intending to continue a journey by bus or train and without preference for any particular class of person and on payment of an appropriate charge, parking space for mechanically propelled vehicles; and

(b) any area under, over or immediately adjoining the building or structure referred to in (a) on which a qualifying premises (as defined in TCA 1997, s 372W or 372AK (see **6.504.3**)) is or is to be situated.

The *relevant local authority*, in relation to the construction or refurbishment of a park and ride facility, or a qualifying premises within the meaning of TCA 1997, s 372W (see **6.403.1**), means—

(a)   in respect of the county boroughs of Cork, Dublin, Galway, Limerick and Waterford, the corporations of the borough concerned;

(b)   in respect of the administrative counties of Clare, Cork, Dún Laoghaire-Rathdown, Fingal, Galway, Kildare, Kilkenny, Limerick, Meath, South Dublin, Waterford and Wicklow, the council of the county concerned;

(c)   an urban district council situated in the administrative county of Kildare, Meath or Wicklow,

in whose functional area the park and ride facility is situated (TCA 1997, s 372U(1)).

6.401.3   Guidelines

Residential

Guidelines for the local authorities to be applied when approving park and ride facilities were issued on 31 August 1999. The guidelines govern the park and ride facility itself and the associated residential accommodation, but not commercial premises related to the park and ride facility. These are to issued later. In the meantime, only applications relating to certification in respect of park and ride facilities and associated residential developments may be processed by relevant local authorities.

Important features of the guidelines issued on 31 August 1999, as they relate to park and ride facilities, are as follows:

(a)   the location of the park and ride facility must be consistent with the local authority's traffic policies and must respect the terms of any transportation/land use plan for the area;

(b)   the facility must incorporate a minimum of—

    (i)   450 car parking spaces in the case of a bus-based facility,

    (ii)   200 car parking spaces in the case of a rail-based facility, or

    (iii)   such other higher number specified by the local authority.

(c)   the facility must incorporate facilities for—

    (i)   pedestrian access to public transport services,

    (ii)   operational requirements for public transport vehicles and ticketing systems,

    (iii)   car passenger drop-off and pick-up facilities including a clean bright, well-serviced waiting area incorporating toilets, litter bins and telephones, and

    (iv)   cycle parking;

(d)   the promoter and operator of the park and ride facility must have submitted a business plan for the provision of an integrated park and ride service;

(e)   the facility must be compatible with the nature of the area in which it is located;

(f)   there must be measures to ensure security of people, cycles and cars and for staffing arrangements at the park and ride facility must be in place;

(g)   access for cars, cycles and public transport vehicles must be designed such that the facility operates smoothly;

(h)   the route alignment of the public transport service must suit travel demands;

(i)   a minimum of 90% of the car park capacity must be available for members of the public;

(j) tickets for the facility should be easy to purchase, understand and use;

(k) provision for reporting on the profile of use of the park and ride facility to ensure continuing compliance with the guidelines must be made.

As regards the residential accommodation, the following criteria must be met:

(a) the development must be wholly within the site of a qualifying park and ride facility;

(b) the development must facilitate the provision and operation of a qualifying park and ride facility;

(c) the development is compatible with the nature of the area in which it is located and construction has been carried out in accordance with appropriate design standards and the local authority's Development Plan.

Commercial

Guidelines relating to commercial development located at a park and ride facility were published in July 2001 and the principal paragraphs of these guidelines are reproduced as follows.

1. Introduction

The guidelines are issued without prejudice to the provisions of the Planning and Development Act 2000, the Building Control Act, 1990, and regulations made under those Acts and the provisions of the relevant local authority's Development Plan.

2. Criteria and Requirements

2.1 When considering whether a commercial development located at a park and ride facility is a development in respect of which a certificate is to be issued to the applicant developer, the relevant local authority must satisfy itself:

(a) that the development is wholly within the site of a qualifying park and ride facility;

(b) that the commercial development facilitates the provision and operation of a qualifying park and ride facility;

(c) that the commercial development is compatible with the nature of the area in which it is located and construction has been carried out in accordance with appropriate design standards and the local authority's Development Plan;

(d) that the commercial development at the park and ride facility serves mainly passing trade and / or trade from those who have parked in the facility. The commercial activities to be carried out in the premises are not designed to be of a type and scale that would attract traffic in their own right. The commercial development may include newsagents, video rental stores, petrol stations, dry cleaners, car valeting, tyre/ exhaust service outlets and other premises in use for the retailing of goods or the provision of services only within the State. However, premises in use as offices or for the provision of mail order or financial services are excluded.

2.2 In the case of a proposed park and ride facility to be located in Dublin County Borough; the administrative counties of Fingal, South Dublin, Dun Laoghaire-Rathdown, Meath, Kildare or Wicklow; or urban districts in Meath, Kildare or Wicklow, the relevant local authority must, prior to a decision to certify a development, consult with, and take into account the views of, the Dublin Transportation Office on the proposed facility.

3. Certification

3.1 Under Chapter 9 of Part 10 of the Taxes Consolidation Act 1997, compliance with the criteria set out in part 2 of these guidelines must be certified by the relevant local authority. The relevant local authority must also certify that the requirements in section 372W(2)(c) of the Taxes Consolidation Act, 1997, in relation to limits on allowable expenditure on commercial development located at a park and ride facility are met. Accordingly, a person wishing to avail of the capital allowances and reliefs provided for under that chapter should make a formal application, in writing, to the relevant local authority. As certification requires the relevant local authority to be satisfied that the commercial development located at a park and ride facility has been undertaken in accordance with the guidelines in part 2, the application for certification can only be decided after the development has been completed.

3.2 However, where the relevant local authority is satisfied that a commercial development located at a park and ride facility, if developed in accordance with the permission granted under the planning process, would comply with the provisions of part 2 of these guidelines, a letter to that effect can, if necessary, issue to the developer concerned. As the relevant local authority can only fully establish compliance with the criteria after the development has been completed, certification can only take place at that stage (see paragraph 3.3).

3.3 The relevant local authority will need to obtain from developers of park and ride facilities the necessary information to allow it to certify that expenditure on commercial development located at a park and ride facility in respect of which allowances are being obtained is within the limits specified in the legislation.

3.4 An application for certification should include—

- name, address and telephone/ fax numbers/ e-mail details of the developer;
- address and description of the commercial development located at a park and ride facility, for which the certification is sought;
- relevant planning permission reference number and date of issue;
- copy of the commencement notice, if applicable, under the Building Control Act 1990 for the relevant development;
- details of the commercial development located at a park and ride facility to be provided including arrangements and responsibilities for the provision of the parking and transport services, proposed level and structure of the charges for the park and ride facility and associated public transport service, ticketing arrangements, etc;
- details of expenditure on the commercial development, and where appropriate, on the park and ride facility and residential development located at a park and ride facility,
- such other documentation and information as the relevant local authority may require for the purposes of its consideration of the certification application.

3.5 Where, on the basis of the information received in an application for certification, the relevant local authority is satisfied that the development has been carried out in accordance with the criteria set out in part 2 of these guidelines, it should issue a certificate to that effect to the applicant developer. Certification is to take the form of a letter from the relevant local authority to the applicant developer:

– confirming that it is satisfied that the relevant commercial development located at a park and ride facility has been developed in accordance with the criteria and requirements set by the Minister for the Environment and Local Government for the purposes of Chapter 9 of Part 10 of the Taxes Consolidation Act 1997; and

– confirming that the requirements in section 372W(2)(c) of the Taxes Consolidation Act 1997 in relation to limits on allowable expenditure on commercial development located at a park and ride facility are met.

6.402   Construction or refurbishment of certain park and ride facilities

6.402.1 Accelerated capital allowances for qualifying park and ride facilities

TCA 1997, s 372V provides for accelerated capital allowances in respect of capital expenditure incurred in the qualifying period on the construction or refurbishment of qualifying park and ride facilities.

See **5.404** regarding the restriction by TCA 1997, s 270(4)-(6) of qualifying expenditure on a qualifying park and ride facility. In the case of expenditure incurred in the period 1 January 2007 to 31 December 2007, only 75% of expenditure incurred is treated as incurred, and in the case of expenditure incurred in the period 1 January 2008 to 31 July 2008, only 50% of expenditure incurred is treated as incurred.

The construction or refurbishment work must be carried out in the qualifying period. An initial allowance of 50% may be claimed by both lessors and owner-occupiers with annual allowances of 4% for the balance up to a maximum of 100% of the expenditure. Alternatively, in the case of owner-occupiers, an accelerated allowance, or free depreciation, of up to 100% may be claimed. Refurbishment expenditure qualifies for allowances only where the amount is at least 10% of the value of the premises before refurbishment. Where a park and ride facility is disposed of after 13 years, there is no clawback of allowances.

TCA 1997, s 372V(1) provides in general that all of the provisions in the Tax Acts relating to the making of allowances or charges in respect of capital expenditure incurred by a company on the construction or refurbishment of an industrial building or structure are, notwithstanding anything to the contrary therein, to apply as if a qualifying park and ride facility were, at all times at which it is a qualifying park and ride facility, a building or structure in respect of which an allowance falls to be made for the purposes of corporation tax under TCA 1997 Part 9 Ch 1 by reason of its use for a purpose specified in TCA 1997, s 268(1)(a) (ie, a mill, factory or other similar premises – see **5.401.1**).

An allowance under TCA 1997, s 372V(1) is to be made in respect of any capital expenditure incurred on the construction or refurbishment of a qualifying park and ride facility only in so far as that expenditure is incurred in the qualifying period (see **6.401.2**).

In general, the entitlement to an industrial building initial allowance arises under TCA 1997, s 271(2) where a person has incurred capital expenditure on the construction of a building or structure which is to be an industrial building or structure occupied for the purposes of a trade by the person who incurs the capital expenditure or by a lessee who occupies the property under a relevant lease (ie, a lease to which the relevant interest, as defined in TCA 1997, s 269, is reversionary). In the case of a company which is an owner-occupier, an initial allowance can be claimed in the accounting period in which the expenditure was incurred. In the case of a lessor company, the initial allowance may be claimed in the accounting period in which the tenancy commences. Where capital expenditure is incurred by a company prior to the commencement of trading, the expenditure is treated as if it were incurred on the day on which the company commences to trade (TCA 1997, s 316(3)).

The entitlement to an industrial building annual allowance arises under TCA 1997, s 272(2) where, at the end of an accounting period, a company is entitled to a relevant interest in the building and the building is in use as an industrial building.

For the purposes of the following discussion on the capital allowances available on industrial buildings under TCA 1997 Part 10 Ch 9, it is assumed that all of the conditions for obtaining the allowances as set out in TCA 1997 Part 9 Ch 1 as well as those in TCA 1997 Part 10 Ch 9 have been satisfied.

6.402.2 Allowances

Where a qualifying park and ride facility is newly constructed or refurbished, the following allowances are available:

owner-occupier:

- industrial building initial allowance 50% plus industrial building annual allowance 4%; or
- free depreciation up to 100% plus industrial building annual allowance 4% on any balance;

lessor:

- industrial building initial allowance 50% plus industrial building annual allowance 4%.

In the case of refurbishment expenditure, however, allowances may by claimed on the amount of expenditure incurred only if the total amount of the expenditure so incurred is not less than an amount which is equal to 10% of the market value of the building or structure immediately before that expenditure was incurred (TCA 1997, s 372V(2)).

In determining whether and to what extent capital expenditure incurred on the construction or refurbishment of a qualifying park and ride facility is or is not incurred in the qualifying period, only such an amount of that capital expenditure as is properly attributable to work on the construction or refurbishment of the qualifying park and ride facility actually carried out during the qualifying period may be treated as having been incurred in that period (TCA 1997, s 372V(5)).

6.402.3   Balancing allowances and charges

TCA 1997, s 274 provides that a balancing allowance or balancing charge is to be computed if, in relation to a qualifying premises in respect of which any capital allowances have been obtained, any of the following events occurs:

(a)   the relevant interest in the building is sold;

(b)   the relevant interest in the building is exchanged (TCA 1997, s 311(3));

(c)   the building is demolished or destroyed;

(d)   the building ceases altogether to be used;

(e)   the relevant interest, if it is a leasehold interest, either:

   (i)   comes to an end, otherwise than on the person entitled to it acquiring the reversionary interest, or

   (ii)   is surrendered for valuable consideration (TCA 1997, s 311(3)).

Where the qualifying park and ride facility is held for a period of at least 13 years from the date it was first used or, where TCA 1997, s 372V(4A) applies (see **6.402.4**), was first used as a qualifying park and ride facility, no balancing charge may be made (TCA 1997, s 372V(4)). The writing down life of the facility is nevertheless 25 years. Accordingly, while a balancing charge may not arise later than 13 years after the facility is first used or, where TCA 1997, s 276 applies (refurbishment expenditure – see **5.407.5**), later than 13 years after the expenditure was incurred, a balancing allowance may still be made at any time up to 25 years after the facility is first used, or, as the case may be, the refurbishment expenditure is incurred. Similarly, a purchaser of the property may still be entitled to capital allowances even where the purchase takes place more than 13 years after first use/expenditure incurred. Furthermore, the cessation of a qualifying trade is not an event requiring a balancing adjustment, provided the owner does not dispose of the relevant interest and so long as the building continues to be used for some purpose. The rules of TCA 1997, s 272(4) (new rate of allowance to write off residue of expenditure evenly over the rest of the writing down period of the expenditure – see **5.410**) apply also to park and ride facilities.

6.402.4   TCA 1997, s 372V in detail

The allowances as detailed above arise under TCA 1997, s 372V(1)-(3). These provisions refer to the underlying legislation of TCA 1997, s 271 (initial allowance) and TCA 1997, s 273 (free depreciation).

   TCA 1997, s 372V(1)(a) provides, subject to:

(a)   TCA 1997, s 372V(2) (minimum refurbishment expenditure incurred to be not less than 10% of market value of qualifying park and ride facility – see **6.402.2** above) and (3)-(4A) (see below);

(b)   TCA s 270(4)-(6) (only 75% of expenditure incurred in the period 1 January 2007 to 31 December 2007 is treated as incurred and only 50% of expenditure incurred in the period 1 January 2008 to 31 July 2008 is treated as incurred – see **5.404**); and

(c)   TCA 1997, s 316(2B) (only the amount of expenditure as is properly attributable to work actually carried out in a period may be treated as having been incurred in that period –see **5.404**), that all of the provisions of the Tax Acts relating to the making of allowances and charges in respect of the construction or refurbishment of an industrial building are to apply as if a qualifying park and ride facility were, at all times at which it is a qualifying park and ride facility, a building or structure in respect of which an allowance is to be made under the provisions relating to the making of industrial building allowances.

An allowance will be available as above in respect of any capital expenditure incurred on the construction or refurbishment of a qualifying park and ride facility only in so far as that expenditure is incurred in the qualifying period (TCA 1997, s 372V(1)(b)).

TCA 1997, s 372V(3)(a) provides that TCA 1997, s 271 is to have effect in relation to capital expenditure incurred in the qualifying period on the construction or refurbishment of a qualifying park and ride facility as if various references (not appropriate for the purposes of TCA 1997, s 372V) were deleted and as if TCA 1997, s 271(4) (rates of industrial building allowances) were substituted by a provision to the effect that the allowance is to be of an amount equal to 50% of the capital expenditure. TCA 1997, s 372V(2) accordingly secures that the 25% initial allowance rate will be available in respect of qualifying expenditure incurred in the qualifying period (see **6.401.2**) on buildings or structures in the qualifying areas.

TCA 1997, s 372V(3)(b) similarly provides that TCA 1997, s 273 is to have effect in relation to capital expenditure incurred in the qualifying period on the construction or refurbishment of a qualifying park and ride facility as if various references and provisions not appropriate for the purposes of TCA 1997, s 372V (eg, TCA 1997, s 273(3)-(7)) were deleted and also as if TCA 1997, s 273(2)(b) (phasing out of free depreciation) were deleted. Accordingly TCA 1997, s 372V(3)(b) secures that free depreciation of up to 100% is available for the purposes of the section.

The allowances available for qualifying park and ride facilities consist of an initial allowance of 50% or (for owner-occupiers) free depreciation of up to 100%, and an annual allowance of 4%. It is not possible to obtain allowances of 50% + 4% in one period. TCA 1997, s 271(5) provides that where an initial allowance has been made under TCA 1997, s 271 for any period, no annual allowance under TCA 1997, s 272 may be made for the same period nor may free depreciation be claimed in any subsequent period in respect of the same expenditure. TCA 1997, s 273(8) provides that where, for any chargeable period, a writing down allowance under TCA 1997, s 272 in respect of qualifying expenditure is increased under TCA 1997, s 273, no initial allowance under TCA 1997, s 271 may be made in respect of that expenditure for that or any subsequent chargeable period.

Delay in building or structure becoming a qualifying park and ride facility

Special provision is made in TCA 1997, s 372V(4A) for a case in which there is a delay in a building or structure becoming a qualifying park and ride facility because the necessary certificate was not received from the relevant local authority by reason of a delay in the provision of a train service to serve the building or structure. The application of the industrial building allowances provisions in these cases is adapted to take account of this delay and the resulting measures are discussed in the following paragraphs.

In a case falling within TCA 1997, s 372V(4A), an industrial building allowance may be claimed for the period in which the building or structure becomes a qualifying park and ride facility (instead of the period in which the expenditure is incurred) (TCA 1997, s 372V(4A)(a)(i)).

It is a condition of entitlement to an industrial building allowance that the building in question is in fact an industrial building when it first comes to be used (TCA 1997, s 271(6) – see **5.405.1**). In the circumstances dealt with in TCA 1997, s 372V(4A) as described above, that condition will be satisfied if the building or structure becomes a qualifying park and ride facility within five years of first becoming used (TCA 1997, s 372V(4A)(a)(ii)).

TCA 1997, s 272(4) provides that where the relevant interest in an industrial building or structure is sold while it is an industrial building or structure, the purchaser of the relevant interest is then entitled, so long as the building continues to be an industrial building, to writing down allowances based on the residue of the expenditure (as adjusted for any balancing allowance/charge). The rate of writing down allowance after the sale is the rate which is necessary to write off the residue of the expenditure on a straight line basis evenly over the rest of the writing down period of the expenditure (see **5.410.2**). For the purposes of TCA 1997, s 372V(4A), this provision applies by taking the full writing down period as commencing at the time the building or structure was first used as a qualifying park and ride facility (instead of at the time it was first used) (TCA 1997, s 372V(4A)(b)).

There can be no balancing allowance or charge on a sale or other event occurring after the end of the writing down period of a building or structure for which industrial building allowances have been given (TCA 1997, s 274(1)(b)(i)(II) – see **5.409.1**). For the purposes of TCA 1997, s 372V(4A), this provision applies on the basis that the writing down period commences at the time the building or structure was first used as a qualifying park and ride facility (instead of at the time it was first used) (TCA 1997, s 372V(4A)(c)(i)).

Where a balancing allowance or charge arises in the case of a building while it is an industrial building, and where there has been any period of non-industrial use since the first use of the building (or since any prior sale as an industrial building), TCA 1997, s 274(5)(b) provides that the balancing allowance or charge is to be reduced to allow for the fact that writing down allowances were not available for the period of non-industrial use. Where this happens, the balancing allowance or charge that would otherwise apply is first computed by comparing the residue of the expenditure (after actual and notional allowances) with the sale, insurance, salvage or compensation moneys. This "provisional" allowance or charge is then adjusted to arrive at the final balancing allowance or balancing charge. For the purposes of TCA 1997, s 372V(4A), this provision applies on the basis that the "relevant period" by reference to which the adjustment is made (see **5.411**) commences at the time the building or structure was first used as a qualifying park and ride facility (instead of at the time it was first used for any purpose) (TCA 1997, s 372V(4A)(c)(ii)).

For the purposes of the calculation of the "residue of expenditure", industrial building allowances are written off at the time the building is first used (TCA 1997, s 277 – see **5.409.2**). For the purposes of TCA 1997, s 372V(4A), the allowance is instead written off at the time the building or structure was first used as a qualifying park and ride facility (TCA 1997, s 372V(4A)(d)(i)).

Under TCA 1997, s 277(4), a notional writing down allowance is made in arriving at the residue of the expenditure if, for any period or periods after the date on which the building or structure "was first used for any purpose", it was not in use for the purposes of a qualifying trade or undertaking (see **5.411**). For the purposes of TCA 1997, s 372V(4A), this provision applies in the case of such non-use after the date on which the building or structure was first used as a qualifying park and ride facility (instead of at after the time it was first used for any purpose) (TCA 1997, s 372V(4A)(d)(ii)).

TCA 1997, s 279(2) permits industrial building allowances to be claimed where the building in question is bought within one year after it is first used (see **5.408.5**). For these allowances to be available, it is a condition that no other person has claimed any industrial building allowance in respect of the same building. For the purposes of TCA 1997, s 372V(4A), this provision applies by taking the one year period as running from the time the building or structure commences to be used as a qualifying park and ride facility (TCA 1997, s 372V(4A)(f)).

6.402.5   Prevention of double relief

Where an allowance is given under TCA 1997, s 372V in respect of capital expenditure incurred on the construction or refurbishment of a qualifying park and ride facility, no allowance may be given in respect of that expenditure under any other provision of the Tax Acts (TCA 1997, s 372V(6)).

6.402.6   Non-application of relief in certain cases

Property developers

Capital allowances may not be claimed under TCA 1997, s 372V by a property developer in respect of expenditure incurred on the construction or refurbishment of a qualifying park and ride facility. This prohibition applies:

(a)   where the property developer is entitled to the relevant interest (see **5.403**) in relation to the expenditure concerned; and

(b)   either the property developer or a person connected with (see **2.3**) the property developer incurred the expenditure on the construction or refurbishment of the qualifying park and ride facility concerned (TCA 1997, s 372V(2A)).

A *property developer* for this purpose is a person carrying on a trade which consists wholly or mainly of the construction or refurbishment of buildings or structures with a view to their sale.

6.403   Construction or refurbishment of commercial premises

6.403.1   Capital allowances for commercial premises

TCA 1997, s 372W provides for capital allowances in respect of capital expenditure incurred on the construction or refurbishment of certain commercial premises located on the site of a park and ride facility. The premises in question and the activity to be carried on there must be certified by the relevant local authority as complying with the guidelines in relation to the development of commercial activity at a qualifying park and ride facility. The scheme of allowances available is the same as that provided for park and ride facilities: an initial allowance of 50% or free depreciation up to 100%. There is, however, an overall restriction on the amount of capital expenditure on commercial premises which may qualify for capital allowances. Only expenditure which, when combined with expenditure on any residential accommodation at a park and ride facility, does not exceed 50% of total allowable expenditure at the facility will qualify for allowances.

See **5.404** regarding the restriction by TCA 1997, s 270(4)-(6) of qualifying expenditure on a qualifying commercial premises on the site of a park and ride facility. In the case of expenditure incurred in the period 1 January 2007 to 31 December 2007, only 75% of expenditure incurred is treated as incurred, and in the case of expenditure incurred in the period 1 January 2008 to 31 July 2008, only 50% of expenditure incurred is treated as incurred.

For the purposes of capital allowances available in respect of commercial premises, TCA 1997, s 372W(1) defines *qualifying premises* as a building or structure the site of which is wholly within the site of a qualifying park and ride facility and:

(a) in respect of which the relevant local authority gives to the person constructing or refurbishing the premises a certificate in writing stating that it is satisfied that the premises and the activity to be carried on in the premises complies with the requirements laid down in the guidelines in relation to the development of commercial activity at a qualifying park and ride facility;

(b) which is not otherwise an industrial building or structure within the meaning of TCA 1997, s 268(1); and

(c) (i) is in use for the purposes of the retailing of goods or the provision of services only within the State but excluding any building or structure in use as offices, or in use for the provision of mail order or financial services, or

    (ii) is let on bona fide commercial terms for such use as is referred to in (i) and for such consideration as might be expected to be paid in a letting of the building or structure negotiated on an arm's length basis,

but does not include any part of a building or structure in use as or as part of a dwelling house.

Although the definition of qualifying premises in TCA 1997, s 372W(1) excludes any part of a building which is in use as a dwelling house, there is no such exclusion in respect of any building or part of a building in use as an office. Where part of a building or structure is, and part is not a qualifying premises, the building or structure and every part of it is treated as a qualifying premises if the capital expenditure incurred in the qualifying period on the construction or refurbishment of the non-qualifying part is not more than 10% of the total capital expenditure which has been incurred in that period on the construction or refurbishment of the building or structure (TCA 1997, s 268(8)).

6.403.2 Basis for capital allowances

TCA 1997, s 372W(2) provides the basis for capital allowances in respect of capital expenditure incurred on the construction or refurbishment of a qualifying premises. That subsection provides that all of the provisions of the Tax Acts relating to the making of allowances or charges in respect of capital expenditure incurred on the construction or refurbishment of an industrial building or structure are to apply to construction or refurbishment expenditure on qualifying premises as defined in TCA 1997, s 372W(1).

The qualifying premises is treated as if it were, at all times at which it is a qualifying building, an industrial building as defined in TCA 1997, s 268(1)(a) (ie, a mill, factory or other similar premises) in respect of which an allowance may be made under TCA 1997, s 271 (initial allowance) or s 272 (annual allowance). Where the property is let, any activity carried on in the property which is not a trade is treated as if it were a trade (TCA 1997, s 372W(2)).

TCA 1997, s 372W(2)(c) provides for the overall restriction on the amount of capital expenditure which may qualify for capital allowances. Only expenditure on commercial premises which, when combined with expenditure on any residential accommodation at a park and ride facility, does not exceed 50% of total allowable expenditure at the facility will qualify for allowances. TCA 1997, s 372W(2)(c)(i) provides that an allowance is to be given under TCA 1997, s 372AP (see **6.504.2**) in respect of any capital expenditure incurred on the construction or refurbishment of a qualifying premises at a park and ride facility only in so far as that expenditure when aggregated with:

(I)   other capital expenditure, if any, incurred on the construction or refurbishment of other qualifying premises and in respect of which an allowance would, or would but for TCA 1997, s 372W(2)(c), be given; and

(II)   other expenditure, if any, in respect of which there is provision for a deduction to be made under TCA 1997, s 372AP (see **6.504**) or 372AR (allowance to individuals as owner-occupiers for certain expenditure on construction),

incurred at that park and ride facility, does not exceed 50% of the total capital expenditure incurred at that park and ride facility in respect of which an allowance or deduction is to be made or would, but for TCA 1997, s 372W(2)(c) or 372AP(5) (see **6.504.2**), be made by virtue of any provision of TCA 1997 Part 10 Chapter 9 (allowances for park and ride facilities and related developments) or Chapter 11 (relief for lessors of rented residential accommodation – see **6.502**).

TCA 1997, s 372W(2)(c)(ii) provides that where a person who has incurred capital expenditure on the construction or refurbishment of a qualifying premises at a park and ride facility and who claims to have complied with the requirements of TCA 1997, s 372(2)(c)(i) in relation to that expenditure, is to be deemed not to have so complied unless that person has received from the relevant local authority a certificate in writing issued by it stating that it is satisfied that those requirements have been met.

Allowances may not be given by virtue of TCA 1997, s 372W(2) in respect of any capital expenditure on the refurbishment of a qualifying premises unless the total amount of capital expenditure so incurred is not less than an amount equal to 10% of the market value of the qualifying premises immediately before that expenditure is incurred (TCA 1997, s 372W(3)).

Allowances may be given in respect of capital expenditure incurred on the construction or refurbishment of a qualifying premises only in so far as that expenditure is incurred in the qualifying period (TCA 1997, s 372W(2)(b)). In determining whether and to what extent capital expenditure incurred on the construction or refurbishment of a qualifying premises is or is not incurred in the qualifying period, only such an amount of that capital expenditure as is properly attributable to work on the construction or refurbishment of the premises actually carried out during the qualifying period may be treated as having been incurred in that period (TCA 1997, s 372W(6)).

6.403.3 Allowances

Where expenditure is incurred on the *construction or refurbishment* of a qualifying premises which is a building situated wholly within a park and ride facility, all of the provisions of the Tax Acts apply to the expenditure incurred as if it were expenditure on which capital allowances would be available under TCA 1997 ss 271 and 272, so that industrial building initial allowances, industrial building annual allowances and free depreciation are available in respect of the expenditure as if the property were a mill, factory or other similar premises. To qualify for the allowances the expenditure must, as already noted above, be incurred in the qualifying period (see **6.401.2**) and the work in respect of which the expenditure has been incurred must actually be carried out within that period.

The capital allowances available by virtue of TCA 1997, s 372W are as follows:

owner-occupier:

– industrial building initial allowance 50% plus industrial building annual allowance 4%; or

– free depreciation 100% plus (to the extent that free depreciation is not claimed) industrial building annual allowance 4%;

lessor:

– industrial building initial allowance 50% plus industrial building annual allowance 4%.

In the case of refurbishment expenditure, allowances may by claimed on the amount of expenditure incurred only if the total amount of the expenditure so incurred is not less than an amount which is equal to 10% of the market value of the building or structure immediately before that expenditure was incurred. Otherwise, no allowances will be available in respect of refurbishment expenditure.

6.403.4 Balancing charges

TCA 1997, s 372W(5) provides that no balancing charge may be made where the qualifying premises is held for a period of at least 13 years from the date it was first used or, where TCA 1997, s 372W(5A) applies (see **6.403.5**), was first used as a qualifying premises. The writing down life of the building is nevertheless 25 years. Accordingly, while a balancing charge may not arise later than 13 years after the building is first used or, where TCA 1997, s 276 applies (see **5.407.5**), later than 13 years after the expenditure was incurred, a balancing allowance may still be made at any time up to 25 years after the building is first used, or, as the case may be, the refurbishment expenditure is incurred. Similarly, a purchaser of the property may still be entitled to capital allowances even when the purchase takes place more than 13 years after first use/ expenditure incurred.

6.403.5 TCA 1997, s 372W in detail

The allowances as detailed above arise under TCA 1997, s 372W(4). This provision refers to the underlying legislative provisions of TCA 1997, s 271 (initial allowance) and TCA 1997, s 273 (free depreciation).

TCA 1997, s 372W(2)(a) provides, subject to:

(a)   TCA 1997, s 372W(2)(b) (need for expenditure to be incurred in qualifying period – see **6.403.2** above), (c) (overall restriction – see **6.403.2** above), (3) (refurbishment expenditure incurred to be not less than 10% of market value of qualifying premises – see **6.403.2** above), (4) and (5A) (see below), and (5) (balancing charges – see **6.403.4** above);

(b)   TCA s 270(4)-(6) (only 75% of expenditure incurred in the period 1 January 2007 to 31 December 2007 is treated as incurred and only 50% of expenditure incurred in the period 1 January 2008 to 31 July 2008 is treated as incurred – see **5.404**); nd

(c)   TCA 1997, s 316(2B) (only the amount of expenditure as is properly attributable to work actually carried out in a period may be treated as having been incurred in that period – see **5.404**),

that all of the provisions of the Tax Acts relating to the making of allowances and charges in respect of the construction or refurbishment of an industrial building are to apply:

(i)   as if a qualifying premises were at all times at which it is a qualifying premises a building or structure in respect of which an allowance is to be made under the provisions relating to the making of industrial building allowances; and

(ii)   where any activity carried on in the qualifying premises is not a trade, as if it were a trade.

TCA 1997, s 372W(4)(a) provides that TCA 1997, s 271 is to have effect in relation to qualifying capital expenditure incurred in the qualifying period on the construction or refurbishment of a qualifying premises as if various references (not relevant for the purposes of TCA 1997, s 372W) were deleted and as if TCA 1997, s 271(4) (rates of industrial building allowances) were substituted by a provision to the effect that the allowance is to be of an amount equal to 50% of the qualifying capital expenditure. TCA 1997, s 372D(4)(a) accordingly secures that the rate of initial allowance in respect of expenditure incurred in the qualifying period on qualifying premises in a park and ride facility will be 50%.

TCA 1997, s 372W(4)(b) similarly provides that TCA 1997, s 273 is to have effect in relation to qualifying capital expenditure as if various references and provisions of TCA 1997, s 273 (ie, TCA 1997, s 273(2)(b) (phasing out of free depreciation) and TCA 1997, s 273(3)-(7)) were deleted. Accordingly TCA 1997, s 372D(4)(b) secures the retention of free depreciation of up to 100% on expenditure in the qualifying period.

TCA 1997, s 271(5) provides that where an initial allowance has been made under TCA 1997, s 271 for any chargeable period, no annual allowance under TCA 1997, s 272 may be made for the same period nor may free depreciation be claimed in any subsequent period in respect of the same expenditure. TCA 1997, s 273(8) provides that where, for any chargeable period, a writing down allowance under TCA 1997, s 272 in respect of qualifying expenditure is increased under TCA 1997, s 273, no initial allowance under TCA 1997, s 271 may be made in respect of that expenditure for that or any subsequent chargeable period.

For the purposes of determining, in relation to a claim under TCA 1997, s 271 or 273 as applied by TCA 1997, s 372W, whether and to what extent capital expenditure incurred on the construction or refurbishment of an industrial building or structure is or is not incurred in the qualifying period, only such amount of that capital expenditure as is properly attributable to work carried out during the qualifying period may be treated as having been incurred in that period (TCA 1997, s 372W(6)).

Delay in building or structure becoming a qualifying premises

Special provision is made in TCA 1997, s 372W(5A) for cases in which a building or structure is not a qualifying premises because the relevant local authority is unable to give the certificate (referred to in **6.403.1** above) relating to compliance with certain requirements at a park and ride facility which would be a qualifying park and ride facility but for a delay in the provision of a train service to serve the facility. The application of the industrial building allowances provisions in these cases is adapted to take account of this delay and the resulting measures are discussed in the following paragraphs.

In a case falling within TCA 1997, s 372W(5A), an industrial building allowance may be claimed for the period in which the building or structure becomes a qualifying park and ride facility (instead of the period in which the expenditure is incurred) (TCA 1997, s 372W(5A)(a)(i)).

It is a condition of entitlement to an industrial building allowance that the building in question is in fact an industrial building when it first comes to be used (TCA 1997, s 271(6) – see **5.405.1**). In the circumstances dealt with in TCA 1997, s 372W(5A) as described above, that condition will be satisfied if the building or structure becomes a qualifying premises within five years of first becoming used (TCA 1997, s 372W(5A)(a)(ii)).

TCA 1997, s 272(4) provides that where the relevant interest in an industrial building or structure is sold while it is an industrial building or structure, the purchaser of the relevant interest is then entitled, so long as the building continues to be an industrial building, to writing down allowances based on the residue of the expenditure (as adjusted for any balancing allowance/charge). The rate of writing down allowance after the sale is the rate which is necessary to write off the residue of the expenditure on a straight line basis evenly over the rest of the writing down period of the expenditure (see **5.410.2**). For the purposes of TCA 1997, s 372W(5A), this provision applies by taking the full writing down period as commencing at the time the building or structure was first used as a qualifying premises (instead of at the time it was first used) (TCA 1997, s 372W(5A)(b)).

There can be no balancing allowance or charge on a sale or other event occurring after the end of the writing down period of a building or structure for which industrial building allowances have been given (TCA 1997, s 274(1)(b)(i)(II) – see **5.409.1**). For the purposes of TCA 1997, s 372W(5A), this provision applies on the basis that the writing down period commences at the time the building or structure was first used as a qualifying premises (instead of at the time it was first used) (TCA 1997, s 372W(5A)(c)(i)).

Where a balancing allowance or charge arises in the case of a building while it is an industrial building, and where there has been any period of non-industrial use since the first use of the building (or since any prior sale as an industrial building), TCA 1997, s 274(5)(b) provides that the balancing allowance or charge is to be reduced to allow for the fact that writing down allowances were not available for the period of non-industrial use. Where this happens, the balancing allowance or charge that would otherwise apply is first computed by comparing the residue of the expenditure (after actual and notional allowances) with the sale, insurance, salvage or compensation moneys. This "provisional" allowance or charge is then adjusted to arrive at the final balancing allowance or balancing charge. For the purposes of TCA 1997, s 372W(5A), this provision applies on the basis that the "relevant period" by reference to which the adjustment is made (see **5.411**) commences at the time the building or structure was first used as a qualifying premises (instead of at the time it was first used for any purpose) (TCA 1997, s 372W(5A)(c)(ii)).

For the purposes of the calculation of the "residue of expenditure", industrial building allowances are written off at the time the building is first used (TCA 1997, s 277 – see **5.409.2**). For the purposes of TCA 1997, s 372W(5A), the allowance is instead written off at the time the building or structure was first used as a qualifying park and ride facility (TCA 1997, s 372W(5A)(d)(i)).

Under TCA 1997, s 277(4), a notional writing down allowance is made in arriving at the residue of the expenditure if, for any period or periods after the date on which the building or structure "was first used for any purpose", it was not in use for the purposes of a qualifying trade or undertaking (see **5.411**). For the purposes of TCA 1997, s 372W(5A), this provision applies in the case of such non-use after the date on which the building or structure was first used as a qualifying premises (instead of at after the time it was first used for any purpose) (TCA 1997, s 372W(5A)(d)(ii)).

TCA 1997, s 279(2) permits industrial building allowances to be claimed where the building in question is bought within one year after it is first used (see **5.408.5**). For these allowances to be available, it is a condition that no other person has claimed any industrial building allowance in respect of the same building. For the purposes of TCA 1997, s 372W(5A), this provision applies by taking the one year period as running from the time the building or structure commences to be used as a qualifying park and ride facility (TCA 1997, s 372W(5A)(f)).

6.403.6 Prevention of double relief

Where an allowance is given under TCA 1997, s 372W in respect of capital expenditure incurred on the construction or refurbishment of a qualifying premises, no allowance may be given in respect of that expenditure under any other provision of the Tax Acts (TCA 1997, s 372W(7)).

6.403.7 Non-application of relief in certain cases

Property developers

Capital allowances may not be claimed under TCA 1997, s 372W by a property developer in respect of expenditure incurred on the construction or refurbishment of a qualifying premises. This prohibition applies:

(a) where the property developer is entitled to the relevant interest (see **5.403**) in relation to the expenditure concerned; and

(b) either the property developer or a person connected with (see **2.3**) the property developer incurred the expenditure on the construction or refurbishment of the qualifying premises concerned (TCA 1997, s 372W(3A)).

A *property developer* for this purpose is a person carrying on a trade which consists wholly or mainly of the construction or refurbishment of buildings or structures with a view to their sale.

6.5 RELIEF FOR LESSORS OF RENTED RESIDENTIAL ACCOMMODATION

6.501 Introduction
6.502 Definitions
6.503 Guidelines on residential developments for third level students
6.504 Rented residential accommodation: relief for lessors

6.501 Introduction

TCA 1997 Part 10, Chapter 11 (ss 372AK-372AT) provide for a "section 23" type relief for newly constructed, refurbished or converted residential property in the qualifying areas ("tax incentive" areas). Whereas reliefs for lessors of residential property were formerly provided for individually in the cases of the various urban renewal and other qualifying areas, TCA 1997 Part 10 Chapter 11, introduced by FA 2002, provides for a single relief for lessors of qualifying residential property in the tax incentive areas. A tax incentive area is:

    (a)   a qualifying urban area;
    (b)   a qualifying rural area;
    (c)   a qualifying town area;
    (d)   the site of a qualifying park and ride facility; or
    (e)   a qualifying student accommodation area.

The kind of expenditure to be incurred in respect of rented residential property and which qualifies for relief ("eligible expenditure") is construction, conversion or refurbishment expenditure and, whereas under the pre-FA 2002 regime, there was separate provision for each of these kinds of expenditure in the case of each of the incentive schemes, a single provision, TCA 1997, s 372AP, provides for the appropriate relief for all three kinds of expenditure and in respect of all of the tax incentive areas. Provision is also made for relief for owner-occupiers of residential property but as this applies to individuals only it is not dealt with here.

6.502 Definitions

Some of the more important definitions relating to the legislation providing for tax relief for lessors of residential accommodation are set out below. Other definitions appear where they are of more specific or direct relevance.

Certificate of compliance

A *certificate of compliance* is a certificate given by the Minister for the purposes of TCA 1997, s 372AP certifying that at the time of the grant and on the basis of the information available to the Minister at that time:

    (a)   the house to which the certificate relates complies—

        (i)   in the case of construction, with such conditions, if any, as may be determined by the Minister from time to time for the purposes of section 4 of the Housing (Miscellaneous Provisions) Act 1979, in relation to standards of construction of houses and the provision of water, sewerage and other services in houses,

    (ii)   in the case of conversion or refurbishment, with such conditions, if any, as may be determined by the Minister from time to time for the purposes of section 5 of the Housing (Miscellaneous Provisions) Act 1979, in relation to standards of improvement of houses and the provision of water, sewerage and other services in houses,

(b)   the total floor area of that house is within the relevant floor area limits specified in TCA 1997, s 372AM(4) (see **6.503** below); and

(c)   in the case of refurbishment, the refurbishment work was necessary for the purposes of ensuring the suitability as a dwelling of any house in the building or the part of the building and whether or not the number of houses in the building or the part of the building, or the shape or size of any such house, is altered in the course of such refurbishment (TCA 1997, s 372AM(1)(a)).

In the case of a house the site of which is wholly within a qualifying town area, the certificate may be given only where an application has been received by the Minister within one year from the day after the end of the qualifying period. In the case of a house the site of which is wholly within a qualifying student accommodation area, the certificate may be given having regard to the relevant guidelines.

Certificate of reasonable cost

A *certificate of reasonable cost* is a certificate given by the Minister for the purposes of TCA 1997, s 372AP certifying that at the time of the grant and on the basis of the information available to the Minister at that time:

(a)   the house to which the certificate relates complies—

    (i)   in the case of construction, with such conditions, if any, as may be determined by the Minister from time to time for the purposes of section 4 of the Housing (Miscellaneous Provisions) Act 1979, in relation to standards of construction of houses and the provision of water, sewerage and other services in houses,

    (ii)   in the case of conversion or refurbishment, with such conditions, if any, as may be determined by the Minister from time to time for the purposes of section 5 of the Housing (Miscellaneous Provisions) Act 1979, in relation to standards of improvement of houses and the provision of water, sewerage and other services in houses,

(b)   the amount specified in the certificate in relation to the cost of construction, conversion or refurbishment of or in relation to the house to which the certificate relates appears to the Minister to be reasonable;

(c)   the total floor area of that house is within the relevant floor area limits specified in TCA 1997, s 372AM(4) (see **6.503** below); and

(d)   in the case of refurbishment, the refurbishment work was necessary for the purposes of ensuring the suitability as a dwelling of any house in the building or the part of the building and whether or not the number of houses in the building or the part of the building, or the shape or size of any such house, is altered in the course of such refurbishment (TCA 1997, s 372AM(1)(a)).

In the case of a house the site of which is wholly within a qualifying town area, the certificate may be given only where an application has been received by the Minister within one year from the day after the end of the qualifying period. In the case of a house the site of which is wholly within a qualifying student accommodation area, the certificate may be given having regard to the relevant guidelines.

Conversion expenditure

Conversion expenditure means expenditure incurred on:

(a) the conversion into a house of—

    (i) a building which fronts on to a qualifying street or the site of which is wholly within a tax incentive area other than the site of a qualifying park and ride facility, or

    (ii) a part of a building which fronts on to a qualifying street or the site of which is wholly within a qualifying urban area or a qualifying town area,

    where the building or the part of the building has not been previously in use as a dwelling, and

(b) the conversion into two or more houses of—

    (i) a building which fronts on to a qualifying street or the site of which is wholly within a tax incentive area other than the site of a qualifying park and ride facility, or

    (ii) a part of a building which fronts on to a qualifying street or the site of which is wholly within a qualifying urban area or a qualifying town area,

    where before the conversion the building or the part of the building had not been in use as a dwelling or had been in use as a single dwelling (TCA 1997, s 372AN(2)).

Expenditure incurred on the conversion of a building or a part of a building includes expenditure incurred in the course of the conversion on either or both of the following:

(a) the carrying out of any works of construction, reconstruction, repair or renewal; and

(b) the provision or improvement of water, sewerage or heating facilities,

in relation to the building or the part of the building or any out office appurtenant to or usually enjoyed with that building or part, but does not include—

    (i) any expenditure in respect of which any person is entitled to a deduction, relief or allowance under any other provision of the Tax Acts; or

    (ii) any expenditure attributable to any part ("non-residential unit") of the building or the part of the building which on completion of the conversion is not a house (TCA 1997, s 372AN(3)).

In relation to (ii) above, where expenditure is attributable to a building or part of a building in general and not directly to any particular house or non-residential unit comprised in the building or the part of the building on completion of the conversion, such an amount of that expenditure is deemed to be attributable to a non-residential unit as bears to the whole of that expenditure the same proportion as the total floor area of the non-residential unit bears to the total floor area of the building or the part of the building (TCA 1997, s 372AN(4)).

Façade

In relation to a house, *façade*, means the exterior wall of the house which fronts on to a street.

House

House includes any building or part of a building used or suitable for use as a dwelling and any out-office, yard, garden or other land appurtenant to or usually enjoyed with that building or part of a building (TCA 1997, s 372AK(1)). Each separate residential unit that is, or may be, the subject of a separate lease is a "house" for the purposes of the relief, provided the maximum and minimum floor area requirements are met. A house may be a house in the normal sense, or a flat or a maisonette. In applying the floor areas limits, each separate residential unit, for example each flat in a block of flats or each apartment in an apartment complex, is considered separately.

Guidelines

Guidelines, in relation to a house the site of which is wholly within the site of a qualifying park and ride facility, has the same meaning as in TCA 1997, s 372U (see **6.401.3**).

Minister

Except where the context otherwise requires, *Minister* means the Minister for the Environment and Local Government.

Qualifying period

Qualifying period, in relation to:

(a)   a qualifying urban area means, subject to TCA 1997, s 372B (Ministerial order – see **6.101.3**), the period commencing on 1 August 1998 and ending on—

    (i)   31 December 2002, or

    (ii)   where TCA 1997, s 372AL(2) applies (certificate from the relevant local authority – see definition below), 31 December 2006, or

    (iii)   where TCA 1997, s 372AL(2) and (3) apply, 31 July 2008;

(b)   a qualifying street, means, subject to TCA 1997, s 372BA (Ministerial order – see **6.101.3**), the period commencing on 6 April 2001 and ending on 31 December 2004 or, where TCA 1997, s 372AL(1A) applies, ending on 31 December 2006 or, where TCA 1997, s 372AL(1A) and (3) apply, ending on 31 July 2008;

(c)   a qualifying rural area, means, for the purposes of TCA 1997 ss 372AP (relief for lessors – see **6.504.2**) and (in so far as it relates to that section) 372AS (determination of expenditure incurred in qualifying period and date expenditure treated as incurred – see **6.504.6**), the period commencing on 1 June 1998 and ending on 31 December 2004 or, where TCA 1997, s 372AL(1A) applies, ending on 31 December 2006 or, where TCA 1997, s 372AL(1A) and (3) apply, ending on 31 July 2008;

(d)   the site of a qualifying park and ride facility, means the period commencing on 1 July 1999 and ending on 31 December 2004 or, where TCA 1997, s 372AL(1A) applies, ending on 31 December 2006 or, where TCA 1997, s 372AL(1A) and (3) apply, ending on 31 July 2008;

(e) a qualifying town area, means, subject to TCA 1997, s 372AB (Ministerial order – see **6.301.3**), the period commencing on 1 April 2000 and ending on 31 December 2004 or, where TCA 1997, s 372AL(1A) applies, ending on 31 December 2006 or, where TCA 1997, s 372AL(1A) and (3) apply, ending on 31 July 2008;

(f) a qualifying student accommodation area, means the period commencing on 1 April 1999 and ending on—

   (i)   31 March 2003, or

   (ii) where TCA 1997, s 372AL(1A) applies, ending on 31 December 2006 or

   (iii) where TCA 1997, s 372AL(1A) and (3) apply, ending on 31 July 2008, and

(g) a special specified building, means the period commencing on 6 April 2001 and ending on 31 July 2008 (TCA 1997, s 372AL(1)).

In relation to (a)(ii) above, TCA 1997, s 372AL(2) applies where the relevant local authority gives a certificate in writing before 30 September 2003 to the person constructing, converting or refurbishing the building or part of the building, the site of which is wholly within the qualifying urban area, stating that it is satisfied that not less than 15% of the total cost of constructing, converting or refurbishing the building or the part of the building and the acquisition of the site thereof had been incurred on or before 30 June 2003, provided the application for the certificate is received by the authority on or before 31 July 2003. In considering whether to give a certificate, the relevant local authority must have regard only to guidelines issued by the Department of the Environment and Local Government in relation to the giving of such certificates (TCA 1997, s 372AL(2)).

TCA 1997, s 372AL(1A) applies, as respects capital expenditure incurred on the construction or refurbishment of a building or structure, if:

(a) (i)   a planning application (not being an application for outline permission within the meaning of section 36 of the Planning and Development Act 2000), in so far as planning permission is required, in respect of the construction or refurbishment work on the building or structure represented by that expenditure, is made in accordance with the Planning and Development Regulations 2001 to 2003,

     (ii) an acknowledgment of the application, confirming that it was received on or before 31 December 2004, is issued by the planning authority in accordance with article 26(2) of the Planning and Development Regulations 2001 (SI 600/2001), and

     (iii) the application is not an invalid application in respect of which a notice is issued by the planning authority in accordance with article 26(5) of those regulations,

(b) (i)   a planning application, in so far as planning permission was required, in respect of the construction or refurbishment work on the building or structure represented by that expenditure, was made in accordance with the Local Government (Planning and Development) Regulations 1994 (SI

86/1994), not being an application for outline permission within the meaning of article 3 of those regulations,

    (ii)   an acknowledgment of the application, confirming that it was received on or before 10 March 2002, was issued by the planning authority in accordance with article 29(2)(a) of the regulations mentioned in (i), and

    (iii)   the application was not an invalid application in respect of which a notice is issued by the planning authority in accordance with article 29(2)(b)(i) of those regulations, or

(c)   where the construction or refurbishment work on the building or structure represented by that expenditure is exempted development for the purposes of the Planning and Development Act 2000 by virtue of section 4 of that Act or by virtue of Part 2 of the Planning and Development Regulations 2001 (SI 600/2001) and—

    (i)   a detailed plan in relation to the development work is prepared,

    (ii)   a binding contract in writing, under which the expenditure on the development is incurred, is in existence, and

    (iii)   work to the value of 5% of the development costs is carried out,

not later than 31 December 2004.

TCA 1997, s 372AL(3) applies in relation to the construction, conversion or refurbishment of a building or part of a building which fronts on to a qualifying street or the site of which is wholly within a tax incentive area where:

(a)   the person constructing, converting or refurbishing the building or part of the building has, on or before 31 December 2006, carried out work to the value of not less than 15% of the actual construction, conversion or refurbishment costs of the building or part of the building; and

(b)   that person or, where the building or part of the building is sold by that person, the person who is claiming a deduction in relation to the expenditure can show that the condition in (a) was satisfied.

See **5.404** regarding the restriction by TCA 1997, s 270(4)-(6) of qualifying expenditure for buildings used for the trade of managing a sports-injury clinic. In the case of expenditure incurred in the period 1 January 2007 to 31 December 2007, only 75% of expenditure incurred is treated as incurred, and in the case of expenditure incurred in the period 1 January 2008 to 31 July 2008, only 50% of expenditure incurred is treated as incurred.

Refurbishment

Refurbishment means:

(a)   in relation to a building or part of a building other than a special specified building, either or both of the following—

    (i)   the carrying out of any works of construction, reconstruction, repair or renewal, and

    (ii)   the provision or improvement of water, sewerage or heating facilities, where the carrying out of such works or the provision of such facilities is certified by the Minister in any certificate of reasonable cost or certificate of compliance,

(b)   in relation to a façade, any works of construction, reconstruction, repair or renewal carried out in the course of the repair or restoration, or maintenance in the nature of repair or restoration, of a façade; and

(c)   in relation to a special specified building, any works of construction, reconstruction, repair or renewal, including the provision or improvement of water, sewerage or heating facilities, carried out in the course of the repair or restoration, or maintenance in the nature of repair or restoration, of the building or for the purposes of compliance with the requirements of the Housing (Standards for Rented Houses) Regulations 1993 (SI 1993/147).

Refurbishment expenditure

Refurbishment expenditure means expenditure incurred on:

(i)   the refurbishment of a specified building and, in the case of a specified building the site of which is wholly within a qualifying town area, the refurbishment of a façade; or

(ii)   the refurbishment of a special specified building (see below),

other than expenditure attributable to any part ("non-residential unit") of the building which on completion of the refurbishment is not a house (TCA 1997, s 372AN(5)(a)).

For the above purposes, where expenditure is attributable to the specified building or, as the case may be, the special specified building in general and not directly to any particular house or non-residential unit comprised in the building on completion of the refurbishment, such an amount of that expenditure is deemed to be attributable to a non-residential unit as bears to the whole of that expenditure the same proportion as the total floor area of the non-residential unit bears to the total floor area of the building or the part of the building (TCA 1997, s 372AN(5)(b)).

A *special specified building* is a building or part of a building:

(a)   in which before the refurbishment to which the refurbishment expenditure relates there is one or more than one house; and

(b)   which on completion of that refurbishment contains, whether in addition to any non-residential unit or not, one or more than one house.

A *specified building* is:

(a)   a building which fronts on to a qualifying street or the site of which is wholly within a tax incentive area other than the site of a qualifying park and ride facility; or

(b)   a part of a building which fronts on to a qualifying street or the site of which is wholly within a qualifying urban area or a qualifying town area, and in which before the refurbishment to which the refurbishment expenditure relates—

(i)   there is one or more than one house—

(I)   in the case of a building the site of which is wholly within a qualifying rural area, or

(II) in the case of a building or part of a building the site of which is wholly within a qualifying town area, and

(ii) there are two or more houses—

(I) in the case of a building or part of a building which fronts on to a qualifying street or the site of which is wholly within a qualifying urban area, or

(II) in the case of a building the site of which is wholly within a qualifying student accommodation area,

and which on completion of that refurbishment contains, whether in addition to any non-residential unit or not—

(A) in the case of a building or part of a building to which (i) above applies, one or more than one house,

(B) in the case of a building or part of a building to which (ii) above applies, two or more houses.

Relevant cost

Relevant cost is defined in TCA 1997, s 372AP(1) as the aggregate of:

(a) (i) where the eligible expenditure is on the construction of the house, the expenditure incurred on the acquisition of, or of rights in or over, any land on which the house is situated, or

(ii) where the eligible expenditure is conversion expenditure or refurbishment expenditure, the expenditure incurred on the acquisition of, or of rights in or over—

(I) any land on which the house is situated, and

(II) any building in which the house is comprised, and

(b) the expenditure actually incurred on the construction of, conversion into, or refurbishment of the house.

Relevant guidelines

The *relevant guidelines*, in relation to a house or building the site of which is wholly within a qualifying student accommodation area, means guidelines entitled "Guidelines on Residential Developments for 3rd Level Students" (see **6.503** below) issued by the Minister for Education and Science in consultation with the Minister and with the consent of the Minister for Finance, or such other guidelines amending or replacing those guidelines issued in accordance with TCA 1997, s 372AM(1)(c). TCA 1997, s 372AM(1)(c) provides that the Minister for Education and Science may, in relation to a house or building the site of which is wholly within a qualifying student accommodation area, in consultation with the Minister and with the consent of the Minister for Finance:

(a) issue guidelines for the purpose of the legislation providing for tax relief for lessors of residential accommodation and such guidelines may include provisions in relation to all or any on one or more of the following—

  (i)   the design and the construction of, conversion into, or refurbishment of, houses,

  (ii)   the total floor area and dimensions of rooms within houses, measured in such manner as may be determined by the Minister,

  (iii) the provision of ancillary facilities and amenities in relation to houses,

  (iv)   the granting of certificates of reasonable cost and of certificates of compliance,

  (v)   the designation of qualifying areas,

  (vi)   the terms and conditions relating to qualifying leases, and

  (vii) the educational institutions and the students attending those institutions for whom the accommodation is provided, and

  (b) amend or replace relevant guidelines in like manner.

Relevant local authority

Relevant local authority:

  (a) in relation to a qualifying urban area, means—

  (i)   the county council or the city council or the borough council or, where appropriate, the town council, within the meaning of the Local Government Act, 2001, in whose functional area the area is situated, or

  (ii)   the authorised company (within the meaning of section 3(1) of the Urban Renewal Act 1998) which prepared the integrated area plan (within the meaning of that section) in respect of the area, and

  (b) in relation to the construction of a house the site of which is wholly within the site of a qualifying park and ride facility and which is a qualifying premises for the purposes of the relief for lessors of residential accommodation, has the same meaning as in TCA 1997, s 372U(1) in relation to the construction or refurbishment of a park and ride facility or a qualifying premises within the meaning of TCA 1997, s 372W (see **6.401.2**).

Replacement building

Replacement building has the same meaning as in TCA 1997, s 372A (see **6.101.2**).

Street

Street includes part of a street and the whole or part of any road, square, quay or lane.

Tax incentive area

Tax incentive area means:

  (a) a qualifying urban area (see **6.101.3**);

  (b) a qualifying rural area (see **6.201.3**),

  (c) the site of a qualifying park and ride facility (see **6.401.2**);

  (d) a qualifying town area (see **6.301.3**); or

  (e) a qualifying student accommodation area (see **6.503**).

Total floor area

Total floor area means the total floor area of a house measured in the manner referred to in section 4(2)(b) of the Housing (Miscellaneous Provisions) Act, 1979.

6.503   Guidelines on residential developments for third level students

The definition of "relevant guidelines" refers to "Guidelines on Residential Developments for 3rd Level Students" and this is reproduced as follows:

Guidelines on Residential Development for Third Level Students

Section 50 of the Finance Act, 1999 provides for a scheme of tax relief for rented residential accommodation for third level students. The relief is along the lines of what is commonly referred to as section 23 relief. The Government attaches significance to this initiative, the purpose of which is the provision of additional rented accommodation to relieve current supply pressures in the private rented sector.

The legislation provides that 'relevant guidelines' may be issued by the Minister for Education and Science, in consultation with the Minister for the Environment and Local Government, with the consent of the Minister for Finance.

The following are the relevant guidelines. They are intended to assist developers and designers in formulating proposals for student residential development. They are not to be regarded as a substitute for appropriate professional advice on any project but should be of assistance in briefing professional advisers engaged on such projects.

The guidelines have been prepared with a view to ensuring that the overall standard of design and construction of accommodation being provided would promote the objectives of the Student Residential Accommodation tax incentives. The guidelines are issued without prejudice to the provisions of the Local Government (Planning and Development) Acts 1963-1998, the Building Regulations Act, 1998, any regulations made under those Acts, regulations under the Housing Acts relating to private rented housing accommodation and the relevant statutory local authority development plan. The design of student residential accommodation should also take into account the following Guides:- Fire Safety in Flats (1994), and Fire Safety in Hostels (1998), which have been published by the Minister for the Environment and Local Government pursuant to the Fire Services Act, 1981.

Planning authorities are asked to have regard to these guidelines in assessing applications received on or after 1 April 1999.

2. Definitions

For the purpose of these Guidelines—

An "educational institution" means:

> an institution in the State which provides courses to which a scheme approved by the Minister for Education and Science under the Local Authorities (Higher Education Grants) Acts 1968 to 1992 applies; or

> an institution which offers an approved course for the purposes of tax relief under section 474 of the Taxes Consolidation Act, 1997.

See Appendix 1 for list of such educational institutions.

A *"student"* means a person who is a registered student of, and is pursuing a course of study on a full-time basis at an educational institution.

A *"qualifying development"* means a development of at least 20 bed spaces which complies with the requirements of these guidelines, and in respect of which a letter has been certified by an educational institution. Such a letter of certification will include—

(a)   the name of the individual/company which owns the development;

(b)   the number of units and bed spaces to be provided for the use of students at the certifying educational institution.

This letter of certification will be requested where any claim for relief is subject to a Revenue audit.

"The scheme" means the scheme of tax relief for rented student accommodation introduced by section 50 of the Finance Act, 1999.

3. Qualifying Areas

Properties qualifying for relief under the scheme should be located within qualifying areas. For the purposes the scheme qualifying areas are:

(1)   Campus areas of the educational institutions; or

(2)   Areas, within an 8 km radius of the main campus, which are approved by the certifying educational institution as being an area within which a qualifying development may take place.

4. Consultation

In order to ensure orderly development there should be early consultation with, and approval by, an educational institution for any proposed development.

5. Qualifying Leases

A lease under the scheme shall comply with the following requirements:

Where the lease is for the whole of an academic year—

(a)   the lease, in writing, governed by the provisions of the Landlord and Tenant code, of a unit in a qualifying development shall be granted to students of the certifying educational institution; or

(b)   the lease shall be granted to the certifying educational institution which subsequently on-lets the units in the qualifying development to students in accordance with the institution's normal policy for letting residential accommodation.

The academic year means the academic year of a course, including any examinations in connection with a course being pursued by the student by whom the unit is occupied.

Owners of qualifying developments should be in a position to provide evidence of letting to students. This evidence will be requested where any claim for relief is subject to a Revenue audit.

Such owners may let the units to non-students for periods outside of the academic year of the certifying institution.

These requirements apply for ten years from the date the property is first let to students.

6. Total Floor Areas of Qualifying Premises

Accommodation under the scheme shall be provided by groupings of study bedrooms in "house" units. Each unit shall consist of a minimum of 3 bed spaces and an overall minimum gross floor area of 55 sq metres, up to a maximum of 8 bed spaces and a maximum of 160 sq metres.

Study bedrooms shall be arranged in units sharing a common entrance hall and kitchen/living room. Rooms shall have reasonable shapes and proportions and have adequate space for normal living purposes. Accurate adult sized furniture shall be indicated on layout plans.

Units shall in turn share common entrances, access stairs and corridors, and ancillary facilities.

6.1 Kitchen/Living room

The provision of shared kitchen/dining/living room space shall be based on a minimum of 4 sq metres per bed space in the unit. This shall be in addition to any shared circulation. At a minimum, basic kitchen units, with sink, cooker and fridge shall be installed.

6.2 Bedrooms

These will be used as study bedrooms requiring desk space, and storage. Therefore, one of the following minimum areas shall apply depending on provision of bathroom facilities:

> Single study bedroom 8 sq metres;
>
> Single study bedroom with en suite shower, toilet and basin 12 sq metres;
>
> Twin study bedroom 15 sq metres;
>
> Twin study bedroom with en suite shower, toilet and basin 18 sq metres;
>
> Single Disabled study bedroom;
>
> with en suite disabled shower, toilet and basin 15 sq metres.

6.3 Bathrooms

These shall be either en suite with the study bedrooms or separately provided to serve a maximum of 3 bed spaces. Bathrooms shall have adult sized sanitary fittings, consisting of wash hand basin, water closet, and shower/bath, with sufficient room to ensure ergonomically adequate spacing in the layout.

6.4 Circulation and Storage

In addition to the above minimum requirements an adequate entrance hallway and circulation space shall be provided within each unit. A hot press/store should also be provided to facilitate use of the unit.

7. Site Planning

The planning and design of developments should take account of the nature and character of the area in which they are located. The completed development should make a positive contribution to the built environment and develop the integration of students into the wider community where located off campus. Necessary security arrangements should be planned in a way which avoids isolating developments from the surrounding community.

The disposition of blocks of residential accommodation on the site and the layout of accommodation within each block should be designed to give optimum orientation in terms of daylight and sunlight to habitable rooms. Regard should be had to the likely level of noise from adjoining sources in determining the optimum location and detailed design of, in particular, study bedrooms within units.

Where not located on campus, adequate open space should be provided within developments for the amenity of students. Where the limitations of sites do not allow for small parks or gardens, alternative provisions should be incorporated in developments through a combination of terraced open space/roof gardens, and/or balconies with good landscaping where appropriate.

Densities should be in line with the draft residential density guidelines with due regard to type of location and to the safeguards set out in the guidelines.

8. Communal Facilities and Amenities

Communal facilities to service the needs of student residents should be provided for. The definition of qualifying developments includes "house" units and ancillary spaces including: caretaker/security office and apartment; centralised storage; laundry facilities; drying rooms and utility rooms; and a seminar room. The floor area of these facilities shall not exceed 12% of the total area of the development, and their cost shall not exceed 12% of the total qualifying expenditure.

Due consideration should be given to the needs of disabled students in the location, layout and design of any communal facilities.

Developments should include reasonable provision for secure bicycle storage within the site.

Facilities for the handling, storage and collection of refuse should be provided with access for frequent collection. Such facilities should be conveniently located, well ventilated and comply with all fire safety and public health requirements. As a general guide in determining storage capacity required, an output of 0.1 cubic metres of refuse per unit per week may be assumed.

9. Internal Design and Layout

Entrance hallways and corridors in developments should be well designed with good lighting and ventilation. Vertical and horizontal circulation should be arranged so that corridors do not extend more than 15 metres from a widened "landing" area which should include natural lighting where possible. Corridors should be widened at entrances to apartments.

Service ducts serving two or more apartments should as far as practicable be accessible from common circulation areas for maintenance purposes.

The number of apartment units per lift/core in a development should not exceed a maximum of 30.

10. Disabled Access and Provision of Accessible Bedrooms

Developments should provide a minimum of one out of every fifty, or part thereof, of the total number of bed spaces in a development designed for students with disabilities. These study bedrooms shall be fully wheelchair accessible complete with ensuite bathroom facilities.

Part M of the Building Regulations, 1997, sets out the legal requirements in relation to access to and use of building facilities by disabled persons. Part M of the regulations applies to public buildings and the common areas of apartment blocks. It is proposed to extend Part M to require new dwellings commencing on or after the 1st January, 2000 to be visitable by the disabled. The design of residential accommodation for students should take this pending development of Part M into account.

11. Data Connection

Internet services shall be made available to each student study bed space, as a standard Ethernet connection (10 BASET). A minimum bandwidth of 64kb/s shall be provided by an Internet Service Provider (ISP) per each 30 student bed spaces.

12. Certificate of Reasonable Cost

Anybody, other than in the case of a new unit purchased from a builder, wishing to claim tax relief under the scheme will require a Certificate of Reasonable Cost in relation to the particular development. The claimant may be required to provide this certificate to the Revenue Commissioners in support of a claim.

A Certificate of Reasonable Cost certifies that the cost of providing the accommodation is reasonable, that the accommodation is within the specified floor area limits (55 to 160 sq metres per unit), and that it complies with the standards set out in these guidelines. In the case of refurbishment projects it also certifies that the work was necessary to ensure the suitability as dwellings of the accommodation.

In the case of refurbishment, to obtain tax relief it is necessary that the Department of the Environment and Local Government certifies that the work was necessary to ensure the suitability as dwellings of the accommodation.

Accordingly, application in respect of a refurbishment project should be made before commencement of work so that a prior inspection of the building can be carried out.

12.1. Application

To apply for a Certificate of Reasonable Cost a completed form HPF/1 must be returned, together with the appropriate documentation and fee, to the Department of the Environment and Local Government, Housing Grants Section, Room F9/10, Government Offices, Ballina, Co. Mayo.

Each application for a Certificate of Reasonable Cost must be accompanied by the following:

(a) Drawings of student residential accommodation to scale 1:50 showing floor plans, sections and elevations (fully dimensioned);

(b) Site plan showing location of site, layout of site numbers and north point, with accommodation units delineated;

(c) Detailed specification of construction;

(d) Copy of planning permission and fire safety certificate;

(e) Breakdown of costs:
1. Where works are executed by the applicant, details of materials and labour cost plus any other expenses incurred.
2. Where work is carried out under contract, details of tender, design fees, etc., and copy of final account.

The Department of the Environment and Local Government, at all times, reserves the right to request a Bill of Quantities.

12.2 Fees

A fee of £50 for unit 1 plus £20 for each additional unit is payable in respect of an application for a Certificate of Reasonable Cost. A separate application is requested for each different construction cost claimed and for each different dwelling type (ie, to which different plans and specifications apply).

Appendix 1

List of Educational Institutions

University College Cork – National University of Ireland Cork;

University College Dublin, National University of Ireland Dublin;
National University of Ireland, Galway;
National University of Ireland, Maynooth;
Trinity College Dublin;
Dublin City University;
University of Limerick;
Pontifical University of Maynooth;
National College of Art & Design, Dublin;
National College of Ireland;
Athlone Institute of Technology;
Institute of Technology, Carlow;
Cork Institute of Technology;
Dundalk Institute of Technology;
Galway-Mayo Institute of Technology;
Letterkenny Institute of Technology;
Limerick Institute of Technology;
Institute of Technology, Sligo;
Institute of Technology, Tallaght;
Institute of Technology, Tralee;
Waterford Institute of Technology;
Dublin Institute of Technology;
Dún Laoghaire Institute of Art, Design & Technology;
Church of Ireland College of Education, Dublin;
Coláiste Mhuire, Marino, Dublin;
Mary Immaculate College, Limerick;
St. Angela's College, Lough Gill, Sligo;
St. Catherine's College, Sion Hill, Dublin;
St. Patrick's College of Education, Drumcondra, Dublin;
Froebel College of Education, Sion Hill, Dublin;
Mater Dei Institute of Education;
Milltown Institute of Theology and Philosophy, Dublin;
All Hallows College, Drumcondra;
St. Patrick's College, Carlow;
Royal College of Surgeons in Ireland;
The Law Society of Ireland, Blackhall Place;
The Honourable Society of Kings Inns;
Montessori College, (AMI) Mount St Mary's, Dundrum Road, Milltown, Dublin 14;
Dublin Business School, Dublin 2;
The American College, Dublin;
Griffith College Dublin, Dublin 8;
Clonliffe College, Dublin;
Holy Ghost College, Kimmage Manor;
HSI College, Limerick;
Portobello College, Dublin 2;
LSB College;
Mid West Business Institute, Limerick;
Montessori Education Centre (North Great George's Street);
Shannon College of Hotel Management;
Skerrys Business College, Cork;
St. John's College, Waterford;
St. Nicholas Montessori College, Dun Laoghaire;
St. Patrick's College, Thurles;

St. Peter's College, Wexford;

6.504 Rented residential accommodation: relief for lessors

6.504.1 Introduction

TCA 1997, s 372AP provides for a "section 23" type relief for newly constructed, converted or refurbished residential property in the tax incentive areas. The relief, first introduced by FA 1981 s 23 and which applied throughout the country until 31 March 1992 (or 31 July 1992 in certain cases) and in areas designated under the various renewals incentive measures, has been retained broadly intact in respect of newly constructed rented residential accommodation in qualifying

6.504.2 The relief

TCA 1997, s 372AP provides, in the case of eligible expenditure on or in relation to a house which is a qualifying premises or a special qualifying premises which is let and which meets all of the requirements of TCA 1997 ss 372AM, 372AP and 372AS, that relief will be given to the lessor of the property in respect of the qualifying cost of the property. Relief is given for so much of the expenditure as is treated under TCA 1997, s 372AP or 372AS(1) as having been incurred in the qualifying period.

Under TCA 1997, s 372AP(2), the qualifying cost of the property is treated, for the purposes of calculating the surplus rent or deficiency arising on the letting of the property, as a deduction authorised by the provisions of TCA 1997, s 97(2). In other words, the qualifying cost of the property is treated in the lessor's Case V computation in the same way as other authorised deductions such as interest on money borrowed for the purchase, improvement or repair of the premises, service charges paid by the lessor, and expenditure on repairs. As provided for in TCA 1997, s 97(1), any deficiency arising on the rental property may be set off against surpluses arising on other rental properties. Under TCA 1997, s 384(2), any remaining deficiency is carried forward to the subsequent accounting period and may be set off against rental income, both from the particular qualifying premises and from other rental properties. The deficiency is carried forward indefinitely until fully utilised against Case V rental surpluses in future periods.

In the case of eligible expenditure which is refurbishment expenditure in relation to a special qualifying premises:

(a) the deduction is to be given—

    (i) for the accounting period in which the expenditure is incurred or, if the special qualifying premises was not let under a qualifying lease during that period, the accounting period in which occurs the date of the first such letting after the expenditure is incurred, and

    (ii) for any subsequent accounting period in which that premises continues to be a special qualifying premises, and

(b) the deduction for each such accounting period will be an amount equal to 15% of the expenditure to which TCA 1997, s 372AP(2) refers (TCA 1997, s 372AP(3)(a)).

For the above purpose, the aggregate amount deductible may not exceed 100% of the expenditure to which TCA 1997, s 372AP(2) refers and, where an accounting period consists of a period of less than one year, the deduction is proportionately reduced (TCA 1997, s 372AP(3)(b)).

In the case of a qualifying park and ride facility, TCA 1997, s 372AP(5)(a) provides that relief for eligible expenditure is to be allowed only in so far as that expenditure, when aggregated with other eligible expenditure, if any, incurred on other qualifying premises at the facility and for which a deduction is or would otherwise be made, does not exceed 25% of the total expenditure incurred at the facility in respect of which an allowance or deduction is to be made or would but for TCA 1997, s 372AP(5)(a) or 372W(2)(c) (see **6.403.2**) be made by virtue of TCA 1997 Part 4 Chapter 9 (Park and Ride Facilities) or 10 (Town Renewal Relief). A company claiming to have complied with this condition will be deemed not to have so complied unless it has received from the relevant local authority (see **6.502**) a certificate in writing issued by that authority stating that it is satisfied that those requirements have been met (TCA 1997, s 372AP(5)(b)).

Where a qualifying premises or a special qualifying premises forms a part of a building or is one of a number of buildings in a single development, or is part of a building which is one of a number of buildings in a single development, TCA 1997, s 372AP(6) allows for such apportionment "as is necessary":

(a)   of the eligible expenditure incurred on the construction, conversion or refurbishment in relation to that building or those buildings; and

(b)   of the amount which would be the relevant cost in relation to that building or those buildings if the building or buildings were a single qualifying premises,

for the purposes of determining the eligible expenditure incurred on or in relation to the qualifying premises or the special qualifying premises and the relevant cost in relation to the qualifying premises or the special qualifying premises.

Expenditure in respect of which relief under TCA 1997, s 372AP is available does not include any expenditure in respect of which any person is entitled to a deduction, relief or allowance under any other provision of the Tax Acts (TCA 1997, s 372AP(11)).

Expenditure will not be regarded as incurred by a person insofar as it has been or is to be met, directly or indirectly, by the State, by any board established by statute or by any public or local authority (TCA 1997, s 372AP(12)).

TCA 1997, s 555 applies (see **3.209.4** and **9.102.17**) as if a deduction under TCA 1997, s 372AP were a capital allowance and as if any rent deemed to have been received by a person were a balancing charge (TCA 1997, s 372AP(13)).

No relief will be available under TCA 1997, s 372AP in respect of any conversion or refurbishment expenditure unless planning permission, in so far as it is required, in respect of the conversion or the work carried out in the course of the refurbishment has been granted under the Local Government (Planning and Development) Acts 1963 to 1999, or the Planning and Development Act 2000 (TCA 1997, s 372AP(14)).

6.504.3   Qualifying premises

A house is a *qualifying premises* where:

(a)   it fronts on to a qualifying street (see **6.101.3**) or is comprised in a building or part of a building which fronts on to a qualifying street, or the site of the house is wholly within a tax incentive area;

(b)   it is used solely as a dwelling;

(c)   it complies with the requirements relating to total floor area (see below);

(d)   in respect of the house, there is in force—

   (i)   a certificate of compliance or,

   (ii)   if it is not a house provided for sale, a certificate of reasonable cost the amount specified in which in respect of the cost of construction, conversion or refurbishment of or in relation to the house is not less than the expenditure actually incurred on such construction, conversion or refurbishment,

   but where refurbishment expenditure relates solely to the refurbishment of a façade, this condition does not apply,

(e)   in the case of a house the site of which is wholly within the site of a qualifying park and ride facility, the relevant local authority gives to the person constructing the house a certificate in writing stating that it is satisfied that the house or, in the case where the house is one of a number of houses in a single development, the development of which it is part complies with the requirements laid down in the guidelines in relation to the development of certain residential accommodation at a park and ride facility; and

(f)   the house—

   (i)   if the eligible expenditure has been incurred on the construction of the house, without having been used is first let in its entirety under a qualifying lease,

   (ii)   if the eligible expenditure incurred is conversion expenditure in relation to the house, without having been used subsequent to the incurring of the expenditure on the conversion is first let in its entirety under a qualifying lease, and

   (iii)   if the eligible expenditure incurred is refurbishment expenditure in relation to the house, on the date of completion of the refurbishment to which the expenditure relates, is let (or, if not let on that date, is, without having been used after that date, first let) in its entirety under a qualifying lease,

   and thereafter throughout the remainder of the "relevant period" (see below) (except for reasonable periods of temporary disuse between the ending of one qualifying lease and the commencement of another such lease) continues to be let under such a lease (TCA 1997, s 372AM(2)).

TCA 1997, s 372AM(4) sets out the requirements relating to *total floor area*. A house is not a qualifying premises unless:

(a)   where the house fronts on to a qualifying street or is comprised in a building or part of a building which fronts on to a qualifying street, or where its site is wholly within—

   (i)   a qualifying urban area, or

   (ii)   the site of a qualifying park and ride facility,

   the total floor area of the house is not less than 38 square metres and not more than 125 square metres,

(b) where the site of the house is wholly within a qualifying rural area, the total floor area of the house is not less than 38 square metres and—

(i) not more than 140 square metres if the eligible expenditure incurred was incurred on the construction of the house before 6 December 2000,

(ii) not more than 150 square metres if the eligible expenditure incurred on or in relation to the house was conversion expenditure or refurbishment expenditure incurred before 6 December 2000, or

(iii) not more than 175 square metres if the eligible expenditure incurred on or in relation to that house was or is incurred on or after 6 December 2000, and

(c) where the site of the house is wholly within a qualifying town area, the total floor area of the house is not less than 38 square metres and—

(i) not more than 125 square metres, or

(ii) not more than 150 square metres if the eligible expenditure incurred on or in relation to the house is conversion expenditure or refurbishment expenditure incurred on or after 6 April 2001, and

(d) where the site of the house is wholly within a qualifying student accommodation area, the total floor area of the house complies with the requirements of the relevant guidelines.

The *relevant period* throughout which the premises must be let for the purposes of (f) in the definition of "qualifying premises" above means—

(a) where the eligible expenditure is incurred on the construction of, or in relation to the conversion of a building into, a qualifying premises, the period of 10 years commencing with the date of the first letting of the qualifying premises under a qualifying lease; and

(b) where—

(i) the eligible expenditure incurred is refurbishment expenditure in relation to a qualifying premises or a special qualifying premises, the period of 10 years commencing with the date of the completion of the refurbishment to which the refurbishment expenditure relates, or

(ii) the qualifying premises or the special qualifying premises was not let under a qualifying lease on the date referred to in (i), the period of 10 years commencing with the date of the first such letting after the date of such completion.

A house which fronts on to a qualifying street, or which is comprised in a building or part of a building which fronts on to a qualifying street, will not be a qualifying premises unless—

(i) the house is comprised in the upper floor or floors of an existing building (see below) or a replacement building (see definition in **6.502**); and

(ii) the ground floor of such building is in use for commercial purposes, or, where it is temporarily vacant, it is subsequently so used (TCA 1997, s 372AM(8)).

An *existing building* is a building or structure which fronts on to a qualifying street and which existed on 13 September 2000.

A house is not a qualifying premises if—

(a)   it is occupied as a dwelling by any person connected with (see **2.3**) the person entitled to a deduction under that section in respect of the eligible expenditure incurred on or in relation to the house; and

(b)   the terms of the qualifying lease in relation to the house are not such as might have been expected to be included in the lease if the negotiations for the lease had been at arm's length (TCA 1997, s 372AM(5)).

A house the site of which is wholly within a qualifying rural area is not a qualifying premises unless, throughout the period of any qualifying lease related to that house, it is used as the sole or main residence of the lessee in relation to that qualifying lease (TCA 1997, s 372AM(7)).

A house the site of which is wholly within a qualifying student accommodation area is not a qualifying premises unless throughout the relevant period it is used for letting to and occupation by students in accordance with the relevant guidelines (TCA 1997, s 372AM(9)).

As an anti-avoidance measure, additional conditions must be satisfied so that a house can be treated as qualifying student accommodation for the purposes of relief. All of the rent in respect of the letting of the house during the ten-year holding period for the relief must be paid to the investor. No other person may receive or be entitled to receive that rent or any part of that rent. Where the expenditure on the provision of the house is incurred by two or more investors, the share of the rent received by each of them must bear the same proportion to the total rent as the expenditure incurred by that investor on the provision of the house bears to the total expenditure incurred on such provision by all the investors.

Where borrowed money is used by an investor to fund the provision of the house, that money must have been borrowed from a financial institution and from no other person. The investor must be personally responsible for the repayment of the loan, the payment of interest on the loan and the provision of any security required in relation to the loan, Furthermore, there must be no arrangement or agreement, whether or not known to the lender, whereby some other person agrees to be responsible for the obligations of the investor in relation to the loan.

Where the investor claims a tax deduction for management or letting fees payable in relation to the letting of the house, such fees must be bona fide fees that reflect the level and extent of the services provided and must not exceed an amount equal to 15% of the rent from the letting of the house.

The detailed provisions of the anti-avoidance measure in TCA 1997, s 372AM(9A), summarised above, are as follows. A house, the site of which is wholly within a qualifying student accommodation area will not be a qualifying premises or a special qualifying premises:

(a)   (i)   if any person other than the person (the "investor") who incurred or, is treated by virtue of TCA 1997, s 372AP(8) (see **6.504.11**), (9) (see **6.504.9**) or (10) (see **6.504.8**), is treated a having incurred eligible expenditure on or in relation to the house, receives or is entitled to receive the rent, or any part of the rent, from the letting of the house during the relevant period in relation to the house, or

    (ii)   where two or more investors have incurred or, by virtue of TCA 1997, s 372AP(8)-(10), are treated as having incurred eligible expenditure on or in relation to the house, unless part of the gross rent received or receivable from the letting of the house during the relevant period in relation to the house that is received or receivable by each investor bears the same proportion to that gross rent as the amount of the eligible expenditure that is incurred, or is so treated as having been incurred, on or in relation to the house by that investor bears to the total amount of the eligible expenditure that is incurred, or is so treated as having been incurred, on or in relation to the house by all such investors,

  (b)   where borrowed money is employed by an investor in the construction of, conversion into, refurbishment of, or, as the case may be, purchase of, the house, unless—

    (i)   that borrowed money is borrowed directly by the investor from a financial institution (see below),

    (ii)   the investor is personally responsible for the repayment of, the payment of interest on, and the provision of any security required in relation to, that borrowed money, and

    (iii)   there is no arrangement or agreement, whether in writing or otherwise and whether or not the person providing that borrowed money is aware of such agreement or arrangement, whereby any other person agrees to be responsible for any of the investor's obligations referred to in (ii),

  (c)   where management or letting fees payable to a person in relation to the letting of the house are claimed by the investor as a deduction under TCA 1997, s 97(2) (see **3.209.3**) for any chargeable period ending in the relevant period in relation to the house, unless—

    (i)   such fees are shown by the claimant to be bona fide fees that reflect the level and extent of the services rendered by the person, and

    (ii)   the aggregate amount of such fees for that chargeable period is not more than an amount equal to 15% of the gross amount of the rent received or receivable by the investor from the letting of the house for that period (TCA 1997, s 372AM(9A)).

Neither (a) nor (b) above will apply as respects eligible expenditure incurred in relation to a house or, where TCA 1997, s 372AP(9) (see **6.504.9**) or (10) (see **6.504.8**) applies, as respects expenditure incurred on the purchase of a house where, before 6 February 2003, the Revenue Commissioners have given an opinion in writing to the effect that the lease between the investor and an educational institution referred to in the relevant guidelines (see **6.503**), or a subsidiary of such an institution, would be a qualifying lease (TCA 1997, s 372AM(9C)).

A *financial institution* for the purposes of (a) above is:

  (i)   a person who holds or has held a licence under s 9 of the Central Bank Act 1971;

  (ii)   a person referred to in s 7(4) of the Central Bank Act 1971; or

  (iii)   a credit institution (within the meaning of the European Communities (Licensing and Supervision of Credit Institutions) Regulations 1992 (SI 1992/

395)) which has been authorised by the Central Bank of Ireland to carry on business of a credit institution in accordance with the provisions of the supervisory enactments (within the meaning of those Regulations).

A house is not a qualifying premises unless persons authorised in writing by the Minister for the purposes of those provisions are permitted to inspect the house at all reasonable times on production, if so requested by a person affected, of their authorisation (TCA 1997, s 372AM(11)).

A house:

(i) which fronts on to a qualifying street or is comprised in a building or part of a building which fronts on to a qualifying street; or

(ii) the site of which is wholly within a qualifying urban area or a qualifying town area,

is not a qualifying premises unless it or, where it is one of a number of houses in a single development, the development of which it is a part complies with such guidelines as may be issued from time to time by the Minister, with the consent of the Minister for Finance, for the purpose of furthering the objectives of urban renewal (TCA 1997, s 372AM(6)(a)). Such guidelines may include provisions in relation to all or any one or more of the following:

(i) the design and the construction of, conversion into, or refurbishment of houses;

(ii) the total floor area and dimensions of rooms within houses, measured in such manner as may be determined by the Minister;

(iii) the provision of ancillary facilities and amenities in relation to houses; and

(iv) the balance to be achieved between houses of different types and sizes within a single development of two or more houses or within such a development and its general vicinity having regard to the housing existing or proposed in that vicinity (TCA 1997, s 372AM(6)(b)).

6.504.4   Special qualifying premises

A *special qualifying premises* is defined in TCA 1997, s 372AM(3) as a house which:

(a) is comprised in a special specified building (see definition in **6.502**);

(b) is used solely as a dwelling;

(c) on the date of completion of the refurbishment to which the refurbishment expenditure in relation to the house relates, is let (or if not let on that date, is, without having been used after that date, first let) in its entirety under a qualifying lease and thereafter throughout the remainder of the relevant period (except for reasonable periods of temporary disuse between the ending of one qualifying lease and the commencement of another such lease) continues to be let under such a lease; and

(d) is not a house on which expenditure has been incurred which qualified, or would qualify, for relief under TCA 1997, s 372AP or any other provision of TCA 1997 Part 10 (Urban and other Renewal Reliefs).

A house is not a special qualifying premises if:

(a)   it is occupied as a dwelling by any person connected with (see **2.3**) the person entitled to a deduction under that section in respect of the eligible expenditure incurred on or in relation to the house; and

(b)   the terms of the qualifying lease in relation to the house are not such as might have been expected to be included in the lease if the negotiations for the lease had been at arm's length (TCA 1997, s 372AM(5)).

A house is not a special qualifying premises if the lessor has not complied with all of the requirements of:

(i)   the Housing (Standards for Rented Houses) Regulations 1993 (SI 147/1993);

(ii)   the Housing (Rent Books) Regulations 1993 (SI 146/1993); and

(iii) the Housing (Registration of Rented Houses) Regulations 1996 (SI 30/1996), as amended by the Housing (Registration of Rented Houses) (Amendment) Regulations 2000 (SI 12/2000) (TCA 1997, s 372AM(10)(a)).

A house is not a special qualifying premises unless the house or, where the house is one of a number of houses in a single development, the development of which it is a part complies with such guidelines (which may include provisions in relation to refurbishment of houses and the provision of ancillary facilities and amenities in relation to houses) as may from time to time be issued by the Minister, with the consent of the Minister for Finance, in relation to the refurbishment of houses as special qualifying premises (TCA 1997, s 372AM(10)(b), (c)).

A house is not a special qualifying premises unless persons authorised in writing by the Minister for the purposes of those provisions are permitted to inspect the house at all reasonable times on production, if so requested by a person affected, of their authorisation (TCA 1997, s 372AM(11)).

6.504.5   Qualifying lease

A lease of a house is a *qualifying lease* where the consideration for the grant of the lease consists:

(a)   solely of periodic payments all of which are or fall to be treated as rents for the purposes of TCA 1997 Part 4 Ch 8 (Case V – see **3.209.2**); or

(b)   of payments of the kind mentioned in (a) together with a payment by means of a premium which—

(i)   in the case of the construction of a house, does not exceed 10% of the relevant cost of the house,

(ii)   in the case of the conversion of a building into a house, does not exceed 10% of the market value of the house at the time the conversion is completed, and

(iii) in the case of the refurbishment of a house—

(I)   is payable on or after the date of the completion of the refurbishment to which the refurbishment expenditure relates or which, if payable before that date, is so payable by reason of or otherwise in connection with the carrying out of the refurbishment, and

(III)   does not exceed 10% of the market value of the house at the time of the completion of the refurbishment to which the refurbishment expenditure relates (TCA 1997, s 372AO(2)).

Market value, in relation to a building, structure or house, means the price which the unencumbered fee simple of the building, structure or house would fetch if sold in the open market in such manner and subject to such conditions as might reasonably be calculated to obtain for the vendor the best price for the building, structure or house, less the part of that price which would be attributable to the acquisition of, or of rights in or over, the land on which the building, structure of house is constructed (TCA 1997, s 372AO(1)).

For the purposes of (b)(ii) or (iii) above, where a house is a part of a building and is not saleable apart from the building of which it is a part, the market value of the house at the time of the conversion is completed or at the time of the completion of the refurbishment to which the refurbishment expenditure relates is taken to be an amount which bears to the market value of the building at that time the same proportion as the total floor area of the house bears to the total floor area of the building (TCA 1997, s 372AO(3)).

Relevant cost is defined in TCA 1997, s 372AP(1) as the aggregate of:

(a)   (i)   where the eligible expenditure is on the construction of the house, the expenditure incurred on the acquisition of, or of rights in or over, any land on which the house is situated, or

(ii)   where the eligible expenditure is conversion expenditure or refurbishment expenditure, the expenditure incurred on the acquisition of, or of rights over—

(I)   any land on which the house is situated, and

(II)   any building in which the house is comprised, and

(b)   the expenditure actually incurred on the construction of, conversion into, or refurbishment of the house.

Example 6.504.5.1

Swift Ltd incurred expenditure of €180,000 on the construction of a new house on a site it had acquired in a tax incentive area for €60,000. The company leases the house for an annual rent of €20,000 plus a premium of €22,000. The "relevant cost" of the house is €240,000 (site cost €60,000 plus actual construction costs €180,000).

As the premium of €22,000 is less than 10% of the relevant cost, the lease will be a qualifying lease, assuming all other conditions are met.

To be a qualifying lease, the terms of the lease must not contain any provisions which would allow the lessee, or any other person, directly or indirectly, at any time to acquire an interest in the house for a consideration which is less than might be expected to be given at that time if the negotiations were conducted in the open market at arm's length (TCA 1997, s 372AO(2)). Where the lease relates to a qualifying rural area, the duration of the lease must not be for a period of less than three months. Where the lease relates to a qualifying student accommodation area, it must comply with the requirements of the relevant guidelines (TCA 1997, s 372AO(4)).

6.504.6   Eligible expenditure

Under TCA 1997, s 372AP(2), relief is given in respect of "eligible expenditure on or in relation to a house which is a qualifying premises or a special qualifying premises".

Expenditure is *eligible expenditure* where it is:

(a)   expenditure incurred on—

    (i)   the construction of a house, other than a house referred to in (ii), or

    (ii)   the necessary construction of a house which fronts on to a qualifying street or is comprised in a building or part of a building which fronts on to a qualifying street,

(b)   conversion expenditure (see definition in **6.502**); or

(c)   refurbishment expenditure (see definition in **6.502**) (TCA 1997, s 372AN(1)).

Necessary construction, in relation to an existing building, means one of more of the following:

(a)   construction of an extension to the building which does not exceed 30% of the floor area of the building immediately before expenditure on the construction, conversion or refurbishment of the building was incurred, where such extension is necessary for the purposes of facilitating access to, or providing essential facilities in, one or more qualifying premises;

(b)   construction of an additional storey or additional storeys to the building which was or were necessary for the restoration or enhancement of the streetscape; or

(c)   construction or a replacement building (see definition in **6.502**); and

any reference to construction in the case of a house which fronts on to a qualifying street applies is if it were a reference to necessary construction unless the context requires otherwise (TCA 1997 ss 372AK(1) and 372A(1)).

Relief under TCA 1997, s 372AP is given for so much of the expenditure as is treated under that section or under TCA 1997 372AS(1) as having been incurred in the qualifying period (see **6.504.2**). Although expenditure might have been incurred within the qualifying period (see definition in **6.502**), only so much of that expenditure as is referable to work actually carried out during the qualifying period may be treated as having been incurred during that period (TCA 1997, s 372AS(1)). This provision would deny relief in a case where, for example, contracts were entered into and expenditure was incurred shortly before the end of the qualifying period but where the work was not carried out until some time after that period.

For the above purposes, where a person incurs eligible expenditure or qualifying expenditure at any time in the period 1 January 2006 to 31 July 2008 on or in relation to a qualifying premises, the amount of eligible expenditure or qualifying expenditure to be treated as having been incurred in the qualifying period for the purposes of entitlement to a deduction under TCA 1997, s 372AP is to be reduced:

(a)   in the case of expenditure incurred in the period from 1 January 2007 to 31 December 2007, to 75%; and

(b)   in the case of expenditure incurred in the period 1 January 2008 to 31 July 2008, to 50%,

of the amount which would otherwise be so treated (TCA 1997, s 372AS(1A)(a)).

For the above purposes and in determining whether and to what extent eligible expenditure or qualifying expenditure is or is not incurred on or in relation to a qualifying premises or a special qualifying premises in—

(i)   the period 1 January 2006 to 31 December 2006;

(ii)   the period 1 January 2007 to 31 December 2007; or

(iii) the period 1 January 2008 to 31 July 2008,

only such an amount of that expenditure as is properly attributable to work done on the construction of, conversion into, or refurbishment of, the qualifying premises or special qualifying premises actually carried out in such period is (notwithstanding the general rule regarding the time any capital expenditure is to be treated as incurred) to be treated as having been incurred in that period (TCA 1997, s 372AS(1A)(b)).

For the purposes of making a claim for the relief, TCA 1997, s 372AS(3)(a) provides that construction or conversion expenditure in relation to a qualifying premises is deemed to have been incurred on the date of first letting of the premises under a qualifying lease.

It is also provided in TCA 1997, s 372AN(7) that, other than in relation to a special qualifying premises, references to construction, conversion or refurbishment in relation to any premises are to be taken as including references to the development of the land on which the premises is situated or which is used in the provision of gardens, grounds, access or amenities in relation to the premises and as including in particular:

(a)   demolition or dismantling of any building on the land;

(b)   site clearance, earth moving, excavation, tunnelling and boring, laying of foundations, erection of scaffolding, site restoration, landscaping and the provision of roadways and other access works;

(c)   walls, power-supply, drainage, sanitation and water supply; and

(d)   the construction of out-houses or other buildings or structures for use by the occupants of the premises or for use in the provision of amenities for the occupants.

Where, by virtue of TCA 1997, s 372AN(7), expenditure on the construction of, conversion into or refurbishment of, a qualifying premises includes expenditure on the development of any land, TCA 1997, s 372AS(1) applies with any necessary modifications as if references to the construction of, conversion into or refurbishment of, the qualifying premises were references to the development of such land (TCA 1997, s 372AS(2)).

In determining the amount of eligible expenditure incurred on or in relation to a building the site of which is situated partly inside and partly outside the boundary of a qualifying urban area or a qualifying town area, and where expenditure incurred in the qualifying period is attributable to the building in general, such amount of that expenditure is deemed to be attributable to the part situated outside the boundary of the area as bears to the whole of that expenditure the same proportion as the floor area of the part situated outside the boundary bears to the total floor area of the building (TCA 1997, s 372AK(2A)).

For the purposes of making a claim for relief under TCA 1997, s 372AP, construction or conversion expenditure in relation to a qualifying premises is deemed to have been incurred on the date of first letting of the premises under a qualifying lease (TCA 1997, s 372AS(3)(a)).

For the purposes of claiming relief under TCA 1997, s 372AP in respect of eligible expenditure, refurbishment expenditure incurred in relation to a qualifying premises or a special qualifying premises is deemed to have been incurred on the date of the commencement of the relevant period in relation to the premises, determined as respects the refurbishment to which the refurbishment expenditure relates. That date will be the date on which the premises are first let after completion of the refurbishment work or, if the premises are already let (ie, tenants are in place and actually occupy the premises before or during the carrying out of the refurbishment), on the date of completion of the work (TCA 1997, s 372AS(3)(b)).

6.504.7 Premiums

The definition of "qualifying lease" in TCA 1997, s 372AO(2) includes the requirement that any premium payable may not exceed 10% of the relevant cost of the house. If a premium is payable, and assuming it does not exceed the 10% limit, an adjustment under TCA 1997, s 372AP(4) may be required in respect of the construction cost which would otherwise qualify for relief under TCA 1997, s 372AP.

TCA 1997, s 372AP(4) provides for a restriction to the amount of the eligible expenditure qualifying for relief under TCA 1997, s 372AP(2), (3) in the case of certain kinds of premium. TCA 1997, s 372AP(4)(a) refers to any premium or other sum which:

(a)   is payable, directly or indirectly, under a qualifying lease or otherwise under the terms subject to which the lease is granted, to or for the benefit of the lessor or to or for the benefit of any person connected with (see **2.3**) the lessor; and

(b)   where the eligible expenditure incurred is refurbishment expenditure in relation to a qualifying premises or a special qualifying premises—

   (i)   is payable on or after the date of completion of the refurbishment to which the refurbishment expenditure relates, or

   (ii)   if payable before that date, is payable by reason of or otherwise in connection with the carrying out of the refurbishment.

Where any such premium or other sum, or any part of such premium or other sum, is not or is not treated as rent for the purposes of TCA 1997, s 97 (see **3.209.2**), the eligible expenditure treated as having been incurred in the qualifying period on or in relation to the qualifying premises or the special qualifying premises to which the qualifying lease relates is deemed to be reduced by the lesser of:

   (i)   the amount of the premium or other sum, or part thereof, not treated as rent; and

   (ii)   a proportion of the amount in (i) arrived at by reference to the amount of the eligible expenditure actually incurred in or in relation to the qualifying premises or the special qualifying premises in the qualifying period divided by the total of the eligible expenditure incurred on or in relation to the qualifying premises or the special qualifying premises (TCA 1997, s 372AP(4)(b)).

In other words, where any amount of eligible expenditure has been incurred after the end of the qualifying period and therefore does not qualify for relief under TCA 1997, s 372AP, the reduction in the amount qualifying for relief will be the lesser of (a) the amount of the premium not treated as rent and (b) a proportion of the premium not treated as rent arrived at by reference to the amount of the eligible expenditure incurred in the qualifying period divided by the total eligible expenditure incurred.

Example 6.504.7.1

Walter Ltd incurs expenditure of €220,000 on the construction of a residence for letting in a tax incentive area. Part of the construction work is carried out after the end of the qualifying period. It is agreed with the inspector of taxes that 90%, or €198,000, of the work was completed within the qualifying period. Walter Ltd lets the residence on a 10-year lease for an annual rent of €24,000 and a premium of €20,000. The cost of acquiring the site on which the residence is built was €60,000.

1. Assuming all other conditions are satisfied, the lease will be a qualifying lease as the premium is less than 10% of the "relevant cost" as defined by TCA 1997, s 372AP(1) (site cost €60,000 plus construction cost €220,000).

2. In accordance with TCA 1997, s 98(1) the amount of the premium which is assessable as rent is €20,000 x (51-10)/50 = €16,400.

Accordingly, the construction cost qualifying for relief under TCA 1997, s 372AP is reduced by the lesser of:

(a) €3,600 (ie, premium €20,000 less €16,400); and

(b) €3,240 (ie, €3,600 x 90%).

Walter Ltd is entitled to relief under TCA 1997, s 372AP in an amount of €194,760 (ie, €198,000 construction cost incurred within the qualifying period less €3,240).

If all of the construction work had been carried out within the qualifying period, the amount by which the construction expenditure would be reduced would be the full amount of the premium not treated as rent.

6.504.8 Developer selling property before use

Where eligible expenditure on a house is incurred by a developer (a person carrying on a trade consisting wholly or partly of the construction, conversion or refurbishment of buildings with a view to their sale) and the house is sold to a company in the course of the developer's trade or part trade, the company is treated by TCA 1997, s 372AP(10) as having incurred in the qualifying period eligible expenditure on or in relation to the house equal to the "relevant price" paid by the company on the purchase (the "first purchase"). This provision applies:

(a) where the eligible expenditure was expenditure on the construction of the house—

   (i) before the house is used, or

   (ii) where a house, the site of which is wholly within a qualifying student accommodation area, is sold on or after 5 December 2001, within a period of one year after it commences to be used, and

(b) where the eligible expenditure was conversion or refurbishment expenditure—

   (i) before the house is used subsequent to the incurring of that expenditure, or

   (ii) where a house, the site of which is wholly within a qualifying student accommodation area, is sold on or after 5 December 2001, within a period of one year after it commences to be used subsequent to the incurring of that expenditure.

The *relevant price*, in relation to the purchase of a house, is the amount which bears to the net price paid on that purchase the same proportion as the amount of the eligible expenditure actually incurred on or in relation to the house, and which is properly attributable to work actually carried out during the qualifying period, bears to the "relevant cost" (see definition in **6.502**) in relation to that house.

The "relevant cost" is the aggregate of the expenditure incurred on the acquisition of, or of rights in or over, any land on which the house is situated (and, in the case of conversion or refurbishment expenditure, of, in or over any building in which the house is comprised) and the expenditure actually incurred on the construction of, conversion into, or refurbishment of the house (see full definition in **6.502**).

The amount of the relevant price attributable to the site would include a portion of the developer's profit. It is not necessary for the sale to take place before the end of the qualifying period.

Example 6.504.8.1

A developer incurs expenditure of €190,000 on the construction of a house on a site which he had acquired, for €30,000, in a tax incentive area. The developer sells the house for €300,000 to Killane Ltd which lets the house under a qualifying lease. The amount of the sale price on which Killane Ltd may claim relief under TCA 1997, s 372AP is €300,000 x 190,000/220,000 = €259,090.

In the case of a house purchased before it is used or, where the eligible expenditure was conversion or refurbishment expenditure, before it is used subsequent to the incurring of the expenditure, from a person who had purchased it from a developer, TCA 1997, s 372AP(10) provides that the amount of the purchase price which qualifies for relief under TCA 1997, s 372AP is to be the relevant price paid on the "first purchase" (see above).

Example 6.504.8.2

The position is as in Example **6.504.8.1** except that Killane Ltd, instead of letting the house which it had purchased from the developer for €300,000, sells it on unused to McNair Ltd for €350,000. McNair Ltd then lets the house under a qualifying lease. The amount of the sale price on which McNair Ltd may claim relief under TCA 1997, s 372AP is €300,000 x 190,000/220,000 = €259.090.

The effect of the above calculation is that all of the profit made by Killane Ltd on the sale of the house to McNair Ltd is excluded from the amount qualifying for relief.

6.504.9 Private sale before use

In the case of a house purchased before it is used or, where the eligible expenditure in relation to the house was conversion or refurbishment expenditure, before the house is used subsequent to the incurring of that expenditure, from a person other than a developer (see **6.504.8**), TCA 1997, s 372AP(9) provides that the amount of the purchase price which qualifies for relief under TCA 1997, s 372AP is to be the lower of (a) the amount of the construction, conversion or refurbishment expenditure actually incurred in the qualifying period and (b) the "relevant price" paid by the purchaser on the purchase. Where the house is sold more than once before it is used or, as the case may be, before the house is used subsequent to the incurring of the expenditure, this provision applies only in relation to the last of those sales.

Example 6.504.9.1

Mr Greusel incurs expenditure of €200,000 in the qualifying period on the construction of a house on a site which he had purchased for €40,000 in a tax incentive area. Without using the house, Mr Greusel, who is not a developer, sells the house to Ector Estates Ltd for €300,000. The company lets the house under a qualifying lease.

The amount of the purchase price on which Ector Estates Ltd is entitled to relief under TCA 1997, s 372AP is €200,000, being the lesser of:

(a) €200,000 (the amount of construction expenditure actually incurred in the qualifying period); and

(b) €300,000 x 200,000/240,000 = €250,000.

The effect of the above calculation is to exclude from the relief the whole amount of the seller's profit on sale; this contrasts with the situation where a developer has sold the property, in which case the developer's profit attributable to the actual construction cost does qualify for the relief.

6.504.10 Clawback of relief

If a house ceases to be a qualifying premises or a special qualifying premises (eg, because it ceases to be let, other than on a temporary basis, or a new lease is granted to a connected person on a non-arm's length basis) or if the house is sold or the ownership of the house otherwise passes to another person while remaining a qualifying premises or a special qualifying premises, and either event occurs within the relevant period (see **6.504.3**), TCA 1997, s 372AP(7) provides that the lessor who obtained relief under TCA 1997, s 372AP(2) will be treated as having received, immediately prior to the sale of the house or immediately before it ceased to be a qualifying premises or a special qualifying premises, an amount of rent equal to the total amount of relief obtained by the lessor. In other words, the relief given to the lessor is clawed back and is assessed on the lessor as rent received on the day before the date of sale. The amount clawed back will, in effect, be the total amount of eligible expenditure which qualified for relief as this would have been the amount allowed as a deduction under TCA 1997, s 97(2) in the year in which the lessor first let the property.

6.504.11 Purchaser or new owner

Where a clawback of relief under TCA 1997, s 372AP has occurred as a result of the sale or the transfer of ownership of the house within the relevant period (see **6.504.9** above), the purchaser or new owner of the house will be entitled to claim relief under the same section.

The amount on which a purchaser will be entitled to claim relief, as provided for in TCA 1997, s 372AP(8)(a), is the lesser of (a) the amount originally qualifying for relief at the date of first letting by the previous owner and (b) the relevant price paid (being the amount which bears to the price paid by the purchaser the same proportion as the amount of eligible expenditure actually incurred on or in relation to the house, and which is properly attributable to work actually carried out during the qualifying period, bears to the relevant cost of the house).

Example 6.504.11.1

Erne Ltd incurred expenditure of €190,000 on the construction of a house on a site which it had purchased for €30,000 in a tax incentive area. The company let the house under a qualifying lease and claimed relief under TCA 1997, s 372AP in the amount of €190,000. Six years after the house was first let, Erne Ltd sold it for €210,000 to Carlton Ltd. Carlton Ltd also lets the house under a qualifying lease and is entitled to relief under TCA 1997, s 372AP on €181,364, being the lesser of:

(a)   €190,000 (the amount of expenditure originally qualifying for relief in the case of Erne Ltd); and

(b)   €210,000 x 190,000/220,000 = €181,364.

Carlton Ltd may claim relief under TCA 1997, s 372AP only in respect of €181,364 notwithstanding that the construction cost originally qualifying for relief was €190,000.

Where a company, being a new owner, has acquired a house otherwise than by way of a purchase, it will be entitled to relief on the amount originally qualifying for relief at the date of first letting.

The first owner's qualifying construction cost may have been reduced due to the fact that an amount by way of premium was payable to him which was not treated as taxable rent in his hands. In calculating a new owner's entitlement to relief under TCA 1997, s 372AP in that case, the amount of the construction cost which originally qualified for relief is to be taken as that cost without reference to the amount of reduction on foot of the premium required by TCA 1997, s 372AP(4)(b) (see **6.504.6** above). This is the position regardless of how the new owner acquired the house, by purchase or otherwise (TCA 1997, s 372AP(8)(a)).

The purchaser obtains the relief in the same way as the previous owner. The purchaser's entitlement is given as a deduction as if it were an allowable expense under TCA 1997, s 97(2). The deficiency arising on that property is aggregated with any surpluses or deficiencies arising on all other rental properties in the State owned by the purchaser. Any aggregate deficiency is carried forward indefinitely for set off in future periods against all Case V rental income until fully utilised.

6.6 MID-SHANNON CORRIDOR TOURISM INFRASTRUCTURE INVESTMENT SCHEME

6.601 Introduction
6.602 Definitions
6.603 Approval, certification and guidelines
6.604 Qualifying mid-Shannon areas
6.605 Registered holiday camps: accelerated capital allowances
6.606 Tourism infrastructure facilities: capital allowances

6.601 Introduction

TCA 1997, Part 10 Chapter 12 (ss 372AW-372AZ) and Schedule 8B provides for a tax-based scheme for tourism facilities in the mid-Shannon area. The purpose of the scheme is to encourage the development of new tourism infrastructure and the refurbishment of existing tourism infrastructure in the area. The qualifying period for the scheme is three years from the date of its commencement (a date fixed by way of Ministerial order).

Relief is available by way of accelerated capital allowances over seven years for qualifying construction and refurbishment expenditure incurred in the qualifying period. In the case of refurbishment, the qualifying expenditure must exceed 20% of the market value of the property before work commences. In areas which are not in the Border, Midlands, West region, only 80% of construction and refurbishment expenditure will qualify for relief.

The nature of the tourism infrastructure buildings and structures which may qualify under the scheme is to be set out in guidelines to be issued by the Minister for Arts, Sport and Tourism in consultation with the Minister for Finance. While relief is available over seven years, a 15-year holding period, during which a clawback of allowances will not be made, applies.

Advance approval, for which an application must be made within one year of the commencement of the scheme, is required for projects wishing to avail of relief. Formal certification after completion is also required. Approval and certification are given, in accordance with the guidelines, by a special board established for the purposes of the scheme. Certain buildings such as those that facilitate gaming or gambling are specifically excluded from the scheme, as are licensed premises (but not restaurants).

Accommodation facilities provided as part of a qualifying project may qualify for relief to the extent that expenditure on such facilities does not exceed 50% of the overall expenditure on the project or such lower percentage as may be specified in the guidelines for the type of project involved. This requirement is subject to the over-riding condition that qualifying expenditure on accommodation facilities may not exceed qualifying expenditure on non-accommodation facilities.

6.602 Definitions

The following definitions are relevant:

In relation to a project, *accommodation building* means a building or structure or part of a building or structure which consists of accommodation facilities or which is to be used or is suitable for use for the provision of such facilities.

In relation to a building or structure, *market value* means the price which the unencumbered fee simple of the building or structure would fetch if sold in the open market in such manner and subject to such conditions as might reasonably be calculated to obtain for the vendor the best price for the building or structure, less the part of that price which would be attributable to the acquisition of, or of rights in or over, the land on which the building or structure is constructed.

The *mid-Shannon corridor* is the corridor of land comprising all qualifying mid-Shannon areas (see **6.604**); the *mid-Shannon Tourism Infrastructure Board* is a board consisting of not more than five persons selected for the purposes of TCA 1997, Part 10 Chapter 12 by the Minister in consultation with the Minister for Finance. The *qualifying mid-Shannon area* is any area described in TCA 1997, Schedule 8B.

The *Minister* is the Minister for Arts, Sport and Tourism.

References to a *project* are to the construction or refurbishment of buildings and structures comprising—

    (a)   a holiday camp of the type referred to in section 372AX(1)(b) (see (b) in **6.605** below), or

    (b)   one or more qualifying tourism infrastructure facilities,

the site or sites of which is or are wholly within a qualifying mid-Shannon area.

A *property developer* is a person carrying on a trade which consists wholly or mainly of the construction or refurbishment of buildings or structures with a view to their sale.

The *qualifying period* is a period of three years commencing on the date on which TCA 1997, Part 10 Chapter 12 comes into effect.

A reference to *qualifying tourism infrastructure facilities* is to such class or classes of facilities, comprising buildings and structures only, as may be approved for the purposes of TCA 1997, Part 10 Chapter 12 by the Minister, in consultation with the Minister for Finance, and published in the relevant guidelines.

In relation to a building or structure, *refurbishment* means any work of construction, reconstruction, repair or renewal, including the provision or improvement of water, sewerage or heating facilities, carried out in the course of—

    (a)   the repair or restoration, or

    (b)   maintenance, in the nature of repair or restoration

of the building or structure.

References to *relevant guidelines* are to guidelines issued in accordance with TCA 1997, s 372AW(3), or any guidelines issued in accordance with that subsection which amend or replace those guidelines.

6.603   Approval, certification and guidelines

Approval and certification

Relief may not be granted under TCA 1997, Part 10 Chapter 12 in respect of capital expenditure incurred in the qualifying period on the construction or refurbishment of a building or structure unless the mid-Shannon Tourism Infrastructure Board has—

    (i)   prior to such expenditure being incurred, but subject to the receipt of an appropriate application (see below), granted approval in principle in relation to the construction or refurbishment of the building or structure, and

    (ii)   after the expenditure is incurred, certified in writing that the construction or refurbishment which was carried out is in accordance with the criteria specified in the relevant guidelines, having regard to any relevant conditions and requirements imposed by the Board in the approval granted in accordance with (i) (TCA 1997, s 372AW(2)(a)).

Approval in principle will not be granted unless an application for such approval, in which the information and details as may be required in accordance with TCA 1997, s 372AW(3)(h) (see below) are included, is received by the mid-Shannon Tourism Infrastructure Board within a period of one year commencing on the date on which TCA 1997, Part 10 Chapter 12 comes into effect (TCA 1997, s 372AW(2)(b)).

Accommodation buildings: qualifying expenditure limits

Accommodation facilities may qualify for relief to the extent that expenditure on such facilities does not exceed 50% of the overall expenditure on the project or such lower percentage as may be specified in the guidelines, but qualifying expenditure may not in any event exceed the amount of qualifying expenditure on non-accommodation facilities.

Approval and certification may not be given or issued by the mid-Shannon Tourism Infrastructure Board in relation to capital expenditure incurred in the qualifying period on the construction or refurbishment of one or more than one accommodation building (see **6.602**) comprised in a project to the extent that such expenditure exceeds (or, where an application for approval is involved, is projected to exceed) an amount (the "limit amount") which is equal to the lesser of—

(i)   50%, or such lower percentage as may be specified (in accordance with TCA 1997, s 372AW(3) (see (e) under *Relevant guidelines* below) in the relevant guidelines for the type of project involved, of the total amount of the capital expenditure incurred in the qualifying period on the construction or refurbishment of all the buildings or structures comprised in the project, and

(ii) the amount of the capital expenditure incurred in the qualifying period on the construction or refurbishment of buildings and structures comprised in the project which are other than accommodation buildings (TCA 1997, s 372AW(4)(a)).

In any case where—

(a)   there is more than one accommodation building comprised in a project, and

(b)   the aggregate of the amounts of capital expenditure incurred in the qualifying period on the construction or refurbishment of each accommodation building exceeds the limit amount, then that aggregate shall, for the purposes of an application for approval or certification, be reduced to an amount equivalent to the limit amount and that equivalent amount is to be apportioned on a just and reasonable basis between all the accommodation buildings comprised in the project (TCA 1997, s 372AW(4)(b)).

Subject to the criteria in the relevant guidelines being satisfied, the mid-Shannon Tourism Infrastructure Board may grant approval or issue certification in relation to an accommodation building—

(i)   where there is one accommodation building comprised in a project, only in relation to the amount of the capital expenditure incurred on the construction or refurbishment of the building in the qualifying period as does not exceed the limit amount, and

(ii)   where TCA 1997, s 372AW(4)(b) applies (see above), provided that it is satisfied with the basis on which the apportionment has been made, only in relation to that part of the equivalent amount (as referred to in TCA 1997, s 372AW(4)(b)) which is attributable to the building following the apportionment made in accordance with that paragraph (TCA 1997, s 372AW(4)(c)).

Where capital expenditure is incurred in the qualifying period on the construction or refurbishment of an accommodation building and TCA 1997 s 372AW(4) applies so as to reduce the amount of such expenditure eligible for certification by the mid-Shannon Tourism Infrastructure Board, the amount of the capital expenditure actually incurred in the qualifying period on the construction or refurbishment of the accommodation building which is to be treated as incurred—

(i)   for the purposes of making industrial building allowances and charges by virtue of TCA 1997 s 372AX and 372AY, but

(ii)   prior to the operation of TCA 1997 s 372AW(4),

is to be reduced to the amount of the capital expenditure which was eligible for certification by the mid-Shannon Tourism Infrastructure Board in relation to that building (TCA 1997, s 372AZ(3)).

Subject to TCA 1997 s 279 as applied by TCA 1997 s 372AZ(5)(b) (treatment of land cost - see **6.606.5** below), for the purposes of making industrial building allowances and charges, references in the Tax Acts to expenditure incurred on the construction or refurbishment of a building or structure are to be construed as references to such expenditure as reduced in accordance with TCA 1997, s 372AZ(3) (TCA 1997, s 372AZ(5)(a)).

Relevant guidelines

For the purposes of approval and certification in accordance with TCA 1997, s 372AW(2) and, as the case may be, certification in accordance with TCA 1997, s 372AX(1)(d) (accelerated capital allowances for construction or refurbishment of certain registered holiday camps - see below) or 372AY(1)(g) (capital allowances for the construction or refurbishment of certain tourism infrastructure facilities - see below), the Minister, in consultation with the Minister for Finance, will issue guidelines to which the mid-Shannon Tourism Infrastructure Board is to have regard in deciding whether to grant approval in principle or to issue certification in relation to any building or structure and which guidelines may include criteria in relation to all or any one or more of the following:

(a)   the nature and extent of the contribution which the project, in which the building or structure is comprised, makes to tourism development in the mid-Shannon corridor or the qualifying mid-Shannon area,

(b)   coherence with national tourism strategy,

(c)   environmental sensitivity, having particular regard to any area which is—

(i)   a European site within the meaning of the European Communities (Natural Habitats) Regulations 1997 (SI No 94 of 1997), or

(ii)   a natural heritage area, a nature reserve or a refuge for fauna for the purposes of the Wildlife Acts 1976 and 2000,

(d)   the amenities and facilities required to be provided in each type of project,

(e)   the nature of and maximum extent to which accommodation buildings (see **6.602**), if any, are allowable in each type of project,

(f)   specific standards of design and construction in relation to buildings and structures which may qualify for relief under TCA 1997, Part 10 Chapter 12,

(g)   relevant planning matters, including the need for consistency with the requirements of a development plan or a local area plan within the meaning of those terms in the Planning and Development Act 2000,

(h)   the details and information required to be provided in an application for approval or certification in accordance with section 372AW(2) and, as the case may be, an application for certification in accordance with section 372AX(1)(d) or 372AY(1)(g), and

(i)   matters relating to the provision of information in accordance with sections 372AX(1)(c) and 372AY(1)(f),

together with such other matters as the Minister, in consultation with the Minister for Finance, may consider are required to be included (TCA 1997, s 372AW(3)).

6.604   Qualifying mid-Shannon areas

Clare

The District Electoral Divisions of Ayle, Ballynahinch, Boherglass, Caherhurley, Cappaghabaun, Carrowbaun, Cloonusker, Coolreagh, Corlea, Derrynagittagh, Drummaan, Fahymore, Feakle, Inishcaltra North, Inishcaltra South, Killaloe, Killokennedy, Killuran, Kilseily, Lackareagh, Loughea, Mountshannon, O'Briensbridge, Ogonnelloe and Scarriff.

Galway

The District Electoral Divisions of Abbeygormacan, Abbeyville, Balinasloe Rural, Ballinasloe Urban, Ballyglass, Ballynagar, Bracklagh, Clonfert, Clontuskert, Coos, Derrew, Drumkeary, Drummin, Eyrecourt, Kellysgrove, Killimor (Portumna rural area), Kilmacshane, Kilmalinoge, Kilquain, Kiltormer, Kylemore, Laurencetown, Leitrim, Lismanny, Loughatorick, Marblehill, Meelick, Moat, Pallas, Portumna, Tiranascragh, Tynagh and Woodford.

Offaly

The District Electoral Divisions of Ballycumber, Banagher, Birr Rural, Birr Urban, Broughal, Cloghan, Clonmacnoise, Derryad, Doon, Drumcullen, Eglish, Ferbane, Gallen, Hinds, Hunston, Killyon, Lumcloon, Lusmagh, Mounterin, Moyclare, Shannonbridge, Shannonharbour, Srah and Tinamuck.

Roscommon

The District Electoral Divisions of Athleague East, Athleague West, Athlone West Rural, Ballydangan, Ballynamona, Castlesampson, Caltragh, Cams, Carnagh, Carrowreagh, Cloonburren, Cloonown, Crannagh, Creagh, Culliagh, Drumlosh, Dysart, Fuerty, Kilcar, Kiltoom, Lackan, Lecarrow, Lismaha, Moore, Mote, Rockhill,

Roscommon Rural, Roscommon Urban, Scregg, Taghmaconnell, Thomastown and Turrock.

Tipperary

The District Electoral Divisions of Aglishcloghane, Ardcrony, Ballina, Ballingarry (in Borrisokane rural area), Ballygibbon, Ballylusky, Ballymackey, Ballynaclogh, Birdhill, Borrisokane, Burgesbeg, Carrig, Carrigatogher, Castletown, Cloghprior, Clohaskin, Cloghjordan, Derrycastle, Finnoe, Graigue (in Borrisokane rural area), Greenhall, Kilbarron, Kilcomenty, Killoscully, Kilkeary, Kilmore, Kilnarath, Knigh, Lackagh, Lorrha East, Lorrha West, Mertonhall, Monsea, Nenagh East Urban, Nenagh Rural, Nenagh West Urban, Newport, Rathcabban, Redwood, Riverstown, Terryglass, Uskane and Youghalarra.

Westmeath

The District Electoral Divisions of Athlone East Rural, Athlone East Urban, Athlone West Urban, Ardnagragh, Auburn, Ballymore, Bellanalack, Carn, Castledaly, Doonis, Drumraney, Glassan, Killinure, Moate, Mount Temple, Moydrum, Muckanagh, Noughaval, Templepatrick, Tubbrit, Umma and Winetown.

6.605 Registered holiday camps: accelerated capital allowances

6.605.1 Qualifying buildings and structures

A building or structure qualifying for accelerated capital allowances in accordance with TCA 1997, s 372AX means a building or structure—

    (a)   the site of which is wholly within a qualifying mid-Shannon area,

    (b)   which is in use as a holiday camp—

        (i)   registered in the register of holiday camps kept under the Tourist Traffic Acts 1939 to 2003, and

        (ii)   which meets the requirements of the relevant guidelines in relation to the types of amenities and facilities that need to be provided in a holiday camp for the purposes of TCA 1997, Part 10 Chapter 12,

    (c)   in relation to which the following data has been provided to the mid-Shannon Tourism Infrastructure Board for onward transmission to the Minister and the Minister for Finance:

        (i)   (I)   the amount of the capital expenditure actually incurred in the qualifying period on the construction or refurbishment of the building or structure, and

             (II) where TCA 1997, s 372AW(4) (see **6.603** above) applies in relation to an accommodation building, the amount of such expenditure which is eligible for certification in accordance with that section,

        (ii)   the number and nature of the investors that are investing in the building or structure,

        (iii) the amount to be invested by each investor, and

        (iv) the nature of the structures which are being put in place to facilitate the investment in the building or structure, together with such other information as may be specified in the relevant guidelines as being of assistance to the Minister for Finance in evaluating the costs, including but not limited to exchequer costs, and the benefits arising from the operation of tax relief for buildings and structures under TCA 1997, Part 10 Chapter 12, and

(d)　in respect of which the mid-Shannon Tourism Infrastructure Board gives a certificate in writing after the building or structure is first used or, where capital expenditure is incurred on the refurbishment of a building or structure, first used subsequent to the incurring of that expenditure—

　　(i)　stating that it is satisfied that the conditions in paragraphs (a), (b) and (c) have been met,

　　(ii)　confirming the date of first use or, as the case may be, first use after refurbishment, and

which includes certification in accordance with section 372AW(2)(a)(ii) (see (ii) under *Approval and certification* in **6.603** above) or a copy of such certification (if previously issued) (TCA 1997, s 372AX(1)).

6.605.2　Accelerated capital allowances

An annual writing-down allowance of 15% may be claimed in respect of the capital expenditure incurred in respect of a qualifying building or structure. Thus, the expenditure may be written off over a period of seven years (15% for six years and 10% for the final year). For industrial building allowances purposes, a building or structure in use for the purposes of a trade of hotel-keeping includes a building or structure in use as a holiday camp registered in the register of holiday camps kept under the Tourist Traffic Acts 1939 to 2003. TCA 1997, s 272(3) (see **5.406**) provides for writing-down allowances over 25 years in respect of buildings in use for the purposes of a trade of hotel keeping. TCA 1997, s 372AX(2)(a)(i) applies TCA 1997, s 272(3) to qualifying buildings and structures as if a seven year write-off period applied in place of that 25 year write-off period.

TCA 1997, s 272(4) (see **5.406**) provides for a writing-down period, or "tax life", of 25 years in respect of buildings in use for the purposes of a trade of hotel keeping. In relation to qualifying buildings and structures, TCA 1997, s 372AX(2)(a)(ii) substitutes a 15 year writing-down period for the normal 25 year tax life. The period begins with the time the building or structure was first used or, where capital expenditure on its refurbishment was incurred, from the time it was first used subsequent to the incurring of that expenditure.

The time beyond which a balancing charge may be made in respect of allowances claimed for expenditure on a qualifying building or structure is 15 years from the time the building or structure was first used or, where capital expenditure on its refurbishment was incurred, from the time it was first used subsequent to the incurring of that expenditure. TCA 1997, s 372AX(2)(b) substitutes this 15 year period for the normal such period provided for by TCA 1997 s 274(1)(b) (see **5.409.1**).

Where capital expenditure is incurred in the qualifying period on the refurbishment of a qualifying building or structure, accelerated allowances will be available only if the total capital expenditure amounts to at least 20% of the market value of the building or structure immediately before the expenditure was incurred (TCA 1997, s 372AX(3)).

In determining for the purposes of this Chapter whether and to what extent capital expenditure incurred on the construction or refurbishment of a building or structure to which this section applies is incurred or not incurred in the qualifying period, such an amount of that capital expenditure as is properly attributable to work on the construction or refurbishment of the premises actually carried out during the qualifying period may be treated as having been incurred in that period (TCA 1997, s 372AX(5)).

In determining whether and to what extent capital expenditure incurred on the construction or refurbishment of a building or structure is or is not incurred in the qualifying period, such an amount of that capital expenditure as is properly attributable to work on the construction or, as the case may be, refurbishment of the building or structure actually carried out during the period is treated as having been incurred in that period (TCA 1997, s 372AX(4)).

6.606   Tourism infrastructure facilities: capital allowances

6.606.1 Qualifying premises

A *qualifying premises* for the purpose of TCA 1997, s 372AY is a building or structure—

(a)   the site of which is wholly within a qualifying mid-Shannon area,

(b)   which apart from this section is not an industrial building or structure within the meaning of TCA 1997, s 268 (see **5.404.1**) or deemed to be such a building or structure,

(c)   which is in use for the purposes of the operation of one or more qualifying tourism infrastructure facilities (see **6.602** above),

(d)   (i)   subject to (ii), which does not include a building or structure or part of a building or structure which is a licensed premises (as defined in section 2 of the Intoxicating Liquor Act 1988), but

    (ii)   which may include a building or structure or part of a building or structure which is a restaurant (as defined in section 6 of the Intoxicating Liquor Act 1988) in relation to which—

        (I)   a wine retailer's on-licence, within the meaning of the Finance (1909-10) Act 1910, is currently in force, or

        (II)   a special restaurant licence, within the meaning of the Intoxicating Liquor Act 1988, has been granted under section 9 of that Act,

(e)   which does not include a building or structure or part of a building or structure in use as a facility in which gambling, gaming or wagering of any sort is carried on for valuable consideration or which supports the carrying on of such activities,

(f)   in relation to which the following data has been provided to the mid-Shannon Tourism infrastructure Board for onward transmission to the Minister and the Minister for Finance:

    (i)   (I) the amount of the capital expenditure actually incurred in the qualifying period on the construction or refurbishment of the building or structure, and

(II) where TCA 1997, s 372AW(4) applies in relation to an accommodation building (qualifying expenditure limit - see **6.603** above), the amount of such expenditure which is eligible for certification in accordance with that section,

(ii) the number and nature of the investors that are investing in the building or structure,

(iii) the amount to be invested by each investor, and

(iv) the nature of the structures which are being put in place to facilitate the investment in the building or structure, together with such other information as may be specified in the relevant guidelines as being of assistance to the Minister for Finance in evaluating the costs, including but not limited to exchequer costs, and the benefits arising from the operation of tax relief for buildings and structures under TCA 1997, Part 10 Chapter 12, and

(g) in respect of which the mid-Shannon Tourism Infrastructure Board gives a certificate in writing after the building or structure is first used or, where capital expenditure is incurred on the refurbishment of the building or structure, first used subsequent to the incurring of that expenditure—

(i) stating that it is satisfied that the conditions in (a), (b), (c), (d), (e) and (f) above have been met,

(ii) confirming the date of first use or, as the case may be, first use after refurbishment, and

(iii) which includes certification in accordance with TCA 1997, s 372AW(2)(a)(ii) (see (ii) under *Approval and certification* in **6.603** above) or a copy of such certification (if previously issued).

6.606.2 Capital allowances

TCA 1997, s 372AY(2) provides the basis for capital allowances in respect of capital expenditure incurred on the construction or refurbishment of a qualifying premises. That subsection provides that all of the provisions of the Tax Acts relating to the making of allowances and charges in respect of the construction or refurbishment of an industrial building or structure are to apply—

(i) as if a qualifying premises were at all times at which it is a qualifying premises a building or structure in respect of which an allowance is to be made under the provisions relating to the making of industrial building allowances, and

(ii) where any activity carried on in the qualifying premises is not a trade, as if, for the purposes of making allowances and charges by virtue of (i), it were a trade.

An allowance may be given by virtue of TCA 1997, s 372AY(2) in respect of any capital expenditure incurred on the construction or refurbishment or a qualifying premises only in so far as that expenditure is incurred in the qualifying period. In determining whether and to what extent capital expenditure incurred on the construction or refurbishment of a qualifying premises is or is not incurred in the qualifying period, only such an amount of that capital expenditure as is properly attributable to work on the construction or refurbishment of the premises actually carried out during the qualifying period may be treated as having been incurred in that period (TCA 1997, s 372AY(5)).

Allowances may not be given in respect of any capital expenditure on the refurbishment of a qualifying premises unless the total amount of capital expenditure so incurred is not less than an amount equal to 20% of the market value of the building or structure immediately before that expenditure is incurred (TCA 1997, s 372AY(3)).

An annual writing-down allowance of 15% may be claimed in respect of the capital expenditure incurred in respect of a qualifying premises. Thus, the expenditure may be written off over a period of seven years (15% for six years and 10% for the final year). TCA 1997, s 272(3) (see **5.406**) provides for writing-down allowances over 25 years in respect of buildings in use for the purposes of a trade carried on in a mill, factory or similar premises etc but TCA 1997, s 372AY(4)(a)(i) applies that provision to a qualifying premises as if a seven year write-off period applied in place of that 25 year write-off period.

TCA 1997, s 272(4) (see **5.406**) provides for a writing-down period, or "tax life", of 25 years in respect of buildings in use for the purposes of a trade carried on in a mill, factory or similar premises etc. In relation to a qualifying premises, TCA 1997, s 372AY(4)(a)(ii) substitutes a 15 year writing-down period for the normal 25 year tax life. The period begins with the time the building or structure was first used or, where capital expenditure on its refurbishment was incurred, from the time it was first used subsequent to the incurring of that expenditure.

The time beyond which a balancing charge may be made in respect of allowances claimed for expenditure on a qualifying premises is 15 years from the time the building or structure was first used or, where capital expenditure on its refurbishment was incurred, from the time it was first used subsequent to the incurring of that expenditure. TCA 1997, s 372AY(4)(b) substitutes this 15 year period for the normal such period provided for by TCA 1997 s 274(1)(b) (see **5.409.1**).

6.606.3 Restrictions on and non-application of relief

The allowances provided for by TCA 1997, ss 372AX and 372AY (**6.605.2** and **6.606.2**) are not available in respect of expenditure incurred on the construction or refurbishment of a building or structure—

(a) where a property developer (see **6.602**) or a person connected with (within the meaning of TCA 1997, s 10 – see **2.3**) the property developer is entitled to the relevant interest (see 5.403) in relation to that expenditure, and

(b) either of the persons in (a) incurred the capital expenditure on the construction or refurbishment of the building or structure concerned, or such expenditure was incurred by any other person connected with the property developer (TCA 1997, s 372AZ(1)(a)).

Neither will the allowances be available where any part of the expenditure incurred has been or is to be met, directly or indirectly, by grant assistance or any other assistance granted by or through the State, any board established by statute, any public or local authority or any other agency of the State (TCA 1997, s 372AZ(1)(b)).

Entitlement to the capital allowances provided for in TCA 1997, ss 372AX and 372AY is subject to the condition that the potential allowances available in respect of the building or structure concerned and the project in which it is comprised comply with the requirements of:

(i) the Guidelines on National Regional Aid for 2007–2013 prepared by the Commission of the European Communities and issued on 4 March 2006 (OJ No C 54 of 4 March 2006, p 13), and

(ii) the National Regional Aid Map for Ireland for the period 1 January 2007 to 31 December 2013 which was approved by the said Commission on 24 October 2006 (OJ No C292 of 1 December 2006, p 11) (TCA 1997, s 372AZ(1)(c)).

Again, the allowances will not be available where the person who is entitled to the "relevant interest" (within the meaning of TCA 1997, s 269 – see **5.403**) in relation to that expenditure is subject to an outstanding recovery order following a previous decision of the Commission of the European Communities declaring aid in favour of that person to be illegal and incompatible with the common market (TCA 1997, s 372AZ(1)(d)).

Mid-Shannon areas other than BMW region

In qualifying mid-Shannon areas which are not in the Border, Midlands, West (BMW) region, only 80% of construction and refurbishment expenditure will qualify for relief. Where industrial building allowances are by virtue of TCA 1997 s 372AX or 372AY (**6.605.2, 6.606.2**) to apply in relation to capital expenditure incurred in the qualifying period on the construction or refurbishment of a building or structure the site of which is wholly within a qualifying mid-Shannon area described in TCA 1997, Schedule 8B Part 1 or Part 5 (Clare or Tipperary in **6.604** above, not being in the BMW region), the amount of that expenditure which is to be treated as incurred for the purposes of the making of industrial building allowances and charges (including the making of balancing allowances and charges under TCA 1997, s 274 and the calculation of the residue of expenditure under TCA 1997, s 277 - see **5.409.2**) is to be reduced to 80% of the amount which would otherwise be so treated (TCA 1997, s 372AZ(4)).

Subject to TCA 1997 s 279 as applied by TCA 1997 s 372AZ(5)(b) (treatment of land cost - see **6.606.5** below), for the purposes of making industrial building allowances and charges, references in the Tax Acts to expenditure incurred on the construction or refurbishment of a building or structure are to be construed as references to such expenditure as reduced in accordance with TCA 1997, s 372AZ(4) (TCA 1997, s 372AZ(5)(a)).

6.606.4 Prevention of double relief

Where any relief is given under TCA 1997, s 372AX or 372AY (**6.605.2** and **6.606.2**) in relation to capital expenditure incurred on the construction or refurbishment of a building or structure, relief may not be given in respect of the same expenditure under any other provision of the Tax Acts (TCA 1997, s 372AZ(2)).

6.606.5 Treatment of land cost

In relation to the cost of acquiring land or a relevant interest in land, which must be excluded in arriving at the expenditure qualifying for industrial building allowances (see **5.404** and **5.408.4**), allowances in respect of buildings purchased unused must be computed by reference to the net price paid as restricted by the land element cost. As respects a building or structure to which TCA 1997, s 372AZ(3) (accommodation buildings – see **6.603**) or s 372AZ(4) (mid-Shannon areas other than BMW region – see

6.606.3) applies, the definition of "the net price paid" provided for in TCA 1997, s 279(1) is modified by TCA 1997, s 372AZ(5)(b) where it is the amount represented by the formula:

$$B \times \frac{C}{D+E}$$

where—

B   is the amount paid by the purchaser of the relevant interest in the building or structure;

C   is the amount of the expenditure actually incurred on the construction of the building or structure as reduced in accordance with TCA 1997, s 372AZ(3) or (4);

D   is the amount of the expenditure actually incurred on the construction of the building or structure; and

E   is the amount of any expenditure actually incurred but disallowed by virtue of TCA 1997, s 270(2) (expenditure on the acquisition of rights in or over land etc – see **5.404**).

In addition, TCA 1997, s 279(2) (relevant interest sold before building or structure is used or within one year after commencement of use) is modified so as to provide that the purchaser of the relevant interest is deemed to have incurred, on the date the purchase price becomes payable, expenditure on the construction of the building equal to the lesser of—

(a)   that expenditure as reduced in accordance with either or both of TCA 1997, s 372AZ(3) and s 372AZ(4), and

(b)   the net price paid (as above).

A purchaser (before first use or within one year of first use) of the relevant interest in a building or structure constructed by a builder is deemed to have incurred capital expenditure on construction equal to the net price paid to the builder for the relevant interest and not by reference to the builder's cost, if less (see **5.408.3**). The builder's actual construction cost is disregarded. In a case where either or both of TCA 1997, s 372AZ(3) and s 372AZ(4) applies, this is also the position except that the wording of TCA 1997, s 279(3)(a) is deemed to be modified so as to be consistent with the modification in TCA 1997, s 279(2) explained above.

Chapter 7

Corporation Tax Incentive Reliefs

7.1 INTRODUCTION

7.101 Incentive reliefs: introduction
7.102 Export sales relief
7.103 Shannon exempted trading operations

7.101 Incentive reliefs: introduction

The most significant tax relief currently available to companies is manufacturing relief whereby the effective corporation tax rate in respect of profits from manufacturing and deemed manufacturing activities is 10%. This relief has been in operation since 1 January 1980 and its scope has been extended in a number of important ways, not least by bringing certain financial services activities, notably those carried on in the International Financial Services Centre in Dublin, within the scope of "manufacturing".

Export sales relief, the predecessor of manufacturing relief, was introduced in 1956. Manufacturing relief, particularly in its earliest form, was modelled to some extent on export sales relief. The basic activity qualifying for relief in both cases was the manufacture in the State of goods and the method of calculating relief was by apportioning trading profits on the basis of turnover from qualifying and non-qualifying activities. Whereas the apportionment formula for export sales relief looked to sales of exported goods as a proportion of total sales of goods, the formula for manufacturing relief apportions trading profits on the basis of sales of manufactured goods ("goods") over sales of "goods" plus sales of "merchandise" (goods not manufactured by the claimant company).

Shannon relief, which applied from 1958, took the form of a complete exemption from tax for companies carrying on qualifying trading operations in the Shannon Airport customs-free area. Like export sales relief, the relief came to an end on 5 April 1990.

As both export sales relief and Shannon relief are of little if any practical relevance today, it will suffice here to provide a very brief outline of these reliefs. The main relief covered in this Chapter is manufacturing relief. Other incentives dealt with are BES relief, the relief introduced in 1995 for research and development expenditure incurred by companies, and relief to companies for investment in films. Although the BES relief is an income tax relief available to individuals, it is appropriate to include some treatment of it here as the relevant legislative provisions include qualifying conditions relating to companies, the relief is of direct relevance to companies, and certain provisions relating to the relief are interconnected with those relating to manufacturing relief.

7.102 Export sales relief

Export sales relief (ESR) was introduced in 1956 and was a relief applied to profits of companies derived from certain export sales for a period of up to twenty years. With certain exceptions, no company commencing to trade on or after 1 January 1980 qualified for ESR and in no case was the relief available in respect of any period after 5 April 1990.

Subject to the 5 April 1990 expiry date, full relief from tax on profits from export sales of manufactured goods was given for a period of fifteen years followed by five years for which relief was given at tapering rates (80%, 65%, 50%, 35% and 15%). Where a company was already exporting manufactured goods at the time the relief was introduced, relief was restricted to the tax attributable to the excess of export sales in the accounting period in question over the export sales in the "standard period", which was the year ended 30 September 1955 or year ended 30 September 1956, at the election of the company claiming the relief.

ESR was originally confined to profits from export sales of goods manufactured in the State but its scope was widened on a number of occasions to include fish production on a fish farm, cultivation of mushrooms, ship repair, engineering services (design and planning services in connection with foreign engineering works), publishing of books and greeting cards, wholesale sales abroad of goods not manufactured by the exporting company, manufacturing processes and export sales of goods manufactured by associated companies.

ESR for an accounting period was, in principle, given by reducing the corporation tax that would otherwise be chargeable for the period on the company's income (ie profits excluding chargeable gains) in the same proportion as the company's trading income attributable to its qualifying export sales bore to the company's total income chargeable to corporation tax. The income attributable to the qualifying export sales was that after excluding the proportion of the Case I trading income attributable to sales in Ireland, whereas the company's total income includes income chargeable to corporation tax under all Schedules and Cases.

To qualify for ESR, it was necessary that a company had either exported Irish manufactured goods from the State prior to 1 January 1981 or, where relevant, had made export sales prior to that date in respect of one of the other types of activity for which export sales relief could be claimed. ESR was not available to any company after 5 April 1990. Furthermore, a company ceased to qualify for export sales relief after it had been entitled to claim the relief for a prescribed period (basically the fifteen years referred to above and the five following "tapering" years, but in no case ending later than 5 April 1990).

To be eligible for ESR after 31 December 1980, a company must either have been exporting goods before 1 January 1981 or, alternatively, must have received before that date an assurance in writing from a person duly authorised by the Minister for Finance to the effect that the company's activities would have qualified for relief if they had been commenced before 1 January 1981 (FA 1980 s 42).

Any company continuing to carry on activities in respect of which the above-mentioned assurance had been given, or which had been exporting goods prior to 1 January 1981, continued to be eligible for relief up to 5 April 1990. However, if the company in question claimed manufacturing relief in respect of any trading operations before 5 April 1990, as it was entitled to do, ESR thereupon ceased to be available and could not be reactivated.

The rules governing the taxation of the recipient of a distribution paid out of export sales relieved income (see **11.115** and **11.119**) are applicable whether the income is derived from the sale by export of goods manufactured in the State or from any of the other activities mentioned above (eg certain engineering services).

7.103   Shannon exempted trading operations

CTA Part V exempted, up to 5 April 1990, a qualified company from corporation tax in respect of income arising from certain types of trading operation carried on in the Shannon Airport customs-free area, provided the activities were certified by the

Minister for Finance as being "exempted trading operations". A qualified company for this purpose was one the whole or the part of the trade of which was carried on within the airport (CTA 1976 s 70(1)).

To obtain the exemption after 31 December 1980, a qualified company must either have been carrying on the exempted trading operations before 1 January 1981 or, alternatively, must have received before that date an assurance in writing from a person duly authorised by the Minister for Finance to the effect that the activities would have qualified for exemption if they had been commenced before 1 January 1981 (FA 1980 s 43); the assurance would have been given in cases where the trading operations in question were considered to contribute significantly to regional or national development.

Any company continuing to carry on activities in respect of which the above-mentioned assurance had been given, or where the activities had commenced before 1 January 1981, continued to be exempted from corporation tax up to 5 April 1990. However, if the company in question claimed manufacturing relief in respect of any exempted trading operations before 5 April 1990, as it was entitled to do, the CTA 1976 Part V exemption thereupon ceased to apply and could not be reactivated.

The types of trading operations for which the Minister for Finance could, up to 1 January 1981, grant an exempted trading operations certificate are set out in CTA 1976 s 70(5). They include the manufacture of goods within the Airport for export from the State and certain other specified types of operations including the repair or maintenance of aircraft within the Airport. They also included other trading operations in regard to which the Minister was of the opinion that they contributed to the use or development of the Airport and other trading operations which were ancillary to any of the other types of operation specified in CTA 1976 s 70(5).

CTA 1976 s 70(6) lists certain other trading operations in respect of which the Minister was not permitted to give an exempted trading operations certificate, eg the rendering within the State of services to embarking or disembarking passengers, including hotel, catering, money changing or transport (other than air transport) services, or services in connection with the landing, departure, loading or unloading of aircraft, the sale of goods by retail, the sale of consumable goods for the fuelling of aircraft or for shipment as aircraft stores, the production or manufacture of goods outside the Airport, and the sale of goods brought or to be brought from the Airport into any other part of the State otherwise than in the course of being exported out of the State.

7.2 MANUFACTURING RELIEF

7.201 Introduction
7.202 Basis of relief
7.203 Trading losses and charges
7.204 Meaning of "manufacture"
7.205 Deemed manufacturing activities
7.206 International financial services
7.207 Transactions between associated persons

7.201 Introduction

7.201.1 General

Manufacturing relief may be claimed by a company carrying on a qualifying trading activity in any accounting period or part of an accounting period (a relevant accounting period) falling within the period beginning on 1 January 1981 and ending (depending on circumstances) on 31 December 2000, 31 December 2002, 31 December 2005 or 31 December 2010.

Manufacturing relief is provided for in Taxes Consolidation Act 1997 (TCA 1997) Part 14 (ss 442-457) and is given effect by way of a reduction, by a fraction, in the amount of corporation tax that would otherwise be chargeable for the relevant accounting period on that part of the company's income that is attributable to its income from the sale of goods manufactured by it. The fraction, by means of which the corporation tax attributable to the income from the sale of the manufactured goods is reduced, varies depending on the standard rate of corporation tax chargeable on the income qualifying for manufacturing relief. The relevant fractions applying since the commencement of manufacturing relief are as follows:

Financial years within period	Rate	Fraction	Legislation
1 Jan 1981 to 31 December 1981	45%	35/45ths	FA 1980 s 41(2)
1 January 1982 to 31 March 1988	50%	40/50ths	FA 1982 Sch 2 Part II para 1
1 April 1988 to 31 March 1989	47%	37/47ths	FA 1988 Sch 3 Part II para 1
1 April 1989 to 31 March 1991	43%	33/43rds	FA 1988 Sch 3 Part II para 1
1 April 1991 to 31 March 1995	40%	30/40ths	FA 1990 Sch 2 Part II para 1
1 April 1995 to 31 March 1997	38%	28/38ths	FA 1995 Sch 4 Part II para 1
			TCA 1997, s 448(2)(b)(i)
1 April 1997 to 31 December 1997	36%	26/36ths	TCA 1997, s 448(2)(b)(ii)
1 Jan 1998 to 31 December 1998	32%	22/32nds	TCA 1997, s 448(2)(b)(iii)
1 Jan 1999 to 31 December 1999	28%	9/14ths	TCA 1997, s 448(2)(b)
1 Jan 2000 to 31 December 2000	24%	7/12ths	TCA 1997, s 448(2)(c)
1 Jan 2001 to 31 December 2001	20%	1/2	TCA 1997, s 448(2)(d)
1 Jan 2002 to 31 December 2002	16%	3/8ths	TCA 1997, s 448(2)(e)
1 Jan 2003 onwards	12.5%	1/5	TCA 1997, s 448(2)(f)

TCA 1997, s 448 provides that manufacturing relief (or the "10% rate of corporation tax") may be claimed in respect a company's income in a relevant accounting period from the sale of goods in the course of a trade which consists of or includes the manufacture of goods. TCA 1997, s 443(1)(a) defines "goods" as goods manufactured within the State in the course of a trade by the company claiming the relief.

In principle only a manufacturing company is entitled to the relief, but TCA 1997, s 443(1)(b) permits a selling company to claim manufacturing relief where it sells goods manufactured within the State by another company where either of the companies is a 90% subsidiary of the other or where both companies are 90% subsidiaries of a third company. A company is a 90% subsidiary of another company if and so long as at least 90% of its ordinary share capital is directly and beneficially owned by that other company (TCA 1997, s 9(1)(c) – see 2.5). TCA 1997, s 443(1)(c) applies the group relief entitlement qualifications of TCA 1997 ss 412-417 (the "profit distribution" and "notional winding up" tests – see **8.304.3** and **8.304.4**) for the purposes of the 90% ownership requirement.

TCA 1997 ss 443, 445 and 446 provide that certain other specified activities are deemed to consist of the manufacture of goods and that the income arising from those activities is deemed to be an amount receivable from the sale of goods (see **7.205**) so that the resulting profits are eligible for the 10% corporation tax rate.

7.201.2 Phasing out of manufacturing relief

Outline

Due to the introduction of the 12.5% corporation tax rate with effect from 1 January 2003, manufacturing relief will in many cases cease to be available before the termination dates indicated above.

For manufacturing trades ("specified trades" – see below) which were approved for grant assistance by an industrial development agency (as defined) on or before 31 July 1998, or other manufacturing trades which were being carried on before 23 July 1998, entitlement to the 10% rate will run to 31 December 2010. For all other manufacturing trades, the 10% corporation tax rate will cease to apply after 31 December 2002.

IFSC licensed operations which were approved on or before 31 July 1998 will be eligible for the 10% corporation tax rate up to 31 December 2005. Those approved after 31 July 1998 will qualify for the 10% rate up to 31 December 2002 and will be taxable thereafter at the 12.5% rate.

Licensed Shannon operations approved on or before 31 May 1998 will be eligible for the 10% corporation tax rate up to 31 December 2005. Those approved after 31 May 1998 will qualify for the 10% rate up to 31 December 2002 and will be taxable thereafter at the 12.5% rate.

The deadline for approval of new IFSC and Shannon projects is 31 December 1999. Any project established in either of these locations after that date will be subject to the standard corporation tax rate ruling at the time.

Certain companies, such as captive insurance and reinsurance companies, captive finance companies, agency fund management companies and securitisation vehicles, may be regarded as extensions of existing IFSC operations (ie, of the manager) and may be approved after 31 December 1999.

Relevant accounting period

Claims to manufacturing relief are made in respect of a "relevant accounting period". Prior to the amendment by FA 1999 of TCA 1997, s 442, a relevant accounting period was an accounting period or part of an accounting period ending on or before 31 December 2000 in the cases of Special Trading Houses and qualifying shipping activities and 31 December 2010 for other manufacturing activities. TCA 1997, s 442(1) now defines *relevant accounting period*, in relation to a trade carried on by a company which consists of or includes the manufacturing of goods, as an accounting period, or part of an accounting period, ending on or before:

(a)   where TCA 1997, s 443(11) or (12) applies (qualifying shipping activities or Special Trading Houses), 31 December 2000;

(b)   in the case of a trade, other than a "specified trade", which is set up and commenced on or after 23 July 1998, 31 December 2002; and

(c)   in any other case, 31 December 2010.

Specified trades

As noted above, a relevant accounting period is an accounting period or part of an accounting period ending on or before 31 December 2010 in the case of a trade already being carried on before 23 July 1998 or, in the case of a trade which commenced on or after that date, in the case of a specified trade.

A *specified trade*, in relation to a company:

(a)   means a trade consisting of or including trading operations specified in a grant agreement ("the relevant grant agreement") entered into between the company and an industrial development agency on foot of an approval of grant assistance for the company made by the agency on or before 31 July 1998; but

(b)   does not include such part of the trade as consists of expansion operations which commenced to be carried on on or after 23 July 1998 other than such of those operations as would fall within the terms of the relevant grant agreement.

Industrial development agency means the Industrial Development Agency in Ireland, Shannon Free Airport Development Company, Údarás na Gaeltachta, the Industrial Development Agency, Ireland, Forbairt, Forfás, or Enterprise Ireland.

Expansion operations, in relation to a company, includes:

(a)   increases in production capacity for existing or directly related product lines of the company; and

(b)   the addition of support functions directly related to the existing trading operations of the company.

A trade which has received the necessary grant assistance as described above is a specified trade. Any part of such a trade which commenced after that date, however, and which consists of expansion operations not within the terms of the grant agreement, is treated as not included in the specified trade.

Arising out of this definition, an accounting period (or part of an accounting period) might fall to be treated as a relevant accounting period in relation to a part of a trade carried on by a company and as not a relevant accounting period in relation to another part of that trade. In any such case, each part is to be treated as a separate trade. Total receipts from sales made or services rendered, and expenses incurred, in the course of the trade are to be apportioned to each part. The apportionment is to be made on a just and reasonable basis (TCA 1997, s 442(3)). Such apportionment would, for example, be made in the case of a company which commenced a specified trade on or after 23 July 1998 and which later began to carry on non-approved expansion operations. As regards any accounting period for which the apportionment is made, that accounting period would be a relevant accounting period as regards the part of the trade which had been grant-approved and would not be a relevant accounting period as regards the part consisting of the expansion operations. Accordingly, profits apportioned to the former part only would be taxable at the 10% rate.

TCA 1997, s 442(4) provides for the situation in which, on or after 23 July 1998, a company ("the successor company") succeeds to a trade or part of a trade which was carried on by another company ("the original company") and in respect of which the original company was entitled to manufacturing relief. Subject to TCA 1997 ss 445 and 446 (IFSC and Shannon), manufacturing relief, in so far as it relates to the trade or part of the trade in question, is to be given to the successor company as regards the remaining relevant accounting periods for which relief could have been claimed by the original company if it had continued to carry on the trade or part of the trade concerned.

Shannon

Prior to FA 1999, TCA 1997, s 445(2) provided that the certificate given by the Minister for Finance to a qualified Shannon company, certifying that the company's trading operations are relevant trading operations, would remain in force until 31 December 2005. TCA 1997, s 445(2) now provides that such a certificate is to remain in force until:

(a)   31 December 2005 in the case of operations which, on or before 31 May 1998, were approved by the Minister to be carried on in the airport; and

(b)   31 December 2002 in the case of those operations so approved after 31 May 1998.

International Financial Services Centre

Prior to FA 1999, TCA 1997, s 446(2) provided that the certificate given by the Minister for Finance to a licensed IFSC company, certifying that the company's trading operations are relevant trading operations, would remain in force until 31 December 2005. TCA 1997, s 446(2) now provides that such a certificate is to remain in force until:

(a)   31 December 2005 in the case of operations which, on or before 31 July 1998, were approved by the Minister to be carried on in the IFSC; and

(b)   31 December 2002 in the case of those operations so approved after 31 July 1998.

7.201.3   Claims

A claim to manufacturing relief for any accounting period is to be made before the date on which the assessment for that period becomes final and conclusive. Under self-assessment, a company will almost always make the claim in its corporation tax return. It is possible to make the claim after the return has been submitted but once an assessment is made which is in accordance with the return, that assessment cannot be amended as a result of a claim made later.

7.202   Basis of relief

7.202.1   General

Income qualifying for manufacturing relief is that arising from the sale of "*goods*", defined in TCA 1997, s 443(1)(a) as "goods manufactured within the State in the course of a trade by the company which is claiming the relief". "Goods", however, does *not* include goods sold by retail (TCA 1997, s 443(5)) and, for this purpose, goods are not regarded as sold by retail if they are sold:

(a)   to a person who carries on a trade of selling goods of the class to which the goods so sold to him belong; or

(b)   to a person who uses goods of that class for the purposes of a trade carried on by him; or

(c)   to a person, other than an individual, who uses goods of that class for the purposes of an undertaking carried on by him.

For the purposes of (b), two types of situation are covered. The sale could be to a person who uses the goods purchased as raw materials or ingredients in a process of manufacturing carried on by him. Alternatively, the goods purchased may constitute machinery or plant used for the purposes of the purchaser's trade.

The basis of manufacturing relief is a reduction, by the appropriate fraction (see **7.201**), in the amount of corporation tax on income from the sale of goods. Where there are sales of *merchandise* (ie, goods other than "goods" as defined in TCA 1997, s 443(1)(a)), *income from the sale of goods* is arrived at by apportioning the income from the sales of both goods and merchandise on a sales ratio basis. Corporation tax (based on the standard rate of 12.5%) is reduced by the following amount:

$$\text{relevant corporation tax} \times \frac{\text{income from sales of goods \& merchandise} \times \dfrac{\text{sales of goods}}{\text{sales of goods \& merchandise}}}{\text{total income}} \times \frac{1}{5}$$

As is seen below (in **7.202.2**), relevant corporation tax is exclusive of corporation tax on any income chargeable at the higher rate of corporation tax and, correspondingly, total income is reduced by the amount of any such income. The basis of manufacturing relief is in TCA 1997, s 448 and is conveniently represented by the above formula.

Thus the different tax rates (standard corporation tax rate and effective 10% rate) will not be applied to the commercial income generated by each activity and this feature would in many instances lead to a dilution of the benefit of the 10% tax rate. In these circumstances, it is usual to segregate non-qualifying activities into a separate legal entity, thus ensuring that the level of taxation arising is in line with the commercial profits basis.

Of course the converse may also be true in that a favourable distorting effect can result from the application of the mandatory sales ratio apportionment method of computing manufacturing income. This will occur where the profitability of the non-manufacturing sales is greater than that of the manufacturing sales. In that case a single company structure gives the more favourable result.

Where the non-qualifying income of a business derives from the provision of a service, there will be no dilution of the 10% rate, since the income from the non qualifying service activity can be determined on a commercial basis.

The important provisions of TCA 1997, s 448 are now examined in more detail.

7.202.2 Relevant corporation tax

Relevant corporation tax is defined in TCA 1997, s 448(1)(d). In short, it means corporation tax on income (but excluding corporation tax on any income taxable at the higher rate of corporation tax – see below). It is described as the corporation tax that would be chargeable on a company's profits for an accounting period, exclusive of the tax chargeable on the part of the profits attributable to chargeable gains (and excluding corporation tax on any income taxable at the higher rate of corporation tax – see below). Where a company's profits include chargeable gains, those gains are to be taken for this purpose as the amount before any deduction for charges on income (see **4.4**), expenses of management (see **12.703**) or other amounts (see below) which can be deducted from or set off against or treated as reducing profits of more than one description.

The "other amounts" would include such amounts as TCA 1997, s 396(2) losses (see **4.101**), excess capital allowances over Case V income (see **4.107** and **5.505.1**) and group relief (see **8.305**); in addition, from 1 January 2007, trading losses, excess trading charges and group relief for trading losses and charges are deductible against certain Case III income (foreign dividends taxable at 12.5% rate – see **3.101.5**) and are accordingly amounts which can be deducted from or set off against or treated as reducing profits of more than one description .

A company's profits may include income taxable at the higher rate of corporation tax in accordance with TCA 1997, s 21A (see **3.101.4**). To prevent distortion in the calculation of manufacturing relief which would otherwise occur if relevant corporation tax included corporation tax calculated at the higher rate as well as at the standard rate, TCA 1997, s 448(5A) provides that relevant corporation tax is not to include any corporation tax calculated at the higher rate. Accordingly, the "relevant corporation tax" of a company for an accounting period is reduced in any such case by an amount determined by the formula:

$$\frac{R}{100} \times S$$

where:

R   is the rate specified in TCA 1997, s 21A(3) (ie, the higher rate of corporation tax) in relation to the accounting period; and

S   is an amount equal to so much of the profits of the company for the accounting period as are charged to tax in accordance with TCA 1997, s 21A.

Again, to prevent distortion in the manufacturing relief formula, it follows that the amount of total income in the denominator must also be reduced by the amount of the company's income which is chargeable at the higher rate for the accounting period. TCA 1997, s 448(5A)(b) provides that notwithstanding TCA 1997, s 4(4)(b), the income of a company, referred to in the expression "total income brought into charge to corporation tax" (see **2.603**), is to be the sum determined by that paragraph reduced by any amounts allowed under TCA 1997, s 243A, 396A or 420A, as well as an amount equal to so much of the profits of the company for the accounting period as are charged to tax in accordance with TCA 1997, s 21A.

Example 7.202.2.1

The income, gains and other relevant information for Harrold Ltd for its latest relevant accounting period are as follows:

	€
Case I	750,000
Case III	130,000
Case V	120,000
Chargeable gains	150,000
Charges (non-trade) on income paid	40,000
Group relief ("relevant trading loss") from fellow group member	120,000

The relevant corporation tax, based on the above details, is as follows:

	€	€
Case I	750,000	
Group relief (TCA 1997, s 420A)	120,000	
	630,000	
Corporation tax @ 12.5%		78,750
Case III	130,000	
Case V	120,000	
	250,000	
Charges	40,000	
	210,000	
Corporation tax @ 25%		52,500
		131,250
Reduced by (TCA 1997, s 448(5B))		52,500
"Relevant corporation tax"		78,750

The charges, which are deductible against profits of more than one description, are in this case attributed entirely to the company's income and not at all to chargeable gains, and then, by concession, to the income chargeable at the higher rate of corporation tax. In this example, the relevant corporation tax is simply the corporation tax attributable to the company's trading income. In accordance with TCA 1997, s 420A, the group relief, being in respect of a relevant trading loss, is set off against the company's trading income (see **8.306**).

Relevant corporation tax for an accounting period is the amount of tax that would be chargeable on income for that period (exclusive of any income chargeable at the higher rate of corporation tax) but ignoring certain specific provisions, including the following:

(a)   TCA 1997, s 448 – manufacturing relief itself;

(b)   TCA 1997, s 22A – 12.5% rate of corporation tax (see **3.101.5**);

(c)   TCA 1997, s 239 – income tax on annual payments (see **4.306**);

(d)   TCA 1997, s 241 – income tax on payments made by non-resident companies (see **4.303.5**);

(e)   TCA 1997 ss 440 and 441 – surcharge on certain undistributed income of close companies (see **10.302** and **10.303**);

(f)   TCA 1997, s 449 – unilateral credit for foreign tax (see **14.4**);

(g)   TCA 1997, s 644B – 20% rate of corporation tax relating to dealing in residential development land (for the year 2000 only);

(h)   TCA 1997, s 827 – double tax relief – application to corporation tax of arrangements under old law affecting corporation profits tax (see **14.202**); and

(i)   TCA 1997 Sch 32 paragraphs 16 and 18 – relief for income tax and corporation profits tax losses (TCA 1997, s 448(1)(d)).

7.202.3   Manufacturing relief formula: income from the sale of goods

The basic manufacturing relief formula is derived from TCA 1997, s 448(2). That subsection provides that where a company sells goods for any accounting period in the course of carrying on a trade which consists of or includes the manufacture of goods, corporation tax payable by the company, to the extent that it is referable to the income from the sale of those goods, is to be reduced by the appropriate fraction. For this purpose, the corporation tax referable to "the income from the sale of those goods" is an amount which bears to the "relevant corporation tax" (see above) the same proportion as the income from the sale of those goods bears to the total income brought into charge to corporation tax. As seen in **7.202.2** above, the "total income brought into charge to corporation tax" for this purpose is reduced by any amounts allowed under TCA 1997, s 243A, 396A or 420A and any income chargeable to tax at the higher rate of corporation tax. At this stage (with a standard corporation tax rate of 12.5%), the product of TCA 1997, s 448(2) can be represented by the formula:

$$\text{relevant corporation tax} \times \frac{\text{income from the sale of goods}}{\text{total income}} \times \frac{1}{5}$$

Where a company's trade consists entirely of the sale of "goods", the required apportionment will be by reference to the company's trading income as a proportion of total income, as in the above formula. It will frequently be the case, however, that the trade will include sales of both "goods" (goods manufactured by the company) and "merchandise" (goods not so manufactured – "bought-in" goods). In a case where no deduction is being claimed for a trading loss, trading charges or group relief, *the income from the sale of those goods* for any accounting period will be the sum which bears to the amount of the company's income from the sale of both goods and merchandise the same proportion as the amount receivable by the company in the period from the sale of goods bears to the total amount receivable in the period from the sale of goods and merchandise (TCA 1997, s 448(3)). In other words, the income from the trade of selling both goods and merchandise is apportioned on a sales ratio basis to arrive at the income from the sale of goods.

Income from the sale of goods can now be represented by the formula:

$$\text{income from sale of goods \& merchandise} \times \frac{\text{sale of goods}}{\text{sale of merchandise}}$$

The previous two formulae can now be combined to produce the following formula:

$$\text{relevant corporation tax} \times \frac{\text{income from sales of goods \& merchandise} \times \dfrac{\text{sales of goods}}{\text{sales of goods \& merchandise}}}{\text{total income}} \times \frac{1}{5}$$

Example 7.202.3.1

Taurus Ltd has the following results for its latest relevant accounting period:

	€
Sales:	
Own manufactured goods	4,000,000
Bought-in goods	2,000,000
	6,000,000
Trading income	600,000
Case III	40,000
Chargeable gain	60,000
Profits	700,000

Corporation tax computation:

Profit as above, excluding chargeable gain	640,000
Corporation tax	
Case I €600,000 @ 12.5%	75,000
Case III €40,000 @ 25%	10,000
	85,000

Less: manufacturing relief:

$$€75,000 \times \frac{600,000 \times 4m/6m}{600,000} \times 1/5 =$$

	10,000
	75,000
Add: corporation tax on chargeable gain €60,000 x 20/12.5 x 12.5% =	12,000
Payable	87,000

Income from the sale of goods: effect of trading losses and charges

The amount arrived at by applying the turnover fraction to the income from the sale of goods and merchandise is referred to as the "relevant sum" (TCA 1997, s 448(3)(a)). In many cases, as explained above, this will also be the amount of the income from the sale of goods. Where, however, for any accounting period ending on or after 18 February 2008 a company has paid any trading charges or has had its income reduced by a trading loss, or has claimed group relief in respect of a trading loss or excess trading charges, the relevant sum is reduced by any such amount to the extent allowed against the company's "income for the relevant accounting period from the sale of those goods" (TCA 1997, s 448(3)(b)).

All relevant trading losses (see **4.103**), relevant trading charges on income (see **4.405**), and such losses and excess charges surrendered by way of group relief (see **8.306**), are deductible from "relevant trading income".

For the purposes of the manufacturing relief formula, however, "income from the sale of goods and merchandise" is calculated as if no relief for any of the above-mentioned losses or charges had been allowed (TCA 1997, s 448(4)). Instead, as mentioned above, the relevant sum is reduced by any such losses or charges to the extent that they have been allowed against the "income for the relevant accounting period from the sale of those goods".

The above procedure results in the following formula:

$$\text{Relief} = 1/5 \times \text{Relevant CT} \times \frac{\text{Income from G} + M \times \dfrac{\text{sales of G}}{\text{sales of G} + M} - \text{s } 448(3)(b)}{\text{Total income}}$$

where–

  G = goods (manufactured by the company; and

  M = merchandise (goods not manufactured by the company).

To summarise, manufacturing relief is one-fifth (where the standard corporation tax rate is 12.5%) of the relevant corporation tax (corporation tax on income excluding income taxable at the 25% rate) multiplied by a formula. The numerator in the formula is trading income (excluding any services type income) multiplied by sales of goods and divided by sales of goods and merchandise, reduced by any amount allowed in respect of trading charges or a manufacturing loss (including any such amount claimed by way of group relief) to the extent that any of these amounts has been allowed against the company's "income for the relevant accounting period from the sale of those goods". The denominator in the formula is the amount of total income less any trade loss, trade charges or group relief in respect of such loss or charges and less any amount that has been taxed at the 25% rate. See **7.203.2**, including Example **7.203.2.1**, for further treatment of this aspect.

7.202.4 Income from the sale of goods and merchandise

So far, it has been assumed that there is no difficulty as regards the meaning of income from the sale of goods and merchandise. Where a company's trade consists only of sales of goods and merchandise, its income from the sale of goods and merchandise is the amount of its trading profits (TCA 1997, s 448(4)). In some cases, however, a company's trade will include other income, which is derived neither from sales of goods nor from sales of merchandise. For example, a company carrying on a trade of selling computer software, comprising both manufactured and bought-in software, might also provide consultancy or training services related to computer software where those activities are regarded as part of the trade which includes the sales of software. In that case, the sales ratio basis cannot be applied to the company's trading profits as a whole.

TCA 1997, s 448(4) provides that where the income from the company's trade for any accounting period is not derived solely from sales of goods and merchandise, its income from the sale of goods and merchandise is to be "such amount of the income from the trade as appears to the inspector or, on appeal, to the Appeal Commissioners, to be just and reasonable". It will be necessary therefore to arrive at the amount of the income from the sale of goods and merchandise and the amount of the other trading income by reference to the facts pertaining to the particular case; the legislation provides no formula for this purpose. In effect, separate profit and loss accounts should be prepared for the sales and services activities. The direct expenses attributable to each part will be allocated accordingly while other expenses should be apportioned on a "just and reasonable" basis. As to how this should be done in any case is entirely dependent on the facts and circumstances of that case.

The company should prepare its own separate profit and loss statements for the sales and services aspects of its trade, allocating non-specific expenses or general overheads on a reasonable basis. Some expenses may reasonably be apportioned on a turnover basis while the most appropriate basis of apportionment in other cases may relate to such factors as usage of floor area, staff time (in the case of employees engaged in both aspects), and use of equipment and facilities. Separate capital allowances computations should be prepared for plant, machinery etc used for the respective activities of the trade. Where any fixed assets are used for both types of activity, capital allowances should be computed for those items in the normal way and the resulting allowances then apportioned by reference to the usage of those items for the respective activities.

In summary, the income from the separate sales and other activities comprised in a company's trade is individually computed for each activity, on a just and reasonable basis, and the sales ratio basis is then applied to the income from sales (ie of goods and merchandise) to arrive at the income from the sale of goods. As will be seen below (**7.205**), certain activities which are not in fact manufacturing activities, including certain service activities, are deemed to be manufacturing activities for the purposes of the relief. In these cases, in arriving (on a just and reasonable basis) at the amount of income from the sale of goods and merchandise, any income from services activities deemed to be the manufacture of goods will be included in the manufacturing relief formula as income from the sale of goods and merchandise and, in the sales ratio part of the formula, any receipts deemed to be receipts from the sale of goods will be included as sales of goods.

For the purposes of calculating manufacturing relief, the amount receivable from the sale of goods and merchandise for any accounting period is deemed to be reduced by the amount of any duty paid or payable by the company in respect of the goods or merchandise or in respect of the materials used in their manufacture and should not include any amount in respect of value-added tax chargeable on the sale of the goods and merchandise (TCA 1997, s 448(5)). A company may be required by notice in writing from the inspector of taxes to furnish him with such information or particulars as may be necessary to ensure that these matters are dealt with correctly.

7.202.5 Total income

The denominator in the manufacturing relief formula is "total income brought into charge to corporation tax". TCA 1997, s 4(4)(b) defines *total income brought into charge to corporation tax* as the amount of the total income from all sources included in any profits brought into charge to corporation tax (see also **2.603**). That amount is to be calculated before any deduction for charges on income, expenses of management or other amounts which can be deducted from or set against or treated as reducing profits of more than one description (see **7.202.2** above).

Where, however, any part of the profits of an accounting period of a company are charged to corporation tax in accordance with TCA 1997, s 21A (higher rate of corporation tax – see **3.101.4**), the total income brought into charge to corporation tax, as well as being reduced by any amounts allowed under TCA 1997, s 243A, 396A or 420A, must be reduced by the amount charged to corporation tax at the higher rate of corporation tax (TCA 1997, s 448(5B)).

7.203 Trading losses and charges

7.203.1 Restriction of trading losses and charges

A trading loss incurred by a company in an accounting period in respect of an activity that is subject to the 10% or 12.5% rate of corporation tax (a "relevant trading loss") may not be offset against profits of that accounting period other than income taxable at the 10% or 12.5% corporation tax rates ("relevant trading income").

A *relevant trading loss*, in relation to a company's accounting period, means a loss incurred by the company in the accounting period in a trade carried on by the company, other than so much of the loss as is a loss incurred in an excepted trade within the meaning of TCA 1997, s 21A (see **3.101.4**).

Relevant trading income, in relation to an accounting period of a company, means the trading income of the company for that period (excluding any income taxable under Case III of Schedule D) other than so much of that income as is income of an excepted trade within the meaning of TCA 1997, s 21A (TCA 1997, s 396A(1) and s 243A(1)).

From the above, it can be seen that a relevant trading loss may consist of, or may include, a manufacturing loss ("loss from the sale of goods", ie a loss incurred in an accounting period in respect of an activity subject to tax at the 10% rate). For any accounting period or part accounting period ending before 1 January 2003, a manufacturing loss could only be set against manufacturing income of that period and, if the company was then carrying on the trade in respect of which the loss arose, against manufacturing income of immediately preceding accounting periods ending within a period equal in length to the period in which the loss was incurred.

(For a more detailed treatment of the position applying before 2003, see the 2003 edition of this book.)

Where any trading loss is being set against manufacturing profits, the loss is to be deducted from the income from the sale of "goods" and not (if there are also sales of merchandise) from the income from the sale of both "goods and merchandise" (TCA 1997, s 448(3)(b)). In the manufacturing relief formula, the "relevant sum" is first derived from income from the sale of goods and merchandise, using the sales ratio basis, and the trading loss to the extent allowed against the company's "income for the relevant accounting period from the sale of those goods" (see *Technical note* on this in **7.203.2** below) is then deducted from the relevant sum.

Charges on income paid by a company in an accounting period in respect of a trading activity ("relevant trading charges on income") may not be offset against profits of that accounting period other than relevant trading income.

Relevant trading charges on income, in relation to a company's accounting period, means the charges on income paid by the company in the accounting period wholly and exclusively for the purposes of a trade carried on by the company, other than so much of those charges as are charges on income paid for the purposes of an excepted trade within the meaning of TCA 1997, s 21A (see **3.101.4**).

It can be seen that relevant trading charges on income may consist of, or may include, "manufacturing" charges ("charges on income paid for the purpose of the sale of goods").

Excess trading charges may be carried forward and set against trading profits, whether from manufacturing profits or not, in accordance with TCA 1997, s 396(7).

A trading loss incurred, or trading charges paid, by a company in respect of an activity that is subject to the 10% or 12.5% rate of corporation tax, may not be offset, for group relief purposes, against profits of a fellow group member of that accounting period other than relevant trading income.

7.203.2   Effect on manufacturing relief

In calculating the amount of a company's "income from the sale of goods" for manufacturing relief purposes, any amount referred to in TCA 1997, s 448(3)(b) is, as indicated in **7.202.3**, deducted from the relevant amount, the amount arrived at after applying the sales ratio apportionment. Furthermore, where any part of the company's profits is charged to corporation tax in accordance with TCA 1997, s 21A (higher rate of corporation tax – see **3.101.4**), the amount charged at the higher rate, together with any amount allowed under TCA 1997, s 243A, 396A or 420A, is also deducted in arriving at the amount of the company's total income chargeable to corporation tax (TCA 1997, s 448(5B)).

Example 7.203.2.1

The results of Cato Ltd for its most recent relevant accounting period (ending after 17 February 2008) are as follows:

	€
Sales of goods (G)	18,000,000
Sales of merchandise (M)	6,000,000
Case I	3,200,000
Group relief for trading loss (TCA 1997, s 420A)	1,000,000
Corporation tax:	
Case I	3,200,000
Group relief	1,000,000
Taxable	2,200,000
Corporation tax @ 12.5%	275,000
Manufacturing relief	41,250
Corporation tax payable	233,750

Manufacturing relief:

$$\text{Relief} = 1/5 \times \text{relevant CT} \times \frac{\left(\text{income from G} + \text{M} \times \dfrac{\text{sale of G}}{\text{sale of G} + \text{M}}\right) - \text{s } 448(3)(b)}{\text{total income}}$$

$$= 1/5 \times €275,000 \times \frac{(3,200,000 \times 18/24) - 750,000}{2,200,000} = €41,250$$

Notes:

1. In the numerator, the trading loss attributable to manufacturing, using the proportion 75%, is deducted from the relevant amount.

2. Total income is €3,200,000 less TCA 1997, s 420A trading loss €1,000,000.

Example 7.203.2.2

The results of Cicero Ltd for its most recent accounting period (ending before 31 January 2007) are as follows:

	€	€
Sales of goods (G)		24,000,000
Sales of merchandise (M)		6,000,000
Case I		4,000,000
Case III		1,600,000
Charges		
– royalties	800,000	
– interest allowed as a charge	400,000	1,200,000
Manufacturing loss from separate trade		900,000
Group relief claimed for manufacturing loss		1,100,000
Group excess manufacturing charges claimed		300,000

Corporation tax computation:

Case I		4,000,000
Loss relief TCA 1997, s 396A	900,000	
Charges (relevant trading charges) TCA 1997, s 243A	1,000,000	
Group relief TCA 1997, s 420A	1,400,000	3,300,000
		700,000
Case III		1,600,000
Total income		2,300,000
Charges (other than relevant trading charges)		400,000
Taxable		1,900,000

Corporation tax:

€1,200,000 (Case III net of non-relevant charges[4]) @ 25%	300,000	
€700,000 @ 12.5%	87,500	387,500
Manufacturing relief		2,500
Corporation tax payable		385,000

Income from the sale goods

Relevant sum (€4m x 80%)		3,200,000
Less TCA 1997, s 448(3)(b) amounts:		
Loss	900,000	
Charges	800,000	
Group relief	1,400,000	3,100,000

	€	€
Income from the sale of goods		100,000

Charges Restriction:

	€	€
Income after sales ratio apportionment		3,200,000
Less: relief under TCA 1997, s 396A		900,000
		2,300,000
Royalties	1,000,000	
Paid for the purpose of sale of goods (sales ratio basis)		800,000
Therefore restriction		Nil

Group relief restriction:

	€	€
Income from sale of goods		3,200,000
TCA 1997, s 396A loss relief[1]	900,000	
Charges TCA 1997, s 243A[1]	800,000	1,700,000
		1,500,000
Group relief	1,100,000	
Excess charges	300,000	1,400,000
Therefore restriction		Nil

Manufacturing Relief:

$$\text{Relief} = 1/5 \times \text{relevant CT} \times \frac{\left(\text{income from G} + \text{M} \times \dfrac{\text{sale of G}}{\text{sale of G} + \text{M}}\right) - \text{s } 448(3)(b)}{\text{total income}}$$

$$= 1/5 \times €87,500^2 \times \frac{(4,000,000 \times 24/30) - 3,100,000}{700,000\,*} = €2,500$$

* Total income is €5,600,000 less TCA 1997 ss 243A/396A/420A (€3,300,000) and as reduced by 21A amount €1,600,000 (see **7.202.5**).

Notes:

1   The order in which reliefs are to be set off against income from the sale of goods is:

   (a)   loss relief (TCA 1997, s 396A(3)),

   (b)   charges on income paid for the purpose of the sale of goods (TCA 1997, s 243A(3)), and

   (c)   group relief (TCA 1997, s 420A(3)).

2   The relevant corporation tax is the corporation tax charged on the company's income less the amount charged at the higher rate, ie the amount charged above at the 12.5% rate.

3   By deducting the corporation tax charged at the higher rate from the relevant amount, and deducting the income charged at that rate from total income, the amount of manufacturing relief should work out the same as it would have had the reduced rate not applied.

4   By concession, these charges may be deducted from income taxable at the 25% rate.

Where, however, there is any TCA 1997, s 243A, 396A or 420A amount, this will produce a distortion in the manufacturing relief formula as effectively the same amounts will be deducted from both the numerator and the denominator. The effect of this distortion is an increased amount of corporation tax resulting from a reduced fraction.

The following example illustrates the position following the FA 2008 amendment to TCA 1997, s 448(3)(b).

Example 7.203.2.3

The results of Cicero Ltd for its most recent accounting period (ending after 17 February 2008) are as follows:

	€	€
Sales of goods (G)		24,000,000
Sales of merchandise (M)		6,000,000
Case I		4,000,000
Case III		1,600,000
Charges		
– royalties	1,000,000	
– interest allowed as a charge	400,000	1,400,000
Manufacturing loss from separate trade		900,000
Group relief claimed for manufacturing loss		1,100,000
Group excess manufacturing charges claimed		300,000

Corporation tax computation:

	€	€
Case I		4,000,000
Loss relief TCA 1997, s 396A	900,000	
Charges (relevant trading charges) TCA 1997, s 243A	1,000,000	
Group relief TCA 1997, s 420A	1,400,000	3,300,000
		700,000
Case III (all taxable at 25%)		1,600,000
Total income		2,300,000
Charges (other than relevant trading charges)		400,000
Taxable		1,900,000

Corporation tax:	€	€
€1,200,000 (Case III net of non-relevant charges[4]) @ 25%	300,000	
€700,000 @ 12.5%	87,500	387,500
Manufacturing relief		14,000
Corporation tax payable		373,500

Income from the sale goods

	€	€
Relevant sum (€4m x 80%)		3,200,000
Less TCA 1997, s 448(3)(b) amounts:		
TCA 1997, s 396A relief	900,000	

	€	€
Charges TCA 1997, s 243A	1,000,000	
Group relief TCA 1997, s 420A	1,400,000	
	3,300,000	
Allowed against manufacturing income 80%		2,640,000
Income from the sale of goods		560,000

Manufacturing Relief:

$$\text{Relief} = 1/5 \times \text{relevant CT} \times \frac{\left(\text{income from G} + \text{M} \times \dfrac{\text{sale of G}}{\text{sale of G} + \text{M}}\right) - \text{s } 448(3)(b)}{\text{total income}}$$

$$= 1/5 \times €87,500 \times \frac{(4,000,000 \times 24/30) - 2,640,000}{700,000 *} = €14,000$$

   *   Total income is €5,600,000 less TCA 1997 ss 243A/396A/420A (€3,300,000) and as reduced by 21A amount €1,600,000 (see **7.202.5**).

Notes:

1   The order in which reliefs are to be set off against income from the sale of goods is:

    (a)   loss relief (TCA 1997, s 396A(3)),

    (b)   charges on income paid for the purpose of the sale of goods (TCA 1997, s 243A(3)), and

    (c)   group relief (TCA 1997, s 420A(3)).

2   The relevant corporation tax is the corporation tax charged on the company's income less the amount charged at the higher rate, ie the amount charged above at the 12.5% rate.

3   By deducting the corporation tax charged at the higher rate from the relevant amount, and deducting the income charged at that rate from total income, the amount of manufacturing relief should work out the same as it would have had the reduced rate not applied.

4   By concession, these charges may be deducted from income taxable at the 25% rate.

5   The TCA 1997, s 448(3)(b) amount is the proportion (80%) of the TCA 1997, ss 243A/396A/420A amounts that is attributable to manufacturing income (but see *Technical note* below on this).

In Example **7.203.2.3**, the final tax payable in respect of the trading income, €73,500, can be seen as comprising €700,000 x 80% @ 10% + €700,000 x 20% @ 12.5% = €73,500. That should also have been the outcome in Example **7.203.2** but, for accounting periods ending before 18 February 2008, the TCA 1997, s 448(3)(b) deduction in the numerator was excessive. The revised TCA 1997, s 448(3)(b) amount (provided for in FA 2008) recognises the amount of trading losses etc effectively allowed against manufacturing income, assumed here to be on a proportionate basis, in contrast with the former position which provided for a deduction for "manufacturing" losses etc regardless of the fact that a part of these could, effectively, have been allowed against non-manufacturing income.

Technical note: The trading losses etc to be deducted from the relevant sum, as seen above, is the amount of such trading loss etc allowed "against the company's income for the relevant accounting period from the sale of those goods". Clearly the intention of this provision, introduced by FA 2008, is to ensure that the correct amount of manufacturing relief is given and this intention is reflected in Example **7.203.2.3** above (see note 5 to that example). It is suggested, however, that what should be deducted is the amount of the losses etc attributable to the relevant sum, such attribution to be determined on a proportionate basis. The "company's income for the relevant accounting period from the sale of those goods" can, it is suggested, only mean the income which is the very income to be determined by TCA 1997, s 448(3)(b).

7.203.3 Change in corporation tax rate

Where an accounting period begins before 1 January in any year and ends on or after that day, and the standard corporation tax rate is altered with effect from that date, the accounting period is to be divided into two periods, one beginning on the date on which the accounting period begins and ending on 31 December, and the other beginning on 1 January (previously 1 April) and ending on the date the accounting period ends.

By virtue of TCA 1997 ss 26(3) and 4(6), the profits of an accounting period straddling 1 January are apportioned between the two parts on a time basis. Where there are any charges on income, they are also effectively apportioned on a time basis (and are not, for example, allocated to the separate periods on the basis of the respective amounts paid in each such period).

7.204 Meaning of "manufacture"

7.204.1 Introduction

"Manufacture" is not defined in tax legislation and its meaning has therefore been taken for tax purposes according to the ordinary usage of the word. As manufacturing is relevant for the purposes of various incentive reliefs, the Irish Revenue authorities had for some time, particularly during the export sales relief regime, tended to interpret "manufacturing" widely.

With the advent of the 10% corporation tax rate, however, the Revenue took the opportunity to make a fresh start with a view to excluding from the scope of the relief certain operations which had previously qualified for other incentives, primarily export sales relief. This in turn resulted in cases being taken before the courts from which have emerged a number of decisions in recent years.

7.204.2 Case law development

The primary requirement of the manufacturing relief legislation is that the claimant company's income must be derived from the sale of product ("goods") which it has manufactured in Ireland. In most instances, it will be quite easy to determine whether a particular process amounts to the manufacture of goods. In the absence of legislative definition of the word "manufacture", however, there have inevitably been occasions when it has been necessary for the courts to decide whether a particular process amounts to manufacturing. The findings of the courts provide a useful guideline on the relevant factors which are indicative of manufacturing operations. These guidelines can be briefly summarised as follows:

(a) the process must result in the production of a commodity which is different from the raw material; this difference may be in terms of content, in quality or in marketability;

(b) the process must bring about a marked change to the physical and commercial characteristics of the product. Commercial changes must be such as to ensure that the manufactured product commands a higher price and conforms to a higher standard;

(c) the setting in which the process is undertaken is a factor in determining whether the process is one of manufacture. Thus a process undertaken in an industrial setting may qualify for relief while a similar process undertaken in a non-industrial setting might not qualify;

(d) the change effected on the raw materials must be as a result of the process undertaken. In this regard, the setting and the degree of physical involvement in effecting this change will be relevant;

(e) in construing the word "manufacture", regard must be had to the scheme and purpose of the relevant incentive legislation.

Examples of processes which the courts or the tax authorities have accepted as constituting the manufacture of goods include volume replication and assembly of software products, the assembly of farm machinery, printing operations and blending of alcoholic drinks. (In addition, tax legislation specifically confirms that newspaper production and processing of meat in an EU approved establishment will constitute industrial manufacturing.)

In *Cronin v Strand Dairy Limited* ITL 135 the company claimed, for the purposes of the 10% corporation tax rate, that its activities of processing of milk constituted manufacturing. The milk was transported in bulk tankers to the company's premises where it was pasteurised and bottled or packaged. The procedure, which was sophisticated and required a high degree of skill, consisted of heating the milk to a particular temperature for a certain period of time. The plant involved was extensive and expensive and included enormous holding tanks with sections for heating, cooling, pumping and filtering.

Mr Justice Murphy, in the course of his judgment, noting that "manufacture" had come to designate an operation by which goods are produced on a larger scale by a combination of man and machine, found that an ordinary man looking at the company's premises and the operation of the plant and equipment would readily accept that a manufacturing process was involved. The relevant test involves comparing the final product with the raw material used. A manufacturing process requires the application of labour and equipment and some change in the substance subjected to the process. The question is to a large extent one of degree.

In this case the milk was changed into pasteurised milk, with the result that harmful and disease causing micro-organisms were killed off. The new product keeps better but is less suitable for other purposes such as making cheese or bread. The value of the new product is much greater insofar as it becomes legally saleable. Consequently it was held that the end product was a commercially different product from that which existed previously and that the company was therefore entitled to the 10% corporation tax rate.

In *Charles McCann Limited v S Ó Culacháin* (HC 1984) the company sought to establish that it was engaged in a manufacturing process for the purposes of a claim to export sales relief. The company's trade involved the importation of unripe bananas from Ecuador and Colombia and the subjecting of them to a complex and costly process of ripening artificially by ethylene gas in specially constructed and equipped ripening rooms. The process required special expertise.

Judgment was given in favour of the company on appeal to the Supreme Court. McCarthy J, referring to the question whether the ordinary person in the street would describe the bananas which had been subjected to the ripening process as "*manufactured goods*" (considered in the High Court), thought that the correct question was whether the ordinary person adequately informed of the relevant facts would so describe that process.

The relevant facts were those discussed by Murphy J in the *Strand Dairy* III ITR (411) case where he stated:

> It seems to me, therefore, that one must look at the goods alleged to have been manufactured and consider what they are, how they appear, what qualities they possess, what value attaches to them. One then looks at the process and seeks to identify to what extent that process conferred on the goods the characteristics which they are found to possess.

That approach was endorsed by McCarthy J subject to the qualification "that one must also, in aid of construction of the particular word as used in the statute look at the scheme and purpose as disclosed by the statute or the relevant part thereof"

McCarthy J went on to note that:

> it is manifest that Part IV of the Act of 1976 was, by tax incentives, to encourage the creation of employment within the State and the promotion of exports, naturally, outside the State, objectives of proper, social and economic kind which the State would be bound to encourage. Employment is created by labour intensive processes and exports by the creation and sale of goods. The operation described in the case stated clearly comes within both categories; in my judgment, it is then a matter of degree, itself a question of law, as to whether or not what the company has done to the raw material makes it goods within the definition of section 54. Applying that test, I am satisfied that the ripened bananas, having been subjected to the process as described, constitute a commercially different product and one within the definition.

In *Kelly v Cobb Straffan Ireland Ltd* IV ITR 526, the High Court (1993) held that a company carrying on the business of producing day old chicks was carrying on a manufacturing process. The company had argued that the product was produced by an artificial, mechanical or manufacturing process and was a standardised product which could not be replicated in a natural process. In *TJ Brosnan v Leeside Nurseries Ltd* V ITR 21 (Supreme Court 1997) it was held that the production of dwarfed chrysanthemum plants did not constitute the manufacture of goods. Distinguishing the conclusion in the *McCann* case which was concerned with the artificial ripening of inanimate objects in the form of bananas which had been severed (and probably limiting somewhat the effect of the *Cobb Straffan* decision), it was observed that the cultivation of living things cannot be a process of manufacturing.

One important question which had been debated for a number of years was whether "manufacture" includes the assembly into a final product of a number of components bought in and not themselves manufactured by the company which carries out the assembly. This issue was addressed in *Irish Agricultural Machinery Ltd v O'Culacháin* III ITR 611. Although the case in question was one decided in the context of the pre-FA

1986 system of stock relief which is no longer applicable (other than for farming trades), it is clear from the judgment in that case that the word "manufacture" has to be considered in the same way for manufacturing relief as it previously applied for stock relief.

The company imported components for agricultural machinery, purchased the necessary additional material locally, and assembled those components into finished machines which it then sold. The assembly operation was on a machine by machine basis. In some cases components or material procured locally were assembled to imported components while in other cases components imported from abroad were adapted, altered and fitted with other parts which may have been imported from different foreign sources.

In the High Court, Mr Justice Murphy noted that it was generally agreed that the company's operations were correctly described as "assembly processes" but that the company claimed that their assembly processes were highly sophisticated requiring the employment of skilled operatives, that the requisite components were not all imported from the one supplier and that some components had to be obtained from other suppliers either domestically or internationally, that the actual work carried out by the operatives was not a mere bolting together but involved a degree of adaptation or alteration to make the machinery "farm worthy" in Ireland.

The Judge found that the process or operation engaged in by the company was such that the components were not subjected to physical forces or chemical reaction, and that the evidence showed that the components remained identifiable in substance and in form on completion of the procedures. The change brought about by the process was a change in the sense that the components were combined or assembled but there was not any significant change in the components themselves.

As to who had manufactured the finished product, it seemed that the only proper way to answer this question was to say that the components had been manufactured by one party and that the machines had been assembled by the company. The Judge stated that "it seems to me that any process which is properly described as one of assembly – however sophisticated – would not be understood by the ordinary well-informed layman as a manufacturing process".

In the judgment delivered in the Supreme Court on 16 March 1989, Mr Justice Griffin stated that "it seems to me that an ordinary adequately informed person would attribute the word 'manufacture' to the process carried on by the company. All the machines have a utility, a quality and a value entirely distinct from the component parts which comprise the whole. Instead of a confusing array of innumerable components (to borrow the phrase used by Murphy J) which would be of no use or value whatever to anyone engaged in agriculture, each of the machines is of immense utility and value, and it seems to me that the fact that they have been 'assembled' rather than fabricated begs the question. It does not necessarily follow that it cannot be described as manufacture". In the judgment, reference was made to *Prestcold (Central) Ltd v Minister for Labour* [1969] 1 All ER 69) where Lord Denning said, in p 71, that:

it seems to me that when a person makes a machine, by getting component parts from elsewhere and assembling them together himself, he can properly be said to be 'manufacturing' that machine. Take some of the large works where motor cars and aircraft are assembled. Those establishments are engaged in 'manufacturing' the machines even though all the components come from other places.

Mr Justice Griffin considered that Lord Denning's statement made good sense and expressed a point of view with which informed members of the public could readily agree. He was further of the view that that view "would equally apply to such as an old-style watchmaker or clockmaker who did not fabricate any of the parts used in his watches or clocks which would nevertheless be 'manufactured' by him".

In his judgment, Griffin J referred to the decision of the Court of Appeal in Northern Ireland in *Samuel McCausland v Ministry of Commerce* [1956] NI 36 where the plaintiff company carried on the business of processing, machining and marketing rye grass seed. The rye grass crop was purchased from the growers and the weeds and impurities, amounting to about one twelfth of the crop, were removed by the company's machining plant. The end product was rye grass seed at least 98% pure. The issue in the case was whether the company was engaged in the manufacture of goods so as to qualify for a grant under the Re-Equipment of Industry Act (Northern Ireland) 1951.

In the *McCausland* case, concluding that the plaintiff company was engaged in the manufacture of goods, Lord MacDermott LCJ noted that the product resulting from the process carried on by the company was a marketable commodity and commercially quite different from the original rye grass crop. He said that it was necessary to look at the matter commercially and see what is being produced for sale. In this case, it was "seed in bulk". He went on to state as follows: "In short the bulk with which we are now dealing is much more than an aggregation of individual seeds; it has a utility, a quality and a worth which are due to and cannot be dissociated from the processes carried out in the company's premises. One cannot, as it seems to me, decide this case merely by looking at the goods and giving them a physical description. One must also consider how they came to be what they are and what the company has done to the crop in order to obtain the finished product. The question is, of course, to a large extent one of degree.

Griffin J (in the *Irish Agricultural Machinery Ltd* case) then commented:

> In my view what was said in that case by the learned Lord Chief Justice can be applied to the present case. The end product produced by the company (the completed machines) are a marketable commodity and commercially are something quite different from the component parts from which they have been assembled. The completed machines are, when completed, much more than an aggregation of the individual component parts and have a utility, a quality and a worth which are due to and cannot be dissociated from the process carried out in the company's premises.

A somewhat different case was that of *Ó Culacháin v Hunter Advertising Ltd* IV ITR 35. Here it was held in the High Court by Murphy J that the production for sale of advertising materials such as TV videos, master negatives and posters was not the manufacture of goods for the purposes of manufacturing relief under TCA 1997 Part 14. It was contended on behalf of the company that it sold a tangible physical product constituting manufactured goods and that these goods were created by it. The blank or unexposed celluloid film (the raw material) was of minimum value whereas the exposed and edited film sold to the customer was of substantial value. On behalf of the inspector, it was contended that no manufacturing process was applied by the company to the blank film or, alternatively, if the filming of the particular sequences shown on the videos etc amounted to a manufacturing process, the work which was actually carried out by the company, ie that of selecting and engaging actors, the creation of the concept and the writing of the script and organisation of the programme generally, was separate from any such manufacturing process.

In his judgment, Murphy J referred to the principles applied as he himself had set out in *Cronin v Strand Dairy Ltd* (see above) and which had since been approved by the Supreme Court in *Charles McCann Ltd v Ó Culacháin*. Applying those principles, the finished product in this case was an exposed and edited film, in contrast with the raw material which was the original blank celluloid film. However, he said that it was difficult to see how the enhanced value due to the activity of the company was conferred on the film by any manufacturing process. He considered that the visual recording of images on the blank film was not a manufacturing process applied by the company.

Manufacturing relief applies to corporation tax referable to "income from the sale of those goods" (TCA 1997, s 448(3) – see **7.202.3**). In *L McGurrin v The Champion Publications Ltd (IV)* ITR (466), the High Court held that the taxpayer company was entitled to manufacturing relief in respect of its income from advertising. In the course of his judgment, Barron J noted that "advertising revenue could not arise without sales [of goods] and such revenue therefore arises in respect of such sales". Thus, it is clearly implied, the central question is not whether an item of sales revenue is proceeds from the sale of a manufactured product but whether the income in question would have arisen were it not for the manufactured product.

7.204.3   Activities deemed not to be manufacturing: general

TCA 1997, s 443(6) deems certain goods as not being manufactured goods for the purposes of the 10% corporation tax rate. The restrictions are intended to counter the effects of certain court decisions, including some of those summarised above. TCA 1997, s 443(6)(a) excludes from the scope of manufacturing relief goods resulting from a process consisting primarily of any one of the following:

(i)   dividing (including cutting), purifying, drying, mixing, sorting, packaging, branding, testing or applying any other similar process to a product, produce or material acquired in bulk so as to prepare that product, produce or material for sale or distribution, or any combination of such processes:

Any activity which is essentially "breaking bulk", ie breaking down large products into smaller parts, to facilitate the preparation of the product for sale or distribution, will not qualify as a manufacturing process. This is designed to exclude activities such as the processing of rye grass seed carried on by the plaintiff in the *McCausland* case, grain drying and the grading and packing of coal. The product must be subjected to real change as a result of the process. Mere commercial, legal or quantitative change will not qualify as manufacturing;

(ii)   applying methods of preservation, pasteurisation or maturation (or other similar treatment) to foodstuffs:

This exclusion counters the effect of the decision in the *Strand Dairy Ltd* case as well as an Appeal Commissioners' decision to the effect that cleansing, purifying and preserving dried fruits constituted a manufacturing activity. Another Appeal Commissioners' decision affected was that which found that the holding of stout (a necessary process before the stout is fit for human consumption) amounted to manufacturing. The ripening of bananas and the freezing of food will also no longer qualify as a manufacturing activity.

Only in cases where the total process consists *primarily* of preservation, pasteurisation or maturation will the exclusion takes effect. Accordingly, companies manufacturing foodstuffs will not be denied manufacturing relief where preservation, pasteurisation or maturation is part only of the process; the company will only be denied relief if the total process consists primarily of such a process;

(iii) cooking, baking or otherwise preparing food or drink for human consumption which is intended to be consumed, at or about the time it is prepared, whether or not in the building or structure in which it is prepared or whether or not in the building to which it is delivered after being prepared:

The fact that the food may have been prepared in a different building is immaterial. This exclusion counteracts devices which, for example, sought to secure manufacturing relief in respect of the profits of the kitchen area of a restaurant in circumstances where the food was sold to a separate company which then sold the "manufactured" food to its customers;

(iv) improving or altering any articles or materials without imposing on them a change in their character:

In the case of a company which slightly modifies goods without changing their essential character, the process will not be regarded as manufacturing. Excluded activities would include, for example, the carrying out of modifications to a motor car such as the installation of a radio or sunroof. The kiln drying of timber, previously held by the Appeal Commissioners in the case of *LM v JB O'Connor* to constitute manufacturing, would now be disqualified under this subsection;

(v) Repairing, refurbishing, reconditioning, restoring or other similar processing of any articles or materials, or any combination of such processes:

Excluded activities here would include the restoration of furniture, the refurbishing of motor vehicles, and the reconditioning of motor parts.

Also generally excluded are goods resulting from a process which is not carried out by the company claiming manufacturing relief (TCA 1997, s 443(6)(b)). This exclusion is intended to cover the case of a manufacturing company which subcontracts a substantial part of its manufacturing activity to an outside party so that the company will not be regarded as carrying on a manufacturing process unless the remaining part of the activity is sufficiently complete in itself to constitute a manufacturing process. TCA 1997, s 443(6)(b) is without prejudice to TCA 1997, s 443(1)(b) which deems a company to be the manufacturer of goods actually manufactured by a 90% associated company (see **7.205.2**).

TCA 1997, s 443(6) is without prejudice to the generality of TCA 1997, s 443(1) and is subject to TCA 1997, s 443(2)–(4) and (8)–(15). Apart from TCA 1997, s 443(1), which deals with actual manufacturing, these provisions deem certain activities to be manufacturing (see **7.205** below). It would seem that the intention of the legislation is that it would be inappropriate that any of these activities should be affected by TCA 1997, s 443(6), eg computer services, shipping activities, film production, meat processing, engineering services. There are indications that the Revenue view is that these activities are protected from TCA 1997, s 443(6)(a) only and not from TCA 1997, s 443(6) as a whole so that the subcontracting prohibition would apply to all manufacturing and deemed manufacturing activities. That view, however, is clearly not in accordance with the relevant wording of the legislation.

TCA 1997, s 443(6) is stated to be for the purposes of TCA 1997, s 443 as a whole and not, as was previously (ie, prior to 1 April 1992) the case, to TCA 1997, s 443(1), the intention being to ensure that the restriction is not confined to actual manufacturing. Thus, for example, it appears to have been intended that contract manufacturing (deemed to be manufacturing by virtue of TCA 1997, s 443(21) – see **7.205.15**) is brought within the ambit of the restriction. In *O'Connell v Fyffes Banana Processing Limited* in May 1999, the High Court found that contract manufacturing had not been brought within the ambit of the restriction but that decision was reversed in the Supreme Court in July 2000 (see below).

TCA 1997, s 443(21) provides that the rendering within the State of manufacturing services is to be regarded as the manufacture within the State of goods. If, for example, a company providing such manufacturing services were to subcontract the manufacturing activity to another party, this would not alter the fact that the company is rendering manufacturing services; the effect of TCA 1997, s 443(21) would then be that the company would be deemed to be manufacturing goods. TCA 1997, s 443(6) is concerned with "goods", and not with any service, and the subsection provides that they (ie, the goods) are not to be regarded as manufactured in certain circumstances. It is far from clear that this has any effect on TCA 1997, s 443(21) which makes no provision affecting goods as such but is concerned only with the characterisation of certain services (the rendering of which is regarded as the manufacture of goods).

The *Fyffes* case mentioned above was concerned with a claim by a company engaged in the business of providing banana ripening services to other companies within the Fyffes group. In his decision in the High Court, Mr Justice Geoghegan pointed out that there was nothing to prevent the Oireachtas deeming any kind of activity to be the "manufacture within the State of goods" and that the definition of "goods" itself becomes irrelevant for the purposes of interpreting any such statutory provision (for example, TCA 1997, s 443(21)) since the entire activity is deemed to be the "manufacture of goods".

In July 2000, however, the Supreme Court found in favour of the Revenue on the point. In arriving at its decision, it invoked the interpretative rule in the UK case *Pryce v Monmouthshire Canal Company* to the effect that an exemption from tax must be given expressly and in clear and unambiguous terms. In applying that rule in the *Fyffes* case, however, the Court adopted a rather novel approach to legislative interpretation by looking at the function of TCA 1997, s 443(21) and deciding that the only function of that subsection was to enable a company providing a manufacturing service to qualify for the 10% corporation tax rate when the process it undertook would be regarded as manufacturing if the goods were owned by that company itself. In other words, the only function of the "manufacturing services" provision is to extend the availability of the 10% tax rate to toll manufacturers where the process involved would qualify under the primary legislation.

The reasoning at the High Court stage of the *Fyffes* case would appear to be impeccable but it has been undermined by the "purposive" approach adopted by the Supreme Court. It is interesting to note that this approach is consistent with, and appears to anticipate, section 5 of the Interpretation Act 2000. Arising from that section, even if not obscure or ambiguous, a literal interpretation of a tax provision in any Act may be departed from if such an interpretation "would fail to reflect the plain intention of the Oireachtas" where that intention can be ascertained from the Act as a whole.

The effect of TCA 1997, s 443(6)(b) would appear to depend on the assumption that a company which subcontracts its manufacturing is not thereby itself carrying out the manufacturing process. That would not necessarily mean that the company may only be regarded as carrying out the manufacturing activity where its own employees are engaged in that activity. The issue which arises here goes to the whole question of corporate personality and the means by which a company can be regarded as carrying out or accomplishing any activity. If the true legal or contractual effect of a company's arrangements is that a particular process is carried out for its own account, can it properly be maintained that the company has not then carried out that process merely because, say, the process has been carried out by another company's employees rather than by its own?

The answer to this question must depend on the precise nature of the contractual arrangements. Should a company contract with a second company for the secondment of some of that company's employees for the purpose of carrying out a manufacturing process on its behalf, the company should nonetheless be regarded as having carried out the manufacturing process itself. If, on the other hand, the company contracts with the second company for the carrying out of the manufacturing process, relief would be denied in accordance with TCA 1997, s 443(6). In the first situation, payment would be made to the second company for the hire of staff whereas, in the second situation, the payment to the second company would be in respect of the carrying out of the manufacturing process. Although the company might still argue that it has manufactured the goods in question, it could probably not successfully claim that it has carried out the manufacturing process since, contractually, another company has agreed to do this.

It is understood that tea blending will qualify for the 10% corporation tax rate notwithstanding the TCA 1997, s 443(6) restrictions. This may have implications for other mixing or blending operations, eg blending of whiskey, coffee, honey etc.

The Revenue Commissioners have issued a statement of practice SP-CT/3/90 setting out the procedures to be followed by companies having doubts as to their continued entitlement to the relief in the light of TCA 1997, s 443(6). Such companies will generally be companies whose entitlement to manufacturing relief was derived from one of the court decisions concerned with the meaning of "manufacture". For the purpose of clarifying its manufacturing relief status, a company may make a submission to the Revenue Commissioners enclosing a detailed description of the inputs to the process in question, the process itself, and the goods resulting from the process. The Revenue Commissioners will then express an opinion as to whether or not the activity is to be regarded as manufacturing. Where additional facts subsequently emerge which, if made available at the time the opinion was expressed would have led to a different Revenue opinion, the first opinion will be disregarded.

7.204.4 Intervention sales

Specifically excluded from the definition of "goods" are sales to the intervention agency (TCA 1997, s 443(7)). For this purpose, the sale of goods to a person other than the intervention agency is deemed to be a sale to the intervention agency if and to the extent that those goods are ultimately sold to the agency. Thus, the exclusion cannot be circumvented by selling indirectly to the intervention agency. The exclusion does not apply to the rendering to the intervention agency of services consisting of the subjecting of meat belonging to the agency to a process of manufacture that is carried out in an establishment specified in TCA 1997, s 443(4)(a), ie an establishment approved and inspected in accordance with the European Communities (Fresh Meat) Regulations, 1987 (SI No 284 of 1987).

For the above purpose, *the intervention agency* means the Minister for Agriculture and Food when exercising or performing any power or function conferred on him by Regulation 3 of the European Communities (Common Agricultural Policy) (Market Intervention) Regulations, 1973 (SI No 24 of 1973), and any other person when exercising or performing any corresponding power or function in any Member State of the European Communities.

7.204.5 Retail sales

Also specifically excluded from the meaning of "goods" are goods sold by retail by the company claiming manufacturing relief. Goods will be regarded as not sold by retail if they are sold:

(a) to a person who carries on a trade of selling goods of the class to which the goods so sold to him belong;

(b) to a person who uses goods of that class for the purposes of a trade carried on by him; or

(c) to a person, other than an individual, who uses goods of that class for the purposes of an undertaking carried on by him.

In relation to (b), the person buying the goods from the company claiming manufacturing relief might use those goods as plant or equipment for the purposes of his trade, or as raw materials or ingredients in a further process carried on by him in the course of his trade. The person referred to in (c) might be, say, a government department where the goods, for example furniture, sold to it would be used for its "undertaking". Individuals are excluded here to rule out the case of an individual purchasing goods for use in an "undertaking", for example the purchase of furniture for use in a holiday home.

It is understand that, concessionally, manufacturing relief will not denied where retail sales arise by export in the context of a grant assisted project. This would be of relevance in relation to certain computer services, eg income from software upgrades.

7.204.6 Mining and construction operations

Mining:

TCA 1997, s 444 provides that "income from the sale of goods" may not include income from:

(a) any mining operations for the purpose of obtaining, whether by underground or surface working, any scheduled mineral, mineral compound or mineral substance, within the meaning of section 2 of the Mineral Development Act 1940; or

(b) any construction operations within the meaning of TCA 1997 Part 18 Ch 2 (ss 530-531).

Matters related to mining and the taxation regime for mining operations are dealt with in **13.4**. The nature of mining, and the meaning of "mine", "minerals", "mineral substance" and other related matters are discussed in **13.402.1** where it was also seen that "mine", in relation to certain capital expenditure, means a mine which is operated for the purpose of obtaining, whether by underground or surface working, any scheduled mineral, mineral compound or mineral substance as defined in section 2 of the Mineral Development Act 1940.

The intention of TCA 1997, s 444 is to exclude from the scope of manufacturing relief any profits arising from mining operations even though the profits may arise in the course of manufacturing activities. Thus, income from mining operations is excluded from the meaning of "income from the sale of goods".

The wording in (a) above is taken from the description of mining operations in FA 1977 s 30. That section was concerned with an identical exclusion of both mining and construction operations from the scope of the incentive provided for by FA 1977 Chapter IV; that incentive was in the form of a 25% corporation tax rate for companies which achieved certain employment targets from the years 1997 to 1980.

TCA 1997, s 444(2) deals with the situation in which a company carries on a trade consisting of or including the manufacture of goods and where, in the course of that trade, it carries on any mining operations as described above from which it obtains any scheduled mineral, mineral compound or mineral substance which is not sold by the company in the course of the trade but which forms the whole or part of the materials used in the manufacture of such goods or is to any extent incorporated in the goods in the course of their manufacture. The subsection provides that the part of the income from the mining operations is to be distinguished from the rest of the income from the sale of goods for the purposes of excluding the former element from the scope of manufacturing relief. For this purpose, the part to be distinguished is to be the amount that appears to the inspector of taxes or, on appeal, to the Appeal Commissioners, to be just and reasonable.

A mining company's activities might involve the carrying on of a trade consisting of mining, as described above, and other activities, such as milling or other processing of the mined product. Arising out of the decision in *Tara Mines Ltd v O'Connell* [Supreme Court, 10 October 2002], the entire activity in any such case is likely to be regarded as mining and therefore ineligible for manufacturing relief.

Construction:

The construction operations excluded from manufacturing relief are those described in TCA 1997, s 530. Accordingly, *construction operations* means operations of any of the following descriptions:

(a)   the construction, alteration, repair, extension, demolition or dismantling of buildings or structures;

(b)   the construction, alteration, repair, extension or demolition of any works forming, or to form, part of the land, including walls, road-works, power-lines, aircraft runways, docks and harbours, railways, inland waterways, pipelines, reservoirs, water mains, wells, sewers, industrial plant and installations for purposes of land drainage;

(c)   the installation in any building or structure of systems of heating, lighting, air-conditioning, sound-proofing, ventilation, power supply, drainage, sanitation, water supply, burglar or fire protection;

(d)   the installation in or on any building or structure of systems of telecommunications;

(e)   the external cleaning of buildings (other than cleaning of any part of a building in the course of normal maintenance); the internal cleaning of buildings and structures, so far as carried out in the course of their construction, alteration, extension, repair or restoration;

(f)   operations which form an integral part of, or are preparatory to, or are for rendering complete, such operations as are described above, including site clearance, earth-moving, excavation, tunnelling and boring, laying of foundations, erection of scaffolding, site restoration, landscaping and the provision of roadways and other access works;

(g)   operations which form an integral part of, or are preparatory to, or are for rendering complete, the drilling for or extraction of minerals, oil, natural gas or the exploration or exploitation of natural resources; and

(h)   the haulage for hire of materials, machinery or plant for use, whether used or not, in any of the above-mentioned construction operations.

The above definition of construction operations is taken from TCA 1997, s 530(1) (tax deductions in respect of payments to sub-contractors in the construction industry). It is most unlikely that many of the construction operations in question could form the basis of a claim to manufacturing relief, even in the absence of TCA 1997, s 444, eg the cleaning of buildings, the dismantling of structures, landscaping or site clearance. The construction of buildings could, however, be construed as a manufacturing operation and sales of such buildings, other than by retail, would qualify for manufacturing relief in the absence of TCA 1997, s 444. Installation, haulage or other kinds of construction operations could, however, be affected where they are concerned with goods manufactured by the company concerned.

An interesting case in point is the activities of road marking companies arising out of the decision in *Judge v Highway Markings Ltd* [Appeal Commissioners 1994]. The view of the Revenue is that the processes involved in the operation of road marking companies include processes which are construction operations as defined in TCA 1997, s 530(1). Accordingly, such operations are precluded from manufacturing relief by virtue of the provisions of TCA 1997, s 444(1)(b).

Arising from a review of the method of operation involved in road marking, however, the Revenue accept that a substantial part of the overall processes would qualify for manufacturing relief. Arising from the review, it is accepted that 55% of overall turnover arises from manufacturing and the remaining 45% from construction operations. These percentages are guidelines based on the review carried out. A company claiming a different breakdown as between manufacturing and construction operations will be required to furnish details in support of its position.

It is understood that the Revenue intends to adopt the above proportionate approach in relation to all companies engaged in road marking. In accordance with self assessment principles, it is expected that road marking companies will submit their corporation tax returns on this basis.

The decision in a Canadian case, *Will Kare Paving & Contracting Limited*, is at odds with this view of manufacturing. The case was concerned with the meaning of "manufacturing or processing goods for sale or lease" and involved a contractor who, in pursuance of a contract to repave a road, produced asphalt and applied it to the road. It was found that the contractor did not derive income from the sale of goods manufactured by him; although the asphalt was undoubtedly manufactured, it was not sold, the contract in question being one for services.

TCA 1997, s 444(3) provides for the situation in which an amount receivable by a company from the sale of goods includes consideration for the carrying out of ancillary construction operations, for example the installation of lighting or air-conditioning manufactured by the company, or the haulage of machinery or plant manufactured by the company. In any such case, a part of the amount receivable by the company as appears to the inspector of taxes or, on appeal, to the Appeal Commissioners, to be just and reasonable is to be deemed to be income from construction operations.

In a Circuit Court case, it was held that a business of extracting sand and gravel from gravel pits followed by further operations consisting of washing, grading and crushing the extracted product was not eligible for the 10% corporation tax rate. The activity was held to comprise construction operations on the basis that it involved the exploitation of natural resources. The activity was contrasted with the production of limestone flour or concrete blocks where it was considered that those products had long passed the natural resource stage. It has been indicated, however, that the "exploration or exploitation of natural resources" test will not generally be used by the Revenue, apparently in view of the denial of manufacturing relief that would follow in many cases where a denial of relief was not intended. Thus, it is understood that the crushing of stone will qualify for the 10% rate. Furthermore, the Revenue have indicated that a company engaged in crushing stone as well as washing and grading sand and gravel will qualify for manufacturing relief on the process as a whole.

The "construction operations" basis of disqualification from manufacturing relief would not normally apply in the case of an activity such as the delivery and pouring of ready-mixed concrete. It is understood that the apportionment provided for in TCA 1997, s 444(3) will not apply in cases where the supplier of the concrete does not have any responsibility for the placement or use of the concrete produced. The position would be otherwise, and an apportionment would be required, where, under a single contract, the supplier has responsibility for the supplying and laying of concrete, for example, in the case of a contract for the laying of a yard or car-park.

7.204.7 Industrial manufacturing

Since the introduction of manufacturing relief in 1981, the question as to what constitutes actual or industrial (as opposed to deemed) manufacturing has, as already mentioned, been the subject of decisions in the courts, but has also been considered on many occasions, and ruled on, by the Revenue Commissioners. It would not be practicable to supply here an exhaustive list of the activities which have been accepted as actual manufacturing but it will be useful to comment on some of the more important of these.

The computer industry

The 10% corporation tax rate is available to virtually all areas of the computer industry, including hardware manufacture, remanufacture and repair of computer equipment, software development and technical support services for software activities. Remanufacture and repair of computer equipment is specifically confirmed as manufacturing by TCA 1997, s 443(15) while software development and technical support services for software activities are deemed to be manufacturing by virtue of TCA 1997, s 443(10) (see **7.205.5** and **7.205.10** below). Hardware manufacture, the production of computers and computer equipment, is of course actual manufacturing and does not require any specific statutory support for eligibility as manufacturing for the purposes of the 10% corporation tax rate.

Thus, computer hardware production such as assembly and manufacture of personal computers, mainframe computers, data storage systems, circuit boards and components qualify for the 10% corporation tax rate as industrial manufacturing. Likewise, income arising to a company from the production and outright sale of programs on punch cards, discs, magnetic tape etc would be eligible for the 10% corporation rate under the industrial manufacture heading.

It has been accepted that the 10% corporation tax rate would apply to a computer manufacturing activity comprising the production of an integrated package involving processor unit assembly, unit and component assembly, notebook and handbook assembly, repair activities, sale of third party software, hardware upgrades and the sale of replacement parts. Sales of incidental software not produced in Ireland, sales of parts out of warranty and hardware upgrades where related revenue did not exceed 5% of total sales revenue.

For computer software operations, there are two potential bases of claim for the 10% corporation tax rate. A company may claim under the industrial or actual manufacturing heading where it is involved in the volume replication and assembly of software (shrink wrapped product) and supplies this software under perpetual use licence agreements; it is accepted that receipts under such licence agreements is tantamount to sales of the manufactured product. An alternative basis of claim (where the activity cannot be established as the sale of manufactured goods) is that under the heading of "software development services". To qualify under this heading, the claimant company must undertake software development operations in Ireland in the course of an undertaking which has received employment grants from a government agency (see **7.205.5** below).

Other activities

The following illustrative list of activities qualifying and not qualifying as actual manufacturing, based on decisions of the courts and evolving practice, may give some insight into the factors to be considered in determining whether a particular activity is likely to be accepted as industrial manufacturing.

> *Qualifying*:
> Rolling of feed barley for animal consumption;
> Production of day-old chicks;
> Manufacture and re-manufacture of blood diagnostic machines, upgrading to current standards using current materials and parts with latest technology, and (possibly) the supply of spare parts therefor;
> Limestone production;

Design, manufacture and sale of range of single patient-use medical products, including tubing sets, protection stations, catheters, custom kits and fluid administration sets, provided certain components manufactured by company within one year of commencing to trade: process involving injection and insert moulding, manual and automatic assembly, sterilisation and packaging;

Generation of electricity for sale to Electricity Supply Board;

Production of membrane filters: cut and shape in "clean" environment and sterile packaging;

Production of laser systems: primarily assembly and testing; repair of laser systems carried out in production plant; and

Production of milk and vegetable powder blends: milling and mixing of ingredients on pre-measured basis.

Not Qualifying:

Production of J-Cloths and nappy liners (TCA 1997, s 443(6)(a));

Production of dwarfed chrysanthemums;

Recycling: sorting, cutting and baling of waste paper for further use in recycling industry; and

Production of toilet paper, production of kitchen paper.

7.205　Deemed manufacturing activities

7.205.1　Outline

The 10% corporation tax regime was introduced in 1980 as a relief for manufacturing activities. Relief was initially applied to industrial or actual manufacturing activities along with a relatively small number of other activities which, however, had some manufacturing connotations. In the ensuing years, legislation was enacted providing for manufacturing relief in respect of a range of activities which had less and less to do with manufacturing (eg financial services) but which nevertheless were regarded as manufacturing for the purposes of the relief. The following trading activities qualify for manufacturing relief in accordance with provisions contained in TCA 1997 Part 14:

(a)　the manufacture in the State of goods (actual manufacturing) (TCA 1997, s 443(1)(a));

(b)　sales by a company of goods manufactured by a 90% related company (TCA 1997, s 443(1)(b));

(c)　the production of fish on a fish farm within the State (TCA 1997, s 443(2));

(d)　the cultivation of plants in the State by "micro-propagation" or "plant cloning" (TCA 1997, s 443(3));

(e)　the processing of meat within the State in an establishment approved and inspected in accordance with the European Communities (Fresh Meat) Regulations, 1987 (SI No 284 of 1987) (TCA 1997, s 443(4)(a)) (including processing on behalf of the Intervention Agency – TCA 1997, s 443(7)(c));

(f)　the processing of fish in the State (TCA 1997, s 443(4)(b));

(g)　ship repairs carried out within the State (TCA 1997, s 443(8));

(h)　engineering services, ie design and planning services the work on the rendering of which is carried out in the State in connection with chemical, civil, electrical or mechanical engineering works outside the territories of the Member States of the European Communities (TCA 1997, s 443(9));

(i)   computer services, ie grant aided or financially assisted data processing and software development services rendered in the State and technical or consultancy services carried on in the State which relate to such data processing and/or software development services (TCA 1997, s 443(10));

(j)   certain qualifying shipping activities involving the use of Irish owned and registered ships (TCA 1997, s 443(11));

(k)   the export sale of Irish manufactured goods by any company qualifying as a "Special Trading House" as defined in TCA 1997, s 443(12);

(l)   the repair or maintenance of aircraft, aircraft engines or components, where the repair or maintenance is carried on within the State and outside the Shannon area (TCA 1997, s 443(13));

(m)   the production of a film on a commercial basis, for exhibition to the public in cinemas or on television, or for training or for documentary purposes, provided at least 75% of the production work is carried out in the State (TCA 1997, s 443(14));

(n)   the remanufacture or repair of computer equipment or of subassemblies within the State by the company which originally manufactured them or by a connected company (within the meaning of TCA 1997, s 10 – see **2.3**) (TCA 1997, s 443(15));

(o)   the wholesale sale by certain agricultural and fishery societies of qualifying goods, being goods purchased from their members who themselves are eligible for the 10% corporation tax rate (TCA 1997, s 443(16));

(p)   the sale by an agricultural society of milk purchased from its members and sold on to a qualifying company (ie a company carrying on a trade of manufacturing milk products) (TCA 1997, s 443(17));

(q)   certain foreign exchange transactions of a company arising in connection with TCA 1997, s 130 ("section 84") loans made to it; profits arising, as specified in TCA 1997, s 80, are regarded as an amount receivable from the sale of goods (TCA 1997, s 443(18));

(r)   the production of a newspaper, including the rendering of advertising services in the course of the production (TCA 1997, s 443(19));

(s)   the rendering in the State of manufacturing services in relation to goods belonging to other persons (provided that one or more actual manufacturing processes are involved) (TCA 1997, s 443(21));

(t)   certain services rendered in the Shannon Airport area (TCA 1997, s 445) (see below);

(u)   the carrying on at the International Financial Services Centre in the Custom House Docks Area of Dublin of certain types of financial services on behalf of non-resident persons (TCA 1997, s 446).

The extension of manufacturing relief as outlined in (*o*) and (*p*) above followed the abolition of the exempt status of agricultural and fishery co-operatives (FA 1992 s 48 – see **12.501**).

Subject to TCA 1997, s 443(19) (see (*r*) above), any amount receivable in respect of the rendering of advertising services in the course of the carrying on of a trade, and which consists wholly or partly of the production of a newspaper, magazine or other similar product, is not to be regarded as an amount receivable from the sale of goods; the resulting trading income is to be regarded for the purposes of TCA 1997, s 448 (see **7.202**) as not derived solely from the sale of goods and merchandise (TCA 1997, s 443(20)).

An essential condition of the availability of the 10% corporation tax rate is that the actual work involved in the manufacturing, repairing, production, cultivation or other activity is performed in the State. Generally, eligibility for the 10% corporation tax rate is determined without regard to whether the sales or services are made on the home or export markets. Exceptions are engineering services, sales of Special Trading Houses, international financial services and, in practice to some extent, computer services. The relief for qualifying shipping activities is given without regard to whether the passengers or other customers are residents or non-residents, but only seagoing transport is covered.

Some of the above listed qualifying activities are discussed further below. International financial services are considered separately in **7.206**. The approach adopted with most of the deemed manufacturing provisions is, firstly, to deem the particular activity in question as involving the manufacture of goods. This enables the company in question to be brought within the scope of TCA 1997, s 448(2) which applies to a company "which carries on a trade which consists of or includes the manufacture of goods". Secondly, it is provided that the income from the process or activity in question is to be treated as "an amount receivable from the sale of goods". This enables the corporation tax attributable to the income to be reduced in accordance with the relieving mechanism of TCA 1997, s 448(2)-(5) (see **7.202.3** above).

7.205.2 Associated companies

Where one company manufactures goods in the State and a second company sells those goods in the course of its trade, the goods will be deemed to have been manufactured by the selling company, provided one of the companies is a 90% subsidiary of the other or both are 90% subsidiaries of a third company (TCA 1997, s 443(1)(b)).

A company is a 90% subsidiary of another company if and so long as not less than 90% of its ordinary share capital is *directly* owned by that other company. For accounting periods ending on or after 1 April 1992, the 90% ownership test also requires (as is the case for group relief purposes – see **7.104**) that the parent company is beneficially entitled to not less than 90% of any profits of the subsidiary available for distribution to equity holders and not less than 90% of any assets of the subsidiary available for distribution to equity holders in a winding up (see also **2.504**).

Sales by a manufacturing company to its 90% related sales associate will be subject to the transfer pricing provisions of TCA 1997, s 453. If all of the sales of both companies qualify for the 10% corporation tax rate, this provision will have no effect. If, on the other hand, the sales of the selling company include sales of goods purchased from the related manufacturing company and other sales, it will be necessary to have regard to TCA 1997, s 453 where there is a transfer pricing arrangement which seeks to maximise the profits of the manufacturing company at the expense of the selling company. (See, however, **7.207** and in particular Example **7.207.1**.)

7.205.3 Meat and fish processing

Meat processed in the State in an approved establishment and fish subjected to a process of manufacture within the State are regarded as the manufacture of *goods*.

TCA 1997, s 443(4) provides that "goods" for the purposes of TCA 1997, s 443(1) includes:

(a) meat produced by a company in the State in an establishment approved and inspected in accordance with the European Communities (Fresh Meat) Regulations, 1987 (SI No 284 of 1987); and

(b) fish which has been subjected by a company to a process of manufacture in the State.

The treatment of fish processing as "goods" is subject to the requirement that the fish are not sold by retail (see **7.204.5**) and to the restriction provided for in TCA 1997, s 443(6)(a)(iii) (cooking, baking or otherwise preparing food or drink for human consumption which is intended to be consumed at or about the time it is prepared – see **7.204.3**).

7.205.4 Engineering services

Engineering services means design and planning services the work on the rendering of which is carried out in the State in connection with chemical, civil, electrical or mechanical engineering works executed outside the territories of the Member States of the European Communities (TCA 1997, s 443(9)).

Where a company carries on a trade which consists of or includes the rendering of engineering services, the rendering within the State of those services is regarded as the manufacture within the State of goods. Any amount receivable in payment for the services is regarded as an amount receivable from the sale of goods. Thus, the company's income is eligible for relief in accordance with TCA 1997, s 448 (see **7.202**).

Manufacturing relief as extended to engineering services contains an "export" element in that the engineering projects serviced by the qualifying activity must be executed abroad, and in fact outside the territories of the European Communities.

7.205.5 Computer services

TCA 1997, s 443(10) extends the availability of the 10% corporation tax rate to the provision of computer services. For this purpose, *computer services* is defined as the provision of:

(a) data processing services;

(b) software development services; and

(c) technical or consultancy services related to either or both of (a) and (b),

the work on the rendering of which is carried out in the State in the course of a service undertaking in respect of which:

(i) (a) an employment grant was made by the Industrial Development Authority under s 25 of the Industrial Development Act 1986, or

(b) an employment grant was made by the Industrial Development Agency (Ireland) or Forbairt under s 12(2) of the Industrial Development Act 1993, or

(ii)   a grant under section 3, or financial assistance under s 4, of the Shannon Free Airport Development Company Limited (Amendment) Act 1970, was made available by the Shannon Free-Airport Development Company Ltd (SFADCO); or

(iii)   financial assistance was made available by Údarás na Gaeltachta under s 10 of the Údarás na Gaeltachta Act 1979.

As respects software development services, qualifying activities include the development of both generic and customised software. The term "software development" is interpreted broadly and encompasses both the development of core software and the modification or upgrading of software developed by third parties. Examples of modification work accepted by the tax authorities as constituting software development include the localisation and translation of US developed software for use on European markets, including the international English market, and translation of software text (involving identification and translation of text within a program, additional programming to ensure compatibility of newly translated text with inbuilt codes and additional modifications). (See also *Call centres* and *Shared services* below.)

The appropriate basis for a claim to relief by a company carrying on an activity which is accepted as involving the sales of goods actually manufactured (see *The computer industry* in **7.204.7** above) is TCA 1997, s 443(1) rather than TCA 1997, s 443(10).

Activities qualifying as "data processing services" include back office functions such as sales administration, credit control, order processing, invoicing and accounting services provided to an overseas distribution company and the processing and payment of insurance claims on behalf of an overseas insurance company. It is usual for the data processing operation to be undertaken through a separate legal entity which then provides services to overseas affiliates in return for a fee. The availability of the 10% corporation tax rate is dependent on the project having obtained an employment grant from a government agency. As regards employment grants receivable from the Industrial Development Agency (Ireland), all such grants are exempt from tax in the hands of the recipient company. Any grant designated by the IDA as an "international services employment grant" will satisfy the computer services qualification requirements.

A further activity eligible for relief under TCA 1997, s 443(10) is the provision of "technical or consultancy services" to the software industry. Examples of such activities are the operation of customer support centres, the provision of consultancy services in relation to the selection or design of software systems, and documentation translation and production (involving translation into foreign languages of computer manuals and similar material. The availability of the 10% corporation tax rate is, again, dependent on the project having been grant aided by a government agency and on substantially all of the work being undertaken directly in Ireland. However, depending on circumstances, the tax authorities may agree to make the 10% corporation tax rate available where the nature of the consulting services is such that on-site visits to locations outside of Ireland are necessary.

TCA 1997, s 443(10) is unaffected by the restrictions in TCA 1997, s 443(6). Once the undertaking has an employment grant and the work is done in Ireland, the income qualifies. This is of relevance primarily in the context of subcontracting software development and translation.

Call centres

Operations qualifying under the heading of "data processing" include telemarketing and telesales, hotel, airline, car hire and similar reservation functions and customer and technical support services for the software and similar industries. The 10% corporation tax rate will apply only where income is derived from the provision of call centre services. Accordingly, call centres are usually conducted through a separate legal entity which provides services and recharges affiliated companies or third parties in respect of those services. An example would be hotel reservation services where the company concerned provides services to an overseas hotel chain; the company would be remunerated by way of a service fee which is taxable at the 10% tax rate. The availability of the 10% corporation tax rate for call centre operations is dependent on the project having obtained an employment grant from a government agency (eg, an IDA international services employment grant).

Shared services

Many multinational organisations arrange cost efficiencies by centralising functions which are replicated in a number of different locations. Where such centralisation takes place in Ireland and the shared services are undertaken as a profit centre, the resulting income may be eligible for the 10% corporation tax rate under the "data processing services" heading. Typical functions which might be centralised for this purpose include financial administration, information technology, personnel administration, sales and marketing and real estate management. The availability of the 10% corporation tax rate for shared services is dependent on the project having obtained an employment grant from a government agency.

Functions of multinationals, under the above headings, which may be centralised include the following (source: Establishing Shared Services Centres in Ireland – IDA Ireland):

Financial administration:

> General ledger maintenance;
> Accounts payable maintenance and processing;
> Fixed asset register maintenance and processing;
> Accounts receivable ledger maintenance;
> Inventory accounts and cash maintenance;
> Statutory reporting;
> Financial systems consolidation and administration;
> Payment processing;
> Procurement processing;

Information technology:

> Data centres;
> Applications software development;
> Systems installation;
> Help desk and technical support;
> User licence maintenance;

Personnel administration:

> Benefit co-ordination and administration;
> Medical claims processing;
> Employer services;
> Compensation and pay related queries;
> Stock option programmes;
> Pensions management;
> Staff development and training;
> Employee record maintenance
> Travel administration

Sales and marketing:

> Telemarketing;
> Customer service;
> Technical support;
> Warranty register;
> Trademark control;

Real estate management:

> Asset register;
> Insurance.

7.205.6 Qualifying shipping trades

A company is entitled to manufacturing relief under TCA 1997, s 443(11) in respect of its trading income from qualifying shipping activities carried on by it in the course of a qualifying shipping trade. TCA 1997, s 407 contains the necessary definitions for the purpose (as well as certain rules restricting the use of capital allowances and losses of qualifying shipping trades – see **5.214**).

A *qualifying shipping trade* is a trade the income from which is within the charge to corporation tax and which consists solely of the carrying on, in the period 1 January 1987 to 31 December 2010 (*the relevant period*), of qualifying shipping activities (TCA 1997, s 407(1)). Where a company carries on a trade consisting partly of qualifying shipping activities and partly of other activities, the trade is treated as two separate trades for all the purposes of the Tax Acts (except for the rules relating to the commencement or cessation of trade). Any necessary apportionments of receipts or expenses may be made to determine respectively the profits, losses, etc of the separate trades.

Qualifying shipping activities carried on by a company in the course of a qualifying shipping trade are regarded as the manufacture within the State of goods (TCA 1997, s 443(11). Any amount receivable from the carrying on of those activities is regarded as an amount receivable from the sale of goods.

Although the definition of "the relevant period" in TCA 1997, s 407(1) refers to the period from 1 January 1987 to 31 December 2010 (previously 31 December 2006), the termination date for eligibility for the 10% corporation tax rate for qualifying shipping activities remains 31 December 2000 (TCA 1997, s 442 – definition of "relevant accounting period" (a)).

See also **13.8** in relation to tonnage tax. For the financial year 2002, tonnage tax profits of a tonnage tax company are chargeable to corporation tax at the rate of 12.5% (see **13.803.1**) (TCA 1997, s 21(1A)(c)).

Qualifying shipping activities is defined in TCA 1997, s 407(1) as any of the following activities carried on by a company in the course of trade:

(a) the use of a qualifying ship for the purpose of carrying passengers or cargo by sea for reward;

(b) the provision, on board the qualifying ship, of services ancillary to such use of the qualifying ship;

(c) the granting of rights to another person (not necessarily a company) to provide such ancillary services on board the qualifying ship (eg the right to provide catering services);

(d) the subjecting of fish to a manufacturing process on board a qualifying ship;

(e) the letting on charter of a qualifying ship for use for the purposes mentioned above, but only where the operation of the ship, and the crew of the ship, remain under the direction and control of the company claiming the relief (referred to as a "wet lease" – see below);

(f) the use of a qualifying ship for transporting supplies or personnel to, or providing services in respect of, offshore installations such as a mobile or fixed rig, platform, vessel or installation of any kind.

Regarding (e) above, this refers to a "wet lease" or a "non-demise" charter where the lessor provides the ship, crew, fuel, provisions etc and is responsible for the direction and control of the ship and crew throughout the period of the charter. This kind of lease contrasts with a "dry lease" or "bare-boat" charter where the lessor provides the ship only and the lessee is responsible for the provision of the crew and the direction and control of the vessel and crew.

For a trade to be a qualifying shipping trade, the ship used must be a qualifying ship. A *qualifying ship* is defined as a sea-going vessel which:

(a) (i) is owned to the extent of not less than 51% by a person or persons resident in the State and is registered in the State under Part II of the Mercantile Marine Act 1995, or

(ii) is the subject of a letting on charter without crew by a lessor not resident in the State and is a vessel in respect of which it can be shown that all the requirements of the Merchant Shipping Acts, 1894 to 1993, have been complied with as if it had been a vessel registered under Part II of the Mercantile Marine Act 1995;

(b) is of not less than 100 tons gross tonnage; and

(c) is self-propelled.

Compliance with the provisions of the Mercantile Marine Act 1995, involves meeting Irish standards as to ship safety and the manning of such ships with seafarers having Irish Certificates of Competency or certificates recognised by the Irish authorities as equivalent certificates.

Vessels which do not qualify for the purposes of the 10% rate, even if otherwise meeting the four conditions for a qualifying ship, and which are therefore not qualifying ships, are tugs (except a tug certified by the Minister for the Marine as being capable of operating in seas outside the territorial seas of the State), fishing vessels (except "factory ships" – see below), vessels used primarily as a floating platform for working machinery or as a diving platform (including dredgers), and any other type of vessel not normally used for the purposes of qualifying shipping activities.

The fact that a qualifying ship must be used to carry passengers or cargo by sea excludes from the scope of the 10% corporation tax rate any income from overland transport of passengers or cargo at either end of the sea voyage; any such income is chargeable to corporation tax at the standard rate under the separate trade rule of TCA 1997, s 407(3).

TCA 1997, s 407(1) treats as a qualifying ship a fishing vessel which is normally used to subject fish to a manufacturing process on board the vessel (a "factory ship"). To be a qualifying shipping activity for the purposes of the 10% corporation tax rate, the process applied to the fish must be of such a nature as to be recognised as manufacturing in the context of the fishing industry. It is understood that processing consisting of two or more of the following activities is likely to be considered manufacturing, namely: sorting, cleaning, filleting, fast freezing, smoking, mincing (eg, for fish meal) and packing.

There are restrictions on the use of "specified capital allowances" and losses related to a qualifying shipping trade (see also **5.214**). *Specified capital allowances* are capital allowances in respect of expenditure incurred in the relevant period on the provision of a qualifying ship which is in use in, or is intended to be used in, a qualifying shipping trade. These capital allowances may be allowed only:

(a)   in computing the income from a qualifying shipping trade; or

(b)   in computing or charging to tax any income from the letting on charter of the qualifying ship to which the specified capital allowances refer, other than letting on charter which is a qualifying shipping activity (ie other than letting on charter where the operation of the ship and crew remain under the direction and control of the letting company – see (e) in the definition of "qualifying shipping activities" above) (TCA 1997, s 407(4)(a)).

The activity described in (b) above (a letting on "dry lease", ie the letting on charter of a qualifying ship in the course of a trade, other than a letting which is a qualifying shipping activity) is deemed to be a trade of leasing for the purposes of TCA 1997, s 403 and to be a separate trade for those purposes (see **5.305**). This is despite the provision in TCA 1997, s 403(1)(c) to the effect that leasing does not include the letting on charter of a ship in the course of a trade of operating ships carried on by a company (TCA 1997, s 407(4)(c)).

Where, however, a binding contract in writing for the acquisition or construction of a ship was concluded on or after 1 July 1996, this provision (ie, TCA 1997, s 407(4)(c)) affecting the letting on charter of a qualifying ship (apart from a letting which is a qualifying shipping activity and which, as explained above, is not treated as a leasing trade where the letting activity is in the course of a trade of operating ships) will not apply, subject to conditions. Such letting on charter will not be subject to the ring-fencing treatment of leasing trades provided for by TCA 1997, s 403 where the terms of the lease comply with the provisions of clauses (I) and (II) of TCA 1997, s 404(1)(b)(i) and where the lessee produces a "relevant certificate" to the Revenue Commissioners (TCA 1997, s 407(5)). A *relevant certificate* is a certificate issued by the Minister for the Marine and Natural Resources, with the consent of the Minister for Finance, certifying, on the basis of a business plan and any other information supplied by the lessee, that the Minister is satisfied that the lease in question:

(a) will result in the upgrading and enhancement of the lessee's fleet leading to improved efficiency and the maintenance of competitiveness;

(b) (i) has the potential to create a reasonable level of additional sustainable employment and other socio-economic benefits in the State, or

    (ii) will assist in maintaining or promoting the lessee's trade in the carrying on of a qualifying shipping activity, and the maintenance of a reasonable level of additional sustainable employment and other socio-economic benefits in the State, and

(c) will result in the leasing of a ship which complies with current environmental and safety standards (TCA 1997, s 407(1)).

The Minister must, before issuing the certificate, be satisfied that the lease is for *bona fide* commercial purposes and is not part of a scheme or arrangement the main purpose, or one of the main purposes, of which is the avoidance of tax (TCA 1997, s 407(2)).

As explained above, one of the conditions for avoiding the ring-fencing treatment provided for in TCA 1997, s 430 is that the terms of the lease must comply with the provisions of clauses (I) and (II) of TCA 1997, s 404(1)(b)(i). This relates to an anti-avoidance measure which counters attempts to gain a tax advantage by deferring taxable lease payments ("balloon leasing") and which is dealt with in **5.306**. The anti-avoidance provision ring-fences capital allowances arising in the cases of such leases of machinery or plant by restricting their set-off to income from the balloon lease. The provision will not apply where the lease payments in the primary period of the lease (the period in which the lessor's expenditure on the leased machinery or plant is recovered) are payable on a broadly even basis.

A loss incurred in the relevant period in a qualifying shipping trade may not be set off:

(a) under TCA 1997, s 396(2) against any profits except to the extent of any income included in those profits which is income from a qualifying shipping trade; or

(b) against total profits of another company under the group relief provisions (TCA 1997, s 420(1)) except to the extent of any income included in those profits which is income from a qualifying shipping trade.

See **5.214** regarding the ring-fencing of qualifying shipping trades.

7.205.7   Special trading houses

The 10% corporation tax rate applies to income of a *Special Trading House*, ie a company which exists solely for the purpose of carrying on a trade consisting solely of the selling of export goods manufactured by a firm which employs less than 200 persons (TCA 1997, s 443(12) and European Communities (Special Trading Houses) Regulations 1988 (SI 61/88)). *Export goods* are Irish manufactured goods which are exported by a Special Trading House (which is not the manufacturer) and where the goods are sold by wholesale.

For the above purpose, goods are exported when they are transported out of the State and are not subsequently transported back into the State in the course of the selling by wholesale of those goods. A Special Trading House which sells export goods in the course of its trade is deemed to have manufactured those goods even though the actual manufacturer is also entitled to the 10% corporation tax rate in respect of its sale of the goods.

The provision came into effect on 25 March 1988, the date appointed by the Minister for Finance. *Selling by wholesale* is defined as selling goods of any class to a person who carries on a business of selling goods of that class or who uses goods of that class for the purposes of a trade or undertaking carried on by him. In other words, the Special Trading House exporting the Irish manufactured goods must not do so by way of retail selling. The goods may, however, be sold to a foreign retailer either for resale by him in the course of a trade in goods of the class in question or for use in his business (eg, as office equipment).

The Export Promotion (Amendment) Act 1987, provides for the licensing of Special Trading Houses by the Minister for Enterprise, Trade and Employment who must be satisfied that the applicant has the structure, organisation and marketing ability to undertake successfully the sale of export goods. The applicant may be required to furnish certain information in support of its application. In the event of a refusal of an application, the Minister is required to provide reasons for the refusal. The applicant may appeal to the Circuit Court within 28 days of the refusal. In accordance with Ministerial guidelines, the information which should accompany a licence application would include the following:

(a)   Memorandum and Articles of Association of the proposed company which, preferably, should be a newly incorporated company and which should reflect in its name its status as a Special Trading House;

(b)   The management structure of the company and details of the promoters' expertise in relation to the chosen target markets and/ or product areas;

(c)   Sources and value of the proposed equity finance and of bank facilities for working capital;

(d)   Cash-flow projections for the first three years;

(e)   Details of any contracts to acquire products from manufacturers;

(f)   Marketing plans.

TCA 1997, s 443(12) effectively provides that the 10% corporation tax rate applies to any qualifying trading income of any accounting period, or part of an accounting period, commencing on or after 25 March 1988. For a company commencing a trade which qualifies for the relief after that date, the 10% corporation tax rate applies from the commencement date. No manufacturing relief is available to Special Trading Houses for any accounting period, or part of an accounting period, ending after 31 December 2000.

7.205.8   Aviation repair and maintenance

The 10% corporation tax rate applies to income derived from the repair or maintenance of aircraft, aircraft engines or components where such work is undertaken in the State.

TCA 1997, s 443(13) provides that the 10% corporation tax rate is available to a company which carries on a trade which consists of or includes the repair or maintenance or aircraft, aircraft engines or components. This provision does not apply to any "relevant trading operation" within the meaning of TCA 1997, s 445(7)(a) (the "repair of maintenance of aircraft" by a company operating within the Shannon Airport area – see below).

Repair or maintenance work as described above is regarded as the manufacture in the State of goods and any amount receivable in payment for such repair or maintenance so carried out is to be regarded as an amount receivable from the sale of goods. Thus, the income arising qualifies for the 10% corporation tax rate.

7.205.9   Film production

The production of a film on a commercial basis, wholly or mainly for exhibition to the public in cinemas or on television or for training or documentary purposes, where at least 75% of the production work is carried out in the State, is regarded as the manufacture of "goods" (TCA 1997, s 443(14)).

A *film* for the purposes of TCA 1997, s 443(13) is a film which is produced

(a)   on a commercial basis with a view to the realisation of profit;

(b)   wholly or principally for exhibition to the public in cinemas or by way of television broadcasting or for training or broadcasting or documentary purposes,

and in respect of which not less than 75% of the work on its production is carried out in the State.

The production of a film by a company is regarded as the manufacture in the State of goods. Any amount receivable for the production is to be regarded as an amount receivable from the sale of goods. Accordingly, the income arising qualifies for the 10% corporation tax rate.

7.205.10 Remanufacturing and repair of computer equipment

The remanufacture or repair by a company within the State of computer equipment or subassemblies, where such equipment or subassemblies were originally manufactured by that company or a connected company, is regarded as the manufacture within the State of "goods" (TCA 1997, s 443(15)).

Any amount receivable in payment for such remanufacture or repair is to be regarded as an amount receivable from the sale of goods so that the resulting income qualifies for the 10% corporation tax rate.

A company is connected with another company if it is so connected within the meaning of TCA 1997, s 10 (see **2.3**).

7.205.11 Agricultural and fishery societies

An agricultural or fishery society which carries on a trade consisting wholly or mainly of the wholesale selling of goods purchased by it from its members (all or a majority of whom are agricultural or fishery societies) is entitled to manufacturing relief on its income from the sale of the goods where the members were entitled to manufacturing relief (or would be so entitled were it not for the fact that the goods are ultimately sold to the intervention agency) in respect of those goods (TCA 1997, s 443(16)).

An agricultural society is a society:

(a)   in relation to which the number of its members is at least 50 and all or a majority of its members are persons who are mainly engaged in, and who derive the principal part of their income from, husbandry; or

(b)   to which a certificate received from the Minister for Finance, on the recommendation of the Minister for Agriculture, relates, being a certificate entitling the society to be treated as an agricultural society for the purposes of TCA 1997, s 443(16).

A *fishery society* is a society:

(a)   in relation to which the number of its members is at least 20 and all or a majority of its members are persons mainly engaged in, and who derive the principal part of their income from, fishing; or

(b)   to which a certificate received from the Minister for Finance, on the recommendation of the Minister for the Marine and Natural Resources, relates, being a certificate entitling the society to be treated as a fishery society for the purposes of TCA 1997, s 443(16).

A *society* is a society registered under the Industrial and Provident Societies Acts 1893 to 1978.

TCA 1997, s 443(16) extends the benefit of the 10% corporation tax rate to profits of a qualifying society in respect of its wholesale sales of qualifying goods. A *qualifying society* is an agricultural or fishery society which carries on a trade which consists wholly or mainly of the sale by wholesale of qualifying goods and all or a majority of whose members are agricultural or fishery societies. Thus a qualifying society may be an agricultural society most of whose members are agricultural societies or are fishery societies, or which comprise both agricultural societies and fishery societies. A similar position applies in the case of a fishery society.

Qualifying goods means goods purchased by a society from its members where the goods are such that the members were entitled to manufacturing relief in respect of those goods, or would have been so entitled were it not for the fact that the goods were ultimately sold to the intervention agency. *Selling by wholesale* means selling goods of any class to a person who carries on a business of selling goods of that class or who uses goods of that class for the purposes of a trade or undertaking carried on by him.

Where in the course of its trade a qualifying society sells qualifying goods by wholesale, the qualifying goods are deemed to have been manufactured by the qualifying society even though the society which actually manufactured those goods has claimed, or was entitled to claim, manufacturing relief in respect of them. Any amount receivable in payment from the sale of the qualifying goods by the qualifying society is to be regarded as an amount receivable from the sale of goods. Accordingly, the resulting income qualifies for the 10% corporation tax rate.

7.205.12 Sales by agricultural societies of milk purchased from their members

An agricultural society which purchases milk from its members and sells it to a qualifying company is deemed to have manufactured the milk and to be entitled to manufacturing relief in respect of the income from sales of that milk. A *qualifying company* for this purpose is one which is certified by the Minister for Agriculture and

Food (after consultation with the Minister for Finance) as a company carrying on a *qualifying trade,* ie a trade consisting wholly or mainly of the manufacture of milk products. Unless the trade consists mainly of milk pasteurisation, however, the manufacture of milk products is deemed for this purpose to be a separate trade. For the above purpose, the Minister must be satisfied that the company carried on, or is carrying on, or intends to carry on, a qualifying trade for a period of at least three years (TCA 1997, s 443(17)).

Agricultural society and *society* have the same meanings as in TCA 1997, s 443(16) (see above).

Milk product means butter, whey-butter, cream, cheese, condensed milk, dried or powdered milk, dried or powdered skim-milk, dried or powdered whey, chocolate crumb, casein, butter-oil, lactose, and any other product which is made wholly or mainly from milk or from a by-product of milk and which is approved for the purposes of TCA 1997, s 443(17) by the Minister for Finance after consultation with the Minister for Agriculture and Food.

The extension of manufacturing relief provided for by TCA 1997, s 443(17) applies to sales of *relevant products,* ie milk purchased by an agricultural society from its members, which milk is sold by the agricultural society to a qualifying company.

Relevant products sold by an agricultural society are deemed to have been manufactured by that society and any amount receivable from the sale of the relevant products by the society is to be regarded as an amount receivable from the sale of goods. Thus, the income arising qualifies for the 10% corporation tax rate.

7.205.13 Foreign exchange profits on foreign currency "section 130" borrowings

Profits or losses from foreign exchange transaction arising in connection with certain "section 84" (TCA 1997, s 130) borrowings (see **11.106**) are deemed to be profits or gains or losses of the borrowing company's trade for which the borrowings are used. Any such profits or gains are regarded as amounts receivable from the sale of "goods" (TCA 1997, s 443(18)).

The profits, gains and losses in question are those dealt with in TCA 1997, s 80. That section provides that a profit or loss from any foreign exchange transaction arising in connection with certain foreign currency denominated TCA 1997, s 130 loans is deemed to be a profit or a loss, as the case may be, of the trade carried on by the company in the course of which trade the loan is used.

The type of TCA 1997, s 130 loan to which TCA 1997, s 80 refers is a *relevant liability* which is defined, in relation to an accounting period, as relevant principal:

(a)   denominated in a currency other than the currency of the State; and

(b)   the interest in respect of which:

   (i)   falls to be treated as a distribution for the purposes of the Corporation Tax Acts and

   (ii)   is computed on the basis of a rate which at any time in that accounting period exceeds 80% of the specified rate at that time.

Relevant principal means a TCA 1997, s 130 loan, ie an amount of money advanced to a borrower by a company the ordinary activities of which include the lending of money where:

(a)   the consideration given by the borrower is a security falling within TCA 1997, s 130(2)(d)(ii), (iii)(I) or (v) (see **11.106**); and

(b)   interest or any other distribution is paid out of the assets of the borrower in respect of that security.

The *specified rate* is the three month Dublin Interbank Offered Rate (DIBOR) or, where a record of that rate is not maintained by the Central Bank, the rate known as the Interbank market three month fixed rate as published in the statistical appendices of the bulletins and annual reports of the Central Bank. With effect from 1 January 1999 (the date appointed by the Minister for Finance – SI 502/1998), the specified rate is the three month European Interbank Offered Rate.

TCA 1997, s 80(2) provides that any profit or loss from any foreign exchange transaction, being a profit or loss which arises in an accounting period

(a)   in connection relevant principal which, in relation to the accounting period, is a relevant liability; and

(b)   to a company which, in relation to that relevant liability, is the borrower,

is deemed to be a profit or gain or loss, as the case may be, of the trade carried on the borrower in the course of which trade the relevant liability is used. Prior to the enactment of TCA 1997, s 80, the correct treatment of foreign exchange gains and losses arising from "section 84" loans was uncertain. The particular question at issue was whether any foreign exchange gain arising was properly a part of the trading profit of the company which was the borrower in relation to the loan. If so, the gain would effectively be taxed at the 10% rate; otherwise the gain would have been taxable at the full standard corporation tax rate. TCA 1997, s 80(2) confirms that any gain, or loss, is a gain or loss of the trade.

TCA 1997, s 443(18) provides that the amount of any profit deemed by TCA 1997, s 80(2) to be a profit or gain of the trade carried on by the company is to be regarded as an amount receivable from the sale of goods. Since TCA 1997, s 80 has application only to companies eligible for the 10% corporation tax rate – TCA 1997, s 130 borrowing is confined to such companies – the profits or gains referred to in TCA 1997, s 443(18) are profits taxable at that rate.

7.205.14 Newspapers

It was provided in FA 1992 that, in respect of accounting periods ending on or after 1 April 1992, advertising receipts of companies carrying on a trade consisting wholly or partly of the production of a newspaper, magazine or other similar product, were not to be regarded as amounts receivable from the sale of goods for the purposes of manufacturing relief.

FA 1993, however, revised this measure by providing that, in respect of accounting periods ending on or after 1 April 1992, the manufacture of a newspaper, including the provision of advertising services in the course of producing the newspaper, is to be regarded as the manufacture of goods (now TCA 1997, s 443(19)). Income from the sales of newspapers and revenue from advertising in the course of the production of a newspaper is treated as income from the sale of manufactured goods. For this purpose, *newspaper* means a newspaper:

(a) the contents of each issue of which consists wholly or mainly, as regards the quantity of printed matter contained therein, of information on the principal current events and topics of general public interest;

(b) whose format is commonly regarded as newspaper format; and

(c) which is:

(i) printed on newsprint,

(ii) intended to be sold to the public, and

(iii) normally published at least fortnightly.

TCA 1997, s 443(19) provides, in the case of a company which carries on a trade consisting of or including the production in the State of a newspaper, that:

(a) the production by the company of the newspaper, including the rendering of advertising services in the course of that production, is to be regarded as the manufacture in the State of goods; and

(b) any amount receivable from the sale of copies of the newspaper, or from the rendering by the company of advertising services in the course of the production of the newspaper, is to be regarded as an amount receivable from the sale of goods.

The resulting income therefore qualifies for the 10% corporation tax rate. This will be the case regardless of whether or not the company prints the newspaper.

7.205.15 Manufacturing services

Where a company carries on a trade which consists of or includes the rendering to another person of services by way of subjecting commodities or materials belonging to that person to any process of manufacturing, the rendering within the State of such services is regarded as the manufacture within the State of goods. Any amount receivable by the company in payment for those services is regarded as an amount receivable from the sale of goods (TCA 1997, s 443(21)). Thus, the company's income is eligible for relief in accordance with TCA 1997, s 448 (see **7.202**).

Contract manufacturing activities are therefore eligible for the 10% corporation tax rate. Thus, a company carrying out manufacturing activities in circumstances where it is not the seller of the goods resulting from those activities may be entitled to manufacturing relief.

As was seen in **7.204.3**, TCA 1997, s 443(6)(b) provides that goods are not to be regarded as manufactured where they result from a process which is not carried out by the company claiming manufacturing relief. This exclusion is intended to apply where a company subcontracts a substantial part of its manufacturing activity to another party; the company will not be regarded as carrying on a manufacturing process unless the part of the activity not subcontracted out is sufficiently complete in itself to constitute a manufacturing process. Although there is an Appeal Commissioners' decision to that effect, it is doubtful that that intention is realised.

TCA 1997, s 443(21) provides that the rendering within the State of manufacturing services is to be regarded as the manufacture within the State of goods. If a company engaged in contract manufacturing services were to subcontract the manufacturing activity to another party, this would not alter the fact that the company is rendering manufacturing services; the effect of TCA 1997, s 443(21) would then be that the company would be deemed to be manufacturing goods. TCA 1997, s 443(6) is concerned with "goods" (and not at all with services) and it provides that they (ie the goods) are not to be regarded as manufactured in certain circumstances. It is far from clear that this has any effect on TCA 1997, s 443(21) which makes no provision in relation to goods as such but is concerned only with the characterisation of certain services (the rendering of which is regarded as the manufacture of goods).

7.205.16 Shannon Free Zone

TCA 1997, s 445 authorises the Minister for Finance to certify that certain types of trading operations of a qualified company are to be treated as "relevant trading operations" so as to qualify for the 10% corporation tax rate. A *qualified company* is a company the whole or part of the trade of which is carried on within the Shannon Customs-Free Airport (the "airport"). *Relevant trading operations* means trading operations specified in a certificate given by the Minister for Finance under TCA 1997, s 445(2) where the certificate certifies that such trading operations of a qualified company are relevant trading operation for the purposes of TCA 1997, s 445. For this purpose, *trading operation* means any trading operation which is not, apart from TCA 1997 ss 445 and 443(13) (repair or maintenance of aircraft, aircraft engines or components carried on within the State and outside the Shannon area), the manufacture of goods and which is carried on by a qualified company.

Since the inception of TCA 1997, s 445, trading activities which involve Irish currency have been excluded from entitlement to the 10% corporation tax rate. This has been provided for in the certificate issued by the Minister for Finance in accordance with TCA 1997, s 445(2). In the light of the change in the currency of the State to the euro on 1 January 1999, however, and from a date to be appointed by Ministerial order, this exclusion will no longer apply. TCA 1997, s 445(2A) provides that an operation which would fall within any class or kind of operation specified in a certificate under TCA 1997, s 445(2) to be a relevant trading operation but for the fact that it involves the currency of the State will be deemed to fall within that class or kind of operation and to have been specified in that certificate as a relevant trading operation.

Relief under TCA 1997, s 445 is available for service type operations only. TCA 1997, s 445(7) limits the type of trading operations which can be certified as relevant trading operations to trading operations carried on within the airport, but only if the trading operations of the qualifying company in question fall within one or more of the following types of trading operation:

(a) the repair or maintenance of aircraft;

(b) trading operations in regard to which the Minister for Finance is of opinion, after consultation with the Minister for Transport, that they contribute to the use or development of the Airport (but excluding any trading operations mentioned below); or

(c) trading operations which are:

(i) ancillary to any of the operations described above, or

(ii) ancillary to any operations consisting of the manufacture of goods.

Examples of operations which may be licensed in Shannon (and which do not qualify elsewhere) include aviation services, distribution activities, mail order and warehousing operations, franchising and licensing of intangible property.

The expiration date for Shannon licensed operations is 31 December 2005, where the operations were approved on or before 31 May 1998, and 31 December 2002 for those approved after 31 July 1998 (see **7.201.2**).

Certain types of trading operation are not eligible for the 10% corporation tax rate whether or not they can be regarded as contributing to the use or development of the airport. TCA 1997, s 445(8) provides that the following trading operations may not be certified by the Minister for Finance under TCA 1997, s 445(2):

(a)   the rendering of—

   (i)   services to embarking or disembarking aircraft passengers, including hotel, catering, money-changing or transport (other than air transport) services, or

   (ii)   services in connection with the landing, departure, loading or unloading of aircraft,

(b)   the operation of a scheduled air transport service;

(c)   selling by retail (otherwise than by mail order or other distance selling (see below) which is regarded by the Minister for Finance, after consultation with the Minister for Transport, as contributing to the use or development of the airport); and

(d)   the sale of consumable commodities for the fuelling of aircraft or for shipment as aircraft stores.

A certificate issued under TCA 1997, s 445, unless revoked, remains in force until 31 December 2005.

Locating in Shannon

Companies licensed to operate in Shannon are eligible for the 10% corporation tax rate. The licensing process involves the submission of a business plan and negotiating with the Shannon authorities, Shannon Free-Airport Development Co Ltd (SFADCO), regarding the scope and nature of the proposed activities. The policy of SFADCO is to assist the establishment of viable businesses that are export oriented and which produce economic benefit, including high quality employment. In considering an application for approval, SFADCO will be primarily concerned to ensure that the operation will contribute to the use of the airport and will generate long term sustainable employment in the Shannon region.

Support for potential projects will accordingly be forthcoming principally on the basis of such criteria as export orientation, job creation (minimum of 15 people over three years), and the contribution of the project to the use and development of the airport (by reference to freight and passenger movements).

There is no specific limitation on the nature of qualifying projects and Shannon can therefore be an attractive location for operations that would not otherwise qualify for the 10% corporation tax rate. Examples of operations which qualify in Shannon, and which would not otherwise qualify, include aviation services, distribution activities, mail order and warehousing operations, franchising and licensing of intangible property. The leasing of aircraft and ships will also qualify if these are undertaken in the course of licensed financial services operations in Shannon.

Activities which have qualified as eligible activities in the Shannon area include:

(a) customer support activities, including distribution and project fulfilment;

(b) international headquarters for sales, accounts and administration;

(c) catalogue and technical documentation publishing;

(d) telemarketing;

(e) import/ export trading;

(f) aircraft management, trading leasing, maintenance and repair;

(g) consultancy and research;

(h) software development;

(i) data processing; and

(j) financial services activities (see **7.206.1**) which contribute to the use of the airport, including:

    (i) international banking,

    (ii) leasing,

    (iii) funds management,

    (iv) treasury management,

    (v) administration services,

    (vi) insurance and reinsurance, and

    (vii) back office operations.

In general, distribution activities will qualify for the 10% corporation tax rate only where they are undertaken in the course of a licensed operation in Shannon. For the purpose of obtaining such a licence, SFADCO would require a commitment that substantially all of the product concerned will physically move through Shannon Airport. It is permissible to sell from a base in Shannon to retail customers by mail order and by distance selling.

Another activity that may be licensed in Shannon is the provision, in consideration of royalty payments, of intra-group intellectual property utilisation on a managed basis, subject to a maximum of €3.81m income per company.

TCA 1997, s 445(2) provides for the giving of a Shannon certificate by the Minister for Finance to a qualifying company. This will certify that such trading operations of a qualified company as are specified in the certificate are relevant trading operations and any such certificate, unless it is revoked, remain in force until:

(a) in the case of operations approved by the Minister on or before 31 May 1998 to be carried on in the airport, 31 December 2005; and

(b) in the case of operations so approved after 31 May 1998, 31 December 2002.

Where the Minister and the qualified company agree to the revocation of a certificate given under TCA 1997, s 445(2), or agree to its revocation and its replacement by another such certificate, the Minister may, by notice in writing served by registered post on the company, revoke the first-mentioned certificate with effect from such date as may be specified in the notice (TCA 1997, s 445(6)).

Other incentives

Apart from the 10% corporation tax rate, licensed Shannon operations also benefit from:

(a) zero withholding tax on interest payments to non residents (irrespective of whether or not a double taxation treaty is in place – see **4.305**);

(b) exemption from income tax in the case of a company not resident in the State or a person not ordinarily resident in the State for interest paid in respect of a "relevant security", ie a security issued by a company in the course of carrying on relevant trading operations on terms which oblige it to redeem the security within 15 years after the date of issue (see also **4.305**) (TCA 1997, s 198(2));

(c) exemption from income tax in the case of a company not resident in the State or a person not ordinarily resident in the State in respect of interest paid by a company in the course of carrying on licensed Shannon operations (TCA 1997, s 198(1));

(d) full deductibility of all business related interest costs (including, in the case of Shannon financial services companies, interest to foreign affiliates – see **11.106**);

(e) free depreciation for machinery and plant and for industrial buildings (see **5.204.3** and **5.407.3**).

As regards (c), the exemption provided is without prejudice to any charge under the Corporation Tax Acts on the profits of a non-resident company. Thus, the possibility of a corporation tax charge on a non-resident company where it operates an Irish branch or agency is preserved.

In relation to (d), interest paid to overseas affiliates is usually treated for Irish tax purposes as a distribution in accordance with TCA 1997, s 130(2)(d)(iv) and is therefore not tax deductible to the paying company. If the affiliated company is resident in a country with which Ireland has a double taxation treaty, a Shannon financial services company may elect to have the payment treated as interest and therefore as deductible against taxable profits. In circumstances where the affiliate is resident in a non-treaty country, the Irish Revenue may in practice agree that interest treatment should apply. Generally, this concessional treatment will be available provided that the borrowed funds are actively used by the Shannon financial services operation and the debt to equity ratio of that operation is in line with that of mainstream financial institutions.

To secure interest treatment, application should be made to Revenue Commissioners and should be accompanied by the following confirmations:

(a) that interest is charged at a commercial rate;

(b) that interest would be deductible, but for TCA 1997, s 130(2)(d)(iv), as a trading expense;

(c) that the funds are borrowed solely for Shannon financial services purposes.

The Revenue may require particulars of the loans and may request that this information be provided annually. They will require that the loans be used for working capital and will not replace permanent capital.

7.205.17 International financial services

A qualified company is entitled under TCA 1997, s 446 to the 10% corporation tax rate in respect of its trading income from relevant trading operations carried out in the Custom House Docks Area in Dublin. *Relevant trading operations* means trading operations specified in a certificate given by the Minister for Finance. A *qualified company* is any company to which the Minister has given a relevant trading operations certificate. The types of activity qualifying for the 10% corporation tax rate under the international financial services heading are described in **7.206**.

Since the inception of TCA 1997, s 446, trading activities which involve Irish currency have been excluded from entitlement to the 10% corporation tax rate. This has been provided for in the certificate issued by the Minister for Finance in accordance with TCA 1997, s 446(2). In the light of the change in the currency of the State to the euro on 1 January 1999, however, and from a date to be appointed by Ministerial order, this exclusion will no longer apply. TCA 1997, s 446(2A) provides that an operation which would fall within any class or kind of operation specified in a certificate under TCA 1997, s 446(2) to be a relevant trading operation but for the fact that it involves the currency of the State will be deemed to fall within that class or kind of operation and to have been specified in that certificate as a relevant trading operation.

7.205.18 10% corporation tax rate – qualifying activities

Below is a summarised list of deemed manufacturing activities for the purposes of the 10% corporation tax rate. The final year for qualification (31 December in each case) is shown for each type of activity.

	Final year
Manufacturing[5]	2010
Deemed manufacturing by related company[5]	2010
Manufacturing services[5]	2010
Engineering services[5]	2010
Computer services[5]	2010
Fish produced on a fish farm[5]	2010
Repair of ships in the State[5]	2010
Shannon operations[1]	2005
Qualifying shipping activities (QSA)[2]	2000
Sales by Special Trading Houses[3]	2000
Custom House Docks Area – international financial services[4]	2005
Plant cultivation[5]	2010
Fish processing on board a factory ship (QSA)[2]	2000
Supply and servicing of offshore installations by Irish ships (QSA)[2]	2000
Wholesale sales by agricultural or fishery societies of goods purchased from agricultural or fishery societies who are its members[5]	2010
Sales by agricultural societies of milk purchased from its members and sold to qualifying companies[5]	2010
Repair and maintenance of aircraft (excluding Shannon operations)[5]	2010
Film production[5]	2010

	Final year
Meat processing in an EU approved establishment[5]	2010
Fish processing[5]	2010
Remanufacture or repair of computer equipment or of subassemblies[5]	2010
Newspaper advertising[5]	2010

Notes:

[1]   Termination date 31 December 2005, if approved on or before 31 May 1998; otherwise 31 December 2002 – TCA 1997, s 445(2).

[2]   Termination date 31 December 2000 – TCA 1997, s 442(1).

[3]   Termination date 31 December 2000 – TCA 1997, s 442(1).

[4]   Termination date 31 December 2005, if approved on or before 31 May 1998; otherwise 31 December 2002 – TCA 1997, s 446(2) (see **7.201.2**).

[5]   Termination date 31 December 2002 if trade, not being a "specified trade", commenced on or after 23 July 1998 (see **7.201.2**).

7.206   International financial services

7.206.1   Introduction

The International Financial Services Centre (IFSC) in the Custom House Docks area of Dublin was established by the Irish government to promote and encourage international financial activities by means of the provision of fiscal incentives. The IFSC is a modern purpose built development with accommodation and telecommunications facilities commensurate with the needs of such a project. The 10% corporation tax rate is available in respect of a wide range of financial services where undertaken by companies in the IFSC and also in the Shannon Airport area. Entitlement to the 10% rate in both cases is dependent on the project having obtained an operating licence from the relevant regulatory authority.

The treatment of international financial services here relates primarily to the IFSC and is governed by the provisions of TCA 1997, s 446. International financial services are, however, also included in the activities in respect of which the Minister may give a certificate for the purposes of TCA 1997, s 445, being activities which are considered to contribute to the use or development of Shannon Airport. Accordingly, the description below of qualifying activities for the purposes of IFSC projects applies also to international financial activities carried on in the Shannon area.

Since the inception of TCA 1997, s 446, trading activities which involve Irish currency have been excluded from entitlement to the 10% corporation tax rate. This has been provided for in the certificate issued by the Minister for Finance in accordance with TCA 1997, s 446(2). In the light of the change in the currency of the State to the euro on 1 January 1999, however, and with effect from 1 January 1999 (the date appointed by Minister – (SI 502/1998), this exclusion will no longer apply. TCA 1997, s 446(2A) provides that an operation which would fall within any class or kind of operation specified in a certificate under TCA 1997, s 446(2) to be a relevant trading operation but for the fact that it involves the currency of the State will be deemed to fall within that class or kind of operation and to have been specified in that certificate as a relevant trading operation.

The primary fiscal incentive available to businesses establishing international financial activities in the IFSC is the 10% corporate tax rate in respect of trading profits arising from those activities. The 10% rate has been approved by the European Commission until 31 December 2005. It is a condition of approval that projects are approved for operation in Ireland in advance of 31 December 1999.

Activities which are subject to corporation tax at the 10% rate are not excluded from the benefit of tax treaties. There are no restrictions on the repatriation of profits and no withholding taxes on interest or capital gains. A comprehensive network of double taxation agreements with other countries is in place (see **14.103**). Under some of these arrangements, profits taxed in Ireland at the 10% rate are not subject to further tax on repatriation.

Qualifying international financial activities are those certified as such by the Minister for Finance. Before the Minister may certify any particular trading operation as a relevant trading operation, he must be satisfied that it will contribute to the development of the area (IFSC) as an international financial services centre or to the use or development of the airport (Shannon).

In the case of the IFSC, the trading operations in question must fall within one or more of the classes of trading operations specified in TCA 1997, s 446 and must, in principle, be carried on within the IFSC except that the Minister may certify as a relevant trading operation any operation which would otherwise be eligible, but which provides qualifying services from temporary accommodation set up outside the IFSC pending suitable accommodation becoming available within the IFSC.

7.206.2   Custom House Docks Area

The Custom House Docks Area is described in TCA 1997 Sch 5 para 2:

> That part of the county borough of Dublin bounded by a line commencing at the point (hereafter in this description referred to as "the first-mentioned point") where a line drawn along the westerly projection of the northerly boundary of Custom House Quay would be intersected by a line drawn along Memorial Road, then continuing in a northerly direction along Memorial Road and Amiens Street to the point where it joins Sheriff Street Lower, then continuing, initially in an easterly direction, along Sheriff Street Lower and Commons Street to the point where it intersects the easterly projection of the northern boundary of Custom House Quay, and then continuing in a westerly direction along that projection and that boundary and the westerly projection of that boundary to the first-mentioned point.

7.206.3   Qualifying activities

TCA 1997, s 446(2) provides that the Minister for Finance may give a certificate certifying that such trading operations of a company (a *qualified company*) as are specified in the certificate are, with effect from a date specified in the certificate, relevant trading operations for the purposes of TCA 1997, s 446. The classes of trading operations which may be certified as relevant trading operations in accordance with TCA 1997, s 446(7) (and also as international financial services for the purposes of TCA 1997, s 445) are as follows:

(a)   the provision for persons not ordinarily resident in the State of services of a type normally provided by a bank in the ordinary course of its trade;

(b) the carrying on on behalf of persons not ordinarily resident in the State of international financial activities including, in particular—

    (i) global money-management,

    (ii) international dealings in currencies and in futures, options and similar financial assets,

    (iii) dealings in bonds, equities and similar instruments,

    (iv) insurance and related activities, or

    (v) the management of the whole or part of the investments and other activities of a specified collective investment undertaking within the meaning of TCA 1997, s 734(1) (see **12.805.2**), of an investment undertaking within the meaning of TCA 1997, s 739B (see **12.806.3**), or of a qualifying company within the meaning of TCA 1997, s 110 ("securitisation" – see **7.206.11**),

(c) the provision for persons not ordinarily resident in the State of services of, or facilities for, processing, control, accounting, communication, clearing, settlement or information storage in relation to financial activities;

(d) dealing by a company in commodity futures or commodity options on behalf of persons not ordinarily resident in the State:

    (i) except on behalf of persons who:

(a) carry on a trade in the types(s) of commodities or futures which are the subject of the futures or options, or

      (b) would be regarded as connected with (within the meaning of TCA 1997, s 10 – see **2.3**) a person or persons described in (a), or

    (ii) where dealing in futures and options, some or all of which are commodity futures or commodity options, as the case may be, is the principal relevant trading operation carried out by the company,

(e) the development or supply of computer software for use in the provision of services or facilities of the type referred to in (c) or for the re-processing, analysing or similar treatment of information in relation to financial activities; and

(f) trading operations which are similar to, or ancillary to, any of the activities mentioned in (a) to (e) above, provided that the Minister for Finance is of the opinion that they contribute to the use of the IFSC as an international financial services centre (or, where appropriate, to the development of the Shannon Airport area).

An important condition for qualifying as a relevant trading operation under any of the classes (a) to (e) above is that the services mentioned must be provided for persons not ordinarily resident in the State. Any service or facility provided for, or any activity carried on on behalf of, a trade carried on in the State by a person not ordinarily resident in the State, is deemed to be provided for a person ordinarily resident in the State and may not therefore be certified as relevant trading operations (TCA 1997, s 446(7)).

The condition that the recipients of international financial services must be persons not ordinarily resident in the State does not apply to the development or supply of computer software mentioned in class (e). A company may carry on in the IFSC a trade of developing or supplying such software for or to other persons trading in the IFSC (who may or may not be resident) to be used by them in providing for non-resident persons services of, or facilities for, processing, control, accounting etc in relation to financial activities. Any such computer software services may be eligible for a relevant trading operations certificate.

Where the trading operations of a qualified company, for the purposes of carrying on its relevant trading operations, include the procurement of services from a person resident in the State and, in the opinion of the Minister for Finance such procurement will contribute to the development of the CHDA as an international financial services centre, that procurement is to be regarded for the purposes of the Tax Acts as part of the relevant trading operations of the qualified company and to have been specified as relevant trading operations in the certificate given to the qualified company under TCA 1997, s 446(2) where they are not so specified (TCA 1997, s 446(8A)).

TCA 1997, s 451 limits the rate of corporation tax to 10% in the case of any income arising from foreign securities or possessions which are investments of a qualifying foreign life assurance business or are investments managed by a qualifying foreign unit trust business. This provision also limits the rate of corporation tax on any chargeable capital gains accruing from the disposal of any such investments to a maximum of 10%. Where any such qualifying income or chargeable gains are liable to income tax or capital gains tax, the maximum rate is again 10% (see **12.603.4**).

To be eligible for the maximum 10% tax rate in respect of the income and chargeable gains from its foreign investments, the foreign life assurance or unit trust business must consist of relevant trading operations certified by the Minister for Finance under TCA 1997, s 446. In the case of foreign life assurance businesses, the maximum 10% tax rate applies only in respect of the income or chargeable gains attributable to the investments of business with policy holders and/or annuitants who reside outside the State. Business with policy holders or annuitants who reside in the State is not prohibited, but if the company's trading operations do not consist solely of foreign life assurance business, the favourable tax regime for policy holders (see **12.603.4**) will not apply.

In the case of a foreign unit trust business, TCA 1997, s 451 does not apply unless *all* the holders of units in the unit trust scheme are resident outside the State. It must also be a registered unit trust scheme within the Unit Trusts Act 1972.

Examples of financial activities which qualify for the 10% corporation tax rate include:

(i) banking, such as lending, deposit taking and asset financing;

(ii) international financial services such as group treasury functions, intra-group lending and sales aid financing;

(iii) insurance, both life and general, and reinsurance, including captive management;

(iv) funds management;

(v) back office operations relating to financial services, such as data processing, information storage and accounting;

(vi) development of software for licensing for use in the financial services industry; and

(vii) other financial operations which contribute to the use and development of the IFSC or Shannon.

The majority of IFSC certificates, with the exception of those for fund management companies, have, prior to the enactment of TCA 1997, s 446(2A) (introduced by FA 1998 Sch 2 paragraph 8 – see **7.206.1** above) required that the trading operations which qualify for the 10% corporation tax rate, or any fee or commission derived from such operations, do not involve Irish currency.

TCA 1997, s 446 also specifically required that certain qualifying activities should involve transactions in foreign currencies. That section did not, however, prevent all qualifying trading operations from trading in Irish currency. The activities for which the legislation applied the "foreign currency" requirement were:

    (a)   banking;

    (b)   dealing in currencies, futures, options etc; and

    (c)   dealing in bonds, equities etc.

This prohibition was removed, with effect from a date to be appointed by Ministerial order, by FA 1998 Sch 2 paragraph 8(b).

No such requirement relating to transactions in foreign currencies has at any time applied in respect of the following activities:

    (a)   global money management;

    (b)   insurance and related activities;

    (c)   investment fund management;

    (d)   computer services in relation to financial activities;

    (e)   dealing in commodity futures and options; and

    (f)   development of computer software.

Furthermore, the "ancillary" clause in TCA 1997, s 446(7)(c)(vi) permits the Minister to certify an operation if it contributes to the development of the IFSC and this clause may be used to permit some Irish pound trading.

The Department of Finance issued two position papers, in April 1990 and October 1994. The October 1994 paper outlines the circumstances in which the Department was prepared to permit some Irish pound trading. The circumstances envisaged are as follows:

    (a)   there is total flexibility as regards UCITSs;

    (b)   in relation to treasury operations, Irish pound trading would be permitted where there would be no loss of tax due to displacement, the scale of the Irish pound element is small and there is no distortion of competition in the Irish economy.

7.206.4   Other incentives

Apart from the 10% corporation tax rate, licensed financial services operations also benefit from:

    (a)   zero withholding tax on interest payments to non residents (irrespective of whether or not a double taxation treaty is in place – see **4.305**);

    (b)   exemption from income tax in the case of a person not ordinarily resident in the State in respect of a "relevant security", ie a security issued by a company in the course of carrying on relevant trading operations on terms which oblige it to redeem the security within 15 years after the date of issue (see also **4.305**) (TCA 1997, s 198(2));

(c) exemption from income tax in the case of a company not resident in the State or a person not ordinarily resident in the State in respect of interest paid by a company in the course of carrying on licensed financial services operations (TCA 1997, s 198(1));

(d) full deductibility of all business related interest costs (including interest to foreign affiliates – see **11.106**);

(e) free depreciation for machinery and plant and for industrial buildings (see **5.204.3** and **5.407.3**); and

(f) a double rent allowance in respect of property rents (available in the IFSC only – see **6.103**).

As regards (c), the exemption provided is without prejudice to any charge under the Corporation Tax Acts on the profits of a non-resident company. Thus, the possibility of a corporation tax charge on a non-resident company where it operates an Irish branch or agency is preserved.

In relation to (d), interest paid to overseas affiliates is usually treated for Irish tax purposes as a distribution in accordance with TCA 1997, s 130(2)(d)(iv) and is therefore not tax deductible to the paying company. If the affiliated company is resident in a country with which Ireland has a double taxation treaty, the IFSC company may elect to have the payment treated as interest and therefore as deductible against taxable profits. In circumstances where the affiliate is resident in a non-treaty country, the Irish Revenue may in practice agree that interest treatment should apply. Generally, this concessional treatment will be available provided that the borrowed funds are actively used by the IFSC operation and the debt to equity ratio of the IFSC operation is in line with that of mainstream financial institutions.

To secure interest treatment, application should be made to Revenue Commissioners and should be accompanied by the following confirmations:

(a) that interest is charged at a commercial rate;

(b) that interest would be deductible, but for TCA 1997, s 130(2)(d)(iv), as a trading expense; and

(c) that the funds are borrowed solely for IFSC trading purposes.

The Revenue may require particulars of the loans and may request that this information be provided annually. They will require that the loans be used for working capital and will not replace permanent capital.

7.206.5 Certification procedure

Entitlement to the 10% rate is dependent on the relevant project having obtained an operating licence from the regulatory authorities. The certification process involves the submission of a business plan to the appropriate industrial development agency (IDA Ireland (for IFSC operations) or Shannon Free-Airport Development Co Ltd (for Shannon operations)) and negotiating with these bodies on employment commitments and other requirements. In the case of managed operations, the approval process will be undertaken by the relevant manager.

Financial services operations in both the IFSC and Shannon may therefore be undertaken either on a stand-alone basis or on a managed basis. In the latter case, the actual conduct of the operation is undertaken by one of the specialist banks or treasury management companies located in the relevant centre. The facility to use a managed structure is generally not available to very large multinational companies or to financial institutions.

Most IFSC certificates include a useful paragraph which provides for the 10% corporation tax rate in respect of the "temporary holding of funds". The word "temporary" in this context has not been defined and each case will be considered separately. The share capital invested should be of an amount which will generate income sufficient to support the contention that trading has commenced.

Certification conditions

The certificate issued by the Minister for Finance is subject to conditions which are normally issued in standard form. The certificate will prescribe the activities which, if undertaken, will qualify for the 10% corporation tax rate, and in addition will define a number of conditions, including:

(a)   the level of economic substance required for the project which will be largely measured by reference to numbers employed: the authorities will seek a commitment to a minimum employment target within a period of three to five years. Typically, the employment requirement will be for employees with appropriate financial qualifications. There will be no requirement that the employees be Irish or EC nationals and work permits are readily available for non EC nationals;

(b)   that transactions between connected persons and connected companies must be concluded on arm's length terms: the applicant must show that procedures have been established to implement an arm's length basis of trading and the auditors will be required to report on the adequacy of these procedures;

(c)   prohibition on applicant regarding surrender of losses incurred in a qualifying financial activity against other income chargeable to Irish tax (but see below); and

(d)   requirement on applicant to abide by regulatory and supervisory requirements imposed by the relevant supervising agency.

Notwithstanding condition (c) above, the Department of Finance has confirmed that the provisions relating to value-based losses (TCA 1997 ss 243B, 396B and 420B – see **4.103**, **4.405** and **8.306.3**) may nevertheless be applied to IFSC certified companies on the same basis that they apply to other companies.

Withdrawal of certificate

The Minister may require a company to desist from carrying on any activity likely to have an adverse effect on the use or development of the IFSC and may revoke a certificate where that requirement is not complied with (TCA 1997, s 446(5)). A certificate may also be revoked where a company's trade has ceased or becomes carried on wholly outside the IFSC (TCA 1997, s 446(4)(a)), or where the company fails to comply with any condition subject to which the certificate was given (TCA 1997, s 446(4)(b)). Unless the certificate is revoked, it remains in force until:

(a)   in the case of operations approved by the Minister on or before 31 July 1998 to be carried on in the IFSC, 31 December 2005; and

(b)   in the case of operations so approved after 31 July 1998, 31 December 2002.

Where in the case of a company which has received a certificate in accordance with TCA 1997, s 446(2) the Minister receives a notification from the Central Bank of Ireland in accordance with section 96 of the Central Bank Act 1989 (the "Act"), as to the non- compliance by the company with any obligation imposed on it by the Central Bank under Chapter VII of the Act, the Minister is required, by notice in writing served by registered post on the company, to revoke the certificate with effect from such date as may be specified in the notice (TCA 1997, s 446(5A)).

Where the Minister and the company agree to the revocation of a certificate given under TCA 1997, s 446(2), or agree to its revocation and its replacement by another such certificate, the Minister may, by notice in writing served by registered post on the company, revoke the first-mentioned certificate with effect from such date as may be specified in the notice. This provision is not, however, to have any effect on TCA 1997, s 446(4) (revocation of certificate in case where the company's trade ceases or becomes carried on wholly outside the IFSC, or where the company fails to comply with conditions of certificate), 446(5) (notice to desist or notice of revocation of certificate where company's activities are deemed to have an adverse effect on the use and development of the IFSC) or 446(5A) (see above) (TCA 1997, s 446(6)).

7.206.6 IFSC corporate treasury operations

Activities which may be carried on as part of an international corporate treasury operation include inter-company lending, discounting or factoring of receivables, hedging foreign currencies, investment of excess cash in market instruments, currency dealing operations and fee-based financial services activities such as loan negotiation. In addition, the treasury operation may undertake asset financing activities through leasing and may co-ordinate the acquisition and provision of assets for group companies.

Several structures have been developed to facilitate operations which, by reason of size, may be unable to make a stand-alone commitment to the IFSC. These structures include stand-alone treasury centres, agency treasury operations and captive finance company (CFC) operations. Of these, only the CFC is of relevance today.

A CFC may provide intra-group financing and the operation is managed by a specialist agent on a fee basis and the agent meets the substance requirements imposed by the regulatory authorities. Because of the restricted activities which may be undertaken (intra-group financing and temporary investment of surplus funds), the substance requirement and the costs of operation will be lower than for the alternative structures. The employment commitment, which is met by the manager, averages 1.5 jobs per certificate.

A CFC is not permitted where the parent company is one of the top 250 companies (ranked by market value) in the Fortune 500 Largest US Industrial Corporations listing, one of the top 300 companies in the Financial Times listing of Europe's Top 500 Companies, or one of the top 75 companies in the Financial Post listing of Canada's Top 500 Companies.

Outsourcing

Although a financial services company may not establish an ATC, it may be permitted to source some staff, equipment and accommodation facilities from an existing IFSC manager.

7.206.7 Leasing/asset financing in the IFSC

Asset financing, particularly through the medium of cross border leases, may be undertaken by a number of entities operating in the IFSC. Features of an international leasing operation set up in the IFSC (or in Shannon) are as follows:

(a)   profits arising are taxable at the 10% corporation tax rate;

(b)   the full cost of equipment leased in the year of acquisition may be written off for tax purposes;

(c)   non-leasing income may be sheltered by excess capital allowances provided the allowances claimed are at the standard writing down rate of 15% per annum;

(d)   virtually all of Ireland's tax treaties provide for the exemption from foreign withholding taxes on lease rentals paid to Ireland; and

(e)   capital allowances are given in respect of capital expenditure on the basis of legal ownership: thus, "double dip" leasing (see below) may be possible with countries which grant depreciation allowances by reference to economic ownership.

Both finance leases and operating leases may be undertaken from the IFSC provided, in the case of operating leases, the individual transactions exceed a minimum value (see below).

In Ireland, a lease is normally understood to refer to a contract between a lessor and a lessee in which the lessee obtains possession and use of the equipment for a period of time in return for a stream of rental payments. If a lease agreement contains a provision enabling the lessee to acquire the asset, it will not be regarded as a true lease either for legal or tax purposes, but will instead constitute a hire purchase agreement. True lease agreements (as opposed to hire purchase arrangements) fall into two categories – finance leases and operating leases. The significant difference between these two types of lease agreement is economic ownership. In the case of a finance lease the risks and rewards inherent in the ownership of the asset pass to the lessee, ie the lessee becomes the economic owner. Under an operating lease agreement, the lessor retains economic ownership.

Companies approved to undertake leasing activities in the IFSC are eligible for the 10% corporation tax rate. The certificate issued to the IFSC company will include conditions which will restrict the 10% incentive tax rate to finance leases. In the case of a finance lease, the term of the lease is normally equivalent to 95% or more of the economic life of the asset. The IFSC company will, therefore, be prohibited from entering into non-finance leases (ie, operating leases) and from undertaking maintenance and service activities as these would not be financial in nature. However, the restrictions on operating leases do not apply to "big ticket" leasing provided that the following conditions are met:

(a)   the total value of assets covered by the lease agreement exceeds €12,700;

(b)   in circumstances where the total value of assets covered by the lease agreement is less than €63,500, the value of the principal asset must be 75% or more of the total assets leased; and

(c)   the lease must be for a term in excess of 12 months and must contain penalties for early cancellation.

From an Irish tax perspective there is no difference between a finance and operating lease. Under both types of agreement, the legal ownership of the asset remains with the lessor and with it the entitlement to capital allowances on the purchase price. Allowances claimed are set primarily against income from leasing but any surplus allowances can be used to shelter non-leasing income.

An IFSC leasing company may claim accelerated allowances of up to 100% on new plant and equipment (other than motor vehicles). These accelerated allowances are, however, ring-fenced and may only be set against income from a leasing trade. The facility to claim accelerated capital allowances on particular assets enables the IFSC company to manage its capital allowances claims so that leasing income is sheltered by accelerated allowances while other, non-leasing, income is sheltered by basic rate allowances.

Where an IFSC company undertakes leasing activities, its foreign affiliates will normally be in a position to secure a tax deduction in respect of the lease payments while the IFSC company can arrange its capital allowances claims so as to secure a deferral of Irish tax on the corresponding lease income.

Additional tax leverage may be achieved for the group if the affiliated lessee is located in a jurisdiction which grants tax depreciation by reference to economic ownership as opposed to legal ownership of the asset. Accordingly, assets leased to affiliates in countries where economic ownership carries an entitlement to tax depreciation (eg Canada, US, Germany, the Netherlands) may give rise to what is known as a "double dip", ie capital allowances are claimed in two jurisdictions in respect of the same asset.

7.206.8 Multi-currency management (reinvoicing)

The Irish regulatory authorities were, up to fairly recently, reluctant to approve multi-currency management activities in the IFSC. Such activities could not be regarded as pure financial services on the basis that reinvoicing would involve an IFSC company having legal title to the underlying goods. However, the Department of Finance now agrees that reinvoicing will be permitted subject to certain conditions. The relevant conditions are set out in a document published by the Department of Finance in December 1995. The text of the document is as follows:

This activity is acceptable to the Department of Finance subject to the following conditions:

(i) that it will be substantive and active and will give rise to employment in the IFSC;

(ii) that this activity will be part of a broadly-based treasury operation in the Centre;

(iii) that the IFSC company will not take any profit on title of goods and that the IFSC company's income from this activity will arise solely from the provision of foreign exchange facilities;

(iv) that the income of the IFSC company from this activity will not exceed a specific amount per annum (to be agreed on a case by case basis) and will arise on a strict arm's length level from dealings with companies in the group. In regard to the latter point, it will be necessary in advance of commencement of this activity, to demonstrate that there is a clear break between the value of the underlying goods and the provision of foreign exchange facilities. It will also be necessary to agree a percentage limit on the fee charged in respect of this activity;

(v) the level of capital involved in this activity will be limited to that agreed with the Department of Finance.

(vi) the Department's preference is for this activity to be part of a stand-alone treasury operation."

The Department of Finance is not at this stage prepared to elaborate on the various limitations referred to in its document and has stressed that each application must be judged on its merits. However, the Department has indicated that while it would have a preference for this activity to be part of a stand-alone treasury operation, it is prepared to consider applications for approval by managed operations.

7.206.9 Funds management in the IFSC

Regulatory environment

The Central Bank of Ireland is the regulatory authority for all funds wishing to establish in the IFSC in Dublin. The Central Bank is the key financial regulator in Ireland. The regulatory framework for funds registered in the IFSC operates on a two tier system. The primary tier consists of the enabling legislation and entrusts the Central Bank with the supervisory and regulatory responsibility for funds seeking registration in Dublin.

The second tier comprises a system of published notices issued by the Central Bank on foot of authority derived from the primary enabling legislation. These notices set out the requirements of the Central Bank on a broad range of matters including information requirements and matters relating to the support of applications for the authorisation of funds, reporting requirements, specific notices on specialists' funds, feeder funds, umbrella funds, and money market funds.

The two tier system is intended to retain with the Central Bank, as regulator and the party closest to developments in the fund industry, the discretion to amend, modify or amplify the published rules which regulate funds.

Funds vehicles

A basic distinction is made in the types of mutual funds which may be established in Ireland. Fund promoters can establish either a UCITS fund (known by its official name as an Undertaking for Collective Investment in Transferable Securities) or a non-UCITS (which in turn can be broken down into different types of non-UCITS funds).

(a) UCITS funds:

The UCITS Directive creates a "single passport" throughout the European Union for the sale of units/shares in UCITS funds authorised in one of the Member States.

The freedom to market units/shares in a UCITS fund in any other Member State is subject to compliance with advertising legislation and other rules and regulations in force in that State which do not fall within the field governed by the UCITS Directive. A UCITS fund is, in theory, an ideal vehicle for distribution of units/shares of a fund throughout the European Union, thereby avoiding the necessity for registration of the fund in each Member State in which units/shares are offered for sale.

The UCITS Directive was implemented in Ireland in 1989. Due to the nature of a UCITS as a retail funds structure (although many UCITS funds are used by institutional investors), the Directive imposes extensive restrictions on the investment and leverage policy of funds that may be authorised as UCITS funds.

A UCITS may be established under the UCITS Regulations in the form of an open-ended unit trust or as an open-ended investment company registered as a public limited company. A UCITS must simultaneously satisfy the following requirements:

(a) the capital of a UCITS must be funded by means of an open offer to the public;

(b) the units/shares of an investor must be redeemed on demand; and

(c) investments may only be made in transferable securities and in accordance with various restrictions.

While a UCITS must principally invest its assets in transferable securities, it may also invest in debt instruments similar to transferable securities, in cash, other UCITSs and in derivative instruments, and use investment techniques subject to restrictions set out in the UCITS Regulations.

(b) Non-UCITS funds:

The Central Bank regulates the establishment and operation of all types of public mutual funds which do not qualify for a UCITS passport under a common series of regulations published by the Central Bank known as the non-UCITS series of notices.

Non-UCITS funds may be established as public retail funds or as public "professional investor" funds or as public "super-professional investor" funds (sometimes referred to as qualifying investor funds).

The non-UCITS notices set out detailed requirements for the authorisation and operation of non-UCITS public retail funds, including restrictions on investment/ leverage policies of those funds. The restrictions on investment/leverage policies of non-UCITS public retail funds are very similar to those of UCITS funds.

Professional investor funds with a minimum subscription requirement per investor of €127,000 may be established under the non-UCITS notices and the restrictions on investment/leverage policies of non-UCITS public retail funds may be disapplied, or relaxed, in the case of professional investor funds on application to the Central Bank. Accordingly, promoters of professional investor funds have more freedom to set the investment/leverage policies for funds in this class (compared to non-UCITS public retail funds).

However, the Central Bank of Ireland has approved an important investment fund category designed for high net worth individuals and institutional investors. In the case of the new "super-professional investor" fund, the conditions and restrictions related to investment objectives on policies, borrowing and leverage set out in the Central Bank's Notices are disapplied in full. The establishment of the super-professional investor fund category represents a significant move from the already existing professional investor fund category where the conditions and restrictions set out in the Central Bank's Notices, in particular those related to investment and borrowings, *may* be disapplied. Each case has to be negotiated on its own merits.

There has been a perceived need for a "high minimum ticket" fund product which would be open only to either high net worth individuals or large professional institutional investors and which would not be subject to the usual investment and borrowing restrictions laid down by the Central Bank for other investor types. The basis for this fund type is that these investors are genuinely sophisticated "professional investors" and have a high degree of knowledge and experience of the relevant markets and understanding of the investment risks involved. Investment in these funds is confined to:

(a)   any natural person who has a minimum net worth (excluding main residence and household goods) in excess of €1.27m; or

(b)   any institution which owns or invests on a discretionary basis at least the equivalent of €25.38m (not necessarily in the super-professional investor fund). The minimum initial subscription per investor in a super-professional investor fund must be the equivalent of €254,000.

Non-UCITS funds may take a number of different legal forms such as a unit trust, a variable capital investment company or an investment limited partnership. Each of these legal forms may be used to create an open-ended fund or a closed-ended fund.

Establishing a fund

To establish a fund it is necessary first to approach the Central Bank, providing details of the promoters of the proposed fund and their track record and financial standing. An outline of the intended investment objectives and policies of the fund should also be given to the Bank. If any deviation from the Bank's published requirements is called for, the issue should be raised and resolved with the Bank at this stage.

Once the Central Bank has given its initial approval to the promoters, the drafts of the documents constituting the fund and the agreements with the various service providers (ie fund administrator, trustee/custodian etc) will need to be submitted to and agreed with the Bank. The Bank will also need to approve the directors of the fund (if a company).

After authorisation, the Central Bank will require to be kept informed of progress of the fund which will have bi-annual review meetings with the manager/administrator of the fund. Changes in the structure of the management of the fund will also require the Bank's prior approval.

Basic requirements

All Irish authorised funds must have a custodian (a trustee in the case of a unit trust), essentially a licensed bank or a subsidiary, or an Irish incorporated subsidiary of an EU credit institution or its equivalent. In addition, unit trusts must have an Irish incorporated company as manager although this is optional in the case of a fund constituted as a variable capital investment company. At least two directors of the management company and variable capital investment company must be resident in Ireland.

A minimum level of administration activities of the fund must be carried on in Dublin. The management of the fund investments can be delegated to advisors located abroad without affecting the tax or regulatory status of the fund.

Listing of funds in the Irish Stock Exchange

A listing on the Irish Stock Exchange is relatively simple and inexpensive to obtain. Provided the criteria of the Stock Exchange are met, any fund may obtain a listing, as the listing facility is not restricted to Irish or EU domiciled funds. A fund must carry out its dealings with the Stock Exchange through a sponsoring stockbroker and it should be possible to obtain a listing within four to six weeks.

IFSC regime – 10% funds

It is possible to establish a non-designated variable capital investment company in the IFSC (but not a 10% unit trust or investment limited partnership) which is not available for marketing to the public but raises funds from a private placement as opposed to the issue of a prospectus to the public. Although the fund is regulated by the Central Bank, it is not subject to the same level of regulation as a tax-exempt fund which is available to the "public". A 10% fund is subject to corporation tax in respect of its qualifying income and gains at the 10% rate. As the fund is liable to taxation in Ireland, its entitlement to tax treaty benefits is clear.

Non-IFSC regime for collective investment funds

Collective investment funds which are not administered from the IFSC (and thus are available to Irish resident investors) are subject to tax at the standard rate of income tax on income and gains. Distributions from the funds are subject neither to advance corporation tax nor to withholding taxes. Funds are entitled to tax treaty benefits.

Funds management

Both public and private funds management may be undertaken in the IFSC. In all cases, the income of the funds manager is taxed at the 10% corporation tax rate. Income and capital gains of certain public funds managed within the IFSC are exempt from tax. These funds include unit trusts authorised under the Unit Trust Act 1990, UCITSs (undertakings for collective investment in transferable securities) authorised under the EU (UCITS) Regulations 1989, designated investment companies with variable capital authorised under the Companies Act 1990, and investment limited partnerships. Neither the income nor the capital gains of such funds are within the charge to Irish tax as long as the funds are for the benefit of non Irish investors. Public funds are regulated, in accordance with domestic legislation and EU regulations, by the Central Bank of Ireland.

Collective investment funds are dealt with in detail in **12.8**.

7.206.10 IFSC insurance activities

Income from insurance and related services are eligible for the 10% corporation tax rate where the services are provided to non-Irish residents. The insurance activities involved include:

(a) commercial insurance and reinsurance of international risks;

(b) reinsurance activities;

(c) captive insurance and reinsurance activities;

(d) insurance management services, including captives management;

(e) investment of funds held for the purposes of qualifying insurance and reinsurance activities;

(f) services of insurance brokers and intermediaries; and

(g) life assurance operations: life companies established in the IFSC may deduct profits which are attributable to policy holders in arriving at taxable income; profits attributable to shareholders are taxed at 10%.

Ireland has implemented all life and non-life EU Directives. The regulatory environment for direct writing insurance companies is in accordance with EU approved guidelines.

Reinsurance companies are not subject to regulation. Responsibility for regulation rests with a single entity, the Department of Enterprise and Employment. The insurance industry can engage in direct writing or reinsurance and in life or non-life services. Captive insurance companies may be established and can avail of a wide range of services offered by captive management companies.

The taxation treatment of life assurance companies as well as that of companies carrying on non-life assurance business is covered in detail in **12.6**.

Foreign life assurance business

Trading profits from carrying on foreign life assurance business qualify for the 10% corporation tax rate. Trading profits for this purpose comprise such part of the profits as belongs or is allocated to, or is expended on behalf of, policy holders or annuitants.

Foreign life assurance business means relevant trading operations within the meaning of TCA 1997, s 446, ie trading operations specified as such, for the purposes of manufacturing relief, in a certificate given by the Minister for Finance, and consisting of life assurance business with policy holders and annuitants who, at the time that business is contracted, reside outside the State (TCA 1997, s 451(1)). For this purpose, as regards any policy issued or contract made with such policy holders or annuitants in the course of such business, that policy must not provide for:

(a)   the granting of any additional contractual rights; or

(b)   an option to have another policy or contract substituted for it,

at a time when the policy holder or annuitant resides in the State. Accordingly, the condition regarding residence outside the State must be fulfilled at the time the policy is written. Thus, the non-residence condition will not be breached, and an IFSC life assurance company will retain its IFSC tax status, where a policy holder or annuitant who commences to be resident in the State continues to keep up, and does not encash, the policy.

TCA 1997, s 446(2B) makes special provision for a case in which, on 31 December 2000, the relevant trading operations of a company are the carrying on of foreign life assurance business and, at any time after that date, the company would be in breach of the conditions under which a certificate was given to it solely by virtue of the company commencing policies or contracts with persons who reside in the State. The trading operations at that time, to the extent that they are trading operations carried on with persons resident outside the State, are deemed to be relevant trading operations and the conditions under which the certificate was given will be deemed not to have been breached. For this purpose, such apportionment as is just and reasonable may be made of any profits arising to the company. This provision is a consequence of the phasing out of the preferential IFSC tax regime discussed in **12.603-607**.

Life assurance: regulatory environment and EU directives

Application for authorisation of life assurance undertakings must be made to the Department of Enterprise, Trade and Employment. The application may be made at the same time as the application for the 10% certificate is being made. The minimum share capital of the company concerned is €635,000. The life insurance undertaking must maintain certain technical and mathematical reserves and satisfy the Department of Enterprise, Trade and Employment that it possesses the solvency margin and minimum guarantee fund required by the Life Regulations (which are in accordance with established EU guidelines).

As a member of the EU, Ireland has implemented the First, Second and Third Life Coordination Directives. The First Life Directive laid down the requirements for the establishment of a Life Insurance Office in a Member State. The Directive also contained various requirements regarding the maintenance of reserves and solvency margins. The Second Life Directive allowed individuals to seek insurance, either directly or indirectly, from companies established in Member States and permits the life companies to sell group insurance (such as supplementary pension schemes) across national borders.

The Third Life Directive is designed to complete the single market by allowing insurance companies establish in one Member State to operate freely throughout the EU, both in terms of setting up branches or offices and in terms of offering their services directly across national borders. The Third Life Directive also aims to establish a degree of harmonisation of the prudential and consumer protection rules between Member States.

Non-life insurance

Underwriting profits from qualifying insurance and reinsurance activities (ie where the insurance services are provided to non-Irish residents) together with related investment income are eligible for the 10% corporation tax rate. Gains or losses arising on the disposal of investments will normally be taxable as income rather than as capital and thus will also be subject to the 10% tax rate.

In general, deductions are available for all specific technical reserves including provisions for claims incurred but not reported, unearned premiums and unexpired risks. Deductions are not available for general or catastrophe reserves or for self-insurance. However, to allow captives to build up reserves on a tax relieved basis, the Revenue authorities will allow tax on the underwriting profits to be deferred for a five year period. This is achieved by allowing captives to prepare their underwriting accounts for tax purposes on a five year funded accounting basis. Investment income and gains do not qualify for the five year deferral and are taxed annually at the 10% rate. The funded accounting basis is not mandatory.

Non-life insurance: regulatory environment and EU directives

The Minister for Enterprise, Trade and Employment is responsible for authorising, regulating and supervising insurance operations in Ireland. A direct writing company must apply to the Department of Enterprise, Trade and Employment for an insurance licence. This application can be made at the same time as the application for the 10% tax rate certificate and both procedures can normally be completed within a period of four months. In order to obtain authorisation, the minimum share capital of the company concerned is €635,000 and the reporting/solvency requirements must be in accordance with established EC guidelines. An insurance company established in the IFSC has access to the EC market.

Reinsurance companies established in Ireland are not subject to regulation. There is no minimum share capital requirement. Such companies are only required to report their establishment to the insurance authorities and to file accounts with the Companies

Registration Office. However, a company writing both insurance and reinsurance is subject to regulation.

As a member of the EC, Ireland has implemented all relevant directives on non-life insurance. The Reinsurance Directive of 1964 recognised the principle of free transaction of reinsurance across national borders. Ireland adopted this Directive into law on 1 January 1973 when it became a member of the EC. Ireland has implemented the First, Second and Third Non-Life Coordination Directives.

The First Non-Life Directive of 1973 coordinated the authorisation procedures allowing non-life companies authorised in their home Member States to establish a base anywhere else in the EC. The Second Non-Life Directive allows companies established in the EC to provide non-life insurance services freely across national borders without having to establish an operation in any other Member State. The Directive distinguished between large risks and mass risks. Large EC risks such as Marine, Aviation and Transport (MAT) and the majority of large commercial and industrial risks could be underwritten by a company established in Ireland.

The Second Non-Life Directive was seen as an intermediate stage in the development of the single market for non-life insurance. The most important feature of the Third Non-Life Directive is the removal of the distinction between large and mass risks thus allowing the majority of non-life insurance services to be provided freely across national borders.

The Third Non-Life Directive is intended to complete the single market by allowing insurance companies established in one Member State to operate freely throughout the EC, both in terms of setting up branches or offices and in terms of offering services directly across national borders. This Directive also aims to establish a degree of harmonisation between the competent authorities in relation to prudential and consumer protection rules.

Captive insurance

Over the years there has been a significant growth in the number of captive insurance companies worldwide. By the end of the century the number of captives is expected to increase significantly accompanied by more than a doubling of premium income. It is expected that the majority of this growth will take place within onshore domiciles (ie low tax approved areas as opposed to pure tax havens) particularly in Europe. To date, the majority of captives have been established by US and to a lesser extent UK companies. Until fairly recently, restrictive exchange controls and lack of suitable captive locations have limited the establishment of captives by such as French, Italian and German companies. This has now changed and it is expected that the number of European owned captives will increase substantially over the next decade.

The growth of captive business in Dublin can be attributed to a number of factors including the availability of the 10% corporation tax rate, access to double taxation treaties, membership of the EC and the trend for captives to locate within onshore as opposed to offshore domiciles. A broad range of captive structures is possible, including:

(i) Pure industrial captive:

Typically the captive is owned by one industrial company/group. The captive writes insurance business only for the company/group.

(ii) Non-pure industrial captive:

These are single/multiple owned captives and/or captives writing third party business. A minimum of 40% of the business of the captive must be from the owners. In return for this added flexibility, the minimum employment requirement will be higher than for that of a pure captive.

(iii) Agency reinsurance captive:

Reinsurance companies may establish a captive reinsurance company managed by a third party IFSC manager. Such captives may write third party business and are effectively treated as stand-alone operations.

Captive management

Captive managers which are already established at the IFSC in Dublin can provide a comprehensive range of insurance related services, as follows:

    (a)   captive feasibility studies;
    (b)   reinsurance and policy issuance arrangements;
    (c)   administration, reporting and claims management; and
    (d)   treasury and investment management services.

Existing captive managers can provide captive insurance and reinsurance companies at minimum cost. Negotiation of the 10% tax rate certificate and insurance operating licence, where appropriate, is undertaken by the manager.

Lending by insurance/reinsurance companies

An IFSC insurance or reinsurance company may be permitted to lend its surplus funds to an IFSC treasury affiliate. Lending to non-Irish affiliates is readily accepted as a qualifying activity but lending to another IFSC company is not within the activities specified in the standard certificate.

    The lending by an insurance or reinsurance company of borrowed funds to affiliates would not be accepted as a qualifying activity; the standard IFSC insurance/reinsurance certificate does not cover borrowed funds and a certificate applicable to an insurance company would not be extended to cover treasury activities. Although the lending of borrowed funds could be regarded as a trading transaction, it would not be accepted as a qualifying activity and profits arising from the lending activity would be taxable at the standard corporation rate.

7.206.11 Securitisation of assets

An entity such as a bank or building society may employ securitisation as a means of realising cash for a block of assets which can then be removed from its balance sheet. The company will sell the assets, typically debts or other receivables with an income stream, to a special purpose vehicle (SPV) which will carry on the business of managing the acquired assets. The SPV will be funded by issuing bonds to investors. To ensure that the transaction is off the balance sheet of the company, a charitable trust may be interposed between the bank and the SPV.

    The level of profits of the SPV is not usually significant as the return is shared between the bank and the investors. A particular advantage associated with the SPV is that withholding tax on interest payments to investors is avoided.

TCA 1997, s 110 provides that the SPV is to be treated for tax purposes as carrying on a trade. Accordingly, the income arising from the assets acquired will be treated for tax purposes in the same way as it would have been treated had the assets been retained by the financial institution which transferred them. An asset which is "securitised" is referred to as a "qualifying asset".

A *qualifying asset*, in relation to a qualifying company, is an asset consisting of, or of an interest (including a partnership interest) in, a financial asset, and *financial asset* includes:

(a)   shares, bonds and other securities;

(b)   futures, options, swaps, derivatives and similar instruments;

(c)   invoices and all types of receivables;

(d)   obligations evidencing debt (including loans and deposits);

(e)   leases and loan and lease portfolios;

(f)   hire purchase contracts;

(g)   acceptance credits and all other documents of title relating to the movement of goods;

(h)   bills of exchange, commercial paper, promissory notes and all other kinds of negotiable or transferable instruments;

(i)   greenhouse gas emissions allowance; and

(j)   contracts for insurance and contracts for reinsurance.

In (j) above, *greenhouse gas emissions allowance* means an allowance, permit, licence or right to emit during a specified period, a specified amount of carbon dioxide or any other greenhouse gas as defined in Directive 10 2003/87/EC of the European Parliament and of the Council of 13 October 2003 (OJ No L 275, 25 October 2003, p 32) establishing a scheme for greenhouse gas emission allowance trading within the Community and amending Council Directive 96/61/EC of 24 September 1996 (OJ No L 257, 10 October 1996, p 26), where such allowance, permit, licence or right is issued by a State or by an intergovernmental or supra-national institution pursuant to a scheme which—

(a)   imposes limitations on the emission of such greenhouse gases, and

(b)   allows the transfer for value of such allowances, permits, licences or rights.

A *qualifying company* (the SPV referred to above) is a company:

(a)   which is resident in the State;

(b)   which—

    (i)   acquires qualifying assets from a person,

    (ii)   as a result of an arrangement with another person holds or manages qualifying assets, or

    (iii)   has entered into a legally enforceable arrangement with another person which arrangement itself is a qualifying asset (such as a derivative);

(c)   which carries on in the State a business of holding, managing, or both the holding and management of, qualifying assets;

(d)   which, apart from activities ancillary to that business, carries on no other activities in the State;

(e) in relation to which the market value of all qualifying assets held or managed, or the market value of all qualifying assets in respect of which the company has entered into legally enforceable arrangements, is not less than €10,000,000 on the day on which the qualifying assets are first acquired or first held, or on the day a legally enforceable arrangement referred to in (b) above is first entered into by the company; and

(f) which has notified in writing the authorised officer in a form prescribed by the Revenue Commissioners that it is or intends to be a company to which (a) to (e) above applies and has supplied such other particulars relating to the company as may be specified on the prescribed form.

A company is not a qualifying company if any transaction or arrangement is entered into by it otherwise than by way of a bargain made at arm's length, except where TCA 1997, s 110(4) (see below under *Interest not treated as a distribution*) applies to any interest or other distribution payable under the transaction or arrangement (unless the transaction or arrangement concerned is excluded from that subsection by virtue of the anti-avoidance provision in TCA 1997, s 110(5) – see below).

An *authorised officer* is an officer of the Revenue Commissioners authorised by them in writing for the purposes of TCA 1997, s 110.

Regarding (c) above, this requirement will be satisfied through the participation of, say, two Irish resident directors in the affairs of the SPV and the appointment of an Irish based corporate administrator to the SPV. The role of the Irish administrator is generally limited (but can be wider if required) to keeping books and records of the SPV, preparing accounts, providing directors etc. The appointment of an Irish based administrator can be dispensed with if the SPV has an "active" board of directors.

It will be noted from (d) above that the SPV must not carry on any other activities (apart from those that are ancillary to the business of the holding and/or management of qualifying assets). This requirement is to ensure that the SPV is only used for particular types of activities so as to confine the favourable tax treatment afforded to Irish SPVs to activities involving qualifying assets.

Tax treatment of qualifying companies

The profits arising to a qualifying company in relation to activities carried out by it in the course of its business are treated as annual profits or gains chargeable to tax under Case III of Schedule D. For this purpose, the profits or gains are to be computed in accordance with the provisions of Case I of Schedule (TCA 1997, s 110(2)(a)). In computing the amount of the profits to be charged, the amount of any debt proved to be bad, and of any doubtful debt to the extent estimated to be bad, is deducted. The deduction may be made to the extent that the amount of the debt is not otherwise deductible and is not recoverable from the original lender or recoverable under any insurance, contract of indemnity or otherwise (TCA 1997, s 110(2)(b)).

Since the profits or gains of a qualifying company are chargeable to tax under Case III, they are taxable at the 25% corporation tax rate (the "higher rate" – see **3.101.4**).

Any amount or part of an amount which had been deducted as an expense in the circumstances described above and which is recovered or is no longer estimated to be bad is, to the extent that it is recovered or no longer estimated to be bad, to be treated as income of the qualifying company at that time (TCA 1997, s 110(2)(c)).

A qualifying company may not surrender any amount eligible for relief from corporation tax under the group relief provisions of TCA 1997 Part 12 Chapter 5 (see **7.303**). Where a qualifying company incurs a loss in an accounting period, it may claim to have the loss set against any profits of the company for any subsequent accounting period as long as it continues to be a qualifying company. A claim to this effect should be included in the company's annual tax return for the subsequent period. The amount of the loss is to be computed in the same way as any profits of the company in that period would have been computed, in the way indicated above (TCA 1997, s 110(3)).

Interest not treated as a distribution

Interest payments, even those that vary with its profits, made by an SPV (on moneys raised to fund the holding or management of qualifying assets) are tax deductible provided the interest does not come within TCA 1997, s 130(2)(d)(iv) (ie, is not paid to a 75% non-Irish tax resident parent or affiliated company). TCA 1997, s 110(4) provides that any interest or other distribution which is paid out of the assets of a qualifying company to another person and is so paid in respect of a security falling within TCA 1997, s 130(2)(d)(iii) (interest on profit participating loans or excessive interest – see **11.106**) is not to be treated as a distribution by virtue only of that provision unless the anti-avoidance provision in TCA 1997, s 110(5) applies.

Even if interest payments come within TCA 1997, s 130(2)(d)(iv), it may still be possible to obtain a tax deduction since most of Ireland's double tax treaties will override the domestic Irish tax provision prohibiting such a deduction and, in addition, there is a statutory override for interest payments to EU resident companies (see **11.106**). If a trustee on behalf of a charitable trust normally holds the SPV's share capital, interest payments to group companies will not arise.

TCA 1997, s 110(5) applies to any interest or other distribution paid or payable out of the assets of a qualifying company if it has been paid as part of a scheme or arrangement the main purpose or one of the main purposes of which is to obtain a tax relief or the reduction of a tax liability, in either case arising from the operation of TCA 1997, s 110(4), by a person within the charge to corporation tax (the "beneficiary") and the beneficiary is the person:

(i)   from whom the assets were acquired by the qualifying company; or

(ii) with whom the qualifying company has entered into an arrangement referred to in (b) of the above definition of "qualifying company" (TCA 1997, s 110(5)(a)).

The anti-avoidance provision will apply only where, at the time of the acquisition of the asset or at the time of entering into the arrangement, the qualifying company concerned is in possession of, or is aware of, information that can reasonably be used by it to identify the beneficiary (TCA 1997, s 110(5)(b)).

IFRS

The provisions of TCA 1997, s 76A (see **3.305**) are to have effect in relation to a qualifying company but on the basis that *generally accepted accounting practice* means Irish generally accepted accounting practice as it applied for a period of account ending on 31 December 2004. A qualifying company may, for any accounting period, elect that TCA 1997, s 76A is not to apply as respects that period or any subsequent accounting period. Such election is irrevocable (TCA 1997, s 110(6)).

7.206.12 IFSC certificates

IFSC Certificates have been issued for the following activities:

(a)   floor trader;

(b)   floor broker and trader;

(c)   special purpose investment company;

(d)   banking company;

(e)   life assurance;

(f)   insurance;

(g)   reinsurance;

(h)   captive insurance;

(i)   captive reinsurance;

(j)   agency reinsurance;

(k)   captive insurance manager;

(l)   insurance broking;

(m)   group treasury;

(n)   agency treasury;

(o)   captive finance;

(p)   captive finance/ agency treasury manager;

(q)   agency fund management;

(r)   group fund management/ administration;

(s)   third party fund administration;

(t)   third party fund management/ administration;

(u)   trustee/custodian;

(v)   special purpose company; and

(w)   asset finance.

7.207   Transactions between associated persons

TCA 1997, s 453 contains anti-avoidance measures designed to ensure that profits of a person taxable at the standard income tax or corporation tax rate may not be diverted to an associated company which benefits from the 10% tax rate. This would, typically, be achieved by arranging for sales of goods from one company to the other company at non-arm's length prices with a view to inflating the profits of the manufacturing company at the expense of its associated company.

TCA 1997, s 453(2) provides that where a company claiming the 10% corporation tax rate (the "buyer") buys from another person (the "seller"), and:

(a)   the seller has control over the buyer or, where the seller is a company or a partnership, the buyer has control over the seller or some other person has control over both the buyer and the seller; and

(b)   the price in the transaction is less than it would be had the parties to the transaction been independent parties dealing at arm's length,

the income or loss of each party is to be computed for any purpose of the Tax Acts as if the price in the transaction were the same as it would have been had the transaction been one between independent parties dealing at arm's length.

Conversely, TCA 1997, s 453(3) provides that where a company claiming the 10% corporation tax rate (the "seller") sells goods to another person (the "buyer"), and:

(a)   the buyer has control over the seller or, where the buyer is a company or a partnership, the seller has control over the buyer or some other person has control over both the seller and the buyer; and

(b)   the goods are sold at a price greater than the price which they might have been expected to fetch had the parties to the transaction been independent parties dealing at arm's length,

the income or loss of each party is to be computed for any purpose of the Tax Acts as if the goods had been sold by the seller to the buyer for the price which they would have fetched had the transaction been one between independent parties dealing at arm's length.

In the second situation above, a company is regarded as selling goods where and to the extent that any amount receivable by it in payment for any trading activity is regarded as an amount receivable from the sale of goods; "seller" and "buyer" are to be construed accordingly. Thus, where an activity is deemed to be the manufacture of goods, eg the rendering of computer services, any amount receivable for the rendering of those services is treated for the purposes of TCA 1997, s 453(3) as an amount receivable for the sale of goods and the company providing the computer services will be regarded as a "seller" for the purposes of that subsection.

For the above purposes, *control* in relation to a company means the power of a person to secure, by means of the holding of shares or the possession of voting power in or in relation to that or any other company, or by virtue of any powers conferred by the articles of association or other document regulating that or any other company, that the affairs of the first-mentioned company are conducted in accordance with the wishes of that person (TCA 1997, s 11).

It will be seen that whereas TCA 1997, s 453(3) deals with the case where a 10% taxed company "sells goods", TCA 1997, s 453(2) is concerned with the situation in which such a company " buys from another person". This is because, where the 10% taxed company is the buyer, it will not necessarily always be buying "goods". Where a manufacturing company is the buyer, it is likely that what it is buying will not be "goods" (ie goods manufactured in the State); it may, for example, be buying raw materials from an associated person and the anti-avoidance provision will apply in that situation.

TCA 1997, s 453 does not extend to transactions between associated persons other than those involving buying and selling, eg inter company charges by way of rent or interest. It may, however, apply in cases of activities deemed to be the sale of goods. For example, any amount receivable from the rendering of computer services is deemed by TCA 1997, s 443(10) to be an amount receivable from the sale of goods. On the other hand, it may also be arguable that since that deeming provision is to apply "for the purpose of relief" under TCA 1997 Part 14, it does not apply for the anti-avoidance purposes of TCA 1997, s 453.

In the practical application of TCA 1997, s 453, it will not always be a simple matter to determine the price which would have been fetched in an arm's length dealing between independent persons.

Example 7.207.1

Tyson Ltd carries on a manufacturing and distribution trade in which its turnover from goods manufactured by it represents 50% of total turnover. The net profit attributable to the manufactured goods is €10m and from other sales €4m and that position is projected to continue for a number of years. In view of the low profitability of the non-manufactured sales, it is decided that that part of the business should be transferred to Garfield Ltd, a wholly owned subsidiary of Tyson Ltd. A comparison of the projected tax positions, based on a single company structure and a two company structure, for a recent relevant accounting period is as follows:

Single company:	€
Annual profit	14,000,000
Corporation tax @ 12.5%	1,750,000
Manufacturing relief:	
€1,750,000 x 50% x 1/5	175,000
Tax payable	1,575,000

Two company structure:

	Tyson Ltd	Garfield Ltd
	€	€
Annual profit	10,000,000	4,000,000
Corporation tax @ 12.5%	1,250,000	500,000
Manufacturing relief x 1/5	250,000	
Tax payable	1,000,000	500,000

Tax under the two-company structure is €1,500,000, resulting in a saving of €75,000.

It is then considered that further savings could be achieved by arranging for Tyson Ltd to sell all of its output to Garfield Ltd which would then sell on those goods to the existing customers of Tyson Ltd. This arrangement would take advantage of the deemed manufacturing provision in TCA 1997, s 443(1)(b) (see **7.205.2**). Accordingly, and to achieve maximum tax savings, it is decided that Tyson Ltd should sell its entire output to Garfield Ltd at the same prices as were being charged to the customers of Tyson Ltd. This would give the following results:

	Tyson Ltd	Garfield Ltd
	€	€
Annual profit	10,000,000	4,000,000
Corporation tax @ 12.5%	1,250,000	500,000
Manufacturing relief x 1/5	250,000	
Manufacturing relief x 1/5 x 50%		50,000
Tax payable	1,000,000	450,000

On the basis of the above computations, the total tax bill would come to €1,450,000, representing a further tax saving of €50,000 which, as can be seen, is attributable to the manufacturing relief now available to Garfield Ltd.

The above position must, however, be considered in the light of TCA 1997, s 453. TCA 1997, s 453(3) is relevant as Tyson Ltd, the "seller", sells goods to Garfield Ltd, a person over whom it has control. The income of both companies will fall to be adjusted if the goods are being sold at a price greater than would be the case had the two companies been independent parties dealing at arm's length.

Since the price being charged to Garfield Ltd is such as to leave it with no profit, it might be considered that an adjustment is inevitable; as an independent party, Garfield Ltd would not agree to buy at a price which would leave it incapable of making a profit. On that basis, the profits of Garfield Ltd should be increased (and the profits of Tyson Ltd correspondingly reduced) by an amount equivalent to what is a commercial profit on the goods purchased from Tyson Ltd.

The problem with this approach is that it takes no account of the position of Tyson Ltd. There is in fact already an objective measure of what the arm's length selling price of the goods is, ie the price at which they are currently being sold to third party customers. The better view must therefore be that no adjustment is required. If the profits of Tyson Ltd were to be reduced only because its sales are to a controlled company, the implied price could not then be an arm's length price.

7.3 INVESTMENT IN FILMS

7.301 Introduction and outline
7.302 Definitions
7.303 The relief
7.304 Capital gains tax
7.305 Revenue notice

7.301   Introduction and outline

In practice, the tax relief for investment in films, known as "section 481 relief", as provided for in TCA 1997, s 481 and introduced to encourage and promote investment in the film industry, is a relief primarily of interest to individuals. The relatively limited amount of tax relief that can be availed of by companies has meant that section 481 investment by companies is somewhat exceptional.

The scheme as outlined below reflects the position following changes introduced by FA 2004 and FA 2005.

The amount of finance which may be raised by an individual production company is governed by a certificate issued by the Minister for Arts, Sport and Tourism ("the Minister") and without such certification no relief may be claimed. Certification is subject to a number of conditions. These conditions include conditions relating to the limits on the percentage of total production costs which may be met by section 481 finance.

The level of production costs which may be met by section 481 financing depends on the total production budget for the film in question. The maximum percentage of production costs which may be met by section 481 financing is 80% but subject to a maximum amount of €50m.

An investor company may not be connected with the film production company (the "qualifying company"). Relief is restricted to 80% of the qualifying investment ("relevant investment"). The amount of tax relief available can differ greatly depending on whether the investor is an individual or a company. Relief for individuals is calculated by reference to investments made in a tax year and the maximum investment permitted to an individual in any one year is €31,750. Unutilised relief may be carried forward to later years (but not beyond the year 2012 in the case of an individual).

For corporate investors, a relevant investment must be made in the period 23 January 1996 to 31 December 2012 (the "qualifying period"). The maximum investment in the twelve- month period ended 22 January 1997 is €7.62m, and for each of the twelve-month periods ending on 22 January 1998 and 22 January 1999, and for the period 23 January 1999 to 5 April 2000 (the "specified period"), is €10.16m. The maximum qualifying investment which may be made by a corporate group, ie a company and its connected companies, in any one film company is €3.81m (€2.54m for a qualifying investment made before 26 March 1997). Where the total investment in any twelve-month period or in the specified period exceeds €3.81m (€2.54m for a period commencing before 23 January 1997), the excess will only qualify for relief if it is invested in qualifying companies with production budgets not exceeding $5.08 m.

A qualifying company must be incorporated and resident in the State or must be carrying on a trade in the State through a branch or agency. It must exist only for the purpose of the production and distribution of one qualifying film. A qualifying film must be made on a commercial basis for cinema or television but not as an advertising programme or commercial. It must be certified by the Minister, with the consent of the Minister for Finance.

Relief for film investment will not be available where the terms of the investment provide for reimbursement to the investor; the moneys invested must constitute risk capital. The investment must be made directly in the qualifying company to provide funds for the production and distribution of the film and must not be withdrawn within two years. The investment must be made for *bona fide* commercial reasons and not for tax avoidance reasons.

The ceiling amount of 80% for a qualifying investment is one of the main features of the section 481. Section 481 relief is available to both individuals and companies; the following paragraphs deal only with the relief as it applies to companies ("allowable investor companies").

7.302   Definitions

7.302.1   Various definitions

The definitions of the following key concepts, provided in TCA 1997, s 481(1), are important for any understanding of the operation of section 481 relief.

Film

Film means:

(a)   a film of a kind which is included within the categories of films eligible for certification by the Revenue Commissioners under TCA 1997, s 481(2A), as specified in regulations made under TCA 1997, s 481(2E); and

(b)   as respects every film, a film which is produced—

(i)   on a commercial basis with a view to the realisation of profit, and

(ii)   wholly or principally for exhibition to the public in cinemas or by way of television broadcasting.

Qualifying film

A *qualifying film* is a film in respect of which the Revenue Commissioners have issued a certificate under TCA 1997, s 481(2A), which has not been revoked under TCA 1997, s 481(2D).

Qualifying company

A *qualifying company* is a company which:

(a)   is incorporated and resident in the State or is carrying on a trade in the State through a branch or agency;

(b)   exists solely for the purposes of the production and distribution of only one qualifying film; and

(c)   does not contain in its name—

(i)   registered under either or both the Companies Acts 1963 to 1999, and the Regulation of Business Names Act 1963, or

(ii)   registered under the law of the territory in which it is incorporated, the words "Ireland", "Irish", "Éireann", "Éire" or "National".

See also **7.302.3** regarding conditions for a qualifying company.

Relevant investment

A *relevant investment* is a sum of money which is:

(a)   paid in the qualifying period to a qualifying company in respect of shares in the company by an allowable investor company on its own behalf or by a qualifying individual on that individual's own behalf, and is paid by the allowable investor company or the qualifying individual directly to the qualifying company;

(b)   paid by the allowable investor company or the qualifying individual to enable the qualifying company to produce a film in respect of which, at the time such sum of money is paid, the authorised officer has given written notice to the qualifying company that the Revenue Commissioners are satisfied for the time being that an application in writing, in the form prescribed by the Revenue Commissioners and containing such information as may be specified in regulations made under TCA 1997, s 481(2E), has been made to enable the Revenue Commissioners to consider whether a certificate should be issued to that company under TCA 1997, s 481(2A); and

(c)   used by the qualifying company within two years of receipt of the sum for the purpose described in (b),

but does not include a sum of money paid to the qualifying company on terms which provide that it will be repaid, other than a provision for its repayment in the event of the Revenue Commissioners not giving a certificate under TCA 1997, s 481(2A).

Allowable investor company

In relation to a qualifying company, an *allowable investor company* is a company not connected (within the meaning of TCA 1997, s 10 – see **2.3**) with the qualifying company.

Qualifying period

In relation to a qualifying investor company, *qualifying period* means the period commencing on 23 January 1996 and ending on 31 December 2012.

Some of these definitions require further elaboration.

7.302.2 Qualifying film

One of the requirements for a "qualifying film" is the receipt of a certificate from the Minister. If the certificate is subsequently revoked, the film will no longer be a qualifying film and any relief given in respect of an investment in that film will be withdrawn.

Authorisation to issue certificate

A qualifying company may make an application to the Revenue Commissioners for a certificate under TCA 1997, s 481(2A) in relation to a film to be produced by it. On request from the Commissioners in relation to the application, the Minister may in accordance with regulations made under TCA 1997, s 481(2E) (see **7.302.4** below) authorise them, subject to TCA 1997, s 481(2A), to issue a certificate under that subsection (TCA 1997, s 481(2)(a)).

In considering whether to give the authorisation, the Minister, in accordance with regulations made under TCA 1997, s 481(2E) (see **7.302.4** below), is to have regard to:

(a)   the categories of films eligible for certification by the Revenue Commissioners under TCA 1997, s 481(2A) (see below under *Conditions for certification as qualifying film*), as specified in those regulations; and

(b)   any contribution which the production of the film is expected to make to either or both the development of the film industry in the State and the promotion and expression of Irish culture,

and where such authorisation is given, the Minister, having regard to those matters, is required to specify in the authorisation such conditions as he may consider proper, including a condition in relation to:

(i)   the employment and responsibilities of the producer, and the producer company, of a film for the production of that film, and

(ii) the employment of personnel, including trainees, (other than the producer) for the production of that film (TCA 1997, s 481(2)(b)).

Specified percentage

The maximum percentage of the total production cost of a film which may be met by section 481 funding, referred to as the *specified percentage*, is 80%. The total cost of production of a film which may be met by relevant investments may, however, not exceed €50m (the limit applying with effect from 17 April 2008 – for details of previous limits, see earlier editions of this book.

Conditions for certification as qualifying film

Where the Revenue Commissioners receive authorisation from the Minister for Arts, Sport and Tourism, they will examine the company's proposal in full and, where they issue a certificate, it will be subject to various conditions which the Commissioners consider proper, having regard to that examination and the conditions specified by the Minister in his authorisation.

On the making of an application by a qualifying company to them, the Revenue Commissioners may, in accordance with regulations made under TCA 1997, s 481(2E) (see **7.302.4** below), issue a certificate to the company stating, in relation to a film to be produced by it, that the film may be treated as a qualifying film for the purposes of section 481 relief (TCA 1997, s 481(2A)(a)). The Revenue Commissioners are required to have received authorisation from the Minister before issuing a certificate. Where, in relation to a film, the principal photography has commenced, the first animation drawings have commenced, or the first model movement has commenced, as the case may be, before application is made by a qualifying company, the Revenue Commissioners may not issue a certificate (TCA 1997, s 481(2A)(c)). An application for a certificate must be in the form prescribed by the Revenue Commissioners and must contain such information as may be specified in regulations made under TCA 1997, s 481(2E).

In considering whether to issue a certificate, the Revenue Commissioners are required, in respect of the proposed production of the film, to examine all aspects of the qualifying company's proposal. They may refuse to issue a certificate if they are not satisfied with any aspect of the qualifying company's application and, in particular, they may refuse to issue a certificate:

(i) if they have reason to believe that the budget or any particular item of proposed expenditure in the budget is inflated; or

(ii) where—

(I) they are not satisfied that there is a commercial rationale for the corporate structure proposed for the production, financing, distribution or sale of the film, or for all of those purposes, or

(II) they are of the opinion that the corporate structure proposed would hinder the Revenue Commissioners in verifying compliance with any of the provisions governing the relief.

A certificate issued by the Revenue Commissioners may be subject to such conditions specified in the certificate as the Commissioners may consider proper, having regard in particular to their examination of the qualifying company's proposal and any conditions specified in the authorisation given by the Minister, and in particular the Commissioners must specify in the certificate a condition:

(a) in relation to the matters (ie, the employment and responsibilities of the producer, and the producer company, of a film for the production of a film, and the employment of personnel, including trainees, for the production of that film) specified by the Minister in the authorisation by virtue of TCA 1997, s 481(2)(b) (see above);

(b) subject to TCA 1997, s 481(2)(c) (see above in relation to "the specified percentage"), that the percentage amount of the total cost of production of the film that may be met by relevant investments may not exceed the amount per cent ("the specified percentage" in TCA 1997, s 481(2)(c)) specified in the certificate;

(c) in relation to the minimum amount of money to be expended on the production of the qualifying film—

(i) directly by the qualifying company on the employment, by the company, of eligible individuals, in so far as those individuals exercise their employment in the State in the production of the qualifying film, and

(ii) directly or indirectly by the qualifying company, on the provision of certain goods, services and facilities, as set out in regulations made under TCA 1997, s 481(E).

(d) where financial arrangements have been approved by the Revenue Commissioners in accordance with TCA 1997, s 481(2C)(ba) (see under *Certain financial arrangements* in **7.302.3** below), in relation to any matter pertaining to those arrangements (TCA 1997, s 481(2A)(g)).

An *eligible individual*, in (d)(i) above, is an individual who is a citizen of Ireland or of another Member State of the EU, or an individual domiciled, resident or ordinarily resident in the state or in another Member state of the EU.

The Revenue Commissioners, having consulted with the Minister as appropriate, may amend or revoke any condition specified in a certificate, or add to such conditions, by giving notice in writing to the qualifying company concerned of the amendment, revocation or addition (TCA 1997, s 481(2A)(h)).

7.302.3   Conditions for qualifying company

A company will not be regarded as a qualifying company:

(a)   unless the company, in relation to a qualifying film, notifies the Revenue Commissioners in writing immediately when the principal photography has commenced, the first animation drawings have commenced, or the first model movement has commenced, as appropriate;

(b)   subject to conditions relating to certain financial arrangements (see below), if the financial arrangements which the company enters into in relation to the qualifying film are—

    (i)   financial arrangements of any type with a person resident, registered or operating in a territory other than a Member State of the EU or a territory with which Ireland has a tax treaty, or

    (ii)   financial arrangements under which funds are channelled, directly or indirectly, to, or through, a territory other than a territory referred to in (i),

(c)   unless the company provides, when requested to do so by the Revenue Commissioners, for the purposes of verifying compliance with the provisions governing the relief or with any condition specified in a certificate issued by them under TCA 1997, s 481(2A)(a) (see under *Conditions for certification as qualifying film* in **7.302.2** above), evidence to vouch each item of expenditure in the State or elsewhere on the production and distribution of the qualifying film, whether expended by the qualifying company or by any other person engaged, directly or indirectly, by the qualifying company to provide goods, services or facilities in relation to such production or distribution and, in particular, such evidence must include—

    (i)   records required to be kept or retained by the company by virtue of TCA 1997, s 886 (see *Obligation to keep certain records* in **15.204**), and

    (ii)   records, in relation to the production and distribution of the qualifying film, required to be kept or retained by that other person by virtue of TCA 1997, s 886, or which would be so required if that other person were subject to the provisions of that section, and

(d)   unless the company, within such time as is specified in the regulations made under TCA 1997, s 481(2E) (see **7.302.4 below)**—

    (i)   notifies the Revenue Commissioners in writing of the date of completion of the production of the qualifying film,

    (ii)   provides to the Revenue Commissioners and to the Minister, such number of copies of the film in such format and manner as may be specified in those regulations, and

    (iii) provides to the Revenue Commissioners, a compliance report, in such format and manner specified in those regulations, which proves to the satisfaction of the Revenue Commissioners that—

(I) the provisions of TCA 1997, s 481 in so far as they apply in relation to the company and a qualifying film have been met, and

(II) any conditions attaching to a certificate issued to the company in relation to a qualifying film under TCA 1997, s 481(2A)(a) (see under *Conditions for certification as qualifying film* in **7.302.2** above) have been fulfilled (TCA 1997, s 481(2C)).

Certain financial arrangements

Regarding film activities in certain non-EU territories, provision is made for the approval by the Revenue Commissioners in limited circumstances of certain financial arrangements involving territories outside the EU with which Ireland does not have a double tax treaty (referred to here as "non-relevant territories"). In this connection, TCA 1997, s 481(2C)(ba) provides as follows.

(i) The condition in (b) above will not apply to financial arrangements in relation to a transaction or series of transactions where such arrangements have been approved by the Revenue Commissioners;

(ii) The Revenue Commissioners may not approve financial arrangements to which condition (b) above would otherwise apply unless:

(I) the arrangements relate to either or both an investment made in a qualifying film and the filming of part of a film in a non-relevant territory,

(II) a request for approval is made by the qualifying company to the Revenue Commissioners before such arrangements are effected,

(III) the qualifying company demonstrates to the satisfaction of the Revenue Commissioners that it can provide, if requested, sufficient records to enable the Commissioners to verify—

(A) in the case of an investment, the amount of the investment made in the qualifying company and the person who made the investment, and

(B) in the case of filming in a territory, the amount of each item of expenditure on the production of the qualifying film expended in the territory, whether expended by the qualifying company or by any other person, and

(IV) they are satisfied that it is appropriate to grant such approval;

(iii) In considering whether to grant an approval in relation to financial arrangements, the Revenue Commissioners may seek any information they consider to be appropriate in relation to any person who is, directly or indirectly, a party to the arrangements;

(iv) Where the Revenue Commissioners have approved financial arrangements, no amount of money expended, either directly or indirectly, as part of the arrangements may be regarded, for the purposes of TCA 1997, s 481(2A)(g)(iv) (see condition (c) of conditions to be specified in certificate to be issued by Revenue under *Conditions for certification as qualifying film* in **7.302.2** above), as an amount of money expended on either the employment of eligible individuals or on the provision of goods, services and facilities as referred to in that condition.

Withdrawal of relief

Where a company fails:

(a)   to comply with any of the provisions of TCA 1997, s 481(2C) or any other provisions governing the relief; or

(b)   to fulfil any of the conditions to which a certificate issued to it under TCA 1997, s 481(2A)(a) is subject, by virtue of TCA 1997, s 481(2A)(g) or (h) (see under *Conditions for certification as qualifying film* in **7.302.2** above),

that failure will constitute the failure of an event to happen by reason of which relief may be withdrawn under TCA 1997, s 481(11) (see **7.303.1** below) and the Revenue Commissioners may, by notice in writing served by registered post on the company, revoke the certificate (TCA 1997, s 481(2D)).

7.302.4   Regulations

The Revenue Commissioners, with the consent of the Minister for Finance, and with the consent of the Minister in relation to the matters to be considered regarding the issue of an authorisation under TCA 1997, s 481(2) (see **7.302.2** above), are required to make regulations with respect to the administration by the them of the section 481 relief and with respect to the matters to be considered by the Minister for the purposes of TCA 1997ss 481(2), and these regulations may include provision:

(a)   governing the application for certification pursuant to TCA 1997, s 481(2A) (conditions for certification as qualifying film – see **7.302.2** above) and the information and documents to be provide in or with such application;

(b)   specifying the categories of films eligible for certification by the Revenue Commissioners under TCA 1997, s 481(2A);

(c)   prescribing the form of such application;

(d)   governing the records that a qualifying company is required to maintain or provide to the Revenue Commissioners;

(e)   governing the period for which, and the place at which, such records must be maintained;

(f)   specifying the time within which a qualifying company must notify the Revenue Commissioners of the completion of the production of a qualifying film;

(g)   specifying the time within which, and the format, number and manner in which, copies of a qualifying film must be provided to the Revenue Commissioners and to the Minister;

(h)   specifying the form and content of the compliance report to be provided to the Revenue Commissioners, the manner in which such report is to be made and verified, the documents to accompany the report and the time within which such report is to be provided;

(i)   governing the type of expenditure that may be accepted by the Revenue Commissioners as expenditure on the production of a qualifying film;

(j)   governing the provision of the goods, services and facilities referred to in TCA 1997, s 481(2A)(g)(iv)(II) (the provision of certain goods, services and facilities – see (d)(ii) in **7.302.2** above), including the place of origin of those goods, services and facilities, the place in which they are provided and the location of the supplier;

(k) specifying the currency exchange rate to be applied to expenditure on the production of a qualifying film;

(l) specifying the criteria to be considered by the Minister, in relation to the matters referred to in TCA 1997, s 481(2)(b)(i) and (ii) (categories of eligible films and contribution which the production of the film is expected to make to either or both the development of the film industry in the State and the promotion and expression of Irish culture – see (a) and (b) under *Authorisation to issue certificate* in **7.302.2** above) –

(i) in deciding whether to give authorisation to the Revenue Commissioners under TCA 1997, s 481(2)(a) (see *Authorisation to issue certificate* in **7.302.2** above), and

(ii) in specifying conditions in such authorisation, as provided for in TCA 1997, s 481(2)(b) (see *Authorisation to issue certificate* in **7.302.2** above), and the information required for those purposes to be included in the application made to the Revenue Commissioners under TCA 1997, s 481(2A) (conditions for certification – see **7.302.2** above) by a qualifying company;

(m) governing the approval of financial arrangements in accordance with TCA 1997, s 481(2C)(ba) (*Certain financial arrangements* above); and

(n) governing the employment of eligible individuals, as referred to in TCA 1997, s 481(2A)(g)(iv) (see (c) under *Conditions for certification as qualifying film* **7.302.2** above), and the circumstances in which expenditure by a qualifying company would be regarded as expenditure on the employment of those individuals in the production of a qualifying film (TCA 1997, s 481(2E)).

7.303   The relief

7.303.1   Outline

The relief available to an allowable investor company is by way of a "relevant deduction" from total profits for the period in which the relevant investment is made. A *relevant deduction* means a deduction equal to 80% of a relevant investment. The maximum investment allowable in any *12 month period* (ie, a period of 12 months ending on the anniversary of 22 January 1996) is €10.16m. This limit is applied to the allowable investor company together with any company or companies which are at any time in that year connected with (within the meaning of TCA 1997, s 10 - see **2.3**) the allowable investor company. The total allowable investment which may be made by an allowable investor company, and its connected companies, in any one qualifying company is €3.81m, whenever invested. Where the total amount of relevant investments (made in all qualifying companies) invested in any of the twelve-month periods exceeds €3.81m, a relevant deduction will be available in respect of the excess amount only to the extent that it is invested in a qualifying company to enable that company to produce a film with a budget not exceeding €5.08m.

Where the amount of the relevant deduction exceeds the company's profits for the period, an amount equal to 125% of the excess may be carried forward to the succeeding accounting period and treated as a relevant investment made in that period (TCA 1997, s 481(3)). Accordingly, the relevant deduction which may be made in that succeeding period will be 80% of the amount carried forward. If there is again an insufficiency of profits to absorb that relevant deduction, the excess is again carried forward in the same manner as previously.

Where any of the limits is exceeded in a case where there are two or more relevant investments, such apportionment of available relief is to be made between the relevant investments by the inspector or, on appeal, the Appeal Commissioners, "as shall be just and reasonable". Where two or more connected companies make relevant investments, it is necessary to apply the various limits to the aggregate amount of those investments. Where any limit is exceeded, the total relief available must be allocated between the companies in proportion to the respective amounts of the relevant investment or investments made by each company.

A claim to relief under TCA 1997, s 481 may be allowed at any time after the time referred to in TCA 1997, s 481(11)(b) (see below) in respect of the payment of a sum to a qualifying company which, if it is used within two years of its being paid, by the qualifying company for the production of a qualifying film, will be a relevant investment, if all the conditions for relief are or will be satisfied. The relief will be withdrawn if, by reason of the happening of any subsequent event including the revocation, under TCA 1997, s 481(2D) (see **7.302.3**), by the Revenue Commissioners of a certificate issued by them under TCA 1997, s 481(2A) (see *Conditions for certification as qualifying film* in **7.302.2** above) or the failure of an event to happen which at the time the relief was given was expected to happen, the company or the individual making the claim was not entitled to the relief allowed (TCA 1997, s 481(11)(a)).

The time referred to above is the time when all of the following events have occurred:

(i)   the payment in respect of which relief is claimed has been made; and

(ii)   in relation to the qualifying film, the principal photography has commenced, the first animation drawings have commenced or the first model movement has commenced, as appropriate (TCA 1997, s 481(11)(b)).

Relief in respect of a relevant investment in a qualifying company will not be available unless the qualifying company has issued a certificate to the investor, in such form as the Revenue Commissioners direct, certifying that the conditions for relief have been, or will be, satisfied in relation to that investment (TCA 1997, s 481(12)). The qualifying company may not issue this certificate until the company has furnished the "authorised officer" (the officer authorised by the Revenue Commissioners for the purposes of TCA 1997, s 481) with a statement confirming that it satisfies the conditions for relief in so far as they apply in relation to the company and a film, and such other information as the Revenue Commissioners may reasonably require (TCA 1997, s 481(13)).

The certificate may not be issued without the written approval of the authorised officer and, where the authorised officer has not received additional information sought in accordance with TCA 1997, s 481(13), or has reason to believe that the conditions for relief are not, or will not be, satisfied, the officer will not give such approval (TCA 1997, s 481(14)(a)). In the event that approval is not so given, the officer will issue a determination to that effect and the provisions of TCA 1997, s 949 (appeals against determinations of certain claims – see **15.209.16**) are to apply to that determination as if it were a determination made on a matter referred to in TCA 1997, s 864 (making of claims etc – see **15.209.16**) (TCA 1997, s 481(14)(b)).

7.303.2 Maximum allowable investment amounts

It might be useful at this point to summarise the position regarding the operation of the various limits, provided for in TCA 1997, s 481(4). These are as follows:

Single investor company

€10.16m limit on total relevant investments in any 12 month period – no carry forward of excess;

€3.81m once only limit on total relevant investments made in one qualifying company – for any excess amount, relief is lost altogether;

where the total of relevant investments (in qualified companies) in any twelve month period exceeds €3.81m, no relief for excess to the extent that it is invested in a film with a budget greater than €5.08m.

Connected investor companies

€10.16m on total relevant investments made by investor company together with connected companies in any 12 month period – no carry forward of excess: where limit is exceeded, relief is allocated to each company in proportion to relevant investments made by each;

€3.81m once only limit on total relevant investments made by investor company together with connected companies in any one qualifying company – for any excess amount, relief is lost altogether: where limit is exceeded, relief is presumably allocated to each company in proportion to the relevant investments made by each;

where the total of relevant investments (in qualified companies) made by investor company together with connected companies in any twelve month period exceeds €3.81m, no relief for excess to the extent that it is invested in a film with a budget greater than €5.08m: where full relief is not available in respect of excess, relief is presumably allocated to each company in proportion to relevant investments made by each.

Single and connected investor companies

where relevant deduction (80% of relevant investment) exceeds profits of an accounting period, 125% of excess is carried forward to succeeding accounting period and treated as relevant investment made in that period;

where aggregate of two or more relevant investments exceeds €10.16m, relief is apportioned to each relevant investment on just and reasonable basis.

7.304 Capital gains tax

The capital gains tax treatment of disposals of shares constituting relevant investments in respect of which section 481 relief was obtained is governed by special rules in TCA 1997, s 481(20). If a relevant investment is made by way of subscription for new ordinary shares of a qualifying company, and none of those shares is disposed of within one year of their acquisition, the full cost will be deductible, for capital gains purposes, from the consideration on disposal of those shares regardless of any section 481 relief which the investor has or could have obtained. Otherwise, if the shares are not new ordinary shares or if a disposal of any of the shares takes place within one year, the allowable cost for capital gains tax purposes is reduced by the amount of the relevant deduction in respect of the shares.

Any capital loss arising on the disposal may, however, be restricted: where the sums allowable as deductions for capital gains tax purposes exceed the consideration on disposal, they will be reduced by the lesser of the amount of the relevant deduction allowed and the amount of the excess.

For the above purposes, *new ordinary shares* means new ordinary shares forming part of the ordinary share capital of a qualifying company which, throughout the period of one year commencing on the date such shares are issued, carry no present or future preferential right to dividends, or to a company's assets on its winding up, and no present or future right preferential right to be redeemed.

7.305   Revenue notice

The following notice was issued by the Revenue Commissioners on 23 December 2004.

Revenue Notice

for the information of film producers and promoters –

on the new administrative arrangements in respect of applications for certification of film projects under Section 481

Key implications of the new procedures:

- With effect from 1st January 2005, all applications for certification of film projects must be submitted to the Revenue Commissioners Office.

- Where a compliance report – due for submission to Department of Arts, Sport and Tourism, under the terms of a certificate issued by that Department – has not been submitted to the Department before 1/1/05, then the compliance report must now be submitted to the Revenue Commissioners. In these cases, Revenue will verify compliance by reference to the compliance requirements specified in the Department's Certificate.

- A full application (as defined) for a certificate, submitted to the Department before 1/1/05, will be processed by the Department, up to and including, where appropriate, the issue of a Certificate stage.

As well as publication on the website of the Regulations and of the prescribed Application Form, the Revenue Commissioners have today published two Guidance Notes – to assist film producers and promoters – as follows:

- The first Guidance Note, incorporating a copy of the Application Form, details the new application procedures prior to issue of a Certificate. If you wish to read this Note now, click on the following link:

  http://www.revenue.ie/doc/pre-certification_21_12.doc

- The second Guidance Note outlines the post-certification procedures and requirements. It should particularly be noted that the requirements of Auditors in regard to the compliance reporting aspects of projects, have not been finally signed off yet with various bodies. However, Revenue expects to have these signed–off very early in the New Year and does not envisage any major changes from what is contained in the second Guidance Note attached. If you wish to read this Note now, click on the following link click on the following link:

http://www.revenue.ie/doc/post_certification_21_12.doc

If you wish to access a copy of the Application Form solely, and applicants are advised – before completing the Form – to read the first Guidance Note referred to above, follow this link:

http://www.revenue.ie/doc/aplcn_form_q_f_cert.doc

If you wish to access a copy of the Regulations, follow this link:

http://www.revenue.ie/doc/s1869_04.docCredit for research and development expenditure

7.4 CREDIT FOR RESEARCH AND DEVELOPMENT EXPENDITURE

7.401 Introduction
7.402 Definitions and related matters
7.403 The relief
7.404 Tax credit for expenditure on buildings or structures used for R&D
7.405 Regulations
7.406 Revenue guidelines

7.401 Introduction

To encourage expenditure on research and development (R&D), a credit of 20% of incremental expenditure incurred by a company may be set against its corporation tax liability for the accounting period in which the expenditure is incurred. Any unused credit may be carried forward indefinitely against the corporation tax liability of subsequent periods until used up.

The scheme is incremental in that expenditure in excess of a defined base amount qualifies for credit. For periods commencing on or after 1 January 2004 and before 1 January 2014, the base amount is the R&D expenditure incurred in a corresponding period ending in 2003. For subsequent periods, there is a rolling one-year base amount. Thus, for the year ended 31 December 2014, the base amount is the amount of the expenditure incurred in the year 2004 while for the year ended 31 December 2015 it is the amount of the expenditure incurred in 2005, and so on. The base amount is calculated and apportioned on a group basis and a group may elect as to the basis on which the credit is to be shared among the group members. An amount equal to 20% of incremental expenditure apportioned to any one company is then available to reduce the corporation tax liability of that company.

Expenditure on R&D in the case of a company means expenditure incurred on R&D activities carried on by that company in the European Economic Area (EEA) in a relevant period. The expenditure must qualify for tax relief in Ireland and, in the case of an Irish resident company, must not qualify for tax relief in any jurisdiction other than Ireland. The credit is not available for royalty payments that constitute exempt royalty income in the hands of the recipient.

While the legislation contains a core definition of what constitutes R&D activities, more detailed guidance as to what activities constitute R&D activities for the purposes of the tax credit is contained in regulations (see **7.405**) made by the Minister for Enterprise, Trade and Employment, in consultation with the Minister for Finance.

The R&D tax credit is in addition to any tax relief that may be available by way of a deduction in computing trading income or as a charge on income, or as a deduction under TCA s 764 (deduction for revenue expenditure on scientific research), or by way of capital allowances in respect of expenditure on plant and machinery under the capital allowances regime.

If group R&D expenditure in a relevant period is less than €50,000, relief will not be available.

Where a company incurring expenditure in carrying out R&D activities also pays a sum to a university or institute of higher academic education in the EEA to enable that university or institute to carry out R&D work on behalf of the company, that sum, up to an amount not exceeding 5% of the expenditure incurred on R&D activities carried out by the company, will qualify for credit. Expenditure by a company on subcontracting research and development work to an unconnected party will qualify for relief up to a limit of 10% of qualifying R&D expenditure incurred by the company in any one year. This will be the case where the sub-contractor carrying out the work does not claim a tax credit in respect of the expenditure.

A company which incurs relevant expenditure on the construction or refurbishment of a building or structure which is to be used for the carrying on by it of R&D activities is entitled to a tax credit of 20% of the cost of construction or refurbishment. The credit is allowed against the company's corporation tax liability over a period of four years. Relevant expenditure means expenditure on the construction of a building or structure which qualifies for capital allowances in Ireland but does not qualify for such relief in any other jurisdiction.

7.402　Definitions and related matters

The following definitions, provided mainly in TCA 1997, s 766(1)(a), are relevant.

Expenditure on research and development

In relation to a company, *expenditure on research and development* means expenditure, other than expenditure on a building or structure, incurred by the company wholly and exclusively in the carrying on by it of research and development activities in a relevant Member State, being expenditure:

(a) (i) which is allowable for tax purposes in Ireland as a deduction in computing trading income (see paragraph 8 in **7.406** below – Revenue guidelines), otherwise than by virtue of TCA 1997, s 307 (allowances for capital expenditure in taxing a trade – see **3.104**), or would be so allowable but for the fact that for accounting purposes it is brought into account in determining the value of an intangible asset, or

(ii) is relieved by TCA 1997 Part 8 (as a charge on income – see **4.4** with reference to patent royalties),

(b) on machinery or plant which qualifies for capital allowances under TCA 1997 Part 9 (see **5.2**) or Part 29 Chapter 2 (allowances for capital expenditure on scientific and research – see **5.601**); or

(c) which qualifies for an allowance under TCA 1997, s 764 (scientific research allowances – see **3.202.10**).

A *relevant Member State* for the above purpose is a state which is a Member State of the European Communities or, not being such a Member State, a state which is a contracting party to the EEA Agreement. In this connection, *EEA Agreement* means the Agreement on the European Economic Area signed at Oporto on 2 May 1992 as adjusted by the Protocol signed at Brussels on 17 March 1993.

Since expenditure on research and development must be expenditure incurred by the company in question in the carrying on by it of research and development activities, these activities cannot be sub-contracted out. (See paragraph 7 in **7.406** below – Revenue guidelines.)

It may appear from (a) above that only expenditure incurred by a trading company will be regarded as expenditure on R&D. Where, however, a company is not a trading company at the time the expenditure is incurred but becomes a trading company later, the expenditure is treated as it would be if the company had commenced to trade at the time the expenditure was incurred (see below under *Company incurring expenditure on R&D before commencing to trade*). Note that, for the purposes of the definition of "expenditure on research and development", the company does not have to be a "qualified company".

Even if the expenditure is incurred by a company that never becomes a trading company, that expenditure may nevertheless be included as expenditure on R&D so that it can be included in arriving at the amount of the group expenditure on R&D (see definition). It would seem reasonable (although not strictly in accordance with the legislation) that the test in relation to such a company would be whether the amounts in (a) – (c) above would be allowable or give rise to allowances *if* the company were a trading company.

As regards (b) above, there is a possible view that expenditure on machinery or plant incurred in an accounting period will not be regarded as expenditure on R&D in that period if the machinery or plant, because not brought into use by the end of the period, does not qualify for capital allowances in that period. The better view, however, must be that the expenditure will qualify as expenditure on R&D in the period in which the expenditure is incurred rather than in the period in which machinery or plant qualifies for capital allowances; otherwise, it would not be possible to qualify for the R&D credit since TCA 1997, s 766(2) provides for relief for an accounting period in respect of qualifying expenditure incurred in that period.

The Revenue have confirmed that they are prepared to accept that expenditure on machinery or plant may be treated as incurred on either (a) the date the machinery or plant is first brought into use for the purposes of a trade or (b) the date the expenditure becomes payable. A condition of opting for (b) is that the credit will be clawed back if the machinery or plant is not brought into use for the purpose of the trade within two years of the expenditure becoming payable.

There is no question that, in order to qualify for credit, a company carrying on R&D activities must hold the intellectual property resulting from that work.

Expenditure on R&D may not include a royalty or other sum paid by a company in respect of the user of the invention:

   (i)   if the royalty or other sum is paid to a person who is connected with the company (see **2.302**) and is income from a qualifying patent within the meaning of TCA 1997, s 234 (see **13.607**), or

  (ii)   to the extent that the royalty or other sum exceeds the amount that would have been paid if the payer and recipient of the royalty or other sum were independent persons acting at arm's length.

Other royalty payments may be included in expenditure on R&D provided they are incurred in the carrying on of R&D activities as defined.

Expenditure by a company on R&D may not include any amount of interest notwithstanding that such interest is brought into account by the company in determining the value of an asset.

Furthermore, expenditure incurred by an Irish resident company will not be treated as expenditure on R&D if it:

   (i)   may be taken into account as an expense in computing income of the company;

(ii)   is expenditure in respect of which an allowance for capital expenditure may be made to the company; or

(iii) may otherwise be allowed or relieved in relation to the company,

for the purposes of tax in a territory other than Ireland.

See paragraph 9 in **7.406** below (Revenue guidelines) regarding information that should be retained, and the type of documentary evidence that should be available, to support claims. In accordance with paragraph 10 of the guidelines, an advance opinion may be obtained from the Revenue as to whether a proposed project would satisfy the requirements of the legislation.

Research and development activities

Research and development activities means systematic, investigative or experimental activities (see paragraph 3.5 in **7.406** below – Revenue guidelines) in a field of science or technology (see paragraph 4 in **7.406** below – Revenue guidelines), being one or more of the following:

(a) basic research, namely, experimental or theoretical work undertaken primarily to acquire new scientific or technical knowledge without a specific practical application in view;

(b) applied research, namely, work undertaken in order to gain scientific or technical knowledge and directed towards a specific practical application; or

(c) experimental development, namely, work undertaken which draws on scientific or technical knowledge or practical experience for the purpose of achieving technological advancement and which is directed at producing new, or improving existing, materials, products, devices, processes, systems or services including incremental improvements thereto, but

activities will not be R&D activities unless they—

(i)   seek to achieve scientific or technological advancement; and

(ii) involve the resolution of scientific or technological uncertainty.

Applied research, as envisaged in (b) above, is usually undertaken either to determine possible uses for the findings of basic research or to determine new methods or ways of creating practical applications.

With regard to (ii) above, it is understood that an actual resolution of scientific or technological uncertainty is not necessary: it is sufficient that the research is carried out with the intention to resolve such uncertainty. Perhaps, therefore, a more appropriate wording would have been: "seek to resolve scientific or technological uncertainty". See paragraphs 2.2, 2.3 and 5 in **7.406** below (Revenue guidelines) for more detailed comments in relation to (i) and (ii) above.

Regulations made by the Minister for Enterprise, Trade and Employment provide that such categories of activities as may be specified in those regulations are not R&D activities and that such other categories of activities as may be specified in the regulations are R&D activities (TCA 1997, s 766(6)). The activities for both of these categories are set out in **7.405** below.

Group expenditure on research and development

The R&D tax credit is based on the amount of group expenditure on R&D. In relation to a relevant period of a group of companies, *group expenditure on research and development* means the aggregate of the amounts of *expenditure on research and development* incurred in the *relevant period* by qualified companies that were members of the group for the relevant period.

However, expenditure incurred by a company that is a member of a group for a part of a relevant period may only be included in group expenditure on R&D if it was incurred when the company is a member of the group.

Expenditure on R&D incurred by a company which has been included in group expenditure on R&D in relation to a group may not be included in group expenditure on R&D in relation to any other group.

In relation to the meaning of group expenditure on R&D, expenditure on R&D by a company that has not yet commenced to trade (which could mean that it is not yet a qualified company), but later does so, may be taken into account as if it had so commenced at the time the expenditure was incurred (TCA 1997, s 766(1)(b)(vi)). Accordingly, the expenditure of that company could be included in group expenditure on R&D. Note also that a qualified company (see definition below) does not have to be a trading company; it may be a 51% subsidiary of a trading company, or a 51% subsidiary of a company whose main business is the holding of stocks etc in one or more trading companies

Qualifying group expenditure on research and development

In relation to a relevant period, qualifying group expenditure on research and development means an amount equal to the excess of the amount of *group expenditure on R&D* in relation to the period over the *threshold amount* in relation to the period.

Qualifying expenditure attributable to a company in relation to a relevant period

In relation to a relevant period, *qualifying expenditure attributable to a company in relation to a relevant period* (the amount on which the tax credit is calculated) means so much of the amount of *qualifying group expenditure on R&D* in the *relevant period* as is attributable to the company in the manner specified in a notice made jointly in writing to the inspector of taxes by the *qualified companies* that are members of the group; where no such notice is given, it is an amount determined by the formula:

$$Q \times \frac{C}{G}$$

where—

Q   is the qualifying group expenditure on R&D in the relevant period;

C   is the amount of expenditure on R&D incurred by the company in the relevant period at a time when the company is a member of the group; and

G   is the group expenditure on R&D in the relevant period (TCA 1997, s 766(3)(a)).

Qualified company

Group expenditure on R&D must be incurred by qualified companies which are members of the group. In relation to a relevant period, *qualified company* means a company which:

   (i)   throughout the relevant period—

       (I)   carries on a trade in the State,

       (II)   is a 51% subsidiary of a company which carries on a trade, or

     (III)   is a 51% subsidiary of a company whose business consists wholly or mainly of the holding of stocks, shares or securities of—

           (A) a company which carries on a trade or

           (B) more than one such company,

   (ii)   carries out R&D activities in the relevant period; and

  (iii)   maintains a record of expenditure incurred by it in the carrying out by it of those activities.

A company (the "subsidiary") will only be regarded as a 51% subsidiary of another company if that other company not only holds the requisite amount of ordinary share capital in the subsidiary but is also entitled to 51% of the profits of the subsidiary available for distribution and 51% of the assets of the subsidiary on a winding up. (See further under *Group* below.)

R&D activities undertaken by a company cannot accordingly be taken into account in ascertaining the amount of group expenditure on R&D unless the company is a trading company, or is a 51% subsidiary of a trading company, or is a 51% subsidiary of a company whose main business is the holding of stocks etc in one or more trading companies.

Relevant period

The meaning of *relevant period* differs depending on whether or not the ends of the accounting periods of companies that are members of a group coincide. Where the group members have accounting periods whose ends coincide, the period of 12 months throughout which one or more group members carries on a trade, and which ends at the end of the first accounting period commencing on or after 1 January 2004, is a relevant period. Each subsequent period of 12 months commencing after the end of the preceding relevant period is also a relevant period.

Thus, in the case of a group of companies whose accounting periods all end on 31 March, the first relevant period is the period from 1 April 2004 to 31 March 2005 and subsequent relevant periods will be the 12 months ending on 31 March 2006 and so on.

Where the group members have accounting periods whose ends do not coincide, the period specified in a notice in writing made jointly by the group members and given to the inspector of taxes within 9 months of end of the period so specified is a relevant period. Each subsequent period of 12 months commencing after the end of the preceding relevant period is also a relevant period. The period of 12 months throughout which one or more group members carries on a trade, and which ends at the end of the first accounting period commencing on or after 1 January 2004, is a relevant period. Each subsequent period of 12 months commencing after the end of the preceding relevant period is also a relevant period.

Threshold amount

In relation to a relevant period of a group of companies, *threshold amount* means:

(i)   where the relevant period is a period commencing at any time after 31 December 2003 and before 1 January 2014 (before 1 January 2010 for accounting periods commencing before 1 January 2008), the aggregate of the amounts of expenditure on R&D incurred in the period of one year (the "threshold period" – see definition below) ending on a date in the year 2003 which corresponds with the date on which the relevant period ends;

(ii)   in any other case, the aggregate of the amounts of expenditure on R&D incurred in the period of one year (the "threshold period") ending on a date which is 10 years (3 years for accounting periods commencing before 1 January 2008) before the end of the relevant period,

by all companies which are members of the group (the "threshold group" – see below) in the threshold period in relation to the relevant period concerned.

For example, where the relevant period of a company is the year ended 31 March 2009, the threshold period in relation to that period is the year ended 31 March 2003 and the threshold amount is the total expenditure incurred in that period by all companies that were members of the group in that period.

Where the relevant period is a period which commences after 31 December 2013, say the year to 30 June 2015, the threshold amount for that period is the amount of the total expenditure on R&D incurred by all group companies in the threshold period in relation to that period, being the 12 month period ending on the date which is 10 years before 30 June 2015, ie the year ended 30 June 2005.

Expenditure incurred by a company that is a member of a group for a part of the threshold period may only be included in the threshold amount if it is incurred at a time when the company is a member of the group.

Threshold period

In relation to a relevant period, threshold period means the period of one year referred to in the definition of "threshold amount".

TCA 1997, s 766(1)(b) explains the meaning of "group" for the purposes of the R&D credit and contains some further provisions relating to what may or may not be regarded as qualifying expenditure.

Group

Two companies are treated as members of a group if one of them is a 51% subsidiary of the other or if both companies are 51% subsidiaries (see **2.502**) of a third company, but, as regards the former case, the other company is treated as not being the owner of:

(a)   any share capital which it owns directly in a company if a profit on a sale of the shares would be treated as a trading receipt; or

(b)   any share capital which it owns indirectly, and which is owned directly by a company for which a profit on a sale of the shares would be treated as a trading receipt (TCA 1997, s 766(1)(b)(i)).

A company and all its 51% subsidiaries form a group and, where that company is a member of a group as being itself a 51% subsidiary, that group comprises all its 51% subsidiaries and the first-mentioned group will be deemed not to be a group (TCA 1997, s 766(1)(b)(iii)). (Contrast the position here with that relating to the meaning of "group" in TCA 1997, s 616(1)(bb) – see **9.202.3**.) Thus, a company and its 51% subsidiaries as well as *their* 51% subsidiaries form a group: and it will be the enlarged group that forms the relevant group for the purposes of the R&D tax credit. Accordingly, a company that is not held as to at least 26.01% (51% x 51%) by the "principal" company in the group cannot be a member of that group.

A company that is not a member of a group is treated as if it were a member of a group consisting of that company alone. Thus, the legislation providing for the R&D credit, which is drafted in terms that are applicable to groups of companies, may apply as appropriate to a single company since it can be treated as constituting a group in its own right (TCA 1997, s 766(1)(b)(iii)).

A company (the "subsidiary") will only be regarded as a 51% subsidiary of another company if that other company not only holds the requisite amount of ordinary share capital in the subsidiary but is also entitled to 51% of the profits of the subsidiary available for distribution and 51% of the assets of the subsidiary on a winding up. For this purpose, the provisions of TCA 1997 ss 412-418 apply as they would apply for the purposes of TCA 1997 Part 12 Chapter 5 (meaning of "group" for group relief purposes: equity entitlement – see **8.304**) if "51% subsidiary" were to be substituted for "75% subsidiary" in that Chapter and TCA 1997, s 411(1)(c) were deleted (TCA 1997, s 766(1)(b)(ii)).

TCA s 411(1)(c) sets out the requirement, in relation to the meaning of "group" for group relief purposes, that any company to be taken into account must be resident in an EU Member State (see **8.302.2**) Thus, for example, there are no residence-related requirements to the effect that a member of a group must be tax resident in a Member State of the EU or in an EEA State. TCA 1997, s 411(1)(c) also excludes any company treated as a share dealing company (see **8.302.3**) but the same exclusion is provided in TCA 1997, s 766(1)(b)(i) in any event – see above.

In determining whether a company was a member of a group of companies (the "threshold group") for the purposes of calculating the threshold amount in relation to a relevant period of a group of companies (the "relevant group"), the threshold group is treated as the same group as the relevant group even if one or more companies in the threshold group is not in the relevant group, or vice versa, where any person or group of persons which controlled the threshold group is the same as, or has a reasonable commonality of identity with, the person or group of persons which controls the relevant group (TCA 1997, s 766(1)(b)(iv)).

As regards what is to be understood by "reasonable commonality of identity", the following would seem to reflect a reasonable view of the type of situation envisaged. Assume that a group comprises 6 companies in the threshold period but only 5 of those companies are in the group in the relevant period. If the same person controls both the 6 and the 5 companies at the respective times, the threshold group of 6 is treated as the same as the relevant group of 5. Again, if the threshold group of 6 companies is controlled by a group of 8 persons and the relevant group of 5 companies is controlled by a group of 7 persons, the group of 6 would be treated as the same as the group of 5 but provided that those 8 persons include the 7 persons and the person who has left the threshold group was not a significant percentage shareholder of the group of 6 companies.

Machinery or plant: apportionment

A proportion of expenditure on machinery or plant used partly for R&D purposes qualifies for the R&D tax credit. Where the machinery or plant provided will not be used wholly and exclusively for R&D activities, a proportionate allocation of the related expenditure is made, on a just and reasonable basis, to determine the amount to be treated as wholly and exclusively incurred on R&D activities. A subsequent apportionment is made in the event that the first apportionment requires revision in the light of the actual usage of the machinery or plant as between R&D and other activities.

Where expenditure is incurred by a company on machinery or plant which qualifies for R&D credit and it will not be used by the company wholly and exclusively for R&D purposes, the amount of the expenditure attributable to R&D will be such portion of the expenditure as appears to the inspector of taxes (or on appeal to the Appeal Commissioners) to be just and reasonable. That portion of the expenditure is treated as incurred by the company wholly and exclusively in carrying on R&D activities (TCA 1997, s 766(1A)(a)).

Where at any time the first or any further apportionment made ceases to be just and reasonable, then:

(a)   such further apportionment is to be made at that time as appears to the inspector of taxes (or on appeal to the Appeal Commissioners) to be just and reasonable,

(b)   any such further apportionment will supersede any earlier apportionment, and

(c)   any such adjustments, assessments or repayments of tax are to be made as are necessary to give effect to any apportionment made (TCA 1997, s 766(1A)(b)).

Expert verification of expenditure incurred

For the purposes of both TCA 1997 ss 766 and 766A, the Revenue may consult with experts to determine whether expenditure incurred by a company was incurred in the carrying on by it of R&D activities. Where the company shows to the satisfaction of the Revenue, or on appeal to the Appeal Commissioners, that disclosure of information to such person could prejudice its business, the Revenue will not make such disclosure.

The Revenue Commissioners may in relation to a claim by a company under TCA 1997, s 766 or 766A:

(i)   consult with any person who in their opinion may be of assistance to them in ascertaining whether the expenditure incurred by the company was incurred in the carrying on by it of R&D activities, and

(ii)   notwithstanding any obligation as to secrecy or other restriction on the disclosure of information imposed by or under the Tax Acts or any other statute of otherwise, disclose any detail in the company's claim under TCA 1997, s 766 of 766A which they consider necessary for the purposes of such consultation (TCA 1997, s 766(7)(a)).

Before disclosing any such information, however, the Revenue must make known to the company the identity of the person they intend to consult and the information they intend to disclose to that person. Where the company shows to the satisfaction of the Revenue (or on appeal to the Appeal Commissioners) that disclosure of such information to that person could prejudice its business, the Revenue may not make such disclosure (TCA 1997, s 766(7)(b)).

Any functions authorised as above to be performed or discharged by the Revenue Commissioners may be performed or discharged by an authorised officer (an officer of the Revenue authorised by them in writing for the purpose) and references to the Revenue Commissioners are, with any necessary modifications, to be construed as including references to the authorised officer (TCA 1997, s 766(8)).

In broad terms, the definition of R&D contained in TCA 1997, s 766 and in the Enterprise Ireland grant-aided scheme for research technology and innovation (RTI) grants are generally comparable. Accordingly, to simplify procedures for smaller claims, the Revenue have indicated that they will not, as a rule, seek independently or separately to have a claim in respect of smaller projects examined by an expert where an Enterprise Ireland RTI grant has been approved in respect of the project. This practice will only apply where—

(a)   the project has been the subject of an RTI grant,

(b)   the R&D tax credit claimed for an accounting period (of not less than 12 months) is €50,000 or less, and

(c)   the project is undertaken in a prescribed field of science or technology, as defined in regulations (SI 434/2004).

Company incurring expenditure on R&D before commencing to trade

Where a company:

(a)   incurs expenditure on R&D at a time when it is not carrying on a trade; and

(b)   it begins to carry on a trade after that time,

the expenditure is treated as if the company had commenced to carry on the trade at the time the expenditure was incurred (TCA 1997, s 766(1)(b)(vi)).

This provision would be of assistance to a non-group company incurring R&D expenditure for some time before it commences to trade. The company would be eligible for credit by reference to the time it incurred the expenditure (being deemed to have commenced trading at that time). The unused credits would then be carried forward would be available for offset against corporation tax on trading profits of later periods. The unused credits could also be used to reduce corporation tax on non-trading income or chargeable gains.

Grant aid and other financial assistance

Expenditure will not be regarded as having been incurred by a company if it has been met directly or indirectly by grant assistance or any other assistance granted by or through the State, any board established by statute, any public authority or any other agency of the State (TCA 1997, s 766(1)(b)(v)).

Cost sharing and pooling arrangements

Expenditure incurred by a company under cost sharing or pooling arrangements will qualify for the tax credit only to the extent that it is incurred by the company in the carrying on by it of qualifying research and development activities. As indicated in the Revenue guidelines in **7.406** below, reimbursements or sharing of costs incurred by another company in the carrying on of research and development activities would not qualify. This follows from the definition of "expenditure on research and development" which requires that the expenditure be "incurred by the company in the carrying on by it of research and development activities".

Payments to University etc

Where a company incurs expenditure on R&D and pays a sum to a university or institute of higher education to enable that university or institute to carry on R&D activities (on its behalf – see Revenue guidelines, no 7, in **7.403** below) in a relevant Member State, that sum, up to a maximum of 5% of the expenditure incurred on R&D, is treated as expenditure incurred by the company on the carrying on by it of R&D activities (TCA 1997, s 766)(1)(b)(vii). (This is an exception to the general position that expense incurred in subcontracting or outsourcing R&D work does not qualify for credit.)

For the above purpose, *university or institute of higher education* means:

(a)   a college or institution of higher education in the State which—

    (i)   provides courses to which a scheme approved by the Minister for Education and Science under the Local Authorities (Higher Education Grants) Act 1968 to 1992 applies, or

    (ii)   operates in accordance with a code of standards which from time to time may, with the consent of the Minister for Finance, be laid down by the Minister for Education and Science, and which the Minister for Education and Science approves for the purposes of TCA 1997, s 473A (relief for fees paid for third level education etc);

(b)   any university or similar institution of higher education in a relevant Member State (other than Ireland) which—

    (i)   is maintained or assisted by recurrent grants from public funds of that or any other relevant Member State (including Ireland), or

    (ii)   is a duly accredited university or institution of higher education in the Member State in which it is situated (TCA 1997, s 766(1)(b)(vii)).

Subcontracting research & development work

Where in any accounting period ending on or after 1 January 2007 a company incurs, on or after 1 January 2007, expenditure on R&D and pays a sum (other than a sum paid to a university etc as described above) to an unconnected (within the meaning of section TCA 1997, s 10 – see **2.302**) person to carry on R&D activities, and provided that person does not claim relief under TCA 1997, s 766 in respect of the expenditure, so much of the sum paid as does not exceed 10% of the expenditure incurred by the company on R&D is treated as if it were expenditure incurred by the company on the carrying on by it of R&D activities (TCA 1997, s 766(1)(b)(viii)).

7.403   The relief

Where for any accounting period a company makes an appropriate claim to the inspector of taxes, the corporation tax liability of the company will be reduced by an amount equal to 20% of the *qualifying expenditure attributable to the company* as is referable to the accounting period (TCA 1997, s 766(2)). For this purpose:

(a) where a relevant period coincides with an accounting period of a company, the amount of qualifying expenditure on R&D attributable to that company as is referable to the accounting period will be the full amount of that expenditure (TCA 1997, s 766(3)(b)); and

(b) where the relevant period does not so coincide—

    (i) the qualifying expenditure on R&D attributable to the company is to be apportioned to the accounting periods which fall wholly or partly in the relevant period, and

    (ii) the amount so apportioned will be treated as the amount of qualifying expenditure on R&D attributable to the company as is referable to the accounting period of the company (TCA 1997, s 766(3)(c)).

A company claiming relief for any accounting period is required to specify the amount of relief claimed in its corporation tax return for that period (TCA 1997, s 766(5)). Where the available tax credit for any accounting period of a company exceeds the company's corporation tax liability for that period, the excess will be carried forward and treated as available for the following accounting period, and so on for succeeding accounting periods (TCA 1997, s 766(4)).

As seen above, the tax credit available to a company for an accounting period is 20% of the *qualifying expenditure attributable to the company* as is referable to the accounting period *(QE)*. From the relevant definitions in **7.402**, it will be seen that QE is derived from qualifying group expenditure on R&D (QGERD), which in turn is derived from group expenditure on R&D (GERD), which in turn is derived from expenditure on R&D (ERD). ERD is expenditure on R&D activities. GERD is the aggregate ERD of qualified companies within a group. QGERD is incremental expenditure, being the excess of GERD over a base amount referred to as the threshold amount. QE, on which the credit available to a company is based, is QGERD apportioned to that company.

Example 7.403.1

The XYZ group comprises three companies, Xanadu Ltd and its wholly owned subsidiary companies Yakima Ltd and Zapata Ltd, each with an accounting year ending on 31 December. Xanadu Ltd and Yakima Ltd are trading companies while Zapata Ltd is a non-trading dedicated group R&D company. The following expenditure was incurred in the year ended 31 December 2008:

	Xanadu Ltd	Yakima Ltd	Zapata Ltd	Total
	€	€	€	€
Patent royalty	100,000			100,000
Expenditure on R&D	4,000,000	1,500,000	5,200,000	10,700,000
Total	4,100,000	1,500,000	5,200,000	10,800,000

The patent royalty is paid to the managing director of Xanadu Ltd who qualifies for exemption from tax on the income. Accordingly, it does not qualify as ERD. Although Zapata Ltd is not a trading company, it is a qualified company so that its expenditure can be included in GERD. GERD is therefore €10,700,000 (€10,800,000-€100,000).

The following example illustrates the calculation of qualifying group expenditure on research and development (QGERD), the incremental expenditure from which QE is derived.

Example 7.403.2

The position is the same as in Example **7.403.1**, and it is ascertained that the threshold amount in relation to the year ended 31 December 2008 is €7.5m, being the aggregate of the amounts of expenditure incurred on R&D activities by group companies in the threshold period, the year ended 31 December 2003.

As was seen in Example **7.403.1**, GERD is €10.7m. QGERD is €3.2m, being the excess of this amount over the threshold amount of €7.5m. It is then necessary to calculate QE for each of the companies. Taking the case of Zapata Ltd, its QE is €1,555,140, being its apportioned share of €3.2, based on its expenditure of €5.2m out of a total of €10.7m.

The tax credit due to Zapata Ltd, based on the formula, is €1,555,140 @ 20% = €311,028. As Zapata Ltd is not liable to corporation tax for the year ended 31 December 2008, its QE would be attributed to one or both of the other group members as specified in a joint notice made to the inspector of taxes. Otherwise, the tax credit would be carried forward for offset against any corporation tax liability of Zapata Ltd in the future. If Zapata Ltd were never to become a trading company, it would nevertheless be entitled to use the credit against its corporation tax liability on any taxable income arising to it.

7.404   Tax credit for expenditure on buildings or structures used for R&D

A company which incurs relevant expenditure on the construction or refurbishment of a building or structure which is to be used for the carrying on by it of R&D activities is entitled, by virtue of TCA 1997, s 766A, to a tax credit of 20% of the cost of construction or refurbishment. The credit is allowed against the company's corporation tax liability over a period of four years.

Definitions

For the purposes of this relief, the meanings of:

    (a)   qualified company;

    (b)   relevant Member State;

    (c)   research and development activities; and

    (d)   group,

are the same as for the purposes of TCA 1997, s 766 (see **7.402** above).

The following definitions of "relevant expenditure" and "refurbishment", specific to the relief for expenditure on buildings, are provided in TCA 1997, s 766A(1)(a).

In relation to a company, *relevant expenditure* on a building or structure means any expenditure incurred by the company on the construction of a building or structure which is to be used wholly and exclusively for the purposes of the carrying on by the company of R&D activities in a relevant Member State, being expenditure which qualifies for an allowance under TCA 1997 Part 9 (relief for capital expenditure – see **5.1-5.5**) or Part 29 (patents (see **13.603**), scientific and certain other research (see **5.601**), know-how (see **3.202.8**), certain training (see **5.602**), research and development (see **7.402**), and transmission capacity rights (see **5.608**)).

However, expenditure incurred by an Irish resident company does not constitute relevant expenditure if it:

    (a)   it may be taken into account as an expense in computing income of the company;

(b)   is expenditure in respect of which an allowance for capital expenditure may be made to the company; or

(c)   may otherwise be allowed or relieved in relation to the company,

for the purposes of tax in territory other than Ireland.

In relation to a building or structure, *refurbishment* means any work of construction, reconstruction, repair or renewal, including the provision of water, sewerage or heating facilities carried out in the course of repair or restoration, or maintenance in the nature of repair or restoration, of a building or structure. This definition is identical to that provided in relation to industrial building allowances (see **5.404** and **5.406**).

For the purposes of relief under TCA 1997, s 766A, expenditure will not be regarded as having been incurred by a company if it has been or is to be met, directly or indirectly, by the State (TCA 1997, s 766A(1)(b)(i))

Any reference to expenditure incurred by a company on the construction of a building or structure includes expenditure on the refurbishment of the building but does not include any expenditure:

(a)   incurred in the acquisition of, or of rights in or over, any land;

(b)   on the provision of machinery or plant or on any asset treated as such; or

(c)   on R&D within the meaning of TCA 1997, s 766 (see **7.402**) (TCA 1997, s 766A(1)(b)(ii)).

Where a building or structure which is to be used for the purposes of carrying on R&D activities forms part of a building or is one of a number of buildings in a single development, or forms part of a building which is itself one of a number of buildings in a single development, there is to be made such apportionment as is necessary of the expenditure incurred on the construction of the whole building or, as the case may be, number of buildings, for the purpose of determining the expenditure incurred on the construction of the building or structure which is to be used for the purposes of carrying on of R&D activities (TCA s 766A(1)(b)(iii)).

R&D tax credit

Where in an accounting period a company incurs relevant expenditure on a building or structure, the corporation tax liability of the company for each accounting period falling wholly or partly into the period of 4 years commencing at the beginning of that accounting period is reduced by an amount determined by a formula—

$$E \times \frac{M}{1460}$$

where—

E   is 20% of the amount of the relevant expenditure on the building or structure, and

M   is the number of days in the accounting period which fall into that period of 4 years (TCA 1997, s 766A(2)).

Example 7.404.1

In the year ended 31 December 2007, Grattan Ltd incurs relevant expenditure of €1m on a building. The credit, being 20% of that amount, is €200,000 and this gives rise to an annual deduction of €50,000 for each of the years ended 31 December 2007, 2008, 2009 and 2010.

Where a building or structure in respect of which a company has received a credit for R&D expenditure:

(a)   is sold; or

(b)   commences to be used for purposes other than the carrying on by the company of R&D activities,

at any time within the period of 10 years commencing with the beginning of the accounting period in which the expenditure is incurred, the company:

(i)   will not be entitled to a tax credit for any accounting period ending after that time; and

(ii)   will be charged to tax under Case IV of Schedule D for the accounting period in which the building or structure is sold or, as the case may be, commences to be used as in (b), in an amount equal to 4 times the aggregate amount by which the corporation tax of the company, or another company, was reduced in relation to that expenditure (TCA 1997, s 766A(3)).

In effect, the full relief obtained to date is clawed back by means of an assessment for four times the credit obtained, taxable under Case IV at the rate of 25%.

Example 7.404.2

The position is as in Example **7.404.1** but in the year ending 31 December 2012 the building is sold. Grattan Ltd will have obtained tax credits totalling €200,000. It is assessed under Case IV for the year ending 31 December 2012 in the amount of €800,000. Tax payable, at 25%, is €200,000.

Where, for any accounting period of a company, the tax credit available to the company for that period exceeds its corporation tax liability for the period, the excess will be carried forward and treated as an available tax credit for the next succeeding period, and so on for succeeding periods (TCA 1997, s 766A(4)(a)). Where, however, the company is a member of a group of companies, it may specify that the excess or any part of it is to be treated as a credit available to another company which is a member of that group for that other company's corresponding accounting period (TCA 1997, s 766A(4)(b)). The amount of the excess so specified may not be carried forward (TCA 1997, s 766A(4)(c)).

For the purposes of group relief, an accounting period of a claimant company that falls wholly or partly within an accounting period of the surrendering company "corresponds to" that accounting period (TCA 1997, s 422(1) – see **8.308**). Presumably the same meaning is intended to apply for the purposes of TCA 1997, s 766A(4)(b).

A company claiming relief under TCA 1997, s 766A for any accounting period is required to specify the amount of relief claimed in its corporation tax return for that period (TCA 1997, s 766A(5)).

7.405   Regulations

In the Taxes Consolidation Act 1997 (Prescribed Research and Development Activities) Regulations, which came into effect on 1 January 2004, it is provided that an activity is not to be regarded as a research and development activity for the purposes of TCA 1997, s 766 unless it is a research and development activity falling within one or more of the following categories:

(1)   an activity undertaken in the field of natural sciences, namely—

    (a)   mathematics and computer sciences, including mathematics and other allied fields, computer sciences and other allied subjects and software development,

    (b)   physical sciences, including astronomy and space sciences, physics, and other allied subjects,

    (c)   chemical sciences, including chemistry and other allied subjects,

    (d)   earth and related environmental sciences, including geology, geophysics, mineralogy, physical geography and other geosciences, meteorology and other atmospheric sciences, including climatic research, oceanography, vulcanology, palaeoecology, and other allied sciences, or

    (e)   biological sciences, including biology, botany, bacteriology, microbiology, zoology, entomology, genetics, biochemistry, biophysics and other allied sciences, excluding clinical and veterinary sciences,

(2)   an activity undertaken in the field of engineering and technology, namely—

    (a)   civil engineering, including architecture engineering, building science and engineering, construction engineering, municipal and structural engineering and other allied subjects,

    (b)   electrical engineering, electronics, including communication engineering and systems, computer engineering (hardware) and other allied subjects, or

    (c)   other engineering sciences such as chemical, aeronautical and space, mechanical, metallurgical and materials engineering, and their specialised subdivisions, forest products, applied sciences such as geodesy and industrial chemistry, the science and technology of food production, specialised technologies of interdisciplinary fields, for example, systems analysis, metallurgy, mining, textile technology and other allied subjects,

(3)   an activity undertaken in the field of medical sciences, namely—

    (a)   basic medicine, including anatomy, cytology, physiology, genetics, pharmacy, pharmacology, toxicology, immunology and immunohaematology, clinical chemistry, clinical microbiology and pathology,

    (b)   clinical medicine, including anaesthesiology, paediatrics, obstetrics and gynaecology, internal medicine, surgery, dentistry, neurology, psychiatry, radiology, therapeutics, otorhinolaryngology and ophthalmology, or

    (c)   health sciences, including public health services, social medicine, hygiene, nursing and epidemiology,

(4)   an activity undertaken in the field of agricultural sciences, namely—

    (a)   agriculture, forestry, fisheries and allied sciences, including agronomy, animal husbandry, fisheries, forestry, horticulture, and other allied subjects, or

    (b)   veterinary medicine.

It is further provided in the regulations that, without prejudice to the generality of clauses (I) and (II) of the definition of "research and development activities" in TCA 1997, s 766 (see (i) and (ii) under *Research and development activities* in **7.402**), an activity falling within any of the following categories shall not be a research and development activity for the purposes of that section:

(a)   research in the social sciences (including economics, business management and behavioral sciences), arts or humanities;

(b)   routine testing and analysis for the purposes of quality or quantity control;

(c)   alterations of a cosmetic or stylistic nature to existing products, services or processes whether or not these alterations represent some improvement;

(d)   operational research such as management studies or efficiency surveys which are not wholly and exclusively undertaken for the purposes of a specific research and development activity;

(e)   corrective action in connection with break-downs during commercial production of a product;

(f)   legal and administrative work in connection with patent applications, records and litigation and the sale or licensing of patents;

(g)   activity, including design and construction engineering, relating to the construction, relocation, rearrangement or start-up of facilities or equipment other than facilities or equipment which is or are to be used wholly and exclusively for the purposes of carrying on by the company concerned of research and development activities;

(h)   market research, market testing, market development, sales promotion or consumer surveys;

(i)   prospecting, exploring or drilling for, or producing, minerals, petroleum or natural gas;

(j)   the commercial and financial steps necessary for the marketing or the commercial production or distribution of a new or improved material, product, device, process, system or service;

(k)   administration and general support services (including transportation, storage, cleaning, repair, maintenance and security) which are not wholly and exclusively undertaken in connection with a research and development activity.

7.406   Revenue guidelines

The following is a re-production of "Revenue Guidelines for Research and Development Tax Credit" published by the Revenue Commissioners in July 2004 and updated as of March 2008.

1. Introduction

TCA 1997, s 766 provides for a tax credit of 20% of incremental expenditure by a company, or group of companies, incurred wholly and exclusively on research and development (R&D).

Expenditure on buildings is not taken into account in calculating the incremental expenditure. TCA 1997, s 766A contains separate rules for the treatment of expenditure on buildings.

2. Research and Development Expenditure: TCA 1997 s 766

The principal features of relief under TCA 1997, s 766 TCA are as follows:

- The tax credit is available to all companies, within the charge to Irish tax, who undertake research and development activities within the European Economic Area (EEA). In the case of an Irish tax resident the expenditure must not qualify for a tax deduction under the law of another territory.

- The tax credit is available on incremental R&D expenditure using a rolling base. For relevant periods commencing between 1 January 2004 and 31 December 2013 the base will be the R&D expenditure incurred in a corresponding period in 2003.

- The relief is calculated as 20% of the qualifying expenditure. The credit is then used to reduce the liability to Corporation Tax.

- Where a company has insufficient corporation tax against which to claim the R&D tax credit in a given year, the tax credit may be carried forward indefinitely, or if a member of a group allocated to other group members. See Section 5.

- The tax credit is in addition to any allowable deductions for R&D expenditure in the accounts of the company.

- Expenditure incurred under cost sharing or pooling arrangements will qualify for the tax credit only to the extent that the expenditure is incurred by the company in the carrying on by it of qualifying research and development activities. Reimbursements or sharing of costs incurred by another company in the carrying on of research and development activities would not qualify.

- Companies claiming the R&D tax credit are not required to hold the intellectual property rights resulting from the R&D work.

Example 1

ABC Ltd incurred qualifying R&D expenditure in year ended 31/12/03 of €10,000. In the year ended 31/12/06 the company incurred qualifying R&D expenditure of €30,000. The tax credit available in 2006 is based on the increase in the amounts of qualifying expenditure in 2006 over the amount of qualifying expenditure in 2003.

	€
Qualifying expenditure 2003	10,000
Qualifying expenditure 2006	30,000
Incremental amount	20,000

ABC Ltd can claim a tax credit in 2006 of €20,000 @ 20% = €4,000.

ABC Ltd can now use €4,000 as a credit against its corporation tax liability.

Example 2

CBA Ltd incurred the following amounts of qualifying R&D expenditure:

Year	€
2003	100,000
2004	300,000
2005	400,000
2006	500,000

Tax credits are calculated as follows:

Year	R&D spend	Calculations	Tax credit
2003	100,000		Nil
2004	300,000	(300,000 - 100,000) @ 20%	€40,000
2005	400,000	(400,000 - 100,000) @ 20%	€60,000
2006	500,000	(500,000 - 100,000) @ 20%	€80,000

2.1 Grants payable

Any expenditure which is met directly or indirectly by any grant from the State, any board established by statute, any public or local authority or any other agency of the State will not qualify for relief.

Example 3

If in the case of CBA Ltd in Example 2 the company was entitled to the following grants.

Year	Grant
	€
2003	40,000
2004	60,000
2005	100,000
2006	Nil

Tax credits are calculated as follows:

Year	R&D spend	Grant	Net cost	Calculations	Tax Credit
2003	100,000	40,000	60,000		Nil
2004	300,000	60,000	240,000	(240,000 - 60,000) @ 20%	36,000
2005	400,000	100,000	300,000	(300,000 - 60,000) @ 20%	48,000
2006	500,000	Nil	500,000	(500,000 - 60,000) @ 20%	88,000

3. Expenditure on Buildings or Structures used for R&D activities: TCA 1997, s 766A

- Section 766A TCA 1997 deals with the tax credit for expenditure on buildings or structures used for research and development. This section was inserted by Finance Act 2004. To qualify the company must be entitled to claim industrial buildings capital allowances on the building/structure.

- The incremental basis does not apply for expenditure on buildings. There is no base year for Section 766A.

- The relief is calculated as 20% of the qualifying expenditure. The credit is then used to reduce the liability to Corporation Tax.

- Relevant expenditure by a qualified company can be claimed over 4 years on a straight-line basis.

- Where a company has insufficient corporation tax to claim the tax credit in a given year, the tax credit may be carried forward indefinitely.

- The tax credit is in addition to Capital Allowances.

- Any expenditure which is met directly or indirectly by the State will not be treated as qualifying expenditure.
- Where a building or structure to be used for R&D is part of a building or structure, or is one of a number of buildings in a single development, such apportionments as is necessary should be used to determine the expenditure on R&D. (See Example 5 below.)

The company should maintain records to show:

1. computation of any apportionment, and
2. the rationale for the use of such basis of apportionment.

Example 4

XYZ Ltd incurred qualifying R&D expenditure in 2006 of €100,000 on an R&D building. The total relief due is (100,000 @ 20%) €20,000. This relief will be allowable over the four years 2006-2009 inclusive. The relief for each year will be (20,000/4) e5,000. For each of the four years XYZ Ltd can use the credit of €5,000 to reduce its Corporation Tax liability.

Example 5

If in the above Example 4 the building was to be used for qualifying R&D activities in addition to other activities, an apportionment of cost is necessary. If the total floor area of the building was 2,500 sq ft, and 1,500 sq ft of that area was used for R&D activities, XYZ could decide to use floor area as a basis of apportionment as follows:

	€
Expenditure incurred	100,000
Qualifying expenditure = 100,000 X 1,500/2,500 =	60,000

The total relief due is €12,000 (60,000 @ 20%). This relief will be allowable over the four years 2006-2009 inclusive. For each of those four years, XYZ Ltd can use the credit of €3,000 to reduce its corporation tax liability

Example 6

ZYX Ltd incurred qualifying expenditure on R&D buildings as follows:

Year		Expenditure
		€
2003		500,000
2004		1,000,000
2005		600,000
2006	(Relief due up to 2009)	1,200,000
2007		Nil
2008	(Relief due up to 2011)	40,000

Tax credits are calculated as follows:

Year	Expenditure	Calculations	Tax credit
2003	500,000		Nil
2004	1,000,000	¼ (1,000,000) @ 20%	50,000
2005	600,000	¼ (1,000,000 + 600,000) @ 20%	80,000
2006	1,200,000	¼ (1,000,000 + 600,000 + 1,200,000) @ 20%	140,000

| 2007 | Nil | ¼ (1,000,000+600,000 + 1,200,000)@ 20% | 140,000 |
| 2008 | 40,000 | ¼ (600,000+1,200,000 + 40,000) @ 20% | 92,000 |

Note: Relief in respect of expenditure incurred of €1,000,000 in 2004 is granted in full over the four years 2004-2007 inclusive.

3.1 Building or Structure sold or ceases to be used for R&D activity

The tax credit is clawed back if, within 10 years of the accounting period for which a credit is claimed, the building or structure is sold or commences to be used for purposes other than the carrying on by the company of R&D activities.

Example 7

In 2004 DEF Ltd incurred relevant R&D expenditure of e100,000 on the construction of a building to be used wholly and exclusively for R&D activities. The building was sold in 2006.

Tax credits granted 2004-2005 are as follows:

	€
2004 (100,000/4) @ 20% =	5,000
2005 (100,000/4) @ 20% =	5,000
Total granted	10,000

In 2006 DEF Ltd will be taxed on the following amount under Schedule D Case IV.

Total relief granted as above	10,000
Multiply by 4 =	40,000
Taxed @ 25% = (40,000 @ 25%) =	10,000

Note: The net effect is that the total relief granted 2004-2005 inclusive is clawed back.

Example 8

The charge to tax under Schedule D Case IV is based on "the aggregate amount by which corporation tax of the company or another company was reduced".

If, in Example 7 above, DEF Ltd used the credits due for 2004-2005 as follows:

> 2004 - €3,000 (carried forward €2,000)
>
> 2005 - €6,000 (carried forward €1,000),

"the aggregate amount by which corporation tax of the company or another company was reduced" would amount to €9,000 (3,000 + 6,000).

In 2006 DEF Ltd would be taxed as follows under Schedule D Case IV:

> Total relief granted 9,000
>
> Multiply by 4 = 36,000
>
> Taxed @ 25% = €9,000

4. Subcontracting out research and development activities

There are two situations where the law provides for relief for a company that has not carried out the research and development itself:

1. A company, which incurs expenditure on research and development, and pays a sum to a university or institute to carry out such activities in a relevant Member State, can claim relief. Relief will be restricted to 5% of the expenditure incurred by the company itself on research and development activities

2. A company, which incurs expenditure on research and development, and pays a sum to another person (other than in 1 above) who is not a connected person, in order for that person to carry on research and development activities, can claim relief. Relief will be restricted to 10% of the expenditure incurred by the company itself on research and development activities. Relief will only be granted where the subcontracted person does not claim this relief. (No 2 effective for accounting periods ending on or after 1 January 2007, in respect of expenditure incurred on or after 1 January 2007)

Example 9

RD Ltd incurred €250,000 expenditure on R&D activities in the period ended 30/6/2007. In addition, it paid €10,000 to a university to carry out R&D activities. RD Ltd also subcontracted some of its R&D work to JK Ltd, an unconnected company. It paid an additional €28,000 to JK Ltd.

(a) As the €10,000 paid to the university is less than €12,500 (250,000 @ 5%), it will also qualify for relief.

(b) As the €28,000 subcontracted out exceeds €25,000 (250,000 @ 10%) by €3,000, the total claim must be restricted to €285,000 (250,000+10,000 + (28,000 - 3,000).

5. Group Expenditure on R&D

Companies will be regarded as members of a group if one is a 51% subsidiary of the other, or both are 51% subsidiaries of a third company, irrespective of the country of residence of each company. In determining whether this is the case, ownership of shares by a company dealing in the shares is to be ignored.

Example 10

ABC Ltd own 60% of the shares of DEF Ltd. DEF Ltd own 90% of the shares of XYZ Ltd. As ABC Ltd effectively controls 60% of DEF Ltd and 54% (60 @ 90%) of XYZ Ltd, all three companies are members of a group for the purpose of claiming the R&D tax credit.

In the case of a group of companies the tax credit is available on a group basis in respect group expenditure on R&D. The principal features of this provision are as follows:

- Group expenditure is defined as "the aggregate of expenditure on R&D incurred by member companies of a group in a relevant period".

- The base period (threshold period) is referred to as the first relevant period. Generally this will be the first period of one year, ending at the end of the first common accounting period of the member companies of the group, that commences on or after 1 January 2004. If the companies do not have a common accounting period, they must jointly elect which accounting date should be used.

- For all relevant periods commencing between 1 January 2004 and 1 January 2013, the base period is one year ending on a date in 2003 that corresponds with the end of the relevant period. (See Example 11.)

- The members of the group that incur expenditure on R&D in the relevant period may allocate the expenditure to group members, in a manner as decided by them. A joint written application must be made to the appropriate Inspector. In the absence of an application, the legislation provides a formula to be used in the allocation of the expenditure.

- Where the group has insufficient corporation tax to claim the tax credit, the credit may be carried forward indefinitely.

Example 11

A group of companies had an aggregate R&D expenditure of €500,000 in the 12 months ended 30/9/2006, and an aggregate R&D expenditure of €30,000 in the 12 months ended 30/9/2003.

The incremental amount for the 12 months ended 30/9/2006 is therefore €470,000 (500,000 - 30,000).

The members of the group who have incurred the R&D expenditure may allocate the tax credit of €94,000 (470,000 @ 20%) to group members, in a manner decided by them.

Example 12

AB USA Corp, AB Ire Ltd and BA Ire Ltd are all members of a group for the purposes of TCA 1997, s 766. AB USA Corp is not within the charge to Irish tax while the other two members of the group are. The companies incurred R&D expenditure as follows:

	2003	2007
	€	€
AB USA Corp	*** 40,000	*** 75,000
AB Ire Ltd	30,000	65,000
BA Ire Ltd	10,000	32,000

*** As AB USA Corp is not within the charge to Irish tax, the R&D expenditure incurred is not taken into account for the purpose of calculating qualifying group expenditure on R&D activities.

Qualifying group expenditure in 2007 is €57,000, calculated as follows:

	€
2007 (65,000 + 32,000) =	97,000
2003 (30,000 + 10,000) =	40,000
Incremental expenditure 2007	57,000

6. Research and Development Activities

Essentially only expenditure on R&D activities may qualify for the tax credit. Qualifying activities must satisfy all of the following conditions. The activities must:

1. be systematic, investigative or experimental activities,

2. be in a field of science or technology,

3. consist of one or more of the following categories of research and development:
    - basic research,
    - applied research, or
    - experimental development.

4. seek to achieve scientific or technological advancement and to involve the resolution of scientific or technological uncertainty.

6.1 Systematic investigative and experimental activities

- The legislation requires R&D activities to be systematic, investigative or experimental in nature. It is expected that activities be to a planned logical sequence, generally to a recognised methodology, with detailed records being maintained.

- Each project should be documented showing clearly why each major element is required, and how it fits into the research activity as a whole. To build on the results of testing in a systematic way requires the organised documentation of work undertaken by way of experimentation or investigation.

- It is important for a company to maintain dated documents of the original scientific or technological goals of the activity, the progress of the work and how it has been carried out, and the conclusions.

- Indicators or measures to be used to determine if the scientific or technological objectives of the research and development activity are met should be identified when forming the concepts for the research and development activity. These measures should also be documented at the early stages of the program. Failure to have such documentation may indicate the absence of a systematic, investigative or experimental approach.

The following are indicative of the existence of a systematic process:

➢ the work is carried out or led by trained or experienced personnel;

➢ the work is conducted under a development protocol or under the direction of a project manager;

➢ the work is documented;

➢ the process by which the work is performed is documented.

6.2 Field of science and technology

The categories of activities that qualify for relief are set out in SI No 434 of 2004, Taxes Consolidation Act 1997 (Prescribed Research and Development Activities) Regulations 2004. The categories are:

1. Natural sciences

2. Engineering and technology

3. Medical sciences

4. Agricultural sciences.

The regulations define each category. Further details are contained in Appendix 3.

6.3 Types of Research

Basic research means "experimental or theoretical work undertaken primarily to acquire new scientific or technical knowledge without a specific practical application in view".

Applied research means, "work undertaken in order to gain scientific or technical knowledge and directed towards a specific practical application". Applied research is usually undertaken either to determine possible uses for the findings of basic research or to determine new methods or ways of creating practical applications.

Experimental development means, "work undertaken which draws on scientific or technical knowledge or practical experience for the purpose of achieving technological advancement and which is directed at producing new, or improving existing, materials, products, devices, processes, systems or services including incremental improvements thereto".

6.4 Scientific or technological advancement

An advance in science or technology means an advance in the **overall knowledge or capability** in the field of **science** or **technology** (not a company's own state of knowledge or capability alone). The test relates to knowledge or capability reasonably available to the company or to a competent professional working in the field. Where knowledge of an advance in science or technology is not reasonably available, for example, where it has not been published, is not in the public domain or it is a trade secret of a competitor, companies would not be disqualified from claiming the credit where they undertake activities seeking to independently achieve the same scientific or technological advancement.

A scientific or technological uncertainty may exist for one company although a competitor has resolved that uncertainty *but retained the resulting knowledge as a trade secret or proprietary information*. A number of companies may be working to resolve the same scientific or technological uncertainty at the same time. Reasonably available scientific or technological knowledge or experience includes information, which is reasonably available to a company from both internal and external sources. Thus if the solution to a scientific or technological uncertainty is reasonably available to a competent professional working in the field, lack of knowledge by a company due to lack of diligence in seeking that solution or lack of appropriate expertise within the company does not constitute scientific or technological uncertainty.

6.4.1. The Act requires that the activity must *seek* to achieve as opposed to succeed in achieving scientific or technological advancement. Even if the advance in science or technology sought by a project is not achieved or not fully realised, R&D still takes place. For example, a particular research and development activity may cease or radically change if the advance originally sought becomes available from a scientific journal or newly published patent. This does not undermine the validity of the activity from the perspective of this test. Equally determining that a hypothesis is incorrect may advance scientific knowledge. Similarly, in experimental development, discovering that a certain technological alternative does not work can advance the technological knowledge base. Such a result would not of itself preclude a claim being made for the R&D credit.

6.4.2 Where a research and development activity is shown to be systematic, investigative or experimental and is undertaken to resolve a clearly defined scientific or technological uncertainty, the requirements of attempting to achieve scientific or technological advancement will generally be met.

Work carried out in incremental stages, the aim of which is the achievement of scientific or technological advancement and involves resolution of scientific or technological uncertainty will qualify as R&D.

6.4.3 New materials/products/systems. Systematic, experimental or investigative activities directed at producing new or improved materials, products, devices, process systems or services can qualify for the tax credit provided the activities seek to achieve the goals set out at 6 above. However a process, material, device, product, service or source of knowledge does not become an *advance* in *science* or *technology* simply because *science* or technology is used in its creation. Work which uses *science* or *technology* but which does not *advance* scientific or technological capability as a whole is not an *advance* in *science* or *technology.* Normal technology transfer, or making improvements to materials, products, devices, processes, systems or services through the purchase of rights or licence, or through the adaptation of known principles or knowledge, would not represent scientific or technological advancement. Neither would solving technical problems or trouble shooting using generally available scientific or technological knowledge or experience meet this test. In addition work in the development of a new or improved product will not of itself constitute research and development activities. The work may, for example, entail the resolution of extensive design issues but may not involve a scientific advancement.

Example

A project which seeks, for example, to:

(a)   extend overall knowledge or capability in a field of science or technology; or

(b)   create a process, material, device, product or service which incorporates or represents an increase in overall knowledge or capability in a field of science or technology; or

(c)   make an *appreciable improvement* to an existing process, material, device, product or service through an advance in science or technology; or

(d)   duplicate the effect of an existing process, material, device, product or service in a new or appreciably improved way through an advance in science or technology(e.g. a product that has exactly the same performance characteristics as existing models, but is built in a fundamentally different manner),

will therefore be R&D.

6.4.4 Scientific or technological uncertainty arises in two situations, viz:

(a)   uncertainty as to whether a particular goal can be achieved, or

(b)uncertainty (from a scientific or technological perspective) in relation to alternative methods that will meet desired cost or other specifications such as reliability or reproducibility.

If, on the basis of reasonably available scientific or technological knowledge or experience such technological or scientific uncertainty exists, research and development activity would aim to remove that uncertainty through systematic, investigative or experimental activity.

Uncertainty as to whether new materials, products, devices, processes, systems or services will be commercially viable *is not scientific or technological uncertainty.* In commercial settings, however, a reasonable cost target is always an objective. As mentioned above, attempting to achieve a particular cost target can require the resolution of a scientific or technological uncertainty. Cost targets may require that scientifically or technologically uncertain alternatives, approaches or configurations etc. have to be attempted, although more costly alternatives exist.

A scientific advance always resolves uncertainty.

6.4.5 Software

The OECD Frascati Manual states: "for software development to be classified as R&D, its completion must be *dependent* on the development of a scientific and/or technical advance, and the aim of the project must be resolution of a scientific and/or technical uncertainty on a systematic basis.

Listing software functions and features at an "end-user" level can rarely describe advancement in technology. Advances are typically made through innovation in software architectures, designs, algorithms, techniques or constructs.

To develop software at the leading edge of today's technologies generally requires the developer to come up with new constructs, such as new architectures, algorithms or database management techniques (ie, make technological advancements), and there are then specific uncertainties as to the viability of these (ie, technological uncertainty). If the software's competitive edge stems from advance in an area other than technology, such as business management, or improvements in financial management techniques, the project is unlikely to be eligible. Almost any software developed for sale is developed systematically and the uncertainties are systematically resolved (ie, technical content).

6.5 Categories of activity that are not research and development activities

SI 434/2004 specifies *a non-exhaustive list* of categories of activities, which are *not* research and development activities. Further details are contained in Appendix 4.

7. When a Research and Development activity ends

The resolution of scientific or technological uncertainty is a determining factor when considering where a research and development activity ceases and activity associated with commercial exploitation begins. Generally this point is reached when the scientific or technological uncertainty, which the research and development activity sought to resolve, has been resolved. The basic criterion for determining when a scientific research and experimental development project has been completed is reaching the point at which the project's initial technological objectives have been achieved. Generally, this occurs when the application of standard operating practices will permit the achievement of the technological performance objectives, which were established for the project.

8. Plant and Machinery

FA 2006 s 66(1)(b) provides, for accounting periods ending on or after 2 February 2006, that where plant and machinery which is used for R&D and other purposes form part of the claim, the cost of the plant and machinery should be apportioned on a just and reasonable basis.

If an apportionment that has already been made in this manner is later shown not to be "just and reasonable" a revised apportionment must be made. The new apportionment then supersedes the previous apportionment. The revised apportionments may give rise to an underpayment or overpayment of corporation tax.

Example 13

QE Ltd had expenditure on R&D of €150,000 in the 12 months ended 30/9/2007. This figure includes plant and machinery at cost of €100,000 to be used for R&D activities and production processing. QE Ltd has analysed the plant and machinery usage on a "machine hour basis" and found that in a typical week it is used 25 hours for R&D and 30 hours for production processing. The plant and machinery is expected to have a useful life of 10 years. The cost of the plant and machinery should accordingly be apportioned as follows:

	€
Cost	100,000
Cost relevant for R&D €100,000 x 25/55 =	45,455
Tax credit due €45,455 @ 20% =	9,091

9. Qualifying expenditure

9.1 Activities undertaken in-house by the claimant company

The tax credit will be available in respect of expenditure incurred in the carrying on of research and development activities under the usual tax rules relating to such expenditure. Under these rules, expenses such as staff and overhead costs can be apportioned and the credit will be available for the portion expended in the carrying on of the research and development activity.

Allowable expenditure would include the cost of the following activities:

(a)   engineering, design, operational research, mathematical analysis, computer programming, data collection, testing, or psychological research;

(b)   indirect supporting activities such as maintenance, security, administration and clerical activities, finance and personnel activities;

(c)   ancillary activities essential to the undertaking of research and development activities such as taking on and paying staff, leasing laboratories and maintaining research and development equipment including computers used for research and development activities;

(d)   the cost of plant and machinery used wholly and exclusively for R&D activity. Please also refer to 8 above.

Expenditure on research and development *will* qualify for the tax credit even though it may be brought into account for accounting purposes in determining the value of an asset.

Interest will *not* be taken into account as expenditure on research and development for the purposes of the tax credit even though, for accounting purposes, it may be included in the value of an asset.

9.2 Royalty payments

Expenditure on research and developments may not include a royalty or other sum paid by a company in respect of the user of an invention if:

(a)   it is paid to a person connected with the company and the royalty is exempt from tax in the hands of the recipient, or

(b)   the payment is not an arm's length fee.

Royalty payments not subject to the above exclusion would qualify provided they are incurred in the carrying on of research and development activities as defined in the law.

10. Information to be retained by the company in support of claims

To avail of the R&D tax credit the company must be in a position to demonstrate that its claim can satisfy two essential tests.

Science test - that the activities under review are consistent with the statutory definition of research and development activities.

Accounting test – that the expenditure claimed as being laid out on qualifying research and development activities are correctly so claimed.

10.1 Records required to be maintained To Satisfy the Science test

(a)   a description of the research and development activities, the methods to be used and what the company seeks to achieve by the undertaking the activities concerned;

(b)   the field of science and technology concerned;

(c)   the scientific or technological advancement that is the goal of the research and development activities; *

(d)   the scientific and technological uncertainty the company is seeking to resolve by those activities; *

(e)   details of systematic investigation outlined at paragraph 6.1 including:
   – the hypothesis advanced,
   – the series of experiments or investigations undertaken to test the hypothesis,
   – documentary evidence of the necessity for each major element and how it fits into the project as a whole,
   – dated documents of the original scientific or technological goals, the progress of the work, how it was carried out and the conclusions, and
   – indicators or measures identified at the commencement of the project to determine if the scientific or technological objectives of the research and development activities are met;

(f)   the qualifications, skill and experience of the project manager;

(g)   the numbers, qualifications and skill levels of other personnel working on the project.

Given the high cost of research and development activities and the requirement for ongoing monitoring inherent in such projects, the records required for Revenue purposes should generally be available within a company for its own internal purposes. The company will, in any event, need to document the project and the information required may be contained in:

- status and/or progress reports;

- notebooks, lab reports, patents, and patent applications;

- notes of problems encountered in the course of the project that identified areas of technological uncertainty and experimental development;

- feasibility plan and/or outline methodology adopted;

- files on personnel involved in the project.

10.2 Records required to be maintained to satisfy the accounting test

TCA 1997, ss 886 and 903, VATA 1972, s 16 VAT Act 1972 and VAT Regulations 1979 all impose obligations on a taxpayer to keep certain books and records. The maintenance of these records is required to enable a taxpayer to make true tax returns and in the event of Revenue audit to demonstrate that the credit claimed is correct.

10.3 Claiming the Credit

Where a company is satisfied that it can comply with the requirements, a claim to relief may be made by completing *Section 12* (headed *Research and Development Tax Credit*) of the form CT1. It is important to note that no supporting documentation is required to be submitted with the return. In this respect, claiming a research and development tax credit is no different from claiming any other corporation tax relief or tax credit.

11. Consultation with other persons (experts)

To ensure compliance with legislation, Revenue may examine the entitlement of certain claims to tax credit for R&D activities. For this Revenue normally require the assistance of qualified individuals with specialised knowledge in the relevant field of science or technology. That individual acts on a consultancy basis for Revenue. They report to Revenue as to whether, in their opinion, the activities examined constitute R&D activities, as defined. Where the opinion of such expert is disputed by a claimant company, the expert may be required to give evidence before the Appeal Commissioners or a court of law.

Before disclosing information to that person, Revenue will notify the company of:

➤ the identity of that person, and

➤ the information they intend to disclose,

and will obtain a signed confidentiality agreement from the expert.

The claimant company may object to the use of that particular expert where they can demonstrate a genuine conflict of interests. In any case of dispute the claimant company will have the right of appeal to The Appeal Commissioners, against the use of a particular expert.

12. RTI grants

As, in broad terms, the definition of R&D contained in TCA 1997, s 766 and used by Enterprise Ireland Research Technology & Innovation (RTI) Grants Scheme are similar, it has been decided that Revenue will not, as a rule, seek to have a claim in respect of smaller projects examined by an expert where an Enterprise Ireland RTI Grant has been approved in respect of the project.

This practice will apply where:

- the project has received an RTI grant,

- the R&D tax credit claimed for an accounting period (of not less than 12 months) is €50,000 or less, and

- the project is undertaken in a prescribed field of science or technology, as defined in regulations (SI No 434 of 2004).

This practice applies only to RTI Grants administered by Enterprise Ireland and not any other grant, whether they are for R&D or otherwise.

As mentioned in 2.1, the amount of the RTI Grant will not qualify for relief.

(See extract from Tax Briefing No 67 at Appendix 2.)

13. Advance Opinion

The Revenue Commissioners would be prepared to give an advance opinion as to whether a proposed project would satisfy the requirements of the legislation. When such requests are received, Revenue normally engage an expert under the conditions set out at paragraph 11.

Applications for an advance opinion containing the information as outlined in paragraph 10 should be made to:

Isolde Hampson

Direct Taxes Interpretation and International Division,

Stamping Building,

Dublin Castle,

Dublin 2. Phone 01 6748103

mailto:ihampson@revenue.ie

Appendix 1

Extract from Tax Briefing No 66, July 2007

Claiming a tax credit for research and development

FA 2004, s 33 introduced a 20% tax credit for companies for expenditure on research and development (R&D) activities. The credit is available on incremental qualifying expenditure over the amount spent in a base year. It has come to Revenue's attention that some uncertainty exists regarding the procedures for claiming such a credit - in particular, the level of documentation required to be submitted with a claim. The procedures were put in place with a view to making the claiming of an R&D tax credit a straightforward process. The purpose of this article is to clarify those procedures.

Definition

The relevant legislation contains a specific definition of research and development, in line with international practice, which is designed to focus the relief on activities involving a high level of innovation across a broad range of industries.

Research and development activities is defined as "systematic, investigative or experimental activities in a field of science or technology, being basic research, applied research or experimental development". A key provision is that activities will not constitute research and development activities for the purposes of the relief unless they:

seek to achieve scientific or technological advancement and

involve the resolution of scientific or technological uncertainty.

Claimant companies are themselves best placed to evaluate whether their activities come within the definition. However, if a company has concerns about a particular aspect of their claim, Revenue is prepared to give an advance opinion as to whether the activities of a specific project constitute research and development activities.

Claiming the Credit

Where a company is satisfied that it can comply with the requirements, a claim to relief may be made by completing Section 12 (headed Research and Development Tax Credit) of the form CT1. It is important to note that no supporting documentation is required to be submitted with the return. In this respect, claiming a research and development tax credit is no different from claiming any other corporation tax relief or tax credit.

Examination by Revenue

Revenue may examine any aspect of a return, including a claim to a research and development tax credit, within four years of the end of the accounting period in which the company has made the return. Revenue may, if necessary, refer the project to an expert in the field of science and technology for an opinion as to whether the activities constitute research and development activities, as defined.

It is the claimant company's responsibility to maintain records which provide sufficient evidence that a project entails research and development activities. The types of records which are required include:

- project title and description

- purpose of the project undertaken (ie, the hypothesis advanced)

- technologically feasible plan and/or methodology adopted

- status and/or progress reports

- problems encountered in the course of the project that identified areas of technological uncertainty and experimental development

- personnel involved in the project

- notebooks, lab reports, patents, and patent applications

In order to reduce the administrative burden on claimant companies, no particular format is specified. Given the high cost of research and development activities and the requirement for ongoing monitoring inherent in such projects, the records required for Revenue purposes should generally be available within a company for its own internal purposes.

Where expenditure is not wholly incurred for research and development purposes, Revenue will accept reasonable apportionment.

Further Information

Please see Revenue Guidelines for Research and Development Tax Credit

http://www.revenue.ie/doc/r&d.doc

Appendix 2

Extract from Tax Briefing No 67, December 2007

Claims for Research and Development (R&D) tax credit in respect of projects approved for Research Technology & Innovation (RTI) grants from Enterprise Ireland.

Background

TCA 1997, s 766 provides for a tax credit of 20% of incremental expenditure by a company or group of companies on research and development (R&D). Expenditure on buildings is not taken into account in calculating the incremental expenditure. Section 766A contains rules for the treatment of expenditure on buildings. The purpose of this article is to simplify administrative procedures, for smaller claims in receipt of Research Technology & Innovation (RTI) grants from Enterprise Ireland.

Definition

Research and development activities is defined as "systematic, investigative or experimental activities in a field of science or technology, being basic research, applied research or experimental development". A key provision is that activities will not be research and development activities for the purposes of the relief unless they:

- seek to achieve scientific or technological advancement, and

- involve the resolution of scientific or technological uncertainty.

Examination of a Claim

The process of examining a claim can be divided into two areas:

The Science test – that the activities under review are consistent with the statutory definition of research and development activities.

The Accounting test – that the expenditure claimed as being laid out on qualifying research and development activities are correctly so claimed.

Experts within a claimant company should have no difficulty in deciding whether the Science test is satisfied. Given that there is no in-house expertise in particular fields of science and technology, it has been necessary for Revenue to employ experts to provide opinion as to whether an activity would satisfy the Science test.

Compatibility with RTI grants

In broad terms, the definition of R&D contained in TCA 1997, s 766 and the Enterprise Ireland grant aided scheme for RTI grants are generally comparable and are both based on the OECD Frascati definition. Unlike the tax credit relief, the RTI scheme does not explicitly require that activities seek to achieve scientific or technological advancement. However, a requirement that a project must represent an advance in the level of technical innovation relative to the company's current products/processes is quite similar. The receipt of such a grant is thus a strong indicator of eligibility for the tax credit.

To simplify administrative procedures for smaller claims and to minimise the need to engage experts, to verify tax credit claims, it has been decided that Revenue would not, as a rule, seek to independently/separately have a claim, in respect of smaller projects examined, by an expert, where an Enterprise Ireland RTI grant has been approved in respect of the project. This practice will apply where:

- the project has been the subject of an RTI grant,

- the R&D tax credit claimed for an accounting period (of not less than 12 months) is €50,000 or less, and

- the project is undertaken in a prescribed field of science or technology, as defined in regulations (SI No 434 of 2004).

Limits to Practice

This treatment applies only to RTI grants administered by Enterprise Ireland and not any other grant, whether they are for R&D or otherwise. Companies may claim a tax credit, up to and including the amount indicated, in respect of activities arising in a number of projects. Not all of those activities or projects will be grant aided. Therefore the receipt of a grant would not be an indication that the entire claim qualifies for the credit.

Moreover, in respect of grant aided and other projects, all the claimed cost will not necessarily qualify. Where an R&D tax credit is claimed for an accounting period all claims examined, in the course of a Revenue audit, must be subjected to the accounting test to ensure that costs correctly attributable to other activities are not included as R&D costs and that any allocations of cost are reasonably and correctly so allocated.

Revenue may from time to time check a number of claims supported by RTI grants on a risk basis.

Further Information

Please see Revenue Guidelines for Research and Development Tax Credit

http://www.revenue.ie/doc/r&d.doc or contact

Isolde Hampson,

Direct Taxes Interpretation and International Division

Stamping Building

Dublin Castle

Dublin

e-mail: ihampson@revenue.ie

Appendix 3

Field of science & technology

Natural sciences

1   Mathematics and computer sciences, including mathematics and other allied fields, computer sciences and other allied subjects, software development

2   Physical sciences including astronomy and space sciences, physics, and other allied subjects

3   Chemical sciences including chemistry and other allied subjects

4   Earth and related environmental sciences including geology, geophysics, mineralogy, physical geography and other geosciences, meteorology and other atmospheric sciences including climatic research, oceanography, vulcanology, palaeoecology, and other allied sciences

5   Biological sciences including biology, botany, bacteriology, microbiology, zoology, entomology, genetics, biochemistry, biophysics, other allied sciences, excluding clinical and veterinary sciences

Engineering and Technology

1.   Civil engineering including architecture engineering, building science and engineering construction engineering, municipal and structural engineering and other allied subjects

2. Electrical engineering, electronics including communication engineering and systems, computer engineering (hardware) and other allied subjects

3. Other engineering sciences such as chemical, aeronautical and space, mechanical, metallurgical and materials engineering, and their specialised subdivisions; forest products; applied sciences such as geodesy and industrial chemistry; the science and technology of food production, specialised technologies of interdisciplinary fields, eg systems analysis, metallurgy, mining, textile technology and other allied subjects

Medical Sciences

1. Basic medicine including anatomy, cytology, physiology, genetics, pharmacy, pharmacology, toxicology, immunology and immunohaematology, clinical chemistry, clinical microbiology, pathology

2. Clinical medicine including anaesthesiology, paediatrics, obstetrics and gynaecology, internal medicine, surgery, dentistry, neurology, psychiatry, radiology, therapeutics, otorhinolaryngology and ophthalmology

3. Health sciences including public health services, social medicine, hygiene, nursing, epidemiology

Agricultural Science

1. Agriculture, forestry, fisheries and allied sciences including agronomy, animal husbandry, fisheries, forestry, horticulture, and other allied subjects

2. Veterinary medicine

Appendix 4

Categories of Activity that are not research and development activities

(a) research in the social sciences (including economics, business management, and behavioural sciences), arts, or humanities;

(b) routine testing and analysis for purposes of quality or quantity control;

(c) alterations of a cosmetic or stylistic nature to existing products, services or processes whether or not these alterations represent some improvement;

(d) operational research such as management studies or efficiency surveys which are not wholly and exclusively undertaken for the purposes of a research and development activity;

(e) corrective action in connection with breakdowns during commercial production of a product;

(f) legal and administrative work in connection with patent applications, records and litigation and the sale or licensing of patents;

(g) activity, including design and construction engineering, relating to the construction, relocation, rearrangement or start-up of facilities or equipment other than facilities or equipment which is to be used wholly and exclusively for the purposes of carrying on by the company of research and development activities;

(h) market research, market testing, market development, sales promotion or consumer surveys;

(i) prospecting, exploring or drilling for, or producing, minerals, petroleum or natural gas;

(j)   the commercial and financial steps necessary for the marketing or the commercial production or distribution of a new or improved material, product, device, process, system or service.

(k)   administration and general support services (such as transportation, storage, cleaning, repair, maintenance and security) which are not wholly and exclusively undertaken in connection with a research and development activity.

Chapter 8

Group Relief

Group Relief

8.1 INTRODUCTION

8.101 Outline
8.102 Subsidiaries
8.103 Groups and holdings of ordinary share capital

8.101 Outline

Recognising that groups of companies usually comprise a single economic entity, Taxes Consolidation Act 1997 (TCA 1997) Part 12 Ch 5 (ss 410-429) provides for the allowance of trading losses and other deficiencies of a group member against the profits of other group members. In addition, it is provided that certain payments between group members, which would normally be made under deduction of tax, are to be made without such deduction. Similar measures are provided in relation to advance corporation tax (ACT) (see **11.206** and **11.207**). Groups are also recognised for certain purposes of corporation tax on chargeable gains. In this case, however, there is no question of permitting the surrender of capital gains tax losses between group members; capital gains tax group treatment allows for the transfer of assets between group members without crystallising a charge to capital gains tax at that point (see **9.203**).

Relief for certain losses or deficiencies may be obtained by a member of a group of companies where surrendered by another company which is a member of the same group (TCA 1997, s 411(2)). The losses or deficiencies are: trading losses, Case V excess capital allowances, excess management expenses and excess charges on income.

Two companies are members of a group of companies if one of them is a 75% subsidiary of the other or both are 75% subsidiaries of a third company, all being resident in the State or, as respects accounting periods ending on or after 1 July 1998, in a Member State of the EU. A company is a *75% subsidiary* of another company where not less than 75% of its ordinary share capital is owned directly or indirectly by that other company.

Relief is also available where the claimant company is a member of a consortium and where the surrendering company is a trading company which is owned by the consortium (and which is not a 75% subsidiary of any company), a trading company which is a 90% subsidiary of a holding company owned by the consortium (and not a 75% subsidiary of any company other than the holding company), or is a holding company which is owned by the consortium (and which is not a 75% subsidiary of any company). All companies must be resident in Ireland or, as respects accounting periods ending on or after 1 July 1998, resident in a Member State of the EU.

Only current losses or deficiencies may be surrendered under the group relief provisions; any loss carried forward can only be used by the company that incurred that loss. Where companies within a group do not make up accounts to the same date, both the profits of the claimant company and the loss of the surrendering company are apportioned on a time basis for the purposes of any claim to relief.

While ownership of ordinary share capital is the primary determinant of a parent-subsidiary relationship, that relationship is also dependent on other tests that look to how the profits and assets of the subsidiary would be distributed.

Losses and certain charges of a manufacturing company may only be surrendered to another company for set off against that other company's manufacturing income. There is nothing to prevent a non-manufacturing loss or other deficiency from being set against manufacturing income.

TCA 1997 Part 12 Ch 5 concerned primarily with group relief but also contains provisions dealing with group payments whereby certain payments which would normally require deduction of tax at source are to be made without such deduction. These provisions apply to both groups and consortia. The meaning of a consortium for this purpose is quite different from that applying in the case of group relief.

8.102 Subsidiaries

For the purposes of the group relief and group payments provisions, three kinds of subsidiaries are defined: a 75% subsidiary, a 51% subsidiary and a 90% subsidiary (see also **2.502-504**).

51% Subsidiaries

A company is a "51% subsidiary" of another company if and so long as more than 50% of its ordinary share capital is owned directly or indirectly by that other company (TCA 1997, s 9(1)(a)). Ownership for this purpose means beneficial ownership. It is not necessary that 51% of the ordinary share capital is held by the other company; a holding of more than 50% of the ordinary share capital is sufficient, eg 50.001%.

51% subsidiaries are relevant in the context of group payments (see **8.2** below).

75% Subsidiaries

A company is a "75% subsidiary" of another company if and so long as not less than 75% of its ordinary share capital is owned directly or indirectly by that other company (TCA 1997, s 9(1)(b)). Ownership for this purpose means beneficial ownership.

The 75% parent-subsidiary relationship is the most important relationship, not only for group relief purposes, but in respect of many other provisions of the Tax Acts, eg capital gains tax groups, distributions to non-resident companies, company reconstructions without change of ownership.

90% Subsidiaries

A company is a "90% subsidiary" of another company if and so long as not less than 90% of its ordinary share capital is directly owned by that other company (TCA 1997, s 9(1)(c)).

An important difference in the definition of a 90% subsidiary, as compared with that for a 51% subsidiary or a 75% subsidiary, is that only direct holdings are recognised.

The meaning of "90% subsidiary" is relevant for the purposes of group relief provisions affecting a consortium.

8.103 Groups and holdings of ordinary share capital

8.103.1 Groups

Two companies are deemed to be members of a "group" of companies if one is the 75% subsidiary of the other or both are 75% subsidiaries of a third company (TCA 1997, s 411(1)(a)), all companies being resident in Ireland or, as respects accounting periods ending on or after 1 July 1998, in a relevant Member State (TCA 1997, s 411(1)(c)). In addition, as will be seen later (see **8.304**), a group relationship will not exist unless the parent company has a corresponding equity entitlement; as well as owning at least 75% of the ordinary share capital of the subsidiary, it must be entitled to at least 75% of the profits distributable to "equity holders" and at least 75% of the assets distributable to equity holders on a winding up. The meaning of "equity holders" involves taking into account the rights of certain loan creditors as well as the shares held by the owners of ordinary share capital.

For the above purposes, *relevant Member State*, means:

(a) a Member State of the European Communities; or

(b) not being such a Member State, an EEA State which is a territory with which Ireland has a tax treaty (TCA 1997, s 616(7)).

EEA State means a state which is a contracting party to the EEA Agreement. *EEA Agreement* means the Agreement on the European Economic Area signed at Oporto on 2 May 1992, as adjusted by the Protocol signed at Brussels on 17 March 1993.

A group may exist within a larger group. Thus, if P Ltd owns 100% of the ordinary share capital of Q Ltd and Q Ltd owns 80% of the ordinary share capital of R Ltd, a group comprising Q Ltd and R Ltd exists within the larger group comprising P Ltd, Q Ltd and R Ltd. There is, however, no particular significance to this fact. On the other hand, a sub-group may exist where, for example, P Ltd owns 80% of the ordinary share capital of Q Ltd and Q Ltd owns 80% of the ordinary share capital of R Ltd. In that case Q Ltd is a member of the group comprising P Ltd and Q Ltd, and of the sub-group comprising Q Ltd and R Ltd; P Ltd and R Ltd are not members of the same group.

8.103.2 Ordinary share capital

TCA 1997, s 2(1) defines "ordinary share capital" in relation to a company as all the issued share capital (by whatever name called) of the company, other than capital the holders whereof have a right to a dividend at a fixed rate, but have no other right to share in the profits in the company.

On the basis of the majority House of Lords decision in *National Westminster Bank plc v CIR* [1994] STC 580, shares are issued when they are registered, ie when the respective shareholders' names are entered in the company's register of members following application and allotment (see also **7.301.2**). The allotment of a share is not the same as the issue of a share.

The rights referred to above are derived from the contract governing the issue of the shares which, in most cases, will be the articles of association as altered from time to time or as varied by agreement (*Tilcon v Holland* [1981] STC 365).

Once the shares give rights to any dividend other than a fixed rate dividend, those shares will be ordinary shares. A dividend does not include the related tax credit; the dividend with (up to 5 April 1999) the addition of the related tax credit, if any, comprises franked investment income (see **4.201** and **11.110**). Because, prior to 6 April 1999, the rate of tax credit will have changed from time to time, the amount of franked investment income resulting from a fixed rate dividend will also have changed but the dividend was nevertheless a fixed rate dividend. If, however, provision was made for the payment of dividends which together with the related tax credit would always amount to a predetermined sum, the dividend was not a fixed rate dividend since it would have varied with each change in the rate of tax credit.

Ordinary share capital may or may not carry voting rights. Shares with rights to dividends not limited to fixed rate dividends but carrying no voting rights are ordinary shares. On the other hand, shares carrying a fixed rate dividend may nevertheless be ordinary shares if they carry voting rights which would enable them to share in the profits of the company in non-dividend form. The right to share in a surplus on a winding up would hardly be such a right although that surplus will have been derived from retained profits. The right to share in profits is more correctly understood to relate to the right to participate in the profits as they arise.

In the unusual case in which shares carry no rights to dividends, it would seem that those shares would be ordinary shares since the fact that the dividend position is constant (ie, no dividend) does not mean that there is a fixed dividend (ie, a zero dividend). The only shares which are preference shares are those which in fact carry a right to a dividend, in the form of a fixed rate dividend.

8.103.3 Percentages of share capital

The various parent-subsidiary relationships for group relief and other purposes are determined by reference to the relevant percentages of ordinary share capital held. A company will own a particular percentage of the ordinary share capital in another company if it holds that percentage of the nominal value of that company's ordinary share capital. The value of the shares held is irrelevant for this purpose.

Since the nominal value of the shares held in a company determines the extent to which another company has a percentage interest in it, it is quite possible for the company to be, say, a 75% subsidiary of that other company even though the economic interest held in it by that other company may be quite small. However, that position is subject to the additional tests prescribed in TCA 1997 ss 412-419 (see below). Those sections look beyond the mere holding of ordinary share capital and have regard to the substance of the matter so that contrivances arranged to produce artificial groups are made ineffective.

8.103.4 Indirect holdings

For the purposes of the definitions of "51% subsidiary" and "75% subsidiary", both direct and indirect holdings of ordinary share capital are taken into account. Where a company owns shares in a second company and the second company owns shares in a third company, the first-mentioned company is regarded as owning shares in the third company. Shares held by the third company in a fourth company are also deemed to be held by the first-mentioned company, and so on indefinitely.

TCA 1997, s 9(5) to (10) set out the rules for ascertaining the percentage of ordinary share capital of a company owned by another company, whether through another company or companies or partly directly and partly through another company or companies. The rules are as follows.

(1) Where, in the case of a number of companies, the first company directly owns ordinary share capital of the second and the second directly owns ordinary share capital of the third, the first company is deemed to own ordinary share capital of the third through the second. If the third directly owns ordinary share capital of a fourth, the first is deemed to own ordinary share capital of the

fourth through the second and the third, and the second is deemed to own ordinary share capital of the fourth through the third, and so on.

(2) (a)   Any number of companies of which the first company directly owns ordinary share capital of the next and the next directly owns ordinary share capital of the next again, and so on, are referred to as a *series*. If there are more than three such companies in the series, any three or more of them also comprise a series;

    (b)   in any series—

        (i)   the company which owns ordinary share capital of another through the remainder is referred to as *the first owner*,

        (ii)   that other company the ordinary share capital of which is so owned is referred to as *the last owned company*,

        (iii)   the remainder, if one only, is referred to as an *intermediary* and, if more than one, are referred to as *a chain of intermediaries*,

    (c)   a company in a series which directly owns ordinary share capital of another company in the series is referred to as an *owner*;

    (d)   any two companies in a series of which one owns ordinary share capital of the other directly, and not through one or more of the other companies in the series, are referred to as being directly related to one another.

(3)   Where every owner in a series owns the whole of the ordinary share capital of the company to which it is directly related, the first owner is deemed to own through the intermediary or chain of intermediaries the whole of the ordinary share capital of the last owned company.

(4)   Where one of the owners in a series owns a fraction of the ordinary share capital of the company to which it is directly related, and every other owner in the series owns the whole of the ordinary share capital of the company to which it is directly related, the first owner is deemed to own that fraction of the ordinary share capital of the last owned company through the intermediary or chain of intermediaries.

(5)   Where—

(a)   each of two or more of the owners in a series owns a fraction, and every other owner in the series owns the whole, of the ordinary share capital of the company to which it is directly related, or

    (b)   every owner in a series owns a fraction of the ordinary share capital of the company to which it is directly related,

    the first owner is deemed to own through the intermediary or chain of intermediaries such fraction of the ordinary share capital of the last owned company as results from the multiplication of those fractions.

(6)   Where the first owner in any series owns a fraction of the ordinary share capital of the last owned company in that series through the intermediary or chain of intermediaries in that series, and also owns another fraction or other fractions of the ordinary share capital of the last owned company, either

(a)   directly, or

(b)   through an intermediary or intermediaries which is not a member or are not members of that series, or

(c)   through a chain or chains of intermediaries of which one or some or all is not a member or are not members of that series, or

(d)   in a case where the series consists of more than three companies, through an intermediary or intermediaries which is a member or are members or the series, or through a chain or chains of intermediaries consisting of some but not all of the companies of which the chain of intermediaries in the series consists,

then, for the purpose of ascertaining the amount of the ordinary share capital of the last owned company owned by the first owner, all those fractions are to be aggregated and first owner is deemed to own the sum of those fractions.

Rule no (4) above can be illustrated as follows (all holdings are of ordinary share capital):

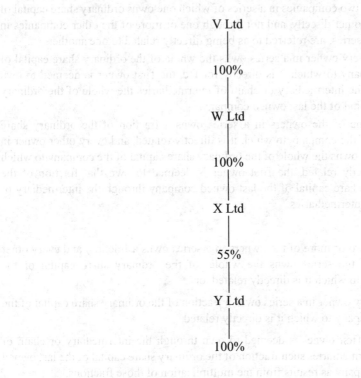

V Ltd

100%

W Ltd

100%

X Ltd

55%

Y Ltd

100%

X Ltd, one of the owners in the series, owns a fraction (55/100ths) of Y Ltd, the company to which it is directly related. Every other owner in the series, V Ltd and W Ltd, owns the whole of the ordinary share capital of the company to which it is directly related. Accordingly, the first owner, V Ltd, is deemed to own 55/100ths of the ordinary share capital of the last owned company, Z Ltd, through the intermediary or chain of intermediaries. This means that both Y Ltd and Z Ltd are 51% subsidiaries of each of V Ltd, W Ltd and X Ltd.

A Ltd

|

100%

|

B Ltd

|

100%

|

C Ltd

|

80%

|

D Ltd

|

70%

|

E Ltd

|

100%

|

F Ltd

Several of the above rules can be illustrated as follows:

Each of C Ltd and D Ltd in the series owns a fraction, and each owner in the series, A Ltd and B Ltd, owns the whole, of the ordinary share capital of the company to which it is directly related. Under rule (5)(a), therefore, the first owner, A Ltd, is deemed to own, through the chain of intermediaries, 56/100ths of the ordinary share capital of F Ltd. F Ltd is therefore a 51% subsidiary of A Ltd.

In accordance with rule (3), C Ltd is both a 51% and a 75% subsidiary of A Ltd. Following rule (4), D Ltd is both a 51% and a 75% subsidiary of each of A Ltd and B Ltd. Under rule (5), E Ltd is a 51% subsidiary of each of A Ltd, B Ltd and C Ltd. Under the same rule, F Ltd is a 51% subsidiary of each of A Ltd, B Ltd and C Ltd while, in accordance with rule (4), it is a 51% subsidiary of D Ltd.

Rule (6) is illustrated as follows:

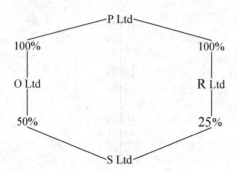

P Ltd owns 75% of the ordinary share capital of s Ltd. s Ltd is therefore both a 51% and a 75% subsidiary of P Ltd.

8.2 GROUP PAYMENTS

8.201 Groups and consortiums
8.202 Group payments

8.201 Groups and consortiums

While TCA 1997, s 410 is headed "group payments", the section does not in fact make any reference to a "group". It deals with companies and their 51% subsidiaries (as well as consortia, as defined) and while the companies affected will in most cases be members of a group in any event, the group payments provisions are not confined to groups as defined in TCA 1997 Part 12 Ch 5.

As mentioned in **8.102**, TCA 1997, s 9(1) defines "51% subsidiary" as a company more than 50% of whose ordinary share capital is owned directly or indirectly by another company. "Ordinary share capital" is defined in TCA 1997, s 2(1) as all of a company's issued share capital "other than capital the holders whereof have a right to a dividend at a fixed rate, but have no other right to share in the profits of the company". For the purposes of these definitions, it is necessary to disregard any share capital held by a company:

(a) directly or indirectly in a company not resident in a relevant Member State; or
(b) indirectly, but held directly by a company for which a profit on the sale of the shares would be a trading receipt (TCA 1997, s 410(3)).

In this connection, *relevant Member State* means:

(a) a Member State of the European Communities; or
(b) not being such a Member State, an EEA State which is a territory with which Ireland has a tax treaty (TCA 1997, s 616(7)).

EEA State means a state which is a contracting party to the EEA Agreement. *EEA Agreement* means the Agreement on the European Economic Area signed at Oporto on 2 May 1992, as adjusted by the Protocol signed at Brussels on 17 March 1993.

A company is owned by a "consortium" if 75% at least of its ordinary share capital is beneficially owned between them by five or fewer companies resident in one or more than one relevant Member State and where none of those companies beneficially owns less than 5% of that capital. The five or fewer companies are referred to as the members of the consortium.

It will be seen that a consortium is defined differently for the purposes of group payments and for group relief. In the latter case, 75% of the share capital must be owned by five or fewer companies but that percentage must be directly so owned. For group payments purposes, ownership may be direct or indirect. A further difference is that the minimum 5% ownership requirement mentioned above does not apply for group relief purposes.

For group payments purposes, a consortium exists as long as 75% of the ordinary share capital of the consortium owned company is owned between them by five or fewer companies resident in relevant Member States, each owning not less than 5%. The remaining 25% of the ordinary share capital could be owned in any other way, even by individuals.

8.202   Group payments

As a general rule, annual payments made by a company (eg, yearly interest other than paid to a bank, annuities) are payable under deduction of tax. In the cases covered in TCA 1997, s 410, these payments are made without deduction of tax.

Where a company which is resident in a relevant Member State makes a payment to another company resident in a relevant Member State and either:

    (a)   the company making the payment is—

        (i)   a 51% subsidiary of the other company or of a company resident in a relevant Member State (see **8.201**) of which the other company is a 51% subsidiary, or

        (ii)   a trading of holding company owned by a consortium the members of which include the company receiving the payment, or

    (b)   the company receiving the payment is a 51% subsidiary of the company making the payment,

the payment is, subject to TCA 1997, s 410(5), to be made without deduction of tax (TCA 1997, s 410(4)).

As mentioned in **8.201**, as to whether a company is a 51% subsidiary of another company for the above purposes, that other company is not treated as being the owner of any share capital that it owns directly or indirectly in a company not resident in a relevant Member State, or any share capital that it owns indirectly and that is owned directly by a company for which a profit on the sale of the shares would be a trading receipt (TCA 1997, s 410(3)). Accordingly, companies connected with each other through a non-EU/EEA resident company will not be members of the same 51% group.

Payments covered by the section are those that:

    (a)   qualify as charges on income (see **4.402**), or would do so if they were not deductible in computing profits, or do not qualify as charges on income by virtue of TCA 1997, s 243(7) (which prevents interest from being a charge on income unless it satisfies the conditions in TCA 1997, s 247(3), (4) – see **4.403**) and,

    (b)   as respects accounting periods ending on or after 1 March 2005, where the company receiving the payments is not resident in the State, are taken into account in computing income of that company chargeable to tax in a relevant Member State (whether in the Member State in which the recipient is resident or in any other Member State).

Not included are any such payments received by a company on any investments if a profit on the sale of those investments would be treated as a trading receipt of the company (TCA 1997, s 410(5)).

A *trading or holding company* is a trading company or a company whose business consists wholly or mainly of the holding of shares in trading companies which are its 90% subsidiaries (see definition in **8.102** above). A *trading company* is a company whose business consists wholly or mainly of the carrying on of a trade or trades.

8.3 GROUP RELIEF

8.301   Introduction

The purpose of the group relief provisions of TCA 1997 Part 12 Ch 5 is to enable groups of companies to offset losses incurred by one or more of its members against profits of one or more of its other members. The effect of these provisions is therefore similar to that in a case where a single company carries on a number of different activities in separate divisions; group relief legislation recognises the fact that the "divisionalisation" of business activities using separate companies is no different economically to the carrying on of such separate activities in a single company. Losses incurred may only be surrendered to fellow group members on a current period basis, just as a loss incurred in one trade carried on by a company may only be offset currently against that company's other profits.

Under the group relief provisions, there is no question of "pooling" profits and losses of group members such as is the case where consolidated tax returns may be made (eg, under the US tax regime); each company makes its own return based on the entity accounts (including the parent company, which should furnish an entity profit and loss account for the purpose). A claim to group relief by any member of the group will form part of its return and will be reflected in the corporation tax computation included with the return.

Group relief is available as between the members of a group or to the members of a consortium. In the latter case, reference is sometimes made to "consortium relief" but the relief is nevertheless group relief; TCA 1997, s 411(3) provides for the various ways in which "group relief" may be claimed in a consortium situation. An important difference between the two forms of group relief is that, whereas within a group any member may claim relief in respect of a loss or other deficiency of any other member, in a consortium situation relief may flow only from the consortium owned company (or one of its 90% subsidiaries) to the members to the consortium; there is no question of group relief being available as between the consortium members themselves.

The losses which may be surrendered under the group relief provisions are trading losses, excess Case V capital allowances, excess management expenses and excess charges on income.

8.302 Claims to group relief

8.302.1 General

TCA 1997, s 411(2) provides that, subject to TCA 1997, s 411(2A), relief for trading losses and other amounts eligible for relief and, as respects accounting periods ending on or after 1 January 2006, trading losses incurred by non-resident companies and other amounts not otherwise eligible for relief, may be surrendered by a company (the surrendering company) which is a member of a group of companies and, on the making of a claim by another company (the claimant company) which is a member of the same group, may be allowed to the claimant company by way of relief from corporation tax called group relief. Losses which may be surrendered are losses incurred in carrying on a trade in respect of which the surrendering company is within the charge to corporation tax (see **8.305.2**).

Two companies are members of a *group* if one is a 75% subsidiary of the other or both are 75% subsidiaries of a third company (TCA 1997, s 411(1)(a)). In addition to satisfying the requirements of the definition of "75% subsidiary" in **8.102**, for group relief purposes a company will not be treated as a 75% subsidiary of another company unless:

(a) the other company is beneficially entitled to at least 75% of any profits available for distribution to equity holders of the subsidiary company (the "profit distribution" test); and

(b) the other company is beneficially entitled to at least 75% of any assets of the subsidiary company available for distribution to its equity holders on a winding up (the "asset distribution" test) (TCA 1997, s 412(1)).

Furthermore, no arrangements of the kind dealt with in TCA 1997, s 424 (arrangements for transfer of company to another group etc) must exist. If the decision in *Pilkington v IRC* [1982] STC 103 (see **8.310.1** below) is to be followed in Ireland, this would mean that it is necessary that the "other company" controls the subsidiary company.

Trading losses and other amounts incurred by a non-resident company are available for surrender only in accordance with TCA 1997, s 420C (see below) and where—

(i) the surrendering company is resident in a relevant Member State (see **8.201**) other than the State and is a 75% subsidiary of the claimant company, and

(ii) the claimant company is resident in the State (TCA 1997, s 411(2A)).

A claim to group relief may be made by any group member in respect of the losses or other deficiencies of any other group member. For any accounting period, two or more group members may make a claim in respect of a loss or other deficiency of a third member of the group but no double allowances may be claimed (see **8.314**).

Example 8.302.1.1

The Falcon group is represented as follows (all three companies being resident in the EU and within the charge to corporation tax):

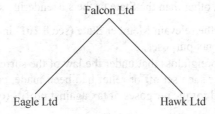

Group relief claims may be made between all three companies where all of the conditions listed below are satisfied. Consequently, Falcon Ltd may surrender losses or other amounts to Eagle Ltd or Hawk Ltd or to both, Eagle Ltd may surrender losses or other amounts to Falcon Ltd or Hawk Ltd or to both, and Hawk Ltd may surrender losses or other amounts to Falcon Ltd or Eagle Ltd or to both. The conditions are as follows:

(a) Falcon Ltd owns at least 75% of the ordinary share capital of Eagle Ltd and Hawk Ltd;

(b) Falcon Ltd is entitled to at least 75% of any profits of Eagle Ltd and Hawk Ltd available for distribution to equity holders;

(c) Falcon Ltd is beneficially entitled to at least 75% of any assets of Eagle Ltd and Hawk Ltd available for distribution to equity holders on a winding up; and

(d) no arrangements exist for the transfer of either Eagle Ltd or Hawk Ltd to another group.

Relief for certain losses of non-resident companies

Where in any accounting period the surrendering company has incurred a "relevant foreign loss", the amount of the loss is to be treated (with any necessary modifications) for the purposes of TCA 1997, ss 420A and 420B (see **8.306**) as a relevant trading loss incurred by the surrendering company in that period.

Relief for a relevant foreign loss is to given after relief for any losses, including relief for losses under TCA 1997, s 397 (terminal loss - see **4.104**) which are not relevant foreign losses (TCA 1997, s 420C(3)). A claim in respect of a relevant foreign loss is to be made within two years from the end of the accounting period in which the loss is incurred. The background to this provision is the opinion of the ECJ in *Marks and Spencer plc v Halsey* [2006 STC 237] (Case C-446/03) referred to in **8.302.2**.

A *relevant foreign loss* is the amount of a foreign loss (ie, a loss or other amount eligible for group relief in accordance with TCA 1997, s 411(2A)) that—

(a) corresponds to an amount of a kind that, for the purposes of TCA 1997, s 420 or 420A, could be available for surrender by means of group relief by a company resident in the State,

(b) is calculated in accordance with the applicable rules under the law of the surrendering state for determining the amount of loss or other amount eligible for relief from tax in that state,

(c) is not attributable to a trade carried on in the State through a branch or agency,

(d) is not otherwise available for surrender, relief or offset in accordance with any provisions of the Tax Acts,

(e) is a "trapped loss" (see below), and

(f) is not available for surrender, relief or offset under the law of any relevant Member State, other than the State or the surrendering state.

A *surrendering state* is the relevant Member State (see **8.201**) in which the surrendering company is resident for tax purposes.

A *trapped loss* is a foreign loss that under the law of the surrendering state cannot be (or, if a timely claim for such set off or relief had been made, could not have been) set off or otherwise relieved for the purposes of tax against profits (of whatever description) of—

(i) that accounting period of the company,

(ii) any preceding accounting period of the company,

(iii) any later accounting period of the company, and

(iv) any period of any other company resident in the surrendering state (TCA 1997, s 420C(2))

If relief for a foreign loss cannot be given solely because, by virtue of condition (iii) above, it is not a trapped loss, the claimant company may make a claim for group relief in respect of the loss at a later time if it proves to the satisfaction of the Revenue Commissioners that that condition is satisfied in relation to the loss at that time. The claim is to be made within two years from the time the condition is satisfied (TCA 1997, s 420C(6)).

A relevant loss may not be used where it arose as the result of any arrangements whatsoever the main purpose, or one of the main purposes, of which was to secure that the loss would qualify for group relief (TCA 1997, s 420C(4)). An example of such an arrangement might be the cessation of the trade of a foreign subsidiary at a time when it has available losses, followed by the recommencement of the trade in another such subsidiary.

An *accounting period* in relation to a company surrendering a relevant foreign loss is a period which would be an accounting period if the company became resident in the State, and accordingly within the charge to corporation tax, at the time when it became a 75% subsidiary of the claimant company (TCA 1997, s 420C(7)).

Group relief for relevant foreign losses may be claimed in relation to an accounting period ending on or after 1 January 2006. An accounting period beginning before and ending after 1 January 2006 is deemed to consist of separate accounting periods, the earlier one ending on 31 December 2005 and the later one commencing on 1 January 2006.

8.302.2 Residence

It is provided in TCA 1997, s 411(1)(c) that "in this section and in the following sections of this Chapter" (ie, for group relief purposes) references "to a company apply only to a company which, by virtue of the law of a relevant Member State, is resident for the purposes of tax in such a Member State". TCA 1997, s 411(1)(c)(iii) provides, for the same purposes, that in determining whether a company is a 75% subsidiary of another company, the other company is to be treated as not being the owner of any share capital which it owns directly or indirectly in a "company, not being a company which, by virtue of the law of a relevant Member State, is resident for the purposes of tax in such a Member State". For this purpose, "tax" in relation to a Member State other than Ireland means any tax imposed in the Member State which corresponds to corporation tax in Ireland.

For the above purposes, *relevant Member State*, means:

(a)   a Member State of the European Communities; or

(b)   not being such a Member State, an EEA State which is a territory with which Ireland has a tax treaty (TCA 1997, s 411(1)(a)).

EEA State means a state that is a contracting party to the EEA Agreement. *EEA Agreement* means the Agreement on the European Economic Area signed at Oporto on 2 May 1992, as adjusted by the Protocol signed at Brussels on 17 March 1993.

For accounting periods ending before 1 July 1998, the residence requirements in TCA 1997, s 411(1)(c) (prior to amendment by FA 1999) were such as to confine group membership to Irish resident companies. The interpretation of this residence requirement, in particular its effect on TCA 1997, s 411, was the subject of the UK case *Imperial Chemical Industries plc v Colmer* [1996] STC 352, [1998] STC 874. Although it is relevant for the purposes of group relief as a whole, the case concerned a claim for group relief by a consortium member and is discussed in that connection also in **8.303.1** below.

The question to be decided in *Colmer* was whether the opening words of [the UK equivalent of] TCA 1997, s 411(1)(c) (prior to amendment by FA 1999 – see above) meant that any reference to a company or companies within the section had to be read as applying only to a company or companies resident in the UK or whether that requirement was independent of [the UK equivalent of] TCA 1997, s 411(1)(a) in which "holding company" is defined. *Holding company* is defined as a company whose business consists wholly or mainly in the holding of shares or securities of companies which are its 90% subsidiaries and which are trading companies. (See further below under *Residence and the EC Treaty*.)

In relation to the definition of "group", TCA 1997, s 411(1)(c)(iii) (as amended by FA 1999 – see above) provides that, in determining whether one company is a 75% subsidiary of another company, that other company is to be treated as not being the owner of any share capital which it owns directly or indirectly in a company which is not resident for tax purposes in a Member State of the EU. Thus, if A Ltd, an Irish company, owns 100% of the ordinary share capital of B Ltd, a Swiss company, and B Ltd owns 100% of the ordinary share capital of C Ltd, an Irish company, the two Irish companies are not members of a group for the purposes of TCA 1997, s 411. This is because the "other company", A Ltd, may not be regarded as being the owner of any share capital that it owns in a company not resident in the EU, B Ltd in this case. If the ownership by A Ltd of B Ltd is to be disregarded, it cannot then be treated as the owner of C Ltd.

Residence and the EC Treaty

The *Colmer* case was concerned with a claim to group relief by a consortium member in respect of losses of a 90% trading subsidiary of a holding company owned by the consortium. Although the trading subsidiary was resident in the UK, most of the trading companies owned by the holding company were not so resident. Furthermore, the majority of the trading companies were resident outside the EU. The UK Revenue view was that since the business of the holding company could not be said to consist wholly or mainly in the holding of shares of UK resident companies, it was not a "holding company" so that group relief could not be claimed in that case.

The Court of Appeal had found in favour of the taxpayer company on the basis that [the UK equivalent of] TCA 1997, s 411(1)(a) and (c) were independent requirements and that the requirement of paragraph (c) should not be read into paragraph (a). In other words, the residence requirement of paragraph (c) relates only to the companies surrendering or seeking to benefit from losses or other amounts under the group relief provisions and does not extend to other companies whose relevance is for the purposes only of the definition of "holding company".

In the House of Lords, this view of the residence requirement was rejected. Such a selective interpretation was seen as not justifiable in the light of the opening words of [the UK equivalent of] TCA 1997, s 411(1)(c) and it was held that the provisions of that subsection must be read into all of the other parts of the section.

The House of Lords, however, additionally found that it is also necessary to construe the group relief provisions in a manner which avoids conflict with Community law, specifically articles 43 and 48 (then 52 and 58 respectively) of the EC Treaty which are directed against restrictions on the freedom of establishment of nationals (including companies) of one Member State in the territory of another (and which prohibition also applies to restrictions on the setting up of agencies, branches or subsidiaries by nationals of any Member State established in the territory of any Member State). The applicability of those articles would be a matter for consideration by the Court of Justice (ECJ) of the European Communities and a reference to that Court under article 234 (then 177) of the EC Treaty would be required to determine the appeal.

In July 1998, the Court of Justice ruled that since consortium relief was available only where the 90% subsidiaries in question were also bodies corporate resident in the UK, the relevant legislative provisions discriminated against companies which had, under article 43 of the EC Treaty, exercised their right of freedom of establishment and which controlled companies mainly resident in other member states. The national court was not, however, required, when deciding an issue that lay outside the scope of Community law, to interpret its legislation so as to comply with Community law. The difference in treatment that depended on whether or not the business of a consortium member holding company consists wholly or mainly in the holding of shares in subsidiaries established outside the EU was a matter that lay outside the scope of Community law. Accordingly, as regards the issue that arose in the *Colmer* case, there was no obligation to apply the relevant tax legislation in such a way as to overlook the non-resident status of the majority of the subsidiary companies in that case.

Having considered the ruling of the Court of Justice, the House of Lords delivered its final judgment on 18 November 1999. This confirmed that the right of a national of an EU Member State to freedom of establishment of companies in another Member State in no way affected the existing group relief provisions in the UK in their application to companies established outside the EU. (See also **9.202.2** in relation to residence and non-discrimination against the framework of EU law.)

Under Irish group relief provisions, relief for trading losses and other deficiencies is available where the relevant group companies are either Irish resident or are trading in

Ireland through a branch (so that they are within the charge to corporation tax – see further in **8.305** below). That the confinement of relief to these situations is compatible with the EC Treaty is consistent with the ECJ decision in *Futura Participations SA v Administration des Contributions* (Case C-250/95) [1997] STC 1301. That decision confirmed the acceptability of the tax rule limiting compensation for losses to losses economically connected with Luxembourg. The taxable profits of a Luxembourg branch of a French company were arrived at by apportioning the company's total income. The company sought to claim losses from earlier years based on an apportionment of its total losses although those losses did not relate to activities carried on in Luxembourg.

In *Bachmann v Belgian State* (Case C-204/90) [1994] STC 855, discriminatory rules were held not to be contrary to the EC Treaty as they were objectively justified by the need to preserve the coherence of the Belgian tax system; as Community law then stood, it was not possible to ensure the cohesion of a tax system, such as that of Belgium, by measures that were less restrictive than those at issue. This "fiscal cohesion" principle can only be invoked where it is shown that there is a direct link between deductibility and taxation involving the same tax and taxpayer.

Marks and Spencer plc v Halsey [2006 STC 237] (Case C-446/03) was concerned with a claim by a UK parent company that it was entitled under EU law to offset losses of subsidiary companies resident in EU countries other than the UK. (See **8.302.1** above regarding TCA 1997, s 420C in response to the outcome of this case.) The matter was referred to the ECJ for its opinion which was delivered on 13 December 2005. Articles 43 & 48 of the EU Treaty do not preclude the tax provisions of a Member State which generally prevent a resident parent company deducting from taxable profits losses incurred in another MS by a subsidiary established in that MS although they allow it to deduct losses incurred by a resident subsidiary. It is, however, contrary to those articles to prevent the deduction of such losses where the subsidiary has exhausted all the possibilities available to it in its own MS to have losses used in the accounting period concerned and for previous accounting periods and where there are no possibilities for losses to be used in its MS for future periods either by subsidiary itself or by a third party.

On 10 April 2006, the High Court in the UK published its decision on the implementation of the ECJ opinion. Agreeing with the UK Revenue approach, the Court found that there was no specific rule disallowing a blanket prohibition on cross-border surrenders of losses but that such a prohibition should be disapplied on a case by case basis where the facts fell within the qualification referred to in the ECJ opinion. As the M&S group's operations in France had been acquired by Galeries Lafayette and the French losses subsequently used in France, M&S was not entitled to group relief for those losses. M&S would only be entitled to use its Belgian and German losses if it had exhausted the possibilities available to it of utilising those losses and there was no possibility to take those losses into account in those countries for future periods. If the group continued to trade in those countries, it would not be sufficient to demonstrate that is was improbable that the losses would be utilised.

An important consideration is the relevant time at which the M&S group could demonstrate that the losses could not be utilised. The criteria outlined in the ECJ opinion must be satisfied at the time the relevant group relief claim is made. Accordingly it would be necessary to decide whether or not all possibilities for utilising the Belgian and German losses had ceased at the time the relevant group relief claim had been made.

In its judgment of 20 February 2007, the Court of Appeal upheld the High Court's view to the effect that the test as to whether all possibilities of utilising overseas losses have been exhausted is to be applied at the date the final group relief claim is made. The CA further stated that where time limits for loss claims under domestic law have expired, the taxpayer should be permitted to lodge claims within a reasonable time from the date of the ECJ opinion of December 2005. The CA has left it to the Special Commissioners to decide what constitutes a "reasonable time". In an Irish context, the facility relating to "untrapped" losses become trapped losses provided for in TCA 1997, s 420C(6) (see **8.302.1** above) would seem to be adequate to meet this requirement.

In the *AMID* case, *Algemene Maatschappij voor Investering en Dienstverlening NV v Belgian State* (Case C-141/99) [2003] STC 356, the ECJ ruled that it was in contravention of the freedom of establishment principle of the EC Treaty to apply a different loss treatment to Belgian residents with a foreign permanent establishment to that afforded to a Belgian company operating solely in Belgium.

Belgium had tax rules for priority of offset under which, inter alia, losses incurred in a treaty protected country had to be offset against treaty protected profits (ie, exempt in Belgium) with only the balance being allowable against Belgian profits. In the converse situation, a Luxembourg subsidiary trading in Belgium would have been allowed to offset its losses against Belgian profits without first having to offset them against any Luxembourg profits. This resulted in the company concerned, a Belgian company with a Luxembourg subsidiary, being denied relief for the losses in question. The fact that the profits of the Luxembourg PE were exempt from Belgian tax did not in the opinion of the ECJ provide sufficient "objective justification" for a different loss treatment and Belgium was obliged to allow tax relief for the losses. Differentiating between the ways in which tax losses can be used on the basis of where they arose amounted to an interference with freedom of establishment.

Profits of foreign subsidiaries of Irish companies (not carrying on a trade in Ireland) are not subject to Irish tax and, where losses arise to such subsidiaries, such losses may not be set against the profits of the Irish parent or fellow subsidiaries. The *AMID* decision would suggest that Ireland is obliged to allow losses of EU resident subsidiaries on the basis that different treatment should not apply as between the case of an Irish parent with non-Irish EU subsidiaries and an Irish parent with Irish subsidiaries.

In *Bosal Holding BV v Staatssecretaris van Financiën* (Case C-168/01) [2003] STC 1483, a Dutch holding company had been denied a deduction for interest paid in connection with the financing of its participations in non-Dutch EU subsidiaries which had no taxable income in the Netherlands. The ECJ held that this prohibition was in conflict with article 52 (now article 43) of the EC Treaty concerning freedom of establishment. Although the Netherlands only taxes profits made in the Netherlands and accordingly prohibited a deduction for interest relating profits made abroad, the costs in question were holding company costs whereas the profits in question were profits of the foreign subsidiaries. There was not therefore a direct link between the costs incurred and the profits generated. The Court did not accept that the prohibition was justified on the basis of the "fiscal cohesion" principle. That principle does not operate to uphold tax measures that link a tax advantage to the parent company (the interest deduction) with the possibility of a tax charge on the subsidiary as different taxpayers are involved, unlike the position relating to a foreign branch/PE of a company, as was the case in *Futura Participations*.

In the *Metallgesellschaft* case – *Metallgesellschaft Ltd and others v IRC and AG, Hoechst AG and another v IRC and AG* (Joint cases C-397/98 and C-410/98) [2001] STC 452, it was held that the cash flow disadvantage that clearly resulted from the inability of UK subsidiaries of non-UK parent companies to make a group income election in respect of advance corporation tax on dividends constituted a discriminatory difference in tax treatment and was contrary to article 52 (now 43) of the EC Treaty. Such difference in treatment was not capable of objective justification on the ground that the situation of resident subsidiaries of resident parent companies was not comparable with that of resident subsidiaries of non-resident parent companies.

8.302.3 Share dealing companies

It is provided in TCA 1997, s 411(1)(c) that in determining whether a company is a 75% subsidiary of another company, the other company is to be treated as not being the owner of any share capital which it owns:

(i) directly in a company if a profit on a sale of the shares would be treated as a trading receipt of its trade; or

(ii) indirectly, and which is owned directly by a company for which a profit on the sale of the shares would be a trading receipt.

Thus, the presence of a share dealing company within a group may have the effect of breaking the group relationship as far as group relief is concerned. Clearly this will not be the case where a share dealing group company owns no shares in any other group member company or at least does not hold shares in other group members on which the group relationship depends.

8.302.4 Beneficial ownership

A company may only be a 75% subsidiary of another company if that other company "beneficially" owns 75% or more of its ordinary share capital. Thus, if a company enters into an unconditional agreement to sell the shares in its subsidiary, it will have lost the beneficial ownership of that subsidiary from that time. Furthermore, arising out of the decision in *Wood Preservation Ltd v Prior* 45 TC 112, if the company had entered into a conditional agreement for the sale of the subsidiary on a basis which would deprive it of all the fruits of ownership of the subsidiary, that would also result in a loss of beneficial ownership of the subsidiary (see also **4.109.8**).

In the *Wood Preservation* case, the owner of certain shares entered into a contract of sale for the shares conditional on the consent of a third party. While that consent was awaited, the owner agreed not to procure the declaration of any dividends in respect of the shares. It was held that the owner ceased to be the beneficial owner of the shares from the contract date although the purchaser could not be regarded as having become the beneficial owner at that time.

On the other hand, if a company grants to another person a call option over its shares, that would not in itself be sufficient to deprive it of the beneficial ownership of those shares. In *Sainsbury plc v O'Connor* [1991] STC 318, it was held that the grant of a call option did not result in the loss of beneficial ownership as long as the registered owner of the shares retained all of the normal benefits associated with share ownership, in particular the right to receive dividends during the option period. By the same token, the grant of a right of pre-emption does not affect beneficial ownership, nor will beneficial ownership be impaired by reason of a shareholders' agreement providing for a restriction on the right to sell shares.

The *Wood Preservation* decision would seem to be relevant only where the rights of the vendor are frozen during the period from the commencement of the agreement to the time it becomes unconditional. Normally, where the vendor continues to be entitled to dividends while the contract is conditional, beneficial ownership of the shares will not be lost.

In summary, where shares are subject to an unconditional contract for sale, the vendor ceases to be the beneficial owner of them from the date of that contract. In the case of a conditional contract, the position will depend on the particular rights of the vendor during the interim period.

Where a parent company goes into liquidation, it ceases at that point to have the beneficial ownership of its assets (see **12.901.1**). There will accordingly be no further entitlement to group relief as between the parent and the companies which were its subsidiaries up to that time.

TCA 1997, s 424 deals with arrangements which may result in a company leaving a group and joining another group and arrangement under which control over a member of a group may pass to persons not controlling other members of the group. In any such case, the section effectively breaks the group connection. It applies to options and to arrangements under which share rights may vary insofar as they may lead to any of the above-described results.

Example 8.302.4.1

Austin Ltd is the owner of 100% of the issued shares in Pontiac Ltd and both companies are members of a group. Austin Ltd enters into a conditional contract for the sale of the Pontiac Ltd shares to Morris Ltd.

Although the conditional contract does not result in the loss of beneficial ownership of the shares in Pontiac Ltd, the group relationship is broken as TCA 1997, s 424 applies.

8.302.5 Control

As noted above, the effect of TCA 1997, s 424 is that it is necessary for group relief purposes for the parent company in any group relationship to control the subsidiary company. TCA 1997, s 424(3)(b)(ii) provides, inter alia, that a company is not to be treated as part of the same group as another company if any arrangements are in existence whereby any person has, or persons together have, control of the first mentioned company but not of the other company. In effect, therefore, the shareholders of the first mentioned company must be able to control the other company.

In *Pilkington v IRC* [1982] STC 103, a company (ML) entered into an arrangement with another company (P) to enable capital allowances in respect of a ship which ML was about to purchase to be surrendered to P by way of group relief. To this end, a reorganisation took place involving HTV and V, initially two wholly owned subsidiaries of P, and GC, initially a wholly owned subsidiary of ML. The reorganisation resulted in the following group structure:

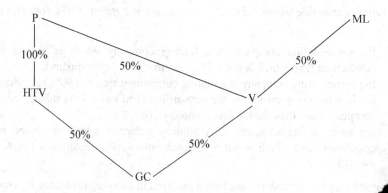

GC therefore became a 75% subsidiary of P (P now having exactly 75% of the ~~share~~ capital of GC) although it was not controlled by P in view of the dead~~lock~~ shareholding position of both V and GC. The House of Lords held that arrange~~ments~~ were in existence whereby the shareholders of P had control of P but not of GC so the claim to group relief failed. The control of P flowed from the articles of association of that company and these were held to be part of the "arrangements", thus giving an extremely wide meaning to the term and not limiting its meaning to, say, a combination of steps taken for a single purpose. It was the effect of arrangements, rather than their purpose, which was relevant. Also irrelevant was the fact that the articles of association had been drawn up many years previously and the fact that the shareholders of P were at no time involved in the group relief proposal. What mattered was that the "arrangements" existed at the time of the group relief scheme.

Although a UK House of Lords decision will usually be persuasive for Irish tax purposes, it is difficult to say whether the Irish courts would follow the decision in this case in view of the surprisingly wide interpretation given to the term "arrangements" and the fact that the decision was a bare majority one. Its logic might appear to mean that in a case where, say, A Ltd wholly owns B Ltd and B Ltd wholly owns C Ltd, there would be some question that losses could not be surrendered under the group relief provisions as between A Ltd and C Ltd, a result that would, plainly, be ridiculous. The group structure here is such that B Ltd has control of C Ltd but not of A Ltd and this is as a result of an "arrangement" (the group structure itself); it will be recalled that TCA 1997, s 424(3)(b)(ii) provides that a company is treated as not being a member of the same group as another company if any person has control of the first company but not of the second. This point was acknowledged by Lord Bridge but did not trouble him in that he was of the opinion that B Ltd could be ignored; the only "person or persons together" who control C Ltd in that situation are, he said, the same as those who control A Ltd. Even if an anomaly existed here, it would not in Lord Bridge's opinion have assisted the appellant's case as it would arise whatever the meaning of "arrangements".

8.303　Consortium claims

8.303.1　General

Group relief is available where the claimant company is a member of a consortium and where:

(a) the surrendering company is a trading company which is owned by the consortium (and which is not a 75% subsidiary of any company);

(b) the surrendering company is a trading company which is a 90% subsidiary of a holding company owned by the consortium (and not a 75% subsidiary of any company other than the holding company); or

(c) the surrendering company is a holding company which is owned by the consortium and which is not a 75% subsidiary of any company (TCA 1997, s 411(3)).

which may be surrendered are losses incurred in carrying on a trade in respect of e surrendering company is within the charge to corporation tax (see **8.305.2**).
aim may be made by a consortium member if a profit on a sale of the shares it the surrendering or holding company would be treated as a trading receipt of mber (TCA 1997, s 411(3)). Neither may a claim be made for any accounting of the surrendering company or holding company if the member's share in the ortium in that period is nil.

For the purposes of TCA 1997, s 411, a company is owned by a *consortium* only if 75% or more of the ordinary share capital of that company is directly and beneficially owned between them by five or fewer companies resident in a relevant Member State (TCA 1997, s 411(1)(a). Prior to 6 April 2000, this share capital requirement was for 100%. The relaxation in the amount of share capital required to be held is intended to facilitate the participation of companies other than those resident in a relevant Member State in consortiums that may be formed as part of Public-Private Partnership projects, or even participation by an individual in a consortium, while not denying to the other member companies the ability to claim reliefs under the consortium relief legislation.

For the above purposes, *relevant Member State*, means:

(a) a Member State of the European Communities; or

(b) not being such a Member State, an EEA State which is a territory with which Ireland has a tax treaty (TCA 1997, s 616(7)).

EEA State means a state which is a contracting party to the EEA Agreement. *EEA Agreement* means the Agreement on the European Economic Area signed at Oporto on 2 May 1992, as adjusted by the Protocol signed at Brussels on 17 March 1993.

The possible group relief claims in a consortium situation as described in (a), (b) and (c) above can be illustrated in the following example.

Example 8.303.1.1

(a)

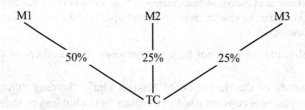

(b)

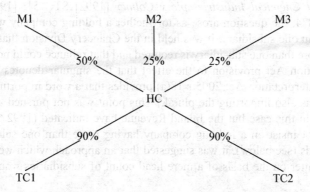

(c)

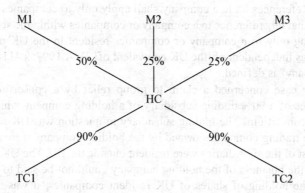

Thus, the following claims are possible:

(a)   M1, a member of the consortium, claims 50% of a trading loss incurred by TC, a trading company owned by the consortium. M2 and M3 could make similar claims in respect of 25% of TC's loss in each case.

(b)   M1, a member of the consortium, claims 50% of a trading loss incurred by TC1, a trading company which is a 90% (direct) subsidiary of HC, a holding company owned by the consortium. M2 and M3 could make similar claims in respect of 25% of the loss of TC1 in each case. All three consortium members could made corresponding claims in respect of any trading loss incurred by TC2.

(c)   M1, a member of the consortium, claims 50% of a loss or other deficiency of HC. M2 and M3 could make similar claims in respect of 25% of the loss or other deficiency of HC in each case.

Consortium relief claims may not be made between the members of the consortium itself.

For the purposes of the definition of "consortium", "holding company" means a company whose business consists wholly or mainly in the holding of shares or securities of companies which are its 90% subsidiaries (see **8.102**) and which are trading companies. A "trading company" is a company whose business consists wholly or mainly of the carrying on of a trade or trades.

In *Imperial Chemical Industries plc v Colmer* [1992] STC 51; [1996] STC 352; [1998] STC 874, the question arose as to whether a holding company was required to have more than one subsidiary. It was held in the Chancery Division that the definition meant that more than one subsidiary is required and that reliance could not be placed on the Interpretation Act provision to the effect that the singular denotes the plural. (In Ireland, the Interpretation Act 2005 s 18(a) provides that a word importing the singular is to be read as also importing the plural.) This point was not pursued at the Court of Appeal stage in this case but the Inland Revenue have indicated (1992 STI 1004) that they would not insist on a holding company having more than one subsidiary. In the House of Lords (see below), it was suggested that an approach which would attempt to decide the matter on the basis of a mere head count of subsidiaries would be an over-simplification.

As indicated in **8.302.2** above, the principal issue in the *Colmer* case was whether a majority of the subsidiaries of a holding company had to be resident in the UK. The question was whether the opening words of [the UK equivalent of] TCA 1997, s 411(1)(c) ("References .... to a company shall apply only to companies resident in the State") meant that *any* reference to a company or companies within the section had to be read as applying only to a company or companies resident in the UK or whether that requirement was independent of [the UK equivalent of] TCA 1997, s 411(1)(a) in which "holding company" is defined.

The *Colmer* case concerned a claim to group relief by a consortium member in respect of losses of a 90% trading subsidiary of a holding company which in turn was owned by the consortium. The trading subsidiary in question was UK resident but the majority of the trading companies owned by the holding company were not so resident and in fact most of the subsidiaries were resident outside the EU. The UK Revenue view was that since the business of the holding company could not be said to consist *wholly or mainly* in the holding of shares of UK resident companies, it was not a "holding company" so that group relief could not be claimed in this case.

The Court of Appeal had found in favour of the taxpayer company on the basis that [the UK equivalent of] TCA 1997, s 411(1)(a) and (c) were independent requirements and that the requirement of paragraph (c) should not be read into paragraph (a). This meant that the residence requirement of paragraph (c) should be confined to the companies surrendering or seeking to benefit from losses or other amounts under the group relief provisions and should not extend to other companies whose relevance was confined to the definition of "holding company". The House of Lords, however, held that the opening words of the provisions of [the UK equivalent of] TCA 1997, s 411(1)(c) must be read into all of the other parts of the section.

In accordance with TCA 1997, s 411(1)(c), as amended by FA 1999, group relief in Ireland would not now be denied in a case involving a consortium owned holding company whose business consists wholly or mainly in the holding of shares in 90% trading subsidiaries resident in Ireland or in one or more Member States of the EU.

8.303.2 Consortium member shares

TCA 1997, s 420(8) provides that in relation to a group relief claim made by a company as a member of a consortium, only a fraction of the loss or other deficiency of the surrendering company may be set off against the member's profits as is equal to its "share in the consortium".

A "member's share in a consortium" in relation to an accounting period of a surrendering company is defined in TCA 1997, s 412(2) as whichever is the lowest in that period of the following percentages, namely:

(a) the percentage of the ordinary share capital of the surrendering company which is beneficially owned by that member;

(b) the percentage to which that member is beneficially entitled of any profits available for distribution to equity holders of the surrendering company; and

(c) the percentage to which that member would be beneficially entitled of any assets of the surrendering company available for distribution to its equity holders on a winding up.

Where, however, the surrendering company is a subsidiary of a holding company owned by a consortium, the percentages to be taken into account are those in the holding company and not in the surrendering company itself.

Where any of the above-described percentages fluctuates during an accounting period, the average over the whole period is to be taken. TCA 1997, s 412(2) does not provide any further details as to how that average should be calculated, for example, whether a weighted average or a simple average would be appropriate. It is suggested that a weighted average would be more "scientific" as this would avoid distortions by allowing for the period of time during which any member's share in the consortium has altered.

As respects (b) and (c) above, these tests correspond to similar tests applying for the purposes of determining whether a company is a 75% or a 90% subsidiary of another company (see **8.304**). For each member of a consortium, the share of the consortium-owned company's loss that may be claimed under the group relief provisions will be the lowest of the three percentages applying. In practice, all three percentages will be the same in most cases. The purpose of the profit and asset distribution tests is to counter attempts to benefit from group relief by artificially arranging for an appropriate percentage of a company's "ordinary share capital" to be held by another company whose true interest in the former company is somewhat less than that percentage.

8.303.3 Arrangements

As with group relief claims made by members of a group (see **8.302**), consortium relief may not be claimed where arrangements of the type dealt with in TCA 1997, s 424 are in existence. This would be relevant to the position of a 90% subsidiary of a holding company. The matter is dealt with in more detail in **8.310**.

8.304   Equity entitlement

8.304.1 Introduction

For group relief purposes, the definitions of "75% subsidiary" and "90% subsidiary" principally relate to holdings of ordinary share capital. "Ordinary share capital" is very widely defined (see **8.103.2**) and it is not difficult to contrive to have a 75% subsidiary or a 90% subsidiary relationship between two companies (typically by the use of non-voting "ordinary" shareholdings) where the real or substantial equity entitlement in the subsidiary concerned is less than 75% or 90%, as the case may be. Accordingly, to counter attempts to arrange for artificial groups based on holdings of ordinary share capital alone, group relief legislation provides for additional tests based on profit and asset entitlements.

In addition to the 75% ordinary share capital ownership requirement (or 90% ordinary share capital ownership requirement for consortium relief purposes), there are two other requirements which must be met before the relevant parent-subsidiary relationship will be recognised.

Firstly, the parent must be beneficially entitled to not less than 75% (or 90%) of any profits available for distribution to equity holders (the "profit distribution" test) and, secondly, the parent must be beneficially entitled to not less than 75% (or 90%) of any assets of the subsidiary available for distribution to equity holders in a winding up (the "notional winding up" test) (TCA 1997, s 412(1)). There is no such test for the purposes of determining the shareholding of a member in a consortium; in a consortium situation, the test is relevant only in relation to 90% subsidiaries of a holding company.

Where either of the two tests ceases to be satisfied during an accounting period, group relief as between the two companies concerned may not be availed of from the relevant time (*Shepherd v Law Land plc* [1990] STC 795).

Equity holder is defined in TCA 1997, s 413(3)(b) as any person holding ordinary shares in the company or a loan creditor in respect of a loan which is not a "normal commercial loan" (as defined in TCA 1997, s 413(3)(a)).

Ordinary shares means all shares other than fixed-rate preference shares. "Fixed-rate preference shares" are shares which:

(a)   are issued for consideration which is or includes "new consideration" (as defined in TCA 1997, s 135(1)(a) – see **11.105.5**),

(b)   do not carry any right either to conversion into shares or securities of any other description or to the acquisition of any additional shares or securities,

(c)   do not carry any right to dividends other than dividends which are of a fixed amount or at a fixed rate of the nominal value of the shares, and represent no more than a reasonable commercial return on the new consideration received by the company in respect of the issue of the shares, and

(d)   on repayment do not carry any rights to an amount exceeding that new consideration (for example, the right to a premium) except in so far as those rights are reasonably comparable with those generally attaching to fixed dividend shares quoted on a stock exchange in the State (TCA 1997, s 413(1)).

The restriction on the right to conversion referred to in (b) above means that the shares may only be convertible into other fixed-rate preference shares. On a narrow reading of (c), it might be thought that shares not carrying any right to a dividend would be fixed-rate preference shares but the correct interpretation must be that some right to dividends is implied and that such rights are confined to dividends of a fixed amount or dividends at a fixed rate. Any right to share in a surplus on a winding up would result in the shares being other than fixed-rate preference shares.

8.304.2 Normal commercial loan

A *normal commercial loan* is a loan of, or a loan including, new consideration and:

(a) which does not carry any right either to conversion into shares or securities of any other description or to the acquisition of additional shares or securities;

(b) which does not entitle the loan creditor to any amount by way of interest which depends to any extent on the results of the company's business or any part of it or on the value of any of the company's assets or which exceeds a reasonable commercial return on the new consideration lent; and

(c) in respect of which the loan creditor is entitled, on repayment, to an amount which either does not exceed the new consideration lent or is reasonably comparable with the amount generally repayable (in respect of an equal amount of new consideration) under the terms of issue of securities quoted on a stock exchange in the State (TCA 1997, s 413(3)(a)).

It may be noted that certain interest is treated by TCA 1997, s 130(2)(d) as a distribution as being in respect of securities with characteristics similar to a loan which would be regarded as a non-commercial loan by virtue of (a) or (b) above. Such interest is described in TCA 1997, s 130(2)(d)(ii) and (iii)(I) (interest on a typical TCA 1997, s 130 ("section 84") loan – see **11.106**). For this reason, a TCA 1997, s 130 loan made (by an outside party) to a subsidiary company which is a member of a group may have the effect of diluting the interest of the parent of that subsidiary for group relief purposes and perhaps breaking the group relationship altogether. This will be the case where the lending bank, an "equity holder" for the purpose, becomes entitled by virtue of the loan, to a return by way of interest which exceeds 25% of the profits available to all equity holders in the company.

Another example of a non-commercial loan is convertible loan stock (even, it would appear, loan stock convertible into fixed-rate preference shares, but not loan stock convertible into other convertible loan stock). A more difficult situation is the case of loan stock issued with warrants entitling the holder to subscribe for shares in the issuing company. It is suggested that such loan stock will not fail to be a normal commercial loan on that count alone as the warrants are a separate asset; it is the warrants, and not the loan stock as such, that are convertible.

Apart from TCA 1997, s 130 loans (as mentioned above), there may be other loans which will be treated as non-commercial loans where the interest payable depends on the results (and not merely the "profits") of the borrowing company's business. For example, interest on a loan made to a property owning company, payable only out of rental income of a specific property, would be dependent on the results of the company's business thus rendering the loan a non-commercial loan. On a very strict reading, a loan made to a company on terms that the lender does not have full recourse to the assets of the company might be considered not to be a normal commercial loan on the basis that entitlement to interest would depend on the value of the assets to which the lender does have recourse. It is doubtful that such a strict interpretation would be followed in practice, particularly where the assets to which the lender has recourse are significant in relation to the amount of the loan.

Interest in respect of a subordinated loan may be suspended in case of default relating to senior debt but this will not result in the loan being a non-commercial loan as long as interest on the subordinated loan continues to accrue.

In order that an index-linked security can be considered to be a normal commercial loan, the amount payable on redemption should be reasonably comparable with the amount repayable in respect of other securities listed on a stock exchange in the State (condition (c) of the definition of "normal commercial loan"). A deep discount security, provided the amount of the discount is reasonably comparable with listed deep discount securities, should rank as a normal commercial loan even though the amount payable on redemption will be in excess of the new consideration lent.

8.304.3 Profit distribution test

Subject to TCA 1997 ss 416 (limited rights to profits – see below) and 417 (diminishing share of profits – see below), the percentage to which a company is beneficially entitled of any profits available for distribution to the equity holders of another company means the percentage to which the first-mentioned company would be so entitled in "the relevant accounting period" (see below) on a distribution (the "profit distribution") in money to those equity holders of:

(a) an amount of profits equal to the total profits of the other company which arise in that period (whether or not any of those profits are in fact distributed); or

(b) if there are no profits of the other company in that period, profits of €100 (TCA 1997, s 414(1)).

It is assumed for the above purposes that no payment is made by way of repayment of share capital or of the principal secured by any loan unless that payment is a distribution; otherwise, where an equity holder is entitled as such to a payment of any description which would not otherwise be treated as a distribution, the payment will nevertheless be treated as an amount to which he is entitled on the profit distribution.

The profits referred to above are the profits as disclosed by the accounts (and not as computed for tax purposes) and are therefore calculated after deducting fixed-rate preference dividends and normal commercial loan interest. In strictness, a shareholder is not entitled to any part of the profits of a company unless and until a dividend is declared, and TCA 1997, s 414 is therefore necessary to provide a profit based means of reckoning a shareholder's interest in the company.

In a case where there are no commercial profits in an accounting period, a token figure of €100 is used as a basis for calculating the underlying entitlements of the equity holders.

8.304.4 Asset distribution test

A company will not at any time be treated, for group relief purposes, as a 75% (or 90% as the case may be) subsidiary of another company unless at that time the other company is beneficially entitled to not less than 75% (or 90%) of any of its assets available for distribution to its equity holders on a winding up ("the notional winding up").

Subject to TCA 1997 ss 416 (limited rights to assets – see below) and 417 (diminishing share of assets – see below), the percentage to which a company is beneficially entitled of any assets of another company available for distribution to its equity holders on a winding up means the percentage to which the first-mentioned company would be so entitled if the other company were to be wound up and on that winding up the value of the assets available for distribution to its equity holders (ie after deducting any liabilities to other persons) were equal to:

(a) the excess, if any, of the total amount of the assets of the company, as shown in the balance sheet relating to its affairs as at the end of "the relevant accounting period" (see below), over the total amount of those of its liabilities as so shown which are not liabilities to equity holders as such; or

(b) if there is no such excess, or if the company's balance sheet is prepared to a date other than the end of the relevant accounting period, €100 (TCA 1997, s 415(1)).

If, on the notional winding up, an equity holder would be entitled as such to an amount of assets of any description which would not otherwise be treated as a distribution of assets, the amount is nevertheless treated as an amount to which the equity holder is entitled on a distribution of assets on the notional winding up (TCA 1997, s 415(3)).

By way of an anti-avoidance measure, TCA 1997, s 415(4) deals with the situation in which an amount ("the returned amount") corresponding to all or any part of the new consideration provided by an equity holder of a company, for any shares or securities in respect of which it is an equity holder, has been returned to it or to a connected company either by way of loan or by the acquisition of shares or securities in the equity holder or in the connected company. In that case, both the total of the assets of the company in question (referred to in (a) above) and the assets entitlement of the equity holder on the notional winding up fall to be reduced by the returned amount.

The reason for this measure is to prevent artificial grouping in a case where the true economic interest of the equity holder in a loss-making company is insubstantial. Otherwise, a "parent" company could, for example, contrive to acquire a 75% subsidiary by increasing its holding of ordinary share capital in that company but then have the cash subscribed returned to it by way of loan from the subsidiary.

TCA 1997, s 415(4)(b) refers to the amount (*the returned amount*) corresponding to the new consideration provided by the equity holder being applied by the company, directly or indirectly, in making a loan to, or in acquiring shares or securities in, the equity holder (or in a connected company). This would, literally, include any loan made, and at any time, by the subsidiary to the parent up to the amount of the new consideration provided by the parent even though the return of any new consideration was not in contemplation at the time it was provided. As a (perhaps extreme) precaution, no loan should be made by a subsidiary to its parent company or to any other group member (connected company). It would have been expected that, to be caught by TCA 1997, s 415(4), the loan made to the equity holder should have some connection or link with the new consideration originally provided, but that position is not confirmed by the subsection.

For the above purposes, *new consideration* has the same meaning as in TCA 1997, s 135 (see **11.105.5**) and any question whether a person is connected with another is to be determined in accordance with TCA 1997, s 10 (see **2.3**).

Example 8.304.4.1

Foremost Ltd holds 60,000 €1 ordinary shares in Northwood Ltd, a company with assets worth €280,000 and issued ordinary share capital of 160,000 €1 ordinary shares. Foremost Ltd subscribes for an additional 340,000 €1 ordinary shares in Northwood Ltd at a price of €1 per share so that it now holds 400,000 out of a total of 500,000 ordinary shares in that company. Northwood Ltd, which now has assets worth €620,000, makes a loan of €340,000 to Foremost Ltd.

While Foremost Ltd has received the return of the entire €340,000 it has subscribed for the additional shares in Northwood, it would on a liquidation of that company be entitled to 80% of its assets totalling €620,000.

TCA 1997, s 415(4) operates to deduct the sum of €340,000 from the value of the assets of Northwood Ltd and from the share of Foremost Ltd in a notional winding up of Northwood Ltd. The net result is that Foremost Ltd ends up with a share of €156,000 (€620,000 x 80% – €340,000) out of a total of €280,000, a share of 55.71%, which is still inadequate to satisfy the asset distribution test of TCA 1997, s 412(1)(b).

Example 8.304.4.2

The position is as in Example **8.304.4.1** except that Northwood Ltd did not make the loan of €340,000 to Foremost Ltd, but did make a loan of €300,000 to Foremost Ltd ten years after the subscription for the additional 340,000 shares. At that time, Northwood Ltd was valued at €1,500,000. There were no changes in the shareholdings in the company during the ten years.

The fact that the loan of €300,000 was made ten years after the subscription for additional shares, and that it was supposedly unrelated to the provision of that new consideration, does not bring the transaction outside the ambit of TCA 1997, s 415(4). Accordingly, a sum of €300,000 must be deducted from the value of the assets of Northwood Ltd (reduced value €1,200,000) and from the share of Foremost Ltd in Northwood Ltd (€1,500,000 x 80% – €300,000). This gives Foremost Ltd a revised share of 75% which is adequate to satisfy the asset distribution test of TCA 1997, s 412(1)(b).

8.304.5 Limited rights to profits or assets

Where the rights of an equity holder in a distribution of profits (dividends or interest) or on a notional winding up are wholly or partly limited by reference to a specified amount or amounts, the percentages to which a company is beneficially entitled to the profits and to the assets of another company are recalculated on the basis that all such limited rights are waived. If, on the basis of the assumed waiver, the entitlement of the equity holder to profits or assets is less than it would otherwise be, that is to be the amount of its entitlement for the purposes of TCA 1997, s 414 or 415, as the case may be (TCA 1997, s 416). This procedure is followed whether the limitation applying is in terms of the capital by reference to which a distribution is calculated or is by reference to an amount of profits or assets or otherwise. For example, an equity holder may be entitled to dividends up to a total of €15,000 or, alternatively, to assets up to €40,000 on a winding up plus 1% of any excess.

Example 8.304.5.1

Tillman Ltd holds 750 participating redeemable preference shares in Orchard Ltd, a leasing company with assets worth €3.5m funded by way of bank borrowings. Orchard Ltd has been set up to lease the assets at an annual rental of €500,000, the lease commencing in the final two weeks of its accounting year; it was previously in receipt of minimal income from a small lease. Tillman Ltd is entitled to all dividends of Orchard Ltd up to a maximum of €25,000 and to all assets on a winding up of that company up to a maximum of €50,000, and to no other rights.

The remaining shares, comprising 250 ordinary shares, in Orchard Ltd are held by Clarion Ltd and that company is entitled to all of the dividends and to all of the assets on a winding up of Orchard Ltd after taking account of the entitlements of Tillman Ltd.

The participating preference shares held by Tillman Ltd are "ordinary" shares for group relief purposes and that company accordingly holds 75% of the ordinary share capital in Orchard Ltd. For the first accounting period of Orchard Ltd, rental income will be negligible and it will therefore have a substantial tax loss resulting from capital allowances available. As its assets are funded by way of bank loan, the value of the company at this time is also negligible. For the first accounting period of Orchard Ltd therefore, the entitlement of Tillman Ltd to all dividends up to €25,000 and all assets up to €50,000 is apparently sufficient to satisfy the profit and asset distribution tests of TCA 1997, s 412(1). On that basis it would be entitled to claim the loss incurred by Orchard Ltd by way of group relief.

However, TCA 1997, s 416 provides that the equity interest of Tillman Ltd in Orchard Ltd is to be calculated as if the former company's limited dividend and asset rights had been waived. On that assumption, Tillman Ltd would have no remaining rights as regards Orchard Ltd and it would therefore fail to satisfy the TCA 1997, s 412(1) tests. Group relief would therefore be denied.

8.304.6 Differing share of profits or assets

Where the rights attaching to any shares or securities of an equity holder may change in a later accounting period, or if those rights will differ with the passing of time, the percentages to which a company is beneficially entitled to the profits and to the assets of another company are recalculated on the basis that effect is given to those arrangements. Where, on the basis of that recalculation, the entitlement of the equity holder to profits or assets is less than it would otherwise be, that is to be the amount of its entitlement for the purposes of TCA 1997, s 414 or 415, as the case may be (TCA 1997, s 417).

TCA 1997, s 417, which is similar in approach to TCA 1997, s 416, is directed at situations in which there are arrangements where, say, shares of an equity holder would lose the right to participate in profits or in assets on a winding-up, or other shares would gain such rights, with a view to enabling a company to establish a 75% entitlement at a time when it would be opportune for group relief purposes to do so. Such an approach would be frustrated by TCA 1997, s 417 which provides that the 75% profits or assets test is to be decided by reference to whichever calculation, present or future, produces the lesser equity entitlement. TCA 1997, s 427(1) defines *arrangements* as arrangements of any kind, whether in writing or not (see also **8.313**).

In any case where both TCA 1997, s 416 (limited rights) and TCA 1997, s 417 (diminishing rights) apply, the relevant calculations are to be carried out on all possible bases and the lowest percentage is to be taken.

As regards any arrangement regarding an entitlement which may differ with the passing of time, it was held in *Sainsbury v O'Connor* [1991] STC 318 that a call option over a part of an equity holder's shareholding would not be affected by this provision (see also **8.302.4**). TCA 1997, s 417 applies only in relation to arrangements affecting the rights attaching to shares and not as respects their ownership.

8.304.7 Beneficial percentage

The beneficial percentage for the purposes of TCA 1997, s 412 and ss 414-417 (see above) may be traced through a chain of companies. For those purposes, the beneficial percentage of a company in another company means its entitlement by reason of any shares which it holds in that other company together with its entitlement by virtue of shares in other companies which themselves hold shares in that other company (TCA 1997, s 418).

TCA 1997, s 418 does not provide rules for determining how indirect entitlements are to be calculated. It might have been expected that rules on the lines of those in TCA 1997, s 9(5) to (10) (see **8.103.4**) would have been adopted here. Such multiplication rules would present no real problem in certain cases, such as where a subsidiary is wholly owned. Thus, if X Ltd holds 50% of the ordinary share capital of Y Ltd and 60% of the ordinary share capital of Z Ltd, while Y Ltd holds the remaining 40% of the ordinary share capital of Z Ltd, the beneficial percentage held by X Ltd in Z Ltd is 80% (50% x 40% + 60%) – provided the profit and asset entitlements are in line with the holdings of ordinary shares and provided neither TCA 1997, s 416 nor TCA 1997, s 417 applies.

The position will be particularly problematic where an intermediate company is partly owned by two or more companies and where it has issued more than one class of ordinary shares and/or where it has a loan which is not a normal commercial loan. Any indirect entitlement in that intermediate company cannot be ascertained simply by multiplying percentages of share capital held. Since no method is prescribed in the legislation, the matter must be dealt with in the most sensible or practical way available, having regard to the circumstances of the particular case. For example, it would be relevant to compute the amount of profits of the subsidiary which would arise to the parent on the assumption that the intermediate company distributed all of its profits including the amount of the profits notionally distributed to it by the subsidiary in accordance with TCA 1997, s 414.

That approach, however, would not be free from difficulty as it would not always be obvious what amount of profits the parent would notionally receive out of the profits notionally received by the intermediate company. A simpler approach might be to look at the percentage of profits of the subsidiary which the parent would receive in the relevant accounting period on the basis that the intermediate company made a single distribution in that period of all of the profits notionally received from the subsidiary.

8.304.8 The relevant accounting period

TCA 1997, s 419 defines the *relevant accounting period* as:

(a) for the purposes of group relief apart from consortium relief, the accounting period current at the time in question; and

(b) for the purposes of consortium relief, the accounting period (of the surrendering company) in relation to which the share in the consortium falls to be determined.

8.304.9 Security

For the purposes of TCA 1997 ss 413-418, a loan to a company is treated as a *security*, whether or not it is a secured loan and, if secured, regardless of the nature of the security.

8.305 Kinds of group relief

8.305.1 Introduction

Relief for—

  (a) trading losses;
  (b) certain excess capital allowances;
  (c) excess management expenses;
  (d) excess charges on income,

may be obtained by a member of a group of companies where surrendered by another company which is a member of the same group (TCA 1997, s 411(2)). Similar relief may be obtained by a member of a consortium (TCA 1997, s 411(3) – see **8.303**).

8.305.2 Trading losses

A loss for an accounting period of a surrendering company, computed as for the purposes of TCA 1997, s 396(2) (see **4.101**), in carrying on a trade (but for accounting periods ending on or after 6 March 2001 only in the case of an excepted trade – see **8.306.2**) in respect of which the company is within the charge to corporation tax, may be set off against the total profits of the claimant company for its "corresponding accounting period" (see **8.308**) (TCA 1997, s 420(1)). Relief is not available in respect of trading losses brought forward from an earlier accounting period. Losses which, by virtue of TCA 1997, s 396(4), are excluded from TCA 1997, s 396(2) (losses in respect of trades falling within Case III of Schedule D – see **3.207.1** and **4.105**) or TCA 1997, s 663 (restriction of relief for losses in farming or market gardening – see **4.101**) may not be surrendered by way of group relief.

Neither may a loss be surrendered so as to reduce the profits of a claimant company which carries on life business within the meaning of TCA 1997, s 706 (see **12.601**) by an amount greater than the amount of such profits computed in accordance with Case I of Schedule D and TCA 1997, s 710(1) (the "I – E" basis – see **12.603.2**). Under the historic I – E basis of taxing life assurance companies, which continues to apply in respect of life policies commenced prior to 1 January 2001, tax is imposed on the profits arising to the shareholders and on the income and gains of the policyholders. TCA 1997, s 420(1)(b) ensures that losses arising to a company that is a fellow group member with a life company will only be available for set off against the part of the profits of the life company that belongs to the shareholders and not the part belonging to the policyholders.

The above reference to the carrying on of a trade "in respect of which the company is within the charge to corporation tax" (inserted by FA 1999) applies in respect of accounting periods ending on or after 1 July 1998 and is a consequence of the extended meaning of "group" and "consortium" for group relief purposes (see **8.302.2**). Although companies resident in one or more Member States of the EU may, for accounting periods ending on or after 1 July 1998, be members of a group and may be taken into account in determining what companies may be treated as members of a group, only losses incurred by companies within the charge to corporation tax may be surrendered under the group relief provisions.

There is no rule, either in a group or in a consortium situation, which requires that losses of the surrendering company must first be applied in reducing other profits arising in the accounting period of the loss. The surrendering company may accordingly choose to be liable to corporation tax on any non-trading income or chargeable gains of the period while surrendering the full amount of the loss sustained in that period. Alternatively, it may of course make any TCA 1997, s 396(2) claim it requires for the period and surrender the balance of the loss after such claim.

Since a trading loss computed as for TCA 1997, s 396(2) will include any capital allowances claimed for the period, losses that may be surrendered by way of group relief will include these capital allowances.

For group relief purposes, a company carrying on life business may not be a surrendering company except to the extent that such life business is new basis business within the meaning of TCA 1997, s 730A (TCA 1997, s 420(9) – see also **12.603.6**).

8.305.3   Excess capital allowances

Capital allowances which are given by way of "discharge or repayment of tax" or in charging the company's income under Case V of Schedule D and which are available primarily against a specified class of income (see **5.105.3**) may also be surrendered by way of group relief (TCA 1997, s 420(2)).

Accordingly, such allowances will include capital allowances in respect of leased buildings and allowances for machinery or plant leased otherwise than in the course of a trade. Although wear and tear allowances made under or by virtue of TCA 1997, s 284(6) (see **3.209.3**) are to be made in charging income under Case V of Schedule D, so that capital allowances in respect of expenditure incurred on fixtures and fittings in rented residential accommodation may be set against rental income, TCA 1997, s 406 prevents any claim for group relief under TCA 1997, s 420(2) in respect of an excess of such allowances (see **5.105.3**).

The amount of the capital allowances which may be surrendered for an accounting period is the excess of such allowances (exclusive of any allowances brought forward from an earlier period) over the related income for the period (before deduction of any losses of any other period or of any capital allowances). Only excess capital allowances arising in the accounting period of the surrendering company which corresponds to the accounting period for which the claimant is claiming relief may be surrendered.

A loss incurred by a company carrying on a trade of leasing, to the extent that it is attributable to "specified capital allowances" (TCA 1997, s 403 – see **5.305**, and TCA 1997, s 404 – see **5.306**), may not be set off under TCA 1997, s 420 against the profits of a fellow group member.

Specified capital allowances are capital allowances in respect of expenditure incurred on machinery or plant provided on or after 25 January 1984 for leasing in a trade of leasing, or capital allowances in respect of the tax written down value of such machinery or plant, other than certain excepted capital allowances in respect of machinery or plant to which TCA 1997, s 403(6), (7), (8) or (9) applies (see below). The leasing of machinery or plant carried on as part of a trade is treated as a separate trade and, for this purpose, any necessary apportionment is to be made of receipts and expenses. A trade of leasing is one consisting wholly of the leasing of machinery or plant or a part of a trade treated as a separate trade of leasing. Leasing includes the letting of any machinery or plant on hire as well as the letting on charter of a ship or aircraft which has been provided for such letting. It does not, however, include the letting of a ship on charter in the course of the carrying on by a company of a trade of operating ships where the letting can be regarded as part of the activities of the trade.

The excepted capital allowances that are excluded from the definition of "specified capital allowances" are capital allowances in respect of:

(a) machinery or plant provided for leasing on or after 25 January 1984 the expenditure on which was incurred under an obligation entered into by the lessor and the lessee—

  (i) before 25 January 1984, or

  (ii) before 1 March 1984 pursuant to negotiations in progress before 25 January 1984 (TCA 1997, s 403(6)),

(b) machinery or plant (other than a film) provided for leasing on or after 25 January 1984 the expenditure on which—

  (i) has been or is to be met directly or indirectly, wholly or partly, by the Industrial Development Authority, Shannon Free-Airport Development Company Ltd or Údarás na Gaeltachta, and

  (ii) was incurred under an obligation entered into between the lessor and the lessee before 13 May 1986, or before 1 September 1986 pursuant to negotiations in progress before 13 May 1986 (TCA 1997, s 403(7)),

(c) machinery or plant (other than a film) provided for leasing on or after 13 May 1986 the expenditure on which is incurred under an obligation entered into by the lessor and the lessee on or after 13 May 1986, or on after 1 September 1986 pursuant to negotiations in progress before 13 May 1986, but subject to the following conditions:

  (i) the terms of the lease include an undertaking by the lessee that during a period ("the relevant period") which is not less than three years and which commences on the day the machinery or plant is first brought into use by the lessee, the machinery or plant so provided will—

   (I) where it is so provided before 4 March 1998, be used by the lessee for the purposes only of a "specified trade" (see **5.305.5** below) carried on in the State by the lessee, and

   (II) where it is so provided on or after 4 March 1998, be used by the lessee for the purposes only of a specified trade carried on in the State by the lessee and, except where the lessor provides the machinery or plant for leasing in the course of a specified trade carried on by the lessor, that it will not be used for the purposes of any other trade, or business or activity other than the lessor's trade (see also **5.305.4**),

  (ii) the lessor and the lessee are not connected persons (within the meaning of TCA 1997, s 10 – see **2.3**),

      (iii)   the machinery or plant is in fact used as provided for in the undertaking referred to in (i) above (TCA 1997, s 403(9)(b)),

    (d)   a film (to which section 6 or 7 of the Irish Film Board Act 1980, applies) provided for leasing, whenever the expenditure was incurred, where the cost of making the film has been or is to be met directly or indirectly, wholly or partly, by the Irish Film Board (TCA 1997, s 403(7)); and

    (e)   machinery or plant provided for leasing, whenever the expenditure was incurred, in the course of the carrying on by the lessor of trading operations qualifying for the 10% corporation tax rate in Shannon Airport (TCA 1997, s 445) or in the International Financial Services Centre (TCA 1997, s 446), and in respect of which no initial allowance or allowance by way of free depreciation has been, or will be, made (TCA 1997, s 403(8)).

An obligation is regarded as having been entered into at any time where there is a binding contract in writing at that time under which the obligation arose. Negotiations pursuant to which an obligation was entered into are regarded as being in progress at any time only where preliminary commitments or agreements in relation to the obligation have been entered into between the lessor and the lessee at that time.

A *specified trade* for the purposes of (c)(i) above is a trade consisting wholly or mainly of the manufacture of goods (including any activity in respect of which the lessee would be entitled to claim manufacturing relief, but with the exception of a qualifying shipping trade – see **7.205.6**). A trade consists "wholly or mainly" of any activities where at least 75% of the amount receivable by the lessee from total sales or services, as the case may be, is derived from sales or services of those activities (see also **5.305.5**).

Since 1986, the main emphasis in the excepted capital allowances test has changed from the availability of grant aid to the nature of the lessee's trade. For expenditure incurred after 12 May 1986 (or, if incurred under negotiations in progress on 12 May 1986, after 31 August 1986), the ring fencing treatment does not apply if the conditions in (c) above are met, whether or not the expenditure on the leased machinery or plant is grant aided. If it appears that the lessee's undertaking has not been fulfilled, any relief obtained by the lessor as a result of having used capital allowances against non-leasing income will be withdrawn retrospectively.

For grant aided expenditure incurred from 25 January 1984 to 12 May 1986, unrestricted capital allowances continue to be available after 12 May 1986 so long as the machinery or plant is provided for leasing in the course of the same lessor's trade (condition (b) above); the position is the same for expenditure incurred under an obligation entered into before 1 September 1986 pursuant to negotiations in progress before 13 May 1986.

A company carrying on a leasing trade will not necessarily have all of the loss incurred by it in an accounting period restricted to its trade of leasing. The restriction applies only to "the relevant amount of the loss". Where all of the company's capital allowances are specified capital allowances, the relevant amount of the loss is the lesser of the amount of the loss incurred and the amount of the specified capital allowances. Where there are both specified capital allowances and other capital allowances, the relevant amount of the loss is the amount of the loss incurred or, if less, the lesser of the amount of the specified capital allowances and the amount by which the loss exceeds the amount of the other capital allowances. If the loss does not exceed the other capital allowances, the relevant amount of the loss is nil.

Non-trading lessors

The entitlement of a company to set off, against its total profits, any excess capital allowances (other than initial allowances) in respect of machinery or plant leased in circumstances in which the leasing income is taxable under Case IV is discussed in **5.302**. Capital allowances available for set off against total profits in any such case must exclude capital allowances in respect of expenditure incurred after 24 January 1984 on the provision of the leased machinery or plant, but with certain exceptions (TCA 1997, s 403(5)). As for a trading lessor, all capital allowances in respect of the leased machinery or plant, including the excepted capital allowances, are available for set-off against the leasing income of the accounting period to which they apply and, where not fully used against that income, for carry forward against the leasing income of the following or any subsequent accounting period. To the extent that they are not fully utilised in the current accounting period, excepted capital allowances may, in accordance with TCA 1997, s 420(2), be surrendered under the group relief provisions.

In the case of machinery or plant provided for leasing before 13 May 1986, the treatment of excepted capital allowances which are available for set-off against total profits to the extent they exceed the Case IV leasing income is similar to that for a trading lessor. There is no restriction in the amount of the set-off under TCA 1997, s 420(2) to the extent that the excess capital allowances are obtained in respect of any grant aided expenditure or, alternatively, in respect of any machinery or plant the expenditure on which was incurred under an obligation entered into between the lessor and the lessee either:

(a) before 25 January 1984; or

(b) before 1 March 1984 if pursuant to negotiations in progress between the lessor and the lessee before 25 January 1984.

For machinery or plant provided for leasing after 12 May 1986, the position of a non-trading lessor differs from that of a trading lessor in that the excepted capital allowances of the former do not include capital allowances in respect of machinery or plant to which TCA 1997, s 403(8) (ie leasing in the course of the carrying on by the lessor of trading operations in Shannon Airport or in the International Financial Services Centre) or TCA 1997, s 403(9)(b) (ie where the terms of the lease include an undertaking by the lessee that the machinery or plant will be used only for the purposes of a "specified trade" for a period of at least three years and the machinery or plant is in fact so used) apply. From 13 May 1986, non-trading lessors' unrestricted capital allowances are limited to those in respect of machinery or plant to which TCA 1997, s 403(6) or (7) apply.

Accordingly, the only capital allowances in respect of machinery or plant provided for leasing after 12 May 1986 which may be included in a claim under TCA 1997, s 420(2) are capital allowances in respect of:

(a) machinery or plant the expenditure on which is incurred under an obligation entered into between the lessor and the lessee:

(i) before 25 January 1984, or

975

   (ii) before 1 March 1984 pursuant to negotiations in progress before 25 January 1984 (TCA 1997, s 403(6)),

   (b) machinery or plant (other than a film) the expenditure on which:

   (i) is incurred under an obligation entered into with the lessee before 13 May 1986, or before 1 September 1986 pursuant to negotiations in progress before 13 May 1986, and

   (ii) has been or is to be met directly or indirectly, wholly or partly, by the Industrial Development Authority, Shannon Free-Airport Development Co Ltd or Údarás na Gaeltachta (TCA 1997, s 403(7)), and

   (c) machinery or plant which is a film made wholly or partly in the State, but only if the cost of making the film has been or is to be met directly or indirectly, wholly or partly, by the Irish Film Board (irrespective of when the expenditure on making the film is incurred) (TCA 1997, s 403(7)).

8.305.4 Excess management expenses

Excess management expenses of an investment company (see **12.7**) may be surrendered under the group relief provisions (TCA 1997, s 420(3)). The amount which may be surrendered for any accounting period is the amount of the expenses of management of the company disbursed for that period (exclusive of any amount brought forward from an earlier accounting period) as exceeds its profits of the period. The amount surrendered may be set against the claimant company's total profits of its corresponding accounting period (see **8.308**). The claimant company does not itself have to be an investment company.

The profits of the surrendering company, for the above purpose, are to be determined without any deduction in respect of management expenses and without regard to any deduction due in respect of losses or allowances for any other period.

In the case of a company carrying on life assurance business, excess management expenses (see **12.603.3**) may not be surrendered by way of group relief (TCA 1997, s 420(5)).

8.305.5 Excess charges on income

Charges on income incurred in an accounting period of a company, to the extent that they exceed its profits for that period, may be surrendered to a fellow group member for set-off by that member against the profits of its corresponding accounting period (TCA 1997, s 420(6)). For this purpose, the surrendering company's profits are to be determined without regard to any deduction in respect of losses or allowances of any other period or any expenses of management brought forward from an earlier period (TCA 1997, s 420(7). It might have seemed obvious that the reference to losses here is to trading losses (as referred to in TCA 1997, s 420(1)) and that the reference to allowances is to capital allowances (as referred to in TCA 1997, s 420(2)). This view, however, was not supported by the decision by the High Court and the Court of Appeal in the UK case *MEPC Holdings Ltd v Taylor* 2002 STC 997. The effect of this interpretation can be illustrated by the following:

	€
Trading profits	100,000
Charges on income	500,000
Chargeable gain	200,000
Capital gains tax losses forward	600,000

On a literal reading of TCA 1997, s 420(7) (taking "losses" as referring to all losses, including capital gains tax losses), the "profits" above are €300,000 (to include the chargeable gain without taking into account CGT losses from an earlier period). Thus, the excess charges available for group relief are €200,000. Since the chargeable gain itself would otherwise have been covered by losses forward, there is no relief for the balance of the charges €200,000, either currently or in any future period. The interpretation contended for by the company in the *MEPC Holdings* case was that the "profits" above are €100,000 so that group relief could be claimed in respect of excess charges of €400,000.

In its judgment delivered on 18 December 2003, and restoring the decision of the Special Commissioners, the House of Lords reversed the decision of the High Court and the Court of Appeal. It was held that on the true construction of the legislation, allowable losses for capital gains tax purposes were not included in the term "losses" in the UK equivalent of TCA 1997, s 420(7). The most natural interpretation of the directive to determine profits without regard to any deduction in respect of losses or allowances was that the deductions to be disregarded were those that the legislation required to be made from what would otherwise be profits. Allowable losses were not deducted from profits but were deducted as part of the computation of chargeable gains that formed one element of profits. Thus, in the above example, "profits" should be €100,000 and the excess charges are €400,000.

The surrender of excess charges in the form of interest may be subject to the anti-avoidance provisions of TCA 1997, s 817A (see **4.403.5**).

8.306 Group relief: treatment of "relevant trading" losses and charges

8.306.1 Manufacturing losses

The ability to surrendering losses and excess charges of manufacturing companies was, up to 31 December 2002 restricted. The part of the loss (*loss from the sale of goods*), or excess charges (*charges on income paid for the purpose of the sale of goods*), of a company for any "relevant accounting period" (see **7.201.2**) which was attributable to the sale of manufactured goods could not, for corporation tax purposes, be set off against the total profits, or against the relevant trading income (see below), of the claimant company for its corresponding period. Such loss or excess charges could be set off, for corporation tax purposes, against the claimant company's income from the sale of goods for its corresponding accounting period, but as reduced by any amounts:

(i)   allowed as deductions in respect of "manufacturing charges) against that income; or

(ii)   set off as manufacturing losses against that income.

For accounting periods ending after 31 December 2002, the treatment of group relief in respect of manufacturing losses and charges is governed by the provisions relating to group relief in respect of relevant trading losses (see **8.306.2** below).

(For a more detailed treatment of the position up to 31 December 2002, see the 2004 edition of this book.) .

In calculating *income from the sale of goods* for manufacturing relief purposes, a deduction is made for any amount for which group relief has been claimed in respect of a trading loss or trading charges to the extent that it has been allowed against the company's "income for the relevant accounting period from the sale of those goods" (TCA 1997, s 448(3)(b) – see **7.202.3** and the *Technical note* in **7.203.2**). A loss from the sale of goods does not include any amount mentioned in TCA 1997, s 407(4)(b), ie a loss in a qualifying shipping trade, since such losses are ring-fenced (see **5.214**).

8.306.2 Relevant trading losses and relevant trading charges

For group relief purposes, a trading loss incurred, or trading charges paid, by a company in an accounting period may not be offset against profits of a fellow group member of that accounting period other than income taxable at the 10% or the standard corporation tax rate, and income of certain insurance business.

For the purposes of this restriction, the following definitions are relevant.

Relevant trading loss, in relation to a company's accounting period, means a loss incurred by the company in the accounting period in a trade carried on by the company, other than:

(a) so much of the loss as is a loss incurred in an excepted trade within the meaning of TCA 1997, s 21A (see **3.101.4**); and

(b) any amount which is or would, if TCA 1997, s 403(8) had not been enacted, be the relevant amount of the loss (see **5.305.6** for the meaning of *the relevant amount of the loss* in the context of the ring-fencing of leasing capital allowances) for the purposes of TCA 1997, s 403(4) (TCA 1997, s 420A(1)).

The purpose of (b) is to ensure that the restriction on the use of certain leasing losses cannot be circumvented by reason of a definition of "relevant trading loss" that would include such losses. If the leasing losses were such relevant trading losses, they could be used to shelter any "relevant trading income", and not just income from a leasing trade, in accordance with TCA 1997, s 396A. The reference to TCA 1997, s 403(8) is to secure that leasing losses from operations in Shannon or the IFSC, which are exempted from the leasing restriction, are nevertheless not to be regarded as relevant trading losses.

Relevant trading charges on income, in relation to a company's accounting period, means the charges on income paid by the company in the accounting period wholly and exclusively for the purposes of a trade carried on by the company, other than so much of those charges as are charges on income paid for the purposes of an excepted trade within the meaning of TCA 1997, s 21A (see **3.101.4**) (TCA 1997 ss 420A(1) and 243A(1)).

Relevant trading income, in relation to an accounting period of a company, means the trading income of the company for that period (excluding any income taxable under Case III of Schedule D) other than so much of that income as is income of an excepted trade within the meaning of TCA 1997, s 21A (TCA 1997 ss 420A(1) and 243A(1)).

Notwithstanding TCA 1997, s 420(1) (group relief for trading losses – see **8.305.2**), TCA 1997, s 420(6) (group relief for excess charges – see **8.305.5**) and 421 (relationship of group relief to other relief – see **8.307**), a relevant trading loss or an excess of relevant trading charges on income of a company for any accounting period may not be set off against the total profits of the claimant company for its corresponding period (TCA 1997, s 420A(2)).

Where in any accounting period the surrendering company incurs a relevant trading loss, computed as for the purposes of TCA 1997, s 396(2) (see **4.101**) or an excess of relevant trading charges on income in carrying on a trade in respect of which the company is within the charge to corporation tax, that loss and/or excess may be set off against:

(i) income specified in TCA 1997, s 21A(4)(b) (certain life, non-life and reinsurance trades – see **3.101.4**);

(ii) relevant trading income, and

(iii) income excluded from TCA 1997, s 21A(3) by virtue of TCA 1997, s 21B (foreign dividends eligible for 12.5% corporation tax rate - see **3.101.5**),

of the claimant company for its corresponding accounting period as reduced by any amounts allowed under TCA 1997, s 243A or 396A (see **4.103** and **4.405**) (TCA 1997, s 420A(3)(a)). Note that only amounts actually allowed under TCA 1997, s 243A or 396A are taken into account so that there is no equivalent here of TCA 1997, s 421(3) which assumes that all relevant claims under certain other provisions have been made (see **8.307.3**).

Such group relief will reduce the trading income of the claimant company for the accounting period concerned:

(a) before any relief under TCA 1997, s 397 (terminal loss – see **4.104**) in respect of a loss incurred in a succeeding accounting period or periods; and

(b) after any relief given under TCA 1997, s 396 (loss forward) in respect of a loss incurred in a preceding accounting period or periods (TCA 1997, s 420A(4)).

TCA 1997, s 420A(3)(a), providing for relief in respect of relevant trading losses against (mainly) relevant trading income, as seen above, does not apply:

(i) to so much of a loss as is excluded from TCA 1997, s 396(2) by TCA 1997, s 396(4) or by TCA 1997, s 663 (Case III and farming and market gardening trades – see **4.101**), or

(ii) so as to reduce the profits of a claimant company carrying on life business (within the meaning of TCA 1997, s 706) by an amount greater than the amount of such profits (before set-off under TCA 1997, s 420A(3) computed in accordance with Case I of Schedule D and TCA 1997, s 710(1) (see **8.305.2** above) (TCA 1997, s 420A(3)(b)).

In the case of a claim to group relief by a company as a member of a consortium, the amount of a relevant trading loss or the excess relevant trading charges on income which may be utilised is the fraction of that loss or excess as is equal to that member company's share in the consortium (TCA 1997, s 420A(5)).

A claim under TCA 1997, s 482(2) (relief for expenditure on significant buildings and gardens – see **3.203.6**) is unaffected by TCA s 420A (TCA 1997, s 482(11)).

The relevant trading income against which a relevant trading loss or an excess of relevant trading charges may be surrendered to a company for any accounting period is the company's relevant trading income for that period, effectively the company's trading income which is taxable at either the 10% or the standard corporation tax rate.

Example 8.306.2.1

Varenne Ltd has the following results for its latest accounting period (ending after 17 February):

	€	€
Sale of goods		15,000,000
Sale of merchandise		5,000,000
Trading income		2,400,000
Case III		1,000,000
Charges		
– patent royalties	800,000	
– interest (allowable under TCA 1997, s 247)	200,000	1,000,000
Trading loss from separate trade		600,000
Group relief claimed for trading loss (TCA 1997, s 420A)		1,400,000
Group excess trading charges claimed (TCA 1997, s 420A)		240,000

Corporation tax computation:		
Trading income		2,400,000
Loss relief – TCA 1997, s 396A	600,000	
Relevant trading charges – TCA 1997, s 243A	800,000	
Group relief – TCA 1997, s 420A	1,000,000	2,400,000
Case I		Nil
Case III		1,000,000
Total income		1,000,000
Charges (non-trading)		200,000
		800,000
Group relief – TCA 1997, s 420		–
Taxable		800,000

Corporation tax:		
Case III	1,000,000	
Less: charges (non-trading)[1]	200,000	
	800,000	
Corporation tax @ 25%[2]		200,000
Income from the sale of goods:	€	€
Income after applying turnover apportionment (€2.4m x 75%)		1,800,000
Less TCA 1997, s 448(3)(b) amounts:		
Trading charges	800,000	
Trading loss – TCA 1997, s 396A(3)	600,000	
Group relief – trading (maximum)	1,000,000	
	2,400,000	
Attributable to manufacturing 75%		1,800,000
Income from the sale of goods		Nil

Notes:

1 In practice, these charges may be deducted from income taxable at the 25% rate.

2 The excess group relief of €640,000 may be used to reduce the corporation tax of €200,000 (TCA 1997, s 420B – relief on a value basis). This topic is covered in **8.306.3**.

Example 8.306.2.2

Onaway Ltd has the following results for its latest accounting period (ending after 17 February):

	€	€
Sale of goods		18,000,000
Sale of merchandise		6,000,000
Trading income		3,200,000
Case III		1,000,000
Charges		
– patent royalties	800,000	
– interest allowed as a charge	200,000	1,000,000
Trading loss from separate trade		600,000
Group relief claimed for trading loss (TCA 1997, s 420A)		800,000
Group excess trading charges claimed (TCA 1997, s 420A)		240,000

Corporation tax computation

	€	€
Trading income		3,200,000
Loss relief – TCA 1997, s 396A(3)	600,000	
Relevant trading charges – TCA 1997, s 243A(3)	800,000	
Group relief – TCA 1997, s 420A	1,040,000	2,440,000
Case I		760,000
Case III		1,000,000
Total income		1,760,000
Charges (non-trading) – TCA s 243		200,000
Taxable		1,560,000
Corporation tax:		
Taxable income excluding Case III – €760,000 @ 12.5%		95,000
Case III	1,000,000	
Less: charges (non-relevant trading)[2]	200,000	
	800,000	
Corporation tax @ 25%		200,000
		295,000
Manufacturing relief		14,250
Corporation tax payable		280,750

Income from the sale goods

Income after turnover apportionment (€3.2m x 75%)		2,400,000
Less TCA 1997, s 448(3)(b) amounts:		
- trading loss	600,000	
- trading charges	800,000	
- group relief – trading	1,040,000	
	2,240,000	
Attributable to manufacturing 75%		1,830,000
Income from the sale of goods		570,000

Manufacturing relief:

$$\text{Relief} = 1/5 \times \text{Relevant CT} \times \frac{\text{Income from G} + \text{M} \times \dfrac{\text{sale of G}}{\text{Sale of G} + \text{M}} - \text{s } 448(3)(b)}{\text{Total income}}$$

$$\text{Relief} = 1/5 \times €95,000 \times \frac{(3,200,000 \times 9/12) - 1,830,000}{760,000^{1}} = €14,250$$

Notes:

1. Total income is exclusive of the Case III income.
2. By concession, these charges may be deducted from income taxable at the 25% rate.
3. See **7.202.3** regarding manufacturing relief formula. The formula was revised for accounting periods ending on or after 18 February 2008 to remove a distortion that previously resulted in an incorrect amount of relief. The tax on trading income can be summarised as €760,000 x 75% @ 10% + €760,000 x 25% @ 12.5% = €80,750.

The order in which reliefs are to be set off against relevant trading income is:

(a) loss relief (TCA 1997, s 396A(3));

(b) charges on income paid for the purposes of the sale of goods (TCA 1997, s 243A(3)); and

(c) group relief (TCA 1997, s 420A(3)(a)).

8.306.3   Group relief on value basis for relevant trading losses and charges

A trading loss (relevant trading loss) incurred, or an excess or trade charges (relevant trading charges) paid, by a company may be used, on a value basis, to reduce the amount of a fellow group member company's corporation tax. The tax which may be so reduced, referred to as the *relevant corporation tax*, is the claimant company's corporation tax otherwise payable for the accounting period in question, after any reduction by virtue of TCA 1997, s 243B or 396B (similar reliefs on value basis for trading charges (see **4.405**) and trading losses (see **4.103**)) but before taking into account any tax payable by virtue of TCA 1997, s 239 (annual payments – see **4.306**), 241 (certain payments by non-resident companies – see **4.303.5**), 440 (surcharge on undistributed estate and investment income – see **10.302**) or 441 (surcharge on undistributed income of service companies – see **10.303**) and, in the case of a company carrying on life business, any corporation tax which would be attributable to policyholders' profits (see **12.603.6**).

The amount, referred to as the *relievable loss*, in respect of which relief may be claimed for an accounting period is the excess of the relevant trading loss and excess of relevant trading charges for that period over the aggregate of the amounts that could, if timely claims had been made for such set off, have been set off in respect of that loss or excess against:

(a) the income of the company for that period in accordance with TCA 1997, s 243A(3);

(b) the income of the company in accordance with TCA 1997, s 396A(3); and

(c) the income of any other company in accordance with TCA 1997, s 420A (TCA 1997, s 420B(2)).

In other words, any claim for value basis relief for an accounting period may only be in respect of the surrendering company's loss arising or charges paid in that period to the extent that that loss or those charges have been used, or could have been used, to reduce the company's income or, in the case of group relief, the income of any other group company.

Where a claim for relief in respect of a relievable loss is made for any accounting period, the relevant corporation tax of the claimant company for that period is reduced:

(a) in so far as the relievable loss consists of a loss from the sale of goods or charges on income paid for the purpose of the sale of goods, by an amount equal to 10% of that loss or those charges; and

(b) in so far as the excess consists of a non-manufacturing loss or non-manufacturing trade charges, by an amount equal to that loss or those charges multiplied by the standard rate of corporation tax for the accounting period (TCA 1997, s 420B(3)).

The amount for a *loss from the sale of goods* (manufacturing loss) is arrived at by apportioning the total amount of loss arising by reference to the amount of the turnover from the sale of "goods" over the amount of turnover from the sale of "goods and merchandise", ie after applying the turnover apportionment method used to calculate manufacturing income. Where the trading loss includes any amount that is not referable to sales of goods and merchandise (eg, services income), that amount must be excluded from the amount of the trading loss before applying the turnover apportionment. A loss from the sale of goods does not include any amount mentioned in TCA 1997, s 407(4)(b), ie a loss in a qualifying shipping trade, since such losses are ring-fenced (see **5.214**).

The amount for *charges on income paid for the purpose of the sale of goods* (manufacturing charges) for any period is arrived at by apportioning the total amount of charges on income paid wholly and exclusively for the purposes of the trade (trade charges) in that period by reference to the amount of turnover from the sale of "goods" over the amount of turnover from the sale of "goods and merchandise", ie on the same basis as manufacturing income is computed where there are sales of both manufactured and non-manufactured goods. Where the trading income of a company includes income other than income from sales of goods and merchandise (eg, services income), any trade charges referable to such income must be excluded from the amount of the trade charges that are to be apportioned on the turnover basis.

Where relief is claimed under TCA 1997, s 420B(3), the surrendering company is treated as having surrendered, and the claimant company is treated as having claimed relief for, trading losses and charges on income of an amount such as would have been utilised had those losses and charges been set against taxable income. Accordingly, that "amount" is the aggregate of (i) 10 times the amount in (a) above and (ii) eight times the amount in (b) above, ie the amount grossed up at 12.5%, being the current standard rate of corporation tax applicable (TCA 1997, s 420B(4)). Effectively, the aggregate is the amount of the loss and charges used for the purposes of the claim for credit under TCA 1997, s 420B(3).

Example 8.306.3.1

The results of group members Archangel Ltd and Resolute Ltd for the year ended 31 March 2008 are as follows:

Archangel Ltd		€	€
Trading income	- non-manufacturing	320,000	
	- manufacturing	80,000	400,000
Trade charges	- non-manufacturing	48,000	
	- manufacturing	12,000	60,000
Non-trade charges			30,000
Case III income			170,000

Resolute Ltd		€	€
Trading loss	- non-manufacturing	480,000	
	- manufacturing	120,000	600,000
Trade charges	- non-manufacturing	60,000	
	- manufacturing	15,000	75,000
Non-trade charges			40,000
Case III income			100,000
Trading income			
2007	- non-manufacturing	36,000	
	- manufacturing	14,000	50,000
Case III 2007			40,000

TCA s 420B(2) – "relievable loss" of Resolute Ltd:

Relevant trading loss:		600,000
(a) allowed TCA s 396A(3) 2005	50,000	
(b) allowed TCA s 420A	340,000	390,000
Excess		210,000
Relevant trading charges:		75,000
- allowed TCA ss 243A		−
Excess		75,000
Relievable loss (210,000 + 75,000)		285,000

Corporation tax computations

Archangel Ltd:

Trading income	400,000
Less trading charges	60,000

	340,000
Less: group relief (TCA s 420A)	340,000
	–

Case III	170,000
Less: non-trade charges	30,000
	140,000
Corporation tax @ 25% ("relevant corporation tax")	35,000
TCA s 420B relief:	
€82,000[2] @ 12.5%	10,250
Payable	24,750

Resolute Ltd:

Case III 2008		100,000
Deduct non-trade charges (TCA s 243A)		40,000
		60,000
Corporation tax @ 25%		15,000
TCA s 243B(3) relief:		
€60,000 @ 12.5%	7,500	
€15,000 @ 10%	1,500	9,000
		6,000

Relevant corporation tax for TCA s 396B(3)[3]	6,000
TCA s 396B(3) relief:	
€48,000 @ 12.5%	6,000
	–

Case 1 2007	50,000
Less: TCA s 396A(3) claim	50,000
	–

Case III 2005 €40,000 @ 25% ("relevant corporation tax")	10,000
TCA s 396B(3) relief 2005:	
€80,000 @ 12.5%	10,000
Payable	–

Notes:

(1) The order in which trading losses, charges etc are to be claimed is: losses (TCA s 396A), charges (TCA s 243A), group relief (TCA s 420A). The order in which tax credits are to be claimed is: charges (TCA s 243B), losses (TCA s 396B), group relief (TCA s 420B).

(2) Balance available – see *Utilisation of losses and charges* below.

(3) Following (1), "relevant corporation tax" against which credits may be claimed is: TCA s 243B (corporation tax before any other credits); TCA s 396B (corporation tax

after any TCA s 243B credits); TCA s 420B (corporation tax after any TCA s 243B or 396B credits).

Utilisation of losses and charges: Resolute Ltd:

	Total	Used	Balance
	€	€	€
1. TCA ss 243A/396A/420A:			
Loss	600,000	50,000	
		340,000	210,000
Trade charges	75,000	–	75,000
Non-trade charges	40,000	40,000	–
2. TCA ss 243B/396B:			
Trade charges (balance)	75,000	75,000	–
Loss (balance)	210,000	48,000	
		80,000	82,000
3. TCA s 420B:			
Loss (balance)	82,000	82,000	–

Reconciliation:	€
Trading losses	600,000
Trade charges	75,000
Non-trade charges	40,000
	715,000

Used:			
Losses 2007		50,000	
Group relief		340,000	
Non-trade charges 2008		40,000	
Credits	- trade charges 2008	75,000	
	- losses 2008	48,000	
	- losses 2007	80,000	
	- group relief	82,000	715,000

8.307 Relationship of group relief to other relief

8.307.1 General

Group relief for an accounting period (where the claim is under TCA 1997, s 420, but not if it is under TCA 1997, s 420A or 420B) is allowed as a deduction from the claimant company's total profits (see **8.307.3** below) for the period *before* reduction by any relief derived from a subsequent accounting period (eg, a TCA 1997, s 396(2) or s 308(4) claim) but as reduced by "any other relief from tax" (see **8.307.2** below under *Total profits*) (TCA 1997, s 421). For this purpose, any available relief under TCA 1997, s 308(4) or 396(2) which has not actually been claimed is to be taken into account as if a claim for that relief had been made (TCA 1997, s 421(3) so that, in practice, any such available relief would be claimed before claiming group relief (see also **8.307.3**). Note, however, that it is not necessary to make a claim under TCA 1997, s 396A (relevant trading loss) or 396B (loss relief on a value basis) before claiming group relief (whether under TCA 1997, s 420, 420A or 420B).

Example 8.307.1.1

Jordan Ltd and Arrow Ltd are both Irish resident trading companies (each trade being an excepted trade) making up accounts to 31 December each year. Jordan Ltd owns all of the ordinary share capital in Arrow Ltd but prior to 1 April 2007 held only 60% of the shares, the remaining shares then being held by Greenville Ltd, another Irish resident company. Jordan Ltd had tax losses forward of €120,000 at 31 December 2006. Greenville Ltd had no taxable profits for the year ended 31 December 2007. The results of the two trading companies for the two years ended 31 December 2007 and 31 December 2008 are as follows:

Year ended	31/12/07	31/12/08
	€	€
Jordan Ltd		
Case I	400,000	(250,000)
Case III	10,000	8,000
Arrow Ltd		
Case I	(160,000)	165,000
Case III	Nil	4,000
Charges on income	Nil	3,500

The taxable profits of the companies for the two accounting periods are computed as follows:

	Jordan Ltd	Arrow Ltd
	€	€
Year ended 31/12/07		
Case I	400,000	Nil
Loss forward	120,000	
	280,000	
Case III	10,000	
Income	290,000	
Group relief:		
1/1/07 – 31/3/07 (consortium 60%)[1]	(24,000)	
1/4/07 – 31/12/07 (group)[1]	(120,000)	
	146,000	
TCA 1997, s 396(2) – from y/e 31/12/08[2]	(146,000)	

Taxable	Nil	
Loss forward[3]	Nil	16,000

Year ended 31/12/08

Case I	Nil	165,000
Loss forward		16,000
	Nil	149,000
Case III	8,000	4,000
	8,000	153,000
Charges on income		3,500
		149,500
Group relief[4]		104,000
Taxable		45,500

Notes:

1 For the period 1 January 2007 to 31 March 2007, Arrow Ltd was owned by a consortium consisting of Jordan Ltd (60%) and Greenville Ltd (40%). Jordan Ltd is entitled, with the consent of Greenville Ltd, to claim 60% of the available loss of Arrow Ltd, ie €160,000 x 3/12 x 60% = €24,000.

For the period 1 April 2007 to 31 December 2007, since Jordan Ltd and Arrow Ltd form a group, Jordan Ltd may claim the full loss, ie €160,000 x 9/12 = €120,000

2 As the TCA 1997, s 396(2) loss is from the following period, it is deducted after group relief.

3 Since Greenville Ltd is not in a position to claim any group relief in the absence of any profits, the balance of the loss in Arrow Ltd is carried forward.

4 The loss for the year ended 31 December 2008 is used as follows:

	€
Total loss	250,000
TCA 1997, s 396(2) y/e 31/12/07	146,000
Available for group relief	104,000

8.307.2   Group relief and consortium relief

Where claims under both the normal group relief and consortium relief provisions are possible, there are no rules which would give one form of relief priority over the other. Thus, if a holding company owned by a consortium has a loss or other deficiency in any accounting period, it may surrender that loss, or any part of it, to one or more members of the consortium. Alternatively, it may surrender all or any part of the loss to one or more of its 90% trading subsidiaries. Similarly, all or any part of a loss incurred by a 90% subsidiary of a holding company in an accounting period may be surrendered to one or more members of the consortium owning the holding company. Alternatively, it may surrender all or any part of the loss to the holding company.

In a consortium situation any group relief claim made by one of the members requires the consent of each of the other members of the consortium. Where a group relief claim (not being a consortium claim) is made, only the consent of the surrendering company is made. This will be true even where the surrendering company is a holding company owned by a consortium and the claim is made by one of its 90% subsidiaries, or where the surrendering company is a 90% subsidiary of a holding company and the claim is made by the holding company. Since the surrendering company in either of those situations is really owned by the consortium members, individual consents of the members are not necessary.

Both group and consortium type group relief claims could be made in respect of parts of the same loss. For example, a holding company could surrender part of a loss incurred in an accounting period against the profits of one of its 90% subsidiaries while the balance of that loss could be surrendered to the members of the consortium, or part of the balance of that loss could be surrendered to some of those members.

8.307.3 Total profits

Group relief (where the claim is under TCA 1997, s 420, but not if it is under TCA 1997, s 420A or 420B) is set against the total profits of the claimant company. TCA 1997, s 421(2) provides that group relief for an accounting period is to be allowed as a deduction against the claimant company's "total profits" for the period before reduction by any relief derived from a subsequent accounting period but as reduced by any other relief from tax (including relief in respect of charges on income under TCA 1997, s 243(2)).

The "other relief from tax" is to be determined on the assumption that all relevant claims under TCA ss 308(4) and 396(2) have been made (TCA 1997, s 421(3)); relief under TCA s 243(2) is automatic and is not claimed.

"Relief derived from a subsequent accounting period" means any of the following, incurred in or falling to be made in an accounting period subsequent to the accounting period the profits for which are being computed:

(a)   a trading loss – TCA 1997, s 396(2);

(b)   capital allowances given by way of discharge or repayment of tax or in charging income under Case V of Schedule D and which are available primarily against a specified class of income (TCA 1997, s 308(4) (see **8.305.3** above).

Accordingly, the above reliefs are to be set off against the total profits of the claimant company after those profits have been reduced by group relief for the period the profits of which are being computed.

"Any other relief from tax", which is to be deducted by the claimant company before group relief, includes:

1.   charges on income paid in the accounting period (which, under TCA 1997, s 243(2), are to be set against total profits as reduced by any other relief from tax other than group relief (see **4.404**)); and

2.   trading losses and capital allowances given by way of discharge or repayment of tax or in charging income under Case V and which are available primarily against a specified class of income (TCA s 308(4) – see **4.107**, **5.105.3**), so far as they arise in the accounting period, and on the assumption that the claimant company makes all relevant claims for that period.

The only claims which are *assumed* to have been made before group relief are any claims in respect of trading losses and capital allowances given by way of discharge or repayment of tax or in charging income under Case V. In respect of any other type of claim, only actual claims made need to be taken into account in reducing total profits before setting off any amount by way of group relief. For example, capital allowances in a trading situation need not be claimed for a particular accounting period. If such a claim is not so made, no amount in respect of capital allowances will be deducted in arriving at total profits for that period, leaving additional scope for claiming group relief if required.

Note also that it is not necessary to assume that a claim under TCA 1997, s 396A (relevant trading loss) or 396B (loss relief on a value basis) has been made before claiming group relief (whether under TCA 1997, s 420, 420A or 420B).

The group relief provisions do not specifically require that trading losses brought forward from an earlier accounting period should be deducted in arriving at total profits before group relief. TCA 1997, s 396(1), however, requires that a loss forward must be claimed against the first available profits of the same trade (see **4.101**). Where a loss forward is not so claimed, it cannot then be claimed against trading profits of a period later than that in which it could first have been claimed; the amount of a loss forward which can be claimed for any accounting period is limited to the amount which could not have been claimed against income or profits of an earlier accounting period. In effect, and unless it is to be abandoned, a loss forward is taken in priority to group relief.

8.308 Corresponding accounting periods

As was seen in **8.305.2**, a trading loss or other deficiency for an accounting period of a surrendering company may be set off under the group relief provisions against the total profits of the claimant company for its "corresponding accounting period" (TCA 1997, s 420). For accounting periods ending on or after 6 March 2001, a loss may be set against total profits only in the case of an excepted trade (see **8.306.2**). Most trading losses are now "relevant trading losses" and as such may be group relieved in accordance with TCA 1997, s 420A and not s 420. (See further below in relation to claims under TCA 1997 ss 420A and 420B.) An accounting period of the claimant company that falls wholly or partly within an accounting period of the surrendering company "corresponds to" that accounting period.

An accounting period of a surrendering company may or may not, however, coincide with a corresponding accounting period of the claimant company. Where the accounting periods of both the claimant and the surrendering companies begin and end on the same dates, as will be the position in the majority of cases, those periods coincide and the procedure is obviously straightforward; any loss of the surrendering company for that period may be set against profits of the claimant company for the same period.

Where the accounting period of the surrendering company and a corresponding accounting period of the claimant company do not coincide, the profits and losses of the overlapping periods must be time-apportioned and group relief is given in respect of the profits or losses as apportioned to the period common to both accounting periods. The procedure to be followed in any such case is:

(a)   time apportion the loss;

(b)   time apportion the profit;

(c)   allow group relief in respect of the lower of (a) and (b).

In this connection, TCA 1997, s 422(2) provides that the amount of the loss (or other deficiency) which may be set off against the total profits of the claimant company for the corresponding accounting period is to be reduced by applying the fraction (if it less than unity):

$$\frac{A}{B}$$

and that the profits against which that loss (or deficiency), as reduced, may be set off is to be reduced by applying the fraction (if it is less than unity):

$$\frac{A}{C}$$

where—
  A   is the length of the period common to the two accounting periods;
  B   is the length of the accounting period of the surrendering company; and
  C   is the length of the corresponding accounting period of the claimant company.

(See also **8.309** regarding the effect on TCA 1997, s 422(2) of companies joining or leaving a group.)

Example 8.308.1

Rodnik Ltd has two wholly owned subsidiaries, Nasir Ltd and Kazhan Ltd. The respective profits and losses of the three companies are as set out below. Kazhan Ltd's loss consists of excess non-trade charges:

	Accounting period	Profit	Loss
		€	€
Rodnik Ltd	1/1/03 - 31/12/03	60,000	
Nasir Ltd	1/1/03 - 31/12/03	120,000	
Kazhan Ltd	1/8/03 - 30/4/04		72,000

The length of the period common to Rodnik Ltd and Kazhan Ltd is five months and the loss of the latter company attributable to this period is €72,000 x 5/9 = €40,000. The profit of Rodnik Ltd attributable to this period is €60,000 x 5/12 = €25,000. Accordingly, Rodnik Ltd may claim €25,000 of the loss of Kazhan Ltd by way of group relief.
The length of the period common to Nasir Ltd and Kazhan Ltd is also five months. The profit of Nasir Ltd attributable to this period is €120,000 x 5/12 = €50,000 so that Nasir Ltd claims €40,000 of the Kazhan Ltd loss. Thus, €65,000 of Kazhan Ltd's loss may be group relieved even though part of its accounting period falls after the accounting periods of the other two companies.
The above feature is an exception to the general group relief rule that only current period losses may be surrendered. This follows from the application of the A/B formula explained above which, in respect of any one group relief claim, merely requires that the surrendering company's loss incurred is to be apportioned on a time basis. Thus, in respect of the claims of Rodnik Ltd and Nasir Ltd, the same loss of €72,000 is apportioned in each case and the only limitation is that the aggregate loss surrendered cannot exceed the loss incurred by Kazhan Ltd.

Group relief (under TCA 1997, s 420) may only be set against the total profits of the claimant company's accounting period that corresponds to the surrendering company's accounting period in which the loss or other deficiency arose. As explained above, these total profits will be time-apportioned if necessary. There can be no carry forward or back by the claimant company of any group relief claimed. The losses or other deficiencies which a surrendering company may surrender in any accounting period are confined to such losses or deficiencies incurred in that accounting period.

A relevant trading loss (a trading loss arising in a trade other than an excepted trade) of a group member may in accordance with TCA 1997, s 420A be set against the relevant trading income (but not against total profits) of another group member, or may be subject to a claim to relief under TCA 1997, s 420B (relief on a value basis against tax on profits other than relevant trading income – see **8.306.3**). As with group relief under TCA 1997, s 420, relief under TCA 1997, s 420A or 420B is to be claimed in respect of income, or tax, of the claimant company's corresponding accounting period. However, TCA 1997, s 422 would appear to have no effect on claims under either TCA 1997, s 420A or 420B. This is because TCA 1997, s 422(2) refers only to the amount that may be set off against "the total profits" of the claimant company whereas such a set-off cannot arise by virtue of a claim under TCA 1997, s 420A or s 420B.

Interestingly TCA 1997, s 420A(5) provides that, in the case of a claim involving a consortium, not only is a relevant trading loss to be reduced by reference to the claimant's share in the consortium but that that reduction is subject to "any further reduction under section 422(2)". The assumption is that s 422(2) applies to s 420A in the first place.

8.309 Companies joining or leaving group or consortium

Group relief is normally available only if the surrendering company and the claimant company are members of the same group (or fulfil the consortium criteria) throughout the whole of the surrendering company's accounting period to which the claim relates and the whole of the corresponding accounting period of the claimant company (TCA 1997, s 423(1)). An accounting period of the claimant company that falls wholly or partly within an accounting period of the surrendering company is a "corresponding accounting period".

Where, however, two companies become or cease at any time to be members of the same group, for group relief purposes (including TCA 1997, s 423(1) – see above) each is to be assumed (unless a true accounting period of the company begins or ends then) to have an accounting period ending and a new one beginning at that time. The new accounting period will then end with the end of the true accounting period (unless before that time there is a further break occasioned by the companies becoming or ceasing to be members of the same group). It is then further to be assumed:

(a) that the losses or other deficiencies of the true accounting period are apportioned to the component accounting periods on a time basis according to their lengths; and

(b) that the amount of total profits of the true accounting period of the claimant company is also so apportioned (ie also on a time basis) to the component accounting periods (TCA 1997, s 423(2)).

Where one company is the surrendering company and the other is the claimant company:

(a) references to accounting periods, profits and losses, allowances, expenses of management, or charges on income of the surrendering company are to be construed in accordance with the above-described rules of TCA 1997, s 423(2) (TCA 1997, s 423(3)(a));

(b) references in TCA 1997 ss 423(1) (see above) and 422 (see **8.308**) to accounting periods are also to be construed in accordance with the rules of TCA 1997, s 423(2) so that, where the two companies are members of the same group in the surrendering company's accounting period, they must also under TCA 1997, s 422 be members of the same group in any corresponding accounting period of the claimant company (TCA 1997, s 423(3)(b));

(c) references in TCA 1997, s 422 to profits, and the amounts to be set off against profits, are also to be construed in accordance with the rules of TCA 1997, s 423(2) so that an amount apportioned under that subsection to a component accounting period may fall to be reduced under TCA 1997, s 422(2), ie the corresponding accounting period rules of TCA 1997, s 422(2) are to be applied as necessary to the component accounting periods (TCA 1997, s 423(3)(c)).

(The above description of TCA 1997, s 423(3) is based on the pre-consolidation wording of that provision which appears to reflect more clearly the intention of the legislation.)

Example 8.309.1

Flint Ltd acquired its wholly owned non-trading subsidiary, Saginaw Ltd, on 1 August 2006. Results for the two companies are as set out below:

	Accounting period	Profit	Excess charges
		€	€
Flint Ltd	1/1/06 – 31/12/06	60,000	
Saginaw Ltd	1/4/06 – 31/3/07		24,000

Of the excess charges of €24,000 incurred by Saginaw Ltd, €16,000 (€24,000 x 8/12) is allocated to its assumed eight-month accounting period 1 August 2006 to 31 March 2007. Of the profit of €60,000 arising to Flint Ltd, €25,000 (€60,000 x 5/12) is allocated to its assumed five-month accounting period 1 August 2006 to 31 December 2006. Having regard to the corresponding accounting period rules of TCA 1997, s 422 (which, as mentioned above, are to be applied to the component accounting periods), the length of the period common to Flint Ltd and Saginaw Ltd is five months and the amount of the excess charges of Saginaw Ltd attributable to this period is €16,000 x 5/8 = €10,000. The profit of Flint Ltd attributable to this period is the €25,000 already apportioned above. Accordingly, Flint Ltd may claim €10,000 of the excess charges of Saginaw Ltd by way of group relief.

Example 8.309.2

Howard Ltd, a non-trading company, acquired two wholly owned subsidiaries, Elmer Ltd and Elba Ltd, on 1 April 2007 and 1 July 2007 respectively. All companies make up accounts to 31 December and the results for the year ended 31 December 2007 are as follows:

	Profit	Excess charges
	€	€
Howard Ltd		72,000
Elmer Ltd	40,000	
Elba Ltd	60,000	

Elmer claims group relief in respect of the excess charges of Howard Ltd. In accordance with TCA 1997, s 423, since an assumed accounting period for both companies commences on 1 April 2007, it is entitled to relief in respect of the smaller of €72,000 x 9/12 = €54,000 and €40,000 x 9/12 = €30,000, ie €30,000.

Elba Ltd also claims group relief in respect of the excess charges of Howard Ltd. Since an assumed accounting period for both companies commences on 1 July 2007, it is entitled to relief in respect of the smaller of €72,000 x 6/12 = €36,000 and €60,000 x 6/12 = €30,000, ie €30,000.

Accordingly, Elmer Ltd and Elba Ltd are entitled to claim €30,000 each by way of group relief.

By reason of TCA 1997, s 428 (exclusion of double allowances – see **8.314**), however, a further restriction applies. Since Howard Ltd was not in group relationship with either Elmer Ltd or Elba Ltd for the three months to 31 March 2007, the aggregate amount of group relief it may surrender, by virtue of TCA 1997, s 428(3), to these companies is restricted to €72,000 x 9/12 = €54,000, whereas a total of €60,000 would have been claimed otherwise. The €54,000 must therefore be divided between the two claimant companies, the division being in accordance with what they themselves decide.

Example 8.309.3

The position is the same as in Example **8.309.2** except that the results for the year ended 31 December 2007 are as set out below. The trade of Elba Ltd is an excepted trade:

	Profit	Excess charges	Trading loss
	€	€	€
Howard Ltd		72,000	
Elmer Ltd	80,000		
Elba Ltd			60,000

Elmer Ltd claims group relief in respect of the excess charges of Howard Ltd and, in accordance with TCA 1997, s 423, is entitled to relief in respect of the smaller of €72,000 x 9/12 = €54,000 and €80,000 x 9/12 = €60,000, ie €54,000.

Elmer Ltd also claims group relief in respect of the trading loss of Elba Ltd and is entitled to relief in respect of the smaller of €60,000 x 6/12 = €30,000 and €80,000 x 6/12 = €40,000, ie €30,000.

As, however, Elmer was not in group relationship with either Howard Ltd or Elba Ltd for the three months to 31 March 2007, the group relief which it may claim is restricted, in accordance with TCA 1997, s 428(4) (see **8.314**), to €80,000 x 9/12 = €60,000, instead of the aggregate amount of €84,000 above. It will be a matter for the companies themselves to agree how the aggregate loss of €60,000 is to be surrendered by the two loss making companies.

The above-described rules also apply in the case of a company joining or leaving a consortium. Where the consortium owned company surrenders a loss or other deficiency to two or more consortium members, the same basis of apportionment must be used for each claim (TCA 1997, s 423(4)).

8.310 Arrangements for transfer of company

8.310.1 Groups

TCA 1997, s 424(3) counters the abuse of group relief where, for example, a parent company cannot, by reason of an insufficiency of profits, benefit from tax losses (attributable to substantial capital allowances available) of a subsidiary and accordingly arranges to transfer the subsidiary to another group which is able to benefit from those losses. The arrangement will include an option enabling the parent to buy back the subsidiary at some time in the future, when its losses have been used up. Where such an arrangement exists, or where the subsidiary may be controlled from outside the group (see **8.302.5**), the subsidiary is treated as having become detached from the group.

TCA 1997, s 424(4) contains similar provisions in relation to trading companies in a consortium situation (see below).

The section provides that a company (*the first company*) is treated as not being a member of the same group as another company (*the second company*) where in an accounting period one of the companies has losses or other reliefs available for surrender under the group relief provisions and arrangements exist by virtue of which, at some time during or after the expiry of that period,

(1) the first company or any "successor" of it could cease to be a member of the same group of companies as the second company and could become a member of the same group of companies as a "third company";

(2) any person has or could obtain, or any persons together have or could obtain, control of the first company, but not of the second; or

(3) a third company could begin to carry on the whole or any part of a trade which, at any time in that accounting period, is carried on by the first company and could do so either as a successor of the first company or as a successor of another company which is not a third company but which, at some time during or after the expiry of that period, has begun to carry on the whole or any part of that trade.

A company is a *successor* of another company if it carries on a trade which, in whole or in part, the other company has ceased to carry on and the circumstances are such that:

(a) TCA 1997, s 400 (company reconstructions without change of ownership – see **4.109**) applies in relation to the two companies as the "predecessor" and the "successor"; or

(b) the two companies are "connected with" each other within the meaning of TCA 1997, s 10 (see **2.3**).

References above to the "the first company" are not confined to a loss making company; TCA 1997, s 424(3)(a) refers to "one of the 2 companies" having trading losses or other amounts eligible for relief so that "the first company" could be a profit making company. A *third company* means, basically, a company which is outside the group to which the loss making company (or the trading company or holding company in a consortium situation) belongs. *Control* has the meaning assigned to it by TCA 1997, s 11 (see **2.402**).

For TCA 1997, s 424 to apply, "arrangements" must exist "by virtue of which" one of the three circumstances described above could result. The section will not apply, therefore, merely because a transfer of shares (the first circumstance) is permitted by a company's articles of association. On the other hand, (see **8.302.5** regarding the decision in the Pilkington case), it would appear that where a person has or could obtain control of one company but not of another (the second circumstance) *is* a result of "arrangements", where control is by virtue of the articles of association.

The fact that the section extends to cases in which one of the three circumstances "could" arise indicates that even the possibility of such an occurrence is taken into account. Thus, at its most literal, the section could be interpreted as applying to a case in which any of the three circumstances could result on the happening of another event, ie that it applies to a situation which is subject to a contingency and is not merely triggered as and when the contingency occurs. For example, the acquisition of shares by a company in another company (which might trigger (1) or (2) above) may be subject to a pre-emption provision prohibiting the shares from being acquired unless the existing shareholders signify an intention to dispose of them. It is suggested that, in practice, such an extreme interpretation is unlikely to be applied in Ireland. It is not, for example, followed in the UK.

As mentioned in **8.304.1** above, it was indicated in *Shepherd v Law Land plc* [1990] STC 795 that where either of the two tests (profit distribution or asset distribution) ceases to be satisfied during an accounting period, group relief as between the two companies concerned may not be availed of from the relevant time. In relation to the UK equivalent of TCA 1997, s 424, it was held in the *Law Land* case that the provision has effect only as long as the "arrangements" in question subsist; as soon as the arrangements no longer exist, the group relationship which had been treated as broken will be restored. The effect of TCA 1997, s 424 does not continue for the part of the accounting period beyond the point at which the arrangements cease to exist.

TCA 1997, s 427(1) defines *arrangements* as arrangements of any kind, whether in writing or not (see also **8.313**). Where arrangements exist, what is relevant is their effect and not their purpose; it does not matter when they originally came into existence as long as they exist at the relevant time (*Pilkington v IRC* [1982] STC 103).

Again, even if arrangements are never implemented, TCA 1997, s 424 may apply to them by reason of their existence alone (*Irving v Tesco Stores (Holdings) Ltd* [1982] STC 881 and *Shepherd v Law Land plc* – see above). Negotiations would not of themselves be sufficient to amount to an arrangement, but an arrangement would probably be created once an offer is accepted on a conditional basis, eg subject to contract, or where a letter of intent is signed, or, where a transaction requires shareholder approval, when such approval is given or when the directors of the company become aware that it will be given.

As seen above, TCA 1997, s 424(3) is concerned with three types of arrangement. The first case, (1) above, involves arrangements which may result in the first company joining another group or in a "successor" of it joining another group.

Example 8.310.1.1

The Pennsauken group is represented as follows:

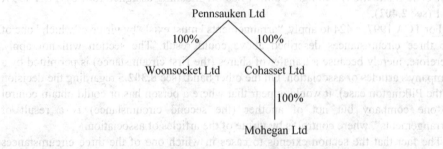

The trade of Cohasset Ltd is transferred to Mohegan Ltd prior to the sale of Mohegan Ltd to Pocasset Ltd, a non-group company (and the "third company"). In the above group, Cohasset Ltd is "the first company" and Mohegan Ltd is the "successor". By reason of the arrangement for the sale of Mohegan Ltd which would involve it becoming a member of the same group as Pocasset Ltd, TCA 1997, s 424 would, in strictness, apply to de-group both Cohasset Ltd and Mohegan Ltd from the Pennsauken group for as long as the arrangement subsisted. This is because Cohasset Ltd, as the first company, will fall to be de-grouped if either it or its successor may be transferred to another group.

In a situation where only Mohegan Ltd may join another group, it does not obviously make sense that Cohasset Ltd as well as Mohegan Ltd should be affected by TCA 1997, s 424. As long as the arrangements subsist, any losses of Cohasset Ltd or of Mohegan Ltd may not be surrendered to Pennsauken Ltd or to Woonsocket Ltd, nor may Cohasset Ltd or Mohegan Ltd claim group relief in respect of any losses of Pennsauken Ltd or Woonsocket Ltd.

In the UK, where there is identical legislation, it is understood that the Inland Revenue would not insist on a de-grouping of Cohasset Ltd where the sale of Mohegan Ltd is not part of the arrangements for the transfer of the trade. The position of the Revenue Commissioners on this point is not known.

The effect of any de-grouping will subsist as long as the "arrangements" are in existence. Thus, once Mohegan Ltd is sold, Cohasset Ltd rejoins the Pennsauken group.

The second case, (2) above, relates to arrangements involving the acquisition of control over a group member and it applies where any persons together have, or could obtain, control of one group member ("the first company") but not of another member ("the second company"). The decision in the *Pilkington* case (see above) would suggest that, for this purpose, those persons need not be acting in concert. Where, for example, shares of a subsidiary are pledged as security under a mortgage or other charge, TCA 1997, s 424 could, in strictness, apply. In the UK, the Inland Revenue would regard [the equivalent of] TCA 1997, s 424 as not applying by reason only of the existence of the mortgage or charge provided the mortgagee's control over the shares is limited to what is necessary to protect his interest. The section would, however, operate on the default or other event giving the mortgagee the right to exercise his rights against the mortgagor. Again, the view of the Revenue Commissioners on this aspect is not known but it is reasonable to suppose that it would not follow the strictest possible interpretation of TCA 1997, s 424.

Another example of the application of the second case of TCA 1997, s 424 would be the situation in which a subsidiary issues preference shares to persons outside its group, carrying voting rights which would result in those persons obtaining control in the event of dividends going into arrear. The mere existence of the preference shares in that case would appear, in strictness, to be sufficient to constitute an "arrangement" whereby the persons concerned could obtain control of the subsidiary, thereby triggering TCA 1997, s 424.

8.3010.2 Consortiums

In a consortium situation, TCA 1997, s 424(4) operates to prevent the trading company concerned (which is owned by the consortium or which is a 90% subsidiary of a holding company owned by the consortium) from surrendering losses or other deficiencies to the consortium members. This will be the case where in any accounting period there are arrangements in existence by virtue of which:

(1)   the trading company or any successor of it could, at some time during or after the expiry of that accounting period, become a 75% subsidiary of a third company;

(2)   any person who owns, or any persons who together own, less than 50% of the ordinary share capital of the trading company has or together have, or could at some time during or after the expiry of that accounting period obtain, control of the trading company;

(3)   any person, other than a holding company of which the trading company is a 90% subsidiary, either alone or together with connected persons, holds or could obtain, or controls or could control the exercise of not less than 75% of the votes which may be cast on a poll taken at a general meeting of the trading company in that accounting period or in any subsequent accounting period; or

(4)   a third company could begin to carry on, at some time during or after the expiry of that accounting period, the whole of any part of a trade which, at any time in that period, is carried on by the trading company and could do so either as a successor of the trading company or as a successor of another company which is not a third company but which, at some time during or after the expiry of that period, has begun to carry on the whole or part of that trade.

Except for the purposes of (4) above, references to the trading company include references to any company of which it is a 90% subsidiary. It will be seen that the four circumstances dealt with in TCA 1997, s 424(4) correspond closely with the three circumstances of TCA 1997, s 424(3). The meanings of "third company", "successor", "connected persons", and "control" are the same for both TCA 1997, s 424(3) and (4).

The above discussion regarding the meaning of "arrangements" also applies equally to both subsections. It will be recalled that, in relation to groups, the wide meaning of the term, strictly construed, could prove to be a considerable restricting factor in relation to group relief claims. In relation to the second circumstance, (2) above, it would seem that any agreement, including an option agreement, between the consortium members providing for a rearrangement of interests in the trading company (or holding company), whereby one or more members owning less than 50% of that company could obtain control of it, would be sufficient to trigger TCA 1997, s 424 and operate to prevent consortium relief claims for the duration of that agreement. In the light of the decision in the *Pilkington* case (see **8.310.1**), where more than one consortium member is involved in this way it is not necessary that they are acting in concert. The Revenue Commissioners have, however, indicated that they would not seek to apply TCA 1997, s 424 in situations in which, by reason of genuine business considerations, provisions are in place which inadvertently result in a group relationship at a later date.

As regards the third circumstance, (3) above, the "connected persons" rule of TCA 1997, s 10(8) (see **2.3**) operates so that any two or more persons acting together to secure or exercise control of a company are treated in relation to that company as connected with each other. This gives rise to particular difficulties of interpretation as regards the scope of TCA 1997, s 424(4).

Example 8.310.2.1

Gansett Ltd, a joint venture trading company, is owned as to 50% each by Eckrium Ltd and Bayard Ltd, which are not otherwise connected. If these two companies are acting together to exercise control over Gansett Ltd, they are connected persons. Since that in turn would mean that Eckrium Ltd, together with Bayard Ltd, would control not less than 75% of the votes which may be cast at a general meeting of Gansett Ltd, the third circumstance of TCA 1997, s 424(4)(b) would apply so that any losses of Gansett Ltd could not be surrendered to either of the other two companies under the consortium provisions.

Clearly, however, this result would defeat the entire purpose of the consortium relief provisions as it is difficult to see how relief could ever be available. The difficulty can only be resolved by regarding the two companies, Eckrium Ltd and Bayard Ltd, as not after all being connected with each other in the above circumstances. Thus, two or more companies together controlling a joint venture company but not otherwise acting "in concert" could be regarded as not connected with each other. In this connection it may be of interest to note, from a published extra statutory concession, that the Inland Revenue would apply the UK equivalent of TCA 1997, s 424(4) in this way.

The situation dealt with in the above example is but one illustration of the difficulty in interpreting the meaning of "acting together" in the context of the connected person rules. It is felt that an Irish court, having regard to the nature and purpose of the consortium relief provisions, might well not regard the consortium members in this example as being connected with each other so as to deny group relief. In practice, the outcome of this question will depend on the particular circumstances in each case, in particular on whether or not there is evidence to show that the shareholders are in fact acting in concert to secure control. The case of *Steele v EVC International NV* [1996] STC 785 was concerned with a situation in which a company was owned as to 50% each by an Italian company and members of a UK group. It was found on the evidence that the company's shareholders were "acting together to secure or exercise control" of the company (see also **2.302.3**).

8.311 Leasing contracts

TCA 1997, s 425 is an anti-avoidance measure relating to capital allowances in respect of machinery or plant purchased for leasing. The section is now practically irrelevant as it relates to schemes involving use of the initial allowance under TCA 1997, s 283 and free depreciation under TCA 1997, s 285 which are no longer in operation other than in excepted cases (see **5.204.3** and **5.205.5**).

The section is directed at schemes typically involving a financial institution which buys machinery which it leases to a loss-making company. The financial institution then claims accelerated allowances in respect of the machinery and, assuming the rental income arising is treated as trading income, sets these allowances against other profits of the period in which the machinery was provided. In the following period, the machinery subject to the lease is transferred to a special purpose subsidiary of the financial institution. As the transfer is within TCA 1997, s 400 (see **4.109**), no balancing charge arises on the disposal. By virtue of a prior arrangement, the loss-making company purchases the shares of the special purpose subsidiary for a discounted price which reflects the benefit of the tax relief obtained by the financial institution. The acquiring company now effectively owns the machinery and its losses are available to shelter profits of the subsidiary.

TCA 1997, s 425, however, provides that losses created by accelerated capital allowances may only be allowed against income from the lease so that they must be carried forward by the financial institution rather than deducted currently.

TCA 1997, s 425(1) provides that:

(a) where a company ("the first company") purchases machinery or plant which it lets to another person by way of a "leasing contract";

(b) apart from TCA 1997, s 425, the first company could claim relief under TCA 1997, s 396(1) or (2) (relief for trading losses other than terminal losses) in respect of losses incurred under the leasing contract; and

(c) in the accounting period for which an allowance under TCA 1997, s 283 or s 285 (see above) in respect of the related expenditure is made to the first company, arrangements are in existence by virtue of which, at some time during or after the expiry of the accounting period, a successor company will be able to carry on any part of the first company's trade which consists of or includes the performance of all or any of the obligations under the leasing contract,

then, in the accounting period mentioned in (c) and in any subsequent accounting period, the first company is not entitled to claim relief under TCA 1997, s 396(1) or (2) except in computing its profits, if any, arising under the leasing contract.

A company is a *successor* to the first company where TCA 1997, s 400 (see **4.109**) applies to the first company and that company as the "predecessor" and "successor" respectively, within the meaning of that section, and the two companies are connected with each other within the meaning of TCA 1997, s 10 (see **2.3**).

For the purposes of TCA 1997, s 425, losses incurred on a leasing contract and profits arising under such a contract are to be computed as if the performance of the leasing contract were a trade begun to be carried on by the first company, separately from any other trade which it may carry on, at the commencement of the letting under the leasing contract.

In determining whether the lessor company would be entitled to claim relief under TCA 1997, s 396(1) or (2), any loss incurred on the leasing contract is to be treated as incurred in a trade carried on by that company separately from any other trade which it may carry on.

TCA 1997, s 427(1) defines *arrangements* as arrangements of any kind, whether in writing or not (see also **8.313**). For the purpose of illustration, the following example assumes that free depreciation is available.

Example 8.311.1

Diamond Trust Bank Ltd, a banking company the activities of which include the leasing of plant and machinery, purchases machinery for €2.5m and leases it to Russ Ltd, an unrelated loss-making company, at a rental of €300,000 payable yearly in advance.

Assuming the circumstances are such that Diamond Trust Bank Ltd is entitled to free depreciation in respect of its capital expenditure on the machinery, it claims capital allowances of €2.5m in the accounting period in which the lease commences. The allowances are first set against the lease income of €300,000, giving rise to an excess allowance of €2.2m. (In the absence of TCA 1997, s 425, the bank would set this excess against its other taxable income.)

In its next accounting period, Diamond Trust Bank Ltd transfers the machinery to Emerald Ltd, a special purpose subsidiary, for €1.95m which is satisfied by the issue of shares at nominal value €1.95m. This gives rise to an overall profit to the bank as follows:

	€
Cost of machinery	2,500,000

Tax relief on excess allowances €2.2m @ 12.5%	275,000
	2,225,000
Lease rental received	300,000
Net cost	1,925,000
Disposal proceeds	1,950,000
Profit on transaction	25,000

As part of a prior arrangement with the bank, Russ Ltd purchases the shares in Emerald Ltd for €1.95m. For an outlay of €2.25m (to include the initial lease rental), Russ Ltd has become the effective owner of machinery worth in the region of €2.5m. It has obtained a cash benefit which, because of its loss position, it could not have obtained through the use of capital allowances. Any continuing losses incurred by Russ Ltd can now be used to shelter the leasing profits of its new subsidiary Emerald Ltd. Even when Russ Ltd returns to making profits, the lease rentals taxable in Emerald Ltd will be cancelled out by an equivalent deduction for rent payable by Russ Ltd.

TCA 1997, s 425 removes the tax advantage that would otherwise arise in this situation by providing that a loss created by excess capital allowances (€2.2m in this case) may only be utilised by way of carry forward against subsequent profits, if any, arising under the leasing contract. On that basis, the arrangement with Russ Ltd could not succeed.

In practice, even if free depreciation were available, a scheme on the above lines would not now be undertaken with a view to creating a benefit of €25,000. TCA 1997 s 425 was introduced at a time not only of accelerated capital allowances but also of much higher tax rates. A corporation tax rate of, say, 45% would have given rise to a profit of €740,000 in these circumstances.

8.312   Partnerships involving companies

TCA 1997, s 426 is an anti-avoidance provision designed to counter abuses arising out of certain partnership situations involving companies. The purpose of the section is to restrict group relief for losses and other deficiencies in respect of a company's share in a partnership profit or loss to cases where that share substantially accrues to or is actually borne by the partner company. The section is directed at schemes in which one partner pays another partner for its right to claim capital allowances or receives compensation for meeting actual losses. In such cases, relief for partnership losses is confined to the partnership trade itself and will not therefore be available to relieve other profits of the partner company.

The provisions of TCA 1997, s 426 apply in relation to a company ("the partner company") which is a member of a partnership carrying on a trade if arrangements exist (whether as part of the terms of the partnership or otherwise) whereby:

(a)   in respect of all or part of the value of the partner company's share in the profits or loss of any accounting period of the partnership, another member of the partnership, or any person connected with another member of the partnership, receives any payment or acquires or enjoys, directly or indirectly, any other benefit in money's worth; or

(b)   in respect of all or part of the cost of the partner company's share in the loss of any accounting period of the partnership, the partner company, or any person connected with that company, receives any payment or acquires or enjoys, directly or indirectly, any other benefit in money's worth, other than a payment in respect of group relief to the partner company by a company which is a member of the same group as the partner company for the purposes of group relief (TCA 1997, s 426(2)).

TCA 1997, s 427(1) defines *arrangements* as arrangements of any kind, whether in writing or not (see also **8.313**). Any question as to whether a person is "connected with" another person is to be determined in accordance with TCA 1997, s 10 – see **2.3**).

Where the provisions of TCA 1997, s 426 apply in relation to the partner company:

(1) the company's share in the loss of the partnership accounting period in question, and its share in any charges on income (within the meaning of TCA 1997, s 243 – see **4.402**) paid by the partnership in that period, may not be set off for the purposes of corporation tax other than against its profits of the several trade (ie, its deemed separate trade by virtue of its membership of the partnership);

(2) other than as in (1), no trading losses are to be available for set-off for the purposes of corporation tax against the profits of the several trade for the partnership accounting period in question; and

(3) other than as in (1) and (2), no amount which would otherwise be available for relief against profits is to be available for set-off for the purposes of corporation tax against so much of the company's total profits as consists of profits of its several trade for the partnership accounting period in question (TCA 1997, s 426(3)).

The provisions of (1) and (2) ensure that the partner company will be unable to use its share of partnership losses or charges to reduce tax in respect of non-partnership profits and will be unable to use non-partnership trading losses to reduce its share of partnership profits. By virtue of (3), the company may not use tax reliefs from non-partnership sources (eg, excess charges, relief for investment in films, relief for research and development) to reduce tax payable on any part of its total profits as consist of profits in respect of its several partnership trade.

Where the partnership profits are chargeable under Case IV or V of Schedule D (see **3.208** and **3.209**), the company's share in the partnership profits or loss is to be treated as if it arose from the carrying on of a several trade of the company and as if any allowance falling to be made by way of discharge or repayment of tax or in charging income under Case V (see **5.105.3**) were an allowance to be made in taxing the profits of the trade (TCA 1997, s 426(4)).

The company's share in the profits or loss of any accounting period of a partnership is the amount determined in accordance with TCA 1997, s 1009 (partnerships involving companies – see **13.701-702**).

TCA 1997, s 426 was enacted at a time of significantly higher company and personal tax rates than are in force today and the tax savings targeted by the provision would accordingly be on a comparatively modest scale as compared with what was formerly the case.

Example 8.312.1

Corinth Ltd and Mr J Monroe carry on business in partnership under the terms of which profits and losses are to be shared equally. Mr Monroe, who is liable to income at the higher rate, formerly carried on business on his own but recently arranged to take Corinth Ltd, a loss-making company, into partnership. Corinth Ltd does not contribute any capital to the partnership.

Arrangements are entered into to the effect that Corinth Ltd agrees to pay 75% of its half share of partnership profits to Mr Monroe.

For a recent accounting period, the partnership profits, as adjusted for tax, are €88,000 of which Corinth Ltd is entitled to €44,000 under the terms of the partnership agreement. Corinth Ltd has incurred a trading loss for the same period and (ignoring TCA 1997, s 426) claims part of that loss against its partnership share of €44,000. As arranged, it then pays €33,000 (€44,000 x 75%) to Mr Monroe.

The position of Corinth Ltd on the above basis is that it has realised a net €11,000 for the year, which exceeds the maximum (undiscounted) tax value of the loss which would otherwise have had to be carried forward – if the loss used could have been used in a later accounting period, it would be worth €5,500 (€44,000 @ 12.5%). It would therefore be better off by at least €5,500 (€11,000 - €5,500) as a result of the arrangement.

The position of Mr Monroe is as follows:

	€
Received from Corinth Ltd	33,000
Tax saving @ 43% on half share of profits €44,000	18,920
	51,920
Less half share of profits ceded to Corinth Ltd	44,000
Gain to Mr Monroe	7,920

The benefit of the arrangement is cancelled by TCA 1997, s 426(3)(b)(ii) (see (2) above) which effectively provides that no trading losses of Corinth Ltd may be set off against the profits of the several partnership trade. It would therefore be liable to corporation tax on €44,000, being its partnership half share, so that the scheme would be ineffective.

In a case where two companies are involved, the potential tax savings (which would have been achievable in the absence of TCA 1997, s 426) are now likely to be no more than marginal.

8.313   Information regarding arrangements

Where a company:

(a)   makes a claim for group relief; or

(b)   being a party to a leasing contract (for the purposes of TCA 1997, s 425 – see **8.311**), claims relief as mentioned in TCA 1997, s 425(1)(b) (ie under TCA 1997, s 396(1) or (2)); or

(c)   being a member of a partnership, claims any relief which, if TCA 1997, s 426(3) applied in relation to it (see **8.312**), it would not be entitled to claim,

and the inspector has reason to believe that any relevant arrangements may exist, or may have existed at any time material to the claim, then at any time after the claim is made he may serve notice in writing on the company requiring it to furnish him, within such time being not less than thirty days from the giving of the notice as he may direct, with—

(i)   a declaration in writing stating whether or not any such arrangements exist or existed at any material time; or

(ii)   such information as he may reasonably require for the purpose of satisfying himself whether or not any such arrangements exist or existed at any material time; or

(iii)   both such a declaration and such information (TCA 1997, s 427(2)).

For this purpose, *relevant arrangements* means, in relation to a claim falling within any of (a) to (c) above, such arrangements as are referred to in the enactment specified in the corresponding provision, ie:

(a)   TCA 1997, s 424(3) or (4) or TCA 1997, s 417(3) (see **8.310** and **8.304.6** respectively);

(b)   TCA 1997, s 425(1)(c) (see **8.311**); or

(c)   TCA 1997, s 426(2) (see **8.312**).

In the case of (a), notice may be served on a company surrendering group relief as well as on the company claiming the relief. In a case within (c), notice may be served on the partners in a partnership.

TCA 1997, s 427(1) defines *arrangements* as arrangements of any kind, whether in writing or not. The term evidently includes arrangements in the form of contractual agreements but is of wider scope. In relation to restrictive trade practices, it has been held to include "the mutual arousal of expectations" (*Re British Basic Slag Ltd's Application* [1963] 1 WLR 727). An arrangement will often and typically consist of a combination of steps for a single purpose but its meaning is not limited to this. Where they exist, what is relevant is their effect and not their purpose; it does not matter when they originally came into existence as long as they exist at the relevant time (*Pilkington v IRC* [1982] STC 103).

8.314   Exclusion of double allowances

Group relief legislation does not restrict claims in respect of any loss or other deficiency to one member of the group. Accordingly, any number of group members may make a group relief claim in respect of the loss or other deficiency of a fellow group member. It is to be expected, therefore, that provision would be made to ensure that relief cannot be given more than once in respect of the same amount.

TCA 1997, s 428 provides for the exclusion of a double allowance in respect of a loss or other deficiency, whether the double allowance would arise by giving group relief more than once or by giving group relief and by giving some other relief (in any accounting period) to the surrendering company. Accordingly, a company may not surrender a trading loss to one or more fellow group members and also carry that loss forward to succeeding accounting periods. Where more than one group member makes a claim for group relief in respect of a loss or other deficiency of another group company, those members may not claim in aggregate more than could have been claimed by a single company whose corresponding accounting period coincided with that of the surrendering company (TCA 1997, s 428(2)).

Example 8.314.1

The following are the results of three members of a group of trading companies:

€

Sunset Ltd – loss for 7 months ended 31 December 2007   700,000

Atholl Ltd – profit for year ended 30 June 2008	2,000,000
Marina Ltd – profits for year ended 31 October 2007	300,000

Group relief claims are made with the following results:

Group relief to Marina Ltd
Common accounting period   1.6.07 – 31.10.07 (5 months)
Loss available (TCA 1997, s 422 – see also **8.308**)

5/7 x €700,000	500,000
Profits eligible for relief	
5/12 x €300,000	125,000
Group relief – lower amount	125,000

Group relief to Atholl Ltd
Common accounting period   1.7.07 – 31.12.07 (6 months)
Loss available

6/7 x €700,000	600,000
Profits eligible for relief	
6/12 x €2,000,000	1,000,000
Group relief – lower amount	600,000
Restricted to (€700,000 – €125,000)	575,000

The maximum relief of €700,000 could of course be allocated on a different basis between the two claimant companies, being a matter for the group to decide on.

If, during some part of a surrendering company's true accounting period, two or more claimant companies do not belong to the same group as the surrendering company, those companies may not between them obtain in all more by way of group relief than would be available to a single claimant company which was not a member of the same group as the surrendering company during that part of the surrendering company's accounting period (but was a member during the remainder of that period (TCA 1997, s 428(3)). Because the situation depicted here involves companies joining or leaving a group, relief will be available in accordance with TCA 1997, s 423(2) and (3). The combined effect of TCA 1997 ss 423 and 428(3) is illustrated in Example **8.309.2**.

Correspondingly, if, during some part of a claimant company's true accounting period, two or more surrendering companies by reference to which the claims are made do not belong to the same group as the claimant company, the claimant company may not obtain in all more by way of group relief for set-off against its profits for the accounting period than it could have obtained if the claim related to a single surrendering company (with unlimited losses or other deficiencies) which was not a member of the same group as the claimant company during that part of the claimant company's accounting period (but was a member during the remainder of that period (TCA 1997, s 428(4)). Because the situation depicted here involves companies joining or leaving a group, relief will be available in accordance with TCA 1997, s 423(2) and (3). The combined effect of TCA 1997 423 and 428(4) is illustrated in Example **8.309.3**.

The provisions of TCA 1997, s 428 apply also in respect of group relief in a consortium situation. As respects a group relief claim made by a company as a member of a consortium, a consortium group relief claim and a group relief claim other than a consortium claim may not both be effective as regards a loss or other deficiency of the same accounting period of the same surrendering company unless each claim relates to a loss or other deficiency apportioned in accordance with TCA 1997, s 423(2)(a) to a component period of the true accounting period (see **8.309**) and the two component periods do not overlap (TCA 1997, s 428(5)(a)).

TCA 1997, s 428(5)(b) provides that consortium claims are to be disregarded in TCA 1997, s 428(3) and (4). In a group situation, two claimant companies may claim to set off the same loss or other deficiency of a surrendering company whereas, in a consortium situation, each company may claim only in respect of its appropriate share of the surrendering company's loss or other deficiency. TCA 1997, s 428(3) and (4) impose an overall limit where two or more companies make claims in respect of one loss (or other deficiency) or where one claimant company makes a claim in respect of more than one loss (or other deficiency). Accordingly, TCA 1997, s 428(3) and (4) are relevant to certain group relief situations but not in a consortium situation.

8.315 Claims and payments for group relief

8.315.1 Claims

A claim for group relief need not be for the full amount available (TCA 1997, s 429(1)(a)). Thus, the claimant company and the surrendering company may decide between themselves how much of any loss or other deficiency is to be surrendered. In practice, this will usually be determined by reference to the quantum of profits available to be reduced by the relief or by reference to the amount of the loss or deficiency available. Even if there is sufficient loss available to cover all of the claimant company's profits, an amount which is less than the amount of those profits may nevertheless be claimed. Although the statutory position is not entirely clear, it is recommended that any group relief claim should be made in respect of a quantified amount, even if the amount stated requires to be adjusted at a later date.

For example, the surrendering company may wish to use some of its loss for the purposes of a TCA 1997, s 396(2) claim, whether against its profits of the current period or against those of the immediately preceding period, leaving the remaining balance to be surrendered to a fellow group member. Again, the surrendering company may decide to carry forward some or all of its trading loss to subsequent accounting period. This might happen, for example, where the surrendering company is less than 100% owned by its immediate parent and the minority shareholder wishes to preserve losses forward to the maximum extent.

A group relief claim must be made within two years from the end of the surrendering company's accounting period to which the claim relates (TCA 1997, s 429(1)(c)). Under the self-assessment regime, the claim will be made by entering the relevant details on the claimant company's corporation tax return.

In this connection, it may seem somewhat anomalous that group relief claims are now required in a return that must be filed within nine months of the end of the relevant accounting period while the statutory deadline for filing such claims is two years from the end the that period. In effect, since the corporation tax returns for both the claimant and the surrendering companies must be filed within nine months, any group relief claim will as a matter of course also be made within that time limit and any decisions regarding the amount to be claimed/surrendered will have been made on behalf of both companies within that time. However, the self-assessment system does not prevent the making of a group relief claim or an amended claim subsequent to the filing of the respective corporation tax returns but within the two-year time limit. An assessment already made on the claimant company on the basis of the return filed may be amended consequent on a group relief claim made within the statutory time limit.

A question may sometimes arise as to whether, after the expiry of the two-year time limit, it is possible to amend or modify a group relief claim already made. In *Farmer v Bankers Trust International Ltd* [1990] STC 564, the taxpayer company lost its case to modify, subsequent to the expiry of the two year time limit, a claim to group relief which it had made within that limit. The modification sought included the substitution of losses of two subsidiaries by the loss of a third subsidiary. It is felt that that decision may be excessively restrictive and that it might not be rigidly applied in Ireland. It may also be considered to be at odds with the general thrust of the *Gallic Leasing* decision which followed (see below).

In relation to the proper form of a group relief claim, in *Gallic Leasing Ltd v Coburn* [1991] STC 699 the company submitted its corporation tax return "subject to group relief", but no further details regarding the claim were provided within the two year time limit. The inspector contended that a valid claim to group relief required an absolute minimum of information, ie the identity of the claimant, the amount of profit against which relief was being claimed, the identity of each surrendering company and the amount and nature of the surrendered amount (the information which is required on a form CT1 in Ireland). Having been unsuccessful in the High Court and the Court of Appeal, the company won its case in the House of Lords where it was held that there was nothing in the relevant UK tax legislation that required a claim to detail the absolute minimum of information referred to above (including the identification of the fellow group members from which losses were to be claimed). Interestingly, it was held that a claim to group relief served no other purpose than to alert the inspector to the fact that reliefs were to be sought. It was considered to be impractical to expect a claimant company, within the two-year time limit, to tie itself to particular amounts in respect of particular reliefs from particular surrendering companies.

The decision in the *Gallic Leasing* case is a clear indication that, at the time of filing a corporation tax return, it is not necessary to be precise concerning the details regarding the amounts and utilisation of any group relief claim to be made. Where these details have still to be worked out, it is recommended that the return should include a statement to the effect that a formal claim will be submitted within the statutory time limit together with the relevant details (although from *Gallic Leasing* it emerges that such details may be furnished even outside that limit).

A claim to group relief requires the consent of the surrendering company notified to the inspector in such form as the Revenue Commissioners may require (TCA 1997, s 429(1)(b)). In practice, notice of consent has for many years been given by letter signed on behalf of the surrendering company but currently, under the self-assessment regime, the consent is signified by way of a simple confirmation in the appropriate place on the corporation tax return. A claim to group relief by a company as a member of a consortium requires the consent of each other member of the consortium, in addition to the consent of the surrendering company.

Although there is a two-year time limit for the making of a claim to group relief, no time limit is prescribed in relation to the notice of consent; the consent requirement is independent from that relating to the claim. It could possibly be argued that, since a claim to group relief requires the consent of the surrendering company, the claim cannot be complete without that consent so that in effect the consent must be notified within the two year time limit also. Nevertheless, the better view is that the notice of consent is not governed by any time limit. While group relief cannot be availed of without the consent of the surrendering company, there is nothing to prevent a claim being made in advance of that consent. Furthermore, in the *Gallic Leasing* case (see above), Lord Oliver of Aylmerton observed (in page 703) that it had been conceded that a consent is not a condition precedent to a claim but only to its acceptance and that the giving of consent is not subject to the mandatory time limit.

On the discovery by the inspector that any group relief given is or has become excessive, he may make an assessment to corporation tax under Case IV of Schedule D in the amount that ought in his opinion to be charged. The inspector may make such other adjustments by way of discharge or repayment of tax or otherwise as may be required where a claimant company has obtained too much relief or a surrendering company has foregone relief in respect of the corresponding period (TCA 1997, s 429(3) and (4)).

8.315.2 Payments for group relief

In relation to losses or other deficiencies surrendered under the group relief provisions, it is common, particularly where there are minority shareholders or where the claim relates to a consortium situation, for the claimant company to make a payment on this account to the surrendering company. A payment for group relief:

(a) is not to be taken into account in computing profits or losses of either the claimant or the surrendering company for corporation tax purposes; and

(b) is not for any purposes of corporation tax to be regarded as a distribution or a charge on income (TCA 1997, s 411(5)).

A *payment for group relief* means a payment made by the claimant company to the surrendering company in pursuance of an agreement between them as respects an amount surrendered by way of group relief, being a payment not exceeding that amount. Where a payment for group relief is made, it will normally equate to the tax value of the loss surrendered. This, however, is not required by the legislation. It is not necessary to make any payment; on the other hand, a payment up to the full amount of the loss or other deficiency may be made.

As to what is the correct tax treatment of a payment not covered by TCA 1997, s 411(5) will not always be clear. Possibly such a payment would have no tax consequences while TCA 1997, s 411(5) merely confirms that position in the case of a payment falling within the subsection. A payment made by a subsidiary to its parent for the surrender of a trading loss and which exceeds the amount surrendered to it could be treated as a distribution under TCA 1997, s 130(2)(b) (see **11.102.3**). A similar payment made by a parent to its subsidiary is not so easily categorised and may in fact have no tax consequence. The fact that TCA 1997, s 411(5)(b) provides, inter alia, that a payment for group relief is not to be regarded as a charge on income would seem to imply that a payment, to the extent that it exceeds the amount surrendered, could be such a charge. The meaning of "charges on income" (see **4.402**), however, does not extend to any payment of this type.

Although a payment for group relief has no tax consequences for either the claimant company or the surrendering company, a payment for group relief which exceeds the tax value of the amount surrendered (and not necessarily an excessive payment) could be categorised as a depreciatory transaction for the purposes of TCA 1997, s 621 (see **9.211**) with the consequence that any loss on a subsequent disposal of the claimant company (or its parent company) could be restricted.

As regards claims under TCA 1997, s 420B (group relief: relief for losses on a value basis), it would seem that TCA 1997, s 411(5) applies to these also so that a payment made by one group company to another in respect of relief obtained is also to be left out of account in computing profits or losses or for any other purpose of corporation tax.

8.316 Late submission of returns: restriction of relief

Where a company fails to deliver a return of income for any accounting period within the time limit prescribed for that purpose, ie nine months after the end of the accounting period, the amount of any group relief being claimed, or the amount of the loss or other deficiency, as the case may be, falls to be restricted by virtue of TCA s 1085.

TCA 1997, s 1085(2)(c) provides that where a company fails to deliver a return of income for an accounting period on or before the "specified return date" (ie, the last day of the period of 9 months commencing on the day immediately following the end of the accounting period), the total amount of the loss referred to in TCA 1997, s 420(1) and the total amount of the excess referred to in TCA 1997, s 420(2), (3) or (6) for the period is to be treated as reduced. If the company whose return is late is the company claiming group relief, the amount of group relief may not exceed 50% of its profits for the period (75% if the return is not more than two months late), subject to a maximum restriction of €158,715 (€31,740 if the return is not more than two months late), as reduced by any relief other than group relief.

If the company whose return is late is the *surrendering* company, the amount of the loss or deficiency is reduced by 50% (25% if the return is not more than two months late), subject to a maximum restriction of €158,715 (€31,740 if the return is not more than two months late).

Similarly, TCA 1997, s 1085(2)(ca) provides that where a company fails to deliver a return of income for an accounting period on or before the specified return date, the total amount of the company's loss or excess referred to in TCA 1997, s 420A(3) for the period is to be treated as reduced by 50% (25% if the return is not more than two months late), subject to a maximum restriction of €158,715 (€31,740 if the return is not more than two months late).

Again, TCA 1997, s 1085(2)(cb) provides that where a company fails to deliver a return of income for an accounting period on or before the specified return date, the total amount of the company's relevant trading loss available for set-off by virtue of TCA 1997, s 420B(2) for the period is to be treated as reduced by 50% (25% if the return is not more than two months late), subject to a maximum restriction of €158,715 (€31,740 if the return is not more than two months late).

In a case where the company that fails to deliver a timely return of income is the company claiming relief under TCA 1997, s 420B, it would seem that there is no requirement to restrict any amount of profits for the purposes of TCA 1997, s 1085; relief in this case is by way of a reduction in tax only.

Example 8.316.1

Seneca Ltd, an Irish resident property rental company, has a wholly owned property rental subsidiary, Metellus Ltd, also resident in Ireland. Both companies make up accounts to 30 April each year. For the year ended 30 April 2007, Seneca Ltd submitted its corporation tax return on 15 April 2008. This return disclosed a deficit of €370,000, being an excess of capital allowances over Case V income, and Case III income of €90,000. Metellus Ltd, which has sufficient profits for the year ended 30 April 2007 to absorb any available losses from Seneca Ltd, makes a claim to group relief in respect of that company's loss.

As provided in TCA 1997, s 421 (see **8.307**), group relief is allowed as a deduction against total profits of the claimant company as reduced by any other relief from tax (other than relief derived from a subsequent period). It is necessary therefore, before considering the group relief position of Seneca Ltd, to deal with its entitlement to claim under TCA 1997, s 308(4). As with group relief claims, a claim under TCA 1997, s 308(4) falls to be restricted where the related corporation tax return is late (TCA 1997, s 1085(2)(a) – see **4.108**). Accordingly, since the return was filed over two months late, the amount of that claim is restricted to 50% of the amount of the profits that would otherwise have been relieved. The TCA 1997, s 308(4) claim therefore reduces the Case III income to €45,000.

In relation to the group relief claim, TCA 1997, s 420(2) provides for relief in respect of a deficiency consisting of excess capital allowances over Case V income. TCA 1997, s 1085(2)(c) provides that the total amount of that loss is to be reduced. That total amount is €370,000.

TCA 1997, s 428 (see **8.314**) is also relevant. It provides, inter alia, that relief is not to be given more than once in respect of the same amount by giving group relief and by giving some other relief (TCA 1997, s 308(4) in this case) to the surrendering company. The total amount of the loss available is, as stated above, €370,000. This amount falls to be restricted by 50% or, if less, by €158,715. The loss is therefore reduced to €211,285 and this is the maximum amount available for the purposes of both TCA 1997 ss 308(4) and 420(2). The amount already claimed under TCA 1997, s 308(4) is €45,000 so that the balance available for group relief purposes is €166,285. For the year ended 30 April 2007 therefore, Metellus Ltd may reduce its profits by €166,285 arising out of its group relief claim.

Where a loss or deficiency is to be restricted (because the tax return of the surrendering company is late), it is the amount of that loss or deficiency itself that is restricted and not necessarily the amount that it is sought to surrender. Accordingly, if the surrendering company has incurred a trading loss that is greater than the amount of the profits in respect of which the group relief claim has been made, it is the amount of the loss arising that is restricted rather than the part of it that is equal to those profits. In certain circumstances that could mean that there would in fact be no restriction as regards the amount of group relief claimed. The restriction in TCA 1997, s 1085(2)(c) applies to "the total amount of the loss" referred to in TCA 1997, s 420(1) and the reference in that subsection is simply to the loss incurred by the surrendering company.

Chapter 9

Companies' Capital Gains and Company Reconstructions

9.1 THE CHARGE TO TAX ON CAPITAL GAINS

9.101 Introduction
9.102 Capital gains tax principles
9.103 Development land gains
9.104 Recovery of capital gains tax
9.105 Double tax relief
9.106 Exit charge

9.101 Introduction

Except for disposals of development land on or after 28 January 1992, an Irish resident company is liable to corporation tax, rather than capital gains tax, on any chargeable gains realised by it. Similarly, a non-resident company is liable to corporation tax in respect of chargeable gains on disposals of certain assets, eg land and buildings in the State, minerals in the State or rights or interests relating to mining or minerals, and unquoted shares deriving their value or the greater part of their value from those assets.

Corporation tax is charged in respect of chargeable gains on an amount which, if charged at the current rate of corporation tax, would produce an amount of tax equal to the amount of capital gains tax which would be payable if the gain were subject to capital gains tax rules. Based on a standard corporation tax rate of 28%, a chargeable gain would accordingly be included in profits subject to corporation tax at 20/28ths of the gain.

For corporation tax purposes, "profits" means income and chargeable gains and "chargeable gains" has the same meaning as in the Capital Gains Tax Acts but does not include a gain accruing on a disposal made before 6 April 1976. Taxpayers other than companies are liable to capital gains tax in respect of chargeable gains while companies are liable to corporation tax in respect of such gains. Taxes Consolidation Act 1997 (TCA 1997), s 21(3) provides that a company "shall not be chargeable to capital gains tax in respect of gains accruing to it so that it is chargeable in respect of them to corporation tax" (ie, is not to be chargeable to capital gains tax in respect of the gains if it is chargeable to corporation tax in respect of them). There is one exception to this. "Chargeable gains" does not include any chargeable gain accruing on a "relevant disposal", ie disposals of "development land" within the meaning of TCA 1997, s 648. In respect of any such disposal, a company is within the charge to capital gains tax rather than corporation tax. It is provided in TCA 1997, s 649(1) that "a company shall not be chargeable to corporation tax in respect of chargeable gains accruing to it on relevant disposals". Accordingly, such gains are not regarded as profits of the company for the purposes of corporation tax but are instead chargeable to capital gains tax. The position of a company in respect of development land gains is the same as for other taxpayers and the capital gains tax provisions regarding the computation of chargeable gains on disposals of development land, the tax returns required, and the time for payment of the resulting tax, apply to a company as they apply to any other person.

In arriving at the amount of a chargeable gain accruing to a company, the computation is carried out in accordance with the rules of the Capital Gains Tax Acts as they apply for the purposes of computing chargeable gains for any other taxpayers. TCA 1997, s 78(5) provides that, except as otherwise provided by the Corporation Tax Acts, chargeable gains and allowable losses are to be computed for corporation tax purposes in accordance with the principles applying for capital gains tax and that all questions as to the amounts which are or are not to be taken into account as chargeable gains or as allowable losses, or in computing gains or losses, or which are to be charged to tax as a person's gain, and all questions as to the time when any such amount is to be treated as accruing, are to be determined in accordance with the provisions relating to capital gains tax as if accounting periods were years of assessment.

Any reference to income tax or to the Income Tax Acts in enactments relating to capital gains tax is, in the case of a company, to be construed as a reference to corporation tax or to the Corporation Tax Acts (TCA 1997, s 78(6). There are two exceptions to this provision:

(a)   TCA 1997, s 554(2) provides that, in a case not involving a trade or profession, there is to be excluded from the sums allowable as a deduction from the consideration in computing a chargeable gain any expenditure which would be allowable as a deduction in computing a trading profit or loss for income tax purposes if a trade were being carried on. The intention is to allow only expenditure of a capital nature. In this context, as is to be expected, TCA 1997, s 78(6) does not operate to substitute a reference to corporation tax for a reference to income tax;

(b)   Capital gains tax provisions which apply only to individuals are not to apply to companies for corporation tax purposes.

Although the rates of corporation tax and capital gains tax at any time may differ, the method by which chargeable gains of a company are included in profits chargeable to corporation tax is such that the amount of tax payable will be the same as it would have been had the company been liable to capital gains tax. The approach is to include the chargeable gain, computed in accordance with capital gains tax principles, at an amount such that tax on that amount at the corporation tax rate applying will be the same as the tax that would have been produced by applying the current capital gains rate to the chargeable gain.

Example 9.101.1

Details of income and chargeable gains of Zabriskie Ltd for the year ended 31 December 2007 are as follows:

	€
Case I	50,000
Case III	30,000
Case V	25,000
Chargeable gains	76,000
Computation:	
Income	105,000
Chargeable gains €76,000 @ 20/12.5 =	121,600
Profits	226,600
Corporation tax @ 12.5% =	28,325

The computation of chargeable gains for corporation tax purposes is provided for in TCA 1997, s 78. That section provides that, for a company with chargeable gains, the amount of capital gains tax in respect of those gains is calculated as if the company were liable to capital gains tax and as if accounting periods were years of assessment. TCA 1997, s 31 provides that capital gains tax is to be charged on the total amount of chargeable gains accruing in the year of assessment after deducting any allowable losses accruing in that year and, so far as not already allowed in any previous year, allowable losses accruing in any previous year of assessment, but not for any year prior to 1974/75. For companies, the reference to allowable losses is to be read as referring to "relevant allowable losses", which means any allowable losses accruing to a company in an accounting period and any allowable losses accruing to the company while it was within the charge to corporation tax and so far as not allowed as a deduction from chargeable gains accruing in any previous accounting period (TCA 1997, s 78(2)).

While chargeable gains of a company are computed for the accounting periods in which the gains arose, the year of assessment in which any gain arises must be taken into account. Except at a time when the rates of capital gains tax and corporation tax are the same, it is necessary to ascertain the amount of capital gains tax which would have been payable by the company had that tax applied in order to compute the amount of the chargeable gain to be included in profits. The capital gains tax amount is arrived at by applying the capital gains tax rate in force for the year of assessment in which the chargeable gain arose. For the purpose of applying the appropriate multiplier in calculating the indexed cost, it is also necessary to identify the year of assessment in which the asset disposed of was acquired.

Having ascertained the amount of capital gains tax which *would* be payable (if capital gains tax applied), the amount to be included in the profits of the company for the accounting period as chargeable gains is the amount which if charged at the standard rate of corporation tax would produce an amount equal to the amount of capital gains tax. That procedure is implicit in Example **9.101.1** and is illustrated using the same facts in the following example.

Example 9.101.2

	€
Corporation tax as in Example **9.101.1**	28,325
Corporation tax on income:	
€105,000 @ 12.5% =	13,125
Therefore corporation tax on chargeable gains	15,200
Corporation tax on chargeable gains (TCA 1997, s 78):	
Chargeable gains	76,000
Capital gains tax @ 20% =	15,200
Amount which would produce corporation tax of €15,200:	
€15,200 x 100/12.5 =	121,600
Corporation tax thereon @ 12.5% =	15,200

Where the accounting period of a company falls into two financial years for which there are different rates of corporation tax, the corporation tax rate applied to the chargeable gains accruing in that accounting period is the rate calculated by the formula:

$$\frac{(A \times C)}{E} + \frac{(B \times D)}{E}$$

where—

A   is the rate for the first financial year;

B   is the rate for the succeeding financial year;

C   is the length of the part accounting period falling within the first financial year;

D   is the length of the part accounting period falling within the succeeding financial year; and

E   is the length of the accounting period.

Example 9.101.3

Assume the facts are the same as in Examples **9.101.1** and **9.101.2** except that the accounting period is the year ended 31 March 2003, a period during which there was a change in the corporation tax rate.

Rate of corporation tax:

$$\frac{(16 \times 9)}{12} + \frac{(12.5 \times 3)}{12} = 15.125\%$$

		€	€
Chargeable gain: €76,000 x 20/15.125 =			100,496
Corporation tax on chargeable gain:			
Period 1.4.02 – 31.12.02 €100,496 x 9/12 @ 16% =		12,059	
Period 1.1.03 – 31.3.03 €100,496 x 3/12 @ 12.5% =		3,141	15,200

It will be seen from these examples that the amount of tax payable is the same regardless of the corporation tax rate.

Where an accounting period falls into two years of assessment for which there are different rates of capital gains tax, the procedure is as already outlined: ascertain the amount of capital gains tax which would be payable if capital gains tax applied, using the capital gains tax rate appropriate for each year of assessment, and calculate the amount which, if charged at the rate of corporation tax then in force, would produce an amount equivalent to the amount of capital gains tax. In the following example, there are two capital gains tax rates and two corporation tax rates in operation.

Example 9.101.4

As in Example **9.101.3**, the chargeable gain arising in the year ended 31 March 2003 is €76,000. The capital gains tax rate for the year 2002 is 20% and it is *assumed* for the purposes of this example that the rate for the year 2003 is 25%. €40,000 of the gains arose in respect of disposals in the year 2002 and €36,000 in the year 2003.

	€	€
Chargeable gains 2002	40,000	
Capital gains tax @ 20% =	8,000	
Amount which would produce corporation tax of €8,000:		
€8,000 x 100/15.125 =		52,893
Chargeable gains 2003	36,000	
Capital gains tax @ 25% =	9,000	

Amount which would produce corporation tax of €9,000:

€9,000 x 100/15.125 =	59,504
Chargeable gains included in profits	112,397
Corporation tax @ 15.125% =	17,000

The result is as it would be had capital gains tax applied:

2002 €40,000 @ 20% =	8,000
2003 €36,000 @ 25% =	9,000
	17,000

The application by TCA 1997, s 78 of capital gains tax rules for corporation tax purposes is not affected in its operation by reason of the fact that capital gains tax and corporation tax are distinct taxes (TCA 1997, s 78(7)). Capital gains tax rules, so far as is consistent with any enactments relating to corporation tax, apply as if the two taxes were one tax. In particular, any matter in a case involving two individuals which is relevant to both of them in relation to capital gains tax will in a similar case involving an individual and a company be relevant to the individual in relation to capital gains tax and to the company in relation to corporation tax. For example, in the case of an acquisition of an asset by a company from an individual who is connected with the company, for the purposes of corporation tax on chargeable gains the acquisition will be deemed to be for a consideration equal to the market value of the asset, while for the purposes of capital gains tax the disposal will also be deemed to be for a consideration equal to that market value.

Where assets of a company are vested in a liquidator, the application by TCA 1997, s 78 of capital gains tax rules is to apply as if the assets were vested in, and the acts of the liquidator in relation to the assets were acts of, the company (see **12.901.3**). Consequently, acquisitions from or disposals to the liquidator by the company are disregarded and any such disposals will not give rise to a chargeable gain or allowable loss.

TCA 1997, s 552(3)(a) provides for the allowability in certain circumstances of interest charged to capital by a company. The sums allowable under TCA 1997, s 552(1) for the purposes of computing a chargeable gain or allowable loss include, in the case of a company, the amount of interest charged to capital other than the amount of such interest which has been taken into account for the purposes of relief under the Income Tax Acts or could have been so taken into account but for an insufficiency of income, profits or gains. Interest charged to capital is allowable where:

(a) a company incurs capital expenditure on the construction of a building, structure or works where that expenditure is deductible under TCA 1997, s 552(1) in computing a chargeable gain or allowable loss on the disposal of that building, structure or works or of any asset comprising it;

(b) the expenditure was defrayed out of borrowed money;

(c) the company charged to capital all or part of the interest on that borrowed money referable to a period ending on or before the disposal; and

(d) the company is chargeable to capital gains tax in respect of the gain.

Since interest is deductible as above only where the company is chargeable to capital gains tax, the deduction provided for here is available only in cases of disposals of development land since in all other cases a company is subject to corporation tax and not capital gains tax. Furthermore, TCA 1997, s 552(3)(b) states that "subject to paragraph (a), no payment of interest shall be allowable as a deduction under this section". However, TCA 1997, s 553 permits a deduction for capitalised interest in the case of a company subject to corporation tax. Its terms are practically identical with those of TCA 1997, s 552(3)(a). The section is as follows:

Where

(a)   a company incurs expenditure on the construction of any building, structure or works, being expenditure allowable as a deduction under section 552 in computing a gain accruing to the company on the disposal of the building, structure or work, or of any asset comprising it, and

(b)   that expenditure was defrayed out of borrowed money, and

(c)   the company charged to capital all or any of the interest on that borrowed money referable to a period or part of a period ending on or before the disposal,

the sums so allowable shall, notwithstanding section 552(3)(b), include the amount of that interest charged to capital.

Whereas TCA 1997, s 552(3)(a) requires the capitalisation of interest "referable to a period ending on or before the disposal", the equivalent wording in TCA 1997, s 553 is "referable to a period or part of a period ending on or before the disposal". Thus, if a company disposes of a building during an accounting period, any interest on borrowings to meet the expenditure on the construction of that building which was capitalised in any accounting period prior to the disposal, or in the part of the current accounting period up to the date of the disposal, is to be included in the sums deductible in computing the chargeable gain or allowable loss on the disposal. TCA 1997, s 552(3) does not refer to interest capitalised for part of a period but this is not necessary; as accounting periods are not involved, the time from the end of the last year of assessment to the date of the disposal is a "period" for this purpose.

The deduction for interest capitalised by a company is available only in connection with the construction, and not for the mere acquisition, of a building, structure or works.

9.102   Capital gains tax principles

9.102.1   Introduction

Capital gains tax legislation is contained in the Capital Gains Tax Acts, ie the enactments relating to capital gains tax in TCA 1997 and in any other enactment. The tax was introduced by the Capital Gains Tax Act 1975, which provided for the taxation of capital gains on disposals of assets on or after 6 April 1974.

9.102.2   Persons chargeable and geographical scope

The charge to capital gains tax applies to individuals, trusts, unincorporated bodies and (in the case of development land gains) companies, while companies are chargeable to corporation tax in respect of chargeable gains other than in respect of development land. TCA 1997, s 78 provides that, for a company with chargeable gains, the amount of capital gains tax in respect of those gains is calculated as if the company were liable to capital gains tax and as if accounting periods were years of assessment. It provides that chargeable gains and allowable losses are to be computed for corporation tax purposes in accordance with the principles applying for capital gains tax and that all questions as to the amounts which are or are not to be taken into account as chargeable gains or as allowable losses, or in computing gains or losses, or which are to be charged to tax as a person's gain, are to be determined in accordance with the provisions relating to capital gains tax as if accounting periods were years of assessment. Accordingly, TCA 1997, s 29, which deals with the circumstances in which certain persons are chargeable to capital gains tax, can be read as applying to companies as well as to other persons. The expression *chargeable period* is used here to denote a year of assessment or an accounting period.

A person who is resident in the State for a chargeable period is chargeable to capital gains tax on chargeable gains made on the disposal of assets wherever situated. A person who is not resident in the State is chargeable to capital gains tax for a chargeable period in respect of gains accruing to him in that period on the disposal of:

(a)   land (including buildings) in the State;

(b)   minerals (as defined in the Minerals Development Act 1940, s 3 – see **3.107.1**) in the State or any rights, interests or other assets in relation to mining or minerals or the searching for minerals;

(c)   assets situated in the State which, at or before the time when the chargeable gains accrued, were used in or for the purposes of a trade carried on by him in the State through a branch or agency, or which at or before that time were used or held or acquired for use by or for the purposes of the branch or agency;

(d)   exploration or exploitation rights in a designated area;

(e)   unquoted shares deriving their value or the greater part of their value directly or indirectly from such assets as are described in (a), (b) or (d) above (TCA 1997, s 29(1), (3), (6)).

A company not resident in the State is not subject to corporation tax unless it carries on a trade in the State through a branch or agency (TCA 1997, s 25(1)). Where a non-resident company does in fact carry on a trade through an Irish branch or agency, it is chargeable to corporation tax on all its chargeable profits wherever arising. In this connection, the definition of "chargeable profits" includes such chargeable gains as would be subject to capital gains tax in the case of a non-resident company (see also **3.107.1**).

The kinds of disposals which can result in a non-resident company being liable to corporation tax in respect of chargeable gains, as detailed in (a) to (e) above, include disposals of exploration or exploitation rights in a designated area. *Exploration or exploitation rights* is as defined in TCA 1997, s 13(1) and means rights to assets produced by exploration or exploitation activities or to interests in or to the benefit of such assets. *Exploration or exploitation activities* are activities carried on in connection with the exploration or exploitation of so much of the sea-bed and sub-soil and their natural resources as are situated in the State or in a designated area. A *designated area* is an area designated by order under the Continental Shelf Act 1968 s 2.

The geographical scope of corporation tax, as well as income tax, in relation to exploration or exploitation activities and rights is extended by TCA 1997, s 13(1) (as applied by TCA 1997, s 23 for corporation tax) and by TCA 1997, s 29(6) in relation to capital gains tax. Profits or gains from exploration or exploitation activities carried on in a designated area are treated as profits or gains from activities in the State and profits or gains from exploration or exploitation rights are treated as profits or gains from property in the State.

TCA 1997, s 13(2) effectively treats the designated areas as part of the State for corporation tax and for capital gains tax purposes. TCA 1997, s 25(2)(b) subjects to corporation tax the chargeable gains of a non-resident company which would be subject to capital gains tax were it not for the fact that the company is subject to corporation tax. TCA 1997, s 29(6) treats gains of a non-resident company on the disposal of exploration or exploitation rights in a designated area as gains on the disposal of assets situated in the State: this brings such gains within the scope of TCA 1997, s 25(2)(b). TCA 1997, s 29(7) treats gains accruing to a person who is not resident and not ordinarily resident in the State on the disposal of assets in (b) or (d) above as gains accruing on the disposal of assets used for the purposes of a trade carried on by that person in the State through a branch or agency. The effect of this provision, as indicated by the Revenue, is that an Irish resident agent of such a non-resident person may be charged to capital gains tax on those gains. It is not obvious, however, that such a provision is necessary for this purpose; TCA 1997, s 1034 provides *inter alia* that a non-resident person may be assessed to tax in the name of any agent, branch or manager on the same basis as if the person were resident in the State.

A gain on the disposal of unquoted shares is subject to capital gains tax in the case of a person not ordinarily resident in the State where the shares derive the greater part of their value from:

(a)   land or buildings in the State;

(b)   minerals in the State or any rights, interests or other assets in relation to mining or minerals or the searching for minerals; or

(d)   exploration or exploitation rights in a designated area (TCA 1997, s 29(1)).

For a non-resident company carrying on a trade in the State through a branch or agency, such gains are accordingly chargeable to corporation tax (TCA 1997, s 25(2)(b)). TCA 1997, s 29(1) effectively provides that a gain on the disposal of shares *"deriving* their value or the greater part of their value" from the above mentioned kinds of assets (for convenience, referred to here as "specified assets") is subject to capital gains tax in the hands of a non-resident. This must mean that the shares are so chargeable where they derive their value or the greater part of their value at the time of disposal. Thus, a company whose main asset was Irish based property might dispose of that property and reinvest the proceeds in quoted shares. If shares in the company owned by a non-resident are later disposed of, no part of the value of those shares would be derived from the property at the time of sale. The fact that the shares derived their value from the property at some time in the past, even where the value of the shares at the disposal date is indirectly attributable to an appreciation in the value of the property formerly held, does not result in those shares deriving their value from that property at the time they are disposed of.

For further comments on the question of shares deriving their value from land in the State see **3.107.1** and Examples **3.107.1.1** and **3.107.1.2**.

9.102.3 Chargeable gains, allowable losses and indexation

Chargeable gains

TCA 1997, s 28 provides that tax is to be charged in accordance with the Capital Gains Tax Acts in respect of "capital gains", that is, in respect of "chargeable gains" computed in accordance with those Acts and "accruing to a person on the disposal of assets". No definition is given as to what for this purpose constitutes a gain of a "capital" nature. That capital gains tax legislation is confined to capital gains is a matter to be inferred from the provisions of the legislation. In principle, all chargeable gains arising on disposals of assets, and as computed according to capital gains tax rules, are chargeable to capital gains tax unless exempted by an express provision to the contrary.

A chargeable gain, if any, arising on the disposal of an asset is computed as the excess of the consideration receivable for the disposal over the aggregate of the permitted deductions comprising

(a)   the amount or value of the consideration in money or money's worth given wholly and exclusively for the acquisition of the asset, together with the incidental costs of the acquisition or, if the asset was not acquired by the person disposing of it, any expenditure wholly and exclusively incurred in providing the asset;

(b)   any additional expenditure, indexed as appropriate, incurred in enhancing the value of the asset ("enhancement" expenditure), being expenditure reflected in the state or nature of the asset at the time of disposal, and any expenditure wholly and exclusively incurred in establishing or preserving title to the asset; and

(c)   any incidental costs of disposal (TCA 1997, s 552(1)).

As regards enhancement expenditure, it was common ground in the case of *Chaney v Watkis* 58 TC 707 that the payment of a sum of money by a landlord to a protected tenant to obtain vacant possession of the property in question, and thereby to increase the value of the landlord's interest in the property, could be qualifying enhancement expenditure. The view of the Revenue Commissioners is that where a freeholder or superior leaseholder pays a sum to his lessee for the surrender of the lease, the sum paid is expenditure allowable under Section 552(1). No apparent distinction is made between the case in which a property is acquired with a protected tenant and the case in which the owner of a property creates a lease and later pays a sum of money to the lessee obtain vacant possession.

The incidental costs of acquiring or disposing of the asset consists of expenditure wholly and exclusively incurred for the purposes of the acquisition or disposal, being fees, commission or remuneration paid for the professional services of any surveyor, valuer, auctioneer, accountant, agent or legal adviser and costs of transfer or conveyance (including stamp duty), together with –

(i)   in the case of the acquisition of an asset, costs of advertising to find a seller, and

(ii)   in the case of a disposal, costs of advertising to find a buyer and costs reasonably incurred in making any valuation or apportionment required for the purposes of the capital gains tax computation arising from the disposal, including in particular expenses reasonably incurred in ascertaining market value where required for those purposes.

In computing the chargeable gain, if any, on the disposal of an asset held by a company on 6 April 1974 (the commencement date for capital gains tax), the cost of acquisition is assumed to be the market value of that asset as held on that date (TCA 1997, s 556(3)). This assumed cost is indexed by reference to the multiplier for the tax year of the disposal as determined by reference to the indexation multiplier appropriate to an acquisition in the year 1974-75. Only additional expenditure incurred in enhancing the value of the asset (or in establishing or preserving title to it) incurred after 5 April 1974 (indexed as appropriate) is brought into the capital gains tax computation.

The 6 April 1974 market value rule does not, however, apply if as a result of applying that rule—

(a)   a gain would accrue on the disposal and either a smaller gain or a loss would accrue otherwise; or

(b)   a loss would accrue on the disposal and either a smaller loss or a gain would accrue otherwise (TCA 1997, s 556(4)).

In either event, the gain or loss is computed without regard to the 6 April 1974 market value rule. If, however, as a result of applying TCA 1997, s 556(4) itself, a loss would be substituted for a gain or a gain would be substituted for a loss, it is to be assumed that the asset in question was acquired by the owner for a consideration such that neither a gain nor a loss accrued to him on making the disposal. In other words, the disposal is deemed to have been made on a no gain/no loss basis.

Indexation

Indexation relief, which was introduced to ensure that only real, as opposed to inflationary, gains would be subject to tax, has been part of the capital gains tax system since 1978. The relief is fundamentally restricted as respects disposals made after 31 December 2003. For disposals made on or after 1 January 2004, deductible expenditure incurred in the year 2003 and subsequent years is not indexed, nor is any earlier deductible expenditure further indexed (2002 accordingly being the latest year for which indexation applies), so that theoretical gains attributable to the effect of inflation after the year 2002 are fully taxable.

For capital gains tax purposes, the cost, or deemed cost, of an asset is multiplied by an indexation factor in arriving at the amount deductible as cost in the computation of the chargeable gain (TCA 1997, s 556(2)). Indexation does not apply in the case of a disposal.

(a)   if as a result of applying it a gain would accrue on the disposal and either a smaller gain or a loss would accrue otherwise; or

(b)   if as a result of applying it a loss would accrue on the disposal and either a smaller loss or a gain would accrue otherwise (TCA 1997, s 556(4)).

In either event, the gain or loss is computed without regard to the indexation rule. If, however, as a result of applying TCA 1997, s 556(4) itself, a loss would be substituted for a gain or a gain would be substituted for a loss, it is to be assumed that the asset in question was acquired by the owner for a consideration such that neither a gain nor a loss accrued to him on making the disposal. In other words, the disposal is deemed to have been made on a no gain/no loss basis.

Indexation does not apply in respect of any expenditure incurred in the twelve months immediately preceding the date of disposal. The indexation factor, or "multiplier", is determined by dividing the Consumer Price Index (CPI) number appropriate to the tax year in which the relevant disposal takes place by the corresponding CPI number appropriate to the tax year in which the expenditure was incurred. The multiplier used for indexing any additional allowable expenditure subsequent to the acquisition of the asset is calculated in the same way, the divisor being the CPI number appropriate to the tax year in which the enhancement expenditure was incurred. The CPI number appropriate to any tax year is the number published for the mid-February date immediately before the beginning of that year.

The Revenue Commissioners make regulations annually specifying the indexation multipliers to be used for disposals of assets made in the current year. Thus, Capital Gains Tax (Multipliers) (2003) Regulations (SI 12/2003) sets out the multipliers to be used, for disposals of assets in the year 2003 (and in fact in all subsequent years since no expenditure for any year after 2002 is indexed), to index the cost of acquisition or other allowable expenditure incurred in any of the years 1974-75 to 2002. For the purpose of calculating the multipliers, the CPI numbers used are those expressed on the basis that the CPI at mid-November 1968 is 100 (CGT(A)A 1978 s 3(7)).

Allowable losses

The disposal of an asset may result in an allowable loss rather than a chargeable gain. In principle, an allowable loss is calculated in the same way as a chargeable gain (TCA 1997, s 546(2)), but with the exception that the indexation adjustment may not create or increase the amount of the loss. In certain cases, the capital gains tax computation using indexation will result in a negative amount while the unindexed amount will be positive. In any such case, the disposal is treated as if it gave rise neither to a chargeable gain nor to an allowable loss (see below).

TCA 1997, s 4(1) provides that an "allowable loss" does not include, for the purposes of corporation tax in respect of chargeable gains, a loss accruing to a company in such circumstances that if a gain accrued the company would be exempt from corporation tax in respect of it. Furthermore, TCA 1997, s 546(3) provides that the provisions of the Capital Gains Tax Acts which distinguish gains that are chargeable gains from those that are not, or which make part of a gain a chargeable gain and part not, are to apply also to distinguish losses that are allowable losses from those that are not, and to make part of a loss an allowable loss and part not.

The gain taxable for any accounting period of a company is the net chargeable gain, being the aggregate of the chargeable gains realised by the company in that period reduced by its allowable losses, if any (TCA 1997, s 31). Where the allowable losses for any period exceed the chargeable gains for the same period, the excess losses are carried forward for set off against chargeable gains of the following period and, if necessary, for succeeding periods until the losses are used up. There are particular rules for the treatment of development land gains (see below).

Subject to other provisions of the Capital Gains Tax Acts, and in particular to TCA 1997, s 540 (options – see below), where an asset is entirely lost, destroyed, dissipated or extinguished, that is to constitute a disposal of the asset whether or not any capital sum is received on that account by way of compensation (TCA 1997, s 538(1)).

Negligible value

Where, on a claim by the owner of an asset, the inspector is satisfied that the value of an asset has become negligible, he may allow the claim and the provisions of the Capital Gains Tax Acts are to have effect as if the claimant had sold and immediately re-acquired the asset for a consideration equal to the value specified in the claim (TCA 1997, s 538(2)). An asset whose value has become negligible may be difficult to dispose of and this provision is intended to facilitate the owner to claim a capital gains tax loss in respect of the loss in the value of the asset as if it had been sold off. The agreement of the inspector is necessary in establishing negligible value. The wording of TCA 1997, s 538(2), taken literally, appears to fix the period for which the negligible value claim is to have effect as the period in which the inspector allows the claim. A more reasonable interpretation, whereby the claim should have effect for the period in which the claim was made, has been held to be permissible (*Williams v Bullivant* [1983] STC 107).

Where a person makes a negligible value claim in respect of a holding of shares in a company which has been dissolved and the person becomes entitled to assets of the company by way of Ministerial waiver, on or after 12 February 1998, under section 31 of the State Property Act 1954, the loss arising to that person cannot be utilised for capital gains tax purposes until such time as the assets are disposed of. TCA 1997, s 538(2A)(a) provides that, where as a result of the dissolution of a body corporate, property of that body corporate becomes property of the State by virtue of Part III of the State Property Act 1954, and the Minister for Finance in accordance with that Part waives the State's right to that property in favour of a person who holds or has held shares in the body corporate, any allowable loss accruing to the person by virtue of a negligible value claim made in respect of those shares will not be allowable as a deduction from chargeable gains in the year of assessment earlier than the year in which the property is disposed of by the person. This restriction applies in the case of a company with no share capital as if references to shares included references to any interest in the company possessed by its members.

For the purposes of TCA 1997, s 538(2A)(a), in the case of a part disposal (within the meaning of TCA 1997, s 534 – see **9.102.8**) of property (ie, shares or an interest in a company), the allowable loss is restricted to a proportionate part of the loss claimed. That part is the part which bears to the amount of the loss claimed the same proportion as the market value, when acquired, of the part of the property which is disposed of bears to the market value of the whole of that property when acquired (TCA 1997, s 538(2A)(c)).

Disposals deemed to be made at market value

In the case of a gift or other transaction involving a transfer of an asset on a non-arm's length basis, so that the person acquiring the asset does not pay its full open market price, the asset is deemed to have been disposed of at its market value at the date of the gift or other transaction (TCA 1997, s 547 – see **9.102.14**).

9.102.4   Rate of capital gains tax

The rate of capital gains tax with effect from 3 December 1997 is 20%, having been 40% up to 2 December 1997 (TCA 1997, s 28(3)). The 40% rate was initially retained for disposals of development land but with effect from 23 April 1998 was reduced to 20% for certain development land disposals (see **9.103.4**). It has already been seen in **9.101** that, apart from a time when the rates of capital gains tax and corporation tax are the same, it is necessary to ascertain the amount of capital gains tax which would have been payable by the company had that tax applied in order to compute the amount of the chargeable gain to be included in profits. The capital gains tax amount is arrived at by applying the capital gains tax rate in force for the year of assessment in which the chargeable gain arose. It is also necessary to identify the years of assessment in which the gain arose and in which the asset disposed of was acquired for the purpose of applying the appropriate factor in calculating the indexed cost.

After calculating the amount of capital gains tax which would be payable (if capital gains tax applied), the amount to be included in the profits of the company for the accounting period as chargeable gains is the amount which if charged at the standard rate of corporation tax would produce an amount equal to the amount of capital gains tax (see Example 9.101.2).

The 40% capital gains tax had been introduced with effect from 6 April 1992. For chargeable gains realised before that date, different rates applied depending on the length of the period of ownership of the asset being disposed of. In addition, disposals of development land, including disposals of unquoted shares deriving their value or the greater value from development land (see **9.103**), were charged at higher rates than other disposals. From 6 April 1994, disposals by individuals of certain shares in Irish resident companies have qualified for a 27% rate, reduced to 26% for disposals made on or after 6 April 1997. The reduction in the general capital gains tax rate from 40% to 20% as from 3 December 1997 meant that this low rate ceased to apply also from that date. The rates of capital gains tax which were in force for disposals from 6 April 1982 to 5 April 1992, as they affected companies, are as follows:

Period of ownership	6/4/82 to 5/4/86	6/4/86 to 5/4/90	6/4/90 to 5/4/92
Development land gains:			
Not more than 1 year	60%	60%	50%
More than 1 year	50%	50%	50%
More than 3 years – compulsory disposal	40%	40%	40%
Other gains:			
Not more than 1 year	60%	60%	50%
More than 1 year – up to 3 years	50%	50%	50%
More than 3 years – up to 6 years	40%	35%	35%
More than 6 years	40%	30%	30%

FA 1986 s 61(2) provided for a special 30% rate of capital gains tax in respect of chargeable gains on disposals on the Smaller Companies Market of the Irish Stock Exchange of shares of a kind dealt in on that market (where not dealt in on the Irish Stock Exchange or on any other stock exchange). This rate applied for disposals made in the period 4 April 1986 to 5 April 1992 and the rate was 30% regardless of the period of ownership. For the same six year period, a 30% rate was also provided for by FA 1986 s 61(3), subject to certain conditions, in respect of chargeable gains on disposals of ordinary shares in qualifying companies for the purposes of the business expansion scheme (see **6.3**) or for the purposes of the former research and development scheme.

9.102.5   Assets and chargeable gains

All forms of property are assets for capital gains tax purposes, whether or not situated in the State, including:

(a)   options, debts and incorporeal property generally;

(b)   any currency, other than Irish currency; and

(c)   any form of property created by the person disposing of it, or otherwise becoming owned without being acquired (TCA 1997, s 532).

In respect of any asset that is not a chargeable asset, no chargeable gain or allowable loss will accrue on its disposal. Although TCA 1997, s 598(5) (disposal of business on retirement) provides a definition of "chargeable asset" (every asset except one on the disposal of which any gain accruing would not be a chargeable gain) for the purposes of that section, there is no such definition for the purposes of capital gains tax generally (see further below). The context of TCA 1997, s 598, however, is such that the reference to "assets" there is to chargeable assets; any property that is an asset for the purposes of the Capital Gains Tax Acts is thereby a *chargeable asset*. Certain assets (eg, government and other securities dealt with in TCA 1997, s 607 – see under *Capital gains tax exemptions* below) are specifically regarded as not being "chargeable assets". Although *assets* is stated as meaning "all forms of property", with the items specified above being examples of what the term includes, it has been held that those items should be taken as providing a limitation to the meaning of "assets".

TCA 1997, s 545(3) provides that, except where otherwise expressly provided by the Capital Gains Tax Acts, every gain is a *chargeable gain*. Examples of gains which, exceptionally, are not chargeable gains are a gain arising on the disposal by an individual of a principal private residence (subject to conditions), a gain accruing on the disposal by an individual of an asset which is tangible movable property where the consideration for the disposal does not exceed €2,540, and a gain on the disposal of a wasting asset. The fact that a gain is a chargeable gain does not necessarily mean that it will be subject to capital gains tax. For example, certain disposals by non-residents (see **9.102.2**) do not result in liability to capital gains tax (or, in the case of a company, to corporation tax in respect of chargeable gains) although the disposal may have resulted in a chargeable gain.

Chargeable assets

The expression "chargeable asset" is not defined in the Capital Gains Tax Acts. Where an asset is referred to as not being a chargeable asset (eg, in relation to TCA 1997, s 607 - as seen above), the effect clearly is that neither a chargeable gain nor an allowable loss will arise on the disposal of that asset for the purposes of the Capital Gains Tax Acts generally. In other capital gains tax contexts, disposals of certain assets are stated not to give rise to a chargeable gain (and consequently will not give rise to an allowable loss either). The significance of the latter approach can be exemplified in relation to debts where no chargeable gain will arise on a disposal but only where the disposal is by the original creditor (so that it is not possible to refer to debts as not being chargeable assets per se). The distinction in approach can also be seen where a reference is made to "chargeable asset in relation to ...." which is a reference to an asset in respect of which a chargeable gain will arise on a disposal made by certain persons, for example, a disposal of Irish based assets giving rise to chargeable gains in the hands of certain non-residents.

Restrictive covenants

A sum received by a person in respect of a non-competition agreement may be treated for capital gains tax purposes as the amount of a chargeable gain accruing to that person on the disposal of a chargeable asset.

TCA 1997, s 541B(1) provides that where—

(a) a person gives an undertaking, whether absolute or qualified and whether legally valid or not, the tenor or effect of which is to restrict that person as to his conduct or activities;

(b) in respect of the giving of that undertaking, or of the total of partial fulfilment of that undertaking, any sum is paid either to the person or to any other person,

the amount of the sum is deemed for capital gains tax purposes to be an amount of a chargeable gain accruing to the person to whom it is paid on the disposal of a chargeable asset.

To be treated as a chargeable gain, the sum must neither be—

(i) treated as profits or gains chargeable to tax under Schedule D or Schedule E; nor

(ii) treated as consideration for the disposal of an asset for capital gains tax purposes.

For the purposes of this provision, where valuable consideration otherwise than in money form is given in respect of the giving of, or the total or partial fulfilment of, any undertaking, a sum equal to the value of that consideration is deemed to have been paid instead (TCA 1997, s 541B(2)).

9.102.6 Assets and disposals of assets

In the important UK case *Kirby v Thorn* [1987] STC 621, as part of an agreement under which it sold three of its subsidiaries, Thorn EMI agreed not to compete with those subsidiaries in the future. The Court of Appeal held that the freedom to trade is not an asset but found that the appellant company did have goodwill in its subsidiaries and that goodwill is an asset from which a chargeable gain could arise. It was also held that there was a disposal of an asset for capital gains tax purposes only where an asset existed before the disposal and which was in the ownership of the person making the disposal. An asset which came into existence only through the disposal itself was not, in relation to that disposal, an asset for the purposes of capital gains tax. On this point, the Crown had argued that, as [the UK equivalent of] TCA 1997, s 532(c) included as an asset any form of property "created by the person disposing of it, or otherwise becoming owned without being acquired ", that was an indication that the legislation contemplated a disposal by the very creation of the asset. That view was rejected by Nicholls LJ who pointed out that the above extract from the legislation made it clear that it is assumed that the person making the disposal was the owner of the property created by him. The legislation does not apply in circumstances where, prior to the disposal, the disponer had no asset.

Nicholls LJ also dealt with the Crown's inference from [the UK equivalent of] TCA 1997, s 534(b) which provides that "there shall be a part disposal of an asset where an interest or right in or over the asset is created by the disposal, as well as where it subsists before the disposal ...". The Crown inferred from this that a disposal could be an act of creation. Nicholls LJ, however, did not agree that it followed that an asset created by a disposal must be assumed to have been intended to fall within the ambit of capital gains tax unless expressly excluded.

The meaning of "otherwise becoming owned without being acquired" in TCA 1997, s 532(c) was considered by Nourse J in *Davenport v Chilver* [1983] STC 426. He expressed the view that the reference here did not extend to the circumstances of a person acquiring a right under a statute but was more likely to refer to, say, the acquisition of the goodwill of a business which had been built up by the person whom it was sought to tax.

In *O'Brien v Benson Hosiery (Holdings) Ltd* [1979] STC 735, the House of Lord held that a sum of money paid to a company by a director in consideration of the company's releasing him from his obligations under a service agreement was a capital sum derived from that agreement and that the agreement was an asset of the company. While it was accepted that the service agreement was not capable of being freely transferred by the company to another party, it was pointed out by Lord Russell that the rights of the employer bear quite sufficiently the mark of an asset which could be turned to account, notwithstanding that its ability to turn it to account is by a type of disposal limited by the nature of the asset.

The question as to whether a right to receive a sum is an asset for capital gains tax purposes was the subject of the appeal in *Marren v Ingles* [1979] STC 637. In that case, the taxpayers sold shares for a cash sum plus the right to a future sum the amount of which depended on certain unpredictable events. It was held that that right was an asset for capital gains purposes and that the nature of the asset was incorporeal property.

The case of *Zim Properties Ltd v Proctor* [1985] STC 90 was concerned with the question as to whether the right to sue was an asset for capital gains tax purposes. The company had entered into a contract to sell certain properties and under its terms the failure to complete various stages of the contract within certain time limits would be a fatal breach of the contract. On failing to produce satisfactory proof of title to the properties on time, the contract was repudiated by the purchaser whereupon the company sued its lawyers for compensation for permitting the contract to state that time was of the essence while not providing for the difficulty of proving title. In his judgment, Warner J held that the "right to sue" was an asset from which the compensation was derived.

Although capital gains tax is a tax on gains realised on disposals of assets, so that a disposal is the event that triggers the charge to tax, capital gains tax legislation provides no definition of "disposal". TCA 1997 ss 534 and 535 provide that certain events are to be regarded as disposals of assets although they may not in reality be disposals.

A disposal of an asset normally includes a part disposal unless the context otherwise requires (TCA 1997, s 534(a)). There is a part disposal of an asset where:

(i)   an interest or right in or over the asset is created by the disposed, as well as where it subsists before the disposal; and

(ii)   generally where, on a person making a disposal, any description of property derived from the asset remains undisposed of (TCA 1997, s 534(b)).

There is a disposal of an asset by its owner where a capital sum is derived from that asset even though no asset is acquired by the person paying the capital sum (TCA 1997, s 535(2)(a)).

Certain transactions do not constitute the disposal of an asset for capital gains tax purposes, eg the transfer by a nominee or trustee of assets to the person for whom he is the nominee or trustee (TCA 1997, s 567(2)), or the conveyance or transfer of an asset to another person by way of security for a liability or obligation (TCA 1997, s 537(1); in the latter case, any dealing with the asset by the person entitled to it by way of security, charge or encumbrance is treated as a dealing by him as nominee for the person entitled to it subject to the security, charge or encumbrance.

A stock loan or repo is, in practice, not treated as involving a disposal/acquisition for capital gains tax purposes – see **3.212**.

9.102.7   Wasting assets

A *wasting asset* is defined in TCA 1997, s 560(1) as an asset with a predictable life not exceeding fifty years, but so that:

(a)   freehold land is not a wasting asset whatever its nature and whatever the nature of the buildings or works on it;

(b)   *life*, in relation to any tangible movable property, means useful life, having regard to the purpose for which the tangible assets were acquired or provided by the person making the disposal;

(c)   plant and machinery is always to be regarded as having a predictable life of less than fifty years, and in estimating that life it is to be assumed that it will end when it is finally put out of use as being unfit for further use, and that it is going to be used in the normal manner and to the normal extent and is going to be so used throughout its life as so estimated; and

(d)   a life interest in settled property is not a wasting asset until the predictable expectation of life of the life tenant is fifty years or less, and the predictable life of life interests in settled property and of annuities is to be ascertained from actuarial tables approved by the Revenue Commissioners.

TCA 1997 Sch 14 provides that a lease of land is not a wasting asset until the time when its duration does not exceed fifty years. Accordingly, a lease of more than fifty years' duration is not a wasting asset at its inception but will become one from the point at which it has fifty years to run.

The general rule affecting the disposal of an asset which is a wasting asset is that its cost and any enhancement expenditure (as reduced by the residual scrap value, if any, at the end of its useful life) are treated as wasting throughout the duration of the life of the asset (TCA 1997, s 560(3)). For the purposes of the computation of the chargeable gain on disposal of a wasting asset, the owner is treated as having used or enjoyed the part of the cost attributable to his ownership during the period of ownership so that only the remaining or unused part of that cost may be deducted. The cost and any enhancement expenditure, less the residual scrap value as estimated at the time the asset is acquired, are wasted on a straight line basis, ie in direct proportion to the expiration of the expected life of the asset.

The allowable cost of all assets, except business assets used solely for the purposes of a trade or profession and which qualify for capital allowances, is restricted in the above way (TCA 1997, s 561). Where an asset is used partly for trading purposes and partly for other purposes, the part apportioned to trade purposes is not restricted.

A wasting asset is usually deemed to be wasted on a straight line basis. In computing the gain on disposal, the cost (less any residual scrap value) is written off at a uniform rate from its full amount at the time it was acquired or provided to nothing at the end of its life (TCA 1997, s 560(3)).

Enhancement expenditure is written off at a uniform rate from the full amount of that expenditure at the time it was first reflected in the state or nature of the asset to nothing at the end of its life. A different treatment applies in the case of expenditure incurred on the acquisition of a lease of land. The amount of the expenditure attributed to the wasted part of that expenditure is arrived at on the basis of a table and fractions provided for in TCA 1997 Sch 14. According to these, the expenditure is weighted towards the later years of the lease. Only the part of the expenditure remaining after wasting is eligible for indexation.

9.102.8 Part disposals

TCA 1997, s 534 provides that, for the purposes of the Capital Gains Tax Acts, references to a disposal of an assets include, except where the context otherwise requires, references to a part disposal of an asset. There is a part disposal of an asset where an interest or right in or over the asset is created by the disposal, as well as where it subsists before the disposal. There is, generally, a part disposal of an asset where, on a person making a disposal, any description of property derived from the asset remains undisposed of.

Special provision is made for the disposal of part of an asset (TCA 1997, s 557). In the case of a part disposal, it is necessary to calculate the part of the cost of that asset which is attributable to the part disposed of. The cost to be deducted from the part disposed of is represented by the formula:

$$\frac{\text{Total cost of asset} \times A}{A + B}$$

where—

A =   the proceeds for the part disposal; and

B =   the market value of the property remaining after the disposal.

Thus the allowable cost, and any enhancement expenditure, is apportioned between the part of the asset disposed of and the remaining part on the basis of the market values of the respective parts at the date of disposal. Where the asset was owned on 6 April, the notional cost is the market value of the asset at that date.

9.102.9 Capital sums derived from assets

The receipt of a capital sum from an asset would not normally be regarded as a disposal of that asset. Subject to certain exceptions, TCA 1997, s 535(2) provides that there is " a disposal of assets by their owner where any capital sum is derived from assets notwithstanding that no asset is acquired by the person paying the capital sum".

TCA 1997, s 535(2) is potentially very wide-ranging and also gives rise to considerable interpretational difficulties, not least in relation to what capital sums are included and in particular as to how a capital sum is to be regarded as being "derived from" assets. The subsection applies in particular to:

(i) capital sums received by way of compensation for any kind of damage or injury to assets or for the loss, destruction or dissipation of assets or for any depreciation or risk of depreciation of an asset;

(ii) capital sums received under a policy of insurance of the risk of any kind of damage or injury to, or the loss or deprecation of, assets;

(iii) capital sums received in return for forfeiture or surrender of rights, or for refraining from exercising rights; and

(iv) capital sums received as consideration for use or exploitation of assets.

In the UK courts, a difference of opinion has arisen as to whether the opening statement of [the UK equivalent of] TCA 1997, s 535(2) to the effect that there is a disposal of assets where a "capital sum is derived from assets" governs the four particular cases which follow ((a) to (d) above), or whether those cases stand on their own feet and prevail over the general words. The former view was favoured by Nourse J in *Davenport v Chilver* [1983] STC 426 and Gibson LJ in *Pennine Raceway v Kirklees Metropolitan Council (No 2)* [1989] STC 122, while Warner J in *Zim Properties v Proctor* [1985] STC 90 and Stuart-Smith LJ also in the *Pennine Raceway* case favoured the narrower interpretation which required that each of the particular cases constituted a disposal of assets only if it involved a capital sum derived from assets. The position in Ireland in relation to this point must remain undecided until such time as the matter is pronounced on by the courts.

The reference in TCA 1997, s 535(2) to a disposal of assets as including the derivation of a capital sum from assets "notwithstanding that no asset is acquired by the person paying the capital sum" was held in *Chaloner v Palliper* [1996] STC 234 to mean "whether or not" an asset was acquired by the person paying the capital sum and it did not therefore exclude the case where the payer of the capital sum received an asset in exchange for that sum.

A capital sum received by way of a gift is an example of a capital sum not being derived from assets. Another example is a capital sum received by way of statutory compensation. In *Drummond v Austin Brown* [1984] STC 331, Fox LJ pointed out that it was the statute alone, under which the compensation in that case was derived, that created the right to the payment. In *Davis v Powell* [1977] STC 32, Templeman J, dealing with a case in which the taxpayer was paid a sum by way of statutory compensation for disturbance of rights under a lease, held that the compensation was not derived from an asset (the lease) but by reason of a statute which provided that it should be paid for expense and loss unavoidably incurred after the lease has gone.

As regards the meaning of *capital sum*, TCA 1997, s 535(1) provides that this means any money or money's worth which is not excluded from the consideration taken into account in the computation of a capital gain under TCA 1997 Part 19 Ch 2 (ss 544-566) (computation of chargeable gains and allowable losses). It is important to note, and this may often be overlooked, that this does not exclude all receipts of an income nature; it merely excludes items specifically excluded by TCA 1997 Part 19 Ch 2. In this connection, TCA 1997, s 551(2) provides that any money or money's worth charged to income tax (or to corporation tax in the case of a company) as income, or taken into account as a receipt in computing income, profits or gains or losses for those purposes, is to be excluded from the consideration for a disposal of assets taken into account in the computation of a chargeable gain.

Furthermore, TCA 1997, s 544(2) provides that references in TCA 1997 Part 19 Ch 2 to sums taken into account as receipts or as expenditure in computing profits, gains or losses for the purposes of income tax (or corporation tax in the case of a company) are to include references to sums which would be so taken into account but for the fact that any profits or gains of a trade, profession or employment are not chargeable to income tax (or corporation tax) or that losses are not allowable for those purposes.

Not every receipt of an income nature, therefore, is excluded from the consideration to be taken into account in computing a gain or loss for the purposes of capital gains tax. Income type receipts which have not been subjected to income tax (or to corporation tax as income, in the case of a company), or which have not been taken into account as income for that purpose, may well (despite TCA 1997, s 551(2), since that subsection applies only to tax exempt receipts of a trade, profession or employment – see above) have to be included in a computation of a chargeable gain for capital gains tax purposes. A receipt from the sale of timber, where received in the context of the management of woodlands on a commercial basis, would not be taken into account for income tax or corporation tax purposes (TCA 1997, s 232(2) – see **3.204.5**). That receipt might not be a trading receipt and it might therefore be arguable that the disposal of timber in this case would not escape liability to capital gains tax. On the other hand, it would be surprising if an Irish court would hold that a receipt falls within the ambit of capital gains tax solely because exempted from income tax.

Three of the four specific cases dealt with by TCA 1997, s 535(2), involving the receipt of various kinds of capital sums, may be dealt with briefly as follows:

Compensation

In *Lang v Rice* [1984] STC 172, the taxpayer received compensation from the Northern Ireland Office arising out of the bombing of his rented business premises in Belfast. The compensation covered loss of trading stock, damage to and loss of contents, loss of profits and tenant's improvements. It was held that the compensation was in respect of the loss of profits which might have been earned but for the destruction caused in the bombing and that it was therefore an income receipt. In *Glenboig Union Fireclay Company Ltd v IRC* 12 TC 427, a company whose business included the mining of fireclay received compensation from a railway company for not working fireclay under or near a railway line. The land continued to be held by the company and the House of Lords held that the compensation was effectively for the loss of a capital asset which had become sterilised.

In *London and Thames Haven Oil Wharves v Attwooll* 43 TC 491, a jetty belonging to the taxpayer was damaged as a result of the negligent handling of an oil tanker arising out of which compensation was received, divided between the physical damage to the jetty and loss of profits. It was held that the compensation was in the nature of income as it was not received in respect of the sterilisation of a capital asset. In *Deeny v Gooda Walker Ltd (in voluntary liquidation)* [1995] STC 299, the principle advanced in the

Attwooll case (the "replacement principle") came under close scrutiny and was eventually upheld by a majority decision. That principle was, briefly, that a sum of money received in lieu of the failure to receive a sum of money which, if it had been received, would have been credited to the amount of profits, if any, arising to the recipient is to be treated in the same way as the sum not received would have been treated for tax purposes. That rule applies irrespective of the source of the legal right of the trader to recover the compensation. The replacement principle was upheld by a bare majority decision and has not to date been tested in the Irish courts.

In *British Transport Commission v Gourley* [1956] AC 185, a substantial part of the damages for personal injuries related to the plaintiff's loss of earnings. These damages would not be subject to tax in the hands of the plaintiff and the House of Lords held that, as the liability to pay income tax on his earnings was a liability established by law, the plaintiff was entitled to claim as a loss only the amount which he would actually have received, ie net of tax. In practice, applying the Gourley principle is likely to be difficult in many cases as it will be necessary first to establish whether the compensation is subject to taxation.

Insurance policies

TCA 1997, s 535(2)(a) provides that there is a disposal of assets where a capital sum is received under a policy of insurance of the risk of any kind of damage or injury to, or the loss or depreciation of, assets. Notwithstanding this, TCA 1997, s 535(2)(b) provides that neither the rights of the insurer nor the rights of the insured under any insurance policy (other than a life policy) are to be regarded as an asset on the disposal of which a gain may accrue. TCA 1997, s 535(2)(b) will not, however, apply where the right to receive compensation under a policy is assigned after the event giving rise to the damage or injury to, or the loss or depreciation of, the asset has occurred; in that case, the assignment is deemed to be a disposal of an interest in the asset concerned.

Forfeiture, surrender and refraining from exercising rights

See below under *Options*, in particular the discussion regarding the abandonment of an option.

9.102.10 Value shifting

Where a person having control of a company exercises his control so that value passes out of shares in the company owned by him or by a person with whom he is connected, or out of rights over the company exercisable by him or by a person with whom he is connected, and passes into other shares in or rights over the company, that exercise of his control is a disposal (or a part disposal) of the shares or rights out of which the value passes by the person by whom they were owned or exercisable (TCA 1997, s 543(2)(a)).

For this purpose, a person is connected with another person if he is so connected within the meaning of TCA 1997, s 10 (see **2.3**), and references to a person include references to two or more persons connected with one another (TCA 1997, s 543(2)(b)).

The above reference to "other shares" into which value might pass would seem to leave open the possibility that the section could apply to a transfer of value from one class of shares into another class of shares owned by the same person. It is suggested that the better, and the only reasonable, view is that the reference to other shares is to shares owned by another person. Furthermore, the references in TCA 1997, s 543(1)(b) to "the parties to the transaction" and "the party making the disposal could have obtained consideration" would seem clearly to support this interpretation.

Any transaction which is treated as a disposal of an asset in accordance with TCA 1997, s 543 is to be so treated (with a corresponding acquisition of an interest in the asset) notwithstanding that there is no consideration for the disposal (TCA 1997, s 543(1)(a)).

Example 9.102.10.1

Silver Ltd and Copper Ltd subscribed for 65,000 and 35,000 respectively of the €1 ordinary shares in Soapstone Ltd at par on the formation of that company.

Later, a resolution of Soapstone Ltd is passed to the effect that all voting control and rights to dividends are to vest in the shares held by Copper Ltd. The market value of the rights passing to Copper Ltd as a result of the resolution is estimated at €250,000 and the market value of the shares held by Silver Ltd at that point is assumed to be €20,000. By virtue of its majority shareholding, Silver Ltd has control of Soapstone Ltd. The passing of the resolution is an exercise of that control by Silver Ltd and results in a part disposal of its shares in Soapstone Ltd. The relevant chargeable gain is computed as follows:

	€
Consideration for part disposal	250,000
Cost €65,000 x 250,000/(250,000 + 20,000)	60,185
Chargeable gain	189,815

As mentioned above, a transaction treated as a disposal of an asset under TCA 1997, s 543 is to be so treated "with a corresponding acquisition of an interest in the asset". Thus, as well as a disposal, there is an equivalent acquisition of the interest with, it would seem, a base cost equal to the deemed consideration for the disposal. In Example **9.102.10.1** above, however, Copper Ltd has not acquired any asset. The effect of TCA 1997, s 543(2) is to tax the transfer of a notional asset consisting of the value that has shifted from some shares into other shares in the company.

A question that then arises is whether Copper Ltd is entitled to include that value as part of the cost of its shares that would be allowable in the event of a future disposal of those shares. The position is not entirely clear, either from TCA 1997, s 543 or elsewhere from the capital gains tax legislation, although it would appear that the intention of TCA 1997, s 543(1)(a) is to provide a basis for a deduction in respect of the value which has passed. The meaning of "assets" (see **9.102.5**) would seem to be sufficiently wide to include the interest in the asset (the shares) which is deemed to have been acquired under TCA 1997, s 543(1)(a). Copper Ltd could therefore be regarded as having acquired an asset arising out of the value shift so that, in the event of a disposal of its shares at a later stage, that asset would also have been disposed of. The technical position nevertheless remains obscure. For example, assuming Copper Ltd later disposes of its shares, it is difficult to say whether the notional asset is a part of a larger asset being disposed of (ie, the shares), or a separate asset disposed of at the same time as the shares. It is difficult to reconcile either position with the provisions of capital gains tax legislation.

A transaction treated as a disposal of an asset is also to be treated as if it had not been at arm's length in so far as the party making the disposal could, on an arm's length basis, have obtained consideration or additional consideration for the disposal. In that event, the amount of the consideration deemed to be receivable added to any consideration actually passing is treated as the market value of what is acquired (TCA 1997, s 543(1)(b)).

The UK case *Floor v Davis* [1979] STC 379 was concerned with the question of value shifting. In this connection it is relevant to note that there is no UK equivalent of TCA 1997, s 543(2)(b) ("person" includes two or more persons – see above) and that the decision is probably incapable of being followed in Ireland as the appeal was largely concerned with the question of control by a number of persons. The case is nevertheless of interest in relation to the concept of value shifting. The facts of the case are, briefly, as follows.

It was arranged that, subject to contract, the share capital of a company (IDM) would be sold at a substantial profit to another company, KDI. The taxpayer and his two sons-in-law, who between them controlled IDM, transferred their shares to a special purpose company, FNW, for preference shares in that company. FNW then sold the IDM shares to KDI for cash. A Cayman Islands company, D, acquired a very small holding of preference shares in FNW. Arising out of a rights issue by FNW, in which rights were taken up by D only, D became the sole shareholder in FNW. FNW was put into liquidation arising out of which D became entitled to six-sevenths of the assets of FNW so that, in effect, the greater part of the proceeds of the share sale accrued to D.

It was held in the House of Lords, upholding the judgment of the Court of Appeal, that value had passed out of the FNW shares and that the taxpayer was assessable accordingly on the grounds that (a) "person" (in the UK equivalent of TCA 1997, s 543(2)) included the plural of that term and (b) the taxpayer and his sons-in-law had exercised their control, notwithstanding that two of them had not voted on the resolution to wind up FNW. In Ireland, the inclusion in the term "person" of two or more persons who are connected with one another is specifically provided for in TCA 1997, s 543(2)(b).

Where, after a transaction which results in the owner of land or of any other property becoming the lessee of the property, any adjustment is made concerning the rights and liabilities under the lease (whether or not involving the grant of a new lease) which is as a whole favourable to the lessor, that adjustment is treated as a disposal of an interest in the property (TCA 1997, s 543(3)).

Example 9.102.10.2

Swan Ltd transfers a freehold building owned by it to Cygnet Ltd, its wholly owned subsidiary, subject to obtaining a 150 year lease of the same building at an annual rent of €50. Clearly, the interest disposed of is all but worthless so that little or no chargeable gain would arise on the disposal.

In the accounting period following the transfer, the terms of the lease are altered so as to provide for a full market value rent with five year rent revisions. As a result of this adjustment, the property regains its full value.

By virtue of TCA 1997, s 543(3), Swan Ltd is treated as making a second disposal, out of the long leasehold, for a consideration equal to the value transferred to Cygnet Ltd. The gain will be the excess of this value over the cost of the freehold, subject to a deduction for any allowable expenses.

Where an asset is subject to any description of right or restriction, the extinction or abrogation, in whole or in part, of the right or restriction by the person entitled to enforce it is treated as a disposal by him of the right or restriction (TCA 1997, s 543(4)).

Example 9.102.10.3

Jacobs Ltd owns a building which it acquired for €200,000. It transfers this building to Mr Jacobs, the managing director, on terms which allow the company to continue to occupy the building. Assuming the market value of the building at that time, and subject to the tenancy, is €280,000, there will be a gain arising to the company by reference to that value.

Jacobs Ltd later gives up the tenancy. This triggers a further disposal, of the remaining rights in the building. Assuming the value of these remaining rights was €50,000 at the time the tenancy came to an end, the chargeable gains are as follows:

Transfer of building:

	€
Market value of building at date of transfer	280,000
$\text{Cost} = \text{€}200,000 \times \dfrac{280,000}{280,000 + 50,000} =$	169,697

Surrender of tenancy:

	€
Market value of tenancy	50,000
Balance of cost €200,000 - €169,697 =	30,303
Chargeable gain	19,697

9.102.11 Debts

The definition of "asset" above includes a specific reference to debts. Although debts are chargeable assets, the general capital gains tax rule is that no chargeable gain accrues on the disposal of a debt by the person (or by his personal representative or legatee) who is or was the original creditor in relation to that debt (TCA 1997, s 541(1)(a)). There are exceptions to this rule. Firstly, the rule does not apply to a disposal of a "debt on a security" (TCA 1997, s 541(1)(b)). For this purpose, *security* includes any loan stock or similar security whether of any government or any public or local authority or of any company and whether secured or unsecured, but excluding securities falling within TCA 1997, s 607 (government and other securities) (TCA 1997, s 1997 585(1)).

Although the general rule to the effect that the disposal of a debt does not give rise to a chargeable gain applies only in a case where the person disposing of it is the original creditor in relation to it, a loss accruing on a disposal of a debt which was acquired by the person disposing of it from the original creditor is not an allowable loss where, at the time the debt was so acquired, that person was connected with (see **2.3**) the original creditor (TCA 1997, s 541(4)).

The meaning of *debt on a security* has been the subject of a number of UK court decisions. It does not mean the same as a secured debt (*Cleveleys Investment Trust v IRC* [1975] STC 457), which is apparent in any event from the above definition of "security". A debt on a security denotes a debt (which may be unsecured) which, if not of a marketable character, has at least such characteristics as enable it to be dealt in and if necessary converted into shares or other securities (*Aberdeen Construction Group v IRC* [1978] STC 127). The intent of the legislation is to distinguish between mere debts which do not normally increase, but may decrease, in value and debts with added characteristics such as enable them to be realised or dealt with at a profit (*WT Ramsay Ltd v IRC* [1981] STC 174).

In *Tarmac Roadstone Holdings Ltd v Williams* [1996] SpC 409, the fact that loan notes required the consent of the issuer for their transfer and were redeemable at the option of the issuer before their due date for redemption was held to mean that they were not in the nature of investments which could be dealt in as such by reason of those features. They were accordingly held not to be debts on a security.

In *Taylor Clarke International v Lewis* [1997] STC 499, a promissory note, although transferable, secured and interest bearing, was held not to be a debt on a security as it lacked a structure of permanence since it had no fixed term and repayment could have been demanded at any time. The loan in that case would not in reality have been marketable without the benefit of security and it had not been established that the security available to the original holder of the note would be transferable with the note. While this did not mean that a debt on a security had to be secured, it was the position in this case that there would be little market for the note in the absence of security.

The general approach of the above UK cases was rejected in the Irish case *Mooney v McSweeney* [1997] ITR 163. This case involved a cash loan convertible into ordinary shares but with no entitlement to interest and with repayment subordinated to the redemption of preference shares and other creditors. In the High Court, Mr Justice Morris considered that convertibility was sufficient in this case to render the loan a debt on a security. The essence of a debt on a security is the additional bundle of rights acquired with the granting of the loan so as to make it marketable and potentially more valuable than the value of the loan on repayment. The potential increase in value must not be illusory or theoretical and it must be realistic at the time the loan and rights are acquired by the lender. A pure loan is exempt from capital gains tax because it can never exceed its value at the time it is made. It is not relevant that the purchaser of a debt might have difficulty, because of local or transient commercial considerations, in finding another purchaser. Once a loan transaction contains the characteristics that would in the ordinary course of commerce render it marketable, it meets the criteria for being a debt on a security.

The intention of the legislature in providing that ordinary loans do not give rise to chargeable gains on their disposal is to ensure that losses, which can easily arise from such loans, may not be set off against gains realised on other transactions. It is not in fact true to say that a pure loan can never exceed its original value. This could easily happen where the borrower's prospects for repaying the loan improve, or where interest rates fluctuate. From the perspective of an original lender, however, any such increase will not give rise to a gain. In the case of a foreign currency loan, on the other hand, where the euro equivalent of the foreign currency amount realised on settlement exceeds the euro equivalent at the time the loan was made, a gain will arise but (assuming it is not a debt on a security) will not be taxable. The *McSweeney* decision is, nevertheless, particularly useful in providing a clear basis for deciding what loans are to be regarded as debts on a security. A loan is or is not, it seems, a debt on a security depending on whether or not the intention of the legislature, to allow losses only in respect of loans that could have realised a gain, is fulfilled.

The above test propounded by Mr Justice Morris was applied by the High Court in *O'Connell v Thomas Keleghan* 1999 No 351R. That case involved the redemption of a loan note on which interest was not initially payable and which was not transferable or assignable. It was held that the loan note was clearly not marketable since it was neither transferable nor assignable (although it was convertible into shares in the event of a public flotation or a placing), being no more than a simple promise to repay a debt. It was also found that the limited conversion rights and interest provisions were not sufficient to enhance the value of the note as an investment so that it was not a debt on a security.

While TCA 1997, s 541(1)(b) refers to a "debt on a security within the meaning of section 585", what is defined in the latter section is "security" and not "debt on a security" as such. As seen above, "security" is defined in that section as "any loan stock or similar security whether of any government or any public or local authority or of any company and whether secured or unsecured, but excluding securities falling within TCA 1997, s 607". On that basis, "debt on a security" could be interpreted as meaning a debt in the form of that kind of security, which would appear to confer on the expression a somewhat narrower meaning than that adopted by the courts, particularly the Irish courts in the light of the *McSweeney* case.

Where a company issues a debenture in the course of a reorganisation to which TCA 1997, s 584(2), s 586(2) or s 587(2) applies (see **9.402**, **9.404** and **9.405**), it is specifically provided in TCA 1997, s 541(7) that that debenture is a debt on a security for capital gains purposes. In addition, where a company issues a debenture in connection with any transfer of assets as is referred to in TCA 1997, s 631 (Mergers Directive: transfers of assets – see **9.302**), TCA 1997, s 632 (Mergers Directive: transfer of asset by company to parent company – see **9.303**) or TCA 1997, s 637 (Mergers Directive: other transactions – see **9.305**), that debenture is also treated by TCA 1997, s 541(7) as a debt on a security for capital gains purposes. Furthermore, a debenture issued in pursuance of rights attached to any debentures issued in any of the foregoing circumstances is treated as a debt on a security.

In relation to the reorganisations referred to above, TCA 1997, s 541(7) applies in respect of the disposal on or after 28 March 1996 of any debentures acquired as above and accordingly will have effect in relation to, say, a "paper for paper" transaction effected before that date in which debentures were acquired for shares. Although the debentures may not have constituted a debt on a security at the time of the transaction, they will be regarded as such if sold on or after 28 March 1996 and the disposal may therefore result in a chargeable gain. As regards the Mergers Directive items, TCA 1997, s 541(7) has effect in relation to disposals of debentures on or after 26 March 1997.

A second exception to the general rule of TCA 1997, s 541(1) relates to a debt owed by a bank which is not in Irish currency and which is represented by a sum standing to the credit of a person in an account in the bank, unless it represents currency acquired by the holder for the personal expenditure outside the State of himself or his family or dependants (TCA 1997, s 541(6)). A credit balance in a foreign currency denominated bank account may give rise to a gain as well as a loss, by reason of fluctuations between the Irish pound and the currency in which the deposit is denominated; hence this further exception.

On 1 January 1999, however, certain bank accounts denominated in foreign currencies were re-dominated in terms of the euro which is also, from that date, Irish currency. In any such case, an exchange gain or loss which would arise on the disposal of the debt (ie, the account) on 31 December 1998 is deemed to arise on that date (TCA 1997, s 541A(1)). Any gain so arising, however, will not be liable to capital gains tax until such time as the debt is disposed of, ie the account is uplifted (TCA 1997, s 541A(2)). The withdrawal of part of the funds in the account would be a disposal of part of the debt and capital gains tax, as appropriate, would be payable accordingly. The satisfaction of the debt or part of the debt is treated as a disposal of the debt or of that part at the time when the debt or that part is satisfied (TCA 1997, s 541(3)).

TCA 1997, s 541A does not for the most part apply in the cases of euro- denominated currency bank accounts held by the life assurance fund or the special investment fund of an assurance company (see **12.603.2** – *Ordinary life business* – *rules for the I-E computation*) or by a company which is an undertaking for collective investment (see **12.805.4** – *Chargeable gains*).

Regarding the location of debts for capital gains tax purposes, see **9.102.24**.

9.102.12 Options

An option is one of the forms of property specifically included in the definition of "asset" for capital gains purposes. An "option" was described by Mr Justice Goff at the Chancery Division stage in *Sainsbury v O'Connor* [1990] STC 156 as an irrevocable offer which is open to acceptance by the exercise of the option. It is not a conditional contract. Once the option is granted, the grantor is contractually obliged not to put it out of his power to do what he has offered to do but otherwise he retains both equitable ownership and the rights of beneficial enjoyment normally attaching to equitable ownership.

An option is not in itself a contract but, once exercised, it becomes a contract. Capital gains tax legislation treats the cost of the asset which is the subject of the option to acquire it (a "call" option) as including both the cost of the option and the cost of acquiring the asset (TCA 1997, s 540(4)(a)). By the same token, the vendor is treated as selling the asset for the total of the amount received for the option itself and the consideration receivable under the option agreement for the sale of the asset (TCA 1997, s 540(3)(a)). Accordingly, the option is treated as being part of the transaction to acquire or dispose of the underlying asset.

In the case of an option requiring the grantor to buy an asset (a "put" option), the cost of the option is treated as an incidental cost of disposal of the asset to the grantor (TCA 1997, s 540(4)(b)). From the grantor's perspective, the consideration for the option is deducted from the cost of acquiring the asset in pursuance of his obligation under the option (TCA 1997, s 540(3)(b)).

The foregoing rules reflect the commercial reality of transactions involving options to buy or sell. The position becomes more difficult in the case of an option which is never exercised, for example because it is abandoned. TCA 1997, s 540(2) provides that, without prejudice to TCA 1997 ss 534 and 535 (capital sums derived from assets – see above), the grant of an option, including:

(a) the grant of an option where the grantor binds himself to sell an asset he does not own, and because the option is abandoned, never has occasion to own; and

(b) the grant of an option where the grantor binds himself to buy an asset which, because the option is abandoned, he does not acquire,

is the disposal of an asset (ie of the option), but subject to the other provisions of TCA 1997, s 540 which treat the grant of an option as part of a larger transaction (as with the exercise of a put or a call option, discussed above). Accordingly, the grant of an option is treated in the first instance as the disposal of a separate asset but subject to a revised treatment if the option is exercised, when the option and the asset merge into a single transaction (so that the option is not then treated as a separate asset).

An option may be abandoned when the person who acquired it does not exercise it (and does not transfer it to someone else). Where it is abandoned, it remains a separate asset for capital gains tax purposes. TCA 1997, s 540(5) provides that the abandonment of an option, by the person who for the time being is entitled to exercise it, constitutes the disposal of an asset (the option) by that person. That abandonment does not, however, give rise to an allowable loss (subject to exceptions discussed below) although, since the grant of an option is a disposal of that option, the grantor is subject to capital gains tax on the gain arising thereon. (The gain is the consideration received less any expenses incurred; since an option is a wasting asset, however, any cost will also be "wasted".)

TCA 1997, s 540(5) has effect in respect of disposals on or after 7 May 1992, the position before that date being that the abandonment of an option did not constitute a disposal for capital gains tax purposes. It is interesting to consider a number of cases which were relevant to the position prior to 7 May 1992 as they were concerned with the questions as to whether "abandonment" for the purposes of TCA 1997, s 540(5) included an abandonment for full consideration and as to whether the abandonment of an option is an exception to TCA 1997, s 535(2)(a) (capital sum derived from an asset – see above).

In the UK case *Golding v Kaufman* [1985] STC 152, the taxpayer had a right under an option agreement to require another party to purchase certain shares at a price determined under the agreement. The other party later decided not to purchase the shares and paid the taxpayer a sum of £5,000 in consideration for the abandonment by the taxpayer of his option. The taxpayer was assessed on the full sum on the basis that it was a capital sum derived from an asset. In the Chancery Division, Vinelott J held that the term "abandonment" was wide enough to include abandonment for value. TCA 1997, s 538(1) treats as a disposal of an asset the occasion of the entire loss, destruction, dissipation or extinction of that asset (see **9.102.3** above) but that subsection is stated to be subject in particular to TCA 1997, s 540. Accordingly, based on the view of Vinelott J, TCA 1997, s 540 (then CGTA s 47) in its pre-7 May 1992 form would have done no more than qualify TCA 1997, s 538(1). TCA 1997, s 535(2), on the other hand, is not expressly made subject to TCA 1997, s 540 so that the abandonment of an option would not be an exception to that provision.

In *Welbeck Securities Ltd v Powlson* [1987] STC 468, the taxpayer company received £2m for its agreement to release and abandon an option to participate in a property development. The effect of the Court of Appeal decision was that the abandonment of an option in such circumstances did not escape being a disposal by virtue of the pre-7 May 1992 version of TCA 1997, s 540 and that the disposal was a chargeable disposal under TCA 1997, s 535(2).

The Irish case, *TA Dilleen v Kearns* Supreme Court [1997], was concerned with an avoidance scheme involving the abandonment of options over shares in a company. The shares were owned between them by the taxpayers, a husband and wife, who, for substantial sums approximating to the value of the shares, had granted options to each other in respect of the shares held by each. The exercise price was relatively small in each case. The shares were sold to an unconnected company, subject to the option and for a sum equal to the exercise price in each case. The company then paid the husband

and wife sums equivalent to the original option prices for the abandonment of their options. Effectively the shares had been sold to the company for market value but with by far the greater part of the proceeds being in respect of the abandonment of options. The taxpayers sought to rely on the pre-7 May equivalent of TCA 1997, s 540, claiming that the abandonment of the options did not constitute a disposal for capital gains tax purposes.

In the High Court, Mr Justice Costello, rejecting the finding of Vinelott J in *Golding v Kaufman*, held that an abandonment for consideration was not a real abandonment of an option; in putting the option to good use and in obtaining an advantage in doing so, a person cannot be said to be abandoning that option. Accordingly, TCA 1997, s 540(5) did not apply. As to whether TCA 1997, s 540(5) was an exception to the general charge under TCA 1997, s 535(2), Mr Justice Costello, agreeing with the conclusions in the above two UK cases, held that the former section merely provided that the abandonment of an option was not a disposal of an asset but that that did not exempt from liability to capital gains tax a transaction involving the receipt of a capital sum on that abandonment. The Supreme Court confirmed the denial of exemption.

An option may bind the grantor to sell or buy shares or securities which have a quoted market value on a stock exchange in the State or elsewhere. Where on option of that kind is disposed of by way of transfer, it is to be regarded as a wasting asset and its life is deemed to end when the right to exercise it ends, or when it becomes valueless, whichever is the earlier (TCA 1997, s 540(6)).

An unresolved question is what, if any, part of the cost of the underlying asset is attributable to an option. TCA 1997, s 559 (assets derived from other assets) provides that where the value of an asset has been derived from another asset in the same ownership, part of the cost of that asset is to be attributed to the first-mentioned asset. Since the value of an option must be derived from the related asset, and since the value of the asset will normally be reduced when an option is granted in relation to it, it would be expected that the option must have some cost. It is understood that that view is not accepted by the Revenue Commissioners and, to date, opinions on the matter remain divided.

Where an option to acquire assets for use in a trade carried on by the person who may exercise it is disposed of or abandoned, then:

(a) where the option is abandoned, that abandonment may give rise to an allowable loss for capital gains tax purposes; this is one of the exceptions to the TCA 1997, s 540(5)(b) rule that the abandonment of an option does not give rise to an allowable loss; and

(b) the general rule whereby expenditure for wasting assets is restricted (TCA 1997, s 560(3)) does not apply (TCA 1997, s 540(7)).

The foregoing treatment applies where the grantee intends to use the assets, if acquired, for the purposes of a trade carried on by him or which he commences to carry on within two years of his acquisition of the option. The effect of this provision is that relief is available in respect of the amount given for the option, and for the full amount since no part of it is wasted.

TCA 1997, s 540(8) makes similar provision for quoted options and traded options. A *quoted option* is an option which, at the time of abandonment or other disposal, is quoted and, in the same way as shares, dealt with on a stock exchange in the State or elsewhere. A *traded option* is an option which, at the time of abandonment or other disposal, is quoted on a stock exchange or a futures exchange in the State or elsewhere. Where a quoted option to subscribe for shares in a company, or a traded option, is disposed of or abandoned, then

(a)   where the option is abandoned, that abandonment may give rise to an allowable loss for capital gains tax purposes; this is another exception to the TCA 1997, s 540(5) rule that the abandonment of an option does not give rise to an allowable loss; and

(b)   the general rule whereby expenditure for wasting assets is restricted (TCA 1997, s 560(3)) and the rule in TCA 1997, s 540(6) (option disposed of by way of transfer treated as wasting asset – see above) do not apply (TCA 1997, s 540(7)).

The following example illustrates how the wasting asset treatment applies in the case of an option.

Example 9.102.12.1

Auburn Ltd purchases an option from Astoria Ltd for €20,000 under which Astoria Ltd binds itself to sell a building to Auburn Ltd for €140,000 if called upon to do so within fifteen months. Auburn Ltd transfers the option to Elliot Ltd three months later for a sum of €17,000. The chargeable gain arising to Auburn Ltd is as follows:

	€	€
Disposal proceeds		17,000
Cost	20,000	
Wasted – €20,000 x 3/15	4,000	16,000
Gain		1,000

In a case where an option binds the grantor both to sell and to buy, TCA 1997, s 540 applies as if it were two separate options with half the consideration being attributable to each (TCA 1997, s 540(9)).

The option rules of TCA 1997, s 540 apply to options binding the grantor to grant a lease for a premium. or to enter into any other transaction which is not a sale (TCA 1997, s 540(1)).

On occasion, a deposit of purchase money will be forfeited where the transaction in question is abandoned. In that event, the amount forfeited is treated as if it were consideration paid for an option binding the grantor to sell and which is not exercised (TCA 1997, s 540(10)). The treatment is the same therefore as in the case of an abandonment of an option (see above). The party retaining the deposit is treated as having disposed of an option. The other party is regarded as having incurred a loss on its disposal but no loss relief is available unless the transaction comes within one of the exceptions described above.

9.102.13   Market value

As respects any assets, *market value* generally means the price which those assets might reasonably be expected to fetch on a sale in the open market (TCA 1997, s 548(1)). In estimating the market value of any assets, no reduction may be made on account of an assumption that the whole of the assets is to be placed on the market at one and the same time (TCA 1997, s 548(2)).

The market value of shares or securities quoted on a stock exchange in the State or in the UK are, except where as a result of special circumstances the quoted prices are by themselves not a proper measure of market value, to be determined in accordance with TCA 1997, s 548(3) as follows:

(a) in relation to shares or securities listed in the Stock Exchange Official List – Irish

    (i) the price shown in that list at which bargains in the shares or securities were last recorded (the previous price), or

    (ii) where bargains, other than bargains done at special prices, were recorded in that list for the relevant date, the price at which the bargains were so recorded, or if more than one such price was so recorded, a price halfway between the highest and the lowest of such prices,

    taking the amount under (i) if less than under (ii) or if no such business was recorded on the relevant date, and taking the amount under (ii) if less than under (i); and

(b) in relation to shares or securities listed in the Stock Exchange Daily Official List—

    (i) the lower of the two prices shown in the quotations for the shares or securities on the relevant date plus one quarter of the difference between those two figures, or

    (ii) where bargains, other than bargains done at special prices were recorded in that list for the relevant date, the price at which the bargains were so recorded, or if more than one such price was so recorded, a price halfway between the highest and the lowest of such prices,

    taking the amount under (i) if less than under (ii) or if no such bargains were recorded on the relevant date, and taking the amount under (ii) if less than under (i).

If, however, the shares or securities are listed in both of the above Official Lists for the relevant date, the lower of the two amounts as ascertained under (a) and (b) is to be taken. The above valuation rules do not apply to shares or securities for which some other stock exchange affords a more active market. If the stock exchange concerned, or one of the stock exchanges concerned, is closed on the relevant date, the market value is to be ascertained by reference to the latest previous date or earliest subsequent date on which it is open, whichever affords the lower market value.

Where shares or securities are not quoted on a stock exchange at the time at which their market value is to be determined under TCA 1997, s 548(1), it is to be assumed for the purposes of such determination that, in the open market which is postulated for the purposes of TCA 1997, s 548(1), there is available to any prospective purchaser of the asset in question all the information which a prudent prospective purchaser of the asset might reasonably require if he were proposing to purchase it from a willing vendor by private treaty and at arm's length (TCA 1997, s 548(4)).

For capital gains tax purposes generally, *market value*, in relation to any rights of unit holders in any unit trust (including any unit trust established outside the State) the buying and selling prices of which are published regularly by the managers of the trust, means an amount equal to the buying price (ie, the lower price) so published on the relevant date, or if none were published on that date, on the latest date before.

If and so far as any appeal against an assessment to capital gains tax (or corporation tax in respect of chargeable gains) or against a decision on a claim under the Capital Gains Tax Acts involves the question of the value of any shares or securities in a company resident in the State, other than shares or securities quoted on a stock exchange, that question is to be determined in the same way as an appeal against an assessment made on the company.

9.102.14 Consideration

As a general rule of capital gains tax, a person's acquisition of an asset is deemed to be for a consideration equal to the market value of the asset where he acquires the asset:

(a)   otherwise than by way of a bargain made at arm's length (including in particular where he acquires it by way of gift);

(b)   by way of distribution from a company in respect of shares in the company (eg by way of a distribution in a winding up); or

(c)   wholly or partly for a consideration which cannot be valued, or in connection with his own or another's loss of office or employment or diminution of emoluments, or otherwise in consideration for or recognition of his or another's services or past services in any office or employment or of any other service rendered or to be rendered by him or another (TCA 1997, s 547(1)).

Correspondingly, a person's disposal of an asset is deemed to be for a consideration equal to the market value of the asset where:

(a)   he disposes of the asset otherwise than by way of a bargain made at arm's length (including in particular where he disposes of it by way of gift); or

(b)   he disposes of the asset wholly or partly for a consideration which cannot be valued (TCA 1997, s 547(4)).

Notwithstanding the market value rule in TCA 1997, s 547(1), where, by virtue of section 31 of the State Property Act 1954, the Minister for Finance waives, in favour of a person, the right of the State to property, any such acquisition on or after 12 February 1998 is deemed to be for a consideration equal to the amount (including a nil amount) of the payment in money made by the person as one of the terms of the waiver (TCA 1997, s 547(1A)).

Without prejudice to the generality of TCA 1997, s 547, where a person acquiring an asset and the person disposing of it are connected with each other, they are to be treated as parties to a transaction otherwise than by way of a bargain made at arm's length (TCA 1997, s 549(1), (2)). TCA 1997, s 10 (see **2.3**) applies for the purpose of determining whether a person is connected with another person.

Transactions between connected persons, therefore, are specifically to be regarded as not being at arm's length so that the market value rule of TCA 1997, s 547 will always be relevant in such cases. Even though the parties to a transaction may not be connected with each other, there may be circumstances in which the transaction will not be at arm's length; this may be due to special factors affecting or related to the transaction which differentiate it from transactions between independent parties. Where a transaction is at arm's length, the market value rule will not apply (other than in certain other particular circumstances: where there is an acquisition of an asset wholly or partly for a consideration that cannot be valued, or in connection with a person's loss of office or employment or diminution of emoluments, or otherwise in consideration for or in recognition of a person's services or past services in any office or employment or of any other service rendered or to be rendered by the person). The circumstances in which the market value of property which is the subject of an arm's length transaction can differ from the consideration given or received for that property will be relatively rare, however, and are likely to occur where, say, either the vendor or the purchaser is not aware of, or is mistaken as to, the true value of the property.

In *Harrison v Nairn Williamson* [1978] STC 67, the taxpayer company paid £210,000 for loan stock issued by a company (the "Company") so that immediately after its issue the aggregate value of loan stock and the share capital of the Company was only £73,500. It was accepted that the loan stock had been issued otherwise than by way of a bargain at arm's length. The loan stock was converted into preferred stock and was later sold by the taxpayer company for £39,900. The taxpayer company argued that the market value rule applied only where there was both an acquisition and a disposal (arguable under the UK version of the market value rule) so that it should be entitled to deduct as the cost of the loan stock the £210,000 it had paid for it and not its market value at the time of acquisition. This view was rejected by the Court of Appeal. Although the acquisition of the loan stock did not involve any disposal by the Company, the court held that the market value rule could be applied to the acquisition. The question that arose in this case would not arise in Ireland as TCA 1997, s 547 deals separately with acquisitions and disposals (see above).

In *Bullivant Holdings Ltd v IRC* [1998] STC 905, it was held that the fact that shares were sold at an undervalue did not necessarily mean that the bargain in that case was otherwise than at arm's length. The sale of the shares was part of a wider transaction, which might have implied that the transaction had been influenced by this factor and was therefore not a bargain made at arm's length. However, Ferris J in the Chancery Division observed that a process under which a party has to yield in respect of one part of a composite transaction in order to obtain the desired benefits of another part of the same transaction is of the essence of a genuine commercial bargain. It should be noted that the circumstances in this case were such that the low sale price for the shares did not fall to be increased by the benefit obtained elsewhere within the wider transaction. Had different evidence been adduced, this might well have been the outcome, introducing consideration that cannot be valued, so bringing the case within TCA 1997, s 547(1) (see (c) above).

It would seem that "consideration that cannot be valued" should be interpreted strictly so that it would not refer to consideration that is merely difficult to value. The case of *Fielder v Vedlynn Ltd* [1995] STC 553 concerned a sale of subsidiary companies for monetary consideration together with a guarantee from the purchaser that the subsidiaries would comply with obligations previously undertaken to pay supplemental sums. In the Chancery Division, Harman J held that the Special Commissioner was entitled to reach the conclusion that no separate and additional monetary value could be placed on the guarantee as part of the consideration for the disposal. Instancing cases in which there was no market, no way of valuing and no comparables that could be referred to in ascertaining something so nebulous as the cash value of a guarantee, he suggested that it must have been that sort of matter at which the legislature were aiming when they enacted this part of the legislation.

Where market value falls to be substituted for the actual consideration, the rule in TCA 1997, s 563 relating to deferred consideration (see **9.102.17** under *Consideration*) will not apply. Since a market value consideration is substituted for the actual consideration, the consideration actually received is no longer relevant and neither, therefore, is any discount on that consideration. For example, where the consideration for the disposal of an asset between connected persons is deferred and, to compensate for the deferral, the amount payable is fixed at an amount above the current market value of the asset, the consideration to be taken will be the market value amount. Thus, because the parties are connected, the effect will (more or less) be that the consideration to be taken into account will be the actual amount of the consideration payable discounted by reason of the deferral.

TCA 1997, s 547(3) disapplies the market value rule of TCA 1997, s 547(1) relating to a person's acquisition of an asset where there is no corresponding disposal of an asset, and

(i)   there is no consideration in money or money's worth given for the asset; or

(ii)   the consideration is of an amount or value which is lower than the market value of the asset.

An interesting question regarding consideration for capital gains tax purposes arose in *Spectros International plc v Madden* [1997] STC 114. As part of the arrangements for the sale of a subsidiary company, it was agreed that the amount of a bank overdraft of the subsidiary should be allocated to the purchase price of the shares so that the purchasing company would discharge the debt to the lending bank. (The overdraft had arisen by reason of a substantial pre-sale dividend and was secured by an equivalent deposit made by the parent company.) It was held that the sale consideration for the shares should include the amount of the overdraft that the purchasing company had agreed to discharge. What was interesting in this decision of the Chancery Division was the observation that the payment of a debt would not ordinarily constitute additional consideration for the shares sold; it did, however, form part of the consideration in the instant case simply because the parties had specifically agreed that it should be allocated to the purchase price.

If the parties to a transaction involving the issue of shares in consideration for the transfer of assets have honestly agreed a value of the new shares for that purpose, that may be taken to be their value for the purpose of fixing the consideration for the asset transfer, even if that agreed value is different from the market value of the shares viewed objectively (*Stanton v Drayton Commercial Investment Co Ltd* [1982] STC 585).

9.102.15 Capital gains tax exemptions

Certain securities are not "chargeable assets" for the purposes of capital gains tax purposes and no chargeable gains or allowable losses arise on their disposal. These are listed mainly in TCA 1997, s 607 and are as follows:

(a) securities (including savings certificates) issued under the authority of the Minister for Finance;

(b) stocks issued by:

  – a local authority, and

  – a harbour authority mentioned in the First Schedule to the Harbours Act 1946;

(c) land bonds issued under the Land Purchase Acts;

(d) debentures, debenture stock, certificates of charge or other forms of security issued by the Electricity Supply Board, Bord Gáis Éireann, Radio Telefís Éireann, Córas Iompair Éireann, Bord na Móna or Dublin Airport Authority;

(e) securities issued by the Housing Finance Agency under section 10 of the Housing Finance Agency Act 1981;

(f) securities issued by a designated body within the meaning assigned by section 4(1) of the Securitisation (Proceeds of Certain Mortgages) Act 1995;

(g) securities issued by the National Development Finance Agency under section 6 of the National Development Finance Agency Act 2002;

(h) securities issued in the State, with the approval of the Minister for Finance, by the European Economic Community, the European Coal and Steel Community, the International Bank for Reconstruction and Development, the European Atomic Energy Community or the European Investment Bank;

(i) securities issued by An Post and guaranteed by the Minister for Finance;

(j) futures contracts, being unconditional contracts for the acquisition or disposal of any of the instruments referred to above and which require delivery of the instrument in respect of which the contracts are made;

(k) rights to winnings obtained by participating in any pool betting or lottery or sweepstake or game with prizes (TCA 1997, s 613(2)).

As regards futures contracts mentioned above, one of the conditions for exemption is that the contract requires delivery of the underlying instrument. This condition would be satisfied where the person who has entered into a contract dealt in or quoted on a futures exchange or stock exchange closes out the contract by entering into another such contract with obligations which are reciprocal to those of the closed out contract, and where both contracts are settled, if necessary, by way of single cash payment or receipt.

By virtue of TCA 1997, s 610, gains are not "chargeable gains" if they arise to the following exempt bodies listed in TCA 1997 Sch 15 Part 1:

(1) an unregistered friendly society whose income is exempt from income tax under TCA 1997, s 211(1);

(2) a registered friendly society whose income is exempt from income tax under TCA 1997, s 211(1);

(3) a registered trade union, to the extent that the proceeds of the disposal giving rise to the gain or, if greater, the consideration for the disposal under the Capital Gains Tax Acts, have been, or will be, applied solely for the purposes of its registered trade union activities;

(4) a local authority within the meaning of section 2(2) of the Local Government Act 1941;

(5)   a body established under the Local Government Services (Corporate Bodies) Act 1971;

(6)   the Central Bank of Ireland;

(7)   The Health Service Executive;

(8)   a vocational education committee established under the Vocational Education Act 1930;

(9)   a committee of agriculture established under the Agriculture Act 1931;

(10)   The National Tourism Development Authority;

(11)   The Dublin Regional Tourism Organisation Ltd;

(12)   Dublin Regional Tourism Authority Ltd;

(13)   The South-East Regional Tourism Authority Ltd;

(14)   South-West Regional Tourism Authority Ltd;

(15)   The Western Regional Tourism Authority Ltd;

(16)   The North-West Regional Tourism Authority Ltd;

(17)   Midlands-East Regional Tourism Authority Ltd;

(18)   Tramore Fáilte Ltd;

(19)   The National Treasury Management Agency;

(20)   Eolas – The Irish Science and Technology Agency;

(21)   Forbairt;

(22)   Forfás;

(23)   The Industrial Development Agency (Ireland);

(24)   The Industrial Development Authority;

(25)   Shannon Free Airport Development Company Ltd;

(26)   Údarás na Gaeltachta;

(27)   The Irish Horseracing Authority;

(28)   Irish Thoroughbred Marketing Ltd;

(29)   Tote Ireland Ltd;

(30)   a designated body within the meaning assigned by section 4(1) of the Securitisation (Proceeds of Certain Mortgages) Act 1995;

(31)   The Dublin Docklands Development Authority;

(32)   The Interim Board established under the Milk (Regulation of Supply) (Establishment of Interim Board) Order, 1994 (SI 1994/408)

(33)   National Rehabilitation Board;

(34)   The National Pensions Reserve Fund Commission;

(35)   National Development Finance Agency;

(36)   Tourism Ireland Limited;

(37)   An approved body (within the meaning of TCA 1997, s 235(1)) (bodies established for the promotion of athletic or amateur games or sports – see also **3.204.7**) to the extent that the proceeds of the disposal giving rise to the gain or, if greater, the consideration for the disposal under the Capital Gains Tax Acts, have been, or will be, applied to the sole purpose of promoting athletic or amateur games or sports;

(38)   any body established by statute for the principal purpose of promoting games or sports and any company wholly owned by such a body, to the extent that the proceeds of the disposal giving rise to the gain or, if greater, the consideration for the disposal under the Capital Gains Tax Acts, have been, or will be, applied for that purpose;

(39) The Courts Service;

(40) The Irish Auditing and Accounting Supervisory Authority;

(41) The Commission for Communications Regulation; and

(42) The Digital Hub Development Agency.

In addition, a gain is not a chargeable gain if it accrues to a body specified in TCA 1997 Sch 15 Part 2 in respect of a disposal by that body of an asset to the Interim Board. The specified bodies are as follows:

(a) The Dublin District Milk Board;

(b) The Cork District Milk Board;

(c) Dairysan Ltd; and

(d) Glenlee (Cork) Ltd.

The following, from TCA 1997, s 613, are not chargeable gains for capital gains tax purposes:

(a) any bonus payable under an instalment saving scheme, within the meaning of FA 1970 s 53;

(b) prizes under F(MP)A 1956 s 22 (Prize Bonds);

(c) sums obtained by way of compensation or damages for any wrong or injury suffered by an individual in his person or in his profession;

(d) winnings from betting, including pool betting, or lotteries or sweepstakes or games with prizes;

(e) gains accruing on disposals of rights to, or to any part of:

– any allowance, annuity or capital sum payable out of any superannuation fund, or under any superannuation scheme, established solely or mainly for persons employed in a profession, trade, undertaking or employment, and their dependants, or

– an annuity granted otherwise than under a contract for a deferred annuity by a company as part of its business of granting annuities on human life, whether or not including instalments of capital, or

– annual payments which are due under a covenant made by any person and which are not secured on any property;

(f) a gain accruing on the disposal of an interest created by or arising under a settlement (including, in particular, an annuity or life interest, and the reversion to an annuity or life interest) by the person for whose benefit the interest was created by the terms of the settlement or by any other person except one who acquired, or derives his title from one who acquired, the interest for a consideration in money or money's worth, other than consideration consisting of another interest under the settlement.

No chargeable gain arises on the disposal of, or of an interest in, an asset which is tangible movable property and which is a wasting asset (see **9.102.7** above) (TCA 1997, s 603(1)). This treatment does not apply in the case of an asset which throughout the entire period of its ownership has been used solely for the purposes of a trade or profession and where the person making the disposal claimed or could have claimed any capital allowances in respect of any expenditure (acquisition or enhancement expenditure) attributable to the asset or interest. Where the asset has been used partly for the purposes of a trade or profession and partly for other purposes, or has been used for the purposes of a trade or profession for part of the period of ownership, the respective amounts of the consideration and expenditure are to be apportioned by reference to the extent to which the expenditure qualified for capital allowances. To that extent, the gain will be a chargeable gain.

No chargeable gain arises on the disposal of, or of an interest in, the rights under any policy of assurance or contract for a deferred annuity on the life of any person except where the person making the disposal is not the original beneficial owner of those rights and acquired them for a consideration in money or money's worth (TCA 1997, s 593 – see **12.604.2**). A disposal for this purpose occurs on the first occasion of:

(a)   the payment of the sum or sums assured by a policy of assurance, including the transfer of investments or other assets to the owner of the policy in accordance with the policy;

(b)   the payment of the first instalment of a deferred annuity;

(c)   the surrender of a policy of assurance; or

(d)   the surrender of the rights under a contract for a deferred annuity.

The consideration for the disposal of a contract for a deferred annuity is deemed to be the market value at that time of the right to receive the first instalment and subsequent instalments of the annuity.

The exemption from capital gains tax in respect of the disposal of, or of an interest in, the rights under any life policy or deferred annuity contract does not apply to a foreign life assurance policy, basically a policy or contract issued by a company with no "trading presence" in the State, or by an IFSC life assurance company to a person who did not reside outside the State for a continuous period of six months from the date the policy or contract was written (TCA 1997, s 594).

A stock loan or repo is, in practice, not treated as involving a disposal/acquisition for capital gains tax purposes – see **3.212**.

9.102.16 Time of disposal

As a general rule of capital gains tax, where an asset is disposed of and acquired under a contract, the time at which the disposal and the acquisition is made is the time the contract is made, and not, if different, the time at which the asset is conveyed or transferred (TCA 1997, s 542(1)(a)). If the contact is conditional (particularly if it is conditional on the exercise of an option), the time at which the disposal and acquisition is made is the time the condition is satisfied.

In *Chaney v Watkis* 58 TC 707, the taxpayer claimed a deduction for enhancement expenditure in respect of a sum agreed to be paid, but which eventually he did not pay, to obtain vacant possession of a property on the ground that the expenditure was expenditure incurred as at the contract date for the disposal of the property and therefore before the disposal. The claim for enhancement expenditure was rejected on the principle that it would be incorrect to apply the enhancement expenditure provision in such a way as to freeze the position as at the date of the contract, thereby ignoring whatever might happen between that date and completion, a view that could clearly lead to absurd results.

There was a similar outcome in *Underwood v HMRC* [2007] SpC 614 which involved a contract for the sale of property with an option for the taxpayer to repurchase the property. The option was duly exercised. The taxpayer claimed that a disposal had taken place on the exchange of the original contract, that no movement in the legal title was necessary, but the Special Commissioners ruled against him on the basis that the purchaser had never acquired beneficial ownership of the property.

What emerges from these cases is the commonsense conclusion that the rule in TCA 1997, s 542(1)(a) does no more than establish the date of an acquisition or disposal which actually takes place; it cannot be a basis for establishing that there has been an acquisition or disposal by reason only of the existence of the contract.

The meaning of "conditional" in this context was considered in *Lyon v Pettigrew* [1985] STC 369. A taxicab proprietor contracted for the sale of six cabs with licences for a sum of £6,000 per taxi/ licence to be paid in instalments of £40 over 150 weeks but with ownership of the licence passing in each case only on payment of the final instalment.

It was held that the taxicabs should not be severed from the disposal of the licences and that both passed under the original agreement. The contract as a whole was not conditional. The underlying principle was set out by Russell LJ in *Eastham v Leigh London and Provincial Properties Ltd* 46 TC 687 where the important distinction was between a condition precedent and a condition subsequent. The former must be fulfilled before there is a binding arrangement between the parties (eg, an option) whereas a condition subsequent is a condition which one of the parties has bound himself to comply with but which does not have to be fulfilled before the parties are contractually bound by the agreement entered into. In a non-tax case, *O'Connor v Coady* [2004] IESC 54 (414/03), which came before the High Court on 12 November 2003, a contract for the sale of a property was contingent on the purchaser securing planning permission. Miss Justice Carroll ruled that the condition providing that the sale was subject to the planning permission being obtained was a condition subsequent and not a condition precedent.

The decision of the High Court was reversed in the Supreme Court (October 2004). The judgment of that Court, however, gives rise to considerable difficulties of interpretation not least in that it would seem to have reduced, if not removed, the importance of the distinction between a condition precedent and a condition subsequent. On the basis of the judgment, it would seem that a contract expressed to be conditional on the obtaining of planning permission should be regarded as a contract capable of being brought to an end by one of the parties if that condition is not fulfilled (as distinct from a contract that would not really come into existence in the first place (hence, condition "precedent") until the condition was satisfied).

In the case of a compulsory disposal, the time of disposal and acquisition is the earlier of the time at which the compensation for the acquisition is agreed or otherwise determined and the time at which the acquiring authority enters on the land in pursuance of its powers (TCA 1997, s 542(1)(c)).

By way of qualification to the position described in the previous paragraph, where a person engaged in farming (within the meaning of TCA 1997, s 654 – see **13.101**) disposes of an interest in land to an authority possessing compulsory powers, for the purposes mentioned in TCA 1997, s 652(5)(a) (construction, widening or extension of a road or part of a road), and immediately before the disposal the land was used for farming purposes, any chargeable gain on the disposal is deemed to accrue in the year of assessment in which the person receives the consideration for the disposal (TCA 1997, s 542(1)(d)).

9.102.17 Computation

General

The computation of a chargeable gain or allowable loss involves the identification of the consideration for the disposal and of the deductible expenditure in relation to that disposal. The relevant rules are mainly contained in TCA 1997 Part 19 Ch 2 (ss 544–566) and these are supported in various parts of the capital gains tax legislation by particular rules which apply to specific circumstances.

TCA 1997, s 28 provides that capital gains are chargeable gains computed in accordance with the Capital Gains Tax Acts and accruing to a person on the disposal of assets. One looks in vain in the legislation for a provision to the effect that a chargeable gain is to be computed by deducting the cost of the asset disposed of (indexed as appropriate) from the proceeds for the disposal. That, however, is the indisputable position regarding the computation of chargeable gains and is to be inferred from the relevant provisions of the legislation.

Consideration

As regards consideration for the disposal of an asset, the position will be quite straightforward in most cases as the amount of the consideration will be evident. The position will be otherwise where, say, there is a non-arm's length disposal at other than market price; the market value rule of TCA 1997, s 547 will then operate by virtue of which it will be necessary to substitute the market value of the asset for the actual sale proceeds received. In other cases where there is no consideration (eg in the case of a gift), the market value rule will again apply.

In *Aberdeen Construction v IRC* [1978] STC 127, the question as to what was the amount of the consideration received on a disposal of shares in a company was less than straightforward. The shares were offered for £250,000 on condition that a loan of £0.5m due from the company to the vendor would be waived. Without the waiver, the shares would have been virtually worthless. It was necessary to decide therefore whether the £250,000 represented consideration solely for the shares or consideration for both the shares and for agreeing to waive the loan. The proper construction of the agreement was crucial to the correct determination of this question. In a majority three-to-two decision in the House of Lords, it was held that the contract had provided for the payment of £250,000 both for the acquisition of the shares and for the waiver of the loan so that it was necessary for the consideration to be apportioned. Undoubtedly, the decision in this case produced the most equitable result. It is difficult to disagree with the minority judgments in the case however (whatever the hardship implied), as it would appear that the contract simply provided for a sale of shares for £250,000 but subject to a condition. It is not easy to see in this an agreement that some of the £250,000 was consideration for the waiver of the loan.

In *Whittles v Uniholdings Ltd (No 3)* [1996] STC 914, a company borrowed US dollars to finance an investment and simultaneously entered into a forward contract to purchase sufficient dollars to repay the loan. The pound sterling depreciated against the dollar during the course of the loan. The Court of Appeal held, by a 2-1 majority, that the loan and the forward contract had to be considered separately, applying *Aberdeen Construction* (see above), so that the company was denied a capital gains tax loss in respect of the loan while being liable in respect of its gain on the disposal of its rights under the forward contract (see also **3.408**).

Receipts which are taxed as income or which are taken into account as income are, in general, not to be included as consideration for a disposal of assets for capital gains purposes (see also **9.102.9** above). TCA 1997, s 551(2) provides that any money or money's worth charged to income tax (or to corporation tax in the case of a company) as income, or taken into account as a receipt in computing income, profits or gains or losses for those purposes, is to be excluded from the consideration for a disposal of assets taken into account in the computation of a chargeable gain.

For this purpose, a reference to sums taken into account as receipts or as expenditure in computing profits, gains or losses for the purposes of income tax (or corporation tax) are to include references to sums which would be so taken into account but for the fact that any profits or gains of a trade, profession or employment are not chargeable to income tax (or corporation tax) or that losses are not allowable for those purposes.

Income receipts which have not been subjected to income tax (or to corporation tax as income), or which have not been taken into account as income for that purpose, may well have to be included in a computation of a chargeable gain for capital gains tax purposes. A receipt from the sale of timber, where received in the context of the management of woodlands on a commercial basis, would not be taken into account for income tax or corporation tax purposes (TCA 1997, s 232(2) – see **3.204.5**). If not treated as a trading receipt, it would be difficult to avoid the conclusion, based on a strict reading of the legislation,that the disposal of timber is not subject to capital gains tax (see also **9.102.9**).

As regards the words "taken into account as a receipt in computing income …", a distinction should be made between amounts taken into account for the purposes of prior calculations affecting a taxpayer and those taken into account as receipts in computing that taxpayer's income (*Hirsch v Crowthers Ltd* 62 TC 759). Thus, for example, amounts taken into account in calculating writing down allowances or a balancing charge would be seen as too far removed from the income tax computation envisaged by TCA 1997, s 551(2). A more direct link is necessary; an example of an amount brought into account directly would be a premium paid on the grant of a lease for less than fifty years. The reasoning in *Hirsch v Crowthers* was applied by the UK Special Commissioners in *Drummond v HMRC* [2007] UKSPC SP00617 in which it was held that the gross proceeds taken into account in the [UK equivalent of] TCA 1997, s 730D calculation (gains arising on a chargeable event - see **12.603.7**) cannot be regarded as taken into account in computing income for the purposes of income tax as envisaged by TCA 1997, s 551. The only amount taken into account for that purpose is the gain as calculated, as a stand-alone figure of income.

The means by which it is provided that income tax (and corporation tax on income) should not overlap with capital gains tax in relation to any particular receipt is simply by requiring the deduction of any income type receipts from the consideration for a disposal for capital gains tax purposes. There is no provision to the effect that the asset or property in question has not been disposed of in the capital gains tax sense. As already pointed out, this leaves open the possibility that occasional receipts of an income nature could be subjected to capital gains tax treatment.

There are corresponding provisions relating to expenditure (see below).

An asset is deemed to be acquired of free of any interest or right by way of security subsisting at the time of any acquisition of it, and as being disposed of free of any such interest or right subsisting at the time of the disposal (TCA 1997, s 537(3)). Where such an interest or right attaches to the asset at the time of acquisition, the full amount of the liability assumed by the person acquiring the asset is to form part of the consideration for the acquisition and disposal in addition to any other consideration.

For the purposes of computing a chargeable gain or allowable loss, the full amount of the consideration received is to be taken into account without regard to any discount for postponing the right to receive any part of the proceeds and without regard to a risk of any part of the consideration being irrecoverable or contingent on the happening of some future event (TCA 1997, s 563(1)(a)). (See, however, **9.102.14** regarding the effect of the market value rule in TCA 1997, s 547.) Where, however, any part of the consideration so taken into account is shown to the satisfaction of the inspector to be irrecoverable, such adjustment is to be made as the case may require (TCA 1997, s 563(1)(b)). The Revenue Commissioners are not prevented by TCA 1997, s 865 from repaying an amount of tax arising out of such adjustment. In a UK case, *Loffland Bros North Sea Inc v Goodbrand* [1997] STC 102, an adjustment was refused to a company which sold assets for a dollar amount where, because of a fall in the value of sterling relative to the dollar, the sterling amount ultimately received was considerably less than the sterling equivalent of the dollar amount at the time of the sale agreement. The exchange loss was considered not to be irrecoverable consideration. This decision of the Chancery Division was upheld in the Court of Appeal (23 June 1998).

Expenditure

The rules relating to the sums allowable as a deduction from the consideration in the computation of a chargeable gain or allowable loss are found principally in TCA 1997, s 552. As regards the sums so allowable, the general rule is that expenditure which is allowable for income tax purposes (or in the computation of income for corporation tax purposes) is to be excluded (TCA 1997, s 554(1)). Excluded also is any expenditure which, although not allowable as a deduction in computing any losses, would be so allowable except for an insufficiency of income or profits. Without prejudice to this position, there is to be excluded from the sums allowable under TCA 1997, s 552 any expenditure relating to assets which, if those assets were and had always been held or used as part of the fixed capital of a trade the profits or gains of which were chargeable to income tax, would be allowable as a deduction in computing the profits or losses of the trade for the purposes of income tax (TCA 1997, s 554(2)). Note, however, that TCA 1997, s 554(2) does not apply for the purposes of corporation tax (TCA 1997, s 78(6) – see **9.101**). (See also under *Interest* below.) The exclusion of expenditure from the sums allowable in computing chargeable gains does not extend to expenditure in respect of which a capital allowance or renewals allowance is made (see under *Capital allowances* below).

Subject to the above, the sums allowable by TCA 1997, s 552(1) as a deduction from the consideration in the computation of a chargeable gain or allowable loss are:

(a) the amount or value of the consideration in money or money's worth given wholly or exclusively for the acquisition of the asset, together with the incidental costs of the acquisition or, if the asset was not acquired, any expenditure incurred wholly and exclusively in providing the asset;

(b) the amount of any expenditure wholly and exclusively incurred on the asset for the purpose of enhancing the value of the asset, being expenditure which is reflected in the state or nature of the asset at the time of the disposal;

(c) any expenditure wholly and exclusively incurred in establishing, preserving or defending title to, or a right over, the asset; and

(d) the incidental costs of making the disposal.

Expenditure on the acquisition of, or for the purpose of enhancing the value of, an asset does not include the notional cost of the taxpayer's own labour (*Oram v Johnson* [1980] STC 222).

Where payment for the acquisition of an asset is in foreign currency, the cost of the asset is the Irish pound equivalent of the foreign currency amount at the time of acquisition. Similarly, foreign currency proceeds received on the disposal of an asset must be converted into Irish pounds at the date of disposal. Where in relation to both the acquisition and disposal of an asset the same foreign currency is used, it is not correct to compute the gain or loss by reference to the Irish pound equivalent of that gain or loss as measured in the foreign currency (*Bentley v Pike* [1981] STC 360); the cost and proceeds amounts must be identified separately in Irish pounds.

The above-described treatment has been given statutory effect in anticipation of the euro becoming the currency of the State. TCA 1997, s 552(1A) (inserted by FA 1998 Sch 2 paragraph 10) provides that where a sum allowable as a deduction was incurred in a foreign currency, it is to be expressed in terms of the currency of the State by reference to the rate of exchange between the two currencies at the time the sum was incurred. For this purpose, *rate of exchange* means a rate at which two currencies might reasonably be expected to be exchanged for each other by persons dealing at arm's length.

As regards the amount deductible by way of enhancement expenditure (see (b) above), in *Aberdeen Construction Group Ltd v IRC* [1977] STC 302 (see also above) a company which had entered into a contract for the disposal of shares in another company had bound itself to waive a loan due to it by that other company. It sought to have the making of the loan and its waiver classified as enhancement expenditure in respect of the shares. It was held, in the Chancery Division, that the making of loans or their waiver could not in any circumstances be regarded as expenditure incurred wholly and exclusively on the shares; much less could either be seen as reflected in the state or nature of the shares at the time of disposal. Although the making of the loan may have enhanced the value of the shares, allowable enhancement expenditure in the sense contemplated by TCA 1997, s 552(1)(b) would have to be expenditure which results in an identifiable change for the better in the state or nature of the asset, a change distinct from the enhancement value.

TCA 1997, s 553(2) elaborates on the meaning of "incidental costs" of an acquisition or disposal (see (a) and (d) above). They must be incurred wholly and exclusively for the purposes of the acquisition or disposal of the asset and must fall into one or more of the following categories:

(a) fees, commission or remuneration paid for the professional services of any surveyor, valuer, auctioneer, accountant, agent, or legal advisor;

(b) costs of transfer or conveyance (including stamp duty);

(c)   in the case of an acquisition of an asset, the costs of advertising to find a seller;

(d)   in the case of a disposal, the costs of advertising to find a buyer and costs reasonably incurred in making any valuation or apportionment required for the purpose of the computation of the chargeable gain or allowable loss, including in particular expenses reasonably incurred in ascertaining market value where required by the Capital Gains Tax Acts.

The question of the deduction available in respect of fees paid to a valuer was considered in the UK case *Couch v Caton's Administrators* [1996] STC 201, where the costs in question were fees paid in connection with the submission of a tax return, subsequent negotiations with the inspector and the conduct of an appeal before the Appeal Commissioners. The High Court upheld the Inland Revenue view that the part of the valuation fee attributable to the negotiations with them and to the conduct of the appeal was not properly deductible as a valuation expense for the purpose of the capital gains tax computation. In what is perhaps a somewhat narrow interpretation, a distinction was made between costs relating to the work of the valuers in respect of the making of a valuation (allowable) and those relating to their work in presenting their client's case on the question of value (not allowable).

Interest

TCA 1997, s 553 provides, in the case of a company, for a deduction in respect of capitalised interest in the computation of a chargeable gain accruing to it on the disposal of a building, structure or works, or of any asset comprising it (see also **8.101**). The deduction is available where the company has incurred expenditure on the construction of the building, structure or works, being expenditure allowable as a deduction under TCA 1997, s 552, and where:

(a)   the expenditure was defrayed out of borrowed money; and

(b)   the company charged to capital all or any of the interest on the borrowed money referable to a period or part of a period ending on or before the disposal.

TCA 1997, s 553 is one of the relatively few provisions in tax legislation which specifically renders the tax treatment of an item dependent on its treatment for accounts purposes. The interest deduction is available to companies only.

TCA 1997, s 552(3)(a) contains a similar provision relating to capital gains of companies (relevant to disposals of development land – see **9.101**).

The availability of a deduction for interest in accordance with TCA 1997, s 553 or s 552(3)(a) is subject to the restriction in TCA 1997, s 554(1) but not the restriction in TCA 1997, s 554(2) (see under *Expenditure* above,)

Grants

Expenditure which has been or is to be met, directly or indirectly, by any government, by any board established by statute or by any public or local authority whether in the State or elsewhere is to be excluded from the computation under TCA 1997 Part 19 Ch 2 (TCA 1997, s 565). Many grants are now paid by the European Union or are paid from EU funds and the question arises as to whether such grants, paid by the EU Commission, are paid by a government or by a body fitting any of the other descriptions above. The fact that such grants are ultimately funded by the governments of the Member States would seem to be too remote a consideration to justify the view that they are made, even indirectly, by those governments.

Foreign tax

For the purposes of giving relief from double taxation in relation to capital gains tax charged under the law of any foreign country, in TCA 1997, s 826 and Sch 24 (see **14.2**) as they apply for the purposes of income tax, for references to income there is to be substituted references to chargeable gains, for references to the Income Tax Acts there is to be substituted references to the Capital Gains Tax Acts and for references to income tax there is to be substituted references to capital gains tax (TCA 1997, s 828(1)). The reference to capital gains tax here is, as the context may require, to tax charged under the law of the State or tax charged under the law of a country outside the State.

In so far as foreign capital gains tax may by virtue of TCA 1997, s 828 be taken into account under TCA 1997, s 826 and Sch 24, that tax, whether or not relief is given by virtue of TCA 1997, s 828 in respect of it, may not be taken into account for the purposes of TCA 1997, s 826 or Sch 24 as they apply apart from TCA 1997, s 828 (TCA 1997, s 828(2)).

Foreign tax on the disposal of an asset which is payable by the person making the disposal is to be allowable as a deduction in computing a chargeable gain or allowable loss (TCA 1997, s 828(4)). The deduction is available subject to the above provisions of TCA 1997, s 828 and to the other provisions of the Capital Gains Tax Acts as regards double taxation relief. In the cases of most double tax treaties, foreign tax payable in respect of the disposal of assets is deductible from the Irish tax payable in respect of the gain.

Capital allowances

Expenditure on assets qualifying for capital allowances (or renewals allowances) is fully allowable as a deduction under TCA 1997, s 552 in computing a chargeable gain or allowable loss in respect of the disposal of those assets (TCA 1997, s 555(1)). For the purposes of computing an allowable loss, however, there is to be deducted from the sums allowable as a deduction under TCA 1997, s 552 any expenditure to the extent to which any capital allowance or renewals allowance has been made in respect of it. Receipts giving rise to balancing charges are, similarly, not excluded from the proceeds taken into account in computing a gain for capital gains purposes, nor are they excluded for the purposes of computing a loss for those purposes (TCA 1997, s 551(3)).

Contingent liabilities

In certain cases, the value of a contingent liability of a person in relation to the disposal of an asset is not deductible under TCA 1997, s 552. No allowance may be made:

(a) in the case of an assignment of a lease of land or other property, for any liability retained or assumed by the assignor which is contingent on a default in respect of liabilities assumed by the assignee under the terms of the lease;

(b) for any contingent liability of the person making a disposal of land or an interest in land by way of sale, lease or option, for any covenant for quiet enjoyment or other obligation assumed;

(c)   for any contingent liability in respect of a warranty or representation made on a disposal by way of sale or lease of any property other than land (TCA 1997, s 562).

Where, however, any of the above contingencies subsequently becomes enforceable and this is so shown within four years from the end of the chargeable period in which this happens, any necessary adjustment is to be made so as to give effect to the deduction of the relevant expenditure incurred. Such adjustment may be made notwithstanding any limitation in TCA 1997, s 865(4) on the time within which a claim to repayment is required to be made.

Assets derived from other assets

In the case of an asset that has derived its value from another asset in the same ownership, part of the cost of the original asset from which it derived that value is to be attributed to it (TCA 1997, s 559). The necessary apportionment is made on the basis of the respective market values of the original asset and the asset that has derived its value from that asset.

In *Aberdeen Construction Group v IRC* [1978] STC 127 (see also above under *Consideration*), the taxpayer company sold shares in another company for £250,000 on condition that a loan of £0.5m due from the company to the vendor would be waived. Without the waiver, the shares would have been virtually worthless. In a majority decision, the House of Lords held that the proceeds of £250,000 should properly be attributed to both the shares and the loan but there was unanimity on the point that it would be incorrect to say that the shares derived value from the loan.

Matched foreign currency assets and liabilities

A company may match foreign currency gains and losses arising on certain assets and liabilities. Matching is by election and it applies to relevant foreign currency assets and foreign currency liabilities.

A *relevant foreign currency asset* is an asset (not being a relevant monetary item within the meaning of TCA 1997, s 79 – see **3.406**) of a company the consideration for the acquisition of which consisted solely of an amount denominated in a foreign currency and which asset consists of shares in another company acquired by the company where immediately after the acquisition—

(i)   the company owns not less than 25% of the share capital of the other company; and

(ii)   the other company is a trading company or a holding company of a trading company (TCA 1997, s 79A(1)(b)(i)).

A *foreign currency liability*, in relation to a company, is—

(i)   a liability (not being a relevant monetary item within the meaning of TCA 1997, s 79); or

(ii)   a sum subscribed for paid up share capital or contributed to the capital,

of the company and which is denominated in a foreign currency (TCA 1997, s 79A(1)(a)).

The inclusion of "contributed to the capital" in (ii) above is to cater for cases in which a capital contribution (in effect, a gift) is made to a company.

A company may, by giving notice in writing to the inspector of taxes, specify that a relevant foreign currency asset denominated in a foreign currency is to be matched with such corresponding foreign currency liability denominated in that currency as is specified by the company. Such notice must be given within three weeks after the acquisition of the relevant foreign currency asset (TCA 1997, s 79A(2)). Accordingly, a company may specify that part only of a relevant foreign currency asset is to be matched with a foreign currency liability. Clearly this will arise where the amount of a company's relevant foreign currency asset in a particular foreign currency is greater than the amount of its foreign currency liabilities in the same currency, but the company may in any event, for whatever reason, specify an amount that is less than the full amount of the relevant foreign currency asset.

For the above purposes, a "corresponding" foreign currency liability simply means a foreign currency liability equal in amount to the relevant foreign currency asset that is the subject of the matching election.

Where in an accounting period a company disposes of a relevant foreign currency asset that has been matched by it with a foreign currency liability, any chargeable gain or allowable loss arising on a disposal of the relevant foreign currency asset is to be computed for capital gains tax purposes as if the consideration received on the disposal—

(a) where the company incurs a loss on the discharge of the liability (see below) and that loss results directly from a change in a rate of exchange, was reduced by an amount equal to the amount of that loss (such reduction not to exceed the amount of any gain on the disposal as results directly from a change in the exchange rate); and

(b) where the company realises a gain on the discharge of the liability and that gain results directly from a change in a rate of exchange, was increased by an amount equal to the amount of that gain (such increase not to exceed the amount of any loss on the disposal as results directly from a change in the exchange rate) (TCA 1997, s 79A(3)).

The amount of a company's gain or loss on the discharge of a foreign currency liability is the amount that would be the gain accruing to, or as the case may be the loss incurred by, the company on the disposal of an asset acquired by it at the time the liability was incurred and disposed of at the time at which the liability was discharged if—

(i) the amount given by the company to discharge the liability was the amount given by it as consideration for the acquisition of the asset (TCA 1997, s 79A(1)(b)(iv)(I)); and

(ii) the amount of the liability incurred by the company was the consideration received by it on the disposal of the asset (TCA 1997, s 79A(1)(b)(iv)(II)).

Example 9.102.17.1
Edson Ltd borrows $1m at a time when the exchange rate is $1:€1. Later, when it repays the borrowing, the exchange rate is $1.1:€1.
There is a gain on the discharge of the foreign currency liability as follows:

	€
Consideration received: amount of liability incurred	1,000,000
Consideration given: amount given to discharge liability	909,091
Gain on discharge of liability	90,909

Where a company disposes of a relevant foreign currency asset that has been matched with a corresponding foreign currency liability but the company does not discharge the liability at that time, the company is deemed to discharge the liability, and to incur a new liability equal to the amount of the liability, at that time (TCA 1997, s 79A(1)(b)(ii)).

If a relevant foreign currency asset has been matched by a company with a corresponding foreign currency liability incurred by it before the time the asset was acquired, the company is deemed to discharge the foreign currency liability, and to incur a new liability equal to the amount of the liability, at that time (TCA 1997, s 79A(1)(b)(iii)). Thus, the "consideration" received on the eventual disposal (or deemed disposal) of the liability will be its euro equivalent at the time the foreign currency asset was acquired.

Example 9.102.17.2

Arantes Ltd has shares in a US trading subsidiary which it had purchased for $2m at which time the exchange rate was $1:€1.08. It also has outstanding borrowings of $2.5m. It now applies to treat the shares as matched by a corresponding amount of $2m of its liabilities. Arantes Ltd later disposes of the shares for $2.3m at which time the exchange rate is $1:€1.1. The borrowings are not discharged at that time.

Arantes Ltd is deemed, at the time the shares were acquired, to have discharged $2m of its foreign currency liability and to have incurred a new such liability of $2m at that time. Accordingly, the consideration deemed to be received (at 1.08) is €2,160,000 (TCA 1997, s 79A(1)(b)(iv)(II)).

At the time of disposal of the shares, Arantes Ltd is deemed to have discharged the corresponding $2m of its foreign currency liability. Accordingly, the consideration deemed to be given (at 1.1) is €2.2m (TCA 1997, s 79A(1)(b)(iv)(I)).

The capital gains tax computation is as follows:

	€	€
Consideration for the disposal ($2.3m @ 1.1)		2,530,000
Loss on discharge of liability:		
Consideration received	2,160,000	
Consideration given	2,200,000	
Loss		40,000
Net consideration		2,490,000
Cost ($2m @ 1.08)		2,160,000
Chargeable gain		330,000

One point on which the legislation is not clear is how matching is to be applied in a case where the amount of the foreign currency liability is less than the amount of the relevant foreign currency asset. The logical approach would be to apply the liability proportionately to the asset.

Example 9.102.17.3

Zagalo Ltd has shares in a US trading subsidiary which it had purchased for $1.5m at which time the exchange rate was $1:€1.05. It has outstanding borrowings of $0.75m. Its issued share capital includes dollar denominated share capital of $0.25m. It now applies to treat the shares as matched by a corresponding amount of foreign currency liability. Zagalo Ltd later disposes of 50% of the shareholding for $0.8m at which time the exchange rate is $1:€0.95. The borrowings are also discharged at that time.

Zagalo Ltd is deemed, at the time the shares were acquired, to have discharged its foreign currency liability of $1m ($0.75m + $0.25m) and at the same time to have incurred a new such liability of $1m. Accordingly, the consideration deemed to be received on the discharge of 50% of that liability (at 1.05) is €525,000 (TCA 1997, s 79A(1)(b)(iv)(II)).

At the time of disposal of the shares, Zagalo Ltd is deemed to have discharged a corresponding $0.5m (50%) of its foreign currency liability. Accordingly, the consideration deemed to be given (at 0.95) is €0.475m (TCA 1997, s 79A(1)(b)(iv)(I)).

The capital gains tax computation is as follows:

	€	€
Consideration for the disposal ($0.8m @ 0.95)		760,000
Gain on discharge of liability:		
Consideration received	525,000	
Consideration given	475,000	
Gain		50,000
Net consideration		810,000
Cost ($750,000 @ 1.05)		787,500
Chargeable gain		22,500

IFSC companies: Revenue practice regarding conduit companies

In certain circumstances, an investment in an IFSC company may be made indirectly through another Irish resident company the sole function of which will be to act as a conduit between the ultimate non-resident investor and the IFSC company. If that investment had been made directly, the investing company would not be subject to capital gains tax on the realisation of the investment whereas, in the case of an investment made indirectly, a capital gains tax liability could arise to the conduit company by reason of currency fluctuations.

In accordance with a Revenue practice, an Irish resident company the sole function of which is to act as a conduit company between the ultimate non-resident investor and an IFSC trading company will not be regarded as realising a chargeable gain or an allowable loss on the redemption of its foreign currency denominated shares in the IFSC company provided—

(a) the balance sheet of the conduit company shows corresponding amounts denominated in the same currency represented by the liability to the ultimate investor and the asset representing the investment in the IFSC company;

(b) no conversion of currency takes place; and

(c) the redemption proceeds per share do not exceed the foreign currency amount subscribed per share (including any capital contribution).

The above-described practice also applies in a case where the conduit company has more than one foreign currency investment but provided the only translation that arises is a translation required for the purposes of preparing its accounts in its functional currency.

9.102.18 Replacement of business and other assets

TCA 1997, s 597 provides for a relief (usually referred to as "roll-over relief"), by way of a deferral of capital gains tax, in the cases of certain business asset disposals. Subject to transitional arrangements (see below), this deferral ceased to be available in respect of disposals on or after 4 December 2002.

To obtain relief from capital gains tax in respect of the disposal of any business assets, the proceeds of disposal must be re-invested in other business assets. Both the asset disposed of and the asset, or assets, acquired must fall within one (not necessarily the same one) of the following categories:

(a) plant or machinery;

(b) except where the trade is a trade of dealing in or developing land, or of providing services for the occupier of land in which the person carrying on the trade has an estate or interest—

    (i) any building or part of a building and any permanent or semi-permanent structure in the nature of a building, occupied (as well as used) only for the purposes of the trade,

    (ii) any land occupied (as well as used) only for the purposes of the trade, and for this purpose a trade of dealing in or developing land will not be treated as such if a profit on a sale of any land held for the purposes of the trade would not form part of the trading profits;

(c) goodwill;

(d) as respects disposals made on or after 11 March 1998, any financial assets (ie, shares of any company and stocks, bonds and obligations of any government, municipal corporation, company or other body corporate) owned by a body of persons established for the sole purpose of promoting athletic or amateur games or sports (TCA 1997, s 597(3)).

TCA 1997, s 597 applies with necessary modifications in relation to—

(i) the discharge of the functions of a public authority;

(ii) the occupation of woodlands where the woodlands are managed by the occupier on a commercial basis and with a view to the realisation of profits;

(iii) a profession, office or employment;

(iv) such of the activities of a body of persons whose activities are carried on otherwise than for profit and are wholly or mainly directed to the protection or promotion of the interests of its members in the carrying on of their trade or profession as are so directed;

(v) the activities of a body of persons, being a body not established for profit whose activities are wholly or mainly carried on otherwise than for profit, but in the case of assets of the kind described in (b) above only if they are both occupied and used by the body and in the case of other specified assets only if they are used by the body;

(vi) such of the activities of a body of persons established for the sole purpose of promoting athletic or amateur games or sports as are directed to that purpose; and

(vii) farming,

as it applies in relation to a trade (TCA 1997, s 597(2)).

In *Temperley v Visibell* [1974] STC 64, it was held that mere visits to a site coupled with the intention to build on it, and the application of planning permission, did not satisfy the requirement that the land had been occupied as well as used for the purposes of the relief. In *Anderton v Lambe* [1981] STC 43, two farmhouses on land farmed in partnership by a husband and wife had qualified for farm capital allowances for income tax purposes. Each house had been occupied as a residence by one of the sons of the couple under a licence from the partnership. It was held that the houses were occupied by the sons in an individual capacity and not by the partnership as such, notwithstanding that they were owned by the partnership and were used as farmhouses, so that they did not meet the test of being occupied and used only for the purposes of the trade.

The question of roll-over relief in relation to goodwill was the subject of the appeal in *Dodd v Mudd* [1987] STC 141. A chargeable gain arose on the disposal of the goodwill of an accountancy practice and the taxpayer claimed roll-over relief against expenditure incurred in acquiring a 75% interest in a large house to be used as a private hotel. The remaining 25% interest was acquired by the taxpayer's wife and the house was held by the couple as tenants in common. A part of the house amounting to 25% was used by them as a private residence. It was held that the gain arising on the disposal of the goodwill could be rolled over only against 75% of the total expenditure on the house.

The main roll-over provision is contained in TCA 1997, s 597(4). To qualify for relief under that subsection, the investment in the replacement asset or assets must take place within the four-year period commencing one year before, and ending three years after, the date of the disposal.

Roll-over relief takes the form of a deferral by treating the gain as not arising until the replacement assets (*the new assets*) cease to be used for the purposes of the trade. There is no question of the gain reducing the cost of the new assets. The relief is not so much a "roll-over" as a "hold-over" of the gain arising on the disposal of the original assets (*the old assets*). In calculating the capital gains tax liability on the deferred gain, on the occasion of the disposal of the new assets, the date of disposal of the old assets is used for the purposes of applying the indexation multiplier.

Where—

(i)   the consideration received by a person carrying on a trade for the disposal, before 4 December 2002, of, or of that person's interest in, assets ("the old assets") used only for the purposes of the trade throughout the period of ownership is applied by that person in acquiring other assets, or an interest in other assets ("the new assets");

(ii) the new assets on their acquisition are taken into use and used only for the purposes of the trade; and

(iii) the old assets and the new assets are assets of a kind specified in TCA 1997, s 597(3) (see (a) to (d) above),

the person carrying on the trade, on making a claim to that effect, is treated as if the chargeable gain accruing on the old assets did not accrue until that person ceases to use the new assets for the purposes of the trade (TCA 1997, s 597(4)(a))

Where the consideration received by a person on the disposal of the new assets is applied in acquiring other new assets which on their acquisition are taken into use and used only for the purposes of the trade and are assets in one of the qualifying categories, the chargeable gain on the disposal of the old assets is treated as not accruing until the person ceases to use—

(a)   the other new assets for the purposes of the trade; and

(b)   any further new assets which are acquired in a similar manner, taken into use, and used only, for the purposes of the trade and are assets in one of the qualifying categories (TCA 1997, s 597(4)(b)).

The termination of roll-over relief for disposals of assets on or after 4 December 2002 does not apply to a disposal on or before 31 December 2003 of an asset used for the purposes of a trade (or activity referred to in TCA 1997, s 597(2) – see above) carried on by the person making the disposal where that person claims that, were it not for the termination of the relief, a claim could have been made such that the chargeable gain accruing on the disposal could not accrue until assets, acquired before 4 December 2002 or acquired under an unconditional contract entered into before that date, ceased to be used for the purposes of the trade (or other activity). Thus, relief can be claimed in respect of disposals from 5 December 2002 to 31 December 2003 but only where sufficient expenditure on replacement assets had been incurred (or committed to) by 3 December 2002. It is not possible to have gains on such disposals deferred further on the occasion of the replacement assets being themselves subsequently replaced.

As seen above, the deferred gain arising on the disposal of the old assets continues to be held over where the consideration received on the disposal of the new assets is applied in acquiring other qualifying new assets (and similarly where the consideration received on the disposal of the other new assets is applied in acquiring further qualifying new assets, and so on). Surprisingly, there is no stipulation here as to how much needs to be expended on the other new assets or further new assets. Where new assets are depreciating assets (typically plant or machinery), the amount of the consideration received on their disposal may be relatively small and may be no more than nominal in many cases. Reinvesting such small or nominal amounts in replacement assets would then be sufficient to secure that the original gain continues to be held over.

Roll-over relief must be claimed; it does not apply automatically. In relation to the three-year period within which replacement assets must be acquired, relief may be claimed at any time only by reference to actual acquisitions and not by reference to anticipated or projected acquisitions within the three-year period. Thus, at the time the relevant return is being filed, a claim may only be made in respect of acquisitions that have taken place up to that time. If further replacement acquisitions are made between that time and the time the tax is due, further relief can be claimed resulting in a reduction in the amount of tax otherwise payable. If yet further replacement acquisitions are made after the date the tax was paid and within the three-year period, additional relief may be claimed. Tax overpaid will then be refunded.

Where roll-over relief has been claimed and the new assets subsequently cease to be used for the purposes of the trade in question, the gain arising on the old assets then crystallises. The capital gains tax rate applicable is the rate in force at the time of the disposal of the old assets. (It is suggested that this is the correct view of the matter despite an Appeal Commissioners' decision to the effect that it is the rate in force at the time of disposal of the new assets. Changes in capital gains tax rates are made by reference to the date of disposal.)

To qualify for full relief under TCA 1997, s 597(4), the entire consideration for the disposal must be re-invested in the new assets. Where part only of the consideration is re-invested, partial deferral is available in accordance with TCA 1997, s 597(5) provided the amount re-invested is greater than the historic cost of the old assets. The arithmetical gain on the sale of the old assets is reduced to the amount not reinvested. The resulting percentage reduction is then applied to the chargeable gain to arrive at the amount of the gain rolled over.

Example 9.102.18.1

On 3 April 14 August 2007, Glencarrig Ltd disposed of premises which it had acquired in June 1973 for €50,000 and which it had used in its manufacturing trade since that time. The market value of the premises as at 6 April 1974 was €72,000. The company realised €600,000 on the disposal and reinvested €500,000 of this amount in new business premises also for purposes of the company's trade.

The chargeable gain is computed as follows:

	€
Disposal proceeds	600,000
Deduct: 6/4/74 market value €72,000 @ 7.528	542,016
Chargeable gain	57,984

In accordance with TCA 1997, s 597(5), the arithmetical gain of €550,000 (€600,000 − €50,000) is reduced to €100,000, the amount not reinvested. This gives a reduction of 81.818% and that reduction is applied to the chargeable gain of €57,984 to arrive at a reduced gain of €10,543. Of the chargeable gain of €57,984 therefore, €10,543 is taxable currently and the balance of €47,441 is deferred or "held over".

Roll-over relief is not available in respect of gains arising on disposals ("relevant disposals") of development land. However, this prohibition does not apply:

(a) to a relevant disposal made by a body of persons established for the sole purpose of promoting athletic or amateur games or sports, being a disposal which is made in relation to such of the activities of that body as are directed to that purpose;

(b) to a relevant disposal where the relevant local authority (see below) gives a certificate in writing to the person making the disposal stating that the land being disposed of is subject to a use which, on the basis of guidelines issued by the Minister for the Environment and Local Development, is inconsistent with the protection and improvement of the amenities of the general area within which that land is situated or is otherwise damaging to the local environment;

(c) to a relevant disposal made to an authority possessing compulsory purchase powers where the disposal is made for the purpose of enabling the authority to construct, widen or extend a road, or part of a road, or for a purpose connected with, or ancillary to, the construction, widening or extension of a road, or part of a road, by the authority;

(d) to a relevant disposal where the old assets (throughout a period of five years ending with the time of disposal) and the new assets are assets of an authorised racecourse (within the meaning of section 2 of the Irish Horseracing Industry Act 1994) (TCA 1997, s 652(3));

(e)   to a relevant disposal made on or after 6 April 1998 where the old assets (throughout a period of five years ending with the time of disposal) and the new assets are assets of an authorised greyhound race track (TCA 1997, s 652(3A));

(f)   to a relevant disposal made on or after 6 April 1998 effected by an order made under section 28(1) of the Dublin Docklands Development Authority Act 1997, ie an order by the Minister for the Environment and Local Government to transfer land in the Dublin Docklands Area from a statutory body to the Dublin Docklands Development Authority (TCA 1997, s 652(3B)).

For the purposes of (b) above, *the relevant local authority*, referred to above, means the county council or the corporation of a county or other borough or, where appropriate, the urban district council in whose functional area the land being disposed of is situated.

For the purposes of (d), *assets of an authorised racecourse* means assets of a racecourse which is an authorised racecourse where the assets are used for the provision of appropriate facilities or services to carry on horseracing at race meetings or to accommodate persons associated with horseracing, including members of the public.

For the purposes of (e), *authorised greyhound race track* means a greyhound race track (within the meaning of section 2 of the Greyhound Industry Act 1958) in respect of which a greyhound race track licence has been granted by Bord na gCon, and that licence has not been revoked. *Assets of an authorised greyhound race track* means assets of a greyhound race track which is an authorised greyhound race track where the assets are used for the provision of appropriate facilities or services to hold greyhound races (within the meaning of section 2 of the Greyhound Industry Act 1958) or to accommodate persons associated with greyhound racing, including members of the public.

In relation to (d) and (e), references to new assets ceasing to be used for the purposes of a trade (in relation to a chargeable gain accruing on the cessation of use of the new assets) include references to new assets ceasing to be assets of an authorised racecourse or, as the case may be, of an authorised greyhound race track.

Time limit for replacement of asset

The proceeds re-invested must be expended within the period of one year before and three years after the disposal (TCA 1997, s 597(7)). The Revenue Commissioners may allow an extension of this time limit. The extension will only be granted in exceptional circumstances where it can be shown that every effort was made to re-invest within the time limit and where such re-investment was prevented by circumstances outside the control of the re-investor. Where it becomes likely that the re-investment will not take place within the time limit, a written explanation should be given detailing the efforts made to re-invest within the time limit, why these failed to secure the re-investment and the likely date the re-investment will take place. That matter would then be considered in the light of the facts. (see also re Chief Inspector's CGT Manual below.)

The UK case *Steibelt v Paling* 1999 STC 594 considered the refusal by the Inland Revenue to exercise the discretion granted to them by the UK equivalent of TCA 1997, s 597(7) to extend the three year period after the disposal of the old assets in which the expenditure on the new asset must occur. The Court held that the Appeal Commissioners, in attempting to overrule the Inland Revenue's decision not to extend the period, acted outside their powers. Only the superior courts, on foot of a judicial review, could overrule the exercise of a discretion statutorily granted to the Revenue.

TCA 1997, s 597(7) provides that the acquisition of (or of an interest in) the new assets must take place, *or* an unconditional contract for such acquisition must be entered into, within the four year time limit referred to above. Accordingly, if an unconditional contract for the acquisition of new assets is entered into, say, more than twelve months before the date of disposal of the old assets, but the new assets are not actually acquired until a time that is within that twelve month period, this condition would be fulfilled. In this case, the general capital gains tax rule to the effect that the date of acquisition of an asset is the time the related (unconditional) contract is made (see **9.102.16**) does not apply.

It is sufficient that an unconditional contract for the acquisition of the replacement assets is entered into within the time limit. Provisional relief will be given where such an unconditional contract is entered into, and any necessary adjustments can be made as *and when, and if, the assets are actually acquired.*

It is necessary that the replacement assets should "on their acquisition" be "taken into use and used only for the purposes of the trade" (TCA 1997, s 597(4)(a)(ii)). In the UK case *Campbell Connelly and Company Limited v Barnett* [1994] STC 50, roll-over relief was denied in part because of a delay in employing the assets acquired in the trade. A company disposed of a premises and shortly afterwards acquired the freehold of another premises. The newly-acquired premises had a sitting tenant and it was not until almost nine months later that vacant possession was obtained and the premises were occupied for the purpose of the trade. The case was complicated by the fact that the freehold was acquired by the taxpayer company, whereas the sitting tenant was bought out by the parent company of the taxpayer so that the new asset was acquired only in part by the taxpayer. But the fact that the delay of the order mentioned occurred before putting the premises into use for the purpose of the trade was in any event fatal to the claim for relief.

The decision in this case is in contrast with that in *Clarke v Mayo* [1994] STC 57, a case concerned with retirement relief in the UK. It was necessary in that case to consider the meaning of the phrase "immediately before the material disposal ... the asset was in use for the purposes of that business". The judge held that the words "immediately before" should not be construed in isolation but in the context of retirement relief as a whole. In that context the words "immediately before" might be construed as meaning "sufficiently proximate in time to the material disposal or cessation so as to justify the conclusion that the transaction in question formed part of it". In *Campbell Connelly,* however, the judge did not apply a similar broad purposive interpretation to the expression "on the acquisition thereof". If a purposive interpretation is appropriate in one case, why is it not equally appropriate in the other? Where an asset is put into use in a business within a reasonably short time after being acquired, especially where it is clear that its acquisition and its use in the business are closely related, it is arguable that the requirement in the words "on the acquisition thereof" is satisfied.

Steibelt v Paling, referred to above, also considered the requirement that the new assets must, on acquisition, be taken into use and used only for the purpose of the trade. The Court concluded that the Inland Revenue statement of practice on roll-over relief correctly interpreted the law in this respect and did not represent a concession. That statement of practice provided that "where a 'new asset' is not, on acquisition, immediately taken into use for the purposes of a trade, it will nevertheless qualify for relief under (TCA 1997, s 597) provided (a) the owner proposes to incur capital expenditure for the purposes of enhancing its value, (b) any work arising from such capital expenditure begins as soon as possible after acquisition and is completed within a reasonable time, (c) on completion of the work the asset is taken into use for the purpose of the trade and for no other purpose, and (d) the asset is not let or used for any non-trading purpose in the periods between acquisition and the time it is taken into use for the purpose of the trade."

In the January 1997 issue of Irish Tax Review (Institute Matters, item 16) it is reported that "the Irish Revenue view was that they would continue to apply the law as it was understood prior to this case (*Campbell Connolly & Co. Ltd v Barnett*) in Ireland".

In the case of *Milton v Chilvers* [1995] STC 57, the UK Special Commissioners held that the meaning of "on the acquisition" in its context was "following on the acquisition". That did not imply immediacy, but it did exclude dilatoriness. The taking into use and the acquisition had to be reasonably proximate to one another.

*   *Revenue/Chief Inspector's CGT Manual*:

    In their capital gains tax manual, the Revenue Commissioners at Paragraph 19.6.2.10 refer to their power to extend the period in which reinvestment must occur in order to avail of the relief. An example of circumstances where the period should be extended is where a local authority uses its compulsory purchase powers to acquire a property in advance of their need to use the property, and allow the former owner to remain in possession for a period of time which may exceed 3 years. The manual states: "In such a case a claim for an extension of the time limit may be allowed by the District Inspector for a period of 12 months after the property ceases to be used by the trader for the trade, if the disposal proceeds are reinvested in qualifying assets within this extended period. Any other claim for extension of the time limit should be submitted to head office."

Assets not used for trade purposes throughout full period of ownership

Where qualifying assets have not been used for the purposes of the trade throughout the entire period of ownership, the cost and sale proceeds are apportioned as if there were two separate assets (TCA 1997, s 597(10)). Any apportionment is to be made "having regard to the time and extent to which it was and was not used for those [trade] purposes". The gain attributable to the use for trading purposes qualifies for relief.

Example 9.102.18.2

On 6 April 1972, Anaconda Ltd purchased a warehouse for €70,000 and used it for the purposes of its trade up to 5 April 1992. The building was let from 6 April 1992 to 5 April 2002 on which date it was sold for €850,000. The market value of the warehouse at 6 April 1974 was €100,000. Anaconda Ltd used the entire proceeds of sale to re-invest in qualifying assets.

	€	€
Sale proceeds		850,000
Market Value 6/4/74	100,000	
Indexation @ 7.18		718,000
Chargeable gain		132,000
Gain attributable to qualifying asset:		
20/30 x €132,000 =		88,000

€88,000 of the gain is eligible for roll-over relief and the balance of the chargeable gain is taxable.

The UK case *Richart v J Lyons & Co Ltd* [1989] STC 8 is authority for the rule that in calculating the periods of trade use and non-trade use, no account is to be taken of any period of time when a chargeable gain was not accruing. Thus, in the above example, the period from 6 April 1970 to 5 April 1974 is ignored.

The *Lyons* case is also authority for the proposition that a deemed disposal and reacquisiton at 6 April 1974 of an asset that was held prior to that date does not interrupt the period of ownership of the asset.

In *O'Coindealbhain EP (Inspector of Taxes) v KN Price* 4 ITR 1, Justice Carroll in the High Court on 29 January 1988 held that a farm of land, which throughout the period of ownership had been let on conacre to a third party and had not otherwise been used by the taxpayer, had not been occupied by the taxpayer for the purpose of a trade, or for farming, and that accordingly an entitlement to roll-over relief did not arise on its disposal, notwithstanding that the proceeds of disposal were invested in the purchase of a new farm.

Justice Carroll held that the taxpayer had neither occupied the old farm nor carried on a trade of farming on it. It was the conacre tenant who occupied the farm and who carried on the trade of farming.

Reinvestment in different trade

As a general rule, the proceeds on disposal must be re-invested in qualifying assets which must be in use for the purpose of the same trade as the trade in which the old assets were used. There are three exceptions to this rule:

(1) where two or more trades are carried on simultaneously by the same taxpayer;
(2) where the taxpayer ceases a trade, and commences a new trade within a specified time period;
(3) where the relief is claimed by a company which is a member of a group (see 5 above – replacement of business assets by group members).

(1) Two or more trades carried on simultaneously (TCA 1997, s 597(11)(a))

Roll-over relief applies where the disposal and re-investment relate to the same trade but also where a person carries on two or more trades, provided—

(a) the trades are in different localities; and
(b) the trades deal wholly or mainly in goods or services of the same kind.

The Revenue Commissioners consider that the reference to carrying on two or more trades applies not only to the carrying on simultaneously of two or more trades but also where one trade ceases and another trade commences (as discussed in *(2)* below). That interpretation must be concessional in that the wording of TCA 1997, s 597(11)(a) seems to apply only to the case of two trades carried on simultaneously. The equivalent UK legislation specifically provides that the two trades may be carried on either successively or at the same time. TCA 1997, s 579(11) provides in separate paragraphs for trades being carried on simultaneously and trades being carried on successively. The latter is subject to time constraints.

Relief is calculated as if the separate trades were a single trade; the disposal of assets may be in one trade and the re-investment in the other.

Example 9.102.18.3

J Pilsbury Ltd operates a supermarket in Rathmines and has a cash-and-carry outlet in Clontarf where the goods dealt with are mainly of the same kind as those sold in Rathmines. The company also has a record store in a shopping centre in Blanchardstown.

The company sells off part of the property in Clontarf for €500,000. €200,000 of these proceeds is then applied in acquiring a unit in the Blanchardstown shopping centre in order to expand the record store there. The balance of €300,000 is applied in acquiring new equipment and fittings for the supermarket in Rathmines.

The three businesses carried on by J Pilsbury Ltd are separate trades. Although the full sale proceeds have been re-invested in qualifying assets, and although all of the new assets are used for the purposes of trades carried on by the company, the €200,000 invested in the extended premises at Blanchardstown does not qualify for roll-over relief. The trade carried on in Blanchardstown is in a different locality to the cash-and-carry trade in respect of which the disposal was made (thereby satisfying one of the conditions for relief) but the trades do not deal wholly or mainly with goods or services of the same kind. Accordingly, relief is not available in respect of any re-investment of proceeds from the cash-and-carry trade in the record store trade.

On the other hand, although the cash-and-carry trade and the supermarket are clearly different in nature, they do deal mainly with goods of the same kind, and they are carried on in different localities. Accordingly the expenditure of €300,000 in Rathmines does qualify for roll-over relief.

Although there is no guidance available as to what "different localities" means, the separate trades in the above example are clearly carried on in different localities. If the supermarket and the cash-and-carry were located in separate units in the same shopping centre in Rathmines, they would be in the same locality and relief would not have been available. As to why it is a condition for relief that the trades should be in different localities is unclear.

Note, however, the published precedent of the Revenue Commissioners as described in *(2)* below.

(2) Cessation of trade – commencement of new trade (TCA 1997, s 597(11)(b))

Roll-over relief also applies to a person who ceases to carry on a trade and subsequently commences to carry on a new trade provided that person—

(a)   carried on the old trade for at least 10 years prior to its cessation; and

(b)   commences a new trade within 2 years of the date of cessation of the old trade.

The relief is calculated as if the two trades were the same trade. There is no requirement in this case that the two trades should be similar.

Example 9.102.18.4

The position is as in Example **9.102.18.3** except that J Pilsbury Ltd ceases its cash-and-carry business in Clontarf, which it had carried on for 20 years, and sells off the fixed assets which had been used in that trade. It re-invests the proceeds in equipment and fixtures required to convert the premises into a snooker hall.

The company is entitled to roll-over relief even though the trade that ceased and the new trade which then commences are in the same locality, and even though they were concerned with goods and services of a very different nature. This is because the roll-over relief being claimed is not in respect of a disposal in a continuing trade, as was the case in Example **9.102.18.3**, but is in respect of a trade which had ceased and a new trade which has then commenced. (The conditions described in (a) and (b) in (1) above do not apply.)

It seems possible to interpret "within a period of 2 years from the date on which the person ceased to carry on the old trade or trades" as including a reference to a situation in which the new trade commences within a period of 2 years *before* the old trade ceases. It is more likely, however, that the provision is intended to cover only a situation in which the new trade commences within a period of 2 years after the old trade ceases. For example, TCA 1997, s 597(11)(b) refers to a person who "commences" to carry on a new trade within 2 years of having "ceased" to carry on the old trade.

Furthermore, the period within which replacement assets may be acquired generally for the purposes of roll-over relief is 12 months before and 3 years after the disposal of the old assets (TCA 1997, s 597(7)). For the purposes of TCA 1997, s 597(11)(b) therefore, if it had been intended that there should be a two-year window both before and after the old trade ceases, the wording of that paragraph would presumably have been similar to that in TCA 1997, s 597(7).

Where a person ceases to carry on more than one trade but not on the same date, it is not clear how the two-year period should be calculated. It would seem reasonable that the period should be reckoned by reference to the later of the two dates.

A person ceasing to carry on a trade within 10 years after commencing to carry it on cannot avail of roll-over relief by re-investing in assets for the purposes of a trade which that person then commences. Relief in that situation would be available only on the basis of carrying on two or more trades in different localities (see (1) above) (or, if the circumstances permit, by reference to group treatment (TCA 1997, s 620)). To be eligible for relief on the basis of (1) above, the person would have to commence the new trade prior to ceasing the old trade and the two trades would have to be carried on in different localities and be concerned wholly or mainly with goods or services of the same kind.

* *Revenue Commissioners – published precedent*:

In a published precedent the Revenue Commissioners state: "Where a trade carried on for less than 10 years ceases and a similar trade commences, strictly, relief is not due as TCA 1997, s 597(11)(b) requires that the old trade be carried on for at least 10 years. However, TCA 1997, s 597(11)(a) allows relief for two trades which are carried on in different localities but which are wholly or mainly concerned with goods or services of the same kind. This is read as applying where the trades are carried on simultaneously or successively, thus covering a cessation of one trade and the commencement of a similar trade."

In effect, the intention of this precedent seems to be to give the best of both worlds in the case of one trade ceasing and another trade commencing. While paragraph (b) denies relief where the old trade was not carried on for at least 10 years, the precedent gives relief on the basis of paragraph (a) which does not have the ten-year requirement. In doing this, however, it ignores the requirements of paragraph (a) in relation to the trades being carried on in different localities and also in relation to the trades dealing wholly or mainly in goods or services of the same kind.

Roll-over relief for certain rental property

TCA 1997, s 600A provides for roll-over relief in respect of disposals of certain rental property (a "qualifying premises") where the consideration received is used to acquire certain other rental property. Each rental property disposed of must have at least three residential units and must comply with certain housing regulations. The gain on the disposal of the first property is deferred where the consideration for its disposal is reinvested in a rental property which contains at least as many residential units as the property disposed of. Subject to transitional arrangements (similar to those discussed above), this deferral ceased to be available in respect of disposals on or after 4 December 2002.Definitions

"Qualifying premises", in relation to a person, means a building or part of a building, or an interest in a building or part of a building—

(a)   in which there is not less than three residential units;

(b)   in respect of which the person is entitled to a rent or to receipts from any easement; and

(b)   in respect of which all the requirements of the Regulations are complied with.

"Regulations" means—

(i)   the Housing (Standards for Rented Houses) Regulations 1993 (SI 1993/14);

(ii)   the Housing (Rent Books) Regulations 1993 (SI 1993/146); and

(iii)   the Housing (Registration of Rented Houses) Regulations 1996, as amended by the Housing (Registration of Rented Houses) (Amendment) Regulations 2000 (SI 2000/12).

"Replacement premises", in relation to a person, means a building or part of a building, or an interest in a building or part of a building—

(a)   which the person acquires with the consideration obtained by him from the disposal of a qualifying premises;

(b)   in which the number of residential units is not less than the number of residential units in the qualifying premises;

(c)   in respect of which the person is entitled to a rent or to receipts from any easement; and

(d)   in respect of which all the requirements of the Regulations are complied with.

"Residential unit" means a separately contained part of a residential premises used or suitable for use as a dwelling.

The relief

The relief takes the form of a deferral by treating the gain from the disposal, on or after 5 January 2001 and before 4 December 2002, of a premises, which was a qualifying premises throughout the period of its ownership by the person disposing of it, as not arising until the replacement premises is disposed of or ceases to be a replacement premises (TCA 1997, s 600A(2)(a)). The gain on disposal does not reduce the cost of the replacement premises and, like the main roll-over relief in TCA 1997, s 597, the relief is not so much a "roll-over" as a "hold-over" of the gain arising on the disposal of the qualifying premises. In calculating the capital gains tax liability on the deferred gain, on the occasion of the disposal of the replacement premises, the date of disposal of the qualifying premises is used for the purposes of applying the indexation multiplier (TCA 1997, s 600A(4)). The termination of roll-over relief for disposals of assets on or after 4 December 2002 does not apply to a disposal on or before 31 December 2003 of a qualifying premises where the person making the disposal claims that, were it not for the termination of the relief, a claim could have been made such that the chargeable gain accruing on the disposal could not accrue until a replacement premises, acquired before 4 December 2002 or acquired under an unconditional contract entered into before that date, was disposed of by that person or ceased to be a replacement premises. Thus, relief can be claimed in respect of disposals from 5 December 2002 to 31 December 2003 but only where sufficient expenditure on a replacement premises has been incurred (or committed to) by 3 December 2002. It is not possible to have gains on such disposals deferred further on the occasion of the replacement premises being themselves subsequently replaced.

Where the consideration received on the disposal of the replacement premises is applied in acquiring further replacement premises, the chargeable gain on the disposal of the qualifying premises is treated as not accruing until the time of the disposal of the further replacement premises, or of any further replacement premises which are acquired in a similar manner, or that further replacement premises or any other further replacement premises acquired in a similar manner cease to be a replacement premises (TCA 1997, s 600A(2)(b)).

For relief to apply, the investment in the replacement premises must take place within the four-year period commencing one year before, and ending three years after, the date of the disposal of the qualifying premises, or at such earlier or later time as the Revenue Commissioners may by notice in writing allow (TCA 1997, s 600A(5)). As with the main relief in TCA 1997, s 597, it is to be expected that this extension will only be granted in exceptional circumstances where it can be shown that every effort was made to re-invest within the time limit and where such re-investment was prevented by circumstances outside the control of the re-investor. It is sufficient that an unconditional contract for the acquisition of the replacement assets is entered into within the time limit. Provisional relief will be given where such an unconditional contract is entered into, and any necessary adjustments can be made as and when, and if, the assets are actually acquired.

In relation to the three-year period within which replacement assets must be acquired, relief applies only by reference to actual acquisitions and not by reference to anticipated or projected acquisitions within the three-year period. Thus, at the time the relevant return is being filed, relief may be obtained only in respect of acquisitions that have taken place up to that time. If further replacement acquisitions are made between that time and the time the tax is due, further relief can be obtained resulting in a reduction in the amount of tax otherwise payable. If yet further replacement acquisitions are made after the date the tax was paid and within the three-year period, additional relief may be obtained. Tax overpaid will then be refunded.

Where roll-over relief has been obtained and the replacement premises is disposed of or subsequently ceases to be a replacement premises, the gain arising on the qualifying premises then crystallises. The capital gains tax rate applicable is the rate in force at the time of the disposal of the qualifying premises.

To qualify for full relief under TCA 1997, s 600A, the entire consideration for the disposal of the qualifying premises must be re-invested in the replacement premises. Where part only of the consideration is re-invested, partial deferral is available in accordance with TCA 1997, s 600A(3) provided the amount re-invested is greater than the historic cost of the qualifying premises. The arithmetical gain on the sale of the qualifying premises is reduced to the amount not reinvested. The resulting percentage reduction is then applied to the chargeable gain to arrive at the amount of the gain rolled over (see Example 9.102.18.1 above in relation to this feature of the relief).

Roll-over relief will not apply if the acquisition of the replacement premises was wholly or partly for the purpose of realising a gain from the disposal of the replacement premises (TCA 1997, s 600A(6)). Thus, the relief is intended to apply only in the case of a "genuine" replacement of a rental property and not where a disposal of rental property is followed by an acquisition of another rental property where there is an intention to dispose of that property at a profit.

If the qualifying premises was not a qualifying premises throughout the period of ownership of the person claiming roll-over relief, relief will apply as if a part of the qualifying premises, representing the period for which it was a qualifying premises, was a separate asset. Relief will then apply in relation to that part. Any necessary apportionments of consideration will then be made in relation to the acquisition or disposal of the interest in the premises (TCA 1997, s 600A(7)). Any apportionment of consideration for the acquisition or disposal of premises some of which qualifies for roll-over relief and some of which does not is to be made in such manner as is just and reasonable (TCA 1997, s 600A(8)).

9.102.19 Trading stock

A chargeable gain or allowable loss may arise where an asset acquired by a person otherwise than as trading stock is "appropriated" by him for the purposes of the trade as trading stock (whether on the commencement of the trade or otherwise). The asset is deemed, for capital gains tax purposes, as having been disposed of at its market value at the time of the appropriation (TCA 1997, s 596(1)).

This treatment is not applied where the person appropriating the asset is chargeable to tax in respect of the profits of the trade under Case I of Schedule D and he elects that, instead, the market value of the asset at the time of the appropriation should, in the computation of trading profits, be treated as reduced by the amount of the chargeable gain or (for appropriations up to 29 May 1990 – see below) increased by the amount of the allowable loss. In that case, the profits of the trade will be computed accordingly, ie the cost of the asset on the appropriation to trading stock will be reduced by the amount of the gain so that the profit on the eventual sale of the asset will be increased by the same amount. The election is not available, however, in the case of an appropriation from trading stock on or after 30 May 1990 where the application of the market value rule would give rise to an allowable loss.

Example 9.102.19.1

Goshen Ltd, a company carrying on a silverware and jewellery trade, purchased a silver statuette which was put on display, but not for sale, in its shop. The statuette cost €15,000. Some time later, when it was valued at €25,000, the company decided to sell the statuette and placed it in its shop window for the purpose. The statuette was later sold for €27,500.

Goshen Ltd is deemed, for capital gains purposes, to have sold the statuette for €25,000 at the time it was put up for sale. The gain is as follows:

	€
Market value at time of appropriation	25,000
Cost	15,000
Gain	10,000

The statuette is brought into stock for trading purposes at €25,000. Accordingly, on its sale for €27,500, the profit for inclusion in the Case I computation is €2,500. Goshen Ltd could elect to have the chargeable gain reduced to nil with the result that the statuette would be brought into trading stock at €15,000. The trading profit realised on its eventual sale would then be €12,500.

In view of the capital gains tax rate of 20%, the election would probably not be made. If the company had available trading losses forward, it might be to its benefit to shelter the chargeable gain.

TCA 1997, s 596(2) deals with the converse situation. Where an asset forming part of the trading stock of a person's trade is appropriated by him for any other purpose, or is retained by him on the cessation of the trade, the asset is treated as having been acquired by that person at that time for a consideration equal to the amount brought into the accounts of the trade in respect of it for the purposes of income tax (or corporation tax in the case of a company) on the appropriation or, as the case may be, on the cessation of the trade.

The precise meaning of "brought into the accounts of the trade" is, perhaps, not obvious from the context of TCA 1997, s 596(2). It would appear to leave open the question as to what value should be put on the asset appropriated from trading stock, and credited to the trading account, at the time of the appropriation for the purposes of the relevant Case I computation. On the basis of the decision in the UK case *Sharkey v Wernher* 36 TC 275, and also perhaps *Petrotim Securities Ltd v Ayrs* 41 TC 389, the asset would be credited to the trading account at its market value but it appears that this treatment is not followed in practice in Ireland. It is understood that the view of the Revenue Commissioners on this matter is that the appropriation should be made at cost.

Example 9.102.19.2

The position is as in Example **9.102.19.1** except that Goshen Ltd originally purchased the statuette for €15,000 for resale in its business. The trade, however, ceased some time later when the statuette remained unsold. Its value at that time was €25,000. The company then commenced a different trade while retaining ownership of the statuette. It later received an offer for the statuette and sold it for €27,500.

At the time the trade ceased, Goshen Ltd is deemed to have acquired the statuette for a non-trading purpose at €15,000. On the eventual sale of the statuette for €27,500, therefore, the company realises a chargeable gain of €12,500.

The deemed appropriation of the asset at cost is, as noted above, in accordance with the view of the Revenue Commissioners. It is not, however, clear that this is what is stated by TCA 1997, s 596(2) and in fact that subparagraph appears to say otherwise. The amount brought into the accounts of the trader "on the appropriation" would seem to require that the amount or value should be taken at the time of the appropriation rather than at the time of the acquisition of the asset by that trader. Where, however, nothing is brought into the accounts at that time, as in the above example, it might be expected that a deemed appropriation at market value would apply. That is the view from *Sharkey v Wernher* but, since that decision is not applied in Ireland, there is probably no option but to regard the appropriation as being made at cost.

9.102.20 Payment of tax

Capital gains tax for any year of assessment is due and payable by 31 October following the end of the year of assessment in which the disposal in question takes place.

Where an assessment to capital gains tax has been raised before 31 October, tax is due on that date. If raised after that date, the tax is due by the date by which the capital gains tax return for the year of assessment in question is due, or 30 days after the assessment is raised, whichever is the later. In the case of an amended assessment, the due date for payment depends on whether the assessment had been raised before or after the capital gains return was delivered. If the assessment had been raised before the return was filed, or if it had already been amended after the return was filed, the due date is 30 days after the date the assessment is amended. Otherwise, tax arising as a result of the amendment is due on the same date that tax in respect of the assessment is due.

For companies, the due date for payment of capital gains tax is largely irrelevant as tax in respect of chargeable gains is part of the corporation tax liability for the accounting period in which the gain arises. As, however, companies are subject to capital gains tax (rather than corporation tax) on gains in respect of development land disposals, the due date for payment by a company of any resulting capital gains tax will be the same as for any other person liable to capital gains tax.

9.102.21 Withholding tax

The sale proceeds in respect of disposals of certain categories of assets are subject, by virtue of TCA 1997, s 980, to a withholding tax of 15% where the consideration for the disposal exceeds €500,000. The assets affected are:

(a)   land (including buildings) in the State;

(b)   minerals (as defined in the Minerals Development Act 1940, s 3 – see **3.107.1**) in the State or any rights, interests or other assets in relation to mining or minerals or the searching for minerals;

(c)   exploration or exploitation rights in a designated area;

(d)   unquoted shares (including stock and any security, eg debentures) deriving their value or the greater part of their value directly or indirectly from such assets as are described in (a), (b) or (c) above;

(e)   unquoted shares to which TCA 1997, s 584 (reorganisation or reduction of share capital – see **9.402**) applies, whether by virtue of that section or any other section, so that, as respects a person disposing of those shares, they are treated as the same shares as those in (d) above, acquired as those shares were acquired; and

(f)   goodwill of a trade carried on in the State.

The purpose of this provision is to ensure that capital gains tax payable in relation to non-residents disposing of certain assets will be collected. The provision applies to all disposals with the qualification that residents disposing of these assets may avoid the tax on obtaining an appropriate clearance certificate.

The withholding provision of TCA 1997, s 980 does not apply to a disposal by a body specified in TCA 1997 Schedule 15 (list of bodies in respect of which, by virtue of TCA 1997, s 610, a gain is treated as not being a chargeable gain – see **9.102.15**).

The obligation to withhold tax applies to the purchaser of the asset who is obliged to deduct the 15% withholding tax on payment of the consideration for acquiring the asset and, within 30 days of the date of the payment, to account to the Revenue Commissioners for the payment and the tax deducted from it and to pay the tax deducted to the Collector-General (TCA 1997, s 980(5)). The capital gains tax payable by the person making the payment is—

(a)   payable by that person in addition to any capital gains tax which by virtue of any other provision of the Capital Gains Tax Acts is payable by him,

(b)   due within 30 days of the time the payment is made, and

(c)   payable without the making of an assessment,

but tax which has become due may be assessed on the person making the payment (whether or it has been paid when the assessment is made) if that tax or any part of it is not paid on or before the due date (TCA 1997, s 980(5A)).

Withholding will not apply where the vendor, or a person acting on the vendor's authority (the "agent"), obtains and produces to the purchaser a clearance certificate from the inspector of taxes authorising the payment to be made gross. The certificate may be obtained on the ground that the vendor is Irish resident, or that no capital gains tax is due in respect of the disposal, or that the capital gains tax has been paid. In practice, most certificates are issued on the first of these grounds. "Capital gains tax" above includes corporation tax in respect of chargeable gains (TCA 1997, s 975(2)).

A clearance certificate may be applied for by the person making the disposal or by an agent acting on that person's authority and the certificate will be issued by the inspector of taxes, on being satisfied that the applicant is either the vendor or the vendor's agent, to the vendor or to the agent, with a copy of the certificate to the person acquiring the asset. An application by an agent should include the name and address of the person making the disposal and, where the person is resident in the State, that person's tax reference number (TCA 1997, s 980(8)).

Alternatively, in the case of a disposal of land on which a new house has been built or land on which a new house is in the course of being built, withholding tax need not be deducted where the vendor provides to the purchaser—

(a)   a current certificate of authorisation issued to the vendor under TCA 1997, s 531 (payments to subcontractors in certain industries);

(b)   a current tax clearance certificate issued to the vendor under TCA 1997, s 1094 (tax clearance certificates in relation to certain licences);

(c)   a current tax clearance certificate issued to the vendor under TCA 1997, s 1095 (tax clearance certificates in relation to public sector contracts); or

(d)   where the vendor does not have any of the above-mentioned certificates, a current tax clearance certificate issued by the Collector-General to the vendor for the purposes of TCA 1997, s 980.

As regards assets within category (e) above, the purpose of the requirement here is to prevent avoidance where, say, shares which would have been subject to the withholding requirement are exchanged for debentures which themselves would not come within one of the categories affected and where the debentures are then sold. Withholding cannot be avoided in this way since the debentures are treated as the same as the shares for which they have been exchanged. Surprisingly, however, although the withholding requirement applies, a non-resident company disposing of assets within category (e) is not chargeable (under TCA 1997, s 29 – see **9.102.2**) to capital gains tax on any gain arising. In practice, the effect of this is to oblige such a non-resident company to apply for a certificate on the ground that no capital gains tax is due.

The withholding requirement of TCA 1997, s 980 applies to the person acquiring the asset even where the consideration for the disposal is in non-monetary form (TCA 1997, s 980(9)). Tax of 15% of the market value of the consideration, estimated to the best of the person's knowledge and belief, must be accounted for although it obviously cannot be withheld from the purchase consideration. In addition, the purchaser is obliged to make a return of information to the Revenue Commissioners with details of the asset acquired, the consideration for acquiring the asset, the best estimate of the market value of the consideration, and the name and address of the person making the disposal. The withholding tax deductible must be accounted for within seven days from the time at which the asset is acquired and is payable without the making of an assessment.

Where the person acquiring the asset has paid over an amount of capital gains tax equal to 15% of the market value of the consideration and has recovered a sum of that amount from the person disposing of the asset, appropriate relief will be given to the person disposing of the asset, on proof being given in that respect, whether by discharge, repayment or otherwise (TCA 1997, s 980(9)(e)).

In computing the vendor's capital gains tax liability in a case where the purchaser has withheld tax, the vendor is entitled, on making a claim, to relief for the tax withheld (TCA 1997, s 980(7)). Relief may be applied for by submitting a completed form CG50B. This form will have been completed by the purchaser and transmitted to the vendor who in turn submits it to the local Revenue office.

9.102.22 Non-resident companies

TCA 1997, s 590 provides for the tax treatment of a chargeable gain realised by a non-resident "closely controlled" company (ie, a non-resident company which would be a close company (see **10.103**) if it were Irish resident). The company is not, of course, liable to capital gains tax (or corporation tax) in respect of the gain (unless it has resulted from the disposal of certain assets located in the State, eg land – see **9.102.2**).

However, every person who, at the time the gain accrues, is resident in the State (and domiciled in the State, if an individual) and who is a participator in the company is liable to tax on his proportionate share of the gain realised (but see **9.204** regarding the deferral of such gains arising on disposals within a non-resident group). See also **9.408** for more detailed treatment of this type.

9.102.23 Share issues

Where shares in a company are issued, the issue itself does not give rise to a chargeable gain on the part of the issuing company. This is because the company is not disposing of any asset (although, in *Stanton v Drayton Commercial Investment Co Ltd* [1982] STC 585, it was held that where shares were issued as consideration for the acquisition of a portfolio of investments, the consideration given was the shares themselves). There cannot be a disposal of an asset for capital gains tax purposes unless the asset existed prior to the disposal. Accordingly, TCA 1997, s 549 (connected persons – see **9.102.14**) has no application in the case of an issue of shares by a company. TCA 1997, s 547 (market value rule) could, however, apply in limited circumstances (eg where a subscription for shares is not by way of a bargain made at arm's length).

Where a person disposes of shares which he has received as a result of a new issue, the base cost for the purposes of any subsequent disposal of those shares will usually be the amount paid (indexed as appropriate) to the company on their issue. If, however, the shares had not been issued by way of a bargain made at arm's length, or if the company and the shareholder are "connected with" each other (within the meaning of TCA 1997, s 10 – see **2.3**), the amount deductible on a later sale of the shares was, up to 23 June 1982, their market value at the time of issue (as provided for in CGTA s 9).

The position for allotments of shares since 24 June 1982 is governed by TCA 1997, s 547(2). Where a company, otherwise than by way of a bargain made at arm's length, allots shares in the company ("the new shares") to a person connected with it, the consideration paid by that person is deemed, for capital gains tax purposes, to be an amount, including a nil amount, equal to the lesser of:

(a)   the amount or value of the consideration given by him for the new shares; and

(b)   the amount by which the market value of the shares in the company which he held immediately after the allotment of the new shares exceeds the market value of the shares in the company which he held immediately before the allotment or, if he held no such shares immediately before the allotment, the market value of the new shares immediately after the allotment.

The background to this provision is the decision in the *Nairn Williamson* case (see above under *Consideration*) which confirmed that the market value rule could be applied in a case involving shares issued other than at market value and otherwise than by way of a bargain made at arm's length. From this evolved a device, to be known as the "reverse Nairn Williamson" scheme, which exploited the market value rule to the advantage of the taxpayer in certain non-arm's length situations. This scheme, as well as the effect of TCA 1997, s 547(2) on it, is discussed in **9.401.1**.

TCA 1997 ss 586(3)(b) and 587(4)(b) are further anti-avoidance measures designed to counter abuses of TCA 1997, s 586 (company reorganisation by exchange of shares) and TCA 1997, s 587 (reconstructions and amalgamations) respectively, discussed in **9.404** and **9.405**.

9.102.24 Location of assets

TCA 1997, s 533 provides certain location or "situs" rules for determining whether, for capital gains tax purposes, an asset is an Irish asset or a foreign asset. Accordingly, the place where an asset is to be regarded as situated under general law, or where it is physically located, will not necessarily be the place where the asset is to be regarded as situated for capital gains tax purposes. The capital gains tax rules described below are largely at variance with the principles derived from a substantial body of case law, relevant to other taxes for which there are no statutory situs rules.

Except where otherwise provided by TCA 1997, s 29 (see **9.102.2** and **9.408**), the location of assets for capital gains tax purposes is to be determined as follows:

(a)   the situation of rights or interests (otherwise than by means of security) in or over immovable property is where that immovable property is;

(b)   subject to TCA 1997, s 533 (see, for example, (f) below), the situation of rights or interests (otherwise than by means of security) in or over tangible movable property is where that tangible movable property is;

(c)   subject to (i) below, a debt, secured or unsecured, is situated in the State only if the creditor is resident in the State;

(d)   shares or securities issued by any municipal or governmental authority, or by any body created by such an authority, are situated in the country of that authority;

(e)   subject to (d), registered shares or securities are situated where they are registered and, if registered in more than one register, where the principal register is situated;

(f)   a ship or aircraft is situated in the State only if the owner is resident in the State, and an interest or right in or over a ship or aircraft is situated in the State only if the person entitled to the interest or right is resident in the State;

(g)   the situation of goodwill as a trade, business or professional asset is at the place where the trade, business or profession is carried on;

(h)   patents, trade marks and designs are be situated where they are registered and, if registered in more than one register, where each register is situated, and copyright, franchises, rights and licences to use any copyright material, patent, trade mark or design are situated in the State if they, or any rights derived from them, are exercisable in the State;

(i)   a judgment debt is situated where the judgment is recorded.

The rule in (c) above, as generally interpreted (but see below), is a reversal of the normal international rule which locates a debt by reference to the residence of the debtor. Accordingly, what would in general law be regarded as a "foreign debt" is treated for Irish capital gains tax purposes as an Irish asset when owned by an Irish resident, and vice versa.

It is suggested, based on a correct literal reading, that (c) is not so much a location rule as such in relation to debts as a qualification to a general rule (to be derived from general or case law). Thus, whatever the location of a debt might otherwise be, it is not to be regarded for capital gains tax purposes as situated in the State unless the creditor is also resident in the State. (Similar remarks apply in relation to the rule in (f) above.) Interestingly, the equivalent pre-consolidation wording is: " … a debt, secured or unsecured, is situated in the State if and only if the creditor is resident in the State". The position there is quite clear whereas the current TCA 1997, s 533 wording says something quite different.

TCA 1997, s 533 does not provide any rule fixing the location a debt where the creditor is not resident in the State. Such an apparent omission seems odd but not so if one accepts the more literal reading referred to above.

9.102.25 Contracts for difference

Introduction

A contract for difference (CFD) is an agreement to exchange the difference between the opening and closing price of the contract position on various financial instruments. CFDs offer all the benefits of trading shares without physically having to own them. CFDs mirror the performance of a share or an index. They are traded "on margin" and the profit or loss is determined by the difference between the buy and the sell price. By trading on margin, there is no need to deposit the full contract value and investors require only a small proportion of the total value of a position in order to trade.

A share CFD enables an investor to take a position in a stock exchange share without owning the share itself. It is an agreement to exchange the difference in the price of a share over a given period of time. Thus, when the contract closes, the holder receives the value of any growth from the time it was opened and will be liable for any loss over the period.

CFDs also mirror corporate actions. The owner of a share CFD receives cash dividends and participates in stock splits. CFDs offer exposure to the markets at a small percentage of the cost of owning the actual share. Thus, an investor can normally buy or sell an instrument at a cost of 10% of the price of the underlying share. CFDs offer considerable opportunities for leverage. A CFD is an effective and convenient speculative instrument for trading shares, indices, futures and commodities.

CFDs enable traders to go "short" (where there is an expectation of a drop in price) as well as long (an increase in price expected), a facility formerly only available to professional investors. With CFDs, in contrast with dealing in shares, short positions become more effective regarding their cost and simpler regarding their establishment.

CFDs permit traders both to achieve speculative profit and to hedge their investment portfolios in the event that they are unprofitable. Hedging is possible where the investor makes a loss from transactions in the shares of some companies but does not want to sell those shares. Risk can be hedged by making a contract for difference, taking a short position, on the shares concerned, thereby affording security against further losses while leaving the investment portfolio intact.

CFDs do not attract stamp duty.

Taxation treatment – Revenue view (e-Brief Issue 36)

CFDs are capital assets to which the CGT rules apply, unless they are held in the course of a financial trade which is subject to Case I treatment, in which instance the charge will be on the accounting profit.

The contracts require two parties to take opposing positions on the future value of a particular asset or index. Investments are often made on a margin of 20% of the contract amount. As well as the difference in value of the asset from beginning to end of the contract period, certain other notional income flows are taken into account in calculating the overall gain or loss.

One of these is notional interest, calculated on the non-margined value of the underlying asset for the contract duration. Another is the notional income which would have been earned by the asset during the contract period.

Where the contract is long, notional interest is a deduction and notional income a credit in the calculation. Where the contract is short, notional interest is a credit and notional income a deduction.

The chargeable gain will be calculated on the gain or loss resulting from the computations above and including a deduction for all necessary broker fees incurred in the full contract.

Actual interest paid, if any, on the margin amount put up will be chargeable under Case III in the ordinary way and does not form part of the CGT calculation.

9.103 Development land gains

9.103.1 Development land: introduction

TCA 1997 Part 22 Ch 2 (ss 648-653) contains provisions relating to capital gains tax on disposals of "development land". TCA 1997, s 648 defines *development land* as land in the State the consideration for the disposal of which, or the market value of which at the time the disposal is made, exceeds the current use value of the land at that time. The term also includes shares of a company which derive their value or the greater part of their value directly or indirectly from such land, other than shares quoted on a stock exchange.

The question as to whether there is a disposal of development land must be considered separately at the time of each disposal of land in the State (or of related shares in unquoted companies). The critical test is whether the sale consideration for the disposal (or, if higher, the market value) exceeds the current use value. The test therefore relates to the price received for the land on its disposal and not to the use to which the land is put. The *current use value*, in relation to land at any time, is the hypothetical market value of the land at that time on the assumption that it is, and will continue in the future to be, unlawful to carry out any development (within the meaning of section 3 of the Planning and Development Act 2000 ("the Act of 2000") in relation to the land other than development of a minor nature. For this purpose, *development of a minor nature* means "development (not being development by a local authority or a statutory undertaker within the meaning of section 2 of the 2002 Act) which, under or by virtue of section 4 of the Act of 2000, is exempted development for the purposes of the Local Government (Planning and Development) Acts 1963 to 1993".

The Act of 2000 lists the following kinds of development as exempted developments:

(a) development consisting of the use of any land for the purposes of agriculture and development consisting of the use for that purpose of any building occupied together with land so used;

(b) development by the council of a county in its functional area, exclusive of any borough or urban district;

(c) development by the corporation of a county or other borough in that borough;

(d) development by the council of an urban district in that district;

(e) development consisting of the carrying out by the corporation of a county or other borough or the council of a county or an urban district of any works required for the construction of a new road or the maintenance or improvement of a road;

(f) development carried out on behalf of, or jointly or in partnership with, a local authority that is a planning authority, pursuant to a contract entered into by the local authority concerned, whether in its capacity as a planning authority or in any other capacity;

(g) development consisting of the carrying out by any local authority or statutory undertaker of any works for the purpose of inspecting, repairing, renewing, altering or removing any sewers, mains, pipes, cables, overhead wires, or other apparatus, including the excavation of any street or other land for that purpose;

(h) development consisting of the carrying out of works for the maintenance, improvement or other alteration of any structure, being works which affect only the interior of the structure or which do not materially affect the external appearance of the structure so as to render the appearance inconsistent with the character of the structure or of neighbouring structures;

(i) development consisting of the thinning, felling and replanting of trees, forests and woodlands, the construction, maintenance and improvement of non-public roads serving forests and woodlands and works ancillary to that development, not including the replacement of broadleaf high forest by conifer species;

(j)   development consisting of the use of any structure or other land within the curtilage of a house for any purpose incidental to the enjoyment of the house as such;

(k)   development consisting of the use of land for the purposes of a casual trading area (within the meaning of the Casual Trading Act, 1995);

(l)   development consisting of the carrying out of any of the works referred to in the Land Reclamation Act 1949, not being works comprised in the fencing or enclosure of land which has been open to or used by the public within the ten years preceding the date on which the works are commenced.

The Minister for the Environment and Local Government may make regulations providing for any class of development being exempted development and such regulations may provide, in the case of structures or other land used for the purpose of any specified class, for their use for any other purpose being exempted development.

The meaning of "exempted developments" for the purposes of the 2000 Act can therefore be a significant factor in ascertaining whether or not certain property is development land for capital gains tax purposes. Thus, if the premium value of land is attributable to exempted development as defined in the 2000 Act, the actual and current use values of that land will probably be the same so that it will not then be development land.

9.103.2   Development

In section 3 of the 2000 Act, *development* means, except where the context otherwise requires, the carrying out of any works on, in, over or under land or the making of any material change in the use of any structures or other land. For this purpose, and without prejudice to the generality of the definition, the use of land is to be taken as having materially changed—

(a)   where any structure or other land or any tree or other object on land becomes used for the exhibition of advertisements; or

(b)   where land becomes used for:

    (i)   the placing or keeping of any vans, tents or other objects, whether or not movable and whether or not collapsible, for the purpose of caravanning or camping or habitation or the sale of goods,

    (ii)   the storage of caravans or tents, or

    (iii)   the deposit of vehicles whether or not usable for the purpose for which they were constructed or last used, old metal, mining or industrial waste, builders' waste, rubble or debris.

The use as two or more dwellings of any house previously used as a single dwelling involves a material change in the use of the structure and of each part thereof which is so used.

In the UK case *Morgan v Gibson* [1989] STC 568, the equating of development value with "hope value", from the earlier case *Watkins v Kidson* [1979] STC 464, was approved.

9.103.3   Development land: implications

Companies are liable to capital gains tax, and not corporation tax, in respect of gains realised on disposals of development land made on or after 28 January 1982 ("relevant disposals"). Other consequences (of diminished significance now in view of the curtailment/phasing out by FA 2003 of indexation and roll-over reliefs) of land being regarded as development land are as follows:

(a) indexation may only be applied to the part of the cost of development land as does not exceed the current use value of the land at the date of acquisition (so that any additional cost of acquisition over that current use value is deductible on an "unindexed" basis);

(b) for development land held on 6 April 1974, the amount which is to be indexed is confined to the current use value of the land on that date;

(c) allowable losses on disposals of assets other than development land may not be set against capital gains on disposals of development land (although the converse does not apply so that any development land losses may be deducted from both development land gains and other capital gains);

(d) roll-over relief was, generally, not available in respect of disposals of development land (but see **9.102.18**).

For disposals of development land from 28 January to 24 March 1982 the capital gains tax rate was 45% (40% for compulsory disposals) and from 25 March 1982 to 5 April 1992 the rate was 50% (40% for compulsory disposals). Development land gains from 6 April 1992 are, generally, subject to tax at 40%. From 23 April 1998, a rate of 20%, ie the rate already applying to any other capital gains from 3 December 1997 (see **9.103.4** below), applies.

Development gains are not to be treated as "profits" of a company so that any reliefs which can be set off against total profits may not be set off against development gains (TCA 1997, s 649(1)), eg loss relief under TCA 1997, s 396(2) and group relief. A loss arising on an asset other than development land cannot be offset against a development gain (TCA 1997, s 653) nor can a development gain be held over under TCA 1997, s 597 (TCA 1997, s 652).

Example 9.103.3.1

Albion Ltd has the following results for its latest accounting period:

	€
Trading profit	50,000
Gain on quoted shares	10,000
Gain on development land	40,000
	100,000
Group relief available (excess management expenses)	75,000
(a) Corporation tax liability	€
Taxable income	50,000
Chargeable gain	10,000
	60,000
Less group relief (restricted)	(60,000)

(b) Capital gains tax liability

Gain on development land:

€40,000 @ 20%   8,000

9.103.4 Development land disposals: capital gains tax rate

Introduction

With effect from 23 April 1998, the 40% capital gains tax rate which had been in force prior to that date was reduced to 20% in respect of disposals of certain development land for residential development. With effect from 1 December 1999, gains arising on disposals of all types of development land are taxable at the rate of 20%.

As originally provided for, the 20% capital gains tax rate for relevant disposals applied in the case of a relevant disposal which, in the period from 23 April 1998 to 5 April 2002, is a disposal of land to a housing authority or is a disposal in respect of which planning permission for residential development exists at the time, except where the contract for the sale of the land is conditional on planning permission, other than for residential development, being obtained.

The conditions under which the 20% capital gains tax rate applies were modified in respect of relevant disposals made on or after 10 March 1999. Whereas for relevant disposals made prior to that date it was necessary that the disposal was to a housing authority or that it was subject to planning permission, from 10 March 1999 a relevant disposal could, alternatively, be to the National Building Agency or to the voluntary housing sector, or could be in respect of land zoned for residential development under a county development plan.

Relevant disposals: disposals up to 30 November 1999

TCA 1997, s 649A(2) provides for a 20% rate of capital gains tax in respect of chargeable gains on certain relevant disposals. The disposals in question, in so far as relevant to companies, are as follows:

(a) a relevant disposal made in the period from 23 April 1998 to 30 November 1999, being a disposal of land to a housing authority (within the meaning of section 23 of the Housing (Miscellaneous Provisions) Act 1992), which land is specified in a certificate given by a housing authority as land required for the purposes of the Housing Acts, 1966 to 1998;

(b) a relevant disposal made in the period from 23 April 1998 to 30 November 1999, being a disposal of land in respect of the whole of which, at the time at which the disposal is made, permission for residential development has been granted under section 26 of the Local Government (Planning and Development) Act 1963, and such permission has not ceased to exist, other than a disposal to which TCA 1997, s 649A(2)(c) (see below) applies;

(c) a relevant disposal made in the period from 10 March 1999 to 30 November 1999, being a disposal of land to the National Building Agency Limited or a body standing approved of for the purposes of section 6 of the Housing (Miscellaneous Provisions) Act 1992, which land is specified in a certificate given by a housing authority or the National Building Agency Limited, as appropriate, as land required for the purposes of the Housing Acts, 1966 to 1998; or

(d)   a relevant disposal made in the period from 10 March 1999 to 30 November 1999, being a disposal of land in respect of the whole of which, at the time at which the disposal is made, is in accordance with a development objective (as indicated in the development plan of the planning authority concerned), for use solely or primarily for residential purposes other than a disposal to which TCA 1997, s 649A(2)(c) (see below) applies (TCA 1997, s 649A(2)(b)).

As regards (c) and (d) above, the 20% rate did not apply in the case of any disposal, up to 30 November 1999, to which TCA 1997, s 649A(2)(c) applies, ie a relevant disposal by any person to a person who is "connected with" (see **2.3**) that person, or a relevant disposal of land under a "relevant contract" in relation to the disposal.

A *relevant contract* in relation to a disposal of land means a contract or other arrangement under which the land is disposed of and which is conditional on permission for development, other than permission for residential development, being granted under section 26 of the Local Government (Planning and Development) Act 1963, in respect of the land.

Residential development includes any development which is ancillary to the development and which is necessary for the proper planning and development of the area in question.

The capital gains tax rate for disposals other than disposals of development land was reduced from 40% to 20% with effect from 3 December 1997. The 20% rate was extended to certain residential development land disposals from 23 April 1998 and 10 March 1999 as detailed above. For the period 3 December 1997 to 30 November 1999, chargeable gains on disposals of development land (apart from the cases mentioned in (a) to (d) above) were taxable at a rate of 40% (TCA 1997, s 649A(1)(a)).

Relevant disposals: disposals from 1 December 1999

In the case of all relevant disposals made on or after 1 December 1999, the capital gains tax rate is 20% (TCA 1997, s 649A(1)(b)).

9.104   Recovery of capital gains tax

To prevent the evasion of corporation tax in respect of chargeable gains, TCA 1997, s 614 provides for the recovery of tax in certain circumstances from a person who is connected with an Irish resident company which has made a chargeable gain where that company has not paid tax for the accounting period in which the gain accrued within six months from the date when it becomes payable. TCA 1997, s 614 applies where a person who is connected with (within the meaning of TCA 1997, s 10 – see **2.3**) an Irish resident company receives or becomes entitled to receive in respect of shares in the company any capital distribution from the company, other than a capital distribution representing a reduction of capital, and

(a)   the capital distributed derives from the disposal, after 5 April 1976, of assets in respect of which a chargeable gain accrued to the company; or

(b)   the distribution constitutes such a disposal of assets.

If the corporation tax assessed on the company for the accounting period in which the chargeable gain accrues includes any amount in respect of chargeable gains, and any of the tax assessed for the period is not paid within six months from the date when it becomes payable by the company, the person in question may, by virtue of an assessment made within two years from that date, be assessed and charged (in the name of the company) to an amount of that corporation tax. The tax may not exceed:

(a) the amount or value of the capital distribution which the person has received or became entitled to receive; or

(b) a proportion, equal to that person's share of the capital distribution made by the company, of corporation tax on the amount and at the rate charged in respect of that gain in the assessment in which the tax was charged (in short, his proportionate share of the tax on the gain).

The person who pays any amount of tax in accordance with TCA 1997, s 614 is entitled to recover a sum equal to that amount from the company (TCA 1997, s 614(4)).

The person's own liability to tax in respect of the capital distribution is not affected by the charge to tax under TCA 1997, s 614. TCA 1997, s 614(5) provides that that charge is without prejudice to any liability of the person receiving or becoming entitled to receive the capital distribution in respect of a chargeable gain accruing to him by virtue of the capital distribution constituting a disposal of an interest in shares in the company.

A *capital distribution* for the above purposes has the same meaning as in TCA 1997, s 583(1) (see **9.401.4** for the meaning of "capital distribution" and the treatment of such a distribution as a disposal of an interest in shares).

TCA 1997, s 614 does not apply in cases where the capital distribution received is in respect of a reduction of capital. The meaning of "reduction of capital" is discussed in **9.402.1**. A reduction of share capital, which for example may include the receipt of new shares in return for the cancellation of existing shares, is treated by TCA 1997, s 584(3) as not involving either a disposal or an acquisition of shares for capital gains tax purposes.

Example 9.104.1

Madoc Ltd realised a chargeable gain of €100,000 in its last accounting period. Corporation tax payable by the company for the period is €62,000, of which €20,000 is in respect of this gain. The company was put into liquidation shortly after the end of the accounting period at which time tax of €25,000 only had been paid in respect of the period.

Lyall Ltd, by virtue of being under the same control, is connected with Madoc Ltd and also has a 35% interest in the company. During the course of the liquidation, Lyall Ltd receives a capital distribution of €8,000, being its share of the total capital distribution made by the liquidator.

Lyall Ltd is liable to be assessed, in the name of Madoc Ltd, to tax of an amount not exceeding the lesser of €8,000 and 35% of the tax in respect of the chargeable gain, ie €7,000.

TCA 1997, s 626 also provides for the recovery of unpaid tax in respect of chargeable gains accruing to a company. If at any time a chargeable gain accrues to a company which at that time is a member of a group of companies (within the meaning of TCA 1997, s 616(1)(b) – see **9.201**) and any of the corporation tax assessed on the company for the accounting period in which the chargeable gain accrues is not paid within six months from the date when it becomes payable by the company, then, if the tax assessed included any amount in respect of chargeable gains, it may be assessed and charged on any company which

(a)   at the time when the gain accrued, was the principal company of the group (within the meaning of TCA 1997, s 616(1)(c) – see **9.202.1**); or

(b)   in any part of the period of two years ending with that time, was a member of that group of companies and owned the asset disposed of or any part of it, or, where the asset is an interest or right in or over another asset, owned either asset or any part of either asset.

The assessment may be made at any time within two years from the time when the tax became payable and is to be assessed and charged in the name of the company to which the chargeable gain accrued. The tax assessed may not exceed the amount of the corporation tax on the amount and at the rate charged in respect of the gain in the assessment on the company to which the chargeable gain accrued (in other words, the amount of the corporation tax attributable to the chargeable gain).

A company which pays any amount of tax in accordance with TCA 1997, s 626 is entitled to recover a sum of that amount:

(a)   from the company to which the chargeable gain accrued; or

(b)   if that company is not the company which was the principal company of the group at the time when the chargeable gain accrued, from that principal company.

Where a company pays any amount in accordance with (b) above, it will be entitled to recover a sum of that amount from the company to which the chargeable gain accrued. To the extent not recovered, it may recover from any company which is for the time being a member of the group and which has, while a member of the group, owned the asset disposed of or any part of it (or where that asset is an interest or right in or over another asset, owned either asset or any part or it), such proportion of the amount unrecovered as is just having regard to the value of the asset at the time when the asset, or an interest or right in or over it, was disposed of by that company.

TCA 1997, s 649(2) provides that TCA 1997, s 626 is to apply, with any necessary modifications, to capital gains tax to which a company is chargeable on chargeable gains accruing to it on a disposal of development land as it would apply in relation to corporation tax on chargeable gains.

9.105   Double tax relief

The question of double tax relief is dealt with in detail in Chapter 14 but some comment may be made here on relevant aspects of that subject and of tax treaties in so far as capital gains tax is concerned.

Tax treaties concluded prior to the enactment of the Capital Gains Tax Act 1975 (unless amended by protocol) do not contain, in the list of Irish taxes covered, a reference to capital gains tax. They do, however, typically include references to income tax and corporation profits tax and to "identical or substantially similar taxes which are subsequently imposed in addition to, or in place of, the existing taxes". Following an application for judicial review concerning the scope of the Ireland-Italy tax treaty, concluded in 1973, the High Court in *Kinsella v Revenue Commissioners* [2007] IEHC

250 held that, by reason of the "identical or substantially similar taxes" reference in article 2, the treaty applies to Irish capital gains tax. This judgment, obviously, has relevance for the older treaties generally.

The issue in the *Kinsella* case involved a claim for exemption from Irish capital gains tax on the basis of tax residence in Italy. Tax treaties provide for relief from double taxation of capital gains - even where the relevant treaty refers simply to "income" (rather than to "income or gains", eg the treaties with Croatia, Chile, Israel); in an international context (in which the position in Ireland and the UK is somewhat exceptional), income tax is a tax on gains whether of an income or a capital nature.

Unilateral credit is available in respect of tax paid on capital gains in certain territories, typically those in respect of which the relevant tax treaties were concluded prior to the introduction of capital gains tax. Where a company chargeable to Irish tax on a capital gain suffers tax on that gain in the other territory concerned, the foreign tax is creditable against Irish tax on the gain (see **14.11**).

Where a capital gains article is included in a tax treaty, the normal approach is to permit the country in which certain categories of assets are situated to impose tax on any capital gains realised on their disposal, but to provide that gains on disposals of other assets are to be taxable only in the country of residence of the person making the disposal. In any case where the country in which the asset was situated prior to its disposal is permitted to tax a capital gain, the country in which the taxpayer is resident is required to provide the necessary relief from double taxation under the "elimination of double taxation" article.

The capital gains article invariably permits the contracting state in which immovable property is situated to impose tax on capital gains arising from the sale, exchange, gift or other form of alienation of that property. For this purpose, "immovable property" is usually given the same meaning as is given in the treaty article dealing with income from immovable property. Later treaties provide that gains from the alienation of shares in companies deriving their value, or the greater part of their value, directly or indirectly from immovable property in one of the states may be taxed in that state. The agreement with the UK, however, excludes from this rule the gains on any such shares that are quoted on a stock exchange; these gains are accordingly treated in the same way as gains from the disposal of shares in companies generally.

It is also usual to permit the country of source to tax capital gains on the alienation of any movable property forming part of the business property of a permanent establishment which an enterprise of the other contracting state has in the country where the permanent establishment is situated. The same treatment usually applies to gains from the disposal of movable property relating to a fixed base which a resident of one of the states has in the other state for the purpose of performing professional services.

The above-described treatment does not apply generally to any capital gains derived by a resident of a contracting state from the alienation of ships or aircraft operated in international traffic. Any such capital gains are taxable only in the country of residence of the person carrying on the international shipping or airline enterprise.

For assets not specifically dealt with, treaties typically provide that gains on their disposal are to be taxable only in the country of residence of the person realising the gain. Thus, a capital gain realised by a resident of Ireland on the disposal of shares in a company resident in, say, Spain, may only be taxed in Ireland, provided that the shares do not owe their value principally to immovable property situated in Spain.

9.106 Exit charge

9.106.1 Introduction

With effect from 21 April 1997, measures contained in TCA 1997 Part 20 Ch 2 (ss 627-629) impose an exit charge on companies which change their residence from Ireland to another jurisdiction. Residence for Irish tax purposes is determined by reference to the location of central management and control of the company concerned, and this determination is unaffected by the place of incorporation of the company. It is not unusual, therefore, to have Irish incorporated companies managed and controlled outside Ireland and thus not Irish resident for tax purposes, and conversely, to have companies incorporated outside Ireland which are managed and controlled in Ireland and thus regarded as resident for Irish corporate tax purposes. Up to 20 April 1997, it has been possible to effect a change of residence from Ireland without a charge to capital gains tax.

TCA 1997, s 627 provides for a deemed disposal and reacquisition of, and hence a charge to capital gains tax in respect of, all the assets of a company which moves its place of residence outside Ireland. The charge to capital gains tax will apply to the entire appreciation in the value of the assets of the company concerned and not merely the appreciation which has arisen during the period of Irish residence. Thus, a company which is Irish resident for a period of, say, one year out of a twenty year lifespan will expose the entire appreciation of its asset portfolio to capital gains tax on a transfer of residence out of Ireland at the end of the one year period.

TCA 1997, s 627 also has a cascade effect when the residence of more than one member of a group of companies moves from Ireland at the same time. Thus, a parent and subsidiary company changing residence abroad with appreciated property at the level of the subsidiary will be taxed twice on the amount of the appreciation; the subsidiary will be subject to capital gains tax on its migration in respect of the appreciated property in the asset while the parent will be subject to capital gains tax on the appreciation in the value of the shares in the subsidiary.

The exit charge will not apply in the case of an "excluded company", ie a company which, broadly, is controlled by residents of jurisdictions with which Ireland has concluded a double tax treaty. Also excluded from the exit charge are assets which are used for the purposes of an Irish trade both before and after the transfer of residence.

9.106.2 The exit charge

The exit charge applies to companies whose tax residence is moved abroad on or after 21 April 1997. The relevant legislation disapplies the hold-over relief provisions of TCA 1997 ss 597 and 620 (see **9.206**) for business assets in circumstances where the new assets are acquired after the change of residence. The exit charge does not apply to assets which are and continue to be used for the purposes of an Irish trade both before and after the change of residence. Under general corporation tax provisions (TCA 1997, s 25), assets in use for the purposes of a trade carried on in Ireland through a branch or agency remain subject to capital gains tax notwithstanding that the company concerned is non-resident (see **9.102.2**). The effect of TCA 1997, s 627, therefore, is to impose a charge to capital gains tax at the point of change of residence on all the corporate assets other than those in use in the Irish trade or business.

The Irish assets used for the trade or business of the company concerned will become subject to capital gains tax in the normal way on a disposal to another party. The legislation in fact imposes a double charge to tax on Irish based real property held for investment. Because the exclusion from the exit charge is confined to trading assets, investment property situated in Ireland is taxable on migration (except in the case of an excluded company – see below) and again on actual disposal. It is difficult to justify such a feature of the legislation. It would appear that it exists because the legislation has been imported uncritically from the UK where, however, there is no general charge to capital gains tax on non-residents in respect of UK based property.

Double taxation will arise, therefore, when the assets concerned are actually disposed of to a third party. For example, if an Irish company migrates through a transfer of its central management and control to the UK and subsequently disposes of the assets concerned, no double taxation relief will be available against the UK capital gains tax which will arise on disposal of the assets in respect of the Irish capital gains tax paid on the migration. The deemed capital gains tax is due in respect of an event which is not within the charge to UK capital gains tax and which is deemed to arise before the transfer of residence.

A company which, at any time on or after 21 April 1997 ("the relevant time"), ceases to be resident in the State is referred to as a *relevant company*. A relevant company is deemed for all capital gains tax purposes to have disposed of all its assets, other than excepted assets (see below), immediately before the relevant time and immediately to have reacquired them at the market value of the assets at that time (TCA 1997, s 627(3)). *Market value* in relation to any assets means the price which those assets might reasonably be expected to fetch on a sale in the open market (see **9.102.13**).

A company is not to be regarded as ceasing to be resident in the State by reason only that it ceases to exist (TCA 1997, s 627(1)(b)). Thus, the liquidation of a company will be unaffected by the charge.

The hold over provisions of TCA 1997, s 597 (see **9.102.18**) do not apply where a relevant company:

(a)   has disposed of the old assets, or of its interest in those assets, before the relevant time; and

(b)   acquires the new assets, or its interest in those assets, after the relevant time,

unless the new assets are excepted as described below (TCA 1997, s 627; FA 1992 s 42(4)). *The new assets* and *the old assets* have respectively the same meanings assigned to them in TCA 1997, s 597.

In the case of a relevant company carrying on a trade in the State through a branch or agency:

(i)   any assets which, immediately after the relevant time (the time at which the company's residence was changed from Ireland to another jurisdiction), are situated in the State and are used in or for the purposes of the trade, or are used or held for the purposes of the branch or agency, are excepted from the exit charge (TCA 1997, s 627(5)(a)); and

(ii)   any new assets which, after that time, are so situated and are so used or so held are excepted from the denial of hold over treatment as described above (TCA 1997, s 627(5)(b)).

In relation to the above-described exception, references to assets situated in the State include references to exploration or exploitation assets and to exploration or exploration rights. *Exploration or exploitation assets* means assets used or intended for use in connection with exploration or exploitation activities carried on in the State or in a designated area. *Designated area, exploration or exploitation activities* and *exploration or exploitation rights* have, respectively the same meanings as they have in TCA 1997, s 13 (see **3.107.1**).

9.106.3   Collection of tax on company migration

To secure collection of tax on the exit charge (particularly since exchange controls are not now in force), TCA 1997, s 629 renders all affiliated companies of the migrating company, together with any controlling director of the migrating group, as secondarily liable for the corporation tax or capital gains tax arising on migration. The Revenue Commissioners may serve notice, within a period of three years from the normal tax return date for the chargeable period (accounting period or year of assessment, as the case may be) in which the migration takes place (the "specified period"), on any of the companies or directors who are secondarily liable, requiring them to pay the tax due.

Where exit charge tax payable by a company (the "taxpayer company") is not paid within six months after the date on or before which the tax is due and payable, the Revenue Commissioners may, at any time before the end of the specified period in relation to the chargeable period concerned, serve on any person with secondary accountability a notice:

(a)   stating the amount which remains unpaid of the tax payable by the taxpayer company for the chargeable period concerned and the date on or before which the tax became due and payable; and

(b)   requiring that person to pay that amount within thirty days of the service of the notice (TCA 1997, s 629(3)).

The secondarily accountable persons are:

(i)   a company which is, or during the period of twelve months ending with the time when the gain accrued was, a member of the same group as the taxpayer company; and

(ii)   a person who is, or during that period was, a controlling director of the taxpayer company or of a company which has, or within that period had, control over the taxpayer company.

Secondary liability applies in any case where the gain accrued before 21 April 1998 in which case the period mentioned in (i) above will be the period beginning on 21 April 1997.

A "controlling director" in relation to a company means a director of the company who has control of it (within the meaning of TCA 1997, s 432 – see **2.401**). A "director", in relation to a company, has the meaning given by TCA 1997, s 116(1) and includes any person falling within TCA 1997, s 433(4). In TCA 1997, s 116(1) "director" means:

(a)   in relation to a body corporate the affairs of which are managed by a board of directors or similar body, a member of that board or similar body;

(b)   in relation to a body corporate the affairs of which are managed by a single director or similar person, that director or person;

(c)   in relation to a body corporate the affairs of which are managed by the members themselves, a member of the body corporate.

As respects the meaning of "director" in TCA 1997, s 433(4), see **10.102**.

Any amount which is payable by virtue of a notice under TCA 1997, s 629 may be recovered from the person as if it were tax due by that person and such person may recover any such amount paid on foot of a notice under TCA 1997, s 629 from the taxpayer company (TCA 1997, s 629(5)). A payment in pursuance of a notice under TCA 1997, s 629 is not to be allowed as a deduction in computing any income, profits or losses for any tax purpose (TCA 1997, s 629(6)).

In (i) above, *group* has the meaning that would be given by TCA 1997, s 616 (see **9.202.1**) but without including references in that section to residence in a relevant Member State and with the substitution of "51% subsidiaries" for "75% subsidiaries". Clearly, therefore, a group has a much wider meaning for the purposes of TCA 1997, s 629 than for the purposes of capital gains tax group treatment.

9.106.4   Postponement of exit charge

Tax arising under TCA 1997, s 627 may be postponed where the company which transfers residence is a 75% subsidiary of an Irish resident company and where both companies so elect in writing to the inspector. A charge to capital gains tax will crystallise if, within ten years, the assets are actually disposed of, the company ceases to be a 75% subsidiary of the other company or the Irish resident parent company changes its residence abroad. No tax charge will arise where none of these events arises.

Postponement of the exit charge will apply where:

(a)   immediately after the change of residence (the "relevant time"), the company in question is a 75% subsidiary of another company (the "principal company") which is resident in the State; and

(b)   the principal company and the company jointly so elect, by notice in writing given to the inspector within 2 years after the relevant time (TCA 1997, s 628(2)).

A company is a 75% subsidiary of another company if and so long as not less than 75% of its ordinary share capital (within the meaning of TCA 1997, s 2(1) – see **8.103.**) is owned directly by that other company.

Where (a) and (b) above apply, any allowable losses accruing to the company on a deemed disposal (ie deemed by virtue of TCA 1997, s 627(3)) of foreign assets are to be set off against the chargeable gains so accruing. The deemed disposal is treated as giving rise to a single chargeable gain equal to the aggregate of those gains after deducting the aggregate of those losses. The whole of the single chargeable gain is treated as not accruing to the company on the deemed disposal but an equivalent amount (the "postponed gain") is to be brought into account as described below (TCA 1997, s 628(3)).

For the above purposes, *foreign assets* of a company means any assets of the company which, immediately after the relevant time, are situated outside the State and are used in or for the purposes of a trade carried on by the company outside the State.

The postponed gain will be crystallised in any of the following circumstances, and to the extent indicated in each case.

1. If at any time within 10 years after the relevant time the company concerned disposes of any assets ("relevant assets") the chargeable gains on which were taken into account in arriving at the postponed gain, a chargeable gain will accrue to the principal company. The gain so accruing will be the whole or the appropriate proportion of the postponed gain so far as not already taken into account. The "appropriate proportion" means the proportion which the chargeable gain taken into account in arriving at the postponed gain in respect of the part of the relevant assets disposed of bears to the aggregate of the chargeable gains so taken into account in respect of the relevant assets held immediately before the time of the disposal (TCA 1997, s 628(4)).

2. If at any time within 10 years after the relevant time, the company concerned ceases to be a 75% subsidiary of the principal company, a chargeable gain will be deemed to have accrued to the principal company. The gain will be the whole of the postponed gain so far as not already taken into account and will be deemed to have accrued at the time the subsidiary ceases to the a 75% subsidiary.

3. If at any time within 10 years after the relevant time the principal company ceases to be resident in the State, a chargeable gain will be deemed to have accrued to it. The gain will be the whole of the postponed gain so far as not already taken into account and will be deemed to have accrued immediately before the time the principal company ceased to be resident.

If at any time:

(a) the company concerned has allowable losses which have not been allowed as a deduction from chargeable gains; and

(b) a chargeable gain accrues to the principal company in any of the three situations described above, then

if and to the extent that the principal company and the company jointly so elect by notice in writing given to the inspector within two years after that time, those losses are to be allowed as a deduction from that gain (TCA 1997, s 628(6)).

9.106.5   Excluded companies

An important exception to the operation of the exit charge is the case of a company (an "excluded company") which is ultimately owned by a foreign company, being a company controlled by persons resident in a country with which the Irish government has concluded a double tax treaty.

The provisions dealing with the exit charge (and with the postponement of the exit charge) do not apply to an excluded company. An *excluded company* is a company of which not less than 90% of its issued share capital is held by a foreign company or foreign companies, or by a person or persons who are directly or indirectly controlled by a foreign company or foreign companies (TCA 1997, s 627(2)(a)). A *foreign company* means a company which:

(i) is not resident in the State;

(ii) is under the control of a person or persons resident in a relevant territory; and

(iii) is not under the control of a person or persons resident in the State.

A *relevant territory* is a territory with the government of which a double tax treaty has been concluded by the Irish government.

For the above purposes, *control* is to be construed in accordance with TCA 1997, s 432(2)-(6) (see **2.401**) except that the reference in TCA 1997, s 432(6) to "5 or fewer participators" is replaced by a reference to "persons resident in a relevant territory". Accordingly, a person has "control" of a company if he exercises, or is able to exercise, or is entitled to acquire, control, direct or indirect, over the company's affairs. In particular, a person has control of a company if he possesses or is entitled to acquire:

(a) the greater part of the share capital or issued share capital of the company;

(b) the greater part of the voting power in the company;

(c) such part of the company's issued share capital as would, on a full distribution of the company's income (but ignoring for this purpose any entitlement of a loan creditor), entitle him to receive the greater part of the amount so distributed; or

(d) such rights as would entitle him to receive the greater part of the company's assets available for distribution, eg on a winding up.

Where two or more persons together satisfy any of the conditions for control, they are to be taken to have control of the company.

Being "entitled to" denotes a present entitlement to acquire something at a future date or a future entitlement to acquire something. There is to be attributed to any person all the rights and powers of any company of which he has, or of which he and his associates have, control, or of any two or more such companies, or of any associate of his or of any two or more associates of his, including the rights and powers of any nominee attributed to a company or associate of the person, but not the rights and powers attributed to an associate by virtue of this paragraph (ie by virtue of control). Such attributions are to be made as will result in the company being treated as under the control of persons resident in a relevant territory if it can be so treated.

The application of the above rules for determining "control" is explained in **10.102** and the rules for attributing rights and powers are illustrated in Examples **10.102.2-6**. The following example deals with a case in which it is necessary to determine whether a company is under the control of persons resident in a relevant territory and accordingly a "foreign company".

Example 9.106.5.1

The central management and control of Moorefield Ltd, an Irish resident wholly owned subsidiary of a US corporation, Meridian Inc, is moved out of Ireland. The issued share capital of Meridian Inc is held as follows:

	A shares	B shares (voting)	Total
R Clanton (US)	900	55	955
J Mc Laury (Canada)	220	80	300
T Rosario (Argentina)	450	25	475
J Rosario (Argentina – T Rosario's wife)	250	25	275

L Rosario (Argentina – J Rosario's brother)	250	25	275
Tallulah Inc (US – controlled by R Clanton)	500	25	525
	2,570	235	2,805

Meridian Inc will be a "foreign company" if more than half of either its issued share capital or its voting shares is controlled by persons resident in a relevant territory (a territory with the government of which Ireland has concluded a double tax treaty). Certain shareholders together will be taken as one person. The shares of Tallulah Inc are attributed to R Clanton giving him a total of 1,480 shares. The shares of Tallulah Inc are, however, included again in their own right.

T Rosario and J Rosario are associates of each other, which gives T Rosario a combined holding of 750 shares. J Rosario is an associate of both T Rosario and L Rosario to give her a combined total of 1,025 (475 + 275 + 275). J Rosario's shares are also attributed to her other associate, L Rosario, to bring his total to 550 (275 + 275). This gives the following position:

Relevant territories (US & Canada)	*No of shares*
R Clanton	1,480
J McLaury	300
Tallulah Inc	525
	2,305

Argentina	
J Rosario	1,025
T Rosario	750
L Rosario	550
	2,325

On the basis of the above, 49.78% of the share capital of Meridian Inc is held by persons resident in a relevant territory so that it is not an excluded company on that basis. An unusual feature of the control rules is that shares of a nominee or associate attributed to a participator may be counted again as shares of that associate or nominee. This accounts for the total deemed shareholdings of T, J and L Rosario. This feature does not arise in the case of shares held by Tallulah Ltd. While its shares are attributed to R Clanton, R Clanton's shares are not attributed to it as the shares of a controlled company are not attributed to the person controlling it.

The position of the B (voting) shares is as follows:

	Held	*Held + Attributed*
Relevant territories		
R Clanton	55	80
J McLaury	80	80
Tallulah Inc	25	25
	160	185
Argentina		
J Rosario	25	75

T Rosario	25	50
L Rosario	25	50
	75	175

On the basis of voting control, persons resident in relevant territories hold 51.39% of the total control. Meridian Inc is therefore a foreign company. This in turn means that Moorefield Ltd is an excluded company and is accordingly not subject to the exit charge.

As explained above, an "excluded company" is a company of which not less than 90% of its issued share capital is held by a foreign company or foreign companies, or by a person or persons who are directly or indirectly controlled by a foreign company or foreign companies.

Example 9.106.5.2

The residence of Schumacher (Ireland) Ltd, a wholly owned Irish resident subsidiary of Schumacher (Holdings) Ltd, another Irish resident company, is moved from Ireland. Schumacher (Holdings) Ltd is owned as to 50% each by Overath GmbH and Klagenfurt GmbH, a German company and an Austrian company respectively, which are both wholly owned subsidiaries of Schoenberg GmbH, a German company.

The issued share capital of Schumacher (Ireland) Ltd is not held by a foreign company or foreign companies. It is, however, held by a person controlled by foreign companies and it is therefore an excluded company and accordingly not subject to the exit charge.

Example 9.106.5.3

The facts are the same as in Example **9.106.5.2** except that Overath GmbH and Klagenfurt GmbH are wholly owned subsidiaries of Kracek Ltd, a Macedonian company. The share capital of Kracek Ltd is widely held, by shareholders in Austria and Germany but principally by residents of Macedonia, Albania and Montenegro.

Schumacher (Ireland) Ltd will be an excluded company if Schumacher (Holdings) Ltd is directly or indirectly controlled by a foreign company or foreign companies. Schumacher (Holdings) Ltd is directly controlled by Overath GmbH and Klagenfurt GmbH which, however, are not foreign companies as they are not under the control of persons resident in a relevant territory. Accordingly, Schumacher (Ireland) is not an excluded company and the exit charge will apply by reason of its change of residence.

9.2   CAPITAL GAINS TAX GROUPS

9.201   Introduction

As in the case of group relief, the legislation dealing with capital gains tax groups acknowledges the reality that the "divisionalisation" of business activities using separate companies is no different economically to the carrying on of such separate activities in a single company. Accordingly, the legislation operates, broadly, by ignoring transactions within a capital gains tax group so that a chargeable gain is computed as the difference between the consideration received when it leaves the group and the consideration given when it was acquired by the group. Because transfers of assets between group members are ignored, it is necessary to make provision for cases in which a company to which an intra-group transfer of an asset has been made later leaves the group. Where this happens, the gain which was previously deferred crystallises at the point at which the company leaves the group and becomes a liability of that company, and not of the company which originally transferred the asset.

Special provision is made for cases in which a capital asset is transferred to a group member so that it becomes trading stock of the transferee company, and for the converse situation in which an asset which was trading stock of the transferor company becomes a capital asset of the transferee company.

The capital gains tax roll over treatment provided for in TCA 1997, s 597 (replacement of business and other assets) is extended in the cases of groups of companies so that all trades carried on by members of the group are treated as a single trade.

There are anti-avoidance provisions which deal with depreciatory transactions in a group, and certain dividend stripping transactions are treated as depreciatory transactions.

9.202   Groups

9.202.1   Meaning of group: general

A "group" for the purposes of companies' capital gains is capable of including a far greater number of companies than a group for the purposes of group relief (TCA 1997, s 411 – see **8.103.1**). The required relationship between members of a capital gains tax group was, up to 10 February 1999, in terms of the percentage of ordinary share capital held and there were no additional tests which had to be satisfied as is the case with group relief (see **8.304** – "equity entitlement").

Up to 10 February 1999, a principal company and all its 75% subsidiaries formed a group for capital gains purposes, and where a principal company was a member of a group as being itself a 75% subsidiary, that group comprised all its 75% subsidiaries (TCA 1997, s 616(1)(b) – prior to amendment by FA 1999). A principal company was defined as a company of which another company is a 75% subsidiary. A company is a 75% subsidiary of another company if and so long as not less than 75% of its ordinary share capital is owned directly or indirectly by that other company (TCA 1997, s 9(1)(b)). Ownership for this purpose means beneficial ownership. In applying this definition, any share capital of a registered industrial and provident society (see **12.101**) is to be treated as ordinary share capital.

In the absence of additional tests on the lines of the equity entitlement provisions relating to group relief, it was, up to 10 February 1999, quite possible to retain a company within a capital gain tax group while disposing of the greater part of the economic interest in the company. Thus, the issued share capital of a subsidiary company might comprise 250 ordinary shares with rights giving them the entire economic interest in the company as well as 750 deferred ordinary shares with negligible rights, all held by the parent company. (It would, however, be necessary that the rights attaching to the deferred shares should not be restricted to the right to a dividend at a fixed rate.) In the event of a disposal of the 250 shares, the subsidiary would remain in the same capital gains tax group as long as the parent retained the 750 deferred shares.

With effect on and from 11 February 1999, the additional equity entitlement tests already in place for group relief purposes apply also for the purpose of defining a capital gains tax group. The required relationship between members of a capital gains tax group is determined by reference to "effective" 75% subsidiaries. Thus, a principal company and all its effective 75% subsidiaries form a group, and where a principal company is a member of a group as being itself an effective 75% subsidiary, that group comprises all its effective 75% subsidiaries (TCA 1997, s 616(1)(bb)). A principal company is a company of which another company is an effective 75% subsidiary.

A company is an effective 75% subsidiary of another company (referred to as the parent) at any time if at that time—

(a)   the company is a 75% subsidiary (see below) of the parent;

(b)   the parent is beneficially entitled to not less than 75% of any profits available for distribution to equity holders of the company; and

(c)   the parent would be beneficially entitled to not less than 75% of the assets of the company available for distribution to its equity holders on a winding up.

A company is a 75% subsidiary of another company if and so long as not less than 75% of its ordinary share capital is owned directly or indirectly by that other company (TCA 1997, s 9(1)(b)). Ownership for this purpose means beneficial ownership. In applying this definition, any share capital of a registered industrial and provident society (see **12.101**) is to be treated as ordinary share capital.

For the purposes of (b) and (c), TCA 1997 ss 413-419 apply as they apply for the purposes of group relief. These "equity entitlement" provisions are discussed fully in **8.304**.

The capital gains tax group legislation does not, however, contain other provisions equivalent to those found in the group relief legislation (for more or less obvious reasons), such as the provisions dealing with the relation of group relief to other reliefs (**8.307**), corresponding accounting periods (**8.308**), joining or leaving a group (**8.309**), arrangements for transfer of company (**8.310**), arrangements involving leasing contracts (**8.311**), arrangements involving partnerships (**8.312**), and exclusion of double allowances (**8.314**).

For the purposes of TCA 1997 ss 616-626A (capital gains tax group treatment), references to a company in any of those sections are to a company which is a resident in a relevant Member State (see **9.202.2** below). (This is subject to TCA 1997, s 621(1) (depreciatory transactions, where "group of companies" may include companies other than companies resident in a relevant Member State – see **9.211**).)

"Group" and "subsidiary" are to be construed with any necessary modifications where applied to a company incorporated under the law of a country outside the State.

References to a company for the purposes the definition of "group" apply only to:

(a) a company within the meaning of the Companies Act 1963;

(b) a company which is constituted under any other Act or a charter or letters patent or is formed under the law of a country or territory outside the State;

(c) a registered industrial and provident society within the meaning of TCA 1997, s 698; and

(d) a building society incorporated or deemed by virtue of s 124(2) of the Building Societies Act 1989, to be incorporated under that Act.

Thus, the meaning of "company" for these purposes is narrower than that in TCA 1997, s 4(1) which applies for the purposes of corporation tax generally (see **1.3**). The effect of (b) above is that a company formed under the law of another country but managed and controlled, and therefore resident, in Ireland (or, as appropriate, in a relevant Member State) may be a member of a group.

As explained above, a group consists of a principal company and all its effective 75% subsidiaries and, where a principal company is a member of a group as being itself an effective 75% subsidiary, that group comprises all its effective 75% subsidiaries. The inclusion in a group of subsidiaries that are less than 75% owned by the principal company is another important feature of a capital gains tax group which distinguishes it from a group for the purposes of TCA 1997, s 411 (group relief).

A capital gains tax group includes a principal company and its effective 75% subsidiaries as well as their effective 75% subsidiaries. That a group may extend to a third tier of effective 75% subsidiaries (and then on to a fourth such tier, and so on) is a matter on which opinion is not unanimous. It would appear that the established view in Ireland is that it is possible only to extend the group to the second tier. The alternative interpretation is that a capital gains tax group comprises a principal company, any 75% subsidiary of the principal company, any 75% subsidiary of a 75% subsidiary, and so on. Thus, one might distinguish between the "restrictive" and the "extended" interpretations of a capital gains tax group. Some comments on each of these interpretations are included below.

Restrictive meaning of "group"

Under the restrictive view of what may constitute a capital gains tax group, a group comprises a principal company and its effective 75% subsidiaries as well as their effective 75% subsidiaries, but not the 75% subsidiaries of those subsidiaries. This is because a company's effective 75% subsidiaries may be included in the group of which that company is a member "as being itself an effective 75% subsidiary" and not as being simply a member of that group. Accordingly, a company cannot be a member of a group if it is effectively held as to less than 56.25% by the principal company. (This is subject to one exception, which arises in the situation dealt with by TCA 1997, s 616(3) and which is covered in **9.202.3** below.) Despite the long-held UK view of the matter prior to 1989, referred to below, the argument for the restrictive view is strong, being based on the words of TCA 1997, s 616(1)(bb). That paragraph commences with the statement that "a principal company and all its effective 75% subsidiaries shall form a group". The statement continues "and where the principal company is a member of a group as being itself an effective 75% subsidiary that group shall comprise all its effective 75% subsidiaries". The second limb of the above statement, where it refers to the principal company being a member of a group must, it would seem, be qualified by the first limb as regards what it is to be a member of a group in the first place. This would appear to be reinforced by the qualification "as being itself an effective 75% subsidiary". If this means anything, it would seem that it must refer to the principal company's membership of the other group by virtue of it being an effective 75% subsidiary, that is, an effective 75% subsidiary of the principal company of that other group.

The fact that a company is an effective 75% subsidiary of another company through an intermediary or a series of companies is irrelevant; it is still an effective 75% subsidiary of that other company (see **8.103.4**).

Example 9.202.1.1

Below are the percentages of ordinary share capital (and equity entitlements) held by and in the various companies in the Aran group. All companies are Irish resident.

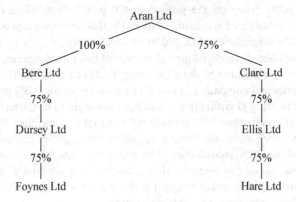

The capital gains tax group comprises Aran Ltd (the principal company), Bere Ltd, Clare Ltd, Dursey Ltd, Ellis Ltd and Foynes Ltd. Hare Ltd is not a member of the Aran group (the group of which Aran Ltd is the principal company). On the restrictive view, that group extends (on the right branch) only as far as Ellis Ltd.

Clare Ltd is also a principal company, of the smaller group comprising Clare Ltd, Ellis Ltd and Hare Ltd. Since Clare Ltd, being a principal company, is a member of the Aran group "as being itself an effective 75% subsidiary", the Aran group comprises all its effective 75% subsidiaries, ie Ellis Ltd in this case. As Hare Ltd is not an effective 75% subsidiary of Clare Ltd, it is not (on the restrictive interpretation) a member of the Aran group.

All companies in the left branch are members of the Aran group. Dursey Ltd, the principal company of the group comprising Dursey Ltd and Foynes Ltd, is itself a member of the Aran group as being itself an effective 75% subsidiary (of Aran Ltd). Its effective 75% subsidiary, Foynes Ltd, is therefore also a member of the group. The fact that Dursey Ltd is an effective 75% subsidiary of Aran Ltd indirectly through Bere Ltd is irrelevant.

Extended meaning of "group"

It may be significant to note that, prior to the introduction in the UK in 1989 (when the relevant legislation was practically identical to the equivalent Irish legislation) of new rules governing the meaning of a group, the accepted interpretation was that a capital gains tax group comprised a principal company, any 75% subsidiary of the principal company, any 75% subsidiary of a 75% subsidiary, and so on indefinitely. This interpretation is referred to here as the extended group view.

As mentioned above, TCA s 616(1)(bb) provides that a principal company and its (effective) 75% subsidiaries form a group (the first limb) and then goes on to say that where a principal company is a member of a group "as being itself an effective 75% subsidiary", the second-mentioned group comprises all of that principal company's (effective) 75% subsidiaries (the second limb). This is interpreted as resulting in an extended group based on the following reasoning.

Assume that D is owned as to 75% by C, which is owned as to 75% by B, which in turn is owned as to 75% by A. By virtue of the first limb, C is the principal company of the CD group. C is also a member of the BC group, "being a 75% subsidiary" of B so that, by virtue of the second limb, the BC group (now in fact the BCD group) comprises C's 75% subsidiary, D. The argument for the extended view then continues as follows.

Since B is a 75% subsidiary of A, A, B and C form a group (the ABC group), by virtue again of the second limb. It is then claimed, however, that D must also be a member of the ABC group on the ground that it is a 75% subsidiary of a principal company, C, that is itself a 75% subsidiary of B. On this reasoning it is possible to go on to include any 75% subsidiaries of D, and so on indefinitely.

Despite the undoubted weight of precedent behind this interpretation, it is difficult to accept that D can be a member of the ABC group in this case. While D is clearly a 75% subsidiary of a principal company (C) and C is a member of the ABC group, to say that that is sufficient to bring D within that group does not seem to be correct. The reference to "as being itself an effective 75% subsidiary" must take its meaning from the context of the first limb which states the basic proposition that a group comprises a principal company and all its 75% subsidiaries. The preferred view here is that C is only a member of the BC group "as being itself an effective 75% subsidiary" (on the basis of the proposition in the first limb) although it is also a member of the ABC group, but then only as being a 75% subsidiary of a 75% subsidiary.

It is acknowledged that, on the restrictive view, if A owns 75% of B, B owns 75% of C and C owns 75% of D (so that D is held as to 42.19% by A), it is nevertheless possible for A to avail of the group treatment provided for by TCA 1997, s 617 (see **9.203**) by transferring an asset to B which may then obtain the same treatment (since B, C and D form a group) by transferring the asset on to D. It would make sense, therefore, to allow A to transfer the asset directly to D. This is not currently possible in the UK by virtue of legislation introduced in 1989 under which D, being less than 51% owned by A, would not be in the A group. Furthermore, a company may only be a member of one UK group so that the indirect transfer of the asset described above would be ineffective.

9.202.2   Residence

For accounting periods ending before 1 July 1998, a non-resident company could not be a member of a capital gains tax group.

By concession, group treatment for capital gains tax purposes is available in relation to the transfer of assets within a non-resident group where the assets are transferred as part of the transfer of a trade carried on in the State and where the profits of the trade, including chargeable gains, are chargeable to corporation tax (see also **9.203.1**).

FA 1999 introduced important changes to the residence requirements of companies for the purposes of the definition of a capital gains tax group. These changes take effect for accounting periods ending on or after 1 July 1998. It will be helpful to deal here with the residence requirements as they relate respectively to accounting periods ending before 1 July 1998 and accounting periods ending on or after that date.

Accounting periods ending before 1 July 1998

"Principal company" in TCA 1997, s 616(1)(c) (prior to FA 1999) means a company of which another company is a 75% subsidiary. Since "company" for the purposes of TCA 1997, s 616 (prior to FA 1999) means only an Irish resident company, both the principal company and the subsidiary must be resident. But what is the effect of the presence of an intermediary company, for example B Ltd above, which is non-resident? Can A Ltd and C Ltd nevertheless be members of a group since both the principal company and the subsidiary in this case are resident?

If B Ltd is non-resident, neither B Ltd nor C Ltd will be in group relationship with A Ltd. The definition of "75% subsidiary" is in TCA 1997, s 9 and in that section the rules for identifying indirect holdings involve numerous references to "company". Accordingly, these references are also relevant "for the purposes of" the definition of "group" and since, for those purposes, only resident companies may be included, any shareholding in or by a non-resident company which is an intermediary or a company in a chain of intermediaries must be ignored.

The Court of Justice of the European Communities has held that discrimination based on fiscal residence may be unlawful. Articles 43 and 48 (formerly 52 and 58 respectively) of the EC Treaty are intended to prevent restrictions on the freedom of establishment of nationals, including companies, of one member state in the territory of another. In *R v Inland Revenue Commissioners, ex parte Commerzbank AG* [1993] STC 605, the denial, on the grounds of non-residence, of a repayment supplement on tax refunded to a German company was held to be incompatible with (what are now) articles 43 and 48 of the EC treaty. The refund had been made to Commerzbank arising out of the earlier case referred to in **14.105**. The UK Revenue contended that the denial of a repayment to a non-resident was not discriminatory since a UK company in the same circumstances would not have been exempted from tax on the income in question. It was held nevertheless that there was no justification for a rule of a general nature withholding the benefit of the repayment supplement.

In *Halliburton Services BV v Staatssecretaris van Financiën* [1994] STC 655, a German subsidiary of Halliburton Inc, a US company, transferred its Dutch permanent establishment to a Dutch subsidiary of Halliburton. The Dutch authorities denied stamp duty group reorganisation relief on the basis that the relevant Dutch exemption applied only where the transferor was a Dutch company. They argued that this involved no breach of Articles 43 and 48 (then 52 and 58 respectively) of the EC Treaty as it was the Dutch company and not the German company that was the taxable entity. The European Court held that Articles 43 and 48 precluded Dutch law from restricting the relief to cases where the company qualifying for exemption acquired immovable property from a company constituted under Dutch law. Otherwise, payment of the tax would make the conditions of sale by the German company more onerous and would therefore amount to discrimination.

On the basis of Articles 43 and 48 of the EC Treaty as interpreted in these cases, it was arguable that a non-Irish company should not be debarred from being a member of a capital gains tax group, including being the principal company of that group. Thus, if an Irish subsidiary of a non-resident parent company transferred an asset to another such Irish subsidiary, it might have claimed that it should be entitled to capital gains tax deferral treatment under TCA 1997, s 617 (intra-group transfers of assets – see **9.203**). Following the *Commerzbank* decision, it was arguable that since that treatment would be available if the parent company were Irish resident, it would be discriminatory to deny relief solely because it is not so resident. In addition, in the light of the *Halliburton* judgment, recourse could have been had to the parent company's right of establishment. If, instead, it was the transferor company that was non-resident and which sought to rely on TCA 1997, s 617, its claim to be taxed as it would be taxed if it were Irish resident would have been supported by Article 43 of the EC Treaty.

The effect of the presence of one or more non-resident companies within a group relationship was the subject of the UK case *Imperial Chemical Industries plc v Colmer* [1996] STC 352, [1998] STC 874. That case was concerned with a group relief consortium claim (see **8.302.2** and **8.303**). TCA 1997, s 411(1)(c) contains a residence requirement similar to that in TCA 1997, s 616(1)(a). It was held in the House of Lords that the UK equivalent of TCA 1997, s 411(1)(c) must be construed strictly; in other words, the presence of a non-resident company in the ownership chain operates to sever any shareholding link that depends on that company. The House of Lords, however, also found that it is necessary to construe the group relief provisions in a manner which does not conflict with Community law, particularly those articles which are directed against the freedom of establishment of nationals, including companies, of one member state in the territory of another.

In July 1998, the Court of Justice ruled that since consortium relief was available only where the 90% subsidiaries of a group holding company were also bodies corporate resident in the UK, the relevant legislative provisions discriminated against companies which had exercised their right of freedom of establishment under Article 43 of the EC Treaty and which controlled companies mainly resident in other member states. The national court was not, however, required, when deciding an issue that lay outside the scope of Community law, to interpret its legislation so as to comply with Community law. Accordingly, in relation to the issue that arose in the *Colmer* case, there was no obligation to apply the relevant tax legislation in such a way as to overlook the non-resident status of the majority of the subsidiary companies in that case. The denial of group relief was upheld on the basis that, since the majority of the trading subsidiaries of the consortium-owned holding company were resident outside the EU, that company did not meet the definition of "holding company" for the purposes of the relief (see **8.302.2**).

Accounting periods ending on or after 1 July 1998

For accounting periods ending on or after 1 July 1998, a capital gains tax group may consist of companies resident in Ireland and companies resident for tax purposes in another Member State of the European Communities (but see below under *Position from 1 January 2002* in relation to "relevant Member State").

TCA 1997, s 616(1)(a) (as amended by FA 1999) provides that a reference to a company or companies in s 616 (ie, for the purpose of defining "group") is to apply to a company or companies which, by virtue of the law of a Member State of the European Communities, is or are resident for tax purposes in such a Member State. For this purpose, "tax" in relation to a Member State other than Ireland means tax imposed in that State and which corresponds to corporation tax in Ireland. TCA 1997, s 616(1)(a) also provides that references to a member or members of a group of companies are to be construed accordingly.

Principal company in TCA 1997, s 616(1)(c) (as amended by FA 1999) means a company of which another company is an "effective 75% subsidiary" (see **9.202.1** above). Since "company" for the purposes of TCA 1997, s 616 means only an EU resident company, both the principal company and the subsidiary must be EU resident.

For accounting periods ended before 1 July 1998, the presence of a non-resident company in a group could have prevented one or more resident companies in that group from being members of that group as a capital gains tax group. For accounting periods ending on or after 1 July 1998, arising out of the amendment, by FA 1999, of TCA 1997 616(1)(a), the presence of a non-EU resident company in a group did not necessarily have a corresponding effect (but does again have such an effect following the enactment of FA 2001 (see below)).

For example, if B Ltd is a wholly owned subsidiary of A Ltd, and C Ltd is a wholly owned subsidiary of B Ltd, C Ltd is an effective 75% subsidiary of A Ltd. If B Ltd is not resident in the EU while both A Ltd and C Ltd are so resident, C Ltd is nevertheless in group relationship with A Ltd because C Ltd is an effective 75% subsidiary of A Ltd. The definition of "75% subsidiary" is contained in TCA 1997, s 9 and in that section the rules for identifying indirect holdings contain references to "company". For accounting periods ended on or after 1 July 1998, the restriction of the meaning of "company" to EU resident companies applied only "where the reference is in this section" (TCA 1997, s 616(1)(a)(i) as it was prior to FA 2001) and since the references to "company" in TCA 1997, s 9 were not "in this section", it was possible to take into account a company whose residence was not in the EU in determining whether or not one or more EU resident companies were members of a capital gains tax group.

The further amendment, by FA 2001, of TCA 1997, s 616(1)(a) effectively restored the pre-FA 1999 position. Accordingly, a company which is an effective 75% subsidiary of the principal company of a capital gains tax group by reason only of shares being held through a non-EU resident company is not a member of that group.

TCA 1997, s 616(1)(a) provides that, subject to TCA 1997, s 621(1) (depreciatory transactions – see **9.211**), a reference to a company is to a company which, by virtue of the law of a Member State of the European Communities (but see below under *Position* *from 1 January 2002* in relation to "relevant Member State"), is resident for the purposes of tax in such a Member State. For this purpose, *tax*, in relation to a Member State other than Ireland, means any tax imposed in the Member State which corresponds to corporation tax in the State and references to members of a group of companies are to be construed accordingly.

Example 9.202.2.1

Below are the percentages of ordinary share capital held by and in the companies in the Mourne group. The relevant equity entitlements match the ordinary shareholdings in all cases. All companies except Camelback Ltd are EU resident.

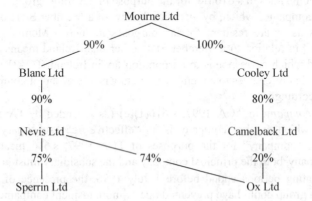

The capital gains tax group comprises Mourne Ltd (principal company), Blanc Ltd, Nevis Ltd, Sperrin Ltd, and Cooley Ltd. Although Sperrin Ltd is not an effective 75% subsidiary of Mourne Ltd (being held as to only 60.75%), it is an effective 75% subsidiary of an effective 75% subsidiary (ie, of Nevis Ltd).

Camelback Ltd, not being an EU resident company, is not a member of the capital gains tax group. Neither can it be taken into account in determining what other companies may be members of the group.

Ox Ltd is held as to 74% only by Nevis Ltd, an effective 75% subsidiary of Mourne Ltd, which is not sufficient to make it a member of the Mourne group. It is, on the other hand, a 75% subsidiary of Mourne Ltd, being held as to 75.94% by the parent company (90% x 90% x 74% + 80% x 20%). The 16% holding through Cooley Ltd and Camelback Ltd cannot, however, be counted for this purpose since Camelback Ltd is not resident in the EU.

9.202.3   Position from 1 January 2002

The position from 1 January 2002 is as the same as that for accounting periods ending on or after 1 July 1998 as described above with the difference that "relevant Member State" is substituted for "Member State of the European Communities". The net effect of this is that Norway is added to the list of countries concerned. In this connection, *relevant Member State*, means—

(a)   a Member State of the European Communities; or

(b)   not being such a Member State, an EEA State which is a territory with which Ireland has a tax treaty (TCA 1997, s 616(7)).

EEA State means a state that is a contracting party to the EEA Agreement. *EEA Agreement* means the Agreement on the European Economic Area signed at Oporto on 2 May 1992, as adjusted by the Protocol signed at Brussels on 17 March 1993.

Mergers Directive

Council Directive No 2005/19/EC amended the 1990 EU Mergers Directive in a number of respects (see **9.301**). Against the background of those amendments, Irish tax legislation includes a measure providing that a capital gains tax group remains the same group in circumstances where a company, being a member of the group, becomes an SE or an SCE.

Where at any time the principal company of a capital gains tax group—

(a) becomes a European Company (SE) by reason of being the acquiring company in the formation of an SE by merger by acquisition (in accordance with Articles 2(1), 17(2)(a) and 29(1) of the SE Regulation (Council Regulation (EC) No 2157/2001 of 8 October 2001, on the Statute for a European Company (SE) (OJ No L 294, 10.11.2001, p1));

(b) becomes a subsidiary of a holding SE (formed in accordance with Article 2(2) of that Regulation); or

(c) is transformed into an SE (in accordance with Article 2(4) of that Regulation),

the group of which it was the principal company before that time and any group of which the SE is a member on formation is to be regarded as the same, and the question of whether or not a company has ceased to be a member of a group is to be determined accordingly (TCA 1997, s 616(3A)(a)).

Treatment identical to the above applies in a case where the principal company of a group becomes a European Cooperative Society (SCE) in the course of a merger in accordance with Article 2 of the SCE Regulation (Council Regulation (EC) No 1435/2003 of 22 July 2003 on the Statute for a European Cooperative Society (SCE) (OJ No L 207, 18.8.2003, p1)) (TCA 1997, s 616(3A)(b)).

If at any time a company ceases to be resident in Ireland in the course of the formation of an SE by merger or the formation of an SCE, then, whether or not it continues after that formation, the Tax Acts and the Capital Gains Tax Acts are to apply to any obligations of the company under TCA 1997 in relation to liabilities accruing and matters arising before that time—

(i) as if the company were still resident in Ireland; and

(ii) where the company has ceased to exist, as if the SE or the SCE were the company (TCA 1997, s 629A).

9.202.4 Principal company and extended group

TCA 1997, s 616(3) is an important provision whose purpose is to ensure that companies will not be regarded as leaving a capital gains tax group in unintended ways. This feature is of particular importance in relation to the operation of TCA 1997, s 623 (crystallisation of tax charge on company leaving group – see **9.209**) but is relevant for other capital gains tax group provisions also. TCA 1997, s 616(3) contains two basic statements (or "limbs"), followed by the third limb stated to be a consequence of each of the first two. The first limb is to the effect that a group remains the same group as long as the same company remains the principal company of the group. The second limb makes provision for the case in which the principal company of a group is acquired by another company. The third limb then goes on to provide that the question as to whether a company has left a group is to be determined in accordance with the first two limbs. It is worth looking at each of the first two limbs in more detail.

TCA 1997, s 616(3) – first limb

A group remains the same group as long as the same company remains the principal company of the group (TCA 1997, s 616(3) – first limb). This is an important provision as, without it, it would often be impossible to know whether a group had ceased to exist and, in particular, whether a company had left a group. The provision should be read in conjunction with TCA 1997, s 623 (see **9.209**).

Example 9.202.3.1

Taking the facts in Example **9.202.2.1** above, if the shares in Blanc Ltd were to be sold, the group would nevertheless continue. It would now comprise Mourne Ltd and Cooley Ltd. The group would remain the same group because Mourne Ltd remains the principal company of it.

If, later, Cooley Ltd were to be sold, the Mourne group would now have ceased to be a group. A group comprising Blanc Ltd, Nevis Ltd and Sperrin Ltd would continue to exist but would not be the same group since Mourne Ltd is not its principal company. These three companies would have left the Mourne group. It might be that there would be tax consequences for one or more of them as a result of leaving the Mourne group which would not be avoided because they continue to be members of the Blanc group (see **9.209**). There might, similarly, be consequences for Cooley Ltd.

Assume that, prior to the sale of Blanc Ltd, that company had transferred an asset to Cooley Ltd. There would be no consequence for Cooley Ltd arising from Blanc Ltd leaving the group because the Mourne group would still be the same group and Cooley Ltd would still be a member of it. When Cooley Ltd later leaves the group, however, it is leaving the same group as that to which Blanc Ltd (the company that had transferred the asset to it) had belonged (so that the consequences of leaving a group described in **9.209** below would follow).

TCA 1997, s 616(3) – second limb

If at any time the principal company of a group becomes an effective 75% subsidiary of another company, the group of which it was the principal company before that time is to be regarded as the same as the group of which that other company is the principal company, or (as the case may be) the same as the group of which that other company is an effective 75% subsidiary (TCA 1997, s 616(3) – second limb), and the question whether or not a company has ceased to be a member of a group is to be determined accordingly (TCA 1997, s 616(3) – third limb). The significance of this provision can usefully be illustrated in the following examples.

Example 9.202.3.2

Megiddo Ltd owns 75% of the ordinary share capital in each of Mordecai Ltd, Micah Ltd and Manasseh Ltd. Manasseh Ltd owns 75% of the ordinary share capital in Lystra Ltd. The equity entitlement in each case is also 75%. Megiddo Ltd is therefore the principal company of the group (the "Megiddo group") comprising Megiddo Ltd, Mordecai Ltd, Micah Ltd, Manasseh Ltd and Lystra Ltd.

Agrippa Ltd owns 75% of the ordinary share capital in each of Amos Ltd, Aquila Ltd and Artemis Ltd. Artemis Ltd owns 75% of the ordinary share capital in Demetrius Ltd. The equity entitlement in each case is also 75%. Agrippa Ltd is therefore the principal company of the group (the "Agrippa group") comprising Agrippa Ltd, Amos Ltd, Aquila Ltd, Artemis Ltd and Demetrius Ltd.

Megiddo Ltd acquires 75% of the ordinary share capital in Agrippa Ltd (and corresponding equity entitlements). The new position can now be represented as follows:

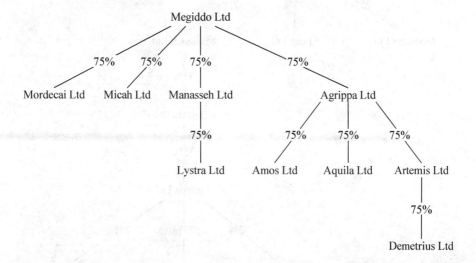

On the acquisition by Megiddo Ltd of its 75% shareholding in Agrippa Ltd, the group of which Agrippa Ltd was the principal company before that time (the Agrippa group) is regarded as "the same as" the group of which Megiddo Ltd is the principal company, the enlarged group (the Megiddo group) now comprising all of the above companies.

In the absence of TCA 1997, s 616(3), the Megiddo group would not (based on the restrictive interpretation of what constitutes a group – see **9.202.1** above) include Demetrius Ltd as that company is not an effective 75% subsidiary of an effective 75% subsidiary of Megiddo Ltd.

The real significance, however, of the second limb of TCA 1997, s 616(3), to the effect that the Agrippa group is the same as the Megiddo group, would be seen in the event that, say, Artemis Ltd later transfers its 75% interest in Demetrius Ltd to Megiddo Ltd. In the absence of the provision, Demetrius Ltd would have left a group (the Agrippa group). Since, however, that group is now "the same as" the Megiddo group, and since Demetrius Ltd remains a member of the Megiddo group, it would be regarded as not having left any group.

Example 9.202.3.3

The position is the same as in Example **9.202.3.2** except that the 75% interest in Agrippa Ltd is acquired by Lystra Ltd. The new structure is now represented as follows:

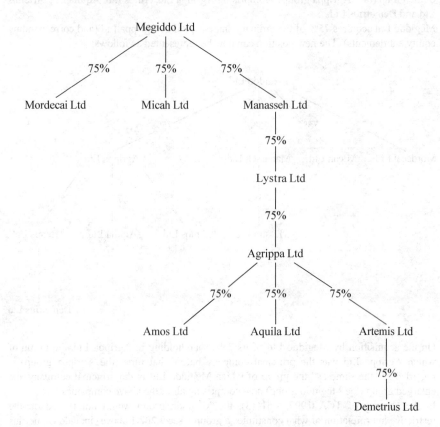

On the acquisition by Lystra Ltd of its 75% shareholding in Agrippa Ltd, the group of which Agrippa Ltd was the principal company before that time (the Agrippa group) is regarded as "the same as" the group of which Lystra Ltd is an effective 75% subsidiary, ie the group of which Manasseh Ltd (Lystra Ltd's "75% parent") is the principal company. The Agrippa group is now regarded as "the same as" the enlarged group (the Manasseh group) comprising Manasseh Ltd, Lystra Ltd, Agrippa Ltd, Amos Ltd, Aquila Ltd, Artemis Ltd and Demetrius Ltd.

In the absence of TCA 1997, s 616(3), the Manasseh group would not (based on the restrictive interpretation of what constitutes a group – see **9.202.1** above) include Amos Ltd, Aquila Ltd, Artemis Ltd or Demetrius Ltd as none of these companies is an effective 75% subsidiary of an effective 75% subsidiary of Manasseh Ltd. Similarly as in Example **9.202.3.2**, the real significance of the second limb of TCA 1997, s 616(3), to the effect that the Agrippa group is the same as the Manasseh group, would be seen in the event that, say, Artemis Ltd later transfers interest in Demetrius Ltd to Manasseh Ltd. In the absence of the provision, Demetrius Ltd would have left a group (the Agrippa group). Since, however, that group is now "the same as" the Manasseh group, and since Demetrius Ltd remains a member of the Manasseh group, it would be regarded as not having left any group.

Again, if Agrippa Ltd were to transfer Artemis Ltd to Manasseh Ltd, neither Artemis Ltd nor Demetrius Ltd would be regarded as having left any group.

A transfer of, say, Artemis Ltd from Agrippa Ltd to Megiddo Ltd would not prevent Artemis Ltd leaving a group since there is no question of the Megiddo group being regarded as "the same as" the Agrippa group. This is because Lystra Ltd (the company that acquired 75% of Agrippa Ltd), is not an effective 75% subsidiary of Megiddo Ltd (although it is a member of the Megiddo group).

If, in the above example, Manasseh Ltd were 100% owned by Megiddo Ltd, the Megiddo group would then have been regarded as "the same as" the Agrippa group so that, for example, a transfer of the 75% interest in Artemis Ltd from Agrippa Ltd to Megiddo Ltd would not result in Artemis Ltd leaving any group. This result follows from the fact that Lystra Ltd (the company that acquired the interest in Agrippa Ltd) is an effective 75% subsidiary of Megiddo Ltd; being indirectly held through Manasseh Ltd is irrelevant for this purpose. In this case, the only reasonable and workable interpretation of the second limb of TCA 1997, s 616(3) is to look to Megiddo Ltd (rather than Manasseh Ltd) as the principal company of the enlarged group – it is still possible to look to Manasseh Ltd (since Lystra Ltd is an effective 75% subsidiary of both Megiddo Ltd and Manasseh Ltd).

A possible technical limitation of the second limb of TCA 1997, s 616(3) can be seen in both of the foregoing examples. Taking Example **9.202.3.3**, it was seen that if the 75% interest in Demetrius Ltd were to be transferred to Manasseh Ltd it would be regarded as not having left a group since it would not be leaving the Manasseh group and as that group is treated as the same as the Agrippa group. It would, however, be leaving the Artemis group (comprising Artemis Ltd and Demetrius Ltd). TCA 1997, s 616(3) does not make any provision to the effect that the Manasseh group is to be regarded as the same as the Artemis group; the acquisition of the 75% interest in Agrippa Ltd by Lystra Ltd does not involve Artemis Ltd (the principal company of the Artemis group) becoming an effective 75% subsidiary of any company so that the Artemis group does not become "the same as" any other group.

One group or groups within a group?

The above discussion on "the same group" and extended groups prompts the question whether a capital gains tax group can include within it one or more capital gains tax groups, each with its own principal company. The first limb of TCA 1997, s 616(3), to the effect that a group remains the same group as long as the same company remains the principal company of the group, might seem to indicate that only one group, being the group of which the ultimate parent is the principal company, exists. This, however, does not necessarily follow and the provision can be applied equally to each sub-group within the larger group.

The reference in TCA 1997, s 616(3) (see above) to "the group of which it *was* the principal company" might at first seem to suggest that a principal company which becomes an effective 75% subsidiary of another company no longer *is*, and has therefore ceased to be, such a principal company. That would, however, seem be to a misconstruction of the real purpose of that subsection which is to prevent certain companies from ceasing to be members of a group after that group is acquired by another company or group. It is for that purpose that the "old" group is deemed to be "the same as" the enlarged group so that the principal company of the old group now becomes a member of the enlarged group. It is in that sense only, and for the purposes only of TCA 1997, s 616(3), that reference is made to the group of which the acquired company "was" the principal company.

Furthermore, TCA 1997, s 616(1)(bb) clearly refers to two groups, one being a group within the other group. It states, firstly, that a principal company and all its 75% subsidiaries form a group, and then goes on to describe a larger group of which that principal company is a member. That aspect of the provision would seem to be more than sufficient to remove any doubts resulting from the somewhat ambiguous wording of TCA 1997, s 616(3) referred to above.

Example 9.202.3.4

Shelley Ltd has a wholly owned subsidiary, Byron Ltd, which in turn has a wholly owned subsidiary, Keats Ltd. Byron Ltd transfers assets to Keats Ltd which transfer, by virtue of TCA 1997, s 617 (see **9.203**), results in neither a gain nor a loss arising to Byron Ltd.

Shelley Ltd sells Byron Ltd to Caldwell Ltd. No charge under TCA 1997, s 623 (company leaving a group – see **9.209.1-3**) arises in respect of the earlier intra-group disposal involving Byron Ltd and Keats Ltd as these two companies are "associated companies".

Three years later, Byron Ltd sells Keats Ltd outside the Caldwell group. The charge under TCA 1997, s 623 will now apply as respects any asset which the company leaving the group acquired from another company "which at the time of acquisition was a member of the group". The intra-group transfer had taken place when the two companies were members of the Shelley group but also, however, while they were members of the Byron group (comprising Byron Ltd and Keats Ltd). Keats Ltd has now left the Byron group so that the TCA 1997, s 623 charge applies.

When Byron Ltd was sold by Shelley Ltd, Byron Ltd and Keats Ltd left the Shelley group but the TCA 1997, s 623 charge was avoided at that time because the companies were associated companies. On joining the Caldwell group, the "old" group (the Byron group comprising Byron Ltd and Keats Ltd) became "the same as" the Caldwell group. Accordingly, neither company is regarded as having left the Byron group at that time (although of course they have left the Shelley group). When Keats Ltd is sold by Byron Ltd, it leaves the Byron group so that the TCA 1997, s 623 charge crystallises.

It is interesting to note that the corresponding UK legislation avoids such ambiguities as exist under the Irish legislation. It provides that a company cannot, generally, be the principal company of a group if it is itself a 75% subsidiary of another company. It further provides that a company may not be a member of more than one group at the same time. See also **7.402** in relation to the meaning of "group" for the purposes of credit relief for research and development. The provision there which corresponds to TCA 1997, s 616(1)(bb) specifically provides that the first-mentioned group will be deemed not to be a group.

The apparent possibility that a company may simultaneously be a member of more than one group (the position under Irish legislation) can have interesting results. This is illustrated in the following example which should be read with TCA 1997, s 617 (see **9.203**) in mind.

Example 9.202.3.5

Welles Ltd owns a building in respect of which it has a potential chargeable gain of €1,500,000. It wishes to sell it to Resnais Ltd, a company in which it owns 74% of the ordinary share capital. Resnais Ltd owns 95% of the ordinary share capital of Vertov Ltd. Welles Ltd is not in a position to acquire any further interest in Resnais Ltd but succeeds in acquiring the remaining 5% interest in Vertov Ltd. All of the ordinary share capital holdings carry equivalent equity entitlements.

The structure can then be represented as follows:

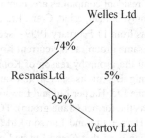

Vertov Ltd is a member of the Resnais group but is also a member of the Welles group since it is an effective 75% subsidiary of Welles Ltd (74% x 95% + 5%). Welles Ltd sells the building to Vertov Ltd for €1.5m, tax free, in accordance with TCA 1997, s 617. Vertov Ltd then sells on the building to Resnais Ltd for €1.5m, again without liability to tax. Welles Ltd has succeeded in transferring the building to Resnais Ltd, a company that is not in group relationship with it.

Enlarged group from 1 July 1998

In many cases a capital gains tax group will have been enlarged for its first accounting period ended on or after 1 July 1998 arising out of the amendment to TCA 1997, s 616(1)(a) (see **9.202.3**) whereby EU resident companies, and not just Irish resident companies, are to be taken into account. For earlier periods there may, for example, have been one or more intra-group transfers within the smaller group (comprising only Irish resident companies) so that TCA 1997, s 617 (see **9.203**) would have applied. As to what is the current impact of the above legislative change on such past transactions may be best dealt with through the use of an example.

Example 9.202.3.6

In the year ended 31 December 1996, the trade and assets of Harper Ltd were transferred to Lawson Ltd. Both companies were Irish resident and wholly owned by a further Irish resident company, Crane Ltd. Crane Ltd was in turn wholly owned by Konig BV, a Dutch resident company. During the year ended 31 December 2007, Konig BV disposed of its shares in Crane Ltd.

Having regard to the rule in TCA 1997, s 616(3) that a group remains the same group as long as the same company remains the principal company of the group, it might seem that from 1 July 1998 there is a new group since the principal company is now Konig BV rather than Crane Ltd. If that is the case, Crane Ltd and its subsidiaries will have left the Crane group on that date.

At first glance, it might appear that the second limb of TCA 1997, s 616(3) (see above) does not operate to treat the former group as being the same as the enlarged group since no acquisition of shares is involved. However, that limb relates to any situation in which a principal company of a group becomes an effective 75% subsidiary of another company. Accordingly, on 1 July 1998 the original Crane group will have become the same group as the enlarged Konig group if on that date Crane Ltd became an effective 75% subsidiary of Konig BV.

For the year ended 31 December 1996, Crane Ltd was not a "75% subsidiary" (as defined in TCA 1997, s 9 – see **2.503**) of Konig BV as only Irish resident companies could then be taken into account for the purpose of determining whether one company was a 75% subsidiary of another. For the year ended 31 December 1998, Crane Ltd was a 75% subsidiary of Konig BV as EU resident companies are, commencing with that period, to be so taken into account. Accordingly, in that period, Crane Ltd became a 75% subsidiary (and an "effective 75% subsidiary" as from 11 February 1999 – see **9.202.1**) of Konig BV. Thus, the former Crane group is "the same group" as the current Konig group.

While no member company left the group by reason of Konig BV becoming the principal company, the disposal by Konig BV of its shares in Crane Ltd in the year ended 31 December 2007 means that Crane Ltd, Harper Ltd and Lawson Ltd have now left the Konig group (deemed to be the same as the former Crane group). TCA 1997, s 623(4) is, however, not triggered by this event as Harper Ltd and Lawson Ltd are associated companies (see **9.209.3** below). Had the position been that Crane Ltd had disposed of Lawson Ltd (or of both Harper Ltd and Lawson Ltd), Lawson Ltd would be regarded as having left the group of which it was a member at the time of the intra-group transfer in the year ended 31 December 1996 thereby triggering a charge under TCA 1997, s 623(4).

9.202.5   Liquidation

On the occasion of a company going into liquidation, it ceases to be the beneficial owner of its assets (*Ayerst v CEK Construction Ltd* [1975] STC 1). However, the passing of a resolution or the making of an order, or any other act, for the winding up of a company is not to be regarded as the occasion of that company, or of any effective 75% subsidiary of that company, ceasing to be a member of a group of companies (TCA 1997, s 616(4)). Accordingly, the capital gains tax group remains in existence until the company in question is wound up.

9.202.6   Nationalised bodies

The provisions of the legislation dealing with capital gains tax groups as to members of a group of companies are extended to the various bodies with related functions under national ownership and control. TCA 1997, s 616(5) provides that TCA 1997 ss 617-629, except in so far as they relate to recovery of tax, are also to have effect in relation to bodies from time to time established by or under any enactment for the carrying on of any industry or part of an industry, or of any undertaking, under national ownership or control as if they were companies within the meaning of those sections, and as if any such bodies charged with related functions and subsidiaries of any of them formed a group, and as if also any two or more such bodies charged at different times with the same or related functions were members of a group.

Thus, for example, chargeable gains on transfers of assets between bodies under national ownership or control and which have related functions, including subsidiaries of any of them, will be deferred in accordance with TCA 1997, s 617 as if such bodies and subsidiaries formed a group.

This extension of capital gains tax group treatment to such bodies is, however, subject to any enactment under which property, rights, liabilities or activities of one such body fall to be treated for corporation tax as those of another.

An example of this qualification to TCA 1997, s 616(5) might be the case of a European Economic Interest Grouping (EEIG). An EEIG registered in Ireland will be a body corporate having a legal personality and, as such, could come within the charge to corporation tax (or income tax or capital gains tax) in its own right. It is not, however, a "company" for the purposes of corporation tax (TCA 1997, s 4(1) – see (b) in definition of "company"). An EEIG is a form of business entity established under Council Regulation (EEC) No 2137/85 of 25 July 1985 on the European Economic Interest Grouping (EEIG) and the European Communities (European Economic Interest Groupings) Regulations, 1989 (SI 1989/191) and can be set up by residents, including companies, of two or more EU states. Under TCA 1997, s 1014, an EEIG is not to be charged to income tax, corporation tax or capital gains tax in respect of profits or gains or chargeable gains arising to it and is not entitled to relief for a loss sustained by it. Any assessment required to be made on such profits or gains or chargeable gains, and any relief for a loss, is to be made instead on, and allowed to, the members of the EEIG. Where the members of an EEIG are companies, properties, rights, liabilities and activities of the EEIG would therefore fall to be treated for corporation tax as those of the members and the extended capital gains treatment provided for by TCA 1997, s 616(5) would not apply in that case.

Another example might be one of the cases dealt with by TCA 1997, s 611 (disposals to State, charities and other bodies). The market value rule of TCA 1997, s 547 does not apply, inter alia, to non-arm's length disposals of assets to any of the bodies falling within FA 1931 s 28(3) (national institutions and other public bodies, eg the National Gallery of Ireland, the National Museum of Science and Art, and any other similar national institution). Where the disposal is for no consideration or for a consideration not exceeding what would be the allowable cost, the disposal and acquisition is treated as being for such consideration as would secure that neither a gain nor a loss accrued on the disposal. Where, however, the asset is later disposed of by the body concerned in circumstances that if a gain accrued it would be a chargeable gain, the capital gains tax which would have been chargeable in respect of the gain on the earlier disposal is to be assessed and charged on the body making the later disposal (in addition to any capital gains tax chargeable in respect of the gain accruing on the later disposal). The extended capital gains treatment provided for by TCA 1997, s 616(5) that might otherwise apply in such a case would not apply in those circumstances.

9.203 Intra-group transfers of assets

9.203.1 Transfers of assets between group members: general

The essential purpose of the capital gains tax group legislation is to ignore intra-group transactions and to compute gains and losses by comparing the amount of the consideration paid when the asset in question comes into group ownership with the amount of the consideration received when the asset leaves the group. Most of the other provisions of that legislation supplement this idea, for example TCA 1997, s 618 which deals with the position where the asset being transferred is trading stock of one of the companies, or TCA 1997 ss 623-624 which ensure that tax is not avoided where a company to which an intra-group asset transfer has been made itself leaves the group. See also **9.213** in relation to stamp duty.

As mentioned in **9.202.2**, a company which, by virtue of the law of a relevant Member State, is resident for the purposes of tax in such a Member State, may be a member of a capital gains tax group.

Where a member of a group of companies disposes, on or after 15 February 2001, of an asset to another member of the group, and in any of the circumstances described below, both members are to be treated (subject to exceptions dealt with below), for the purposes of corporation tax on chargeable gains, as if the asset acquired by the member to whom the disposal is made were acquired for a consideration of such amount as would secure that on the disposal by the first mentioned company neither a gain nor a loss would accrue to that company (TCA 1997, s 617(1)).

The circumstances referred to above are that—

(a) the company making the disposal is resident in the State at the time of the disposal or the asset is a chargeable asset in relation to that company immediately before that time; and

(b) the other company—

    (i) is resident in the State at the time of the disposal or the asset is a chargeable asset in relation to that company immediately after that time, and

    (ii) is not an authorised investment company (within the meaning of Part XIII of the Companies Act 1990) which is an investment undertaking within the meaning of TCA 1997, s 739B (see **12.806.3**).

An asset is a "chargeable asset" in relation to a company at any time if, were it to be disposed of by the company at that time, any gain accruing to the company would be a chargeable gain. A chargeable gain will arise to a non-resident company only in respect of disposals of certain categories of assets (eg, Irish based land, shares deriving their value or the greater part of their value from such land, Irish based assets used in an Irish branch trade – see **9.102.2**). However, since TCA 1997, s 617(1) applies only "for the purposes of corporation tax on chargeable gains", only such assets as are being disposed of or acquired by companies carrying on a trade in the State through a branch or agency (and which are accordingly subject to corporation tax) are chargeable assets in relation to the company and then only (subject to the position relating to development land, discussed below) where the assets are used in or for the purposes of the trade or are used or held by, or are acquired for, the purposes of the branch or agency (see **3.107.1**).

As explained in **9.203.5** below, as regards disposals of development land (including shares deriving their value or the greater part of their value from such land), TCA 1997, s 617 applies in relation to capital gains tax to which a company is chargeable on chargeable gains as it applies in relation to corporation tax on chargeable gains. Accordingly, TCA 1997, s 617 applies so as to defer a chargeable gain arising on an intra-group disposal of development land until such time as the development land is disposed of outside the group. This provision has the interesting result that, whereas a non-resident member of a group transferring development land (including shares deriving their value etc) intra-group benefits from TCA 1997, s 617 treatment, no such benefit is available where the intra-group transfer relates to land, or shares, other than development land.

From the above, it can be seen that TCA 1997, s 617(1) can apply to an intra-group transfer of assets in any of the following circumstances—

    (i) the transfer of an asset by an Irish resident company to another Irish resident company;

(ii)   the transfer by an Irish resident company to a non-resident company of an asset which immediately after the transfer was a chargeable asset in relation to the non-resident company;

(iii)   the transfer by a non-resident company to an Irish resident company of an asset which immediately before the transfer was a chargeable asset in relation to the non-resident company; and

(iv)   the transfer by a non-resident company to another non-resident company of an asset which immediately before the transfer was a chargeable asset in relation to the transferor company and immediately after the transfer is a chargeable asset in relation to the transferee company; and

(v)   the transfer of development land (including the transfer of shares deriving their value or the greater part of their value from such land) between group members.

In the cases of (ii), (iii) or (iv), where certain assets subsequently cease to be chargeable assets in relation to a company, there is a deemed sale and reacquisition of those assets at market value at that time (TCA 1997, s 620A). The assets in question are those assets which were used or held by, or were acquired for, the purposes of the company's Irish branch or agency and which now cease to be chargeable assets by virtue of their becoming situated outside the State (TCA 1997, s 620A(1)(a)(ii)). The deemed sale and reacquisition does not apply to assets ceasing to be chargeable assets in relation to the company as a result of their ceasing to be used for the purposes of the branch or agency (provided of course that that does not result in the assets being transferred outside the State).

There is also a deemed sale and reacquisition by a company of assets that cease to be chargeable assets in relation to the company and which, at the time of their acquisition by the company, consisted of shares deriving their value or the greater part of their value from assets specified in TCA 1997, s 29(3)(a) or (b) (see **9.102.2**), but only in circumstances where they cease to be such chargeable assets because they no longer derive their value or the greater part of their value from those specified assets (TCA 1997, s 620A(1)(a)(i)). The inclusion of this provision could relate to a situation of the kind covered in (v) above, where TCA 1997, s 617 has applied in the case of a non-resident member of a group transferring shares deriving their value or the greater part of their value from development land. Otherwise, the reason for including the provision is not clear since the acquisition of such shares would not have been as a result of a disposal to which TCA 1997, s 617 (which refers to "corporation on chargeable gains") applied.

TCA 1997, s 617 would of course apply to the transfer, from one Irish resident company to another, of shares deriving the greater part of their value from Irish based land. If the residence of the transferee company in that situation were later to be moved outside the State, say to another EU Member State, the shares would then cease to be a chargeable asset in relation to that company. But this would not result in a deemed sale and reacquisition of the shares since it would not have been by virtue of the shares ceasing to derive their value or the greater part of their value from Irish land that they would have ceased to be chargeable assets in relation to the company; they would have so ceased only because the company is no longer Irish resident. (It is also clear that the shares would not have ceased to be chargeable assets in relation to the company by virtue of their becoming situated outside the State.)

In relation to a company that becomes a member of a group of companies on or after 1 March 1999, capital gains tax group treatment cannot be availed of to take advantage of certain "pre-entry" losses and certain subsequent losses of that company on the disposal of "pre-entry assets" (see **9.212**).

By concession, the group treatment provided for in TCA 1997, s 617(1) is extended to cases involving the transfer of assets within a group where one, or both, of the companies involved in the transfer is, or are, not Irish resident. The concession applies where the assets are transferred as part of the transfer of a trade carried on in the State and where the profits of the trade, including chargeable gains, are chargeable to corporation tax.

Where it is assumed for any purpose that a group member has sold or acquired an asset, it is to be assumed also that it was not a sale to or acquisition from another member of the group; in other words, TCA 1997, s 617(1) is concerned only with actual disposals and not with situations in which a disposal is deemed to be made. For example, a principal company having control of another (non-group) company might exercise that control with the result that value passes out of its shares in that company and into other such shares held by another group member (see also **9.102.10**). Where that exercise of control is deemed by TCA 1997, s 543 to be a part disposal of the shares in the non-group company, it is not to be regarded for the purposes of TCA 1997, s 617 as a sale to the other group member.

Group treatment does not apply to:

(a) the disposal of a debt effected by its repayment or part repayment by the group member concerned;

(b) a disposal involving the redemption of redeemable shares held by a fellow group member;

(c) anything which under TCA 1997, s 583 is to be treated as a disposal of an interest in shares in a company in consideration for a capital distribution from that company (see **9.401.4**), whether or not involving a reduction of capital (TCA 1997, s 617(2)); or

(d) a disposal for consideration in money or money's worth by way of compensation for any kind of damage or injury to assets, or for the destruction or dissipation of assets or for anything which depreciates or might depreciate an asset, the disposal being treated as made to the person, normally an insurer, who effectively bears the cost of the compensation (TCA 1997, s 617(3)).

An example of the exception at (a) above would be where one group member owes a sum of money to another group member where the debt was acquired from the original creditor, and the debt is paid off, either in full or in part.

Example 9.203.1.1

Camden Ltd issues debentures for €1,000,000. The debentures are subsequently purchased by Arundel Ltd, a fellow group member, for €900,000. Camden Ltd eventually redeems the debentures for the full €1,000,000 resulting in a gain of €100,000 to Arundel Ltd.

As the debt has been purchased from the original creditor, its disposal now at a profit gives rise to a chargeable gain (see **9.102.11**). The gain is not deferred under TCA 1997, s 617(1) as the debt was owed by a fellow group member.

The type of situation envisaged in (b) above is similar in principle to that in (a).

The exception listed at (c) is concerned with the case in which, say, the principal company of a group receives a capital distribution in respect of the disposal on liquidation of its shares in a subsidiary. The concept of a capital distribution is explained in **9.401.4**.

While a transfer by the liquidator of a company of an asset *in specie* to the parent company would fall within TCA 1997, s 617(1), so that neither a gain nor a loss would result on the disposal, a different position applies in relation to the part disposal by the parent company of its shares in the company in liquidation in consideration for a capital distribution.

The latter disposal is another exception to the general rule in TCA 1997, s 617(1). Accordingly, the transfer of the asset by the liquidator, and its acquisition by the parent, are assumed to be for a consideration of an amount that would secure that neither a gain nor a loss accrues to the subsidiary on the disposal, but the disposal by the parent of its shares in the subsidiary is subject to capital gains tax treatment at that point (see *Innocent v Whaddon Estates Ltd* [1982] STC 115).

Example 9.203.1.2

Shelburne Ltd formed a subsidiary, Flanders Ltd, which it capitalised for €100,000 by way of subscribing for 100,000 €1 ordinary shares. Both companies are Irish resident. Using the proceeds of the share subscription, Flanders Ltd purchased a property for €100,000. Some years later, when the property was worth €300,000, Flanders Ltd was put into liquidation. The liquidator transferred the property *in specie* to Shelburne Ltd in satisfaction of its entitlement in the liquidation. Some years later again, Shelburne Ltd sold the property for €500,000.

The transfer of the property gives rise to three events. Firstly, there is a disposal of the property by the liquidator. This is a TCA 1997, s 617(1) disposal and, as such, is regarded as having taken place at no gain/ no loss. Secondly, Shelburne Ltd acquires the property for a consideration of an amount that would secure that neither a gain nor a loss would arise on the disposal by the liquidator. The deemed acquisition price is therefore €100,000.

Thirdly, Shelburne Ltd has made a deemed disposal of its shares in Flanders Ltd in consideration for a capital distribution of the property worth €300,000. A chargeable gain of €200,000 arises in respect of this disposal.

On the ultimate disposal of the property by Shelburne Ltd, the chargeable gain arising is €400,000 (€500,000 – €100,000).

The aggregate of the chargeable gains arising to Shelburne Ltd is €600,000, although the economic gain is only €400,000. This is an example of the operation of the classical capital gains tax "double bite", where tax accumulates on a trapped gain.

Had the TCA 1997, s 617(1) deferral not operated, a gain of €200,000 would have accrued to the liquidator on the transfer of the property to Shelburne Ltd. The base cost of the property to Shelburne Ltd would then have been €300,000 and its later gain on the disposal of the property would have been €200,000. The gain on the disposal of the shares in Flanders Ltd on liquidation would, as before, have been €200,000. The aggregate chargeable gain would again have been €600,000.

In a third scenario, Flanders Ltd holds the property up to the time of its disposal for €500,000. The gain accruing to it is €400,000. Assuming corporation tax on the chargeable gain at an effective rate of 20%, the after tax proceeds are €420,000. The company is now worth €420,000. If Shelburne Ltd sells off or liquidates Flanders Ltd, the resulting chargeable gain would be €320,000 (€420,000 – €100,000). The aggregate chargeable gain would then amount to €720,000 (€400,000 + €320,000), giving rise to additional tax of €24,000 ((€720,000 − €600,000) x 20%) as compared to the other two scenarios.

In a fourth scenario, Flanders Ltd could have transferred the property to Shelburne Ltd at cost. No chargeable gain would have arisen at that point. Flanders Ltd would then be wound up with the €100,000 being distributed to Shelburne Ltd. No gain would arise on the disposal of the Flanders Ltd shares. Although the group would now have come to an end, Shelburne Ltd would not be regarded as having left the group as the group would have ceased in consequence of Flanders Ltd being wound up (TCA 1997, s 623(1)(d) – see **9.209**). On the disposal of the property by Shelburne Ltd for €500,000, the chargeable gain would be €400,000, which would equate with the actual gain.

The exception at (c) above refers to a disposal of an interest in shares for a capital distribution "whether or not involving a reduction of capital". As discussed in **9.401.4** below, a capital distribution normally means a distribution on a winding up but may also refer to a payment made by a company on the redemption, repayment or purchase of its own shares. A reduction of capital is a form of repayment of share capital (see **9.402.1**) and may therefore give rise to a capital distribution. In any such case, references in TCA 1997, s 617(1) to a member of a group of companies disposing of an asset do not apply to anything treated as a disposal of shares in consideration for a capital distribution which is in the form of a payment made on a reduction of capital. As explained in **9.402.1**, a reduction of share capital would normally constitute a disposal of the shares cancelled. A reduction of share capital is, however, treated by TCA 1997, s 584 in the same way as a reorganisation of share capital and therefore as not involving either a disposal or an acquisition of shares for capital gains tax purposes. It is appropriate therefore that TCA 1997, s 617(1) should not apply to a reduction of capital.

As regards the exception at (d) above, this refers to a disposal for consideration in money or money's worth by way of compensation for damage or injury to, or other loss in value of, assets. The disposal is treated as made to the person who, whether as an insurer or otherwise, bears the cost of furnishing the consideration. An asset owned by a group member and which has been damaged might be transferred to another group member at a reduced price to reflect the reduction in value occasioned by the damage. The transferor company might then claim and receive compensation from an insurer in respect of the loss of value. Being an exception to TCA 1997, s 617(1), that disposal of the asset would not be treated as having been made on a no gain/ no loss basis and is treated as having been made to the insurer.

Certain tax implications of companies purchasing their own shares are discussed in **11.3**. Where a company purchases its own shares it may cancel them (see **11.302**). One result of the cancellation is that the amount of the company's issued share capital must be reduced by the nominal value of the shares purchased. In the case of a purchase of its own shares by a company from a fellow group member, the shares purchased are treated as cancelled on purchase. Accordingly, although the shares have been "purchased", there is no acquisition of shares. On that basis, TCA 1997, s 617 would have no application in the case of an intra-group purchase by a company of its own shares.

As already explained, the intra-group asset transfer provision of TCA 1997, s 617 operates on the basis that gains and losses are to be computed by comparing the amount of the consideration paid when the asset in question comes into group ownership with the amount of the consideration received when the asset leaves the group. Nevertheless, it has been sought to limit this principle in cases where an intra-group transfer of shares had been made in respect of an issue of shares. The point arose in *Westcott v Woolcombers Ltd* [1987] STC 600 and in *NAP Holdings UK Ltd v Whittles* [1994] STC 979 and is fully discussed in **9.404.3** and to some extent in **9.210**. It is sufficient to say here that the TCA 1997, s 617 principle was reinforced as was the view that there is no difference in tax consequences between a transfer of shares within a group in consideration for an issue of shares, being a reorganisation for the purposes of TCA 1997, s 586, and a transfer for some other consideration.

The tax effect of TCA 1997, s 617(1) is that the intra-group asset transfer is treated as having been made on the basis that neither a gain nor a loss accrues to the company making the transfer. This follows regardless of what consideration is given for the asset and whether or not any consideration is so given. From this it might appear that the matter of consideration is of no consequence at all for tax purposes. If the asset is transferred at undervalue by a group member to another group member, it may be considered that the company making the transfer has made a distribution in accordance with TCA 1997, s 130(3)(a) to the extent of the amount of the undervalue (see **10.107**). TCA 1997, s 130(3)(b), however, provides that where the transferring company is a subsidiary of the other company or both companies are subsidiaries of a third company (the transferor and transferring companies being Irish resident and the third company being resident for tax purposes in a relevant Member State – see **9.202**), the amount is not to be treated as a distribution. Neither will the transfer constitute a distribution "in respect of shares"; it is specifically provided in TCA 1997, s 130(5)(c) that any amount which *would* be a distribution by virtue of TCA 1997, s 130(3)(a) may not be treated as a distribution "out of assets" by virtue of TCA 1997, s 130(2)(b).

There then remains the question as to whether the transfer at undervalue could amount to a capital distribution in respect of shares (see **9.401.4**) so that, in accordance with TCA 1997, s 583(2), the recipient company would be regarded as having disposed of an interest in shares. It is unlikely that the transfer is in respect of shares merely because the transferee is the parent company. TCA 1997, s 135(10) provides that a thing is to be regarded as done in respect of a share if it is done to a person as being the holder of the share (see **11.105.7**). Although the transfer would not have been made had the transferee not held the shares in the transferring company (the holding of shares being the *causa sine qua non* in relation to the transfer), it is arguable that something more is necessary to make the transfer a distribution "in respect of shares" (the *causa causans*). On the other hand, unless it is possible to point to some other reason for the transfer of the asset in question, it may be difficult to resist the contention that the transfer is one in respect of shares.

Whatever the outcome of this question, it is relevant to note that, by virtue of a Revenue precedent, a capital distribution generated purely as a result of an internal group restructuring undertaken for bona fide commercial purposes does not result in a part disposal under TCA 1997, s 583(2).

An intra-group transfer of an asset other than to the parent company would not be a transfer to a member, and so could not come within TCA 1997, s 130(3)(a). As to whether the transfer could be in respect of shares, and so come within TCA 1997, s 130(2)(b), would depend on whether the transfer is something which has been done to the shareholder (the parent company) as being the holder of the shares. The point has been made in **11.105.7** that it is possible for a benefit provided by a company to a person other than a shareholder to be "in respect of shares", for example where the benefit is provided at the request of or according to the wishes of a shareholder and where there was no commercial reason for the benefit other than the connection between the shareholder and the recipient of the benefit. In this sense, there would appear to be some possibility, however remote, that the transfer would amount to a distribution in accordance with TCA 1997, s 130(2)(b). As against this, it might be contended that an asset transfer in such circumstances would not normally amount to something which has been "done to" the shareholder.

9.203.2   Controlled company transferring assets at undervalue

As explained in **9.407**, where a close company transfers an asset to any person otherwise than by way of a bargain made at arm's length and at less than the market value of the asset, an amount equal to the difference is to be apportioned among the issued shares of the company (TCA 1997, s 589). For the purposes of computing a chargeable gain accruing on the disposal of any of those shares by the person owning them on the date of transfer of the asset, the amount apportioned to those shares must be excluded from the expenditure allowable as a deduction from the consideration for the disposal. TCA 1997, s 589 applies also in the case of a non-resident company that is a "closely controlled" company, ie a non-resident company which would be a close company if it were resident in the State.

If the person owning any of the shares at the date of the transfer of the asset is itself a close company, an amount equal to the amount apportioned to it is to be apportioned among the issued shares of that close company, and the holders of those shares are to be treated in the same way as described above, and so on through any number of close companies.

Where, however, the transfer is a disposal to which TCA 1997, s 617(1) applies, TCA 1997, s 589 does not apply (TCA 1997, s 616(6)(b)). Consequently, the apportionment prescribed by TCA 1997, s 589 will not apply where a closely controlled company which is a member of a group transfers an asset at undervalue to another member of the group. The transfer will normally have the effect of reducing the value of the shares in the transferor company so that, on a later sale of any of those shares, there will be a correspondingly reduced gain. The purpose of TCA 1997, s 589 is to offset that reduction in the gain by providing for a corresponding reduction in the allowable cost of shares. Where the reduction in value has passed elsewhere within a group, however, TCA 1997, s 589 will not apply. Any reduction in the value of the shares in the transferor company should be offset by a corresponding increase in the value of the shares in the transferee company.

9.203.3   Part disposals

TCA 1997, s 617(1) applies to part disposals (see also **9.102.8**) as well as to disposals of assets. Although the provision deals with cases in which there is both a disposal by a group member and an acquisition by another group member, it is nowhere stated that the asset acquired must be the same as the asset which is the subject of the disposal. A disposal consisting of, say, the grant of a leasehold by one group member to another would involve a part disposal of the freehold (the entire interest held by the company prior to making the disposal) and the acquisition by the other company of the leasehold and the disposal should come within the intra-group capital gains tax treatment provided by TCA 1997, s 617(1). Example **9.203.3.1** below illustrates how the computation would be carried out.

A member of a group may have a leasehold interest in a property the freehold of which is held by another member of the group. If the lease is surrendered, the company owning the freehold will have made no acquisition on the surrender. It is unlikely therefore that TCA 1997, s 617 would apply to the surrender. The lessee company could, alternatively, assign the benefit of the leasehold to the other company in which case TCA 1997, s 617 would appear to apply. Although the effect of the assignment will be that the leasehold interest will merge with the freehold, the assignee will undoubtedly have acquired an asset, ie the benefit of the leasehold, for however short a time.

TCA 1997, s 557 caters for situations involving a disposal of part of an asset (which would include such a disposal within a group). In the case of a part disposal, it is necessary to calculate the part of the cost of the asset concerned which is attributable to the part disposed of. The cost to be deducted from the part disposed of is represented by the formula

$$\text{Total Cost of Asset} \times \frac{A}{A + B}$$

where—

A = the proceeds for the part disposal; and
B = the market value of the property remaining after the disposal.

TCA 1997, s 616(6)(a) provides that the apportionment of the allowable cost in the case of a part disposal must be made before, and without regard to, TCA 1997, s 617(1) and any other enactment the effect of which is to secure that neither a gain nor a loss accrues on a disposal. The purpose of this provision is to prevent distortions which would otherwise result. In applying the part disposal fraction, the question arises as to whether "A" is the actual proceeds, as would normally be the case, or the market value of the part disposed of. In the absence of TCA 1997, s 616(6)(a), since invariably the parties to the transaction would be connected with another, TCA 1997 ss 547 and 549 would operate to substitute market value for actual proceeds where the disposal is made for a price other than the market value price.

Example 9.203.3.1

Elmyra Ltd and Sparta Ltd are Irish resident members of a capital gains tax group. Elmyra purchased land for €1,200,000 and some years later, when the land was valued at €1,800,000, transferred a part of it to Sparta Ltd for €600,000. The value of the part transferred was €750,000 at the time. The cost of the part of the land transferred is:

$$€1,200,000 \times \frac{750,000}{750,000 + 1,050,000} = €500,000$$

Under TCA 1997, s 617(1), the consideration for the transfer of the land is to be taken as the amount which would result in neither a gain nor a loss accruing to Elmyra Ltd. That amount, arising out of the apportioned cost above, is €500,000.

Some time later, Elmyra Ltd sells the remaining part of the land outside the group for €1,400,000 while, later again, Sparta Ltd sells its part of the land outside the group for €900,000. The chargeable gain arising to Elmyra Ltd is €700,000 (€1,400,000 – €700,000) while the gain to Sparta is €400,000 (€900,000 – €500,000). The aggregate gain from the two disposals is €1,100,000 which is equal to the aggregate proceeds less the original cost to the group (€1,400,000 + €900,000 – €1,200,000).

In the absence of TCA 1997, s 616(6)(a), requiring that the apportionment is to be carried out before applying TCA 1997, s 617(1), it is difficult to see what different result could ensue. As Elmyra Ltd and Sparta Ltd, being members of the same group, must be connected persons, TCA 1997 ss 547 and 549 would ensure that market value would be taken as the value of "A" in the part disposal fraction and not, if different, the actual sale price.

9.203.4   Indexation

The deferral of chargeable gains on the occasion of an intra-group transfer of an asset is given effect by treating the disposal as having taken place at a price such that neither a gain nor a loss accrues to the company making the disposal. That being the case, it might seem that the notional price should be arrived at by taking the allowable cost as increased by the appropriate indexation multiplier. On the other hand, TCA 1997, s 619(2) provides that, in computing the chargeable gain or allowable loss on the eventual disposal outside the group of an asset which has been transferred from one group member to another, TCA 1997, s 556 (indexation relief – which, as noted from **9.102.3**, is fundamentally restricted as regards disposals made after the year 2003) is to apply as if all group members were a single person. The member disposing of the asset outside the group is deemed to be the company which originally acquired it when it was acquired by the group (see **9.208** below). Furthermore, the reference to a "gain" is not necessarily to the chargeable gain but, in accordance with the better view, to the arithmetical gain. (In this connection, see Example **9.102.18.1** in which the concept of an arithmetical gain in another context arises.)

If, therefore, the cost to the member acquiring the asset on the occasion of an intra-group transfer were to be the transferor's cost indexed up to the date of the transfer, that position would be in direct conflict with what is provided in TCA 1997, s 619(2). It must be that the intention of the legislation is that in arriving at the amount which would produce a no gain/no loss result on the part of the transferor, the transferor's acquisition cost and enhancement expenditure should be taken into account without any adjustment for indexation. Otherwise, on the transferee's eventual disposal outside the group, the chargeable gain arising would be computed by reference to the indexed cost at the time of the intra-group transfer but as indexed again by reference to the date the asset came into the group. In dealing with any dispute on this question, the courts would surely follow the clear directive of TCA 1997, s 619(2) as against the more problematic and uncertain alternative.

Example 9.203.4.1

Lempira Ltd and Quetzal Ltd are Irish resident members of a capital gains tax group. On 1 August 1993, Lempira Ltd purchased shares for €60,000 and transferred them to Quetzal Ltd on 16 April 2003 at a time when their value was €130,000. On 1 April 2008, Quetzal Ltd sold the shares outside the group for €210,000.

If, in line with TCA 1997, s 619(2), the notional disposal and acquisition price for the intra-group transfer is to be taken without regard to indexation, that price will be €60,000. On the ultimate disposal of the shares by Quetzal Ltd, this cost is indexed using the multiplier for an acquisition in the tax year 1993-94 and a disposal in the year 2008, ie 1.331, to give an indexed cost of €79,860. The chargeable gain to Quetzal Ltd is therefore €130,140 (€210,000 - €79,860).

In accordance with TCA 1997, s 556, the multiplier to be used relates to the consumer price index number "relevant to the year of assessment in which the deductible expenditure was incurred". In the above example, that year is 1993-94. The multiplier 1.331 for a disposal in the year 2008 is the same as for a disposal in the year 2003; for disposals in years after 2003, deductible expenditure is not further indexed.

9.203.5 Development land

Companies are liable to capital gains tax, rather than corporation tax, in respect of gains on "relevant disposals", ie disposals of development land made on or after 28 January 1982. Other consequences of land being regarded as development land are discussed in **9.103.3**.) Allowable losses on disposals of assets other than development land may not be set against capital gains on disposals of development land. Development gains are not included as "profits" of a company (TCA 1997, s 649(1)) and accordingly any reliefs which may be set against total profits may not be set off against development gains, eg loss relief under TCA 1997, s 396(2) or s 420 (group relief). A loss arising on the disposal of an asset other than development land cannot be offset against a development land gain (TCA 1997, s 653) nor, as respects relevant for disposals made before 4 December 2002, could a development land gain be held over under TCA 1997, s 597 (TCA 1997, s 652).

For disposals of development land from 28 January 1982 up to 24 April 1992, the deferral, under TCA 1997, s 617, of chargeable gains on intra-group disposals did not apply. In respect of relevant disposals made after 24 April 1992, TCA 1997, s 649(2) provides that TCA 1997, s 617 is to apply, with any necessary modifications, in relation to capital gains tax to which a company is chargeable on chargeable gains accruing to it as it applies in relation to corporation tax on chargeable gains, with references to corporation tax being construed as including references to capital gains tax. Accordingly, although companies continue to be liable to capital gains tax rather than corporation tax in respect of relevant disposals made on or after 24 April 1992, TCA 1997, s 617 applies so as to defer a chargeable gain arising on an intra-group disposal of development land until such time as the development land is disposed of outside the group.

Although TCA 1997, s 617 is stated to apply to "both members" involved in an intra-group disposal, it seems possible to read TCA 1997, s 649(2) as applying that section only to the company making the disposal: it provides that TCA 1997, s 617 is to apply "in relation to capital gains tax to which a company is chargeable ... on a relevant disposal". On the other hand, the section must be intended to apply to both members as otherwise the essential purpose of the section, ie the deferral of a chargeable gain, would not be fulfilled.

Where a company that is, or has been, a member of a group disposes of development land which it had acquired intra-group at a time when that land was not development land, so that the intra-group disposal was not a relevant disposal and TCA 1997, s 617 applied, the chargeable gain on the disposal of the development land, and the capital gains tax on that gain, are computed as if the group members were a single person and as if the acquisition of the land by the group taken as a single person had been its acquisition by the member disposing of it (TCA 1997, s 649(3)(a)).

Example 9.203.5.1

Jervis Ltd acquired land on 1 July 1988 for €100,000 and on 1 July 1991 transferred it to Hazlet Ltd, a fellow group member. The market value of the land at this time was €250,000 but the land was not development land so that the disposal by Jervis Ltd was not a relevant disposal. By virtue of TCA 1997, s 617, the disposal by Jervis Ltd was regarded for corporation tax purposes as being at neither a gain nor a loss.

The land later became development land and on 1 July 2007 Hazlet Ltd disposed of it outside the group for €2m. At no time was Hazlet Ltd engaged in a trade of land dealing.

For the purposes of the computation of the chargeable gain on the disposal of the development land, Hazlet Ltd is regarded as having acquired that land on 1 July 1988 for €100,000. Without TCA 1997, s 649(3)(a), however, it seems that Hazlet Ltd would be regarded as having acquired the land on 1 July 1988 in any event, by virtue of TCA 1997, s 649(2).

Example 9.203.5.2

The position is as in Example **9.203.5.1** except that the land had become development land at the time of the intra-group disposal on 1 July 1991. Accordingly, that disposal is also subject to capital gains tax rules and is treated as taking place at market value for the purposes of both the disposal by Jervis Ltd and the acquisition by Hazlet Ltd.

Example 9.203.5.3

The position is as in Example **9.203.5.1** except that the intra-group disposal took place on 1 July 1993 at which time the land had become development land. Its market value was then €750,000.

For the purposes of the disposal by Jervis Ltd, since it took place after 24 April 1992, TCA 1997, s 617 applies so that neither a gain nor a loss arises (TCA 1997, s 649(2)). In relation to the disposal by Hazlet Ltd, since its intra-group acquisition was the result of a disposal that *was* a relevant disposal, TCA 1997, s 649(3)(a) does not apply. Since TCA 1997, s 649(2) applies, however, it is still treated as having acquired the land at the time Jervis Ltd acquired it.

If, by virtue of TCA 1997, s 618(2) (transfer of asset from trader to non-trader – see **9.205.3**) or 623 (company leaving group – see **9.209**), another date of acquisition by a member of the group is provided for which date is later than the date the asset was acquired by the group as a whole, that later date is treated as the date the group commenced to own the asset (TCA 1997, s 649(3)(b)). This is intended to prevent an excessive period of ownership that might otherwise result from TCA 1997, s 649(3)(a).

Example 9.203.5.4

The position is as in Example **9.203.5.1** except that on 1 July 2007 Hazlet Ltd ceased to be a member of the capital gains tax group.

By virtue of TCA 1997, s 623, Hazlet Ltd is treated as having disposed of and reacquired the land at market value on 1 July 1991. This date of acquisition is taken instead of 1 July 1988, the date that would otherwise apply on the basis of TCA 1997, s 649(3)(a). Presumably the market value rule in TCA 1997, s 623 is also followed so that the deemed acquisition cost for Hazlet Ltd is €250,000, the amount for which it is deemed to have disposed of the land.

9.204   Non-resident groups

TCA 1997, s 590 (see **9.102.22** and **9.408**) is concerned with the tax treatment of a chargeable gain realised by a non-resident "closely controlled" company (ie, a non-resident company that would be close if it were resident). Such gains are not assessable on the company itself (unless it has resulted from the disposal of certain assets located in the State, eg land).

However, every person who, at the time the gain accrues, is resident in the State (and, if an individual, is domiciled in the State) and who is a participator in the company is liable to tax on his proportionate share of the gain realised (TCA 1997, s 590(4)).

The group provisions are extended, however, by TCA 1997, s 590(16) to cover transfers of assets between members of a non-resident group. TCA 1997, s 590(16)(a) defines *non-resident group* as:

(i)   in the case of a group, none of the members of which is resident in the State, that group; and

(ii) in the case of a group, two or more members of which are not resident in the State, the members which are not resident in the State.

The term "group" where used in (i) and (ii) above is to be construed in accordance with the provisions of TCA 1997, s 616(1), (3) and (4), but without the requirement in TCA 1997, s 616(1)(a) to the effect that a company must be a company resident in the State or as the case may be, resident in a relevant Member State.

In short, a non-resident group means a group comprised of non-resident companies, or the non-resident members of a group.

The main consequence of TCA 1997, s 590(16) is to apply the provisions of TCA 1997, s 617 (other than s 617(1)(b) and (c) – which can apply to non-resident companies – see **9.203**) so as to defer the apportionment (to Irish resident shareholders) by TCA 1997, s 590(4) of chargeable gains arising to non-resident closely controlled companies where such gains are the result of transfers between members of a non-resident group.

Example 9.204.1

Park (CI) Ltd is a non-resident company controlled by a small number of shareholders. Park (IOM) Ltd is a non-resident wholly owned subsidiary of Park (CI) Ltd. Park Ltd, an Irish resident company, holds 40% of the ordinary share capital of Park (CI) Ltd.

Park (CI) Ltd transfers shares that it acquired some years ago for €50,000, and that are now worth €180,000, to Park (IOM) Ltd. Subject to TCA 1997, s 590(16), the chargeable gain on the disposal is €130,000. By virtue of TCA 1997, s 590(4), 40% of this gain, or €52,000, would be attributed to Park Ltd which would be treated as if a gain of €52,000 had accrued to it.

TCA 1997, s 590(16), however, provides that TCA 1997, s 617 is to apply to Park (CI) Ltd and Park (IOM) Ltd as members of a non-resident group (comprising those two companies) as it applies to resident companies which are members of a group of companies. The transfer of the shares is treated therefore as if the shares were acquired for a consideration that would secure that no gain arose on their disposal by Park (CI) Ltd. Accordingly, no chargeable gain is attributed to Park Ltd. Any such gain, as well as any consequential apportionment, is deferred until such time as the shares are disposed of outside the non-resident group.

For the purposes of TCA 1997, s 590, capital gains tax group provisions other than TCA 1997, s 617 will also apply to non-resident companies which are members of a non-resident group in the same way as they apply to resident companies which are members of a group. Thus, TCA 1997, s 618 (group transfers involving trading stock – see **9.205**), TCA 1997, s 619 (disposal or acquisition outside of group – see **9.208**) and TCA 1997, s 620 (replacement of business assets – see **9.206**) will apply as appropriate (but ignoring anything which applies those provisions to non-resident companies) to non-resident groups in so far as any of those provisions may be relevant for the purposes of TCA 1997, s 590 (TCA 1997, s 590(16)(b)(i)). In addition, TCA 1997, s 623 (apart from s 623(2)(c) and (d) which can apply to non-resident companies – see **9.209.1**) (company leaving group – see **9.209**) and TCA 1997, s 625 (shares in subsidiary member of group – see **9.210**) also apply as if references to a group of companies were to a non-resident group and as if references to resident companies were to non-resident companies (TCA 1997, s 590(16)(b)(ii)).

9.205   Stock in trade

9.205.1   Introduction

In a group of companies, an asset that would be a capital asset of one member might be trading stock if transferred to another, for example shares transferred from an investment company to a share dealing company. TCA 1997, s 618 provides for the tax treatment both of an intra-group transfer of assets that become trading stock of the transferee company and the transfer of assets that cease to be trading stock following an intra-group transfer. TCA 1997, s 618 is accordingly concerned with the treatment of trading stock of a trade, being either—

(a)   a trade carried on by a company which is resident in the State; or

(b)   a trade carried on in the State through a branch or agency by a company which is not so resident (TCA 1997, s 618(3)).

9.205.2   Transfer to trader

TCA 1997, s 618(1) provides that where—

(a)   a company which is a member of a group of companies acquires an asset as trading stock of a trade to which TCA 1997, s 618 applies (being either a trade carried on by an Irish resident company or by a non-resident company through an Irish branch or agency);

(b)   the acquisition is from another company which is a member of the group; and

(c)   the asset did not form part of the trading stock of any such trade (ie, as described in (a)) carried on by the other company,

the company acquiring the asset is to be treated for the purposes of TCA 1997, s 596 (appropriations to and from stock in trade) as having acquired the asset otherwise than as trading stock and as having immediately appropriated it for the purposes of the trade as trading stock.

TCA 1997, s 596 provides that where an asset acquired by a person otherwise than as trading stock is appropriated by him for the purposes of the trade as trading stock, it is deemed, for capital gains tax purposes, as having been disposed of at its market value at the time of the appropriation (TCA 1997, s 596(1) – see Example **9.102.19.1**). Accordingly, any necessary capital gain or loss calculation is made at that point. The asset is then taken into the profit and loss account at its market value. In this connection, it is to be noted that TCA 1997 ss 618(1) and 596(1) apply for the purposes of the Capital Gains Tax Acts only and not in relation to the computation of profits and losses for Case I purposes. The treatment whereby the transferred asset is taken into the profit and loss account at its market value for Case I purposes either follows the assumption that the above provisions apply for Case I purposes (which is not the case) or that it is to be taken that assets are generally appropriated for trading purposes at market value. The practice in Ireland, however, appears to be that such appropriations are, at least generally, to be made at cost (see **3.202.16**).

TCA 1997, s 596(3) permits an election to be made by the person appropriating an asset for trading purposes whereby TCA 1997, s 596(1) is not to apply but instead the market value of the asset, to be included in the computation of trading profits, is reduced by the amount of the chargeable gain. (TCA 1997, s 596(3) therefore appears to assume that the effect of TCA 1997, s 596(1) is that, for Case I purposes, and not just for capital gains tax purposes, the asset is appropriated at market value, although subsection (1) makes no provision for the Case I treatment.) Unlike TCA 1997, s 596(1), TCA 1997, s 596(3) does indeed provide for the Case I treatment of an asset appropriated to stock-in-trade. In this case also, however, the underlying assumption must be that the appropriation would, apart from the subsection, be at market value (and not, as suggested in **3.202.16**, at cost). By disapplying TCA 1997, s 596(1), the capital gains tax treatment reverts to that provided for in TCA 1997, s 617 so that the asset is treated as passing on a no gain/no loss basis, ie at cost.

Example 9.205.2.1

Epsilon Ltd, a company which carries on a trade and which holds a number of investments, and Lambda Ltd, a share dealing company, are Irish resident members of a capital gains tax group. On 4 November 2006, Epsilon Ltd sold to Lambda Ltd 5,000 Kappa plc shares that it had purchased on 3 January 2005 for €9,500. The shares were sold to Lambda Ltd for €15,000 and their market value at that time was €17,500.

In accordance with TCA 1997, s 617(1), Epsilon Ltd is treated as having disposed of the shares on the basis that neither a gain nor a loss accrued to it. Lambda Ltd is treated as having acquired the shares for the same consideration and as other than stock in trade. It is also, however, treated under TCA 1997, s 618(1) as having then, for capital gains tax purposes, immediately appropriated the shares for the purposes of its share dealing trade as trading stock and as having done so at the market value of the shares at the time, ie €17,500. The chargeable gain arising to Lambda Ltd is as follows:

	€
Deemed sale proceeds	17,500
Cost	9,500
Gain	8,000

On 26 September 2007, the shares are sold by Lambda Ltd for €24,000, resulting in a profit of €6,500 (€24,000 - €17,500) and this amount will be included in the Case I computation of the share dealing trade for the accounting period in which the shares are sold, say, the year ended 31 March 2008. The inclusion of the amount of €17,500 as the cost price for Case I purposes appears to be based on the assumption that appropriations from stock-in-trade are to be taken at market value.

Lambda Ltd considers the possibility of an election under TCA 1997, s 596(3) to treat the market value of the shares at the time of their acquisition from Epsilon Ltd as reduced by €8,000, the amount of the gain arising. If an election were to be made, TCA 1997, s 596(1) would not apply, the chargeable gain would be reduced to nil and the shares would be treated as having been appropriated to the trade as trading stock at the reduced amount of €9,500 (€17,500 - €8,000), in effect at the original cost of the shares. The amount to be included in the Case I computation would then be €14,500 (€24,000 - €9,500).

Given the capital gains tax rate of 20%, and a corporation tax rate of 12.5%, an election would be to the benefit of the company.

Up to 29 May 1990, a person appropriating an asset for the purposes of a trade could have elected under CGTA 1975 Sch 1 paragraph 15(3) to have the market value of the asset at the time of the appropriation treated as increased by the amount of an allowable loss. In that case, the asset would have been brought into trading stock at market value increased by the amount of the allowable loss. The election would have been made, for example, where the acquiring company was unlikely to have a chargeable gain in the foreseeable future and would therefore be unable to use the allowable loss. It would then elect to bring in the asset for Case I purposes at the increased amount thereby reducing the amount of the profit on its later disposal. An election under CGTA Sch 1 paragraph 15(3) (now TCA 1997, s 596(3)) may not be made, however, in the case of an appropriation from trading stock on or after 30 May 1990 where the application of the market value rule would give rise to an allowable loss. Accordingly, an election in those circumstances may not be made for the purposes of TCA 1997, s 618(1).

The reason for the withdrawal of the election option in CGTA Sch 1 paragraph 15(3) where an allowable loss has arisen can be seen from a number of UK cases. In *Coates v Arndale Properties Ltd* [1984] STC 637, the taxpayer company sought to create a substantial Case I loss from a capital loss while retaining the asset concerned, a leasehold property, within the group of which it was a member. The property had fallen in value from the time it had been acquired by an investment company within the group. It was sold to a dealing company within the group and was then sold on at a small accounting profit by the dealing company to a third member of the group. The dealing company elected to treat the investment company's base cost of the property as its own cost for Case I purposes (ie, by electing to increase the market value of the property, at the time it acquired it from the investment company, by the amount of the loss). It was held, however, that the election was ineffective on the ground that the dealing company had not acquired the property as trading stock but for the purposes of establishing a loss for fiscal purposes. It was found that there had been no element of speculation and that the accounting profit realised by the dealing company was window-dressing resulting from a sale at a deliberate under-value by the investment company. The point at issue here would be academic since a TCA 1997, s 596(3) election may not be made to transmute a capital loss into a Case I loss.

In the later case *Reed v Nova Securities* [1985] STC 124, the taxpayer company acquired from a fellow group member shares in and debts due from a third company. The third company was insolvent at the time although some part of the debts was considered to be recoverable and, on the basis of the amount paid for them, a small profit would have been realised by reference to the amount considered to be recoverable. In the House of Lords, it was held that there could have been no commercial justification for the purchase of the shares and that they were therefore not acquired as trading stock. It was held that there was sufficient evidence of commerciality relating to the purchase of the debts and it was accepted that they were acquired as trading stock. The House of Lords held that, to be regarded as trading stock, an asset acquired should be acquired with a view to resale at a profit.

In *New Angel Court Ltd v Adam* [2004] STC 779, a property dealing company that acquired certain investment properties from a non-dealing fellow group member was found by the Special Commissioners not to have appropriated those properties to stock in trade following the acquisition. This was because, although the company was a property dealing company, it did nothing in relation to the properties in question that was in any way different to what the investment company had done. It brought no new expertise to the table, it initiated no marketing campaign and did nothing to render the properties more attractive to potential buyers. Mere formal appropriation was not sufficient to convert the properties into trading stock.

The company's appeal against this decision was rejected in the High Court, which held that the tax-planning element was so predominant in the transaction as to deprive it of a commercial purpose, but was allowed by the Court of Appeal. It was held there that the company had satisfied the condition that there should be a trading purpose as regards its acquisition of the properties and the mere fact that the group had set out to avail itself of the opportunity to obtain a fiscal advantage provided for in the legislation had no effect on the requirement (being a requirement of the company and not the group) that the properties should have been acquired as trading stock. The properties were of a kind that were sold in the ordinary course of the company's trade and had been acquired by it for the purpose of resale at a profit.

9.205.3   Transfer by trader

Where an asset is disposed of by a member of a group to another member and the asset formed part of the trading stock of a trade to which, as respects a disposal on or after 15 February 2001, TCA 1997, s 618 applies (see below) carried on by the member disposing of it but is acquired by the other member otherwise than as trading stock, the member disposing of the asset is treated for the purposes of TCA 1997, s 596(2) as having immediately before the disposal appropriated the asset for a purpose other than the purpose of use as trading stock (TCA 1997, s 618(2)).

For the above purposes, a trade to which TCA 1997, s 618 applies is either—

(a)   a trade carried on by a company which is resident in the State; or
(b)   a trade carried on in the State through a branch or agency by a company which is not so resident (TCA 1997, s 618(3)).

TCA 1997, s 596(2), referred to above, provides that where an asset forming part of the trading stock of a person's trade is appropriated by him for any other purpose, it is treated as having been acquired by that person at that time for a consideration equal to the amount brought into the accounts of the trade in respect of it for the purposes of income tax (or corporation tax in the case of a company) on the appropriation (see Example **9.102.19.2**).

In this connection, the phrase "brought into the accounts of the trade ... for the purposes of income tax on the appropriation" gives rise to some difficulties. It would appear to leave open the question as to what value should be put on the asset appropriated from trading stock, and credited to the trading account, at the time of the appropriation for the purposes of the relevant Case I computation. On the basis of the decision in the UK case *Sharkey v Wernher* 36 TC 275, the asset would be credited to the trading account at its market value but this treatment is not followed in Ireland. The view of the Revenue Commissioners on this point, based on long-standing practice relating to the approach to be taken in relation to appropriations out of trading stock, appears to be that the appropriation would be made at cost (see **3.202.16**).

For the purposes of TCA 1997, s 618(2) therefore, the transferor is treated as having appropriated the asset from stock in trade and as having acquired it for capital gains tax purposes, at cost. Accordingly, the transferor would be treated as having disposed of the asset at neither a gain nor a loss, while the base cost to the transferee, for the purpose of computing a gain or a loss on a subsequent disposal of the asset, would be the original cost to the transferor.

The absence of any market value rule on the lines of *Sharkey v Wernher* 36 TC 275 (which is not followed in Ireland) must indeed mean that an appropriation at cost is the only remaining option. In *Sharkey v Wernher*, it was held that an appropriation from trading stock for personal use should be credited in the accounts of the trade at market value. This view is inconsistent with that in *Dublin Corporation v McAdam* 2 TC 387 which held that "no man ... can trade with himself: he cannot ... make in what is its true sense of meaning, taxable profits by dealing with himself".

The interpretation of TCA 1997, s 618(2) to the effect that the deemed appropriation from trading stock is to be taken at the cost price of the asset concerned may give rise to problems of inconsistency resulting in potential double taxation of certain gains. TCA 1997 ss 596(2) and 618(2) are concerned with capital gains tax only; although the capital gains tax treatment provided for is determined by the hypothetical income tax treatment relating to an appropriation of trading stock, the actual income tax treatment of a transfer by one company to another company (and which does not involve an appropriation of trading stock) is not influenced by these provisions. Accordingly, for Case I purposes, it may well be that the Case I treatment of the transferring company will be based on the actual sale price in the transaction, Alternatively, if the decision in *Ridge Securities Ltd v CIR* 44 TC 373 (see **3.202.16**) is found to apply, the sale will be deemed to have taken place for a market value consideration

Again, for example, if the intra-group sale is a sale of development land, by a dealer and developer of land, to a fellow group company so that TCA 1997, s 642(2) (see **13.306.2**) applies, the seller will be regarded, for the purposes of computing its trading profits, as having made the sale at market value. This, however, will have no effect for the purposes of TCA 1997, s 618(2) so that the buyer will be regarded for the purposes of corporation tax on chargeable gains as having acquired the land at original cost to the seller; the deemed cost for this purpose will still be the amount that would have been recognised on an appropriation by the seller from stock in trade.

Example 9.205.3.1

The position involves the same two companies as in Example **9.205.2.1** but in this case, on 6 October 2006, the share dealing company, Lambda Ltd, sells to Epsilon Ltd 7,000 Gamma plc shares which it had purchased on 8 January 2005 for €12,000. The shares were sold intra-group for €18,000 and their market value at that time was €21,000. They are sold by Epsilon Ltd on 17 September 2007 for €27,000.

Lambda Ltd is regarded as having on 6 October 2006 appropriated the shares from trading stock at the amount brought into the accounts of its trade in respect of them "for the purposes of income tax on the appropriation" and as having, for capital gains tax purposes, reacquired them at that price. It is therefore treated as having disposed of the shares at cost, ie for €12,000.

For capital gains tax purposes, Lambda Ltd is also treated as having reacquired the shares for €12,000 before disposing of them to Epsilon Ltd. Epsilon Ltd is then treated as having acquired the shares for €12,000 also and, on its subsequent disposal of them for €27,000, realises a chargeable gain of €15,000.

It might be assumed here that Lambda Ltd is treated for Case I purposes as having sold the Gamma plc shares to Epsilon Ltd for €12,000, the amount that would have been brought into the accounts of its trade for income tax purposes on an appropriation of the shares, thereby resulting in a nil profit on the sale. Such a result would be the equitable outcome as far as the group is concerned. But the actual Case I treatment is not governed by TCA 1997 ss 618(2) and 596(2) which have effect only as respects the capital gains tax treatment. Accordingly, the sale price of the shares for Case I purposes would appear to be either €18,000, the actual price in the transaction, or, if *Ridge Securities* were to apply, €21,000, being the market value of the shares.

9.206   Replacement of business assets by group members

TCA 1997, s 597 provides for a relief (usually referred to as "roll-over relief"), by way of a deferral of capital gains tax, in the cases of certain business asset disposals (see **9.102.18**). To obtain relief, the proceeds of disposal must be re-invested in other business assets. Both the asset disposed of and the asset, or assets, acquired must fall within one (not necessarily the same one) of the following categories:

(a)   plant or machinery;

(b)   except where the trade is a trade of dealing in or developing land, or of providing services for the occupier of land in which the person carrying on the trade has an estate or interest—

    (i)   any building or part of a building and any permanent or semi-permanent structure in the nature of a building, occupied (as well as used) only for the purposes of the trade,

    (ii)   any land occupied (as well as used) only for the purposes of the trade, and for this purpose a trade of dealing in or developing land will not be treated as such if a profit on a sale of any land held for the purposes of the trade would not form part of the trading profits;

(c)   goodwill.

To qualify for relief under TCA 1997, s 597, the asset disposal in question must have taken place before 4 December 2002 (or by 31 December 2003 in certain cases – see **9.102.18**) and the investment in the replacement asset or assets must take place within the four-year period commencing one year before, and ending three years after, the date of the disposal.

The relief takes the form of a deferral by treating the gain as not arising until the replacement asset ceases to be used for the purposes of the trade. The gain does not reduce the cost of the replacement asset. The relief results in a "hold-over" (rather than a roll-over) of the gain arising on the disposal of the original asset. In calculating the capital gains tax liability on the deferred gain, on the occasion of the disposal of the replacement asset, the date of disposal of the original asset is used for the purposes of applying the indexation multiplier.

To qualify for relief under the main roll-over provision in TCA 1997, s 597(4), the entire consideration for the disposal (which, unless new assets have been acquired before 4 December 2002, must take place before that date – see above) must be re-invested in the new assets. Where part only of the consideration is re-invested, partial deferral is available in accordance with TCA 1997, s 597(5) provided the amount re-invested is greater than the historic cost of the old assets. The arithmetical gain on the sale of the old assets is reduced to the amount not reinvested. The resulting percentage reduction is then applied to the chargeable gain to arrive at the amount of the gain rolled over.

Subject to conditions, for the purposes of TCA 1997, s 597, all the trades to which TCA 1997, s 620 applies carried on by members of a group of companies are to be treated as a single trade (TCA 1997, s 620(2)).

A trade to which TCA 1997, s 620 applies is any trade carried on by a company that is resident in the State and any trade carried on in the State through a branch or agency of a company that is not so resident (TCA 1997, s 620(3)).

The conditions subject to which TCA 1997, s 620(2) applies are that—

(a) the company disposing of the "old assets" (within the meaning of TCA 1997, s 597 – see **9.102.18**) is resident in the State at the time of the disposal, or the assets are chargeable assets in relation to that company immediately before that time; and

(b) the company acquiring the "new assets" (within the meaning of TCA 1997, s 597) is resident in the State at the time of the acquisition, or the assets are chargeable assets in relation to that company immediately after that time (TCA 1997, s 620(4)).

TCA 1997, s 620(4) would naturally be read as applying to two companies, one being the company disposing of the old assets and the other being the company acquiring the new assets. It seems possible, however, to read the subsection as applying to a single company, the company disposing of the old assets and the company acquiring the new assets being the same company. If that were not the case, TCA 1997, s 620 would, ironically, be prevented by the subsection from applying to a single company. Technically, as is explained below, TCA 1997, s 620(2), strictly read, applies only to a single company.

An asset is a "chargeable asset" in relation to a company at any time if, were it to be disposed of by the company at that time, any gain accruing to the company would be a chargeable gain. A chargeable gain will arise to a non-resident company only in respect of disposals of certain categories of assets (eg, Irish based land, shares deriving their value or the greater part of their value from such land, Irish based assets used in an Irish branch trade – see **9.102.2**). In the case of a non-resident company, TCA 1997, s 620 is concerned only with a company carrying on a trade in the State through a branch or agency, and then only where the assets in question are used in or for the purposes of that trade (see also **9.203.1**).

The above conditions apply where (a) either the disposal or acquisition is on or after 15 February 2001 or (b) both the disposal and acquisition are on or after that date. In the case of (a), any question as to whether a company was, at the time of the acquisition or disposal corresponding to the disposal or acquisition, a member of a group is to be determined in accordance with TCA 1997, s 616 following its amendment by FA 2001 (see in particular **9.202.2**).

From the above, it can be seen that TCA 1997, s 620(2) can apply in any of the following circumstances, the companies concerned being members of the same group—

(i) where there is a disposal of old assets by an Irish resident company and an acquisition of new assets by another Irish resident company;

(ii) where there is a disposal of old assets by an Irish resident company and an acquisition of new assets by a non-resident company in relation to which the new assets are chargeable assets immediately after the acquisition;

(iii)   where there is a disposal of old assets by a non-resident company in relation to which those assets were chargeable assets immediately before the disposal and an acquisition of new assets by an Irish resident company; and

(iv)   where there is a disposal of old assets by a non-resident company in relation to which those assets were chargeable assets immediately before the disposal and an acquisition of new assets by a non-resident company in relation to which the new assets are chargeable assets immediately after the acquisition.

In the cases of (ii), (iii) or (iv), where certain new assets subsequently cease to be chargeable assets in relation to a company, there is a deemed sale and reacquisition of those assets at market value at that time (TCA 1997, s 620A). The new assets in question are those assets which were used or held by, or were acquired for, the purposes of the company's Irish branch or agency and which now cease to be chargeable assets by virtue of their becoming situated outside the State (TCA 1997, s 620A(a)(ii)). The deemed sale and reacquisition does not apply to assets ceasing to be chargeable assets in relation to the company as a result of their ceasing to be used for the purposes of the branch or agency.

Surprisingly, there is a deemed sale and reacquisition by a company of assets that cease to be chargeable assets in relation to the company and which, at the time of their acquisition by the company, consisted of shares deriving their value or the greater part of their value from assets specified in TCA 1997, s 29(3)(a) or (b) (see **9.102.2**) (TCA 1997, s 620A(a)(i)). It is not clear why such assets are included here since it is not apparent that they would have constituted new assets for the purposes of TCA 1997, s 597 (assets used solely for trading purposes).

The effect of TCA 1997, s 620(2) is that that the use, for trading purposes, by one group member of assets acquired by another group member may be taken into account for the purposes of a hold over claim by that other member. Accordingly, a group member may avail of the relief where it uses the proceeds from the disposal of qualifying assets to purchase assets used for the purposes of the trade of another group company. For example, sale proceeds from the disposal by group member X of a building which had been used for its trade could be reinvested in another building which is then leased to group member Y for the purpose of the latter company's trade. This is possible because the trades of both X and Y are treated by TCA 1997, s 620 as a single trade thus enabling company X to claim relief under TCA 1997, s 597 as if the new building had been put into use for the purposes of its own trade.

There is no requirement that the company claiming hold over relief by virtue of TCA 1997, s 620 should have been a member of the group in question at the time its gain is realised. If it realises a chargeable gain and subsequently becomes a member of a group, it would still be entitled to make a claim under TCA 1997, s 597 where the proceeds related to the gain are reinvested in other assets within the required time limit and where those assets are used for the trade of another group member.

TCA 1997, s 620 does not, however, go so far as to treat the various group members as a single person. Accordingly, it does not in strictness permit the proceeds of a sale of assets by one group member to be held over against a purchase of assets by another group member (so that, technically, the section cannot apply in the circumstances listed in (i) to (iv) above). TCA 1997, s 597 clearly confines relief to situations in which the consideration for the disposal of assets used for the purposes of a trade of a person is "applied by that person" in acquiring other assets which are taken into use and used only for the purposes of the trade. Nothing in TCA 1997, s 620 changes this except to relax the trade requirement to include all of the trades carried on by the group members. To enable the sale proceeds of assets by one group member to be held over against a purchase of assets by another group member, the section would have had to provide that all the trades carried on by the group members are to be treated as a single trade and that all the group members are to be treated as a single person.

In this connection, it is interesting to note that the equivalent UK legislation specifically provides to this effect and that the relevant FA 1995 amendment was introduced to give statutory effect to what had been a long-standing published practice. Section 175(2A) of the Taxation of Chargeable Gains Act 1992 is as follows:

Section 152 or 153 [TCA 1997, s 597 in Ireland] shall apply where—

(a)   the disposal is by a company which, at the time of the disposal, is a member of a group of companies;

(b)   the acquisition is by another company which, at the time of the acquisition, is a member of the same group; and

(c)   the claim is made by both companies,

as if both companies were the same person.

In practice, the Revenue Commissioners admit hold over claims on the wider basis so that gains of one group member may be held over against acquisitions of other group members. In fact, it would appear to be the Revenue interpretation of TCA 1997, s 620 (rather than any concession) that claims may be made on that basis, as can be seen from the insertion, by FA 2001, of TCA 1997, s 620(4) as discussed above and, furthermore, the following excerpt from the Revenue Guidance Notes on Taxes Consolidation Act 1997:

"This section [TCA 1997, s 620] extends roll-over relief (section 597) to members of a group, such that all the trades carried on by the members are treated as a single trade. Thus the roll-over relief extends to a case where one company in a group disposes of an asset and another member acquires a new asset provided the other conditions of the relief are met. The relief allows for the re-investment of the proceeds from the sale of an asset, by one member of the group, in another asset, by any member of the group. This relief does not apply where the proceeds are re-invested in an asset which itself is acquired from a group member."

Also of interest is the following from the Chief Inspector's Instructions in relation to TCA 1997, s 620:

The following rules apply to a claim for roll-over relief (TI 19.6.2 Par 2 et seq) made by a member of a group of companies:

(a)   Subject to (b) below, all the trades carried on by the members of a group are treated as a single trade carried on by the same person. For example, a group will not lose the benefit of Section 597 where, on a reorganisation of its business, one company of the group acquires new machinery from outside the group in order to take over a process previously carried on by another company in the group that has disposed of its machinery outside the group. Similarly, if one trading company in a group disposes of an asset outside the group and another company in the group acquires an asset from outside the group, roll-over relief is available (subject to the other conditions of Section 597 – see TI 19.6.2 Par 2 et seq) even though there is no transfer of funds between the members of the group and, therefore, no direct application of the disposal proceeds by the company which made the disposal.

(b) The single trade concept outlined in (a) above does not apply where either the person acquiring the old asset (from the group member who acquired it) is also a member of the same group. For example, if A, B and C are trading members of a group and A has a gain from the disposal of a qualifying asset to a company which is not in the group, whilst B acquires another qualifying asset from C, A's trade is not treated as one with B's for the purpose of rolling over A's gain against the asset which B has acquired from C, so that there is no postponement of the charge on A's gain.

An interesting consequence of the above-described defect in TCA 1997, s 620 (whereby the group members are not treated as a single person) is that it seems possible to avoid a recapture of roll-over relief which has been claimed by one group member on the basis of replacement assets acquired by another group member. The relief will be recaptured only if the "person" (ie, the first group member) ceases to use the replacement assets (TCA 1997, s 597(4)(a)), which is most unlikely ever to happen where those assets have been acquired by the second group member. If both companies were treated as the same person, the position would be otherwise.

In practice, a property holding company within a group should, in relation to properties used for the purposes of any of the trades carried on by trading members of the group, itself be treated as if it were a trading company. Consequently, if land held by a holding company in a group and used for trade by a trading company in the group is sold and replaced by land similarly used, then relief under section 597 is available (subject to the other conditions of the section) whether the purchase is made by the holding company or by a trading company within the group and whether or not funds are transferred between the companies concerned.

If any gain becomes assessable, it is assessable on the member of the group which holds the asset on the occurrence of the occasion of a charge. Any case where such member claims that it is not the proper person to be assessed should be reported to Head Office.

In the situation described in (b) above from the Chief Inspector's Instructions, roll-over relief should not in any event be available, based on a strict reading of TCA 1997, s 620, since, as already stated, that section does not treat the various group members as a single person. Even if B had acquired the other qualifying asset from outside the group instead of from C, relief would not in strictness be due. The Revenue, however, interpret the section as though it treats all group members as a single person.

It will be seen also from the above excerpt from the Chief Inspector's Instructions that roll-over relief may be claimed by a company which is not carrying on a trade or profession. Thus, the Revenue accept that a property holding company within a group should, in relation to properties used for the purposes of any of the trades carried on by trading members of the group, itself be treated for the purposes of roll-over relief as if it were a trading company.

The extension of hold over relief by TCA 1997, s 620 applies "except in a case of one member of the group acquiring, or acquiring the interest in, the new assets from another member or disposing of, or disposing of the interest in, the old assets to another member". This anti-avoidance measure is intended to prevent hold over relief being obtained where a group member disposes of an asset and reinvests the proceeds in another asset which it acquires from another group member where the other member continues to use the asset for the purposes of its trade. In that case, the TCA 1997, s 620 rule that all trades carried on by the group members are to be treated as a single trade will not apply. There is nothing, however, to prevent the first-mentioned company using the proceeds in acquiring another group member's assets that it then uses in *its own* trade. For this purpose, TCA 1997, s 620 is not needed to obtain hold over relief as only the trade of the first-mentioned company is in question.

TCA 1997, s 620 will not apply either where the assets disposed of are disposed of within the group. This would prevent relief being obtained where a group member disposes of an asset to another group member, even where the asset is then leased back to the first-mentioned group member for use in its trade. However, since the disposal would come within TCA 1997, s 617, any chargeable gain at that point would be deferred in accordance with that section.

9.207 Company reconstructions and amalgamations

9.207.1 Introduction

A reconstruction or amalgamation involves the transfer of part or all of the business of one company to another company. TCA 1997, s 615 provides for the tax-free transfer of a business or part of a business between two (not necessarily related) Irish or other EU resident companies in connection with a scheme of reconstruction or amalgamation. An essential requirement for this treatment is that the transferor company should receive no part of the consideration for the transfer (otherwise than by the other company taking over the whole or part of the liabilities of the business).

The reconstruction or amalgamation will (although this is not specifically stated in the section) involve the issue by the transferee company of shares or debentures to the shareholders of the transferor company in respect of and in proportion to their holdings of shares or debentures in the transferor company. Accordingly, it is to be expected that the shares or debentures issued would have a value equal to the value of the transferred business and that the value of the shareholders' interests in the transferee company following the transfer would correspond to the value of their former interests in the business transferred. (See also **9.409** in relation to stamp duty relief for reconstructions or amalgamations of companies.)

It is understood that the Revenue would accept that TCA 1997, s 615 (as well as the equivalent stamp duty relief – see **9.409.3**) may apply in the case of the incorporation of a partnership involving two corporate partners. Thus, the partnership trade and assets would be transferred to a company in return for an issue of shares to the two companies. Technically, what would be involved is a transfer by each company of its "several" trade (and its corresponding interest in the trade assets) to the company in return for an issue to it of shares in the company.

Assets transferred are taken over by the transferee company at the original cost and acquisition date of the transferor company. The relief does not extend to any asset which, up to the time of the transfer, formed part of the trading stock of a trade carried on by the transferor company, or to an asset which is acquired as trading stock for the purposes of a trade carried on by the transferee company (TCA 1997, s 615(3)). *Trading stock* means property of any description, whether real or personal, which is either:

(a)   property such as is sold in the ordinary course of the trade in relation to which the expression is used or would be so sold if it were mature or if its manufacture, preparation, or construction were complete; or

(b)   materials such as are used in the manufacture, preparation, or construction of property such as is sold in the ordinary course of the said trade (TCA 1997, s 89(1)(a)).

TCA 1997, s 615 should be considered in tandem with TCA 1997, s 587 (company reconstruction and amalgamations – see **9.405**). As TCA 1997, s 615 envisages the transfer by a company of its assets for no consideration, it is necessary to have regard to company law requirements in accordance with which the divestment by a company of its assets may be permitted. Accordingly, any such arrangement must be on the basis of some form of agreement involving the shareholders (and debenture holders) whereby assets that would normally be distributed to them are instead distributed to a company in which they have an interest. Any such distribution not involving the issue of shares by the transferee company would constitute a capital distribution (unless, being "in respect of shares", a distribution in accordance with TCA 1997, s 130 is involved - see **9.401.4**) and would therefore give rise to a part disposal for capital gains tax purposes. If, however, the transferee company issues shares to the shareholders in the transferor company, TCA 1997, s 587 operates to secure that no such part disposal will result.

For the purposes of TCA 1997, s 615, a reference to a *company* applies only to a company which, by virtue of the law of a relevant Member State, is resident for the purposes of tax in such a Member State. For this purpose, *tax*, in relation to a relevant Member State other than Ireland, means any tax imposed in the Member State that corresponds to corporation tax in the State (TCA 1997, s 615(2)(b)(ii)).

Relevant Member State, means—

(a)   a Member State of the European Communities; or

(b)   not being such a Member State, an EEA State which is a territory with which Ireland has a tax treaty (TCA 1997, s 616(7)).

EEA State means a state that is a contracting party to the EEA Agreement. *EEA Agreement* means the Agreement on the European Economic Area signed at Oporto on 2 May 1992, as adjusted by the Protocol signed at Brussels on 17 March 1993.

Whereas TCA 1997, s 615 provides that the assets being transferred in the course of a reorganisation or amalgamation are treated as having been disposed of on a no gain/ no loss basis, TCA 1997, s 587 treats the issue of shares as a share for share exchange to which TCA 1997, s 586(1) applies.

TCA 1997, s 615(2) provides, as respects disposals on or after 15 February 2001, that where:

(i)   any scheme of reconstruction or amalgamation involves the transfer of the whole or part of a company's business to another company;

(ii)   the company acquiring the assets is resident in the State at the time of the acquisition or the assets are chargeable assets in relation to that company immediately after that time;

(iii)   the company from which the assets are acquired is resident in the State at the time of the acquisition or the assets are chargeable assets in relation to that company immediately before that time;

(iv)   the first-mentioned company receives no part of the consideration for the transfer (otherwise than by the other company taking over the whole or part of the liabilities of the business), and

(v)   the company acquiring the assets is not an authorised investment company (within the meaning of Part XIII of the Companies Act 1990) which is an investment undertaking within the meaning of TCA 1997, s 739B (see **12.806.3**),

then, for the purposes of corporation tax in respect of chargeable gains, the two companies are to be treated as if the assets included in the transfer had been acquired by one company from the other for a consideration of an amount as would secure that, on the disposal by way of transfer, neither a gain nor a loss would accrue to the company making the disposal. For the purposes of TCA 1997, s 556 (indexation relief), the acquiring company is to be treated as if the respective acquisitions of the assets by the other company had been its own acquisitions of them.

An asset is a "chargeable asset" in relation to a company at any time if, were it to be disposed of by the company at that time, any gain accruing to the company would be a chargeable gain. A chargeable gain will arise to a non-resident company only in respect of disposals of certain categories of assets (eg, Irish based land, shares deriving their value or the greater part of their value from such land, Irish based assets used in an Irish branch trade – see **9.102.2**). However, since TCA 1997, s 615(2) applies only "in so far as relates to corporation tax on chargeable gains", only such assets as are being disposed of or acquired by companies carrying on a trade in the State through a branch or agency (and which are accordingly subject to corporation tax) are chargeable assets in relation to the company and then only where the assets are used in or for the purposes of the trade or are used or held by, or are acquired for, the purposes of the branch or agency (see **3.107.1**).

From the above, and except where the acquiring company is an authorised investment company which is an investment undertaking, it can be seen that TCA 1997, s 615(2) can apply in any of the following circumstances—

(i)   the acquisition of assets by an Irish resident company from another Irish resident company;

(ii)   the acquisition by an Irish resident company from a non-resident company of assets which were chargeable assets in relation to the non-resident company immediately before the acquisition;

(iii)   the acquisition by a non-resident company from an Irish resident company of assets which are chargeable assets in relation to the non-resident company immediately after the acquisition; and

(iv)   the acquisition by a non-resident company from another non-resident company of assets which are chargeable assets in relation to the company immediately after the acquisition and which were chargeable assets in relation to that other non-resident company immediately before the acquisition.

In the cases of (ii), (iii) or (iv), where certain assets subsequently cease to be chargeable assets in relation to a company, there is a deemed sale and reacquisition of those assets at market value at that time (TCA 1997, s 620A). The assets in question are those assets which were used or held by, or were acquired for, the purposes of the company's Irish branch or agency and which now cease to be chargeable assets by virtue of their becoming situated outside the State (TCA 1997, s 620A(a)(ii)). The deemed sale and reacquisition does not apply to assets ceasing to be chargeable assets in relation to the company as a result of their ceasing to be used for the purposes of the branch or agency.

Surprisingly, there is a deemed sale and reacquisition by a company of assets that cease to be chargeable assets in relation to the company and which, at the time of their acquisition by the company, consisted of shares deriving their value or the greater part of their value from assets specified in TCA 1997, s 29(3)(a) or (b) (see **9.102.2**) (TCA 1997, s 620A(a)(i)). It is not clear why such assets are included here since they would not have been acquired by the company as a result of a disposal to which TCA 1997, s 615 (which refers to "corporation tax on chargeable gains") applied.

9.207.2　Scheme of reconstruction or amalgamation

TCA 1997, s 615(1) defines *scheme of reconstruction or amalgamation* as a scheme for the reconstruction of any company or companies or the amalgamation of any two or more companies. The definition is identical to that in TCA 1997, s 587(1). The definition provided is not comprehensive and perhaps not very helpful. Neither "reconstruction" nor "amalgamation" is defined in company law, nor have these terms any precise legal meaning. Long-standing practice and usage would indicate that they have a wide meaning and they can be taken to include any form of internal reorganisation of a company or its affairs, and any scheme for amalgamating two or more companies.

In most cases where it is necessary for a company to rearrange its capital structure, the agreement of the shareholders will be forthcoming but it will nevertheless often be necessary, particularly where the process is complex, to obtain the sanction of the courts. Where proposals for rearrangement are opposed by some shareholders, it will be necessary to have a means whereby dissentient (and perhaps untraceable) shareholders cannot be enabled to frustrate the process and which will bind those shareholders. One such rearrangement would be a reconstruction in which all or part of a company's undertaking is transferred to another company without any substantial change in the persons who are ultimately interested in that undertaking (*Brooklands Selangor Holdings Ltd v IRC* [1970] 1 WLR 429). It will be sufficient that there is substantial identity of interest immediately before and after the transfer, even, it appears, where the shares in the transferee company are then sold. (There are some echoes here of TCA 1997, s 400 which, while it does not mention the term "reconstruction", is headed "company reconstructions without change of ownership – see **4.109**.) The Revenue Commissioners have stated that it is not necessarily significant that as a next step the shares in the transferee company are sold. The reconstruction must not, however, be contingent on the subsequent sale or other transfer of the shares. Furthermore, in the opinion of the Revenue, a contract for the subsequent sale of the shares must not be in existence before the reconstruction takes place.

For the purposes of certain reliefs from stamp duty, the concept of a reconstruction is relevant. In that context, it is necessary that the companies involved be owned by the same shareholders in identical terms. Otherwise, a substantial identity of ownership is sufficient. An "amalgamation" is the converse of a reconstruction in that it involves the bringing together of two or more businesses within a single company. The single company may be a newly formed company to which the businesses are transferred or may be a company carrying on one of the businesses and to which the other business is transferred. An example of an amalgamation would be the case in which a company ("X" Ltd) transfers a business to another company ("Y" Ltd) in exchange for the issue of shares in Y Ltd to the X Ltd shareholders: the shareholders of Y Ltd are now an amalgamation of the shareholders of the participating companies. The acquisition by a company of the shares in another company does not by itself result in an amalgamation (*Swithland Investments Ltd and another v IRC* [1990] STC 448). (See more detailed discussion on this topic in **9.409.3** and **9.410.2** in relation to stamp and capital duty reliefs for reconstructions or amalgamations of companies.)

In the cases of both reconstructions and amalgamations, there will be a continuity of interest. An amalgamation involves the shareholders of the transferee company being substantially the combined shareholders of the two companies. An amalgamation could be effected, for example, where one company is put into liquidation and its business, including liabilities, is transferred by the liquidator to the other company with that company issuing shares to the shareholders of the liquidated company.

9.207.3   Transfer of business

TCA 1997, s 615 envisages the transfer of the whole or part of a company's business. A business includes a trade but obviously denotes something much wider. The carrying on of a business has been described as "any gainful use to which [a company] puts any of its assets" and as usually calling for "some activity on the part of whoever carried it on, though, depending on the nature of the business, the activity may be intermittent with long intervals of quiescence in between" (*American Leaf Blending Co Sdn Bhd v Director of Inland Revenue* [1978] STC 561). The ownership of property which is let and the holding of shares, whether by way of portfolio investment or in wholly owned subsidiaries, would amount to the carrying on of business. The Revenue will accept that the transfer of a 100% shareholding constitutes the transfer of a business (or undertaking). (For a discussion on the meaning of "business", see **13.304**.)

Difficulties are more likely to arise as regards what constitutes the transfer of a part of a business; it may be that the part transferred is substantially less than the whole of which it had formed a part and what is transferred may not be sufficient of itself to constitute a business. Although an asset may be acquired in the course of a business, it does not necessarily represent a part of a business; an "undertaking" (which can be taken to mean the same as "business", as confirmed, for example, in the *Swithland* case) is something more than the sum of its parts (*Baytrust Holdings Ltd v IRC* [1971] 1 WLR 1333). Although a housebuilder's business is to construct and sell houses, it would obviously not be correct to say that a house purchased from him represented the acquisition of a part of his business. On the other hand, if another person acquired part of that builder's land bank, with some plant and machinery and perhaps work in progress, and took on some of his employees with a view to commencing a building business, that would constitute the acquisition of part of the housebuilder's business. Again, the disposal of the retail part of a combined wholesale and retail business would be a disposal of a part of that business.

The essential test is whether the severed part is capable of continuing as a business in its own right. The same would be true of an investment business carried on by a company where it is possible to identify a separate part of that business, eg where particular employees are responsible for a specific category of investments managed by the company.

The question becomes even more difficult in the case of a business which does not require much in the way of activity or organisation. For example, the business of a company holding a small number of properties from which it merely derives rents, and which involves no other activity, would consist of no more than the holding of those properties. Yet if the company disposed of one of the properties, it would not be correct to say that it had disposed of part of its business.

That position should be distinguished from a company's business of holding shares in active subsidiaries where it would be more correct to say that each holding would constitute a part of the company's business. It was held in *CIR v Tyre Investment Trust Ltd* 12 TC 646 that the holding of investments can of itself constitute a business. In practice, it would probably be accepted that the transfer by a holding company of the shares in even one active trading subsidiary would constitute the transfer of part of a business. This emerges from the decision in the *Baytrust* case referred to above, which was concerned with UK stamp duty reconstruction relief and in particular with the question whether an undertaking or part of an undertaking had been transferred. The case is often referred to on the question as to what constitutes an "undertaking", whether in a stamp duty context or otherwise. Since, however, some confusion followed in the wake of the decision in this case, it is appropriate to look at the facts in a little more detail.

The taxpayer company (F) had a number of wholly owned subsidiaries which were engaged in steel manufacturing as well as a subsidiary (N) whose business was to exploit patents relating to a process of steel-hardening, and two minority holdings in companies involved in the steel industry. The minority shareholdings were transferred to N in consideration for the issue of shares by N. The shares in N, together with some cash, were then transferred to a new company as part of an arrangement which involved that company issuing shares to the shareholders in F. It was claimed that each of the two transactions involved the transfer of part of an undertaking. Nevertheless, it was held that all that had happened was that certain assets of F which were not required for employment "in its business" had been passed on to its shareholders in the form of shares in the new company. The inference to be drawn from this is that the "business" of F was the holding of shares in the operating subsidiaries but that what was transferred was not a part of that business but merely certain assets employed in that business. The holding of shares in wholly owned subsidiaries carrying on active businesses would therefore appear to be capable of being regarded as the carrying on of a business but not the holding of other investments, such as those in N and the minority shareholdings in the *Baytrust* case.

9.207.4 Tax treatment

As mentioned above, TCA 1997, s 615 provides for the tax-free transfer of a business or part of a business between two Irish or other EU resident companies in connection with a scheme of reconstruction or amalgamation. The section applies where the transferor company receives no part of the consideration for the transfer (otherwise than by the other company taking over the whole or part of the liabilities of the business). Assets transferred are treated as taken over by the transferee company for a consideration of such amount as would secure that neither a gain nor a loss would accrue to the transferor company. Although TCA 1997, s 615 is a relatively short provision, its application in practice can be somewhat complicated.

A reconstruction involves a transfer of some or all of a company's undertaking to another company without any substantial change in the persons ultimately interested in that undertaking (see **9.207.2**). A scheme of reconstruction involves the transferee company carrying on substantially the same business, and having substantially the same members, as the transferor company.

Example 9.207.4.1

The share capital of Newton Ltd is owned as to 50% each by Joule Ltd and Hertz Ltd. Under a proposed reconstruction, part of the trade of Newton Ltd is to be transferred to a new company, Weber Ltd. The part of the trade is duly transferred in consideration for the issue of shares in Weber Ltd that results in Joule Ltd and Hertz Ltd acquiring 50% each in the equity of that company.

The transfer of the trade on the above terms is a reconstruction within the meaning of TCA 1997, s 615. The assets relating to the part of the trade transferred by Newton Ltd are treated as having been acquired by Weber Ltd for a consideration of such amount as would secure that, on the disposal by way of transfer, neither a gain nor a loss would accrue to Newton Ltd.

TCA 1997, s 615 has no relevance in relation to the tax positions of Joule Ltd and Hertz Ltd. Newton Ltd has transferred trading assets to Weber Ltd for no consideration (other than by way of the assumption by Weber Ltd of the liabilities attaching to the part of the trade). A transaction of this nature is likely to have certain company law implications but it is assumed that these would not prevent it from proceeding. In accordance with TCA 1997, s 587 (see **9.405**), Joule Ltd and Hertz Ltd are treated as having exchanged their shares in Newton Ltd for shares in Newton Ltd and Weber Ltd. TCA 1997, s 586(1) then applies to these exchanges so that they are deemed to be a reorganisation of capital.

It is sometimes considered that a transaction of the kind dealt with in the foregoing example gives rise to a distribution to the persons who receive shares in the transferee company. TCA 1997, s 130(2)(b) provides that a "distribution" includes any other distribution out of assets of a company, whether in cash or otherwise, in respect of shares in the company (see **11.102.3** and **11.105.7**). In the example, Joule Ltd and Hertz Ltd have received shares without providing any new consideration. While no cost has fallen on Weber Ltd (since it has received assets of equivalent value), the cost of issuing the shares has effectively been incurred by Newton Ltd. TCA 1997, s 135(5) provides that a distribution is to be treated as made out of assets of a company if the cost falls on the company. On that basis, Newton Ltd might be thought to have made distributions to Joule Ltd and Hertz Ltd. No such distributions arise, however, since no actual transfer has been made by Newton Ltd to Joule Ltd or Hertz Ltd, the persons who hold the shares in Newton Ltd. No transfer of value has been made to those two companies and it cannot be correct to regard them as having receiving distributions when no benefit has arisen to them.

The transfer of assets to Weber Ltd (for no consideration other than the assumption of liabilities) is arguably not a distribution to that company on the basis that, not having any shares in Newton Ltd, it has not received the assets "in respect of shares". It is, however, possible that something can be regarded as having been done in respect of shares if it is done at the request or wishes of a shareholder so that in that sense "it is done to" the shareholder (see **11.105.7**). It might be difficult to contend that the transfer of the part trade to Weber Ltd took place other than at the request of, or in accordance with the wishes of, the shareholders in Newton Ltd. On that basis, assuming Newton Ltd is Irish resident, it might be that a distribution has been made to Weber Ltd. By virtue of TCA 1997, s 129, however, any such distribution would not be taken into account in computing income for corporation tax purposes. The distribution could, however, give rise to an investment income surcharge under TCA 1997, s 440 (see **10.302**).

That a transfer of a trade in the above circumstances could be construed as giving rise to a distribution would be consistent with a certain UK provision regarding "exempt distributions". Section 213 Income and Corporation Taxes Act 1988 (which has no counterpart in TCA 1997) provides that references to distributions of a company are not to apply, inter alia, to a distribution consisting of the transfer by a company ("the distributing company") to another company of a trade and the issue of shares by the transferee company to the members of the distributing company. The distribution which is exempted here must be the distribution of the trade assets, by the "distributing" company, to the transferee company (there apparently being no question of the share issue by the transferee company giving rise to a distribution).

Division or "partition"

As mentioned above, a reconstruction involves a transfer of some or all of a company's undertaking to another company without any substantial change in the persons ultimately interested in that undertaking, and a scheme of reconstruction involves the transferee company carrying on substantially the same business, and having substantially the same members, as the transferor company.

On that basis, a division of a company's undertaking into two or more companies owned by different groups of shareholders would not meet the requirement for a reconstruction. This type of transaction is referred to as a "partition". (Both the *Brooklands Selangor* and *Swithland* cases were concerned with partitions.) In practice, however, relief will be extended to a case involving a partition carried out for bona fide commercial reasons where, as would frequently be the case, the separate groups involved are separate family groups.

A reconstruction would accordingly be treated as including a scheme under which a company's shares are reorganised into separate classes, the separate parts of its undertaking are allocated to the separate classes, new companies are used to acquire the separate parts of the undertaking so allocated, and the group of shareholders for each class of shares receives shares in a separate new company, even though the new companies have no common shareholder. In this context, it is necessary that there is a separation of trades, and not merely a separation of assets.

Example 9.207.4.2

Danforth Ltd is a company owned as to 50% each by two brothers, Millhouse and Quincy Jones. The trade of Danforth Ltd comprises two divisions, the "Millhouse" division and the "Quincy" division, reflecting the respective involvements of the two brothers. The brothers want to "demerge" the trade of Danforth Ltd as they wish to carry on the Millhouse and Quincy trades separately, each on his own account.

As a preliminary to the "demerger", new articles are adopted by Danforth Ltd whereby the shares held by Millhouse and Quincy are redesignated as "A" ordinary and "B" ordinary shares respectively, and on terms that respectively attribute the interests in the Millhouse and Quincy divisions to those two classes of shares.

Millhouse forms Millhouse Ltd and Quincy forms Quincy Ltd. Danforth Ltd is put into liquidation. The liquidator transfers the Millhouse division to Millhouse Ltd in consideration for the issue of shares in Millhouse Ltd to Millhouse and also transfers the

Quincy division to Quincy Ltd in consideration for the issue of shares in Quincy Ltd to Quincy. Millhouse now has ownership, through Millhouse Ltd, of the former Millhouse division and a similar position applies in relation to Quincy.

The respective values of the Millhouse and Quincy divisions are similar but, as would be expected, are not exactly the same. Accordingly, just before the new articles are adopted, there is a transfer of cash from one of the divisions to the other resulting in the equalisation of the respective values of the two divisions.

The transactions concerned will be treated as reconstructions and will therefore not result in chargeable gains. In accordance with TCA 1997, s 615, the assets of the Millhouse and Quincy divisions transferred to Millhouse Ltd and to Quincy Ltd respectively are treated as having been acquired by those companies for a consideration of such amount as would secure that, on the disposal by way of transfer, neither a gain nor a loss would accrue to Danforth Ltd.

The tax position of the brothers also needs to be considered. Without specific provision to the contrary, the transfers of the divisions to Millhouse Ltd and Quincy Ltd are capital distributions and, as such, would give rise to part disposals (TCA 1997, s 583 – see **9.401.4**). TCA 1997, s 587, however, provides that Millhouse and Quincy are to be treated as having exchanged their shares in Danforth Ltd for shares in Millhouse Ltd and Quincy Ltd respectively. TCA 1997, s 586(1) is then treated as applying to these exchanges so that they are deemed to be a reorganisation of capital. That, in turn, means that there have been no disposals of the original shares and no acquisitions of the new holdings and that the new holding in each case is treated as the same asset as the original shares.

If at later date there is a disposal of the shares in, say, Millhouse Ltd, that would result in a chargeable gain to Millhouse. For this purpose, the base cost of the shares in Millhouse Ltd is a proportion of the cost to Millhouse of his shares in Danforth Ltd. That proportion will be by reference to the respective market values of the shares in Danforth Ltd and Millhouse Ltd at the date of disposal of the shares in Millhouse Ltd (TCA 1997, s 584(6)).

The above treatment would appear to be in accordance with a Revenue precedent whereby TCA 1997 ss 587 and 615 are applied as though the partition or division were a reconstruction. The precedent is as follows: "Where a family trading company (or group of companies) is broken up into separate individual trading companies, such an event will not be regarded as a disposal for CGT purposes provided that the value of each individual's holding in the company or group remains strictly unaltered and also provided certain other conditions are met." The conditions are that—

(a)   no money or money's worth changes hands;

(b)   there is no value shift, so that the value of each shareholding before and after the partitioning is identical;

(c)   it is accepted that assets transferred between companies pass in each case to the transferee company at the original date of acquisition and cost to the transferor company;

(d)   it is accepted that the new shares received in exchange (plus the original shares where they are retained) assume the original date of acquisition and cost of the original shares;

(e)   the partition is a "family" partition (see below re "family");

(f)   the partition relates to a 100% family company (see below);

(g)   all parties must be Irish resident;

(h)   the partition relates to the separation of trading companies only, ie trades capable of division into separate trading entities, eg a number of retail outlets, two distinct trading activities such as manufacturing and distribution/sales – but, in practice, where the value of non-trade assets does not exceed 10% of the value of the trading entity as a whole, this condition is regarded as satisfied;

(i)   the separate trades must continue after the partition, must not be available as an alternative to a partial winding up or to be used as a mere separation into trade assets and investment assets;

(j)   where the partition involves the division of a group of companies, the entity to be transferred may be a 100% trading subsidiary of a 100% family company (in which case, TCA 1997, s 623 will be relevant);

(k)   there is no equivalent stamp duty relief;

(l)   the partition must be for bona fide commercial reasons and not to secure a tax advantage of any kind.

In relation to (f) above, *family company*, in relation to an individual, is defined in TCA 1997, s 598(1)(a) as "a company the voting rights in which are—

(i)   as to not less than 25% exercised by the individual; or

(ii)   as to not less than 75% exercisable by the individual or a member of his or her family and, as to not less than 10%, exercisable by the individual himself or herself".

Family, in relation to an individual, means the husband or wife of the individual, and a relative of the individual or of the individual's husband or wife, and *relative* means brother, sister, ancestor or lineal descendant.

Regarding condition (b) above, it will often be difficult if not impossible to satisfy the requirement that the value of each shareholding before and after the partition should be identical. In the above example, it is assumed that an intra-divisional transfer of cash prior to the partition is sufficient to avoid any value shift resulting from the partition.

Advance approval should be sought for the above treatment and requests should identify the parties involved and outline the existing structure, the reasons for the partitioning and the proposed new structure together with the proposed steps to achieve the new structure. Undertakings may be sought in relation to some of the conditions.

The following example is a variation on Example **9.207.4.2** and assumes that Danforth Ltd is owned by two companies.

Example 9.207.4.3

Danforth Ltd is a joint venture company owned as to 50% each by Millhouse Ltd and Quincy Ltd. The trade of Danforth Ltd comprises two divisions, the "Millhouse" division and the "Quincy" division, reflecting the original input of Millhouse Ltd and Quincy Ltd respectively. The partners have now decided that they wish to "demerge" the trade of Danforth Ltd, particularly as Millhouse Ltd wishes to be in a position to sell off the Millhouse division on its own account should a suitable offer materialise.

As a preliminary to the "demerger", new articles are adopted by Danforth Ltd whereby the shares held by Millhouse Ltd and Quincy Ltd are redesignated as "A" ordinary and "B" ordinary shares respectively, and on terms which respectively attribute the interests in the Millhouse and Quincy divisions to those two classes of shares. The respective values of the two divisions are similar but not equal, and full equalisation is achieved by arranging for an appropriate cash transfer between the divisions, prior to adopting the new articles.

Millhouse Ltd forms Millhouse (New) Ltd and Quincy Ltd forms Quincy (New) Ltd. Danforth Ltd is put into liquidation. The liquidator transfers the Millhouse division to

Millhouse (New) Ltd in consideration for the issue of shares in Millhouse (New) Ltd to Millhouse Ltd and also transfers the Quincy division to Quincy (New) Ltd in consideration for the issue of shares in Quincy (New) Ltd to Quincy Ltd. Millhouse Ltd now has ownership, through Millhouse (New) Ltd, of the former Millhouse division and a similar position applies to Quincy Ltd and the Quincy division.

If the transactions concerned could be treated as reconstructions, they would not result in chargeable gains. In accordance with TCA 1997, s 615, the assets of the Millhouse and Quincy divisions transferred to Millhouse (New) Ltd and to Quincy (New) Ltd respectively would be treated as having been acquired by those companies for a consideration of such amount as would secure that, on the disposal by way of transfer, neither a gain nor a loss would accrue to Danforth Ltd.

As the transactions bring about a partition, but not a "family" partition, however, they may not be treated as reconstructions, at least in accordance with the above-mentioned Revenue precedent. It might then be argued that the transactions are reconstructions since a reconstruction involves a transfer of some or all of a company's undertaking to another company without any substantial change in the persons ultimately interested in that undertaking. In this example, each of the two transactions involving the transfer of a division results in the same person owning the division immediately before and after the transaction. As against this, however, it seems that it is necessary, in line with the approach taken in *Swithland Investments Ltd v IRC* [1990] STC 448, to look at the transactions as a whole and that what must be compared is the ownership position before the adoption of the new articles and the ownership following the transfers of the divisions to the new companies.

9.208 Disposal outside a group

TCA 1997, s 619 provides for the computation of gains and losses in cases where an asset which was acquired by a member of a group of companies from another group member is ultimately disposed of outside the group. Any restriction of a loss by reference to capital allowances under capital gains tax rules is to take account of allowances given while the asset was owned by any member of the group. Where ownership of the asset has passed between members of a group before being disposed of outside the group, TCA 1997, s 556 (indexation relief) is to apply as if the asset had been acquired and disposed of by the same company.

Expenditure on assets qualifying for capital allowances (or renewals allowances) is fully allowable as a deduction under TCA 1997, s 552 in computing a chargeable gain in respect of the disposal of those assets (TCA 1997, s 555). However, any expenditure to the extent to which any capital allowance or renewals allowance has been made in respect of it is to be deducted from the sums allowable as a deduction for the purposes of computing an allowable loss. For this purpose, the amount of any capital allowances to be taken into account is to include any balancing allowance arising on the disposal and is net of any balancing charge arising on that disposal.

Where a company which is or has been a member of a group of companies disposes of an asset which it acquired from another group member and, as respects an acquisition on or after 15 February 2001, where that acquisition was in the course of a disposal to which TCA 1997, s 617 applies (see **9.203.1**), the restriction of losses by reference to capital allowances obtained by the company (as provided for in TCA 1997, s 555 – see above) is also to apply in relation to any capital allowances made to the other member (so far as not taken into account in relation to a disposal of an asset by that other member), and so on as respects previous transfers of the asset between members of the group (TCA 1997, s 619(1)).

The chargeable gain or allowable loss on the eventual disposal outside the group of an asset which was acquired by one group member from another and, as respects an acquisition on or after 15 February 2001, where the acquisition was in the course of a disposal to which TCA 1997, s 617 applies (see **9.203.1**), is calculated under TCA 1997, s 556 (indexation relief) as if all group members were a single person (TCA 1997, s 619(2)). The member disposing of the asset outside the group is deemed to be the company which originally acquired it when it was acquired by the group. The 6 April 1974 market value rule (where relevant) and the indexation provisions are applied on this basis. (See **9.203.4** regarding the apparent conflict with TCA 1997, s 617 on this point.)

Example 9.208.1

Mallett Ltd owns 60% of the issued share capital of Marson Ltd and all of the issued share capital of Maxse Ltd. On 1 November 1971, Mallett Ltd purchased a building for €190,000. The market value of the building on 6 April 1974 was €350,000. On 1 October 1992 Mallett Ltd sold the building to Maxse Ltd for €1,200,000. Maxse Ltd incurred expenditure of €100,000 on extensions and improvements to the building which were completed at the end of February 1994. On 2 April 2007, Maxse Ltd sold the building to Marson Ltd for €3,000,000. It is established that the building is not development land.

The sale of the building to Maxse Ltd is treated for capital gains tax purposes as giving rise to neither a gain nor a loss to Mallett Ltd. The base cost of the building to Mallett Ltd is its market value on 6 April 1974, ie €350,000. As the sale of the building to Marson Ltd is a non-group sale, a chargeable gain arises to Maxse Ltd as follows:

	€	€
Sale proceeds		3,000,000
Cost (MV 6 April 1974) €350,000		
Indexed @ 7.528 (see **9.203.4**)	2,634,800	
Enhancement expenditure €100,000		
Indexed @ 1.331	133,100	2,767,900
Gain		232,100

As seen in **9.203**, TCA 1997, s 617 applies so as to defer a chargeable gain arising on an intra-group disposal of development land occurring on or after 24 April 1992 until such time as the development land is disposed of outside the group. Where at any time after an asset was acquired or provided by a group taken as a single person in accordance with TCA 1997, s 619(2), and before 24 April 1992 there was an acquisition ("the later acquisition") of that asset by a member of a group from another member of the group as a result of a relevant disposal (ie, because the asset consisted at that time of development land), TCA 1997, s 619(2) applies as if the reference to the acquisition or provision of the land by the group were a reference to the later acquisition (or the last such acquisition where there was more than one). Thus, where there has been an intra-group disposal of development land at any time from 28 January 1982 to 23 April 1992, the chargeable gain on a subsequent disposal of that land outside the group is to be computed on the basis that the group member disposing of the land acquired it when it actually acquired it, ie on its acquisition of the land on the intra-group disposal.

9.209 Company leaving group

9.209.1 Tax charge on company leaving group

In the absence of special provisions, it would be possible to avoid a chargeable gain on the disposal of an asset by first transferring the asset within a capital gains tax group and then disposing of the company to which the asset had been transferred. A chargeable gain would have been avoided on the intra-group transfer in accordance with TCA 1997, s 617(1) which, in the absence of a disposal of the asset by the transferee company, would not be "clawed back". By way of variation, where the asset to be sold is a member of the group, that member could first be sold to a special purpose subsidiary within the group for full consideration left on loan account, followed by a sale of the special purpose company to the vendor. The vendor would then arrange for the repayment of the inter-company indebtedness. TCA 1997, s 623 counters this type of avoidance by securing that the intra-group disposal is taxed retrospectively when the group member leaves the group.

The retrospective charge to tax applies where a company ("the chargeable company") which is a member of a group of companies—

    (a)   acquires an asset from another company which at the time of the acquisition was a member of the group;

    (b)   the company ceases to be a member of the group within 10 years after the time of the acquisition;

    (c)   the company is resident in the State at the time of acquisition of the asset, or the asset is a chargeable asset in relation to that company immediately after that time; and

    (d)   the other company is resident in the State at the time of that acquisition, or the asset is a chargeable asset in relation to that company immediately before that time (TCA 1997, s 623(2)).

An asset is a "chargeable asset" in relation to a company at any time if, were it to be disposed of by the company at that time, any gain accruing to the company would be a chargeable gain. A chargeable gain will arise to a non-resident company only in respect of disposals of certain categories of assets (eg, Irish based land, shares deriving their value or the greater part of their value from such land, Irish based assets used in an Irish branch trade – see **9.102.2**). However, only such assets as are held by a non-resident company carrying on a trade in the State through a branch or agency (and which is accordingly subject to corporation tax) are chargeable assets in relation to the company and then only where the assets are used in or for the purposes of the trade or are used or held by, or are acquired for, the purposes of the branch or agency (see **3.107.1** and **9.203.1**).

From the above, it can be seen that TCA 1997, s 623(2) can apply in any of the following circumstances—

    (i)   the company ceasing to be a group member and the company from which it had acquired the asset intra-group were both Irish resident companies at the time of acquisition;

    (ii)   the company ceasing to be a group member was an Irish resident company at the time it acquired the asset intra-group and the asset acquired was immediately before that time a chargeable asset in relation to the company from which it was acquired;

(iii) immediately after it was acquired intra-group, the asset acquired was a chargeable asset in relation to the company ceasing to be a group member and the company from which it acquired the asset was an Irish resident company at that time of the acquisition; and

(iv) the asset acquired was a chargeable asset in relation to the company ceasing to be a group member immediately after, and a chargeable asset in relation to the company from which it was acquired immediately before, the time of the intra-group acquisition.

The charge under TCA 1997, s 623 does not apply where a company ceases to be a group member by reason of being wound up or dissolved or in consequence of another group member being wound up or dissolved (TCA 1997, s 623(1)(d)). Where a company ceases to be a member of a group of companies on or after 28 March 1996, this exception will apply only where the winding up or dissolution is for *bona fide* commercial reasons and is not part of a scheme or arrangement the main purpose or one of the main purposes of which is the avoidance of tax.

When the chargeable company ceases to be a member of the group, it is treated for capital gains tax purposes as if immediately after its acquisition of the asset it had sold, and immediately reacquired, the asset at market value at that time (TCA 1997, s 623(4)). The retrospective charge applies only where, at the time the chargeable company leaves the group, that company, or an associated company also leaving the group, owns, otherwise than as trading stock:

(i) the asset; or

(ii) property on the acquisition of which a chargeable gain in relation to the asset has been deferred on a replacement of business assets.

For the above purposes, two or more companies are associated companies if, by themselves, they would form a group of companies.

Example 9.209.1.1

Kaiser Ltd, an Irish resident company, purchased shares in Strindberg plc some years ago for €50,000. The shares now have a market value of €450,000. Kaiser Ltd forms an Irish resident subsidiary, Toller Ltd, and subscribes for 450,000 €1 shares in that company. The Strindberg plc shares are sold to Toller Ltd for €450,000. In accordance with TCA 1997, s 617, the sale is on the basis that neither a gain nor a loss arises to Kaiser Ltd.

Kaiser Ltd sells the shares in Toller Ltd to Capek Ltd for €450,000. No chargeable gain arises on the sale of the Toller Ltd shares. Under TCA 1997, s 623(4), however, Toller Ltd is deemed to have sold the Strindberg plc shares at the time it acquired them from Kaiser Ltd and to have immediately reacquired them at their then market value, €450,000. Toller Ltd is therefore liable to corporation tax in respect of a chargeable gain of €400,000 (€450,000 – €50,000) in respect of this deemed disposal.

As respects (i) above, an asset acquired by the chargeable company is treated as the same as an asset owned at a later time by that company or an associated company if the value of the second asset is derived in whole or in part from the first asset, and in particular where the second asset is a freehold, and the first asset was a leasehold and the lessee has acquired the reversion (TCA 1997, s 623(1)(c)).

Example 9.209.1.2

Sedan Ltd, Laurel Ltd and Hardy Ltd are Irish resident members of a capital gains tax group. Sedan Ltd holds the freehold in a building that it purchased some years ago for €750,000. Sedan Ltd received €100,000 from Laurel Ltd in respect of the grant of a lease of the building to that company. Under TCA 1997, s 617, the part disposal (the grant of the lease) did not give rise to a chargeable gain.

The value of the freehold is now €900,000 and the leasehold is valued at €175,000. The leasehold is purchased by Hardy Ltd for €175,000. Again under TCA 1997, s 617, Hardy Ltd is deemed to have acquired the leasehold (and Laurel Ltd to have disposed of it) for €100,000, the original cost to Laurel Ltd.

Shortly afterwards, the reversion (the freehold subject to the leasehold) is purchased by Hardy Ltd from Sedan Ltd for €900,000. Hardy Ltd is deemed under TCA 1997, s 617 to have acquired, and Sedan Ltd to have disposed of, the freehold at €750,000, the cost to Sedan Ltd.

The termination of the leasehold has increased the market value of the freehold by an amount equal to the market value of the leasehold, ie by €175,000, so that it is now worth €1,075,000.

If Hardy Ltd ceases to be a member of the group while owning the freehold, it will be treated as having sold and immediately reacquired the freehold at its market value at the time it acquired it from Sedan Ltd. Its chargeable gain will then be as follows:

	€
Deemed disposal proceeds	1,075,000
Deemed cost (cost to Sedan Ltd)	750,000
Chargeable gain	325,000

It will be seen that the gain of €325,000 equates to the aggregate of gains not taxed at the times of the two intra-group disposals, as follows:

	€
Grant of leasehold to Laurel Ltd	100,000
Sale of leasehold to Hardy Ltd	75,000
Sale of reversion to Hardy Ltd (€900,000 - €750,000)	150,000
Aggregate gains	325,000

For the purposes of (ii) above, a chargeable gain is deferred on a replacement of business assets if, by virtue of one or more claims under TCA 1997, s 597 (see **9.206**), a chargeable gain on the disposal of those assets is treated as not accruing until the time the replacement assets cease to be used for the purposes of a trade carried on by the company making the claim (TCA 1997, s 623(1)(b)).

Example 9.209.1.3

Heron Ltd acquires a business premises for €100,000. It later sells the building, when its market value is €240,000, to its wholly owned subsidiary Nightjar Ltd. Both companies are Irish resident. Under TCA 1997, s 617, Heron Ltd is treated as having disposed of the building, and Nightjar Ltd as having acquired it, for €100,000.

Nightjar Ltd uses the building for the purposes of its trade but later sells it – assume before 4 December 2002 – outside the group for €320,000. A chargeable gain accrues to Nightjar Ltd in an amount of €220,000 (€320,000 - €100,000). However, Nightjar applies the full €320,000 in purchasing a replacement building, at a cost of €400,000, for the purposes of its trade and it accordingly claims under TCA 1997, s 597 (replacement of business assets –

see **9.206**) to have the chargeable gain deferred until such time as the replacement building ceases to be used in its trade (and is not further replaced in accordance with TCA 1997, s 597).

Still later (but within 10 years of the date it disposed of the building to Nightjar Ltd), Heron Ltd disposes of its shares in Nightjar Ltd to a non-group company. As Nightjar Ltd has now left the group of which it was a member when it acquired the first building from Heron Ltd, it becomes liable under TCA 1997, s 623(4) in respect of a chargeable gain as if it had sold that building, and immediately reacquired it, for €240,000 at the time it acquired it from Heron Ltd. The gain that would have arisen had Nightjar Ltd sold the building for €240,000 at that time is €140,000 (€240,000 - €100,000), and that gain now crystallises.

Assume further that Nightjar Ltd eventually sells the second building, without replacing it, for €500,000. The amount of the gain originally held over was €220,000. Since in the meantime, however, Nightjar Ltd was deemed to have sold and reacquired the first building for €240,000, the gain held over must be revised to €80,000 (€320,000 - €240,000) and that is the amount of the deferred gain which now crystallises. The gain on the disposal of the second building is €180,000 (€500,000 - €400,000 + €80,000).

An assessment under TCA 1997, s 623 may be made at any time within ten years from the time the chargeable company ceased to be a member of the group (TCA 1997, s 623(6)).

Where the chargeable company is treated under TCA 1997, s 623 as having disposed of and reacquired an asset, all such re-computations of liability in respect of other disposals, and all such adjustments of tax, whether by way of assessment or by way of discharge or repayment of tax, as may be required under TCA 1997, s 623 are to be carried out (TCA 1997, s 623(6)). This provision would apply where there is a subsequent part disposal of an asset in respect of which a charge under TCA 1997, s 623(4) arose.

Time at which charge accrues

As to the time when tax arising by virtue of TCA 1997, s 623 becomes due and payable, the section is unclear. It might seem to follow from TCA 1997, s 623(4) that this will be by reference to the accounting period in which the intra-group disposal took place. This is because that subsection provides that, for the purposes of the Capital Gains Tax Acts, the chargeable company is deemed to have sold the asset in question at that time. The more obvious consequences of that treatment are that indexation is calculated, and the capital gains tax rate is determined, by reference to that earlier time. Similarly, only capital gains tax losses available at that earlier time would be available for offset against the gain arising. But it surely cannot be correct that tax is treated as due and payable by reference to the earlier date so that, for example, interest on overdue tax will accrue by reference to that date.

In the equivalent UK legislation (from which TCA 1997, s 623 was originally taken), the gain (or loss) does not accrue until the later of the time immediately after (a) the intra-group transfer and (b) the beginning of the chargeable company's accounting period in which that company leaves the group. This would seem to be a clear acknowledgment that it would be fundamentally wrong that the gain or loss should accrue at the time of the original intra-group transfer.

It is arguable that TCA 1997, s 623 does not clearly result in the gain or loss accruing at the time of the intra-group transfer. If the event triggering the charge is the chargeable company leaving the group, so that there can have been no liability arising before that time, the liability must arise by reference to that event so that to infer that the charge to tax accrues from an earlier date, which may be many years earlier, would amount to retrospective taxation and would probably be vulnerable to a constitutional challenge. Does the fact that there is a deemed disposal at that earlier time necessarily mean that the gain or loss is also deemed to accrue from that time? Perhaps, but it is suggested that the section should include a provision fixing a date related to the date the chargeable company leaves the group. In the absence of such a provision, the precise effect of TCA 1997, s 626(4) must remain in doubt.

Furthermore, TCA 1997, s 623(5), dealing with the question of secondary liabilities (see **9.209.4** below) provides that where corporation tax assessed on a company by reason of TCA 1997, s 623 is not paid within six months from the date on which it becomes payable, another company within the same group may, at any time within two years from the time the tax became payable, be assessed and charged, in the name of the chargeable company, to all or any part of that tax. If the tax becomes due and payable at the time of the intra-group transfer, this two-year period will have expired in many cases before the chargeable company leaves the group and it is hardly credible that this is the intention of the legislation. There is surely here a strong indication that the tax is considered to have become payable only by reference to the more recent event, ie the chargeable company leaving the group.

9.209.2   Leaving a group

Since a charge under TCA 1997, s 623 may be triggered on the occasion of a company ceasing to be a member of a group, an understanding of the factors which determine the existence or otherwise of a capital gains tax group is of particular importance. This matter is dealt with in detail in **9.202** (meaning of "group"). Some difficulties of interpretation are discussed in **9.202.3** and these, as well as Examples **9.202.3.1** to **9.202.3.4**, are especially relevant for the purposes of TCA 1997, s 623.

As discussed also in **9.202**, EU resident companies may be members of a capital gains tax group, but the presence of a non- EU resident company in the ownership chain may mean that certain EU resident companies may also fail to qualify as members of the group. Consequently, changes of residence can have implications for groups as regards retrospective charges to tax under TCA 1997, s 623. For example, in the case of two companies comprising a capital gains tax group, if one of the companies had transferred an asset to the other and the management and control of one or both of the companies is later moved to a jurisdiction outside the EU, any tax charge deferred at the time of the intra-group transfer would be triggered at that point.

In the UK case *Lion v Inspector of Taxes* [1997] SpC 115, the Special Commissioners held that where a holding company resident in the UK ceased to be a member of a group of companies by reason of its subsidiaries becoming non-resident, it was deemed to dispose of assets then held by it and which it had obtained as a result of an earlier intra-group transfer. The exception relating to companies ceasing to be members of a group at the same time (TCA 1997, s 623(3) – see below) did not apply as the subsidiaries were no longer "associated" once they became non-resident. This decision was endorsed by the High Court in another UK case, *Dunlop International AG v Pardoe* [1998] STC 459, and subsequently by the Court of Appeal.

In the case of a group consisting of a parent and a subsidiary, the disposal of the subsidiary would result in both companies ceasing to be members of a group. If the parent had previously acquired an asset from the subsidiary, any chargeable gain deferred at that time under TCA 1997, s 617 would be triggered in accordance with TCA 1997, s 623. The TCA 1997, s 623 charge can be avoided in such circumstances by forming a new subsidiary prior to the disposal of the older subsidiary.

Where a company which was a member of a group of companies is sold, the time at which it ceases to be a member of the group is the time its parent ceases to have beneficial ownership of it. That will generally be the time the parent contracts to dispose of it – see also **8.302.4** in relation to groups for group relief purposes.

Effective 75% subsidiaries – companies ceasing to be group members

As from 11 February 1999, for the purpose of ascertaining whether or not a capital gains tax group exists, and in determining what companies are members of such a group, the provisions relating to "equity entitlement" for the purposes of group relief (see **8.340**) are applied by TCA 1997, s 616(1). Only "effective 75% subsidiaries" may be taken into account for that purpose (see **9.202.1**).

The more restricted definition of a capital gains tax group may mean that certain companies which qualified as members of a group under the old definition (before the amendment of TCA 1997, s 616(1) by FA 1999) may cease to qualify because of failure to satisfy the equity entitlement tests. This will be true particularly of companies which never satisfied those tests and which, on 11 February 1999, ceased to be members of a capital gains tax group for that reason.

TCA 1997, s 623A is a transitional provision which deals with the case of a company ceasing to be a member of a group of companies by virtue only of the amendment of the definition of a capital gains tax group. The section applies where the company at that time owns, otherwise than as trading stock, an asset which it had acquired from another company which was at the time of acquisition a member of that group of companies, or property which replaced that asset and on the acquisition of which a chargeable gain has been deferred on a replacement of business assets. In those circumstances, TCA 1997, s 623(4) will not apply so that the company will not be treated as having sold and immediately reacquired that asset at the time it had acquired it from the fellow group member.

The TCA 1997, s 623(4) charge will not, however, be disapplied where, on the basis of the old definition of a group of companies (TCA 1997, s 616(1) before its amendment by FA 1990),

(a)   the company ceases to be a member of the group;

(b)   at that time the company (or an associated company also ceasing at that time to be a member of the group) owns, otherwise than as trading stock, the asset, or property which replaced that asset and on the acquisition of which a chargeable gain has been deferred on a replacement of business assets; and

(c)   the asset had been acquired within the period of ten years ending with the time the company ceases to be a group member.

In other words, the transitional relief will apply unless the company in question ceases to be a group member in accordance with the old definition (ie, as a result of some or all of its shares being disposed of to a non-group acquirer). Without this qualification, the TCA 1997, s 623(4) charge would not apply where, say, a company is deemed by virtue of the new definition to have ceased to be a member of a group of companies (the first event) but its shares are later disposed of outside the group (the second event). Since the company can only have left the group once, the TCA 1997, s 623(4) charge would not apply on the occasion of the second event. The qualification secures that the TCA 1997, s 623(4) charge will in fact apply on the happening of the second event.

Example 9.209.2.1

The position is as in Example **9.209.1.3** except that on 11 February 1999, by virtue of the operation of TCA 1997, s 616(1) (as amended by FA 1999), Nightjar Ltd ceases to be a member of the group. As before, Heron Ltd later disposes of its shares in Nightjar Ltd to a non-group company.

Although Nightjar Ltd ceases to be a member of the group on 11 February 1999, TCA 1997, s 623(4) is not triggered at that time. On the subsequent disposal of its shares by Heron Ltd, however, Nightjar Ltd is then treated under TCA 1997, s 623(4) as having sold the building, and immediately reacquired it, for €240,000 at the time it acquired it from Heron Ltd.

9.209.3   Associated companies leaving group

Where two or more associated companies (ie, companies which by themselves would form a group of companies) cease to be members of a group at the same time, TCA 1997, s 623(2) does not have effect as respects an acquisition of an asset by one from another of those companies (TCA 1997, s 623(3)). This is a relieving measure which excludes from the operation of TCA 1997, s 623(4) a case in which an asset has been transferred between two group members and both leave the group later and at the same time while continuing to be in group relationship with each other. For the provision to apply, it is necessary that the companies are associated at the point at which they leave the group, and not just immediately prior to that point. The decision in the *Dunlop International* case mentioned in **9.209.2** above refers. The UK Special Commissioners' decision in *Johnston Publishing (North) Ltd & Others v HMRC* [2006] SPC 564 suggests that the companies should also have been associated at the time the assets had been transferred intra-group. The decision was upheld in the Chancery Division on 14 March 2007. Despite this endorsement of the earlier decision of the Special Commissioners, some may find the reasoning advanced by the court as less than convincing.

Example 9.209.3.1

Emerald Ltd and its wholly owned subsidiary company Ruby Ltd, both Irish resident companies, are members of the Diamond group. Emerald Ltd transfers a property to Ruby Ltd during the year ended 31 December 2003. By reason of TCA 1997, s 617, no chargeable gain arises in respect of this transfer.

During the year ended 31 December 2007, Diamond Ltd, the principal company of the Diamond group, disposes of the shares in Emerald Ltd to a non-group company. No charge under TCA 1997, s 623(4) is triggered in relation to the earlier transfer of property between Emerald Ltd and its subsidiary Ruby Ltd as the two companies are associated companies which have ceased to be members of the Diamond group at the same time.

Example 9.209.3.2

The facts are as in Example **9.209.3.1** except that the property transferred from Emerald Ltd to Ruby Ltd had earlier been acquired from Diamond Ltd during the year ended 31 December 2002.

By virtue of TCA 1997, s 617, no chargeable gain arose in respect of the transfer of the property from Diamond Ltd to Emerald Ltd. The occasion of Emerald Ltd leaving the Diamond group triggers a charge under TCA 1997, s 623(4) in respect of the transfer of the property from Diamond Ltd to Emerald Ltd. At the date Emerald Ltd ceases to be a member of the group, it is deemed to have disposed of and reacquired the property at its market value at the date on which it acquired it from Diamond Ltd.

The exception in TCA 1997, s 623(3) may apply in certain cases even where the two companies involved in the earlier intra-group transfer would not by themselves form a group.

Example 9.209.3.3

The position is as in Example **9.209.3.1** except that Emerald Ltd and Ruby Ltd are both owned by Amethyst Ltd, all three companies being members of the Diamond group. Emerald Ltd transfers a property to Ruby Ltd during the year ended 31 December 2003. By reason of TCA 1997, s 617, no chargeable gain arises in respect of this transfer.

During the year ended 31 December 2007, Diamond Ltd, the principal company of the Diamond group, disposes of the shares in Amethyst Ltd to a non-group company. No charge under TCA 1997, s 623(4) is triggered in relation to the earlier transfer of property between Emerald Ltd and Ruby Ltd as two or more companies (three in this case) have ceased to be members of the Diamond group at the same time and the earlier intra-group transfer involved two of those companies.

TCA 1997, s 623(3) contains an anti-avoidance measure directed at attempts to reduce the value of a subsidiary before its disposal outside a group. The measure applies where two or more associated companies cease to be members of a group of companies at the same time and a dividend has been paid or a distribution was made by one of those companies to another company (not being one of the associated companies) wholly or partly out of profits derived from the disposal of any asset by one to another of the associated companies. To the extent that the dividend or distribution was derived from those profits, it is deemed for capital gains tax purposes to be consideration (or additional consideration as the case may be) received by the company that disposed of the shares in the company which paid the dividend or made the distribution.

This provision is unclear in one respect. The circumstances in which it applies are where a dividend is paid or a distribution is made "to a company which is not one of the associated companies". It is not stated that that company must be a group company but the intention presumably is that it would be such a company. This would appear to be confirmed by the wording which follows to the effect that the dividend or the value of the distribution is deemed to be consideration "received by the member of the group or former member of the group in respect of a disposal, which disposal gave rise to or was caused by the associated companies ceasing to be members of the group". Such a disposal could only have been made by another group company.

The amount deemed to be consideration or additional consideration is the amount of the dividend or value of the distribution to the extent that it is paid or made out of the profits derived from the disposal of the asset between the associated companies. The profit for this purpose is presumably the actual profit realised, ie net consideration received less cost, and not the profit or gain as computed for capital gains tax purposes.

Example 9.209.3.4

As in Examples **9.209.3.1** and **9.209.3.2**, Emerald Ltd and its wholly owned subsidiary company Ruby Ltd are members of the Diamond group. Emerald Ltd transfers a property to

Ruby Ltd during the year ended 31 December 2003 for €1,000,000, giving rise to a profit of €450,000.

During the year ended 31 December 2007, Diamond Ltd, the principal company of the Diamond group, disposes of the shares in Emerald Ltd to a non-group company for €600,000. Before this happens, a dividend of €500,000 is paid by Emerald Ltd to Diamond Ltd.

No charge under TCA 1997, s 623 is triggered in relation to the earlier transfer of property between Emerald Ltd and Ruby Ltd as these two companies are associated companies which have ceased to be members of the Diamond group at the same time.

Of the dividend of €500,000, €450,000 is derived from the profit made on the disposal of the asset between the associated companies. The consideration of €600,000 received by Diamond Ltd for the disposal of the Emerald Ltd shares is therefore increased by €450,000 and the chargeable gain on the disposal is computed by reference to sale proceeds of €1,050,000.

In the foregoing example, the disposal of the shares in Emerald Ltd "gave rise to" the associated companies ceasing to be members of the group. TCA 1997, s 623(3) also envisages a situation in which a disposal "was caused by" the associated companies ceasing to be members of the group.

Example 9.209.3.5

The position is the same as in Example **9.209.3.4** except that Diamond Ltd does not sell any shares. Instead, Sapphire Ltd, an unrelated company, subscribes for shares giving it 26% of the ordinary share capital of Emerald Ltd.

The acquisition of the 26% interest in Emerald Ltd by Sapphire Ltd results in Emerald Ltd ceasing to be a 75% subsidiary of Diamond Ltd and therefore ceasing to be a member of the Diamond group. Since there is no disposal, however, it might appear that TCA 1997, s 623(3) does not apply. The possible ambiguity in the interpretation of this subsection is discussed following this example. The effect of TCA 1997, s 623(3), assuming it applies, is that €450,000 of the dividend is deemed to be consideration received by Diamond Ltd "in respect of a disposal" caused by the associated companies, Emerald Ltd and Ruby Ltd, ceasing to be members of the group. A chargeable gain would accordingly be computed by reference to disposal proceeds of €450,000.

The above example attempts to deal with the position in which a disposal "was caused by" the associated companies ceasing to be members of the group. Taken literally, this might suggest that such a disposal would have to be an actual disposal that was caused by the associated companies ceasing to be members of the group. No such actual disposal, however, can be identified in this case. The reference may on the other hand be to a hypothetical or deemed disposal resulting from the associated companies leaving the group.

A hypothetical disposal could possibly be inferred from the words "shall be deemed ... to be consideration ... received ... in respect of a disposal.... being a disposal which ... was caused by the associated companies ceasing to be members of the group". Thus, the words "shall be deemed" would be seen as referring, not only to the consideration, but to the words "a disposal ... being a disposal which was caused by the associated companies ceasing to be members of the group". It is not at all clear that such an interpretation can be supported.

Alternatively, the reference could be to a deemed disposal, being a deemed disposal (by Diamond Ltd) of the asset previously transferred intra-group between Emerald Ltd and Ruby Ltd. This interpretation also gives rise to difficulties, not least since it would seem to be necessary to take this deemed disposal into account again should Emerald Ltd (within ten years) dispose of its shares in Ruby Ltd.

The following example considers the position of companies changing groups. It also illustrates a consequence of the view that it is possible to have a group within a group. (In this regard, see also **9.202.3**.)

Example 9.209.3.6

Helsing Ltd has a wholly owned subsidiary, Skagerrak Ltd, which in turn has a wholly owned subsidiary, Kattegat Ltd. Skagerrak Ltd sells a property to Kattegat Ltd which, under TCA 1997, s 617, results in neither a gain nor a loss arising to Skagerrak Ltd.

Three years later, Helsing Ltd sells Skagerrak Ltd to Murmansk Ltd. No charge under TCA 1997, s 623 arises in respect of the earlier intra-group disposal involving Skagerrak Ltd and Kattegat Ltd as these companies are "associated" within the meaning of TCA 1997, s 623(1).

Two years later, Skagerrak Ltd sells Kattegat Ltd outside the Murmansk group. The charge under TCA 1997, s 623(4) will apply as respects any asset which the company leaving the group acquired from another company "which at the time of acquisition was a member of the group". The intra-group transfer had taken place when the two companies were members of the Helsing group but also, however, while they were members of the Skagerrak group (comprising Skagerrak Ltd and Kattegat Ltd). Kattegat Ltd has now left the Skagerrak group so that the charge under TCA 1997, s 623(4) applies.

When Skagerrak Ltd was sold by Helsing Ltd, Skagerrak Ltd and Kattegat Ltd left the Helsing group but the charge was avoided at that time because the two companies were associated.

9.209.4 Secondary liabilities

Where corporation tax assessed on a company by reason of TCA 1997, s 623 is not paid within six months from the date on which it becomes payable, then:

(a) a company which on the due date for payment, or immediately after the chargeable company ceased to be a member of the group, was the principal company of the group; or

(b) a company which owned the asset on that date, or when the chargeable company ceased to be a member of the group,

may, at any time within two years from the time the tax became payable, be assessed and charged, in the name of the chargeable company, to all or any part of that tax. The company paying any amount of such tax will be entitled to recover a sum of that amount from the chargeable company (TCA 1997, s 623(5)).

9.209.5 Exemption in cases of certain mergers

TCA 1997, s 623 does not have effect where a company (referred to as "company A") ceases to be a member of a group of companies (referred to as "the A group") as part of a merger where the merger is shown to have been carried out for *bona fide* commercial reasons and that the avoidance of liability to tax was not the main, or one of the main, purposes of the merger (TCA 1997, s 624).

The definition of *merger* for this purpose is lengthy and somewhat complex and is given in full here. It means an arrangement, including a series of arrangements:

(a)   whereby one or more companies ("the acquiring company" or "the acquiring companies") none of which is a member of the A group acquires or acquire, otherwise than with a view to their disposal, one or more interests in the whole or part of the business which, before the arrangement took effect, was carried on by company A; and

(b)   whereby one or more members of the A group acquires or acquire, otherwise than with a view to their disposal, one or more interests in the whole or part of the business which, before the arrangement took effect, was carried on either by the acquiring company or acquiring companies or by a company at least 90% of the ordinary share capital of which was then beneficially owned by two or more of the acquiring companies; and

(c)   in respect of which certain conditions (detailed below) are fulfilled.

For the above purposes, a member of a group is to be treated as carrying on as one business the activities of that group.

The conditions referred to in (c) above are that:

(1)   not less than 25% by value of each of the interests acquired as mentioned in (a) and (b) above consists of a holding of ordinary share capital, and the remainder of the interest or, as the case may be, of each of the interests, acquired as mentioned in (b) above consists of a holding of share capital (of any description) or debentures, or both;

(2)   the value or, as the case may be, the aggregate value of the interest or interests acquired as mentioned in (a) is substantially the same as the value or, or as the case may be, the aggregate value of the interest or interests acquired as mentioned in (b) above; and

(3)   the consideration (ie, in cash) received by any member of the A group for the acquisition of the interest or interests acquired by the acquiring company or acquiring companies as mentioned in (a) above, disregarding any *de minimis* amounts, either consists of, or is applied in acquiring, or consists partly of and as to the balance is applied in acquiring, the interest or interests acquired by members of the A group as mentioned in (b) above.

For the above purposes, the value of an interest is to be determined as at the date of its acquisition.

Notwithstanding the provisions of TCA 1997, s 616(1)(a) (see **9.202.2**), references to a company for the purposes of TCA 1997, s 624 includes references to a company which is not resident in a relevant Member State (TCA 1997, s 624(5)).

To summarise, to qualify as a merger, an arrangement must be on terms whereby a company ceases to be a member of a group, that the interest in the company's business is acquired by an outside company or companies, and that an interest or an equivalent value in the business or businesses of the acquiring company or companies is acquired by a member or members of the A group. At least 25% of the value of those interests must consist of ordinary shares with the remainder, in the case of the acquisition by the A group, consisting of share capital of any kind or debentures, or both.

Example 9.209.5.1

Hummingbird Ltd is the principal company of the Hummingbird group, comprising Hummingbird Ltd, Thrush Ltd and Sparrow Ltd. Hawk Ltd is the principal company of the

Hawk group, comprising Hawk Ltd, Kestrel Ltd and Peregrine Ltd. All companies are Irish resident and both groups are capital gains tax groups.

Under a merger arrangement, which is being entered into for *bona fide* commercial reasons not connected with tax avoidance, businesses valued at around €3.5m in each case and carried on by the subsidiaries of each group are to be merged and carried on as a joint venture. For this purpose, Hummingbird Ltd forms a new subsidiary, Robin Ltd and Hawk Ltd forms a new subsidiary, Harrier Ltd.

Thrush Ltd and Sparrow Ltd transfer to Robin Ltd the businesses carried on by them which are to be merged while Kestrel Ltd and Peregrine Ltd transfer to Harrier Ltd the businesses carried on by them which are to be merged.

Hummingbird Ltd exchanges 50% of its ordinary shares in Robin Ltd for 50% of the ordinary shares held by Hawk Ltd in Harrier Ltd.

The transfers of businesses to Robin Ltd and Harrier Ltd involve intra-group transfers which, by virtue of TCA 1997, s 617, give rise to neither a gain nor a loss. The exchange of the 50% shareholding interests is a merger within the meaning of TCA 1997, s 624. Accordingly, although this results in Robin Ltd leaving the Hummingbird group and Harrier Ltd leaving the Hawk group, there will be no retrospective charge under TCA 1997, s 623 in respect of the intra-group transfers.

9.209.6 Development land

TCA 1997, s 649(2) provides, *inter alia*, that TCA 1997 ss 623 and 624 are to apply, with any necessary modifications, to capital gains tax to which a company is chargeable on chargeable gains accruing to it on a disposal of development land as it would apply in relation to corporation tax on chargeable gains.

9.210 Shares in subsidiary member of group

TCA 1997, s 625 provides for situations involving tax avoidance similar to those dealt with by TCA 1997, s 623. A typical situation envisaged by the section would be a case in which a company (H) has a wholly owned subsidiary (S) the disposal of the shares in which would give rise to a chargeable gain. To avoid this charge, the company forms a further subsidiary (T) and transfers its shares in S to T in exchange for shares in T. No charge would arise in respect of this transfer and T would acquire the shares in S at their then market value (following TCA 1997, s 547). T then disposes of the shares in S without giving rise to a chargeable gain. The disposal proceeds would normally be passed back to H by way of loan.

TCA 1997, s 625 counters this device by providing that where a company leaves a group after its shares have been the subject of a share exchange within the group, the company which had on the earlier occasion disposed of the shares is deemed to have disposed of them and immediately reacquired them at that time at their then market value. In the above case, therefore, when the shares in S are sold by T, H would be deemed to have sold and immediately reacquired them at their market value at the time it had transferred them to T, thus crystallising the chargeable gain it had sought to avoid (but see below regarding the decision in *NAP Holdings*).

TCA 1997, s 625 applies where a company ("the subsidiary") ceases to be a member of a group of companies and, on "an earlier occasion", shares in the subsidiary were disposed of by another company ("the chargeable company") which was then a member of that group "in the course of an amalgamation or reconstruction in the group", provided the earlier occasion fell within the period of ten years ending with the date on which the subsidiary ceases to be a member of the group.

A company is not regarded as ceasing to be a member of a group for the purposes of TCA 1997, s 625 by being wound up or dissolved or in consequence of another member of the group being wound up or dissolved.

The chargeable company is treated for capital gains tax purposes as if immediately before the earlier occasion it had sold, and immediately reacquired, the shares in question at market value at that time (TCA 1997, s 625(2)).

Where, before the subsidiary ceases to be a member of the group, the chargeable company has ceased to exist (or a resolution has been passed or an order made for the winding up of the company, or any other act has been done for a similar purpose), any corporation tax to which it would have become chargeable under TCA 1997, s 625 had it continued in existence may be assessed and charged, in the name of the chargeable company, on the company which is, at the time when the subsidiary ceases to be a member of the group, the principal company of the group. If any such tax remains unpaid within six months from the date when it becomes payable, all or any part of that tax may within two years from the time it became payable be assessed and charged, in the name of the chargeable company, on:

(a)   a company which is, on the date the tax becomes due and payable, or was on the earlier occasion, the principal company of the group; or

(b)   any company taking an interest in the subsidiary as part of the amalgamation or reconstruction in the group (TCA 1997, s 625(4)).

A company which pays any amount of tax under TCA 1997, s 625(4) will be entitled to recover a sum of that amount from the chargeable company or, as the case may be, from the company assessed as above.

An assessment to corporation tax in accordance with TCA 1997, s 625 may be made at any time within ten years from the time when the subsidiary ceased to be a member of the group.

For the purposes of TCA 1997, s 625, there is a disposal of shares *in the course of an amalgamation or reconstruction in a group* of companies if TCA 1997, s 586 or 587 (see **9.404** and **9.405**) applies to shares in a company so as to equate them with shares or debentures of another company, and the companies are members of the same group, or become members of the same group as a result of the amalgamation or reconstruction.

Where, by virtue of TCA 1997, s 587, shares are to be treated as cancelled and replaced by a new issue, references to a disposal of shares include references to the occasion of their being so treated.

Interestingly, one implication of the decision in *NAP Holdings UK Ltd v Whittles* [1994] STC 979 would appear to be that TCA 1997, s 625 is for the most part an unnecessary measure. The point was taken up at the Court of Appeal stage in that appeal but was adequately addressed by Lord Keith in the House of Lords. (See **9.404.3** for a more detailed discussion on the interpretational difficulties of the relevant statutes.) In the situation discussed above involving H, S and T, the implication of the *NAP Holdings* decision is that the base cost of the S shares to T would be the same as their cost to H, so that T's disposal of them would result in a chargeable gain to T. This point was acknowledged by Nolan LJ in the Court of Appeal where he referred to apparent anomalies that would arise if the Crown's argument were correct (which, following the decision in the House of Lords, it subsequently proved to be). He referred in particular to [the UK equivalent of] TCA 1997, s 625 which he noted was designed as an anti-avoidance measure and which would be largely superfluous if the Crown's argument were to succeed.

TCA 1997, s 625 specifically provides that H is to be treated as having, at the time it transferred the S shares to T, disposed of them at their then market value thereby giving rise to a chargeable gain. That should mean that T would after all have acquired the shares at the same market value, which is in direct conflict with the position that emerges from the *NAP Holdings* judgment. A further consequence would be that H would then be deemed to have acquired its shares in T at market value. These anomalies cannot be dismissed but Lord Keith considered that the draftsman of TCA 1997, s 625 mistakenly believed that TCA 1997, s 617 did not apply to an intra-group share exchange, and that any anomalies do not disturb the overriding principle that gains and losses should be computed by reference to the consideration paid when an asset comes into the group and the consideration received when it goes out.

TCA 1997, s 649(2) provides, *inter alia*, that TCA 1997, s 625 is to apply, with any necessary modifications, to capital gains tax to which a company is chargeable on chargeable gains accruing to it on a disposal of development land as it would apply in relation to corporation tax on chargeable gains.

Effective 75% subsidiaries – company ceasing to be a group member

As from 11 February 1999, for the purpose of ascertaining whether or not a capital gains tax group exists, and in determining what companies are members of such a group, the provisions relating to "equity entitlement" for the purposes of group relief (see **8.340**) are applied by TCA 1997, s 616(1). Only "effective 75% subsidiaries" may be taken into account for that purpose (see **9.202.1**).

The more restricted definition of a capital gains tax group may mean that certain companies which were members of a group under the old definition (before the amendment of TCA 1997, s 616(1) by FA 1999) may cease to be such members by reason of not satisfying the equity entitlement tests. This will be true particularly of companies that never satisfied those tests and which, on 11 February 1999, ceased to be members of a capital gains tax group for that reason.

TCA 1997, s 625A is a transitional provision which deals with the case of a company ("the subsidiary" in TCA 1997, s 625(1)) ceasing to be a member of a group of companies by virtue only of the amendment of the definition of a capital gains tax group. The section applies where the "chargeable company" (in TCA 1997, s 625(1)) would for that reason be treated by TCA 1997, s 625(2) as selling shares in the subsidiary at any time. In those circumstances, TCA 1997, s 625(2) will not apply so that the chargeable company will not be treated as having sold and immediately reacquired the shares in the subsidiary at market value immediately before the time ("the earlier occasion") it had disposed of them by way of a share exchange within the group.

The TCA 1997, s 625(2) charge will not, however, be disapplied where, *on the basis of the old definition* of a group of companies (TCA 1997, s 616(1) before its amendment by FA 1990),

(a) the subsidiary ceases to be a member of the group; and

(b) the time of the earlier occasion fell within the period of ten years ending with the time the company ceases to be a group member.

In other words, the transitional relief will apply unless the company in question ceases to be a group member in accordance with the old definition (ie, as a result of some or all of its shares being disposed of to a non-group acquirer). Without this qualification, the TCA 1997, s 625(2) charge would not apply where, say, a company is deemed by virtue of the new definition to have ceased to be a member of a group of companies (the first event) but its shares are later disposed of outside the group (the second event). Since the company can only have left the group once, the TCA 1997, s 625(2) charge would not apply on the occasion of the second event. The qualification secures that the TCA 1997, s 625(2) charge will in fact apply on the happening of the second event.

9.211   Depreciatory transactions

9.211.1   Restriction of losses

A loss on the disposal of shares in a subsidiary company could, in the absence of anti-avoidance measures, be created artificially by transferring assets out of the company at an under-value or by "stripping" value out of it by means of a dividend prior to liquidation or before a sale of the shares in that subsidiary. TCA 1997 ss 621 and 622 are designed to deny such losses for corporation tax purposes.

Where a disposal of shares in a company results in a loss and, prior to the disposal and on or after 6 April 1974, there was an intra-group "depreciatory transaction" which materially reduced the value of the shares, the loss on the disposal may be reduced to such an amount as to the Inspector seems "just and reasonable". Where a gain subsequently arises on a disposal of the shares of the company that was party to the depreciatory transaction, the gain may be reduced by reference to the adjustment to the earlier loss, where the second disposal takes place within ten years after the depreciatory transaction.

TCA 1997, s 621 applies as respects a disposal of shares in, or securities of, a company (an "ultimate disposal") if the value of the shares or securities has been materially reduced by a depreciatory transaction effected on or after 6 April 1974. A *depreciatory transaction* means:

(a)   any disposal of assets at other than market value by one member of a group of companies to another; or

(b)   any other transaction satisfying the following conditions, namely, that:

  (i)   the company the shares in which, or securities of which, are the subject of the ultimate disposal, or any effective 75% subsidiary of that company, was a party to the transaction, and

  (ii)   the parties to the transaction were, or included, two or more companies which at the time of the transaction were members of the same group of companies (TCA 1997, s 621(3)).

The cancellation of any shares in or securities of one member of a group of companies under section 72 of the Companies Act 1963, is, to the extent that immediately before the cancellation those shares or securities were the property of another member of the group, to be taken to be a transaction satisfying the conditions in (b) above. Section 72(2)(b) of the Companies Act 1963, permits a limited company, subject to confirmation by the High Court and if so authorised by its articles, by special resolution to reduce its share capital by cancelling any paid up share capital which is lost or unrepresented by available assets. This may be done either with or without extinguishing or reducing the liability on any of its shares.

A transaction will not be treated as a depreciatory transaction to the extent that it consists of a payment which is required to be, or has been, brought into account for the purposes of corporation tax on chargeable gains, in computing a chargeable gain or allowable loss accruing to the person making the ultimate disposal (eg a capital distribution).

For the above purposes, *securities* includes any loan stock or similar security whether secured or unsecured (TCA 1997, s 621(1)). References to a disposal of shares or securities include references to the occasion of the making of a claim under TCA 1997, s 538(2) that the value of shares or securities has become negligible (see **9.102.3**), and references to a person making a disposal are to be construed accordingly (CTA 1976 s 138(8)).

A *group of companies* may consist of companies some or all of which are not resident for the purposes of tax in a relevant Member State (TCA 1997, s 621(1)). This is an exception to the rule that a group of companies for the purposes of companies' capital gains may consist only of companies resident in a relevant Member State (see **9.202.2**).

The tax consequences of a depreciatory transaction are dealt with in TCA 1997, s 621(6). If the company making the ultimate disposal is, or at any time has been, a member of the group of companies referred to above in the definition of "depreciatory transaction", any allowable loss accruing on the disposal is to be reduced to such extent as appears to the inspector, or on appeal the Appeal Commissioners, or on a rehearing by a judge of the Circuit Court, that judge, to be just and reasonable having regard to the transaction.

If, however, the company making the ultimate disposal is not a member of the group when it disposes of the shares or securities, no reduction of the loss is to be made by reference to a depreciatory transaction which took place when the company was not a member of the group. To be excluded from the effect of TCA 1997, s 621, therefore, the company making the ultimate disposal must not be a member of the group concerned in the depreciatory transaction either at the time of the transaction or at the time it makes the disposal.

As respects the opinion of the inspector, the Appeal Commissioners or the Circuit Court judge, as the case may be, as to what reduction should be made to the loss arising, TCA 1997, s 621(7) directs that the decision based on that opinion is to be made on the footing that the allowable loss ought not to reflect any diminution in the value of the company's assets which was attributable to a depreciatory transaction. Allowance may, however, be made for any other transaction which has enhanced the value of the company's assets and depreciated the value of the assets of any other member of the group.

Example 9.211.1.1

Frigate Ltd acquires a 75% interest (including equivalent equity entitlements) in Schooner Ltd for €250,000, the purchase price being based on the net value of the assets of that company. Shortly afterwards, Schooner Ltd transfers assets worth €150,000 to Sloop Ltd, another effective 75% subsidiary of Frigate Ltd, for €45,000. Frigate Ltd then sells its shares in Schooner Ltd for €145,000 thereby realising a loss of €105,000 on its cost of shares in that company.

The intra-group sale of the assets is a depreciatory transaction. The disposal of the shares in Schooner Ltd by Frigate Ltd is an "ultimate disposal". The allowable loss stands to be reduced by €105,000, the amount which represents the diminution in value of the shares in Schooner Ltd which is attributable to the depreciatory transaction.

Example 9.211.1.2

Harwood Ltd subscribed for 500,000 €1 shares in Ellwood Ltd, a newly formed subsidiary. Ellwood Ltd used the proceeds of the share issue to purchase a building for €500,000. Some years later, when the building is worth €800,000, it is transferred to Harwood Ltd for €100,000. Harwood Ltd then sells its shares in Ellwood Ltd for €100,000. It makes a claim in respect of an allowable loss of €400,000 on the disposal of the shares.

The transfer of the land worth €800,000 to Harwood Ltd for €100,000 is a depreciatory transaction. On the sale of the shares in Ellwood Ltd (an "ultimate disposal"), the loss of €400,000 stands to be reduced by €400,000 so that there is no allowable loss. Although the reduction in the value of the shares in Ellwood Ltd attributable to the depreciatory transaction is €700,000, TCA 1997, s 621 operates only to reduce an allowable loss so that the adjustment to be made is restricted to €400,000.

It should follow, where a depreciatory transaction occurs within a group of companies, that there will be a corresponding increase in value elsewhere in the group. To prevent an effective double charge to tax, it is provided that where a reduction to an allowable loss has been made, any chargeable gain accruing on a disposal of the shares or securities of any other company which was a party to the depreciatory transaction by reference to which the reduction was made, being a disposal not later than ten years after the transaction, is to be reduced to such extent as appears to the inspector, or on appeal the Appeal Commissioners, or on a rehearing by a judge of the Circuit Court, that judge, to be just and reasonable having regard to the effect of the depreciatory transaction on the value of those shares or securities at the time of their disposal (TCA 1997, s 621(8)). For this purpose, the total amount of any one or more reductions in chargeable gains made by reference to a depreciatory transaction may not exceed the amount of the reductions in allowable losses made by reference to that depreciatory transaction.

Example 9.211.1.3

The facts are as in Example **9.211.1.2** where it is seen that the depreciatory transaction results in an increase in value of €700,000 in the value of Harwood Ltd. If shares or securities in Harwood Ltd are subsequently disposed of, any chargeable gain accruing will fall to be reduced to such an extent as appears just and reasonable having regard to the effect of the depreciatory transaction on those shares or securities. It is not provided that the reduction should equal the reduction in the allowable loss on the earlier disposal.

The reduction in the allowable loss available to Harwood Ltd was €400,000, the maximum amount in this case since that was the amount of the loss. A just and reasonable reduction in the amount of any gain accruing on the disposal of the shares or securities in Harwood Ltd would also presumably be €400,000.

If a shareholder company holding 25% of the equity in Harwood Ltd disposes of its shares resulting in a gain of, say, €250,000, it would seem reasonable that that gain should be reduced by €100,000 (25% of the reduction in the earlier allowable loss) so that the final chargeable gain accruing to that company would be €150,000.

TCA 1997, s 649(2) provides, *inter alia*, that TCA 1997, s 621 is to apply, with any necessary modifications, to capital gains tax to which a company is chargeable on chargeable gains accruing to it on a disposal of development land as it would apply in relation to corporation tax on chargeable gains.

9.211.2 Dividend stripping

The dividend stripping anti-avoidance provision, TCA 1997, s 622, applies where 10% or more of the shares of any one class of a company are held on capital account (ie, other than in a share dealing capacity) by a corporate shareholder and where a dividend paid out prior to a disposal of the shares materially reduces their value. The obvious purpose of such a device is to create an artificial loss or to reduce a gain on the disposal of the shares. As with TCA 1997, s 621, however, TCA 1997, s 622 operates only to restrict a loss on the disposal of shares and it has no effect where a gain accrues. TCA 1997, s 622 provides that a dividend paid in the above-described circumstances is to be regarded as a depreciatory transaction under TCA 1997, s 621 and any loss arising on the disposal of the shares falls to restricted accordingly.

Since according to TCA 1997, s 616(1)(a) a reference to a "company" in TCA 1997 Part 20 Chapter 1 (which includes TCA 1997, s 622) is to a company tax resident in an EU Member State, it would seem to follow that holdings in EU resident companies, and those companies only, are affected. Prior to FA 2001, the corresponding reference was to Irish resident companies. It is doubtful that the change was intended as it is not clear why holdings in EU and non-EU resident companies should be distinguished for the purposes of TCA 1997, s 622.

TCA 1997, s 622 applies where one company ("the first company") has a holding in another company ("the second company") and the following conditions are fulfilled:

(a) the holding amounts to, or is an ingredient in a holding (see below) amounting to, 10% of all holdings of the same class in the second company;

(b) the first company is not a dealing company in relation to the holding (see below);

(c) a distribution is or has been made on or after 6 April 1974 to the first company in respect of the holding; and

(d) the effect of the distribution is that the value of the holding is or has been materially reduced.

As respects (d), no description is supplied as to what constitutes "materially reduced". Where, in the manner described above, TCA 1997, s 622 applies in relation to a holding, TCA 1997, s 621 is to apply in relation to any disposal of any shares or securities comprised in that holding, whether the disposal is by the first company or by any other company to which the holding is transferred by a transfer to which TCA 1997, s 617 applies, as if the distribution were a depreciatory transaction and, if the companies concerned are not members of a group of companies, as if they were group members (TCA 1997, s 622(2)).

A distribution will not be treated as a depreciatory transaction to the extent that it consists of a payment which is required to be, or has been, brought into account for the purposes of corporation tax on chargeable gains, in computing a chargeable gain or allowable loss accruing to the person making the ultimate disposal (eg a capital distribution).

In (b) above, a company is a *dealing company* in relation to a holding if a profit on the sale of the holding would be taken into account in computing the company's trading profits (TCA 1997, s 622(4)).

References to a *holding* in a company are to a holding of shares or securities by virtue of which the holder may receive distributions made by the company but:

(1)   a company's holdings of different classes in another company are to be treated as separate holdings; and

(2)   holdings of shares or securities which differ in the entitlements or obligations they confer or impose are to be regarded as holdings of different classes (TCA 1997, s 622(5)).

For the purposes of (a) above:

(i)   all of a company's holdings of the same class in another company are to be treated as ingredients constituting a single holding; and

(ii)   a company's holding of any one class is to be treated as an ingredient in a holding amounting to 10% of all holdings of that class if the aggregate of that holding and other holdings of that class held by "connected persons" (within the meaning of TCA 1997, s 10 – see **2.3**) amount to 10% of all holdings of that class (TCA 1997, s 622(6)).

Example 9.211.2.1

Steiger Ltd owns all of the issued share capital in Cooper Ltd. The shares were purchased for €220,000 but are now worth €620,000. Steiger Ltd intends to dispose of Cooper Ltd but first procures that a dividend of €500,000 is paid out of that company. By virtue of TCA 1997, s 129, Steiger Ltd is not taxable in respect of the dividend (see **3.205**). If Steiger Ltd is a close company, the dividend may give rise to a surcharge on undistributed investment income (see **10.302**).

Steiger Ltd then sells the shares in Cooper Ltd to an outside company for €120,000. It claims an allowable loss of €100,000 (€220,000 - €120,000).

The effect of the dividend payment undoubtedly is that the value of Steiger Ltd's holding in Cooper Ltd is materially reduced. As such the dividend payment constitutes a depreciatory transaction and the loss of €100,000 will not be an allowable loss of Steiger Ltd.

It is notable in the above example that the potential chargeable gain of €400,000 is avoided as only losses are affected by TCA 1997, s 622. There are indications that the stripping of genuine post-acquisition reserves constitutes "acceptable" tax planning. Of course it will not always be practicable to arrange for a subsidiary to pay the required pre-sale dividend as it may not have sufficient distributable reserves for the purpose. A device which could formerly have been availed of would involve the subsidiary itself acquiring a subsidiary to which it would then transfer assets for the purpose of generating liquid reserves in order to facilitate the payment of the pre-sale dividend. This strategy would now effectively be blocked by the operation of TCA 1997, s 623(3).

As discussed in **9.209.3**, TCA 1997, s 623(3) contains an anti-avoidance measure directed at attempts to reduce the value of a subsidiary before its disposal outside a group. It applies where two or more associated companies cease to be members of a group of companies and a dividend has been paid by one of those companies to another company wholly or partly out of profits derived from the disposal of any asset by one to another of the associated companies. To the extent that the dividend or distribution was derived from those profits, it is deemed for capital gains tax purposes to be consideration (or additional consideration as the case may be) received by the company which disposed of the shares in the company which paid the dividend or made the distribution.

TCA 1997, s 649(2) provides, *inter alia*, that TCA 1997, s 622 is to apply, with any necessary modifications, to capital gains tax to which a company is chargeable on chargeable gains accruing to it on a disposal of development land as it would apply in relation to corporation tax on chargeable gains.

9.211.3   Pre-sale dividend

Certain dividends paid, or distributions made, on or after 19 February 2008 in connection with the sale of shares may be regarded as part of the consideration for the disposal of those shares. This treatment applies to so-called "abnormal" dividends or distributions and is not confined to dividends or distributions to the shareholders of the company whose shares are being disposed of.

A dividend paid, or a distribution made, by a company to a person in respect of shares or securities of a company in connection with a disposal of shares in that company will be treated as being *abnormal* if the amount or value of the dividend or distribution exceeds the amount that could reasonably have been expected to be paid, or made, in respect of the shares or securities of the company if there were no such disposal of those shares or securities (TCA 1997, s 591A(1)).

Where, in connection with the disposal by a person of any shares or securities of a company, there exists any scheme, arrangement or understanding by virtue of which, either directly or indirectly, an abnormal dividend is paid, or an abnormal distribution is made—

(a)   where the person is a company, to that person or to any company connected (within the meaning of TCA 1997, s 10 – see **2.302**) with that person, and

(b)   where the person is not a company, to any company connected with the person,

the amount or value of the dividend or distribution will be treated for the purposes of the Capital Gains Tax Acts (ie, enactments relating to capital gains tax – see **2.2**) as consideration received by the person for the disposal of the shares or securities, and will be ignored for the purposes of the Tax Acts (ie, enactments relating to income tax and corporation tax – see **2.2**) (TCA 1997, s 591A(2)).

The above-described treatment will not apply if it is shown that the scheme, arrangement or understanding is effected for bona fide commercial reasons and is not, or does not form part of, any scheme, arrangement or understanding of which the main purpose or one of the main purposes is avoidance of liability to tax (TCA 1997, s 591A(3)).

9.212   Pre-entry losses

9.212.1   Introduction

TCA 1997, s 626A and Schedule 18A restrict the use of capital gains tax losses incurred by and subsequently brought into a group by a new member, as well as losses realised by a company after joining a group which result from disposals of assets ("pre-entry assets") brought into the group. Both kinds of loss are referred to as "pre-entry losses". TCA 1997, s 626A applies in the case of a company which becomes a member of a group of companies on or after 1 March 1999.

The restrictions on the use of pre-entry losses apply whether the company which has incurred the losses is acquired by a group for tax avoidance reasons or for purely commercial reasons. Prior to 1 March 1999, it was possible for a group to take advantage of the TCA 1997, s 617 treatment of intra-group transfers of assets (no gain/

no loss – see **9.230**) by transferring assets with potential gains to a newly acquired capital loss company and subsequently disposing of those assets outside the group.

A pre-entry loss may be set against a gain—

(a) on a disposal made by the loss company before the date it entered the group (the "entry date") but made within the same accounting period in which the entry date falls;

(b) on a disposal of an asset held by that company immediately before the entry date; or

(c) on a disposal by the company of an asset acquired from a non-group member on or after the entry date if the asset has been used or held only for the purposes of a trade carried on by the company immediately before the entry date and carried on continuously up to the date of disposal. (See **9.212.5** for more detailed treatment.)

Example 9.212.1.1

Raleigh Ltd becomes a member of the Saladin group at a time when it has unused capital gains tax losses of €320,000. Rudge Ltd, another member of the Saladin group, is about to dispose of an asset with a potential capital gain of €220,000 but instead transfers it to Raleigh Ltd. The disposal to Raleigh Ltd results in neither a gain nor a loss for tax purposes. Raleigh Ltd then disposes of the asset to the intended buyer outside the group.

The chargeable gain on the disposal by Raleigh Ltd is €220,000. No part of the loss of €320,000 may be set against this gain.

Where a new member of a capital gains tax group disposes of a pre-entry asset at a loss, the loss is apportioned (see **9.212.4**) and the pre-entry loss, being the proportion of the loss attributed to the pre-entry period, is restricted in the way indicated above.

Example 9.212.1.2

The position is as in Example **9.212.1.1** except that, instead of having a loss at the time it joins the Saladin group, Raleigh Ltd has an asset with an unrealised loss. Some time after joining the group, it disposes of the asset at a loss of €290,000. The pre-entry proportion of this loss is €180,000.

Only €110,000, the post-entry proportion of the loss, may be set against the chargeable gain of €220,000.

TCA 1997 Sch 18A has no effect in relation to gains arising from disposals of pre-entry assets.

Example 9.212.1.3

The position is as in Example **9.212.1.2** except that, at the time of joining the Saladin group, Raleigh Ltd has an asset with an unrealised gain and Rudge Ltd has existing capital gains tax losses of €80,000. After joining the group, Raleigh Ltd transfers its asset to Rudge Ltd and Rudge Ltd disposes of the asset outside the group. The gain arising on the disposal is €170,000.

The loss of €80,000 is set against the gain of €170,000 resulting in a chargeable gain of €90,000.

Neither does TCA 1997 Sch 18A prevent the use of a capital gains tax loss in a situation in which a company with an unrealised gain is acquired by a group (or company) which has unrealised losses.

Example 9.212.1.4

Assume that Rudge Ltd in the preceding examples has an asset with an unrealised capital gains tax loss. Raleigh Ltd is acquired by the Saladin group at a time when it has an asset with an unrealised capital gain of €430,000. Shortly afterwards, Rudge Ltd transfers its asset to Raleigh Ltd and Raleigh Ltd disposes of both assets outside the group realising a loss of €360,000 and a gain of €430,000.

The loss of €360,00 may be set against the gain of €430,000.

Even where a gain has been realised by the new group member before it joins the group, a group loss may be set against the gain but provided both the gain and the loss arise (to the new member) in the same accounting period.

Example 9.212.1.5

Assume that Rudge Ltd in the preceding examples has an asset with an unrealised capital gains tax loss. Raleigh Ltd disposes of an asset realising a chargeable gain of €430,000. In the same accounting period in which this gain is realised, Raleigh Ltd is acquired by the Saladin group. Again in the same accounting period, Rudge Ltd transfers its asset to Raleigh Ltd. Still later in the accounting period, Raleigh Ltd disposes of the asset outside the group realising a loss of €360,000.

The loss of €360,000 may be set against the gain of €430,000.

9.212.2 Definitions

Relevant group

The pre-entry loss rules concern losses that arise to a company prior to that company becoming a member of a capital gains tax group. The rules therefore require that any pre-entry loss must relate to some group and that group is the relevant group. Accordingly, the relevant group means the group of companies of which the loss-making company is or has been a member (TCA 1997 Sch 18A paragraph 1(1)).

The reference to the group of which the loss-making company "has been" a member is important as former membership of a group may be significant in certain circumstances.

Example 9.212.2.1

Glen Ltd incurs a capital gains tax loss and later becomes a member of the Valley group. Glen Ltd then acquires an asset from Dale Ltd, another member of the Valley group. Later still, both Glen Ltd and Dale Ltd are acquired by the Delta group. Glen Ltd disposes of the asset it had acquired from Dale Ltd, resulting in a gain.

If the Delta group were the only relevant group, there would be no restriction on the use of the pre-entry loss of Glen Ltd against the gain realised by it (since that gain would have arisen prior to Glen Ltd becoming a member of the relevant group – see (b) in **9.212.1**). Because the Valley group is a group of which Glen Ltd has been a member, however, it is also a relevant group and the loss falls to be restricted.

Pre-entry loss

A pre-entry loss in relation to a company means—

    (a)   an allowable loss that accrued to the company at a time before it became a member of the relevant group in so far as the loss has not been allowed as a deduction from chargeable gains accruing to the company prior to that time; or

(b)   the pre-entry proportion of an allowable loss (see **9.212.4**) accruing to the company on the disposal of a pre-entry asset (TCA 1997 Sch 18A paragraph 1(2)).

In determining whether an allowable loss accruing to a company on a disposal under TCA 1997, s 719 (deemed disposal and reacquisition of certain assets by life assurance companies – see **12.603.2**) or 738(4)(a) (deemed disposal and reacquisition of assets by undertakings for collective investment – see **12.805.4**) is a loss that accrued before the company became a member of the relevant group, the provisions of TCA 1997, s 720 or 738(4)(b) (gain or loss spread over seven years), as the case may be, are to be disregarded (TCA 1997 Sch 18A paragraph 1(9)). Accordingly, the loss so accruing is deemed to have accrued at the time of the transaction in question.

9.212.3   Pre-entry asset

In relation to a disposal, a *pre-entry asset* means an asset that was held at the time immediately before the relevant event occurred in relation to it by a company which is or was a member of the relevant group (TCA 1997 Sch 18A paragraph 1(3)).

References to *the relevant event occurring in relation to a company*—

(i)   in a case in which—

(I)   the company was resident in the State at the time when it became a member of the relevant group, or

(II)   the asset was a chargeable asset in relation to the company at that time,

are references to the company becoming a member of that group, and

(ii) in a case in which (whether or not (i)(I) above also applies)—

(I)   the company is an SE (European Company – see **9.301**) or an SCE (European Cooperative Society – see **9.301**) resident in Ireland, and

(II)   the asset was transferred to—

(A)   the SE as part of the process of its formation by the merger by acquisition of two or more companies in accordance with Articles 2(1) and 17(2)(a) or (b) of the SE Regulation (within the meaning of TCA 1997, s 630) (Council Regulation (EC) No 2157/2001 of 8 October 2001, on the Statute for a European Company (SE)), or

(B)   the SCE as part of the process of its formation by merger in accordance with Article 2 of the SCE Regulation (within the meaning of TCA 1997, s 630) (Council Regulation (EC) No 1435/2003 of 22 July 2003 on the Statute for a European Cooperative Society (SCE)),

are references to the asset becoming a chargeable asset in relation to the SE or the SCE or, if at the time of the formation of the SE or the SCE the asset was a chargeable asset in relation to a company which ceased to exist as part of the process of the formation of the SE or the SCE, to the asset becoming a chargeable asset in relation to that company,

(iii)   in any other case, are references to whichever is the first of—

    (I)   the company becoming resident in the State, or

    (II)   the asset becoming a chargeable asset in relation to the company (TCA 1997 Sch 18A paragraph 1(3A)).

An asset is a *chargeable asset* in relation to a company at any time if, were it to be disposed of by the company at that time or, if the company is an SE or an SCE, by reason of the asset having been transferred to the SE or the SCE on its formation, any gain accruing to the company would be a chargeable gain. A chargeable gain will arise to a non-resident company only in respect of disposals of certain categories of assets (eg, Irish based land, shares deriving their value or the greater part of their value from such land, Irish based assets used in an Irish branch trade – see **9.102.2**).

In the majority of cases, the concept of a pre-entry asset relates to an asset held by a company just before it became a member of a group. Where, however, the company was not an Irish resident company and the asset was not a chargeable asset in relation to it, a pre-entry asset is an asset held by the company just before it became Irish resident or the asset became a chargeable asset in relation to the company, whichever is the earlier.

The above definition, however, is subject to TCA 1997 Sch 18A paragraph 1(4) which provides that an asset is not a pre-entry asset in relation to a disposal where—

(a)   the company which held the asset at the time the relevant event occurred in relation to it is not the company which makes the disposal; and

(b)   since that time the asset has been disposed of (otherwise than by way of an intra-group disposal to which TCA 1997, s 617 (see **9.203**) applies);

but (without prejudice to TCA 1997 Sch 18A paragraph 1(8) – see Assets derived from other assets below) where, on a disposal to which TCA 1997, s 617 does not apply, an asset would otherwise cease to be a pre-entry asset and the company making the disposal retains any interest in or over the asset, that interest will be a pre-entry asset.

A pre-entry asset is one that was held by "a company" and therefore not necessarily the company making the disposal. The definition is therefore sufficiently wide to cover a situation in which a pre-entry asset may be disposed of within a group before being disposed of outside the group at a loss, so that the company which disposed of it was not the company which brought it into the group.

The exception in TCA 1997 Sch 18A paragraph 1(4) takes into account the possibility that an asset disposed of outside a group might later be re-acquired by the group and later again be disposed of outside the group at a loss. In that case, provided the company making the second disposal is not the company that brought the asset into the group on the first occasion, the asset is not a pre-entry asset in relation to that disposal.

Example 9.212.3.1

At the time of joining the Nobel group, Mujen Ltd has a property with an unrealised loss. After joining the group, Mujen Ltd disposes of the property to Bosch Ltd, another member of the Nobel group. Bosch Ltd sells the property to a non-group member, Warren Ltd, for €240,000 realising a loss of €560,000. The pre-entry proportion of the loss is €500,000. Of the loss of €560,000, €500,000 may not be set against any chargeable gain of Bosch Ltd.

Later, Bosch Ltd re-acquires the property from Warren Ltd for €240,000. Some years later, Bosch Ltd disposes of the property outside the group for €80,000.

In relation to this second disposal, the property is not a pre-entry asset. The loss of €160,000 may therefore be set against any chargeable gain of Bosch Ltd.

The qualification to TCA 1997 Sch 18A paragraph 1(4) envisages a part disposal. If the first disposal outside the group is a part disposal, so that the company making the disposal retains an interest in it, that interest is a pre-entry asset.

Example 9.212.3.2

The position is as in Example **9.212.3.1** except that, after joining the Nobel group, Mujen Ltd sells a half interest in the property to a non-group purchaser, Hutton Ltd, for €120,000. The disposal of the half interest is a part disposal and the resulting loss is calculated at €280,000 of which the pre-entry proportion is €250,000.

Of the loss of €280,000, €30,000 may be set against any chargeable gain of Mujen Ltd but the remaining €250,000 may only be utilised by Mujen Ltd in one of the circumstances referred to in (a) to (c) in **9.212.1** above (and **9.212.5** below).

Later, Bosch Ltd purchases the half interest in the property from Hutton Ltd for €130,000 as well as the other half interest from Mujen Ltd. Some time later, Bosch Ltd disposes of the entire property outside the group for €80,000.

In relation to this second disposal of the property, one half interest is, and one half interest is not, a pre-entry asset. Only the loss resulting from the disposal of the half interest acquired from Hutton Ltd (€130,000 – €40,000) may be set against a chargeable gain of Bosch Ltd.

Assets derived from other assets

Where the value of an asset held in a group of companies (or held by a former member of the group) is derived wholly or partly from the value of a pre-entry asset, both assets are pre-entry assets. This applies in particular where a lease is a pre-entry asset and the lessee acquires the reversionary interest. It will also apply in a case where, under capital gains tax "reorganisation" provisions, an asset held at a later time and an asset held at an earlier time are treated as the same asset (see **9.402-405**).

TCA 1997 Sch 18A paragraph 1(8) provides that for the purposes of TCA 1997 Sch 18A—

(a) an asset (the "first asset") acquired or held by a company at any time and an asset (the "second asset") held at a later time by the company (or by any company which is or has been a member of the same group of companies as the company) is to be treated as the same asset if the value of the second asset is derived in whole or in part from the first asset; and

(b) where—

    (i) an asset is treated (whether by virtue of (a) or otherwise) as the same as the asset held by a company at a later time, and

    (ii) the first asset would have been a pre-entry asset in relation to the company,

the second asset is to be treated as a pre-entry asset in relation to the company.

The treatment described in (a) above is to apply in particular where the second asset is a freehold and the first asset is a leasehold the lessee of which acquires the reversion.

The relevant time

In relation to a pre-entry asset, *the relevant time* means the time when the relevant event occurred in relation to that company by reference to which that asset is a pre-entry asset and for the purposes of TCA 1997 Sch 18A—

(a) where a relevant event has occurred in relation to a company on more than one occasion, an asset is a pre-entry asset by reference to the company if the asset would be a pre-entry asset by reference to the company in respect of any one of those occasions; and

(b) references to the time when a relevant event occurred in relation to a company, in relation to assets held on more than one such occasion as is mentioned in (a), are references to the later or latest of those occasions (TCA 1997 Sch 18A paragraph 1(5)).

9.212.4 Pre-entry proportion of loss

The pre-entry proportion of an allowable loss cannot exceed an amount calculated by reference to the market value of the pre-entry asset at the relevant time (the time the loss company becomes a member of the relevant group).

Where an allowable loss accrues on the disposal by a company of any pre-entry asset, the pre-entry proportion of that loss is the lesser of—

(a) the amount of the allowable loss which would have accrued if the asset had been disposed of at the relevant time at its market value at that time; and

(b) the amount of the allowable loss accruing on the disposal (TCA 1997 Sch 18A paragraph 2).

9.212.5 Gains from which pre-entry losses are deductible

The kinds of gains from which pre-entry losses may be deducted were outlined in **9.212.1** and are described in more detail here. The position governing a pre-entry loss and that governing the pre-entry proportion of an allowable loss are dealt with separately.

Pre-entry loss

A pre-entry loss that accrued to a company on a disposal before the company became a member of the relevant group may only be deducted from a chargeable gain accruing to the company where the gain is one accruing—

(a) on a disposal made by the company before the date ("the entry date") on which the company became a member of the relevant group and made in the same accounting period in which the entry date falls;

(b) on the disposal of an asset which was held by the company (or by an associated company – see under *Associated companies* below) immediately before the entry date; or

(c) on the disposal of an asset which—

(i) was acquired by the company (or by an associated company – see under *Associated companies* below) on or after the entry date from a person who was not a member of the relevant group at the time of the acquisition, and

(ii)   since its acquisition from that person has not been used or held for any purposes other than those of a trade which was being carried on by the company at the time immediately before the entry date and which continued to be carried on by the company until the disposal (TCA 1997 Sch 18A paragraph 3(1)).

Pre-entry proportion of allowable loss

Similarly, the pre-entry proportion of an allowable loss accruing to a company on the disposal of a pre-entry asset may only be deducted from a chargeable gain accruing to the company where—

(a)   the gain is one accruing on a disposal made by the company before the entry date and made in the same accounting period in which the entry date falls and the company is the one ("the initial company") by reference to which the asset disposed of at a loss is a pre-entry asset;

(b)   the pre-entry asset and the asset on the disposal of which the gain accrues were each held by the same company (or by associated companies – see under *Associated companies* below) at a time immediately before the company became a member of the relevant group; or

(c)   the gain is one accruing on the disposal of an asset which—

(i)   was acquired by the initial company (or by an associated company – see under *Associated companies* below) (whether before or after the initial company became a member of the relevant group) from a person who, at the time of the acquisition, was not a member of that group, and

(ii)   since its acquisition from that person has not been used or held for any purposes other than those of a trade which was being carried on, immediately before the entry date, by the initial company and which continued to be carried on by that company until the disposal (TCA 1997 Sch 18A paragraph 3(2)).

The application of the above rules is illustrated in Examples **9.212.1.1–9.212.1.5**.

For the purposes of (c) above (both in relation to a pre-entry loss and the pre-entry proportion of an allowable loss), if within three years a company becomes a member of a relevant group and there is a major change in the nature or conduct of the trade, or if the loss company's trade was small or negligible at the time it joined the group, the trade is disregarded. This provision is similar to that in TCA 1997, s 401 (disallowance of trading losses on change of ownership – see **4.110** for this and references to relevant case law relating to "major change" in a company's trade).

TCA 1997 Sch 18A paragraph 4(1) provides that, for the purposes of (c) above (both in relation to a pre-entry loss and the pre-entry proportion of an allowable loss), where—

(a)   within any period of three years a company becomes a member of a group of companies and there is (either earlier or later in that period, or at the same time) a major change in the nature or conduct of a trade carried on by the company; or

(b)   at any time after the scale of the activities in a trade carried on by a company has become small or negligible and, before any considerable revival of the trade, the company becomes a member of a group of companies, the trade carried on before the change mentioned in (a) or, as the case may be, the trade mentioned in (b), is to be disregarded in relation to any time before the company became a member of the group in question.

A major change in the nature or conduct of a trade includes—

(a) a major change in the type of property dealt in, or services or facilities provided, in the trade; or

(b) a major change in customers, markets or outlets of the trade,

and this will be the case even if the change is the result of a gradual process which began outside the period of three years mentioned above.

In (c) above (both in relation to a pre-entry loss and the pre-entry proportion of an allowable loss), it is seen that (c)(ii) in each case requires that the asset disposed of must have been "used or held" only for a trade carried on by the company which acquired it. That condition would not, it appears, be fulfilled in a case where the asset is disposed of intra-group and leased back to the acquiring company. Although the asset would continue to be used for the trade of that company, it would now also be "held" for the purposes of the lessor company's business. (This problem would not, however, arise in some circumstances involving certain associated companies – see *Associated companies* below)

Associated companies

TCA 1997 Sch 18A paragraph 3(3) deals with the situation in which two or more companies join a relevant group at the same time and those companies (for convenience, referred to here as "associated companies") were all members of the same group of companies immediately before they became members of the relevant group. In any such case—

(a) an asset is to be treated for the purposes of TCA 1997 Sch 18A paragraph 3(1)(b) (see (b) above under *Pre-entry loss*) as held, immediately before the company became a member of the relevant group, by the company to which the pre-entry loss in question accrued if the company is one of those companies and the asset was in fact so held by another of those companies;

(b) two or more assets are to be treated for the purposes of TCA 1997 Sch 18A paragraph 3(2)(b) (see (b) above under *Pre-entry proportion of allowable loss*) as assets held by the same company immediately before the company became a member of the relevant group wherever they would be so treated if all those companies were treated as a single company; and

(c) the acquisition of an asset is to be treated for the purposes of TCA 1997 Sch 18A(1)(c) and (2)(c) (see (c) above in each of *Pre-entry loss* and *Pre-entry proportion of allowable loss*) as an acquisition by the company to which the pre-entry loss in question accrued if the company is one of those companies and the asset was in fact acquired (whether before or after those companies became members of the relevant group) by another of those companies.

Example 9.212.5.1

Leigh Ltd and Gable Ltd are members of the Academy group. Both companies become members of the Templeton group at the same time and at which time Leigh Ltd owns an asset with an unrealised loss and Gable Ltd owns an asset with an unrealised gain. Leigh Ltd disposes of its asset to Gable Ltd. Gable Ltd sells both assets outside the Templeton group, realising a loss on the asset originally owned by Leigh Ltd and a gain on the other asset.

The pre-entry proportion of the loss may be set against the gain on the other asset.

The position would have been the same had Gable Ltd disposed of its asset intra- group to Leigh Ltd with Leigh Ltd disposing of both assets outside the group.

As was seen in **9.212.3**, the definition of "pre-entry asset" is sufficiently wide to cover the situation in which a pre-entry asset may be disposed of within a group before being disposed of outside the group at a loss, so that the company which disposes of it is not the company which brought it into the group. The following example is a slight variation on the previous example and considers the position where the company disposing of the asset outside the relevant group is neither of the associated companies.

Example 9.212.5.2

Leigh Ltd and Gable Ltd, members of the Academy group, become members of the Templeton group at the same time and when Leigh Ltd owns an asset with an unrealised loss and Gable Ltd owns an asset with an unrealised gain. Both assets are transferred to Finch Ltd, a member of the Templeton group. Finch Ltd later sells the assets outside the Templeton group, realising a loss on the pre-entry asset and a gain on the other asset.

The pre-entry proportion of the loss may be set against the gain on the other asset.

It is important to note, in relation to (a) above, that the legislation does no more than to treat the asset in question (on the disposal of which the gain arises) as having been held by the company which incurred the pre-entry loss at the time that company joined the relevant group (thus enabling the pre-entry loss to be set against the gain on that asset). It does not, for example, treat the chargeable gain arising on the disposal of the asset as arising to any company other than the company to which it actually arises. Accordingly, where two associated companies join a group together and one has a pre-entry loss, that loss may not be set against a gain arising to the other company in respect of an asset held by it at the entry date.

Example 9.212.5.3

Leigh Ltd and Gable Ltd, members of the Academy group, become members of the Templeton group at the same time and when Leigh Ltd has a pre-entry loss and Gable Ltd owns an asset with an unrealised gain. Gable Ltd sells its asset outside the Templeton group, realising a gain on the disposal.

The pre-entry proportion of the loss may not be set against the gain on the other asset. This is because the loss and the gain have arisen to different companies; there is no question of the gain realised by Gable Ltd being treated as having been realised by Leigh Ltd.

9.212.6   Companies changing groups on certain transfers of shares etc

Two kinds of reconstruction are treated for the purposes of TCA 1997 Sch 18A as not resulting in the creation of a relevant group. One of these involves a new shell company becoming a holding company by means of a share for share exchange (see **9.212.7**). In the other kind of reconstruction, shares in a subsidiary company within a group are transferred to another company in consideration, say, for that company issuing shares to the company which owned the shares in that subsidiary. Alternatively, both the subsidiary and its holding company might be transferred to another company in consideration for the issue of shares by the acquiring company to the owners of the shares in the holding company.

TCA 1997 Sch 18A paragraph 5 provides that where—

(a)   a company which is a member of a group of companies becomes at any time a member of another group of companies as the result of a disposal of shares in or other securities of the company or any other company; and

(b)   that disposal is one on which, by virtue of any provision of the Tax Acts or the Capital Gains Tax Acts, neither a gain nor a loss would accrue,

the pre-entry loss provisions are to apply in relation to the losses that accrued to the company before that time and the assets held by the company at that time as if any time when the company was a member of the first group were included in the period during which the company is treated as having been a member of the second group.

As seen in (b) above, the disposals in question are those on which neither a gain nor a loss would accrue. Provisions which operate in this way include TCA 1997 ss 615 (reconstruction or amalgamation involving transfer of undertaking – see **9.207.2-9.207.4**), 617 (intra-group transfers of assets – see **9.203**) and 702 (union or amalgamation of societies – see **12.201**). Of these, it would seem that only TCA 1997, s 615 is relevant here.

As was noted in **9.207.3**, an undertaking may include shares held by a company in active subsidiaries. Accordingly, TCA 1997 Sch 18A paragraph 5 would be relevant in a case where, say, the shares in a member of a group of companies are transferred to a company in another group in consideration for the issue of shares by the acquiring company to the company which held the shares in the company being transferred. Alternatively, the shares in the holding company ("any other company" in (a) above) of a member of a group of companies (with of course the shares in the member company itself) might be so transferred, the consideration being the issue of shares in the acquiring company to the shareholders of the holding company. If in the course of a scheme of reconstruction or amalgamation, that transaction would result in neither a gain nor a loss accruing on the disposal of the shares in question.

As regards any pre-entry losses and any pre-entry assets of the member company which had accrued before, or were held at, the time it became a member of the second group, any time when the company was a member of the first group is treated as included in the period during which it is treated as having been a member of the second group. In other words, the occasion of the company becoming a member of the second group is not treated as involving the creation of a relevant group. The same position would apply in relation to any pre-entry losses or assets of the holding company mentioned above.

9.212.7   Takeovers

It is important, in the context of the legislation on pre-entry losses, to be able to identify the point (the "relevant time") at which a company has joined a relevant group. This will be necessary for the purpose of determining whether a loss has accrued before the company joined that group or, where a loss arises on the disposal of an asset which the company had before the entry date, the pre-entry proportion of that loss.

Where the principal company of a capital gains tax group is acquired by another company, so that the members of the first-mentioned group become members of the enlarged group, TCA 1997, s 616(3) (see **9.202.3**) or, in a case involving an SE or an SCE, 616(3A) (see **9.202.2**), treats the first group and the enlarged group as the same group. That provision, if not qualified in the context of the pre-entry loss rules, would make those rules unworkable in certain circumstances. Accordingly it is provided in TCA 1997 Sch 18A paragraph 1(6) that where—

(a)   the principal company of a group of companies ("the first group) has at any time become a member of another group ("the second group") so that the two groups are treated as the same by virtue of TCA 1997, s 616(3) or (3A); and

(b)   the second group, together in pursuance of TCA 1997, s 616(3) with first group, is the relevant group,

then, except where TCA 1997 Sch 18A paragraph 1(7) applies (see below), the members of the first group are to be treated as having become members of the relevant group at that time, and not by virtue of TCA 1997, s 616(3) at the times when they became members of the first group.

Since the effect of TCA 1997, s 616(3) is to treat the first group and the enlarged group as the same group, the members of the first group would, in the absence of special provision, not be treated as joining any group at the time they became members of the second group. The intention of the pre-entry loss rules is that they should in fact be so treated as joining the relevant group, being the second group in this instance.

Example 9.212.7.1

Saxon Ltd, the principal company of the Saxon group, disposes of an asset resulting in a capital gains tax loss. Later, the shares in Saxon Ltd are acquired by Hausen Ltd, a member of the Uhlan group. TCA 1997, s 616(3) treats the Saxon group and the new Uhlan group as the same group. Accordingly, since Saxon Ltd would not then have joined any group, its realised loss would not be subject to the pre-entry loss rules.

TCA 1997, Sch 18A paragraph 1(6), however, treats the members of the Saxon group as having joined the deemed enlarged group at the time Saxon Ltd was acquired by Hausen Ltd (and not when it had joined the Saxon group).

The following example deals with the kind of situation that arose in the case of *Five Oaks Properties Ltd and others v HMRC* SCD 2006 769.

Example 9.212.7.2

Saxon Ltd disposes of an asset resulting in a capital gains tax loss and in year 2 becomes a member of the Uhlan group. In year 3, Hausen Ltd, already a member of that group, disposes of an asset resulting in a capital gains tax loss. In year 4, the Uhlan group is acquired by the Masurian group. TCA 1997, s 616(3) treats the Uhlan group and the Masurian group as the same group (the "relevant group") but TCA 1997, Sch 18A paragraph 1(6) treats the members of the former Uhlan group as having joined the relevant group in year 4 (and not when they had joined the Uhlan group).

The loss realised by Hausen Ltd is a pre-entry loss relative to the Masurian group: despite TCA 1997, s 616(3), deeming both groups to be the one group, Hausen Ltd is treated as having joined the relevant group only in year 4 so that the use of the loss within that group is restricted.

What then is the position relating to the earlier loss, the loss incurred by Saxon Ltd? The use of that loss would have been restricted within the Uhlan group. But TCA 1997, Sch 18A paragraph 1(6) appears to say that Saxon Ltd only joined the relevant group (that being the only group) in year 4. It would appear therefore that, retrospectively, Saxon Ltd had not joined the Uhlan group in year 2. On that basis, its loss could now be used to shelter profits of the former Uhlan group. But that would not be the correct outcome if the Five Oaks decision were to be followed.

The Special Commissioners in the *Five Oaks* case, taking a purposive approach, held that only losses realised by a company in the position of Saxon Ltd after it joined the Uhlan group were prevented from being used by companies already in the Masurian group and that losses realised before Saxon Ltd joined the Uhlan group remained ring-fenced from the members of that group. In effect, the Commissioners said that a company like Saxon Ltd was not in fact deemed to have joined the relevant group in year 4. To follow any other interpretation would not make sense although the wording of the relevant legislation seems clearly to give the result contended for by the taxpayer.

In the more recent case *Limitgood Ltd and others v HMRC* [2007] UKSPC SPC00612, where the issue was essentially the same as in *Five Oaks,* Counsel for the taxpayer submitted that the earlier case had been wrongly decided. Accepting that the broad purpose of the legislation was to prevent pre-entry losses being set against group gains such as those that were at issue, the correct course nevertheless was to interpret and apply the words used in the statute. The Special Commissioners found in favour of the taxpayer and considered that it was clear that the words used in the legislation could not be interpreted as HMRC contended without doing undue violence to the language used.

It may be noted that the *Limitgood* judgment included discussion on parts of the UK legislation not replicated in the Irish legislation (a rather concise version of its much more complex UK equivalent) and which were somewhat unhelpful to the Revenue's case.

The rule in TCA 1997 Sch 18A paragraph 1(6) does not apply where a new holding company is superimposed on the existing group. Specifically, it will not apply where—

(a)   the persons who, immediately before the time when the principal company of the first group became a member of the second group, owned the shares comprised in the issued share capital of the principal company of the first group are the same as the persons who, immediately after that time, owned the shares comprised in the issued share capital of the principal company of the relevant group; and

(b)   the company which is the principal company of the relevant group immediately after that time—

  (i)   was not the principal company of any group immediately before that time, and

  (ii)   immediately after that time had assets consisting entirely, or almost entirely, of shares comprised in the issued share capital of the principal company of the first group (TCA 1997 Sch 18A paragraph 1(7)).

Where this exception applies, the pre-entry loss rules will not operate in relation to any realised or unrealised losses of a member of the first group at the time it becomes a member of the enlarged group. The exception recognises that a takeover in these circumstances does not result in any change in the ultimate ownership of the member companies concerned.

9.213   Substantial shareholdings relief ("participation exemption")

9.213.1   Introduction and outline

TCA 1997 ss 626B and 626C, together with Schedule 25A, provide for an exemption from capital gains tax for companies in Ireland in respect of disposals, on or after 2 February 2004, from substantial shareholdings in their trading subsidiaries, or in trading sub-groups, where the subsidiary whose shares are disposed of is tax resident in an EU Member State (including Ireland) or in a country with which Ireland has a tax treaty.

To qualify for the relief, or "participation exemption", the company disposing of the shares (the investor company) should hold or have held—

(a)   for a period of 12 months within which the date of the disposal falls; or

(b)   for a period of 12 months ending in the 24 months preceding the date of disposal,

at least 5% of the ordinary share capital of the investee company.

The full 12-month ownership period does not have to fall within the 24-month period preceding the disposal; it is sufficient that part of it does.

A further condition of relief is that, at the time of the disposal of the shares, either—

(i)   the investee company's business consists wholly or mainly of the carrying on a trade or trades; or

(ii)   the business of the investor company, each company of which the investor company is the parent company, the investee company (where the investor company is not its parent) and any company of which the investee company is the parent company, taken together consists wholly or mainly of the carrying on of a trade or trades.

The exemption does not apply to disposals of shares deriving the greater part of their value from Irish based land or from minerals or rights or interests relating to mining or minerals or the searching for minerals.

A secondary exemption applies to options to acquire shares and to certain convertible securities related to shares in circumstances similar to those in which a gain is exempt under the main exemption provision.

The ownership period relating to the shares disposed of can, if necessary, be extended where the shares were acquired in a transaction that was treated as giving rise to neither a gain nor a loss, for example, where the shares had previously been acquired from another company which was a member of the same capital gains tax group. In those circumstances, the company now disposing of the shares may include in its ownership period the time during which the shares had been held by the previous owner.

There are special provisions dealing such matters as a previous deemed disposal and reacquisition of the shares now being sold, repurchase agreements where a company transfers shares to another company subject to an agreement that the original owner will buy them back, stock lending arrangements, company reconstructions whereby a company that held shares in one company exchanges them for shares in a second company, and the appropriation of shares as trading stock.

9.213.2 Parent company

Central to the purposes of the substantial shareholdings relief is the meaning of "parent company" and the time or times at which a company is treated as another company's parent company. A company is a *parent company* in relation to another company at any time only if that time falls within an uninterrupted period of not less than 12 months throughout which it directly or indirectly holds shares in that company by virtue of which—

(a)   it holds not less than 5% of the company's ordinary share capital;

(b)   it is beneficially entitled to not less than 5% of the profits available for distribution to equity holders of the company; and

(c)   it would be beneficially entitled on a winding up to not less than 5% of the assets of the company available for distribution to equity holders,

and, for the above purposes—

(i)   TCA 1997, s 9(2)-(10) (determination of amount of capital held indirectly – see **2.505**) applies with any necessary modifications; and

(ii)   TCA 1997 ss 413-419 apply as they apply for the purposes of Part 12 Chapter 5 (group relief: equity entitlement – see **8.304**) except that in TCA 1997, s 413(3)(a) "in a relevant territory" is to be read instead of "in the State", and as if TCA 1997, s 411(1)(c), other than its application by virtue of subparagraphs (i) and (ii) of that paragraph, were deleted (TCA 1997, s 626B(1)(b)(i)).

The reference in (ii) above to TCA 1997, s 413(3)(a) is to the definition of "normal commercial loan" in which there is a reference to securities quoted on a stock exchange in the State (see **8.304.2**). It should be noted that the existence of a "non-commercial" loan could result in failure to satisfy the parent company requirement; a mere holding of 10% of the ordinary shares in a company may not be sufficient for this purpose. In this connection see **8.304.1-2**.

Also in relation to (ii), TCA s 411(1)(c) sets out the requirement, in relation to the meaning of "group" for group relief purposes, that any company to be taken into account must be resident in an EU Member State (see **8.302.2**). Thus, for the purposes of TCA 1997, s 626B, there are no residence-related requirements to the effect that a member of a group must be tax resident in a Member State of the EU or in an EEA State. TCA 1997, s 411(1)(c), in subparagraphs (i) and (ii), also excludes any company treated as a share dealing company (see **8.302.3**) and for the purposes of TCA 1997, s 626B these subparagraphs are not disregarded.

Example 9.213.2.1

Throughout the year ended 30 June 2007, Bonaventure Ltd held 5% of the ordinary share capital of Camargo Ltd (and satisfied the corresponding profit distribution and asset distribution tests). Bonaventure Ltd was a parent company in relation to Camargo Ltd on 30 June 2007. It was also such a parent company at any time during the year.

Example 9.213.2.2

Throughout the year ended 30 June 2007, Bonaventure Ltd held 100% of the ordinary share capital of Alpine Ltd (and satisfied the corresponding profit distribution and asset distribution tests). Also throughout that year, Alpine Ltd held 5% of the ordinary share capital of Camargo Ltd (and satisfied the corresponding profit distribution and asset distribution tests). Bonaventure Ltd was, indirectly, a parent company in relation to

Camargo Ltd on 30 June 2007. It was also such a parent company at any time during the year.

Deemed holdings of group member

In determining whether the conditions in TCA 1997, s 626B(2) are satisfied, a company that is a member of a group is treated as holding so much of any shares held by any other company in the group and as having so much of the entitlement of any such company to any rights enjoyed by virtue of holding shares—

(a) as the company would not otherwise hold or have; and

(b) as are not part of a life business fund within the meaning of section 719 (see **12.603.2**),

and, for this purpose, *group* means a company which has one or more 51% subsidiaries (see **2.502**) together with those subsidiaries (TCA 1997, s 626B(1)(b)(ii)). TCA 1997, s 616 (meaning of "group" for capital gains tax group treatment – see **9.202**) does not apply for the purposes of the substantial shareholdings relief (TCA 1997, s 626B(1)(b)(v)).

> **Example 9.213.2.3**
>
> Throughout the year ended 30 June 2007, Bonaventure Ltd held 60% of the ordinary share capital of Alpine Ltd and 2% of the ordinary share capital of Camargo Ltd (and satisfied the corresponding profit distribution and asset distribution tests in each case). Alpine Ltd held 4% of the ordinary share capital of Camargo Ltd (and satisfied the corresponding profit distribution and asset distribution tests).
>
> For the purposes of TCA 1997, s 626B(2), Alpine Ltd and Bonaventure Ltd are members of the same group. Alpine Ltd is deemed to hold the shares and other interests held by Bonaventure Ltd in Camargo Ltd. Accordingly, Alpine Ltd was a parent company in relation to Camargo Ltd on 30 June 2007. It was also such a parent company at any time during the year.

TCA s 626B(1)(b)(ii) also operates in the following way. If the investor company holds the required shareholding percentage in the investee company at the date of disposal and if it had acquired that shareholding from a fellow group member less than twelve months before the date of disposal, the parent company condition would also be satisfied provided the fellow group member had held the shareholding for a period such that the combined periods of ownership by the two companies was at least twelve months.

> **Example 9.213.2.4**
>
> Angkor Ltd disposes of its 5% interest in Quemoy Ltd at which time it had held that interest for one month. Matsu Ltd, another group member, had held the 5% interest for the eleven months immediately preceding the transfer of the shareholding to Angkor Ltd. Angkor Ltd is deemed to have held 5% of Quemoy Ltd for the entire twelve month period prior to disposal.

> **Example 9.213.2.5**
>
> Matsu Ltd held a 5% interest in Quemoy Ltd for a period of 11 months but disposed of 2% to Angkor Ltd which then disposed of that 2% one month later. Angkor Ltd is deemed (a) to have held 5% (2% + 3%) on the date of disposal and (b) also to have held 5% (0% + 5%) throughout the immediately preceding 11 month period. Thus, Angkor Ltd would be regarded as the parent company of Quemoy Ltd on the date of disposal even though on that date it had itself only held 2% of that company and then only for one month.

9.2013.3 The relief

A gain accruing to a company (the *investor company*) on a disposal of shares in another company (the *investee company*) is not a chargeable gain if—

(a) the disposal by the investor company is at a time—

    (i) when the investor company is a parent company (see **9.213.2** above) of the investee company, or

    (ii) within the two-year period (see below) beginning on the most recent day on which the investor company was a parent company of the investee company,

(b) the investee company is, by virtue of the law of a relevant territory, resident for the purposes of tax in the relevant territory at the time of the disposal; and

(c) at the time of the disposal—

    (i) the investee company is a company whose business consists wholly or mainly of the carrying on of a trade or trades, or

    (ii) the business of—

        (I) the investor company,

        (II) each company of which the investor company is the parent company, and

        (III) the investee company, if it is not a company as described in (II), and any company of which the investee company is the parent company,

taken together consists wholly or mainly of the carrying on of a trade or trades (TCA 1997, s 626B(2)).

In connection with (b) above, a *relevant territory* is—

(i) a Member State of the European Communities; or

(ii) not being such a Member State, a territory with which Ireland has concluded a tax treaty.

In relation to a relevant territory other than the State, *tax* means any tax imposed in that territory which corresponds to income tax or corporation tax in the State.

For the above purposes, *two-year period* means a period ending on the day before the second anniversary of the day on which the period began.

As regards the time at which the parent company requirement must be satisfied, this should be a straightforward matter in most cases; the requirement will be satisfied if the investor company is a parent company of the investee company at the date of disposal. Where this is not the case, the requirement may still be satisfied by virtue of the two-year extension to the time period in which the requirement must be satisfied.

Regarding (c) above, while it was hardly to be expected that a precise trading test would be provided by the legislation, it can be taken that "wholly or mainly" means more than 50% and that the factors of primary importance in applying the test would be the proportion of trading profits to total profits or the proportion of trading assets to total assets. Factors such as the number of hours spent by employees on trading activities, or the total turnover from trading, would be of secondary importance in this context. Where the businesses of a number of companies "taken together" are being considered, transactions between those companies, such as the payment of dividends, interest or management charges and any trading transactions, would be ignored.

In the following examples, it is assumed that the investee company satisfies the conditions regarding tax residence and nature of business.

Example 9.213.3.1

Morgan Ltd held 6% of the ordinary share capital of Ralston Ltd (and satisfied the corresponding profit distribution and asset distribution tests) for a number of years. It disposed of part of this shareholding on 31 December 2005 so that it then held 4%. The 4% interest was disposed of on 30 December 2007.

In relation to the disposal on 30 December 2007, Morgan Ltd was not a parent company of Ralston Ltd on that date. The most recent day on which it was such a parent company is 31 December 2005. The two-year period beginning on that day ended on 30 December 2007 so that the disposal of the 4% interest in Ralston Ltd qualifies for exemption; the two-year period ended on the day before the second anniversary of the day on which the period began – see definition of "two-year period" above.

Note that the effect of TCA 1997, s 626B is to deem certain gains as not being "chargeable gains". The tax charge imposed by TCA 1997, s 590 (chargeable gains of closely controlled non-resident companies – see **9.408**) relates to a chargeable gain realised by a non-resident "closely controlled" company. Except where otherwise expressly provided, every gain is a chargeable gain (TCA 1997, s 545(3), including a chargeable gain realised by a non-resident company. Accordingly, if a gain realised by a closely controlled non-resident company results from the disposal of shares in a trading company (or group), and provided the conditions prescribed by TCA 1997, s 626B are satisfied, the gain will not be a chargeable gain and there will be no attribution by virtue of TCA 1997, s 590.

The liquidation of an investee company will constitute a disposal of the shares in that company so that relief under TCA 1997, s 626B may be available to one or more corporate shareholders in that company. Since, however, it will usually be the case that the company in liquidation will have ceased to trade before the date on which it is finally wound up, this may have a bearing on the trading requirement referred to in (c) above.

Effect of share for share transaction

In determining whether the relief provided for in TCA 1997, s 626B(2) applies, the question as to whether there is a disposal is to be determined without regard to TCA 1997, s 584 or that section as applied by any other section (see **9.402-405**); and, to the extent to which an exemption under TCA 1997, s 626B(2) does apply in relation to a disposal, TCA 1997, s 584 will not apply in relation to the disposal (TCA 1997, s 626B(1)(b)(iii)).

Thus, the relief provided for in TCA 1997, s 626B takes precedence over any reorganisation treatment that would otherwise have applied by virtue of TCA 1997 ss 584-587.

Example 9.213.3.2

Colonial Ltd sold its ordinary shares in Keystone Ltd to Airway Ltd in consideration for an issue of shares in Airway Ltd. By virtue TCA 1997, s 586, no disposal of shares is deemed to have taken place; for the purposes of capital gains tax on any later disposal by Colonial Ltd of the shares it acquired in Airway Ltd, the base cost of those shares would be the same as the base cost of the shares now disposed of.

It is determined that the disposal of the shares in Keystone Ltd qualifies for exemption under TCA 1997, s 626B. Accordingly, TCA 1997, s 586 (and therefore TCA 1997, s 584) does not operate, as it would normally do, to deem that disposal as not being a disposal. The gain on the disposal is then exempt by virtue of TCA 1997, s 626B.

As regards any later disposal by Colonial Ltd of the shares in Airway Ltd (which will not necessarily qualify for exemption under TCA 1997, s 626B), the base cost of those shares will be their market value at the time of the exchange (since TCA 1997, s 584, which would treat the original shares and the new holding as the same asset, does not apply to the disposal).

The cost to Airway Ltd of the shares in Keystone Ltd is, as it would normally be, the current market value of those shares at the time of the exchange.

Assets vested in liquidator

Where assets of a company are vested in a liquidator under section 230 of the Companies Act 1963 or otherwise, the assets will be deemed to be vested in, and the acts of liquidation in relation to the assets will be deemed to be the acts of, the company (and acquisitions from, and disposals to, the liquidator will be disregarded accordingly) (TCA 1997, s 626B(1)(b)(iv)). Accordingly, an investor company in liquidation may be entitled to exemption in respect of disposals of shareholdings made by the liquidator.

Allowable losses

An allowable loss, for the purposes of corporation tax in respect of chargeable gains, does not include a loss accruing to a company in such circumstances that, if a gain accrued, the company would be exempt from corporation tax in respect of the gain (TCA 1997, s 4(1) – see **9.102.3**), Accordingly, a capital loss resulting from a disposal of shares such that, if a gain had arisen on that disposal, that gain would be exempt under TCA 1997, s 626B will not be an allowable loss.

Relief not to apply in certain cases

The relief provided for under TCA 1997, s 626B (and correspondingly under TCA 1997, s 626C – see **9.213.4** below) does not apply in a number of circumstances. The treatment of a gain as not being a chargeable gain does not apply in the case of—

(a) a disposal which by virtue of any provision relating to chargeable gains is deemed to be for a consideration such that no gain or loss accrues to the person making the disposal;

(b) a disposal a gain on which, by virtue of any provision other than TCA 1997, s 626B or s 626C, would not be a chargeable gain;

(c) disposals, including deemed disposals, of shares which are part of a life business fund within the meaning of section 719 (see **12.603.2**);

(d) a disposal of shares deriving their value or the greater part of their value directly or indirectly from assets specified in TCA 1997, s 29(3)(a) or (b) (see **3.107.1** and **9.408**) (TCA 1997, s 626B(3)) ; or

(e) a deemed disposal under TCA 1997, s 627 (exit charge – see **9.106**).

With regard to (a) above, relevant provisions would include TCA 1997 ss 615 (see **9.207.2**) and 617 (see **9.203**). TCA 1997, s 617 recognises that the members of a group of companies are, in a commercial sense, a single person so that any gains or losses arising on transfers of assets between them are ignored for capital gains tax purposes. It is appropriate therefore that a provision exempting a gain arising on a disposal should not apply to a disposal treated as giving rise to neither a gain nor a loss. The exclusion at (d) is directed at companies dealing in Irish-based properties. The exclusion at (e) is to prevent an unintended interaction between the exit charge and the participation exemption. Accordingly, the exemption does not apply in the case of a disposal subject to the exit charge.

Where a company transfers shares in a subsidiary company to another company within the same capital gains tax group and the consideration is the issue of shares by the transferee company, TCA 1997 ss 584 and 586 will be relevant. If the disposal satisfies the conditions for exemption under TCA 1997, s 626B, however, TCA 1997, s 584 will not apply. (It was seen above under *Effect of previous share for share transaction* that, to the extent to which an exemption under TCA 1997, s 626B(2) applies in relation to a disposal, TCA 1997, s 584 does not apply in relation to that disposal.) The transaction will also be subject to TCA 1997, s 617 so that neither a gain nor a loss arises on the disposal. This being the case, TCA 1997, s 626B does not apply to that disposal (in accordance with (a) above). Since TCA 1997, s 626B does not apply, it follows that TCA 1997 ss 584 and 586 are not disapplied on that count.

Where, however, TCA 1997, s 617 applies to a disposal, TCA 1997, s 584 does not apply so as to treat the disposal as not being a disposal (see **9.404.3** in relation to the *Woolcombers* and *NAP Holdings* decisions), albeit the disposal is at no gain/no loss.

Example 9.213.3.3

The position is as in Example **9.213.3.2** except that Colonial and Airway Ltd are members of the same capital gains tax group. Colonial Ltd sells its ordinary shares in Keystone Ltd to Airway Ltd in consideration for an issue of shares in Airway Ltd. As TCA 1997, s 617 applies and notwithstanding TCA 1997 ss 584 and 586, there is a disposal of shares by Colonial Ltd; Airway Ltd acquires the shares in Keystone Ltd at their cost to Colonial. For the purposes of capital gains tax on any later disposal by Colonial Ltd of the shares it acquires in Airway Ltd, the base cost of those shares will, by virtue of TCA 1997 ss 584/ 586, be the same as the base cost of the Keystone Ltd shares.

It is determined that the disposal of the shares in Keystone Ltd satisfies the conditions for relief under TCA 1997, s 626B. Since the disposal is one in respect of which neither a gain nor a loss arises, however, the relief will not apply. Accordingly, TCA 1997 ss 584/586 are not disapplied for that reason. Those provisions do not, however, operate so as to treat the disposal by Colonial Ltd of the shares in Keystone Ltd as not being a disposal; there is a disposal for the purposes of TCA 1997, s 617 albeit for a consideration giving rise to neither a gain nor a loss.

In summary, for the purposes of capital gains tax on any future disposals, Airway Ltd acquires the Keystone Ltd shares at their cost to Colonial Ltd while Colonial Ltd acquires its shares in Airway Ltd at its cost of the Keystone Ltd shares.

9.213.4   Assets related to shares

A secondary exemption from capital gains tax applies to options to acquire shares and to certain convertible securities related to shares in circumstances similar to those in which a gain is exempt under TCA 1997, s 626B.

An asset is *related to shares* in a company if it is—

(a) an option to acquire or dispose of shares in that company;

(b) a security to which are attached rights by virtue of which the holder is or may become entitled to acquired or dispose of (whether by conversion or exchange or otherwise)—

    (i) shares in that company,

    (ii) an option to acquire or dispose of shares in that company, or

    (iii) another security, or

(c) an option to acquire or dispose of any security within (b) or an interest in any such security (TCA 1997, s 626C(1)(a)).

In determining whether a security is within (b) above, no account is to be taken—

(i) of any rights attached to the security other than rights relating, directly or indirectly, to shares of the company in question; or

(ii) of rights as regards which, at the time the security came into existence, there was no more than a negligible likelihood that they would in due course be exercised to a significant extent (TCA 1997, s 626C(1)(a)).

A gain accruing to a company (the "first-mentioned company") on the disposal of an asset related to shares in another company is not a chargeable gain if—

(a) (i) immediately before the disposal the first-mentioned company holds shares in the other company, and

    (ii) any gain accruing to the first-mentioned company on a disposal at that time of the shares would, by virtue of TCA 1997, s 626B, not be a chargeable gain, or

(b) (i) immediately before the disposal the first-mentioned company does not hold shares in the other company but is a member of a group and another member of that group does hold shares in the other company; and

    (ii) if the first-mentioned company, rather than the other member of the group, held the shares, any gain accruing to the first-mentioned company on a disposal at that time of the shares would, by virtue of TCA 1997, s 626B, not be a chargeable gain (TCA 1997, s 626C(2)).

For the above purposes, *group* means a company that has one or more 51% subsidiaries (see **2.502**) together with those subsidiaries. TCA 1997, s 616 (meaning of "group" for capital gains tax group treatment – see **9.202**) does not apply for those purposes (TCA 1997, s 626B(1)(b)(v)).

Relief not to apply in certain cases

See **9.213.3** above.

9.213.5 Supplementary provisions

TCA 1997 Sch 25A contains various provisions for the purposes of supplementing TCA 1997 ss 626B and 626C. Their purpose is to resolve difficulties that would otherwise result from the interaction of TCA ss 626B and 626C with other provisions of the Capital Gains Tax Acts.

Previous no gain/no loss transfer: extension of ownership period

The period during which a company has held shares is treated as extended by any earlier period during which the shares concerned, or shares from which they are derived (see below), were held—

(a)   by a company from which the shares concerned were transferred to the company on a no-gain/no-loss transfer (see below); or

(b)   by a company from which the shares concerned, or shares from which they are derived, were transferred on a previous no-gain/no-loss transfer—

    (i)   to a company within (a), or

    (ii)   to another company within (b) (TCA 1997 Sch 25A paragraph 1(2)).

Shares are "derived" from other shares only where—

(a)   one holding of shares is treated by virtue of TCA 1997, s 584 (see **9.402**) as the same asset as another; or

(b)   there is a sequence of two or more of the occurrences mentioned in (a) (TCA 1997 Sch 25A paragraph 1(1)).

A *no-gain/no-loss transfer* means a disposal and corresponding acquisition that, by virtue of the Capital Gains Tax Acts, are deemed to be for a consideration such that no gain or loss accrues to the person making the disposal, for example by virtue of TCA 1997, s 617 (see **9.203**) (TCA 1997 Sch 25A paragraph 1(3)). Other examples of the no-gain/no-loss treatment involving shares are TCA 1997, s 615 (company reconstruction or amalgamation – see **9.207.1**) and s 701 (reorganisation of cooperative societies – see **9.404.6**).

Where a company (the "first-mentioned company") is treated as having held any shares for an extended period as described above, the first-mentioned company is treated, for the purposes of the shareholding requirement under TCA 1997, s 626B(2), as having had at any time the same entitlement—

(a)   to shares; and

(b)   to any rights enjoyed by virtue of holding shares,

as the company (the "other company") that at that time held the shares concerned or, as the case may be, the shares from which they are derived (TCA 1997 Sch 25A paragraph 1(4)).

The shares and rights to be attributed to the first-mentioned company include any holding or entitlement attributed to the other company under section 626B(1)(b)(ii) (TCA 1997 Sch 25A paragraph 1(5)).

Example 9.213.5.1

Krull Ltd sold shares comprising 15% of the ordinary share capital in Felix Ltd (which shares satisfied the corresponding profit distribution and asset distribution tests) having held them for a period of 3 months. It had acquired the shares from a fellow-group member, Kroger Ltd, which company had held them (and had satisfied the corresponding profit distribution and asset distribution tests) for the immediately preceding 10 months.

Krull Ltd is regarded as having held the shares in Felix Ltd for a period of 13 months ending on the date it disposed of them. It is accordingly, for the purposes of relief under TCA 1997, s 626B(2), regarded as a parent company of Felix Ltd on that date.

Example 9.213.5.2

Krull Ltd sold shares comprising 15% of the ordinary share capital in Felix Ltd (which shares satisfied the corresponding profit distribution and asset distribution tests) having held them for a period of 3 months. It had acquired the shares from a fellow-group member, Kroger Ltd, which company had held them (and had satisfied the corresponding profit distribution and asset distribution tests) for the immediately preceding 4 months. Kroger Ltd had in turn acquired the shares from another fellow-group member, Klinger Ltd, which company had held them (and had satisfied the corresponding profit distribution and asset distribution tests) for the immediately preceding 5 months

Krull Ltd is regarded as having held the shares in Felix Ltd for a period of 12 months ending on the date it disposed of them. It is accordingly, for the purposes of relief under TCA 1997, s 626B(2), regarded as a parent company of Felix Ltd on that date.

Had it been necessary for the purposes of the relief, any earlier intra-group transfers of the Felix Ltd shares (prior to their transfer from Klinger Ltd to Kroger Ltd) could also have been taken into account in the same way.

As mentioned above, shares are "derived" from other shares where one holding of shares is treated by virtue of TCA 1997, s 584 as the same asset as another, or there is a sequence of two or more occurrences in which that treatment applies.

Example 9.213.5.3

Krull Ltd sold shares comprising 15% of the ordinary share capital in Felix Ltd (which shares satisfied the corresponding profit distribution and asset distribution tests) having held them for a period of 3 months. It had acquired the shares from a fellow-group member, Kroger Ltd, which company had held them (and had satisfied the corresponding profit distribution and asset distribution tests) for the immediately preceding 5 months.

Kroger Ltd had acquired the Felix Ltd shares in consideration for the disposal of a 60% interest in Ferdinand Ltd which disposal was treated as not being a disposal by virtue of TCA 1997 ss 584 and 586. (Assume that the disposal of the Ferdinand interest did not qualify for TCA 1997, s 626B treatment.) The 60% interest in Ferdinand Ltd was comprised of ordinary shares (with corresponding profit distribution and asset distribution entitlements) and had been held for the immediately preceding 7 months.

The shares in Felix Ltd are treated as derived from the Ferdinand Ltd shares. Krull Ltd is regarded as having held the shares in Felix Ltd for a period of 15 months ending on the date it disposed of them. It is accordingly, for the purposes of relief under TCA 1997, s 626B(2), regarded as a parent company of Felix Ltd on that date.

Had it been necessary for the purposes of the relief, any earlier intra-group transfers of the Ferdinand Ltd shares (prior to their transfer from Kroger Ltd to Krull Ltd) could also have been taken into account in the same way.

It is assumed above that the disposal of the shares in Ferdinand Ltd did not qualify for TCA 1997, s 626B treatment. If it had so qualified, TCA 1997, s 586/584 would not have applied (see *Effect of share for share transaction* in **9.213.3** above). Accordingly, it would seem that in that event the period of ownership of the Ferdinand shares could not be taken into account in determining the period of ownership of the Felix shares.

Investee company and earlier company reconstruction

A company holding shares in one company may exchange those shares for shares in another company so that the exchange is a reconstruction and therefore not a disposal for capital gains tax purposes. The cost of the original shares becomes the cost of the new shares. In any such case, the period of ownership of the new shares may include the period of ownership of the old shares for the purposes of relief under TCA 1997, s 626B.

The above-described treatment applies where shares in one company (the "first company")—

(a) are exchanged (or are deemed to be exchanged) for shares in another company (the "second company") (see **9.404**); or

(b) are deemed to be exchanged by virtue of TCA 1997, s 587 (see **9.405**) for shares in the first company and shares in the second company,

in circumstances such that, under TCA 1997, s 584 (see **9.402**) as that section applies by virtue of TCA 1997, s 586 or 587, the original shares and the new holding are treated as the same asset (TCA 1997 Sch 25A paragraph 5(2)).

Where the second company—

(a) is an investee company, and is accordingly the company by reference to which the shareholding requirement under section 626B(2) falls to be met; or

(b) is a company by reference to which, by virtue of this paragraph, that requirement may be met,

that requirement may instead be met, in relation to times before the exchange (or deemed exchange) by reference to the first company (TCA 1997 Sch 25A paragraph 5(3)).

If in any case that requirement can be met by virtue of this paragraph, it is to be treated as met (TCA 1997 Sch 25A paragraph 5(4)).

Example 9.213.5.4

Stellar Ltd has held a 20% equity interest in Galaxy Ltd, a trading company, for a number of years. It exchanges its Galaxy Ltd shares for shares in Cosmos Ltd, the holding company of a trading group, as part of an arrangement qualifying as a reorganisation of share capital for the purposes of TCA 1997, s 586. (Assume that the disposal of the Galaxy interest does not qualify for TCA 1997, s 626B treatment.) A few weeks later, Stellar Ltd disposes of its shares in Cosmos Ltd for €50m and realises a gain by reference to the excess of sale proceeds over the cost of the shares (that cost being deemed to be equal to the cost of the Galaxy Ltd shares).

For the purpose of determining whether Stellar Ltd is a parent company of the investee company, Cosmos Ltd, it can satisfy the ownership period requirement in relation to the Cosmos Ltd shares for the period prior to the share exchange by reference to its ownership period in relation to the Galaxy Ltd shares. On that basis, it is treated as a parent company of Cosmos Ltd at the time it disposes of the shares in that company.

It is assumed above that the disposal of the shares in Galaxy Ltd did not qualify for TCA 1997, s 626B treatment. If it had so qualified, TCA 1997, s 586/584 would not have applied (see *Effect of share for share transaction* in **9.213.3** above). Accordingly, it would seem that in that event the period of ownership of the Galaxy shares could not be taken into account in determining the period of ownership of the Cosmos shares.

The following example involves the application of both paragraphs 5(3) and 1(2) (see above under *Previous no gain/no loss transfer: extension of ownership period*) of TCA 1997 Sch 25A.

Example 9.213.5.5

Krull Ltd sold shares comprising 15% of the ordinary share capital in Felix Ltd (which shares satisfied the corresponding profit distribution and asset distribution tests) having held them for a period of 3 months. It had acquired the Felix Ltd shares in consideration for the disposal of a 60% interest in Ferdinand Ltd which disposal was treated as not being a disposal by virtue of TCA 1997 ss 584 and 586. (Assume that the disposal of the Ferdinand interest did not itself qualify for TCA 1997, s 626B treatment.) The 60% interest in Ferdinand Ltd was comprised of ordinary shares (with corresponding profit distribution and asset distribution entitlements) and had been held by Krull Ltd for the immediately preceding 5 months. By virtue of TCA 1997 Sch 25A paragraph 5(3), Krull Ltd may satisfy the ownership period requirement in relation to the Felix Ltd shares for the period before the share exchange by reference to its ownership period in relation to the Ferdinand Ltd shares. That ownership period is therefore deemed to be 8 months.

Krull Ltd had acquired the Ferdinand Ltd shares from a fellow-group member, Kroger Ltd, which company had held them (and had satisfied the corresponding profit distribution and asset distribution tests) for the immediately preceding 6 months. By virtue of TCA 1997 Sch 25A paragraph 1(2), Krull Ltd's period of ownership of the shares in Ferdinand Ltd is extended to 11 months. Thus, its total ownership period of the shares in Felix Ltd is deemed to be the 14 months ending on the date it disposed of them. It is accordingly, for the purposes of relief under TCA 1997, s 626B(2), regarded as a parent company of Felix Ltd on that date.

Had it been necessary for the purposes of the relief, any earlier intra-group transfers of the Ferdinand Ltd shares (prior to their transfer from Kroger Ltd to Krull Ltd) could also have been taken into account in the same way.

It is assumed above that the disposal of the shares in Ferdinand Ltd did not qualify for TCA 1997, s 626B treatment. If it had so qualified, TCA 1997, s 586/584 would not have applied (see *Effect of share for share transaction* in **9.213.3** above). Accordingly, it would seem that in that event the period of ownership of the Ferdinand shares could not be taken into account in determining the period of ownership of the Felix shares.

The following example involves the application of paragraph 5 where there has been a deemed exchange of shares by virtue of TCA 1997, s 587.

Example 9.213.5.6

Kramer Holdings Ltd has been the parent company of Riviere Ltd, a trading company, for some years. Riviere Ltd transfers its trade and assets to Renfrew Ltd in consideration for an issue of shares in Renfrew Ltd to Kramer Holdings Ltd. Four months later, Kramer Ltd disposes of the shares in Renfrew Ltd to a third party.

In accordance with TCA 1997, s 587, Kramer Holdings Ltd is treated as having exchanged its shares in Riviere Ltd for those held by it in consequence of the arrangement, the shares in Riviere Ltd being regarded as if they had been cancelled and replaced by a new issue, ie the shares in Riviere Ltd together with the shares in Renfrew Ltd. TCA 1997, s 586 (and therefore s 584) accordingly applies to this exchange.

The transaction falls within TCA 1997 Sch 25A paragraph 5(2) and, accordingly, for the purpose of determining whether Kramer Holdings Ltd is a parent company of the investee company, Renfrew Ltd, it can satisfy the ownership period requirement in relation to the Renfrew Ltd shares for the period prior to the transaction by reference to its ownership period in relation to the Riviere Ltd shares. On that basis, it is treated, for the purposes of TCA 1997, s 626B, as a parent company of Renfrew Ltd at the time it disposes of the shares in that company.

Effect of deemed disposal and reacquisition

A company is not regarded as having held shares throughout a period if at any time during that period there is a deemed disposal and reacquisition of—

(a)   the shares concerned; or

(b)   shares from which those shares are derived (see above for meaning of "derived") (TCA 1997 Sch 25A paragraph 2(2)).

For this purpose, *deemed disposal and reacquisition* means a disposal and immediate reacquisition treated as taking place under the Capital Gains Tax Acts.

The purpose of this provision is to prevent a possible duplication or overlapping of relief. Thus, where a company is deemed at any time to have disposed of and reacquired shares in an investee company, the resulting gain at that time may well be eligible for substantial shareholding relief. Accordingly, in relation to the eventual actual disposal of those shares, the period of ownership for the purposes of any relief on that disposal will only commence at the time of the deemed market value reacquisition and not at the time of the earlier actual acquisition: the period prior to the deemed disposal and reacquisition will already have been taken into account for the purposes of relief in relation to that disposal.

Example 9.213.5.7

On 1 August 2007, Magner Ltd acquired 25% of the ordinary shares in Alex Ltd from Jason Ltd, a fellow capital gains tax group member. Jason Ltd had held these shares throughout the preceding twelve months. Magner Ltd ceased to be a member of the group on 31 October 2007. On 31 December 2007, Magner Ltd sold its shares in Alex Ltd.

There is in accordance with TCA 1997, s 623 a deemed disposal and reacquisition of the Alex Ltd shares at market value on 31 October 2007, the date Magner Ltd left the group. Any gain arising on this (deemed) disposal is eligible for relief under TCA 1997, s 626B as the ownership period of the shares is extended from three months to 15 months.

In relation to the actual disposal on 31 December 2007, however, Magner Ltd is not regarded as having held the Alex Ltd shares throughout the 17-month period as there was a deemed disposal and reacquisition during that period. The period of ownership is restricted to three months.

Degrouping: time deemed sale and reacquisition treated as taking place

Where—

(a)   a company that had acquired an asset on a no-gain/no loss basis (because transferred intra-group) ceases at any time (the "time of degrouping") to be a member of the group, so that, by virtue of TCA 1997, s 623(4) (see **9.209.1**), there is a deemed disposal and reacquisition of the asset immediately after the earlier intra-group acquisition; and

(b)   if the company had disposed of the asset immediately before the time of degrouping any gain accruing on the disposal would, by virtue of TCA 1997, s 626B, not have been a chargeable gain,

TCA 1997, s 623(4) will apply as if the deemed sale and reacquisition had taken place immediately before the company ceased to be a member of the group rather than at the time of the intra-group transfer (TCA 1997 Sch 25A paragraph 7). Thus, the exemption from capital gains tax will apply at the time the company leaves the group even if the conditions for exemption were also satisfied at the earlier date. If the conditions for relief are not satisfied at the time the company leaves the group but were satisfied at the time of the intra-group transfer, the time of disposal is at that earlier time.

Example 9.213.5.8

On 1 May 2007, Magner Ltd acquired 25% of the ordinary shares in Alex Ltd, a trading company, from its fellow group member, Jason Ltd. Jason Ltd had held these shares throughout the preceding ten months and is deemed to have disposed of them to Magner Ltd for neither a gain nor a loss. Magner Ltd ceased to be a member of the group on 31 March 2008.

At the time immediately prior to leaving the group, Magner Ltd satisfies the conditions for relief under TCA 1997, s 626B in relation to the disposal of the Alex Ltd shares.

Normally TCA 1997, s 623(4) would operate so that Magner Ltd would be treated as having disposed of and as having immediately reacquired the Alex Ltd shares on 1 May 2007 and a chargeable gain (or loss) would arise on that basis since the shares would then be deemed to have been held for ten months only. TCA 1997 Sch 25A paragraph 7, however, provides that, since Magner Ltd now satisfies the conditions for relief under TCA 1997, s 626B, it is deemed to have made the disposal on 31 March 2008, immediately before it ceased to be a group member, and any gain arising is an exempt gain in accordance with TCA 1997, s 626B.

Example 9.213.5.9

The position is as in Example **9.213.5.8** except that at the time Magner Ltd ceased to be a member of the capital gains tax group Alex Ltd had ceased to be a trading company so that one of the conditions necessary for exemption was not satisfied. Accordingly, the deemed date of disposal and reacquisition of the shares is 1 May 2007, the date of the intra-group acquisition, in accordance with TCA 1997, s 623(4). At that date, Magner Ltd is deemed to have held the shares for a period of ten months only so that it does not qualify for exemption.

Negligible value

A company may not claim relief for a loss in value of shares (negligible value – see **9.102.3**) if a gain on disposal of the shares would be exempt under TCA 1997, s 626B.

TCA 1997 Sch 25A paragraph 6 provides that a claim for relief under TCA 1997, s 538(2) may not be made in relation to shares held by a company if, by virtue of TCA 1997, s 626B, any loss accruing to the company on a disposal of the shares at the time of the claim, or at any earlier time at or after which the value of the shares becomes negligible, would not be an allowable loss. If, by virtue of TCA 1997, s 626B, a gain resulting from a disposal would not be a chargeable gain, a loss arising from a disposal in the same circumstances cannot be an allowable loss (see **9.102.3** under *Allowable losses*). A loss arising on a deemed disposal at the time of a negligible value claim (or at any earlier time when the value of the shares was negligible) is not an allowable loss if the conditions of TCA 1997, s 626B apply at that time and accordingly a negligible value claim cannot be made in that case.

Effect of repurchase agreement

A repurchase agreement (or "repo") is an arrangement whereby a company transfers shares to another company subject to an agreement that the original owner will buy them back. Recognising the substance of these transactions, the Revenue do not in practice regard such transaction as involving a disposal/acquisition for tax purposes (see **3.212**). Shares transferred in that way are also, for the purposes of TCA 1997, s 626B, regarded as remaining with the original holder in determining whether the shareholding requirement for the purposes of the exemption has been met.

A *repurchase agreement* is an agreement under which—

(a)   a person (the "original owner") transfers shares to another person (the "interim holder") under an agreement to sell them; and

(b)   the original owner or a person connected with (see **2.303**) the original owner is required to buy them back either—

  (i)   in pursuance of an obligation to do so imposed by that agreement or by any related agreement, or

  (ii)   in consequence of the exercise of an option acquired under that agreement or any related agreement.

For the purposes of (b), agreements are related if they are entered into in pursuance of the same arrangements (regardless of the date on which either agreement is entered into) (TCA 1997 Sch 25A paragraph 3(1)).

Any reference to the period of a repurchase agreement is a reference to the period beginning with the transfer of the shares by the original owner to the interim holder and ending with the repurchase of the shares in pursuance of the agreement.

For the purposes of the shareholding requirement in TCA 1997, s 626B(2), but subject to TCA 1997 Sch 25A paragraph 3(5) (see below), where a company that holds shares in another company transfers those shares under a repurchase agreement—

(a)   the original owner is treated as continuing to hold the shares transferred and accordingly as retaining entitlement to any rights attached to them; and

(b)   the interim holder is treated as not holding the shares transferred and as not becoming entitled to any such rights,

during the period of the repurchase agreement (TCA 1997 Sch 25A paragraph 3(4)).

If, at any time before the end of the period of the repurchase agreement, the original owner, or another member of the same group as the original owner, becomes the holder—

(a)   of any of the shares transferred; or

(b)   of any shares directly or indirectly representing any of the shares transferred,

TCA 1997 Sch 25A paragraph 3(4) will not apply after that time in relation to those shares or, as the case may be, in relation to the shares represented by those shares.

For the above purposes, *group* means a company that has one or more 51% subsidiaries (see **2.502**) together with those subsidiaries (TCA 1997 Sch 25A paragraph 3(5)).

Effect of stock lending arrangements

A stock lending arrangement is similar to a repurchase agreement except that under the latter there is a pre-agreed return date. As in the case of a repo, the Revenue do not in practice regard such transaction as involving a disposal/acquisition for tax purposes (see **3.212**). Shares transferred under a stock lending arrangement are also, for the purposes of TCA 1997, s 626B, regarded as remaining with the original holder in determining whether the shareholding requirement for the purposes of the exemption has been met.

A *stock lending arrangement* is an arrangement between two persons ("the borrower" and "the lender") under which—

(a) the lender transfers shares to the borrower otherwise than by way of sale; and

(b) a requirement is imposed on the borrower to transfer those shares back to the lender otherwise than by way of sale (TCA 1997 Sch 25A paragraph 4(1)).

Any reference to the period of a stock lending arrangement is a reference to the period beginning with the transfer of the shares by the lender to the borrower and ending—

(a) with the transfer of the shares back to the lender in pursuance of the arrangement; or

(b) when it becomes apparent that the requirement for the borrower to make a transfer back to the lender will not be complied with.

For the purposes of the shareholding requirement in TCA 1997, s 626B(2), but subject to TCA 1997 Sch 25A paragraph 4(5) (see below), where a company that holds shares in another company transfers those shares under a stock lending arrangement—

(a) the lender is treated as continuing to hold the shares transferred and accordingly as retaining entitlement to any rights attached to them; and

(b) the borrower is treated for those purposes as not holding the shares transferred and as not becoming entitled to any such rights,

during the period of the stock lending arrangement (TCA 1997 Sch 25A paragraph 4(4)).

If at any time before the end of the period of the stock lending arrangement the lender, or another member of the same group as the lender, becomes the holder—

(a) of any of the shares transferred; or

(b) of any shares directly or indirectly representing any of the shares transferred.

TCA 1997 Sch 25A paragraph 4(4) will not apply after that time in relation to those shares or, as the case may be, in relation to the shares represented by those shares.

For the above purposes, *group* means a company that has one or more 51% subsidiaries (see **2.502**) together with those subsidiaries (TCA 1997 Sch 25A paragraph 4(5)).

Appropriations to stock in trade

In a case where shares are appropriated by a company to stock in trade and where the gain on those shares at that time is exempt from tax by virtue of TCA 1997, s 626B, the company is treated as acquiring the shares at market value for the purposes of computing the profits of the trade to which they are appropriated.

Where—

(a) an asset acquired by a company otherwise than as trading stock of a trade carried on by it is appropriated by the company for the purposes of the trade as trading stock (whether on the commencement of the trade or otherwise); and

(b) if the company had then sold the asset for its market value, a chargeable gain or allowable loss would have accrued to the company but for the provisions of section 626B, the company is treated for capital gains tax purposes as if it had thereby disposed of the asset for its market value (TCA 1997 Sch 25A paragraph 8(1)).

TCA 1997, s 618 (intra-group transfer from non-trader to trader – see **9.205.2**) applies in relation to this paragraph as it applies in relation to TCA 1997, s 596 (see **9.102.19**) (TCA 1997 Sch 25A paragraph 8(2)).

9.214   Stamp duty: transfers between associated companies

Stamp duty is not chargeable under or by reference to the following headings in Schedule 1 of the Stamp Duties Consolidation Act 1999 (SDCA 1999)—

(a) "CONVEYANCE or TRANSFER on sale of any stocks or marketable securities";

(b) "CONVEYANCE or TRANSFER on sale of a policy or insurance or a policy of life insurance where the risk to which the policy relates is located in the State"; or

(c) "CONVEYANCE or TRANSFER on sale of any property other than stocks or marketable securities or a policy of insurance or a policy of life insurance",

on any instrument to which SDCA 1999 s 79 applies (SDCA 1999 s 79(1)).

Relief will not apply in the case of any instrument unless the instrument has been stamped with a particular stamp denoting that it is not chargeable with any duty or that it is duly stamped (SDCA 1999 s 79(2)).

SDCA 1999 s 79 refers throughout to bodies corporate. A company is a body corporate but "body corporate" has a somewhat wider meaning than "company" (see **1.3**). For convenience, the relief is referred to here as "associated companies relief" and references are to "company" and "companies" instead of to "body corporate" and "bodies corporate".)

SDCA 1999 s 79 applies to any instrument effected for the purposes of conveying or transferring a beneficial interest in property from one company to another where at the time of execution of the instrument the companies in question were associated. The companies in question are associated at the time where one is the beneficial owner of not less than 90% of the ordinary share capital (see **2.601**) of the other or a third company is the beneficial owner of not less than 90% of the ordinary share capital of each.

Ordinary share capital, in relation to a company, means all the issued share capital, by whatever name called, of the company other than capital the holders of which have a right to a dividend at a fixed rate but have no other right to share in the profits of the company (SDCA 1999). Thus, fixed rate preference shares would not be taken into account for the purpose of determining whether or not companies are associated.

Beneficial ownership for the above purpose may be direct or indirect through another company or other companies, or may be partly direct and partly indirect through another company or other companies. For the purpose of identifying beneficial ownership through indirect holdings of ordinary share capital, TCA 1997, s 9(5) to (10) apply (see **8.103.4**) (SDCA 1999 s 79(3)). (In applying TCA 1997, s 9(5)-(10), references to "company" and to "companies" are to be read as references to "body corporate" and "bodies corporate" respectively.)

In addition to the 90% share capital ownership requirement, there are two other requirements that must be met before two companies may be regarded as being associated.

Firstly, one company must be beneficially entitled to not less than 90% of any profits available for distribution to the shareholders of the other company or, as the case may be, a third company must be beneficially entitled to not less than 90% of any profits available for distribution to the shareholders of each of the two companies. Secondly, it is necessary that one company would be beneficially entitled to not less than 90% of any assets available for distribution to the shareholders of the other company in a winding-up or, as the case may be, a third company would be beneficially entitled to not less than 90% of any assets available for distribution to the shareholders of each of the two companies in a winding-up.

The beneficial percentages of distributable profits or assets distributable on a winding-up may be traced through a chain of companies. For those purposes, the beneficial percentage entitlement of a company in another company means the percentage to which the first-mentioned company is, or would be, so entitled, either directly or through another company or other companies or partly directly and partly through another company or other companies (SDCA 1999 s 79(4)). The provisions of TCA 1997 ss 414 and 415 apply, with necessary modifications, for the purposes of determining the beneficial percentages (SDCA 1999 s 79(8)) (see **8.304.3-7**).

Associated companies relief may also apply in cases involving foreign companies that do not have a capital structure based on share capital but provided they have a capital structure that is equivalent to a share capital structure. SDCA 1999 s 79(9) provides that the associated companies relief is to be available notwithstanding that a body corporate is incorporated outside the State and corresponds, under the law of the place of its incorporation, to a body corporate having an ordinary share capital and subject to any necessary modifications for the purpose of so corresponding, and provided that all the other provisions of TCA 1999 s 79 are met.

Associated companies relief will not be available unless the instrument in question can be shown not to have been executed in pursuance of or in connection with an arrangement under which—

(a)   the consideration, or any part of the consideration, for the conveyance or transfer was to be provided or received, directly or indirectly, by any person (an "outsider") other than a company which, at the time of the execution of the instrument, was associated with either the transferor or the transferee company;

(b)   the beneficial interest was previously conveyed or transferred, directly or indirectly, by an outsider; or

(c)   the transferor and the transferee were to cease to be associated (SDCA 1999 s 79(5)).

The purpose of (a) is to prevent relief being claimed in a case where an outside party would ultimately be responsible for the payment of the purchase money for the transfer of the property in question. The purpose of (b) is to prevent relief being claimed in a case involving a transfer of property to an unrelated purchaser company effected by way of transferring the property firstly to a specially formed associated company (with the consideration being left on loan account) which would then be sold to the purchaser following which the property would be transferred from the sold company to the purchaser. The sold company would be paid for the property and would use the proceeds to pay its outstanding debt to the vendor. Condition (b) prevents associated companies relief from being claimed on the second transfer of the property while condition (a) prevents relief from being claimed on the first transfer, making the overall transaction doubly expensive in stamp duty terms.

For the purposes of SDCA 1999 s 79, the Revenue Commissioners may require the delivery to them of a statutory declaration in such form as they may direct and made by a responsible officer of a company or by a solicitor of the Courts of Justice, or by both, and of such further evidence as they may require (SDCA 1999 s 79(6)(a)).

Associated companies relief ceases to be applicable, with stamp duty becoming chargeable as if the relief had never applied, if—

(a)   in the case where any relief had been allowed, it is subsequently found that any declaration or other evidence furnished in support of the claim was untrue in any material particular; or

(b)   the transferor and the transferee cease to be associated within a period of two years from the date of the conveyance or transfer (SDCA 1999 s 79(7)).

Where relief ceases to apply, interest on the stamp duty in question, at the rate of 0.0273% per day or part of a day, becomes payable for the "period of delay" (to the day on which the duty is paid, from, in the case of (a), the date of the conveyance or transfer and, in the case of (b), the date the transferor and the transferee ceased to be associated).

An example of (b) above would be the liquidation of either the transferor or the transferee company within the two-year period, or the liquidation of any other company on which the associated companies relationship depends.

9.3 THE MERGERS DIRECTIVE

9.301 Introduction

TCA 1997 Part 21 (ss 630-638) implements Council Directive No 90/434/ EEC of 23 July 1990 (the "Mergers Directive") which seeks to remove barriers occasioned by the absence of a common taxation system, generally by deferring capital gains tax which would otherwise accrue, to mergers, divisions, transfers of assets and exchanges of shares between companies from different Member States of the European Communities. Article 1 of the Directive provides that "each Member State shall apply this Directive to mergers, divisions, transfers of assets and exchanges of shares in which companies from two or more Member States are involved". As regards exchanges of shares, TCA 1997 ss 584-588 already provides the necessary reliefs under Irish tax legislation. Mergers and divisions are as yet not provided for under Irish company law (see below). TCA 1997 Part 21, accordingly, is mainly concerned with transfers of assets. The legislation extends the benefits of the Directive, which apply to transactions between companies from two Member States, to transactions between companies which are Irish resident.

Broadly, a merger is an arrangement in which one or more companies is dissolved without being wound up and in which the company (or companies) transfers all of its assets and liabilities to another company in exchange for shares in the transferee company issued to its shareholders or to its parent company. The consideration may consist partly of cash, but any cash is limited to 10% of the total consideration.

A division is an arrangement in which a company is dissolved without going into liquidation and where the company transfers all of its assets and liabilities to two or more companies in exchange for a proportionate issue by those companies of shares to its shareholders. Again, there is a 10% limit on any consideration consisting of cash.

Council Directive No 2005/19/EC amends the 1990 Directive in a number of respects. The Directive—

(a) broadens the scope of the 1990 Directive to cover a larger range of companies, including the European Company (a European public limited liability company, *Societas Europaea*, or "SE") and the European Co-operative Society (*Societas Cooperativa Europaea*, or "SCE");

(b) provides for a tax neutral regime for the transfer of the registered office of an SE or an SCE between Member States;

(c) confirms that tax neutrality applies where a company of a Member State converts its branch in another Member State into a subsidiary company there;

(d) provides for tax neutral treatment in respect of a transaction covered by the Directive where, unusually, one of the parties to the transaction is regarded as a company in one Member State but as a transparent entity, such as a partnership, for tax purposes in the other Member State; and

(e)   provides for tax neutrality in the case of a "partial division".

These changes are incorporated, to the extent appropriate, into domestic provisions of Irish tax legislation. As regards (b), a change of registered office does not of itself result in the SE or SCE ceasing to be tax resident in Ireland (see **3.106.2**). Irish tax legislation had already provided for the tax neutrality referred to in (c). As respects (d), provision is made for the exceptional case in which an entity is treated in one Member State as a company but as a "look through" entity in another Member State. Irish legislation includes a measure (see **14.8**) providing for credit relief in circumstances where, say, an Irish resident is a member of a company of another Member State which under Irish law would be regarded as a partnership. In relation to (e), since, as stated above, cross border divisions (and mergers) are not provided for under Irish law, there is no corresponding tax provision to be made in respect of divisions.

The tax consequences of forming an SE or SCE by merger are dealt with in TCA 1997 ss 633A, 633B and 633C (see **9.307**). The occasion of the formation by merger of an SE or an SCE may have implications for the legislation on pre-entry losses in the context of a capital gains tax group becoming part of an enlarged group (see **9.212.7**).

Company

For the purposes of TCA 1997 Part 21, company means a company from a Member State of the European Communities (TCA 1997, s 630). In this context, company from a Member State takes its meaning from Article 3 of the Directive. Thus, it means any company which:

(a)   takes one of the forms listed in the Annex to the Directive (see below);

(b)   according to the tax laws of a Member State is considered to be resident in that State for tax purposes and, under the terms of a double tax agreement concluded with a third State, is not considered to be resident for tax purposes outside the Community; and

(c)   is subject to one of the taxes listed below, without the possibility of an option or of being exempt, or to any other tax which may be substituted for any of the above taxes.

The forms of company listed in the Annex are:

Austria	Aktiengesellschaft, Gesellschaft mit beschränkter Haftung (GmbH)
Belgium	société anonyme/naamloze vennootschap, société en commandite par actions/commanditaire vennootschap op aandelen, société privé à responsabilité limitée/besloten vennootschap met beperkte aansprakelijkheid, and those public bodies that operate under private law
Denmark	aktieselskab, anpartsselskab
Finland	osakeyhtiö/aktiebolag, osuuskunta/andelslag, säästöpankki/sparbank, vakuutusyhtiö/försäkringsbolag
France	société anonyme, société en commandite par actions, société à responsabilité limitée, and industrial and commercial public establishments and undertakings

Germany	Aktiengesellschaft, Kommanditgesellschaft auf Aktien, Gesellschaft mit beschränkter Haftung (GmbH), bergrechtliche Gesellschaft
Greece	anonume etairia
Ireland	public companies limited by shares or by guarantee, private companies limited by shares or by guarantee, bodies registered under the Industrial and Provident Societies Acts or building societies registered under the Building Societies Acts
Italy	società per azioni, società in accomandita per azioni, società a responsabilità limitata and public and private entities carrying on industrial and commercial activities
Luxembourg	société anonyme, société en commandite par actions, société à responsabilité limitée
Netherlands	naamloze vennootschap, besloten vennootschap met beperkte aansprakelijkheid
Portugal	commercial companies or civil law companies having a commercial form as well as other legal persons that carry on commercial or industrial activities and are incorporated in accordance with Portuguese law
Spain	sociedad anónima, sociedad comanditaria por acciones, sociedad de responsabilidad limitada and those public law bodies which operate under private law
Sweden	aktiebolag, bankaktiebolag, försäkringsbolag
UK	companies incorporated under the law of the United Kingdom

The list of taxes referred to in (c) above is as follows:

Austria	Körperschaftsteuer
Belgium	impôt des sociétés/ vennootschapsbelasting
Denmark	Selskabsskat
Finland	yhteisöjen tulovero/inkomstskatten för samfund
France	impôt sur les sociétés
Germany	Körperschaftsteuer
Greece	phoros eisodematos nomikon prosopon kerdoskopikou charaktera
Ireland	corporation tax
Italy	imposta sul reddito delle persone giuridiche
Luxembourg	impôt sur le revenue des collectivités
Netherlands	Vennootschapsbelasting
Portugal	imposto sobre o rendimento das pessoas colectivas
Spain	impuesto sobre sociedados
Sweden	statlig inkomstskatt
UK	corporation tax

Accordingly, any reference to a company in connection with any of the reliefs discussed covers both Irish incorporated and EU incorporated companies (provided that any such company is tax resident in a Member State and, under the terms of a double tax agreement concluded between that State and a third State, is not considered to be resident for tax purposes outside the Community). A company incorporated in, say,

Switzerland and managed and controlled, and therefore tax resident, in Ireland is not a "company" for the purposes of TCA 1997 Part 21 (because it is not listed in the Annex). A company in that position might, however, be entitled to succeed in a case arising from the anti-discrimination article of the relevant tax treaty which extends to nationals of one of the Contracting States (including companies incorporated in that state) benefits equivalent to those available to nationals of the other Contracting State.

9.302   Transfer of assets

TCA 1997, s 631 provides certain reliefs in respect of the transfer by a company of the whole or a part of a trade carried on by it in the State to another company where the transfer consideration consists entirely of the issue of securities (the *new assets*) to the transferring company. A company that transfers part of a trade to another company is treated as having carried on that part of its trade as a separate trade. *Securities* means shares and debentures while *shares* includes stock. The consequences of the transfer are as follows:

(1)   No balancing allowance or balancing charge will arise under TCA 1997, s 307 or s 308 as a result of the disposal of the assets by the transferring company.

(2)   The acquiring company takes over the assets transferred at their tax written down values. All allowances and charges in respect of those assets are made to or on the acquiring company on the same basis as if the transferring company had continued to carry on the trade and had continued to use the assets for the purposes of the trade and as if the acquiring company had been carrying on the trade since the transferring company began to do so.

(3)   For capital gains tax purposes, the transfer is treated as not involving any disposal by the transferring company and the acquiring company is treated as if the assets transferred to it were acquired at the same time as, and for the same consideration for which, they are acquired by the transferring company and as if all things done by the transferring company relating to the assets transferred had been done by it.

(4)   Where at any time within six years from the date of the transfer of the assets, the transferring company disposes of the "new assets", then, for the purposes of computing any chargeable gain on the disposal of the new assets—

(a)   the aggregate of the chargeable gains less allowable losses which would have been chargeable (had they not been deferred at the time of the transfer) are to be apportioned between the new assets as a whole, and

(b)   the sums allowable as a deduction under TCA 1997, s 552(1)(a) (see **9.102.17**) are to be reduced by the amount apportioned to the new assets under (a),

and if the securities comprising the new assets are not all of the same type, the apportionment between the securities under (a) is to be in accordance with their market value at the time they were acquired by the transferring company.

As regards (1) and (2) above, TCA 1997, s 631 will not apply in any case where, as respects the assets transferred, TCA 1997, s 400 applies. For example, if the trade transferred is substantially owned (to the extent of 75% at least) by the same person or persons before and after the transfer, TCA 1997, s 400 will apply instead of TCA 1997, s 631. The tax consequences are, however, the same (see also **4.109.10** in relation to the provisions of TCA 1997 ss 400 and 631(2)).

The provisions of TCA 1997, s 631 will not apply if immediately after the time of the transfer:

(a) the assets transferred in the course of the transfer are not used for the purposes of a trade carried on by the acquiring company in the State;

(b) the acquiring company would not be chargeable to tax on chargeable gains accruing to it on a disposal (if it were to make such a disposal) of any assets (other than cash – which would not result in a chargeable gain in any event) acquired in the course of the transfer; or

(c) any assets are assets of a kind specified in a double tax treaty so that the acquiring company falls to be regarded as not liable to tax in the State on the disposal of those assets.

Neither will TCA 1997, s 631 apply if the transferring company and the acquiring company jointly elect, by notice in writing to the inspector, that the provisions of the section should not apply. The notice is to be made by the time by which the transferring company's corporation tax return for the accounting period in which the transfer takes place falls to be made.

TCA 1997, s 631 will not have effect as respects a transfer of assets unless it is shown that the transfer is effected for *bona fide* commercial reasons and does not form part of any arrangement or scheme of which the main purpose, or one of the main purposes, is the avoidance of liability to income tax, corporation tax or capital gains tax.

Example 9.302.1

Under the terms of an agreement between the boards of Iberia Ltd and Roseland Ltd, Iberia Ltd transfers its trade, which is carried on in Ireland, to Roseland Ltd in return for an issue of new ordinary shares in Roseland Ltd giving it a 25% equity interest in that company. Both companies are incorporated and resident in the EU.

As regards any assets transferred with the trade, the transfer is treated for capital gains tax purposes, and for corporation tax in respect of chargeable gains, as not involving any disposal by Iberia Ltd.

Roseland Ltd is treated as if the assets transferred to it in the course of the transfer were acquired by it at the same time and for the same consideration at which they were acquired by Iberia Ltd and as if everything done by Iberia Ltd relating to the assets transferred had been done by it. On the disposal of any of these assets by Roseland Ltd, the cost date and acquisition cost in each case will be what it was to Iberia Ltd, for the purposes of computing chargeable gains or allowable losses arising to Roseland Ltd.

As indicated in (4) above, if the transferring company disposes of the "new assets" within a period of six years from the date of the transfer, any chargeable gain arising to it is computed by deducting from the consideration given for those assets the whole or the part of the relieved gain, ie the gain which would otherwise have arisen at the time of the transfer. Where all of the new assets are disposed of, the full relieved gain is deducted from the cost. Where some only of the new assets are disposed of, the appropriate proportion of the relieved gain is deducted. The relieved gain in any case will be the net gain after any allowable losses that would have arisen at the time of transfer.

Where the transferring company is not resident in Ireland, however, any gain arising on the disposal of the new assets will not be subject to capital gains tax unless those assets are unquoted shares deriving their value or the greater part of their value from land in Ireland or other assets which are subject to capital gains tax in the case of a non-resident person (see **9.102.2**).

Example 9.302.2

The facts are as in Example **9.302.1** with the additional information that the assets transferred in the course of the transfer of the trade had an allowable cost of €280,000 and that the deemed disposal proceeds of the business transferred (the value of the 25% interest in Roseland Ltd) was €400,000. Of that amount, €340,000 relates to the value of the assets included (the balance being attributable to net current assets).

Some months after the transfer, Iberia Ltd disposed of 60% of its interest in Roseland Ltd for €300,000.

The chargeable gain accruing to Iberia Ltd is computed as follows:

	€
Relieved gain	
Proceeds attributable to assets	340,000
Allowable cost of assets	280,000
Relieved gain	60,000
Reduced cost of new holding	
Appropriate proportion of relieved gain 60%	36,000
Cost of part of new holding sold – €400,000 x 60%	240,000
Deduct proportion of relieved gain	36,000
Adjusted cost	204,000
Chargeable gain on disposal of new holding	
Sale proceeds	300,000
Allowable cost, as adjusted	204,000
Gain[1]	96,000

Note:

[1]   If Iberia Ltd is not resident in Ireland, it will not be chargeable in respect of the gain unless the shares in Roseland Ltd derive their value or the greater part of their value from Irish based land or certain other assets on the disposal of which a non-resident person would be subject to capital gains tax.

The relief provided for by TCA 1997, s 631 is available to companies incorporated in any EU Member State and solely tax resident in a Member State. Thus, capital gains may be deferred where, for example, a Portuguese (resident and incorporated) company transfers its Irish branch trade to a Spanish company, or to an Irish company, or where an Irish company transfers its trade, or part of its trade, carried on in Ireland to a branch of a Finnish company.

One of the circumstances in which relief under TCA 1997, s 631 (see (b) above) would be denied is where the acquiring company would not be chargeable to tax on chargeable gains accruing to it on a disposal of any assets (other than cash) acquired in the course of the transfer. Basically, the assets transferred must remain within the charge to corporation tax. This condition will be fulfilled in the case of land and certain other categories of assets which are subject to capital gains tax regardless of the residence of the company making the disposal (see **9.102.2**).

A non-resident company is chargeable to corporation tax on chargeable gains accruing on the disposal of assets situated in the State which, at or before the time when the chargeable gains accrued, were used in or for the purposes of a trade carried on by it in the State through a branch or agency, or which at or before that time were used or held or acquired for use by or for the purposes of the branch or agency. Otherwise, where a non-resident company would not be chargeable to tax on chargeable gains accruing to it on a disposal of assets acquired in the course of the transfer, the TCA 1997, s 631 relief will not apply.

Under condition (c) above, the acquiring company must not be protected by the operation of a double tax treaty from liability to corporation tax on chargeable gains accruing on a disposal of the assets transferred. The relevant article in each of the tax treaties to which Ireland is a contracting party (see **9.105.2**) effectively provides that capital gains from the alienation of movable property (including goodwill) forming part of the business property of a permanent establishment which a non-resident company has in the State, including such gains from the alienation of such permanent establishment, may be taxed in the Ireland. Accordingly, since condition (a) above requires that the acquiring company must, immediately after the transfer, use the transferred assets for the purposes of a trade carried on by it in the State, it is unlikely that there are any circumstances in which that company could be protected from tax on chargeable gains by virtue of the provisions of a tax treaty.

9.303   Transfer of asset to parent company

TCA 1997, s 632 extends the application of TCA 1997, s 617 to a situation in which a company disposes of an asset used for the purposes of a trade carried on by it in the State to a company which holds all of the securities (shares, including stock, and debentures) representing its capital and where TCA 1997, s 617 (see **9.203**) would not otherwise apply, ie where the condition to the effect that the companies must be Irish resident, or that the asset being transferred is a chargeable asset in relation to either of the companies if it is not so resident, is not satisfied. (Since this condition would be satisfied in any case involving the transfer of an asset used for the purposes of a trade, so that TCA 1997, s 617 would apply, the circumstances in which TCA 1997, s 632 could then apply are not immediately apparent.) The section applies where, immediately after the disposal, the acquiring company commences to use the asset for the purposes of a trade carried on by it in the State and the disposal is not, or does not form part of, a transfer to which TCA 1997, s 631 applies.

Where TCA 1997, s 632 applies, TCA 1997, s 617 (transfers of assets within group), TCA 1997, s 618 (transfers within a group: trading stock – see **9.205**) and TCA 1997, s 619 (disposal or acquisition outside a group – see **9.208**) are to apply with any necessary modifications as if the two companies were Irish resident.

As with TCA 1997, s 631, the benefit of this section is not to apply in any of the three circumstances (a) to (c) described in **9.302** above in relation to that section or where, as with TCA 1997, s 631, the transferring company and the acquiring company jointly elect, by notice in writing to the inspector, that the provisions of the section should not apply. The notice is to be made by the time by which the transferring company's corporation tax return for the accounting period in which the transfer takes place falls to be made.

Example 9.303.1

Keene Ltd, an Irish resident and incorporated company, has a wholly owned UK resident and incorporated subsidiary, Williston Ltd. Williston Ltd carries on a manufacturing trade through its Irish branch. It transfers a factory building that had been used in the trade to Keene Ltd and uses the proceeds to acquire a new premises in which it continues to carry on its trade. Keene Ltd immediately commences to use the building acquired for the purposes of its own trade, also carried on in Ireland.

The disposal is not, and does not form part of, a transfer to which TCA 1997, s 631 applies because Williston Ltd has not transferred any part of its trade to Keene Ltd.

The disposal is, however, a disposal to which TCA 1997, s 617 applies since the building is a chargeable asset in relation to Williston Ltd, a non-Irish but EU resident company, immediately before the transfer. Accordingly, TCA 1997, s 632 does not apply but on the basis of TCA 1997, s 617 the building is in any event transferred so that neither a gain nor a loss accrues to Williston Ltd. Keene Ltd is treated as if the cost of the building to Williston Ltd and the date of its acquisition by that company were its own cost price and acquisition date.

TCA 1997, s 632 will not have effect as respects a transfer of assets unless it is shown that the transfer is effected for *bona fide* commercial reasons and does not form part of any arrangement or scheme of which the main purpose, or one of the main purposes, is the avoidance of liability to income tax, corporation tax or capital gains tax.

9.304　Development land

The relief provided for in TCA 1997, s 615 in respect of company reconstructions or amalgamations (see **9.207**) did not apply to gains on disposals of development land ("relevant disposals") made before 24 April 1992. FA 1992 s 67 (now TCA 1997, s 633) extended the benefit of CTA 1976 s 127 (now TCA 1997, s 615) to development land in cases of disposals made on or after 24 April 1992. *Development land* is defined in TCA 1997, s 648 (see **9.103.1**).

TCA 1997, s 633 applies for the purposes of or in connection with a "scheme of reconstruction or amalgamation", ie a scheme for the reconstruction of any company or companies or the amalgamation of any two or more companies (see **9.207**).

Where TCA 1997, s 633 applies, the companies are treated in accordance with TCA 1997, s 615 and therefore as if the land transferred were acquired by the acquiring company for a consideration of such amount as would secure that on its disposal neither a gain nor a loss would accrue to the transferring company. For the purposes of indexation relief, the acquiring company is treated as if the acquisition of the asset by the transferring company had been its own acquisition of it.

TCA 1997, s 633 applies in cases of disposals to which TCA 1997, s 631 does not apply, for example, where the consideration for the transfer of the property does not consist solely of the issue of securities in the transferee company to the transferring company.

TCA 1997, s 649(2) extends the benefit of TCA 1997, s 617 to cases involving disposals of development land. (Prior to 24 April 1992, development land was specifically excluded from the benefit of group capital gains tax treatment).

TCA 1997, s 649(2) also extends the application of TCA 1997, s 623 (company ceasing to be a member of a group – see **9.209**) and TCA 1997, s 624 (exemption from charge under TCA 1997, s 623 in the case of certain mergers) to disposals of development land.

9.305 Other transactions

TCA 1997, s 637 provides that a transaction which is covered by the Directive and which is not specifically relieved under TCA 1997 Part 21 may be relieved on application to the Revenue Commissioners, who may then give such relief as appears to them to be just and reasonable for the purposes of giving effect to the provisions of the Directive. The section could have application, for example, in the cases of mergers or divisions (see **9.301**).

9.306 Returns

Where TCA 1997 ss 631, 632, 633, 663A, 663B, 663C or 634 (credit relief – see **14.8**) applies in relation to a transfer or disposal, the transferring company is obliged by TCA 1997, s 636 to make a return of the transfer or disposal to the appropriate inspector in such form as the Revenue Commissioners may require. For this purpose, *appropriate inspector* has the same meaning as in TCA 1997, s 950 (see **15.104.2**). The return is required to be made within 9 months from the end of the accounting period in which the transfer occurs.

Tax Briefing Issue 32 contains an article prepared by the Revenue Commissioners in relation to the obligation to file a return in accordance with TCA 1997, s 636. The text of this article is as follows:

> A separate return is required where relief from capital gains tax is sought, on the transfer assets within an EU group, as specifically provided for in TCA 1997 Part 21 (ss 631-634).
>
> TCA 1997 636 obliges the participating companies to file a return within 9 months from the end of the accounting period in which the transfer occurs.

Because the group structure in each case is unique to that group, it has not been possible to devise a specific form for this purpose. Accordingly, to assist practitioners in meeting their clients' return filing obligations, it has been decided that a statement containing the following details will suffice:

> the name, country of tax residence and tax reference number of the transferor company;
>
> the name, country of tax residence and tax reference number of the transferee company;
>
> a brief description of the nature, location and value of the assets which are the subject of the transfer.

In addition, practitioners are requested to:

> specify the section under which relief applies, ie TCA 1997 ss 631, 632, 633 or 634.
>
> support the application with a "relevant certificate" vouching the quantity and date of payment of tax incurred in another Member State [including the

equivalent IR£/euro amount paid] where credit is being sought for foreign tax suffered at source in respect of the same transaction (see TCA 1997, s 643).

identify the ultimate parent company and its tax residency (albeit the parent company itself may not have been directly involved in the asset transfer).

Note TCA 1997, s 980 applies to intra-group asset transfers where the value of the asset(s) being transferred exceeds €500,000.

For convenience, practitioners may wish to note that this statement can be submitted when filing their client's corporation tax return for the relevant accounting period. (Legislative reference: EU Council Directive 90/34/EEC: OJ L225 20/8/1990 as enacted in TCA 1997 Part 21 ss 630-638).

9.307   Formation of SE or SCE by merger

The formation of an SE or SCE by merger has certain tax consequences relating to the transfer of assets by the companies being merged. These are dealt with in TCA 1997 ss 633A and 633B. The treatment is similar to that provided for in TCA 1997, s 400 (company reconstructions without change of ownership – see **4.109.4**)

For the purposes of TCA 1997 ss 633A and 633B, a company is treated as resident for tax purposes in a Member State (other than Ireland) if—

(a)   it is so treated by virtue of the law of the Member State; and

(b)   it is not treated, for the purposes of double tax arrangements to which a Member State is a party, as resident for tax purposes in a territory which is not a Member State, and for this purpose *tax* in relation to a Member State (other than Ireland) means any tax imposed in the Member State which corresponds to corporation tax in Ireland (TCA 1997, s 633A(2)).

9.307.1   Formation by merger: leaving assets in Ireland

Assets may be transferred to an SE or an SCE as part of the process of the merger forming it. The "qualifying assets" so transferred are treated as being acquired by the SE or SCE for a consideration resulting in neither a gain nor a loss. For this purpose, an asset is a *qualifying transferred asset* if—

(a)   it is transferred to an SE or an SCE as part of the process of the merger forming it;

(b)   either the transferor is resident in Ireland at the time of transfer or any gain that would have accrued to the transferor in respect of the asset, had it disposed of it immediately before the transfer, would have been a chargeable gain; and

(c)   either the transferee SE or SCE is resident in Ireland on its formation or any gain that would have accrued to the transferee SE or SCE in respect of the asset, if it disposed of the asset immediately after the transfer, would be a chargeable gain (TCA 1997, s 633A(1)).

Where TCA 1997, s 633A applies, qualifying transferred assets are treated for the purposes of the Capital Gains Tax Acts and, as regards chargeable gains, the Corporation Tax Acts, as if acquired by the SE or the SCE for a consideration resulting in neither a gain nor a loss for the transferor (TCA 1997, s 633A(4)). TCA 1997, s 633A applies where—

(i) an SE is formed by the merger of two or more companies in accordance with Articles 2(1) and 17(2)(a) or (b) of the SE Regulation (Council Regulation (EC) No 2157/2001 of 8 October 2001, on the Statute for a European Company (SE)), or an SCE is formed by a merger in accordance with Article 2 of the SCE Regulation (Council Regulation (EC) No 1435/2003 of 22 July 2003 on the Statute for a European Cooperative Society (SCE));

(ii) each merging company is tax resident in a Member State;

(iii) the merging companies are not all tax resident in the same Member State; and

(iv) TCA 1997, s 615 (company reconstruction or amalgamation: transfer of assets – see **9.207**) does not apply to any qualifying transferred assets (TCA 1997, s 633A(3)).

Where TCA 1997, s 633A applies—

(a) the transfer of assets in the course of the merger is treated as not giving rise to any balancing allowance or charge provided for by TCA 1997, s 307 or 308 (see **5.105.2-3**, also **4.109.10**); and

(b) there is to be made to or on the SE or the SCE all such allowances and charges as are provided for by TCA 1997, s 307 and 308 as would, if the transferring company had continued to use the transferred assets for the purposes of its trade, have been made to or on that company in respect of any assets transferred in the course of the merger, and the amount of any such allowance or charge is to be computed as if the SE or the SCE had been carrying on the trade carried on by the transferring company since that company began to do so and as if everything done to or by that company had been done to or by the SE or the SCE (TCA 1997, s 633A(5)).

9.307.2 Formation by merger: not leaving assets in Ireland

Where TCA 1997, s 633B applies, for the purposes of the Capital Gains Tax Acts and, as regards chargeable gains, the Corporation Tax Acts—

(a) the allowable losses accruing to the company resident in Ireland on the transfer are to be set off against the chargeable gains so accruing; and

(b) the transfer is to be treated as giving rise to a single chargeable gain equal to the aggregate of those gains after deducting the aggregate of those losses (TCA 1997, s 633B(2)).

Where TCA 1997, s 633B applies, TCA 1997, s 634 also applies (credit for tax that would be payable in the Member State in which the acquiring company is resident – see **14.8**) (TCA 1997, s 633B(3)).

TCA 1997, s 633B applies where—

(i) an SE is formed by the merger of two or more companies in accordance with Articles 2(1) and 17(2)(a) or (b) of the SE Regulation (Council Regulation (EC) No 2157/2001 of 8 October 2001, on the Statute for a European Company (SE)), or an SCE is formed by a merger in accordance with Article 2 of the SCE Regulation (Council Regulation (EC) No 1435/2003 of 22 July 2003 on the Statute for a European Cooperative Society (SCE));

(ii) each merging company is tax resident in a Member State;

(iii)   the merging companies are not all tax resident in the same Member State; and

(iv)   in the course of the merger an Irish tax resident company transfers to an EU resident company (not resident in Ireland) all assets and liabilities of a trade which the Irish resident company carried on in a Member State (other than Ireland) through a branch or agency; and

(v)   the aggregate of the chargeable gains accruing to the company resident in Ireland on the transfer exceeds the aggregate of any allowable losses so accruing (TCA 1997, s 633B(1)).

9.307.3   Formation by merger: treatment of securities

Where TCA 1997, s 633C applies, the merger is treated for the purposes of TCA 1997, s 587 (company reconstructions and amalgamations: company issuing shares or debentures to holders of shares or debentures in target company – see **9.405**) as if it were a scheme of reconstruction (TCA 1997, s 633C(2)). TCA 1997, s 633C applies where—

(a)   an SE is formed by the merger of two or more companies in accordance with Articles 2(1) and 17(2)(a) or (b) of the SE Regulation (Council Regulation (EC) No 2157/2001 of 8 October 2001, on the Statute for a European Company (SE)), or an SCE is formed by a merger in accordance with Article 2 of the SCE Regulation (Council Regulation (EC) No 1435/2003 of 22 July 2003 on the Statute for a European Cooperative Society (SCE));

(b)   each merging company is tax resident in a Member State;

(c)   the merging companies are not all tax resident in the same Member State; and

(d)   the merger does not constitute or form part of a scheme of reconstruction or amalgamation within the meaning of TCA 1997, s 587 (TCA 1997, s 633C(1)).

9.308   Anti-avoidance

TCA 1997 ss 631, 632, 633, 633A, 633C and 634 will not have effect as respects a transfer, disposal or the formation of an SE or an SCE by merger unless it is shown that the transfer, disposal or merger is effected for *bona fide* commercial reasons and does not form part of any arrangement or scheme of which the main purpose, or one of the main purposes, is the avoidance of liability to income tax, corporation tax or capital gains tax (TCA 1997, s 635).

9.4 COMPANIES AND SHAREHOLDERS

9.401   Share transactions

9.402   Reorganisation or reduction of share capital

9.403   Conversion of securities

9.404   Company amalgamations by exchange of shares

9.405   Company reconstructions and amalgamations

9.406   Transfer of business to a company

9.407   Controlled company transferring assets at undervalue

9.408   Chargeable gains of non-resident companies

9.409   Stamp duty: significant reliefs

9.401   Share transactions

9.401.1   Share issues: cost of acquisition

As noted in **9.102.23**, the issue of shares in a company does not of itself give rise to a chargeable gain on the part of the issuing company since the company is not disposing of any asset. There cannot be a disposal of an asset unless the asset existed prior to the disposal. TCA 1997, s 549 (connected persons – see **9.102.14**) does not apply, therefore, in the case of an issue of shares by a company. On the other hand, where, for example, a subscription for shares is not by way of a bargain made at arm's length, TCA 1997, s 547 (market value rule) could apply.

Where a person disposes of shares received as a result of a new issue, the base cost of those shares for the purposes of any subsequent disposal of them will usually be the amount paid (indexed as appropriate) to the company on their issue. If the shares had not been issued by way of a bargain made at arm's length, however, and if the company and the shareholder are "connected with" each other (as in TCA 1997, s 10 – see **2.3**), the amount deductible on a later sale of the shares was, up to 23 June 1982, their market value at the time of issue, as provided for in CGTA 1975 s 9 (now TCA 1997, s 547).

Where a company, otherwise than by way of a bargain made at arm's length, allots shares in the company ("the new shares") to a person connected with it, the consideration paid by that person is deemed, for capital gains tax purposes, to be an amount, including a nil amount, equal to the lesser of:

(a)   the amount or value of the consideration given by him for the new shares; and

(b)   the amount by which the market value of the shares in the company which he held immediately after the allotment of the new shares exceeds the market value of the shares in the company which he held immediately before the allotment or, if he held no such shares immediately before the allotment, the market value of the new shares immediately after the allotment (TCA 1997, s 547(2)).

Example 9.401.1.1

Wilbur Ltd owns all of the issued share capital of €1,000 in Wright Ltd. In addition, it has made loans of €99,000 to that company. Wright Ltd has carried on a trade since its formation but has fared badly and currently its balance sheet position is as follows:

	€	€
Fixed assets		25,000
Current assets	8,000	
Current liabilities	7,500	
Net current assets		500
		25,500
Loan from parent company		99,000
Net liabilities		73,500
Represented by:		
Issued share capital		1,000
Profit and loss account – deficit		74,500
		73,500

Wilbur Ltd has received an offer to purchase Wright Ltd for a nominal sum on condition that the loan of €99,000 is written off. Realising that the allowable loss on disposal of the shares will be €1,000 only, whereas Wilbur Ltd stands to lose an additional €99,000 in respect of the loan, it is decided to capitalise the loan before the shares are disposed of. Wright Ltd now has net assets of €25,500 (the loan of €99,000 having been discharged) represented by share capital €100,000 and the P&L deficit of €74,500. Wilbur Ltd claims an allowable loss of €100,000 (less, say, €1 received for the shares).

However, Wilbur Ltd and Wright Ltd are connected with each other and the new shares have been issued otherwise than by way of a bargain made at arm's length. TCA 1997, s 547(2) restricts the allowable cost of the new shares to the lesser of

(a)   the amount subscribed by Wilbur Ltd for the new shares, ie €99,000; and

(b)   the excess of the market value of the shares held by it immediately after the new issue over the market value of the shares held by it immediately before that issue.

As the market value of the shares held by Wilbur Ltd both before and after the capitalisation is nil, the excess amount from (b) is nil, and it will not be entitled to claim anything in respect of the cost of those shares for capital gains tax purposes.

The relevance of TCA 1997, s 547(2) to a situation in which it is sought to reduce or eliminate a chargeable gain (as opposed to creating an allowable loss) can be illustrated in the following example.

Example 9.401.1.2

The latest balance sheet of Pierce Ltd is as follows:

	€	€
Fixed assets		85,000
Current assets	20,000	
Current liabilities	5,000	
Net current assets		15,000
		100,000
Long term liabilities		20,000
Net assets		80,000
Represented by:		

Issued share capital	1,000
Profit and loss account	79,000
	80,000

The sole shareholder, Clay Ltd, which acquired its shares some years ago, has received an offer of €80,000 for the shares. If the offer is accepted, Clay Ltd will be liable to tax in respect of a chargeable gain computed as follows:

	€
Proceeds	80,000
Cost of shares – €1,000	1,000
Gain	79,000

To reduce this gain, it is decided to issue a further 5,000 shares of €1 each at par to Clay Ltd before disposing of the company. This increases the net assets of Pierce Ltd to €85,000 and the issued share capital to €6,000. Clay Ltd and Pierce Ltd are connected with each other and the new issue of shares is other than by way of a bargain made at arm's length. It is hoped, therefore, that TCA 1997, s 547(1) will operate to the effect that the new shares will be treated as having been acquired at their market value rather than at actual cost. This, however, does not take account of TCA 1997, s 547(2) in the absence of which the capital gains tax liability of Clay Ltd would be as follows:

	€	€
Proceeds		85,000
Cost of original shares – €1,000	1,000	
"Cost" of additional shares		
– market value €85,000 x 5,000/6,000	70,833	71,833
Gain		13,167

The effect of TCA 1997, s 547(2) is to confine the allowable cost of the additional shares issued to Pierce Ltd to the lesser of the amount paid for them and an amount equal to the increase in value of the shareholder's total holding in the company arising from the issue, in this case the amount paid. The chargeable gain would therefore stand at €79,000 (€85,000 – €6,000).

The background to TCA 1997, s 547(2) is the decision in *Harrison v Nairn Williamson* [1978] STC 67 (see also **9.102.14**) in which it was held that the market value rule could be applied in a case involving shares issued other than at market value and otherwise than by way of a bargain made at arm's length. From this evolved the "reverse Nairn Williamson" scheme which exploited the market value rule to the advantage of the taxpayer in certain non-arm's length situations.

In the *Nairn Williamson* case, the taxpayer company paid £210,000 for loan stock issued by a company (the "Company") so that immediately after its issue the aggregate value of loan stock and share capital of the Company was only £73,500. It was agreed on both sides that the loan stock had been issued otherwise than by way of a bargain at arm's length. The loan stock was converted into preferred stock and was later sold by the taxpayer company for £39,900. The company contended that the market value rule (TCA 1997, s 547 in Ireland) applied only where there was both an acquisition and a disposal (a position which could be argued under the UK version of TCA 1997, s 547) so that it was entitled to deduct as the cost of the loan stock the £210,000 it had paid for it and not its market value at the time of acquisition. The Court of Appeal did not accept this argument and held that, although the acquisition of the loan stock did not involve any disposal by the Company, the market value rule could be applied to the acquisition. The question which arose in this case would not arise in Ireland as TCA 1997, s 547 deals separately with acquisitions and disposals (see separate deemed market value rules for acquisitions and disposals **9.102.14**).

The reverse Nairn Williamson scheme, which could be implemented in the absence of TCA 1997, s 547(2), is illustrated in the following example.

Example 9.401.1.3

The entire issued share capital of Madox Ltd is owned between them by Rockland Ltd, Lagan Ltd and Omagh Ltd, each company owning 6,000 €1 ordinary shares which had been issued some years ago when Madox Ltd was formed. The three shareholding companies now receive an offer of €4.5m for their shares.

On the basis of the offer, the gain arising to each company would be as follows:

	€
Sale proceeds – €4.5m/3	1,500,000
Cost – €6,000	6,000
Gain	1,494,000

To avoid the substantial chargeable gain, a further issue of 200,000 €1 shares by the company is arranged, Rockland Ltd, Lagan Ltd and Omagh Ltd receiving 65,000, 66,000 and 69,000 shares respectively. On this basis, the shares have not been issued under a bargain made at arm's length so that, under TCA 1997, s 547(1), the companies are regarded as having acquired them at market value. Based on the offer for shares and the new share issue, the market value of Madox Ltd would now be €4.7m. If the shares are now sold, the gain arising to, say, Lagan Ltd, would be as follows:

	€	€
Sale proceeds – €4.7m x 72,000/218,000		1,552,294
Cost – €6,000	6,000	
Market value of new shares issued		
– €4.7m x 66,000/218,000	1,422,936	1,428,936
Gain		123,358

If the new shares issued to the three companies had been in proportion to the shares already held by them, the issue would have been a reorganisation within TCA 1997 586 (see **9.402**). That would mean that the new shares would be treated as not having been acquired now, but when Madox Ltd was formed, and the amount paid for them would be treated as enhancement expenditure in respect of the original shares. For this reason, the shares are issued in differing amounts and not in proportion.

If TCA 1997, s 547(2) is now applied, the consideration given by Lagan Ltd for the new shares will be the lesser of—

(a)   the amount given by it for the new shares, ie €66,000; and

(b)   the excess of the market value of the shares held by it immediately after the new issue over the market value of the shares held by it immediately before that issue, ie €1,552,294 - €1,500,000 = €52,294.

The revised chargeable gain would therefore be as follows:

	€	€
Sale proceeds		1,552,294
Cost – €6,000	6,000	
Deemed cost of new shares issued	52,294	58,294
Gain		1,494,000

It will be seen that the effect of TCA 1997, s 547(2) is to restore the chargeable gain to what it would have been had the reverse Nairn Williamson scheme not been put in place. In effect, the uplift in the cost of the shares sold is restricted to the increase in the amount receivable on their sale.

The market value rule of TCA 1997, s 547(1) does not apply to the acquisition of an asset where:

(a)   there is no corresponding disposal of the asset; and

(b)   (i)   there is no consideration in money or money's worth for the asset, or

(ii)   the consideration for the asset is of an amount or value which is lower than the market value of the asset (TCA 1997, s 547(3)).

The issue of shares by a company involves an acquisition of an asset (ie the shares) without a corresponding disposal. Accordingly, where a company issues shares for a nil consideration or for a consideration which is less than the market value of the shares, the market value rule of TCA 1997, s 547(1) does not apply. The purpose of TCA 1997, s 547(3) is to counter certain tax avoidance schemes involving pre-1986 share option schemes. In these situations, shares could have been purchased at a price which was significantly lower than their market price at the date the option was exercised. Prior to 1986, the benefit obtained was free of income tax. In addition, it was possible to argue that the transaction was at arm's length but that the shares were acquired in consideration for services in an office or employment so that, while TCA 1997, s 547(2) did not apply, TCA 1997, s 547(1)(c)(iii) did apply. Accordingly, on a disposal of the shares, their cost for capital gains tax purposes was their market value at the time of acquisition.

9.401.2   Calls on shares

Where, as respects an issue of shares in or debentures of a company, a person gives any consideration on a date which is more than twelve months after the date on which the shares or debentures were allotted, that consideration is deemed, for the purposes of applying indexation in the capital gains tax computation of a gain accruing to the person on the disposal of the shares or debentures, to be expenditure incurred (ie, enhancement expenditure) on the date on which the consideration was given (TCA 1997, s 582).

Example 9.401.2.1

On 1 July 2001, Crabtree Ltd applied for and was allotted 25,000 €1 ordinary shares in Miller Ltd, 75c per share being payable on application and the remaining 25c per share being paid on due call by the company on 1 October 2002. Crabtree Ltd sold its shares in Miller Ltd on 18 August 2007 for €75,000. The computation of the chargeable gain arising is calculated as follows:

	€	€
Proceeds of disposal		75,000

Cost 1/7/01 €18,750		
Indexed @ 1.087		20,381
Enhancement expenditure 1/10/02 €6,250		
Indexed @ 1.049	6,556	26,937
Gain		48,063

9.401.3   Shares: identification

Where some of the shares of the same class in the same company are sold, it is necessary to identify the shares sold so that their cost can be ascertained and the correct indexation multiplier applied. The general identification rule, contained in TCA 1997, s 580, is that shares acquired at an earlier time are deemed to have been disposed of before shares acquired at a later time. In other words, the first-in first-out (FIFO) rule applies and it is irrelevant as to what shares have actually been disposed of. Shares are treated as being of the same class only where they would be so treated if they were dealt in on a stock exchange.

The four-week rule is an exception to the FIFO provision. Where shares are disposed of within four weeks of the acquisition of other shares of the same class, those shares are regarded as the same as the shares so acquired within that four weeks (TCA 1997, s 581(1)). The rule does not identify shares disposed of with shares subsequently acquired, even within four weeks.

In a case where a loss accrues to a person on the disposal of shares and shares of the same class in the same company are acquired by that person within four weeks of the disposal, the loss will be allowed as a deduction only against a gain arising on the disposal of the shares so acquired (TCA 1997, s 581(3)). Where part only of the shares disposed of are replaced, the loss is restricted to the extent that the shares were replaced.

Example 9.401.3.1

Beryl Ltd purchases 50,000 €1 ordinary shares in Caine Ltd at a price of €2.50 per share. Some time later, the value of the shares has fallen to 30c per share. Beryl Ltd wishes to retain the shares but, to crystallise an allowable loss now, sells them on the market and buys them back a week later.

Although a loss of €110,000 (50,000 x €2.20) has been realised, no deduction may be made against any chargeable gain realised by Beryl Ltd other than any gain eventually realised on a disposal of the shares which were bought back within the week as above.

Example 9.401.3.2

The position is the same as in Example **9.401.3.1** except that only 20,000 of the shares disposed of were repurchased.

As 2/5ths of the shares were repurchased, that fraction of the loss, ie €44,000, may only be offset against any future gain on the disposal of the shares repurchased. The balance of the loss, €66,000, may be deducted against any chargeable gain accruing to Beryl Ltd.

In the event of a taxpayer seeking to avoid the impact of TCA 1997, s 581(3) by purchasing shares just *before* disposing of the shares giving rise to the loss, the FIFO rule will operate to secure that the shares disposed of are identified with those shares. The cost price of the shares sold will therefore be the cost of the shares purchased just prior to their sale so that no (or almost no) loss will result.

9.401.4   Capital distributions

TCA 1997, s 583 provides that where a person receives or becomes entitled to receive in respect of shares in a company any capital distribution from the company (except a new holding – see **9.402.1**), he is to be treated as if for that capital distribution he had disposed of an interest in the shares.

For this purpose, *capital distribution* means any distribution from a company, including a distribution in the course of dissolving or winding up the company, in money or money's worth, except a distribution which in the hands of the recipient constitutes income for the purposes of income tax.

Distributions from Irish resident companies (see **11.1**) are subject to income tax under Sch F (TCA 1997, s 20 – see **11.110**). TCA 1997, s 130 defines the term *distribution* and this includes a capital dividend (a dividend out of capital profits, not the same thing as a capital distribution) but not distributions made in respect of share capital in a winding up. Being subject to income tax, anything treated by TCA 1997, s 130, or otherwise, as a distribution should not be a capital distribution. As a working rule, any distribution made out of a company's assets that falls outside the meaning of "distribution" is likely to be a capital distribution.

TCA 1997, s 20 states that for the purposes of income tax all such distributions as are not specially excluded from income tax are to be "regarded as income however they are to be dealt with in the hands of the recipient". This is sometimes seen (for example by HMRC - the UK Revenue) as support for the view that a capital distribution for the purposes of TCA 1997, s 583 excludes anything described as a distribution in TCA 1997, s 130 and that this position is not affected by, say, TCA 1997, s 130(3)(b) which disapplies TCA 1997, s 130(3)(a) (transfers of assets to members treated as distributions). But the exclusion mentioned in TCA 1997, s 583 refers to any "distribution which in the hands of the recipient constitutes income for income tax purposes". Is it necessary therefore, to be excluded, that the distribution be not only regarded as income but that it should constitute income for income tax purposes "in the hands of the recipient"? It would surely be meaningless, however, to regard something as income but not as income in the hands of the recipient of that income.

Taking the case of a transfer of assets from company A to company B, where there are common shareholders, it will usually be the case that such a transfer will be "in respect of shares", giving rise to a distribution within the meaning of TCA 1997, s 130 and as such taxable under Schedule F. Even if the distribution is not actually taxable (as would be the case where received by a company), TCA s 20 seems to treat the item as income anyway. If the view expressed by HMRC in this context is correct, any dividend or other distribution as defined in TCA 1997, s 130 (including any transfer of assets as described in TCA 1997, s 130(3)(a)) is not a capital distribution (because of the closing words of TCA 1997, s 583(1) quoted above).

In certain circumstances (see **11.303**), a payment made on the redemption, repayment or purchase of its own shares by an unquoted company is treated as not being a distribution (as it would normally be under TCA 1997, s 130(2)(b) – see **11.102.3**). In addition, any disposal of shares consequent on the redemption, repayment or purchase by a quoted company of its own shares is not to be treated as a distribution and is instead subject to capital gains tax treatment. In summary therefore, a capital distribution refers to a distribution on a winding up or, in some circumstances, to a payment made by a company on the redemption, repayment or purchase of its own shares (TCA 1997, s 175), or to the disposal of rights following a rights issue (see **9.402.7**).

TCA 1997, s 534(b) provides that there is a part disposal of an asset where, on a person making a disposal, any description of property derived from the asset remains undisposed of. An interim distribution by a liquidator, and any distribution up to the time the company is struck off the register of companies and the shares cease legally to exist, is a part disposal. TCA 1997, s 583, however, specifically treats a capital distribution by a company as a disposal of an interest in the shares (which comes to the same thing). The fact that a redemption or reduction of capital (being, in certain cases at least, a capital distribution) is treated by TCA 1997, s 583 as a disposal could, it might be argued, imply that it is merely a notional and not an actual disposal. (It appears to be the view of the UK Inland Revenue that a redemption of shares does not involve an actual disposal of the shares, although the precise basis for this view remains obscure). A purchase of its own shares by a company, which may also come within the meaning of "capital distribution", clearly involves an actual disposal so that it is not a disposal by virtue of TCA 1997, s 583.

Example 9.401.4.1

Taber Ltd, a wholly owned subsidiary of Dundee Ltd, was formed on 1 February 2006 when it issued 250,000 €1 ordinary shares at par. The proceeds of the shares issued were invested in equities, gilts and other investments. On 1 March 2007, it was decided to wind up the company. At that time, the investments were valued at €700,000 and the company also had cash of €20,000. On 15 April 2007, the liquidator had disposed of some of the investments and made a distribution of €150,000.

By 20 August 2007, all of the investments had been realised and all taxes and expenses accounted for. The liquidator paid out the balance of €425,000 as a final liquidation distribution to Dundee Ltd and, on 10 March 2008, Taber Ltd was struck off the register of companies.

A computation of the chargeable gain in respect of each distribution is necessary and, for this purpose, the value of the investments remaining after the interim distribution, less a provision for tax and other expenses, is €450,000. The chargeable gains computations are as follows:

	€
Distribution on 15 April 2007	
Capital distribution	150,000
Attributable cost of part disposal:	
$€250,000 \times \dfrac{150,000}{150,000 + 450,000} =$	62,500
Chargeable gain	87,500
Distribution on 20 August 2007	
Capital distribution	425,000
Balance of cost after interim distribution:	
€250,000 - €62,500 =	187,500
Chargeable gain	237,500

Disposals by a liquidator of a company's assets in the course of the winding up, whether to discharge liabilities or to realise cash to pay the shareholders, are disposals for capital gains tax purposes. Distributions of assets in specie to the shareholders are also such disposals. Winding up distributions received by the shareholders are part disposals of their shares for capital gains tax purposes. The shares are extinguished at the point at which the company is struck off the register of companies and any disposal before that time is, technically at least, a part disposal. In practice, a final distribution by the liquidator before the company is struck off would not require a computation in accordance with part disposal formula (see Example **9.401.4.1** above) as the shares would have no remaining value at that point.

A transfer by the liquidator of an asset *in specie* to the parent company of the company in liquidation would fall within TCA 1997, s 617(1) and would accordingly be on the basis that neither a gain nor a loss had resulted. This is not one of the exceptions to group treatment listed in TCA 1997, s 617(2). The transfer of the asset by the liquidator is to be distinguished from the part disposal by the parent company of its shares in the company in liquidation in consideration for a capital distribution and which *is* one of the exceptions so listed (see *Innocent v Whaddon Estates Ltd* [1982] STC 115 and **9.203.1**). Consequently, the transfer of the asset by the liquidator is assumed to be for no gain and no loss but the share disposal by the parent company is subject to capital gains tax treatment at that point.

9.402 Reorganisation or reduction of share capital

9.402.1 Reorganisation etc results in no disposal, no acquisition

A reorganisation of a company's share capital, in contrast to a disposal of shares or a capital distribution in respect of shares (see **9.401.4**), does not involve any real disposal of an interest in the shares held. In a reorganisation, the shareholders may receive new shares in exchange for their existing shares and the new shares may be of a different type from the shares exchanged and may have rights which are different from the exchanged shares. Capital gains tax legislation recognises that in such situations the shareholders have not made any real disposal since they will not have derived consideration in any tangible form from the company, and that they should therefore be treated as not having made any disposal which would be subject to capital gains tax.

As regards shares in a single company, shareholders may receive a bonus issue, or may subscribe for a rights issue, or may exchange shares in the company for other shares, stock or debentures in the company. Again, existing shares may be retained but the rights attaching to them may be altered. All of these kinds of changes are regarded as reorganisations of share capital, the feature common to all being that the shareholders (more or less) retain their interests in the company.

In the case of a single company, the provisions of TCA 1997, s 584-588 are concerned with reorganisations and reductions (see below) of share capital. Where more than one company is involved, the provisions of TCA 1997, s 584-588 deal with situations in which, for example, the share or debenture holders exchange their shares or debentures in one company for shares or debentures in another company (see **9.404**).

Although TCA 1997, s 584 provides specific examples of what is to constitute a reorganisation (see below) for capital gains tax purposes, no such guidance is given in relation to a *reduction* of a company's share capital. A reduction of capital is a form of repayment of share capital. The share capital in question is paid off in accordance with s 72 of the Companies Act 1963. To bring about a reduction of share capital, the articles of association of the company concerned must contain power to do so; it is not sufficient for this purpose that the memorandum contains such a provision. Where the necessary power is not contained in the articles, they may be altered as necessary by means of a special resolution. A further special resolution must then be passed to give effect to the reduction.

A reduction of share capital is distinct from a redemption of share capital but is a form of repayment of capital (see also **11.105.1-105.3**). TCA 1997, s 584(1) provides that a reduction of share capital does not include the paying off of redeemable share capital (a redemption of shares, otherwise than in a liquidation, being treated as a disposal of those shares at the time of the redemption). A reduction of share capital may involve a reduction in the nominal capital of a company as well as in its issued capital. Again, a reduction of share capital may take the form of a reduction in the paid up share capital of a company or in the share capital which has been issued but not paid up. To be effective, a reduction of share capital must be carried out with the permission of the High Court. The company may then proceed with the reduction, for example by cancelling some of the shares held by each shareholder.

A reduction of share capital may be sought by a company where its existing capital is in excess of its requirements. Alternatively, it may want to reduce its share capital where it requires to raise new share capital but is unable to do so due to its inability to pay dividends, which in turn is due to a loss of capital or to the fact that its capital is no longer represented by available assets and there is a substantial deficit in its profit and loss account. By cancelling a sufficient number of shares, the deficit can be eliminated thus enabling the company to resume paying dividends from profits as they arise.

A reorganisation or reduction of share capital involves a disposal of "original shares" in exchange for a "new holding". A new holding, in relation to original shares, means the shares in and debentures of the company which as a result of the reorganisation or reduction of capital represent the original shares (including such, if any, of the original shares as remain). Original shares means shares held before and concerned in the reorganisation or reduction of capital (TCA 1997, s 584(1)).

A reduction of share capital would normally constitute a disposal of the shares cancelled but is treated by TCA 1997, s 584 as not involving either a disposal or an acquisition of shares for capital gains tax purposes. The *new holding* (ie, the shares remaining after the reduction) is treated as the same asset acquired as the original shares were acquired. In other words, the reduced shares comprising the new holding are regarded, for capital gains tax purposes, as the same as the original shares in terms of their acquisition date and acquisition cost.

A reduction of share capital may take the form of, or include, the receipt of new shares in return for the cancellation of existing shares. For example, each preference shareholder might receive one new ordinary share in return for the cancellation of a given number of preference shares held. Again, the exchange of shares is treated as not involving a disposal of the preference shares and the ordinary shares acquired take on the acquisition date and cost of the cancelled preference shares.

TCA 1997, s 584(1) defines a *reorganisation* of a company's share capital as including—

    (a)   any case where persons are, whether for payment or not, allotted shares in or
            debentures of the company in respect of and in proportion to (or as nearly as

may be in proportion to) their holdings of shares in the company or of any class of shares in the company; and

(b)   any case where there are more than one class of shares and the rights attached to shares of any class are altered.

For the above purposes, "shares" includes stock. For the meaning of *debentures*, see **9.404.1**.

As a consequence of (a) above, a reorganisation may consist of the issue of shares in or debentures of a company in respect of shares in the company, the issue of ordinary shares in return for the cancellation of preference shares (which may also constitute a reduction of share capital – see above), or a bonus or a rights issue of shares. The definition of "reorganisation" is not exhaustive and merely describes the more obvious and important forms, and allows for other possible forms, of reorganisation as was confirmed in *Dunstan v Young Austen Young Ltd* [1989] STC 69. A reorganisation may include any arrangement involving the issue of shares by a company to its shareholders by virtue of their existing shareholdings in the company and in proportion to those holdings. It would seem therefore that an increase in the issued share capital of a company, where the additional shares are taken up by the existing shareholders in their capacity as shareholders and in proportion to their shareholdings, would be a reorganisation.

TCA 1997, s 584(3) provides that a reorganisation or reduction of a company's share capital is not to be treated as involving any disposal of the original shares or any acquisition of the new holding or any part of it, and that the original shares (taken as a single asset) and the new holding (taken as a single asset) are to be treated as the same asset acquired as the original shares were acquired. The new holding, consisting of the shares held both before and after the reorganisation or reduction, are treated as the same as the shares held before the reorganisation or reduction as regards their acquisition date and their base cost for capital gains tax purposes.

TCA 1997, s 584(3) does not apply to the extent that the new holding comprises debentures, loan stock or other similar securities issued or allotted on or after 4 December 2002, unless—

(a)   they were so issued or allotted pursuant to a binding written agreement made before that date; or

(b)   TCA 1997, s 584 has application by virtue of TCA 1997, s 586 (in which case deferral may still apply if the debentures etc are issued by one company to another company within the same capital gains tax group – see **9.404.1**) (TCA 1997, s 584(9)).

9.402.2   Paper for paper

A reorganisation for the purposes of TCA 1997, s 584 includes a case in which shares in a company are disposed of in exchange for other shares in the same company (referred to as a "paper for paper" or a "share for share" transaction). The exchange does not involve any disposal of the original shares or any acquisition of the replacement shares. The new holding is treated as the same asset as the original shares in terms of their acquisition date and cost.

9.402.3   Additional consideration given for new holding

A reorganisation or reduction of a company's share capital may be carried out on the basis that a shareholder gives, or becomes liable to give, new consideration for his new holding or any part of it. That consideration is treated, for the purposes of indexation relief in the computation of a gain accruing to him on the disposal of the new holding (or part of it), as expenditure incurred on the date the consideration was given.

Thus, for the acquisition of the new holding, the shareholder may be required to surrender his existing shares and in addition to give further consideration. This does not involve any disposal of the original shares (since a reorganisation is involved) but the shareholder, on the eventual disposal of the new holding (or part of it), will now have two separate expenditure items to be deducted from the consideration received, ie the cost of the original shares, indexed by reference to the multiplier appropriate to the year of assessment in which the shares were acquired, and expenditure comprising the new consideration given (in effect, "enhancement expenditure"), indexed by reference to the multiplier appropriate to the year of assessment in which that expenditure was incurred (TCA 1997, s 584(4)).

For the above purposes, consideration given for the new holding does not include:

(a)   any surrender, cancellation or other alteration of the original shares or of the rights attached thereto; or

(b)   any consideration consisting of any application, in paying up the shares or debentures or any part of them, of any assets of the company, or of any dividend or other distribution declared out of those assets but not made.

Where TCA 1997, s 816 (taxation of shares issued in lieu of cash dividends – see **3.208.5**) applies as respects an issue of shares, the cash which the shareholder might have received instead of the shares is treated as consideration given for those shares.

9.402.4   Other consideration received with new holding

A reorganisation or reduction of a company's share capital may be on terms under which a shareholder receives, or is deemed to receive, or becomes entitled to receive, consideration other than the new holding for the disposal of an interest in the original shares. Where this is the case, TCA 1997, s 584(5) provides that the other consideration is deemed to be consideration for a part disposal of the original shares. This is without prejudice to the original shares and the new holding being treated as the same asset in accordance with TCA 1997, s 584(3) (see above). Thus, the new holding acquires the same acquisition date as the original shares and the same cost, but subject to an adjustment to exclude the part of the cost attributable to the part disposal. TCA 1997, s 584(5) applies in particular:

(a)   where the shareholder is to be treated as if he had in consideration of a capital distribution disposed of an interest in the original shares (see **9.401.4**); or

(b)   where the shareholder receives, or is deemed to receive, consideration from the other shareholders in respect of a surrender of rights derived from the original shares.

Example 9.402.4.1

Redbrick Ltd acquired 12,000 €1 ordinary shares at par in Yellowstone Ltd on 15 February 2007. Arising out of a reorganisation on 31 December 2007, Redbrick Ltd received 6,000 non-voting preference shares in Yellowstone Ltd and €10,500 cash. At the date of their issue, the market value of the preference shares was €7,000. On 10 March 2008, Redbrick Ltd disposed of the preference shares for €4,000.

The cash of €10,500 is deemed to be consideration for a part disposal of the original 12,000 ordinary shares held by Redbrick Ltd. The chargeable gains arising on this part disposal and on the disposal of the shares are calculated as follows:

	€
Cash consideration e10,500	
Consideration received	10,500
Attributable cost:	
$€12,000 \times \dfrac{10,500}{10,500 + 7,000} =$	7,200
Chargeable gain	3,300
Disposal of shares	
Disposal proceeds	4,000
Attributable cost €12,000 - €7,200	4,800
Loss	800

9.402.5 Apportionment

A reorganisation, as already explained, is treated as not involving any disposal of the original shares or any acquisition of the new holding so that the original shares and the new holding are treated as the same asset acquired as the original shares were acquired. Thus, the new holding is treated as the same as the original shares held before the reorganisation as regards their acquisition date and their base cost for capital gains tax purposes.

In computing the gain or loss accruing to a person from the acquisition and disposal of any part of a new holding where no part of the holding is quoted, it will sometimes be necessary (ie, where the new holding consists of more than one class of shares or of shares and debentures) to apportion the cost of acquisition (treated as the cost of the original shares) between the part which is disposed of and the part which is retained. TCA 1997, s 584(6) provides that this apportionment is to be made by reference to market value at the date of the disposal (with such adjustment of the market value of any part of the new holding as may be required to offset any liability attaching to it but which forms part of the cost to be apportioned – see further below). Any corresponding apportionment is to be made in the same way where this is required for the purposes of TCA 1997, s 584(5) (other consideration received with new holding – see above).

If any liability is attached to part of the new holding and that liability forms part of the cost being apportioned, the market value is to be adjusted to take that factor into account. The amount of the liability, which is also added to the base cost of the new holding, is added to the market value of the relevant part of the new holding.

Example 9.402.5.1

On 1 May 2006, Marlin Ltd purchased 5,000 €1 ordinary shares at par in Hamlin Ltd. On 1 July 2007, Marlin Ltd received 2,500 "A" ordinary shares and 2,500 preference shares in exchange for its original holding. On 15 March 2008, it sold the preference shares for €3,500. At that time, the market value of the "A" ordinary shares was €5,000. Neither the ordinary shares nor the preference shares were quoted at any time. The chargeable gain on the disposal of the preference shares is computed as follows:

	€
Disposal proceeds	3,500
Attributable cost:	
$€5,000 \times \dfrac{3,500}{3,500+5,000} =$	2,059
	1,441

Where the new holding—

(a) consists of more than one class of shares or debentures and one or more of those classes is of shares or debentures which, at any time not later than the end of three months from the date of the reorganisation or of such longer period as the Revenue Commissioners allow, are quoted on a recognised stock exchange in the State or elsewhere; or

(b) consists of more than one class of rights of unit holders one or more of which is of rights the prices of which were published regularly by the managers of the scheme at any time not later than three months from the date of the reorganisation (or longer period if allowed),

the following procedure applies.

Where, for the purpose of computing the gain or loss from the acquisition and disposal of all or part of any class of shares or debentures or rights of unit holders forming part of the new holding, it is necessary (because there is more than one class) to apportion the cost of acquisition between the part disposed of and the part retained, the cost of the new holding is first to be apportioned between the entire classes of shares or debentures or rights included in the new holding by reference to their respective market values on the first day (whether published before or after the reorganisation took effect) on which the market values or prices of the shares or debentures or rights were quoted or published (with such adjustment of the market value of any part of the new holding as may be required to offset any liability attaching to it but which forms part of the cost to be apportioned). The day on which a reorganisation of share capital involving the allotment of shares or debentures or unit holders' rights takes effect is the day following the day on which the right to renounce any allotment expires (TCA 1997, s 584(7)).

Shares or debentures are *quoted* for this purpose if they have a quoted market value on a recognised stock exchange at any time up to the end of the three month period beginning with the date on which the reorganisation or reduction took effect, or within such longer period as the Revenue Commissioners may by notice in writing allow. A reorganisation of share capital involving the allotment of shares or debentures takes effect on the day following the day on which the right to renounce any allotment expires.

9.402.6   Bonus issues

A bonus issue is an issue of shares in or debentures of a company, made to the existing shareholders other than for consideration in money or money's worth. A bonus issue involves the capitalisation of the company's reserves, or, more usually, a part of them, resulting in the replacement of those reserves by additional share capital or loan stock. The amount of the reserves which have been capitalised may not subsequently be paid out by way of dividend.

Following a bonus issue, the value of the shareholders' interests in the company remains unchanged although the composition of their holdings will have altered. Because of this, a bonus issue is treated for capital gains tax purposes as a reorganisation, which means that the shareholders are not regarded as having acquired any new shares. The new holding, consisting of the shares held both before and after the bonus issue, is treated as the same as the shares held before the bonus issue as regards the acquisition date and base cost for capital gains tax purposes.

9.402.7   Rights issues

A rights issue of shares normally involves an issue, for new consideration, of shares by a company to its shareholders in proportion to their existing shareholdings, eg one new ordinary share for each five ordinary shares held. Accordingly, a rights issue is a reorganisation within the meaning of TCA 1997, s 584 so that the new shares acquired are treated as not involving an acquisition of any asset for capital gains tax purposes. A rights issue takes the form of an offer by a company to its members of a right to subscribe for new shares in the company, normally at a favourable price. Some shareholders may not wish to provide additional consideration and may therefore decide not to take up their rights or to take up only a part of those rights.

A rights issue does not result in any acquisition of an asset although new consideration will have been provided by the shareholders taking up their rights. Instead, the consideration provided is treated as enhancement expenditure on the shares already held (the "original shares"). The original shares (taken as a single asset) and the new holding (taken as a single asset) are to be treated as the same asset acquired as the original shares were acquired. The new holding, consisting of the shares held both before and after the rights issue, is treated as the same as the shares held before the rights issue as regards the acquisition date and base cost for capital gains tax purposes.

Accordingly, the allowable cost of the shares when disposed of will comprise the original cost indexed by reference to the multiplier appropriate to the year of assessment in which the shares were acquired, and the enhancement expenditure comprising the amount paid for the rights taken up indexed by reference to the multiplier appropriate to the year of assessment in which that expenditure was incurred.

The above-described treatment of a rights issue of shares was confirmed by the decision in the UK case *IRC v Burmah Oil Co Ltd* [1982] STC 30. That case involved an arrangement in which the taxpayer company (Burmah) sought to create an allowable loss arising out of a substantial loan it had made to its subsidiary company. The subsidiary incurred a deficit represented by the amount of the loan. The arrangement involved a loan, indirectly provided by Burmah through another company, to the subsidiary to enable it to repay its loan to Burmah, followed by the payment by Burmah of an equivalent sum to take up a rights issue of shares by the subsidiary. The proceeds of the rights issue were used by the subsidiary to repay its loan from the other company. The subsidiary was then liquidated and Burmah claimed an allowable loss in respect of the cost of its shares.

The Revenue sought to deny the loss on the basis that the rights shares should be regarded as having been acquired at market value at the date of issue. That view was rejected. As the rights shares were the result of a reorganisation, there was no acquisition and the amount paid for those shares must be treated as additional consideration for the original shares. Burmah, however, was ultimately denied its loss on other grounds which, in view of the decision in *McGrath and Others v JE MacDermott* 3 ITR 683, would probably not apply in Ireland. TCA 1997, s 547(2) would now prevent a loss being claimed in Ireland in a situation similar to that in the Burmah case (see **9.401.1**).

Where members of a company making a rights issue do not take up their rights, it is usual to offer those rights to members who do take up their rights, or to sell them to third parties. Since in such circumstances the allotment of shares to members taking up the further rights would not then be in proportion (and, probably, not "as nearly as may be in proportion") to their existing holdings, it would seem that one of the necessary conditions for a reorganisation would not then be fulfilled. The additional shares taken up as a result of rights originally offered to other members would then amount to the acquisition of an asset. Where rights are sold on to third parties, any shares thereby acquired would, clearly, not be acquired as part of a reorganisation.

Where a person receives or becomes entitled to receive in respect of any shares or debentures in a company a provisional allotment of shares in or debentures of the company and he disposes of his rights, the consideration received is treated as a capital distribution received by him from the company in respect of the first-mentioned shares (or debentures) and as if he had, instead of disposing of the rights, disposed of an interest in those shares (or debentures) (TCA 1997, s 584(8)). The following example shows how a disposal of rights is treated as a part disposal of the shares to which the rights are attached, and also deals with the disposal of shares which include shares taken up under a rights issue.

Example 9.402.7.1

On 2 November 2007, Fillmore plc announced a rights issue in which one new ordinary share would be allotted for every five ordinary shares then held, at an issue price of €3 per share. Millard Ltd held 2.5m ordinary shares in Fillmore plc on 2 November 2007 and on 22 November 2007 sold to another company for €20,000 the rights to subscribe for 200,000 new shares. On 4 December 2007, Millard Ltd took up the remaining rights and acquired 300,000 new shares in Fillmore plc for €900,000. The ex-rights price of the Fillmore plc shares was then €3.15.

On 10 March 2008, Millard Ltd sold 1.75m shares for €3.30 per share.

The 2.5m shares had been acquired by Millard Ltd as follows:

	€
Purchase of 500,000 shares on 1 January 2003	500,000
Bonus issue 2:1 on 31 March 2004 – 1,000,000 shares	
Purchase of 1,000,000 shares on 1 September 2005	2,800,000

The cost history of the shareholdings by Millard Ltd in Fillmore plc can be represented as follows:

		1 January 2003			*1 September 2005*	
	No of Shares	*Cost*	*Enh Exp*	*No of Shares*	*Cost*	*Enh Exp*
		€	€		€	€
Purchase	500,000	500,000				
Bonus issue	1,000,000					
Balance	1,500,000	500,000				
Purchase				1,000,000	2,800,000	
Balance	1,500,000	500,000		1,000,000	2,800,000	
Rights sold[1]		3,155				
Balance	1,500,000	496,845		1,000,000	2,800,000	
Rights issue[2]	100,000		300,000	200,000		600,000
Balance	1,600,000	496,845	300,000	1,200,000	2,800,000	600,000
Sold 10/3/08	1,600,000	496,845	300,000	150,000	350,000	75,000
Balance	–	–	–	1,050,000	2,450,000	525,000

Sale of rights:

	€
Proceeds	20,000

$$\text{Cost:} \quad €500{,}000 \times \frac{20{,}000}{20{,}000 + (1{,}000{,}000 \times 3.15)} = \qquad 3{,}155$$

Gain	16,845

Sale of 1,750,000 shares on 10 March 2008:
The 1,750,000 shares sold on 10 March 2008 comprise the following:

	€	€
(a) Shares to which the rights sold were attached (FIFO basis): 200,000 x 5 =		1,000,000
(b) Balance of shares purchased in 2003 (1,500,000 - 1,000,000)		500,000
Rights shares attached (1/5):		100,000
		600,000
(c) Shares purchased in 2005:		
Balance sold 1,750,000 - (1,000,000 + 600,000) =	150,000	
Comprising: rights shares attached (1/6)	25,000	
Shares to which rights attached (5/6)	125,000	150,000

The chargeable gains are computed for these blocks of shares as follows:

	(a) 1 January 2003		(b) 1 January 2003		(c) 1 September 2005	
	€	€	€	€	€	
Sale proceeds:						
1,000,000 @ €3.30	3,300,000					
600,000 @ €3.30			1,980,000			
150,000 @ €3.30					495,000	
Cost:						
3	330,178					
4			166,667			
5					350,000	
Enhancement exp:			300,000		75,000	
				466,667		425,000
Chargeable gain	2,969,822			1,513,333		70,000

Notes:

1   Part disposal (FIFO basis) – see calculation under *Sale of rights.*

2   The number of shares taken up under the rights issue is apportioned, on the basis of the numbers of shares held, between the existing shareholdings acquired on different dates. The costs, which are treated as enhancement expenditure, are similarly apportioned. Of the 1,500,000 shares purchased in 2003, the rights shares attaching to 1,000,000 shares were sold on 22 November 2007 so that the rights shares attaching to the remaining shares are 500,000 x 1/5 = 100,000. The rights shares attaching to the 2005 shares are 1,000,000 x 1/5 = 200,000 shares. Enhancement expenditure in each case is at €3 per share.

3   The cost is the apportioned cost less cost of rights sold, ie €500,000 x 1,000/1,500 – €3,155 = €330,178.

4   The cost is the apportioned cost, ie €500,000 x 500/1,500 = €166,667.

5   The cost is the apportioned cost, ie €2,800,000 x 125/1,000 = €350,000.

A rights issue, as envisaged by TCA 1997, s 584, may involve an issue of shares or debentures. The rights issue need not be of shares of the same class as those in respect of which it is made and, where debentures are issued, would not involve any issue of shares. In either case, the apportionment of the consideration for the rights taken up, as between the shares held before the rights issue and new shares or debentures acquired, must be carried out by reference to the respective market values of the original shares and the rights shares or debentures. The date by reference to which the market value is to be taken depends on whether or not the shares or debentures are quoted (see **9.402.5**).

Example 9.402.7.2

On 1 September 2007, Lenoir Ltd announced details of a rights issue in which one unit of 9% Debenture Stock would be allotted for every five ordinary shares held, at an issue price of €1.5 per unit. Othello Ltd held 1,500,000 ordinary shares in Lenoir Ltd at the date of the rights issue entitling it to subscribe for 300,000 units of Debenture Stock. On 1 October 2007, Othello Ltd acquired the Debenture Stock for €450,000.

On 1 October 2007, the ex-rights market price of the ordinary shares was €1.75 per share and the Debenture Stock was valued at €2 per unit. On 10 March 2008, Othello Ltd sold

250,000 units of Debenture Stock for €2.20 per unit. The market value of the ordinary shares on that day was €1.95 per share.

Othello acquired its ordinary shareholding in Lenoir Ltd as follows:

Purchase of 1,000,000 shares on 1 July 2003 for €1,000,000

Purchase of 500,000 shares on 1 December 2005 for €1,200,000

The cost history of the shareholding of Othello Ltd in Lenoir Ltd, including the position after the sale of the Debenture Stock, can be represented as follows:

	No of Shares	Cost	Enh Exp	No of Shares	Cost	Enh Exp
			1 July 2003			1 December 2005
		€	€		€	€
Ordinary shares	1,000,000	1,000,000				
Ordinary shares				500,000	1,200,000	
Balance	1,000,000	1,000,000		500,000	1,200,000	
Rights issue						
Deb stock	200,000		300,000	100,000		150,000
Balance	1,200,000	1,000,000	300,000	600,000	1,200,000	150,000
Cost re-apportioned:						
Ordinary shares	1,000,000	815,900	244,770	500,000	979,079	122,385
Debenture Stock	200,000	184,100	55,230	100,000	220,921	27,615
Sold 10/3/08	200,000	184,100	55,230	50,000	110,460	13,808
Balance	Nil	Nil	Nil	50,000	110,461	13,807

Cost re-apportioned:	*Cost of "new holding"*	*MV at date of disposal*
	€	€
1 July 2003		
Ordinary shares	1,000,000	1,950,000
Debenture Stock	300,000	440,000
Apportioned on basis of MV:		
Ordinary shares		
- cost €1,000,000 x 1,950/ 2,390 =	815,900	
- enh exp €300,000 x 1,950/ 2,390 =	244,770	
Debenture Stock		
- cost €1,000,000 x 440/ 2,390 =	184,100	
- enh exp €300,000 x 440/ 2,390 =	55,230	
1 December 2005		
Ordinary shares	1,200,000	975,000
Debenture Stock	150,000	220,000
Apportioned on basis of MV:		
Ordinary shares		
- cost €1,200,000 x 975/1,195 =	979,079	
- enh exp €150,000 x 975/1,195 =	122,385	
Debenture Stock		

- cost €1,200,000 x 220/ 1,195 =   220,921
- enh exp €150,000 x 220/ 1,195 =   27,615

Computation of chargeable gain on disposal of 250,000 Debenture Stock:

	€	€	€	€
Sale proceeds 10 March 2008 (FIFO)		440,000		110,000
Cost:				
200,000 units	184,100			
200,000 units (enh exp)	55,230			
50,000 units			110,460	
50,000 units (enh exp)			13,808	
		239,330		124,268
Gain		200,670		ng/nl

As already explained (see **9.402.5**), where the new holding includes shares or debentures which are quoted, the cost is apportioned between the classes of shares or debentures included in the new holding by reference to their respective market values on the first day on which market values were quoted or published for the shares or debentures. There may be some ambiguity as regards the precise meaning of "the first day" in TCA 1997, s 584(7). It may appear at first sight to mean the first day on which any shares or debentures included in the new holding were quoted, even if that means a date long before the date of the reorganisation. This, however, would lead to an unworkable situation and it must be that the reference is to the first day on which prices are first quoted for any of the elements making up the new holding but only *as* elements of the new holding. The reason for the reference to "whether published before or after the reorganisation took effect" would then be to allow for the fact that prices could be quoted at any time after the first rights shares or debentures were issued but before the day following the day on which the right to renounce any allotment expires. The market values of both the quoted and unquoted classes of shares or debentures in the new holding must then be taken as at that day.

Example 9.402.7.3

The position is the same as in Example **9.402.7.2** except that the shares and debentures are quoted.

On 1 September 2007, Lenoir plc announced details of a rights issue in which one unit of 9% Debenture Stock would be allotted for every five ordinary shares held, at an issue price of €1.5 per unit. Othello Ltd held 1,500,000 ordinary shares in Lenoir plc at the date of the rights issue entitling it to subscribe for 300,000 units of Debenture Stock. On 1 October 2007, Othello Ltd acquired the Debenture Stock for €450,000.

Both the shares and debenture stock of Lenoir plc were first quoted on the Dublin Stock Exchange on 1 October 2007. On that date, the ex-rights price of the ordinary shares was €1.75 per share and the Debenture Stock was quoted at €2 per unit. On 10 March 2008, Othello Ltd sold 250,000 units of Debenture Stock for €2.20 per unit. Othello acquired its ordinary shareholding in Lenoir plc as follows:

Purchase of 1,000,000 shares on 1 July 2003 for €1,000,000

Purchase of 500,000 shares on 1 December 2005 for €1,200,000

The cost history of the shareholding of Othello Ltd in Lenoir plc, including the position after the sale of the Debenture Stock, is represented as follows:

	No of Shares	Cost €	Enh Exp €	No of Shares	Cost €	Enh Exp €
			1 July 2003		*1 December 2005*	
Ordinary shares	1,000,000	1,000,000				
Ordinary shares				500,000	1,200,000	
Balance	1,000,000	1,000,000		500,000	1,200,000	
Rights issue debenture stock	200,000		300,000	100,000		150,000
Balance	1,200,000	1,000,000	300,000	600,000	1,200,000	150,000
Cost re-apportioned:						
Ordinary shares	1,000,000	813,953	244,186	500,000	976,744	122,093
Debenture stock	200,000	186,047	55,814	100,000	223,256	27,907
Sold 10/3/08	200,000	186,047	55,814	50,000	111,628	13,954
Balance	Nil	Nil	Nil	50,000	111,62 8	13,953

Cost re-apportioned:	Cost of "new holding" €	MV at date of rights issue €
1 July 2003		
Ordinary shares	1,000,000	1,750,000
Debenture Stock	300,000	400,000
Apportioned on basis of MV:		
Ordinary shares		
- cost €1,000,000 x 1,750/ 2,150 =	813,953	
- enh exp €300,000 x 1,750/ 2,150 =	244,186	
Debenture Stock		
- cost €1,000,000 x 400/ 2,150 =	186,047	
- enh exp €300,000 x 400/ 2,150 =	55,814	
1 December 2005		
Ordinary shares	1,200,000	875,000
Debenture Stock	150,000	200,000
Apportioned on basis of MV:		
Ordinary shares		
- cost €1,200,000 x 875/1,075 =	976,744	
- enh exp €150,000 x 875/1,075 =	122,093	
Debenture Stock		
- cost €1,200,000 x 200/ 1,075 =	223,256	
- enh exp €150,000 x 200/ 1,075 =	27,907	

Computation of chargeable gain on disposal of 250,000 Debenture Stock:

	€	€	€	€
Sale proceeds 10 March 2008 (FIFO)		440,000		110,000
Cost:				
200,000 units	186,047			
200,000 units (enh exp)	55,814			
50,000 units			111,628	
50,000 units (enh exp)			13,954	
		241,861		125,582
Gain		198,139		ng/nl

9.403   Conversion of securities

TCA 1997, s 584 applies "with any necessary modifications" in relation to the conversion of securities as it applies in relation to the reorganisation or reduction of a company's share capital (TCA 1997, s 585(1)). For this purpose, *conversion of securities* includes:

(a)   a conversion of securities of a company into shares in the company;

(b)   a conversion at the option of the holder of the securities converted as an alternative to the redemption of those securities for cash where the conversion takes place before 4 December 2002, or where the conversion takes place after that date pursuant to a binding written agreement made before that date; and

(c)   any exchange of securities effected in pursuance of any enactment which provides for the compulsory acquisition of any shares or securities and the issue of securities or other securities instead.

Security includes any loan stock or similar security whether of any government or of any public or local authority or of any company and whether secured or unsecured but excluding securities falling within TCA 1997, s 607 (see **9.102.15**).

Example 9.403.1

Ringgold Ltd subscribed €40,000 for 7% convertible loan stock in Baker Ltd. The loan stock was convertible into ordinary shares of Baker Ltd at the end of three years at the option of Ringgold Ltd. At the end of the three years, Ringgold Ltd exercised its option and received 40,000 €1 ordinary shares in Baker Ltd in exchange for its loan stock.

The exchange of loan stock for shares is a conversion of securities within the meaning of TCA 1997, s 585 and is therefore a reorganisation for the purposes of TCA 1997, s 584. The exchange does not involve any disposal of the loan stock or any acquisition of the ordinary shares. The ordinary shares (new holding) are treated as the same asset as the loan stock in terms of their acquisition date and cost.

9.404 Company amalgamations by exchange of shares

9.404.1 "Share for share" exchanges

A reorganisation may involve shares or debentures in more than one company so that shareholders may receive shares or debentures in one company in respect of their holdings of shares or debentures in another company. TCA 1997, s 586 provides, subject to TCA 1997, s 587 (see **9.405** below), that where a company issues shares or debentures to a person in exchange for shares in or debentures of another company, TCA 1997, s 584 is to apply "with any necessary adaptations" as if the two companies were the same company and the exchange were a reorganisation of its share capital. The exchange will, however, be treated as a reorganisation only where the company issuing the shares or debentures has, or in consequence of the exchange will have, control of the other company, or where the first-mentioned company issues the shares or debentures in exchange for shares as the result of a general offer made to members of the other company or any class of them (with or without exceptions for persons connected with the first-mentioned company), the offer being made in the first instance on a condition such that, if it were satisfied, the first-mentioned company would have control of the other company. For the above purposes, *control* is to be construed in accordance with TCA 1997, s 432 (see **2.401.1**) (TCA 1997, s 5(1)) and any question as to whether a person is "connected with" another person is to be determined in accordance with TCA 1997, s 10 (see **2.3**).

In practice, the Revenue have accepted that TCA 1997, s 586 will apply where the company acquiring the target company is not the company issuing the shares or debentures but is rather a subsidiary of that company.

A *debenture* is defined in company law as including debenture stock, bonds and any other securities of a company whether or not constituting a charge on the assets of the company. A debenture is a document containing an acknowledgment of indebtedness by a company that need not be, but usually is, under seal, that need not give, but usually does give, a charge on the assets of the company by way of security, and that may or may not be one of a series. A debenture is always for a specified sum that can only be transferred in its entirety. A holder of a debenture is not a member of the company concerned and in this respect is different from a share in the company. Debentures may be issued at a discount. Interest at the specified rate on the debentures may be paid out of capital. A company may purchase its own debentures.

TCA 1997, s 586 does not apply where, on or after 4 December 2002, a company issues debentures, loan stock or other similar securities to a person in exchange for shares of another company unless—

(a) the issue is pursuant to a binding written agreement made before that date;

(b) the company issuing the debentures, loan stock or other similar securities and the person to whom they are issued are members of the same capital gains tax group throughout the period commencing one year before and ending one year ending after the day the debentures, loan stock or other similar securities are issued; or

(c) the other company is a company quoted on a stock exchange and its board of directors had, before 4 December 2002, made a public announcement that they had agreed the terms of a recommended offer to be made for the company's entire issued, and to be issued, ordinary share capital (TCA 1997, s 586(3)(c)).

Although TCA 1997, s 586 is headed "Company amalgamations by exchange of shares", the word "amalgamation" does not appear in any place in that section. The section is concerned with transactions known as "share for share" exchanges where shares or debentures of one company are exchanged for shares or debentures of another company as a result of which one company obtains control of the other company. TCA 1997, s 587 (see **9.405**), on the other hand, deals with "company reconstructions and amalgamations" where "amalgamation" essentially means the bringing together of the undertakings of two (or more) companies into the ownership of one company, without any change in the ultimate ownership of those undertakings other than that the ownership interests become merged.

The application and interpretation of TCA 1997, s 586, regarding share for share arrangements involving two companies, is considerably more problematic than is the case with single company transactions as dealt with in TCA 1997 ss 584 and 585. The direction in TCA 1997, s 586(1) to treat the two companies as if they were the same company (albeit "with any necessary adaptations") poses its own problems, not least as the two companies will continue in existence after the share exchange.

A share for share exchange, in its most straightforward form, involves the receipt of shares or debentures by the shareholders in the target company as the full consideration for their shares or debentures.

Example 9.404.1.1

Pike Ltd holds 10,000 €1 ordinary shares, valued at €10,000, in Sturgeon Ltd. Congar Ltd plans to make a takeover bid for the shares in Sturgeon Ltd. Its shares are valued at €2.50 per share.

The shareholders of Sturgeon Ltd are offered two shares in Congar Ltd for every five shares in Sturgeon Ltd. Accordingly, Pike Ltd would receive 4,000 shares in Congar Ltd for its shareholding in Sturgeon Ltd. The offer is accepted as a result of which Pike Ltd now holds 4,000 shares in Congar Ltd having a value of €10,000.

Pike Ltd is treated as not having disposed of its shares in Sturgeon Ltd and as not having acquired any shares in Congar Ltd. This is because a share for share exchange is treated as being a reorganisation of share capital for the purposes of TCA 1997, s 584 and Congar Ltd and Sturgeon Ltd are treated, with any necessary adaptations, as if they were the same company.

Arising out of the judgment in *Westcott v Woolcombers Ltd* [1987] STC 600 (see discussion below), the assumption that the two companies are the same company, and that there has been no disposal or acquisition of shares, should be made only for the purposes of dealing with the capital gains tax position of Pike Ltd, the person disposing of shares in this case. No such treatment is extended to Congar Ltd so that it is regarded as having acquired the shares in Sturgeon Ltd at the date of the share for share exchange and at the value of the shares at that time.

On the eventual disposal by Pike Ltd of its shares in Congar Ltd, the cost price and acquisition date of those shares, for the purposes of the relevant computation of the chargeable gain arising, will be taken as the same as the original cost price and acquisition date of the shares formerly held by it in Sturgeon Ltd.

In a case where a takeover involves the receipt by the target company shareholders of shares or debentures in the acquiring company plus consideration in cash, the shareholders are treated as having made a part disposal of their shares in the target company. TCA 1997, s 584(5), which applies in that case (see **9.402.4** above), provides that the cash consideration is deemed to be consideration for a part disposal of the original shares. This is without prejudice to the original shares and the new holding being treated as the same asset. The shares acquired as a result of the exchange take on the same acquisition date and base cost as the shares exchanged, but subject to an adjustment to exclude the part of the cost attributable to the part disposal (see also Example 9.402.4.1).

A takeover by share exchange may also involve the target company shareholders receiving shares or debentures in the acquiring company in exchange for their shares or debentures plus the payment of a cash amount to the acquiring company. That position is provided for in TCA 1997, s 584(4) (see **9.402.3**). The cash consideration is treated, for the purposes of indexation relief in the computation of any gain accruing to them on the disposal of the new shares, as expenditure incurred on the date the consideration was given (in effect, "enhancement expenditure").

The share exchange in this case does not involve any disposal of the original shares (since a reorganisation is involved) but the shareholders, on the eventual disposal of any of the shares acquired in the exchange, will have two separate expenditure items to be deducted from the consideration received, ie the cost of the original shares, indexed by reference to the multiplier appropriate to the year of assessment in which the shares were acquired, and expenditure comprising the cash consideration given, indexed by reference to the multiplier appropriate to the year of assessment in which the share exchange took place.

9.404.2 Anti-avoidance

TCA 1997, s 586(3)(b) provides that TCA 1997, s 586 is not to apply in the case of a share for share exchange unless it is shown that the exchange is effected for *bona fide* commercial reasons and does not form part of any arrangement or scheme of which the main purpose, or one of the main purposes, is avoidance of liability to tax. For this purpose, *shares* includes stock, debentures and any options in relation to such shares.

As might be expected, the precise meaning and scope of a provision of this nature is a matter that is likely to remain uncertain. There is no mechanism for obtaining a Revenue clearance in advance of a reorganisation to the effect that it will not fail to meet the requirements of TCA 1997, s 586(3)(b). It is considered that the section will not apply unless the overall purpose of the reorganisation is the avoidance of liability to Irish taxation. As will often be the case, a reorganisation may be carried out to achieve a commercial purpose while employing steps which individually will be designed to avoid or minimise tax. It is unlikely that such a reorganisation would fall foul of TCA 1997, s 586(3)(b).

9.404.3 Share exchanges and capital gains tax group treatment

TCA 1997, s 617 (see **9.203.1**) provides that a transfer of an asset between members of a capital gains tax group is to be deemed to be for a consideration of such amount that neither a gain nor a loss arises on the transfer. The UK case *Westcott v Woolcombers Ltd* [1987] STC 600 was concerned with an apparent conflict between the UK equivalent provision and that providing for the treatment of a share for share exchange as a reorganisation (TCA 1997, s 586). In that case, a company (H) had acquired the issued share capital of three companies for £1.27m which it later transferred to a wholly owned subsidiary (T) in exchange for ordinary shares in T, credited as fully paid. Some years later, T sold the shares in the three companies to W, another wholly owned subsidiary of H, for £601,235. A short time later, the three subsidiaries were put into liquidation arising from which W received assets of a market value of £601,235 on the winding up distribution. W claimed a capital gains tax loss on the disposal of its shares in the three companies by reference to the excess of £1.27m, the cost price of the shares to the group, over £601,235, the amount realised. That position was based on the view that each of the transfers of shares in the three companies (from H to T, and from T to W) was an intra-group transfer for the purposes of capital gains tax group treatment (TCA 1997, s 617 in Ireland) and that it was correct therefore, on the ultimate disposal of the shares on liquidation, to take as their cost the original cost to W, the first group member to acquire them.

The Revenue position in this case was that [the UK equivalent of] TCA 1997, s 617 did not apply to the transfer by H of the shares in the three companies to T as that transfer was governed by [the UK equivalent of] TCA 1997, s 586. That meant that the transfer of the shares from H to T was not a disposal at all for tax purposes so that capital gains tax intra-group treatment (TCA 1997, s 617) did not apply. The Court of Appeal found in favour of W, the taxpayer company.

It is worthwhile to look in some detail at the reasoning (using the equivalent Irish references) behind this decision, as it provides a useful insight into the correct approach to be taken in interpreting TCA 1997, s 586(1). TCA 1997, s 584(3) provides that a reorganisation is not to be treated as involving any disposal of the original shares or any acquisition of the new holding, the original shares and the new holding being treated as the same asset. TCA 1997, s 586(1) then provides that where a company issues shares to a person in exchange for shares of another company, TCA 1997, s 584 is to apply with any necessary modifications as if the two companies were the same company and the exchange were a reorganisation of its share capital. TCA 1997, s 617 provides that where a member of a group of companies disposes of an asset to another member of the group, both members are to be treated as if the asset acquired were acquired by the member acquiring it for a consideration of such an amount as would secure that on the other member's disposal of it, neither a gain nor a loss would accrue to that member.

The combined effect of TCA 1997 ss 584(3) and 586(1) is to impose two fictions. The first of these is the "no disposal fiction" and the words of TCA 1997, s 584(3) seem to assume that a reorganisation can give rise to a disposal but that that is subject to TCA 1997, s 584(3). The second fiction, also of TCA 1997, s 584(3), is the "composite single asset fiction" whereby the original shares and the new holding are treated as the same asset. Significantly, however, these two fictions are only applicable to a case that is within the provisions of TCA 1997, s 586(1) "with any necessary modifications". The identification of the necessary modifications is crucial to the correct resolution of the kind of situation that arose in the *Woolcombers* case.

In a "one company" situation with which TCA 1997, s 584(3) is concerned, the shareholder begins and ends with shares in the same company whereas, in the "two company situation" of TCA 1997, s 586(1), the shareholder begins with shares in one company and ends with shares in another company. Whereas in the one company situation the single asset fiction can be applied without difficulty (simply by treating the new holding as if it were the original shares), its application in a two company situation is more problematical. TCA 1997, s 584(3) was designed for the one company situation and its provisions must be modified to meet the requirements of the two company situation. In fact, the composite single asset fiction cannot be fully applied in a two company situation. TCA 1997, s 586(1) does not require the exchange of shares to be disregarded; the exchange is to be treated as a reorganisation.

Following the exchange of shares as between H and T in the *Woolcombers* case, T became the owner of the shares in the three companies and it could not be correct to say that these shares were "the same asset" as the shares issued by T itself and which were now in the ownership of H. (This aptly demonstrates the need to limit the application of the single asset fiction in a two company situation.) The position of H, however, as the transferor of the original shares, was different. From its standpoint, the original shares and the new holding can indeed be treated as the same asset and as having been acquired when the original shares were acquired. A person's ownership of successive assets can, therefore, be merged as required by TCA 1997, s 584(3) but that cannot apply to successive ownership of the same asset by *different* persons. In summary, therefore, while it was correct to treat the transfer of the shares in the three companies as involving neither a disposal nor an acquisition of an asset from the standpoint of H, T clearly cannot be treated as owning the shares that it has issued in consequence of the exchange. The fact that T had now become the owner of the shares in the three companies is a factor that has no counterpart in a one company situation. The composite single asset fiction cannot operate, therefore, in relation to T.

The purpose of the hypothesis in TCA 1997 ss 584(3) and 586(1) is to relieve the shareholder (in a one company situation) and the transferor (in a two company situation) from liability to tax. In a two company situation, that purpose can be achieved by limiting the fictions to the tax consequences of the transaction to the owner of the original shares. The single asset fiction cannot be applied to the transferee and to apply the no disposal fiction to it would produce a situation in which it would be assumed to have acquired the asset without any disposal to it at all. Such an unreal result should not be accepted when the purpose of the legislation can be achieved by limiting the effect of both fictions to the position of the transferor of the assets. This approach seems obviously preferable to an approach that would assume that an actual transfer of assets which undeniably took place was something that never took place at all. In short, there is in fact no conflict between the operation of TCA 1997, s 617 and TCA 1997, s 586(1) and a share for share exchange involving two members of a group does not interfere with the application of TCA 1997, s 617 as regards the subsequent treatment of the shares transferred.

Following the decision in the *Woolcombers* case, legislation was introduced in the UK which, in terms of equivalent legislation in Ireland, was to the effect that TCA 1997, s 617 may not apply to a transaction treated by virtue of TCA 1997 ss 584(3) and 586 as not involving a disposal by the transferor company. That legislation took effect as respects transactions on or after 15 March 1988 whereas the transactions dealt with in the *Woolcombers* case (and in the *NAP Holdings* case – see below) had taken place earlier. No such legislation has been introduced in Ireland. It is worth observing, however, that the effect of the *Woolcombers* and *NAP Holdings* judgments is simply that intra-group transactions are to be ignored and that gains and losses are to be computed by comparing the amount of the consideration paid when the asset in question comes into group ownership with that received when the asset leaves the group.

The decision in *Woolcombers* was approved by the House of Lords in *NAP Holdings UK Ltd v Whittles* [1994] STC 979. In that case, the decision in the Court of Appeal was at variance with that in the *Woolcombers* case but that decision was overturned in the House of Lords. The taxpayer company (N) had realised a substantial gain on the disposal of shares that it had acquired from its holding company (O) as part of a share for share exchange. The Revenue contended that the original price paid for the shares by O should be treated as N's acquisition cost while N maintained that its acquisition cost should be taken to be the market value of the shares at the time it acquired them from O. Somewhat ironically therefore, the Revenue were taking the opposite view to that adopted by them in the *Woolcombers* case but this proved to be the correct stance on this occasion. Echoing the *Woolcombers* line of reasoning, Lord Keith, in the leading judgment, observed that "gains and losses should be compared by reference to the consideration paid when an asset comes into the group and the consideration received when it goes out".

The decision in *NAP Holdings* (like the *Woolcombers* decision, leaves a troublesome legacy of ambiguity and uncertainty of interpretation when considered in the wider context of intra-group transfers of shares. TCA 1997, s 625 (see **9.210**) seems clearly to have been designed to prevent precisely the kind of result sought by the taxpayer company in *NAP Holdings*, which leads to the possible inference that, in its absence, the taxpayer should have succeeded, ie that N's acquisition cost of the shares should be taken to be the market value of the shares at the time it acquired them from O. In the Court of Appeal, Nolan LJ referred to this apparent anomaly and also thought that if the Crown's case was correct, the position of a taxpayer failing the *bona fide* test in TCA 1997, s 586(3) would be rendered more favourable. Lord Keith's judgment in the House of Lords is worth considering further on this and other points relating to the combined effect (using Irish statute references) of TCA 1997 ss 617, 625, 584(3) and 586(1), (3).

Assuming that *Woolcombers* was correctly decided, he was of the view that the construction it placed on TCA 1997 ss 617, 584(3) and 586 was not displaced by TCA 1997, s 625 or by the anti-avoidance measure in TCA 1997, s 586(3). As regards the dilemma that this might seem to pose, Lord Keith observed that it was likely that the draftsman of TCA 1997 ss 625 and 586(3) believed that TCA 1997, s 617 did not apply to an intra-group share exchange. That belief could not, however, have the effect of altering the true construction of the enactment in question, ie TCA 1997, s 617. This is an interesting comment on attempts, apparently unjustified, to interpret a statute by drawing an inference from the purpose or effect of another statute. The correct approach must be to derive the true construction of an enactment from the words of the enactment itself.

It was plain that TCA 1997 ss 584(3) and 586 were intended to affect only the tax position of the shareholder who disposes of his shares in one company in exchange for shares in another company. The overriding principle in the case of a group of companies is that gains and losses should be computed by reference to the consideration paid when an asset comes into the group and the consideration received when it goes out. Indeed, it is difficult to see why there should be a difference in tax consequences between the transfer of shares within a group in consideration of an issue of shares and transfers for some other consideration.

The *NAP Holdings* and *Woolcombers* judgments might well be followed by the Irish courts should the matter ever come to be tested there. TCA 1997, s 617 must mean that the same tax consequences should follow for a transfer of shares within a group whether the consideration is by way of an issue of shares or is in the form of some other consideration. If that is the correct interpretation of the section, within the terms of the section itself, it would be wrong not to follow that interpretation simply because it is somehow inconsistent with the apparent motivation behind TCA 1997, s 625.

9.404.4   Share exchange not involving capital gains tax group

It is important to recall what the correct capital gains treatment is where TCA 1997, s 586 applies but where the transaction in question is not one taking place within a group so that TCA 1997, s 617 has no application. That position is illustrated in Example 9.404.1.1 above. A company disposing of shares to another company in exchange for shares in that other company is treated as not having made a disposal of its original shares. The position of the transferee company is not, however, governed by TCA 1997, s 586 (which was confirmed by the *Woolcombers* judgment) and its acquisition of the shares from the first-mentioned company is treated as an acquisition of them at their market value at that time. Essentially this follows the basic consideration rule of TCA 1997, s 547, the acquisition of the shares being otherwise than by way of a bargain made at arm's length. Only where the two companies are members of a group would this acquisition cost be set aside and replaced by the cost of the shares at the time they came into the ownership of the group.

9.404.5   Building societies and trustee savings banks: reorganisation

TCA 1997, s 703 provides for the conversion of a building society or trustee savings bank into a company while TCA 1997 ss 704 and 705 provide respectively for the amalgamation of trustee savings banks and the reorganisation of trustee savings banks into companies. These matters are governed by the above-mentioned provisions rather than by TCA 1997 ss 584-587 and are dealt with in **12.205**, **12.302** and **12.303**.

9.404.6   Reorganisation of co-operative societies

Following the transfer of agri-food undertakings from the ownership of co-operative societies ("societies") to quoted companies, such societies became the owners of shares in those companies. TCA 1997, s 701 contains provisions which facilitate the transfer (or "spin-off") of those shares by the societies to their members and the consequential reduction, by way of cancellation, of the share capital of the societies. The effect of the provision is to enable the shares to be transferred without giving rise to distributions from the societies and on the basis that neither a gain nor a loss accrues to the society on that transfer. The members are treated as not having disposed of their society shares while the shares acquired take on the base cost and acquisition date of the cancelled shares.

Where, on or after 6 April 1993, a society that controls, or has had control of, a company transfers to its members shares owned by it in the company, TCA 1997, s 701 makes certain provisions for relief. These provisions apply where:

(i)   the transfer, in so far as it relates to any member, is in respect of and in proportion to, or as nearly as may be in proportion to, that member's holding of shares in the society immediately before the transfer (the "original shares");

(ii)   no consideration (apart from the consideration given by the members represented by the cancellation of the original shares) for, or in connection with, the transfer is given to, or received from, any member (or any person connected with the member) by the society (or any person who is connected with the society); and

(iii)   on the transfer, or as soon as possible thereafter, the original shares (or the appropriate number of those shares) of each member are cancelled without any consideration (apart from the transfer of the shares in the company to them) for, or in connection with, such cancellation being given to, or received from, any member (or any person connected with that member), and, where the original shares (or the appropriate number of those shares) have been issued to a member at different times, any cancellation of such shares is to involve those issued earlier rather than those issued later.

Where the above conditions apply, the transfer of shares to the members is treated as not being a distribution within the meaning of TCA 1997 Part 6 Ch 2 (see **11.102**) and as being for a consideration of such amount as would secure that, for the purposes of charging the gain on the disposal by the society of the shares in the company, neither a gain nor a loss would accrue to the society.

For capital gains purposes:

(a)   the cancellation of the original shares (or the appropriate number of them) is not to be treated as involving any disposal of those shares; and

(b)   each member is to be treated as if the shares transferred to him had been acquired by him at the same time and for the same consideration at which the original shares (or the appropriate number of them) were acquired by him and, for this purpose, where the original shares (or the appropriate number of them) have been issued to a member at different times, all such apportionments as are just and reasonable are to be made.

TCA 1997, s 701 will not apply or have effect unless it is shown that the transfer is effected for *bona fide* commercial reasons and does not form part of any arrangement or scheme of which the main purpose, or one of the main purposes, is avoidance of liability to corporation tax or capital gains tax.

For the purposes of TCA 1997, s 701, *consideration* means money or money's worth. *Control* has the meaning assigned to it by TCA 1997, s 9 (see **2.4**). Any question as to whether a person is "connected with" another person is to be determined in accordance with TCA 1997, s 10 (see **2.3**). *Society* means a society registered under the Industrial and Provident Societies Acts, 1893 to 1978, which is an agricultural society or a fishery society within the meaning of (see **12.501**).

References above to *the appropriate number* of the original shares means such portion (or as near as may be to such portion) of the total number of the referable shares owned by the member at the time of the transfer as bears to that number the same proportion as the total number of shares in the company which are subject to the transfer bears to the total number of shares in the company owned by the society immediately before the transfer. The number of the referable shares owned by a member is an amount determined by the formula:

$$\frac{A \times B}{C} \times \frac{D}{B}$$

where—

A   is the market value of the shares in the company owned by the society immediately before the transfer;

B   is the total number of the shares in the society that are in issue immediately before the transfer;

C   is the market value of the total assets (including the shares in the company) of the society immediately before the transfer; and

D   is the number of shares in the society owned by the member immediately before the transfer.

Based on the above formula, the number of a member's referable shares can be stated to be the number of his shares in the society reduced proportionately by reference to the value of the shares in the company over the value of the society's total assets. Condition (iii) above therefore envisages the cancellation of members' shares of an amount not greater than the number of them that corresponds to the value of the shares which the society holds in the company.

9.405   Company reconstructions and amalgamations

A company reconstruction or amalgamation is treated for capital gains purposes as a reorganisation of share capital. TCA 1997, s 587 deals with the position of the shareholders affected by a company reconstruction or amalgamation while the position of the company involved in a reconstruction or amalgamation is dealt with in TCA 1997, s 615 (company reconstruction or amalgamation: transfer of assets – see **9.207**).

As explained in **9.207.1**, a reconstruction involves the transfer of part or all of the undertaking of one company to another company. Whereas TCA 1997, s 615 provides that the assets being transferred in the course of a reconstruction or amalgamation are treated as having been disposed of on a no gain/ no loss basis, TCA 1997, s 587 treats the issue of shares as a share for share exchange to which TCA 1997, s 586(1) applies. It is understood that the Revenue would accept that TCA 1997, s 587 may apply in the case of the incorporation of a partnership involving two corporate partners where the partnership trade and assets would be transferred to a company in return for an issue of shares to the two companies (see also **9.207.1**).

TCA 1997, s 587 provides that where, under an arrangement between a company and the persons holding shares in or debentures of the company or any class of such shares or debentures, being an arrangement in connection with a scheme of reconstruction or amalgamation,

(a)   another company issues shares or debentures to those persons in respect of and in proportion to (or as nearly as may be in proportion to) their existing holdings of shares or debentures; but

(b)   the original shares or debentures are either retained (including being retained with altered rights or in an altered form whether as the result of reduction, consolidation, division or otherwise) by those persons or cancelled, those persons are treated as exchanging the original shares or debentures for those held by them in consequence of the arrangement. Any shares or debentures retained are regarded for this purpose as if they had been cancelled and replaced by the new issue. TCA 1997, s 586 (company share for share exchanges), apart from subsection (2) of that section, then applies to the exchange of shares or debentures as if the two companies were the same company and the exchange were a reorganisation of its share capital for the purposes of TCA 1997 ss 584/ 586. TCA 1997, s 584(3) provides that a reorganisation of share capital is treated as not involving any disposal of the original shares or any acquisition of the new holding, the original shares and the new holding being treated as the same asset acquired as the original shares were acquired (see Example **9.207.4.1**).

For the above purposes, "shares" includes stock, debentures and interests in a company with no share capital, held by members of the company, and also includes options in relation to such shares. For the meaning of *debentures*, see **9.404.1** above.

For the treatment of a disposal of part of a new holding, see **9.402.5**.

TCA 1997, s 587 does not apply to any person to whom, under a scheme of reconstruction or amalgamation, a company issues debentures, loan stock or other similar securities on or after 4 December 2002, unless—

(a)   the issue is pursuant to a binding written agreement made before that date;

(b)   the company and the person are members of the same capital gains tax group throughout the period commencing one year before and ending one year ending after the day the debentures, loan stock or other similar securities were issued; or

(c)   they were issued pursuant to a scheme or arrangement, the principal terms of which had been brought to the attention of the Revenue Commissioners and the Commissioners had acknowledged in writing, before 4 December 2002, to the effect that the scheme or arrangement was a scheme of reconstruction and amalgamation (TCA 1997, s 587(4)(c)).

The situation envisaged in TCA 1997, s 587 is that in which a company (Y) issues shares or debentures to the persons holding shares in or debentures of another company (X) under a scheme of reconstruction or amalgamation between those persons and X which in fact (see **9.207** re TCA 1997, s 615) involves the transfer of the whole or part of the business of X to Y, with no consideration passing to X other than the assumption by Y of all or part of the liabilities of the business.

TCA 1997, s 587(1) defines *scheme of reconstruction or amalgamation* as a scheme for the reconstruction of any company or companies or the amalgamation of any two or more companies, which is in fact the same definition as provided in TCA 1997, s 615(1). (See **9.207.2** and **9.207.4** for the meaning of "reconstruction" and "amalgamation" and in relation to a division or "partition".)

Anti-avoidance

TCA 1997, s 587(4)(b) provides that TCA 1997, s 587 is not to apply in the case of a scheme of reconstruction or amalgamation unless it is shown that the exchange is effected for *bona fide* commercial reasons and does not form part of any arrangement or scheme of which the main purpose, or one of the main purposes, is avoidance of liability to tax. For this purpose, *shares* includes stock, debentures and any interests in a company possessed by members of the company, and any options in relation to such shares. (See **9.404.1** above regarding the meaning of *debentures*).

As might be expected, the precise meaning and scope of a provision of this nature is a matter that is likely to remain uncertain. There is no mechanism for obtaining a Revenue clearance in advance of a reorganisation to the effect that it will not fail to meet the requirements of TCA 1997, s 587(4)(b). It is considered that the section will not apply unless the overall purpose of the reorganisation is the avoidance of liability to Irish taxation. As will often be the case, a reorganisation may be carried out to achieve a commercial purpose while employing steps that individually will be designed to avoid or minimise tax. It is unlikely that such a reorganisation would fall foul of TCA 1997, s 587(4)(b).

9.406   Transfer of business to a company

Where a person who is not a company transfers a business as a going concern to a company, relief from liability to capital gains tax on the disposal is available to the extent that the proceeds are received in the form of shares in the company. The relief is by way of a deferral of the tax payable on the amount of the consideration comprising shares.

TCA 1997, s 600(2) provides that the deferral applies where a person who is not a company transfers to a company a business as a going concern, together with the whole of the assets of the business, or together with the whole of those assets other than cash, and the business is so transferred wholly or partly in exchange for shares (the "new assets") issued by the company to the person transferring the business.

Relief is by way of a deduction from the aggregate of the net chargeable gains (chargeable gains less allowable losses), ie the gains calculated in the normal way, and referred to as the gain on the "old assets". The amount of the deduction is such portion of the gain on the old assets as bears the same proportion to the total of such gains as the cost of the new assets bears to the value of the whole of the consideration received by the transferor in exchange for the business. In this context, *the cost of the new assets* means any sums which would be allowable as a deduction under TCA 1997, s 552(1)(a) if the new assets were disposed of as a whole in the circumstances giving rise to a chargeable gain (ie, their allowable cost for capital gains tax purposes).

Any question as to whether a business was transferred as a going concern is to be decided as at the date of the transfer. In *Gordon v IRC* [1991] STC 174, a farming partnership comprising a husband and wife transferred the farm business and assets to a company at a time when negotiations were in progress for the sale of the farm. The farm was in fact sold within a short time after the transfer. It was held that the business had been transferred as a going concern as the farming business was a going concern at the date of the transfer.

Example 9.406.1

Martin O'Neill, who had carried on business as a sole trader since 1 January 1985, transferred the business and its assets on 1 January 2008, to a company, Maron Ltd, in exchange for 200,000 €1 ordinary shares in the company and €400,000 cash. The assets and liabilities of Martin O'Neill on the transfer date were as follows:

	€	€
Premises at cost (value €1,750,000)		250,000
Goodwill (agreed value at 1/1/08)		600,000

Debtors (realisable value €60,000)		80,000
Stock-in-trade		165,000
Cash		75,000
		1,170,000
Creditors	170,000	
Taxation	45,000	215,000
		955,000

The value of the business being transferred is accordingly as follows:

		€
Premises		1,750,000
Goodwill		600,000
Debtors		60,000
Stock-in-trade		165,000
Value of whole consideration		2,575,000
Less to be paid by Maron Ltd on behalf of Martin O'Neill:		
Creditors	170,000	
Taxation	45,000	215,000
Net amount due to Martin O'Neill		2,360,000

Of the net amount due to Martin O'Neill, €400,000 is met by way of cash leaving, as the balance, an amount of €1,960,000 in respect of shares (and which is "the cost of the new assets").

The chargeable gains on the disposals of the premises and goodwill are as follows:

	€	€
Premises:		
Consideration on disposal		1,750,000
Cost 1 January 1985	250,000	
Indexed @ 1.819		454,750
Gain		1,295,250
Goodwill:		
Consideration on disposal (= gain)		600,000
Aggregate gain on "old assets"		1,895,250
Gain deferred 1,960,000/ 2,575,000[1] x €1,895,250		1,442,598
The taxable gain is €1,895,250 - €1,442,598 =		452,652

Notes:

[1]   The amount of €2,575,000 is the value of the whole consideration receivable. This is because the assumption of liabilities is essentially the same as the payment of additional cash consideration equal to the value of those liabilities. In practice, in a case where a business is transferred to a company for shares only, the Revenue agree that bona fide trade creditors taken over will not be treated as consideration.

Example 9.406.2

The facts are as in Example **9.406.1** with the additional information that Martin O'Neill sells the shares in Maron Ltd on 31 March 2008 for €2,300,000.

The cost of the shares, €1,960,000, is reduced by the amount of the deferred gain €1,442,598, to give a reduced cost of €517,402. The chargeable gain is as follows:

	€
Sale proceeds	2,300,000
Cost (as adjusted)	517,402
Gain	1,782,598

9.407   Controlled company transferring assets at undervalue

Where a close company (see **10.103**) transfers an asset to any person otherwise than by way of a bargain made at arm's length and for a consideration of an amount or value less than the market value of the asset, an amount equal to the difference is to be apportioned among the issued shares of the company (TCA 1997, s 589). For the purposes of computing a chargeable gain accruing on the disposal of any of those shares by the person owning them on the date of transfer of the asset, an amount equal to the apportioned amount must be excluded from the expenditure allowable as a deduction from the consideration for the disposal. TCA 1997, s 589 applies also in the case of a non-resident company which is a "closely controlled" company, ie a non-resident company which would be a close company if it were resident in the State.

If the person owning any of the shares at the date of the transfer of the asset is itself a close company, an amount equal to the amount apportioned to it is to be apportioned among the issued shares of that close company, and the holders of those shares are to be treated in the same way as described above, and so on through any number of close companies.

Multiple tax charges

TCA 1997, s 589 applies to transfers of assets not only to its members or "in respect of shares" (see **11.105.7**), but to "any person" where the transfer is made other than by way of a bargain made at arm's length. In most cases, however, any such transfer is likely to be made in respect of shares. By virtue of TCA 1997, s 130(3), any transfer of an asset to members at undervalue gives rise to a distribution (see **11.108**). Where TCA 1997, s 589 has effect therefore, TCA 1997, s 130(3) is also likely to result in a distribution to the person to whom the asset has been transferred. There is then nothing to prevent the additional consequence, by virtue of TCA 1997, s 589, that all of the shareholders will suffer a diminution in the capital gains tax base cost of their shares in the company. Furthermore, since the asset transfer will have been at less than market value and not by way of a bargain made at arm's length, the company will be regarded, under TCA 1997, s 547, as having disposed of the asset at market value with a consequential liability in respect of the chargeable gain arising.

9.408   Chargeable gains of non-resident companies

TCA 1997, s 590 contains provisions relating to the tax treatment of a chargeable gain realised by a non-resident "closely controlled" company (ie, a non-resident company which would be a close company (see **10.103**) if it were resident in the State).

Any person who, at the time the chargeable gain accrues, is resident or ordinarily resident in the State (and, if an individual, who is domiciled in the State) and who is a participator (within the meaning of TCA 1997, s 433(1) – see **2.401.2**) in the company is treated for capital gains tax purposes as if a part of the chargeable gain arising to the company had accrued to that person (TCA 1997, s 590(4)). That part is an amount equal to the proportion of the gain that corresponds to the extent of the participator's interest as a participator in the company (TCA 1997, s 590(5)).

A person's interest as a participator in a company means the interest in that company that is represented by all the factors by reference to which the person falls to be treated as such a participator (TCA 1997, s 590(1)(b)). References to "the extent" of such an interest are to the proportion of the interests, as participators, of all the participators in the company (including any who are not resident or ordinarily resident in the State) which on a just and reasonable apportionment is represented by that interest (TCA 1997, s 590(1)(c)).

Where—

(a)   the interest of any person in a company is wholly or partly represented by an interest which that person has under any settlement (the "person's beneficial interest"); and

(b)   that beneficial interest is the factor, or one of the factors, by reference to which the person would otherwise be treated as having an interest as a participator in the company,

the interest as participator in the company which would be that person's interest is deemed, to the extent that it is represented by the person's beneficial interest, to be an interest of the trustees of the settlement and not an interest of the person's. References, in relation to a company, to a participator are to be construed accordingly (TCA 1997, s 590(2)).

The charge under TCA 1997, s 590(4) does not apply in the case of any participator in the company to which the gain accrues where the aggregate amount falling to be apportioned to the participator, and to persons connected with the participator, does not exceed 5% of the gain (TCA 1997, s 590(6)).

TCA 1997, s 590 does not apply in respect of—

(i)   a chargeable gain accruing on the disposal of assets, being tangible property, whether movable or immovable, or a lease of such property, where the property was used, and used only, for the purposes of a trade carried on by the company wholly outside the State;

(ii)   a chargeable gain accruing on the disposal of currency or of a debt within TCA 1997, s 541(6) (a credit balance in a foreign currency denominated bank account – see **9.102.11**), where the currency or debt is or represents money in use for the purposes of a trade carried on by the company wholly outside the State; or

(iii) a chargeable gain in respect of which the company is chargeable to capital gains tax by virtue of TCA 1997, s 29 (charge to capital gains tax on non-residents – see **9.102.2**) or is chargeable to corporation tax by virtue of TCA 1997, s 25(2)(b) (see below) (TCA 1997, s 590(7)).

As respects (iii) above, this recognises that certain chargeable gains are taxable in any event even where they accrue to a non-resident. As explained in **9.102.2**, a person not resident in the State is chargeable to capital gains tax in respect of gains on disposals of specific categories of assets, ie

(a) land (including buildings) in the State;

(b) minerals (as defined in the Minerals Development Act 1940, s 3 – see **3.107.1**) in the State or any rights, interests or other assets in relation to mining or minerals or the searching for minerals;

(c) assets situated in the State which, at or before the time when the chargeable gains accrued, were used in or for the purposes of a trade carried on by him in the State through a branch or agency, or which at or before that time were used or held or acquired for use by or for the purposes of the branch or agency;

(d) exploration or exploitation rights in a designated area;

(e) unquoted shares deriving their value or the greater part of their value directly or indirectly from such assets as are described in (a), (b) or (d) above;

(f) assets situated outside the State of an overseas life assurance company (within the meaning of TCA 1997, s 706(1) – see **12.603.11**), being assets that were held in connection with the life business (within the meaning of TCA 1997, s 706(1)) carried on by the company, which at or before the time the chargeable gains accrued were used or held by or for the purposes of that company's branch or agency in the State (TCA 1997, s 29(3)).

Also in relation to (iii) above, TCA 1997, s 29(7) treats gains accruing to a person who is not resident and not ordinarily resident in the State on the disposal of assets in (b) or (d) above as gains accruing on the disposal of assets used for the purposes of a trade carried on by that person in the State through a branch or agency. The effect of this provision, as indicated by the Revenue, is that an Irish resident agent of such a non-resident person may be charged to capital gains tax on those gains (see also **9.102.2**).

Finally as respects (iii) above, TCA 1997, s 25(2)(b) subjects to corporation tax the chargeable gains of a non-resident company which would be subject to capital gains tax were it not for the fact that the company is subject to corporation tax (see **3.107.1**). TCA 1997, s 29(6) treats gains of a non-resident company on the disposal of exploration or exploitation rights in a designated area as gains on the disposal of assets situated in the State: this brings such gains within the scope of TCA 1997, s 25(2)(b).

Where any amount of capital gains tax is paid by a person under TCA 1997, s 590(4) and an amount in respect of the chargeable gain is distributed (by way of dividend or distribution of capital or on the dissolution of the company) within two years from the time when the chargeable gain accrued to the company, relief is to be given to that person in respect of that tax. The amount of the tax, in so far as it is neither reimbursed by the company nor applied as a deduction under TCA 1997, s 590(9) (see below), is to be applied in reducing or extinguishing any liability of the person to income tax in respect of the distribution or (in the case of a distribution falling to be treated as a disposal on which a chargeable gain accrues to the person) to any capital gains tax in respect of the distribution (TCA 1997, s 590(8)).

Similarly, the amount of capital gains tax paid by a person by virtue of TCA 1997, s 590(4), to the extent that it has neither been reimbursed by the company nor applied under TCA 1997, s 590(8) in reducing any liability to tax (see above), is to be allowed as a deduction in the computation of a gain accruing on the disposal by that person of any asset representing the person's interest as a participator in the company (TCA 1997, s 590(9)).

For the purposes of TCA 1997, s 590(8), in ascertaining the amount of any income tax chargeable on any person for any year of assessment on or in respect of a distribution, any such distribution falling to be treated as income of that person for that year is to be regarded as forming the highest part of the income on which he is charged to tax for the year (TCA 1997, s 590(10)). Accordingly, credit in respect of tax paid under TCA 1997, s 590(4) is given to the maximum extent against income charged at the higher rate.

It may happen that the disposal of an asset by the non-resident closely controlled company results in a loss. In that event TCA 1997, s 590 also applies, so that a part of the loss in the year of assessment in question will be attributed to certain shareholders, but only for the purposes of reducing or extinguishing any gain which also arose in the same year of assessment to those shareholders by virtue of that section (TCA 1997, s 590(11)).

Where the person who is a participator in the non-resident company at the time the chargeable gain accrued to the company is itself a company which is not resident in the State but is a closely controlled company (the "participating company"), an amount equal to the amount apportioned out of the chargeable gain to the participating company's interest as a participator in the company to which the gain accrues is to be further apportioned among the participators in the participating company. This apportionment is to be made according to the extent of the respective interests of those participators as participators, and TCA 1997, s 590(4) is to apply to them accordingly in relation to the amounts further apportioned, and so on through any number of companies (TCA 1997, s 590(12)).

The persons treated by TCA 1997, s 590 as if a part of a chargeable gain accruing to a company had accrued to them include trustees who are participators in the company (or in any company which is one of the participators amongst which the gain is apportioned under TCA 1997, s 590(12)), if when the gain accrued to the company the trustees are neither resident nor ordinarily resident in the State (TCA 1997, s 590(13)). This provision counters devices that would otherwise avoid the consequences of TCA 1997, s 590 by interposing a non-resident trust between an Irish resident or ordinarily resident person and the non-resident closely controlled company.

If any tax payable by any person in accordance with TCA 1997, s 590 is paid by the company to which the chargeable gain accrues, or by any such company as is dealt with by TCA 1997, s 590(12), the amount so paid is not to be regarded, for income tax or capital gains tax purposes, as a payment to the person by whom the tax was originally payable (TCA 1997, s 590(14)). Payment by the company of the capital gains tax otherwise due by the shareholder concerned will not therefore result in any "grossing up" to take account of a benefit thereby received from the company.

For the purposes of TCA 1997, s 590, the amount of the gain or loss accruing at any time to a company which is not resident in the State (and which is not within the charge to corporation tax on capital gains) is to be computed as if the company were within the charge to corporation tax on capital gains (TCA 1997, s 590(15)).

TCA 1997, s 590 makes no provision for allowing any of the tax payable by the non-resident company in respect of the gain in question as a credit against the tax payable in accordance with TCA 1997, s 590(4).

TCA 1997, s 626B: avoidance of TCA 1997, s 590 charge

The tax charge imposed by TCA 1997, s 590 relates to a chargeable gain realised by a non-resident "closely controlled" company. Except where otherwise expressly provided, every gain is a chargeable gain (TCA 1997, s 545(3), including a chargeable gain realised by a non-resident closely controlled company. That gain might consist of a gain on the disposal of shares in a trading company (or group). Provided the conditions prescribed by TCA 1997, s 626B (see **9.213**) are satisfied, the gain will not be a chargeable gain so that there would then be no attribution by virtue of TCA 1997, s 590.

9.409 Stamp duty: significant reliefs

9.409.1 Charge of stamp duty

Any instrument which—

(a) is specified in TCA 1999 Schedule 1; and

(b) is executed in the State or, wherever executed, relates to any property situated in the State or any matter or thing done or to be done in the State,

is chargeable with stamp duty (SDCA 1999 s 2).

SDCA 1999 Schedule 1 lists the headings under which the charge to stamp duty arises. Some of the more important charge headings include the following: AGREEMENT or CONTRACT accompanied with a deposit, LEASE, AGREEMENT for a lease, ASSIGNMENT, BILL OF EXCHANGE or PROMISSORY NOTE, BOND, CONVEYANCE or TRANSFER on sale of any stocks or marketable securities, CONVEYANCE or TRANSFER on sale of any property other than stocks or marketable securities or a policy of insurance or a policy of life insurance, COVENANT for securing the payment or repayment of any money, DEPOSIT of title deeds, EQUITABLE MORTGAGE, LETTER OF CREDIT, MORTGAGE, BOND, DEBENTURE, COVENANT, POLICY OF INSURANCE, PROMISSORY NOTE, RELEASE or RENUNCIATION.

In relation to (b), the words "relates to any property situated in the State or any matter or thing done or to be done in the State" should be interpreted widely. Thus, it has been held that a transfer executed in France of French property in exchange for shares in an English company was subject to stamp duty in the UK (*IRC v Maple & Co (Paris) Ltd*, 1908 AC 22); the issue of shares in an English company was "a thing done or to be done" in England. Similarly, a deed of covenant executed in Canada relating to the carrying out of his profession in England by an engineer in consideration for the issues of shares and debentures of a Canadian company was held to relate to something to be done in the UK (*Faber v IRC* (1936) 155 LT 228).

9.409.2 Intellectual property

Stamp duty legislation provides for an exemption, with effect from 1 April 2004, from duty on the sale, transfer or other disposition of intellectual property.

Intellectual property

SDCA 1999 s 101(1) defines *intellectual property* as—

(a)   any patent, trademark, registered design, design right, invention or domain name;

(b)   any copyright or related right within the meaning of the Copyright and Related Rights Act 2000;

(c)   any supplementary protection certificate provided for in Council Regulation (EEC) No 1768/92 of 18 June 1992 (OJ No L 8.8.1996, p 30);

(d)   any supplementary protection certificate provided for in Regulation (EC) No 1610/96 of the European Parliament and of the Council of 23 July 1996 (OJ No L 182, 2.7.1992, p 1);

(e)   any plant breeders' rights within the meaning of section 4 of the Plant Varieties (Proprietary Rights) Act 1980, as amended by the Plant Varieties (Proprietary Rights) (Amendment) Act, 1998;

(f)   any application for the grant of registration of anything within (a) to (e) above;

(g)   any licence or other right in respect of anything within (a) to (f) above;

(h)   any rights granted under the law of any country, territory, state or area, other than the State, or under any international treaty, convention or agreement to which the State is a party, that correspond to or are similar to those within (a) to (g) above;

(i)   goodwill to the extent that it is inherent in anything within (a) to (h) above.

Exemption from stamp duty

Subject to SDCA 1999 s 101(3) (which provides for apportionment where part of the property being transferred consists of intellectual property), stamp duty is not chargeable under or by reference to any heading in Schedule 1 on an instrument for the sale, transfer or other disposition of intellectual property (SDCA 1999 s 101(2)).

In a case where stamp duty is chargeable on an instrument under or by reference to any heading in Schedule 1 and part of the property concerned consists of intellectual property—

(a)   the consideration in respect of which stamp duty would otherwise be chargeable is to be apportioned, on a just and reasonable basis, as between the part of the property consisting of intellectual property and the part that does not; and

(b)   the instrument will be chargeable only in respect of the consideration attributable to such of the property as is not intellectual property (SDCA 1999 s 101(3)).

There are further provisions in SDCA 1999 s 101(5)–(8) dealing with apportionment in cases involving property referred to in SDCA 1999 s 45(1), ie property contracted to be sold for one consideration for the whole of it and conveyed to the purchaser in separate parts or parcels by different instruments.

9.409.3   Reconstructions or amalgamations of companies

SDCA 1999 s 80 provides for exemption from stamp duty in the cases of certain reconstructions or amalgamations of companies (including a society registered under the

Industrial and Provident Societies Act 1893). The exemption applies where there is a scheme for the bona fide reconstruction of any company or companies or the amalgamation of any companies and that, in connection with such a scheme, a company (the "acquiring company") is to be registered, or has been established, or has increased its capital, with a view to the acquisition of either the undertaking another company (the "target company"), or not less than 90% of the issued share capital of a target company. The consideration for the acquisition must consist as to not less than 90%, where an undertaking is being acquired, in the issue of shares to the target company or to the holders of shares in the target company, or, where shares are being acquired, in the issue of shares to the holders of shares in the target company.

Reconstruction

Reconstruction is not defined in stamp duty legislation but was stated by Pennycuick J in *Brooklands Selangor Holdings Ltd v IRC* [1970] 1 WLR 429 to be "used to describe the refashioning of any object in such a way as to leave the basic character of the object unchanged. In relation to companies, it has a fairly precise meaning which corresponds, so far as the subject matter allows, to its meaning in ordinary speech. It denotes the transfer of the undertaking or part of the undertaking of an existing company to a new company with substantially the same persons as members as were members of the old company" (see also **9.207.2**). He disagreed that the term should be so narrowly construed as to suggest that the new company must consist of the same shareholders.

Pennycuick J went on to describe as the usual mode of reconstruction a situation in which "a company resolves to wind itself up, and proposes the formation of a new company, which is to consist of the old shareholders, and to take over the old undertaking, the old shareholders receiving shares in the new company. In that case the old company ceases to exist in point of law, and there is in form a sale to the members of a new corporation. But the company is in substance, and may be fairly said to be, reconstructed."

In the case *In re South African Supply and Cold Storage Co Ltd* (1904) 2 Ch 268, Buckley J described a reconstruction as occurring where an undertaking of some definite kind is being carried on where it is not desirable to kill it off but to preserve it in some form, not by selling it to an outsider to carry it on (which would be a mere sale) "but in some altered form to continue the undertaking in such a manner as that the persons now carrying it on will substantially continue to carry it on. It involves, I think, that substantially the same business shall be carried on and substantially the same persons shall carry it on. But it does not involve that all the assets shall pass to the new company or resuscitated company, or that all the shareholders of the old company shall be shareholders in the new company or resuscitated company. Substantially the business and the persons interested must be the same."

Citing the above remarks of Buckley J, Plowman J in *Baytrust Holdings Ltd v IRC* [1971] 1 WLR 1333 added that "a reconstruction normally involves the transfer of a company's undertaking (or part of it) to a new company which is going to carry on substantially the same business as the business transferred to it."

A reconstruction is not the same as an amalgamation (which is rather the converse of a reconstruction). In this connection it has been explained (Lindley on the *Law of Companies*) that "reconstruction differs from amalgamation in that, as a rule, there is only one transferring company, and the company to which the property in question is transferred is practically the same company with some alterations in its constitution."'

From the above, the following would be examples of a reconstruction:

1. The shares in A are transferred to B, a newly formed company, in consideration for the issue of shares by B to the shareholders of A.
2. The trade of A is transferred to B, a newly formed company, in consideration for the issue of shares by B to the shareholders of A.
3. A is put into liquidation and its trade is transferred to B, a newly formed company, in which the shareholders are, or are substantially, the same as the shareholders in A.

Amalgamation

Neither is *amalgamation* defined in stamp duty legislation. It refers to the fusion of the businesses of two companies, the acquiring company and the target company. An amalgamation is the converse of a reconstruction. It may involve a newly formed company to which the businesses are transferred or a company carrying on one of the businesses and to which the other business is transferred. The acquisition by a company of the shares in another company does not by itself result in an amalgamation (*Swithland v IRC* [1990] STC 448). (See also **9.207.2**in relation to capital gains tax.)

Distinguishing an amalgamation from a reconstruction, Buckley J in the *South African Supply* case, said that "you must have the rolling .... of two concerns into one. You must weld two things together and arrive at an amalgam – a blending of two undertakings. It does not necessarily follow that the whole of the two undertakings should pass – substantially they must pass – nor need all the corporators be parties, although substantially all must be parties. The difference between reconstruction and amalgamation is that in the latter is involved the blending of two concerns one with the other, but not merely the continuance of one concern. An amalgamation may take place, it seems to me, either by the transfer of undertakings A and B to a new corporation, C, or by the continuance of A and B by B upon terms that the shareholders of A shall become shareholders in B. It is not necessary that you should have a new company. You may have a continuance of one of the two companies upon the terms that the undertakings of both corporations shall substantially be merged in one corporation only."

Based on the above, the following transactions can be considered:

1. The trade of A is transferred to B, a previously unrelated trading company, in consideration for the issue by B of shares to the shareholders of A. This is an amalgamation as it involves the coming together of two undertakings. It is not a reconstruction as there has been a change in the ownership of the A trade.
2. The trades of A and B are transferred to C in consideration for the issue of shares in C to the shareholders of A and B. This is an amalgamation rather than a reconstruction for reasons similar to those in 1.
3. The shares in A, a trading company, are transferred to B, a previously unrelated trading company, in consideration for the issue of shares to the shareholders of A. Based on the relevant case law, this is an amalgamation.

With regard to 3, since the ownership of the A trade has changed, the transaction is not a reconstruction. Although the trades continue to be carried on separately by the two companies, however, it is an amalgamation as the trades have been brought together by reason of the shareholders in the two companies, through their holdings in B, having an interest in the two trades equivalent to their former interests in the separate trades (see further regarding *Crane Freuhauf* below).

The fact that the transaction in question is a share for undertaking or a share for share transaction, as envisaged by SDCA 1999 s 80, does not in itself mean that it is an amalgamation: note that the section envisages either of these types of transaction being carried out "in connection with the scheme" (ie, of reconstruction or amalgamation) so that something more than the share for share etc would seem to be required. Thus, in the case of a share for share transaction, this should be part of a scheme in which there would be a bringing together of the undertakings of the two companies concerned.

The case of *Re Walker's Settlement* [1935] Ch 567 was concerned with the question whether a transaction in which a holding company acquired at least 90% of the share capital of various trading companies in exchange for shares in itself was an amalgamation. Maugham J said that "I think we have to answer this question: can an acquisition of shares by a holding company properly be described as an amalgamation of the company whose shares .... are being acquired by the holding company? For my part, I must answer that in the negative." In the same case, Romer LJ pointed out that if an acquisition of shares was sufficient to constitute an amalgamation, the legislature would not have included in the relevant statue the opening words: "If in connection with a scheme for the ... amalgamation of any companies it is shown".

In *Crane Freuhauf Ltd v IRC* [1975] STC 51, the shares in one company, Boden, were acquired by another company, Crane, in return for an issue of shares, and a small amount of cash, to the Boden shareholders. The two companies were carrying on similar trades. The Court of Appeal upheld the decision of Templeman J in the High Court to the effect that there was an amalgamation as soon as Boden's shareholders were registered as the holders of the new shares in Crane and Boden's shares were transferred to Crane. That this was an indication that a share for share transaction could amount of itself to an amalgamation was rejected in *IRC v Ufitec Group Ltd* [1977] STC 363 where May J allowed that he was startled by the submission that what Templeman J said could be seen as support for that view.

Nevertheless *Crane Freuhauf* is authority for the view that a share for share transaction can be an amalgamation, provided that there has been a coming together of the undertakings of two companies. It is worth quoting Scarman LJ from the Court of Appeal:

> "Templeman J held that the scheme was a scheme for amalgamation because it brought together in one company ... the share capital of two companies ... I agree with this analysis and conclusion. Although "amalgamation" is a technical term in the sense that it is frequently used by technicians in the field of company law, it is not a legal term of art; it has no statutory definition. It is frequently used to describe a merging of the undertakings of two or more companies into one undertaking. Such a merger can be achieved in several ways; and the resultant one undertaking may become that of one of the companies concerned or of a new company altogether. In the present case the scheme contemplated the amalgamation of the Crane and Boden undertakings into one by the issue to the Boden shareholders of Crane shares in exchange for their Boden shares. On its completion the Boden and Crane separate undertakings were united in the one undertaking of Crane."

Stamp LJ in the same case envisaged two forms of amalgamation, one in which the business of one company is acquired by another company in return for an issue of shares in the transferee company to the transferor company or to its shareholders, and one in which the transferee company acquires shares in the existing company in exchange for shares in the transferee company issued to the shareholders of the existing company. In either case, the value of the issued shares will correspond to the value of the business or, as the case may be, the shares transferred, with the result that the shareholders in the two companies, through their holdings in the transferee company, will have an interest in the two businesses equivalent to their former interests in the separate businesses.

Although some commentators have expressed a difficulty in reconciling the decisions in *Crane Freuhauf* and *Swithland*, it is noteworthy that Ferris J in *Swithland*, having considered the various transactions under consideration there noted that the circumstances were different from those in *Crane Freuhauf* where, "prior to the share exchange, both Crane and Boden had their own separate well-established undertakings". That this was not the case in *Swithland*, where the facts were more complex and involved a fragmented series of transactions, was decisive in arriving at the conclusion that there was nothing that could properly be described as an "amalgamation" as there was no coming together of two entities nor any welding or blending of two undertakings or concerns into one.

Exemption

Exemption from stamp duty in the cases of a reconstruction or amalgamation applies where it is shown to the satisfaction of the Revenue Commissioners that there exists a scheme for the bona fide reconstruction of any company or companies or the amalgamation of any companies and that, in connection with the scheme, the following conditions exist—

(a) a company with limited liability is to be registered, or a company has been established by Act of the Oireachtas, or the nominal share capital of a company has been increased (or any of its unissued share capital is issued);

(b) the company (the "acquiring company") is to be registered, or has been established, or has increased its capital, with a view to the acquisition of either—

    (i) the undertaking (including part of the undertaking) of a particular existing company (the "target company"), or

    (ii) not less than 90% of the issued share capital of a target company;

(c) the consideration for the acquisition (except such part of that consideration as consists in the transfer to, or discharge by, the acquiring company of liabilities of the target company) consists as to not less than 90% of that consideration—

    (i) where an undertaking is being acquired, in the issue of shares in the acquiring company to the target company ("shares for undertaking two-party swap") or to the holders of shares in the target company ("shares for undertaking three-party swap"), or

    (ii) where shares are being acquired ("share for share"), in the issue of shares in the acquiring company to the holders of shares in the target company in exchange for the shares held by them in the target company.

Regarding the meaning of *undertaking*, see **9.207.3**. It is understood that the Revenue would accept that SDCA 1999 s 80 may apply in the case of the incorporation of a partnership involving two corporate partners where the partnership trade, or "undertaking", and assets would be transferred to a company in return for an issue of shares to the two companies (see also **9.207.1**).

Shares includes stock (SDCA 1999 s 80(1)(a)). Any reference to an acquiring company is a reference only to a company with limited liability (SDCA 1999 s 80(1)(b)).

A company will not be treated as a target company unless it is provided by the memorandum of association of, or Act establishing, the acquiring company that one of the objects for which the company is formed is the acquisition of the undertaking of, or shares in, the target company, or unless it appears from the resolution, Act or other authority for the increase of the capital of the acquiring company that the increase is authorised for the purpose of acquiring the undertaking of, or shares in, the target company (SDCA 1999 s 80(6)).

Where the above conditions are satisfied, stamp duty is not chargeable under or by reference to the following headings in Schedule 1 of the Stamp Duties Consolidation Act 1999 (SDCA 1999)—

(a)   "CONVEYANCE or TRANSFER on sale of any stocks or marketable securities";

(b)   "CONVEYANCE or TRANSFER on sale of a policy or insurance or a policy of life insurance where the risk to which the policy relates is located in the State"; or

(c)   "CONVEYANCE or TRANSFER on sale of any property other than stocks or marketable securities or a policy of insurance or a policy of life insurance",

on any instrument made for the purposes of or in connection with the transfer of the undertaking or shares, or on any instrument made for the purpose of or in connection with the assignment to the acquiring company of any debts, secured or unsecured, of the target company (SDCA 1999 s 80(2)).

Relief in accordance with SDCA 1999 s 80(2) will not apply to an instrument made for the purposes of, or in connection with, the transfer of an undertaking of a target company that includes any property an instrument for the conveyance of which is chargeable to stamp duty under or by reference to the heading in (c) above, where a conveyance of that property has not been obtained by the target company prior to the date of the execution of the instrument (SDCA 1999 s 80(2A)).

Relief will not apply in the case of any instrument unless it has been stamped with a particular stamp denoting that it is not chargeable with any duty or that it is duly stamped (SDCA 1999 s 80(3)(a)). In the case of an instrument made for the purposes of or in connection with a transfer to a company, relief will not apply unless the instrument is either—

(i)   executed within a period of 12 months from the date of the registration of the acquiring company or the date of the resolution for the increase of the nominal share capital of the acquiring company; or

(ii)   made for the purpose of effecting a conveyance or transfer in pursuance of an agreement which has been filed, or particulars of which have been filed, with the registrar of companies within that period of 12 months (SDCA 1999 s 80(3)(b)).

Relief will not be available unless the scheme of reconstruction or amalgamation is effected for bona fide commercial reasons and does not form part of a scheme or arrangement of which the main purpose, or one of the main purposes, is avoidance of liability to stamp duty, income tax, corporation tax, capital gains tax or capital acquisitions tax (SDCA 1999 s 80(4)).

For the purposes of SDCA 1999 s 80, the Revenue Commissioners may require the delivery to them of a statutory declaration in such form as they may direct and made by a solicitor of the Courts of Justice, and of such further evidence as they may require (SDCA 1999 s 80(7)(a)).

Relief ceases to be applicable, with stamp duty becoming chargeable as if the relief had never applied, if—

(a) in the case where any relief had been allowed, it is subsequently found that any declaration or other evidence furnished in support of the claim was untrue in any material particular or that the conditions specified in SDCA 1999 s 80(2) are not fulfilled in the reconstruction or amalgamation as actually carried out;

(b) in a case where shares in the acquiring company have been issued to the target company (shares for undertaking two-party swap), the target company within a period of two years from the date of the registration or establishment, or of the authority for the increase of the capital, of the acquiring company ceases, otherwise than in consequence of reconstruction, amalgamation or liquidation, to be the beneficial owner of the shares so issued to it; or

(c) in a case where shares in the target company are acquired by the acquiring company (share for share), the acquiring company within a period of two years from the date of its registration or establishment or of the authority for the increase of its capital, ceases, otherwise than in consequence of reconstruction, amalgamation or liquidation, to be the beneficial owner of the shares so acquired (SDCA 1999 s 80(8)).

Where relief ceases to apply, interest on the stamp duty in question, at the rate of 1% per month or part of a month, becomes payable up to the day on which the duty is paid, from, in the case of (a), the date of the conveyance or transfer, in the case of (b), the date the target company ceased to be the beneficial owner of the shares so issued to it and, in the case of (c), from the date the acquiring company ceased to be the beneficial owner of the shares so acquired.

For the purposes of (b) and (c) above, the condition continues to be satisfied where the shares in question cease to be held within the two year period by reason of the liquidation of either the acquiring or the target company within the two year period, or by reason of a further reconstruction or amalgamation (not necessarily qualifying for relief under SDCA 1999 s 80).

Where, in the case of any scheme of reconstruction or amalgamation, the Revenue Commissioners are satisfied that at the proper time for making a claim for exemption from duty there existed all the necessary conditions for exemption other than the condition that not less than 90% of the issued share capital of the target company would be acquired by the acquiring company, they may—

(a)   if it is proved to their satisfaction that not less than 90% of the issued share capital of the target company has, under the scheme, been acquired within a period of six months from—

   (i)   the last day of the period of one month after the first allotment of shares made for the purposes of the acquisition, or

   (ii)   the date on which an invitation was issued to the shareholders of the target company to accept shares in the acquiring company,

   whichever first occurs, and

(b)   on production of the instruments on which the duty paid has been impressed,

repay such an amount of duty as would have been remitted if that condition had been originally fulfilled (SDCA 1999 s 80(9)).

Relief under SDCA 1999 s 80 applies provided the acquiring company is incorporated in the State or in another Member State of the European Union. As regards the other parties involved, the target company and the vendor (if a company), there is no requirement governing the place of incorporation. It is necessary, however, that the acquiring company or the target company incorporated outside the State corresponds, under the law of the place where it is incorporated, to an acquiring company or target company within the meaning of SDCA 1999 s 80 and, subject to any necessary modifications for the purposes of so corresponding, that all the other provisions of the section are met (SDCA 1999 s 80(10)).

9.409.4   Transfers between associated companies

See **9.214**.

9.410   Capital duty

9.410.1   Capital companies: charge of stamp duty

The charge to stamp duty, referred to as *capital duty*, arises in the case of a capital company where, at the date of a transaction effected on or before 6 December 2005, or as a result of such a transaction—

(a)   the effective centre of management of the capital company is in the State; or

(b)   if the effective centre of management of the capital company is in a third country, the registered office of the capital company is in the State (SDCA 1999 s 116(2)).

Capital duty was abolished by FA 2006 in respect of transactions effected on or after 7 December 2005.

Capital duty applies in the cases of the following transactions—

(a)   the formation of a capital company (see below);

(b)   the conversion into a capital company of a company, firm, association or legal person which is not a capital company (for example, where a company limited by guarantee is converted into a company limited by shares);

(c)   an increase in the (issued, not nominal or authorised) capital of a capital company by the contribution of assets of any kind other than an increase in capital through the capitalisation of profits or reserves (eg, a bonus issue), whether temporary or permanent reserves, but including the conversion of loan stock of a capital company into share capital;

(d)   an increase in the assets of a capital company by the contribution of assets of any kind in consideration, not of shares in the capital or assets of the company, but of rights of the same kind as those of members of the company such as voting rights, a share in the profits or a share in the surplus on liquidation;

(e)   the transfer from a third country to the State of the effective centre of management of a capital company whose registered office is in a third country;

(f)   the transfer from a third country to the State of the registered office of a capital company (which, however, is not possible in most countries) whose effective centre of management (see below) is in a third country;

(g)   the transfer from a Member State to the State of the effective centre of management of a capital company which is not considered to be a capital company in the other Member State;

(h)   the transfer from a Member State to the State of the registered office of a capital company whose effective centre of management is in a third country and which is not considered to be a capital company in the Member State from which the registered office is being transferred (SDCA 1999 s 116(1)).

Capital duty is charged at the rate of 0.5% and is charged, in the cases of the transactions described in (a), (c) and (d) above, on the amount of the actual value, at the date of the transaction, of the assets of any kind contributed or to be contributed in connection with the transaction by the members of the capital company concerned after the deduction of liabilities attaching to such assets and assumed by the capital company and of the expenses incurred by the capital company in connection with such contributions. In the cases of the transactions described in (b), (e), (f), (g) and (h), the duty is charged on the amount of the actual value, at the date of the transaction, of the assets of any kind of the capital company after the deduction of its liabilities on that date and of the expenses incurred by the company in connection with the transaction (SDCA 1999 s 118(1)).

The amount on which duty is chargeable, however, may not be less than the nominal value of the shares, if any, in the capital company concerned allotted to the members of the company in connection with the transaction or belonging to the members immediately after the transaction (SDCA 1999 s 118(2)(a)). The memorandum and articles of a company limited by shares is required to state the amount of share capital with which the company proposes to be registered and the division thereof into shares of a fixed amount. The amount thus stated is the company's *nominal* capital.

In arriving at the amount of the actual value in respect of which capital duty is charged, the amount of any assets contributed in connection with the transaction by a member with unlimited liability, or the shares of such a member in the assets of the company, is excluded (SDCA 1999 s 118(2)(b)).

A statement of assets, liabilities and expenses must be delivered to the Registrar of Companies and stamped prior to the formation of a capital company. For all other chargeable transactions, the statement must be delivered within 30 days of the chargeable transaction. Where difficulties arise in ascertaining the exact amount on which duty is chargeable, the statement will be charged in the first instance with duty on an amount considered by the Revenue Commissioners to be appropriate and if it is later established that too little duty has been paid additional duty will be payable and treated as duty in arrear (SDCA 1999 s 117(2), (4)). Where it is established that too much duty has been paid, the excess will be repaid, with interest.

Simple interest at the rate of 0.0273% per day or part of a day is payable in respect of the amount of capital duty chargeable and remaining unpaid for each day from the expiration of one month from the date of the transaction giving rise to the charge. In a case where additional duty is found to be payable as explained above, the interest runs from the date of the transaction (SDCA 1999 s 117(3), (4)).

A *capital company* means—

(a) a company incorporated with limited liability, or a limited partnership formed under the law of the State or a company or partnership which is incorporated or formed in any other Member State and which, under the law of that State, corresponds to any such company or partnership;

(b) any other company, firm, association or legal person the shares in whose capital or assets can be dealt in on a stock exchange; or

(c) any other company, firm, association or legal person operating for profit whose members have the right to dispose of their shares to third parties without prior authorisation and are responsible for the debts of the company, firm, association or legal person only to the extent of their shares (SDCA 1999 s 114(1)).

Member State means a Member State of the European Communities.

Third country means any state other than a Member State.

Effective centre of management is not defined in stamp duty or other tax legislation. It would appear not to be coterminous with "central management and control" (relevant in determining the tax residence of companies for corporation tax purposes – see **3.106.2**) but might be considered to amount to the same thing. It would accordingly mean the place where key management and commercial decisions that are necessary for the conduct of a company's business are in substance made and would therefore ordinarily be the place where the most senior person or group or persons, for example, the board of directors, makes its decisions, the place where the actions to be taken by the company as a whole are determined. In some countries, eg Italy, the place of effective management is taken to include the place where the main and substantial activity of a company is carried on.

In their booklet entitled "Companies Capital Duty", the Revenue Commissioners state that the effective centre of management of a company is located where the day to day management of the company takes place. On this view, it would be quite possible for a company to have its tax residence located in one jurisdiction, because its board meetings take place there, while having its effective centre of management located in another jurisdiction, on the basis that that is where its day to day management takes place. As to which view of the matter might be expected to prevail in any case remains unclear.

9.410.2 Reconstructions or amalgamations of capital companies

SDCA 1999 s 119 provides for a zero rate of capital duty in the cases of certain reconstructions or amalgamations of companies. (See **9.409** above in relation to the meaning of "reconstruction" and "amalgamation".) Exemption applies where, in the case of a transaction, a capital company or a capital company which is in the process of being formed (the "acquiring company") acquires either—

(a)   the undertaking or part of the undertaking of another capital company (the "target company"); or

(b)   share capital of another capital company to the extent that, after that transaction, but not necessarily as a result of that transaction, the acquiring company owns at least 75% of the issued share capital of the target company (SDCA 1999 s 119(1)).

Where the 75% target is reached by means of two or more transactions, the zero rate of capital duty applies only to the transaction which results in that percentage being acquired and to any transaction subsequent to the achievement and retention of that percentage (SDCA 1999 s 119(2)).

The zero rate of capital duty will apply only where the consideration for the acquisition (except for such part as consists of the transfer to or discharge by the acquiring company of liabilities of the target company) consists—

(a)   where the undertaking or part of the undertaking of the target company is acquired, of the issue of shares in the acquiring company to the target company or to the holders of shares in the target company; or

(b)   where shares of the target company are acquired, of the issue of shares in the acquiring company to the holders of shares in the target company in exchange for shares held by them in the target company,

with or without a payment in cash, but where there is a payment in cash, that payment may not exceed 10% of the nominal value of the shares in the acquiring company which are comprised in the consideration (SDCA 1999 s 119(3)).

The statement that would otherwise be chargeable at the zero rate of capital duty becomes chargeable with duty, at 0.5%, if the acquiring company does not, for a period of five years from the date of the transaction, retain—

(a)   at least 75% of the issued share capital of the target company; and

(b)   all the shares which it held following that transaction, including shares acquired whether by means of a transaction or otherwise before that transaction and held at the time of the transaction (SDCA 1999 s 119(4)).

The zero rate will, however, continue to apply if the transfer, as a result of which the shares in question are not held for the required five-year period, was—

(i)   a transfer forming part of a transaction, taking place before 7 December 2005, which would of itself qualify for the zero rate in accordance with SDCA 1999 s 119;

(ii)   a transfer forming part of a transaction, taking place on or after 7 December 2005, which would of itself so qualify had the transaction taken place before 7 December 2005, or

(iii) a transfer in the course of the liquidation of the acquiring company (SDCA 1999 s 119(5)).

Relief will also not be lost where the target company goes into liquidation within five years. This follows a declaration made on 9/10 April 1973 at a meeting of the EEC Council.

If capital duty becomes chargeable where the acquiring company fails to satisfy either of the conditions in (a) and (b) above, the statement delivered in respect of which the zero rate of duty was charged will be charged at the normal rate of duty (0.5%). For the purposes of charging interest on overdue capital duty (see **9.410.1**), however, the date of the transaction is the date on which the event occurred (SDCA 1999 s 119(6)).

Relief under SDCA 1999 s 119 applies only where the effective centre of management (see **9.410.1** above) or the registered office of the target company concerned is in a Member State of the European Union (SDCA 1999 s 119(7)). A company, partnership, firm, association or legal person considered to be a capital company in another Member State is deemed to be a target company notwithstanding that it is not considered to be a capital company (SDCA 1999 s 119(8)).

Chapter 10

Close Companies

Close Companies

10.1 CLOSE COMPANY: DEFINITIONS

10.101 Introduction

The objective of the close companies legislation is an anti-avoidance one and is mainly designed to neutralise attempts to escape or reduce personal taxation at the higher rate. Close company provisions extend the meaning of "distribution", for example to certain benefits provided by companies that are not caught by the legislation on benefits in kind. The legislation penalises companies that make loans to proprietors and other persons interested in such companies by obliging them to pay a temporary tax which is retained until the loans are repaid. To counter the device whereby income tax at the higher rate is avoided or postponed by allowing profits of close companies to accumulate rather than to be distributed, a 20% surcharge is imposed on the undistributed investment and rental income, and a 15% charge on certain undistributed income of service companies. See also **9.407** as regards close companies transferring assets at undervalue.

In determining whether or not a company is close, the principal test is one of control. Control by five or fewer participators or by participators who are directors, whatever the number, is the basic determinant of close company status. The objective is to restrict opportunities to avoid tax that would otherwise be available in the cases of companies whose relationships with their shareholders and other interested parties are not at arm's length.

10.102 Definitions

A number of important definitions are provided in Taxes Consolidation Act 1997 (TCA 1997), s 433.

Participator

A *participator*, in relation to a company, is any person having a share or interest in the capital or income of the company and also includes:

(a) any person who possesses or is entitled to acquire share capital or voting rights in the company;

(b) any loan creditor of the company;

(c) any person who possesses, or is entitled to acquire, a right to receive or participate in distributions (ignoring any amounts treated as distributions under close company rules only) of the company or any amounts payable (in cash or in kind) to loan creditors by way of a premium on redemption; and

(d) any person entitled to secure that the income or assets (whether present or future) of the company will be applied directly or indirectly for his benefit (TCA 1997, s 433(1)).

The reference to "having a share or interest in the capital or income of the company" is probably sufficiently wide to apply to shares in a company held by a discretionary trust.

The objects of that trust have an interest in the capital of the company and would therefore be participators in that company. The interest of a person who has received an unspecific legacy or who has a general interest in an estate would hardly be sufficient to result in that person being a participator in any company whose shares are comprised in the estate assets. On the other hand, a specific legacy of shares received by a person would constitute an interest sufficient to render that person a participator in the company concerned as long as the estate remains in a position to discharge that legacy.

The wide meaning of "participator" can result in overlapping interests in the same asset. A person who does not currently hold shares in a company but who has an option over such shares held by another person is clearly a person "who is entitled to acquire share capital" in the company and is therefore a participator in that company. At the same time, the current holder of those shares is also a participator. The position is the same whether the option is exercisable immediately or at some time in the future since being "entitled to" includes having a future entitlement. That would not be the case, however, with a contingent entitlement. Thus if Mr A may acquire shares in a company contingent on his marrying Ms B, the managing director's daughter, there is no actual entitlement, whether present or future, and Mr A would not be a participator on that account.

The definition of "participator" includes persons "possessing" share capital, voting rights and certain other rights. Thus the concept extends beyond beneficial ownership so that nominee holders of share capital and other entitlements are included as participators.

The above references to a person being entitled to do anything include a present entitlement to do that thing at a future date as well as a future entitlement to do that thing.

There is no provision which deems a participator in a company which controls another company as being a participator in that other company also, such as is the case with the legislation dealing with loans to participators (see **10.204** below). In fact, the definition of "participator" includes the provision that that definition is without prejudice to any other close company provision requiring a participator in one company to be treated as being also a participator in another company.

Associate

The relevance of identifying "associates" of participators arises in a number of ways. It is particularly important in relation to the question of control as interests of associates are attributed to the persons with whom they are associated for that purpose. Provisions dealing with expenses of participators and loans to participators extend to associates of participators while the legislation on excessive interest paid to certain directors extends also to their associates.

An *associate*, in relation to a participator or any other person (eg, a director), is:

(a) any relative of the participator or other person (ie, spouse, ancestor, lineal descendant, brother or sister – not including the spouse of a relative or the relative of a spouse);

(b) the trustee or trustees of a settlement (including any disposition, trust, covenant, agreement, or arrangement, and any transfer of money or other property or of any right to money or other property) of which the participator or other person or any relative of his (living or dead) is or was the settlor;

(c)   where the participator or other person has an interest in any shares or obligations of the company which are subject to any trust or are part of the estate of a deceased person, any other person interested therein; or

(d)   any partner (which could include a company) of the participator or other person.

A *settlor* for the purposes of paragraph (b) above means any person by whom the settlement was made or entered into and in particular includes any person who provided or undertook to provide funds for the settlement or who has made reciprocal arrangements with another person for that other person to make or enter into the settlement. It was held in *IRC v Buchanan* 37 TC 365 that a trust created by a will is not a disposition, and therefore not a settlement. It followed that a testator of a will is not a settlor.

The effect of paragraph (b) of the definition of "associate" is confined to settlements, which, as seen above, does not apply to wills. Paragraph (c), which refers to trusts and estates, is evidently broader in scope in this respect. Where shares or obligations (eg, voting rights) of a company are the subject of a trust or deceased person's estate, any two or more persons interested in those shares are associates of one another.

Example 10.102.1

Anne Wilson and Joan Berry, who are not relatives of one another, are beneficiaries under the will of the late Mrs Philpot. The settlement arrangements include provision for separate funds designated for the two beneficiaries, included in which are shares in various companies. Shares in Mascot Ltd are included in each fund but no other company shares are included in both funds.

Anne Wilson and Joan Berry are associates of one another by virtue of their each being interested in Mascot Ltd shares. Had there not been some shares of the same company held in each fund, Anne and Joan would not have been associates of one another.

The meaning of "associate" was the subject of discussion in the UK case *Willingale v Islington Green Investment Co* 48 TC 547. Interestingly, the decision in that case turned on an aspect of the definition of "associate" which was subsequently removed from the relevant UK legislation but is still part of the definition in TCA 1997, s 433(3). Shares in the company were at the relevant time the subject of an unadministered estate; the shares remained registered in the name of the deceased. The three executors of the estate were a solicitor and two sons of the deceased and they were made the trustees of the will.

One of the sons, C, was a participator in the company through his ownership of most of the shares and was also a director but not a whole-time service director. The residuary estate, which included shares in the company, was bequeathed to the sons on trusts of which they were beneficiaries; a legacy was bequeathed to the solicitor. Interest was paid by the company to the executors and the Revenue contended that this interest was a distribution; at that time a distribution included interest paid to a director who was a participator but not a whole-time service director, or to an associate of such a director. The Revenue case was that the executors were associates of C so that the interest paid to them in that capacity was a distribution.

It was found that paragraph (b) of the definition of "associate" (trustees of a settlement treated as associates of the settlor or his relative) did not treat the executors (in their capacity as executors) as associates of C as an executor of a will is not a trustee of a settlement (following Buchanan).

Paragraph (c), however, which treats persons interested in shares subject to a trust or estate as associates of one another, applied; "interested in" in that paragraph refers both to beneficial and fiduciary interests. This followed the decision in *Gartside v CIR* [1968] AC 553 where the meaning of "interest" was held to take its colour from the context in which it was found, and the decision in *J Bibby & Sons Ltd v CIR* 29 TC 167 where it was observed that the distinction between a legal and a beneficial interest was sufficiently well known to lead to the conclusion that if the legislature had intended to draw it in the context of paragraph (c) it would have done so expressly. The context of paragraph (c) is such that the interests of executors are clearly included and the reference to "the estate of a deceased person" is particularly apt to an unadministered estate. The position of an administered estate would be different because the shares would be vested either in the trustees (the executors becoming trustees on completion of the administration of the estate) or in the beneficiaries. Paragraph (c) therefore envisaged both beneficial and fiduciary interests and on that basis the executors were associates of C.

For the purposes of paragraph (c), an individual will not be treated as an associate by reason of being entitled or eligible to benefit under a trust which relates exclusively to an exempt approved scheme (TCA 1997 Part 30 Ch 1). Nor will an individual be treated as an associate by reason of being entitled or eligible to benefit under a trust (disregarding any charitable trusts which could arise on the failure or determination of any other trusts) which is exclusively for the benefit of the employees, or employees and directors, of the company or their dependants (and not wholly or mainly for the benefit of directors or their relatives) provided the individual is not, and could not through the operation of the trust become, either alone or with his relatives, the beneficial owner of more than 5% of the ordinary share capital of the company.

Loan creditor

A *loan creditor*, in relation to a company, is a creditor in respect of any debt incurred by the company for:

(a)   money borrowed or capital assets acquired by the company;

(b)   any right to receive income created in favour of the company;

(c)   consideration the value of which to the company, at the time the debt was incurred, was substantially less than the amount of the debt,

or a creditor in respect of any redeemable loan capital issued by the company. A loan creditor is also any person who has received or will receive substantially more from the company than the value of the consideration he has given to the company. TCA 1997, s 433(6)(b) excludes a bank which has lent money in the ordinary course of its business.

A loan creditor is also any person who is not a creditor but who has a beneficial interest in any of the above-mentioned debts or loan capital. The meaning of loan creditor is thus very widely defined and includes persons who have not lent any money to the company, such as a vendor awaiting payment for a capital asset sold to the company or any person with a beneficial interest in a debt due from a company.

Director

A *director* in relation to a company includes any person occupying the position of director, by whatever name called, and any person in accordance with whose directions or instructions the directors are accustomed to act. Also included is any person who:

(a) is a manager of the company or who is involved in the management of the company's trade or business; and

(b) alone or with one or more associates is the beneficial owner of, or is able, directly or through the medium of other companies or by any other indirect means, to control, 20% or more of the ordinary share capital of the company.

The above reference to "either on his or her own or with one or more associates" is to be taken as meaning that a person will be treated as owning or controlling what any associate owns or controls, even if he or she does not own or control share capital on his or her own (TCA 1997, s 433(5)).

The reference to "directions or instructions" should be construed narrowly and as not including mere advice even where such advice is normally acted on. It may often happen that the influence of an individual who has control of a company is such that the board of directors finds itself carrying out known policies of that individual in relation to the company, but that in itself would also seem to fall short of the directors acting on his directions or instructions.

It should be pointed out that the above is in accordance with the relevant pre-consolidation legislation and is not, literally, as provided for in TCA 1997, s 434(4). What that subsection actually states is that a director includes any person:

(a) occupying the position of director, by whatever name called;

(b) in accordance with whose directions or instructions the directors are accustomed to act;

(c) who is a manager of the company or otherwise concerned in the management of the company's trade or business; and

(d) who is, either on his or her own or with one or more associates, the beneficial owner of, or is able, directly or through the medium of other companies or by any other indirect means, to control, 20% or more of the ordinary share capital of the company.

It will be seen that the provision in its present form is ambiguous and could, for example, be read as meaning that a director will only include a person who fulfils each of the conditions in (a) to (d) above, though, clearly, that is not the intention.

Control

A person has *control* of a company if he exercises, or is able to exercise, or is entitled to acquire, control, direct or indirect, over the company's affairs (TCA 1997, s 432). In particular, a person has control of a company if he possesses or is entitled to acquire:

(a) the greater part of the share capital or issued share capital of the company;

(b) the greater part of the voting power in the company;

(c) such part of the company's issued share capital as would, on a full distribution of the company's income (but ignoring for this purpose any entitlement of a loan creditor), entitle him to receive the greater part of the amount so distributed; or

(d) such rights as would entitle him to receive the greater part of the company's assets available for distribution, eg on a winding up.

Where two or more persons together satisfy any of the conditions for control, they are to be taken to have control of the company. This provision is particularly relevant as it will be seen that close company status is determined by reference to the control exercised by persons taken together. (In this connection, see also the attribution rules below as regards control exercised by five or fewer participators.)

Being "entitled to" denotes a present entitlement to acquire something at a future date or a future entitlement to acquire something.

There is to be attributed to any person all the rights and powers of:

(a) any company of which he has control;

(b) any company of which he and his associates have control;

(c) any two or more companies of which he has control;

(d) any two or more companies of which he and his associates have control;

(e) any associate of his; or

(f) any two or more associates of his (TCA 1997, s 432(6)).

The rights and powers of a company or associate that may be attributed to a person in accordance with (a)-(f) above include those attributed to that company or associate by virtue of TCA 1997, s 432(5), ie, the rights and powers of any nominee for the company or associate. The rights and powers of a company or associate attributable to a person in accordance with (a)-(f) do not, however, include any rights or powers attributed to an associate by virtue of TCA 1997, s 432(6) itself. In other words, there is no double attribution. Thus, for example, an interest in company A, attributed to an associate of a participator in company A by virtue of that associate's control of another company having an interest in company A, is not then in turn attributed to the participator (see examples below).

Such rights and powers attributed under TCA 1997, s 432(6) are to be attributed so as to result in the company being treated as under the control of five or fewer participators if it can be so treated (see Example **10.103.1** below).

The rather convoluted attribution rules in the previous paragraph can best be explained in the following five examples in which it is required to determine what level of control Mr Albert possesses in relation to Crest Ltd.

Example 10.102.2

Mr Albert owns 60% of the share capital in Xavier Ltd and 10% of the share capital in Crest Ltd. Xavier Ltd owns 25% of the share capital in Crest Ltd.

As Xavier Ltd is controlled by Mr Albert, its 25% interest in Crest Ltd is attributed to him. Accordingly, Mr Albert's interest in Crest Ltd is 35% (10% + 25%).

Example 10.102.3

Mr Albert owns 40% and Ms Seymour, his sister, owns 20% of the share capital in Xavier Ltd. Mr Albert owns 10% and Xavier Ltd owns 25% of the share capital in Crest Ltd.

Mr Albert and his associate, Ms Seymour, have control of Xavier Ltd (60%). Accordingly, the 25% interest which Xavier Ltd has in Crest Ltd is attributed to Mr Albert giving him a 35% (10% + 25%) interest in Crest Ltd.

Ms Seymour's 25% interest in Crest Ltd through Xavier Ltd is not further attributed to Mr Albert.

Example 10.102.4

Mr Albert owns 40% and Ms Seymour, his sister, owns 20% of the share capital in Xavier Ltd. Mr Albert owns 10% of the share capital in Crest Ltd. Mr Albert owns 25% and Ms Seymour owns 30% of the share capital in Tyler Ltd. Xavier Ltd owns 25% and Tyler Ltd owns 15% of the share capital in Crest Ltd.

Mr Albert and his associate, Ms Seymour, have control of both Xavier Ltd (60%) and Tyler Ltd (55%). Accordingly, the 25% and 15% interests respectively held by Xavier Ltd and Tyler Ltd in Crest Ltd are attributed to Mr Albert giving him a 50% (10% + 25% + 15%) interest in Crest Ltd.

Ms Seymour's interests in Crest Ltd, 25% through Xavier Ltd and 15% through Tyler Ltd, are not further attributed to Mr Albert.

Example 10.102.5

Mr Albert owns 10% and 60% of the share capital in Crest Ltd and Xavier Ltd respectively. Mr Neville holds 15% of the share capital in Crest Ltd as nominee for Ms Seymour, Mr Albert's sister. Mr Neville also holds 5% of the share capital in Crest Ltd as nominee for Xavier Ltd. Ms Seymour holds 55% of the voting power in Tyler Ltd and Tyler Ltd owns 7% of the share capital in Crest Ltd.

Mr Neville's 15% and 5% interests in Crest Ltd are attributed to Ms Seymour and Xavier Ltd respectively and therefore to Mr Albert. Mr Albert's interest in Crest Ltd is therefore 30% (10% + 15% +5%).

Ms Seymour, through her control of Tyler Ltd, has attributed to her the share capital of 7% in Crest Ltd. That interest is, however, not attributed to Mr Albert.

The wide definition of control can result in a concept of overlapping control in the sense that control of a company may be held simultaneously and independently by different people or groups of people. For example, three individuals owning between them 60% of the issued share capital would control that company but so would, say, three other individuals who between them own sufficient shares to give them majority voting control over the company.

A company is treated as another company's *associated company* at any time if, at that time or at any time within the previous year, one of the two has control of the other or both are under the control of the same person or persons.

10.103 Meaning of close company

The close company legislation is directed at family companies and other companies which are owned or controlled by a small number of people. A close company is a company which is under the control of five or fewer participators (together with associates) or of any number of participators (plus associates) who are directors (TCA 1997, s 430).

A peculiar feature of the legislation is that the interests of associates can be counted twice in determining who has control of a company. By reason of the attribution rules, the interests of associates are attributed to the participator but there is nothing which prevents their interests being taken into account in their own right and therefore twice.

Example 10.103.1

Mr Albert owns 10% and Ms Seymour, his sister, owns 15% of the issued share capital in Crest Ltd. Mr Phoenix, who is a business partner of Mr Albert, has 10% of the share capital but 20% of the voting control in Crest Ltd. The remaining 65% of the share capital and the remaining 80% of the voting control are held by a large number of unconnected shareholders. The substantial interests in Crest Ltd held by these unconnected shareholders might suggest that Mr Albert and Ms Seymour could not have control of the company. However, as the interests held by Ms Seymour and Mr Phoenix are attributed to Mr Albert, it appears that Mr Albert and Ms Seymour between them have control of the company based on share capital owned, as follows: :

	%
Mr Albert (10% + attributed 25%)	35
Ms Seymour (15% + attributed 10%)	25
	60

Although they may be closely controlled, it is specifically provided that companies in the following categories are to be regarded as not being close companies:

(a) a non-resident company (TCA 1997, s 430(1)(a));

(b) a registered industrial and provident society registered under the Industrial and Provident Societies Acts, 1893-1978, or a building society within the meaning of the Building Societies Acts,1874-1989 (TCA 1997, s 430(1)(b), (c));

(c) a company controlled by or on behalf of the State and *not otherwise* a close company (TCA 1997, s 430(1)(d));

(d) a company which is controlled by a non-close company or companies, and which could not otherwise be treated as a close company except by including as one of the five or fewer participators a company which is not a close company (TCA 1997, s 430(4)(a));

(e) a company controlled by or on behalf of—

    (i) a Member State of the EC (other than Ireland), or

    (ii) the government of a territory with which Ireland has a tax treaty in force (TCA 1997, s 430(1)(da));

(f) a company with quoted shares, as in **10.104** below;

(g) a company that comes within the definition of a close company only by including as one of its participators a loan creditor, being a non-close company, as a result of that creditor being entitled to assets of the company distributable among the participators (see definition of *control* in **10.102** above) (TCA 1997, s 430(4)(b)).

A company is controlled by or on behalf of the State only where it is under the control of the State or of persons acting on behalf of the State (eg, the Minister for Finance), independently of any other person (TCA 1997, s 430(2)). The exception in paragraph (c) applies only if the company could not be treated as a close company under some other test. For example, a company could be controlled by the State by virtue of a "golden share" issued to the Minister for Finance. Simultaneously, more than 50% of the issued shares might be held by five individuals. The company would be a close company in that case despite being controlled on behalf of the State. The separate control by the five individuals would be relevant here, however, only if exercised by them acting independently of the State.

With regard to (e) above, this refers only to a company that is under the control of the Member State in question or the government of the territory in question, or of persons acting on behalf of that Member State or the government of that territory, independently of any other person. Where a company is so controlled, it will not be treated as a close company otherwise unless it can be treated as such by reason of being under the control of persons acting independently of that Member State or the government of that territory (TCA 1997, s 430(2A)).

In paragraph (d) above, the reference to a non-close company is to a company that would not be a close company even if it were resident in the State. Furthermore, shares held in trust for an approved superannuation scheme or retirement benefits scheme are deemed for the purposes of (d) above to be in the beneficial ownership of a non-close company. Depending on the extent of that shareholding, this could mean that the company in which the shares are held would itself be regarded as a non-close company. It is necessary for this purpose that the scheme is not wholly or mainly for the benefit of employees, directors, past employees or directors (or their dependants) of the company in which the shares are held, or of an associated company of that company, or of a company controlled by the directors or associates of that company, or of any close company.

Example 10.103.2

60% of the issued share capital of Radiator Ltd is held by the trustees of an approved pension fund established for the benefit of Compack plc, a non-close company having no connection with Radiator Ltd. Three directors of Radiator Ltd hold shares giving them 55% of the voting control in the company.

The shares held by the pension fund are deemed to be in the beneficial ownership of a non-close company and Radiator Ltd is therefore controlled by a non-close company. That control, however, is disregarded as Radiator Ltd can otherwise be treated as a close company by reason of being controlled by the three directors with voting control. Radiator is therefore a close company.

The purpose of the exception in (g) above is to prevent a company from being a close company merely because of substantial indebtedness to one or more non-close companies, typically banks. The rights of such companies as loan creditors are ignored for this purpose.

The requirement for control by five or fewer unrelated shareholders (not being directors) in most cases means that it would require at least ten unrelated shareholders to avoid close company status. Assuming that the share capital and control in a company is held as to 10% each by ten such shareholders, the company will avoid close company status only if no special provision, such as for a casting vote to one shareholder to prevent a deadlock, has been made. Where shareholdings or voting rights are not evenly distributed, it will take an even larger number of shareholders to render the company "open".

It will be appreciated from the discussion on "control" above that, for the purpose of counting the number of persons exercising control, any one person together with any associate or nominee of his, and certain controlled companies, will be aggregated and will count as one person only. Control on any basis is sufficient. If attributions of interests can be made in more than one way, it may be necessary to consider each possibility.

As the rights of a nominee of a participator are to be attributed to that participator, such rights cannot at the same time be taken into account as belonging to the nominee. For the purposes of determining control, the correct procedure is to look through nominees to the beneficial owners. Accordingly, a nominee (or nominees) cannot have control of a company even though a nominee can be a participator (as noted in **10.102**).

In this respect, the position relating to the rights of a nominee is different to that for the rights of an associate.

Example 10.103.3

The issued share capital of Bendigo Ltd is as follows (all amounts representing shares of €1 each):

	A shares	B shares	Total
		(voting)	
R Smyth	800	35	835
J Kelleher	240	60	300
T Robinson	300	80	380
J Robinson (T Robinson's wife)	230	70	300
L Flaherty (J Robinson's sister)	210	100	310
B Sherwin	550	90	640
11 individuals – 50 shares each	Nil	550	550
188 individuals – 25 shares each	4,700	Nil	4,700
Capstan Ltd (controlled by R Smyth)	470	15	485
	7,500	1,000	8,500

Bendigo Ltd will be close if more than half of either its issued share capital or its voting shares is controlled by five or fewer shareholders. Certain shareholders together will be taken as one person. The five largest shareholdings are those held by R Smyth, B Sherwin, Capstan Ltd, T Robinson and L Flaherty. The shares of Capstan Ltd are attributed to R Smyth giving him a total of 1,320 shares. The shares of Capstan Ltd are, however, included again in their own right.

T Robinson and J Robinson are associates of one another as are J Robinson and L Flaherty, with combined shareholdings of 680 and 610 respectively. T Robinson's holding is therefore counted as 680. However, there is nothing to prevent J Robinson's shares being attributed also to her other associate L Flaherty, to bring her total up to 610.

J Robinson, who so far has not been included as one of the five largest shareholders, has two associates, T Robinson and L Flaherty, and when their shares are attributed to her she has a total of 990 shares, which brings her into the top five with Capstan Ltd dropping out. The top five shareholdings, counting attributions, are now:

R Smyth	1,320
J Robinson	990
T Robinson	680
B Sherwin	640
L Flaherty	610
	4,240

This represents a total of 49.88% of the total shareholding so that the company is not a close company on this basis. One of the peculiarities of the control rules is that shares of a nominee or associate attributed to a participator may be counted again as shares of that associate or nominee. If that person is to be counted as one of the top five participators, the attribution rules will be applied again, in reverse. This accounts for the total deemed shareholdings of T and J Robinson. (It is questionable as to whether such a bizarre result could have been intended and as to whether in practice it would be insisted on by the

Revenue.) This feature does not arise in the case of shares held by Capstan Ltd. While its shares are attributed to R Smyth, R Smyth's shares are not attributed to it as the shares of a controlled company are not attributed to the person controlling it. The five largest B shareholdings (voting) are as follows:

	Held	*Held + Attributed*
L Flaherty	100	170
B Sherwin	90	90
T Robinson	80	150
J Robinson	70	250
J Kelleher	60	60
	400	720

When the voting control of associates is attributed, the five top participators are deemed to exercise 72% of the total. On that count, Bendigo Ltd is a close company.

A company is a close company if, on a full distribution of its distributable income, more than half of that income would be paid to five or fewer participators or any number of participators who are directors. Thus, a company that is not under the control of five or fewer participators, or of its directors who are participators, is not necessarily "open".

The definition of "participator" in relation to a company includes "any loan creditor" of the company and the potential for control on that basis should not be overlooked. The entitlement of any loan creditor (as loan creditor) to receive part of the income of a company on a full distribution among the participators is ignored for the purpose of ascertaining the level of control held by participators. The other entitlements are taken into account, including the rights of a loan creditor (apart from any non-close company – see (g) in categories of non-close companies above) to assets available for distribution to participators in a winding up (TCA 1997, s 432(2)(c)).

Example 10.103.4

Assume that no combination of participators or directors of Ayers Ltd has the greater part of the issued share capital, voting power or share capital conferring rights to receive the greater part of the company's income available for distribution to participators. Summarised balance sheets are as follows:

	31/12/06	*31/12/07*
	€	€
Total assets	1,000,000	775,000
Financed by:		
Loans (1)	450,000	100,000
P&L account	150,000	275,000
Issued share capital (2)	400,000	400,000
	1,000,000	775,000
(1)		
Banks	75,000	100,000
J Craft	375,000	–
	450,000	100,000

J Craft's loan was repaid on 31/12/06 following the sale of fixed assets.

(2) 20,000 €1 shares each held by 5 shareholders including J Craft, and 15,000 €1 shares each held by 20 other shareholders.

	€	€
Total assets	1,000,000	775,000
Due to banks	75,000	100,000
Available to participators	925,000	675,000
5 greatest asset entitlements:		
J Craft – as shareholder	20,000	20,000
– as loan creditor	375,000	–
4 shareholders x 20,000	80,000	80,000
	(51.35%) 475,000	(14.8%) 100,000

Craft was a close company at 31/12/06 as the five largest asset entitlements of participators accounted for more than half of the total of such entitlements. The banks are not "loan creditors" as it can be assumed that their loans were made in the ordinary course of business. As at 31/12/07 the company is no longer close due to the effect of the repayment of J Craft's loan.

10.104 Companies with quoted shares

A company is not a close company if shares (including stock) carrying not less than 35% of the voting power (not being shares with a fixed dividend rate) are beneficially held by "the public", provided the shares have been quoted in the official list of a recognised stock exchange within the preceding twelve months and have been traded on the exchange in that period (TCA 1997, s 431(3)). Shares are regarded as beneficially held by *the public*:

(a) if they are beneficially held by a non-close resident company or by a non-resident company that would not be a close company if it were resident;

(b) if they are held on trust for an approved superannuation or retirement benefits scheme; or

(c) if they are *not* comprised in a principal member's holding, but *not* if they are held:

   (i) by a director of the company or any associate of a director,

   (ii) by a company under the control of a director or director's associate or of two or more such persons,

   (iii) by an associated company of the company, or

   (iv) as part of a fund for the benefit of the employees, directors, past employees or directors (or their dependants) of the company or of a company within (ii) or (iii) above (TCA 1997, s 431(5), (6), (7)).

References in (i) to (iv) above to shares being held by any person include references to their being held by a nominee of that person.

Shares and securities admitted to trading on the Alternative Investment Market (AIM) of the London Stock Exchange are not admitted to the "official list" of that exchange and accordingly are not regarded as listed for the purposes of TCA 1997, s 431(3).

In determining the voting power which any person has, there is to be attributed to that person any voting power of a nominee of his, or of any company of which he has, or of which he and his associates have, control, or of any two or more such companies, or of any associate of his or of any two or more associates of his, including the rights and powers of any nominee attributed to a company or associate of the person, but not the rights and powers attributed to an associate by virtue of this paragraph (ie, by virtue of control) (TCA 1997, s 431(2)(c)). This attribution rule is derived from the meaning of "control" and is illustrated in some detail in Examples **10.102.2-6**.

The exception under TCA 1997, s 431(3) does not apply where more than 85% of a company's voting power is held by the *principal members"* (TCA 1997, s 431(4)). Generally, a person is a *"principal member"* if he holds more than 5% of the voting power of the company and, if there are more than five such persons, is one of the five members who hold the greatest percentages of voting power. If two or more such persons have equal percentages of voting power and they are included in the six (or more, if appropriate) persons with the greatest percentages, the principal members comprise those six (or more) persons. A principal member's holding means the shares which carry the voting rights possessed by him (TCA 1997, s 431(2)(a), (b)).

Example 10.104.1

The percentages of voting power in Atlantic Ltd, Pacific Ltd and Arctic Ltd are as follows:

	Atlantic Ltd	*Pacific Ltd*	*Arctic Ltd*
	%	%	%
A	30*	30*	30*
B	30*	15*	10*
C	30*	15*	10*
D	4	10*	10*
E	3	10*	10*
F	2	8	10*
G	1	8	10*
H	Nil	4	10*
	100	100	100

* principal members

Atlantic Ltd has only three principal members as only three have more than 5%. All eight shareholders in Arctic Ltd are principal members as nine of them have equal percentages of voting power and obviously none of them can be excluded.

At first glance, the concept of 35% of a company's voting power being held by the public may seem straightforward enough but it will be apparent by now, given the qualifications, and qualifications to qualifications, that the matter can be complex.

Example 10.104.2

The percentages of voting power in Doheny Ltd and Sunset Ltd are as follows:

	Doheny Ltd	Sunset Ltd
	%	%
Magnetics plc pension fund	28* #	
P Ryan – director	18*	39*
J Purcell "	15*	13*
R Cleary "	15*	13*
S Doyle "	12*	4
Sundry members of the public	12 #	31#
	100	100

Doheny Ltd

Percentage held by the public (#)	40%
Percentage comprised in principal members' holdings (*)	88%

Although it might initially seem that the company is not a close company since at least 35% of the voting power is beneficially held by the public, the fact that more than 85% of the voting power is held by the principal members means that Doheny Ltd is a close company.

Sunset Ltd

Percentage held by the public (#)	31%
Percentage comprised in principal members' holdings (*)	65%

Sunset Ltd is a close company as less than 35% of its voting power is beneficially held by the public; the 4% of voting power held by S Doyle, a director of the company, is not regarded as held by the public. S Doyle's resignation from the board of directors would result in Sunset Ltd becoming an open company.–

As is the case with the control rules, voting control of one person attributed as associate to another person would appear to be attributable in reverse also. Thus, strange and perhaps unintended results may follow.

Example 10.104.3

Shares carrying voting power in Waldo plc are held as follows:

Art Ltd	18
Brush Ltd	18
Colour Ltd	18
Daub Ltd	16
Mr Elegant	6
Ms Fine	6
Ms Gayle	6
Mrs Hill	6
Mr Ian	6
Total	100

The five shareholders owning 6 shares each are all related to one another. None of the other four shareholders is an associate of any other shareholder.

Mr Elegant's four relatives are associates of his and their voting power is attributed to him. He is deemed therefore to have shares giving him 30% of the total voting control. Each of his relatives is also deemed to have 30% of the voting power – a somewhat bizarre outcome! The five relatives are therefore the principal members of Waldo plc. They are accordingly not members of the public so that the company would not be able to avoid close company status by reason of 35% or more of its voting power being held by the public.

10.105 Information

The vast majority of Irish companies are close companies and in most cases it will be readily apparent as to whether or not a company is a close company. A family company or one which is owned by a small number of individuals will evidently be a close company while most quoted companies will be "open". Most of the detailed and complicated provisions dealt with in **10.102-104** above will therefore usually be of little practical relevance.

Inevitably, there will be cases where it is necessary to investigate the position in detail, for example, the circumstances of a company whose share structure is complex, particularly where shares are held abroad or through trusts, or a quoted company in which there are large shareholdings held by family members. Borderline cases may need to be reviewed periodically as it is quite possible for a company to become or to cease to be a close company at various times.

It will be obvious that the Revenue will in certain cases require detailed information for the purpose of determining whether a company is a close company. Inspectors of taxes are accordingly, under CTA s 104, empowered to require any company which is or appears to be a close company to furnish such particulars as are deemed necessary for that purpose. A registered shareholder is obliged, when required by notice in writing issued by an inspector, to state whether he is the beneficial owner of the shares registered in his name and to supply the name and address of the beneficial owner of any shares not beneficially held by him. A similar requirement exists in relation to loan capital.

An inspector may also, by notice in writing, require a company which appears to him to be a close company to furnish details of any bearer securities issued by the company with the names and addresses of the persons to whom the securities were issued and the respective amounts issued to each person. Where any person has sold or transferred securities, he may be required by notice in writing to furnish such information as is necessary to enable the inspector to ascertain the names and addresses of the persons beneficially interested in the securities. *Securities* for this purpose includes shares, stocks, bonds, debentures and debenture stock and any promissory note or instrument evidencing indebtedness issued to a loan creditor of the company.

10.2 DISTRIBUTIONS AND OTHER ISSUES FOR PARTICIPATORS AND DIRECTORS

10.201   Introduction
10.202   Expenses for participators and associates
10.203   Interest paid to directors and associates
10.204   Loans to participators and associates
10.205   Anti-avoidance

10.201   Introduction

As stated at the beginning of this chapter, the objective of the close companies legislation is mainly to counter attempts to escape or reduce personal taxation at the higher rate. For example, certain benefits provided by companies that are not within the ambit of the benefit in kind legislation, because they are not provided to employees or directors, are treated as distributions by the close company rules. The legislation penalises companies that make loans to proprietors and other persons interested in such companies ("participators") by obliging those companies to pay a temporary tax which is retained until the loans are repaid. Benefits for participators are treated as distributions, as is excessive interest to certain directors.

The effect of treating a benefit or interest to an individual as a distribution is that it becomes taxable under Schedule F at the marginal income tax rate. As the paying company cannot obtain a tax deduction for the amount paid (TCA 1997, s 76(5)), the designation of interest as a distribution is unfavourable; in a close company situation, the participators will be concerned with the tax consequences both for the company and for themselves. The treatment of a benefit provided by a company as a distribution has the twofold effect that the value of the benefit is taxable in the hands of the recipient (whereas it might not otherwise have been), while the company is denied a tax deduction for the cost of providing the benefit.

10.202   Expenses for participators and associates

TCA 1997 Part 6 Ch 2 (ss 130-135) deals with the meaning of *distribution* in relation to all companies (see **11.1**). TCA 1997 Part 13 (ss 430-441), which is concerned with matters affecting close companies only, includes two provisions that extend the meaning of *distribution* in the cases of these companies.

TCA 1997, s 436 treats as a distribution the amount of any expense incurred by a close company in or in connection with the provision of certain benefits for any participator. An associate of a participator is treated as a participator for this purpose. Furthermore, a participator of a company that controls another company is also a participator of that other company.

This provision does not apply in the case of any expense incurred in providing benefits or facilities to any director or employee of the company which, being treated as benefits in kind by virtue of TCA 1997, s 118, are liable to income tax under Schedule E. Neither does it apply to the provision of any pension, annuity, lump sum, gratuity or similar benefit to the spouse, children or dependants of a director or employee on their death or retirement.

The benefits to which the section applies are living or other accommodation, entertainment, domestic or other services and any *other benefits or facilities of whatever nature*. The amount of the distribution in any such case is so much of the expense incurred by the company as is not reimbursed to it by the participator or associate.

Example 10.202.1

The following transactions relate to Travel Agency Ltd:

(a) The company paid €5,000 for a foreign holiday for Mr Carroll who owns 40% of the equity in the company.

(b) Ms Dunne, a 10% shareholder, bought a car worth €28,000 from Blue Bayou Ltd, a subsidiary of Travel Agency Ltd, for €10,000.

(c) The company paid €4,500 by way of rent subsidy on behalf of Mr O'Brien, a 5% shareholder and a senior employee of the firm.

(d) Ms Murphy's college fees €3,500 were funded by the company. Her father has lent €150,000 to the company.

The tax consequences are as follows:

(a) Mr Carroll is a participator in Travel Agency Ltd and the cost of his holiday is a distribution. He is taxable on an amount of €5,000. The cost of the holiday is not tax deductible to the company.

(b) Ms Dunne, a participator, is also a participator in Blue Bayou Ltd, and is liable to income tax on a distribution of €18,000. The cost to Blue Bayou Ltd is not tax deductible.

(c) Since Mr O'Brien is an employee, the rent subsidy is taxable under Schedule E and is therefore not a distribution.

(d) Mr Murphy, as a loan creditor of the company, is a participator, and the benefit received by his daughter is a distribution; being an associate of his, she is treated as a participator also (TCA 1997, s 436(2)). She is liable to income tax on €3,500. The cost to the company is not tax deductible.

Where a close company incurs expense partly in providing benefits or facilities to a participator or associate and partly for other purposes, the amount of the expense properly apportioned to the provision of those benefits or facilities is a distribution. TCA 1997, s 436(4) applies the provisions of TCA 1997, s 119 for the purposes of valuing certain benefits or facilities provided by a close company. Thus, if the company provides living accommodation, by way of transferring property which it has used, to a participator or associate, it is deemed to have incurred expense, and to have made a distribution, equal to the value of the property at the time it is transferred.

An anti-avoidance measure counters attempts to escape distribution treatment on the part of close companies acting in concert, or acting as a result of arrangements made by any person, to provide benefits to each other's participators. TCA 1997, s 436(7) provides that where each of two or more such companies makes a payment, or gives any consideration, or provides any facilities, to a participator of one of the other companies, each company is deemed to have made a distribution to its own participator by reference to the benefit received by that participator.

Example 10.202.2

Red Ltd, Blue Ltd and Green Ltd agree to the following:

(a) Red Ltd provides a car, which it had purchased for €28,000, to Mr Green Participator.

(b)   Blue Ltd makes a gift of a painting, which it had purchased for €15,000, to Ms Red Participator.

(c)   Green Ltd sells an apartment valued at €80,000 to Ms Blue Participator for €60,000.
The tax result is as follows:

(a)   Red Ltd has made a distribution of €15,000 to Ms Red Participator.

(b)   Blue Ltd has made a distribution of €20,000 to Ms Blue Participator.

(c)   Green Ltd has made a distribution of €28,000 to Mr Green Participator.

No deduction will be made in respect of any distribution (TCA 1997, s 76(5)) but it is unlikely that the companies would have arranged matters with a view to securing such deductions or with a view to avoiding dividend withholding tax. With the abolition of ACT from 6 April 1999, TCA 1997, s 436(7) is unlikely to have much if any practical effect.

Where both the company and the participator are Irish resident companies and one is a subsidiary of the other, or both are subsidiaries of another Irish resident company, any benefit to the participator as a result of the transfer of assets or liabilities by the company to the participator, or by the participator to the company, will not be treated as a distribution by virtue of TCA 1997, s 436 (TCA 1997, s 436(5)). (Nor, incidentally, will the benefit be treated as a distribution by virtue of TCA 1997, s 130, as a practically identical exception is provided for in TCA 1997, s 130(3).) In this connection, *subsidiary* means a 51% subsidiary (TCA 1997, s 436(6)) and a company is a *51% subsidiary* of another company if more than 50% of its ordinary share capital is owned directly or indirectly by that other company (TCA 1997, s 9(1)). The other company will not for this purpose be regarded as the owner of any share capital which it owns—

(a)   directly in a company if a profit on a sale of the shares would be treated as a trading receipt;

(b)   indirectly, but which is owned directly by a company for which a profit on a sale of the shares would be treated as a trading receipt; or

(c)   directly or indirectly in a company not resident in Ireland.

Example 10.202.3
Albinoni Ltd holds 100% and 75% of the ordinary share capital of Byrd Ltd and Corelli Ltd respectively. Byrd Ltd, a share dealing company, holds 75% of the ordinary share capital of Dowland Ltd while Corelli Ltd holds 80% of the ordinary share capital in Capella Ltd. All companies are Irish resident companies.

Benefits arising as a result of assets or liabilities passing between Albinoni Ltd, Byrd Ltd, Corelli Ltd and Capella Ltd will not attract distribution treatment. Distribution treatment will, however, apply to benefits to either Albinoni Ltd or Byrd Ltd resulting from transfers of assets or liabilities involving Dowland Ltd, which is not a 51% subsidiary of either.

Example 10.202.4
The facts are as in Example **10.202.3** except that Corelli Ltd is not Irish resident. Corelli Ltd and Capella Ltd have both transferred assets to Albinoni Ltd at undervalue. Capella Ltd has also transferred assets at undervalue to Corelli Ltd.

Since Corelli Ltd is not an Irish resident company, the TCA 1997, s 436(5) exception does not apply. Being a non-resident company, however, it is not a close company so that TCA 1997, s 436 does not apply in any event and no distribution arises.

The benefit arising to Albinoni Ltd is not a distribution by virtue of TCA 1997, s 436. It could, however, be said to be something arising from a foreign possession. If that benefit were income in nature, it would be taxable under Schedule D Case III. Since the benefit arises from the transfer of assets, however, the benefit is likely to be capital in nature.

Capella Ltd is indirectly owned as to 60% by Albinoni Ltd and it might appear that it is therefore a 51% subsidiary of that company. It is necessary, however, to treat Albinoni Ltd as not owning any share capital in Corelli Ltd for this purpose (since that company is non-resident) so that   Albinoni Ltd could not then be regarded as owning any share capital indirectly in Capella Ltd. Accordingly, transfers of assets at undervalue by Capella Ltd to Albinoni Ltd give rise to distributions in amounts represented by the excess of the value of the assets over the consideration paid in each case. Albinoni Ltd is not subject to corporation tax in respect of any distributions received, being distributions received from an Irish resident company.

10.203   Interest paid to directors and associates

TCA 1997, s 437 is directed at tax avoidance transactions that seek to withdraw profits from a close company under the guise of interest. The section treats excessive interest paid to certain directors or their associates as a distribution, thereby denying the company a tax deduction for the excess amount.

A director to which TCA 1997, s 437 applies is any director of the close company or of a company that controls, or is controlled by, the close company and where the director has a material interest in the close company or, where the close company is controlled by another company, in that other company. A person has a *material interest* in a company if he, either alone or with one or more associates, or if any associate of his with or without any such other associates:

(a)   is the beneficial owner of more than 5% of the ordinary share capital of the company; or

(b)   is able to control, directly or indirectly, more than 5% of the ordinary share capital of the company.

Example 10.203.1

Weiss Ltd, a close company, controls Wolf Ltd which in turn controls Zeller Ltd – see meaning of "control" in **10.102**.

Mr Weiss owns 10% of the equity in Weiss Ltd and Mr Zeller owns 15% of the equity in Zeller Ltd.

Mr Weiss is a director of Weiss Ltd and Mr Zeller is a director of Zeller Ltd.

Wolf Ltd pays excess interest to Mr Weiss and also to a sister of Mr Zeller.

The excess interest paid to Mr Weiss is a distribution because –

(a)   Wolf Ltd is a close company;

(b)   Mr Weiss is a director of Weiss Ltd which controls Wolf Ltd; and

(c)   Mr Weiss has a material interest in Weiss Ltd which controls Wolf Ltd, the interest paying company.

The excess interest paid to Mr Zeller's sister is not a distribution because, although

(a)   Mr Zeller's sister is his associate and he is a director of Zeller Ltd; and

(b)   Zeller Ltd is controlled by Wolf Ltd, the interest paying company.

Mr Zeller does not have a material interest in Wolf Ltd or in a company which controls Wolf Ltd.

Example 10.203.2

The circumstances are as in Example **10.203.1** except that Mr Weiss owns no shares in Weiss Ltd; his brother and sister, however, each controls 3% of the ordinary share capital of the company.

The tax consequences are exactly the same as in Example **10.203.1**. Mr Weiss is deemed to have a material interest in Weiss Ltd because his associates between them have control of more than 5% of the ordinary share capital of the company.

The excess interest for any accounting period is reckoned by reference to the rate of 13% pa, or such other rate as the Minister for Finance may prescribe. An overall limit is first calculated on all of the interest paid in the period to the directors and associates concerned, and this limit is then apportioned between the recipients in accordance with the amounts paid to them. The overall limit is 13% of the lesser of:

(a) the total of the loans, advances and credits on which the company paid interest in the accounting period, or, if the total amount varied during the period, the average total for the period; and

(b) the nominal amount of the issued share capital of the company, with the addition of any share premium account (or other comparable account by whatever name called), as at the beginning of the period.

The 13% rate to be applied is an annual rate. Accordingly, if the accounting period in question is a period of less than 12 months, it will be necessary to reduce the amount of interest proportionately. If the total of the loans made is different at different times in the period, the average total for the period is to be taken. For example, if the total was €500,000 for the first six months of the period and was €900,000 for the remaining six months, the 13% rate would be applied to the average amount of €700,000. Similarly, if there were no loans for part of the period, say, for the first six months, and there were loans for the remainder of the period, say, €500,000 for the remaining six months, the 13% rate would be applied to the average amount of €250,000 for that period.

Example 10.203.3

The latest balance sheet of Winemakers Ltd is as follows:

	€
Assets	600,000
Ordinary shares (no change during year)	1,000
Reserves	499,000
Directors' loans:	
A Cork	50,000
O Bung	30,000
T Camden	20,000
	600,000
Interest paid on loans @ 16% =	16,000
Overall limit is 13% of the lesser of:	
(a) €100,000 and	
(b) €1,000 =	130
Treated as a distribution	15,870
Treated as interest	130

Standard rate income tax must be withheld on payment of the interest of €130 and accounted for to the Revenue under TCA 1997, s 239. The interest is allowable as a trading expense assuming the borrowings from the directors were wholly and exclusively for the purposes of the company's trade.

The directors are liable to income tax on interest and distributions as follows:

	Amount paid	*Interest*	*Distribution*
	€	€	€
A Cork	8,000	65	7,935
O Bung	4,800	39	4,761
T Camden	3,200	26	3,174
	16,000	130	15,870

Both the interest and the distribution in each case will be subject to income tax at the marginal rate for each director.

For the purposes of TCA 1997, s 437, *interest* includes any consideration paid or given for the use of the money advanced or credit given to the close company.

The section is stated to have effect subject to TCA 1997, s 436(7). Thus the provision directed at reciprocal arrangements in that section applies also to arrangements intended to circumvent the provisions of TCA 1997, s 437.

TCA 1997, s 246(3)(g) confirms that the withholding tax provisions of TCA 1997, s 246 (see **4.305**) do not apply to interest treated as a distribution under TCA 1997, s 437.

10.204   Loans to participators and associates

TCA 1997, s 438 attacks the practice of withdrawing profits from close companies in the form of loans. Without this measure, it would be possible for shareholders in a close company to borrow from the company in place of taking remuneration or dividends. The borrowings could be left outstanding for long periods and in some cases never repaid.

TCA 1997, s 438 provides that where a close company, other than in the ordinary course of carrying on a business which includes the lending money, makes a loan or advances money to an individual who is a participator, or an associate of a participator, in the company, the company is deemed to have made, in the year of assessment in which the loan was made, an annual payment which after the deduction of income tax at the standard rate for that year is equal to the amount of the loan.

A registered industrial and provident society is excluded by TCA 1997, s 430(1)(b) from the definition of *close company*. In relation to any loan or advance made on or after 23 May 1983, this exclusion does not apply for the purposes of TCA 1997, s 438.

The deemed annual payment is a *relevant payment* for the purposes of TCA 1997, s 239 (see **4.306**) and the company is accordingly obliged to remit to the Revenue the tax appropriate to that payment. The deemed annual payment is to be included on the return of annual payments required by TCA 1997, s 239 (now incorporated in the corporation tax return, form CT1) which is due within nine months (but not later than the 21st of the ninth month) of the end of the accounting period in which the loan was made. The tax due is payable by the date by which corporation tax for the period is due (TCA 1997, s 239(5)) and is treated, for the purposes of the charge, assessment, collection and recovery from the company of that tax, and of any interest or penalties on the tax, as corporation tax for that period (TCA 1997, s 239(11). The tax will therefore form part of the company's preliminary tax obligation in respect of the period (see **15.103**).

Example 10.204.1

Maple Leaf Ltd, a close company carrying on a retailing business, advances €16,000 on 1 November to Mr Mc Donald whose wife is a shareholder in the company. The company's year end is 31 March.

	€
As Mr McDonald is an associate of his wife, who is a participator in the company, Maple Leaf Ltd is deemed to have made an annual payment of	20,000
which after deduction of income tax @ 20%	4,000
is equal to the amount of the advance	16,000

The company must return the €20,000 as a *relevant payment* in its return of annual payments under TCA 1997, s 239 which is due by the date on which the company's corporation tax return is due (see **15.104.1**). The income tax of €4,000 is treated as corporation tax for the accounting period in which the loan is made and is accordingly payable on the date(s) by reference to which that corporation tax is payable. Mr McDonald has no liability to tax in respect of the loan made to him.

Although the *grossed up* amount of a loan made by a close company to an individual who is a participator or associate is deemed to be an annual payment, it is not treated as a charge on income. TCA 1997, s 243(4) includes annual payments in the definition of *charges on income* but TCA 1997, s 438(1)(c) states that the annual payments dealt with in that subsection are not charges on income for the purposes of TCA 1997, s 243 (allowance of charges on income – see **4.404**).

A participator in a company that controls another company is treated as being also a participator in that other company. Only loans or advances to those borrowers who are participators, or associates of participators, at the time of the loan or advance are affected by TCA 1997, s 438. The fact that a borrower who was not a participator or associate in relation to the lending company at the time of the loan or advance subsequently becomes such a participator or associate does not trigger any liability under the section.

A close company is regarded as making a loan to a person for the purposes of TCA 1997, s 438 where the person incurs a debt to that company, except in the case of a debt incurred in connection with the supply by the company of goods or services in the ordinary course of its trade or business, and then only if the credit given is not for more than six months and is not for a period longer than is normally allowed by the company to its customers.

The concept of "making a loan" is obviously fairly widely drawn for TCA 1997, s 438 purposes. A sum of money misappropriated by a participator, however, has been held not to constitute a loan (*Stephens v T Pittas Ltd* [1983] STC 576). It was held in *Ramsden v IRC* 937 TC 169 that purchase moneys left outstanding did not constitute the making of a loan but, since the incurring of a debt is specifically included in TCA 1997, s 438 as the making of a loan, that decision has no effect in this context; no distinction can be made here between a loan and a debt.

A close company is deemed to have made a loan to a person where a debt due from that person to another person is assigned to the company.

Example 10.204.2

J Simpson, a shareholder in Colt Ltd, a close company, is indebted to O Fuhrman, who has no connection with the company, for €8,000. O Fuhrman assigns the debt to Colt Ltd for consideration. Colt Ltd is regarded as having made a loan to J Simpson. It is therefore deemed to have made an annual payment of €10,000 (assuming a standard income tax rate of 20%) and the provisions of TCA 1997, s 438 apply. Tax of €2,000 must be remitted in accordance with TCA 1997, s 239.

More serious problems could be encountered as a result of this provision. It would not be unusual for a sole trader transferring his business to a newly incorporated company to include his outstanding liabilities in the transfer. If the liabilities relate to long-term loans the problem is that the new company, to which the loans have been assigned, will be regarded as having made a loan to the sole trader of an amount equal to those liabilities. To avoid any TCA 1997, s 438 consequences, the sole trader might be advised to repay the loans, although in many cases this might not be practicable.

The uncovering of a deficiency in the funds of a close company in the course of a Revenue audit would quickly raise a presumption of a prior extraction of funds by the proprietors. If such a presumption could not be rebutted, the shortage might have to be acknowledged as a debt due to the company in which case a liability under TCA 1997, s 438 would arise.

Certain loans are exempted from the tax charge under TCA 1997, s 438. Loans made by a company in the ordinary course of a business which includes the lending money are not affected. In this connection, the lending of money would seem to denote the lending of money in the sense in which moneylending is part of the ordinary business of a registered moneylender or bank. That would clearly not be true in the case of a single loan made to a participator, or where only a few such loans are made, even if made on commercial terms. Even where the lending company can show that it operates a commercially constituted business of lending money, any loan to a participator must be made on terms and conditions consistent with its overall lending business (*Steen v Law* [1964] AC 287).

Loans to certain employees of the close company are also left out of account, provided that:

(a)   any such loan, together with any outstanding loans made by the company or by any of its associated companies (within the meaning of TCA 1997, s 432(1) – see **2.401.5**) to the borrower, or to the spouse of the borrower, does not exceed €19,050;

(b)   the borrower works full-time for the close company or for any of its associated companies; and

(c)   the borrower does not have a material interest in the company or in any of its associated companies.

In relation to condition (c), a *material interest* has the same meaning as it has for the purposes of TCA 1997, s 437(2) (see **10.203** and Example **10.203.1** above). If the borrower does not have a material interest in the close company at the time the loan is made but he acquires such an interest before the loan is repaid in full, the company is deemed to have made to him at that time a loan equal to the amount of the sum then outstanding.

The effect of TCA 1997, s 438 is to discourage companies from making loans to participators in the circumstances described. The obligation on the company to remit tax at standard rate on the grossed up amount of the loan is a sufficient deterrent in this respect. The tax charge is not intended to amount to a permanent cost to the company and it is repayable according as the loan is repaid. If the loan or any part of it is repaid, the company may claim, within ten years of the end of the year of assessment in which the repayment is made, to have the tax, or a proportionate part of the tax in the case of a part repayment, refunded to it (TCA 1997, s 438(4)). Although tax payable by a company under TCA 1997, s 438 is part of the company's preliminary tax, interest will not be paid on the amount of any such tax repaid to it (TCA 1997, s 953(7)(a)(ii)).

TCA 1997, s 438(4) provides that a refund is to be made where the loan or advance or any part of it is repaid "after a company has been assessed to tax under this section". It would seem in strictness, therefore, that a company must be assessed under TCA 1997, s 239 before any repayment is made to it if it is to be entitled to a refund. An assessment would be made as a matter of course under the self assessment regime where the annual payment has been included in the return of relevant payments required under TCA 1997, s 239. A refund can then be claimed in respect of any subsequent repayment or part repayment of the loan.

This raises interesting questions as to what happens where a loan is repaid in whole or in part before an assessment is made. An advance made by a close company to an individual who is a participator will often be repaid within a short time, perhaps within the same accounting period. There would appear to be a technical difficulty in these situations in the matter of claiming the appropriate refund since, clearly, the repayment will not have been made after the company has been assessed to tax. In fact, the company will probably not even have paid over the tax.

In practice, the approach of the Revenue appears to be that no assessment will, generally, be made, and tax need not be paid, where the loan or advance is repaid within six months of the end of the accounting period in question. (But see also under *Revenue practice in relation to preliminary tax* below.) The loan or advance should nevertheless be disclosed in the usual way. The decision in *Earlspring Properties Ltd v Guest* [1993] STC 473 is interesting in this respect as it decided that where a loan to a participator has been repaid, an assessment cannot then be raised in respect of tax which ought to have been paid. Although, taken literally, the TCA 1997, s 438 liability remains even after a participator's loan has been repaid, Vinelott J in his judgment was adamant that this result cannot possibly have been intended by the legislature. The UK equivalent of TCA 1997, s 438 therefore must be taken as impliedly limited to cases in which the loan has not been repaid at the time an assessment is made.

Notwithstanding any limitation prescribed by TCA 1997, s 865(4) on the time within which a repayment claim must be made (see **15.204.2**), the refund claim to be made under TCA 1997, s 438(4) is to be made within four years from the end of the year of assessment in which the loan or advance, or any part of it as the case may be, is repaid to the company.

Attempts to circumvent TCA 1997, s 438 by means of "bed and breakfast" tactics are likely to attract Revenue attention, particularly since the relevant details must be disclosed in the company's corporation tax return. Having such loans repaid shortly before year end and advanced again at the beginning of the next period would leave the company open to a charge under TCA 1997, s 438, taken literally, so that an assessment could be raised in respect of each such advance while a refund of the tax could be denied on the basis that repayment took place before any assessment was made.

If the Revenue are prevented from making an assessment in any case where the participator's loan has been repaid, the bed and breakfast approach may be viable. That this is possible is in fact acknowledged in the *Earlspring Properties* case. The equivalent UK legislation as amended in 1986 now provides that the tax is assessable whether or not the whole or any part of the loan or advance in question has been repaid and, appropriately, also provides that, on repayment (not necessarily *after* the company has been assessed to tax) of the loan or advance or any part of it, the related tax is refundable.

Example 10.204.3

Merville Ltd, a close company, carries on its business as a recruitment agency from the home of its managing director, Ms Kilmer. It uses one room in the house as its office and recently spent €80,000 on a major renovation of that part of the house.

As the entire building, including the renovated office, is the property of Ms Kilmer, the €80,000 spent by the company represents a benefit from the company to her. It could be a distribution under TCA 1997, s 130(2) – "any other distribution out of assets of the company (whether in cash or otherwise) in respect of shares" – which would give rise to significant tax costs in terms of an income tax liability for Ms Kilmer.

Before the dust has settled, however, the potential problem is identified and it is decided to treat the €80,000 as a loan from the company. The company will then be obliged to remit €20,000 (assuming a 20% standard rate of income tax) to the Revenue as required by TCA 1997, s 438. This tax may only be recovered according as the loan is repaid. The repayment might be made over a period with the assistance of a rent paid to Ms Kilmer, giving rise, however, to a residual tax liability (her Case V liability less the company tax saving).

Although TCA 1997, s 438 deals only with loans or advances made to individuals, the section also applies to certain companies. For this purpose, a company receiving a loan in a fiduciary or representative capacity, or a company not resident in a Member State of the European Communities, is treated as an individual. A loan made to such a company, as well as a loan made to a third party in consideration of any payment or transfer of property to, or the release or satisfaction of any debt due by, the company will result in the close company which made the loan being deemed to have made an annual payment equal to the amount of the loan.

A company is regarded as being a resident of a Member State of the EC if it is, by virtue of the law of that Member State, resident for the purposes of tax (being, in the case of the State, corporation tax and, in any other case, being any tax imposed in the Member State that corresponds to corporation tax in the State) in such Member State (TCA 1997, s 438(6)).

Revenue practice in relation to preliminary tax

For the purposes of satisfying a close company's preliminary tax obligations (see also **15.103.3**) for an accounting period, Revenue will not require the company to take account of the provisions of TCA 1997, s 438 with regard to the imposition of the charge to income tax in circumstances where the participator or associate repays the loan or advance in question by the due date for filing of the company's corporation tax return.

This practice should be relied on only to the extent that the loan arrangements concerned are undertaken in good faith and for purposes other than tax avoidance. It will not apply in the case of "bed and breakfast" type of arrangements where a new loan/advance is taken out on, or shortly after, repayment of an existing loan/advance. In such cases, Revenue will insist that the provisions of TCA 1997, s 438 be taken into account for preliminary tax purposes. [The correctness of this approach may be open to argument in the light of the decision in *Earlspring Properties referred to above*.] However, in circumstances where it is the practice of a director to operate a current account with the company and this account is cleared annually from the director's own resources (eg, the director's remuneration), such an arrangement will not be regarded as a "bed and breakfast" type arrangement.

In addition, and without prejudice to Revenue's entitlement to review, amend or withdraw its practices from time to time as appropriate, the practice set out above will be subject to ongoing review by the Revenue Commissioners, and Revenue reserves the right to amend or withdraw this practice on foot of such review as respects preliminary tax payments due after such amendment or withdrawal.

Anti-avoidance

TCA 1997, s 438 includes an anti-avoidance measure that counters the use of an intermediary company between a close company and a borrower. The measure applies where under arrangements made by any person other than in the ordinary course of business:

(a)   a close company makes a loan or advance which would not otherwise be caught by TCA 1997, s 438 (because not made to a participator in the company); and

(b)   a person other than the company makes a payment or transfers property to, or releases or satisfies in whole or in part a liability of, an individual who is a participator in the company or an associate of a participator.

In these circumstances the loan or advance made by the company is deemed to have been made to the participator or associate. An exception to this provision is the case where the participator or associate is taxable on the full amount represented by the payment, transfer or release referred to in (b) above. In a case heard before the Appeal Commissioners, it was held that the reference in (b) above to a person other than the company relates to payments etc which are gratuitous and not to such payments made for full consideration.

Example 10.204.4

Carville Ltd, a close company, places €32,000 with Torville Ltd, a related company, interest free and on an indefinite basis on the understanding that Torville Ltd will write off a loan of the same amount due from Mr Potter, a shareholder in Carville Ltd (but who has no interest in Torville Ltd).

Carville Ltd is regarded as having made an annual payment of €40,000 (assuming a 20% standard rate of income tax) and it must account for tax of €8,000 in a return under TCA 1997, s 239.

In the light of the Appeal Commissioners' decision referred to above, it might be argued that Torville Ltd has received full consideration for writing off the loan to Mr Potter. Since, however, the amount lent to it remains as a debt due to Carville Ltd, it would be difficult to establish that Torville Ltd has received full consideration for writing off the loan to Mr Potter.

Example 10.204.5

The facts are as in Example **10.204.4** except that the debt that Torville Ltd agrees to write off is in respect of the supply of goods to Mr Potter for his business. The €32,000 written off will be treated as a trading receipt of Mr Potter's business under TCA 1997, s 87 and will therefore be subject to tax in his hands. The loan to Torville Ltd would not therefore be caught by TCA 1997, s 438.

There is a further anti-avoidance measure aimed at the use of a non-close company to circumvent TCA 1997, s 438. Where a non-close company controlled by a close company makes a loan that would otherwise not give rise to a charge under the section, the close company is treated as having made that loan (TCA 1997, s 438A(2)). This approach is extended by TCA 1997, s 438A(3) to the situation in which a non-close company that makes a loan not caught by TCA 1997, s 438 subsequently comes under the control of a close company. In that case, the section applies as if the loan had been made by the close company immediately after the time it acquired control. For the purposes of TCA 1997, s 438A, a "loan" includes an advance.

Example 10.204.6

Clusener Ltd, a close company, acquires control of Callis Ltd, a company resident in the Isle of Man and therefore not itself a close company. Clusener Ltd makes a capital contribution of €100,000 to Callis Ltd. Callis Ltd then makes loans amounting to €100,000 to various individual shareholders of Clusener Ltd. Clusener Ltd is treated as having made these loans to its participators and TCA 1997, s 438 accordingly applies.

Before Clusener Ltd had acquired control of Callis Ltd, Callis Ltd had made a loan of €25,000 to one of the shareholders in Clusener Ltd. Clusener Ltd is also treated as having made this loan immediately following the acquisition of control and, again, TCA 1997, s 438 applies to the loan.

Where two or more close companies together control a non-close company that makes, or has made, a loan. TCA 1997, s 438A(2) and (3) apply as if each of them controlled that company and as if the loan had been made by each of them (TCA 1997, s 438A(4)). In that case, however, the loan is apportioned between the close companies in such proportion "as may be appropriate" having regard to the nature of their respective interests in the non-close company.

The above anti-avoidance provisions will not apply if it is shown that no person has made any arrangements (otherwise than in the ordinary course of a business carried on by that person) as a result of which there is a connection between the making of the loan and the acquisition of control, or between the making of the loan and the provision by the close company of funds for the company making the loan (TCA 1997, s 438A(5)). The close company will be regarded as providing funds for the company making the loan if it directly or indirectly makes any payment or transfers any property to, or releases or satisfies (in whole or in part) a liability of, that company.

In applying TCA 1997, s 438A, any question whether the company making the loan did so otherwise than in the ordinary course of a business carried on by it which includes the lending of money, whether the loan or any part of it has been repaid to the company, or whether the company has released or written off the whole or part of the debt in respect of the loan, is to be determined by reference to the company that makes the loan (TCA 1997, s 438A(6)).

References in TCA 1997, s 438A to a company making a loan include references to cases in which the company is, or if it were a close company would be, regarded as making a loan by virtue of TCA 1997, s 438(2) (TCA 1997, s 438A(7)).

Release of debt etc in respect of TCA 1997, s 438 loan

There is no question of a liability to tax arising out of TCA 1997, s 438 on the part of the participator or associate to whom the loan or advance is made. Where, however, the debt created by a loan or advance to which TCA 1997, s 438 applied is released or written off in whole or in part, the borrower is regarded, for the purposes of computing total income, as having received income which, after deduction of income tax at the standard rate in force for the year of assessment in which the release or write off took place, is equal to the amount released or written off (TCA 1997, s 439).

A debt would not be released where it is satisfied by being repaid but would be regarded as being released where the borrower transfers the liability to another party. In *Collins v Addies; Greenfield v Bains* [1992] STC 746 the taxpayers unsuccessfully argued that their liability had been satisfied by arranging for a third party to assume it. Where a company simply allows a debt due to it to become statute-barred, TCA 1997, s 439 would not apply; a release or write-off of a debt requires some act on the part of the company.

In computing the tax liability of the borrower who has benefited from the release or write-off, tax will by payable on the amount of income included in total income as described above, subject to credit for the tax deemed to have been deducted from that amount. Tax deemed to have been so deducted will not, however, be eligible for any repayment (TCA 1997, s 439(1)(b) – but see below in relation to certain non-residents). The income will not for the purposes of TCA 1997 ss 237 or 238 (see **4.302** and **4.303**) be regarded as income "brought into charge to income tax", which means that it will not be available to relieve the borrower of any obligation to account for tax on any annual payments made.

TCA 1997, s 59 provides that, where income from which tax is deductible by virtue of Schedule C or D or from which tax is deducted by virtue of TCA 1997, s 237 or 238 is to be taken into account in computing total income of an individual for any year of assessment, credit is to be given, in determining the amount of tax payable on that total income, for the tax deducted from the income in question. The amount of the credit is the amount of tax deducted from that income. For this purpose, any part of the amount released or written off which has been treated under TCA 1997, s 439 as income is to be treated as if income tax had been deducted from that amount at the standard rate for the year of assessment in which the whole or part of the debt was released or written off. Where the amount (or, as the case may be, the amounts) exceeds the amount of the individual's taxable income charged to income tax at the standard rate or higher rate of income tax, the tax credit referred to in TCA 1997, s 59 may not exceed the amount of the income tax, if any, charged on that excess (TCA 1997, s 439(1)(d)). This provision is intended to deal with a situation in which the standard rate of income tax at the time the loan or part of the loan is released or written off is not the same as the standard rate at the time the loan was originally made.

Where TCA 1997, s 439 has effect on the release or write-off of a loan, the close company has no further liability to tax, but the tax previously paid over by it under TCA 1997, s 438 will not be refunded. This is logical as the result is what it would have been had the company simply paid interest to the participator under deduction of tax except, however, that the participator might in that case have been entitled to a refund of the tax. It could happen, however, that a loan to a participator has been written off in the books of the lending company while not being forgiven or released, in which case the loan could eventually be repaid. Such repayment would, for example, be made by the personal representatives of a deceased borrower in the absence of a formal waiver of the debt due. In that event, there would be nothing to prevent the company from claiming repayment of the tax paid under TCA 1997, s 438 on the occasion of the making the loan. Unfortunately, however, any tax paid under TCA 1997, s 439 could not be reclaimed.

The provisions dealing with loans to participators do not apply to any loan made before 27 November 1975. Where the debt represented by such a loan is released or written off in whole or in part on or after 27 November 1975, the resulting benefit may still be a distribution. TCA 1997, s 130(3) treats as a distribution the benefit arising from a transfer of assets or liabilities between a company and its members and the write off of a loan made to a member (who would be a participator) might therefore, arguably, give rise to a distribution. As against this, it is doubtful whether the write off would constitute the *transfer* of an asset or a liability.

Example 10.204.7

In 2001, Abbey Ltd made a loan of €2,400 to A Baldwin, a participator in the company, and tax under TCA 1997, s 438 was duly accounted for. On 18 December 2007 the loan was forgiven. Mr Baldwin is subject to income tax at the 41% rate. He paid a covenanted annuity of €1,000 on 1 November 2007.

Income of €3,000 is included in Mr Baldwin's total income for tax purposes for the year 2007. His tax liability on the income is €3,000 @ 41% = €1,230 less credit for €600, net liability €630. He is also liable to account for tax under TCA 1997, s 238 on the annuity, ie €1,000 @ 20% = €200.

If, instead of having his loan forgiven, Mr Baldwin had received interest of €3,000 under deduction of tax, the annuity would have been paid out of income brought into charge to income tax. He would have been entitled to deduct tax of €200 on payment but could have set that tax against the tax of €630 deducted from interest received and would not have had to account for it to the Revenue under TCA 1997, s 238. The balance of tax deducted on interest received, €430, would have been eligible for credit in computing Mr Baldwin's income tax liability.

On the basis of TCA 1997, s 439(1)(b) (see above), where the borrower whose loan is forgiven or written off is a non-resident, the tax paid by virtue of TCA 1997, s 438 by the company which made the loan is not refundable. TCA 1997, s 439 would then have no practical effect on the non-resident company. While it would be deemed to have received income equivalent to the "grossed up" amount of the sum forgiven or written off, it would not have an Irish tax liability in respect of that amount. Where, however, the borrower is resident in a country with which Ireland has a tax treaty and where that treaty has an "income not expressly mentioned" article (see **14.109.9**) whereby liability to tax is confined to the country of residence of the borrower, the borrower would, arguably, be entitled to reclaim the income tax deemed to have been deducted. On the other hand, it could be contended that the reference to "income" in the relevant treaty article must bear its ordinary meaning and that it does not extend to deemed income.

The fact that a borrower has ceased to be a participator, or an associate of a participator, in a company at the time a loan made to him by the company is released or written off does not prevent TCA 1997, s 439 from having effect.

Where the person to whom a loan to which TCA 1997, s 438 has applied has died, or where such a loan was made to trustees of a trust which has been terminated, and the debt represented by the loan or any part of it is released or written off, TCA 1997, s 439 applies to the person from whom the debt was due at the time of the release or write off. The grossed up equivalent of the sum released or written off is treated as income of the estate or of the beneficiary as the case may be. In a case where the debt released or written off was due by the personal representative of a deceased person whose estate is under administration, the deemed income is treated as chargeable to income tax in accordance with the provisions of TCA 1997 Part 32 Ch 1(ss 799-804). In effect, the deemed income is included in the total income of the estate and is treated as income from which standard rate income tax has been deducted.

10.205 Anti-avoidance

TCA 1997, s 817 applies for the purpose of counteracting schemes or arrangements involving close companies and their shareholders intended to avoid distribution treatment by extracting money or money's worth from the company (TCA 1997, s 817(2)). Such schemes or arrangements would be entered into to eliminate or reduce a charge to tax under Schedule F in respect of a dividend from a close company.

TCA 1997, s 817 will operate if, following such a disposal or following the carrying out of a scheme or arrangement of which the disposal is part, the interest of the shareholder in question in any trade or business of the close company is not significantly reduced (whether or not that trade or business continues to be carried on by the company after the disposal) (TCA 1997, s 817(3)).

A disposal for the above purposes includes any disposal of shares or deemed disposal of shares under the provisions of the Capital Gains Tax Acts, and any part disposal of shares. For the purposes of TCA 1997, s 817, *shares* includes loan stock, debentures and any interest or rights in or over, or any option in relation to, shares, loan stock or debentures, and references to *shareholder* are to be construed accordingly. Thus, the section applies to any disposal of an interest in a company as part of a scheme or arrangement for avoiding a charge to tax under Schedule F.

The effect of the anti-avoidance provision is to treat as a distribution received by the shareholder, the proceeds received in respect of the disposal of shares or, if less, the excess of those proceeds over any "new consideration" (as defined in TCA 1997, s 135(1)(a) – basically, consideration provided by the shareholder and not provided directly or indirectly by the company) received by the company for the issue of the shares and which has not already been taken into account for similar purposes (TCA 1997, s 817(4)).

The deemed distribution is treated as received at the time the shares are disposed of. The amount to be treated as a distribution at that time, however, may not exceed the amount of the capital receipt, or the aggregate of capital receipts, which has or have been received by the shareholder. Any capital receipt received on or after the disposal results in a distribution being deemed to have been received at the time of the disposal, the amount to be treated as a distribution being limited to the amount of the capital distribution or distributions received. For the purpose of calculating interest in relation to any tax unpaid in respect of a distribution, the tax will be treated as due from the date on which the shareholder received the capital receipt.

Capital receipt means the amount of money or money's worth, or, as the case may be, the amount of money *and* money's worth (other than shares issued by the close company), received by a shareholder in respect of the disposal of shares or in respect of anything arising out of a scheme or arrangement of which the disposal of shares was a part, and which is not otherwise subject to income tax in the hands of the shareholder (TCA 1997, s 817(5)(a)). Thus, the proceeds of a disposal of shares is not a capital receipt in so far as they consist of additional shares in the company carrying on the trade or business from which the distributable profits first arose. Where a shareholder exchanges one form of share ownership of a trade or business for another, this will not give rise to a "capital receipt".

As mentioned above, TCA 1997, s 817(2) sets out the purpose of the anti-avoidance provision, which is aimed at schemes or arrangements undertaken or arranged by or involving a close company the purpose of which, or one of the purposes of which, is to secure that any shareholder in the company avoids or reduces a charge or assessment to income tax under Schedule F by directly or indirectly extracting, or enabling such extracting of, either or both money and money's worth from the company for the benefit of the shareholder, without the company paying a dividend, or (apart from TCA 1997, s 817(4) – see above) making a distribution, chargeable to tax under Schedule F. A question which then arises is whether this limits the application of TCA 1997, s 817(3). In other words, if there is no scheme or arrangement to extract money or money's worth, is it then unnecessary to have regard to TCA 1997, s 817(3) which also applies the provision but without regard to the question of a scheme or arrangement? The argument would be that what is being done is not something which it is the purpose of the section to counteract. As against this it could be said that the section could have a general anti-avoidance purpose (as may be inferred from TCA 1997, s 817(7) – see below) apart from the particular purpose described in TCA 1997, s 817(2).

The provision will not apply where it can be shown that the disposal of shares was effected for *bona fide* commercial reasons and not as part of a scheme or arrangement the purpose, or one of the purposes, of which was the avoidance of tax (TCA 1997, s 817(7)). If in any case TCA 1997, s 817(2) does not apply, it would seem that this *bona fide* test would equally have to have been satisfied (unless some form of avoidance other than the extraction of money or money's worth is involved).

As already mentioned, the anti-avoidance provision operates where there has *not* been a significant reduction in a shareholder's interest in a trade or business following a share disposal or the carrying out of a scheme or arrangement. A significant reduction will be deemed to have occurred where, subject to TCA 1997, s 817(1)(ca) (see below), the percentages of:

(a) the ordinary share capital of the close company beneficially owned by the shareholder; and

(b) any profits available for distribution to equity holders of the close company to which the shareholder is beneficially entitled; and

(c) any assets available for distribution to equity holders on a winding up of the close company to which the shareholder would be entitled, are significantly less than the respective percentages beneficially owned by the shareholder, or to which the shareholder was beneficially entitled, at any time prior to the disposal (TCA 1997, s 817(1)(c)).

As respects disposals of shares made on or after 1 March 2005, TCA 1997, s 817(1)(ca) makes provision for a number of situations in which a holding in a close company is to be treated as significantly reduced. In determining whether a person's interest in a business has been significantly reduced following a disposal of shares, the interests of connected persons, such as family members, are taken into account. Also taken into account is the disposal of a holding company by a person without a significant reduction in his interest in the entire business. A person's interest in a company is deemed not to have been significantly reduced following a disposal of shares in that company where any gain realised is wholly or mainly attributable to a prior transfer of value to the company from another company that is controlled by the same person, either directly or in association with persons connected to him.

Following a disposal of shares in a close company by a shareholder or the carrying out of a scheme or arrangement of which the disposal is a part, the interest of the shareholder in any trade or business which was carried on by the close company is deemed:

(i) to include the interest or interests in that trade or business or one or more persons connected with (see **2.3**) the shareholder if increasing the shareholder's interest by such interest or interests would result in the shareholder's interest not having been significantly reduced;

(ii) notwithstanding TCA 1997, s 817(1)(c) (see above), not to have been significantly reduced where—

(I) the business carried on by the close company, taking account of any trade carried on by that company, consisted wholly or mainly of the holding of shares in another company carrying on a trade or business or in more than one such other company, and

(II) the interest of the shareholder in any such trade or business last-mentioned in (I), whether or not that trade or business continues to be carried on by such other company after the disposal, is not significantly reduced, and

(iii) notwithstanding TCA 1997, s 817(1)(c) (see above), not to have been significantly reduced where the gain realised by the shareholder on that disposal is wholly or mainly attributable to payments or other transfers of value from another company or companies, being a company or companies that is or are controlled by (see **2.401**) that shareholder or by that shareholder and persons connected with him, to the close company; and

(iv) not to have been significantly reduced where:

(I) it would not have been so reduced if the shareholder were to be treated as beneficially entitled to any shares to which he could at any time become so entitled by the exercise of a discretion by trustees,

(II) the acquisition of those shares by the trustees was directly or indirectly related to a disposal, including a prior or subsequent disposal, of such shares by the shareholder, and

(III) the shares were acquired by the trustees with the direct or indirect financial assistance of a company or companies which is or are controlled by (see **2.401**) the shareholder or by the shareholder and persons connected with (see **2.3**) the shareholder (TCA 1997, s 817(1)(ca)).

TCA 1997, s 817 gives no indication, however, as to what constitutes "significantly less" as respects the percentage of ordinary share capital, distributable profits or assets available for distribution. In the legislation dealing with purchases by companies of their own shares (TCA 1997, s 178 – see **11.304** and **11.306**), the "substantially reduced" test refers to a reduction of 25% or more in the interest held in a company, but there is no mathematical guideline in the close company anti-avoidance provision. "Significant" would probably denote a lesser reduction than is indicated by "substantial" so that a reduction of, say, 5% could possibly be regarded as significant. The group relief provisions dealing with profits or assets available for distribution and related matters (TCA 1997 ss 413-415 and 418 – see **8.304**) apply for the purposes of determining the above-mentioned percentages as they apply for group relief purposes.

With regard to (i) above, whereas one would expect, for the purpose of the comparison, that any such aggregation of interests should apply both before and after the disposal, a strict reading suggests that where the interests of connected persons are to be taken into account, they are to be taken into account in relation to the position following the disposal only. Thus, it will be much more difficult than was formerly the case to ensure that a significant reduction in a shareholder's interest in a trade or business has taken place; it is now in fact quite possible for a shareholder whose interest has been reduced following a disposal of shares to be treated as if his interest has increased.

TCA 1997, s 817 also counters attempts to avoid distribution treatment by way of arrangements involving one close company issuing shares to the shareholders of the other close company. This anti-avoidance aspect relates to the situation in which there is an arrangement, similar to an arrangement for the purposes of a scheme of reconstruction of amalgamation, between a close company and some or all of its shareholders whereby a second close company issues shares to those shareholders in respect of or in proportion to their shareholdings in the first mentioned company and where those shareholdings are either retained or cancelled. In that event, the shareholders are treated, for the purposes of TCA 1997, s 817, as making a disposal, or a part disposal as the case may be, of their original shareholdings in exchange for the newly issued shares (TCA 1997, s 817(1)(b)(ii)). The result accordingly is that the shareholders are treated as having received a capital receipt in money's worth and therefore as having received distributions in amounts equal to the market value of the shares received in the second close company.

An example of the type of avoidance being targeted above might be a reorganisation involving the transfer of a profitable trade from one company to another in exchange for shares issued to the transferring company's shareholder. Cash and other liquid assets would be retained by the transferring company which would then be liquidated with the proceeds being distributed to the shareholder. TCA 1997, s 817 will apply to a subsequent disposal of shares in the transferee company by deeming the disposal not to have involved a significant reduction in the shareholder's interest in the underlying trade.

Another example would be a case in which a shareholder transfers his shares in the close company to a discretionary trust of which he is one of the objects and where the transfer has been facilitated by way of financial assistance from a company or companies controlled by the shareholder, or by the shareholder and persons connected with the shareholder. The interest of the shareholder in the shares in such a case will include what that interest would be on the assumption that the trustees had appointed the shares to him.

10.3 SURCHARGE

10.301 Introduction
10.302 Surcharge on undistributed investment and estate income
10.303 Surcharge on service companies

10.301 Introduction

To discourage the practice of allowing profits of close companies to accumulate, thereby avoiding income tax at the higher rate on distributions from such profits, a surcharge of 20% is imposed on the undistributed investment and rental income of close companies, and a 15% surcharge on certain undistributed income of close service companies.

The surcharge applies to the "distributable estate and investment income" and to one-half of service company income of close companies that is not distributed within eighteen months of the end of the accounting period in which the income arose. Once a company is a service company, the surcharge applies to one-half of all of its undistributed professional and trading income, and to all of its undistributed investment and estate income. For other companies, the surcharge applies to undistributed estate and investment income. For small amounts undistributed, not exceeding €635 per annum, no surcharge is made, and where the undistributed amount does not exceed €847, the surcharge is limited to 4/5ths of the amount in excess of €635. Where a company has associated companies, the €635 limit is divided by the number of associated companies, including the company itself.

10.302 Surcharge on undistributed investment and estate income

TCA 1997, s 440 imposes a 20% surcharge on certain undistributed investment and rental income of close companies. Where the "distributable estate and investment income" of a close company for an accounting period exceeds the distributions of the company for the same period, the excess is liable to a surcharge of 20% (TCA 1997, s 440(1)(a)). There are some exceptions to this treatment:

(a) Where the excess is €635 or less, no surcharge arises. For this purpose the €635 limit is reduced proportionately where the accounting period of the close company is less than twelve months, and, where the close company has one or more associated companies (within the meaning of TCA 1997, s 432(1) – see **2.401.5**), is divided by one plus the number of associated companies (TCA 1997, s 440(1)(b)(i)). For this purpose, an associated company is to be taken into account for an accounting period even if it was an associated company for part only of that period, and two or more associated companies are to be counted even if they were associated companies for different parts of that period (TCA 1997, s 440(4)).

(b) Where the accumulated undistributed income of the company (ie, as disclosed in the company's financial statements) at the end of the accounting period (plus any amount which, on or after 27 November 1975, was transferred to capital reserves or was used to issue shares, stock or securities as paid up otherwise than for new consideration, or was otherwise used artificially to reduce the amount of the accumulated undistributed income) is less than the excess mentioned above, the amount liable to the surcharge is restricted to the balance available for distribution (TCA 1997, s 440(2)).

(c)   In determining the amount of income on which a surcharge arises, account is to be taken of any restriction in law affecting the making of distributions (TCA 1997, s 434(7)). As to how this provision would operate in practice would presumably be determined by reference to the particular circumstances in each case. Generally, if a close company can show that it would have made a distribution sufficient to avoid or reduce a surcharge were it not for the fact that it was legally prevented from making such a distribution, no surcharge or a reduced surcharge should be made. The fact that a distribution cannot be made after a liquidator has been appointed does not prevent the making of a surcharge (see **12.901**).

For the purposes of the UK close company legislation relating to shortfall assessments, a company successfully contended that it was prevented under company law provisions from distributing an amount brought to its share premium account and which had resulted from acquiring trading companies with substantial undistributed profits (*Shearer v Bercain* [1980] STC 359). A company whose articles of association imposed restrictions on the payment of dividends contended that it was prevented from paying dividends by reason of a restriction imposed by law but a shortfall assessment on the company was upheld as it was held that it was free to alter its articles if it wished (*Noble v Laygate Investments Ltd* [1978] STC 430).

The amount of the surcharge may not be greater than 80% of the amount by which the excess is greater than €635 (or €635 reduced as in (a) above). This marginal relief operates in respect of excess amounts up to €847 (TCA 1997, s 440(1)(b)(ii)).

The *distributions of a company for an accounting period* are all dividends declared for or in respect of the accounting period and which are paid or payable during the accounting period or within eighteen months after the end of the accounting period. The expression also includes all distributions (other than dividends) made in the accounting period (TCA 1997, s 434(2)). A payment made by an unquoted company on the redemption, repayment or purchase of its shares which avoids distribution treatment generally by virtue of TCA 1997, s 176 (see **11.304**) does not do so for the purposes of TCA 1997, s 440 (TCA 1997, s 176(1)).

TCA 1997, s 440 does not apply to dividends and other distributions of an overseas company that is relevant shipping income of a tonnage tax company (TCA 1997, s 697H(3) – see **13.803.3**).

Distributions made in respect of share capital in a winding up are not distributions for the purposes the definition of *distribution* in TCA 1997, s 130(1). Such distributions have been held not to be distributions of an accounting period for the purposes of reducing or eliminating a surchargeable amount (*Rahinstown Estate Company Ltd (In Liquidation) v Hughes,* HC [1986]) (See also **12.901.3**).

Provision is made for the situation in which a company's period of account (the period for which it has made up accounts) falls partly within an accounting period (as defined in TCA 1997, s 27) and where the company pays or declares a dividend by reference to that period of account. In that case a proportion of the dividend is treated as being in respect of the accounting period and that proportion is the proportion which the part of the period of account falling within the accounting period bears to the full period of account.

Example 10.302.1

Etowah Ltd, a close company, makes up accounts for the period 1 January 2006 to 31 March 2007. It declares a final dividend of €300,000 for that period in May 2007 and this is paid in June 2007.

Etowah Ltd has two accounting periods, the year ended 31 December 2006 and the period ended 31 March 2007. The distributions for the two accounting periods are €240,000 and €60,000 respectively.

To understand the meaning of "distributable estate and investment income" it is necessary first to define *income* and *distributable income*.

The *income* of an accounting period is the income for that period, exclusive of franked investment income (FII), before deducting any losses, deficiencies, charges on income or expenses of management carried forward from an earlier accounting period or carried back from a later accounting period, and after deducting any losses, deficiencies and relevant trading charges on income in so far as allowed against relevant trading income. No deduction is made for group relief claimed. Thus, the "income" of a company for an accounting is defined as the income for that period, computed for corporation tax purposes, exclusive of franked investment income, before deducting:

(a) any loss incurred in any trade or profession carried on by the company which is carried forward from an earlier, or carried back from a later, accounting period;

(b) any loss which if it were a profit would be chargeable to corporation tax on the company under Case III or IV of Schedule D and which is carried forward from an earlier accounting period or any expenses of management or any charges on income which are so carried forward; and

(c) any excess of deficiencies over surpluses which if such excess were a surplus over deficiencies would be chargeable to corporation tax under Case V of Schedule D, and which is carried forward from an earlier, or carried back from a later, accounting period;

and after deducting—

(d) any loss incurred in the accounting period in any trade or profession carried on by the company,

(e) any loss incurred in the accounting period which if it were a profit would be chargeable to corporation tax on the company under Case III or IV of Schedule D;

(f) any excess of deficiencies over surpluses which if such excess were an excess of surpluses over deficiencies would be chargeable to corporation tax on the company under Case V of Schedule D; and

(g) any amount which is an allowable deduction against relevant trading income by virtue of TCA 1997, s 243A (see **4.405**) (TCA 1997, s 434(4)).

The Revenue are prepared to accept that in computing income of an accounting period for the purposes of "section 23" type reliefs (see **6.5**), any amount which is carried forward from an earlier period may be deducted. In effect therefore, any unused amounts arising out of these provisions may be taken into account in calculating "estate income" and "distributable income" of the accounting period.

Distributable estate and investment income of a company for an accounting period means the estate and investment income of the company for that period after deducting the amount of corporation tax which would be payable by the company for the accounting period if the tax were computed on the basis of that income (TCA 1997, s 434(5A)(a)). In the case of a trading company, the distributable estate and investment income for an accounting period is the amount so determined reduced by 7.5% (TCA 1997, s 434(5A)(b)).

The *estate and investment income* of a company for an accounting period is the amount by which the sum of:

(i) the franked investment income for the period; and

(ii) an amount determined by applying to the amount of the income of the company for the accounting period the fraction:

$$\frac{A}{B}$$

where:

A is the aggregate of the estate income and investment income taken into account in computing income for the accounting period; and

B is the amount of the company's income before taking account of any amount specified in TCA 1997, s 434(4)(d) to (g) (see (d) to (g) above – trading and other losses, Case V deficiencies, relevant trading charges),

exceeds the aggregate of:

(I) the amount of relevant charges; and

(II) the amount which is an allowable deduction in computing total profits for the accounting period in respect of expenses of management by virtue of TCA 1997, s 83(2) (see **12.703**) (TCA 1997, s 434(5)(a)).

The above definition secures that a trading loss incurred by a close company will be taken into account to reduce, or eliminate, the amount of surchargeable estate and investment income. Where there are trading losses, "income" will be net of such losses (see (d) in the definition of "income" above). The value of B, on the other hand, is the company's income *before* deducting any trading loss (as well as other losses, deficiencies etc). (See Example **10.302.2** below.)

In practice, the Revenue accept that the legislation permits the use of a negative amount where that is the result of applying the fraction A/B (in circumstances where the "income" itself is a minus amount and A has some positive value). It is clear from the meaning of "income" that a trade loss can reduce or eliminate investment and/or rental income and it makes sense that it should have a similar effect as regards franked investment income. Taking a negative amount into account in this way reduces or eliminates the amount of any franked investment income. Where, however, the value of A is nil, because there is no untaxed interest or estate income, applying the fraction A/B will produce a nil amount so that there would be no negative amount to set against the franked investment income.

Investment income is essentially interest and dividend income, not including any interest or dividends in the nature of trading receipts but which have not (at the option of the Revenue) been assessed as part of trading income under Case I or II of Schedule D or which have not been assessed as part of trading income because they comprise franked investment income (TCA 1997, s 434(1)). Also excluded are any dividends or other distributions received in respect of shares at a time when any gain on a disposal of those shares would not have been a chargeable gain by virtue of TCA 1997, s 626B (exemption from tax on gains of certain disposals of shares – see **9.213**). Note, however, that dividends and other distributions from Irish resident companies are not excluded; there is no equivalent exclusion in respect of "franked investment income".

Estate income is, basically, rental income. It means income assessable under Case III, IV or V of Schedule D and which arises from the ownership of land or any interest in or right over land or from the letting furnished of any building or part of a building (TCA 1997, s 434(1)).

Franked investment income is defined in TCA 1997, s 156(1) as income of a company resident in the State consisting of a distribution made by another company resident in the State, but, for the purposes of TCA 1997, s 434, such distributions do not include:

(a) a distribution made out of exempt profits within the meaning of TCA 1997, s 140 (stallion fees, stud greyhound service fees and occupation of woodlands – see **11.114.4**);

(b) a distribution made out of disregarded income within the meaning of TCA 1997, s 141 (patent distributions – see **11.114.2**) and to which TCA 1997, s 141(3)(a) applies (see **13.607.6**); and

(c) a distribution made out of exempted income within the meaning of TCA 1997, s 142 (distributions from profits of certain mines – see **11.112.1**) (TCA 1997, s 434(1)).

Relevant charges, in relation to an accounting period of a company, means charges on income paid in the accounting period by the company and which are allowed as deductions under TCA 1997, s 243 other than so much of those charges as is paid for the purposes of an excepted trade within the meaning of TCA 1997, s 21A (see **3.101.4**) (TCA 1997, s 434(1)). Trade charges, apart from excepted trade charges, are not allowed as deductions under TCA 1997, s 243 (TCA 1997, s 243A – see **4.405**) so that that section provides for the allowance of non-trade charges plus excepted trade charges. "Relevant charges", however, excludes excepted trade charges. In effect, therefore, the result of this slightly convoluted definition is that "relevant charges" means charges other than trade charges.

A *trading company*, for the purposes of the 7.5% reduction mentioned above, means a company which exists wholly or mainly for the purpose of carrying on a trade but also includes any company whose income does not consist wholly or mainly of investment income or estate income (TCA 1997, s 434(1)).

The meaning of "distributable estate and investment income" may appear to be complex, based on the various definitions and the formula above. Essentially it is the aggregate of the estate income and investment income, less charges other than any trade charges, less tax at 25% of that net amount, plus franked investment income.

Example 10.302.2

Dacca Ltd, a close company, has the following results for its latest accounting period:

	€
Rental income	50,000
Interest income	30,000

	€
Dividends from Irish resident companies	15,000
Trading income	120,000

The distributable estate and investment income is (€50,000 + €30,000) x 75% + €15,000 = €75,000. From this a deduction of €5,625 (7.5%) is made, since the company is a trading company, leaving a net amount of €69,375. The surcharge is 20% of this amount, or €13,875.

In the above case, it is not necessary to apply the fraction A/B to arrive at the amount of the distributable estate and investment income. Suppose, however, that the company had incurred a trading loss of €100,000. In that case, "income" would be nil and, after applying the fraction A/B, estate and investment income would also be nil so that the distributable estate and investment income would be confined to the franked investment income of €15,000 (less 7.5%).

Alternatively, if the company had incurred a trading loss of €25,000, "income" would now be €55,000 (€50,000 + €30,000 - €25,000). The estate and investment income would then be €55,000 x 80,000/80,000 = €55,000 (effectively €80,000 – €25,000).

Example 10.302.3

Bart Ltd is a close trading company with the following results for its latest accounting period:

	€	€
Case I		1,200,000
Income of excepted trade included in Case I		200,000
Loss forward		400,000
Bank interest received		300,000
Franked investment income		100,000
Charges:		
- interest	50,000	
- royalties		
– excepted trade	10,000	90,000
– other trading	30,000	Nil
Distributions for period		

The 20% surcharge will be charged on the company's distributable estate and investment income less 7.5%. It is necessary first to calculate the estate and investment income. This is arrived at on the basis of the formula (expanding the meanings of "A" and "B"):

$$FII + I \times \frac{EI + II}{I} - (RC + ME)$$

where—

FII = franked investment income;

I   = "income";

EI   = estate income;

II   = investment income;

RC   = relevant charges; and

ME   = management expenses.

"I" is €1,200,000 + €300,000 = €1.5m.

The estate and investment income is therefore:

$$€100,000 + €1.5m \times \frac{0 + 300,000}{1.5m} - €50,000 = €350,000$$

Distributable estate and investment income is €350,000 less corporation tax computed on the basis of that amount, ie €250,000 (to exclude FII) @ 25% = €62,500, net €287,500 and less a deduction of 7.5%, or €21,563, as Bart Ltd is a trading company. The surcharge is accordingly 20% of €265,937 = €53,187.

In short, distributable estate and investment income is 75% of the Case III income less charges other than trade charges (including excepted trade charges), plus franked investment income, reduced by 7.5%.

Example 10.302.4

The position is the same as in Example **10.302.3** except that Bart Ltd pays a dividend of €265,200 in respect of the accounting period. Bart Ltd has no associated companies.

	€
Distributable estate and investment income, as before	265,937
Distribution for the accounting period	265,200
Excess	737
Surcharge @ 20%	147
Maximum:	
Excess greater than €635 by €102	102
80% thereof	82
Final surcharge payable	82

Example 10.302.5

The position is as in Example **10.302.3** except that the accounts of Bart Ltd for the accounting period disclose distributable reserves of €50,000. Some years ago, the company capitalised reserves of €150,000 for the purpose of issuing new shares.
The maximum amount on which a surcharge may be made is:

	€
Distributable reserves	50,000
Add back amount capitalised	150,000
Surchargeable amount	200,000
Surcharge @ 20%	40,000

A company may be a close company for part only of an accounting period. As to what income would then be subject to the surcharge is not clear; there is, for example, no provision here for deemed separate accounting periods. There would appear to be some support in *CHW (Huddersfield) Ltd v CIR* 41 TC 92 for the view that the surcharge position of a company for any accounting period should be decided by reference to the company's status at balance sheet date. It is understood that that position is accepted by the Revenue Commissioners. On the other hand, Revenue guidance notes indicate that the matter is covered by TCA 1997, s 434(6), which provides that the amount for part of an accounting period of any description of income for surcharge purposes is to be a proportionate part of the amount for the whole period. It is stated that this provision would cover the case of a company that is a close company for part only of an accounting period. This, however, seems less than satisfactory. For that to be correct would require a provision to the effect that the surcharge is to apply only to the income of the part of the accounting period for which the company was a close company. In accordance with TCA 1997, s 434(6), the amount of that income would then be the proportionate part.

A company which incurs a surcharge liability by failing to distribute certain distributable investment or estate income may subsequently decide to distribute some or all of the income in respect of which the surcharge was made. There is no provision whereby the company can recover any part of the related surcharge paid.

Any surcharge arising is treated as corporation tax chargeable for the earliest accounting period ending on or after a day which is twelve months after the end of the accounting period (TCA 1997, s 440(6)). Normally, ie where the company's following accounting period is for twelve months, the surcharge will be treated as corporation tax due for that accounting period. Otherwise, where a shorter accounting period follows, the surcharge will be treated as corporation tax due for a later period – whichever is the first such period ending not earlier than twelve months after the end of the accounting period in respect of which the surcharge arose.

In the event that there is no accounting period ending on a date as indicated above, the surcharge will be treated as corporation tax due for the accounting period in respect of which it is made.

Example 10.302.6

Apple Ltd, Berry Ltd, Cherry Ltd and Damson Ltd all made up accounts for the year ended 31 March 2006. Each company incurred a surcharge liability in respect of that period. Apple Ltd maintained its 31 March yearend subsequently, Berry Ltd changed its accounts year end to 31 December, while Cherry Ltd made up accounts to 31 July 2006, to 31 January 2007, and then to 31 December 2007. Damson Ltd ceased trading on 31 March 2006 and was completely dormant after that date.

The surcharge liabilities are treated as corporation due for the following accounting periods:

Apple Ltd	year ended 31 March 2007
Berry Ltd	year ended 31 December 2007
Cherry Ltd	period ended 31 December 2007
Damson Ltd	year ended 31 March 2007

The surcharge on undistributed investment or estate income does not apply in the case of a collective investment undertaking (TCA 1997, s 734(9)(b) – see **12.805**).

Disregard of inter-company distributions

As respects dividends paid, or distributions made, on or after 31 January 2008, a joint election may be made, by a company paying and a company receiving a distribution to have the distribution disregarded for the purposes of the close company surcharge. This will facilitate the payment of a dividend or other distribution to a close company, in practice typically a holding company, without giving rise to a close company surcharge. The election will secure that distributions between Irish resident companies will obtain the same treatment as those received from a non-resident subsidiary. The effect of the election is that the distribution concerned will be treated as not being a distribution received by the holding company and as not being a distribution made by the subsidiary.

Where a close company pays a dividend, or makes a distribution, to another close company, the companies may jointly elect, by giving notice to the Collector-General in such manner as the Revenue Commissioners may require, that the dividend or distribution is to be treated for the purposes of TCA 1997, s 440 as not being a distribution (TCA 1997, s 434(3A)(a)).

Where notice is given as above, the dividend, or distribution, will be treated—

(a)   for the purposes of TCA 1997, s 440 as not being a distribution, and

(b)   for the purposes of TCA 1997, s 434(5) as not being franked investment income (TCA 1997, s 434(3A)(b)).

As regards (a), any such dividend or distribution will not rank as a distribution made by the paying company so that it will not be taken into account in calculating the excess of the distributable estate and investment income over the distributions of the company for the period in question. The effect of (b) is that the surchargeable amount will not include, as franked investment income, any dividends or other distributions in respect of which the election is made.

An election made by a close company should be included with the company's corporation tax return for the accounting period in question.

10.303   Surcharge on service companies

Undistributed income of service companies is also liable to a corporation tax surcharge. The surcharge rate for the distributable trading income of these companies is 15% while the 20% rate applicable to the distributable estate and investment income of close companies generally applies in the cases of service companies also.

Distributable trading income of a company for an accounting period means the trading income of the company for that period after deducting the amount of corporation tax which, apart from TCA 1997 ss 22A(2) (the 12.5% corporation tax rate where "net relevant trading income" does not exceed a ceiling amount – see **3.101.5**) and 448(2) (the 10% corporation tax rate – see **7.202**), would be payable by the company for the accounting period if the tax were computed on the basis of that income (TCA 1997, s 434(5A)(a)).

The *trading income* of a company for an accounting period is the income of the company for the period after deducting:

(i)   an amount equal to the amount specified in (ii) of the definition of *estate and investment income* (ie, "income" x A/B - see **10.302** above);

(ii)   where the aggregate of the amounts in (I) and (II) in the definition of "estate and investment income" (relevant charges and expenses of management – see **10.302** above) exceeds the sum of the amounts specified in (i) and (ii) of that definition (franked investment income plus the amount in (i) above ("income" x A/B)), the amount of the excess; and

(iii) charges on income paid for the purposes of an excepted trade within the meaning of TCA 1997, s 21A (higher rate of corporation tax – see **3.101.4**) (TCA 1997, s 434(5)(b)).

Example 10.303.1

The income and outgoings of Acre Ltd, a close company, are as follows:

	€
Professional earnings	320,000
Rental income	50,000

Deposit interest			40,000
Franked investment income (FII)			10,000
Charges – interest			120,000

"Income" is €320,000 + €50,000 + €40,000 = €410,000.

"Trading income", in accordance with the definition in TCA 1997, s 434(5)(b), is as follows:

	€	€	€
Income			410,000
Less:			
Income x A/B (410,000 x 90,000/410,000) ("X")		90,000	
Excess of:			
relevant charges	120,000		
over FII + X (10,000 + 90,000)	100,000	20,000	
			110,000
Trading income			300,000

A *service company* is defined as a close company:

(a) whose business consists of, or includes, the carrying on of a profession or the provision of professional services;

(b) which holds or exercises an office or employment; or

(c) whose business consists of, or includes, providing services or facilities to a company described in (a) or (b), to an individual or partnership carrying on a profession, to a person holding or exercising an office or employment, or to a person or partnership connected with any person or partnership of any of the foregoing descriptions. Services provided to an unconnected person or partnership are, however, ignored.

To determine whether a person is connected with another person for the above purposes, the provisions of TCA 1997, s 10 (see **2.3**) apply. A partnership is connected with a company or individual, and vice versa, where any of the partners is connected with that company or individual. A partnership is connected with another partnership where any of its partners is connected with any of the partners in the other partnership.

An example of a service company in this context would be a company formed by an employee to take on his role as employee with a view to substituting corporation tax for personal tax at the higher rate; the level of personal tax on emoluments to be taken from the company could be controlled as required. Another example would be a service company formed to supply staff and other services to a professional partnership. In this way the level of profits arising to the partnership, and therefore the incidence of personal taxation, could be controlled. Devices such as these are rendered less attractive by means of the surcharge provided by TCA 1997, s 441 in respect of undistributed service company income.

Always likely to be controversial is the question as to whether a company is carrying on a profession. It will be a question of fact as to whether a profession is being carried on in any case. Tax Briefing, Issue 48 (June 2002), states that the following (to which some case law references have been inserted, where appropriate) are regarded as being professions and as falling within the provisions of section 441:

Held to be carrying on a profession:

Accountant	
Actor	*Davies v Braithwaite* 18 TC 198
Actuary	
Archaeologist	
Architect	*Durant v CIR* 12 TC 245
Auctioneer/Estate agent	
Barrister	*Seldon v Croom-Johnson* 16 TC 740
Computer programmer	
Dentist	
Doctor	
Engineer	
Journalist	*CIR v Maxse* 12 TC 41
Management consultant	
Optician	*CIR v North and Ingram* [1918] 2 KB 705
Private school	
Quantity surveyor	
Solicitor	
Veterinary surgeon	

The statement to the effect that all of the above are regarded as being professions and as falling within the provisions of TCA 1997, s 441 is surprising. The relevance of most of them to the position of a company is far from clear and it might well be asked in what circumstances a company could fall within TCA 1997, s 441 by reason of the activities of, say, a doctor, a dentist, an actor, an archaeologist, a barrister, a solicitor. While an individual practising as a doctor, dentist etc would undoubtedly be exercising a profession, a company employing any of these could hardly be regarded on that account as carrying on a profession. That a company carrying on activities as a private school might thereby be regarded as carrying on a profession does not seem to make sense. Neither does it seem correct that a computer programmer should be regarded as carrying on a profession.

Held not to be carrying on a profession:

Advertising	*MacGiolla Mhaith v Brian Cronin and Associates Ltd* (III) ITR (211)
Auctioneers of livestock in cattle mart	
Chartered secretary firm	*Burt & Co v CIR* [1919] 2 KB 650
Dance band leader	*Loss v CIR* [1945] 2 All ER 683
Insurance broker	*Durant v CIR* 12 TC 245
Photographer	*Cecil v CIR* [1919] 36 TLR 164
Professional gambler	*Graham v Green* 2 TC 309
Public relations company	
Retail pharmacy	

Stockbroker	*Christopher Barker & Sons v CIR* [1919] 2 KB 222
Tax agent	*Currie v CIR* 12 TC 245

It will be seen that many of the activities involved in the above two lists are unlikely to be carried on by a company. The only case included above which dealt with the question of the carrying on of a profession for surcharge purposes was the lone Irish case, involving an advertising company. In *CIR v Maxse,* some clue is given as to what might be the determining factors in deciding when a profession is being exercised. Indicative of a profession would be a requirement for either purely intellectual skill or for a manual skill controlled by the intellectual skill of the operation, such as in painting, sculpture or surgery, as distinct from an occupation which is substantially the production or sale, or arrangements for the production or sale, of commodities.

A company is not a service company where the principal part of its income which is chargeable under Schedule D, Cases I and II, and Schedule E, is not derived from the activities described in (a) to (c) above or from any two or more of those activities.

The surcharge applies to the excess of one-half of the distributable trading income and all of the distributable estate and investment income over the distributions of the company for the accounting period. To the extent that the distributable estate and investment income exceeds the distributions of the company, the excess is subject to a surcharge of 20%. Any other excess is liable to a 15% surcharge. Where the excess is €635 or less, no surcharge arises. For this purpose the €635 limit is reduced proportionately where the accounting period of the close company is less than twelve months, and, if the close company has one or more associated companies (within the meaning of TCA 1997, s 432(1) – see **2.401.5**), is divided by one plus the number of associated companies.

The amount of the surcharge may not be greater than four-fifths of the amount by which the excess is greater than €635 (or €635 reduced as in (a) above). This marginal relief operates in respect of excess amounts up to €847.

The provisions in TCA 1997, s 434 dealing with such matters as the meaning of income, distributable estate and investment income and the distributions for an accounting period, (see **10.302**), apply for the purposes of the services company surcharge as they do for the purposes of the surcharge on undistributed investment and estate income, with references to a trading company being taken as references to a service company where appropriate. Also applicable in the same way are the provisions in TCA 1997 ss 434 and 440 dealing with apportionment of dividends and income, the effect of any legal restriction on the payment of dividends, the limitation of the surchargeable amount to the amount of accumulated undistributed income, and the treatment of the surcharge as corporation tax due for an accounting period.

Example 10.303.2

Bolt Ltd is a service company with the following results for its latest accounting period (for which period it paid a dividend of €150,000):

	€
Professional earnings	1,200,000
Other trading profits	300,000
Deposit interest	300,000
	1,800,000

The "estate and investment income" is €300,000 and the "distributable estate and investment income" is 75% of that amount, or €225,000, less 7.5% = €208,125.

The "trading income" is the income less the estate and investment income, ie €1,800,000 – € 300,000 = €1,500,000. The "distributable trading income" is the trading income less the amount of corporation tax payable on the basis of that income, ie €1,500,000 less €1,500,000 @ 12.5% = €1,312,500.

Surcharge calculation:

	€	€
Distributable estate and investment income	208,125	
Dividend paid	150,000	
	58,125	
Surcharge @ 20%		11,625
Distributable trading income €1,312,500 x 50%	656,250	
Surcharge @ 15%		98,438
Total surcharge		110,063

Any surcharge arising is treated as corporation tax chargeable for the earliest accounting period ending on or after a day that is twelve months after the end of the first-mentioned accounting period (see Example **10.302.6** and before).

Disregard of inter-company dividends

See **10.302**.

Chapter 11

Distributions, Buy-back of Shares

11.1 DISTRIBUTIONS

11.101 Meaning of distribution: general

Dividends and other distributions paid by Irish resident companies, together with (for distributions paid before 6 April 1999) the related tax credits, are treated as income chargeable to income tax under Schedule F (Taxes Consolidation Act 1997 (TCA 1997), s 20). Subject to specific exceptions, corporation tax is not chargeable on dividends and other distributions of an Irish resident company nor are any such dividends or distributions taken into account in computing income for the purposes of corporation tax (TCA 1997, s 129). For tax purposes, any item deemed to be a distribution is treated in the same way as a dividend and in that sense could be regarded as a "quasi-dividend". Thus, as in the case of a dividend, an item treated as a distribution is not allowable as an expense in computing income from any source (TCA 1997, s 76(5) – see **3.102.2**) nor may any such item be treated as a charge on income (TCA 1997, s 243(1) – see **4.402**).

The consequences of any item being treated as a distribution are therefore basically threefold. Firstly, the item is subject to income tax under Schedule F; it might otherwise not have been subject to tax at all (for example the transfer of an asset at undervalue by a company to one of its members), or would have been taxable in a different way (for example interest treated as a distribution which would otherwise normally have been taxed under Case III of Schedule D). Secondly, the item is not deductible for the purposes of computing income for corporation tax purposes; it might not have been deductible in any event (for example the above-mentioned transfer of an asset to a company member) or it might otherwise have been so deductible (for example interest payable by a company). Thirdly, any item treated as a distribution is generally not taxable where the recipient is a company; this is the basis of the once popular and widely used "section 84 loan" (now TCA 1997, s 130) (see **11.106**).

For tax purposes, the term "distribution" refers to distributions of profits which, when made by an Irish resident company, are taxable under Schedule F in the hands of a person chargeable to income tax. A company dividend is a distribution, but the term is given a much wider meaning to include a number of other payments, mainly to the shareholders and other "participators" in a company. It includes, for example, interest and certain other payments in respect of certain types of securities of a company paid to persons who may or may not be shareholders of that company. A distribution is not necessarily a payment of money, and may consist of the transfer of an asset to a shareholder or to a holder of a certain type of security.

The meaning of "distribution" is determined by provisions in TCA 1997 Part 6 Ch 2 (ss 130-135) (which are relevant to companies generally) and in TCA 1997, ss 436-437 (relevant only to close companies – see **10.202** and **10.203**). TCA 1997, s 4(1) also provides that "distribution" has the meaning assigned to it by TCA 1997 Part 6 Ch 2 and ss 436, 436 (close companies – see **10.202-203**) and 816(2)(b) (see **3.208.5** under *Shares issued in lieu of cash dividends*). In considering whether any payment made by a company is a distribution, therefore, it is necessary to have regard to such one or more of the above-mentioned provisions as may be relevant.

TCA 1997, s 130(1) confirms that any payment, transfer of assets or other distribution made in respect of share capital in a winding up is not a distribution for the purpose of the above-mentioned provisions.

TCA 1997, s 130 provides that the term *distribution* means:

(a)   any dividend including a capital dividend (**11.102.2**);

(b)   any other distribution made out of the assets of the company (whether in cash or otherwise) "in respect of" shares (except, subject to TCA 1997, s 132, a repayment of capital, or a payment equalled by "new consideration" received by the company) (**11.102.3**);

(c)   any amount met out of the assets of a company (whether in cash or otherwise) in respect of the redemption of "securities" (defined in TCA 1997, s 135(8) – see **11.106**) which were issued in respect of shares or securities of the company, other than for new consideration (see **11.103.2**);

(d)   interest paid on securities:

    (i)   as described in (c),

    (ii)   convertible into shares in the company (not being quoted securities),

    (iii) in respect of which the interest depends on the results of the company,

    (iv)   in respect of which the interest represents more than a reasonable commercial return (when the excess only is treated as a distribution),

    (v)   held by a non-resident 75% parent company (or non-resident 75% fellow subsidiary except a fellow subsidiary 90% of whose ordinary share capital is owned directly by an Irish resident company), or

    (vi)   which are "connected with" shares (see **11.106**);

(e)   the transfer of assets (or liabilities) by a company to a member (or to a company by a member) where the benefit received by the member exceeds the value of any new consideration given by him (see **11.108**);

(f)   any amount treated as a distribution under TCA 1997, s 131 (bonus issue following repayment of share capital – see **11.103.3**).

A distribution may arise under TCA 1997, s 132(2) in the case of certain repayments of share capital after an earlier bonus issue (see **11.103.4**) or under TCA 1997, s 132(4) on a premium paid on the redemption of share capital (see **11.104**). Certain payments made by close companies are treated as distributions under TCA 1997, s 436 (provision of benefits in kind for company members or other participators, or under TCA 1997, s 437 (interest paid to certain company directors or their associates in excess of a prescribed limit (see **10.202** and **10.203**).

11.102 Distributions in respect of shares

11.102.1 Introduction

TCA 1997, s 130(2)(a) treats as a distribution any dividend paid by a company, including a capital dividend. Distributions of resident companies have been taxable under Schedule F since 6 April 1976. Prior to 6 April 1976, only dividends paid out of profits of a revenue nature were taxable as income in the hands of the shareholder. Capital dividends (ie, those paid out of capital profits) were not, generally, subject to any taxation.

The very much wider definition of a distribution, which became effective from 27 November 1975, operates to prevent shareholders of a company from extracting funds from the company in a tax-free manner. The current position for distributions in respect of shares may be considered separately under two headings, namely dividends and other distributions, as follows:

11.102.2 Dividends

Dividend means a distribution made to a shareholder out of a company's profits by way of a return on the shares held by that shareholder in the company. A dividend is expressed in terms of a sum of money. Accordingly, a dividend in specie will be expressed as a sum of money to be satisfied by the transfer of assets; the mere transfer of an asset expressed as the payment of a dividend will not be sufficient to constitute a dividend.

Irrespective of the nature of the shares on which the dividend is paid, a recipient of a dividend who is liable to income tax is taxable under Schedule F in respect of that dividend.

In general, a dividend (and any other distribution) from an Irish resident company is not subject to tax in the hands of a company liable to corporation tax nor is it to be taken into account in computing income for corporation tax purposes. Essentially this is because the dividend has been paid out of profits which have already borne corporation tax and is therefore "franked" for the purposes of that tax. By way of exception, dividends on certain preference shares are subject to tax (see below) under Case IV of Schedule D.

11.102.3 Other distributions in respect of shares

TCA 1997, s 130(2)(b) treats as a distribution any other distribution out of the assets of a company (whether in cash or otherwise) which is made in respect of shares (other than one in a winding up), except where it constitutes a repayment of capital or where the company receives "new consideration" in respect of the distribution. An example of a distribution of this kind is a premium on the redemption of shares except where a premium was payable on the issue of those shares. This provision has particular relevance to a reduction of capital, the redemption of shares and the purchase by a company of its own shares (see **11.105.4** and **11.3**). TCA 1997, s 130(2)(b) would also apply to transfers of assets to company members for no consideration or for inadequate consideration (see **11.108**).

"New consideration" means consideration not provided directly or indirectly out of the assets of the company (but see **11.105.5** below for more detailed meaning). A distribution is treated as made "out of assets of the company" if the cost falls on the company (TCA 1997, s 135(5) – see **11.105.6**). A distribution is regarded as being made "in respect of" shares if it is made to the recipient in his capacity as shareholder (TCA 1997, s 135(10) – see **11.105.7**).

The purpose of TCA 1997, s 130(2)(b) is to treat as a distribution any payment or other distribution (not being a dividend and not being in respect of share capital in a winding up), the cost of which falls on the company, regardless of its nature and whether it is in the form of income or capital, unless it can be shown to be a repayment of capital or to be in respect of new consideration received by the company.

The question as to whether any particular distribution out of the assets of a company is a repayment of capital (and, therefore, not taxable on the recipient as income) is determined in accordance with TCA 1997, s 132 (see **11.103**). That section restricts the circumstances in which transactions normally regarded as repayments of capital may be treated as such for the purposes of the definition of "distribution".

11.102.4 Dividends on certain preference shares

TCA 1997, s 138 contains an exception to the general rule that dividends paid in respect of the shares of a company are treated as distributions not chargeable to corporation tax in the hands of a company. The section is directed primarily against certain types of preference shares (including stock) issued by a company to another company ("the subscriber") on terms under which the funds provided are more in the nature of loan finance than shares in the company. Dividends paid on preference shares dealt with by TCA 1997, s 138 are taxable under Case IV of Schedule D as income in the hands of the subscriber rather than as a distribution.

TCA 1997, s 138 applies to dividends paid in respect of preference shares of the issuer where all of the following circumstances apply:

(a) the dividend is paid by a company ("the issuer") to another company ("the subscriber") which is within the charge to corporation tax; and

(b) the shares are not excluded from the definition of "preference shares" by TCA 1997, s 138(1) (see below).

The subscriber referred to above is the company to which the particular dividend is paid (and not necessarily the original subscriber for the preference shares). The subscriber may well be the person to whom the shares were issued, but the same treatment will apply if the dividend is received by any company within the charge to corporation tax where all of the above circumstances are present.

TCA 1997, s 138 does not apply to the following types of preference shares (referred to here as the "excluded preference shares"):

(a) preference shares which are quoted on a stock exchange in the State;

(b) preference shares not quoted on an Irish stock exchange and which carry rights in respect of dividends and capital which are comparable with the rights generally attaching to fixed-dividend shares quoted on an Irish stock exchange; or

(c)   non-transferable preference shares issued after 5 April 1989 by a company carrying on "relevant trading operations" within the meaning of TCA 1997, s 445 or 456 to a company which is entirely foreign owned and which would not be chargeable to corporation tax otherwise than under TCA 1997, s 138 (see also below).

In relation to the first two exclusions, a "normal" preference share should not be affected by the provisions of TCA 1997, s 138 so that any dividend paid to another company in respect of such a share would be treated as a distribution not chargeable to corporation tax. An unquoted preference share will only be an excluded preference share if the rights it carries as to dividends, repayment of capital (eg, right to a premium, priority etc) are comparable to the rights attaching to preference shares (or other fixed-dividend shares) quoted on an Irish stock exchange. In determining whether the unquoted shares are so comparable, the combined effect of all the rights to dividends and capital should be taken into account.

The purpose of (c) is to enable a company carrying on certain non-manufacturing trading operations in the Shannon Airport area or in the Custom House Docks area of Dublin to obtain finance through preference shares subscribed for by persons not resident in the State. In this case, the exclusion applies whether or not the shares carry dividend/capital rights comparable to shares quoted on an Irish stock exchange. The relevant trading operations which entitle the "borrower" company to obtain such "foreign source" preference share financing are the kinds of operations which may be certified by the Minister for Finance as qualifying for the 10% rate of corporation tax under TCA 1997, s 445 (Shannon Airport area) or TCA 1997, s 446 (Custom House Docks area) (see **7.205.16-17**).

The company which has subscribed for the preference shares (the only company which can benefit since the shares must be non-transferable) must satisfy two further conditions. Firstly, none of the shares of the subscriber can be beneficially owned, directly or indirectly, by any person resident in the State.

Secondly, the subscriber must be a company which is not chargeable to corporation tax in respect of any profits (other than dividends which would be chargeable under TCA 1997, s 138 if the preference shares were not excluded preference shares). This means that any company which carries on a trade in the State through a branch or agency cannot be a subscriber, but an entirely foreign-owned company is not disqualified through having income from Irish sources if it has no Irish trading branch or agency (since any such income would only be chargeable to income tax and not corporation tax).

Exclusion (c) is not relevant in the case of dividends on preference shares which were issued before 6 April 1989. Unless such preference shares are within either of exclusions (a) or (b), the subscriber company remains liable to corporation tax under TCA 1997, s 138 in respect of the dividends on those shares whenever paid (indefinitely into the future).

If none of the foregoing exclusions is relevant, TCA 1997, s 138(3)(b) requires any dividend on the preference shares of the issuer company paid by it to the subscriber company to be charged to corporation tax under Schedule D Case IV. Accordingly, the preference dividend is not treated as a distribution from the standpoint of the subscriber.

From the standpoint of the issuer, TCA 1997, s 138 does not alter the fact that the preference dividend is a distribution (TCA 1997, s 130(2)(a)). Consequently, the dividend is not deductible in arriving at the taxable profits of the issuer notwithstanding that the dividend is taxed in the hands of the subscriber.

11.103 Bonus issues and repayments of capital

11.103.1 Introduction

A bonus issue of shares is made where a company capitalises profits otherwise available for distribution by transferring the whole or part of any balance standing to the credit of its profit and loss account and/or reserves to its share capital account and issues shares to its shareholders without the payment by them of any new consideration. The company may also apply the capitalised profits by way of issuing to the shareholders a bonus issue consisting of a different class of shares or a security (eg a loan stock) of the company.

A bonus, or "capitalisation", issue as such does not give rise to a distribution of the company. This is because the bonus issue is not a dividend within TCA 1997, s 130(2)(a) and because it does not involve any other distribution of cash or any other asset of the company within TCA 1997, s 130(2)(b); there is no distribution "out of assets" and a bonus issue is merely a matter of balance sheet movement so far as the issuing company is concerned. There is no cost to the company and its assets remain undisturbed. The result of the bonus issue is that the shareholder simply has a larger number of shares, or perhaps the same number of shares with the addition of a new security of the company, without any immediate change in the value of his total holding.

Without TCA 1997, ss 130(2)(c), 131 and 132, it would be possible for a company to make a tax-free distribution of profits by capitalising profits followed by a repayment of capital, or by capitalising profits following a repayment of capital. TCA 1997, s 130(2)(c) deals with the redemption of a security that was previously issued in respect of shares in the company otherwise than for full consideration, ie the redemption of bonus shares or bonus debentures (up to the amount redeemed). TCA 1997, s 131 deals with the case in which a company repays share capital and subsequently capitalises profits so as to replace that share capital with new shares without receiving any new consideration from the shareholders, ie with bonus shares. TCA 1997, s 132(2) deals with the reverse situation in which there is first a bonus issue and then a repayment of capital.

11.103.2 Redemption of bonus shares/debentures

TCA 1997, s 130(2)(c) treats as a distribution assessable under Schedule F any amount met out of the assets of a company (whether in cash or otherwise) in respect of the redemption of any security that had been issued by the company in respect of shares in or securities of the company (bonus shares or securities), otherwise than wholly for new consideration. If the security being redeemed was issued partly for new consideration, a part of the amount applied to redeem the security is treated as a distribution, being the part corresponding to the part of the security issued otherwise than for new consideration.

TCA 1997, s 130(2)(c) is directed at attempts by companies to avoid making taxable distributions by capitalising profits by way of a bonus issue of shares or loan stock followed by the repayment of the capital of the security. Only so much of the amount applied to redeem the security as is properly attributable to any new consideration given for the security will be regarded as received by the holder in the form of capital. The full amount applied to redeem the security, whether in cash or otherwise, and whether or not involving a premium on redemption, must be brought into account.

Example 11.103.2.1

On 1 February 2001 Rintoul Ltd issued €50,000 9.25% unsecured loan stock to its shareholders for cash of €14,000. At that time it capitalised €36,000 then standing to the credit of its profit and loss account, which was applied in paying up the balance due in respect of the loan stock. On 15 September 2007 the company redeemed the 9.25% loan stock in full at a premium of €10,000. This was effected by dividing among the holders of the loan stock its investment of €67,700 9.5% Exchequer Stock which then had a market value of €60,000. Mr Ralph, the holder of €5,000 of the loan stock received €6,770 9.5% Exchequer Stock (market value €6,000) in respect of his holding.

The effect of TCA 1997, s 130(2)(c) on the above transactions is as follows:

	€
Amount met out of assets of Rintoul Ltd to redeem unsecured loan stock	
- market value of €67,700 9.5% Exchequer Stock at 15/9/07	60,000
Part of 9.25% unsecured loan stock issued otherwise than for new consideration (1/2/01)	36,000
Value of 9.25% unsecured loan stock when issued (1/2/01)	50,000
Amount treated by TCA 1997, s 130(2)(c) as distribution on 15/9/07:	
€60,000 x 36/50	43,200

Mr Ralph is taxable under Schedule F in respect of his share of the total redemption value as follows:

	€
Amount of distribution under TCA 1997, s 130(2)(c):	
€6,000 x 36/50	4,320

The fact that Mr Ralph may not have been the original holder of the €5,000 9.25% unsecured loan stock when it was issued, and may not be a shareholder of the company, at the time of its redemption is irrelevant.

11.103.3 Bonus issue following repayment of share capital

TCA 1997, s 131 is concerned with the situation in which, at or after the time a company has repaid share capital at any time after 26 November 1975, it issues any share capital as paid up otherwise than for new consideration (eg, as a bonus issue). Subject to certain exceptions, TCA 1997, s 131(2) treats the amount so paid up as a distribution in respect of the shares in respect of which the bonus issue is made so that it becomes taxable as a distribution under TCA 1997, s 130(2)(b). However, if and to the extent that the amount of the profits capitalised by the bonus issue exceeds the amount of the share capital previously repaid, this excess is not a distribution for Schedule F or any other purpose.

For TCA 1997, s 131 to have effect, it is not necessary that there is a connection between the repayment of capital and the bonus issue; it is not necessary that the repayment of capital should be of the shares in respect of which the bonus issue was made.

The effect of the provision is not confined to a bonus issue out of undistributed profits, and would apply equally if the new shares issued after the repayment of capital are paid up out of, say, a share premium account arising out of an earlier share issue. What is relevant is whether the shareholder provides any new consideration for the new shares issued after the capital repayment. If part but not all of the new share capital is paid up by way of new consideration, the remaining part is taken into account in determining the amount of the distribution taxable under TCA 1997, s 131(2).

TCA 1997, s 131 does not apply to treat a bonus issue as a distribution where the repaid share capital consists of fully paid up preference shares which existed as such on 27 November 1975 or if the shares were issued after 27 November 1975 as fully paid preference shares wholly for new consideration not derived from ordinary shares provided that, in either case, the shares continued to be fully paid preference shares until the date of their repayment (TCA 1997, s 131(3)). Furthermore, in the case of a company other than a close company, TCA 1997, s 131 does not apply if the bonus shares are issued more than 10 years after the repayment of the share capital, and if the bonus shares are not redeemable share capital (TCA 1997, s 131(4)). In the case of a close company, once there has been a repayment of capital there is no 10 year let-out provision so that a later bonus issue at any time after a post-26 November 1975 repayment of capital is taxable as a distribution.

Example 11.103.3.1

On 19 October 1975, Zelda Ltd repaid to its shareholders €80,000 of its ordinary share capital by way of a capital reduction. On 12 March 1997, it made a further capital repayment of €90,000 to the same shareholders. The company subsequently traded successfully for a number of years resulting in a substantial credit balance on its profit and loss account. It then capitalised profits and applied them in issuing new fully paid shares as bonus issues to its ordinary shareholders as follows:

13 August 2006

50,000 new ordinary shares of €1 each fully paid by the capitalisation of €50,000 out of the balance then standing to the credit of the profit and loss account

2 September 2007

80,000 new cumulative 15% redeemable preference shares of €1 each fully paid by the capitalisation of €80,000 out of the profit and loss account balance at that date.

The effect of TCA 1997, s 131(1) on the above transactions is as follows:

(1) The share capital repayment of €80,000 on 19 October 1975 is ignored as it took place before 27 November 1975 but the €90,000 repayment of capital made on 12 March 1997 is relevant in relation to the subsequent bonus issues.

(2) The company is treated as making a distribution of €50,000[1] to its ordinary shareholders on 13 August 2006 equal to the full amount treated as paid up on the new ordinary shares issued on that date and without any new consideration being received.

(3) The company is treated as making a distribution of €40,000[2] to its ordinary shareholders on 2 September 2007, as follows:

	€	€
Amount treated as paid up on the new preference shares issued on that date without the payment of new consideration		80,000
Amount of share capital previously repaid after 26/11/1978	90,000	
Less: amount of previous bonus issue treated as distribution by TCA 1997, s 131(1)	50,000	
		40,000
Therefore amount treated as distribution on 2/9/07 limited to		40,000

Notes:

[1] The bonus issue of ordinary shares made on 13 August 2006 is a distribution as it was made within 10 years of the repayment of share capital of €90,000.

[2] The bonus issue made on 2 September 2007 is a distribution as it consisted of the issue of redeemable share capital.

Although TCA 1997, s 131 clearly implies that a redemption of shares involves a repayment of share capital, a purchase of shares does not involve any repayment of capital. Accordingly, TCA 1997, s 131 does not treat as a distribution a bonus issue which follows a purchase of shares (see **11.105.4** below and also **11.304**).

11.103.4   Bonus issue followed by repayment of share capital

TCA 1997, s 132(2) is an exception to the rule that a payment made by a company in repaying share capital is not to be treated as a distribution. It is relevant where a distribution out of the assets of a company is made (other than in a winding up) in repaying shares representing any share capital that was issued as paid up otherwise than for new consideration (eg, a previous bonus issue). In any such case TCA 1997, s 132(2)(a) provides that, for the purposes of TCA 1997, ss 130 and 131, the amount applied in repaying the shares is not to be treated as a repayment of capital. Accordingly, the amount so applied is a distribution within TCA 1997, s 130(2)(b) subject, however, to certain exceptions.

TCA 1997, s 132(2)(a) does not apply to prevent the treatment of the amount used in repaying the shares as a repayment of capital in any of the following circumstances:

(a) if the earlier bonus issue was made before 27 November 1975;

(b) if the earlier bonus issue was itself treated as a distribution when it was made (eg under TCA 1997, s 131(2) following a previous repayment of share capital – see above);

(c) if the amount of the capital repaid exceeds the amount of the earlier bonus issue (in which case only the latter amount is treated as a distribution while the excess capital repaid is treated as a repayment of capital); or

(d) if, where the company is not a close company:

(i) the repayment of capital is made more than 10 years after the relevant bonus issue, and

(ii) the repayment is not one of redeemable share capital.

Where a company which has previously issued bonus shares makes a repayment of capital, in applying TCA 1997, s 132(2)(a) it is necessary first to deduct from the amount so paid up (on the earlier bonus issue) the part, if any, of that amount which was treated as a distribution at the time. Only the balance of the earlier bonus issue is then relevant in treating as a distribution any part of the subsequent capital repayment. For example, if the company in Example **11.103.3.1** above were to make any repayment in respect of the €80,000 redeemable preference share capital issued without the receipt of any new consideration on 2 September 2004, the €40,000 treated by TCA 1997, s 131(2) as a distribution on that date would have to be excluded from the computation of any distribution arising under TCA 1997, s 132(2)(a) on the subsequent repayment. The balance of the amount paid up without new consideration on the 80,000 preference shares, ie €40,000, remains liable to be treated as a distribution in the event of a later repayment of share capital.

For the purposes of TCA 1997, s 132(2)(a), all shares of the same class are treated as representing the same share capital (TCA 1997, s 132(2)(b)). Furthermore, if shares are issued in respect of other shares, or are directly or indirectly converted into or exchanged for other shares, both the original shares and the new shares are treated as representing the same share capital. Accordingly, once there has been a post-26 November 1975 bonus issue, a subsequent repayment of any part either of the original shares or the new shares, or both, is treated as a distribution. However, once TCA 1997, s 132(2)(a) has had effect to treat one or more subsequent repayments of share capital as distributions up to the full amount of any earlier bonus issues available, any additional capital repaid in excess of that amount is received by the shareholder as capital and not as a distribution.

Example 11.103.4.1

On 26 November 1999 Dumas Co, an unlimited liability company, had ordinary paid up share capital consisting of 30,000 shares of €1 each. Mr Alexander, the controlling shareholder, held 20,400 of these shares. On 7 March 2005, the company capitalised €15,000 then standing to the credit of its profit and loss account by issuing 15,000 new ordinary shares of €1 each as fully paid up shares. No part of this bonus issue was treated as a distribution and no new consideration was received.

On 8 November 2009, Dumas Co repaid share capital by way of redeeming 27,000 of the then existing 45,000 ordinary shares at par. At that time, Mr Alexander held 30,600 shares so that the company paid him €18,360 in respect of the redemption.

Under TCA 1997, s 132(2)(b), both the original 30,000 shares and the 15,000 bonus issue shares are treated as representing the same share capital. The effect of TCA 1997, s 132(2) on the distribution of €27,000 (the capital repayment) made in respect of the total share capital of €45,000 is as follows:

	€
Amount paid up otherwise than for new consideration on March 2005 bonus issue	15,000
Less: part of that issue treated as a distribution in March 2005	Nil
Amount remaining available under TCA 1997, s 132(2)	15,000
Amount of capital repaid on 8/11/09	
(27,000 ordinary shares redeemable at par)	27,000

Less: total of earlier capital repayments re bonus issue (7/3/05)	
previously treated as distributions by TCA 1997, s 132(2)	Nil
	27,000
Amount treated as distribution (8/11/09) by TCA 1997, s 132(2)	15,000

Mr Alexander's capital repayment of €18,360 is treated as follows:	€
Part of capital repaid on 8/11/09 treated as distribution to be	
included in Schedule F income for the year 2009:	
€15,000 x 30,600/45,000	10,200

Balance remaining: a repayment of capital not subject to income tax	
€18,360 – €10,200	8,160

11.104 Premiums on redemption of share capital

TCA 1997, s 132(4) is intended to prevent the tax-free extraction of assets from a company by means of the payment of a premium on the occasion of the redemption of share capital; the premium on redemption is treated as not being a repayment of share capital with the result that it becomes a distribution under TCA 1997, s 130(2)(b).

As an exception, TCA 1997, s 132(3) provides that, if share capital is issued at a premium representing new consideration, the amount of the premium is treated as forming part of that share capital. In that case, a premium paid on a subsequent repayment of that share capital is not a distribution within TCA 1997, s 132(4), but this will be the case only to the extent that the premium on the redemption does not exceed the premium previously subscribed in the form of new consideration. Furthermore, if and to the extent that the premium paid on the issue of the shares has been applied to pay up any share capital (ie, as a bonus issue), it ceases to be available to render a premium on redemption as a repayment of capital.

Example 11.104.1

On 10 August 1999, Lafayette Company, an unlimited liability company, had an initial share capital of 45,000 ordinary shares of €1 each fully paid up at a premium of €90,000. The company's three shareholders each subscribed €45,000 for 15,000 shares.

At 31 December 2007 the company had an undistributed credit balance of €180,000 on its profit and loss account. On 1 April 2008 the company redeemed 27,000 shares at a premium of €4.50 per share, resulting in a total payment to the shareholders of €148,500, comprising €27,000 on share capital account and a premium on redemption of €121,500. Each shareholder received €49,500 (being €9,000 in respect of share capital and €40,500 by way of premium on redemption).

As the premium of €90,000 paid on the original issue of the shares represented new consideration, and since no part of that premium had been applied subsequently in paying up any share capital, it is treated by TCA 1997, s 132(3) as part of the original share capital. The treatment of the total distribution of €148,500 made on 1 April 2008 is as follows:

	Share capital	Share premium
	€	€
Amounts subscribed originally for 45,000 shares	45,000	90,000

Amounts subscribed for part of share capital		
(including premium) now redeemed – 27/45ths	27,000	54,000
Amounts repaid on 1/4/08 (27,000 shares):		
- share capital	27,000	
- premium	_____	121,500
Premium on redemption not treated as repayment of		
share capital (TCA 1997, s 132(4))	Nil	67,500

Lafayette Company is accordingly treated under TCA 1997, s 130(2)(b) as making a distribution of €67,500, while the €27,000 repaid on share capital account and the €54,000 of the premium on redemption covered by the share premium paid on 10 August 1999 are repayments of capital and are not treated as distributions. Each shareholder is taxable for the year 2008 as follows:

	€
Amount treated as distribution: €67,500 x 1/3 (on 9,000 shares)	22,500

11.105   Some key concepts and definitions

11.105.1   Repayment of share capital

The expression "repayment of share capital", which is crucial to much of the legislation on distributions and is relevant also to the legislation on companies purchasing their own shares (see **11.3**), is not defined although there are specific provisions dealing with matters which are not to be regarded as repayments of share capital, as dealt with in **11.103** above. Apart from these provisions, the expression must therefore take its ordinary meaning. A repayment of share capital denotes the return of the nominal amount represented by the share capital in question (and not, if different, of the amount paid on subscription). It also includes amounts representing premiums paid on subscription for the share capital.

11.105.2   Reduction of capital

A company can reduce its share capital only with the sanction of the court. The reduction can take two forms. The amount involved may simply be returned to the shareholders in either cash or asset form, or, if there is a liability for uncalled capital, this can be reduced or extinguished. Alternatively, instead of returning any cash or assets to the shareholders, the balance sheet may be adjusted to bring the capital into line with the company's assets.

The former method would be adopted where the company is over-capitalised or where it wishes to raise alternative capital more cheaply. The second type of reduction would be effected where the company has lost a significant part of its capital: due to trading losses, the assets may have been significantly reduced, the actual value of company's capital will have fallen below the nominal value of the issued shares, and the profit and loss account may be in debit thereby preventing the payment of dividends. A reduction in capital facilitates the writing off of the debit balance and the balance sheet will better reflect the true asset position of the company.

Subject to court approval, the company may pass a special resolution reducing its share capital by paying off any paid up capital that is in excess of the its requirements or by extinguishing or reducing the liability of the shareholders in respect of uncalled share capital.

The memorandum and articles of a company limited by shares is required to state the amount of share capital with which the company proposes to be registered and the division thereof into shares of a fixed amount. The amount thus stated is the company's *nominal* capital. A reduction of capital is a form of repayment of share capital; the share capital in question is paid off in accordance with section 72 of the Companies Act 1963. There would appear to be no such concept as the payment of a premium on the paying off of share capital. If, however, the share capital is reduced or paid off other than in cash form, the value of the assets transferred in payment may well exceed the nominal value of the shares paid off. The reduction will not be a distribution by virtue of TCA 1997, s 130(2)(b) (see **11.102.3**) since it is a repayment of capital (and assuming it is not caught by TCA 1997, s 131 or 132 – see **11.103.3-103.4** relating to bonus issues and repayments of capital).

A reduction of capital by way of a transfer of an asset *in specie* may, however, give rise to a distribution by virtue of TCA 1997, s 130(3) (assets transferred to members for less than full consideration – see **11.108**). The consideration given by the members in such circumstances would be their agreement to extinguish their shares, being "new consideration" up to the amount received by the company on the original issue of the shares. In short, the taxable distribution would be the market value of the assets transferred over the amount originally subscribed for the shares. The market value of the shares themselves at the time of the reduction would be irrelevant in this context.

A reduction of capital is the most obvious form of repayment of capital (the capital being "paid off" in accordance with section 72 of the Companies Act 1963). It is sometimes contended that a reduction can also include a redemption or a repurchase of capital (see below under *Redemption*).

11.105.3 Redemption

If authorised by its articles to do so, a company limited by shares or by guarantee and having a share capital may issue shares and redeem them accordingly. No redeemable shares may be issued or redeemed at any time when the nominal value of the issued share capital that is not redeemable is less than one-tenth of the nominal value of the total issued share capital of the company. Redemption may only be effected if the shares are fully paid up. The terms of the redemption must provide for payment on redemption. The shares must be redeemed out of distributable profits (when an amount equal to the nominal amount of the shares redeemed must be transferred to a capital redemption reserve fund), or, where the company proposes to cancel shares on redemption, may be redeemed out of the proceeds of a fresh issue of shares made for the purposes of the redemption, so that the capital of the redeemed shares is replaced by the capital of the new shares.

Any premium paid on redemption must be paid out of distributable profits but where the redeemable shares have been issued at a premium, the premium on redemption may be paid out of the proceeds of a fresh issue of shares made for the purposes of the redemption up to an amount equal to the aggregate of the premiums received on the issue of the redeemed shares or, if less, the current amount of the company's share premium account (including any sums transferred to that account in respect of premiums on the new shares).

A redemption of capital does not in itself involve the return of the nominal amount represented by the share capital. If, following the redemption, the shares are retained as treasury shares, the issued share capital of the company will remain the same. If the shares are cancelled, on the other hand, the amount of the issued share capital will be reduced by the nominal value of the cancelled shares. The intent of company law is to ensure that redemption does not lead to any reduction of capital so that, as mentioned above, a redemption may only be effected when the shares are fully paid up and only out of profits or out of the proceeds of a fresh issue in which case the capital represented by the new shares replaces the capital represented by the redeemed shares. In the latter case, an amount equal to the nominal amount of the redeemed shares must be transferred to the capital redemption reserve fund which fund is treated as if it were paid up capital.

A redemption of capital is sometimes regarded as being distinct from a repayment of capital (and therefore also as not being a reduction of capital). References to "the redemption, repayment or purchase of its own shares" in the Tax Acts (in TCA 1997, s 176(1) (see **11.301**) would seem to confirm this distinction. On the other hand, TCA 1997, s 132(4) provides that "premiums paid on redemption of share capital shall not be treated as repayments of capital", which would appear to imply that a redemption of shares would amount to a repayment of share capital up to the amount originally paid on the issue of the shares. (See also in **11.105.4** below the view of the UK Inland Revenue to the effect that part of a payment to redeem shares should be viewed as a repayment of share capital.) The stronger indication would seem to be that the intention of the tax legislation, and indeed its effect, is that a redemption of shares can involve a repayment of capital. Only the excess of the redemption price over the original price paid on their issue will constitute a distribution.

The technical position relating to a purchase by a company of its own shares, as to whether it involves a repayment of capital, is less clear (probably due to the fact that the legislation governing distributions for tax purposes pre-dates the time from which it became possible for a company to buy back its own shares). In practice (see further below), the payment of an amount equal to the new consideration received on the issue of the shares, together with any premium, appears to be accepted as a repayment, and as a form of reduction, of capital. For this purpose, it is assumed that the repurchased shares, as with redeemed shares, are cancelled and are not held as treasury shares.

11.105.4 Purchase of own shares

The legislation dealing with the purchase by a company of its own shares (see **11.3**) does not define or describe what is meant by that expression, and the normal usage of the expression will therefore presumably apply. The payment by a company of any sum on the purchase of its own shares does not, accordingly, include anything by way of a repayment of share capital. An exception may, however, be a case in which a company purchases its own shares out of capital. This could be effected, for example, by way of a return of the premium paid in on the occasion of the issue of the shares, where the share premium account would be correspondingly reduced. To the extent of the amount of the premium returned, there would be a repayment of share capital (TCA 1997, s 132(3)).

In practice, it seems to be accepted that the amount paid for the purchase by a company of its own shares is not treated as a distribution up to the amount originally paid on their issue, thereby implying, in contrast with what is stated in **11.105.2** above, that a purchase of own shares involves a repayment of capital. (For example the view of the UK Inland Revenue (COT 1751) is that part of a payment by a company to redeem or purchase its own shares should be viewed as a repayment of share capital, and therefore not a distribution. The basis for this view is not supplied.)

It is suggested, however, that a technically more satisfactory view of the matter is that (apart from the case in which the purchase is made out of capital) the shares re-acquired by the company in the buy-back represent new consideration received, up to the nominal amount originally paid on their issue, and to that extent there is not a distribution. A consequence of this view is that TCA 1997, ss 131 and 132(2) (bonus issue following, and followed by, repayment of capital – see **11.103.3–4**) would not be in question in the case of a purchase by a company of its own shares. In addition, the amount to be treated as a distribution may not be the same since the amount not to be so treated is that equal to the nominal amount rather than the amount originally subscribed which may be different.

11.105.5 New consideration

New consideration means consideration not provided, directly or indirectly, out of the assets of the company making the distribution or other payment. It does not include any amount retained by the company by way of capitalising a distribution (TCA 1997, s 135(1)(a)), for example, a bonus issue or stock dividend.

However, shares paid for from a share premium account are regarded as having been issued for new consideration unless the premium has already been taken into account as a repayment of share capital under TCA 1997, s 132(3). TCA 1997, s 135(1)(b) states that if any share capital has been issued at a premium for new consideration, any part of that premium subsequently applied in paying up share capital is treated as new consideration also for that share capital so paid up, except in so far as the premium has been taken into account (see **11.104**) so as to enable a distribution to be treated as a repayment of capital.

Example 11.105.5.1

The facts are as in Example **11.104.1** above from which the movements on the share premium account of Lafayette Company from 10 August 1999 to 1 April 2008 can be summarised as follows:

	€
10/8/99:	
New consideration paid as premium on issue of 45,000 ordinary shares	90,000
1/4/08:	
Amount of premium treated by TCA 1997, s 132(3)	
as forming part of share capital repaid (and therefore not a distribution)	54,000
Balance of new consideration (10/8/99) on share premium	36,000

On 12 June 2008, the company capitalised €50,000 then standing to the credit of its profit and loss account by issuing 50,000 fully paid up bonus shares of €1 each to its ordinary shareholders. Since this is a bonus issue following the repayment of share capital on 1 April 2008, TCA 1997, s 131(2) applies to treat as a distribution that part of the €50,000 that is paid up otherwise than by the receipt of new consideration (see **11.103.3**).

Since €36,000 of the new consideration paid as share premium on 10 August 1999 has not been used up for the purposes of TCA 1997, s 132(3), it is treated by TCA 1997, s 135(1) as new consideration also for the 50,000 bonus shares issued on 12 June 2008. TCA 1997, s 131(2) therefore applies as follows:

	€
Amount paid up on bonus shares (after earlier repayment of capital)	50,000
Less: balance of new consideration on share premium account	36,000
Amount treated as distribution (12/6/08)	14,000

Share capital or securities of a company may be derived from other shares or securities, or from voting or other rights, of the company. TCA 1997, s 135(2)(a) provides that no consideration derived from the value of any share capital or security of a company, or from voting or other rights in a company, is to be regarded as new consideration received by the company, unless the consideration consists of:

(a)   money or value received from the company as a distribution;

(b)   money received from the company as a payment which constitutes a repayment of that share capital or of the principal secured by that security; or

(c)   the surrender of the right to that share capital or security on its cancellation, extinguishment or acquisition by the company.

Thus the proceeds of a dividend or other amount treated as a distribution taxable under Schedule F may be reinvested as new consideration for shares or securities in the company. Again, where loan stock is issued to the holder of preference shares in consideration for the cancellation of those shares, the consideration derived from the cancelled shares would be regarded as new consideration given for the loan stock. As regards (b) and (c) above, no amount is to be treated as new consideration to the extent that it exceeds any new consideration received by the company for the issue of the share capital or security in question or, in the case of share capital which constituted a distribution on issue (bonus issue – see **11.103.3**), the nominal value of that share capital (TCA 1997, s 135(2)(b)).

It is sometimes considered that a company does not receive any consideration, new or otherwise, on the purchase of its own shares since the shares are automatically cancelled at the time so that the company receives nothing. It is clear, however, that TCA 1997, s 135(2)(a) presupposes that a company receives new consideration on the *acquisition* (see (c) above) of its shares (and even on their cancellation or extinguishment).

It has already been seen (see **11.105.4***)* that a sum paid by a company in the purchase of its own shares does not normally include anything by way of a repayment of share capital. The surrender of the right to share capital on its cancellation or acquisition does, however, amount to new consideration received by the company. The *amount* of that new consideration is the nominal value of the shares cancelled or acquired, even where the shares were issued at a premium, because that is the value that the shareholder has surrendered on the cancellation or acquisition of the shares. Although, as noted above, TCA 1997, s 135(2)(b) provides that the amount of any new consideration may not exceed the amount of any new consideration originally received by the company for the issue of the share capital in question, including the amount of any premium paid in, that is not to say that that is the measure of the new consideration; it is merely setting an upper limit as to the amount of the new consideration.

The concept of a company receiving consideration on the occasion of its shares being cancelled (as in (c) above) may appear somewhat obscure. In the sense that the shares to be cancelled represent a liability of the company, so that their cancellation results in the discharge of that liability, that discharge must be assumed to be a form of consideration. It must further be assumed, since the legislation so implies, that it is "new" consideration. If, however, the market value of the cancelled shares at the time they are cancelled is greater than the amount given for them on subscription, the excess amount cannot represent new consideration (as provided for by TCA 1997, s 135(2)(b) – see above).

Example 11.105.5.2

Plimsoll Ltd has an issued share capital of 100,000 €1 ordinary shares which were subscribed for at par. The company purchases 60,000 of the shares for €3,000,000.

The new consideration derived from the value of the company's share capital cannot exceed the new consideration received by it at the time the shares were issued. The new consideration given by the shareholders is accordingly €60,000, being the nominal value of the shares acquired by the company. Unless TCA 1997 Part 6 Ch 9 (companies purchasing their own shares – see **11.3**) applies, Plimsoll Ltd will be regarded as making a distribution of €2,940,000.

Example 11.105.5.3

The position is as in Example **11.105.5.2** except that only 25,000 of the shares have been issued at par, the balance being comprised of bonus shares. Plimsoll Ltd arranges a reduction of its share capital and pays off 60,000 shares.

In the absence of specific provisions, the shares subscribed for at par and the bonus shares should be regarded as having been paid off rateably. Accordingly, of the 25,000 shares subscribed for at par, 15,000 (25,000 x 6/10ths) would be regarded as having been paid off at nominal value. The company has therefore received new consideration of €15,000. If TCA 1997 Part 6 Ch 9 does not apply, the distribution is €45,000 (€60,000 – €15,000).

Example 11.105.5.4

The position is as in Example **11.105.5.3** except that the 25,000 shares were subscribed for at a premium of €75,000, the additional shares having been paid for out of the share premium account.

There is a repayment of share capital of €60,000 (TCA 1997, s 135(1)(b)).

11.105.6 "Out of assets"

TCA 1997, s 135(5) provides that a distribution is to be treated as made, or consideration as provided, out of assets of a company if the cost falls on the company.

If a company pays or reimburses a third party in connection with the making of a distribution to the company's shareholders, the amount comprised in the distribution is regarded as having been provided out of the assets of the company since the related cost will have fallen on the company.

11.105.7 "In respect of shares"

TCA 1997, s 135(10) provides that a thing is to be regarded as done in respect of a share if it is done:

(a)   to a person as being the holder of the share;

(b)   to a person as having at a particular time been the holder the share;

(c)   in pursuance of a right granted or offer made in respect of a share, and anything done in respect of shares by reference to shareholdings at a particular time is to be regarded as done to the then holder of the shares or the personal representatives of any shareholder then dead.

It is the capacity in which a benefit has been received that will be relevant in determining whether the benefit is a distribution. In practice, to avoid distribution treatment, it will be a matter for the shareholder (or other person receiving the benefit – see below) to show in what capacity, other than his capacity as shareholder in the company, the benefit was received.

TCA 1997, s 135(10) may appear to mean that "in respect of shares" requires that a distribution must be something that passes to the shareholder. Thus, when it says that a thing is done in respect of a share "if it is done to a person as being the holder of the share", it seems to be saying that only a distribution passing to a shareholder can be a distribution for the purposes of TCA 1997, s 130(2)(b). A close reading of the subsection, however, does not bear out this interpretation: a distribution made to a shareholder is a distribution in respect of shares but this kind of distribution does not exhaust all of the possibilities for having a distribution for the purposes of TCA 1997, s 130(2)(b). As was explained in the Special Commissioners' decision in *Noved Investment Company v Commissioners of HM Revenue and Customs* [2006] SpC00521, [the UK equivalent of] TCA 1997, s 135(10) applies a sufficient but not a necessary condition – it provides that "if it is done ..." and not "only if it is done..." - so that a wider enquiry is permissible as to whether something has been done in respect of shares.

It is possible for a benefit provided by a company to a person other than a shareholder to be "in respect of shares", for example where the benefit was provided at the direction of a shareholder and there was no commercial reason for the benefit other than the connection between the shareholder and the recipient of the benefit. This view is consistent with the decision in the *Noved Investment* case where it was stated that, on the exercise by a shareholder of a right to require a payment to a third party (and it appears to have been of some relevance that the shareholder had that right), the subsequent payment out of the assets of the company to that party would be a payment in respect of shares even though it is not made to the shareholder.

Anything done "in respect of shares" in a company which is a member of a "90% group" includes anything done by that company in respect of shares in any other member of the group. In particular, anything distributed out of assets of one member of the group in respect of shares in another member is a "distribution" (TCA 1997, s 135(4)(b)), but this is not to mean that a company is to be treated as making a distribution to another 90% group member which is resident in the State (TCA 1997, s 135(4)(c)).

A *90% group* is a group comprised of a principal company and all its 90% subsidiaries, "principal company" meaning a company of which another company is a subsidiary. A company is a *90% subsidiary* of another company if and so long as not less than 90% of its ordinary share capital is directly and beneficially owned by that other company (TCA 1997, s 9(1)(c), (3)).

Where, say, company C is wholly owned by company B and company B is wholly owned by company A, companies C and A are not in the same 90% group since the relationship between them is indirect only. Accordingly, if something is distributed out of the assets of company C to the shareholders in company A (ie, in respect of shares of company A), that would not be a distribution since it is not in respect of shares in a company in the same 90% group as company C. Suppose, however, something is distributed by company C to company A in respect company A's shares in company B, that would be a distribution even if company A is resident in the State; although companies C and B are in the same 90% group, so that anything done by company C in respect of shares in company B must be taken into account, the distribution is from company C to company A and, since those companies are not in the same 90% group, the exception in TCA 1997, s 135(4)(c) for a distribution made to a resident company does not apply.

If company B and company C were wholly-owned subsidiaries of company A, a distribution out of the assets of company B to company C could be a distribution, not by virtue of TCA 1997, s 135(4) but in consequence of TCA 1997, s 130(2)(b) since the distribution is likely to have been made at the direction of the parent company A and therefore in respect of that company's shareholding in company B.

All of the above comments concerning the meaning of "in respect of shares" apply equally to the meaning of "in respect of securities".

11.105.8 Member

Section 31 of the Companies Act 1963, defines *member* in relation to a company. The subscribers to the memorandum of a company are deemed to have agreed to become members of the company and, on its registration, are to be entered as members in its register of members. (They are in law members of the company even if the company fails to place them on the register, subject to the exception that if the company allots all of the authorised share capital to others it is not possible to treat the subscribers as members.) Every other person who agrees to become a member of a company and whose name is entered in its register of members is a member of the company.

Accordingly, a person may become a member of a company by subscribing to the memorandum of association on the registration of the company, by agreeing to take a share and being placed on the register of members, by taking a transfer of a share and being placed on the register of members, by succeeding to the estate of a bankrupt or deceased member and being placed on the register of members, or by allowing his name to be on the register of members or otherwise holding himself out or allowing himself to be held out as a member.

The term "member" is therefore not synonymous with "shareholder", nor could it be in view of the existence of companies which do not have a share capital. However, for the vast majority of companies, which do have a share capital, the shareholders will in fact be the members.

11.106 Interest on certain securities

TCA 1997, s 130(2)(d) treats as a distribution any interest or other distribution out of the assets of a company in respect of securities of the company where the securities are:

(a) securities issued after 26 November 1975, otherwise than wholly for new consideration, in respect of shares in or securities of the company (eg, as the result of a bonus issue);

(b) securities convertible directly or indirectly into shares in the company, or securities carrying any right to receive shares in or securities of the company, not being (in either case) securities quoted on a recognised stock exchange or issued on terms reasonably comparable with the terms of issue of such quoted securities;

(c) securities under which:

   (i) the consideration given by the company for the use of the principal secured is to any extent dependent on the results of the company's business, or

   (ii) the consideration so given represents more than a reasonable commercial return for the use of the principal secured (in which case only so much of the interest in respect of the security as exceeds a reasonable commercial return is treated as a distribution) (but see **7.206.11** regarding exception for interest paid by securitisation vehicle);

(d) securities issued by the company and held by a company not resident in the State, where:

   (i) the company which issued the securities is a 75% subsidiary of the other company,

   (ii) both companies are 75% subsidiaries of a third company which is not resident in the State, or

   (ii) except where at least 90% of the ordinary share capital of the company which issued the securities is directly owned by an Irish resident company, both the company which issued the securities and the company not resident in the State are 75% subsidiaries of a third company which is resident in the State; and

(e) securities which are "connected with" shares in the company.

Security would normally suggest that some form of document creating or evidencing a charge on assets is involved, usually as security for money borrowed (see **2.605** regarding the meaning of "securities" generally). However, in relation to the meaning of "distribution" for the purposes of TCA 1997, s 130, the term includes a security not creating or evidencing a charge on assets (TCA 1997, s 135(8)) and interest paid by a company on money advanced without the issue of a security for the advance is treated as if paid in respect of a security issued for the advance. For the purposes of TCA 1997, s 130(2)(d), "security" would seem to cover any loan or advance made to a company, regardless of whether or not the loan or advance is secured.

In (c)(i) above, the expression "the results of the company's business or any part of it" presumably refers to the results as disclosed by the accounts of the company. This would mean the profits of the company's business or the profits of a particular part of that business, as disclosed by the accounts but could also, it would seem, refer to other aspects of the company's business, for example, the value of properties held.

Consideration given by a company for the use of principal received is treated as not being to any extent dependent on the results of the company's business or any part of it by reason only of the fact that the terms (however expressed) of the security provide:

(a) for the consideration to be reduced in the event of the results improving; or

(b) for the consideration to be increased in the event of the results deteriorating (TCA 1997, s 130(2A)).

Thus, the rule in (c)(i) above is disapplied in the case of a loan providing for higher levels of interest where the borrower's profits fall and lower levels of interest where the borrower's profits rise. For the purposes of (e) above, securities are *connected with* shares in the company where, owing to the nature of the rights attaching to the securities or shares, in particular of any terms or conditions attaching to the right to transfer the shares or securities, it is necessary or advantageous for a person who has, or disposes of or acquires, any of the securities also to have, or to dispose of or to acquire, a proportionate holding of the shares.

As regards interest described in TCA 1997, s 130(2)(d)(iv) (see (d) above), a "qualified company" paying such interest in an accounting period may make a written election, which should be submitted to the inspector of taxes with the company's corporation tax return for that period, to have the interest treated as not being a distribution (TCA 1997, s 452(3)). The election may be made in respect of interest which:

(i) is payable by the company in the course of carrying on relevant trading operations;

(ii) would, except for TCA s 130(2)(d)(iv), be deductible as a trading expense in computing the company's trading income for the period; and

(iii) represents no more than a reasonable commercial return for the use of the principal in respect of which the interest is paid.

A *qualified company* for the above purpose is an international financial services company or a Shannon financial services company. *Relevant trading operations* means financial services operations in respect of which a qualified company is entitled to the 10% corporation tax rate. TCA 1997, s 246(3)(c) permits interest paid by a company in the course of carrying on qualifying IFSC or Shannon operations to a person whose usual place of abode is outside the State to be paid without deduction of income tax (see **4.305**).

As regards certain interest described in TCA 1997, s 130(2)(d)(iv) (see (d) above), a company paying such interest in an accounting period may make a written election, which should be submitted to the inspector of taxes with the company's corporation tax return for that period, to have the interest treated as not being a distribution (TCA 1997, s 452(2)). The election may be made in respect of interest which:

(i) is payable by the company in the ordinary course of carrying on a trade;

(ii) would, except for TCA s 130(2)(d)(iv), be deductible as a trading expense in computing the company's trading income for the period; and

(iii) is interest payable to a company resident in a relevant territory, ie a Member State of the EC other than Ireland or a country with which Ireland has a tax treaty.

A company is regarded as being resident in a *relevant territory* if:

(a) in a case where the territory is a country with which Ireland has a tax treaty, the company is regarded as being a resident of that country in accordance with the relevant treaty; and

(b) in any other case, the company is by virtue of the law of the territory resident for tax purposes in that territory (where "tax" refers to tax imposed in that territory which corresponds to corporation tax in Ireland).

A bank paying interest described in TCA 1997, s 130(2)(d)(iv) (see (d) above) in an accounting period may make a written election, which should be submitted to the inspector of taxes with the bank's corporation tax return for that period, to have the interest treated as not being a distribution (TCA 1997, s 845A). The election may be made in respect of interest which:

(i)   is payable by the bank in the course of carrying on a bona fide banking business in the State;

(ii)   would, except for TCA s 130(2)(d)(iv), be deductible as a trading expense in computing the bank's income from its banking business for the period; and

(iii) represents no more than a reasonable commercial return for the use of the principal in respect of which the interest is paid by the bank.

Bank for the above purposes means:

(a)   a person who is the holder of a licence granted under section 9 of the Central Bank Act 1971; or

(b)   a person who holds a licence or other similar authorisation under the law of any other Member State of the EC which corresponds to a licence granted under section 9.

In certain circumstances interest paid by a company to a non-resident 75% parent or associated company will not be treated as a distribution. In certain cases double taxation can arise where the interest is disallowed as a trading expense under the distribution rule and is also taxed in the hands of the recipient as interest. Subject to certain conditions being met, a company paying yearly interest to a non-resident 75% parent or associated company may treat such interest as not being a distribution. The conditions are that the interest is yearly interest which is—

(i)   a distribution by virtue only of TCA 1997, s 130(2)(d)(iv),

(ii)   is payable by a company in the ordinary course of a trade carried on by it and would but for TCA 1997, s 130(2)(d)(iv) be deductible as a trading expense in computing its trading income, and

(iii) is not interest to which TCA 1997, s 452(2) (trade interest payable to a company resident in a relevant territory - see above) applies.

Where the conditions are satisfied in respect of any yearly interest payable by a company for an accounting period, and which is paid on or after 1 February 2007, and the company makes an election, which should be submitted to the inspector of taxes with the company's corporation tax return for the period, to have that interest treated as not being a distribution, TCA 1997, s 130(2)(d)(iv) will not apply to that interest (TCA 1997, s 452(3A)).

The election can be made only in respect of yearly interest. Not being a distribution by reason of the election, the interest will accordingly be payable subject to deduction of tax at the standard rate of income tax in accordance with TCA 1997, s 246. Since the interest will be payable to a company not resident in a relevant territory, the exemption provided for by TCA 1997, s 246(3)(h) (see **4.305**) will not be available. Only exceptionally, therefore, will it be in the interests of a company to make the election.

In respect of any interest paid or other distribution made on or after 6 February 2003, interest (apart from interest to which TCA 1997, s 452 or 845A applies – see above) paid to a company resident in a Member State of the European Communities and not resident in Ireland is treated as not being a distribution by virtue of TCA 1997, s 130(2)(d)(iv). A company is a resident of a Member State of the EC if, by virtue of the law of that State, it is resident for the purposes of tax (being any tax imposed in the Member State which corresponds to corporation tax in Ireland) in that State (TCA 1997, s 130(2B)). Thus, interest claimed as a charge on income and paid to an affiliated company resident in the EC will not be treated as a distribution by virtue only of the residence position of the recipient. The withholding requirement of TCA 1997, s 246 in relation to such interest is disapplied by virtue of TCA 1997, s 246(3)(h) (interest paid … "in the ordinary course of a … business").

1997, s The position regarding the withholding tax requirement of TCA 1997, s 246(2) and interest within TCA 1997, s 130(2)(d)(iv) generally was the subject matter of the 1986 Supreme Court case *Asahi Synthetic Fibres (Ireland) Ltd v Murphy* 3 ITR 246. The point at issue was whether interest paid by an Irish company to its Japanese parent company was correctly charged with tax under Schedule D and therefore subject to deduction of income tax in accordance with TCA 1997, s 246(2) (then FA 1974 s 31), and at the rate (10%) prescribed by article 12 paragraph 2 of the Ireland/Japan double tax treaty. The Revenue view in that case was that Schedule F did not apply because of the provisions of TCA 1997, s 826(1) (then ITA 1967 s 361) and those of the tax treaty; that the treaty takes precedence over any other enactment; that article 11 paragraph 3 of the treaty specifically excludes from the meaning of the term "dividend" income arising out of debt claims; that article 12 paragraph 2 of the treaty provides that interest may by taxed in the state in which it arises; and that a charge to tax is imposed by TCA 1997, s 246(2) in respect of interest.

It was held in the Supreme Court that the interest in question was not a dividend within the meaning of article 11 of the treaty but a payment of interest to which article 12 applied (which was common ground in any event). It was, however, further held that the payment was nevertheless a distribution within the meaning of TCA 1997, s 130(2)(d)(iv) and that, in this respect, there was no conflict between that provision and the tax treaty. Tax was chargeable, therefore, under Schedule F and not under Schedule D and TCA 1997, s 246(2) did not apply so that there was no obligation to withhold tax on payment.

Arising out of that decision, it is appropriate to distinguish between cases involving tax treaties containing a definition of "dividends" which reflects the wider meaning of "distributions" in TCA 1997, s 130(2)(d)(iv) (mainly those treaties which have been concluded or amended following that enactment). Thus, the later treaties generally contain in the definition of "dividends" wording such as "... any income or distribution assimilated to income from shares under the taxation law of the Contracting State of which the company paying the dividends or income or making the distribution is resident". This is in contrast with older treaties where the typical wording is "...income from other *corporate rights* assimilated to income from shares by the taxation laws of the Contracting State of which the company making the distribution is a resident". The older wording is narrower in scope and by confining the reference to "income ... assimilated to income from shares" to income from "corporate rights", does not cover the case of interest treated as a distribution by virtue of TCA 1997, s 130(2)(d)(iv). There are now, however, a number of newer treaties which contain the narrower definition of "dividends".

Revenue practice in the cases of pre-1976 tax treaties containing the narrower definition of "dividends" is to treat interest falling within TCA 1997, s 130(2)(d)(iv) as interest for tax deductibility purposes. Thus, interest satisfying the usual conditions for deductibility as a trading expense will be deductible to the paying company for Case I purposes while interest satisfying the requirements of TCA 1997, s 247 (see **4.403**) will be deductible to the paying company as a charge on income.

Treaties that contain the narrower definition of "dividends" (including some post-1976 treaties – China, India, Israel, Romania) are Belgium, Canada, China, Cyprus, France, Germany, India, Israel, Italy, Japan, Luxembourg, Netherlands, Pakistan, Romania and Zambia.

Interest in all of the above cases is subject to dividend withholding tax (DWT) on payment at the appropriate treaty rate *applicable to interest* in each case; since under domestic legislation the interest will always be a distribution in accordance with TCA 1997, s 130(2)(d)(iv), it will not be charged to tax under Schedule D and TCA 1997, s 246(2) cannot apply. The procedure to be followed by the paying company in these cases (except where, in accordance with TCA 1997, s 172D (see **11.116.6**), there is complete exemption from DWT in the case of a distribution to a qualifying non-resident person) is to deduct DWT at the full rate; the recipient is then entitled to claim repayment of the excess DWT by reference to the treaty rate applicable to interest.

Since interest in the cases discussed above will not be paid subject to deduction of income tax, a technical difficulty may arise in situations where such interest is being claimed as a charge on income. This is because, to qualify as a charge on income, the interest may be subject to the requirement in TCA 1997, s 243(5) to deduct income tax on payment. It is understood that in practice this requirement would not in such circumstances prevent a deduction as a charge on income.

Certain of the later tax treaties, although containing the wider definition of "dividends", also contain a non-discrimination article the effect of which is that interest within the meaning of TCA 1997, s 130(2)(d)(iv) will be tax deductible in determining the taxable profits of the paying company (whether as a trading expense or as a charge on income) where it otherwise satisfies the normal criteria for deductibility. The treaties in question are those with Bulgaria, Canada, Croatia, the Czech Republic, Denmark, Estonia, Finland, Hungary, Korean Republic, Latvia, Lithuania, Malaysia, Mexico, New Zealand, Norway, Portugal, Romania, the Slovak Republic, Slovenia, South Africa, Spain and the US. In addition, the protocol to the treaty with the Russian Federation confirms the allowability of interest on a similar basis.

In the cases of the treaties with Sweden and Switzerland, non-discrimination articles provide for the deductibility of interest for the purpose of determining the taxable profits of the paying company but this is qualified in each case. The relieving measure in each case has effect except where the paragraph that defines "dividends" in the relevant Dividends article applies. Since that paragraph has application in any case where an Irish company pays interest to a 75% related overseas affiliate, the non-discrimination provision dealing with deductibility of interest cannot then have effect. It is difficult, however, to understand why it would be intended that interest paid by an Irish company and treated as a distribution under Irish domestic law should not be deductible to the paying company in accordance with the non-discrimination article. A somewhat similar situation arises in the cases of the treaties with Israel and Poland. Several treaties, those with Belgium, China, India and Romania, although they contain the narrow definition of "dividends", also have non-discrimination articles that provide for the deductibility of interest as a trading expense. Interest falling within TCA 1997, s 130(2)(d)(iv) will in these cases be tax deductible to the paying company on the same basis as any other interest.

In the light of the above, the remaining treaties which confirm the unfavourable treatment (ie, non deductibility for tax purposes) of interest to which TCA 1997, s 130(2)(d)(iv) applies are those with Australia, Israel, Poland and Switzerland (although interest is deductible in any event where paid to companies resident in Poland, an EU Member State from 1 May 2004.

Interest payable to companies resident in other EU Member States is deductible for tax purposes on the basis of the non-discrimination principle of the Treaty of Rome. However, all such interest is now deductible in any event by virtue of TCA 1997, s 130(2B) or, where applicable, TCA 1997, s 452 or 845A.

It is important to note that interest falling within TCA 1997, s 130(2)(d)(iv), whether deductible as interest in accordance with the Revenue practice relating to pre-1976 treaty definitions of "interest, the non-discrimination article of a tax treaty, or the non-discrimination principles of the Treaty of Rome, is generally subject to DWT (see **11.116**). In practice, returns of such interest in accordance with the requirements of TCA 1997, s 172K need only be made on an annual basis. Interest as described in TCA 1997, s 130(2)(d)(iv) but which, by virtue of TCA 1997, s 452 or 845A is not a distribution (see above), is not subject to DWT.

The position relating to interest falling within TCA 1997, s 130(2)(d)(iv), as dealt with above, is now quite complex and the following table may therefore be helpful in identifying the appropriate tax treatment in individual cases.

Treaty Country	*"Dividends" definition*	*Treaty override*[9]	*Deductible*[2]	*DWT rate*[1,3]	*Condition for lower DWT rate*[8]
Australia	Broad			0%[4]	
Austria	Broad		Yes[5]	0%[4]	
Belgium	Narrow	Yes	Yes[5,6]	15%[7]	
Bulgaria	Broad	Yes	Yes	5%/10%[4]	25% of capital
Canada	Broad		Yes[11]	5/15%[4]	10% voting power
China	Narrow	Yes	Yes	10%[7]	
Croatia	Broad	Yes	Yes	5%/10%[4]	10% voting power
Cyprus	Narrow		Yes[5,6]	0%[7]	
Czech Republic	Broad	Yes	Yes[5]	5%/15%[4]	25% voting power
Denmark	Broad	Yes	Yes[5]	0%[4]	
Estonia	Broad	Yes	Yes[5]	5%/15%[4]	25% voting power
Finland	Broad	Yes	Yes[5]	0%[4]	
France	Narrow		Yes[5,6]	0%[7]	
Germany	Narrow		Yes[5,6]	0%[7]	
Greece	Broad	Yes	Yes[5]	5%/15%[4]	25% voting power
Hungary	Broad	Yes	Yes[5]	5%/15%[4]	10% of capital
Iceland	Broad	Yes	Yes	5%/15%[4]	25% of capital

India	Narrow	Yes	Yes	10% [7]	
Israel	Narrow			10% [7]	
Italy	Narrow		Yes [5,6]	10% [7]	
Japan	Narrow		Yes [6]	10% [7]	
Korean Republic	Broad	Yes	Yes	0% [4]	
Latvia	Broad	Yes	Yes [5]	5%/15% [4]	25% voting power
Lithuania	Broad	Yes	Yes [5]	5%/15% [4]	25% voting power
Luxembourg	Narrow		Yes [5,6]	0% [7]	
Malaysia	Broad	Yes	Yes	10% [4]	
Mexico	Broad	Yes	Yes	5%/10% [4]	25% voting stock
Netherlands	Narrow		Yes [5,6]	0% [7]	
New Zealand	Broad	Yes	Yes	0% [4]	
Norway	Broad	Yes	Yes	5%/15% [4]	25% of capital
Pakistan	Narrow		Yes [6]	0% [7]	
Poland	Broad		Yes [5]	0%/15% [4]	25% voting power
Portugal	Broad	Yes	Yes [5]	15% [4]	
Romania	Narrow	Yes	Yes	3% [7]	
Russia	Broad	Yes	Yes	10% [4]	
Slovakia	Broad	Yes	Yes [5]	0%/10% [4]	25% voting power
Slovenia	Broad	Yes	Yes [5]	5%/15% [4]	25% of capital
South Africa	Broad	Yes	Yes	0% [4]	
Spain	Broad	Yes	Yes [5]	0% [4]	
Sweden	Broad		Yes [5]	0% [4]	
Switzerland	Broad			0% [4]	
UK	Broad		Yes [5]	5%/15% [4]	10% voting power
USA	Broad	Yes	Yes	0% [7]	10% voting stock
Zambia	Narrow		Yes [6]	0% [7]	

Notes:

[1] Where an election under TCA 1997, s 452 or 845A is in force, or where TCA 1997, s 130(2B) applies, interest is not treated as a distribution. Accordingly, interest is tax deductible in accordance with basic principles and DWT does not apply. Exceptionally, an election in respect of interest to which TCA 1997, s 452 or 845A applies may not in fact be made. In any such case, the rate of DWT, as indicated in the table, applies.

[2] Interest is deductible, either as a trading expense or as a charge on income.

[3] Except where exemption is claimed in respect of a distribution paid to a qualifying non-resident person, paying company deducts DWT at full standard income tax rate and recipient company claims refund of excess DWT as per treaty. The current standard income tax rate is 20%.

[4] Final tax is at rate provided for in dividends article of tax treaty. DWT is deducted at standard rate and recipient claims refund of excess DWT as per treaty. Treaty rate does not apply where recipient has a permanent establishment in Ireland that is effectively connected with holding from which dividend arises.

5. Deductible on basis of TCA 1997, s 130(2B) unless TCA 1997, s 452 or 845A applies. Applicable from 1 May 2004 in the cases of the 10 new Member States included above.

6. Deductible on basis of Revenue practice for pre-1976 tax treaties.

7. Final tax is at rate provided for in interest article of tax treaty. (Regarding US treaty, see protocol re paragraph 5 of article 10.) DWT is deducted at standard rate and recipient claims refund of excess DWT as per treaty. Treaty rate is available except where recipient has a permanent establishment in Ireland that is effectively connected with indebtedness (but this condition does not apply in case of Pakistan).

8. Minimum percentage of voting power, or holding of capital, required for lower DWT rate in previous column. UK treaty allows for direct or indirect control of voting power.

9. Non-discrimination article (exchange of letters in case of Russia) of treaty provides that interest paid by Irish company is to be deductible in determining that company's taxable profits on same basis as interest paid to a resident of Ireland.

10. In accordance with the Parent-Subsidiary Directive, and subject to conditions, distributions made to a parent company resident in another EU country are exempt from DWT.

11. On basis of article 24(4), interest deductible where paid to a Canadian 75% parent (but not to a fellow subsidiary).

Interest treated as a distribution under TCA 1997, s 130(2)(d) has for many years been referred to as "section 84" interest and the related securities as "section 84" loans or "section 84 financing". A recipient of any such interest, where assessable to income tax, is taxable under Schedule F rather than under Schedule D Case III (since for tax purposes it is a distribution rather than interest).

Apart from interest payments, TCA 1997, s 130(2)(d) treats as a distribution any "other distribution out of assets of the company" in respect of any of the types of securities referred to in (a) to (e) above, unless and to the extent that the amount distributed represents the principal of the loan, debt or other advance secured. For this purpose, no amount is to be regarded as the principal secured by a security in so far as it exceeds any new consideration received by the company for the issue of the security, for example, a premium paid on the redemption of a security or on the repayment of an unsecured loan or advance.

Example 11.106.1

On 1 January 2003, Ms N Rowley advanced €40,000 to Cardigan Ltd in consideration for which she would be paid interest at the rate of 2.5% per annum with a further payment equal to 0.5% of the company's pre-tax profits for a 5 year period ending on 31 December 2007. The company also agreed to pay her a premium of €5,000 on the redemption of the loan.

Since the consideration payable by Cardigan Ltd for the use of the money advanced by Ms Rowley includes an element which varies with the profits of the company, the loan is a security for the purposes of TCA 1997, s 130(2)(d)(iii)(1) so that the combined interest and profit share element is treated as a distribution.

On 31 December 2007, Cardigan Ltd redeemed the loan and paid Ms Rowley €45,000 to include the premium. Being a payment out of the assets of the company in respect of a security within TCA 1997, s 130(2)(d), the premium is a distribution. The first €40,000 of the redemption proceeds is not a distribution since it represents no more than the principal amount of the loan.

Based on the interest and other payments received as set out below and assuming pre-tax profits of €960,000 and €310,000 for the years ended 31 December 2005 and 31 December 2006 respectively, Ms Rowley is taxable under Schedule F for the final two years 2006 and 2007 as follows:

		2006	*2007*
		€	€
31/3/06	Interest at 2.5% for 6 months	500	
30/9/06	Interest at 2.5% for 6 months	500	
31/3/06	0.5% x €960,000	4,800	
31/3/07	Interest at 2.5% for 6 months		500
30/9/07	Interest at 2.5% for 6 months		500
31/3/07	0.5% x €310,000		1,550
31/12/07	Excess of €45,000 over principal €40,000		5,000
Amount of distribution under TCA 1997, s 130(2)(d)		5,800	7,500

11.107 Restrictions on section 130 financing

11.107.1 Introduction

TCA 1997, ss 133-134 restrict the circumstances in which interest or any other distribution falling within TCA 1997, s 130(2)(d)(ii), (iii)(I) or (v), and paid to another company that is within the charge to corporation tax, is to be treated as a distribution. The interest in question here is interest on the types of securities described in (b), (c)(i) and (e) above included in the securities listed in TCA 1997, s 130(2)(d). The restriction, introduced by FA 1984 and extended by subsequent Finance Acts, was intended to curtail so-called "section 84" financing and has resulted in the removal of this form of financing except in a limited number of situations for which specific provision is made. In practice, the various and somewhat complex measures introduced by FA 1984 and later Finance Acts, restricting the availability of section 84 (now section 130) financing, are of somewhat esoteric interest but the following outline of the legislation, and of the circumstances in which section 130 loans may still be availed of, may be useful.

11.107.2 Limitation on meaning of "distribution": general

TCA 1997, s 133 provides that any interest or other distribution paid out of assets of a company ("the borrower") to another company within the charge to corporation tax and which is paid in respect of a security within TCA 1997, s 130(2)(d)(ii), (iii)(I) or (v) is not to be a distribution for the purposes of the Corporation Tax Acts, subject to exceptions. This limitation on the meaning of "distribution" does not apply where certain conditions relating to the lender and the borrower are satisfied.

The restriction on the meaning of "distribution" is contained in TCA 1997, s 133(2). That subsection provides that any interest or other distribution paid out of assets of a company ("the borrower") to another company within the charge to corporation tax and which is paid in respect of a security within TCA 1997, s 130(2)(d)(ii), (iii)(I) or (v) (a *relevant security*) is not to be regarded as a distribution for the purposes of the Corporation Tax Acts, subject to exceptions. The restriction is not applicable:

(a) in the case of "foreign" section 130 loans, ie loans advanced by a company out of money subscribed for the share capital of the company where that share capital is beneficially owned, directly or indirectly, by a non-resident or non-residents (TCA 1997, s 133(3)): these loans are also excepted from a similar restriction as provided for in TCA 1997, s 134, subject to certain conditions (see below);

(b) where the consideration given by the borrower for the use of the moneys borrowed represents more than a reasonable commercial return for the use of the money borrowed – in which case only so much of the interest in respect of the security (the amount borrowed) as exceeds a reasonable commercial return is treated as a distribution (TCA 1997, s 133(4)); or

(c) to any interest paid by the borrower, in an accounting period of the borrower, to another company in respect of "relevant principal" (see below) advanced by that other company, where

    (i) in that accounting period the borrower carries on in the State a "specified trade",

    (ii) the relevant principal is used in the course of the specified trade:

        (I) for the activities of the trade consisting of the manufacture of goods within the meaning of "specified trade" (see below), or

        (II) where the borrower is an agricultural society or a fishery society, for the activities of the trade consisting of "selling by wholesale" referred to in the definition of "specified trade", and

    (iii) the interest, if it were not a distribution, would be treated as a trading expense of that trade for that accounting period (TCA 1997, s 133(5)).

A *specified trade* is a trade which consists "wholly or mainly" (see below) of:

(i) the manufacture of goods, including activities which would qualify as manufacturing for the purposes of the 10% tax rate (but not those in respect of which a certificate has been given by the Minister for Finance under TCA 1997, s 445 – see **7.205.16** – or those of a qualifying shipping trade within the meaning of TCA 1997, s 407 – see **7.205.6**); or

(ii) where the borrower mentioned in (c) above is a 75% subsidiary of an agricultural society or a fishery society (see below), either or both of:

    (I) the manufacture of goods as described in (i) above, and

    (II) the selling by wholesale of agricultural products (in the case of an agricultural society) or fish (in the case of a fishery society).

Relevant principal means an amount of money advanced to a borrower by a company which is within the charge to corporation tax and the ordinary activities of which include the lending of money, where:

(i) the consideration given by the borrower for that amount is a relevant security (see above); and

(ii) interest or any other distribution is paid out of the assets of the borrower in respect of that security.

Agricultural society and *fishery society* have the meanings assigned to them by TCA 1997, s 443(16) (see **7.205.11**). *Selling by wholesale* means selling goods of any class to a person who carries on a business of selling goods of that class or uses goods of that class for the purposes of a trade or undertaking carried on by the person.

A trade is regarded, as respects an accounting period, as consisting *wholly or mainly* of particular activities only if the total amount receivable by the borrower from sales made or, as the case may be, in payment for services rendered in the course of the activities in the accounting period is not less than 75% of the total amount receivable by the borrower from all sales made in the course of the trade in that period.

TCA 1997, s 443(6) provides that certain manufactured goods are to be treated as not being manufactured goods for the purposes of the 10% corporation tax rate (see **7.204.3**). As respects interest paid in respect of relevant principal advanced before 20 April 1990 to a company which carries on in the State a trade which would be a specified trade but for TCA 1997, s 443(6), that trade is treated as a specified trade for the purposes of TCA 1997, s 133.

110% Limit

Notwithstanding the exception in TCA 1997, s 133(5) (see above – loans to borrowers carrying on a specified trade), where at any time on or after 12 April 1989 the total of the amounts of relevant principal advanced by a company in respect of relevant securities held directly or indirectly by it at that time exceeds 110% of the total corresponding amount on 12 April 1989, such part of any interest paid at that time to the company in respect of relevant principal as bears, in relation to the total amount of interest so paid to the company, the same proportion as the excess bears in relation to the current amounts of relevant principal is not to be treated as a distribution for the purposes of the Corporation Tax Acts in the hands of the company (TCA 1997, s 133(7)). That interest, however, remains a distribution from the standpoint of the borrower.

75% Limit

TCA 1997, s 133(8) provides for a 75% ceiling in respect of section 130 loans (apart from "foreign" section 130 loans and loans with interest in excess of a reasonable commercial return – see (a) and (b) above) made on or after 31 January 1990. Such loans made in excess of that ceiling are permitted in certain exceptional cases, ie new grant-aided manufacturing projects where certain specified conditions are met.

Where at any time on or after 31 January 1990 the total of the amounts of relevant principal advanced by a company in respect of relevant securities held directly or indirectly by it at that time exceeds 75% of the total corresponding amount on 12 April 1989, interest paid on relevant principal advanced on or after 31 January 1990 is not to be treated as a distribution for the purposes of the Corporation Tax Acts in the hands of the company (TCA 1997, s 133(8)(b)). That interest, however, remains a distinction form the standpoint of the borrower.

The restriction in TCA 1997, s 133(8)(b) as described above does not apply where the interest is within the terms of TCA 1997, s 133(8)(c). That interest is such interest as is paid for a *specified period* (ie the period beginning on the date on which the relevant principal was advanced and ending on the date on which it is to be repaid or, if earlier, 11 April 2001 where the relevant principal was advanced before 11 April 1994 and, in any other case, at the end of seven years from the date the relevant principal was advanced) in respect of relevant principal advanced and which was, at the time the relevant principal was advanced, specified in the list referred to in TCA 1997, s 133(8)(c)(iv) ((iv) below) where:

(i) the relevant principal is advanced by the company to a borrower who was in negotiation before 31 January 1990 with any company for an amount of relevant principal;

(ii) the borrower had, prior to 31 January 1990, received a written offer of grant aid from the Industrial Development Authority (IDA), the Shannon Free Airport Development Company Ltd (SFADCO) or Údarás na Gaeltachta (ÚnaG) in respect of a specified trade or a proposed specified trade for the purposes of which trade the relevant principal was borrowed;

(iii) the specified trade is one which the borrower commenced on or after 31 January 1990 or is one in respect of which the borrower was committed, under a business plan approved by the IDA, SFADCO or ÚnaG to the creation of additional employment;

(iv) the specified trade of the borrower was, before 25 March 1992, included in a list prepared by the IDA and approved before that day by the Minister for Enterprise, Trade and Employment and the Minister for Finance, being a list specifying a particular amount of relevant principal in respect of each trade as is considered to be essential for the success of that trade; and

(v) the borrower, or a company connected with the borrower, did not commence to carry on international financial services activities (within the meaning of TCA 1997, s 446 – see **7.206**) after 20 April 1990 and did not intend to do so (TCA 1997, s 133(8)(c)).

The above exception to the 75% ceiling is not to apply in respect of any interest on relevant principal advanced after the time when the total amount, within the terms of the exception, advanced by all lenders exceeds €215,855,473.33.

For the purposes of TCA 1997, s 133(8) (and also for the purposes of TCA 1997, s 133(9), (10) – see below), relevant principal advanced at any time on or after a day includes any relevant principal advanced on or after that day under an agreement entered into before that day (TCA 1997, s 133(8)(d)(i)). Where on or after 6 May 1993 the period of repayment of relevant principal was extended, whether or not in accordance with the terms of the loan agreement, the lending company is treated as having received repayment of the relevant principal and as having advanced a corresponding amount of relevant principal on the date on which the relevant principal originally fell to be repaid (TCA 1997, s 133(8)(d)(ii)). Extending the repayment period at any time on or after 6 May 1993 will accordingly have the effect that the relevant principal in question will be regarded as having been advanced at that time (and therefore on or after 31 January 1990) so that interest paid in respect of it may be treated as not being a distribution if the 75% limit is exceeded.

Where, at any time after an amount of relevant principal is specified in a list as described above (or in a list in accordance with TCA 1997, s 133(9)(c)(ii) or (10)(b)(ii) – see below), a company advances, or is treated as advancing, to a borrower relevant principal the interest on which is treated as a distribution by virtue only of the exception in TCA 1997, s 133(8)(c) (or the exceptions in TCA 1997, s 133(9)(c), (10)(b) – see below), the amount of relevant principal specified in the list is treated as reduced by the amount of the relevant principal so advanced, or treated as advanced, to a borrower and the amount so reduced is treated as the amount specified on the list (TCA 1997, s 133(8)(d)(iii)). In other words, any amounts of relevant principal advanced after an amount of relevant principal has been specified on a list will go to use up the amount so specified.

However, in the case of relevant principal which, before 7 December 1993, was repaid before the scheduled repayment date for that relevant principal, and in respect of which interest was treated as a distribution by virtue only of TCA 1997, s 133(8)(c) (or TCA 1997, s 133(9)(c), (10)(b)), any further amount or amounts of relevant principal advanced by way of replacement (up to the amount repaid) will not be treated as reducing the amount specified on the IDA list in the way described above. In any such case, the lender will be treated as having received repayment of the relevant principal on the scheduled repayment date of the first loan and as having at the same time advanced a corresponding amount of relevant principal (TCA 1997, s 133(12)(b), (c)). In short, a replacement loan made before 7 December 1993 and made not later than the scheduled repayment date of the original loan will not have the effect of reducing the amount specified in the IDA list.

In this connection, where there is more than one further advance of relevant principal, the amount to which the restriction in TCA 1997, s 133(8)(d)(iii) will not apply is to be as far as possible an earlier rather than a later further advance (TCA 1997, s 133(12)(d)).

Interest which would otherwise fail to be treated as a distribution by virtue only of TCA 1997, s 133(8)(d)(iii) will nevertheless be treated as a distribution if paid in respect of relevant principal advanced before 7 December 1993 (TCA 1997, s 133(12)(e)).

Where, for the purposes of TCA 1997, s 133(8), (9) or (10), a company on or after 31 January 1990 has advanced relevant principal to a borrower under the terms of an agreement and, under those terms or under the terms of any other agreement, it assigns to another company part or all of its rights and obligations under the first-mentioned agreement in relation to the relevant principal, such assignment will be deemed not to have taken place (TCA 1997, s 133(8)(e)). This measure prevents lending companies from switching amounts of relevant principal between them with a view to avoiding excess amounts being held by one of them in the context of the 75% limit.

40% Limit

A 40% limit applies in respect of section 130 loans (apart from "foreign" section 130 loans and loans with interest in excess of a reasonable commercial return) made on or after 31 December 1991. Such loans made in excess of that limit are permitted in certain exceptional cases, ie new manufacturing projects where certain specified conditions are met. Where, however, at any time after 31 December 1991 the volume of loans outstanding in the case of any lender is less than the 40% ceiling amount, that lender is required make, as far as possible, any section 130 loans to the exceptional cases. Where, at any time in the period from 18 April 1991 to 31 December 1991, a section 130 loan is repaid by a non-manufacturing Shannon company, the 40% limit will apply to the lending company in question on and from the date of that repayment.

TCA 1997, s 133(9) provides, as respects relevant principal advanced before 20 December 1991, that where at any time on or after 31 December 1991 the amounts of relevant principal advanced by a company in respect of relevant securities held directly or indirectly by it at any time exceeds 40% of the total corresponding amount on 12

April 1989, interest paid on advances made on or after 31 December 1991 is not to be treated as a distribution for the purposes of the Corporation Tax Acts in the hands of the company. That interest, however, remains a distribution from the standpoint of the borrower.

Furthermore, if the total amount of relevant principal outstanding at any time on or after 31 December 1991 is less than the 40% ceiling amount, the ceiling amount is reduced at that time to that lower amount – unless the lending bank could prove that at all times on or after 1 April 1990 it had as far as possible made advances to borrowers of relevant principal in respect of the interest on which the 40% limit does not or would not apply by reason of TCA 1997, s 133(9)(c) (see below).

Where at any time during the period from 18 April 1991 up to the time immediately before 31 December 1991 a company carrying on one or more trading operations within the meaning of TCA 1997, s 445(1) (ie a non-manufacturing Shannon company eligible for the 10% corporation tax rate) repaid an amount of relevant principal, the operative date for the purposes of the 40% limit has effect from the date of that repayment.

As respects interest paid to a company in respect of relevant principal advanced on or after 31 December 1991, the restriction in TCA 1997, s 133(9)(b) as described above does not apply where the interest is within the terms of TCA 1997, s 133(9)(c). Accordingly, the restriction will not apply where:

(i) the specified trade is one which the borrower commenced to carry on after 31 January 1990 or is one in respect of which the borrower is committed, under a business plan approved by the Industrial Development Authority, Shannon Free Airport Development Company Ltd or Údarás na Gaeltachta, to the creation of additional employment;

(ii) the specified trade was selected by the IDA for inclusion on a list, approved by the Minister for Enterprise, Trade and Employment and the Minister for Finance, which list specifies a particular amount of relevant principal in respect of each trade which amount is considered to be essential for the success of that trade; and

(iii) the borrower, or a company connected with the borrower, did not commence to carry on relevant trading operations within the meaning of TCA 1997, s 446 (international financial services activities) after 20 April 1990 and does not intend to do so.

The foregoing exception does not to apply in respect of interest on relevant principal advanced after the time when the total of the amounts, within the terms of the exception, advanced by all lenders exceeds €317,434,519.61 plus any remaining balance from the earlier €215,855,473.33 limit referred to in TCA 1997, s 133(8)(c) (see above) (TCA 1997, s 133(11)).

For the purposes of TCA 1997, s 133(9), relevant principal advanced at any time on or after a day includes any relevant principal advanced on or after that day under an agreement entered into before that day (TCA 1997, s 133(8)(d)(i)). Where on or after 6 May 1993 a period of repayment of relevant principal was extended, whether or not in accordance with the terms of the loan agreement, the lending company is treated as having received repayment of the relevant principal and as having advanced a corresponding amount of relevant principal on the date on which the relevant principal originally fell to be repaid (TCA 1997, s 133(8)(d)(ii)). Extending the repayment period at any time on or after 6 May 1993 will accordingly have the effect that the relevant principal in question will be regarded as having been advanced at that time so that interest paid in respect of it may be treated as not being a distribution if the 40% limit is exceeded.

Where, at any time after an amount of relevant principal is specified in a list as described above, a company advances, or is treated as advancing, to a borrower relevant principal the interest on which is treated as a distribution by virtue only of the exception in TCA 1997, s 133(9)(c), the amount of relevant principal specified in the list is treated as reduced by the amount of the relevant principal so advanced, or treated as advanced, to a borrower and the amount so reduced is treated as the amount specified on the list (TCA 1997, s 133(8)(d)(iii)). In other words, any amounts of relevant principal advanced after an amount of relevant principal has been specified on a list will go to use up the amount so specified.

However, in the case of relevant principal which, before 7 December 1993, was repaid before the scheduled repayment date for that relevant principal, and in respect of which interest was treated as a distribution by virtue only of TCA 1997, s 133(9)(c), any further amount or amounts of relevant principal advanced by way of replacement (up to the amount repaid) will not be treated as reducing the amount specified on the IDA list in the way described above. In any such case, the lender will be treated as having received repayment of the relevant principal on the scheduled repayment date of the first loan and as having at the same time advanced a corresponding amount of relevant principal (TCA 1997, s 133(12)(b), (c)). In short, a replacement loan made before 7 December 1993 and made not later than the scheduled repayment date of the original loan will not have the effect of reducing the amount specified in the IDA list.

In this connection, where there is more than one further advance of relevant principal, the amount to which the restriction in TCA 1997, s 133(8)(d)(iii) will not apply is to be as far as possible an earlier rather than a later further advance (TCA 1997, s 133(12)(d)).

Interest which would otherwise fail to be treated as a distribution by virtue only of TCA 1997, s 133(8)(d)(iii) will nevertheless be treated as a distribution if paid in respect of relevant principal advanced before 7 December 1993 (TCA 1997, s 133(12)(e)).

Where, for the purposes of TCA 1997, s 133(9), a company on or after 31 January 1990 has advanced relevant principal to a borrower under the terms of an agreement and, under those terms or under the terms of any other agreement, it assigns to another company part or all of its rights and obligations under the first-mentioned agreement in relation to the relevant principal, such assignment will be deemed not to have taken place (TCA 1997, s 133(8)(e)). This measure prevents lending companies from switching amounts of relevant principal between them with a view to avoiding excess amounts being held by one of them in the context of the 40% limit.

11.107.3   Loans made on or after 20 December 1991

Subject to certain exceptions, interest paid in respect of section 130 loans (apart from "foreign" section 130 loans and loans with interest in excess of a reasonable commercial return) made on or after 20 December 1991 will not be treated as a distribution.

TCA 1997, s 133(10)(a) provides that any interest paid to a company in respect of relevant principal advanced by the company on or after 20 December 1991 is not to be treated as a distribution for the purposes of the Corporation Tax Acts in the hands of the company. The restriction in TCA 1997, s 133(10)(a) as described above does not apply where the interest is within the terms of TCA 1997, s 133(10)(b). That interest is such interest as is paid for a *specified period* (ie the period beginning on the date on which the relevant principal was advanced and ending on the date it is to be repaid or, if earlier, 11 April 2001 where the relevant principal was advanced before 11 April 1994 and, in any other case, at the end of seven years from the date the relevant principal was advanced) in respect of relevant principal advanced and which was, at the time the relevant principal was advanced, specified in the list referred to in (ii) below where:

(i)   the specified trade is one which the borrower commenced to carry on after 31 January 1990 or is a specified trade in respect of which the borrower is committed under a business plan approved by the Industrial Development Authority (IDA), the Shannon Free Airport Development Company Ltd or Údarás na Gaeltachta to the creation of additional employment;

(ii)   prior to 25 March 1992 the specified trade of the borrower was included in a list prepared by the IDA and approved before that day by the Minister for Enterprise, Trade and Employment and the Minister for Finance, being a list specifying a particular amount of relevant principal in respect of each trade which amount is considered to be essential for the success of that trade; and

(iii)   the borrower is not a company which carries on relevant trading operations within the meaning of TCA 1997, s 446 (international financial services activities) and does not intend to do so.

The foregoing exception does not to apply in respect of interest on relevant principal advanced after the time when the total of the amounts, within the terms of the exception, advanced by all lenders exceeds €317,434,519.61 plus any remaining balance from the earlier €215,855,473.33 limit referred to in TCA 1997, s 133(8)(c) (see above).

For the purposes of TCA 1997, s 133(10), relevant principal advanced at any time on or after a day includes any relevant principal advanced on or after that day under an agreement entered into before that day (TCA 1997, s 133(8)(d)(i)). Where on or after 6 May 1993 a period of repayment of relevant principal is extended, whether or not in accordance with the terms of the loan agreement, the lending company is treated as having received repayment of the relevant principal and as having advanced a corresponding amount of relevant principal on the date on which the relevant principal originally fell to be repaid (TCA 1997, s 133(8)(d)(ii)). Extending the repayment period at any time on or after 6 May 1993 will accordingly have the effect that the relevant principal in question will be regarded as having been advanced at that time.

Where, at any time after an amount of relevant principal is specified in a list as described above, a company advances, or is treated as advancing, to a borrower relevant principal the interest on which is treated as a distribution by virtue only of the exception in TCA 1997, s 133(10)(b), the amount of relevant principal specified in the list is treated as reduced by the amount of the relevant principal so advanced, or treated as advanced, to a borrower and the amount so reduced is treated as the amount specified on the list (TCA 1997, s 133(8)(d)(iii)). In other words, any amounts of relevant principal advanced after an amount of relevant principal has been specified on a list will go to use up the amount so specified.

However, in the case of relevant principal which, before 7 December 1993, was repaid before the scheduled repayment date for that relevant principal, and in respect of which interest was treated as a distribution by virtue only of TCA 1997, s 133(10)(b), any further amount or amounts of relevant principal advanced by way of replacement (up to the amount repaid) will not be treated as reducing the amount specified on the IDA list in the way described above. In any such case, the lender will be treated as having received repayment of the relevant principal on the scheduled repayment date of the first loan and as having at the same time advanced a corresponding amount of relevant principal (TCA 1997, s 133(12)(b), (c)). In short, a replacement loan made before 7 December 1993 and made not later than the scheduled repayment date of the original loan will not have the effect of reducing the amount specified in the IDA list.

In this connection, where there is more than one further advance of relevant principal, the amount to which the restriction in TCA 1997, s 133(8)(d)(iii) will not apply is to be as far as possible an earlier rather than a later further advance (TCA 1997, s 133(12)(d)).

Interest which would otherwise fail to be treated as a distribution by virtue only of TCA 1997, s 133(8)(d)(iii) will nevertheless be treated as a distribution if paid in respect of relevant principal advanced before 7 December 1993 (TCA 1997, s 133(12)(e)).

Where, for the purposes of TCA 1997, s 133(10), a company on or after 31 January 1990 has advanced relevant principal to a borrower under the terms of an agreement and, under those terms or under the terms of any other agreement, it assigns to another company part or all of its rights and obligations under the first-mentioned agreement in relation to the relevant principal, such assignment will be deemed not to have taken place (TCA 1997, s 133(8)(e)). This measure prevents lending companies from switching amounts of relevant principal between them with a view to avoiding excess amounts being held by one of them in the context of the 40% limit.

11.107.4   Foreign currency section 130 loans

TCA 1997, s 133(13) provides that interest paid to a company in respect of foreign currency denominated relevant principal for a *relevant period* (ie basically a period between interest payment dates) beginning on or after 30 January 1991 is not to be treated as a distribution for the purposes of the Corporation Tax Acts in the hands of the company if, at any time during the period, the rate applicable exceeds 80% of EIBOR ("the three month European Interbank Offered Rate"), except interest paid to a company in respect of relevant principal advanced by the company:

    (i)   before 30 January 1991 under an agreement made before that date and where the rate on that date exceeded 80% of EIBOR, but not as respects any relevant period commencing on or after 20 December 1991 if in that relevant period the rate exceeds the rate that would have applied if the loan had remained in the currency it was denominated in on 30 January 1991;

    (ii)   on or after 30 January 1991 which is included in the lists referred to in TCA 1997, s 133(8)(c), (9)(c) or (10)(b) (see above) and which was for the purposes of a specified trade of a borrower certified by the Minister for Enterprise, Trade and Employment as having received an undertaking that the interest would be treated as a distribution, but provided that this exception is not to apply for any relevant period commencing on or after 20 December 1991 if in that relevant period the rate of interest applicable to the relevant principal exceeds:

        (a)   a rate (currently 25%) approved by the Minister for Finance in consultation with the Minister for Enterprise, Trade and Employment, or

(b) where it is lower than the rate so approved and the relevant principal was advanced on or after 30 January 1991 and before 20 December 1991, the rate that would have applied if the relevant principal had continued to be denominated in the currency in which it was denominated when it was advanced;

(iii) on or after 18 April 1991 where the interest rate applicable exceeds 80% of EIBOR by reason only that the relevant principal is denominated in sterling; or

(iv) to a borrower which is a company carrying on one or more trading operations within the meaning of TCA 1997, s 445(1) (non-manufacturing Shannon activities eligible for the 10% corporation tax rate).

In relation to the undertaking, mentioned in (ii) above, to the effect that the interest will be treated as a distribution, it is understood that all of the undrawn balances on the 1990 list (€215,855,473.33 limit) have been certified by the Minister for Enterprise, Trade and Employment as having received that undertaking. In relation to the 1991 list (€317,434,519.61 limit), it is necessary in individual cases to check that the undertaking has been received. In the list this is indicated by the comment "yes" in the column headed "high coupon undertaking".

11.107.5 "Foreign" section 130 financing

TCA 1997, s 134 applies to "foreign" section 130 loans, ie loans advanced by a company out of money subscribed for the share capital of the company where that share capital is beneficially owned, directly or indirectly, by a non-resident or non-residents (TCA 1997, s 134(2)).

TCA 1997, s 134(3) provides that any interest or other distribution paid out of assets of a company ("the borrower") to another company within the charge to corporation tax and which is paid in respect of a security (*relevant security*) within TCA 1997, s 130(2)(d)(ii), (iii)(I) or (v) is not to be regarded as a distribution for the purposes of the Corporation Tax Acts, subject to exceptions. The restriction is not applicable:

(a) where the consideration given by the borrower for the use of the moneys borrowed represents more than a reasonable commercial return for the use of the money borrowed – in which case only so much of the interest in respect of the security (the amount borrowed) as exceeds a reasonable commercial return is treated as a distribution; or

(b) to any interest paid by the borrower, in an accounting period of the borrower, to another company the ordinary trading activities of which include the lending of money, where

(i) in that accounting period the borrower carries on in the State a specified trade, and

(ii) the interest, if it were not a distribution, would be treated as a trading expense of that trade for that accounting period.

A *specified trade* is a trade which consists "wholly or mainly" (see below) of:

(i) the manufacture of goods, including activities which would qualify as manufacturing for the purposes of the 10% tax rate (but not those of a

qualifying shipping trade within the meaning of TCA 1997, s 407 – see
7.205.6); or

(ii)   where the borrower mentioned in (b) above is a 75% subsidiary of an
       agricultural society or a fishery society, either or both of:

   (I)   the manufacture of goods as described in (i) above, and

   (II)   the selling by wholesale of agricultural products (in the case of an
          agricultural society) or fish (in the case of a fishery society), or

(iii) in the case of any interest or other distribution paid by a borrower under an
       obligation entered into before 13 May 1986, or before 1 September 1986 in
       accordance with negotiations in progress between the borrower and a lender
       before 13 May 1986, the rendering of services in the course of a service
       undertaking in respect of which an employment grant was made by the
       Industrial Development Authority under section 2 of the Industrial
       Development (No 2) Act 1981.

Agricultural society and *fishery society* have the meanings assigned to them by TCA
1997, s 443(16) (see **7.205.11**). *Selling by wholesale* means selling goods of any class to
a person who carries on a business of selling goods of that class or uses goods of that
class for the purposes of a trade or undertaking carried on by the person.

A trade is regarded, as respects an accounting period, as consisting *wholly or mainly*
of particular activities only if the total amount receivable by the borrower from sales
made or, as the case may be, in payment for services rendered in the course of the
activities in the accounting period is not less than 75% of the total amount receivable by
the borrower from all sales made in the course of the trade in that period.

11.107.6   New loans qualifying as section 130 loans

In the light of the various restrictions on the meaning of "distribution" for the purposes
of section 130 lending, and the complex legislation described above, it will be useful to
identify what loans may still be made as section 130 loans. These are:

(a)   all "foreign" section 130 loans, ie where the section 130 funds lent have been
      advanced out of money subscribed for the share capital of the lending company
      and that share capital is beneficially owned directly or indirectly by a person or
      persons resident outside Ireland, but subject to the conditions of TCA 1997,
      s 134;

(b)   Irish pound denominated section 84 loans provided (i) the specified trade was
      one which the borrower commenced to carry on after 31 January 1990 or is a
      trade in respect of which the borrower was committed to the creation of
      additional employment, (ii) the trade was included, before 25 March 1992, in
      the list prepared by the IDA and approved by the Minister for Enterprise, Trade
      and Employment and the Minister for Finance, and (iii) the borrower was not a
      company which commenced to carry on IFSC operations after 20 April 1990
      and did not intend to do so – subject to the limit of €317,434,519.61 plus any
      remaining balance from the earlier €215,855,473.33 limit;

(c)   foreign currency denominated section 130 loans provided they comply with the
      conditions in (b) and provided the interest rate at no time exceeded 80% of
      EIBOR;

(d)   foreign currency denominated section 130 loans, other than those in (c), provided they comply with the conditions in (b), are for the purposes of a specified trade in respect of which an undertaking has been received that the interest will be treated as a distribution, and in respect of which the interest rate does not exceed the approved rate (25%);

(e)   sterling denominated section 130 loans provided they comply with the conditions in (b) and in respect of which the interest rate exceeds 80% of EIBOR only because the loan is denominated in sterling; and

(f)   foreign currency denominated section 130 loans, other than those in (c), (d) and (e), made to borrowers carrying on non-manufacturing Shannon activities eligible for the 10% corporation tax rate, and which comply with the conditions in (b).

11.108   Assets transferred between company and members

Where on the transfer of assets or liabilities of a company to its members, or to a company by its members, the amount or value of any benefit received by a member (taken according to its market value) exceeds the amount of any new consideration given by him, the company is treated by TCA 1997, s 130(3) as making a distribution to that member. The reference to assets or liabilities being transferred by a company "to its members" followed by the reference to any benefit received by "a member" could, it would seem, be interpreted as meaning that TCA 1997, s 130(3) deals only with transfers involving the members as a class and not transfers involving individual members. It was surely intended that transactions with individual members are covered but, on the other hand, it would then have been a simple matter to refer to a transfer of assets or liabilities "to any member".

Assuming that TCA 1997, s 130(3) refers to transfers to one or more members of a company, it envisages four kinds of possibility: a transfer of an asset by the company to a member, a transfer of an asset by a member to the company, a transfer of a liability by the company to a member, and a transfer of a liability by a member to the company. In any of these cases, it is provided that where the amount or value of any benefit received by the member exceeds the amount of any new consideration given by him, the company is treated as making a distribution.

From the wording of TCA 1997, s 130(3), it would seem that each of the four possibilities should be capable of giving rise to a benefit to the member *before* the amount or value of any new consideration is taken into account. Clearly, if an asset of a company is transferred to one of its members, there is a benefit to the member by reference to the value of that asset. If the member gives no consideration for the asset or consideration which is less than the value of the asset, the company is treated as having made a distribution to the member in an amount equal to the net benefit passing to that member. It is not, however, apparent how the transfer of a liability of the company to a member could of itself benefit that member. Furthermore, it would be unusual for the transfer of an asset by a member to the company to result in a benefit to that member; perhaps in exceptional circumstances a member would so benefit, for example where due to special circumstances the continued ownership of the asset would prove burdensome to the member.

Obviously, if an asset is transferred by the member to the company for consideration which exceeds the value of that asset, a benefit results to the member, but TCA 1997, s 130(3) only envisages consideration passing *from* the member *to* the company. Similarly, the transfer of a liability by the company to the member, where the member receives excessive consideration for assuming that liability, would confer a benefit on that member but, again, TCA 1997, s 130(3) refers only to consideration given *by* the member. In this connection, it is interesting to compare the wording of TCA 1997, s 130(3) with that in TCA 1997, s 436 which treats as a distribution the incurring by a close company of expense in or in connection with the provision for any participator of any benefits or facilities (see **10.202**).

Where the value of any benefit received by a member of a company as a result of the company assuming responsibility for a debt or liability of his exceeds the amount of any new consideration provided by him, the excess is treated as a distribution.

Example 11.108.1

Marathon Ltd sells a car to one of its shareholders, Mr Miles, for €15,000 when the market value of the car was €23,500. At the same time, the company assumes a liability of €11,000 due by another shareholder, Ms Davis, to a third party; in consideration, Ms Davis transfers to the company a holding of government stock having a market value of €7,600.

Consequent on the above transactions, Marathon Ltd is treated under TCA 1997, s 130(3) as making distributions to Mr Miles and Ms Davis as follows:

	Mr Miles	Ms Davis
	€	€
Market value of car transferred	23,500	
Amount of liability assumed by company		11,000
Consideration given by member:		
Mr Miles – cash	15,000	
Ms Davis – market value of stock		7,600
Amount of distribution received – Schedule F	8,500	3,400

From the context of TCA 1997, s 130(3), it has been argued that the reference to "assets" must be confined to assets other than cash. The reference to the amount or value of the resulting benefit "taken according to its market value" would be inappropriate in the case of a cash benefit. Furthermore, there is no reference in TCA 1997, s 130(3) to transfers of assets "whether in cash or otherwise" as there is for matters treated as distributions by TCA 1997, s 130(2)(b) and (c) (see **11.102.3** and **11.103**); it would have been a simple matter to include identical wording in TCA 1997, s 130(3) if the inclusion of transfers in cash form had been intended.

These arguments were considered in *Noved Investment Company v Commissioners of HM Revenue and Customs* [2006] SpC00521 in which the Special Commissioners held that as "assets" would normally include cash and since there was nothing in the context of the legislative provision which dictated otherwise, cash should be so included. While acknowledging the force of the "market value" argument and accepting the phrase to be a clumsy one when applied to cash, and noting that a cash benefit in the form of a foreign currency has a "market value", the Commissioners found sufficient evidence of an apparent intention to include cash. The phrase "whether in cash or otherwise", necessary in the context of TCA 1997, s 130(2)(b) which dealt with "any other distribution" where it could otherwise have been argued that cash distributions were not included, did not need to be included in TCA 1997, s 130(3).

It would generally be understood that the typical application of TCA 1997, s 130(3) is to transfers of assets to members, as envisaged in Example **11.108.1** above. Many such transfers would be caught anyway by TCA 1997, s 130(2)(b) as a distribution "out of the assets of the company ... in respect of shares in the company" (see **11.102.3**) but not all transfers to members would necessarily be "in respect of shares". A reduction of capital effected by way of a transfer of assets, the value of which exceeds the nominal value of the shares concerned, would seem to be another example of a distribution triggered by TCA 1997, s 130(3), but not by any other provision of TCA 1997, s 130 since it would not be "out of the assets" of the company.

A company may grant to a member an option over some of its assets. Since no assets are transferred at that point, there would be no distribution. Although an option is itself an asset, there would again be no distribution as the option would have been created, not transferred.

A situation which may arise in practice would be that in which an asset is sold by a company to a member for what is agreed between the parties to be its market value. If it should subsequently emerge that the market value is in fact greater than that agreed amount, the difference would give rise to a distribution. The member might then make good the difference to the company thereby eliminating the distribution. In practice, it is to be hoped that in any such case, provided the original sale of the asset was not effected for tax avoidance reasons, there would be no charge under TCA 1997, s 438 (loans to participators – see **10.204**) by reference to the period from the sale of the asset to the time the shortfall is made good.

Exception: certain inter-company transactions

Where the company and the member receiving the benefit (resulting from a transfer of assets or liabilities) are both Irish resident companies and either the former is a subsidiary of the latter or both are subsidiaries of a third company, being a company which, by virtue of the law of a relevant Member State, is resident for tax purposes in such a Member State, the amount of the benefit is not treated for the purposes of TCA 1997, s 130(3) as a distribution (TCA 1997, s 130(3)(b)). It is specifically provided that any amount which *would* be a distribution *apart from this exception* may not be treated as a distribution "out of assets" by virtue of TCA 1997, s 130(2)(b) (see – **11.102.3**). If the view taken above to the effect that transfers of cash are not treated as "distributions" under TCA 1997, s 130(3), distributions in cash between group members cannot be included in the exception so that they may still be treated as distributions "out of assets" within TCA 1997, s 130(2)(b).

For the above purposes, *relevant Member State*, means:

(a) a Member State of the European Communities; or

(b) not being such a Member State, an EEA State which is a territory with which Ireland has a tax treaty (TCA 1997, s 616(7)).

EEA State means a state which is a contracting party to the EEA Agreement. *EEA Agreement* means the Agreement on the European Economic Area signed at Oporto on 2 May 1992, as adjusted by the Protocol signed at Brussels on 17 March 1993.

A company is a subsidiary of another company if it is a 51% subsidiary (as defined in TCA 1997, s 9 – see **2.502**) of that company. For this purpose, however, the other company is treated as not being the owner of any share capital:

    (a)   owned directly by it and held as "trading stock", ie in respect of which any profit on a sale of the shares would be treated as a trading receipt;

    (b)   owned indirectly by it and which is owned directly by a company holding it as "trading stock"; or

    (c)   owned directly or indirectly by it in a company that is not a company which, by virtue of the law of a relevant Member State, is resident for tax purposes in such Member State.

As regards the above references to being resident for tax purposes in a relevant Member State, tax means any tax imposed in the Member State which corresponds to corporation tax in the State (TCA 1997, s 130(3)(c)).

    TCA 1997, s 130(5)(a) provides for a second exception involving distributions between resident, but unrelated, companies. A transfer of assets (other than cash) or of liabilities from one of the companies to the other is not to be treated as constituting or giving rise to a distribution by reason of TCA 1997, s 130(2)(b) or (3) provided they are companies:

    (i)   both of which are resident in the State and neither of which is a 51% subsidiary of a company not so resident; and

    (ii)   which neither at the time of the transfer nor as a result of it, are under common control.

Two companies are under common control if they are under the control of the same person or persons. For this purpose, *control* in relation to a company means the power of a person to secure, by means of the holding of shares or the possession of voting power in or in relation to the company or any other company, or by virtue of any powers conferred by the articles of association or other document regulating that or any other company, that the affairs of the company are conducted in accordance with the wishes of that person.

    It can be seen that only transfers of assets other than cash are exempt distributions for the purposes of TCA 1997, s 130(5)(a). Transfers in cash form between unrelated resident companies are therefore not excluded from being distributions "out of assets" for the purposes of TCA 1997, s 130(2)(b). By the same token, TCA 1997, s 130(5)(a) does not provide an exception for such cash transfers for the purposes of TCA 1997, s 130(3), which may seem to be inconsistent with the view that such transfers are not within the scope of that subsection in the first place. The inclusion in TCA 1997, s 130(5)(a) of the reference to "(other than cash)" can, however, simply be seen as relevant in relation to TCA 1997, s 130(2)(b) without being relevant to TCA 1997, s 130(3).

    See also **9.407** regarding transfers by closely controlled companies of assets at undervalue.

11.109 Disallowance of reliefs for bonus issues

The entitlement to recover tax in respect of certain kinds of distributions is denied by TCA 1997, s 137. This provision may accordingly operate to deny recovery of dividend withholding tax in respect of those distributions.

    TCA 1997, s 137 has effect in relation to amounts treated as distributions under the following provisions:

(a) TCA 1997, s 130(2)(c) – redemption of "bonus securities" (**11.103.2**);

(b) TCA 1997, s 130(2)(d) – interest in respect of certain securities (**11.106**);

(c) TCA 1997, s 131 – bonus issue following repayment of capital (**11.103.3**); or

(d) TCA 1997, s 132(2) – repayment of capital following earlier bonus issue (**11.103.4**).

For the purposes of TCA 1997, s 137, any distribution of the above kind is referred to as a *bonus issue* (although only some are actual bonus issues).

A bonus issue is treated as not being franked investment income within the meaning of TCA 1997, s 156 (see **3.205**) (TCA 1997, s 137(3)).

The recipient of a bonus issue may not claim a refund of dividend withholding tax (see **11.116.10**).

Recovery of tax in the case of bonus issue is restricted by TCA 1997, s 137(2). Before dealing with this provision, it is useful to refer to TCA 1997, s 137(5) which limits the application of TCA 1997, s 137(2) and (3). That subsection provides that the rules disallowing the reliefs concerned, and providing that a bonus issue is not to be treated as franked investment income, do not apply to the proportion, if any, of any bonus issue which, if it were declared as a dividend, would represent a normal return to the recipient on the consideration given by him for the relevant shares or securities.

Accordingly, in the case of any bonus issue it is necessary, for the purposes of TCA 1997, s 137, to determine how much of the bonus issue can be considered to be attributed to a normal return on the recipient's investment in the relevant shares and securities. For this purpose, *relevant shares or securities* is described in TCA 1997, s 137(5) as the shares or securities in respect of which the bonus issue was made or, if those securities are derived from shares or securities previously acquired by the recipient, the shares or securities which were previously acquired.

The actual cost of acquisition of the relevant shares or securities is taken as the consideration on which the normal return on the investment is based, unless the actual cost exceeded the market value of the relevant shares or securities on the date acquired or no consideration was given for any of those shares or securities. In either of these events, the normal return is computed by reference to the market value on the date acquired.

For the purpose of determining whether an amount received exceeds what would be a normal return if received as a dividend, regard is to be had to the length of time since the recipient first acquired any of the relevant shares or securities to the time the amount was received, and to any dividends and other distributions made in respect of them during that time. The normal return due in respect of the relevant shares or securities will be the difference between the normal return for the period mentioned less the amount of any dividends and other distributions already received. If and to the extent that the amount of the bonus issue does not exceed this balance, it is not affected by TCA 1997, s 137(2) or (3) and only the excess, if any, of the bonus issue remains subject to those provisions.

A shareholder within the charge to income tax who has borne dividend withholding tax in relation to a relevant distribution in a year of assessment may claim to have that withholding tax set against income tax chargeable for that year and, where the withholding tax exceeds that liability, to have the excess refunded. Where the shareholder is not within the charge to income tax, a refund of the withholding tax may be claimed. A person who has borne dividend withholding tax in relation to a relevant distribution, and who is a non-liable person (ie, an excluded person or a qualifying non-resident person – see **11.116.5** and **11.116.6**) in relation to that distribution, may claim to have the dividend withholding tax refunded (TCA 1997, s 172J(2) – see **11.116.10**).

TCA 1997, s 137(2) provides that where the recipient of a bonus issue is entitled by reason of:

(a) any exemption from tax;

(b) the setting-off of losses against profits or income; or

(c) the payment of interest,

to recover tax in respect of any distribution which the recipient has received, no account is to be taken, for the purposes of any such exemption, set-off or payment of interest, of any bonus issue which the recipient has received. In any such case, the relevant computation takes into account only the part of the bonus issue excluded from the effect of TCA 1997, s 137(2) by TCA 1997, s 137(5). For an individual recipient of a bonus issue, however, the full amount of the bonus issue is nevertheless included in the income taxable under Schedule F.

It will be seen that the circumstances in which dividend withholding tax may be refunded in accordance with TCA 1997, s 172J include those referred to in (a) to (c) above. Accordingly, an entitlement to a refund of dividend withholding tax in these circumstances may be restricted in the case of a bonus issue by reason of the operation of TCA 1997, s 137(2). For bonus issues after 5 April 1999, since only exceptionally will dividend withholding tax be deducted from distributions made to companies, TCA 1997, s 137 will be of relevance almost exclusively to individual recipients.

11.110 Schedule F

Dividends and other distributions of a company resident in the State are charged to income tax under TCA 1997, s 20(1), unless specifically excluded from income tax. Where received by or on behalf of a person liable to income tax, almost all such distributions are within the Schedule F charge but distributions paid out of certain types of income which are exempted from corporation tax may be excluded from income tax by reason of specific provisions in the Tax Acts (see **11.112**). Distributions of a non-resident company are taxable under Schedule D Case III, and are not within the charge to tax under Schedule F.

As has been seen from **11.101-108**, the term "distribution" is very widely defined so as to bring within the Schedule F charge not only all dividends paid by a resident company, but most other distributions of profits in whatever form, apart from distributions in respect of share capital on a winding up.

In principle, distributions made before 6 April 1999 by a resident company carried a tax credit the amount of which was computed as a fraction of the distribution paid, but which was at a lower rate for distributions out of certain types of tax relieved income. The tax credit was not an additional payment made by the company to the shareholder, but represented the part of the corporation tax paid by the company that was "imputed" to the person receiving the distribution. The recipient in this case was said to be "entitled to" the attaching tax credit (TCA 1997, s 136(1) – repealed by FA 2000 s 69(2).

In the case of a resident person other than a company, the income charged under Schedule F is the amount of distributions received and the recipient of the distribution is required to include in his total income for any year the amount or value of all distributions received in that year.

Schedule F income, consisting of distributions received from Irish resident companies, has always been chargeable to income tax on a current year basis; the taxpayer is chargeable for any year of assessment in respect of the amount of his Schedule F income received in that year. For the purposes of the Corporation Tax Acts, and except as otherwise provided, a dividend is treated as paid on the date it becomes due and payable (TCA 1997, s 4(5)). Any other distribution is taxable by reference to the date on which it is paid or otherwise made.

A final dividend is normally due and payable on the date it is declared, unless it is expressed as being payable at a future date (*Re Kidner* [1929] 2 Ch 121). An interim dividend is normally due on the date on which it is actually paid; this is because it is possible for the directors, by resolution, to rescind payment at any time up to then (*Potel v IRC* 46 TC 658).

In *Murphy v The Borden Co Ltd* 3 ITR 559, a dividend was held to be received when a set-off through an inter-company account was agreed, and not when the accounting entries were made after year end; the making of an accounting entry is a mere record of the actual underlying transaction and not the transaction itself. There was sufficient evidence of the intention to pay the dividend before year end and its effective payment by set-off.

Corporation tax is not normally charged on distributions made by a resident company, whether or not the recipient company is resident in Ireland (TCA 1997, s 129).

Non-residents in receipt of distributions

With effect from 6 April 1999, certain non-residents are exempted from Irish income tax in respect of distributions made to them by Irish resident companies. The exemption applies to those non-residents who are exempted from dividend withholding tax (see **11.116.6**). Up to 5 April 1999, there was an effective exemption from income tax for all non-resident shareholders in respect of distributions made by Irish resident companies.

TCA 1997, s 153(4) provides that where the income of a qualifying non-resident person (as defined – see below) includes an amount in respect of a distribution made by an Irish resident company:

(a)   income tax is not to be chargeable in respect of that distribution; and

(b)   the amount or value of the distribution is to be treated for the purposes of TCA 1997, ss 237 and 238 (see **4.302** and **4.303**) as not brought into charge to income tax.

For this purpose, a *qualifying non-resident person* in relation to a relevant distribution is a person beneficially entitled to the relevant distribution and who is:

(a)   a person, other than a company, who—

    (i)   is neither resident nor ordinarily resident in the State; and

    (ii)   is, by virtue of the law of a relevant territory, resident for the purposes of tax in that territory, or

(b)   a company which is not resident in the State and—

(i)   is, by virtue of the law of a relevant territory, resident for tax purposes in that territory, but is not under the control, directly or indirectly, of a person or persons who is or are resident in the State,

(ii)   is under the control, directly or indirectly, of a person or persons who, by virtue of the law of a relevant territory, is or are resident for tax purposes in that territory and who is or are not under the control, directly or indirectly, of a person or persons who is or are not so resident, or

(iii)   the principal class of the shares of which, or—

    (I)   where the company is a 75% subsidiary (see **2.503**) of another company, of that other company, or

    (II) where the company is wholly-owned by two or more companies, of each of those companies,

is substantially and regularly traded on one or more than one recognised stock exchange in a relevant territory or territories, or on such other stock exchange as may be approved by the Minister for Finance for the purposes of TCA 1997, s 153 (TCA 1997, s 153(1)).

In determining whether or not a company is a 75% subsidiary or another company for the purposes of (b)(iii)(I) above, the equity entitlement provisions of TCA 1997, ss 412-418 (see **8.305**) apply as they would apply for the purposes of group relief if TCA 1997, s 411(1)(c) were deleted (ie, ignoring requirements relating to EU residence and to shares held as "trading stock" – see **8.302.2-302.3**) (TCA 1997, s 153(3)).

In determining whether a company is wholly-owned by two or more companies for the purposes of (b)(iii)(II) above, the company (referred to as an "aggregated 100% subsidiary") is to be treated as being wholly-owned by two or more companies (referred to as the "joint parent companies") if and so long as 100% of its ordinary share capital is owned directly or indirectly by the joint parent companies, and for this purpose:

(a)   subsections (2) to (10) of TCA 1997, s 9 are to apply as they apply for the purpose of that section (meaning of "subsidiary" – see **2.505**); and

(b)   TCA 1997, ss 412-418 (see **8.305**) apply with any necessary modifications as they would apply for the purposes of group relief—

(i)   if TCA 1997, s 411(1)(c) were deleted (ie, ignoring requirements relating to EU residence and to shares held as "trading stock" – see **8.302.2-302.3**), and

(ii)   if TCA 1997, s 412(1) (the wording in which would be inappropriate to the position of joint parent companies – see **8.304.1**) were substituted by a subsection to the following effect:

Notwithstanding that at any time a company is an aggregated 100% subsidiary of the joint parent companies, it is not to be treated at that time as such a subsidiary unless additionally at that time—

    (I)   the joint parent companies are between them beneficially entitled to not less than 100% of any profits available for distribution to equity holders of the company, and

    (II)   the joint parent companies would be beneficially entitled between them to not less than 100% of any assets of the company available for distribution to its equity holders on a winding up (TCA 1997, s 153(3A)).

A *relevant territory* means a Member State of the European Communities other than Ireland, or a territory (not being such a Member State) with the government of which arrangements having the force of law by virtue of TCA 1997, s 826(1) have been made (ie, with which Ireland has concluded a tax treaty).

Tax in relation to a relevant territory means any tax imposed in that territory which corresponds to income tax or corporation tax in the State.

Control in the definition of *qualifying non-resident person* in (b)(i) above is to be construed in accordance with TCA 1997, s 432(2)-(6) as if in TCA 1997, s 432(6) (see **2.401.4**) "five or fewer participators" were substituted by "persons resident in the State" (TCA 1997, s 153(1A)).

Control in the definition of *qualifying non-resident person* in (b)(ii) above is to be construed in accordance with TCA 1997, s 432(2)-(6) as if in TCA 1997, s 432(6) (see **2.401.4**) "five or fewer participators" were substituted by:

(a)   as regards the first mention of "control" in (b)(ii), "persons who, by virtue of the law of a relevant territory … are resident for the purposes of tax in such a relevant territory" (TCA 1997, s 153(2)(a); and

(b)   as regards the second mention of "control" in (b)(ii), "persons who are not resident for the purposes of tax in a relevant territory …" (TCA 1997, s 153(2)(b)).

Where, by virtue of TCA 1997, s 831(5), dividend withholding tax (see **11.116**) does not apply to a distribution made to a parent company which is not resident in the State by its subsidiary which is resident in the State (see **14.702**):

(a)   income tax is not to be chargeable in respect of that distribution; and

(b)   the amount or value of the distribution is to be treated for the purposes of TCA 1997, ss 237 and 238 (see **4.302** and **4.303**) as not brought into charge to income tax (TCA 1997, s 153(5)).

Where for any year of assessment the income of an individual who for that year is neither resident nor ordinarily resident in the State, but is not a qualifying non-resident person, includes an amount in respect of a distribution made by an Irish resident company, then:

(a)   notwithstanding TCA 1997, s 15(2) (which provides for a charge to income tax at the standard and higher rates, as appropriate), income tax is not to be chargeable in respect of that distribution at a rate in excess of the standard rate; and

(b)   the amount of value of the distribution is to be treated for the purposes of TCA 1997, ss 237 and 238 (see **4.302-303**) as not brought into charge to income tax (TCA 1997, s 153(6)).

11.111   Tax Credits: distributions paid before 6 April 1999

11.111.1   Entitlement to tax credit

With effect from 6 April 1999, dividends and other distributions from Irish resident companies do not carry a tax credit (FA 1998 Sch 5 paragraph 1). What follows in **11.111**, therefore, is of relevance only as regards distributions paid by companies before that date.

TCA 1997, s 2(3A) (introduced by FA 2000 Sch 2) provides that a reference in the Tax Acts to a tax credit in relation to a distribution is to be construed as a reference to a tax credit as computed in accordance with those Acts as they applied at the time of the making of the distribution.

The recipient of a distribution paid, before 6 April 1999, by a company resident in the State was entitled to the tax credit attaching to that distribution. Residents and non-residents were entitled to the tax credit; non-residents were not so entitled prior to 6 April 1992.

Where a distribution was, or fell to be treated as, or was deemed under any provision of the Tax Acts to be, the income of a person other than the recipient, it was that other person rather than the recipient who was entitled to the tax credit

Where a distribution from a resident company was the income of a trust or settlement resident in the State, the trustees were entitled to the tax credit if no other person fell to be treated as receiving the distribution. For example, if the trustees of an Irish resident settlement received distributions from Irish resident companies but the income of the settlement was deemed to be the income of the settlor, the trustees were not entitled to the tax credits attaching to those distributions. In that case, the settlor was the person entitled to the tax credits, being the person who was taxable in respect of the distributions.

A _trust resident in the State_ is a trust administered under the law of the State, not being a trust the general administration of which is ordinarily carried on outside the State and the trustees, or a majority of the trustees, of which are resident or ordinarily resident outside the State. In other words, a trust or settlement administered under Irish law would have been regarded as resident in the State and as entitled to the tax credits in question if either its general administration was ordinarily carried on in the State or all, or a majority of, the trustees were resident and ordinarily resident in the State.

11.111.2   Types of tax credit

The Irish corporation tax system was up to 5 April 1999, an imputation system; corporation tax paid by a company was "imputed" to its shareholders by way of the tax credit on distributions made. A shareholder in receipt of a distribution was entitled to a credit in respect of tax paid by the company on the profits out of which the distribution had been made, the credit being available against the shareholder's income tax liability.

Where the standard tax credit in respect of distributions was, say, 21/79ths (ie, for the year 1997-98, but only up to 2 December 1997) that fraction represented 21% of the aggregate of the distribution and tax credit. Dividends were declared and paid "_net_", unlike the pre-6 April 1976 position where a gross dividend was declared and paid net of a deduction for income tax.

The tax credit was not normally restricted by reference to the amount of corporation tax on the profits out of which the dividend or other distribution was paid. Thus, a dividend paid by a company with all of its profits in a particular year relieved by capital allowances nevertheless carried a full tax credit.

The imputed tax credit represented a part of the corporation tax payable by the distributing company. A shareholder subject to income tax was treated as if he had already suffered a part of the corporation tax payable by the company on the profits out of which the distribution was made. It was this part of the corporation tax that was imputed to the shareholder and from which was derived the tax credit which was included with the distribution in the shareholder's total income and which was deducted from the tax liability on that income.

The amount of the tax credit attaching to a distribution varied depending on whether the distribution was made out of profits which had been taxed at the standard corporation tax rate or which had been wholly or partly relieved or exempted from corporation tax by reason of any of the special tax incentive reliefs or exemptions mentioned below. The tax credits which could arise were:

(a) standard tax credit, which arose where the distribution was made wholly out of income in respect of which the distributing company was taxable at the standard corporation tax rate;

(b) tax credit equal to 1/18th of the distribution which arose where the distribution was made out of income on which the rate of corporation tax has been reduced to 10% as the result of "manufacturing" relief;

(c) reduced tax credit under which arose where the distribution was made out of income in respect of which the normal corporation tax liability had been reduced by reason of export sales relief; and

(d) "Nil" tax credit which arose where the distribution was made out of income which had been wholly exempted form corporation tax by reason of any of the following:

    (i) Shannon trading operations exemption;

    (ii) exemption in respect of income from qualifying patents (see **13.607**);

    (iii) exemptions in respect of income from certain stallion fees and in respect of income from certain greyhound fees;

    (iv) exemption in respect of income from commercial woodlands (see **3.204.5**);

    (v) the exemption in respect of income from farming in the State earned before 6 April 1974: it is possible for a farming company to have such income remaining undistributed.

The distributable income of the company making a distribution might have included one or more distributions received from other resident companies. The computation of the amount of the tax credit attaching to the distribution made depended on the extent to which any distributions received carried a standard tax credit, a 1/18th tax credit or a Nil tax credit by reason of one of the exemptions from tax.

Where the distributable income for the relevant accounting period out of which a distribution was made consisted only of income which had been charged at the standard corporation tax rate (including any distributions from income of other resident companies taxed at the standard corporation rate), the position was straightforward; a standard tax credit attached to the full distribution. Likewise, if the distribution was made out of income consisting entirely of any one of the other categories mentioned above (including distributions received out of another resident company's income of the same category), the attaching credit would have been a 1/18th tax credit, a reduced tax credit or a Nil tax credit depending on the category of the income received by the distributing company.

Where the income from which the distribution was made consisted of more than one of the above categories, the position was more complex and it was necessary to allocate the distribution to the relevant categories of income for the purpose determining the correct tax credit. Except where the income consisted only of standard rate taxed income and export sales relieved income, a distribution from two or more categories of income was treated as if it were two or more separate distributions each with a different type of tax credit.

11.111.3   Calculation of tax credit

The amount of a tax credit was determined by reference to the following formula:

$$D \times \frac{A}{100 - A}$$

where—

A =   the standard credit rate per cent for the year of assessment in which the distribution was made; and

D =   the amount or value of the distribution.

For the above purposes, the standard credit rate per cent was not necessarily the standard rate of income tax but an amount derived from the corporation tax rate. The standard credit rate per cent represented (up to 2 December 1997) the imputed part of the corporation tax paid by the distributing company. The following were the standard credit rates for the years 1976-77 to 1998-99:

Years of assessment	*Standard credit rate*
1976-77 to 1977-78	35%
1978-79 to 1982-83	30%
1983-84 to 1987-88	35%
1988-89	32%
1989-90 to 1990-91	28%
1991-92 to 1994-95	25%
1995-96 to 1996-97	23%
1997-98 (to 2/12/97)	21%
1997-98 (from 3/12/97)	11%
1998-99	11%

The tax credit formula for a distribution made on or after 3 December 1997 and before 6 April 1999 was:

$$D \times \frac{11}{100 - 11}$$

11.111.4 Effect of tax credits

A resident person, other than a company, receiving Schedule F distributions before 6 April 1999 could claim to have the tax credits attaching to those distributions set off against the income tax chargeable on his taxable income for the year of assessment in which the distributions were made. The person entitled to the tax credits was required to include in his total income, as Schedule F income, the aggregate of the distributions received with the addition of the tax credits attaching to those distributions.

If the aggregate of the tax credits to which the claimant was entitled in respect of all Schedule F distributions received by him in any year of assessment, up to the year 1998-99, exceeded the income tax chargeable in respect of his total income, he was entitled to have the excess repaid to him. The normal procedure for making the set off or repayment claim was for the relevant person to include the amount of the distributions and related tax credits in his income tax return for the tax year in question; in the resulting assessment, the appropriate credit was given against the income tax chargeable. In fact, no repayment of income tax was made to an individual unless the aggregate of his tax credits for the year of assessment exceeded the aggregate of the individual's liabilities to income tax, health contribution, employment levy, income levy and any self-employed PRSI contribution.

The provisions governing the taxation of a person chargeable to income tax in respect of Schedule F distributions varied in certain respects depending on the type of tax credit attaching to the distribution.

11.112 Treatment of distributions from exempt income

11.112.1 Introduction

Distributable income of a company may be wholly exempted from corporation tax under one of more of the following provisions:

(a) Shannon exemption (CTA 1976 Part V, see **7.103**);

(b) TCA 1997, s 234 exemption for qualifying patents (see **13.607**);

(c) TCA 1997, s 231 exemption for certain stallion fees (see **3.204.4** and **13.107.7**);

(d) TCA 1997, s 233 exemption for stud greyhound fees (see **3.204.4**)

(e) TCA 1997, s 232 exemption for commercial woodlands (see **3.204.5**);

(f) FA 1969 s 18 former exemption for farming in the State – prior to 6 April 1974 (to the extent income not yet distributed).

A distribution made by an Irish resident company out of income of any of these exempt categories is referred to here as a "tax exempt distribution". Furthermore, if a distribution made out of exempt income is received by another resident company, it is generally treated in the hands of that company as tax exempt income of the same category.

For example, if a distribution made by a company out of exempt stallion fee income is received by a second company which then makes a distribution out of that distribution, the distribution made by the second company is also treated as an exempt distribution from stallion fee income. That process may be continued through any number of companies with the same tax effect. However, a distribution received after 23

April 1992 by a company out of another company's tax exempt patent income can only be used to pay a tax exempt distribution if the distribution received is one in respect of "eligible shares" (see **11.112.3**).

Prior to the Finance Act 1992, all distributions made out of a company's tax exempt income (or out of tax exempt distributions) were fully exempted from income tax in the hands of any individual or other person chargeable to income tax. The relevant statutory provisions are:

(a)   TCA 1997, s 144 – distributions out of Shannon tax exempt income;

(b)   TCA 1997, s 141 – distributions out of income from qualifying patents within TCA 1997, s 234;

(c)   TCA 1997, s 140 – distributions out of tax exempted income from stallion fees, stud greyhound fees and commercial woodlands;

(d)   TCA 1997, s 142 – distributions out of profits of certain mines (ie, exempted income, being income in respect of which a company has obtained relief under Finance (Profits of Certain Mines) (Temporary Relief from Taxation) Act 1956, or Chapter II (Profits of Certain Mines) of Part XXV of the Income Tax Act 1967.

The full exemption for distributions out of Shannon tax exempt income received after 28 January 1992 was terminated by FA 1992 s 35; a partial exemption applied for Shannon distributions received from 29 January 1992 to 5 April 1994. With certain exceptions, the full income tax exemption for distributions out of exempt income from qualifying patents received after 23 April 1992 was withdrawn by FA 1992 s 19 with partial exemption for patent distributions received from 24 April 1992 to 5 April 1994. For distributions out of tax exempted income from stallion fees and commercial woodlands there has been no change, so that the full exemption remains for such distributions (as well as for distributions out of income from stud greyhound fees).

The specific rules relating to Shannon distributions and patent distributions are now discussed as follows.

11.112.2   Shannon distributions

(a) General

The full income tax exemption for Shannon distributions applies only in respect of such distributions received before 29 January 1992. For Shannon distributions received from 29 January 1992 to 5 April 1994, there was a partial exemption from income tax. For Shannon distributions received after 5 April 1994, there is no income tax exemption and the distributions are taxable in full (see (b) below).

CTA 1976 s 76(2)(a)(i) provided that so much of any distribution as has been made out of income from Shannon "exempted trading operations" (see **7.103**) was not to be regarded as income for any purpose of the Income Tax Acts (except, where relevant, under FA 1974 s 54 in the case of certain employees and directors). TCA 1997, s 144(3)(a) provides that if the recipient of a Shannon exempted distribution is a company, the distribution is to be treated in the hands of that company as income from Shannon exempted trading operations (so that any distribution made by it out of the distribution received is also treated as a Shannon exempt distribution in the hands of the recipient).

The term "Shannon distribution" is used here to refer to any distribution made by a company out of either:

(a)   income earned by the company from activities carried on in the Shannon Airport Customs-free Area which was exempted from corporation tax under CTA Part V (not applicable for income after 5 April 1990); or

(b)   income deemed by TCA 1997, s 144(3)(a) to be income from exempted trading operations (ie, distributions from another company out of its income from exempted trading operations).

Accordingly, once a distribution or part of a distribution received before 29 January 1992 by a person subject to income tax had been identified as a Shannon distribution, the distribution was completely disregarded and no income tax was chargeable in respect of it (apart from the exceptional case where FA 1974 s 54 applied). It followed that the Shannon distribution was not liable to the health contribution, employment levy, self-employed PRSI contribution or any other levy charged on income as determined by the Income Tax Acts (except to the extent that FA 1974 s 54 applied to treat the distribution as income liable to income tax).

Although the exemption from corporation tax under CTA 1976 Part V does not apply to income from exempted trading operations earned after 5 April 1990, a company may have undistributed income after that date consisting of income from exempted trading operations earned before that date. Any such income continues to be distributable as a Shannon distribution and, if received by another company, is available to be distributed by that company as a Shannon distribution. Consequently, the provisions relating to Shannon distributions discussed here can continue to be relevant for a number of years after 5 April 1990.

TCA 1997, s 144(2) provides that any distribution for an accounting period that is made partly out of income from Shannon exempt trading income and/or Shannon distributions received, and partly out other profits, is to be treated as if it consisted of two separate distributions, being a Shannon exempt distribution and a distribution other than a Shannon exempt distribution.

TCA 1997, s 144 contains provisions for determining the extent to which any distribution for an accounting period is to be regarded as made out of income from exempted trading operations (including any Shannon distributions received) and out of other profits. The term "other profits" is taken as including all dividends or other distributions received from other companies (other than Shannon distributions).

These provisions, and those which deal with the attribution of the various types of distributions to accounting periods, are dealt with in **11.114**. It is assumed here that the Shannon distributions have already been identified. In addition, in any case where only a part of a distribution is deemed by TCA 1997, s 144(2) to be a "separate" distribution out of exempted Shannon trading income, that part is also included in any reference to a Shannon distribution.

Originally, all Shannon distributions received by an individual or other person chargeable to income tax were fully exempted from income tax under CTA 1976 s 76(2)(a)(i). However, CTA 1976 s 76A removed that exemption for Shannon distributions received after 5 April 1994 and restricted the exemption to a part only of Shannon distributions received from 29 January 1992 to 5 April 1994.

(b) Shannon distributions: 6 April 1994 onwards

The income tax exemption provided for in CTA 1976 s 76(2)(a)(i) does not apply to any Shannon distributions received on or after 29 January 1992 (subject to the partial exemption regime which was in operation for the period 29 January to 5 April 1994). A Shannon distribution received in the tax year 1994-95 or any later year is therefore fully chargeable to income tax. It follows that all such distributions are also fully subject to the health contribution, the self-employed PRSI contribution and any levies based on income as determined under the Income Tax Acts).

11.112.3 Patent distributions

By virtue of TCA 1997, s 234, an Irish resident company is exempted from corporation tax in respect of any income from qualifying patents. A *qualifying patent* is a patent in relation to which the research, processing, designing and other work leading to the invention the subject of the patent has been carried out in a state of the European Economic Area (EEA) (in the State as regards work carried out before 1 January 2008). A more detailed discussion on the subject of exempted income from qualifying patents is included in **13.607**. In general, income from qualifying patents must be received from a manufacturer or from an unconnected person other than a person involved in any arrangements intended to obtain a tax exemption. Where received from a manufacturer, the royalty income arising will, with effect from 23 April 1996, be tax exempt only if the amount involved does not exceed an amount arrived at by applying an arm's length rate.

TCA 1997, s 141 provides for an exemption from income tax in respect of "patent distributions", ie distributions made by an Irish resident company from exempt patent income or from patent distributions received by it from other resident companies. Exempt patent income is income exempted by virtue of TCA 1997, s 234(2) or, in the case of a company, TCA 1997, s 234(2) together with TCA 1997, s 76(6), and is referred to as "disregarded income". For many years, all patent distributions were exempted from income tax, but the exemption provided for in TCA 1997, s 141 was restricted by FA 1992 s 19 as regards distributions received on or after 24 April 1992 (which must be made in respect of "eligible shares" or out of "relevant income") and is further restricted by TCA 1997, s 141(1)(a) as regards distributions made out of patent income accruing on or after 28 March 1996.

(a) Disregarded income

Exemption from income tax in respect of certain distributions received from Irish resident companies is provided for in TCA 1997, s 141. The exemption applies in the cases of distributions made out of one or more of the following categories of income, referred to as *disregarded income*:

(a) income from qualifying patents earned by the distributing company itself;

(b) distributions which the distributing company has received on or after 24 April 1992 in respect of "eligible shares", or which is made out of "relevant income" (see below), and paid out of the qualifying patent income of another company;

(c) distributions which the distributing company has received before 24 April 1992 on any type of shares or securities and made out of the qualifying patent income of another company; or

(d)   distributions which the distributing company has received before 24 April 1992 on any type of shares or securities and made out of another company's distributions received from a third company's income from qualifying patents: this process may be repeated through a series of distribution payments, however long, where the ultimate source is income from qualifying patents.

Relevant income means income which is referable to a qualifying patent in relation to which the person receiving the distribution carried out, either solely or jointly with another person, the research, planning, processing, experimenting, testing, devising, designing, development or other similar activity leading to the invention which is the subject of the qualifying patent.

Distributions made on or after 24 April 1992 in respect of shares which are not eligible shares, and which are not made out of "relevant income", are not disregarded income when received by another company. For example, a dividend paid on 29 April 1993 by a company to another company in respect of preference shares (which are not eligible shares) out of income from qualifying patents (which is not "relevant income") is not disregarded income in the hands of the recipient company. Consequently, any distribution which the second company makes out of the preference dividend received does not qualify for income tax exemption.

Income from a qualifying patent which is received by a company from a person with whom it is connected (within the meaning of TCA 1997, s 10 – see **2.3**) is not disregarded income; such income is instead treated as "specified income". A distribution or distributions made out of the specified income accruing to a company on or after 28 March 1996 is treated as made out of disregarded income to the extent that it does not exceed the amount of the aggregate expenditure incurred by it, and by fellow group members, on research and development activities in that period and in the two previous accounting periods. Distributions made out of the excess over the matching element are fully taxable but subject to exemption in respect of "innovative" patents (see below).

A distribution made (after 23 April 1992) by one company out of its disregarded income is not disregarded income in the hands of a second company unless it is received in respect of shares which are eligible shares (TCA 1997, s 141(4)(a)(i) or is made out of relevant income (TCA 1997, s 141(4)(a)(ii)). A distribution made by the second company out of such a distribution, therefore, is not treated as a distribution made out of disregarded income (whether or not the second company's distribution is in respect of eligible shares).

(b) Eligible shares

"Eligible shares" are shares which form part of a company's ordinary share capital and which:

(a)   are fully paid up;

(b)   carry no preferential right to dividends or to the company's assets on a winding up and no present or future right to be redeemed; and

(c)   are not subject to any treatment different from the treatment which applies to all shares of the same class, and in particular are not subject to different treatment in respect of:

   (i)   dividends payable,

   (ii)   repayment,

(iii)   restrictions attaching to the shares, or

(iv)   any offer of substituted or additional shares, securities or rights of any description in respect of the shares (TCA 1997, s 141(1)).

For the above purpose *ordinary share capital* is defined in TCA 1997, s 2(1) and means all the share capital (by whatever name called) of a company, other than capital the holders whereof have a right to a dividend at a fixed rate, but have no other right to share in the profits of the company. In other words, ordinary shares are usually eligible shares whereas preference or any other class of shares (eg, deferred shares) are not eligible shares.

(c) Distributions from qualifying patent income received from connected persons

Specified income

As explained above, distributions made on or after 28 March 1996 out of the specified income (ie, income from a qualifying patent which is received by a company from a person with whom it is connected) of a company is treated as made out of disregarded income to the extent only that it is matched by expenditure incurred by it, and by fellow group members, on research and development activities in that period and in the two previous accounting periods.

Specified income is defined in TCA 1997, s 141(1) as income from a qualifying patent which would not be such income were it not for TCA 1997, s 234(1)(a) of the definition of "income from a qualifying patent". In other words, patent royalties and similar sums treated as income from a qualifying patent because received from a manufacturer are no longer treated as disregarded income, but as specified income. Only income under TCA 1997, s 234(1)(b) received by a distributing company continues to qualify as disregarded income, ie royalties and similar amounts received from a person unconnected with the distributing company and who has not entered into any arrangement for the purpose, or mainly for the purpose, of obtaining the exemption by avoiding being "connected with" the company (see also **13.607.5**).

Specified income is treated by TCA 1997, s 141(1), in the first instance, as not being disregarded income but that position is then qualified in that distributions out of such income *are* treated as being out of disregarded income to the extent that they are matched by certain research and development expenditure (TCA 1997, s 141(5)(c)). To the extent that the distributions are not so matched, they are treated as not being made out of disregarded income but, by way of another exception, they may still be so treated if the patent in question involved "radical innovation" (see below).

Expenditure on research and development

The research and development expenditure the level of which is compared with the distributions made by a company out of specified income for an accounting period means non-capital expenditure incurred by the company "in relation to the accounting period" (see below) and which comprises:

(a)   such part of the emoluments paid to its employees engaged in carrying out research and development activities related to the company's trade as are paid to them for the purposes of those activities;

(b)   expenditure on materials or goods used solely by it in carrying out research and development activities related to its trade; and

(c)   any amount paid to another person (unconnected with the company) to carry out research and development activities related to the company's trade.

Where a company is a member of a group (see below), the amount of expenditure on research and development activities incurred in an accounting period by another company which, in the accounting period, is a member of the group is, on a joint election in writing made by the two companies, treated as expenditure incurred on research and development activities in the period by the first-mentioned company and not by the fellow group member (TCA 1997, s 141(5)(a)).

The meaning of *research and development activities* is as defined in TCA 1997, s 766(1)(a) (but prior to the amendment by FA 2004 of that paragraph), ie systematic, investigative or experimental activities which are carried on wholly or mainly in the State (ie, where not less than 75% of the total amount expended in the course of such activities is expended in the State), which involve innovation or technical risk, and are carried on for the purpose of:

(a)   acquiring new knowledge with a view to that knowledge having a specific commercial application; or
(b)   creating new or improved materials, products, devices, processes or services,

as well as other activities carried on wholly or mainly in the State for a purpose directly related to the carrying on of the above-mentioned activities.

Specifically excluded are activities carried on by way of market research, market testing, market development, sale promotion or consumer surveys, quality control, the making of cosmetic modifications or stylistic changes to products, processes or production methods, management studies or efficiency surveys, and research in social sciences, arts or humanities.

For the purposes of ascertaining what companies are members of the same group, the meaning of *group* is the same as for the purposes of group relief (see **8.103.1**) except that no company is required to be Irish resident. In addition, two companies are members of a group if both are wholly or mainly under the control of the same individual or individuals, that is, where at least 75% of the ordinary share capital of each company is owned directly or indirectly by the same individual or individuals. TCA 1997, ss 412-418 contain anti-avoidance provisions which counter attempts to create artificial groups (see **8.304**). The additional tests for group relationship as prescribed by these sections, the "profit distribution test" and the "asset distribution test", are applicable here also. In cases where companies are under the control of the same individual or individuals, they apply as if references to "parent company" were references to an individual or individuals.

The amount of research and development expenditure incurred by a company *in relation to the accounting period* and which is compared to the amount of distributions made out of specified income is the amount of the aggregate expenditure incurred by the company and by fellow group members on research and development activities in that period and in the two previous accounting periods. Thus, the same research and development expenditure could be taken into account more than once, in fact typically three times, where distributions made for three periods are being considered.

As to the accounting period for which a distribution is regarded as made, see **11.114.2**.

Radical innovation

Where a company makes a distribution out of specified income, all of that income will be treated as disregarded income if the company can show in writing to the satisfaction of the Revenue Commissioners that the specified income is income from a qualifying patent in respect of an invention which:

(a)   involved radical innovation; and

(b)   was patented for bona fide commercial reasons and not primarily for the purpose of avoiding liability to tax (TCA 1997, s 141(5)(d)).

An EU Green Paper published at the end of 1995 defined "radical innovation" as "completely new and qualitatively different". The concept can apply at different category levels as follows:

1.   incremental change in existing products and/ or processes;
2.   modest improvement in existing products/ or processes;
3.   completely new products and/ or processes.

In the view of the Revenue, it seems that innovation at the first level would not amount to radical innovation. As regards the second level, innovation involves real but small-scale innovation and while innovation relating to products would probably be regarded as innovative, it is doubtful that that would hold true of processes. Innovation at the third level would be regarded as innovative, whether in relation to products or processes.

The following view on the matter was expressed by the Minister for Finance in the course of the passage of the 1995 Finance Bill through the Dáil:

"The term 'radical innovation' means the creation of something which is fundamentally novel. The degree of novelty cannot be other than a subjective judgment. However, there is an OECD precedent for classifying innovation as 'completely new', 'modestly improved' and 'merely a differentiation of an existing product or process'. In viewing the foregoing categories in the context of 'radical innovation' something completely new would come within its scope but a mere differentiation would not. The modestly improved product which is not a mere differentiation is more likely to be considered radical innovation than a modestly improved process.

A body of precedents exists to which inspectors can refer and the interpretation of 'radical' or 'innovative' can be reasonably adduced. This matter will be clarified with the taxation administration committee and guidelines will be given to domestic tax practitioners."

There is, however, no information as to the nature or location of the "body of precedent" referred to above and, to date, no guidelines have been issued. Until such time as these matters are progressed, persons requiring clarification will need to obtain advance Revenue agreement in individual cases by submitting all relevant data and information concerning the invention, including a copy of the patent application, a memorandum explaining how the product in question involves radical innovation, and any technical or trade literature substantiating that contention.

For the purpose of making their determination, the Revenue will consider any evidence submitted to them and may consult with any person who may be of assistance to them in the matter. The Revenue Commissioners' determination may be appealed to the Appeal Commissioners and all of the provisions relating to appeals against income tax assessments, the rehearing of appeals, and the stating of a case for the opinion of the

High Court on a point of law, will apply in the case of such an appeal and with any necessary modifications.

As regards the requirement in (b) above that the invention in question should have been patented for *bona fide* commercial reasons and not primarily for the purpose of avoiding liability to tax, it is difficult to see how this requirement would in practice operate to deny exemption. It is not easy to see how an invention involving radical innovation would have been patented primarily for tax reasons rather than for commercial reasons. Even if it appeared that the desire to obtain the benefit of the tax exemption was the primary motive for patenting the invention, it is not clear that tax would have been *avoided* since the result would be an exemption from tax specifically provided for in the relevant legislation; in other words, since the intention of the legislation is that there should be no tax liability in respect of certain income resulting from the patenting of certain inventions, there is no tax to be avoided.

(d) Distributions out of disregarded income and other profits

It is provided in TCA 1997, s 141(2) that a distribution made for an accounting period of the distributing company partly out disregarded income, and partly out other profits, is to be treated as consisting of two separate distributions respectively made out of exempt profits and out of other profits.

Example 11.112.3.1

Details of the income of Haynes & Co Ltd, an Irish resident company, for its accounting year ended 31 December 2007 are as follows:

	€	€
Case I		313,477
Less: corporation tax at 12.5%		39,185
		274,292
Exempt income from qualifying patents		46,000
Distributions from other companies:		
2/5/07 – ordinary dividend from Jon Ltd		
(from disregarded income)[1]	60,000	
3/4/07 – preference dividend from Rob Ltd		
(from qualifying patent income)[2]	18,000	
1/2/07 – dividend from Mag Ltd		
(from taxable income)	12,000	90,000
Distributable income		410,292

On 4 January 2008, Haynes & Co Ltd paid a dividend €410,292 on its ordinary shares out of its profits for the year ended 31 December 2007, made up as follows:

	€	€
Disregarded income:		
Exempt income from qualifying patents	46,000	
Exempt patent distributions received	60,000	106,000
Other profits:		
Case I (after tax)	274,292	

Distributions	30,000	304,292
Distribution		410,292

Accordingly, under TCA 1997, s 141(2) the dividend is to be treated as two distributions as follows:

	€
Distribution out of disregarded income	106,000
Distribution out of other profits	304,292

If the dividend of €410,292 includes a dividend of €4,103 to Mr Byrne, one of the shareholders, he is treated as having two distributions as follows:

	€
Patent distribution	1,060
Other distribution	3,043

Notes:

1 The ordinary shares in respect of which Haynes & Co Ltd received the dividend of €60,000 from Jon Ltd are taken to have satisfied the conditions for "eligible shares".

2 The preference shares in respect of which the company received the dividend of €18,000 from Rob Ltd are not eligible shares.

The provisions dealing with the attribution of distributions made by a company to the appropriate accounting periods and their allocation as between disregarded patent income and the other income of the accounting periods are dealt with in **11.114.2**. It as assumed here that the patent distributions have already been identified.

(e) The income tax exemption

For distributions received up to 23 April 1992, CTA 1976 s 170(3)(a)(i) provided that so much of any distribution as has been made by a company out of its disregarded income was not to be regarded as income for any purpose of the Income Tax Acts. To the extent that a distribution was a patent distribution, it was exempted from income tax in the hands of the recipient; to the extent that a patent distribution was exempt from income tax, it was exempt also from the health contribution, the self-employed PRSI contribution and any other income levies based on income as determined under the Income Tax Acts.

TCA 1997, s 141(4)(a) restricts the benefit of the income tax exemption (as regards distributions received after 23 April 1992) to:

(a) patent distributions in respect of "eligible shares" in the distributing company; and

(b) patent distributions made out of "relevant income", ie such distributions received by the inventor in relation to the qualifying patent, whether in respect of eligible shares or other shares or securities.

For the purposes of (b), the "inventor" in relation to a qualifying patent is any person who, either solely or jointly with another person, carried out the research, planning, processing, experimenting, testing, devising, designing, development or other similar activity leading to the invention which is the subject of the qualifying patent.

Example 11.112.3.2

The position is as in Example **11.112.3.1** where the dividend received by Mr Byrne from Haynes & Co Ltd comprises two deemed distributions, as follows:

	€
Patent distribution	1,060
Other distribution	3,043

Mr Byrne is not the "inventor" in relation to any of the patents giving rise to the disregarded income of Haynes & Co Ltd from which the dividend of 4 January 2008 was paid. However, it is established that the ordinary shares meet all the conditions to be eligible shares within TCA 1997, s 141.

Accordingly, Mr Byrne is fully exempt in respect of the patent distribution of €1,060 in respect of these shares and is liable to tax in respect of the distribution of €3,043. His position in respect of the full €4,103 distribution is therefore as follows:

Schedule F income – distribution	€3,043

Example 11.112.3.3

Mr Gradgrind, as a result of research, planning, experimenting and development activities carried out solely by him in the State, created a new formula for a product to be used in the remediation of polluted rivers and lakes. The product is patented in the State and in certain other countries.

The patents are transferred to an Irish resident company, Clearwater Ltd, which exploits the patent through licensing in the State and abroad. The company issues 25,000 ordinary shares and 200,000 10% preference shares, all at €1 each fully paid, as follows:

	Ordinary	Preference
	€	€
Mr Gradgrind	10,000	20,000
Mr Tulliver	5,000	80,000
Others	10,000	100,000

Clearwater Ltd derives royalty and other income from the licensing of the qualifying patents to Mr Gradgrind's invention. All of the income is exempt from corporation tax under TCA 1997, s 234 (as applied by TCA 1997, s 76(6)). Although the patents are licensed to connected parties in certain cases, the company has been able to demonstrate that the soil remediation process involved radical innovation and that it was not patented primarily for tax avoidance reasons. The company has no other income.

Clearwater Ltd pays dividends on its shares as follows:

	Ordinary	Preference
	€	€
Amounts paid	125,000	20,000

As Mr Gradgrind is the inventor in relation to the qualifying patent income out of which the dividends were paid, he is fully exempt from income tax (and the levies on income) in respect of his ordinary and preference dividends. Accordingly he receives the following amounts as disregarded income fully exempt from income tax (and levies):

	€

Ordinary dividend	50,000
Preference dividend	2,000

As Mr Tulliver is not the inventor, he will be exempt from tax in respect of his dividends to the extent that the related shares are eligible shares. It is assumed that the ordinary shares are such shares so that the ordinary dividend of €25,000 received by him is fully exempt from tax (including levies). As the preference shares are not eligible shares, Mr Tulliver is taxable in respect of his preference dividend of €8,000.

11.113   Distributions from exempt income: overview

11.113.1   Introduction

It was for many years necessary to ascertain whether and to what extent distributions were to be treated as having been made out of income taxed at the standard corporation tax rate, the various kinds of tax exempt income, manufacturing income, and export sales relieved income. This feature of the legislation became less relevant with changes in legislation dating from the early 1990s. Distributions from Shannon exempt and export sales relieved profits have been taxable since 6 April 1994. Tax credits were abolished for distributions made by companies after 5 April 1999. Numerous provisions referring to tax credits, relevant distributions and distributions from export sales relieved profits were repealed by FA 2000 s 69(2) with effect from 6 April 1999 for income tax purposes and as respects accounting periods commencing on or after that date for corporation tax purposes.

To put the post-5 April 1999 position relating to distributions into perspective, the following points can be made:

1. Distributions made by companies essentially fall into two main groups, those which are subject to tax under Schedule F and those which are exempt from tax. Exempt distributions are those paid out of exempted profits from stallion fees, stud greyhound fees, profits from commercial woodlands and exempt patent income. Taxable distributions are those paid from manufacturing profits, export sales relieved profits, Shannon exempt income, as well as distributions from profits subject to corporation tax.

2. Prior to 6 April 1999, it was necessary to attribute distributions to appropriate accounting periods for the purpose of ascertaining what distributions or parts of distributions were taxable and non-taxable, and also for the purpose of determining the appropriate tax credits attaching to the distributions.

3. After 5 April 1999, it is necessary to attribute distributions to accounting periods but only for the purpose of determining what distributions or parts of distributions are taxable and non-taxable. Taxable distributions are chargeable in full to income tax under Schedule F.

4. It is necessary to attribute distributions to accounting periods other than those for which they are declared where there is an insufficiency of distributable income, or as a result of an election under TCA 1997, s 154.

5. For the purposes of attributing distributions to accounting periods, "distributable income" is as defined in TCA 1997, s 144(8) (see **11.114.3**).

6. Essentially, it is now only necessary to distinguish between the exempt profits and any other profits of any accounting period to which distributions made on or after 6 April 1999 are attributed.

7. Although TCA 1997, s 154 (election to attribute distributions to one or more accounting periods – see **11.114.5**) refers to an attribution as being "for the purposes of sections 140, 141 and 144", it would seem that the only practical purpose of the s 154 election is to fix the extent to which a distribution is to be regarded as made respectively out of exempt income and out of taxable income, rather than for any specific purpose of any of these sections.

11.113.2 "Distributable income"

Before considering whether and to what extent a distribution is of any particular category, it is necessary first to determine the distributable income of the company in question for each accounting period to which the distribution is or may be attributed. "Distributable income" is defined in TCA 1997, s 144(8) (see **11.114.3**). For convenience, it may be worth repeating the definition here and, accordingly, the *distributable income* of a company for an accounting period is the amount determined by the formula:

$$(R - S) + T$$

where:

R is the amount of the company's income charged to corporation tax for the period plus any amount of the company's income that would be charged to corporation tax for the period but for TCA 1997, s 231 (stallion fee income – see **3.204.4**, **11.112.1** and **13.107.7**), 232 (occupation of woodlands – see **3.204.5** and **11.112.1**), 233 (stud greyhound service fees – see **3.204.4** and **11.112.1**) or 234 (income from qualifying patents – see **3.204.3** and **11.112.1-3**), or section 71 of the Corporation Tax Act 1976 (Shannon exempt income – see **7.103**), and for this purpose—

  (a) the income of a company for an accounting period is the amount of its profits for that period on which corporation tax falls finally to be borne (see **2.604**) exclusive of the part of the profits attributable to chargeable gains, and

  (b) the part referred to in (a) is the amount brought into the company's profits for the period for corporation tax purposes in respect of chargeable gains before any deduction for charges on income, expenses of management or other amounts which can be deducted from, or set against, or treated as reducing, profits of more than one description,

S is the amount of the corporation tax which, before any set-off of or credit for tax, including foreign tax, and after any relief under TCA 1997, s 448 (manufacturing relief – see **7.202**) or paragraph 16 or 18 of Schedule 32 (income tax or corporation profits tax losses), or section 58 of the Corporation Tax Act 1976 (export sales relief), is chargeable for the accounting period, exclusive of the corporation tax, before any credit for foreign tax, chargeable on the part of the company's profits attributable to chargeable gains for the period; and that part is the amount brought into the company's profits for the period for corporation tax purposes in respect of chargeable gains before any

> deduction for charges on income, expenses of management or other amounts which can be deducted from, or set against, or treated as reducing, profits of more than one description; and
>
> T   is the amount of the distributions received by the company in the accounting period which is included in its franked investment income of the period, plus any amount received by the company in the period to which TCA 1997, s 140(3)(a) (distributions from certain exempt profits – see **3.204.4-5**), 141(3)(a) (distributions from disregarded patent income – see **13.607.6**), 142(4) (distributions from profits of certain mines) or 144(3)(a) (Shannon distributions – **11.112.2**) applies.

Each distribution must in the first instance be treated as a distribution "for" (ie, attributed to) an accounting period, whether or not the distributable income of that accounting period is sufficient to cover the amount of the distribution concerned (and any other distribution previously attributed to the same accounting period).

TCA 1997, s 140(9) provides that any distribution not expressed to be for or in respect of a specified period must be attributed first to the accounting period in which it is actually made. This implies that any distribution expressed to be for or in respect of a specified period is attributed first to that specified period even if paid in a different period. For the purpose of this provision, a company may express a distribution as being paid for or in respect of the profits of a period considerably earlier than the period in which it is being made.

When a distribution is expressed to be for or in respect of a specified period, that period will usually coincide with an accounting period of the distributing company. On the other hand, a distribution may be expressed as being paid for a period of account which is not itself an accounting period and where part of that period of account is within an accounting period. In that case, TCA 1997, s 140(8) provides that the distribution is to be apportioned to the accounting period in the proportion that the part which is within the accounting period bears to the whole period of account.

Example 11.113.2.1

Kingman Ltd, an Irish resident company, has for many years carried on a manufacturing trade in respect of which it was eligible for the 10% corporation tax rate.

In addition to its trading income, Kingman Ltd has interest income and income earned directly from patents in respect of which the invention work was carried out in Ireland and giving rise to exempt income for corporation tax purposes. The company also receives various kinds of distributions from other resident companies.

Based on the information provided, the company's distributable income for two of its accounting periods, years ended 31 December 2004 and 31 December 2007, is as set out below.

	y/e 31/12/04 €	y/e 31/12/07 €
Case I:		
Income from manufacturing trade	110,000	210,000
Case III:		
Interest income	30,000	70,000
Total income	140,000	280,000

Corporation tax:		
€30,000 @ 25%	7,500	
€110,000 @ 12.5%	13,750	
€70,000 @ 25%		17,500
€210,000 @ 12.5%		26,250
Less:		
Manufacturing relief	(2,750)[1]	(5,250)[2]
Corporation tax payable	18,500	38,500
Income net of corporation tax payable	121,500	241,500
Add:		
Income exempt from corporation tax:		
Income from qualifying patents	18,600	19,500
Distributions from other companies:		
Distributions from manufacturing companies	15,000	24,000
Exempt Shannon distributions	6,000	4,000
Exempt distributions from patent income	4,000	7,000
ESR distributions	28,000	25,000
Other distributions	16,000	17,000
Distributable income	209,100	338,000

The amounts of distributable income, €209,100 and €338,000, are relevant to the later breakdown of distributions which may be attributed to the above accounting periods (see Example **11.113.3.1**).

Notes:

[1]   €13,750 x 1/5 = €2,750

[2]   €26,250 x 1/5 = €5,250

11.113.3   Analysis of distributable income

Total distributable income of an accounting period may be analysed under one or more of the following two categories:

(a)   tax exempt income (including any distributions received from any other resident company's tax exempt income or tax exempt distributions received); and

(b)   the aggregate of—

(i)   Case I income from "manufacturing" profits as reduced by the 10% corporation tax payable thereon,

(ii)   distributions received from income taxed at the 10% rate,

(iii)   Shannon exempt income,

(iv)   distributions received from Shannon exempt income,

(v)   any profits eligible for export sales relief,

(vi)   any ESR distributions received from any other company,

(vii)   other income chargeable to corporation tax (ie, the total income chargeable to corporation tax as reduced by the corporation tax payable thereon, and

(viii)   any other distributions received.

Example 11.113.3.1

From Example **11.113.2.1**, the total distributable income of Kingman Ltd for the years ended 31 December 2004 and 31 December 2007 is broken down as follows:

			y/e 31/12/04	y/e 31/12/07
			€	€
(1)	Tax exempt income			
	Income from qualifying patents		18,600	19,500
	Exempt distributions received:			
	Patent distributions (TCA 1997, s 141)		4,000	7,000
			22,600	26,500
(2)	Other income			
	Income after corporation tax		121,500	241,500
	ESR distributions		28,000	25,000
	Shannon distributions (TCA 1997, s 144)		6,000	4,000
	Distributions received from manufacturing companies		15,000	24,000
	Standard distributions received		16,000	17,000
			186,500	311,500
	Distributable income (1) + (2)		209,100	338,000

For the use of the above breakdown of the distributable income, see Examples **11.113.4.1** to **11.113.5.2**.

11.113.4   Attribution of distributions to accounting periods

The aggregate of the distributions attributed to any one accounting period can never exceed the total distributable income of that period. Once the total of the distributable income has been exhausted by way of distributions attributed to that income, any additional amount of distributions must be attributed to a different accounting period. Furthermore, if the latest distribution made exceeds the balance of distributable income remaining just prior to that distribution, the excess must be attributed to another accounting period.

Example 11.113.4.1

From Example **11.113.3.1** the distributable income of Kingman Ltd for the two years ended 31 December 2004 and 31 December 2007 was analysed as follows:

	y/e 31/12/04	y/e 31/12/07
	€	€
Tax exempt income	22,600	26,500
Other income	186,500	311,500
	209,100	338,000

Kingman Ltd declares dividends on its share capital as detailed below. It is assumed that no distributions paid before that of 17 May 2008 (see below) have been attributed to either of the two accounting periods so that the total distributable income for each period is still fully available for distribution.

(i) dividend on "A" ordinary shares of €40,000 payable on 17 May 2008 expressed to be a dividend in respect of the year ended 31 December 2004, and

(ii) dividend on "B" ordinary shares of €240,000 payable on 14 July 2008 expressed to be a dividend in respect of the year ended 31 December 2007.

Kingman Ltd makes two further distributions as follows:

(i) dividend of €130,000 on the "A" ordinary shares payable on 5 November 2008, and

(ii) dividend of €75,000 on the "B" ordinary shares payable on 12 November 2008.

In accordance with TCA 1997, s 154, the company initially decides to attribute both of these distributions to its year ended 31 December 2004. However, it is necessary first to ascertain whether it has sufficient distributable income for that period to cover both distributions. The following calculation is made:

	€
Distributable income for year ended 31/12/04:	209,100
Less: amount utilised by dividend of 17 May 2008	40,000
Amount remaining undistributed at 4 November 2008	169,100

Accordingly, the full 5 November 2008 dividend of €130,000 can be attributed to the year ended 31 December 2004, but that will leave only €39,100 remaining from the distributable income for the purposes of any later distribution. The remaining €35,900 of the €75,000 dividend of 12 November 2008, therefore, must be attributed to a different accounting period.

Kingman Ltd therefore decides to attribute the €130,000 dividend and €39,100 of the €75,000 dividend to the year ended 31 December 2004 and the balance of €35,900 of the later dividend to the year ended 31 December 2007 (for which there is a balance of €98,000 by way of distributable income remaining undistributed following the €240,000 dividend of 14 July 2008).

11.113.5 Analysis of distribution

A distribution made by a company may be analysed to ascertain whether and to what extent it is a distribution from tax exempt income and a distribution from other income. Distributable income may consist entirely of standard rate taxed income (including any "standard" distributions received), export sales relieved income (including any ESR distributions received), manufacturing income (including any distributions received from manufacturing income), exempt Shannon income (including any exempt Shannon distributions received) or tax exempt income (including distributions received from tax exempt income). Alternatively, it may comprise a mix of two or more of those categories of income.

1. Determination of tax exempt distribution

For the purpose of analysing a distribution in any case where the distributable income of a company for accounting period includes any tax exempt income, the relevant legislation does not specify what part of the income is to be regarded as exempt income but it has been the practice that any distribution attributed to that accounting period is made first out of the exempt income (so as to be a tax exempt distribution).

For the purpose of identifying the amounts of tax exempt distributions for any accounting period (whether patent distributions under TCA 1997, s 141 or exempt stallion fee, stud greyhound fee or commercial woodlands distributions under TCA 1997, s 140, the term *distributable income* is as defined in TCA 1997, s 144(8) (see **11.113.2** above).

In respect of distributable income that includes more than one category of exempt income, there are no provisions indicating which category of exempt income is to be treated as being distributed first. As a practical matter, however, this does should not present a difficulty as it is only necessary to identify how much of a distribution made by a company as consists of exempt income. If the amount of a distribution is greater than the aggregate of the exempt income for the relevant accounting period, each category of exempt income will in any event be allocated in full to the distribution (eg, as a patent distribution equal to the exempt patent income and as a stallion fee distribution equal to the exempt stallion fee income etc).

Example 11.113.5.1

In Example **11.113.4.1**, it was seen that the dividends of 17 May 2008 and 14 July 2008, as attributed respectively to the accounting periods ended 31 December 2004 and 31 December 2007 of Kingman Ltd, were as follows:

	€
Dividend of 17 May 2008 (attributed to y/e 31/12/04)	40,000
Dividend of 14 July 2008 (attributed to y/e 31/12/07)	240,000

The distributable income for each of the two accounting periods from which the two other distributions are made were as follows:

	y/e 31/12/04	*y/e 31/12/07*
	€	€
Exempt income	22,600	26,500
Other income	186,500	311,500
	209,100	338,000

Treating the tax exempt income as distributed before the other income, the other distribution amounts are now re-analysed between exempt distributions and distributions out of other income as follows:

	€	€
Distribution of 17 May 2008 (€40,000):		
Exempt distribution	22,600	
Distribution out of other income (balance)	17,400	
Distribution of 14 July 2007 (€240,000):		
Exempt distribution		26,500
Distribution out of other income (balance)		213,500

2. Determination of other distribution

Having ascertained the amount of the tax exempt distribution included in a given distribution, any remaining part will be a normal or "standard" distribution.

Example 11.113.5.2

In Example **11.113.5.1** it was seen that the "other distribution" balances remaining were as follows:

	€
Dividend of 17 May 2008	
Balance out of year ended 31 December 2004	17,400
Dividend of 14 July 2008	
Balance out of year ended 31 December 2007	213,500

The "distributable income" for the two years ended 31 December 2004 and 31 December 2007, after excluding tax exempt income, and which is therefore relevant for the purposes of identifying the standard distributions included in the above balances, is as follows:

	y/e 31/12/04	y/e 31/3/07
	€	€
Distributable income	209,100	338,000
Exempt distributions	22,600	26,500
Balance for payment of standard distributions	186,500	311,500
Paid as follows:		
Dividend of 17/5/08 (balance)	(17,400)	
Dividend of 14/7/08 (balance)		(213,500)
Dividend of 5/11/08	(130,000)	
Dividend of 12/11/08	(39,100)	(35,900)
Balance remaining	–	62,100)

11.114 Patent, Shannon and other exempt distributions

11.114.1 Introduction

The taxation of distributions made out of income exempted from corporation tax was dealt with in **11.112**. It is also necessary to consider when and to what extent distributions made by a company are treated as coming out of income which has been exempted from corporation tax (or out of distributions received from another company's exempted income).

The different types of distribution which may be made out of income exempted from corporation tax ("exempt income") or out of distributions received out of another resident company's exempt income ("exempt distributions") have been identified in **11.112**. These are "Shannon distributions" under TCA 1997, s 144, "patent distributions" under TCA 1997, s 141 and "stallion fee distributions", "stud greyhound fee distributions" and "commercial woodlands" distributions under TCA 1997, s 140.

In all cases, the rules for identifying and quantifying a company's exempt distributions are almost identical. In practice, the most relevant of the exempt distributions is the patent distribution as the corporation tax exemption for income from exempted trading operations in Shannon ceased to apply after 5 April 1990 (although some companies may still have undistributed exempt income from before 6 April 1990 from which to source exempt Shannon distributions). It is appropriate therefore to deal here mainly with the provisions relating to patent distributions and to refer more briefly to the other kinds of exempt distribution.

Consequent on the repeal by FA 2000 s 69(2) of TCA 1997, ss 145-151 (and other repeals and amendments arising out of the abolition of tax credits from 6 April 1999), the current treatment of distributions from exempt income, as dealt with principally in **11.114.2**, contrasts significantly with that for distributions made before 6 April 1999. In particular, the more complicated treatment for cases involving both manufacturing income and disregarded patent income no longer features. Reference can be made to the 1999-2000 edition of this book for the position that obtained in respect of distributions made before 6 April 1999.

11.114.2 Patent distributions

(a) General

TCA 1997, s 141 provides for the determination of the amount of any distribution which is to be regarded as made respectively out of exempt patent income and/or exempt patent distributions received from other companies (referred to together as "disregarded patent income") and out of other profits. For this purpose, the term "other profits" includes dividends or other distributions received from other resident companies except that it does not include any exempt patent distributions (TCA 1997, s 141(1)).

A distribution received by a company out of the disregarded patent income of another company is not disregarded patent income in the hands of the receiving company unless that distribution is paid in respect of "eligible shares" (ordinary shares meeting certain further conditions – see **11.112.3**) or is made out of "relevant income" (see below). Distributions out of qualifying patent income of another company are not "disregarded income" (ie, tax exempt income) if the patent income was received from a connected person (see *(c) Distributions from qualifying patent income received from connected persons* in **11.112.3**).

Relevant income means income which is referable to a qualifying patent in relation to which the person receiving the distribution carried out, either solely or jointly with another person, the research, planning, processing, experimenting, testing, devising, designing, development or other similar activity leading to the invention which is the subject of the qualifying patent.

TCA 1997, s 141(2) provides that a distribution for an accounting period that is made partly out of disregarded patent income and partly out other profits is to be treated as if it consisted of two separate distributions. The part of the distribution made out of the disregarded income is a "patent distribution"). The part paid out of other profits was, where paid before 6 April 1999, a distribution carrying a normal tax credit or a reduced tax credit (or one of the other types of distribution without a tax credit), depending on the nature and composition of those other profits.

To determine how much, if any, of a distribution is a patent distribution it is necessary first to attribute the distribution concerned to a particular accounting period or periods. The distribution can then be analysed into "separate" distributions by reference to the make up of the company's distributable income of the accounting period or periods to which it is attributed.

(b) Attribution to accounting periods

TCA 1997, s 141(10) applies the provisions of TCA 1997, s 140(8), (9) for the purpose of attributing each distribution to its appropriate accounting period. (A distribution is in the first instance attributed to a particular accounting period, whether or not the distributable income of that period is sufficient to cover the total distributions attributed to it.) A distribution attributed to an accounting period under these rules is said to be a distribution "for" that accounting period.

TCA 1997, s 140(9) provides that any distribution not expressed to be for or in respect of a specified period must be attributed first to the accounting period in which it is actually made; accordingly, a distribution expressed to be for or in respect of a specified period is attributed first to that period even if paid in a different period. For the purpose of this provision, it is possible for a distribution to be expressed to be paid for or in respect of the profits of a period considerably earlier than the period in which it is being made.

When a distribution is expressed to be for or in respect of a specified period, that period will usually coincide with an accounting period of the distributing company. On the other hand, a distribution may be expressed as being paid for a period of account which is not itself an accounting period and where part of that period of account is within an accounting period. In that case, TCA 1997, s 140(8) provides that the distribution is to be apportioned to the accounting period in the proportion that the part which is within the accounting period bears to the whole period of account.

Example 11.114.2.1

Jethro Ltd, an Irish resident company in receipt of income from qualifying patents and income from patent distributions and other distributions received from other resident companies, makes up accounts annually to 31 March. During its year ended 31 March 2008, it pays the following distributions:

	€
Ordinary dividend paid 21 September 2007, expressed to be paid out of the1475 company's profits of the year ended 31 March 2004	80,000
Section 130 distribution paid 15 November 20077 expressed to be paid for the 8 months ended 31 August 2007	12,000
Dividend paid 6 November 2007 not expressed to be paid for any period	17,500

The accounting periods to which these distributions are attributed are as follows:

(1)	Dividend paid 21 September 2007:	
	Treated as distribution for year ended 31 March 2004	80,000
(2)	Section 130 distribution paid 15 October 2007:	
	Treated partly as distribution for year ended 31 March 2007	
	3 months to 31 March 2007 12,000 x 3/8ths	4,500
	and partly as distribution for year ended 31 March 2008	
	5 months to 31 August 2007 12,000 x 5/8ths	7,500
(3)	Dividend paid 6 November 2007	
	Treated as distribution for year ended 31 March 2008	
	(period in which paid)	17,500

(c) Distributable income

In connection with patent income distributions, it is provided in TCA 1997, s 141(9) that a distribution attributed to an accounting period is treated as having been made out of the "distributable income" of that accounting period up to the amount of the distributable income for the period. If the amount of any distribution (excluding any relevant distribution) exceeds the distributable income of the accounting period to which it is attributed, the excess must be treated as paid out of the company's "most recently accumulated income" (see below), referred to here as the "excess distribution".

For the purpose of quantifying how much of the distribution concerned is a patent distribution, TCA 1997, s 141(9) provides that the term "distributable income" is to have the same meaning as that given in TCA 1997, s 144(8) (see **11.114.3**). Accordingly, the distributable income of a company for any relevant accounting period is arrived as follows:

(a) ascertain the amount of the income for the accounting period on which corporation tax falls finally to be borne (see **2.604**), in effect, the total chargeable income as reduced by charges on income, expenses of management and other amounts which can be deducted from or set against or treated as reducing profits of more than one description, and excluding any chargeable gains (before any such deductions);

(b) add any amounts of income that would be chargeable to corporation tax but for the fact that they are treated as exempt for that purpose, ie stallion fee income, stud greyhound service fee income, income from the occupation of woodlands, income from qualifying patents, Shannon exempt income (earned before 6 April 1990);

(c) deduct from the sum of (a) and (b) the amount of corporation tax payable, before any set-off of tax or credit for tax (including foreign tax) for the accounting period which is attributable to that income;

(d) add an amount equal to the total of all distributions received by the company in the accounting period which are included in the company's franked investment income; and

(e) add any amount received by the company in the period by way of distributions from exempt stallion fee, stud greyhound services or exempt commercial woodlands income, distributions from disregarded patent income, distributions from exempt profits of certain mines, and distributions from Shannon exempt income.

Example 11.114.2.2

Monroe Ltd, an Irish resident company owns a number of qualifying patents for the purposes of TCA 1997, s 234 (patents in respect of products connected with inventions devised in Ireland). It also owns non-qualifying patents, related to inventions devised in the United States. It derives exempt income from the licensing of the qualifying patents and also has certain income chargeable to corporation tax (including royalties from the non-qualifying patents) and receives distributions from other resident companies.

On 4 January 2008, the company pays a dividend of €260,000 on its ordinary shares expressed as payable for year ended 31 December 2007. TCA 1997, s 141(9) provides that the dividend is to be treated as paid out of the company's distributable income of this accounting period (to the extent of the distributable income).

Based on the information provided below, the company's distributable income for the year ended 31 December 2007 is computed in accordance with TCA 1997, s 144(8) as follows:

	€	€
Case III:		
Income from non-qualifying patents (licensed abroad)		50,000
Untaxed interest		38,000
Case IV:		
Income from non-qualifying patents (licensed in the State)		16,000
Total income chargeable to corporation tax		104,000
Less: corporation tax @ 25%		26,000
Total chargeable income after corporation tax		78,000
Exempt income from qualifying patents		95,000
Distributions received from other companies:		
Patent distributions within TCA 1997, s 141	45,000	
Other distributions	19,700	64,700
Distributable income		237,700

Since the dividend of €260,000 exceeds the distributable income of the accounting period, only the first €237,700 of the dividend can be attributed to the year ended 31 December 2007 while the remaining €22,300 must be treated as paid out of the most recently accumulated income (see Example **11.114.2.3**).

(d) Most recently accumulated income

The "most recently accumulated income", referred to in TCA 1997, s 141(9), out of which any "excess distribution" occurring in one accounting period is deemed to be paid is not defined. To ascertain a company's most recently accumulated income, however, it is evidently necessary to look first at the accounting period (the "first preceding period") immediately preceding that to which the distribution is first attributed to determine whether there is sufficient undistributed income in the first preceding period available to absorb the excess distribution carried back.

If the distributable income of the first preceding period exceeds the total of any earlier distributions attributed or carried back to that period, the amount of that accumulated income of the first preceding period is the most recently accumulated income for the purpose of TCA 1997, s 141(9). The excess distribution is then treated as coming out of the accumulated income of the first preceding period, to the extent of that income.

If, however, the amount of the accumulated income of the first preceding period is insufficient to cover the excess distribution brought back, the part of that excess distribution which exceeds that accumulated income is carried back to the next preceding accounting period (the "second preceding period") to be covered by the undistributed income of that period. This process is repeated, as far as is necessary, to a third and subsequent accounting periods. The accumulated income of any accounting period is the distributable income of that period less the total of any earlier distributions treated as paid out of that income.

In practice, the procedure can be made less tedious by expressing the current distribution as being payable in respect of an accounting period for which it is clear that there is sufficient undistributed income left to cover the current distribution.

Example 11.114.2.3

The position is as in Example **11.114.2.2** in which it was ascertained that €22,300 of the dividend paid by Monroe Ltd on 4 January 2008 exceeded the company's distributable income for the year ended 31 December 2007 to which the full dividend of €260,000 was initially attributed.

The excess distribution of €22,300 must be treated as paid out of the most recently accumulated income. The preceding accounting period, year ended 31 December 2006, must be looked at first and then, if necessary, the year ended 31 December 2005, and so on as necessary. It is also necessary to take into account any previous distributions taken from the distributable income of these periods.

The distributable income for the purposes of TCA 1997, s 141, based on the income details set out below, is calculated for each of the two preceding accounting periods as follows:

	y/e 31/12/05	y/e 31/12/06
	€	€
Total income chargeable to corporation tax	85,000	60,000
Less: corporation tax (assume all at standard rate):		
85,000 x 12.5%	10,625	
60,000 x 12.5%		7,500
Total chargeable income after corporation tax	74,375	52,500
Exempt income from qualifying patents	76,300	38,800
Distributions received from other companies:		
Patent distributions within TCA 1997, s 141	28,000	15,000
Other distributions	11,000	12,000
Distributable income for purposes of TCA 1997, s 141	189,675	118,300

Treatment of previous distributions

To ascertain the "most recently accumulated income" to cover the €22,300 excess distribution brought back from the year ended 31 December 2007, the amounts of previous distributions already deducted from the above amounts of distributable income must be identified.

It is learned that the company's only previous distributions attributable to any of the relevant accounting periods are as follows:

(1)   dividend of €100,000 paid on 6 March 2006 expressed to be for the year ended 31 December 2005, and

(2)   dividend of €150,000 paid on 18 March 2007 expressed to be for the year ended 31 December 2006.

For the purposes of TCA 1997, s 141, the dividend of €100,000 paid on 6 March 2006 is treated as a distribution for the year ended 31 December 2005 (the period for which it is expressed to be payable).

Likewise, the dividend of €150,000 paid on 18 March 2007 is expressed to be for the year ended 31 December 2006 and is treated as a distribution for that period.

However, the distributable income for the year ended 31 December 2006 is €118,300 so that only the first €118,300 of the dividend of €150,000 is treated as a distribution for that period for the purposes of TCA 1997, s 141. The balance of the dividend, €31,700, is an "excess distribution".

Accumulated income

For the purposes of the patent distribution provisions of TCA 1997, s 141, the dividend of €100,000 paid on 6 March 2006 and the distributions of €118,300 and €31,700 included in the dividend of €150,000 paid on 18 March 2007 are finally treated as paid out of the two accounting periods (to reduce the "accumulated" or undistributed income of the periods), as follows:

	y/e 31/12/05	y/e 31/12/06
	€	€
Distributable income for TCA 1997 s141	189,675	118,300
Less: dividend of 6 March 2006 (paid first)	100,000	
	89,675	
Less: dividend of 18 March 2007 (limited to distributable income y/e 31 December 2006)		118,300
Distribution carried back and deemed		
paid out of most recently accumulated income	31,700	_____
Accumulated income as at 19 March 2007 (TCA 1997 s141)	57,975	Nil

As regards the "excess distribution" part (€22,300) of the dividend of 4 January 2008, the most recently accumulated income available to absorb that amount is the €57,975 undistributed income of the year ended 31 December 2005 (since all the distributable income of the year ended 31 December 2003 has been used up by the dividend of 18 March 2008).

Summary

Based on the above figures and those in Example **11.114.2.2**, the dividend of €260,000 paid on 4 January 2008 is finally attributed to distributable income of accounting periods as follows:

	€
Treated as distribution for year ended 31 December 2007 (Example **11.114.2.2**)	237,700
Treated as distribution for year ended 31 December 2005	22,300
	260,000

(e) Determination of patent distribution

Having established the accounting period or periods out of which the distribution concerned has been made, and the breakdown of the total distributable income of each of these periods, the amount to be treated as a patent distribution under TCA 1997, s 141 is calculated.

There is, however, no provision in TCA 1997, s 141 (similar to the apportionment formula provided by the repealed TCA 1997, s 147 for identifying "manufacturing" distributions) for ascertaining the amount of a distribution treated as made out of the disregarded patent income. If the company's only income is exempt patent income and/ or patent distributions received, the full amount of the distribution is a patent distribution. The position is more difficult where a company has both disregarded patent income and other types of income.

In practice, the Revenue Commissioners will accept a claim that a distribution deemed by TCA 1997, s 140(8) or (9) to be a distribution "for" an accounting period in which there is any disregarded patent income may be treated as coming first out of that exempt income (up to the full amount of that income) and, as respects any balance remaining, out of other income.

In the case of a patent distribution made on or after 24 April 1992 in respect of shares which are not "eligible" shares (see **11.112.2**) to any person liable to income tax, that person (unless the inventor in relation to the relevant patents) is taxable on the amount of the distribution. However, it will be in the interest of ordinary shareholders (holders of eligible shares), who continue in most cases to enjoy tax exemption, that there is no change in the practice of treating distributions as paid first out of any disregarded patent income.

Example 11.114.2.4

The position is as in Example **11.114.2.3** where it was seen in the case of Monroe Ltd that the balance of the dividend of €260,000 dividend paid by the company on 4 January 2008 was to be treated for the purposes of TCA 1997, s 141 as paid out of the distributable income of two accounting periods as follows:

	€
y/e 31 December 2005	22,300
y/e 31 December 2007	237,700

The patent distribution content of each of these two amounts is computed as follows:
Amount paid out of income of y/e 31 December 2005
The distributable income for the year ended 31 December 2005 may now be analysed as follows:

	€	€
Disregarded patent income:		
Exempt income from qualifying patents	76,300	
Patent distributions received	28,000	104,300
Other taxed income/ distributions:		
Total chargeable income after corporation tax	71,400	
Other distributions received	11,000	82,400
Distributable income for purposes of TCA 1997, s 141		186,700

Before dealing with the €22,300 amount included in the 4 January 2008 distribution attributed to the year ended 31 December 2005, it is necessary to determine how much of the disregarded patent income has been paid out already by previous distributions attributed to the same accounting period. The distributions to date out of the €189,675 distributable income are broken down as follows:

	Disregarded income	Other income
	€	€
Totals for year ended 31 December 2005 (as above)	104,300	82,400
Less: part of dividend of 6 March 2006 (€100,000) taken first out of disregarded income with balance out of other income	(100,000)	Nil
Part (€31,700) of dividend of 18 March 2007 taken first out of disregarded income with balance out of other income	(4,300)	(27,400)
Balances left at 19 March 2007	Nil	55,000

Since there is no disregarded patent income remaining undistributed, no part of the €22,300 dividend paid on 4 January 2008 and attributed to the year ended 31 December 2005 will come out of disregarded patent income. Accordingly, the distribution of €22,300 is fully attributable to standard taxed income and does not give rise to any patent distribution.

Amount paid out of income of y/e 31 December 2007

To determine the amount of the patent distribution, in accordance with TCA 1997, s 141, the "distributable income" for the year ended 31 December 2007 (shown in detail in Example **11.114.2.2**), is restated here as follows:

	€	€
Disregarded patent income:		
Exempt income from qualifying patents	95,000	
Patent distributions received	45,000	140,000
Other taxed income/ distributions:		
Total chargeable income after corporation tax	78,000	
Standard distributions received	19,700	97,700
Distributable income for TCA 1997, s 141		237,700

The dividend of 4 January 2008 is the first distribution to be attributed to the year ended 31 December 2007. Since the full distributable income of €237,700 is being paid out as part of the dividend of 4 January 2008, the breakdown of this part of the dividend from this accounting period is as follows:

	€
Patent distribution (TCA 1997, s 141) out of disregarded income	140,000
Other distribution out of other income (all standard rate taxed)	97,700

Final make up of dividend

The dividend of €260,000 paid on 4 January 2008 may now be reassembled into its separate distributions, as follows:

	€	€
Patent distribution:		
Paid out of year ended 31 December 2007		140,000
Other distribution:		
Paid out of year ended 31 December 2007	97,700	
Paid out of year ended 31 December 2005	22,300	120,000
		260,000

11.114.3 Shannon distributions

The provisions for determining when and how much of a distribution is to be regarded as made out of income from Shannon exempted trading operations ("exempted trading income") and how much out of other profits are contained in TCA 1997, s 144. For the purposes of these provisions, a distribution received out of another company's exempted Shannon trading income (a "Shannon exempt distribution") is deemed to be made out of income from exempted trading operations (so that any distribution made out of Shannon exempt distributions received is itself a Shannon exempt distribution).

Although a distribution may still be categorised by TCA 1997, s 144 as being made from "exempted trading operations" (and is accordingly referred to here as a Shannon exempt distribution), it is important to note that such a distribution is not in fact exempt.

As pointed out in **11.113.1**, distributions from Shannon exempt profits have been taxable under Schedule F since 6 April 1994.

For convenience, references to "Shannon exempt income" are used here to include income from Shannon exempted trading operations and/or Shannon exempt distributions received from other companies. Exempted trading income does not arise to any company after 5 April 1990, but a company may well have undistributed exempted trading income earned before that date which is still available to be paid out as a Shannon exempt distribution after that date.

The term "other profits", for the purpose of TCA 1997, s 144, includes all dividends and other distributions received from other resident companies which are not Shannon exempt distributions (TCA 1997, s 144(1)), for example, patent distributions within TCA 1997, s 141 and income from those trading operations in Shannon which are taxed at the 10% corporation tax rate (as well as any other 10% taxed income). In other words, any kind of income apart from that from Shannon exempted trading operations and Shannon exempt distributions received are included in a company's "other profits" for the purposes of TCA 1997, s 144.

TCA 1997, s 144(2) provides that a distribution for an accounting period which is made partly out of Shannon exempt income and partly out other profits is to be treated as if it consisted of two separate distributions. The part of the distribution made out of the exempt income is a "Shannon distribution".

For the purpose of analysing a distribution to determine how much, if any, of it is a Shannon distribution, it is necessary first to attribute the distribution concerned to a particular accounting period or periods. The distribution can then be broken down into separate distributions by reference to the make up of the company's distributable income of the accounting period or periods to which it is attributed.

A distribution made for an accounting period is regarded as having been made out of the distributable income of that period to the extent of that income and, in relation to the excess of the distribution over that income, out of the most recently accumulated income (TCA 1997, s 144(7)). For this purpose, the *distributable income* of a company for an accounting period is defined in TCA 1997, s 144(8) as the amount determined by the formula:

$$(R - S) + T$$

where:

R   is the amount of the company's income charged to corporation tax for the period plus any amount of the company's income that would be charged to corporation tax for the period but for TCA 1997, s 231 (stallion fee income – see **3.204.4**, **11.112.1** and **13.107.7**), 232 (occupation of woodlands – see **3.204.5** and **11.112.1**), 233 (stud greyhound service fees – see **3.204.4** and **11.112.1**) or 234 (income from qualifying patents – see **3.204.3** and **11.112.1-3**), or section 71 of the Corporation Tax Act 1976 (Shannon exempt income – see **7.103**), and for this purpose—

    (a)   the income of a company for an accounting period is the amount of its profits for that period on which corporation tax falls finally to be borne (see **2.604**) exclusive of the part of the profits attributable to chargeable gains, and

(b)   the part referred to in (a) is the amount brought into the company's profits for the period for corporation tax purposes in respect of chargeable gains before any deduction for charges on income, expenses of management or other amounts which can be deducted from, or set against, or treated as reducing, profits of more than one description,

S   is the amount of the corporation tax which, before any set-off of or credit for tax, including foreign tax, and after any relief under TCA 1997, s 448 (manufacturing relief – see **7.202**) or paragraph 16 or 18 of Schedule 32 (income tax or corporation profits tax losses), or section 58 of the Corporation Tax Act 1976 (export sales relief), is chargeable for the accounting period, exclusive of the corporation tax, before any credit for foreign tax, chargeable on the part of the company's profits attributable to chargeable gains for the period; and that part is the amount brought into the company's profits for the period for corporation tax purposes in respect of chargeable gains before any deduction for charges on income, expenses of management or other amounts which can be deducted from, or set against, or treated as reducing, profits of more than one description; and

T   is the amount of the distributions received by the company in the accounting period which is included in its franked investment income of the period plus any amount received by the company in the period to which TCA 1997, s 140(3)(a) (distributions from certain exempt profits – see **3.204.4-5**), 141(3)(a) (distributions from disregarded patent income – see **13.607.6**), 142(4) (distributions from profits of certain mines) or 144(3)(a) (Shannon distributions – **11.112.2**) applies.

TCA 1997, s 144(9) applies the provisions of TCA 1997, s 140(8), (9) for the purpose of attributing the distribution concerned to its appropriate accounting period or periods. Each distribution must in the first instance be treated as a distribution "for" (ie, attributed to) an accounting period, whether or not the distributable income of that accounting period is sufficient to cover the amount of the distribution concerned (and any other distribution previously attributed to the same accounting period).

TCA 1997, s 145(9) provides that any distribution not expressed to be for or in respect of a specified period must be attributed first to the accounting period in which it is actually made. This implies that any distribution expressed to be for or in respect of a specified period is attributed first to that specified period even if paid in a different period. For the purpose of this provision, a company may express a distribution as being paid for or in respect of the profits of a period considerably earlier than the period in which it is being made.

It will be seen that the above described provisions of TCA 1997, s 144 for identifying and quantifying Shannon distributions also those which apply for the purposes of TCA 1997, s 141 in identifying and quantifying patent distributions. The position as it applies to Shannon distributions can therefore be summarised as follows:

(a)   ascertain the amount of the income for the accounting period on which corporation tax falls finally to be borne (see **2.604**), in effect, the total chargeable income as reduced by charges on income, expenses of management and other amounts which can be deducted from or set against or treated as reducing profits of more than one description, and excluding any chargeable gains (before any such deductions);

(b)　add any amounts of income that would be chargeable to corporation tax but for the fact that they are treated as exempt for that purpose, ie stallion fee income, stud greyhound service fee income, income from the occupation of woodlands, income from qualifying patents, Shannon exempt income (earned before 6 April 1990);

(c)　deduct from the sum of (a) and (b) the amount of corporation tax payable, before any set-off of tax or credit for tax (including foreign tax) for the accounting period which is attributable to that income;

(d)　add an amount equal to the total of all distributions received by the company in the accounting period which are included in the company's franked investment income; and

(e)　add any amount received by the company in the period by way of distributions from exempt stallion fee, stud greyhound services or exempt commercial woodlands income, distributions from disregarded patent income, distributions from exempt profits of certain mines, and distributions from Shannon exempt income.

Exemption from income tax was phased out for Shannon distributions received after 28 January 1992, but the "eligible shares" treatment which applies to patent distributions has no relevance for Shannon distributions. All distributions wholly or partly paid out of any Shannon exempt income (whether exempt trading income earned before 6 April 1990 or Shannon exempt distributions received) continue indefinitely to be Shannon exempt income in the hands of a recipient company (available to be distributed as a Shannon distribution), whatever the type of shares in respect of which they are received.

11.114.4　Other exempt distributions

The provisions of TCA 1997, s 140 relating to distributions made out of the other types of exempt income – exempt income from stallion or stud greyhound fees or commercial woodlands – are identical with those of TCA 1997, s 144 in relation to Shannon.

11.114.5　Attribution to accounting periods: TCA 1997, s 154 election

For the purpose of fixing how much, if any, of a distribution has been made by a company out of income which has benefited from Shannon exemption, exemption in respect of income from stallion or stud greyhound fees, the management of woodlands, patent royalty exemption or export sales relief, the company may make an election under TCA 1997, s 154 specifying the extent to which the distribution is to be treated as made for any accounting period or periods.

The company making the election must furnish a written notice to the inspector of taxes, specifying the accounting period(s) for which it requires the distribution concerned to be allocated. If more than one accounting period is specified, the notice must also specify how much of the distribution is to be allocated to each of the periods chosen. This notice must be given within six months after the end of the accounting period in which the distribution is made (TCA 1997, s 154(1)(a)). The election should normally be made separately for each distribution concerned.

The right of a company to specify an accounting period in relation to a distribution is subject to the following limitations:

(a)   the amount specified as a distribution may not exceed the amount of the undistributed income of the accounting period chosen as at the date of the distribution (ie, it cannot exceed the distributable income as reduced by any earlier distributions which have been attributed to the same accounting period);

(b)   no part of the distribution may be attributed to an accounting period which ended more than nine years before the date of the distribution unless, at the date of the distribution, there is no remaining undistributed income in any accounting period ended in the nine years before the date of the distribution;

(c)   subject to the exceptions listed in TCA 1997, s 154(3) (see below), the company may not attribute any part of a distribution to the accounting period in which the distribution is made.

The amount of the *undistributed income* for any accounting period on any day (which limits the amount of any distribution which may be allocated to that period) is defined by TCA 1997, s 154(6) (as amended by FA 2000) as the amount determined by the formula—

$$(R - S) + T - W$$

reduced by the amount of each distribution, or part or each distribution, made before the day in question and on or after 6 April 1989, which is to be treated under TCA 1997, s 154 (or which was treated under the repealed TCA 1997, s 147) as made for that accounting period,

where—

R, S and T have the same meanings respectively as in TCA 1997, s 144(8) (see **11.114.3** above), and W is the amount of the distributions made by the company before 6 April 1989 which—

(a)   were made for the accounting period,

(b)   are, by virtue of TCA 1997, s 154(7) (see below), deemed to have been made for the accounting period, or

(c)   would be deemed to have been made for the accounting period if TCA 1997, s 140(9) applied for the purposes of TCA 1997, s 154.

TCA 1997, s 140(9) provides that any distribution not expressed to be for or in respect of a specified period must be attributed first to the accounting period in which it is actually made (see **11.114.3** above).

Where the total amount of the distributions made by a company for an accounting period exceeds the amount represented by "(R - S) + T" (same meaning as above) for that period, the excess is deemed to be a distribution for the immediately preceding accounting period (TCA 1997, s 154(7)(a)).

Where the total amount of the distributions made, or deemed under paragraph (a) of TCA 1997, s 154(7) to have been made, by a company for the immediately preceding accounting period referred to in paragraph (a) exceeds the amount represented by "(R - S) + T" (see above) for that period, the excess is deemed to be a distribution for the immediately preceding accounting period and so on (TCA 1997, s 154(7)(b)).

A company may attribute the distribution concerned in any proportion it specifies between any of the accounting periods within the nine year period (but limited to the undistributed income of any accounting period specified).

Normally, the latest period to which a distribution can be attributed is the accounting period most recently ended before the date of the distribution. However, TCA 1997, s 154(3) permits a company to attribute any of the following types of distribution to the accounting period in which the distribution is made:

(a) an interim dividend paid before 1 January 2003 by the directors of a company, pursuant to powers conferred by its articles of association, in respect of the profits of the accounting period in which it is paid;

(b) a payment which is a distribution by virtue only of TCA 1997, s 130(2)(d)(ii), (iii)(I) or (v) (see **11.106**);

(c) a distribution made in respect of shares of the kind referred to in TCA 1997, s 138(1)(c) of the definition of "preference shares" (see **11.102.4**);

(d) a distribution made in the accounting period in which the company commences to be chargeable to corporation tax; or

(e) a distribution made in the accounting period in which the company ceases to be chargeable to corporation tax.

The fact that a distribution may be expressed to be payable for a particular period of account has no effect on the right of the company under TCA 1997, s 154 to specify the accounting period to which it is to be attributed.

Example 11.114.5.1

Austin Holdings Ltd, an Irish resident holding company receives dividends from a number of other resident companies and also certain untaxed interest income. Details of the company's income for the three years ended 31 December 2002, 2003 and 2004 are as follows:

	y/e 31/12/02	y/e 31/12/03	y/e 31/12/04
	€	€	€
Case III – untaxed interest income	160,000	200,400	320,000
Less: corporation tax @ 25%	40,000	50,100	80,000
Income after corporation tax (R - S)	120,000	150,300	240,000
Distributions received (T):			
Exempt patent distributions (TCA 1997, s 141)	Nil	120,000	160,000
Normal distributions	400,000	280,000	180,000
Distributable income ((R - S) + T)	520,000	550,300	580,000

Austin Holdings Ltd pays the following dividends in respect of its year ended 31 December 2004:

	€
Interim dividend for y/e 31/12/04 paid 30 December 2004	460,000
Final dividend for y/e 31/12/04 paid 26 March 2005	620,000

The company intends to make elections under TCA 1997, s 154 in respect of these distributions. It ascertains that its distributable income for the above three periods, as at 29 December 2004 (the day before the first of these dividends is paid), is as follows:

	y/e *31/12/02*	*y/e* *31/12/03*	*y/e* *31/12/04*
	€	€	€
Distributable income (as above)	520,000	550,300	580,000
Distributions already attributed:			
Dividend for y/e 31/12/02 paid 11/4/03	280,000		
Dividend for y/e 31/12/03 paid 15/3/04		300,000	
	240,000	250,300	580,000

The company also has undistributed income from earlier accounting periods back to the year ended 31 December 1988 (the first accounting period for which it had exempt income, in the form of an exempt patent distribution received from a subsidiary company on 3 December 1988). As some of these earlier accounting periods commenced before 6 April 1989, the distributable income of such periods was determined by reference to the formula "(R – S) + T – W", but it is not necessary to show the computations of these amounts here.

For the three years ended 31 December 1999, 2000 and 2001, it is ascertained that the undistributed income at 29 December 2004 is as follows:

	y/e *31/12/99*	*y/e* *31/12/00*	*y/e* *31/12/01*
	€	€	€
Distributable income ("(R - S) + T – W")	Nil	260,000	285,000
Distributions after 5 April 1989 attributed[1]:			
Dividend paid 16 April 2001 for y/e 31/12/00		148,000	
Dividend paid 6 May 2002 for y/e 31/12/01			166,000
Undistributed income at 29 December 2004	Nil	112,000	119,000

The total amounts of undistributed income at 29 December 2004 for each of the years ended 31 December 1988 to 31 December 1998 are ascertained to be as follows:

	€
y/e 31 December 1988	60,000
y/e 31 December 1989	80,000
y/e 31 December 1990	140,000
y/e 31 December 1991	110,000
y/e 31 December 1992	150,000
y/e 31 December 1993	170,000
y/e 31 December 1994	210,000
y/e 31 December 1995	148,000
y/e 31 December 1996	110,000
y/e 31 December 1997	Nil
y/e 31 December 1998	Nil

Election for 30 December 2004 dividend

This is an interim dividend but, as it was not paid before 1 January 2003, the company may not attribute any part of it to the current accounting period, year ended 31 December 2004. The company elects under TCA 1997, s 154 to attribute the dividend as follows:

	€
To y/e 31/12/95 (ended less than 9 years before 30/12/04)[2]	148,000
To y/e 31/12/02	240,000
To y/e 31/12/01	72,000
	460,000

Election for 26 March 2005 dividend

The undistributed income of the accounting periods which ended not more than nine years before 26 March 2005, following the attribution of the interim dividend of 30 March 2004, is as follows:

Year ended	€
31 December 2004	580,000
31 December 2003	250,300
31 December 2002 (€240,000 - €240,000)	Nil
31 December 2001 (€119,000 - €72,000)	47,000
31 December 2000	112,000
31 December 1997-99	Nil
31 December 1996	110,000
	1,099,300

The undistributed income for the three earlier accounting periods is as follows:

Year ended	€
31 December 1995 (€148,000 - €148,000)	Nil
31 December 1994	210,000
31 December 1993	170,000

Austin Holdings Ltd decides to clear out the undistributed income of the earlier accounting periods as far as possible. However, as the undistributed income for the nine years ended 31 December 1996 to 31 December 2004 (€1,099,300) exceeds the dividend of €620,000 now being paid, it cannot use the income of any period prior to the year ended 31 December 1996.

The company therefore elects to attribute the dividend of €620,000 of 26 March 2005 as follows:

	€
y/e 31 December 1996	110,000
y/e 31 December 2000	112,000
y/e 31 December 2001	47,000
y/e 31 December 2003	211,300
y/e 31 December 2004	139,700
	620,000

Notes:

1   "W" for each accounting period is the amount of distributions made before 6 April 1989 which were attributed to that period by applying TCA 1997, s 154(6), (7).

2   The year ended 31 December 1995 is the earliest accounting period to which the dividend paid on 30 March 2004 may be attributed since any earlier period ends more than nine years before that date and as the undistributed income at 29 December 2004 for the nine years ended 31 December 2003 totals €979,300 (which is greater than the dividend amount of €460,000).

Two or more distributions made on same day

It may happen that a company makes two or more distributions on the same day so that more than one dividend may be attributed to the same accounting period, or because the company decides to make that attribution by virtue of an election under TCA 1997, s 154.

Where the undistributed income of an accounting period immediately before the date of the distribution exceeds the total of two or more distributions being paid on the day in question, the distributions will be absorbed by that income so that each distribution remains a distribution for that accounting period. The position is more complex where the aggregate of the distributions exceeds the undistributed income of the accounting period.

A company is entitled to elect under TCA 1997, s 154 to attribute one of the distributions (or any part of that distribution) being made on the same day to an accounting period (up to the amount of the undistributed income of that period) in priority to the other distribution. In that case, and if there is insufficient undistributed income remaining to absorb all of the other distribution (or distributions), the excess of the other distribution (or distributions) over the remaining income may be attributed to a different accounting period by a further election under TCA 1997, s 154. If no such further election is made, the excess is attributed to the accounting period for which it was expressed to be made.

11.115 Supplementary distributions

Prior to the introduction of corporation tax, preference and certain types of shares were usually issued on terms providing for a gross dividend at a fixed percentage or of a fixed amount each year or half year and it was to be expected that income tax would be deducted at the standard rate (or at a reduced rate if any tax incentive relief applied). For dividends paid on or after 6 April 1976, and before 6 April 1999, in respect of preference and any other shares issued before 6 April 1976 on terms which entitled the shareholder to a dividend expressed as a fixed percentage or fixed amount, it was necessary to adjust the shareholder's dividend entitlement to reconcile with the corporation tax method which provides for dividends carrying tax credits, instead of dividends net of income tax.

For this purpose TCA 1997, s 139 (repealed by FA 2000 s 69(2)) provided, in the case of any dividend paid on or after 6 April 1976 (and before 6 April 1999) in respect of a right existing before 6 April 1976 to a dividend to which the shareholder was entitled was to be a lower amount (or "net" equivalent amount) to reflect the fact that the lower amount will carry a tax credit. TCA 1997, s 139 provided that the amount of the dividend in respect of any such pre-6 April 1976 fixed rate shares was to be an amount equal to the gross dividend originally provided for under the terms of issue as reduced by an amount equal to the standard tax credit rate in force at the date of the dividend. TCA 1997, s 139 is dealt with fully in previous editions of this book.

11.116   Dividend withholding tax

11.116.1   Introduction

Prior to 5 April 1999, dividends and other distributions paid by Irish resident companies had never been subject to deduction of tax on payment. This statement, however, needs to be qualified to some extent as regards the position governing dividends paid by Irish companies before 6 April 1976 (see **1.2**). Prior to the introduction of corporation tax, such dividends were payable subject to income tax at standard rate but that income tax was no more than a proportion of the income tax already paid by the company on the profits out of which the dividend was paid. Thus, there was no question of the paying company being obliged to account to the Revenue for income tax on payment of any dividend and all of the profits of an accounting period, net of income tax and corporation profits tax, were available for payment by way of dividend.

On the introduction of corporation tax, which replaced income tax and corporation profits tax, the two taxes formerly payable by most companies up to 5 April 1976, the concept of income tax as it related to dividends was no longer appropriate. In that respect, income tax was replaced by tax credits which represented part of the corporation tax paid by the dividend paying company in respect of the profits out of which the dividend was paid. Thus, some of the tax paid by the company was "imputed to" the shareholders who were thereby entitled to a credit attaching to their dividends. In the case of individual resident shareholders, that tax credit was credited against the income tax liability on the dividends receivable by them or was payable to them in certain circumstances.

The reduction, in 1988, in the standard corporation tax rate from 50% to 47% was to prove to be the commencement of a process of reducing corporation tax rates that is set to continue up to 1 January 2003 when the rate will be fixed at 12.5%. In line with this, the rate of the standard tax credit has also been reduced and had fallen from an initial 35/65ths to 11/89ths by 5 April 1999 following which tax credits were abolished altogether.

It is against the background of the abolition of tax credits on dividends that the dividend withholding tax was introduced with effect from 6 April 1999. Although referred to in the legislation as "dividend withholding tax", the tax applies to "relevant distributions" which has a somewhat wider meaning than "dividends".

11.116.2   Dividend withholding tax: outline

With effect from 6 April 1999, a withholding tax, at the standard rate on income tax, applies to dividends and other profit distributions (relevant distributions) paid by Irish resident companies. Certain shareholders are exempt from the dividend withholding tax. These are: Irish resident companies, charities, pension funds, certain amateur or athletic sporting bodies, designated brokers receiving dividends on behalf of holders of special portfolio investment accounts, certain collective investment undertakings and certain employee share ownership trusts, certain residents of Member States of the EU or of tax treaty countries, companies resident in another EU Member State or in a tax treaty country and which are not controlled by Irish residents, companies controlled by residents of EU Member States or tax treaty counties, and companies the principal class of the shares of which is substantially and regularly traded on a recognised stock exchange in an EU Member State or in a tax treaty country or which are 75% subsidiaries of such a company or which are wholly owned by two or more such companies.

It is necessary to declare exemption from the dividend withholding tax and documentary evidence is required in appropriate cases. For the first year of operation of the withholding tax, exemptions for certain non-resident shareholders may be based on a shareholder's address on the share register of the dividend paying company or, where the dividend is paid through an intermediary, the address of the non-resident person in the records of the intermediary.

Distributions which are not liable to income tax in the hands of the recipients (eg, certain patent dividends, dividends paid out of profits or gains from stallion fees, stud greyhound services or the occupation of woodlands and dividends from profits of certain mines) are exempt from dividend withholding tax. Paying companies are, however, obliged to return details of such distributions in their dividend withholding tax returns.

The obligation to withhold tax on relevant distributions falls on the paying company or on the authorised withholding agent acting for the company. That agent is entitled to receive distributions from the company without deduction of withholding tax and is obliged to apply withholding tax on payment of amounts representing those distributions on the same basis as if the distributions had been made directly by the company.

Relevant distributions may be made by a company or a withholding agent directly to the beneficial owners of those distributions, or indirectly to such owners through one or more qualifying intermediaries.

Where a distribution is to be made by a company or an authorised withholding agent directly to an exempt person, that person is obliged to provide evidence of entitlement to the exemption to the company or the agent. Where the distribution is made through a qualifying intermediary, evidence of entitlement to exemption must be furnished to the intermediary whereupon the intermediary will notify the company of the amount of the distribution to be received on behalf of exempt persons.

Where a distribution is to be made to an exempt person through a series of qualifying intermediaries, evidence of entitlement to exemption must be given to the qualifying intermediary from whom that person will finally receive payment. The intermediary will in that event convey to the intermediary next before in the series the amount to be received on behalf of exempt persons. The intermediary next before will then convey details of the amount of the distribution to be received by it, which will ultimately be passed on to exempt persons, to the company or, where there is another intermediary involved, to that intermediary. This process is repeated through any number of qualifying intermediaries. If any intermediary in the series is not a qualifying intermediary, withholding tax must be applied where the distribution is paid by that intermediary. Special arrangements are made for intermediaries being depositary banks which receive distributions on behalf of the holders of American depositary receipts.

Qualifying intermediaries and qualifying withholding agents must be authorised by the Revenue Commissioners with whom they must enter into formal agreements for that purpose. Qualifying withholding agents must be resident in the State or be carrying on a trade in the State through a branch or agency.

Qualifying intermediaries may be resident outside Ireland in a Member State of the EU or in a tax treaty country but in that event must enter into an agreement with the

Revenue Commissioners with a view to protecting the Exchequer. A person may not be an authorised withholding agent or a qualifying intermediary unless the person is, or is a subsidiary of, a licensed bank, a member of a recognised stock exchange in a Member State of the EU or in a tax treaty country or is otherwise considered by the Revenue Commissioners to be suitable to be such an agent or intermediary. Special arrangements are made for intermediaries being depositary banks which receive distributions on behalf of the holders of American depositary receipts.

Tax withheld from a relevant distribution must be paid to the Collector-General by the 14th of the month following the month in which the distribution is made. A return of all distributions must be made by companies, or withholding agents, and by qualifying intermediaries, indicating details of recipients, payments made and the amount of withholding tax deducted.

In the case of market claims, ie where dividends are incorrectly paid to a person by reason of delays in updating share registers, brokers and other intermediaries who are involved in settling such claims are legally obliged to deduct dividend withholding tax where that tax was not deducted at the time the distribution was originally made. They are obliged to pay all amounts so deducted to the Revenue Commissioners and to make an annual return containing details of dividend withholding tax so deducted during the previous year.

11.116.3 Definitions

TCA 1997, s 172A contains a number of important definitions relating to the legislation dealing with dividend withholding tax as provided for in Part 6 Chapter 8A. Some of the more important definitions are dealt with below.

TCA 1997, s 172A(1)(a) defines *dividend withholding tax* in relation to a relevant distribution as a sum representing income tax on the amount of the relevant distribution at the standard rate in force at the time the relevant distribution is made. A *relevant distribution* is:

(i) a distribution within the meaning of Schedule F paragraph 1 in TCA 1997, s 20(1), other than such a distribution made to a Minister of the Government as such Minister; and

(ii) any amount assessable and chargeable to tax under Case IV of Schedule D by virtue of TCA 1997, s 816 (taxation of shares issued in place of cash dividends – see **3.208.5**).

As regards (i) above, TCA 1997, s 20(1) refers in turn to TCA 1997 Part 6 Chapter 2 and ss 436, 437 and 816(2)(b). Part 6 Chapter 2 (ss 130-135) contains the basic legislation dealing with the meaning of "distribution" and is dealt with fully in **11.101-108**. TCA 1997, ss 436 and 437 deal respectively with distributions made by close companies by way of expenses for participators (see **10.202**) and interest paid to directors (see **10.203**). It is noteworthy that relevant distributions include distributions which are exempt from taxation by reason of being paid out of exempt profits, for example, exempt patent distributions and distributions from exempt stallion fees.

The operation of the dividend withholding tax is to a significant extent governed by the roles of the authorised withholding agent and the qualifying intermediary and these terms are defined in TCA 1997, ss 172G and 172E (see **11.116.7** and **11.116.8**).

An *intermediary* is a person who carries on a trade consisting of or including:

(a) the receipt of relevant distributions from a company or companies resident in the State; or

(b) the receipt of amounts or other assets representing such distributions from another intermediary or intermediaries.

A non-liable person in relation to a relevant distribution means the person beneficially entitled to the relevant distribution, being an excluded person or a qualifying non-resident person. The key terms excluded person and qualifying non-resident person are defined in TCA 1997, ss 172C and 172D(3) respectively and are dealt with in **11.116.5** and **11.116.6** below.

A *relevant territory* is a Member State of the European Communities other than Ireland, or a territory (not being such a Member State) with the government of which arrangements having the force of law by virtue of TCA 1997, s 826(1) have been made (ie, with which Ireland has concluded a tax treaty).

American depositary receipt has the same meaning as in FA 1992 s 207. It is an instrument:

(a) which acknowledges—

   (i)   that a depositary or a nominee acting on his behalf holds stocks or marketable securities which are dealt in and quoted on a recognised stock exchange, and

   (ii) that the holder of the instrument has rights in or in relation to such stocks or marketable securities including the right to receive such stocks or marketable securities from the depositary or his nominee, and

(b) which—

   (I)   is dealt in and quoted on a recognised stock exchange which is situated in the US, or

   (II) represents stocks or marketable securities which are so dealt in and quoted.

An *auditor* in relation to a company is the person or persons appointed as auditor of the company for the purposes of the Companies Acts 1963 to 1990, or under the law of the territory in which the company is incorporated and which corresponds to those Acts.

A *collective investment undertaking* is a collective investment undertaking within the meaning of TCA 1997, s 734 (see **12.802.1**), an undertaking for collective investment within the meaning of TCA 1997, s 738 (see **12.805.4**), an investment undertaking within the meaning of TCA 1997, s 739B (see **12.806.3**) or a common contractual fund within the meaning of TCA 1997, s 739I(a) (see **12.810.2**).

Pension scheme means an exempt approved scheme within the meaning of TCA 1997, s 774 (see **3.202.5**) or a retirement annuity contract or a trust scheme to which TCA 1997, s 784 or s 785 applies (see Pension business in **12.602**).

A *qualifying employee share ownership trust* is an employee share ownership trust which the Revenue Commissioners have approved of as a qualifying employee share ownership trust in accordance with TCA 1997 Schedule 12 (see **3.203.3**) and which approval has not been withdrawn.

The persons making and receiving relevant distributions are respectively referred to as the "relevant person" and the "specified person". A relevant person in relation to a relevant distribution means:

(a) where the relevant distribution is made by a company directly to the person beneficially entitled to it, that company; and

(b) where the relevant distribution is not made by the company directly to the person beneficially entitled to it but is made to that person through one or more qualifying intermediaries, the qualifying intermediary from whom the distribution, or an amount or other asset representing the distribution, is receivable by the person beneficially entitled to the distribution.

The *specified person* in relation to a relevant distribution is the person to whom the distribution is made, whether or not that person is beneficially entitled to the distribution.

The amount of a relevant distribution is an amount equal to:

(a) where the relevant distribution consists of a payment in cash, the amount of the payment;

(b) where the relevant distribution consists of an amount which is treated under TCA 1997, s 816 as a distribution made by a company, the amount so treated;

(c) where the relevant distribution consists of an amount which is assessable and chargeable to tax under Case IV of Schedule D by virtue of TCA 1997, s 816, the amount so assessable or chargeable; and

(d) where the relevant distribution consists of a non-cash distribution, other than a distribution referred to in (b) or (c), an amount equal to the value of the distribution (TCA 1997, s 172A(2)).

Tax in relation to a relevant territory means any tax imposed in that territory which corresponds to income tax or corporation tax in the State.

References to the making of a relevant distribution by a company, to a relevant distribution to be made by a company, or to the receipt of a relevant distribution from a company do not include, respectively, references to the making of a relevant distribution by a collective investment undertaking, to a relevant distribution to be made by a collective investment undertaking, or to the receipt of a relevant distribution from a collective investment undertaking (TCA 1997, s 172A(1)(b)).

11.116.4 Dividend withholding tax

With effect from 6 April 1999, a withholding tax, at the standard income tax rate, to dividends and other profit distributions paid by Irish resident companies. TCA 1997, s 172B(1) provides that where, on or after 6 April 1999, a company resident in the State makes a relevant distribution to a specified person:

(a) the company is required to deduct dividend withholding tax in relation to the relevant distribution out of the amount of that relevant distribution;

(b) the specified person must allow such deduction on receipt of the residue (ie, the balance after withholding tax) of the relevant distribution; and

(c) the company is to be acquitted and discharged of so much money as is represented by the deduction as if that amount of money had actually been paid to the specified person.

TCA 1997, s 172B(2) deals with the situation in which a relevant distribution is made by a company by way of giving additional share capital in the company (scrip dividends).

In short, the company is required to reduce the amount of additional share capital it issues by an amount equal to the amount of the dividend withholding tax.

Where, on or after 6 April 1999, an Irish resident company makes a relevant distribution to a specified person and the distribution consists of an amount referred to in TCA 1997, s 172A(2)(b) or (c) (see amount of a relevant distribution, (b) and (c), in **11.116.3** above), the dividend withholding requirement of TCA 1997, s 172B(1) is not to apply but, instead:

(a) the company is required to reduce the amount of the additional share capital to be issued to the specified person by such amount as will secure that the value at that time of the additional share capital issued to the specified person does not exceed an amount equal to the amount which the person would have received, after deduction of dividend withholding tax, if the person had received the distribution in cash instead of in the form of additional share capital of the company;

(b) the specified person must allow such reduction on receipt of the additional share capital;

(c) the company is to be acquitted and discharged of so much money as is represented by the reduction in the value of the additional share capital as if that amount of money had actually been paid to the specified person;

(d) the company becomes liable to pay to the Collector-General an amount (treated as a deduction of dividend withholding tax in relation to the relevant distribution) equal to the dividend withholding tax that would otherwise have been deductible from the relevant distribution; and

(e) the company becomes liable to pay that amount in the same manner in all respects as if it were the dividend withholding tax which would otherwise have been deductible from the relevant distribution.

TCA 1997, s 172B(3) is concerned with cases in which a relevant distribution is made by a company in non-cash form, other than a relevant distribution in the form of a scrip dividend (see above).

Where, on or after 6 April 1999, an Irish resident company makes a relevant distribution to a specified person and the distribution consists of a non-cash distribution, not being a relevant distribution to which TCA 1997, s 172B(3) applies, the dividend withholding requirement of TCA 1997, s 172B(1) is not to apply but, instead:

(a) the company becomes liable to pay to the Collector-General an amount (treated as a deduction of dividend withholding tax in relation to the relevant distribution) equal to the dividend withholding tax that would otherwise have been deductible from the relevant distribution;

(b) the company becomes liable to pay that amount in the same manner in all respects as if it were the dividend withholding tax which would otherwise have been deductible from the relevant distribution; and

(c) the company will be entitled to recover a sum equal to that amount from the specified person as a simple contract debt in any court of competent jurisdiction.

It will not always be possible to know with certainty whether or not a relevant distribution being made by a company is one to which the dividend withholding provisions of TCA 1997 Chapter 8A apply. For example, it will sometimes be difficult to know with certainty whether or not a particular shareholder is an excluded person or a qualifying non-resident person. TCA 1997, s 172B(4) accordingly permits a company which has satisfied itself that a relevant distribution to be made by it to a specified person is one to which the withholding provisions do not apply to treat it as such until such time as it has information to the effect that the distribution is or may be a relevant distribution to which the withholding provisions apply.

Subject to TCA 1997, s 129 (distributions from Irish resident companies not generally liable to corporation tax – see **3.205**), the computation of profits or gains of persons who are beneficially entitled to relevant distributions is not affected by the deduction for dividend withholding tax (TCA 1997, s 172B(5)). Accordingly, the amount of any such distributions received by such persons is to be taken into account in computing for tax purposes the profits or gains of those persons. The inclusion of relevant distributions for this purpose is subject to TCA 1997, s 129. Generally therefore, relevant distributions will not be included in the computation of profits or gains of companies for corporation tax purposes. By the same token, of course, relevant distributions paid to most resident companies, and to many non-resident companies, will not be subject to dividend withholding tax in any event.

Dividend withholding tax does not apply in the case of a relevant distribution made by an Irish resident company to its Irish resident parent company (TCA 1997, s 172B(8)). A parent company for this purpose is a company of which the dividend paying company is a 51% subsidiary (see **2.502**).

Dividend withholding tax does not apply in the case of a distribution made by an Irish resident subsidiary company to its parent company in another Member State of the EU where such withholding tax is prohibited under the Parent-Subsidiary Directive. TCA 1997, s 172B(6) provides that dividend withholding tax is not to apply to a relevant distribution where TCA 1997, s 831(5) applies in relation to that distribution. There is a similar exemption in respect of distributions paid to a parent company that is tax resident in Switzerland (see *Exemption from withholding tax* and *Exemption from withholding tax:Switzerland* in **14.702**).

Dividend withholding tax does not apply where a relevant distribution is made by an Irish resident company and the distribution is:

(a) a distribution made out of exempt profits within the meaning of TCA 1997, s 140 (profits or gains from stallion fees, stud greyhound services fees and the occupation of certain woodlands – see **11.112.1**);

(b) a distribution made out of disregarded income within the meaning of TCA 1997, s 141 (income from patent royalties) and to which TCA 1997, s 141(3)(a) applies (ie, which is treated as disregarded income – see **11.112.3**, **13.607.6**); or

(c) a distribution made out of exempted income within the meaning of TCA 1997, s 142 (profits of certain mines – see **11.112.1**) (TCA 1997, s 172B(7)).

DWT and TCA 1997, s 130(2)(d)(iv)

The question as to what distributions falling within TCA 1997, s 130(2)(d)(iv) are subject to DWT is somewhat complex and can depend on any of a number of factors, for example, the provisions of the "dividend" article or the non-discrimination article of a tax treaty. This matter is discussed in detail in **11.106**. Interest as described in TCA

1997, s 130(2)(d)(iv) but which, by virtue of TCA 1997, s 452 is not a distribution, is not subject to DWT.

11.116.5 Excluded persons

Distributions made to Irish resident companies, pension schemes, qualifying employee share ownership trusts, collective investment undertakings and charities are exempt from the dividend withholding tax, subject to the recipient in each case making a declaration regarding entitlement to exemption.

TCA 1997, s 172C(1) provides that dividend withholding tax is not to apply where an Irish resident company makes a relevant distribution to an excluded person. A person is an *excluded person* in relation to a relevant distribution where that person is beneficially entitled to the distribution and is:

(a)   without prejudice to the operation of TCA 1997, s 172B(8) (non-application of dividend withholding tax to dividends paid by a 51% subsidiary), a company resident in the State which has made a declaration (see below) to the relevant person in relation to the relevant distribution in accordance with TCA 1997 Sch 2A paragraph 3;

(b)   a pension scheme which has made a declaration to the relevant person in relation to the relevant distribution in accordance with TCA 1997 Sch 2A paragraph 4;

(c)   a qualifying fund manager or qualifying savings manager who—

(i)   is receiving the relevant distribution as income arising in respect of assets held:

(I)   in the case of a qualifying fund manager, in an approved retirement fund (ARF) or an approved minimum retirement fund (AMRF) (within the meanings respectively of TCA 1997, ss 784A and 784C – see **12.806.7**), and

(II)   in the case of a qualifying savings manager, in a special savings incentive account (see **12.603.7**), and

(ii)   has made a declaration to the relevant person in relation to the relevant distribution in accordance with TCA 1997 Sch 2A paragraph 4A,

(d)   a PRSA administrator (the PRSA ("Personal Retirement Savings Account") provider or a person to whom a PRSA provider delegates in pursuance of Part X of the Pensions Act, 1990, its administrative functions in relation to a PRSA, including a person resident in the State appointed by a non-resident PRSA provider to be responsible for the discharge of duties and obligations relating to PRSAs imposed on the PRSA administrator or provider) who is receiving the relevant distribution as income arising in respect of PRSA assets (assets held on behalf of a contributor in a PRSA and includes the value of any contributions made to that PRSA by any employer of the contributor) and has made a declaration to the relevant person in relation to the relevant distribution in accordance with TCA 1997 Sch 2A paragraph 10;

(e)   a qualifying employee share ownership trust (ESOT – see **3.203.3**) which has made a declaration to the relevant person in relation to the relevant distribution in accordance with TCA 1997 Sch 2A paragraph 5;

(f) a collective investment undertaking which has made a declaration to the relevant person in relation to the relevant distribution in accordance with TCA 1997 Sch 2A paragraph 6;

(g) a person who—

    (i) is entitled to exemption from income tax under Schedule F in respect of the relevant distribution by virtue of—

        (I) TCA 1997, s 189(2) (permanently incapacitated individuals who are exempt from income tax in respect of income arising from the investment of compensation payments made by the courts, or out of court settlements, in respect of personal injuries),

        (II) TCA 1997, s 189A(2) (trustees of "qualifying trusts", being trusts the funds of which were raised by public subscriptions on behalf of individuals who are permanently incapacitated from maintaining themselves) who are exempt from income tax in respect of income arising from the investment of trust funds),

        (III) TCA 1997, s 189A(3)(b) (permanently incapacitated individuals who are exempt from income tax in respect of payments received from such qualifying trusts and in respect of income arising from the investment of such payments), or

        (IV) TCA 1997, s 192(2) (payments in respect of thalidomide victims who are exempt from income tax in respect of income arising from the investment of compensation payments made by the Minister for Health and Children or the "thalidomide victims foundation"), and

    (ii) has made a declaration to the relevant person in relation to the relevant distribution in accordance with TCA 1997 Sch 2A paragraph 6A,

(h) a unit trust to which TCA 1997, s 731(5)(a) applies (see **12.806.3** under *(a) Unit trusts*) and which has made a declaration to the relevant person in relation to the relevant distribution in accordance with TCA 1997 Sch 2A paragraph 11;

(i) a person who—

    (i) is entitled to exemption from income tax under Schedule F in respect of the relevant distribution by virtue of TCA 1997, s 207(1)(b) (exemption for hospitals and other charities – see **12.1002**), and

    (ii) has made a declaration to the relevant person in relation to the relevant distribution in accordance with TCA 1997 Sch 2A paragraph 7 (TCA 1997, s 172C(2)),

(j) an approved body of persons which—

    (i) is entitled to exemption from income tax under Schedule F in respect of the relevant distribution by virtue of TCA 1997, s 235(2) (exemption for income of athletic or other sporting bodies – see **3.204.7**), and

    (ii) has made a declaration to the relevant person in relation to the relevant distribution in accordance with TCA 1997 Sch 2A para 7A, or

(k) a designated broker who—

(i) is receiving the relevant distribution as all or part of the relevant income or gains (within the meaning of TCA 1997, s 838 – see **12.602**) or a special portfolio investment account (SPIA), and

(ii) has made a declaration to the relevant person in relation to the relevant distribution in accordance with TCA 1997 Sch 2A para 7B (TCA 1997, s 172C(2)).

Approved body of persons has the same meaning as in TCA 1997, s 235 (see **3.204.7**).

For the purposes of TCA 1997, s 172C(2), certain persons who receive a relevant distribution are treated as being beneficially entitled to that distribution. These are: a collective investment undertaking, a designated broker receiving the distribution as all or part of the relevant income or gains of a special portfolio investment account (see **12.602**), a qualifying fund manager receiving the distribution as income in respect of assets held in an ARF or an AMRF (see (c)(i)(I) above), a qualifying savings manager receiving the distribution as income in respect of assets held in a special savings incentive account (see (c)(i)(II) above), and the trustees of a qualifying trust (within the meaning of TCA 1997, s 189A – see (g)(i)(II), (III) above) receiving the distribution as income in respect of the trust funds (TCA 1997, s 172C(3)).

Designated broker has the same meaning as in TCA 1997, s 838, ie a person which is a dealing member firm of the Irish Stock Exchange or a member firm (which carries on a trade in the State through a branch or agency) of a stock exchange of any other Member State of the European Communities, and which has sent to the Revenue Commissioners a notification of its name and address and of its intention to accept specified deposits (sums of money invested to acquire assets to be held in a special portfolio investment account).

For the purposes of TCA 1997, s 172C(2) and Sch 2A:

(a) a collective investment undertaking (see **11.116.3**) which receives a relevant distribution;

(b) a designated broker who receives a relevant distribution as all or part of the relevant income or gains (within the meaning of TCA 1997, s 838 – special portfolio accounts) of a special portfolio account;

(c) a qualifying fund manager or a qualifying savings manager who receives a relevant distribution as income arising in respect of assets held—

(i) in the case of a qualifying fund manager, in an approved retirement fund or an approved minimum retirement fund, and

(ii) in the case of a qualifying savings manager, in a special savings incentive account,

(d) a PRSA administrator who receives a relevant distribution as income arising in respect of PRSA assets;

(e) a unit trust to which TCA 1997, s 731(5)(a) applies (see **12.806.3** under *(a) Unit trusts*) which receives a relevant distribution in relation to units in that unit trust; and

(f) the trustees of a qualifying trust (within the meaning of TCA 1997, s 189A – special trusts for permanently incapacitated individuals) who receive a relevant distribution as income arising in respect of the trust funds, are treated as being beneficially entitled to the relevant distribution (TCA 1997, s 172C(3)).

There is a special tax regime in force in relation to SPIAs (essentially equity/gilt investment products) operated by designated stockbrokers on behalf of Irish resident individuals. Income and gains, whether realised or unrealised, arising from the investments are subject to an annual 20% tax charge which accounts for the full tax liability. In keeping with the intention of the SPIA legislation, distributions made to designated brokers for the benefit of the holders of SPIAs are exempt from dividend withholding tax.

Declaration by Irish resident companies

The declaration in accordance with TCA 1997 Sch 2A paragraph 3, to be made by an Irish resident company, is a declaration in writing to the relevant person in relation to relevant distributions which:

(a) is made by the person ("the declarer") beneficially entitled to the relevant distributions in respect of which the declaration is made;

(b) is signed by the declarer;

(c) is made in such form as may be prescribed or authorised by the Revenue Commissioners;

(d) declares that, at the time the declaration is made, the person beneficially entitled to the relevant distributions is a company resident in the State;

(e) contains the name and tax reference number of the company;

(f) contains an undertaking by the declarer that, if the person mentioned in (d) ceases to be an excluded person, the declarer will, by notice in writing, advise the relevant person in relation to the relevant distribution accordingly; and

(g) contains such other information as the Revenue Commissioners may reasonably require for the purposes of dividend withholding tax.

11.116.6 Exemption for certain non-residents

Relevant distributions made to certain non-residents are exempt from dividend withholding tax, being relevant distributions made to residents of foreign countries with which Ireland has a tax treaty (tax treaty countries), residents of EU Member States other than Ireland, companies not resident in the State which are ultimately controlled by residents of tax treaty countries or EU Member States other than Ireland, and companies the principal class of shares of which are substantially and regularly traded on a recognised stock exchange in such countries or Member States. In each case, an appropriate declaration must be made and evidence of entitlement to exemption provided

TCA 1997, s 172D(2) provides that dividend withholding tax is not to apply where, on or after 6 April 2000, a company resident in the State makes a relevant distribution to a qualifying non-resident person. A *qualifying non-resident person* in relation to a relevant distribution is a person beneficially entitled to the relevant distribution and who is:

(a) a person, other than a company, who—

(i) is neither resident nor ordinarily resident in the State,

(ii)   is, by virtue of the law of a relevant territory, resident for the purposes of tax in that territory, and

(iii)   has made a declaration (see **11.116.13**) to the relevant person in relation to the relevant distribution in accordance with TCA 1997 Sch 2A paragraph 8 and in relation to which declaration the certificate (see below) referred to in TCA 1997 Sch 2A paragraph 8(f) is a current certificate at the time the relevant distribution is made, or

(b)   a company which is not resident in the State and—

(i)   is, by virtue of the law of a relevant territory, resident for tax purposes in that territory, but is not under the control, directly or indirectly, of a person or persons who is or are resident in the State,

(ii)   is under the control, directly or indirectly, of a person or persons who, by virtue of the law of a relevant territory, is or are resident for tax purposes in that territory and who is or are not under the control, directly or indirectly, of a person or persons who is or are not so resident, or

(iii)   the principal class of the shares of which, or—

(I)   where the company is a 75% subsidiary (see **2.503**) of another company, of that other company, or

(II)   where the company is wholly-owned by two or more companies, of each of those companies,

is substantially and regularly traded on a stock exchange in the State, on one or more than one recognised stock exchange in a relevant territory or territories, or on such other stock exchange as may be approved by the Minister for Finance for the purposes of dividend withholding tax,

and which has made a declaration (see below) to the relevant person in relation to the relevant distribution in accordance with TCA 1997 Sch 2A paragraph 9 and in relation to which declaration each of the certificates referred to in clause (i), the certificate referred to in clause (ii) or, as the case may be, the certificate referred to in clause (iii), of subparagraph (f) of paragraph 9 (see (f)(i), (ii) and (iii) in relation to declaration below) is a current certificate at the time the relevant distribution is made (TCA 1997, s 172D(3)).

In determining whether or not a company is a 75% subsidiary or another company for the purposes of (b)(iii)(I) above, the equity entitlement provisions of TCA 1997, ss 412-418 (see **8.305**) apply as they would apply for the purposes of group relief if TCA 1997, s 411(1)(c) were deleted (ie, ignoring requirements relating to EU residence and to shares held as "trading stock" – see **8.302.2-302.3**) (TCA 1997, s 172D(5)).

In determining whether a company is wholly-owned by two or more companies for the purposes of (b)(iii)(II) above, the company (referred to as an "aggregated 100% subsidiary") is to be treated as being wholly-owned by two or more companies (referred to as the "joint parent companies") if and so long as 100% of its ordinary share capital is owned directly or indirectly by the joint parent companies, and for this purpose:

(a)   subsections (2) to (10) of TCA 1997, s 9 are to apply as they apply for the purpose of that section (meaning of "subsidiary" – see **2.505**); and

(b)   TCA 1997, ss 412-418 (see **8.305**) apply with any necessary modifications as they would apply for the purposes of group relief—

  (i)   if TCA 1997, s 411(1)(c) were deleted (ie, ignoring requirements relating to EU residence and to shares held as "trading stock" – see **8.302.2-302.3**), and

  (ii)   if TCA 1997, s 412(1) (the wording in which would be inappropriate to the position of joint parent companies – see **8.304.1**) were substituted by a subsection to the following effect:

Notwithstanding that at any time a company is an aggregated 100% subsidiary of the joint parent companies, it is not to be treated at that time as such a subsidiary unless additionally at that time—

  (I)   the joint parent companies are between them beneficially entitled to not less than 100% of any profits available for distribution to equity holders of the company, and

  (II)   the joint parent companies would be beneficially entitled between them to not less than 100% of any assets of the company available for distribution to its equity holders on a winding up (TCA 1997, s 172D(6)).

The certificate referred to in TCA 1997 Sch 2A paragraph 8(f) (non-resident other than a company) is a certificate given by the tax authority of the relevant territory in which the person is, by virtue of the law of that territory, resident for the purposes of tax certifying that the person is so resident in that territory.

Control in the definition of *qualifying non-resident person* in (b)(i) above (and in (f)(i) below) is to be construed in accordance with TCA 1997, s 432(2)–(6) (see **2.401**) as if in TCA 1997, s 432(6) (see **2.401.4**) "five or fewer participators" were substituted by "persons resident in the State" (TCA 1997, s 172D(3A)).

Control in the definition of *qualifying non-resident person* in (b)(ii) above is to be construed in accordance with TCA 1997, s 432(2)-(6) (see **2.401**) as if in TCA 1997, s 432(6) (see **2.401.4**) "five or fewer participators" were substituted by:

(a)   as regards the first mention of "control" in (b)(ii), "persons who, by virtue of the law of a relevant territory ... are resident for the purposes of tax in such a relevant territory" (see Example **11.116.6.3** below) (TCA 1997, s 172D(4)(a); and

(b)   as regards the second mention of "control" in (b)(ii), "persons who are not resident for the purposes of tax in a relevant territory ..." (TCA 1997, s 172D(4)(b)).

Example 11.116.6.1

Rhinestone Ltd is tax resident in the Cayman Islands and is wholly owned by Lodestar Inc, a US company whose shareholders are all resident in the US.

Rhinestone Ltd is a qualifying non-resident person as it is under the control of a person who is tax resident in a relevant territory, the US, and because that person, Lodestar Inc, is not under the control of a person or persons not resident in a relevant territory.

The relevance of the second mention of "control", referred to in (b) above, is illustrated in the following example.

Example 11.116.6.2

Rhinestone Ltd is tax resident in the Cayman Islands and is wholly owned by Lodestar Inc, a US company wholly owned by a Brazilian company whose shareholders are all resident in Brazil.

Rhinestone Ltd is not a qualifying non-resident person as, although it is under the control of a person who is tax resident in a relevant territory, that person, Lodestar Inc, is under the control of persons not resident in a relevant territory.

The wide meaning of "control" as defined in TCA 1997, s 432 can have surprising results, as can be seen in the following example.

Example 11.116.6.3

Kleber GmbH, a company incorporated and tax resident in Liechtenstein, is owned as follows:

	%
Matthew Ronan	20
Patricia Ronan	10
Frances McCarthy	20
Joseph McCarthy	10
Four unrelated individuals owning 10% each	40
	100

All shareholders are Irish resident and ownership refers to both equity holdings and voting rights. Gillian Ronan, a daughter of Matthew and Patricia Ronan, has been living in Switzerland for a number of years. Patrick McCarthy, a son of Frances and Joseph McCarthy, has been living in Greece for a number of years. Neither Gillian Ronan nor Patrick McCarthy has any interest in or connection with Kleber GmbH.

Kleber GmbH is about to receive a dividend from Garryowen Ltd, an Irish resident company, and it is necessary to ascertain whether or not dividend withholding tax should be deducted from the dividend.

In accordance with TCA 1997, s 432(6), the shareholdings of Matthew and Patricia Ronan are attributed to Gillian Ronan (an associate of each) so that she is deemed to own 30% of Kleber GmbH. Similarly, the shareholdings of Frances and Joseph McCarthy are attributed to Patrick McCarthy so that he is also deemed to own 30% of the company.

TCA 1997, s 432(6) (as applied by TCA 1997, s 172D(4)(a)) provides that such attributions are to be made under the subsection as will result in the company being treated as under the control of persons tax resident in a relevant territory if it can be so treated. In fact, the company can be so treated by virtue of TCA 1997, s 432(3) which provides that, where two or more persons satisfy any of the conditions for control, they are to be taken to have control of the company. Accordingly, Gillian Ronan and Patrick McCarthy, who are residents of relevant territories but who have no connection with the company, are treated as having control of Kleber GmbH and the company is therefore a qualifying non-resident person in relation to the dividend to be paid by Garryowen Ltd.

A condition of Kleber GmbH being a qualifying non-resident person is that it has made a declaration to Garryowen Ltd in accordance with TCA 1997 Sch 2A paragraph 9 (see (a) to (h) below) and in relation to which declaration the certificate referred to in clause (ii) of paragraph 9(f) is a current certificate at the time the dividend is paid.

The declaration in accordance with TCA 1997 Sch 2A paragraph 9, to be made by a non-resident company, is a declaration in writing to the relevant person in relation to relevant distributions which:

(a)   is made by the person ("the declarer") beneficially entitled to the relevant distributions in respect of which the declaration is made;

(b)   is signed by the declarer;

(c)   is made in such form as may be prescribed or authorised by the Revenue Commissioners;

(d)   declares that, at the time the declaration is made, the person beneficially entitled to the relevant distributions is a company which is a qualifying non-resident person;

(e)   contains—

  (i)   the name and address of that company,

  (ii)   the name of the territory in which the company is resident for the purposes of tax,

(f)   is accompanied by—

  (i)   a certificate given by the tax authority of the relevant territory in which the company is, by virtue of the law of that territory, resident for tax purposes certifying that the company is so resident in that territory, and a certificate signed by the auditor of the company certifying that in the auditor's opinion the company is not under the control (within the meaning of TCA 1997, s 172D(3A) – see above), directly or indirectly, of a person or persons who is or are resident in the State,

  (ii)   a certificate signed by the auditor of the company certifying that in the auditor's opinion the company is a company which is not resident in the State and is under the control (within the meaning of TCA 1997, s 172D(4)(a) – see above), directly or indirectly, of a person or persons who, by virtue of the law of a relevant territory, is or are resident for the purposes of tax in such a relevant territory and who is or are not under the control (within the meaning of TCA 1997, s 172D(4)(b) – see above), directly or indirectly, of a person or persons who is or are not so resident, or

  (iii)   a certificate signed by the auditor of the company certifying that in the auditor's opinion the principal class of the shares of the company or—

    (I)   where the company is a 75% subsidiary (within the meaning of TCA 1997, s 172D(5) – see above) of another company, of that other company, or

    (II)   where the company is wholly owned (within the meaning of TCA 1997, s 172D(6) – see above) by two or more companies, of each of those companies,

    is substantially and regularly traded on a stock exchange in the State, on one or more than one recognised stock exchange in a relevant territory or territories or on such other stock exchange as may be approved of by the Minister for Finance for the purposes of dividend withholding tax,

(g)   contains an undertaking by the declarer that, if the person mentioned in (d) ceases to be a qualifying non-resident person, the declarer will, by notice in writing, advise the relevant person in relation to the relevant distribution accordingly; and

(h) contains such other information as the Revenue Commissioners may reasonably require for the purposes of dividend withholding tax.

As noted in **2.401.1** and **2.401.5**, the particular meanings of "control" are without prejudice to the general meaning of control. The general definition of control in TCA 1997, s 432(2) refers both to direct and indirect control over the company's affairs. The reference to "control" is to control at the level of general meetings of shareholders since it is that control that confers on its holder the power to make the ultimate decisions as to the business of the company and in that sense to control its affairs.

Example 11.116.6.4

Elm Ltd, an Irish resident company pays a dividend to its Kenyan parent, Thika Ltd. The equity and voting control interests in Thika Ltd are as represented below. A Flynn and G Cross are unconnected Irish resident individuals, Details regarding beneficial interests and other matters relating to the M Mann Trust are unclear. Sitka Ltd holds the entire equity and voting control in Thika Ltd. It can be assumed that Lodge Ltd is not controlled by persons who are not resident in relevant territories.

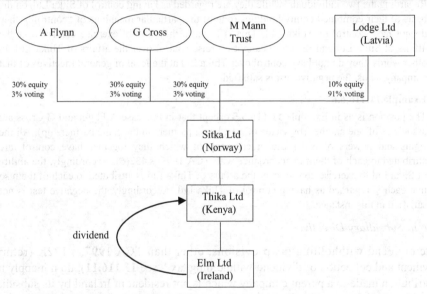

It is required to establish that Thika Ltd is a qualified non-resident person in accordance with TCA 1997, s 172D(3)(b)(ii) (see (b)(ii) in relation to the meaning of *qualifying non-resident person* above). Thika Ltd must satisfy a "positive" test to the effect that it is controlled by persons who are resident in a relevant territory and who themselves are not controlled by persons who are not so resident. Thika Ltd is controlled by Sitka Ltd, a person resident in a relevant territory (Norway). Sitka Ltd is itself not controlled by persons not so resident. On the one hand, it is controlled by Lodge Ltd, a person resident in a relevant territory (Latvia) and it has been confirmed that that company is not controlled by persons not resident in a relevant territory. Sitka Ltd is also controlled by the two Irish resident individuals so, on this basis also, it is controlled by persons resident in a relevant territory.

An alternative and simpler approach to satisfying this "positive" test would, in the first instance, identify Lodge Ltd as the person controlling Thika Ltd; Lodge Ltd is resident in a relevant territory and is not itself controlled by persons not so resident.

Example 11.116.6.5

The facts are as in Example **11.116.6.4** but in this case it is required to establish that Thika Ltd is a qualified non-resident person in accordance with TCA 1997, s 172D(3)(b)(i) (see (b)(i) in relation to the meaning of *qualifying non-resident person* above), Specifically, Thika Ltd must satisfy a "negative" test to the effect that it is not controlled, directly or indirectly, by persons resident in Ireland. Clearly, Thika Ltd is controlled by Sitka Ltd. It is clear also that Sitka Ltd, as well as being controlled by Lodge Ltd on the basis of voting control, is also controlled by the two Irish resident individuals since between them they hold more than 50% of the ordinary shares in the company. The question which then arises is whether the two individuals have control of Thika Ltd.

Since Sitka Ltd can exercise control over the affairs of Thika Ltd, it controls that company (in accordance with the general meaning of "control"). In view of the extent of its voting control in Sitka Ltd, Lodge Ltd controls Sitka Ltd since, again, it can exercise control over its affairs. Lodge Ltd therefore also (indirectly) controls Thika Ltd since it can exercise control over the affairs of the company (Sitka Ltd) which in turn can exercise control over the affairs of Thika Ltd. In other words, Lodge Ltd has control of Thika Ltd at the level of general meetings of that company.

Regarding the two individuals, while they are regarded as having control of Sitka Ltd, on the basis of their combined equity holdings (one of the particular meanings of "control"), they do not have control of Thika Ltd. This is because they do not exercise control over the affairs of Sitka Ltd and therefore cannot exercise control over the affairs of Thika Ltd. In other words, they do not have control over Thika Ltd at the level of general meetings of that company. Thus, the negative test is satisfied.

Example 11.116.6.6

The position is as in Example **11.116.6.5** except that in this case A Flynn and G Cross are associates of one another (by virtue of, say, being partners in the same partnership). All the rights and powers of Sitka Ltd, a company of which they together have control, are attributed to each of them in accordance with TCA 1997, s 432(6). Accordingly, the ability of Sitka Ltd to exercise control over the affairs of Thika Ltd is attributed to each of them so that each is regarded as having control of Thika Ltd. Accordingly, the negative test is not satisfied in this instance.

Parent-Subsidiary Directive

The dividend withholding tax provisions, other than TCA 1997, s 172K (returns, payment and collection of dividend withholding tax – see **11.116.11**), do not apply to a distribution made to a parent company which is not resident in Ireland by its subsidiary which is a company resident in Ireland (TCA 1997, s 831(5) – see also **14.702**).

This exclusion from the withholding provisions will not, however, apply in the case of a distribution to a parent company if the majority of the voting rights in the parent are controlled directly or indirectly by persons other than persons who, by virtue of the law of any relevant territory, are resident for the purposes of tax in such a territory, unless it is shown that the parent company exists for bona fide commercial reasons and does not form part of any arrangement or scheme of which the main purpose, or one of the main purposes, is the avoidance of liability to income tax (including dividend withholding tax), corporation tax or capital gains tax (TCA 1997, s 831(6)).

Where dividend withholding tax does not apply by virtue of TCA 1997, s 831(5), income tax is not chargeable in respect of the distribution, and the amount or value of the distribution is treated for the purposes of TCA 1997, ss 237 and 238 (see **4.302-3**) as not brought into charge to income tax (TCA 1997, s 153(5)). Accordingly, where for any reason dividend withholding tax has been deducted in a case coming within TCA 1997, s 831(5), the recipient of the distribution will be entitled to reclaim the amount of that tax. (See also **11.116.10** – credits or repayments in respect of dividend withholding tax).

Tax in relation to a relevant territory means any tax imposed in that territory which corresponds to income tax or corporation tax in the State.

Tax Treaties

Certain tax treaties provide for taxation of dividends only in the country in which the beneficial owner of the dividends is a resident. In some of these cases, this provision is dependent on, say, the recipient holding a minimum percentage of the voting power of the dividend paying company; in other cases there are no conditions (apart from residence) relating to the recipient.

The recipient of a dividend paid by an Irish resident company may not be a "qualifying non-resident person" within the meaning of TCA 1997, s 172D(3) but may be taxable, by virtue of a tax treaty, in the country of residence only. A practical question which arises in such a case is whether or not the dividend paying company may pay the dividend without deduction of withholding tax. That in turn raises the question as to whether the Revenue may authorise the payment of the dividend without withholding tax. In fact, the dividend paying company should deduct withholding tax at the full rate and the recipient should then make an appropriate refund claim.

11.116.7   Authorised withholding agent

The obligation to deduct withholding tax on relevant distributions falls on the paying company or on the authorised withholding agent acting for the company. That agent generally receives distributions from the company for the benefit of the person beneficially entitled to them without deduction of withholding tax (TCA 1997, s 172G(1)) and is obliged to apply withholding tax on payment of amounts representing those distributions on the same basis as if the distributions had been made directly by the company.

Authorised withholding agent

An authorised withholding agent in relation to relevant distributions to be made by an Irish resident company is an intermediary who:

(a)   is resident in the State or, if not so resident, is, by virtue of the law of a relevant territory, resident for the purposes of tax in that territory, and carries on through a branch or agency in the State a trade consisting of or including the receipt of relevant distributions from an Irish resident company or companies on behalf of other persons;

(b)   has entered into an authorised withholding agent agreement (see below) with the Revenue Commissioners; and

(c)   has been authorised by the Revenue Commissioners, by way of notice in writing, to be an authorised withholding agent in relation to relevant distributions to be made to the person by Irish resident companies for the benefit of other persons who are beneficially entitled to the relevant distributions, which authorisation has not been revoked under TCA 1997, s 172G(6) (TCA 1997, s 172G(2)).

The Revenue Commissioners may not authorise an intermediary to be an authorised withholding agent unless the intermediary is:

(a) a company which holds a licence granted under section 9 of the Central Bank Act 1971, or a person who holds a licence or other similar authorisation under the law of any relevant territory which corresponds to that section;

(b) a person who is wholly owned by a company or person referred to in (a);

(c) a member of the Irish Stock Exchange Limited or of a recognised stock exchange in a relevant territory; or

(d) a person suitable, in the opinion of the Revenue Commissioners, to be an authorised withholding agent for the purposes of TCA 1997 Chapter 8A (TCA 1997, s 172G(4)).

Authorised withholding agent agreement

An *authorised withholding agent agreement* is an agreement entered into between the Revenue Commissioners and an intermediary under the terms of which the intermediary undertakes:

(a) to accept and retain all declarations, with accompanying certificates, and notifications (other than any notice given to the intermediary by the Revenue Commissioners) made or given to the intermediary in accordance with TCA 1997 Part 6 Chapter 8A (dividend withholding tax) and Schedule 2A (declarations by resident companies and other persons, for the longer of the following periods—

　　(i) six years,

　　(ii) a period which, in relation to the relevant distributions for which the declaration or notification is made or given, ends not earlier than three years after the date on which the intermediary has ceased to receive relevant distributions on behalf of the person who made the declaration or, as the case may be, gave the notification to the intermediary,

(b) on being so required by notice in writing given to the intermediary by the Revenue Commissioners, to make available to the Commissioners, within the time specified in the notice—

　　(i) all declarations, certificates or notifications referred to in (a) above which have been made or, as the case may be, given to the intermediary, or

　　(ii) such class or classes of such declarations, certificates or notifications as may be specified in the notice,

(c) to inform the Revenue Commissioners if the intermediary has reasonable grounds to believe that any such declaration or notification made or given by any person was not, or may not have been, a true and correct declaration or notification at the time of the making of the declaration or the giving of the notification;

(d) to inform the Revenue Commissioners if the intermediary has at any time reasonable grounds to believe that any such declaration made by any person would not, or might not, be a true and correct declaration if made at that time;

(e) to operate the provisions of TCA 1997, s 172H (obligations of authorised withholding agent in relation to relevant distributions – see below) in a correct and efficient manner;

(f) to provide to the Collector-General the return referred to in TCA 1997, s 172K(1) (see **11.116.11** below) and to pay to the Collector-General any dividend withholding tax required to be included in such a return, within the time specified in that section;

(g) to provide to the Revenue Commissioners, not later than three months after the end of the first year of the operation of the agreement by the intermediary, a report on the intermediary's compliance with the agreement in that year, which report is to be signed by—

    (i) if the intermediary is a company, the auditor of the company, or

    (ii) if the intermediary is not a company, a person who, if the intermediary were a company, would be qualified to be appointed auditor of the company,

and thereafter, on being required by notice in writing given to the intermediary by the Revenue Commissioners, to provide to the Commissioners, within the time specified in the notice, a similar report in relation to such other period of the operation of the agreement by the intermediary as may be specified in the notice, and

(h) to allow for the verification by the Revenue Commissioners of the intermediary's compliance with the agreement and the provisions of TCA 1997 Chapter 8A in any other manner considered necessary by the Commissioners (TCA 1997, s 172G(3)).

The Revenue Commissioners may examine or take extracts from or copies of any declarations, certificates or notifications made available to the Commissioners as described in (b) above (TCA 1997, s 172G(3A)).

The authorisation by the Revenue Commissioners of an intermediary as an authorised withholding agent for the purposes of dividend withholding tax will cease to have effect on the day before the seventh anniversary of the date from which such authorisation applied, but this is not to prevent:

(a) the intermediary and the Revenue Commissioners from agreeing to renew the authorised withholding agent agreement entered into between them or to enter into a further such agreement; and

(b) a further authorisation by the Revenue Commissioners of the intermediary as an authorised withholding agent for the purposes of dividend withholding tax (TCA 1997, s 172G(8)).

List of authorised withholding agents

A list of authorised withholding agents is required to be maintained by the Revenue Commissioners. Notwithstanding any obligation as to secrecy or other restriction on disclosure, the Commissioners may make available to any person the name and address of any such authorised withholding agent (TCA 1997, s 172G(5)). If the Commissioners are satisfied at any time that an authorised withholding agent has failed to comply with the authorised withholding agent agreement or the provisions of TCA 1997 Chapter 8A, or is otherwise unsuitable to be an authorised withholding agent, they may, by notice in writing served by registered post on the agent, revoke the authorisation with effect from such date as may be specified in the notice (TCA 1997, s 172G(6)). Notice of the revocation is to be published in Iris Oifigiúil.

As at November 2004, the Governor and Company of the Bank of Ireland, together with its nominee companies, IBI Nominees Ltd and Bank of Ireland Nominees Ltd, have been listed as authorised withholding agents.

Obligations of authorised withholding agent

TCA 1997, s 172H imposes certain obligations on authorised withholding agents in relation to relevant distributions. Where an authorised withholding agent is to receive, on behalf of other persons, any relevant distributions to be made by an Irish resident company, it must notify that company by notice in writing that it is an authorised withholding agent in relation to those distributions. An authorised withholding agent essentially steps into the shoes of the company making the relevant distribution. Where the agent receives, on behalf of another person, a relevant distribution from an Irish resident company, and gives that distribution, or any amount or other asset representing that distribution, to that other person, the dividend withholding tax as provided for in TCA 1997 Chapter 8A is to operate with any necessary modifications as if:

(a)   the authorised withholding agent were the company making the distribution; and

(b)   the giving by the authorised withholding agent of the relevant distribution, or other amount or other asset representing that distribution, to that other person were the making of the relevant distribution by the authorised withholding agent to that other person at the time the relevant distribution was made by the company to the authorised withholding agent,

so that, except where otherwise provided, TCA 1997, s 172B (dividend withholding tax on relevant distributions) is to apply in relation to that relevant distribution and the authorised withholding agent will be obliged to pay and account for the dividend withholding tax, if any, due in relation to the relevant distribution (TCA 1997, s 172H(2)).

Where at any time an Irish resident company makes a relevant distribution to a person and the relevant distribution would otherwise be treated as being made to an authorised withholding agent for the benefit of another person, the distribution is to be treated as not being made to the authorised withholding agent for that purpose unless, at or before that time, the authorised withholding agent has notified the company in accordance with TCA 1997, s 172H(1) (see above) that it is an authorised withholding agent in relation to the relevant distribution. In the absence of such notification, TCA 1997, s 172B will accordingly apply in relation to the relevant distribution (TCA 1997, s 172H(3)).

11.116.8   Qualifying intermediary

Relevant distributions may be made by a company or a withholding agent directly to the beneficial owners of those distributions, or indirectly to such owners through one or more qualifying intermediaries.

Where a distribution is to be made by a company or an authorised withholding agent directly to an exempt person, that person is obliged to provide evidence of entitlement to the exemption to the company or the agent. Where the distribution is made through a qualifying intermediary, evidence of entitlement to exemption must be furnished to the intermediary whereupon the intermediary will notify the company of the amount of the distribution to be received on behalf of exempt persons.

Withholding tax not to apply

TCA 1997, s 172E(1) provides that, subject to TCA 1997, s 172F(6) (see below), dividend withholding tax is not to apply where a company resident in the State makes a relevant distribution through one or more than one qualifying intermediary for the benefit of a person beneficially entitled to that distribution who is a non-liable person in relation to the distribution.

Qualifying intermediary

A person is a qualifying intermediary in relation to relevant distributions to be made to the person by a company resident in the State, and in relation to amounts or other assets representing such distributions to be paid or given to the person by another qualifying intermediary, if the person is an intermediary who:

(a) is resident in the State or who, by virtue of the law of a relevant territory, is resident for the purposes of tax in the relevant territory;

(b) has entered into a qualifying intermediary agreement (see below) with the Revenue Commissioners; and

(c) has been authorised by the Revenue Commissioners, by way of notice in writing, to be a qualifying intermediary in relation to relevant distributions to be made to the person by Irish resident companies, and in relation to amounts or other assets representing such distributions to be paid or given to the person by another qualifying intermediary, for the benefit of other persons who are beneficially entitled to the relevant distributions, which authorisation has not been revoked under TCA 1997, s 172E(6) (TCA 1997, s 172E(2)).

The Revenue Commissioners may not authorise an intermediary to be a qualifying intermediary unless the intermediary is:

(i) a company which holds a licence granted under section 9 of the Central Bank Act 1971, or a person who holds a licence or other similar authorisation under the law of any relevant territory which corresponds to that section;

(ii) a person who is wholly owned by a company or person referred to in (i);

(iii) a member firm of the Irish Stock Exchange Limited or of a recognised stock exchange in a relevant territory; or

(iv) a person suitable, in the opinion of the Revenue Commissioners, to be a qualifying intermediary for the purposes of TCA 1997 Part 6 Chapter 8A (TCA 1997, s 172E(4)).

American depositary receipts

The dividend withholding tax legislation makes special arrangements for Irish companies using American depositary receipts (ADRs) through American depositary banks. ADRs are dollar denominated negotiable instruments which enable US investors to trade in non-US securities. They are traded on the principal US stock exchanges (New York, AMEX, NASDAQ) and afford non-US companies easy access to the US capital markets. Many quoted companies and some emerging new companies in Ireland have raised substantial amounts of capital in the US through the use of ADRs.

An *American depositary receipt* is an instrument which acknowledges that a depositary, or a nominee acting on his behalf, holds stocks or marketable securities and that the holder of the ADR has rights in or in relation to such stocks or marketable securities, including the right to receive such stocks or marketable securities from the depositary or his nominee. A *depositary* is a person who holds stocks or marketable securities in trust for or on behalf of holders of ADRs and who maintains a register of ownership of such ADRs. A depositary will market shares which are the subject of ADRs by creating American depositary shares (ADSs) which are essentially bundles of issued shares. The depositary creates the ADRs which are notes or pieces of paper which evidence or are secured on the ADSs. The holder of an ADR may demand the transfer to him of the underlying ADSs.

To secure the payment of a dividend free of withholding tax, it is generally necessary to arrange for a series of certifications from the individual shareholder through all relevant intermediaries up to the company paying the dividend. Thus, only genuine residents of tax treaty countries will be able to benefit from the exemption from withholding. The scale of US investment in Irish companies through the use of ADRs, however, is such that the burden of certification necessary to secure exemption from the withholding tax would be unduly onerous. Accordingly, American depositary banks in receipt of dividends from Irish banks for transmission to US based holders of ADRs are facilitated through a less burdensome certification procedure.

An American depositary bank may receive and pass on Irish dividends without deduction of withholding tax where the bank's ADR register shows that the direct beneficial owner of the dividends has a US address on that register, even though this is not supported by a certificate of US tax residence. If there is a further intermediary, for example a mutual fund, between the bank and the beneficial owner, dividends may also be paid gross where the bank receives confirmation from the intermediary to the effect that the owner's address in the intermediary's records is in the US, again without being supported by a certificate of tax residence in the US.

Qualifying intermediary agreement

A *qualifying intermediary agreement* is an agreement entered into between the Revenue Commissioners and an intermediary under the terms of which the intermediary undertakes:

(a) to accept and retain all declarations, with accompanying certificates, and notifications (other than any notice given to the intermediary by the Revenue Commissioners) made or given to the intermediary in accordance with TCA 1997 Part 6 Chapter 8A (dividend withholding tax) and Schedule 2A (declarations by resident companies and other persons, for the longer of the following periods—

   (i) six years,

   (ii) a period which, in relation to the relevant distributions for which the declaration or notification is made or given, ends not earlier than three years after the date on which the intermediary has ceased to receive relevant distributions on behalf of the person who made the declaration or, as the case may be, gave the notification to the intermediary,

(b) on being so required by notice in writing given to the intermediary by the Revenue Commissioners, to make available to the Commissioners, within the time specified in the notice—

    (i) all declarations, certificates or notifications referred to in (a) above which have been made or, as the case may be, given to the intermediary, or

    (ii) such class or classes of such declarations, certificates or notifications as may be specified in the notice,

(c) to inform the Revenue Commissioners if the intermediary has reasonable grounds to believe that any such declaration or notification made or given by any person was not, or may not have been, a true and correct declaration or notification at the time of the making of the declaration or the giving of the notification;

(d) to inform the Revenue Commissioners if the intermediary has at any time reasonable grounds to believe that any such declaration made by any person would not, or might not, be a true and correct declaration if made at that time;

(e) to operate the provisions of TCA 1997, s 172F (see *Obligations of qualifying intermediary* below) in a correct and efficient manner and provide to the Revenue Commissioners the return referred to in TCA 1997, s 172F(7) within the time specified in TCA 1997, s 172F(8) (see *Returns by qualifying intermediaries* below);

(f) to provide to the Revenue Commissioners, not later than three months after the end of the first year of the operation of the agreement by the intermediary, a report on the intermediary's compliance with the agreement in that year, which report is to be signed by—

    (i) if the intermediary is a company, the auditor of the company, or

    (ii) if the intermediary is not a company, a person who, if the intermediary were a company, would be qualified to be appointed auditor of the company,

(f) and thereafter, on being required by notice in writing given to the intermediary by the Revenue Commissioners, to provide to the Commissioners, within the time specified in the notice, a similar report in relation to such other period of the operation of the agreement by the intermediary as may be specified in the notice;

(g) if required by the Revenue Commissioners, to give a bond or guarantee to the Commissioners sufficient to indemnify them against any loss arising by virtue of the fraud or negligence of the intermediary in relation to the operation by the intermediary of the agreement and the provisions of TCA 1997 Chapter 8A;

(h) where the intermediary is a depositary bank holding shares in trust for, or on behalf of, the holders of American depositary receipts—

    (i) if authorised to do so by the Revenue Commissioners, to operate the provisions of TCA 1997, s 172F(3)(d) (obligations of qualifying intermediary, being a depositary bank: persons to be included in Exempt Fund – see *Exempt fund* under *Obligations of qualifying intermediary* below), and

  (ii) to comply with any conditions in relation to such operation as may be specified in the agreement, and

 (i) to allow for the verification by the Revenue Commissioners of the intermediary's compliance with the agreement and the provisions of TCA 1997 Chapter 8A in any other manner considered necessary by the Commissioners (TCA 1997, s 172E(3)).

The Revenue Commissioners may examine or take extracts from or copies of any declarations, certificates or notifications made available to the Commissioners as described in (b) above (TCA 1997, s 172E(3A)).

The authorisation by the Revenue Commissioners of an intermediary as a qualifying intermediary for the purposes of dividend withholding tax will cease to have effect on the day before the seventh anniversary of the date from which such authorisation applied, but this is not to prevent:

 (a) the intermediary and the Revenue Commissioners from agreeing to renew the qualifying intermediary agreement entered into between them or to enter into a further such agreement; and

 (b) a further authorisation by the Revenue Commissioners of the intermediary as a qualifying intermediary for the purposes of dividend withholding tax (TCA 1997, s 172E(8)).

List of qualifying intermediaries

A list of qualifying intermediaries is to be maintained by the Revenue Commissioners. Notwithstanding any obligation as to secrecy or other restriction on disclosure, the Commissioners may make available to any person the name and address of any such qualifying intermediary (TCA 1997, s 172E(5)). If the Commissioners are satisfied at any time that a qualifying intermediary has failed to comply with the qualifying intermediary agreement or the provisions of TCA 1997 Chapter 8A, or is otherwise unsuitable to be a qualifying intermediary, they may, by notice in writing served by registered post on the intermediary, revoke the authorisation with effect from such date as may be specified in the notice (TCA 1997, s 172E(6)). Notice of the revocation is to be published in Iris Oifigiúil.

The following is a list of qualifying intermediaries, together with associated nominee companies, as authorised by the Revenue Commissioners by November 2004.

Company	Associated nominee company
Ulster Bank Markets (Nominees) Ltd	None
Davy Stockbrokers	Davy Nominees Ltd
	Davycrest Nominees Ltd
Bank of Ireland Securities Services Limited	IBI Nominees Ltd
	Bank of Ireland Nominees Ltd
Bloxham Stockbrokers	Mole Nominees Ltd
	Tusker Holdings Ltd
	Bloxham Nominees Ltd
Dolmen Butler Briscoe	Scoti Co Ltd
	College Green Nominees Ltd
Goodbody Stockbrokers	Skerries Nominees Ltd
	Goodbody Nominees Ltd

Company	Associated nominee company
Campbell O'Connor & Co	Camocon SPIA Ltd
	Ashdale Investment Trust Services Ltd
ABN AMRO Stockbrokers (Ireland) Ltd	Riada Nominees
NCB Stockbrokers Ltd	Aurum Nominees
	Russell Nominees
	Quince Nominees
	NCB Broking Nominees
	Harlequin Nominee
BCP Stockbrokers	Relko Nominees Ltd
AIB Investment Managers Ltd	None
Union Bank of California Global Custody	None
Allied Irish Nominees Ltd	None
Mars Nominees Limited	None
Merrion Stockbrokers Ltd	Merrion Stockbrokers Nominee Ltd
Societe Generale	Hambros Bank (Nominees) Ltd
The Bank of New York	See below * attached schedule to Letter of Authorisation and additional letters dated 21/10/02 and 15/04/03 issued to the Bank of New York
Delta Lloyd Bank NV	None
Carr Sheppards Crosthwaite	Ferlim Nominees Ltd
	R & R Nominees Ltd
	Bell Nominees Ltd
	Tudor Nominees Ltd
	PEP Services Nominees Ltd
	Investment Administration Nominees Ltd
	Carr Investment Services Nominees Ltd
	Carr PEP Nominees Ltd
Brown Brothers Harriman & Company	Brown Brothers Harriman Trustee Services (Ireland) Ltd
Bank of Tokyo-Mitsubishi	Tokyotrust Nominees Ltd
Royal Trust Corporation of Canada	Roy Nominees Ltd
Sumitomo Trust and Banking Co (USA)	None
Investors Bank & Trust Co	None
Boston Safe Deposit & Trust Company	None
Quilter & Co. Ltd	Morgan Stanley Quilter Nominees Ltd
Quilter Co. Ltd	(formerly Commercial Union Quilter
Dublin Branch t/a Morgan Stanley Quilter	Nominees Ltd)
	Quilpep Nominees Ltd
	Coastal Nominees Ltd
	Morgan Stanley Quilter (Ireland) Nominees Ltd
State Street Bank & Trust Company	State Street Nominees Ltd.
Deutsche Bank Trust Company Americas (formerly Bankers Trust Company)	None
Northern Trust Company	Nortrust Nominees Ltd

Company	Associated nominee company
Paine Webber Inc	None
Redmayne Bentley	Redmayne (Nominees) Ltd
	Redmayne Nominees PEP Ltd
C Hoare & Co	Hoares Bank Nominees
	Messrs Hoare Trustees
Deutsche Bank AG London Branch	Morgan Nominees Ltd
	Channel Nominees Ltd
	Pembol Nominees Ltd
	BT CTAG Nominees Ltd
	BT Globenet Nominees Ltd
Daiwa Securities Trust & Banking (Europe) plc	None
Reyker Securities plc	Reyker Nominees Ltd
	Appleby House Nominees Ltd
Bank of Ireland Trustee Company Ltd	None
HSBC Bank plc	See attached schedule to Letter of Authorisation issued by the RevenueCommissioners to HSBC Bank plc on 09/01/02
JP Morgan Chase Bank – London Branch (Investor Services)	None
JP Morgan Chase Bank – London Branch (Institutional Trust Services)	Guaranty Nominees Ltd Hanover Nominees Ltd
KAS Bank NV	KAS Nominees Ltd
Hapoalim Nominees Ltd	None
Citibank NA, London Branch	Citibank Nominees (Ireland) Ltd
	Scottish Provident (Irish Holdings) Ltd
	NCB Trust Ltd
	National City Nominees Ltd
	CUIM Nominee Ltd
	Citifriends Nominee Ltd
	Citibank London Nominees Ltd
	Vidacos Nominees Ltd
BNP Paribas Securities Services London	Securities Services Nominees Ltd
	Harewood Nominees Ltd
	Victoire Nominees Ltd
BNP Paribas Securities Services with the following branches also covered: BNP Paribas Securities Services Milano Branch; BNP Paribas Securities Services Frankfurt Branch; BNP Paribas Securities Services London Branch – Global Custody Operations	
Staal Bank NV	Staal Bewaarbedrijf BV
Mellon Bank NA Ldn Branch	Mellon Nominees (UK) Ltd
	Mellon Grafton Nominees Ltd

Company	Associated nominee company
Northern Trust Global Services Ltd	None
Pilling & Co. Stockbrokers	St. Anns Square Nominees Ltd
Pershing Ltd	Pershing Keen Nominees Ltd
	Pershing International Nominees Ltd

* **Schedule to letter of authorisation issued by the Revenue Commissioners to the Bank of New York on 31 May, 2000**

The authorisation covers the following entities:

The Bank of New York, New York

The Bank of New York, Brussels Branch

The Bank of New York (Europe) Ltd

The Bank of New York (Luxembourg) SA

In addition, the following nominee companies are covered by the letter dated 31 May 2000, issued by the Revenue Commissioners, authorising The Bank of New York to act as a Qualifying Intermediary for the purposes of Chapter 8A of Part 6 of the Taxes Consolidation Act, 1997 as amended.

Bank of New (Nominees) Ltd

BNY CTOC Nominees Ltd. (formerly Retail Nominees Ltd)

The Bank of New York International Nominees

Class Nominees Ltd

Collateral Nominees Ltd

Direct Nominees Ltd

Europe Nominees Ltd.

Falcon (External Clients) Nominees Ltd

Falcon Nominees Ltd

Imperial Pensions Nominees Ltd

INS Nominees Ltd

KWS Nominees Ltd

Names Nominees Ltd

Nutraco Nominees Ltd

RBSTB Nominees Ltd

Rowan Nominees Ltd

SCOT Nominees Ltd

Waterhouse Nominees Ltd

Willstock Nominees Ltd

Additional letter issued to The Bank of New York on 21 October 2000

The authorisation issued to the Bank of New York on 31 May 2000 also covers the following nominee company with effect from close of business on 6 September 2002:

BNY Custodial Nominees (Ireland) Ltd

Additional letter issued to the Bank of New York on 15 April 2003

The authorisation issued to the Bank of New York on 15 April 2000 also covers the following entity:

The Bank of New York, London Branch.

Schedule to letter of authorisation issued by the Revenue Commissioners to HSBC Bank plc on 9 January 2002

The following nominee companies are covered by the letter dated 9 January, 2002, issued by the Revenue Commissioners, authorising HSBC Bank plc to act as a Qualifying Intermediary for the purposes of Chapter 8A of Part 6 of the Taxes Consolidation Act, 1997, as amended.

> HSBC Issuer Services Depositary Nominee (UK) Ltd
>
> HSBC Issuer Services Common Depositary Nominee (UK) Ltd
>
> HSBC Client Holding Nominees Ltd
>
> HSBC Equity Nominee No. 2 (UK) Ltd
>
> HSBC Equity Nominee No. 33 (UK) Ltd
>
> HSBC Equity Nominee No. 34 (UK) Ltd
>
> HSBC Equity Nominee No. 35 (UK) Ltd
>
> HSBC Equity Nominee No. 65 (UK) Ltd
>
> HSBC European Clients Depositary Receipts Nominee (UK) Ltd
>
> HSBC Global Custody Nominee (UK) Ltd
>
> HSBC Marking Name Nominee (UK) Ltd
>
> HSBC Overseas Nominee (UK) Ltd
>
> HSBC SOC Lloyds Clients Nominee (UK) Ltd
>
> HSBC SPMS Nominee (UK) Ltd
>
> MAGIM Client HSBC GIS Nominee (UK) Ltd
>
> Midland Bank (Finch Lane) Nominees Ltd
>
> Prudential Client HSBC GIS Nominee (UK) Ltd
>
> AMP Client HSBC Custody Nominee (UK) Ltd

Schedule to letter of authorisation issued by the Revenue Commissioners to Brown Brothers Harriman & Company on 12 September, 2002

The following entities are now covered by the letter dated 12th September 2002 issued by the Revenue Commissioners, authorising affiliated entities of Brown Brothers Harriman & Company to operate as Qualifying Intermediaries for the purposes of Chapter 8A of part 6 of the Taxes Consolidation Act, 1997, as amended.

> Brown Brothers Harriman & Co, Boston
>
> Brown Brothers Harriman & Co, New York
>
> Brown Brothers Harriman (Luxembourg) SCA

Obligations of qualifying intermediary

TCA 1997, s 172F sets out the obligations of a qualifying intermediary. A qualifying intermediary is required to maintain a record of two categories of shareholders, an Exempt Fund and a Liable Fund. The Exempt Fund will contain details of non-liable persons or other intermediaries who will receive amounts from the first intermediary on behalf of non-liable persons. Non-liable persons may be included in this fund only if the first intermediary receives declarations and evidence of exemption from the non-liable persons or from another intermediary to whom payments will be made on behalf of non-liable persons. The Liable Fund will contain details of all other shareholders. The first intermediary will notify the company making the distribution of the Exempt and Liable Funds and the company will then apply withholding tax to the distributions relating to the Liable Fund. The qualifying intermediary is obliged to make a return to the Revenue

Commissioners of all amounts received by it as well as details of persons to whom it makes payments, distinguishing which persons are non-liable.

TCA 1997, s 172F(1) provides that a qualifying intermediary which is to receive on behalf of another person:

(a)   any relevant distributions to be made by any company resident in the State; or

(b)   from another qualifying intermediary amounts or other assets (referred to here as "payments") representing such distributions

is to create and maintain, in relation to such distributions and payments, two separate and distinct categories to be known respectively as the "Exempt Fund" and the "Liable Fund", and is to notify that company or that other qualifying intermediary by notice in writing whether the relevant distributions or the payments representing such distributions to be made to it are to be received by it for the benefit of a person included in the Exempt Fund or a person included in the Liable Fund.

Exempt fund

A qualifying intermediary is required, subject to TCA 1997, s 172F(3), (5) (see below), to include in its Exempt Fund, in relation to relevant distributions to be made to it by an Irish resident company and payments representing such distributions to be made to it by another qualifying intermediary, only those persons on whose behalf it is to receive such distributions or payments, being:

(a)   persons beneficially entitled to such distributions or payments who are non- liable persons in relation to such distributions; and

(b)   any further qualifying intermediary to whom such distributions or payments (or amounts or other assets representing such distributions or payments) are to be given by the qualifying intermediary and are to be received by that further qualifying intermediary for the benefit of persons included in that further qualifying intermediary's Exempt Fund (TCA 1997, s 172F(2)).

A qualifying intermediary may not include a person mentioned in (a) above in its Exempt Fund unless it has received from that person:

(i)   a declaration made by the person in accordance with TCA 1997, s 172C(2) (excluded persons – see **11.116.5** above); or

(ii)   a declaration made by the person in accordance with TCA 1997, s 172D(3) (qualifying non- resident persons – see **11.116.6** above) in relation to which—

(I)   the certificate referred to in TCA 1997 Sch 2A para 8(f) is a current certificate, or

(II)   the certificates referred to in TCA 1997 Sch 2A para 9(f) are current certificates

at the time the relevant distributions are made (TCA 1997, s 172F(3)(a)).

A qualifying intermediary may not include a further qualifying intermediary, referred to in (b) above, in its Exempt Fund unless it has received from that further qualifying intermediary a notification in writing in accordance with TCA 1997, s 172F(1) (see above) to the effect that the:

(i)   relevant distribution made by the Irish resident company or, as the case may be;

(ii)   the payments representing such distributions,

which are to be given by the qualifying intermediary to that further qualifying intermediary are to be received by that further qualifying intermediary for the benefit of a person included in that further qualifying intermediary's Exempt Fund (TCA 1997, s 172F(3)(b)).

Notwithstanding TCA 1997, s 172F(3)(a) and (b), a qualifying intermediary, being a depositary bank holding shares in trust for, or on behalf of, the holders of American depositary receipts, is required, if provided for in the qualifying intermediary agreement and subject to any conditions specified in that agreement, to operate the provisions of TCA 1997, s 172F(3)(d) as set out below (TCA 1997, s 172F(3)(c)).

The qualifying intermediary, in the circumstances referred to in TCA 1997, s 172(3)(c), is required to include in its Exempt Fund:

(i)   any person on whose behalf it is to receive any relevant distribution to be made by a company resident in the State, or on whose behalf it is to receive from another qualifying intermediary payments representing such distributions, being a person who is beneficially entitled to such distributions or payments, who is the holder of an American depositary receipt and whose address on the qualifying intermediary's register of depositary receipts is located in the United States of America; and

(ii) any specified intermediary (see below) to which such distributions or payments (or amounts or other assets representing such distributions or payments) are to be given by the qualifying intermediary and are to be received by that specified intermediary for the benefit of—

    (I)   persons who are beneficially entitled to such distributions or payments, who are the holders of American depositary receipts, whose address on that specified intermediary's register of depositary receipts is located in the United States of America, and who in accordance with TCA 1997, s 172F(3)(e)(iii)(I) (see (iii)(I) in relation to definition of "specified intermediary" below) are to be included in that specified intermediary's Exempt Fund, or

    (II) any further specified intermediary to which such distributions or payments (or amounts or other assets representing such distributions or payments) are to be given by the first-mentioned specified intermediary and are to be received by that further specified intermediary for the benefit of persons who in accordance with TCA 1997, s 172F(3)(e)(iii)(I) or (II) (see (iii)(I), (II) in relation to definition of "specified intermediary" below) are to be included in that further specified intermediary's Exempt Fund (TCA 1997, s 172F(3)(d)).

For the purposes of TCA 1997, s 172F, but subject to paragraphs (g) and (h) of that section, an intermediary is a specified intermediary if it:

(i)   is not a qualifying intermediary but is a person referred to in TCA 1997, s 172E(4)(a), (b), (c) or (d) (see (i)-(iv) under Qualifying intermediary above) who is operating as an intermediary in an establishment situated in the United States of America;

(ii) creates and maintains, in relation to such distributions or payments (or amounts or other assets representing such distributions or payments) to be received by it on behalf of other persons from a qualifying intermediary or another specified intermediary, an Exempt Fund and a Liable Fund in accordance with TCA 1997, s 172F(1), (5), but subject to (iii) and (iv) below, as if it were a qualifying intermediary;

(iii) includes in its Exempt Fund in relation to such distributions or payments (or amounts or other assets representing such distributions or payments), only—

    (I) those persons who are beneficially entitled to such distributions or payments, being persons who are the holders of American depositary receipts and whose address on its register of depositary receipts is located in the US, and

    (II) any further specified intermediary to which such distributions or payments (or amounts or other assets representing such distributions or payments) are to be made by the intermediary and are to be received by that further specified intermediary for the benefit of persons who are to be included in that further specified intermediary's Exempt Fund,

(iv) includes in its Liable Fund in relation to such distributions or payments (or amounts or other assets representing such distributions or payments), all other persons (being persons who are holders of American depositary receipts) on whose behalf such distributions or payments (or amounts or other assets representing such distributions or payments) are to be received by it from a qualifying intermediary or a further specified intermediary, other than those persons included in its Exempt Fund;

(v) notifies, by way of notice in writing or in electric format, the qualifying intermediary or, as the case may be, the further specified intermediary from whom it is to receive, on behalf of other persons, such distributions or payments (or amounts or other assets representing such distributions or payments), whether such distributions or payments (or amounts or other assets representing such distributions or payments) are to be so received by it for the benefit of persons included in its Exempt Fund or persons included in its Liable Fund; and

(vi) enters into an agreement with the qualifying intermediary or further specified intermediary, as the case may be, under the terms of which it agrees that if and when required to comply with TCA 1997, s 172F(7A) it will do so (TCA 1997, s 172F(3)(e)).

Where, by virtue of TCA 1997, s 172F(3)(a)-(e) (see above), any person, being a person who would not otherwise be a non-liable person in relation to the distributions or payments (or amounts or other assets representing such distributions or payments) to be received on that person's behalf by a qualifying intermediary or a specified intermediary, is included in the Exempt Fund of the qualifying intermediary or, as the case may be, of the specified intermediary, that person is to be treated as a non-liable person in relation to such distributions (TCA 1997, s 172F(3)(f)).

Notwithstanding TCA 1997, s 172E(3)(e), where the Revenue Commissioners are satisfied that an intermediary, being a specified intermediary or other specified intermediary referred to in TCA 1997, s 172E(7A), has failed to comply with that subsection:

(i) they may, by notice in writing given to the intermediary, notify it that it will cease to be treated as a specified intermediary for the purposes of TCA 1997, s 172E from such date as may be specified in the notice; and

(ii)   they may, notwithstanding any obligations as to secrecy or other restriction on disclosure of information imposed by or under statute or otherwise, make available to any qualifying intermediary (being a depositary bank holding shares in trust for, or on behalf of, the holders of ADRs) or specified intermediary a copy of such notice (TCA 1997, s 172E(3)(g)).

Where subsequently the Revenue Commissioners are satisfied that the intermediary has furnished the information required under subsection (7A) of TCA 1997, s 172F and will in future comply with that subsection if and when requested to do so, they may, by further notice in writing given to the intermediary, revoke the notice given under subsection (3)(g) of that section from such date as may be specified in the further notice, and a copy of that further notice is to be given to any person to whom a copy of the notice under subsection (3)(g) was given (TCA 1997, s 172E(3)(h)).

A qualifying intermediary is required to update its Exempt Fund in relation to relevant distributions to be made to it by an Irish resident company and payments representing such distributions to be made to it by another qualifying intermediary, as often as may be necessary to ensure that the provisions of TCA 1997, ss 172E(1) (Withholding tax not to apply – see above) and 172F(2), (3) are complied with, and to notify the company or, as the case may be, that other qualifying intermediary, by way of notice in writing, of all such updates (TCA 1997, s 172F(5)).

Liable fund

A qualifying intermediary is required, subject to TCA 1997, s 172F(5) (see below), to include in its Liable Fund, in relation to relevant distributions to be made to it by an Irish resident company and payments representing such distributions to be made to it by another qualifying intermediary, all persons on whose behalf it is to receive such distributions or payments, other than those persons included in its Exempt Fund in relation to such distributions and payments (TCA 1997, s 172F(4)).

A qualifying intermediary is required to update its Liable Fund in relation to relevant distributions to be made to it by an Irish resident company and payments representing such distributions to be made to it by another qualifying intermediary, as often as may be necessary to ensure that the provisions of TCA 1997, s 172E(1) (Withholding tax not to apply – see above) and 172F(4) are complied with, and to notify the company or, as the case may be, that other qualifying intermediary, by way of notice in writing, of all such updates (TCA 1997, s 172E(5)).

In addition, as was seen above, a specified intermediary is required to include in its Liable Fund in relation to such distributions or payments (or amounts or other assets representing such distributions or payments) to be received by it on behalf of other persons from a qualifying intermediary or another specified intermediary, all other persons (being persons who are holders of American depositary receipts) on whose behalf such distributions or payments (or amounts or other assets representing such distributions or payments) are to be received by it from a qualifying intermediary or a further specified intermediary, other than those persons included in its Exempt Fund (TCA 1997, s 172F(3)(e)(iv)).

A company must deduct dividend withholding tax from a relevant distribution where it has not been notified by a qualifying intermediary as to the inclusion in the Exempt Fund of the person beneficially entitled to the distribution. Where at any time an Irish resident company makes a relevant distribution to a qualifying intermediary and the distribution would otherwise be treated as being made to the qualifying intermediary for the benefit of a person beneficially entitled to it who is a non-liable person in relation to it, the distribution is to be treated as if it were not made to the qualifying intermediary for the benefit of that person unless, at or before that time, the qualifying intermediary has notified the company in accordance with TCA 1997, s 172F(1) or (5), as the case may be, that the distribution is to be received by the qualifying intermediary for the benefit of a person included in the qualifying intermediary's Exempt Fund in relation to relevant distributions to be made to the qualifying intermediary by the company. Otherwise, dividend withholding tax is to apply to the distribution in accordance with TCA 1997, s 172B (TCA 1997, s 172F(6)).

Returns by qualifying intermediaries

A qualifying intermediary is required by TCA 1997, s 172F(7), for years of assessment commencing with the year 1999-2000, to make a return to the Revenue Commissioners showing:

(a) the name and address of—

    (i) each company resident in the State from which the qualifying intermediary received, on behalf of another person, a relevant distribution made to that company in the year of assessment to which the return refers, and

    (ii) each other person from whom the qualifying intermediary received, on behalf of another person, an amount or other asset representing a relevant distribution made by a company resident in the State in the year of assessment to which the return refers,

(b) the amount of each such relevant distribution;

(c) the name and address of each person to whom such a relevant distribution, or an amount or other asset representing such a relevant distribution, has been given by the qualifying intermediary; and

(d) the name and address of each person referred to in (d) in respect of whom a declaration under TCA 1997, s 172C(2) (excluded persons – see **11.116.5**) or 172D(3) (qualifying non- resident persons – see **11.116.6** above) has been received by the qualifying intermediary (TCA 1997, s 172F(7)(a)).

A return made by a qualifying intermediary under paragraph (a) of TCA 1997, s 172F(7) may be confined to such class or classes of relevant distributions as may be specified in the notice given to that intermediary by the Revenue Commissioners under that paragraph (TCA 1997, s 172F(7)(b)).

TCA 1997, s 172F(7A) sets out further requirements of qualifying intermediaries and specified intermediaries where a qualifying intermediary has been obliged to make a return under TCA 1997, s 172F(7)(a) and a relevant distribution (or an amount or other asset representing such a relevant distribution), the details of which are required to be included in that return, has been given by the qualifying intermediary to a specified intermediary.

The qualifying intermediary must, immediately on receipt of the notice referred to in TCA 1997, s 172F(7)(a), request the specified intermediary, by way of notice in writing or in electronic format, to notify the qualifying intermediary or the Revenue Commissioners of the name and address of each person to whom the specified intermediary gave such a distribution (or an amount or other asset representing such a distribution) and of the amount of each such distribution (TCA 1997, s 172F(7A)(b)).

The specified intermediary must, within 21 days of the receipt of a notice under paragraph (b) of TCA 1997, s 172F(7A), furnish to the qualifying intermediary or, at the discretion of the specified intermediary, to the Revenue Commissioners, by way of notice in writing or in electronic format, the information required under that paragraph (TCA 1997, s 172F(7A)(c)).

Where the specified intermediary furnishes the information required under paragraph (b) of TCA 1997, s 172F(7A):

(i)   to the qualifying intermediary, the qualifying intermediary must include that information in the return to be made by it under TCA 1997, s 172F(7)(a); or

(ii)   to the Revenue Commissioners, the specified intermediary must, by way of notice in writing or in electronic format, immediately advise the qualifying intermediary of that fact and the qualifying intermediary must include in the return to be made by it under TCA 1997, s 172F(7)(a) a statement to the effect that it has been so advised by the specified intermediary (TCA 1997, s 172F(7A)(d)).

If any person to whom a specified intermediary gave such a distribution (or an amount or other asset representing such a distribution) is another specified intermediary, the specified intermediary must, immediately on receipt of a notice under paragraph (b) of TCA 1997, s 172F(7A), request the other specified intermediary, by way of notice in writing or in electronic format, to notify the specified intermediary or the Revenue Commissioners of the name and address of each person to whom it gave such a distribution (or an amount or other asset representing such a distribution) and of the amount of each such distribution (TCA 1997, s 172F(7A)(e)).

The other specified intermediary must, within 21 days of the receipt of a notice under paragraph (e) of TCA 1997, s 172F(7A), furnish to the specified intermediary or, at the discretion of the other specified intermediary, to the Revenue Commissioners, by way of notice in writing or in electronic format, the information required under that paragraph (TCA 1997, s 172F(7A)(f)).

Where the other specified intermediary furnishes the information required under paragraph (e) of TCA 1997, s 172F(7A):

(i)   to the specified intermediary, the specified intermediary must, by way of notice in writing or in electronic format, immediately transmit that information to the person referred in paragraph (d) of TCA 1997, s 172F(7A) (being the qualifying intermediary or the Revenue Commissioners, as the case may be) to whom it furnishes the information required under paragraph (b), and—

(I)   if that person is the qualifying intermediary, the qualifying intermediary must include that information in the return required to be made by it under TCA 1997, s 172F(7)(a), or

(II)   if that person is the Revenue Commissioners, the specified intermediary must, by way of notice in writing or in electronic format, immediately advise the qualifying intermediary of the fact that the information required to be furnished by the other specified intermediary under paragraph (e) of TCA 1997, s 172F(7A) has been furnished to the specified intermediary and transmitted by the specified intermediary to the Revenue Commissioners in accordance with this paragraph and the qualifying intermediary must include in the return to be made by it under TCA 1997, s 172F(7)(a) a statement to the effect that it has been so advised by the specified intermediary, or

(ii) to the Revenue Commissioners, the other specified intermediary must, by way of notice in writing or in electronic format, immediately advise the specified intermediary of that fact, the specified intermediary must in turn, by way of similar notice, immediately advise the qualifying intermediary of that fact and the qualifying intermediary must include in the return to be made by it under TCA 1997, s 172F(7)(a) a statement to the effect that it has been so advised by the specified intermediary (TCA 1997, s 172F(7A)(g)).

Where, in accordance with TCA 1997, s 172(7A), the specified intermediary or the other specified intermediary furnishes information to the Revenue Commissioners in electronic format, such format must be agreed in advance with the Revenue Commissioners (TCA 1997, s 172F(7A)(h)).

Every return by a qualifying intermediary must be made in an electronic format approved by the Revenue Commissioners, and must be accompanied by a declaration made by the qualifying intermediary, on a form prescribed or authorised for that purpose by the Revenue Commissioners, to the effect that the return is correct and complete (TCA 1997, s 172F(8)).

Where the Revenue Commissioners are satisfied that a qualifying intermediary does not have the facilities to make a return in the format referred to in TCA 1997, s 172F(8), the return is to be made in writing in a form prescribed or authorised by the Revenue Commissioners and must be accompanied by a declaration made by the qualifying intermediary, on a form prescribed or authorised for that purpose by the Revenue Commissioners, to the effect that the return is correct and complete (TCA 1997, s 172F(9)).

11.116.9 Statement to be given to recipients of relevant distributions

TCA 1997, s 172I provides for the giving of a statement to a shareholder by a company making relevant distributions, or, where applicable, by an authorised withholding agent, setting out details of the distributions and the tax withheld. The requirement may be satisfied by including details on the relevant dividend counterfoil.

Every person ("the payer") who makes, or who (being an authorised withholding agent) is treated as making, a relevant distribution must, at the time the relevant distribution is made or, in the case of an authorised withholding agent, at the time of the giving by the agent of the relevant distribution, or an amount or other asset representing that distribution, to another person, give the recipient of the relevant distribution or, as the case may be, that other person, a statement in writing showing:

(a) the name and address of the payer and, if the payer is not the company making the relevant distribution, the name and address of that company;

(b) the name and address of the person to whom the relevant distribution is made;

(c) the date the relevant distribution is made;

(d) the amount of the relevant distribution; and

(e) the amount of the dividend withholding tax, if any, deducted in relation to the relevant distribution (TCA 1997, s 172I(1)).

A statement delivered by means of electronic communications to an intermediary will satisfy the above requirements where—

(i) the statement contains an ISI Number, a recipient ID code, the information referred to in (c)–(e) above and an electronic number,

(ii) the intermediary has consented to the statement being delivered by means of electronic communications and has not withdrawn that consent, and

(iii) the Revenue Commissioners have agreed to accept the statement for DWT purposes (TCA 1997, s 172I(1A)).

An *ISI Number*, in relation to a security issued by a company, means that security's unique International Securities Identification Number (ISIN) issued by the Irish Stock Exchange Limited or by an equivalent authority in a relevant territory.

A *recipient ID code*, in relation to the recipient of a dividend, means the unique code on an electronic dividend voucher that identifies that recipient. An *electronic dividend voucher* is a statement in electronic format that satisfies the requirements the requirements in (i) above. An *electronic number* is a unique number on an electronic dividend voucher.

The requirements of TCA 1997, s 172I(1) may be satisfied by the inclusion of the particulars listed above in a statement in writing made in relation to the distribution in accordance with TCA 1997, s 152(1) (dividend warrants etc – see **11.117** below).

Where a person fails to comply with any of the provisions of TCA 1997, s 172I(1), TCA 1997, s 152(2) (see **11.117**) is to apply as it applies where a company fails to comply with any of the provisions of TCA 1997, s 152(1) (TCA 1997, s 172I(3)).

11.116.10 Credits or repayments in respect of dividend withholding tax

Dividend withholding tax deducted in a year of assessment may be set off against a shareholder's tax liability for that year. Where the withholding tax exceeds that liability, the excess may be repaid. A non-liable person who has been charged withholding tax will be entitled to a refund of the tax withheld.

Where a person is within the charge to income tax in relation to a year of assessment and has borne dividend withholding tax in relation to a relevant distribution to which he is beneficially entitled and which is referable to that year, he may claim to have that dividend withholding tax set against income tax chargeable for that year. Where the withholding tax exceeds the income tax, a claim may be made to have the excess refunded (TCA 1997, s 172J(1)).

Where a person is not within the charge to income tax in relation to a year of assessment and has borne dividend withholding tax in relation to a relevant distribution to which he is beneficially entitled and which is referable to that year, he may claim to have that dividend withholding tax refunded (TCA 1997, s 172J(2)).

Where, in a year of assessment or in an accounting period of a company (as appropriate), a person has borne dividend withholding tax in relation to a relevant distribution to which that person is beneficially entitled and the person:

(a) is a non-liable person in relation to the relevant distribution;

(b) would have been a non-liable person in relation to the relevant distribution if the requirement for the person to make the appropriate declaration referred to in TCA 1997 Sch 2A (see **11.116.5** and **11.116.6**) had not been necessary,

a claim may be made to have the amount of the dividend withholding tax refunded to that person (TCA 1997, s 172J(3)).

Relevant distributions include distributions which are exempt from taxation by reason of being paid out of exempt profits, for example, exempt patent distributions, distributions from exempt stallion or stud greyhound fees, and distributions out of income from commercial woodlands. Accordingly, dividend withholding tax may be deductible from these distributions although they are exempt from taxation. The recipient of such a distribution may then make a claim for a refund of the tax deducted.

A person making a claim for a credit or a refund is required to furnish, in respect of each amount of dividend withholding tax to which the claim relates, the statement in writing given to that person in accordance with TCA 1997, s 172I(1) (see **11.116.9** above) by the person who made, or who (being an authorised withholding agent) was treated as making, the relevant distribution in relation to which the dividend withholding tax was deducted (TCA 1997, s 172J(4)).

The Revenue Commissioners may not authorise the setting-off of dividend withholding tax against income tax chargeable on a person for a year of assessment, or make a refund of dividend withholding tax to a person, unless they receive such evidence as they consider necessary that the person is entitled to that setting-off or refund (TCA 1997, s 172J(5)).

11.116.11 Returns, payment and collection of dividend withholding tax

TCA 1997, s 172K provides for the making of returns and payment of tax withheld in respect of relevant distributions to the Revenue Commissioners by the company making the distribution (or by the authorised withholding agent if appropriate). Any tax withheld from a distribution made in a calendar month must be paid to the Revenue Commissioners by the 14th of the following month. A return must be furnished to the Commissioners at the same time showing the name and address of each recipient, the amount paid to each and whether tax was withheld.

A person ("the accountable person"), being a company resident in the State which makes, or an authorised withholding agent treated under TCA 1997, s 172H as making, any relevant distribution to specified persons in any month must, within 14 days of the end of that month, make a return to the Collector-General containing details of:

(a) the name and tax reference number of the company which actually made the relevant distribution;

(b) if different from the company which actually made the relevant distributions, the name of the accountable person, being an authorised withholding agent, in relation to those distributions;

(c) the name and address of each person to whom a relevant distribution was made or, as the case may be, was treated as being made by the accountable person in the month to which the return refers;

(d) the date on which the relevant distribution was made to that person;

(e) the amount of the relevant distribution made to that person;

(f)   the amount of the dividend withholding tax, if any, in relation to the relevant distribution deducted by the accountable person or, as the case may be, the amount (if any) to be paid to the Collector-General by the accountable person in relation to that distribution as if it were a deduction of dividend withholding tax;

(g)   the aggregate of the amounts referred to in (f) in relation to all relevant distributions made or treated under TCA 1997, s 172H (see Obligations of authorised withholding agent in **11.116.7**) as being made by the accountable person to specified persons in the month to which the return relates; and

(h)   in a case where TCA 1997, s 172B has not applied to a relevant distribution due to the operation of subsection (7) of that section, whether the relevant distribution is a distribution within paragraph (a), (b) or (c) of that subsection (dividend withholding tax not applicable in respect of distributions out of certain exempt profits and income – see **11.116.4**) (TCA 1997, s 172K(1)).

Dividend withholding tax which is required to be included in a return is due at the time by which the return is to be made and is payable by the accountable person to the Collector-General. The tax so due is payable without the making of an assessment. Dividend withholding tax which has become due may, however, be assessed on the accountable person (whether or not paid at the time the assessment is made) if that tax or any part of it is not paid on or before the due date (TCA 1997, s 172K(2)).

Where it appears to the inspector of taxes that any amount of dividend withholding tax in relation to a relevant distribution which ought to have been, but has not been, included in a return, or where the inspector is dissatisfied with any such return, he may make an assessment on the accountable person in relation to the relevant distribution to the best of his judgment. Any amount of dividend withholding tax due by reason of such an assessment is to be treated for the purposes of interest on unpaid tax as having been payable at the time when it would have been payable if a correct return had been made (TCA 1997, s 172K(3)).

Where any item has been incorrectly included in a return as a relevant distribution in relation to which dividend withholding tax is to be deducted, the inspector may make such assessments, adjustments or set-offs as may in his judgment be required to secure that the resulting liabilities to tax, including interest on unpaid tax, whether of the accountable person in relation to the relevant distribution or any other person, are so far as is possible the same as they would have been if the item had not been so included (TCA 1997, s 172K(4)).

Any dividend withholding tax assessed on an accountable person will be due within one month after the issue of the notice of assessment (unless the tax is due earlier under TCA 1997, s 172K(2)), subject to any appeal against the assessment. No such appeal may affect the date when any amount is due under TCA 1997, s 172K(2) (TCA 1997, s 172K(5)).

The provisions of the Income Tax Acts relating to:

(i)   assessments to income tax;

(ii)   appeals against such assessments (including the rehearing of appeals and the statement of a case for the opinion of the High Court – see **15.209**); and

(iii)   the collection and recovery of income tax,

are, in so far as they are applicable, to apply to the assessment, collection and recovery of dividend withholding tax (TCA 1997, s 172K(6)(a)).

Any amount of dividend withholding tax payable without the making of an assessment carries interest at 0.0322% for each day or part of a day from the date when the amount becomes due and payable until payment (TCA 1997, s 172K(6)(b)).

The provisions of TCA 1997, s 1080(3)-(5) (interest on overdue tax – see **15.106.2** and **15.207**) are to apply in relation to interest payable under TCA 1997, s 172K(6)(b) as they apply to interest payable under TCA 1997, s 1080 (TCA 1997, s 172K(6)(c)). In its application to any dividend withholding tax charged by assessment, TCA 1997, s 1080 is to apply as if TCA 1997, s 1080(2)(b) were deleted (TCA 1997, s 172K(6)(d)). That paragraph provides that interest on unpaid tax is to run on any tax charged by an assessment to income tax notwithstanding any appeal against the assessment, from the date it would run if there had been no assessment (see **15.207**).

Subject to TCA 1997, s 172K(8), every return by an accountable person is to be made in an electronic format approved by the Revenue Commissioners and must be accompanied by a declaration made by the accountable person, on a form prescribed or authorised for that purpose by the Commissioners, to the effect that the return is correct and complete (TCA 1997, s 172K(7)).

Where, however, the Revenue Commissioners are satisfied that an accountable person does not have the facilities to make a return in electronic format as required above, the return is to be made in writing in a form prescribed or authorised by the Commissioners and must be accompanied by a declaration made by the accountable person, on a form prescribed or authorised for that purpose by the Commissioners, to the effect that the return is correct and complete (TCA 1997, s 172K(8)).

11.116.12 Reporting of distributions made under stapled stock arrangements

In cases where, under "stapled stock" arrangements, shareholders of an Irish resident company opt to take a dividend from a non-resident company, the Irish resident company must make a return to the Revenue Commissioners containing details of the shareholders and of the distributions received.

Stapled stock, or "dual share", arrangements have been adopted in a number of cases involving Irish public companies with overseas subsidiaries. Shareholders holding stapled stock have the choice of taking their dividends from the Irish holding company or from one of the overseas companies. Conversely, Irish corporate shareholders might hold stapled stock in an overseas company owning one or more Irish subsidiaries. Irish corporate shareholders of, say, UK public companies might have been at a potential disadvantage as regards the sourcing of dividends from the UK. By taking their dividends from an Irish company within the UK group, such companies were enabled to receive franked investment income and (up to 5 April 1999) to "frank" their own dividends for ACT purposes and thereby control the ACT cost of dividend payments.

TCA 1997, s 172L(1) provides that a distribution made to a person by a company not resident in the State ("the non-resident company") is to be treated for the purposes of TCA 1997, s 172L as made under a stapled stock arrangement where:

(a)　the person has, under any agreement, arrangement or understanding, whether made or entered into on, before or after 6 April 1999, exercised a right, whether directly or through a nominee or other person acting on behalf of the person, to receive distributions from the non-resident company instead of receiving relevant distributions from a company resident in the State ("the resident company"); and

(b)   that right has not been revoked.

Where, on or after 6 April 1999, the non-resident company makes distributions to persons under a stapled stock arrangement, the resident company is obliged, within 14 days of the end of each month in which those distributions were made, to make a return to the Revenue Commissioners containing details of:

(a)   the name and tax reference number of the resident company;

(b)   the name and address of the non-resident company which made those distributions;

(c)   the name and address of each person to whom such a distribution was made in the month to which the return refers;

(d)   the date on which such distribution was made to that person; and

(e)   the amount of such distribution made to that person (TCA 1997, s 172L(2)).

Subject to TCA 1997, s 172L(4), every return by a company is to be made in an electronic format approved by the Revenue Commissioners and must be accompanied by a declaration made by the company, on a form prescribed or authorised for that purpose by the Commissioners, to the effect that the return is correct and complete (TCA 1997, s 172L(3)).

Where, however, the Revenue Commissioners are satisfied that a company does not have the facilities to make a return in electronic format as required above, the return is to be made in writing in a form prescribed or authorised by the Commissioners and must be accompanied by a declaration made by the company, on a form prescribed or authorised for that purpose by the Commissioners, to the effect that the return is correct and complete (TCA 1997, s 172L(4)).

11.116.13 Settlement of market claims

It will sometimes be the case, due to delays in updating share registers of companies, that dividends will be paid to persons who are not the current beneficial owners of the relevant shares. It will accordingly be necessary to settle the consequential "market claims" arising out of the incorrect payment of these dividends. Brokers and other intermediaries who are involved in settling such claims are legally obliged, as on and from 10 February 2000, to deduct dividend withholding tax where that tax was not deducted at the time the distribution was originally made. They are obliged to pay all amounts so deducted to the Revenue Commissioners and to make an annual return containing details of dividend withholding tax so deducted during the previous year.

Market claim

A *market claim* will be deemed to have arisen in relation to a relevant distribution where:

(a)   an Irish resident company has made a relevant distribution to a person (the "recorded owner") on the basis of the information on the share register of the company at a particular date;

(b) it subsequently transpires, as a result of an event (the "specified event"), being—

  (i) the sale or purchase of, or

  (ii) the happening, or failure to happen, of another event in relation to,

the shares or other securities in respect of which the relevant distribution was made, that another person (the "proper owner") had actually been entitled to receive the relevant distribution, and

(c) a person (an "accountable person"), being—

  (i) the relevant stockbroker who has acted for the recorded owner in the specified event, or

  (ii) if the recorded owner is a qualifying intermediary or an authorised withholding agent,

is obliged to pay the relevant distribution to the proper owner or, as may be appropriate, to the relevant stockbroker who acted for the proper owner in the specified event (which action is referred to here as the "settlement of the market claim") (TCA 1997, s 172LA(2)).

A *stockbroker* is a member firm of the Irish Stock Exchange or of a recognised stock exchange in another territory (TCA 1997, s 172LA(1)).

Deduction of dividend withholding tax on settlement of market claim

Where, in the event of a market claim, dividend withholding tax had not already been deducted from the amount of the relevant distribution made by the Irish resident company to the recorded owner:

(a) the accountable person must, on settlement of the market claim, deduct from the amount of the relevant distribution dividend withholding tax in relation to that distribution;

(b) the proper owner or, as may be appropriate, the relevant stockbroker who has acted for the proper owner in the specified event must allow such deduction on the receipt of the residue of the relevant distribution; and

(c) the accountable person will be acquitted and discharged of so much money as is represented by the deduction as if that amount had actually been paid to the proper owner or, as may be appropriate, to the relevant stockbroker who has acted for the proper owner in the specified event (TCA 1997, s 172LA(3)).

Where TCA 1997, s 172LA(3) applies, the accountable person must, on the settlement of the market claim, give the proper owner or, as may be appropriate, the relevant stockbroker who has acted for the proper owner in the specified event a statement in writing showing:

(a) the name and address of the accountable person;

(b) the name and address of the company which made the relevant distribution;

(c) the amount of the relevant distribution; and

(d) the amount of the dividend withholding tax deducted in relation to the relevant distribution (TCA 1997, s 172LA(4)).

Payment of dividend withholding tax by accountable person

Dividend withholding tax which is required to be deducted by the accountable person under TCA 1997, s 172LA(3) must be paid by the accountable person to the Collector-General within 14 days of the end of the month in which that tax was required to be deducted. The tax so due is payable without the making of an assessment but dividend withholding tax so due may be assessed on the accountable person if the tax, or any part of it, is not paid on or before the due date (TCA 1997, s 172LA(5)).

Dividend withholding tax which is required to be paid under TCA 1997, s 172LA(5) must be accompanied by a statement in writing from the accountable person making the payment showing:

(a)   the name and address of that accountable person;

(b)   the name and address of the company or companies which made the relevant distribution or distributions to which the payment relates; and

(c)   the amount of the dividend withholding tax included in the payment (TCA 1997, s 172LA(6)).

Annual return

An accountable person must, as respects each year of assessment commencing with the year 1999-2000 in which TCA 1997, s 172LA(3) applied in relation to the accountable person and not later than 15 February following that year, make a return to the Revenue Commissioners showing:

(a)   the name and address of the accountable person;

(b)   the following details in relation to each market claim to which subsection (3) applied in that year:

(i)   the name and address of the Irish resident company which made the relevant distribution to which the market claim relates,

(ii)   the amount of the relevant distribution concerned, and

(iii) the amount of the dividend withholding tax in relation to the relevant distribution deducted by the accountable person (TCA 1997, s 172LA(7)).

Subject to subsection (9) of TCA 1997, s 172LA, every return by an accountable person under subsection (7) of that section is to be made in electronic format approved by the Revenue Commissioners and is to be accompanied by a declaration made by the accountable person, on a form prescribed or authorised for that purpose by the Revenue Commissioners, to the effect that the return is correct and complete (TCA 1997, s 172LA(8)).

Where the Revenue Commissioners are satisfied that an accountable person does not have the facilities to make a return under subsection (7) of TCA 1997, s 172LA in electronic format as referred to in subsection (8), the return is to be made in writing in a form prescribed or authorised by the Revenue Commissioners and must be accompanied by a declaration made by the accountable person, on a form prescribed or authorised for that purposes by the Revenue Commissioners, to the effect that the return is correct and complete (TCA 1997, s 172LA(9)).

Retention of records by accountable person

An accountable person must keep and retain for a period of six years the accountable persons documents and records relating to market claims arising from relevant distributions made by Irish resident companies. An accountable person must allow the Revenue Commissioners to inspect such documents and records and to verify the accountable persons compliance with TCA 1997, s 172LA in any other manner considered necessary by the Commissioners (TCA 1997, s 172LA(10)).

11.116.14 Delegation of powers of Revenue Commissioners

The Revenue Commissioners may delegate the operation of the dividend withholding tax to any of their officers. TCA 1997, s 172M provides that the Revenue Commissioners may nominate any of their officers to perform any acts and discharge any functions authorised by TCA 1997 Part 6 Chapter 8A or Schedule 2A to be performed or discharged by the Revenue Commissioners.

11.116.15 Declarations

TCA 1997 Schedule 2A contains details of declarations that must be provided by non-liable persons to companies or authorised withholding agents. (See **11.116.5** for declaration to be made by Irish resident companies.) All non-liable persons claiming exemption from dividend withholding tax are required to give a declaration in writing declaring their entitlement to exemption. A declarations made by a non-resident person must be accompanied by a certificate of residence from the tax authority in the country of residence of that person. A declaration by a non-resident company must be accompanied by a certificate from the company's auditors certifying that it is ultimately controlled by residents of EU Member States (other than Ireland) or tax treaty countries, and by a certificate from the Revenue Commissioners certifying that they have received a copy of the auditor's certificate and are satisfied that it is true and correct.

11.116.16 Retention period for documentation

An Irish resident company is obliged to keep and retain for a minimum prescribed period all declarations, with accompanying certificates, and notifications (other than any notice given to the company by the Revenue Commissioners) made or given to the company in accordance with TCA 1997 Part 6 Chapter 8A (dividend withholding tax) and Schedule 2A (which deals mainly with declarations by resident companies, pension schemes, ESOTs, collective investment undertakings, charities and qualifying non-resident persons).

The retention period is a period of six years or, if longer, a period which, in relation to the relevant distributions for which the declaration or notification is made or given, ends not earlier than three years after the date on which the company has ceased to make relevant distributions to the person who made the declaration or, as the case may be, gave the notification to the company (TCA 1997, s 172B(4A)(a)).

An Irish resident company must, on being so required by notice in writing given to it by the Revenue Commissioners, make available to the Commissioners, within the time specified in the notice:

(a)   all declarations, certificates or notifications referred to above which have been made or, as the case may be, given to the company; or

(b)   such class or classes of such declarations, certificates or notifications as may be specified in the notice (TCA 1997, s 172B(4A)(b)).

The Revenue Commissioners may examine or take extracts from, or copies of, any declarations, certificates or notifications made available to the Commissioners (TCA 1997, s 172B(4A)(c)).

11.117   Dividend warrants, cheques and other orders

Every warrant, cheque or other order drawn or made in the payment by any company of any dividend, or of any interest treated as a distribution must have attached to it a statement in writing showing certain particulars. It will usually be necessary for the recipient of a dividend or other distribution to have adequate information as to the exact nature of that distribution. In the case of an individual or other person chargeable to income tax, this information will be required so that the distribution can be correctly returned in the relevant income tax return and the resulting tax liability correctly calculated.

TCA 1997, s 152(1) requires the following particulars to be disclosed in relation to each dividend or other distribution:

(a)   the amount of the distribution (dividend or interest) made;

(b)   in the case of a dividend that is paid wholly or partly out of capital profits, the part so paid; and

(c)   the period for which the dividend or interest is paid.

Where a company fails to comply with any of the provisions of TCA 1997, s 152(1), it will incur a penalty of €10 in respect each offence. The aggregate amount of the penalties imposed on any company in respect of offences connected with any one distribution of dividends or interest may not exceed €125 (TCA 1997, s 152(2)).

Public companies paying dividends usually furnish the necessary information in a detachable counterfoil with the dividend warrant, but the requirement may be satisfied in any form of written statement as long all of the relevant particulars are provided. A company which makes a distribution other than as a payment by warrant, cheque or other order mentioned in TCA 1997, s 152(1) must, if the recipient requests it in writing, furnish a statement in writing showing the amount or value of the distribution (TCA 1997, s 152(3)).

Additional information must be given in the statement attached to a distribution, or in the statement provided at the recipient's request under TCA 1997, s 152(3), for certain types of distribution, as follows:

Type of distribution	*Additional information*
Shannon exempt distribution	That the distribution is made out of income from exempted trading operations (TCA 1997, s 144(5))

Type of distribution	*Additional information*
Distribution out of income from stallion under fees, stud greyhound fees or commercial woodlands	That the distribution is out of exempt profits TCA 1997, ss 231-233 (TCA 1997, s 140(5))
Distribution out of patent income to be disregarded for income tax purposes	That the distribution is out of disregarded income under TCA 1997, s 234 (TCA 1997, s 141(7))

A company may pay a dividend or other distribution partly out of income which has benefited from one of the special corporation tax exemptions or reliefs and partly out of other income. Except in the case of such a distribution made partly out of export sales relieved income and partly out of standard taxed profits, such distributions are treated as consisting of two separate distributions so that the appropriate particulars must be given separately in respect of each part. In practice, this is usually done on the one dividend counterfoil, with the total dividend payment analysed between their separate parts.

11.2 ADVANCE CORPORATION TAX

11.201   Introduction: liability to ACT
11.202   Set-off of ACT
11.203   Surplus ACT
11.204   ACT payable where distributions received
11.205   Surrender of ACT
11.206   Change in ownership of companies
11.207   Distributions to certain non-resident companies

11.201   Introduction: liability to ACT

Advance corporation tax (ACT) ceased to apply in respect of distributions paid by Irish resident companies on or after 6 April 1999. ACT was repealed in line with the abolition of tax credits which also ceased to apply in respect of distributions paid on or after 6 April 1999. What follows in this section is a brief summary of the main features of ACT. For a detailed treatment of ACT, please refer to earlier (2000-2001 or earlier) editions of this book.

ACT was introduced by FA 1983 primarily to deal with a weakness in tax law under which a shareholder receiving a dividend was entitled to the benefit of the attaching tax credit even where the distributing company had paid no tax. ACT ceased to apply after 5 April 1999, in line with the abolition of tax credits on distributions made on or after 6 April 1999.

Irish resident companies making distributions on or after 9 February 1983 and before 6 April 1999 were required to account to the Revenue Commissioners for an amount of ACT equivalent to the tax credit attaching to the distributions. Generally, this resulted in a liability to ACT equal to the amount of the standard tax credit attaching to the distribution paid where the income out of which that distribution had been paid was taxable at the standard corporation tax rate.

A lower rate of ACT resulted where the underlying income had been taxed at a lower rate, for example, due to manufacturing relief (see **7.2**). Distributions paid out of certain tax exempted income carried a Nil tax credit so that no ACT was payable following distributions made out of such income. Where the distributing company had received one or more dividends from other Irish companies in the accounting period in which the distribution was made, the amount of the resulting ACT, if any, was the excess of the tax credit attaching to the distributions less the amount of the tax credits attaching to the distributions received, subject to some restrictions.

ACT in respect of a distribution made was payable within 6 months of the end of the accounting period in which that distribution was made. Where, however, the payment date would have fallen after the 28th day of a month, ACT was payable not later than the 28th of that month.

11.202   Set-off of ACT

ACT paid by a company (and not repaid) in respect of any distribution made by it in an accounting period was set, in so far as possible, against the company's liability to corporation tax (referred to as "mainstream corporation tax") on any income charged to corporation tax for that period, that is, the amount of its profits for that period on which corporation tax falls finally to be borne excluding the part of the profits attributable to chargeable gains.

11.203 Surplus ACT

Surplus ACT (ie, ACT in excess of the mainstream corporation tax against which it was being set off in the first instance) could be set off against corporation tax for *any* accounting period *ending within* the twelve months preceding the accounting period in which the surplus ACT arose and had to be set off against the tax of most recent accounting periods in priority to tax of other periods. ACT so carried back was treated, for the purposes of setting ACT paid against mainstream corporation tax, as if it had been ACT paid in respect of distributions made in the period to which it was carried back. ACT so carried back to an earlier period was not, however, treated as paid in respect of a distribution made in that period for the purpose of enabling any surplus amount of it arising in that period to be carried back yet again.

Surplus ACT paid by a company for any accounting period and which had not been carried back to an earlier period, as described above, was treated as ACT paid in respect of distributions made by the company in the following accounting period. If this treatment resulted in surplus ACT arising for that following accounting period, that surplus was treated as ACT paid in respect of distributions made by the company for the next following period and so on until all surplus ACT is utilised.

The legislative provisions dealing with ACT were deleted by FA 2003 which, however, introduced a provision enabling companies having surplus ACT carried forward from earlier years to continue to offset such surplus ACT against their corporation tax in future accounting periods. For this purpose, *surplus advance corporation tax*, in relation to a company's accounting period, means an amount of ACT:

(a) to which the company was liable under the legislation dealing with ACT in respect of a distribution made before 6 April 1999;

(b) which was paid by the company and not repaid to it; and

(c) which was not set against the company's liability to corporation tax for any preceding accounting period (TCA 1997, s 845B(1)).

Where a company has an amount of surplus ACT in an accounting period, that amount is to be set against the company's liability to corporation tax on any income charged to corporation tax for that period (TCA 1997, s 845B(2)).

For the above purposes, the income of a company charged to corporation tax for any accounting period is the amount of its profits for that period on which corporation tax falls finally to be borne, not including the part of the profits attributable to chargeable gains. The part of the profits attributable to chargeable gains is the amount brought into the company's profits for the purposes of corporation tax in respect of chargeable gains before any deduction for charges on income, expenses of management or other amounts that can be deducted from or set against or treated as reducing profits of more than one description (TCA 1997, s 845B(3)).

A notice under TCA 1997, s 884 (return of profits – see **15.104.6** and **15.205**) may require the inclusion in the return to be delivered by the company in question of particulars of any surplus ACT carried forward in relation to the company (TCA 1997, s 845B(4)).

Where any set-off of surplus ACT ought not to have been made, or is or has become excessive, an assessment may be made for the purpose of recovering any tax that ought to have been paid and generally to secure that the resulting liabilities to tax, including interest on unpaid tax, of the company concerned are what they would have been if only the correct set-off had been made (TCA 1997, s 845B(5)).

11.204   ACT payable where distributions received

Where a company received one or more distributions in an accounting period, ACT was payable in respect of a distribution made in that period only to the extent that the tax credit attaching to the distribution exceeded the tax credits on the distributions received. Where the aggregate amount of the tax credits in respect of distributions received by a company in an accounting period exceeded the sum of:

(a)   the aggregate amount of the tax credits, if any, in respect of distributions made by it in the period; and

(b)   the amount of any payment to the company of the tax credits in respect of distributions received by it in the period,

the excess was carried forward to the following accounting period and treated for the purposes of calculating liability to ACT as a tax credit in respect of a distribution received by the company in that period.

11.205   Surrender of ACT

Where ACT had been paid by a company (the "surrendering company") in respect of dividends paid by it in an accounting period and that ACT had not been repaid to it, the benefit of the ACT could be surrendered to any company (the "recipient company") which was a member of the same group of companies throughout that accounting period. ACT the benefit of which had been surrendered ("the surrendered amount") was treated as if it had arisen in respect of a dividend paid by the recipient company itself on the same date as the surrendering company's dividend had actually been paid. The surrendered amount, however, could not be used by the recipient company for any period earlier than the period in which it had been surrendered. On the other hand, the surrendered amount could be set against the recipient company's mainstream corporation tax before any ACT paid in respect of a distribution it had made itself, possibly leaving that ACT available for relief in a subsequent accounting period or available for carry- back to a period ending within the twelve months preceding the accounting period in which that ACT arises.

A surrendering company could elect to surrender the benefit of ACT arising in an accounting period to more than one group member. For this purpose, it was entitled to determine the proportions in which the surplus ACT was to be surrendered to those companies.

Where in the case of a surrendered amount the related ACT was paid by the surrendering company in respect of one dividend, or in respect of more than one dividend all of which were paid on the same date, the recipient company was treated as having paid an amount of ACT equal to the surrendered amount in respect of a distribution made by it on that date. Where the related ACT was paid in respect of dividends paid on different dates, the recipient company was treated as having paid an amount of ACT equal to the appropriate part of the surrendered amount in respect of a distribution made by it on each of those dates. The *appropriate part of the surrendered amount* means the part of the amount as bears to the whole the same proportion as the tax credit in respect of that dividend bears to the total amount of the tax credits in respect of the dividends.

11.206　Change in ownership of companies

ACT paid could not be used for set-off against mainstream corporation tax in certain cases of change of ownership of companies. This prohibition was aimed at cases involving the purchase of companies with surplus ACT where the intention was to use that ACT to shelter tax payable on profits which would arise in the purchased company as a result of the creation of or the diversion of profits into the company.

11.207　Distributions to certain non-resident companies

It was possible to treat the following kinds of distribution as not being distributions for the purposes of liability to ACT:

(a)　a distribution which was a distribution by virtue only of TCA 1997, s 130(2)(d)(iv) (interest paid to foreign parent or foreign fellow subsidiary); or

(b)　a *dividend* paid by a company to another company:

    (i)　of which the first-mentioned company is a 75% subsidiary, or

    (ii)　which is a member of a consortium which owns the first-mentioned company, and

which is a resident of a country with which Ireland has a tax treaty.

Where a company made a distribution falling within either (a) or (b) above, it was entitled to claim to have it treated as not being a distribution for the purposes of liability to ACT. The recipient company was not then entitled to a tax credit in respect of the distribution.

A company is owned by a *consortium* if at least 75% of its ordinary share capital is beneficially owned between them by five or fewer companies (the "members of the consortium") of which none beneficially owns less than 5% of that capital. The meaning of "consortium" here is similar to that applying for the purposes of TCA 1997, s 410 (group payments) but differs in one important respect in that the members of the consortium did not need to be Irish resident.

11.3   BUY-BACK OF SHARES

11.301   Introduction

Prior to the enactment of FA 1991 Pt I Ch VIII, the redemption, repayment or purchase by a company of its own shares was generally treated as a distribution under CTA 1976 ss 84–86 (now TCA 1997, ss 130–132 – see **11.102** and **11.103**) to the extent that the amount paid out exceeded the amount subscribed for the shares. The amount treated as a distribution was taxable under Schedule F in the case of an individual shareholder while it constituted franked investment income in the hands of a corporate shareholder.

> **Example 11.301.1**
>
> Grodny Ltd issues 80,000 ordinary shares of €1 each on 29 May 2003 at par and no premium is payable. It redeems the shares on 23 February 2008 for €170,000.
>
> The premium on redemption €90,000 is a distribution under TCA 1997, s 130(2)(b).
>
> In the hands of an individual shareholder, the redemption would result in an income tax liability on €90,000.

With effect from 1 July 1990, following the enactment of Part XI (ss 206-234) of the Companies Act 1990, companies have been permitted to acquire their own shares. A company may buy back any of its issued shares, whether or not those shares were originally issued as "redeemable" shares. Where a company acquires some of its own shares it may cancel them or hold them as "treasury shares". A company may purchase its own shares out of its distributable profits.

So as not to inhibit the purchase of shares which was facilitated by the Companies Act 1990, TCA 1997 Part 6 Ch 9 (ss 173-186) provides for special treatment for the purchase or redemption of shares in certain circumstances. Although the main treatment applies to shares in unquoted companies, it may be useful to consider first the position governing quoted companies.

Quoted companies

Quoted company is defined in TCA 1997, s 173(1) as "a company whose shares, or any class of whose shares, are listed in the official list of a stock exchange or dealt in on an unlisted securities market".

The position of a quoted company repaying, purchasing or redeeming its own shares up to 25 March 1997 was that it was deemed to have made a distribution of the amount of the premium, if any, paid on the purchase or redemption and was obliged to account for ACT at the appropriate rate.

The treatment of the premium payable by a quoted company in the hands of the vendor shareholder was less clear. There was no statutory exception to the distribution treatment and the premium was therefore in theory chargeable to income tax under Schedule F. If a share had been issued at, say, a nominal value of £1, was purchased by an individual some years later for £5 on the open market and was sold, again on the open market, for £6. If in this instance the company which issued the share was the purchaser it would, in strictness, have made a distribution of £5 (£6 – £1).

In practice there was generally no problem as the vendor would normally sell through a broker and would not be aware of the identity of the buyer. The seller would return the transaction as a chargeable gain of £1 and account for any capital gains tax due.

Any payment made by a quoted company, on or after 26 March 1997, on the redemption, repayment or purchase of its own shares is not to be treated as a distribution for the purposes of the Tax Acts. A quoted company for this purpose includes a company which is a member (see **11.105.8**) of a group of which a quoted company is a member (TCA 1997, s 175(2)). A *group* is a company which has one or more 51% subsidiaries (see *The company* in **11.305**) together with those subsidiaries (TCA 1997, s 173(1)).

From 26 March 1997 therefore, all disposals of shares consequent on the redemption, repayment or purchase by a quoted company of its own shares will be subject to capital gains tax treatment.

For accounting periods ending on or after 31 January 2008, a deduction for the cost to a company in buying back its own shares in circumstances where the payment made is treated as not being a distribution is specifically prohibited. TCA 1997, s 176A states that, for the purpose of computing the amount of the profits or gains charged to tax under Case I or II of Schedule D, a deduction may not be made for any sum in respect of any payment that is treated by virtue of TCA 1997, s 175 or 176 as not being a distribution.

The prohibition does not apply to so much of any payment as consists of expenditure incurred by a company to the extent that it is incurred on shares acquired by it and given by it as consideration for goods or services, or to an employee or director of the company. This exception is itself subject to TCA 1997, s 81(2)(n) (see **3.305.5**) which prohibits a deduction being made for any consideration given for goods and services, or consideration given to an employee or director of a company, consisting of shares in the company, or a connected company, except to the extent (i) of the amount of the expenditure incurred by the company on the acquisition of the shares at an arm's length price, (ii) where the shares are shares in a connected company, of any arm's length payment by the company to the connected company for the issue or transfer by that company of the shares, or (iii) of certain other expenditure incurred or payment made to the connected company in connection with the right to receive such shares.

The need for the prohibition is not clear. Other than in the circumstances of a claim in accordance with TCA 1997, s 81(2)(n), a deduction for trading purposes could hardly have been justified having regard to basic principles.

Distribution v capital gains tax

In the case of an individual shareholder, the capital gains tax treatment will usually be more favourable than distribution treatment due to the personal exemption and the probable lower rate of tax.

Where the vendor is a corporate or institutional shareholder, distribution treatment may be more favourable as franked investment income is not normally brought into charge to corporation tax.

While distribution treatment will therefore usually be more favourable for a vendor company, that treatment may not be applied as there will be no indication that the shares were purchased by the company which issued them. In the case of quoted companies, most share dealings are carried out on the market and the identity of the purchaser will not normally be known to the vendor.

Redemption, repayment and purchase of shares

The relieving provisions of TCA 1997 Part 6 Ch 9 set aside to some extent the effect of TCA 1997, s 20 and Part 6 Ch 2 (Schedule F and company distributions) as they would otherwise apply to the redemption, repayment or purchase by a company of its own shares.

If authorised by its articles to do so, a company limited by shares or by guarantee and having a share capital may issue shares and redeem them accordingly. No redeemable shares may be issued or redeemed at any time when the nominal value of the issued share capital that is not redeemable is less than one-tenth of the nominal value of the total issued share capital of the company. Redemption may only be effected if the shares are fully paid up. The terms of the redemption must provide for payment on redemption. The shares must be redeemed out of distributable profits or, where the company proposes to cancel shares on redemption, may be redeemed out of the proceeds of a fresh issue of shares made for the purposes of the redemption.

Any premium paid on redemption must be paid out of distributable profits but where the redeemable shares have been issued at a premium, the premium on redemption may be paid out of the proceeds of a fresh issue of shares made for the purposes of the redemption up to an amount equal to the aggregate of the premiums received on the issue of the redeemed shares or, if less, the current amount of the company's share premium account (including any sums transferred to that account in respect of premiums on the new shares).

A redemption of shares, like the purchase by a company of its own shares, since it does not involve the return of the nominal amount represented by the shares, is regarded as a matter of normal usage as different to a repayment of capital (see below) and the distinction would appear to exist for corporation tax purposes as evidenced by the phrase "redemption, repayment or purchase" used in TCA 1997, s 176. TCA 1997, s 132(4), however, provides that "premiums paid on redemption of share capital shall not be treated as repayments of capital", which would seem to imply that a redemption of shares would normally amount to a repayment of share capital up to the amount originally subscribed for the shares. The intention of the tax legislation, and clearly its effect, is that a repayment of capital may include a redemption of shares. The technical position relating to a purchase by a company of its own shares, as to whether it involves a repayment of capital, is less clear (probably due to the fact that the legislation governing distributions for tax purposes pre-dates the time from which it became possible for a company to buy back its own shares). In practice (see further below), the payment of an amount equal to the new consideration received on subscription, together with any premium, appears to be accepted as a repayment of capital.

Repayment, as it applies to share capital, is not defined although certain provisions of TCA 1997 Part 6 Ch 2 deal with matters which are not to be regarded as being repayments of share capital (see **11.103.4**). Otherwise it is necessary to look to the ordinary meaning of the expression "repayment of share capital". A repayment of share capital is generally understood to refer to the return of the nominal amount represented by that share capital, including amounts representing premiums paid on subscription for the share capital, and not, if different, of the amount paid on subscription (see also **11.105.1**).

A "reduction" of capital is the most obvious form of repayment of share capital involving the paying off of that capital in accordance with section 72 of the Companies Act 1963. There is no question of the payment of a premium on the paying off of share capital, although a payment in non-cash form may be in excess of the amount originally subscribed for the shares. (See **11.105.2** for a more detailed explanation of a reduction of capital.)

The legislation dealing with the *purchase* by a company of its own shares (see **10.3**) does not define or describe what is meant by that term, and its normal usage will therefore apply. The payment by a company of any sum on the purchase of its own shares does not, as normally understood, include anything by way of a repayment of share capital. The purchase by a company of its own shares out of capital may, however, be an exception. This might be achieved by way of a return of the premium paid in on the occasion of the issue of the shares, resulting in a corresponding reduction in the share premium account. To the extent of the amount of the premium returned, there would be a repayment of share capital (TCA 1997, s 132(3) – see **11.104** regarding the treatment of premiums on redemption as repayments of share capital) and, as seen above, the payment of an amount equal to the new consideration received on subscription, together with any premium, appears to be accepted for tax purposes at least as a repayment of capital. In this context, shares redeemed or repurchased should be cancelled, and not held as treasury shares.

While there have for long been clear indications as to the differences between the redemption, repayment and the purchase of shares, those differences become somewhat blurred in the relevant tax legislation.

11.302 Purchase of shares: company law

If authorised by its articles of association, a company may purchase its own shares, including any redeemable shares. In this connection, a distinction is made between "market" and "off-market" purchases. Off-market purchases are purchases made other than on a recognised stock exchange (and purchases on a recognised stock exchange that are not subject to a marketing arrangement on that exchange).

An off-market purchase may only be effected where the terms of the proposed contract of purchase are authorised by special resolution before the contract is entered into. This authority may be varied, revoked or from time to time renewed by special resolution.

There are certain company law provisions governing notices of a proposed contract of purchase before a special resolution is passed. A copy of the contract, or where the contract is not in writing, a written memorandum of its terms, must be available for inspection by members of the company at its registered office for at least twenty-one days before the meeting at which the resolution is passed, and at the meeting itself. It is not possible to hold the extraordinary general meeting on short notice, and even if members and auditors agree to hold a meeting on short notice it is still necessary to give twenty-one days notice since a copy of the contract of purchase (or memorandum of its terms) must be available at the registered office of the company for twenty-one days prior to the date of the meeting.

Any memorandum of the terms of the contract of purchase made available for this purpose must include the names of any members holding shares to which the contract relates and any copy of the contract must have annexed to it a written memorandum specifying those names if the names do not appear in the contract itself.

A company may agree to a variation of an existing contract of purchase but only where the variation is authorised by special resolution of the company. The same notice requirements as outlined above apply in respect of the special resolution in this case. However, a copy or memorandum of the original contract should be available as well as a copy of the memorandum of the proposed varied contract.

There are particular procedures required by company law with respect to voting on a special resolution. Notwithstanding anything contained in the company's articles of association, any member of the company may demand a poll on a special resolution. A special resolution is not effective if any member holding shares to which the resolution relates exercises the voting rights carried by any of those shares in voting on the resolution and the resolution would not have been passed if he had not done so.

The procedures outlined above apply also in relation to so-called contingent purchase contracts. A contingent purchase contract is one not amounting to an actual contract to purchase the shares but under which, subject to certain conditions, a company may become entitled or obliged to purchase its own shares. Examples of contingent purchase contracts would be put or call options on shares. The purchase of shares pursuant to a contingent purchase contract is permissible only if the terms of the proposed contract are authorised by special resolution before the contract is entered into. The procedural requirements which apply to off-market purchase contracts, as described above, apply also to contingent purchase contracts.

There is an absolute prohibition on the assignment of the rights acquired by a company under a contract to purchase its own shares. This is to prevent a company from speculating on its own share price by buying and selling purchase rights.

Prior to the enactment of the Companies Act 1990, a company, if authorised by its articles, could issue redeemable preference shares and could also issue shares which could be redeemed at the option of the company. The 1990 Act allows for the issue of redeemable equity shares and for the conversion of existing non-redeemable shares to redeemable shares. The Act also permits a company to buy back its own shares whether or not those shares had been issued as redeemable shares.

The power to redeem shares and the power to purchase shares, both provided for in the 1990 Act, are separate powers although in practice they may not always be distinguished. The company may adopt both powers in its memorandum and articles of association. Where a company has both powers, its power to purchase its own shares applies to all shares, including redeemable shares.

Section 211 of the Companies Act 1990, provides that a company may, if so authorised by its articles, purchase its own shares, including any redeemable shares. A company may not purchase any of its shares if, as a result of such purchase, the nominal value of the issued share capital which is not redeemable would be less than one-tenth of the nominal value of the total issued share capital of the company. Certain provisions dealing with the redemption of shares are applied equally to the purchase of shares. These are summarised as follows:

(i)   shares may not be purchased unless they are fully paid;

(ii)   the terms of purchase must provide for payment on purchase (ie not by instalments);

(iii)   no shares may be purchased otherwise than out of profits available for distribution;

(iv)   if the shares are to be cancelled on purchase (see below), the purchase may also be made out of the proceeds of a fresh issue of shares made for the purposes of the purchase;

(v)   if the shares were issued at a premium, any premium payable on the purchase (in the case of a purchase made out of the proceeds of a fresh issue of shares) may be paid out of the proceeds of a fresh issue of shares up to a certain amount. That amount is a sum equal to the aggregate of the premiums received by the company on the issue of the shares or the current amount of the company's share premium account, including any sum transferred to that account in respect of premiums on the new shares, whichever is the less.

Shares which are purchased by a company may be cancelled on purchase, in which case the following provisions apply:

(a)   the amount of the company's issued share capital is to be reduced by the nominal value of the shares purchased (but the cancellation does not have the effect of reducing the amount of the authorised share capital);

(b)   where the shares were purchased wholly out of profits available for distribution, an amount equal to the nominal value of the shares purchased must be transferred to a capital redemption reserve fund (to maintain the principle that a limited liability company may not reduce the value of its capital);

(c)   where the shares were purchased partly or wholly out of the proceeds of a fresh issue of shares and the aggregate amount of the proceeds is less than the nominal value of the shares redeemed, the difference is to be transferred to the capital redemption reserve fund;

(d)   the capital redemption reserve fund may be applied by the company in paying up unissued shares of the company, other than redeemable shares, to be allotted to members of the company as fully paid bonus shares.

Instead of cancelling shares on their purchase, a company may retain them as *treasury shares*. The total amount of treasury shares held by a company at any time may not exceed 10% of the nominal value of the issued share capital of the company. For this purpose, shares held in the company by a subsidiary, shares held in the company by a nominee on behalf of the company, and shares held by a subsidiary in pursuance of section 9, Insurance Act 1990, are deemed to be shares held by the company. As long as the company holds treasury shares the following conditions apply:

(a)   no voting rights may be exercised in respect of the shares;

(b)   no dividend or other payment (including any payment in a winding up of the company) may be payable to the company in respect of the shares;

(c)   treasury shares may subsequently be cancelled as if they had been cancelled on their purchase;

(d)   treasury shares may subsequently be re-issued as shares of any class or classes.

Where treasury shares are reissued, the reissue is not treated as an increase in share capital (so that no stamp duties are payable). Where the shares are to be reissued "off-market", the company must, in general meeting, determine in advance the maximum and minimum prices at which such shares or classes of shares are to be issued. In addition, a special resolution requiring a 75% majority of the members voting is required to determine the price range and the special resolution must be passed at the same meeting as that at which the resolution authorising the purchase was passed.

The terms of any special resolution governing the price range may be varied or altered by a further special resolution. Such resolution must be passed prior to any contract being entered into for the reissue of the treasury shares in question. Any special resolution passed is effective for a maximum period of 18 months from the date on which it is passed. A similar period of 18 months applies in the case of any varying resolution.

The following is a suggested checklist of matters to be taken into account and attended to by a company which proposes to purchase any of its shares from a shareholder.

(i)   Review the articles of association to ensure that the company has the necessary power to purchase its own shares.

(ii)   In the event that the company does not have that power, propose a special resolution at an extraordinary general meeting of the company (see (vi) below) to alter the articles accordingly.

(iii) Agree the proposed contract between company and vendor.

(iv)   Convene a board meeting prior to the extraordinary general meeting, for the purpose of proposing the convening of the extraordinary general meeting and to approve the notice of the meeting.

(v)   Issue notice of the extraordinary general meeting at least twenty-one clear days in advance.

(vi)   Convene the extraordinary general meeting to deal with:

   (a)   the alteration of the articles, if necessary, and

   (b)   the authorisation of the contract of purchase, or memorandum of terms of such contract.

(vii) File a copy of the special resolution(s) on Form G1(16) with the Registrar of Companies within fifteen days of being passed.

(viii) Where the purchase of shares is being effected wholly out of distributable profits, proceed with the purchase of shares following the passing of the resolution and the signing of the contract.

(ix) Within twenty-eight days of the purchase, file Form H5 with the Registrar of Companies.

(x) If the shares are to be cancelled following purchase, convene extraordinary general meeting to propose ordinary resolution to that effect and file Form 16A within one month of the passing of the resolution.

(xi) Retain the contract of purchase for ten years after completion of the sale of the shares and retain for inspection by members during business hours at company's registered office.

11.303 Tax consequences: general

As a "distribution" includes any distribution out of assets of a company, except so much, if any, as represents a repayment of capital on the shares or is equal in amount or value to any new consideration received by the company for the distribution (TCA 1997, s 130(2)(b)), any payment made by the company to a shareholder in excess of the original share purchase price is treated as a distribution. Similarly, any amount met in cash or otherwise out of the assets of the company in respect of the redemption of bonus shares or securities, otherwise than wholly for new consideration, or in the redemption of such part of such bonus shares or securities as is not properly referable to new consideration, is treated as a distribution (TCA 1997, s 130(2)(c)). TCA 1997, s 131-132 treat as distributions the use of bonus shares to replace share capital already repaid or a bonus issue in advance of a repayment of share capital (see **11.102-103**).

TCA 1997, s 176 provides that where the company and the shareholder satisfy certain conditions, any reference to a distribution in any of the foregoing provisions is to be taken as not including a reference to a payment made on the redemption, repayment or purchase of its own shares by a company which is an unquoted trading company or the unquoted holding company of a trading group.

Example 11.303.1

Millwood Ltd was incorporated with an issued share capital of €50,000 comprising 50,000 ordinary shares of €1 each. At that time, Mr Wright subscribed for 20,000 of those shares.

The company traded profitably and some years later the value of Mr Wright's share of the company's net worth was €60,000, representing an increase in the value per share from €1 to €3.

The shareholders now decide to reduce the share capital of the company to €150,000 by way of purchasing Mr Wright's shares.

Without TCA 1997, s 176, the tax consequences for Mr Wright would be:

	€
Amount subscribed for shares:	
20,000 shares at €1 each	20,000
Shares purchased:	
20,000 shares at €3 each	60,000
Premium	40,000

As the premium is a distribution, Mr Wright would be liable to income tax, for the year in which the shares are repurchased, in respect of a distribution of €40,000.

Where a company, being an unquoted trading company or an unquoted holding company of a trading group, purchases its own unquoted shares, TCA 1997, s 176 provides that, notwithstanding TCA 1997 Part 6 Ch 2, the payment made by the company is not to be treated as a distribution for the purposes of that chapter. Accordingly, the buy-back of the shares falls to be treated as a capital payment and, in the hands of the vendor shareholder, a capital receipt.

Example 11.303.2

The position is as in Example **11.303.1** except that TCA 1997, s 176 applies.

The premium is not regarded as a distribution, and Mr Wright is liable to capital gains tax on the following gain:

	€
Proceeds on sale of shares to company	60,000
Less: purchase price	20,000
Chargeable gain	40,000

Capital gains tax treatment will usually be preferred due to the combined effects of indexation (albeit that there is no further indexation after 2002), the low capital gains tax rate and the annual exemption. Where distribution treatment is, however, more beneficial, it is a relatively simple matter to ensure that at least one of the conditions required for TCA 1997, s 176 treatment will not be fulfilled.

A payment made in respect of the cancellation, redemption or repurchase of a share in a collective investment undertaking which is a company is not treated as a distribution for any purpose of the Tax Acts (TCA 1997, s 734(9)(a) – see **12.805**). Thus, a payment of the above kind made by an authorised investment company within the meaning of Part XIII of the Companies Act 1990, which is a collective investment undertaking, is not treated as a distribution for any purpose.

For accounting periods ending on or after 31 January 2008, a deduction for the cost to a company in buying back its own shares in circumstances where the payment made is treated as not being a distribution is specifically prohibited. TCA 1997, s 176A states that, for the purpose of computing the amount of the profits or gains charged to tax under Case I or II of Schedule D, a deduction may not be made for any sum in respect of any payment that is treated by virtue of TCA 1997, s 175 or 176 as not being a distribution. (See also **11.301**.)

11.304   The relief

Provided the necessary conditions applying to the company and the vendor shareholder are fulfilled, TCA 1997, s 176 provides that the proceeds arising on the redemption, repayment or purchase of its own shares by a company will not be regarded as a distribution. If the conditions are not satisfied, the proceeds will amount to a distribution except to the extent that they represent a repayment of capital on the shares or are, when made, equal in amount or value to any new consideration received by the company in respect of the amount paid out (TCA 1997, s 130(2)(b) and (c)). For the meaning of *new consideration*, see **11.105.5**.

It is important to note that TCA 1997, s 176 does not cancel the effect of TCA 1997, s 131 which treats as a distribution a bonus issue of shares which replaces an earlier repayment of share capital. That section treats as a distribution the issue itself of the bonus shares ("the amount so paid up") up to the amount of the share capital previously repaid, whereas TCA 1997, s 176 deals only with payments made on redemption, repayment or purchase.

In this connection, it was seen in **11.301** that although a redemption of shares is not normally understood as including a repayment of capital, it does appear to include a repayment of capital in the tax sense at least. A purchase of shares, on the other hand, does not involve any repayment of capital. Accordingly, TCA 1997, s 131 does not treat as a distribution a bonus issue which follows a purchase of shares.

The benefits of TCA 1997, s 176 are intended to include such matters as the provision of a ready market for shares which might not otherwise easily be disposed of and the retention of control by family shareholders on the occasion of the departure of a family member from the company. Although the family would normally have pre-emption rights over the shares of that member, the actual exercise of those rights might be inhibited by a shortage of funds for the purpose. A purchase of shares by the company from the parting member can, with the assistance of TCA 1997, s 176, be effected so as to ensure retention of family control. The beneficial tax treatment also makes it possible for a shareholder to sell shares to the company where the proceeds are the only means of discharging an inheritance tax liability arising in respect of those shares.

The essential purpose of a buy-back of shares is to benefit the trade of the company concerned. The benefit may result from the buying out of a dissident shareholder, the retirement of the owner of a company to allow new management to be introduced, or the buying out of an outside shareholder who had provided equity finance but who now wishes to realise his investment.

As already seen above, where TCA 1997, s 176 has effect, the payment by the company is not treated as a distribution for the purposes of TCA 1997 Part 6 Ch 2. The payment will still, however, continue to be a distribution for the purposes of TCA 1997, ss 440 and 441 (surcharge on certain undistributed income of close companies – see **10.3**) and may therefore be instrumental in avoiding or reducing a close company surcharge.

Relief under TCA 1997, s 176 may also be available in respect of a payment made by a company which is a subsidiary (within the meaning of section 155 of the Companies Act 1963) of another company on the acquisition of shares of that other company. The relief will be available if it would be available on the assumption that the payment is one made by the other company on the purchase of its own shares and the acquisition of the shares is a purchase by the other company of its own shares (TCA 1997, s 176(2)).

Under section 155 of the Companies Act 1963, a company is deemed to be a *subsidiary* of another company if:

(a) that other company:

    (i) is a member of it and controls the composition of its board of directors, or

    (ii) holds more than half in nominal value of its equity share capital, or

    (iii) holds more than half in nominal value of its shares carrying voting rights (other than voting rights which arise only in specified circumstances), or

(b) the first-mentioned company is a subsidiary of any company which is that other company's subsidiary.

For the meaning of *member* see **11.105.8**.

11.305 Conditions for relief: the company

As regards a redemption, repayment or purchase of shares in a company, the conditions for relief (ie, non-distribution treatment) are contained in TCA 1997, s 176. Although the treatment discussed here refers mainly to the purchase of its own shares by a company, the relevant tax provisions apply equally to the redemption or repayment of shares. The relevant conditions relate to the type of company concerned, the reason for the purchase of the shares by the company, and the vendor shareholder from whom the shares are being purchased. Where shares are being sold by a vendor for the purpose of facilitating the payment of inheritance tax, certain conditions relating to the company and the reason for the sale are relaxed.

The company

TCA 1997, s 176(1) provides that the company must be an "unquoted" company and either a "trading company" or the "holding company" of a "trading group". An *unquoted company* is a company none of whose shares, or any class of them, are listed in the official list of a stock exchange or dealt in on an unlisted securities market; TCA 1997, s 173(4) provides that an unquoted company is a company which is neither a quoted company nor a 51% subsidiary of a quoted company.

A trading company is a company whose business consists wholly or mainly of the carrying on of a trade or trades. Trade does not include dealing in shares, securities, land, futures or traded options.

A holding company is a company whose business, disregarding any trade carried on by it, consists wholly or mainly of the holding of shares or securities of one or more companies which are its 51% subsidiaries.

The relevant legislation does not define "wholly or mainly" for the purposes of the above two definitions. There is nothing to suggest that an income type test is to be adopted; such a yardstick would in any event be quite inappropriate in the case of a holding company. The better view would be to take the test as being a functional one having regard to the time, effort and resources expended by the company concerned in relation to its holding company or trading role.

A company is a 51% subsidiary of another company if and so long as more than 50% of its ordinary share capital is owned directly or indirectly by that other company (TCA 1997, s 9(1)(a)). The reference to "disregarding any trade carried on by it" allows for a company which holds shares in 51% subsidiaries and which also carries on a trade.

A *trading group* means a group the business of whose members, taken together, consists wholly or mainly of the carrying on of a trade or trades, where *group* means a company together with its 51% subsidiaries. In view of this definition of "group", the presence of one or more non-trading subsidiaries within a group could mean that the group is not a trading group. It is understood, however, that non-trading activities of a company could be regarded as forming part of the trade or trades of other trading group members, for example, the holding by one group company of property occupied for trading purposes by trading members of the group. It is also possible to treat a sub-group as a trading group where its members between them fulfil the necessary conditions although the larger group of which that sub-group is a part does not satisfy them.

Purpose of buy-back

The buy-back (or redemption or repayment) of shares must be wholly or mainly for the purpose of benefiting a trade carried on by the company or by any of its 51% subsidiaries and must not form part of a scheme or arrangement the main purpose or one of the main purposes of which is to enable the shareholder to participate in profits of the company or of any of its 51% subsidiaries, without receiving a dividend (TCA 1997, s 176(1)(a)).

As to how it may be established in individual cases whether or to what extent a trade of a company will be benefited by a purchase of its shares could present difficulties. In the narrowest sense, it seems possible to argue that a purchase of shares cannot benefit a trade at all. The legislation provides no assistance on this aspect. The Revenue Commissioners have published their views on this matter in *Tax Briefing – Issue 25* and the position regarding the operation of the trade benefit test is accordingly as follows.

The test requires that it be shown that the sole or main purpose of the buy-back is to benefit a trade carried on by the company or of one of its 51% subsidiaries. The test would not be met where, for example, the sole or main purpose of the buy-back is to benefit the shareholder or to benefit a business purpose of the company other than a trade, eg an investment activity.

The Revenue will normally regard a buy-back of shares as benefiting the trade where, for example:

(a) there is disagreement between the shareholders over the management of the company and that disagreement is having or is expected to have an adverse effect on the company's trade and where the effect of the share purchase transaction is to remove the dissenting shareholder; or

(b) the purpose of the buy-back is to ensure that an unwilling shareholder who wishes to end his association with the company does not sell the shares to someone who might not be acceptable to the other shareholders.

Examples of the above-described situations would include the following:

(a) an outside investor who had provided equity finance but who now wishes to realise his investment;

(b) the wish of a proprietor or controlling shareholder to retire and make way for new management;

(c) the wish of the personal representatives of a deceased shareholder not to retain inherited shares; and

(d) a legatee of a deceased shareholder who does not wish to hold shares in the company.

The above examples envisage the shareholder selling his entire shareholding and making a complete break from the company. If the company is not purchasing all of the shares owned by the vendor, or if the vendor is selling all the shares but retaining some connection with the company, eg in the form of a directorship, it would seem unlikely that the transaction would benefit the company's trade. There may, however, be situations where:

(a) for sentimental reasons a retiring director of a company wishes to retain a small shareholding in the company; or

(b)   a controlling shareholder in a family company is selling his shares to allow control to pass to his children but remains on as a director for a specified period purely because his immediate departure from the company at that time would otherwise have a negative impact on the company's business.

In circumstances such as these, it may still be possible for the company to show that the main purpose of the share buy-back is to benefit the trade.

Where a company is unsure whether a proposed buy-back is for the benefit of the trade and where all the other legislative requirements have been met, the Revenue will, if requested, give an advance opinion on the question of whether the proposed buy-back satisfies the trade benefit test. Applications for an advance ruling should:

(a)   confirm that all the other requirements of the legislation have been met;

(b)   list the current shareholders in the purchasing company together with particulars of their shareholdings and their relationship, if any, with each other. In a group situation, a statement or diagram of the group structure would be helpful;

(c)   state the reason for the share buy-back and the trading benefit expected to accrue to the company (or its 51% subsidiary);

(d)   state the name(s) of the person(s) disposing of the shares, the number and type of shares involved in the buy-back and the date(s) the shares were acquired;

(e)   state the amount to be paid for the shares, how this is to be financed and how the latter will impact on the financial position of the company; and

(f)   forward a copy of the most recent accounts of the company.

In practice, therefore, the disposal of his *entire* interest in the company by any shareholder would be accepted as being effected for the benefit of the company's trade. This will apply to disposals on a phased basis, which may be the only means by which a company is in a position to buy out a shareholder. This is compatible with TCA 1997, s 178 which provides for minimum levels of reduction in a shareholding in respect of which the TCA 1997, s 176 relieving provision will apply. A buy-back of a part shareholding with a minimum shareholding being retained by the vendor, however, would need to be carried out for a particular and demonstrable commercial reason to satisfy the purpose test.

As already mentioned, the buy-back of shares must not be effected as part of a scheme or arrangement the main purpose or one of the main purposes of which is to enable the shareholder to participate in profits of the company or of any of its 51% subsidiaries, without receiving a dividend (TCA 1997, s 176(1)(a)(i)(II)). It will be readily apparent in certain cases that the intention of a purchase of shares from a shareholder is to facilitate the receipt in capital form by that shareholder of payments that are essentially dividends in disguise; no relief will then be available. In other cases, it may be difficult to apply any objective test in ascertaining whether the securing of capital gains tax treatment rather than distribution treatment was the main, or one of the main, purposes of the transaction. Where the vendor retains an interest in the company, the need to point to some commercial justification for the transaction becomes more important.

There would appear to be considerable justification for the view that if the "benefiting the trade" test can be satisfied, it is almost axiomatic that relief will not be denied by reason of the "scheme or arrangement" test. Each of the two tests may, in a manner, be a function of the other. If, therefore, it appears that a buy-back of shares has been effected for the purpose of facilitating a shareholder to receive payment in capital form so as to avoid income receipts, it is most unlikely that the transaction could be shown to have been carried out for the benefit of the company's trade. Where all of the shareholder's interest is purchased by the company, and provided that shareholder is no longer connected with the company (see below), it is virtually certain that no "scheme or arrangement" will be adduced. It is also practically certain in that case that the purchase would be accepted as being for the benefit of the company's trade. The mere fact that the vendor obtains a tax benefit by receiving payment in capital form cannot, clearly, be sufficient reason for denying that benefit.

11.306 Conditions for relief: the vendor

11.306.1 Introduction

TCA 1997, ss 177-181 prescribe a number of conditions relating to the vendor if relief under TCA 1997, s 176 is to be secured. These conditions relate to the residence of the vendor, the period of ownership of the shares before being purchased by the company, and the reduction of the vendor's interest as a shareholder in the company.

11.306.2 Residence

The vendor must be resident and, in the case of a person other than a company, ordinarily resident in the State for the chargeable period (year of assessment or accounting period for individuals and companies respectively) in which the purchase (or redemption or repayment) takes place. If the shares are held through a nominee, the nominee must also be resident and ordinarily resident – to ensure that capital gains tax can be collected from the vendor (TCA 1997, s 177(2)).

In the case of trustees, residence and ordinary residence is to be determined in accordance with TCA 1997, s 574 so that they will be regarded as resident and ordinarily resident in the State unless the general administration of the trust in question is ordinarily carried on outside the State and the trustees or a majority of them for the time being are not resident or not ordinarily resident in the State.

The residence and ordinary residence of personal representatives is to be taken as being the same as the residence and ordinary residence of the deceased immediately before his death.

11.306.3 Period of ownership

The vendor must have beneficially owned the shares throughout the period of five years ending with the date of their purchase by the company except that that holding period is three years where the shares were appropriated to a vendor under an approved profit sharing scheme (APSS) and where the provisions of TCA 1997, s 515(4)-(7) do not apply (see **3.203.2**) (TCA 1997, s 177(6)). "Purchase" means the redemption, repayment or purchase and "vendor" refers to the owner of the shares immediately before the purchase. Where there has been a reorganisation of share capital under which, for the purposes of TCA 1997, s 584-558 (see **9.402-405**), a "new holding" is deemed to have been acquired at the same time as the original holding was acquired, that provision will apply also in determining the time when a person acquired shares for the purposes of the relief under TCA 1997, s 176 (TCA 1997, s 177(10)).

Under capital gains tax rules, a vendor would lose beneficial ownership of the shares at the date of the (unconditional) contract for their sale to the company. On that basis, the shares would not have been owned by him for any period ending with the date of the purchase for the purposes of TCA 1997, s 177(6); that date is the date when the shares are actually redeemed, repaid or purchased pursuant to the contract. It is unthinkable, however, that relief could be lost on this technical point.

In determining the period of beneficial ownership of shares in the case of an individual, the period of ownership of the shares by that individual's spouse may be taken into account where the shares had been gifted to the individual by the spouse and provided the spouses were living together at the time of the gift and, unless the spouse who made the gift has died in the meantime, at the date of the purchase (TCA 1997, s 177(7)). TCA 1997, s 1015 applies in determining whether the spouses were living together at any date. Thus, a wife is to be treated as living with her husband unless either they are separated under an order of a court of competent jurisdiction or by deed of separation, or they are in fact separated in such circumstances that the separation is likely to be permanent.

Where the vendor became entitled to the shares under the will or on the intestacy of a previous owner, or is the personal representative of a previous owner, any period during which the shares were owned by that previous owner or his personal representatives is to be treated as a period of ownership by the vendor. In addition, the required period of ownership by the vendor in that case is three years instead of five years.

TCA 1997, s 177(9) deals with the period of ownership requirement in cases where the vendor acquired shares of the same class at different times. Shares acquired earlier are to be taken into account before shares acquired later. For the purpose of applying the ownership requirement in the case of a later disposal, however, any previous disposal of shares of the same class is assumed to be a disposal of shares acquired *later* rather than of shares acquired earlier.

Example 11.306.3.1

In 1999, John Moran purchased 5,000 ordinary shares of €1 each in Marsh Ltd and a further 3,000 shares in that company in 2007. Marsh Ltd proposes to buy back 3,000 of John Moran's shares in February 2009 and the other 5,000 shares in February 2010.

For the purposes of the first buy-back, in 2009, the shares to be purchased are assumed to be from the 5,000 bought by John Moran in 1999 since shares acquired earlier are assumed to be disposed of before shares acquired later. The five-year ownership test is therefore satisfied in this case.

For the purposes of the second buy-back, in 2010, since there will have been a previous disposal by John Moran of 3,000 ordinary shares in 2009, that earlier disposal is assumed to be a disposal of shares acquired *later* (the 3,000 shares acquired in 2007) rather than a disposal out of the 5,000 shares acquired earlier (in 1999). Accordingly, the 5,000 shares to be disposed of in 2010 are assumed to be the 5,000 shares acquired in 1999 so that the five-year ownership test is also satisfied in respect of this disposal.

11.306.4 Reduction in vendor's interest

TCA 1997, s 178 deals with purchases (including redemptions and repayments) of shares where only a part buy-back of a complete shareholding is being effected. The relief provided for in TCA 1997, s 176 will be available where the combined interests of the vendor and his associates (see **11.307** below for meaning of "associate") in the company has been "substantially reduced". Where any associate of the vendor owns shares in the company immediately after the purchase, the combined interests of the vendor and his associates as shareholders in the group must be substantially reduced. The question whether those combined interests have been substantially reduced is to be determined in the same way as the question whether a vendor's interest as a shareholder is substantially reduced, except that the vendor is assumed to have the interests of his associates as well as his own.

The substantial reduction issue will be relevant therefore not only where less than a complete shareholding of a vendor has been purchased by a company (perhaps because the company has insufficient funds to purchase the entire shareholding), but also where the entire shareholding of the vendor is being purchased while associates of the vendor are retaining their shareholdings.

The vendor's interest is taken to be substantially reduced if the total nominal value of the shares owned by him immediately after the purchase, expressed as a fraction of the issued share capital of the company at the time, does not exceed 75% of the corresponding fraction immediately before the purchase (TCA 1997, s 178(4)).

Example 11.306.4.1

The position is as in Example **11.306.3.1** where it is ascertained that John Moran is disposing of his shareholding to facilitate the introduction of new management by his two older children. The following information relating to the shareholdings in Marsh Ltd is available:

	€1 ord shares
John Moran	8,000
Ann Moran (wife – 3,000 shares acquired at each of same two dates as John Moran)	6,000
Jane Moran (age 26)	7,000
Mary Moran (age 24)	7,000
Jim Moran (age 17 – shares acquired 2003)	3,000
	31,000

The proposed purchase of 3,000 of John Moran's shares in 2009 would reduce his shareholding from 25.81% (8,000 out of 31,000) to 17.86% (5,000 out of 28,000). His shareholding as a fraction would be reduced to 69.2% of what it had been immediately before. When, however, the interests of his associates (wife and minor child) are taken into account, it is seen that the combined interest would not have dropped to 75% of what it had been immediately before the purchase. The combined interests before and after would be 54.84% and 50% respectively, ie a reduction to 91.17% only.

Since the effect of a buy-back of shares is to reduce both the shareholding of the vendor and the amount of the issued share capital of the company, it is necessary to ascertain the minimum reduction required by use of a simultaneous equation. In this case, the minimum reduction works out at 7,220 shares. The combined interest of John Moran and his associates, after a total reduction of 7,220 shares owned by them, would be 41.13% (9,780 out of 23,780) which represents 75% of their original holding.

Accordingly, it is agreed that Ann Moran will also sell 3,000 of her shares (the maximum amount for the purposes of the five-year rule), and Jim Moran 1,220 of his shares, to the company. It would not be sufficient, for the purposes of relief under TCA 1997, s 176, for John Moran to sell any more than 5,000 of his shares at this time since (as seen in Example

11.306.3.1) the remaining 3,000 shares have been held by him for less than the requisite five-year period. (By selling only 3,000 shares now, he retains a "cushion" of 2,000 shares for this purpose.)

11.306.5   Profit distribution test

In addition to the "substantially reduced" test, TCA 1997, s 178 prescribes a profit distribution test which must also be satisfied by a vendor wishing to obtain relief under TCA 1997, s 176. The vendor must show that on a full distribution by the company of its profits available for distribution immediately after the purchase, his entitlement to a share of those profits, expressed as a fraction of the total of those profits, would not exceed 75% of the corresponding fraction immediately before the purchase (TCA 1997, s 178(5)). As with the "substantially reduced" test, this test applies in relation to the vendor together with his associates. The test complements the "substantially reduced" test by ensuring that that test cannot be circumvented by the use of different classes of shares with different rights to dividends.

Example 11.306.5.1

The position is as in Example **11.306.4.1** with the additional information that the shares held in Marsh Ltd by John and Ann Moran are "A" ordinary shares while those held by the other members of the family are "B" ordinary shares. After the buy-back of the 7,220 shares indicated in the previous example, the shareholdings are as follows:

	"A" ordinary shares	*"B" ordinary shares*
John Moran	5,000	
Ann Moran	3,000	
Jane Moran		7,000
Mary Moran		7,000
Jim Moran		1,780
	8,000	15,780

If both classes of shares rank pari passu in all respects, the profit distribution test will have been satisfied as the profits available for distribution to John Moran and his associates immediately after the purchase, expressed as a fraction of the total of those profits, would not exceed 75% of the corresponding fraction immediately before the purchase.

If, however, the "A" ordinary shares carry any advantage, for example in relation to dividends, it will be necessary to calculate the distributable profits available to John Moran and his associates as a fraction of the total such profits before and after the share purchase. Assuming that the "A" shares have a right to a dividend of €1.05 for every €1 dividend on the "B" shares, the position is as follows.

Prior to any buy-back of shares, the shares held by John, Ann and Jim Moran were entitled to 17,700/ 31,700, or 55.84%, of the distributable profits and to 10,180/ 24,180, or 42.1%, after the buy-back. The new fraction represents 75.4% of the previous fraction so that the profit distribution test would not be satisfied.

The necessary step to be taken to satisfy this test has the added complication that any further disposals of "A" shares will trigger distribution treatment since, for both John and Ann Moran, all of their remaining shares have been held for less than five years. Accordingly, Jim Moran is prevailed on to sell a further 93 shares to the company. His reduced shareholding is now 1,687 shares and the total number of "B" shares in issue is reduced to 15,687. The shares held by John, Ann and Jim Moran would now give them an entitlement of 10,087/ 24,087, or 41.88%, of the distributable profits. This represents 75% of the original fraction so that the profit distribution test is now satisfied.

In determining the division of profits among the persons entitled to them, a person entitled to periodic distributions calculated by reference to fixed rates or amounts is regarded as entitled to a distribution of the amount or maximum amount to which he would be entitled for a year.

For the above purposes, *profits available for distribution* has the same meaning as it has for the purposes of Part IV of the Companies (Amendment) Act 1983, but subject to some adjustments as explained below. A company's profits available for distribution, as defined in section 45 of the Companies (Amendment) Act 1983, are its accumulated realised profits, so far as not previously utilised by distribution or capitalisation, less its accumulated realised losses, so far as not previously written off in a reduction or reorganisation of capital. TCA 1997, s 178(7) adopts this meaning of profits available for distribution but also provides that the amount of such profits (whether immediately before or immediately after the purchase) is to be treated as increased:

(a) in the case of every company, by €100; and

(b) in the case of a company from which any person is entitled to periodic distributions calculated by reference to fixed rates or amounts, as referred to in the previous paragraph, by a further amount equal to that required to make the distribution to which he is so entitled.

Where the aggregate of the sums payable by the company on the purchase, and on any redemption, repayment or purchase of other shares of the company made at the same time, exceeds the amount of the profits available for distribution immediately before the purchase, that amount is to be treated as further increased by an amount equal to the excess.

11.306.6 Buy-back by group member

Where the purchasing company is a member of a group, the vendor's interest in the group as a whole must be taken into account in ascertaining whether or not a substantial reduction has taken place (TCA 1997, s 179)). Accordingly, the "substantially reduced" and profit distribution tests apply also where the company purchasing the shares is a member of a group and where, either before or after the buy-back, the vendor owns shares in more than one group company.

Where the company purchasing the shares is immediately before the purchase a member of a group and immediately after the purchase:

(a) the vendor owns shares in one or more group members (whether or not he then owns shares in the company making the purchase); or

(b) the vendor owns shares in the company making the purchase and immediately before the purchase he owned shares in one or more group members,

the vendor's interest as a shareholder in the group must be substantially reduced.

Where the company purchasing the shares is, immediately before the purchase, a member of a group and where at the same time an associate of the vendor owns shares in any member of the group, the combined interests of the vendor and his associates as shareholders in the group must be substantially reduced. The question whether those combined interests have been substantially reduced is to be determined in the same way as the question whether a vendor's interest as a shareholder in a group is substantially reduced, except that the vendor is assumed to have the interests of his associates as well as his own.

The meaning of *group* was discussed in **11.305** above but has a wider meaning for the purposes of TCA 1997, s 179. It means a company which has one or more 51% subsidiaries, but is not itself a 51% subsidiary of any other company, together with those other companies (TCA 1997, s 179(1)). Where, however, the whole or a significant part of the business carried on by an unquoted company (the "successor company") was previously carried on by the company purchasing the shares or by a company which is a member of a group (in the normal sense) to which the purchasing company belongs, the successor company and any company of which it is a 51% subsidiary is treated as being a member of the same group as the company making the purchase, whether or not the company making the purchase is a member of a group (in the normal sense). This extended meaning of "group" does not apply if the successor company first carried on the business more than three years before the time of the purchase (TCA 1997, s 179(2), (3)).

A company which ceases to be a 51% subsidiary of another company before the time of the buy-back is treated as continuing to be such a subsidiary if, at the time of the buy-back, there exist arrangements under which it could again become such a subsidiary (TCA 1997, s 179(4)).

The purpose of the foregoing measures is to defeat attempts to prevent part of the profits, or the vendor's interest in those profits, from being considered by transferring a part of the trading activities carried on within a group to a non-group company before the buy-back of the shares.

The vendor's interest (including that of any associates) as a shareholder in a group is ascertained by:

(a) expressing the total nominal value of the shares owned by him in each relevant company as a fraction of the issued share capital the company;

(b) adding together the fractions so obtained; and

(c) dividing the result by the number of relevant companies (including any relevant companies in which the vendor owns no shares) (TCA 1997, s 179(9)).

A *relevant company* for the above purpose means the company making the purchase and any other company in which the vendor owns shares and which is a member of the same group as the company making the purchase, immediately before or immediately after the purchase.

The vendor's interest ascertained as above is substantially reduced if and only if it does not exceed 75% of the corresponding interest immediately before the purchase (TCA 1997, s 179(10)).

In addition, the entitlement of the vendor, with associates, to share in distributable profits of the group must similarly be reduced. Profits available for distribution are calculated on the basis that every group member distributes all its distributable profits immediately after the buy-back of shares, including profits received on any distribution from another member. The aggregate of the vendor's (and of any associate's) share of those profits, expressed as a fraction of the aggregate of distributable profits of each group member which is a relevant company or which is a 51% subsidiary of a relevant company, must not exceed 75% of the corresponding fraction immediately before the purchase.

In determining the division of profits among the persons entitled to them, a person entitled to periodic distributions calculated by reference to fixed rates or amounts is regarded as entitled to a distribution of the amount or maximum amount to which he would be entitled for a year.

11.306.7 Severance of vendor-company connection

For TCA 1997, s 176(1) to apply, the vendor must not, immediately after the purchase of the shares, be "connected" with the purchasing company or with any company which is a member of the same group as that company (TCA 1997, s 180(2)). *Group* has the same meaning here as it has for TCA 1997, s 179 (see above in relation to buy-back by group member). A person may be connected with a company in any of a number of ways, as detailed below, and for this purpose a person is to be assumed to have the rights or powers of his associates (see meaning of "associate" below) as well as his own (TCA 1997, s 186(4)(b)). A person is connected with a company if he directly or indirectly possesses or is entitled to acquire more than 30% of:

(a) the issued ordinary share capital of the company; or

(b) the loan capital and issued share capital of the company; or

(c) the voting power in the company (TCA 1997, s 186(1)(a)).

A person is treated as entitled to acquire anything that he is entitled to acquire at a future date or will at a future date be entitled to acquire.

Loan capital includes any debt incurred by the company:

(a) for any money borrowed or capital assets acquired by the company; or

(b) for any right to receive income created in favour of the company; or

(c) for consideration the value of which to the company was, at the time when the debt was incurred, substantially less than the amount of the debt, including any premium thereon.

Loan capital may be ignored where it has been advanced to the company in the ordinary course of a business which includes the lending of money and where the lender takes no part in the management or conduct of the company (TCA 1997, s 186(2)).

A person is also connected with a company where he directly or indirectly possesses or is entitled to acquire such rights as would, on a winding-up of the company or in any other circumstances, entitle him to receive more than 30% of the assets of the company which would then be available for distribution to equity holders of the company. The meaning of "equity holders" and the percentage of the assets of the company to which a person would be entitled are determined in accordance with TCA 1997, ss 413 and 415 (see **8.304**); references in TCA 1997, s 415 to the "first company" are to be construed as references to an "equity holder" and references to a winding up are to be construed as including references to other circumstances in which the assets of a company are available for distribution to its equity holders.

Equity holder means any person who holds ordinary shares in the company or who is a loan creditor of the company in respect of a loan which is not a normal commercial loan (TCA 1997, s 413(3)(b)). A *normal commercial loan* is a loan of new consideration, or a loan including new consideration:

(a)   which does not carry any right either to conversion into shares or securities of any other description or to the acquisition of additional shares or securities; and

(b)   which does not entitle the loan creditor to any amount by way of interest which depends to any extent on the results of the company's business or any part of it or on the value of any of the company's assets or which exceeds a reasonable commercial return on the new consideration lent; and

(c)   in respect of which the loan creditor is entitled on repayment to an amount which either does not exceed the new consideration lent or is reasonably comparable with the amount generally repayable (in respect of an equal amount of new consideration) under the terms of issue of securities quoted on a stock exchange in the State.

Some of the above characteristics recall those of a "section 130" loan (see **11.106**) and it will be seen that a section 130 loan is a particularly relevant example of a non-commercial loan.

A person is regarded as connected with a company if "the person has control of it" (TCA 1997, s 186(1)(c)). In this connection, *control* has the meaning given to it by TCA 1997, s 11 where, in relation to a company, it means the power of a person to secure, by means of the holding of shares or the possession of voting power in or in relation to that or any other company, or by virtue of any powers conferred by the articles of association or other document regulating that or any other company, that the affairs of the first-mentioned company are conducted in accordance with the wishes of that person.

Example 11.306.7.1

The position is as in Example **11.306.5.1** where the shareholdings after the purchases of shares from John, Ann and Jim Moran were as follows:

	"A" ordinary shares	"B" ordinary shares
John Moran	5,000	
Ann Moran	3,000	
Jane Moran		7,000
Mary Moran		7,000
Jim Moran		1,687
	8,000	15,687

It is seen that although John Moran now owns only 21.11% of the ordinary shares in the company, he and his associates between them own 40.9% so that he is still connected with Marsh Ltd. The aggregate shareholding must once again be reduced to sever the connection with the company as required by TCA 1997, s 180(2).

The aggregate shareholdings of John Moran and his associates must be further reduced by 3,687 shares. This can be achieved by a further reduction of 2,000 shares in the case of John Moran (the "cushion" amount already identified in Example **11.306.4.1**) and by the purchase of the remaining shares of Jim Moran (who will be "looked after" at a later date).

The final combined shareholding of John Moran and Ann Moran (now his only associate) is 6,000 out of a total of 20,000, or 30%, thus satisfying the "not connected" test.

It will be seen that the reduction in the fractional shareholding of Ann Moran is from 19.35%, or 6,000 out of 31,000 shares, to 15%, or 3,000 out of 20,000 shares, ie to 77.52% of the fraction before the buy-back. See **11.306.9** below in relation to this aspect.

11.306.8 "Scheme or arrangement"

A further condition for treatment in accordance with TCA 1997, s 176(1) is that the buy-back must not be part of a scheme or arrangement which is designed or likely to result in the vendor or any associate of his having interests in any company such that, if he had those interests immediately after the purchase, any of the conditions relating to the reduction in the vendor's interest or the buy-back by a group member, as discussed above, could not be satisfied (TCA 1997, s 180(3)). Any transaction occurring within one year after the buy-back is deemed to be part of a scheme or arrangement of which the purchase is part (TCA 1997, s 180(4)).

What this measure is intended to deal with is the situation in which a vendor of shares enters into arrangements to acquire shares from another party after obtaining the benefit of TCA 1997, s 176. What, however, is to be the result where, say, a shareholder who is not an associate of the vendor sells his shares to the company within one year of the buy-back so that the vendor's interest in the company is increased to more than 30%? Since the interest of the vendor is now such that he is connected with the company and since, if he had that interest immediately after the purchase, one of the conditions for TCA 1997, s 176 relief would not be satisfied, the benefit of that relief would in fact be withdrawn.

The problem is that TCA 1997, s 180(4) applies to *any* transaction occurring within one year of the buy-back and deems such a transaction to be part of a scheme or arrangement, whether or not the vendor had any control over that transaction. The same result would also occur if, say, the vendor subsequently inherited shares in the company which brought his interest above the 30% mark except that in that case the vendor might have the opportunity to waive his entitlement to the inheritance (which he might well do if the value of the shares was small but sufficient to bring his shareholding above 30%).

On the other hand, if in the first place there is no scheme or arrangement "of which the purchase is also part", it can be argued that a transaction cannot be deemed to be part of such a scheme or arrangement. Although TCA 1997, s 180(4) deems the transaction to be part of a scheme or arrangement of which the purchase is also part, it is not clear that the subsection goes so far as to deem the scheme or arrangement itself to exist. This view would seem to derive some support from the reference in TCA 1997, s 180(3) to a scheme or arrangement which is *designed* or *likely to result* in the vendor having certain interests in the company (such that relief would be denied if he possessed those interests immediately after the share purchase). If in fact nothing has been "designed", and nothing is "likely to result" for the simple reason that there is no scheme or arrangement, it may be extending the hypothesis in TCA 1997, s 180(4) somewhat too far to transmute any transaction into one which is part of a scheme or arrangement of which the purchase is also part.

11.306.9 Relaxation of conditions

TCA 1997, s 181 deals with the situation in which a vendor has not satisfied certain conditions necessary for relief under TCA 1997, s 176 where shares have been sold for the purpose of facilitating an associate to qualify for that relief. This was the position at the end of Example **11.306.7.1** where Ann Moran was seen to have reduced her fractional interest in Marsh Ltd to 77.52% of the interest held by her before the buy-back. On that basis, her interest has not been substantially reduced.

TCA 1997, s 181 effectively provides that where a vendor (Ann Moran in this case) proposed or agreed to the purchase of her shares in order to satisfy the condition that there would be a substantial reduction in the combined interests of an associate (John Moran) of the vendor and that vendor, or the condition that the combined interests of the associate and the vendor in a group are substantially reduced, and the condition is in fact satisfied as a result of that purchase, the vendor is to be treated as having satisfied the conditions in TCA 1997, ss 178-180. Those conditions relate to the substantial reduction of shareholdings and of share of profit distribution in relation to the company making the purchase, substantial reduction of shareholdings and of share of profit distribution in relation to all companies in a group, and severance of connection between the vendor and the company or group and prohibition regarding schemes or arrangements to acquire future interests in the company or group.

Where a vendor is selling shares to facilitate the entitlement of an associate to relief under TCA 1997, s 176 (capital gains tax rather than distribution treatment), that vendor will also qualify for the same relief by satisfying the conditions in TCA 1997, s 177 only, ie in relation to residence and period of ownership of the shares. The relief will apply only to so much of the purchase of shares from the vendor as was necessary to facilitate the purchase of shares from the associate.

It may of course be the case that capital gains tax treatment is less favourable to the vendor than distribution treatment would be. In that case, the remedy for that vendor is to arrange for the sale of shares to the company independently of the sale by the associate. To achieve the required result for the associate, the sale should take place at the same time as the associate's sale (albeit independently and without any acknowledgement that it is being effected to assist the associate's sale) since the associate's relief is conditional on the combined interests of both parties being substantially reduced "immediately after the purchase" (TCA 1997, s 178(2)).

11.307 Meaning of "associate"

The following relationships result in the persons concerned being *associates* of one another (TCA 1997, s 185):

(a) a husband and wife living together;

(b) parents and their children aged under 18;

(c) a company and the person who controls it, and two or more companies that are controlled by the same person;

(d) where shares in a company are held by trustees (other than bare trustees), then, in relation to that company, the trustees; and

  (i) any person who directly or indirectly provided property to the trustees or has made a reciprocal arrangement for another to do so,

  (ii) any person who is, by virtue of (a) above, an associate of a person within (i), and

  (iii) any person who is or may become beneficially entitled to more than 5% in value of all shares held on the trusts (excluding any shares in which he is not and cannot become beneficially entitled to an interest);

(e) where shares in a company are comprised in the estate of a deceased person, then, in relation to that company, the deceased's personal representatives and any person who is or may become beneficially entitled to more than 5% in value of all the shares comprised in the estate (excluding any shares in which he is not and cannot become beneficially entitled to an interest);

(f) a person who is accustomed to act (though not in his capacity as employee) under the directions of another person in relation to the affairs of a company, and that other person.

The reference to shares in a company held on trust in (d) above does not apply to shares held under an approved pension scheme or held exclusively for the benefit of employees, or employees and directors, of the company or of companies in a group (a company which has one or more 51% subsidiaries together with those subsidiaries) to which the company belongs, or their dependants, and are not wholly or mainly for the benefit of directors or their relatives.

It is worth noting that the definition of "associate" for the purposes of the legislation dealing with the buy-back of shares is significantly narrower than that in TCA 1997, s 433(3) in relation to close companies. In that case, a relative includes a husband, wife, ancestor, lineal descendant, brother or sister but in TCA 1997, s 185 only husbands, wives and minor children are included. The aggregation rule will not therefore prove to be as restrictive as might appear to be the case at first. Thus, shares in a company held by, say, an individual, his adult children, and his brothers and sisters will not be aggregated for the purposes of determining whether the individual is connected with the company for the purposes of entitlement to relief under TCA 1997, s 176.

11.308 Discharging liability to inheritance tax

The strict requirement that the share buy-back must benefit the company's trade will not be applied where a shareholder, for reasons of hardship, sells the shares to the company to facilitate the payment of inheritance tax arising on his inheritance of those shares (TCA 1997, s 176(1)(b)). However, the tax must be paid within four months of the valuation date for inheritance tax purposes, that is, within four months of the date on which the legatee became entitled to the shares. Alternatively, if the inheritance tax has already been paid from borrowed money, the requirement that the buy-back should benefit the company's trade will not apply provided the borrowed money is repaid within one week of the receipt of the payment for the shares.

Relief under TCA 1997, s 176 will be available where the whole, or substantially the whole, of the sale proceeds (apart from any sum applied in discharging any resulting capital gains tax liability) arising from the buy-back must be applied in discharging the inheritance tax (including any probate tax) liability or, as the case may be, the debt incurred for the purpose of discharging that liability, and where the liability or debt could not without undue hardship have otherwise been discharged. Accordingly, capital gains tax treatment will apply without the vendor having to satisfy the other conditions for that treatment, ie residence and ordinary residence, period of ownership of the shares, substantial reduction requirements and severance of connection with the company, and without the need for the company to show that the buy-back was for the benefit of the company's trade. Neither will the anti-avoidance provisions dealing with such matters as schemes or arrangements have application in such cases.

There is no statutory or other guidance as to the meaning of "undue hardship" for the above purposes. To satisfy this requirement, it would not be necessary to prove inability to pay the inheritance tax but rather to show that payment would involve considerable difficulty or sacrifice were it necessary to discharge the inheritance tax liability from resources other than the proceeds from the sale of the shares to the company. The test is likely to be applied fairly stringently and the sale of the shares would probably need to be seen as a last resort to enable payment of the inheritance tax to be made.

Uncertainties concerning this matter are bound to remain, however, and it might be wondered whether, for example, a case in which inheritance tax could be discharged only by means of borrowing would amount to a last resort situation. That in turn might depend on whether the necessary borrowings could be arranged and in particular whether those borrowings could be serviced having regard to the financial position of the vendor. The fact that TCA 1997, s 176(1)(b) makes specific provision for the use of the sale proceeds to discharge a debt incurred for the purposes of discharging a liability to inheritance tax, whatever the circumstances, would suggest that it is reasonable to use such proceeds to avoid the need to incur such a debt in the first place.

The legislation makes no reference to undue hardship relating to part only of an inheritance tax liability. It may be supposed therefore that where the full inheritance tax liability cannot be discharged without undue hardship, the condition for relief will have been fulfilled.

Where a legacy comprises shares in the company and other assets, it will be necessary for the purposes of TCA 1997, s 176(1)(b) to calculate the amount of inheritance attributable to the shares. No guidance is available in relation to this matter. In practice, it is likely that the overall inheritance tax liability would be apportioned by reference to the respective values of the shares and the other assets.

11.309 Share dealers

TCA 1997, s 174 provides that where a company purchases its own shares, or a company which is a subsidiary (within the meaning of section 155 of the Companies Act 1963 – see **11.304**) of another company purchases the other company's shares, from a dealer in shares, the purchase price is to be taken into account in computing the profits of the dealer chargeable to tax under Case I or II of Schedule D. The dealer will therefore be charged to tax only on his actual gain on the transaction, that is, on the excess of sale proceeds over the price he paid for those shares, and not on the excess of sale proceeds over the issue price. Distribution treatment therefore does not apply, nor does the payment fall to be treated as a capital gain.

A dealer who is an individual will not have a liability to Schedule F in respect of any distribution represented by any part of the price paid for the shares. TCA 1997, s 129, which provides that distributions received from Irish resident companies are not subject to corporation tax (see **3.205**), does not apply to a distribution in this case.

A person is a *dealer* in relation to shares of a company if the price received on their sale by him other than to the company, or to a company which is a subsidiary of the company (within the meaning of section 155 of the Companies Act 1963 – see **11.304**) would be taken into account in computing his profits chargeable to tax under Case I or II of Schedule D.

The provisions regarding dealers apply to transactions in shares of both quoted and unquoted companies. The provisions of TCA 1997, s 174 apply only to the treatment of the payment in the hands of the dealer and do not affect the purchasing company's position.

The reference to a purchase of shares in this context includes a reference to the redemption or repayment of shares and the purchase of rights to acquire shares, and the reference to the purchase price includes a reference to any sum payable on redemption or repayment.

The above-described treatment of share dealers does not apply in relation to the redemption of fixed-rate preference shares or the redemption, on binding terms settled before 18 April 1991, of other preference shares issued before that date, provided the shares were issued to and were held continuously by the person from whom they are redeemed. *Preference shares* means shares which:

(a) were issued wholly for new consideration (see **11.105.5**);

(b) do not carry any right either to conversion into shares or securities of any other description or to the acquisition of any additional shares or securities;

(c) do not carry any right to dividends other than dividends which are of a fixed amount or at a fixed rate per cent of the nominal value of the shares; and

(d) carry rights in respect of dividends and capital which are comparable with those general for fixed-dividend shares quoted on a stock exchange in the State.

11.310   Treasury shares

As was seen in **11.302**, instead of cancelling shares on their purchase, a company may retain them as *treasury shares*. As long as the company holds treasury shares, no voting rights may be exercised in respect of the shares and no dividend or other payment (including any payment in a winding up of the company) may be payable to the company in respect of the shares. Treasury shares may subsequently be cancelled as if they had been cancelled on their purchase and treasury shares may subsequently be re-issued as shares of any class or classes. Where treasury shares are re-issued, the re-issue is not treated as an increase in share capital.

TCA 1997, s 184 provides that, for the purposes of the Tax Acts and the Capital Gains Tax Acts, any shares which are held by the company as treasury shares and not cancelled by the company are to be deemed to be cancelled immediately on their acquisition by the company. Shares purchased by the company, whether they are cancelled or deemed to be cancelled, are treated as giving rise to neither a chargeable gain nor an allowable loss in the hands of the company. A re-issue by the company of treasury shares is treated as an issue of new shares by it so that there is an acquisition of them by the shareholder but no disposal by the company.

11.311   Advance corporation tax

Advance corporation tax (ACT) was abolished as respects distributions paid on or after 6 April 1999. What follows is therefore of somewhat limited interest now in relation to the question of buy-back of shares.

Dividends paid between companies did not attract ACT where the paying company was:

(a) a 51% subsidiary of the other or of a third resident company of which the recipient is also a 51% subsidiary; or

(b)   a trading or holding company owned by a consortium of which the recipient company is a member.

Such dividends were treated as not being distributions for the purposes of liability to ACT. The related tax credits were not available for payment to the recipient company. Distributions made on or after 6 April 1999 do not carry a tax credit and do not give rise to any liability to ACT.

For this purpose *dividends* includes distributions made by (mainly quoted) companies on the redemption, repayment or purchase of their own shares or by subsidiaries of such companies on the acquisition of those shares.

The following are treated as not being distributions for ACT purposes:

(a)   a deemed distribution under TCA 1997, s 130(2)(d)(iv) (interest paid to foreign parent or foreign fellow subsidiary); or

(b)   a *dividend* paid to a 75% foreign parent resident in a treaty country. For this purpose, *dividend* includes a distribution made by a company on the redemption, repayment or purchase of its own shares, or by a subsidiary of that company on the acquisition of those shares.

11.312   Returns and information

Where a company makes a payment which it treats as one to which TCA 1997, s 176 applies, so as not to be regarded as a distribution, it is required to make a return in a prescribed form to the inspector of taxes to include particulars of the payment, the circumstances by reason of which TCA 1997, s 176(1) or (2), whichever is appropriate, is regarded as applying to it and such further particulars as may be required by the prescribed form. A *prescribed form* is a form prescribed by the Revenue Commissioners or a form used under their authority, and includes a form which involves the delivery of a return by any electronic, photographic or other process approved by the Revenue Commissioners (TCA 1997, s 950(1)).

The inspector to whom the return is to be made is the *appropriate inspector* which, in relation to a person chargeable to tax, means:

(a)   the inspector who has last given notice in writing to the chargeable person that he is the inspector to whom that person is required to deliver a return or statement of income or profits or chargeable gains;

(b)   in the absence of such an inspector as is referred to in (a), the inspector to whom it is customary for the chargeable person to deliver such return or statement; or

(c)   in the absence of such an inspector as is referred to in (a) and (b), the inspector of returns (TCA 1997, s 950(1)).

The *inspector of returns* is the inspector specifically nominated by the Revenue Commissioners under TCA 1997, s 951(11) to be the inspector of returns and who is required to take delivery of tax returns from any chargeable person who does not otherwise have an inspector to whom a return should be sent. The name and address of the inspector of returns is published annually in Iris Oifigiúil.

The return is due within 9 months from the end of the accounting period in which the company makes the payment for the share purchase, or if at any time after the payment is made the inspector by notice in writing requests such a form, within the time, which may not be less than 30 days, limited by such notice. Generally therefore, the return is due at the same time as the company's corporation tax return is due, but may be due by an earlier date where requested in writing by the inspector.

The requirement to furnish the return is governed by TCA 1997, s 1071(1) which specifies penalties for failure to make returns and for the delivery of incorrect returns.

Where a company treats a payment made by it as one to which TCA 1997, s 176(1)(a) or (2) applies (see below), any person who is connected with the company and who knows of any such scheme or arrangement affecting the payment as is mentioned in TCA 1997, s 180(3) (see **11.306.8**) is required, within 60 days after he first knows of both the payment and the scheme or arrangement, to give notice to the inspector containing particulars of the scheme or arrangement.

It will be recalled that TCA 1997, s 176(1)(a) deals with the condition that the share purchase is made for the purpose of benefiting the trade and is not made as part of a scheme or arrangement designed to enable the vendor to participate in profits of the company without receiving a dividend, and that TCA 1997, s 176(2) is concerned with a payment made by a subsidiary of another company on the acquisition of shares of that company.

The scheme or arrangement referred to in TCA 1997, s 180(3) is that involving a temporary reduction in the interests of the vendor or any associates with a view to taking advantage of the relief provided for by TCA 1997, s 176.

Where an inspector has reason to believe that a payment treated by a company as one to which TCA 1997, s 176(1)(a) or (2) applies may form part of a scheme or arrangement of the kind referred to in TCA 1997, s 180(3), he may by notice require the company or any person connected with the company to furnish him within such time, not being less than 60 days, as may be specified in the notice with:

(a)   a declaration in writing stating whether or not, according to information which the company or the person has or can reasonably obtain, any such scheme or arrangement exists or has existed; and

(b)   any other information which the inspector may reasonably require to establish whether a scheme or arrangement exists.

The recipient of a payment for a buy-back of shares which is treated by the company as one to which TCA 1997, s 176(1)(a) or (2) applies, as well as any person on whose behalf such a payment is received, may be required to state whether the payment received by him or on his behalf is received on behalf of any person other than himself and, if so, the name and address of that person.

11.313 Other matters

11.313.1 General

The greater part of the legislation contained in TCA 1997 Part 6 Ch 9 is concerned with the conditions under which a payment made by a company for the purchase (including redemption or repayment) of its shares will not be treated as a distribution. Certain difficulties may arise for vendors in cases where distribution treatment applies because the conditions for treatment under TCA 1997, s 176 cannot be fulfilled. The position of a corporate vendor of shares in these circumstances is considered below. Also considered is the question of capital losses involving connected persons and problems associated with the obtaining of interest relief where borrowings are undertaken by a company to purchase shares. Finally, the question of stamp duty is discussed briefly.

11.313.2   Corporate vendor of shares

Where the conditions for treatment under TCA 1997, s 176 are not satisfied, the part of the consideration paid by the company purchasing its shares over the amount of the new consideration received by it on the issue of the shares is treated as a distribution. Where the vendor is a company, it may at first appear that the position is quite straightforward in that the distribution received is franked investment income in its hands and, as such, not subject to corporation tax.

The distribution is included in the investment income of a close company for the purposes of the surcharges provided for by TCA 1997, ss 440 and 441 (see **10.302** and **10.303**).

The vendor company may incur a capital loss as a result of a buy-back of shares. The company might, for example, have purchased 4,000 €1 ordinary shares from a third party for €15,000 which shares are now bought back by the issuing company for €20,000. The capital receipt included in the €20,000 is the issue price of €4,000 and the balance of €16,000 is a distribution. The capital gains tax loss, on that basis, is €11,000 and the company may utilise this loss against any chargeable gains arising to it in the current or any subsequent accounting period (but see below).

The distribution of €16,000 is franked investment income and, as noted above, is not chargeable to corporation tax. TCA 1997, s 129 states: "except as otherwise provided by this Act, corporation tax shall not be chargeable on dividends and other distributions of a company resident in the State, nor shall any such dividends or distributions be taken into account in computing income for corporation tax". The reference to "except as otherwise provided" is to exceptions, such as an election made to include pre-6 April 1999 distributions in taxable income with a view to claiming payment of the related tax credits, and to certain other provisions such as TCA 1997, s 174(2)(iii) which provides that TCA 1997, s 129 does not apply to a distribution received by a share dealer as a result of a buy-back of shares (see **11.309**). Otherwise, a distribution received from an Irish resident company is not chargeable to corporation tax nor is it to be taken into account in computing income for corporation tax purposes.

The conclusion reached above to the effect that the corporate vendor of shares had sustained a capital gains tax loss of €11,000 may be open to question. It assumes that the distribution of €16,000 did not form part of the consideration for the disposal of shares. The grounds for that assumption are, however, somewhat fragile.

There is no general provision in capital gains tax law to the effect that proceeds of a revenue nature cannot be brought in for capital gains tax purposes. The usual basis for not including such proceeds is TCA 1997, s 551(2). The effect of that subsection is to exclude from the consideration for a disposal of assets in computing a chargeable gain any money or money's worth charged to income tax as income of, or taken into account as a receipt in computing income, profits, gains or losses for income tax purposes of, the person making the disposal.

By virtue of TCA 1997, s 78(6), the foregoing references to "income tax" and "income tax purposes" are to be read as including references to "corporation tax" and "corporation tax purposes". Since a distribution received by a corporate vendor from a buy-back of shares is not (except in the case of a share dealer) charged to corporation tax or taken into account in computing income of that vendor for corporation tax purposes, there would appear to be no basis for excluding it from the consideration received for the disposal of the shares for capital gains tax purposes.

TCA 1997, s 129 provides that a dividend or other distribution (i) is not to be chargeable to corporation tax and (ii) that it is not to be taken into account in computing income for corporation tax. While the second limb here mentions "income" (and is therefore presumably not intended to refer to chargeable gains), the first simply takes a dividend or other distribution out of the charge to corporation tax altogether and might therefore appear to apply to corporation tax on chargeable gains as much as to corporation tax on income. This was the basis for the conclusion by the UK High Court before being reversed in the Court of Appeal in the case of *Strand Options and Futures Ltd v Vojak* [2004] STC 64. The case concerned the purchase by a company of its own shares and the distribution arising therefrom and the question as to whether that distribution should be included in the consideration for the disposal of shares for the purposes of corporation tax on chargeable gains.

The High Court considered that it would be highly anomalous and an unlikely consequence of the relevant legislation that a deemed distribution resulting from a sale of shares should potentially be subject to income tax (eg, dividend withholding tax in Ireland) and to corporation tax on the distribution giving rise to a capital gain. That conclusion was, however, overturned by the Court of Appeal on the basis that the words "shall not be chargeable on dividends and other distributions" was intended to refer to a charge to tax on distributions as such rather than to tax charged indirectly as part of the computation of a taxable amount. In the latter context, the distribution was not directly subject to tax but was merely one element taken into account in computing a chargeable gain.

TCA 1997, s 583 provides that where a person receives a capital distribution in respect of shares in a company, that person is to be treated as if he had in consideration of that distribution disposed of an interest in the shares (see **9.401.4**). For that purpose, a *capital distribution* means any distribution from a company in money or money's worth except a distribution which in the hands of the recipient constitutes income for the purposes of income tax. If it is maintained that a distribution received by a company resulting from the buy-back of shares of an Irish resident company is not excluded, by virtue of TCA 1997, s 551(2), from the consideration for a disposal of assets on the ground that it is not income charged to tax as income in its hands, it would equally have to be conceded that such a distribution (and indeed any other distribution from an Irish resident company) is a "capital distribution" for the purposes of TCA 1997, s 583. The receipt of any such distribution by a company would therefore result in that company being treated as having made a part disposal of its interest in the shares in respect of which the distribution is received. This, surely, cannot be correct.

Distributions from Irish resident companies generally are not capital distributions and this is surely the case regardless of the fact that they do not constitute income in the hands of a company for corporation tax purposes. The extension by TCA 1997, s 78(6), in enactments relating to capital gains tax, of references to income tax to corporation tax would seem to be an incorrect use of that provision, and contrary to the scheme of the legislation, if applied to TCA 1997, s 583 and equally to TCA 1997, s 551(2). TCA 1997, s 78(6) is an interpretative provision and, it is suggested, should yield to the context of the above-mentioned capital gains tax provisions.

For capital gains tax purposes, there is a deemed disposal of an asset by virtue of TCA 1997, s 535(2) "where any capital sum is derived from the asset". TCA 1997, s 535(1) provides that *capital sum* means money or money's worth "not excluded from the consideration taken into account in the computation of the gain" under TCA 1997 Part 19 Ch 2". If a distribution received by a company from an Irish resident company is to be regarded as not excluded from the consideration so taken into account (in TCA 1997, s 551(2)), it is accordingly a capital sum for the purposes of TCA 1997, s 535(1) so that, again, this must involve a (part) disposal of assets for capital gains purposes. It is extremely doubtful that that conclusion would be supported by the courts but it can only be set aside if one accepts the view that a distribution from an Irish resident company is properly to be excluded from the consideration taken into account in the computation under TCA 1997, s 551(2).

11.313.3 Capital losses involving connected persons

Where a loss accrues to a person making a disposal of an asset in circumstances where the person acquiring the asset is "connected with" (within the meaning of TCA 1997, s 10 – see **2.3**) that person, the loss may be deducted only from a chargeable gain accruing to that person on some other disposal of an asset to the same connected person and provided the parties are still connected at that time (TCA 1997, s 549(3)).

Where TCA 1997, s 176 does not apply so that there is a distribution on the buy-back of shares, a capital loss may arise on the disposal in a case where the vendor was not the original subscriber for the shares. If the vendor was connected with the company at the time of the buy-back, the loss incurred may never be deductible as the vendor and the company are most unlikely to be connected again in the future. It may be argued that TCA 1997, s 549(3) does not apply in the case of a buy-back of shares on the ground that the purchasing company has not "acquired" anything since the shares (apart from any treasury shares) are cancelled on their purchase.

This line of argument is not easy to sustain, however, as it is difficult to envisage a purchase of something without an acquisition. Cancellation of shares must require some action by the company since it has the choice of doing this or retaining the shares as treasury shares. Section 208 of the Companies Act 1990, which applies to a purchase of shares as well as to a redemption, provides that shares redeemed *may be* cancelled on redemption. Furthermore, TCA 1997, s 184 provides that treasury shares that are not cancelled are deemed to be cancelled "immediately on their acquisition" so that, clearly, an acquisition is envisaged before any cancellation.

11.313.4 Interest on borrowings

In some cases, it may be necessary for a company purchasing its own shares to discharge the purchase price out of borrow money. The question then arises as to whether the company is entitled to a tax deduction in respect of interest on those borrowings. The only grounds for such a deduction are that the borrowings were incurred wholly and exclusively for the purposes of the company's trade or that the interest paid qualifies as a charge on income within the meaning of TCA 1997, s 243 (see **4.4**).

Although in most cases a company will have established that the buy-back of shares was for the purpose of benefiting its trade, that would seem to fall somewhat short of the strict requirement that the buy-back, and therefore the related borrowings, should have been effected *wholly and exclusively* for the purposes of that trade.

Interest on the borrowings could qualify as a charge on income provided the conditions in TCA 1997, s 247 (interest on borrowings to acquire shares in certain companies – see **4.403**) are satisfied. Relief on this basis would not be available in a single company situation, where a company borrows to purchase its own shares. Where, in accordance with TCA 1997, s 176(2) (see **11.304**), a subsidiary borrows money to acquire shares of the company of which it is the subsidiary (the "parent"), the conditions in TCA 1997, s 247 could be satisfied. For this purpose, the parent should be a trading company, a rental company or a holding company, and the subsidiary should, at the time the interest is paid, have a material interest (more than 5% of the ordinary share capital) in the parent or in a company connected with the parent. The material interest in the parent would consist of the shares acquired.

11.313.5 Stamp duty

Some uncertainty attaches to the question of stamp duty in relation to the buy-back of shares by a company. It has been contended that stamp duty does not arise in the case of a buy-back of shares on the basis that the company secretary or registrar may amend the share register without requiring that any statement of delivery is to be stamped with ad valorem duty.

There are two possible methods of effecting a buy-back transaction. The shares may be bought-back by means of a standard transfer form in which case duty is assessable in the normal way. Alternatively, the shares may be bought back on foot of a contract or share purchase agreement. If the shareholder and the company enter into an agreement and the shareholder simply hands over the share certificates to the company there is no need for a stock transfer form and no duty can be charged. The Revenue have confirmed that the share purchase agreement is not chargeable to duty as it falls outside the scope of SDCA s 31 (stamp duty on contracts).

Chapter 12

Special Types of Companies

12.1 INDUSTRIAL AND PROVIDENT SOCIETIES

12.101   Introduction

The history of industrial and provident societies goes back to the earlier part of the nineteenth century. The term "industrial and provident societies" derives from societies that were established to trade with a view to earning profits and to distribute their profits by way of provident provisions for the future of their members. The original Act of 1834 permitted friendly societies to be established for any legal purpose and the object of investing the savings of their members was added in the Act of 1846.

The first Industrial and Provident Societies Act was enacted in 1852 thereby setting industrial and provident societies apart from friendly societies. The scope of this Act extended only to cooperatives and it was provided that one third only of their trading profits could be divided amongst the members, the balance to be retained or applied for provident purposes. Members obtained limited liability through the incorporation of registered societies in 1862.

An industrial and provident society is a society registered under the Industrial and Provident Societies Acts, 1893 to 1978 (the Acts). The legislation on industrial and provident societies was codified in 1893 with rules providing that the Registrar of Friendly Societies could authorise societies to carry on a wide variety of trades and businesses.

In general, a society carrying on any trade or business authorised by or specified in its rules, whether wholesale or retail, and including dealings of whatever description with land, may register under the Acts. Registration under the Acts renders a society a body corporate with limited liability, with perpetual succession and a common seal. Since "company" means "any body corporate" (Taxes Consolidation Act 1997 (TCA 1997), s 4(1)) – see **1.3**), an industrial and provident society is a company for the purposes of corporation tax and is therefore chargeable to corporation tax on its income and chargeable gains. Industrial and provident societies are, however, subject to special rules contained in TCA 1997 ss 698- 700. TCA 1997, s 698 contains definitions, including the definition of *society* which means a society registered under the Industrial and Provident Societies Acts, 1893 to 1978.

A registered industrial and provident society, being a society within the meaning of TCA 1997, s 698, is not a close company (TCA 1997, s 430(1)(b)).

12.102   Share and loan interest paid

Share or loan interest paid by an industrial and provident society (a "society"):

(a)   is payable without deduction of income tax and is charged to tax under Case III of Schedule D; and

(b)   is not to be treated as a distribution (TCA 1997, s 700(1)).

but (a) above does not apply to any share or loan interest payable to a person whose usual place of abode is outside the State unless payment may be made gross in accordance with the provisions of a tax treaty. For this purpose, "society" includes a credit union which is registered as such under the Credit Union Act 1997, or is deemed to be so registered by virtue of section 5(3) of that Act.

Deduction of tax at source, where it applies, is provided for in TCA 1997, s 246. *Share interest* is defined in TCA 1997, s 698 as any interest, dividend, bonus, or other sum payable to a shareholder of a society by reference to the amount of his holding in the share capital of the society; it is therefore similar in this respect to "distributions" paid by other companies (although not treated like a distribution in the hands of the recipient). *Loan interest* is defined in the same section as any interest payable by the society in respect of any mortgage, loan, loan stock, or deposit.

12.103 Computation of profits

TCA 1997, s 699 contains provisions for the deduction of certain expenses in computing trading income of an industrial and provident society for the purposes of Case I of Schedule D. Discounts, rebates, dividends and bonuses granted by the society to its members or other persons in respect of amounts payable by or to them on account of their transactions with the society, being transactions taken into account in the computation of the society's trading income, are deductible as expenses in computing trading income. To be deductible, any such payment should be calculated by reference to the amounts payable in respect of the transactions and by reference to the magnitude of the transactions, and not by reference to the amount of any share or interest in the capital of the society.

Share or loan interest paid by the society, being interest wholly and exclusively laid out or expended for the purposes of the society's trade is deductible as an expense.

Any amount deductible as a charge on income in accordance with TCA 1997, s 243 is similarly deductible against the total profits of a society except that the interest mentioned in TCA 1997, s 243(4)(a) (see **4.402**) need not be yearly interest. No interest may be deducted as a charge on income unless it satisfies the conditions of TCA 1997, s 247 (see **4.403**).

Income of a society other than trading income is assessable according to the appropriate rules applying, eg untaxed interest and other investment income (apart from franked investment income) is assessable under Case III and rental income is assessable under Case V of Schedule D. In the latter case, any loan interest in respect of money borrowed for the purpose of the purchase, repair or improvement of the premises in respect of which the rent is receivable is deductible (TCA 1997, s 97(2)(e), (f)). Share interest, not being interest on borrowed money, is not deductible for Case V purposes.

12.104 Returns of interest paid

Every society is required to deliver to the inspector of taxes, on or before 1 May each year, a return of the share and loan interest paid by it in that year together with details of the name and place of residence of every person to whom such interest amounting to €90 or more was paid in the year of assessment ending before 1 May (TCA 1997, s 700(3)). The penalty for failure to comply with this requirement is a loss of a deduction (as a trading expense, as interest deductible against rental income, or as a charge on income) in respect of the interest in question.

12.105 Other matters

An industrial and provident society is not a close company (see **10.103**). A society is, however, treated as a close company for the purposes of the close company provisions dealing with loans to participators (TCA 1997, s 438(8)).

The definition of "75 per cent subsidiary" for the purposes of group relief is based on ownership of ordinary share capital. For this purpose, the share capital of a registered industrial and provident society is treated as ordinary share capital (TCA 1997, s 411(1)(b)). An industrial and provident society is a "company" for the purposes of the definition of a "group" in relation to companies' capital gains (TCA 1997, s 616(2)(c)).

12.2 BUILDING SOCIETIES

12.201   Introduction
12.202   Corporation tax rate
12.203   Share and loan interest
12.204   Disposals of government securities
12.205   Change of status

12.201   Introduction

Building societies are subject to corporation tax on the same basis as other companies, with some minor differences. Formerly, building societies were taxable under a special administrative arrangement agreed with the Revenue Commissioners under which interest and dividends in respect of shares, deposits and loans were paid net of tax. The societies accounted for tax at a composite rate and the interest and dividends were deductible in computing profits. This arrangement was put on a statutory basis by means of legislation contained in CTA s 31 (now TCA 1997, s 702) but, with the introduction of deposit interest retention tax, that regime ceased to have effect for the tax year 1986/87 and later years (FA 1986 s 34).

Building society is defined for the purposes of TCA 1997, s 702(1) as a building society within the meaning of the Building Societies Acts, 1874 to 1989. A company carrying on the business of advancing loans was held not to be a building society by reason of making housing loans to employees (*Property Loan and Investment Co Ltd v Revenue Commissioners* 2 ITR 25).

A building society, within the meaning of TCA 1997, s 702(1), is not a close company (TCA 1997, s 430(1)(c)).

TCA 1997, s 702(2) provides for cases in which assets are transferred from one building society to another, whether in the course of a union or amalgamation of two or more building societies or a transfer of engagements by a building society to another building society. Both societies are treated for the purposes of corporation tax in respect of chargeable gains as if the assets had been transferred for a consideration such that neither a gain nor a loss would accrue to the society making the disposal.

12.202   Corporation tax rate

Building societies are subject to corporation tax at the standard corporation tax rate.

CTA 1976 s 79 provided for a 35% corporation tax rate for certain classes of income. CTA 1976 s 31(9) applied that section to the profits of building societies which had entered into arrangements with the Revenue Commissioners as provided for in that section, in so far as those profits consisted of income. The arrangements were to the effect that in respect of certain sums a society was liable to account for and pay an amount representing income tax partly at the standard rate and partly at a reduced rate. CTA s 31(1), which provided for these arrangements, ceased to have effect for 1986/87 and later years. Both CTA 1976 s 31(1) and CTA 1976 s 79 ceased to have effect for accounting periods ending on or after 1 April 1989.

12.203 Share and loan interest

No interest paid on or after 6 April 1986 by a building society in respect of shares in the society is treated as a distribution for corporation tax purposes. Neither is such interest treated as franked investment income in the hands of an Irish resident company (TCA 1997, s 261(a)). In fact CTA 1976 s 31(2), which ceased to have effect from 6 April 1986, had made similar provision in respect of interest payable in respect of shares or loans, where a society had entered into an arrangement with the Revenue Commissioners.

For the purposes of deposit interest retention tax (DIRT), a building society is a "relevant deposit taker" and, as such, is obliged to deduct appropriate tax from any payment of relevant interest made by it.

Relevant interest is interest paid in respect of a "relevant deposit", ie a deposit held by a building society or other relevant deposit taker, subject to specific exclusions such as deposits made by companies, pension funds and non-residents. A *deposit* means a sum of money paid to a relevant deposit taker on terms that it will be repaid with or without interest and either on demand or at a time or in circumstances agreed by or on behalf of the person making the payment and the person to whom it is made. *Interest* means any interest however described, whether yearly or otherwise, paid in consideration of the making of a deposit, including any dividend or other distribution in respect of shares in a building society. Accordingly both share and loan interest paid by a building society is subject to DIRT; share interest would be "interest" on this basis, being a distribution in respect of shares.

Appropriate tax which is deducted from relevant interest is a sum representing income tax, in the case of relevant deposits held in special savings accounts, at the rate of 15%, and in any other case, at the standard income tax rate in force at the time of payment. A relevant deposit taker must, within 15 days of the end of each year of assessment, make a return to the Collector-General of the relevant interest paid by it in that year and of the appropriate tax in relation to the payment of that interest. The appropriate tax is due for payment to the Collector-General at the time the return is due. However, an amount on account of appropriate tax must be paid within 15 days from 5 October in the year of assessment, that amount being not less than the amount which would be due and payable based on the amount of relevant interest accrued up to 5 October on all relevant deposits held.

A building society for the purposes of DIRT is defined as a building society within the meaning of the Building Societies Act 1989, or a society established in accordance with the law of any other Member State of the European Communities which corresponds to that Act. This extension of the definition of a building society secures that foreign building societies operating in Ireland under the provisions of EC Directive 89/ 646 are not required to deduct standard rate income tax from payments of yearly interest in accordance with TCA 1997, s 246; TCA 1997, s 257(3) provides that any payment of relevant interest is treated as not being within TCA 1997, s 246.

Interest paid by a building society, whether in respect of shares or loans, is deductible as a trading expense in computing income for the purposes of Case I of Schedule D.

12.204   Disposals of government securities

Gains arising on disposals by Irish incorporated building societies of government securities were formerly treated as capital gains and therefore as exempt from capital gains tax. As from 29 January 1992, these gains are taxable as part of the trading income of a building society. No liability arises in respect of accrued interest in the cases of such disposals; accrued interest was taxable prior to 29 January 1992. The treatment of gains as part of trading income was phased in for the period up to 31 December 1994 when the taxation of accrued income was phased out. Since 1 January 1995, gains on disposals of government securities are taxable in full and no liability arises from that date in respect of accrued interest.

12.205   Change of status

A building society may convert itself into a company in accordance with Part XI of the Building Societies Act 1989. Once registered as a company, it ceases to be a building society. For this purpose, a building society is defined as a building society incorporated or deemed by section 124(2) of the Building Societies Act 1989, to be incorporated under that Act.

The taxation consequences of the conversion of a building society into a company are dealt with in TCA 1997, s 703 and Schedule 16.

Capital allowances

TCA 1997 Sch 16 provides that the conversion is not to be treated, for the purposes of capital allowances and balancing charges, as the permanent discontinuance of the society's trade and that the successor company is not treated as having commenced to carry on a new trade. This treatment is similar to that provided for in TCA 1997, s 400 (see **4.109**). The conversion is not treated as an event giving rise to a balancing allowance or balancing charge. The capital allowances and balancing charges made to or on the successor company are made on the basis that that company had been carrying on the trade of the building society from the time that the society commenced to carry on its trade and as if everything done to or by the society had been done to or by the company.

Capital gains

The financial trading stock of a society (its financial assets the gains or losses on the disposal of which would be chargeable to tax under Case I of Schedule D) is valued at cost for the purposes of TCA 1997, s 89 (which provides for the valuing of trading stock belonging to a trade on its discontinuance). The transfer of financial trading stock by the society to the company is therefore not treated as a disposal of assets by the society. The company is treated as acquiring the financial assets at their cost to the society and any profit or loss on the subsequent disposal of the assets by the company is calculated on the basis that they were acquired at that cost. *Financial assets* are assets held by the society in accordance with the provisions of s 39(1) and (3) of the Building Societies Act 1989.

For capital gains tax purposes, the conversion of a society into a company does not constitute a disposal by the society of the assets owned by it up to the time of the conversion or an acquisition by the company of those assets. There is therefore no charge to capital gains tax arising out of the conversion. Any gain or loss on the subsequent disposal of the assets by the company is calculated on the basis that the assets were acquired at the same time and at the same cost as they were acquired by the society, and as if the company had existed as a company since the society was incorporated and as if everything done by the society, including everything done in relation to the acquisition and disposal of the assets, had been done by the company.

Where, in connection with the conversion, members of the society are conferred with rights to acquire shares in the company in priority to other persons, or to acquire such shares for less than their market value, or to receive free shares in the company, the rights are treated for capital gains tax purposes as an option (within the meaning of TCA 1997, s 540) granted to and acquired by each member for no consideration and having no value at that time. In effect, the members are treated as having acquired the shares at no cost or, as the case may be, at the value of any consideration given.

Where, in connection with the conversion, shares in the company are issued to the members of the society, the shares are treated for the purposes of capital gains tax as having been received for no consideration and accordingly as having no value at that time, or for the value of any new consideration given and as therefore having a value at that time equal to the value of that consideration.

Shares in the company may also be issued to trustees, in whose hands they constitute settled property, in connection with the conversion, on terms providing for their transfer to members of the society for no new consideration. In these circumstances, the shares are treated as having been acquired by the trustees for no consideration and the interest of any member in the settled property constituted by the shares is regarded as acquired by him for no consideration and as having no value at that time. Where a member becomes absolutely entitled as against the trustees to any of the settled property, both the trustees and the member are treated as if at that time the shares had been disposed of and immediately reacquired for a consideration such that neither a gain nor a loss arises. In this instance, the provision in TCA 1997, s 576(1) giving rise to a deemed disposal and reacquisition by a trustee at market value does not apply.

New consideration means consideration other than consideration provided directly or indirectly out of the assets of the society or the company, or consideration derived from a member's shares or other rights in the society or the company.

The Revenue Commissioners may, for capital gains tax purposes, request information regarding the issue of shares to the members of a mutual building society on the occasion of its ceasing to be a mutual company (TCA 1997 Sch 16 paragraph 4(7)).

12.3 TRUSTEE SAVINGS BANKS

12.301 Introduction
12.302 Amalgamation
12.303 Change of status

12.301 Introduction

Savings banks licensed under the Trustee Savings Bank Act 1989 s 10 were exempted from tax in respect of interest and dividends from investments of moneys to the credit of the special account with the Minister for Finance, interest and dividends from investments in securities of the government as determined by the Central Bank of Ireland in accordance with the provisions of section 32 of the Trustee Savings Bank Act 1989, and in respect of profits or gains from disposals of those government securities (ITA 1967 s 337). This exemption was terminated with effect from 1 April 1993 (FA 1993 s 43) so that trustee savings banks are liable to corporation tax in respect of their profits.

12.302 Amalgamation

Part IV of the Trustee Savings Bank Act 1989, provides for the amalgamation of trustee savings banks. Where any assets or liabilities of a trustee savings bank are transferred or deemed to be transferred to another trustee savings bank in accordance with the provisions of that Act, those banks are treated for tax purposes as if they were the same person (TCA 1997, s 704(2)). Accordingly, an amalgamation does not result in the cessation of a trade so that no balancing allowances or balancing charges will arise where capital allowances have been claimed. Nor will the provisions dealing with trading stock on the discontinuance of a trade (TCA 1997, s 89) apply (TCA 1997 Sch 17 para 4).

Since the two banks are treated as the same person, the amalgamation will not give rise to any disposal or acquisition of assets for capital gains tax purposes.

12.303 Change of status

In accordance with section 57 of the Trustee and Savings Bank Act 1989, the Minister for Finance may authorise the reorganisation of one or more trustee savings banks into a company, or the reorganisation of a company referred in subsection (3)(c)(i) of that section into a company referred to in subsection (3)(c)(ii) of that section. The tax consequences of any such reorganisation are provided for in TCA 1997, s 705 and Schedule 17.

Capital allowances

The transfer (as defined below) is not treated as giving rise to any balancing allowance or charge on the part of the transferor (the trustee savings bank or, as the case may be, the company within the meaning of section 57(3)(c)(i) of the Trustee Savings Bank Act 1989). The same capital allowances and balancing charges are made to or on the successor (the company to which the property, rights, liabilities and obligations are transferred) as would have been made to or on the transferor had it continued to carry on its trade and as if the successor had been carrying on the trade of the transferor from the time that it commenced to carry it on and as if everything done to or by the transferor had been done to or by the successor (TCA 1997 Sch 17 paragraph 2).

The successor is not, however, entitled to any capital allowances which were unused by the transferor and would have been carried forward.

Transfer means the transfer by a trustee savings bank of all or part of its property and rights and all of its liabilities or obligations under an order made by the Minister for Finance in accordance with the provisions of section 57 of the Trustee Savings Bank Act 1989, authorising the reorganisation of one or more trustee savings banks into a company, or the reorganisation of a company referred to in subsection (3)(c)(i) of that section into a company referred to in subsection (3)(c)(ii) of that section.

Trading losses

Trading losses cannot be carried forward by a company referred to in section 57(3)(c)(i) of the Trustee and Savings Bank Act 1989, which becomes a company referred to in section 57(3)(c)(ii) of that Act. A company referred to in section 57(3)(c)(ii) of the Trustee and Savings Bank Act 1989, is not entitled to losses forward under TCA 1997, s 396(1) in respect of losses incurred by a company referred to in section 57 (3)(c)(i) of that section (TCA 1997 Sch 17 paragraph 3). The effect of this restriction is that losses forward of a trustee savings bank while it was under the control of the Minister for Finance may not be availed of by a company which is not or is no longer under his control after the reorganisation.

Financial assets

The financial trading stock of the transferor (assets the gains or losses on the disposal of which would be chargeable to tax under Case I of Schedule D) is valued at cost for the purposes of TCA 1997, s 89 (which provides for the valuing of trading stock belonging to a trade on its discontinuance). The acquisition by the successor of any assets the profits or gains on the disposal of which would be chargeable to tax under Case I of Schedule D is treated as not constituting a disposal of assets by the transferor. The successor is treated as acquiring the financial assets at their cost to the transferor and any profit or loss on the subsequent disposal of the assets by the successor is calculated on the basis that they were acquired at that cost (TCA 1997 Sch 17 paragraph 4).

Capital gains

The disposal of assets by the transferor to the successor in the course of the transfer is deemed to be for a consideration such that neither a gain nor a loss arises on the disposal by the transferor (TCA 1997 Sch 17 paragraph 5). On a subsequent disposal of any of these assets, the successor is treated as if the acquisition or provision of those assets by the transferor were the successor's acquisition of them. Any allowable losses accruing at that time to, and not allowed to, the transferor are treated as accruing to the successor.

For the purposes of roll-over relief (TCA 1997, s 597), the transferor and the successor are treated as if they were the same person. In respect of assets subject to the transfer, therefore, any gains of the transferor which have been deferred in accordance with that relief will accrue at the time they cease to be used by the successor (unless deferred again in accordance with TCA 1997, s 597).

12.4 MUTUAL BUSINESS AND TRADE ASSOCIATIONS

12.401 Introduction
12.402 Mutuality: case law
12.403 Arrangement with Revenue Commissioners

12.401 Introduction

A business in which the "customers" and the persons carrying on the business are the same persons is not subject to tax. The result of any such business is that no real profit arises since the "profit" from dealings with the persons as customers arises to the same persons as traders. Any surplus arising merely reflects the extent to which contributions received from the members or participators exceed requirements. Any surplus for the time being belongs to the members and is returnable to them.

As to whether a surplus arising is exempt from taxation in any case depends on whether or not the body concerned, usually designated as a trade association or trade protection association and which may or may not be incorporated, is engaged in mutual trading. That question has been the subject of a considerable number of decided cases in the UK, principally involving insurance companies and societies, where the main issue was whether or not the profits of the insurance company or society were made from insuring its members; the question therefore was whether any surplus arising was derived from business done with the persons entitled to share in that surplus.

Income received from members in respect of mutual transactions are not liable to tax. Any expenditure related to such transactions is of course not tax deductible. A mutual trading concern is taxable in the ordinary way in respect of any income not derived from its mutual activities. Liability will therefore arise to a trade association under Case III of Schedule D in respect of its interest income, or under Case V in respect of any letting income. Liability under Case I of Schedule D could also arise; this would follow where the association has income or profits from any non-mutual activities, eg the provision of services to unconnected parties.

A surplus distributed to the members on the liquidation of a mutual trading company is not taxable as a trading receipt in their hands. The case of *Stafford Coal and Iron Co Ltd v Brogan* 41 TC 306 concerned a company which received a share of the surplus on the voluntary liquidation of a mutual insurance company of which it was a member. The insurance company's articles of association directed that on a liquidation of the company its surplus assets should be divided among its members, including past members, in proportion to the total premiums paid in the last five financial years before 1 January 1947. The premiums were allowed as deductions in computing the member company's profits for tax purposes while the insurance company was not assessed on its excess of receipts over expenses. It was held that the sum received on the winding up of the insurance company was a share of the surplus in a liquidation and not a trading receipt.

A trade association may enter into an arrangement with the Revenue Commissioners under which it agrees to pay tax on surpluses arising from mutual trading with a view to ensuring that its members' subscriptions are allowable for tax purposes (see **12.403** below).

12.402   Mutuality: case law

In *New York Life Insurance Co v Styles* 2 TC 460, membership of a mutual life insurance company was confined to the holders of participating life insurance policies amongst whom the annual surpluses of receipts over expenses and estimated liabilities were divided. (These holders of policies were referred to as members of the corporation, not shareholders; the corporation had no share capital.) The surpluses were partly derived from profits from non-participating policies and other business and it was held that the part of the surplus from the excess contributions of the holders of participating policies only were not subject to tax.

The case of *Equitable Life Assurance Society of United States v Bishop* 4 TC 147 concerned an assurance society whose dividend rate was limited by local law. The society's earnings above the amount of the dividend, losses and expenses were required to be accumulated and credited every five years to the participating policyholders. The society's surplus was derived from its business of writing both participating and non-participating policies and from other business. Not all the participating policyholders were members of the society. It was found that a part of the trading surplus was used to pay a dividend to the shareholders who were not the same persons as the members of the mutual insurance body and that the society was not therefore a mutual trading organisation.

In the case of *IRC v Sparkford Vale Co-operative Society Ltd* 12 TC 891, a society which purchased milk exclusively from its members and sold the milk in the open market was held, not surprisingly, to be taxable on its profits as these were derived from sales to the public and not from purchases from its members.

In *National Association of Local Government Officers v Watkins* 18 TC 499, all of the property of an association which owned a holiday camp belonged to the members as a whole. While the profits from the holiday camp were for the benefit of all the members, the holiday camp was used only by a limited number of members, as well as by non-members. The association was held to be taxable in respect of its profits derived from non-members.

The profits of a mutual insurance company which conducted fire insurance business with its members only were held not to be taxable (*Municipal Mutual Insurance Ltd v Hills* 16 TC 430). The company did, however, conduct other insurance business with both members and non-members. It was held that the profits of this other business were not derived from mutual business.

The principle that a mutual concern incorporated as a company is no less a mutual concern for being incorporated was established in *Jones v South-West Lancashire Coal Owners' Association Ltd* 11 TC 790. The purpose of the association in this case was the indemnification of its members only, all coal owners, against liability for workmen's compensation. Funds were built up from members' contributions in proportion to wages paid and calls were made on members for payment of the company's liabilities for compensation and other expenses. The calls formed a general fund and surpluses from this fund were transferred annually to a reserve fund. The reserve fund was deemed to belong to the members in proportion to their respective contributions and any member's share would be returned to him on his retirement from membership or on the company being wound up. It was held that the surplus, represented by the excess of the association's income from calls on its members and from its investment income over the expense of meeting claims and reinsuring risks, was not a trading profit.

In the same case, Viscount Cave, commenting on the nature of mutuality, observed that sooner or later "the whole of the company's receipts must go back to the policy holders as a class, though not precisely in the proportions in which they have contributed to them; and the association does not in any true sense make a profit out of their contributions".

The decision in *Liverpool Corn Trade Association Ltd v Monks* 10 TC 442 suggests that where a company trades with its shareholders, it does not follow that it is trading mutually. The company in that case was formed to protect the interests of the corn trade and to provide a clearing house and other facilities for corn traders. Members (ie shareholders) solely comprised persons engaged in the corn trade in their own right. Each member was obliged to acquire one share and to pay an entrance fee and an annual subscription. Non-members could also become subscribers and payments were made to the association by members and non-members in respect of services rendered to them. It was held that the profit arising to the association from its transactions with its members was liable to tax.

The basis for the decision in this case is not entirely clear. Rowlatt J appears to have based his decision on the fact that the company had a share capital, and attributed considerable importance to the fact that the association was incorporated as a company. In this regard, he distinguished the *New York Life Insurance* decision pointing out that in that case, although it involved a corporation, there was no share capital, "nothing belonging to the corporation which is severable from what belongs to the aggregation of the individuals – nothing". On the other hand, where there is a share capital, with a possibility of dividends being paid to the owners of that share capital, and at the same time a dealing with people who happen to be the shareholders whereby they receive benefits in return for the payment of subscriptions and entrance fees, it is necessary to take account of the incorporation and to treat as profits the surplus which arises from dealings with people who happen to be the shareholders. The decision in the *South-West Lancashire* case (see above), which followed a little later, would suggest that incorporation is not a significant matter in relation to the question of mutuality.

Although concerned with UK legislation which was never relevant in Ireland, the case of *IRC v Ayrshire Employers Mutual Insurance Association Ltd* 27 TC 331 is nevertheless interesting in what is said there about the significance of mutual trading in a tax context. The association's function was to insure its members, who were all colliery owners, on the mutual principle and to indemnify them against liability for workmen's compensation. Its transactions were exclusively with its members. Each member was obliged to contribute a certain sum in the event of the association being wound up and the association's funds came from monthly premiums paid by the members and from calls made on them in the event of a deficiency in the ordinary income. A reserve fund was built up from income and the income generated by the fund was credited to members' accounts in proportion to their contributions. A separate account was kept for each member which was cleared annually. Premiums paid by each member and his share of income from funds invested were credited, and compensation actually paid and estimated as required to settle claims arising against him during the year and his share of expenses were debited, to the account.

The Inland Revenue sought to tax the surplus arising each year on the footing that the surplus was a profit chargeable to income tax by virtue of FA 1933 s 31(1). That subsection sought tax on surpluses arising from transactions carried on by a company with its members in circumstances where those surpluses would have been taxable if they had arisen from transactions carried on with non-members.

FA 1933 s 31(1) provided that:

> ... any reference to profits or gains shall be deemed to include a reference to a profit or surplus arising from transactions of the company or society with its members which would be included in profits or gains for the purposes of that provision or rule if those transactions were transactions with non-members ...

In the House of Lords, Lord Macmillan observed that FA 1933 s 31(1) assumed that a surplus arising from the transactions of an incorporated company with its members is not taxable as profits or gains but that the subsection then enacted that the surplus, although in fact arising from transactions with members, is to be deemed to be something which it is not, namely, a surplus arising from transactions of the company with non-members. The underlying hypothesis was that a surplus arising from the transactions of a mutual insurance company with non-members is taxable but that hypothesis was wrong. It is not membership or non-membership which determines immunity from or liability to taxation but rather the nature of the transactions. If the transactions are of the nature of mutual insurance, the surplus arising is not taxable whether the transactions were with members or non-members. It was incorrect to say that a mutual transaction could not take place with a non-member. A mutual insurance company can enter into a contract of mutual insurance with a person who is not a member of the company. Accordingly, the effect of FA 1933 s 31(1) on the transactions of a mutual insurance company was merely to deem mutual transactions with members to be treated as if they were mutual transactions with non-members. The subsection was therefore ineffective in seeking to tax profits or surpluses arising from mutual insurance transactions.

As the basis for the decision in this case may still be somewhat elusive, it is worth noting that some difficulty arose as to how the reference to "member" should be understood in the context of the case. The Inland Revenue view was that a non-member was a person who was not a contributor to and participator in a mutual insurance scheme, rather than a person who was not a member of the company or society according to its constitution. In that way it was possible to interpret FA 1933 s 31(1) as deeming a mutual transaction not to be a mutual transaction. This understanding of the meaning of "member" was rejected as it would render the subsection meaningless; it would envisage a transaction in which mutuality is essential and at the same time a party to that transaction who by virtue of the meaning of "non-member" is excluded from any transaction involving just that element of mutuality.

The decision in the *Ayreshire Employers* case underlines the importance, in the case of a company, of the correct understanding of mutuality. While in other contexts, it may be correct to refer to transactions between the body concerned and its members as being of a mutual nature, transactions between a company and its members (usually shareholders) are not necessarily mutual transactions. This also emerged from the decision in the *Liverpool Corn Trade Association* case, as discussed above, although in a quite different light. Mutuality focuses on the nature of the transactions involved and is not a matter of whether or not the transactions are carried on between a company and its members. In the *Ayreshire Employers* case, the element of mutuality inhered in the transactions between the company and the persons who on the one hand contributed to, and on the other hand were participators in, a mutual insurance scheme.

In *Faulconbridge v National Employers' Mutual General Insurance Association Ltd* 33 TC 103, an association was incorporated as a company limited by guarantee to provide for the mutual insurance of its members against employers' liability and workmen's compensation. Following a change in its constitution, the association was entitled to carry on other kinds of insurance of its members apart from life assurance. All policyholders had to be members of the association and ceased to be members when they ceased to be insured by it. Profits were ascertained on the basis of a valuation made every three years. The surplus for each department, after suitable transfers to reserves, was divided among the members insured in that department in proportion to their surplus premiums. On a winding up of the company, the surplus in any department was distributable among the members insured in that department.

The Inland Revenue contended that from the time the company's constitution had been amended it was operating as a trading company. The court disagreed with that view and held that the company's business had continued to be a mutual one. It was not essential for this purpose that every policy holder should be entitled to share in the assets on a winding up and that it was sufficient that any surplus should ultimately go back to the contributors in a winding up or otherwise. The court also found that it was not necessary that losses be made good by the members; it was sufficient that there was a common fund which was liable for losses.

12.403 Arrangement with Revenue Commissioners

A trade protection association or similar organisation may enter into an arrangement with the Revenue Commissioners under which it will pay tax on its surpluses while its members will be entitled to relief in respect of their contributions to the association. In the absence of any such arrangement, deductions for contributions are allowable to the extent only that the expenditure incurred by the association would have been tax deductible had it been incurred by the members themselves. Alternatively, where the function of the association is to provide specific services to its members, deductibility will depend on the nature of the services provided. Entering into an arrangement with the Revenue secures that members' contributions are tax deductible in any event.

The following conditions apply to an arrangement approved by the Revenue Commissioners under which members' contributions are deductible in computing profits for tax purposes:

(a) the association will furnish to the Revenue Commissioners copies of its rules and regulations and copies of any additions or amendments thereto as and when they are made:

(b) the association will furnish accounts of its income and expenditure and will be assessed to corporation tax in accordance with TCA 1997, s 76(1), (3) (application of income tax principles in computing income) insofar as the provisions of that section are not expressly excluded by or are not inconsistent with the terms of the arrangement;

(c) in computing income assessable to corporation tax under Case I of Schedule D:

  (i) receipts will include all entrance fees, subscriptions, levies and other payments whatever (other than loans or payments of a capital nature) paid by members, and all other receipts of the association, other than income otherwise chargeable to corporation tax, and

(ii) expenditure will include all administrative expenses, all payments of any kind (other than loans or payments of a capital nature) to members, and all payments for legal charges in cases taken on behalf of members of the association;

(d) if any member has received or will receive from the association payment of any kind (other than loans or payments of a capital nature)—

(i) it will bring the amount received to the credit of its trading account and, for the purposes of computing its profits for assessment to tax, the amount will be treated as a trade receipt of the member for the period in which payment was or will be received;

(ii) if a member neglects of refuses to bring the amount received to account, the amount will be disallowed as an expense of the association;

(iii) the association will furnish immediately after the end of every period, particulars of all sums paid within the period to members, specifying the members to whom payments have been made and the amount of the payments;

(e) contributions or subscriptions by the association to any other organisation may only be allowed as an expense on production of the accounts of such organisation and on evidence that it has entered into similar arrangements with the Revenue Commissioners or has no surplus income which ought, on the lines of these arrangements, to be subjected to tax;

(f) the existing and future accumulated funds of the association will be regarded as taxed income in the event of the association being wound up and the funds being distributed amongst the members;

(g) the provisions of the Corporation Tax Acts, except as specifically mentioned above, will not apply to any association entering into an arrangement;

(h) in the event of any dispute as to the admissibility of otherwise of any item of expenditure, the matter will be dealt with by way of appeal to the Appeal Commissioners subject to the provisions of the Income Tax Acts (including the provisions relating to the statement of a case for the opinion of the High Court), on the understanding that these arrangements or the validity of the assessment made in accordance therewith will not otherwise be impugned;

(i) the association will give an undertaking to abide by these arrangements;

(j) these arrangements may be determined by the Revenue Commissioners or by the association on twelve months' notice expiring on 5 April in any year.

12.5 AGRICULTURAL AND FISHERY SOCIETIES

12.501   Introduction

The tax treatment of industrial and provident societies was discussed in **12.1**. Agricultural and fishery societies, which are also industrial and provident societies, were formerly exempt from income tax in respect of a large range of transactions. This exemption was removed, with effect from 6 April 1976, by FA 1976 s 33 but that section was in turn repealed by FA 1978 s 52 in line with the introduction, by FA 1978 s 18, of an exemption from corporation tax in respect of certain classes of transactions engaged in by these societies.

An *agricultural society* for this purpose is defined as a society whose members number not less than fifty and a majority of whose members are persons who are mainly engaged in, and who derive the principal part of their income from, husbandry. A *fishery society* is a society whose members number not less than twenty and a majority of whose members are persons who are mainly engaged in, and who derive the principal part of their income from, fishing.

The exemption in FA 1978 s 18 was terminated in respect of transactions carried on by any society on or after 1 April 1992 (FA 1992 s 48). *Society* here means a society registered under the Industrial and Provident Societies Acts, 1893 to 1978, which is an agricultural society or a fishery society within the meaning of FA 1978 s 18.

The transition from exemption to full corporation tax liability was phased in over the period 1 April 1992 to 1 January 1994. The phasing in process did not apply in respect of profits from the sale of goods and which profits were therefore eligible for the 10% effective corporation tax rate.

12.502   Manufacturing relief

An agricultural or fishery society which carries on a trade consisting wholly or mainly of the wholesale selling of goods purchased by it from its members (all or a majority of whom are agricultural or fishery societies) is entitled by virtue of TCA 1997, s 443(16) to manufacturing relief on its income from the sale of the goods where the members were entitled to manufacturing relief (or would be so entitled were it not for the fact that the goods are ultimately sold to the intervention agency) in respect of those goods (see **7.205.11**).

An *agricultural society* is one whose members number at least 50 and all or a majority of whose members are persons mainly engaged in, and who derive most of their income from, husbandry. A *fishery society* is one whose members number at least 20 and all or a majority of whose members are persons mainly engaged in, and who derive most of their income from, fishing. Alternatively, a society will be treated as an agricultural society or a fishery society if it obtains a certificate to that effect from the Minister for Finance, on the recommendation of the Minister for Agriculture and Food or, as the case may be, the Minister for the Marine and Natural Resources.

An agricultural society which purchases milk from its members and sells it to a qualifying company is deemed by TCA 1997, s 443(17) to have manufactured the milk and to be entitled to manufacturing relief in respect of the income from sales of that milk. A qualifying company is one which is certified by the Minister for Agriculture and Food (after consultation with the Minister for Finance) as a company carrying on a qualifying trade, ie a trade consisting wholly or mainly of the manufacture of milk products. Unless the trade consists mainly of milk pasteurisation, however, the manufacture of milk products is deemed for this purpose to be a separate trade. For the above purpose, the Minister must be satisfied that the company carried on, or is carrying on, or intends to carry on, a qualifying trade for a period of at least three years.

Milk product means butter, whey-butter, cream, cheese, condensed milk, dried or powdered milk, dried or powdered skim-milk, dried or powdered whey, chocolate crumb, casein, butter-oil, lactose, and any other product which is made wholly or mainly from milk or from a by-product of milk and which is approved by the Minister for Finance after consultation with the Minister for Agriculture and Food.

The provisions of TCA 1997, s 443(16), (17) apply in respect of any accounting period or any part of an accounting period commencing on or after 1 April 1992.

12.503 Transfer of shares to members

Certain transfers of shares by an agricultural or fishery society to its members are treated as not being distributions within the meaning of TCA 1997 Part 6 Ch 2 (see **11.101**) and as being made for consideration of an amount as would result in neither a gain nor a loss accruing to the society making the transfer (TCA 1997, s 701(3)). This treatment applies to a transfer by a society of shares in a company controlled by it (within the meaning of TCA 1997, s 432 – see **2.401**) to its members where:

(a) the transfer is in proportion to, or as near as may be in proportion to, the members' holding of shares immediately before the transfer ("the original shares");

(b) no consideration for or in connection with the transfer is given to or received by any member, by the society; and

(c) on or as soon as possible after the transfer, the original shares (or an appropriate number of those shares) of each member are cancelled without any consideration for or in connection with the transfer being given to or received from any member by the society.

For the above purposes, consideration means consideration in money or money's worth but does not include (in respect of (b)) consideration represented by the cancellation of members' shares in the society or (in respect (c)) consideration by way of shares in the company. References to a person or to the society include references to any person connected with (within the meaning of TCA 1997, s 10 – see **2.3**) that person or society. Where original shares have been issued at different times, those issued earlier will be regarded as cancelled before those issued later.

For capital gains tax purposes, the cancellation of the original shares (or the appropriate number of those shares) is not treated as involving any disposal of those shares. The shares transferred to each member are treated as having been acquired at the same time and for the same consideration as the original shares in respect of which they were transferred. For this purpose, where those original shares were issued at different times, any such apportionments as are just and reasonable are to be made.

The relief provided for in TCA 1997, s 701 will be available only where it is shown that the transfer was made for *bona fide* commercial reasons and did not form part of any arrangement or scheme of which the main purpose, or one of the main purposes, was the avoidance of liability to corporation tax or capital gains tax.

For any accounting period in which a society has made a transfer of shares to which TCA 1997, s 701 applies, it is required to include in its corporation tax return for that period a statement of the total number of shares cancelled.

12.504 Exhibitions and shows

Profits or gains arising to an agricultural society (but not to a fishery society) from an exhibition or show held for the society's purposes are exempt from tax where such profits are applied solely to the purposes of the society (TCA 1997, s 215). An agricultural society for this purpose means any society or institution established for the purpose of promoting the interests of agriculture, horticulture, livestock breeding, or forestry.

It will be seen that the definition of "agricultural society" here is quite different to that pertaining to the matters discussed elsewhere in this section. The question as to whether a company qualified as an agricultural society by reason of being in the business of livestock breeding was considered in *The Trustees of the Ward Union Hunt Races v Hughes* 2 ITC 152. A committee comprised of the trustees, set up to hold annual horse races, was found to be a society which was established but not to be a society established for the purpose of breeding livestock and therefore not to be an agricultural society.

12.6 INSURANCE COMPANIES

12.601   Life companies: introduction
12.602   Life assurance business
12.603   Taxation of life assurance business
12.604   Capital gains tax issues involving life assurance
12.605   General insurance business

12.601 Life companies: introduction

The rules governing the taxation of life companies, contained in TCA 1997 Part 26 (ss 706-730), are unique and complex. Life companies are companies which carry on "life business", a term which covers life assurance business and industrial assurance business. TCA 1997, s 706(1) provides that *life business* includes "life assurance business" (ordinary branch) and "industrial assurance business" (industrial branch), which have the meanings assigned to them in section 1 of the Insurance Act 1936, and, where a company carries on both businesses, may mean either.

Life assurance business, as defined in section 1 of the Insurance Act 1936, is the business of effecting contracts of assurance on human life, but excludes industrial assurance. *Industrial assurance* means the business of effecting assurances on human life where the premiums are payable at intervals of less than two months and are collected by means of collectors. This branch of life business is of little importance today.

Where the life business of an assurance company includes both ordinary branch and industrial branch, each such class of business is treated as a separate business and the rules in TCA 1997, s 707 pertaining to the deduction of management expenses are applied separately to each class (TCA 1997, s 710(4)).

An *assurance company* is:

(a)   an assurance company within the meaning of section 3 of the Insurance Act 1936, or

(b)   a person that holds an authorisation within the meaning of the European Communities (Life Assurance) Framework Regulations 1994 (SI No 360 of 1994) (TCA 1997, s 706(1)).

12.602 Life assurance business

An assurance company carrying on life assurance business writes contracts to provide different forms of life assurance in return for the receipt of premiums from policyholders. It also conducts pension business by receiving contributions from individuals under retirement annuity contracts and from the trustees of approved occupational pension schemes to secure the obligations of such schemes to pay future pensions. An assurance company also carries on general annuity business by entering into contracts to provide annuities or deferred annuities, otherwise than as pensions, in consideration for the receipt of premiums or lump sum payments.

The premium income (including premiums, contributions and lump sums) of an assurance company is invested by it in a wide range of investments including government stocks, other stocks and shares, industrial and commercial property, and other investments. The returns from the investments, whether in the form of income or gains (net of losses) resulting from changes in investments or from their realisation, are accumulated as additions to the life assurance funds and are reinvested to meet the company's current and future liabilities to policyholders under its life assurance, pension and general annuity contracts.

For corporation tax purposes, just as the life assurance business and the industrial assurance business of assurance companies are treated as separate businesses, so too are the three classes of life assurance business carried on by these companies. Consequently, the rules in TCA 1997, s 707 providing for the deduction of management expenses are applied separately to each class (TCA 1997, s 707(2). The three classes of life assurance business, as defined in TCA 1997, s 706, are listed in TCA 1997, s 707(2) as follows:

(a) pension business;

(b) general annuity business, meaning any business of granting annuities on human life which is not excluded annuity business (see below) or pension business (see below); and

(c) other life assurance business, referred to here as ordinary life business.

Excluded annuity business, in relation to an assurance company, is annuity business which:

(a) is not pension business, or the liability of the company in respect of which is not taken into account in determining the foreign life assurance fund (within the meaning of TCA 1997, s 718(1) – see below) of the company; and

(b) arises out of a contract for the granting of an annuity on human life, and which arises out of a contract for the granting of an annuity on human life which contract was effected, extended or varied on or after 6 May 1986 and which fails to satisfy any one or more of the following conditions:

(i) the annuity is to be payable until the end of a human life or is payable for a period ascertainable only by reference to the end of a human life (whether or not continuing after the end of a human life);

(ii) the amount of the annuity is to be reduced only on the death of a person who is an annuitant under the contract or by reference to a *bona fide* index of prices or investment values, and

(iii) the policy document evidencing the contract must expressly and irrevocably prohibit the company from agreeing to commutation, in whole or part, of any annuity arising from the contract.

Pension business means the writing of:

(a) any contract approved under TCA 1997, s 784 to provide retirement annuities and related benefits for self employed individuals and employees in non-pensionable employments, and any contract approved under TCA 1997, s 785 to provide such benefits for their dependants or to provide life assurance;

(b) any contract, including an assurance contract, to underwrite the provision of pensions and related benefits under exempt approved pension schemes within TCA 1997 Part 30 Ch 1 (ss 770-782);

(c) any contract with the trustees or other persons managing a scheme approved under TCA 1997, s 784 or 785, or under both of those sections, being a contract entered into for the purposes only of that scheme and framed such that the liabilities undertaken by the assurance company correspond with liabilities against which the contract is intended to secure the scheme; or

(d) any PRSA (personal retirement savings account) contract and any contract with a PRSA provider (within the meaning of Part X of the Pensions Act, 1990), being a contract entered into for the purposes only of the PRSA concerned.

TCA 1997, s 706(2) provides that the division of a company's life assurance business between general annuity business, pension business and other life assurance business ("ordinary life business") is to be carried out:

(a) by referring to pension business all premiums, including any consideration for an annuity, payable under contracts approved under TCA 1997 ss 784 and 785 to provide retirement annuities and related benefits or under contracts relating to exempt approved pension schemes within TCA 1997 Part 30 Ch 1, together with the incomings, outgoings and liabilities referable to those premiums, and the policies and contracts under which they have been or are to be paid;

(b) by allocating to general annuity business the premiums and related incomings, outgoings and liabilities in respect of all other annuity business, except excluded annuity business; and

(c) by allocating the remaining premiums and related incomings, outgoings and liabilities (including those relating to excluded annuity business) to ordinary life business.

References to *pension fund* and *general annuity fund* are to be construed accordingly whether or not such funds are kept separately from the assurance company's life assurance fund. An assurance company's pension fund, therefore, is that part of its life assurance fund which has been built up from premiums received in respect of contracts to provide retirement annuities, pensions and related benefits, with the addition of income from investments and net gains from changes to and disposals of investments acquired for the fund, and which is available to meet current and future liabilities to policyholders under pension and retirement annuity contracts.

An assurance company may also have a foreign life assurance fund for which there are special rules contained in TCA 1997, s 718. The charge to corporation tax under Case III of Schedule D in the case of income from foreign investments of a foreign life assurance fund is confined to the amount of such income remitted to Ireland. Income from government stocks and government guaranteed stocks, the income from which is exempt in the cases of persons not domiciled or not ordinarily resident in the State, is exempt from corporation tax where it arises from investments forming part of the foreign life assurance fund of a life company and is applied for the purposes of the fund or is reinvested so as to form part of it. An assurance company may, if it wishes, keep its foreign life assurance fund separately from its other life assurance funds.

Foreign life assurance fund, where the fund is kept separately from other life assurance funds, means any fund representing the amount of the liability of an assurance company in respect of its life business with policyholders and annuitants resident outside the State whose proposals were made to, or whose annuity contracts were granted by, the company at or through a branch or agency outside the State. Where the fund is not kept separately it means such part of the life assurance fund as represents the company's liability under policies and annuity contracts made or granted to non-residents as estimated in the same manner as it is estimated for the purposes of the periodical returns of the company.

Notwithstanding the above references to pension business and general annuity business, these are no longer dealt with in any detail in the present edition of this book as they are now, together with ordinary life business written on or after 1 January 2001, included in new basis business (see **12.603.6**).

12.603 Taxation of life assurance business

12.603.1 Introduction

Life assurance companies are subject to the corporation tax regime applying to companies generally but the calculation of their trading profits is carried out in accordance with special rules provided for in the corporation tax legislation. The legislation is, however, not comprehensive and case law provides little in the way of guidance with the result that the taxation regime for life companies is governed to a large extent by practice. The corporation tax regime governing life assurance companies can be considered by reference to the "old basis" which has operated up to 31 December 2000, and which continues beyond that date in respect of old basis business, and by reference to the "new basis" which applies to ordinary life business written on or after 1 January 2001 and to all general annuity and pension annuity business. The old basis is dealt with in **12.603.1-6** while the new basis is considered in **12.603.7**.

Old basis

The inspector of taxes has the option to assess a life company on the basis of its trading profits (*Liverpool & London & Globe Insurance v Bennett* 6 TC 327) or on the basis of income less expenses, which involves taking as income the investment income and chargeable gains together with the underwriting profits of the general annuity and pension businesses and deducting the management expenses and charges on income.

The special tax treatment of life companies derives largely from the fact of mutual trading within proprietary life offices. An assurance company which reserves its profits for the policyholders is doing no more than trading with its own members and there can be no taxation liability in respect of those profits (see **12.4** above). Only the balance of profits transferred to the shareholders (often referred to as the surplus transferred to shareholders) is subject to taxation. The part of the profits transferred to shareholders is computed under the rules of Case I of Schedule D and the resulting tax is the minimum tax payable by the company. This computation is a notional computation which is carried out to ascertain what adjustment is required to the "income less expenses" computation so as to produce the required minimum taxation liability.

As an assessment on a life company's investment income usually generates a greater liability than one on its actuarial surplus, the Revenue exercise their right, derived from case law (see above), to base assessments on investment income but subject to their option to assess the company's profits under Case I if this produces a higher liability. For a time in the early 1900s, life companies sought to overturn this method of assessment, arguing that assessments should be based on Case I profits, inclusive of investment income. The option to base assessments on investment income prevailed but, by way of mitigation, relief by way of management expenses was introduced in 1915. It was acknowledged that without the ability to deduct its expenses of management from income assessed on that basis, the burden of tax on assurance companies would be excessive. This was subject to a proviso that tax in respect of investment income less management expenses could not produce a result which was less favourable to the Revenue than one based on Case I profits.

A subsequent amendment in 1923 accordingly provided that the minimum tax payable should be based on the profits retained for the shareholders, ie the notional Case I profit. This amendment was enacted, for Irish tax purposes, in FA 1947. It is now provided in TCA 1997, s 707 that management expenses may be deducted, subject to the overall limitation that the tax payable by the company on that basis may not be less than would have been payable if the profits of the company's life business, to the extent transferred to shareholders, had been assessed under Case I of Schedule D.

An assurance company carrying on life business is treated for corporation tax purposes as an investment company. It is accordingly subject to tax on the income and chargeable gains from its investments. TCA 1997, s 717, however, provides for exemption from corporation tax in respect of the income from, and chargeable gains in respect of, investments and deposits of an assurance company's life assurance fund and separate annuity fund, if any, as is referable to pension business, ie the income and gains arising to the company's pension fund.

Investment companies are entitled to a deduction in respect of management expenses as provided for by TCA 1997, s 83 and this treatment is extended to life assurance companies by TCA 1997, s 707(1) but subject to the provisions of TCA 1997, s 708-710. Charges on income are deductible as they are for other companies.

A company carrying on life assurance business must prepare two tax computations. Although the company is assessable under Cases III, IV and V of Schedule D in respect of its investment income and under Schedule F in respect of distributions from Irish resident companies, with deductions for management expenses and charges on income, a Case I computation must nevertheless be made because the management expenses deduction may, as indicated above, require to be restricted. The restriction is provided for in TCA 1997, s 707(4) and it ensures that the deduction for management expenses will not result in the corporation tax on the company's income and gains from its life business being lower than it would be if the company had been charged to tax under Case I at the standard rate of corporation tax.

New basis

TCA 1997, s 730A provides for a new regime, effective from 1 January 2001, for taxing life assurance companies, whether in respect of those life companies operating in the IFSC or in respect of domestic assurance companies.

Profits of a life assurance company are computed and charged under provisions applicable to Case I of Schedule D where they arise from "new basis business". Case I treatment already applied, and continues to apply, to IFSC companies (see **12.603.4**). From 1 January 2001, new basis business of an existing domestic assurance company also comes within the Case I regime (see **12.603.6**). Existing ordinary life business of a domestic assurance company continues to be taxed on an annual basis on a measure of income and gains (the "I-E" basis).

12.603.2 " I–E" computation: general

The method of computing the profits of a life assurance company for corporation tax purposes is that appropriate to an investment company with some modifications. The approach is to ascertain income, which comprises investment income, chargeable gains and distributions from Irish resident companies and to deduct from that total the company's management expenses and charges on income. This is referred to as the "income less expenses" computation, or the "I-E" computation.

Management expenses must be applied to each class of business as if it were the only business of the company (TCA 1997, s 707(2)). The company's charges on income are allocated to the three classes of business (TCA 1997, s 706(4)).

A second computation is then carried out for the purpose of ascertaining whether any restriction to management expenses must be made. This is the computation under Case I and, being for the aforementioned purpose only, it is referred to as the "notional Case I" computation, or the "NCI" computation.

The method of computing income ("I" in the I-E computation) differs for each of the three classes of business. The following points may be made in relation to the computation of income of life assurance business generally.

As an exception to the rule in TCA 1997, s 129 that corporation tax is not chargeable on distributions of Irish resident companies, such distributions are taxable in the hands of assurance companies to the extent attributable to ordinary life business, and are included in income chargeable to corporation tax.

Both the income and the chargeable gains from an assurance company's life business, after deducting management expenses and charges on income, are taxable at a corporation tax rate equivalent to the standard income tax rate.

In computing chargeable gains on disposals of assets of a company's life business, no indexation relief is allowed. The exemption in TCA 1997, s 607 from capital gains tax in respect of government and other securities does not apply to investments of a fund or funds of an assurance company's life business (TCA 1997, s 711(1)(a)(ii)). Accordingly, in the case of a life fund, gains arising on disposals of these securities are chargeable gains and losses arising are allowable losses. These provisions appear to apply only to policyholder assets so that shareholder gilts continue to be exempt while indexation relief would continue to be available for other shareholder assets. (Note that indexation relief was essentially frozen with effect from 2003 – see **9.102.3**.)

With certain exceptions, the assets of an assurance company's "life business fund" (ie, the fund or funds maintained by the company in respect of its life business) are "marked to market", that is, they are deemed to be disposed of and reacquired at market value at the end of each accounting period of the company (TCA 1997, s 719). This treatment does not apply in respect of government and other securities dealt with in TCA 1997, s 607, the assets of a foreign life assurance fund (as defined in **12.602** and **12.603.10**) and assets which are strips within the meaning of TCA 1997, s 55 (see **3.207.3**). The resulting gains, net of losses, are spread over seven years, one-seventh in the current accounting period and one-seventh in each of the succeeding accounting periods until the whole amount of the loss or gain has been accounted for (TCA 1997, s 720).

Where any accounting period in the seven-year period is a period of less than one year, the fraction of one seventh is proportionately reduced and the fraction for the last period over which the gain or loss is spread is reduced so that no more than the full amount of the gain or loss is accounted for.

The rules for computing "I" in the I-E computation in respect of the ordinary life business carried on by an assurance company are outlined as follows.

Ordinary life business – rules for the I-E computation

The ordinary life business of an assurance company comprises all of its life assurance business apart from its pension business and general annuity business. For any accounting period, "I" for ordinary life business comprises:

(a) investment income and distributions for the period from Irish resident companies to the extent attributable to ordinary life business;

(b) chargeable gains (net of allowable losses) from actual disposals in the period of investments attributable to ordinary life business; and

(c) the amount of unrealised chargeable gains (net of allowable losses) "marked to market" for the period (based on the seven year spread rule) in respect of deemed disposals of investments attributable to ordinary life business.

The total investment income of the company's life funds is arrived at under the normal tax rules for ascertaining investment income, subject to certain modifications. It will therefore be made up of the various items assessable under Cases III, IV and V of Schedule D as well as distributions received from Irish resident companies. The investment income attributable to ordinary life business is the income from investments which are specifically linked to policies related to the liabilities of that class of business as well as a proportion of other investment income, based on the average of the actuarial liabilities of the class as a proportion of the average of the actuarial liabilities for the entire business.

An example of investments being linked to policies would be the case of unit-linked policies where a life company's liability to the policyholders varies with the value of the underlying investments identified in the company's records as investments by reference to the value of which the benefits to the policyholders are determined. Income from investments linked to policies or other contracts related to the liabilities of ordinary life business is attributed to that class of business.

For investments other than linked investments, a proportion of investment income is attributed to ordinary life business. For the purposes of this apportionment, the concept of the "mean actuarial liabilities" is relevant. The mean actuarial liabilities for an accounting period, as applied to a company's life business or any class of assurance business, is the average of the actuarial liabilities of the business or class at the commencement and at the end of that period. The apportionment of the investment income (excluding linked investment income) of a company's entire life funds to ordinary life business is made in the proportion which the mean non-linked actuarial liabilities of the ordinary life business bear to the mean non-linked actuarial liabilities of the entire life assurance business.

Notwithstanding TCA 1997, s 129 (corporation tax not charged on distributions made by an Irish resident company – see **11.110**), distributions from Irish resident companies received by a life company and which are attributable to its ordinary life business are included in investment income of that class of business. As with other investment income, such distributions from investments linked to policies or other contracts related to the liabilities of the ordinary life business are attributed to that class of business, while a proportion of other such distributions not so linked is attributed to the class on the basis of the mean actuarial liabilities.

Chargeable gains both in respect of actual disposals and deemed (mark to market) disposals are also included in "I". As already mentioned, in computing chargeable gains on actual or deemed disposals of assets of a life business, no indexation is applied to the cost of those assets (TCA 1997, s 711(1)(a)(i)). Chargeable gains arising on disposals of investments of the life business are therefore computed by reference to the excess of disposal proceeds, or deemed market value proceeds, over the cost of those investments, or the market value price at which the investments were deemed to have been reacquired in the previous accounting period. Only in the case of actual disposals will any costs of disposal be included in the computation of a chargeable gain.

TCA 1997, s 711(2) provides for an adjustment to be made to the profit or loss arising on *ex div* disposals of securities (ie, where the right to the next interest payment is retained) of a fund maintained in respect of the life business of an assurance company. Where in any accounting period an assurance company disposes of securities so that in the following period it receives interest in respect of those securities, the gain or loss accruing on the disposal is to be computed as if the price paid by the company for the securities was reduced by a proportion of the interest.

The purpose of TCA 1997, s 711(2) is to disallow the element of accrued interest in the original purchase price of the securities sold. The subsection is intended to apply only where the securities in question are held for a period not exceeding six months; the calculation of the disallowed interest element is taken from TCA 1997, s 749 (and Sch 21) which applies to dealers in securities in cases where the securities are held for six months or less, but it is not clear that this reference achieves the objective of confining the application of TCA 1997, s 711(2) to those cases. If a life company purchases securities *cum div* for, say, €10,500 which includes an interest element of €500, a sale of those securities *ex div* for €10,000 close to its year end would produce a loss of €500 which could then be offset, under TCA 1997, s 711(3), as management expenses against other income of that period. The accrued interest would not arise to the company until the following period.

The purpose of TCA 1997, s 711(2) is to ensure that any capital losses arising on *ex div* disposals of securities within six months are not allowed in an accounting period earlier than the period in which the final interest in respect of those securities is received by the life company. The loss arising is reduced by the "appropriate proportion of the interest" but the amount of the reduction is then treated as a loss arising in the following period. The appropriate proportion of the interest is:

$$\text{interest} \times \frac{\text{length of period 1}}{\text{length of period 2}}$$

where—

period 1 = the number of days beginning with the earliest date on which the securities could have been quoted *ex div* in respect of the last interest paid before the interest included in the purchase price began to accrue (in short, the last *ex div* date before purchase), and ending with the day before the company purchased the securities; and period 2 = the number of days beginning with the first date referred to in the definition of period 1, and ending with the day before the earliest date on which the securities could have been quoted *ex div* in respect of the interest received by the company in the following period (in short, the day before the first *ex div* date for the interest in the following period).

The exemption from capital gains tax in TCA 1997, s 607 in respect of disposals of government and other securities (eg, securities issued by the Housing Finance Agency, Bord Gáis Éireann, An Post or Bord Telecom Éireann) do not apply to investments of a fund or funds of an assurance company's life business (TCA 1997, s 711(1) (a)(ii)). Gains on disposals of these securities of a life fund are therefore chargeable gains and losses arising are allowable losses.

The assets of an assurance company's life business fund (ie, the fund or funds maintained by the company in respect of its life business) are, with certain exceptions, deemed to be disposed of and immediately reacquired at market value on the last day of each accounting period of the company (TCA 1997, s 719). The exceptions are:

(a) (i)   assets to which TCA 1997, s 607, other than where such assets are held in connection with a contract or other arrangement which secures the future exchange of the assets for other assets to which TCA 1997, s 607 does not apply (ie other than government securities held under an arrangement for the swapping of those securities for assets which are not such securities), or

  (ii) assets which are strips within the meaning of TCA 1997, s 55 (ie, securities under which the right to receive each interest payment and to the redemption of capital can be traded separately – see **3.207.3**),

(b)   assets linked solely to pension business; and

(c)   the assets of a foreign life assurance fund.

The capital gains tax treatment of investments (apart from the exceptions mentioned in the preceding paragraph) depends on whether or not they are linked solely to ordinary life business. Where they are linked solely to ordinary life business, mark to market treatment applies to the resulting gains or losses on those investments. Where they are not so linked, mark to market treatment applies to a fraction of each category of asset. The result of applying the fraction to each category (not linked solely to ordinary life business) is to isolate the ordinary life business element on a modified mean fund basis. This basis involves the use of "the relevant chargeable fraction", the meaning of which depends on whether or not it relates to linked assets. Some assets may not be linked solely to one class of business. For example, certain assets of a life assurance company may be linked both to life and pension business. Applying the fraction "Life/ Life + Pension" in that case will isolate the life business element.

Linked assets is defined in TCA 1997, s 719(1) as assets of an assurance company which are identified in its records as assets by reference to the value of which benefits provided for under a policy or contract are to be determined. References to assets which are "linked solely to" any business or class of business have a corresponding meaning.

The detailed meaning of *the relevant chargeable fraction* is as follows. In the case of assets which are linked assets it is the fraction of which:

(a) the denominator is the average of such of the opening and closing life business liabilities as are liabilities in respect of benefits determined by reference to the value of linked assets (other than assets linked solely to ordinary life business or pension business and assets of the foreign life assurance fund); and

(b) the numerator is the average of such of the opening and closing liabilities within (a) which are liabilities of business the profits of which are not charged to tax under Case I or Case IV of Schedule D (ie, not general annuity business or pension business) – note, however, that from 1 January 2001 these items are part of new basis business and are therefore taxable under Case I.

In the case of assets other than linked assets the relevant chargeable fraction is the fraction of which:

(a) the denominator is the aggregate of the average of the opening and closing life business liabilities (excluding liabilities in respect of benefits determined by reference to the value of linked assets and liabilities of foreign life assurance business) and the average of the opening and closing amounts of the investment reserve; and

(b) the numerator is the aggregate of the average of the opening and closing liabilities within (a) which are liabilities of business the profits of which are not charged to tax under Case I or Case IV of Schedule D (ie, not general annuity business or pension business), and the average of the appropriate parts of the opening and closing amounts of the investment reserve.

The references to opening and closing amounts in relation to an accounting period are references to amounts at the beginning and end respectively of the valuation period (the period for which an actuarial report is made) which coincides with the accounting period or in which the accounting period falls. The *investment reserve* is the excess of the value of the assets of the life business fund (excluding assets of the foreign life assurance fund) over the liabilities of the life business (excluding liabilities of the foreign life assurance business). *Average* in relation to two amounts means one-half of the aggregate of those two amounts. The *appropriate part* in relation to the investment reserve in (b) above means:

(a) where there are no or insignificant with-profits liabilities (ie, liabilities in respect of policies or contracts under which the policyholders or annuitants are eligible to participate in surplus) included in the liabilities of the life business, the part of the reserve which bears to the whole the same proportion as the amount of the liabilities of business, the profits of which are not charged to tax under Case I or Case IV of Schedule D (ie, not general annuity business or pension business), which are not linked liabilities bears to the whole amount of the liabilities of the life business which are not linked liabilities; and

(b) in any other case, the part of the reserve which bears to the whole the same proportion as the amount of the with-profits liabilities of business, the profits of which are not charged to tax under Case I or Case IV of Schedule D (ie, not general annuity business or pension business), bears to the whole amount of the with-profits liabilities of the life business.

"Liabilities" in (a) and (b) above does not include the liabilities of the foreign life assurance business.

The assets of an assurance company's life business fund are deemed to be disposed of and reacquired at market value at the end of each accounting period of the company (TCA 1997, s 719(2)). This treatment does not apply in respect of government and other securities dealt with in TCA 1997, s 607, assets linked solely to pension business, the assets of a foreign life assurance fund (as defined in **12.602** and **12.603.10**) and assets which are strips within the meaning of TCA 1997, s 55 (see **3.207.3**).

The difference between the aggregate gains and aggregate losses (the "net amount") for the ordinary life business, resulting from the application of the mark to market rule, is spread over seven years. One-seventh of the net amount is treated as a gain or loss of the accounting period to which the deemed disposals relate. A further one-seventh of the net amount is similarly included in each of the succeeding accounting periods until the whole amount of the gain or loss has been accounted for (TCA 1997, s 720). Where any accounting period in the seven-year period is a period of less than one year, the fraction of one-seventh is proportionately reduced and the fraction for the last period over which the gain or loss is spread is reduced so that no more than the full amount of the gain or loss is accounted for. If the company ceases to carry on life business in an accounting period, any unaccounted for balance of the net amount for any earlier periods is treated as a chargeable gain or allowable loss of that period.

On 1 January 1999, certain bank accounts formerly denominated in foreign currencies were re-denominated in terms of the euro which is also, from that date, Irish currency. As a general rule, an exchange gain or loss that would arise on the disposal of the account on 31 December 1998 is deemed to arise on that date (TCA 1997, s 541A(1)). Any gain so arising, however, will not be liable to capital gains tax until such time as the account is wholly or partly disposed of (TCA 1997, s 541A(2)). As this deemed disposal and re-acquisition treatment would be in conflict with TCA 1997, s 719(2) as described above, different treatment is provided for in relation to a euro-denominated currency bank account held as an asset of the life business fund of an assurance company.

Where an accounting date of the assurance company falls on 31 December 1998, the provisions of TCA 1997, s 541A are disapplied (TCA 1997, s 541A(4)(b)(i)). This ensures that the normal disposal and re-acquisition rule and the seven year spread treatment will apply in such cases.

Where an accounting date of the assurance company does not fall on 31 December 1998, TCA 1997, s 719(2) applies as if an accounting period of the company ended on 31 December 1998 so that gains and losses in respect of a euro-denominated currency bank account are crystallised on that date. TCA 1997, s 541A(2) is, however, disapplied and the gains and losses arising are treated, for the purposes of the seven year spread rule, as accruing at the end of the accounting period in which 31 December 1998 falls (TCA 1997, s 541A(4)(b)(i)(I)).

The benefits under a life policy may consist of or include the transfer to the policyholder of assets other than cash, for example, stocks, shares and securities. In the event of such a transfer by an assurance company, the company is deemed to have disposed of the asset, and the policyholder to have acquired it, at its market value at the time of transfer (TCA 1997, s 721).

The overall amount to be included in "I" for an accounting period in respect of chargeable gains is the aggregate of gains or losses in respect of actual disposals in the period, one-seventh (or lesser fraction if appropriate) of the net amount in respect of deemed disposals for the period, and the one-seventh (or lesser fraction if appropriate) of each net amount brought forward from earlier periods in respect of deemed disposals of those periods. Where there is an overall gain, the amount is included in "I". If an overall loss results, the amount of that loss is treated by TCA 1997, s 711(3) as an additional amount of management expenses deductible under TCA 1997, s 707(1), rather than as an allowable loss deductible from chargeable gains under TCA 1997, s 31. For this purpose, gains or losses arising in any accounting period as a result of the seven year spreading of gains or losses are taken into account in determining the amount, in any, of the excess of allowable losses over chargeable gains (TCA 1997, s 711(4)).

Where an asset in respect of which deemed gains or losses have arisen by virtue of the mark to market rule is actually disposed of, a gain or loss is calculated by reference to the difference between the proceeds of disposal and the last marked to market value. The gain or loss is recognised in the accounting period in which the disposal took place while the spreading of the net amounts continues until they are fully accounted for. If a loss arises on disposal, it can be set against other income of the period. However, for disposals on or after 28 March 1996, the part of the loss (ie, the incremental loss by reference to the last mark to market value) which exceeds the overall *actual* loss in respect of the asset must be spread forward over seven years. In other words, the excess loss is treated in the same way as a deemed loss under the mark to market rule.

IFRS

There may be instances in which "fair value" under IFRS (see **3.305**) does not equal market value under Irish GAAP. For example, IFRS may require a bid price valuation whereas existing Irish GAAP would use a mid price valuation. Such differences will give rise to a prior year adjustment on the changeover to IFRS. As seen above, at the end of each accounting period, life assurance companies are deemed by TCA 1997, s 719 to dispose of all old basis assets, and immediately to reacquire them, at market value. TCA 1997, s 720 then taxes any deemed gain under capital gains tax rules over a seven year period. For this purpose, companies will heretofore have used "market value" as per the accounts but on the introduction of IFRS may wish to use "fair value" per IFRS accounts, which may differ slightly from "market value" under current Irish GAAP.

In accordance with an IFRS guidance note issued by the Revenue Commissioners in February 2008, it is pointed out that where a particular arrangement is already in place to give effect to the provisions of TCA 1997, ss 719 and 720, the position post-IFRS must be tax neutral in that nothing should fall out of charge or be doubly taxed as a result of the change to IFRS. This outcome is to be achieved by ensuring that the first computation of gains post-IFRS is based on opening values of the assets concerned which are the same as the closing market values of those assets which were used to compute unrealised gains for tax purposes directly before the move to IFRS. This will give effect to the requirement of TCA 1997, s 719(2) that the assets concerned are deemed to be disposed of and immediately reacquired at the same value.

12.603.3 " I–E" computation: management expenses and charges

TCA 1997, s 707 provides for the deduction of management expenses of assurance companies. These expenses are "E" in the "I-E" computation and they essentially comprise the normal running and administration costs of the assurance company's business, such as staff salaries, office rents, commissions to brokers and other suppliers of services, and other overheads. TCA 1997, s 707 applies TCA 1997, s 83 (deduction for management expenses for investment companies) to assurance companies except that the following items are deducted from the amount treated as management expenses for any accounting period:

(a) any repayment or refund receivable in the period in respect of any sum previously disbursed by the company as expenses of management, including commissions however described;

(b) reinsurance commissions earned by the company in the period;

(c) any fines or fees receivable in the period or profits arising from reversions in the period: in calculating profits from reversions, the company may set off any unrelieved losses from reversions in any previous accounting period;

(d) a part of management expenses attributable to relieved income of an assurance company's foreign life assurance fund;

(e) any income not charged to tax (other than premium income) which, if the profits of the company were chargeable to corporation tax under Case I of Schedule D, would be taken into account in computing those profits. Any such deduction is treated as reducing expenses other than acquisition expenses.

No relief under TCA 1997, s 707 is given in respect of stamp duty known as the premium levy, charged under FA 1982 s 92(8)(c), except for any amount of such stamp duty as is referable to pension business. The management expenses available to an overseas life assurance company are limited to the expenses attributable to the life assurance business carried on by the company at or through its Irish branch or agency (TCA 1997, s 728). An overseas life assurance company is an assurance company whose head office is outside the State but which carries on life assurance business through a branch or agency in the State.

Deductible management expenses include sums allowable by virtue of TCA 1997, s 519 (payments made in establishing an approved employee share ownership trust or in making contributions to the trustees of the trust – see **3.203.3**).

Income from foreign securities and possessions forming part of the investments of the foreign life assurance fund of an assurance company is subject to corporation tax by reference to the amount remitted into Ireland. Where certain tax exempt securities (securities issued by the Minister for Finance with exemption from tax in accordance with TCA 1997, s 43 and stocks or other securities exempt from tax as provided for by TCA 1997, s 49) form part of the investments of the foreign life assurance fund of an assurance company, the income from those stocks or securities is not liable to tax provided the income is applied for the purposes of the fund or is reinvested so as to form part of the fund. Income from a foreign life assurance fund remitted to Ireland and invested in such stocks or securities is also exempt from tax. To the extent that income has been relieved from tax for any of the above reasons, a corresponding reduction is made in respect of management expenses.

Income from sources not charged to tax (apart from franked investment income) is deducted from the expenses of management of an investment company but no such deduction is, generally, made in the case of an assurance company. As seen in (e) above, such deduction is, however, made in respect of the amount of any income (other than receipts from premiums) which, if the assurance company's profits were chargeable to corporation tax under Case I, would be taken into account in computing those profits. This provision was introduced by FA 1999 to clarify that certain miscellaneous income earned by life assurance companies, such as underwriting commission, is to be deducted from management expenses and therefore effectively taxed in the I-E computation.) Any such deduction from expenses of management is not to be regarded as reducing acquisition expenses within the meaning of TCA 1997, s 708 (see below).

Certain acquisition expenses of assurance companies are spread over a period of seven years. This treatment applies to the acquisition expenses for any period of an assurance company carrying on life assurance business comprising certain expenses of management, including commissions however described, as are for that period attributable to the company's ordinary life business. There is no statutory definition of "acquisition expenses" and it is therefore possible that most expenses incurred by a life company could, in part at least, be considered to be acquisition expenses. It is understood that capital allowances would not be regarded as acquisition expenses. The expenses affected are:

(a)   expenses of management disbursed solely for the purpose of the acquisition of business; and

(b)   so much of any other expenses of management disbursed partly for the purpose of the acquisition of business and partly for other purposes to the extent attributable to the acquisition of business, but *as reduced by*:

(i)   any repayment or refund receivable in the period in question of the whole or part of management expenses falling within (a) or (b) which were disbursed by the company for that or for an earlier period, and

(ii)   reinsurance commission earned by the company in the period which is referable to ordinary life insurance business.

The "acquisition of business" in the above context includes the securing of the payment of increased or additional premiums in respect of an insurance policy already issued. Genuine renewal commissions do not come within the scope of the acquisition of business and are therefore not affected. The expenses of management for any period which are attributable to an assurance company's ordinary life business are those disbursed for that period (not including such expenses carried forward from an earlier period and treated by TCA 1997, s 83(3) as disbursed in the current period) and which (ignoring the seven year spreading rule) are deductible as expenses of management of ordinary life business in accordance with TCA 1997, s 707 (the expenses comprising "E" as described above). The spreading treatment is provided for in TCA 1997, s 708(5)-(7) and is applied as follows:

(a)   an amount equal to one-seventh of the acquisition expenses incurred in any accounting period is deductible for that period (the "base period"), even where the accounting period is a period of less than one year;

(b)   a further amount of one-seventh of the acquisition expenses is deductible for each succeeding accounting period after the base period until the full amount of the expenses has been allowed, except that where the period is for less than one year the fraction is proportionately reduced;

(c)   the fraction of the expenses to be allowed for the final period of the spreading will, if necessary, be reduced to ensure that no more than the balance of expenses remaining to be allowed will be deducted for that period.

To summarise, the total amount of expenses of management which will fall to be deducted for any accounting period in the case of ordinary life business will be the full amount of management expenses of that business disbursed for that period, apart from acquisition expenses, plus one-seventh (or other appropriate fraction) of the acquisition expenses of that business disbursed for the period, plus the appropriate fraction of acquisition expenses of that business incurred in previous periods. For the other classes of life business, general annuity business and pension business, the full amount of the expenses of management incurred for each class is deductible for the period in which they are incurred.

Deductible expenses of management may also be reduced by the amount of a reverse premium (see **3.209.2**). Deductible management expenses are deducted from the amount making up "I".

Charges on income for corporation tax purposes are described in TCA 1997, s 243 (see **4.402**). They include yearly interest, annuities and other annual payments.

Having deducted the appropriate expenses of management and charges on income from "I", the result is a profit or an excess of management expenses and charges. In the latter case, the excess is carried forward to the succeeding accounting period and treated under TCA 1997, s 83(3) as expenses of management disbursed in that period.

Before calculating the corporation tax on the I-E profit, it is necessary to carry out the notional Case I computation ("NCI" computation) for the purpose of ascertaining what corporation tax would be payable on that basis; that tax is the minimum amount of corporation tax payable by the assurance company. Where the NCI computation has effect, there is an appropriate restriction to the expenses of management so as to bring the amount of the corporation tax computed on the I-E basis up to the minimum amount (TCA 1997, s 707(4)).

For the purposes of that computation, TCA 1997, s 751A (exchange of shares held as "trading stock") applies "with the necessary modifications". Briefly, that section is concerned with transactions involving a disposal of shares ("original shares") in a company, which are held as "trading stock" of a trader, in exchange for other shares (a "new holding"). Any such exchange of shares which occurs as part of a merger or reconstruction will not give rise to a tax charge at that time. (See **3.211** for more detailed treatment of this provision.)

Excess management expenses of a company carrying on life assurance business may not be surrendered by way of group relief (TCA 1997, s 420(5) – see **8.305.4**).

For group relief purposes generally, a company carrying on life business may not be a surrendering company except to the extent that such life business is new basis business within the meaning of TCA 1997, s 730A (see **12.603.6**).

12.603.4   Notional Case I computation

The calculation of profits on the notional Case I (NCI) basis gives rise to technical difficulties due to the absence of legislative guidance on the matter. In practice the approach adopted has largely been derived from the 1941 agreement between the UK Inland Revenue and the Life Offices Association. Thus, the practice which has become established is to base the calculation on the surplus derived from the actuarial valuation carried out by the life companies themselves. The NCI profit taken into account is that part attributable to the company's shareholders (the surplus transferred to shareholders). It is also accepted that any unallocated surplus carried forward may be regarded as reserved for the policyholders.

The profits computed on the NCI basis are reduced by the part of the profit belonging or allocated to, or expended on behalf of, the company's policyholders or annuitants. Profits reserved for policyholders and annuitants are also excluded but if any such profits cease at any time to be so reserved, and are not allocated to, or expended on behalf of, policyholders or annuitants, those profits are treated as profits of the company for the accounting period in which they cease to be so reserved (TCA 1997, s 710(1)).

Although the NCI computation is carried out on a Case I basis, it is also subject to special rules appropriate to life assurance companies provided for in TCA 1997 ss 709(2), 710 and 714. The following are the main features of the NCI computation:

(a) the computation commences with the amount of the company's actuarial surplus for the period, transferred to shareholders. The actuarial surplus is the excess of the book value of the life funds over the total actuarial liabilities at the end of the accounting period in question and the shareholders' portion is re-grossed for any tax deducted in arriving at the surplus;

(b) in arriving at the actuarial surplus in (a), the figures used are those appearing in the Department of Enterprise and Employment returns. These are likely to differ from the shareholders' profit included in the company's statutory accounts, following implementation of the Insurance Accounts Directive (No 91/674/EEC of 23 December 1991);

(c) franked investment income of a company resident in the State which is attributable to the investments of the life assurance fund is included (TCA 1997, s 714);

(d) any expenses not allowable in accordance with normal Case I rules, and which were deducted in arriving at the actuarial surplus, such as capital expenditure, excess motor expenses, entertainment expenses, are added back;

(e) in ascertaining the amount, if any, of a loss incurred by a company in respect of its life business for the purposes of loss relief under TCA 1997, s 396 or 397, the profits from the investments of its life assurance fund, including franked investment income where the company is Irish resident, are treated as part of the profits of that business (TCA 1997, s 709(2) – see below);

(f) capital allowances are deducted, and balancing charges are added;

(g) expenses of management which are deductible in the I-E computation may not be deducted in computing a trading loss (TCA 1997, s 396(5)) but for the purposes of the NC1 computation this restriction does not apply.

The purpose of TCA 1997, s 709(2), as outlined in (e) above, relates to the fact that actuarial reserves include the reservation of investment income for policyholders and annuitants and that if investment income were to be excluded and taxed separately, as it normally is, a loss would generally occur. A trading loss would normally be available for offset against the insurance company's non-trading income, such as investment income, and could therefore be used, by way of a claim under, say, TCA 1997, s 396 against the company's investment income, thereby frustrating the purpose and effect of the I-E computation. The use of the I-E computation recognises the fact that the investment income of a life company normally generates a greater tax liability than one based on its actuarial surplus (see also **12.603.1** above).

Where a company's trading operations consist solely of foreign life assurance business (carried on in the International Financial Services Centre), the company is chargeable to tax in respect of the profits of that business under Case I of Schedule D. The procedure for calculating tax on the I-E basis, subject to possible adjustment by reference to the NC1 computation, does not apply in the case of a company carrying on only a foreign life assurance business. The taxable profits are calculated on a Case I basis and are subject to tax, by virtue of TCA 1997, s 451(2), at a maximum rate of 10% (see also **7.206.10**). There is no exclusion in respect of profits reserved for policyholders and annuitants but the part of the profits belonging or allocated to or expended on behalf of policyholders and annuitants is excluded as it is for other life companies. Income from "shareholders' investments" (investments which are not investments of a fund representing the liability to the policyholders and annuitants) are chargeable to tax under Case III, IV or V (normally Case III), of Schedule D and not under Case I. In addition, management expenses disbursed for the purpose of managing shareholders' investments are deductible under TCA 1997, s 83 without the restrictions provided for in TCA 1997, s 707 in the cases of other life assurance companies (see **12.603.3**).

A *foreign life assurance business* means relevant trading operations within the meaning of TCA 1997, s 446, ie trading operations specified as such, for the purposes of manufacturing relief, in a certificate given by the Minister for Finance, and consisting of life assurance business with policyholders and annuitants who, at the time that business is transacted, reside outside the State (TCA 1997, s 451(1)). For this purpose, as regards any policy issued or contract made with such policyholders or annuitants in the course of such business, that policy must not provide for:

(a) the granting of any additional contractual rights; or

(b) an option to have another policy or contract substituted for it,

at a time when the policyholder or annuitant resides in the State. Accordingly, the condition regarding residence outside the State must be fulfilled at the time the policy is written. Thus, the non-residence condition will not be breached, and the IFSC life assurance company will retain its IFSC status, where the policyholder or annuitant does not cash in the policy on commencing to be resident in the State.

Franked investment income is apportioned between the company's policyholders and annuitants and its shareholders (TCA 1997, s 713(5)). This is done by allocating the franked investment income between the two categories in the same proportion as the total surplus is divided between policyholders/ annuitants and shareholders.

Example 12.603.4.1

City Life plc has a surplus, as computed on the NCI basis, of €2.2m and franked investment income of €900,000. The surplus is apportioned between policyholders/ annuitants and shareholders as to €1.8m and €0.4m respectively. Franked investment income as apportioned is follows:

		€
Policyholders/ annuitants	€900,000 x 1.8/ 2.2 =	736,364
Shareholders	€900,000 x 0.4/ 2.2 =	163,636

Where the amount of franked investment income for an accounting period exceeds the surplus of that period, only the franked investment income up to the amount of those profits is apportioned, the excess being attributed entirely to the policyholders and annuitants (see TCA 1997, s 713(5)).

> **Example 12.603.4.2**
>
> Boyne Life Ltd has a surplus of €1.1m and franked investment income of €1.2m. The surplus is apportioned as to €0.9m and €0.2m between the policyholders/ annuitants and shareholders. Franked investment income is apportioned as follows:
>
> | | | € |
> | --- | --- | ---: |
> | | | € |
> | Franked investment income | | €1.2m |
> | Apportionment restricted to surplus | | €1.1m |
> | Policyholders/ annuitants | €1.1 x 0.9/ 1.1 = | 900,000 |
> | | + excess (€1.2m - €1.1m) = | 100,000 |
> | | | 1,000,000 |
> | | | |
> | Shareholders | €1.1 x 0.2/ 1.1 = | 200,000 |

At this point, an NCI profit figure, distinguishing between the shareholders' part of franked investment income and the remaining shareholders' profits, is available. The shareholders' part of the franked investment income is not included in computing corporation tax on the NCI basis.

12.603.5   Computation of corporation tax

The NCI computation will now have produced a notional corporation tax figure which is to be compared with the corporation tax resulting from the I-E computation so far. That tax (resulting from the I-E computation) is the sum of:

(a)   corporation tax at the standard corporation tax rate on the part of the "unfranked" investment income included in the NCI profit as is attributable to the shareholders; and

(b)   corporation tax, at a rate equal to the standard income tax rate for the year of assessment in which the accounting period ends, on the I-E profit (including franked investment income) and excluding the part of the NCI profit taxable at the standard corporation tax rate as in (a) (TCA 1997, s 713(6)(a)).

In relation to (b) above, TCA 1997, s 713(3) provides that the profits are taxed at a rate of tax, generally referred to as the "pegged rate", equal to the standard income tax rate.

The basis for the pegged rate is in TCA 1997, s 713. The rate is applied, on a claim by the assurance company, to a part of the "unrelieved profits". *Unrelieved profits* means "the amount of profits on which corporation tax falls finally to be borne" (TCA 1997, s 713(1)(a)), ie the amount of profits after making all deductions and giving all reliefs due (TCA 1997, s 4(4)(c)). For the purposes of TCA 1997, s 713, the unrelieved profits are the profits computed on the I-E basis. The part of the unrelieved profits taxed at the pegged rate is specified in TCA 1997, s 713(6). Corporation tax at the pegged rate is charged on the amount of the unrelieved profits or, if it is less, on the excess of:

(a) the aggregate of the unrelieved profits and the shareholders' part of franked investment income; over

(b) the NCI profits.

The result of the above is that the shareholders' "unfranked" part of the NCI profit is taxable at the standard rate of corporation tax and the balance of the I-E profit is taxed at the pegged rate. There is no amount taxed at the pegged rate where the amount in (b) equals or exceeds the amount in (a) (TCA 1997, s 713(6)(b)).

For the above purposes, the NCI profits must be reduced by the aggregate of the amounts of any relevant trading charges on income (TCA 1997, s 243A – see **4.405**), relevant trading loss (TCA 1997, s 396A – see **4.103**) or a loss or excess for the purposes of group relief claim (TCA 1997, s 420A – see **8.306**) to which the company concerned is entitled. This ensures that life companies may only benefit from these reliefs at the 12.5% corporation tax rate and not to any extent at the 20% rate.

Example 12.603.5.1

For the year ended 31 December 2007, Sherbrooke Insurance Co Ltd has a surplus of €1.4m of which €190,000 is allocated to shareholders and €1,210,000 to policyholders and annuitants. Franked investment income is €1.5m and untaxed interest income is €200,000. The profit computed on Case I principles ("NCI") is €190,000, the surplus transferred to shareholders, but no assessment is made on this amount. The unrelieved profits ("I-E") are €100,000.

Franked investment income must be apportioned between shareholders and policyholders/ annuitants. Since the amount of that income is greater than the surplus, the maximum amount to be apportioned is the latter amount (TCA 1997, s 713(5)). €1,400,000 is apportioned as to €210,000 to shareholders and €1,190,000 to policyholders/ annuitants with the balance of €100,000 being allocated to policyholders/ annuitants.

Unrelieved profits	100,000
Shareholders' franked investment income	210,000
	310,000
Profits on Case I basis	190,000
Excess	120,000

The €100,000 is taxed at a rate equal to the standard rate of income tax for the year of assessment 2006.

Example 12.603.5.2

The position is as in Example **12.603.5.1** except that the surplus is €1.6m, allocated as to €240,000 to shareholders and €1,360,000 to policyholders/ annuitants.

Franked investment income is apportioned between shareholders and policyholders/ annuitants. Since the amount of that income is not greater than the surplus, €1,500,000 is apportioned as to €225,000 to shareholders and €1,275,000 to policyholder/ annuitants.

	€
Unrelieved profits	100,000
Shareholders' franked investment income	225,000
	325,000

Profits on Case I basis	240,000
Excess	85,000

The amount of €85,000 is subject to corporation tax at a rate equal to the standard income tax rate for the year 2007. The balance of €15,000 is taxable at the standard corporation tax rate, 12.5%.

Example 12.603.5.3

The position is as in Example **12.603.5.2** except that the unrelieved profits amount of €100,000 is net of a new basis trading loss of €10,000.

	€	€
Unrelieved profits		100,000
Shareholders' franked investment income		225,000
		325,000
Profits on Case I basis	240,000	
Less: TCA s 396A loss	10,000	230,000
Excess		95,000

The amount of €95,000 is subject to corporation tax at a rate equal to the standard income tax rate for the year 2007. The balance of €5,000 is taxable at the standard corporation tax rate, 12.5%.

Example 12.603.5.4

The position is as in Example **12.603.5.1** except that franked investment income is €1.2m. The surplus is again €1.4m, apportioned as to €210,000 to shareholders and €1,190,000 to policyholders/ annuitants. Unrelieved profits are €20,000.

Franked investment income is apportioned between shareholders and policyholders/ annuitants. Since the amount of that income is not greater than the surplus, €1,200,000 is apportioned as to €180,000 to shareholders and €1,020,000 to policyholder/ annuitants.

	€
Unrelieved profits	20,000
Shareholders' franked investment income	180,000
	200,000
Profits on Case I basis	210,000

As there is no excess in this case, no amount is taxed at the pegged rate and the full €20,000 is taxed at the standard corporation tax rate, 12.5%.

The corporation tax computed on the NCI basis is the minimum amount of corporation tax payable. If this is not greater than the amount of tax on the I-E basis, no adjustment is required to the amount of tax on the I-E basis. If it is greater, however, that is the amount of tax payable. Accordingly, the I-E computation must be revised so as to produce the minimum corporation tax liability by restricting the amount of expenses of management which may be deducted. That restriction will be such as to ensure that corporation tax on the revised I–E profit, computed in the same way as before but with reduced management expenses, will equal the minimum corporation tax payable.

In the revised computation, the deduction for expenses of management must be restricted first. To the extent that expenses of management are restricted in any accounting period, the disallowed amount is carried forward for each class as expenses of management of that class for the purposes of relief in the following accounting period (TCA 1997, s 707(4)).

12.603.6   Taxation of assurance companies: new basis

TCA 1997, s 730A provides for a new regime, effective from 1 January 2001, for taxing life assurance companies, whether in respect of those life companies operating in the IFSC or in respect of domestic assurance companies. In effect, from 1 January 2001, the IFSC regime is extended to all assurance companies. Accordingly, the annual tax, at the standard rate of income tax, is no longer imposed on policyholders' funds. Where an assurance company makes a payment to a policyholder, it is required to deduct tax on the investment return to the policyholder at the standard rate of income tax plus three percentage points. That tax is the final tax liability although, under the "gross roll-up system" which is common in other EU countries, tax is not deductible in the case of a payment to a person who is neither resident nor ordinarily resident in the State and who has complied with certain declaration formalities (see **12.603.7**).

In accordance with TCA 1997, s 730A, the profits of a life assurance company are to be computed and charged under provisions applicable to Case I of Schedule D where they arise from "new basis business". Case I treatment already applied, and continues to apply, to IFSC companies (see **12.603.4**). From 1 January 2001, however, new basis business of an existing domestic assurance company also comes within the Case I regime. Existing ordinary life business of a domestic assurance company continues to be taxed on an annual basis on a measure of income and gains (the "I-E" basis – see **12.603.2-603.3**).

An *assurance company* for the purposes of the new basis is defined simply as an assurance company chargeable to corporation tax (TCA 1997, s 730A(1)).

New basis business means:

(a)   where the assurance company was carrying on life business on 1 April 2000, other than where the assurance company's trading operations at that time consisted solely of foreign life assurance business within the meaning of TCA 1997, s 451(1) (life assurance business carried on in the IFSC – see **7.206.10** and **12.603.4**)—

    (i)   all policies and contracts commenced by the assurance company on or after 1 January 2001 except those that refer to industrial assurance business (see **12.601**), and

    (ii)   all policies and contracts commenced by the assurance company before 1 January 2001 in so far as they relate to pension business and general annuity business, and permanent health insurance in respect of which the profits arising to the assurance company were before 1 January 2001 charged to tax under Case I of Schedule D,

(b)   where the assurance company was carrying on life business on 1 April 2000, and the company's trading operations at that time consisted solely of foreign life assurance business (within the meaning of TCA 1997, s 451(1), all policies and contracts commenced on or after 1 January 2001; and

(c)   where the assurance company was not carrying on life business on 1 April 2000, subject to election under TCA 1997, s 730A(2) (see below), all policies and contracts commenced by the assurance company from the time it began to carry on life business.

Where an assurance company begins to carry on life business after 1 April 2000 and before 31 December 2000, the company may elect that all policies and contracts commenced by it before 31 December 2000 be treated as not being new basis business in so far as they relate to life business (other than pension business and general annuity business) (TCA 1997, s 730A(2)).

Life business of an assurance company, in so far as it comprises new basis business, is treated for corporation tax purposes as though it were a business separate from any other business carried on by the company (TCA 1997, s 730A(3)). An assurance company is chargeable to corporation tax in respect of the profits of new basis business under Case I of Schedule D. Those profits are to be computed in accordance with the provisions applicable to that Case (TCA 1997, s 730A(4)).

In this regard, however, where all or part of the profits of an assurance company are to be computed in accordance with the provisions applicable to Case I:

(a)   such part of those profits as belongs to or is allocated to, or is expended on behalf of, policyholders or annuitants is to be excluded in making the computation; and

(b)   any remaining part of those profits *reserved* for policyholders or annuitants is not to be excluded in making the computation (TCA 1997, s 730A(5)).

Where an assurance company incurs a loss in respect of new basis business, the amount of the loss that may be set off against the profits of any other business of the company may not exceed the amount of those profits computed under the provisions of Case I of Schedule D and TCA 1997, s 710 (TCA 1997, s 730A(6)). Thus, the loss may not be set against profits belonging to policyholders under the I-E regime.

For group relief purposes, a company carrying on life business may not be a surrendering company except to the extent that such life business is new basis business within the meaning of TCA 1997, s 730A (TCA 1997, s 420(9)).

Neither may a loss be surrendered so as to reduce the profits of a claimant company which carries on life business within the meaning of TCA 1997, s 706 by an amount greater than the amount of such profits computed in accordance with Case I of Schedule D. Under the I-E basis, which continues to apply in respect of ordinary life business policies commenced prior to 1 January 2001, tax is imposed on the profits arising to the shareholders and on the income and gains of the policyholders. TCA 1997, s 420(1)(b) ensures that losses arising to a company which is a fellow group member with a life company will only be available for set off against the part of the profits of the life company which belong to the shareholders and not the part belonging to the policyholders.

Under the new basis, mutual life assurance companies (see **12.401-2** and **12.603.1**) are assessable to tax on a measure of unallocated profits. For any accounting period of a mutual life company, a fraction of the increase in value of the funds for which an allocation to policyholders has not been determined is treated as annual profits or gains and chargeable to corporation tax under Case III of Schedule D (TCA 1997, s 730A(7)(b)). The fraction is one-twentieth of:

(i)   the total value at the end of the accounting period; less

(ii)   the total value at the beginning of the accounting period,

of all funds the allocation of which to policyholders has not been determined (TCA 1997, s 730A(8)(c)).

In the case of an overseas life assurance company, the values in (i) and (ii) at a given time are apportioned to arrive at the amounts relating to its Irish branch business and are accordingly multiplied by the fraction A/B where:

A   is the liabilities at that time to policyholders whose proposals were made to the company at or through its branch or agency in the State; and

B   is the liabilities at that time to all the company's policyholders (TCA 1997, s 730A(8)(c)).

Where for any accounting period the value arrived at in (ii) above is not less than such value at 31 December 2000 but exceeds the value referred to in (i) above, an amount equal to one-twentieth of the excess may be deducted from the annual profits or gains chargeable to corporation tax by virtue of TCA 1997, s 730A(7)(b) of the previous accounting period (where that period commences on or after 1 January 2001) or a subsequent accounting period (TCA 1997, s 730A(7)(c)).

For the above purposes, the liabilities of an assurance company attributable to any business at any time are to be ascertained by reference to the net liabilities of the company valued by an actuary for the purposes of the statutory accounts in relation to the company (TCA 1997, s 730A(8)(b)).

Statutory accounts, in relation to a company, means:

(i)   in the case of a company resident in the State (the "resident company"), the profit and loss account and balance sheet of that company; and

(ii)   in the case of a company not resident in the State but carrying on a trade in the State through a branch or agency (the "non-resident company"), the profit and loss account and balance sheet of the company,

a report in respect of which is required to be made to the members of the company by an auditor appointed under section 160 of the Companies Act, 1963, or under the law of the state in which the resident company or non-resident company is incorporated and which corresponds to that section (TCA 1997, s 730A(8)(a)).

New basis – computation

The following is based on various issues of Tax Briefing published by the Revenue Commissioners, principally Issue 43.

Case I computation – proprietary companies

The basis of computation is the transfer to the non-technical account. The technical account records all income and expenditure flows including those relating to policyholders so that it includes all premium income, investment income and gains, claims paid to policyholders, expenses (including taxation) incurred by the life company, and the movement in the liability to policyholders. The amount remaining for the shareholders, being the shareholders' profit from the life business, is transferred from the technical to the non-technical account. Thus, the non-technical account shows all of the shareholders' flows commencing with the "transfer to non-technical account" and including investment income and gains on assets owned by the shareholders. Taxation relating to the shareholders is deducted.

A proportion of the transfer to the fund for future appropriation (FFA) is regarded as taxable shareholder profits with the balance being treated as belonging to policyholders. Technically, the FFA, which includes only with-profit items, represents amounts that have not been finally allocated between policyholders and shareholders. In the case of a with-profits business, there will be an investment reserve (usually representing gains on investments) that have not been finally declared as bonuses to policyholders or transferred as profit to shareholders and these amounts are shown in the FFA. The proportion of the transfer to FFA which is regarded as shareholder profits is that proportion which represents the upper limit under the company's constitution which may be allocated to shareholders out of any surplus, but subject to a minimum or ' floor' of 5% of the transfer. In the case of negative transfers to the fund, the same proportion is deductible but only to the extent that the cumulative transfers from 1 January 2001 exceed the value of the fund as at 31 December 2000.

The annual transfer to the shareholder non-distributable reserve is taxable – it is allocated fully to shareholders.

Normal add-backs/deductions for tax purposes are made.

A deduction is allowed in respect of Irish dividend income included in shareholder profits. This is calculated as follows:

$$\frac{\text{total Irish dividend income}}{\text{total technical income}} \times \text{profit on activities (per non - technical account)}$$

The following illustrates the position:

Transfer from technical account		X
Add: Taxation		X
		X
Add: Investment Income		X
Profit on ordinary activities		X
Add: Transfer to fund for future appropriations (relevant proportion)		X
Normal add-backs		X
		X
Less: Normal deductions		X
Capital allowances	X	
Irish dividend Income	X	X
Taxable profits		X
Tax payable		X
Less: Tax deducted at source	X	
Double tax relief (net basis)	X	X
Net tax liability		X

Notes:

  (i)   Technical income: non-technical

        This is the gross income per the technical account, comprised of the following:

Earned premiums net of reinsurance

Investment income

Gains on investments

Any other technical income

(ii) The above reference to 'investment income' is a reference to the investment income taken directly to the non-technical account.

(iii) Total profits are assessed under Case I of Schedule D, except in the exceptional circumstances where shareholder assets are disposed of. In that case capital gains tax applies (eg, disposal of assets that are not part of the insurance funds).

Case I computation – mutual companies

Under the old basis, mutual companies were taxable on the I-E basis, and therefore at the income tax rate, without any adjustment by reference to an NCI computation. This followed the mutual trading principle whereby it is not possible for a company to derive profits, even notional profits, from trading with itself. The simple abolition of the I-E basis would have resulted in no tax, other than exit tax, being derived from mutual companies. Accordingly, the new regime as it applies to mutual companies involves an arbitrary basis whereby they are taxed on a proportion of the transfer to FFA under Case III at the trading rate of corporation tax.

5% of the transfer to the fund for future appropriations is deemed to be profits chargeable under Case III at the trading corporation tax rate.

5% of negative transfers from the FFA may be carried forward against the deemed profits of the following year or carried back against the deemed profits of the preceding year.

In the case of a company trading in the State through a branch/agency, the Irish deemed profits are:

$$5\% \text{ of transfer} \times \frac{\text{Irish mean liabilities}}{\text{world-wide mean liabilities}}$$

In view of the fact that the FFA is concerned solely with "with-profits" policies, the numerator and denominator in the above fraction will exclude non with-profits business.

Capital Allowances may be set against deemed profits under Case III.

Mix of new basis and old basis business

Case I computation – proprietary companies:

Total Case I income is calculated on the basis outlined above. However, the computation is adjusted to extract the profits attributable to the "old basis" business. This is achieved by attributing income and expenditure to each category to the extent that such income/expenditure is identifiable. Where income/expenditure cannot be the subject of specific attribution, for example general expenses or capital allowances, they are allocated on the basis of an actuarial valuation. In practice, each company will submit a computation with accompanying notes on specific items, as appropriate.

The example below illustrates the computational approach to be adopted. For old basis business, involving the transfer in accordance with the DETE return, the first column is relevant while for new basis business, where the starting point is the profit per Accounts, the fifth column is the appropriate column.

	Old Basis	New Basis	DETE Total	Old Basis	New Basis	Accounts Total
	€m	€m	€m	€m	€m	€m
Premiums	70	30	100	70	30	100
Investment income	40	10	50	40	10	50
Expenses	(5)	(25)	(30)	(5)	(10)	(15)
Claims	(20)	(5)	(25)	(20)	(5)	(25)
Movement in reserves	(65)	(20)	(85)	(65)	(20)	(85)
Surplus/profit	20	(10)	10	20	5	25
DETE transfer	25	(10)	15	N/a	N/a	N/a

Assume that the above example represents the position after a few years into the new regime by which time, say, shareholder tax is 12.5% and standard rate tax is 20%. The company only writes Old Basis life business and New Basis life business, ie no pensions or PHI business. The totals for DETE and for the Accounts bases are from the respective audited annual returns. It is assumed for simplicity that the only material difference between the two bases is in the treatment of acquisition expenses, these being deferred under the Accounts basis. (Note that, based in this practice, the tax treatment follows the accounts and a deduction for deferred expenses is denied.) Any FFA complications are also ignored.

The following comments are made in respect of the allocation between Old Basis and New Basis:

> Premiums are actual.
> Investment income is actual or mean fund based, or a mixture of both. (It is necessary to have a methodology for allocating items between old basis and new basis business for the purpose of computing the profits for each business. Certain items, for example premiums, will be allocable on an actual basis but this will not be possible for other items and the preferred allocation in these cases is by reference to mean liabilities or "mean fund".)
> Expenses are attributed using similar techniques as have traditionally been used to attribute between pension and life business.
> Claims are actual.
> Movement in reserves are actual.
> Surplus or profit will then fall out from the above allocations.
> It is appropriate that the DETE transfer would be allocated in proportion to surplus, but restricting any negative transfer on the new basis to the level of negative surplus.

In carrying out the tax computation, second order adjustments (depreciation etc) are ignored and in particular it is assumed that the NCI would equal the DETE transfer. Accordingly the tax computation would be as follows:

Old Basis: I-E = 35 of which 25 (NCI) is taxed at 12.5% and 10 is taxed at 20%.

New Basis: 5 is taxed at 12.5% (of course policyholders will have been debited with any exit taxes due).

Tax deducted at source – this follows the relevant attribution of investment income.

Double Taxation Relief (DTR)

Again, this follows the relevant attribution of investment income and therefore the amounts of DTR available under each system should be readily available. For new basis business DTR is available at the corporation tax rate only in respect of the following:

(i)   investments attributable to new basis life business investments;

(ii)   investments attributable to pension, annuity, and PHI (if already Case I).

Any excess credit are treated in accordance with the general rules applicable to DTR.

Pension (PAB) and General Annuity Business (GAB) – Case IV

PAB and GAB are integrated into Case I going forward. These, whenever written, are new basis business to be included in the Case I computation with effect from 1 January 2001. The question of the allowability of pre-31 December 2000 losses arises and these are dealt with as follows:

> To allow for carry forward of PAB losses to the extent that they can be shown to relate to "unit-linked" business. In the case of non-linked business losses will only be allowed forward to the extent that the valuation of assets in the Case IV tax computation is consistent with the valuation of liabilities in the tax computation. Any other PAB losses are seen as essentially due to timing and therefore adequately covered by the untaxed portion of the FFA.

> To allow carry forward of GAB losses as reduced by any foreign fund relief previously allowed. (Foreign fund relief – under the old basis, investment income attributable to the foreign branch business of an Irish life company is not taxable until remitted to Ireland.)

Permanent Health Insurance (PHI)

To allow any losses forward into the new regime, where PHI previously assessed under Case I of Schedule D.

Mutual Companies

Deemed profits chargeable under Case III (as outlined above) to be reduced by the proportion of the FFA transfer attributable to "old basis" business. In practice, each company should submit notes outlining the methodology used for attribution between new and old business.

> PAB & GAB losses to be allowed on the same basis as for proprietary companies.

> 5% of negative transfers to the FFA will be deductible only to the extent that the cumulative transfer from 1 January 2001 exceed the value of the fund as at 31 December 2000 and in so far as they relate to new basis business.

I-E Basis

This continues for 'old basis' life business. The pre-existing law and practice continues to apply and in particular the Notional Case I will be calculated by reference to the position outlined in the *Tax Briefing* article in Issue 24.

IFSC Companies

The pre-existing practice ceased on 31 December 2000.

The new basis for calculation of Case I profits is effective from 1 January 2001. The separate charge for shareholders' investment income no longer applies from 1 January 2001 and accordingly the losses forward at that date are available against all IFSC profits.

IFSC and domestic business continue to be treated as separate trades for tax purposes. The provisions of Section 730A(3) TCA 1997 as they apply to IFSC companies have the effect of preventing the set-off of IFSC losses against domestic business written from 1 January 2001, but not over-riding the legislation already in place as regards business written under the IFSC certificate. There is no such effect as regards loss relief under TCA 1997, s 396B or 420B (relief on a value basis – see **4.103** and **8.306.3**).

Industrial Branch Business (IB)

All IB business falls within "old basis" business, including business written on or after 1 January 2001.

The following example illustrates the approach to be taken in applying the new basis which is appropriate for all pension and annuity business, whenever written, and ordinary life business written on or after 1 January 2001. Also included is the old basis computation in respect of ordinary life business written before 1 January 2001.

Example 12.603.6.1

The following information is relevant to Hardwicke Life Assurance Co Ltd for its most recent accounting period. Accounts are prepared in accordance with Irish GAAP.

	New basis business	Ordinary life assurance business pre - 2001	Overall total
	NBB	OLAB	
	€000	€000	€000
Technical account			
Premium income	8,000	5,000	13,000
Investment income			
– franked	200	120	320
– unfranked	1,000	700	1,700
Realised profits	500	350	850
Unrealised profits	900	770	1,670
Total income	10,600	6,940	17,540
Claims	2,500	1,300	3,800
Expenses	900	450	1,350
Increase in actuarial liabilities	4,400	3,700	8,100
Transfer to FFA (1)	1,250	670	1,920
Total outgo	9,050	6,120	15,170
Transfer to non-technical account	1,550	820	2,370

Non-technical account

Transfer from technical account	1,550	820	2,370
Taxation	221	117	338
Investment income	50	130	180
Profit for year before tax	1,821	1,067	2,888
Taxation	227	133	360
Profit for year after tax	1,594	934	2,528
Profit b/f from previous period	2,068	3,521	5,589
Profit c/f	3,662	4,455	8,117
DETE transfer to shareholders	800	550	1,350
DETE policyholders surplus	350	250	600

(1)   The upper limit that may be allocated to shareholders out of funds held within the FFA is 5%.

Other information

	New basis business	Ordinary life assurance business pre-2001
	NBB	OLAB
	€000	€000
Chargeable gains (realised) (1)	N/A	700
Unrealised chargeable gains (2)	N/A	210
Expenses	800	400
Disallowable expenses	160	80
Capital allowances	40	45

(1)   Realised gains €700,000 (OLAB) are net of incremental losses of €450,000 by reference to the last mark to market value in respect of which the aggregate loss over the period of ownership is €350,000.

(2)   This is one-seventh of unrealised gains based on the mark to market rule. In addition, there is an amount of €120,000 (OLAB), being one-seventh of unrealised gains brought forward from earlier periods.

The New Basis Business (NBB) computation is as follows:

	€000	€000
Profit for year before tax		1,821
Add 5% of transfer to FFA	63	
Add disallowable expenses	160	223
Less – capital allowances	40	
– Irish dividend income (Note)	34	(74))
Taxable profits		1,970
Corporation tax liability @ 12.5%		246

Note: Irish dividend income attributable to shareholder profits =

Profit before tax $\times \dfrac{\text{total Irish dividend income}}{\text{total technical a/c income}}$

= 200/10,600 x 1,821 = 34

The NCI computation is as follows:

	Policyholders	Shareholders	Total
	€000	€000	€000
Transfer to DETE	250	550	800
Disallowable expenses	Nil	80	80
	250	630	880
Capital allowances	Nil	(45)	(45)
Adjusted surplus	250	585	835
Tax gross up	Nil	71	71
Adjusted gross surplus	250	656	906
Shareholders' FII €0.12m x 656/906 =		87	
Shareholders' unfranked income (balance)		569	
		656	

Notional corporation tax payable:

	€
€0.087m @ 0% =	Nil
€0.569m @ 12.5% =	71
€0.656m	71

The I-E computation is as follows:

OLAB	€000	€000
Unfranked income		700
Franked investment income		120
Chargeable gains (see below)		1,116
		1,936
Management expenses	400	
- disallowed	80	
	320	
Capital allowances	45	365
		1,571

Chargeable gains:	€000	€000
Realised gains	700	
Add: excess of incremental loss over aggregate loss in respect of investments previously marked to market	100	800
One-seventh of excess of incremental loss over aggregate loss*		(14)

One-seventh of unrealised gains in current period**	210
One seventh of unrealised gains brought forward**	120
Chargeable gains	1,116

*   one-seventh x (450,000 - 350,000) – see note (1) above

**   see note (2) above

Tax on the I-E basis is now as follows:

	€
Unrelieved profits from life business (as above)	1,571,000
Add: shareholders' franked investment income	87,000
	1,658,000
Deduct: NCI profits	656,000
Excess for purposes of s 713(6)	1,002,000

The liability on the I-E basis is therefore:

	€		€
OLAB	1,571,000		
Excess (TCA 1997, s 713(6))	1,002,000	@ 20%	200,400
Balance	569,000	@ 12.5%	71,125
			271,525

Tax on the NCI basis is less than tax on the I-E basis. It is therefore not necessary to increase the latter amount of tax by restricting management expenses. (For an example in which tax on the NCI basis exceeds tax on the I-E basis, see Example **12.603.5.4** in the second edition (1998-99)).

The overall amount to be included in "I" for an accounting period in respect of chargeable gains is the aggregate of gains or losses in respect of actual disposals in the period, the appropriate fraction (one-seventh or lesser fraction if appropriate in the case of OLAB) of the net amount in respect of deemed disposals for the period, and the one-seventh (or lesser fraction if appropriate) of each net amount brought forward from earlier periods in respect of OLAB deemed disposals of those periods. Where there is an overall gain, the amount is included in "I". If an overall loss results, the amount of that loss is treated by TCA 1997, s 711(3) as an additional amount of management expenses deductible under TCA 1997, s 707(1), rather than as an allowable loss deductible from chargeable gains under TCA 1997, s 31. For this purpose, gains or losses arising in any accounting period as a result of the seven year spreading of OLAB gains or losses are taken into account in determining the amount, in any, of the excess of allowable losses over chargeable gains (TCA 1997, s 711(4)).

Where an asset in respect of which deemed gains or losses have arisen by virtue of the mark to market rule is actually disposed of, a gain or loss is calculated by reference to the difference between the proceeds of disposal and the last mark to market value. The gain or loss is recognised in the accounting period in which the disposal took place while, in the case of OLAB assets, the spreading of the net amounts continues until they are fully accounted for. If a loss arises on disposal, it can be set against other income of the period. However, for OLAB disposals on or after 28 March 1996, the part of the loss which exceeds the overall actual loss in respect of the asset must be spread forward over seven years. In other words, the excess loss is treated in the same way as a deemed loss under the mark to market rule.

IFRS

Regarding IFRS, see **3.305**. The following is based on a guidance note on the taxation of insurance companies issued by the Revenue Commissioners in February 2008.

Shareholder gains on investments:

Given that the new basis Case I computation is accounts-based, it follows that shareholder gains on investments chargeable under Case I should also follow the accounts. The TCA 1997, Schedule 17A transitional rules (see **3.305.6**) on changeover to IFRS will apply.

Accounting for insurance contracts as investment contracts:

Under IFRS, certain unit-linked and similar contracts are treated as investment contracts so that they are not accounted for in the Income Statement but rather as balance sheet items. Prior to the move to IFRS, unit-linked premiums and claims were regarded as trading receipts and expenses respectively and reflected in the technical account. Any end of year surplus was transferred to unit-linked policyholders and reflected in the balance sheet as "unit-linked policyholder liabilities". Post IFRS, unit-linked premiums are treated as investments made and repaid (much the same as deposits in a bank). The current value of these investments is carried in the balance sheet as a separate liability on "investment contracts". The change is one of form as opposed to substance and as such has no impact on the trading profit of the company. As a consequence of this, the Case 1 computation will continue to be based on accounting profit, but within the scope of IFRS. Any transitional adjustments will be dealt with under TCA 1997, Schedule 17A, ensuring the elimination of any double taxation or non-taxation.

Valuation issues, Case 1

There may be instances in which "fair value" under IFRS does not equal market value under local GAAP. For example, IFRS may require a bid price valuation whereas existing Irish GAAP would use a mid price valuation. The items in the technical account would relate to policyholders and therefore would be taken care of in the taxation of policyholders. Any adjustments would be referable to shareholders' interests and therefore the transitional measures in TCA 1997, Schedule 17A paragraph 4 (see **3.305.6** – *Financial instruments: transitional*), including the "bed and breakfast" provisions of Schedule 17A paragraph 4(5), would have application in that regard only.

12.603.7 Policyholders: new basis

TCA 1997 Part 26 Chapter 5 (ss 730B-730G) provides for the taxation treatment of life insurance policies that are essentially investment products with a life cover element. Life assurance policies commenced on or after 1 January 2001 are subject to an exit tax regime under which funds are allowed to accumulate without the imposition of an annual tax charge on income and gains (the "gross roll-up" basis). Accordingly, a charge to tax (exit charge) is imposed only at the time when payment is made, following the surrender or encashment of the policy, to a policyholder. The investment return or growth is liable to tax at the standard rate of income tax increased by 3 percentage points.

Gains arising from personal portfolio life policies are subject to an additional charge of 20%. The additional charge applies to proceeds paid out, on or after 26 September 2001, by a life assurance company in respect of policies. It does not apply in cases where the normal exit charge is not to arise in respect of particular classes of policyholders, eg policyholders who are non-resident and non-ordinarily resident, or charities and investment undertakings.

Tax arises at the time of payment of the investment return and is deductible, and is to be accounted for, by the assurance company. A tax liability may also arise where the benefits conferred by a life assurance policy are assigned for value. Life assurance companies that commenced business in the period 1 April 2000 to 31 December 2000 were entitled to elect to have their profits of the policies commencing in that period taxed on the "I-E" basis (see **12.603.2**). In the absence of an election, the growth in value of these policies from commencement to 31 December 2000 is taxable at 40%.

Chapter 5 imposes certain charges to tax in respect of a policy (a "life policy") that is:

(a) a policy of assurance on the life of any person; or

(b) a policy in respect of a sinking fund or capital redemption business,

where the life policy is new basis business (see **12.603.6**) of the assurance company which commenced the life policy (TCA 1997, s 730B(2)).

Sinking fund or capital redemption business has the same meaning as in section 3 of the Insurance Act 1936.

The Chapter does not, however, apply to a life policy relating to pension business, general annuity business or permanent health insurance business of an assurance company (TCA 1997, s 730B(3)).

Courts Service

The Courts Service (the "Service"), which administers the investment of funds lodged in Court, is exempted from the exit tax in respect of Court funds invested in life assurance products (see (b)(vi) under *Gains treated as not arising* below). The Service is required to operate the exit tax on payments made to it by the life assurance company when it allocates those payments to the beneficial owners.

TCA 1997, s 737B(4) provides that:

(a) where a policyholder is a person entrusted to pay all premiums ("group premiums") in respect of a life policy ("group policy") out of money under the control or subject to the order or any Court, the provisions relating to policyholders: new basis apply as if the group policy comprised separate life policies ("separate life policies");

(b) each person beneficially entitled to any part of the rights conferred by the group policy is to be treated as being the policyholder of a separate life policy;

(c) the premiums paid for each separate life policy will be such amount of the money referred to in (a) included in group premiums paid that is beneficially owned by the policyholder of the separate life policy;

(d)   a gain which, but for TCA 1997, s 730D(2) (gains treated as not arising – see below), would have arisen on the happening of a chargeable event in relation to the group policy is treated as if it were a gain arising on the happening of a chargeable event in relation to any separate policy where, and to the extent that, the gain is beneficially owned by the policyholder of that separate policy;

(e)   TCA 1997 ss 730F(2), (3) and (4) (various provisions relating to deduction of appropriate tax – see under *Appropriate tax* below), 730G (see under *Returns and collection of appropriate tax below*) and 730GA (see under *Repayment of exit tax* below), and 904C (power of inspection in relation to returns and collection of appropriate tax: assurance companies) apply as if references to an assurance company were to references to the Service; and

(f)   the Service is required, in respect of each year of assessment, on or before 28 February in the following year, to make a return (including a nil return if appropriate) to the Revenue Commissioners in approved electronic format which—

   (i)   specifies the total amount of gains ("total gains") arising in respect of the group policy, and

   (ii)   specifies in respect of each policyholder of a separate policy, where available, the name and address of the policyholder, the amount of the total gains to which the such person has beneficial entitlement, and such other information as the Revenue Commissioners may require.

Chargeable event

A *chargeable event* in relation to a life policy (ie, the occasion on which a tax charge may arise in relation to a life policy) means:

(a)   the maturity of the life policy (including where payments are made on death or disability, which payments result in the termination of the life policy);

(b)   the surrender in whole or in part of the rights conferred by the life policy (including where payments are made on death or disability, which payments do not result in the termination of the life policy);

(c)   the assignment in whole or in part of the rights conferred by the life policy;

(d)   the ending of a relevant period, where such ending is not otherwise a chargeable event, *relevant period* in relation to a life policy meaning a period of eight years beginning with the inception of the policy and each subsequent period of eight years beginning immediately after the preceding relevant period (TCA 1997, s 730C(1)(a)).

The inclusion of (d) as a chargeable event (by virtue of TCA 1997, s 730C(1)(a)(iv)) means that in relation to new basis business there will be an exit charge every eight years whether or not a policy is encashed or realised. The eight-year relevant period applies in relation to a chargeable event occurring on or after the passing of FA 2006, 31 March 2006. The first relevant period will end on 1 January 2009, ie eight years after the commencement of the gross roll-up regime which applies to life assurance policies commenced on or after 1 January 2001. For the seven-year relevant period which previously applied, see the 2005 edition of this book.

In the case of a life policy issued by an assurance company which could have made, but did not make, an election under TCA 1997, s 730A(2) (see **12.603.6**), a chargeable event is deemed to happen on 31 December 2000 where the life policy was commenced before that date (TCA 1997, s 730C(1)(b)).

For the purposes of the definition of "chargeable event", no account is to be taken of an assignment in whole or part effected:

(a) by way of security for a debt, or the discharge of a debt secured by the rights concerned, where the debt is a debt due to a financial institution (see below);

(b) between a husband and wife who at the time of such assignment were living together;

(c) between the spouses or former spouses concerned (as the case may be), by virtue or in consequence of an order made under Part III of the Family Law (Divorce) Act 1996, on or following the granting of a decree of divorce;

(d) between the spouses concerned, by virtue or in consequence of an order made under Part II of the Family Law Act 1995, on or following the granting of a decree of judicial separation within the meaning of that Act; or

(e) between the spouses or former spouses concerned (as the case may be), by virtue of an order or other determination of like effect, which is analogous to an order referred to in (c) or (d), of a court under the law of a territory other than the State made under or in consequence of the dissolution of a marriage or the legal separation of the spouses, being a dissolution or legal separation that is entitled to be recognised as valid in the State (TCA 1997, s 730C(2)).

A *financial institution* for the purposes of (a) above is—

(i) a person who holds a licence under s 9 of the Central Bank Act 1971;

(ii) a person referred to in s 7(4) of the Central Bank Act 1971; or

(iii) a credit institution duly authorised by virtue of Directive No 2000/12/EC of 20 March 2000 (OJ No L126, 26.5.2000, p1) (TCA 1997, s 730A(1)).

The inclusion of the above meaning of "credit institution" in the definition of "financial institution" permits the assignment of a policy to a financial institution in the EU, and not only an assignment to a domestic bank, to be made without triggering exit tax.

Where at any time a life policy, or an interest in a life policy, gives rise to benefits in respect of death or disability, the amount of value of those benefits to be taken into account in determining the amount of a gain under TCA 1997, s 730D (the gain arising on the chargeable event) is the excess of the value of the policy or interest therein immediately before that time over the value of the policy or interest therein immediately after that time (TCA 1997, s 730C(3)(a)).

For this purpose, the value of a policy or of an interest therein at a time means—

(a) in the case of a policy with a surrender value, the surrender value of the policy or of the interest therein at that time; and

(b) in the case of a policy not having a surrender value, the market value of the rights or other benefits conferred by the policy or interest therein at that time (TCA 1997, s 730C(3)(b)).

In determining the amount or value of benefits payable under a life policy for the above purposes, no account is to be taken of any amount of "appropriate tax" (see below) which may be required to be deducted from such benefits (TCA 1997, s 730C(3)(c)).

Gain arising on a chargeable event

The amount of the gain arising on a chargeable event in relation to a life policy is set out in TCA 1997, s 730D. No gain arises where the policyholder is not resident (and, in the case of a policyholder who is not a company, not ordinarily resident) in Ireland.

The computation of a gain which arises on the happening of a chargeable event in relation to a life policy depends on which of the four kinds of chargeable event (see definition above) is in question. The computation of the gain for each kind of chargeable event (distinguishing whole and part surrenders and whole and part assignments) is described as follows:

(a) maturity of life policy or the surrender of the whole of the policy rights:
Where the chargeable event is the maturity of the life policy or the surrender in whole of the rights thereby conferred, the gain is the amount determined by the formula—

$$B-P$$

(b) assignment of the whole of the policy rights:
Where the chargeable event is an assignment of the whole of the rights conferred by the life policy, the gain is the amount determined by the formula—

$$V-P$$

(c) surrender of part of policy rights:
Where the chargeable event is the surrender of part of the rights conferred by the life policy, the gain is the amount determined by the formula—

$$B - \frac{(P \times B)}{V}$$

(d) assignment of part of policy rights:
Where the chargeable event is the assignment of part of the rights conferred by the life policy, the gain is the amount determined by the formula—

$$A - \frac{(P \times A)}{V}$$

(e) ending of relevant period:
Where the chargeable event is the ending of a relevant period (eight or, as the case may be, twelve year period), the gain, subject to TCA 1997, s 730D(1A) (see below), is the amount determined by the formula—

$$V-P$$

(f) transfer of moneys:
Where the chargeable event is the transfer of moneys invested from one fund to another, the gain is the amount determined by the formula—

$$T - \frac{(P \times T)}{V}$$

(g) deemed chargeable event on 31 December 2000:
Where the chargeable event is deemed to happen on 31 December 2000, the gain is the amount determined by the formula—

$$V - P$$

where—

B   is the amount or value of the sum payable and other benefits arising by reason of the chargeable event,

P   is, subject to TCA 1997, s 730D(4) (see below), an amount of premiums ("allowable premiums") being the total of all premiums paid in respect of the life policy immediately before the chargeable event, to the extent that they have not been taken into account in determining a gain on the previous happening of a chargeable event (other than an event which is a chargeable event by reason only of being the ending of a relevant period),

V   is the value of the rights and other benefits conferred by the life policy immediately before the chargeable event,

T   is the value of the benefits arising by reason of the chargeable event to the extent that they have not been taken into account in determining a gain on the previous happening of a chargeable event, and

A   is the value of the part of the rights and other benefits conferred by the life policy, which has been assigned,

without regard to any amount of appropriate tax (within the meaning of TCA 1997, s 730F – see below) in connection with the chargeable event (TCA 1997, s 730D(1), (3)).

TCA 1997, s 730D(1A) provides that where a chargeable event occurs in relation to a life policy and is preceded by another chargeable event in relation to that policy, being a chargeable event within the meaning of TCA 1997, s 730C(1)(a)(iv) (a chargeable event by reason only that it is the ending of a relevant period), the gain arising on the later event is to be determined as if the earlier event had not been a chargeable event. Where the earlier chargeable event is not the surrender or assignment of part of the rights conferred by the policy, any "first tax" (the appropriate tax accounted for in respect of the earlier event and which has not been repaid) is to be added to the value of the rights or other benefits conferred by that policy immediately before the chargeable event. Where the earlier chargeable event is the surrender or assignment of part of the rights conferred by the policy, any first tax is to be deducted from the amount of premiums taken into account in determining the gain on the happening of the chargeable event.

In relation to the value of P above, it was seen that this is subject to TCA 1997, s 730D(4) and this is for the purpose of reducing that value by reference to the amount of allowable premiums already taken into account in determining a gain, if any, on the happening of an earlier chargeable event. So, for example, in calculating the gain on a surrender of a part of the rights under a life policy ((c) above), the deductible amount is the proportion of the premiums paid to date as is represented by the amount received for the surrender over the value of the policy at the time of surrender. If, however, there had been a similar such surrender at an earlier date, P must first be reduced by the amount of the premiums allowed on the earlier occasion, which will be the proportion of the premiums paid up to that earlier date as is represented by the amount received for the earlier part surrender over the value of the policy at the time of that earlier part surrender. The amount to be deducted from P, for the purposes of (c) above, is accordingly an amount equal to the lesser of B and—

$$\frac{(P \times B)}{V}$$

and, likewise, for the purposes of (d) above, it is an amount equal to the lesser of A and—

$$\frac{(P \times A)}{V}$$

where P, A, B and V have the same meanings as above (TCA 1997, s 730D(4)(a)).

Where there is a deemed chargeable event in relation to a life policy at 31 December 2000, the premiums allowable in arriving at the amount of the gain (V-P) on a subsequent chargeable event will be deemed to be the greater of—

(i)   the value of the policy immediately after 31 December 2000; and

(ii) the allowable premiums immediately before 31 December 2000 (TCA 1997, s 730D(4)(b)).

Where a chargeable event in relation to a life policy is the assignment of the whole of the rights under the policy, the allowable premiums immediately after the time of the assignment in arriving at the amount of the gain (V-P) on a subsequent chargeable event are deemed to be the greater of—

(i)   an amount equal to the value of the policy immediately after the time of the assignment; and

(ii) the allowable premiums immediately before the assignment (TCA 1997, s 730D(4)(c)).

Where a chargeable event in relation to a life policy is the assignment of part of the rights under the policy, the policy will, for the purposes of arriving at the amount of the gain (A - (P x A)/V) on a subsequent chargeable event, be deemed to consist of two policies, that is:

(i)   one policy conferring the part of the rights assigned, the allowable premiums for which immediately after the assignment are an amount equal to the value of the policy immediately after the assignment; and

(ii) the other policy conferring the rights which were not assigned, the allowable premiums for which immediately after the assignment are the amount of the allowable premiums immediately before the assignment reduced by the amount of premiums taken into account in determining a gain on the assignment (TCA 1997, s 730D(4)(d)).

Where at any time:

(i)   a chargeable event, being the ending of a relevant period (a *relevant event*), occurs in relation to a life policy that commenced before 1 May 2006;

(ii) immediately before that time the assurance company that commenced the life policy does not have in its possession an appropriate declaration in relation to the policy (see *Declarations* below); and

(iii) the permanent address of the policyholder, as stated in the policy, is not in the State and the assurance company does not have reasonable grounds to believe that the policyholder is resident in the state, the assurance company may elect to be treated in relation to that chargeable event as if, immediately before that time, it was in possession of the declaration (TCA 1997, s 730D(5)(a)).

Where at any time:

(i) a relevant event occurred in relation to a life policy and a chargeable event, not being a relevant event, subsequently occurs in relation to the policy;

(ii) TCA 1997, s 730D(5)(a) (as above) applied to the relevant event; and

(iii) immediately before that time the assurance company that commenced the life policy does not have in its possession an appropriate declaration.

TCA 1997, s 730D(5)(a) is deemed not to have applied to the relevant event and any appropriate tax payable by virtue of a gain arising on a chargeable event is will be due and payable as if TCA 1997, s 730D(5)(a) had not been enacted (TCA 1997, s 730D(5)(b)).

Example 12.603.7.1

A policy holder assigns his life policy at its then value, €12,000, at which time premiums of €10,000 had been paid in respect of the policy. Later, the assignee receives €18,000 from the life company on the maturity of the policy at which time premiums of €15,000 had been paid on the policy.

The gain ("V-P") on the assignment, the first chargeable event, is €12,000 - €10,000 = €2,000. The gain ("B-P") on the second chargeable event, the maturity of the policy, is as follows:

	€	€
Proceeds		18,000
(A) value of policy immediately after assignment	12,000	
(B) premiums immediately before assignment	10,000	
Greater of (A) and (B) (TCA 1997, s 730D(4)(c))	12,000	
Premiums paid by purchaser	5,000	
Deductible		17,000
Taxable		1,000

Without the qualification in TCA 1997, s 730D(4)(c), the value of "P" would be the total premiums paid less the premiums of €10,000 taken into account for the previous chargeable event. The effect of the qualification is that, for the purpose of determining the gain on the second event, the amount of the allowable premiums immediately after the assignment is the greater of (A) and (B). To this is added the amount of the premiums paid subsequently.

The aggregate gains taxable as between the two holders is €3,000 which is equal to the overall gain represented by the excess of the proceeds on maturity €18,000 and the total premiums paid €15,000.

Example 12.603.7.2

The position is as in Example **12.603.7.1** except that the first chargeable event is one within TCA 1997, s 730C(1)(a)(iv), ie the end of a relevant period, and the policyholder receives €17,540 (reflecting a deduction of €460 made by the company in respect of the first chargeable event) from the life company on the maturity of the policy. The value of the policy at the time of the first chargeable event is €12,000.

The gain ("V-P") on the ending of the relevant period, the first chargeable event, is €12,000 - €10,000 = €2,000, resulting in tax payable, at 23%, of €460.

The gain ("B-P") on the maturity of the policy, the second chargeable event, is as follows:

	€
Proceeds ("B") (before exit tax)	17,540
Add: "first tax"	460
	18,000
Less: total premiums paid in respect of policy ("P")	15,000
Taxable	3,000
Tax @ 23%	690
Less: credit for first tax	460
Tax payable	230

The value of "P" is determined as if TCA 1997, s 730C(1)(a)(iv) had not been enacted. Accordingly, it is the amount of the total premiums paid without regard to the premiums taken into account in respect of the first chargeable event. Regarding the availability of credit in respect of tax on the first event, see below under *Offset of tax paid on chargeable event*.

The aggregate tax payable as between the two chargeable events is €690 which represents the tax payable on a gain consisting of pre-tax proceeds of €18,000 less total premiums paid.

Gains treated as not arising

A gain is treated as not arising on the happening of a chargeable event in relation to a life policy where:

(a) immediately before the chargeable event, the assurance company which commenced the life policy—

    (i) is in possession of a declaration, in relation to the life policy, of a kind referred to in TCA 1997, s 730E(2) (see *Declarations* below), and

    (ii) is not in possession of any information which would reasonably suggest that—

        (I) the information contained in that declaration is not, or is no longer, materially correct,

        (II) the policyholder (within the meaning of TCA 1997, s 730E(1) – see below) failed to comply with the undertaking referred to in TCA 1997, s 730E(2)(f) (to the effect that if the policyholder becomes resident in the State, the policyholder will notify the assurance company accordingly), or

        (III) immediately before the chargeable event the policyholder (within the meaning of TCA 1997, s 730E(1)) is resident or ordinarily resident in the State (TCA 1997, s 730D(2)(a)),

(b) immediately before the chargeable event, the policyholder is—

    (i) a company carrying on life business,

    (ii) an investment undertaking (within the meaning of TCA 1997, s 739B – see **12.806.3**),

    (iii) a person who is entitled to exemption—

(I) from income tax by virtue of TCA 1997, s 207(1)(b) (charitable exemption – see **12.1002**), or

(II) from corporation tax by virtue of TCA 1997, s 207(1)(b) as it applies for corporation tax purposes under TCA 1997, s 76(6) (application of income tax principles to corporation tax – see **3.102.2**),

(iv) a PRSA provider (within the meaning of Part X of the Pensions Act, 1990),

(v) a credit union (within the meaning assigned in section 2 of the Credit Union Act, 1997), or

(vi) a person entrusted to pay all premiums payable, in respect of the life policy, out of money under the control or subject to the order or any Court (thereby exempting the Courts Service from the exit tax),

and the assurance company which commenced the life policy is in possession of a declaration in relation to the life policy, of a kind referred to in TCA 1997, s 730E(3) (TCA 1997, s 730D(2)(b)); or

(c) where the life policy is an asset held in a special savings incentive account within the meaning of TCA 1997, s 848B (see below) and the assurance company which commenced the life policy is in possession of a declaration of a kind referred to in TCA 1997, s 730E(3A) (TCA 1997, s 730D(2)(c)).

A *special savings incentive account* is an account which may be opened by a qualifying individual with a "qualifying savings manager" in the period 1 May 2001 to 20 April 2002 and to which the Revenue Commissioners pay a tax credit equal to income tax at the standard rate on the grossed up amount of subscriptions made by the individual.

Policyholder , in relation to a life policy, at any time means:

(i) where the rights conferred by the life policy are vested at that time in a person as beneficial owner, that person;

(ii) where the rights conferred by the life policy are held at that time on trusts created by a person, that person; and

(iii) where the rights conferred by the life policy are held at that time as security for a debt owed by a person, that person (TCA 1997, s 730E(1)).

A gain is not to be treated as arising on the happening of a chargeable event in relation to a life policy where:

(i) (I) the assurance company which commenced the policy has established a branch in an offshore state, and the commitment represented by that life policy is covered by that branch; or

(II) the assurance company which commenced the life policy underwrites the business from the State on a freedom of services basis under Regulation 50 of the European Communities (Life Assurance) Framework Regulations 1994 (SI No 360 of 1994) or other equivalent arrangement in an EEA state, and the policyholder resides in an offshore state, and

(ii) the assurance company has received written approval from the Revenue Commissioners (who may give the approval subject to such conditions as they consider necessary), to the effect that the provisions of TCA 1997, s 730D(2)(a) (see (a)(i) and (ii) above) need not apply to the life policy, and that approval has not been withdrawn (TCA 1997, s 730D(2A)(b)).

In this connection, *offshore state* means a state, other than the State, which is:

(a)   a Member State of the European Communities; or

(b)   a state which is an EEA State (TCA 1997, s 730D(2A)(a)).

EEA State means a state, other than the State, which is a contracting party to the EEA Agreement. EEA Agreement means the Agreement on the European Economic Area signed at Oporto on 2 May 1992, as adjusted by the Protocol signed at Brussels on 17 March 1993.

Thus, TCA 1997, s 730D(2A) provides that a gain will not arise on the happening of a chargeable event under the gross roll-up regime in relation to a life policy where the assurance company has established a branch in an EU or EEA Member State and has received written approval from the Revenue Commissioners that exit tax will not apply.

The exemption is extended so as to apply where the life company carries on business on a freedom of services basis or under an equivalent arrangement in an EEA state and the policy holder resides in an EU or EEA Member State other than Ireland. Written approval from the Revenue Commissioners is also be required for this purpose.

Declarations

TCA 1997, s 730E provides for three kinds of declaration, these relating to the three situations described in (a) to (c) above.

The declaration, referred to in (a) under *Gains treated as not arising* above, in relation to a life policy is, subject to TCA 1997, s 730D(4) (see below), a declaration in writing to the assurance company which:

(a)   is made by the policyholder at or about the time of the inception of the life policy;

(b)   is signed by the policyholder;

(c)   is made in such form as may be prescribed or authorised by the Revenue Commissioners;

(d)   declares that the policyholder is not resident and not ordinarily resident in the State at the time the declaration is made;

(e)   contains the name of, and the address of the principal place of residence of, the policyholder;

(f)   contains an undertaking by the policyholder that if the policyholder becomes resident in the State, the policyholder will notify the assurance company accordingly;

(g)   contains such other information as the Revenue Commissioners may reasonably require (TCA 1997, s 730E(2)).

The declaration, referred to in (b) under *Gains treated as not arising* above, in relation to a life policy is, subject to TCA 1997, s 730D(4) (see below), a declaration in writing to the assurance company which:

(a)   is made, and signed, by the policyholder;

(b)   is made in such form as may be prescribed or authorised by the Revenue Commissioners;

(c)   contains the name and address of the policyholder;

(d)   declares that the policyholder, at the time the declaration is made, is—

    (i)   a company carrying on life business,

    (ii)   an investment undertaking (within the meaning of TCA 1997, s 739B – see **12.806.3**), or, as the case may be,

    (iii)   a person who is entitled to exemption from income tax by virtue of TCA 1997, s 207(1)(b) (charitable exemption – see **12.1002**), or is entitled to exemption from corporation tax by virtue of TCA 1997, s 207(1)(b) as it applies for corporation tax purposes under TCA 1997, s 76(6) (application of income tax principles to corporation tax – see **3.102.2**),

    (iv)   a PRSA provider (within the meaning of Part X of the Pensions Act, 1990),

    (v)   a credit union (within the meaning assigned in section 2 of the Credit Union Act, 1997), or

    (vi)   a person entrusted to pay all premiums payable, in respect of the life policy, out of money under the control or subject to the order or any Court),

(e)   contains an undertaking that should the policyholder cease to be a person referred to in (i), (ii), (iii), (iv), (v) or, as the case may be, (vi), the assurance company will be advised accordingly; and

(f)   contains such other information as the Revenue Commissioners may reasonably require (TCA 1997, s 730E(3)).

The insurance company is obliged to keep and retain declarations referred to above for a period of six years from the time the life policy concerned ceases (TCA 1997, s 730E(5)).

The declaration, referred to in (c) under *Gains treated as not arising* above, in relation to a life policy is a declaration in writing to the assurance company which:

(a)   is made by a qualifying savings manager (the "declarer") within the meaning of TCA 1997, s 848B, in respect of the life policy which is an asset held in a special savings incentive account (see above);

(b)   is signed by the declarer;

(c)   is made in such form as may be prescribed or authorised by the Revenue Commissioners;

(d)   declares that, at the time the declaration is made, the life policy in respect of which the declaration is made, is—

    (i)   an asset held in a special savings incentive account, and

    (ii)   is managed by the declarer for the individual who is beneficially entitled to the life policy,

(e)   contains the name and address, and the PPS Number (within the meaning of section 262 of the Social Welfare Consolidation Act 2005), of the individual referred to in (d);

(f)   contains an undertaking by the declarer that if the life policy ceases to be an asset held in the special savings incentive account, the declarer will notify the assurance company accordingly; and

(g) contains such other information as the Revenue Commissioners may reasonably require (TCA 1997, s 730E(3A)).

Where, immediately before the happening of a chargeable event, the rights conferred by a life policy were vested beneficially in two or more persons, or were held on trusts created, or as security for a debt owed, by two or more persons, TCA 1997 ss 730D and 730E (provisions dealing with gains arising on chargeable event and with declarations) are to have effect in relation to each of those persons as if the person had been the sole owner, settlor or, as the case may be, debtor. Accordingly, any reference to the amount of a gain is to be read as a reference to the part of the gain proportionate to the persons share in the rights at the time of the event or, as the case may require, when the trusts were created (TCA 1997, s 730E(4)).

Personal portfolio life policies

Under the tax regime applying to life policies from 1 January 2001, funds can accumulate without the imposition of an annual tax charge on income and gains (the "gross-roll-up" basis). Accordingly, a charge to tax (exit charge) is imposed only at the time when payment is made to a policyholder.

With effect from 26 September 2001, the exit charge relating to personal portfolio life policies is increased by 20 percentage points (see under *Appropriate tax* below). A personal portfolio life policy is, broadly, a policy under the terms of which the policyholder, or a person connected with the policyholder, may select or influence the selection of the assets that determine the policy benefits. A policy will not be treated as a personal portfolio life policy where the only property that can be selected is property consisting of units in a unit trust and similar undertakings, property allocated by the assurance company to an internal fund so as to fund policy benefits, cash or a combination of these.

The above exceptions apply only where the opportunity to select the property in question (ie, property of the exact same description as that which is available for selection at any particular time) is widely available to the public at the time the property is actually being selected. This wide availability must be evidenced in marketing or promotional material published by the assurance company at the time of the selection of the property providing the policy benefits. In the case of an index or a basket of indices, a similar rule applies as to general availability to the public at the time the selection of the index is being made. This availability must be evidenced through marketing or promotional material published by the assurance company at the time the selection is being made.

For the purpose of ensuring that there would be no abuse or exploitation of the exceptions, there are additional requirements relating to policies taken out or marketed from 5 December 2001. The life company must deal with every person interested in selecting the property available for selection on a non-discriminatory basis. Where the property to be selected is primarily land or buildings and the life company is seeking to raise a pre-determined amount in investments, each investment by a policyholder will be limited to 1% of the amount being sought by the company.

Policyholder has the same meaning as in TCA 1997, s 730E (see above under *Gains treated as not arising*).

A *personal portfolio life policy* is a life policy or a foreign life policy (as *foreign life policy* is defined in TCA 1997, s 730H – see **12.603.8**), as the case may be, under whose terms:

(a)   (i)   some or all of the benefits conferred by the policy are or were determined by reference to the value of, or the income from, property of any description (whether or not specified in the policy), or

      (ii)   some or all of the benefits conferred by the policy are or were determined by reference to fluctuations in, or fluctuations in an index of, the value of property of any description (whether or not specified in the policy), and

(b)   some or all of the property or the index may be or was selected by, or the selection of some or all of the property or index may be or was influenced by—

      (i)   the policyholder,

      (ii)   a person acting on behalf of the policyholder,

      (iii)   a person connected (within the meaning of TCA 1997, s 10 – see **2.3**) with the policyholder,

      (iv)   a person connected with a person acting on behalf of the policyholder,

      (v)   the policyholder and a person connected with the policyholder, or

      (vi)   a person acting on behalf of both the policyholder and a person connected with the policyholder (TCA 1997, s 730BA(2)).

For the purposes of (b) above and without prejudice to the application of the definition of "personal portfolio life policy", the terms of a life policy or a foreign life policy are to be treated as permitting the selection referred to where:

(a)   the terms of the policy or any other agreement between any person referred to in (b) above and the assurance company concerned—

      (i)   allow the exercise of an option by any person referred to in (b) above to make the selection referred to there,

      (ii)   give the assurance company discretion to offer any person referred to in (b) above the right to make the selection referred to there, or

      (iii)   allow any of the persons referred to in (b) above the right to request, subject to- the agreement of the assurance company, a change in the terms of the policy such that the selection referred to there may be made by any of those persons, or

(b)   the policyholder is unable under the terms of the policy to select any of the property so as to determine the benefits under the policy, but any of the persons referred in (b) above has or had the option of requiring the assurance company to appoint the investment advisor (no matter how such a person is described) in relation to the selection of the property which is to determine the benefits under the policy (TCA 1997, s 730BA(3)).

A life policy is not a personal portfolio life policy if:

(a)   (i)   the only property which may be or has been selected is—

      (I)   property which the assurance company concerned has appropriated to an internal linked fund (see below),

(II) property consisting of any of the following—

    (A) units in an investment undertaking (as defined in TCA 1997, s 739B – see **12.806.3**), or

    (B) cash, including cash deposited in a bank account or similar account (including cash deposited in a share account with a building society – see below) except where the acquisition of the cash was made wholly or partly for the purpose of realising a gain from the disposal of the cash, or

(III) property consisting of a combination of the property specified in (I) and (II), and the property satisfies the conditions specified in TCA 1997, s 730BA(5) (see below), or

(ii) the only index which may be or has been selected is of a description specified in TCA 1997, s 730BA(6) (see below), and

(b) as respects a life policy or a foreign life policy commenced on or after 5 December 2001 (other than a policy in respect of which the only property which may be selected is property described in (II)(B) above or a policy in respect of which marketing or other promotional literature was published before that date) the terms under which the policy is offered meet the requirements of TCA 1997, s 730BA(7) (see below) (TCA 1997, s 730BA(4)).

An *internal linked fund* means a fund maintained by an assurance company to which fund the company appropriates certain linked assets and which fund may be subdivided into subdivisions the value of each of which is determined by the company be reference to the value of such linked assets. A *linked asset* is an asset of an assurance company which is identified in its records as an asset by reference to the value of which the benefits provided for under a life policy are to be determined (TCA 1997, s 730BA(1)).

Building society means a building society within the meaning of the Building Societies Acts, 1989, or a society established in accordance with the law of any other Member State of the European Communities which corresponds to that Act (TCA 1997 ss 730BA(1) and 256(1)).

The condition specified in TCA 1997, s 730BA(5) is that at the time when the property is or was available to be selected, the opportunity to select:

(a) in the case of land (see below), that property; and

(b) in any other case, property of the same description as the first-mentioned property,

is or was available to the public (see below) on terms which provide or provided that the opportunity to select the property is or was available to any person falling within the terms of the opportunity and that opportunity is or was clearly identified to the public, in marketing or other promotional literature published at that time by the assurance company concerned, as available generally to any person falling within the terms of the opportunity.

Land includes an interest in land as well as shares deriving their value or the greater part of their value directly or indirectly from land, other than shares quoted on a recognised stock exchange (TCA 1997, s 730BA(1)).

Public means individuals generally, companies generally, or a combination of these, as the case may be (TCA 1997, s 730BA(1)).

The index description specified in TCA 1997, s 730BA(6) is an index consisting or a prices' index (see below) or a combination of prices' indices where, at the time the index is or was available to be selected, the opportunity to select the same index is or was available to the public on terms which provide or provided that the opportunity to select the index is or was available to any person falling within the terms of the opportunity and that opportunity is or was clearly identified to the public, in marketing or other promotional literature published at that time by the assurance company concerned, as available generally to any person falling within the terms of the opportunity.

A *prices' index* means:

(a)   the all items consumer price index compiled by the Central Statistics Office;

(b)   any general index of prices corresponding to such consumer price index and duly published by or on behalf of any state other than the State; or

(c)   any published index of prices of shares listed on a recognised stock exchange (TCA 1997, s 730BA(1)).

The requirements of TCA 1997, s 730BA(7) are that:

(a)   the assurance company concerned does not subject any person to any treatment in connection with the opportunity which is different or more burdensome than any treatment to which any other person is or may be subject; and

(b)   where the terms of the opportunity referred to in TCA 1997, s 730BA(5) include terms—

(i)   which set out the capital requirement of the opportunity and this requirement is identified to the public in the marketing or other promotional material published by the assurance company at the time the property is available to be selected, and

(ii)   indicating that 50% or more by value of the property referred to in that subsection is or is to be land,

the amount any one person may invest in the policy may not represent more than 1% of the capital requirement (exclusive of any borrowings) of the opportunity as so identified.

Appropriate tax

TCA 1997, s 730F provides for the rate of appropriate tax ("exit tax") to be applied to a gain in the case of a payment by an assurance company to a policy holder. The rate of tax in most cases is the standard rate of income tax increased by three percentage points. The tax which is to be deducted on the occurrence of a chargeable event is referred to as appropriate tax.

Where the chargeable event happens on or after 1 January 2001, and subject to the position relating to chargeable events happening on or after 26 September 2001 in the case of a personal portfolio life policy, the appropriate tax is a sum representing income tax on the amount of the gain arising at a rate determined by the formula: $(S + 3)$ per cent – where S is the standard rate per cent for the year of assessment in which the gain arises (TCA 1997, s 730F(1)(a)).

Where, in the case of a personal portfolio life policy, the chargeable event happens on or after 26 September 2001, the appropriate tax is a sum representing income tax on the amount of the gain arising at a rate determined by the formula: $(S + 23)$ per cent – where S is the standard rate per cent for the year of assessment in which the gain arises (TCA 1997, s 730F(1)(b)).

Where the chargeable event occurs on or before 31 December 2000, the appropriate tax is a sum representing income tax on the amount of the gain arising at a rate 40% (TCA 1997, s 730F(1)(c)).

An assurance company is obliged to account for appropriate tax in accordance with TCA 1997, s 730G (see *Returns and collection of appropriate tax below*).

Where an assurance company is liable to account for appropriate tax in connection with a chargeable event in relation to a life policy, it will be entitled to pass on the cost of that tax to the relevant policyholder. Thus, where the chargeable event is the maturity, transfer, ending or surrender in whole or in part of the rights under the life policy, the assurance company will be entitled to deduct from the proceeds payable to the policyholder on maturity, transfer, ending or surrender, as the case may be, an amount equal to the appropriate tax. Where the chargeable event is the assignment in whole or in part of the rights under the policy, is the ending of a relevant period, or is deemed to happen on 31 December 2000, the assurance company will be entitled to appropriate and realise sufficient assets of the underlying life policy to meet the amount of appropriate tax for which it liable to account (TCA 1997, s 730F(3)(a)).

In either of the above cases, the assurance company is acquitted and discharged of such deduction or, as the case may be, such appropriation as if the amount of the deduction or the value of the appropriation had been paid to the policyholder. The policyholder is obliged to allow such deduction or, as the case may be, such appropriation.

Offset of tax paid on chargeable event

Appropriate tax paid on a chargeable event which is the ending of a relevant period in relation to a life policy may be offset against appropriate tax paid on the subsequent maturity, surrender or assignment of the policy. In certain circumstances, where the final amount of tax due is less than the amount already collected, tax overpaid may be refunded.

Where at any time there is a chargeable event by reason of the occurrence of an event, not being the ending of a relevant period, which has been preceded by another chargeable event which *was* the ending of a relevant period, a proportion of the appropriate tax accounted for in respect of that earlier event and which has not been repaid (*first tax*) will be set off against appropriate tax (*second tax*) in respect of the gain (*new gain*) on the later event (TCA 1997, s 730F(1A)(b)(i)). The proportion, referred to as the *relevant proportion*, of the appropriate tax to be set off is an amount determined by the following formula—

$$A \times \frac{B}{C}$$

where:

A   is the first tax,

B   is the new gain, and

C   is a gain determined in accordance with TCA 1997, s 730D on the assumption that the policy matured at that time (TCA 1997, s 730F(1A)(c)).

If the second event is the maturity of the policy, the formula will produce a value equivalent to the tax on the first event since the values of B and C will be the same. Otherwise, where the new gain arises on, say, an assignment of part of the rights under the policy, the creditable tax will only be a proportion of the tax on the first event.

If the relevant proportion exceeds the second tax, the excess amount is to be paid by the assurance company to the policy holder concerned. The excess amount is also to be included in the return required by TCA 1997, s 730G(2) (see below) and is to be treated as an amount which may be set off against appropriate tax payable by the assurance company in respect of any chargeable event in the period for which such return is to be made, or any subsequent period (TCA 1997, s 730F(1A)(b)(ii)).

Repayment of exit tax

Exit tax may be repaid where a policyholder is entitled to exemption from tax in certain circumstances.

For the purposes of a claim to relief under TCA 1997, s 189 (payments in respect of person injuries), 189A (trusts for permanently incapacitated individuals) or 192 (payments in respect of thalidomide children), or a repayment of income tax in consequence of any of those provisions, the amount of a payment made to a policyholder by an assurance company is to be treated as a net amount of income from the gross amount of which has been deducted income tax, of an amount equal to the amount of appropriate tax deducted from the payment, and that gross amount is to be treated as chargeable to tax under Case III of Schedule D (TCA 1997, s 730GA). Provision is made in each of the three sections referred to whereby income that would be chargeable to tax under Case III is to be exempt from income tax and not reckoned in computing total income for income tax purposes. Appropriate tax treated as income tax deducted from the gross payments will accordingly be repayable in such cases.

Returns and collection of appropriate tax

An assurance company is required for each financial year (calendar year) to make to the Collector-General a return of the appropriate tax, and amounts which may be credited under TCA 1997, s 730F(1A) (see above), in connection with chargeable events happening on or prior to 30 June, within 30 days of that date and a return of appropriate tax, and amounts which may be credited under TCA 1997, s 730F(1A), in connection with chargeable events happening in the period 1 July to 31 December, within 30 days of that later date. Where appropriate, the return should specify that there is no appropriate tax for the period in question (TCA 1997, s 730G(2)). A return is to be in the form prescribed by the Revenue Commissioners and must include a declaration to the effect that the return is correct and complete.

Appropriate tax required to be included in a return (reduced by any amount which is to be credited under TCA 1997, s 730F(1A)) is due at the time by which the return is to be made and is payable by the assurance company to the Collector-General.

An inspector who is of the opinion that an amount of appropriate tax due has been omitted from a return made by an assurance company, or is dissatisfied with any return, may make an appropriate assessment on the assurance company. Any appropriate tax assessed becomes due within one month after the issue of the notice of assessment, unless it is due earlier by reference to the time by which the relevant return is due.

Any amount of appropriate tax carries interest at 1% per month or part of a month from the date when the amount becomes due and payable until the date of payment.

12.603.8   Policyholders: certain foreign life policies

With effect from 1 January 2001, a new system of taxing policyholders of certain foreign life assurance policies came into force. Instead of the 40% rate that applies to gains on the disposals of such policies (TCA 1997, s 594(2)(f) – see **12.604.3**), a new rate of 23% applies in respect of policyholders other than companies; the 25% corporation tax rate applies in the case of policyholders that are companies. In the cases of foreign life policies not covered by the new system, the 40% capital gains rate continues to apply.

The policies to which the new system applies are those issued from another Member State of the EU, a Member State of the EEA, or a member of the OECD and with which Ireland has a tax treaty.

Irish residents taking out policies to which the new regime applies are deemed to be chargeable persons for self-assessment purposes and are required to include details of the policies in their tax returns. Profits from the investment in these policies are taxed at the 23% rate of tax (20% in the case of an income payment) or, in the case of a company, at 25%. (The 23% rate is also the exit tax rate applying to investment in domestic life assurance policies – see **12.603.7**.) The 23% rate or, in the case of companies, the 25% rate, only applies where details of the payment from the foreign policy are included in a tax return made on time by the policyholder; otherwise, the 40% capital gains rate applies to the profit on the policy.

Definitions

A *deemed disposal* is a disposal of the type provided for in TCA 1997, s 730K(6) (see below).

A *foreign life policy* is a policy of assurance on the life of a person commenced:

(a)   by a branch or agency, carrying on business in an offshore state, of an assurance company; or

(b)   by an assurance company carrying on business in an offshore state, other than by its branch or agency carrying on business in the State (TCA 1997, s 730H(1)).

Thus, a foreign life policy may be a policy commenced by the foreign branch of an Irish company or by a non-Irish company except where the policy is commenced by its Irish branch. An *offshore state* is a state other than the State which is:

(i)   a Member State of the European Communities;

(ii)   a state which is an EEA State; or

(iii)   a state which is a member of the OECD, the government of which has entered into a tax treaty with Ireland.

OECD means the organisation known as the Organisation for Economic Co-operation and Development.

EEA state means a state, other than the State, which is a Contracting party to the EEA Agreement. *EEA Agreement* means the Agreement on the European Economic Area signed at Oporto on 2 May 1992, as adjusted by the Protocol signed at Brussels on 17 March 1993.

A *relevant event* in relation to a foreign life policy is the ending of a relevant period, where *relevant period* means a period of eight years beginning with the inception of the policy and each subsequent period of eight years beginning immediately after the preceding relevant period.

A *relevant payment* is any payment made to a person in respect of a foreign life policy where such payments are made annually or at more frequent intervals, other than a payment made in consideration of the disposal, in whole or in part, of the foreign policy.

Payment in respect of foreign life policy

With effect on and from 1 January 2001, a person, other than a company, who has a foreign life policy and who receives a payment in respect of that policy is subject to tax as follows. If the income represented by the payment is correctly included in a return of income, the income is taxable:

(a) where the payment is a relevant payment, the standard rate of income tax in force at the time of the payment; and

(b) where the payment is not a relevant payment and is not made in consideration of the disposal, in whole or part, of the policy—

 (i) in the case of a foreign life policy which is a personal portfolio life policy (see **12.603.7**), at the rate determined by the formula: $(S + 23)$ per cent – where S is the standard rate per cent for the year of assessment in which payment is made, and

 (ii) in any other case, at a rate determined by the formula: $(S + 3)$ per cent – where S is the standard rate per cent for the year of assessment in which payment is made.

Where the income represented by the payment is not correctly included in a return of income, the income is taxable:

(i) in the case of a foreign life policy which is a personal portfolio life policy, at the rate determined by the formula: $(H + 20)$ per cent – where H is a rate per cent determined in relation to the person by TCA 1997, s 15 for the year of assessment in which payment is made; and

(ii) in any other case, at a rate determined in relation to the person by TCA 1997, s 15 for the year of assessment in which payment is made (TCA 1997, s 730J(1)(a)).

In the case of a company with a foreign life policy and which receives a payment in respect of that policy, the income represented by the payment is chargeable to tax under Case III of Schedule D (TCA 1997, s 730J(1)(b)). Accordingly, the rate at which the income is taxed is 25% (see **3.101.4**).

Disposal of foreign life policy

With effect on and from 1 January 2001, where a person disposes in whole or in part of a foreign life policy and the disposal results in a gain computed as described below, and if details of the disposal have been correctly included in a return of income made on time, the gain is treated as an amount of income chargeable to tax under Case IV of Schedule D (TCA 1997, s 730K(1)).

Where the person making the disposal is not a company, the rate of income tax to be charged on that income is a rate determined by the formula—

(a) where the foreign life policy is a personal portfolio life policy, $(S + 23)$ per cent:

 – where S is the standard rate per cent for the year of assessment in which the disposal is made and,

(b) in any other case, $(S + 3)$ per cent:

 – where S is the standard rate per cent for the year of assessment in which the disposal is made (TCA 1997, s 730K(1)(a)).

Where the disposal is made by a company, since the income is taxable under Case IV of Schedule D, the applicable corporation tax rate is 25% (see **3.101.4**).

The amount of the gain accruing on a disposal of a foreign life policy is the amount of the relevant gain (within the meaning of TCA 1997, s 594(2) – see **12.604.3**) which would be computed if the gain on the disposal were computed for the purposes of that section (so that, for example, it would be computed without regard to TCA 1997, s 556(2) (indexation – see **9.102.3**)) (TCA 1997, s 730K(2)). Where, however, a capital gains computation would result in a loss, and notwithstanding TCA 1997 ss 538 and 546 (assets lost or destroyed; negligible value; allowable losses – see **9.102.3**), a gain on the disposal of a foreign life policy is, subject to TCA 1997, s 730K(3)(b), to be treated as nil and no loss will be treated as accruing on the disposal (TCA 1997, s 730K(3)(a)).

The concept of a "deemed disposal" of a foreign life policy is explained in TCA 1997, s 730K(6). It is a disposal which is deemed to have been made when there is a relevant event (the ending of an eight-year period). Where there is such a deemed disposal, the owner of the policy is deemed to have disposed of the whole policy immediately before the time of that event and immediately to have reacquired it at its market value at that time.

Where, in respect of a foreign life policy:

(i) a gain on a disposal is treated as nil in accordance with TCA 1997, s 730K(3)(a),

(ii) that disposal is *not* a deemed disposal, and

(iii) a person was chargeable to tax in respect of an earlier deemed disposal on the policy,

then the provisions of TCA 1997, s 865 (repayment of tax – see **15.204.2**), apart from subsection (4) (time within which a repayment claim may be made), are to apply and the inspector of taxes may make such repayment or set-off as is necessary to secure that the aggregate of tax payable in respect of the policy does not exceed the tax that would have been payable if TCA 1997, s 730K(6) had not been enacted (TCA 1997, s 730K(3)(b)). Accordingly, where the computation discloses a loss, the overall tax payable in respect of the policy is not to exceed the amount that would be payable on the assumption that there had not been a deemed disposal and reacquisition of the policy at market value at the time of the earlier event mentioned in (iii) above.

The above-described position relates to relevant events occurring on or after the date of the passing of FA 2006, 31 March 2006, in respect of foreign policies taken out on or after 1 January 2001.

In a case where a disposal by a company results in an amount of income being chargeable to tax under Case IV of Schedule D, that amount may not be reduced on foot of a claim made by the company under TCA 1997, s 396 (relief for trading losses – see **4.101**) or 399 (Case IV losses – see **4.106**) (TCA 1997, s 730K(4)).

Returns on acquisition of foreign life policy

A person acquiring a foreign life policy in any chargeable period (a year of assessment or, in the case of a company, an accounting period – see **15.102.3**) is deemed to be a chargeable person for that period for the purposes of TCA 1997 ss 951 (obligation to make a return – see **15.104**) and 1084 (surcharge for late returns – see **15.103.5**). The return of income to be delivered for that period should include the following particulars:

(a)   the name and address of the person who commenced the foreign life policy;

(b)   a description of the terms of the foreign life policy including premiums payable; and

(c)   the name and address of the person through whom the foreign life policy was acquired (TCA 1997, s 730I).

12.603.9   Foreign life assurance business: deduction of tax from certain proceeds

As noted earlier (see **12.603.4** above), where a company's trading operations consist solely of foreign life assurance business, the company (which will be an IFSC company) is chargeable to tax in respect of the profits of that business under Case I of Schedule D and tax is payable at a maximum rate of 10%. Foreign life assurance business is life assurance business with policyholders and annuitants who, at the time that business is transacted, reside outside the State. It was seen that, for this purpose, non-resident holders of policies who subsequently come to reside in the State may retain their policies.

In this connection, TCA 1997, s 710(3) provides that when such a policy matures at a time when the holder is resident or ordinarily resident in the State, the life assurance company is obliged to account for tax, which it can deduct from the sum payable, being tax at the standard rate of income tax on the amount (the "relevant amount") by which the benefits under the policy increased while the holder was resident in the State. In the case of a retirement benefits policyholder, tax is deductible at the standard rate of income tax on 75% of that amount.

The obligation to account for tax applies to a *policy of assurance* which is defined as:

(a)   a policy of assurance issued by an IFSC company to an individual who, on the date the policy was issued, resides outside the State and who continuously so resides throughout a period of at least six months commencing on that date; or

(b)   a policy issued or a contract made which is not a retirement benefits policy solely by virtue of the age condition not being complied with (see below).

The obligation also applies to a *retirement benefits policy*, which means a policy issued or a contract made by a company:

(a)   to or with an individual who, on the date the policy is issued or the contract is made, resides outside the State and who continuously so resides throughout a period of at least six months commencing on that date; and

(b)   on terms which include the condition ("age condition") that the main benefit secured by the policy or contract is the payment by the company, otherwise than on the death or disability of the individual, of a sum to the individual on or after he attains the age of sixty years and before he attains the age of seventy years and that condition is complied with.

Where in the case of a policy of assurance or a retirement benefits policy a sum is payable, otherwise than by reason of death or disability of the policyholder, to a policyholder who is resident in the State:

(i)   the company is deemed to have made, in the year of assessment in which the sum is payable, an annual payment of an amount equal to the "relevant amount" (see below) in relation to the policy;

(ii)   TCA 1997, s 239 (income tax on annual payments – see **4.306**) applies as regards the charge, assessment and recovery of tax in respect of the payment;

(iii)   the company is entitled to deduct the tax out of the sum in question;

(iv)   the recipient may not claim repayment of, or credit for, the tax deducted; and

(v)   the sum paid is not to be taken into account in computing total income of the recipient for the purposes of the Income Tax Acts.

The *relevant amount* means, in relation to a policy of assurance, the amount determined by the formula "V-P" and, in relation to a retirement benefits policy, 75% of that amount, where:

V   is the amount or the aggregate of amounts by which the market value of all the entitlements under the policy increased during any period or periods in which the policyholder was residing in the State; and

P   is the amount of premiums or like sums paid in respect of the policy during any period or periods in which the policyholder was residing in the State.

Where a policy or contract is taken out by a person who did not continuously reside outside Ireland for a period of six months after the policy or contract was taken out, the life company will not be obliged to withhold tax from proceeds of that policy/contract but the holder will be fully liable to Irish capital gains tax on those proceeds. The company will be obliged to file an annual return with the Revenue showing details of such cases including the tax reference numbers of the individual policyholders concerned.

12.603.10 Foreign life assurance funds (old basis only)

Where foreign investments are held by the foreign life assurance fund of a life assurance company, the corporation tax liability on the income from such investments is computed by reference to the amount remitted to Ireland (TCA 1997, s 718). *Foreign life assurance fund*, where the fund is kept separately from other life assurance funds, means any fund representing the amount of the liability of an assurance company in respect of its life business with policyholders and annuitants resident outside the State whose proposals were made to, or whose annuity contracts were granted by, the company at or through a branch or agency outside the State. Where the fund is not kept separately it means such part of the life assurance fund as represents the company's liability under policies and annuity contracts made or granted to non-residents as estimated in the same manner as it is estimated for the purposes of the periodical returns of the company (TCA 1997, s 718(1)). An assurance company may, if it wishes, keep its foreign life assurance fund separately from its other life assurance funds.

Where certain tax exempt securities (securities issued by the Minister for Finance with exemption from tax in accordance with TCA 1997, s 43 and stocks or other securities exempt from tax as provided for by TCA 1997, s 49) form part of the investments of the foreign life assurance fund of an assurance company, the income from those stocks or securities is not liable to tax provided the income is applied for the purposes of the fund or is reinvested so as to form part of the fund. Income from a foreign life assurance fund remitted to Ireland and invested in such stocks or securities is also exempt from tax.

To the extent that income has been relieved from tax for any of the above reasons, a corresponding reduction is made in respect of management expenses. A corresponding reduction is also made in the amount of investment income included in the computation of profits under TCA 1997, s 715 in respect of general annuity business and pension business. Where income is reduced or relieved in any of the above-described ways, there is a similar reduction in the amount of chargeable gains arising on the disposals of the investments in respect of which that income arose. Any losses arising from disposals of those investments are similarly reduced.

12.603.11 Overseas life assurance companies (old basis only)

TCA 1997 ss 726-730 contain special rules for the taxation of overseas life assurance companies. These rules relate to the taxation of investment income, the computation of profits of pension and general annuity business under TCA 1997, s 715, the offset of income tax, foreign tax and tax credits against corporation tax, and the allowance of tax credits in respect of distributions received from Irish resident companies. An *overseas life assurance company* is an assurance company having its head office outside the State but which is carrying on life assurance business through a branch or agency in the State. An *assurance company* is:

(a) an assurance company within the meaning of section 3 of the Insurance Act 1936, or

(b) a person that holds an authorisation within the meaning of the European Communities (Life Assurance) Framework Regulations 1994 (SI No 360 of 1994) (TCA 1997, s 706(1)).

1 Investment income

In relation to investment income, a proportion of the worldwide income of a foreign life assurance company from the investments of its ordinary life business fund (ie, excluding investments of the funds of its general annuity and pension businesses) is chargeable to corporation tax under Case III of Schedule D. The proportion is the amount of the mean actuarial liabilities of the company in respect of its Irish business relative to its total liabilities.

For the foregoing purposes, distributions received from Irish resident companies are taken into account notwithstanding their exclusion by virtue of TCA 1997 ss 129 and 25(2)(a) from the charge to corporation tax. In the case of a distribution received from a non-resident company, an overseas life assurance company may be entitled to an amount corresponding to a tax credit. Any such distribution is treated as consisting of income equal to the distribution and that amount.

The proportion of the income from the investments of an overseas life assurance company's ordinary life business fund which is chargeable to corporation tax for any accounting period is, as stated above, the proportion which the mean actuarial liabilities of the company in respect of its Irish business bears to its total liabilities (TCA 1997, s 726(4)). The proportion is determined by the formula:

where—

$$\frac{A \times B}{C}$$

A   is the total income from the investments for the period;

B   is the average of the liabilities in respect of the company's ordinary life business for the period to Irish resident policyholders and to non-resident policyholders whose proposals were made to the company at or through its Irish branch or agency; and

C   is the average of the liabilities for the period to all the company's policyholders.

The liabilities referred to here are to be ascertained by reference to the net liabilities as valued by an actuary for the relevant periodical return, ie the return deposited with the Minister for Enterprise, Trade and Employment under the Assurance Companies Act 1909, and the Insurance Act 1936. The average of the liabilities for an accounting period is one-half of the aggregate of the liabilities at the beginning and end of the valuation period (the period for which an actuarial report is made under section 5 of the Assurance Companies Act 1909, as extended by the Insurance Act 1936) which coincides with that accounting period or in which that accounting period falls.

In the worldwide investment income that is to be apportioned to the Irish branch of an overseas life assurance company, amounts corresponding to tax credits attaching to foreign dividends received by the company are to be included (TCA 1997, s 726(3)). These amounts are essentially imputation credits similar to those formerly attaching to Irish dividends (see **11.111**).

The amount to be included in profits in respect of chargeable gains accruing to an overseas life assurance company is determined by TCA 1997, s 726(6). This provision is intended to ensure an acceptable level of charge in respect of chargeable gains in the case of an overseas life assurance company that does not invest in Ireland to an extent commensurate with its Irish business and it applies only in cases of such under-investment. The under-investment arises where "the average of branch liabilities for an accounting period" exceeds the mean value of certain assets (see below) for that period. *The average of branch liabilities for an accounting period* means the average liabilities of the entire Irish business, specifically the aggregate for that period of:

(a)   the average of the liabilities in respect of the company's ordinary life business for the period to Irish resident policyholders and to non-resident policyholders whose proposals were made to the company at or through its Irish branch or agency;

(b)   the average of the liabilities attributable to general annuity business in respect of contracts with Irish residents and with non-residents whose proposals were made to the company at or through its Irish branch or agency; and

(c)   the average of liabilities attributable to pension business.

The assets in question are all Irish assets, whether or not chargeable to capital gains tax. It is necessary to include non-chargeable assets for this purpose as otherwise such assets held by the company would not be available to cover a corresponding amount of liabilities with the result that the charge in respect of chargeable gains would be excessive. The assets comprise those assets in respect of which a person neither resident nor ordinarily resident in the State is liable by virtue of TCA 1997, s 29 (land in the State, minerals in the State and related rights and assets, assets used for the purposes of a trade carried on in the State through a branch or agency, exploration or exploitation rights in a designated area, and unquoted shares deriving their value or the greater part of their value from those assets) (see **9.102.2**) as well as assets not chargeable by virtue of TCA 1997, s 607 (government and other securities), TCA 1997, s 613 (miscellaneous exemptions, such as prize bonds) and TCA 1997, s 551 (money or money's worth charged to income tax or taken into account as a receipt in computing income). In relation to TCA 1997, s 551, the intention is to ensure the inclusion of gains from investments referable to general annuity and pension business that are otherwise not chargeable because they form part of trading income.

Where there is an under-investment in Irish assets, as determined above, the amount to be included in profits in respect of chargeable gains for an accounting period is an amount determined by the formula:

$$\frac{A \times B}{C}$$

where—

A   is the amount which would normally be included in profits;

B   is the average of branch liabilities for the period; and

C   is the mean value for the period of the assets.

For example, if the mean value of assets for an accounting period represented 90% of the average branch liabilities for that period, the amount to be included in respect of chargeable gains would be the amount of the chargeable gains arising for the period increased by one-ninth.

The Case III profits are taxable at the "pegged rate", ie at a corporation tax rate equivalent to the standard rate of income tax. This treatment is subject to the qualification that the amount so taxable is the amount of the unrelieved profits or, if less, the excess of the aggregate of the unrelieved profits and the shareholders' part of franked investment income over the NCI profits, as described under **12.603.5** above. The availability of the pegged rate here is in accordance with the view of the Revenue Commissioners although, technically, there must be some doubt that it follows from TCA 1997, s 713.

2 Deductions for income tax, foreign tax and tax credits

In computing the income or gains of an overseas life assurance company in respect of the investment income of its ordinary life business fund for the purposes of TCA 1997, s 726, no deduction may be made in respect of foreign tax (TCA 1997, s 729(1)) notwithstanding the provision in TCA 1997, s 77(6) that income from foreign securities and possessions is to be reduced by any sum paid in respect of income tax in the jurisdiction in which the income arises.

TCA 1997, s 25(3) provides for the set-off against corporation tax of income tax deducted from payments received by non-resident companies. The income tax which may be set off against corporation tax chargeable in respect of the investment income of an overseas life assurance company's ordinary life business is restricted by TCA 1997, s 729(3) to an amount of income tax at the standard rate on the proportion of investment income chargeable to corporation tax in accordance with TCA 1997, s 726(4).

Foreign tax in respect of gains on the disposal of investments held in connection with the life business of an overseas life assurance company is not allowed as a deduction in computing chargeable gains under TCA 1997, s 726(6).

Where an overseas life assurance company receives a distribution from an Irish resident company, and it is not entitled to, or disclaims, a tax credit under the terms of a double tax treaty, it is deemed to be entitled to the tax credit in respect of the distribution that it would be entitled to if it were a company resident in the State. It follows that the income represented by the distribution is the aggregate of the distribution and the tax credit. Any disclaimer of a tax credit available under the terms of a double tax treaty must be made in writing to the inspector of taxes.

12.604 Capital gains tax issues involving life assurance

12.604.1 Introduction

The treatment of chargeable gains of life companies has been discussed in **12.603.2** where it was seen that gains are included in income ("I" in the "I – E" computation) and are taxable at the standard income tax rate. Other features of the tax treatment of chargeable gains of life companies are the inclusion of gains on actual disposals of government stocks, the deemed disposal and reacquisition of certain investments at market value at year-end, the seven-year spreading of certain gains and losses, and the denial of indexation. Other capital gains tax issues related to life companies contained in the Capital Gains Tax Acts, although of little relevance to the taxation of life companies, are outlined in the following paragraphs

12.604.2 Life assurance and deferred annuities

No chargeable gain arises on the disposal of, or of an interest in, the rights under any policy of assurance or contract for a deferred annuity on the life of any person except where the person making the disposal is not the original beneficial owner of those rights and had acquired them for a consideration in money or money's worth (TCA 1997, s 593). A disposal for this purpose occurs on the first occasion of:

(a) the payment of the sum or sums assured by a policy of assurance, including the transfer of investments or other assets to the owner of the policy in accordance with the policy;

(b)   the payment of the first instalment of a deferred annuity;

(c)   the surrender of a policy of assurance; or

(d)   the surrender of the rights under a contract for a deferred annuity.

The consideration for the disposal of a contract for a deferred annuity is deemed to be the market value at that time of the right to receive the first instalment and subsequent instalments of the annuity.

12.604.3   Foreign life assurance and deferred annuities

The exemption from capital gains tax in respect of the disposal of, or of an interest in, the rights under any life policy or deferred annuity contract does not apply to a foreign life assurance policy, basically a policy or contract issued by a company with no "trading presence" in the State, or by an IFSC life assurance company to a person who did not reside outside the State for a continuous period of six months from the date the policy or contract was written. Specifically, the exemption is denied in the case of a policy or contract:

(a)   issued by a company which is not a "relevant company" (see below); or

(b)   which is an "excluded policy" (see below) issued or made by a relevant company to which TCA 1997, s 710(2) applies (ie, whose trading operations consist solely of foreign life assurance business carried on in the International Financial Services Centre or, as respects the financial year 2001 and subsequent financial years, whose trading operations on 31 December 2000 consisted solely of foreign life assurance business).

TCA 1997, s 594(2) provides that in any such case the minimum amount of chargeable gains arising to the person making the disposal in any year of assessment is to be an amount equal to the total amount of any relevant gains accruing to that person in that year. *A relevant gain* is a chargeable gain arising on a disposal of, or of an interest in, the rights under any policy of assurance (including where benefits are payable under the policy) or contract for a deferred annuity which is issued or made otherwise than by a relevant company or which is an excluded policy issued or made by an IFSC company. A disposal for this purpose includes a disposal by a person who is not the original beneficial owner of the rights and who acquired them, or an interest in them, for a consideration in money or money's worth. A relevant gain is to be computed without any relief by way of indexation (TCA 1997, s 594(2)(c)).

For the purposes of TCA 1997, s 594(2), there is a disposal of, or of an interest in, the rights of a policy of assurance where benefits are payable under the policy (TCA 1997, s 594(1)(iv)(I)). Where a policy of assurance, or an interest therein, gives rise to benefits in respect of death or disability, either on or before maturity of the policy, the amount or value of such benefits to be taken into account in determining the amount of the gain is the excess of the value of the policy or, as the case may be, the interest therein, immediately before that time, over the value of the policy or, as the case may be, the interest therein, immediately after that time (TCA 1997, s 594(1)(iv)(II)).

The value of a policy or of an interest therein at any time, for the above purposes, means:

(a)   in the case of a policy which has a surrender value, the surrender value of the policy or, as the case may be, of the interest therein, at that time; and

(b)   in the case of a policy which does not have a surrender value, the market value of the rights or other benefits conferred by the policy or, as the case may be, the interest therein, at that time (TCA 1997, s 594(1)(v)).

The rate of capital gains tax applicable to disposals of foreign life assurance policies is 40%. In this connection, TCA 1997, s 594(2)(f) provides that, notwithstanding TCA 1997 28(3) (which provides for a capital gains tax rate of 20%), the rate of capital gains tax in respect of a relevant gain accruing to a person is to be 40%. With effect from 1 January 2001, however, a new system of taxing policyholders of certain foreign life assurance policies came into effect (see **12.603.8**). Instead of the 40% rate which applies to gains on the disposals of such policies, a new rate of 23% applies in respect of policyholders other than companies; the 25% corporation tax rate applies in the case of policyholders that are companies. In the cases of foreign life policies not covered by this system, the 40% capital gains rate continues to apply.

In the case of a policy issued or a contract made before 20 May 1993, only the amount of the gain on disposal as accrued on or after 20 March 2001 is a chargeable gain (TCA 1997, s 594(2)(g)).

A *relevant company* is a company which is within the charge to corporation tax in respect of its life assurance fund by reason of being resident in the State or, being an overseas life assurance company, by reason of being chargeable to tax under Case III of Schedule D by virtue of TCA 1997, s 726 (see **12.603.11**) in respect of its income from investments of its ordinary life business fund (a foreign life assurance policy).

An *assurance company* is:

(a)   an assurance company within the meaning of section 3 of the Insurance Act 1936, or

(b)   a person that holds an authorisation within the meaning of the European Communities (Life Assurance) Framework Regulations 1994 (SI 360/1994).

An *excluded policy* is a policy of assurance or contract for a deferred annuity on the life of any person which is issued to or made with a person who did not continuously reside outside the State throughout the period of six months commencing on the date of the policy or contract.

Where the chargeable gains accruing to any person in a year of assessment include any relevant gains, the total amount of chargeable gains, after deducting any allowable losses, may not be less than the amount of the relevant gains. Any allowable losses may therefore not exceed the amount of chargeable gains other than relevant gains. The personal exemption threshold will be restricted or disregarded if necessary to ensure the minimum charge referable to relevant gains.

12.604.4   Foreign reinsurance contracts

TCA 1997, s 594(4) contains provisions relating to foreign reinsurance contracts under which a life assurance company reinsures its liabilities (and is therefore an "insured company") in respect of life insurance policies or deferred annuity contracts. A *reinsurance contract* is any contract or other agreement for reassurance or reinsurance in respect of:

(i)   any policy of assurance on the life of any person; or

(ii)   any class of such policies,

not being new basis business within the meaning of TCA 1997, s 730A (see **12.603.6**).

Since profits on reinsurance are included in the new basis of taxing life companies, it is appropriate, in order to prevent double taxation, to remove the capital gains tax charge relating to reinsurance of policies commenced under that basis. That charge is removed with effect on and from 1 January 2001.

A reinsurance contract is deemed to be a life assurance policy for the purposes of the Capital Gains Tax Acts. However, TCA 1997, s 594(4)(c) provides that TCA 1997, s 594(2) (see **12.604.3**) and, in the case of a reinsurance contract with a foreign re-insurer, TCA 1997, s 595 (see **12.604.5**) is not to apply to a reinsurance contract. Instead, TCA 1997, s 594(4)(*d*) provides that gains or losses accruing to an insured company on disposals or deemed disposals (in accordance with TCA 1997, s 720 – see **12.603.2** above) of, or of any interest in, rights under foreign reinsurance contracts are chargeable gains or allowable losses. A foreign reinsurance contract is one with an assurance company that is not within the charge to corporation tax in respect of its life assurance fund.

Effectively a chargeable gain is the excess of the amount paid on maturity of the reinsurance policy over the reinsurance premium. This treatment does not apply to any disposal resulting directly from the death, disablement or disease of a person, or one of a class of persons, specified in the terms of the policy. It applies to the extent that the insured company could receive (other than on the death, disablement or disease of any person, or one of a class of persons, to whom the policy refers) payment on a disposal of those rights the aggregate amount of which would exceed the aggregate amount of payments made by it in respect of those rights. In other words, gains or losses are recognised for corporation tax purposes where the insured company could, apart from payments on the death, disablement or disease of the insured person, receive an amount for the rights which is in excess of the amount payable for them.

In computing chargeable gains or allowable losses in respect of the rights under a reinsurance contract, no benefits receivable by the company in respect of death, disablement or disease are brought into account. Nor is any payment made by the insured company, to the extent referable to any entitlement to such benefits, brought into account as a deduction from the consideration receivable in computing a gain or loss. The computation will include as additional consideration the market value of an entitlement to a payment on the death, disablement or disease of an insured person to the extent that the insured company held the entitlement in place of any return which would otherwise have accrued under the reinsurance contract and increased the consideration. For example, if part of the investment return is taken in the form of free life cover on separate business, there will be included, as additional consideration on the disposal of the reinsurance contract, the value of the free insurance or reinsurance cover.

The above-described provisions apply to disposals or deemed disposals on or after 20 May 1993 of the rights of an insured company:

(a) under a reinsurance contract made or modified on or after 1 January 1995; or

(b) where a reinsurance contract was made before 1 January 1995 and is not modified on or after that date, to the extent that it relates to life assurance policies which were issued on or after 1 January 1995 or which were varied on or after that date (TCA 1997, s 594(4)(*d*)).

Formerly, gains by reference to the excess of the proceeds of a reinsurance policy over the reinsurance premium would have been included in the notional Case I computation only but they are now included in the "I-E" computation subject to the deemed disposal rules and subject to spreading. The provision does not apply to business ceded by IFSC life companies (which are outside the scope of the I-E system) nor to reinsurance contracts with other Irish life companies. In the latter case, such reinsurance contracts will be within the scope of capital gains tax under TCA 1997, s 595 (TCA 1997, s 594(4)(c)), but the standard (income tax) rate tax liability on gains under TCA 1997, s 595 will be offset by a standard rate credit (TCA 1997, s 595(3)(a)).

TCA 1997, s 594(4) is essentially aimed at reinsurance contracts which are based on life assurance policies which can and do mature otherwise than on death, disability or disease, ie policies which have an investment dimension.

12.604.5 Life assurance policies held by companies

TCA 1997, s 595 provides for special treatment in respect of a gain arising on the disposal of a "relevant policy". A *relevant policy* is a life assurance policy or a contract for a deferred annuity on the life of a person, entered into or acquired by a company on or after 11 April 1994, which is not:

(a) a policy to which TCA 1997, s 594 applies (a "foreign life assurance policy", ie which is issued otherwise than by a company within the charge to corporation tax in respect of its life assurance fund); or

(b) new basis business within the meaning of TCA 1997, s 730A (see **12.603.6**).

Since any policy taken out currently would be new basis business, TCA 1997, s 595 is now of little relevance. A disposal of a relevant policy is referred to as a "relevant disposal" and a chargeable gain arising on a relevant disposal is a "relevant gain". A relevant disposal does not include a disposal by a person who is not the original beneficial owner of the rights under the policy and who acquired them, or an interest in them, for a consideration in money or money's worth. Nor does it include a disposal resulting directly from the death, disablement or disease of a person, or one of a class of persons, specified in the terms of the policy.

The provision whereby no chargeable gain arises on the disposal of, or of an interest in, the rights under any life policy or deferred annuity contract does not apply in the case of a relevant disposal (TCA 1997, s 595(2)).

A relevant gain arising to a company is treated as a sum from which corporation tax has been deducted at the standard rate of income tax. The company is chargeable to corporation tax on the grossed up amount of the relevant gain subject to a credit for the deemed corporation tax deducted. Where the deemed corporation tax cannot be set off in this way, it is to repaid to the company. The rule in TCA 1997, s 546(2) whereby losses are computed in the same way as gains are computed is not affected in any way by the treatment of gains in TCA 1997, s 595.

12.604.6 Demutualisation of assurance companies

A demutualisation of a life assurance company results in certain tax consequences that are provided for in TCA 1997, s 588. TCA 1997, s 587 deals with the reconstruction and amalgamation of companies generally while TCA 1997, s 588 is concerned with the taxation consequences of rights which a member of an assurance company carrying on mutual life business receives as a result of a reconstruction to which TCA 1997, s 587 applies.TCA 1997, s 587 (see **9.405**) provides that where under an arrangement between a company and persons holding shares or debentures of the company or any class of such shares or debentures, being an arrangement in connection with a scheme of reconstruction or amalgamation, another company issues shares or debentures to those persons in respect of and in proportion to their existing holdings of shares or debentures, but the original shares or debentures are either retained by those persons or cancelled, those persons are treated as exchanging the original shares or debentures for those held by them in consequence of the arrangement. Any shares or debentures retained are regarded for this purpose as if they had been cancelled and replaced by the new issue.

TCA 1997, s 586 (company reorganisation by exchange of shares – see **9.404**), apart from subsection (2), then applies to the exchange of shares or debentures as if the two companies were the same company and the exchange were a reorganisation of its share capital in accordance with TCA 1997, s 584 (see **9.402**). That section provides that a reorganisation of share capital is treated as not involving any disposal of the original shares or any acquisition of the new holding, the original shares and the new holding being treated as the same asset acquired as the original shares were acquired. In short, the exchange is ignored for capital gains tax purposes at that time while the new holding takes on the cost basis and acquisition date of the original shares for the purposes of any later disposal of that holding.

The rights that a member of a mutual assurance company obtains on a reconstruction to which TCA 1997, s 587 applies are rights to acquire:

(a)   shares in another company (the "successor company") in priority to other persons;

(b)   shares in the successor company for consideration of an amount or value lower than the market value of the shares; or

(c)   free shares in the successor company.

Where such rights are received by a member, they will be regarded as an option (within the meaning of TCA 1997, s 540) granted to and acquired by the member for no consideration and having no value at the time of the grant and acquisition (TCA 1997, s 588(3)). This means that for capital gains tax purposes the reorganisation is ignored and the right and the acquisition of the shares when the right is exercised are treated as a single transaction.

An *assurance company* for the purposes of TCA 1997, s 588 is:

(a)   an assurance company within the meaning of section 3 of the Insurance Act 1936, or

(b)   a person that holds an authorisation within the meaning of the European Communities (Life Assurance) Framework Regulations 1994 (SI 360/1994).

Where a member of an assurance company that demutualises receives shares in the successor company, the cost of those shares is restricted for capital gains purposes to the amount of any new consideration paid by that person. On a disposal of those shares therefore, the gain arising will be computed by reference to the actual amount paid for them. Specifically, TCA 1997, s 588(4) provides that where as a result of the demutualisation the shares issued by the successor company are treated by TCA 1997, s 587 as having been exchanged by the member concerned for the interest in the company which he possessed, those shares will, notwithstanding TCA 1997, s 584, be regarded for the purposes of TCA 1997, s 585(2) (conversion of securities – see **9.403**) as having:

(a)   been issued to the member for a consideration given by him of an amount or value equal to the amount or value of any new consideration given by him for the shares or, if no consideration is given, as having been issued for no consideration; and

(b)   at the time of their issue to the member, a value equal to the amount or value of the new consideration so given or, if no consideration is given, as having no value.

Accordingly, free shares will have a nil base cost for capital gains tax purposes while "discounted" shares will be treated as having been acquired at the actual price paid for them. For the above purposes, *free shares*, in relation to a member of the assurance company, means any shares issued by the successor company to that member in connection with the arrangement but for no consideration. *Member*, in relation to the assurance company, means a person who is or has been a member of it, in that capacity, including a member of any class or description.

New consideration means consideration other than:

(a)   consideration provided directly or indirectly out of the assets of the assurance company or the successor company; or

(b)   consideration derived from a member's shares or other rights in the assurance company or the successor company.

Where a person acquires both free and discounted shares as a result of the demutualisation and subsequently disposes of part of the holding, the disposal is dealt with on the basis of the first-in first-out rule provided for in TCA 1997, s 580 (see **9.401.3**). In practice, it may not be possible to identify which shares were acquired before other shares held and in the circumstances the Revenue will accept computations based on the taxpayer's nomination of the block of shares from which the disposal is to be treated as made.

Where the arrangement provides for the issue by the successor company of shares to trustees on terms which provide for the transfer of those shares to members of the assurance company for no new consideration and the circumstances are such that in the hands of the trustees the shares constitute settled property, the consequences are as follows:

(i)   the shares are regarded as acquired by the trustees for no consideration;

(ii)   the interest of any member in the settled property constituted by the shares is to be regarded as acquired by the member for no consideration and as having no value at the time of its acquisition; and

(iii) when the member becomes absolutely entitled as against the trustees to any of the settled property, both the trustees and the member are treated as if, on the member becoming so entitled, the shares in question had been disposed of and immediately reacquired by the trustees, in their capacity as trustees (ie, as nominees only), for a consideration of such an amount as would secure that on the disposal neither a gain nor a loss would accrue to the trustees and, accordingly, TCA 1997, s 576(1) (deemed disposal and reacquisition at market value) will not apply in relation to that occasion.

The Revenue Commissioners may, for capital gains tax purposes, request information regarding the issue of shares to the members of a mutual life assurance company on the occasion of its ceasing to be a mutual company. The information, to be contained in a return in such electronic format as the Revenue may require, is to be provided within 30 days of the arrangements being effected, or within such longer period as the Revenue may on request allow (TCA 1997, s 588(7)).

12.605 General insurance business

12.605.1 Introduction

General or non-life insurance business is taxed as a trade under the rules of Case I of Schedule D. It is therefore taxed in the same way as other trades but with some differences which result from the application of practical rules rather than because of any statutory provisions.

The main differences in the taxation regime for general insurance companies, as compared to other companies, relate to the treatment of investment income, the realisation of investments, the funded basis of accounting, technical reserves, and branches.

12.605.2 Investment income

Where investment income can be taxed under Case I or under some other Case of Schedule D, the inspector of taxes has the option of choosing which Case is to be applied. This follows the decision in *Liverpool & London & Globe Insurance Co v Bennett* 6 TC 327 where it was held that the Crown were not obliged to assess certain investment income of an insurance company under Case IV or V where they preferred to assess under Case I. The normal practice of the Irish Revenue is to compute income under the rules of Case III, IV or V as appropriate but to assess the income in question under Case I. Receipts brought into the computation of trading profits are properly included on the accruals basis. Certain kinds of investment income will inevitably be received under deduction of income tax. Such income is normally assessable under Case IV of Schedule D on a receipts basis with credit for the corresponding tax deducted at source. Where such income is assessed for any accounting period under Case I at the option of the Revenue, it makes sense to include the amounts received in the accounting period and, in practice, this is accepted by the Revenue.

As regards franked investment income, TCA 1997, s 129 provides that such income arising to a resident company is not chargeable to corporation tax nor is it to be taken into account in computing income for corporation tax. The position is no different for general insurance companies.

12.605.3 Realisation of investments

For the same reason that income from investments would normally be included as receipts of the trade of a general insurance company, profits or gains arising from the disposal of its investments will also be included as part of trading income. The investments subject to this treatment would be those "at risk" or held for the purposes of the business of the insurance company, ie portfolio investments, as distinct from assets held as permanent or semi-permanent investments such as office buildings used by the company or shares in certain subsidiary companies. As regards shares in subsidiaries, the Revenue view appears to be that these may also be regarded as trading assets where the businesses of the subsidiaries in question are not insurance related. Again, the view here is that such shares are at risk in the context of an insurance business. Losses incurred on disposals of investments treated as trading assets are deductible as expenses of the trade.

Although investments held by an insurance company are generally treated as trading assets, an insurance company is not regarded as a dealer in investments nor do these investments constitute trading stock. There is no question therefore of unrealised losses in respect of investments held being deducted in computing a trading profit or loss of a general insurance company (see *AB Ltd v MacGiolla Riogh* 3 ITC 301).

Although not trading stock in the general sense, investments held by an insurance company would appear, following the decision in *Alherma Investments Ltd v Tomlinson* 48 TC 81, to constitute "trading stock" for the purposes of TCA 1997, s 89 where the term is defined, inter alia, as property of any description which is sold in the ordinary course of a trade. In the event of a cessation or transfer of the trade of a general insurance company, the amount to be included in computing the profit or loss of the trade will be the amount received for the investments where they are being acquired by a person entitled to deduct the cost of those investments as a trading expense of the trade being acquired. Otherwise, the amount to be included in the computation will be the market value of the investments at the time of the cessation or transfer.

12.605.4 Funded basis of accounting

General insurance companies may use the funded basis of accounting to defer recognition of profit until such time as the extent of associated claims can be established with reasonable certainty. This accounting treatment is particularly appropriate where significant delays occur in reporting claims such as is the case with marine, aviation and transport (MAT) business as well as long-tail reinsurance business.

The funded basis of accounting involves the creation of a fund for each underwriting year and the allocation to that fund of the premiums written on all policies and contracts written or made in that year. All payments in respect of related claims as well as related management expenses are also allocated to the fund. The fund cannot be closed until the company is in a position to determine the underwriting result with a reasonable degree of accuracy. Any foreseen losses relating to the underwriting year should however be recognised immediately.

When the company's statutory accounts are prepared on the funded basis, this treatment will generally be followed for tax purposes. However, where the statutory accounts are prepared on an annual basis, the Revenue are prepared concessionally to accept tax computations of certain insurance companies on a funded basis. This concessional treatment is confined to IFSC captive insurance and reinsurance companies.

The current concessional practice is for a five year funded basis which involves the recognition of the underwriting profit or loss for any year after five years and the recognition of investment income and related expenses as these arise. For example, in the case of a company commencing on 1 January 2001 to operate the funded basis for taxation purposes, the underwriting profit for the year 2001 would be allocated to the fund in that year but would not be released for the purposes of the company's corporation tax computation until the year 2006. Similarly, the underwriting profit for 2002 would be allocated to the fund in 2002 and brought into the corporation tax computation in the year 2007. Any items arising during the period of the fund but which relate to the period prior to 2001 would be excluded from the fund. Amounts which are not material are ignored for this purpose.

Where it is necessary to translate foreign currency amounts for inclusion in income, amounts that have been deferred under the funded basis should be translated using the average exchange rate for each of the periods in which the income was deferred.

12.605.5   Irish branches of non-resident companies

A non-resident company is subject to corporation tax if it carries on a trade in the State through a branch or agency and, if it does so, it will be chargeable to corporation tax on all its chargeable profits wherever arising. The chargeable profits are any trading income arising directly or indirectly through or from the branch or agency and any income from property or rights used by, or held by or for, the branch or agency. In tax treaty cases, liability to corporation tax in Ireland in the case of a non-resident will depend on whether or not the company carries on a trade in Ireland through a permanent establishment (see **3.107**). The position is no different in the case of a non-resident insurance company. Such a company, however, may have a representative office in Ireland.

An Irish representative or contract office of a foreign insurance company would typically be used in connection with the provision of information and with marketing activities and would not be involved in the transmission of proposal terms for consideration by the company's head office abroad or the issue of policies by the head office. Where the activities of the representative office are confined to such representative activities and other incidental or ancillary activities, the company will not be regarded as carrying on a trade in Ireland and will not therefore be liable to corporation tax.

Where the insurance company is resident in a country with which Ireland has a tax treaty, the question to be addressed is whether the company is carrying on a trade through a permanent establishment situated in Ireland. A permanent establishment means a fixed place of business in which the business of the company is wholly or partly carried on, including especially such items as a branch or an office. Specifically excluded are facilities used only for the purposes of collecting information, for advertising, for the supply of information and for similar activities having a preparatory or auxiliary character. An Irish representative office of a foreign insurance company whose activities would come within those descriptions should not amount to a permanent establishment.

The position would, evidently, be different if underwriting activities were to be carried on at the Irish based office or if contracts were concluded at, or policies issued from, that office. A permanent establishment also includes an Irish based agent of the foreign insurance company who has and habitually exercises authority to conclude contracts in the name of the company, regardless of whether or not that agent operates through a fixed place of business.

An important case in this context is *Sun Life Assurance Co of Canada v Pearson* [1986] STC 335 which involved a Canadian insurance company with a branch in the UK and regional offices, essentially representative offices, in a number of other countries. Sales representatives from the regional offices assisted customers in the completion of proposal forms that were then transmitted to London for acceptance or rejection. The UK branch was held to include the regional offices outside the UK.

As seen above, the profits of a non-resident insurance company that are chargeable to corporation tax are any trading income arising directly or indirectly through or from the branch or agency and any income from property or rights used by or held by or for the branch or agency (TCA 1997, s 25(2). The relevant legislation however provides no guidance as to how the investment income of an Irish branch is to be computed. It might be appropriate simply to take the figures as disclosed in the company's Irish branch records. Alternatively, TCA 1997, s 25(2) might support a case for taxing a proportion of worldwide income and in practice this is the approach adopted with investment income being attributed to the Irish branch in proportion to the level of technical reserves or premiums relevant to the Irish branch.

12.605.6 Provisions and reserves

Insurance companies are required by the regulatory authorities to maintain a minimum solvency margin and to establish and maintain adequate technical reserves. Such technical reserves can be categorised, for company law and statutory accounting purposes, between provisions and reserves. Sums retained by way of providing for known liabilities the amounts of which cannot be established with substantial accuracy are known as provisions. Reserves are sums retained which are in excess of what is reasonably necessary for the purpose of providing for known liabilities. In accordance with long established tax principles, provisions are normally tax deductible while amounts set aside by way of reserves are not so deductible. Provisions and reserves may be calculated in accordance with traditionally accepted practices and will include amounts held in respect of outstanding claims, including claims reported and claims incurred but not reported, unearned premiums, and unexpired risks. Catastrophe and equalisation reserves are also made in the accounts of general insurance companies.

1 Outstanding claims

Accounts of general insurance companies will reflect the amount of claims settled in the period covered by the accounts and will include provisions in respect of claims which have not yet been settled. Some of these claims will have been notified by the end of the accounting period in question while other claims identified will have been incurred but not reported. In all cases, the claims for which provision is made in the accounts should relate to events which have occurred before the end of the period covered by the accounts.

(a) Claims notified

The principle that a provision for a known liability is deductible for tax purposes followed the decision in *Owen v Southern Railway of Peru Ltd* 36 TC 602. In that case, the company had provided for statutory sums due to employees on the termination of their employment. The provisions, being in respect of known liabilities that could be estimated at year end with reasonable certainty, were held to be allowable. The provisions were deductible, although the amounts in respect of which they were made were payable in future years, provided a reasonable method for estimating the liabilities was employed. That principle was approved in the subsequent case *IRC v Titaghur Jute Factory Co Ltd* 53 TC 675 where it was held that an actuarially estimated liability for the cost of future retirement payments to employees was deductible in the year in which the liability arose.

In estimating its likely liability for claims notified but not settled by year end, an insurance company may take account of the effect of inflation on the amount of future settlements, sums recoverable under reinsurance contracts and anticipated expenses of settling the claims. An additional contingency reserve may also be made which, being general in nature, is not strictly tax deductible. Statistical evidence is usually relied on in making claims estimates and this may be supported by industry evidence, particularly in the cases of new companies. The objective will be to have due regard to the requirements of prudence while not erring on the side of excessive caution. Success in resisting some disputed claims should not be discounted. Salvage recoveries should not be ignored. It is incorrect to anticipate future losses (*BSC Footwear Ltd v Ridgeway* 47 TC 495).

In the cases of exceptionally large claims, it is particularly important that provisions are both specific and supportable by statistical evidence.

(b) Incurred but not reported

Provisions for claims incurred but not reported (IBNR) will usually be based on statistical evidence and may include a contingency margin to take account of variations from past experience or as a general reserve. Such provisions are tax deductible provided they are calculated with substantial accuracy but, to the extent that they include a reserve over the amount based on statistical evidence, they will not generally be allowable. A general reserve will not be deductible but a case may be made for contingency provisions computed with a high degree of reliability particularly in the case of long tail business.

2 Unearned premium and unexpired risk provisions

The proportion of premiums relating to a period of risk falling after a particular accounting date is deferred to subsequent periods by way of an unearned premium provision. Where it is expected that claims and expenses in respect of business in force at the end of an accounting period will exceed related premiums, an unexpired risk provision will usually also be made to provide for the anticipated loss. It was held in *Sun Insurance Office v Clarke* 6 TC 39 that a tax deduction should be made in respect of a reserve of 40% of the yearly premiums carried forward in the accounts of the company. The practice of carrying forward a reserve of 40% of premiums became established with general insurance companies following the *Sun Insurance* case but the correct construction of the decision in that case remains a matter of fundamental difficulty and the divergent views which emerged from the decision remain unreconciled.

The view described as the "unearned premium approach" is that the part of the premium relating to the post balance sheet period of the risk is not earned in the accounting period and so need not be brought into account for tax purposes. This view is in accordance with the accounting practice recommended by the Statement of Recommended Practice (SORP) – Accounting for Insurance Business, issued by the

Association of British Insurers and approved by the Accounting Standards Committee. The view taken by the Inland Revenue in the UK, known as the "unexpired risks approach", is that a premium is fully earned at the inception of a policy and that the effect of the *Sun Insurance* decision is that a provision is permissible for the unexpired risks on business written in the accounting period. That would mean that an unearned premium provision is allowable insofar as it represents a provision for unexpired risks.

For example, if an annual premium of €1,200 is received three quarters way during the year, €900 will have been earned in the year and €300 will be carried forward as unearned. If the underwriting is at break-even, claims and expenses of €300 can be expected to arise in the future in respect of the unearned premium. Under the unearned premium approach, a deduction would be allowed for the unearned premium of €300. The unexpired risk is €300 and a deduction of €300 would therefore also be allowed under the unexpired risks approach. Where the underwriting is not at break even, differences will arise depending on which approach is taken. If the loss ratio is less than 100% (where premiums exceed expected claims and expenses), the deduction allowed under the unexpired risks approach will be less than the amount of the unearned premium. The corollary is that a greater deduction would be allowed where the loss ratio exceeds 100%.

The practice of the Irish Revenue is to allow a deduction for provisions included in the accounts of an insurance company in respect of unearned premiums and unexpired risks. The practice of allowing a provision equal to 40% of premiums is probably now redundant what with the current availability of computer generated statistical evidence of underwriting experience and enhanced scientific assessment of unexpired risks.

3 Catastrophe and equalisation reserves

Insurance companies may establish, in addition to technical claims provisions, reserves to meet solvency requirements or reserves to provide against an uneven incidence of claims, especially isolated claims for catastrophic events. These reserves are generally not allowable for tax purposes.

Equalisation reserves do not conform with the tax rule that profits of a period may not be reduced by anticipated losses of a future period where they are designed to balance or equalise the underwriting results from year to year. These reserves are not tax deductible except to the extent that they represent provisions for claims which have arisen; they are not deductible where they are no more than a means of eliminating undue fluctuations in the results of the underwriting business from year to year.

Catastrophe reserves are not deductible for tax purposes where they relate to anticipated future events or, in cases where they relate to the period of risk covered by in-force business, where they lack the degree of accuracy of calculation required for allowability; catastrophe reserves built up over a period of years tend to be of a round sum nature.

4 Deferred acquisition expenses

Under the accruals concept it is appropriate, where unearned premiums are deferred, to defer an equivalent proportion of related acquisition expenses. This is recognised in the SORP issued in 1990 (and in the draft SORP of 1995) which also recommends that the provisions for unearned premiums and deferred acquisition expenses should be calculated and disclosed separately in the company's accounts. The view of the Irish

Revenue is that the deferral of acquisition costs is in effect a restriction on the unearned premium provision since that provision should be calculated net of acquisition expenses. The argument here would be that the portion of the premium covered by initial expenses is earned at the inception of the relevant policy when the expenses were incurred. Otherwise it would be possible to claim a deduction for the full amount of acquisition expenses, including those deferred to a later period, since expenses are deductible when incurred (*Vallambrosa Rubber Co Ltd v Farmer* 5 TC 529). The Revenue view accordingly is that an immediate deduction for deferred acquisition expenses may be taken provided a corresponding restriction is made for unearned premium provision.

5 Discounting claims provisions

In estimating the provision required for outstanding claims, the SORP recommends that account be taken of possible inflation in claims costs so as to determine the amount ultimately required to settle. It is recognised, however, that provisions may properly be discounted so as to take account of the investment income expected to be earned in the period before the claims are settled. The SORP therefore permits explicit discounting (involving a disclosed accounting policy) at the discretion of the company but not implicit (undisclosed) discounting. A similar approach is taken by the EC Accounts Directive where explicit discounting is permitted but subject to more stringent conditions. Thus, discounting would apply only to claims expected to be settled on average at least four years after the accounting date and where the discount rate does not exceed the rate of return represented by the lower of the actual investment income achieved during the current period and the average for the five preceding five years.

In the UK, the Inland Revenue view is that discounting of provisions for long-tail claims is supported by the view of Lord Radcliffe in the Southern Railway of Peru case. Thus, discounting is appropriate for long tail business in order to cancel the effect of inflation in claims estimates so as to arrive at the current value of claims. The counter argument here is that discounting is an anticipation of future investment income although the Revenue would say that discounting is merely an adjustment to a provision for a liability and is not anticipating income. Again, this view would not appear to be in accordance with the conclusion in *Willingale v International Commercial Bank Ltd* 52 TC 242 to the effect that discounts are taxable on a realisation basis only. Although it can be said that the 30 to 40 year period of deferral in the Southern Railway case contrasts sharply with the much shorter periods involved in insurance business and that the event giving rise to an insurance claim occurs at the outset so that a claim can be made at any time, the Revenue in the UK point to the fact that the liability in the Southern Railway case was vested whereas the liability in insurance cases is more remote, being contingent on a number of factors.

In the relatively recent case *IRC v Lo & Lo* [1984] STC 366, an undiscounted provision in respect of retirement benefits was allowed on the basis that the amount provided was not set aside to a specific fund in which investment income would be earned. In *Southern Pacific Insurance Co (Fiji) Ltd v CIR* [1986] STC 178, an undiscounted provision for claims incurred but not reported (IBNR) was allowed based on evidence that the majority of the claims were notified in the twelve months following the period in which the provision was made.

The issue of discounting insurance claims has not to date been the subject of litigation in either the UK or the Irish courts and, while the issue has been controversial in the UK, the practice of the Irish Revenue in relation to discounting has been to follow the treatment adopted in the statutory accounts.

6 Claims handling expenses

Another controversial area has been that concerning the inclusion of claims handling and settlement expenses in the provisions for outstanding claims whether notified or not. These expenses comprise direct expenses attributable to particular claims, for example, the costs of surveyors, assessors and legal advisers, as well as the indirect expenses of running the claims administration department such as salaries, rent, rates and telephone. The SORP recommends the inclusion of claims handling expenses and provides that provisions be included in the period in which the claims occur. The EC Insurance Accounts Directive has now made it compulsory that claims provisions include a provision for both direct and indirect claims settlement costs.

The inclusion of indirect claims handling expenses has been resisted in the past by the UK Revenue insofar as they comprised internal costs, for example, staff salaries as opposed to the costs of using the services of third parties. Such costs, it was argued, should only be allowed on an incurred basis as, otherwise, to allow such costs would be tantamount to anticipating losses. The argument for allowing all claims handling expenses is that they are part of outstanding provisions, that accounts drawn up in accordance with the SORP may reflect this treatment and that the amounts of the provision can be calculated with a sufficient degree of accuracy. Furthermore, the anticipation of an expense relating to an insurance loss incurred within an accounting period is not tantamount to the anticipation of a loss. In the *Vallambrosa Rubber* case, expenses were held to be deductible no later than in the period in which they were incurred and did not have to be deferred under the matching principle, ie they did not have to be deferred until such time as the related income was earned. The decision did not, however, attempt to state that expenses may not be deducted prior to being incurred.

The decision in the *Southern Railway* case would support a deduction for internal claims handling expenses; a contingent liability for future payments to employees was allowed on the basis that the profits for a year would be overstated in the absence of such a provision. Internal settlement expenses will relate to an insurance claim which has been made in an accounting period and, as such, should be brought into that period. The current UK Revenue view on this matter is that provisions for claims handling and settlement expenses made in accordance with the SORP will be allowed and the Irish Revenue in practice also accept that view.

12.605.7 Equalisation reserves

Certain credit insurance companies may take account of a statutory reserve when calculating profits or losses for tax purposes. A tax deduction may be taken for the transfer of any amounts into this equalisation reserve. Transfers from the reserve are treated as income for tax purposes.

Under Regulation 24 of the European Communities (Reinsurance) Regulations 2006 (SI No 380 of 2006), it became compulsory for certain credit insurance companies to create and maintain an equalisation reserve. This treatment has effect as and from 15 July 2006, being the date on which the obligations under the above Regulations came into operation.

The tax treatment relating to the making of equalisation reserves is subject to rules specified in TCA 1997, s 81B(3). These in turn contain references to the *relevant rules*, ie the rules as set out in point D, as inserted by Council Directive 87/343/EEC of 22 June 1987 (OJ No L 185, 4 July 1987, p72), to the Annex to the First Council Directive 73/239/EEC of 24 July 1973 (OJ No L 228, 16 August 1973, p3). The specified rules are that—

(a) amounts which, in accordance with the relevant rules, are transferred to the equalisation reserve in respect of a company's business in a period are to be deductible in that period,

(b) amounts which, in accordance with the relevant rules, are transferred from the reserve in respect of a company's business in a period are to be treated as receipts of that business in that period, and

(c) it is to be assumed that all such transfers as are required by the Reinsurance Regulations to be made to or from the reserve in respect of a company's business for any period are made as required.

Reinsurance Regulations means the European Communities (Reinsurance) Regulations 2006 (SI 380/2006);

Full account is to be taken of all amounts in accordance with the specified rules in making any computation, for the purposes of Case I of Schedule D, of the profits or losses for any accounting period of an insurance company whose business has at any time been or included business in respect of which it was required, by virtue of Regulation 24 of the Reinsurance Regulations, to establish and maintain an equalisation reserve (TCA 1997, s 81B(2)).

Where an insurance company having any business in respect of which it is required, by virtue of Regulation 24 of the Reinsurance Regulations, to maintain an equalisation reserve ceases to trade—

(a) any balance which exists in the reserve at that time for corporation tax purposes will be treated as having been transferred out of the reserve immediately before the company ceases to trade, and

(b) that transfer out will be treated as a transfer in respect of the company's business for the accounting period in which the company ceases to trade and as having been required by virtue of the Reinsurance Regulations (TCA 1997, s 81B(4)).

To the extent that any actual or assumed transfer in accordance with the Reinsurance Regulations of any amount to an equalisation reserve is attributable to arrangements entered into wholly or mainly for tax purposes—

(a) the treatment provided for by TCA 1997, s 81B(2) will not apply to that transfer, and

(b) the making of the transfer will be disregarded in determining, for tax purposes, whether and to what extent there is subsequently any requirement to make a transfer to or from the reserve in accordance with the Reinsurance Regulations, and irrespective of whether or not the insurance company in question is a party to the arrangements (TCA 1997, s 81B(5)).

For the above purposes, the transfer of an amount to an equalisation reserve is attributable to arrangements entered into wholly or mainly for tax purposes to the extent that the arrangements to which it is attributable are arrangements—

(a)   the sole or main purpose of which is, or

(b)   the sole or main benefit accruing from which might, apart from TCA 1997, s 81B(7), be expected to be,

the reduction by virtue of TCA 1997, s 81B of any liability to tax (TCA 1997, s 81B(6)). Where—

(a)   any transfer made to or from an equalisation reserve maintained by an insurance company is made in accordance with the Reinsurance Regulations in respect of business carried on by that company over a period (the *equalisation period*), and

(b)   parts of the equalisation period are in different accounting periods,

the amount transferred is to be apportioned between the different accounting periods in the proportions that correspond to the number of days in the equalisation period that are included in each of those accounting periods (TCA 1997, s 81B(7)).

12.605.8   IFRS

Regarding IFRS, see **3.305**. The following is based on a guidance note on the taxation of insurance companies issued by the Revenue Commissioners in February 2008.

Treatment of interest on gilts:

Prior to the introduction of TCA 1997, s 76A (company profits or gains: accounting standards – see **3.305.2**), certain investment income of non-life insurance companies was taxed on a cash receipts basis even though such income was accounted for on an earning or accruals basis. TCA 1997, s 76A(1) confirms that the accounts basis is now the starting point of the computation of profits or gains for tax purposes: it provides that: "For the purposes of Case I or II of Schedule D, the profits or gains of a trade or profession carried on by a company shall be computed in accordance with generally accepted accounting practice subject to any adjustment required or authorised by law in computing such profits or gains for those purposes". Under IFRS and Irish GAAP, interest from Irish gilts is accounted for on an accruals basis. In the absence of any legal requirement or authorisation providing otherwise, the accounting result should be carried into the Case 1 computation without adjustment.

The amount of interest accrued immediately before the change in treatment should be included in the Case 1 computation but may be regarded as an amount to which the spreading provisions of TCA 1997, Schedule 17A paragraph 4 (see **3.305.6** – *Financial instruments: transitional*) apply.

12.7 INVESTMENT COMPANIES

12.701 Introduction
12.702 Meaning of "investment company"
12.703 Expenses of management
12.704 Deduction of management expenses

12.701 Introduction

TCA 1997, s 83 provides for the deduction, in the computation of profits for corporation tax purposes, of the expenses of management of Irish resident investment companies (including savings banks). The income of an investment company will consist, or consist mainly of, investment income subject to tax under Case III of Schedule D, or franked investment income being dividends or other distributions from other Irish resident companies. As such, the income of an investment company will comprise, or mainly comprise, income in the nature of "pure income profit" (see **4.301**). As such, the income subject to tax will be the actual amount received without any deduction for expenses; the nature of pure income profit is such as to consist of the amount received, which does not require any expense to be incurred in earning it.

It is, however, recognised that investment companies are obliged to incur certain expenses in managing their investment activities and the allowance of such expenses against the companies' total profits is accordingly provided for in TCA 1997, s 83; the allowance of management expenses against the investment income of life assurance companies is provided for in TCA 1997, s 707 (see **12.603.3**).

An *investment company* is defined as any company whose business consists wholly or mainly in the making of investments, and the principal part of whose income is derived from those investments. The definition specifically includes any savings bank or other bank for savings.

12.702 Meaning of "investment company"

In ascertaining whether a company is an investment company, two tests are applied. It is necessary to determine first whether the business of the company consists wholly or mainly of the making of investments and then, if that is the case, whether the company's income is principally derived from those investments.

In the case of *Howth Estate Co v Davis* 2 ITC 74, a company was formed, inter alia, to acquire a large estate in land near Dublin with a view to its management and development, and a life interest in land in England and in investments representing "capital monies" from sales of estates there. The consideration for the properties acquired was the issue of shares in the company and a life annuity in favour of the vendor. The company was held not to be an investment company, not being a company whose business consisted mainly in the making of investments. The decision in that case was followed in *Casey v Monteagle Estate Co v Davis* 3 ITC 313, which also involved a company formed to acquire an estate in land. The company sold part of the estate and reinvested the proceeds in stock exchange securities. For the year which was the subject of the appeal, the main part of the company's income consisted of income from the running of the estate, including income from lettings and leases made and granted out of the estate lands. It was held that the company was not an investment company for that year.

One point which emerges from the judgments in the above two Irish cases is that income from landed property may be treated as income from investment and that the purchase or holding of such property may be treated as investment for the purposes of what was at the time the equivalent of TCA 1997, s 83. The company in each case nevertheless failed to establish that it was an investment company. It appears to have been of some significance that the landed estates were acquired for shares issued (as opposed to acquiring them for cash) and that no subsequent such investments were acquired; in the *Monteagle Estate* case, Teevan J referred extensively to the *Howth Estate* decision and noted that the acquisition of the property there was not an investment in itself and that the company "made no investment for it had nothing to invest".

In his judgment, Teevan J pointed out that what must be looked at is the nature of the operations or functions of the company and that what is sought is not a company making investments but one whose main business is the making of investments. Furthermore, for the year in question, the greater part of the company's income comprised rents and other income from lands in respect of leases and lettings existing before the estate was acquired by the company (as opposed to income from stocks and other securities and rents from leases granted by the company) so that the greater part of the income did not arise from investments *made by* the company.

In the UK case *Cook v Medway Housing Society Ltd* [1997] STC 90, reference was made to the above two Irish cases but the society, which made an investment in houses which it rented at a below market rent, was held to be an investment company. Once the houses were purchased, the company did no more than hold and manage its investment. It was found that the making of investments included the holding of investments.

That an investment company should be in the business of *the making of investments* might appear to suggest that the company must have an active involvement in the making of investments so as to be more than a mere investment holding company. That, however, is not the case. The making of a single investment, acquired for cash, may be sufficient to enable a company to be regarded as an investment company provided its income is mainly derived from that investment and it continues to manage that investment. The decision in *CIR v Tyre Investment Trust Ltd* 12 TC 646, a UK case concerned with excess profits duty, included the finding that "the making of investments" did not require the "turning over" of investments. In this connection, Rowlatt J noted that "making investments" does not mean making profits by the purchase and re-sale of investments. He added that "making" is nothing and that it means no more than investing, that "before you can hold an investment you have to acquire it, in other words, to make it". The precise meaning of "the making of investments" remains less than fully clear. While the turning over of investments is not a necessary condition of making investments, the concept may imply at least some level of activity. This might be satisfied by arranging for regular directors' meetings at which the investments of the company are discussed and reviewed and in the course of which the possible acquisition or disposal of investments would be considered.

In practice, to be an investment company it is not necessary to apply the investment and income tests for each accounting period of a company. If a company is already established as an investment company, the fact that its investment income in a particular period is less than half of its total income (which could happen, for example, because one or more companies in which it has investments did not pay any dividends) will not of itself prevent the company being an investment company for that period. In the *Monteagle* case, the company failed to establish that it was an investment company in the year in which it derived income from investments which it had acquired from the sale proceeds of part of its landed estate. The amount of the investment income for the year was not sufficient for this purpose and the company had not previously been regarded as an investment company.

In the case of *Macniven v Westmoreland Investment Ltd* [1997] STC 1103, the Chancery Division upheld the decision of the UK Special Commissioners to the effect that a company which once had a major property portfolio, but which had wound down and was now inactive and holding only deposits and gilts, had not lost the character of being an investment company. It was not necessary continually to make new investments. (This case subsequently went to the House of Lords but on a subsidiary point.)

It is accepted that a property rental company may be an investment company for the purposes of TCA 1997, s 83(1). While it is difficult to identify precisely what characteristics would render a property rental company an investment company, it can be said, generally speaking, that a rental company which holds more than one property would be regarded as an investment company. A rental company holding only one property but which also holds any other classes of investments in more than nominal amounts (eg, government bonds, quoted shares) would also be regarded as an investment company.

It is understood that the Revenue will not seek to distinguish between the "making of" and the "holding of" investments in the cases of such companies. It would, however, be necessary in the case of a property rental company to show clearly that the nature of the operations of the company is such that it can be accepted that its main business is the making of investments and that the principal part of its income is derived from those investments.

There is no definition of *investments* for the purposes of TCA 1997, s 83. Stocks, shares, bonds, debentures, loan stocks and any similar securities would be included. An investment in land would also be an investment for the purposes of TCA 1997, s 83. This would seem to be confirmed in the *Howth Estate* and *Monteagle Estate* cases and to be implied by the provision in TCA 1997, s 83(2)(a) to the effect that expenses deductible in computing income under Case V of Schedule D are not included in management expenses. A deposit account would not normally be regarded as an investment.

12.703 Expenses of management

TCA 1997, s 83(2) provides that expenses of management which are deductible in computing total profits include commissions, but not any such expenses as are deductible in computing income for the purposes of Case V of Schedule D (see **3.209**). TCA 1997, s 83 does not define *expenses of management* but the term has been considered in some decided cases. In *Sun Alliance Assurance Co v Davidson* 37 TC 330, Viscount Simonds expressed the view that the term "is unsusceptible of precise definition and there must be a border line or twilight area".

The quest for the true meaning of "expenses of management" has given rise to significant divergence of judicial opinion. On the narrow view, expenses of management are distinguished from expenses *by* management and are seen as not extending to executive action. Thus, "expenses of management" refers to expenses in shaping policy and in other matters of managerial decision and not to expenses subsequently and consequently incurred at lower levels of a company's executive structure. That was the basis of the decision in *Capital & National Trust Ltd v Golder* 31 TC 265.

In that case, brokerage and stamp duties incurred by an investment company in connection with changes in its investments were held not to be expenses of management. The same conclusion was reached in the *Sun Alliance* case, which involved management expenses of a life assurance society, but for a different reason. The reasoning in this case was that the expenses involved were really part of the cost of investments being acquired and for that reason could not be expenses of management. A distinction is drawn between costs incurred up to the point at which a commitment is made to acquire an investment and any costs incurred subsequently, the latter being costs of the investment and therefore not expenses of management. The reasoning in the *Capital & National Trust Ltd* decision was disapproved of; Lord Somervell was of the view that the words "expenses of management" would cover expenses normally deductible in respect of its life assurance business if an assurance company carrying on such business was assessed as a trader, and rejected the distinction drawn between the management and the carrying on of the business where management was restricted to the head management.

In *Stephen Court Ltd v Browne* 5 ITR 680, the broader view of the meaning of "expenses of management" was followed. Although that case was concerned with expenses allowable under TCA 1997, s 97(2) for the purposes of Case V, the decision is relevant also to an understanding of the meaning of "expenses of management" for the purposes of TCA 1997, s 83 (see also **3.209.3**). In this case, Justice McWilliam quoted with approval Lord Reid's dissenting judgment from the *Capital & National Trust* case where it was suggested that work performed by a member of the staff of a business, and which may be regarded as an expense of management, should be no less an expense of management where the work is performed by independent qualified persons. For example, if consultants were to be employed to deal with a matter involving value added tax, the related expense would be an expense of management. Justice McWilliam expressed the view that expenses of management are not confined to decision making but extend also to executive action.

The Supreme Court judgment of 20 January 2000 in *Hibernian Insurance Company Ltd v MacUimis* essentially builds on that in the *Sun Alliance* case. The issue here related to abortive acquisition costs (due diligence etc) incurred by the company in relation to a proposed investment acquisition. Judgment was in favour of the Revenue and its effect is to narrow the scope for claiming, as management expenses, costs relating to acquisition and disposals of investments. It would appear that expenses of management would cover expenses involved in, say, reviewing a particular industry sector with a view to identifying specific acquisitions but, once a specific investment is identified, any costs incurred from that point onwards would be regarded as part of the cost of the investment and not as an expense of management.

In the *Hibernian Insurance* case judgment, Murphy J said that it would be impossible to justify any distinction regarding the nature of the costs in question by reference to whether the work done on behalf of the purchaser was carried out before any agreement was reached. The relationship between the disputed expenses and the potential purchases was such as to deprive the expenditure of the character of expenses of management. In his view, the very substantial costs incurred by the group in procuring the expert and specific evaluation of the three investments opportunities involved did not constitute management expenses. He was satisfied that from the date on which the group focused its attention on the acquisition of the prospect of investments, the expenditure incurred in respect of them would probably have been considered to be costs of acquisition of an investment in the event of the purchase being completed and that it would not have a different characterisation simply because the plans to purchase were frustrated or aborted.

The above-described narrow view as to what may constitute expenses of management was not followed in the UK case *Camas v Atkinson* [2004] STC 860. In that case it was held that the correct test to be applied was the "severability" test whereby it was appropriate to distinguish between costs incurred on the transaction which were properly deductible as management expenses and those costs which represented part of the acquisition costs of the asset and that were therefore disallowable. On that analysis, all costs incurred up to the point at which a company makes a definitive decision to acquire the target are deductible as expenses of management (including, for example, the due diligence work leading up to the making of this decision). Costs incurred beyond that point would be capital in nature and would therefore be disallowable. The acquisition did not proceed but, even if it had, the nature of the services rendered would be the same; the fees were payable regardless of whether or not the purchase took place. The position relating to a success fee, which can only become payable if the acquisition proceeds to completion, would be different as such an expense, like brokerage fees, cannot be severed from the costs of the acquisition itself. Unfortunately, the outcome of the *Camas* case, a UK decision, is no more than persuasive as against the binding nature of the *Hibernian Insurance* judgment.

An interesting difference between the judgments of Murphy J and Justice Barron J in the *Hibernian Insurance* case is that whereas the former was of the view that capital expenditure is not deductible as an expense of management, Barron J considered that capital expenditure was not a bar to its deductibility. It would appear (whatever the true position in relation to expenses of management) that abortive expenditure can be capital in nature. The case law definition of capital expenditure (see **3.201.3**) as expenditure "... with a view to bringing into existence an asset or an advantage for the enduring benefit of a trade" might seem to suggest otherwise but perhaps the essential test here is the purpose of the expenditure rather than its eventual result.

The essential difference emerging from the Irish and UK judgments above would seem to be that, whereas the Irish view is that management expenses cannot be incurred once a specific target is identified, the UK view is that the time at which expenses become expenses of acquisition would tend to be at a very late date, possibly as late as the point at which there is a legally binding obligation to acquire. Since in practice most expenses in this area would be incurred in relation to the possibility of acquiring a specific target, with relatively few relating to the carrying out of a general survey of an industry, the impact of the Irish view would seem to be to prevent the allowance of professional costs in most instances.

The expression "expenses of management" should be seen as referring to management in its ordinary sense and includes all the ordinary expenses of management of a company's investments. Thus, in *Southern v Aldwych Property Trust Ltd* 23 TC 707, the expenses of a property owning company in advertising for tenants were held to be an expense of management of the property and it was not correct to restrict the meaning of "management" by reference to its association with the words "maintenance", "repairs" and "insurance".

The expenses incurred by an investment company in issuing debenture stock to replace other debentures and indebtedness were held not to be management expenses (*London County Freehold & Leasehold Properties Ltd v Sweet* 24 TC 412). In *Bennet v Underground Electric Railways Co of London Ltd* 8 TC 475, an exchange loss arising out of the payment of interest on foreign owned bonds issued by the company was held not to be an expense of management.

Commissions paid by a UK company to its German parent for guaranteeing the payment of principal and interest of redeemable loan stock raised by the company were held not to be expenses of management (*Hoechst Finance Ltd v Gumbrell* [1983] STC 150).

Interest will not normally be deductible as an expense of management. Thus, interest on borrowings to finance an investment company's investment acquisitions will not be regarded as expenses of management; such interest is an expenses of acquiring the investments but is not an expense "of management". In certain cases, interest on an investment company's borrowings to finance day to day expenses of running the company, may qualify as an expense of management but any such amounts are likely to be relatively small.

Expenses such as office rent and rates, secretarial expenses, audit fees, and stationery, will normally be accepted as expenses of management of an investment company. In the case of directors' salaries and fees, these will be allowable to the extent that they are considered to be commensurate with the services rendered by the directors (*Berry (LG) Investments Ltd v Attwooll* 41 TC 547). In practice, an amount of 10% of the investment income for the period in question will be accepted as expenses of management. Any sum paid or valuable consideration given by an investment company which is chargeable to tax in the hands of an individual under TCA 1997, s 127 (consideration for certain restrictive covenants etc) is treated as expenses of management for the accounting period in which the sum is paid or valuable consideration is given.

Expenses admissible as maintenance expenditure (for the purposes of the former Schedule A) were held not to be admissible as expenses of management (*London and Northern Estates Co Ltd v Harris* 21 TC 197). Excessive service charges were held in *Fragmap Developments v Cooper* 44 TC 366 not to be allowable as management expenses. Entertainment expenses are specifically disallowed by TCA 1997, s 840(2)(b) in computing management expenses.

TCA 1997, s 83(4) provides for the inclusion as management expenses of any lump sums paid under the Redundancy Payments Act 1967, and allowed to the company under TCA 1997, s 109, and any employer's contributions under an approved superannuation scheme allowed to the company by virtue of TCA 1997, s 774.

In relation to directors' remuneration in the case of property rental companies, the Revenue view is that the remuneration is admissible to the extent that it is reasonable having regard to the services rendered or the duties performed. In practice no objection will be raised to payments which do not exceed 10% of the gross rents. Where the directors devote a substantial part of their time to the management of a company's properties and there is not a separate management charge, payments which do not exceed 15% of gross rents will not be questioned.

In relation to investment companies generally, there has been a long standing Revenue practice to accept as admissible an amount of directors' remuneration which does not exceed 10% of the company's gross income (including franked investment income). It is not intended to disturb this approach in relation to non-rental income. Accordingly, where the income of an investment company includes rental income to which the 15% limit would be applicable, this percentage limit will be applied to the rental income only and the 10% limit will be applicable to the other income of the company.

It is important to note that directors' remuneration within limits mentioned will not be aggregated with other admissible expenses of management, irrespective of whether or not the rental company comes within the definition of investment company in TCA 1997, s 83(1). In other words, the percentage limits of 10% or 15%, as appropriate, are to be applied only in determining the level of directors' remuneration which would be regarded as admissible. Those limits are not to be regarded as inclusive of other expenses of management and neither are they to be applied to other expenses of management.

Example 12.703.1

Wood Estates Ltd is an investment company whose income includes rental income and whose directors devote a substantial part of their time to the management of the company's properties. The company's income for its most recent accounting period is as follows:

	€
Gross rents	300,000
Other income (gross)	70,000
	370,000
Admissible directors' remuneration is as follows:	
Gross rents €300,000 x 15%	45,000
Other income €70,000 x 10%	7,000
Admissible	52,000

Where a property rental company is regarded as an investment company, it will be entitled to claim deductions in respect of any expenses of management which are additional to expenses deductible as costs of management of premises under TCA 1997, s 97(2)(d) in computing rental income. However, in the case of companies which derive all their income from rents, no additional deductions for the costs of management of premises should be due. Accountancy fees would be allowed as a deduction under ITA 1967 s 81 in computing rental income.

12.704 Deduction of management expenses

TCA 1997, s 83(2) provides for the deduction of management expenses of an investment company incurred in an accounting period against the company's total profits for that period. (Despite the wording of the subsection to the effect that the expenses are to be deducted "in computing ...... the total profits", it is suggested that it must be correct that they are deductible *against* those profits: otherwise, for example, the concept of management expenses in excess of the profits "from which they are deductible", as dealt with below, would not make sense.) The amount of the management expenses is reduced by the amount of any income (other than franked investment income) in the period which is derived from sources not charged to tax. In effect, expenses of management are to be deducted in the first instance from non-taxable income.

Where in any accounting period the expenses of management, together with any charges on income (see **4.4**) paid wholly and exclusively for the company's business, exceed the profits from which they are deductible, the excess amount is carried forward to the succeeding accounting period and treated as expenses of management of that period. Where the excess management expenses carried forward cannot be set off fully against the profits of the succeeding period, due to an insufficiency of such profits, the amount unused is carried forward again, and so on until fully used (TCA 1997, s 83(3)).

Example 12.704.1

Fortune Investments Ltd has the following income and expenses for its latest accounting period:

	€	€
Dividends from Irish companies		19,400
National loan interest		3,200
UK government stock interest		1,200
UK dividends		16,200
Chargeable gains (as adjusted)		5,200
		45,200
Expenses:		
Office rent and rates	1,500	
Secretarial expenses	3,300	
Travel expenses	720	
Audit	1,400	
Directors' fees	7,500	
Stockbrokers' fees[1]	850	
Stamp duty	870	
Interest	2,100	18,240
		26,960
Case III computation:		
National loan interest		3,200
UK government stock interest		1,200
UK dividends		16,200
		20,600
Management expenses:		
Office rent and rates	1,500	
Secretarial expenses	3,300	
Audit	1,400	
Directors' fees, say €40,000 @ 12.5%[2]	5,000	11,200
		9,400
Corporation tax @ 25%		2,350
Chargeable gains	5,200	

Corporation tax @ 12.5%   650

Total tax   3,000

Notes:

1   Even on the wider meaning of "expenses of management", it is unlikely that the term
    would extend to stockbrokers' fees. As in the *Sun Alliance* case, these expenses are
    more likely to be regarded as part of the cost of the investments to which they relate.

2   Assume that a limit of 12.5% is accepted. The limit is applied to the company's
    income, including dividends from Irish companies.

12.8 FUNDS AND FUNDS MANAGEMENT COMPANIES

12.801   Introduction: collective investment undertakings

A collective investment undertaking (CIU) is, as the name would suggest, a vehicle for the investment of pooled moneys which facilitates investment in a wide range of company shares. Investors having relatively limited amounts available may wish to minimise their risk by spreading their investments over a large number of companies. The investment of relatively large amounts of "collective" or "mutual" funds is a more efficient means of investing in a wide range of securities than is such investment by individuals or companies on their own who would thereby incur disproportionately high costs, such as minimum brokerage fees, in attempting to spread limited funds over a large number of investments.

In Ireland for many years, the recognised vehicle for the making of collective investments was the unit trust. In the case of a unit trust, the trustees are obliged to redeem the units of any unit holder at his request for the holder's proportionate share of the trust assets. It is accordingly necessary that the value of each unit of a unit trust will approximate to the value of the proportionate share of the underlying assets. This feature is in contrast with the position of an investment trust, which, unlike a unit trust, is a company. In the case of an investment trust, there is no obligation to redeem shares for a proportionate part of the company's underlying assets so that the market price of its shares may vary significantly from the value of its assets.

Because the capital of a unit trust can easily fluctuate, it is an example of what is referred to as an "open-ended" vehicle. An open-ended fund is one which provides for the redemption or repurchase of shares or units, at the request of the investors, from the assets of the investment fund. An investment trust, on the other hand, is an example of a "closed-ended" vehicle; its share capital remains relatively fixed. A closed-ended fund is one in respect of which the investors may not recover their investment out of the fund assets, usually over a predetermined period of time.

Unlike Ireland and the UK, continental European countries did not develop the concept of the unit trust and instead resorted to corporate vehicles to facilitate the collective investment function. The relevant company law permitted companies there to redeem share capital in return for a proportionate share of assets where requested by the shareholders. A company having this feature of varying capital is known as a SICAV. The equivalent in continental Europe of the investment trust (primarily a UK vehicle and relatively little known in Ireland) is the fixed capital investment company, or SICAF.

Directive No 85/611/EEC (the "UCITS Directive") published by the European Union enabled an Undertaking for Collective Investment in Transferable Securities (UCITS) formed in any Member State to be marketed freely in any other Member State. The various Member States of the EU have adopted the Directive as part of their domestic law, in the case of Ireland by SI No 78 of 1989.

The publication of the UCITS Directive was followed by the marketing of UCITSs from the International Financial Services Centre (IFSC) in Dublin. It soon became apparent that investors, who did not welcome the investment constraints under which a UCITS is required to operate, wished to have the opportunity to participate in the types of investment company equivalent to the SICAV and the SICAF in mainland Europe. As a result, legal provision was made in the form of Part XIII of the Companies Act 1990, which came into operation on 1 January 1991. The result was a new legal entity, an investment company not subject to the UCITS Regulations.

In 1994, the Investment Partnership Act 1994 was enacted. This facilitated mutual investment by institutional investors primarily through a form of limited partnership rather than through a trust or corporate vehicle.

12.802 CIU structures

12.802.1 Introduction

A *collective investment undertaking* (CIU) is defined in TCA 1997, s 734(1) and means any of the following:

(a) A UCITS within the meaning of the UCITS Regulations;

(b) a unit trust scheme authorised under the Unit Trusts Act 1990;

(c) an authorised investment company within the meaning of Part XIII of the Companies Act 1990;

(d) an investment limited partnership established under the Investment Limited Partnership Act 1994.

UCITS funds, as the name suggests, invest primarily in transferable securities (see **12.803.4** below). The other three forms of CIU mentioned above may invest in a wider variety of assets.

12.802.2 (a) Undertakings for Collective Investment in Transferable Securities

A UCITS is defined in the UCITS Regulations, ie the European Communities (Undertakings for Collective Investment in Transferable Securities) Regulations 1989 (SI 1989/78 1989) as:

(a) an undertaking the sole object of which is the collective investment in transferable securities of capital raised from the public and which operates on the principle of risk-spreading; and

(b) the units of which are, at the request of holders, repurchased or redeemed, directly or indirectly, out of that undertaking's assets.

Transferable securities are securities in respect of which the right to transfer is unrestricted. A UCITS is free to promote its shares to members of the public in Europe. *Repurchase* means the purchase of shares by a management company or investment company and *redemption* denotes the purchase of units or shares from a holder by a management company or investment company. The requirement to repurchase or redeem units is regarded as satisfied by action taken by the UCITS to ensure that the stock exchange value of its units does not significantly vary from their net asset value. A UCITS may not be a closed-ended vehicle. As provided in the UCITS Regulations, a UCITS comprises any of the following entities:

(1)   a unit trust;
(2)   a variable capital investment company;
(3)   a fixed capital investment company.

(1) Unit trust

The unit trust in Ireland is similar to the US "mutual fund". Unit trusts were originally legislated for in Ireland in the form of the Unit Trusts Act 1972, but were not widely used as an investment medium until the enactment of the Unit Trusts Act 1990, and the implementation of the UCITS Directive. A unit trust operates as an investment fund established under a trust deed between a management company and a trustee. The assets of the fund are beneficially owned by the investors but are held legally by the trustee on their behalf. The fund and its investments are managed by the management company with the assistance of an investment adviser. The management function is sometimes delegated to an investment manager.

The relationship between the unit holders, the management company and the trustee is regulated by the trust deed which also defines the investment policy and sets out procedures for such matters as the issue and redemption of units, meetings of unit holders and the termination of the fund.

The management company may be incorporated as a private limited company and must have its registered office and head office in the State. It must in the opinion of the Central Bank have sufficient financial resources at its disposal to enable it to conduct its business effectively and meet its liabilities. The company must have a minimum share capital of €127,000 (or the equivalent in a non-euro currency) and a minimum of two directors who are Irish residents. It must satisfy the Central Bank that it possesses adequate experience and expertise to carry out its functions.

The trustee has a supervisory role in ensuring that the activities of the fund are carried on in accordance with the law and the provisions of the trust deed. The trustee is the financial institution responsible for the safe keeping and custody of the fund assets. The custodial function may be, and usually is, delegated to a sub-custodian.

(2) Variable capital investment company

A variable capital investment company (VCIC) must be registered as a public limited company and, like any other company incorporated in Ireland, is governed by the Companies Acts but subject to the provisions of the UCITS Regulations. It must in the opinion of the Central Bank have sufficient paid up share capital to enable it to conduct its business effectively and meet its liabilities. If the company does not have the services of a management company, its paid up share capital must be at least €127,000, or its non-euro currency equivalent, within three months of authorisation; otherwise the minimum paid up share capital is €38,100.

A VCIC is free, if so authorised by its articles, to repurchase its own shares provided such shares are fully paid. The VCIC is an open-ended vehicle, ie the company must, if requested to do so by a shareholder, repurchase some or all of that shareholder's shares. Shares repurchased are then treated as cancelled and the company's share capital is reduced accordingly. The articles of the company provide that the amount of the paid up share capital shall at all times be equal to the net asset value of the company; its shares may not have a nominal or par value.

A VCIC must include the words "Investment company with Variable Capital" or "cuideachta infheistíochta le caipiteal athraitheach" on all its deeds, announcements, publications, letters and other documents.

No stamp duties or capital duties are payable on the subscription, redemption or transfer of shares of a VCIC.

(3) Fixed capital investment company

A fixed capital investment company (FCIC) must also be registered as a public limited company and, like any other company incorporated in Ireland, is governed by the Companies Acts but subject to the provisions of the UCITS Regulations. It must in the opinion of the Central Bank have sufficient paid up share capital to enable it to conduct its business effectively and meet its liabilities. If the company does not have the services of a management company, its paid up share capital must be at least €127,000, or its non-euro currency equivalent, within three months of authorisation; otherwise the minimum paid up share capital is €38,100.

The FCIC is similar to the SICAF mentioned earlier. The FCIC is an open-ended vehicle, ie it may, if authorised by its articles, issue redeemable preference shares which are liable at the option of the shareholder to be redeemed, and redeem them accordingly. No redeemable shares may be redeemed unless fully paid and redemption must be made out profits available for distribution or out of the proceeds of a fresh issue of shares made for the purpose of redemption.

Where redeemable shares are redeemed wholly out of profits available for distribution, a sum equal to the nominal amount of the shares redeemed must be transferred to the capital redemption reserve fund. Where the shares are redeemed wholly or partly out of the proceeds of a fresh issue and the aggregate amount of those proceeds is less than the aggregate nominal value of the shares redeemed, an amount equal to the difference must be transferred to the capital redemption reserve fund.

Any premium paid on redemption must have been provided for out of the profits of the company or out of the company's share premium account before the shares are redeemed. Shares so redeemed are treated as cancelled on redemption and the amount of the company's issued share capital is reduced by the nominal value of those shares accordingly. No such cancellation may have the effect of reducing the company's authorised share capital. By far the greater part of the capital of an FCIC is comprised of redeemable preference shares.

An FCIC must include the words "investment company" or "cuideachta infheistíochta" on all its deeds, announcements, publications, letters and other documents.

No stamp duties or capital duties are payable on the subscription, redemption or transfer of shares of an FCIC.

12.802.3 (b) Unit trusts

As mentioned above in relation to the UCITS type of unit trust, the law up to 1990 relating to unit trusts was contained in the Unit Trusts Act 1972, but the Unit Trusts Act 1990, was enacted on 26 December 1990 to cope with demands created by developments in the mutual funds industry. A CIU does not include a unit trust which is a special investment scheme (TCA 1997, s 737(6)(a)); a special investment scheme is by definition an authorised unit trust scheme – see **12.806.3** above under *(a) Unit Trusts*. Neither does a CIU include a unit trust scheme which requires a life assurance policy to be effected as a requirement for participation in the unit trust scheme (TCA 1997, s 735).

12.802.4 (c) Authorised investment companies

An authorised investment company (AIC), formed under Part XIII of the Companies Act 1990, is also similar to the SICAV (and is therefore also a variable capital investment company, but is conveniently referred to here as an AIC to distinguish it from the VCIC, the UCITS version of a variable capital investment company). It is an open-ended vehicle whose capital can be redeemed at will. Its sole object is the collective investment of its funds with the aim of spreading investment risk and providing its members with the benefits of the management of those funds. It can invest in real property as well as in other securities.

Designated AICs

An AIC may be designated (may be marketed to the public) or non- designated (restricted to private investors, and therefore not generally a CIU). An AIC may be designated by the Central Bank as a company permitted to raise capital by promoting the sale of its shares to members of the public. Not being a UCITS, the company's shares may not be promoted freely in Europe. A designated AIC is a tax-free vehicle and is found only in the IFSC.

Companies capital duty is not payable in the case of a designated AIC. Neither are transfers of shares in a designated AIC subject to stamp duty.

The transfer of shares in a non-designated AIC is not subject to gift or inheritance tax provided that, at the time of the disposition, neither the disponer nor the beneficiary is resident or ordinarily resident Ireland and provided that at the time of the gift or inheritance the shares are not situated in Ireland. A foreign domiciled person is not considered to be resident or ordinarily resident in Ireland until 1 December 2004 and then only if that person has been resident in Ireland for the five consecutive years preceding the date of the disposition.

Non-Designated AICs

A non-designated AIC is not authorised to promote the sale of its shares to members of the public and is therefore not normally a collective investment vehicle (see exception below). It may operate within or outside the IFSC. In the latter case, it is subject to corporation tax in the same way as any other company operating outside the IFSC. Where it is licensed to operate within the IFSC, it is entitled to the 10% corporation tax rate.

Companies capital duty is not payable in the case of a non-designated AIC. Transfers of shares in a non-designated AIC (other than shares in bearer form and denominated in a non-Irish currency), whether the company is a limited or an unlimited liability company, are subject to stamp duty at 1% of the value of the shares.

The transfer of shares in a non-designated AIC is not subject to gift or inheritance tax provided that, at the time of the disposition, the disponer is not domiciled in Ireland and provided that at the time of the gift or inheritance the shares are not situated in Ireland.

A non-designated AIC may also be a CIU where it is a specified collective investment undertaking (see below) and where all the holders of units who are required to be non-resident (so that the company may be such a specified collective investment undertaking) are collective investors. This treatment will facilitate the establishment in the IFSC of companies set up for investment by institutional investors on behalf of clients. A *collective investor* is a life assurance company, a pension fund, or other investor:

(a) which invests in securities or any other property with moneys contributed by fifty or more persons:

   (i)   none of whom has at any time, directly or indirectly, contributed more than 5% of such moneys, and

   (ii) each of a majority of whom has contributed moneys to the investor so as to be entitled (otherwise than on the death of any person or by reference to any risk to any person or property) to receive from the investor a payment which, or payments the aggregate of which, exceeds those moneys by a part of the profits or income arising to the investor, and

(b) which invests in the AIC primarily for the benefit of the above mentioned fifty or more persons.

Payment for cancellation etc of shares not treated as distribution

A payment made in respect of the cancellation, redemption or repurchase of a share in a collective investment undertaking which is a company, including an authorised investment company within the meaning of Part XIII of the Companies Act 1990, is not treated as a distribution for any purpose of the Tax Acts (TCA 1997, s 734(9)(a)).

12.802.5   (d) Investment limited partnerships

An investment limited partnership is a partnership of two or more persons and whose principal business is the investment of its funds in property of all kinds. The partnership consists of at least one general partner and at least one limited partner. The position of a general partner would broadly be analogous to that of a manager in a unit trust structure or in an investment company, while a limited partner would be similar to a unit holder in a unit trust or a shareholder in an investment company.

The limited partnership structure is well recognised in the international funds industry. It is found in a number of offshore locations and its presence in the IFSC as a tax transparent pooled investment vehicle exhibits a structure which is familiar to the international funds industry.

Participation in an investment limited partnership is not required to be promoted to the public and the structure is accordingly suitable as a private investment vehicle.

12.802.6 Open-ended and closed-ended funds

The distinction between closed-ended and open-ended funds has already been explained in **12.801** above but may be worth repeating here. An open-ended fund is one which provides for the redemption or repurchase of shares or units from the assets of the investment fund, at the request of the investors. A unit trust, whose capital can easily fluctuate, is an example of an open-ended fund. A closed-ended fund is one in respect of which the investors may not recover their investment out of the fund assets, usually over a predetermined period of time. An investment trust, because its share capital remains relatively fixed, is an example of a closed-ended fund.

12.802.7 Public and private investment funds

Public investment funds include all of the above-mentioned structures apart from the non-designated authorised investment company (AIC) which may not promote the sale of its shares to members of the public. Private investment funds, where public or collective investment is not appropriate, may take the following forms:

(a) non-designated authorised investment company (AIC) within the meaning of Part XIII of the Companies Act 1990;

(b) special purpose investment company; and

(c) investment limited partnership established under the Investment Limited Partnership Act 1994.

It will be seen that an investment limited partnership may be a public or a private investment fund. As with a non-designated AIC, a special purpose investment company (SPIC), which is tax resident in Ireland (but not necessarily incorporated in Ireland), is not a collective investment vehicle but rather an investment company used by the private investor. Apart from the case of a non-designated AIC which qualifies as a specified collective investment undertaking, the tax treatment of the non-designated AIC and the SPIC is the same: the 10% corporation tax rate applies where it is located in the IFSC while the company is otherwise taxable at the standard corporation tax rate.

12.802.8 Non-UCITS retail funds

The three forms of CIU investments apart from UCITS funds (ie the unit trust scheme authorised under the Unit Trusts Act 1990, the authorised investment company within the meaning of Part XIII of the Companies Act 1990, and the investment limited partnership established under the Investment Limited Partnership Act 1994) may invest in a wider variety of assets than is the case with a UCITS. Retail funds established in any of these three forms are subject to a common series of regulations issued by the Central Bank, known as the Non-UCITS series of notices. Retail funds are subject to greater restrictions as regards their investments than are professional investor funds.

Where any of these restrictions is breached, the fund may be terminated or the manager and trustee may be removed and replaced by the Bank. The investment policy of the fund must be clearly defined in its prospectus and the fund must, unless specifically exempted, comply with the general investment restrictions summarised in the following paragraphs.

Acceptable investments

Acceptable investments include exchange traded securities and warrants, in respect of which not more than 10% of the fund's net assets may be invested in securities of the same issuer. Investments in other open-ended CIUs are not subject to this restriction. The restriction may be relaxed in the cases of securities of certain sovereigns and public bodies. Except where a fund invests primarily in warrants (when prominent disclosure of risks in the fund prospectus is required) a restriction of 5% of net assets may apply to investments in warrants.

Investments in cash deposits may be made of up to 10% of net assets, and in some cases (cash deposits with an EU credit institution, a bank authorised by a signatory state to the Basle Capital Convergence Agreement of 1988, the trustee/custodian of the fund, or a bank which is an associated company of the trustee/custodian) up to 30% (see also **12.803.6**).

Investments in other open-ended funds may be made of up to 20% of net assets. The 20% restriction may be subject to derogation if the other fund is established in a non-EU state and investment made through that fund is the only effective means of investing in securities in that state. Sales charges on investments in any related fund must be waived.

Subject to approval by the Bank, a non-UCITS retail fund may have investments in wholly owned subsidiary companies.

Investments may be made in exchange traded and over-the-counter derivative instruments. These instruments must be traded on a regulated market in continuous operation which is recognised and open to the public. Derivative instruments must be economically appropriate to the efficient portfolio management of the fund and may be used only in accordance with the investment objectives of the fund. The fund's prospectus must disclose the intention to use derivative instruments. The trust deed, articles of association or partnership agreement of the fund must specify detailed valuation procedures.

In the case of exchange traded futures and options, there is a general restriction by way of a limit of 10% of net assets on the amount which may be paid or received by way of premium for options plus the initial margin for futures contracts. In the case of transactions in over-the-counter derivatives, initial outlay to any one counterparty may not exceed 5% of the net asset value of the fund and the counterparty must have shareholders' funds in excess of €1.27bn, or its non-euro currency equivalent.

A non-UCITS retail fund may enter into stock lending agreements. The collateral obtained from the lending transaction cannot be sold or pledged and its value must at all times exceed the value of the amount invested. The collateral must be marked to market daily and must be transferred into the name of the trustee, or its agents, until the expiration of the agreement. Collateral may be in the form of cash, government or other public securities, certificates of deposit, unconditional and irrevocable letters of credit and certificates issued by securities exchange clearing systems. Collateral in the form of cash may not be invested other than in government or other public securities, certificates of deposit or letters of credit with maturities of less than three months. The aggregate nominal value of stock lending agreements may not exceed 50% of the fund's net asset value. The nominal value of agreements outstanding with any one counterparty must not exceed 10% of the fund's net asset value.

Repurchase contracts may be effected by a fund only in accordance with normal market practice. The fund must at all times be able to meet its repurchase obligations. Securities obtained under a repurchase contract may not be sold or pledged and their value must at all times exceed the value of the amount invested. The securities must be transferred into the name of the trustee or its agents until the expiration of the agreement and must be marked to market daily. The nominal value of repurchase contracts outstanding with any one counterparty may not exceed 10% of the fund's net asset value.

Unacceptable investments

Investments which are not acceptable investments for non-UCITS retail funds include securities carrying voting rights enabling the fund to exercise significant influence over the management of the issuing body.

Borrowings and leverage

Borrowings of a non-UCITS retail fund may not exceed 25% of net assets at any time. For the purposes of the efficient portfolio management of the fund, leverage is permitted through the use of derivative instruments. The maximum potential exposure through leverage and borrowings may not exceed 125% of net assets.

12.802.9 Professional investor funds

Public funds marketed to professional investors only (funds with an initial investment requirement of at least €127,000, or non-euro currency equivalent, per investor, and which may be spread across sub-funds of an umbrella fund structure) may be established in any one of the three legal forms of non-UCITS retail funds, ie a unit trust scheme authorised under the Unit Trusts Act 1990, an authorised investment company within the meaning of Part XIII of the Companies Act 1990, or an investment limited partnership established under the Investment Limited Partnership Act 1994. For the purpose of the minimum subscription, an institution may pool together investors subscribing less than €127,000 (or its non-euro currency equivalent) as long as the institution provides discretionary investment management to those investors.

The organisation and activities of professional investor funds are, like non-UCITS retail funds, subject to regulation by the Central Bank under the Non-UCITS series of notices but, in contrast with the retail funds, the promoters of professional investor funds have wide discretion, subject to Central Bank approval, in designing the investment or borrowing objectives and policies of the funds. The flexibility of professional investor funds in relation to these matters depends on the experience and background of the promoters and of the investment manager and/or investment advisers.

Super-professional investor funds

In the case of the more recently approved "super-professional investor fund", the conditions and restrictions set out in the Central Bank series of notices, particularly those in relation to investment and borrowing, may be disapplied. This development follows the perceived need for a "high minimum ticket" investment product restricted to high net worth individuals and large institutional investors and which would not be subject to the usual investment and borrowing restrictions that apply in other cases. Investors qualifying for these funds are confined to:

(a)   natural persons having a minimum net worth (excluding main residence and household goods) in excess of €1.27m, or non-euro currency equivalent; and

(b)   institutions owning or investing on a discretionary basis at least €25.4m, or non-euro currency equivalent, or the beneficial owners of which are qualifying investors in their own right.

The minimum initial subscription per investor is the equivalent of €254,000. This subscription may be spread across sub-funds of an umbrella fund structure. Institutions may not pool together amounts of less than the equivalent of €254,00 for individual investors. There is no minimum amount for subsequent subscriptions.

12.802.10 Types of funds

Within the basic CIU structures, a number of investment fund types can be accommodated. These include the following.

A. UCITS fund structures:

Single funds

The most commonly used UCITS fund is the structure in which investors invest in a single fund.

Umbrella funds

An umbrella fund is a collective investment scheme that comprises a number of sub-funds in which investors may exchange rights in one sub-fund for rights in another. In this structure, additional sub-funds may be established at a relatively low cost. Umbrella funds may be operated for both unit trust and investment company structures. In the case of an umbrella fund established as a unit trust the third party liabilities of each sub-fund may be ring fenced from those of the other sub-funds. Such ring fencing is not, however, possible in the case of an investment company umbrella fund.

Central Bank approval of an umbrella fund is dependent on all of the sub-funds falling within the relevant regulations pertaining to investment and borrowing policies.

The charges applying to the switching of investments between sub-funds must clearly be stated in the prospectus of the umbrella fund. In the case of an investment company, the prospectus must also confirm that as between all of the sub-funds there is joint and several liability to third parties.

For capital gains tax purposes, the switching of assets between sub-funds is not regarded as a disposal apart from the case of sub-funds of a unit trust where the switch consists of a transfer to a capital gains tax exempt fund.

Parent-Subsidiary funds

An investment company may acquire investments through a wholly owned subsidiary company whether established in Ireland or elsewhere. A parent-subsidiary fund structure would be useful in gaining access to tax treaty benefits in the case of a treaty between the country in which the subsidiary is resident and the country in which the fund assets are located. For example, UCITS funds which have invested in Indian-based assets have used this type of structure where the subsidiary company is tax resident in Mauritius. (A tax treaty between Ireland and India is currently under negotiation.)

Holding company funds

A fund may invest in securities through the medium of a holding company established in a country outside the European Union where it is otherwise not possible to invest in securities of issuers resident in that country.

Multi-class funds

A multi-class fund is a single-pooled vehicle with different classes of shares for the purpose of providing flexibility as regards such matters as currencies different to the currency of the investment portfolio, and different fee structures. Essentially only one fund, or pool of assets, is involved.

B. Non-UCITS fund structures:

Non-UCITS funds may be established as single funds, umbrella funds, parent-subsidiary funds, holding company funds or multi-class funds, with structures essentially the same as the above described UCITS funds. In addition, the following types of funds may be used.

Fund of funds

A fund of funds is one whose principal investment objective is the investment in shares or units in other funds; ancillary liquid assets may also be held. The fund may only invest in funds authorised in Ireland or in another jurisdiction with investor protection regulations supervised by a regulatory authority similar to that in Dublin or in respect of which the Central Bank is satisfied that the management and custodial arrangements, constitution and investment objectives of the underlying fund can provide protection to investors which is equivalent to that available under Irish law. These requirements may be relaxed in the case of a professional investor fund (see above).

A retail fund of funds may not normally invest in the shares or units of another fund of funds and may not invest more than 20% of its net assets in the shares or units of any one fund, but a 30% limit may be available in respect of one fund only. A retail fund of funds may invest up to 10% of its net assets directly in transferable securities. A professional investor fund may exceed these percentages but on a limited basis.

Where the manager of the fund of funds is also the manager of the underlying fund, or is a related entity of that manager, any preliminary or initial sales charge on subscription by the fund of funds in the underlying fund must be waived and any sales commission received by the manager of the fund of funds must be paid back to the fund. The types of charges and other costs chargeable to a fund of funds relating to the underlying funds must be adequately disclosed.

Feeder funds

A feeder fund is one whose principal objective is investment in another fund. Although a feeder fund may be established as a non-UCITS fund only, it may "feed into" a UCITS fund established anywhere in the EU.

A feeder fund may be used as a single vehicle for investment in another fund. It is more usual, however, for the feeder fund to be one of a number of feeder funds investing into a master fund. The Central Bank will not, as a policy matter, authorise a retail feeder fund if the identified master fund is domiciled in an unregulated jurisdiction where the protection of investors' interests is not provided for.

There must be adequate disclosure in the prospectus of the feeder fund as to the relationship, if any, between the fund and the master fund, including detailed information as to charges and expenses imposed by the master fund. The prospectus and periodic reports of the master fund must be attached to the prospectus and periodic reports, respectively, of the feeder fund.

Restrictions relating to charges and commissions apply to feeder funds as they do to funds of funds. Any sales commission received by the manager of a feeder fund from the master fund must be paid into the feeder fund.

Master feeder fund

A retail or professional investor fund may be authorised as the master fund or as a feeder fund in a master fund/ feeder fund structure. The manager of the master fund must waive any sales charges relating to the issue of units or shares to a feeder fund.

Although feeder funds are specifically regulated for in the IFSC in Dublin, it is not possible to establish a UCITS master fund in any EU jurisdiction (except where such a fund is itself publicly marketed). As regards a non-UCITS master fund, the only form possible in the IFSC at present is the investment limited partnership.

Money market funds

A money market fund is a CIU whose sole object is investment in money market instruments. Money market funds are subject to regulations additional to those applying to funds generally.

At least 80% of the assets of the fund must be invested in short-term securities or deposits, ie with a maturity of less than one year. Not more than 5% of the total fund assets may be invested in companies (other than banks) whose shareholders' funds are less than €1.27bn.

Property funds

A property fund is one whose sole object is the investment in property, either directly or indirectly through securities issued by a company the principal activity of which is investment in, dealing in, or development of, property.

Such investments must conform with the concept of risk spreading and with the requirement for adequate independent controls over the management company. Conditions applying to property funds included the following:

(a)   Not more than 20% of the fund assets may be invested in a single property; for this purpose, property whose economic viability is linked to property invested in is taken into account.

(b)   The fund must reach a minimum of €3.81m within six months of its commencement; otherwise it will be obliged to wind up its activities.

(c)   The fund may borrow up to 50% of the amount of its net assets. Not more than 25% of the assets may be invested in specific properties which are subject to a mortgage. Borrowings may be secured generally on up to 50% of the value of the fund assets.

(d)   The properties must be valued at least twice yearly by a qualified independent valuer.

(e)   The valuation of a property being purchased must be carried out on the basis that it is capable of being disposed of within a reasonable period. The property must be acquired within six months of the date of the report and at a price which is within 5% of the valuation.

(f)   The manager or investment advisory company must have specific property experience.

(g)   The fund prospectus must draw attention to the risks of investing in property and the possible difficulty from time to time of raising finance to meet redemptions.

12.803   Regulatory environment

12.803.1   Central Bank

The Central Bank of Ireland is the principal regulator of the financial services and banking sector in Ireland. It is responsible for authorising and supervising UCITSs authorised under the UCITS Regulations, units trusts established under the Unit Trusts Act 1990, authorised investment companies established under Part XIII of the Companies Act 1990, and investment limited partnerships established under the Investment Limited Partnership Act 1994. The Bank is also responsible for supervising the marketing of overseas based UCITSs into Ireland.

Under a system of published Notices, the Central Bank retains discretion to amend, modify or amplify the published rules which regulate investment funds being established in Dublin. The Notices are updated regularly in response to developments in the investment funds industry. Derogations from the strict application of certain provisions in the Notices may be granted in individual cases subject to the Central Bank being satisfied as to the justification for such derogation and subject to the Bank having the necessary discretion in the particular matter.

12.803.2   IDA Ireland

The Irish industrial development authority, IDA Ireland, is responsible for the promotion of the IFSC internationally and is the body through which all applications for authorisation to establish in the IFSC must be routed.

12.803.3   UCITS funds

Compliance with the UCITS Directive results in the ability of the relevant UCITS to sell its units or shares throughout the EU. An Irish based UCITS fund may distribute units or shares in any Member State without the need to register the fund in each state in which the units or shares are offered for sale. The Central Bank is the designated competent authority for authorising and supervising UCITS funds established in Ireland while the regulatory framework of the UCITS Regulations, which implements the UCITS Directive, forms the basis for the regulation of mutual funds generally in Ireland.

As is to be expected, a UCITS, being by nature a retail fund structure, is governed by extensive restrictions on investment and leverage policies imposed by the UCITS Directive. In 1993, a draft UCITS 2 Directive was published but agreement on its terms was never agreed. A further draft may be published which would incorporate the right of a UCITS to choose a foreign depositary and which would permit a UCITS feeder fund to invest all of its assets in another UCITS master fund.

12.803.4 Investment policies of UCITSs

Investments of a UCITS are restricted to any one or more of the following:

(a) transferable securities admitted to the official listing on the stock exchange in a Member State or transferable securities which are dealt in on another regulated market in a Member State which operates regularly and which is recognised and open to the public;

(b) transferable securities admitted to official listing on a stock exchange in a non-Member State or dealt in on another regulated market in a non-Member State which operates regularly and is recognised and open to the public where the stock exchange or market has been approved by the Central Bank or provided for in the trust deed or in the investor company's articles of association;

(c) recently issued transferable securities for which an application for admission to official listing on the same terms as in either (a) or (b) has been made provided such admission is secured within one year of issue.

A UCITS may invest no more than 10% of its assets in transferable securities other than those in (a) to (c) above. It may invest no more than 10% of its assets in debt instruments equivalent to transferable securities and which are, inter alia, transferable, liquid and of a value which can be accurately determined at any time or at least regularly, being in most cases at least twice a month. The total of investments referred to in this paragraph may not under any circumstances amount to more than 10% of the assets of the UCITS.

An investment company may acquire real and personal property which is required for the purpose of its business. A UCITS may not acquire either precious metals or certificates representing them.

A UCITS may hold ancillary liquid assets and may employ techniques and instruments relating to transferable securities subject to the restrictions set out in the UCITS Regulations.

The objective of the UCITS Regulations is to ensure a spread of investment risk. For this purpose, the Regulations may restrict the proportion of the assets of a fund that may be invested with any one issuer, by restricting the proportion of any one issue which a UCITS may take up, and by restricting the level of control which a management company may exercise over the markets.

A UCITS is generally prohibited from investing more than 10% of its assets in transferable securities issued by the same body. The total value of transferable securities held by it in the issuing bodies in each of which it invests more than 5% of its assets may not exceed 40% of the value of its assets. There are relaxations to these limits:

(a) the limit of 10% is increased to 35% in the case of investments by the UCITS in transferable securities issued or guaranteed by an EU Member State, by its local authorities, by a non-Member State or by public international bodies of which one or more Member States are members. These securities are disregarded in applying the 40% limit;

(b) a UCITS may invest up to 25% of its assets in bonds issued by a credit institution whose registered office is in a Member State and which is subject by law to special public supervision designed to protect bondholders. Where the UCITS invests more than 5% of its assets in such bonds issued by one issuer, their total value may not exceed 80% of the value of the assets of the UCITS. These securities are also disregarded in applying the 40% limit.

If the Central Bank is satisfied that unit holders have protection equivalent to that resulting from the above described limits, it may authorise a UCITS to invest up to 100% of its assets in different transferable securities issued or guaranteed by any EU Member State or its local authorities, by any non-Member State or by any of the public international bodies of which one or more Member States are members, provided the UCITS:

(i)   holds securities from at least six different issues where the securities from any one issue do not account for more than 30% of its total assets;

(ii)   specifies in its trust deed or articles the names of the States, local authorities or public international bodies issuing or guaranteeing securities in which it intends to invest more than 35% of its assets; and

(iii)   includes a prominent statement in its prospectus and any promotional literature drawing attention to the Bank's authorisation and indicating the States, local authorities and public international bodies in the securities of which it intends to invest or has invested more than 35% of its assets.

A UCITS may invest a maximum of 5% of its assets in the units of other UCITSs. Investment in the units of a unit trust managed by the same or a connected management company is permitted only where the unit trust, in accordance with its trust deed, has specialised in investment in a specific geographical area or economic sector, and provided the investment has been authorised by the Bank. The Bank will only authorise such investment if the unit trust has announced its intention to make such investment in its trust deed.

An investment company or a management company acting in connection with all of the UCITSs which are unit trusts which it manages may not acquire any voting shares which would enable it to exercise significant influence over the management of the issuing body.

A UCITS may not acquire more than:

(a)   10% of the non-voting shares of any single issuing body;

(b)   10% of the debt securities of any single issuing body;

(c)   10% of the units of any single UCITS.

12.803.5 UCITS: borrowings and other matters

Generally, neither an investment company nor a management company or trustee acting on behalf of a unit trust may borrow money. A UCITS may, however, borrow up to 10% of its assets (investment company) or of the value of the fund (unit trust) provided the borrowing is on a temporary basis. An investment company may borrow up to 10% of its assets to facilitate the acquisition of real property required for the purposes of its business but provided the total borrowing referred to in this paragraph does not exceed 15% of the company's assets.

A UCITS may acquire foreign currency by means of a "back to back" loan.

Neither an investment company nor a management company or trustee acting on behalf of a unit trust may grant loans or act as guarantor on behalf of third parties but this does not prevent such undertakings from acquiring transferable securities which are not fully paid.

Neither an investment company nor a management company or trustee acting on behalf of a unit trust may sell transferable securities which it does not own.

12.803.6 Non-UCITS investment policies

In the cases of non-UCITS unit trusts and designated authorised investment companies (AICs), the Central Bank obliges managers to follow the principles of risk spreading, by regulating the permitted bodies in which investments may be made, by limiting the size of the investments and by regulating the proportion of any issue which may be taken up by a fund. The control of a manager over a company or institution in which investments are made is also restricted. A non-designated AIC is not subject to any investment restrictions but the Bank reserves the right to comment on the company's investment and borrowing policies. The following limits apply:

(a) Not more than 10% of the assets of the undertaking may be invested in securities which are not traded in a market approved by the Bank or in a market which is not specifically mentioned in the memorandum and articles or trust deed of the undertaking.

(b) Not more than 10% of the assets of the undertaking may be invested in securities or deposits with the same body. That limit is 30%, however, where the funds are maintained with a credit institution whose registered office is in a Member State, a bank authorised in an EFTA state, a bank authorised by a state which is a signatory to the Basle Capital Conveyance Agreement of July 1988 or, on a case by case basis, with a bank which is an associated company of an approved trustee.

(c) Not more than 10% of a particular issue of securities, or of an issue of a similar nature by the same body, may be acquired by the undertaking.

(d) Up to 100% of the assets of the undertaking may be invested in different transferable securities issued or guaranteed by any state, its constituent states, its local authorities, or by public international bodies of which one or more states are members.

(e) Up to 20% of the assets of an undertaking may be invested in units of other CIUs but, where that investment is made in a CIU managed by the same or a connected company, no fees or costs may be charged to the undertaking. Any commission received by the manager must be paid into the assets of the undertaking.

(f) The Bank may in certain circumstances relax some of the above limits if an investment could not otherwise be made in the securities of a particular country.

(g) An investment company or a management company, acting in connection with all of the schemes which it manages, may not acquire any voting shares which would enable it to exercise significant influence over the management of an investment.

An undertaking may be permitted by the Bank to engage in futures and options contracts and stock lending and repurchase agreements in the interests of efficient portfolio management. Techniques may also be employed to reduce the exposure of the assets of the undertaking to foreign exchange risk. Any proposal to use such techniques must be disclosed in the prospectus and the manner in which they were utilised must be explained in the periodic reports to the Bank.

The following conditions apply generally in relation to the use of futures and options contracts:

(i)   Futures and options may only be used in accordance with the investment objectives of the undertaking and only where the transactions are conducted on an organised exchange.

(ii) Futures and options may not, generally, be used for the purpose of gearing the fund. Uncovered put and call options may, however, be purchased provided their exercise value does not exceed 10% of the net assets of the undertaking.

(iii) The exercise value of put and call options and futures contracts must, except as provided above, be held by the undertaking in cash or liquid assets with a maturity of no more than three months.

(iv) The undertaking may use index put and call options contracts.

(v)   The total premium paid or received for an option, or the initial margin paid for a futures contract, may not exceed 10% of the net asset value of the undertaking.

(vi) The security which is the subject of an options contract must remain at all times in the ownership of the undertaking. This condition may be satisfied in the case of a futures contract through the holding of assets of equal value whose prices can reasonably be expected to move in line with the assets which are the subject of the contract.

12.803.7   Management company

Effective control and management of a CIU is provided by the management company. Its functions include the drafting, filing and issuing of the prospectus, the raising of funds and their vesting in the trustee/custodian, the provision or procurement of investment advice, the administration of the sale and redemption of units/shares, the valuation of the fund assets and units/shares, the preparation of the annual report and accounts, the maintenance of books of account, the updating of the prospectus, the marketing of units/shares, and compliance on behalf of the CIU with all relevant regulatory and legal requirements.

The day to day operations of a unit trust are carried out by a management company. An investment company normally delegates its management functions to the management company in return for an annual fee. The management of an investment limited partnership is, however, conducted by one or more of the general partners.

A management company must have a minimum paid up share capital of €127,000, or its non-euro currency equivalent. At least two directors of the management company must be Irish resident. Adequate information as to the expertise and reputation of the proposed directors and managers must be provided to the Bank. The names of the company secretary and of the shareholders must be furnished. The management company is required to submit annual and half-yearly audited accounts to the Bank. In addition, the Bank requires the submission to it of annual audited accounts of the shareholders in the management company and, where relevant, the investment adviser. The management company must be incorporated in the State or under the law of a

Member State of the EU. It must have sufficient financial resources at its disposal to conduct its business effectively and to meet its liabilities. It is required to satisfy the Central Bank that it is a suitable body for the purpose of performing its functions as required by law. The activities of a management company are restricted to the management of units trusts and investment companies and such ancillary activities as would enable it to administer its own assets. A management company may not also act as trustee in relation to a CIU. Although they may be under common control, the management company and the trustee must act independently and solely in the interests of the unit holders or shareholders.

A management company may delegate certain of its functions to third parties. Any application for authorisation as a CIU must include information concerning the name of any entity which has been contracted by the management company to carry out its functions, together with copies of the relevant agreements. Adequate information regarding any such third party must be furnished to satisfy the Bank as to its expertise, integrity and adequacy of financial resources.

A management company may delegate or subcontract its investment advisory function to an investment adviser. In that event, the Bank must be informed as to the name of the adviser, information as to its expertise, integrity and adequacy of financial resources, its the latest audited accounts, details of its overseas regulatory status, if any, and a copy of the investment advisory agreement.

12.803.8   Trustee/custodian

The assets of a CIU must be entrusted to a trustee/custodian for safe keeping except where the Central Bank has expressly waived this requirement. Provision for the safe keeping of the assets must be made in the trust deed (unit trust), articles of association (investment company) or partnership agreement (investment limited partnership). The assets of a unit trust are beneficially owned by the unit holders but are held in the name of the trustee/custodian. In the case of an investment company or limited partnership, the assets are beneficially owned by the company or partnership and are held in the name of the custodian.

A trustee/custodian must be a body corporate incorporated in the State or under the laws of any other Member State of the EU. Additionally, it must be:

(a)   a bank licensed in the State;

(b)   a company which is wholly owned and which has its liabilities guaranteed by such a licensed bank; or

(c)   a company which has been granted a certificate under TCA 1997, s 446 to trade from the IFSC and which is:

   (i)   wholly owned by an EU credit institution being an undertaking whose business it is to receive deposits from the public and to grant credit for its own account,

   (ii)   wholly owned by an institution in a non-Member State which is deemed by the Bank to be the equivalent of an EU credit institution, or

   (iii)   wholly owned by an institution or company which is deemed by the Bank to be an institution or company which provides unit holders or shareholders with protection equivalent to that provided by any of the above mentioned institutions.

A trustee/custodian, or its parent company which guarantees its liabilities, must have a minimum paid up share capital of €6.35m, or its non-euro currency equivalent. The trustee/ custodian must satisfy the Bank that it has the appropriate expertise and experience to carry out its functions, which are summarised as follows. The trustee/ custodian must:

(a) ensure that the sale, issue, repurchase, redemption and cancellation of units or shares effected on behalf of the CIU are carried out in accordance with the UCITS Regulations, the Unit Trusts Act 1990, the Investment Limited Partnership Act 1994, or Part XIII of the Companies Act 1990, as the case may be, in accordance with any conditions imposed by the Bank, and in accordance with the trust deed, memorandum and articles of association or partnership agreement, as the case may be;

(b) respect any other obligations imposed by the UCITS Regulations, Unit Trusts Act 1990, the Investment Limited Partnership Act 1994, or Part XIII of the Companies Act 1990, or by the Bank;

(c) ensure that the value of units or shares is calculated in accordance with the UCITS Regulations (in the case of a UCITS), the trust deed (units trust) or memorandum and articles of association (investment company) or partnership agreement (investment limited partnership);

(d) ensure that the income of the CIU is applied in accordance with the UCITS Regulations, trust deed, the Investment Limited Partnership Act 1994 or the partnership agreement, or the memorandum and articles of association, as appropriate;

(e) ensure that any consideration arising in connection with transactions involving the assets of the CIU is remitted to it within the time limits which are acceptable market practice in relation to the transactions in question;

(f) carry out the instructions of the management company of general partner, as appropriate, unless they are in conflict with the UCITS Regulations, the Unit Trusts Act 1990, the Investment Limited Partnership Act 1994, the trust deed or the partnership agreement;

(g) enquire into the conduct of the management company, general partner or investment company, as appropriate, in each annual accounting period and report thereon to the unit holders or shareholders. The report must be delivered to the management company, general partner or investment company in good time to enable that body to include a copy of the report in its annual report. The report of the trustee/custodian must state whether in its opinion the CIU has been managed in the period:

(i) in accordance with the limitations imposed on the investment and borrowing powers of the management company or investment company and the trustee/custodian by the trust deed, partnership agreement or memorandum and articles of association and by the Bank under the powers granted to it under the UCITS Regulations, the Unit Trusts Act 1990, the Investment Limited Partnership Act 1994 and Part XIII of the Companies Act 1990,

(ii)   otherwise in accordance with the provisions of the trust deed or memorandum and articles of association, partnership agreement and UCITS Regulations, the Unit Trusts Act 1990, the Investment Limited Partnership Act 1994 or Part XIII of the Companies Act 1990,

and if not, the trustee/custodian should state why this is the case and outline the steps taken by it to rectify the situation,

(h)   transmit to the Bank any information and returns which the Bank considers it necessary to receive.

The following additional supervisory requirements are imposed on trustees/custodians by the Bank:

1. The trust deed or custodian agreement must state that the trustee/custodian will indemnify the management company or investment company and the unit holders or shareholders for any loss suffered by them resulting from its unjustifiable failure to perform its obligations or its improper performance of them. This liability may be enforced by the unit holders or shareholders either directly or indirectly through the management company depending on the legal relationship between the trustee/custodian, the management company and the unit holders or shareholders.

2. In the case of an investment limited partnership, the custodian agreement must provide that the custodian will be liable to the general partner(s) for any loss suffered by them resulting from its unjustifiable failure to perform its obligations or its improper performance of them.

3. The trust deed, in the case of a unit trust, or custodian agreement in the case of an investment company or investment limited partnership, must state that the liability of the trustee or custodian will not be affected by the fact that it has entrusted some or all of the assets to a third party for safe keeping.

4. No single company may act as both trustee/custodian and management company, general partner or investment company.

5. The trustee/custodian and the management company, general partner or investment company must act independently and solely in the interests of the unit holders or shareholders. A trustee/custodian may nevertheless, subject to certain conditions set out in Central Bank Notices, have a parent company in common with a management company or general partner.

6. A trustee/custodian may not carry out sales of transferable securities when such securities are not in the ownership of the CIU.

7. The trustee/custodian may issue registered certificates or bearer securities, representing one or more portions of the scheme, or, in accordance with the provisions of the trust deed, partnership agreement or memorandum and articles of association, may issue written confirmations of entry in the register of units or shares or fractions of units or shares without limitation as to the splitting-up of units or shares.

Any provision in the trust deed of a unit trust which would exempt or indemnify the trustee/custodian from or against liability for breach of trust will be void where it fails to show the degree of care and diligence required of it as trustee/custodian. A release may nevertheless be given to a trustee/custodian in respect of anything done or omitted to be done by it, or a provision may be included enabling such a release to be given, with the agreement of unit holders or shareholders holding not less than 75% in value of the units or shares in issue.

12.804   Taxation of management companies and custodians

Management companies and companies acting as trustees/custodians in relation to CIUs, and accordingly established in the IFSC or Shannon, are entitled to be taxed at the effective 10% rate of corporation tax in respect of their income from fees, commissions and other charges. TCA 1997, s 446 provides that the Minister for Finance may give a certificate to a company (a "qualified company") certifying that such trading operations of a company as are specified in the certificate are "relevant trading operations" (see **7.206.3**).

Relevant trading operations are regarded as the manufacture within the State of goods and any amount receivable in respect of anything sold or any services rendered in the course of those operations are regarded, for the purposes of manufacturing relief (see **7.202**), as an amount receivable from the sale of goods. *Relevant trading operations* means trading operations carried on by a qualified company in the IFSC within the Custom House Docks Area (CHDA) in Dublin and includes (see TCA 1997, s 446(7)(c)) the carrying on on behalf of persons not ordinarily resident in the State of international financial activities, including:

(a)   the management of investments and other activities of a specified collective investment collective undertaking (see **12.805**) or, where at any time after 31 March 2000 the specified collective investment undertaking becomes an in investment undertaking (see **12.806.3**), the management of and other activities of that investment undertaking (see below);

(b)   the provision for persons not ordinarily resident in the State of services of, or facilities for, processing, control, accounting, communication, clearing, settlement or information storage in relation to financial activities; and

(c)   trading operations which, though not provided for persons not ordinarily resident in the State, are similar to or ancillary to financial activities which are so provided and in regard to which the Minister for Finance is of the opinion that they contribute to the use of the CHDA as an international financial services centre.

Clearly, a company which manages a CIU which is a specified collective investment undertaking will qualify for the 10% corporation tax rate under (a) above, provided it has received the necessary certificate from the Minister for that purpose. A company which manages a CIU other than a specified collective investment undertaking would qualify under (b) or possibly (c). For the purposes of (b), although the CIU which is being managed will usually be Irish resident, the fact that the unit holders or shareholders are not so resident will be taken as satisfying the condition that the services are being provided for persons not ordinarily resident in the State.

TCA 1997, s 446(2A) makes special provision for a case in which, on 31 March 2000, the business of a qualifying management company is the managing of the activities or the whole or part of the assets of a specified collective investment undertaking (SCIU) and, at any time after that date, the SCIU ceases to be a SCIU but is an investment undertaking within the meaning of TCA 1997, s 739B (see **12.806.3**). The business at that time, to the extent that the management can be directly attributed to be for the benefit of unit holders (within the meaning of TCA 1997, s 739B – see **12.806.4**) in the investment undertaking who are persons resident outside the State, is deemed to be relevant trading operations and to have been specified as such in the certificate given to the management company. For this purpose, such apportionment as is just and reasonable may be made of any profits arising to the management company.

In the same vein, by virtue of TCA 1997, s 446(7)(c)(ii)(V)(B), "relevant trading operations" includes the carrying on on behalf of persons not ordinarily resident in the State of international financial activities consisting of the management of the activities or the whole or part of the assets of an investment undertaking to the extent that the management can be directly attributed to be for the benefit of unit holders in the investment undertaking who are persons resident outside the State. For this purpose, such apportionment as is just and reasonable may be made of any profits arising to a qualified company.

The definition of *qualifying management company* in TCA 1997, s 734(1) in relation to a CIU envisages such a company as being a qualified company for the purposes of the 10% corporation tax rate. It means a qualified company (basically a 10% taxed Shannon or IFSC company) which in the course of relevant trading operations (ie, as specified in a certificate given by the Minister for Finance) manages the whole or any part of the investments and other activities of the business of a CIU. For this purpose, the 31 December 2005 or, as the case may be, 31 December 2002, termination date which applies to IFSC and Shannon financial services operations is assumed not to apply to qualifying management companies in so far as this is relevant to the meaning of a specified collective investment undertaking (see **12.805.2**). In so far as the management company itself is concerned, however, the 31 December 2005 or 31 December 2002 termination date remains.

The position for companies acting as custodians would broadly be similar to that described above in relation to management companies.

Where the company is established in Shannon Airport, eligibility for the 10% corporation tax rate derives from TCA 1997, s 445. *Relevant trading operations* for the purposes of that section includes (see TCA 1997, s 445(7)(b)) trading operations which are regarded as contributing to the use or development of the airport and which are certified to that effect in a certificate given by the Minister for Finance.

The requirement in TCA 1997, s 246(2) to withhold income tax at the standard rate from interest paid to non-residents does not apply to such interest paid by a company in the course of carrying on international financial services activities in the CHDA or Shannon (see **4.305**).

The disposal of shares held by non-residents in a management or custodian company will not result in a liability to capital gains tax since the greater part of the value of such shares at any time will not be derived from land in the State (see **9.102.2**).

The value added tax (VAT) position of fund managers/ administrators and trustee/ custodians is not entirely clear but, in general, services provided by a management or administrator company to Irish investment funds are exempt from VAT. Although safe custody services are not exempt from VAT, where these services are provided in the context of an overall trustee service, including the safe-keeping of assets, collection of dividends and interest etc, the trustee service will in practice be VAT exempt.

12.805 Taxation of collective investment companies

12.805.1 Introduction

The taxation treatment of a CIU depends on whether or not it is a specified collective investment undertaking (SCIU – see **12.805.2** below). For CIUs which are not SCIUs, the tax treatment up to 5 April 1994 was not much different to that for SCIUs in that they were not subject to tax on their income and gains. The tax exemption was removed for these "domestic" CIUs with effect from 6 April 1994 with exemption on a transitional basis up to 5 April 1998 being extended to certain CIUs established on or before 24 May 1993. From 6 April 1994, the tax treatment of SCIUs is dealt with in TCA 1997, s 734 while the tax treatment of other CIUs (including, principally, "undertakings for collective investment") is governed mainly by TCA 1997, s 738. A non-designated AIC is not (subject to one exception) a CIU as it is not authorised to promote the sale of its shares to members of the public (see **12.802.4**). A non-designated AIC is eligible for the 10% corporation tax rate where it is licensed to carry on business within the IFSC; otherwise it is subject to corporation tax at the standard corporation tax rate.

A *unit* in relation to a CIU is defined as including any investment, such as a subscription for shares or a contribution of capital, in the CIU, giving the holder of the unit an entitlement to a share of the investments or relevant profits (see below) of, or to receive a distribution from, the CIU. References to a *unit holder* are accordingly references to a person holding units or, in the case of a company which is a CIU, shares who is thereby entitled to a share of any of the investments or relevant profits of, or to receive a distribution from, the CIU.

The definition of "relevant payment" is important in relation to the tax treatment of CIUs and their unit holders. A *relevant payment* means a payment made to a unit holder by a CIU by reason of rights conferred on the unit holder as a result of holding a unit or units in the CIU, other than a payment made in respect of the cancellation, redemption or repurchase of a unit.

Also important are the definitions of "relevant income" and "relevant gains" which together comprise the *relevant profits* in relation to a CIU. *Relevant income* means any amounts of income, profits or gains which arise to, or are receivable by a CIU being amounts of income, profits or gains:

(a) which are, or are to be, paid to unit holders as relevant payments; or

(b) out of which relevant payments are, or are to be, made to unit holders; or

(c) which are, or are to be, accumulated for the benefit of, or invested in transferable securities for the benefit of, unit holders,

and which would be taxable as income if they arose to an individual resident in the State.

Relevant gains means gains accruing to a CIU being gains which would constitute chargeable gains in the hands of a person resident in the State.

12.805.2 Specified collective investment undertakings

TCA 1997, s 734 provides for the taxation of collective investment undertakings. In that section, definitions of "collective investment undertaking" (see **12.802.1**) and "specified collective investment undertaking" are provided. A specified collective investment undertaking (SCIU) is, evidently, a form of collective investment undertaking (CIU). As already seen above, the tax treatment of all CIUs up to 5 April 1994 was broadly similar in that they were not subject to tax on their income and gains. From 6 April 1994, however, the tax exemption no longer applies to CIUs which are not SCIUs. TCA 1997, s 734 contains certain provisions dealing with CIUs (which accordingly apply to SCIUs) and certain other provisions which apply only to SCIUs. From 6 April 1994, TCA 1997, s 734, apart from subsections (7)-(9) of that section (see below), applies to SCIUs only.

A *specified collective investment undertaking* is a collective investment undertaking:

(a) most of the business of which, to the extent that it is carried on in the State:

  (i) is carried on in the CHDA by the undertaking, or by a qualifying management company (see definition in **12.804** above) of the undertaking, or by the undertaking *and* the qualifying management company, or is not so carried on in the CHDA but is carried on in the State, would be carried on in the CHDA except for circumstances outside the control of the person or persons carrying on the business, and is so carried on in the CHDA as soon as circumstances permit, or

  (ii) is carried on in Shannon Airport by the undertaking, or by a qualifying management company of the undertaking, or by the undertaking *and* the qualifying management company, and

(b) all the holders of units in the undertaking are persons resident outside the State, except to the extent that such units are held by the undertaking itself, the qualifying management company of the undertaking, a company whose trading operations consist entirely of foreign life assurance business (see **12.602**), a "specified company" (see below) or another SCIU,

and includes any company limited by shares or guarantee which:

(c) is wholly owned by such a CIU or its trustees, if any, for the benefit of the holders of units in that undertaking;

(d) is so owned solely for the purpose of limiting the liability of that undertaking or its trustees in respect of futures contracts, options contracts or other financial instruments with similar risk characteristics, by enabling it or its trustees to invest or deal in such investments through the said company; and

(e) would satisfy the conditions set out in (a) above if "company limited by shares or guarantee" were to be read for "undertaking" (TCA 1997, s 734(1)).

A *specified company* is, broadly, an IFSC or a Shannon financial services company not more than 25% of the share capital of which is owned directly or indirectly by persons resident in the State, or all of the share capital of which is owned directly by another company resident in the State and not more than 25% of the share capital of that other company is owned directly or indirectly by persons resident in the State.

TCA 1997, s 734(3) provides that a CIU (and therefore a SCIU) is not to be chargeable to tax in respect of relevant profits (relevant income and relevant gains – see above). Any relevant profits are instead taxable in the hands of any unit holder (including the undertaking itself – since it can be a unit holder), to whom a relevant payment of relevant profits, or a relevant payment out of the relevant profits, is made. That tax charge arises if and to the extent that the unit holder would be chargeable to tax in the State on such relevant profits, or on such part of the relevant profits as is represented by the relevant payment, as if the relevant profits, or that part, had arisen directly to the unit holder. In other words, the CIU is treated for tax purposes as a transparent vehicle. As noted in **12.804** above, for the purposes of the definition of a CIU, the 31 December 2005 or, as the case may be, 31 December 2002, termination date which applies to IFSC and Shannon financial services operations is assumed not to apply to a qualifying management company. Thus, the tax transparency of collective funds managed by a certified IFSC or Shannon company is permitted to continue beyond the year 2002 or 2005, as the case may be. This extension relates only to the position of the CIU itself so that the 10% corporation tax entitlement of the management company does not extend beyond that date.

TCA 1997, s 734(7) provides that TCA 1997, s 732, which charges a qualifying unit trust (a registered unit trust scheme within the meaning of the Unit Trusts Act 1972) to capital gains tax at one-half of the capital gains tax rate, is not to apply to such a unit trust or to the disposal of units of such a trust where the unit trust is also a CIU.

Distributions from a SCIU to its unit holders are not subject to withholding tax. Neither is the undistributed income of a SCIU subject to withholding tax (TCA 1997, s 734(3)).

A person not resident in the State will not be taxable through an Irish based agent (under TCA 1997, s 1034 – which income tax provision can apply to corporation tax by virtue of TCA 1997, s 1040 (see also **3.107.2** regarding the exclusion of certain independent agents)) in respect of any relevant payment made out of the relevant profits of a CIU (734(10)).

A relevant payment made out of the relevant profits of a CIU which is a company, or a payment made in respect of the cancellation, redemption or repurchase of a share in the CIU, is not treated as a distribution for any purpose of the Tax Acts (TCA 1997, s 734(9)(a) – see also **12.802.4**).

No surcharge on undistributed investment income may be made under TCA 1997, s 440 (see **10.302**) in respect of any income of a CIU (TCA 1997, s 734(9)(b)).

The surcharge on certain undistributed income of the trustees of a discretionary trust, as provided for in TCA 1997, s 805, does not apply to a CIU (TCA 1997, s 734(8)).

The holding of shares in a SCIU will not result in the holder, other than a qualifying management company, being treated as carrying on a trade in the State through a branch or agency or otherwise, where the unit holder would not be so treated if he did not hold any units in a SCIU (TCA 1997, s 734(11)).

FA 1989 s 85 provides that, subject to certain conditions, the recipient of units in a SCIU by way of a gift or inheritance is not subject to capital acquisitions tax, and is not to be taken into account in computing tax on any gift or inheritance taken by that recipient. The conditions to be satisfied are:

(a) that the recipient is neither domiciled nor ordinarily resident in the State at the date of the gift or the date of the inheritance;

(b) that the units are comprised in the gift or inheritance at the date of the gift or at the date of the inheritance, and at the valuation date; and

(c) that at the date of the disposition the disponer is neither domiciled nor ordinarily resident in the State *or* the proper law of the disposition is not the law of the State.

No stamp duties or capital duties are payable on the subscription, redemption or transfer of units of a SCIU.

Exemption for interest paid to certain non-residents

TCA 1997, s 198(1)(c) provides for an exemption from income tax in the case of a company not resident in the State or a person not ordinarily resident in the State in respect of interest paid by a specified collective investment undertaking. The exemption provided is without prejudice to any charge under the Corporation Tax Acts on the profits of a non-resident company. Thus, the possibility of a corporation tax charge on a non-resident company where it operates an Irish branch or agency is preserved.

12.805.3 Domestic CIUs (excluding non-designated AICs) up to 5 April 1994

Income and gains

For accounting periods (accounting periods for companies, or basis periods for years of assessment in other cases) ending on or before 5 April 1994, UCITSs, authorised unit trusts and designated AICs established before 25 May 1993 and which are not SCIUs (accordingly, "domestic" CIUs) are, like SCIUs, not subject to tax on their income or gains. TCA 1997, s 734(3) provides that a CIU is not to be chargeable to tax in respect of relevant profits (relevant income and relevant gains).

The relevant profits are instead taxable in the hands of any unit holder (including the undertaking itself) to whom a "relevant payment" (as defined above) of relevant profits, or a relevant payment out of the relevant profits, is made. That tax charge arises if and to the extent that the unit holder would be chargeable to tax in the State on such relevant profits, or on such part of the relevant profits as is represented by the relevant payment, as if the relevant profits, or that part, had arisen directly to the unit holder. A domestic CIU established before 25 May 1993 is therefore treated as a tax transparent entity.

Taxation of unit holders

Where a unit holder is chargeable to tax on a relevant payment, to the extent that that payment is made out of relevant income, the charge to tax is made under Case IV of Schedule D as if the payment were an amount of income arising at the time of the payment (TCA 1997, s 734(4)(a)). To the extent that the payment is made out of relevant gains, it is treated as a capital distribution, within the meaning of TCA 1997, s 731(1), made by a unit trust and as if the unit or units in respect of which it is paid were a unit or units in a unit trust. (TCA 1997, s 731(4) provides that a person receiving a capital distribution from a unit trust is treated as if he had in consideration of that capital distribution disposed of an interest in the units.)

Withholding tax

Unlike a SCIU, a pre-25 May 1993 domestic CIU is obliged under TCA 1997, s 734(5) to withhold income tax at the standard rate from relevant payments out of relevant profits (income or capital gains) made to unit holders and from any undistributed relevant income (but not capital gains) at the end of each accounting period. *Undistributed relevant income* is any relevant income receivable by the CIU in an accounting period and which at the end of the accounting period has not been paid to the unit holders and from which appropriate tax has not previously been deducted. The tax which is to be withheld is the *appropriate tax* which means income tax at the standard rate in force at the time of payment in the case of a relevant payment, and in the case of undistributed income in force at the end of the accounting period to which the undistributed income relates, less certain deductions (TCA 1997, s 734(1)). The tax withheld must be accounted for to the Collector General within 15 days of the end of each year of assessment.

The deductions which may be made in arriving at the amount of the appropriate tax take into account the fact that appropriate tax may already have been deducted. Accordingly, a relevant payment may be made wholly or partly out of income which previously comprised or was part of the undistributed income of the CIU. In that case, a deduction is made in respect of appropriate tax deducted from that income or, where the relevant payment (or the part of the relevant payment which is made out of that income) is less than the amount of that income, appropriate tax deducted from the part of the income represented by the relevant payment, ie the amount of the tax which bears to the total amount of the tax deducted from the income the same proportion as the amount of the payment bears to the amount of the income.

Where any tax other than appropriate tax was deducted from the relevant profits out of which the relevant payment is made, and is not repayable to the CIU, a deduction is made also for that tax or, where the relevant payment is less than the relevant profits, for the tax on the part of the profits represented by the relevant payment. The tax on that part is the amount which bears to the total amount of the tax deducted from the relevant profits the same proportion as the amount of the payment bears to the amount of the relevant profits.

In the case of undistributed income, any tax other than appropriate tax deducted from such income, and which is not repayable to the CIU, is also deductible in arriving at the amount of the appropriate tax.

Where a non-resident unit holder receives a relevant payment from a CIU from which appropriate tax has been deducted from the payment or from any part of the relevant profits out of which the payment was made, he will be entitled to claim repayment of the appropriate tax, or of so much of it as is referable to the relevant payment. If the unit holder is resident in the State at the time the payment is made, he may claim to have any tax liability in respect of the payment reduced by a sum equal to so much, if any, of the appropriate tax as is referable to the amount of the relevant payment; if that appropriate tax exceeds the tax liability in respect of the relevant payment, the unit holder may claim repayment of the excess amount.

Other matters

A person not resident in the State is not to be taxable through an Irish based agent (under TCA 1997, s 1034 – which income tax provision can apply to corporation tax by virtue of TCA 1997, s 1040 (see also **3.107.2** regarding the exclusion of certain independent agents)) in respect of any relevant payment made out of the relevant profits of a CIU (TCA 1997, s 734(10)).

A relevant payment made out of the relevant profits of a CIU which is a company, or a payment made in respect of the cancellation, redemption or repurchase of a share in the CIU, is not treated as a distribution for any purpose of the Tax Acts.

No surcharge on undistributed investment income may be made under TCA 1997, s 440 (see **9.3**) in respect of any income of a CIU (TCA 1997, s 734(9)(b)).

The surcharge on certain undistributed income of the trustees of a discretionary trust, as provided for in TCA 1997, s 805, does not apply to a CIU (TCA 1997, s 734(8)).

12.805.4 Domestic CIUs (excluding non-designated AICs) from 6 April 1994

The tax treatment of domestic CIUs (apart from non-designated AICs) for accounting periods ending on or before 5 April 1994 was similar to that for specified collective investment undertakings in that they were not subject to tax on their income and gains. Where a domestic CIU was carrying on a collective investment business on 25 May 1993, the tax exemption was removed for that CIU with effect from 6 April 1994; if it was not carrying on such a business on 25 May 1993, the tax exemption had no effect from that date (TCA 1997, s 738(2)(a)). For example, a domestic CIU which began to carry on a collective investment business on 2 August 1993 would not be exempt from income tax and capital gains tax by virtue of TCA 1997, s 734 in respect of any part of its profits.

For the foregoing purposes, where an accounting period of a domestic CIU which is a company began before 6 April 1994 and ended on or after that day, it was treated as two separate accounting periods, one ending on 5 April 1994 followed by a second period beginning on 6 April 1994. (No such provision is made in relation to the 25 May 1993 cut-off date.) Any attribution of income or chargeable gains to periods treated as separate periods was to be made on the basis of the time the income arose to the CIU, or the disposal of the assets concerned took place, as appropriate, and not by reference to the usual time apportionment method as provided for in TCA 1997, s 4(6).

Transitional provisions

The provisions of TCA 1997, s 738 replace those of TCA 1997, s 734 in relation to domestic CIUs (apart from non-designated AICs) but with the exception of TCA 1997, s 734(7)-(9). These subsections deal with the non-application of TCA 1997, s 732 to a qualifying unit trust (but only where the unit trust is also a SCIU), the surcharge on certain undistributed income of trustees, the treatment of relevant payments and payments for the cancellation, redemption or repurchase of units in a CIU as not being distributions, and the non-application of the surcharge on undistributed investment and estate income (see above in relation to the position up to 5 April 1994).

Exemption on a transitional basis is provided for in TCA 1997, s 738(9) up to 5 April 1998 for certain domestic CIUs established on or before 24 May 1993. The provisions of TCA 1997, s 734 continue to apply to designated undertakings for collective investment and to guaranteed undertakings for collective investment for accounting periods ending on or before 5 April 1998 (instead of 5 April 1994); accounting periods of a CIU which is a company and which begin before 6 April 1998 and ended on or after that day will again be treated as two separate periods, one ending on 5 April 1998 followed by a second period beginning on 6 April 1998.

If, however:

(i)   at any time after 25 May 1993 and before 5 April 1997, the 80% designated assets test is not satisfied in the case of a designated undertaking for collective investment (see definition below); or

(ii) at any time before 5 April 1997 a guaranteed undertaking for collective investment makes any payment to unit holders in the CIU which is not a payment in cancellation of units, the reference to 5 April 1998 is to be read as a reference to 5 April next subsequent to that time.

A *designated undertaking for collective investment* is a CIU which, on 25 May 1993, owned designated assets for which it gave aggregate consideration of not less than 80% of the aggregate of the consideration it gave for all assets owned by it on that day. *Designated assets* means land or shares in an Irish resident company excluding shares listed in the official list, or dealt in on the smaller companies market, or the unlisted securities market, of the Irish Stock Exchange.

For the purposes of the 80% rule above, the amount of any consideration given is to be determined in accordance with TCA 1997, s 547 (consideration deemed to be for market value of asset where acquired otherwise than by way of a bargain made at arm's length or for a consideration that cannot be valued etc).

A *guaranteed undertaking for collective investment* is a CIU all of the issued units of which on 25 May 1993 are units in respect of each of which the CIU will make one payment only, being a payment:

(a)   to be made on a specified date in cancellation of those units; and

(b)   which is the aggregate of a fixed amount and an amount (which may be nil) determined by a stock exchange index or indices.

A *unit* includes a share and any other instrument granting an entitlement to a share of the investments or relevant profits of, or, to receive a distribution from, a CIU. References to a *unit holder* are accordingly references to a person holding units or (in the case of a company which is a CIU) shares who is thereby entitled to a share of any of the investments or relevant profits of, or to receive a distribution from, the CIU.

Meaning of undertaking for collective investment

For the purposes of TCA 1997, s 738, a CIU is an "undertaking for collective investment", which is almost the same as a "collective investment undertaking" as defined in TCA 1997, s 734 (see **12.802.1**). One difference is that an undertaking for collective investment does not include any unit trust scheme which is a special investment scheme within the meaning of TCA 1997, s 737 (see below) or a unit trust scheme mentioned in TCA 1997, s 731(5) (a unit trust, not being, nor being deemed to be, an authorised unit trust scheme within the meaning of the Unit Trusts Act, 1990, in respect of all of the issued units in which are assets such that any gain accruing on the disposal of them by the unit holder would be wholly exempt from capital gains tax, so that gains accruing to the unit trust itself are not chargeable gains).

A second difference is that the definition of "undertaking for collective investment" does not include a non-designated AIC; it will be recalled that a non-designated AIC may also be a CIU for the purposes of TCA 1997, s 734 where it is a specified collective investment undertaking and in respect of which all the holders of units who are required to be non-resident (so that the company may be such a specified collective investment undertaking) are collective investors. Since this type of non-designated AIC is in fact a SCIU, it is not dealt with in TCA 1997, s 738; a SCIU is specifically excluded (see below).

A *special investment scheme* is an authorised unit trust scheme in respect of which certain conditions are satisfied. The beneficial interests in the assets subject to any trust created under the authorised unit trust scheme concerned must be divided into special investment units. Units in a special investment scheme may not be issued after 31 December 2000. An *undertaking for collective investment* (which is a form of CIU but, to avoid confusion, is referred to here as a UCI), as defined in TCA 1997, s 738, means any of the following:

(a)   a unit trust scheme, not including any unit trust scheme which is a special investment scheme within the meaning of TCA 1997, s 737 or a unit trust scheme mentioned in TCA 1997, s 731(5)(a), which is or is deemed to be an authorised unit trust scheme within the meaning of the Unit Trust Act 1990, and has not had its authorisation revoked;

(b)   any other undertaking which is a UCITS within the meaning of the UCITS Regulations, being an undertaking which holds an authorisation, which has not been revoked, issued pursuant to those Regulations;

(c)   any authorised investment company within the meaning of Part XIII of the Companies Act 1990, which has not had its authorisation revoked and which has been designated in that authorisation as an investment company which may raise capital by promoting the sale of its shares to the public and has not ceased to be so designated.

References to a UCI are to be construed as including a reference to a trustee, management company or other person who is authorised to act on behalf of, or for the purposes of, the UCI and who habitually does so, to the extent that that construction brings into account any matter relating to the UCI which would not otherwise be brought into account (TCA 1997, s 738(1)(b)). Specifically excluded from the definition of a UCI for the purposes of TCA 1997, s 738 is a SCIU, as defined in TCA 1997, s 734, as well as an offshore fund within the meaning of TCA 1997, s 743(1) (see **3.210.1**).

Taxation of undertakings for collective investment: corporation tax

TCA 1997, s 738 introduced a new regime for the taxation of undertakings for collective investment (UCIs) (CIUs other than SCIUs and non-designated AICs). A UCI which is a company is liable to corporation tax for any accounting period, in respect of income and chargeable gains, at a rate equal to the standard rate of income tax for the year of assessment in which the accounting period falls. Where the accounting period falls into two tax years for which there are different standard rates of tax, the rate of corporation tax is a composite of the two standard income tax rates arrived at by time apportioning the accounting period between the parts falling into the two tax years. In computing profits for the purposes of this provision, the rate of capital gains tax is deemed to be the same as the standard corporation tax rate. This ensures that the corporation tax rate applicable to all profits, including chargeable gains, will be equal to the standard rate of income tax (TCA 1997, s 738(2)(b)). As the undertaking is taxed as described above, the investor has no further liability either in respect of the income or the chargeable gains.

In the case of a company which is a UCI, TCA 1997, s 129 does not apply so that distributions received from Irish resident companies are not disregarded for corporation tax purposes (TCA 1997, s 738(3)(a)(i)). Accordingly, any such distributions are to be included in the income of the UCI.

Chargeable gains

For chargeable periods ending on or after 6 April 1994, in computing chargeable gains on disposals of assets of a UCI, no indexation relief is allowed (TCA 1997, s 738(5)(a)(i)). The exemption in TCA 1997, s 607 from capital gains tax in respect of government and other securities does not apply to investments of such a UCI (TCA 1997, s 738(5)(a)(ii)).

With certain exceptions, the assets of a UCI are "marked to market", that is, they are deemed to be disposed of and reacquired at market value on the last day of each chargeable period (accounting period in the case of a company (TCA 1997, s 738(4)(a)(i)). The exceptions are:

(a)   assets to which TCA 1997, s 607 applies by virtue of any provisions of the Capital Gains Tax Acts, other than where such assets are held in connection with a contract or other arrangement which secures the future exchange of the assets for other assets to which TCA 1997, s 607 does not apply (ie, other than government securities held under an arrangement for the swapping of those securities for assets which are not such securities); or

(b)   assets which are strips within the meaning of TCA 1997, s 55 (ie, securities under which the right to receive each interest payment and to the redemption of capital can be traded separately – see **3.207.3**) (TCA 1997, s 738(4)(a)(iii)).

The resulting gains, less losses, are spread over seven years, one seventh in the current chargeable period and one seventh in each of the succeeding chargeable periods until the whole amount of the gain or loss has been accounted for.

The difference between the aggregate gains and aggregate losses (the "net amount") of the UCI, resulting from the application of the mark to market rule, is spread over seven years. One-seventh of the net amount is treated as a gain or loss of the chargeable period to which the deemed disposals relate. A further one-seventh of the net amount is similarly included in each of the succeeding chargeable periods of the UCI until the whole amount of the gain or loss has been accounted for (TCA 1997, s 738(4)(b)). Where any chargeable period in the seven year period is a period of less than one year, the fraction of one-seventh is proportionately reduced and the fraction for the last period over which the gain or loss is spread is reduced so that no more than the full amount of the gain or loss is accounted for (TCA 1997, s 738(4)(c)). Where the UCI ceases to carry on its collective investment business in a chargeable period, any unaccounted for balance of the net amount for any earlier periods is treated as a chargeable gain or allowable loss of that period (TCA 1997, s 738(4)(d)).

Where an asset in respect of which deemed gains or losses have arisen by virtue of the mark to market rule is actually disposed of, a gain or loss is calculated by reference to the difference between the proceeds of disposal and the last marked to market value. The gain or loss is recognised in the chargeable period in which the disposal took place while the spreading of the net amounts continues until they are fully accounted for. If a loss arises on disposal, it can be set against other income of the period of disposal. However, for disposals on or after 28 March 1996, the part of the loss which exceeds the overall actual loss in respect of the asset must be spread forward over seven years. In other words, the excess loss is treated in the same way as a deemed loss under the mark to market rule (TCA 1997, s 738(4)(e)).

On 1 January 1999, certain bank accounts formerly denominated in foreign currencies were re-denominated in terms of the euro which is also, from that date, Irish currency. As a general rule, an exchange gain or loss which would arise on the disposal of the account on 31 December 1998 is deemed to arise on that date (TCA 1997, s 541A(1)). Any gain so arising, however, will not be liable to capital gains tax until such time as the account is wholly or partly disposed of (TCA 1997, s 541A(2)). Different treatment is, however, provided for in relation to a euro-denominated currency bank account held as an asset of a company which is an undertaking for collective investment.

Where an accounting date of the company falls on 31 December 1998, the provisions of TCA 1997, s 541A are disapplied (TCA 1997, s 541A(4)(b)(ii)). This ensures that the normal disposal and re-acquisition rule and the seven year spread treatment will apply in such cases.

Where an accounting date of the company does not fall on 31 December 1998, TCA 1997, s 738(4)(a) applies as if an accounting period of the company ended on 31 December 1998 so that gains and losses in respect of a euro-denominated currency bank account are crystallised on that date. TCA 1997, s 541A(2) is, however, disapplied and the gains and losses arising are treated, for the purposes of the seven-year spread rule, as accruing at the end of the accounting period in which 31 December 1998 falls.

If a UCI was carrying on a collective investment business on 25 May 1993, it is deemed to have acquired each of the assets it held on 5 April 1994, apart from any assets consisting of government or other securities referred to in TCA 1997, s 607, at its market value at that date (TCA 1997, s 738(5)(c)).

Subject to the 7 year spreading rule explained above, where a UCI incurs allowable losses on disposals or deemed disposals of assets in a chargeable period, the amount if any by which the aggregate of such allowable losses exceeds the aggregate of chargeable gains on such disposals in the period are to be:

(a) disregarded for the purposes of setting off allowable losses in arriving at the amount of the chargeable gains charged to capital gains tax as provided for in TCA 1997, s 31;

(b) treated as reducing the income chargeable to income tax or corporation tax arising to the undertaking in the period; and

(c) to the extent that it is not treated as reducing income in (b), treated for capital gains tax purposes as an allowable loss incurred on a disposal of an asset deemed to be made in the next subsequent chargeable period.

The provisions of TCA 1997, s 584, which allow for a reorganisation or reduction of the share capital of a company without giving rise to a disposal for capital gains tax purposes (see **9.402**) are extended to unit trusts by virtue of TCA 1997, s 733. The extended treatment applies to any unit trust scheme registered under the Unit Trusts Act 1972, or authorised under the UCITS Regulations. It is therefore possible to switch units from one sub-fund to another sub-fund of an umbrella fund, whether the umbrella fund is a company or a unit trust. The "switching relief" does not apply in the cases of unit trusts where the new units are units which are deemed not to be chargeable assets for capital gains tax purposes.

A UCI (the "first undertaking") is permitted to exchange some or all of its assets (the "transferred assets") for units in another such UCI without triggering a capital gains tax charge (TCA 1997, s 739A(1)). When the units so acquired are disposed of, however, they are treated as having the same base cost as the assets they replaced. For the purposes of computing a gain accruing to the first undertaking on a disposal, or on the first deemed disposal under TCA 1997, s 738(4)(a)(ii) (deemed disposal and reacquisition on last day of chargeable period – see above), of those units, the amount or value of the consideration in money or moneys worth given by the first undertaking for the acquisition of the units is:

(a) where the transferred assets fell within TCA 1997, s 738(4)(a)(i), the value of the transferred assets on their latest deemed disposal by the first undertaking; and

(b) where the transferred assets did not fall within TCA 1997, s 739(4)(a)(i), the cost incurred by the first undertaking in acquiring the transferred assets (TCA 1997, s 739A(2)).

Disposals of securities ex div

TCA 1997, s 738(7) provides for an adjustment to be made to the profit or loss arising on *ex div* disposals of securities (ie, where the right to the next interest payment is retained) of a UCI. Where in any chargeable period a UCI disposes of securities so that in the following period it receives interest in respect of those securities, the gain or loss accruing on the disposal is to be computed as if the price paid by the UCI for the securities was reduced by a proportion of the interest.

The purpose of this provision is to disallow the element of accrued interest in the original purchase price of the securities sold. The subsection is intended to apply only where the securities in question are held for a period not exceeding six months; the calculation of the disallowed interest element is taken from TCA 1997, s 749 (and Sch 21) which applies to dealers in securities in cases where the securities are held for six months or less, but it is not clear that this reference achieves the objective of confining the application of TCA 1997, s 738(7) to those cases. If a UCI purchases securities *cum div* for, say, €10,500 which includes an interest element of €500, a sale of those securities *ex div* for €10,000 close to the end of its chargeable period would produce a loss of €500 which could then be offset against income of that period (see treatment of allowable losses above). The accrued interest would not arise to the company until the following period.

The purpose of TCA 1997, s 738(7) is to ensure that any capital losses arising on *ex div* disposals of securities within six months are not allowed in a chargeable period earlier than the period in which the final interest in respect of those securities is received by the UCI. The loss arising is reduced by the "appropriate proportion of the interest" but the amount of the reduction is then treated as a loss arising in the following period. The appropriate proportion of the interest is:

$$\text{interest} \times \frac{\text{length of period 1}}{\text{length of period 2}}$$

where—

period 1 = the number of days beginning with the earliest date on which the securities could have been quoted *ex div* in respect of the last interest paid before the interest included in the purchase price began to accrue (in short, the last *ex div* date before purchase), and ending with the day before the CIU purchased the securities; and period 2 = the number of days beginning with the first date referred to in the definition of period 1, and ending with the day before the earliest date on which the securities could have been quoted *ex div* in respect of the interest received by the UCI in the following period (in short, the day before the first *ex div* date for the interest in the following period).

Other matters

Unit holders in a UCI are not entitled to any credit for, or repayment of, income tax, capital gains tax or corporation tax paid by the UCI in respect of any of its income, capital gains or profits.

TCA 1997, s 815(3) excludes UCITSs and unit trusts from the bond washing provisions of TCA 1997, s 815 (see **3.208.7**). This is because, by virtue of TCA 1997, s 738, tax is charged at the standard rate on both income and chargeable gains, thereby rendering the bond washing provisions unnecessary in this context. TCA 1997, s 815(3) relieves the burden of calculating TCA 1997, s 815 interest and also simplifies the accounting and administration of government gilt gains and interest.

12.805.5 Taxation of unit holders

Introduction

Up to 5 April 1994, unit holders in a CIU were chargeable to tax on payments made by the CIU out of its income and gains. TCA 1997, s 739 deals with the taxation of payments made on or after 6 April 1994 in money or money's worth to a unit holder by reason of rights conferred on the holder as a result of holding units in an undertaking for collective investment (UCI). Such payment might consist of a distribution from the UCI or a payment in respect of the cancellation, redemption or repurchase of a unit or units. In the case of a unit holder which is not a company, a payment is not to be taken into account in computing the total income of the holder for income tax purposes.

Companies: charge under Case IV

In the case of a unit holder that is a company, a payment is treated as a net amount from which income tax has been deducted at the standard rate. The amount grossed up at the standard rate of income tax is accordingly taxed at the standard corporation tax rate under Case IV of Schedule D, subject to a credit for tax at the standard rate of income tax. Where the credit exceeds the total corporation tax liability of the company, the excess amount is refundable to it. This treatment ensures that such income is taxed at the standard corporation tax rate whether the investments are held directly by a company or indirectly through a UCI.

Financial concerns

In the case of payments of a kind normally chargeable to corporation tax under Case I (which arise to financial traders, such as banks and insurance companies), the treatment outlined in the previous paragraph does not apply. Instead, the "income" attributable to the payments made by the UCI is charged to tax. For any accounting period, that income consists of the amount of the payments received in the period, less a deduction in respect of certain consideration given, and as then grossed up at the standard rate of income tax.

In computing the amount of income attributable to a payment, where the payment arises on a sale or other transfer of ownership, or on a cancellation, redemption or repurchase by the UCI of units, or an interest in units, a deduction is made for the consideration in money or money's worth given by or on behalf of the unit holder for the acquisition of units, or an interest in units, for which the payment is made. Where units are acquired before 6 April 1994 in a UCI which was carrying on business on 25 May 1993, the consideration given for the units is deemed to be an amount equal to their market value on 6 April 1994 if that value is greater than the actual consideration given. Where units are acquired for a consideration which is less than their market value, the consideration given is deemed to be that market value. The amount of consideration given for units is to be determined in accordance with TCA 1997, s 580 (identification of shares, commodities etc – "first in, first out" rule – see **9.401.3**).

The amount computed in accordance with the previous paragraph is "grossed up" at the standard rate of income tax for the year of assessment in which the payment is made. TCA 1997, s 739(2)(*d*) provides that the amount is to be increased by an amount determined by the following formula:

$$I \times \frac{A}{100 - A}$$

where—

I   is the income computed as above; and

A   is the standard rate per cent of income tax for the year of assessment in which the payment is made.

Chargeable gains

In the case of a disposal by a company on or after 6 April 1994 of units in a UCI, the following treatment applies for corporation tax purposes:

(a)   any chargeable gain accruing on the disposal is treated as an amount net of a gross amount from which capital gains tax at the standard rate of income tax has been deducted;

(b)   the amount in respect of chargeable gains brought into the computation of profits for the accounting period in which the units are disposed of is the gross amount in (a); and

(c)   the capital gains tax treated as deducted from the gross amount is to be set off against the corporation tax assessable for that accounting period or, in so far as it cannot be so set off, repaid to the company.

Where the units disposed of were acquired before 6 April 1994 in a UCI which was carrying on business on 25 May 1993, however, the above-described treatment applies only to the amount of the chargeable gain as does not exceed the chargeable gain which would have accrued had the company sold and immediately reacquired the units on 5 April 1994 at their market value on that date.

The treatment described in (a) to (c) above is subject to TCA 1997, s 739(5) which applies where in relation to an acquisition, on or after 6 April 1994, of units in a UCI, both the person acquiring the units and the person from whom they were acquired were treated for capital gains tax purposes as if the acquisition had been for a consideration which secured that neither a gain nor a loss accrued to the previous owner. In any such case, the previous owner's date of acquisition of the units and their cost are to be treated as the date of acquisition and cost for the person now acquiring the units. An example would be the acquisition by a company of units from a company within the same capital gains tax group (see **9.202**). The above treatment is not, however, to apply where the no gain/ no loss rule in TCA 1997, s 556(4) applied (deemed disposal of assets on no gain/ no loss basis in place of indexation rule or rule regarding deemed acquisition of assets held at 6 April 1974 at market value – see **9.102.3**).

The treatment outlined in the previous paragraph is applied also in relation to the previous owner if he acquired the units in circumstances similar to those of the person now acquiring them. Accordingly, the date of acquisition and cost of the units for the predecessor to that previous owner will be taken as the date of acquisition and cost for the person now acquiring the units, and so on as necessary for any previous acquisitions in similar circumstances until the first such acquisition before 6 April 1994 or, as the case may be, until an acquisition on a disposal on or after that date.

12.805.6   Reorganisation of undertakings for collective investment

An undertaking for collective investment may exchange some or all of its assets for units in another such undertaking without triggering a tax liability. When units so acquired are disposed of, however, they are treated for capital gains tax purposes as having the same base cost as the assets they replaced.

Where an undertaking for collective investment (the "first undertaking") disposes of assets ("transferred assets") to another undertaking for collective investment in exchange for the issue of units to the first undertaking by that other undertaking, no chargeable gains accrue to the first undertaking on that disposal (TCA 1997, s 739A(1)).

For the purposes of computing a gain accruing to the first undertaking on a disposal or first deemed disposal, under TCA 1997, s 738(4)(a) (ie, the mark to market rule – see *Chargeable gains* in **12.805.4**), of the units referred to in TCA 1997, s 739A(1), the amount or value of the consideration in money or moneys worth given by the first undertaking for the acquisition of the units is:

(a)   where the transferred assets were subject to the mark to market rule, the value of the transferred assets on their latest deemed disposal by the first undertaking; and

(b)   where the transferred assets were not subject to mark to market treatment, the cost incurred by the first undertaking in acquiring the transferred assets (TCA 1997, s 739A(2)).

12.806   Taxation of investment undertakings

12.806.1   Introduction

In the context of Ireland's negotiations with the EU to move to a uniform 12.5% rate of corporation tax on trading profits from 1 January 2003, the Irish government made a commitment to a parallel phasing out of the 10% corporation tax rate for IFSC activities. This commitment led to the introduction of a uniform taxation system for both IFSC tax-exempt funds and taxable domestic funds. The appropriate legislation is contained in TCA 1997 Part 27 Chapter 1A (ss 739B-739H) and Schedule 2B (introduced by FA 2000 s 58).

Prior to the enactment of FA 2000 s 58, the legislative position governing the taxation of collective investment funds was that IFSC funds (specified collective investment funds, or "SCIUs" – see **12.805.2**) were tax exempt (subject to satisfying certain conditions – for example, that there should be no Irish resident investors) whereas domestic funds were taxed annually on a measure of income and gains. TCA 1997 Part 27 Chapter IA introduced a new common tax regime for both IFSC funds (whether existing or new) and domestic Irish funds established after 31 March 2000, referred to jointly as "investment undertakings".

The legislation dealing with investment undertakings permits Irish residents to invest in all Irish funds. In addition it removes the requirement to appoint an IFSC-based manager/administrator (although under Central Bank regulations it is required to appoint an Irish-based, but not necessarily IFSC-based, manager/administrator). The regime provides for tax to be levied on the occasion of the payment of an investment return to a unit holder where the unit holder is resident or ordinarily resident in the State. Tax will also generally be levied on the occasion of the transfer, on sale or otherwise, of units held by a unit holder in an investment undertaking.

The legislation sets out the amount of the "gain" which arises to a fund on the happening of a chargeable event in respect of a unit holder. A gain will arise if the unit holder is neither resident nor ordinarily resident in the State at the time of the chargeable event, provided the necessary declarations are in place. An undertaking may incorporate the information required by the Revenue in the standard form of application for units.

Establishing the status of an individual's place of residence is governed by a declaration procedure. In the absence of a signed declaration there is a presumption that the investor is resident or ordinarily resident in Ireland. A facility is provided for an intermediary or nominee to make a declaration on behalf of clients. There is an exemption in respect of fund units/shares held in a Revenue-recognised clearing system. An exemption from tax is provided in respect of certain categories of Irish resident unit holders. Certain events are not regarded as chargeable events.

See **4.305** regarding exemption from withholding tax on interest paid to investment undertakings.

12.806.2 Taxation of investment undertakings: outline

Taxation of an investment undertaking arises in respect of the "gain" arising to the undertaking on the happening of a "chargeable event in respect of a unit holder". The taxation position of the unit holder as such is a separate matter (see **12.806.10**). In describing the taxation treatment of investment undertakings, it is necessary to distinguish between IFSC funds in existence on 31 March 2000 and new funds established after that date.

IFSC funds existing on 31 March 2000

Non-Irish residents who, on 31 March 2000, were investors in IFSC funds existing on that date are unaffected by the investment undertakings legislation introduced by FA 2000 s 58 subject to the fund making and filing a specific declaration to the Revenue authorities by 30 June 2000. (This general rule does not apply in a limited number of particular circumstances relating to certain Irish resident shareholders who, by concession, were permitted to invest in IFSC funds.) Failure by an existing IFSC fund to make the necessary declaration results in its existing non-Irish resident investors coming within the terms of the new regime.

Investors on and from 1 April 2000, being non-Irish unit holders as at 31 March 2000, are required to file a declaration stating that they are neither resident nor ordinarily resident in Ireland. In the absence of such a declaration, the fund is obliged to charge Irish tax on the happening of a "chargeable event" (even though such investors are neither resident nor ordinarily resident). Even where an IFSC fund continues to exclude Irish resident investors, it is not exempt from the requirement to have the necessary new declaration process in place (TCA 1997, s 739D(7)).

In accordance with transitional arrangements agreed by the Revenue, existing IFSC funds have until 1 October 2000 to put the new declaration procedures in place. An undertaking may incorporate the information required by the Revenue in the standard form of application for units. Investors will already have confirmed their non-resident status as part of the application process and, since applications are retained by the fund, such confirmations will have been in the possession of the fund. The transitional arrangements allow for the use, up to 1 October 2000, of these applications as evidence of non-residence.

Under the transitional arrangements, existing funds are also required to forward to the Collector-General, on or before 30 November 2000, a list containing the names and addresses of all resident or ordinarily resident persons who were issued with units on or after 1 April 2000 and before 1 October 2000.

New funds established after 31 March 2000

In the case of funds established after 31 March 2000, the declaration process as described above will also be in operation. New funds are obliged to apply the declaration procedures immediately; there are no transitional rules for them.

Former unit trusts

The regime for taxing investment undertakings applies to an investment undertaking which was a unit trust mentioned in TCA s 731(5)(a) (see **12.806.3**) from the day on which the unit trust became an investment undertaking (TCA 1997, s 739B(3)).

Tax exemption

The tax position of both existing IFSC funds and new funds is as follows:

(a) funds are exempt from tax in respect of their income and gains;

(b) investors who make a correct declaration to the effect that they are neither resident nor ordinarily resident in Ireland, or who are exempt from making a declaration, will not be liable to Irish tax on the income or gains arising from their investments in the funds;

(c) in relation to investors who have made a correct declaration of non-residence or non-ordinary residence for tax purposes, or who are exempt Irish investors entitled to exemption on the making of a declaration, no tax is deductible on distributions from the funds or on payments made by the fund in respect of the redemption or other disposal of investments in the fund.

Exempt Irish Investors

Provided they have completed the necessary statutory declarations, the following categories of Irish resident persons may invest in a fund without giving rise to a charge to tax on the fund on "gains" arising in respect of their investments (see **12.806.7**):

  (a) a tax exempt pension scheme;

  (b) an authorised life assurance company;

  (c) an investment undertaking, which may consist of any of the following—

  (i) an authorised unit trust scheme;

  (ii) a UCITS;

  (iii) an authorised non-UCITS fund;

  (iv) a non-designated investment company with collective investors;

  (v) an investment limited partnership;

  (vi) certain 100% subsidiaries of qualifying funds;

  (d) a special investment scheme (see **12.806.3** under *(a) Unit Trusts*);

  (e) a unit trust scheme confined to tax exempt pension schemes and charities;

  (f) a tax-exempt charity;

  (g) an IFSC fund manager investing in the fund it manages;

  (h) an IFSC company which is not owned as to more than 25% by Irish residents;

  (i) a qualifying fund manager of an approved retirement fund;

  (j) a qualifying fund manager of an approved minimum retirement fund;

  (k) a qualifying savings manager of a special savings incentive account;

  (l) a PRSA administrator;

  (m) a credit union;

  (n) a money market fund;

  (o) the National Pensions Reserve Fund;

  (p) a securitisation vehicle within the meaning of TCA 1997, s 110 (see **7.206.11**).

In accordance with transitional arrangements agreed by the Revenue, existing IFSC funds have until 30 June 2000 to put the new declaration procedures relating to Irish tax exempt investors in place. In the light of the definition of "specified collective investment undertaking", as respects the unit holders who may be Irish resident (see **12.805.2**), affected investors in existing IFSC funds are: the qualifying management company in relation to the fund, an IFSC life assurance company, a specified company (an IFSC company which is not owned as to more than 25% by Irish residents), and another IFSC fund.

Non-Chargeable events

While a chargeable event includes any payments to unit holders or any encashment, redemption or transfer of units, it does not include:

  (a) any transactions in relation to units held in a recognised clearing system (as designated by order of the Irish Revenue Commissioners);

  (b) a transfer arising on the death of a unit holder;

  (c) an exchange of units in a sub-fund of an umbrella fund for units in another sub-fund of that same umbrella fund; or

(d) an exchange of units arising from a reconstruction or amalgamation of two or more Irish funds.

The exemption for units held in a recognised clearing system means that funds which are satisfied that all units are held in a recognised clearing system will not have to implement a declaration process as no declarations will be required from investors. An initial list of approved clearing systems issued by the Revenue includes Clearstream Banking SA, Clearstream Banking AG, Euroclear, Crest-UK, National Securities Clearing System, Sicovam SA and SIS Sega Intersettle AG.

Calculation of tax due and payment date

The calculation of tax is such that fund administrators need to ensure that their systems can track the cost of investors units. The legislation permits the use of average cost or FIFO (if a fund makes an irrevocable election).

The rates of tax arising in the fund in respect of taxable investors are 22% on distributions and 25% on gains arising on redemption, cancellation and transfers of units.

A fund is required to make a twice-yearly return of any tax due within 30 days of 30 June and 31 December.

All funds must obtain a tax reference number.

Period 1 April 2000 to 31 December 2000: transitional arrangements

Existing non-Irish resident investors at 31 March 2000 and 1 April 2000 in an IFSC fund are unaffected by the provisions of the investment undertaking regime provided the fund makes and files a specific declaration with the Collector-General by 30 June 2000 (TCA 1997, s 739D(8)).

In respect of any Irish tax resident investors who were investors in the IFSC fund on 31 March and 1 April 2000, who cannot or do not avail of exemption from the tax due in respect of a chargeable event by completing an appropriate declaration, the fund is subject to a tax of 40% on any chargeable event (other than a distribution, which is subject to tax of 22%, or deemed disposal at 31 December 2000) occurring on or before 31 December 2000 (TCA 1997, s 739E(1)(c)).

Such investors are taxable at 40% on any deemed gain arising on the deemed disposal of their units as at 31 December 2000, unless the IFSC fund fails to file a specified declaration with the Collector-General on or before 30 June 2000. (Failure to file results in the tax liability arising to the IFSC fund – TCA 1997, s 739D(8)(a)(ii)). Any deemed gain arising is computed as the difference between the value of the investors investment in the IFSC Fund at 31 December 2000 and the cost of the investment as calculated under special rules.

In respect of any Irish tax resident or Irish ordinarily tax resident investors, who were not investors in an IFSC fund on 31 March and 1 April 2000, investing in the fund prior to 31 December 2000, who cannot or do not avail of exemption from the tax due on a chargeable event by completing an appropriate declaration, the fund is subject to a tax of 40% on any chargeable event (other than a distribution, which is subject to tax of 22%, or deemed disposal at 31 December 2000) occurring on or before 31 December 2000 (TCA 1997, s 739E(1)(c)).

In respect of those same investors, who were not investors in the fund on 31 March and 1 April 2000, the fund is taxable at 40% on any deemed gain arising on the deemed disposal of their units as at 31 December 2000. Any deemed gain arising will be computed as the difference between the value of the investors investment in the fund at 31 December 2000 and the cost of the investment as calculated under special rules (TCA 1997, s 739D(2)(e)).

Refunds of Irish Tax

The legislation does not provide for any refunds of tax to be made to non-Irish investors where tax is deducted in the absence of the necessary statutory declarations. Refunds of tax will only be made to corporate investors who are within the charge to Irish corporation tax. Thus it is critical for all funds to have the necessary declaration procedure in place for all investors.

12.806.3 Meaning of "investment undertaking"

An "investment undertaking" is similar to an "undertaking for collective investment" (UCI) as defined in TCA 1997, s 738 (see **12.805.4**). It is also somewhat similar to a "collective investment undertaking" as defined in TCA 1997, s 734 (see **12.802.1**) but, as with a UCI, with certain differences. One such difference is that it does not include any unit trust scheme which is a special investment scheme within the meaning of TCA 1997, s 737 or a unit trust scheme mentioned in TCA 1997, s 731(5)(a) (see below).

An investment undertaking (like a UCI) also differs from a collective investment undertaking as defined in TCA 1997, s 738 in that it does not include a non-designated AIC; it was seen in **12.802.4** that a non-designated AIC may also be a CIU for the purposes of TCA 1997, s 734 where it is a specified collective investment undertaking (SCIU) and in respect of which all the holders of units who are required to be non-resident (so that the company may be such a SCIU) are collective investors. An investment undertaking has a somewhat broader meaning than a UCI. It can include an AIC whose shareholders are all collective investors, an investment limited partnership, or a company limited by shares or guarantee which is wholly owned by an investment undertaking or its trustees.

An *investment undertaking* is defined in TCA 1997, s 739B(1) and means any of the following:

(a)　a unit trust scheme, not including any unit trust scheme which is a special investment scheme within the meaning of TCA 1997, s 737 (see below under *(a) Unit Trusts*) or a unit trust scheme mentioned in TCA 1997, s 731(5)(a), which is or is deemed to be an authorised unit trust scheme within the meaning of the Unit Trust Act, 1990, and has not had its authorisation revoked;

(b)　any other undertaking which is a UCITS within the meaning of the UCITS Regulations, being an undertaking which holds an authorisation, which has not been revoked, issued pursuant to those Regulations;

(c)　any authorised investment company within the meaning of Part XIII of the Companies Act, 1990, which has not had its authorisation revoked, and

(i)　which has been designated in that authorisation as an investment company which may raise capital by promoting the sale of its shares to the public and has not ceased to be so designated, or

(ii)　each of the shareholders of which is a collective investor (see below); and

(d) an investment limited partnership (within the meaning of the Investment Limited Partnership Act, 1994,

which is not an offshore fund (within the meaning of TCA 1997, s 734 – see **3.210.1**), but includes any company limited by shares or guarantee which:

(A) is wholly owned by such an investment undertaking or its trustees, if any, for the benefit of the holders of units in that undertaking; and

(B) is so owned solely for the purpose of limiting the liability of that undertaking or its trustees, as the case may be, in respect of futures contracts, options contracts or other financial instruments with similar risk characteristics, by enabling it or its trustees, as the case may be, to invest or deal in such investments through the company,

which is not an offshore fund (within the meaning of TCA 1997, s 743).

References to an investment undertaking are to be construed as including a reference to a trustee, management company or other person who is authorised to act on behalf of, or for the purposes of, the investment undertaking and who habitually does so, to the extent that that construction brings into account any matter relating to the investment undertaking which would not otherwise be brought into account. Such construction may not, however, render the trustee, management company or other such person liable in a personal capacity to any tax imposed on an investment undertaking (TCA 1997, s 739B(2)).

A *collective investor*, in relation to an AIC, means an investor, being a life assurance company, a pension fund, or other investor:

(a) which invests in securities or any other property with moneys contributed by 50 or more persons:

(i) none of whom has at any time, directly or indirectly, contributed more than 5% of such moneys, and

(ii) each of a majority of whom has contributed moneys to the investor so as to be entitled (otherwise than on the death of any person or by reference to any risk to any person or property) to receive from the investor a payment which, or payments the aggregate of which, exceeds those moneys by a part of the profits or income arising to the investor, and

(b) which invests in the AIC primarily for the benefit of the above mentioned fifty or more persons (TCA 1997, s 739B(1)).

(a) Unit trusts

The law up to 1990 relating to unit trusts was contained in the Unit Trusts Act 1972, but the Unit Trusts Act 1990, was enacted on 26 December 1990 to cope with demands created by developments in the mutual funds industry. An investment undertaking does not include a unit trust scheme which is a special investment scheme within the meaning of TCA 1997, s 737; a special investment scheme is by definition an authorised unit trust scheme – see below. Neither does an investment undertaking include a unit trust mentioned in TCA 1997, s 731(5)(a) (a unit trust which neither is, nor is deemed to be, an authorised unit trust scheme within the meaning of the Unit Trusts Act, 1990, in respect of all of the issued units in which are assets such that any gain accruing on the disposal of them by the unit holder would be wholly exempt from capital gains tax, so that gains accruing to the unit trust itself are not chargeable gains).

A *special investment scheme* is an authorised unit trust scheme in respect of which certain conditions are satisfied. The beneficial interests in the assets subject to any trust created under the authorised unit trust scheme concerned must be divided into special investment units. Units in a special investment scheme may not be issued after 31 December 2000.

(b) Undertakings for collective investment in transferable securities

A UCITS is defined in the UCITS Regulations, ie the European Communities (Undertakings for Collective Investment in Transferable Securities) Regulations 1989 (SI 78/1989) as:

(a)   an undertaking the sole object of which is the collective investment in transferable securities of capital raised from the public and which operates on the principle of risk-spreading; and

(b)   the units of which are, at the request of holders, repurchased or redeemed, directly or indirectly, out of that undertakings assets.

Transferable securities are securities in respect of which the right to transfer is unrestricted. A UCITS is free to promote its shares to members of the public in Europe. *Repurchase* means the purchase of shares by a management company or investment company and *redemption* denotes the purchase of units or shares from a holder by a management company or investment company. The requirement to repurchase or redeem units is regarded as satisfied by action taken by the UCITS to ensure that the stock exchange value of its units does not significantly vary from their net asset value. A UCITS may not be a closed-ended vehicle. As provided in the UCITS Regulations, a UCITS comprises any of the following entities:

(1)   a unit trust;

(2)   a variable capital investment company;

(3)   a fixed capital investment company.

(1) Unit trust

The unit trust in Ireland is similar to the US "mutual fund". Unit trusts were originally legislated for in Ireland in the form of the Unit Trusts Act 1972, but were not widely used as an investment medium until the enactment of the Unit Trusts Act 1990, and the implementation of the UCITS Directive. A unit trust operates as an investment fund established under a trust deed between a management company and a trustee. The assets of the fund are beneficially owned by the investors but are held legally by the trustee on their behalf. The fund and its investments are managed by the management company with the assistance of an investment adviser. The management function is sometimes delegated to an investment manager.

The relationship between the unit holders, the management company and the trustee is regulated by the trust deed which also defines the investment policy and sets out procedures for such matters as the issue and redemption of units, meetings of unit holders and the termination of the fund.

The management company may be incorporated as a private limited company and must have its registered office and head office in the State. It must in the opinion of the

Central Bank have sufficient financial resources at its disposal to enable it to conduct its business effectively and meet its liabilities. The company must have a minimum share capital of €127,000 (or the equivalent in a non-euro currency) and a minimum of two directors who are Irish residents. It must satisfy the Central Bank that it possesses adequate experience and expertise to carry out its functions.

The trustee has a supervisory role in ensuring that the activities of the fund are carried on in accordance with the law and the provisions of the trust deed. The trustee is the financial institution responsible for the safe keeping and custody of the fund assets. The custodial function may be, and usually is, delegated to a sub-custodian.

(2) Variable capital investment company

A variable capital investment company (VCIC) must be registered as a public limited company and, like any other company incorporated in Ireland, is governed by the Companies Acts but subject to the provisions of the UCITS Regulations. It must in the opinion of the Central Bank have sufficient paid up share capital to enable it to conduct its business effectively and meet its liabilities. If the company does not have the services of a management company, its paid up share capital must be at least €127,000, or its non-euro currency equivalent, within three months of authorisation; otherwise the minimum paid up share capital is €38,100.

A VCIC is free, if so authorised by its articles, to repurchase its own shares provided such shares are fully paid. The VCIC is an open-ended vehicle, ie the company must, if requested to do so by a shareholder, repurchase some or all of that shareholders shares (see **12.802.6**). Shares repurchased are then treated as cancelled and the company's share capital is reduced accordingly. The articles of the company provide that the amount of the paid up share capital shall at all times be equal to the net asset value of the company; its shares may not have a nominal or par value.

A VCIC must include the words "Investment company with Variable Capital" or "cuideachta infheistíochta le caipiteal athraitheach" on all its deeds, announcements, publications, letters and other documents.

No stamp duties or capital duties are payable on the subscription, redemption or transfer of shares of a VCIC.

(3) Fixed capital investment company

A fixed capital investment company (FCIC) must also be registered as a public limited company and, like any other company incorporated in Ireland, is governed by the Companies Acts but subject to the provisions of the UCITS Regulations. It must in the opinion of the Central Bank have sufficient paid up share capital to enable it to conduct its business effectively and meet its liabilities. If the company does not have the services of a management company, its paid up share capital must be at least €127,000, or its non-euro currency equivalent, within three months of authorisation; otherwise the minimum paid up share capital is €38,100.

The FCIC is similar to the SICAF mentioned in **12.801**. The FCIC is an open-ended vehicle, ie it may, if authorised by its articles, issue redeemable preference shares which are liable at the option of the shareholder to be redeemed, and redeem them accordingly (see **12.802.6**). No redeemable shares may be redeemed unless fully paid and redemption must be made out profits available for distribution or out of the proceeds of a fresh issue of shares made for the purpose of redemption.

Where redeemable shares are redeemed wholly out of profits available for distribution, a sum equal to the nominal amount of the shares redeemed must be transferred to the capital redemption reserve fund. Where the shares are redeemed wholly or partly out of the proceeds of a fresh issue and the aggregate amount of those proceeds is less than the aggregate nominal value of the shares redeemed, an amount equal to the difference must be transferred to the capital redemption reserve fund.

Any premium paid on redemption must have been provided for out of the profits of the company or out of the company's share premium account before the shares are redeemed. Shares so redeemed are treated as cancelled on redemption and the amount of the company's issued share capital is reduced by the nominal value of those shares accordingly. No such cancellation may have the effect of reducing the company's authorised share capital. By far the greater part of the capital of an FCIC is comprised of redeemable preference shares.

An FCIC must include the words "investment company" or "cuideachta infheistíochta" on all its deeds, announcements, publications, letters and other documents.

No stamp duties or capital duties are payable on the subscription, redemption or transfer of shares of an FCIC.

(c) Authorised investment companies

An authorised investment company (AIC), formed under Part XIII of the Companies Act, 1990, is also similar to the SICAV (see **12.801**) (and is therefore also a variable capital investment company, but is conveniently referred to here as an AIC to distinguish it from the VCIC, the UCITS version of a variable capital investment company). It is an open-ended vehicle whose capital can be redeemed at will. Its sole object is the collective investment of its funds with the aim of spreading investment risk and providing its members with the benefits of the management of those funds. It can invest in real property as well as in other securities.

Designated AICs

An AIC may be designated (may be marketed to the public) or non- designated (restricted to private investors, and therefore not generally a collective investment undertaking). An AIC may be designated by the Central Bank as a company permitted to raise capital by promoting the sale of its shares to members of the public. Not being a UCITS, the company's shares may not be promoted freely in Europe. A designated AIC is a tax-free vehicle and is found only in the IFSC.

Companies capital duty is not payable in the case of a designated AIC. Neither are transfers of shares in a designated AIC subject to stamp duty.

Non-designated AICs

A non-designated AIC is not authorised to promote the sale of its shares to members of the public and is therefore not normally a collective investment vehicle. A non-designated AIC cannot be an investment undertaking.

(d) Investment limited partnerships

An investment limited partnership is a partnership of two or more persons and whose principal business is the investment of its funds in property of all kinds. The partnership consists of at least one general partner and at least one limited partner. The position of a general partner would broadly be analogous to that of a manager in a unit trust structure or in an investment company, while a limited partner would be similar to a unit holder in a unit trust or a shareholder in an investment company.

The limited partnership structure is well recognised in the international funds industry. It is found in a number of offshore locations and its presence in the IFSC as a tax transparent pooled investment vehicle exhibits a structure which is familiar to the international funds industry.

Participation in an investment limited partnership is not required to be promoted to the public and the structure is accordingly suitable as a private investment vehicle.

12.806.4 "Chargeable event" and related definitions

The occasion on which a tax charge may arise to a unit holder is referred to as a chargeable event. A *chargeable event*, in relation to an investment undertaking in respect of a unit holder, means:

(a) the making of a relevant payment by the investment undertaking;

(b) the making of any other payment by the investment undertaking to a person, by virtue of that person being a unit holder (whether or not in respect of the cancellation, redemption or repurchase of a unit);

(c) the transfer by a unit holder, by way of sale or otherwise, of entitlement to a unit in the investment undertaking;

(d) the appropriation or cancellation of units of a unit holder by an investment undertaking for the purposes of meeting the amount of appropriate tax payable on any gain arising by virtue of (c) (see under *Recovery of appropriate tax by investment undertaking* in **12.806.9**) (so that where an investment undertaking discharges its tax liability on the transfer of units by cancelling units belonging the unit holder, the tax liability arising on the cancelled units is taken into account);

(e) the ending of a relevant period where such ending is not otherwise a chargeable event within the meaning of TCA 1997, s 730B, *relevant period,* in relation to a unit in an investment undertaking, meaning a period of eight years beginning with the acquisition of that unit by the unit holder and each subsequent period of eight years beginning immediately after the preceding relevant period, and

(f) the chargeable event deemed to happen on 31 December 2000 in respect of all unit holders (if any) at that date in relation to an investment undertaking—

    (i) which commenced on or after 1 April 2000, or

    (ii) which was on 31 March 2000 a specified collective investment undertaking,

but does not include:

(I) any exchange by a unit holder, effected by way of a bargain made at arm's length by an investment undertaking which is an umbrella scheme, of units in a sub-fund of the investment undertaking, for units in another sub-fund of the investment undertaking;

(II) any exchange by a unit holder, effected by way of a bargain made at arm's length by an investment undertaking, of units in the investment undertaking for other units in the investment undertaking;

(III)   any transaction in relation to, or in respect of, relevant units (units in an investment undertaking acquired with moneys under the control or subject to the order of any Court) in an investment undertaking which transaction arises only by virtue of a change of court funds manager (a person appointed by the Courts Service to set up and administer an investment undertaking with money under the control or subject to the order of any Court) for that undertaking (thus ensuring that these beneficiaries will only be subject to the exit charge in respect of any payments made to them out of the funds and will not inadvertently become subject to the charge on such funds where no proceeds flow directly to them such as on a change of investment manager);

(IV)   any transaction in relation to, or in respect of, units which are held in a recognised clearing system (see below); and

(V)   the transfer by a unit holder of entitlement to a unit where the transfer is—

(A)   between a husband and wife,

(B)   between the spouses or former spouses concerned (as the case may be), by virtue or in consequence of an order made under Part III of the Family Law (Divorce) Act 1996, on or following the granting of a decree of divorce,

(C)   between the spouses concerned, by virtue or in consequence of an order made under Part II of the Family Law Act 1995, on or following the granting of a decree of judicial separation within the meaning of that Act, or

(D)   between the spouses or former spouses concerned (as the case may be), by virtue of an order or other determination of like effect, which is analogous to an order referred to in (B) or (C), of a court under the law of a territory other than the State made under or in consequence of the dissolution of a marriage or the legal separation of the spouses, being a dissolution or legal separation that is entitled to be recognised as valid in the State,

but on the happening of a chargeable event following such a transfer, the then unit holder is to be treated as having acquired the unit transferred at the same cost as the person who transferred the unit (TCA 1997, s 739B(1)).

The inclusion of (e) as a chargeable event (by virtue of TCA 1997, s 739B(1)(ccc)) means that there will be an exit charge every eight years whether or not a payment is made by an investment undertaking to a unit holder, thereby preventing the indefinite postponement of an exit charge. The eight-year relevant period applies in relation to a chargeable event occurring on or after the passing of FA 2006, 31 March 2006. The first relevant period will end on 1 January 2009, eight years after the commencement of the gross roll-up regime which applies to units acquired on or after 1 January 2001.

Recognised clearing system, referred to in (III) above, means the following clearing systems:

(i)   Bank One NA, Depository and Clearing Centre;
(ii)   Central Moneymarkets Office;
(iii) Clearstream Banking SA;
(iv)   Clearstream Banking AG;

(v)   CREST;

(vi)   Depository Trust Company of New York;

(vii)   Euroclear;

(viii)   Monte Titoli SPA;

(ix)   Netherlands Centraal Instituut voor Giraal Effectenverkeer BV;

(x)   National Securities Clearing System;

(xi)   Sicovam SA;

(xii)   SIS Sega Intersettle AG; and

(xiii)   any other system for clearing securities which is for the time being designated, for the purposes of TCA 1997, s 246A or any other provision of the Tax Acts or the Capital Gains Tax Acts which applies that section, by order of the Revenue Commissioners as a recognised clearing system (TCA 1997 ss 246A(2)(a), 739B(1A)).

For the above purpose, the Revenue Commissioners may by order designate one or more than one system for clearing securities as a "recognised clearing system" (TCA 1997, s 246A(2)(b)). That order may contain such transitional and other supplemental provisions as appear to the Revenue Commissioners to be necessary or expedient and may be varied or revoked by a subsequent order (TCA 1997, s 246A(2)(c)).

A *relevant payment* is a payment including a distribution (see **11.1**) made to a unit holder by an investment undertaking by reason of rights conferred on the unit holder as a result of holding a unit or units in the investment undertaking, where such payments are made annually or at more frequent intervals, other than a payment made in respect of the cancellation, redemption or repurchase of a unit.

A *unit holder*, in relation to an investment undertaking, is any person who by reason of the holding of a unit, or under the terms of a unit, in the investment undertaking is entitled to a share of any of the investments or relevant profits of, or to receive a relevant payment from, the investment undertaking.

A *unit* includes any investment made by a unit holder, such as a subscription for shares or a contribution of capital, in an investment undertaking, being an investment which entitles the investor:

(a)   to a share of the investments or relevant profits; or

(b)   to receive a relevant payment from,

the investment undertaking.

Relevant profits, in relation to an investment undertaking, means the relevant income and relevant gains of the undertaking.

Relevant income, in relation to an investment undertaking, means any amounts of income, profits or gains which arise to or are receivable by the investment undertaking, being amounts of income, profits or gains:

(a)   which are or are to be paid to unit holders as relevant payments;

(b)   out of which relevant payments are or are to be made to unit holders; or

(c)   which are or are to be accumulated for the benefit of, or invested for the benefit of, unit holders,

and which if they arose to an Irish resident individual would in the hands of that individual constitute income for income tax purposes.

Relevant gains, in relation to an investment undertaking, means gains accruing to the investment undertaking, being gains which would constitute chargeable gains in the hands of an Irish resident person including gains which would so constitute chargeable gains if all assets concerned were chargeable assets and no exemption from capital gains tax applied.

A *specified collective investment undertaking* is a collective investment undertaking

(a) most of the business of which, to the extent that it is carried on in the State:

  (i) is carried on in the IFSC by the undertaking, or by a qualifying management company (see definition in **12.804** above) of the undertaking, or by the undertaking and the qualifying management company, or is not so carried on in the IFSC but is carried on in the State, would be carried on in the IFSC except for circumstances outside the control of the person or persons carrying on the business, and is so carried on in the IFSC as soon as circumstances permit, or

  (ii) is carried on in Shannon Airport by the undertaking, or by a qualifying management company of the undertaking, or by the undertaking and the qualifying management company, and

(b) all the holders of units in the undertaking are persons resident outside the State, except to the extent that such units are held by the undertaking itself, the qualifying management company of the undertaking, a company whose trading operations consist entirely of foreign life assurance business (see **12.602**), a "specified company" (see below) or another specified collective investment undertaking, and includes any company limited by shares or guarantee which—

(c) is wholly owned by such collective investment undertaking or its trustees, if any, for the benefit of the holders of units in that undertaking;

(d) is so owned solely for the purpose of limiting the liability of that undertaking or its trustees in respect of futures contracts, options contracts or other financial instruments with similar risk characteristics, by enabling it or its trustees to invest or deal in such investments through the said company; and

(e) would satisfy the conditions set out in (a) above if "company limited by shares or guarantee" were to be read for "undertaking" (TCA 1997, s 1997 734(1)).

An *umbrella scheme* (or "umbrella fund") is an investment undertaking which is divided into a number of sub-funds and in which the unit holders are entitled to exchange units in one sub-fund for units in another (see also **12.802.7**).

A *specified company* is, broadly, an IFSC or a Shannon financial services company not more than 25% of the share capital of which is owned directly or indirectly by persons resident in the State, or all of the share capital of which is owned directly by another company resident in the State and not more than 25% of the share capital of that other company is owned directly or indirectly by persons resident in the State.

Where a holder of units in an investment undertaking is:

(a) an investment undertaking;

(b) a special investment scheme; or

(c) a unit trust to which TCA 1997, s 731(5)(a) applies,

the unit holder is to be treated as being entitled to the units held (TCA 1997, s 739B(6)).

12.806.5   Charge to tax

TCA 1997, s 739C(1) provides that an investment undertaking to which TCA 1997 Part 27 Chapter 1A applies is not to be chargeable to tax in respect of relevant profits otherwise than to the extent provided for in that Chapter. The provisions of Chapter 1A apply to existing IFSC funds (specified collective investment funds, or "SCIUs") from 1 April 2000 and to any new funds established on or after that date. Existing domestic funds continue to be taxed on the same basis as previously, ie by way of an annual tax on a measure of income and gains accruing to the fund (see **12.805.4**).

Chapter 1A of TCA 1997 Part 27 applies to an investment undertaking and the unit holders in relation to that undertaking—

(a)   where the undertaking is on 31 March 2000 a specified collective investment undertaking, from 1 April 2000; or

(b)   where the undertaking first issued units on or after 1 April 2000, from the day of such first issue (TCA 1997, s 739B(3)).

The provisions of TCA 1997 Part 8 Chapter 4 (deposit interest retention tax) apply to a deposit to which an investment undertaking is for the time being entitled as if such deposit were not a relevant deposit within the meaning of that Chapter. In other words, such deposits are not subject to DIRT as long as they are held by an investment undertaking.

Where TCA 1997 Part 27 Chapter 1A applies to an investment undertaking, TCA 1997 ss 734, 738 and 739 will not apply to that investment undertaking or to unit holders in relation to that investment undertaking (TCA 1997, s 739B(4)). Those provisions set out the tax treatment respectively of collective investment undertakings, undertakings for collective investment, and unit holders in undertakings for collective investment and are dealt with in **12.805**. An investment undertaking is a form of collective investment undertaking (CIU) and, as was mentioned in **12.806.3**, is similar in many respects to an undertaking for collective investment (UCI). As is to be expected, many UCIs will come within the definition of "investment undertaking" and TCA 1997, s 739B(4) is intended to avoid any overlap in relation to the legislative provisions dealing with CIUs, UCIs and investment undertakings, and between the provisions dealing with the taxation of unit holders in UCIs and investment undertakings.

12.806.6   Gain arising on chargeable event

The amount of the gain arising to an investment undertaking on the happening of a chargeable event in respect of a unit holder is set out in TCA 1997, s 739D. No gain arises where the unit holder is neither resident nor ordinarily resident in Ireland at the time of the chargeable event. Exemption from tax is provided for in respect of certain categories of unit holder, such as pension funds, charities, authorised unit trust schemes.

A reference to an investment undertaking being associated with another investment undertaking is to both investment undertakings being set up and promoted by the same person (TCA 1997, s 739D(1)(a)).

Where a unit acquired by a unit holder (the "original unit") is a unit in a sub-fund of an umbrella fund and that unit has been exchanged for a unit or units of another sub-fund of the umbrella fund, a reference to "an amount invested by a unit holder in an investment undertaking for the acquisition of a unit" is to be taken as a reference to the amount invested by the unit holder for the acquisition of the original unit (TCA 1997, s 739D(1)(b)).

References to "an amount invested by a unit holder in an investment undertaking for the acquisition of a unit" (the "original unit"), where the original unit has been exchanged for a unit or units in a transaction of the type referred to in paragraph (IIa) of the definition of "chargeable event" in TCA 1997, s 739B(1) (item (III) of the events not included in "chargeable event" in **12.806.4**), are references to the amount invested by the unit holder for the acquisition of the original unit (TCA 1997, s 739D(1)(bb)).

In the case of an amount invested by a unit holder in an investment undertaking for the acquisition of a unit, where the investment undertaking was on 31 March 2000 an IFSC fund (SCIU), a reference to "an amount invested by a unit holder in an investment undertaking for the acquisition of a unit" is to be taken as a reference to the amount invested by the unit holder for the acquisition of the unit of the SCIU, or where that unit was otherwise acquired by the unit holder, the value of that unit at its date of acquisition by the unit holder (TCA 1997, s 739D(1)(c)). In this context, "unit" and "unit holder" are as defined in TCA 1997, s 734(1) (see **12.805.1**).

The computation of a gain which arises to an investment undertaking in respect of a unit holder depends on which kind of chargeable event (see kinds of "chargeable event" listed in (a) to (f) in **12.806.4** above) is in question. The computation of the gain for each kind of chargeable event is described as follows.

(a) Relevant payment

Where the chargeable event in relation to an investment undertaking in respect of a unit holder is the making of a relevant payment, the gain arising to the investment undertaking is the amount of the relevant payment.

(b) Any other payment otherwise than on the cancellation, redemption or repurchase of a unit

Where the chargeable event in relation to an investment undertaking in respect of a unit holder is the making of any other payment by the investment undertaking otherwise than on the cancellation, redemption or repurchase of a unit, the gain arising to the investment undertaking is the amount of the payment.

(c) Payment on cancellation, redemption or repurchase of a unit

Where the chargeable event in relation to an investment undertaking in respect of a unit holder is the making of a payment by the investment undertaking on the cancellation, redemption or repurchase of a unit, the gain treated as arising to the investment undertaking is—

  (i)   the amount determined by the formula—

$$P - \frac{(C \times P)}{V}$$

     where—

       P   is the amount in money or money's worth payable to the unit holder on the cancellation, redemption or repurchase of units, without regard to any amount of appropriate tax (within the meaning of TCA 1997, s 739E – see **12.806.9**) thereby arising,

C   is the total amount invested by the unit holder in the investment undertaking to acquire the units held by the unit holder immediately before the chargeable event, reduced by any amount of first tax (appropriate tax accounted for in respect of an earlier event – see **12.806.9**), and—

   (a) where any unit was otherwise acquired by the unit holder, or

   (b) where a chargeable event was deemed to happen on 31 December 2000 in respect of the unit holder of that unit,

the amount so invested to acquire the unit is—

   (i) in the case of (a), the value of the unit at the time of its acquisition by the unit holder, and

   (ii) in the case of (b), the greater of the cost of first acquisition of the unit by the unit holder and the value of the unit on 31 December 2000, without regard to any amount of appropriate tax thereby arising, and

V   is the total value of the units held by the unit holder immediately before the chargeable event, or

(ii) where the investment undertaking has made an election under TCA 1997, s 739D(5) (see below), the gain arising is the amount of the payment reduced by the amount invested by the unit holder in the investment undertaking in acquiring the unit, and where the unit was otherwise acquired by the unit holder, the amount so invested is the value of the unit at the time of its acquisition by the unit holder (TCA 1997, s 739D(2)(c), (3)).

(d) Transfer of entitlement to a unit

Where the chargeable event in relation to an investment undertaking in respect of a unit holder is the transfer, by way of sale or otherwise, of entitlement to a unit in the investment undertaking, the gain arising to the investment undertaking is—

(i)   the amount determined by the formula—

$$V1 - \frac{(C \times V1)}{V2}$$

where—

V1   is the value of the units transferred, at the time of transfer, without regard to any amount of appropriate tax (within the meaning of TCA 1997, s 739E – see **12.806.9**) thereby arising,

C   is the total amount invested by the unit holder in the investment undertaking to acquire the units held by the unit holder immediately before the chargeable event, reduced by any amount of first tax (appropriate tax accounted for in respect of an earlier event – see **12.806.9**), and—

   (a) where any unit was otherwise acquired by the unit holder, or

   (b) where a chargeable event was deemed to happen on 31 December 2000 in respect of the unit holder of that unit, the amount so invested to acquire the unit is—

> (i) in the case of (a), the value of the unit at the time of its acquisition by the unit holder, and
>
> (ii) in the case of (b), the greater of the cost of first acquisition of the unit by the unit holder and the value of the unit on 31 December 2000 without regard to any amount of appropriate tax thereby arising, and

V2 is the total value of the units held by the unit holder immediately before the chargeable event, or

(ii) where the investment undertaking has made an election under TCA 1997, s 739D(5) (see below), the gain arising is the value of the unit transferred at the time of transfer reduced by the amount invested by the unit holder in the investment undertaking in acquiring the unit, and where the unit was otherwise acquired by the unit holder, the amount so invested is the value of the unit at the time of its acquisition by the unit holder (TCA 1997, s 739D(2)(d), (4)).

(e) Appropriation or cancellation of units to meet appropriate tax

Where the chargeable event is the appropriation or cancellation of units by an investment undertaking as a consequence of the transfer by a unit holder of entitlement to a unit, except as a consequence of a gain arising on a chargeable event which is the ending of a relevant period – (e) in the definition of "chargeable event" in **12.806.4**), the gain arising is the amount determined by the following formula:

$$A \times G \times \frac{100}{100 - (G \times (S+3))}$$

where—

A is the appropriate tax payable on the transfer by a unit holder of entitlement to a unit holder in accordance with (d) above;

G is the amount of the gain on that transfer of that unit divided by the value of that unit; and

S is the standard rate per cent (within the meaning of TCA 1997, s 4 – see **2.601**).

(f) Ending of relevant period

Where the chargeable event is the ending of a relevant period in relation to a unit of a unit holder, the gain arising is—

(i) the excess (if any) of the value of the unit, without regard to any amount of appropriate tax thereby arising, held by the unit holder on the day of that ending over the total amount invested in the investment undertaking by the unit holder for the acquisition of the unit, and where the unit was otherwise acquired by the unit holder, the amount so invested to acquire that unit is the value of the unit at the time of its acquisition by the unit holder, or

(ii) where the investment undertaking has made an election under TCA 1997, s 730D(5B) (see below), the amount determined under that subsection.

(g) Deemed chargeable event on 31 December 2000

Where the chargeable event in relation to an investment undertaking in respect of a unit holder is deemed to happen on 31 December 2000, the gain arising to the investment undertaking is the excess if any of the value of the units held by the unit holder on that day over the total amount invested in the investment undertaking by the unit holder for the acquisition of the units, and where any unit was otherwise acquired by the unit holder, the amount so invested to acquire that unit is the value of the unit at the time of its acquisition by the unit holder.

Where a chargeable event in relation to an investment undertaking is preceded by a chargeable event which is the ending of a relevant period, the gain arising on the later event is to be determined as if the earlier event had not been a chargeable event (TCA 1997, s 739D(2A)).

Elections

The election referred to in (c)(ii) and (d)(ii) above permits an investment undertaking to adopt, in place of the average cost basis prescribed, a first-in first-out (FIFO) method of arriving at the deductible cost of units cancelled, redeemed or repurchased or, as the case may be, transferred. The election is an irrevocable election made by the investment undertaking in respect of all its unit holders at the time of the election or at any other time, so that, for the purposes of identifying units acquired with units subsequently disposed of by a unit holder, units acquired at an earlier time are deemed to have been disposed of before units acquired at a later time (TCA 1997, s 739D(5)(a)).

On the first occasion that an investment undertaking is required to compute a gain on the happening of a chargeable event in respect of a unit holder on the cancellation, redemption, repurchase or transfer of a unit, and—

(i)   the gain is computed on the basis of the above-described election, the investment undertaking will be deemed to have made that election; or

(ii)   the gain is not so computed, that election may not be made (TCA 1997, s 739D(5)(b)).

Thus, whether the average cost method or the FIFO method is used to calculate the exit tax, the method used on the occasion of the first calculation is the method to be used for all subsequent such calculations.

Example 12.806.6.1

A unit holder transfers units in an investment undertaking at their then value, €12,000, at which time a total of €30,000 had been invested by the holder in acquiring units in that undertaking. The total value of units held immediately prior to the transfer was €36,000. Later, the transferee receives €18,000 from the investment undertaking on the redemption of the units acquired from the original unit holder.

The gain ("V1 - (C x V1)/V2") on the transfer, the first chargeable event, is €12,000 - (€30,000 x 12,000/36,000) = €2,000.

The gain ("P - (C x P)/V") on the second chargeable event, the redemption of the units, is as follows:

	€	€
Proceeds on redemption (P)		18,000
(C): value of units at time of acquisition	12,000	

(V): value of units held immediately before redemption	18,000
(C x P)/V: 12,000 x 18,000/18,000)	<u>12,000</u>
Taxable	<u>6,000</u>

The aggregate gains taxable as between the two unit holders is €8,000 which is equal to the overall gain represented by the excess of the proceeds on redemption €18,000 over the €10,000 paid to the investment undertaking in respect of the units transferred, ie one third of €30,000.

Example 12.806.6.2

The position is the same as in Example **12.806.6.1** except that the total amount paid by the unit holder to acquire units is €10,000 and the first chargeable event is the end of a relevant period at which time the value of the units held is €12,000. The units are later redeemed for €18,000.

The gain on the ending of the relevant period, the first chargeable event, is €12,000 - €10,000 = €2,000 (value of units less amount paid in by unit holder at that time). Tax payable @ 23% is €460.

The gain ("P - (C x P)/V") on the second chargeable event, the redemption of the units, is as follows:

	€	€
Proceeds on redemption (P)		18,000
(C): total amount invested to acquire units	10,000	
(V): value of units held immediately before redemption	18,000	
(C x P)/V: 10,000 x 18,000/18,000		<u>10,000</u>
Taxable		<u>8,000</u>
Tax @ 23%		1,840
Less: credit for tax on first event		460
Net tax payable		<u>1,380</u>

The aggregate tax payable as between the two chargeable events is €1,840 which represents the tax payable on a gain consisting of proceeds less total amount paid to the investment undertaking. Regarding the availability of credit in respect of tax on the first event, see **8.806.8** below, under *Offset of tax paid on chargeable event*.

The election referred to in (f)(ii) permits an investment undertaking, in place of using a valuation of the units at the date of the chargeable event (the date on which the relevant period ended), to use their valuation on the later of 30 June and 31 December prior to the date of the chargeable event. The election is an irrevocable election made by an investment undertaking in respect of all its unit holders at the time of the election or at any other time and the amount is as determined by the formula—

$$A1 - A2$$

where—

A1 is the value of the unit at the later of 30 June or 31 December prior to the date of the chargeable event, and

A2 is—

(i) the total amount invested in the investment undertaking by the unit holder for the acquisition of the unit, and where the unit was otherwise acquired by the unit holder, the amount so invested to acquire that unit is the value of the unit at the time of its acquisition by the unit holder, or

(ii) if a chargeable event being the ending of a relevant period ((e) in the definition of "chargeable event" in **12.806.4**) has previously occurred, the value of the unit at the later of 30 June or 31 December prior to the date of the latest of such chargeable events (TCA 1997, s 739D(5B)(a)).

On the first occasion that an investment undertaking is required to compute a gain on the happening of a chargeable event in respect of a unit holder on the cancellation, redemption, repurchase or transfer of a unit, and—

(i) the gain is computed on the basis of the above-described election, the investment undertaking will be deemed to have made that election; or

(ii) the gain is not so computed, that election may not be made (TCA 1997, s 739D(5B)(b)).

12.806.7 Gains treated as not arising

A gain is treated as not arising to an investment undertaking on the happening of a chargeable event in respect of a unit holder in certain circumstances. This treatment in any case is dependent on the making to the investment undertaking of one of the appropriate declarations provided for in TCA 1997 Schedule 2B.

Declarations

An investment undertaking is obliged to keep and retain declarations made to it for a period of six years from the time the unit holder of the units in respect of which a declaration was made ceases to be both such a unit holder and a unit holder in all investment undertakings which are associated with the investment undertaking (ie, other investment undertakings which have been set up and promoted by the same person – see **12.806.6**) (TCA 1997, s 739D(10)).

The declarations provided for in paragraphs 2-9B of TCA 1997 Schedule 2B relate to exempt Irish investors and follow a fairly uniform format. A declaration of this kind:

(a) is made and signed by the "declarer", who is the person entitled to the units or, in the case of an approved retirement fund or an approved minimum retirement fund, the qualifying fund manager;

(b) is in such form as may be prescribed or authorised by the Revenue Commissioners;

(c) declares that at the time the declaration is made, the person entitled to the units is the appropriate kind of exempt person (eg, pension scheme, special investment scheme, unit trust, beneficial owners of assets in an ARF, AMRF or special savings incentive account, credit union etc);

(d) contains the name and tax reference number of the person entitled to the units;

(e) contains such other information as the Revenue Commissioners may reasonably require.

Additional information is required in the cases of certain declarations. For example, in the case of a pension scheme, the declaration must contain a certificate by the appropriate person in relation to the pension scheme that the declaration and the information furnished in relation to the name and tax reference number of the scheme are true and correct. The *appropriate person* in relation to a pension scheme means—

(a) in the case of an exempt approved scheme (within the meaning of TCA 1997, s 774 – see **3.202.5**), the administrator (within the meaning of TCA 1997, s 770 – the person or persons having the management of the scheme) of the scheme;

(b) in the case of a retirement annuity contract to which TCA 1997, s 784 or 785 applies (see **12.602**), the person lawfully carrying on in the State the business of granting annuities on human life with whom the contract is made; and

(c) in the case of a trust scheme to which TCA 1997, s 784 or 785 applies, the trustees of the trust scheme.

In the case of a charity, the declaration must contain a statement to the effect that the units in respect of which the declaration is made are held for charitable purposes only and form part of the assets of a body or persons or trust treated by the Revenue Commissioners as a body or trust established for charitable purposes only. An undertaking is required to the effect that if the person entitled to the units ceases to be entitled to exemption from income tax, the declarer will notify the investment undertaking accordingly.

In the case of an approved retirement fund (ARF) (a fund which is managed by a qualifying fund manager and which complies with certain conditions (TCA 1997, s 784A(1)(a))) or an approved minimum retirement fund (AMRF) (a fund managed by a qualifying fund manager and which complies with certain conditions (TCA 1997, s 784C(1)), the declaration must confirm that the units in respect of which the declaration is made are all assets of an ARF or AMRF and are managed by the declarer for the individual beneficially entitled to the units. An undertaking is required to the effect that if the units cease to be assets of the ARF or, as the case may be, the AMRF, including a case where the units are transferred to another such fund, the declarer will notify the investment undertaking accordingly.

Paragraphs 10 and 11 of Schedule 2B set out the formats of declarations respectively of a non-resident corporate and non-corporate unit holder. The details described in (a), (b) and (e) above, as well as the name and address of the declarer, are required on these declarations together with a declaration to the effect that the declarer at the time of the declaration is not resident in the State or, as the case may be, is neither resident nor ordinarily resident in the State. An undertaking is required to the effect that if the declarer becomes resident in the State, the declarer will notify the investment undertaking accordingly.

A paragraph 12 declaration is a declaration to the Collector-General which contains the information set out in (a), (b) and (e) above and the name, address and tax reference number of the investment undertaking. It also contains a declaration to the effect that no units in the investment undertaking were held on 1 April 2000 by a person who was resident in the State at that time, other than such persons whose names and addresses are set out in the schedule to the declaration. The schedule sets out the name and address of each person who on 1 April 2000 was a unit holder in the investment undertaking and who was on that date resident in the State.

A paragraph 13 declaration is a declaration made by intermediaries which contains the information set out in (a) and (b) above and the name and address of the intermediary. It also contains a declaration to the effect that at the time of making the declaration, the person beneficially entitled to each of the units in respect of which the declaration is made is, in the case of a company, not resident in the State and, where the person is not a company, is neither resident nor ordinarily resident in the State. An undertaking is required to the effect that where the intermediary becomes aware that the declaration is no longer correct, the intermediary will notify the investment undertaking accordingly.

Exempt Irish investors

A gain is treated as not arising to an investment undertaking on the happening of a chargeable event in respect of a unit holder where, immediately before the chargeable event, the unit holder:

(a) is a pension scheme which has made an appropriate declaration (paragraph 2) to the investment undertaking;

(b) is a company carrying on life business within the meaning of TCA 1997, s 706 (see **12.602**) and which company has made an appropriate declaration (paragraph 3) to the investment undertaking;

(c) is another investment undertaking which has made an appropriate declaration (paragraph 4) to the investment undertaking;

(d) is a special investment scheme (within the meaning of TCA 1997, s 737 – see **12.806.3** above under *(a) Unit Trusts*) which has made an appropriate declaration (paragraph 5) to the investment undertaking;

(e) is a unit trust to which TCA 1997, s 731(5)(a) applies (see **12.806.3** above under *(a) Unit Trusts*) which has made an appropriate declaration (paragraph 6) to the investment undertaking;

(f) is a person who—

  (i) is exempt from income tax under TCA 1997, s 207(1)(b) (charitable exemption), or

  (ii) is exempt from corporation tax by virtue of TCA 1997, s 207(1)(b) as it applies for corporation tax purposes under TCA 1997, s 76(6) (application of income tax principles to corporation tax – see **3.102.2**),

  and has made an appropriate declaration (paragraph 7) to the investment undertaking,

(g) is a qualifying management company or a specified company (within the meaning of TCA 1997, s 734(1) – see below) and has made an appropriate declaration (paragraph 8) to the investment undertaking;

(h) is a person exempt from income tax and capital gains tax by virtue of TCA 1997, s 784A(2) (exemption for beneficial owners of assets in an approved retirement fund) and the units held are assets of an approved retirement fund (ARF), an approved minimum retirement fund (AMRF) (within the meaning of TCA 1997, s 784C – a fund managed by a qualifying fund manager and which complies with certain conditions) or, as the case may be, a special savings incentive account (see **12.603.7**), and the qualifying fund manager or, as the case may be, the qualifying savings manager has made an appropriate declaration (paragraph 9) to the investment undertaking;

(i) is a person exempt from income tax and capital gains tax by virtue of TCA 1997, s 787I (as inserted by the Pensions (Amendment) Act, 2002) and the units held are assets of a PRSA under the terms of a PRSA contract and the

PRSA administrator had made an appropriate declaration (paragraph 9A) to the investment undertaking;

(j)   is a credit union (within the meaning of section 2 of the Credit Union Act 1997) that has made an appropriate declaration (paragraph 9B) to the investment undertaking;

(k)   is, where the investment undertaking is a money market fund (as defined in Regulation (EC) No 2423/2001 of the European Central Bank of 22 November 2001 (OJ No L333, 17.12.2001, p1)), a company that is or will be within the charge to corporation tax in accordance with TCA 1997, s 739G(2) in respect of payments made to it by the investment undertaking (see **12.806.10** below under *Companies*) and has made an appropriate declaration to that effect and has provided the investment undertaking with the company's tax reference number,

(l)   is the National Pensions Reserve Fund Commission and has made a declaration to that effect to the investment undertaking, or

(m)   is a company that—

    (i)   is or will be within the charge to corporation tax in accordance with TCA 1997, s 110(2) (securitisation – see **7.206.11**) in respect of payments made to it by the investment undertaking, and

    (ii)   has made a declaration to that effect and has provided the investment undertaking with the company's tax reference number,

and the investment undertaking is in possession of the declaration immediately before the chargeable event (TCA 1997, s 739D(6)).

A *PRSA* is a personal retirement savings account established by a contributor with a PRSA provider (within the meaning of Part X of the Pensions Act, 1990).

A *PRSA contract* is a contract entered into between a PRSA provider and a contributor in respect of a PRSA product (within the meaning of Part X of the Pensions Act, 1990).

A *PRSA administrator* is a PRSA provider or a person to whom a PRSA provider delegates, in pursuance of Part X of the Pensions Act, 1990, its administrative functions in relation to a PRSA, including a person appointed by the PRSA provider in accordance with TCA 1997, s 787G(5). TCA 1997, s 787G(5) applies where the administrator or provider is not resident in the State or is not trading in the State through a branch or agency and is accordingly obliged to ensure that there is a resident person appointed by the PRSA provider to be responsible for the discharge of all duties and obligations relating to the PRSAs that are imposed on the PRSA administrator or provider by virtue of TCA 1997 Part 30 Chapter 2A (Personal Retirement Savings Accounts)).

A *specified company* referred to in (g) above is, broadly, an IFSC or a Shannon financial services company not more than 25% of the share capital of which is owned directly or indirectly by persons resident in the State, or all of the share capital of which is owned directly by another company resident in the State and not more than 25% of the share capital of that other company is owned directly or indirectly by persons resident in the State.

Declaration held by investment undertaking

Subject to TCA 1997, s 739D(8) in relation to IFSC funds (see below), a gain is treated as not arising to an investment undertaking on the happening of a chargeable event in respect of a unit holder where, immediately before the chargeable event, the investment undertaking:

(a)   is in possession of an appropriate declaration (paragraphs 10 (company) and 11 (non-company)); and

(b)   is not in possession of any information which would reasonably suggest that—

   (i)   the information contained in that declaration is not, or is no longer, materially correct,

   (ii)   the unit holder failed to comply with the undertaking (to the effect that if the declarer becomes resident in the State, the declarer will notify the investment undertaking accordingly) referred to in the declaration, or

   (iii)   immediately before the chargeable event the unit holder is resident or ordinarily resident in the State (TCA 1997, s 739D(7)).

Where an investment undertaking is in possession of:

(a)   a declaration made by a unit holder who is a person referred to in TCA 1997, s 739D(6) (see *Exempt Irish investors* above); or

(b)   a declaration made by a unit holder of the kind referred to in TCA 1997, s 739D(7) (see above) and the conditions in (b)(i) to (iii) above are satisfied,

and that unit holder is entitled to the units in respect of which the declaration was made, a gain will not be treated as arising—

   (i)   to an investment undertaking on the happening of a chargeable event in respect of the unit holder in relation to any other units in the investment undertaking to which the unit holder becomes entitled; or

   (ii)   to another investment undertaking which is associated with the investment undertaking (ie, where both investment undertakings have been set up and promoted by the same person – see **12.806.6**) referred to in (i), on the happening of a chargeable event in respect of the unit holder in relation to units in that other investment undertaking to which the unit holder becomes entitled (TCA 1997, s 739D(7A)).

Accordingly, where an investment undertaking is in possession of a declaration from a unit holder which entitles that unit holder to exit tax exemption, that declaration will have effect not only in respect of the units in respect of which the declaration is made, but also in respect of any other units that the unit holder acquires in the same fund or any associated fund.

IFSC funds at 31 March 2000

Subject to the position relating to an "excepted unit holder" (see below), a gain is treated as not arising to an investment undertaking on the happening of a chargeable event in respect of a unit holder where the investment undertaking was on 31 March 2000 an IFSC fund (specified collective investment undertaking) and:

(i) the unit holder was a unit holder in relation to that fund at that time, and on or before 30 June 2000 the investment undertaking makes a declaration to the Collector-General in accordance with TCA 1997 Schedule 2B paragraph 12; or

(ii) the unit holder otherwise became a unit holder on or before 30 September 2000 and the investment undertaking forwarded to the Collector-General, on or before 1 November 2000, a list containing the name and address of each such unit holder who is resident in the State,

otherwise than, subject to TCA 1997, s 739D(8)(b) (see below), in respect of a unit holder (an "excepted unit holder"):

(I) whose name is included in the schedule to the declaration referred to in TCA 1997 Sch 2B paragraph 12(d) or the list referred to in (ii) above; and

(II) who has not made a declaration of a kind referred to in TCA 1997, s 739D(6) to the investment undertaking (TCA 1997, s 739D(8)(a)).

The declaration to be made to the Collector-General in accordance with paragraph 12 is to the effect that no units in the investment undertaking were held on 1 April 2000 by a person who was resident in the State at that time, other than such persons whose names and addresses are set out in the schedule to the declaration (paragraph 12(d)). The schedule sets out the name and address of each person who on 1 April 1 2000 was a unit holder in the investment undertaking and who was on that date resident in the State.

In other words, the provision to the effect that a gain is treated as not arising to an investment undertaking on the happening of a chargeable event in respect of a unit holder is disapplied (subject to TCA 1997, s 739D(8)(b)) in a case involving an excepted unit holder. An *excepted unit holder* is a unit holder whose name is included in the schedule to the declaration referred to above and who has not made (whether because that unit holder was not entitled to do so or because of failure to do so) a declaration of a kind referred to in TCA 1997, s 739D(6) (see *Exempt Irish investors* above) to the investment undertaking.

A gain is, however, treated as not arising to an investment undertaking on the happening of a chargeable event in respect of an excepted unit holder where the chargeable event is deemed to happen on 31 December 2000 (TCA 1997, s 739D(8)(b)). In the case of any other kind of chargeable event, therefore, such gain is treated as arising to an investment undertaking on the happening of a chargeable event in respect of an excepted unit holder. As regards a chargeable event which is deemed to happen on 31 December 2000 and which is in respect of an excepted unit holder, TCA 1997, s 739G provides for a tax charge at 40% in respect of the gain (see **12.806.10**).

Where in accordance with TCA 1997, s 739D(8)(a) (see above) a gain is not treated as arising to an investment undertaking on the happening of a chargeable event in respect of a unit holder who acquires units on or before 30 September 2000, a gain will not be treated as arising:

(a) to an investment undertaking on the happening of a chargeable event in respect of the unit holder in relation to any other units in the investment undertaking to which the unit holder becomes entitled; or

(b) to another investment undertaking which is associated with the investment undertaking (ie, where both investment undertakings have been set up and promoted by the same person – see **12.806.6**) referred to in (a), on the happening of a chargeable event in respect of the unit holder in relation to units in that other investment undertaking to which the unit holder becomes entitled (TCA 1997, s 739D(8A)).

Thus, in a case where the transitional arrangements for IFSC funds coming within the investment undertaking regime are extended so that their existing declaration procedure suffices for unit holders up to 30 September 2000, those arrangements will apply not only in respect of the units held by any such unit holder on or before that date, but also in respect of any other units that the unit holder acquires in the same fund or any associated fund.

Other transitional arrangements

Transitional arrangements are also provided for certain unauthorised exempt unit trusts which, on becoming authorised, come within the investment undertaking regime. A gain is not to be treated as arising to an investment undertaking on the happening of a chargeable event in respect of a unit holder where:

(a) the investment undertaking was a unit trust mentioned in TCA 1997, s 731(5)(a) (see **12.806.3**);

(b) the unit holder held units in that trust at the time it became an investment undertaking; and

(c) within 30 days of that time, the investment undertaking forwards to the Collector-General a list containing the name and address of each such unit holder and such other information as the Revenue Commissioners reasonably require (TCA 1997, s 739D(8B)).

Scheme of amalgamation

A gain is not to be treated as arising to an investment undertaking on the happening of a chargeable event in respect of a unit holder where—

(i) the unit holder acquires units in the investment undertaking in exchange for units held in a unit trust referred to in TCA 1997, s 731(5)(a) (see **12.806.3**), under a scheme of amalgamation; and

(ii) within 30 days of the scheme of amalgamation taking place, the investment undertaking forwards to the Collector-General a list containing, in respect of each unit holder who so acquired units in the investment undertaking, the name and address and such other information as the Revenue Commissioners may reasonably require (TCA 1997, s 739D(8C)).

Scheme of amalgamation means an arrangement whereby a unit holder in a unit trust referred to in TCA 1997, s 731(5)(a) exchanges units so held for units in an investment undertaking.

Scheme of migration and amalgamation

A gain is not to be treated as arising to an investment undertaking on the happening of a chargeable event in respect of a unit holder where:

(i) under a scheme of migration and amalgamation the unit holder acquires units in the investment undertaking in exchange for the unit holder's interest in an offshore fund; and

(ii)   within 30 days of the scheme of migration and amalgamation taking place, the investment undertaking forwards to the Collector-General a declaration of the kind described below,

otherwise than in respect of a unit holder whose name is included in the schedule referred to below (TCA 1997, s 739D(8D)(b)).

Scheme of migration and amalgamation means an arrangement whereby the assets of an offshore fund are transferred to an investment undertaking in exchange for the issue by the investment undertaking of units to each of the persons who has an interest in the offshore fund, in proportion to the value of that interest, and as a result of which the value of that interest becomes negligible (TCA 1997, s 739D(8D)(a)).

An *offshore fund* is any of the following:

(a)   a company not resident in the State;

(b)   a unit trust scheme, the trustees of which are neither resident nor ordinarily resident in the State; and

(c)   any arrangements not within (a) or (b) which take effect by virtue of the law of a territory outside the State and which under that law create rights in the nature of co-ownership (without restricting that expression to its meaning in the law of the State),

in which persons have an interest and which is established for the purposes of collective investment by such persons, and references to an offshore fund are accordingly to be construed as references to any such arrangements in which such persons have an interest (TCA 1997, s 739D(8D)(a)).

The declaration referred to above is a declaration in writing made and signed by the investment undertaking which:

(i)   declares to the best of the investment undertaking's knowledge and belief that at the time of the scheme of migration and amalgamation it did not issue units to a person who was resident in the State at that time, other than such persons whose names and addresses are set out on the schedule to the declaration; and

(ii)   contains a schedule which sets out the name and address of each person who was resident in the State at the time that the person was issued units by the investment undertaking under the scheme of a migration and amalgamation (TCA 1997, s 739D(8D)(c)).

Declarations made by intermediaries

A gain is not to be treated as arising to an investment undertaking on the happening of a chargeable event in respect of a unit holder, where immediately before the chargeable event the investment undertaking or an investment undertaking associated with the first-mentioned investment undertaking:

(a)   is, in relation to the units concerned, in possession of an appropriate declaration (declaration by intermediary – Schedule 2B, paragraph 13); and

(b)   is not in possession of any information which would reasonably suggest that—

(i)   the information contained in that declaration is not, or is no longer, materially correct,

    (ii)   the intermediary failed to comply with the undertaking (see undertaking in (e) below) referred to in the declaration, or

    (iii)   any of the persons on whose behalf the intermediary holds units of, or receives payments from, the investment undertaking, is resident or ordinarily resident in the State (TCA 1997, s 739D(9)).

The declaration in Schedule 2B paragraph 13 is a declaration in writing to the investment undertaking which:

(a)   is made and signed by the intermediary;

(b)   is made in such form as may be prescribed or authorised by the Revenue Commissioners;

(c)   contains the name and address of the intermediary;

(d)   declares that—

    (i)   at the time of making the declaration, to the best of the intermediary's knowledge and belief, the person who has beneficial entitlement to each of the units in respect of which the declaration is made—

        (I) is not resident in the State, where that person is a company, and

        (II) where that person is not a company, the person is neither resident nor ordinarily resident in the State, and

    (ii)   unless the investment undertaking is notified in writing to the contrary, every subsequent application by the intermediary to acquire units in the investment undertaking, or an investment undertaking associated with the first-mentioned investment undertaking, is to be on behalf of such person,

(e)   contains an undertaking that where the intermediary becomes aware at any time that the declaration is no longer correct, the intermediary will notify the investment undertaking in writing accordingly; and

(f)   contains such other information as the Revenue Commissioners may reasonably require.

A gain is not to be treated as arising to an investment undertaking on the happening of a chargeable event in respect of a unit holder, where immediately before the chargeable event the investment undertaking or an investment undertaking associated with the first-mentioned investment undertaking:

(a)   is, in relation to the units concerned, in possession of an appropriate declaration (declaration by intermediary: certain resident entities – Schedule 2B, paragraph 14); and

(b)   is not in possession of any information which would reasonably suggest that—

    (i)   the information contained in that declaration is not, or is no longer, materially correct,

    (ii)   the intermediary failed to comply with the undertaking (see undertaking in (e) below) referred to in the declaration, or

    (iii)   any of the persons on whose behalf the intermediary holds units of, or receives payments from, the investment undertaking, is not a person referred to in TCA 1997, s 739D(6)(a)-(k) (see (a)-(k) under *Exempt Irish investors* above) (TCA 1997, s 739D(9A)).

The declaration in Schedule 2B paragraph 14 is a declaration in writing to the investment undertaking which:

(a) is made and signed by the intermediary;

(b) is made in such form as may be prescribed or authorised by the Revenue Commissioners;

(c) contains the name and address of the intermediary;

(d) declares that—

    (i) at the time of making the declaration, to the best of the intermediary's knowledge and belief, the person who has beneficial entitlement to each of the units in respect of which the declaration is made is a person referred to in TCA 1997, s 739D(6)(a)-(k) (see (a)-(k) under *Exempt Irish investors* above), and

    (ii) unless the investment undertaking is notified in writing to the contrary, every subsequent application by the intermediary to acquire units in the investment undertaking, or an investment undertaking associated with the first-mentioned investment undertaking, is to be on behalf of such person,

(e) contains an undertaking that where the intermediary becomes aware at any time that the declaration is no longer correct, the intermediary will notify the investment undertaking in writing accordingly; and

(f) contains such other information as the Revenue Commissioners may reasonably require.

12.806.8 Personal portfolio investment undertakings

Special anti-avoidance rules provide for the taxation of personal portfolio investment undertakings in relation to payments made to unit holders. Income and gains had been allowed to be rolled up tax-free within a fund. Payments made from the fund to unit holders were generally subject to an exit tax of 23% and no further charge to tax applied. This feature had given rise to a practice whereby certain investors placed personal asset investments into investment undertakings with a view ultimately to achieving a final tax liability based on a rate of 23% (instead of the investor's marginal tax rate).

With a personal portfolio investment undertaking, the location of the property of the undertaking or offshore fund in an EU Member State, an EEA state, or a state which is a member of the OECD with which Ireland has a tax treaty ("offshore states" - see **3.210.10** regarding more favourable tax treatment from 1 January 2001 for certain offshore funds) can be influenced by the unit holder or by certain connected persons.

Under the special rules, where a chargeable event occurs in relation to an investment undertaking which is a personal portfolio investment undertaking on or after 20 February 2007, the gain arising is taxable at the standard rate of income tax plus 23%.

Where a payment is made in respect of an offshore fund in an EU Member State, an EEA state, or a member of the OECD with which Ireland has a double taxation agreement, and the fund is a personal portfolio investment undertaking, the payment is taxable at the standard rate plus 23% where the income was correctly included in the individual's tax return. Where the payment was not correctly so included, the payment is taxable at the individual's marginal rate plus 23%.

A *personal portfolio investment undertaking*, for the purposes of TCA 1997, Part 27 Chapter 1A (investment undertakings) and Chapter 4 (certain offshore funds - see **3.210.10**) is—

   (a)   in relation to an investor in an investment undertaking, an investment undertaking, and

   (b)   in relation to an investor in an offshore fund (within the meaning of TCA 1997, s 743 - see **3.210.1**) to which TCA 1997, Part 27 Chapter 4 (see **3.210.10**) applies, such an offshore fund,

under the terms of which some or all of the property of the undertaking or, as the case may be, the offshore fund, may be, or was, selected by, or the selection of some or all of the property may be, or was, influenced by—

   (i)   the investor,

   (ii)   a person acting on behalf of the investor,

   (iii)   a person connected with (within the meaning of TCA 1997, s 10 - see **2.3**) the investor,

   (iv)   a person connected with a person acting on behalf of the investor,

   (v)   the investor and a person connected with the investor, or

   (vi)   a person acting on behalf of both the investor and a person connected with the investor (TCA 1997, s 739BA(2)).

An *investor* for the above purpose is—

   (a)   in relation to an investment undertaking, a unit holder in the undertaking who is an individual, and

   (b)   in relation to an offshore fund to which TCA 1997, Part 27 Chapter 4 applies, an individual who has a material interest (within the meaning of TCA 1997, s 743 - see **3.210.2**) in the offshore fund (TCA 1997, s 739BA(1)).

In relation to the definition of "personal portfolio investment undertaking", the terms of an investment undertaking, or offshore fund, as the case may be, are treated as permitting the selection referred to where—

   (a)   the terms of such undertaking or offshore fund, or any other agreement between any person referred to in that definition and such undertaking or offshore fund concerned—

      (i)   allow the exercise of an option by any person referred to in the definition to make the selection referred to there,

      (ii)   give such undertaking or offshore fund discretion to offer any person referred to in the definition the right to make the selection referred to there, or

      (iii)   allow any of the persons referred to in the definition the right to request, subject to the agreement of such undertaking or offshore fund, a change in those terms such that the selection referred to may be made by any of those persons, or

   (b)   the investor is unable under those terms to select any of the property but any of the persons referred to in the definition has or had the option of requiring such undertaking or offshore fund to appoint an investment advisor (no matter how such a person is described) in relation to the selection of the property (TCA 1997, s 739BA(3)).

An investment undertaking or an offshore fund, as the case may be, is not a personal portfolio investment undertaking if—

(a) the only property which may be or has been selected satisfies the condition specified in TCA 1997, s 739B(5), and

(b) the terms under which such undertaking or offshore fund is offered meet the requirements of TCA 1997, s 739B(6) (see below).

The condition specified in TCA 1997, s 739B(5) is that at the time the property is or was available to be selected, the opportunity to select—

(i) in the case of land (including an interest in land and unquoted shares deriving their value or the greater part of their value directly or indirectly from land - TCA 1997, s 730BA(1)), that property, and

(ii) in any other case, property of the same description as the first-mentioned property,

is or was available to the public (individuals generally, companies generally, or a combination of these - TCA 1997, s 730BA(1)) on terms which provide or provided that the opportunity to select the property is or was available to any person falling within the terms of the opportunity and that opportunity is or was clearly identified to the public, in marketing or other promotional literature published at that time by the investment undertaking or offshore fund concerned, as available generally to any person falling within the terms of the opportunity.

The requirements of TCA 1997, s 739B(6) are that—

(a) the investment undertaking or offshore fund concerned does not subject any person to any treatment in connection with the opportunity which is different or more burdensome than any treatment to which any other person is or may be subject, and

(b) where the terms of the opportunity referred to in TCA 1997, s 739B(5) include terms—

(i) which set out the capital requirement of the opportunity and this requirement is identified to the public in the marketing or other promotional material published by the investment undertaking or offshore fund at the time the property is available to be selected, and

(ii) indicating that 50% or more by value of the property referred to in TCA 1997, s 739B(5) is or is to be land,

then, the amount that any one person may invest in the investment undertaking or offshore fund may not represent more than 1% of the capital requirement (exclusive of any borrowings) of the opportunity as so identified.

TCA 1997, s 739BA applies, as respects the occurrence of a chargeable event in relation to an investment undertaking, the receipt by a person of a payment in respect of a material interest in an offshore fund and the disposal of a material interest in an offshore fund, on or after 20 February 2007.

12.806.9   Appropriate tax

TCA 1997, s 739E provides for the rate of tax to be applied to a gain. In the case of a payment by an investment undertaking to a unit holder which is a normal annual or more frequent income distribution, the rate of tax is the standard rate of income tax at the time in question. Where the payment is not of that kind, the rate of tax is the standard rate of income tax increased by three percentage points. The tax which is to be deducted on the occurrence of a chargeable event is referred to as *appropriate tax*.

Amount of appropriate tax

Subject to TCA 1997, s 739E(1)(ba), where the amount of the gain is the amount of the relevant payment (see (a) in **12.806.6**), appropriate tax is a sum representing income tax on the amount of the gain arising to the investment undertaking at the standard rate for the year of assessment in which the gain arises (TCA 1997, s 739E(1)(a)).

Subject to TCA 1997, s 739E(1)(ba), where the chargeable event happens on or after 1 January 2001 and the amount of the gain is any of the other amounts described in (b), (c), (d) and (e) in **12.806.6**, appropriate tax is a sum representing income tax on the amount of the gain arising to the investment undertaking at a rate determined by the formula: (S + 3) per cent – where S is the standard rate per cent for the year of assessment in which the gain arises (TCA 1997, s 739E(1)(b)).

Where, in the case of a personal portfolio investment undertaking, the chargeable event happens on or after 20 February 2007, the appropriate tax is a sum representing income tax on the amount of the gain arising at a rate determined by the formula: (S + 23) per cent – where S is the standard rate per cent for the year of assessment in which the gain arises (TCA 1997, s 739E(1)(ba)).

Where the chargeable event happens in the period 1 April 2000 to 31 December 2000 and the amount of the gain is any of the other amounts described in (b), (c), (d) and (e) in **12.806.6**, appropriate tax is a sum representing income tax on the amount of the gain arising to the investment undertaking at a rate of 40% (TCA 1997, s 739E(1)(c)).

Offset of tax paid on chargeable event

Appropriate tax accounted for, paid and not repaid on a chargeable event which is the ending of a relevant period in relation to a unit of a unit holder (referred to as *first tax*) may be offset against appropriate tax paid on a subsequent chargeable event. In certain circumstances, where the final amount of tax due is less than the amount already collected, tax overpaid may be refunded.

Where at any time a chargeable event is preceded by another chargeable event which *was* the ending of a relevant period, a proportion of *first tax* will be set off against appropriate tax (*second tax*) in respect of the gain (*new gain*) on the later event (TCA 1997, s 739E(1A)(b)(i)). The proportion, referred to as the *relevant proportion*, of the appropriate tax to be set off is an amount determined by the following formula:

$$A \times \frac{B}{C}$$

where—

   A   is the first tax in relation to the unit,

   B   is the new gain, and

C   is a gain determined in accordance with TCA 1997, s 739D on the assumption that the unit to which the first tax applied was cancelled at that time (TCA 1997, s 739E(1A)(c)).

If the second event is, say, the redemption of the units, the formula will produce a value equivalent to the tax on the first event since the values of B and C will be the same. Otherwise, where the new gain arises on, say, the making of a relevant payment, the creditable tax will only be a proportion of the tax on the first event.

If the relevant proportion exceeds the second tax, the excess amount is to be paid by the investment undertaking to the unit holder concerned. The excess amount is also to be included in the return required by TCA 1997, s 739F(2) (see below) and is to be treated as an amount which may be set off against appropriate tax payable by the investment undertaking in respect of any chargeable event in the period for which such return is to be made, or any subsequent period.

Alternatively, where the undertaking elects in writing to the Revenue Commissioners, the excess amount may be paid to the unit holder in respect of the unit on receipt of a claim by the unit holder but only if immediately before the chargeable event the value of the number of units of the investment undertaking in respect of which, if a gain had arisen, would be treated as arising to the investment undertaking on the happening of a chargeable event does not exceed 15% of the value of the total number of units of the investment undertaking at that time. In other words, where the percentage of the value of chargeable units in an investment undertaking does not exceed 15% of the value of the total units and the investment undertaking so elects, the amount of any excess tax arising, on a deemed disposal, will be repaid directly to the unit holder by the Revenue Commissioners, rather than by the investment undertaking, on receipt of a claim by the unit holder.

Where the investment undertaking has advised the unit holder that the excess is being repaid in accordance with the election procedure and has supplied the unit holder with the necessary information to enable the claim to be made to the Revenue, it will be deemed to have made the election; otherwise the election may not be made (TCA 1997, s 739E(1A)(b)(ii)).

Recovery of appropriate tax by investment undertaking

Where an investment undertaking is liable to account for appropriate tax in connection with a chargeable event in relation to a unit holder, it will be entitled to pass on the cost of that tax to that unit holder. Thus, where the chargeable event is the making of a payment to the unit holder, the investment undertaking will be entitled to deduct from the payment an amount equal to the appropriate tax. Where the chargeable event is the transfer by a unit holder of entitlement to a unit, the appropriation or cancellation of units as a consequence of the transfer by a unit holder of entitlement to a unit, the ending of a relevant period, or where the chargeable event is deemed to happen on 31 December 2000, the investment undertaking will be entitled to appropriate or cancel such units of the unit holder as are required to meet the amount of appropriate tax.

In any of the above cases, the investment undertaking is acquitted and discharged of such deduction or, as the case may be, such appropriation or cancellation as if the amount of appropriate tax had been paid to the unit holder. The unit holder is obliged to allow such deduction or, as the case may be, such appropriation (TCA 1997, s 739E(3)).

Returns and collection of appropriate tax

An investment undertaking is required to account for the appropriate tax in connection with a chargeable event in relation to a unit holder in accordance with TCA 1997, s 739F, as set out below (TCA 1997, s 739E(2)). A de minimis limit applies to the effect that the investment undertaking will not, in respect of a deemed disposal only, be required to deduct exit tax where the value of the number of chargeable units in the investment undertaking (or in the sub-fund within an umbrella scheme) is less than 10% of the value of the total units and the investment undertaking, or sub-fund, elects to report annually certain details for each unit holder. As provided by TCA 1997, s 739G(2A), the unit holder will, instead, be required to return the gain, constituting profits or gains chargeable to tax under Case IV of Schedule D at the rate specified in TCA 1997, s 739E(1)(b) (the standard rate of tax for the year of assessment in which the gain arises plus three percentage points - see above under *Amount of appropriate tax*), directly to the Revenue Commissioners and to account for the appropriate tax. The gain is not to be reckoned in computing total income for the purposes of the Tax Acts.

In relation to a chargeable event which is the ending of a relevant period, the obligation to account for appropriate tax will not apply where—

(a)　immediately before the chargeable event the value of the number of units in the investment undertaking, or if an umbrella scheme exists in the sub-fund concerned, in respect of which any gains arising would be treated as arising to the investment undertaking, or the subfund as the case may be, on the happening of a chargeable event is less than 10% of the value of the total number of units in the investment undertaking, or the sub-fund as the case may be, at that time, and

(b)　the investment undertaking has made an election in writing to the Revenue Commissioners that it will make, in respect of "each year of assessment", a statement (including, where appropriate, a statement with a nil amount) to the Revenue Commissioners in electronic format approved by them, on or before 31 March in the year following the year of assessment, which specifies in respect of each person who is a unit holder—

　　(i)　the name and address of the person,

　　(ii)　the value at the end of the year of assessment of the units to which the person is entitled at that time, and

　　(iii)　such other information as the Revenue Commissioners may require (TCA 1997, s 739E(2A)(a)).

Where the appropriate tax obligation does not apply by reason of (a) and (b) above, the investment undertaking must advise the unit holder concerned in writing to that effect and must make the statement described in (b). The unit holder will be deemed for "that chargeable period" (presumably the year of assessment in question or, in the case of a unit holder which is a company, the accounting period in which the chargeable event occurs) to be a chargeable person for the purposes of TCA 1997, ss 951 (see **15.104.1**) and 1084 (late return surcharge – see **15.104.10**), and the return of income to be delivered by the person for that period is to include the name and address of the investment undertaking, and the gains arising on the chargeable event (TCA 1997, s 739E(2A)(b)).

Subject to TCA 1997, s 739E(2A), an investment undertaking (including the Courts Service - see below) is required for each financial year (calendar year) to make to the Collector-General a return of the appropriate tax, and amounts which may be credited under TCA 1997, s 739E(1A) (see above), in connection with chargeable events happening on or prior to 30 June, within 30 days of that date and a return of appropriate tax, and amounts which may be credited under TCA 1997, s 739E(1A), in connection with chargeable events happening in the period 1 July to 31 December, within 30 days of that later date. Where appropriate, the return should specify that there is no appropriate tax for the period in question (TCA 1997, s 739F(2)). A return is to be in the form prescribed by the Revenue Commissioners and must include a declaration to the effect that the return is correct and complete.

Appropriate tax required to be included in a return (reduced by any amount which is to be credited under TCA 1997, s 739E(1A)) is due at the time by which the return is to be made and is payable by the investment undertaking company to the Collector-General.

The Courts Service, which administers the investment of funds lodged in Court, is required to operate the exit tax on payments made to it by the collective fund when it allocates those payments to the beneficial owners. For this purpose, the Service is treated as if it were an investment undertaking so that, in respect of payments by an investment undertaking to the Service, the obligation to operate the exit charge is transferred from the undertaking to it (TCA 1997, s 739B(2A)(a)). The Service is obliged, in respect of each year of assessment, on or before 28 February in the following year, to make a return (including a nil return if appropriate) to the Revenue Commissioners in approved electronic format which—

(i) specifies the total amount of gains arising to the investment undertaking in respect of "relevant units" (units acquired by the Service out of money under the control or subject to the order of any Court); and

(ii) specifies, where available, the name and address of each person beneficially entitled to those units, the amount of the total gains to which each such person has beneficial entitlement, and such other information as the Revenue Commissioners may require (TCA 1997, s 739B(2A)(b)).

Appropriate tax required to be included in a return is due at the time by which the return is to be made and is payable by the investment undertaking to the Collector- General (TCA 1997, s 739F(3)).

An inspector who is of the opinion that an amount of appropriate tax due has been omitted from a return made by an investment undertaking, or is dissatisfied with any return, may make an appropriate assessment on the investment undertaking (TCA 1997, s 739F(4)). Any appropriate tax assessed becomes due within one month after the issue of the notice of assessment, unless it is due earlier by reference to the time by which the relevant return is due (TCA 1997, s 739F(6)).

If any item has been incorrectly included in a return as appropriate tax, an inspector may make any assessments, adjustments or set-offs necessary to secure that the resulting liabilities to tax, including interest on unpaid tax, are the same as they would have been if the item had not been included (TCA 1997, s 739F(5)(a)). The Revenue Commissioners may repay any exit tax correctly paid by an investment undertaking but where subsequent events indicate that had the procedures been properly followed at that time, such tax would not have been paid (TCA 1997, s 739F(5)(b)).

Any amount of appropriate tax carries interest at 0.0322% for each day or part of a day from the date when the amount becomes due and payable until the date of payment (TCA 1997, s 739F(7)(b)).

12.806.10 Taxation of unit holders

Where appropriate tax has been deducted by an investment undertaking from a payment made to an individual unit holder, that individual (except where a Case IV liability arises in relation to a chargeable event which is the ending of a relevant period - see under *Returns and collection of appropriate tax* in **12.806.9**) has no further liability to income tax or capital gains tax. Where tax has not been deducted, the payment is treated as if it were a payment from an offshore fund. Where an individual is neither resident nor ordinarily resident in Ireland, no tax liability arises.

There are various circumstances in which a payment may be made by an investment undertaking to a company. Where a company is not Irish resident, no tax liability arises.

Excepted unit holder: deemed chargeable event on 31 December 2000

Where a chargeable event in relation to an investment undertaking in respect of a unit holder is deemed to happen on 31 December 2000 and the unit holder is an "excepted unit holder", that unit holder is treated for capital gains tax purposes as if the amount of the gain which would have arisen to the investment undertaking on the happening of the chargeable event were a chargeable gain accruing to the unit holder at that time. The rate of capital gains tax in respect of that chargeable gain is 40%. (TCA 1997, s 739D(8)(b) provides that a gain is treated as not arising to an investment undertaking on the happening of a chargeable event in respect of an excepted unit holder where the chargeable event is deemed to happen on 31 December 2000 – see **12.806.7** under *IFSC funds at 31 March 2000*.)

Unit holders other than companies

As respects a payment in money or money's worth to a unit holder other than a company by reason of rights conferred on that unit holder as a result of holding units in an investment undertaking, the tax consequences, as set out in TCA 1997, s 739G(2), are as follows. (References to payments from which appropriate tax has not been deducted, made to a unit holder by an investment undertaking, include references to payments made to a unit holder who holds units which are held in a recognised clearing system (TCA 1997, s 739G(3)).)

(a) Payment from which appropriate tax deducted

Where the payment is a payment from which appropriate tax has been deducted, the payment is not to be reckoned in computing the total income of the unit holder for income tax purposes and is not to be treated as giving rise to a chargeable gain for capital gains tax purposes.

(b) Payment from which appropriate tax not deducted

In the case of a payment from which appropriate tax has not been deducted, the payment is to be treated for income tax purposes as consideration for the disposal of an interest in a material interest in an offshore fund (see **3.210.2**) and the provision of TCA 1997, s 747E will apply accordingly (charge to tax under Case IV in respect of disposal of interest in offshore fund – see **3.210.10**).

Companies

As respects a payment in money or money's worth to a unit holder which is a company by reason of rights conferred on that company as a result of holding units in an investment undertaking, the tax consequences are set out in TCA 1997, s 739G(2) and are as follows. (References below to payments from which appropriate tax has not been deducted, made to a unit holder by an investment undertaking, include references to payments made to a unit holder who holds units which are held in a recognised clearing system (TCA 1997, s 739G(3)).)

(c) Relevant payment: appropriate tax deducted

In the case of a relevant payment from which appropriate tax has been deducted, the amount received by the unit holder is, subject to (e) below, treated for tax purposes as the net amount of an annual payment chargeable to tax under Case IV of Schedule D from the gross amount of which income tax has been deducted at the standard rate.

(d) Relevant payment: appropriate tax not deducted

In the case of a relevant payment from which appropriate tax has not been deducted, the amount of the payment is, subject to (e) below, treated for tax purposes as income arising to the unit holder constituting profits or gains chargeable to tax under Case IV of Schedule D.

(e) Not a relevant payment: appropriate tax deducted

In the case of a payment which is not a relevant payment from which appropriate tax has been deducted, the payment is, subject to *(g)* below, not otherwise to be taken into account for tax purposes.

(f) Not a relevant payment: appropriate tax not deducted

In the case of a payment which is not a relevant payment and from which appropriate tax has not been deducted, the amount of the payment is, subject to *(g)* below, treated for tax purposes as income arising to the unit holder constituting profits or gains chargeable to tax under Case IV of Schedule D. Where, however, the payment is in respect of the cancellation, redemption, repurchase or transfer of units, that income is to be reduced by the amount of the consideration in money or money's worth given by the unit holder for the acquisition of those units.

(g) Companies chargeable to tax under Case I of Schedule D

Where the unit holder is a company chargeable to tax under Case I of Schedule D, or is a qualifying company within the meaning of TCA 1997, s 110 (securitisation – see **7.206.11**) that is chargeable to tax on the payment under Case III of Schedule D—

(i)   subject to (ii), the amount received by the unit holder increased by the amount, if any, of appropriate tax deducted is treated as income of the unit holder for the chargeable period in which the payment is made;

(ii) where the payment is made on the cancellation, redemption or repurchase of units by the investment undertaking, such income is to be reduced by the amount of the consideration in money or moneys worth given by the unit holder for the acquisition of those units; and

(iii) the amount, if any, of appropriate tax deducted is to be set off against corporation tax assessable on the unit holder for the chargeable period in which the payment is made.

(h) Non-resident companies

The amount of a payment made to a unit holder by an investment undertaking, where the unit holder is a non-resident company, is not chargeable to income tax or capital gains tax.

Repayment of appropriate tax

Repayment of appropriate tax may not, otherwise than by virtue of TCA 1997, s 739F(5) (see *Returns and collection of appropriate tax* in **12.806.9**) or *(j)* below, be claimed by any person other than a company that is within the charge to corporation tax.

Exceptions for claims under TCA 1997 ss 189, 189A and 192

Notwithstanding *(a)* above, for the purposes of a claim to relief under TCA 1997, s 189 (payments in respect of person injuries), 189A (trusts for permanently incapacitated individuals) or 192 (payments in respect of thalidomide children), or a repayment of income tax in consequence of any of those provisions, the amount of a payment made to a unit holder is to be treated as a net amount of income from the gross amount of which has been deducted income tax, of an amount equal to the amount of appropriate tax deducted in making the payment, and that gross amount is to be treated as chargeable to tax under Case III of Schedule D (TCA 1997, s 739G(2)(j)). Thus, exit tax may be repaid in the case of a unit holder entitled to exemption from tax under any of the above three sections.

Foreign currency denominated units

Where the units of an investment undertaking are denominated in a currency other than the currency of the State (a "foreign currency"), the amount of foreign currency given by a unit holder to the investment undertaking for the acquisition of a unit in the undertaking is deemed for capital gains tax purposes to have been disposed of and reacquired by the unit holder:

(a) immediately before it was so given; and

(b) immediately after the unit holder receives payment for the cancellation, redemption or repurchase of, or as the case may be, transfer of his units (TCA 1997, s 739G(4)).

In other words, where units in an investment undertaking are denominated in a foreign currency, a currency gain made by the unit holder on the original investment is liable to capital gains tax in the period in which the units are disposed of.

12.806.11   Reconstructions and amalgamations

The cancellation of old units arising from an exchange in relation to a scheme of reconstruction or amalgamation is not to be a chargeable event. The amount invested by a unit holder for, and the date of, the acquisition of the new units is to be taken as the amount invested by the unit holder for, and the date of, the acquisition of the old units (TCA 1997, s 739H(2)).

A *scheme of reconstruction or amalgamation* means a scheme for the reconstruction of any investment undertaking or the amalgamation of any two or more investment undertakings.

An *exchange*, in relation to a scheme of reconstruction or amalgamation, means the issue of units ("new units") by an investment undertaking (the "new undertaking") to the unit holders of another investment undertaking (the "old undertaking") in respect of and in proportion to (or as nearly as may be in proportion to) their holdings of units ("old units") in the old undertaking in exchange for the transfer by the old undertaking of all its assets and liabilities to the new undertaking where the exchange is entered into for the purposes of or in connection with a scheme of reconstruction or amalgamation.

A reference in the above definition of "exchange" to an investment undertaking includes a reference to a sub-fund of an umbrella scheme where the exchange concerned is between two or more subfunds of different umbrella schemes, but only where the exchange concerned is effected for bona-fide commercial reasons and not primarily for the purpose of avoiding liability to taxation (TCA 1997, s 739H(1A), (1B)).

The above treatment is extended to common contractual funds. TCA 1997, s 739H is applied to a scheme for the reconstruction of a common contractual fund or funds (within the meaning of TCA 1997, s 739I(1)(a)(i) (see **12.810**) or to the amalgamation of two or more such funds as it would apply to a scheme of reconstruction or amalgamation (TCA 1997, s 739H(3)(a)). For this purpose, "investment undertaking" is to be read as including a common contractual fund.

The definitions of "investment undertaking", "unit" and "unit holder" apply, with any necessary modifications, to a common contractual fund as they apply to an investment undertaking within the meaning of paragraph (b) of the definition of "investment undertaking" (TCA 1997, s 739H(3)(b)). Paragraph (b) of that definition refers to "any other undertaking which is a UCITS within the meaning of the UCITS Regulations, being an undertaking which holds an authorisation, which has not been revoked, issued pursuant to those Regulations" (see **12.806.3**).

12.807   Special purpose investment companies

Special purpose investment companies (SPICs) are, like non-designated AICs, intended to operate on behalf of private investors and may not be marketed to the public. The trading profits and gains of a SPIC are subject to corporation tax at the effective 10% rate, subject to holding the required certificate under TCA 1997, s 446 from the Minister for Finance.

Companies capital duty at the rate of 1% of the share capital subscribed is payable in the cases of SPICs which are limited liability companies; no such duty arises in the cases of unlimited liability companies. Transfers of shares in a SPIC (other than shares in bearer form and denominated in a non-Irish currency), whether the company is a limited or an unlimited liability company, are subject to stamp duty at 1% of the value of the shares.

The transfer of shares in a SPIC is not subject to gift or inheritance tax provided that, at the time of the disposition, neither the disponer nor the beneficiary is resident or ordinarily resident Ireland and provided that at the time of the gift or inheritance the shares are not situated in Ireland. A foreign domiciled person is not considered to be resident or ordinarily resident in Ireland until 1 December 2004 and then only if that person has been resident in Ireland for the five consecutive years preceding the date of the disposition.

12.808   Double tax agreements

Up to 6 April 1993, the provisions of any double tax treaty were not applicable to a CIU but this restriction was removed with effect from 6 April 1993. Ireland has double tax treaties with many countries (see **14.103**), including treaties with all of the EU Member States and all of the major economic countries.

Despite the removal of the above-mentioned restriction on the accessibility of tax treaties in the case of CIUs, the fact that some treaties to which Ireland is a party include in the relevant article a requirement that a "resident" of a contracting state should be "liable to tax" in that state, would appear to deny treaty benefits to SCIUs which are tax exempt entities in Ireland. The matter is not, however, free from doubt. There is a persuasive school of thought to the effect that "liable to tax", in the context of the definition of "resident" in tax treaties, denotes no more than a requirement that the body in question should have the kind of personal attachment to the contracting state (management and control in many states, including Ireland) which *can* result in liability to taxation, whether at the current time or at any future time. In practice, the Korean authorities have agreed to allow SCIUs, on a case-by-case basis, to benefit from the provisions of the Ireland/ Korea tax treaty.

Another typical requirement of double tax treaties is that a person must be "beneficially entitled" to income or gains as a prerequisite to entitlement to treaty benefit in respect of that income. For unit trusts and limited partnerships, therefore, where beneficial ownership vests in the unit holders and the partners respectively, treaty access would appear not to be available to the entities themselves. In practice, treaty benefits may nevertheless be obtained in certain cases involving unit trusts, depending on the practice or treatment in the treaty partner country.

CIUs subject to tax in Ireland, such as CIUs taxable on or after 6 April 1994 at the reduced corporation tax rate (equal to the standard income tax rate), non-designated AICs which are taxable either at the standard corporation tax rate or at the effective 10% rate (where operating in the IFSC or Shannon), and SPICs taxable also at the 10% rate are in a position to benefit from tax treaties.

12.809   Returns in relation to foreign UCITSs

TCA 1997, s 893 requires persons acting in Ireland ("intermediaries") on behalf or foreign UCITSs to furnish details of transactions engaged in by Irish residents in relation to such UCITSs.

An intermediary, if required by notice in writing from an inspector, is obliged to prepare and deliver within the time specified in the notice, being not less than 30 days, a return of the names and addresses and tax reference numbers of all persons resident in the State in respect of whom the intermediary has in the course of providing relevant facilities in relation to a relevant UCITS during the period specified in the notice:

(a) acted as an intermediary in the purchase by or on behalf of any of those persons of units in the relevant UCITS or in the sale to such persons of such units;

(b) provided facilities for the making of payments by the relevant UCITS to any persons who hold units of the relevant UCITS; and

(c) provided facilities for the repurchase or redemption of units of the relevant UCITS held by any of those persons.

A *relevant UCITS* is an undertaking which is situated in a Member State of the European Communities other than the State, is a UCITS for the purposes of the relevant Directives, and markets its units in the State (TCA 1997, s 893(1)). A *UCITS* is an undertaking for collective investment in transferable securities to which the relevant Directives relate. *Units* includes shares and any other instruments granting an entitlement to share in the investments or income of, or to receive a distribution from, a relevant UCITS. The *relevant Directives* means Council Directive 85/611/EEC of 20 December 1985 (being a Directive on the coordination of laws, regulations and administrative provisions relating to undertakings for collective investment in transferable securities (UCITS) and any Directive amending that Directive. *Relevant facilities* means, in relation to a relevant UCITS:

(a) the marketing in the State of the units of the relevant UCITS;

(b) the acting in the State as an intermediary in the purchase of the units of the relevant UCITS by or on behalf of persons resident in the State or in the sale to such persons of such units; and

(c) the provision in the State on behalf of the relevant UCITS of facilities for the making of payments to holders of its units, the repurchase or redemption of its units or the making available of the information which the relevant UCITS is duly obliged to provide for the purposes of the relevant Directives.

An *intermediary* is any person who provides relevant facilities in relation to a relevant UCITS.

Where appropriate, the return to be made by an intermediary should also include, in respect of each resident person mentioned above:

(i) the name and address of each relevant UCITS:

   (I) the units of which have been so purchased by, or on behalf of, or sold to that person in the period specified in the notice,

   (II) on whose behalf facilities have been provided for the making of payments by the relevant UCITS to that person in the period, and

   (III) on whose behalf facilities have been provided for the repurchase or redemption by the relevant UCITS in the period of units in the relevant UCITS held by that person, and

(ii) (I) the value or total value of the units so purchased by, or on behalf of, or sold to that person,

(II)   the amount of the payments so made by the relevant UCITS to that person, and

(III)   the value or total value of the units held by that person which were so repurchased or redeemed by the relevant UCITS.

Any resident person availing of relevant facilities from an intermediary in relation to a relevant UCITS is obliged to furnish to the intermediary details of which the intermediary is required to include in a return to an inspector. The intermediary must take all reasonable care, if necessary by requesting documentary evidence, to confirm that the details furnished are true and correct.

12.810   Common contractual funds

12.810.1   Introduction

The common contractual fund (CCF), introduced at the beginning of 2004 within the EU, allows pension assets to be pooled in a tax-transparent structure. To date, a limited type of CCF, formed under the UCITS regulations, has been available in Ireland but legislation is to be introduced allowing for a general CCF not confined by the UCITS regulations. TCA 1997, s 739I is designed to allow for a non-UCITS version of the CCF, thereby broadening the products in which a CCF may invest, and to extend the range of qualifying investors to include all forms of institutional investment.

Some of the cost inefficiencies associated with the need to maintain multiple pension schemes can be mitigated by pooling the assets of a number of pension funds in a single regulated vehicle. Asset pooling is of particular interest to institutional money managers and multinational companies with multiple occupational pension plans. The CCF is designed to facilitate pooling while ensuring that the tax treaty benefits normally enjoyed by pension funds are not affected. Each investor in a CCF is treated for tax purposes as being the direct owner of the underlying investments while the CCF itself is treated as a regulated entity and managed accordingly. A CCF is accordingly tax transparent but only where the unit holders are institutional investors and where certain reporting requirements are met.

12.810.2   Common contractual fund

A *common contractual fund* is:

(i)   a collective investment undertaking being an unincorporated body established by a management company under which the participants by contractual arrangement participate and share in the property of the collective investment undertaking as co-owners, where it is expressly stated under its deed of constitution to be established pursuant to the Investment Funds, Companies and Miscellaneous Provisions Act 2005 and which holds an authorisation issued in accordance with that Act and which is not established pursuant to Council Directive No 85/611/EEC of 20 December 1985 (OJ No L375/3, 31.12.1985), as amended from time to time, or

(ii)   an investment undertaking within the meaning of paragraph (b) of the definition of "investment undertaking" in TCA 1997, s 739B(1) (ie, any other undertaking which is a UCITS within the meaning of the UCITS Regulations, being an undertaking which holds an authorisation, which has not been revoked, issued pursuant to those Regulations – see **12.806.3**), which is constituted otherwise than under trust law or statute law (TCA 1997, s 739I(1)(a)).

The entity described in (i) above is the proposed general form of CCF vehicle while the description in (ii) relates to the existing UCITS CCF vehicle.

12.810.3 Tax treatment

A CCF is not chargeable to tax and is accordingly tax transparent. Thus, profits (income and gains) arising or accruing to the fund are treated as arising or accruing to the unit holders in proportion to the value of the units held by them, as if such profits did not arise or accrue to the CCF.

Notwithstanding anything in the Tax Acts, but subject to TCA 1997, s 739I(3) and (4) (see below), a CCF is not to be chargeable to tax in respect of relevant profits (TCA 1997, s 739I(2)(a)). For the purposes of the Tax Acts, relevant income and relevant gains in relation to a CCF are to be treated as arising or accruing to each unit holder of the CCF in proportion to the value of the units beneficially owned by the holder as if the relevant income and relevant gains had arisen or accrued to the unit holders in the CCF without passing through the hands of the CCF (TCA 1997, s 739I(2)(b)).

For the above purposes, the definitions in TCA 1997, s 739B(1) of *relevant profits*, *relevant income*, *relevant gains*, *relevant payment*, *unit* and *unit holder* (see **12.806.4**) are to apply with any necessary modifications to a collective investment undertaking within the meaning of (i) of the definition of "common contractual fund" in **12.810.1** above.

The above-described tax treatment is confined to institutional investors such as pension funds and life assurance companies. TCA 1997, s 739I(3) provides that the treatment applies only where each unit of the CCF:

(a) is an asset of a pension fund or is beneficially owned by a person other than an individual; or

(b) is held by a custodian or trustee for the benefit of a person other than an individual.

Any deposit to which a CCF is for the time being entitled is treated as if it were not a "relevant deposit" for the purposes of TCA 1997 Part 9 Chapter 4 (TCA 1997, s 739I(5)). As with other collective investment undertakings, interest arising on such a deposit will accordingly not be subject to DIRT.

12.810.4 Reporting requirement

For each year of assessment, each CCF is required, on or before 28 February in the year following that year, to make a statement to the Revenue Commissioners in electronic format approved by them specifying for each year of assessment:

(a) the total amount of relevant profits arising to the CCF in respect of units in that fund; and

(b)   in respect of each person who is a unit holder—

    (i)   the name and address of the person,

    (ii)   the amount of the relevant profits to which the person is entitled, and

    (iii)   such other information as the Revenue Commissioners require (TCA 1997, s 739I(4)).

12.9 COMPANIES IN LIQUIDATION, RECEIVERSHIP

12.901 Liquidation
12.902 Receivership
12.903 Examinership

12.901 Liquidation

12.901.1 Winding Up of a company

When a company commences to be wound up, it ceases to be the beneficial owner of its assets and the custody and control of those assets pass to the liquidator. A winding up commences with the passing of a resolution to wind up the company or, if no such resolution has previously been passed, on the presentation of a petition to the courts resulting in the granting of a winding up order, or on the doing of any other act for a like purpose in the case of a winding up otherwise than under the Companies Act 1963 (as amended), for example, a winding up under some foreign enactment (TCA 1997, s 27(7)). A company ceases to exist on the completion of the winding up procedures under the Companies Act 1963, or by being struck off the register of companies as a defunct company, in accordance with the provisions of section 12(1) of the Companies (Amendment) Act 1982. The dissolution of a company is confirmed by the publication of this fact in Iris Oifigiúil.

Under section 206 of the Companies Act 1963, two types of winding up are recognised:

(a) compulsory winding up by a court; and

(b) voluntary winding up initiated by the shareholders or creditors.

Since the company's assets cease to belong to it when it commences to be wound up, it is no longer the beneficial owner of any shares it may have in subsidiary companies so that it would no longer be a parent company within a group (*IRC v Olive Mill Spinners Ltd (in liquidation)* 41 TC 77 and *Ayerst v CEK Construction Ltd* [1975] STC 1).

In most cases involving a members' voluntary liquidation, the decision to wind up is occasioned by retirement or by a reorganisation. All the creditors will be paid, as the liquidator is obliged to do, and there is no obligation on the company or on the liquidator to inform creditors of the winding up by way of public advertisement. The resolution to put the company into liquidation and to appoint the liquidator must be registered with the Companies Registration Office and must be advertised in Iris Oifigiúil. A declaration of solvency, signed by a majority of directors, must be furnished to the Companies Registration Office, together with the winding up resolution, within 15 days of the shareholders' meeting at which the decision to wind up is made. The final meeting must be advertised by the liquidator.

In the case of a creditors' voluntary liquidation, the company directors call a shareholders' meeting and a creditors' meeting. The latter must be advertised at least ten days prior to the meeting and specific notice given in writing; the shareholders' meeting must be held on the same day as, or on the day before, the creditors' meeting. It is usual for the shareholders to resolve to appoint, by resolution, a liquidator at the shareholders' meeting (which precedes the creditors' meeting) but the creditors have the absolute right to appoint a liquidator of their own choosing in which case the appointment of the shareholders' nominee lapses.

In a court liquidation, the directors may apply to the Court for a compulsory winding up order. This kind of liquidation is most usually the result of a creditor's application. The Court appointed liquidator advertises for claims of creditors under the auspices of the Court. In a court liquidation, proof of debt is usually a relatively cumbersome procedure and, compared to a creditors' liquidation, the liquidation process will generally take much longer to complete.

In a voluntary liquidation, the liquidator must call annual meetings not less than 12 months and not more than 15 months after the date of his appointment and thereafter in each successive year of the liquidation. At each annual meeting, the liquidator presents a copy of his receipts and payments for the past year. At the conclusion of the liquidation, the liquidator must call a final meeting of the shareholders and creditors to which he presents a copy of his total receipts and payments. Notice of the meeting must appear in two daily newspapers at least 28 days before the meeting.

12.901.2   Status of liquidator

Unlike a receiver, a liquidator is not an agent of the company or of the creditors. Neither is he an officer of the company. In *Re Oriental Inland Steam Co, ex parte Scinde Rail Co* 1874 9 Ch App 22 WR 810, Mellish J stated that a winding up makes the property of the company clearly trust property which ceases to be beneficially the property of the company. From the time of the winding up order, all the powers of the directors to carry on trading or to deal with the company's assets are to be "wholly determined" and only the official liquidator has power to deal with them. Thus the liquidation constitutes a trust for the benefit of all the creditors.

In *Ayerst v CEK Construction,* Lord Diplock pointed out that this kind of trust differs from the normal trust in that the custody and control are taken out of the hands of the legal owner (the company) and vested in the liquidator, a third party, over whom the company has no control. The property of a company in liquidation is trust property in the sense that it is distinguished from other property in that it cannot be used or disposed of by the company, the legal owner, for its own benefit but must be used or disposed of for the benefit of other persons. Accordingly, when a company goes into liquidation, it ceases to be the beneficial owner of its assets.

Prior to liquidation, a company is both the legal and beneficial owner of its assets whereas when it is put into liquidation it ceases to be the beneficial owner, while remaining the legal owner, of the assets. As such, it no longer retains the custody and control of those assets. Except in the case of a court order, the assets do not vest in the liquidator. The liquidator holds the assets for the purpose of distributing them or what remains of them to the ultimate beneficial owners. A liquidator may be described as a quasi trustee for all those persons who have a claim on the assets of the company, including the creditors and shareholders. Provisions in the Tax Acts dealing with trustees do not apply to a liquidator as such.

12.901.3 Tax consequences of winding up

The appointment of a liquidator has a number of tax consequences:

(i) When a company commences to be wound up, an accounting period ends and a new one begins; thereafter, an accounting period may not end otherwise than on the expiration of twelve months from its beginning or by the completion of the winding up.

(ii) The appointment of a liquidator to a group member company is the occasion of that company ceasing to be the owner of its assets thereby breaking the group relationship between it and any of its subsidiaries, direct or indirect. This will be relevant for group payments and group relief purposes (see **8.202** and **8.302**) but not for capital gains tax group treatment (see **9.203**). The retention of trading losses and tax written down values provided for in TCA 1997, s 400 (company reconstructions without change of ownership – see **4.109**) may be affected.

(iii) Disposals of assets by the liquidator in the course of the winding up are subject to capital gains tax (but subject to (v) below).

(iv) Distributions of the proceeds of the liquidation to the shareholders are subject to capital gains tax; a distribution on liquidation is not a distribution for the purposes of corporation tax, including advance corporation tax (TCA 1997, s 130(1)).

(v) Where assets of a company are vested in a liquidator, they are treated for corporation tax purposes in relation to chargeable gains as vested in, and the acts of the liquidator in relation to the assets are treated as acts of, the company; acquisitions from, or disposals to, the liquidator are accordingly disregarded (TCA 1997, s 78(8)).

(vi) Whereas a company leaving a group may result in the crystallisation of previously deferred chargeable gains on intra-group transfers of assets, the occasion of a company leaving a group as a result of that company or another company going into liquidation does not have this effect, provided the winding up is effected for *bona fide* commercial reasons and is not part of a scheme or arrangement the main purpose or one of the main purposes of which is the avoidance of tax (TCA 1997, s 623(1)(*d*) – see **9.209**).

(vii) Where the company being wound up is insolvent and is a party to a group VAT registration, each member of the VAT group is jointly and severally liable for the VAT debts of that company.

(viii) Where a company has undistributed investment or estate income at the time it commences to be wound up, a surcharge under TCA 1997, s 440 or 441 would seem to be unavoidable (see **10.3** and below). A distribution in the course of a winding up is not a distribution for the purposes of TCA 1997, s 440(1) and so cannot, with a view to avoiding the surcharge, operate to reduce the company's undistributed investment or estate income earned up to the time the liquidation commenced.

(ix) Certain liabilities, including certain tax liabilities, become preferential.

The ending of an accounting period (see (i) above) can affect the following:

(a)   the due date for payment of preliminary tax/corporation tax – this is fixed by reference to the final day of the accounting period concerned;

(b)   the date by which the company's corporation tax return must be submitted;

(c)   the extent to which trading losses may be offset against the total profits of the immediately preceding period or against a fellow group member's total profits on a claim to group relief.

With regard to (a), this gives rise to the practical necessity to ensure that preliminary tax is paid some six weeks before the date on which the winding up commences.

As regards (b), in a case where an accounting period ends on or before the date of commencement of the winding up of a company and the "specified return date" in respect of that period would otherwise fall on a date after the date of commencement of the winding up but not within a period of 3 months after that date, the specified return date (the date by which the return should be made) is the date which falls 3 months after the date of commencement of the winding up, but in any event not later than the 21st of the month in which that period of three months ends (TCA 1997, s 950(1) – (c) in the meaning of "specified return date for the chargeable period" – see also **15.104.1**).

The above provision has potentially bizarre consequences when TCA 1997, s 958(3)(d) is taken into account. This is the general rule whereby corporation tax for an accounting period is due and payable on or before the specified return date for that period (TCA 1997, s 958(3)(d) – see **15.106.3**). Accordingly, the mere act of putting a company into liquidation will typically have the effect of bringing forward the payment date for corporation tax (in practice, the balance of tax due after taking account of preliminary tax paid) for the period ending on the date of commencement of the winding up and, for accounting periods ending before 1 January 2006, payment could have fallen due some three months prior to the date on which the second instalment of preliminary tax was due. Conceivably this could have been the case even where the preliminary tax paid was such as to have satisfied the full corporation tax liability for the period.

For the purposes of the close companies surcharges, TCA 1997, s 434(7) provides that where a company is subject to any restriction "imposed by law" as regards the making of distributions, regard shall be had to this restriction in determining the amount of income on which the surcharge is to be imposed. It has been held in the courts that "regard shall be had" is to be interpreted in a reasonable way. It can reasonably be argued that a surcharge should not be imposed for any accounting period in which a company is in liquidation since the liquidator is legally prevented from making a distribution of an income nature. Prior to the commencement of the winding up, however, there is no such restriction so that if a surcharge on any investment or estate income is to be avoided, it will be necessary to distribute that income (or most of it) before the commencement of the winding up (see *Rahinstown Estate Company Ltd (In Liquidation) v Hughes,* HC [1986] and **10.302**).

Investment or estate income arising within the liquidation period cannot be distributed. It is understood, however, that the Appeal Commissioners and the Circuit Court have accepted that in the case of a members' voluntary liquidation a surcharge could be made on the basis that the company could be removed from liquidation on application to the High Court so that it is within the power of the directors/shareholders to make a distribution. In practice, the surcharge would not be pursued by the Revenue where it is obvious that a genuine liquidation is involved; the Revenue had been concerned that companies were being left in liquidation for prolonged periods during which substantial passive income was being accumulated.

The appointment of a liquidator does not result in the company ceasing to trade although, of course, a cessation of trading will often occur at that point. It will be a question of fact as to whether a company's trade ceases on the appointment of a liquidator. The relevant issue will be whether the liquidator is carrying on a trade or merely realising assets (*Armitage v Moore* 4 TC 199, *CIR v The Old Bushmills Distillery Co Ltd (in liquidation)* 12 TC 1148, *Wilson Box (Foreign Rights) Ltd (in liquidation) v Brice* 20 TC 736, *Baker (as liquidator of First National Pathe Ltd) v Cook* 21 TC 337). If the trade then ceases, the usual tax consequences will follow, eg losses forward cease to be used, terminal loss relief may arise, balancing allowances or charges may arise. Unused capital gains tax losses continue to be available and may be set against chargeable gains arising at any time up to the completion of the liquidation.

12.901.4 Chargeable gains

As the appointment of a liquidator does not result in the company's assets vesting in him, there is no disposal of those assets to the liquidator for the purposes of corporation tax on chargeable gains. However, under section 230 of the Companies Act 1963, which applies to court liquidations only, the Court, on the application of the liquidator, may direct that all or part of the company's assets are to vest in him. Where the assets are so vested, TCA 1997, s 78(8) provides that for the purposes of corporation tax on chargeable gains it is to be assumed that the assets are vested in, and the acts of the liquidator in relation to the assets are acts of, the company and that acquisitions from or disposals to him by the company are to be disregarded.

A distribution made by a liquidator in the course of the winding up of a company is a capital distribution, being a distribution in specie to the shareholders. TCA 1997, s 583(1) defines *capital distribution* as "any distribution from a company (including a distribution in the course of dissolving or winding up the company) in money or money's worth except a distribution which in the hands of the recipient constitutes income for the purposes of income tax". TCA 1997, s 20, which charges income tax under Schedule F on dividends and other distributions of companies resident in the State which are not specially excluded from income tax, provides that all such distributions are to be regarded as income however they are to be dealt with in the hands of the recipient.

TCA 1997, s 130 (see **11.101**) deals with the meaning of *distribution*, which includes capital distributions, but TCA 1997, s 130(1) provides that references to distributions of a company do not apply to distributions in respect of share capital in a winding up. In *CIR v George Burrell, CIR v William Burrell* 9 TC 27, it was held that in a liquidation undistributed profits can no longer be distinguished from capital and that such portion of the assets distributed by the liquidator as represents undistributed profits is not income in the hands of the shareholders. For capital gains tax purposes, therefore, capital distributions are mainly confined to distributions made in the dissolution or winding up of a company; capital distributions also arise in connection with the purchase by a company of its own shares (see **11.3**).

The payment by a liquidator of arrears of preference dividends is a distribution in respect of share capital under TCA 1997, s 130(1) and, being made in respect of share capital in a winding up, is a capital distribution giving rise to a disposal or part disposal in the hands of the shareholders.

The capital gains tax consequences of a winding up are illustrated in the following example.

Example 12.901.4.1

On 1 August 1996, Mr R O'Leary transferred his holiday cottage worth €20,000 to his company Robol Ltd in consideration for the issue of shares. The cottage was used only by him and his family and no income was earned at any time by the company, whether from the cottage or from any other source. The company did not acquire any other asserts.

On 31 March 2008, Robol Ltd was wound up and the cottage, which was then worth €120,000, was transferred *in specie* to Mr O'Leary.

As the liquidator has disposed of the cottage otherwise than by way of a bargain made at arm's length, he is deemed to have sold it at its market value, €120,000, to Mr O'Leary (TCA 1997, s 547). The tax is computed as follows:

	€	€
Disposal at market value		120,000
Cost	20,000	
Indexed @ 1.251		25,020
Chargeable gain		94,980
Adjusted for corporation tax (20/12.5)		151,968
Corporation tax @ 12.5%		18,996

The transfer of the cottage *in specie* to Mr O'Leary is a capital distribution received by him and as such is treated as a disposal by him of his shares in Robol Ltd for €120,000 being the market value of the asset received in specie (TCA 1997, s 583(2)). The resulting capital gains tax is as follows:

	€	€
Disposal proceeds		120,000
Cost of shares	20,000	
Indexed @ 1.251		25,020
Capital gain		94,980
Exemption		1,270
Chargeable		93,710
Capital gains tax @ 20%		18,742

The capital gains tax cost of the cottage, for the purpose of any future disposal of it by Mr O'Leary, is €120,000.

In practice, there is a problem in that the liquidator will not be able to pay the tax on the first chargeable gain. Unless Mr O'Leary provides the necessary funds for this purpose, the liquidator will be forced to sell the cottage and pay the capital gains tax (and his fees and expenses) out of the proceeds. The position in that case would be as follows. Assuming the costs of liquidating the company are €10,000, the value of the distribution is €91,004 (€120,000 less tax as above €18,996 and less expenses €10,000). The resulting capital gains tax is as follows:

	€	€
Disposal proceeds		91,004
Cost of shares	20,000	

Indexed @ 1.251	25,020
Capital gain	65,984
Exemption	1,270
Chargeable	64,714
Capital gains tax @ 20%	12,943

Again, the capital gains tax cost of the cottage, for the purpose of any future disposal of it by Mr O'Leary, is €120,000.

Where the liquidator makes a series of distributions, as will often be the case, each such distribution constitutes a capital distribution, being a distribution *in specie* to the shareholders. As respects any shareholder, each distribution is a part disposal of his shares and the resulting capital gains tax computation will be in accordance with the part disposal formula in TCA 1997, s 557 so that the cost of each part disposal is:

$$\text{total cost of shares} \times \frac{\text{capital distribution}}{\text{capital distribution} + \text{value of shares after distribution}}$$

In practice, any reasonable estimate of the residual value of the shares, based on the value of the remaining assets, is likely to be accepted by inspectors of taxes.

12.901.5 Charge to tax

TCA 1997, s 26(2) provides, inter alia, that a company is to be chargeable to corporation tax on profits arising in the winding up of the company. This provision is necessary to overcome the difficulty of dealing with the income or gains of a company in liquidation; because the company has ceased to be the beneficial owner of its assets, it could otherwise be treated as not being beneficially entitled to the income or gains arising from those assets.

An assessment on the profits of a company for an accounting period which falls after the commencement of the winding up of that company is not invalid because made before the end of the accounting period (TCA 1997, s 919(6)). This provision facilitates the early agreement of liabilities of companies in liquidation. During the course of the winding up, the liquidator has the responsibility of accounting for corporation tax on income received and on capital gains arising on disposals of chargeable assets. Tax liabilities have been held to be a necessary disbursement of the liquidator and to rank for payment in priority to the liquidator's remuneration (*In re Mesco Properties Ltd* 1979 STC 788).

That judgment was, however, not followed in the case *In re Van Hool McArdle Ltd (in liquidation), Revenue Commissioners v Donnelly* [1983] ILRM 329, in which the Supreme Court considered the question of liability to corporation tax in respect of chargeable gains arising on the sales of certain properties in the case of a court liquidation. The Court held that rule 129 of the Winding Up Rules 1966 (SI 28/1966) of the Superior Courts, which is concerned with the priority of different creditors in a liquidation, was intended to deal with "expenses properly incurred in preserving, realising or getting in the assets" and not with the liabilities of a company, and that the expenses covered did not include a company's liability to corporation tax.

TCA 1997, s 571 deals with the type of situation which was the subject of the *Van Hool* case. In respect of chargeable gains on disposals of assets by the liquidator, capital gains tax ("referable capital gains tax") or corporation tax ("referable corporation tax") may be assessed on and collected from the liquidator as the person with possession of the sale proceeds. The section applies to disposals by a liquidator, by any person entitled to the assets of the company by way of security, and by any person appointed to enforce or give effect to that security, such as a receiver (see below).

The tax is assessable under Case IV of Schedule D as income of the year in which the disposal occurs and is treated as a necessary disbursement out of, and recoverable out of, the proceeds of the disposal. The Case IV assessment will be in an amount the income tax on which at the standard rate is equal to the amount of the referable corporation tax, ie the amount of capital gains tax which would be payable by the company if it were liable to capital gains tax rather than corporation tax and as if accounting periods were years of assessment. Tax paid by the liquidator is treated as discharging a corresponding amount of the liability of the company to corporation tax on chargeable gains.

TCA 1997, s 571(2), (3), (4) contain rules for apportioning capital gains tax or corporation tax on chargeable gains between the liquidator (or receiver) and the company where there have been disposals by both parties (see Example **12.902.3.1** in relation to a receiver).

In the case of a court liquidation (*In re Hibernian Transport Ltd (in liquidation) & Others* [1984] ILRM 583), the High Court found that there is no statutory obligation to pay corporation tax in respect of periods after the commencement of the winding up. The case concerned the liability to tax in respect of deposit interest earned during the course of the liquidation. In his judgment, Mr Justice Costello pointed out that there is no statutory provision for the payment of a debt due to the Revenue for a liability to tax incurred in the post liquidation period; TCA 1997, s 571 (then FA 1983 s 56) is such a provision but only in respect of corporation tax on chargeable gains arising from disposals by a liquidator. He went on to state that if the Revenue cannot recover tax under rule 129 of the Winding Up Rules 1966, although there is a statutory obligation on the company to pay the tax, there are no assets out of which the tax can be paid because they would have been used to pay other creditors, when the company is insolvent, and other creditors and contributors, when the company is solvent.

The position in a voluntary liquidation contrasts with that for a court liquidation. In the case of a members' or creditors' winding up, income of the liquidation period is subject to corporation tax which is payable by the liquidator (*A Noyek & Sons Ltd (in voluntary liquidation), Burns v Hearne* 3 ITR 523). It was held that a company in voluntary liquidation could not avoid a charge to tax on deposit interest earned in the course of the liquidation, nor was there anything to prevent collection of that tax.

The Supreme Court held that payments made by an insolvent company as part of an arrangement to settle liabilities of associated companies were *ultra vires* and to be regarded as held in trust for the general body of creditors (*Frederick Inns Ltd, The Rendezvous Ltd, The Graduate Ltd, Motels Ltd (in liquidation) v The Companies Acts 1983-1986* 4 ITR 247).

12.901.6 Ranking of creditors and Revenue priority

On the occasion of a company being put into liquidation, the ranking of creditors in respect of payments due to them is as follows:

    (i)   secured creditors under fixed charges;

   (ii)   all costs, charges and expenses properly incurred in the winding up;

  (iii)   remuneration and expenses of the liquidator;

  (iv)   employee deductions in relation to PRSI ("super-preferential" creditors);

   (v)   preferential creditors;

  (vi)   floating charges;

 (vii)   unsecured creditors;

(viii)   shareholders.

In a court liquidation the Court may, if the assets are insufficient to satisfy the liabilities, make an order as to payment out of the assets of the costs, charges and expenses incurred in the winding up in such order of priority as the Court thinks fit (section 244 Companies Act 1963). Section 281 of the same Act provides, in the case of any voluntary winding up, that all costs, charges and expenses properly incurred in the winding up, including the remuneration of the liquidator, are to be payable out of the assets of the company in priority to all other claims.

It was held that the liability of a company to tax which arose during the period of a liquidation formed part of the costs, charges and expenses of the winding up (*In re Beni-Felkai Mining Co Ltd* 18 TC 632). In the *Mesco Properties* case (see above), it was held that corporation tax in respect of chargeable gains arising on the disposals of assets by the liquidator are costs, charges and expenses of the liquidator and are accordingly payable in priority to his remuneration. However, the position in Ireland arising out of the *Hibernian Transport* decision (see also above) is that the costs, charges and expenses do not include a company's liability to corporation tax in cases involving a winding up as a court liquidation.

Preferential creditors, as set out in sections 98 and 285 of the Companies Act 1963, include all assessed taxes including income tax and corporation tax assessed on the company up to 5 April (whether the assessment was made before or after that date – *Gowers & Others v Walker & Others* 15 TC 165) next before the "relevant date" (normally the date of the passing of the resolution for the winding up of the company) but not exceeding in the whole one year's assessment. It is specifically provided in TCA 1997, s 974 that the priority attaching to assessed taxes under sections 98 and 285 of the Companies Act 1963, shall apply to corporation tax. For this purpose, the Revenue may select whichever year they wish for each tax (*CIR v Liquidators of Purvis Industries Ltd* 38 TC 155). It was held in *Re Cushla Ltd* [1979] STC 615, that the Revenue have the right to set off any tax owing to the company in liquidation against tax due by the company; the amount effectively recovered by way of set off, therefore, does not have to rank with other preferential or non-preferential creditors.

Interest chargeable on late payment of the tax also ranks as a preferential payment; in relation to interest on overdue tax, TCA 1997, s 1080(3) states that the provisions of every enactment relating to the recovery of any tax and the provisions of every rule of court relating thereto, and the provisions of section 81 of the Bankruptcy Act 1988, and sections 98 and 285 of the Companies Act 1963, are to apply to the recovery of interest on that tax as if the interest were a part of the tax.

Where authorised by the Collector-General, an employer may remit PAYE deducted from employees at intervals longer than the normal one month remittance period, provided the extended period does not exceed one year. To secure the preferential status of the Revenue in company liquidations in respect of PAYE, TCA 1997, s 995 provides that the preferential creditor amounts referred to in section 285(2)(a)(iii) of the Companies Act 1963, are to include amounts in respect of PAYE which would, in the absence of the above-mentioned authorisation, be due for remittance by the employer at the date of liquidation.

TCA 1997, s 995 also provides that the Revenue may take into account, for the purposes of calculating the preferential PAYE debt of a company in liquidation, any PAYE deducted by the company for the income tax month in which the liquidation commenced. Section 285(2)(a)(iii) of the Companies Act 1963, provides that the amounts which are to be paid in priority to all other debts in a winding up are to include any amount due at the relevant date in respect of sums which an employer is liable to remit under the PAYE regulations in respect of emoluments paid in the 12 months up to the relevant date. The "relevant date" may be the date of appointment of a provisional liquidator, the date of the winding up order or the date of the passing of the resolution for the winding up. TCA 1997, s 995(b), however, provides that for the purposes of Section 285(2)(a)(iii) of the Companies Act 1963, the relevant date is to be the ninth day after the end of the income tax month in which the relevant date occurred; this ensures the priority of any PAYE due by the end of the month in which the liquidation of a company commences.

12.902 Receivership

12.902.1 Nature of receivership

Unlike a liquidator, a receiver is an agent of the company. The concept of receivership derives from bankruptcy law. Lending institutions advancing money to a company will normally require to be repaid out of the assets of the company in priority to other creditors. It is normal practice for a loan agreement or debenture deed to include provisions for the appointment of a receiver in the event of certain contingencies, typically that the company will be unable to pay interest or to repay principal within a specified period.

A receiver will act as agent of the company within the terms of the lending agreement but in certain circumstances may act as the lender's agent. The objective of the receiver will be to realise sufficient assets to discharge his own remuneration, to settle the outstanding amount due to the lender and to maintain the company's business and employment as far as possible. He has no obligation to advise unsecured creditors regarding the likely outcome of the receivership but would normally list their claims for the attention of the directors or of a liquidator, where appropriate, after the loan creditor or debenture has been paid. A receivership normally comes to an end on the occasion of the handing back by the receiver of the company's assets to the directors or by his petitioning the court to appoint a liquidator.

12.902.2 Charges

A receiver may be given a charge over the assets of the company. A fixed charge is one which is secured on specific company assets or property while a floating charge will be given in respect of the company's assets generally, or in respect of certain categories of company assets such as debtors or inventories. A charge must be registered within 21 days to be effective as security.

Where a receiver is appointed on behalf of the holders of a debenture secured by a floating charge, section 98 of the Companies Act 1963, provides that debts which would rank as preferential in a winding up (see **12.901**) are to be paid by the receiver out of any funds *coming into his possession* before any claim for principal or interest relating to the debenture.

12.902.3 Tax consequences of receivership

As compared with the position in a winding up, the tax consequences of the appointment of a receiver are not significant. The appointment of a receiver is not an occasion of the ending of an accounting period. More importantly, the appointment does not result in the company losing beneficial ownership of its assets; thus, a receivership does not have any effect on the structure of a group of which the company is a member so that the company continues to be a member of the group for the purposes of group payments and group relief. Neither does the appointment of a receiver have any effect on a capital gains tax group of which the company is a member (notwithstanding that under TCA 1997, s 571 corporation tax in respect of chargeable gains may be assessed on and collected from the receiver – see below).

Losses of the company in receivership may, under the group relief provisions, be claimed by other group companies. This would require the consent of the receiver as agent for the company. The receiver could accordingly refuse to surrender the losses or to demand payment for the losses. Such payments received are not taxable (TCA 1997, s 411(5)). The receiver is therefore in a position to obtain value for any losses incurred during the period of the receivership.

In the event of a cessation of trading during the course of the receivership, a trading loss incurred in the final twelve months may be offset against trading profits, if any, for the immediately preceding 36 months (TCA 1997, s 397 – see **4.104**). Losses forward may only be set against future trading profits of the same trade.

If the trade is to be transferred to another company, however, such losses may be preserved if the conditions in TCA 1997, s 400 are satisfied (see **4.109**). For this purpose, the important requirement is that *at any time* within two years after the transfer the trade or an interest of at least 75% in the trade belongs to the same persons as the trade or such interest belonged at some time within one year before the transfer. Ownership of a trade is, broadly, determined by reference to the beneficial ownership of ordinary share capital in the company carrying on the trade. If the trade is to be transferred to another group company therefore, any losses forward should be available to the company acquiring the trade.

If the receiver intends to sell off the trade as a going concern while preserving the losses forward, the trade should first be transferred to a subsidiary company in anticipation of a later sale of that company to a prospective buyer. The transfer would usually be effected in consideration for the issue of shares in the subsidiary company. In that way, relief from capital duty on the issue of the shares, and from stamp duty on any dutiable assets passing as part of the transfer of trade, can be availed of. To preserve the stamp duty relief, the subsequent sale of the subsidiary should not take place until after the end of two years from the date the trade was transferred.

In was held in *CIR v Thompson (as receiver for the First and Second Debenture Holders of John A Wood Ltd)* 20 TC 422 that the receiver had not succeeded to the company's trade but that he was properly assessable to tax as the person receiving or entitled to receive income of the company. This finding was based on the then UK equivalent of TCA 1997, s 52 which provides that "tax under Schedule D shall be charged on and paid by the persons or bodies of persons receiving or entitled to the income in respect of which tax under that Schedule is in this Act directed to be charged".

A receiver will, as a matter of course, dispose of assets of the company and may therefore realise capital gains in respect of such disposals. TCA 1997, s 537(2) provides that where a person entitled to an asset by way of security, or to the benefit of a charge or encumbrance on an asset, including a person appointed as receiver for the purpose of enforcing or giving effect to the security, deals with the asset for that purpose, his dealings are to be treated as if they were done through him as nominee of the company. The provisions of the Capital Gains Tax Acts apply as if the property were vested in the company and as if the acts of the receiver were acts of the company, and acquisitions from or disposals to the receiver by or from the company are to be disregarded (TCA 1997, s 567(2) as applied for corporation tax purposes by TCA 1997, s 78(5)). Accordingly, chargeable gains arising on disposals by the receiver are subject to corporation tax in the hands of the company.

TCA 1997, s 571, which is relevant for the purposes of the assessment of capital gains tax on disposals of assets by a liquidator (see **12.901.5**), applies in the same way as respects disposals by a receiver. For this purpose, an *accountable person* includes "any person entitled to an asset by way of security or to the benefit of a charge or encumbrance on an asset, or, as the case may be, any person appointed to enforce or give effect to the security, charge or encumbrance". In respect of chargeable gains on disposals of assets by the receiver, corporation tax may be assessed on and collected from him as the person with possession of the sale proceeds.

The tax is assessable under Case IV of Schedule D as income of the year in which the disposal occurs and is treated as a necessary disbursement out of, and is recoverable out of, the proceeds of the disposal. The Case IV assessment will be in an amount the income tax on which at the standard rate is equal to the amount of the referable corporation tax, ie the amount of capital gains tax which would be payable by the company if it were liable to capital gains tax rather than corporation tax and as if accounting periods were years of assessment. The tax paid by the receiver is treated as discharging a corresponding amount of the liability of the company to corporation tax on chargeable gains.

Where there have been disposals of assets by the receiver (ie in respect of assets secured, charged or encumbered) and by the company (in respect of other assets) in an accounting period within the period of the receivership, it will be necessary to identify the part of the total corporation tax liability which must be paid by the receiver as accountable person. In that case, TCA 1997, s 571(2), (3), (4) apply to apportion capital gains tax or corporation tax on chargeable gains between the receiver and the company. The approach to be taken is illustrated in the following example.

Example 12.902.3.1

During its latest accounting period, the following chargeable gains arose to Diogenes Shipping Ltd (in receivership):

	€
Sale of shipping vessels charged in favour of debenture holders	4,275,000
Sale of other assets	5,890,000

	10,165,000
Capital gains tax losses forward	7,915,000
Taxable	2,250,000
Adjusted for corporation tax (20/12.5)	3,600,000
Corporation tax @ 12.5%	450,000

The liability is apportioned as follows:

Receiver:	€450,000 x 855,000[1]/ 2,033,000[2]	189,252
Company:	€450,000 x 1,178,000[3]/ 2,033,000	260,748
		450,000

[1] 4,275,000 @ 20% = 855,000
[2] 10,165,000 @ 20% = 2,033,000
[3] 5,890,000 @ 20% = 1,178,000

The apportionments are done on the basis of the respective amounts of capital gains tax that would be payable in respect of the full chargeable gain (ie, before losses).

As regards corporation tax due by a company in receivership, other than in respect of chargeable gains, tax legislation does not include any provision for the collection or corporation tax assessed (see *Wayte (Holdings) Ltd (in receivership), Burns v Hearne* HC [1986]). Any amount assessed remains a liability of the *company*. (However, an amount so assessed may be claimed by the Revenue in a subsequent liquidation of the company; tax assessed for any one year during the course of the receivership may be deemed a preferential debt in the liquidation – see *H Williams (Tallaght) Limited (in receivership and liquidation)* 5 ITR 387. There are no specific provisions governing the collection of tax from a receiver who may possibly retain the full proceeds of income earned during the receivership for the benefit of the debenture holder, leaving the company without funds to discharge the relevant tax liability.

12.903 Examinership

The role and functions of an examiner are governed by the Companies (Amendment) Act 1990. During the course of an examinership, the liabilities of the company are frozen. There is no preferential ranking of creditors. Under a "scheme of arrangement", liabilities of the company are written down.

For the purposes of corporation tax, the appointment of an examiner does not result in the ending of an accounting period nor is there any question of the company losing beneficial ownership of its assets. Where liabilities are reduced under a scheme of arrangement, amounts consequentially credited to the profit and loss account may by subject to tax or may use up losses forward if available.

12.10 CHARITABLE COMPANIES

12.1001 Introduction
12.1002 Income
12.1003 Chargeable gains

12.1001 Introduction

Corporation tax legislation does not contain any special provisions for charitable companies, nor does it include any definition of a charitable company. CTA s 79(3)(*g*) refers to a company which is established solely for the advancement of religion or education and which under its memorandum or articles of association is prohibited from distributing any part of its profits to its members. Such a company could be described as a charitable company. CTA s 79, which provided for a 30% corporation tax rate in respect of certain income including the income of charitable companies, ceased however to have effect from 1 April 1989.

12.1002 Income

TCA 1997, s 208 provides for the exemption from income tax chargeable under Case I(b) of Schedule D (see **3.103.6**) where the profits or gains so chargeable arise out of lands, tenements or hereditaments which are owned and occupied by a charity.

Exemption is also provided from income tax chargeable in respect of the profits of a trade carried on by a charity if the profits are applied solely to the purposes of the charity and either the trade is exercised in the course of the actual carrying out of a primary purpose of the charity or the work in connection with the trade is mainly carried on by beneficiaries of the charity. Where a trade of farming is carried on by a charity, exemption is available whether or not the profits from the trade are applied to the purposes of the charity.

A *charity* for the above purposes means any body of persons or trust established for charitable purposes only (TCA 1997, s 208(1)). Thus a company may be a charity, as long as it is established for charitable purposes only. As regards the meaning of "for charitable purposes", in *Special Commissioners of Income Tax v Pemsel* 3 TC 53 Lord MacNaghten instanced as the purposes which the law considers to be charitable as the relief of poverty, the advancement of religion or education, and other purposes of a charitable nature beneficial to the community.

The relief of the poor of a particular church (*Re Wall, Pomeroy v Willway* (1889) 43 Ch D 774), the encouragement of choral singing (*Royal Choral Society v IRC* 25 TC 263), the promotion of an annual chess tournament for boys (*Re Dupree's Deed Trusts* [1944] 2 All ER 443), the establishment of a rest home for nurses (*Re White's Will Trusts, Tindall v United Sheffield Hospital Board of Governors* [1951] 1 All ER 528), the relief of poor widows and orphans of deceased bank officers (*Re Coulthurst* [1951] All ER 774) and the publication of law reports (*Incorporated Council of Law Reporting v AG* 47 TC 341) have all been held to come within the description of "charitable purposes".

Charitable purposes were, on other hand, held not to include the formation of a council to secure legislative and other temperance reform (*IRC v Temperance Council of the Christian Churches of England and Wales* 10 TC 748), the advancement of education in political matters in the interests of one political party (*Bonar Law*

Memorial Trust v IRC 17 TC 508), the setting up of a private body to develop industry and enterprise and to provide vocational education to the public (*IRC v Oldham Training and Enterprise Council* [1996] STC 1218) and the suppression of vivisection (*IRC v National Anti-Vivisection Society* 28 TC 311).

In *Beirne v St Vincent de Paul Society, Wexford (*1) ITR (393), a business which was bequeathed to a society established for charitable purposes, and which employed a man who would otherwise have been an object of the society, was refused charitable exemption. In *Davis v Mater Misericordiae Hospital (*1) ITR (387), a hospital entitled to charitable exemption was held to be taxable in respect of profits derived from an annexe used as a private nursing home.

TCA 1997, s 76(6) (see **3.102.2**) provides, inter alia, that any provision of the Income Tax Acts or of any other statute conferring an exemption from income tax is, except as otherwise provided, to have effect for corporation tax purposes. Thus the income tax exemptions provided for in TCA 1997, s 208 in respect of charities apply also for corporation tax purposes.

Although only trading income of a charitable company is exempt under TCA 1997, s 208, the exemption extends in practice to other income of such a company, such as interest and dividends.

A charity is exempt from tax in respect of offshore income gains provided the gains are applied for charitable purposes only (TCA 1997, s 745(5) – see **3.210.3**).

Various exemptions from income tax in the cases of charities are provided for by TCA 1997, s 207. These exemptions are extended to corporation tax by virtue of TCA 1997, s 76(1) (see **3.102.2**). Exemption is provided for in respect of the following:

(a) income tax chargeable under Schedule D in respect of rents and profits of any property belonging to any hospital, public school or almshouse, or vested in trustees for charitable purposes, in so far as those rents and profits are applied to charitable purposes only (TCA 1997, s 207(1)(a));

(b) income tax chargeable:

(i) under Schedule C in respect of any interest, annuities, dividends or shares of annuities,

(ii) under Schedule D in respect of any yearly interest or other annual payment, and

(iii) under Sch F in respect of any distribution,

forming any part of the income of any body of persons or trust established for charitable purposes only or which, according to the rules or regulations established by statute, decree, deed of trust or will, are applicable to charitable purposes only, and in so far as those items of income are applied to charitable purposes only (TCA 1997, s 207(1)(b));

(c) income tax chargeable under Sch C in respect of any interest, annuities, dividends or shares of annuities in the names of trustees applicable solely towards the repairs of any cathedral, college, church or chapel, or any building used solely for the purposes of divine worship, and in so far as those items of income are applied to those purposes (TCA 1997, s 207(1)(c)).

12.1003 Chargeable gains

A gain accruing to a charity is not a chargeable gain if it accrues to a charity and is applicable and applied for charitable purposes (TCA 1997, s 609(1)). For capital gains tax purposes, *charity* has the meaning assigned to it by TCA 1997, s 208(1) (see **12.1002** above).

If property held on charitable trusts ceases to be subject to charitable trusts:

(a)   the trustees are treated as if they had disposed of, and immediately reacquired, the property for a consideration equal to its market value, and any gain on the disposal is treated as not accruing to a charity; and

(b)   if and so far as any of that property represents, directly or indirectly, the consideration for the disposal of assets by the trustees, any gain accruing on that disposal is to be treated as not having accrued to a charity.

The question whether a donation from one charity to another is the application of the amount of the donation for charitable purposes was considered in *IRC v Helen Slater Charitable Trust Ltd* [1980] STC 150. It was held that a charitable corporation acting *intra vires* and making an outright transfer of money applicable for charitable purposes to another charitable corporation, so that full title to the money passes to the other corporation, must be taken by the transfer to have applied the money for charitable purposes unless the transferor knows or ought to know that the money will be misapplied by the transferee. The transferor corporation would therefore be entitled to claim exemption from capital gains tax without having to show how the money has been dealt with by the transferee.

Subject to TCA 1997, s 848A (donations to approved bodies – see **3.203.8**), where a disposal of an asset is made to a charity, otherwise than under a bargain at arm's length, the deemed market value rule in TCA 1997, s 547 (see **9.102.14**) does not apply and the disposal and acquisition are treated as being made for such consideration as to secure that neither a gain nor a loss accrues on the disposal. TCA 1997, s 611(1)(a)(II) deals with the situation in which there is a disposal of an asset to a charity and the asset is later disposed of by the charity in such circumstances that if a gain accrued on that disposal it would be a chargeable gain (ie, the gain is not one which is applicable and applied for charitable purposes only). In that case, the capital gains tax which would have been chargeable in respect of the gain accruing on the earlier disposal, if the market value rule in TCA 1997, s 547 had applied to it, is to be assessed and charged on the charity in addition to any capital gains tax chargeable in respect of the gain accruing to it on the later disposal.

Chapter 13

Special Types of Business

13.1 FARMING

13.101 Introduction

A company carrying on a trade of farming is liable to corporation tax on the profits arising from that trade. The profits subject to corporation tax are computed in the same way as the trading profits of companies generally but with some differences, principally in the areas of capital allowances, losses, stock relief, stallion fee exemption and woodlands exemption. In addition, stud farms are subject to certain practical rules for determining the closing value of broodmares and their progeny. Some features of the taxation regime which apply to farming trades apply only to individuals, eg income averaging and the exemption of certain income from the leasing of farm land.

Farming means farming land in the State wholly or mainly occupied for the purposes of husbandry, other than market garden land (Taxes Consolidation Act 1997 (TCA 1997), s 654). *Occupation* in this context means having the use of the land or having the right by virtue of any easement to graze livestock on the land. An *easement* is defined in TCA 1997, s 96(1) as including "any right, privilege or benefit in, over or derived from premises". *Premises* means "any lands, tenements or hereditaments in the State".

Special rules have for many years applied to the taxation of profits from the ownership and occupation of farming land in the State. Farming profits were exempt from income tax up to 5 April 1974 prior to which tax was charged under Schedule A in respect of the ownership of land and under Schedule B in respect of the occupation of land. Schedule A and B assessments were based on a fixed but notional annual value of the land. For the period 6 April 1969 to 5 April 1976, companies were liable to corporation profits tax in respect of profits or gains from farming. They were liable to income tax for the years 1974/75 and 1975/76. Farming profits of a company became liable to corporation tax from 6 April 1976.

Farming is distinguished from market gardening, which refers to the occupation of market garden land, ie land in the State occupied as a nursery or garden for the sale of the produce (other than land used for the growth of hops) (TCA 1997, s 654). Market gardening profits are taxable under Case I of Schedule D in the same way as other trading profits and without special rules.

All farming in the State is treated as the carrying on of a trade, or part of a trade as the case may be, the profits or gains of which are charged to tax under Case I of Schedule D (TCA 1997, s 655). All farming carried on by one person whether solely or in partnership is treated as the carrying on of a single trade. This is despite the rule in TCA 1997, s 1008(1) that the profits arising to a partner from a partnership trade are treated as a separate trade ("several trade") carried on solely by that partner. Thus, a person who carries on some farming activities solely and other farming activities in partnership is treated as carrying on a single farming trade.

As seen above, farming involves the occupation of farm land for the purposes of husbandry. *Husbandry* is not defined for taxation purposes but can be taken to denote the working of land for the purpose of extracting the produce of the land. It includes the growing and harvesting of crops, the breeding and rearing of livestock on the land and the sale of milk, butter, wool and other animal produce. As already mentioned, farming does not include market gardening. Nor does it refer to such activities as mink farming, intensive production of poultry, and cattle or milk dealing. If produce such as vegetables, fruit and flowers which are normally associated with market gardening are grown on farm land as part of a farming activity, they will normally be treated as part of the farming trade.

The concept of "occupation" is central to the meaning of farming. It denotes having the use of the land or having the right by virtue of any easement (meaning any right, privilege or benefit in, over or derived from premises) to graze livestock on the land. Occupation is not confined to owners or lessees of land although that is how land is occupied in the vast majority of cases. A person engaged in husbandry on land used for that purpose with the permission of the owner or lessee is farming. Occupation also refers to grazing livestock on land by virtue of an easement. Thus a person having grazing rights, whether for a period of less than or more than a year, is regarded as occupying that land and may therefore be carrying a trade of farming.

The position of cattle and milk dealers is governed by TCA 1997, s 53. The occupation of farm land by a dealer in cattle or a dealer in or a seller of milk, where the land is insufficient for the keep of the cattle brought onto it, is treated as the carrying on of a trade taxable under Case I of Schedule D. As to whether land is sufficient for the keep of cattle brought onto it is a question of fact in each particular case. In *Huxham v Johnson* 11 TC 266, the appellant kept milch cows on land whose soil was so poor that large sums had to be expended to feed the cattle. Milk was sold both from the cattle and from purchases and the cows were sold when they became dry. It was held that the activity in question was one of cattle dealing and not farming.

With a view to giving relief to persons carrying on certain qualifying trades to take account of the effect of inflation on the cost of carrying trading stocks, stock relief in the form of a deduction against trading may be claimed by those persons. In the cases of manufacturing and construction operations and trades of supplying goods to other qualifying trades, the relief given is a percentage of the opening trading stock value for an accounting period. For farming trades, the relief is by reference to the increase, if any, in the value of the trading stock during the accounting period in question. Where there is a decrease in the value of trading stock during an accounting period, previous stock relief deductions are clawed back to the extent of that decrease.

With the exception of farming trades, no stock relief has been given in respect of profits chargeable to income tax for 1986/87 or later years of assessment and in respect of profits chargeable to corporation tax for accounting periods ending after 5 April 1985.

Stock relief for farming companies is available to companies carrying on a trade of farming in the State and is confined to Irish resident companies. A stock relief deduction may be claimed for an accounting period in which a company's closing trading farming stock value exceeds its opening stock value. The amount of the deduction is treated as a trading expense. For accounting periods ending after 5 April 1995, there is no clawback of relief given in earlier periods where there is a decrease in stock value during the period; for earlier periods a clawback resulted in any such case. Obviously, no stock relief is available where there is a decrease in stock value.

13.102   Computation of farming profits

13.102.1   Introduction

The computation of farming taxable profits or tax losses for any period is, in principle, carried out in exactly the same way as for any other trade; the farmer is required to prepare accounts in the same way as any other trader and to submit them each year to the inspector of taxes together with the necessary supporting data.

Since farming is treated as the carrying on of a trade, the Case I computational rules contained in the Income Tax Acts and relevant court decisions affecting their interpretation apply equally to the computation of farming profits under Case I. The principles discussed in **3.201-204** relating to items to be included in or excluded from trading receipts and deductible expenses, as well as the other computational matters dealt with there, are relevant for the purposes of the computation of farming profits and losses.

There are, however, certain statutory as well as practical differences in the taxation of farming profits and in relation to the capital allowances that may be set off against the farmer's Case I profits. One area requiring separate discussion concerns the practical approach adopted in arriving at the cost of a farmer's trading stock to be used for tax purposes; this is covered in **13.104**. Stock relief for farming companies is discussed in **13.103**). For the capital allowances that are available against farming profits, see **13.2**.

As with other trades, the pre-tax farming profit or loss as disclosed by the accounts is adjusted by adding back any disallowable items charged in the accounts (eg capital expenditure, depreciation, personal and other non-farming expenses) and, to the extent relevant, deductions are made for items credited in the accounts which are not taxable or are chargeable to tax under some other heading, eg capital profits. Any stock relief deduction should be taken at the end of the computation.

13.102.2   Disallowance of certain wages

Employees of a farming company may sometimes be employed to carry out improvements or other work of a capital nature on the farm or in work totally unrelated to the farming activities. For example, farm labour may be used for erecting new fences (as distinct from repairing or replacing existing ones), for constructing or extending farm buildings or for such works as land reclamation or new drainage. The employee may also carry out work on non-farm land (eg, separate woodlands). To the extent that farm wages have been charged in the accounts for such capital works or for such non-farm purposes, an appropriate disallowance must be made in the Case I tax computation.

To the extent that any such farm wages and other expenses are disallowed in the Case I computation due to their being of a capital nature, the company is entitled to claim the appropriate capital allowances available, depending on the nature of the expenditure.

For example, expenditure on the construction of farm buildings (other than farm dwelling houses), land reclamation, drainage, new fencing etc qualifies for the farm buildings allowance (see **13.202**), while any such capital expenditure in relation to farm machinery (eg on the installation of new milking equipment) attracts the usual wear and tear allowances. It is a matter of fact in each case as to whether the work on which the wages are incurred is of a capital nature or whether it is properly deductible as a trading expense.

13.103 Stock relief

13.103.1 Introduction

Stock relief has been available for farming trades since it was first introduced for companies by FA 1975 s 31 and extended to individuals and other non-corporate persons by FA 1976 s 12. Originally, the system of stock relief applied also for certain other types of "qualifying trades" (manufacture, construction and the supply of machinery, plant and other goods to any of the qualifying trades including farming). The relief, introduced as a temporary measure, has since its inception been extended by numerous Finance Acts but, for qualifying trades other than farming, the final period for which the relief was available was 1983-84 or, for companies, the last accounting period ending before 6 April 1994.

For the trade of farming only, stock relief has continued to be extended for one or two years at a time by Finance Acts from FA 1984 to date. The latest extension, provided in TCA 1997, s 666(4)(a), is to the effect that stock relief is available, in the case of farming companies, for accounting periods ending not later than 31 December 2008.

Stock relief legislation is now contained in TCA 1997 Part 23 Ch 2 (ss 665-669). The relief entitles a company chargeable to corporation tax and which carries on the trade of farming to a stock relief deduction for any accounting period in which there is an increase in the value of the trading stock of its farming trade. The calculation of the deduction is explained in **13.103.6** below. The deduction is allowed by treating the amount so determined as if it were a trading expense in computing the company's Schedule D Case I profits from its trade of farming for the accounting period concerned.

TCA 1997, s 666(1) entitles a resident company carrying on a trade of farming in the State to claim a stock relief deduction for an accounting period in which the company's closing farming stock value exceeds its opening value in that period (the "increase in stock value"). The deduction is 25% of the amount of the increase in stock value. The amount of the deduction is treated as if it were a trading expense in computing the company's Case I profits from the farming trade for the accounting period in which the increase in stock value occurs.

A company claiming stock relief for any accounting period is required by TCA 1997, s 666(5) to make a written claim for the deduction no later than the return filing date ("specified return date") for that period. A company's corporation tax return for an accounting period is required to be made within nine months of the end of the accounting period (but in any event not later than the 21st of the month in which that period of nine month ends) (TCA 1997, s 950(1)).

13.103.2 Farming

Stock relief is available only to companies carrying on the trade of farming. *Farming* is defined in TCA 1997, s 654 as farming land in the State wholly or mainly occupied for the purposes of husbandry, other than market garden land (see **13.101**). For the "wholly or mainly" condition to be met in any accounting period, the test prescribed in FA 1975 s 31A(11) (now repealed) was that at least 75% of the company's total sales in the course of its trade in that accounting period was derived from sales made in the course of its farming operations. No such clarification is, however, provided in TCA 1997, s 654. Assuming that a company would still be accepted as carrying on a trade of farming on the basis of the 75% test, it is possible for up to a maximum of one-quarter of the sales of the trade to be derived from operations other than farming without rendering the company ineligible for stock relief in the accounting period concerned. "Sales" in an accounting period, whether from farming or other operations, are measured in terms of the amounts receivable in the accounting period from sales in the course of trade.

13.103.3   Partnerships

TCA 1997, s 666(6) applies the provisions of TCA 1997, s 666 to a farming trade carried on by a partnership as those provisions apply to a trade carried on by any other person. Consequently, a partnership carrying on a trade of farming is also entitled to claim stock relief in arriving at the partnership profits (which profits, after any stock relief deduction, are allocated between the several trades of the partners in the normal way – see **13.701**).

Stock relief is available to a "person", which means a person resident in the State and not resident elsewhere. It is likely therefore that stock relief was intended to apply in the cases of partnerships only where all the partners are resident in the State. However, the legislation contains no such requirement. TCA 1997, s 666(6) simply provides that the stock relief provisions apply to a trade of farming carried on by a partnership as they apply to a trade of farming carried on by a person. Generally, a partnership does not have a residence for tax purposes, nor does the stock relief legislation contain any stipulation regarding residence.

13.103.4   Accounting period

For the purpose of the rules for stock relief for farming companies, the term *accounting period* is given the same meaning as it has for corporation tax purposes generally (as defined in TCA 1997, s 27 – see **3.105**) (TCA 1997, s 665). Briefly, some of the main rules for defining the accounting period of a company for corporation tax generally, and which are therefore applicable in applying the rules providing stock relief for companies, may be restated here:

(a)   The accounting period of a company is normally the period for which it makes up its accounts, but in no case can there be an accounting period which is longer than 12 months.

(b)   A company may make up accounts for a period shorter than 12 months and, if it does so, that period is normally the accounting period for stock relief purposes. Unlike the position for income tax, there is no question of the Revenue Commissioners having the right to select a given period of 12 months as the accounting period.

(c)   If a company makes up accounts for a period longer than 12 months, the period of accounts is divided into two accounting periods consisting respectively of the first 12 months of that period and the balance of that period (eg a period of accounts of 15 months ending 31 March 2000 is divided into an accounting period of 12 months ending 31 December 1997 and an accounting period of 3 months ending 31 March 2000.

(d) An accounting period always ends on the date on which a resident company ceases to be resident, whether or not this coincides with the end of a period of account. For the effect on stock relief of an accounting period ending due to a company ceasing to be resident, see below.

(e) An accounting period always ends when a company goes into liquidation and, thereafter, the company has accounting periods for each succeeding period of 12 months so long as the liquidation continues, but the last accounting period ends on the date the liquidation is completed.

(f) An accounting period always ends on the date on which the company's trade ceases (except where the trade has been continued into the period of liquidation in which case the accounting period ends on the date determined by the rule in (e).

13.103.5   Trading stock: definition and valuation

TCA 1997, s 665 defines *trading stock* for stock relief purposes, in relation to the farming trade of a company, by giving the term the same meaning as it has in TCA 1997, s 89, which is:

(a) property of any description, whether real or personal, which is sold in the ordinary course of the trade, or would be sold if it were mature or if its manufacture, preparation or construction were complete; or

(b) materials that are used in the manufacture, preparation or construction of property of a type that is sold in the ordinary course of the trade.

In relation to a trade of farming, this definition clearly includes all livestock, poultry etc kept on the farm land either for rearing for sale or for producing offspring or farm produce (milk, eggs etc), all farm produce, crops etc, as well as all fertilisers, seeds etc held to be used on the farm itself. These items do not of course constitute an all-inclusive list of what may be included in a farmer's trading stock.

The values of the farmer's opening and closing trading stock used to determine the increase (if any) in trading stock value by reference to which the stock relief is calculated are normally taken as being the trading stock figures used in the farmer's accounts. This assumes that the method of valuing the trading stock for the accounts follows normal principles for stock valuations for tax purposes, but if any adjustments to the accounting figures are required to reflect proper tax principles, the same adjustments need to be made in the opening and closing stock values which are used in calculating stock relief.

In the event that any payments on account have been received by the farmer in respect of a forthcoming sale of any item(s) still included in either the opening or closing trading stock, the relevant stock value is to be reduced by the amount(s) of the payment(s) on account, as required by the definition of trading stock in TCA 1997, s 665.

For the special rules of TCA 1997, s 669(5)(a) which may apply for the valuation of the opening stock for the first accounting period in which a person carries on a trade of farming, see *Opening stock of new business* below.

In addition, in some circumstances it is necessary to apply certain special rules in the determining the opening and/or closing stock values from which the increase (if any) in stock value for an accounting period is calculated (but without changing the stock values for other purposes). The special rules may be required in the following circumstances:

(a) where the company was not carrying on the farming trade immediately before the beginning of an accounting period, the rule in TCA 1997, s 669(5)(a) may apply to require the inspector to fix the opening stock value for that accounting period at such value as the inspector considers reasonable and just;

(b) where the company has acquired or disposed of trading stock otherwise than in the normal conduct of the farming trade in question, TCA 1997, s 669(1)(a) requires the opening and/or closing stock values, as appropriate, of the relevant period of account to be determined at such values as the inspector considers reasonable and just; and

(c) where the basis of valuing the company's trading stock at the end of a period of account has been changed compared with the basis of valuing the trading stock at the beginning of the period of account, TCA 1997, s 669(1)(b) requires the opening stock value for that period to be revised to the same basis as that used for valuing the closing stock value.

(a) Opening stock of new business

When a person commences to carry on a farming trade, the opening stock at the start of the first accounting period is often very low or perhaps there is no opening stock. In order to provide a reasonable measure of stock relief for the first accounting period, TCA 1997, s 669(5)(a) requires stock relief to be calculated as if the farmer had a trading stock at the beginning of the accounting period of such value as the inspector of taxes considers reasonable and just. This rule applies where, immediately before the beginning of an accounting period for which a stock relief deduction is claimed, the trade was not being carried on by the person claiming the relief.

The above described rule is therefore always relevant for a person starting a new farming trade, but may also be relevant for a person succeeding to an existing farming trade previously carried on by another person. For the circumstances in which an exception to this rule applies, ie in the case of a person commencing a trade who takes over trading stock from the person previously carrying on the trade, see below.

Where the inspector is required to make a valuation under the rule in TCA 1997, s 669(5)(a), the "reasonable and just" valuation of the opening stock is relevant only for the purposes of determining the increase in stock value (if any) for the stock relief computation. No adjustment is made to the opening trading stock value which is used in arriving at the taxable trading profits of the accounting period.

In making the "reasonable and just" valuation under TCA 1997, s 669(5)(a), the inspector is required to have regard to all the relevant circumstances of the case. In particular, the inspector is required to take account of movements during the accounting period in the costs of items of a kind included in the farmer's trading stock during the period, and of changes during the period in the volume of the trade carried on (TCA 1997, s 669(5)(b)). On any appeal against the decision of the inspector, the Appeal Commissioners are similarly directed to have regard to all the relevant circumstances (TCA 1997, s 669(5)(c)).

While no other directions are given to the inspector as to how the notional opening trading stock valuation should be made, the particular circumstances mentioned in the section do suggest a line of approach which can best be explained by the following example.

Example 13.103.5.1

Kingston Farms Ltd commenced a farming trade with an opening trading stock of €5,000. At the end of its first accounting period, trading stock is valued at €170,000. Prices for the company's products have increased by about 10% during the year. At the end of the first year, the company's farm sales are running at an average of €55,000 a month compared with €20,000 per month for the first three months.

The opening stock value which appears to the inspector to be reasonable and just might be arrived at on the following lines, based on TCA 1997, s 669(5)(b):

	€
Closing stock value	170,000
Comparable opening value based on lower prices: €170,000 x 100/110	154,545
Monthly sales at year end adjusted by reference to opening sales prices	
(say 10% higher): €55,000 x 100/110 = €50,000	
Adjust €154,545 to allow for lower sales levels in opening months:	
€154,545 x 20,000/ 50,000	61,818

Assuming the company accepts this opening figure, the increase in stock value by reference to which its stock relief deduction for the accounting period is calculated as follows:

	€
Closing stock value	170,000
Less: opening stock value	61,818
Increase in stock value for period	108,182

The "reasonable and just" estimate of the opening stock value is not made, if:

(a) the company commencing to carry on the trade of farming has acquired the initial trading stock on a sale or transfer from another person on that other person's ceasing to carry on the trade; and

(b) the stock acquired from the other person is, or is included in, the opening trading stock of the company commencing to carry on the trade.

Where this exception applies, the opening stock value for the company's stock relief computation for the accounting period in which it commences to carry on the farming trade is determined under the ordinary rules. Thus, the opening stock value will normally be taken as the amount of the consideration paid by the company for the stock or, if no consideration was given, the market value of the stock at the date of transfer.

(b) Abnormal transactions

Where a farming company has acquired or disposed of trading stock other than in the normal course of the farming trade, TCA 1997, s 669(1)(a) requires the value of the opening and/or closing trading stock of an accounting period to be treated as having such value as appears to the inspector or, on appeal, the Appeal Commissioners to be reasonable and just in all the circumstances.

The purpose of this rule is to counter excessive stock relief claims made on the basis of artificial changes in the level of trading stock. An inspector of taxes might, for example, invoke this rule if a company claiming stock relief has abnormally increased its closing trading stock value for an accounting period by an usually large purchase of cattle from a related person just before the relevant date and has sold the cattle back to the same person or another related person at the beginning of the next period.

Before allowing a stock relief claim, the inspector of taxes may well enquire of the company whether the trading stock includes any items acquired other than in the course of normal trading (eg, from a connected person) and if so, to give particulars of the value of such stock. The rule is not, however, directed against the case where the farm trading stocks may be built up towards the end of an accounting period in the normal course of the trade.

(c) Change in basis of stock valuation

TCA 1997, s 669(1)(b) deals with the case where a farming company changes the basis of valuing the farm trading stock so that the basis on which the closing stock of an accounting period is valued is different from that used to value the opening stock. In any such case, the opening stock must be revalued on the same basis as was used for the closing stock.

13.103.6   Amount of deduction

The amount of a company's stock relief deduction for an accounting period is the lower of:

(a)   25% of the increase in stock value for that accounting period (TCA 1997, s 666(1); or

(b)   the company's "net" Case I trading income for that accounting period (TCA 1997, s 666(2)(a)).

The amount of the deduction is accordingly 25% of the increase in stock value in the accounting period, subject to the restriction that it cannot exceed the net Case I trading income from the farming activity. The net trading income for this purpose is income *before* any stock relief deduction but *after* reducing the income by the capital allowances attributable to the farm trade and by any trading losses carried forward to the accounting period or, if relevant, any terminal loss carried back from a later accounting period (TCA 1997, s 666(2)(a)).

Example 13.103.6.1

Johnstown Estates Ltd, an Irish resident company, carries on a trade of farming in the State. It has for many years made up its annual accounts to 30 June but after 30 June 2007 makes up its next accounts for the nine month period to 31 March 2008.

The following information is relevant for the last two accounting periods:

	Year ended 30/6/07 €	Period ended 31/3/08 €
Value of trading stock:		
At 1 July 2006	111,000	
At 30 June 2007	149,000	
Increase in period	38,000	

At 1 July 2007		149,000
At 31 March 2008		183,000
Increase in period		34,000
Case I trading income (before stock relief)	47,500	55,700
TCA 1997, s 396(1) loss forward from y/e 30 June 2006	41,600	
Net Case I profit (before stock relief)	5,900	55,700

The stock relief deductions for these accounting periods are calculated as follows:

	Year ended 30/6/07	Period ended 31/3/08
	€	€
Lower of:		
(a)		
25% x €38,000	9,500	
25% x €34,000		8,500
and		
(b)		
Net Case I profit	5,900	55,700
Stock relief deduction	5,900	8,500

The final Case I profits from the company's farming trade for inclusion in its profits chargeable to corporation tax are as follows:

	Year ended 30/6/07	Period Ended 31/3/08
	€	€
Case I profits	47,500	55,700
Less: stock relief deduction	5,900	8,500
	41,600	47,200
Less: loss forward from y/e 30/6/06	41,600	Nil
Final Case I profits from farming	Nil	47,200

13.103.7   Reference periods

TCA 1997, s 669(2), (3) provide rules relating to the determination of a company's stock relief deduction in any case where a company's accounting period does not coincide with a "period of account" (ie, a period for which accounts are made up) or with two or more such periods.

In such cases, any increase in stock value for stock relief purposes is first determined as the excess of the value of the trading stock at the end of the "reference period" over the trading stock value at the commencement of the reference period. A reference period, as defined in TCA 1997, s 669(2)(a), will always be longer than the accounting period in question, and it is therefore necessary to attribute to the accounting period a proportion only of the increase in stock value in the reference period. The stock relief deduction is then calculated for the accounting period by reference to the part of the increase in stock value so attributed to the accounting period. A period of account which exceeds 12 months cannot coincide with a corporation tax accounting period so that, for stock relief purposes, the reference period rules become relevant.

These rules are as follows:

(a) if the accounting period relevant for the stock relief calculation does not commence on the first day of a period of account, the reference period begins on the first day of the period of account which is "current" (ie still running) at the start of that accounting period;

(b) if the accounting period does not end on the last day of a period of account, the reference period ends on the last day of the period of account which is current at the end of the accounting period;

(c) if the accounting period commences on the first day of a period of account, the reference period commences on that day;

(d) if the accounting period ends on the last day of a period of account, the reference period ends on that day.

Once the reference period has been determined, the farming company's increase in stock value for the relevant accounting period is calculated in accordance with the following formula:

$$\frac{A(C-O)}{N}$$

where

A = the number of months in the accounting period,

C = the value of the company's trading stock at the end of the reference period,

O = the value of the company's trading stock at the start of the reference period, and

N = the number of months in the reference period.

The company's stock relief deduction for the accounting period is the lower of:

(a) 25% of the part of the increase in stock value in the reference period apportioned to the accounting period; or

(b) the net Case I trading income for the accounting period.

Example 13.103.7.1

The facts are as in Example **13.103.6.1**, except that instead of having two separate periods of account covering the period 1 July 2006 to 31 March 2008, Johnstown Estates Ltd made up only one set of accounts covering the 21 month period. Accordingly the stock value at 30 June 2007 will not figure in the stock relief calculation.

For corporation tax purposes, TCA 1997, s 27 requires the 21 month period of account to be divided into two separate accounting periods, ie year ended 30 June 2007 and nine months ended 31 March 2008.

Since neither of these accounting periods coincides with a period for which accounts are made up, it is necessary to apply the reference period rules of TCA 1997, s 669(2), (3) for the stock relief deduction for each accounting period.

The reference period to be used for the stock relief deduction for the year ended 30 June 2007 is the 21 month period beginning on 1 July 2006 (rule (c) above) and ending on 31 March 2008 (rule (b)). The reference period for the 9 month accounting period 1 July 2008 to 31 March 2008 is also the period from 1 July 2006 (rule (a) above) and ending on 31 March 2008 (rule (d)).

The following figures relevant to stock relief are taken using the results of the 21 months period of account (the reference period for each accounting period):

	€
Value of trading stock:	
At 1 July 2006 (= O)	111,000
At 31 March 2008 (= C)	183,000
Case I adjusted profits (after capital allowances, but before stock relief)	103,200
TCA 1997, s 396(1) loss forward from y/e 30 June 2006	41,600

The increase in stock value attributable to each accounting period is determined as follows:

		€
(a) Year ended 30 June 2007		
Number of months in accounting period (= A)	12	
Number of months in reference period (= N)	21	
Increase in stock value in reference period (C – O)		72,000
Increase in stock value attributable to this period:		
€72,000 x 12/21		41,143
(b) Period 1 July 2007 to 31 March 2008		
Number of months in accounting period (= A)	9	
Number of months in reference period (= N)	21	
Increase in stock value in reference period (C – O)		72,000
Increase in stock value attributable to this period:		
€72,000 x 9/21		30,857

For the purposes of the stock relief restriction, if any, the Case I adjusted profit of €103,200 for the 21 months period of account must first be apportioned on a time basis between the two accounting periods. The net Case I profits (before stock relief) for each accounting period is accordingly calculated as follows:

	Year ended 30/6/07	Period ended 31/3/08
	€	€
Year ended 30/6/07:		
€103,200 x 12/21	58,971	
Nine months ended 31/3/08:		
€103,200 x 9/21		44,229
TCA 1997, s 396(1) loss forward from y/e 30/6/06	41,600	
Net Case I profits (before stock relief)	17,371	44,229

The stock relief deductions for each of the two accounting periods can be now calculated as follows:

	Year ended	Period ended
	30/6/07	31/3/08
	€	€
Lower of:		
(a)		
25% x €41,143	10,286	
25% x €30,857		7,714
and		
(b)		
Net Case I profit (before stock relief)[1]	17,371	44,229
Stock relief deduction	10,286	7,714

The company's final Case I profits from its farming trade for inclusion in its profits chargeable to corporation tax are as follows:

	Year ended	Period ended
	30/6/07	31/3/08
	€	€
Case I profits (before stock relief)	58,971	44,229
Less: stock relief deduction	10,286	7,714
	48,685	36,515
TCA 1997, s 396(1) loss forward from year ended 30/6/06	41,600	Nil
Final Case I profits from farming	7,085	36,515

Note:

1. There is no restriction in either accounting period as the net Case I profits (before stock relief) exceed the deduction otherwise available for each period.

13.103.8 Effect of cessation of trade etc

TCA 1997, s 669(4)(a) provides that a company is not entitled to any stock relief deduction for any accounting period which ends by virtue of the company:

(a)   ceasing to carry on its trade of farming; or

(b)   ceasing to be resident in the State; or

(c)   ceasing to be within the charge to corporation tax under Schedule D Case I.

TCA 1997, s 669(4)(b) extends the effect of subsection (4)(a) to cover the case where it is necessary to determine a farming company's increase in stock value for an accounting period by reference to the increase in stock value over a reference period. In any such case, a stock relief deduction is denied if the cessation of trade or other event occurs at the end of any of the accounting periods comprised in the reference period.

13.104   Valuation of farm trading stock

13.104.1   Introduction

The valuation of a farming company's trading stock at the beginning and end of each period of account is an important element in arriving at its profit or loss for that period. The same principles apply to the valuation of farm trading stock as are used in valuing the trading stocks of other businesses. Livestock, harvested crops and other trading stock must be valued at its "cost" to the farming company, except for any trading stock which has a market value (ie net realisable value) of less than its cost. In examining any farm accounts submitted, the inspector of taxes will need to be satisfied that the company has not only included all items of trading stock, but also that the different items have been correctly valued in accordance with the lower of cost and market value principle.

In practice, due to the nature of farming, it may be more difficult than for most other trades to put an accurate cost figure on many items of farm stock. In order to deal with this problem, the Revenue has devised a rule of thumb approach which deems the cost of livestock (except horses) bred on the farm or purchased as immature stock to be a certain percentage of their market values as estimated at the year end accounting date.

The same approach is used to arrive at the cost value of harvested crops, but crops still in the ground at the year end date need not be valued and may therefore be excluded from farm trading stock. A company will normally have sufficiently accurate costing records to do so and may, if it wishes, value trading stocks at their actual cost, but in practice the Revenue's rule of thumb approach is widely accepted.

In accordance with guidance notes issued by the Revenue Commissioners, farmers are required to carry out an accurate stocktaking on each accounting date and to have the stock analysed and recorded under the classifications set out at sections E (livestock) and F (crops) of form AG 3 (see Tables 2 and 3 in **13.106.2**). Although section E provides spaces for horses (stallions, brood mares, foals etc), the guidance notes state that the percentage of market values does not apply to the valuation of horses. If any horses are included in a farmer's trading stock, it is generally necessary to produce actual cost figures. For the method of valuing bloodstock in a stud farm, see **13.107.2-107.5**.

13.104.2   Livestock

A farming company's livestock may be either animals bred by it as part of its farming activities or animals that it has purchased either for fattening and resale or for breeding purposes either immediately or at a future time when fully reared. For stock valuation purposes, it is necessary to distinguish between immature and mature animals. For this purpose, a cow, ewe or sow only becomes mature following the birth of its first calf, lamb or bonham; a bull, ram or boar becomes mature when it goes into service for the first time. All other animals, whether bred on the farm or purchased after birth, are regarded as immature. For example, an in-calf heifer is immature until after the birth of its first calf, while a bullock is always immature.

Strictly, the "cost" of an immature animal (eg a calf) bred on the farm includes any sire's fee paid by the company for the services of the bull (if not its own), the keep of the cow while in calf, the keep of the calf from its birth to the relevant accounting date of the valuation, and any other direct expenses during this period. For an animal purchased while immature, eg a calf acquired for fattening and resale, its cost is its purchase price plus the cost of its keep from the date of purchase to the accounting date and any other direct costs incurred in this period.

Instead of taking such actual cost figures, the Revenue's rule of thumb method is to assume that the cost value of each immature animal at the relevant accounting date is, for the different types of animal, arrived at as follows:

cattle:	60% of market value (at the accounting date),
sheep:	75% of market value,
pigs:	75% of market value.

This method of valuation must, whenever it is adopted, be applied each year for all immature stock, whether bred on the farm or purchased after birth. If the same immature animal is in stock at two or more accounting dates, its cost value on each occasion automatically varies in accordance with changes in its market value, but the percentage applied to that value always remains the same. Clearly, when cost is determined in this manner, there can never be any question of writing it down to a lower market value.

Mature animals, ie breeding stock, differ from immature livestock in that their cost value once established remains the same at all subsequent accounting dates until they are either sold or until they die. However, if the company can show that the market value of any animal falls below its cost at any accounting date after that cost was established, the lower market value is substituted in the trading stock valuation at that accounting date.

Any animal purchased as breeding stock in a mature state, ie after previously giving birth, has a cost value equal to its purchase price. An animal bred by the farming company on its own farm which develops from an immature animal to a mature one, ie on giving birth for the first time, is assumed to acquire a cost value as breeding stock equal to the appropriate percentage of its market value at the first accounting date after it becomes mature. This cost value continues to be used until it is sold or until it dies. For this purpose the same percentages are used as noted above for immature animals – ie, 60% for cattle, 75% for sheep and pigs.

The determination of the market values of livestock at each accounting date is therefore a most important matter in farm accounting. There are no tax rules as to who should estimate the market value of livestock. While it may assist the farming company in agreeing the farm accounts with the inspector if the animals are valued by a professional valuer used to valuing livestock, it is perfectly valid for the company to make its own valuations.

Irrespective of who makes the valuation, the inspector is likely to scrutinise carefully the market values placed on the livestock used as part of the formula for determining their cost or, in the case of mature animals, to be satisfied as to the validity or otherwise of any writing down to a market value below cost. The inspector is likely to have available various published data regarding livestock prices; if the values placed on any farmer's livestock show material variations from comparable published statistics of livestock prices, the inspector may query the stock valuations produced by or on behalf of the company. Since the available statistical data tend to relate to average prices, it may in appropriate cases be possible for the company concerned to establish that the animals or some of them are below average quality or, perhaps, not all in good health.

13.104.3   Crops, fertilisers etc

The guidance notes adopt a similar approach to arrive at the cost of production of harvested crops remaining unsold at the accounting date. "Cost" is to be taken as 75% of the market value of the crops in question. Effectively, this assumes that the market value at which it is expected the crops can be sold is such as to give a farming company a 33.3% mark up on the assumed cost figure.

The guidance notes also state that crops in the ground, ie still growing at the accounting date need not be valued, nor feed fertilisers which have been spread but which are still unexhausted. However, any fertiliser that has been purchased, but which has not yet been spread must be taken into the farm stock valuation at its cost of purchase. Similarly, any hay, silage, feeding stuffs etc that have been purchased and which remain unconsumed at the accounting date must also be taken into trading stock at their purchase price unless it can be shown that their market value at the accounting date has fallen below that price.

13.104.4   Discontinuance of trade

TCA 1997, s 89 (see **3.202.11**) provides that where trading stock is sold or transferred for valuable consideration on the discontinuance of a trade to a person carrying on or intending to carry on a trade in the State and who is entitled to a deduction against trading profits in respect of the cost of that stock, the value of the trading stock is to be taken to be:

(a)   where the person to whom the stock is sold or transferred is not connected with the seller, the amount realised on the sale or, as the case may be, the amount which is the value of the consideration given for the transfer; and

(b)   where those persons are connected, what would have been the price received had the sale or transfer been a transaction between independent persons dealing at arm's length.

Where the trading stock is sold or transferred on the discontinuance of a trade but not in the circumstances described in the previous paragraph, its value is to be taken as the amount which it would have realised if sold in the open market on the discontinuance.

In the case of a transfer of stock in the circumstances described in (b) above but where the arm's length price is more than the "acquisition value" (essentially, the book value) of the stock and is also more than the price received for it, and subject to a joint election by both parties, the value of the stock sold is to be taken to be an amount equal to the greater of its acquisition value and the price received for it (TCA 1997, s 89(4)).

TCA 1997, s 656(2) provides, in the case where trading stock of a trade of farming is transferred by a farmer (the transferor) to another farmer (the transferee), the two parties may jointly elect that the market value rule described above will not apply and that, for the purposes of computing the profits or gains from farming, both the transferor and the transferee will include the stock at the value at which it is included in the accounts of the transferor at the date of the discontinuance. The effect of the election, therefore, is that the stock is transferred at its book value instead of at its market value. The election provided for by TCA 1997, s 656(2) is available to farming companies by virtue of TCA 1997, s 76 (computation of income: application of income tax principles).

13.105   Compulsory disposal of cattle

13.105.1   General

A farming company carrying on a trade of farming in the State may elect under TCA 1997, s 668 for certain tax benefits if it is compulsorily required, under any statute relating to the eradication or control of diseases in livestock, to dispose of its entire herd of cattle or stock of animals and poultry. The benefits of the section are confined to compulsory disposals of stock as defined.

The stock to which TCA 1997, s 668 applies is:

(a) all cattle forming part of the trading stock of the trade of farming, where such cattle are compulsorily disposed of on or after 6 April 1993, under any statute relating to the eradication or control of diseases in livestock, all cattle being regarded as compulsorily disposed of where, in the case of any disease eradication scheme, all eligible cattle for the purposes of any such scheme, together with such other cattle as are required to be disposed of, are disposed of; or

(b) animals and poultry of a kind specified in Parts I and II, respectively, of the First Schedule to the Diseases of Animals Act 1966, forming part of the trading stock of the trade of farming, where all animals or poultry of the particular kind forming part of that trade of farming are disposed of on or after 6 December 2000, in such circumstances that compensation is paid by the Minister for Agriculture and Food respect of that disposal.

A claim under TCA 1997, s 668 requires that the disposal is of all the cattle and other animals and poultry forming part of the trading stock of the company's trade of farming. A company carrying on a trade of farming, however, would be treated for this purpose as disposing of all of its cattle if the disposal is of all eligible cattle for the purpose of the said scheme, together with such other cattle as are required to be disposed of (TCA 1997, s 668(1)). In other words, if any cattle are not "eligible cattle" for the purposes of, or are not other cattle required to be disposed of by, an order under the eradication scheme, their retention does not prevent the farming company electing for the benefits of TCA 1997, s 668.

For the benefits of TCA 1997, s 668 to be available to a farming company, it must make an election to avail of the section by giving notice in writing to the inspector no later than the "specified return date" for the chargeable period in which the compulsory disposal is made. For example, if a farming company chargeable to corporation tax makes a compulsory disposal of its herd in the year ended 31 December 1997, the election must be made no later than 30 September 1997.

There are two types of benefit available under TCA 1997, s 668 relating to any profit realised from the compulsory disposal of stock. Firstly, taxable income is deferred for a four year period. Secondly, a special 100% stock relief deduction may be elected for during the same four year deferral period provided that expenditure is incurred in replacing cattle disposed of.

13.105.2   Deferral of taxable income

entitles A farming company which has realised a "profit" (as defined below) from the compulsory disposal of stock, may, in accordance with TCA 1997, s 668(2), (3), elect to ignore that profit in arriving at its Case I farming profit or loss of the accounting period in which the compulsory disposal is made and, instead, to include one-quarter of the profit in each of the four immediately succeeding accounting periods.

The option to spread the profit over the following four accounting periods is not available where there is a permanent discontinuance of the trade. TCA 1997, s 668(3A) provides that where a trade of farming is permanently discontinued, tax is to be charged under Case IV of Schedule D, for the accounting period in which the discontinuance takes place, in respect of the amount of the excess which would, but for the discontinuance, be treated under the deferral option as arising in an accounting period or periods ending after the discontinuance.

Example 13.105.2.1

Agricola Enterprises Ltd, a farming company which makes up accounts to 31 December each year, is required to dispose of its herd of cattle under a disease eradication order. The company realises a "profit" of €116,000 from the compensation received on foot of a compulsory disposal of its herd of cattle in April 2004. It is entitled to elect under TCA 1997, s 668(2), (3)(a) to deal with this profit as follows:

(1)   to ignore the full €116,000 in arriving at the adjusted Case I farming profit or loss for the year ended 31 December 2004; and

(2)   to include €29,000 of the said "profit" in computing the adjusted profit or loss for each of the four years ending 31 December 2005 to 31 December 2008.

Alternatively, and subject to TCA 1997, s 668(3A) (see above), a company may elect, under TCA 1997, s 668(3)(b), to include one-quarter of the profit from the compulsory disposal in the accounting period in which the disposal is made and the other three-quarters in the three immediately succeeding accounting periods. In effect, this is a deferral of three-quarters of the profit to the following three accounting periods.

Example 13.105.2.2

Instead of making an election as in Example **13.105.2.1**, Agricola Enterprises Ltd may elect to include the €116,000 profit from the compulsory disposal in April 2004 as follows:

(1)   to include €29,000 in computing the adjusted Case I farming profit or loss for the year ended 31 December 2004; and

(2)   to include €29,000 in computing its adjusted profit or loss for each of the three years ended 31 December 2005 to 31 December 2007 inclusive.

As indicated above, and subject to TCA 1997, s 668(3A), the deferral period may comprise either the four accounting periods following that of the compulsory disposal or, if so elected, the accounting period of the compulsory disposal and the three immediately following accounting periods.

The "profit" on the compulsory disposal (referred to in TCA 1997, s 668 as the "excess") is defined as the excess of:

(a)   the "relevant amount" over;

(b)   the value of the stock included in the farming company's trading stock on the first day of the accounting period in which the compulsory disposal takes place.

The *relevant amount* is the amount of any income received as a result, or in consequence, of the compulsory disposal of the stock. A Revenue precedent states that the reference to "income" is to the total proceeds received in respect of the cattle which are compulsorily disposed of. This does not deal with the question of expenses, for example expenses that might be incurred directly in connection with the compulsory disposal, but it would nevertheless seem reasonable to assume that the reference to income should be to the net proceeds received after such expenses. Elsewhere (in the Guidance Notes on Legislation), the Revenue state that the "excess" is, in effect, the profit arising on the compulsory disposal; this would seem to strengthen the view that disposal expenses should indeed be taken into account.

The exclusion of the "profit" in arriving at the taxable profit of the accounting period in which the compulsory disposal is made may result in a Case I farming loss for that accounting period; the "excess" is to be disregarded as respects the accounting period in which the disposal is made. All the normal loss reliefs are available for any loss resulting from the deferral of the profit on the compulsory disposal.

In deciding which four accounting periods should comprise the deferral period over which the "excess" is to be spread, the farming company should have regard to the requirement for the stock relief deduction, discussed below, to the effect that the target amount of expenditure on replacing cattle which are the subject of the compulsory disposal has to be incurred before the end of the deferral period actually elected for. Thus it may be preferable to elect for the four accounting periods immediately succeeding that in which the compulsory disposal is made since this gives a longer period in which to incur the necessary replacement expenditure.

Example 13.105.2.3

Resulting from an outbreak of cattle disease, Rhode Island Ltd, a farming company, is required to have its herd of cattle destroyed during the twelve month accounting period ended 31 December 2004. The company is entitled to compensation of €230,000 under the relevant disease eradication scheme, but it incurs expenditure of €25,000 directly in connection with the disposal. The stock value of the herd of cattle at 1 January 2004 is assumed to have been €110,000 (which value excludes all other trading stock). The "excess" for which the benefit of TCA 1997, s 668(3)(a) is available is calculated as follows:

	€
Compensation for compulsory disposal	230,000
Less: expenses of the disposal	25,000
"Relevant amount" (income from disposal)	205,000
Less: value of cattle at 1 January 2004	110,000
"Excess" from disposal in year ended 31/12/04	95,000

Rhode Island Ltd elects under TCA 1997, s 668(2), (3)(a) to defer the €95,000 excess so that it is to be included in four equal instalments for the next four accounting periods ending 31 December 2005 to 31 December 2008 inclusive. The election must be made no later than 30 September 2005.

The adjusted profit/ (loss) Case I figures (before stock relief) are as set out below. Based on these, the result of the election in respect of the "excess" for each of the five accounting periods concerned is as follows:

	Year ended 31/12/04 €	Year ended 31/12/05 €	Year ended 31/12/06 €	Year ended 31/12/07 €	Year ended 31/12/08 €
Case I profits/(loss)	102,620	(12,460)	49,880	(6,430)	62,480
Less: excess deferred by election	95,000				

	Year ended 31/12/04 €	Year ended 31/12/05 €	Year ended 31/12/06 €	Year ended 31/12/07 €	Year ended 31/12/08 €
Add: excess treated as income		23,750	23,750	23,750	23,750
Revised profits (before stock relief)	7,620	11,290	73,630	17,320	86,230

The above assessable profits are subject to any stock relief deductions (including any under TCA 1997, s 668(4) – see below) and capital allowances. For the year ended 31 December 2004, no stock relief is due since there is a decrease in stock value following the compulsory disposal. For the stock relief position for the succeeding accounting periods, see Example **13.105.3.1**.

13.105.3 Deemed stock relief

TCA 1997, s 668(4) provides for a further benefit arising out of a compulsory disposal due to a disease eradication or control scheme. This is in the form of a stock relief deduction equal to the amount treated under TCA 1997, s 668(3)(a) or (3)(b), as appropriate, as arising in each accounting period (instead of the usual 25% deduction). It entitles the farming company, if it incurs or intends to incur expenditure on replacing stock which was the subject of the compulsory disposal, to a stock relief deduction in each of the four accounting periods which together comprise the four year deferral period. TCA 1997, s 666 (stock relief – see **13.103**) applies with "any necessary modifications" in order to give effect to the relief.

TCA 1997, s 668(4) provides that the stock relief deduction is to be an amount equal to the amount treated as arising in each accounting period under TCA 1997, s 668(3)(a) or (3)(b), as the case may be, but subject to the normal stock relief restriction that the amount of the deduction cannot exceed the "net" Case I trading income for the accounting period (see **13.103.6**).

In applying the restriction to the Case I trading profits (or net Case I trading income) of each of the accounting periods in the deferral period, it is to be noted that the Case I trading profits (or trading income) are taken after including the one-quarter of the "excess" as additional income of each accounting period.

Replacement expenditure not less than relevant amount

To obtain the maximum deduction, it is a condition that the expenditure on replacing the stock is of a total amount at least equal to the "relevant amount" (the amount of income received by the farming company as a result, or in consequence, of the compulsory disposal). It is a further condition that this replacement expenditure is incurred no later than the end of the deferral period.

Example 13.105.3.1

The position is as in Example **13.105.2.3** where Rhode Island Ltd elected to have the excess (the profit from the compensation for the compulsory disposal) spread over a deferral period comprising the years ended 31 December 2005 to 31 December 2008. (It is assumed that stock relief continues to be available for accounting periods ending on or before 31 December 2008.)

The following results from the compensation for the compulsory disposal in the accounting period ending 31 December 2004 are, again, as follows:

	€
"Relevant amount" (the income from the disposal)	205,000
"Excess" (the profit from the disposal)	95,000

Rhode Island Ltd has incurred expenditure in purchasing cattle to replace the herd destroyed, as follows:

	€
Expenditure on replacement of cattle:	
Prior to 31/12/04	Nil
From 1/1/05 to 31/12/05	80,400
From 1/1/06 to 31/12/06	148,600
Total replacement expenditure by 31/12/08	229,000

Rhode Island Ltd wishes to take the stock relief deduction provided for by TCA 1997, s 668(4) by reference to the increases in stock values for each of the four accounting periods in the deferral period. Since it has incurred replacement expenditure in excess of the €205,000 relevant amount by 31 December 2008, it is entitled to the full deduction for each of the four accounting periods (subject to the trading profits restriction, if relevant).

The other figures relevant for the computation of the stock relief deductions are:

	Year ended 31/12/05 €	Year ended 31/12/06 €	Year ended 31/12/07 €	Year ended 31/12/08 €
Opening stock value:				
Cattle	Nil	80,400	172,100	188,600
Other livestock and sundry stocks	20,800	17,600	18,500	16,100
	20,800	98,000	190,600	204,700
Closing stock value:				
Cattle[1]	80,400	172,100	188,600	196,500
Other livestock and sundry stocks	17,600	18,500	16,100	19,300
	98,000	190,600	204,700	215,800
Increase in stock value in period	77,200	92,600	14,100	11,100
Case I farming profits (before stock relief)[2]	11,290	73,630	17,320	86,230

The result of the stock relief election under TCA 1997, s 668(4) is as follows:

	Year ended 31/12/05 €	Year ended 31/12/06 €	Year ended 31/12/07 €	Year ended 31/12/08 €
Increase in stock value in period	77,200	92,600	14,100	11,100
TCA 1997, s 668(3)(a) amount	23,750	23,750	23,750	23,750

	Year ended 31/12/05 €	Year ended 31/12/06 €	Year ended 31/12/07 €	Year ended 31/12/08 €
Case I farming profits (before stock relief)	11,290	73,630	17,320	86,230
Stock relief deduction for period (lower amount)	11,290	23,750	17,320	23,750

The final assessable profits (subject to capital allowances) for the five periods affected are therefore as follows:

	Year ended 31/12/04 €	Year ended 31/12/05 €	Year ended 31/12/06 €	Year ended 31/12/07 €	Year ended 31/12/08 €
Farming profits (before stock relief)	7,620	11,290	73,630	17,320	86,230
Less: stock relief deduction	Nil	11,290	23,750	17,320	23,750
Final farming profits (after stock relief)	7,620	Nil	49,880	Nil	62,480

Notes:

1   All the replacement cattle acquired in the year ended 31 December 2005 are still in stock at that date, but some were sold during the following year.

2   The farming profits (before stock relief) for the four accounting periods in the deferral period are the figures after adding the respective instalments of the excess resulting from the compulsory disposal in the year ended 31 December 2004 (see Example **13.105.2.3**).

Replacement expenditure less than relevant amount

It may transpire that the farming company which has compulsorily disposed of the herd of cattle did not incur replacement expenditure equal to the relevant amount before the end of the deferral period. In these circumstances, TCA 1997, s 668(4A) requires that the aggregate stock relief deduction that would otherwise be allowable for the four accounting periods in the deferral period is to be reduced proportionately, the proportion being that which the replacement expenditure actually incurred in the four accounting periods bears to the relevant amount. The reduction to be made should as far as possible be made in a later period in priority to an earlier period.

Example 13.105.3.2

The position is as in Examples **13.105.2.3** and **13.105.3.1**, except that the expenditure incurred by Rhode Island Ltd to the end of the deferral period on replacing the cattle is as follows:

	€
From 1/1/05 to 31/12/05	50,100
From 1/1/06 to 31/12/06	30,300
From 1/1/07 to 31/12/07	49,600

From 1/1/08 to 31/12/08	52,800
Total	182,800

Since the total of this expenditure, €182,800, is less than the relevant amount €205,000, the stock relief deduction in each accounting period in the deferral period must be reduced so that it does not exceed the appropriate proportion of the "excess", €95,000.

However, before computing the upper limits to the 100% stock relief deductions, it is necessary to look again at the results for each accounting period based on the new replacement expenditure in the year ended 31 December 2006. It is assumed that the results for the year ended 31 December 2005 are the same as in Example **13.105.3.1**.

The results for the years ended 31 December 2006 to 31 December 2008, having regard to the lower amount of restocking expenditure and other consequential changes, are now assumed to be as follows:

	Year ended 31/12/06 €	Year ended 31/12/07 €	Year ended 31/12/08 €
Opening stock value			
Cattle	80,400	131,300	154,500
Other livestock and sundry stocks	17,600	18,500	16,100
	98,000	149,800	170,600
Closing stock value			
Cattle	131,300	154,500	161,400
Other livestock and sundry stocks	18,500	16,100	19,300
	149,800	170,600	180,700
Increase in stock value in period	51,800	20,800	10,100
Case I farming profits (before stock relief)	53,560	6,180	52,700

The ceilings to the stock relief deductions may now be computed, by reference to the €95,000 excess for the two accounting periods, as follows:

	Year ended 31/12/05 €	Year ended 31/12/06 €	Year ended 31/12/07 €	Year ended 31/12/08 €
Replacement expenditure	50,100	30,300	49,600	52,800
Relevant amount	205,000	205,000	205,000	205,000
Excess	95,000	95,000	95,000	95,000

Provisional (subject to TCA 1997, s 668(4A)) stock relief deductions for each accounting period are now as follows:

	Year ended 31/12/05 €	Year ended 31/12/06 €	Year ended 31/12/07 €	Year ended 31/12/08 €
Increase in stock value in period	77,200	51,800	20,800	10,100
TCA 1997, s 668(3)(a) amount	23,750	23,750	23,750	23,750

	Year ended 31/12/05 €	Year ended 31/12/06 €	Year ended 31/12/07 €	Year ended 31/12/08 €
Case I farming profits (before stock relief)	11,290	53,560	6,180	52,700
Stock relief deduction for period (lower amount)	11,290	23,750	6,180	23,750

These stock relief deductions are subject to reduction by virtue of TCA 1997, s 668(4A). The aggregate amount is €64,970 and this falls to be reduced by applying the fraction 182,800/205,000, giving a reduction of €7,036. The reduction is to be made from later periods in priority to earlier periods. In this case, the reduction is made entirely from the stock relief amount for the year to 31 December 2008. The revised deduction for that period is therefore €16,714

The final assessable profits (subject to capital allowances) for the two accounting periods are as follows:

	Year ended 31/12/05 €	Year ended 31/12/06 €	Year ended 31/12/07 €	Year ended 31/12/08 €
Farming profits (before stock relief)	11,290	53,560	6,180	52,700
Less: stock relief	11,290	23,750	6,180	16,714
Farming profits (after stock relief)	Nil	29,810	Nil	35,986

13.106   Farm records and accounts

TCA 1997, s 886 (obligation to keep certain records) applies, as it does for any person carrying on a trade or profession, to require all farmers to keep such books of account and other records as will enable true returns of their farming profits to be made. The Revenue Commissioners or any of their duly authorised officers have powers to inspect the farmer's books, to enter the farming premises, and to obtain information from other persons regarding transactions with the farmer in relation to any person carrying on a trade or business.

Apart from keeping full and accurate records of all farming receipts and payments, a farming company should make a detailed stocktaking at the end of each period for which it makes up accounts to enable the inspector of taxes to be given the required analysis of its opening and closing trading stocks, as well as of changes in livestock held during the period (see below).

In principle, every farmer is now required to prepare and submit to the inspector of taxes a set of accounts of the farming activities each year and to provide the inspector with such additional information as is necessary to enable the farmer's Case I profit or loss to be determined. A farming company's accounts will normally consist of a full and audited profit and loss account and balance sheet.

In addition to the farm accounts, a farmer is normally required to provide the inspector with certain minimum additional information as set out in the form AG 3, but it is not essential to use the form if the necessary data is given in another manner, eg in schedules to the accounts or in covering or explanatory notes sent in with the accounts.

In the case of farming carried on in partnership, the precedent acting partner is required to give a separate form AG 3 (or the data in some other form) for the partnership trade.

13.107   Bloodstock activities

13.107.1   Introduction

The use of land as a stud farm for the breeding of thoroughbred racehorses, hunters etc has for many years been regarded as husbandry or farming. Consequently, all of the legislation relative to the taxation of farming profits are applicable to the taxation of stud farms as it is to farming generally. While a number of stud farm operations are run mainly or wholly as such, it is not unusual for an ordinary farmer or farming company to carry on stud farm activities as part of the one trade. Similarly, a specialised stud farming company may also carry on some general farming activities in conjunction with its stud farm business. Irrespective of the mix between stud farming and general farming carried on by a company, and whether or not all the activities are being conducted in the same place, TCA 1997, s 655(2) applies to treat all the stud farming and general farming as a single trade (see **13.101**).

The object of a stud farm is usually to breed horses suitable for racing either for sale or, in many instances, for the owner of the stud farm's own racing activities, or for both purposes. Apart from the case of a racehorse trainer (see below), an individual's, and generally also a company's, racing activities are treated as activities outside the scope of the tax system. For an individual, racing activities have always been regarded as a hobby or as recreational activities, and therefore outside the scope of income tax. In practice, racing activities of a company are also generally treated as being outside the scope of corporation tax. Profits which are derived from racing are accordingly not taxable and, correspondingly, racing losses are not eligible for any form of tax relief and are not deductible in arriving at taxable income for any period. Consequently, if a stud company also races horses, it is necessary to separate the financial results of its horse breeding (and other farming) activities from those of its racing activity. Any expenses of racing, including those of training its horses, must be excluded from the stud farm accounts, as must any prize monies or other receipts from the racing activity.

In the case of a company which owns and races horses as well as carrying on the trade of stud farming, it is possible in certain circumstances for its racing activities to be regarded as part of the one trade of breeding and racing. If this can be established in any particular case, any losses on the racing side of the business may be deductible from profits from the breeding activities, and vice versa. This conclusion is not free from doubt, but an argument in its favour is that a company can hardly be said to have a hobby or to indulge in recreational activities. On the other hand, for racing to be accepted as part of the company's overall trade, it would seem that the racing must be closely linked to the breeding activities and organised and managed in the way a trade is normally operated.

Apart from the distinction between breeding and racing, it may sometimes be necessary to distinguish a stud farm company from a company operating as a dealer in bloodstock. The latter buys and sells bloodstock with the intention of making a profit, but without using the animals for breeding. While stud farmers and dealers in bloodstock are each taxable on their profits under Case I as traders, the distinction remains important as a dealer is not entitled to benefit from stock relief for which a farming company may be eligible.

In general, the adjusted Case I profits or losses of a stud farm are arrived at in the same way as for other farming profits or losses (see **13.102**). Stock relief is available to a stud farmer under the rules relating to farming (see **13.103**). The farm buildings capital allowances, the rules restricting the extent to which initial allowances or free depreciation may be claimed on farming machinery or plant, and the rules relating to relief for farming losses, are applied to stud farms in the same way as to other farming trades (see **13.2**).

In considering the taxation treatment of stud farms there are, however, several aspects which require separate discussion. Firstly, the rules for the valuation of a stud farmer's trading stock, ie mares, foals, yearlings etc, differ from those used to value an ordinary farmer's livestock. Secondly, if animals bred in the stud are transferred to the stud company's racing activities, it is necessary to consider the values at which they are transferred out of the stud and, if relevant, the values at which animals may be transferred back to the stud for breeding purposes after they have finished racing. Thirdly, it is necessary to consider the treatment of stallions and of income received for the services of stallions.

13.107.2   Valuation of bloodstock as trading stock

The accounts of stud farm companies are generally made up annually to 31 December. The company's trading stock at 31 December in any year normally consists of its brood mares (most of whom will be in foal), foals, yearlings and, sometimes, two year olds and three year olds. Under the Rules of Racing (flat racing) and the National Hunt Rules (steeplechasing), a horse is treated as becoming a year older on 1 January in each year, irrespective of its actual date of birth.

Consequently, taking a stud company's closing stock included in its balance sheet at, say, 31 December 1997, the foals included are all animals born at any time in the calendar year 1997, the yearlings those born in 1996, the two year olds in 1995 etc. Any foal born in 1997 becomes a yearling on 1 January 1998 and, if not intended to be retained for the company's own racing establishment, may well be sold at one of the yearling sales in 1998, thus ceasing to be part of trading stock before the 31 December 1998 balance sheet date.

In practice, horses intended for the owner's racing activities are generally transferred out of the stud farm and sent for training prior to racing while two year olds, although expected to be steeplechasers, ie under National Hunt rules, are more likely to be retained at the stud for a further year; they are likely to remain in stud farm trading stock until after becoming three year olds. This outline describes the general position concerning the times at which animals bred on the stud farm cease to be trading stock. Two year olds and three year olds are sometimes kept in stud farm trading stock after the time at which the progeny of the stud are normally sold or transferred to racing.

The valuation of all animals in the closing trading stock at any relevant balance sheet date should be made under the normal rule for valuing trading stock generally, ie each animal should be brought into stock at its "cost" unless its market value at the balance sheet date is lower, in which case the lower market value figure should be used. Due to the special nature of a stud farm business, it may not be easy to arrive at an accurate figure for the cost of any animal, but the Revenue Commissioners have drawn up a number of principles which are, in general, accepted by stud farmers as providing a reasonable approach to the determination of the cost of the animals within each category. These are now discussed as follows:

Brood mares

Normally, the trading stock of a company carrying on a stud farming business is principally comprised of its stock of brood mares, some of which may have high stock values attaching to them, particularly if purchased for the stud farm from another owner after a successful racing career. Each mare must be brought into trading stock at the lower of cost or market value. Each mare has her own base cost which, if the mare is in foal at the balance sheet date, must be increased to reflect the cost of producing the foal. For the "cost" value as trading stock of the mare at any later balance sheet date, the same base cost is taken, but the addition in respect of any foal conceived in the later year is the cost of producing that foal. In short, each mare retains the same base cost until she is sold, dies or otherwise ceases to be stud farm trading stock.

The base cost of any mare purchased from another owner, whether the mare was acquired by the stud farming company first for racing (or hunting) or was purchased directly for the stud, is the actual purchase price paid. The cost of any mare that was originally bred by the company itself, and which it has continued to own, is her cost of production as previously determined in the stud farm accounts, whether or not the mare has been raced in the meantime. This cost of production should be taken as the "cost" value of the animal concerned as credited to the stud farm accounts at the time she was transferred out to racing (see **13.107.4** below). Should the own-bred mare not have been raced, but retained throughout as stud farm trading stock, her base cost as a brood mare is her cost of production up to the 1 January in the year she became a three year old (see below).

For the mare in foal at the balance sheet date, the addition to the base cost of the mare to reflect the cost of producing the foal may be taken as the sum of the following items:

(a)   the stud fee (if any) paid for the services of a stallion;

(b)   the cost of keep of the mare while at stud with the stallion;

(c)   the costs of carriage of the mare from the stud farm to where the stallion was standing and of her return to the stud farm;

(d)   the costs of keep of the mare at the stud farm from the date of her return from the stallion to the accounting date; and

(e)   the cost of insurance of the mare (and the foal) over the period covered by (a) to (d).

In practice, the addition to the mare's base cost in respect of the foal is often taken as the sum of (a) the stud fee (if any) paid for the stallion and (b) the cost of keep of the mare from the time she goes to the stallion to the end of the accounting period (ie, items (a), (b) and (d) above). This simpler formula is normally accepted by inspectors of taxes in cases where it is used, although it is understood that the Revenue consider the more detailed costing approach indicated above as technically more correct. Whichever method is used, it should be applied consistently in each successive year.

If, instead of paying a stud fee for the stallion, the stud company purchases a "nomination" to the stallion from another person entitled to the use of the stallion's services (see below), the cost of that nomination is taken as part of the cost of the foal instead of the stud fee. If the stud company uses the stallion free of charge, either because it owns the stallion or owns a stallion share which entitles it to a free service, no addition is made under (a) above as only actual costs incurred may be brought in. In practice, a deduction will be allowed for the advertised stud fee for the stallion but subject to two conditions.

Firstly, this notional cost may not be deducted until the resulting progeny is sold, which will normally be in the accounting period following the period in which the free nomination was used, or in the next following period. In practice, this condition has no effect as actual stud fees paid must be included in the closing cost of the relevant mare, and subsequently in the closing cost of the offspring produced, and are therefore also not allowed until the offspring is sold. Secondly, the notional cost may not be used to create a loss, or to increase a loss, on the sale of the progeny. See further discussion below on this aspect, in particular Example **13.107.6.1**.

For the cost of keep of the mare, a round sum estimate is usually taken instead of an exactly costed figure, particularly if there are a number of mares involved. Currently, there are no guideline figures as to what would be an acceptable figure but it is suggested that a cost of keep figure of, say, €2,300 to €2,550 per annum would be reasonable.

Finally, if the mare has proved barren after being with the stallion, there is of course no addition to be made in respect of a foal in her "cost" for the next balance sheet stock valuation. In practice, if a mare has been barren for a few years, this may be accepted by the inspector of taxes as a good reason for justifying a market value below cost, especially if the mare was one bought in at a high figure. Otherwise, inspectors of taxes tend to resist the writing-down of a mare to a claimed market value below cost so long as the mare continues to be used for breeding purposes. It is of course open to the taxpayer to produce evidence to satisfy the inspector that a lower market value is justified in any particular case.

Mares bought in foal

Where a stud farming company purchases a mare already in foal, the purchase price is treated as if it included the advertised stallion fee and the relevant costs of keep of the mare up to the date of purchase. Consequently, the "cost" of the mare at the year-end is taken as its full purchase price plus the further costs of keep from the date of purchase to the year-end. In arriving at the base cost of the mare for all subsequent years, the purchase price is reduced by the advertised stallion fee and the cost of keep to the date of purchase which were treated as included in the purchase price. This deduction of the advertised stud fee is made even if the previous owner did not in fact pay any stud fee or purchase any nomination to the stallion, which would be the case, say, where that owner had the free use of the stallion's services. The advertised stud fee for any stallion is normally published each year by its owner(s).

Foals

The "cost" of each foal in trading stock at the first year end following its birth is taken as being the sum of its cost of production as included in the stock value of its mother at the previous year end and the cost of keep for the whole of the year to the current balance sheet date. In fact, part of the cost of keep is for the mare before the birth of the foal during the year just ended and the rest is for the keep of the foal itself after its birth.

However, as it is normal practice to assume the same annual cost of keep for a mare as for a foal, only one yearly figure is normally added. Strictly, the cost of insurance of the foal for the year should probably be included also in its stock cost value, but in practice this is not always done.

Yearlings, two year olds etc

The "cost" of each yearling in trading stock is normally the sum of its cost value as a foal at the end of the previous year and a further yearly addition for the cost of its keep in the year just ended (again usually taken at the same figure used for the cost of keep of a mare or foal). Similarly, the cost of a two year old is the previous year's cost value as a yearling plus a further annual charge for the cost of keep in the year just ended. The reason for this yearly addition for the cost of keep is that it is regarded as a further cost of producing the animal until it becomes mature. Bloodstock are regarded for tax purposes as becoming mature when they become three year olds and no further cost of keep addition is made for any time after the year as a two year old. The cost of keep addition only applies so long as the animal continues to be maintained at the stud. It is not, however, relevant for, say, a two year old after the time it is taken out of stud for training or racing.

13.107.3 Valuation of broodmares: agreement with Revenue Commissioners

Following an agreement reached between the Irish Horseracing Authority and the Revenue authorities, it is now accepted that a thoroughbred broodmare may be valued at balance sheet date for tax purposes at the lower of cost and net realisable value. This agreement is effective in respect of accounting periods ending on or after 31 December 1994. In respect of registered thoroughbred broodmares, the following principles have been agreed:

(1) broodmares will be valued in accordance with accounting principles at the lower of cost and net realisable value;

(2) where a taxpayer is unable to agree with a Revenue auditor on the value at which a mare is carried in the books, the case will be reviewed, at the taxpayer's request, at the Technical Services Unit of the Office of the Chief Inspector of Taxes;

(3) the review will be in addition to the right to an independent review, eg by a senior inspector of taxes in the relevant district, as laid down in the Charter of Rights, and to any statutory right of appeal to the Appeal Commissioners.

Cost

Where the broodmare is purchased from a third party, cost is simply the purchase price paid. Where the broodmare is bred from a mare belonging to the stud, cost is the sum of:

(a) the nomination fee paid in respect of the broodmare's sire,

(b) the cost of maintenance of the broodmare's dam while at the sire's stud,

(c) the cost of carriage of the dam to and from the sire's stud,

(d) the cost of maintenance of the broodmare as a foal, yearling and two year old, and,

(e)   insurance associated with the carriage of the dam when in foal with the broodmare.

In this respect, the position regarding cost is as set out already under *Broodmares* above.

Realisable value

Net realisable value is the price the broodmare's owner objectively estimates the broodmare would fetch if sold on the open market at the end of the accounting period. As noted earlier, the former practice of the Revenue was to accept values at below cost only in exceptional circumstances, probably only where the mare had been barren for a few years. As the question of valuations below cost will tend to give rise to disagreement between the Revenue auditor and the taxpayer, the procedure for referring the matter to the Technical Services Unit of the Chief Inspector of Taxes has been introduced to give the taxpayer an additional opportunity to settle the matter without having to resort to the statutory appeal procedure.

Stock records

Where thoroughbred broodmares are carried in the annual accounts as fixed assets (ie, at cost less accumulated depreciation), bloodstock breeders will be required to maintain detailed records of tax "cost", ie lower of cost and net realisable value. This will involve the keeping of a separate annual statement showing the valuation of the broodmares for tax purposes, for inclusion with the stud's tax returns.

Where the broodmares are carried in the accounts as trading stock, and therefore valued from year to year at the lower of cost and net realisable value, it will not, in theory at least, be necessary to maintain a separate annual valuation statement for tax purposes. This is because the value for both accounts and tax purposes should be the same.

In practice, it may nevertheless be necessary to continue to maintain separate cost records for tax purposes as the method of arriving at cost for accounts purposes may not always be the same as that required for tax purposes. For any particular period, it will be appropriate to compare cost (incorporating the items at (a) to (e) under *Cost* above) with realisable value for each broodmare. Where net realisable value is less than (or not greater than) the actual purchase price in any case, it will clearly not be necessary to compute cost for tax purposes in that case. In certain cases, net realisable value may exceed the original purchase cost of the broodmare but may be less than cost for tax purposes (ie, with the addition of the (a) to (b) items); in any such case, it will be necessary to include the broodmare at cost for tax purposes.

In this connection, it will be recalled that cost figures which do not include carriage and insurance (items (c) and (d)) will in practice be accepted by the Revenue where the method of calculating cost is consistently applied from year to year. Accordingly, this approach may be adopted in practice for the purpose of including the closing cost of thoroughbred broodmares at the lower of cost and net realisable value.

13.107.4   Transfers between stud farm and racing

Where horses bred in the stud farm business are transferred to the company's racing stable or are sent to a trainer prior to racing, the stud farm accounts must be credited with the cost value of each animal concerned at the date of its transfer. Cost for this purpose is the trading stock cost value at the balance sheet date preceding the transfer to racing/training plus, in the case of any animal younger than a three year old, the cost of its keep from the previous year end to the date of the transfer. For example, if a colt which was in trading stock as a yearling on 31 December 2007 at a cost value of €14,900 (cost as foal at 31 December 2006 €12,000 plus year 2007 keep, say, €2,900) is transferred to the company's racing stable on 31 March 2008, the amount to be credited to the stud farm account for the year to 31 December 2008 would be arrived at as follows:

	€
Cost value of yearling at 31/12/07	14,900
Add: cost of keep 1/1/08 to 31/3/08:	
€3,000 per annum (say) x 3/12	750
Transfer price	15,650

When racehorses are transferred back to the stud farm for breeding purposes after their racing careers, the stud farm trading account is then debited with the cost of the animal to its owner, irrespective of its actual market value at the time of the transfer. This is normally relevant only for mares as it is the exception rather than the rule for a stallion to become trading stock of a stud farm. In the case of a mare purchased while still in racing, it is the cost of this purchase that is taken as the transfer price to be charged to the stud farm account when the animal is brought back to stud. On the other hand, if the animal is one bred originally by the stud company itself prior to her transfer to its own racing activity, her original cost value, as credited to the stud farm account at the earlier transfer to racing, is debited. In this latter case, the fact that the own-bred filly may have appreciated many times in value due to a highly successful racing career is irrelevant.

Once an animal has been transferred out of the stud to racing/training, any profit on a subsequent sale by the owner company is related to the racing activity and is (usually) not subject to any liability to corporation tax. Correspondingly, no loss on such a sale or on the death of the animal after it leaves the stud is deductible for tax purposes. This position applies notwithstanding that the market value of the animal at the time it left the stud may have been substantially in excess of its cost value credited to the stud farm accounts on the transfer out. This practice of crediting transfers from stud farm to racing at cost, and of debiting transfers back at cost, is in contrast to that used in the UK where, as a result of the House of Lords decision in *Sharkey v Wernher* [1953] 2 All ER 791, 36 TC 275, the accounts of a UK stud farm have to be credited or debited, whichever is the case, with the market value of the animals transferred to or from the same person's racing activities. The Irish Revenue have made it clear that it does not apply the decision in *Sharkey v Wernher* and that it considers that the proper treatment for Irish tax purposes is to make the transfers at cost.

The principle that these transfers to and from racing are at cost does not apply if the stud farm and the racing establishment are owned by different persons. For example, a racehorse owner may set up a company to carry on the stud farm business, but may race in his own name. In this case, there is normally a sale by the company to the individual shareholder or, perhaps, to the shareholder's spouse, or even to a racing partnership in which one or more of the shareholders are partners. The stud farm accounts should in any such case reflect the actual sale that takes place and, usually, it is to be expected that the sale price in the transaction will be a reasonably commercial one.

13.107.5   Illustrations of bloodstock valuations

The above described principles for the valuation of bloodstock as trading stock, and for the "transfer values" on transfers from stud farm to racing and from racing back to stud farm, may be more easily understood with the assistance of the following examples.

Example 13.107.5.1

Moyglachan Stud Ltd, a company carrying on a stud farm business, has three mares – Azalea, Dogwood and Magnolia – in foal at its 31 December 2006 balance sheet date. Relevant facts regarding the acquisition of these mares are:

Azalea

Born on the stud farm on 14/2/00, transferred to the company's racing stable as a two-year old on 1/5/02, raced for several years before being transferred back to stud on 31/3/06.

Dogwood

Purchased for racing by the company on 25/6/03 for €40,000, raced in 2003 and 2004 and was then transferred to the company's stud farm on 1/4/06. Its value at that time was estimated at €150,000.

Magnolia

Purchased directly for the company's stud farm on 30/9/02 for €190,000 and has since remained one of the stud farm's brood mares (although it proved barren in 2003 and 2004).

The trading stock "base costs" of Dogwood and Magnolia are respectively €40,000 and €190,000, ie their costs of purchase. The fact that Dogwood won several important races after being acquired by Moyglachan Stud Ltd and had an estimated market value of €150,000 when transferred to stud on 1/4/02 is irrelevant. The base cost of Azalea as trading stock is her cost of production as an own bred filly up to the date of her transfer to racing (1/5/02); this is determined as follows based on the figures assumed below:

	€
Sire's fee paid in 1999	9,600
Mare's keep while with stallion and carrying foal:	
- say €1,700 per annum for 12 months	1,700
Carriage of mare to and from stallion, insurance etc	4,000
Cost to date of birth (14/2/00)	15,300
Keep as foal (15/2/00 to 31/12/00) say €2,300 per annum x 10.5/12	2,013
Keep as yearling (year 2001) – say €2,400	2,400
Keep as two year old (1/1/02 to 1/5/02): say €2,600 per annum x 4/12	867
Cost when sent to racing (1/5/02)	20,580

Since Azalea has continued in the company's ownership from 1/5/02 until her transfer back to the stud farm as trading stock on 31/3/06, her base cost as a stud farm brood mare is her "cost" up to the date of transfer to racing, ie €20,580.

Example 13.107.5.2

The facts are as in Example **13.107.5.1** with the additional information that the three mares were each sent to stallions on 1/4/06 and that after servicing they were returned to the stud farm each in foal. They were serviced as follows:

Azalea:

with stallion Coimbra for a stud fee of €50,000;

Dogwood:

with stallion Bayard owned by a syndicate of which Moyglachan Stud Ltd was not a member; nomination to the stallion purchased by company for €30,200;

Magnolia:

with stallion Sartain owned by a syndicate of which Moyglachan Ltd was a member; right to service obtained free of charge.

The trading stock "cost" values of each mare in foal at 31/12/06 are determined as follows:

	Azalea	Dogwood	Magnolia
	€	€	€
(a) Cost of foal (up to 31/12/06):			
Sire's fee	50,000		
Cost of stallion nomination		30,200	
Free stallion service			
Mare's keep (1/4/06 to 31/12/06):			
say €2,700 per annum x 8/12	1,800	1,800	1,800
Carriage of mares, insurance etc to 31/12/06, say	3,100	2,900	2,600
	54,900	34,900	4,400
(b) Base cost of mare (per Example **13.107.5.1**)	20,580	40,000	190,000
Cost of mare in foal	75,480	74,900	194,400

The trading stock values of Azalea and Dogwood are taken as these cost values of €75,480 and €74,900 respectively. However, in view of Magnolia's previous two barren services, and also having regard to her only being expected to have a few breeding years left, Moyglachan Stud Ltd obtains expert opinion that Magnolia's market value as a mare in foal at 31/12/06 is only €60,000. Since this figure is less than its cost as a mare in foal, €194,400, the lower market value of €60,000 is taken into the closing stock valuation. Assuming that the inspector of taxes is satisfied that €60,000 is a valid market value, the Case I computation will follow this accounting treatment.

Example 13.107.5.3

Moyglachan Stud Ltd purchased a mare already in foal for €76,000 on 15 September 2006. The previous owner had serviced the mare with his own stallion and had not therefore paid any stallion fee. The mare had been brought to the stallion on 1 March 2006 and the previous owner had met the cost of the mare's keep from that date to the sale on 15 September 2006. Moyglachan Stud Ltd charges the keep of the mare in foal from 15 September 2006 onwards in its stud farm accounts. The previous owner had advertised the services of the stallion for €8,700 for the 2006 mating season.

The mare in foal's "cost" value for inclusion in the company's trading stock at 31 December 2006 is arrived at as follows:

	€
Purchase price paid (15/9/06)	76,000
Keep of animal (16/9/02 to 31/12/02) say €2,700 per annum x 3.5/12	788
Insurance (16/9/06 to 31/12/06)	825
Cost as trading stock	77,613

The mare's base cost for future trading stock valuations is arrived at as follows:

	€	€
Purchase price paid (15/9/06)		76,000
Less: advertised stud fee	8,700	

Keep (1/3/06 to 15/9/06) €2,700 X 7.5/12   <u>1,688</u>

                                                      <u>10,388</u>

Base cost of mare (ex foal)   <u><u>65,612</u></u>

Example 13.107.5.4

The following events occur in the cases of the three mares in Example **13.107.5.2** included in the farm trading stock of Moyglachan Stud Ltd at 31 December 2006. Azalea gives birth to a colt and Dogwood to a filly, each new foal being born towards the end of February 2006. The mare Magnolia dies in January 2007 and there is no foal. The trading stock "cost" values of the two foals at 31 December 2006 are determined as follows:

	Colt	*Filly*
	(ex Azalea)	*(ex Dogwood)*
	€	€
Cost of foal (up to 31/12/06) (as per Example **13.107.5.2**)	54,900	34,900
Keep for whole of 2006, say €2,400 each	<u>2,700</u>	<u>2,700</u>
Cost as trading stock 31/12/06	<u><u>57,600</u></u>	<u><u>37,600</u></u>

Since the 31 December 2006 closing stock value of €60,000 for Magnolia with foal (see Example **13.107.5.2** above) is also debited as part of the opening stock value at 1 January 2007, the death of the mare results in the inclusion of a gross loss of €60,000 in the stud farm accounts for the year 2007.

13.107.6 Treatment of stallions, stallion fees etc

A stud farming company may own one or more stallions for the service of its mares, or it may send its mares to the stallions of other owners to be serviced for a stud or stallion fee. The company may acquire a share in a syndicate stallion, ie one owned jointly by a number of persons under a syndication agreement. Since thoroughbred racing stallions are very expensive, especially those that have been successful in racing so as to be much sought after for breeding, the practice of acquiring stallion shares through a syndicate is widespread. Even where a stallion is owned by a single person, it is more than likely that it will be used to service not only its owner's mares, but also the mares of other owners in consideration for stud fees.

In theory, a stallion owned by a stud farming company, kept on its land and used mainly for the servicing of its own mares might be regarded as trading stock in the same way as the mares used for breeding. In practice, even where a stallion is wholly owned by the company, it is more than likely that the stallion will be used to a significant extent to service also the mares of other owners. The fact that fees earned for such services may be tax exempt (up to 31 July 2008 - see below) is generally a strong reason for using the stallion in this way, particularly as the stud company can charge in its accounts (and therefore in its Case I computation) any stud fees it pays itself for using another person's stallion. Consequently, there are few, if any, cases where stallions are owned and used in such a way as to require them to be treated as trading stock.

The more usual form of stallion syndicate is one where the ownership of the stallion is divided into 40 shares and the members of the syndicate own one or more shares each. The original owner of the stallion, often the person who had previously raced it, may well have retained a number of shares, but this is not essential. Depending on the exact terms of the syndication agreement, each share usually entitles its holder to have a mare owned by that holder serviced by the stallion each year. Any member of the syndicate not wishing to use this right to the stallion's services in any year is entitled to sell that right (the "nomination") to another person for the purpose of servicing one of that person's mares in that year.

A stallion owned by a syndicate is usually kept on the land of one of the members, although it may sometimes be kept on the land of another person in consideration for an appropriate charge and the reimbursement of its keep and other expenses. The expenses relating to the stallion, eg keep, veterinary, insurance, any rent or other charge paid to the person on whose land it stands, must be shared by the members of the syndicate in proportion to the number of shares held by each. In practice, there are often one or two additional nominations to the stallion available and the syndicate may itself sell those nominations and use the proceeds to offset the syndicate expenses. To the extent that there are excess expenses, however, each member is required to contribute the appropriate share of the excess. If the syndicate income for any year should exceed its expenses, the excess income is usually divided among the members in proportion to their shares.

Stallion fees paid by a stud company, or the cost of purchase of any right to a nomination to a stallion, for the purpose of servicing its mares are a deductible expense in computing profits or losses for tax purposes. As mentioned in **13.107.2**, any stallion fee paid for the servicing of a mare is included in arriving at that mare's trading stock cost value if the mare is in foal at the following year end and, after the foal is born, becomes part of the foal's cost for trading stock purposes. The stallion fee or cost of purchasing a nomination is effectively carried forward in the trading stock valuation until the progeny is sold or transferred out of the stud to training/racing. Any stallion fee or cost of a nomination paid for a service that proves to be barren is not included in any trading stock valuation, so that the effect of the deduction for the expense is reflected in arriving at the stud farm profit or loss for the year in which the expense is incurred.

While a stud farming company which pays a stallion fee or purchases a nomination to a syndicate stallion deducts the amount paid as a trading expense, the cost of acquiring a share in a stallion is treated as capital expenditure for which no deduction is available under normal Case I principles. The fact that the company's objective in acquiring a stallion share is almost invariably to enable it to have the use of the stallion's services each year does not alter this treatment. Further, it has been held that capital expenditure on the purchase of a stallion does not qualify as expenditure on machinery or plant for which a wear and tear allowance can be claimed. In *Earl of Derby v Aylmer* [1915] 3 KB 374, 6 TC 665, Rowlatt J held that a stallion kept for breeding purposes was a wasting source of production which, although his value might diminish year by year as it grew older, did not diminish in value by reason of wear and tear.

As already mentioned, in practice, a special deduction is allowed to the stud company which uses a free service from a syndicate stallion in which it has acquired a share. The same deduction is also given where it uses its own stallion to service a particular mare or mares in its own stud farm. In either of these cases, the deduction is given in the computation of the stud farm profit, or loss, for the year in which the colt or filly resulting from the particular stallion service is sold. It is not given at all if the mare does not produce a foal as a result of the service or if the foal dies before it is sold, but the death of the mare after giving birth does not prevent the giving of the deduction if the colt or filly survives and is sold while still stud farm trading stock.

The deduction given is of an amount equal to the fee that was being advertised for the services of the particular stallion at the time the service took place, but may be restricted to ensure that no loss (or greater loss if there is already a loss) arises on the sale of the colt or filly. In effect, therefore, the amount deductible is the lower of the advertised stallion fee and the excess of the sale price for the colt or filly over its "cost" as trading stock at the date of the sale. This means that no deduction is available if the colt or filly is transferred to the stud farmer's racing stable since, in that case, as the transfer price is credited to the accounts at "cost", any deduction at all would result in a loss.

Example 13.107.6.1

The facts are as in Example **13.107.5.2** except that Moyglachan Stud Ltd was entitled to deduct as a trading expense, in its stud farm accounts for the year ended 31 December 2006, the sire fee of €50,000 paid in that year to have its mare Azalea serviced by the stallion Coimbra. It was also entitled to deduct in the same year the €30,200 paid for the nomination to the stallion Bayard used to service its mare Dogwood. The company was not entitled to any expense deduction in 2006 for the cost of purchasing its share in the stallion Sartain, nor for any proportion of that cost.

Assume that the mare Magnolia had not died (as was the case Example **13.107.5.4**) but had lived to produce a colt born on 1 March 2007. This colt is in due course sold as a yearling for €28,000 on 30 September 2008. On the assumption that the stallion fee advertised by the syndicate for the services of Sartain in 2006 was €25,000, the tax treatment of the colt is as follows:

	€
Cost as a foal (up to 31/12/06) as per Example **13.107.5.2**	4,400
Keep as foal to 31/12/07, say	2,900
Keep as yearling (1/1/08 to 15/9/08), say €3,000 per annum x 9/12	2,250
Cost up to date of sale	9,550
Sale as yearling	28,000
Gross profit on sale	18,450

Moyglachan Stud Ltd may take a deduction in its stud farm Case I computation for the year to 31 December 2008, as follows:

	€
Advertised stud fee for Sartain in 2006	25,000
Limited to gross profit (deduction cannot produce a loss on sale)	18,450

A stud farming company which acquires a share in a stallion is regarded as holding a capital asset so that any profit or loss arising on its sale is treated as a capital profit or loss. Any such profit or loss, therefore, must be excluded from the Case I computation. Further, since a stallion is a "wasting asset" for capital gains tax purposes, no question of any tax on a capital gain arises.

Similarly, any profit or loss on the sale of a stallion owned outright by a stud company is almost invariably treated as a capital profit not subject to any tax either as income or as a capital gain. One possible exception might be a profit on the sale of a stallion owned solely by the stud company that is kept on its own land and used to service only its own mares. Such a stallion might be treated as trading stock so long as he is held and used in this way in which case any sale proceeds would have to be taken in as trading receipts in the stud farm accounts.

13.107.7 Stallion fee exemption

TCA 1997, s 231(1) (as extended by TCA 1997, s 76(6)) exempts from corporation tax the profits or gains arising to a stallion owning company from the sale of services of mares by the stallion, but only if the stallion is ordinarily kept on land in the State and if the servicing of the mares takes place in the State. The exemption ceases to apply in respect of profits or gains arising after 31 July 2008 (TCA 1997, s 231(4)). For the position applying after that date, see **13.107.8** below. In respect of accounting periods commencing on or after 1 January 2004, the exempt profits arising to a company from its stallion services activities are required to be included in the company's annual return of income. Where a notice under TCA 1997, s 951(6) (exclusion from obligation in relation to making of a tax return – see **15.104.3**) has been issued to any person to whom stallion services income has arisen, that person is treated as if such a notice had not been issued. The obligations relating to the keeping records (TCA 1997, s 886 – see **13.106.1**) apply as if the exempt profits were taxable profits (TCA 1997, s 231(2)). For the above purposes, profits and losses are to be computed in accordance with the Tax Acts as if the exemption from tax were not available (TCA 1997, s 231(3)).

TCA 1997, s 231 gives a corresponding exemption to the part owner of a stallion in respect of any profits or gains from either the sale of the stallion's services or the sale of rights (nominations) to his services. Any company which is a part owner is entitled to this exemption if both conditions mentioned above are met, ie if the stallion in which it has a share is ordinarily kept in the State and if the servicing of the mares takes place in the State.

In the case of a stallion ordinarily kept on land outside the State, a part owner (but not a sole owner) is also entitled to the exemption in respect of the profits from the sale of the stallion's services or of rights to those services, but only if:

(a) the part owner carries on in the State a trade consisting of or including bloodstock breeding; and

(b) it is shown to the satisfaction of the inspector or, on appeal, the Appeal Commissioners, that the part ownership of the stallion was acquired, and is held, primarily for the purposes of the service of mares owned or partly owned by the part owner of the stallion in the course of that trade.

The current rules denying the exemption for stallions kept abroad (except in the case of a part owner meeting conditions (a) and (b) above) became effective for a company chargeable to corporation tax for any accounting period ending after 5 April 1985; stallion fees arising before 6 April 1985 were exempted in all circumstances under the old rules.

The Revenue, however, accept that nomination income from a stallion that is ordinarily kept on land in the State but which is temporarily exported for genuine commercial reasons, and for a period that will not exceed two years, will be regarded as exempt from tax. This position will apply to so-called dual hemisphere or shuttle stallions. These stallions normally stand in Ireland but are sent abroad to the Southern hemisphere at the end of the Irish breeding season. Only profits derived from the service of mares within the State by dual hemisphere stallions are regarded as exempt from tax in accordance with TCA 1997, s 231; profits from the servicing of mares outside the State by these stallions are not so exempted.

13.107.8   Taxation of stallion profits and gains

Introduction

TCA 1997, Part 3 Chapter 4 (ss 669G-669K) provides for the taxation from 1 August 2008 of profits and gains arising from stallion stud fees. During the period, up to 31 July 2008, for which stallion stud fees were tax exempt (see **13.107.7** below), costs together with stallion stud fee income were not taken into consideration for taxation purposes. With effect from 1 August 2008, stallions are treated as stock in trade and income or gains arising from stallion stud fees or from the sale of stallions are subject to taxation. Normal expenses for the upkeep of stallions are allowable for tax purposes and a deduction for the purchase cost of a stallion is provided for over a four year period at 25% per annum.

Stallions purchased on the open market after 31 July 2008 are to be valued, for the purposes of the four year deduction, at their purchase price. Where a stallion is standing at stud prior to the termination date of the exemption, or is transferred to stud from racing or training, or is bred on the farm or held as stock in trade, its cost for the purposes of the four year deduction is its prevailing market value as of 1 August 2008 or the date it first stands at stud, as appropriate. The Revenue Commissioners may consult with any person as they see fit in determining the market value of a stallion.

The above-described treatment applies also to syndicated owners of stallions. In a cases in which a syndicate member is not wholly or mainly engaged in farming, however, costs and losses arising from the ownership of the stallion will be offset solely against profits and gains from horse-breeding.

Charge to tax

The profits or gains arising in any accounting period to a company as owner or part-owner of a stallion from the sale of services of mares by the stallion or rights to such services are chargeable to corporation tax. Where the owner or part-owner carries on in that period a trade of farming in respect of which it is within the charge to tax under Case I of Schedule D, the profits or gains, and any amount chargeable under TCA 1997, 669I(3)(c) (amounts receivable on disposal or death of a stallion - see below regarding TCA 1997, 669I(3), under (c)), are chargeable under Case I as part of that trade. Otherwise, the profits or gains and any amount chargeable under TCA 1997, 669I(3)(c) are chargeable under Case IV of Schedule D (TCA 1997, s 669H).

Deductions

If a company acquires ownership or part-ownership of a stallion the profits or gains in relation to which are chargeable as above, the company, in computing the amount of income to be charged to tax for any accounting period, will not be entitled to any deduction in respect of expenditure incurred on such acquisition except as follows.

Where the profits or gains are chargeable under Case I, the owner or part-owner of the stallion will, in computing the trading income of the trade of farming, be entitled for each of four consecutive accounting periods, the first of which begins with the chargeable period in which—

(i)   1 August 2008 occurs, in a case where the stallion is owned or part-owned on that day, or

    (ii)   in any other case, the stallion is either acquired for, or appropriated to, stud activities, as the case may be,

to a deduction equal to 25% of the initial value of the stallion, as if the deduction were a trading expense incurred in the chargeable period (TCA 1997, s 669I(2)(a)).

Subject to section 669K(3) (restriction on use of Case IV losses - see below), where the profits or gains are chargeable under Case IV, in determining the amount of income to be charged to tax, that income is to be computed in accordance with the provisions applicable to Case I of Schedule D, taking into account TCA 1997, Part 3 Chapter 4 (TCA 1997, s 669I(2)(b)).

Where, in any accounting period a stallion is disposed of or dies, then—

    (a)   no deduction which would otherwise be allowed for the purposes of Case I or Case IV in respect of the initial value of that stallion will be allowed for that or any subsequent period,

    (b)   a deduction of an amount equal to the residual value of the stallion at the time of its disposal or death is to be allowed for that period as if it were a deduction for Case I purposes, and

    (c)   a company, being the owner or part-owner of the stallion, will be chargeable to corporation tax on—

        (i)   the amount received in money or money's worth, in respect of its disposal or death, or

        (ii)   in the case of a disposal, if greater, the price which the stallion might reasonably have been expected to fetch at the time of its disposal on a sale, at arm's length between persons who are not connected (within the meaning of TCA 1997, s 10 – see **2.3**), in the open market (TCA 1997, s 669I(3)).

In relation to a stallion, *initial value* means its market value on 1 August 2008 or on the day it is either acquired for, or appropriated to, stud activities, as the case may be, whichever is later, and any reference to a stallion includes a reference to an interest in a stallion. A reference to a stallion's *market value* at any time is to the price which the stallion might reasonably be expected to fetch on a sale in the open market or, in a case where a purchaser acquires the stallion from another person at arm's length and the purchaser and the vendor are not connected persons (within the meaning of TCA 1997, s 10 – see **2.3**), the price paid. In determining the market value of a stallion, the Revenue Commissioners may consult which such persons or body of persons as in their opinion may be of assistance to them.

For the purposes of (b) above, *residual value* in relation to a stallion means—

    (a)   an amount equal to the initial value of the stallion, or

    (b)   if less, the amount by which the initial value exceeds—

        (i)   the amount allowed as a deduction under TCA 1997, s 668I for an accounting period ending before that time, or

        (ii)   where there is more than one such amount, the aggregate of such amounts.

For all purposes of stock relief (see **13.103**), trading stock comprising stallions is to be disregarded (TCA 1997, s 669K(2)).

Where for any accounting period of a company the computation of income for Case IV purposes results in a loss, the amount of the loss may not be deducted from or set off against other income charged to tax under that Case for that period. Any such loss carried forward to a subsequent period may only be deducted from or set off against stallion fee income chargeable under Case IV for that period (TCA 1997, s 669K(3)).

13.108   Losses: non-commercial farming and market gardening

TCA 1997, s 663 provides rules which may prevent a company chargeable to corporation tax from setting off losses in a trade of farming or market gardening against its total profits chargeable to corporation tax; trading losses are normally available for set off against total profits under TCA 1997, s 396(2) – see **4.101**. (Since farming losses are now "relevant trading losses", however, denial of relief under TCA 1997, s 396(2) has no real effect – see *Farming losses as relevant trading losses* below.)

In order that a trading loss may be set off against its total profits, the company must be carrying on the relevant activity, farming or market gardening, as the case may be, on a commercial basis and with a view to the realisation of profits. In interpreting this rule, if the farming or market gardening was in fact being carried on in an accounting period in such a way as to afford a reasonable expectation of profit, this fact is to be taken as conclusive evidence that the trade was then being carried on with a view to the realisation of profits.

By itself, this "commercial" test might sometimes be difficult to apply in practice. It is, therefore, supported by a "prior three years" losses rule which is capable of more objective interpretation. This rule provides that, without limiting the general application of the main rule, no TCA 1997, s 396(2) relief is to be given in respect of a farming or market gardening loss incurred in an accounting period if, in all of the accounting periods wholly or partly comprised in the prior three years (the last three years before the beginning of the accounting period in which the loss was incurred), there was also a farming or market gardening loss. The question as to whether or not there is a loss in any period is determined by applying the normal Case I computational rules; regard is had to the actual adjusted Case I loss, if any, for that period after adding back depreciation and other disallowable items, but before taking account of capital allowances or balancing charges (TCA 1997, s 663(2)(b)).

Although, under TCA 1997, s 307(1), capital allowances are deducted as an expense in computing trading profits or losses for the purposes of Case I, no account is taken of any such allowances in ascertaining whether or not a loss has been incurred for the purposes of TCA 1997, s 663(2). Equally, no account is taken of any balancing charges so that, while there may be a taxable profit after including any such charge, a loss may nevertheless have arisen, for the purposes of TCA 1997, s 663(2), when the balancing charge is ignored.

The main commercial test can be applied on its own to prevent TCA 1997, s 396(2) loss relief for any accounting period, even if losses have not been incurred in prior periods. The onus is on the company to satisfy the inspector, if required, that the farming or market gardening is being undertaken on a commercial basis in the period of the loss for which relief is sought. On the other hand, the prior three years losses rule only operates to deny TCA 1997, s 396(2) relief from the accounting period immediately following the prior three years if there have been losses in the periods wholly or partly comprised in the prior three years. It does not prevent the making of a TCA 1997, s 396(2) claim in respect of the losses for any of the accounting periods wholly or partly within the prior three years for which the main commercial test is met.

There are three exceptions to both the main commercial test and the prior three years losses rule. A claim under TCA 1997, s 396(2) for a farming or market gardening loss incurred in any accounting period may still be made if any of the following exceptions applies:

(a) the company shows that the whole of its farming or market gardening activities in the year immediately following the prior three years are of such a nature, and are carried on in such a way, as would have justified a reasonable expectation of the realisation of profits in the future if they had been undertaken by a competent farmer or market gardener, but where, if that farmer or market gardener had carried on those activities at the beginning of the "prior period of loss", he could not reasonably have expected the activities to become profitable until after the end of the year immediately following the prior period of loss;

(b) the farming or market gardening trade forms part of, and is ancillary to, a larger trading undertaking; or

(c) the farming or market gardening trade was set up and commenced within the prior three years.

In determining whether exception (a) applies, it is necessary to establish that, if the hypothetical competent farmer or market gardener had carried on the relevant activities during the prior period of loss, that person could not reasonably have expected those activities to have become profitable until at least a year after the end of that prior period of loss. For this purpose, the *prior period of loss* means the last three years before the beginning of the accounting period in question or, if losses were incurred in successive accounting periods amounting in all to a period longer than three years and ending when those last three years end, that longer period.

If a farming or market gardening loss is prevented by TCA 1997, s 663 from being set off against a company's total profits under TCA 1997, s 396(2), that loss is also unavailable for set off against the total profits of any other company under the group relief provisions (TCA 1997, s 420(1) second limb).

Example 13.108.1

Leisurely Farms Ltd commenced farming on 1 November 1997 and prepared its first farm accounts for the three months ended 31 January 1998 and has since then prepared accounts to 31 January in each year. It incurs farming losses for the three months ended 31 January 1998 and for each of the next four years ended 31 January 1999, 2000, 2001 and 2002. The company claims to set these farming losses against total profits of each of the four accounting periods to date.

Claims for periods ended 31/1/98, 31/1/99, 31/1/00 and 31/1/01

The inspector of taxes is of the view that the company's trade was not carried on commercially and with a view to the realisation of profits. However, as the farming trade was set up within the last three years prior to each of these four periods, exception (c) applies so that the TCA 1997, s 396(2) claims for these periods will be allowed. It is not necessary to consider the prior three years losses rule for any of these accounting periods as losses have not been incurred in each of the accounting periods comprised in the three years prior to any of these periods; for example, in relation to the year ended 31 January 2001, the prior three year period extends back to 1 February 1997 while the company's first accounting period only commenced on 1 November 1997.

Although the inspector of taxes may be prepared to accept that Leisurely Farms Ltd is farming on a commercial basis and with a view to the realisation of profits, the company did not commence trading within the last three years prior to this period so that exception (c) does not apply, and it incurred farming losses in each of the accounting periods wholly or partly comprised in the prior three years. It is, however, possible that exception (a) applies.

In this connection, it is necessary to establish the "prior period of loss" in relation to the year ended 31 January 2002. This is the period from 1 November 1997 to 31 January 2001 (which is longer than the prior three years). Exception (a) will apply if the company can show that a competent farmer, who had undertaken the same farming activities from 1 November 1997, could not reasonably have expected those activities to become profitable until after 31 January 2002, ie until after the year following the prior period of loss.

The application of the main commercial test and the prior three years losses rule is not course limited to the years following the commencement of farming or market gardening activities. A farming or market gardening company which has traded on a commercial basis for a number of years may cease to do so without actually ceasing to trade. Alternatively, it may incur losses in consecutive accounting periods. If the inspector considers that the company is not farming on a commercial basis in any such period, a TCA 1997, s 396(2) claim may be resisted for that period, even if there was not a loss in one or more prior periods. Alternatively, if there are losses in each of the accounting periods falling wholly or partly within the prior three years, even after one or more previous profitable periods, the rule will operate to deny TCA 1997, s 396(2) relief for the following period.

TCA 1997s 663 does not restrict or deny loss relief by way of carry forward under TCA 1997, s 396(1) or by way of terminal loss under TCA 1997, s 397 (or by say of a claim under TCA 1997, s 396A(3) – see below). Thus, a company which has carried on farming unsuccessfully for a number of years is still entitled to carry forward all Case I farming losses (other than losses not eligible for carry forward, for example, because already used in a TCA 1997, s 396(2) claim) for relief under TCA 1997, s 396(1) against farming profits of subsequent periods, provided there has not been a cessation of the company's single trade of farming in the meantime.

13.108.1   Farming losses as relevant trading losses

Losses incurred in a trade of farming are "relevant trading losses" (see **4.103**) and as such cannot, from 6 March 2001, be used for the purposes of a claim under TCA 1997, s 396(2). Relief may instead be claimed under TCA 1997, s 396A(3) and then only against relevant trading income and not against total profits. TCA 1997, s 663 makes no provision for denying relief claimed under TCA 1997, s 396A(3).

13.2 FARMING: CAPITAL ALLOWANCES

13.201   Introduction
13.202   Capital allowances: farm buildings and works
13.203   Capital allowances: farm machinery and plant
13.204   Milk quotas
13.205   Notional wear and tear allowances

13.201   Introduction

The capital expenditure regime for the trade of farming is the same as that applicable to other trades but with additional features. A farming company chargeable to tax under Case I is entitled to claim capital allowances in respect of capital expenditure on machinery or plant incurred for the purpose of its trade of farming. The company is also entitled to claim capital allowances in respect of qualifying expenditure on farm buildings, fences and other farm works, a form of capital allowance relevant only to farming. In principle, the rules relating to capital allowances and balancing charges on machinery or plant apply to farming in the same way as to other trades, but with modifications.

The allowances for capital expenditure on farm buildings and other farm works are covered in **13.202**. As with the allowances for farm machinery and plant, certain accelerated capital allowances were available for many years, but these have ceased to be available for expenditure incurred after 31 March 1992 so that only normal annual writing down allowances are now available.

For expenditure incurred on farm buildings (except dwellings), fences and other farm works on or after 27 January 1994 the writing down period is seven years (ie 15% in the first six years and 10% in the seventh year).

From 6 April 1982 to 26 January 1994, farm buildings capital allowances were calculated at 10% on the straight line basis over 10 years, but with the right to claim an increased (free depreciation) allowance, when available, at the farmer's option. For qualifying expenditure incurred before 1 April 1989 on farm buildings and other works, a free depreciation allowance could be claimed of up to 100% of the qualifying expenditure in the first chargeable period related to the expenditure (and of up to 100% of any balance in the second or any subsequent chargeable period).

For capital expenditure incurred from 1 April 1989 and 31 March 1991, the maximum free depreciation claim for any chargeable period was 50% of the expenditure incurred. The rules for farm buildings allowances are discussed in **13.202**.

Capital allowances for farm machinery and plant have comprised annual wear and tear allowances, free depreciation, initial allowances and balancing allowances as discussed in Chapter 5 in the context of trades and professions. However, as with such other trades or professions, accelerated allowances (free depreciation and initial allowances) ceased to apply in respect of machinery or plant provided after 31 March 1992 for which only annual writing down allowances are available.

An important former difference between farming and other trades was the restriction of the amount of accelerated allowances that could be claimed by a farming company for certain machinery or plant in any 12 month accounting period, so as not to exceed 30% of the Case I profits. This restriction (imposed by FA 1980 s 26 affecting chargeable periods commencing after 5 April 1980) was removed by FA 1988 s 52(3) and had ceased to apply for any chargeable period commencing after 5 April 1989.

13.202 Capital allowances: farm buildings and works

13.202.1 Introduction

Capital allowances are provided for by TCA 1997, s 658 in respect of capital expenditure on the construction of farm buildings (other than dwellings) and certain farm works incurred by any person carrying on the trade of farming the profits of which are charged to tax under Schedule D Case I. These capital allowances referred to as "farm buildings allowances".

Farm buildings allowances are given in respect of capital expenditure incurred on:

    (a)   the construction of farm buildings (excluding a building or part of a building used as a dwelling);

    (b)   fences;

    (c)   roadways, holding yards, drains or land reclamation or other works.

Farm buildings qualifying for the allowance may be cattle sheds, milking parlours, pighouses or any other buildings of any kind used for the purposes of the trade of farming. Apart from fences and the other works specifically mentioned in (b) and (c), any other works of a capital nature on the farm land to improve that land for the purpose of the farmer's farming activities of any kind, or to provide other facilities for the purposes of the farming, attract the farm buildings allowances. For example, capital expenditure on the control of farm pollution qualifies as "other works". Clearly, farm buildings allowances do not apply to capital expenditure on machinery or plant in respect of which other capital allowances are available (eg tractors, harrows, milking machinery).

To qualify for farm buildings allowances, capital expenditure must have been incurred for the purposes of a trade of farming land in the State occupied by the person claiming the allowances (but see **13.202.6** below). Any capital expenditure met directly or indirectly by the State or by any public or local authority grant or otherwise does not qualify for allowances and must be excluded (TCA 1997, s 658(13)).

Capital expenditure incurred by a company about to carry on a trade of farming, but before it commences to farm, is deemed to be incurred on the day on which the trade commences (TCA 1997, s 658(5)). Where any expenditure is incurred partly for the purposes of farming and partly for other purposes, the part of that expenditure fairly apportioned to the farming purposes qualifies for the allowances (TCA 1997, s 658(11)).

13.202.2 The writing down period

TCA 1997, s 658(2) provides for the granting of farm buildings allowances in respect of qualifying expenditure over a writing down period of seven years which begins with the "chargeable period related to the expenditure". This seven years writing down period applies where the expenditure on the farm buildings, fences, roadways, holding yards, drains, land reclamation or other works is incurred on or after 27 January 1994. For expenditure which was incurred before 27 January 1994, the allowances are given over a ten year writing down period (TCA 1997 Sch 32 para 23). "Chargeable period", for a company carrying on a farming trade, means the relevant accounting period of the company.

The "chargeable period related to" any particular farm buildings or other expenditure is, in the case of a company chargeable to corporation tax, the accounting period in which the expenditure in question is incurred (TCA 1997, s 321(2) – see Chapter 5).

For a company chargeable to corporation tax, the writing down period begins on the first day of the accounting period in which the qualifying expenditure is incurred and continues until the last day of the seven years commencing on that first day. For example, if a company incurs qualifying farm buildings expenditure in its accounting period 1 January 2001 to 31 December 2001, the writing down period for that expenditure is the seven years commencing on 1 January 2001 and ending on 31 December 2008.

13.202.3 Writing down rates

Farm buildings allowances are, in principle, made at the rate necessary to write off the full expenditure on a straight line basis over the duration of the writing down period, currently seven years. For expenditure incurred after 31 March 1992, only annual writing down allowances are available; accelerated allowances had been available for expenditure incurred up to that date.

Farm buildings allowances, for capital expenditure incurred on or after 27 January 1994 on farm buildings or farm works, are in the form of an annual writing down allowance over a seven year writing down period, as follows:

(a)   an allowance of 15% of the expenditure for each of the first six years of the writing down period; and

(b)   an allowance 10% of the expenditure for the seventh and final year of the writing down period (TCA 1997, s 658(2)).

Example 13.202.3.1

Rolling Meadows Ltd, a company carrying on a farming trade, incurs capital expenditure of €92,000 on the construction of new farm buildings in its first accounting period from 1 July 2003 to 31 December 2003. The company thereafter made up accounts to 31 December each year.

The company's seven year writing down period for the qualifying expenditure incurred in its initial accounting period commences on 1 July 2003 and ends on 30 June 2010. The seventh and final year of the writing down period for which a 10% writing down allowance applies is the year commencing on 1 July 2009 and ending on 30 June 2010.

The company's farm buildings allowances for the period ended 31 December 2003 (the chargeable period related to the expenditure of €92,000) and the following periods up to 31 December 2010, assuming it continues to carry on the farming trade throughout, are as follows:

	€
Six months 31/12/03:	
15% x €92,000 x 6/12ths[1]	6,900
Year ended 31/12/04:	
15% x €92,000	13,800
Years ended 31/12/05 to 31/12/08:	
15% x €92,000 x 4	55,200

Year ended 31/12/09:

15% x €92,000 x 6/12²	6,900
10% x €92,000 x 6/12³	4,600

Year ended 31/12/10

10% x €92,000 x 6/12³	4,600

Notes:

¹   The 15% writing down allowance is reduced proportionately for a six month period.

²   Since only the first six months of the year ended 31 December 2009 is within the 6th year of the writing down period, only 6/12ths of the allowance at 15% is due for that period.

³   The allowance at 10% for the 7th year of the writing down period is split between the two final accounting periods.

Farm buildings allowances in respect of capital expenditure incurred from 1 April 1992 to 26 January 1994 on farm buildings or farm works were at a rate 10% for each chargeable period over a ten year writing down period (TCA 1997 Sch 32 paragraph 23(1)). Thus, expenditure was written off by means of a straight-line writing down allowance of 10% of the qualifying expenditure for each chargeable period of 12 months falling within the writing down period. No free depreciation or any other accelerated capital allowances are available in respect of expenditure on farm buildings or works incurred from 1 April 1992 to 26 January 1994.

For capital expenditure on farm buildings and farm works incurred before 1 April 1992, a farming company could elect to increase the amount of the 10% writing down allowance then available for any chargeable period by such amount as the company specified, subject to certain limits. For expenditure incurred in the period 1 April 1991 to 31 March 1992, the limit was 25%. For expenditure in the period 1 April 1989 to 31 March 1991, the limit was 50% while any amount up to 100% could be claimed in respect of expenditure incurred prior to 1 April 1989 (TCA 1997 Sch 32 paragraph 23(1)). References in the Tax Acts to a farm buildings allowance are deemed to include a writing down allowance as increased under any such "free depreciation" election.

13.202.4   Manner of making allowances

Farm buildings allowances are made "in taxing a trade" of a company. Accordingly, the company ceases to be entitled to any allowance for any accounting period after that in which it has ceased to carry on farming trade. This is true even where the writing down period may not have expired. The farming trade of a farming company does not, however, cease until it has ceased to carry on all farming activities in the State.

Farm buildings allowances are available to a farming company in the same way as any other capital allowances, ie by way of a deduction as an expense in the Schedule D Case I computation of the taxable profit or allowable loss (TCA 1997, s 307(2)).

13.202.5   No balancing allowances or balancing charges

It might be expected that on the sale or other disposal of farm buildings or farm works for which farm buildings allowances had been obtained, a balancing allowance of balancing charge would arise. There are, however, no provisions to this effect. Nor is there any balancing allowance or balancing charge in the event of a farming company ceasing to use the land for farming.

Consequently, a company which incurred the original qualifying expenditure is entitled to the normal writing down allowance for each chargeable period in the writing down period up to and including the sale, transfer or other disposal of the land, while there is no clawback of the allowances obtained whatever the amount of the profit that might be realised on the disposal.

13.202.6   Disposal of farm land: new owner's allowances

TCA 1997, s 658(9) deals with the situation in which a farming company sells or otherwise transfers to another person its interest in any farm land on which the company had incurred any capital expenditure qualifying for farm buildings allowances. The subsection provides that that other person becomes entitled, to the exclusion of the transferring company, to claim farm buildings allowances on any part of the original expenditure not already written off, provided that that person farms the land. The company which incurred the expenditure is, however, allowed to claim the allowances for the accounting period in which the transfer of the interest in the land took place.

Should the company transfer a part only of its farm land, it will be necessary to distinguish the part of any previous expenditure on farm buildings or farm works which is referable to the part of the land transferred. The new owner is then entitled to farm buildings allowances, on the part of the qualifying expenditure properly referable to the land acquired, for the unexpired part of the writing down period. If the company continues to farm the land retained, it remains entitled to the allowances on the balance of the expenditure referable to the land retained until the end of the writing down period.

The expenditure in respect of which the new owner is entitled to farm buildings allowances may have been incurred by the transferring company in two or more accounting periods. In that event, the new owner acquires different unexpired writing down periods over which the balance of the expenditure may be written off as allowances for the new owner.

The new owner's entitlement to farm buildings allowances by reference to the amount of the qualifying expenditure incurred by the transferring company is totally unaffected by the amount paid for the purchase or transfer of the land. Clearly, if the purchase or transfer occurs after the end of the writing down period in respect of the transferring company's expenditure (or where that expenditure was completely written off due to free depreciation in one or more earlier years), the purchaser is not entitled to any farm buildings allowances in respect of that expenditure.

Example 13.202.6.1

Pasturas del Cielo Ltd, a company which has carried on a trade of farming on two farms for many years, makes up accounts to 31 December each year. On 1 January 2004, it sells one of the farms, including the land, farm buildings and other works on that land, to Llano Estacado Ltd, which continues to farm that land. Pasturas del Cielo Ltd also continues to farm the land retained by it.

No capital expenditure on farm buildings and farm works on the farm sold to Llano Estacado Ltd had been incurred for a number of years up to 31 December 1999, but Pasturas del Cielo Ltd had incurred the following capital expenditure on that farm from 1 January 2000 to 31 December 2003:

	€
Year ended 31 December 2000:	
Extension to milking parlour	16,400
New fencing	5,800
New cattle sheds	11,200
	33,400
Year ended 31 December 2002	
New farm road	7,900
New fencing	5,200
New drainage	11,800
	24,900
Year to 31 December 2003	
Capital improvements to general farm buildings	8,900
Drainage improvements	3,900
	12,800

Pasturas del Cielo Ltd has claimed farm buildings allowances in respect of all the foregoing capital expenditure for the periods up to and including the year ended 31 December 2003. The capital allowances claimed and the resulting amounts of expenditure still unallowed at 1 January 2004 are as follows:

		€
Expenditure in year ended 31/12/00		33,400
Writing down allowance (WDA) y/e 31/12/00 (15%)	5,010	
WDAs years ended 31/12/01 to 31/12/03		
€33,400 x 15% x 3	15,030	20,040
Amount unallowed at 1/1/04		13,360
Expenditure in year ended 31/12/02		24,900
WDAs years ended 31/12/02 and 31/12/03		
€24,900 x 15% x 2		7,470
Amount unallowed at 1/1/04		17,430
Expenditure in year ended 31/12/03		12,800
WDA year ended 31/12/03		
€12,800 x 15%		1,920
Amount unallowed at 1/1/04		10,880

Since Llano Estacado Ltd acquired the farm from Pasturas del Cielo Ltd on 1 January 2004, it is entitled to farm buildings allowances in respect of the capital expenditure incurred by the vendor company in the periods mentioned above, but only for accounting periods after 31 December 2003. The allowances available are as follows:

	€
Expenditure in year ended 31/12/00 (€33,400)	
WDAs years ended 31/12/04 to 31/12/06 – €33,400 x (15% x 2 + 10%)	13,360
Expenditure in year ended 31/12/02 (€24,900)	
WDAs years ended 31/12/04 to 31/12/08 – €24,900 x (15% x 4 + 10%)	17,430
Expenditure in year ended 31/12/03 (€12,800)	
WDAs years ended 31/12/04 to 31/12/09 – €12,800 x (15% x 5 + 10%)	10,880

13.202.7 Farm pollution control allowances

TCA 1997, s 659 provides for a scheme of capital allowances to farmers who incur expenditure on necessary pollution control measures. The scheme applies for the period from 6 April 1997 to 31 December 2008. For expenditure incurred from 6 April 1997 to 5 April 2000, qualifying expenditure is written off over eight years and allowances available comprise a first year allowance of 50% of expenditure incurred up to an expenditure limit of €38,100 with the balance of the expenditure being written off in accordance with the normal wear and tear rules, ie 15% per annum for the following six years and 10% in the eighth year.

For expenditure incurred on or after 6 April 2000 and before 1 January 2005, the qualifying expenditure is written off over seven years at 15% per annum for six years and 10% for the final year. The person claiming the allowances may, however, irrevocably elect to have the allowances made on an alternative basis. Accordingly, a claim may be made in respect of 50% of the expenditure incurred up to a maximum of €31,750. The whole or any part of that amount (the "residual amount") may be claimed in any year of the writing-down period. Where the election is in force, writing-down allowances are made in respect of the balance of the expenditure (the "specified amount") so as to write off that balance at 15% per annum for six years and 10% in the seventh year.

For expenditure incurred on or after 1 January 2005, the qualifying expenditure is written off over three years at 33% per annum over a three year writing down period. The alternative basis election described above applies also in this case.

The allowances under TCA 1997, s 659 are available to a farmer who has a farm nutrient management plan in place in respect of his farm and who incurs necessary capital expenditure for the control of pollution on buildings or structures of the type listed below.

TCA 1997, s 659 applies to any person:

(a) carrying on farming, the profits or gains of which are chargeable to tax in accordance with TCA 1997, s 655 (see **13.101**);

(b) for whom, in respect of capital expenditure referred to in (c) below and in respect of farm land occupied by him, a farm nutrient management plan has been drawn up by an agency or planner approved to draw up such plans by the Department of Agriculture, Food and Rural Development, and drawn up in accordance with:

(i)   the guidelines in relation to such plans entitled "Farm Nutrient Management Plan" issued by the Department of Agriculture, Food and Rural Development on 21 March 1997, or

(ii)   a plan drawn up under the scheme known as the Rural Environment Protection Scheme (REPS) or the scheme known as the Erne Catchment Nutrient Management Scheme, both being schemes administered by the Department of Agriculture and Food, and

(c)   who incurs capital expenditure on or after 6 April 1997 and before 1 January 2009 on the construction of those farm buildings (excluding a building or part of a building used as a dwelling) or structures specified below in the course of a trade of farming land occupied by such person where such buildings or structures are constructed in accordance with that farm nutrient management plan and are certified as being necessary by that agency or planner for the purpose of securing a reduction in or the elimination of any pollution arising from the trade of farming (TCA 1997, s 659(1)).

The buildings or structures referred to above are as follows:

(1)   Waste storage facilities including slurry tanks;

(2)   Soiled water tanks;

(3)   Effluent tanks.

(4)   Tank fences and covers;

(5)   Dungsteads and manure pits;

(6)   Yard drains for storm and soiled water removal;

(7)   Walled silos, silage bases and silo aprons;

(8)   Housing for cattle, including drystock accommodation, byres, loose houses, slatted houses, sloped floor houses and kennels, roofed feed or exercise yards where such houses or structures eliminate soiled water;

(9)   Housing for sheep and unroofed wintering structures for sheep and sheep dipping tanks.

Where a company which is a person referred to in TCA 1997, s 659(1) delivers a farm nutrient management plan to the Department of Agriculture, Food and Rural Development and has incurred the capital expenditure referred to in (c) above, writing-down allowances in respect of the expenditure, referred to as *farm pollution control allowances*, will be made to that company during the specified writing-down periods (see below). The allowances are to be made in taxing the company's trade (TCA 1997, s 659(2)) and are subject to the provisions of Article 6 of Council Regulation (EEC) No 2328/91 of 15 July 1991 (OJ No L218 of 6.8.91, p 1) on improving the efficiency of agricultural structures, as amended.

The specified *writing-down periods* are as follows:

(i)   in respect of capital expenditure incurred before 6 April 2000, 8 years beginning with the accounting period in which that expenditure is incurred;

(ii)   in respect of capital expenditure incurred on or after 6 April 2000 and before 1 January 2005, 7 years beginning with the accounting period in which that expenditure is incurred; and

(iii) in respect of capital expenditure incurred on or after 1 January 2005, 3 years beginning with the accounting period in which that expenditure is incurred (TCA 1997, s 659(2)(b)).

As regards the farm pollution control allowances to be made, it is necessary to distinguish the treatment of capital expenditure incurred up to 5 April 2000, expenditure incurred on or after 6 April 2000 and before 1 January 2005, and expenditure incurred on or after 1 January 2005. This is dealt with below.

Where a person entitled to farm pollution control allowances in respect of farm land occupied by him transfers his interest in that land or any part of that land to another person, the other person will then become entitled to the allowances (to the exclusion of the first-mentioned person) for the chargeable periods following the chargeable period in which the transfer took place (TCA 1997, s 659(8)). Where the transfer relates to part of the farm land, the foregoing treatment will apply to so much of the allowances as is properly referable to that part of the land as if it were a separate allowance.

In the case of expenditure incurred partly for a purpose for which a farm pollution control allowance is to be made and partly for other purposes, allowances are to be made in respect of the related expenditure by reference to a just apportionment of that expenditure (TCA 1997, s 659(10)). No farm pollution control allowance may be made for any expenditure if for the same or any other chargeable period an allowance is or has been made in respect of that expenditure under TCA 1997, s 658 (farm building and works – see above) or under the general capital allowances (industrial building allowances and allowances in respect of machinery or plant) regime (TCA 1997, s 659(11)).

For the purposes of farm pollution control allowances, expenditure is regarded as not having been incurred by a person in so far as it has been or is to be met directly or indirectly by the State or by any other person (TCA 1997, s 659(12)).

In determining, for the purposes of farm pollution control allowances, whether and to what extent capital expenditure has been incurred on the construction of a building or structure in any period, only so much of that expenditure as is properly attributable to work on the building or structure actually carried out during the period may be treated as having been incurred in that period (TCA 1997, s 659(13)).

The treatment of capital expenditure incurred for the separate periods 6 April 1997 to 5 April 2000, 6 April 2000 to 31 December 2004 and 1 January 2005 onwards is as follows.

Expenditure incurred from 6 April 1997 to 5 April 2000

The farm pollution control allowances to be made are as follows:

(a) as respects the first year of the writing-down period referred to in (i) above, where the capital expenditure was incurred—

  (i) before 6 April 1998, 50% of that expenditure or €12,700, whichever is the lesser,

  (ii) on or after 6 April 1998 and before 6 April 2000, 50% of the that expenditure or €19,050, whichever is the lesser;

(b) for the next 6 years of the writing-down period, 15% of the balance of that expenditure after deducting the amount of any allowance made under (a), and

(c) for the final year of the writing-down period, 10% of the balance of that expenditure after deducting the amount of any allowance made under (a) (TCA 1997, s 659(3)(a)).

Expenditure incurred from 6 April 2000 to 31 December 2004

In relation to expenditure incurred on or after 6 April 2000, the definitions of "residual amount" and "specified amount" are relevant.

The *residual amount*, in relation to capital expenditure incurred by a company in an accounting period, means an amount equal to 50% of that expenditure or €31,750, whichever is the lesser. The *specified amount*, in relation to capital expenditure incurred by a company in an accounting period, means the balance of that expenditure after deducting the residual amount.

The farm pollution control allowances to be made in respect of capital expenditure incurred on or after 6 April 2000 are to be made on the following basis:

(a) subject to (b), the allowances to be made in respect of the capital expenditure incurred are—

    (i) 15% of that expenditure for each of the first 6 years of the writing-down period, and

    (ii) 10% of that expenditure for the last year of the writing-down period;

(b) notwithstanding (a), a company to which farm pollution control allowances are to be made may elect to have the following allowances made to it—

    (i) 15% of the specified amount for each of the first 6 years of the writing-down period, and

    (ii) 10% of the specified amount for the last year of the writing-down period, and

    (iii) subject to (c), the whole or any part of the residual amount as is specified by the company, in any year of the writing-down period;

(c) the election referred to in (b), which cannot be altered or varied during the writing-down period to which it refers, is to be made in writing on or before the specified return for the accounting period date (see **15.104.1**) in which the expenditure is incurred (TCA 1997, s 659(3)).

The allowances to be made in accordance with (b)(i) and (iii) above may not in the aggregate exceed the residual amount.

Expenditure incurred on or after 1 January 2005

In relation to expenditure incurred on or after 1 January 2005, the definitions of "residual amount" and "specified amount" are relevant.

The *residual amount*, in relation to capital expenditure incurred by a company in an accounting period, means an amount equal to 50% of that expenditure or:

(i) €31,750 where incurred in an accounting period ending before 1 January 2006; and

(ii) €50,000 in any other case,

whichever is the lesser.

The *specified amount*, in relation to capital expenditure incurred by a company in an accounting period, means the balance of that expenditure after deducting the residual amount.

The farm pollution control allowances to be made in respect of capital expenditure incurred on or after 1 January 2005 are to be made on the following basis:

(a) subject to (b), the allowances to be made in respect of the capital expenditure incurred are 33% of that expenditure for each of the three years of the writing-down period;

(b) notwithstanding (a), a company to which farm pollution control allowances are to be made may elect to have the following allowances made to it—

   (i) 33% of the specified amount for each of the three years of the writing-down period, and

   (iii) subject to (c), the whole or any part of the residual amount as is specified by the company, in any year of the writing-down period;

(c) the election referred to in (b), which cannot be altered or varied during the writing-down period to which it refers, is to be made in writing on or before the specified return for the accounting period date (see **15.104.1**) in which the expenditure is incurred (TCA 1997, s 659(3)).

The allowances to be made in accordance with (b) above may not in the aggregate exceed the residual amount.

13.203   Capital allowances: farm machinery and plant

13.203.1   General

For accounting periods ended after 5 April 1989, the capital allowances regime for farming companies is the same as that for other companies. As for other trades, accelerated capital allowances were available in respect expenditure incurred by a farming company up to 31 March 1992 on machinery or plant. The subject of capital allowances for machinery or plant is dealt with fully in **5.2** and, since farming companies are treated no differently to other companies in this respect, an outline will suffice here.

As with non-farming trades, the capital allowances treatment of motor vehicles, purchased before 1 January 2001, for a farming trade differed from that relating to other types of machinery or plant used in the trade. Accelerated capital allowances were never available for capital expenditure on motor vehicles. For all machinery or plant provided up to 31 March 1992, wear and tear allowances were given on the reducing balance basis but after that date allowances for machinery or plant (other than motor vehicles purchased before 1 January 2001) have been allowed on a straight-line basis (FA 1992 s 26) while the reducing balance basis continued to apply for expenditure on such machinery or plant provided before 1 April 1992. To provide a uniform method of claiming capital allowances for all machinery or plant (apart from motor vehicles purchased before 1 January 2001), it is provided in TCA 1997, s 241(1A) that, for accounting periods ended after 5 April 1996, the straight-line basis would apply to machinery or plant provided before 1 April 1992 also. For this purpose, the starting point is the tax written value at the end of the last accounting period ending before 6 April 1996.

13.203.2 Farm machinery or plant

For capital expenditure on machinery or plant provided for use for the purposes of a trade of farming, TCA 1997, s 284(1) provides for an annual wear and tear allowance of 12.5% of the expenditure for each chargeable period until the full amount of the expenditure is written off. For expenditure incurred before 1 January 2001 on machinery or plant (other than certain road vehicles) and provided for use on or after 1 April 1992, the rate was 15% and, for expenditure incurred from 1 January 2001 to 3 January 2002, 20%. For a farming company, a chargeable period is an accounting period.

In the case of a farming company, the expenditure is normally allowed over five accounting periods beginning with the period in which the expenditure is incurred. Apportionment will be necessary where an accounting period is a period of less than twelve months. So that the annual wear and tear allowances are available for the full five years, it is of course necessary that the item of machinery or plant continues to be used for the farming trade throughout that period.

For capital expenditure on machinery or plant provided for use on or after 1 April 1992, the former free depreciation allowance for owner-users is not available. Likewise, the former initial allowance cannot be claimed for any capital expenditure that is incurred on or after 1 April 1992. Thus, the only capital allowances available for farm machinery or plant first used in the trade after 31 March 1992 are the ordinary annual or wear and tear allowances described above.

Example 13.203.2.1

Ackerbau Ltd, a company which has carried on a farming trade since 1 January 2000, incurs capital expenditure of €18,800 on 6 August 2003 on new farm machinery (not including motor vehicles). A grant of €1,800 was obtained in respect of the cost of the machinery. The machinery is brought into use for the farming trade in the company's year ended 31 December 2003.

Ackerbau Ltd is entitled to writing down allowances on the net amount of expenditure incurred (TCA 1997, s 317) commencing with the year ended 31 December 2003 and the capital allowances available in respect of the expenditure, assuming the company continues to carry on the trade, are as follows:

€

Years ended 31/12/03 to 31/12/10:

12.5% x €17,000 x 8   17,000

Where an accounting period is a period shorter than twelve months, the rate of wear and tear allowance for that period in respect of any capital expenditure is proportionately reduced by reference to the number of months in the period (TCA 1997, s 284(2)(b). Accordingly, for expenditure on machinery or plant provided for use in an accounting period of less that twelve months duration, the amount of the wear and tear allowance for that period will be a proportionate part (number of months in the period as a proportion of 12) of 12.5% of the expenditure. The amount to be written off in the seventh period will comprise apportioned amounts to be written off at 15% and at 10%, while the amount to be written off in the eighth period will be an apportioned amount at 10%.

Example 13.203.2.2

Valley Farms Ltd, which commenced a trade of farming on 1 April 2003, incurs expenditure of €30,000 on machinery in its first accounting period 1 April 2003 to 31 December 2003. The company makes up its accounts for all subsequent periods to 31 December.

Writing down allowances for all periods (assuming the company continues to trade throughout) in respect of the machinery are as follows:

	€
Years ended 31/12/03 to 31/12/10:	
€30,000 x 12.5% x 8	<u>30,000</u>

Example 13.203.2.3

The position is the same as in Example **13.803.2.2** except that Valley Farms Ltd made up its accounts to 31 March each year up to 31 March 2005, after which date account were made up to 31 December. Wear and tear allowances for all periods are as follows:

	€
Years ended 31/3/04 to 31/3/05:	
€30,000 x 12.5% x 2	7,500
Period ended 31/12/05:	
€30,000 x 12.5% x 9/12	2,813
Years ended 31/12/06 to 31/12/10:	
€30,000 x 12.5% x 5	18,750
Year ended 31/12/11:	
€30,000 x 12.5% x 3/12	<u>937</u>
	<u>30,000</u>

13.203.3 Motor vehicles

For capital expenditure incurred before 1 January 2001 on a "road vehicle", ie a vehicle suitable for the conveyance by road of persons or goods or the haulage by road of other vehicles and used for the farming trade, wear and tear allowances for any chargeable period was 20% of the value of the vehicle at the commencement of that period.

In respect of expenditure incurred on or after 1 January 2001, the position for motor vehicles is the same as for machinery or plant generally, ie, for expenditure incurred up to 3 January 2002, wear and tear allowances at 20% of cost and, for expenditure incurred on or after 4 January 2002, 12.5% of cost, on a straight line basis.

13.203.4 Balancing allowances and balancing charges

Under TCA 1997, s 288, a balancing allowance or balancing charge arises to a company carrying on a trade of farming in the same way as a company carrying on any other trade (see **5.207**). The events requiring the calculation of a balancing adjustment (allowance or charge) in respect of machinery or plant are as follows:

(a) the sale of the machinery or plant;

(b) the machinery or plant ceasing to belong to the company other than by way of sale (eg, gift, complete loss through fire, flood or other mishap);

(c) the machinery or plant, while continuing to belong to the company, being is permanently withdrawn from its farming trade;

(d) the company ceasing permanently to carry on any farming in the State (ie, on the permanent cessation of the farmer company's single trade of farming; or

(e) the company being deemed to cease permanently to carry on the trade by reason of the rule in TCA 1997, s 77(2)(a) (see **3.102.2**).

The most usual event requiring the calculation of a balancing allowance or balancing charge is the sale by the farming company of an item of machinery or plant in respect of which it has obtained capital allowances for one or more previous accounting periods. A balancing allowance or charge is made for the accounting period in which the machinery or plant is sold.

The amount of the balancing allowance or charge is determined by comparing the tax written down value of the item of machinery or plant in question with the "sale, insurance, salvage or compensation moneys" receivable by the company arising out of the sale or other event. For certain events, the company may be deemed to have received consideration equal to the market value of the machinery or plant at the date of the event.

In the majority of cases, where the machinery or plant had been purchased, the tax written down value is the amount arrived at after deducting from the original cost price (including any installation or similar costs) the aggregate of all capital allowances previously obtained. In certain cases, it may be necessary to write down a deemed cost equal to the market value of the plant when acquired. In certain other circumstances, it may be necessary to deduct also notional wear and tear allowances (see **13.204**).

A balancing allowance is made if the net proceeds of sale, after deducting any expenses of the sale, are less than the tax written down value of the item sold at the end of the previous accounting period. The amount of the balancing allowance is the amount by which the net proceeds of sale fall short of the tax written down value.

If the net proceeds of sale exceed the tax written down value of the item of machinery or plant sold, a balancing charge of an amount equal to that excess is made, except that the balancing charge cannot exceed the aggregate of all the capital allowances actually obtained for previous accounting periods in respect of the company's cost of providing that machinery or plant for its trade. While in some cases notional wear and tear allowances may have been deducted in arriving at the tax written down value prior to the sale, any such notional allowances are ignored in calculating this upper limit to the balancing charge; the purpose of a balancing charge is to claw back the amount of allowances actually obtained.

The rules relating to balancing allowances and balancing charges apply in principle in the same way without regard to the date on which the machinery or plant sold was provided for use in the farming trade, or to when the original expenditure was incurred.

Example 13.203.4.1

In the years ended 31 December 2004 and 2007, High Plains Ltd, a farming company, purchased a trailer and a sprayer for €10,000 and €7,000 respectively, and used these items entirely in its farming trade. The sprayer was purchased in a liquidation sale. During the year ended 31 December 2008, the trailer was sold for €5,520 less €120 selling expenses and the sprayer for €7,200. The balancing adjustments on these sales are calculated as follows:

	Trailer 12.5%	Sprayer 12.5%
	€	€
Original cost	10,000	7,000

Less: capital allowances to 31/12/07:		
W & T y/e 31/12/04	1,250	
	8,750	
W & T y/e 31/12/05	1,250	
	7,500	
W & T y/e 31/12/06	1,250	
	6,250	
W & T y/e 31/12/07	1,250	875
	5,000	6,125
Net sale proceeds	5,400	7,200
Excess of proceeds over WDV	400	1,075
Balancing charge[1]	400	875

Note:

[1] The balancing charge in the case of the trailer is the excess of sale proceeds over tax written value. In the case of the sprayer, the balancing charge is limited to the amount of allowances obtained. The limit will apply where sale proceeds exceed the original cost.

Example 13.203.4.2

Belle Fourche Ltd, a farming company, purchased an excavator for €64,000 on 6 June 2004. It incurred further expenditure of €4,800 in respect of transport and installation related to the excavator.

The company had made up accounts to 30 September each year but, after 30 September 2004, made up accounts to 31 December 2004 and maintained a 31 December year end thereafter. The excavator continued to be used in the company's farming trade until it was sold on 31 August 2007 for a net consideration of €35,000 after extensive damage caused by fire. No insurance proceeds were received in respect of the fire damage and, apart from the sales proceeds of €35,000, no other proceeds were received.

The capital allowances and balancing adjustment on sale are as follows:

	€	€
Purchase cost (including transport and installation)		68,800
W & T allowances:		
Year ended 30/9/04		
€68,800 x 12.5%	8,600	
Three months ended 31/12/04		
€68,800 x 12.5% x 3/12	2,150	
Year ended 31/12/05		
€68,800 x 12.5%	8,600	
Year ended 31/12/06		
€68,800 x 12.5%	8,600	
		27,950
WDV 31/12/06		40,850
Net proceeds of sale		35,000
Balancing allowance year ended 31/12/07		5,850

13.203.5   Manner of making balancing allowances and charges

In the case of a farming company chargeable to corporation tax, any balancing allowance is added to the other farming capital allowances and the total is deducted as a trading expense in arriving at the Case I farming profit or loss for the relevant accounting period. Correspondingly, any balancing charge on a company is treated as if it were an additional trading receipt to be taking into account in computing the farming profit or loss for corporation tax purposes.

13.203.6   Capital grants

A farming company may receive grants or other subventions towards the capital cost of acquiring machinery or plant for use in its trade. Grants may come through the State, from a board established by statute or from some other public authority or a local authority. Occasionally, a farmer may receive a capital sum from some other person to be applied towards its cost of acquiring machinery or plant.

For capital expenditure on machinery or plant, TCA 1997, s 317 (formerly FA 1986 s 52) provides that, for the purpose of wear and tear allowances, the claimant is not to be regarded as having incurred expenditure in so far as it has been met, directly or indirectly, by the State or by any person other than the claimant. The grant or subsidy must accordingly be deducted from the capital expenditure otherwise incurred with the result that capital allowances are based on the net of grant cost of the machinery or plant.

Where capital expenditure on machinery or plant was incurred in the period from 29 January 1986 to 5 May 1993, FA 1986 s 52 provided for the deduction of grants or other subsidies obtained directly or indirectly from the State, any board established by statute, or any public or local authority, but made no reference to grants or subsidies from non-public sources. If a grant or subsidy was received from a private or commercial source to help meet capital expenditure on machinery or plant incurred between the above-mentioned dates, there was no requirement to deduct such receipt from the expenditure on which the wear and tear allowances were given.

13.204   Milk quotas

13.204.1   Introduction

Arising out of the EU phasing out of milk quota leasing, a scheme for giving capital allowances in respect of expenditure on milk quotas under the National Quota Restructuring Scheme has been introduced with effect from 6 April 2000. The allowances apply to milk quotas purchased from co-operatives or dairies as well as to certain milk quotas purchased by lessees of quotas directly from the lessors of those quotas where the lessee is not connected with the lessor. Under this scheme, expenditure on the purchase of certain milk quotas qualifies for writing-down allowances. Allowances are available only to farmers and the capital expenditure amount on which allowances may be claimed is controlled by the Minister for Agriculture and Food.

TCA 1997 Part 23 Chapter 3 (ss 669A-669F), introduced by FA 2000 s 61, provides for capital allowances in respect of qualifying expenditure incurred on the purchase of qualifying milk quotas. Allowances are on a straight-line basis over a seven year period. Although the legislation relates to expenditure incurred on or after 6 April 2000, it is to come into operation only on such day as the Minister for Finance may by order appoint.

The commencement order was signed on 1 November 2001 but is backdated to 6 April 2000.

13.204.2 Definitions

A *qualifying quota* means:

(a) a milk quota purchased by a person on or after 1 April 2000 under a Milk Quota Restructuring Scheme; or

(b) any other milk quota purchased on or after 1 April 2000.

A *milk quota* means:

(a) the quantity of a milk or other milk products which may be supplied by a person carrying on farming, in the course of a trade of farming land occupied by such person, to a purchaser in a milk quota year without that person being liable to pay a levy; or

(b) the quantity of a milk or other milk products which may be sold or transferred free for direct consumption by a person carrying on farming, in the course of a trade of farming land occupied by such person, in a milk quota year without that person being liable to pay a levy.

Milk means the produce of the milking of one or more cows and *other milk products* includes cream, butter and cheese.

Milk quota year means a twelve month period beginning on 1 April and ending on the following 31 March.

Milk quota restructuring scheme means a scheme introduced by the Minister for Agriculture and Food under the provisions of Article 8(b) of Council Regulation (EEC) No 3950 of 28 December 1992, as amended.

Levy means the levy referred to in Council Regulation (EEC) No 3950 of 28 December 1992, as amended.

Purchaser has the same meaning assigned to it under Council Regulation (EEC) No 3950 of 28 December 1992.

Qualifying expenditure means:

(a) in the case of milk quota to which paragraph (a) of the definition of "qualifying quota" refers, the amount of the capital expenditure incurred on the purchase of that qualifying quota; and

(b) in the case of milk quota to which paragraph (b) of the definition of "qualifying quota" refers, the lesser of—

(i) the amount of capital expenditure incurred on the purchase of that qualifying quota, or

(ii) the amount of capital expenditure which would have been incurred on the purchase of that milk quota if the price paid were set otherwise than by the Minister for Agriculture and Food for the purposes of a Milk Quota Restructuring Scheme in the area in which the land with which that quote is associated is situated.

A *writing-down period* is a period of seven years commencing with the beginning of the chargeable period related to the qualifying expenditure (TCA 1997, s 669B(2)).

The legislative provisions dealing with milk quotas includes important references to chargeable periods and related concepts. In this connection, TCA 1997, s 321(2) explains certain relevant phrases (see **5.101**) as follows:

(a) *chargeable period*: either an accounting period of a company or a year of assessment;

(b) *chargeable period or its basis period*: either the basis period for a year of assessment or the accounting period of a company;

(c) *chargeable period related to expenditure*: the year of assessment in the basis period for which the expenditure is incurred or the accounting period of a company in which the expenditure is incurred;

(d) *chargeable period related to a sale or other event*: the year of assessment in the basis period for which the sale or other event takes place or the accounting period in which the sale or other event occurs.

13.204.3 Writing-down allowances

Where, on or after 6 April 2000, a person incurs qualifying capital expenditure on the purchase of a qualifying quota, writing-down allowances during the writing-down period. The writing-down allowance is determined by the formula:

$$A \times \frac{B}{C}$$

where—

A is the amount of the qualifying expenditure incurred on the purchase of the milk quota,

B is the length of the part of the chargeable period falling within the writing-down period, and

C is the length of the writing-down period (TCA 1997, s 669B(3)).

In other words, the amount of the writing-down allowance is the fraction of the qualifying expenditure incurred represented by the length of the chargeable period (or, as the case may be, the length of the part of that period falling within the writing-down period) for which the allowance is being made over the length of the writing-down period.

No writing-down allowance may be made in respect of any qualifying expenditure to the person who incurred it unless the allowance is to be made to that person in taxing the persons trade of farming (TCA 1997, s 669B(1)).

13.204.4 Effect of sale or lapse of quota

TCA 1997, s 669C deals with a number of events involving a sale of a qualifying quota or the coming to an end of the quota. The tax consequences of the events in question, as they relate to the position of a company, are as follows.

Discontinuance of writing-down allowances

Where a company incurs capital expenditure on the purchase of a qualifying quota and any of the following events occurs within the writing-down period:

(a) the company sells the qualifying quota or so much of the quota as it still owns;

(b) the qualifying quota comes to an end;

(c)   the qualifying quota ceases altogether to be used;

(d)   the company sells part of the qualifying quota and the net proceeds of the sale (in so far as they consist of capital sums) are not less than the amount of the qualifying expenditure remaining unallowed;

no writing-down allowance may be made to the company for the accounting period in which the event occurred or for any subsequent accounting period (TCA 1997, s 669C(1)).

Example 13.204.4.1

In its year ended 31 December 2005, Pastures New Ltd, a farming company specialising in milk production, incurs capital expenditure of €210,000 on the purchase of a milk quota under a milk quota restructuring scheme. On 1 January 2007 the company sells off part of the quota for a sum of €175,000.

The writing-down period in relation to the milk quota purchased is the period of 7 years from 1 January 2005 to 31 December 2011. The writing-down allowance for each of the years ended 31 December 2005 and 31 December 2006 is €210,000 x 12/84 = €30,000. The amount of the expenditure remaining unallowed at the date of sale is €150,000. The amount of the net proceeds of sale is not less than this amount.

Pastures New Ltd is not entitled to claim any writing-down allowances in respect of its expenditure on the milk quota for the year ended 31 December 2007 or for any subsequent period.

See also Example **13.204.4.4** below in relation to the balancing charge arising.

Lapse of quota or outright sale where proceeds less than unallowed expenditure

Where a company incurs qualifying expenditure on the purchase of a qualifying quota and any of the following events occurs within the writing-down period:

(a)   the qualifying quota come to an end;

(b)   the qualifying quota ceases altogether to be used;

(c)   the company sells all of the qualifying quota or so much of it as it still owns and the amount of the net proceeds of the sale (in so far as they consist of capital sums) is less than the amount of the qualifying expenditure remaining unallowed;

a "balancing allowance" is to be made to the company for the accounting period in which the event occurs equal to:

(i)   in the case of (a) or (b), the amount of the qualifying expenditure remaining unallowed; and

(ii)   in the case of (c), the amount of the qualifying expenditure remaining unallowed less the net proceeds of the sale (TCA 1997, s 669C(2)).

Example 13.204.4.2

The position is as in Example **13.204.4.1** except that on 1 January 2007 Pastures New Ltd sells all of its qualifying quota for €140,000. As before, the amount of the expenditure remaining unallowed at the date of sale is €150,000.

Pastures New Ltd is entitled to a balancing allowance of €150,000 - €140,000 = €10,000.

Example 13.204.4.3

The position is as in Example **13.204.4.1** except that on 1 January 2007 the qualifying quota comes to an end. The amount of the expenditure remaining unallowed at the date the quota comes to an end is €150,000.

Pastures New Ltd is entitled to a balancing allowance of €150,000.

Sale of all or part of quota for proceeds in excess of unallowed expenditure

Where a company which has incurred capital expenditure on the purchase of a qualifying quota sells all or any part of that quota and the amount of the net proceeds of the sale (in so far as they consist of capital sums) exceeds the amount of the qualifying expenditure remaining unallowed, if any, a "balancing charge" is to be made on the company for the accounting period in which the sale took place on an amount equal to:

(a) the excess; or

(b) where the amount of the qualifying expenditure remaining unallowed is Nil, the amount of net proceeds of the sale (TCA 1997, s 669C(3)).

Example 13.204.4.4

The position is as in Example **13.204.4.1**. It was seen in that example that Pastures New Ltd ceased to be entitled to any further writing-down allowances after the year ended 31 December 2006.

In addition, a balancing charge is made on the company in an amount of €175,000 - €150,000 = €25,000.

Sale of part of quota for proceeds not in excess of unallowed expenditure

Where a company which has incurred capital expenditure on the purchase of a qualifying quota sells a part of that quota and TCA 1997, s 669C(3) does not apply (ie, where the amount of the sale proceeds does not exceed the amount of the qualifying expenditure remaining unallowed), the amount of any writing-down allowance to be made in respect of that expenditure for the accounting period in which the sale takes place or for any subsequent accounting period is to be an amount determined by:

(a) subtracting the amount of the net proceeds of the sale (in so far as they consist of capital sums) from the amount of the qualifying expenditure remaining unallowed at the time of the sale; and

(b) dividing the result by the number of complete years of the writing-down period which remained at the beginning of the accounting period in which the sale took place,

and so on for any subsequent sales (TCA 1997, s 669C(4)).

Example 13.204.4.5

The position is as in Example **13.204.4.1** except that on 1 January 2007 Pastures New Ltd sells the part of its quota for €125,000. As before, the amount of the expenditure remaining unallowed at the date of sale is €150,000.

The number of complete years of the writing-down period remaining on 1 January 2007 is 5. For the year ended 31 December 2008 and subsequent periods within the writing-down period, Pastures New Ltd is entitled to a writing-down allowance, in respect of its expenditure on the quota, of €150,000 - €125,000/5 = €5,000.

The amount of the capital expenditure remaining unallowed

The "amount of the capital expenditure remaining unallowed" in all of the above situations is the amount of the capital expenditure less the amount of any writing-down allowances made in respect of that expenditure for accounting periods before the accounting period in which the event in question occurred and less also the amount of the net proceeds of any previous sale, by the company which incurred the expenditure, of any part of the qualifying quota acquired by the expenditure in so far as those proceeds consist of capital sums (TCA 1997, s 669C(5)).

The second deduction mentioned above takes account of a case in which a company had previously disposed of a part of its qualifying quota for a capital sum in circumstances where no balancing allowance or charge had been made.

Example 13.204.4.6

The position is as in Example **13.204.4.5** where on 1 January 2007 Pastures New Ltd had sold a part of its quota for €125,000. These proceeds were less than €150,000, the amount of the expenditure remaining unallowed at the date of that sale. For the year ended 31 December 2007 and subsequent periods, Pastures New Ltd was entitled to a writing-down allowance of €5,000.

Assume that on 1 January 2008 Pastures New Ltd sold a further part of its milk quota for €28,000.

The amount of the capital expenditure remaining unallowed on 1 January 2008 is as follows:

	€	€
Cost of qualifying quota		210,000
Less:		
Writing-down allowances for 2 years to 31.12.06 (€30,000 x 2)	60,000	
Writing-down allowances for 2 years to 31.12.08 (€5,000 x 2)	10,000	70,000
		140,000
Proceeds of previous sale		125,000
Expenditure remaining unallowed		15,000
Proceeds of second sale		28,000
Balancing charge (TCA 1997, s 669C(3))		13,000

A balancing allowance may not be made in respect of any expenditure unless a writing-down allowance has been made in respect of that expenditure, or unless such an allowance could have been made in respect of that expenditure but for the happening of the event giving rise to the balancing allowance (TCA 1997, s 669C(6)(a)). Accordingly, a balancing allowance may be made in a situation in which, say, a company sells all of its qualifying quota in the same accounting period in which it bought that quota. Assuming the proceeds of sale are less than the amount of the qualifying expenditure incurred by the company in acquiring the quota, the amount of the balancing allowance will be the amount of the expenditure incurred less the sale proceeds.

The total amount on which a balancing charge is made in respect of any expenditure may not exceed the total writing-down allowances actually made in respect of that expenditure less, if a balancing charge has previously been made in respect of that expenditure, the amount on which that charge was made (TCA 1997, s 669C(6)(b)).

13.204.5 Manner of making allowances and charges

An allowance or charge made on a company in connection with qualifying expenditure incurred by it on the purchase of a qualifying quota is to be made to or on the company in taxing the profits or gains from its trade of farming but only if at any time in the accounting period concerned the qualifying quota in question was used for the purposes of that trade.

Although the legislation providing for capital allowances in respect of qualifying expenditure on a qualifying milk quota is contained in TCA 1997 Part 23 Chapter 3, TCA 1997 Part 9 Chapter 4 is to apply as if the legislation were contained in that chapter. Accordingly, Part 9 Chapter 4 will be relevant in relation to such matters as the manner of making allowances and charges, the treatment of grants, control and "main benefit" sales, and the time at which expenditure is incurred (see **5.1** generally (TCA 1997, s 669E(1)).

In TCA 1997 Part 9 Chapter 4 (as applied by virtue of TCA 1997, s 669E(1) to a qualifying quota), the reference in TCA 1997, s 312(5)(a)(i) to the sum mentioned in paragraph (b) of that subsection is, in the case of a qualifying quota, to be construed as a reference to the amount of the qualifying expenditure on the acquisition of the qualifying quota remaining unallowed, computed in accordance with TCA 1997, s 669C (TCA 1997, s 669E(2)). In TCA 1997, s 312(5)(b), the reference is to the amount of the expenditure "still unallowed" (the tax written down value – see **5.103.3**) but the amount of the capital expenditure remaining unallowed as defined in TCA 1997, s 669C (see **13.204.4** and Example 13.204.4.6 above) has a meaning somewhat different to that in TCA 1997, s 312(5).

13.205 Notional wear and tear allowances

In certain circumstances, a farming company may not actually obtain any wear and tear allowance in respect of machinery or plant for one or more accounting periods during its period of ownership of that machinery or plant. For example, the company may not use the plant at all for the farming trade in an accounting period or it may be that the company only uses the plant for farming for a part of an accounting period so that only part of the normal wear and tear allowance is obtained.

In any such circumstances, the company would, in the absence of any other provision, obtain a benefit to the extent that a higher tax written down value would result so that it would then be entitled to an increased wear and tear allowance in a subsequent accounting period, or would benefit from a higher balancing allowance or a lower balancing charge when the plant is disposed of.

TCA 1997, s 660 applies specifically in the case of a farming trade and requires the writing off of notional or deemed wear and tear allowances for any accounting period during the farming company's period of ownership for which a normal wear and tear allowance is not obtained due to certain specified circumstances. In addition, TCA 1997, s 287 (which is applicable in similar circumstances in relation to all types of trades, including the trade of farming) provides for the writing off of notional wear and tear allowances.

In effect, the provisions of TCA 1997 ss 660 and 287 are more or less identical except that the latter is relevant only in relation to later wear and tear allowances and is supported by TCA 1997, s 296 in relation to the balancing allowance or charge computation, whereas TCA 1997, s 660 affects both later wear and tear allowances and the balancing allowance or charge computation.

The apparent reason for a separate section applicable to farming only was to cover situations where, at one time, certain individuals carrying on the trade of farming were exempted from income tax (up to 1982-83) or where certain individuals could opt to be taxed on a special notional basis, and not on actual farming profits (up to 1979-80). Without TCA 1997, s 660 (formerly FA 1974 s 25), such individuals who later became subject to normal taxation on their farming profits would have benefited from higher amounts of capital expenditure "unallowed" carried forward for use in a period of normal taxation.

Application of TCA 1997, s 660

TCA 1997, s 660(2) requires a notional wear and tear allowance to be written off the cost of any item of farm machinery or plant belonging to a person for every chargeable period which is a "chargeable period to be taken into account for the purpose of this section".

The section is applicable for the purpose of determining whether any, and if so what, wear and tear allowance, balancing allowance or balancing charge is to be given or made for a particular accounting period in respect of any item of machinery or plant. In dealing with this question for a particular accounting period, it is necessary to consider the position for all previous relevant accounting periods, ie those periods from the time the company owning the plant or machinery acquired it, whether or not it was then carrying on its single trade of farming. It is first necessary to ascertain for each previous accounting period whether or not it is a chargeable period to be taken into account for the purpose of TCA 1997, s 660.

TCA 1997, s 660(3) provides that an accounting period is, in relation to a company, a chargeable period to be taken into account for the purpose of this section if it is an accounting period in which the following circumstances existed:

(a)   the machinery or plant belonged to the company in question; and

(b)   (i)   the machinery or plant was not used by that company for the purposes of farming during the accounting period, or

(ii)   farming was not carried on by that company during the accounting period.

The above-described circumstances relate to cases in which no wear and tear allowance was obtained for an accounting period. The circumstances described in (b)(i) and (ii) are capable of being met for plant acquired either currently or at any time in the past.

In determining the wear and tear allowance, balancing allowance or balancing charge for a particular accounting period, TCA 1997, s 660 provides that, for every previous accounting period in which the machinery or plant belonged to the company and which is a chargeable period for the purposes of the section (an accounting period), the company is to be deemed to have obtained a normal wear and tear allowance. To the extent that the wear and tear allowance, if any, actually obtained in respect of the item of machinery or plant for a relevant accounting period falls short of the normal wear and tear allowance for that period, a "notional" wear and tear allowance is deducted from the tax written down value of the machinery or plant.

The amount of the notional allowance to be deducted is the amount by which the wear and tear allowance actually obtained in respect of the item of machinery or plant for the relevant accounting period falls short of the normal wear and tear allowance for that period. If no wear and tear allowance was actually obtained for a relevant accounting period, for example, because the company did not engage in farming activities at any time during the period, the notional allowance to be deducted is an amount equal to the normal wear and tear allowance.

In fact, the phrase "normal wear and tear allowance" comes from TCA 1997, s 287(1) and does not appear in TCA 1997, s 660 although the wording used in the definition of that phrase is very similar to wording used for the same purpose in TCA 1997, s 660. TCA 1997, s 287(1) deems a normal wear and tear allowance to be made in circumstances similar to those described in the previous paragraph. TCA 1997, s 660 provides that there is to be deemed to be made (in the case of a company) such wear and tear allowance or greater wear and tear allowance, if any, in respect of the machinery or plant as would have fallen to be made to the company if, in relation to every previous chargeable period in which the machinery or plant belonged to the company:

(a)   the profits or gains from farming had been chargeable to tax under Case I of Schedule D;

(b)   farming had been carried on by the company ever since the date on which it acquired the machinery or plant;

(c)   the machinery or plant had been used by the company solely for the purposes of farming ever since that date; and

(d)   a proper claim had been duly made by the company for wear and tear allowance in respect of the machinery or plant for each of the previous chargeable periods.

The reference above to "such wear and tear allowance" refers to the case where no wear and tear allowance at all was obtained for the relevant period. The reference to "such greater wear and tear allowance" refers to the case where a wear and tear allowance was obtained but which is one which is less than the normal wear and tear allowance.

Example 13.205.1

Clover Farms Ltd, a farming company, purchased a new machine for €20,000 on 5 July 2006 which was immediately put into use for the farming trade. During the year ended 31 December 2007 the company lent this machine to another party for the seven months 1 April to 31 October 2007. The actual wear and tear allowance for the year ended 31 December 2007 is accordingly reduced to 5/12ths of the normal wear and tear allowance. The machine was used only in the farming trade of Clover Farms Ltd prior to 1 April 2007 and after 31 October 2007.

The year ended 31 December 2007 is a chargeable period for the purposes of TCA 1997, s 660 so that a notional allowance has to be made for that period. The capital allowances computations for the machine in question for the periods are:

	€	€
Cost of machine		20,000
W & T y/e 31/12/06		2,500
WDV 31/12/06		17,500
W & T y/e 31/12/07 (actual):		
€20,000 x 12.5% x 5/12	1,042	
Notional W & T allowance y/e 31/12/07		
(€20,000 x 12.5%) - actual €1,042[1]	1,458	2,500

WDV 31/12/07	15,000
W & T y/e 31/12/08	2,500
WDV 31/12/08[2]	12,500

Notes:

[1] Since the actual wear and tear allowance for the year ended 31 December 2007 is less than the normal 12.5% allowance, TCA 1997, s 660 requires that the excess amount of €1,458 be deducted in the writing down calculation so that it will affect the wear and tear allowance for the last period in which such an allowance is to be made or, as the case may be, to affect the calculation of a balancing allowance or balancing charge.

[2] Assuming that no balancing event (sale etc) occurs first, the €12,500 will be written off as follows:

	€
WDV at 31/12/08	12,500
W & T years ended 31/12/09 to 31/12/13	12,500
WDV 31/12/13	Nil

Example 13.205.2

The position is as in Example **13.205.1** except that the machine in question is sold for €18,000 during the year ended 31 December 2009.

TCA 1997, s 660 applies for the purpose of calculating the resulting balancing allowance or balancing charge. As the notional allowance for the year ended 31 December 2007 has been deducted in arriving at the written down value of €12,500, however, no further adjustment is required so that the balancing allowance/ charge computation is as follows:

	€
WDV 31/12/08	12,500
Sale proceeds	18,000
Excess of sale proceeds over WDV	5,500
Balancing charge year ended 31/12/09[1]	5,500

Notes:

[1] Since the €5,500 excess of sale proceeds over tax written down value (and after the notional allowance) is not greater than the amount of the actual wear and tear allowances obtained (€6,042), there is no restriction to the amount of the balancing charge.

13.3 LAND DEVELOPMENT ACTIVITIES

13.301 Introduction and outline

This section deals with companies engaged in dealing in and developing land. "Land" in this context includes all real property or real estate and therefore refers to buildings as well as to land in the narrow sense. As in the case of any other trade, a company carrying on a trade of dealing in or developing land is chargeable to corporation tax under Schedule D Case I on the profits or gains of its trade. There are, however, particular legislative provisions which identify the types of activity which may be taxed under Case I as part of a trade or business of dealing in or developing land and which deal with the computation of the amount of the taxable profits or gains.

The particular rules governing transactions involving land dealing or development are in addition to the normal Case I rules, and are contained in TCA 1997 Part 22 Ch 1 (ss 639-647) (formerly F(MP)A 1968 Part IV (ss 16-24). TCA 1997, s 639 contains a number of important definitions and other interpretational rules. The meaning of *connected with* is set out in TCA 1997, s 10 and in relation to companies is dealt with in TCA 1997, s 10(6)-(8) (see **2.3**).

TCA 1997, s 640 brings within the charge to tax under Case I certain activities of a business of dealing in or developing land which activities would not otherwise be treated as a trade so as to be taxable under Case I. TCA 1997 ss 641-642 provide certain specific rules for land dealing and development transactions, which are in addition to the normal Case I computational rules. These rules are applied, where relevant, in computing the Case I profits or losses of any trade or business of dealing in or developing land. TCA 1997, s 646 provides for the payment by instalments of the tax on the profits from certain types of sale and leaseback transactions.

TCA 1997 ss 643-645 charge to tax under Case IV certain gains of a capital nature (not otherwise taxable as income) realised from the disposal of land or from certain other property deriving its value from land. In particular, TCA 1997, s 643 taxes as income gains which would otherwise be capital gains, for example gains resulting from the sale of shares in a land dealing or developing company.

The rules in TCA 1997 22 are directed mainly at tax avoidance schemes and have been modified on several occasions to counter further avoidance schemes designed to circumvent the legislation as it developed. In their present form, these rules are derived from FA 1981 ss 28 and 29 which substantially amended the previous legislation. The current rules became effective as regards profits, gains or losses in any period ending after 5 April 1981.

TCA 1997 Part 22 in its present form evolved with not a little difficulty and it is necessary for a full appreciation of this legislation to consider the earlier legislative provisions from which it is derived.

13.302 Legislative background

FA 1935 s 6 was enacted to counter the effect of the decision in *Birch v Delaney* 1 ITR 515. This case concerned a builder who acquired by lease certain plots of ground, each for a term of 500 years and subject to a ground rent, on which he built houses which he disposed of by way of sublease for periods varying from 450 to 495 years in consideration of "fines", comprising lump sums and ground rents. The builder was assessed under Case I of Schedule D for the years 1929-30 to 1932-33 on the footing that the fines received plus the capitalised value of the excess of the ground rents receivable under the subleases over the original ground rents were trading receipts. It was held in the Supreme Court that neither the fines nor the capitalised excess ground rents were taxable as the builder had not disposed of the entire interests, ie the 500 year leases, he had acquired in the lands. It was found that he had only sublet the houses and, to the extent that he derived any income from the development, it could only be taxable under Schedule A in respect of the ownership of land, ie by reference to a notional annual value.

In the wake of this decision, FA 1935 s 6 was enacted to provide for the taxation, under Case I, of the profits or gains from any building operation or from the sale or demise of any lands acquired by the trader with the intention either of selling, demising or developing by any building operation. This section also provided that in the event of a disposal by way of demise or lease, the capitalised value of the rent reserved on the demise should be included as a trading receipt in addition to any fine, premium or other amount actually included in the consideration for the demise.

Substantial changes to this legislation were introduced in FA 1965 to deal with the outcome of *Swaine v VE II* ITR (472). In that case, an individual had purchased certain lands in 1937 at which time he was a builder. Shortly afterwards he ceased building activities and used the lands for farming purposes. It was found that at the time of purchase he had the intention of retiring from the building business and that he did not purchase the lands with the intention of selling or demising them nor with the intention of developing them by the erection or reconstruction of buildings. In 1948, however, having decided to develop the lands and to resume building activities, he built a number of houses and shops on the lands and disposed of them by way of long term subleases in consideration of fines and ground rents.

The Supreme Court held that, because he had not acquired the lands with the intention of selling, demising or developing them, FA 1935 s 6 could not be applied to tax him either on the fines or the capitalised value of the ground rents. In the course of his judgment Walsh J stated:

> Section 6 of the Finance Act 1935 was clearly enacted to deal with gains arising from some speculative building adventures. Prior to the enactment of that section the gains or profits of a speculative builder were assessable under Schedule D as the gains and profits arising from a trade when the building operation was carried out in the course of a trade as such and the builder in selling disposed of the entire of his interest in the land or the site after he had built upon it and the site itself had been a trading asset of the builder. So far as

this latter point is concerned, in practice it meant that to become a trade asset or part of the stock in trade of the builder the land had to be acquired for that purpose.

It was found that the situation in which land was acquired other than as trading stock of a business was not within the scope FA 1935 s 6. The above quoted excerpt highlighted two weaknesses in the 1935 legislation – failure to deal with land disposals other than disposals of the entire interest therein, and failure to deal with cases involving the acquisition of land where there was no intention at the time of acquisition of selling, demising or developing that land.

FA 1965 Third Schedule repealed FA 1935 s 6 and introduced, in ss 41-48 (later ITA 1967 ss 96-103), a new set of rules for taxing profits from dealing in or developing land. Broadly, the 1965 changes imposed a liability to income tax on all profits or gains arising or accruing from any business of dealing in or developing land. The definitions, particularly of "business", contained in this legislation were very wide with the result that real capital gains as well as the types of gain intended to be caught were taxed as income. This unsatisfactory situation was brought to an end with the repeal of the legislation and its substitution by the new rules of F(MP)A 1968 Part IV).

F(MP)A 1968 Part IV, in its original form, introduced rules which extended the charge to tax under Case I to cover the profits from certain activities of a business of dealing in or developing land which would otherwise escape tax for the reasons identified in *Birch v Delaney* and *Swaine v V E*. It also included a provision which taxes as income the profits of a business of dealing in or developing land realised in the course of the winding up of a company.

F(MP)A 1968 Part IV contained additional rules for the computation of the profits taxable under Case I in respect of any trade of dealing in or developing land as well as for any business treated by that legislation as a trade of dealing in or developing land. F(MP)A 1968 s 20 introduced a new charge to tax under Case IV which applied, in certain circumstances, to profits derived from the sale of shares in a company the activities of which included the construction or the securing of the construction of any building. FA 1974 s 63 broadened the scope of F(MP)A 1968 s 20 to include profits on the sale of shares in a company the activities of which include the development or the securing of the development of land, and not only the construction of buildings.

FA 1981 ss 28 and 29 substituted a new F(MP)A 1968 s 17(1) and completely replaced F(MP)A 1968 ss 18 and 20-22 (now TCA 1997 ss 641 and 643-645). The new F(MP)A 1968 s 17(1) (now TCA 1997, s 640(2)) also remedied a weakness in the original subsection which prevented its applying in a case where the full interest in the land, rather than merely a part interest in the land, was disposed of. TCA 1997, s 640 is dealt with in **13.304**.

The substituted F(MP)A 1968 s 18 (TCA 1997, s 641) modifies the normal rules of Case I for calculating the taxable profits of trades of dealing in or developing land, as well as those of activities deemed by TCA 1997, s 640 to be such trades. The new F(MP)A 1968 s 20 (TCA 1997, s 643) substituted entirely new legislation which deals with gains realised directly or indirectly through the sale of shares in companies engaged in construction and land dealing activities, as well as gains realised through selling an interest in a trust or in a partnership.

The present F(MP)A 1968 ss 21-22 (TCA 1997 ss 644-645) contain additional administrative and information rules. They did not replace the former F(MP)A 1968 ss 21-22 since the matters contained in these sections (provisions applying F(MP)A

1968 s 20 to sales of shares in holding companies and provisions dealing with certain arrangements attempting to circumvent the former s 20) are included in the new F(MP)A 1968 s 20 (TCA 1997, s 643).

13.303 Definitions

TCA 1997, s 639 contains definitions of terms and interpretational rules relevant for the purposes of TCA 1997 part 22 and provides that that Part is to apply where there is a business of dealing in or developing land notwithstanding any provisions to the contrary in TCA 1997 Part 4 Ch 8 (ss 96-106) dealing with the taxation of rents and certain other payments (TCA 1997, s 639(3)).

Development in relation to any land means (a) the construction, demolition, extension, alteration or reconstruction of any building on the land or (b) the carrying out of any engineering or other operation in, on, over or under the land to adapt it for materially altered use. The words "developing" and "developed" are to be construed accordingly. Apart from the case where a house, factory or other building is constructed, there is a development of land where, for example, farming land is cleared and drains suitable for housing are laid. If the land is subsequently sold, whether the work is wholly or partly completed, the sale is treated as a sale of land that has been developed even if all the main construction work is subsequently undertaken by another party.

A *disposal of an interest in land* clearly arises where a company sells, gifts or otherwise transfers its entire interest held in that land. It is also treated as arising where the owner of the interest creates any other interest in the same land, apart from the case where a lease of the land is granted on terms which do not require the payment of any fine, premium or similar lump sum. The conveyance or transfer of an interest in land by way of security, eg where the land is mortgaged as security for a loan, is not to be regarded as a disposal.

An option or other right to acquire or dispose of any interest in land is deemed to be an interest in the land. Consequently, if a company owning a freehold interest grants an option to another person on certain terms either to buy the freehold or to take a lease of the land, this is treated as a disposal of an interest in the land by the company.

Example 13.303.1

Ashford Ltd, which owns the freehold interest in certain developed lands, grants a 35 year lease to Bond Ltd in consideration of a premium of €350,000 and an annual rent of €20,000. The grant of the lease constitutes a disposal of an interest in the land for the purposes of TCA 1997 Part 22.

If Ashford Ltd had granted the lease in consideration solely of an annual rent of, say, €150,000, there would have been no disposal within the meaning of TCA 1997 since no payment of a fine, premium or similar sum had been required.

The term *trading stock* is given the same meaning as that in TCA 1997, s 89(1)(a), ie property of any description, whether real or personal, which is either:

(a) property sold in the ordinary course of a trade or which would be so sold if it were mature or if its manufacture, preparation, or construction were complete; or

(b) materials such as are used in the manufacture, preparation, or construction of property such as is sold in the ordinary course of a trade.

In the case of a trade of dealing in or developing land or of a business treated by TCA 1997 Part 22 as such a trade, trading stock accordingly includes any land or interest in land, including buildings on the land, sold, or intended to be sold, in the ordinary course of the trade or business, whether in its existing state or on the completion or part completion of the development. Trading stock also includes building and other materials used or intended to be used in the development of the land and buildings in the course of the trade or business.

Market value, in relation to any property, means the price which that property might reasonably be expected to fetch if sold in the open market.

13.304   Extension of Case I tax charge

TCA 1997, s 640(2) extends the charge to tax under Schedule D Case I to the profits of certain activities undertaken by a business of dealing in or developing land. TCA 1997, s 640(2) charges to tax any activities of such a business which:

(a)   would not otherwise be regarded as carried on in the course of a trade within Case I; but

(b)   would be so regarded if every disposal of an interest in land included among the activities of the business (including a disposal which apart from this provision is a disposal of the full interest in the land which the person carrying on the business had acquired) were treated as fulfilling two conditions:

   (i)   that the disposal was a disposal of the full interest in the land which the person carrying on the business had acquired, and

   (ii)   that the interest had been acquired in the course of the business by that person.

TCA 1997, s 640(2) is intended to cover cases where the only reason why the particular activities would not normally be regarded as carried on in the course of a trade taxable under Case I is that some, or all, of the disposals of interests in land do not meet either or both of the above two conditions. If that is the position, it is necessary to ask whether the disposal of the interest in land is one of a business of dealing in or developing land. If, but only if, it is such a business, it is then assumed that both conditions are met for every disposal in the course of that business (and this assumption is also to be made even where the conditions are met as, otherwise, it would be possible to read the legislation, as happened in the *Hummingbird* case (see below), so as to exclude cases where the conditions are in fact met). If, having made those assumptions, there is no other reason why all the activities of the business should not be treated as being in the course of a trade, the resulting profits are taxable under Case I.

The requirement to assume that each disposal of an interest in land is a disposal of the full interest meets the defect identified in *Birch v Delaney* (see **13.302**). In the light of what is now TCA 1997, s 640(2), it would be indisputable that the kind of disposal by the builder in that case, being a disposal of the houses by way of sublease, must be treated as a trading activity. On the *assumption* that the disposal is of the full interest in the land, ie of the long leasehold interest acquired in that case, the business activity, one of developing land, must be regarded as the carrying on of a trade.

The second assumption that the interest in land was acquired in the course of a business of dealing in or developing land meets the type of argument successfully advanced by the taxpayer in the case of *Swaine v VE*. By *assuming* that the taxpayer had acquired his interest in the lands in the course of a business of developing land (which was not actually the position in that case), there is no remaining reason why his activity of building and selling houses is not to be regarded as carried on in the course of a trade.

It will have been seen that TCA 1997, s 640(2) does not operate unless the activities in question are undertaken in the course of a business of dealing in or developing land. The term "business" is not defined in the Tax Acts. In *IRC v Marine Steam Turbine* 12 TC 174, "business" was defined by Rowlatt J as "an active occupation ... continuously carried on" but, in *South Behar Railway Co* 12 TC 657, he qualified this by pointing out that "when I said business involved activity, I merely meant something you describe by way of an active verb – something positive". In the latter case, Lord Simons noted that the term "business" implied a "repetition of acts" and the references to continuity and repetition above would suggest that an isolated transaction would not constitute a business as such.

In *Rolls v Miller* [1884] 27 Ch D 71, a useful definition of "business" (cited by Sheridan J in the Irish case *AE v Revenue Commissioners* (V) ITR (686) was provided by Lindley J when he stated that "the word [business] means almost anything which is an occupation, as distinguished from a pleasure – anything which is an occupation or duty which requires attention is a business". Thus, the term "business" appears to be capable of including all types of activity carried out on a commercial basis (as distinct from being carried on in a personal or private capacity). For example, a person who has bought a house as a residence, and who carries out work on extending or adapting it and who later sells it on the occasion of purchasing a new residence, could not normally be regarded as disposing of the house in the course of a business. If, however, the house is converted into flats which are then rented out, whether or not involving any fine or premium, this activity would normally be regarded as a business activity.

In the case of a company, this approach needs to be adapted somewhat since a company cannot act in a personal capacity but, instead, generally acts for the benefit of its shareholders. In *American Leaf Blending Co Sdn Bhd v Director of Inland Revenue* [1978] STC 561, Lord Diplock said:

> In the case of a private individual it may well be that the mere receipt of rents from property that he owns raises no presumption that he is carrying on a business. In contrast, in their Lordships' view, in the case of a company incorporated for the purpose of making profits for its shareholders any gainful use to which it puts any of its assets prima facie amounts to the carrying on of a business.

The case of *Spa Estates v OhArgáin* [HC, 1975] illustrates the significance of continuity in relation to the meaning of "business". In that case, a company acquired land for development with a view to its eventual disposal. However, the land was sold off before development commenced. In that connection, Kenny said:

> It is an oversimplification to say that Spa was formed to carry on business as builders. The trade which the directors of Spa intended to carry on was that of developing lands, building houses on them and selling houses. The purchase of the lands and the applications for planning permission seem to me to have been acts preparatory to the carrying on of a trade and not to be evidence that a trade was being carried on. This view is supported by the decision in *The Birmingham District Cattle By-Products Co Ltd v IRC* 12 TC 92. It is true that houses cannot be sold without selling the lands on which the houses are situated. But when no development has been done and no houses have been built, the purchase of the land

for the purpose of building does not involve the consequence that the taxpayer was dealing in land. In my view, the only possible conclusion on the facts of this case was that Spa never commenced to carry on the trade of developing lands, building houses on them and selling the houses nor did they commence the business of dealing in land.

In the UK case *Shadford v Fairweather Ltd* 43 TC 291, on the other hand, where the facts were somewhat similar, the taxpayer company's original intention was to exploit developed land in the most profitable manner possible but it had not decided whether to proceed by way of lease or by way of sale. In the absence of a definite intention to hold the land as an investment, it was held that the company had undertaken an adventure in the nature of trade.

While a situation such as arose in the *Spa* case, involving an isolated transaction which would be unlikely to constitute a "business of dealing", would probably be outside the scope of TCA 1997, s 640, it would probably be caught by TCA 1997, s 643, assuming the land was situated in Ireland. The charge under TCA 1997, s 640 is more likely to apply in the case of a person who would have acquired land with no intention of trading but who subsequently disposes of it in a business-like way, for example by obtaining planning permission and selling off the land in smaller and more marketable units.

As to whether a particular business is one of dealing in or developing land is one to be considered in the light of the relevant facts. Even in a case where the business involves the construction of buildings or some other form of development, it may still be possible to argue that the activities carried out are done in the course of a business of investing in property or as part of an entirely different type of business, eg manufacturing. In other words, while there may be an activity of development carried out in the course of business, it remains necessary to determine whether the business is one of dealing in or developing land.

Example 13.304.1

Ampere Ltd, a manufacturing company, owns a house in which its managing director has resided for many years. On his retirement, the company takes the decision to redevelop the house as an office block with a view to disposing of it in the manner best calculated to maximise profits. On completion of the redevelopment, the company grants a 99 year lease of the property to an insurance company in consideration for a lump sum of €700,000 and a nominal rent. Without TCA 1997, s 640(2), the profits realised by Ampere Ltd from the development and sublease would not be taxable as income under Case I, because:

(a)   Ampere Ltd had not acquired its freehold interest in the house as trading stock of any trade or business of dealing in or developing land; and

(b)   it did not dispose of its full freehold interest when granting the 99 year lease.

However, it is fairly clear that the redevelopment and sublease of the house was undertaken as part of a "business" of developing land and it is reasonable to suppose that the company has set about the development in an organised way. Ampere Ltd might argue that any "business" involved in the redevelopment and sublease was not the business of dealing in or developing land, but was merely the optimum means of realising an asset no longer required in its trade.

If, as seems reasonable, it is accepted that the company has been involved in a business of developing land, the relevant question then is whether the granting of the 99 year lease is to be regarded as an activity carried on in the course of a trade. If both of the assumptions (conditions (i) and (ii) in (b) above) required by TCA 1997, s 640(2) are made, there is a strong case for the view that the development and sublease of the property must be treated as carried on in the course of a trade. That being the case, Ampere Ltd would be taxable under Case I on its profits derived from the redevelopment and sublease.

It is only necessary to consider TCA 1997, s 640(2) where the activities of dealing in or developing land are not all capable of being treated as a trade or as an adventure in the nature of trade under the ordinary meanings of those terms (see **3.103**). In any case in which land or an interest in land is acquired with the intention of selling it or developing it with a view to sale, and where the sale involves the disposal of the full interest acquired in the land, the activity would normally be treated as a trade without the need to invoke TCA 1997, s 640.

On the other hand, the fact that an interest in land, whether the full interest held or an interest derived from the full interest, is sold in the course of a business of dealing in or developing land does not necessarily mean that the profit is taxable under Case I. If the necessary business requirement is met and the two conditions required by TCA 1997, s 640(2) are assumed to be met, it is then necessary to decide whether on the basis of all of the facts of the case the sale of the interest in land may be regarded as a transaction in the course of a trade. Unless that is the case, there can be no charge to tax under Case I.

Example 13.304.2

The position is as in Example **13.304.1** except that Ampere Ltd redeveloped the house as offices with the intention of using some offices for its business and letting other offices on short leases. After a few years, the company acquired new offices and sold the redeveloped building at a profit.

On this basis, the redevelopment of the house can properly be regarded as a business activity. It is assumed that the redevelopment undertaken is part of a business of developing land. Making the two assumptions required by TCA 1997, s 640(2), the relevant question is whether the profit realised on the eventual sale of the building is properly taxable under Case I as the profits of a trade?

It remains necessary to ask whether the underlying transactions can be regarded as carried out in the course of a trade or as an adventure in the nature of trade. On the basis of the facts outlined above, Ampere Ltd can make the case that the redevelopment of the property was carried out with the intention partly of providing a fixed asset (company offices) and partly as a property investment. If there was no intention to develop the house for resale, TCA 1997, s 640 could not then operate to bring the profit realised on disposal within the charge to tax under Case I.

In *Mara v Hummingbird Ltd* II ITR (667), which was decided before F(MP)A 1968 s 17 was amended by FA 1981 s 28 (to what is now TCA 1997, s 640), a company had acquired property intending to develop it and subsequently to let it as a long-term investment. Shortly after commencing development, however, it received an attractive offer resulting in the sale of the property at a substantial profit. It was held in the Supreme Court that the acquisition and sale of the property did not, on general principles, represent an "adventure in the nature of trade".

Mr Justice Kenny stated that the activity which is brought within the tax net by the section is one in which the taxpayer has disposed of a lesser interest than he had whereas in the case before him the sale was of the whole of the taxpayer's interest in the land so that the section did not apply to the sale of that land. To deal with that point, what is now TCA 1997, s 640 specifically provides that the two conditions (see (b)(i), (ii) above) are to be treated as being satisfied even where the disposal by the person carrying on the business of dealing in or developing land is in fact a disposal of the full interest, as well as where it is the disposal of a lesser interest and is then *deemed* to be a disposal of the full interest.

Normally, the question of whether or not there is a "dealing in land" or a "development of land" is clear and these terms do not require any definition. TCA 1997, s 640(1) makes it clear that, for the purposes of TCA 1997, s 640, a dealing in land is regarded as taking place in any case where a person, having an interest in any land, disposes either of that interest or of any interest derived from it. This applies whether the interest disposed of relates to the whole or any part of the land in which the interest is held. Thus, for example, if a company takes a 35 year leasehold interest in land, it can be treated as dealing in that land either where it disposes of the lease or where it grants a sublease for, say, 15 years, out of the lease.

TCA 1997, s 640(1) also provides that any person who secures the development of any land can be treated for the purposes of the provision as if he developed the land himself. Consequently, if a company secures the development of land as part of the activity of a business not otherwise treated as a trade within Case I, TCA 1997, s 640(2) can operate, assuming all of the other necessary conditions apply, to charge to tax under Case I the profit realised by the company from securing the development. Thus, property developers generally, and not just speculative builders, would be brought within the scope of TCA 1997, s 640.

It is arguable that TCA 1997, s 640(2) applies only in the case of a business of developing property which is undertaken with a view to disposal at a profit. It was held in the *Hummingbird* case that the acquisition and sale of the property did not, on general principles, represent an adventure in the nature of trade. The Revenue had contended that F(MP)A 1968 s 17 (before it was amended – in its amended form now TCA 1997, s 640) applied to transactions which would be regarded as trading transactions but for the fact that the interest in the land disposed of had not been acquired with a view to its disposal at a profit (a point which did not need to be decided on in view of the conclusion that the section as it then stood only applied to disposals of less than the full interest in the land). TCA 1997, s 640(2)(a), however, only applies where the disposal in question is "included amount" the activities of a business of dealing in or developing land; the business of the company in the *Hummingbird* case was the development of the property for investment purposes and the sale of the property was an unanticipated event and not a part of that business.

13.305 Disposals of land in course of winding up

A trade carried on by a company is normally regarded as ceasing when the company goes into liquidation, whether compulsorily due to the company's being insolvent or voluntarily by a resolution of its shareholders. While it is possible in certain circumstances for a liquidator to be held to be trading, this is unusual and, generally, the liquidator is doing no more than realising the assets of the company to the best possible advantage. It was formerly possible, therefore, for the profits of a trade of dealing in or developing land to escape a charge to tax if the relevant disposal did not take place until after a company had gone into liquidation.

TCA 1997, s 640(3) deals with this situation by providing that where an interest in land is disposed of in the course of the winding up of a company, the company is deemed for the purposes of TCA 1997, s 640 not to have ceased to carry on the trade or business which it carried on before the commencement of the winding up. The trade or business is deemed to continue until the completion of the last disposal of an interest in land by the liquidator. It requires the question whether any such disposal was made in the course of the business of dealing in or developing land to be determined without regard to the fact that the company is being wound up. This position applies whether the business is itself a trade or is deemed by TCA 1997, s 640(2) to be a trade.

It follows that in any case where tax would have been charged either under the normal rules of Case I, or by those rules as extended by the provisions of TCA 1997, s 640(2), the charge to tax cannot be avoided by arranging for the company to go into liquidation. However, it remains necessary to ask the question as to whether that business was a trade or, if not, whether it would be regarded as a trade if the two conditions of TCA 1997, s 640(2) are assumed to be met.

13.306 Computation of taxable profits

13.306.1 Introduction

Particular rules for the computation, under Schedule D Case I, of taxable profits or allowable losses of a business of dealing in or developing land are contained in TCA 1997, s 641. These rules apply whether the business is itself a trade within Case I or is deemed by TCA 1997, s 640 to be a such a trade. Two further rules are provided by TCA 1997, s 642 and these are relevant in the case of any transfer of an interest in land between the person carrying on the trade or business and any other person connected with him. Otherwise, the normal computational rules of Case I apply in computing profits and losses for tax purposes in these cases.

TCA 1997, s 641(2) contains the rules (additional to those applying for Case I purposes generally) which are likely to be relevant in the general run of cases involving a business of dealing in or developing land, while anti-avoidance measures (discussed in **13.307**) are included in TCA 1997, s 641(3), (4) which are intended to prevent certain artificial deductions in computing profits and losses. The following matters, dealt with mainly in TCA 1997 ss 641(2) and 642, are now considered:

(a) trading receipts, including treatment of lease premiums;

(b) trading stock, its acquisition and retention; and

(c) valuation of trading stock after disposal of part of interest in land.

13.306.2 Trading receipts

Trading receipts brought into the computation of profits under Case I must include the full consideration received in respect of every disposal of an interest in land made in the course of the trade or, as the case may be, in carrying on the activities treated by TCA 1997, s 640 as a trade or part of a trade. To the extent that the consideration for any disposal includes rent or any part of a lease premium or other sum treated as rent by TCA 1997, s 98 (see **3.202.13**), however, that rent or deemed rent must be excluded in the Case I computation. Where part of a premium, or other sum treated as a premium, is taxable as rent under TCA 1997, s 98, the balance of the premium or other sum excluded from the Case V income by TCA 1997, s 98(1) must be included as a trading receipt (TCA 1997, s 641(2)(a)).

Example 13.306.2.1

Bauer Ltd, a property development company, grants a 35 year lease of a building that it has developed in consideration of a premium of €200,000 and an annual rent of €15,000. In accordance with TCA 1997, s 641(2)(a), the company includes an amount of €136,000 as a trading receipt in its Case I computation, calculated as follows:

	€
Premium on grant of lease	200,000

Less: amount treated as rent by TCA 1997, s 98(1):

$$€200,000 \times \frac{51-35}{50} =$$ | 64,000

Trading receipt	136,000

Note:

The annual rent excluded from the Case I computation is taxable under Case V, as well as the amount of €64,000 deducted above.

In the case of a company subject to tax under Case I in respect of its trade or business of dealing in or developing land and which disposes of an interest in land at less than its market value to a person connected with it, it is necessary to substitute that market value for the actual price paid for the purpose of computing the profit assessable under Case I. Where the disposal to the connected person is by way of gift, a trading receipt in the amount of the market value must be brought into the Case I computation. This market value rule is not, however, applied where the person connected with the vendor also carries on a trade or business of dealing in or developing land and the actual purchase price paid may be debited in computing that person's own profit or loss for the purposes of Case I (TCA 1997, s 642(2)).

Prior to 6 April 1981, it was necessary for a person carrying on a business of dealing in or developing land to include as a trading receipt the capitalised value of any rents or ground rents created on a sublease. Under current legislation, any consideration received by the trader for the granting of any right in relation to the development of any land must be included as a trading receipt (TCA 1997, s 641(2)(e)). Thus, for example, if instead of developing land owned by it, a company obtains valuable consideration for disposing of its right to develop the land, it will not escape a charge to tax under Case I in respect of that consideration.

13.306.3　Trading stock

Where a company carrying on a taxable trade or business has acquired an interest in land before the trade or business commenced, or where it has acquired land otherwise than as trading stock and appropriates it as trading stock at a later time, the interest in land must be brought into the accounts as trading stock at an assumed cost equal to its market value at the time of that appropriation (TCA 1997, s 641(2)(d)). If land, or an interest in land, is acquired otherwise than for a consideration in money or money's worth, its cost as trading stock is treated as being equal to its market value at the time of its acquisition or, if later, at the time it is appropriated as trading stock (TCA 1997, s 641(2)(c)).

Where a company carrying on a taxable trade or business purchases any interest in land, at a price greater than the market value of that interest, from another person with whom it is connected, that interest is treated as trading stock acquired at its market value

(TCA 1997, s 642(1)). The market value rule is not applied, however, where the sale consideration is brought into the vendor's Case I computation as a trading receipt of a business of dealing in or developing land. In the case of an acquisition at less than market value, the actual price paid in the transaction must be used as the cost of the trading stock acquired and the purchaser is not entitled to substitute the market value.

Example 13.306.3.1

In 2002, Mr Fedor Golovin purchased the freehold interest in a house which he converted into offices to be used in his travel agency business. The combined cost of acquisition and conversion was €90,000. On 21 December 2007, Mr Golovin transferred his business to another location and sold the original premises for €500,000 to Golovin Enterprises Ltd, a company controlled by him and carrying on a building trade. At that time the market value of the premises was €360,000.

Golovin Enterprises Ltd acquired the premises with the purpose of demolishing them and building retail shop premises for resale.

As Golovin Enterprises Ltd is controlled by Mr Golovin, he is connected with the company. Golovin Enterprises Ltd must therefore bring in the premises acquired as trading stock at the market value of €360,000, rather than at €500,000, as required by TCA 1997, s 642(1).

An interest in land acquired as trading stock, or appropriated as trading stock subsequent to its acquisition, continues to be regarded as trading stock until it is fully disposed of in the course of the trade or business of dealing in or developing land or, if earlier, when the trade or business is permanently discontinued (TCA 1997, s 641(2)(b)). Thus, if a company carrying on that trade or business withdraws land or any interest in land from its trading stock, applies it for some non-trading purpose and then sells it at a later date while the trade or business continues, it must bring in the full sale proceeds realised as a trading receipt. Where the trade is discontinued before the land is fully disposed of, the land must be included in the closing trading stock valuation on the date of the discontinuance of the trade (TCA 1997, s 89(2)).

In the case of a trade or business of dealing in or developing land carried on by a company which, under the rule of TCA 1997, s 640(3), is regarded as still continuing notwithstanding that the company is being wound up (see **13.305**), TCA 1997, s 641(2)(b) treats all unsold interests in land acquired as trading stock as continuing to be trading stock until finally disposed of by the liquidator.

13.306.4 Valuation of retained interest

Where a company carrying on a trade or business disposes of an interest in land that has been acquired or appropriated as trading stock, but does not dispose of the entire interest, the interest that is retained continues to be trading stock of the business. For example, if a building company which has developed houses on land held freehold demises them on long leases under which it remains entitled to ground rents, the freehold interest in the land retained must continue to be included at an appropriate value.

TCA 1997, s 641 does not provide any rule for valuing the interest retained (unlike the former s 18 which did provide such a rule). It is therefore necessary to apply the normal Case I rules for valuing the interest retained as trading stock at the lower of cost or net realisable value at the balance sheet date. In determining the "cost" of the interest retained for this purpose, the formula (reminiscent of the part disposal formula for capital gains tax) introduced in the case of *John Emery & Sons v IRC* [1937] AC 91, 20

TC 213 and first applied in *Hughes v BC Utting & Co Ltd* [1939] 2 All ER 126, 23 TC 174 is used:

$$\text{"cost" of interest retained} \, \frac{A}{A+B} \times D$$

"cost" of interest retained

where—

A =   the market value of the interest retained at the date the inferior interest is created;

B =   the consideration received for the part of the interest in land disposed of;

D =   the cost to the trader of the entire interest acquired including the development costs allocated to it.

Example 13.306.4.1

Mondale Developments Ltd, a building company, acquired the freehold interest in a plot of land for €210,000 and built offices on it at a cost of €430,000. The company granted a 99 year lease of the offices for a lump sum of €700,000 and the right to receive an annual rent of €12,000. The market value of the rent reserved at the time the lease was granted is €100,000.

The taxable profit on the development of the offices and their disposal by way of the 99 year lease is calculated as follows:

	€	€
Consideration for 99 year lease		700,000
Add: trading stock – value of interest retained:		
$€640,000 \times \dfrac{100,000}{100,000+700,000} =$		80,000
		780,000
Less:		
Cost of development		
Site cost	210,000	
Building costs	430,000	
		640,000
Taxable profit		140,000

Note:

[1]   The freehold interest retained must continue to be brought forward as trading stock at its "cost" of €80,000 (or at net realisable value, if lower, at any balance sheet date) as long as the company's building trade continues.

13.307   Prevention of certain deductions

TCA 1997, s 641(3), (4) contain anti-avoidance rules intended to prevent artificial deductions in the computation of profits or losses for Schedule D Case I purposes in the case of a trade or business of dealing in or developing land. TCA 1997, s 641(3) provides that no account is to be taken in the Case I computation of any sum (the "relevant sum") which is paid or payable at any time by the trader as consideration for the forfeiture or surrender of the right of any person to an annuity or other annual payment, unless that payment arises under a testamentary disposition (eg, a will or an intestacy) or arises under a liability incurred for:

(a) valuable and sufficient consideration all of which is treated as taxable income of the person to whom the payment is made; or

(b) consideration given to a person who

    (i) has not at any time carried on a business of dealing in or developing land which is, or is to be regarded as, a trade or a part of a trade; and

    (ii) is not, and was not at any time, connected with any of the following persons:

        (I) the trader,

        (II) a person who is, or was at any time, connected with the trader, or

        (III) any other person who, in the course of a business of dealing in or developing land which is or is regarded as a trade or part of a trade, holds or held an interest in land upon which the annuity or other annual payment was charged or reserved.

Alternatively, a deduction will be allowed where the relevant sum must be brought into account in the recipient's computation of tax in respect of the profits or gains of a trade of dealing in or developing land.

Without such a provision, it would be possible for a trader to claim a deduction as a business expense for the payment of a lump sum to another person in consideration for the forfeiture of that person's right to an annuity in circumstances where the annuity had been charged on some artificial or non-arm's length basis. TCA 1997, s 641(3) prevents a deduction being made in these circumstances.

A similar measure is provided for in TCA 1997, s 641(4) to deal with the case where a person other than the trader pays a sum to another person as consideration for that person's forfeiting or surrendering his right to an annuity or other annual payment. This provision applies where:

(a) the trader has incurred any expenditure ("the cost") in acquiring any interest in land upon which the annuity or other annual payment in question has been reserved or charged; and

(b) the sum paid for the forfeiture or surrender is not a sum which the person to whom it is payable must bring into account as a trading receipt in computing the Case I profits of his trade or business of dealing in or developing land.

Where these circumstances apply, TCA 1997, s 641(4) treats the trader as if the cost of acquiring the interest in land subject to the annuity or other annual payment is equal to the cost he would have incurred if the right to the payment had not been forfeited or surrendered. Further, the excess of the cost of the interest in land over what the cost would have been, if the right had not been forfeited or surrendered, has to be dealt with under TCA 1997, s 641(3) as if payable by the trader as consideration for the forfeiture or surrender of the right so that it is not deductible in the Case I computation.

Example 13.307.1

Acme Construction Ltd proposes to purchase an interest in land having a market value of €500,000 and on which an annuity with a capitalised value of €100,000 is charged. In the meantime, Alton Ltd, an associated company of Acme Construction Ltd, pays the annuitant

€110,000 for giving up his right to the annuity charged on the land. Acme Construction Ltd buys the land for €500,000.

The acquisition cost to Acme Construction Ltd must be taken to be the amount it would have paid if the right to the annuity had not been surrendered; the allowable cost is therefore €500,000 – €100,000 = €400,000.

In addition, the excess of the actual price paid, €100,000, is treated as an amount paid by Acme Construction Ltd in consideration of the surrender of the annuity by the annuitant so that the company is not entitled to deduct that amount in computing its profits assessable under Case I, unless the annuity surrendered satisfies one of the conditions in **13.307** above, ie it arose under a testamentary disposition, or under a liability incurred for valuable and sufficient consideration etc.

13.308   Postponement of tax: certain leasebacks

TCA 1997, s 647 entitles a company carrying on a trade of dealing in or developing land to pay by instalments over a ten year period a part of the corporation tax in respect of the profits from certain types of sale and leaseback transactions. The instalment arrangement may be availed of only where all of the following conditions, specified in TCA 1997, s 646(2), are satisfied:

(a)   the disposal by the company is made in the course of its trade and consists of the full interest in the land previously acquired by it;

(b)   the purchaser is not a person connected with the company;

(c)   the vendor's right to the leaseback must be contained in the terms of the disposition;

(d)   a sum representing the value of the company's right to be granted a lease falls to be taken into account as consideration for the disposal in computing the profits or gains of the trade;

(e)   the leaseback must actually be granted by the purchaser to the vendor within six months after the date of the sale;

(f)   the company retains the leasehold interest acquired by it from the purchaser; and

(g)   the company does not dispose of any interest derived from that leasehold interest (eg, by granting a sublease), whether of the whole or of any part of the land concerned.

The tax payable by instalments is not that payable on the total profit from the sale and leaseback transaction, but rather the additional tax payable resulting from the inclusion in the sale consideration of the sum representing the value of the company's right to a leaseback. The remaining corporation tax for the accounting period concerned is payable on its normal due date.

An amount of corporation tax equal to 90% of the additional tax attributable to the vendor's right to the leaseback is postponed. The tax postponed is payable in nine equal instalments at yearly intervals commencing on the expiration of twelve months from the date on which the corporation tax on the profits of the trade would normally be payable in full. In the context of the current rules relating to the due date for payment of corporation tax, including preliminary tax (see **15.103.2** and **15.106**), it is not clear what is to be regarded as the date on which corporation tax would normally be payable. The relevant legislation does not set down what is to be the amount of the first instalment (but rather what is the minimum amount payable to avoid certain adverse consequences).

Example 13.308.1

Magellan Ltd, a property development company, purchases a site freehold and arranges for a builder to erect a block of apartments on the site for a total cost of €750,000. On completion, in the year ended 31 December 2006, Magellan Ltd disposes of the freehold interest in the developed property to an insurance company for a cash payment of €850,000 plus the right to be granted a 35 year lease at an annual rent of €40,000 for the first 7 years (with 5 year rent reviews on an arm's length basis thereafter). The insurance company grants the 35 year lease to Magellan Ltd within the six-month limit.

The company's taxable profits, after capital allowances, for the year ended 31 December 2006 are €150,000 after crediting the sale price of €850,000, but before including the value of the company's right to the leaseback as a trading receipt. This right is valued at €200,000, thereby increasing the final Case I amount for the period to €350,000. The corporation tax liability of Magellan Ltd for the period is determined on the bases of including and excluding the additional €200,000 as follows:

	Including €200,000	*Excluding* €200,000
	€	€
Case I profits	350,000	150,000
Other income, say	10,000	10,000
	360,000	160,000
Deductions in arriving at total income, say	95,000	95,000
	265,000	65,000
Corporation tax @ 16%	42,400	10,400

Tax postponed: 90% x (€42,400 - €10,400) = €28,800

Accordingly, the company's corporation tax liability for the year ended 31 December 2006 is payable on the following dates (and ignoring the issue relating to the first instalment of preliminary tax referred to above):

	€	€
21 June 2007 (normal due date):		
Liability for period	42,400	
Less: tax postponed	28,800	
		13,600
21 June 2008 - €28,800 x 1/9 (= €3,200)		3,200
Eight further instalments on 21 June each year subsequently		
€3,200 x 8		25,600
		42,400

TCA 1997, s 646(4) provides that, after there has been any postponement of tax under the section, the balance of the income tax still unpaid becomes due and payable forthwith if any of the following events occurs:

(a) the company ceases to retain the leasehold interest acquired by it;

(b) as regards the whole or any part of the land, the company disposes of any interest derived from that leasehold interest; or

(c) the company commences to be would up.

13.309   Gains of a capital nature

13.309.1   General

Certain gains of a capital nature realised on the disposal of land, or of other property deriving its value from land, are charged to tax as income under TCA 1997, s 643. The resulting charge to corporation tax is under Schedule D Case IV and is made on a company, whether or not resident in the State, where all or any part of the land is situated in the State, but subject to three tests as outlined below.

The Case IV charge applies where the land or any part of the land which is the subject of the disposal is situated in the State, but does apply in the case of a disposal of any foreign property that derives its value from land in the State (TCA 1997, s 643(3), (17)).

The section is directed at persons dealing in or developing land who arrange their activities with a view to realising a gain of a capital nature instead of a profit which would be taxable as income under Case I; transactions involving the realisation of genuine capital gains are not caught. While the legislation refers to direct disposals, it is aimed primarily at indirect disposals of land, since a direct disposal would normally come within the scope of Case I as extended by the rules of TCA 1997, s 640 (see **13.304**). The legislation is of particular relevance in cases where control over land in the State changes hands through the disposal of shares in companies or other property deriving their value from the land.

The three tests (considered in more detail below), subject to which TCA 1997, s 643 applies, are as follows:

(a)   land must have been acquired, held or developed for one of three specified purposes (see below), or property deriving its value from land must have been acquired with the object of realising a gain from a disposal of the land (the "purpose" test);

(b)   a gain of a capital nature must have been obtained from a disposal of land (the "disposal" test); and

(c)   the person who "obtains" the gain must be either the person who acquired, held or developed the land or a person connected with that person or, in the case of an arrangement or scheme involving the land, a person concerned in the arrangement or scheme (the "obtained" test).

For these purposes "land" is defined as including any interest in land and any reference to land includes a reference to all or any part of the land. TCA 1997, s 643(1) provide that *property deriving its value from land* includes:

(a)   any shareholding in a company, any partnership interest, or any interest in settled property deriving its value, or the greater part of its value, directly or indirectly, from land; and

(b)   any option, consent or embargo affecting the disposition of land.

A shareholding in a company, a partnership interest or an interest in settled property is accordingly treated as property deriving its value from land if more than 50% of its value is attributable to land. In determining whether and to what extent the value of any property or right is derived from land or any other property or right, value may be traced through any number of companies, partnerships and trusts; and the property held by any company, partnership or trust is to be attributed to its shareholders, partners or beneficiaries at each stage in whatever manner is considered just and reasonable (TCA 1997, s 643(4)).

There may be considerable difficulty in deciding what is the correct approach in ascertaining the extent to which shares in a company derive their value from land. Where the assets of a company wholly or mainly comprise land there will be no difficulty and, due to the nature of their businesses, the matter may be relatively straightforward in many property or land development companies. As suggested in **3.107.1**, difficulties may arise where company indebtedness has to be taken into account and it is necessary to decide how that indebtedness is to be attributed to a company's assets or whether any such attribution is to be made. For companies whose shares are most appropriately valued on a going concern basis, the extent to which those shares are derived from any underlying land may be difficult to ascertain. In practice, however, in the cases of companies for which the provisions of TCA 1997, s 643 are relevant, it is much more likely that the value of their shares is directly attributable to land held by them.

13.309.2   The three tests

The three tests, each one of which must be satisfied before tax can be charged under Case IV as a result of TCA 1997, s 643, have already been referred to above, as the purpose test, the transaction test and the person test. These are now considered individually.

The purpose test

The purpose test, provided for in TCA 1997, s 643(3), is satisfied in relation to the disposal of any land if any of the following conditions is met:

(a)   the land, or any property deriving its value from land, was acquired with the sole or main object of realising a gain from disposing of the land;

(b)   the land was held as trading stock;

(c)   the land was developed by a company with the sole or main object of realising a gain from disposing of the land when developed.

The effect of condition (a) is that if land or property deriving its value from land was acquired for another purpose, for example for farming, and the decision to dispose of the land to realise a gain was made later, TCA 1997, s 643 cannot be applied. However, irrespective of the intention at the time of acquisition, the purpose test is satisfied under condition (b) if the land is subsequently appropriated as trading stock before the disposal or, under condition (c) if the land is developed by a company for the purpose of realising a gain from the disposal of the land when developed.

Condition (c) is necessary as it might otherwise be possible to avoid the effect of TCA 1997, s 643 by a disposal made by way of selling shares in the company which developed the land (see the "transaction" test below). If the land or the shares in the company had been acquired originally without any object of realising a gain from the disposal of the land, the purpose test would not have been satisfied under condition (a); alternatively, the company itself might be an investment company not holding the land as trading stock so as to meet condition (b).

The disposal test

The disposal test is satisfied if there is a disposal of land and that disposal results in the obtaining of a gain of a capital nature by any person.

There is a *disposal of land* if either the property in the land or control over the land is effectually disposed of (TCA 1997, s 643(5)). This is regarded as taking place whether it occurs as a result of either one or more transactions or any arrangement or scheme. The transactions, arrangement or scheme may concern the land itself or any property deriving its value from the land in question. Any number of transactions may be regarded as constituting a single arrangement or scheme if a common purpose is discerned in them, or if there is other sufficient evidence of a common purpose (TCA 1997, s 643(6)(b)).

Accordingly, a disposal of land is regarded as taking place not only if the land or any interest in the land is sold or otherwise disposed of, but also if there is an effective transfer of control over the land as a result of any transaction, arrangement or scheme concerning property deriving its value from the land. For example, if a person holds shares in a company which derive the greater part of their value from an interest in land held by the company, and if these shares give the holder "control" (as defined TCA 1997, s 432 – see **2.401**) of the company, any disposal of the shareholding is treated as a disposal of the land. The same position would apply to the disposal of the controlling interest in a partnership owning land, provided that the interest in the partnership is property deriving its value from land (ie any land and not just the land the subject of the particular tax charge considered here).

In fact, a disposal of land could also be regarded as taking place if the majority shareholder in a landowning company sells sufficient of his shares to reduce his holding to a point where he can no longer exercise control of the company. For example, if Mr Alport owns 51% of the controlling shares in Alport Ltd and Mr Clyde owns 49%, a sale by Mr Alport to Mr Clyde of 1.1% of these shares would transfer control over the land and, therefore, amount to a disposal of the land. On the other hand, if Mr Alport owned 73% and Mr Clyde owned 27%, a sale by Mr Alport to Mr Clyde of 22.9% of his holding would not result in a change of control over the land so that, if this is the only transaction, it does not amount to a disposal of the land.

Where the transaction, arrangement or scheme concerns a shareholding in a company or an interest in a partnership or in settled property, TCA 1997, s 643 only applies if both control over the land changes and the greater part of the value of the shareholding or interest actually arises from the land. It is possible, for example, for a person to sell a controlling interest in a partnership that carries on a trade of dealing in land, but which also carries on other activities not relating to land. Should the greater part of the value of the partnership be attributable to its non-land assets, the sale of the controlling interest is not treated as a disposal of land and the transaction test is not met.

A disposal of land or of control over land may take place in any manner whatsoever. TCA 1997, s 643(7) provides that account must be taken of any method, direct or indirect, by which any property or right is transferred or transmitted to another person, or by which the value of any property or right is enhanced or diminished. Consequently, the occasion of the transfer or transmission of any property or right, or the occasion on which the value of any property or right is enhanced or diminished, may be treated as an occasion on which tax becomes chargeable under TCA 1997, s 643 (assuming of course that both the "purpose" and "obtained" tests are also met).

TCA 1997, s 643(8) lists a number of ways in which property may be transferred to another person or in which the value of any property or right may be enhanced or diminished (so as to constitute a disposal). The subsection confirms that TCA 1997, s 643(7) is to apply, in particular, to:

(a) sales, contracts and other transactions made for less than full consideration or for more than full consideration;

(b) any method by which any property or the control over any property may be transferred to any person by assigning—

    (i) share capital or other rights in a company,

    (ii) rights in a partnership, or

    (iii) an interest in settled property;

(c) the creation of any option, consent or embargo affecting the disposition of any property; and

(d) the disposal of any property on the winding up, dissolution or termination of any company, partnership or trust.

The meaning of *gain of a capital nature* can be inferred from the definition of *capital amount,* in TCA 1997, s 643(1), as any amount in money or money's worth which, apart from TCA 1997, s 643, would not be included in any computation of income for the purposes of the Tax Acts; any other expressions in TCA 1997, s 643 or s 644 which include the word "capital" are to be given a corresponding meaning.

In *Yuill v Wilson* (see below), the sale of land by a share dealing company resident in Guernsey was regarded as giving rise to a gain of a capital nature. As the proceeds of the sale were not included in any computation of income for UK tax purposes, due to the non-residence of the company, the gain arising was regarded as a capital gain. The fact that the Guernsey company would, if resident in the UK, have been taxed on the gain as the income profit of a share dealing company did not prevent the attribution of the character of "capital" to the gain under the corresponding UK legislation.

The obtained test

Assuming it has been established that there has been a gain of a capital nature obtained from the disposal of land, and that the purpose test has also been satisfied. TCA 1997, s 643 imposes a charge to tax if the gain has been "obtained" from the disposal by :

(a) the person acquiring, holding or developing the land;

(b) a person connected with that person; or

(c) any person who is a party to, or is concerned in, any arrangement or scheme effected as respects the land which enables the gain to be realised directly or indirectly by any transaction or by a series of transactions.

In determining whether a gain has been obtained by a person connected with the person acquiring, holding, or developing the land, the "connected persons" rules of TCA 1997, s 10(6)-(8) (see **2.3**) are applied. A company may obtain a gain on its own behalf but TCA 1997, s 643(6)(a) deals also with the case in which a person obtains a gain for another person. This occurs if one person "makes available" to another person "the opportunity of realising a gain". This opportunity may be provided directly in any manner whatsoever, but one particular method, ie a premature sale, is envisaged in TCA 1997, s 643(6)(a). Where this arises, the person who obtained the gain for the other person, ie by providing the opportunity for that other person to realise the gain, is the person who will be subject to tax under Case IV (TCA 1997, s 643(11)).

The circumstances envisaged by TCA 1997, s 643(6)(a) are exemplified in *Yuill v Wilson* [1980] STC 460, [1980] 3 All ER 7. That case concerned an individual (Mr Y) who held a controlling interest in Y Ltd, a building company, by virtue of his shares together with the shares of trustees of family settlements created by him. A number of years before the transactions giving rise to the case occurred, two other companies (the "land holding companies") controlled by Mr Y and his family interests acquired various interests in land expected to be used in due course by Y Ltd in its building business. In September 1972, Mr Y created a new settlement with trustees resident in Guernsey for the benefit of members of his family. These trustees formed two companies resident in Guernsey, M Ltd and C Ltd; and the trustees held all the shares in, and had complete control of, these two companies.

Between December 1972 and March 1974, M Ltd and C Ltd acquired several holdings of land from the two land holding companies and sold these lands to Y Ltd at substantial profits. These profits fell to be treated as gains of a capital nature since, due to the residence of M Ltd and C Ltd in Guernsey, the profits were not taxable as income in the UK. The Inland Revenue assessed Mr Y under TA 1970 s 488 (the UK equivalent of TCA 1997, s 643) on the grounds that he, either directly or through his companies and with the help of his Guernsey trustees, obtained the gains for M Ltd and C Ltd by making available to them the opportunity for realising the gains. The House of Lords unanimously held that this was the correct view of the whole matter.

TCA 1997, s 643 is most likely to be of relevance where the gain of a capital nature is obtained by the person acquiring, holding or developing the land or by some other person connected with him. Unless there is an arrangement or scheme, it is not possible for any unconnected person to be charged under this section in respect of the gain. In any case where there is, or has been, an arrangement or scheme carried out as respects the land, two further conditions would have to apply before such an unconnected person can be charged by the section.

Firstly, the person who has obtained the gain of a capital nature from the disposal of the land should either be a party to the arrangement or scheme, or be concerned in it. Secondly, the arrangement or scheme must enable the gain to be realised directly or indirectly. Clearly, a person is a party to an arrangement or scheme if he is either a transferor or a transferee in any one or more of the transactions which together make up the scheme, but a person may sometimes be concerned in a scheme even if he is not a party to any of the transactions in the scheme or is not involved in its documentation.

In the UK case of *Winterton v Edwards* [1980] STC 206, [1980] 2 All ER 56, the ownership of land acquired with the sole or main object of realising a gain was transferred by a Mr L to a company in which he held 90.5% of the share capital. The transfer was accomplished by a series of transactions in a manner designed to defer Mr L's income tax liability on the disposal of the land. After the acquisition of the land, but before execution of the scheme, Mr L agreed with the taxpayer, Mr W, that he would be given a 4.5% share in the proceeds of the sale. The scheme was in due course implemented and Mr W was paid his share of the sale proceeds.

Mr W was assessed under the UK equivalent of TCA 1997, s 643 on his share of the proceeds. Although he was not a party to any of the documentation related to the sale of the land to the company, it was held that he was "concerned in" the scheme, since it had been agreed he would receive a share of the proceeds and as Mr L had by letter executed a declaration of trust confirming Mr W's interests. On the second question as to whether the scheme effected by Mr L had enabled Mr W to realise a gain, the fact that he subsequently received a proportionate share of the proceeds of sale was held to be sufficient to answer the question in the affirmative. The taxpayer was held to be correctly assessable.

13.309.3 Exceptions

TCA 1997, s 643 provides for two exceptions to the full charge to tax under Case IV, notwithstanding that the three tests described above are all satisfied. Firstly, if the "purpose" test is satisfied in the case of the development of land by a company with the object of realising a gain from disposing of the land when developed, the Case IV charge does not apply to the part of the gain that is fairly attributable to the period before the intention to develop the land was formed (TCA 1997, s 643(10)). This exception does not, however, apply if the land was previously acquired with the object of realising a gain from its disposal or if it was held as trading stock. In other words, if the land was acquired to realise a dealing gain or was held as trading stock of a land dealing business, the fact that a subsequent decision is made to develop the land before its disposal does not operate to exclude any part of the gain from the charge to tax under Case IV.

Secondly, the Case IV charge will not be made in certain circumstances where there is a disposal of shares either in a company which holds land as trading stock or in a company which owns directly or indirectly 90% or more of the ordinary share capital of another company which holds land as trading stock (TCA 1997, s 643(12)). For the excluded to apply in any such case, three further conditions must be met, namely:

(a)   all the land held as trading stock by the company concerned, at the time the shares are disposed of, must be disposed of (subsequently) in the normal course of its trade by that company;

(b)   the disposal of the land must be made in such a way as to ensure that all opportunity of profit in respect of the land arises to that company only; and

(c)   the gain must not be one obtained by any person who is a party to, or is concerned in, any arrangement or scheme effected as respects the land.

In practice, the condition in (a) above can be satisfied by obtaining, from the purchaser of the shares, an undertaking that the company will dispose of the land in the normal course of trading.

13.309.4   Charge to tax

All of the gain of a capital nature from the disposal of the land by a company is treated as income chargeable to corporation tax arising at the time the gain is realised (TCA 1997, s 643(4)). Accordingly the gain is taxable under Case IV in the year of assessment in which the gain is realised.

Person chargeable

The person chargeable to tax under Case IV is normally the person by whom the gain is realised on the particular disposal of land giving rise to the gain. Since the person who acquired, held or developed the land with the object of realising a gain its disposal would, in the event of making an actual disposal of the land (as distinct from a deemed disposal), almost always be directly assessable under Case I, either directly or as a result of TCA 1997, s 640 (see **13.304**), that person would not normally be the person subject to the Case IV charge. The Case IV charge is more likely to apply to a person who disposes of land by selling or otherwise transferring property deriving its value from the land in question, eg by selling a controlling interest in an investment company, being the parent company of another company that has developed the land with the object of realising a gain.

TCA 1997, s 643(11) provides an exception to the normal rule that it is the person who actually realises the gain who is chargeable. The exception applies in any case where the gain accrues to any person so that all or any part of the gain is derived from value, or from an opportunity to realise a gain, provided directly or indirectly by some other person. In any such case, TCA 1997, s 643(4) applies to tax the person who provided the value or made available the opportunity of realising a gain for the other person; the person actually realising the gain is not then taxable.

In *Yuill v Wilson* (see above), the assessment under the corresponding UK legislation was made on Mr Y who had provided the two Guernsey companies with the opportunity of realising the gains of a capital nature from the disposal of land in the UK; the Guernsey companies were not, therefore, charged. The House of Lords approved the assessment on Mr Y, although in that case the Inland Revenue failed to enforce most of its claim as it was held that only a very small part of the gain was actually realised in the year in which it was sought to assess it.

The failure of the Inland Revenue on this point appears to have been due mainly to a provision in TA 1970 s 489(13) regarding the time when the capital amount is deemed to be receivable. The Irish legislation does not contain any corresponding provision defining the time of receipt so that the time when a gain is realised must be determined in accordance with the normal meaning of these words.

Computation of taxable gain

There are no precise rules for computing the amount of the gain of a capital nature chargeable under Case IV. TCA 1997, s 643(9) requires that such method of computing the gain should be adopted as is just and reasonable in the circumstances, taking into account the value of what is obtained for disposing of the land and allowing only such expenses as are attributable to the land disposed of. From the definition of "capital amount" (see above), it can be inferred that any part of the consideration falling to be included in the computation of any income otherwise chargeable under the Tax Acts should be excluded in computing the amount of the gain.

The consideration or other capital amount received may be in respect of the disposal of shares in a company or of other property deriving its value from the land. In this context, the deductible expenses should normally include the cost of acquiring the property disposed of (eg, the shares), as well as any reasonable expenses incurred in connection with the disposal. However, the requirement to use such method as is just and reasonable may result in the disallowance of any deduction not considered to be appropriate in all the circumstances of the case.

In view of the very wide scope of TCA 1997, s 643, and the possible circumstances in which a gain of a capital nature may therefore arise, it would not be possible to provide for all matters to be taken into account in the computation of the taxable gain in all circumstances. Several other points are, however, mentioned. Firstly, TCA 1997, s 643(9)(a) provides that, if a transaction involves or includes the acquisition of an interest in land and the retention of the reversion on a subsequent disposal, account may be taken of the way in which the profits or gains are computed under Case I (ie, the "Emery" formula – see **13.306.4** above). In certain cases, it may well be necessary to attribute a value to the reversion retained (to be credited in the Case IV computation in the manner of closing trading stock).

Secondly, in any case where the "purpose" test is met due only to the development of land by a company with the sole or main object of realising a gain from disposing of the land when developed, TCA 1997, s 643(10) requires the computation of the taxable amount of the gain to exclude any part of the gain that is "fairly" attributable to the period, if any, before the intention to develop the land was formed. In applying this rule, account is to be taken of the treatment under Case I of a person who appropriates land as trading stock. In effect, the opening value of the land (or of the property deriving its value from the land) that is debited as the "acquisition cost" in the computation of the taxable gain should be its market value at the date the intention to develop the land is formed.

Example 13.309.4.1

Mr Apraxin owns 65% of the ordinary share capital of Yaroslavl Ltd, having acquired this shareholding in August 1993 for €350,000. The remaining 35% of the shareholding is held by a bank. The only asset of Yaroslavl Ltd is a 75% holding in the ordinary share capital of Pereslavl Ltd, a company carrying on a trade of wholesaling.

On 1 February 2004, Pereslavl Ltd ceased to trade and at 16 July 2004 it had disposed of all its trading assets and discharged most of its liabilities. Its only remaining assets were its land and buildings valued in July 2004 at €500,000 and a bank balance of €390,000. Its liabilities were €35,000. On 12 September 2004, it was decided that Pereslavl Ltd would demolish the existing buildings on its freehold land and redevelop the site by erecting three modern factory units with the intention of selling them off at a profit.

The development is completed on 30 November 2008 at which date the balance sheet of Pereslavl Ltd is as follows:

	€	€
Freehold land and buildings:		
– at cost	300,000	
– cost of redevelopment	920,000	
		1,220,000
Balance at bank		49,000
		1,269,000
Less: liabilities (including loan to finance development)		455,000
Net assets		814,000
Represented by:		
Share capital and reserves		814,000

On 1 December 2008, the market value of the developed factory units, as certified by professional valuers, was €1,500,000. Disposal of the units was, however, postponed due to the difficult market conditions then prevailing. However, Mr Apraxin, wishing to realise his investment in Yaroslavl Ltd, sold his 65% holding in that company to the 35% shareholder for €725,000. The tax consequences are as follows:

(a)   Although there has been no actual disposal of the developed factory sites, the sale by Mr Apraxin of his controlling interest in Yaroslavl Ltd (which controls Pereslavl Ltd, the company which developed the land) is a sale of property deriving its value from land; control over the land has effectively been disposed of and the disposal is therefore a disposal of land within TCA 1997, s 643(5). Thus, the "disposal" test is satisfied;

(b)   Since the land was developed by Pereslavl Ltd, with the object of realising a gain on its disposal when developed, the "purpose" test is satisfied;

(c)   Since the gain from the deemed disposal of the land (the sale of the Yaroslavl Ltd shares) is obtained by Mr Apraxin as a person "connected with" the company which developed the land, the "obtained" test is also met;

(d)   TCA 1997, s 643(10) limits the amount chargeable to the part of Mr Apraxin's gain attributable to the period after 12 September 2004, ie after the intention to develop the land was formed. In determining the amount of this part of the gain, the market value of the land at that date (when it was appropriated as trading stock by Pereslavl Ltd) must be brought into the computation;

(e)   The following is a suggested method of computing the gain taxable under TCA 1997, s 643 in respect of the sale of Mr Apraxin's 65% holding in Yaroslavl Ltd:

	€	€
Sale price of 65% holding		725,000
Assumed cost of 65% holding:		
– taken as equal to market value of the holding July 2004[1]	355,000	
Expenses of negotiating sale, say	25,000	
		380,000
Gain taxable under Case IV		345,000

Notes:

[1]   The value of Mr Apraxin's holding in Yaroslavl Ltd in July 2004 has been determined, after bringing in the land held by Pereslavl Ltd at its market value at that time (ie, applying the Case I rule for land appropriated as trading stock), as follows:

	€
Value of Pereslavl Ltd:	
Land and buildings at market value July 2004	500,000
Balance in bank	390,000
Less: liabilities	(35,000)
Value of 100% holding	855,000
Value of Yaroslavl Ltd:	
Market value of 75% holding in Pereslavl Ltd	
€855,000 x 75%	641,250

Value of Mr Apraxin's shares in July 2004:

Market value of 65% holding in Yaroslavl Ltd	
€641,250 x 65%	416,813
Less: discount - approximately 15%[2]	(62,522)
Market value July 2004	354,291

[2]   15% discount (approx) suggested for 65% holding.

[3]   The exclusion from the tax charge provided by TCA 1997, s 643(12) (see *Exceptions* above) is not available as Yaroslavl Ltd (the company whose shares are disposed of) is not the company that holds the land as trading stock and as it does not own 90% or more of the ordinary share capital of Pereslavl Ltd.

13.309.5   Recovery of tax from person realising gain

Where TCA 1997, s 643(11) operates so that the person who provided value, or who made available an opportunity for another person to realise a gain, is taxable in respect of a gain realised by that other person (see the "obtained" test above), TCA 1997, s 644(1) entitles the person so taxable (the first-named person) to recover from the other person (the second-named person) any of the tax so charged that the first named person has paid. In calculating the amount of tax so recoverable, it is assumed that the amount charged as income under TCA 1997, s 643 was taxed as the highest part of the first named person's income for the tax year in question.

The first-named person is entitled to request the inspector of taxes to furnish him with a certificate specifying the amount of income in respect of which he has paid tax, and the amount of tax so paid. He may present this certificate to the second-named person when seeking to recover the tax. On the other hand, if any part of the tax assessable on the first-named person has not been paid by him within six months from the due date of the tax, the Revenue Commissioners are entitled to recover the tax from the person who actually realised the gain.

13.309.6   Non-residents

A non-resident company may be charged to tax under Case IV in the same circumstances and in the same manner as a resident company, but only if the land actually disposed of is situated in the State (TCA 1997, s 643(17)). It is the situation of the land that is the determining factor for liability, but a non-resident person remains chargeable even if the disposal is made through the sale of any property deriving its value from the land in the State. The fact that this property, eg the shares in a company or an interest in a partnership, may be an asset situated outside the State does not of itself prevent the non-resident company from being assessable.

However, if TCA 1997, s 643 would normally operate to tax a non-resident company in respect of a gain realised through the sale, or "alienation" of any property deriving its value from land (eg shares in a company, resident or non-resident), the double tax treaty with the foreign country of which the person in question is a resident should be consulted. It may be that the treaty article dealing with the alienation of assets (other than land) will apply to exempt the non-resident from any Irish tax on the gain. It is not unusual for a double tax agreement to provide that the resident of the other country is not to be subject to Irish tax on gains realised from the sale of shares in companies.

However, not all of the agreements provide for this exemption if the gain is from shares deriving the greater part of their value from land in the State (see **9.105** and **14.109.7**).

In any case where a person chargeable to tax under TCA 1997, s 643 is resident outside the State, enforcement of payment by direct assessment is likely to be difficult. Accordingly, TCA 1997, s 644(2) empowers the Revenue Commissioners to direct that the collection procedure in TCA 1997, s 238 (see **4.303.6**) is to be applied to any payment due to be made to the non-resident person that forms parts of any consideration or amount that is chargeable to tax under these provisions. There is, however, no specific requirement for any person making such a payment to a non-resident to withhold income tax under this rule, unless the Revenue Commissioners actually make this direction.

Where the direction is made, the person making the payment is required to deduct income tax at the standard rate from the actual amount being paid. The non-resident person who suffers the withholding of tax at source is entitled to recover any excess of the tax withheld over the amount of his actual liability to tax under the provisions of TCA 1997, s 643. The recovery can, however, only be made after the non-resident has submitted the necessary returns and other information and has agreed the actual liability with the inspector of taxes.

A non-resident person who claims that, due to a relevant provision in the double tax agreement between the State and his country of residence, he is exempted from any Irish tax in respect of a gain from the alienation of an asset other than land in the State, should apply to the Revenue Commissioners for the withdrawal of any direction under TCA 1997, s 644(2) (if such a direction is made). If the Revenue Commissioners are satisfied that the non-resident is in fact entitled to such an exemption, it is to be expected that they would withdraw the direction (or refrain from making it if advised in advance).

13.309.7   Power to obtain information

TCA 1997, s 645 empowers an inspector of taxes by notice in writing to require any person to furnish such particulars as the inspector may think necessary for the purpose of applying TCA 1997, s 643 or s 644. The information which may be so requested includes particulars related to various matters as set out in TCA 1997, s 645(2). These matters include information as to whether the person served with the notice has taken part in any transactions or arrangements of a kind specified in the notice and whether the person is or was acting on his own account or on behalf of other persons.

TCA 1997, s 645(3) provides an exception which excludes a solicitor from having to furnish information as regards any transactions or arrangements in respect of which his only involvement was to give professional advice to a client in connection with the transactions or arrangements. However, if the solicitor has done more than give professional advice and has otherwise involved himself in any way, he is not excused from giving full information in relation to his other involvement. In relation to anything done on behalf of a client, the solicitor cannot be compelled to do more than state that he is or was acting on behalf of the client, but need not give the name and address of the client.

13.309.8   Tax on capital gains

A transaction involving the disposal of land (including property deriving its value from land) coming within the charge to tax under Case IV is generally also a disposal of an asset for capital gains tax purposes. In a more straightforward case, where the person charged under Case IV is also the person subject to a charge to tax on capital gains as the disponer of the asset in question, the normal rules of capital gains tax apply to prevent a double assessment to tax. Any amount in money or money's worth that is included as a receipt in calculating an amount of income chargeable as income under Case IV is excluded from the consideration receivable in computing the chargeable gain (TCA 1997, s 551(2)). Similarly, any expenditure deductible in the TCA 1997, s 643 calculation cannot be deducted again in the computation of the capital gain (TCA 1997, s 554(1)).

TCA 1997, s 644(5) extends these capital gains tax rules preventing double assessment to cover the case where, say, a company assessed to corporation tax under these provisions is not the person who actually realises the gain. This is relevant where the company is so charged due to having provided value to another person or an opportunity for another person to realise the gain. In making any computation for capital gains purposes in such a case, any receipt or expenses included or deducted in the computation under these provisions of the company providing the value or the opportunity to realise the gain is excluded from the capital gains computation of the person who actually disposed of the asset and realised the gain.

TCA 1997, s 644(4) deals with the case where TCA 1997, s 643(10) has applied to exclude from the computation of the gain under that section the part attributable to the period before the intention to develop the land was formed. The subsection provides that any land or other property appropriated as trading stock in the computation of the gain at the time the intention to develop (and to realise a gain from the developed land) was formed is to be regarded, in applying the capital gains tax computational rules of TCA 1997, s 596, as having been appropriated as trading stock at the same time. In effect, this means that the company treated as appropriating the land as trading stock may be charged to tax on a capital gain computed by reference to a deemed disposal of the asset at its market value at that date.

13.4 MINING ACTIVITIES

13.401   Introduction and rate of tax

It has been argued many times within the industry that mining activities cannot be taxed in the same way as other production activities and that a special basis for the taxation of mining profits is necessary. There are important factors which are unique to the mining industry. It will probably always be in a country's national interest to give priority to the establishment of a supply of raw materials and, in doing this, it has to be recognised that there are extraordinary risks attached to mining. Given the scale and dimensions of mining operations, the capital required will come from the international sector where assessments will be made of the comparative fiscal climates. The means of attracting the necessary capital will inevitably be in the form of tax incentives which should take account of the high risks involved and the capital intensive nature of the industry and, in particular, the long lead time between commencement of exploration and the first realisation of mining profits.

In Ireland, tax relief for certain mining activities was first provided for in Finance (Profits of Certain Mines) (Temporary Relief from Taxation) Act 1956. The relief took the form of exemption from income tax and corporation profits tax for four years followed by a 50% exemption for a further four years in the cases of new mines coming into production before April 1961. The April 1961 deadline was extended twice subsequently to accommodate mines commencing to be worked at any time in the 30 year period up to 5 April 1986. With a view to activating projects which would result in significant additional employment, it was recognised that significant further expansion in exploration and development could be stimulated by additional tax incentives. The original tax relief was accordingly replaced with a twenty-year period of complete exemption, provided for in ITA ss 382-392.

The twenty year tax holiday was replaced by the provisions of Finance (Taxation of Profits of Certain Mines) Act 1974 ("F(TPCM)A 1974"), now contained in TCA 1997 Part 24 Ch 1 (ss 670-683), the intention being to instal a scheme of tax allowances to meet the specific needs of the Irish mining industry on lines similar to those operating in comparable economies. Under the 1967 legislation, a mine commencing on 5 April 1986 would have been eligible for tax exemption up to the year 2006. F(TPCM)A 1974 withdrew the income tax exemption for all tax years after 1973/74 and the corporation profits tax exemption for all accounting periods or parts of accounting periods after 5 April 1974.

The regime contained in TCA 1997 Part 24 Ch 1 is essentially an incentive based on capital allowances for expenditure on exploration and development. Up to 1990, any relief for exploration expenditure could only be effective from the time the trade of working a qualifying mine was carried on; FA 1990 introduced measures (now in TCA 1997, s 679) which deem a company engaged in exploring for scheduled minerals to be carrying on a trade of working a qualifying mine so that tax relief may be obtained in respect of exploration expenditure prior to commencement of a mining trade.

Prior to the enactment of F(TPCM)A 1974, legislation providing for allowances in respect of exploration and development expenditure was confined to ITA 1967 s 245 (now TCA 1997, s 670). Under that section, which is still in operation, qualifying expenditure on exploration and development and construction costs of mineworks are allowed over the useful life of the mine on a straight-line basis, with a maximum write-off period of 20 years. Only expenditure referable to the particular working mine is relieved so that no abortive expenditure could ever be allowed, whether in the case of a company already working a qualifying mine or which later commences to work a qualifying mine. In effect, the working of each qualifying mine is treated as a separate trade under TCA 1997, s 670. A weakness in the regime provided for by TCA 1997, s 670 is that interest related to the cost of financing exploration and development is not tax deductible. A further disability is the termination of all exploration allowances in a situation where a company engaged in exploration transfers its interest in a mine before commencing to work it.

Under TCA 1997, s 673, a company may take an immediate deduction for all exploration and development expenditure incurred after 5 April 1974 provided it is carrying on trade of working a qualifying mine. Expenditure is not identified with a particular mine as is the case in TCA 1997, s 670.

Article 10 of the Constitution of 1937 provides that all natural resources, including the air and all forms of potential energy, within the jurisdiction of the Parliament and government belong to the State, subject to all estates and interests therein for the time being lawfully vested in any person or body. The State is enabled to manage mines and minerals acquired by the State and the State owns some mineral rights by virtue of certain legislation, eg the Irish Land Acts of 1903, 1907 and 1909, the Land Act 1923, and the Minerals Development Act 1940. The Minerals Development Act 1979 vests in the Minister for Communications, Energy and Natural Resources the exclusive right to work minerals. The precise extent of State ownership of minerals is, however, unknown; it has been estimated that between 60% and 65% of the total of potential minerals are State owned.

25% tax rate

Mining profits (profits from the trade of working a mine) are subject to corporation tax at the higher rate of 25%.

TCA 1997, s 21A provides that corporation tax is to be charged on the profits of companies in so far as those profits consist, inter alia, of income of an excepted trade (see 3.101.4). An *excepted trade* is a trade consisting only of trading operations or activities which are excepted operations (TCA 1997, s 21A(1)). If a trade consists partly of excepted operations and partly of other operations or activities, each part is treated as a separate trade for the purposes of TCA 1997, s 21A. *Excepted operations* includes "working minerals". *Working*, in relation to minerals, includes digging, searching for, mining, getting, raising, taking, carrying away and treating minerals and the sale or other disposal of minerals. *Minerals* means all substances (other than the agricultural surface of the ground and other than turf or peat) in, on or under land, whether obtainable by underground or by surface working, and includes all mines, whether or not they are already opened or in work, and also includes the cubic space occupied or formerly occupied by minerals.

13.402   Mine development allowance

13.402.1   Introduction

TCA 1997, s 670 provides for a mining development allowance to a person, in practice probably always a company, carrying on a trade of working a mine and who has incurred capital expenditure on the development of that mine and on the construction of certain works for the purpose of that mining operation. TCA 1997 Part 24 Ch 1, apart from TCA 1997, s 670, provides for capital allowances in respect of mining development expenditure and for exploration expenditure, as well as certain other allowances, to a company carrying on the trade of working a qualifying mine.

The following are some important definitions relating to the allowances for exploration and development expenditure.

A *qualifying mine* is a mine that is being worked for the purpose of obtaining scheduled minerals. The word "mine" originally meant an underground excavation for the purpose of getting minerals and also includes a stratum or vein (*Abinger (Lord) v Ashton* [1873] LR 17 EQ 358 and *Midland Railway Co v Haunchwood Brick and Tile Co* [1882] 20 Ch D 522). For the purposes of the Mines and Quarries Act 1965, "mine" means an excavation or system of excavation made for the purpose of, or in connection with, the getting wholly or substantially by means involving the employment of persons below ground of minerals, whether in their natural state or in solution or suspension, or products of minerals. There is no requirement that the mine should be located in the State.

"Mine" is not defined in the Minerals Development Acts of 1940 to 1979 but can be understood as meaning any underground working. "Mine" is defined in TCA 1997, s 670 as an underground excavation made for the purpose of getting minerals. In relation to capital expenditure incurred on or after 6 April 1960, "mine" means a mine which is operated for the purpose of obtaining, whether by underground or surface working, any scheduled mineral, mineral compound or mineral substance as defined in section 2 of the Mineral Development Act 1940.

The *scheduled minerals* are listed in the Table in TCA 1997, s 672 as follows:

> Barytes
> Felspar
> Serpentinous marble
> Quartz rock
> Soapstone
> Ores of copper
> Ores of gold

Ores of iron
Ores of lead
Ores of manganese
Ores of molybdenum
Ores of silver
Ores of sulphur
Ores of zinc

There is no definition of "minerals" and its meaning is exhaustive. Primarily, it means all substances, other than the agricultural surface of the ground (*Hext v Gill* [1872] 7 Ch App 699 and *Midland Railway Co v Haunchwood Brick and Tile Co* [1882] 20 Ch D 522). The words "mineral" and "mineral substance" are largely synonymous.

A *scheduled mineral asset* is a deposit of scheduled minerals or land comprising such a deposit or an interest in or right over such deposit or land. Since the definition includes certain land, the question arises as to whether it includes land under which there are deposits of scheduled minerals, having regard to the fact that ownership of such deposits vest in the State. It would seem that only land the title to which includes title to the underlying minerals would be included in the definition.

Development expenditure is defined as capital expenditure:

(a)   on the development of a qualifying mine; or

(b)   on the construction of any works in connection with a qualifying mine which are of a nature that, when the mine ceases to be operated, they are likely to have little or no value,

and includes interest on money borrowed to meet such capital expenditure. Development expenditure does not include any expenditure on the acquisition of the site of the mine or of rights in or over the site, or any expenditure in acquiring any scheduled mineral asset. Also excluded is expenditure on works constructed wholly or mainly for subjecting the raw product of the mine to any process except a process designed for preparing the raw product for use as such.

Development expenditure would typically include expenditure on excavating for minerals at the site of the mine, and expenditure on constructing mineshafts and installing lifts and other installations (apart from machinery or plant) directly related to the mining activity, which are usually or little or no value at the time the mining operation comes to an end.

The cost of constructing a mill for crushing, grading and other processing of ore extracted from the mine is arguably development expenditure. An important requirement in this regard is that the mill can be regarded as "works" and as being of such a *nature* that when the mine ceases to be operated it (the mill) is likely to have little or no value. The reference to "nature" here would seem to impose a requirement that the mill should have so diminished in value because of the type of building or structure it is and not, for example, because of such factors as age or dilapidation.

Furthermore, for the expenditure to quality as development expenditure, it should not fall within any of the excluded categories of expenditure described above, thus it is relevant to consider whether the expenditure might be regarded as expenditure on works constructed wholly or mainly for subjecting the raw product of the mine to any process except a process designed for preparing the raw product for use as such. Undoubtedly, the mill would be used for subjecting the raw product of the mine to a process but the expenditure will not be disallowed if that process is designed for preparing the raw product for use as such. In practice, it is likely that the purpose of a mill operation is to prepare the raw product for further processing, eg, smelting. It certainly seems arguable that the end product of the mill operation is not only a raw product but one which is designed for use as such, ie, as an input to a smelting process.

Assuming the expenditure on the mill qualifies as development expenditure, it will not be eligible for industrial building allowances also. Although a mill is a building or structure in use for the purposes of a trade carried on in a mill, factory or similar premises (see **5.401.2**), expenditure on such a building which jellifies as development expenditure will not qualify for industrial building allowances on the basis of TCA 1997, s 270(2)(c); that paragraph rules out any expenditure in respect of which an allowance is or may be made under TCA 1997, s 670 (mine development allowance).

The cost of constructing a mill for crushing, grading and other processing of ore extracted from the mine is unlikely to be development expenditure on the basis that the process is not carried out for preparing the product extracted for use as such; it is more likely that the purpose of the mill operation is to prepare the raw product for further processing, eg smelting. In that connection, a mill would be an industrial building (a building or structure in use for the purposes of a trade carried on in a mill, factory or similar premises – see **5.401.2**) in respect of which industrial building allowances could be claimed.

Exploration expenditure means capital expenditure on searching in the State for deposits of scheduled minerals, or on testing such deposits or winning access thereto or on systematic searching for areas containing scheduled minerals and searching by drilling or other means for scheduled minerals within those areas, but does not include expenditure on operations in the course of working a qualifying mine or expenditure which is development expenditure.

Unlike development expenditure, exploration expenditure does not include interest on money to finance the costs of exploration. A company already deriving profits from mining activities and which allocates interest costs to ongoing exploration will not be in a position to claim a tax deduction for the allocated interest.

Mine development allowance has the same meaning as in TCA 1997, s 670.

The main relief section is TCA 1997, s 673. The section provides for relief in respect of both exploration and development expenditure. TCA 1997, s 674 provides for relief in respect of certain abortive exploration expenditure.

13.402.2   Allowance for development expenditure

A company carrying on the trade of working a qualifying mine is entitled under TCA 1997, s 673 to claim a mine development allowance in respect of development expenditure incurred by it on or after 6 April 1974. The allowance is given in taxing the profits of the trade of working that mine. The allowance is presumably intended to be given for the accounting period in which the expenditure is incurred but, surprisingly, this is not confirmed by TCA 1997, s 673 nor indeed by TCA 1997, s 670. The company in question may make an application under TCA 1997, s 670 for the allowance "for a chargeable period" but TCA 1997, s 673(1) does not state what that period is. TCA 1997, s 670(9) provides that expenditure incurred by a person about to carry on the trade of working a mine but before commencing such trade is to be treated as incurred on the day the trade commenced. That provision does not, however, state that the allowance is to be given for or by reference to the period in which the expenditure is incurred. As mentioned above, it would appear that the intention of the legislation is that the allowance is to be made to a company for the accounting period in which the expenditure was incurred or, if later, in the accounting period in which the trade commenced.

The amount of the allowance made in respect of development expenditure in the relevant accounting period is equal to the total amount of the development expenditure as reduced by the amount which, in the opinion of the inspector, the assets representing that expenditure are likely to be worth at the end of the estimated life of the qualifying mine. To be entitled to the allowance, the company working the qualifying mine must make an application for the allowance under TCA 1997, s 670, which is required not later than 24 months after the end of the accounting period for which it is claimed.

TCA 1997, s 673(1)(c) provides that any reference in the Tax Acts to an allowance made under TCA 1997, s 670 is to be construed as including a reference to an allowance made under that section by virtue of TCA 1997, s 673.

The allowance for development expenditure is given in taxing the trade of working the qualifying mine (TCA 1997, s 670(6)). If the profits of the trade for the relevant accounting period are insufficient to absorb the allowance fully, any unused part of the allowance is carried forward and treated as a mine development allowance for the next accounting period and, if necessary, for the next following accounting period, and so on (TCA 1997 ss 670(6) and 304(4)).

Expenditure met directly or indirectly by the Oireachtas, or by any person other than the company carrying on the trade of working the mine, is regarded as not having been incurred by the company.

13.402.3 Allowance for exploration expenditure

A company carrying on a trade of working a qualifying mine is also entitled by virtue of TCA 1997, s 673 to claim a mine development allowance under TCA 1997, s 670 equal to the full amount of the exploration expenditure incurred by it on or after 6 April 1974. The allowance may be claimed whether or not a deposit of scheduled minerals is found as a result of the exploration expenditure in question. Prior to FA 1990, relief for such abortive exploration expenditure was restricted to such expenditure incurred on or after 6 April 1967 and no more than ten years before the company commenced to carry on the trade of working a qualifying mine. The ten year limit was removed with effect from 1 April 1990 so that, from that date, all abortive exploration expenditure incurred is allowable.

The mine development allowance in respect of the exploration expenditure is presumably to be made for the accounting period in which the expenditure is incurred or, if the company claiming the allowance has not yet commenced a trade of working a qualifying mine, for the accounting period in which the trade commenced; as mentioned above in relation to the allowance for development expenditure, however, this does not appear to be confirmed by the legislation. The allowance is made on foot of an application to the inspector no later than 24 months after the end of the relevant accounting period.

The allowance is given in taxing the trade of working the qualifying mine (TCA 1997, s 670(6)).

Expenditure met directly or indirectly by the Oireachtas, or by any person other than the company carrying on the trade of working the mine, is regarded as not having been incurred by the company.

Where a company commences to carry on the trade of working a qualifying mine but did not incur the exploration expenditure incurred in connection with that mine, no allowance may be made in respect of exploration expenditure incurred by that company before it commenced to carry on that trade (TCA 1997, s 674(3)). In other words, a company which has abortive exploration expenditure cannot utilise it for tax purposes simply by buying into a working mine.

Where there has been a change in the ownership of a company, a deduction under TCA 1997, s 674 for abortive exploration expenditure may not be made in respect of such expenditure incurred before the change of ownership. This provision mirrors the loss buying anti-avoidance legislation in TCA 1997, s 401 and "change in ownership" is as defined in TCA 1997 Schedule 9 – see **4.110.2**). For this purpose, any shares acquired by a Minister of State are to be disregarded in determining whether or not there has been a change of ownership.

13.403   Sale of results of exploration

TCA 1997, s 676 deals with the case in which a company incurs exploration expenditure which results in the finding of a deposit of scheduled minerals but, without ever getting to work the deposit and without obtaining any allowance under TCA 1997 ss 672-683 in respect of the expenditure, sells any assets representing that expenditure to another person. If that other person, say a company, carries on a trade consisting of or including the working of that deposit, it is deemed for the purposes of TCA 1997 ss 672-683 to have incurred, in connection with the deposit, exploration expenditure equal to the amount of expenditure represented by the assets or the price paid by it for the assets, whichever is the smaller. The expenditure is deemed to have been incurred by the purchasing company on the date on which it commences to carry on the trade (ie the trade consisting of or including the working of the deposit).

The purchasing company will be deemed to have incurred the exploration expenditure only where its working of the deposit results in the production of scheduled minerals in reasonable commercial quantities. It will not, however, be entitled to an exploration investment allowance (see **13.406**) in respect of the exploration expenditure deemed to have been incurred by it.

The phrase *assets representing that expenditure* is not defined. In the legislation on petroleum taxation, TCA 1997, s 684 defines "development expenditure" (see **13.402.1**) and then provides that "assets representing development expenditure" is to be construed accordingly and is to include any results obtained from any search or enquiry upon which the expenditure was incurred. In respect of assets representing exploration expenditure, as envisaged by TCA 1997, s 676(1), it is reasonable to adopt a similar approach so that the phrase would include any valuable assets brought into existence or otherwise obtained as a result of the exploration activity, such as scientific data, geological information, plans, blueprints etc.

13.404   Deemed exploration companies

TCA 1997, s 679 treats a company which is engaged in exploring for scheduled minerals and which is not carrying on a trade of working a qualifying mine as if it were a carrying on such a trade. This enables the company to offset its exploration expenditure against other income on a current basis. The section has effect in respect of exploration expenditure incurred on or after 1 April 1990.

TCA 1997, s 679(2) provides that *for as long as* a company:

(i)   is an exploration company;

(ii)   does not carry on a trade of working a qualifying mine; and

(iii)   incurs capital expenditure (including capital expenditure on acquiring plant and machinery) for the purpose of exploring for scheduled minerals,

that company is deemed for the purposes of TCA 1997 ss 673, 674(3), 677 and 678 and other provisions of the Tax Acts, but not for the purposes of TCA 1997 ss 672, 674(1), (2), (4), 675 676 and 680-683:

(a)   to be carrying on a trade of working a qualifying mine;

(b)   to come within the charge to corporation tax in respect of that trade when it first incurs that capital expenditure: thus, a new accounting period will begin on that date;

(c)   to the extent that the expenditure was incurred on acquiring plant and machinery, to incur the expenditure for the purposes of the trade: thus, it will be entitled to the 20% investment allowance for plant and machinery (see **13.408**).

An *exploration company* is a company the business of which consists primarily of exploring for scheduled minerals. *Exploring for scheduled minerals* means searching in the State for deposits of scheduled minerals or testing such deposits or winning access thereto, and includes the systematic searching for areas containing scheduled minerals and searching by drilling or other means for scheduled minerals within those areas but does not include operations which are operations in the course of developing or working a qualifying mine. This definition mirrors the definition of "exploration expenditure" (see **13.402.1**).

As stated above, the purposes for which TCA 1997, s 679(2) applies include those of TCA 1997 ss 673, 674(3), 677 and 678. Any allowance which falls to be made under TCA 1997, s 673 (exploration allowance), 677 (investment allowance) or 678 (allowance for machinery or plant) is to be made to an exploration company as if the allowance were an expense of the deemed trade of that company. Similarly, any balancing charge is treated as a trading receipt of that trade.

TCA 1997, s 679(2) also applies for the purposes of TCA 1997, s 674(3). This is to prevent an exploration company from being denied a deduction for exploration expenditure in certain circumstances. For example, an exploration company might use exploration expenditure incurred by it to shelter its investment income. Should it later buy into a qualifying mine, it could be denied (retrospectively) any allowances for that expenditure as expenditure incurred before it commenced to carry on the trade of working that mine (see **13.402.3**). Since, however, TCA 1997, s 679(2) applies for the purposes of TCA 1997, s 674(3), the company is deemed for the purposes of that subsection to be carrying on the trade of working a qualifying mine at the time it incurred the exploration expenditure so that the subsection would not then operate to deny relief in respect of that expenditure.

Where, as a result of TCA 1997, s 679(2), an exploration company incurs a loss in its trade (the deemed trade of working a qualifying mine), TCA 1997, s 679(3) provides that the company:

(a) may utilise the loss for the purposes of TCA 1997 ss 396(1)-(3), 397(1) and (2)(see **4.101** and **4.104**) except that for the purposes of TCA 1997 ss 396(1) and 397, the loss may be set off against total profits rather than against the income from the trade;

(b) may not otherwise use the loss or surrender the loss under TCA 1997, s 420(1) (group relief).

TCA 1997, s 670(11) provides that where a company (the vendor) carrying on a trade of working a mine sells to another person (not being a person who succeeds the vendor in the trade) any asset representing capital expenditure incurred in connection with the mine for which mine development allowances (MDAs) have been made:

(a) if the total of the MDAs and the sum received for the sale of the asset is less than the amount of the capital expenditure (so that there is an unexhausted allowance), further MDAs may be made to the vendor for the accounting period in which the sale took place or for any previous accounting period, up to the amount of the unexhausted allowance;

(b) if the total of the MDAs and the sum received for the sale of the asset exceeds the capital expenditure, the amount of the excess or the total of the MDAs, whichever is the less, is treated as a trading receipt of the trade accruing immediately before the sale.

In this connection, TCA 1997, s 679(4)(a) provides that any asset representing exploration expenditure (see **13.403** above), for which an exploration allowance has been made to a company by virtue of TCA 1997, s 679(2), is treated for the purposes of TCA 1997, s 670(11) as an asset representing capital expenditure incurred in connection with the mine which the company is deemed to be working. Accordingly, on a sale of any asset representing exploration expenditure, the position would be as described in (a) and (b) above. Furthermore, in the event of any such sale, the company will continue to be within the charge to corporation tax in respect of a (deemed) trade of working a qualifying mine up to the time the asset is sold. This latter provision is to ensure that the result in (a) or (b) above, whichever is appropriate, will follow the sale of the asset as it could happen that the company would otherwise cease to be treated as carrying on a trade or working a qualifying mine, eg if it was no longer incurring capital expenditure for exploration purposes, as required by (iii) above.

Where a company begins at any time ("the relevant time") to carry on a trade of working a qualifying mine so that it is no longer *deemed* to be carrying on such a trade, it is treated under TCA 1997, s 679(4)(b) as carrying on the same trade before and after the relevant time for the purposes of:

(i) any allowance, charge or trade receipt treated as arising in connection with any capital expenditure incurred before the relevant time; and

(ii) relief (other than by virtue of TCA 1997, s 679(3) – see above) under TCA 1997, s 396(1) for any unutilised loss arising before the relevant time.

In effect, any losses arising as a result of an excess of exploration allowances, and which are still unused at the time the company commences to work a qualifying mine, may be carried forward for offset against the trading profits from working the mine. While the company is deemed to be carrying on a trade of working a qualifying mine, any such losses arising in an accounting period may be used against total profits arising in the same or succeeding periods. Once the company is actually working a qualifying mine, these losses may be used as losses forward in the normal way, ie against trading profits only.

Losses may not be carried forward as described in the previous paragraph, however, where there is a change of ownership in the company within the three year period beginning 12 months before the relevant time and ending 24 months after that time. For the purposes of determining whether or not a change of ownership has occurred, the provisions of TCA 1997 Sch 9 (see **4.110.2**) are to have effect.

As was seen above, TCA 1997, s 679(2) provides that *for as long as* a company is an exploration company and does not carry on a trade of working a qualifying mine, it is deemed for certain purposes to be carrying on a trade of working a qualifying mine. In practice, such a company might make a discovery of scheduled minerals following a period of exploration, at which point its exploration activities would cease while it became engaged in developing a qualifying mine. At the end of the development period, the company would then commence to work the mine. It is understood that the intervention of such a period of development would not prevent the application of TCA 1997, s 679(4)(b) for the purposes set out in (i) and (ii) above so that, for example, losses incurred in the deemed trade could be carried forward against profits of the actual trade.

To prevent the possibility of a double allowance being available, TCA 1997, s 679(5)(a) provides that where any allowance or deduction is given by virtue of TCA 1997, s 679 in respect of any expenditure, no other allowance or deduction may be given for the same expenditure under any provision of the Tax Acts, including TCA 1997, s 679.

While a company is deemed to be carrying on a trade of working a qualifying mine, it is not entitled to any repayment of deposit interest retention tax (DIRT) by virtue of TCA 1997, s 24(2) and TCA 1997, s 261(1)(b).

13.405 Surrender of exploration expenditure

TCA 1997, s 675 permits exploration expenditure to be surrendered between certain associated companies. The section will facilitate a group in which there is a producing and an exploration company so that the latter can elect to surrender its exploration expenditure to the former. The effect of the election is that the exploration expenditure is deemed to have been incurred by the producing company which can then take a deduction for the amount involved.

The election may be made in respect of both successful and abortive exploration expenditure, in respect of which deductions may be claimed under TCA 1997 ss 673-674. It may also be made in respect of exploration expenditure allowable under TCA 1997, s 673 as applied by TCA 1997, s 679 (by a deemed exploration company).

For the purposes of the election, the required relationship between the two companies is as follows. The company which incurs the exploration expenditure (the exploration company) is or is deemed to be a wholly owned subsidiary of the other company, or the other company is or is deemed to be a wholly owned subsidiary of the exploration company. A company is deemed to be a wholly owned subsidiary of another company if and as long as all of its ordinary share capital is owned by that other company, whether directly or through another company or companies, or partly directly and partly through another company or companies. For the purposes of determining the amount of ordinary share capital held in a company through other companies, the provisions of TCA 1997 Schedule 9 have effect (see **2.505**).

The fact that part of the ordinary share capital of a company is held by a Minister of State is ignored for the purposes of the previous paragraph. If, for example, the ordinary share capital of B Ltd is held as to 60% by A Ltd and as to 40% by the Minister for Finance, B Ltd is deemed to be a wholly owned subsidiary of A Ltd.

The surrender of exploration expenditure is at the election of the exploration company which may surrender all of the expenditure it has incurred or such lesser amount of it as it specifies. The exploration expenditure may be surrendered in any of the following three ways:

(1) Where another company is or is deemed to be a wholly owned subsidiary of the exploration company, the exploration expenditure specified may, at the election of the exploration company, be deemed to have been incurred by that other company.

(2) Where the exploration company is or is deemed to be a wholly owned subsidiary of another company, the exploration expenditure specified is deemed, at the election of the exploration company, to have been incurred by the company (the parent company) of which the exploration company was a wholly owned subsidiary at the time the expenditure was incurred.

(3) Where the exploration company is or is deemed to be a wholly owned subsidiary of another company, the exploration expenditure specified is deemed, at the election of the exploration company, to have been incurred by such other company specified by it as is, or is deemed to be, a wholly owned subsidiary of the parent company referred to in (2).

Where exploration expenditure was incurred prior to the incorporation of a company specified by an exploration company as a company deemed to have incurred that expenditure, that company is treated as if it had been in existence at the time the expenditure was incurred and as if it had incurred the expenditure at that time.

TCA 1997, s 675 is not to have the effect that the same expenditure could be taken into account in relation to more than one trade. Neither may a deduction or allowance be made in respect of the same expenditure both by virtue of the section and under some other provision of the Tax Acts.

Example 13.405.1

Skagway Ltd, a mining exploration company, is a 100% subsidiary of Klondyke Ltd which in turn is a 100% subsidiary of Wrangell Ltd. Yukon Ltd is also a 100% subsidiary of Klondyke Ltd. Apart from Skagway Ltd, each of the companies in the group is carrying on a trade of working a qualifying mine. In the latest accounting period of the group, Skagway Ltd incurred exploration expenditure of €1,200,000. Klondyke Ltd, Wrangell Ltd and Yukon Ltd have mining profits of €450,000, €300,000 and €70,000 respectively in the same period. Skagway Ltd elects that its exploration expenditure of €1,200,000 is deemed to have been incurred as follows:

	€
Klondyke Ltd (parent company)	700,000
Wrangell Ltd (parent company)[1]	430,000
Yukon Ltd	70,000
	1,200,000

Klondyke Ltd uses the €700,000 deemed exploration expenditure to cover its profits of €450,000 for the accounting period with the balance of €250,000 being carried forward. The election in this case is in accordance with (2) above – exploration expenditure deemed to be incurred by parent company.

Yukon Ltd uses deemed exploration expenditure of €70,000, as specified by Skagway Ltd, to reduce its profits of €70,000 for the accounting period to nil. The present circumstances relating to the mine being worked by Yukon Ltd are such that it is not likely to be profitable in the foreseeable future. The election in this case is in accordance with (3) above – exploration expenditure deemed to be incurred by wholly owned subsidiary of parent company.

Wrangell Ltd may also be deemed to have incurred exploration expenditure[1] of €430,000 to reduce its profits of €300,000 to nil, the balance of €130,000 being carried forward. The election in this case is also in accordance with (2) above.

Note:

[1] Although the legislation might appear to distinguish (see wording in (2) above) between a company which is a wholly owned subsidiary of another company and one which is *deemed* to be such, TCA 1997, s 675(3) *deems* as wholly owned subsidiaries both directly and indirectly owned subsidiaries. Thus, in the above example, Skagway Ltd may be regarded as a wholly owned subsidiary of Wrangell Ltd (which is therefore also a parent company of Skagway Ltd).

13.406 Investment allowance

A company carrying on a trade of working a qualifying mine and which incurs, on or after 5 April 1974, exploration expenditure which qualifies for relief under TCA 1997, s 673, may claim an exploration investment allowance in respect of that expenditure. The amount of the allowance is 20% of the exploration expenditure incurred (TCA 1997, s 677). The allowance is made in addition to any mine development allowance obtained in respect of the expenditure and is made for the same accounting period as that for which the mine development allowance is available.

Accordingly, the combined investment allowance and mine development allowance in respect of the exploration expenditure in question results in a total allowance of 120% of the amount of the exploration expenditure incurred. Any part of the total allowance which is not utilised in the accounting period in which the expenditure was incurred is available for carry forward for set-off against future taxable profits from the qualifying mine. There is no investment allowance in respect of development expenditure.

An exploration investment allowance is given in taxing the trade of working the qualifying mine. If the profits of the trade for the relevant accounting period are insufficient to absorb the allowance fully, any unused part of the allowance is carried forward and treated as a mine development allowance for the next accounting period, and so on.

No exploration investment allowance may be made in respect of any exploration expenditure incurred before 6 April 1974, including any such expenditure deemed to have been incurred on or after that date. Nor will the allowance be made to a person who is deemed to have incurred exploration expenditure actually incurred by another person. The allowance would therefore not be made to the purchaser of the results of exploration expenditure as described in **13.403** above. On the other hand, it is specifically provided that a company deemed by TCA 1997, s 675 (see **13.405**) to have incurred exploration expenditure actually incurred by another company is not prevented from claiming an investment allowance in respect of that exploration expenditure.

13.407 Mineral depletion allowance

A company carrying on the trade of working a qualifying mine is entitled under TCA 1997, s 680 to an annual allowance for capital expenditure incurred after 31 March 1974 on the acquisition of a scheduled mineral asset entitling it to work deposits of scheduled minerals where it commences to work those deposits in connection with that trade (TCA 1997, s 680(1)). Where a company which commences to carry on such a trade at any time on or after 6 April 1974 incurred capital expenditure before that time on the acquisition of a scheduled mineral asset in connection with that mine, it is deemed, for the purposes of TCA 1997, s 680(1), to have incurred the expenditure on the day it commences to carry on the trade (TCA 1997, s 680(2)).

The mineral depletion allowance is made as a mine development allowance under TCA 1997, s 670. The allowance is on a straight line basis over the estimated life of the mine, such life being limited to 20 years. The qualifying expenditure is the total amount paid less the likely residual value at the end of the estimated life. The mineral depletion allowance for each accounting period during the estimated life of the deposits is computed as the appropriate proportion, on a time basis, of the excess of the acquisition cost of the scheduled minerals over their estimated residual value at the end of the estimated life.

TCA 1997, s 680(1) refers to the acquisition of a scheduled mineral asset entitling the purchaser to work deposits of scheduled minerals. In the case of a person commencing to carry on the trade of working a qualifying mine on or after 6 April 1974 and who incurred capital expenditure before the time of that commencement on acquiring a scheduled mineral asset, TCA 1997, s 680(2) makes no reference to an entitlement to work deposits of scheduled minerals. The position of the former purchaser might therefore appear to be somewhat more restrictive than in the case of the purchaser who incurred the expenditure before commencing to work a qualifying mine. In practice, this may not amount to any real difference as the acquisition of the scheduled mineral by a person who had commenced to work a qualifying mine is to be "in connection with that mine" and must, presumably, entitle that person to work the qualifying mine.

A person who commences at any time on or after 6 April 1974 to carry on the trade of working a qualifying mine is entitled to a mineral depletion allowance in respect of the related cost where the asset was acquired before that time in connection with that mine. It would seem, however, that the expenditure in that case should have been incurred after 31 March 1974; TCA 1997, s 680(2) states that "for the purposes of this section" the person is deemed to have incurred the expenditure on the day the trade commences. The reference to "for the purposes of this section" brings this provision within the ambit of TCA 1997, s 680(1) which applies only to expenditure incurred after 31 March 1974.

Example 13.407.1

In February 1998, at which time it had been carrying on a trade of working a qualifying mine, Armadale Ltd acquired a scheduled mineral asset entitling it to work deposits of scheduled minerals. As part of that trade, the company brought the deposit into production on 30 May 2004. Armadale Ltd is entitled to a mineral depletion allowance in respect of the expenditure.

Hopetoun Ltd acquired a scheduled mineral asset in February 1974 but did not (due to exceptional and protracted difficulties) commence to carry on the trade of working that deposit until 30 May 2004. The company is not entitled to a mineral depletion allowance in respect of the expenditure on acquiring the asset as the expenditure was not incurred after 31 March 1974 (TCA 1997, s 680(1)).

Onslow Ltd acquired a scheduled mineral asset on 30 April 1988 and commenced to work the deposit on 12 August 2004. It had not already been carrying on a trade of working a qualifying mine. The company is deemed to have incurred the expenditure on the scheduled mineral asset on 12 August 2004 and is entitled to a depletion allowance in respect of its expenditure (TCA 1997, s 680(2)).

Unusually, there is no requirement to calculate a balancing charge where the scheduled mineral assets are subsequently sold for more than their tax written down value, but no balancing allowance may be claimed if they are sold for less than that written down value. The charge to tax under Case IV on the sale of scheduled mineral assets for a capital sum in excess of their acquisition cost (unaffected by any mining depletion allowances previously obtained) is discussed in **13.410**. In computing the amount of the capital sum taxable on such a sale, no deduction is allowed for any part of any mine development or exploration expenditure.

13.408 Machinery and plant

TCA 1997, s 678 provided for free depreciation in respect of capital expenditure incurred on new machinery or new plant provided for use on or after 6 April 1974 for the purposes of a trade of working a qualifying mine. The allowance was made by deeming the machinery or plant to be qualifying machinery or plant for the purposes of free depreciation available, under FA 1967 s 11 (TCA 1997, s 285), in the designated areas. This free depreciation regime came to an end on 1 April 1992.

A company carrying on a trade of working a qualifying mine is entitled to an investment allowance of 20% of the expenditure on new machinery or new plant (other than vehicles suitable for the conveyance by road of persons or goods or the haulage by road of other vehicles) acquired by it for the purposes of the trade. The company may obtain this allowance only where it incurs the expenditure itself; it is not available for leased machinery or plant. The allowance is made for the accounting period in which the expenditure is incurred.

13.409 Mine rehabilitation expenditure

13.409.1 Introduction

TCA 1997, s 681 provides for relief for expenditure incurred in connection with the closure of a mine. Where such expenditure is incurred after the mine has closed, it is treated as incurred on the date of closure so that it is allowable in the final accounting period of trading. There are also tax allowances for contributions to a mine rehabilitation fund made on the basis of certified payments into the fund. The aggregate of the payments required under the certification process is allowed over the estimated life of the mine but cumulative allowances at any time may not exceed the total of payments made to the fund at or before that time. Payments made out of the fund to a company for rehabilitation purposes are treated as taxable income while the actual expenditure on the rehabilitation is allowed.

13.409.2   Allowance for rehabilitation expenditure

In the case of a company, TCA 1997, s 681(3) provides that an allowance for rehabilitation expenditure, up to the amount of the "net cost of the rehabilitation of the site of a mine", is to be made to a company for the accounting period in which the expenditure is incurred. Expenditure incurred by a company after it ceases to carry on the trade of working a qualifying mine is treated as having been incurred on the last day on which the company carried on the trade.

The net cost of the rehabilitation of the site of a mine means the excess, if any, of rehabilitation expenditure over any receipts which are attributable to the rehabilitation, whether for spoil or other assets removed from the site or for tipping rights or otherwise.

A *qualifying mine* is a mine being worked for the purpose of obtaining scheduled minerals, dolomite and dolomitic limestone, fireclay, coal, calcite and gypsum, or any of those minerals. The definition is therefore broader in scope than that applying generally for the purposes of TCA 1997 Part 24 Ch 1 (see **13.402.1**). Accordingly, a company carrying on a trade of working a mine for the purpose of obtaining, say, dolomitic limestone would be entitled to the rehabilitation allowance but not, for example, to the development allowance provided for in TCA 1997, s 673 as the mine would not be a qualifying mine for the latter purpose.

Rehabilitation expenditure, in the case of a company which has ceased to work a mine, means expenditure incurred by the company in connection with the rehabilitation of the site of the mine, or part of the mine, to comply with any condition:

(a)   of a State mining facility;

(b)   subject to which planning permission was granted for development consisting of the mining and working of minerals; or

(c)   subject to which an integrated pollution control licence for an activity specified in the First Schedule to the Environmental Protection Agency Act 1992, was granted

Accordingly, if a company is operating only one mine, it will get no allowance until its mining trade ceases. If a company carries on a trade or operating two or more mines, rehabilitation expenditure will be allowed as it is incurred.

Rehabilitation is defined as including landscaping and the carrying out of any activities which take place after the mine ceases to be worked and which are required by a condition subject to which planning permission for development consisting of the mining and working of minerals, or an integrated pollution control licence, was granted.

An *integrated pollution control licence* is a licence granted under section 83 of the Environmental Protection Agency Act 1992.

A *State mining facility* means a State mining lease, a State mining licence or a State mining permission granted by the Minister for Communications, Energy and Natural Resources ("the Minister").

References to the site of a mine include references to land used in connection with the working of the mine.

13.409.3 Allowance for payments to rehabilitation fund

Where the Minister has issued a certificate to a company in relation to a mine rehabilitation fund related to a qualifying mine, an allowance will be made to the company where it is working the qualifying mine and is obliged to make "relevant payments" (see below) to the fund holder in relation to the fund (TCA 1997, s 681(4)). The allowance is made for any accounting period falling wholly or partly into the *funding period*, ie the period commencing on the date the certificate is issued and ending at the end of the estimated life of the mine. The amount of the allowance is the amount determined by the formula:

$$E \times \frac{N}{12} \times \frac{1}{L}$$

where—

E is the aggregate of scheduled payments (payments required under the certificate to be paid to the fund holder);

N is the number of months in the accounting period, or the part of the accounting period, falling into the funding period; and

L is the number of years in the estimated life of the mine.

In other words, the allowance for any accounting period is a fraction of the total scheduled payments, the fraction being the number of months in the accounting period, or part of the accounting period, within the funding period over the number of months in the estimated life of the mine.

The amount of the allowance for an accounting period may, however, be restricted by reference to cumulative payments to date. In arriving at the amount to be allowed for any accounting period, the aggregate of allowances for that period and all preceding periods (in accordance with the above formula) may not exceed the aggregate of relevant payments made in the period and in all preceding periods; *relevant payments* means payments specified in the certificate given by the Minister and paid at or about the time specified in that certificate. The certificate will specify the amounts of scheduled payments to be made to the fund as well as the times at which they are to be paid and the relevant payments are the amounts actually paid at or about the time specified (and may therefore differ from the amount of the specified payments). The cumulative restriction therefore ensures that allowances will not be made in advance of payments actually made.

Where the restriction described in the previous paragraph applies for any accounting period, the amount not allowed for that period is added to the amount of the allowance, if any, for the following period and is then deemed to be part of the allowance (or comprises the full allowance, as the case may be) for that period, but subject again to the cumulative restriction.

The definition of *mine rehabilitation fund* is lengthy. In relation to a qualifying mine being worked by a company in the course of a trade, it means a fund:

(a) consisting of payments made by the company to an unconnected person (the "fund holder");

(b) which must be maintained under the terms of a State mining facility, or of any other written agreement to which the Minister is a party and to which the State mining facility is subject;

(c) the sole purpose of which is to have available, when the mine ceases to be worked, an amount specified in a certificate given by the Minister, being an amount which in his opinion is necessary to meet rehabilitation expenditure in relation to the qualifying mine; and

(d) no part of which may be paid to the company (or a person connected with company) which is working or has worked the qualifying mine except where—

    (i) the fund holder has been authorised in writing by the Minister, and by either or both the relevant local authority and the Environmental Protection Agency, to make a payment to the company (or the connected person as the case may be), for the purposes of incurring rehabilitation expenditure in relation to the qualifying mine, or

    (ii) an amount may be paid to the company (or the connected person as the case may be), after a certificate of completion of rehabilitation in relation to the qualifying mine has been submitted to, and approved by, the Minister and either or both the relevant local authority and the Environmental Protection Agency.

The *relevant local authority*, in relation to a qualifying mine, means the council of a county or the corporation of a county or other borough or, where appropriate, the urban district council, in whose functional area the mine is situated. TCA 1997, s 10 applies for the purposes of determining when a company is connected with another person (see **2.3**).

The Minister may issue a certificate where, in relation to the rehabilitation fund, he is of the opinion that the matters contained in (a), (b) and (d) in the above definition of "mine rehabilitation fund" are satisfied and that the sole purpose of the fund is to have available, when the mine ceases to be worked, an amount which may reasonably be expected to be necessary to meet rehabilitation expenditure in relation to the qualifying mine.

The certificate must additionally specify:

(i) the number of years, being the Minister's opinion of the life of the mine remaining at the time the certificate is issued – the "estimated life of the mine";

(ii) the amount which in the Minister's opinion could reasonably be expected to be necessary to meet rehabilitation expenditure in relation to the qualifying mine; and

(iii) the amounts of the scheduled payments, being the amounts required to be paid to the fund holder, and the times at which such amounts are to be paid so as to have available, when the mine ceases to be worked, an amount which may reasonably be expected to be necessary to meet rehabilitation expenditure in relation to the qualifying mine.

The Minister may, by written notice given to a company to whom a certificate has been given, amend the certificate in any accounting period of that company. Where such written notice is given:

(a) if the aggregate of allowances made for the period and for all preceding periods exceeds the aggregate of allowances that would have been made for those periods in accordance with the amended certificate, the excess amount is treated as a trading receipt of the accounting period in which the certificate was amended; and

(b) if the aggregate of allowances made for the period and for all preceding periods is less than the aggregate of allowances that would have been made for those periods in accordance with the amended certificate, the allowance for the accounting period in which the certificate was amended is treated as increased by the difference.

13.409.4 Payments from fund

Payments made out of a mine rehabilitation fund to a company for rehabilitation purposes are treated as taxable income. An amount received by a company which is working, or which has worked, a qualifying mine (or received by a person connected with that company) from the fund holder of the related mine rehabilitation fund is treated as trading income of that company (TCA 1997, s 681(6)). The amount treated as trading income for any accounting period may not, however, be greater than the excess of the aggregate of the amounts of allowances made in that period and in any preceding periods (as adjusted by reason of any amended certificate – see (a) above) over the aggregate amounts treated as trading income for all preceding periods, whether as a result of TCA 1997, s 681(6) or of an amended certificate.

Where the amount treated as trading income is received by a company at a time when it is working the qualifying mine, it is treated as trading income of the accounting period in which the amount is received; otherwise it is treated as trading income of the accounting period in which the mine ceases to be worked. In the latter case, although the amount is treated as income of the accounting period in which the mine ceases to be worked, it is assessable for the accounting period in which the amount is received. For this purpose, details of the receipt of the amount must be included in the company's corporation tax return for that period. The effect of this provision is that the amount treated as taxable income will not become taxable until it is received but, by treating it as income of the period in which the mine ceases to be worked, it will be subject to tax by reference to the circumstances pertaining to that period, so that, for example, the corporation tax rate then in force will apply and any unused trading losses will be available for offset against the amount.

While a company falls to be taxed in respect of amounts paid to it from a mine rehabilitation fund, it will obtain a corresponding deduction for the amount to the extent that it is expended on rehabilitation, as outlined above.

13.409.5 Transfer of obligations

Where a company ceases to work a qualifying mine and any obligations it has to rehabilitate the site of the mine are transferred to any other person, that other person is treated, for the purposes of the previous paragraph, as if he had worked the qualifying mine and as if everything done to or by the company had been done to or by him.

13.409.6 Manner of giving allowances

Any allowance made under TCA 1997, s 681, whether as rehabilitation expenditure or as a payment to a rehabilitation fund, to a company carrying on the trade of working a qualifying mine is to be made "in taxing that trade", ie as an allowance made in computing the trading income, to be given effect by treating the amount of the allowance as a trading expense of the trade (TCA 1997 ss 307(2)(a) and 321(4) – see **5.105.2**). Unused allowances for any accounting period will therefore form part of, or will comprise, a trading loss of that period which may therefore be carried forward under TCA 1997, s 396(1) for offset against the company's trading profits of succeeding periods.

13.410   Capital sums for sale of scheduled mineral assets

A company which realises a capital sum as the whole or part of the net proceeds of sale of any scheduled mineral asset is liable to tax under Schedule D Case IV (TCA 1997, s 683). The taxable amount is the amount of the capital sum which comprises or which forms part of the consideration for the sale, reduced by the amount of any capital sum paid by the company which comprised or formed part of the consideration for the acquisition of the scheduled mineral asset. Where any part of the consideration for the sale consists of a royalty or similar payment that is already taxable as income, that part is excluded from the Case IV computation. The same position applies to deny a deduction for any part of the vendor's previous acquisition cost which consisted of a royalty.

TCA 1997, s 683 charges to tax in the same way any capital sum received as consideration, or as part of the consideration, for the grant of a licence to work scheduled minerals (TCA 1997, s 683(1)). In other words, the granting of a licence by a company which holds rights to work scheduled minerals is treated as a sale of part of its rights if, but only if, a capital sum is included in the consideration received. If the only consideration for the licence is a royalty, the provision has no application.

The rules for taxing capital sums in respect of the sale of scheduled mineral assets, or for the grant of a licence to work scheduled minerals, are similar to those applicable for the sale of patent rights or for the licensing of patents, as discussed in **13.605** (resident vendor) and **13.606** (non-resident vendor). However, under TCA 1997, s 683 a vendor company is assessable in respect of the capital sum for the accounting period in which it receives the sum.

A non-resident company, being the vendor of a scheduled mineral asset, is also chargeable under Case IV, but the person paying the capital sum to it is required to deduct income tax at the standard rate and to account for that tax, under TCA 1997, s 238, to the Revenue Commissioners. On making any necessary returns to the inspector of taxes, the non-resident company is entitled to have its liability in respect of the capital sum adjusted to allow for the deduction of any capital sum previously paid by it on its acquisition of the asset.

Where any compensation is paid to a company by the Minister by reason of an order made under section 14 of the Minerals Development Act 1940, for the acquisition of scheduled minerals or the right to work such minerals, the company is deemed for the purposes of TCA 1997, s 683 to have sold a scheduled mineral asset for a capital sum equal to the amount of the compensation paid to it.

13.411   Marginal mine allowance

The Minister for Finance, after consulting with the Minister for Communications, Energy and Natural Resources, may direct that the tax chargeable for any accounting period in respect of the profits of a marginal mine is to be reduced to such an amount, including nil, as may be specified by him (TCA 1997, s 682(2)).

A *marginal mine* is a qualifying mine in respect of which the Minister for Communications, Energy and Natural Resources gives a certificate stating that he is satisfied that the profits derived or to be derived from the working of that mine are such that, if tax is to be charged on those profits in the normal way, the mine is unlikely to be worked or to continue to be worked.

A company carrying on a trade of working a qualifying mine and in respect of which the Minister for Finance has given a direction, as described above, for an accounting period, may obtain an allowance, called a marginal mine allowance, as a deduction in charging the profits of its trade for that period. The amount of the deduction will ensure that the tax charged in respect of the profits of the trade will equal the amount specified by the Minister.

13.412   Expenses allowance for mineral rights

TCA 1997, s 111 entitles a company which owns rights to work minerals in the State, and which derives rents or royalties from leasing or otherwise allowing another person to work those minerals, to claim a deduction for expenses which it incurs wholly, exclusively and necessarily in managing or supervising the minerals. This allowance is given effect by way of repayment of the tax which the company has paid or suffered in respect of the rent or royalties in question. The allowance is given for the expenses incurred in the relevant accounting period against the actual rents or royalties receivable in that year.

No repayment of tax is, however, made under this section:

(a)   unless the company proves that it has actually paid tax on the aggregate amount of the rent or royalties receivable in the accounting period; or

(b)   if, and to the extent that, the said expenses have in any other way been allowed to the company as a deduction in computing its income for corporation tax purposes.

The company must specifically claim this allowance by giving notice in writing to the inspector within 24 months of the end of the relevant accounting period. The normal rights of appeal to the Appeal Commissioners and for a case stated for the opinion to the High Court are open to the company if the inspector objects to its claim under this section.

13.413   Rents from mining, quarrying etc concerns

Tax under Case IV of Schedule D is charged by TCA 1997, s 104 on rents, royalties and certain other payments received in respect of premises or easements used, occupied or enjoyed in connection with any of the types of concern enumerated in Case I(b) (TCA 1997, s 18(2)). The concerns in question are those which derive profits or gains arising out of lands, tenements and hereditaments which are taxable under Case I(b) in respect of any of the activities enumerated in that Case, including:

quarries of stone, slate, limestone etc, mines of coal, tin, lead, copper etc, ironworks, gasworks, waterworks, docks, canals, inland navigations and other concerns of a like nature having profits from or arising out of any lands, tenements or hereditaments.

These rents, royalties and other payments are the sole exception to the normal rule that all rents and receipts from easements from lands, tenements and hereditaments in the State are taxable under Case V. The charge to tax under Case IV in respect of these items is, therefore, relevant where the owner of the lands etc in question derives a rent, royalty or any yearly interest, annuity, or other annual payment for allowing the lands to be used in connection with mining, quarrying, inland waterways, docks and other concerns.

Although chargeable to tax under Case IV, a company receiving these payments normally receives them as taxed income and they are dealt with as such in its corporation tax computations. Any rent in respect of the premises or easements in question that is paid in kind, in produce of the concern in question (eg in limestone quarried), is taxed under Case IV on its market value as the nature of the consideration given in respect of the rent is such that tax cannot be withheld at source.

13.5 PETROLEUM ACTIVITIES

13.501 Petroleum companies: introduction and outline

TCA 1997 Part 24 Ch 2 (ss 684-697) contains special measures which deal with the taxation of petroleum activities. The main provision is an effective corporation tax rate of 25% in respect of income from certain petroleum leases. Qualification for the 25% rate depends on a lease being granted before a certain date and there are different such dates for various categories of petroleum lease.

All petroleum activities carried on in areas subject to the 1975 licensing terms are included within the scope of the legislation.

On the commencement of petroleum extraction activities by a company, all of its past exploration expenditure is deductible against petroleum profits except that, in the case of abortive exploration expenditure, a 25 year time limit applies. Companies within the same ownership may, for tax purposes, transfer entitlements to exploration expenditure.

Capital expenditure on production or development is deductible from the date production or development in commercial quantities commences in the field in respect of which the assets in question are brought into use. A deduction is allowed for expenditure on the abandonment of a field and in respect of the dismantling or removal of structures and plant or machinery used to transport petroleum to dry land. Losses attributable to such allowances (abandonment losses) may be set against profits of the period in which the loss was incurred and of the three years immediately preceding that period. Unused abandonment losses at the time a person ceases to carry on a petroleum trade may be used against the profits of a new petroleum trade subsequently carried on by that person.

Petroleum activities are ring fenced from other trading activities mainly to prevent erosion of the tax base which would result from non-petroleum profits being sheltered by the substantial allowances attributable to petroleum development.

Relief may not be claimed in respect of interest on borrowings used to finance exploration activities. Interest payable to connected persons is allowable as a trading expense provided it does not exceed an arm's length amount. Interest (other than in respect of borrowings to finance exploration activities) on money borrowed to acquire petroleum rights from connected persons is not deductible. Charges on income paid to connected persons are not deductible against petroleum profits. Interest payable to a foreign parent or fellow subsidiary resident in a country with which Ireland has a tax treaty is allowable as a trading expense.

Changes in licence interests at the pre-production stage (farm-ins and farm-outs) do not give rise to chargeable gains provided they are approved by the Minister for Communications, Energy and Natural Resources and their sole purpose is the furtherance of exploration or development of licensed acreage.

13.502   Definitions

The petroleum tax legislation contains many definitions and it is necessary to look at these in detail at the outset. Many of the definitions contain terms which themselves require further definitions.

It will be seen that the 25% corporation tax rate applies to certain *petroleum profits,* which means the income of a company from petroleum activities and any amounts to be included in profits in respect of chargeable gains from disposals of petroleum-related assets. *Petroleum activities* means any one or more of the following:

    (a)   petroleum exploration activities;

    (b)   petroleum extraction activities; or

    (c)   the acquisition, enjoyment or exploitation of petroleum rights.

Petroleum exploration activities in relation to a company means activities carried on by the company or on its behalf in searching for deposits of petroleum in a licensed area (an area in respect of which a licence is in force), in testing or appraising such deposits or winning access thereto for the purposes of such searching, testing or appraising, where the activities are carried on under a licence (other than a petroleum lease) authorising the activities and held by the company or by an associated company.

Petroleum means petroleum within the meaning of section 2(1) of the Petroleum and Other Minerals Development Act 1960, won or capable of being won under the authority of a licence. Section 2(1) of that Act provides that "petroleum" includes "any mineral oil or relative hydrocarbon and natural gas and other liquid or gaseous hydrocarbons and their derivatives or constituent substances existing in its natural condition in strata (including, without limitation, distillate, condensate, casinghead gasoline and such other substances as are ordinarily produced from oil and gas wells) and includes any other mineral substance contained in oil and natural gas brought to the surface with them in the normal process of extraction, but does not include coal and bituminous shales and other stratified deposits from which oil can be extracted by distillation".

A *licence* is:

    (a)   an exploration licence;

    (b)   a lease undertaking;

    (c)   a licensing option;

    (d)   a petroleum prospecting licence;

    (e)   a petroleum lease; or

    (f)   a reserved area licence,

        granted in respect of an area in the State or a designated area under the Petroleum and Other Minerals Development Act 1960, and which was granted subject to—

(i) the licensing terms set out in the Notice entitled "Ireland Exclusive Offshore Licensing Terms" presented to each House of the Oireachtas on 29 April 1975, or

(ii) licensing terms presented to each House of the Oireachtas after 29 April 1975, or

(iii) licensing terms as in (i) or (ii) as amended or varied.

A *licensed area* is an area in respect of which a licence is in force. A *designated area* is an area standing designated by order under section 2 of the Continental Shelf Act, 1968. Licences are granted in respect of areas in the State, which includes the territorial seas, or in a designated area.

References in the Tax Acts to "the State" are to the Republic of Ireland, its islands and its territorial seas. The law governing the extent of the territorial seas is partly derived from international law and practice. The Maritime Jurisdiction Act, 1959, provides that the territorial seas extend to the three-mile limit. The rights of coastal states in regard to the exploitation of the sea and sea-bed well beyond territorial waters is dependent on such concepts as the "economic zone" and the "continental shelf". The Geneva Convention on the Continental Shelf defines the "continental shelf" as extending to the point where exploitation of the natural resources is admitted by the depth of superjacent waters. The "economic zone" would extend no further than two hundred miles from the coastline. The right to natural resources in designated areas of the continental shelf is vested, in the case of Ireland, in the Minister for Communications, Energy and Natural Resources under the Continental Shelf Act, 1969.

The geographical scope of income tax, capital gains tax and corporation tax in relation to exploration or exploitation activities and rights was extended by TCA 1997, s 13 (as applied by TCA 1997, s 23 for corporation tax). Profits or gains from exploration or exploitation activities carried on in a designated area are treated as profits or gains from activities in the State and profits or gains from exploration or exploitation rights are treated as profits or gains from property in the State.

As noted above, "petroleum profits" also refers to amounts to be included in profits in respect of chargeable gains from disposals of petroleum-related assets. *Petroleum-related assets* means any of the following assets or any part of such an asset:

(a) any petroleum rights;

(b) any asset representing exploration expenditure or development expenditure;

(c) shares deriving their value or the greater part of their value, directly or indirectly, from petroleum activities, other than shares quoted on a stock exchange.

Petroleum rights means rights to petroleum to be extracted, or rights to interests in petroleum, or rights to the benefit of petroleum, and includes an interest in a licence.

The above definition of "petroleum exploration activities" includes a reference to an associated company. Two companies are associated with one another if one is a 51% subsidiary of the other, each is a 51% subsidiary of a third company, or one is owned by a consortium of which the other is a member. A company is owned by a consortium if all of its ordinary share capital is directly and beneficially owned between them by five or fewer companies (TCA 1997, s 684(2)). There is no requirement, as there is in the group relief legislation (see **8.303.1**), that the consortium members should be Irish resident. A company is a 51% subsidiary of another company as long as more than 50% of its ordinary share capital is owned directly or indirectly by that other company (TCA 1997, s 9(1)(a)).

Petroleum extraction activities in relation to a company means activities carried on by the company or on its behalf under a petroleum lease authorising the activities and held by the company or by an associated company, being activities in:

(a) winning petroleum from a relevant field, including searching in that field for, and winning access to, such petroleum;

(b) transporting as far as dry land (land not permanently covered by water) petroleum won from a place not on dry land; or

(c) effecting the initial treatment and storage of petroleum that is won from the relevant field.

A *relevant field* is an area in respect of which a licence, being a petroleum lease, is in force. *Initial treatment and storage* in relation to petroleum won from a relevant field means any of the following:

(a) subjecting the petroleum to any process of which the sole purpose is to enable it to be safely stored, safely loaded into a tanker or safely accepted for refining;

(b) separating petroleum consisting of gas from other petroleum;

(c) separating petroleum won, and consisting of gas that is of a kind that is transported and sold in normal commercial practice, from other petroleum consisting of gas;

(d) liquefying petroleum consisting of gas of such a kind as is described in (c) for the purposes of transporting it;

(e) subjecting petroleum to any process to secure that petroleum disposed of without having been refined has the quality that is normal for petroleum disposed of from the relevant field;

(f) storing petroleum prior to its disposal or prior to its appropriation to refining or to any use except use in—

(i) winning petroleum from a relevant field, including searching in that field for, and winning access to, such petroleum, or

(ii) transporting as far as dry land petroleum won from a place not on dry land,

but does not include any activity carried on as part of, or in association with, the refining of petroleum.

A *petroleum trade* is a trade

(a) consisting only of trading activities which are petroleum activities; or

(b) where a trade consists partly of such activities and partly of other activities, the part of the trade consisting only of trading activities which are petroleum activities.

Where petroleum activities are carried on as part of a trade, they are treated for tax purposes as a separate trade, provided they would be treated as a trade if carried on alone. For this purpose, any necessary apportionment is to be made of receipts and expenses (TCA 1997, s 685).

For the purposes of the 25% effective corporation tax rate, the definition of a relevant petroleum lease is important as the rate applies to income arising under that kind of lease. A *relevant petroleum lease* is a petroleum lease in respect of a relevant field discovered as a result of petroleum exploration activities carried on under a licence (other than a petroleum lease) authorising the carrying on of those activities for a period which (apart from any extension of the period or revision or renewal of the licence):

(a)   is not longer than 10 years, where the petroleum lease is granted by the Minister for Transport, Energy and Communications before 1 June 2003;

(b)   is longer than 10 years and not longer than 15 years where the petroleum lease is granted before 1 June 2007; or

(c)   is longer than 15 years where the petroleum lease is granted before 1 June 2013.

A petroleum lease in respect of a relevant field is, however, a relevant petroleum lease where:

(i)   the field was discovered under a lease which is not a licence;

(ii)   the lease under which the field was discovered expired before the petroleum lease is granted; and

(iii) the petroleum lease is granted by the Minister for Communications, Energy and Natural Resources before 1 June 2003.

The inclusion of this last category in the definition of a relevant petroleum lease effectively permits the development and exploitation of fields which were discovered under a lease which had been issued before the 1975 licensing terms where that lease had expired without a petroleum lease having been issued in respect of the field. This 1995 amendment to the definition of a petroleum lease is intended to encourage exploration in marginal fields which would otherwise remain undeveloped.

TCA 1997, s 685 contains other definitions which are dealt with later in relation to particular provisions of the petroleum tax regime.

13.503   Corporation tax rate

TCA 1997, s 686 provides for a reduction of corporation tax on certain income from petroleum activities to produce an effective rate of 25%. Since 1 January 2000 the standard rate of corporation tax has been lower than 25% but from that date the higher rate of corporation tax, 25%, provided for in TCA 1997, s 21A, applies, inter alia, to the income of trades consisting of petroleum activities. The definition of "petroleum activities" in TCA s 21A is identical to that in TCA 1997, s 684(1) but the effective 25% rate of tax provided for in TCA s 686 relates to income from a defined part of a company's activities from petroleum activities whereas the 25% rate of tax in TCA 1997, s 21A relates simply to income from petroleum activities. The essential difference between the two provisions is that TCA 1997, s 686 is concerned with the income from activities related to Irish licences whereas TCA s 21A relates to petroleum activities generally. Thus, for example, the 25% rate provided for in TCA 1997, s 21A will apply regardless of whether or not there is a "relevant petroleum lease".

Furthermore, TCA 1997, s 686 ceases to have effect as respects accounting periods ending on or after 3 February 2005. In the light of what is outlined above, TCA 1997, s 686 is of practical relevance only in relation to profits arising on or before 31

December 1999. TCA 1997, s 686(2) provides a formula for calculating the income of a company in respect of which the 25% rate is charged and its provisions are dealt with in previous editions of this book.

13.504 Ring fencing

13.504.1 Introduction

To prevent the erosion of the tax base which would otherwise occur from the sheltering of non-petroleum profits by the substantial allowances attributable to petroleum development, losses from petroleum activities are ring fenced from other trading activities. In addition, if a company carries on any petroleum activities as part of a trade and those activities would on their own constitute a trade, they are to be treated as a separate trade for tax purposes, distinct from all other activities carried on by the company. Any necessary apportionment of receipts and expenses is to be made for the purpose of arriving at the profits of the separate trade (TCA 1997, s 685(1)).

13.504.2 Trading losses

For the purposes of TCA 1997, s 396(2) (see **4.101**), a loss incurred in a petroleum trade may only be set off against petroleum profits (income from petroleum activities and chargeable gains from disposals of petroleum-related assets). With the exception of losses from a mining trade, no losses other than from a petroleum trade may be set against petroleum profits (TCA 1997, s 687(1)). There is thus a "two-way" ring fencing of trading losses for the purposes of TCA 1997, s 396(2)); petroleum (and mining) losses may only be set against petroleum profits and petroleum profits may only be relieved by petroleum losses.

The working of a qualifying mine as part of a trade carried on by a company is also treated for the purposes of the petroleum tax legislation as a separate trade, distinct from all other activities carried on by the company. Other activities carried on by such a company could, for example, include the production of petroleum under a licence not governed by the 1975 or subsequent licensing terms or might consist of petroleum refining or distribution. Any necessary apportionment of receipts and expenses is to be made for the purpose of arriving at the profits of the separate trade (TCA 1997, s 685(2). A *mining trade* is a trade consisting only of working a qualifying mine (see **13.402.1**) or, where a trade consists partly of such an activity and partly of one or more other activities, the part of that trade consisting only of working such a mine which is treated under TCA 1997, s 685 as a separate trade (TCA 1997, s 684(1)).

13.504.3 Non-trading losses

A loss incurred in an accounting period by a company in a transaction any profits from which would be chargeable to tax under Case IV of Schedule D (see **3.208.1** and **4.106**) may under TCA 1997, s 399 be set off against any other profits or gains on which the company is assessed under Case IV for the same period. Where a company has income chargeable to tax under Case IV and which arises from petroleum activities, for example royalties from an interest in a petroleum deposit, that income may not be reduced by virtue of TCA 1997, s 399(1) other than by a loss incurred in petroleum activities.

Capital allowances which are to be given by way of discharge or repayment or tax, or in charging income under Case V of Schedule D, may not be given effect under TCA 1997, s 308(4) (see **5.105.3**) against petroleum profits (TCA 1997, s 687(3)).

13.504.4   Group relief

Where a claim for group relief under TCA 1997, s 411 is made (see **8.302**), group relief may not be given against any petroleum profits of the claimant company except to the extent that the claim relates to:

(a)   a loss incurred by the surrendering company in a petroleum trade or a mining trade; or

(b)   charges on income paid, other than to a connected person, by the surrendering company and consisting of payments made wholly and exclusively for the purposes of the trade (TCA 1997, s 688).

Where any such group relief is allowed in respect of a loss or charges, it is to be allowed only against the profits of the claimant company which consist of petroleum profits. As with TCA 1997, s 396(2) losses, there is a two-way ring fencing of losses and charges for the purposes of group relief; petroleum (and mining) losses and charges may only be set against petroleum profits and petroleum profits may only be relieved by petroleum losses.

13.504.5   Chargeable gains

For the purposes of corporation tax in respect of chargeable gains, an allowable loss arising on the disposal of an asset other than a petroleum-related asset may not be deducted from the amount of a chargeable gain accruing on a disposal of a petroleum-related asset. An allowable loss arising on the disposal of a petroleum-related asset may not be deducted from the amount of a chargeable gain arising on the disposal of any asset other than a petroleum-related asset. Again, a two-way ring fence applies (TCA 1997, s 689).

The relief provided for by TCA 1997, s 597 (replacement of business assets – "roll-over" relief – see **9.102.18**) applies in relation to a person carrying on two or more trades in different localities which are concerned wholly or mainly with goods or services of the same kind as if, in relation to the assets used for the purposes of the trade, the trades were the same trade. That provision applies also in relation to the disposal of assets which have been used by the person disposing of them for the purposes of a petroleum trade.

13.505   Interest and charges on income

In computing the income of a company arising from a petroleum trade, no deduction may be made, for corporation purposes, in respect of:

(i)   any interest payable by the company to a connected person (see **2.3**) to the extent that the amount of the interest exceeds, for whatever reason, the amount which might have been expected to be payable if the lender and the borrower had been independent persons dealing at arm's length;

(ii)   interest payable by the company on any money borrowed to meet expenditure incurred on petroleum exploration activities; or

(iii)   interest payable by the company on any money borrowed to meet expenditure incurred in acquiring petroleum rights from a connected person (TCA 1997, s 690(1)).

TCA 1997, s 130(2)(d)(iv) treats as a distribution (see **11.106**) interest paid by a company in respect of securities held by a non-resident 75% parent company or by a non-resident 75% fellow subsidiary company (except a fellow subsidiary 90% of whose ordinary share capital is owned directly by an Irish resident company). That provision does not apply to so much of any interest as:

(a)   would otherwise be deductible in computing the company's income from a petroleum trade (ie, if it is wholly and exclusively paid for the purposes of that trade);

(b)   would not be prevented by (i), (ii) or (iii) above from being so deducted; and

(c)   is interest payable to a company which is resident in a country which has a double tax treaty with Ireland (TCA 1997, s 690(2)).

Certain restrictions, including a two-way ring fencing provision, apply in relation to the allowance of charges on income against petroleum profits. No such deduction may be made from that part of a company's profits which consists of petroleum profits in respect of any charge on income paid by the company to a connected person, or in respect of any other charge paid by it unless it is a payment made wholly and exclusively for the purposes of a petroleum or mining trade carried on by the company. Neither may any deduction be allowed from that part of a company's profits which consists of profits other than petroleum profits in respect of any charge on income paid by the company which is a payment made wholly and exclusively for the purposes of a petroleum trade carried on by the company (TCA 1997, s 690(3)). (The part of a company's profits which consists of profits other than petroleum profits may, however, be reduced by charges paid wholly and exclusively for the purposes of a mining trade carried on by the company; mining trade charges may be deducted from any profits of the company.)

Charges on income may accordingly be restricted for any accounting period either by way of restricting petroleum trade charges to the petroleum part of a company's profits, or by restricting charges other than petroleum and mining trade charges to the non-petroleum part of its profits. In either case, it may happen that the amount of the charges allowable against only one part, say the non-petroleum part, of the company's profits exceeds that part, and the excess is greater than the amount, if any, by which the total amount of charges on income exceeds the total profits of the company. In that event, for the purposes of group relief in respect of excess charges (see **8.305.5**), the excess non-petroleum charges may be surrendered to another group company on the basis that the amount of the charges paid by the company was the amount of the non-petroleum charges and that the profits of the company were its non-petroleum profits only (TCA 1997, s 690(6)).

Example 13.505.1

Baku Oil (Ireland) Ltd has the following results, adjusted for tax purposes, for its latest accounting period:

	€
Petroleum profits	80,000
Profits other than petroleum profits	100,000

Charges paid for petroleum trade	70,000
Charges paid for purposes other than petroleum (or mining) trade	120,000

The excess charges paid in the period which are restricted to the non-petroleum profits are €20,000. This excess is greater than €10,000, the excess of the total charges €190,000 over total profits €180,000. The excess of €20,000 may be surrendered to another group company by way of group relief. The profits against which the €20,000 may be allowed must, however, be other than petroleum profits (see **13.504.4** above).

Were it not for TCA 1997, s 690(6), the amount which could have been surrendered by way of group relief would have been limited to €10,000.

The charges of €120,000 paid other than for the purposes of the petroleum trade could include charges paid for a mining trade carried on by the company.

Example 13.505.2

The position is as in Example **13.505.1** except that the charges paid for purposes other than the petroleum trade include an amount of €5,000 in respect of a mining trade carried on by the company.

The charges now allowable against petroleum profits are €75,000 and those allowable against other profits are €115,000. The excess charges relating to the non-petroleum profits amount to €15,000 which, again, is greater than the excess of total charges over total profits. The company may surrender the excess €15,000 to the other group company.

Excess charges on income (see **4.404**) paid in any accounting period by a company to a connected person may not be carried forward for the purposes of TCA 1997, s 396(7) so as to augment a trading loss, where paid wholly and exclusively for the purposes of a petroleum trade (TCA 1997, s 690(5)).

13.506 Development expenditure

TCA 1997, s 692 provides for an allowance of 100% of capital expenditure on production and development in connection with a relevant field being worked in the course of carrying on a petroleum trade. A company may not claim any allowance in respect of assets representing development expenditure for any accounting period ending before the commencement of production of petroleum in commercial quantities in the field in respect of which the assets in question are provided.

The provisions of the Tax Acts relating to allowances and charges for capital expenditure have effect in relation to a petroleum trade as if assets representing development expenditure, other than machinery or plant, were machinery or plant and on the basis that a 100% allowance is to be made instead of the normal rate allowance (see **5.203.3**) provided for in TCA 1997, s 284(1) (TCA 1997, s 692(1)). In this connection, TCA 1997, s 284(2) applies as if the references in TCA 1997, s 284(2)(a)(i), (aa) and (ad) to 15%, 20% and 12.5% (see **5.203.3**) were a reference to 100% (TCA 1997, s 692(2)).

The following provisions have no effect as respects development expenditure:

(a) TCA 1997 Part 9 Ch 1 (industrial building allowances) and Ch 3 (initial and annual allowances for dredging);
(b) TCA 1997, s 283 (initial allowances for expenditure on machinery or plant);
(c) TCA 1997, s 670 (mine development allowance);
(d) TCA 1997 Part 29 Ch 1 (annual allowances and balancing allowances and charges in respect of patents);

(e)   TCA 1997 ss 763-765 (allowances for expenditure on scientific research); and

(f)   TCA 1997, s 768 (allowance for know-how).

For the above purposes, capital expenditure on the provision of leased assets is deemed to be development expenditure.

Development expenditure is defined in TCA 1997, s 684(1) as capital expenditure incurred in connection with a relevant field on the provision for use in carrying on petroleum extraction activities of:

(a)   machinery or plant;

(b)   any works, buildings or structures; or

(c)   any other assets,

which are likely to be of little or no value when the relevant field ceases to be worked, but does not include—

(i)   expenditure on any vehicle suitable for the conveyance by road of persons or goods or the haulage by road of other vehicles;

(ii)   expenditure on any dwelling house, shop or office or for any purpose ancillary to the purposes of such a building;

(iii) expenditure on petroleum exploration activities and payments made to the Minister for Energy in connection with the application, granting or holding of a licence (other than a petroleum lease);

(iv) expenditure on the acquisition of the site of a relevant field, or of the site of any works, buildings or structures or of rights in or over any such site;

(v)   expenditure on the acquisition of, or of rights in or over, deposits of petroleum,

(vi) expenditure on machinery or plant, or works, buildings or structures, which are provided for the processing or storage of petroleum won in the course of carrying on petroleum extraction activities, other than the initial treatment and storage of such petroleum; or

(vii) any interest payment.

Assets representing development expenditure is to be construed accordingly and includes any results obtained from any search or enquiry in respect of which the expenditure was incurred.

It is specifically provided in TCA 1997, s 692 that, for the purposes of that section, assets ("leased assets") provided for leasing to a person carrying on a petroleum trade are to be deemed to be "assets representing development expenditure" where they would be so regarded if they had been provided by that person. In any such case, capital allowances will be available to the lessor under TCA 1997, s 284 as if the trade for which the leased assets are in use (the lessee's trade), or the deemed lessor's trade for which they *would* under TCA 1997, s 298(1) (burden of wear and tear falling directly on the lessee) be regarded as being in use, were a petroleum trade carried on by the lessor. Furthermore, TCA 1997, s 403 (see **5.305** – restriction of lessor's capital allowances) is to have effect in relation to assets representing development expenditure as it has in relation to machinery or plant.

In respect of assets used for the purposes of a petroleum trade which do not fall within the description of assets representing development expenditure, the normal capital allowances provisions will apply.

13.507   Exploration expenditure

Where a company carrying on a petroleum trade has incurred any exploration expenditure it will be entitled, for the accounting period in which the expenditure is incurred, to an allowance equal to the amount of that expenditure. Expenditure which is met directly or indirectly by any person other than the company (for example, on a "farm-in" – see **13.511**) is disregarded for this purpose (TCA 1997, s 693(1)).

Where an allowance in respect of exploration expenditure has been made to a company carrying on a petroleum trade, and the company disposes of assets representing any amount of that expenditure, a balancing charge equal to the amount or value of the consideration in money or money's worth received by the company on the disposal will be made for the accounting period in which the disposal takes place. If the disposal occurs after the trade is permanently discontinued, the charge is made for the accounting period in which the discontinuance occurred. The maximum amount of any balancing charge is the amount of the allowance made to the company in respect of the amount of exploration expenditure represented by the assets so disposed of (TCA 1997, s 693(2)).

For the purpose of computing a balancing charge, any assets representing exploration expenditure which have been destroyed are treated as having been disposed of immediately before their destruction. Any sale, insurance, salvage or compensation moneys received in respect of the assets by the company carrying on the petroleum trade are treated as consideration received on that disposal (TCA 1997, s 693(3)).

Exploration expenditure means:

(a)   capital expenditure incurred on petroleum exploration activities; and

(b)   payments made to the Minister for the Marine and Natural Resource on the application for, or in consideration for the granting of, a licence (other than a petroleum lease) or other payments made to him in respect of the holding of the licence,

but does not include any interest payment (TCA 1997, s 684(1)). The term *assets representing exploration expenditure* is to be construed accordingly and includes any results obtained from any search, exploration or enquiry in respect of which the expenditure was incurred. The mere fact that exploration expenditure is capitalised in the accounts of a company does not give rise to such assets. Assets in this context would consist of such items as plans, blueprints, drawings, seismic data or any other items to which value can be attributed and which have resulted from exploration activities. Assets representing exploration expenditure are treated as including a part or share in any such assets (TCA 1997, s 693(17)).

Where a company disposes of any assets representing exploration expenditure incurred by it in an area which at the time of the disposal is, or subsequently becomes, a relevant field, or part of such a field, a company acquiring those assets will be deemed to have incurred exploration expenditure in relation to those assets if it carries on a petroleum trade which consists of or includes the working of the relevant field (or the part of the relevant field). The exploration expenditure will be deemed to have been incurred on the day the acquiring company acquires the assets or, if later, on the day on which it commences to work the area connected with the assets as a relevant field (or part of a relevant field). The amount of exploration expenditure deemed to have been incurred by the acquiring company will be the lesser of the amount of the exploration expenditure represented by the assets (ie, the part of the exploration expenditure incurred by the first company as was incurred in respect of the assets) and the amount or value of the consideration given by it on the acquisition of the assets (TCA 1997, s 693(4)).

A company may claim relief not only in respect of successful exploration expenditure but also for abortive exploration expenditure, but not in respect of any such expenditure incurred more than 25 years before the date on which the petroleum trade commenced. On the commencement of petroleum extraction activities by a company, all of its past exploration expenditure, subject to the 25 year time limit for abortive expenditure, is deductible against petroleum profits; that expenditure is deemed to have been incurred on the day the trade commences (TCA 1997, s 693(5)). Abortive exploration expenditure is expenditure which was incurred in connection with an area which is not a relevant field (ie, which is not eventually worked by the company as a producing field).

Where a company incurs exploration expenditure before it commences to carry on a petroleum trade (so that it will be deemed to have incurred the expenditure on the day the trade commences), but before the trade commences it disposes of assets representing any amount of that expenditure, the allowance falling to be made to the company in respect of its exploration expenditure is reduced by the net amount or value of any consideration in money or money's worth received on the disposal (TCA 1997, s 693(6)).

The day on which exploration expenditure is incurred is to be taken as the day on which the amount in question becomes payable (TCA 1997, s 693(7)). This rule is, however, subject to TCA 1997, s 693(4), (5) (see above) where, for example, expenditure may be treated as incurred on the date trading commences.

An allowance or balancing charge made to or on a company in connection with exploration expenditure is to be made in taxing the company's petroleum trade (TCA 1997, s 693(8)). Apart from the situation dealt with by TCA 1997, s 693(4) (where a company disposes of assets representing exploration expenditure to another company which then qualifies for allowances in respect of the same expenditure), an allowance may not be made in respect of the same expenditure in taxing more than one petroleum trade.

An allowance or charge made in respect of exploration expenditure for any accounting period in taxing a trade of a company is to be given effect by treating the amount of any allowance as a trading expense of the trade in that period and by treating any charge as a trading receipt of the trade in the period (TCA 1997, s 693(10)). The treatment is therefore the same as that applying for the purposes of capital allowances generally in the case of a company (see **5.105.2**).

The provisions of TCA 1997, s 312 (control and main benefit sales – see **5.103**) and the definition of "sale, insurance, salvage or compensation moneys" in TCA 1997, s 318 (see **5.104**) apply, with any necessary modifications, to allowances made for exploration expenditure as they apply for the purposes of capital allowances and balancing charges generally (TCA 1997, s 693(13)).

For certain capital gains tax purposes, allowances and charges made in respect of exploration expenditure are treated as if they were allowances or charges arising under the general capital allowances regime (TCA 1997, s 693(14)). TCA 1997, s 551(2) provides that for the purposes of computing a capital gain on the disposal of an asset, any amount charged to income tax (or corporation tax) as income or taken into account as a receipt in computing income of the person making the disposal, is to be excluded from the consideration for the disposal. Any amount which is taken into account in making a balancing charge, however, is not so excluded (TCA 1997, s 551(3)). That exception applies to balancing charges in respect of exploration expenditure as it does in relation to capital allowances generally (TCA 1997, s 693(14)(a)).

TCA 1997, s 555(1) provides that in computing a capital gains tax loss on the disposal of an asset, any expenditure which has attracted capital allowances is to be excluded. That provision applies to allowances made in respect of exploration expenditure as it applies in respect of capital allowances generally (TCA 1997, s 693(14)(b)) (see also **9.102.17**). Balancing charges are not, however, excluded for the purposes of computing either a gain or a loss for capital gains tax purposes (TCA 1997, s 551(3)). Again, that position also applies in relation to allowances made in respect of exploration expenditure (TCA 1997, s 693(14)(b)).

For the purposes of computing allowances in respect of exploration expenditure, the amount of any such expenditure incurred by a company may not include any amount in respect of value-added tax for which the company is entitled to claim input credit or to claim a refund. Similarly, in computing a balancing allowance or charge in respect of exploration expenditure, the amount of any sale, insurance, salvage or compensation moneys to be taken into account may not include any value-added tax chargeable to the company in respect of those moneys (TCA 1997, s 693(15)).

For the purposes of any claim in respect of exploration expenditure, a company will be deemed to be carrying on a petroleum trade only if and when it is carrying on, in the course of that trade, trading activities which are petroleum extraction activities (TCA 1997, s 693(16)). It will be recalled that the definition of a petroleum trade refers to trading activities which are petroleum activities and that petroleum activities comprise petroleum exploration activities, petroleum extraction activities and the acquisition, enjoyment or exploitation of petroleum rights. Only when a company is carrying on petroleum extraction activities will it be treated as carrying on a petroleum trade for the purposes of entitlement to allowances in respect of exploration expenditure.

13.508 Surrender of exploration expenditure

TCA 1997, s 694 permits exploration expenditure (other than expenditure which has been or is to be met directly or indirectly by another person) to be surrendered between certain associated companies. This facility is similar to that available in respect of mining operations (see **13.405**). The section will facilitate a group in which there is a producing and an exploration company so that the exploration company can elect to surrender its exploration expenditure to the producing company. The effect of the election is that the exploration expenditure is deemed to have been incurred by the producing company which can then take a deduction for the amount involved.

The election may be made in respect of both successful and abortive exploration expenditure, in respect of which a deduction may be claimed under TCA 1997, s 693.

For the purposes of the election, the required relationship between the two companies is as follows. The company which incurs the exploration expenditure (the "exploration company") is, at the time the exploration expenditure is incurred, a wholly owned subsidiary of the other company ("the parent company"), or the other company is a wholly owned subsidiary of the exploration company. A company is deemed to be a wholly owned subsidiary of another company if and as long as all of its ordinary share capital is owned by that other company, whether directly or through another company or companies, or partly directly and partly through another company or companies (TCA 1997, s 694(5)). For the purposes of determining the amount of ordinary share capital held in a company through other companies, the provisions of TCA 1997 Schedule 9 paragraph 6, and thereby TCA 1997, s 9(5)-(10), have effect (see **2.505**).

The surrender of exploration expenditure is at the election of the exploration company which may surrender all of the expenditure it has incurred or such lesser amount of it as it specifies. The exploration expenditure may be surrendered in any of the following three ways:

(1)   Where another company is a wholly owned subsidiary of the exploration company, the exploration expenditure specified may, at the election of the exploration company, be deemed to have been incurred by that other company;

(2)   Where the exploration company is, at the time the exploration expenditure is incurred, a wholly owned subsidiary of the parent company, the exploration expenditure specified is deemed, at the election of the exploration company, to have been incurred by the parent company;

(3)   Where the exploration company is, at the time the exploration expenditure is incurred, a wholly owned subsidiary of the parent company, the exploration expenditure specified is deemed, at the election of the exploration company, to have been incurred by such other company specified by it as is a wholly owned subsidiary of the parent company.

Expenditure incurred by an exploration company and which is deemed to have been incurred by another company is deemed to have been incurred by that other company at the time it was incurred by the exploration company. Where exploration expenditure was incurred prior to the incorporation of a company specified by an exploration company as a company deemed to have incurred that expenditure, that company is treated as if it had been in existence at the time the expenditure was incurred. As regards exploration expenditure deemed to have been incurred by another company which is carrying on a petroleum trade, that expenditure is deemed to have been incurred for the purposes of that trade and not to have been met directly or indirectly by the exploration company.

TCA 1997, s 694 is not to have the effect that the same expenditure could be taken into account in relation to more than one trade. Neither may a deduction or allowance be made in respect of the same expenditure both by virtue of the section and under some other provision of the Tax Acts.

Example 13.508.1

Qatar Resources Ltd, a petroleum exploration company, is a 100% subsidiary of Barranquilla Oil Ltd which in turn is a 100% subsidiary of Houma Ltd. Tupelo Ltd is also a 100% subsidiary of Barranquilla Oil Ltd. Apart from Qatar Resources Ltd, each of the other companies in the group is carrying on an oil producing trade. In the latest accounting period of the group, Qatar Ltd incurred exploration expenditure of €2,700,000. Barranquilla Oil Ltd, Houma Ltd and Tupelo Ltd have petroleum profits of €1,100,000, €750,000 and €50,000 respectively in the same period. Qatar Resources Ltd elects that its exploration expenditure of €2,700,000 is deemed to have been incurred as follows:

	€
Barranquilla Oil Ltd (parent company)	1,600,000
Houma Ltd (parent company)	1,050,000
Tupelo Ltd	50,000
	2,700,000

Barranquilla Oil Ltd uses the €1,600,000 deemed exploration expenditure to cover its profits of €1,100,000 for the accounting period with the balance of €500,000 being carried forward. The election in this case is in accordance with (2) above – exploration expenditure deemed to be incurred by parent company.

Tupelo Ltd uses deemed exploration expenditure of €50,000, as specified by Qatar Resources Ltd, to reduce its profits of €50,000 for the accounting period to nil. The circumstances pertaining to the field being worked by Tupelo Ltd are such that it is not likely to be profitable in the foreseeable future. The election in this case is in accordance with (3) above – exploration expenditure deemed to be incurred by wholly owned subsidiary of parent company.

Houma Ltd may also be deemed to have incurred exploration expenditure of €1,050,000 to reduce its profits of €750,000 to nil, the balance of €300,000 being carried forward. The election in this case is also in accordance with (2) above.

13.509   Abandonment expenditure

TCA 1997, s 695 provides for an allowance in respect of *abandonment expenditure* which, in relation to any field or any part of it, means expenditure incurred on abandonment activities in relation to the field or the part of it. *Abandonment activities*, in relation to any field or any part of it and as respects a company, means the activities of the company, whether carried on by it or on its behalf, which comply with the requirements of a petroleum lease held by it or by a company associated with it, in respect of:

(a)   the closing down, decommissioning or abandonment of the relevant field or the part of it; or

(b)   the dismantling or removal of the whole or part of any structure, plant or machinery which is not situated on dry land and which has been brought into use for the purposes of transporting as far as dry land petroleum won from the relevant field or from the part of it.

Two companies are associated with one another if one is a 51% subsidiary of the other, or each is a 51% subsidiary of a third company, or one is owned by a consortium of which the other is a member. A company is owned by a consortium if all of its ordinary share capital is directly and beneficially owned between them by five or fewer companies ("the consortium members").

An allowance is provided for under TCA 1997, s 695 in respect of abandonment expenditure incurred by a company which is or has been carrying on petroleum extraction activities, other than the initial treatment and storage of petroleum won. The abandonment expenditure is available for expenditure incurred in respect of the field, or the part of it, in relation to which the petroleum extraction activities are or were being carried on. The allowance, of an amount equal to the amount of the expenditure incurred, is to be made for the accounting period in which the company incurred the expenditure. Expenditure which is or is to be met directly or indirectly by any person other than the company is not taken into account for this purpose.

TCA 1997, s 396(2), (3) apply to the amount of any loss incurred by a company in an accounting period, to the extent that it is an "abandonment loss", as if the period specified in subsection (3) were a period of three years ending immediately before the accounting period in which the loss is incurred. TCA 1997, s 396(2), (3) provide (see **4.101**) that a trading loss may be offset:

(a) against profits of any description (before charges) of the same accounting period; and

(b) provided the company was then carrying on the trade, against profits of any description (before charges) of immediately preceding accounting periods ending within a period equal in length to the period in which the loss was incurred.

As applied to an abandonment loss, the effect of TCA 1997, s 396(3) is that the loss may be set against profits of any description of the accounting periods ending within the three year period immediately before the period in which the loss is incurred.

An *abandonment loss* means so much of a loss in a petroleum trade incurred by a company in an accounting period as does not exceed the total amount of allowances which:

(i) fall to be made to the company for that period under TCA 1997, s 695 (ie, in respect of abandonment expenditure); and

(ii) have been brought into account in determining the amount of the said loss in the petroleum trade.

In short, an abandonment loss of a company for an accounting period is the part of a trading loss incurred by that company in that period which is attributable to abandonment expenditure incurred by it.

In a case where a company permanently ceases to carry on a petroleum trade and subsequently carries on another petroleum trade, any unused allowances for abandonment expenditure of the first-mentioned trade are deductible as a trading expense of the new trade (TCA 1997, s 695(4)). The deduction is made for the first accounting period of the first petroleum trade to be carried on by the company after the permanent discontinuance of the first-mentioned trade. Abandonment expenditure incurred by a company after a petroleum trade has been discontinued is treated, for the purposes of the making of allowances in respect of abandonment expenditure, as if it had been incurred by it on the last day on which it carried on the trade (TCA 1997, s 695(5)).

The day on which exploration expenditure is incurred is to be taken as the day on which the amount in question becomes payable (TCA 1997, s 695(6)). This is subject to the situations dealt with by TCA 1997, s 695(4), (5), referred to in the previous paragraph.

An allowance made to a company in connection with abandonment expenditure is to be made in taxing the company's petroleum trade (TCA 1997, s 695(7). An allowance may not be made in respect of the same expenditure in taxing more than one petroleum trade.

The following provisions have no effect as respects expenditure which is abandonment expenditure:

(a)   TCA 1997 Part 9 (relief in respect of capital expenditure);

(b)   TCA 1997, s 670 (mine development allowance);

(c)   TCA 1997 Part 29 Ch 1 (annual allowances and balancing allowances and charges in respect of patents); and

(d)   TCA 1997 ss 763-765 (allowances for expenditure on scientific research).

However, TCA 1997, s 316(1), (2) (interpretation of certain references to expenditure and time when expenditure is incurred), and TCA 1997, s 317(2) (treatment of grants) and TCA 1997, s 320(5) (setting up or permanent discontinuance of trade) are, with any necessary modifications, to apply for the purposes of TCA 1997, s 695 as they apply for the purposes of TCA 1997 Part 9 and Part 29 Ch 1 (see **5.102**, **5.203.3**, **5.205.2**, **5.405.2** and **13.601**).

For the purposes of computing an allowance in respect of abandonment expenditure, the amount of any such expenditure incurred by a company may not include any amount in respect of value-added tax for which the company is entitled to claim input credit or to claim a refund (TCA 1997, s 695(9)).

13.510   Valuation of petroleum

Petroleum which is acquired by a company by virtue of petroleum activities and which is disposed of otherwise than by way of a sale at arm's length is treated, as respects both the disposal and the acquisition by the person to whom the disposal was made, as having been for a consideration equal to the market value of the petroleum at the time the disposal was made (TCA 1997, s 696(1)).

TCA 1997, s 696(2) provides another market value rule in the cases of certain appropriations. The rule will apply where a company carrying on petroleum activities and other activities in the course of a trade appropriates any petroleum won, or otherwise acquired in the course of carrying on petroleum activities, to refining or to any use except use for petroleum extraction activities carried on by it. Where this happens, the company is treated as having at the time of the appropriation:

(a)   sold the petroleum in the course of the petroleum trade carried on by it; and

(b)   bought it in the course of a separate trade consisting of the activities other than the petroleum activities,

and as having sold and bought the petroleum at a price equal to its market value at the time the petroleum was appropriated.

For the above purposes, the market value at any time of any petroleum is the price which that petroleum might reasonably be expected to fetch on a sale at that time if the parties to the transaction were independent parties dealing at arm's length.

The transfer pricing rules are necessary for a proper determination of the respective amounts of profits from activities on each side of the "ring fence", such as, respectively, petroleum extraction and refining. The market value rule affecting sales of petroleum would be relevant, for example, in the case of a petroleum production company selling petroleum to an associated company carrying on a refining trade. The market value appropriation rule would apply in the case of a company carrying on both production and refining activities in which case the company would be treated as carrying on two separate trades so that appropriations of petroleum to refining would be treated as sales at market value.

13.511 Changes in licence interests

In the cases of changes in licence interests at the pre-production stage ("farm-ins and farm-outs") which are approved by the Minister for Communications, Energy and Natural Resources, TCA 1997, s 696A operates to secure that such disposals will not give rise to chargeable gains where their sole purpose is the furtherance of exploration, delineation or development of acreage licensed under the 1975 or subsequent licensing terms.

TCA 1997, s 696A(2) provides that the exemption from tax on a chargeable gain will apply where a person, with the consent of the Minister for Communications, Energy and Natural Resources, makes a disposal of an interest in a licensed area (including the part disposal of such an interest, or the exchange of an interest owned by him in one licensed area for an interest in another licensed area – known as "unitisation") and the disposal is shown to the satisfaction of the Minister to have been made for the sole purpose of ensuring the proper exploration, delineation or development of any licensed area.

In the case of a disposal by a company qualifying for capital gains tax exemption (other than one involving an exchange of interests and, therefore, normally a part disposal on a farm-out), TCA 1997, s 696A(3) provides for a form of roll-over treatment. The consideration received for the disposal might be cash or might, as is usual in a farm-out, be in the form of a drilling commitment or work programme.

Where the consideration received by the company in the "relevant period" is wholly and exclusively applied, whether by it or on its behalf by the person acquiring the asset disposed of, for the purposes of petroleum exploration activities, or the searching for or winning access to petroleum in a relevant field, or for the purposes of both, the disposal will not, on a claim to that effect by the company, be treated as involving any disposal of an asset. In that case, however, as regards any subsequent disposal of any asset acquired or brought into existence or enhanced in value by reason of the application of that consideration, the consideration will not be deductible from the consideration for that subsequent disposal for the purposes of computing the chargeable gain on that disposal (TCA 1997, s 696A(3)).

The *relevant period* mentioned above is the period beginning 12 months before and ending 3 years after the disposal, or such longer period as the Minister may, on the application of the person making the disposal, certify to be in his opinion reasonable having regard to the proper exploration, delineation or development of any licensed area.

Exchanges of licence interests are dealt with in TCA 1997, s 696A(4). Such arrangements are generally treated as not involving any disposal or acquisition for capital gains tax purposes and the assets exchanged are treated as a single asset. Where a company making an exchange makes an appropriate claim, the exchange is treated as not involving any disposal or acquisition by it of an asset but the asset given and the asset acquired by it in the exchange are treated as the same asset, and as acquired as the asset given by it was acquired.

Where, however, a company, being one party to the exchange, receives consideration in addition to the licence interest taken by it, and that additional consideration is applied in the same way as discussed above in the case of a part disposal, TCA 1997, s 696A(4) will apply, on a claim to that effect by the party making the disposal, to such part of the licence interest given by it as is equal in value to the licence interest taken by it; the disposal of the balance of the original interest is then treated as a part disposal to which the roll-over treatment provided for in TCA 1997, s 696A(3) applies.

Where, conversely, a company *gives* consideration in addition to the interest in a licensed area given by it in the exchange, it is treated as acquiring a part only of the asset received by it and the provisions relating to the treatment as a single asset will apply only to that part; on a subsequent disposal, the other part is treated as having been acquired for the amount of the additional consideration.

13.512   Profit resource rent tax

13.512.1   Introduction

TCA 1997, Part 24 Chapter 3 gives effect to the Government decision of 30 July 2007 that a Profit Resource Rent Tax will apply in the case of any petroleum lease entered into following on from a licensing option or from an exploration licence, or a reserved area licence, awarded by the Minister for Communications, Energy and Natural Resources after 1 January 2007. The tax, which applies where profits exceed certain defined levels, is in addition to the corporation tax charge, at 25%, that applies to profits from petroleum activities.

A key feature of the new tax is that it is based on the profit ratio of a petroleum field, which is defined as the rate of profits (net of 25% corporation tax) for the field, divided by the accumulated level of capital investment in the field. Different rates of profit resource rent tax will apply, depending on the ratio, as follows:

Profit ratio	Profit resource rent tax rate
4.5 or more	15%
3 or more and less than 4.5	10%
1.5 or more and less than 3	5%
less than 1.5	Nil

13.5012.2 Definitions

TCA 1997, s 696B(1) contains a number of definitions relevant to the profits resource rent tax regime and these are set out below:

cumulative field expenditure (in the profit ratio equation), in relation to an accounting period of a company in respect of a taxable field, means the aggregate of the taxable field expenditure of the company in respect of the taxable field—

(a)   for that accounting period, and

(b)   for any preceding accounting period beginning on or after 1 January 2007;

for any accounting period, this figure is the sum of the capital expenditure (as defined) incurred by a company in relation to a taxable field from 1 January 2007 up to the end of that period;

cumulative field profits (the numerator in the profit ratio equation), in relation to an accounting period of a company in respect of a taxable field, means the aggregate of the net taxable field profits of the company in respect of the taxable field—

(a)   for that accounting period, and

(b)   for any preceding accounting period beginning on or after 1 January 2007, after deducting the amount of any loss incurred in respect of the taxable field for any such period.

For any accounting period, this figure will be the sum of net profits (as defined) of the company in relation to a taxable field from 1 January 2007 up to the end of that period;

net taxable field profits, in relation to an accounting period of a company, means the taxable field profits of the company for the accounting period after deducting the amount of corporation tax (if any) which would, apart from TCA 1997, Part 24 Chapter 3, be payable by the company for the accounting period if the tax were computed on the basis of those profits;

profit ratio, in relation to an accounting period of a company in respect of a taxable field, means an amount determined by the formula—

$$\frac{A}{B}$$

where—

A   is the cumulative field profits of the company in respect of the taxable field in relation to that accounting period, and

B   is the cumulative field expenditure of the company in respect of the taxable field in relation to that accounting period;

specified licence means an exploration licence, or a reserved area licence (see also **13.502** regarding the meaning of "licence"), granted on or after 1 January 2007, or a licensing option;

taxable field means an area in respect of which a petroleum lease entered into following on from a specified licence is in force;

taxable field expenditure, in relation to an accounting period of a company, means the aggregate of the amounts of capital expenditure which consist of—

(a)   abandonment expenditure (see **13.509**),

(b)   development expenditure (see **13.506**), and

(c)   exploration expenditure (see **13.507**), incurred by the company for the accounting period in respect of a taxable field;

taxable field profits, in relation to an accounting period of a company, means the amount of the petroleum profits of the company in respect of a taxable field, after making all deductions and giving or allowing all reliefs that for the purposes of corporation tax are made from, or are given or allowed against, or are treated as reducing—

(a)   those profits, or

(b)   income or chargeable gains, if any, included in those profits.

13.512.3   Interpretation

A number of interpretational principles relevant to the profits resources rent tax are contained in TCA 1997, 696B(2) and (3) and are set out as follows.

The interpretations in TCA 1997, s 684 (see **13.502**, **13.504.2**, **13.506** and **13, 507**) are to apply, with any necessary modifications, in relation to expenditure and activities carried on under a specified licence as they would apply in relation to expenditure and activities carried on under a licence within the meaning of that section if such a licence was a specified licence.

Capital expenditure incurred on or after 1 January 2007 by a company in an area which is not a taxable field but which subsequently becomes a taxable field (or part of such a field) is to be treated as if it had been incurred by the company on the day on which the area first becomes a taxable field (or part of such a field).

Petroleum activities in respect of each taxable field are "ring-fenced" to ensure, for example, that a company cannot offset losses from any other activities against profits of a taxable field. Where a company carries on a petroleum trade and that petroleum trade includes petroleum activities carried on under a specified licence, such activities are treated in respect of each taxable field as a separate petroleum trade distinct from all other activities carried on by the company as part of the trade. For this purpose, any necessary apportionment is to be made in computing taxable field profits or taxable field expenditure of a company and the method of apportionment adopted is to be such method as appears to the inspector or on appeal the Appeal Commissioners to be just and reasonable.

The provisions of TCA 1997, ss 687 (treatment of losses - see **13.504.2**), 688 (treatment of group relief - see **13.504.4**), 689 (restriction of relief for losses on certain disposals - see **13.504.5**) and 690 (interest and charges on income - **13.505**) apply for the purposes of the profits resources rent tax in relation to any activities treated above as a separate petroleum trade as they apply to a petroleum trade within the meaning of those sections. However, in relation to an accounting period of a company in respect of a taxable field, no account is to be taken of any charges paid, interest payable or a loss incurred—

   (i)   by any other company, or

   (ii) by the first mentioned company, in respect of activities other than activities in relation to that field.

13.512.4 Charge to profit resources rent tax

TCA 1997, s 696C contains the core rules concerning what the profit resources rent tax is and on what it is charged. The tax is an additional duty of corporation tax which applies when the profit ratio, calculated for an accounting period of a company in respect of a taxable field, is greater than or equal to 1.5.

Where for an accounting period of a company the profit ratio of the company in relation to a taxable field is equal to 1.5 or more, an additional duty of corporation tax (referred to as a "profit resource rent tax") is chargeable on the profits of the company (TCA 1997, s 696C(1)). The tax is charged on the profits, as determined below, for an accounting period at the rate of—

   (a)   5%, where the profit ratio is less than 3,

   (b) 10%, where the profit ratio is equal to or greater than 3 and less than 4.5,

   (c) 15%, where the profit ratio is equal to or greater than 4.5 ((TCA 1997, s 696C(2))).

The profits to which the tax applies are profits in respect of any petroleum lease entered into following on from an exploration licence where that licence was awarded by the

Minister for Communications, Energy and Natural Resources after 1 January 2007. As respects any taxable field for an accounting period of a company, those profits—

(a) in respect of any accounting period in relation to which—

(i) the profit ratio is equal to or greater than 1.5, and

(ii) the profit ratio for the immediately preceding accounting period was less that 1.5,

are to be determined by the formula—

$$\{A - (B \times 1.5)\} \times \frac{100}{100 - R}$$

where—

A is the cumulative field profits of the company in respect of the taxable field in relation to the accounting period,

B is the cumulative field expenditure of the company in respect of the taxable field in relation to the accounting period, and

R is the rate per cent specified in TCA 1997, s 21A(3) (see **3.101.4**), and

(b) in respect of any other accounting period of the company, are the taxable field profits of the company in respect of the taxable field for the accounting period ((TCA 1997, s 696C(3))).

13.512.5 Groups

TCA 1997, s 696D contains provisions relating to groups of companies and provides, inter alia, for the situation in which capital expenditure incurred by one company can be deemed to have been incurred by another company for the purposes of determining the cumulative expenditure, where one company is a subsidiary of the other or both are subsidiaries of a third company.

Where taxable field expenditure in respect of a taxable field is incurred by a company (the "first company") and

(a) another company is a wholly-owned subsidiary of the first company, or

(b) the first company is, at the time the taxable field expenditure is incurred, a wholly-owned subsidiary of another company (the "parent company"),

the expenditure, or so much of it as the first company specifies, may at the election of that company be deemed to be taxable field expenditure in respect of the taxable field incurred—

(i) where (a) applies, by that other company as the first company specifies, and

(ii) where (b) applies, by the parent company or by such other company (being a wholly-owned subsidiary of the parent company) as the first company specifies (TCA 1997, s 696D(1)).

Regarding the meaning of *wholly-owned subsidiary* for the above purposes, see below.

Where, as above, taxable field expenditure incurred by a first company is deemed to have been incurred by another company (the "other company")—

(a)   the expenditure will be deemed to have been incurred by the other company at the time at which the expenditure was actually incurred by the first company, and

(b)   will—

    (i)   be deemed to have been incurred by the other company for the purposes of determining the cumulative field expenditure of that company, and

    (ii)   be deemed not to have been incurred by the first company for the purposes of determining the cumulative field expenditure of that company (TCA 1997, s 696D(2)).

The same expenditure may not be taken into account in relation to the determination of cumulative expenditure for more than one taxable field by virtue of TCA 1997, s 696D (TCA 1997, s 696D(3)).

TCA 1997, s 694(5) (exploration expenditure incurred by certain companies - see **13.508**) applies for the purposes of subsection (1) as it applies for the purposes of that subsection (TCA 1997, s 696D(4)). Thus, a company is deemed to be a wholly owned subsidiary of another company if and as long as all of its ordinary share capital is owned by that other company, whether directly or through another company or companies, or partly directly and partly through another company or companies. For the purposes of determining the amount of ordinary share capital held in a company through other companies, the provisions of TCA 1997 Schedule 9 paragraph 6, and thereby TCA 1997, s 9(5)-(10), have effect (see **2.505**).

13.512.6   Returns and collection etc

TCA 1997, s 696E provides for the submission of returns by companies in respect of the new licences granted on or after 1 January 2007. The returns are to be submitted with the annual corporation tax return.

A company carrying on petroleum activities under a specified licence is required, in addition to the corporation tax return required to be delivered under TCA 1997, s 951 (see **15.104**), to prepare and deliver to the Collector-General at the same time as, and together with, the corporation tax return, on or before the specified return date for the chargeable period a full and true statement in a prescribed form of the details required by the form in respect of—

(a)   the amounts constituting the aggregate of the cumulative field expenditure for each field,

(b)   the amounts constituting the aggregate of the cumulative field profits for each field,

(c)   the breakdown of the amounts in (a) and (b), and

(d)   the amount of profit resource rent tax, if any, payable in respect of each field,

and of such further particulars as may be required by the prescribed form (TCA 1997, s 696E(2)).

A *prescribed form* is a form prescribed by the Revenue Commissioners or a form used under the authority of the Revenue Commissioners, and includes a form which involves the delivery of a statement by any electronic, photographic or other process approved of by the Revenue Commissioners.

TCA 1997, s 1052 (penalties for failure to make returns etc - see **15.104.4**) applies to a failure by a person to deliver a statement under, or the details or particulars referred to in, TCA 1997, s 696E as it applies to a failure to deliver a return referred to in that section (TCA 1997, s 696E(5)).

TCA 1997, s 696F contains the collection and general provisions in respect of the profit resource rent tax. The normal corporation tax provisions for assessment, appeals, collection and recovery also apply to the tax. Interest charges will also apply in the case of late payment of the tax.

The provisions of the Corporation Tax Acts relating to—

(a) assessments to corporation tax,

(b) appeals against such assessments (including the rehearing of appeals and the statement of a case for the opinion of the High Court), and

(c) the collection and recovery of corporation tax,

apply in relation to a profit resource rent tax as they apply to corporation tax charged otherwise.

Any amount of profit resource rent tax payable without the making of an assessment carries interest at the rate of 0.0273% for each day or part of a day from the date when the amount becomes due and payable until payment. TCA 1997, s 1080 (interest on overdue tax - see **15.106.2**) applies in relation to interest payable in respect of profit resource rent tax as it applies in relation to interest payable under that section.

13.6 PATENT INCOME

13.601 Introduction

A person to whom an Irish patent is granted has the sole and exclusive right to exploit commercially the invention which is the subject of the patent. This right will also vest in any party to whom the person assigns the patent rights. The person may also exploit the patent indirectly through licensing arrangements. Patents may also be taken out in other countries where it is required to ensure that the invention cannot be exploited outside the State by other parties other than in cases where this is done under a proper licensing arrangement. Where the original patent is taken out in another country, the person to whom it was granted may obtain an Irish patent to prevent its unauthorised use in the State.

A patent is the right, deriving from letters patent, to the exclusive use and benefit of a new invention. An application for an Irish patent in respect of a new invention may be made to the Patents Office either by the first inventor or by an assignee to whom the first inventor has assigned his right to make the application for the patent. The application must be accompanied by a specification giving details of the invention. Where the specification is provisional, a complete specification must be filed within 12 months from the date of the application. The date of filing the complete specification becomes the date of the patent, even if the letters patent are not actually granted until several years later. The normal term or life of an Irish patent is 16 years from the date of the patent, ie from the date the complete specification is filed.

A company which owns a patent may use the patented invention for the purposes of its trade. The company may license another person to use the invention or it may sell the patent outright so that all of its rights under it pass to the purchaser who may exploit it for his own benefit. The current owner of the patent may also use it in his own trade and at the same time license one or more other persons to use it, but generally such licensees are only given the right to exploit the invention in countries in which the owner of the patent is not trading. Depending on the terms of the licence, a licensee may be able to sublicense a third party to use the invention in any of the countries for which he himself has the right of user. He may also be able to sell the licence to another person who then fully assumes all the rights which the original licensee possessed under the patent in question.

The approach of the Tax Acts is to tax as income all types of profits or gains derived from a patent and from any rights under a patent, whether received as royalties for the licensing or sublicensing of the right to use the patented invention or as a capital sum for the sale of the patent or for the granting of a licence or any other rights under the patent (but subject to a deduction for any capital cost of purchase). TCA 1997 Part 29 Ch 1 (ss

754-762) contains particular provisions (apart from the normal taxation rules which apply to royalties) relating to the taxation of patent income, including a regime of capital allowances for capital expenditure on the purchase of patent rights and certain other expenses. For the exemption from tax provided for in TCA 1997, s 234 for income from certain patents, and the corresponding treatment of dividends paid out of such income as dealt with in TCA 1997, s 141, see **13.607**.

The following definitions in TCA 1997, s 754 are relevant both for the purposes of the rules relating to capital allowances for patent rights expenditure and for the taxation of capital sums received for the sale of patent rights.

Patent rights means the right to do or authorise the doing of anything which would, but for that right, be an infringement of a patent. It follows that not only does the owner for the time being of a patent have patent rights, but so also does any other person currently entitled to use the patented invention under a licence or a sub-licence. Furthermore, since the filing of a complete specification of an invention in connection with the application for a patent operates to prevent the unauthorised use of the invention, the person who has made this application is treated as having patent rights capable of being sold (see *Green v Brace* 39 TC 281).

Any reference to *the sale of part of patent rights* includes a reference to the grant of a licence (or a sub-licence) in respect of the patent in question (TCA 1997, s 754(2)). This is relevant in any case where the granting of the licence (or sub-licence) is made for a consideration that consists of or includes a capital sum. If the only consideration given by the grantee of the licence or sub-licence is a royalty or other non-capital sum for the use of the patent, the royalty is taxable normally and there are no other tax implications for the person granting the licence.

Where, however, the terms of the licence are such that the licensee is to have the sole use of the patent concerned to the exclusion of the grantor and of all other persons for the remaining life of the patent, the grant is treated as equivalent to the sale by the grantor of the whole of the rights (TCA 1997, s 754(2)).

A reference to *the purchase of patent rights* includes a reference to the acquisition of a licence (or sub-licence) in respect of a patent (TCA 1997, s 754(2)). Consequently, if and to the extent that the grantee of the licence or sub-licence gives consideration consisting of or including a capital sum, he is treated as having incurred capital expenditure on the purchase of patent rights.

If an invention which is the subject of a patent is made for the service of, or is used by, the State under section 77 of the Patents Act, 1992, the making or using of the invention is treated as taking place under a licence. A similar position applies in the case of an invention made for the service of, or used by, the government of another country under any corresponding legal provisions of that country (TCA 1997, s 754(3)).

TCA 1997, s 316(1) provides that *capital expenditure* and *capital sums* are to be understood as not including:

(a)   in relation to the person incurring the expenditure or paying the sums, any expenditure or sum allowed as a deduction in computing the profits or gains of a trade, profession, office or employment carried on or held by him, or any royalty or other sum payable for the use of a patent, or any annuity or other annual payment of other sum from which income tax is deductible under TCA 1997, s 237 or 238; or

(b)   in relation to the person receiving the capital sum, any amounts or sums which fall to be taken into account as receipts in computing the profits or gains of any trade, profession, office or employment carried on or held by him, or any royalty or other sum payable for the user of a patent, or any annuity, other annual payment or any other sum from which income tax is deductible under TCA 1997, s 237 or 238.

However, the requirement of TCA 1997, s 757(2) for income tax to be deducted under TCA 1997, s 238 from a capital sum paid to a non-resident seller of Irish patent rights (see **13.606**) does not change the status of what is otherwise a capital sum.

Capital expenditure on the purchase of patent rights is regarded as not having been incurred by a person in so far as it has been met by grant or otherwise by the State, any statutory board, or public or local authority or by any person other than the person concerned (TCA 1997, s 317(3)). Again, the requirement of TCA 1997, s 757(2) to deduct income tax under TCA 1997, s 238 from a capital sum paid to a non-resident seller does not affect the status of that capital sum.

The expression *net proceeds of sale* is not expressly defined, but may be taken as referring to the amount of any capital sum received for the sale of any patent rights as reduced by any expenses incurred by the seller directly for the purposes of the sale. Deductible expenses of sale may include such items as the costs of advertising the patent rights for sale or any patent agent's fees in connection with the sale. Any royalty or other payment that is not a capital sum (see above), even if receivable as part of the consideration for the sale of any patent rights, is always excluded in determining the net proceeds of sale.

13.602   Taxation of patent income

TCA 1997, s 754(1) defines *income from patents* as any royalty or other sum paid in respect of the user of a patent, and any amount on which tax is payable for any chargeable period by virtue of TCA 1997 Part 29 Ch 1 (ss 754-762). In effect, income from patents may comprise any one or more of the following items:

(a)   any royalty or other sum received from an Irish source for the use of a patent (normally received subject to deduction of income tax at the standard rate in accordance with TCA 1997, s 237 or s 238 – see **4.302** and **4.303**);

(b)   any royalty or other sum received from a foreign source for the use of a patent (taxable as income from a foreign possession under Schedule D Case III – see **3.207.2**);

(c)   any capital sum received for the sale of any patent rights to the extent taxable under Case IV in accordance with the provisions of TCA 1997, s 757 (see **13.605-606**); and

(d)   any balancing charge arising on the sale of any patent rights which is taxable under Case IV (TCA 1997, s 761(2)) (see **13.604**).

In taxing a company's income from patents for any accounting period, TCA 1997 Part 29 Ch 1 effectively provides for allowances in respect of the following:

(a)   capital allowances (including any balancing allowances) for the accounting period in respect of capital expenditure on the purchase of patent rights (see **13.603, 13.604**);

(b) notwithstanding anything in TCA 1997, s 81 (disallowance of capital expenditure), any fees paid or expenses incurred by the company in the accounting period in obtaining, for the purposes of a trade, the grant of a patent or an extension of the term of a patent; and

(c) otherwise than for the purposes of a trade, any fees paid or expenses incurred by the company in the accounting period in connection with the grant or maintenance of a patent or the obtaining of an extension of the term of the patent (TCA 1997, s 758(2)).

Except where made in taxing the profits of a trade, these allowances are made by way of discharge or repayment of tax and are available against income from patents (TCA 1997, s 761(2)). Accordingly, the total of these allowances for any accounting period must be set off in the first instance against the company's income from the patents for that period. For this purpose, all of the company's income from patents for the period is aggregated, even if assessable under different Cases or if received as taxed income. If the total of the allowances for any accounting period exceeds the company's income from patents for that period, the unused allowances are carried forward for set-off against its income from patents in the following accounting period, and so on without time limit until fully used (TCA 1997, s 308(3)). There is no right to set off any of the unused allowances for any accounting period against income from any other source; TCA 1997, s 308(4), which provides for that treatment, applies only to allowances available *primarily* against income of a specified class whereas TCA 1997, s 761(2) provides for allowances to be available simply "against income from patents".

Capital allowances and any relevant balancing charges in respect of capital expenditure on the purchase of patent rights are made in taxing the trade of the company concerned if, at any time in the relevant accounting period, the patent rights in question, or any other rights out of which they were granted, were used for the purposes of that trade (TCA 1997, s 761(1)). In such a case, any fees paid or expenses incurred in obtaining, for the purposes of the trade, the grant of a patent or an extension of the term of a patent are allowed as expenses, and not as capital allowances (TCA 1997, s 758(1)).

Example 13.602.1

Some years ago, Edison Ltd purchased the Irish and UK patents to an invention devised abroad for use in its trade. It also owns other patents, taken out in the State and in a number of foreign countries, to inventions not used in its trade but from which it derives royalty income from licences to other parties (taxable under Case IV). The company claims writing down allowances in respect of the capital expenditure in purchasing all these patent rights (trade and non-trade).

During its most recent accounting period, Edison Ltd sold the UK patents as well as some Italian (and non-trade) patent rights, the sale in each case resulting in a balancing charge (see **13.604**) and a charge to tax under Case IV in respect of the capital sums received for the sales (see **13.605**). In the same period, the company paid fees and certain other expenses in connection with its application for two new patents, one for use in its trade and the other to be licensed outside its trade.

Based on the figures given below, the company's income from patents, patent rights capital allowances, balancing charges and other allowances for the accounting period are dealt with as follows:

A. In taxing the profits of the trade under Case I

	€	€
Balancing charge:		
sale of UK patent (trade)		2,000
Capital allowances:		
writing down allowances (all trade patents)	6,220	
Fees and other expenses for applications for new patents (trade)		
- deduct as trade expenses (TCA 1997, s 758 (1))	2,340	8,560
Loss forward		6,560

B. Taxable separately as income from patents

	€	€
Royalties received		
Case III: licences of various foreign patents (non-trade)		10,100
Irish taxed royalties: licences of Irish patents (non-trade)		1,400
Capital sums for sales of patent rights		
Case IV: net amount taxable for year		
- sale of UK patent (trade)[1]		1,000
- sale of Italian patent rights (non-trade)		750
Balancing charge (Case IV)		
Sale of Italian patent rights (non-trade)		2,700
		15,950
Capital etc allowances for year (non-trade):		
writing down allowances	4,300	
Fees and expenses re applications for new patent (non-trade)	2,290	6,590
Taxable income from patents		9,360

Note:

[1] Although the balancing charge on the sale of the UK patent used for the trade is included in the Case I assessment (TCA 1997, s 761(1)), the "income" arising from the capital sum for the sale of the rights is nevertheless taxable under Case IV (see **13.605**).

13.603 Capital allowances for patent rights

A company incurring capital expenditure on the purchase of patent rights is entitled under TCA 1997, s 755 to a writing-down allowance in respect of that expenditure. Where the consideration given by the company consists both of a capital payment and an undertaking to pay a royalty, the capital payment only (see "capital expenditure" and "capital sums" in **13.601**) qualifies for the writing down allowance.

TCA 1997, s 755 is understood (including by the Revenue, as indicated in their Guidance Notes: reference is made to "capital allowances in respect of expenditure incurred on the acquisition of a patent or patent rights") to mean that capital allowances are due whether the purchase relates to the acquisition of patent rights (including the acquisition of a licence or sub-licence) or to the acquisition of the patent itself.

The writing down allowance is made for each accounting period during a prescribed writing down period related to the normal life of the patent in question or, if shorter, to the length of the period for which the rights have been acquired. The writing down period commences with the accounting period in which the capital expenditure on the purchase of the patent rights in incurred. Where the accounting period is a period of less than 12 months, the allowance for that period is proportionately reduced.

The length of the writing down period is whichever of the following periods is appropriate:

(a) 17 years (the 16 years' normal life of a patent plus one year), unless the patent rights are acquired for a specified period or unless they begin at least one complete year after the commencement of the patent; or

(b) in the case of patent rights purchased for a specified period, the number of years comprised in that period; or

(c) where the rights purchased begin one complete year or more after the commencement of the patent (and where not purchased for a specified period), 17 years as reduced by the number of complete years between the commencement of the patent and the date on which the rights purchased begin (TCA 1997, s 755(2)).

The length of the writing down period determines the rate of the writing down allowance. For patent rights purchased at the commencement of a patent (or within one year of that time), the writing down allowance is one-seventeenth of the expenditure for each relevant accounting period except where the rights are acquired for a specified period of less than 17 years. For patent rights acquired for such shorter specified period, or where the rights purchased begin more than one complete year after the commencement of the patent, the rate of the writing down allowance is adjusted by reference to the number of years in the writing down period.

The commencement of the patent is defined, in relation to any patent, as the date from which the patent rights become effective (TCA 1997, s 754(1)). This commencement date is the date of the patent, ie the date on which the complete specification was filed (see **13.601**), irrespective of the date on which the patent was actually granted. The fact that the maximum writing down period is 17 years while the normal life of a patent is 16 years from the date of the patent may be due to the fact that the first application for the patent may be made up to one year before the complete specification is lodged, thus giving up to 17 years between the original application and the end of the normal life of the patent.

Example 13.603.1

Marconi Ltd purchased the following patent rights in the year ended 31 December 2007:

	Capital expenditure
	€
Irish patent in respect of Irish invention	
(date of patent 1/6/07 – purchased 1/10/07)	17,000
Licence to exploit (including sublicensing) Irish patent to	
foreign invention for 10 years to 31/3/17	
(date of patent 1/4/02 – purchased 1/4/07)	14,000

UK patent in respect of German invention

(date of patent 1/5/03, but company's rights to use

patent begin on date of purchase 1/5/07)   19,500

Since Marconi Ltd does not use these patent rights in any trade or profession, the writing down allowances for the above capital expenditure are given by way of discharge or repayment of tax and are available against the company's income from patents (see **13.602**). The writing down periods for the various patent rights purchased in the year ended 31 December 2007 are as follows:

Irish patent in respect of Irish invention

17 years from 1/1/07 to 31/12/23

– writing down allowance y/e 31/12/07 (and following periods)

1/17 x €17,000   1,000

Licence for Irish patent of foreign invention

10 years from 1/1/07 to 31/12/16

(specified period for which rights acquired, ie from date of

purchase 1/4/07 to 31/3/17)

- writing down allowance y/e 31/12/07 (and following periods)

1/10 x €12,000   1,200

UK patent in respect of German invention

13 years from 1/1/07 to 31/12/19[1]

- writing down allowance y/e 31/12/07 (and following periods)

1/13 x €19,500   1,500

Notes:

1. Since the company's rights under the UK patent did not commence until 1/5/07 (four years after the commencement of the patent), the writing down period must be reduced to 13 years.

2. Each writing-down allowance commences with the first day of the relevant accounting period, even if the patent rights are not purchased until near the end of that period.

Capital allowances in respect of patent rights expenditure may, in certain circumstances, have to be based on the open market value of the patent rights acquired rather than on the actual capital expenditure incurred. TCA 1997, s 312 applies in the same way to capital expenditure on patent rights as it does for other assets qualifying for capital allowances (see **5.103**). For example, if a company sells patent rights to another company at a price which is other than the open market price and the companies are under common control, TCA 1997, s 312(3) requires both companies to be treated as if the sale had taken place at the market price for those rights.

13.604   Balancing allowances and charges

13.604.1   Introduction

Balancing allowances and charges on disposals of patent rights may arise as they do in the case of other assets qualifying for capital allowances and TCA 1997, s 756 provides for these but with some differences. In the case of machinery or plant or industrial buildings, once the item is sold the seller no longer has an interest in it. This contrasts with the position for patent rights where it is possible for the owner to make a sale of part of his rights while retaining other rights in the same patent. For example, the owner of a patent may grant a non-exclusive licence to another person for a capital payment or a royalty, or both, while retaining the continued use and benefit of the patent subject only to non-infringement of the rights granted to the licensee. Accordingly, there are rules dealing with the sale of part of a person's rights under a patent.

Whether in the case of a partial or a total sale of patent rights, the question of a balancing allowance or charge arises only if the seller had previously incurred capital expenditure on their acquisition (or was deemed to have incurred such expenditure under the market value rule of TCA 1997, s 312 – see **13.603**). If a company selling patent rights had simply acquired the rights in consideration for the payment of a royalty, no balancing allowance or charge will arise, even if the consideration for sale consists of or includes a capital sum, but a liability to tax may arise under TCA 1997, s 757 if the consideration includes a capital sum (see **13.605**).

13.604.2 Sale of whole of patent rights

To the extent that they consist of capital sums, the net proceeds of sale of patent rights are compared with the amount of the capital expenditure remaining unallowed (the tax written down value of the patent rights concerned). If the net proceeds are less than the tax written down value, a balancing allowance is made to the seller in an amount equal to the difference. Conversely, if the net proceeds exceed the tax written down value, a balancing charge is made on the seller in an amount equal to the excess (but subject to the limit prescribed in TCA 1997, s 756(6), mentioned below).

The balancing allowance or charge, whichever is the case, is made for the accounting period in which the patent rights are sold. The tax written down value for the purposes of the computation is the amount of the capital expenditure previously incurred on the acquisition of the patent rights as reduced by the total of the writing down allowances made in respect of that expenditure for previous accounting periods and the net proceeds, to the extent that they consist of capital sums, of any previous sale of any part of the rights acquired as a result of that expenditure (TCA 1997, s 756(5)).

TCA 1997, s 312 (control sales - see **5.103.2**) should also be considered in relation to patent rights since this section, and in fact the provisions of Part 9, Chapter 4 (ss 304-321 – miscellaneous capital allowances provisions) are applied by virtue of TCA 1997, s 762. TCA 1997, s 762(2) specifically provides that the election to substitute tax written down value in place of open market value is to apply as if the reference to tax written down value were a reference to the amount of the capital expenditure on patent rights remaining unallowed.

Patent rights held by a company may come to an end otherwise than by a sale. If the company owns a patent or has been licensed to use it for the remainder of its term, its patent rights automatically lapse at the end of the life of the patent (normally 16 years after the date of the patent). If it has been licensed to use the patent for a specified period, it ceases to have any rights under that patent at the end of that period. In any such case where a company's patent rights come to an end without being subsequently revived, it is entitled to a balancing allowance equal to the tax written down value of those rights immediately before they came to an end.

Example 13.604.2.1

On 24 March 1993, in its accounting year to 31 December 1993, Bell Ltd incurred capital expenditure of €15,300 for the acquisition of all of the rights to a new invention. The relevant patent application had been filed, with a complete specification of the invention, on 1 November 1992. The patent was later granted with retrospective effect from 1 November 1992 so that its term ran for the period of 16 years to 31 October 2008. Bell Ltd also took out patents to the invention in a number of other countries.

Bell Ltd was accordingly in receipt of income from the patent rights since 24 March 1993 by way of royalties under various licensing arrangements. No part of the income resulted in the company receiving any capital sums nor did the company receive any sum from the sale of the whole of its rights under the patents. It first obtained the patent rights writing down allowance in respect of the capital expenditure of €15,300 for the year ended 31 December 1993, the period in which the expenditure was incurred.

The capital allowances for the years ended 31 December 1993 to 31 December 2008 are as follows:

	€	€
Capital expenditure (24/3/93)		15,300
Writing down allowances:		
y/e 31/12/93: €15,300 x 1/17	900	
ys/e 31/12/94 – 31/12/08: €15,300 x 1/17 x 15	13,500	14,400
WDV 31/12/08		900
y/e 31/12/09:		
Balancing allowance[2]		900

Notes:

[1] Since the patent rights were purchased less than one year after the date of the patent (1/11/92), the writing down period is 17 years.

[2] The balancing allowance is equal to the tax written down value of the patent rights immediately before they terminated on 31 October 2008.

13.604.3   Sale of part of patent rights

In a case where only part of the rights under a patent are sold, say, where a company that has purchased a patent subsequently grants a licence for part of the territory covered by the patent, the net proceeds of sale (so far as consisting of capital sums) are deducted from the tax written down value of those patent rights immediately before the sale. The tax written down value is the original capital expenditure on the purchase of the rights under the patent in question as reduced by all writing down allowances previously made and, if relevant, by the net proceeds of any earlier part sales of those patent rights. If the net proceeds of sale exceed the tax written down value, a balancing charge is made on the amount of the excess (subject to the balancing charge limit); no further writing down allowance may be claimed in respect of the unsold rights (TCA 1997, s 756(1)(c), (3)).

Where the net proceeds of a sale of part of the rights under a patent are less than the tax written down value, no balancing allowance or charge arises but the net proceeds are deducted from the tax written down value and a new writing down allowance is calculated to write off this reduced written down value over the remainder of the original writing down period. The new writing down allowance, which is made to a company for the accounting period in which the sale occurs, and for subsequent accounting periods, is computed as follows:

$$\text{writing down allowance (12 months)} = \frac{\text{tax written down value (as reduced)}}{n}$$

where—

n = the number of complete years of the writing down period remaining at the beginning of the accounting period in which the sale occurs (TCA 1997, s 756(4)).

Thus, in the case of a company carrying on a trade which sells part of certain patent rights used in that trade, if the sale is made in the company's year ended 31 December 1997, the writing down allowance for that period and subsequent periods is calculated by reference to the number of complete years comprised in the period from 1 January 1997 to the end of the original writing down period. If the company had previously purchased the patent rights for, say, a specified ten-year period in its year ended 31 December 1991, the original writing down period would have been the ten years from 1 January 1992 to 31 December 2000. Since there are four complete years remaining, ie 1 January 1997 to 31 December 2000, the new writing down allowance is one quarter of the tax written down value (as reduced by the net proceeds of sale); this allowance is first made for the year ended 31 December 1997.

13.604.4 Limit to balancing charge

The amount of any balancing charge made in respect of capital expenditure on patent rights, whether as a result of a sale of the whole or a part of those rights, may not exceed the total writing down allowances previously made in respect of that expenditure (TCA 1997, s 756(6)). If a balancing charge has already been made in respect of an earlier sale of part of the rights under the same patent, the balancing charge on the sale of the remainder of those rights (or a further partial sale) may not exceed the total writing down allowances as reduced by the previous balancing charge.

13.605 Capital sums: resident vendor

A charge to tax under Case IV of Schedule D arises by virtue of TCA 1997, s 757(1) in the case of a resident company which sells (or grants a licence in respect of – see **13.601**) a part or all of its rights under a patent for a capital sum. In computing the amount chargeable, however, TCA 1997, s 757(4) allows the capital expenditure, if any, in acquiring those patent rights to be deducted from the net sale proceeds. The charge is made under Case IV even if the patent rights sold had previously been used in the trade of the vendor; furthermore, the charge arises whether or not any writing down or other capital allowances have been obtained in respect of the patent rights in question. If capital allowances have been obtained in a case where the net proceeds of the sale exceed the original capital expenditure, there is both a balancing charge to write back the earlier capital allowances and a Case IV charge under TCA 1997, s 757(1) to tax the excess sale proceeds.

Sums chargeable under TCA 1997, s 757 are of the kind treated as capital receipts (see above) and do not include royalties or other sums paid for the user of patent rights. If, for example, a patentee were to receive a lump sum for the future unlimited user of a defined portion of the property in a patent, the transaction would be treated as a sale for a capital sum.

As seen in **13.601** above, *patent rights* means the right to do or authorise the doing of anything which, without such right, would be an infringement of a patent. Thus, any person entitled to use a patented invention under a licence or a sub-licence has acquired patent rights as of course also has the owner (the "patentee") of the patent. Ownership of patent rights is distinct from ownership of the patent itself (even though ownership of the patent may involve ownership of the underlying patent rights, and even where the value of the patent is no more than the value of those rights).

The background to TCA 1997, s 757 can be traced to such cases as *CIR v British Salmson Aero Engines Ltd* 22 TC 29. In this case a company, formed to acquire the sole licence to manufacture and sell in the UK and dependent territories the aeroplane engines made by a French company, acquired such a licence for ten years for the payment of a sum of £25,000, payable in instalments, as well as sums of £2,500 payable as royalties during each year of the currency of the licence. It was held that the sum of £25,000, being a lump sum payment, was a capital payment and that the royalty payments were royalties or other sums paid in respect of the user of a patent with the result that tax was deductible on payment of the latter but not the former.

One argument that was rejected in the Court of Appeal was that any sum paid for the user of a patent, even a lump sum, is necessarily stamped with the character of income. It was pointed out that the agreement in question was more than one for the right to use a patent, being also an agreement entitling the payer to restrain the patentees from exercising the patent in the designated territories as well as to call on the patentees to prevent others doing so. Thus, the Crown's contention that both sums were payable in respect of the user of a patent was not upheld.

The Court, however, went on to clarify that not every payment in respect of the user of a patent is necessarily of an income nature: it will be necessary in any case to establish whether the payment is capital or income which question must be decided by reference to the particular facts of the case, including the contractual relationship between the parties. In *Constantinesco v Rex* 11 TC 730 (see also **4.301**), a lump sum payment to inventors for the use of a patented invention was held to be "in respect of the user of" a patent and to be of an income nature. An influential factor in that case was the finding that the corpus of the patent had not been taken away from the patentee.

The purpose of TCA 1997, s 757 is to tax as income the receipt of such payments of the above kind that would be considered to be capital. (See also **13.607** below regarding the exemption for income from qualifying patents.)

From the foregoing, it follows that the payment of a sum for the outright acquisition of patent rights, for the exclusive user of a patented invention for the full remaining life of a patent, or for the future unlimited user of an invention for a defined period and within a defined area, would be examples of capital sums being received in respect of the sale of patent rights. The payment of a sum for the outright acquisition of the patent itself would also be capital but (even though this would usually involve acquiring ownership of the underlying patent rights) would not be for the acquisition of patent rights as such; it is understood that the Revenue accept this distinction and that TCA 1997, s 757 does not apply to a sale of the patent itself.

The amount chargeable under Case IV by TCA 1997, s 757(1) is not normally all subjected to tax in the one accounting period but is spread equally over six years. Where the seller of the patent rights is a company, one-sixth of the excess or the net sale proceeds over the capital expenditure in acquiring those rights is charged under Case IV for the accounting period in which the capital sum is received and a further one-sixth of the excess is taxed in each of the next five periods. Where any accounting period in question is less than twelve months, however, the amount taxed for that and each subsequent period will be a fraction of the full amount equal to the fraction represented by the length of each period over six years, until the full amount is taxed.

Example 13.605.1

Logie Ltd is granted patent rights in Ireland and certain other countries in respect of a new invention it has devised. After granting licences and receiving royalties for the use of these patents for several years, the company sells the patent rights outright for a capital sum of €79,000 on 10 September 2002. Since the company did not incur any capital expenditure on purchasing the patents, it does not obtain any writing down allowances.

Assuming Logie Ltd makes up accounts to 31 December each year up to 31 December 2005 and thereafter to 30 June, and incurred expenses of €1,000 in advertising its patent rights for the sale, it is liable to tax under Case IV as follows:

	€
Capital sum for sale (10/9/02)	79,000
Less: expenses of sale	1,000
Net proceeds of sale	78,000
Less: capital expenditure on purchase	Nil
Total amount assessable (net gain)	78,000

Taxable y/e 31/12/02:	
1/6th of net gain €78,000	13,000
Taxable 3 ys/e 31/12/03 – 31/12/05:	
€13,000 x 3	39,000
Taxable p/e 30/6/06:	
€13,000 x 6/12	6,500
Taxable y/e 30/6/07	13,000
Taxable y/e 30/6/08:	
€13,000 x 6/12	6,500
Total	78,000

Successive sales

A company which has sold some of the rights under a patent (for example, by granting, for a lump sum, a licence for part of the territory covered by the patent) may subsequently sell some or all of the remaining rights under that patent. On the occasion of that subsequent sale, if the consideration received for any previous sale consisted of or included a capital sum, the amount of the capital expenditure to be deducted from any capital sum received currently must itself be reduced by any capital sum on any previous sale. If any previous capital allowances have not been fully clawed back on the earlier sale(s), a balancing charge is made on the current sale.

Example 13.605.2

On 1 January 2001, Foyle Ltd incurred expenditure of €80,000 on the acquisition of the entire rights to a Czech patent for a 16 year period; the writing down period commenced in the company's year ended 31 December 2001. Foyle Ltd obtains writing down allowances totalling €30,000 for the six years ended 31 December 2001 to 31 December 2006 following which, on 1 October 2007, it grants a licence to another company to use the Czech patents (due to expire on 31 December 2016) up to 31 December 2012. It receives a capital sum of €60,000 for the sale of part of its patent rights. The tax treatment of the sale is as follows:

	€
Capital expenditure (1/1/01)	80,000
Writing down allowances:	
Years ended 31/12/01 to 31/12/04	
€80,000/16 x 6	30,000
WDV 31/12/06	50,000
Sale of part of rights (1/10/07)	60,000
Balancing charge y/e 31/12/07	10,000

There is no charge to tax under TCA 1997, s 757 as the capital sum of €60,000 is less than the previous capital expenditure of €80,000.

On 1 April 2008, Foyle Ltd sells its remaining rights under the patents for a capital sum of €22,000. The total amount on which it now becomes chargeable to tax under the successive sales rule of TCA 1997, s 757, to be spread over the six accounting periods commencing with the year ending 31 December 2008, is computed as follows:

	€	€
Capital sum on sale (1/4/08)		22,000
Less: capital expenditure on purchase (1/1/01)	80,000	
Reduced by capital sum on previous sale (1/10/07)	60,000	
		20,000
Total amount assessable		2,000

In addition, a balancing charge of €20,000 is made for the year ended 31 December 2008 to recapture the balance of the writing down allowances not covered by the previous balancing charge of €10,000.

Election for single year assessment

A company chargeable under TCA 1997, s 757(1) in respect of a capital sum received for the sale of the whole or a part of any patent rights is entitled to elect to have the total amount chargeable in the one accounting period instead of having it spread over six years (TCA 1997, s 757(1)(b)). The election must be made by notice in writing to the inspector no later than 12 months after the end of the accounting period in which the capital sum was received. A company might make this election, for example, if its taxable income for the period is lower than normal or if it has a trading loss, or excess capital allowances for the purposes of Case V, available for set off against its total profits (including the amount assessable under TCA 1997, s 757) for that period.

Alternatively, the company may apply, by notice in writing to the inspector within the same time limit, to have the total amount chargeable under TCA 1997, s 757(1) spread over a number of years other than six. In that event, if it appears to the Revenue Commissioners that hardship is likely to arise to the company if it is taxed over the six-year period, they may direct that the taxable amount should be spread over such other number of years as they consider appropriate. In making their decision on this matter, the Commissioners are required to have regard to all the circumstances of the case (TCA 1997, s 757(1)(c)).

13.606 Capital sums: non-resident vendor

A company which is not resident in the State may, by virtue of TCA 1997, s 757(2), be subject to tax under Case IV of Schedule D where it sells any patent rights for a capital sum, but only if the patent in question is an Irish patent. An *Irish patent* is a patent granted under the laws of the State (TCA 1997, s 754(1)); the term therefore includes any patent taken out under the Patents Act 1992, whether the invention protected by the patent was devised in the State or in any foreign country. The tax charge under this subsection applies whether the non-resident company sells its Irish patent rights outright or grants a licence or sub-licence for a capital sum to any other person to use its Irish patent (or any rights it possesses under an Irish patent). The subsection does not of course charge tax on any part of the consideration for the sale that is not a capital sum, for example, a royalty.

The way in which a non-resident is taxed under TCA 1997, s 757(2) differs from that provided for in TCA 1997, s 757(1) in the cases of resident persons (see **13.605**). TCA 1997, s 757(2) requires the person paying the capital sum to the non-resident vendor to deduct Irish income tax at the standard rate from the amount of that sum and to account to the Revenue Commissioners under TCA 1997, s 238 for the tax deducted. Income tax must be deducted from the full amount of any capital sum paid by the purchaser without making any allowance for the fact that the vendor may be able to claim a deduction in respect of his capital expenditure on his original acquisition of the Irish patent rights (TCA 1997, s 757(4)(b)).

A non-resident company which has received any capital sum from which Irish income tax has been deducted under the foregoing rule, may elect by notice in writing to the Revenue Commissioners to be taxed in respect of its sale of the Irish patent rights over a six year period on its "net gain" on the sale, rather than on the full capital sum. The effect of the election is to leave the non-resident company liable to Irish income tax (corporation tax if the company is carrying on a trade in Ireland) on one-sixth of its net gain on the sale in the tax year or accounting period in which it received the capital sum, and on a further one-sixth of that profit for each of the next five tax years. In computing the net gain that is chargeable over these six tax years, the same deduction is given in respect of capital expenditure as applies in computing the total amount taxable under TCA 1997, s 757(1) for a resident vendor.

In any case where the non-resident company elects to be taxed over the six year period, it obtains the benefit of that election by obtaining a repayment of the excess of the income tax deducted under TCA 1997, s 238 over its final Irish tax liability for each relevant tax year or accounting period in the six year spreading period. The election to be taxed over the six-year period does not avoid the requirement of the payer of any capital sum to deduct and account for income tax under TCA 1997, s 238.

Effect of double taxation agreement

The above-described position of a non-resident vendor of patent rights may be modified where that vendor is resident in a country which has a tax treaty with Ireland (see **14.103**). The majority of the tax treaties with other countries provide that a resident of the other country in receipt of royalties and other income from patents is to be exempted from Irish income tax or corporation tax in respect of such income. If a non-resident vendor company may benefit under a treaty, it is entitled, on making the appropriate claim, to be repaid all the Irish income tax deducted by the payer of any capital sum for the sale of the Irish patent rights.

13.607 Exemption for certain income from patents

13.607.1 Introduction

A person who is a resident of the State and not resident elsewhere may claim to have certain patent income exempted (treated as "disregarded income") for all purposes of the Income Tax Acts (TCA 1997, s 234). Such income is also disregarded for corporation tax purposes by virtue of TCA 1997, s 76(6). In the case of a company, "a resident of the State" means a company which is managed and controlled in the State. The income which is disregarded is *income from a qualifying patent*, meaning any royalty or other sum paid in respect of the use of the invention to which the qualifying patent relates. (The legislation refers to "the *user* of the invention", which might have the appearance of a reference to the person using the invention but is no more than a reference to the use of the invention.) "Other sum" includes any sum paid for the grant of a licence to exercise rights under the patent. This appears to be taken as meaning that even a capital sum received for the grant of a licence to use an invention which is the subject of a qualifying patent is not taxable under TCA 1997, s 757 (see **13.605**). On the other hand, a sum received in respect of the outright sale of patent rights, not being, or not being merely, for the *use* of the invention concerned, would be so taxable.

With effect from 1 January 2008, the amount of disregarded income arising to any person in a "relevant period" may not exceed €5m (see **13.607.7** below).

A *qualifying patent* is a patent in respect of which the work leading to the invention which is the subject of the patent was carried out in an EEA state (a state which is a contracting party to the EEA Agreement, ie the Agreement on the European Economic Area signed at Oporto on 2 May 1992, as adjusted by the Protocol signed at Brussels on 17 March 1993). (For patents developed before 1 August 2008, the work leading to the invention etc has to be carried out in Ireland. Where not all of the work is carried on in Ireland, the Revenue take a reasonable approach regarding compliance with this condition where they are satisfied that the spirit of the legislation is fulfilled.) The work would include research, planning, processing, experimenting, testing, devising, designing and developing. The exemption applies in respect of income received for the use of an invention in respect of which a patent application has been made even where the patent has not yet been granted. If, however, the patent application proves to be unsuccessful, any exemption previously availed of is withdrawn and any necessary additional assessments will be made to recover the tax in question.

An individual who has devised an invention that is the subject of a patent, or for which an application for a patent has been made, may wish to exploit the invention through the use of a limited company, which is probably a more effective means of entering into licensing arrangements, possibly in a number of different countries as well as in the State. If the individual sells the patent rights to the company outright for a capital sum, he is taxable under TCA 1997, s 757(1) without the benefit of the exemption. However, this liability may be avoided by granting a licence to the company to exercise all the rights under the patent to the exclusion of the individual himself and of all other persons for the whole of the remaining term of the patent. Although this is effectively a sale of all his rights under the patent, the individual is nevertheless only receiving a sum for the grant of the licence and is accordingly not taxable.

The exemption applies whether the qualifying income is derived from the use of the patent or from its licence for use within the State or abroad. It is not an essential requirement that the patent be an Irish one and income from any foreign patent is covered by the exemption, provided that the research, planning, processing and other work leading to the invention was carried out in an EEA state (or the State for pre-1 August 2008 developed patents). If income from a qualifying patent is received from a source outside the State, the fact that it is to be disregarded for all purposes of income tax is subject to one exception. TCA 1997, s 234(5) provides that the person in receipt of the income is not to be treated, by reason of the income being disregarded, as having ceased to possess the whole of a single source of income chargeable under Case III of Schedule D (see **3.207.1**).

A company may derive some income from patents qualifying for exemption and other income which does not. In any such a case, any expenses which may be incurred that are attributable to the company's patent income generally must be allocated as between patent income qualifying for the exemption and income which does not qualify. It is possible that the company will receive only one payment for the use of several patents not all of which qualify for the exemption. An allocation of expenses would also be necessary where royalties from qualifying patents for a relevant period exceed the €5m limit (see **13.607.7** below). To compute the amount of the income to be disregarded for tax purposes in that case, the Revenue Commissioners may make such apportionments of receipts and expenses as may be necessary (TCA 1997, s 234(6)). Only so much of any deductible expenses as are not attributable to the exempted income may be used to reduce income from patents not covered by the exemption.

In practice, it is not unusual for letters of patent to be granted several years after an application for a patent is made. This gives rise to the question as to whether the exemption from tax under TCA 1997, s 234 extends to any royalties or other income earned from allowing other persons to use the invention for which the patent application has been made, before the patent is granted. Once the patent has been granted, it has retrospective effect from the date on which the complete specification was filed (see **13.601**).

Assuming that a qualifying patent applied for is ultimately granted, therefore, any royalties or other income accruing after the date on which the complete specification was filed qualify for the exemption and any tax previously paid on the exempted income may be reclaimed. On the other hand, should the patent application be refused, there would be no exemption for any royalties or other payments made for the use of the invention, whether earned prior to the rejection of the patent application or subsequently.

13.607.2 Restrictions on individuals

Patent income arising to individuals may not be disregarded other than in the case of an individual who carried out, alone or with others, the research, planning, processing, experimenting, testing, devising, designing, development or other similar activity leading to the invention which is the subject of the qualifying patent (TCA 1997, s 234(3)).

13.607.3 Excessive royalties

To prevent the unintended use of patent income exemption, the definition of *income from a qualifying patent* in TCA 1997, s 234(1) provides that where a royalty or other sum, paid on or after 23 April 1996 between connected persons (within the meaning of TCA 1997, s 10 – see **2.3**), exceeds the amount which would have been paid if the payer and the payee were independent persons acting at arm's length, the excess amount does not qualify as income from a qualifying patent. In practice, to ensure that all such income from a qualifying patent will be exempted for tax purposes, professional advice should be sought as to what level of royalty or other income may reasonably be taken in respect of the use of the patent.

13.607.4 Restrictions on companies

For companies, the meaning of "income from a qualifying patent" is restricted to sums paid:

(a) for the purposes of activities which would be regarded, otherwise than by virtue of TCA 1997, s 445(7)(b) or (c) or TCA 1997, s 446, as the manufacture of goods for the purposes of relief under TCA 1997 Part 14 (ie, other than Shannon operations, apart from the maintenance or repair of aircraft, qualifying for the 10% corporation tax rate, and international financial services operations);

(b) for the purposes of activities which, although not carried out in the State, would fall within (a) if they were carried out in the State; or

(c) by a person who is not connected (within the meaning of TCA 1997, s 10 – see **2.3**) with the recipient of the royalty or other sum, and who has not entered into any arrangement for the purpose, or mainly for the purpose, of avoiding being "connected with" the recipient.

The phasing out of manufacturing relief is given effect by the definition of "relevant accounting period" in TCA 1997, s 442(1) (see **7.201.2**). A company that commenced to trade on or after 23 July 1998 is not entitled to manufacturing relief after 31 December 2002. This does not affect a company's entitlement to patent income exemption under TCA 1997, s 234 which continues to apply where it receives royalties from a connected company engaged in manufacturing activities within the meaning of TCA 1997 Part 14 but which is precluded from claiming manufacturing relief by virtue of TCA 1997, s 442(1).

13.607.5 Further restriction: distributions out of "specified income"

Distributions made out certain income ("specified income") accruing to a company on or after 28 March 1996, where the specified income is income from a qualifying patent in respect of an invention which was patented for *bona fide* commercial reasons and not primarily for the purpose of avoiding liability to taxation, are not regarded as distributions out of disregarded income unless certain conditions are satisfied. For this purpose, the meaning of "disregarded income" is restricted where the person paying the royalty or other sum is connected with the person who is beneficially entitled to that sum. Income from a qualifying patent which is received by a company from a person with whom it is connected is not disregarded income (TCA 1997, s 141(1)); such income is instead treated as "specified income" for which different treatment is prescribed.

Specified income is income from a qualifying patent received from a connected person and which would not be regarded as income from a qualifying patent except for the fact that the patent is used for the purpose of manufacturing activities (ie, by virtue of the exceptions in (a) and (b) **13.607.4** above).

Exception: expenditure on research and development

A distribution or distributions made for an accounting period out of specified income accruing to a company on or after 28 March 1996 is *treated as* made out of disregarded income to the extent that it does not exceed "the amount of aggregate expenditure on research and development incurred by a company in relation to an accounting period" (TCA 1997, s 141(5)(c)).

For this purpose, *the amount of aggregate expenditure on research and development incurred by a company in relation to an accounting period* means the amount of expenditure on research and development activities incurred in the State by the company in that period and the two previous accounting periods. Where, however, a company incurs expenditure on research and development activities in an accounting period and at least 75% of that expenditure was incurred in the State, all of that expenditure is deemed to have been incurred in the State (TCA 1997, s 141(5)(a)).

The *amount of the expenditure on research and development activities* is non-capital expenditure incurred by a company and comprises:

(a) such part of the emoluments paid to its employees engaged in carrying out research and development activities related to the company's trade as are paid to them for the purposes of those activities;

(b) expenditure on materials or goods used solely by it in carrying out research and development activities related to its trade; and

(c) any amount paid to another person (unconnected with the company) to carry out research and development activities related to the company's trade.

Where a company is a member of a group (see below), the amount of expenditure on research and development activities incurred in an accounting period by another company which, "in the accounting period", is a member of the group is, on a joint election in writing made by the two companies, treated as expenditure incurred on research and development activities in the period by the first-mentioned company and not by the fellow group member. On the narrowest reading, it would seem that research and development expenditure of companies that have been fellow group members at any time during the accounting period in question may be aggregated for the above purpose.

Research and development activities means systematic, investigative or experimental activities which are carried on wholly or mainly in the State (ie, where not less than 75%

of the total amount expended in the course of such activities is expended in the State), which involve innovation or technical risk, and are carried on for the purpose of:

(a) acquiring new knowledge with a view to that knowledge having a specific commercial application; or

(b) creating new or improved materials, products, devices, processes or services

as well as other activities carried on wholly or mainly in the State for a purpose directly related to the carrying on of the above-mentioned activities (as defined in TCA 1997, s 766 before its amendment by FA 2004).

Specifically excluded are activities carried on by way of market research, market testing, market development, sale promotion or consumer surveys, quality control, the making of cosmetic modifications or stylistic changes to products, processes or production methods, management studies or efficiency surveys, and research in social sciences, arts or humanities.

For the purposes of ascertaining what companies are members of the same group, the meaning of *group* is the same as for the purposes of group relief (see **8.103.1**) except that there is no requirement that any company should be Irish resident. In addition, two companies are members of a group if both are wholly or mainly under the control of the same individual or individuals, that is, where at least 75% of the ordinary share capital of each company is owned directly or indirectly by the same individual or individuals. TCA 1997, s 412–418 contain anti-avoidance provisions which counter attempts to create artificial groups (see **8.304**). The additional tests for group relationship as prescribed by these sections, the "profit distribution test" and the "asset distribution test", are applicable here also. In cases where companies are under the control of the same individual or individuals, they apply as if references to "parent company" were references to an individual or individuals.

Alternative exception: radical innovation

Where a company makes a distribution out of specified income, all of that income will be treated as disregarded income if the company can show in writing to the satisfaction of the Revenue Commissioners that the specified income is income from a qualifying patent in respect of an invention which:

(a) involved radical innovation, and

(b) was patented for bona fide commercial reasons and not primarily for the purpose of avoiding liability to tax (TCA 1997, s 141(5)(d)).

The purpose of the patent income exemption is to encourage and reward effort leading to worthwhile inventions and the development of genuinely new products. The legislative provisions restricting the availability of patent income exemption are intended to confine the benefits of the exemption to those situations. This accounts for the requirement, where the parties are connected, that the amount of exempt dividends paid by a patent company should be related back to expenditure on research and development. As an alternative to meeting that requirement, the company in receipt of the royalties may apply in writing to the Revenue Commissioners for a determination to the effect that they are satisfied that the invention which is patented involved radical innovation and that it was patented for *bona fide* commercial reasons and not mainly to avoid liability to tax.

An EU Green Paper published at the end of 1995 defined "radical innovation" as "completely new and qualitatively different". Where an invention has resulted in a completely new product or process, there would be little doubt but that radical innovation has been involved. There is less certainty where the result of an invention is a modest improvement in an existing product or process. Where a product is involved, it is likely that a small but real improvement would qualify as radical innovation but the position relating to a small improvement to a process remains doubtful; there are indications that the Revenue would take a more rigid line in relation to process, as compared with product, innovation, probably because the evaluation of a process is likely to necessitate a greater amount of analysis and is much less amenable to objective verification. It is most unlikely that an incremental change to an existing product or process would be regarded as radical innovation.

The fact that an invention must have involved radical innovation means that the production of something completely new, involving a break with the past, must have been in mind at the time the work on the invention was taking place. (This should not, however, preclude a case in which the inventor's research accidentally or fortuitously results in an innovation different from the one originally envisaged.) It is not sufficient that the innovative character of what is produced only becomes apparent as a result of its subsequent commercialisation. It is understood that the Revenue are likely to take a more favourable view as to what constitutes radical innovation against a background of slow-moving technology where any change in technology following a relatively long period of no change can more easily be justified as being radical.

The following view on the matter was expressed by the Minister for Finance in the course of the passage of the Finance Bill through the Dáil:

> "The term 'radical innovation' means the creation of something which is fundamentally novel. The degree of novelty cannot be other than a subjective judgment. However, there is an OECD precedent for classifying innovation as 'completely new', 'modestly improved' and 'merely a differentiation of an existing product or process'. In viewing the foregoing categories in the context of 'radical innovation' something completely new would come within its scope but a mere differentiation would not. The modestly improved product which is not a mere differentiation is more likely to be considered radical innovation than a modestly improved process.

> A body of precedents exists to which inspectors can refer and the interpretation of 'radical' or 'innovative' can be reasonably adduced. This matter will be clarified with the taxation administration committee and guidelines will be given to domestic tax practitioners."

There is, however, no information as to the nature or location of the "body of precedent" referred to above and, to date, no guidelines have been issued. Until such time as these matters are progressed, persons requiring clarification will need to obtain advance Revenue agreement in individual cases by submitting all relevant data and information concerning the invention, including a copy of the patent application, a memorandum explaining how the product in question involves radical innovation, and any technical or trade literature substantiating that contention. Inventions in respect of which favourable "radical innovation" rulings have been received include an interactive system, methods of processing bivalve molluscs, jointed optic fibres, and improvements to bag-making apparatus.

For the purpose of making *their* determination, the Revenue will consider any evidence submitted to them and may consult with any person who may be of assistance to them in the matter. The Revenue Commissioners' determination may be appealed to the Appeal Commissioners and all of the provisions relating to appeals against income tax assessments, the rehearing of appeals, and the stating of a case for the opinion of the High Court on a point of law, will apply in the case of such an appeal and with any necessary modifications.

To the above indications regarding what might constitute radical innovation can now be added a view from the judiciary. The case of *Revenue Commissioners v Wen-Plast (Research & Development) Ltd* [2007] IEHC 66 (9 March 2007) involved abstruse argument on a point of law concerning the correct meaning of the phrase "income from a qualifying patent in respect of an invention which ... involved radical innovation". The reasoning that led to the Court's conclusion will give some insight into the correct approach to be taken in relation to this question. The High Court found that the exemption applied to patent royalty income relating to the development of a hygienic fire door set. The development of the door set was such that it was considered not necessary to show that radical innovation was part of the process leading to a patent but that it was sufficient that a combination of known technology could, and did, result in an invention which involved radical innovation.

The Revenue had contended that it was immaterial whether or not an invention is in itself a radical innovation and that the innovation which must be identified is radical innovation in the process leading to the invention that has been patented. The Court rejected this view, the essential question for determination being whether the invention itself involved radical innovation.

The Revenue view was largely based on the fact that TCA 1997, s 141(5)(d) refers to an invention which "involved" (ie, past tense) radical innovation so that the innovation must be part of the process leading to the invention. But this was to ignore the fact that the definition of "qualifying patent" distinguishes the invention from the process leading to it and that in the above paragraph both the invention and the patenting are events which occurred in the past.

The relevance of the above distinctions derived from the nature of the patented product. Previously, two door sets were required for pharmaceutical clean rooms, one to provide fire-resistant capabilities but which could not meet the required hygiene standards, and a second set which met those standards. The invention permitted the production of a single door set with the necessary fire-resistant and hygienic qualities. The inventive aspect of the door set was the encasing of a fire resistant intumescent strip in a specific type of door frame made from cured plastic materials.

The Revenue case rested on expert evidence produced on their behalf to the effect that it was the introduction of the intumescent strip within the cured plastic material that constituted the invention. The type of strip used and the technology governing the cured plastic materials were, it was claimed, each "part of the prior art" at the time the patent was granted. Consequently, and in the light of the interpretation of TCA 1997, s 141(5)(d) to the effect that the innovation must be part of the process leading to the invention, it was not necessary to consider whether the resulting product was itself a radical innovation.

The invention in question involved bringing together in a new and creative way several scientific principles already well established so that what was involved was a new product rather than a "new science". In effect, the Revenue view was that there could be no radical innovation in the case of a new product that did not involve "new science". The Court disagreed with this conclusion, based as it was on an incorrect interpretation of the legislation. In any event, the term "radical innovation" should not be seen as a term of art or as having any special connotation and is to be given its ordinary colloquial meaning, ie "root change".

The Revenue had also argued, as a central plank of its case, that the concept of invention can exist separately from the concept of the product that incorporates it. It had been accepted on both sides, however, that the invention was the introduction of the intumescent strip within the cured plastic. The material manifestation of the invention was the door set which incorporated the product and any normal assessment of the quality of the invention would be conducted by reference to that manifestation. The Court confirmed that the proper question for determination was whether the invention itself involved radical innovation in the sense that it involved a change which was original and fundamental, a question which it answered in the affirmative.

Anti-avoidance: franchising, licensing etc between unconnected parties

In cases involving franchising, licensing or other similar arrangements between unconnected parties, any tax exemption in respect of distributions, made by a company on or after 2 February 2006, from exempt patent royalty income of the company from a person with whom it has also entered into such an arrangement is limited by reference to research and development expenditure incurred by the company, as well as by its fellow group companies, over a three year period. This limited exemption applies provided the patent in question was taken out for *bona fide* commercial reasons and not primarily for tax avoidance purposes.

A number of definitions are relevant in connection with this measure.

An *arrangement* is any arrangement, agreement, understanding, promise or undertaking whether express or implied.

Relevant income is income to which paragraph (b) of the definition of "income from a qualifying patent" in TCA 1997, s 234 applies, ie sums paid by a person who is not connected (within the meaning of TCA 1997, s 10 – see **2.3**) with the recipient of the royalty or other sum, and who has not entered into any arrangement for the purpose, or mainly for the purpose, of avoiding being "connected with" the recipient (see (c) in **13.607.4** above).

The amount of aggregate expenditure on research and development incurred by a company in relation to an accounting period has the same meaning as in TCA 1997, s 234(5)(a) (see definitions above).

A *payment in respect of the use of intellectual property* is any payment made, directly or indirectly, in respect of:

(a) any franchise, trade mark, registered design, design right, invention or domain name;

(b) any copyright or related right within the meaning of the Copyright and Related Rights Act 2000;

(c) any licence or other right in respect of anything within (a) or (b) above;

(d) any rights granted under the law of any country, territory, state or area, other than the State, or under any international treaty, convention or agreement to which the State is a party, that correspond to or are similar to those within (a) to (c) above;

(e) goodwill to the extent that it is directly attributable to anything within (a) to (d) above.

Where TCA 1997, s 141(5A) applies to a company for an accounting period and the company makes for that period one or more distributions out of relevant income, then so much of the amount of that distribution, or the aggregate of such distributions, as does not exceed the amount of aggregate expenditure on research and development incurred by the company in relation to the accounting period is to be treated as a distribution made out of disregarded income. A distribution will not, however, be so treated unless the relevant income is income from a qualifying patent in respect of an invention that was patented for *bona fide* commercial reasons and not primarily for the purpose of avoiding liability to tax (TCA 1997, s 141(5A)(d)).

TCA 1997, s 141(5A) applies to a company for an accounting period if under any arrangement:

(i) a person becomes, or could become, liable to make to the company any payment in respect of the use of intellectual property by virtue of the fact that any payment that is relevant income made by the person to the company was, or, as the case may be, could have been, insufficient for the purposes of the arrangement; or

(ii) the company becomes, or could become, liable to make to any person any payment in respect of the use of intellectual property by the person by virtue of the fact that any payment that is relevant income made by the person to the company was, or, as the case may be, could have been, excessive for the purposes of the arrangement (TCA 1997, s 141(5A)(c)).

13.607.6   Distributions out of disregarded income

A dividend or other distribution received by a person and made by a company out of disregarded patent income is itself treated as not being income for income tax purposes provided it is a distribution in respect of "eligible shares" or is made out of disregarded income referable to a qualifying patent in relation to which the person carried out, either solely or jointly with another person, the research, planning, processing, experimenting, testing, devising, designing, development or other similar activity leading to the invention which is the subject of the qualifying patent (TCA 1997, s 141(3)(a)(i), (4)(a)). Where received by a company in respect of eligible shares, the distribution is treated as disregarded income (TCA 1997, s 141(3)(a)(ii)).

Eligible shares means shares which are fully paid up, which carry no preferential right to dividends or assets on a winding up and no preferential right to be redeemed, and which are not the subject of any treatment different from the treatment applying to all shares of the same class.

Where the income out of which the distribution is made consists partly of exempted income and partly of other income, the distribution is treated as two distributions, one being from exempted income and the other being from income which is not exempted (see also **11.112**). The legislation does not, however, prescribe a method for apportioning the distribution for this purpose. It might be expected that a distribution out of mixed income should be apportioned in the ratio of exempted and non-exempted income. In practice, however, it seems that the Revenue Commissioners normally accept that a distribution for an accounting period in which there is any disregarded patent income may be treated as coming first out of that exempt income up to its full amount and, as respects any balance remaining, out of other income (see also **11.114**).

From 6 April 1994, distributions out of disregarded income are not treated as disregarded income for income tax purposes except where received by:

(a) an individual who carried out, alone or with others, the research, testing or other work which led to the invention which is the subject of the patent in respect of which the disregarded income arose; or

(b) an individual in receipt of a distribution in respect of eligible shares.

Example 13.607.6.1

Pantheon Ltd receives royalty income from Heraclitus Ltd in respect of the use of a qualifying patent. Magnus Pijksson receives distributions from Pantheon Ltd. All parties are solely Irish resident. The distributions received will be exempted ("disregarded") income of Mr Pijksson in the circumstances outlined below. It is necessary first that the royalty income of Pantheon Ltd is disregarded income. Being in respect of a "qualifying patent", the royalty payments made by Heraclitus Ltd can be taken to have been set at an arm's length price.

Any distribution made by Pantheon Ltd is treated as a distribution made out of disregarded income if, for the accounting period in which it is made:

(a) Heraclitus Ltd is not connected with Pantheon Ltd, *or*

(b) the royalty is paid for the purposes of manufacturing or deemed manufacturing activities of Heraclitus Ltd, *and either*

    (i) the amount of the distribution does not exceed the amount of non-capital expenditure on research and development activities incurred by Pantheon Ltd and any of its fellow group members in the accounting period and in the two previous accounting periods: otherwise, only the amount of the distribution up to that amount of expenditure is treated as made out of disregarded income, *or*

    (ii) it can be shown to the satisfaction of the Revenue Commissioners that the invention which is the subject of the patent involved radical innovation and was patented for genuine commercial reasons..

Assuming that, on the above basis, any distributions made to Mr Pijksson are made out of disregarded income of Pantheon Ltd, those distributions will be exempted income of Mr Pijksson if—

(a) he was involved in carrying out the research, planning, testing, designing or other work leading to the invention which is the subject of the patent, *or*

(b) the distributions received are in respect of "eligible shares" in Pantheon Ltd.

13.607.7 Disregarded income: €5m ceiling amount

With effect from 1 January 2008, the amount of disregarded income arising to any person in a "relevant period" may not exceed €5m. A *relevant period* is the period of 12 months commencing on 1 January 2008 and each subsequent twelve month period. The €5m ceiling is applied to the combined qualifying patent income of a company and all other persons connected with the company.

The aggregate amount of income from qualifying patents arising to a person in a relevant period that can be disregarded for tax purposes may not exceed €5m. For this purpose, the €5m ceiling is applied to the aggregate amounts of income from qualifying patents arising to a company and to one or more persons who are connected with (within the meaning of TCA 1997, s 10 – see **2.302**) that company (TCA 1997, s 234(3A)(a), (b)).

Where the aggregate amounts exceed €5m, the disregarded income of €5m is allocated between the company and the connected persons The allocation of the €5m ceiling amount for a relevant period may be effected in a manner specified in a notice made jointly in writing to the inspector of taxes by the company and the connected persons on or before the tax return filing date relative to the latest chargeable period (accounting period or year of assessment) of the company or any of the connected persons which falls wholly or partly into the relevant period. The aggregate of the amounts allocated may not exceed €5m. Where no such notice is given, the €5m is to be allocated in proportion to the respective amounts of income from qualifying patents arising to the company and the connected persons (TCA 1997, s 234(3A)(c)).

The excess qualifying patent income of a company will be subject to corporation tax, the rate depending on whether or not it arises from the carrying on of a trade. In a case where, say, the aggregate qualifying patent income of two connected companies exceeds €5m and where only one of those companies is a trading company, it will be possible to allocate the €5m to the maximum extent against the patent income of the non-trading company. (Obviously, where one or more of the connected persons are individuals, the €5m will nearly always be allocated to the maximum extent to them.)

Where a relevant period does not coincide with a company's accounting period, the qualifying patent income of the company for the relevant period will be the aggregate of the amounts of such income arising in any accounting period, or part of an accounting period, falling within the relevant period (TCA 1997, s 234(3A)(d)).

Income arising in a relevant period that is to be treated as disregarded will be treated as representing income of an accounting period only to the extent that it cannot be treated as representing income of an earlier period or part of such period (TCA 1997, s 234(3A)(d)(iii)).

Example 13.607.7.1

Chandler Ltd had income from qualifying patents as follows:

Year to	*€000*
30 September 2008	4,800
30 September 2009	9,600
30 September 2010	11,600

For the relevant period 1 January 2008 to 31 December 2008, the company's income from qualifying patents is the aggregate of the amounts of such income arising to it in the parts of its accounting periods falling within that period. The qualifying patent income arising in the first two accounting periods is treated as arising in the parts of those periods falling within the year ended 31 December 2008 on a time basis:

		€000
1.1.08 - 30.9.08	9/12 x €4.8m =	3,600
1.10.08 - 31.12.08	3/12 x €9.6m =	2,400
Aggregate		6,000

For the relevant period 1 January 2009 to 31 December 2009, the company's income from qualifying patents is the aggregate of the amounts of such income arising to it in the parts of its accounting periods falling within that period:

		€000
1.1.09 – 30.9.09	9/12 x €9.6m =	7,200
1.10.09 – 31.12.09	3/12 x €11.6m =	2,900
Aggregate		10,100

All but €1m of the qualifying patent income arising in the first relevant period is disregarded income. For the second relevant period, the disregarded income is €5m and the remaining €5.1m is taxable.

It is then necessary to identify the disregarded income of the accounting periods. All of the qualifying patent income of €4.8m for the year ended 30 September 2008 is disregarded. Since TCA 1997, s 234(3A) applies only from 1 January 2008, income of €1.2m referable to the period 1 October 2007 to 31 December 2007 is disregarded income without any reference to that provision and only €3.6m forms part of the disregarded income of €5m for the first relevant period. Accordingly, the balance of the disregarded income for the first relevant period is €1.4m and this is allocated to the year ended 30 September 2009 as is the €5m for the second relevant period. Accordingly, the taxable income for the year ended 30 September 2009 is €9.6m - €6.4m = €3.2m.

Since the qualifying patent income of the year ended 30 September 2010, net of the amount of €2.9m included for the relevant period 2008, exceeds €5m, the income of that period will be treated as including disregarded income of €5m.

13.608 Spreading of royalty income

A royalty or other sum may be received for the use of a patent that extends over a period of years. Normally any such payment to a company is taxable as taxed income for the accounting period in which it is received or, if it is from a foreign source, under the rules for Schedule D Case III. A company in receipt of such royalty or other sum is entitled under TCA 1997, s 759 to require its tax liability to be computed as if it had been paid over a number of years, but only in the case of a royalty or other sum to which TCA 1997, s 237 or 238 apply.

In effect, the right to have the royalty income spread over a number of years is only available to such income from Irish sources as is subject to the rules on deduction of income tax at source. If the period over which the use of the patent has extended is six complete years or more, the company is entitled to require the inspector to re-compute its tax liability for the relevant accounting periods on the assumption that the royalty was paid in six equal instalments at yearly intervals, the last of which was paid on the date on which the payment was in fact made.

In the event that the royalty or other sum is paid in respect of the use of a patent for two complete years or more, but less than six complete years, the company's tax liability may be recomputed as if the royalty had been paid in equal annual instalments of a number equal to the number of complete years comprised in the period over which the use of the patent extended.

The years over which the royalty is spread are the actual years working back from the date on which the particular royalty payment was made. For example, if a single royalty payment of €17,000 was made on 1 June 1999 in respect of the use of a patent for the five years ended 31 March 1999, the company in receipt of the royalty may have its tax liabilities recomputed on the assumption that it had received five royalty payments of €3,400 each on 1 June 1999, 1 June 1998, 1 June 1997, 1 June 1996 and 1 June 1995. If the company makes up accounts to 31 December each year, this would result in its corporation tax liabilities for the years ended 31 December 1995 to 31 December 1999 being recomputed by including royalty income of €3,400 for each of those periods, and by excluding from its income for the year ended 31 December 1999 the €17,000 actually received.

The spreading backwards of royalty payments is relatively unusual. It is not applicable to the case where the royalties are paid annually on a regular basis or for any royalty payable for a period of use of less than two complete years. Spreading treatment may not be claimed at all if the royalty payment arises from a foreign source not subject to the deduction of Irish income tax under either TCA 1997, s 237 or 238.

13.7 COMPANIES IN PARTNERSHIP

13.701 Partnership taxation rules
13.702 Capital allowances
13.703 Limited partnerships: restriction of reliefs
13.704 Partnership returns

13.701 Partnership taxation rules

13.701.1 Introduction

Although most partnerships are formed by individuals, a partnership trade can just as easily be carried on by two or more companies. It is also possible, and it is not infrequently the case, that a partnership would have both individual and corporate members. A partnership is defined in the Partnership Act 1890, as "two or more persons carrying on business in common with a view to profit".

In the commercial world, a partnership has rights and obligations distinct from those of its members. Partners are never indebted to each other in respect of partnership transactions; any such relationship is between an individual partner and the firm. In law, however, the firm as such has no legal recognition; it is not recognised as distinct from the members comprising it. The firm does not enter into contracts in the firm name but in the names of its partners. Although a partnership profit and loss account and balance sheet would be made up for the firm, the assets usually belong jointly to the persons making up the partnership and the partners are jointly and severally liable. In law, it would not be correct to say that the firm carries on business. Under Irish law, a (partnership) firm as such has no existence and the partners carry on the business both as principals and as agents for each other within the scope of the partnership business. The partnership name is a mere expression rather than a legal entity, although "it may be used for the sake of suing and being sued" (Farwell LJ in *Sadler v Whiteman*).

13.701.2 Taxation of partnership profits

For taxation purposes, TCA 1997 Part 43 (ss 1007-1013) provides for the taxation of the members of a partnership rather than the firm itself. A determination of partnership profits and of partnership capital allowances is made for each relevant year of assessment and is made on the precedent partner of the firm. The *precedent partner* in relation to a partnership is a partner resident in the State who is first named in the partnership agreement or, if there is no such agreement, is named singly or with precedence to the other partners in the usual name of the firm, or is the precedent acting partner if the person named with precedence is not an acting partner. The partnership is required to make annual tax returns, through the precedent partner, of the partnership income and capital gains. Each partner is, however, liable to tax in respect of his separate share of the firm's trading profits and other income and in respect of his share of any chargeable gains realised on disposals of property and assets held jointly.

The profits of the partnership firm for the purposes of Case I or II of Schedule D are ascertained in accordance with the normal rules for those Cases and are then allocated to the partners. There are specific partnership rules relating to capital allowances. The capital allowances computation is prepared for the partnership and allowances are divided between the partners in accordance with the terms of the partnership. Any excess capital allowances would be carried forward to following periods for the partnership as a whole. Although a partnership tax return with tax computation will be filed with the tax authorities, assessments are never made on the partnership as such. Each partner is assessed separately in respect of his individual profit share, determined by reference to how the partnership agreement provides for the division of profits and losses.

13.701.3 The relevant period

A *partnership trade* is defined in TCA 1997, s 1007(1) as one which is carried on by two or more persons in partnership. As a means of regulating the commencement and cessation of a partnership trade taking account of the admission and retirement of partners from time to time, the concept of the "relevant period" is important. The *relevant period* is the entire period during which the partnership trade is treated as continuing irrespective of the changes in the members of the partnership. The relevant period commences on the date on which the trade is first carried on by two or more persons in partnership, and ends when the trade is permanently discontinued, or when it is no longer carried on by at least two persons, or when there is a complete change in the partners carrying on the trade (TCA 1997, s 1007(2)).

A trade is first carried on by two or more persons at the time the trade itself is carried on from its commencement by two or more persons in partnership, or at the time a person who had been carrying on the trade alone admits one or more partners, or when there is a complete change in the partners carrying on the trade.

13.701.4 Partners' several trades

TCA 1997, s 1008(1) provides that each partner is to be taxed on his share of profits or gains from the partnership trade as if that share were profits or gains of a "several" trade, ie a trade carried on solely by him. Where a partnership loss arises, each partner is entitled to claim any available relief in respect of his share of that loss as if it were a loss sustained in his several trade. Similarly, each partner is entitled to his share of the partnership capital allowances and is taxable on his share of any partnership balancing charges for each year of assessment for which he is a partner.

The amount of profits arising to a partner from his several trade for any period of account of the partnership, or the amount of any loss sustained for that period, is to be taken to be so much of the full profits or loss of the partnership trade as would fall to his share on an apportionment made in accordance with the terms of the partnership agreement as to the sharing of profits or losses (TCA 1997, s 1008(2)(a)(i)).

Where for any year or period within the relevant period the aggregate of the respective amounts (the "aggregate") of the profits or gains which under TCA 1997, s 1008(2)(a)(i) are taken as arising to each partner in the partnership is less than the full amount of the profits or gains of the partnership trade for that year or period, the amount of the difference (the "balance") between that full amount and the aggregate is for the purposes of TCA 1997, s 1008(1) to be apportioned in full between the partners—

(a)   in the ratio which is expressed between the partners in relation to the apportionment of the balance, or

(b)   where there is no such ratio expressed—

(i)   in the same ratio as the ratio which applies between the respective amounts of the profits or gains which, under TCA 1997, s 1008(2)(a)(i), were taken as arising to each partner, or

(ii)   where no amount of profits or gains was under that subparagraph taken as arising to any individual partner, in equal shares (TCA 1997, s 1008(2)(a)(ii)).

Before the taxable profit, or allowable loss, of each partner's several trade can be ascertained, the profit or loss of the partnership firm as a whole must be determined for each period for which the firm makes up accounts. The full amount of the firm's taxable profit or tax adjusted loss for each such period must be determined as if the trade had commenced at the beginning of the relevant period and as if it had continued to be carried on at all times in the relevant period by one person (TCA 1997, s 1008(3)).

The significance of the relevant period concept therefore is that partnership profits or losses are calculated for tax purposes on the same basis throughout the relevant period regardless of what changes may take place during that period as regards the admission of new partners or the retirement of existing partners. No deduction may be made in computing the profits or losses of a partnership trade for any expenses incurred before the commencement of the relevant period. Thereafter, the question of the non-allowability of pre-trading expenses does not arise as long as the relevant period does not come to an end. TCA 1997, s 89, which contains provisions regarding the valuation of closing stock on the cessation of a trade, has no application to a partnership trade unless and until the relevant period for the partnership comes to an end.

When the Case I or Case II profit or loss for the partnership has been determined for any period of account, the profit or loss is allocated between the persons who were partners during that period. That allocation is made in accordance with the terms of the partnership agreement as to the sharing of profits or losses, ie profits or losses as disclosed by the firm's accounts (TCA 1997, s 1008(2)(a) – see above). In some cases, the partners may agree at times to vary the terms of the partnership agreement as to the sharing of profits and losses. Where the accounting profit or loss is divided between the partners for any period in a manner different to that provided for in the partnership agreement, the allocation for tax purposes will follow that division for that period.

The share of the profit or loss allocated to each partner is treated as a profit or loss of his several trade. TCA 1997, s 1009(2) provides that TCA 1997, s 1008(1), (2)(a) and (3) are to have effect for the purposes of corporation tax in relation to a partner company in the same way as for income tax in relation to an individual partner. For a partner company, unlike an individual partner for whom it would then be necessary to apply the income tax basis period rules, the apportionment of the share of profit or loss to the company's accounting period is a straightforward matter. Where the partnership period of account coincides with the company's accounting period, obviously no apportionment is required. Otherwise, the apportionment is made on a time basis (TCA 1997, s 1009(3), (5)). Any apportionment, whether to a part of an accounting period of the company, to a part of the period of account of the partnership, or to a part of a year of assessment, is to be made by reference to the number of months or fractions of months contained in that part and in the remainder of that period or year. The allocation of partnership profits to a corporate partner and the apportionment to the company's accounting period are subject to the deduction of the company's share of capital allowances and to the addition of the share of any balancing charge arising (see **13.702**).

Example 13.701.4.1

Repnin Ltd, which makes up accounts to 31 December each year, is a partner in Adam Weide & Associates. Partnership accounts are made up to 31 March each year. The partnership's trading profit for the year ended 31 March 2007, as adjusted for tax purposes, is €80,000 and the partnership share of Repnin Ltd for that period, in accordance with the terms of the partnership agreement, is 25%.

The share of the partnership profit for the year ended 31 March 2007 allocated to Repnin Ltd is €20,000. Of this amount, 3/12 ths, or €5,000, is apportioned to the company's year ended 31 December 2007; the remaining €15,000 will have been apportioned to the year ended 31 December 2006. For the year ended 31 December 2007, it will be necessary to await the partnership results for the year ended 31 March 2008, so as to apportion the company's share of the profit (or loss) for that period, before the corporation tax return can be completed.

It is common practice for the terms of a partnership agreement to provide for the payment of salaries to one or more partners before any division of profits or losses is made and also for interest to be paid or credited to partners on their respective current or capital account balances. The agreement will also provide for the payment of interest by any partner whose current or capital account is overdrawn. In these circumstances, salaries and interest are treated as appropriations of profit and will be added back in the computation of the partnership's taxable profit or loss. In allocating the resulting adjusted profit or loss between the partners, the respective amounts for salaries and interest will be taken into account. Where interest is paid by or charged to any partner, the amount in question is deducted from his profit share; it is not included as a partnership trading receipt.

It will often be the case that a partner owns an asset which is used in the partnership trade. The asset may accordingly be rented or hired to the partnership and, assuming the amount charged is fair and reasonable and therefore incurred wholly and exclusively for the purposes of the trade, it will be deductible in arriving at the amount of the partnership profit of loss (see *Heastie v Veitch* 18 TC 305). The partner who owns the asset should include the amount receivable (eg as rent taxable under Case V or as miscellaneous income under Case IV) in his individual tax return. Instead of making a charge for the use of the asset, the partner may contribute it as part of his capital contribution to the firm. If no specific charge is made for its use by the firm, there will be nothing to be included in the partner's individual tax return in respect of the asset, the return to the partner merely being reflected in his share of the partnership profit.

Example 13.701.4.2

Magnus Stenbock and Otto Vellinck have been carrying on a trade in partnership for some years, sharing profits equally, and make up accounts of the firm to 28 February each year. On 1 March 2006, the partners admit an unlimited liability company, Danzig & Co, as a new partner. The company is to contribute capital of €120,000 carrying an interest rate of 10%, and the individual partners are to receive annual salaries of €10,000 each. The new profit sharing ratios, after allowing for interest and salaries, are 30% each for Stenbock and Vellinck and 40% for Danzig & Co.

Danzig & Co makes up accounts to 30 November each year and has been carrying on its own separate trade for a number of years. The following are the computations of taxable profits for the years ended 28 February 2007 and 29 February 2008 for the partnership:

	Year ended 28 February 2007	Year ended 29 February 2008
	€	€
Profit (loss) per accounts	110,000	(73,000)
Disallow:		
Depreciation	35,000	36,000
Sundry non-allowable items	11,000	12,000
Partners' salaries	20,000	20,000
Interest on capital	12,000	12,000
	188,000	7,000
Allow:		
Profit on sale of fixed assets	8,400	5,600
Adjusted profit before capital allowances	179,600	1,400

The profit is allocated between the partners as follows:

	Magnus Stenbock	Otto Vellinck	Danzig & Co
	€	€	€
Year ended 28 February 2007			
Salary	10,000	10,000	Nil
Interest			12,000
Balance of €147,600 allocated:			
M Stenbock and O Vellinck – 30% each	44,280	44,280	
Danzig & Co - 40%			59,040
Total profit allocated	54,280	54,280	71,040
Year ended 29 February 2008			
Salary	10,000	10,000	Nil
Interest			12,000
Balance of (€30,600) allocated:			
M Stenbock and O Vellinck – 30% each	(9,180)	(9,180)	
Danzig & Co - 40%			(12,240)
Total profit (loss) allocated	820	820	(240)

It is then necessary to apportion the profits (loss) to the accounting periods of Danzig & Co as follows:

	Year ended 30 November 2006	Year ended 30 November 2007
	€	€
Share from y/e 28/2/07 – profit €71,040:		
Allocated to y/e 30/11/06		
€71,040 x 9/12	53,280	
Allocated to y/e 30/11/07		
€71,040 x 3/12		17,760
Share from y/e 29/2/08 – loss €240:		
Allocated to y/e 30/11/07		
€240 x 9/12		(180)
Total taxable profit	53,280	17,580

The computations, incorporating capital allowances, are completed in Example **13.702.1**.

The share of profit or loss allocated to a partner company, as apportioned to the company's accounting period, may require further adjustment for the purposes of the corporation return for the that period. Expenses incurred by the company itself may be deductible in arriving at the final amount of assessable profits. For example, audit fees incurred by the company in respect of the accounts for the period may be deductible.

A company may also wish to obtain a tax deduction for interest on borrowings used in purchasing a share in a partnership or in contributing money to the partnership by way of capital or otherwise for use for the purposes of the partnership trade. TCA 1997, s 253 makes provision for the allowance of interest for tax purposes in these circumstances but only in the case of an individual partner. In the absence of a specific provision for companies, the entitlement of a company to relief for such interest is doubtful. To obtain relief, it would seem that the company would have to rely on being able to show that the interest has been incurred wholly and exclusively for the purposes of its trade. This position would, however, be difficult to support. For example, assuming that the money borrowed and paid into the partnership is used for the purposes of the partnership trade, it could then be said that it has been used wholly and exclusively for the purposes of the partnership trade rather than for the several trade of the partner company.

The amount received by each partner is then included in that partner's taxable income at the grossed up equivalent of the sum received and the income tax paid is deducted from the final tax liability. A partner company would be liable to corporation tax in respect of any such receipt subject to a deduction in respect of the income tax paid (TCA 1997, s 24(2))

13.701.5 Losses

A trading loss in the case of a partnership is computed for tax purposes in the same way as a trading profit. To the extent that a partnership loss is allocated to a partner company, the amount is treated as a trading loss of its several trade (TCA 1997, s 1008(2)(a)). The loss can be used as if the company was carrying on the trade on its own (see **4.101**) so that, for example, it may be offset against the company's total profits for the period of the loss, with any necessary apportionment where the company's accounting period differs from the partnership period of account.

A partnership profit may not be allocated with the result that any partner sustains a loss in respect of his several trade. By the same token, a partner may not have a profit for tax purposes where a loss has been sustained by the partnership as a whole; the combined losses allocated to partners may not exceed the tax adjusted partnership loss. The partnership profit or loss for this purpose is the profit or loss after making any necessary adjustments for salaries and interest on capital. Where the initial allocation of a partnership loss results in one or more partners having a profit, those partners are treated as having made neither a profit nor a loss and their profits are reallocated so as to reduce the losses of the loss making partners proportionately according to their own profit sharing ratios.

Where a partner company's several trade ceases on the occasion of its retirement from the firm, it may make a terminal loss claim under TCA 1997, s 397 (see **4.104**) in respect of any loss sustained in its several trade, as increased by its share of capital allowances, for the final 12 months ending with the date of the retirement.

Where the relevant period comes to an end (because, say, the partnership trade ceases altogether or because there is a complete change in the persons making up the partnership), terminal loss claims may be made by the partners where a partnership loss is incurred in the final 12 months of trading.

13.701.6 Partnership or joint venture?

Because, as seen above, there are particular rules governing the tax treatment of partnerships, it will sometimes be necessary to decide whether a business arrangement involving two or more parties is truly a partnership or is a joint venture. The distinction can be difficult to make, not least as it would appear that in some instances it is possible to have a relationship which is both a partnership and a joint venture. A partnership denotes the relationship which subsists between two or more persons carrying on business in common with a view to profit. The distinction between a partnership and a joint venture (not being a partnership) can often be difficult to draw. A joint venture has been defined as a partnership confined to a particular venture, speculation, course of trade or voyage, and in which the partners use no firm or social name and incur no responsibility beyond the limits of the venture. In short, a joint venture is a kind of partnership, one of a specially limited character.

The essential elements of a partnership are that business is being carried on, that it is being carried on by two or more persons in common, and that there is a profit motive. In relation to the last mentioned element, this would denote an intention to share both profits *and* losses. However, it would appear that these elements could also be present in the case of a joint venture.

The distinction is probably most easily seen in relation to how the parties to either arrangement would account for their transactions. In the case of a partnership, accounts for the firm as a whole are drawn up and, depending on the terms of the partnership, each partner takes a share of the net profit, or loss. In the case of a joint venture, there would appear to be a number of possibilities. A joint venture account (basically an income and expenditure account) might be maintained for the joint venture. In that case other accounts would also be maintained such as the partners' capital accounts, joint cash account, and joint bills receivable and bills payable accounts. A special banking account might be opened for the joint venture. Where no separate banking account is opened, each party to the venture would disburse sums on behalf of the joint account from its banking account into which would also be paid cash received by it from time to time.

In certain cases, no separate books would be opened for the joint venture transactions so that each party would record its own transactions on behalf of the joint venture. There would be no joint banking account and, to ascertain profits or losses, each party would render to the other a complete statement of all transactions entered into by it which would then be combined into a memorandum joint venture account.

The distinction between a partnership and a joint venture is reflected to some extent in Irish tax law. In a partnership situation, as already explained, the firm would submit a partnership tax return. The relevant tax computation would commence with the partnership profit or loss as disclosed by the accounts and adjustments would be made in the normal way to arrive at the profit or loss for tax purposes. There are specific partnership rules relating to capital allowances. The capital allowances computation is prepared for the partnership and allowances are divided between the partners in accordance with the terms of the partnership (see **13.702**). Any excess capital allowances would be carried forward to following periods for the partnership as a whole. Although a partnership tax return with a tax computation is filed with the inspector of taxes, assessments are never made on the partnership as such. Each partner is assessed separately in respect of the individual profit share, determined by reference to how the partnership agreement provides for the division of profits and losses.

In the case of a joint venture, there is no question of submitting a joint venture tax return; each party to the joint venture would include the results of the joint transactions in its own tax return. Capital allowances would be computed separately by reference to the plant and equipment, fixtures and fittings etc owned by each party.

A written partnership agreement will almost invariably exist in the case of a firm carrying on a business in partnership. The existence or otherwise of a partnership, however, does not depend on such an agreement. There are many instances in case law in which it has been found that a partnership business was being carried on where no partnership agreement existed and, in some cases, despite a written declaration by the parties that their relationship was not to be construed as amounting to a partnership (*Weiner v Harris* [1910] 1 KB 285, 290). The courts will always look to the facts and circumstances of each case and will not necessarily be guided by what the parties to the joint transactions themselves say. An important principle to be observed in deciding whether a partnership exists is that regard is to be had to the true contract and intention of the parties as appearing from all of the facts of the case (*Cox v Hickman* 8 HCL 268).

An arrangement entered into and intended to operate as a joint venture could be found to constitute a partnership. This possibility emerges from the relevant case law. In certain cases, arrangements which at first sight appeared to amount to no more than a joint transaction falling short of a partnership, were nevertheless found to constitute a partnership. The common factor in these cases was the sharing of profits and losses. Where a number of persons jointly buy goods for resale with the intention of dividing the profits resulting from the transaction, that amounts to a partnership (*Reid v Hollinshead* 4 B & C 867, and *Oppenheimer v Frazer and Wyatt* [1907] 1 KB 519; [1907] 2 KB 50). Persons agreeing to share the profits of an adventure in which they are engaged are prima facie partners even though they stipulate that they are not liable for losses beyond the sums they agree to subscribe (*Brown v Tapscott* 6 M & W 119). A sharing of gross returns, as distinct from profits, would not of itself create a partnership (section 2(2) Partnership Act 1890). That difference is important. While the sharing of gross returns would not of itself be sufficient to denote a partnership arrangement, the sharing of profits and losses almost always creates a partnership, even if the participants bear some expenses or enjoy some receipts individually.

13.701.7 Manufacturing relief

In certain circumstances, the availability of manufacturing relief to a company could depend on whether it is carrying on business in a manufacturing partnership or merely carrying on business as part of a joint venture. For example, in the case of two companies acting together in a manufacturing venture, one company might contribute, say, finance and technical expertise while the other carries out the actual manufacturing process. In that situation, the second company would clearly be entitled to manufacturing relief (the 10% corporation tax rate) in respect of its joint venture activities. The first company would not, however, be entitled to the relief on this basis. To be so entitled, it would be necessary that the company is engaged in manufacturing operations.

Although the joint venture as a whole would be a manufacturing venture, the company would not itself be involved in the manufacturing process. TCA 1997, s 443(6)(b) specifically provides that where the manufacturing process is not carried out by the company claiming relief, the goods in question are not to be regarded as manufactured; they would be regarded as manufactured for the purposes of relief being claimed by the company which does carry out the process, the second company in this case (see **7.204.3**). It would be necessary therefore to vary the arrangements so as to involve the first company in the manufacturing process.

In this connection, ownership of premises and ownership of plant and equipment for the purposes of manufacturing is not of particular significance; a manufacturer would be no less a manufacturer where the premises are rented and the plant and equipment hired. Where the manufacturing process is not carried out, whether wholly or partly, by the claimant company's employees, it will not be possible to contend that the company is in any way carrying out the manufacturing process.

The manufacturing relief difficulty associated with a joint venture arrangement can be avoided in a partnership arrangement. In the case of two companies carrying on a manufacturing trade in partnership, each partner will be entitled to manufacturing relief. The concept of a "partnership trade" is recognised in Irish tax legislation (see above) which provides that the profits arising to each partner are deemed to be profits of a separate trade carried on by that partner. Where the partnership trade as a whole is a manufacturing trade, each partner would be taxable in respect of its share of the manufacturing profit and would accordingly be entitled to manufacturing relief.

13.701.8 Chargeable gains

TCA 1997, s 30 provides that where two or more persons carry on a trade in partnership, tax in respect of chargeable gains accruing to them on the disposal of any partnership assets are to be assessed and charged on them separately and that any partnership dealings in assets are to be treated as dealings by the partners and not by the partnership firm as such. Capital gains made by a partnership are therefore not assessed on the partnership but are to be apportioned between the partners and assessed separately on each partner.

Legally, a partnership is not a person in itself. Insofar as assets are concerned, there is no person consisting of a partnership which can be said to own the assets; they are jointly owned by all of the partners in the firm. A partner, however, is entitled to have each partnership asset employed for the purposes of the partnership business and, on a dissolution of the partnership, to have the assets sold and the proceeds applied primarily to discharge the partnership liabilities and to have any remaining surplus distributed between the partners in accordance with the terms of the partnership agreement (Partnership Act 1890, ss 20 and 39).

A partner's share in a partnership is not itself a distinct legal asset; the concept refers to his interest (being a joint interest) in each of the partnership assets and to his rights under the partnership agreement vis-à-vis the other partners. It is that interest or those rights which are the assets for capital gains tax purposes. It is to be noted that only assets jointly owned by the partners as partnership assets are partnership assets; it is not uncommon for assets owned by one or more partners individually to be used in the partnership trade. Furthermore, property may be owned jointly by partners as individual investors, and even used in the partnership trade, without being partnership property if the property was acquired with that intention. The distinction between assets owned by a partnership and assets not so owned (whether owned individually or jointly by partners) is important since, for example, the commencement or dissolution of a partnership, or a change in partnership interests, or the admission or retirement of a partner will be an occasion of a disposal (or part disposal) and of an acquisition of interests by the individual partners in the partnership assets.

Application of the capital gains tax rules in these situations can result in tedious capital gains tax calculations. For example, on the creation of a partnership, the contribution of an asset to the partnership by one of the partners amounts to a part disposal of that asset by that partner with a corresponding acquisition of a part interest in the asset by each of the other partners. If the transaction is not at arm's length, the contributing partner will be deemed to have received consideration equal to the market value of the interest disposed of. A similar position would result on the admission of a new partner and, where no payment is made by the incoming partner, part disposals based on market values would arise. A new partner may contribute assets to the partnership in which case there will be a part disposal of those assets to the existing partners. The corresponding acquisitions of interests in these assets would also be deemed to have been at market value.

13.701.9 Other income and charges on income

Where income other than trading or professional income arises to a partnership, it is divided between the partners according to their entitlements, ie as provided under the terms of the partnership agreement. Each partner's share of interest, dividends, rents or other income of the partnership is included in his return of income in the same way as other such income earned by him solely. Where there are deductible expenses, eg in respect of rental income, they are similarly divided between the partners.

TCA 1997, s 26(2) provides that a company is to be chargeable to corporation tax on profits arising under any partnership in any case in which it would be so chargeable if the profits accrued to it directly.

The appropriate proportion of any "annual payment" paid by the partnership in a period of account is treated as paid by each partner (TCA 1997, s 1008(1)(b)). *Annual payment* is defined for this purpose as any payment from which, apart from any insufficiency of profits or gains of the persons making it, tax is deductible under TCA 1997, s 237 (see **4.301** and **4.302**). The term therefore includes annuities, patent royalties and certain mining and other rents and royalties coming within TCA 1997, s 104. For a partner company, an annual payment would constitute a charge on income within the meaning of TCA 1997, s 243 (see **4.402**) so that a partner company's share of any such payment should be deductible in the same way as any such charge paid solely by it.

13.702 Capital allowances

Where capital allowances are to be claimed in the case of a partnership trade, the precedent partner must first make a claim for a "joint allowance", ie the capital allowances due to the partnership as a whole. Details of the claim should be included in the annual partnership tax return (TCA 1997, s 880(2)) and that claim is treated as a proper claim by each partner for his share of the allowances falling to made to him for the year concerned (TCA 1997, s 1010(9)). Balancing charges, as determined for the partnership as a whole, are allocated to the individual partners in the same way, each partner's share being a share of a "joint charge" (TCA 1997, s 1010(3)).

Capital allowances in the case of a partnership trade are calculated as they would be in the case of any other trade. For this purpose, the partnership trade commences at the beginning of the relevant period (see above) and continues as long as the relevant period continues.

Plant or machinery belonging to any partner which is not partnership property may be used for the purposes of the partnership trade. Where a hire or lease charge is made for such use, the partner may claim capital allowances in respect of the expenditure on the plant or machinery which will be allowed against the hire or lease income assessable under Case IV of Schedule D. Where no such charge is made, the related capital allowances are included in the joint allowance which is allocated to the partners as if the plant or machinery were partnership property (TCA 1997, s 293(2)). Use of excess capital allowances, where the plant or machinery is hired or leased to the partnership, is subject to the restrictions provided for by TCA 1997, s 403 – see **5.305)**.

Joint allowances and charges for a year of assessment are allocated between the partners for that year. The allocation is made in accordance with the terms of the partnership agreement as to the sharing of profits and losses for the year of assessment. As with profits, the allocation is made by reference to the way in which the balance of profits after salaries, interest, or any other entitlement of any partner, is shared (TCA 1997, s 1010(7)(b)).

Where a new partner is admitted to, or an existing partner retires from, the partnership, or if the profit sharing ratios are changed, during the year of assessment, any joint allowance or charge for that year is apportioned on a time basis between the respective parts of that year. The joint allowances or charges as apportioned to the parts of the year before and after the change took place are allocated between the partners in the ratios in which they share profits and losses for the respective parts.

The share of the joint allowance for any partner for a year of assessment is set off against that partner's share of the partnership profits as allocated to his several trade for that year. The share of any joint charge is treated as a trading receipt for the year. Where a partner's share of a joint allowance for any year of assessment exceeds his share of the partnership profits, and his share of any joint charge, for that year, the excess may be used, in the case of an individual partner, to reduce total income on a claim under TCA 1997, s 381, and in the case of a company, to reduce total profits on a claim under TCA 1997, s 396(2) or, as is more likely, to make a claim under TCA 1997, s 396A(3) or 396B(3). To the extent that it cannot be fully used in that way, the excess is carried forward to the following year of assessment and if necessary to any subsequent year of assessment as long as the partnership trade is carried on.

It is in relation to this aspect of capital allowances legislation that the position is somewhat unique. It might be expected that the excess capital allowances carried forward would be available against the profits of the individual partner's several trade but that is not the case. The excess is in fact treated as a joint allowance which must therefore be allocated between the persons who are partners in the year of assessment following the year in which the excess arose; TCA 1997, s 1010(8)(b) provides that the aggregate of all partnership capital allowances brought forward from a year of assessment is deemed to be a joint allowance for the following year when it is allocated in accordance with the profit sharing ratios applicable for that year. Any such deemed joint allowance will effectively be added to any joint allowance arising for the following year but, unlike that joint allowance, the deemed joint allowance may not be allowed for the purposes of a claim under TCA 1997, s 381.

Since, however, capital allowances are treated as trading expenses for corporation tax purposes, the question of unused capital allowances as such does not arise for companies; instead, any excess amount is treated as a trading loss or part of a trading loss. For this reason, TCA 1997, s 1009(4)(d), in relation to partnerships involving companies (see below), provides that, notwithstanding TCA 1997, s 1010(8), a joint allowance for a year of assessment does not include any capital allowance that is or could be brought forward from a previous year of assessment.

The manner in which a corporate partner obtains relief for its share of the joint partnership capital allowances, and is taxed on its share of the joint partnership balancing charges, for any year of assessment is provided for in TCA 1997, s 1009(4). For this purpose it is necessary to determine the "relevant amount", which is treated as a trading expense, or as a trading receipt, as the case may be, of the company's several trade for the accounting period any part of which falls within that year of assessment. The *relevant amount*, as defined in TCA 1997, s 1009(4)(a), means:

(i)   where the year of assessment and the accounting period of the company coincide, the full amount of the share of the joint allowance or joint charge; and

(ii)   where part only of the year of assessment falls within the company's accounting period, such portion of the share of the joint allowance or charge as is apportioned to that part of the year of assessment which falls within the accounting period.

The procedure for ascertaining the relevant amount of an allowance for an accounting period can be summarised as follows:

(1)   The joint partnership capital allowances are calculated for each year of assessment into which the accounting period falls;

(2)   The company's share of the joint allowance for each year of assessment is calculated as the share of the joint allowance based on the ratio in which the company shares in the firm's profits for that year;

(3)   The amount calculated for each year of assessment is time apportioned to the accounting period in the ratio which the number of months in the year of assessment falling within the accounting period bears to twelve;

(4)   The relevant amount for the accounting period is the sum of the amounts in 3.

The procedure for calculating the relevant amount of a balancing charge is the same as described above.

Example 13.702.1

The position is as in Example **13.701.4.2** and the following are details of capital allowances and balancing charges for the tax years 2006 and 2007:

	2006	2007
	€	€
Plant & machinery – WDA	35,000	39,000
Industrial building annual allowance	5,000	7,000
Joint allowances	40,000	48,000
Joint charges	18,000	7,000

Danzig & Co became a partner on 1 March 2006 so that no capital allowances are due to it for the year 2005, although part of its accounting period ended 30 November falls within that year. Consequently, capital allowances and charges for the following two years only need to be taken into account.

Of the joint allowance for 2006, Danzig & Co is entitled to a 40% share and this is apportioned to the part of that year for which it was a partner, ie 10/12ths. On the basis that the company was a partner throughout the year 2007, it is entitled to the full share of its joint allowance for that year, again apportioned on a time basis. The shares of joint allowances and charges for the two tax years are as follows:

	2006	2007
	€	€
Allowances:		
2002 €40,000 x 40% x 10/12	13,333	
2003 €48,000 x 40%		19,200
Charges:		
2002 €18,000 x 40% x 10/12	6,000	
2003 €7,000 x 40%		2,800

These allowances and charges are then apportioned to the company's accounting periods as follows:

	Year ended 30 November 2006	Year ended 30 November 2007
	€	€
Share of 2006 joint allowance:		
€13,333 x 9/10[1] (1/3/06 – 30/11/06)	12,000	

€13,333 x 1/10[1] (1/12/06 – 31/12/06)		1,333
Share of 2007 joint allowance:		
€19,200 x 11/12 (1/1/07 – 30/11/07)		17,600
Relevant amounts – capital allowances	12,000	18,933

Share of 2006 joint charge:		
€6,000 x 9/10[1]	5,400	
€6,000 x 1/10[1]		600
Share of 2007 joint charge:		
€2,800 x 11/12		2,567
Relevant amounts – balancing charges	5,400	3,167

The final Case I computations can now be completed as follows:

	Year ended 30 November 2006	Year ended 30 November 2007
	€	€
Profits before capital allowances (Example **13.701.4.2**)	53,280	17,580
Relevant amounts – balancing charges	5,400	3,167
	58,680	20,747
Relevant amounts – capital allowances	12,000	18,933
Case I profits	46,680	1,814

Note:

[1] Danzig & Co is entitled to capital allowances for 10/12ths of the year 2006. Accordingly, in apportioning the share of the joint allowance for that year to the company's accounting periods, the denominator in the fraction is 10 rather than the usual 12. The position is the same for the share of joint charges.

As seen above, although unused capital allowances from an earlier year are treated under TCA 1997, s 1010(8)(b) as joint allowances of the year to which they are brought forward, no such capital allowances may be treated as joint allowances for the purposes of TCA 1997, s 1009(4). Because capital allowances are deducted as trading expenses in the case of a company, the company will always receive the benefit of any share of allowances for the accounting period to which they are apportioned, whether the amount apportioned reduces trading profits or becomes a loss or part of a loss. For this reason, TCA 1997, s 1009(4)(d) provides that, notwithstanding TCA 1997, s 1010(8), a joint allowance for a year of assessment does not include any capital allowance that is or could be brought forward from a previous year of assessment.

13.703   Limited partnerships: restriction of reliefs

Capital allowances made by way of discharge or repayment of tax, or in charging income under Case V of Schedule D (see **5.105.3**), to which a partner company is entitled by virtue of its participation in a trade and which, to the extent that they exceed the income of the class to which they relate, may normally be set off against total profits in accordance with TCA 1997, s 308(4). Similarly, where a partner company has excess charges under TCA 1997, s 243 (see **4.404**), or trading losses under TCA 1997, s 396(2) (see **4.101**), these may normally be offset against the company's total profits. These kinds of losses or deficiencies may also be surrendered by the company under the group relief provisions of TCA 1997, s 420(1), (2), (6) (see **8.305**). TCA 1997, s 1013(2)(b) restricts the extent to which a limited partner company may avail of any of these provisions, together referred to as *the specified provisions*, by restricting the use of the loss or deficiency to the profits or gains of the partnership trade and then only to the extent of the partner company's contribution to the trade. (Incidentally, TCA 1997, s 1013 contains no reference to TCA 1997, s 243A, 243B, 396A, 396B, 420A or 420B and so apparently has no effect on any of these provisions.)

TCA 1997, s 1013 was enacted to counter the effect of arrangements whereby certain partnership losses available against other income of a limited partner exceeded the amount invested in the partnership (see *MacCarthaigh v Daly* 3 ITR 253).

In its initial form, TCA 1997, s 1013 (then FA 1986 s 46) restricted the use of the limited partnership losses to the amount of the contribution by the limited partner to the partnership trade. The use of the specified provisions is further restricted by TCA 1997, s 1013(2)(b)(II). The losses and other deficiencies from 24 April 1992, as well as being restricted by reference to the amount of capital contributed by the limited partner to the partnership trade, may only be offset against profits arising from the partnership trade. The time by reference to which the amount of capital contributed is to be considered in any case is the end of the accounting period in which the loss is incurred, or in which the charges are paid, or for which the allowance falls to be made, as the case may be; if, however, the company ceases to carry on the trade during that accounting period, the time is the time it so ceased.

In so far as any of the amounts in TCA 1997, s 420(1), (2), (6) is concerned, the effect of TCA 1997, s 1013 is that a partner company may not surrender the amount to a fellow group member to the extent that the amount is in excess of the amount contributed by it to the partnership trade. From 24 April 1992, however, the application of TCA 1997, s 1013 to TCA 1997, s 420 is no longer necessary since the amount of the loss or deficiency is confined to profits from the partnership trade.

A *limited partner*, in relation to a trade, is defined in TCA 1997, s 1013(1) as:

(a) a person who is carrying on the trade as a limited partner in a limited partnership registered under the Limited Partnerships Act 1907;

(b) a person who is carrying on the trade as a general partner in a partnership who:

    (i) is not entitled to take part in the management of the trade, and

    (ii) who is entitled to have his liabilities, or his liabilities beyond a certain limit, for debts or obligations, incurred for the purposes of the trade, discharged or reimbursed by some other person,

(c) a person who carries on the trade jointly with others and who, under the law of any territory outside the State, is not entitled to take part in the management of the trade and is not liable beyond a certain limit for debts or obligations incurred for the purposes of the trade;

(d) a person who carries on the trade as a general partner in a partnership otherwise than as an active partner;

(e) a person who carries on the trade as a partner in a partnership registered under the law of any territory outside the State, otherwise than as an active partner; or

(f)   a person who carries on the trade jointly with others under any agreement, arrangement, scheme or understanding which is governed by the law of any territory outside the State, otherwise than as a person who works for the greater part of his time on the day-to-day management or conduct of that trade.

An *active partner* for the purposes of (d) above means a partner who works for the greater part of his time on the day-to-day management or conduct of the partnership trade.

Under the Partnership Act 1907, a limited partner is not entitled to take part in the management of the partnership firm and has his liability for the debts of the firm limited to his capital contribution to it. The above definition of "limited partner" includes such persons but also extends to a person who, while not legally a limited partner, is in a similar position by reason of being prevented from taking part in the management of the firm and by virtue of having his joint and several liability for the firm's debts limited in the way described above.

TCA 1997, s 1013(4) treats a general partner as also being a limited partner in the following circumstances:

(a)   where there is an agreement, arrangement, scheme or understanding requiring the partner to cease to be a partner in the partnership at any time before he is entitled to recover the full amount of his contribution to the partnership trade; and

(b)   where there is an agreement, arrangement, scheme or understanding by virtue of which a creditor of the partner or the partnership has limited recourse to any asset of the partner for the purpose of recovering his debt.

In those circumstances, the partner is treated as a person not entitled to take part in the management of the partnership trade and as a person who is entitled to have his liabilities, or his liabilities beyond a certain limit, for debts or obligations, incurred for the purposes of the trade, discharged or reimbursed by some other person; in other words that partner is treated as a limited partner.

For the purposes of TCA 1997, s 1013, a contribution of a partner company to a partnership trade at any time is defined as the aggregate of:

(i)   all amounts contributed by the company to the trade as capital, as reduced by any amount subsequently withdrawn or received back, directly or indirectly, from the partnership, or from a person connected with the partnership (but not as reduced by any amount it is entitled to withdraw or receive, or have reimbursed to it by another person, while it is carrying on the trade as a limited partner, in relation to expenditure it has incurred on behalf of, or in providing facilities for, the partnership trade); and

(ii) the amount of any profits or gains of the trade to which it is entitled but which it has not received in money or money's worth.

In relation to (i) above, the company will be regarded as having received back an amount which it has contributed if:

(a)   it receives consideration of that amount or value for the sale of its interest, or any part of its interest, in the partnership;

(b)   the partnership or any person connected with the partnership repays that amount of a loan or advance from it; or

(c)   the company receives that amount of value for assigning any debt due to it from the partnership or from any person connected with the partnership.

For the purposes of (b) and (c) above, TCA 1997, s 10 applies in determining whether a person is regarded as connected with a partnership (see **2.3**).

13.704   Partnership returns

TCA 1997, s 880(2) provides that the precedent partner, when required to do so in a notice issued by the inspector of taxes in relation to any year of assessment, must prepare and deliver a return in the prescribed form of:

(a)   all the sources of income of the partnership for the year of assessment in relation to which the notice is given;

(b)   the amount of income from each source for the year of assessment computed in accordance with TCA 1997, s 880(3); and

(c)   such further particulars for tax purposes as may be required by the notice or indicated by the prescribed form.

The amount of income from any source to be included in a return, in accordance with (c) above, is to be computed in accordance with the Income Tax Acts. Where, in the case of a trade or profession, an account has been made up to a date within the year of assessment or more accounts than one have been made up to dates within that year, the computation is to be made by reference to the period, or to all the periods if more than one, for which accounts have been made up (TCA 1997, s 880(3)).

In addition, the return must include details of any chargeable gains realised in the year of assessment for which the return is made and details of any chargeable assets acquired by the partnership in that year (TCA 1997, s 913(7)).

Under the self-assessment provisions, a return for any year must by forwarded to the inspector by 31 January in the year of assessment following the year (TCA 1997, s 951(2)). The partners must also complete and forward their own returns to include their shares of partnership trading income and shares of other income. A partner company will include in its corporation tax return the share of profits from the partnership trade as apportioned to that period for which the return is made. Where relevant, the return should also include the company's share of any other income, charges on income paid, capital allowances and chargeable gains.

13.8 SHIPPING: TONNAGE TAX

13.801   Introduction

TCA 1997 Part 24A (ss 697A-697Q), with Schedule 18B, provides for an alternative method, in the form of a so-called tonnage tax, for calculating the profits of shipping companies for corporation tax purposes. The commencement date for the tonnage tax is 28 March 2003.

Profits calculated under the tonnage method are subject to corporation tax at the 12.5% rate in the same way as shipping profits are taxed under normal rules. Tonnage tax profits are calculated by reference to the tonnage of the ships used in the shipping trade. As mentioned above, the tonnage tax system is an alternative method (to that based on accounting profits) of computing profits for corporation tax purposes and is applied at the option of the shipping company concerned.

The tonnage tax regime is intended to result in certain advantages to shipping companies electing into the regime. By providing certainty regarding the level of tax payable, the need to make provision for deferred taxation in the financial statements is obviated thereby helping to increasing earnings per share. Companies will have more freedom to choose when to purchase vessels and how to finance them, thereby introducing greater flexibility in the matter of making decisions to purchase which will largely be determined by commercial rather than by tax considerations. The tax position of companies within the regime will be clearer and more easily understood thereby making them more attractive to investors and potential business partners. Electing into the tonnage tax system will render the fiscal regime of shipping companies more compatible with and competitive with those in other countries.

Companies may themselves decide whether or not to enter the tonnage tax system. Once an election is made, a company must remain within the system for at least 10 years. All qualifying companies within a group making an election must enter the scheme. To be eligible to enter the scheme, a company must be within the charge to corporation tax, must operate qualifying ships, and must carry on the strategic and commercial management of those ships in the State.

Among the key income sources benefiting from tonnage tax regime are:

(a)   income from activities related to the actual operation of a qualifying ship (eg, the carriage of cargo or passengers, marine research, etc);

(b)   income from activities carried out on board qualifying ships that are ancillary to those activities, such as the operation of cinemas, bars, shops, restaurants;

(c)   income from activities undertaken to enable the activities in (a) to be undertaken, such as embarkation/disembarkation services, ticket sales, hire of containers; and

(d)   income from the provision of ship management services for qualifying ships.

Although capital allowances and capital gains are not part of the tonnage tax regime, they are relevant in relation to certain transitional arrangements so that balancing charges may arise in some cases while capital gains tax charges may arise in relation to assets acquired before entry into tonnage tax. Such charges will not arise, however, until such time as the ship in question is sold. Available reliefs may then operate to defer any balancing charge where there is re-investment in a new ship. Charges may be reduced or eliminated by reference to the time a company has been in tonnage tax or through the use of unrelieved losses incurred before entry into tonnage tax.

Ring fencing provisions ensure that advantage is not taken of the tonnage tax regime by including income from non-tonnage tax activities or by seeking to obtain tax relief for losses incurred on tonnage tax activities against other sources of income. Other measures ensure that the tonnage tax regime cannot be used for tax avoidance activities or transactions.

13.802   Definitions

The following definitions are provided in TCA 1997, s 697A(1).

A _tonnage tax company_ and a _tonnage tax group_ mean, respectively, a company or group in relation to which a tonnage tax election has effect.

Tonnage tax activities, in relation to a tonnage tax company, means activities carried on by the company in the course of a trade which consists of one or more than one of the activities described in (a) to (i) of the definition of "relevant shipping income" below. The term is of relevance in relation to the ring-fencing of losses incurred in the carrying on of tonnage tax activities (see **13.803.1**) and in relation to the separate trade provisions (see **13.803.4**). See also **13.803.3** regarding the general exclusion from tonnage activities of activities giving rise to investment income, and the exclusion from the exemption from capital gains tax of assets used for tonnage tax activities.

Tonnage tax asset means an asset used wholly and exclusively for the purposes of the tonnage tax activities of a tonnage tax company. (See **13.803.3** regarding the capital gains tax exemption in respect of tonnage tax assets.)

Tonnage tax profits, in relation to a tonnage tax company, means the company's profits for an accounting period calculated in accordance with TCA 1997, s 697C. It is these profits that take the place, in the tonnage tax regime, of a company's normal profits for corporation tax purposes.

Tonnage tax trade, in relation to a tonnage tax company, means a trade carried on by the company the income from which is within the charge to corporation tax and which consists solely of the carrying on of tonnage tax activities or, in the case of a trade consisting partly of the carrying on of such activities and partly of other activities, that part of the trade consisting solely of the carrying on of tonnage tax activities and which is treated under TCA 1997, s 697L as a separate trade carried on by the company.

A _qualifying company_ is a company:

(a)   within the charge to corporation tax;

(b)   that operates qualifying ships; and

(c)   which carries on the strategic and commercial management of those ships in the State.

Not surprisingly, the legislation does not attempt to elaborate on what constitutes strategic and commercial management of ships but the Revenue have provided some guidance on the matter. As to what constitutes strategic and commercial management of ships may mean different things depending on the context. Strategic and commercial management of ships in the context of providing ship management services would be quite different to strategic and commercial management of ships in the context of owning the ships that are operated.

Essentially, the carrying on strategic and commercial management of ships in the State would involve such matters as the taking of decisions in Ireland on significant capital expenditure and disposals, the awarding of major contracts and concluding agreements on strategic alliances. In evaluating such matters, the extent to which foreign based personnel work under the direction of, and report to, personnel based in Ireland would be important. As to whether the strategic function in any case is carried out in Ireland is likely to depend largely on where the company headquarters is located, including where senior managers are based, where decisions of the board of directors are made, and where decisions of the operational board are taken, In the case of commercial management, matters relating to route planning, the taking of bookings for passengers or cargo, managing bunkers, provisioning and victualling requirements of ships, personnel management, training, and the technical management of ships including the taking of decisions on their repair and maintenance, should take place in Ireland.

Other matters likely to be relevant to the requirement in (c) above would include the maintenance of support facilities such as training centres, terminals etc in Ireland and the extent to which foreign offices or branches work under the direction of Irish based personnel. The fact that a ship is flagged, classed, insured or financed in Ireland may be further influential factors. It is necessary to comply with both the strategic and the commercial management aspects of the requirement.

A *qualifying group* means a group of companies of which one or more members are qualifying companies.

Income from a ship that is not a qualifying ship, whatever its activities, cannot be "relevant shipping income" (see below). A *qualifying ship* is, subject to TCA 1997, s 697A(2) (see below), a self-propelled seagoing vessel (including a hovercraft) of 100 tons or more gross tonnage which is certified for navigation at sea by the competent authority of any country or territory, but does not include a vessel (*vessel of an excluded kind*) which is:

(a) a fishing vessel or a vessel used for subjecting fish to a manufacturing or other process on board the vessel (a fish factory vessel);

(b) a vessel, other than a vessel operated for *bona fide* commercial purposes and with an overnight passenger capacity (not including crew) of not less than 50 persons, of a kind whose primary use is for the purposes of sport or recreation (see below);

(c) a harbour, estuary or river ferry;

(d) an offshore installation, including a mobile or fixed rig, a platform or other installation of any kind at sea (essentially offshore installations not designed for the transportation of cargo or passengers by sea);

(e) a tanker used for petroleum extraction activities (within the meaning of TCA 1997 Chapter 2 of Part 24 – see **13.502**);

(f) a dredger, including a vessel used primarily as a floating platform (such as a seagoing crane) for working machinery or as a diving platform (for cable laying); or

(g) a non-ocean going tug, ie a tug in respect of which a certificate has not been given by the Minister for Communications, Energy and Natural Resources certifying that in the opinion of the Minister the tug is capable of operating in seas outside the portion of the seas which are, for the purposes of the Maritime Jurisdiction Act 1959, the territorial seas of the State.

Thus, a qualifying ship should be of a size sufficient to engage in reasonable commercial operations and should comply with all of the requirements for navigation at sea imposed by the competent authorities of any country or territory. Acceptance of a ship as seagoing will normally require that it be certified as such under the International Load Line or the SOLAS (Safety of Life at Sea) Convention.

Regarding (b) above, it is understood that cruise liners taking fare-paying passengers will not be excluded. The exclusion would apply to a vessel, such as a holiday yacht, that is chartered as a whole by its passengers acting together or by a third party on behalf of one or more of the passengers.

Regarding (e) above, this refers to oil tankers used for the purpose of delivering oil from an offshore oilfield to an on-shore storage facility. Such vessels are excluded as the profits attributable to their activities are subject to the special petroleum taxation regime (see **13.502–3** in relation to petroleum activities and petroleum extraction activities).

A vessel is not a qualifying ship if the main purpose for which it is used is the provision of goods or services of a kind normally provided on land (TCA 1997, s 697A(2)). The kinds of activities in question would include retailing, restaurants, hotels, radio stations, casinos, financial services.

Relevant shipping income, in relation to a tonnage tax company, means the company's income from:

(a) the carriage of passengers by sea in a qualifying ship operated by the company (which would include any income from the transport of passengers by land where there is a single contract for the transport and the land element is priced at arm's length);

(b) the carriage of cargo by sea in a qualifying ship operated by the company (which would include any income from the transport of cargo by land where there is a single contract for the transport and the land element is priced at arm's length);

(c) towage, salvage or other marine assistance (which does not include income from the sale of salvaged goods) by a qualifying ship operated by the company, but not including income from any such work undertaken in a port or an area under the jurisdiction of a port authority;

(d) transport services in connection with other services of a kind necessarily provided at sea by a qualifying ship operated by the company (eg, diving support, cable laying, construction work in the marine environment,); profits or losses will need to be apportioned, on a just and reasonable basis, as between those attributable to these other services those attributable to the transport activities;

(e)   the provision on board a qualifying ship operated by the company of goods or services ancillary to the carriage of passengers or cargo (such as cinemas, bars, restaurants, shops), but only to the extent that such goods or services are provided for consumption on board the qualifying ship;

(f)   the granting of rights by virtue of which another person provides or will provide such ancillary services on board a qualifying ship operated by the company (ie, the franchising or contracting out of such on-board services to specialist operators);

(g)   other ship-related activities that are a necessary and integral part of the business of operating the company's qualifying ships (see below);

(h)   the letting on charter of a qualifying ship for use for the carriage by sea of passengers and cargo where the operation of the ship and the crew of the ship remain under the direction and control of the company;

(i)   the provision of ship management services (as described in TCA 1997 Sch 18B paragraph 8(6) – see **13.804.2**) for qualifying ships operated by the company;

(j)   a dividend or other distribution of a company not resident in the State (*overseas company*) in respect of which the conditions set out in TCA 1997, s 697H(1) (see **13.803.3** below) are met;

(k)   gains treated as income by virtue of TCA 1997, s 697J (foreign currency gains – see **13.803** and **3.406** in relation to TCA 1997, s 79).

As regards (g) above, "necessary and integral" is understood to denote activities that are both required for the business of operating a company's qualifying ships and that enable it to carry on its business of operating those ships, including:

(i)   ship management operations such as purchasing fuel and hiring crew;

(ii)   commercial management operations such as booking cargo or passengers;

(iii)   administrative and insurance services related to the transport of passengers or cargo;

(iv)   transport on another ship if there is a single contract that includes transport on a qualifying ship operated by the company;

(v)   the provision of excursions for passengers on qualifying ships operated by the company;

(vi)   the sale of a holiday under a single contract that includes transport on a qualifying ship operated by the company;

(vii)   embarkation and disembarkation of passengers from a qualifying ship operated by the company;

(viii)   loading and unloading of cargo on a qualifying ship operated by the company, including the moving of containers within a port area immediately before or after a voyage;

(ix)   consolidation or breaking of cargo carried on on a qualifying ship operated by the company immediately before or after a voyage;

(x)   rental or provision to customers of containers for goods to be carried on a qualifying ship operated by the company.

The Revenue may consider it necessary to look at the facts in relation to a particular company to decide whether or not certain activities are necessary and integral to its core business. It may be necessary for them to specify limits in relation to particular activities. If the limit has been breached, none of the income from that activity would be considered to be relevant shipping income.

Furthermore, services (provided to third parties) which, if carried out in relation to qualifying ships operated by the company, would be an activity that is necessary and integral to the company's business are also regarded as other ship-related activities but only to the extent that the relevant staff and assets are needed by it to carry out its main function and the services are undertaken to make full use of those staff and assets. This will be the case only where the third party services provided are minimal compared to the company's core business and its ancillary business. It may be necessary for the Revenue to specify limits as to the level of such activities.

Relevant shipping profits, in relation to a tonnage tax company, means:

(a)   the company's relevant shipping income; and

(b)   so much of the company's chargeable gains as are excluded from the charge to tax by TCA 1997, s 697N.

Accordingly, relevant shipping profits consist of the amount that would normally be brought within the charge to corporation tax in respect of the income from activities sheltered by tonnage tax and the gains on assets used for the purposes of those activities disposed of by the company.

13.803   Tonnage tax

13.803.1   Calculation of tonnage tax profits

TCA 1997, s 697B provides that, notwithstanding any other provision of the Tax Acts or the Capital Gains Tax Acts, TCA 1997 Part 24A and Sch 18B are to apply to provide an alternative method, referred to as *tonnage tax*, for computing the profits of a qualifying company (see **13.802**) for the purposes of corporation tax. (Note that "tonnage tax" is a method for computing taxable profits, and not a tax as such. The profits so computed are then subjected to corporation tax in the same way as profits of a shipping company computed under normal rules.) Subject to an election having been made in accordance with TCA 1997, s 697D, the tonnage tax profits of a tonnage tax company are to be charged to corporation tax in place of the company's "relevant shipping profits" (see definition in **13.802** above) (TCA 1997, s 697C(1)). It will accordingly be necessary, in the case of any company electing for the tonnage tax, to ascertain the amount of that company's relevant shipping profits as only those profits are replaced by the profits computed under the tonnage tax method; any other profits of the company are taxable under normal rules.

TCA 1997, s 21(1A)(c) states that, for the financial year 2002, tonnage tax profits of a tonnage tax company are chargeable to corporation tax at the rate of 12.5%.

The basis for a company's tonnage tax is the net tonnage (see **13.807.1**) of each qualifying ship operated by that company with the net tonnage of a ship being rounded down if necessary to the nearest multiple of 100 tons (TCA 1997, s 697C(3)). The profit attributable to each qualifying ship for an accounting period is found by multiplying the daily profit by the number of days in the period or, if the ship was operated by the company as a qualifying ship for part only of the period, by the number of days in that part (TCA 1997, s 697C(5)). The amount of the tonnage tax profits of a company for an accounting period is the aggregate of the profits determined in respect of each qualifying ship operated by the company (TCA 1997, s 697C(6)). The "daily profit" attributable to each qualifying ship is determined by reference to the net tonnage of the ship as follows:

(a)   for each 100 tons up to 1,000 tons, €1.00;

(b)   for each 100 tons between 1,000 and 10,000 tons, €0.75;

(c)   for each 100 tons between 10,000 and 25,000 tons, €0.50; and

(d)   each 100 tons above 25,000 tons, €0.25 (TCA 1997, s 697C(4)).

Example 13.803.1.1

Rhodes Line Ltd, a shipping company, operates two qualifying ships, one with a tonnage of 25,000 tons and the other having a tonnage of 30,000 tons. The profit per day per ship is first calculated, followed by the profit per ship for the company's latest accounting period. From this it is possible to calculate the tonnage tax profits and the resulting corporation tax.

	€
First ship (25,000 tons):	
Each 100 tons up to 1,000 tons @ €1	10.00
Each 100 tons in the range 1,000 to 10,000 tons @ €0.75	67.50
Each 100 tons in the range 10,000 to 25,000 tons @ €0.50	75.00
Daily profit	152.50
Second ship (30,000 tons):	
Each 100 tons up to 1,000 tons @ €1	10.00
Each 100 tons in the range 1,000 to 10,000 tons @ €0.75	67.50
Each 100 tons in the range 10,000 to 25,000 tons @ €0.50	75.00
Each 100 tons in the range 25,000 to 30,000 tons @ €0.25	12.50
Daily profit	165.00
For two ships	317.50
For accounting period €317.50 x 365	115,887.50
Corporation tax @ 12.5%	14,485.94

If two or more companies are to be regarded as operators of a ship by virtue of a joint interest in the ship, or in an agreement for the use of the ship, the tonnage tax profits of each company are to be computed as if each were entitled to a share of the profits proportionate to its share of that interest (TCA 1997, s 697C(7)). If two or more companies are otherwise to be treated as the operator of a ship (so that it is not possible to ascertain the proportionate share of each company's interest in the ship), the tonnage tax profits of each company are to be computed as if each were the only operator (TCA 1997, s 697C(8)).

As mentioned above, the tonnage tax profits of a tonnage tax company that has made an appropriate election are to be charged to corporation tax in place of the company's relevant shipping profits. Where the taxable profits of a tonnage tax company would, but for the making of that election, be relevant shipping income, any loss accruing to it in respect of its tonnage tax activities, or any loss that would otherwise be taken into account by virtue of TCA 1997, s 79 (foreign currency: computation of income and chargeable gains – see **3.406**), in computing the trading income of the company may not be brought into account for corporation tax purposes (TCA 1997, s 697C(2)). As seen in **13.802**, a company's "tonnage tax activities" are the activities carried on by it in the course of a trade which consists of one or more of the activities described in (a) to (j) of the definition of "relevant shipping income" in **13.802**.

13.803.2   Election for tonnage tax

Tonnage tax applies only where a tonnage tax election has been made. *Tonnage tax election* means an election made by a qualifying single company (a *company election*) or by a qualifying group of companies (a *group election*) (TCA 1997, s 697D(1)). A *group of companies* means all the companies of which an individual has control or, where a company that is not controlled by another person controls one or more other companies, that company and all the companies of which that company has control, and references to membership of a group and to a group are to be construed accordingly. *Control* is to be construed in accordance with TCA 1997, s 432(2)-(6) (see **2.401**). Tonnage tax applies only to a company that is a member of a group of companies if the company joins in a group election which is to be made jointly by all the qualifying companies in the group. A group election has effect in relation to all qualifying companies in the group (TCA 1997, s 697D(2)).

   All qualifying companies that are members of a group must elect for tonnage tax as a group so that it is not possible for some qualifying companies not to enter tonnage tax while other qualifying group members elect in. Thus, extensive provision is made in Schedule 18B Part 4 (see **13.806**) in relation to groups of companies.

   A tonnage tax election may only be made if the conditions in TCA 1997, s 697F, relating to a requirement not to enter into tax avoidance arrangements, are met. This provision is aimed at deliberate cases of serious or repeated abuse of the tonnage tax regime. It will not be invoked in the cases of minor computational errors or genuine misunderstandings. Nor will it be used to attack legitimate pre-election restructuring such as that required to permit a group to elect into the regime, for example, the division of activities into shipping and non-shipping activities. The conditions are as follows:

(1)   It is a condition of remaining within tonnage tax (ie, continuing to be a tonnage tax company) that a company is not a party to any transaction or arrangement that is an abuse of the tonnage tax regime;

(2)   A transaction or arrangement is regarded as being an abuse of the tonnage tax regime if in consequence of its being, or having been, entered into, the provisions of TCA 1997 Part 24A and Schedule 18B may be applied in a way that results (or would but for this anti-avoidance provision result) in—

    (a)   a tax advantage (within the meaning of TCA 1997, s 811 (transactions to avoid liability to tax – the general anti-avoidance provision of TCA 1997)) being obtained for—

        (i)   a company other than a tonnage tax company, or

        (ii)   a tonnage tax company in respect of its non-tonnage tax activities, or

    (b)   the amount of the tonnage tax profits of a tonnage tax company being artificially reduced;

(3)   If a tonnage tax company is a party to any such transaction or arrangement as is referred to in (1) above, the Revenue Commissioners may—

    (a)   if it is a single company, give notice excluding it from tonnage tax (ie, excluding it from being a tonnage tax company),

    (b)   if it is a member of a group, subject to TCA 1997 Sch 18B paragraph 22, give notice to the tonnage tax company excluding the group from tonnage tax (ie, excluding the group from being a tonnage tax group);

(4)   The effect of a notice referred to in (3)—

    (a)   in the case of a single company, is that the company's tonnage tax election will cease to be in force from the beginning of the accounting period in which the transaction or arrangement was entered into, and

    (b)   in the case of a group, is that the group's tonnage tax election will cease to be in force from such date as may be specified in the notice, but the date so specified may not be earlier than the beginning of the earliest accounting period in which any member of the group entered into the transaction or arrangement in question;

(5)   The provisions of TCA 1997, s 697P (withdrawal of relief etc on company leaving tonnage tax – see below) apply where a company ceases to be a tonnage tax company by virtue of TCA 1997, s 697F.

A company aggrieved by the giving of a notice under TCA 1997, s 697F (tax avoidance arrangements) may appeal to the Appeal Commissioners within 30 days from the date of the giving of the notice, the appeal to be made by notice in writing to that effect to the Revenue Commissioners. In the case of a notice given to a tonnage tax company that is a member of a group of companies, only one appeal may be brought, but such notice may be brought jointly by two or more members of the group concerned (TCA 1997, s 697G).

Method of making and giving effect to an election

A tonnage tax election is to be made by notice in writing to the Revenue Commissioners and is to be made by means of a form prescribed for that purpose (TCA 1997 Sch 18B paragraph 1(1)). The notice must contain such information, particulars and documentation ("information") as the Revenue Commissioners may require and the election will not take effect until such information is provided to the satisfaction of the Revenue Commissioners (TCA 1997 Sch 18B paragraph 1(2)).

    The information that may be requested from an applicant company (the company making the election by notice to the Revenue Commissioners) by the Revenue Commissioners includes:

    (i)   documentation on legal status, memorandum and articles of association, and certificate of incorporation of the company;

    (ii)   business plans or similar documents of the company;

    (iii)   the name and address of each of the directors of the company;

    (iv)   the name and address of each of the beneficial shareholders of the company and the number and class of shares held by each;

    (v)   details of the qualifying ships owned or leased by the company;

    (vi)   particulars of how the strategic and commercial management of the qualifying ships is carried on by the company in the State;

    (vii)   in the case of a group election, particulars of all the companies in the group, their respective shareholdings, and the flow of funds between all of the companies in the group (TCA 1997 Sch 18B paragraph 1(3)).

When election may be made

A tonnage tax election may be made at any time before the end of the period (the *initial period*) of 36 months beginning on the commencement date (the day appointed by the Minister for Finance by order as the day the provisions of the tonnage tax come into operation) (TCA 1997 Sch 18B paragraph 2(1)). After the end of the initial period, a tonnage tax election may only be made in certain specified circumstances. These circumstances are:

(a)   where a single company becomes a qualifying company and was not previously a qualifying company at any time on or after the commencement date; such election must be made before the end of the period of 36 months beginning with the day on which the company became a qualifying company (TCA 1997 Sch 18B paragraph 2(3));

(b)   where a group of companies becomes a qualifying group of companies by virtue of a member of the group becoming a qualifying company, not previously having been a qualifying company, at any time on or after the commencement date; such election must be made before the end of the period of 36 months beginning with the day on which the group of companies became a qualifying group of companies. Such election may not, however, be made if the group of companies—

     (i)   was previously a qualifying group at any time on or after the commencement date, or

     (ii)   is substantially the same as a group that was previously a qualifying group of companies at any such time (TCA 1997 Sch 18B paragraph 2(4)).

When election takes effect

A tonnage tax election has effect from the beginning of the accounting period in which it is made (TCA 1997 Sch 18B paragraph 3). A tonnage tax election has no effect in relation to an accounting period beginning before 1 January 2002. The Revenue Commissioners may allow a tonnage tax election made before the end of the initial period to have effect from the beginning of an accounting period earlier than that in which it is made (but not one beginning before 1 January 2002) and may allow an election made before the end of the initial period to have effect from the beginning of the accounting period following that in which it is made or, where the Revenue Commissioners determine that due to exceptional circumstances, unrelated to the avoidance or reduction of tax, it is commercially impracticable for the election to take effect, the beginning of the next following period (TCA 1997 Sch 18B paragraph 3(3), (4)).

Period for which election is in force

A tonnage tax election remains in force until it expires at the end of the period of 10 years beginning:

(a)   in the case of a company election, with the first day on which the election has effect in relation to the company; and

(b)   in the case of a group election, with the first day on which the election has effect in relation to any member of the group (TCA 1997 Sch 18B paragraph 4(1)).

A tonnage tax election ceases to be in force:

(a)   in the case of a company election, if the company ceases to be a qualifying company, and

(b)   in the case of a group election, if the group of companies ceases to be a qualifying group (TCA 1997 Sch 18B paragraph 4(2)).

Effect of election ceasing to be in force

A tonnage tax election that ceases to be in force ceases to have effect in relation to any company (TCA 1997 Sch 18B paragraph 5).

Renewal election

As seen above, a *renewal election*, being a tonnage tax election by a single company or group of companies further to a tonnage tax election already in force, may be made. The renewal election may be made at any time when a tonnage tax election is in force. As with a tonnage tax election, a renewal election is to be made by notice to the Revenue Commissioners. TCA 1997, s 697D and the above-described provisions of TCA 1997 Sch 18B paragraphs 4 and 5 apply in relation to a renewal election as they apply in relation to an original tonnage tax election. A renewals election supersedes the existing tonnage tax election (TCA 1997 Sch 18B paragraph 6).

13.803.3   Relevant shipping profits: supplementary provisions

Relevant shipping income: distributions of overseas shipping companies

The conditions referred to in (j) of the definition of "relevant shipping income" in **13.802** above (so that distributions from overseas companies are to be treated as relevant shipping income) are that:

(a)   the overseas company (company not resident in the State) operates qualifying ships;

(b)   more than 50% of the voting power in the overseas company is held by a company resident in a Member State, or that two or more companies each of which is resident in a Member State hold in aggregate more than 50% of that voting power;

(c)   all the income of the overseas company is such that, if it were a tonnage tax company, it would be relevant shipping income;

(d)   the distribution is paid entirely out of profits arising at a time when—

    (i)   the conditions in (a) to (c) above were met, and

    (ii)   the tonnage tax company was subject to tonnage tax, and

(e)   the profits of the overseas company out of which the distribution is paid are subject to a tax on profits (in the country of residence of the company or elsewhere, or partly in that country and partly elsewhere) (TCA 1997, s 697H(1)).

A dividend or other distribution of an overseas company which is made out of profits that are referable to a dividend or other distribution in relation to which the above conditions (a) to (f) are met is deemed to be a dividend or other distribution in respect of which those conditions are met (TCA 1997, s 697H(2)). Thus, a distribution will qualify even where it is received through a chain of companies as long as it can be traced back to income which would have been qualifying shipping income if the overseas company earning it were a tonnage tax company.

TCA 1997, s 440 (surcharge on undistributed investment and estate income – see **10.302**) does not apply to dividends and other distributions of an overseas company that is relevant shipping income of a tonnage tax company (TCA 1997, s 697H(3)).

Relevant shipping income: foreign currency gains

Foreign exchange gains referable to a company's trading activities are included in the definition of "relevant shipping income" A gain is treated as income for the purposes of the definition of "relevant shipping income" (see **13.802**) if it is a gain, whether realised or unrealised, attributable to:

(a)   a relevant monetary item (within the meaning of TCA 1997, s 79 – see **3.406**) which would but for TCA 1997 Part 24A be taken into account in computing the trading income of a company's tonnage tax trade in accordance with TCA 1997, s 79; or

(b)   a relevant contract (within the meaning of TCA 1997, s 79 – see **3.406**) which would but for TCA 1997 Part 24A be taken into account in computing the trading income of a company's tonnage tax trade in accordance with TCA 1997, s 79 (TCA 1997, s 697J(1)).

General exclusion of investment income

Income from investments, including any income chargeable to tax under Case III (see **3.207**), IV (see **3.208**) or V (see **3.209**) of Schedule D or under Schedule F (see **11.110**), is treated as not being relevant shipping income (TCA 1997, s 697K(1)). An exception to this exclusion is income that is relevant shipping income under TCA 1997, s 697H (distributions of overseas shipping companies – see above) (TCA 1997, s 697K(3)). To the extent that an activity gives rise to income from investments, it is not regarded as part of a company's tonnage tax activities (TCA 1997, s 697K(2)).

Chargeable gains

Where, for one or more continuous periods of at least 12 months, part of an asset has been used wholly and exclusively for the purposes of the tonnage tax activities of a tonnage tax company and part has not, the part so used is treated as a separate asset (TCA 1997, s 697N(1)). This provision applies where an asset is used partly for a company's tonnage tax trade and partly for other purposes; it envisages separate parts of the asset being used respectively for the tonnage tax and non-tonnage tax activities. For this purpose, any necessary apportionment of the gain or loss on the disposal of the whole asset is to be made on a just and reasonable basis (see **13.806.3**) (TCA 1997, s 697N(2)).

Where an asset (or part of an asset treated as a separate asset) that has been a tonnage tax asset (ie, an asset used wholly and exclusively for the purposes of the tonnage tax activities of a tonnage tax company) is disposed of—

(a) any gain or loss on the disposal which would otherwise have been the chargeable gain or allowable loss on the disposal is to be treated as a chargeable gain or allowable loss only to the extent (if any) to which it is referable to periods during which the asset was not a tonnage tax asset; and

(b) any such chargeable gain or allowable loss on a disposal by a tonnage tax company is to be treated as arising otherwise than in the course of the company's tonnage tax trade (TCA 1997, s 697N(3)(a)).

For the above purposes, the proportion of the gain or loss referable to periods during which the asset was not a tonnage tax asset is determined by the formula:

$$(P-T)/P$$

where—

P   is the total length of the period since the asset was created or, if later, the last third-party disposal; and

T   is the length of the period (or the aggregate length of the periods) since—

  (i)   the asset was created, or

  (ii)   if later, the last third-party disposal,

during which the asset was a tonnage tax asset (TCA 1997, s 697N(3)(b)).

Third-party disposal means a disposal or deemed disposal that is not treated as one on which neither a gain nor a loss accrues to the person making the disposal (TCA 1997, s 697N(3)(c)).

A tonnage tax election does not affect the deduction under TCA 1997, s 31, as applied by TCA 1997, s 78(2), of relevant allowable losses (within the meaning of TCA 1997, s 78 – see **9.101**) that accrued to a company before it became a tonnage tax company (TCA 1997, s 697N(4)). In other words, capital losses referable to periods outside of tonnage tax are available for set off against any capital gains arising on a tonnage tax asset that is referable to periods outside of tonnage tax.

13.803.4   Tonnage tax trade: ring fence

Separate trade

The activities of a company which are subject to the tonnage tax method of calculating profits (tonnage tax trade) are ring-fenced so that the corporation tax treatment of that company, including all provisions relating to the computation of tax and the keeping of records separate from any other activity carried on by the company, is separated from the treatment of its other, non-tonnage tax related, activities. The effect of the ring-fencing is that the benefits of the tonnage tax regime are confined to qualifying activities and that the normal corporation tax rules continue to apply to activities outside of the ring fence even if carried on by the same company.

Where in any accounting period a tonnage tax company carries on tonnage tax activities as part of a trade, those activities are, subject to TCA 1997, s 697M (see **13.803.5** below), treated for corporation tax purposes (other than for the purposes of any provision relating to the commencement or cessation of a trade) as a separate trade distinct from all other activities carried on by the company as part of the trade. An accounting period ends (if it would not otherwise then end) when the company enters or leaves tonnage tax, ie when it becomes or ceases to be a tonnage tax company (TCA 1997, s 697L).

Exclusion of reliefs, deductions and set-offs

As seen in **13.803.1** above, tonnage tax profits of a company are calculated solely by reference to the net tonnage of each qualifying ship operated by that company. No relief, deduction or set-off of any description is allowed against the amount of a company's tonnage tax profits (TCA 1997, s 697M(1)). Furthermore, when a company enters tonnage tax (ie, when it becomes a tonnage tax company), any losses accruing to it before entry that are attributable:

(a) to activities that, under tonnage tax, become part of its tonnage tax trade; or

(b) to a source of income that, under tonnage tax, becomes relevant shipping income,

are not available for loss relief (including any means by which a loss might be used to reduce the amount in respect of which the company, or any other company, is chargeable to tax) in any accounting period beginning on or after the company's entry into tonnage tax (TCA 1997, s 697M(2)(a), (c)). Such losses are therefore effectively extinguished, although they may be utilised against a balancing charge made on the company (see **13.805.8** below). Any apportionment necessary to determine the losses so attributable are to be made on a just and reasonable basis (see **13.806.3**) (TCA 1997, s 697M(2)(b)).

Any relief or set-off against a company's tax liability for an accounting period may not apply in relation to so much of that tax liability as is attributable to the company's tonnage tax profits. Such relief includes, but is not limited to, any relief or set-off under TCA 1997, s 826 (double tax relief), 828 (double tax relief: capital gains tax – see **9.102.17** and **14.202**) or Part 2 of Schedule 24 (double tax relief: unilateral relief – see **14.209-210** and **14.212**), but does not include any set-off under TCA 1997, s 24(2) (income tax on payments made or received by non-resident companies – see **3.206**) or 25(3) (taxed payments received by non-resident companies – see **3.107.1** and **3.206**) (TCA 1997, s 697M(3)).

Capital allowances: general

Ring-fence provisions relating to capital allowances apply from the time a company enters tonnage tax. When a company leaves tonnage tax, its trade again becomes subject to the normal corporation tax rules so that capital allowances are again available for set-off against its trading profits.

A company's tonnage tax trade is not treated as a trade for the purposes of determining its entitlement to capital allowances under TCA 1997 Part 9 (relief for capital expenditure) or under any other provision which is to be construed as one with that Part. This does not, however, prevent the making of a balancing charge, where this is appropriate, under those provisions as applied by TCA 1997 Schedule 18B (TCA 1997, s 697O(1)). Notwithstanding any other provision of the Tax Acts, TCA 1997 Part 9, insofar as it relates to machinery or plant, does not apply to machinery or plant provided for leasing by a lessor (within the meaning of TCA 1997, s 403 – a person providing machinery or plant for leasing, including a successor in title to such person) who is an individual to a lessee (within the meaning of TCA 1997, s 403 – a person to whom machinery or plant is or is to be leased, including a successor in title to such person) for use in a tonnage tax trade carried on or to be carried on by the lessee (TCA 1997, s 697O(2)). Thus, individual lessors are prevented from obtaining capital allowances that would otherwise be available in respect of capital expenditure on plant and machinery used in a company's tonnage tax trade.

A tonnage tax trade is ring-fenced from whatever other activities the company may be carrying on. Thus, as regards a company's tonnage tax trade, the capital allowances provisions do not apply – the trade is treated as not being a trade for that purpose. Any other activities of the company are treated in the normal way, so that the provisions relating to capital allowances are relevant for those activities.

As noted above, however, this does not prevent the making of a balancing charge. Thus, a balancing charge will apply in respect of disposals, while the company is in tonnage tax, of assets acquired before the company entered tonnage tax (ignoring any capital allowances claims related to the company's non-tonnage tax activities); there would be no balancing charge in respect of any assets acquired for the tonnage tax trade since no capital allowances could have been claimed in respect of these. A tonnage tax company may elect in certain circumstances to have the balancing charge reduced, deferred or eliminated (see **13.805.7-9**).

13.803.5 Transactions between associated persons etc

Goods and services provided to a tonnage tax company by an associated non-tonnage tax company, or by a tonnage tax company to an associated non-tonnage tax company, must be on an arm's length basis.

TCA 1997, s 697LA applies in cases where the results of certain transactions, whereby provision is made or imposed as between a tonnage tax company and another company, are taken into account in computing the tonnage tax company's relevant shipping income. The transactions in question may include any agreement, arrangement or understanding of any kind, and whether or not they are, or are intended to be, legally enforceable. Where at the time of such a transaction:

(a) one of the companies is directly or indirectly under the control (within the meaning of TCA 1997, s 11 – see **2.402**) of the other company; or

(b) both companies are, directly or indirectly, under the control of the same person or persons,

and the relevant shipping income of the tonnage tax company is greater than it would be if the parties to the transaction had been independent parties dealing at arm's length, the income or losses of both companies are to be computed for tax purposes as if the consideration in the transaction had been what it would have been if the transaction had been one between independent parties dealing at arm's length (TCA 1997, s 697LA(2)).

Losses, for the above purposes, include any amounts in respect of which relief may be given in accordance with TCA 1997, s 83(3) (excess management expenses and charges of an investment company – see **12.704**) and Part 12 (trading losses, capital allowances and group relief).

The arm's length treatment described above is also applied where provision is made or imposed as between a tonnage tax company's trade and other activities carried on by the company on the basis that:

(a) that trade and those other activities were carried on by two different persons;

(b)   those persons had entered into a transaction; and

(c)   the two persons were both controlled by the same person at the time of the making or imposition of the provision (TCA 1997, s 697LA(3)).

A company in respect of which TCA 1997, s 697LA(2) or (3) is relevant is required to keep, for a period of at least six years, sufficient documentation to prove how prices and terms have been determined in a relevant transaction, including a written and detailed explanation of the pricing principles it has applied in relation to any such business transaction (TCA 1997, s 697LA(4)). A company may be required, by notice in writing from an officer of the Revenue Commissioners, to furnish information, particulars or documentation as may be necessary to establish whether or not it has complied with the requirements of TCA 1997, s 697LA (TCA 1997, s 697LA(5)).

13.803.6 Finance costs

TCA 1997, s 697LB counters a device, sometimes referred to as "thick" capitalisation, whereby a tonnage tax company or trade is capitalised with a preponderance of equity so that other companies or activities are capitalised by means of borrowings giving rise to excessive tax deductions in respect of finance costs. It is generally recognised that the shipping industry is capital intensive due to the high cost of the assets involved so that the amount of required debt funding would be seen as greater than would be the case for many other activities.

In relation to a company, *finance costs* means the cost of debt finance for that company, including:

(a)   any interest expense giving rise to a deduction as a trading expense or as a charge on income;

(b)   any gain or loss referred to in TCA 1997, s 79 (foreign currency: computation of income and chargeable gains – see **3.406**) in relation to debt finance;

(c)   the finance cost implicit in a payment under a finance lease;

(d)   the finance cost payable on debt factoring or on any similar transaction; and

(e)   any other costs arising from what would be considered on generally accepted accounting practice to be a financing transaction (TCA 1997, s 697LB(1)(a)).

A *finance lease*, in relation to finance costs, is any arrangement that provides for machinery or plant to be leased or otherwise made available by a person (the "lessor") to another person such that, in a case where the lessor and persons connected (see **2.302**) with the lessor are all companies resident in the State:

(i)   the arrangements; or

(ii)   the arrangements in which they are comprised,

fall, in accordance with generally accepted accounting practice, to be treated in the accounts (including any consolidated group accounts relating to two or more companies of which that company is one) of one or more of those companies as a finance lease or as a loan (TCA 1997, s 697LB(1)(a)).

Where it is apparent that a tonnage tax company (not being a member of a tonnage tax group) carrying on tonnage tax activities and other activities in an accounting period has deductible finance costs outside the tonnage tax trade in excess of what would be a fair proportion of its total finance costs, an adjustment may be made for the purposes of computing the company's profits for corporation tax purposes for that period (TCA 1997, s 697LB(2)). For this purpose, *deductible finance costs outside the tonnage tax trade* means the total of the amounts that may be taken into account in respect of finance costs in calculating the company's profits, other than relevant shipping profits, for corporation tax purposes (TCA 1997, s 697LB(1)(a)).

The proportion of the company's "deductible finance costs outside the tonnage tax trade" to be treated as excessive is determined on a just and reasonable basis (TCA 1997, s 697LB(3)(a)). No precise method for calculating excess finance costs is set out in the legislation but the underlying principle is that individual items of finance should not be seen as linked to individual activities, financing instead being viewed as relating to the totality of all tonnage tax and non-tonnage tax activities.

TCA 1997, s 697LB(3)(b) indicates how the "just and reasonable" determination of the excessive non-tonnage tax trade finance costs should be made. The company's total finance costs (see definition below), being those actually deducted with the addition of those that would have been deductible but for the tonnage tax election, are apportioned between the tonnage and non-tonnage activities by reference to the extent to which the total debt finance of the company is actually applied in earning relevant shipping profits. The resulting amount referable to the non-tonnage activities can then be compared with the amount allocated to those activities in the accounts.

An amount equal to the excess of the actual finance costs allocated to the non-tonnage activities over the above-apportioned amount is taken into account (effectively included as taxable profits) in computing the trading income of the company's non-tonnage tax activities for the accounting period in respect of which the adjustment arises (TCA 1997, s 697LB(4)).

In relation to a tonnage tax company, *total finance costs* means so much of the company's finance costs as could, if there were no tonnage tax election, be taken into account in calculating the company's profits for corporation tax purposes (TCA 1997, s 697LB(1)(a)).

TCA 1997, s 697LB(5) deals with the case of a tonnage tax company which is a member of a tonnage tax group and where the activities carried on by the members of the group in an accounting period include activities other than the activities of a tonnage tax trade or trades. Where it appears that the group's deductible finance costs outside the tonnage tax trade exceed what would be a fair proportion of the group's total finance costs, an adjustment may be made for the purposes of computing the company's profits for corporation tax purposes for that period. For this purpose, *deductible finance costs outside the tonnage tax trade* means so much of the group's finance costs as may be taken into account in calculating for corporation tax purposes:

(i) in the case of a group member that is a tonnage tax company, the company's profits, other than relevant shipping profits; and

(ii) in the case of a group member that is not a tonnage tax company, the company's profits (TCA 1997, s 697LB(1)(a)).

The proportion of the group's "deductible finance costs outside the tonnage tax trade" to be treated as excessive in relation to the company is determined on a just and reasonable basis (TCA 1997, s 697LB(6)(a)).

TCA 1997, s 697LB(6)(b) indicates how the "just and reasonable" determination of the excessive non-tonnage tax trade finance costs should be made. The group's total finance costs (see definition below), being those actually deducted with the addition of those that would have been deductible but for the tonnage tax election, are apportioned between the tonnage and non-tonnage activities by reference to the extent to which the total debt finance of the group is actually applied in earning relevant shipping profits. The resulting amount referable to the non-tonnage activities can then be compared with the amount allocated to those activities in the accounts.

An amount equal to a proportion of the excess of the actual finance costs allocated to the non-tonnage activities over the above-apportioned amount is taken into account (effectively included as taxable profits) in computing the trading income of the company's non-tonnage tax activities for the accounting period in respect of which the adjustment arises. The proportion is the amount of the excess which the company's tonnage tax profits bears to the tonnage tax profits of all members of the group (TCA 1997, s 697LB(7)).

In relation to a group of companies, *total finance costs* means so much of the group's finance costs as could, if there were no tonnage tax election, be taken into account in calculating the profits of any group member for corporation tax purposes (TCA 1997, s 697LB(1)(a)).

No adjustment under TCA 1997, s 697LB will be made if, in calculating the "deductible finance costs outside the tonnage tax trade" of a company or a group, the amount taken into account in respect of costs and losses is exceeded by the amount taken into account in respect of profits and gains (TCA 1997, s 697LB(8)). In other words, in calculating "finance costs" (see above), if the total of the profits or gains included (ie, foreign exchange gains) is not less than the total of the costs and losses included, no adjustment will arise.

13.803.7 Withdrawal of relief, deduction or set-off on company leaving tonnage tax

Certain provisions withdrawing relief apply where a company ceases to be a tonnage tax company on ceasing to be a qualifying company (see definition in **13.802**) for reasons relating wholly or mainly to tax, or under TCA 1997, s 697F (requirement not to enter tax-avoidance arrangements – see **13.803.2** above). Any exemption received in respect of chargeable gains on the disposal of tonnage tax assets, and any relief from a balancing charge arising in the period during which a company was subject to tonnage tax, is clawed back on ejection from tonnage tax.

Where a company ceases to be a tonnage tax company in either of the above-mentioned circumstances, TCA 1997, s 697N (see under *Chargeable gains* in **13.803.3** above) applies in relation to chargeable gains, but not in relation to losses, on all "relevant disposals" as if the company had never been a tonnage tax company (so that any gain on the disposal is treated as a chargeable gain notwithstanding that it is referable to a period or periods during which the asset was a tonnage tax asset).

A *relevant disposal* is a disposal:

(a)   on or after the day on which the company ceases to be a tonnage tax company; or

(b)   at any time during the period of 6 years immediately preceding that day when the company was a tonnage tax company (TCA 1997, s 697P(2)).

Where the amount of a chargeable gain on a disposal made at a time within the period mentioned in (b) is increased as described above, the gain is treated to the extent of the increase:

(a)   as arising immediately before the company ceased to be a tonnage tax company; and

(b)   as not being relevant shipping profits of the company (TCA 1997, s 697P(3)) – so that such profits are subjected to corporation tax in the normal way rather than in accordance with the tonnage tax method).

No relief, deduction or set-off of any description may be allowed against the amount of the increase or the corporation tax charged on that amount (TCA 1997, s 697P(4)).

Where a relief, deduction or set-off is denied in accordance with TCA 1997, s 697P, and in a relevant accounting period during which the company in question was liable to a balancing charge in relation to which TCA 1997 Sch 18B paragraph 16 or 17 (see **13.805.7** and **13.805.8** below), as appropriate, applied to reduce the amount of the charge, the company is treated as having received an additional amount of profits chargeable to corporation tax equal to the aggregate of the amounts by which those balancing charges were reduced (TCA 1997, s 697P(5)).

A *relevant accounting period* means an accounting period ending not more than 6 years before the day on which the company ceased to be a tonnage tax company (TCA 1997, s 697P(6)).

The additional profits deemed to have been received as above are treated:

(a)   as arising immediately before the company ceased to be a tonnage tax company; and

(b)   as not being relevant shipping profits of the company (TCA 1997, s 697P(7)) – so that such additional profits are subjected to corporation tax in the normal way rather than in accordance with the tonnage tax method.

No relief, deduction or set-off of any description may be allowed against the deemed additional profits or the corporation tax charged on them (TCA 1997, s 697P(8)).

There are provisions for the treatment of a company that leaves tonnage tax for reasons other than the expiry of the company's election. These provisions impose exit tax charges or result in disqualification from tonnage tax for a ten-year period.

13.803.8   Disqualification from re-entry into tonnage tax

Where a company leaves tonnage tax other than on the expiry of its election, a disqualification in the form of a ten-year exclusion from the tax applies. There is, however, currently no provision for entry into tonnage tax other than by way of election, or mechanism for re-entry where a company exits after the expiry of the ten-year election period without making a renewals election, so that the question of re-entry is of little practical relevance at the moment. In accordance with TCA 1997 Sch 18B paragraph 2(6), however, the Minister for Finance may provide for additional periods within which a company may elect for tonnage tax. A company that has been excluded from tonnage tax under TCA 1997, s 697Q will be unable to re-enter tonnage tax under any election procedure that may be provided for until the expiry of a ten-year period.

In every case where a company ceases to be a tonnage tax company otherwise than on the expiry of a tonnage tax election:

(a)   a company election made by a former tonnage tax company (a company that is not a tonnage tax company but has previously been such a company) is rendered ineffective if made before the end of the period of 10 years beginning with the date on which the company ceased to be a tonnage tax company; and

(b)   a group election that—

  (i)   is made in respect of a group whose members include a former tonnage tax company, and

  (ii)   would result in that company becoming a tonnage tax company,

is rendered ineffective if made before the end of the period of 10 years beginning with the date on which the company ceased to be a tonnage tax company (TCA 1997, s 697Q(2)).

A company is not, however, prevented by reason of the above provisions from becoming a tonnage tax company under and in accordance with the rules in TCA 1997 Part 4 of Sch 18B (groups, mergers and related matters) (TCA 1997, s 697Q(3)).

13.804   Matters relating to qualifying ships

13.804.1   Company temporarily ceasing to operate qualifying ships

If a company which temporarily ceases to operate any qualifying ships (but not where the company continues to operate a ship that temporarily ceases to be a qualifying ship) gives notice to the Revenue Commissioners stating:

(a)   its intention to resume operating qualifying ships; and

(b)   its wish to remain within tonnage tax,

the company will, for the purposes of tonnage tax, be treated as if it had continued to operate the qualifying ship or ships it operated immediately before the temporary cessation.

The above provision ceases to apply if and when the company abandons its intention to resume operating qualifying ships or again in fact operates a qualifying ship (TCA 1997 Sch 18B paragraph 7).

13.804.2   Meaning of operating a ship

A company is regarded, for tonnage tax purposes, as operating any ship owned by, or chartered to, that company but subject to the provisions of TCA 1997 Sch 18B paragraph 8.

A company is not regarded as the operator of a ship where part only of the ship has been chartered to it and, for this purpose, the company is not regarded as having part only of a ship chartered to it by reason only of the ship being chartered to it jointly with one or more other persons (TCA 1997 Sch 18B paragraph 8(2)).

A company is not regarded as the operator of a ship that has been chartered out by it on bareboat charter terms (TCA 1997 Sch 18B paragraph 8(3)). It will, however, be regarded as the operator of a ship that has been chartered out by it on bareboat charter terms if the person to whom it is chartered is not a third party, where *third party* means:

(a)   in the case of a single company, any other person;

(b)   in the case of a member of a group companies—

(i) any member of the group that is not a tonnage tax company (and does not become a tonnage tax company by virtue of the ship being chartered to it) or

(ii) any person who is not a member of the group (TCA 1997 Sch 18B paragraph 8(4)).

Bareboat charter terms, in relation to the charter of a ship, means the letting on charter of a ship for a stipulated period on terms which give the charterer possession and control of the ship, including the right to appoint the master and crew (TCA 1997, s 697A(1)). In the case of a bareboat charter, therefore, the owner has no responsibilities for crewing, provisioning or directing the ship, these being assumed by the person chartering the ship.

A company is not regarded as the operator of a ship where part only of the ship has been chartered to it and, for this purpose, the company is not regarded as having part only of a ship chartered to it by reason only of the ship being chartered to it jointly with one or more other persons (TCA 1997 Sch 18B paragraph 8(2)).

A company is not regarded as ceasing to operate a ship that has been chartered out by it on bareboat charter terms if:

(a) the ship is chartered out because of short-term over-capacity; and
(b) the term of the charter does not exceed 3 years (TCA 1997 Sch 18B paragraph 8(5)).

A company will be regarded as operating a qualifying ship for the purposes of the activity described in (j) of the definition of "relevant shipping income" (see **13.802**) if that company has entered contractual arrangements in relation to the provision of ship management services for the qualifying ship for a stipulated period and the terms of those arrangements give the company:

(a) possession and control of the ship;
(b) control over the day to day management of the ship, including the right to appoint the master and crew and route planning;
(c) control over the technical management of the ship, including decisions on its repair and maintenance;
(d) control over the safety management of the ship, including ensuring that all necessary safety and survey certificates are current;
(e) control over the training of the officers and crew of the ship; and
(f) the management of the bunkering, victualling and provisioning of the ship;

and those terms are actually implemented for the period in which the company provides ship management services in respect of that ship (TCA 1997 Sch 18B paragraph 8(6)).

13.804.3 Qualifying ship used as vessel of an excluded kind

A qualifying ship that begins to be used as a vessel of an excluded kind ceases to be a qualifying ship when it begins to be so used, but if:

(a) a company operates a ship throughout an accounting period of the company; and
(b) in that period the ship is used as a vessel of an excluded kind on not more than 30 days (with that figure being proportionately reduced in the case of an

accounting period shorter than a year), that use will be disregarded in determining whether the ship is a qualifying ship at any time during that period (TCA 1997 Sch 18B paragraph 9(1), (2)).

If a company operates a ship during part only of an accounting period of the company, the 30 days mentioned above (as reduced proportionately in the case of a short accounting period) are substituted by the number of days that bear to the length of that part of the accounting period the same proportion that 30 days bears to a year (TCA 1997 Sch 18B paragraph 9(3)).

13.805   Capital allowances, balancing charges and related matters

13.805.1   Plant and machinery used wholly for tonnage tax trade

On entering tonnage tax (ie, on becoming a tonnage tax company) a company may have incurred capital expenditure on machinery or plant before its entry into tonnage tax, where that machinery or plant is to be used wholly and exclusively for the purposes of the company's tonnage tax trade. In such a case:

(a)   no balancing charge or balancing allowance will arise under TCA 1997, s 288 (see **5.207**) as a result of the machinery or plant being used for the purposes of the company's tonnage tax trade (TCA 1997 Sch 18B paragraph 10(1)(b)(i));

(b)   any allowance attributable to the machinery or plant referred to in (a) which would otherwise have been made to the company under the capital allowances legislation, or under any other provision construed with that legislation, for any accounting period in which the company is a tonnage tax company may not be made (TCA 1997 Sch 18B paragraph 10(1)(b)(ii)); and

(c)   TCA 1997, s 287 (wear and tear allowances deemed to have been made – see **5.206** re notional wear and tear allowances) will not apply as respects any accounting period during which the machinery or plant has been used wholly and exclusively for the purposes of a company's tonnage tax trade (TCA 1997 Sch 18B paragraph 10(1)(b)(iii)).

Where the machinery or plant referred to above begins to be used wholly or partly for purposes other than those of a company's tonnage tax trade and where the asset begins to be *wholly* used for purposes other than the company's tonnage tax trade:

(a)   no balancing allowance may be made on the company under TCA 1997, s 288(2) for any period in which the company is subject to tonnage tax;

(b)   for the purposes of making a balancing charge under TCA 1997, s 288 on the happening of the events referred to in TCA 1997, s 288 (1) (see **5.207.1**)—

(i)   TCA 1997, s 296 (wear and tear allowances deemed to have been made – see **5.207.5** re notional allowances) is not to apply as respects any accounting period of a company in which it is subject to tonnage tax,

(ii)   where the event occurs at a time when the company is subject to tonnage tax, the amount of its capital expenditure still unallowed at the time of the event will, notwithstanding TCA 1997, s 296, be the amount of its capital expenditure on the provision of the machinery or plant which was still unallowed at the time the company's election into tonnage tax had effect, and

(iii) where the event occurs at a time when the company is subject to tonnage tax, the references in TCA 1997, s 288 to sale, insurance, salvage or compensation moneys and the reference in TCA 1997, s 289(3)(b) (see **5.207.4**) to the open market price of the machinery or plant are to be taken to be references to the least of _

(A) the actual cost to the company of the machinery or plant for the purpose of the trade carried on by the company,

(B) the price the machinery or plant would have fetched if sold in the open market at the time the company's election into tonnage tax had effect, and

(C) the sale, insurance, salvage or compensation moneys arising from the event or, where TCA 1997, s 289(3)(b) (see **5.207.4**) applies, the open market price of the machinery or plant at the time of the event (TCA 1997 Sch 18B paragraph 10(2)(b)).

Where machinery or plant referred to above begins to be used wholly or partly for purposes other than those of a company's tonnage tax trade and the asset begins to be *partly* used for purposes other than the company's tonnage tax trade:

(a) the machinery or plant is treated as two separate assets, one in use wholly and exclusively for the purposes of the tonnage tax trade and the other in use wholly and exclusively for purposes other than the company's tonnage tax trade;

(b) TCA 1997 Sch 18B paragraph 10(2)(b) (see above) is to apply in relation to the part of the asset treated as in use wholly and exclusively for the purposes of the tonnage tax trade as it applies in relation to machinery or plant which begins to be used wholly for purposes other than the company's tonnage tax trade;

(c) in determining the amount of any capital allowances or balancing charge to be made under the capital allowances legislation, or under any other provision construed with that legislation, in relation to the part of the asset treated as in use wholly and exclusively for purposes other than the company's tonnage tax trade, regard is to be had to all relevant circumstances and, in particular, to the extent of the use, if any, of the machinery or plant for the purposes of a trade, and there is to be made to or on the company, in respect of that trade, an allowance of such an amount or a balancing charge of such an amount, as may be just and reasonable (see **13.806.3**) (TCA 1997 Sch 18B paragraph 10(2)(c)).

13.805.2 Plant and machinery used partly for tonnage tax trade

On entry into tonnage tax, machinery or plant in respect of which capital expenditure was incurred by a company before its entry may be used partly for the purposes of the company's tonnage tax trade and partly for purposes other than its tonnage tax trade. In those circumstances, the following rules will apply:

(a) The machinery or plant is to be treated as two separate assets, one in use wholly and exclusively for the purposes of the tonnage tax trade and the other in use wholly and exclusively for the purposes of the other trade of the company (TCA 1997 Sch 18B paragraph 11(2)(a)).

(b) Subject to (c) below, in determining the amount of—

(i) any capital allowances or balancing charges to be made in respect of that part of the asset treated as in use wholly and exclusively for purposes other than the company's tonnage tax trade under the capital allowances legislation, or under any other provision construed with that legislation, or

(ii) the amount of any balancing charge to be made for the purposes of the tonnage tax trade under the capital allowances legislation, or under any other provision construed with that legislation, as applied by TCA 1997 Schedule 18B,

regard is to be had to all relevant circumstances and, in particular, to the extent of the use of the machinery or plant for the purposes of a trade other than the tonnage tax trade and, in respect of that trade, an allowance will be made to the company or, in respect of both the tonnage tax trade and the other trade, a balancing charge will be made on the company, of such an amount as may be just and reasonable (see **13.806.3**) (TCA 1997 Sch 18B paragraph 11(2)(b)), and

(c) TCA 1997 Sch 18B paragraph 10(1)(b) and TCA 1997 Sch 18B paragraph 10(2)(b) will apply in relation to the part of the asset treated as in use wholly and exclusively for the purposes of the tonnage tax trade as they apply in relation to the machinery or plant referred to in **13.805.1** (TCA 1997 Sch 18B paragraph 11(2)(c)).

13.805.3 Plant and machinery: new expenditure partly for tonnage tax purposes

A company subject to tonnage tax may incur capital expenditure on the provision of machinery or plant partly for the purposes of its tonnage tax trade and partly for the purposes of another trade carried on by it. In any such case, the machinery or plant will be treated as two separate assets one in use wholly and exclusively for the purposes or the tonnage tax trade and the other in use wholly and exclusively for the purposes of the other trade of the company.

In determining the amount of any capital allowance or the amount of any charge to be made under the capital allowances legislation, or under any other provision construed with that legislation, in the case of that part of the asset treated as a separate asset for the purposes of the other trade, regard is to be had to all relevant circumstances and, in particular, to the extent of the use of the machinery or plant for the purposes of the other trade and, in respect of that other trade, an allowance will be made to, or a balancing charge made on, the company of such an amount as may be just and reasonable (see **13.806.3**) (TCA 1997 Sch 18B paragraph 12).

13.805.4 Plant and machinery: change of use of tonnage tax asset

The following rules apply where, at any time when a company is subject to tonnage tax, machinery or plant acquired after the company became subject to that tax, and which is used wholly and exclusively for the purposes of the company's tonnage tax trade, begins to be used wholly or partly for the purposes of another trade:

(a) If the asset begins to be used wholly for the purposes of another trade, the capital allowances legislation is to apply as if capital expenditure had been incurred by the person carrying on the other trade on the provision of machinery or plant for the purposes of that trade in that person's chargeable period in which the machinery or plant is brought into use for those purposes, and the amount of that expenditure is to be taken to be the lesser of—

(i) the amount of the capital expenditure actually incurred by the person, and

(ii) the price which the machinery or plant would have fetched if sold on the open market on the date on which it was brought into use:

(b) If the asset begins to be used partly for the purposes of another trade of the company and partly for the purposes of the tonnage tax trade—

(i) the machinery or plant is to be treated as two separate assets, one in use wholly and exclusively for the purposes of the tonnage tax trade and the other in use wholly and exclusively for the purposes of the other trade of the company,

(ii) the capital allowances legislation is to apply as if the company had incurred capital expenditure on the provision of that part of the asset treated as in use wholly and exclusively for the other trade of the company in the accounting period of the company in which that part of the asset is brought into use for those purposes, and

(iii) in determining the amount of any capital expenditure incurred on the provision of that part of the asset treated as in use as a separate asset for the purposes of the other trade of the company, regard is to be had to all relevant circumstances as is just and reasonable (see **13.806.3**) (TCA 1997 Sch 18B paragraph 13).

13.805.5 Plant and machinery: change of use of non-tonnage tax asset

The following rules apply where, at any time when a company is subject to tonnage tax, machinery or plant wholly and exclusively used for the purposes of another trade carried on by the company, not being a tonnage tax trade, begins to be used wholly or partly for the purposes of the company's tonnage tax trade:

(1) Where the asset begins to be wholly used for the purposes of the company's tonnage tax trade—

(a) no balancing allowance or balancing charge is to be made as a consequence of the change of use, and

(b) for the purposes of making a balancing charge under TCA 1997, s 288 on the happening, subsequent to the change in use, of any of the events referred to in TCA 1997, s 288(1) (see **5.207.1**)—

(i) TCA 1997, s 296 (wear and tear allowances deemed to have been made – see **5.207.5** re notional allowances) is not to apply as respects any accounting period of a company in which the asset is used wholly and exclusively for the purposes of the company's tonnage tax trade,

(ii) where the event occurs at a time when the asset is so used, the amount of the capital expenditure of the company still unallowed at the time of the event will, notwithstanding TCA 1997, s 296, be the amount of the capital expenditure on the provision of the machinery or plant which was still unallowed at the time the asset began to be used, and

(iii) where the event occurs at a time when the asset is so used, the references in TCA 1997, s 288 to sale, insurance, salvage or compensation moneys and the reference in TCA 1997, s 289(3)(b) (see **5.207.4**) to the open market price of the machinery or plant are to be taken to be references to the least of–

   (A) the actual cost to the company of the machinery or plant for the purpose of the trade carried on by the company,

   (B) the price the machinery or plant would have fetched if sold in the open market at the time the asset began to be so used, and

   (C) the sale, insurance, salvage or compensation moneys arising from the event or, where TCA 1997, s 289(3)(b) (see **5.207.4**) applies, the open market price of the machinery or plant at the time of the event (TCA 1997 Sch 18B paragraph 14(2)).

(2) Where the asset begins to be partly used for the purposes of the company's tonnage tax trade—

(a) the machinery or plant is to be treated as two separate assets, one in use wholly and exclusively for the purposes of the other trade of the company and the other in use wholly and exclusively for the purposes of the tonnage tax trade of the company,

(b) no balancing charge or balancing allowance may be made in respect of the part treated as wholly and exclusively for the purposes of the tonnage tax trade as a consequence of the change in use,

(c) the rules in (1)(b)(i) to (iii) above are to apply in relation to the part of the asset treated as in use wholly and exclusively for the purposes of the tonnage tax trade as they apply for the purposes of the machinery or plant wholly used for the purposes of the company's tonnage tax trade (TCA 1997 Sch 18B paragraph 14(3)).

13.805.6 Plant and machinery: provisions relating to balancing charges

A balancing charge arising under capital allowances legislation, as applied by TCA 1997 Schedule 18B or under Schedule 18B, is to be:

(a) treated as arising in connection with a trade carried on by the company other than the company's tonnage tax trade; and

(b) made in taxing that trade (TCA 1997 Sch 18B paragraph 15(1)).

Subject to TCA 1997 Sch 18B paragraphs 16 and 17 (see **13.805.7** and **13.805.8** below), the balancing charge will have effect in the accounting period in which it arises (TCA 1997 Sch 18B paragraph 15(2)).

On the first occasion of the happening of an event that gives rise to a balancing charge on a tonnage tax company (including such an event arising in respect of more than one asset on the same date) under capital allowances legislation as applied by TCA 1997 Schedule 18B, or under Schedule 18B, the company should elect, by notice in writing to the Revenue Commissioners, for relief against that charge either under paragraph 16 or, if applicable, paragraph 17 of Schedule 18B but not for relief under both. Any such election will be irrevocable. The election is to be included in the company's tax return under TCA 1997, s 951 for the accounting period in which the charge arises (TCA 1997 Sch 18B paragraph 15(3)).

Where, under the capital allowances legislation as applied by TCA 1997 Schedule 18B, or under Schedule 18B, a balancing charge arises on a tonnage tax company subsequent to any charge on the company such as is referred to in TCA 1997 Sch 18B paragraph 15(3), relief against that charge will only be available under the paragraph for which the company elected for relief in accordance with that subparagraph (TCA 1997 Sch 18B paragraph 15(4)). Relief under TCA 1997 Sch 18B paragraph 16 or 17 will not be available to a company unless it has made an election under TCA 1997 Sch 18B paragraph 15(3) (TCA 1997 Sch 18B paragraph 15(5)).

13.805.7 Reduction in balancing charge by reference to time in tonnage tax

The amount of any balancing charge, in accordance with the legislation on capital allowances as applied by TCA 1997 Schedule 18B or under Schedule 18B, is to be reduced by 20% of the amount of the charge for each whole year in which the company liable to the charge has been subject to tonnage tax calculated by reference to the time of the event giving rise to the charge (TCA 1997 Sch 18B paragraph 16). (See also **13.803.4**.)

13.805.8 Set-off of accrued losses against balancing charge

Where a balancing charge under the legislation on capital allowances, as applied by TCA 1997 Schedule 18B or under Schedule 18B, arises in connection with the disposal of a qualifying ship, the company in question may set off against any balancing charge so arising any losses (including any losses referable to capital allowances treated by virtue of TCA 1997, s 307 (see **3.104**) or 308 (see **5.105.3**) as trading expenses of the company) which accrued to the company before its entry to tonnage tax and which are attributable to—

(a) activities which under tonnage tax became part of the company's tonnage tax trade; or

(b) a source of income which under tonnage tax becomes relevant shipping income (TCA 1997 Sch 18B paragraph 17).

13.805.9 Deferment of balancing charge on re-investment

Where a balancing charge under the legislation on capital allowances, as applied by TCA 1997 Schedule 18B, arises in connection with the disposal by a company of a qualifying ship and, within the period beginning on the date the company's election for tonnage tax takes effect and ending five years after the date of the event giving rise to the balancing charge, the company, or another qualifying company which is a member of the same tonnage tax group as the company, incurs capital expenditure on the provision of one or more other qualifying ships (the "new asset"), then:

(i) if the amount on which the charge would have been made, as reduced under TCA 1997 Sch 18B paragraph 16 or 17 (see **13.805.7** and **13.805.8** above), if applicable, is greater than the capital expenditure on providing the new asset, the balancing charge is to be made only on an amount equal to the difference; and

(ii) if the capital expenditure on providing the new asset is equal to or greater than the amount on which the charge would have been made, as reduced under TCA 1997 Sch 18B paragraph 16 or 17, if applicable, the balancing charge may not be made (TCA 1997 Sch 18B paragraph 18(1)).

Where an event referred to in TCA 1997, s 288(1) (see **5.207.1**) occurs in relation to the new asset in the period in which the company which incurs the expenditure on the new asset is subject to tonnage tax, a balancing charge under TCA 1997 Sch 18B paragraph 18 is to be made on that company (TCA 1997 Sch 18B paragraph 18(2)).

Subject to any reduction under TCA 1997 Sch 18B paragraph 16 or 17 and to any further application of TCA 1997 Sch 18B paragraph 18, the amount of the charge referred to in TCA 1997 Sch 18B paragraph 18(2) (see above) will be:

(a) where Sch 18B paragraph 18(1)(i) (see (i) above) applies, the difference between the balancing charge which, but for Sch 18B paragraph 18(1), would have been made on the disposal referred to in that subparagraph and the actual charge made;

(b) where Sch 18B paragraph 18(1)(ii) (see (ii) above) applies, the amount of the charge which, but for Sch 18B paragraph 18(1), would have been made on the disposal referred to in that subparagraph (TCA 1997 Sch 18B paragraph 18(3)).

For the purposes of TCA 1997 Sch 18B paragraph 18(1), where machinery or plant is let to a tonnage tax company on the terms of the company being bound to maintain the machinery or plant and deliver it over in good condition at the end of the lease, and if the burden of the wear and tear on the machinery or plant will in fact fall directly on the company, the capital expenditure on the provision of the machinery or plant is deemed to have been incurred by that company and the machinery or plant is deemed to belong to that company (TCA 1997 Sch 18B paragraph 18(5)).

13.805.10 Exit: plant and machinery

Where a company leaves tonnage tax (ie, when it ceases to be a tonnage tax company), the amount of capital expenditure incurred on the provision of machinery or plant in respect of each asset used by the company for the purposes of its tonnage tax trade, which asset was acquired at a time the company was subject to tonnage tax and was held by it at the time it leaves tonnage tax, will be the lesser of:

(a) the capital expenditure actually incurred by the company on the provision of that machinery or plant for the purposes of the company's tonnage tax trade; and

(b) the price the machinery or plant would have fetched if sold in the open market at the date the company leaves tonnage tax (TCA 1997 Sch 18B paragraph 19(1)).

For the purposes of the making of allowances and charges under the legislation on capital allowances, or any provision construed as one with that legislation, the capital expenditure on the provision of the machinery or plant as determined in accordance with TCA 1997 Sch 18B paragraph 19(1) is deemed to have been incurred on the day immediately following the date the company leaves tonnage tax (TCA 1997 Sch 18B paragraph 19(1)).

TCA 1997 Sch 18B paragraph 19(3) applies where a company:

(i) leaves tonnage tax having incurred expenditure on the provision of machinery or plant for the purposes of a trade carried on by the company before entry into tonnage tax;

(ii) has used that machinery or plant for the purposes of its tonnage tax trade;

(iii) has been denied allowances in respect of that machinery or plant by virtue of TCA 1997, s 697O (see **13.803.4** under *Capital allowances: general*) and the provisions of TCA 1997 Schedule 18B paragraph 10(1)(b)(ii) (see **13.805.1**) or 11(2)(c) (see **13.805.2**); and

(iv) on leaving tonnage tax, starts, recommences or continues to use that machinery or plant for the purposes of a trade carried on by it.

Where TCA 1997 Sch 18B paragraph 19(3) applies, and subject to TCA 1997 Sch 18B paragraph 19(3)(c) and (d) (see below), any allowance which, but for TCA 1997, s 697O and TCA 1997 Schedule 18B paragraph 10(1)(b) or 11(2)(c), would have been made under the capital allowances legislation, or any provision construed as one with that legislation, to the company for any accounting period in which it was subject to tonnage tax will, subject to compliance with that legislation, be made instead for such accounting periods immediately after the company leaves tonnage tax as will ensure, subject to that legislation, that all such allowances are made to the company in those accounting periods as would have been made to it in respect of that machinery or plant if the company had never been subject to tonnage tax (TCA 1997 Schedule 18B paragraph 19(3)(b)).

No wear and tear allowance may be made by virtue of TCA 1997 Schedule 18B paragraph 19(3) in respect of any machinery or plant for any accounting period of a company if such allowance, when added to the allowances in respect of that machinery or plant made to that company for any previous accounting period, will make the aggregate amount of the allowances exceed the actual cost to the company of the machinery or plant, including in that actual cost any expenditure in the nature of capital expenditure on the machinery or plant by means of renewal, improvement or repair (TCA 1997 Schedule 18B paragraph 19(3)(c)).

A wear and tear allowance in respect of any machinery or plant made by virtue of TCA 1997 Schedule 18B paragraph 19(3) for any accounting period may not exceed the amount appropriate to that machinery or plant as set out in TCA 1997, s 284(2) (see **5.203.3**) (TCA 1997 Schedule 18B paragraph 19(3)(d)).

13.805.11 Industrial buildings

Where any identifiable part of a building or structure is used for the purposes of a company's tonnage tax trade, that part is treated for the purposes of TCA 1997 Chapter 1 of Part 9 (see **5.4**) as used otherwise than as an industrial building or structure (TCA 1997 Sch 18B paragraph 20(1)).

Where in an accounting period during which a company is subject to tonnage tax, an event giving rise to a balancing charge occurs in relation to an industrial building or structure in respect of which capital expenditure was incurred by the company before its entry into tonnage tax, the following provisions apply:

(i) the sale, insurance, salvage or compensation moneys to be brought into account in respect of any industrial building or structure is to be limited to the market value of the relevant interest (see **5.403**) when the company entered tonnage tax; and

(ii) the amount of any balancing charge under Part 9 will, subject to TCA 1997 Sch 18B paragraph 15(3)-(5) (see **13.805.6**), be reduced in accordance with TCA 1997 Sch 18B paragraphs 16 or 17 (see **13.805.7** and **13.805.8** above), as appropriate (TCA 1997 Sch 18B paragraph 20(2)).

Where a company subject to tonnage tax disposes of the relevant interest in an industrial building or structure, TCA 1997 277 (see **5.409.2**) is to apply to determine the residue of expenditure in the hands of the person who acquires the relevant interest, as if:

(a) the company had not been subject to tonnage tax; and

(b) all writing down allowances and balancing allowances and charges had been made as could have been made if the company had not been subject to tonnage tax (TCA 1997 Sch 18B paragraph 20(3)).

Where a company leaves tonnage tax (ie, where it ceases to be a tonnage tax company), the amount of capital expenditure qualifying for relief under TCA 1997 Chapter 1 of Part 9 (see **5.4**) is to be determined as if:

(a) the company had never been subject to tonnage tax; and

(b) all such allowances and charges under Part 9 had been made as could have been made (TCA 1997 Sch 18B paragraph 20(4)).

13.806 Groups, mergers and related matters

13.806.1 Company not to be treated as member of more than one group

Where a company is a member of both a tonnage tax group and a non-tonnage tax group which, if a group election (see **13.803.2**) had been made, would have been a tonnage tax group (a "qualifying non-tonnage tax group"), the company is treated as a member of the tonnage tax group and not of the qualifying non-tonnage tax group (TCA 1997 Sch 18B paragraph 21(1)).

Where a company is a member of two tonnage tax groups, it is treated as a member of the group whose tonnage tax election was made first and not of the other tonnage tax group. In the case of group elections made at the same time, the company must choose which election it joins in and, for the purposes of TCA 1997 Part 24A and 18B, it will be treated as a member of the group in respect of which that election is made and not of any other tonnage tax group (TCA 1997 Sch 18B paragraph 21(2)).

13.806.2 Arrangements for dealing with group matters

The Revenue Commissioners may enter into arrangements with the qualifying companies within a group for one or more of those companies to deal on behalf of the group in relation to matters arising under TCA 1997 Part 24A and Schedule 18B that may conveniently be dealt with on a group basis (TCA 1997 Sch 18B paragraph 22(1)).

13.806.3 Meaning of "merger" and "demerger"

A *merger* is a transaction by which one or more companies become members of a group, and a *demerger* is a transaction by which one or more companies cease to be members of a group (TCA 1997 Sch 18B paragraph 23(1)).

References to a merger to which a group is a party include any merger affecting a member of the group (TCA 1997 Sch 18B paragraph 23(2)).

13.806.4 Merger: between tonnage tax groups or companies

Where there is a merger between:

    (a)   two or more tonnage tax groups;

    (b)   one or more tonnage tax groups and one or more tonnage tax companies; or

    (c)   two or more tonnage tax companies,

the group resulting from the merger is a tonnage tax group as if a group election had been made (TCA 1997 Sch 18B paragraph 24(1), (2)).

This deemed election continues in force, subject to the provisions of TCA 1997 Part 24A, until whichever of the existing tonnage tax elections had the longest period left to run would have expired (TCA 1997 Sch 18B paragraph 24(3)).

13.806.5 Merger: tonnage tax group/company and qualifying non-tonnage tax group/company

Where there is a merger between a tonnage tax group or company and a qualifying non-tonnage tax group (see **13.806.1** above) or company, the group resulting from the merger may elect that:

    (a)   it be treated as if a group election had been made which deemed election will continue in force until the original election made by the tonnage tax group or company would have expired; or

    (b)   the tonnage tax election of the group or company ceases to be in force as from the date of the merger (TCA 1997 Sch 18B paragraph 25(1), (2)).

Any such election must be made jointly by all the qualifying companies in the group resulting from the merger and by way of notice in writing to the Revenue Commissioners within 12 months of the merger (TCA 1997 Sch 18B paragraph 25(3)).

13.806.6 Merger: tonnage tax group or company and non-qualifying group or company

Where there is a merger between a tonnage tax group or company and a non-qualifying group or company, the group resulting from the merger is a tonnage tax group by virtue of the election of the tonnage tax group or company (TCA 1997 Sch 18B paragraph 26).

13.806.7 Merger: non-qualifying group or company and qualifying non-tonnage tax group or company

Where there is a merger between a non-qualifying group or company and a qualifying non-tonnage tax group or company, the group resulting from the merger may make a tonnage tax election having effect as from the date of the merger (TCA 1997 Sch 18B paragraph 27(1), (2)).

Any such election must be made jointly by all the qualifying companies in the group resulting from the merger, by notice in writing to the Revenue Commissioners within 12 months of the merger (TCA 1997 Sch 18B paragraph 27(3)).

13.806.8   Demerger: single company

Where a tonnage tax company ceases to be a member of a tonnage tax group and does not become a member of another group:

(a)   the company remains a tonnage tax company as if a single company election had been made; and

(b)   the deemed election continues in force, subject to the provisions of TCA 1997 Schedule 18B, until the group election would have expired (TCA 1997 Sch 18B paragraph 28(1), (2)).

If two or more members of a previous group remain, and any of them is a qualifying company, the group consisting of those companies are treated as a tonnage tax group by virtue of the previous group election (TCA 1997 Sch 18B paragraph 28(3)).

13.806.9   Demerger: group

Where a tonnage tax group splits into two or more groups, each new group containing a qualifying company that was a tonnage tax company before the demerger is treated as a tonnage tax group as if a group election had been made. The deemed election continues in force, subject to the provisions of TCA 1997 Sch 18B, until the group election would have expired (TCA 1997 Sch 18B paragraph 29).

13.806.10 Duty to notify Revenue Commissioners of group changes

A tonnage tax company that becomes or ceases to be a member of a group, or of a particular group, is required to give notice in writing to the Revenue Commissioners of that fact. The notice should be given within the period of 12 months beginning with the date on which the company became or ceased to be a member of the group (TCA 1997 Sch 18B paragraph 30).

13.807   Miscellaneous

13.807.1   Measurement of tonnage ship

References to the gross or net tonnage (see **13.803.1**) of a ship are to that tonnage as determined:

(a)   in the case of a vessel of 24 metres in length or over, in accordance with the IMO International Convention on Tonnage Measurement of Ships 1969;

(b)   in the case of a vessel under 24 metres in length, in accordance with tonnage regulations.

A ship will not be treated as a qualifying ship for the purposes of TCA 1997 Part 24A and Sch 18B unless there is in force:

(a)   a valid International Tonnage Certificate (1969); or

(b)   a valid certificate recording its tonnage as measured in accordance with tonnage regulations.

Tonnage regulations means regulations under section 91 of the Mercantile Marine Act 1955 or the provisions of the law of a country or territory outside the State corresponding to those regulations (TCA 1997 Sch 18B paragraph 31).

13.807.2 Second or subsequent application of TCA 1997 ss 687P and 697Q

Where TCA 1997 ss 697P and 697Q (see **13.803.7** and **13.803.8**) apply on a second or subsequent occasion on which a company ceases to be a tonnage tax company (whether or not those sections applied on any of the previous occasions):

(a) the references to the company ceasing to be a tonnage tax company are to be read as references to the last occasion on which it did so; and

(b) the references to the period during which the company was a tonnage tax company do not include any period before its most recent entry into tonnage tax (TCA 1997 Sch 18B paragraph 32).

13.807.3 Appeals

Where in TCA 1997 Part 24A and in Schedule 18B there is provision for the determination of any matter on a just and reasonable basis (see **13.803.3**, **13.803.4**, **13.805.1**, **13.805.2**, **13.805.3** and **13.805.4**) and it is not possible for the company concerned and the appropriate inspector (within the meaning of TCA 1997, s 950) to agree on what is just and reasonable in the circumstances, there is to be a right of appeal to the Appeal Commissioners in the like manner as an appeal would lie against an assessment to corporation tax, and the provisions of the Tax Acts relating to appeals will apply accordingly (TCA 1997 Sch 18B paragraph 34).

Chapter 14

Double Taxation Relief

14.1 DOUBLE TAX TREATIES: GENERAL

14.101 Introduction

A person resident in Ireland is normally liable to Irish tax in respect of his worldwide income. In the case of foreign source income, the country in which the income arises will usually tax that income so that in the absence of any other provisions in the tax law of either country, the foreign source income of an Irish resident would be taxed twice.

A person not resident in Ireland who has Irish source income is, under general principles of Irish tax law, liable to Irish tax in respect of that income and also to tax in his country of residence. Again, in the absence of any relieving provisions in either country, the income may be doubly taxed. To prevent such double taxation arising, the Irish government has negotiated a range of double taxation treaties with governments of other countries. Each such treaty alters the tax treatment provided for by the respective laws of Ireland and the other country concerned insofar as they affect persons who are to be relieved from double taxation. Tax treaties, or "conventions", are bilateral agreements between the governments of the two countries concerned, having the objective of avoiding the double taxation of income from sources in one of the countries which arises to residents of the other. A tax treaty may also contain measures to relieve or prevent the double taxation of capital gains.

Tax treaties apply, as a general rule, to persons who are residents of either of the two countries concerned ("the contracting states").

The taxation rights of each contracting state in relation to any category of income, where a resident of one of the countries has income of the class in question in the other country, or in relation to capital gains, are set out in the relevant treaty article, as well as the limitations imposed by the treaty on those rights. With a view to preventing tax evasion, tax treaties usually contain an article providing for the exchange of information between the tax authorities of the respective countries.

In general, double taxation treaties negotiated by the Irish government entitle a resident of Ireland to have the foreign tax suffered on foreign source income credited against the Irish tax payable in respect of that income. The entitlement to the credit for foreign tax is provided for in the relevant treaty but the method by which the credit is computed is set out in the domestic legislation, in Ireland mainly in Taxes Consolidation Act 1997 (TCA 1997) Sch 24. The rules for calculating foreign tax credits are discussed in **14.2**.

14.102   Legislative authority for tax treaties

TCA 1997, s 826 provides the statutory authority for the government to make double taxation agreements with other countries. TCA 1997, s 826(1) states as follows:

Where—

(a)   the Government by order declare that arrangements specified in the order have been made with the government of any territory outside the State in relation to—

   (i)   affording relief from double taxation in respect of—

   (I)   income tax,

   (II)   corporation tax in respect of income and chargeable gains (or, in the case of arrangements made before the enactment of the Corporation Tax Act 1976, corporation profits tax),

   (III)   capital gains tax,

   (IV)   any taxes of a similar character, imposed by the laws of the State or by the laws of that territory, and

   (ii)   in the case of taxes of any kind or description imposed by the laws of the State or the laws of that territory—

   (I)   exchanging information for the purposes of the prevention and detection of tax evasion, or

   (II)   granting relief from taxation under the laws of that territory to persons who are resident in the State for the purposes of tax,

and that it is expedient that those arrangements should have the force of law, and

(b)   the order so made is referred to in Part 1 of Schedule 24A (reproduced below),

then, subject to this section and to the extent provided for in this section, the arrangements shall, notwithstanding any enactment, have the force of law as if each such order were an Act of the Oireachtas on and from the date of—

(A)   the insertion of Schedule 24A into the Principal Act by paragraph (b), or

(B)   the insertion of a reference to the order into Part 1 of Schedule 24A,

whichever is the later.

The reference to "notwithstanding anything in any enactment" confirms that for Irish tax purposes the provisions of tax treaties take precedence over domestic law. All the tax treaties currently in force between Ireland and other countries derive their legal status from statutory orders made by the government under the authority conferred by TCA 1997, s 826. In the case of each agreement, its terms are first negotiated between officials of the respective governments and are then put before the respective parliaments for ratification. On the Irish side, the full terms of the treaty to be ratified are set out in a draft statutory order that is laid before Dáil Éireann. On the approval of this draft by a resolution of Dáil Éireann, and following ratification also by the other country, the agreement acquires the force of law on the publication of the final statutory order as a statutory instrument.

A new treaty was signed on behalf of the governments of Ireland and the US on 28 July 1997. This treaty, having been ratified by the Dáil and the US Senate, came into force on 1 January 1998. The new treaty contains transitional provisions so that, for example, the old treaty can continue to apply for a further period of twelve months.

Several phrases in TCA 1997, s 826(1) merit further comment. Firstly, the authority given by the section is for the government to make arrangements in relation to "affording relief from double taxation". Then, when the required statutory order setting out the agreement with a particular country has been made, the terms contained therein are given the force of law "notwithstanding any enactment".

In effect, this means that the terms of a tax treaty may vary or override any rules that would otherwise apply under the Tax Acts, but usually only if the result is to provide a relief from Irish tax for a person who is "a resident of" (see **14.106**) the country with which the treaty in question has been made.

The terms of a treaty may override provisions of domestic legislation to the effect that they provide relief from taxation, whether for the benefit of a resident of Ireland or for a resident of the other country, but they cannot impose any new taxation or taxation additional to that already provided for under domestic legislation. It is common for certain articles in tax treaties to state that one, or both, of the contracting states "may" tax specified income in a particular way. This means that the country in question has the right to tax the income in that way, should it wish to do so, but it does not of itself impose any additional taxation to that already existing under domestic legislation.

TCA 1997, s 826 (1A) provides that where—

(a) the Government by order declare that arrangements specified in the order have been made with the government of any territory outside the State in relation to affording relief from double taxation of air transport undertakings and their employees in respect of all taxes which are or may become chargeable on profits, income and capital gains imposed by the laws of the State or the laws of that territory, and that it is expedient that those arrangements should have the force of law, and

(b) the order so made is referred to in Part 2 of Schedule 24A,

then, subject to this section and to the extent provided for in this section, the arrangements shall, notwithstanding any enactment, have the force of law as if each such order were an Act of the Oireachtas on and from the date of—

(i) the insertion of Schedule 24A into the Principal Act by paragraph (b), or

(ii) the insertion of a reference to the order into Part 2 of Schedule 24A,

whichever is the later.

TCA 1997, s 826 (1B) provides that where—

(a) the Government by order declare that arrangements specified in the order have been made with the government of any territory outside the State in relation to—

> (i) exchanging information for the purposes of the prevention and detection of tax evasion in the case of taxes of any kind or description imposed by the law of the State or the laws of that territory,

> (ii) such other matters relating to affording relief from double taxation as the Government considers appropriate, and that it is expedient that those arrangements should have the force of law, and

(b) the order so made is specified in Part 3 of Schedule 24A

then, subject to this section, the arrangements shall, notwithstanding any enactment, have the force of law as if each such order were an Act of the Oireachtas on and from the date of the insertion of a reference to the order into Part 3 of Schedule 24A.

TCA 1997, Schedule 2A is as follows:

SCHEDULE 24A

ARRANGEMENTS MADE BY THE GOVERNMENT WITH THE GOVERNMENT OF ANY TERRITORY OUTSIDE THE STATE IN RELATION TO AFFORDING RELIEF FROM DOUBLE TAXATION AND EXCHANGING INFORMATION IN RELATION TO TAX

PART 1

ARRANGEMENTS IN RELATION TO AFFORDING RELIEF FROM DOUBLE TAXATION IN RESPECT OF THE TAXES REFERRED TO IN SECTION 826(1), MADE BY THE GOVERNMENT AND SPECIFIED IN ORDERS MADE BY THE GOVERNMENT

1. The Double Taxation Relief (Taxes on Income and Capital) (Australia) Order 1983 (SI No 406 of 1983).

2. The Double Taxation Relief (Taxes on Income) (Republic of Austria) Order 1967 (SI No 250 of 1967) and the Double Taxation Relief (Taxes on Income and Capital Gains) (Republic of Austria) Order 1988 (SI No 29 of 1988).

3. The Double Taxation Relief (Taxes on Income) (Kingdom of Belgium) Order 1973 (SI No 66 of 1973).

4. The Double Taxation Relief (Taxes on Income and Capital Gains) (The Republic of Bulgaria) Order 2000 (SI No 372 of 2000).

5. The Double Taxation Relief (Taxes on Income and Capital Gains) (Government of Canada) Order 2004 (SI No 773 of 2004).

5A. The Double Taxation Relief (Taxes on Income and Capital Gains((Republic of Chile) Order 2005 (SI No 815 of 2005).

6. The Double Taxation Relief (Taxes on Income) (People's Republic of China) Order 2000 (SI No 373 of 2000).

7. The Double Taxation Relief (Taxes on Income and Capital Gains) (Republic of Croatia) Order 2002 (SI No 574 of 2002).

8. The Double Taxation Relief (Taxes on Income) (Cyprus) Order 1970 (SI No 79 of 1970).

9. The Double Taxation Relief (Taxes on Income and Capital) (Czech Republic) Order 1995 (SI No 321 of 1995).

10. The Double Taxation Relief (Taxes on Income) (Kingdom of Denmark) Order 1993 (SI No 286 of 1993).

11. The Double Taxation Relief (Taxes on Income and Capital Gains) (Republic of Estonia) Order 1998 (SI No 496 of 1998).

12. The Double Taxation Relief (Taxes on Income and Capital Gains) (Republic of Finland) Order 1993 (SI No 289 of 1993).

13. The Double Taxation Relief (Taxes on Income) (Republic of France) Order 1970 (SI No 162 of 1970).

14. The Double Taxation Relief (Taxes on Income and Capital and Gewerbesteuer (Trade Tax)) (Federal Republic of Germany) Order 1962 (SI No 212 of 1962).

15. The Double Taxation Relief (Taxes on Income and Capital Gains) (Government of the Hellenic Republic) Order 2004 (SI No 774 of 2004).

16. The Double Taxation Relief (Taxes on Income) (Republic of Hungary) Order 1995 (SI No 301 of 1995).

17. The Double Taxation Relief (Taxes on Income and on Capital) (Republic of Iceland) Order 2004 (SI No 775 of 2004).

18. The Double Taxation Relief (Taxes on Income and Capital Gains) (Republic of India) Order 2001 (SI No 521 of 2001).

19. The Double Taxation Relief (Taxes on Income) (Italy) Order 1973 (SI No 64 of 1973).

20. The Double Taxation Relief (Taxes on Income) (State of Israel) Order 1995 (SI No 323 of 1995).

21. The Double Taxation Relief (Taxes on Income) (Japan) Order 1974 (SI No 259 of 1974).

22. The Double Taxation Relief (Taxes on Income and Capital Gains) (Republic of Korea) Order 1991 (SI No 290 of 1991).

23. The Double Taxation Relief (Taxes on Income and Capital Gains) (Republic of Latvia) Order 1997 (SI No 504 of 1997).

24. The Double Taxation Relief (Taxes on Income and Capital Gains) (Republic of Lithuania) Order 1997 (SI No 503 of 1997).

25. The Double Taxation Relief (Taxes on Income and on Capital) (Grand Duchy of Luxembourg) Order 1973 (SI No 65 of 1973).

26. The Double Taxation Relief (Taxes on Income) (Malaysia) Order 1998 (SI No 495 of 1998).

27. The Double Taxation Relief (Taxes on Income and Capital Gains) (The United Mexican States) Order 1998 (SI No 497 of 1998).

28. The Double Taxation Relief (Taxes on Income and Capital) (Kingdom of the Netherlands) Order 1970 (SI No 22 of 1970).

29. The Double Taxation Relief (Taxes on Income and Capital Gains) (New Zealand) Order 1988 (SI No 30 of 1988).

30. The Double Taxation Relief (Taxes on Income and on Capital) (Kingdom of Norway) Order 2001 (SI No 520 of 2001).

31. The Double Taxation Relief (Taxes on Income) (Pakistan) Order 1974 (SI No 260 of 1974).

32. The Double Taxation Relief (Taxes on Income) (Republic of Poland) Order 1995 (SI No 322 of 1995).

33. The Double Taxation Relief (Taxes on Income) (Portuguese Republic) Order 1994 (SI No 102 of 1994) and the Double Taxation Relief (Taxes on Income) (Portuguese Republic) Order 2005 (SI No 816 of 2005).

34. The Double Taxation Relief (Taxes on Income and Capital Gains) (Romania) Order 1999 (SI No 427 of 1999).

35. The Double Taxation Relief (Taxes on Income) (Russian Federation) Order 1994 (SI No 428 of 1994).

36. The Double Taxation Relief (Taxes on Income and Capital Gains) (The Slovak Republic) Order 1999 (SI No 426 of 1999).

37. The Double Taxation Relief (Taxes on Income and Capital Gains) (Republic of Slovenia) Order 2002 (SI No 573 of 2002).

38. The Double Taxation Relief (Taxes on Income and Capital Gains) (Republic of South Africa) Order 1997 (SI No 478 of 1997).

39. The Double Taxation Relief (Taxes on Income and Capital Gains) (Kingdom of Spain) Order 1994 (SI No 308 of 1994).

40. The Double Taxation Relief (Taxes on Income and Capital Gains) (Sweden) Order 1987 (SI No 348 of 1987) and the Double Taxation Relief (Taxes on Income and Capital Gains) (Sweden) Order 1993 (SI No 398 of 1993).

41. The Double Taxation Relief (Taxes on Income and Capital) (Swiss Confederation) Order 1967 (SI No 240 of 1967) and the Double Taxation Relief (Taxes on Income and Capital) (Swiss Confederation) Order 1984 (SI No 76 of 1984).

42. The Double Taxation Relief (Taxes on Income and Capital Gains) (United Kingdom) Order 1976 (SI No 319 of 1976), the Double Taxation Relief (Taxes on Income and Capital Gains) (United Kingdom) Order 1995 (SI No 209 of 1995) and the Double Taxation Relief (Taxes on Income and Capital Gains) (United Kingdom of Great Britain and Northern Ireland) Order 1998 (SI No 494 of 1998).

43. The Double Taxation Relief (Taxes on Income and Capital Gains) (United States of America) Order 1997 (SI No 477 of 1997) and the Double Taxation Relief (Taxes on Income and Capital Gains) (United States of America) Order 1999 (SI No 425 of 1999).

44. The Double Taxation Relief (Taxes on Income) (Republic of Zambia) Order 1973 (SI No 130 of 1973).

45. The Double Taxation Relief (Taxes on Income) (Adjustment of Profits of Associated Enterprises) (European Community) Order 1994 (SI No 88 of 1994) as amended by the Double Taxation Relief (Taxes on Income) (Adjustment of Profits of Associated Enterprises) (European Communities) Order 2004 (SI No 40 of 2004), the Double Taxation Relief (Taxes on Income) (Adjustment of Profits of Associated Enterprises) (Republic of Austria, Republic of Finland and Kingdom of Sweden) Order 2004 (SI No 41 of 2004) and the Double Taxation Relief (Taxes on Income) (Adjustment of Profits of Associated Enterprises) (Accession States) Order 2006 (SI No 112 of 2006).

PART 2

ARRANGEMENTS, PURSUANT TO SECTION 826(1A) IN RELATION TO AFFORDING RELIEF FROM DOUBLE TAXATION OF AIR TRANSPORT UNDERTAKINGS AND THEIR EMPLOYEES, MADE BY THE GOVERNMENT AND SPECIFIED IN ORDERS MADE BY THE GOVERNMENT

Double Taxation Relief (Air Transport Undertakings and their Employees) (Union of Soviet Socialist Republics) Order 1987 (SI No 349 of 1987)

PART 3

ARRANGEMENTS, PURSUANT TO SECTION 826(1B) IN RELATION TO EXCHANGE OF INFORMATION RELATING TO TAX AND IN RELATION TO OTHER MATTERS RELATING TO TAX

TCA 1997, s 826(2) requires the rules of TCA 1997 Sch 24 to be applied in connection with the calculation of any foreign tax credit permitted under a relevant treaty. TCA 1997, s 826(3) approves any provision in a treaty which allows relief from tax for a period prior to the actual conclusion of that treaty. TCA 1997, s 826(5) permits the government to revoke any existing treaty by a subsequent statutory order (which must first be approved by a resolution of Dáil Éireann).

TCA 1997, s 826(9) authorises the Revenue Commissioners, if they think fit, to make regulations relating to the implementation of any double taxation agreement made under their enabling powers given by TCA 1997, s 826. To date, the Revenue Commissioners have not, it would appear, thought it necessary to make any regulations affecting any double taxation agreement covered by TCA 1997, s 826.

14.103 Tax treaties in force

Full double taxation agreements are in force with the following countries:

Country	Statutory Instrument
Australia	SI 1983/406
Austria (protocol SI 1988/29)	SI 1967/250
Belgium	SI 1973/66
Bulgaria	SI 2000/372
Canada	SI 2004/733
China	SI 2000/373
Croatia	SI 2002/574
Cyprus	SI 1970/79
Czech Republic	SI 1995/321
Denmark	SI 1993/286
Estonia	SI 1998/496
Finland	SI 1993/289
France	SI 1970/162
Germany	SI 1962/212
Greece	SI 2004/774
Hungary	SI 1995/301
Iceland	SI 2004/775
India	SI 2001/521
Israel	SI 1995/323
Italy	SI 1973/64
Japan	SI 1974/259
Korean Republic	SI 1991/290
Latvia	SI 1997/504
Lithuania	SI 1997/503
Luxembourg	SI 1973/65
Malaysia	SI 1998/495
Mexico	SI 1998/497
Netherlands	SI 1970/22
New Zealand	SI 1988/30

Country	Statutory Instrument
Norway	SI 2001/520
Pakistan	SI 1974/260
Poland	SI 1995/322
Portugal (protocol)	SI 1994/102
Romania	SI 1999/427
Russian Federation	SI 1994/428
Slovakia	SI 1999/426
Slovenia	SI 2002/573
South Africa	SI 1997/478
Spain	SI 1994/308
Sweden (protocol SI 1993/398)	SI 1987/348
Switzerland (protocol SI 1984/76)	SI 1967/240
UK (protocols SI 1995/209, SI 1998/494)	SI 1976/319
USA (protocol SI 1999/1425)	SI 1997/477
Zambia	SI 1973/130

New treaties with Georgia, Macedonia and Moldova, as well as a protocol to the existing treaty with South Africa, have been agreed and will be brought into force on completion of the appropriate legal requirements. New treaties with Argentina, Egypt, Kuwait, Malta, Morocco, Serbia, Singapore, Thailand, Tunisia, Turkey and the Ukraine are being negotiated. A treaty with Chile was signed in June 2005 but has not yet been ratified. A treaty with Vietnam was signed in 2008. The existing treaties with Cyprus, France, Germany, Italy and Korea are in the process of re-negotiation. Re-negotiation of the treaty with Switzerland is being considered. The treaty with the United States is due for re-negotiation in 2008.

Treaties which were in force prior to the enactment of the Corporation Tax Act 1976, and the Capital Gains Tax Act 1975, and which have not been replaced, or amended by protocols, continue to apply notwithstanding the substitution of corporation tax for income tax in the case of companies and the introduction of capital gains tax. These older treaties therefore have the disadvantage of not providing adequately for the Irish taxation system now in operation, principally in relation to capital gains tax.

Treaties coming into force or which were amended following the introduction of corporation tax and capital gains tax are those with Australia, Austria, Bulgaria, Canada (effective from 1 January 2006), China, Croatia, the Czech Republic, Denmark, Estonia, Finland, Hungary, India, Israel, the Republic of Korea, Latvia, Lithuania, Malaysia, Mexico, New Zealand, Norway, Poland, Portugal, Romania, Russia, the Slovak Republic, Slovenia, South Africa, Spain, Sweden, Switzerland, the UK and the US. (See **9.105** in relation to capital gains tax.)

A treaty signed on 17 December 1986 between the governments of Ireland and the former Soviet Union (USSR) is an agreement for the avoidance of double taxation of air transport undertakings and their employees.

14.104 OECD Model Double Taxation Convention

The Organisation for Economic Cooperation and Development ("OECD") approved in 1963 the text of a Draft Double Taxation Convention on Income and Capital that had been prepared by its Fiscal Committee. In 1977, the OECD Council approved the new

Model Double Taxation Convention on Income and on Capital – 1977 and recommended that OECD member countries should conclude any new tax conventions in accordance with the 1977 Model Convention.

In 1991, the Committee on Fiscal Affairs adopted the concept of an ambulatory Model Convention, providing periodic and timelier updates and amendments, and without waiting for a complete revision. In 1992, a version of the Model Convention in loose-leaf format was published. Rather than being the outcome of a comprehensive revision, this version was the first step of an ongoing process intended to produce periodic updates so as to ensure that the Model Convention would continue to reflect accurately the views of member countries at any point in time. In the update produced in 1997, the positions of a number of non-member countries on the Model Convention were added in a second volume in recognition of the growing influence of the Model Convention outside the OECD countries.

Double taxation treaties to a large extent adopt principles having fairly wide international acceptance regarding the manner in which relief for double taxation is to be implemented.

The fact that the OECD Convention is a model for tax treaties negotiated between different countries does not prevent variations in individual treaties negotiated between countries that accept its general principles; it is always necessary to have regard to the particular tax laws and the policies of the governments concerned in any bilateral treaty negotiations.

The Model Convention of 12 January 2003 is published, as were its predecessors, with a detailed commentary on each of its articles and is useful in elaborating on and explaining the intention behind each article. In some places, it refers to possible alternative approaches that certain countries may wish to adopt in treaties concluded by them. In the discussion that follows, any reference to the OECD Convention or to its commentary is, unless indicated otherwise, a reference to the 2003 Model Convention.

The OECD published an updated version of the Model Tax Convention in 2005 incorporating the latest changes to the Model which were approved by the OECD Council on 15 July 2005. This latest version includes changes made by a number of OECD and non-OECD countries to their observations, reservations or positions on the OECD Model Tax Convention. In addition, the positions of Serbia and Montenegro on the Model Tax Convention have been included.

14.105 Scope of agreements and taxes covered

Double taxation treaties generally adopting the principles of the OECD Model Convention commence with a "personal scope" article which provides that the agreement applies to persons who are residents of one or both of the contracting states. The effect of this article was generally considered to apply also for the purposes of most of the older treaties that do not contain a personal scope article. On that basis, unless any article in a treaty dealing with a particular class of income or capital gain provides otherwise, a resident of a third country, not being a party to the treaty, cannot claim any benefit from it.

In *IRC v Commerzbank* [1990] STC 285, however, it was held that a person resident in a third country could benefit from a tax treaty although the country of residence of that person was not a party to the treaty. (The treaty in question was the then UK-US tax treaty and the benefit in question, an exemption from tax on interest, would not be available under the current treaty in force.) The situation that arose in that case is unlikely to arise in connection with any of the more recent treaties which contain an express provision to the effect that the treaty in question is to apply to persons who are residents of one or both of the contracting states. Furthermore, TCA 1997 Sch 24 paragraph 3 provides that, subject to paragraphs 9A, 9B and 9C (which paragraphs, in the light of the *Saint-Gobain* case, extend the availability of credit relief to Irish branches of EU resident companies – see **14.209-10),** credit relief is confined to persons resident in the State.

In *Compagnie de Saint-Gobain, Zweigniederlassung Deutschland v Finanzamt Aachen-Innenstadt* (Case C-307/97) [2000] STC 854, a French company with a German branch claimed that certain provisions of German tax law were contrary to articles 43 and 48 (then 52 and 58 respectively) of the EC Treaty on the grounds that the related benefits were available to a German resident company but not to a German branch of a company resident in another EU country and that that position amounted to discrimination. The provisions in question included the exemption from German corporation tax in respect of dividends received from non-EU resident companies provided for under tax treaties and the tax credit available against German corporation tax in respect of underlying corporation tax on the profits of a foreign subsidiary. The European Court of Justice found in favour of the company.

Each tax treaty contains an article specifying the particular taxes of each of the two contracting states to which the agreement is to apply. The treaties concluded or amended from 1976 onwards specify the Irish taxes covered as being income tax, corporation tax and capital gains tax. The earlier treaties still in force specify the Irish taxes as being income tax (including surtax) and corporation profits tax, but provide that the treaty is to apply also to any identical or substantially similar taxes that may subsequently be imposed in addition to or in place of those in existence at the date the treaty was made.

In applying any existing treaty concluded prior to the introduction of corporation tax, references to the Irish surtax and corporation profits tax are no longer relevant. Corporation profits tax, previously relevant to the taxation of the income (but not capital gains) of companies, has been replaced by corporation tax since 6 April 1976. To the extent that it applies to the income of companies, corporation tax is regarded as a substantially similar tax to the former corporation profits tax, even though there were significant differences in the manner in which the former tax was levied. Irish capital gains tax is not generally considered to be a tax substantially similar to the taxes on income that are the only Irish taxes covered in the older treaties. Until these treaties are renegotiated and either amended or replaced by new treaties, therefore, they do not provide relief from double taxation in respect of capital gains.

However, in some of the renegotiated treaties, the double taxation relief in respect of taxes on capital gains may be given retrospectively from 6 April 1974. Thus, for example, the treaty of 2 June 1976 with the UK and the amended Swiss agreement of 24 October 1980 apply from 6 April 1974 as respects Irish capital gains tax and are also effective as regards corporation tax from the financial year 1974 onwards, thus providing double taxation relief in respect of corporation tax on capital gains (as well as on income) with effect from the first financial year for which such gains could be subject to that tax. On the other hand, the treaty of 18 May 1983 with Australia applies to Irish capital gains tax from 1984/85, ie for the tax year beginning in the calendar year following that in which the agreement was concluded; it does not apply to Australian capital gains tax.

Some countries subject income and/or capital gains to taxation at the state, provincial or municipal level in addition to that levied under the federal or national law. For example, most of the states in the US, provinces and territories in Canada and the cantons and municipalities in Switzerland impose income taxes on the basis of residence or source of income, or both. As to whether a resident of Ireland will be entitled to any relief in respect taxes at these levels depends on what taxes are covered in the "taxes covered" article in the relevant treaty. The treaty with Switzerland includes the Swiss cantonal and municipal taxes in the same way as it does the Swiss federal tax. Consequently, a person resident in Ireland who suffers Swiss federal, cantonal and/or municipal tax on any Swiss source income is entitled to include all these taxes in the Swiss tax for which he is entitled to a credit for set off against his Irish tax on the same income.

14.106 Definitions

Each tax treaty contains definitions of terms used for the purposes of the treaty. Generally, these definitions follow a standard format but there are variations which make it necessary to look to the individual treaty to ascertain the precise meaning of any word or expression which is relevant to the position of any person claiming relief under that treaty.

Resident of a contracting State

A feature common to most tax treaty articles is the regulation of the tax treatment of income or gains from sources in one of the contracting states which arises to a resident of the other contracting state. The definition in a treaty of the term "resident" in relation to each contracting state is applied for the purposes of the treaty generally. The treaty definition of "resident of Ireland" is not necessarily the same as the meaning of that term under Irish domestic tax law. It is possible for a person to be resident in Ireland under domestic tax law while not being so resident for the purposes of a tax treaty, and vice versa. While the treaty definition has to be used where it is applied in any relevant treaty article, it does not alter either state's domestic tax law definition of "resident" for other purposes.

The treaties which came into force prior to 1976, except that with Japan, define a "resident of Ireland" as a person who is resident in Ireland for the purposes of Irish tax and who is not resident in the other contracting state for the purposes of taxation in that country. Accordingly, it is necessary first to apply the Irish rules governing residence and then to ascertain whether or not the person in question is considered by the other state to be resident in its territory according to its rules. If resident on the basis of both tests, that person is not a resident of either country for the purposes of the treaty and will not benefit from any treaty article in respect of which residence is a requirement.

The treaty with Japan allows Ireland and Japan to apply their respective domestic tax laws first, but if that approach results in an individual being considered resident in both countries, the treaty then requires the "Competent Authorities" of the two countries to determine, by mutual agreement, the country of residence that is to apply for the purpose of the treaty. Unlike the later agreements (see below), the treaty with Japan does not prescribe any specific tests to determine the issue, but it is thought that in practice tests similar to those in the later treaties would probably be applied by the respective Competent Authorities.

Most of Ireland's tax treaties contain a "fiscal domicile" article in the form used in the OECD Model Convention. This commences by defining "resident of a contracting state" as meaning any person who under the laws of that state is liable to tax there by reason of his domicile, residence, place of management or any other criterion of a similar nature. A person is not, however, treated as a resident of a contracting state if the only reason he is liable to tax in that state is because he derives income (or capital gains) from sources there. This definition is generally read as meaning that, to be resident, the person in question must actually be liable to tax. Accordingly, in the cases of treaties containing this definition, entities not subject to Irish taxation, for example specified collective investment undertakings (see **12.805.2**), are denied treaty benefits.

There is an alternative view, cogently argued in *Klaus Vogel on Double Taxation Conventions*, to the effect that what the definition means is that a resident of a contracting state is a person who meets the locality-related criteria which, under the domestic law of that state, attract taxation as a resident. Thus, it is not a condition of residence that the person concerned is actually taxed but that the person has that personal attachment to the state that *might* result in him becoming subject to full tax liability. The fact that a person is actually subjected to taxation in a contracting state is no more than a strong indication of the legal pre-requisites for residence having been satisfied.

In the older treaties, the general approach is to treat a company as a resident of Ireland if its business is managed and controlled in Ireland, irrespective of the country of its incorporation. In some treaties, the reference is to the country in which the effective management of the company is situated, but this usually amounts to the same thing. The treaty with Japan is slightly different. Each country is to apply its own tests of residence first, and should these result in a company being resident in both Japan and Ireland, it is deemed for the purposes of the treaty to be a resident of the country in which its head office or main office is situated.

The main rule of the fiscal domicile article in the later treaties treats a company or other body corporate as being a resident of the contracting state in which it is liable to tax by reason of its domicile, residence, place of management or other criterion of a similar nature. In the event that the application of this main rule would result in a company being a resident of both contracting states, the place of residence is deemed to be the state in which its place of effective management is situated.

In the UK, the view of the Inland Revenue is that the place of effective management may differ from the place of central management and control. Thus, for example, a company run by executives who are based abroad would have its place of effective management abroad but, if the final directing power is exercised from the UK, the place of central management and control would be in the UK. The position in Ireland in this regard is less clear but, although the place of effective management and the place in which central management and control is exercised will be the same in most instances, it is unlikely that it could be held that they mean the same thing.

Territory of contracting State

The territory of a contracting state is defined in each treaty for each of the two contracting states. The definition usually consists of the name of the country concerned, but in some of the treaties, eg those with Australia and France, the foreign country is stated as including specified overseas departments or territories. A number of the treaties contain definitions that extend the territories of the contracting states to include that part of the continental shelf within which each state is entitled to exercise exploration and exploitation rights with respect to the seabed and subsoil and their natural resources. It has become normal practice to include this extension in treaties concluded from the early 1970s onwards. In the absence of any specific extension to bring in the continental shelf or any overseas territories, the territory of a country for purposes of a treaty is limited to its recognised land area (including any islands included therein) and its territorial waters.

Enterprise of a contracting State

"Enterprise of" in relation to a contracting state is defined simply as an enterprise carried on by a resident of either one of the states, depending on the context. For example, the reference in article 6 of the Ireland/ Switzerland tax treaty to an enterprise of a contracting state carrying on business in the other contracting state through a permanent establishment situated there may be taken as applying either to (a) an enterprise carried on by a resident of Ireland through a permanent establishment in Switzerland or (b) an enterprise carried on by a resident of Switzerland through a permanent establishment in Ireland.

In the Commentary to the Model Convention, it is stated that the question as to whether a commercial activity is to be considered to be part of an enterprise, or to be an enterprise, is a matter of domestic law. In *Thiel v FCT* [1990] 90 ATC 4717, the Australian High Court effectively held that an adventure in the nature of trade carried on by a resident of a treaty state could amount to an enterprise. In that case, because the resident carrying on the activity in question did not have a permanent establishment in Australia, he was entitled to exemption from Australian tax in accordance with the relevant treaty.

Contracting State

"Contracting state" is defined in each treaty as meaning either of the states whose governments have concluded the treaty, as the context may require.

Person

A "person" includes an individual, a company and any other body of persons.

Company

A "company" is defined in most of the treaties as including any body corporate or any entity which is treated as a body corporate for tax purposes. The commentary to article 3 of the OECD Convention indicates that it is the treatment as a body corporate according to the tax laws of the contracting state in which the entity is organised that determines the matter. For example, a building society organised under the Irish Building Societies Acts is a company for the purposes of Ireland's tax treaties as it is treated as a company under the Corporation Tax Act 1976.

Under Irish law, an overseas entity having a separate legal personality under its own legal system would generally be regarded as a body corporate for tax purposes (*Dreyfus v IRC* 14 TC 560, *Memec v IRC* [1998] STC 754). In other circumstances, where an entity is treated by the other treaty state as a body corporate tax resident in that state, the entity should qualify as a resident of that state for treaty purposes (see under *Resident of a contracting state* above).

Nationals

The term "national" is generally defined as including any legal person deriving its status as such from the laws in force in a contracting state. A company incorporated in Ireland, therefore, would be an Irish national, regardless of where it is resident.

Irish tax

"Irish tax" refers to any or all of the Irish taxes listed in the "taxes covered" article. For example, if a particular treaty article provides a relief from Irish tax in respect of capital gains, the article may be taken as applying either to capital gains tax or to corporation tax on chargeable gains. If the "taxes covered" article applies the treaty to any identical or substantially similar taxes introduced after the treaty was signed, the term "Irish tax" may be given a similar extended meaning.

Tax treaties usually contain a corresponding definition of "tax" in relation to the other treaty country. For example, the term "Swiss tax" in article 2 of the Ireland/ Switzerland agreement refers to the Swiss federal, cantonal and communal taxes listed in that article.

Terms not defined

As a general principle and unless the context otherwise requires, any term not specifically defined in a treaty is to be given the meaning which it has under the laws of the contracting state relating to the taxes which are the subject of that treaty. For example, if a resident of Belgium is affected by a treaty provision relating to the Irish taxation of an Irish item of income, the Irish meaning of the term is applied.

In *Padmore v IRC* [1989] STC 493, it was indicated that the context of the treaty concerned was such that the wider legal definition of "body of persons" might have to be applied in preference to the narrower tax definition. Where a domestic tax law definition is to be applied in any case, the appropriate definition is the one that is relevant to the particular tax provision which is the subject of treaty relief. The commentary to article 2 of the Model Convention suggests that where a tax law definition is altered subsequent to the conclusion of a treaty, it is the definition which is in force at the time the treaty is being applied which should be used (the "ambulatory" approach). On the other hand, an altered definition should not be applied where the context of the treaty indicates that the incorporation of a new definition would impair the balance or affect the substance of the treaty. It is also suggested that any difficulties arising by reason of the incorporation of a new tax definition into a tax treaty should be capable of resolution under the mutual agreement procedure.

It may happen that the tax systems of the two states that are parties to a tax treaty contain conflicting tax law definitions. The Irish Revenue have indicated that if the country of source in a treaty situation has exerted taxing rights on the basis of having classified income in a manner which is at variance with its Irish tax law definition, treaty relief will nevertheless be given.

In certain treaties, there will be an express provision to the effect that a term is to be defined by reference to the general law or to the tax law of one of the treaty states. For example, article 6 of the Model Convention provides that immovable property is to have the meaning it has under the law of the treaty state in which such property is situated.

In *Travers v O' Síocháin* 5 ITR 54, in connection with article 18 of the Ireland/UK treaty and the meaning of the expressions "local authority in the UK" and "functions of a governmental nature", Carroll J observed that neither was defined in the treaty but that the "terms not defined" article was not relevant as neither expression was defined in the context of Irish law. As the status of a "local authority" is dependent on the laws of the state in which it is established, the expression should be interpreted in the light of its legal meaning in the UK. On the other hand, the concept "functions of a governmental nature" did not bear a technical meaning and it was held that it must be interpreted generally so as to give it the same meaning in both treaty states; this is in accordance with article 33(3) of the Vienna Convention where it is stated that the terms of a treaty are presumed to have the same meaning in each text.

14.107 Elimination of double taxation

The elimination of double taxation through tax treaties is effected in two stages. Firstly, treaty articles which deal with specific classes of income or capital gains arising from sources in either of the two treaty countries and earned by a person who is a resident of the other country prescribe rules defining whether and to what extent the country of source may tax a resident of the other country in respect of the type of income or capital gain covered. Depending on the particular treaty and the type of income or gain, the country of source may be permitted by the treaty to tax the income or gain in full or up to a specified maximum rate of tax or, alternatively, may be required to exempt it from its tax regime altogether.

Secondly, the treaty article, usually headed "elimination of double taxation", sets out the way in which each contracting state grants double taxation relief to a person resident in its territory who has borne or paid tax in the other state in respect of income arising there. In general, the country of residence is only required to give relief for tax which the other country is entitled to charge in accordance with the particular articles in the treaty. Irish tax law applies this article, where appropriate, to give double taxation relief for the relevant foreign tax if the person claiming the relief is resident in Ireland (and also, in certain circumstances, to Irish branches of EU resident companies), even if not a "resident of" Ireland within the treaty definition of that term (TCA 1997 Sch 24 paragraph 3).

The OECD Model Convention provides two principal ways in which the elimination of double taxation article in a tax treaty may operate. These are referred to as the "exemption" and "credit" methods of double taxation relief. Under the exemption method, the country of residence does not tax any item of income that, in accordance with the treaty article dealing with the type of income in question, may be taxed in the country of source. Under the credit method, the country of residence includes the full income arising in the other country in the resident person's total income chargeable to income tax or corporation tax, but grants a credit for the foreign tax paid in the other country on the income. It is not necessary that the two contracting states should adopt the same method. It may be provided that one country will apply the exemption method, while the other will give relief under the credit method.

All the double taxation treaties adopted by the Irish government apply the credit method of granting double taxation relief to Irish resident persons who have paid tax in the other treaty country, but only for taxes properly paid in accordance with that country's taxing rights as provided for in the specific treaty articles. On the other hand, the method used by the other country in giving its residents relief for Irish taxes properly paid in accordance with the relevant treaty varies with the practice and law of the country concerned. For example, the UK, the US and Canada all adopt the credit method, while Belgium, Germany and Switzerland apply the exemption method.

The "elimination of double taxation" article in the tax treaties concluded by the Irish government requires the Irish Revenue to grant credit in respect of the relevant foreign tax against Irish tax on the foreign income in question "subject to the provisions of the law of Ireland regarding the allowance as a credit against Irish tax of tax payable in a territory outside Ireland". Irish tax law dealing with the way in which credits are given in respect of foreign tax against the corresponding Irish tax is contained mainly in TCA 1997 Sch 24. TCA 1997, Sch 24 paragraph 7 contains rules affecting the computation of income and chargeable gains in respect of which credit for foreign tax is to be allowed against Irish tax on that income or those chargeable gains.

The foreign tax credit rules in TCA 1997 Sch 24, in relation to any case in which a tax treaty applies, do not permit a credit against Irish tax for any tax paid in the other country that is not one of the taxes mentioned in the "taxes covered" article in the treaty with that country Any tax levied by the other country on any income in excess of the tax which that country is permitted to charge under the relevant treaty article is not eligible for credit against Irish tax. The Irish resident must seek a refund from the tax authorities of the other country in respect of any such excess tax paid.

14.108 Tax sparing

Some tax treaties contain "tax sparing" provisions which provide that income which has not borne tax in the source country because of economic incentive reliefs is not subject to further tax in the country of residence. TCA 1997, s 829 permits a credit against Irish tax to be given to a resident person in respect of tax under the law of a territory outside the State which would have been payable but for an incentive relief. This type of credit is given only in respect of foreign income received from another country with which there is a double taxation agreement specifically providing for this treatment.

The foreign tax which may be eligible for this treatment is tax normally payable under the domestic tax laws of the country concerned, but which is not in fact paid due to any relief from tax available in that country that is given with a view to promoting industrial, commercial, scientific, educational or other development in that country (TCA 1997, s 829(1), (2)). In other words, tax is "spared" by the foreign country under special tax incentive relief provisions broadly comparable with the Irish incentive reliefs such as manufacturing relief. The Irish government has sought to include in tax treaties, on a reciprocal basis, tax sparing articles which would enable residents of the other country to receive favourable treatment there in respect of income from investments in Irish tax relieved business operations. However, such reciprocation appears to be the exception rather than the rule. Tax sparing or "matching credit" is provided for in respect of income received in Ireland in four treaties.

In article 21 of the Ireland/ Cyprus tax treaty, Cyprus tax available for credit against Irish tax is deemed to include, inter alia, the Cyprus tax which would have been payable on any profit or interest normally taxable under Cyprus law, but which has been relieved from Cyprus tax due to certain specified tax incentive exemptions or reliefs. Similarly, the article grants a resident of Cyprus a credit against Cyprus tax for the Irish tax spared under certain of the Irish tax incentive reliefs (eg, manufacturing relief).

In the treaty with Pakistan, article 15 provides that creditable tax is deemed to include tax which would have been payable as Pakistan tax but for an exemption granted or a rebate in tax allowed under specified statutory provisions in force at the time the treaty came into force, or exemptions of a similarly character subsequently agreed.

The treaty with Korea has a general provision in article 23 under which creditable tax in Ireland may include tax reduced or eliminated as a result of economically based time limited incentives, but so that the deemed tax is limited to a maximum of 15% of profits.

In article 23 of the Ireland/ Denmark treaty, creditable tax in Ireland may include tax relieved on the profits of an enterprise that has benefited from a tax reduction for a limited period with the objective of encouraging economic development in Denmark.

14.109   Articles in tax treaties

14.109.1   Permanent establishment

Following the usage of the OECD Model Convention, each double taxation agreement contains an article dealing with "business profits". This article should be read in conjunction with the definition of "permanent establishment" which is usually dealt with in a separate article.

The general principle adopted in all the treaties is that the industrial or commercial or business profits of an enterprise carried on by a resident of one of the contracting states is not subject to tax in the other state, unless that enterprise carries on business in that other state through a permanent establishment situated therein. Accordingly, a company resident in Ireland is not taxable in respect of any business profits earned in the other country unless it carries on business in that country through a permanent establishment situated there. Conversely, a company resident in the other country must carry on business through a permanent establishment in Ireland before it can be subject to Irish corporation tax on its business profits. Thus, a non-resident company resident in a country having a tax treaty with Ireland might sell goods in Ireland under contracts made in Ireland, but if those transactions are not part of a trade carried on in Ireland through a permanent establishment that company will not be taxable in Ireland in respect of the profits arising.

The term *permanent establishment* as defined in each tax treaty means a fixed place of business through which the business of an enterprise is wholly or partly carried on. According to the Commentary to the OECD Model Convention, this general definition requires three factors to be present before there can be a permanent establishment in any country. Firstly, a place of business must exist in the country in question, but this may include any place or facility for doing business such as premises or, in certain instances, machinery or equipment. Secondly, the place of business must be "fixed", that is, it must be established at a distinct place with a certain degree of permanence. Thirdly, the enterprise must carry on at least some business through the fixed place of business (see also **3.107.2-107.3**) which means, usually, that persons who are dependent on the enterprise (personnel) conduct the business of the enterprise in the State in which the fixed place is situated.

Each treaty lists the items which can be regarded as a permanent establishment, for example, a place of management, a branch, an office, a factory or a workshop; a mine, an oil or gas well, a quarry or other place of extraction of natural resources; or a building site or construction or assembly project which exists for more than a stated number of months. It should be noted that any such fixed place will not amount to a permanent establishment unless the business of the company concerned is carried on through that place.

As to whether business is being carried on through a permanent establishment in a particular country will be determined by reference to the domestic laws of that country. Each country will have regard to its own legislation in deciding what constitutes the carrying on of a business in that country. The circumstances in which Irish tax law regards a non-resident company as exercising a trade within the State are discussed in **3.107**.

The permanent establishment rule is in fact reminiscent of the provision in TCA 1997, s 25 which is to the effect that a non-resident company is not chargeable to Irish corporation tax unless it carries on a trade through a branch or agency in the State. In most cases, a non-resident company which carries on a trade in the State through a branch or agency would be chargeable to Irish corporation tax under Irish tax law as well as under the permanent establishment definition in the relevant tax treaty.

It can happen, however, that a non-resident company that would be taxable under Irish law may not be subject to Irish corporation tax where that company is resident in a country with which Ireland has a tax treaty. This would be the case where the company sells goods in Ireland under contracts concluded in Ireland but where the sale transactions are not carried on through an Irish based permanent establishment.

All treaties provide that an agent or other person acting in one of the contracting states on behalf of an enterprise of the other contracting state may, depending on circumstances, be deemed to be a permanent establishment of that enterprise in the first mentioned State. An agent for this purpose does not include a broker, general commission agent or any other agent of independent status who acts for the foreign enterprise in the ordinary course of his business. Otherwise, an agent or other representative of the foreign company is deemed to be a permanent establishment of that company in the first-mentioned state if he has and habitually exercises in that state an authority to conclude contracts in the name of the company. However, if he does no more than purchase goods or merchandise for the enterprise, that is not on its own sufficient to make him a permanent establishment.

The "acting in the ordinary course of their business" test referred to above has been the source of much confusion and, indeed, the object of considerable criticism. The Commentary attempts to clarify this test but it still remains the case that the final position may depend on the legal tradition of the jurisdiction in question. The test has been interpreted to mean that an otherwise independent agent performing a business activity that is unusual for that agent will constitute a permanent establishment. This may be the case even where the activity in question, although unusual for the agent, is normal for the industry in question. Conversely, although the point is not as clear, it is probably correct that an independent agent will not constitute a permanent establishment where the activity is not usual for the industry in question but is customary for the agent.

For a company resident in one treaty country to be taxable in the other country, the Commentary to the OECD Model Convention indicates that the authority of the agent acting in the second mentioned country should extend to concluding contracts other than contracts relating to matters which are merely incidental to the non-resident's business. For example, if the agent's authority only extends to engaging employees for the non-resident's business, this would not be sufficient in itself to result in the agent being a permanent establishment. Generally, it may be taken that the agent's authority must extend to concluding contracts for sales. The OECD Commentary also concludes that before a permanent establishment may be said to exist the authority to conclude contracts must be habitually exercised.

Some treaties deem an agent to be a permanent establishment of the foreign enterprise if either he has and habitually exercises authority to conclude contracts for the enterprise or he has a stock of goods or merchandise from which he regularly fills orders on its behalf. For example, if a Japanese company has an agent in Ireland without any authority to conclude contracts, but who holds a stock of the Japanese company's goods within the country from which he fills orders from the company's customers, then the company is deemed to carry on business through a permanent establishment in the State, ie through the agent. A similar position applies in relation to the treaty with Pakistan.

"Permanent establishment" does not include the use of facilities solely for the purpose of storage, display or delivery of goods or merchandise belonging to the enterprise in question nor to the maintenance of a stock of goods or merchandise belonging to the enterprise solely for the purpose of storage, display or delivery. Neither will it include the maintenance of a fixed place of business solely for the purpose of carrying on, for the enterprise, any other activity of a preparatory or auxiliary character.

Most of the treaties to which Ireland is a party refer to a mine, oil well or other place of extraction or exploitation of natural resources within the State as being a permanent establishment. While some of the treaties do not mention a mine or oil well or other place of extraction, it is considered that the exploitation of natural resources carried out through a mine or quarry in the State is clearly an activity carried on through a fixed place of business since these items clearly amount to a fixed place of business.

Irish tax rules regarding the taxation of non-resident persons carrying out exploration or exploitation activities on the Irish sector of the Continental Shelf are dealt with in **3.107.1**. A non-resident person carrying on such activities on the Continental Shelf outside Irish territorial waters may by virtue of a tax treaty be exempted from Irish tax on his trading profits from those activities, depending on the terms of the treaty with his country of residence. The question depends on how the particular treaty defines the "territory of Ireland" or "Ireland".

Certain treaties provide that the term "Ireland" includes any area outside Irish territorial waters which in accordance with international law has been or may be designated, under the laws of Ireland concerning the Continental Shelf, as an area within which Ireland may exercise rights with respect to the seabed and subsoil of the Continental Shelf.

The permanent establishment article in these cases either includes in its definition a mine, quarry or other place of extraction of natural resources, or specifically provides that activities carried on in the State in connection with the exploration or exploitation of the seabed, subsoil or their natural resources in the State are to be treated as activities of a business carried on through a permanent establishment in the State. Where this approach is adopted therefore, the resident of the other treaty country remains liable to Irish taxation under TCA 1997, s 13 on the profits derived from its Irish continental shelf activities.

Other tax treaties do not extend the definition of the territory of Ireland to include the Irish sector of the continental shelf outside Irish territorial waters. In these cases, a company resident in the other treaty country is not liable to Irish corporation tax by virtue of TCA 1997, s 13, or under any other provision, in respect of the profits which may arise to it from any exploration or exploitation activities carried on by it outside Irish territorial waters, even where these activities are conducted in the Irish sector of the Continental Shelf. This of course assumes that the particular non-resident company does not have any fixed base or other place of business in the State itself from which the Continental Shelf activities are carried on. In the absence of any such fixed place of business within the State, a company resident in a country with which Ireland has a tax treaty does not have a permanent establishment in Ireland.

Electronic commerce: web-sites and servers

Members of the OECD Committee on Fiscal Affairs reached a consensus on how to apply one of the conditions that, under tax treaties, determine the right of a country to tax profits from electronic commerce. The Committee had been mandated to clarify how the definition of "permanent establishment" in the Model Convention applies in the context of electronic commerce, particularly in relation to the use of web-sites and servers. The consensus reached is reflected in amendments to the Commentary and the main elements are summarised below. The amendments deal exclusively with the definition of permanent establishment as it currently appears in article 5 of the Model Tax Convention.

While fixed automated equipment operated by an enterprise and located in a country may constitute a permanent establishment in that country, it is necessary to distinguish computer equipment which could in such circumstances constitute a permanent establishment and the data and software used by that equipment. Thus, for example, in the case of an internet web-site consisting of a combination of software and electronic data stored on and operated by a server, since the web-site would not involve any tangible property it could not of itself constitute a "place of business". The server through which the web-site is operated, however, is a piece of equipment requiring a physical location and therefore may well constitute a "fixed place of business". As regards being "fixed", what matters is not the possibility that the equipment in question may be moved around but whether in fact it is so moved. Accordingly, for a server to constitute a permanent establishment, it would need to be located at a certain place for a sufficient period of time so as to become fixed in the sense of being established at a distinct place with a certain degree of permanence.

It will frequently be the case that the enterprise that operates a server on which a web-site is hosted will not be the enterprise that carries on business through that web-site. If the server itself is not a fixed place of business of the enterprise carrying on the business, for example where it is rented to that enterprise, the mere operation of the web-site of that enterprise from a server located in that country cannot constitute a permanent establishment of the enterprise. It is common for the web-site through which an enterprise carries on its business to be hosted on the server of an internet service provider (ISP). In that case, the server and its location are not at the disposal of the enterprise, even if it may decide that its web-site should be hosted on that particular server. Since the web-site does not involve any tangible assets, the enterprise does not have any physical presence at the place in question.

Other than in very unusual circumstances, an ISP will not constitute an agent of an enterprise carrying on business through a web-site hosted on the ISPs server; either the ISP will not have authority to conclude contracts in the name of that enterprise and will not regularly conclude such contracts, or the ISP will be an independent agent acting in the ordinary course of its business of hosting web-sites of many different enterprises. Neither will the web-site itself constitute an agent of the enterprise since it is not itself a "person".

Automated equipment that does not require on-site human intervention for its operation may constitute a permanent establishment. Thus, it is not relevant as to whether equipment used for electronic commerce operations in a country is or is not operated and maintained by personnel who are residents of that country or who visit that country for that purpose.

A permanent establishment will not exist where the electronic commerce operations carried on through computer equipment located in a country are restricted to preparatory or auxiliary activities. Where the functions performed through the computer equipment include activities which in themselves form an essential and significant part of the commercial activity of an enterprise as a whole, they would be more than "preparatory or auxiliary" and, if the equipment constitutes a fixed place of business, it would accordingly amount to a permanent establishment.

A summary of the consensus reached by the members of the OECD Committee, as referred to above, is as follows:

* a web-site cannot, in itself, constitute a permanent establishment;
* a web-site hosting arrangement typically does not result in a permanent establishment for the enterprise that carries on business through that web-site;
* an internet service provider will not, except in very unusual circumstances, constitute a dependent agent of another enterprise so as to constitute a permanent establishment of that enterprise;
* a server located at a particular place long enough to be considered "fixed" can by itself constitute a permanent establishment depending on the specific nature of the business and the functions the server performs.

In the case of France, the view is that servers alone are auxiliary in character and cannot give rise to a taxable permanent establishment without further human activity. Sometimes, however, if a server alone completely performs the enterprise's core functions, it will constitute a permanent establishment.

It is understood that comments received from non-OECD countries indicate that the amendments to the Commentary reflect interpretations that have wide support among these countries.

Outsourcing of support services

The Authority for Advance Rulings ("AAR") in India handed down a landmark judgment in the case of Morgan Stanley & Co, a US investment bank ("Morgan Stanley") in the business of providing financial advisory services, corporate lending and securities underwriting services. Morgan Stanley outsources a wide range of high-end support services to its captive group company, Morgan Stanley Advantage Services Private Limited ("MSAS").

One of the daunting questions which the outsourcing industry has been confronted with is whether outsourcing to Indian companies, particularly to captive service providers/manufacturers would cause a permanent establishment ("PE") to come into existence. If Indian tax authorities were to hold that such activities would be tantamount to a PE, the global profits attributable to the PE would be taxable in India at the rate of approximately 41 % in the hands of the foreign entity. Further, the availability of tax credit for such tax paid in the home jurisdiction may be uncertain, thus potentially leading to double taxation and wiping out the economic advantage of outsourcing to India. On the other hand, if no PE exists, no profits can be subjected to Indian corporate tax.

Certain questions regarding the outsourcing arrangement were raised before the AAR, including:

1. Whether, in case it were to be held that there was indeed a PE in India, there would be anything further attributable to the PE if the PE were compensated at arm's length?

2. Whether the Applicant had a PE in India under the India-US tax treaty by virtue of MSAS being regarded as (i) its fixed place of business, (ii) a dependent agent, or (iii) constituting a service PE on account of deputation of its employees in India?

   The AAR held that the captive service provider, MSAS, was not a fixed place of business PE of Morgan Stanley, as it was not the business of Morgan Stanley that was carried out from there. It also held that MSAS would not constitute an agency PE of Morgan Stanley, one of the factors for this being that it did not have the authority to conclude contracts on behalf of Morgan Stanley.

As to whether, if a PE were held to exist, a portion of global profits of Morgan Stanley would be subject to tax in India where the Indian company was compensated at arm's length, the AAR responded in the negative. This finding will provide a welcome degree of certainty (for multinationals with operations in India at least) given that companies doing business with an associated company in India are required to comply with transfer pricing, and to compensate that company on an arm's length basis.

With regard to the exposure to a service PE arising out of the proposed deputation of personnel, the AAR held that the presence of employees for over 90 days would constitute a service PE in India. It rejected the contention that, as the deputed personnel were assigned to oversee the functioning of MSAS and to perform quality control and risk management services, they could not be said to be the employees of the Applicant even though their salaries were borne by the Applicant.

The outsourcing industry in India will welcome the assurance that outsourcing in itself does not expose the business income of multinationals to corporate tax in India. Though in India, an advance ruling is binding only on the Applicant it has significant persuasive value and plays a critical role in the evolution of international tax jurisprudence.

14.109.2 Business profits

Where a company resident in a country with which Ireland has a tax treaty carries on a trade through a permanent establishment in Ireland, the business profits article in the relevant treaty allows Ireland to tax that foreign company on its business profits, but only on so much of them as are attributable to the permanent establishment. In principle, the amount of the taxable profits of the business is ascertained under the ordinary rules of Schedule D Case I , but the business profits article in the treaty may apply some additional rules for this purpose.

All Ireland's treaties require the taxable profits of the permanent establishment of the foreign enterprise to be calculated on the assumption that the business of the permanent establishment is carried on as a distinct and separate enterprise, ie as one dealing wholly independently with the enterprise of which it is the permanent establishment. In other words, the taxable profits are computed on the basis that the prices charged to, or by, the permanent establishment for goods or services supplied by, or to, its foreign head office are the same as would apply in dealings between independent unconnected parties.

In most cases, there will be a provision that, for the purpose of calculating the taxable profits of the permanent establishment, deductions may be made for expenses incurred for the purposes of the permanent establishment including executive and general administration expenses, irrespective of whether incurred in the taxing state or elsewhere. For example, the Commentary to the OECD Model Convention indicates that in the case of general administration expenses incurred at the head office of the enterprise, it may be appropriate to deduct a proportionate part based on an appropriate ratio, eg the ratio of the turnover of the establishment to that of the enterprise as a whole. In practice, the taxation authorities of the country in which the permanent establishment is situated usually require to be satisfied that the amount charged for these expenses is fair and reasonable having regard to all the circumstances of the particular case.

The term "industrial and commercial profits" is separately defined in some treaties, but in the absence of any special reference in a treaty, it may be taken as including the taxable profits of all forms of trading activity except for types of income covered in separate articles. Almost all the treaties deal with the profits from ships and aircraft operated in international traffic under a separate article (see below).

While items of income dealt with under other articles in a treaty are not normally treated as business profits, most of the treaties provide that dividends, interest or royalties received by a resident of one of the countries are to be taxed as part of the profits of that permanent establishment under the business profits article if they are effectively connected with a permanent establishment in the other country In these cases, the business profits article operates in priority to the relevant dividend, interest or royalty article. For example, interest income earned by an Irish branch of a French banking company is chargeable to Irish corporation tax as part of that branch's banking profits. Consequently, the exemption from Irish tax otherwise given to a resident of France under the interest article in the Ireland/France treaty does not apply to that branch's interest income.

On April 10, 2007, the OECD released a draft of revised Commentary language on Article 7 of the Model Tax Convention relating to the attribution of business profits to permanent establishments ("PE"). The release follows the finalization of Part I, II and III of its Report on the Attribution of Profits to Permanent Establishments ("the Report") in December 2006. The draft is intended to reflect those changes and clarifications in the interpretation of Article 7 of the OECD Model Treaty that can be implemented without modification of the existing treaty language. The OECD intends to release later in 2007 a revised version of Article 7 and related Commentary that will incorporate all of the changes reflected in the Report.

The importance of this version of the draft commentary lies in the fact that the process of changing actual bilateral treaty language to reflect the consensus views set out in the Report will take many years. The final version of the revised Commentary is likely to guide tax authorities, including the Competent Authorities, in interpreting

Article 7 for some years to come, including how and to what extent the conclusions of the Report will be applied under existing treaties that contain OECD Model Treaty language. The intention to obtain consensus on the revised Commentary and applying the new agreed Commentary to existing treaties could be seen as potentially inconsistent with the approach to treaty interpretation followed by US Courts under reasoning in *National Westminster Bank plc v US*, No 95-758T (Fed Cl 2003) and other cases. In the *National Westminster* case, the US Federal Court of Claims stated that the 2001 draft version of the Report was "ultimately irrelevant" to the subject litigation because the document did not reflect the understandings and intent of the treaty partners at the time of ratification.

Separate entity approach

Article 7, paragraph 2, provides that the profits to be attributed to a PE are those which it would have made if, instead of dealing with the rest of the enterprise, it had been dealing with an entirely separate enterprise engaged in the same or similar activities under the same or similar conditions and dealing wholly independently with the rest of the enterprise of which it is a PE (the "separate entity approach"). This is referred to as the "central directive" on which the attribution of profits to a PE is intended to be based.

The draft Commentary confirms the applicability of the Report's two-step approach in calculating the profits attributable to a PE: the identification of the activities carried on through the PE, in particular the economically significant activities; and the determination of the remuneration to be attributed to those dealings with other parts of the enterprise applying, by analogy, the principles developed for the application of the arm's length principle to associated enterprises. According to the Report's two-step approach, in the area of financial services risks and assets are based on the "key entrepreneurial risk taking functions"; otherwise they are allocated as between PE and head office based on the "significant people functions".

The draft Commentary rejects the "force of attraction" approach whereby income, such as other business profits, dividends, interest and royalties, arising from sources in a territory is fully taxable even though not attributable to the PE in that territory. The generally accepted principle in double taxation conventions, the draft Commentary notes, is based on the view that the fiscal authorities of a country from which an enterprise of another country derives profits should look at the separate sources of profit that the enterprise derives from their country and should, without prejudice to other articles, apply the permanent establishment test to each such source. It also rejects an interpretation of Article 7 that would limit the attribution of income to a PE to the amount of the profits of the enterprise as a whole and confirms that there may be cases where the application of the article on a hypothetical separate entity basis may result in profits being attributed to a PE even though the enterprise as a whole has never made profits.

Profits attributable to dependent agent PE

The draft Commentary includes a new paragraph on the calculation of profits attributable to a dependent agent PE. Consistently with the Report, it indicates that the principles to be applied to dependent PEs are those used for other PEs. The activities of the dependent agent are identified through a functional and factual analysis that will determine the functions undertaken by the agent both on its own account and on behalf of the enterprise. The dependent agent and the enterprise constitute two separate potential taxpayers. The enterprise derives its own income or profits from its activities on its own account, the amount being determined under Article 9 and the arm's length principle. Thereafter, the profits attributable to the dependent agent PE are derived as follows: to the PE will be attributed the assets and risks of the enterprise relating to the functions performed on its behalf by the dependent agent, together with sufficient capital to support those assets and risks; profits will be attributed to the PE on the basis of those assets, risks and capital. Those profits will be separate from and will not include the income or profits properly attributable to the dependent agent itself.

Deductions

Article 7, paragraph 3, provides for the allowance, as deductions, of expenses incurred for the purposes of a PE, including executive and general administrative expenses so incurred (for example, a proportion of head office administrative expenses calculated on a turnover or other suitable basis). The draft Commentary notes that this provision only determines which expenses should be attributed to the PE but does not state that those expenses, once attributed, are deductible when computing the taxable income of the PE since the conditions for deductibility are a matter to be determined by domestic law.

Article 7, paragraph 2, establishes the "separate entity" approach to allocating income to a PE while paragraph 3, on the other hand, appears to suggest that deductions are most appropriately dealt with by allocating administrative and other head office costs to the PE at cost, normally without adding any profit element. The draft Commentary, while acknowledging that the application of paragraph 3 may raise some practical difficulties, especially in relation to the separate enterprise and arm's length principles underlying paragraph 2, sees no inherent conflict between these paragraphs and suggests that there is no difference in principle between them. Some costs are best charged at cost while others are best charged at a profit. The draft Commentary on paragraph 3 relating to expenses is mostly left unchanged, except for the part relating to interest expense (discussed below). There is no clear conclusion as to when companies must charge a profit mark-up on head office expenses charged to a PE.

Interest expense

The treatment of the attribution of interest expense in the Commentary is revised to reflect the approach taken in the Report. Apart from the case of financial enterprises such as banks, it is generally agreed that internal "interest" charged by a head office to its PE with respect to internal "loans, such interest need not be recognised because, from a legal standpoint, such an approach is incompatible with the true legal nature of a PE. Furthermore, internal debts and receivables may prove to be non-existent: if an enterprise is solely or predominantly equity funded, it should not be permitted to deduct interest charges that it has clearly not had to pay.

The draft Commentary takes account of the fact that, in order to carry out its activities, a PE requires a certain amount of funding made up of "free" capital and interest-bearing debt. An arm's length amount of interest should accordingly be attributed to the PE after attributing an appropriate amount free capital to support the functions, assets and risks of the PE. As in the Report, the Commentary suggests that there are different acceptable approaches for attributing "free" capital.

Intangible assets

The draft Commentary leaves virtually unchanged the paragraph on intangible rights (with their related development costs). It is suggested that it is difficult to allocate "ownership" of intangible rights solely to a single part of an enterprise and to argue that this part should receive royalties from the other parts as if it were an independent enterprise, and that it would be appropriate to allocate between the various parts of the enterprise the actual costs of the creation or acquisition of such intangible rights, as well as the costs subsequently incurred with respect to these intangible rights, without any mark-up for profit or royalty.

Given the general approach of the Report envisaging the implementation of personnel related principles in other areas, it might have been expected that such principles would be applied also in relation to intangible property so as to provide for the allocation of assets and risks by reference to the location of personnel related activities. The retention of the status quo in this regard may amount to an invitation to some countries to seek to allocate income related to intangibles to a dependent agent PE even where that PE plays no part in the development of the intangible assets in question.

14.109.3   Shipping and air transport

In most tax treaties, the business of operating ships or aircraft in international traffic is dealt with separately from other types of trade. The permanent establishment rule is considered inappropriate to the circumstances of that kind of business. An international shipping or air transport operation usually involves the enterprise in having offices and/ or other facilities in a number of countries and in concluding contracts in more than one country to carry passengers and/ or cargo between two or more countries. In the absence of special treatment in double taxation agreements, an international transport enterprise could be liable to tax on its profits in a number of countries in respect of the same activities (due to having permanent establishments, such as a booking office, in each).

Most of the treaties provide that the profits of ships and aircraft in international traffic are to be taxable only by the state in which the place of effective management of the enterprise is located, but several of the treaties differ in this respect. The treaty with Pakistan, for example, gives the sole taxing right to the country of residence of the enterprise but, in the case of shipping, makes this conditional on the presence in the country of residence of the port of registry of the ships involved.

Alternatively to referring to the place of effective management, some of the treaties (eg, the treaty with Sweden) provide that profits from the operation of ships or aircraft in international traffic derived by an enterprise of one of the contracting states are to be taxable only in that state. In most cases, the effect is the same due to the definition of an enterprise of a contracting state as being an enterprise carried on by a resident of that state, with the definition of residence being related, in the case of a company, to the country in which its place of effective management is situated.

The shipping and air transport article in a treaty normally applies only where international traffic is involved. Most treaties apply the article only to transport operations that are not solely between places in one of the contracting states.

The Commentary to the OECD Model Convention indicates that the phrase "profits from the operation of ships or aircraft in international traffic" is intended to cover not only profits from the carriage of passengers or cargo, but also profits obtained by leasing a ship or aircraft on charter fully equipped, manned and supplied. On the other hand, the article is not intended to apply to profits from leasing a ship or aircraft on a "bareboat charter" basis (to which, therefore, the Business Profits article applies), except where this is only an occasional source of income for an enterprise engaged in the international operation of ships or aircraft. Where the international transport includes the delivery of goods directly to the consignee in a different country, the inland transportation necessary to effect this delivery is also intended to be covered by the article, as are certain other activities, eg the leasing of containers, if supplementary or incidental to the international traffic operations.

14.109.4 Associated enterprises

The associated enterprises article may be relevant in any case where two associated enterprises trade or have other commercial or financial dealings with each other on terms different from those that would apply in similar transactions or dealings between independent enterprises. An enterprise of one contracting state is treated, for the purposes of this article, as associated with the enterprise of the other state if:

(a) either one of the two enterprises participates directly or indirectly in the management, control or capital of the other enterprise; or

(b) the same persons participate directly or indirectly in the management, control or capital of each of the two enterprises.

If the result of any non-arm's length transactions between two such associated enterprises is that a lesser amount of profits accrues to one of the enterprises than would have accrued if the dealings had been at arm's length, the "associated enterprises" article permits the state which would otherwise lose tax as a result of the understatement of profits to adjust the amount of the taxable profits of its resident enterprise. This rule is most likely to have effect in relation to the pricing of goods transferred between associated enterprises in the course of their trading activities, but it may apply also to any other business transactions such as inter-company services, interest on loans, royalties for the use of patents and leasing of equipment.

While an article in a tax treaty may permit a contracting state to tax income in a particular way, it is also necessary that the domestic tax law of the state in question contains rules under which the income is taxable in that state. Irish tax legislation does not, generally, contain transfer pricing provisions and for this reason the Irish tax authorities may not be in a position to invoke the associated enterprises article to adjust profits where it is considered that the related transactions have not been conducted using arm's length prices.

Assuming the associated enterprises article has been used to adjust the profits of a company for Irish corporation tax purposes, double taxation will occur if the profits of the company in the other country are not correspondingly reduced. Not all of Ireland's tax treaties require the other contracting state to make a compensating adjustment to the taxable profits of the associated enterprise resident in its territory. Those which do contain such a requirement include the treaties with Australia, Canada (new treaty), the Czech Republic, Denmark, Finland, Greece, Hungary, Israel, Latvia, Lithuania, Malaysia, Mexico, New Zealand, Poland, Portugal, Romania, the Slovak Republic, South Africa, Spain, Sweden, the UK and the US, in each of which there is a provision requiring the other country to give such relief.

The treaty with the UK requires the contracting state in the other country to make the compensating adjustment by a reduction in the tax payable by the associated enterprise resident in its territory. The adjustment is made through an extension of the foreign tax credit rules under the elimination of double taxation article (article 21) in the agreement. This is explained in **14.110.4**.

14.109.5   Dividends

Most countries impose withholding taxes on dividends paid by companies within their territories to persons resident in other countries. From 6 April 1999, dividends and other distributions paid by Irish resident companies to certain non-residents are subject to withholding tax (see **11.116**). Where a tax treaty is not in force, a non-resident individual in receipt of Irish source dividends is liable to tax on such dividends at the higher rate of income tax.

Tax treaties contain articles which vary the domestic rules of taxation in each of the contracting states in respect of dividends. In general, these articles provide that the contracting state in which the dividend arises should either exempt the dividend from its taxes or tax the dividend at a reduced rate, if the person beneficially entitled to it is a resident of the other state. In practice, some countries operate a procedure whereby the treaty relief or exemption may be obtained in advance so as to obviate the need to withhold tax at the time of payment of the dividend, whereas in other cases the normal withholding taxes are imposed and the resident of the other country is obliged to claim repayment of the tax from the country from which the dividend arose.

There are specific procedures in force for the purpose of enabling dividends and other distributions to be paid by Irish companies to certain non-residents free of withholding tax (see **11.116.6**).

Position up to 5 April 1999

Prior to 6 April 1999, a tax charge under Schedule F (see **11.110**) was imposed on non-residents in respect of the aggregate amount of dividends and related tax credits received from Irish resident companies (TCA 1997, s 20(1)). There was a theoretical income tax liability in these cases but this was eliminated by way of a reduction in the amount of tax equal to that liability (TCA 1997, s 153(1)). A more detailed treatment of the position obtaining prior to 6 April 1999 is contained in earlier editions of this book.

Dividends: position from 6 April 1999

With effect from 6 April 1999, certain non-residents are exempted from Irish income tax in respect of distributions made to them by Irish resident companies. The exemption applies to those non-residents who are exempted from dividend withholding tax (see **11.116.6**).

TCA 1997, s 153(4) provides that where the income of a non-resident person (as defined – see below) includes an amount in respect of a distribution made by an Irish resident company—

(a)   income tax is not to be chargeable in respect of that distribution; and

(b)   the amount or value of the distribution is to be treated for the purposes of TCA 1997 ss 237 and 238 (see **4.302** and **4.303**) as not brought into charge to income tax.

For this purpose, a *qualifying non-resident person* in relation to a relevant distribution is a person beneficially entitled to the relevant distribution and who is—

(a)   a person, other than a company, who—

    (i)   is neither resident nor ordinarily resident in the State, and

    (ii)   is, by virtue of the law of a relevant territory, resident for the purposes of tax in that territory, or

(b)   a company which is not resident in the State and—

    (i)   is, by virtue of the law of a relevant territory, resident for tax purposes in that territory, but is not under the control, directly or indirectly, of a person or persons who is or are resident in the State,

    (ii)   is under the control, directly or indirectly, of a person or persons who, by virtue of the law of a relevant territory, is or are resident for tax purposes in that territory and who is or are not under the control, directly or indirectly, of a person or persons who is or are not so resident, or

    (iii)   the principal class of the shares of which, or—

        (I)   where the company is a 75% subsidiary (see **2.503**) of another company, of that other company, or

        (II)   where the company is wholly-owned by two or more companies, of each of those companies,

is substantially and regularly traded on one or more than one recognised stock exchange in a relevant territory or territories, or on such other stock exchange as may be approved by the Minister for Finance for the purposes of TCA 1997, s 153 (TCA 1997, s 153(1)).

In determining whether or not a company is a 75% subsidiary or another company for the purposes of (b)(iii)(I) above, the equity entitlement provisions of TCA 1997 ss 412-418 (see **8.305**) apply as they would apply for the purposes of group relief if TCA 1997, s 411(1)(c) were deleted (ie, ignoring requirements relating to EU residence and to shares held as "trading stock" – see **8.302.2-302.3**) (TCA 1997, s 153(3)).

In determining whether a company is wholly-owned by two or more companies for the purposes of (b)(iii)(II) above, the company (referred to as an "aggregated 100% subsidiary") is to be treated as being wholly-owned by two or more companies (referred to as the "joint parent companies") if and so long as 100% of its ordinary share capital is owned directly or indirectly by the joint parent companies, and for this purpose—

(a)   subsections (2) to (10) of TCA 1997, s 9 are to apply as they apply for the purpose of that section (meaning of "subsidiary" – see **2.505**); and

(b)   TCA 1997 ss 412-418 (see **8.305**) apply with any necessary modifications as they would apply for the purposes of group relief—

    (i)   if TCA 1997, s 411(1)(c) were deleted (ie, ignoring requirements relating to EU residence and to shares held as "trading stock" – see **8.302.2-302.3**), and

    (ii)   if TCA 1997, s 412(1) (the wording in which would be inappropriate to the position of joint parent companies – see **8.304.1**) were substituted by a subsection to the following effect:

Notwithstanding that at any time a company is an aggregated 100% subsidiary of the joint parent companies, it is not to be treated at that time as such a subsidiary unless additionally at that time—

(I) the joint parent companies are between them beneficially entitled to not less than 100% of any profits available for distribution to equity holders of the company, and

(II) the joint parent companies would be beneficially entitled between them to not less than 100% of any assets of the company available for distribution to its equity holders on a winding up (TCA 1997, s 153(3A)).

A *relevant territory* means a Member State of the European Communities other than Ireland, or a territory (not being such a Member State) with the government of which arrangements having the force of law by virtue of TCA 1997, s 826(1) have been made (ie, with which Ireland has concluded a tax treaty).

Tax in relation to a relevant territory means any tax imposed in that territory which corresponds to income tax or corporation tax in the State.

See **11.116.6** for more detailed treatment of this topic.

General

Where an Irish resident receives a dividend from a company resident in the other treaty country, most treaties permit the country of source to tax the dividend, but subject to a maximum rate. A number of the treaties prescribe a lower maximum rate of tax, or provide for complete exemption, in the case of an Irish resident company holding a minimum proportion of share capital in the dividend paying company. For example, the maximum rate of Swiss tax payable on Swiss company dividends to shareholders who are residents of Ireland is 15%, but if the recipient is a company which controls directly or indirectly at least 25% of the voting power in the Swiss company, the Swiss tax is limited to a maximum rate of 10%.

Most treaties, particularly the later treaties, exclude from the operation of the "dividends" article any amounts paid in respect of shares the holding of which is "effectively connected with" or "attributable to" a business which the shareholder carries on through a permanent establishment in the country from which the dividends are derived. In any such case, the dividends are taxable in the country of source under the "business profits" article in the relevant treaty. Consequently, the non-resident, in the case of a dividend received before 6 April 1999, would not have been entitled to any payment of the Irish tax credit that might otherwise have been available.

Example 14.109.5.1

Rehnskjold AB, a Swedish resident company, owns 7.5% of the voting power in Corona Ltd, an Irish resident company liable to tax at the standard corporation tax rate. Rehnskjold AB, which carries on a trade in Ireland through a permanent establishment, receives various dividends from Corona Ltd. The acquisition of the 7.5% interest in Corona Ltd was sourced out of profits generated by the permanent establishment trade.

Assuming that the business of Corona Ltd is similar to that carried on through the permanent establishment and that the decision to invest in that company was occasioned by that fact, it may be concluded that the shareholding is effectively connected with the permanent establishment trade. The dividends received are treated as income of the Irish trade and are covered by the business profits article of the Ireland/ Sweden tax treaty.

Although article 8, by virtue of article 11, of the Ireland/ Sweden tax treaty permits Ireland to tax Rehnskjold AB on the dividend as income effectively connected with its Irish permanent establishment, distributions from Irish resident companies are not chargeable to corporation tax (TCA 1997, s 129) so that Rehnskjold AB is not taxable in respect of the dividend received from Corona Ltd.

Later treaties define the term "dividend", as it is to be applied in relation to Irish tax, as including any item which under the law of Ireland is treated as a distribution, or as income from shares, including any income or distribution "assimilated to" income from shares under Irish tax law. The definition therefore brings within the term "dividend" any distribution of an Irish resident company that is treated as such by TCA 1997, s 130 (see discussion in **11.106** on this point). A "dividend" received by an Irish company from a company resident in a foreign country includes any payment treated as such under the law of the country in question.

In article II of the Ireland/ Germany tax treaty, *dividends* is stated to include, in the case of Germany, profits distributed by a "Gesellschaft mit beschränkter Haftung" (GmbH), or limited liability company, and distributions on investment trust certificates and income derived by a sleeping partner from his participation as such. In relation to the last-mentioned item, the question arose in *Memec plc v IRC* [1998] STC 754 as to whether that meaning of "dividends", which appears in identical terms in article VI of the UK/ Germany treaty, could be applied for the purposes of article XVIII (credit relief for underlying tax) of that treaty, although the definition in article VI was not expressly made applicable to article XVIII.

In the *Memec* case, a UK parent company, Memec plc, and its wholly owned German subsidiary, Memec GmbH, had entered into a silent partnership arrangement under which Memec plc, the "silent" partner (sleeping partner), was entitled to most of the profits of Memec GmbH which in turn consisted of dividends from two wholly owned German trading companies. It had been held in the Chancery Division that "dividends" for the purposes of article XVIII included the distribution of silent partnership profits but this conclusion was rejected in the Court of Appeal. Memec plc failed in its appeal (both in the Chancery Division and in the Court of Appeal) to obtain credit for underlying tax (consisting of corporation tax and trade tax paid by the two German trading subsidiaries). That tax had not been paid by Memec GmbH itself and, to obtain relief for such tax, it was necessary to rely on domestic UK legislation (as well as on the treaty). For the purposes of that legislation, "dividends" could not be given the wider treaty meaning to include a distribution of silent partnership profits; the term would have to be confined to the commonest form of distributions made by companies.

14.109.6 Interest and royalties

Most countries impose withholding taxes on interest and royalties paid from sources within their territories to persons resident in other countries. Irish tax law follows this practice in the case of annual interest paid to a person whose usual place of abode is outside the State and for patent royalties paid to a non-resident (see **4.303**, **4.304** and **4.306**). Where a tax treaty is not in force, a non-resident individual in receipt of Irish source interest or royalties is liable to tax on such income at the higher rate of income tax.

Tax treaties contain articles which vary the domestic rules of taxation in each of the contracting states in respect of interest and royalties. In general, these articles provide that the contracting state in which the income arises should either exempt the income from its taxes or tax the income at a reduced rate if the person beneficially entitled to it is a resident of the other state. In practice, some countries operate a procedure whereby the treaty relief or exemption may be obtained in advance so as to obviate the need to withhold tax at the time of payment of the income in question, whereas in other cases the normal withholding taxes are imposed and the resident of the other country is obliged to claim repayment of the tax from the country from which the income arose.

In the case of Irish source interest and royalties, the Revenue Commissioners are prepared to authorise the Irish resident person making the payment not to withhold tax on payment or to apply a lower treaty rate, where appropriate. For this purpose, a company resident in the other country should complete an appropriate claim form and have it certified by the tax authorities of its country of residence to the effect that it is resident there and entitled to benefit from the relevant article in the treaty. On presentation of the certified form to the residence branch of the Irish tax authorities, that branch will, if satisfied that the claim is in order, authorise the payer of the interest or royalty to make the payment gross or subject to withholding at the appropriate reduced rate.

Interest

In the cases of most of the tax treaties concluded by the Irish government, interest income is taxable in the country in which the recipient is resident. Some treaties, for example, those with Australia, Belgium, Italy and Japan give the source country a restricted right to impose tax in respect of interest. In the case of the Ireland/ Belgium tax treaty, instead of the more usual provision whereby interest arising in one of the countries is totally exempt from tax there, a resident of one country deriving interest income from the other country is subject to tax in that other country at a maximum rate of 15%. The treaty with New Zealand allows each contracting state to impose tax at a rate not exceeding 10% on New Zealand source interest arising to a resident of Ireland.

The treaty with Pakistan requires the country of residence of the recipient to exempt interest income from its tax if the interest has been taxed in the source country. In the case of interest paid or guaranteed by the government of the country of source, the treaty gives the sole taxing right to that country. Since Ireland does not impose any taxation on interest on government securities beneficially owned by a person not ordinarily resident in the State, a resident of Pakistan may be exempt from both Irish and Pakistan tax in respect of interest from Irish government securities.

A typical definition of "interest" in tax treaties is that appearing in the Ireland/ Sweden treaty which is as follows:

> income from debt-claims of every kind, whether or not secured by mortgage and whether or not carrying a right to participate in the debtor's profits, and in particular, income from government securities and income from bonds or debentures, including premiums and prizes attaching to such securities, bonds or debentures, but does not include any income dealt with in article 11 [dividends].

It is usual in later treaties, as in the above case, to find that "interest" does not include any income which is treated as a dividend in the relevant dividends article. The dividends article will then include in the meaning of "dividends" any item which under the law of Ireland is treated as a distribution, such as interest on certain securities treated as a distribution by TCA 1997, s 130.

In the absence of a provision on the above lines, the treaty provisions relating to interest will continue to apply, even where the interest is treated as a distribution for Irish tax purposes (*Murphy v Asahi Synthetic Fibres* ITR Vol III 246). The fact that the interest article applies for treaty purposes does not affect the treatment of that interest for domestic Irish tax purposes. Tax treaties do not oblige the contracting states to re-characterise transactions for the purposes of applying their domestic tax provisions. Each country will in the first instance apply its own tax rules in relation to the transaction in question and then have regard to the treaty for the purpose of ascertaining the tax credit or exemption position in relation to that transaction. In practice, however, where the relevant tax treaty was concluded prior to the enactment of the Corporation Tax Act 1976, and has not been amended so as to include a provision as described above, the Revenue Commissioners treat interest paid by an Irish resident company to a company resident in the other treaty state, for corporation purposes generally, as not being a distribution (see also **11.106**).

Most of the tax treaties to which Ireland is a party exclude from the operation of the "interest" article any interest on a debt claim that is "effectively connected with" or "attributable to" any business which the recipient of the interest carries on through a permanent establishment in the country of source. In any such case, the interest is taxable under the "business profits" article and the treaty exemption, or reduced tax rate as the case may be, available in respect of interest does not apply.

A resident of one of the contracting states is generally entitled to the treaty exemption or reduced rate of tax if the interest arises in the other state. In later treaties, it is usually necessary that the resident person is the "beneficial owner" of the interest. It is not, generally, necessary that the person making the payment should be a resident of the source country. For example, a UK resident is entitled to receive without liability to Irish tax interest which is paid by an Irish branch of another UK company, or even an Irish branch of, say, of a Slovakian company.

In the case of the Ireland/Sweden tax treaty, however, it is provided in the interest article that interest is normally deemed to arise in the country of residence of the payer but that, if the payer has a permanent establishment or fixed base in the other country, it is deemed to arise in that country if it arises on indebtedness connected with that permanent establishment or fixed base and if the interest is borne by the permanent establishment or fixed base. If, for example, a Slovakian company carrying on a trade through a fixed base in Ireland pays interest to a Spanish resident company on a loan obtained by that fixed base for the purposes of the trade, and provided the interest is borne by the fixed base, the interest is within the scope of the Ireland/ Spain tax treaty and the Spanish company is not liable to Irish tax in respect of the interest.

Where there is a special relationship between the payer and the recipient of interest, the application of the relevant interest article may be restricted. In such cases, most treaties provide that any interest which is in excess of a fair and reasonable consideration for the use of the money or of the other benefits provided is not entitled to benefit from the treaty, so that the excess amount of interest is subject to normal taxation in the country of source.

In later treaties, it is becoming usual to include an anti-avoidance provision in the interest article. For example, in article 12 (interest) of the Ireland/ UK treaty, it is provided that the article will not apply if the debt-claim in respect of which the interest is paid was created or assigned mainly for the purpose of taking advantage of that article and not for *bona fide* commercial reasons. A similar article appears in the Ireland/ New Zealand treaty. A notable example is the limitation on benefits article in the new Ireland/ US treaty (see **14.111.10**).

The anti-avoidance treaty provisions are directed primarily at so-called "treaty-shopping" arrangements. For example, if A Ltd in Country A would have to withhold tax on interest payable to B Ltd in Country B, in the absence of a tax treaty with Country B, it might be arranged to use I Ltd in Ireland as a conduit for the interest payment on the basis that the Country A and Country B treaties with Ireland allow for the payment of interest without deduction of tax. Accordingly, borrowings would be re-arranged so that A Ltd would pay interest to I Ltd which would in turn pay equivalent interest to B Ltd. Where included in a tax treaty, the anti-avoidance provision will deny treaty benefits in such situations.

Royalties

With some exceptions, the treatment of royalties in tax treaties is to allow them to be taxed only in the country in which the recipient of those royalties is resident. The source country is given a restricted right to impose tax in a number of treaties, for example, the treaties with Australia and Japan which permit the country of source to charge tax at a maximum rate of 10%. The treaties with Pakistan and the US allow the country of source to tax royalties receivable by a resident of the other country, but only where that person is engaged in trade or business in the country of source and where the royalties are attributable to that trade or business.

In later treaties, it is usually necessary that the resident person is the "beneficial owner" of the of the royalties. It is not, generally, necessary that the person making the payment should be a resident of the source country. For example, a Portuguese resident is entitled to receive without liability to Irish tax royalties which are paid by an Irish branch of another Portuguese company, or even an Irish branch of, say, of a Brazilian company.

As with most items of income dealt with in a treaty article, the definition of "royalty" generally follows a fairly standard form. The following definition from the Ireland/ Norway treaty is typical:

> payments of any kind received as consideration for the use of, or the right to use, any copyright of literary, artistic or scientific work (including cinematograph films and films or tapes for radio or television broadcasting), any patent, trademark, design or model, plan, secret formula or process, or for the use of, or the right to use, industrial, commercial, or scientific equipment, or for information concerning industrial, commercial, or scientific experience.

This definition broadly follows the definition in the OECD Model Convention. The commentary to that Convention confirms that the definition is intended to include not only patent and copyright royalties, but also lease rentals for the use of plant, machinery, equipment or other industrial properties. In fact, Irish tax law does not require income tax to be withheld on payment of copyright royalties or lease rentals paid to non-residents. The only royalties in respect of which Irish tax is to be withheld are patent royalties and any other payments which can be considered to be "annual payments" (see **4.301**). Most other payments normally described as royalties, however, are probably not annual payments.

As with interest, most treaties exclude from the operation of the "royalty" article any royalty arising from any right or property effectively connected with or attributable to a business carried on by the recipient through a permanent establishment in the source country. The royalty is taxable in accordance with the "business profits" article and the treaty exemption or reduced tax rate for royalties does not apply.

Again, as in the case of interest, a resident of one of the contracting states is generally entitled to the treaty exemption or reduced rate of tax if the royalty arises in the other state. It is not necessary that the person making the payment should be a resident of the source country.

Where there is a special relationship between the payer and the recipient of a royalty, the application of the relevant royalty article may be restricted. In such cases, most treaties provide that any royalty which is in excess of a fair and reasonable consideration for the use of the money or of the other benefits provided is not entitled to benefit from the treaty, so that the excess amount of royalty is subject to normal taxation in the country of source.

Thus, if a Japanese parent company charges a royalty of 12% (amounting to €60,000) to its Irish resident subsidiary in respect of the use of a patent, and it is ascertained that a proper arm's length royalty for the patent concerned would be at 7% only (or €35,000), article 13(2), (5) of the Ireland/ Japan tax treaty allows the Irish Revenue to tax the Japanese parent as follows:

	€	€
Arm's length royalty	35,000	
Withholding tax @ 10%		3,500
Excess royalty (€60,000 – €35,000)	25,000	
At standard income tax rate 20%		5,000
Total		8,500

As with interest, in later treaties it is usual to have an anti-avoidance provision incorporated in the royalty article. For example, article 14 (royalties) of the Ireland/New Zealand treaty, provides that the article will not apply if the obligation in respect of which the royalty is paid was created or assigned mainly for the purpose of taking advantage of that article and not for *bona fide* commercial reasons.

14.109.7 Income from immovable property

Ireland's tax treaties include an article dealing with income from immovable property. The article provides that the state in which the immovable property is situated has the right to tax the income under its own laws without any restriction. This article applies to all income from immovable property, including income derived from the direct use, letting, or use in any other form of the property.

"Immovable property" is to be given the meaning that it has under the law of the contracting state in which the property is situated, thus avoiding difficulties of interpretation as to what constitutes immovable property in different countries.

14.109.8 Capital gains

Tax treaties concluded prior to the introduction of capital gains tax in the Capital Gains Tax Act 1975, do not provide for the relief of double taxation in respect of capital gains.

Later treaties contain articles applicable to tax on capital gains in each of the contracting states, although Australia does not at present charge tax on capital gains as such. Similarly, in the Russian Federation, no distinction is made between income and capital gains. While some of the older treaties contain an article on "capital gains" or "alienation of immovable property", this is generally for the purposes only of taxing a resident of Ireland in respect of capital gains realised on the disposal of assets situated in the other country. These treaties do not entitle a person resident in Ireland to any credit against Irish capital gains tax for any tax paid in the other country in respect of capital gains. Where a capital gains article is included in a tax treaty, the normal approach is to permit the country in which certain categories of assets are situated to impose tax on any capital gains realised on their disposal, but to provide that gains on disposals of other assets are to be taxable only in the country of residence of the person making the disposal (see also **9.105**). In any case where the country in which the asset was situated prior to its disposal is permitted to tax a capital gain, the country in the taxpayer is resident is required to provide the necessary relief from double taxation under the "elimination of double taxation" article.

The capital gains article invariably permits the contracting state in which immovable property is situated to impose tax on capital gains arising from the sale, exchange, gift or other form of alienation of that property. For this purpose, "immovable property" is usually given the same meaning as is given in the treaty article dealing with income from immovable property (see above). The later treaties, in line with the current version of the OECD Model Treaty, all provide that gains from the alienation of shares in companies deriving their value, or the greater part of their value, directly or indirectly from immovable property in one of the states may be taxed in that state. The agreement with the UK, however, excludes from this rule the gains on any such shares that are quoted on a stock exchange; these gains are accordingly treated in the same way as gains from the disposal of shares in companies generally.

It is also usual to permit the country of source to tax capital gains on the alienation of any movable property that forms part of the business property of a permanent establishment which an enterprise of the other contracting state has in the country where the permanent establishment is situated.

The above-described treatment does not apply in the later treaties to any capital gains derived by a resident of a contracting state from the alienation of ships or aircraft operated in international traffic. Any such capital gains are taxable only in the country of residence of the person carrying on the international shipping or airline enterprise.

For assets not specifically dealt with, the later treaties provide that gains on their disposal are to be taxable only in the country of residence of the person realising the gain. Thus, a capital gain realised by a resident of Ireland on the disposal of shares in a company resident in, say, Switzerland can only be taxed in Ireland, provided that the value of the shares are not derived principally from immovable property situated in Switzerland.

14.109.9 Income not expressly mentioned

Most treaties contain an article which provides that where a resident of one of the contracting states derives an item of income that is not expressly mentioned in the treaty, that income is to be taxable only in the state of which the recipient is a resident. Some of the treaties provide that this article only applies to items of income arising in the other contracting state (eg, the treaties with Belgium, Cyprus and Japan). Other treaties (eg, with Austria, France, Switzerland and the UK) do not make this stipulation. Under the latter type treaties, only the country of residence of the taxpayer is entitled to tax the otherwise unspecified income, whether it arises in the other state or in a third country.

Article 21 of the treaty (of 2004)with Canada provides that if income not otherwise dealt with in the treaty is derived by a resident of a contracting state from sources in the other contracting state, such income may also be taxed in the state in which it arises and according to the laws of that state. Where the income is from an estate or trust, other than a trust to which contributions were deductible, the rate of tax on the gross amount of the income may not exceed 15%.

The case of *Beame v The Queen* [2001-3210(IT)G12, Oct 2002] was concerned with the question of Canadian tax assessed on a gain from the disposal by an Irish resident of Canadian shares. It was held that the 15% maximum tax permitted by the 1967 treaty (which provided for a 15% Canadian tax on income from sources within Canada) applied to the actual gain rather than the taxable gain. For the purposes of that treaty, it was not correct to substitute for the ordinary or broad meaning of "income" another meaning derived from the operation of domestic law in force at the time in question. This was notwithstanding Article 2(1) of the 1967 treaty where it is stated that a term not otherwise defined in the treaty is generally to have the meaning it has under the laws of the contracting state that is applying the provisions of the treaty. While this might have seemed to suggest that "income" in Article 6 of the treaty was to have the meaning it has under Canadian tax law, the court's view, citing *The Queen v Melford Developments* [82 DTC 6281 (SCC)] and other Canadian cases, was that laws enacted by Canada that redefine tax procedures and mechanisms with reference to income were not incorporated in the expression "the laws of [Canada]" in the general definitions article of the treaty.

If a treaty does not contain an "income not expressly mentioned" article, it generally follows that the country of source is entitled to tax any such income according to its domestic tax laws. In such a case, the country of residence is required to give the appropriate double taxation relief either by the credit or the exemption method (whichever applies). The agreement with Australia does contain an article dealing with income not expressly mentioned, but permits the country of source to tax any such income. It appears in this case, therefore, that the article is only of relevance to income arising in a third country.

The treaty with New Zealand is different in that it permits either contracting state to tax any income not expressly mentioned in the treaty only where that income arises from a source in its territory. If the recipient of the income is a resident of the other state, that state is required to give double taxation relief (by way of credit in both countries). Subject to this provision, the income not expressly mentioned is only taxable in the recipient's country of residence. The effect of giving the country of residence the sole taxing right is, therefore, limited to income arising in third countries. The country of residence has, under normal principles, the right to tax its own residents on income arising in its own territory.

It is usual for later treaties to exclude "other income" which is derived by a resident of one of the contracting states through a permanent establishment or fixed base which it has in the other contracting state where that income is effectively connected with the permanent establishment or fixed base. Such other income, for example income arising in a third country, may be taxed in the contracting state in which the permanent establishment or fixed base is situated. Tax would be imposed in accordance with the business profits article or the independent personal services article of the treaty. For example, a Swedish resident company carrying on a trade through a permanent establishment in Ireland may be taxed in Ireland in respect of interest income arising to that permanent establishment from Norway.

14.109.10 Non-discrimination

Most tax treaties contain a non-discrimination article providing that the nationals of either contracting state are not to be subjected in the other contracting state to any taxation, or to any related requirement, which is more burdensome than the taxation or related requirements to which nationals of that other state are or may be subjected to in the same circumstances. The term "nationals" is usually defined separately, in relation to each country, as all citizens of that country and all legal persons, partnerships and associations deriving their status as such from the law in force in the country concerned. Accordingly, in the case of a company, the non-discrimination principle will be applied by reference to its place of incorporation rather than by reference to where it is tax resident.

This article generally provides also that the taxation of a permanent establishment which an enterprise of one of the contracting states has in the other state may not be less favourably levied in that other state than the taxation levied on an enterprise of the other state carrying on the same activities.

Another provision which usually appears in tax treaties is to the effect that an enterprise of a contracting state the capital of which is wholly or partly owned or controlled, directly or indirectly, by one or more residents of the other state may not be subjected in the first-mentioned state to any taxation, or any connected requirement, which is more burdensome than the taxation and connected requirements to which other similar enterprises of the first-mentioned state are or may be subjected.

The Commentary to the OECD Model Convention confirms that the clause dealing with nationals in the "non-discrimination" article is solely designed to prevent discrimination in tax treatment on the grounds of nationality, and not on the grounds of residence. Under EC law, however, discrimination against non-residents may be regarded as no different to discrimination against non-nationals and such discrimination may be prohibited in the absence of an acceptable justification (*R v IRC ex parte Commerzbank* [1991] STC 271; [1993] STC 605).

The Commentary also notes that, if one of the contracting states should grant special taxation privileges either to its own public bodies or public service, or to private non-profit making institutions whose activities are performed for purposes of public benefit specific to its own territory, the "non-discrimination" article is not to be construed as obliging that state to extend the same privileges to the public bodies or public services of the other state or to any such private institutions in the other state.

In relation to the clause relating to permanent establishments, the Commentary states that its purpose is to end all discrimination in the treatment in one of the states of the permanent establishment there of the enterprise of the other state, but only as compared with the treatment of resident enterprises belonging to the same sector of activities. It indicates that the clause does not mean that the state in question may not apply a different practical approach to the taxation of the permanent establishment, provided that the final result is not to impose more burdensome taxation than is imposed on similar resident enterprises.

The Commentary acknowledges that experience in applying "non-discrimination" articles in tax treaties has shown that it is often difficult to define clearly how precisely this principle of equal tax treatment should operate. The main reason for the difficulty appears to lie in the actual nature of the permanent establishment, which is not a separate legal entity but only a part of an enterprise that has its head office in another state.

14.109.11 Mutual agreement procedure

Most tax treaties contain a mutual agreement procedure article which entitles a resident of either of the contracting states to invoke the assistance of the "competent authority" of the state of which he is a resident to adjudicate on any problems in the application of any of the provisions in the relevant treaty to his own particular case. This article is normally designed to give the resident of the state in question the right to seek this assistance if he considers that the actions of the competent authority of either or both of the contracting states result, or will result, in his being taxed other than in accordance with the terms of the particular treaty.

Under this article, the taxpayer in question is required to present his case to the competent authority of his country of residence. That authority is then required to examine the case and, if the claim appears to it to be justified and if it is not itself able to arrive at an appropriate solution, the authority should endeavour to resolve the case with the competent authority of the other contracting state. This recourse to the mutual agreement procedure is usually available to the taxpayer aggrieved in addition to any of the remedies provided by the national laws of the two states, for example, in addition to the normal appeal in Ireland. In practice, the Revenue Commissioners would probably allow an appeal or similar claim to remain open until such time as the mutual agreement process has been exhausted.

Ireland is one of a number of countries that have entered a reservation in respect of article 25 of the Model Convention to the effect that the granting of reliefs and refunds on foot of the mutual agreement procedure should be subject to the time limits applying generally to appeals and claims under domestic tax law.

The Commentary to the OECD Model Convention mentions, inter alia, that the most frequent applications of the procedure in practice are likely to relate to the interpretation of articles in the normal treaty designed specifically to avoid double taxation. Such problems might relate, for example, to the rules for the attribution to a permanent establishment in one country of a proper proportion of the executive and general administration expenses incurred by the head office of the enterprise in the other country. Problems might relate also to cases where lack of information as to the taxpayer's actual position has led to misapplication of the agreement, eg as to the determination of residence or as to the existence of a permanent establishment.

The Commentary also indicates that the right of the taxpayer to seek the assistance of the competent authority of his country of residence should be available, whether or not he has exhausted all the remedies available to him under the domestic law of each of the two states. The Commentary notes that the competent authority in question is obliged, if it appears that the taxpayer's complaint is justified, to take the appropriate action.

If the complaint is justified and if the competent authority accepts that it is due wholly or in part to the laws of the state of residence, the Commentary requires that authority to take the necessary action as speedily as possible and to make such adjustments or allow such reliefs (in order to prevent double taxation) as appear to be justified. If the complaint is due to tax provisions in the country of source, the competent authority of the state of residence must make every effort to resolve the matter with the competent authority of the other country.

Mutual agreement articles often contain a provision directing the two treaty states to resolve by mutual agreement any difficulties or doubts arising as to the interpretation or application of the treaty concerned. The Commentary to the Model Convention indicates that this provision authorises the two states to complete or clarify the definition of doubtful terms in the treaty, to settle any difficulties arising out of changes to the internal tax laws of either state, and to determine the application of "thin capitalisation" rules.

In *IRC v Commerzbank* [1990] STC 285, the High Court in the UK held that an interpretation agreed by the revenue authorities of the two contracting states under the mutual agreement procedure of the UK/US tax treaty did not "confer any binding or authoritative effect on the view or statements of the competent authorities in the English courts".

14.109.12 Exchange of information

Tax treaties which follow the OECD Model Convention contain an article providing for the exchange of information between the competent authorities of the two contracting states under two broad headings. Firstly, the two contracting states to a treaty undertake to exchange such information as is necessary for carrying out the provisions of the tax treaty in question. Secondly, they agree to exchange such information as is necessary for carrying out the provisions of their respective domestic tax laws.

All of Ireland's tax treaties (except that with Switzerland) contain an article under which the two contracting states agree to exchange such information as is necessary for carrying out the provisions of the relevant treaty. Some treaties, mainly the later ones, follow the OECD Model Convention and provide also for the exchange of such information as is necessary for the carrying out of the domestic laws of the two states. The article containing this latter provision generally limits the exchange of information under it to the taxes covered by the agreement in question and then only in so far as the taxation under the relevant domestic laws is not contrary to anything in the agreement.

The OECD Model Convention, and the treaties following its approach, each contains a supplementary clause in the "exchange of information" article which limits the application of the article so that it does not impose on either contracting state any obligation:

(a) to carry out administrative measures at variance with its own laws and administrative practice or with those of the other state,

(b) to supply information which is not obtainable under its own laws or in the normal course of its administration or of those of the other state, or

(c) to supply information which would disclose any trade, business, industrial, commercial or professional secret or trade process, or information the disclosure of which would be contrary to public policy.

Some of the treaties (eg, that with Australia) contain an additional sub-clause to the effect that the information that may be exchanged is not to be restricted by the "personal scope" article in the treaty. In other words, although the treaty may contain an article providing that the agreement as a whole is to apply to persons who are residents of one or both of the contracting states, the inclusion of that sub-clause permits either state to seek information from the other state regarding persons not resident in either state. Such information about non-residents may, however, only be sought within the same limitations of the article as apply to information about residents of either state.

It is normal for the "exchange of information" article to require each contracting state to observe the same requirements as to secrecy regarding the information exchanged as must be observed under the respective domestic tax laws of the two states. The information must not be disclosed other than to persons or authorities (including courts and administrative bodies) involved in the assessment or collection of the taxes covered by the treaty, or to persons involved in the enforcement of, or in the determination of appeals in relation to, those taxes.

TCA 1997, s 826(7) authorises the Revenue Commissioners to disclose to any authorised officer of the government of another contracting state to a treaty such information as is required to be disclosed under the terms of that treaty. See also **14.202** regarding the provision in TCA 1997, s 826(1) for the exchange of information for the purposes of preventing and detecting tax evasion.

14.110 UK tax treaty

14.110.1 Introduction

The double tax treaty between the Irish government and the government of the United Kingdom was concluded on 2 June 1976 and was supplemented by a Protocol signed on 28 October 1976. Both the convention and the protocol entered into force on 23 December 1976. A further protocol, providing for a new Article 17A dealing with occupational pension schemes, was signed in November 1994.

Article 1 of the treaty states that the treaty is to apply to persons who are residents of one or both of the Contracting States. *Resident of a Contracting State* is given the meaning assigned to it by article 4 (fiscal domicile) which adopts the form of that article used in the OECD Model Convention (see **14.104**). Accordingly, the treaty may apply to affect the taxation in either country of any individual, company and any other body of persons regarded as resident in either country by its domestic tax laws. However, in applying any particular article which refers to either a "resident of Ireland" or a "resident of the United Kingdom", article 4(3) provides that where by reason of article 4(1) a company is a resident of both Contracting States, it is to be deemed to be a resident of the state in which its place of effective management is situated.

Article 2 specifies the taxes covered by the treaty as being:

(a) in Ireland: income tax, corporation profits tax, corporation tax and capital gains tax;

(b) in the United Kingdom: income tax, corporation tax, petroleum revenue tax and capital gains tax.

Thus, in the case of an Irish resident company with income chargeable to the UK petroleum revenue tax, the elimination of double taxation article, which gives a credit against Irish tax for any UK tax paid on UK source income, entitles that company to a credit for the UK petroleum revenue tax.

Article 3 (general definitions) contains other definitions similar to those already discussed in **14.106**. The definitions of *Ireland* and *United Kingdom*, as these terms are used throughout the treaty, are stated to include any area outside the territorial waters of the respective Contracting States which, in accordance with international law is designated, under the respective laws of each country concerning the Continental Shelf, as an area within which that country may exercise its rights with respect to the sea bed and subsoil and their natural resources.

In relation to Ireland, the term "nationals" is defined as meaning all citizens of Ireland and all legal persons, associations or other entities deriving their status as such from the laws in force in the Republic of Ireland. In relation to the United Kingdom, "nationals" means citizens of the United Kingdom and Colonies, British subjects under specified provisions in the British Nationality Acts, British protected persons within the British Nationality Act 1948 (now repealed), and all legal persons, associations or other entities deriving their status as such from the law in force in the United Kingdom.

14.110.2 Elimination of double taxation

With a few exceptions, the Ireland/ UK tax treaty follows closely the general form of the OECD Model Convention. The articles dealing with the various items of income and with capital gains define, mainly following the general principles of the Model Convention, the circumstances in and the extent to which the country of source may tax income and capital gains arising there to a resident of the other state. The "elimination of double taxation" article (article 21) then requires the country of residence to provide relief from double taxation by way of the foreign tax credit method in respect of income or gains which the other articles in the treaty allow to be taxed in the country of source.

This approach is similar to that for other treaties generally, as discussed in **14.107**. It may be useful, however, to examine further the treatment in the Ireland/ UK treaty of certain key articles affecting companies. The rules of TCA 1997 24, under which the credits for foreign tax to be allowed against Irish tax on any foreign income are to be computed, are discussed in some detail in **14.2**. The principles discussed there are equally applicable to the computation for Irish tax purposes of UK source income in respect of which a resident of Ireland claims credit for UK tax payable in accordance with the rules of the Ireland/ UK treaty.

14.110.3 Business profits

Article 8 (business profits) of the Ireland/ UK treaty follows the general form of the corresponding article in the OECD Model Convention. It permits the Irish Revenue to tax the profits derived by a resident of the UK from any business carried on through a permanent establishment in Ireland. Such profits of a UK resident as may arise in Ireland otherwise than through a permanent establishment in Ireland may not be subjected to Irish corporation tax. The article also applies the normal additional "business profits" article rules in determining the amount of the taxable profits attributable to the permanent establishment (see **14.109.2**).

The term "permanent establishment" is defined in article 5 as being a fixed place of business in which the business of the enterprise (the resident of the other Contracting State) is wholly or partly carried on. This follows the normal tax treaty concept of a permanent establishment as already discussed in some detail in **14.109.1**. Accordingly, a UK resident company is taxable on its business profits to the extent that they are properly attributable to any branch, agency or other fixed place of business it may have in Ireland. The term "permanent establishment" especially includes a place of management, a branch, an office, a factory, a workshop, a mine, oil well, quarry or other place of extraction of natural resources, an installation or structure used for the exploration of natural resources, and a building site or construction or installation project which lasts for more than six months.

Article 5(5) deems a person carrying on activities offshore in a Contracting State in connection with the exploration or exploitation of the sea bed and subsoil and their natural resources situated in that Contracting State to be carrying on a business in that State through a permanent establishment there. Since the Irish sector of the Continental Shelf is included in the territory of Ireland for purposes of the treaty (article 3(1)(a)), any profits earned by a UK resident company from exploration or exploitation activities on the Irish sector of the Continental Shelf are chargeable to Irish tax under the rules of TCA 1997, s 13 (see **3.107.1**). The same principle applies in the reverse situation of an Irish resident company carrying on any exploration or exploitation activities on the UK sector of the Continental Shelf.

Articles 8(4) and 9 of the treaty provide for specific treatment for certain kinds of businesses. Article 8(4) provides that the normal business profits rules are not to affect the liability to tax in either of the Contracting States, under its own domestic tax laws, of a life assurance company not having its head office in that state. Both Ireland and the UK have special rules for taxing an "overseas" life assurance company. In Ireland, "overseas life assurance company "is defined (TCA 1997, s 706 – **12.603.8**) as a life assurance company having its head office outside the State but carrying on a life assurance business through a branch or agency in the State. Article 8(4) preserves each country's right to tax any such life assurance company that is a resident of the other country under the former country's rules to the exclusion of the normal permanent establishment rules contained in article 8.

The nature of a life assurance company's general life and annuity business makes it impracticable to allocate its investment income and/or business profits specifically to a branch or agency in any particular country as distinct from the rest of its worldwide business. Irish corporation tax law taxes the Irish branch of an overseas life assurance company on the proportion of its investment income (less expenses) represented by the ratio that the actuarial liabilities of the branch bears to the actuarial liabilities of the company's worldwide business. UK tax law applies in a similar way, in reverse, to tax any branch or agency which an Irish life assurance company may have in the UK. These rules are not disturbed by any provision of the tax treaty between the two countries.

Article 9 excludes from the normal business permanent establishment rule the profits from the operation of ships or aircraft in international traffic. Any such profits derived by a resident of one of the states is exempted from tax in the other state so as to be taxable only in the taxpayer's country of residence. However, any profits from voyages of ships or aircraft confined solely to places in the other state may be taxed there (so that the country of residence, which also taxes those profits, is required to grant credit relief under article 21).

14.110.4   Associated enterprises

The rules contained in article 10, regarding commercial or financial dealings between associated enterprises resident in Ireland and the UK, are similar to those referred to in **14.109.4**. Accordingly, if the result of any non-arm's length transactions between two such associated enterprises is that a lesser amount of profits accrues to one of the enterprises than would have accrued if the dealings had been at arm's length, article 10 permits the state which would otherwise collect less tax by reason of the understatement of profits to adjust the amount of the taxable profits of its resident enterprise. This rule is most likely to have effect in relation to the pricing of goods transferred between associated enterprises in the course of their trading activities, but it may apply also to any other business transactions such as inter company services, interest on loans, royalties for the use of patents and leasing of equipment.

While an article in a tax treaty may permit a Contracting State to tax income in a particular way, it is also necessary that the domestic tax law of the state in question must contain rules under which the income is taxable in that state. Irish tax legislation does not, generally, contain transfer pricing provisions and for this reason the Irish tax authorities would be prevented from invoking the associated enterprises article to adjust profits where it is considered that the related transactions have not been conducted using arm's length prices.

Assuming the associated enterprises article has been used to adjust the profits of a company for UK corporation tax purposes, double taxation will occur if the profits of the company in Ireland are not correspondingly reduced. Article 21(4) of the treaty requires Ireland to make the compensating adjustment by way of a reduction in the tax payable by the associated enterprise resident in Ireland. The adjustment is made through an extension of the foreign tax credit rules under article 21.

To the extent that profits have been understated for UK purposes, the amount by which they have been understated is included in the accounting and taxable profits of the Irish company and subjected to Irish corporation tax as a result of the way in which the commercial or financial transactions have been priced. Article 21(4) deems an amount equal to the understatement taxed by the UK to be income which the Irish company has earned in the UK.

The Irish company is then assumed to have paid the additional UK corporation tax on the amount understated which was actually paid by the UK company as a result of the adjustment made under article 10. The Irish Revenue are required to allow the Irish company credit for the UK corporation tax which it is deemed to have borne on the understated profits. For this purpose, Ireland applies its normal rules for determining the amount of the credit for the foreign tax against its own tax. Thus, the computational rules of TCA 1997 Sch 24 are applied (see **14.207**).

Example 14.110.4.1

Westport Ltd, an Irish resident company, and Bedford Ltd, a UK resident company are both wholly owned subsidiaries of a Dutch company. Part of the turnover of Westport Ltd is derived from sales of goods to Bedford Ltd.

The profits of Westport Ltd for its current accounting period are €540,000 and corporation tax at 12.5% results in tax payable of €67,500.

Following enquiries by the UK inspector of taxes, it is established that the prices charged for goods sold by Westport Ltd to Bedford Ltd are in excess of the normal arm's length prices for the goods in question. As a result, the taxable profits of Bedford Ltd for the period are adjusted upwards as follows:

	Stg£
Actual price paid for goods purchased from Westport Ltd	620,000
Arm's length price for same transactions	500,000
Understated profits chargeable to UK tax	120,000
Additional UK tax payable Stg£120,000 @ 30% (ignore marginal relief)	36,000

Due to the transfer pricing policies adopted by the group, the taxable profits of Westport Ltd for Irish tax purposes include the euro equivalent of Stg£120,000 (€180,000), the understated profits of Bedford Ltd. In accordance with article 21(4) of the Ireland/ UK treaty, Westport Ltd is treated as if €180,000 of its taxable profits were earned in the UK and had suffered UK corporation tax of €54,000 (Stg£36,000). It is necessary to calculate the credit to be given against the Irish corporation tax liability of Westport Ltd in respect of the UK tax borne, €54,000. The computation is as follows:

	€
Profits deemed to be earned in UK	180,000
Less: UK tax deemed paid	54,000
Net "foreign" income	126,000
Gross up at the lower rate – 12.5%	
€126,000 x 100/(100 - 12.5)	144,000
Credit for UK tax on doubly taxed income:	
€144,000 x 12.5%	18,000

In the final corporation tax computation for Westport Ltd, the re-grossed profits deemed to have been earned in the UK are substituted for the actual profits made in respect of the sales to Bedford Ltd:

	€
Case I profits:	
Manufacturing profits as before	540,000
Less: profits deemed earned in UK	180,000
	360,000
Regrossed profits deemed earned in UK	144,000
Total profits	504,000
Corporation tax payable:	
€504,000 x 12.5%	63,000
Credit relief as above	18,000
Final corporation tax payable	45,000

The final amount of corporation tax payable compares with the original amount of €67,500, a reduction of €22,500. In effect, this is the understated profits of €180,000 @ 12.5%. Had the UK rate of tax been lower than the Irish rate, the amount by which the corporation tax liability of Westport Ltd would have been reduced would have been by reference to the UK rate.

14.110.5 Dividends

Article 11 of the treaty deals with dividends which a resident of either Contracting State derives from companies which are residents of the other State. The term "dividend" is defined in article 11(3) as including, for Irish tax purposes, any item which under the law of Ireland is treated as a distribution and as including, for UK tax purposes, any item which under the law of the UK is treated as a distribution. Thus, credit relief in accordance with article 21 (see **14.110.2** above) would be due in the case of certain interest payments. For example, interest paid by a UK company to its Irish parent company (or Irish company which controls at least 10% of the voting power in the UK company) might be such as to fall within TCA 1997, s 130(2)(d) (see **11.106**) because, say, the interest rate varies with the results of the UK company. Such interest, even if paid by a foreign company, is regarded for Irish tax purposes as a distribution and would accordingly be a "dividend" for the purposes of the treaty.

Article 11(1) contains provisions which, up to 5 April 1999, had no effect as they had no application under the tax laws of either country. The position prior to 6 April 1999 was that the provisions of paragraph (1) were not to be applied by either country as long as an individual in a Contracting State was entitled to a tax credit in respect of dividends paid by companies resident in the other Contracting State (article 11(2)). This provision of the treaty ceased to have effect from 6 April 1999 thus bringing paragraph (1) into force for the first time. This was in line with the abolition of tax credits in Ireland; from 6 April 1999, the tax laws of Ireland no longer give such an entitlement although tax credits still attach to dividends payable by UK companies (at 10/90ths of the amount of the dividend).

Article 11(1) provides that dividends received by a resident of one of the countries from a company resident in the other country may be taxed in the first-mentioned country. Such dividends may also be taxed in the other country according to the laws of that country but, where the beneficial owner of the dividends is a resident of the first-mentioned country, the tax charged may not exceed:

(a) 5% of the gross amount of the dividends if the beneficial owner is a company which controls directly or indirectly 10% or more of the voting power in the company paying the dividends;

(b) 15% of the gross amount of the dividends in all other cases.

As far as dividends from Irish resident companies are concerned, the reference to "gross" dividends is no longer relevant. Up to 5 April 1999, a "gross" dividend denoted a dividend with the addition of the related tax credit.

Prior to 5 April 1999, neither Ireland nor the UK imposed a withholding tax on the payment of dividends. From 6 April 1999, dividend payments made by Irish resident companies to certain shareholders (resident individuals and certain non-resident persons) are subject to a withholding tax at the standard rate of income tax (see **11.121**). This withholding tax does not apply to dividends paid to shareholders resident in the UK or in any other EU Member State or in a jurisdiction with which Ireland has a tax treaty. The 5% and 15% maximum tax liabilities, as provided for in article 11(1), accordingly have no application as regards such dividends. There are currently no provisions under UK law which impose a withholding tax on the payment of dividends.

In the case of an Irish company receiving a dividend from a UK company in which it controls at least 10% of the voting power, the fact that the maximum UK tax on the dividend is 5% would seem to allow for a payment to that company of one-half of the related tax credit (one-half of 10% of the "gross" dividend). There is now, however, no mechanism for any such repayment under the treaty. For other shareholders, although UK tax of up to 15% of the gross dividend may be imposed, no such tax is provided for currently. In either case, liability in Ireland is calculated on the amount of the cash dividend received and without any credit for UK tax (other than in respect of underlying tax in the case of a direct investor – see below).

An Irish resident company receiving dividends from a UK company in respect of which it controls, directly or indirectly, 10% or more of the voting power (a "direct investor") is entitled to a foreign tax credit under the rules of TCA 1997 Sch 24 (see **14.202**) in respect of the underlying UK tax paid by the distributing company on its relevant profits (art 21(1)(*b*)). The converse applies in the case of a UK company in receipt of dividends from an Irish resident company.

The procedure for determining the "relevant profits" of the dividend paying UK resident company, for computing the underlying tax rate, and for granting credits for foreign taxes (including, where relevant, the foreign underlying tax) against an Irish resident company's corporation tax payable in respect of foreign source income, is discussed in **14.207** and **14.208**.

Strictly, the euro/pound sterling rate of exchange to be used is that ruling on the date the dividend is payable and this rate should be applied for each separate dividend. In practice, however, the Irish inspector of taxes normally permits an average exchange rate for each year to be used in translating all UK dividends received. Whether an actual or an average exchange rate is used, a consistent approach should be adopted and the same rate should be applied for each dividend and for the UK tax attributable to that dividend.

Article 11(5) of the treaty provides that a Contracting State may not impose any tax on the dividends paid by a company that is a resident of the other State where that company has derived profits or income from sources in the territory of the first-mentioned State, except to the extent that such dividends are paid to its own residents or where the holding in respect of which the dividends are paid is effectively connected with a permanent establishment situated in the first-mentioned State. Article 11(5) also prevents either Contracting State from imposing any tax on the undistributed profits of a resident company of the other State, even if those undistributed profits consist wholly or partly of profits arising in the first-mentioned State.

14.110.6 Interest

Interest derived and beneficially owned by a resident of a Contracting State is taxable only in that State. Article 12(2) states that the term "interest" means:

> "income from Government securities, bonds or debentures, whether or not secured by mortgage and whether or not carrying a right to participate in profits, and other debt-claims of every kind as well as all other income assimilated to income from money lent by the taxation law of the State in which the income arises but shall not include any income which is treated as a distribution under Article 11".

It is usually the case in the more recent treaties that "interest" does not include any income which is treated as a dividend in the relevant dividends article. The dividends article will then include in the meaning of "dividends" any item which, for example, under the law of Ireland is treated as a distribution, such as interest on certain securities treated as a distribution by TCA 1997, s 130 (see **14.110.5** above).

Excluded from the operation of the "interest" article is any interest on a debt claim that is "effectively connected with" a business which the recipient of the interest carries on through a permanent establishment in the country of source. In any such case, the interest is taxable under article 8 (business profits) and the treaty exemption otherwise available in respect of interest does not apply.

A resident of one of the contracting states is entitled to the treaty exemption if the interest arises in the other state. It is not necessary that the person making the payment should be a resident of the source country. Thus, for example, a UK resident is entitled to receive without liability to Irish tax interest which is paid by an Irish branch of another UK company, or even an Irish branch of a company resident in a third company.

Where there is a special relationship between the payer and the beneficial owner of the interest, or between both of them and some other person, the provisions of article 12 are not to apply to any interest to the extent that it is in excess of the amount that would have been paid in the absence of that relationship. The excess amount remains subject to normal taxation in the country of source.

Article 12 will not apply if it was the main purpose or one of the main purposes of any person concerned with the creation or assignment of the debt-claim in respect of which the interest is paid to take advantage of the article by reason of that creation or assignment.

14.110.7   Capital gains

Article 14 of the Ireland/ UK tax treaty provides that capital gains from the alienation of certain types of assets realised by any person who is a resident of one of the Contracting States may be taxed in the other state, but only if the assets in question are situated in that other State. Apart from gains on the disposal of the types of asset specified, capital gains from the alienation of all other types of asset may only be taxed in the Contracting State of which the person disposing of the assets is a resident.

Under article 14, a resident of Ireland may be taxed in the UK in accordance with the relevant UK domestic tax law on capital gains from the disposal of any of the following assets:

(a) immovable property situated in the UK, including any property accessory to such immovable property – see article 7(2)(b);

(b) shares deriving their value or the greater part of their value directly or indirectly from immovable property situated in the UK, apart from shares in which there is a substantial and regular trading on a Stock Exchange;

(c) an interest in a partnership or trust the assets of which consist principally of immovable property situated in the UK, or of shares referred to in (b);

(d) movable property forming part of the business property of a permanent establishment which an Irish resident enterprise has in the UK; and

(e) the permanent establishment or fixed base itself (including any goodwill) which the resident of Ireland has in the UK.

The above position applies in reverse to a resident of the UK in respect of capital gains from assets situated in Ireland. There are two exceptions to rule (c) above. If the movable property of the UK permanent establishment or fixed base consists either of shares in a company owing the greater part of their value to immovable property situated in Ireland or of property pertaining to the operation of ships and/or aircraft used in international traffic, any resulting capital gains may be taxed only in Ireland.

Apart from the types of assets listed in (a) to (e) above, capital gains realised by a resident of Ireland from the disposal of assets situated in the UK are exempted from any tax which the UK may impose on capital gains.

TCA 1997, s 590 provides that a person resident in Ireland is subject to capital gains tax in respect of capital gains realised by non-resident closely held companies in which that person is a participator (see **9.408**). Except where the non-resident company realises gains from assets which may be taxed in Ireland (eg, immovable property in Ireland), article 14 overrides the provisions of TCA 1997, s 590 if the company is resident in the UK.

In this respect, article 14(5) provides that any gain from the alienation by the UK resident company of assets not listed in (a) to (e) above are to be taxable only in the Contracting State of which the alienator is a resident. This prevents a capital gains tax charge from being levied on the Irish resident participator under TCA 1997, s 590.

In any case where an Irish resident company is chargeable to UK tax on capital gains from any property (eg, immovable property) situated in the UK, article 21(1) entitles the company to a credit for the UK tax properly payable in accordance with the rules of the treaty against the corporation tax chargeable on the capital gains in question.

The preceding paragraphs describe the provisions of article 14 of the Ireland/ UK tax treaty in relation to capital gains. As may also be the case with other tax treaty provisions, certain limitations on the taxing rights Contracting States may not in any event impose tax on the gains in question. UK capital gains tax law does not impose a capital gains tax charge on non-residents except in the case of assets used for the purposes of a trade carried on in the UK through a branch or agency which a non-resident has in the UK. Assets of a person who is neither resident nor ordinarily resident in Ireland which are subject to capital gains tax in Ireland are:

(a)   land (including buildings) in the State;

(b)   minerals in the State or rights, interests or other assets in relation to mining or minerals or the searching for minerals;

(c)   assets in the State which, at or before the time the chargeable gains accrued, were used in or for the purposes of a trade carried on by the person in the State through a branch or agency, or which at or before that time were used or held or acquired for use by or for the purposes of the branch or agency;

(d)   exploration or exploitation rights in a designated area (see **3.107.1**); and

(e)   shares deriving their value or the greater part of their value directly or indirectly from assets mentioned in (a) or (b) above, except shares quoted on a stock exchange.

It will be seen that these classes of assets correspond somewhat with the earlier list (a) to (e) above so that the treaty position reflects to a large extent the position under domestic law in Ireland.

14.111   US tax treaty

14.111.1   Introduction

The current double tax treaty between the Irish government and the government of the United States was signed on behalf of both governments on 28 July 1997 and, following ratification later in 1997, the treaty, including a protocol also signed on 28 July 1997, came into force on 1 January 1998.

Article 1 of the treaty provides that the treaty is to apply to persons who are residents of one or both of the Contracting States, except as otherwise provided by the treaty. "Resident of a Contracting State" is given the meaning assigned to it by article 4 which provides that the term applies to any person who, under the laws of that State, is liable to tax therein by reason of his domicile, residence, place of management, place of incorporation, or any other criterion of a similar nature. Accordingly, the treaty may apply to affect the taxation in either country of any individual, company and any other body of persons regarded as resident in either country in accordance with its domestic tax laws. However, in applying any particular article which refers to either a "resident of Ireland" or a "resident of the United States", article 4 paragraph 4 provides that where by reason of article 4 paragraph 1 a company is a resident of both Contracting States, the competent authorities of the Contracting States are to endeavour by mutual agreement to deem the company to be a resident of one Contracting State only.

Article 2 specifies the taxes covered by the treaty as being:

(a)   in Ireland: income tax, corporation tax and capital gains tax;

(b)   in the United States: the Federal income taxes imposed by the Internal Revenue Code of 1986 (excluding the accumulated earnings tax, the personal holding company tax and social security taxes) and the Federal excise taxes imposed on insurance premiums paid to foreign insurers and with respect to private foundations.

Article 3 (general definitions) contains other definitions similar to those already discussed in **12.106**. The definitions of "Ireland" and "United States", as these terms are used throughout the treaty, are stated to include any area outside the territorial waters of the respective contracting states, which, in accordance with international law has been or may be designated, under the respective laws of each country concerning the Continental Shelf, as an area within which that country may exercise its rights with respect to the sea bed and subsoil and their natural resources.

In relation to a Contracting State, the term "national" is defined as any citizen of that state and any legal person, association or other entity deriving its status as such from the laws in force in that state.

The terms "enterprise of a Contracting State" and "enterprise of the other Contracting State" mean respectively an enterprise carried on by a resident of a Contracting State and an enterprise carried on by a resident of the other Contracting State.

14.111.2   Relief from double taxation

With a few exceptions, the Ireland/US tax treaty follows the general form of the OECD Model Convention. The articles dealing with the various items of income and with capital gains define, mainly following the general principles of the Model Convention, the circumstances in and the extent to which the country of source may tax income and capital gains arising in that country to a resident of the other state. Article 24 (relief from double taxation) then requires the country of residence to provide relief from double taxation by way of credit for foreign tax in respect of income or gains which, by virtue of other treaty articles, are permitted to be taxed in the country of source.

This approach is similar to that for other treaties generally, as discussed in **14.107**. It may be useful, however, to examine further the treatment in the Ireland/ US treaty of certain key articles affecting companies. The rules of TCA 1997 Sch 24, under which the credits for foreign tax to be allowed against Irish tax on any foreign income are to be computed, are discussed in some detail in **14.2**. The principles discussed there are equally applicable to the computation for Irish tax purposes of US source income in respect of which a resident of Ireland claims credit for US tax payable in accordance with the rules of the Ireland/ US treaty.

14.111.3 Business profits

Article 7 (business profits) of the Ireland/US treaty follows the general form of the corresponding article in the OECD Model Convention. It permits the Irish Revenue to tax the profits derived by an enterprise of the US from any business carried on through a permanent establishment in Ireland. Such profits of a US enterprise as may arise in Ireland other than through a permanent establishment in Ireland may not be subjected to Irish corporation tax. The article also applies the normal additional "business profits" article rules in determining the amount of the taxable profits attributable to the permanent establishment (see **14.109.2**).

The term "permanent establishment" is defined in article 5 as a fixed place of business through which the business of the enterprise (the resident of the other Contracting State) is wholly or partly carried on. This follows the normal tax treaty concept of a permanent establishment as already discussed in some detail in **14.109.1**. Article 5 paragraph 3 provides that a building site or construction or installation project constitutes a permanent establishment only if it lasts more than twelve months. A US resident company is taxable on its business profits to the extent that they are properly attributable to any branch, agency or other fixed place of business it may have in Ireland.

Article 21 provides that an enterprise of a Contracting State carrying on exploration or exploitation activities in the other Contracting State is, subject to article 21 paragraph 3, to be deemed to be carrying on business in that other state through a permanent establishment situated therein. "Exploration activities" are activities carried on offshore in connection with the exploration of the sea bed and subsoil and their natural resources situated in a Contracting State, and "exploitation activities" are activities carried on offshore in connection with the exploitation of the sea bed and subsoil and their natural resources situated in a Contracting State.

Exploration activities carried on by an enterprise of a Contracting State in the other Contracting State for a period or periods not exceeding 120 days within any period of twelve months will not constitute the carrying on of business through a permanent establishment situated therein (article 21 paragraph 3). Since the Irish sector of the Continental Shelf is included in the territory of Ireland for purposes of the treaty (article 3 paragraph 1(g)), any profits earned by a US resident company from exploration or exploitation activities on the Irish sector of the Continental Shelf are chargeable to Irish tax under the rules of TCA 1997, s 13 (see **3.107.1**). The same principle applies in the reverse situation of an Irish resident company carrying on any exploration or exploitation activities on the US sector of the Continental Shelf.

Article 8 excludes from the normal business permanent establishment rule the profits from the operation of ships or aircraft in international traffic. Any such profits derived by an enterprise of a Contracting State is exempted from tax in the other state so as to be taxable only in that enterprise's country of residence. Profits from the operation of ships or aircraft in international traffic includes profits derived from the rental of ships or aircraft on a full (time or voyage) basis and profits from the rental of ships or aircraft on a bareboat basis if such ships or aircraft are operated in international traffic by the lessee, or if the rental income is incidental to profits from the operation of ships or aircraft in international traffic.

Irish branches of US corporations will in future be taxed based on OECD norms and the archaic "force of attraction" principle of the 1949 treaty has been removed. This provision rendered all Irish source income taxable in Ireland if the entity concerned had a permanent establishment in Ireland. In practice, however, this change will be of no consequence to the vast majority of US owned operations in Ireland.

14.111.4 Associated enterprises

The rules in article 9, regarding commercial or financial dealings between associated enterprises resident in Ireland and the US, are similar to those referred to in **14.109.4**. Accordingly, if the result of any non-arm's length transactions between two such associated enterprises is that a lesser amount of profits accrues to one of the enterprises than would have accrued if the dealings had been at arm's length, article 9 permits the state which would otherwise collect less tax by reason of the understatement of profits to adjust the amount of the taxable profits of its resident enterprise. This rule is most likely to have effect in relation to the pricing of goods transferred between associated enterprises in the course of their trading activities, but it may apply also to any other business transactions such as inter company services, interest on loans, royalties for the use of patents and leasing of equipment.

While an article in a tax treaty may permit a Contracting State to tax income in a particular way, it is also necessary that the domestic tax law of the state in question must contain rules under which the income is taxable in that state. Irish tax legislation does not, generally, contain transfer pricing provisions and for this reason the Irish tax authorities may not be in a position to invoke the associated enterprises article to adjust profits where it is considered that the related transactions have not been conducted using arm's length prices.

Assuming the associated enterprises article has been used to adjust the profits of a company for US tax purposes, double taxation will occur if the profits of the company in Ireland are not correspondingly reduced. Article 9 paragraph 2 of the treaty requires Ireland, where it agrees that the profits additionally included for US purposes are profits that would have accrued to the US enterprise if the conditions applying were those applying to independent enterprises, to make a compensating adjustment by way of a reduction in the tax payable by the associated enterprise resident in Ireland. In making the adjustment, due regard is to be had to the other provisions of the treaty and the competent authorities of the two states are, if necessary, to consult each other. (See also **15.204** re TCA 1997, s 865(1)(b)(iii) – repayment of tax in connection with correlative adjustment.)

14.111.5   Dividends

Article 10 of the Ireland/ US treaty deals with the treatment of dividends which a resident of either Contracting State derives from companies which are residents of the other state. The term "dividend" is defined in article 10 para 5 as income from shares or other rights, not being debt-claims, and as including any income or distribution treated as income from shares under the taxation laws of the Contracting State of which the company paying the dividends or income or making the distribution is a resident.

Para 5 of the Protocol to the Ireland/ US treaty confirms, however, that the term "dividends" is not to include any interest which, by reason of the fact that it was paid to a non-resident company, is treated as dividends under the domestic laws of either Contracting State, to the extent that such interest does not exceed the amount which would be expected to be paid between independent parties dealing at arm's length.

Interest falling within TCA 1997, s 130(2)(d)(iv) (see **11.106**) paid to a US resident company will, under the Ireland/ US treaty, accordingly be dealt with under article 11 (interest) of the treaty and not under article 10. As regards the deductibility of such interest for corporation tax purposes (not a treaty matter), TCA 1997, s 76(5)(a) provides that no deduction may be made in computing income from any source in respect of dividends or other distributions. TCA 1997, s 243(1) contains a similar prohibition as regards the allowability of interest as a charge on income. Article 25 of the treaty (non-discrimination), however, provides in paragraph 3 that interest and other disbursements paid by a resident of a Contracting State to a resident of the other Contracting State are, for the purposes of determining the taxable profits of the first mentioned resident, to be deductible under the same conditions as if they had been paid to a resident of the first mentioned state.

In summary, therefore, interest falling within TCA 1997, s 130(2)(d)(iv) is treated as interest for the purposes of the treaty but otherwise is, technically, a distribution. By virtue of the non-discrimination article of the treaty, such interest will not be disallowed in computing profits (whether as a trading deduction or as a charge on income) by reason solely of being a distribution. Such interest remains a distribution for the purposes of Irish domestic taxation (unless such treatment is avoided by virtue of an appropriate election – see **11.106**), however, so that it is subject to the dividend withholding tax (see **11.121**).

Article 10 paragraph 2 provides that dividends paid by a company resident in one of the Contracting States to a resident of the other Contracting State may be taxed in the country of which the dividend paying company is a resident and according to the laws of that state. A dividend paid by a US resident company to an Irish resident is subject to US withholding tax and *vice versa* but, in accordance with article 10 paragraph 2, that tax may not exceed:

(a)   5% of the gross amount of the dividend if the beneficial owner is a company owning at least 10% of the voting stock of the dividend paying company; and

(b)   15% of the gross amount of the dividend in all other cases.

Credit for any such withholding tax is given in the country of residence.

Article 10 paragraph 3 provides that the provisions of paragraphs 1 and 2 are not to be applied, in the case of a dividend paid by a company resident in Ireland, as long as an individual resident in Ireland is entitled under Irish law to a tax credit in respect of dividends paid by an Irish resident company. The tax laws of Ireland gave such an entitlement in respect of dividends paid before 6 April 1999. For dividends paid on of after that date, the provisions of article 10 paragraph 2 apply.

US direct investors

For the purposes of computing its liability to US tax in respect of a dividend received by it from an Irish company, a US resident company controlling directly or indirectly 10% or more of the voting power in the Irish company is entitled to a credit against the US tax for the underlying Irish tax paid by or on behalf of the Irish company in respect of the profits out of which the dividend is paid (art 24 para 1(b)).

Treatment of US dividends

Article 10 paragraph 3 has no application to the case of an Irish resident general investor; the question of tax credits is not a feature of dividends paid by US companies. The position of the Irish recipient of a dividend from a US company is governed by treaty article 24 paragraph 4. US tax payable under US law and in accordance with the Ireland/ US treaty, whether directly or by deduction, on income from sources within the US (excluding underlying tax related to a dividend) is to be allowed as a credit against any Irish tax computed by reference to the same income (see below) by reference to which the US tax is computed (article 24 para 4(a)). As seen above, a dividend paid by a US resident company to an Irish resident is subject to US withholding tax but, in accordance with article 10 para 2, that tax may not exceed a certain percentage of the gross dividend (5% if the beneficial owner of the dividend is a company owning at least 10% of the voting stock of the US dividend paying company, and 15% in other cases). The Irish recipient of the dividend is taxable on the gross amount of the dividend (ie, before withholding tax) but subject to a credit for the withholding tax in computing the Irish tax liability thereon.

As regards the "same income" against tax on which credit for US tax is to be allowed, the judgment in *Legal & General Assurance Society Ltd v HMRC* [2006] EWHC 1770 (Ch) – see also **14.201**) would suggest that this is the Irish company's total Case III income and not the US dividend itself. The connection being made by the treaty article is between the fund charged to US tax (the dividend) and the fund chargeable to Irish tax which includes the dividend (ie, the company's Case III income).

Where the recipient of the dividend controls directly or indirectly 10% or more of the voting power in the US dividend paying company, the credit allowable is to take into account (in addition to any US tax creditable under article 24 paragraph 4(a)) the US tax payable by the dividend paying company in respect of the profits out of which the dividend was paid (article 24 para 4(b) – see **14.207** for treatment of foreign underlying tax: direct investments).

The procedure for determining the "relevant profits" of the dividend paying US resident company, for computing the underlying tax rate, and for granting credits for foreign taxes (including, where relevant, the foreign underlying tax) against an Irish resident company's corporation tax payable in respect of foreign source income, is discussed in **14.207** and **14.208**.

As indicated above, a direct investor for the purposes of article 10 of the Ireland/ US treaty is a company which is a resident of Ireland, is the beneficial owner of the dividend, and which controls directly or indirectly 10% or more of the voting power of the US dividend paying company. Article 10 paragraph 3(c) extends the meaning of direct investor to include the case where the required 10% or more of the voting power is held, directly or indirectly, by the Irish resident company and by one or more associated companies. For this purpose, two companies are deemed to be associated with each other either if one is controlled directly or indirectly by the other or if both are controlled directly or indirectly by a third company. The associated company need not necessarily be a resident of Ireland.

Permanent establishment

The provisions of article 10 paragraphs 1-3 have no application where a company receiving a dividend, being a resident of one Contracting State, carries on business in the other Contracting State (in which the dividend paying company is resident) through a permanent establishment there and the dividend is attributable to such permanent establishment. In any such case, the provisions of article 7 (business profits) will apply so that the dividend will be included in the business profits subject to tax under that article (article 10 para 6).

A company which is a resident of a Contracting State and which has a permanent establishment in the other Contracting State or which is subject to tax on a net basis in that other state on items of income or gains that may be taxed there under article 6 (real property) or article 13 paragraph 1 (capital gains) may be subject in that other state to a tax in addition to the tax which may be imposed in accordance with the other provisions of the treaty. Such additional tax may be imposed only on the portion of the business profits of the company attributable to the permanent establishment and the portion of the income or gains which may be taxed under articles 6 or 13, and, in the case of Ireland, representing an amount which would, if those profits, income or gains arose to a subsidiary company incorporated in Ireland, would be distributed as a dividend and, in the case of the US, representing the "dividend equivalent amount" as that term is defined under the laws of the US.

14.111.6 Royalties

Royalties paid from Ireland to the US, and vice versa, are not subject to withholding tax, to the extent that the royalties do not exceed arm's length amounts.

14.111.7 Interest payments to US

Provided it is not excessive, interest paid to a US lender can be paid without deduction of withholding tax. Furthermore, provisions of Irish domestic law (TCA 1997, s 130) which treat interest paid to a foreign parent company or affiliate as a dividend, and therefore as not tax deductible in Ireland, are superseded by the treaty. Interest to a US parent or affiliate will be tax deductible in Ireland to the extent that the interest does not exceed a normal arm's length rate of interest (see also under *Dividends* above). Such interest, although tax deductible, may still be treated as a dividend (distribution) unless this treatment is superseded by other domestic law provisions.

14.111.8 Immovable property

Income derived by a resident of a Contracting State from immovable property (real property), including income from forestry, situated in the other Contracting State may be taxed in that other State. "Immovable property" for this purpose has the meaning it has under the law of the Contracting State in which the property in question is situated (article 6).

14.111.9 Capital gains

Gains derived by a resident of a Contracting State from the alienation of immovable property situated in the other Contracting State may be taxed in that other State (article 13). "Immovable property" for this purpose includes, in the US, a US real property interest and, in Ireland, shares (including stock and any security), other than shares quoted on a stock exchange, deriving the greater part of their value directly or indirectly from immovable property situated in Ireland.

Gains from the alienation of movable property that are attributable to a permanent establishment that an enterprise of a Contracting State has in the other Contracting State, or that are attributable to a fixed base available to a resident of a Contracting State in the other Contracting State for the purpose of performing independent personal services, and gains from the alienation of such permanent establishment (alone or with the whole enterprise) or of such a fixed base, may be taxed in the other state. Gains arising to a resident of a Contracting State from the disposal of goodwill (regarded as movable property) attaching to a business carried on through a permanent establishment in the other Contracting State may be taxed in that state.

Gains derived by an enterprise of a Contracting State from the alienation of ships, aircraft or containers operated in international traffic or personal property pertaining to the operation of such ships, aircraft or containers, are to be taxable only in that state.

Gains derived from the alienation of any property other than property referred to above is to be taxable only in the Contracting State of which the alienator is resident.

Where, under the terms of the treaty, gains are chargeable in both countries, double tax relief is given by way of credit. Tax payable in respect of a gain arising in one Contracting State is allowed as a credit against the tax liability on the same gain arising to a resident (or citizen in the case of the US) of the other Contracting State.

In the US, Irish tax paid by or on behalf of a citizen or resident of the US is to be allowed as a credit against the US tax on income (which includes gains). In Ireland, US tax payable on chargeable gains from sources within the US is to be allowed as a credit against any Irish tax computed by reference to the same chargeable gains by reference to which the US tax is computed. Relief is given by deducting the amount of the credit from the amount of the tax payable in the country of residence. Credit may not be given at a rate which exceeds the effective overall rate of tax payable in the country of residence in respect of the gain on which foreign tax has been paid. That rate is calculated by dividing the total tax payable in the country of residence for the year or period by the total gain for that year or period.

TCA 1997, s 590 provides that a person resident in Ireland is subject to capital gains tax in respect of capital gains realised by non-resident closely held companies in which that person is a participator (see **9.408**). Except where the non-resident company realises gains from assets which may be taxed in Ireland (eg immovable property in Ireland), article 13 overrides the provisions of TCA 1997, s 590 if the company is resident in the US.

14.111.10 Limitation on benefits

For some years, arising out of US Treasury concerns regarding the abuse known as "treaty shopping" (residents of third countries gaining access to treaty benefits), the US has insisted on the inclusion of an article in its tax treaties to confine the benefits of the treaty to certain residents of the other Contracting State. That article is intended to prevent residents of non-treaty countries, or of countries with unfavourable treaties with the US, forming a company in an intermediate jurisdiction with a more favourable treaty and routing income from the US to the intermediate jurisdiction, subject to favourable withholding rates. The article in question is headed "limitation on benefits" and appears in the Ireland/ US treaty as article 23. Limitation on benefits (LOB) articles have been a normal part of US treaty provisions for some years and the article is included in the US model treaty but, from an Irish perspective, the inclusion of such a treaty article is a unique feature.

LOB article: introduction

The purpose of article 23 is to confine the benefits of the treaty to residents who are "qualified persons" and to prescribe conditions under which residents who are not qualified persons may nevertheless qualify for treaty benefits. The article is a two-way limitation on benefits provision but, as the prospect of third country investors routing Irish income through the US is somewhat remote, the article is mainly relevant for Irish companies with income arising in the US. The provisions of article 23 differ in a number of ways from the equivalent provisions in the US treaties with the Netherlands, Switzerland and Luxembourg so that, for example, there is no headquarters company exclusion in article 23.

There are many non-Irish companies operating in the IFSC which enter into transactions with the US and the LOB provisions will primarily be of interest to those companies. Under the treaty, an Irish company, including an IFSC company taxable in Ireland at the 10% corporation tax rate, will suffer no withholding tax on interest income from the US. Many IFSC companies in particular are engaged in lending funds to US customers, either as banks to third party customers or as group treasury companies to related parties. Although the treaty retains the zero withholding provision for US interest paid to Irish resident companies, it is necessary for this purpose to determine whether an Irish company in any case will be regarded as a qualifying person and therefore entitled to treaty benefits. In applying the LOB provision, which may result in a denial of zero withholding to companies that are not qualified persons, it is necessary to distinguish the different categories of Irish investors.

Irish and US owned Irish companies

Irish companies that are owned by Irish or US investors are largely unaffected by the LOB provisions. Ultimate ownership of a company by Irish individuals, US residents or listed companies or funds in the US or Ireland ensures that the company is a qualified person and is therefore not affected by LOB as long as the company satisfies the "base reduction" test.

Qualified person exception

Article 23 paragraph 2 provides that a resident of a Contracting State will be entitled to all the benefits of the treaty only if that resident is a qualified person. A "qualified person" is a resident of one of the Contracting States, being—

 (a) an individual;

 (b) a qualified government entity (as defined in article 3 paragraph 1 of the treaty);

 (c) a person other than an individual in respect of whom the ownership and base reduction tests (see below) are satisfied;

 (d) a listed fund in Ireland or the US, ie a person other than an individual or a company—

  (i) where the principal class of units in that person is listed on a recognised stock exchange in one of the Contracting States and is substantially and regularly traded (see below) on one or more such exchanges, or

  (ii) where the direct or indirect owners of at least 50% of the beneficial interests in that person are persons referred to in (i) above or in (e) below;

 (e) a listed company, ie a company (resident in one of the Contracting States), where—

  (i) the principal class of its shares is substantially and regularly traded on one or more recognised stock exchanges, or

  (ii) at least 50% of the aggregate vote and value of its shares is owned directly or indirectly by companies described in (i) above or by persons referred to in (b) above, or by companies more than 50% of the aggregate vote and value of which is owned by persons referred to in (b) above, or by any combination of the above;

 (f) a person described in article 4 paragraph 1(c) of the treaty (ie, pension trust or similar entity, a charitable or other exempt organisation, subject to conditions regarding use of assets) provided more than half of the beneficiaries, members or participants, if any, in such organisation are qualified persons.

The ownership test in (c) requires that at least 50% of the beneficial interest in the person or, where the person is a company, at least 50% of the aggregate vote and value of the company's shares, is owned directly or indirectly by other qualified persons or by residents or citizens of the US. Where indirect ownership is involved, the ownership test must be satisfied by the last owners in the chain of ownership. In effect, intermediate owners in a chain will generally be disregarded and ownership will need to be traced to a person entitled to treaty benefits without reference to its owners (eg, a publicly traded company). Thus, the test will be satisfied where the (ultimate) owners are qualified persons as described in (a), (b), (d), (e) or (f), since such persons are entitled to treaty benefits without reference to their ownership (if any), or residents or citizens of the US, since the treaty partners would not be concerned with treaty-shopping through such persons.

The purpose of the base reduction test mentioned in (c) above is to secure that, say, an Irish resident company cannot access treaty benefits in respect of US source income in circumstances where a significant part of its gross income is used to make certain kinds of payments to persons who would have been subject to US taxation had they received those payments directly. The test will be satisfied if amounts paid or accrued by the company during its fiscal year—

(a) to persons that are neither qualified persons nor residents or citizens of the US; and

(b) that are deductible for income tax purposes in that fiscal year in the company's state of residence (but not including arm's length payments in the ordinary course of business for—

    (i) services or tangible property, and

    (ii) payments in respect of financial obligations to a bank, provided that where such bank is not a resident of either Contracting State the payment is attributable to a permanent establishment of the bank and the permanent establishment is located in either Contracting State),

do not exceed 50% of the gross income of the company.

The term "gross income" in the above context is understood to take its meaning from US rules and accordingly refers to gross receipts less cost of goods sold. It is also understood that financing costs, if any, would not be deductible in ascertaining gross income. "Gross income", in relation to a current fiscal year, is defined in article 23 as gross income of the fiscal year preceding that year but the amount of that income may not be less than the average of the annual amounts of gross income of the four fiscal years preceding the current year. (In the case of a newly established company, it is likely that the averaging requirement would be dealt with by way of mutual agreement between the competent authorities of the Contracting States.)

Under the base reduction test, a third country resident would, for example, be prevented from arranging for an Irish company owned, say, by two Irish individuals to have its taxable income reduced by payments to a country not having a tax treaty with the US. Under the test, not more than 50% of the gross income of the Irish company may be paid in tax deductible payments outside Ireland and the US.

Whereas the exclusion in the base reduction test for arm's length payments in respect of services or tangible property is a standard feature of modern US treaties, the exclusion of payments in respect of financial obligations to banks is unique to the Ireland/ US treaty. The inclusion of that provision results from the nature of the banking market in Ireland where banks which are not Irish owned (or indeed EU owned) operate on the Irish domestic market and provide finance for Irish businesses. Interest and other financial obligation payments to banks resident in Ireland and the US, and to Irish branches of foreign banks, are not taken into account for the purposes of the base erosion test. The residence requirement for banks in the base reduction test does not include a requirement that the banks concerned would be "qualified persons" for purposes of the treaty.

For the purposes of (d) above, the protocol to the treaty confirms that shares in a class of shares, or the units in a class of units, are considered to be substantially and regularly traded on one or more recognised stock exchanges in a fiscal year if—

(a) trades in such class are effected on one or more of such stock exchanges, other than in de minimis quantities, during every quarter; and

(b) the aggregate number of shares or units of that class traded on such stock exchange or exchanges during the previous fiscal year is at least 6% of the average number of shares or units outstanding in that class during that taxable year, provided that if such class was not listed on a recognised stock exchange in the previous fiscal year the shares or units will be considered to have satisfied this requirement.

Alternative exception

Article 23 paragraph 5 provides for an alternative basis whereby a resident of a Contracting State may be entitled to the benefits of the Ireland-US tax treaty. To be entitled to treaty benefits under this paragraph, an Irish company must satisfy a number of tests: an ownership test, a "base reduction" test and, as respects access to the 5% dividend withholding tax rate, an "equivalent benefits" test. These are considered in turn as follows.

1. Ownership test:

To qualify for treaty benefit, at least 95% of the aggregate vote and value of all of the shares of the Irish company should be owned, directly or indirectly, by seven or fewer qualified persons or persons that are residents of Member States of the EU or of parties to the North American Free Trade Agreement (NAFTA), or any combination of these. (The parties to NAFTA are the US, Canada and Mexico.)

For the purposes of the ownership test, article 23 of the treaty defines "resident of a Member State of the European Union" as a person that would be entitled to the benefits of a comprehensive tax treaty between its own EU Member State and the US provided that, if that treaty does not contain a comprehensive LOB article (including provisions similar to paragraphs 2(c) and (e) of the Ireland-US treaty – see (c) and (e) under *Qualified person exception* above), the person would be entitled to the benefits of the Ireland-US treaty in accordance with article 23 paragraph 2 if that person were resident in Ireland in accordance with article 4 (residence) of the treaty.

2. Base reduction test:

An Irish company must meet the base reduction test in article 23 paragraph 2(c)(ii), described above under *Qualified person exception*. The test will accordingly be satisfied if amounts paid or accrued by the company during its fiscal year—

(a) to persons that are neither qualified persons (a resident of an EU Member State or a party to NAFTA being regarded as a qualified person for this purpose) nor residents or citizens of the US; and

(b) that are deductible for income tax purposes in that fiscal year in Ireland (but not including arm's length payments in the ordinary course of business for—

  (i) services or tangible property, and

  (ii) payments in respect of financial obligations to a bank, provided that where such bank is not a resident of either Contracting State the payment is attributable to a permanent establishment of the bank located in either Contracting State),

do not exceed 50% of the gross income of the Irish company. Regarding the term "gross income" in the above context, see above under *Qualified person exception*.

For the purposes of the base reduction test, a resident of a Member State of the EU (see definition of "resident of a member state of the European Union" under Ownership test above) or a party to NAFTA is treated as a qualifying person so that any payments to such a resident may be ignored. The definition of "resident of a party to NAFTA" is very similar to that for a resident of an EU Member State and refers to a person that would be entitled to the benefits of a comprehensive tax treaty between its own NAFTA member state and the US provided that, if that treaty does not contain a comprehensive LOB article (including provisions similar to paragraphs 2(c) and (e) of the Ireland-US treaty – see (c) and (e) under *Qualified person exception* above), the person would be entitled to the benefits of the Ireland-US treaty in accordance with article 23 paragraph 2 if that person were resident in Ireland in accordance with article 4 of the treaty.

3. Equivalent benefits test:

Failure to satisfy the equivalent benefits test results in a denial of treaty benefits in relation to certain kinds of US source income (dividends, interest and royalties) but, provided the ownership and base reduction tests are satisfied, does not affect any other treaty benefits. The equivalent benefits test is to be applied separately in respect of any dividend, interest or royalty income so that, for example, a company may be entitled to treaty benefits in respect of one of these income sources but not in respect of the others.

In relation to, say, US source dividends received by an Irish company, the company will be entitled to the reduced 5% withholding tax on such dividends if at least 95% of its shares (not 95% of the "vote and value" as for the ownership test) are held, directly or indirectly, by one or more residents of a Member State of the EU (see meaning of "resident of a Member State of the European Union" under Ownership test above) or of parties to NAFTA, or any combination thereof, who under the tax treaty between their state of residence and the US would be entitled to benefits that are at least equivalent to those provided for under the Ireland-US tax treaty with respect to dividend income.

Non-EU/NAFTA owned Irish companies

Under article 23, the benefits of the Ireland/ US treaty are denied to Irish companies owned by shareholders outside the EU and NAFTA. Thus, non-EU/NAFTA owned Irish companies do not qualify for zero withholding from the US on interest so that the normal 30% rate applies in these cases.

EU/NAFTA owned Irish companies

In an intermediate category (ie, not US or Irish owned but EU/ NAFTA owned) are Irish companies owned by EU and NAFTA shareholders. This category contains two sub-categories.

1. EU/NAFTA owned companies with equivalent home treaty benefits

Treated similarly to US and Irish owned companies, and therefore fully entitled to the benefits of the treaty, are companies owned from EU and NAFTA countries with equivalent home treaty benefits (article 23 paragraph 5). In this sub-category are Irish companies owned from Austria, the Czech Republic, Denmark, Finland, France, Germany, Greece, Hungary, Luxembourg, Netherlands, Poland, Slovakia, Sweden and the UK. As long as the Irish resident company is at least 95% owned by seven or fewer shareholders resident in these countries, the full benefits of the US treaty will be available and the company will continue to qualify for zero withholding in respect of interest paid from the US.

The base reduction provisions in paragraph 2(c)(ii) (see above) apply so that certain tax deductible payments may not exceed 50% of gross income. These anti-conduit provisions prevent an Irish company owned by relevant EU/ NAFTA shareholders from eroding the tax base through tax deductible payments to third countries. In determining whether a company meets the base reduction test for EU/ NAFTA ownership, it is necessary to take into account payments that are not excluded from the base reduction provisions and made to persons that are not EU/ NAFTA residents, not Irish qualified persons and not residents or citizens of the US. The excluded base reduction payments are those mentioned above, ie arm's length payments in the ordinary course of business for services or tangible property, and payments in respect of financial obligations to a bank which is either resident in Ireland or the US, or is a bank with a permanent establishment in Ireland or the US to which the financial obligation payment is attributable.

Where base reduction payments not excluded by the above provisions exceed 50% of the gross income of the Irish resident company, the EU/NAFTA ownership test is not met and the company will not be entitled to treaty benefits.

Irish companies satisfying the base erosion test and which are at least 95% owned by seven or fewer shareholders from the countries mentioned above (or from Ireland or the US) will be eligible for treaty benefits.

2. EU/NAFTA owned companies without equivalent home treaty benefits

In the second sub-category are companies owned from the remaining EU and NAFTA countries which have no treaty with the US or whose treaties with the US allow for higher withholding tax on interest payments than is the case under the US/ Ireland treaty, ie Belgium, Canada, Cyprus, Estonia, Italy, Latvia, Lithuania, Malta, Mexico, Portugal, Slovenia and Spain. Under the Ireland-US treaty, Irish companies owned from these countries will not be entitled to the benefits of the articles dealing with interest, dividends and royalties (but may qualify under the remaining articles). For example, an Irish company 94% of the shares in which are owned by qualified residents of Germany (under the US/ German treaty) and 6% of the shares of which are owned by a Belgian company will not qualify for treaty benefits on interest. A similar position will apply in the case of, say, an Irish subsidiary of a Canadian parent.

The above-described "derivative benefits" test, provided for in article 23 paragraph 5(b), must be met by an Irish resident company that satisfies the ownership and base reduction tests in paragraph 5(a) but which requires to obtain the benefit of any of the articles dealing with dividends, interest or royalties. The company may not benefit under these articles unless at least 95% of its shares are held by EU or NAFTA residents where the treaties between the home countries of those residents and the US provide for benefits equivalent to those required under the Ireland-US treaty. The derivative benefits test could therefore be satisfied by a company in relation to one of the three income items (for example, dividends) but not in relation to the other items (interest and royalties). Apart from the position pertaining to dividends, interest and royalties, the company will be entitled to all other benefits under the treaty.

Active business exception

Even where an Irish company is not a qualified person, it may nevertheless, based on other tests, qualify for treaty benefits with respect to income derived from the US.

Treaty benefits may be available if the business of the Irish resident qualifies as an active trade or business article 23 paragraph 3). To qualify in this way, the Irish resident—

(a) must be engaged in the active conduct of a trade or business in Ireland (other than the business of making or managing investments unless such business is carried on by a bank or insurance company acting in the ordinary course of its business); and

(b) the US source income in question must be connected with or be incidental to the trade or business in Ireland, provided, where the income item is connected with a trade or business in Ireland and the Irish resident has an ownership interest in the activity in the US which generated the income, the Irish trade or business must be substantial in relation to the US activity.

Thus two determinations must be made: (1) whether the business undertaken in Ireland constitutes "the active conduct of a trade or business" and (2) whether the income items arising in the US (eg, interest or dividend income) is connected with the Irish trade or business. The treaty requires the activity in the US which generates the income item to be a line of business which forms a part of, or is complementary to, the trade or business conducted in Ireland.

In the case of income derived from an activity in which the Irish resident has an ownership interest, "all relevant facts and circumstances" will be taken into account in determining whether the Irish trade or business is substantial. The usual "safe harbour" rules apply, requiring that, in the three preceding fiscal years or in the preceding year, the asset value, gross income and payroll expense of the trade or business of the Irish resident in Ireland is at least 7.5% of the asset value, gross income and payroll expense, respectively, of the activity that generated the income in the US and that the average of the three ratios exceeds 10%.

The active trade or business provisions are further qualified in the protocol to the treaty, as follows:

1. a determination is to be made based on an analysis of all the relevant facts and circumstances. It is understood that the purpose of this provision is to ensure that the matter is not exclusively considered under the US domestic law provisions;

2. there is a safe haven for banks which are considered to be engaged in the active conduct of a trade or business if they regularly accept deposits from the public or make loans to the public. All banks licensed at the date of signature of the treaty will satisfy this requirement. This will be particularly relevant to non-EU/ NAFTA licensed banks in the IFSC, and those from EU/ NAFTA countries without equivalent home treaty benefits;

3. an insurance company will be considered to be engaged in the active conduct of a trade or business if its gross income consists primarily of insurance or reinsurance premiums and investment income attributable to such premiums;

4. activities conducted by a partnership in which a person is a partner and activities conducted by persons connected to such person are deemed to be conducted by such person: a person is connected with another person if one possesses at least 50% of the beneficial interest in the other (in the case of a company, 50% of the aggregate vote and value of the company's shares or of

the beneficial equity interest in the company) or another person possesses directly or indirectly at least 50% of the beneficial interest (in the case of a company, at least 50% of the aggregate vote and value of the company's shares or of the beneficial equity interest in the company) in each person;

5. the protocol confirms that an ownership interest in an activity in the US is not created by the supply of goods or provision of services. For example, in the case of a lessor leasing property to a business in which the lessor does not otherwise have an ownership interest, the leased property does not constitute an ownership interest.

Subjective test, discretionary qualification

Article 23 paragraph 6 of the treaty provides for a subjective test for qualification for treaty benefits where the qualified person test is not met. The provision enables treaty benefits to be granted if the establishment, acquisition or maintenance of the Irish company and the conduct of its operations did not have as one of its principal purposes the obtaining of treaty benefits. The relevant determination is made by the Internal Revenue Service in the US, who must consult with the Irish competent authorities in making the determination.

Exempt foreign branches

Even where an Irish company satisfies the principal LOB requirements, higher US withholding taxes may be imposed if the US source income is attributable to a non-Irish branch of the company (article 23 paragraph 7). If the foreign branch is exempt from Irish tax (under TCA 1997, s 847 – see **14.9**), dividends, interest and royalties from the US will be subject to a 15% withholding tax unless the branch tax rate is more than 50% of the corresponding Irish rate. There is an exclusion from the higher withholding tax if the US source income is connected with or incidental to the active conduct of a trade or business undertaken in the foreign branch (including banking and insurance, but not other investment activities).

Mutual funds

Relevant in an IFSC context is the entitlement to treaty benefits of mutual fund structures. Specifically included as Irish residents for purposes of the treaty are Irish collective investment undertakings (CIUs) including unit trusts, UCITSs, investment limited partnerships and investment companies under Part XIII of the Companies Act 1990 (see **12.802**). US residents include Regulated Investment Companies (RICs) and Real Estate Investment Trusts (REITs). The funds will of course be subject to normal LOB provisions.

Insurance

In the case of the US, the treaty applies to US Federal income tax and Federal excise tax. Both insurance and reinsurance premiums are covered by the treaty. However, the usual anti-conduit provisions of US treaties are included and the treaty applies only to the extent that the risks covered by the insurance premiums are not reinsured with a person who is not entitled to exemption from Federal excise tax under the Irish or any other treaty. The protocol to the treaty provides that an insurer in receipt of premiums and claiming exemption from Federal excise tax must be subject to "the generally applicable tax imposed on insurance corporations in the state of residence".

14.2 CREDIT FOR FOREIGN TAX

14.201 Introduction

All of the tax treaties to which Ireland is a party are given the force of law by TCA 1997, s 826(1). TCA 1997, s 826(2) provides that TCA 1997 Sch 24 ("Relief from income tax and corporation tax by means of credit in respect of foreign tax") is to apply where a credit for a foreign tax is to be given against Irish tax under any double taxation agreement given the force of law by a government order made under that section. TCA 1997, s 826A provides for unilateral relief to be given in accordance with TCA 1997, Sch 24 in cases not covered by TCA 1997, s 826. TCA 1997 Sch 24 provides for credits to be given against income tax, corporation tax and, by virtue of TCA 1997, s 828, capital gains tax.

Credit for foreign tax against Irish tax chargeable in respect of any income is given by reducing the relevant Irish tax by the amount of the credit (TCA 1997 Sch 24 paragraph 2(1)). It was widely thought that the credit for foreign tax paid in respect of any foreign income item is only given against the Irish tax payable on the same income. The judgment in *Legal & General Assurance Society Ltd v HMRC* [2006] EWHC 1770 (Ch) would, however, suggest that the Irish tax against which credit is to be allowed is the tax on the company's total income chargeable to tax under the appropriate Case of Schedule D. It is a fundamental principle of UK tax law, the judgment notes, that tax is charged by reference to various kinds of income identified according to their source under the Schedules and Cases with each case having its charging provisions which identify the income to be taxed. Thus, it is incorrect in principle to refer to UK tax as being "chargeable in respect of" a fund of income, being a part of the income chargeable under the relevant Case, which corresponds to the amount of the income which has borne the foreign tax.

Notwithstanding the above view of TCA 1997, Sch 24 paragraph 2(1), *Legal & General* is unlikely to have any real effect for Irish tax purposes. This is because of the limit imposed on the foreign credit tax itself as provided for in TCA 1997, Sch 24 paragraph 4(1) (TA 1998, s 797(1) in the UK) which restricts the amount of foreign tax creditable against Irish tax to an amount calculated by applying the Irish tax rate to the amount of the foreign income (see 14.202 and 14.212). Thus, while the Irish tax against which the creditable tax is allowable may be the tax on the full income charged under the appropriate Case of Schedule D, the creditable tax itself is restricted by reference to the foreign income.

In the absence of any provision equivalent to TCA 1997, Sch 24 paragraph 4(2), the foreign tax credit limit in the UK is by reference to the gross foreign income. Providing for a "net basis" (see 14.202), paragraph 4(2) explains what, "for the purposes of this paragraph", is meant by corporation tax "attributable to any [foreign] income". For Irish tax purposes, that explanation of paragraph 4(1) must be preferred to any alternative explanation that might be derived from the *Legal & General* case.

TCA 1997 Sch 24 paragraph 9E provides for the pooling of tax credits in the cases of certain dividends (see **14.214**).

Credit relief may be disclaimed at the option of the taxpayer (TCA 1997 Sch 24 paragraph 10).

For the purposes of TCA 1997 Sch 24, "foreign tax" is limited to any foreign tax properly chargeable under the laws of another country with which Ireland has a double tax treaty and is a tax in respect of which the treaty permits a credit against Irish tax (TCA 1997 Sch 24 paragraph 1(1), (2)). In most treaties, the article dealing with the elimination of double taxation provides that the credit is for taxes paid in the other treaty country "in accordance with this Convention". Accordingly, if a treaty permits one country to levy tax on an item of income at a maximum rate of tax, but a higher rate of tax is withheld on payment of that item, the maximum foreign tax creditable against Irish tax is tax at the rate stated in the treaty. It will then be for the taxpayer in question to claim repayment of the excess tax from the country in which the tax was withheld.

It is a requirement that credit for foreign tax against Irish corporation tax on income or chargeable gains for an accounting period is given, subject to Sch 24 paragraphs 9A, 9B and 9C (which paragraphs, in the light of the *Saint-Gobain* case, extend the availability of credit relief to Irish branches of EU resident companies – see **14.209-10**), only to a company which is "resident in the State" for that period (TCA 1997 Sch 24 paragraph 3).

Double taxation may be avoided either by exemption in the source country or by way of credit in the home country (country of residence of the recipient of the income). Under a credit system, foreign income is subjected to tax in the home country but a credit is allowed against home country tax in respect of the foreign tax attributable to the foreign income. Creditable tax may be limited to the amount withheld or may include underlying tax ("deemed paid tax") of the foreign company. Entitlement to credit is derived from the relevant tax treaty but the rules for calculating the relief are to be found in domestic legislation, principally in TCA 1997 Sch 24. Under the deduction system, tax in the home country is reduced by foreign tax paid or payable. This method is less favourable than either the exemption or the credit method and produces a higher overall effective rate of tax on foreign income. The system of reducing the burden of double taxation in Ireland contains both exemption and credit elements but also provides for deduction to some extent.

Irish companies may incur foreign taxation in a number of ways. Interest, royalties, dividends and rents received from abroad may be payable subject to deduction of foreign tax at source (withholding tax). An Irish company may suffer foreign tax on the profits of its foreign branch or permanent establishment. Even where no foreign branch trade is being carried on, receipts of a domestic Irish trade, such as royalties or licence fees, or interest earned by a bank, may be subjected to foreign withholding tax.

The terms of a tax treaty take precedence over domestic law to the extent that they provide for relief from double taxation. A treaty cannot impose or increase a charge to tax.

14.202 Computation

TCA 1997, s 826(1) gives the force of law to tax treaties negotiated by the Irish government. These sections are supplemented by TCA 1997 Sch 24. TCA 1997, s 826(1) makes provision for the purposes of affording relief from double taxation in respect of income tax and corporation tax.

TCA 1997, s 827 provides, subject to any express amendments made by the Corporation Tax Acts and except in so far as arrangements made on or after 31 March 1976 provide otherwise, that arrangements made under ITA 1967 s 361, or any earlier enactment corresponding to that section, in relation to corporation profits tax are to apply in relation to corporation tax and income and chargeable gains chargeable to that tax as they are expressed to apply in relation to corporation profits tax and profits chargeable to that tax, and not as they apply to corporation tax (TCA 1997, s 827). TCA 1997, s 827 is not, however to affect the operation, as they apply to corporation tax, of TCA 1997, s 826(7) (obligation as to secrecy not to prevent disclosure to any authorised officer of government of country with treaty arrangements are made) and TCA 1997 Sch 24 para 12 (claim to credit for foreign tax to be made within six years from the end of the accounting period in which the income, foreign tax on which credit relief is to be given, is charged to corporation tax).

A case in point here might be paragraph II of the Protocol to the Ireland-Netherlands tax treaty which provides for the deduction of interest paid by an Irish resident to a Dutch resident in the corporation profits tax computation of the payer. As to whether or not this gives a right to an automatic deduction for interest for corporation tax purposes is doubtful in the light of TCA 1997, s 130 which presumably is an instance of "any express amendments made by the Corporation Tax Acts". As regards the Ireland-Netherlands treaty, the point is somewhat academic now in the light of the statutory treatment of interest paid to affiliates in fellow EU Member States.

TCA 1997, s 826(1) provides that where the Government by order declare that arrangements specified in the order have been made with the government of any territory outside the State in relation to—

(a) affording relief from double taxation in respect of income tax, corporation tax in respect of income and chargeable gains (or for corporation profits tax where the arrangements pre-dated the introduction of corporation tax), capital gains tax, any taxes of a similar character imposed by the laws of the State or by the laws of that territory, and

(b) in the case of taxes of any kind or description imposed by the laws of the State or the laws of that territory—

(i) exchanging information for the purposes of the prevention and detection of tax evasion, or

(ii)   granting relief from taxation under the laws of that territory to persons who are resident in the State for the purposes of tax,

and that it is expedient that those arrangements should have the force of law ..... "the arrangements shall, notwithstanding any enactment, have the force of law". The reference to "notwithstanding any enactment" confirms the precedence of tax treaty provisions over domestic law. TCA 1997, s 826(2) accordingly provides that TCA 1997 Sch 24 is to apply where arrangements which have the force of law by virtue of the section provide that tax payable under the laws of the territory concerned are to be allowed as a credit against Irish tax. TCA 1997 Sch 24 provides the rules for the determination of the foreign tax credit that is given under the terms of a double tax treaty.

TCA 1997 Sch 24 paragraph 1(1) confirms which taxes are taken into account for the purposes of giving double taxation relief. Thus, *the Irish taxes* means income tax and corporation tax and *foreign tax* means, in relation to the foreign country concerned, any tax chargeable under the laws of that country for which credit may be allowed in accordance with the relevant tax treaty. Credit is allowed in respect of national or federal taxes on income but may also be available in respect of other foreign taxes, such as municipal taxes, tax on immovable property and tax in respect of undistributed income.

Two fundamental aspects of credit relief are dealt with in TCA 1997 Sch 24 Part I, namely, the determination of the amount of the income in respect of which the foreign tax credit is claimed (paragraph 7) and the limit to the amount of the credit for the foreign tax (paragraph 4). TCA 1997 Sch 24 paragraph 4 sets down the fundamental principle that the amount of the credit to be allowed against corporation tax for foreign tax in respect of any income may not exceed "the corporation tax attributable to that income". TCA 1997 Sch 24 paragraph 7 contains the rules for computing that income. It will be recalled that TCA 1997, s 828(1) extends the application of certain provisions as they apply for income tax purposes, particularly TCA 1997, s 826(1) and TCA 1997 Sch 24, for the purposes of giving relief from double taxation in relation to capital gains tax charged under the law of any foreign country.

TCA 1997 Sch 24 paragraph 4(2) clarifies the meaning of "corporation tax attributable to any income or gain" of a company. It is the corporation tax attributable to so much of the income or chargeable gains of the company ("the relevant income" or, as the case may be, "the relevant gain"), computed in accordance with the Tax Acts and the Capital Gains Tax Acts, as is attributable to that income or gain. In respect of a particular income (or gain) item, it is necessary to allocate the total income (or gain) of the company as computed for Irish corporation tax purposes to the item that has borne foreign tax. The income so allocated is sometimes referred to as "the Irish measure" of the foreign income.

The allocation is to be done on a "turnover" basis, by reference to the amount of the foreign income item over total receipts of the trade. TCA 1997 Sch 24 paragraph 4(2A) (introduced by FA 2006) provides that, subject to TCA 1997 Sch 24 paragraph 4(3) (computer services/ software and IFSC/Shannon income eligible for the 10% rate – see below), where credit is to be allowed against corporation tax for foreign tax in respect of any income, being income (other than income from a trade carried on by the company through a branch or agency in a territory other than the State - see further below) included as part of a company's trading income for an accounting period, the relevant income is that part of the trading profits for the period as is determined by the following formula—

$$P \times \frac{I}{R}$$

where—

P   is the amount of the profits or gains of the trade for the accounting period before deducting any amount under Sch 24 paragraph 7(3)(c) (deduction for excess foreign tax – see below);

I   is the amount of that (ie, foreign) income for the period before deducting any disbursements or expenses of the trade; and

R   is the total amount receivable by the company in the carrying on of the trade in the period.

It was never intended that the above-described approach was to apply for the purposes of calculating credit relief in respect of foreign tax paid by an overseas branch. Although this could be inferred from the wording of paragraph 4(2A), which seems somewhat inappropriate to the position of a foreign branch, it may nevertheless have been possible to interpret the subparagraph so as to apply to foreign branches. That is no longer possible with effect from 31 January 2008; hence the exception mentioned above. To cater for the position of companies that may have, to their disadvantage, filed their tax returns using the formula basis to calculate credit relief for tax paid by an overseas branch, an election may be made to have the relief calculated on the pre-formula basis as on and from 1 January 2006.

In computing the Irish measure of foreign income (for the purposes of the limitation on foreign credit imposed by TCA 1997 Sch 24 paragraph 4(1)), it was considered for many years that this computation could be carried out by a company on a "gross" basis, ie without making any deduction from the foreign income in respect of expenses incurred generally by the company. This question became topical for banking and other IFSC companies that suffered foreign withholding taxes on gross receipts, particularly interest. The Irish measure of the foreign income was simply the gross amount received with no deduction for attributable expenses such as cost of funds or share of overheads. The gross basis was replaced by a net basis for accounting periods ended after 31 December 1994 and this is reflected in the meaning of "corporation tax attributable to any income or gain" as defined above. This topic is considered further in **14.212**.

TCA 1997 Sch 24 paragraph 4(4) explains "corporation tax attributable to" in relation to foreign income or gains. It is the amount of the foreign income or gains multiplied by the rate of corporation tax payable by the company (before any credit for double tax relief) for the accounting period in which the income or gain arises (referred to hereafter as "the effective rate of corporation tax"). This definition is amplified by TCA 1997 Sch 24 paragraph 4(5) which is relevant where a company is entitled to any deduction in respect of charges on income, management expenses or other amounts which are deductible in arriving at the company's total profits (see **14.208**).

In computing the foreign income in respect of which the effective rate of corporation tax is applied—

(a) no deduction is to be made for foreign tax, whether in respect of the same or any other income (but subject to (c) below) (TCA 1997 Sch 24 paragraph 7(3)(a));

(b) where the income includes a dividend in respect of which there is an entitlement to a credit for underlying tax ("foreign tax not chargeable directly or by deduction", ie withholding tax), the amount of the income is to be increased by that tax (TCA 1997 Sch 24 paragraph 7(3)(b));

(c) the amount of the (doubly taxed) income is reduced by any foreign tax which cannot be allowed as a credit ("excess foreign tax") including any indirect foreign tax (TCA 1997 Sch 24 paragraph 7(3)(c)).

Application of the above rules poses a momentary problem. While the amount of foreign income to be included for the purposes of the computation of credit is to be reduced by any excess foreign tax, it is necessary to know the amount of the foreign income finally to be included in the computation to ascertain whether there is any excess foreign tax. This riddle is solved by a practical approach which incorporates "grossing up" the "net foreign income", ie the foreign income as computed for Irish tax purposes after deducting the foreign taxes paid or payable in respect of that income, and before adding any foreign indirect taxes which may be available for credit (see Example **14.202.2** below). Where the company is entitled to a deduction for charges on income or other amount which is deductible against its total profits, any such amount must be allocated against the different items of income and gains as discussed later (see **14.208**). The computation involves the following steps.

(a) identify the net foreign income (see **14.208**) (see above);

(b) ascertain the amount of the foreign taxes available for credit in respect of the foreign income (see **14.203**);

(c) calculate the effective rate of foreign tax, ie the rate of foreign tax available for credit, expressed as a percentage of the Irish measure of the foreign income, ie the sum of the foreign tax and the amount of the net foreign income, as computed for Irish tax purposes (see **14.204**);

(d) ascertain the effective rate of corporation tax payable by the company for the accounting period in which the foreign income arises;

(e) gross up the net foreign income at the lower of

  (i)   the effective rate of foreign tax, and

  (ii) the effective rate of corporation tax,

(f) the amount of the credit for foreign tax is the amount by which the net foreign income has been grossed up in (e), or, the excess of the amount in (e) over the amount in (a).

The net foreign income grossed up at (e) is the amount after deducting any charges or other amounts deductible from total profits, allocated to the foreign income in question.

Example 14.202.1

The trading profits of Winslow Ltd for its most recent accounting period include €1,200,000, as computed for Irish tax purposes, from its branch in the Czech Republic.

Czech tax of €300,000 has been paid in respect of these profits. All of the company's profits are subject to Irish corporation tax at 12.5%. The computation of credit for Czech tax is as follows:

	€
Net foreign income	900,000
Foreign tax	300,000
Effective rate of foreign tax	25%
Gross up net foreign income at 12.5%	1,028,571
Corporation tax @ 12.5%	128,571
Less: credit for foreign tax (maximum)	128,571
	Nil

The excess foreign tax, as disclosed using the "gross up" method, is €171,429 (300,000 - 128,571). The credit relief computation could therefore, alternatively, be set out as follows:

	€
Foreign income	1,200,000
Deduct: excess foreign tax credit	171,429
	1,028,571
Corporation tax @ 12.5%	128,571
Less: credit for foreign tax	128,571
	Nil

It can be seen that grossing up is not necessary where the foreign tax rate is clearly lower than the effective corporation tax rate. In that case, the foreign income in respect of which credit relief is due is that income computed in accordance with Irish tax rules.

The following example deals with a situation in which the gross up method is appropriate.

Example 14.202.2

The trading profits of Midway Ltd are €60,000, being gross receipts €100,000 less expenses €40,000. Receipts include foreign income of €20,000 from which withholding tax of €2,000 was deducted. The profits of Midway Ltd are taxable at 10% in Ireland.

The credit relief computation could be carried out in the following way, using a process of iteration to recalculate the unallowed credit until the resulting amount stabilises:

	€
"Irish measure" of foreign income – €60,000 x 20/100	12,000
Foreign tax	2,000
Foreign tax rate	16.67%
Credit = Irish tax on foreign income – €12,000 @ 10%	1,200
Unallowed credit (€2,000 - €1,200)	800
Foreign income adjusted (€12,000 - €800)	11,200
Credit = Irish tax on revised foreign income @ 10%	1,120
Unallowed credit	880

Foreign income adjusted (€12,000 - €880)	11,120
Credit = Irish tax on revised foreign income @ 10%	1,112
Unallowed credit	888
Foreign income adjusted (€12,000 - €888)	11,112
Credit = Irish tax on foreign income @ 10%	1,111
Unallowed credit	889
Foreign income adjusted (€12,000 - €889)	11,111
Credit = Irish tax on foreign income @ 10%	1,111
Unallowed credit	889

Corporation tax computation:

Profit as finally adjusted (€60,000 - €889)	59,111
Corporation tax @ 10%	5,911
Less: credit relief	1,111
Tax payable	4,800

Using the gross up approach, the computation can more conveniently be carried out as follows:

	€
"Irish measure" of foreign income – €60,000 x 20/100	12,000
Net foreign income – €12,000 - €2,000	10,000
Gross up net foreign income at 10%	11,111
Corporation tax @ 10%	1,111
Less: credit for foreign tax	1,111

Corporation tax computation:

Profit	60,000
Deduct: unallowed credit (€2,000 - €1,111)	889
	59,111
Corporation tax @ 10%	5,911
Less: credit relief	1,111
Tax payable	4,800

TCA 1997 Sch 24 paragraph 4(3) deals with the computation of foreign income which qualifies in Ireland for the effective 10% corporation tax rate, being income from qualifying activities carried on in the IFSC or Shannon, income from computer services or income derived from sales of computer software which has been manufactured in Ireland ("an amount receivable from the sale of goods" within the meaning of TCA

1997, s 449). Income in these cases is to be computed on the sales apportionment basis provided for in TCA 1997, s 449(2)(b), (c) – see **14.403**).

As regards the corporation tax attributable to the foreign income or gain (the "relevant income or gain"), this is an amount equal to the percentage of that income or gain as corresponds to the rate of corporation tax payable by the company "on its income or chargeable gains" (in effect, the 25% or the 12.5% rate, as appropriate) except that where the corporation tax payable by the company for the relevant accounting period on the relevant income or gain—

(a) is charged at the rate specified in TCA 1997, s 21A (higher rate of corporation tax – see **3.101.4**), the rate of corporation tax payable on the income and chargeable gains is that rate;

(b) is reduced by virtue of TCA 1997, s 448 by any fraction (in arriving at the effective 10% corporation tax rate or a mixed rate between the 10% rate and the standard rate – see **7.202**), the rate of tax payable on the income or gains is to be reduced by that fraction;

(c) is to be computed in accordance with TCA 1997, s 713(3) (in the case of a life assurance company – see "pegged rate" in **12.603.5**) or 738(2) (in the case of an undertaking for collective investment – see Taxation of CIUs: corporation tax in **12.805.4**), the rate of corporation tax payable on the income and chargeable gains is to be treated as the standard rate of income tax;

(d) is reduced by virtue of TCA 1997, s 644B by a fraction (the one-fifth fraction to produce the effective 20% rate for trading income from dealing in residential development land – see **3.101.6**), the rate of corporation tax payable on the income and chargeable gains is treated as reduced by that fraction (TCA 1997 Sch 24 paragraph 4(4)).

As regards (a) and (d), the position described above in relation to them applies in respects accounting periods ending on or after 1 January 2000. In this connection, where an accounting period of a company begins before 1 January 2000 and ends on or after that day, it is to be divided into two parts, one beginning on the day on which the accounting period begins and ending on 31 December 1999 and the other beginning on 1 January 2000 and ending on the day on which the accounting period ends, and both parts are to be treated as separate accounting periods of the company.

14.203 Foreign taxes available for credit

To ascertain the foreign taxes available for credit in any case, it is necessary to consult the relevant tax treaty. Foreign taxes comprise both direct and indirect taxes. Direct taxes are the taxes which the company claiming credit itself suffers. Direct taxes consist of taxes deducted from income received by the company (withholding taxes) and those paid in respect of foreign income arising, eg tax in respect of foreign branch profits. All tax treaties provide for credits in respect of direct taxes and also specify the extent to which the government of the other contracting state may impose direct taxes. Thus, direct taxes in respect of interest or royalties are in most cases reduced to nil and are limited to a maximum percentage in other cases.

Indirect taxes, or "underlying taxes", are those taxes which the company resident in the other contracting state pays or is liable to pay in respect of the profits out of which dividends are paid. Credit for indirect foreign tax against Irish tax only arises therefore where the Irish resident company receives dividends and where the relevant tax treaty specifically provides that an indirect tax credit may be given. In addition to the credit for foreign direct taxes, most of Ireland's tax treaties permit the Irish resident company to claim a credit for these taxes.

Trading income is generally taxed on the accruals basis. This can give rise to timing differences in relation to a claim for relief for foreign withholding taxes (or underlying taxes in the case of dividends) where such taxes have not yet been paid on the profits taxable in Ireland on the accruals basis. To overcome the effects of this mismatch for credit relief purposes, the Revenue in practice allow relief for foreign taxes not yet paid on the accruals basis in so far as this treatment is consistent with the recognition of income.

Certain treaties provide for an indirect tax credit in respect of any dividends paid to an Irish resident company, but in the most cases this credit is only given in respect of an ordinary dividend or any participating element in a participating preference dividend. Certain treaties provide for a credit for indirect taxes only where the foreign dividends are received by an Irish resident company holding a minimum percentage of the voting share capital or of the ordinary share capital in the company paying the dividend.

Some treaties provide that the taxes available for credit include not only national or federal taxes on income but also other taxes, such as municipal or local authority taxes, tax on immovable property and tax in respect of undistributed income, to the extent payable on the distributing company's profits. For example, the Ireland/ Germany tax treaty provides that the credit for foreign tax includes the German trade tax (*Gewerbesteuer*) to the extent that it is based on profits.

14.204 Effective rate of foreign tax

The effective rate of foreign tax in respect of any item of income is the amount of the foreign taxes available for credit in respect of that item as a percentage of the aggregate of the net foreign income and the foreign taxes available for credit. Where a credit is available for direct taxes only, and the income is such that the only foreign tax is a withholding tax, eg dividends, interest or royalties, the foreign tax rate is simply the tax withheld as a percentage of the gross (ie, before deducting the foreign tax) income. The tax withheld will itself usually be limited, and will often be nil, in accordance with the treaty.

Where a company carries on trading activities through a foreign branch, the direct foreign tax will consist of the corporate tax levied on those profits by the foreign jurisdiction. In that case, the effective rate of foreign tax is the amount of the foreign tax payable as a percentage of the foreign branch profits computed under Irish tax rules. Sometimes the rate is expressed in accordance with the following formula:

$$\frac{FT}{NFI + FT}$$

where—

FT   is the foreign tax paid in respect of the branch profits; and

NFI   is the net foreign income as computed under Irish tax rules, less the foreign tax paid.

Example 14.204.1

The Italian branch results of Blackhill Ltd, an Irish resident company, show a trading profit of €60,000. For Italian tax purposes, the adjusted profits and tax payable thereon are €65,000 and €21,500 respectively..

The assessable Italian branch profits of Blackhill Ltd for Irish corporation tax purposes are computed for the relevant accounting period as follows:

	€
Profits per Italian branch accounts	60,000
Add: disallowable expenses	8,600
	68,600
Capital allowances	7,500
Branch profits	61,100

The net foreign income is €61,100 less the Italian tax paid €21,500 = €39,600.

The Italian tax available for credit is €21,600. The effective rate of Italian tax payable is as follows:

$$\frac{21,500}{39,600+21,500} = 35.19\%$$

The net foreign income of €39,600 is grossed up at the lower effective rate, the Irish rate of 12.5%, to give a taxable profit of €45,257. The Irish corporation tax computation is as follows:

	€
Italian branch profits assessable	45,257
Corporation tax @ 12.5%	5,657
Less: credit	5,657
Net payable	Nil

Calculation of the effective foreign rate is less straightforward where the foreign income is a dividend in respect of which an Irish company is entitled to include the foreign underlying tax in the tax credit computation. In that case, the effective rate of foreign tax is a function of the direct tax withheld by the dividend paying company and the underlying tax payable by it in respect of its profits out of which the dividend has been paid. Credit for underlying tax is allowed in some tax treaties only in cases of direct investments.

Before looking at the question of how credit for underlying taxes is calculated, it is useful to distinguish between direct investments and other ("portfolio") investments.

14.205 Portfolio and direct investments

A portfolio investment in a company is generally a shareholding representing a small proportion of the company's issued share capital. It is usually an investment in a quoted company and, in many cases, as the name "portfolio" suggests, is part of a shareholding of such investments held by the company concerned. A direct investment, on the other hand, is a larger shareholding in a company, normally one representing 10% or more of the company's issued share capital or, where the company has more than one class of share capital, of its ordinary or voting shares. Direct investments are often controlling shareholdings or shareholdings sufficiently large to confer significant voting control in relation to the company's affairs.

Where under the terms of a tax treaty a withholding tax has been deducted, the credit available against Irish tax includes that withholding tax, whether in relation to a portfolio or a direct investment. Dividends received by Irish resident companies from abroad are usually subject to foreign withholding taxes although some countries do not impose withholding taxes due to a tax treaty provision or because of a provision in their own domestic tax laws.

Credit against Irish tax for underlying foreign tax is sometimes allowed only where the resident company is a direct investor, and then usually only if the direct investor holds a minimum percentage of the voting power in the dividend paying company. Furthermore, the approach taken by the Irish Revenue to the determination of the rate of the foreign underlying tax usually differs depending on whether the resident company is a portfolio or a direct investor.

14.206 Effective foreign rate: portfolio dividends

14.206.1 Introduction

For Irish portfolio investors, the most important source of foreign dividends is the UK and the treatment of UK dividends is dealt with separately in **14.110.5**. The effective rate of foreign tax in the case of UK source dividends of a portfolio investor is 15% since the Ireland/ UK tax treaty limits the credit for underlying tax to companies controlling 10% or more of the voting power in the dividend paying company. The position relating to dividends from other countries is outlined below.

14.206.2 US dividends

Under article 10 of the Ireland/ US treaty, the rate of US withholding tax on US company dividends paid to residents of Ireland is reduced to 15% (other than in a case in which the recipient is a company owning at least 10% of the voting stock of the dividend paying company, when the maximum rate is 5%). Article 24 paragraph 4 provides for the allowance of US direct tax in respect of a dividend paid by a US company by way of credit against any Irish tax payable on that dividend and, where the recipient of the dividend is a company resident in Ireland and controlling directly or indirectly 10% or more of the voting power in the dividend paying company, to a credit in respect of the underlying US tax on the profits out of which the dividend is paid.

14.206.3 Canadian dividends

The Ireland/Canada tax treaty restricts the rate of Canadian withholding tax in respect of a Canadian dividend paid to a resident of Ireland to 15% of the amount of the dividend or, in the case of a dividend paid to a company that controls, directly or indirectly, at least 10% of the voting power in the Canadian company, 5%. Article 23(2) of the treaty entitles an Irish resident company that controls, directly or indirectly, at least 10% of the voting power in the Canadian dividend paying company to a credit against Irish tax for both the Canadian direct tax and the Canadian tax on the profits out of which the dividend is paid.

An abatement of 10% against the Canadian federal corporation tax is given in respect of income earned in a province (the abatement being proportionately reduced where income is earned through a permanent establishment outside Canada).

Provincial taxes vary from 9.9% in Quebec to 16% in Nova Scotia and Prince Edward Island (with lower rates for active business income below a threshold amount). The Ontario provincial rate is 14% (12% for manufacturing and processing). The Ireland/ Canada treaty does not provide for credit for the provincial taxes against Irish taxes. """"

The Canadian federal corporation tax rate, net of the 10% abatement, is 28%, less a general rate reduction, for certain active business income over a threshold amount, of 8.5% from 1 January 2008 (increasing incrementally to a 13% reduction by 1 January 2012).

14.206.4   Germany

Under German tax reform proposals which became effective in the business year 2001 (or 2001/02 for companies with financial years ending other than on 31 December), a uniform rate of 25% replaced the former split-rate system incorporating rates of 40% and 30%. The effect of the current system is to produce an aggregate tax rate (to include the trade tax) of about 40% on business income of German companies. There is also a solidarity surcharge on business income calculated at 5.5% of the amount of the corporate tax on that income.

German companies are also liable to the business or trade tax (*Gewerbesteuer*), a local or municipal tax, which is levied separately each year on income. The business tax is deducted in arriving at taxable profits for the corporate income tax and for the purposes of its own calculation. Effective rates vary from just under 12% (or, theoretically, even lower) to 20.5% and are about 20% for most large cities.

Article 6 of the Ireland/ Germany tax treaty restricts the German withholding tax of 25% (20% from 2000) plus 5.5% solidarity surcharge, if any, on dividends paid to a resident of Ireland to 20% or 15%. A resident of Ireland is entitled under article 22(1) of the treaty to a credit against Irish tax for German direct tax as well as for underlying taxes consisting of the national corporation tax and the trade tax to the extent payable in respect of the dividend paying company's income (but not in respect of any such tax that might be levied in respect of its capital).

By virtue of the Parent-Subsidiary Directive, dividends paid by a German resident company to an Irish resident company are exempt from German withholding tax where the Irish company holds at least 25% of the share capital of the German company (see **14.7**). This exemption is also a feature of German domestic legislation provided the Irish company has not been interposed for tax reasons.

In practice, for portfolio investors, the Irish Revenue allow credit by reference to an underlying rate of 37% (see **14.206.6**), apparently a combination of the corporation tax rate of 25% and the 15% treaty withholding tax rate ((100 - 25) x 15% + 25% = 36.25%, say 37%).

14.206.5   Dividends from other countries

In cases involving dividends from countries other than the UK, the US and Canada, the portfolio investor will not normally be in a position to ascertain the effective rates of foreign tax for dividends carrying the right to a credit for the foreign underlying tax against Irish tax.

It should normally be possible to identify the rate of the foreign withholding tax, if any, as this is usually indicated on the counterfoil or other document accompanying the dividend. In most cases, this rate is the maximum rate specified in the relevant tax treaty. In practice, however, some countries deduct a rate of tax higher than that permitted by the relevant treaty leaving it to the recipient of the dividend to reclaim any excess tax withheld.

The maximum withholding tax permitted by a treaty is not always deducted. For example, although the Ireland/ Australia tax treaty allows Australia to withhold tax of 15% from franked dividends paid, no withholding tax is in fact deducted. The Australian withholding tax applies only to unfranked dividends (dividends paid out of profits not taxed at the full company rate). For other franked dividends paid after 30 June 1987, there is no withholding tax and the effective Australian rate for the portfolio investor is nil%.

The foreign underlying taxes to be included in the Irish resident's foreign tax credit computation may, if permitted by the relevant treaty, include local taxes (eg municipal tax, state tax) payable in respect of the dividend paying company's profits. This can result in a significant increase in the underlying foreign tax rate, as was seen above in the case of Germany.

The treaties with Belgium, Cyprus, Germany, Japan, Luxembourg, Pakistan and Zambia also provide for a credit to an Irish resident portfolio investor in respect of the indirect tax (in addition to the direct tax) on ordinary dividends from companies resident in the country in question, and a credit for indirect tax on the part of any participating preference share dividend from such companies which exceeds the fixed rate part of the dividend.

The treaties with France and Italy allow an Irish resident portfolio investor a credit for the underlying tax on any dividend. Similarly, the treaty with the Russian Federation provides for a credit for the tax paid on the profits out of which a dividend is paid by a Russian company, in proportion to the participation held by an Irish company in the Russian company.

14.206.6 Summary of effective rates

As suggested above, a portfolio investor will not normally be in a position to ascertain the effective rates of foreign tax in relation to dividends in respect of which credit for underlying tax is available. The table below gives approximate effective rates, applicable from 1 January 2005, for countries in respect of which credit for underlying tax is provided for in tax treaties. The table is based on *Tax Briefing* Issue 67 (November 2007) in which the Revenue Commissioners have indicated that they will accept these rates.

Effective rates of foreign tax: portfolio dividends

Country	Effective foreign tax rate %
Belgium	44
France	43
Germany	37
Italy	43
Japan	44
Luxembourg	35

Note:
Credit for underlying tax paid on the profits from which dividends are paid to portfolio investors is also provided for in the treaties with Cyprus, Pakistan, Russia and Zambia. In the cases of these countries, however, because of the number of potential rates of withholding/ underlying tax applying, effective rates have not been published by the Revenue.

14.207 Foreign underlying tax: direct investments

In cases of direct investments in a foreign dividend paying company, it is usually necessary to calculate the rate of the foreign underlying tax on a case by case basis. As explained in **12.305**, a direct investment in a company is generally taken as one representing 10% of more of the issued share capital or voting capital in that company. There is no hard and fast rule on this matter and the approach outlined in **14.206** may be accepted for holdings of 10% or even more where the dividend in question is not substantial.

TCA 1997 Sch 24 paragraphs 8 and 9 contain special rules for the computation of credit in respect of foreign dividends. These paragraphs provide for underlying or "deemed paid" credit in respect of dividends received from companies resident in other tax treaty contracting states. Foreign tax not chargeable directly or by deduction (ie, underlying tax) is to be taken into account in computing the credit against Irish tax, but subject to conditions relating to minimum shareholdings or voting power as prescribed by the treaties.

The underlying foreign tax is taken to be the tax attributable to the proportion of the relevant profits which is represented by the dividend (TCA 1997 Sch 24 paragraph 8). Accordingly, the appropriate procedure is to calculate the rate per cent which the total foreign company tax (including, where provided for by treaty, any sub-national taxes on the company's income) bears to the relevant profits. The resulting effective or average rate of underlying tax is combined with any direct tax deducted from the dividends to give the final effective foreign rate in respect of the dividend.

To ascertain the rate of foreign indirect or underlying tax in respect of any dividend, it is necessary to identify the foreign tax borne by the dividend paying company in respect of the relevant profits and the amount of the "relevant profits" out of which the dividend is paid. The rate of foreign underlying tax may be found by using the following formula:

$$\frac{FT}{RP+FT}$$

where—
FT   is the foreign tax borne on the relevant profits; and
RP   is the relevant profits

TCA 1997 Sch 24 paragraph 8 provides that the underlying taxes to be taken into account are those attributable to the profits ("relevant profits") out of which the dividend is paid. The foreign tax is taken as the tax attributable to the proportion of the relevant profits as is represented by the dividend. Detailed rules are provided for attributing relevant profits to specific periods or items of income. Accordingly, the relevant profits are—

(a)   if the dividend is paid for a specified period, the profits of that period;
(b)   if the dividend is not paid for a specified period but is paid out of specified profits, those profits, and

(c) if the source of the dividend is not specified (ie, if the dividend is paid neither for a specified period nor out of specified profits), the profits of the last period for which accounts of the company ("body corporate") were made up before the dividend became payable.

In the cases of (a) and (c), if the total dividend exceeds the profits available for distribution of the period mentioned, the relevant profits will be the profits of that period together with so much of the profits available for distribution of preceding periods (other than profits already distributed or previously treated as distributed) as is equal to the excess. For this purpose, the profits of more recent preceding periods must be taken into account before profits of earlier periods.

It will be seen that the requirement to take account of profits of earlier periods applies only in the cases of (a) and (c). In the case of (b), it is accordingly permissible to source a dividend payment out of any specified profits without regard to the quantum of profits available for distribution for the period in which those specified profits arose.

Example 14.207.1

Lima Ltd, an Irish resident company has a wholly owned German subsidiary, Delbac GmbH, which in turn has a wholly owned Spanish subsidiary, Segundo Lda. In its latest accounting period, Segundo Lda pays a dividend of €500,000 to Delbac GmbH and in the same period Delbac GmbH pays a dividend of €450,000 to Lima Ltd.

Also in the same period, Delbac GmbH incurred a loss of €400,000 so that its profits for that period, being the dividend from its subsidiary less the amount of the loss, are €100,000. Delbac GmbH also has distributable reserves of €800,000 from earlier periods.

The profits of Delbac GmbH available for distribution for the current period are €900,000 (€500,000 - €400,000 + €800,000) so that it has adequate reserves out of which to pay the dividend of €450,000. The appropriate dividend resolution declares that the dividend is being paid out of specified profits consisting of the dividend of €500,000 from Segundo Lda. (The fact that the profits for the period amount to €100,000 only is irrelevant.)

The foreign tax credit rate applicable to the dividend of €500,000 will be calculated by reference to the tax position of Segundo Lda for the period out of which that dividend has been paid.

Where it is necessary to take into account the profits of any preceding period, the underlying tax appropriate to that period (on the basis of the above formula) will be included as part of the underlying tax.

If a tax treaty provides that underlying foreign tax is to be taken into account as regards dividends of some classes but not of other classes, then if a dividend of one of the latter classes is paid to a company which controls directly or indirectly at least 50% of the voting power in the dividend paying company, credit is to be allowed as if the dividend were a dividend of one of the former classes (TCA 1997 Sch 24 para 9).

As to what profits are to be taken as the relevant profits, are these the profits as computed for tax purposes or the profits as shown in the accounts of the dividend paying company? This issue was decided in *Bowater Paper Corporation Ltd v Murgatroyd* 46 TC 37 where it was held that the relevant profits are the profits shown by the company's accounts as being available for distribution. In this case, due to accelerated capital allowances, the taxable profits of the dividend paying company were substantially lower than the accounting profits. A higher foreign tax credit would have resulted if those profits had been used as the denominator in the above fraction.

Example 14.207.2

Erne Ltd received a dividend of €5,000 from Tejo Lda, a subsidiary resident in a treaty country. No tax was withheld on payment of the dividend. The following information is relevant to Tejo Lda:

	€
Accounts profit (before depreciation)	10,000
Depreciation	1,300
Capital allowances	2,900
"Relevant profits" (per Bowater)	8,700
Taxable profits	7,100
Foreign tax payable @ 35% (and as provided for in the accounts)	2,485
Profits available for distribution	6,215

Rate of underlying tax:

$$\frac{\text{overseas tax charge}}{\text{accounting profits for distribution} + \text{foreign tax}} = \frac{2,485}{8,700} = 28.6\%$$

Credit in respect of dividend €5,000 x 28.6/71.4   = €2,003

Following the *Bowater* decision, uncertainties remained as to the exact method of calculating the profits available for distribution. The matter was negotiated between the Inland Revenue in the UK and the Consultative Committee of Accountancy Bodies following which an agreed statement on the matter was issued. It is understood that the Irish Revenue follow the *Bowater* decision and the main points arising out of the agreement between the Inland Revenue and the CCAB, but that there may some difficulty regarding the treatment of deferred taxation in the dividend paying company's accounts.

The distributable profits for a period of account are normally taken as the profits shown in the company's audited accounts, after deducting taxation as provided in those accounts, but before any transfers to or from reserves. It would be expected that the accounting profits of a company for this purpose would include capital profits, although such profits may not always appear in the company's profit and loss account. It is understood that the Revenue Commissioners are likely to contend that capital profits should be included in distributable profits even where credited direct to reserves. It might be difficult to sustain this view in a case where capital profits are not distributable under the law of the foreign country in question.

The taxation charge in the accounts of the dividend paying company may include an adjustment for tax underprovided or overprovided in prior years and may also include a provision for deferred taxation. While normal adjustments for under-provisions or over-provisions related to prior years are accepted, the position of the Revenue Commissioners traditionally has been that distributable profits are those before any transfers to or from the deferred tax account. In practice, however, they will accept that account may be taken of deferred tax if that treatment is consistently followed.

Example 14.207.3

Bridgeport Ltd, an Irish resident company, receives a dividend of £330,000 (equivalent to €490,000) from its UK wholly owned subsidiary company Bridgeport (UK) Ltd in the current accounting period. The profit and loss account of Bridgeport (UK) Ltd for the period is as follows:

	£000	£000
Profits before tax		1,200
Provision for corporation tax	350	
Deferred tax	100	
Underprovision for prior year	20	470
Distributable profits		730
Dividend to Bridgeport Ltd		330
Retained		400

Bridgeport (UK) Ltd – corporation tax computation:

	£000
Profits per accounts	1,200
Disallow: depreciation	350
	1,550
Capital allowances	150
	1,400
Corporation tax at, say, 27.1% effective	380

Underlying rate of UK tax:

$$\frac{FT}{RP+FT} = \frac{380}{730+380} = 34.23\%$$

Gross up dividend at Irish rate – assume 12.5%:

$$€490,000 \times \frac{100}{100-12.5} = €560,000$$

Bridgeport Ltd – corporation tax computation:

	€
"Gross" dividend received	560,000
Corporation tax @ 12.5%	70,000
Less: credit for UK tax	70,000
Net Irish corporation tax	Nil

In the above calculations, the relevant profits were taken as the distributable profits after adjusting for deferred tax. If the traditional approach applied by the Revenue Commissioners had been used, the relevant profits would have been £830,000 and the effective rate would have been:

$$\frac{FT}{RP+FT} = \frac{380}{830+380} = 31.4\%$$

Since this rate is again higher than the Irish effective rate, the computation of the foreign credit is unaffected.

The foreign tax borne (FT in the above formula) does not include any tax apart from the tax suffered in the country in which the dividend paying company is resident. Such additional taxes could arise, for example, in the case of a UK subsidiary of an Irish resident company where the subsidiary carries on a trade in the UK as well as through a branch in Denmark. The subsidiary also receives dividends from Germany in respect of which withholding tax at 15% is deducted. The Danish and German taxes are creditable against the subsidiary's UK tax. In computing the underlying UK tax rate, however, for the purpose of ascertaining the UK credit available in respect of dividends paid to its Irish parent, the figure for foreign tax borne will not include the Danish or German taxes. Even if the UK subsidiary paid Irish corporation tax on profits from an Irish branch trade, the foreign tax borne would not include that Irish tax.

Example 14.207.4

Slaney Ltd, an Irish resident company, owns 25% of the ordinary share capital and of the voting rights of Severn Ltd, a UK resident company. On 28 April 2008, Severn Ltd declared a dividend of £280,000 on its ordinary shares in respect of the year ended 31 March 2008. The dividend of £70,000 paid to Slaney Ltd is equivalent to, say, €110,000. In accordance with the Ireland/ UK tax treaty, Slaney Ltd is entitled to a credit in respect of the underlying UK corporation tax of Severn Ltd

It is necessary to determine the relevant profits for the year ended 31 March 2008 and the UK tax borne on those profits. The audited accounts of Severn Ltd for the year ended 31 March 2008 show the following results:

	Stg£	Stg£
Profits before tax		720,000
Less: provision for tax:		
Corporation tax	210,000	
Overseas tax	52,000	
Underprovision for previous years	15,000	
Transfer to deferred taxation	40,000	317,000
		403,000
Extraordinary item:		
Profit on sale of premises net of UK tax £35,000		80,000
Net profits available for distribution		483,000

UK corporation tax payable for the year ended 31 March 2008 is computed as follows:

	Stg£
Profits per accounts	720,000
Disallowable items (net)	90,000
	810,000
Corporation tax at, say, 30% (assume no small companies/ marginal relief)	243,000
Less: credit relief for overseas tax, as agreed	51,000
	192,000
Corporation tax on chargeable gains	35,000
UK corporation tax	227,000

On the basis that the transfer to deferred tax must be reversed (in contrast to the position taken in Example **14.207.2**), the relevant profits for the year ended 31 March 2008 are computed as follows:

	Stg£
Profits available for distribution	483,000
Add back transfer to deferred tax	40,000
Relevant profits	523,000

Rate of underlying UK tax
The rate of underlying UK corporation tax is as follows:

$$\frac{FT}{RP + FT} = \frac{227,000}{523,000 + 227,000} = 30.27\%$$

Irish Tax Computation

	€
Dividend from Severn Ltd	110,000
Irish corporation tax rate	12.5%
UK effective rate	30.27%
Gross up dividend at lower rate 12.5% (110,000 x 100/(100 - 12.5))	125,714
Corporation tax @ 12.5%	15,714
Less: credit for UK tax (max)	15,714
Final corporation tax payable	Nil

Example 14.207.5
The position is as in Example **14.207.4** except that on 28 August 2008 Severn Ltd declares a further dividend £430,000 in respect of the year ended 31 March 2008. Slaney Ltd accordingly receives a further dividend of £107,500, equivalent to, say, €170,000.
The available reserves of Severn Ltd are insufficient to pay the full dividend of £430,000 and it will therefore be necessary to take part of this dividend from the distributable profits of one or more previous years. The remaining distributable reserves for the year ended 31 March 2007 are £120,000 (after a dividend of £260,000 paid for that year) and for the year ended 31 March 2006 £270,000 (after a dividend of £100,000 for that year). The distributable profits for the relevant periods are accordingly as follows:

	Distributable profits	Previous dividends	Relevant profits
	£	£	£
Year ended 31 March 2008	523,000	280,000	243,000
Year ended 31 March 2007	380,000	260,000	120,000
Year ended 31 March 2006	370,000	100,000	270,000
			633,000

The effective rates of tax for the two years to 31 March 20072 and 2006 are, say, 29.84% and 30.15% respectively. The further dividend of £430,000 is regarded as paid out of distributable profits as follows:

	UK underlying rate (1)	Relevant profits (2)	(2) x (1) (100 - (1))
	%	£	£
Year ended 31 March 2008	30.27	243,000	105,487
Year ended 31 March 2007	29.84	120,000	51,038
Year ended 31March 2006 (part)	30.15	67,000	28,920
		430,000	185,445

The underlying UK rate in respect of the dividend of £430,000 is 185,445/615,445 = 30.13%.

To substantiate a claim for foreign underlying tax, it will usually be necessary to provide a copy of the relevant accounts of the foreign subsidiary and evidence, such as an official receipt or written confirmation from the tax authorities in the country in which the subsidiary is resident. The foreign tax computations may also be required.

Tax treaties to which Ireland is a party provide for the availability to an Irish resident company of a credit for foreign underlying tax where the company has a controlling interest in the voting power or in the share capital of the dividend paying company. Certain treaties provide for underlying credit, regardless of the extent of the holding, in respect of ordinary dividends and in respect of the participating element of participating preference dividends. The underlying tax credit is confined in some cases to Irish resident companies holding a minimum percentage of the voting power, or in certain cases the share capital, in the dividend paying company. A list of those countries, showing the minimum percentage of voting power in each case, is included below.

The underlying tax credit is available for all dividends paid to a company having the required minimum percentage of voting power (or minimum shareholding in certain cases). The entitlement to a credit for any direct foreign taxes deducted from dividends is available to all Irish resident shareholders..

Country	Minimum percentage of voting power/share capital
Australia	10%
Austria	25%
Belgium[1]	10%
Bulgaria	10%
Canada	10%
China	10%
Croatia	10%
Czech Republic	10%
Denmark	25%
Estonia	10%
Finland	10%
Greece	10%
Hungary	10%
Iceland	10%
India	25%

Country	Minimum percentage of voting power/share capital
Israel	10%
Latvia	10%
Lithuania	10%
Malaysia	10%
Mexico	10%
Netherlands	50%
New Zealand	10%
Norway	25%
Poland	25%
Portugal	25%
Romania	10%
Slovakia	10%
Slovenia	10%
South Africa	10%
Spain[2]	25%
Sweden	10%
Switzerland	10%
United Kingdom	10%
United States	10%

Notes:

[1] The treaty with Belgium also provides for a credit in respect of underlying tax to any Irish resident shareholder in receipt of ordinary dividends or dividends on participating preference shares to the extent that they exceed a fixed rate.

[2] The treaty with Spain provides that the 25% participation must be held on a continuous basis during at least the two years before the dividend was paid.

Example 14.207.6

Redfern Ltd, an Irish resident trading company, has a 35% holding in the ordinary share capital of a UK resident company and a holding of less than 10% of the ordinary share capital in a New Zealand company, as well as holdings in German and Japanese companies.

Details of Redfern Ltd's income chargeable to corporation tax for its latest accounting period are as follows:

	Gross dividend €	Foreign direct tax €	Net dividend €
Foreign dividends (Case III)			
UK dividend[1]	50,000	Nil	50,000
German dividend (15% tax withheld)	10,000	1,500	8,500
Japanese dividend (15% tax withheld)	12,000	1,800	10,200
New Zealand dividend (15% tax withheld)	15,000	2,250	12,750
	87,000	5,550	81,450
Adjusted trading profits – Case I			400,000

The effective rates of foreign tax are agreed with the inspector of taxes as follows (see also **14.206**):

UK dividend[1]	27.25%
German dividend	37.00%
Japanese dividend	44.00%
New Zealand dividend[2]	15.00%

The final corporation tax computation requires the net amount of each foreign dividend to be grossed up at the lower of the Irish rate of corporation tax, assume 12.5% for each dividend, and the effective foreign rate appropriate to the dividend:

	Regrossed	Credit
	€	€
Foreign dividends regrossed:		
UK dividend (at 12.5%)		
€50,000 x 100/(100 - 12,5)	57,143	7,143
German dividend (at 12.5%)		
8,500 x 100/(100 - 12.5)	9,714	1,214
Japanese dividend (at 12.5%)		
€10,200 x 100/(100 - 12.5)	11,657	1,457
New Zealand dividend (at 12.5%)		
€12,750 x 100/(100 - 12.5)	14,572	1,822
Final Case III income	93,086	11,636

Final corporation tax computation:

	€
Case I	400,000
Case III	93,085
Total income chargeable to corporation tax	493,085
Corporation tax @ 12.5%	61,636
Less: credits for foreign tax	11,636
Corporation tax payable	50,000

Notes:

[1] The holding in the UK company is a direct investment and Redfern Ltd is entitled to a credit against Irish tax for the underlying UK tax. The underlying rate is assumed to be 27.25%.

[2] As the voting power held in the New Zealand company is less than 10%, there is no credit for New Zealand underlying tax.

Where a foreign branch of an Irish company sells goods manufactured by the company in Ireland, the company is entitled to manufacturing relief for Irish corporation tax purposes. One result of this relief is that the Irish effective rate will probably be lower than the foreign rate and it will be necessary to compute the effective Irish rate in respect of the branch profits.

Example 14.207.7

Greenfield Ltd, an Irish resident company entitled to manufacturing relief, sells some of the goods manufactured by it to UK customers through its branch in the UK. The branch is subject to UK corporation tax in respect of profits from the carrying on of a trade through a permanent establishment in the UK. The company's profits for its current accounting period for Irish corporation tax purposes are €1,600,000.

The UK branch profits for the period are £270,000 (equal to, say, €400,000) for UK tax purposes, after capital allowances, and €430,000 for Irish tax purposes.

Greenfield Ltd has no associated companies. UK corporation tax is £270,000 x 19%[1] = £51,300 (€76,000). For foreign tax credit purposes, the net foreign income and the effective UK tax rate are based on the UK branch profits as computed under Irish tax rules as follows:

	€
Branch profits	430,000
Less: UK tax thereon	76,000
Net foreign income	354,000
Effective UK tax rate 76/430	17.67%

The effective Irish corporation tax rate is 10% and, being lower than the UK effective rate, is the rate used to gross up the branch profits:

	€
€354,000 x 100/(100-10)	393,333

The final corporation tax computation for the period is as follows:

	€	€
Case I profits – as provisionally computed		1,600,000
Less: deduction for excess UK tax credit (€76,000 - €39,333)[2]		36,667
Case I profits finally chargeable		1,563,333
Corporation tax x 12.5% =	195,416	
Less: manufacturing relief €195,416 x 1/5	38,083	
		156,333
Less: credit for UK tax		39,333
Corporation tax payable		117,000

Notes:

[1] The small companies' rate is normally available to a UK resident company but a non-resident company trading in the UK through a branch (permanent establishment) is entitled to this rate by reason of the non-discrimination article in the relevant tax treaty, in this case article 23 of the Ireland/ UK treaty. The 19% rate is available provided the worldwide profits of the claimant company (and any associated companies it may have) are taken into account.

[2] The excess UK credit (the part of the UK tax for which no credit can be taken because it exceeds the Irish corporation tax attributable to the branch profits) is the excess of the UK tax paid (€76,000) over the amount of the available credit. The available credit is €393,333 - €354,000. (See also Example **14.202.1**.)

The relief for the total UK tax on the branch profits may be reconciled as follows:

	€
Deducted in computing branch profits finally chargeable to Irish tax	36,667
Allowed as credit against Irish tax	39,333
Total UK tax payable	76,000

14.208   Corporation tax deductions

In arriving at the profits in respect of which corporation tax is finally payable, certain amounts may be deducted from, or set against, or treated as reducing, profits of more than one description. Accordingly, these amounts are not deductible in computing any particular type of income or in computing chargeable gains. The amounts in question comprise charges on income (TCA 1997, s 243), trading losses for which a claim under TCA 1997, s 396(2) is made, capital allowances in excess of rental income assessable under Case V of Schedule D (TCA 1997, s 308(4)), and management expenses of an investment company (TCA 1997, s 83) or life assurance company (TCA 1997, s 707). Since trading losses and charges, including group relief for such losses and charges (see **3.101.5**, **4.103**, **4.405**, and **8.306.2**), may now be offset against foreign dividends taxable at the 12.5% corporation tax rate, these are also available for relief against profits of more than one description.

For credit relief purposes, TCA 1997 Sch 24 paragraph 4(5) provides rules for the treatment of these deductions, as follows:

(a)   a company may, for the purposes of paragraph 4, paragraph 9D and TCA 1997 ss 449 and 450, allocate any deduction arising in an accounting period in such amounts and against such of its profits for the period as it thinks fit;

(b)   to the extent that any such deduction is allocated against any item of foreign source income, the amount of that income brought into the computation of the foreign tax credit is reduced accordingly;

(c)   to the extent that any such deduction is allocated against income treated as manufacturing income within TCA 1997, s 449 (see **14.4**), the amount of that income brought into the computation of the foreign tax credit is reduced accordingly;

(d)   to the extent that any such deduction is allocated against income attributable to "relevant payments" within the meaning of TCA 1997, s 450 (interest from sources in tax treaty countries taxable in Ireland under the 10% tax regime in the IFSC or in Shannon – see **14.5**), the amount of that income brought into the computation of the foreign tax credit is reduced accordingly; and

(e)   to the extent that any such deduction is allocated against income treated for the purposes of TCA 1997 Sch 24 paragraph 9D (see **14.212**) as referable to an amount of relevant interest, the amount of that income brought into the computation of the foreign tax credit is reduced accordingly.

See **4.403.5** regarding the allocation of certain interest qualifying for relief under TCA 1997, s 247 against "relevant income".

For accounting periods ending on or after 6 March 2001, but before 18 February 2008, it was not possible to offset a trading loss incurred, charges on income paid, or a trading loss incurred, or trading charges paid, by a group surrendering company, in respect of an activity subject to the 10% or the standard rate of corporation tax, against profits other than income taxable at the 10% or the standard corporation tax rates (see **3.101.5**, **4.103**, **4.405** and **8.306**). Accordingly, such losses or deficiencies ("relevant trading losses" and "relevant trading charges on income") could not be deducted from, or set against, or treated as reducing, "profits of more than one description".

""In most cases it would be advantageous (where foreign income has borne foreign tax) to allocate amounts that may be deducted from, or set against, or treated as reducing, profits of more than one description against Irish income so as to preserve, to the maximum extent, the benefits of double tax relief.

Normally, the deductions should be applied first to reduce the company's income, and any chargeable gains, that are subject to Irish tax without credit relief. The company will then wish to allocate any remaining deductions as far as possible against foreign income carrying effective foreign tax rates (ie, rates before allocating the deductions) which are lower than the Irish rate applying to that income. Where the foreign income carrying such lower rates exceeds the amount of the deductions available, the deductions should be applied first to those items of income carrying the lowest effective foreign rate, then against the foreign income carrying the next lowest rate, and so on. This leaves the taxable foreign income consisting, to the greatest extent, of the income carrying the highest rates of foreign tax credit.

Where income not eligible for credit relief (say, trading income) is taxable at a rate lower than the rate applying to the foreign income eligible for credit (eg, dividends taxable at 25%), it will sometimes be beneficial for a company to allocate deductions against the foreign income but only to the extent necessary ("in such amounts … as it thinks fit") to secure that corporation tax on the resulting reduced foreign income equates to the foreign tax.

Deductions allocated in accordance with TCA 1997 Sch 24 paragraph 4(5) to items of foreign income are allocated against foreign income in each case; this follows TCA 1997 Sch 24 paragraph 4(5)(b) (see **14.202**). The procedure whereby that income is grossed up at the lower of the Irish and foreign effective rates is by reference to the foreign income as reduced by the amount of the deduction allocated to it (the "Irish measure"), and net of the foreign tax.

Example 14.208.1

Conrad Ltd, an Irish resident distributing company, had the following results for its latest accounting period:

	€
Untaxed interest	9,000
Chargeable gains (as adjusted)	4,700
Management expenses	40,000
Foreign dividends	99,000

Details of foreign tax credits relating to the dividends are given below. The UK and NZ dividends are subject to corporation tax at the 25% rate and the other dividends are taxable at the 12.5% rate. Conrad Ltd holds a 20% interest in the UK dividend paying company. The underlying corporation tax rate on the profits out of which the UK dividend was paid was 30%. The underlying credit rates for the dividends from Belgium and France are 44% and 43% respectively (see table for portfolio dividends in **14.206**). Conrad Ltd holds less than

10% of the voting power in the Swiss dividend paying company and there is therefore no underlying credit for the dividend in that case (see table in **14.207**).

	Gross dividend	Foreign direct tax	Net dividend
	€	€	€
Dividend from UK company	35,000	Nil	35,000
Dividend from Swiss company	8,000	1,200	6,800
Dividend from Belgian company	10,000	1,500	8,500
Dividend from French company	40,000	6,000	34,000
Dividend from New Zealand company	6,000	900	5,100
	99,000	9,600	89,400

In accordance with TCA 1997 Sch 24 paragraph 4(5), Conrad Ltd allocates €13,700 of the management expenses against the untaxed interest and chargeable gain. It then allocates the balance of the management expenses, €26,300, against the dividends as follows:

Dividend	Foreign tax rate	Gross dividend	Mgt expenses	Irish measure	Foreign tax	Net foreign income
		€	€	€	€	€
NZ	15%	6,000	5,100	900	900	Nil
Swiss	15%	8,000	6,800	1,200	1,200	Nil
UK	30%	35,000	14,400	20,600	-	20,600
Belgian	44%	10,000	Nil	10,000	1,500	8,500
French	43%	40,000	Nil	40,000	6,000	34,000
		99,000	26,300	72,700	9,600	63,100

The above foreign tax rates are the rates before allocating any management expenses. Management expenses are accordingly applied firstly to the NZ dividend, where the foreign rate (15%) is lower than the Irish rate (25%). The final corporation tax computation, including the calculation of the foreign tax credits now remaining, is as follows:

	€
Case III	
Untaxed interest	9,000
Foreign dividends – covered by management expenses	26,300
Foreign dividends - balance:	
UK (gross up at 25%)[1] €20,600 x 100/(100 - 25)	27,467
Belgian (gross up at 12.5%)[1] €8,500 x 100/(100 - 12.5)	9,714
French (gross up at 12.5%)[1] €34,000 x 100/(100 - 12.5)	38,857
Income	111,338
Chargeable gains	4,700
Total profits	116,038
Management expenses (TCA 1997, s 83)	40,000
	76,038

Corporation tax payable:

UK dividends €27,467 @ 25%	6,867
Belgian and French dividends €48,571 @ 12.5%	6,071
	12,938
Less: credits for foreign tax[2]	12,938
Final corporation tax payable	Nil

Notes:

[1] In accordance with TCA 1997 Sch 24 paragraph 4(1), the UK, Belgian and French dividends are grossed up at the Irish effective rate, 25% or 12.5%, which in each case is lower than the foreign effective rate.

[2] The credits for foreign tax are as follows:

	€
Foreign dividends as re-grossed:	
UK (27,467 - 20,600)	6,867
Belgian (9,714 - 8,500)	1,214
French (38,857 - 34,000)	4,857
	12,938

In the above example, there is no net corporation tax liability because the foreign income gross up is at the appropriate Irish corporation tax rate. The resulting corporation tax liability is accordingly matched by the foreign tax credits which are also determined by the appropriate Irish rate in each case. The allocation of the management expenses is such that the foreign dividends remaining taxable carry a foreign tax rate equal to or greater than the Irish corporation tax rate. Thus there is no net liability.

The following example shows what the result would have been had the management expenses been allocated proportionately against all items.

Example 14.208.2

The facts are as in Example **14.208.1** except that the management expenses are not allocated against any specific items of income. The allocation is therefore as follows:

	Income/ gain	Mgt expenses	Foreign direct tax	Foreign tax rate	Income/ gain after deduction
	€	€	€		€
Untaxed interest	9,000	3,194	-		5,806
New Zealand dividend (15%)	6,000	2,130	900	23.26%	2,970
Swiss dividend (15%)	8,000	2,840	1,200	23.26%	3,960
UK dividend (30%)	35,000	12,422	-	> 30.00%	22,578
Belgian dividend (44%)	10,000	3,549	1,500	> 44.00%	4,951
French dividend (44%)	40,000	14,197	6,000	> 44.00%	19,803
Chargeable gain	4,700	1,668	-		3,032
	112,700	40,000	9,600		63,100

For credit relief purposes, the foreign tax rate is calculated by reference to the foreign tax as a percentage of the Irish measure of the foreign income (ie, net of allocated management expenses) in each case. Thus, in the case of the Swiss dividend, the rate is 1,200/5,160 = 23.26%.

The final corporation tax computation, including the calculation of the foreign tax credits, is as follows:

	€
Case III	
Untaxed interest	5,806
Net foreign dividends:	
UK dividend (gross up at 25%) 22,578 x 100/(100 - 25)	30,104
New Zealand dividend (gross up at 23.26%) 2,970 x 100/(100 - 23.26)	3,870
Swiss dividend (gross up at 12.5%) 3,960 x 100/(100 - 12.5)	4,526
Belgian dividend (gross up at 12.5%) 4,951 x 100/(100 - 12.5)	5,658
French dividend (gross up at 12.5%) 19,803 x 100/(100 – 12.5)	22,632
Income	72,596
Chargeable gain	3,032
Total profits	75,628
Corporation tax payable:	
€39,780 @ 25%	9,945
€35,848 @ 12.5%	4,481
	14,426
Less: credits for foreign tax[1]	12,528
Final corporation tax payable[2]	1,898

Note:

[1]   The credits for foreign tax are as follows:

	€
Foreign dividends as re-grossed:	
New Zealand (3,870 - 2,970)	900
Swiss (4,526 - 3,960)	566
UK (30,104 - 22,578)	7,526
Belgian (5,658 - 4,951)	707
French (22,632 - 19,803)	2,829
	12,528

[2]   The tax liability can be summarised as follows:

	€	€
Interest €5,806 @ 25%		1,452
Chargeable gain €3,032 @ 12.5%		379
NZ dividend €3,870 @ 25%	967	
- less credit	900	67
		1,898

Example 14.208.3

The facts are as in Example **14.208.1** except that Conrad Ltd does not have any management expenses but has available to it a trading loss of €80,000 from a fellow group member, for the accounting period.

Since trading losses are now available for offset against certain foreign dividends (see **3.101.5**), they are for the purposes of TCA 1997, Schedule 24 paragraph 4(5) available for relief against "profits of more than one description". Accordingly, Conrad Ltd may allocate the trading loss against "such of its profits for that period as it thinks fit". For this purpose, however, since trading losses and charges may not be offset against non-trading income generally, presumably the only non-trading income to which this allocation may be made is that consisting of foreign dividends taxable at the 12.5% rate (ie, paid out of trading profits and received from companies resident in EU or tax treaty countries).

In practice, group relief would not be claimed. The loss of the tax value, at 12.5%, resulting from the surrender of the group trading loss would exceed the amount of tax saved by covering the 12.5% taxable dividends; in fact, no such tax would be saved in view of the credit relief available in respect of those dividends.

Neither would a TCA 1997, s 420B claim be made in respect of the untaxed interest and chargeable gain. Such a claim could only be made after making any possible TCA 1997, s 420A claim.

14.209   Unilateral relief

14.209.1   Introduction

Up to 1994, Irish tax legislation contained no provision for the allowance of any form of unilateral credit relief in respect of foreign tax not creditable under the terms of a double tax treaty. The form of unilateral credit relief introduced by FA 1994 (and now provided for in TCA 1997, s 449 – see **14.4**) is limited to cases involving "relevant foreign tax", meaning tax which cannot be credited by virtue of a double tax treaty and which consists of a withholding tax applied by a foreign territory in respect of an amount receivable from the sale of computer software, or an amount treated as receivable from the sale of goods, being in respect of the rendering of computer services, Shannon operations, or international financial services.

As respects accounting periods ending on or after 1 April 1998, TCA 1997 Sch 24 paragraph 9A provides for a general form of unilateral relief whereby credit is available for foreign tax in respect of dividends received, consisting of withholding taxes and taxes paid on the profits of the dividend paying company. An Irish resident company, or an EU resident company where the dividend forms part of that company's Irish branch profits (see **14.209.2** below), which receives a dividend from a foreign company in which it owns, directly or indirectly, at least 5% of the ordinary share capital, is entitled to a credit against the Irish tax on the dividend for any withholding tax paid on payment of the dividend and for an appropriate part of the foreign tax on the underlying profits.

Unilateral relief as provided for in TCA 1997 Sch 24 paragraph 9A is available for accounting periods ending on or after 1 April 1998.

14.209.2   Taxes creditable

Unilateral relief is described in TCA 1997 Sch 24 paragraph 9A(2) as such relief as would be available under Sch 24 if a tax treaty were in force with the territory under the law of which the foreign tax in question is payable. Subparagraph (2) goes on to state "a reference in this Schedule to credit under arrangements shall be construed as including a reference to unilateral relief".

Unilateral relief is given by way of credit for "tax paid under the law of a territory other than the State in relation to a relevant dividend paid by a company resident in the territory to a company falling within TCA 1997 Sch 24 paragraph 9A(3A)" (TCA 1997 Sch 24 paragraph 9A(3)). Such tax means:

(a)   tax directly charged on the dividend, whether by charge to tax, deduction of tax at source or otherwise, and the whole of which tax neither the company nor the recipient would have borne if the dividend had not been paid, and

(b)   tax paid in respect of its profits under the law of the territory by the company paying the dividend in so far as that tax is properly attributable to the proportion of the profits represented by the dividend (TCA 1997 Sch 24 paragraph 9A(4)(a)).

A company falls within TCA 1997 Sch 24 paragraph 9A(3A) if—

(i)   it is resident in the State, or

(ii)   it is, by virtue of the law of a relevant Member State (see below) other than the State, resident for the purposes of "tax in such Member State" (ie, tax imposed in the Member State which corresponds to corporation tax in the State) and the dividend referred to above forms part of the profits of a branch or agency of the company in the State.

As regards (a) above, this will usually refer to withholding taxes. The reference to "charge to tax" is to a form of taxation on dividends paid which is other than one effected by deduction at source but it is presumably similar in effect. In relation to (b), tax paid on the profits of the dividend paying company will include the usual company tax on profits (federal, national etc) but also sub-national type taxes such as state, city or provincial taxes. The creditable tax will be a proportion of the tax on profits equal to the amount of the dividend as a percentage of those profits.

For the above purposes, *relevant Member State*, means—

(a)   a Member State of the European Communities, or

(b)   not being such a Member State, an EEA State which is a territory with which Ireland has a tax treaty (TCA 1997, s 616(7)).

EEA State means a state that is a contracting party to the EEA Agreement. *EEA Agreement* means the Agreement on the European Economic Area signed at Oporto on 2 May 1992, as adjusted by the Protocol signed at Brussels on 17 March 1993.

Relevant dividend means a dividend paid by a foreign resident company to a company falling within TCA 1997 Sch 24 paragraph 9A(3A) (see above) where that company:

(a)   directly or indirectly owns not less than 5% of the ordinary share capital of the foreign company, or

(b)   is a subsidiary of a company which directly or indirectly owns not less than 5% of the ordinary share capital of the foreign company (TCA 1997 Sch 24 paragraph 9A(4)(b)).

For the above purposes, a company is a subsidiary of another company if the other company owns, directly or indirectly, not less than 50% of the ordinary share capital (see **2.601** and **8.103.2**) of the first-mentioned company.

Unilateral relief is specifically denied for the following taxes:

(a)   tax paid under the law of a territory with which Ireland has a tax treaty (except to the extent that credit may not be given for that tax under the treaty – see **14.209.3** below);

(b) tax which is "relevant foreign tax" within the meaning of TCA 1997, s 449 (the limited form of unilateral relief referred to in **14.209.1** above) or within the meaning of TCA 1997 Sch 24 paragraph 9D (the limited form of unilateral relief referred to in **14.212**); and

(c) tax in respect of which credit may be allowed under TCA 1997, s 831 (the "Parent-Subsidiary Directive" – see **14.7**).

For the purposes of unilateral relief, references to tax payable or paid under the law of a territory outside the State are confined to taxes which are charged on income or capital gains and which correspond to corporation tax and capital gains tax (TCA 1997 Sch 24 paragraph 9A(7)).

14.209.3 The relief

Unilateral relief is a relief from corporation tax "in respect of profits represented by dividends" (the part of the recipient company's profits consisting of dividends received from a company resident in a non-treaty country) and is given in respect of "tax paid under the law of a territory other than the State in relation to a relevant dividend paid by a company" (see **14.209.2** above), ie withholding taxes and taxes on the profits of the dividend paying company in so far as attributable to the part of the profits represented by the dividend (TCA 1997 Sch 24 paragraph 9A(3)). The creditable tax is allowed against corporation tax of the company receiving the dividends notwithstanding that there is for the time being no tax treaty in force between Ireland and the other territory (TCA 1997 Sch 24 paragraph 9A(1)).

Example 14.209.3.1

Pharmaceuticals Ltd, an Irish resident company, owns 25% of the ordinary share capital of Benellin Lda, a Colombian resident company. For its latest accounting period, the profits of Pharmaceuticals Ltd, as adjusted for tax, were €320,000 including a dividend of Ps100m (equal to €65,000 at the time of receipt) from which Colombian withholding tax at 7% was deducted. The dividend was paid out of profits of Ps550m on which Colombian profits tax of Ps150m had been paid. The distributable profits of Benellin Lda for the period were Ps400m.

The foreign taxes for the purposes of credit relief are the corporate income tax of Ps150m and the withholding tax of Ps7m. The rate of underlying tax of Benellin Lda for the period for which the dividend to Pharmaceuticals Ltd was paid is as follows:

$$\frac{FT}{RP+FT} = \frac{150,000,000}{400,000,000+150,000,000} = 27.27\%$$

Including the withholding tax of Ps 7m, the overall effective rate of tax in respect of the dividend is 7% x 72.72% + 27.27% = 32.36%. Accordingly, the net dividend received, €60,450, is grossed up at the lower Irish rate of 25%, ie €60,450 x 100/75 = €80,600. The corporation tax computation of Pharmaceutical Ltd for the period is as follows:

	€
Adjusted profits	320,000
Add: credit for foreign dividend (€80,600 - €65,000)	15,600
	335,600
Corporation tax:	
trading income €255,000 @ 12.5%	31,875

dividend income €80,600 @ 25%	20,150
	52,025
Less: credit relief (€80,600 - €60,450)	20,150
Net corporation tax	31,875

As seen in **14.209.2**, the company receiving the dividend may be an Irish resident company or a company resident in a relevant Member State where the dividend forms part of the profits of that company's Irish branch or agency. This extension of credit relief to EU resident companies (prior to the subsequent extension of the relief to relevant Member State companies) follows the decision in the *Saint-Gobain* case (see **14.105**) and takes effect for accounting periods ending on or after 15 February 2001.

As mentioned in **14.209.2** above, unilateral relief is not given in respect of tax paid under the law of a territory with which Ireland has a tax treaty. Unilateral relief will, however, be available in respect of tax paid where credit for that tax is denied under a treaty (because, for example, of an insufficient holding in the dividend paying company). The exception secures that the existence of a tax treaty will not in itself result in a denial of credit relief. Prior to FA 2004, the exception did not apply to, and unilateral relief was accordingly not available for, sub-national taxes (city, state, provincial etc) paid under the law of a territory with which Ireland had a tax treaty if credit for such taxes was not provided for in that treaty. Unilateral relief may now, for example, be claimed in respect of city, state or provincial taxes levied on profits of dividend paying companies in the US or Canada; the treaties in these cases do not provide for credit for such taxes.

14.210   Relief for third country taxes

14.210.1   Introduction

An Irish resident company, or an EU resident company where the dividend forms part of that company's Irish branch profits (see **14.210.2** below), which receives a dividend from a foreign company to which it is related is entitled:

(1)   to credit for "third country" (including Irish) taxes paid in respect of the profits of that foreign company, and

(2)   where the foreign company itself is related to another company ("third company"), to treat as third country taxes for the purposes of (1) any underlying tax of the third company to the extent that it would be taken into account if the dividend had been paid by a foreign company to an Irish company in accordance with a tax treaty (TCA 1997 Sch 24 paragraph 9B).

The treatment of third country taxes of a related company of an Irish company as in (1) above, and the extension of this treatment to include taxes of a third company as in (2) above, are dealt with respectively in **14.210.2** and **14.210.3** below.

14.210.2   Relief for third country taxes of a foreign company

Where a company resident outside the State ("foreign company") pays a dividend to a company falling within TCA 1997 Sch 24 paragraph 9B(1A) (the "relevant company") and the foreign company is related to the relevant company, then, in computing the amount of underlying credit relief in respect of the dividend, there is to be taken into account, as if it were tax payable under the law of the country in which the foreign company is resident:

(a)   any Irish income tax or corporation tax payable by the foreign company in respect of its profits (TCA 1997 Sch 24 paragraph 9B(1)(a)), and

(b)   any tax which, under the law of any other country (a "third country"), is payable by the foreign company in respect of its profits (TCA 1997 Sch 24 paragraph 9B(1)(b)).

A company falls within TCA 1997 Sch 24 paragraph 9B(1A) if—

(i)   it is resident in the State, or

(ii)   it is, by virtue of the law of a relevant Member State other than the State, resident for the purposes of "tax in such Member State" (ie, tax imposed in the Member State which corresponds to corporation tax in the State) and the dividend referred to above forms part of the profits of a branch or agency of the company in the State.

For the above purposes, relevant Member State, means—

(a)   a Member State of the European Communities, or

(b)   not being such a Member State, an EEA State which is a territory with which Ireland has a tax treaty (TCA 1997, s 616(7)).

EEA State means a state that is a contracting party to the EEA Agreement. *EEA Agreement* means the Agreement on the European Economic Area signed at Oporto on 2 May 1992, as adjusted by the Protocol signed at Brussels on 17 March 1993.

Accordingly, the company receiving the dividend may be an Irish resident company or a company resident in a relevant Member State where the dividend forms part of the profits of that company's Irish branch or agency. This extension of credit relief to EU resident companies (prior to the subsequent extension of the relief to relevant Member State companies) follows the decision in the *Saint-Gobain* case (see **14.105**) and takes effect for accounting periods ending on or after 15 February 2001.

A company is *related to* another company if that other company controls directly or indirectly, or is a subsidiary of a company that controls directly or indirectly, not less than 5% of the voting power of the first-mentioned company. A company is a *subsidiary* of another company if the other company owns, directly or indirectly, not less than 50% of the ordinary share capital of the first-mentioned company (TCA 1997 Sch 24 paragraph 9B(5)(b)).

Any tax which, under the law of any other country (a third country), is payable by the foreign company in respect of its profits includes—

(i)   tax in respect of profits of a branch of the foreign company in the third country (TCA 1997 Sch 24 paragraph 9B(1)(b)),

(ii)   withholding tax imposed by the third country in respect of interest or royalties (or other payments from which tax is withheld) paid to that company – since such tax can be regarded as tax paid (by way of deduction at source) by the foreign company on its profits (ie, on the interest, royalties etc) (TCA 1997 Sch 24 paragraph 9B(1)(b)), and

(iii)   withholding tax imposed by the third country on dividends paid to the foreign company (TCA 1997 Sch 24 paragraph 9B(2)(b) – see **14.210.3** below).

Example 14.210.2.1

On 3 April 2008 Longwood Ltd, an Irish resident company which makes up accounts to 31 December each year, received a dividend of £107,000 (equal to €160,000 on the date of receipt) from Fleetwood Ltd, a UK a company in which it owns 30% of the share capital. The dividend is paid out of the profits of Fleetwood Ltd for its year ended 31 December 2007.

The profits of Fleetwood Ltd for the year ended 31 December 2007, as disclosed in its accounts, were £1,650,000, and these included profits of £300,000 from its Irish branch on which Irish corporation tax equivalent to £90,000 had been paid, and profits of £500,000 from its German branch on which German tax equivalent to £220,000 had been paid. The distributable profits, after providing for taxation, are £980,000. The corporation tax computation for Fleetwood Ltd for the year ended 31 December 2007 is as follows:

	£	£
Profits, as adjusted for tax		1,800,000
Corporation tax @ 30%		540,000
Less credit - Irish	90,000	
- German (max £500,000 @ 30%)	150,000	240,000
Net UK tax payable		300,000

For Irish corporation tax purposes, foreign tax is £610,000 (£300,000 + £90,000 + £220,000) and the rate of foreign tax is therefore:

$$\frac{610,000}{980,000+610,000}=38.36\%$$

The dividend is grossed up at the lower effective rate (assumed Irish rate 12.5%):

$$€160,000 \times \frac{100}{100-12.5}=€182,857$$

Longwood Ltd: corporation tax computation year ended 31 December 2008

	€
Gross dividend received	182,857
Corporation tax @ 12.5%	22,857
Less credit	22,857
Net Irish corporation tax	Nil

14.210.3   Relief for taxes of a third company

Where a foreign company has received a dividend from a third company which is related to the foreign company (see **14.210.2**) and which is connected with the relevant company (see **14.210.2**), then, subject to certain conditions (see below), tax paid by the foreign company in respect of its profits is deemed to include—

(a) any underlying tax paid by the third company, and

(b) any tax directly charged on the dividend which neither company would have borne had the dividend not been paid (ie, withholding tax on dividends paid abroad),

to the extent that it would be taken into account under TCA 1997 Sch 24 if the dividend had been paid by a foreign company to a relevant company and arrangements (ie, a tax treaty) had provided for underlying tax to be taken into account: and for this purpose, there is to be taken into account as if it were tax payable under the law of the territory in which the third company is resident—

(i)   any income tax or corporation tax payable in the State by the foreign company in respect of its profits, and

(ii)   any tax which, under the law of any other territory, is payable by the foreign company in respect of its profits (TCA 1997 Sch 24 paragraph 9B(2)).

A company is *connected with* another company if that other company controls directly or indirectly, or is a subsidiary (see **14.210.2**) of a company which controls directly or indirectly, not less than 5% of the voting power of the first-mentioned company.

It is sometimes mistakenly thought that the above words "to the extent that it would be taken into account ..." mean that any relief for the underlying tax paid by the foreign company is itself limited to the Irish rate of corporation tax under the limit on total credit provided for in TCA 1997 Sch 24 paragraph 4 (see **14.202**). Thus, where a second tier company with an underlying rate of, say, 35% pays a dividend to a first tier company, the amount of underlying tax that may be attributed to the first tier company would be limited to 25% (applying the limit on credit for a dividend paid to a relevant company). However, the wording refers to the tax which is to be "taken into account" rather than to the *amount* for which credit is to be allowed. Accordingly, the underling tax to be taken into account is the full amount of the underlying tax as if the second tier company were paying the dividend to an Irish resident company.

The withholding tax in (b) above, since it is borne by the foreign company by deduction from the dividend received by it, is in fact a third *country* tax paid by it (rather than a third company tax) and is the tax referred to in (iii) in **14.210.2** above.

As regards (a) above, *underlying tax* in relation to a dividend means tax borne by the dividend paying company in respect of the relevant profits (within the meaning of TCA 1997 Sch 24 paragraph 8 – see **14.207**) in so far as that tax is properly attributable to the proportion of the relevant profits represented by the dividend. In short, it is the proportion of the tax on the profits out of which the dividend is paid represented by the amount of the dividend as a percentage of those profits.

Following FA 2004 (see **14.209.3** above), underlying tax includes any sub-national (city, state, provincial etc) taxes payable in respect of the profits of the third (or fourth etc) company.

Where a third company has received a dividend from a fourth company which is related to the third company and which is connected with the relevant company, then, again subject to conditions (see below), tax paid by the fourth company (fourth company tax), or tax directly charged on the dividend (fourth country tax), is treated for the purposes of paragraph 9B(2) as tax paid by the third company; accordingly, that tax is also included as tax paid by the foreign company (TCA 1997 Sch 24 paragraph 9B(3)).

The above procedure is continued as necessary for successive companies each of which is connected with the relevant company (TCA 1997 Sch 24 paragraph 9B(3)).

Both as regards the foreign company and the third (or fourth etc) company (which may include a company resident in Ireland), relief for underlying tax of the *latter* company is available regardless of whether or not either of the companies is resident in a country with which Ireland has a tax treaty.

As seen above, the underlying tax must be such tax as would qualify as underlying tax had the dividend been paid by a foreign company to a relevant company under the terms of a tax treaty. Treaty-based credit for tax paid by a foreign company to an Irish company does not include any tax suffered in a country other than that in which the dividend paying company is resident. For the purposes of the relief provided for by paragraph 9B(2) and (3), however, tax suffered in the country in which the dividend paying company is resident is deemed to include both Irish tax (tax payable by the company in respect of its Irish branch profits) and tax payable under the law of any other country (tax payable by the company in respect of the profits of a branch in some other country).

The position whereby tax payable under the law of a country other than that in which the dividend paying company is resident follows an amendment introduced by FA 2004. In the light of this amendment, however, it would seem that the wording "to the extent that it would be taken into account ....", following (b) above, is no longer necessary; that wording does not now appear to qualify in any way the extent to which credit may be claimed.

Paragraph 9B does not provide for any relief in respect of tax paid by the foreign company itself; if that company is resident in a treaty country, credit will be available in accordance with TCA 1997 Sch 24 Part 1(paragraphs 1-9) whereas, if it is not so resident, unilateral relief in accordance with TCA 1997 Sch 24 paragraph 9A would be available.

The conditions mentioned above are that—

(a) no tax may be taken into account in respect of a dividend paid by a relevant company except Irish corporation tax and any tax for which that company is entitled to credit under TCA 1997 Sch 24 (eg, foreign tax paid by a foreign branch of the relevant company) (TCA 1997 Sch 24 paragraph 9B(4)(a)); and

(b) no tax may be taken into account in respect of a dividend paid by a foreign company to another foreign company unless it could have been taken into account under TCA 1997 Sch 24 had the other foreign company been a relevant company (TCA 1997 Sch 24 paragraph 9B(4)(b) (see **14.210.2** re "relevant company")).

The need for condition (b) is not apparent. Without the condition, credit relief would be confined in any event to foreign tax paid by the foreign company in question in respect of its profits. If such tax were creditable in accordance with the provisions of a tax treaty, it could only consist, apart from withholding taxes, of taxes paid in respect of the profits of the subsidiary paying the dividend. If creditable under unilateral rules, it could consist only of taxes on income or capital gains which correspond to corporation tax and capital gains tax (TCA 1997 Sch 24 paragraph 9A(7) – see **14.209.2**). It is difficult therefore to see what further restriction is imposed by condition (b).

Example 14.210.3.1

McDonnell International Ltd, an Irish resident company, owns 30% of the ordinary share capital of Tilburg BV, a Dutch resident company, which in turn has a wholly owned Dutch subsidiary, Kampen BV. During its most recent accounting period, McDonnell International Ltd received a dividend of €150,000 from Tilburg BV paid out of profits of €800,000 on which tax of €250,000 had been paid. The profits of €800,000 include a dividend of €100,000 received from Kampen BV out of profits of €500,000 net of tax €200,000.

Assuming the tax charge in the accounts of Tilburg BV is also €250,000, the distributable profits are €550,000.

For the purposes of credit relief in the case of McDonnell International Ltd, the tax paid by Tilburg BV is treated as including the tax paid by Kampen BV. The amount to be taken into account for this purpose is the amount which would be taken into account if the dividend paid by Kampen BV had been paid to a relevant company, in effect the proportion of the tax of €200,000 represented by the dividend of €100,000 as a percentage of that company's profits, ie €200,000 x 100,000/500,000 = €40,000.

In relation to the dividend of €150,000 paid by Tilburg BV to McDonnell International Ltd, the total tax to be taken into account is therefore €250,000 + €40,000 = €290,000. The effective rate of foreign tax is therefore:

$$\frac{290,000}{550,000 + 290,000} = 34.52\%$$

Since this rate is higher than the Irish effective rate, assumed to be 12.5%, the dividend received by McDonnell International Ltd will be grossed up at 12.5%. The corporation tax computation of McDonnell International Ltd for the period is now as follows:

	€
Dividend received	150,000
Gross up at Irish effective rate – €150,000 x 100/87.5	171,429
Corporation tax @ 12.5%	21,429
Less credit relief	21,429
Net corporation tax payable	Nil

The calculation of underlying tax of a foreign dividend paying company may be quite complex due to such factors as the need to take into account taxes other than the federal or national tax of the country in question or the requirement, in calculating federal or national taxes, to make a deduction for other taxes, for example the trade tax in Germany. Underlying tax calculations for such countries as Germany and Japan are particularly complex.

As pointed out in **14.206.6**, the Revenue Commissioners have published a list of effective tax rates that will be accepted in practice in the cases of countries for which credit for underlying tax is provided in tax treaties. Use of these rates is particularly useful for portfolio investors who would not normally be in a position to ascertain the precise rate of underlying tax. In a case in which a relevant company receives a dividend from a foreign company which in turn has received a dividend from a company in a third country, the treatment of third country tax cannot be illustrated using the approximate effective rates in the Revenue list where such tax is creditable against the tax payable by the foreign company. It will be necessary therefore in such cases to calculate the actual underlying rate of tax.

In the case of Germany, for example, the accepted rate of underlying tax in the Revenue list is 37%. The computation of the actual effective rate of German tax is complex and subject to change. In the following example, the treatment of German underlying tax takes account of the 2008 tax reform whereby the overall company tax rate works out at about 30% as compared with the previous 40%. (In this respect, the example is merely illustrative and is included only to show the working of TCA 1997 Sch 24 para 9B where a German company receives a dividend from a third country.)

Example 14.210.3.2

Barrow Ltd, an Irish resident company, is a wholly owned subsidiary of Furness Ltd, a UK resident company, which in turn is a wholly owned subsidiary of Rapidan Inc, a US company. Barrow Ltd owns 30% of the ordinary share capital of a German resident company, Jena GmbH, which in turn holds 25% of the ordinary share capital of a Dutch company, Zandvoort BV. Furness Ltd and Rapidan Inc each owns 2% of the ordinary share capital in Zandvoort BV.

Rapidan Inc holds, directly and indirectly, 11.5% (30% x 25% + 2% + 2%) of the ordinary share capital of Zandvoort BV and, since Barrow Ltd is a subsidiary of Rapidan Inc, Zandvoort BV is connected with Barrow Ltd. Accordingly, since Zandvoort BV is also related to Jena GmbH, third country credit as provided for in TCA 1997 Sch 24 paragraph 9B will be available in respect of any dividend paid by Zandvoort BV to Jena GmbH.

During its most recent accounting period, Barrow Ltd receives a dividend of €240,000 from Jena GmbH paid out of profits of €2m. No withholding tax is deducted from this dividend. The profits of €2m include a dividend of €248,505 received from Zandvoort BV and paid out of profits of €1,242,525 on which tax of €443,759 had been paid. By virtue of the tax treaty between Germany and the Netherlands, and in any event the Parent-Subsidiary Directive, no withholding tax is deducted from the dividend.

For the purposes of credit relief in the case of Barrow Ltd, the tax paid by Jena GmbH is treated as including the tax paid by Zandvoort BV (TCA 1997 Sch 24 paragraph 9B). The amount to be taken into account for this purpose is the amount which would be taken into account if the dividend paid by Zandvoort BV had been paid to a relevant company, in effect the proportion of the tax of €443,759 represented by the dividend of €248,505 as a percentage of that company's profits, ie €443,759 x 248,505/1,242,525 = €88,752.

In relation to the dividend of €240,000, paid by Jena GmbH to Barrow Ltd and taxable at the 12.5% corporation tax rate, the total tax to be taken into account is €656,500 (see calculation of underlying German tax below) + €88,752 = €745,252. The rate of foreign tax is 30.68% (see calculation below).

The corporation tax computation of Barrow Ltd for the period is as follows:

	€
Dividend received	240,000
Effective rate of foreign tax 30.68%	
Therefore gross up at lower Irish effective rate – €240,000 x 100/87.5	274,286
Corporation tax @ 12.5%	34,286
Less credit relief	34,286
Net corporation tax payable	Nil

Underlying tax relating to dividend from Jena GmbH

The suggested calculation of underlying tax in respect of the dividend of €240,000 received from Jena GmbH is as follows (see also **14.206.4**):

	€	€
Profits of Jena GmbH		2,000,000
Corporation tax €2m x 15%	300,000	
Solidarity surcharge @ 5.5%	16,500	316,500
Available for distribution		1,683,500

Dividend	800,000
Retained	883,500

In calculating the rate of underlying tax, the foreign tax borne includes only the foreign taxes eligible for credit under the Ireland/ Germany treaty:

	€	€
Business tax (income element) €2m @ 17%		340,000
Corporation tax @ 15%	300,000	
Solidarity surcharge @ 5.5%	16,500	316,500
Eligible for credit		656,500
Add: Dutch tax eligible for credit (TCA 1997 Sch 24 para 9B)		88,752
		745,252

In calculating the relevant profits of the German subsidiary, the actual profits available for distribution must be taken, ie €1,683,500. As the dividend of €248,505 received by Jena GmbH is exempt from tax in Germany, there is no credit in Germany for Dutch underlying tax in respect of it. The underlying rate of tax (for Irish tax purposes), taking into account underlying Dutch tax, is as follows:

$$\frac{FT}{RP+FT} + \frac{745,252}{1,683,500+745,252} = 30.68\%$$

Example 14.210.3.3

Fortwilliam Ltd, an Irish resident company, has a wholly owned UK subsidiary, Tavistock Ltd, which in turn has a wholly owned US subsidiary, Carlsbad Inc.

During its latest accounting period, Fortwilliam Ltd received a dividend of £250,000 (equal to €375,000 at the date of receipt) from Tavistock Ltd. The dividend is liable to Irish corporation tax at 25%. The profits before tax, from which the dividend was paid, were £800,000, including a dividend of $59,000 (equal to £30,000) received from Carlsbad Inc from which US withholding tax at 5% had been deducted (ie, net dividend received £28,500). The dividend of $50,000 had been paid out of profits of $160,000 on which US federal tax of $60,800 had been paid. For convenience, it is assumed that the tax charge in the accounts of Carlsbad Inc for the relevant period is the same as the tax payable so that the distributable profits are $99,200 ($160,000 – $60,800).

The profit and loss account of Tavistock Ltd for the relevant period is as follows:

	£	£
Profits before tax		800,000
Provision for corporation tax	240,000	
Overprovision for prior year	25,000	215,000
Distributable profits		585,000
Dividend to Fortwilliam Ltd		250,000
Retained		335,000

For the purposes of the relevant UK corporation tax computation of Tavistock Ltd, it is necessary to ascertain the effective US rate of tax relating to the dividend of £30,000. On the basis of federal tax of $60,800 on profits of $160,000 and withholding tax at 5%, the effective rate is 41.1% (5% x 62% + 38%). Accordingly the dividend, net of withholding tax at 5%, is grossed up at the lower UK rate of 30%, ie £28,500 x 100/70 = £40,714.

Based on relevant information, the UK corporation tax computation of Tavistock Ltd is as follows:

	£	£
Profit per accounts		800,000
Add: Depreciation	120,000	
other disallowable items	30,000	
foreign tax credit (£40,714 - £30,000)	10,714	160,714
		960,714
Less: capital allowances		180,000
		780,714
Corporation tax @ 30% (assume no small companies/marginal relief)		234,214
Less: credit (£40,714 - £28,500)		12,214
Net UK corporation tax		222,000

Carlsbad Inc is related to Tavistock Ltd and is connected with Fortwilliam Ltd. For Irish corporation tax purposes therefore, the foreign tax to be taken into account for credit relief purposes will include US underlying tax and also US withholding tax. US federal tax is taken to be the proportion of the dividend of £30,000 received by Tavistock Ltd represented by the US tax as a proportion of US distributable profits:

$$£30,000 = \frac{60,800}{99,200} = £18,387$$

Accordingly, the total tax to be taken into account for Irish corporation tax purposes is £241,887 (£222,000 + £18,387 + £1,500). The effective rate of foreign tax is as follows:

$$\frac{FT}{RP+FT} = \frac{241,887}{585,000+241,887} = 29.25\%$$

The dividend from Tavistock Ltd is therefore grossed up at the lower Irish rate of 25%.

Fortwilliam Ltd: corporation tax computation

	€
Dividend of €375,000 grossed up at 25%	500,000
Corporation tax @ 25%	125,000
Less: credit	125,000
Net corporation tax payable	Nil

Example 14.210.3.4

Killeen Ltd, an Irish resident company, owns 40% of the ordinary share capital in a Dutch company, Koopman BV, which in turn holds 30% of the ordinary share capital in a US company, Bismarck Inc.

During its latest accounting period, Killeen Ltd received a dividend of €280,000 from Koopman BV. No withholding tax arises in respect of the dividend by virtue of the Parent-Subsidiary Directive (see **14.7**). The dividend is taxable in Ireland at 12.5%. The profits before tax, from which the dividend was paid, were €1m, including a dividend of $160,000 (equal to €120,000) received from Bismarck Inc from which US withholding tax at 5% had been deducted (ie, net dividend received €114,000). The dividend of $160,000 had been paid out of profits of $620,000 on which US federal tax of $215,000 had been paid.

The profit and loss account of Koopman BV for the period is as follows:

	€	€
Profits before tax		1,000,000
Provision for corporation tax	420,000	
Underprovision for prior years	15,000	405,000
Distributable profits		595,000
Dividend to Killeen Ltd		280,000
Retained		315,000

For Dutch tax purposes, the dividend from Bismarck Inc is excluded in accordance with the Dutch "participation exemption". Assume the Dutch corporation tax computation is as follows:

		€	€
Profit per accounts			1,000,000
Less: US dividend			120,000
			880,000
Add:	depreciation	230,000	
	other disallowable items	40,000	270,000
			1,150,000
Less: capital allowances			310,000
			840,000
Corporation tax @, say, 25%			210,000

Bismarck Inc is related to Koopman BV (at least 25%) and is connected with Killeen Ltd (at least 10%). For Irish corporation tax purposes, therefore, the foreign tax to be taken into account for credit relief purposes will include US underlying tax and also US withholding tax. US federal tax can be taken to be the proportion of the dividend of €120,000 received by Koopman BV represented by the US federal tax as a proportion of the US distributable profits

$$€120,000 \times \frac{215,000}{405,000} = €63,704$$

For Irish corporation tax purposes, therefore, the foreign tax, including the US underlying and withholding taxes, is €279,704 (€210,000 + €63,704 + €6,000). The effective rate of foreign tax is therefore:

$$\frac{FT}{RP + FT} = \frac{279,704}{595,000 + 279,704} = 31.98\%$$

The dividend from Koopman BV is therefore grossed up at the lower Irish rate of 12.5%.

	€
Dividend of €280,000 grossed up at 12.5%	320,000
Corporation tax @ 12.5%	40,000
Less: credit	40,000
Net corporation tax payable	Nil

Dividends paid from transferred profits

TCA 1997, Schedule 24 paragraph 9H extends the circumstances under which a foreign tax credit may be availed of by an Irish company in receipt of a dividend, paid on or after 31 January 2008, from a foreign company. Where the foreign company itself receives a dividend from another foreign company, the Irish company is entitled to a credit in respect of the foreign tax paid by the other foreign company on the profits out of which it paid the dividend.

Credit relief will also be available when the profits of the other foreign company become profits of the foreign company other than by way of paying a dividend, for example, where there is a merger of the two companies. Credit relief will be given where a dividend is paid by a company following a merger in respect of the underlying tax paid by its predecessor companies. The credit will be limited, where appropriate, to the amount that would have been given had the profits been transferred instead by way of a dividend, and will not apply where the profits transfer is a result of a tax avoidance scheme.

TCA 1997, Schedule 24 paragraph 9H applies in any case where—

(a) under the law of a territory outside the State, tax is paid by a company (the "first company") resident outside the State in respect of any of its profits,

(b) some or all of those profits become profits of another company (the "second company") resident outside the State otherwise than by paying a dividend to that company, and

(c) the second company pays a dividend out of those profits to another company, wherever resident (TCA 1997, Schedule 24 paragraph 9H(1)).

For the purposes of allowing credit under TCA 1997, Schedule 24 for foreign tax in respect of profits of the first company attributable to any dividends paid—

(i) by any foreign resident company (whether or not the second company),

(ii) to a company resident in the State,

TCA 1997, Schedule 24 applies with any necessary modifications as if the second company had paid the tax paid by the first company in respect of those profits of the first company which became profits of the second company (TCA 1997, Schedule 24 paragraph 9H(2)).

The foregoing treatment is subject to two limitations, so that—

(a) the credit against corporation tax allowable to an Irish resident company may not exceed what it would have been had the transferred profits become profits of the second company by virtue of the payment of a dividend, and

(b) no tax may be taken into account in respect of profits which became profits of the second company by virtue of a scheme or arrangement the purpose, or one of the main purposes, of which is the avoidance of tax (TCA 1997, Schedule 24 paragraph 9H(3)).

14.211 Credit relief for Irish branches of EU companies

Credit relief may be claimed in respect of foreign tax suffered on income of the Irish branch of a company resident in a relevant Member State (apart from any tax suffered in the company's home country). This extension of credit relief to EU resident companies follows the decision in the *Saint-Gobain* case (see **14.105**) and takes effect for accounting periods ending on or after 15 February 2001.

For the above purposes, *relevant Member State*, means—

(a)   a Member State of the European Communities; or

(b)   not being such a Member State, an EEA State which is a territory with which Ireland has a tax treaty (TCA 1997, s 616(7)).

EEA State means a state which is a contracting party to the EEA Agreement. *EEA Agreement* means the Agreement on the European Economic Area signed at Oporto on 2 May 1992, as adjusted by the Protocol signed at Brussels on 17 March 1993.

TCA 1997 Sch 24 paragraph 9C provides for the extension of any credit relief available under Sch 24 to a relevant company. A *relevant company* is a company which—

(i)   is not resident in the State;

(ii)   is, by virtue of the law of a relevant Member State other than the State, resident for the purposes of "tax in such Member State" (ie, tax imposed in the Member State which corresponds to corporation tax in the State); and

(iii)   carries on a trade in the State through a branch or agency (TCA 1997 Sch 24 paragraph 9C(1)).

A relevant company is entitled, in respect of an accounting period, to such relief under TCA 1997 Sch 24 in respect of relevant tax as would, if the branch or agency in the State had been an Irish resident company, have been given in accordance with a tax treaty to that resident company (TCA 1997 Sch 24 paragraph 9C(2)). The credit is available to a company that receives dividends which form part of the profits of the branch or agency.

For the above purposes, *relevant tax* means foreign tax paid in respect of the income or chargeable gains of an Irish branch or agency of a relevant company, except such tax paid in a territory in which the company is liable to tax by reason of domicile, residence, place of management or other similar criterion (TCA 1997 Sch 24 paragraph 9C(1)).

14.212   Treasury companies

TCA 1997 Sch 24 paragraph 4(2) provides that foreign income for credit relief purposes is to be arrived at by allocating the total income of a company as computed for Irish corporation tax purposes to the item which has borne foreign tax (see **14.202**). The income so allocated is sometimes referred to as "the Irish measure" of the foreign income. Where the foreign income for which credit is to be allowed is taken into account in computing a company's trading income, a formula-based allocation is prescribed by TCA 1997 Sch 24 paragraph 4(2A) (introduced by FA 2006). As mentioned in **14.202**, TCA 1997 Sch 24 paragraph 4(3) provides that the sales ratio basis is to be followed for the purpose of determining the amount of income attributable to receipts from the sales of goods within the meaning of TCA 1997, s 449 (computer services/software and IFSC/Shannon income). The sales ratio approach derives basically from the method for calculating manufacturing relief (see **7.202**). It has already been pointed out that a sales ratio basis applied to a services activity deemed to be the manufacture of goods suffers from a technical weakness resulting from the need to assume that non-qualifying services income constitutes "merchandise". Further difficulties arise from the application of the sales ratio basis to income of treasury companies.

The sales ratio basis is prescribed by TCA 1997, s 449(2)(b) for the purposes of TCA 1997, s 449 and its application is illustrated in Example **14.403.1**. TCA 1997 Sch 24 paragraph 4(3) prescribes this method of identifying the Irish measure of foreign income for credit relief purposes also, for companies with income attributable to receipts from the sales of goods within the meaning of TCA 1997, s 449. This income includes income from financial services activities carried on in the IFSC. Companies in receipt of such income must therefore use this basis for allocating expenses and may not have regard to the actual expenses incurred in earning the income in question.

As mentioned in **14.202**, the Irish measure of foreign income (for the purposes of the limitation on foreign credit imposed by TCA 1997 Sch 24 paragraph 4) was computed on a "gross" basis, ie without making any deduction from the foreign income in respect of expenses incurred generally by a company. The availability, in the context of the IFSC, of the 10% tax rate in respect of interest and other financial income from abroad focussed attention on the facility for eliminating any Irish tax liability by the use of the gross basis. The Irish measure of the foreign income was simply the gross amount received with no deduction for attributable expenses such as cost of funds or share of overheads.

Example 14.212.1

Worldwide Finance Ltd, an IFSC company eligible for the 10% corporation tax rate in respect of its profits from treasury operations, receives annual interest of €100,000, subject to 10% withholding tax, from Australian customers. The loans made to Australia have been funded partly from share capital and partly from borrowings on which interest of €30,000 is payable. Annual overheads are €10,000.

Later, loans are made to customers in Germany. These loans produce interest income of €200,000. Annual funding costs of €150,000 are incurred in connection with the German loans. There is no increase in overheads.

On a "gross" basis, the corporation tax computation is as follows:

	€	€
Gross interest receivable		300,000
Funding cost	180,000	
Overheads	10,000	190,000
Profit		110,000
Corporation tax @ 10%		11,000
Less: credit relief (10% of €100,000)		10,000
Payable		1,000

Before the German loans were made, the position was:

	€	€
		100,000
Funding cost	30,000	
Overheads	10,000	40,000
Profit		60,000
Corporation tax @ 10%		6,000
Less: credit relief (max)		6,000
Payable		Nil

The introduction of the German business permitted some of the German interest to be sheltered by credit in respect of the Australian interest. The incremental profit on the German business is €50,000 but this results in tax of €1,000 only.

The scope for "arbitrage" on the above lines led to a reassessment of the basis on which the Irish measure of foreign income should be computed, eventually resulting in the introduction of a "net" basis for accounting periods ended after 31 December 1994 (as now provided for in TCA 1997 Sch 24 paragraph 4(2), (2A)). Thus, the computation in Example **14.212.1** would now be as in the following example. In applying the net basis, it is necessary to employ the sales ratio method since the income in question comes within TCA 1997, s 449. The example includes an alternative computation in which, in arriving at the amount of the net income, the expenses deductible are taken to include the foreign withholding tax. There appears to be some support for this approach to the net basis but the first computation reflects the preferred view here.

Example 14.212.2

The facts are as in Example **14.212.1** but the computation here illustrates the "net" basis to be used in calculating the Irish measure of foreign income, incorporating the sales ratio method.

	€
Profit	110,000
Irish measure of Australian income:	
€110,000 x 100,000/300,000	36,667
Foreign tax rate: 10,000/36,667 = 27.27%	
Net foreign income (Irish measure less foreign tax)	26,667
Gross up at Irish rate 10%	29,630
Creditable tax (€29,630 - €26,667)	2,963
Non-creditable tax (€10,000 - €2,963)	7,037
Corporation tax computation:	
Net income as above	110,000
Less: non-creditable tax	7,037
	102,963
Corporation tax @ 10%	10,296
Less: credit for foreign tax	2,963
Payable	7,333

Alternative computation:

	€
Profit	110,000
Credit relief:	
Irish measure of Australian income	
€100,000 x 100,000/300,000	33,333
Gross up at Irish rate 10%	37,037
Creditable tax (€37,037 - €33,333)	3,704
Non-creditable tax (€10,000 - €3,704)	6,296

Corporation tax computation:

Net income as above	110,000
Less: non-creditable tax	6,296
	103,704
Corporation tax @ 10%	10,370
Less: credit for foreign tax	3,704
Payable	6,666

As previously mentioned, the foreign income for which the sales ratio basis is prescribed comprises income from qualifying activities carried on in the IFSC or Shannon, income from computer services and income from sales of Irish manufactured computer software. For software companies in particular, income may be derived from both Irish manufactured and foreign manufactured sales and an initial apportionment on a sales basis is made for the purpose of ascertaining "income from the sale of goods" which will be taxable at the 10% rate. A further apportionment is then made, also on a sales ratio basis, to ascertain the income that has borne foreign tax (the "Irish measure of foreign income"). The position for treasury companies is similar. Assuming all income qualifies for the 10% rate, the Irish measure of foreign income is arrived at on a sales ratio basis where the numerator is the foreign income that has borne withholding tax and the denominator comprises total receipts.

The sales ratio basis obviously fails to recognise the principle of matching costs with revenue and is likely to result in distortions in the computation of foreign tax credits. Treasury companies in particular are likely to engage in transactions giving rise to certain receipts that must be brought into the sales ratio formula in a manner that greatly distorts the allocation of income. For IFSC operations, the effect of TCA 1997, s 446(10)(b) is that the denominator in the sales ratio formula is "any amount receivable in payment for anything sold, or any services rendered, in the course of the relevant trading operations". This description would seem to include, for example, non-interest type receipts such as swap income and foreign currency sales proceeds and where these arise to a treasury company could greatly dilute the foreign credit available. Proceeds of sale of foreign currency would bear no relationship to the income from the related financial transaction. Similarly, where swap transactions are undertaken to hedge income streams in various currencies into the functional currency of the company concerned, the denominator in the sales ratio formula may include the swap receipt.

Example 14.212.3

Global Finance Ltd, an IFSC treasury company, is in receipt of Australian bond interest income from which Australian withholding tax of 10% has been deducted. The company's functional currency is the US dollar and the Australian income is swapped into US dollars. The accounts of the company for the relevant accounting period show the following:

	$
Bond interest (net of withholding tax)	90,000
Swap receipts	80,000
Swap payments	(100,000)
Profit	70,000

Calculation of credit relief:

Foreign tax ($100,000 @ 10%)	10,000
Income	70,000
Total income	80,000
Irish measure of foreign income (sales ratio):	
$80,000 x 100,000/180,000	44,444
Foreign tax rate:	
10,000/44,444	22.5%
Irish rate of tax on foreign income	10%
"Net foreign income" (Irish measure less foreign tax)	34,444
Gross up at lower rate of tax (10%):	
$34,444 x 100/(100 – 10)	38,271
Creditable tax ($38,271 - $34,444)	3,827
Non-creditable tax ($10,000 - $3,827)	6,173
Income less non-creditable tax ($80,000 - $6,173)	73,827
Corporation tax computation:	
$73,827 @ 10%	7,383
Less: credit for foreign tax	3,827
Payable	3,556

If the denominator in the sales ratio were to include only the net gain, if any, on a swap transaction, the same anomaly would remain although on a much reduced scale. In this example, there is no net gain. The credit calculation without including any swap amount in the denominator would be as follows:

	$
Total income	80,000
Irish measure of foreign income (sales ratio):	
$80,000 x 100,000/100,000	80,000
Foreign tax rate:	
10,000/80,000	12.5%
Irish rate of tax on foreign income	10%
"Net foreign income" (Irish measure less foreign tax)	70,000
Gross up at lower rate of tax (10%):	
$70,000 x 100/(100 - 10)	77,778
Creditable tax ($77,778 - $70,000)	7,778
Non-creditable tax ($10,000 - $7,778)	2,222
Income less non-creditable tax ($80,000 - $2,222)	77,778
Corporation tax computation:	
$77,778 @ 10%	7,778
Less: credit for foreign tax	7,778
Payable	Nil

It is understood that, in practice, the Irish Revenue would accept that the net proceeds of a hedging contract, being either a net swap gain or the net proceeds on a foreign exchange transaction, may be included in the denominator for the sales ratio formula.

Where a net payment results, there is no effect as can be seen from the alternative computation in Example **14.212.3**. This is the equitable result which recognises that the real gross revenue has borne tax at 10% so that no further tax should be paid in Ireland. As noted above, the inclusion of any net swap or foreign exchange gain (where the functional currency is weaker than the currency in which the loans are made) in the denominator, rather than the corresponding gross proceeds, alleviates the distortion problem but does not remove it entirely since the denominator is still increased.

A further problem remains in the case of a treasury company which is in receipt of interest some of which has suffered foreign withholding tax and some of which has been received gross. If, for example, only the income subject to the foreign tax has been swapped, any net swap expense will be allocated proportionately between the two interest streams despite the fact that the swap relates entirely to the foreign taxed income. In that case, the Irish measure of foreign income will be disproportionately increased to the advantage of the company concerned. Obviously, a disadvantage will result in the converse situation where only the income received gross has been swapped.

The following example illustrates another facet of the sales ratio basis used for calculating the Irish measure of foreign income for credit relief purposes.

Example 14.212.4

International Finance Company Ltd, a treasury company operating in the IFSC and whose functional currency is the US dollar, has the following income (all qualifying for the 10% corporation tax rate) and expenses:

	$	$
Australian bond interest (net of 10% withholding tax)		2,250,000
US dollar loan interest		4,000,000
Other foreign source interest		100,000
		6,350,000
Less:		
Hedging costs		
- Australian	1,200,000	
- US	1,100,000	
Other operating costs	50,000	2,350,000
Net profit		4,000,000

For credit relief purposes, the Irish measure of foreign (Australian) income is calculated on the sales ratio basis as follows:

$$\text{Net income} \times \frac{\text{Australian interest}}{\text{total receivable}} = \$4,000,000 \times \frac{2,500,000}{6,600,000} = \$1,515,152$$

The points made here regarding the sales ratio basis are also relevant to the calculation of the form of unilateral credit relief discussed in **14.4**.

See also **3.212** in relation to stock lending/sale and repo transactions, in particular as regards the question of direct attribution and apportionment of "manufactured payments".

14.213 Credit for withholding tax on certain interest

TCA 1997 Sch 24 paragraph 9D provides for unilateral credit relief for withholding tax deducted, in countries with which Ireland does not have a tax treaty, from interest ("relevant interest") received by a company where the interest forms part of its trading income. The mechanism of the relief is similar to that provided for in TCA 1997, s 449, as described in **14.403**. Relief is not to apply in respect of any accounting period of a company which is not a relevant accounting period within the meaning of TCA 1997, s 442 (see **7.201.2**); an accounting period part of which is a relevant accounting period is to be apportioned on a time basis for the purpose of ascertaining any amount to be taken into account for the relevant accounting period (TCA 1997 Sch 24 paragraph 9D(3)). Thus, the relief is directed at non-IFSC treasury companies.

The tax which qualifies for credit relief (*relevant foreign tax*) is tax—

(a)   which under the laws of any foreign territory has been deducted from the amount of the interest;

(b)   which corresponds to income tax or corporation tax;

(c)   which has not been repaid to the company in question;

(d)   for which credit is not available under a double tax treaty; and

(e)   which is not otherwise treated under TCA 1997 Sch 24 as reducing the amount of any income.

Relevant interest means interest receivable by a company which interest falls to be taken into account in computing the trading income of a trade carried on by the company and from which relevant foreign tax is deducted.

The requirement that the tax must correspond with income tax or corporation tax in Ireland followed questions as to whether any kind of tax suffered on payment, such as premium taxes in the case of insurance business, might be included. Only withholding type taxes qualify and not taxes levied by direct assessment or underlying taxes.

The purpose of (e) above is to confirm that credit relief will not be available in respect of any amount of foreign tax which, in accordance with TCA 1997 Sch 24 ("Relief from income tax and corporation tax by means of credit in respect of foreign tax"), is allowed as a deduction in computing income (see **14.202**).

The relief is a percentage of the foreign tax or, if smaller, the corporation tax attributable to the amount of relevant interest from which the foreign tax has been withheld. The attributable corporation tax is calculated on the income referable to the relevant interest which has suffered the foreign tax, and that income is the proportion of the total trading income, as increased by the relevant foreign tax (TCA 1997 Sch 24 paragraph 9D(1)(b)(ii)), as is represented by the amount of relevant interest which has suffered the foreign tax over the total amount receivable in the course of the trade.

Because the foreign tax will already have been deducted in computing trading income (see **14.301**), the unilateral credit relief is confined to an appropriate percentage of that foreign tax. Accordingly, the credit takes the form of a deduction from corporation tax of—

(a)   in so far as the corporation tax is charged on profits apportioned to the financial year 2002, 84%; and

(b)   in so far as the corporation tax is charged on profits apportioned to the financial year 2003 or any subsequent year, 87.5%.

The credit allowable will be the lesser of the amount calculated as above and the amount of the Irish tax attributable to the foreign income. In nearly all cases, credit will be limited to the Irish tax so attributable (TCA 1997 Sch 24 paragraph 9D(2)).

Irish corporation tax attributable to the income computed as above is fixed by TCA 1997 Sch 24 paragraph 9D(1)(b) at—

(a) in so far as it is corporation tax charged on profits apportioned to the financial year 2002, 16%; and

(b) in so far as it is corporation tax is charged on profits apportioned to the financial year 2003 or any subsequent year, 12.5%.

The legislation does not appear to deny relief in cases where the financial trade is a foreign trade of an Irish resident company and therefore taxable under Case III. The mechanism of the relief, however, since it involves a deduction of 87.5% of the corporation tax charged, and corporation tax at 12.5% attributable to the foreign income, suggests that only Case I trades are in question.

The corporation tax rate in (a) or (b), as appropriate, is applied to the income referable to the relevant interest, computed as above, as reduced by the amount of the relevant foreign tax (TCA 1997 Sch 24 paragraph 9D(1)(b)(i))

The foreign taxes in respect of which the unilateral credit is allowed for any period comprise any relevant foreign tax suffered in that period. These taxes may have been suffered in more than one country. Relief at the appropriate percentage of the relevant foreign taxes, or the Irish corporation tax attributable to the foreign income in question, whichever is less, is then allowed as a deduction from the company's corporation tax liability. There is no question of relating any amount creditable to a particular income item or to income from a particular country. In this respect, the credit differs from the treaty based credit relief which allows for credit on an item by item basis. In practice, this difference is unlikely to have any impact since, as already noted, unilateral credit will nearly always be given at the Irish corporation tax rate which will tend to be lower than any foreign withholding tax on gross income.

The unilateral credit relief is available to Irish branches (or permanent establishments) of foreign companies. In this respect also, the relief is different to the treaty-based relief which is only available to Irish resident companies. Since an Irish branch of a non-resident company is not entitled to treaty relief for foreign taxes, such taxes can qualify for the unilateral relief. It is irrelevant whether or not the foreign taxes in these cases arise in a treaty country.

Example 14.213.1

The following information is relevant to Ballarmin Ltd for its latest accounting period:

	€
Gross receipts (interest)	100,000
Interest subject to foreign tax	20,000
Withholding tax deducted	2,000
Expenses	60,000
Profit	40,000
Corporation tax computation:	€
Profit	40,000

Deduct: foreign tax		2,000
		38,000
		€
Irish tax @ 12.5%		4,750
Unilateral credit (lesser of A and B below)		750
		4,000

	€	€
A: Foreign tax €2,000 x 87.5%		1,750
B: Amount from which foreign tax was withheld	20,000	
Income referable thereto[1]:		
$€40,000 \times \dfrac{20,000}{100,000} =$		8,000
Less: relevant foreign tax [2]		2,000
		6,000
€6,000 @ 12.5% =		750
Smaller of A and B		750

Note:

1. The total income €38,000 in the formula is increased by the amount of the relevant foreign tax €2,000 (TCA 1997 Sch 24 paragraph 9D(b)(ii)).

2. The income referable to the relevant interest is reduced by the relevant foreign tax (TCA 1997 Sch 24 paragraph 9D(b)(i))).

14.214 Unrelieved foreign tax on dividends: pooling of tax credits

A company receiving a foreign dividend may set the foreign tax on the dividend against Irish tax on that dividend. In certain circumstances, in accordance with pooling arrangements, where the foreign tax related to a dividend exceeds the Irish tax on that dividend, the excess may be offset against Irish tax on the remaining foreign dividends received in the same accounting period. Any balance still unused may be carried forward for offset in subsequent accounting periods. In respect of dividends received on or after 31 January 2008, two pools of tax credits are available, one for foreign dividends subject to tax at the 25% rate and one for "specified" dividends, ie foreign dividends taxable at the 12.5% rate.

The tax credit pooling arrangements apply in a case where a company receives a relevant dividend. A *relevant dividend* is a dividend received by a company from a foreign company, ie a company that is not resident in the State, where that company is related to the company receiving the dividend. For this purpose, a company is *related to* another company if that other company controls directly or indirectly, or is a subsidiary of a company that controls directly or indirectly, not less than 5% of the voting power of the first-mentioned company. A company is a *subsidiary* of another company if the other company owns, directly or indirectly, not less than 50% of the ordinary share capital of the first-mentioned company (TCA 1997 Sch 24 paragraph 9B(5)(b)).

Where, in the case of a relevant dividend received by a company in an accounting period and which is taxable at the 25% rate in accordance with TCA 1997, s 21A, any part of the foreign tax cannot otherwise be allowed as a credit against Irish tax on the dividend so that the income representing the dividend is reduced in accordance with TCA 1997 Sch 24 paragraph 7(3)(c) (see **14.202**), the aggregate amount of corporation tax payable by the company for that period in respect of relevant dividends (including any specified dividends) received from foreign companies in the period is to be reduced by the unrelieved foreign tax of that period (TCA 1997 Sch 24 paragraph 9E(2)(a), (b)).

The aggregate amount of corporation tax payable by a company for an accounting period in respect of any dividends received by the company in the accounting period from foreign companies is the amount of corporation tax that would otherwise be payable by the company for that period had those dividends not been received (TCA 1997 Sch 24 paragraph 9E(1)(b)(ii)).

The *unrelieved foreign tax* of an accounting period is the amount determined by the formula—

$$\frac{100-R}{100} \times D$$

where—

R   is the rate per cent specified in TCA 1997, s 21A(3), and

D   is the amount of the part of the foreign tax by which the income is to be treated under TCA 1997 Sch 24 paragraph 7(3)(c) as reduced (1997 Sch 24 paragraph 9E(2)(a).

The rate specified in TCA 1997, s 21A(3) is the higher rate of corporation tax, currently 25% – see **3101.4**.

Where the unrelieved foreign tax in relation to an accounting period exceeds the aggregate amount of corporation tax payable by the company for the period in respect of relevant dividends received by it in that period from foreign companies, the excess is carried forward and treated as unrelieved foreign tax of the next succeeding period, and so on for succeeding accounting periods (TCA 1997 Sch 24 paragraph 9E(2)(c)).

Example 14.214.1

In its latest accounting period, Thomas Ltd, an Irish resident company, received dividends of €50,000 and €60,000, both taxable at the 25% corporation tax rate, from Pierre SA and Bartok Ltd respectively. The subsidiaries are resident in France and Hungary respectively and are wholly owned subsidiaries of Thomas Ltd. The corporation tax computation is as follows:

	€	*Pierre Ltd* €	€	*Bartok Ltd* €
Profits before tax		100,000		100,000
Tax paid		30,000		20,000
After tax profits		70,000		80,000
Dividend to Thomas Ltd		50,000		60,000
Foreign tax attributable to dividend		21,429		15,000
Gross dividend		71,429		75,000
Gross dividend for Irish purposes		66,667		75,000
Corporation tax @ 25%		16,667		18,750

Credit for foreign tax	16,667		15,000
Unrelieved foreign tax	Nil		3,572
		16,667	18,572
Irish tax payable		Nil	178

The unrelieved tax is as follows:

$$\frac{100 - 25}{100} \times \text{€}4,762 = \text{€}3,572$$

It will be seen that the unrelieved tax is 75% of the amount by which the dividend is reduced for the purposes of the Irish corporation tax computation. Grossing up the French dividend by the lower Irish rate of 25% produces taxable income of €66,667, effectively reducing the income of €71,429 by €4,762. Since relief of €1,190 is already obtained by virtue of this reduction (€4,762 @ 25%), the further relief of €3,572 provided for by TCA 1997 Sch 24 paragraph 9E brings the aggregate relief up to the full amount of the unrelieved foreign tax of €4,762. Taking the credit relief of €16,667 into account, credit has now been obtained for the full foreign tax of €21,429.

A relevant dividend which is not charged to corporation tax at the 25% rate, but at the 12.5% rate by virtue of TCA 1997, s 21B (see **3.101.5**) is a *specified dividend* (TCA 1997 Sch 24 paragraph 9E(3)(a)) Where, in the case of a specified dividend received by a company in an accounting period, any part of the foreign tax cannot otherwise be allowed as a credit against Irish tax on the dividend so that the income representing the dividend is reduced in accordance with TCA 1997 Sch 24 paragraph 7(3)(c) (see **14.202**), the aggregate amount of corporation tax payable by the company for that period in respect of specified dividends received from foreign companies in the period is to be reduced by the unrelieved foreign tax in respect of specified dividends of that period (TCA 1997 Sch 24 paragraph 9E(3)(b), (c)).

The aggregate amount of corporation tax payable by a company for an accounting period in respect of any dividends received by the company in the accounting period from foreign companies (and which are specified dividends) is the amount of corporation tax that would otherwise be payable by the company for that period had those dividends not been received (TCA 1997 Sch 24 paragraph 9E(1)(b)(ii)).

The *unrelieved foreign tax* of an accounting period in respect of specified dividends is the amount determined by the formula—

$$\frac{100-R}{100} \times D$$

where—

R   is the rate per cent specified in TCA 1997, s 21, and
D   is the amount of the part of the foreign tax by which the income is to be treated under TCA 1997 Sch 24 paragraph 7(3)(c) as reduced (1997 Sch 24 paragraph 9E(3)(b).

The rate specified in TCA 1997, s 21 is the standard rate of corporation tax, currently 12.5% – see **3101.1**.

Where the unrelieved foreign tax in respect of specified dividends in relation to an accounting period exceeds the aggregate amount of corporation tax payable by the company for the period in respect of specified dividends received by it in that period from foreign companies, the excess is carried forward and treated as unrelieved foreign tax in respect of specified dividends of the next succeeding period, and so on for succeeding accounting periods (TCA 1997 Sch 24 paragraph 9E(3)(d)).

Example 14.214.2

In its latest accounting period, Thomas Ltd, an Irish resident company, received dividends of €50,000 and €75,000 from Pierre SA and Bartok Ltd respectively, of which dividends of €30,000 and €50,000 respectively are taxable at the 25% corporation tax rate. The subsidiaries are resident in France and Hungary respectively and are wholly owned subsidiaries of Thomas Ltd. The corporation tax computation is as follows:

		Pierre Ltd		*Bartok Ltd*
	€	€	€	€
Profits before tax		100,000		110,000
Tax paid		30,000		10,000
After tax profits		70,000		100,000
Dividends to Thomas Ltd				
- 25% taxable	30,000		50,000	
- specified	20,000		25,000	
		50,000		75,000
Foreign tax attributable to dividends				
- 25% taxable	12,857		5,000	
- specified	8,572		2,500	
		21,429		7,500
Gross dividends				
- 25% taxable	42,857		55,000	
- specified	28,572		27,500	
		71,429		82,500
Gross dividends for Irish purposes				
- 25% taxable	40,000		55,000	
- specified	22,857		27,500	
		62,857		82,500
Dividends taxable @ 25%:				
Gross dividends for Irish purposes		40,000		55,000
Corporation tax @ 25%		10,000		13,750
Credit for foreign tax	10,000		5,000	
Unrelieved foreign tax	Nil		2,143	
		10,000		7,143
Irish tax payable		Nil		6,607

The unrelieved tax is as follows:

$$\frac{100-25}{100} \times €2,857 = €2,143$$

The unrelieved tax is 75% of the amount by which the dividend is reduced for the purposes of the Irish corporation tax computation. Grossing up the French dividends by the lower Irish rate of 25% produces taxable income of €40,000, effectively reducing the income of €42,857 by €2,857. Since relief of €714 is already obtained by virtue of this reduction (€2,857 @ 25%), the further relief of €2,143 brings the aggregate relief up to the full amount of the unrelieved foreign tax of €2,857. Taking the credit relief of €10,000 into account, credit has now been obtained for the full foreign tax of €12,857.

Specified dividends:	€	€	€	€
Gross dividends for Irish purposes		22,857		27,500
Corporation tax @ 12.5%		2,857		3,438
Credit for foreign tax	2,857		2,500	
Unrelieved foreign tax	Nil		938	
		2,857		3,438
Irish tax payable		Nil		Nil
Unrelieved foreign tax carried forward (€5,001 - €938)	4,063			

The unrelieved tax is as follows:

$$\frac{100-12.5}{100} \times €5,715 = €5,001$$

The unrelieved tax is 87.5% of the amount by which the dividend is reduced for the purposes of the Irish corporation tax computation. Grossing up the French dividends by the lower Irish rate of 12.5% produces taxable income of €22,857, effectively reducing the income of €28,572 by €5,715. Since relief of €714 is already obtained by virtue of this reduction (€5,715 @ 12.5%), the further relief of €938 brings the aggregate relief up to €1,652. Taking the credit relief of €2,857 into account, and the unrelieved foreign tax of €4,063 carried forward, the full foreign tax of €8,572 is accounted for.

14.215   Unrelieved foreign tax on interest: enhanced tax credit

In the light of the expiry of the IFSC regime on 31 December 2005, it was regarded as necessary to replace the enhanced credit relief provided for in TCA 1997, s 450 (see **14.501**) with a new form of enhanced credit with effect from 1 January 2006. The relevant legislation is contained in TCA 1997 Schedule 24 paragraph 9F. The relief is not confined to companies previously eligible for the TCA 1997, s 450 relief and is available to a broad range of companies in the financial sector.

A company receiving relevant interest, ie interest from a related company and sourced from a country with which Ireland has a tax treaty, in circumstances where the interest forms part of its trading profits, may set foreign tax withheld from the interest under the laws of any tax treaty country against Irish tax on that interest. In certain circumstances, where the foreign tax related to the interest exceeds the creditable tax on that interest, an amount equal to 87.5% (100-12.5) of the excess may be offset as an additional credit against the Irish tax attributable to all relevant interest received in the same accounting period. Unlike the position for the similar relief in respect of dividends (see **14.214** above), any unused balance of unrelieved foreign tax in an accounting period may not be carried forward to subsequent periods.

For the above purpose, *foreign tax* in relation to interest receivable by a company means tax which—

(i)   under the laws of any foreign territory has been deducted from the amount of that interest;

(ii)   corresponds to income or corporation tax; and

(iii) has not been repaid to the company.

The enhanced credit is available in a case where a company receives relevant interest. *Relevant interest* is interest received by a company from a source within a territory with which Ireland has concluded a tax treaty, which interest falls to be taken into account in computing the trading income of a trade carried on by the receiving company, and where the interest is received from a company such that one of the companies is a 25% subsidiary of the other company or both companies are 25% subsidiaries of a third company. (See **4.304** regarding the determination of the source of interest income.)

For this purpose, a company is a *25% subsidiary* of another company if and so long as not less than 25% of its ordinary share capital would be treated as owned directly or indirectly by that other company if TCA 1997, s 9, other than s 9(1) (which does not include a reference to a 25% subsidiary – see **2.5**), applied (TCA 1997 Sch 24 paragraph 9F(1)(b)). A company will not be deemed to be a 25% subsidiary of another company (the "parent company") at any time if the percentage—

(a)   of any profits available for distribution to equity holders of the company at that time to which the parent company is then beneficially entitled; or

(b)   of any assets available for distribution to equity holders on a winding up of the company at that time to which the parent company would then be beneficially entitled,

is less than 25% of those profits or assets at that time.

TCA 1997 ss 413, 414, 415 and 418 are to apply, with any necessary modifications but without regard to TCA 1997, s 411(1)(c) (which refers to EU resident companies), to the determination of the percentage of those profits or assets to which a company is beneficially entitled as they apply for the purposes of group relief (see **8.304**) (TCA 1997 Sch 24 paragraph 9F(1)(b)).

Where, as respects any relevant interest received by a company in an accounting period, any part of the foreign tax cannot otherwise be allowed as a credit against corporation tax on that interest so that the income representing the interest is reduced in accordance with TCA 1997 Sch 24 paragraph 7(3)(c) (see **14.202**), the aggregate amount of corporation tax payable by the company for that period in respect of relevant interest of the company for the period from foreign companies is to be reduced by the unrelieved foreign tax of that period (TCA 1997 Sch 24 paragraph 9F(3)).

The aggregate amount of corporation tax payable by a company for an accounting period in respect of relevant interest of the company in the accounting period from foreign companies is the amount of corporation tax payable by the company for that period as would not have been payable by it for the period had that interest not been chargeable to tax. A *foreign company* for this purpose is a company resident outside the State (TCA 1997 Sch 24 paragraph 9F(1)(a)).

The *unrelieved foreign tax* of an accounting period is the amount determined by the formula—

$$\frac{100-R}{100} \times D$$

where—

R   is the rate per cent specified in TCA 1997, s 21(1) (standard rate of corporation tax – see **3.101.1**), and

D   is the amount of the part of the foreign tax by which the income is to be treated under TCA 1997 Sch 24 paragraph 7(3)(c) as reduced (TCA 1997 Sch 24 paragraph 9F(2)).

Example 14.215.1

Aungier Ltd, an Irish resident company, has 25% subsidiaries Yang Ltd and Stelean Ltd, resident in China and Romania respectively. In the most recent accounting period, the taxable profits of Aungier Ltd are €600,000: gross receipts €1.8m less deductible expenses €1.2m. The gross receipts include relevant interest of €30,000 and €60,000 from Yang Ltd and Stelean Ltd respectively, from which tax of 10% and 3% respectively was withheld. The non-creditable tax is first ascertained:

	Yang Ltd	Stelean Ltd
	€	€
Interest to Aungier Ltd	30,000	60,000
Irish measure of foreign income (1/3)	10,000	20,000
Foreign tax withheld	3,000	1,800
Net foreign income	7,000	18,200
Foreign tax rates 30% and 9%		
Gross up at lower of foreign and Irish rate	8,000	20,000
Corporation tax @ 12.5%	1,000	2,500
Credit relief (before enhanced credit)	1,000	1,800
Non-creditable tax (deductible from taxable interest)	2,000	-

The enhanced credit will be the lesser of (A) the unrelieved tax and (B) the tax that would not have been payable had the relevant interest not been chargeable to tax.

A.   Unrelieved foreign tax in relation to the interest from Yang Ltd:

$$\frac{100-12.5}{100} \times €2,000 = €1,750$$

The unrelieved foreign tax is 87.5% of the non-creditable tax. Since relief of €250, at 12.5%, has already been obtained by reducing the taxable interest from €10,000 to €8,000, the further amount of €1,750 provided for by TCA 1997 Sch 24 paragraph 9F brings the aggregate potential relief up to the full amount of the non-creditable tax of €2,000.

B.   Tax not payable if no relevant interest:

	€	€
Actual corporation tax (before enhanced credit):		
Profit		600,000
Deduct non-creditable tax		2,000
		598,000
Corporation tax @ 12.5%		74,750
Less: credit relief as above (1,000 + 1,800)		2,800
Tax payable		71,950
Tax payable if relevant interest not chargeable:		
Net profit		600,000
Exclude relevant interest		90,000
Net profit		510,000

Corporation tax @ 12.5%		63,750
Tax not payable if no relevant interest		8,200
Corporation tax computation:		
Profit (net of non-creditable tax)		598,000
Corporation tax @ 12.5%		74,750
Less: credit relief as above (1,000 + 1,800)	2,800	
Enhanced credit – lesser of A and B	1,750	
Total credit		4,550
Tax payable		70,200

14.216   Dividends from companies taxed as a group

A feature of the tax system of certain overseas countries (the consolidated filing regime in the US being a case in point) is that tax on the profits of one or more companies in a group is remitted by a group member designated for that purpose. Accordingly, the tax on profits earned by one group member will be paid by another group member. In the context of the rules governing credit relief for underlying tax in respect of dividends, this gives rise to a technical problem in that the creditable tax is the tax paid by the company paying the dividend (see **14.207** regarding TCA 1997 Sch 24 paragraph 8(2)). TCA 1997 Sch 24 paragraph 9G addresses this issue by treating the foreign tax paid by the "remitting" company as, effectively, tax paid by one or more of the companies that earned the profits giving rise to the foreign tax.

TCA 1997 Sch 24 paragraph 9G applies where—

(a)   under the law of a foreign territory tax is payable by a company (the "responsible company") resident in that territory in respect of the aggregate profits, or aggregate profits and aggregate gains, of that company and one or more other companies (the "consolidated companies"), taken together as a single taxable entity; and

(b)   a dividend is paid—

(i)   by any one of the consolidated companies (the "paying company") to a company other than a consolidated company (the "recipient company"), or

(ii)   by a company that is not one of the consolidated companies (the "third company") to any one of the consolidated companies (TCA 1997 Sch 24 paragraph 9G(1)).

Where TCA 1997 Sch 24 paragraph 9G applies, for the purposes of allowing credit for foreign tax in respect of profits attributable to dividends, the rules governing the allowance of a credit for foreign taxes set out in TCA 1997 Sch 24 are to apply with any necessary modifications on the assumption that—

(i)   the consolidated companies taken together are a single company (the "single company");

(ii)   any dividend paid by any of the consolidated companies to a recipient company is paid by the single company;

(iii)   any dividend paid by a third company to any one of the consolidated companies is paid to the single company;

(iv)   the single company is related to (5% voting power requirement – see **14.210.2**) the recipient company if the paying company is related to it;

(v)   the third company is related to the single company if it is related to the consolidated company to which it paid the dividend; and

(vi)   the single company is resident in the territory in which the responsible company is resident,

so that the relevant profits for the purposes of TCA 1997 Sch 24 paragraph 8 (the profits on which the creditable foreign tax has been paid – see **14.207**) is a single aggregate figure in respect of the single company and the foreign tax paid by the responsible company is foreign tax paid by the single company (TCA 1997 Sch 24 paragraph 9G(2)(a)).

A single company treated as paying a dividend is treated as connected with (5% voting power requirement – see **14.210.3**) a relevant company (ie, the company receiving the dividend – see **14.210.2**) in relation to the dividend if the company paying the dividend is connected with that relevant company (TCA 1997 Sch 24 paragraph 9G(2)(b)(i)).

A relevant dividend (ie, the dividend paid to the relevant company – see **14.209.2**) paid by any one of the consolidated companies to a recipient company is treated as a relevant dividend paid by the single company to that recipient company (TCA 1997 Sch 24 paragraph 9G(2)(b)(ii)).

References to a "body corporate" in TCA 1997 Sch 24 paragraph 8 (the dividend paying company – see **14.207**) include references to a single company within the meaning of TCA 1997 Sch 24 paragraph 9G (TCA 1997 Sch 24 paragraph 9G(2)(b)(iii)).

Example 14.216.1

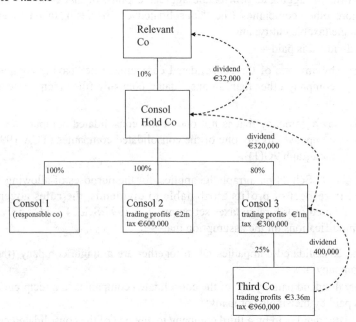

In the above structure, Relevant Co is an Irish company and the recipient company in respect of a dividend of €32,000 from its overseas 10% subsidiary. The four "Consol" companies are "consolidated companies" on whose behalf one of them, Consol 1, is responsible for paying the taxes on their aggregate taxable profits. The dividend of €32,000 is paid out of the profits of Consol HoldCo which comprises a dividend of €320,000 received from Consol 3.

The trading profits of Consol 2 and Consol 3, and tax payable thereon, are as shown above. Consol 3 has a tax liability of €8,000, net of credit relief, in respect of the dividend from Third Co, its 25% subsidiary resident in a third country.

Consol 1, which has no income of its own, remits the aggregate tax of €908,000 on behalf of the four consolidated companies.

Third Co paid the dividend of €400,000 out of distributable profits of €2,400,000 which is the amount of its trading profits net of tax €960,000.

In accordance with TCA 1997 Sch 24 paragraph 9G, the four "Consol" companies are treated as a "single company". Accordingly, Relevant Co is treated as receiving the dividend of €32,000 from the single company which in turn is deemed to have received the dividend of €400,000 from Third Co.

The single company is treated as being related to Relevant Co while Third Co is treated as being related to the single company. The single company is also treated as being connected with Relevant Co. Accordingly, TCA 1997 Sch 24 paragraph 9B (relief for third country taxes – see **14.210.3**) will apply.

In accordance with TCA 1997 Sch 24 paragraph 9B, Consol 3 is deemed to have paid underlying tax of €160,000 (€960,000 x 400,000/2,400,000) in respect of its dividend of €400,000.

The single company is treated as having paid the taxes paid by Consol 1 on the aggregate profits of all four consolidated companies, as well as the underlying tax of €160,000. The distributable profits of the single company are €3,400,000 – €908,000 = €2,492,000. Total underlying tax is €908,000 + €160,000 = €1,068,000.

Consol HoldCo is deemed to have paid underlying tax of €137,143 (€1,068,000 x 320/2,492) in respect of its dividend of €320,000.

For credit relief purposes, Relevant Co is deemed to have paid underlying tax of €13,714 in respect of the dividend of €32,000.

14.217 Exchange rates

Since some foreign income will be received in a currency other than the euro, it is generally necessary to translate that income into euro for the purpose of computing the Irish tax liability on that income. In computing that liability, it will also be necessary to translate foreign currency denominated income and taxes into euro for the purpose of calculating any credit in respect of foreign taxes.

For companies subject to Irish corporation tax and whose functional currency is other than the euro, foreign income will often be in a currency other than that functional currency so that amounts representing foreign income and taxes will have to be translated into the functional currency concerned.

In the case of a foreign branch of an Irish company, where the currency of the foreign country in question is a currency other than the company's functional currency, the profits for any period are translated into the company's functional currency at the average rate of exchange for the two currencies for that period. This procedure is based on long-standing practice and is always applied.

For income items which arise on a particular date, such as dividends, royalties and interest payments, translation will be by reference to the relevant exchange rate on the date the income is received. An exception would be the case of an IFSC company in receipt of foreign interest which forms part of its trading profits. The taxation treatment in that case would follow the accounting treatment which would recognise the interest income on an accruals basis.

Foreign withholding taxes are normally translated at the exchange rate appropriate to the income item from which they have been deducted. In other words, they would be translated at the exchange rate applying at the time the net income is paid.

Direct foreign tax available for credit, such as tax paid by a foreign branch, is translated at the exchange rate ruling on the date the tax becomes due and payable (*Greig v Ashton* 36 TC 581) or, by convention, at the average exchange rate for the period in which the branch profits arise.

14.3 DEDUCTION FOR FOREIGN TAX

14.301   Foreign tax as a trading expense
14.302   'Deduction against investment income

14.301   Foreign tax as a trading expense

In cases where a double tax treaty is not in force, and unless covered by unilateral provisions, there can be no credit relief. It is sometimes thought that foreign tax suffered by an Irish company in a country in which the company is carrying on business may be claimed as an expense incurred wholly and exclusively for the purposes of the company's trade. In *Harrods (Buenos Aires) Ltd v Taylor-Gooby* 41 TC 450, Argentinian tax (which, incidentally, was not a profits tax but an annual percentage tax on the capital tax of companies incorporated outside Argentina but carrying on business there) paid by a UK company was held to be deductible as a trading expense on the basis that it was an expense incurred wholly and exclusively for the purposes of the company's trade and not, as the Inland Revenue argued, incurred by the company merely in its capacity as taxpayer. In fact, however, it was precisely because the tax which arose in the Harrods case was not a profits tax but rather a tax incurred to enable the company to carry on business in Argentina that it was held to be deductible on Case I principles. A profits tax on the other hand is not incurred for that purpose but is an expense that arises consequent on doing business, and is more in the nature of an appropriation of profits.

In this connection, the fundamental question that arises is whether the foreign tax is charged on the profits of the trade or whether it is incurred in the carrying on of the trade. If incurred in carrying on the trade it will be deductible provided it satisfies the other criteria for deductibility, ie that it is wholly and exclusively incurred for trading purposes and is not capital expenditure. If the tax is a tax on profits, on the other hand, it is essentially a portion of the profit and cannot be something that is deducted in calculating the quantum of the profit (*Ashton Gas Co v A-G* [1906] AC 10, HL).

Foreign tax may be suffered by a foreign branch of an Irish trading company. This tax may be tax imposed by the jurisdiction in which the branch is based or may be tax levied by a third country, eg withholding taxes imposed on third country source royalty income received by the branch. Credit relief will be available in the normal way (even, by virtue of unilateral provisions (see **14.901.2**), where a tax treaty is not in place). To the extent that credit cannot be claimed in respect of the full amount of the foreign tax, the excess tax may, in accordance with TCA 1997 Sch 24 paragraph 7(3)(c), be deducted from the foreign income in question.

If there is no treaty in place, and where unilateral provisions do not apply, foreign tax levied by the country in which the foreign income arises, if it is a tax on income or otherwise not a cost incurred to enable the company to carry on its trade, will not be deductible as a trading expense. A foreign withholding tax deducted from a trading receipt, such as interest or royalties, is not a tax on profits in the same sense as a foreign branch profits tax. Neither, however, is it clearly an expense incurred wholly and exclusively for the purposes of a trade, being a tax necessarily suffered to enable the foreign income item to be repatriated. As against that, it could be argued that it is a tax necessarily incurred to enable the foreign income to be *received* and that income that cannot be received is not truly income that has arisen in the first place. Revenue practice is to permit, concessionally, a deduction for such tax on the same basis as applies in treaty cases, accordingly only up to the amount of the Irish measure of the foreign income (the "net basis" approach - see **14.202**).

14.302 'Deduction against investment income

In the case of a company chargeable to tax under Case III of Schedule D, a deduction for foreign taxes is also available under TCA 1997, s 77(6). The deduction applies in respect of "income arising from securities and possessions in any place outside the State" which would normally refer to foreign source investment or rental income which is charged to tax in Ireland under Case III.

TCA 1997, s 77(6) provides that such income is to be treated as reduced by any sum which has been paid in respect of income tax in the place where the income has arisen. This treatment applies where a deduction cannot be made under, and is not forbidden by, any provision of Irish tax law.

Case III income would also include the profits of a foreign trade (see **4.105**). In this connection, TCA 1997, s 77(5) provides that the income from a trade the profits of which are chargeable under Case III is to be computed in accordance with the provisions applicable to Case I.

14.4 Credit for Foreign Tax not Otherwise Credited

14.401   Introduction
14.402   Taxes qualifying for relief
14.403   Mechanism of relief

14.401   Introduction

Although the effect of the non-availability, up to 1994, of any form of unilateral credit relief in respect of foreign tax not creditable under the terms of a double tax treaty was greatest in the cases of companies subject to corporation tax at the standard rate, the call for such relief came principally from companies operating in the International Financial Services Centre (IFSC) and to some extent from software companies subject to foreign withholding taxes on royalty income.

The form of unilateral credit relief (not to be confused with the main unilateral relief introduced by FA 1998 and provided for in TCA 1997 Sch 24 paragraph 9A – see **14.209**) introduced by FA 1994 (and now provided for in TCA 1997, s 449) is limited to cases involving "relevant foreign tax" which means tax which has not been repaid, which cannot be credited by virtue of a double tax treaty, and which has been withheld, under the laws of any foreign territory, from an amount receivable from the sale of goods. For this purpose, *an amount receivable from the sale of goods* means an amount which, being—

(a)   receivable from the sale of computer software; or
(b)   treated as receivable from the sale of goods, being in respect of:

  (i)   the rendering of computer services,

  (ii)   Shannon operations, or

  (iii)   international financial services,

is regarded as receivable from the sale of goods for the purposes of manufacturing relief (see **7.2**).

"Computer services" means data processing services, software development services and technical and consultancy services related to data processing and/ or software development services, which are undertaken in Ireland in the course of a service undertaking for which an employment grant was made by the Industrial Development Authority, the Industrial Development Agency (Ireland) or Forbairt, a grant or financial assistance was made available by Shannon Free Airport Development Co Ltd (SFADCO), or financial assistance was made available by Údarás na Gaeltachta (TCA 1997, s 443(10) (see also **7.205.5**).

14.402   Taxes qualifying for relief

The foreign tax qualifying for unilateral credit relief ("relevant foreign tax") is specified in TCA 1997, s 449. *Relevant foreign tax* means—

(a)   withholding tax deducted from receipts, such as interest, software royalties or other gross receipts;
(b)   which corresponds to income tax or corporation tax;
(c)   which has not been repaid to the company in question;
(d)   for which credit is not available under a double tax treaty; and

(e)   which is not treated under TCA 1997 Sch 24 as reducing the amount of any income.

The requirement that the tax must correspond with income tax or corporation tax in Ireland followed questions as to whether any kind of tax suffered on payment, such as premium taxes in the case of insurance business, might be included. Only withholding type taxes qualify and not taxes levied by direct assessment or underlying taxes.

The purpose of (e) above, introduced by FA 1998 s 59, is to confirm that credit relief will not be available in respect of any amount of foreign tax which, in accordance with TCA 1997 Sch 24 ("Relief from income tax and corporation tax by means of credit in respect of foreign tax"), is allowed as a deduction in computing income (see **14.202**).

14.403   Mechanism of relief

The relief is nine-tenths of the foreign tax or, if smaller, the corporation tax attributable to the amount from which the foreign tax has been withheld. The attributable corporation tax is calculated on the income referable to the amount which has suffered the foreign tax, and that income is the proportion of the income from the sale of goods as is represented by the amount which has suffered the foreign tax over the total amount receivable from the sale of goods. The attributable corporation tax is the corporation tax on that income after manufacturing relief, ie at the 10% rate.

The relief is therefore confined to trading companies eligible for the 10% corporation tax rate and then only to certain such activities. Because the foreign tax will already have been deducted in computing trading income (see **14.301**), the unilateral credit relief is confined to nine-tenths of that foreign tax. In the context of an effective 10% rate of tax, the value of the deduction in computing trading income under Case I will equate to 10% of the foreign tax. Accordingly, the unilateral credit is given for nine-tenths only of the foreign tax subject, however, to the credit being limited to the Irish tax attributable to the foreign income. In nearly all cases, due to the low 10% rate, credit will be limited to the Irish tax so attributable.

Income attributable to the receipts that have borne foreign tax is arrived at on a "sales ratio" basis (sales or receipts from which the foreign tax was deducted over total amount receivable from the "sale of goods"). (The sales ratio basis may result in unintended distortions in arriving at the amount of the income – see **14.212**.) This sales ratio basis is applied to the income from the sale of goods that is itself to be taken as increased by the amount of the relevant foreign tax (TCA 1997, s 449(2)(b)).

In fact, two apportionments are necessary. Firstly, as indicated above, TCA 1997, s 449(2)(b) provides that the income referable to the amount which has suffered foreign tax is the proportion of the income from the sale of goods (as increased by the relevant foreign tax) as is represented by the amount which has suffered the foreign tax over the total amount receivable from the sale of goods. (This income amount is also the amount by reference to which the limit on total credit is determined (TCA 1997 Sch 24 paragraph 4(3) – see **14.202**).) Secondly, the income from the sale of goods is itself also arrived at on a "sales ratio" basis (where the company has sales or receipts giving rise to income not eligible for the 10% tax rate); TCA 1997, s 449(2)(c) provides that the apportionment in this case is that provided for in TCA 1997, s 448(3), the basis which applies generally (see **7.202**) to determine the amount of income from the sale of goods for manufacturing relief purposes. The product of this sales ratio apportionment is, as already mentioned above, increased by the amount of the relevant foreign tax before applying the sales ratio apportionment provided for in TCA 1997, s 449(2)(b).

The sales apportionment basis in TCA 1997, s 448(3) is, however, technically inappropriate in cases involving services income, such as financial services or computer services income. While receipts from the qualifying part of such service activities are regarded as amounts received from the sale of manufactured goods, there is no provision which regards non-qualifying receipts as being from the sale of "merchandise" (meaning goods other than goods manufactured in the State). In practice, revenues are apportioned as if they comprised receipts from goods and merchandise.

Irish tax attributable to the income computed as above, but as reduced by the amount of the relevant foreign tax, is fixed by TCA 1997, s 449(2)(a) at 10% of that net amount.

The foreign taxes in respect of which the unilateral credit is allowed for any period comprise any relevant foreign tax suffered in that period. These taxes may have been suffered in more than one country. Relief at nine-tenths of the relevant foreign taxes, or the Irish corporation tax attributable to the foreign income in question, whichever is less, is then allowed against the company's corporation tax liability. There is no question of relating any amount creditable to a particular income item or to income from a particular country. In this respect, the unilateral credit differs from the treaty based credit relief which allows for credit on an item by item basis. In practice, this difference is unlikely to have any impact since, as already noted, unilateral credit will nearly always be given at the Irish 10% rate which will tend to be much lower than any foreign withholding tax on gross income.

Unilateral credit relief is available to Irish branches (or permanent establishments) of foreign companies. In this respect also, the unilateral relief is different to the treaty-based relief which is only available to Irish resident companies. Since an Irish branch of a non-resident company is not entitled to treaty relief for foreign taxes, such taxes can qualify for the unilateral relief. It is irrelevant whether or not the foreign taxes in these cases arise in a treaty country.

Example 14.403.1

The following information is relevant to Xanadu Ltd for its latest accounting period:

	€
Sales of computer software	3,200,000
Sales of other manufactured goods	800,000
Receipts in respect of computer services	6,000,000
Sales of non-manufactured goods	2,000,000
	12,000,000
Expenses	7,000,000
Profit	5,000,000

Computer services receipts include an amount of €1,200,000 from which Brazilian withholding tax of €210,000 was deducted.

Corporation tax computation:	€
Profit	5,000,000
Deduct: foreign tax	210,000
	4,790,000

	€
Irish tax @ 12.5%	598,750
Manufacturing relief (1)	99,792
	498,958
Unilateral credit (2)	29,420
Net corporation tax	469,538

(1)

$$€598,750 \times 1/5 \times \cfrac{4,790,000 \times \cfrac{10,000,000}{12,000,000}}{4,790,000} = €99,792$$

	€	€
(2)		
A: Foreign tax €210,000 x 9/10		189,200
B: Amount from which foreign tax was withheld	1,200,000	
Income referable thereto[1]:		
$(€4,790,000 \times \cfrac{10,000,000}{12,000,000} + 210,000) \times \cfrac{1,200,000}{10,000,000} =$	504,200	
Less: relevant foreign tax[2]	210,000	
	294,200	
€294,200 @ 10% =		29,420
Smaller of A and B		29,420

Note:

1. The income from the sale of goods (€4,790,000 x 10/12) is increased by the amount of the relevant foreign tax €210,000 (TCA 1997, s 449(2)(b)).
2. The corporation tax is calculated on an amount as reduced by the relevant foreign tax (TCA 1997, s 449(2)(a)).

In the above example, income from the sale of goods is €4,790,000, ie the amount net of the foreign tax of €210,000. If the company had excess foreign tax credits as a result of having other taxed foreign income subject to treaty-based credit relief, these excess credits should not be deducted in arriving at the amount for income from the sale of goods for the purposes of the unilateral credit calculation so that the amount of €4,790,000 is unaffected.

14.5 ENHANCED CREDIT RELIEF FOR CERTAIN COMPANIES

14.501 Introduction

The impact of the "net" basis (see **14.212**) of computing the Irish measure of foreign income for credit relief purposes was seen as leading to a significant increase in the tax liabilities of some companies. The impact of this is mitigated for certain companies operating in the International Financial Services Centre (IFSC) and is therefore mainly of relevance to companies taxable at the 10% corporation tax rate. The relief, provided for in TCA 1997, s 450, is in the form of a treaty based enhanced credit relief for "stand-alone" (as opposed to "managed") treasury operations carried on in the IFSC. The enhanced credit is available by way of election which must be made for any accounting period within nine months of the end of that period.

In the light of the expiry of the IFSC regime on 31 December 2005, a replacement form of enhanced credit was introduced with effect from 1 January 2006. The relevant legislation is contained in TCA 1997 Schedule 24 paragraph 9F. This relief is not confined to companies previously eligible for the TCA 1997, s 450 relief and is available to a broad range of companies in the financial sector (see **14.215**).

14.502 Qualifying companies

The enhanced credit relief is available to a "relevant company" which broadly refers to a limited category of companies operating in the IFSC and to certain companies carrying on financial activities in Shannon. As mentioned above, the relief is intended to apply to stand-alone treasury operations which essentially refers to companies carrying on treasury operations other than under the terms of a management agreement with one of the specialised IFSC companies which provide fee based management services to agency treasury centres and captive finance companies.

A *relevant company* is defined as a qualified company (an IFSC licensed company) other than a credit institution, or a 25% subsidiary of a credit institution, the relevant trading operations of which:

(a) are wholly carried on by persons:

  (i)   who are employees of the qualified company or a company related to it and who are not employees of any other person, and

  (ii) concerning whom there is no understanding or arrangement the purpose of which, or one of the purposes of which, is to provide for the engagement of the services of those persons, whether as employees or otherwise, should they cease to be employed by the qualified company or a related company, as the case may be, and

(b) are not managed or directed, directly or indirectly, by another qualified company other than a company related to the first-mentioned company (TCA 1997, s 450(1)).

Relevant trading operations are trading operations specified in a certificate given to an IFSC licensed company, ie in respect of which the 10% corporation tax rate applies. Also included are financial services operations carried on by Shannon licensed companies, ie trading operations which could be licensed for IFSC purposes if they were being carried on in the IFSC.

A company is treated as *related to* another company if one of the companies is a 25% subsidiary of the other or both are 25% subsidiaries of the same company. A company is a 25% subsidiary of another company if not less than 25% of its ordinary share capital is beneficially owned, whether directly or indirectly, by that other company. Being "owned directly or indirectly" is to be construed in accordance with TCA 1997, s 9(2) (see **2.505**). In determining whether a company is a 25% subsidiary of another company, the profit distribution and notional winding up tests applicable to the definition of a 75% subsidiary for group relief purposes (see **8.304**) are applied with necessary modifications but without regard to TCA 1997, s 411(1) which limits the reference to a company to a company resident in Ireland.

A *credit institution* is an undertaking whose business it is to receive deposits or other repayable funds from the public and to grant credit on its own account. This prevents banks and their 25% subsidiaries from availing of the relief. If a credit institution is not a company, another company will not be prevented from being its 25% subsidiary by reason only that the credit institution is itself not a company.

In summary, the enhanced credit relief is available to IFSC licensed companies which are not credit institutions and whose business is wholly carried on by direct employees, where the employment of those employees is not guaranteed by a third party, and which are not managed by another IFSC company.

14.503   The relief

As explained in **14.212**, foreign withholding taxes deducted from (gross) interest received by Irish treasury companies are creditable only against the Irish corporation tax attributable to the net interest income, ie after funding costs of loans made to the foreign customers, and other overheads. Furthermore, treaty based credit relief allows for credit on an item by item basis only. TCA 1997, s 450 relaxes this condition by increasing (subject to an overall limit) the Irish corporation tax attributable to interest income receivable from 25% related companies resident in treaty countries. This increases the limit on foreign creditable tax prescribed by TCA 1997 Sch 24 paragraph 4 (see **14.202**). All foreign tax, subject to a maximum rate of 10%, deducted from interest receivable from 25% affiliates is creditable up to the overall limit.

The tax which is increased is the Irish corporation tax attributable to "group relevant payments" from which foreign tax has been deducted. A *group relevant payment* is a relevant payment made to a relevant company by a related company. A *relevant payment* is a payment of interest:

(a)   received from a source within a country which has a tax treaty with Ireland; and

(b)   which is subject to Irish corporation tax under the 10% tax regime in the IFSC or the equivalent Shannon regime.

The increase is limited to 35% of the corporation tax which would be payable without the enhanced credit relief and which is attributable to all relevant payments received by the company in question (TCA 1997, s 450(2)(b)). The increased amount may be allocated by the company to such parts of the income attributable to the group relevant payments as it thinks fit (TCA 1997, s 450(2)(a)).

The corporation tax which would be payable in the absence of the enhanced credit relief is determined by the formula:

$$A - B$$

where—

A   is 10% of the income attributable to relevant payments, and
B   is the credit which would be allowed in respect of the foreign tax in the absence of the enhanced credit relief.

The income attributable to relevant payments is arrived at by apportioning the total income qualifying for the 10% rate in the proportion which the amount of relevant payments bears to total receipts from activities qualifying for the 10% tax rate.

The foreign tax which qualifies for enhanced credit relief ("relevant foreign tax") is tax creditable under the terms of a tax treaty, subject to an upper limit of 10%, and which has been deducted from relevant payments. The enhanced credit is ignored in calculating the deduction available under TCA 1997 Sch 24 paragraph 7(3)(c) for non- creditable foreign tax (TCA 1997, s 450(3)). In other words, the excess of the foreign tax available over the amount creditable, which is allowed as a deduction in computing taxable income, is not reduced as a result of the increase in the amount of the creditable tax. This factor increases the value of the enhanced credit since that credit is effectively deductible at 10% and is also creditable in full.

Example 14.503.1

Coolgordie Ltd, a stand-alone IFSC treasury company and whose functional currency is the Australian dollar, has the following income and expenses:

	A$
Interest from Australian 25% related companies (net of 10% tax)	180,000
Interest from German loans	100,000
	280,000
Interest payable	100,000
Profit	180,000

Credit relief calculation:

	A$
Foreign tax (A$200,000 @ 10%)	20,000
Income	180,000
Total income	200,000
Irish measure of foreign income (sales ratio):	
A$200,000 x 200,000/300,000	133,333
Foreign tax rate:	
20,000/133,333	15%
Irish rate of tax on foreign income	10%
"Net foreign income" (Irish measure less foreign tax)	113,333
Gross up at lower rate of tax (10%):	
A$113,333 x 100/(100 – 10)	125,926
Creditable tax (A$125,926 – A$113,333)	12,593
Non-creditable tax (A$20,000 – A$12,593)	7,407
Income less non-creditable tax (A$200,000 – A$7,407)	192,593

Corporation tax computation:

	A$	A$
A$192,593 @ 10%		19,259
Less: credit for foreign tax	12,593	
enhanced credit:[1]	2,333	14,926
Payable		4,333

Note:

[1] Enhanced foreign tax credit:

	A$	A$
Foreign tax deducted from group relevant payments		20,000
Limit 35% x (A – B)		
A = 10% x A$192,593 x 300,000/300,000	19,259	
B = treaty based credit	12,593	
	6,666	
Enhanced credit 35% x A$6,666		2,333

14.6 RELIEF FOR CERTAIN DIVIDENDS FROM FOREIGN SUBSIDIARIES

14.601 Introduction
14.602 The relief

14.601 Introduction

Repatriation by companies of profits earned abroad can result in significant incremental taxation particularly where the profits have not been taxed in the foreign jurisdiction in which they arise. Where such profits are repatriated for the purpose of reinvesting them in Ireland, a limited relief from taxation is provided for by TCA 1997, s 222 but only where an appropriate certificate was received from the Minister for Finance before 15 February 2001.

14.602 The relief

TCA 1997, s 222(3) provides that relevant dividends received by a company in an accounting period are not to be taken into account in computing income for corporation tax purposes for that period.

Relevant dividends are dividends, received by an Irish resident company from a foreign subsidiary, which are specified in a certificate given before 15 February 2001 by the Minister for Finance in accordance with TCA 1997, s 222(2), and which are applied for the purposes of an approved investment plan. An *"approved investment plan"* is a plan in respect of which the Minister has given a certificate, being a plan of an Irish resident company which is directed towards the creation or maintenance of employment in Ireland in trading operations carried on, or to be carried on, in Ireland, and which has been submitted to the Minister either before its implementation or, where the Minister is satisfied that it was reasonable that the plan was submitted later, within one year from the commencement of its implementation.

The procedure outlined above would envisage the submission to the Minister of a schedule of dividends, identifying the dividend paying company, and the amounts and due dates of payment. In the certificate given by the Minister, dividends will be identified as relevant dividends. Inclusion of these dividends in the certificate means that the a claim for exemption from tax may be made when the related funds are applied for the purposes of the investment plan.

The Minister may give the required certificate, certifying that the dividends referred to in the certificate are relevant dividends, where he has received the claimant company's investment plan and is satisfied that the plan is directed towards the creation or maintenance of employment in Ireland in trading operations carried on, or to be carried on, in Ireland.

Foreign subsidiary means a 51% subsidiary of the claimant company and which is resident in a country with which Ireland has a tax treaty (residence being determined for this purpose in accordance with the particular treaty provision). A company is a 51% subsidiary of another company where more than 50% of its ordinary share capital is owned directly or indirectly by that other company. The meaning of "owned directly or indirectly" is explained in TCA 1997, s 9(2) (see **2.505**).

Relevant dividends must be applied for the purposes of the approved investment plan within the period beginning one year before the first day on which the dividends specified in the certificate are received in Ireland, or at such earlier time as the Revenue may allow, and ending two years after the first day referred to, or at such later time as the Revenue may allow. It is not necessary that the investment plan be implemented by the company receiving the dividends. It will often be the case that these dividends are received by an Irish holding company and it is only necessary that they be applied for purposes of an approved investment plan, which would include the use of the dividend proceeds for the purposes of the acquisition by any group member of an Irish business resulting in the creation or maintenance of employment. The employment must be created or maintained in trading operations and not, for example, in an investment activity.

If the Minister considers that all or part of the relevant dividends have not been applied for the purposes of the approved investment plan within the time permitted, he may by notice reduce the amount of relevant dividends specified in the certificate by the amount not so applied. Any relief already granted in respect of the amount of dividends so reduced is to be clawed back by way of assessment or additional assessment.

A claim for relief under TCA 1997, s 222 is to be made in writing to the inspector of taxes and should be submitted with the company's return of income for the period in question.

The exemption provided by TCA 1997, s 222 will be of particular benefit to companies whose foreign subsidiaries have paid no tax or relatively little tax, for whatever reason. Repatriation of dividends from such subsidiaries would normally result in immediate taxation in Ireland in the absence of any, or worthwhile, credit relief. Circumstances accounting for the payment of little or no tax in the foreign jurisdiction would include losses incurred by the subsidiary, an exemption from tax on the lines of the "participation exemption" in the Netherlands, or the reduction or elimination of tax due to foreign taxes incurred in a third country.

14.7 THE PARENT-SUBSIDIARY DIRECTIVE

14.701   Introduction
14.702   The relief

14.701   Introduction

TCA 1997, s 831 gives legal effect in Ireland to Council Directive No 90/435/EEC of 23 July 1990 (OJ No L 225 of 20.8.1990, p 6), as amended. The purpose of this measure is to reduce taxation on distributions of profits between companies in different Member States of the European Union. The Directive requires relief to be given in the paying company's Member State by way of exemption from withholding tax (article 5). This relief is relevant in the case of Ireland as respects dividend withholding tax on distributions paid on or after 6 April 1999 (see **11.116**).

TCA 1997, s 831 provides for credit in respect of underlying tax of the dividend paying company to the extent that that tax exceeds the amount of any tax credit in respect of the distributions as is payable to the Irish parent company by the Member State in which the dividend paying company is resident.

As well as dealing with distributions from subsidiaries to their parents, TCA 1997, s 831 deals with distributions paid by a company in a Member State to the permanent establishment, situated in another Member State, of the paying company's parent company where the parent and the subsidiary are in the same or are in different Member States.

14.702   The relief

The form of relief required in the Member State of the recipient company is provided for, in the case of Ireland, in TCA 1997, s 831(2)(a) and (2A). The subsection provides that where a parent company receives a distribution (other than on a winding up) from its subsidiary, being a company that is not resident in the State, credit is to be allowed for—

(i)   any withholding tax charged on the distribution by a Member State pursuant to a derogation given from Article 5.1 (which generally prohibits such withholding tax) of the Directive,

(ii)   foreign tax (see further below under *Credit for underlying tax*), not chargeable directly or by deduction in respect of the distribution, and

(iii)   any foreign tax borne by a company that *would* be allowed under TCA 1997 Sch 24 paragraph 9B (see **14.210.3**) *if* the dividend paying company (at whatever tier) were connected with the relevant company,

against the Irish corporation tax payable in respect of the distribution to the extent that that credit would not otherwise be allowed, ie by virtue of the provisions of a double tax treaty or, for accounting periods ending on or after 1 April 1998, for third country taxes by virtue of TCA 1997 Sch 24 paragraph 9B – see below under *Credit for underlying tax*.

Distribution is defined as income from shares or from other rights, not being debt claims, to participate in a company's profits, and includes any amount assimilated to income from shares under the taxation laws of the State of which the company making the distribution is resident. This definition echoes the typical definition of "dividend" in current tax treaties. The reference to any amount "assimilated to income from shares" under the taxation laws of a state means that any amount treated as a distribution under TCA 1997, s 130 (see **11.101**) would rank as a distribution for the purposes of TCA 1997, s 831.

TCA 1997, s 831(2)(b) provides, following the Directive, that withholding tax must not be deducted in accordance with TCA 1997 Part 4 Ch 2 (ss 60-64) ("encashment tax") in the case of dividends being paid into Ireland from a subsidiary to a parent company through paying agents.

Parent company means a company (the "first-mentioned company") being—

(i)   a company which owns (directly) at least 5% of the share capital of another company which is not resident in the State; or

(ii) a company not resident in the State which owns (directly) at least 5% of the share capital of another company which is resident in the State (TCA 1997, s 831(1)(a)).

However, this definition is to have effect subject to, and is to be construed according to, any provision in a bilateral agreement (a tax treaty to which Ireland is a party) to the effect—

(I)   that the first-mentioned company may only be a parent company during any continuous period of at least two years throughout which it owns at least 5% of the share capital of the other company, or

(II) that a requirement (being a requirement for the purposes of the definition of "parent company") that—

    (A)   the first-mentioned company own at least 5% of the share capital of another company is to be treated as a requirement that it holds at least 5% of the voting rights in the other company, or

    (B)   the first-mentioned company own at least 5% of the share capital of another company is to be treated as a requirement that it holds at least 5% of the voting rights in the other company and that it may only be treated as a parent company during any continuous period of at least two years throughout which it holds at least 5% of the voting rights in the other company.

A company is a subsidiary of another company which owns shares or holds voting rights in it where the other company's ownership of those shares or holding of those rights is sufficient for that other company to be the parent company (TCA 1997, s 831(1)(b)).

The qualification in (I) and (II) above means that the requirement on the parent company to own at least 5% of the share capital of the Irish resident company may be replaced by an alternative requirement: where a tax treaty provides that (a) a parent company must hold the necessary 5% shareholding for an uninterrupted period of two years, or (b) the 5% shareholding requirement must be treated as a 5% voting power requirement, or (c) the 5% shareholding requirement must be treated as a 5% voting power requirement and the parent company must also hold at least 5% of the voting power for an uninterrupted period of at least two years, then the relevant alternative requirement is to apply.

To date, except in the case of the Ireland-Spain tax treaty (see article 23 paragraphs 1(b) and 2(b)), none of the tax treaties to which Ireland is a party contains any such requirement, apart from the voting power requirement in (b) above, which appears in certain treaties. Where a treaty prescribes a voting power requirement in excess of 5%, only a 5% requirement, as provided for in TCA 1997, s 831, will apply.

Company

For the purposes of TCA 1997, s 831, *company* means a company of a Member State, while *company of a Member State* takes its meaning from article 2 of the Directive (Council Directive No 90/435/EEC of 23 July 1990 as amended by Council Directive No 2003/123/EC of 22 December 2003). Thus, it means any company which:

(a)   takes one of the forms listed in the Annex to the Directive (see below);

(b)   according to the tax laws of a Member State is considered to be resident in that State for tax purposes and, under the terms of a double tax agreement concluded with a third State, is not considered to be resident for tax purposes outside the Community; and

(c)   is subject to one of the taxes listed below, without the possibility of an option or of being exempt, or to any other tax which may be substituted for any of the above taxes.

In the case of Ireland, both limited and unlimited liability companies are included. The forms of company listed in the Annex are:

Austria	Aktiengesellschaft, Gesellschaft mit beschränkter Haftung (GmbH), Versicherungsvereine auf Gegenseitigkeit, Erwerbs- und Wirtschaftsgenossenschaften, Betriebe gewerblicher Art von Körperschaften des öffentlichen Rechts, Sparkassen, and other companies constituted under Austrian law subject to Austrian corporate tax
Belgium	société anonyme/naamloze vennootschap, société en commandite par actions/commanditaire vennootschap op aandelen, société privé à responsabilité limitée/besloten vennootschap met beperkte aansprakelijkheid, société coopérative à responsabilité limitée/coöperatieve vennootschap met beperkte aansprakelijkheid, société coopérative à responsabilité illimitée/coöperatieve vennootschap met onbeperkte aansprakelijkheid, société en nom collectif/vennootschap onder firma, société en commandite simple/gewone commanditaire vennootschap, public undertakings which have adopted one of the above-mentioned legal forms, and other companies constituted under Belgian law subject to Belgian corporate tax
Cyprus	Etairias
Czech Republic	Akciová společnost, společnost s ručením omezeným
Denmark	aktieselskab, anpartsselskab and other companies subject to tax under the Corporation Tax Act, insofar as their taxable income is calculated and taxed in accordance with the general tax legislation rules applicable to aktieselskaber
Estonia	täisühing, usaldusühing, osaühing, aktsiaselts, tulundusühistu
Finland	osakeyhtiö/aktiebolag, osuuskunta/andelslag, säästöpankki/sparbank, vakuutusyhtiö/försäkringsbolag

France	société anonyme, société en commandite par actions, société à responsabilité limitée, sociétés par actions simplifiées, sociétés d'assurances mutuelles, caisses d'épargne et de prévoyance, sociétés civiles which are automatically subject to corporation tax, coopératives, unions de coopératives, industrial and commercial public establishments and undertakings, and other companies constituted under French law subject to French corporate tax
Germany	Aktiengesellschaft, Kommanditgesellschaft auf Aktien, Gesellschaft mit beschränkter Haftung (GmbH), Versicherungsverein auf Gegenseitigkeit, Erwerbs- und Wirtschaftsgenossenschaft, Betriebe gewerblicher Art von juristischen Personen des öffentlichen Rechts, and other companies constituted under German law subject to German corporate tax
Greece	anonymi etairia, etairia periorismenis efthinis (EPE), and other companies constituted under Greek law subject to Greek corporate tax
Hungary	Közkereseti társaság, betéti társaság, közös vállalat, korlátolt felelősségű társaság, részvénytársaság, egyesülés, szövetkezet
Ireland	Companies incorporated or existing under Irish law, bodies registered under the Industrial and Provident Societies Acts, building societies incorporated under the Building Societies Acts, and trustee savings banks within the meaning of the Trustee Savings Banks Act, 1989
Italy	società per azioni, società in accomandita per azioni, società a responsabilità limitata, società cooperative, società di mutua assicurazione, and private and public entities whose activity is wholly or principally commercial
Latvia	Akciju sabiedrība, sabiedr ba ar ierobežotu atbildību
Lithuania	companies incorporated under Lithuanian law
Luxembourg	société anonyme, société en commandite par actions, société à responsabilité limitée, société coopérative, société coopérative organisée comme une société anonyme, association d'assurances mutuelles, association d'épargne-pension, entreprise de nature commerciale, industrielle ou minière de l'Etat, des communes, des syndicats de communes, des établissements publics et des autres personnes morales de droit public, and other companies constituted under Luxembourg law subject to Luxembourg corporate tax
Malta	Kumpaniji ta' Responsabilita' Limitata, Sojetajiet en commandite li l-kapital taghom maqsum f'azzjonijiet
Netherlands	naamloze vennootschap, besloten vennootschap met beperkte aansprakelijkheid, Open commanditaire vennootschap, Coöperatie, onderlinge waarborgmaatschappij, Fonds voor gemene rekening, vereniging op coöperatieve grondslag, vereniging welke op onderlinge grondslag als verzekeraar of kredietinstelling optreedt, and other companies constituted under Dutch law subject to Dutch corporate tax
Poland	Spółka akcyjna, spółka z ograniczoną odpowiedzialnością
Portugal	commercial companies or civil law companies having a commercial form and cooperatives and public undertakings incorporated in accordance with Portuguese law
Slovakia	Akciová spoločnost, spoločnost s ručením obmedzeným, komanditná spoločnost

Slovenia	delniška družba, komanditna družba, družba z omejeno odgovornostjo
Spain	sociedad anónima, sociedad comanditaria por acciones, sociedad de responsabilidad limitada, public law bodies which operate under private law, and other entities constituted under Spanish law subject to Spanish corporate tax ("Impuesto sobre Sociedades")
Sweden	aktiebolag, försäkringsaktiebolag, ekonomiska föreningar, sparbanker, ömsesidiga försäkringsbolag
UK	companies incorporated under the law of the United Kingdom

companies incorporated under Council Regulation (EC) No 2157/2001 of 8 October 2001 on the Statute for a European company (SE) and Council Directive 2001/86/EC of 8 October 2001 supplementing the Statute for a European company with regard to the involvement of employees and cooperative societies incorporated under Council Regulation (EC) No 1435/2003 of 22 July 2003 on the Statute for a European Cooperative Society (SCE) and Council Directive 2003/72/EC of 22 July 2003 supplementing the Statute for a European Cooperative Society with regard to the involvement of employees

The list of taxes referred to in (c) above are set out under *Credit for underlying tax* below).

Accordingly, any reference to a company in TCA 1997, s 831 is to both Irish incorporated and EU incorporated companies (provided that any such company is tax resident in a Member State and, under the terms of a double tax agreement concluded between that State and a third State, is not considered to be resident for tax purposes outside the Community). A company incorporated in, say, Norway and managed and controlled, and therefore tax resident, in Ireland is not a "company" for the purposes of TCA 1997, s 831 (because it is not listed in the Annex). A company in that position might, however, be entitled to succeed in a case arising from the anti-discrimination article of the relevant tax treaty which extends to nationals of one of the Contracting States (including companies incorporated in that state) benefits equivalent to those available to nationals of the other Contracting State.

Credit for underlying tax

The *foreign tax* in respect of which credit is to be allowed means any tax which is payable by the distributing company under the laws of a Member State other than Ireland, and which is specified in paragraph (c) of Article 2 of the Directive or is substituted for, or is substantially similar to, a tax so specified. The tax creditable is the tax attributable to the proportion of the company's profits represented by the distribution, and it will be allowed to the extent that it exceeds the amount of any tax credit attaching to the distribution as is payable to the parent company by the Member State in which the paying company is resident.

Tax specified in Article 2 paragraph (c) of the Directive for each Member State is as follows:

Austria	Körperschaftsteuer
Belgium	Impôt des sociétés/ vennootschapsbelasting
Denmark	Selskabsskat
Finland	yhteisöjen tulovero/inkomstskatten för samfund
France	Impôt sur les sociétés
Germany	Körperschaftsteuer

Greece	phoros eisodematos nomikon prosopon kerdoskopikou charaktera
Ireland	corporation tax
Italy	imposta sul reddito delle persone giuridiche
Luxembourg	Impôt sur le revenu des collectivités
Netherlands	Vennootschapsbelasting
Portugal	imposto sobre o rendimento das pessoas colectivas
Spain	impuesto sobre sociedados
Sweden	statlig inkomstskatt
UK	corporation tax

Where a company is to be allowed a credit in accordance with the Directive (as implemented by TCA 1997, s 831(2)(a)) or (2A) (see below), the provisions of TCA 1997 Sch 24 ("Relief from income tax and corporation tax by means of credit in respect of foreign tax") are to have effect as if the provisions of TCA 1997, s 831(2) were arrangements (ie, tax treaties) providing for that credit and as if references to dividends in TCA 1997 Sch 24 were references to distributions as defined above. The definition of "foreign tax" (see above) which is creditable in Ireland is such that it may be payable under the law of a Member State other than the Member State in which the distributing company is resident. Thus (for accounting periods ending before 1 April 1998 – see below), credit would be available in Ireland in respect of third country taxes not creditable by virtue of a tax treaty (provided the third country is a Member State). For example, an Irish parent company receiving a dividend from a Dutch subsidiary with a permanent establishment in Italy would be entitled to a credit against Irish tax on the dividend in respect of Italian tax payable by the subsidiary's permanent establishment as well as in respect of the Dutch tax paid by the subsidiary.

However, by virtue of TCA 1997 Sch 24 paragraph 9B (effective for accounting periods ending on or after 1 April 1998 – see **14.210**), a general relief for third country taxes is available, subject to conditions, so that such relief will be by reference to that paragraph rather than by reference to TCA 1997, s 831 – the latter form of relief is available only to the extent that credit "would not otherwise be so allowed".

As was seen above, credit is also available in respect of any foreign tax borne by a company that is not allowed under TCA 1997 Sch 24 paragraph 9B (see **14.210.3**) but would be so allowed if the dividend paying company in each case were connected with the relevant company. Accordingly, where a foreign company has received a dividend from a third company (and similarly where a third company has received a dividend from a fourth company, and so on) which is related to the foreign company but which is not connected with the relevant company, such credit may, subject to conditions, include tax paid by the third company (or fourth company, etc, as the case may be) in respect of its profits to the extent that it would be taken into account under TCA 1997 Sch 24 if the dividend had been paid by a foreign company to an Irish company (see **14.210.2**). Creditable tax for this purpose also includes any sub-national (city, state, provincial etc) taxes payable in respect of the profits of the third (or fourth etc) company (see **14.209.3**).

A general unilateral relief is available for foreign tax in respect of dividends, consisting of withholding taxes and taxes paid on the profits of the dividend paying company (see **14.209**). An Irish resident company which receives a dividend from a company resident in a country with which Ireland does not have a tax treaty, and in respect of which it owns, directly or indirectly, not less than 5% of the ordinary share capital, is entitled to a credit against the tax on the dividend for an appropriate part of the foreign tax on the underlying profits. In relation to this relief, however, it would seem that TCA 1997, s 831 would have priority since it is specifically provided that the unilateral relief is not available "for any tax in respect of which credit may be allowed under section 831" (TCA 1997 Sch 24 paragraph 9A(5)(c)).

As explained above, the "foreign tax" credit under TCA 1997, s 831 is available in cases where relief is not otherwise allowable and is restricted to tax payable under the laws of a Member State. The credit is in respect of underlying tax payable in the country of residence of the dividend paying company. Certain treaties allow credit for underlying taxes only where the Irish company receiving a dividend has a minimum percentage of voting power in the dividend paying company (see **14.207**). The credit for "foreign tax" provided for in TCA 1997, s 831 is available where the Irish parent holds at least 5% of the share capital in the distributing company (but this 5% requirement must be read as referring to voting rights where the relevant treaty so prescribes).

In a case where, due to the legal characteristics of a non-resident subsidiary of a parent company, the parent company is chargeable to tax in Ireland on its share of the subsidiary's profits as they arise, credit will be allowed for the amount of—

(a)   any foreign tax that is borne by the subsidiary; and

(b)   any foreign tax that would be treated as tax paid by the subsidiary under TCA 1997 Sch 24 paragraph 9B (see **14.210**) if—

    (i)   the subsidiary were the foreign company for those purposes, and

    (ii)   there were no requirement in paragraph 9B whereby the dividend paying company should be connected with the relevant company,

as is properly attributable to the proportion of the subsidiary's profits which are chargeable on the parent company in the State against corporation tax in respect of the profits chargeable on the parent company to the extent that credit for such foreign tax would not otherwise be so allowed (TCA 1997, s 831(2A)).

The purpose of this provision is to cater for the possibility whereby, from an Irish perspective, a foreign subsidiary is not regarded as a company but is rather a transparent entity such as a partnership. In those circumstances, credit relief for Irish tax purposes will take into account tax paid by that entity on its profits as well as tax treated as paid by it on the basis of TCA 1997 Sch 24 paragraph 9B, ie tax paid on the profits of any subsidiary of the entity (and, so far as applicable, on the profits of a subsidiary of that subsidiary, and so on). The subsidiary should be "related to" (within the meaning of TCA 1997 Sch 24 paragraph 9B – see **14.210.2**) the entity but there is no requirement that the subsidiary should be "connected with" the parent company.

In the above connection, Article 4 paragraph 1(a) of the Directive is as follows:

"Nothing in this Directive shall prevent the State of the parent company from considering a subsidiary to be fiscally transparent on the basis of that State's assessment of the legal characteristics of that subsidiary arising from the law under which it is constituted and therefore from taxing the parent company on its share of the profits of its subsidiary as and when those profits arise. In this case the State of the parent company shall refrain from taxing the distributed profits of the subsidiary.

When assessing the parent company's share of the profits of its subsidiary as they arise the State of the parent company shall either exempt those profits or authorise the parent company to deduct from the amount of tax due that fraction of the corporation tax related to the parent company's share of profits and paid by its subsidiary and any lower-tier subsidiary, subject to the condition that at each tier a company and its lower-tier subsidiary meet the requirements provided for in Articles 2 and 3, up to the limit of the amount of the corresponding tax due."

Where a company is entitled to credit by virtue of TCA 1997, s 831(2)(a) or ((2A), as described above, TCA 1997 Sch 24 is to apply for the purposes of that subsection as if its provisions were arrangements providing that tax so payable is to be allowed as a credit against Irish tax and as if references in that Schedule to a dividend were references to a distribution within the meaning of TCA 1997, s 831 (TCA 1997, s 831(3)).

The relief provided for in TCA 1997, s 831(2) and (2A) applies without prejudice to any provision of a bilateral agreement (TCA 1997, s 831(4)).

Exemption from withholding tax

The dividend withholding tax provisions of TCA 1997 Part 6 Chapter 8A (see **11.116**), other than TCA 1997, s 172K (returns, payment and collection of dividend withholding tax – see **11.116.11**), are not to apply to a distribution made to a parent company (note meaning of "parent company" above) which is not resident in Ireland by its subsidiary which is a company resident in Ireland (TCA 1997, s 831(5)).

This exclusion from the dividend withholding provisions will not, however, apply in the case of a distribution to a parent company if the majority of the voting rights in the parent are controlled directly or indirectly by persons, other than persons who by virtue of the law of any relevant territory (as defined in TCA 1997, s 172A – see **11.116.3**) are resident for the purposes of tax in such a territory, unless it is shown that the parent company exists for bona fide commercial reasons and does not form part of any arrangement or scheme of which the main purpose, or one of the main purposes, is the avoidance of liability to income tax (including dividend withholding tax), corporation tax or capital gains tax (TCA 1997, s 831(6)).

Where dividend withholding tax does not apply by virtue of TCA 1997, s 831(5), income tax is not chargeable in respect of the distribution, and the amount or value of the distribution is treated for the purposes of TCA 1997 ss 237 and 238 (see **4.302-3**) as not brought into charge to income tax (TCA 1997, s 153(5)). Thus, where for any reason dividend withholding tax has been deducted in a case coming within TCA 1997, s 831(5), the recipient of the distribution will be entitled to reclaim the amount of that tax. (See also **11.116.10** – credits or repayments in respect of dividend withholding tax).

Tax in relation to a relevant territory means any tax imposed in that territory which corresponds to income tax or corporation tax in the State. States.

Exemption from withholding tax: Switzerland

Provisions equivalent to those in the Parent-Subsidiary Directive ("the Directive") are extended to Swiss companies as part of an agreement between the EU and Switzerland providing for measures in Switzerland equivalent to the EU Savings Directive. TCA 1997, s 831A provides for exemption from dividend withholding tax in respect of distributions made by an Irish company to a Swiss resident company.

In respect of distributions made on or after 1 July 2005, TCA 1997, s 831A(2) provides that the dividend withholding tax provisions of TCA 1997 Part 6 Chapter 8A (see **11.116**), other than TCA 1997, s 172K (returns, payment and collection of dividend withholding tax – see **11.116.11**), are not to apply to a distribution made to a parent company which is, by virtue of the law of Switzerland, resident for tax purposes in Switzerland by its subsidiary which is a company resident in Ireland.

The following definitions are relevant for the above purposes.

In relation to a company that is resident for tax purposes in Switzerland, *company* means a company which—

   (i)   takes one of the forms specified in Article 15 of the Agreement attached to the Council Decision (2004/911/EC) of 2 June 2004 on the signing and conclusion of the Agreement between the EC and the Swiss Confederation providing for measures equivalent to those in Council Directive 2003/48/EC of 3 June 2003 on taxation of savings income in the form of interest payments and the accompanying Memorandum of Understanding – OJ No L381, 28.12.2004, p 32); and

   (ii)   is subject to tax in Switzerland without being exempt.

A *parent company* is a company that controls not less than 25% of the voting power in another company.

In relation to Switzerland, *tax* means any tax imposed in Switzerland that corresponds to income tax or corporation tax in Ireland.

A company is a *subsidiary* of another company which holds voting rights in it where the other company's holding of those rights is sufficient for it to be a parent company.

There is no anti-avoidance provision in TCA 1997, s 831A equivalent to TCA 1997, s 831(6) as described under *Exemption from withholding tax* above.

14.8 CREDIT RELIEF: MERGERS DIRECTIVE

14.801 Introduction
14.802 The relief

14.801 Introduction

TCA 1997 Part 21 (ss 630-638) implements Council Directive No. 90/434/EEC (the "Mergers Directive") which seeks to remove barriers, generally by deferring capital gains tax which would otherwise arise, to mergers, divisions, transfers of assets and exchanges of shares between companies from different Member States. The legislation extends the benefits of the Directive, which apply to transactions between companies from two Member States, to transactions between companies which are Irish resident.

TCA 1997, s 634 applies to cases in which an Irish resident company transfers the whole or part of a trade which, immediately before the transfer, was carried on in a Member State other than Ireland, to a company resident in another Member State where the consideration for the transfer consists wholly or partly of the issue to the transferring company of securities in the acquiring company. The section applies where the transfer includes all of the assets of the transferring company used for the purposes of the trade or the part of the trade, or all of the assets other than cash. The section also deals with the case in which a non-resident company transfers the whole or part of a trade to another company for an issue of securities and where income or gains of the transferring company are treated as income or chargeable gains of a person chargeable to Irish tax.

Company

For the purposes of TCA 1997 Part 21, *company* means a company from a Member State of the European Communities (TCA 1997, s 630). In this context, *company from a Member State* takes its meaning from article 3 of the Directive. Thus, it means any company which:

(a)   takes one of the forms listed in the Annex to the Directive (see below);

(b)   according to the tax laws of a Member State is considered to be resident in that State for tax purposes and, under the terms of a double tax agreement concluded with a third State, is not considered to be resident for tax purposes outside the Community; and

(c)   is subject to one of the taxes listed below, without the possibility of an option or of being exempt, or to any other tax which may be substituted for any of the above taxes.

The forms of company listed in the Annex are:

Austria	Aktiengesellschaft, Gesellschaft mit beschränkter Haftung (GmbH)
Belgium	société anonyme/naamloze vennootschap, société en commandite par actions/commanditaire vennootschap op aandelen, société privé à responsabilité limitée/besloten vennootschap met beperkte aansprakelijkheid, and those public bodies that operate under private law
Denmark	aktieselskab, anpartsselskab
Finland	osakeyhtiö/aktiebolag, osuuskunta/andelslag, säästöpankki/sparbank, vakuutusyhtiö/försäkringsbolag

France	société anonyme, société en commandite par actions, société à responsabilité limitée, and industrial and commercial public establishments and undertakings
Germany	Aktiengesellschaft, Kommanditgesellschaft auf Aktien, Gesellschaft mit beschränkter Haftung (GmbH), bergrechtliche Gesellschaft
Greece	anonume etairia
Ireland	public companies limited by shares or by guarantee, private companies limited by shares or by guarantee, bodies registered under the Industrial and Provident Societies Acts or building societies registered under the Building Societies Acts
Italy	società per azioni, società in accomandita per azioni, società a responsabilità limitata and public and private entities carrying on industrial and commercial activities
Luxembourg	société anonyme, société en commandite par actions, société à responsabilité limitée
Netherlands	naamloze vennootschap, besloten vennootschap met beperkte aansprakelijkheid
Portugal	commercial companies or civil law companies having a commercial form as well as other legal persons that carry on commercial or industrial activities and are incorporated in accordance with Portuguese law
Spain	sociedad anónima, sociedad comanditaria por acciones, sociedad de responsabilidad limitada and those public law bodies which operate under private law
Sweden	aktiebolag, bankaktiebolag, försäkringsbolag
UK	companies incorporated under the law of the United Kingdom

The list of taxes referred to in (c) above is as follows:

Austria	Körperschaftsteuer
Belgium	impôt des sociétés/ vennootschapsbelasting
Denmark	Selskabsskat
Finland	yhteisöjen tulovero/inkomstskatten för samfund
France	impôt sur les sociétés
Germany	Körperschaftsteuer
Greece	phoros eisodematos nomikon prosopon kerdoskopikou charaktera
Ireland	corporation tax
Italy	imposta sul reddito delle persone giuridiche
Luxembourg	impôt sur le revenue des collectivités
Netherlands	Vennootschapsbelasting
Portugal	imposto sobre o rendimento das pessoas colectivas
Spain	impuesto sobre sociedados
Sweden	stattlig inkomstskatt
UK	corporation tax

Accordingly, any reference to a company in connection with any of the reliefs discussed covers both Irish incorporated and EU incorporated companies (provided that any such company is tax resident in a Member State and, under the terms of a double tax agreement concluded between that State and a third State, is not considered to be resident for tax purposes outside the Community).

14.802 The relief

Where the section applies, Irish capital gains tax arising on the disposal of the assets is to be reduced by the amount of tax which would be payable in the Member State in which the acquiring company is resident (TCA 1997, s 634(2)). The credit is given in respect of "tax specified in a relevant certificate" given by the tax authorities of the other Member State, ie a certificate which states:

(a) whether the gains accruing to the transferring company would have been chargeable under the law of the Member State but for the Directive or any provision of the law of the Member State which has the effect of deferring a charge to tax on a gain in the case of such a transfer; and

(b) if the gains in question would have been so chargeable, the amount of tax which would have been payable under the said law, and on the assumption that any losses arising on the transfer are set against any gains so arising (TCA 1997, s 634(1).

The reference above to any provision of the law of the Member State which has the effect of deferring a charge to tax means any law which provides:

(a) that the gain accruing is to be treated as not accruing until the disposal of the assets by the acquiring company; or

(b) that the acquiring company is to be treated as having acquired the assets for a consideration of such amount as would secure that neither a gain nor a loss would accrue to the transferring company on the transfer and that the acquiring company is to be treated as if the acquisition of the assets by the transferring company had been its own acquisition of them; or

(c) any other deferral of a charge to tax corresponding to (a) or (b) (TCA 1997, s 634(1)).

This relieving provision will not to have effect unless it can be shown that the transfer in question is effected for *bona fide* commercial reasons and does not form part of any arrangement or scheme of which the main purpose, or one of the main purposes, is avoidance of liability to corporation tax or capital gains tax.

Provision is made for tax neutral treatment in respect of a transaction covered by the Mergers Directive, as amended by EU Directive No 2005/19/EC (see **9.301**), in which, unusually, one of the parties to the transaction is regarded as a company in one Member State but as a transparent entity, such as a partnership, for tax purposes in the other Member State.

Where—

(a) a company not resident in Ireland transfers the whole of a trade carried on by it, or a part of such a trade, to another company and the consideration for the transfer consists solely of the issue to the transferring company of securities in the receiving company; and

(b) for the purposes of computing the income or gains of any person (the "relevant person") who is chargeable to tax in Ireland, income or gains of the transferring company are treated as being income or chargeable gains of the relevant person and not of the transferring company,

then, in computing any liability to tax of the relevant person in respect of the transfer, an appropriate part of tax specified in a relevant certificate given by the tax authorities of the Member State in which the trade was so carried on is treated for the purposes of TCA 1997 Part 35 Chapter 1 (double tax relief: principal reliefs – see **14.201-2**) as tax—

(i) payable under the law of that Member State; and

(ii) in respect of which credit may be allowed under a double tax treaty (TCA 1997, s 634(3)(a)).

For the above purpose, the *appropriate part of tax* on income or gains specified in a certificate in relation to a relevant person is so much of that tax as bears to the amount of that tax the same proportion as the part of any income or gains of the transferring company in respect of the transfer which is treated as income or gains of the relevant person bears to the amount of that income or gains of the transferring company (TCA 1997, s 634(3)(b)). In other words, it is the part of the transferring company's tax liability on the transfer as is proportionately attributable to the relevant person by reference to the amount of the company's income or gains that are attributable to the relevant person.

Thus, for example, a transferring company with an Irish resident shareholder, although treated as a company in the Member State in which it is resident, may be regarded as a partnership from an Irish perspective. The transferring entity receives shares in the transferee company as consideration for the transfer of a trade to that company. Being a partnership for Irish tax purposes, a proportion of the transferring entity's gain on the disposal of the chargeable assets is attributable to the Irish shareholder in accordance with that shareholder's ownership interest. A proportionate part (reflecting the shareholder's "partnership" interest) of the transferring entity's tax liability in respect of the disposal (as certified by the tax authorities of the country in question) is treated for Irish tax purposes as tax payable by the Irish resident under the law of that country and is available as a credit against capital gains tax, or corporation tax on chargeable gains, payable in Ireland in respect of the disposal.

Where corporation tax or capital gains tax payable by a company is reduced by virtue of TCA 1997, s 634, the return required by TCA 1997, s 636 (see **9.306**) must include a relevant certificate given by the authorities of the Member State in which the trade was carried on immediately before the time of the transfer (TCA 1997, s 636(3)).

14.9 FOREIGN BRANCH PROFITS

14.901 Unilateral relief
14.902 Exemption for foreign branch profits

14.901 Unilateral relief

14.901.1 Introduction

Provision is made for unilateral credit relief for foreign tax suffered by a company that has a branch or agency in a country with which Ireland does not have a tax treaty. The company can reduce its corporation tax liability by the foreign tax paid in respect of the profits of the branch or agency. Without the relief, the company would only be entitled to a deduction for the foreign tax in computing its taxable income.

14.901.2 Unilateral relief

TCA 1997, Sch 24 paragraph 9DA(1) provides that relief (referred to as "unilateral relief") from corporation tax in respect of profits of a company from a trade carried on by the company through a branch or agency in a territory other than the State is to be given in respect of tax payable under the law of any territory other than the State by allowing that tax as a credit against corporation tax, notwithstanding that there is not for the time being in force any tax treaty providing for such relief. *Unilateral relief* is such relief as would fall to be given under TCA 1997, Sch 24 if arrangements (ie, a treaty) with the government of the territory in question containing the provisions in TCA 1997, Sch 24 paragraph 9DA(3)-(5) (see below) were in force, and a reference in Sch 24 to credit under arrangements shall be construed as including a reference to unilateral relief (TCA 1997, Sch 24 paragraph 9DA(2)).

Credit for tax paid under the law of a territory other than the State, and computed by reference to income of a qualifying company from a trade carried on by it through a branch or agency in that territory, is allowable against Irish corporation tax computed by reference to that income (TCA 1997, Sch 24 paragraph 9DA(3)). A qualifying company for this purpose is a company that is tax resident in Ireland or which is, by virtue of the law of a relevant Member State (an EU/EEA state) other than Ireland, resident in that state for tax purposes and provided the foreign branch income concerned forms part of the income of a branch or agency of the company. In this connection, *tax* means any tax imposed in the Member State which corresponds to corporation tax in Ireland (TCA 1997, Sch 24 paragraph 9DA(4)).

References to tax payable or paid under the laws of a territory outside the State include only references to taxes that are charged on income or capital gains and which correspond to corporation tax and capital gains tax (TCA 1997, Sch 24 paragraph 9DA(7)).

Unilateral relief will not be allowed for—

(i) tax paid under the law of a territory where there are arrangements with the government of that territory except to the extent that credit may not be given for that tax under those arrangements, or

(ii) for any tax which is "relevant foreign tax" within the meaning of TCA 1997, s 449 (see **14.402**) or TCA 1997, Sch 24 paragraph 9D (see **14.213**) (TCA 1997, Sch 24 paragraph 9DA(5)).

Where—

(a)   unilateral relief may be given in respect of any profits, and

(b)   it appears that the assessment to corporation tax made in respect of the profits is not made in respect of the full amount thereof, or is incorrect having regard to the credit, if any, falling to be given by way of unilateral relief,

any such assessment may be made or amended as is necessary to ensure that the total amount of the profits is assessed, and the proper credit, if any, is given in respect thereof (TCA 1997, Sch 24 paragraph 9DA(6)).

14.901.3   Pooling

Under "pooling" provisions, where the foreign tax on the branch profits in one country (whether or not a tax treaty is in place) exceeds the Irish tax on those profits, thereby limiting the foreign tax credit to the amount of that tax, the unallowed foreign tax relative to that branch is available to be credited against tax on branch profits in other countries in the year concerned. There is no provision for the carry forward of excess foreign tax (as with the position relating to unrelieved foreign tax on certain interest (see **14.215**) but in contrast to the position relating to unrelieved foreign tax on dividends (see **14.214**)).

The aggregate amount of corporation tax payable by a company for an accounting period in respect of foreign branch income of the company for the accounting period is to be reduced by the unrelieved foreign tax (see formulae below) of the period (TCA 1997, Sch 24 paragraph 9FA(3)). The *aggregate amount of corporation tax payable by a company for an accounting period in respect of foreign branch income of the company for the accounting period* means so much of the corporation tax which would otherwise by payable by the company for that period as would not have been payable had that income been disregarded for tax purposes (TCA 1997, Sch 24 paragraph 9FA(1)).

In relation to a company, *foreign branch* means a branch or agency of the company in a territory other than the State through which the company carries on a trade in that territory, and *foreign branch income* means so much of the company's income as is attributable to a foreign branch. In relation to foreign branch income of a company, *foreign tax* means tax which—

(i)   is paid under the laws of the territory in which the foreign branch is situated on income attributable to that branch, and

(ii)   corresponds to corporation tax.

Unrelieved foreign tax

Where any part of the foreign tax on foreign branch income for an accounting period cannot otherwise be allowed as a credit against corporation tax, so that that income is treated under TCA 1997, Sch 24 paragraph 7(3)(c) (see **14.202**) as reduced by that part of the foreign tax, an amount equal to the aggregate of—

(a)   where income chargeable to tax at the rate specified in TCA 1997, s 21(1) (standard rate of corporation tax - see **3.101.1**) for the accounting period is treated under TCA 1997, Sch 24 paragraph 7(3)(c) as reduced, an amount determined by the formula—

$$\frac{100-R}{100} \times D$$

where—

R   is the rate per cent specified in TCA 1997, s 21(1), and

D   is the amount by which that income is treated as so reduced, and

(b)   where income chargeable to tax at the rate specified in TCA 1997, s 21A(3) (higher rate of corporation tax - see **3.101.4**) for the accounting period is treated under TCA 1997, Sch 24 paragraph 7(3)(c) as reduced, an amount determined by the formula—

$$\frac{100-R}{100} \times D$$

where—

R   is the rate per cent specified in TCA 1997, s 21A(3), and

D   is the amount by which that income is treated as so reduced.

is treated as unrelieved foreign tax of that accounting period (TCA 1997 Sch 24 paragraph 9FA(2)).

Use of the second formula above will be extremely rare, being confined to situations in which trading profits are taxable at 25%.

Example 14.901.3.1

Spencer Ltd, an Irish resident company, has trading branches in Serbia and Slovenia. For its most recent accounting period, the taxable profits of Spencer Ltd are €2m and the profits, as computed under Irish tax rules, of the Serbian and Slovenian branches are €200,000 and €100,000 respectively, on which profits taxes of €20,000 and €25,000 respectively were paid. The non-creditable tax is first ascertained:

	Serbia	Slovenia
	€	€
Profits	200,000	100,000
Foreign tax	20,000	25,000
Net foreign income	180,000	75,000
Foreign tax rates 10% and 25%		
Gross up at lower of foreign and Irish rate	200,000	85,714
Corporation tax @ 12.5%	25,000	10,714
Credit relief (before additional credit)	20,000	10,714
Non-creditable tax		14,286

The additional credit is the lesser of (A) the unrelieved foreign tax and (B) the tax that would not have been payable had the foreign branch profits not been chargeable to tax.

A.   Unrelieved foreign tax in relation to Slovenian profits:

$$\frac{100-12.5}{100} \times €14,286 = €12,500$$

The unrelieved foreign tax is 87.5% of the non-creditable tax. Since relief of €1,786 (at 12.5%) has already been obtained by reducing the branch profits from €100,000 to €85,714, the further amount of €12,500 brings the aggregate potential relief up to the full amount of the non-creditable tax of €14,286.

B. Tax not payable if no foreign branch profits:

	€	€
Corporation tax otherwise payable (before additional credit):		
Profit		2,000,000
Deduct non-creditable tax		14,286
		1,985,714
Corporation tax @ 12.5%		248,214
Less: credit relief as above (20,000 + 10,714)		30,714
Tax payable		217,500
Tax payable if foreign branch profits not chargeable:		
Profit	2,000,000	
Exclude foreign branch profits	300,000	
Net profit	1,700,000	
Corporation tax @ 12.5%		212,500
Tax not payable if no foreign branch profits		5,000
Corporation tax computation:		
Profit (net of non-creditable tax)		
Corporation tax @ 12.5%		1,985,714
Less: credit relief as above	30,714	248,214
Additional credit – lesser of A and B	5,000	
Total credit		35,714
Tax payable		212,500

The rules for calculating the additional credit are intended to result in an aggregate credit equivalent to what would have been available had the foreign branches been a single branch with aggregate profits and tax paid equal to the aggregate of the actual profits of the branches and taxes paid by them. The following example deals with the same position as in the previous example but assumes that the Serbian tax rate on profits is only 5%. In this example, the average tax rate for the two branches is below the Irish 12.5% rate and, in contrast with the above example, the value for "A"" is lower than that for "B". Where "B" is lower, as in the above example, the unrelieved foreign tax is restricted, indicating that the average foreign tax rate is above 12.5%.

Example 14.901.3.2

	Serbia	Slovenia
	€	€
Profits	200,000	100,000
Foreign tax	10,000	25,000
Net foreign income	190,000	75,000

	Serbia	Slovenia
	€	€
Foreign tax rates 5% and 25%		
Gross up at lower of foreign and Irish rate	200,000	85,714
Corporation tax @ 12.5%	25,000	10,714
Credit relief (before additional credit)	10,000	10,714
Non-creditable tax		14,286

The additional credit is the lesser of (A) the unrelieved foreign tax and (B) the tax that would not have been payable had the foreign branch profits not been chargeable to tax.

A.   Unrelieved foreign tax in relation to Slovenian profits:

$$\frac{100-12.5}{100} \times €14,286 = €12,500$$

The unrelieved foreign tax is 87.5% of the non-creditable tax. Since relief of €1,786 (at 12.5%) has already been obtained by reducing the branch profits from €100,000 to €85,714, the further amount of €12,500 brings the aggregate potential relief up to the full amount of the non-creditable tax of €14,286.

B.   Tax not payable if no foreign branch profits:

	€	€
Corporation tax otherwise payable (before additional credit):		
Profit		2,000,000
Deduct non-creditable tax		14,286
		1,985,714
Corporation tax @ 12.5%		248,214
Less: credit relief as above (10,000 + 10,714)		20,714
Tax payable		227,500
Tax payable if foreign branch profits not chargeable:		
Profit	2,000,000	
Exclude foreign branch profits	300,000	
Net profit	1,700,000	
Corporation tax @ 12.5%		212,500
Tax not payable if no foreign branch profits		15,000
Corporation tax computation:		
Profit (net of non-creditable tax)		1,985,714
Corporation tax @ 12.5%		248,214
Less: credit relief as above	20,714	
Additional credit – lesser of A and B	12,500	
Total credit		33,214
Tax payable		215,000

14.902 Exemption for foreign branch profits

14.902.1 Introduction

TCA 1997, s 847 provides for an incentive by way of exemption from corporation tax and capital gains tax in respect of the income and gains of a foreign branch of an Irish company which creates substantial new employment in Ireland resulting from a substantial new investment of permanent capital in Ireland. The exemption is given to a company (a "qualified company") which holds a certificate which it received before 15 February 2001 from the Minister for Finance where the Minister is satisfied that an investment plan submitted to him will result in the creation of substantial new employment in the State and that the maintenance of that employment is dependent on the carrying on of trading operations by the company through a foreign branch or branches.

The relief will cease to apply in respect of accounting periods ending after 31 December 2010. For this purpose, an accounting period beginning before 31 December 2010 and ending after that date is to be divided into two parts, one ending on 31 December 2010 and the other commencing on 1 January 2011, and those parts are to be treated as separate accounting periods.

14.902.2 Conditions for exemption

The exemption relates to profits and gains from *qualified foreign trading activities*, which means trading activities undertaken by a qualified company through a branch or agency outside Ireland in a country specified in a qualification certificate held by the company. The certificate is issued by the Minister for Finance following consultation with the Minister for Enterprise, Trade and Employment. The certificate, which must have been issued by the Minister before 15 February 2001, certifies that a company is a qualified company with effect from a date specified in the certificate. It is issued to a company, being an Irish resident company, which has submitted a plan to the Minister. The Minister may issue the certificate where he is satisfied that:

(a) the plan is an investment plan;

(b) the company, or its associated company, will, before the date approved by the Minister and specified in the plan, make a substantial permanent capital investment in the State under the investment plan for the purposes of the creation of substantial new employment in the State;

(c) the creation of substantial new employment in the State under the investment plan will be achieved; and

(d) the maintenance of the employment so created in trading operations in the State will be dependent on the carrying on by the company of qualified foreign trading operations.

An *investment plan* is a plan of an Irish resident company:

(a) which involves the investment by the company, or by its associated company, of substantial permanent capital in the State for the purposes of the creation, before the date specified in the plan, of substantial new employment in the State in trading operations carried on, or to be carried on, in the State by the company or associated company; and

(b)   which has been submitted before the commencement of its implementation to the Minister by the company for the purpose of enabling it to obtain the relief under TCA 1997, s 847.

In accordance with guidelines issued by the Minister on 10 October 1995, the minimum sustainable employment requirement is 40 new incremental jobs which must be achieved within a three year period. The employment condition here is much more demanding than in the case of the "approved investment plan" for the purposes of TCA 1997, s 222 (see **14.602**); that plan is one directed towards the creation or maintenance of employment in Ireland in trading operations carried on, or to be carried on, in Ireland. There is no minimum amount specified in relation to the substantial permanent capital investment in Ireland and this will accordingly be a matter to be determined by reference to the requirements of each project. Neither is the nature of the permanent capital investment specified and there is no guidance as to whether this is to be in the form of an equity investment or otherwise.

The investment plan to be submitted to the Minister must contain details of the promoters of the investment, the nature of the Irish trading operations, including the structure, ownership, board of directors, funding, employment and location, the location and activities of the foreign branch and details of any supervisory or regulatory authorities in Ireland with responsibility for supervising the branch trading operations.

A certificate may be revoked where the conditions relating to its issue are not complied with. Revocation will be from a date specified in a notice in writing served on the company by registered post.

A company is associated with another company where one of the companies is a 75% subsidiary of the other or both are 75% subsidiaries of a third company. In determining whether one company is a 75% subsidiary of another company, the other company will not for this purpose be regarded as the owner of any share capital which it owns:

(a)   directly in a company if a profit on a sale of those shares would be treated as a trading receipt; or

(b)   indirectly, but which is owned directly by a company for which a profit on sale of the shares would be treated as a trading receipt.

In determining whether a company is a 25% subsidiary of another company, the profit distribution and notional winding up tests applicable to the definition of a 75% subsidiary for group relief purposes (see **8.102**) are applied with necessary modifications but without regard to TCA 1997, s 411(1)(c) which limits the reference to a company to a company resident in Ireland.

14.902.3   The exemption

TCA 1997, s 847(6) provides for the disregarding of profits, gains or losses arising from "qualified foreign trading activities". As might be expected, no deduction is allowed in respect of charges on income, management expenses or other amounts which can be deducted from or set off against profits of more than one description insofar as these are attributable to the qualified foreign trading activities.

A qualified company is therefore exempt from corporation tax on its trading profits derived from foreign branches in the territories specified in its qualification certificate. It is also exempt in respect of chargeable gains on disposals of assets used wholly and exclusively for the purposes of the qualified foreign trading activities, with some exceptions. These are assets specified in TCA 1997, s 980(2)(a) to (d), ie land in the State, minerals in the State or any rights, interests or other assets in relation to mining or minerals or the searching for minerals, exploration or exploitation rights in a designated area, and shares in an unquoted company deriving their value or the greater part of their value, directly or indirectly, from those assets.

The tax exemption in respect of branch profits applies both to companies liable to corporation tax at the standard rate and to International Financial Services Centre (IFSC) companies liable to corporation tax at the effective 10% rate. In practice, since the exemption relates to branches, the most widespread use of the exemption is likely to be made by banks and insurance companies which are accustomed to conduct overseas business through branches.

TCA 1997, s 847(1)(b)(iii) provides that a trade carried on by a qualified company which consists partly of qualified foreign trading activities and partly of other trading activities is to be treated as comprising two distinct trades. TCA 1997, s 847(1)(b)(iv) provides that there shall be attributed to each trade (or each deemed trade) carried on, such profits or gains or losses as would have resulted if each had been carried on by independent persons acting at arm's length. This provision is necessary to prevent excessive profits being allocated to the exempt foreign trading activities. There are to be made, in the case of trade carried on, or treated as carried on, by a qualified company, all necessary apportionments as are just and reasonable for the purpose of computing profits or gains or losses as well as charges on income, expenses of management or other amounts deductible against total profits.

14.10 CREDIT RELIEF: INTEREST AND ROYALTIES DIRECTIVE

14.1001 Introduction
14.1002 Definitions
14.1003 Credit relief

14.1001 Introduction

TCA 1997 Part 8 Chapter 6 (ss 267G-267I) gives effect to Council Directive No 2003/49/EC, providing for a common system of taxation applicable to interest and royalty payments made between associated companies of different Member States. Interest and royalties to which this legislation applies are exempt from corporation tax and income tax. Accordingly, payments of royalties and interest are exempt from the withholding provisions that would otherwise apply. In any case in which tax is deducted at source, the recipient company in question (which will be tax resident in a Member State other than Ireland) will be entitled to a refund of the tax deducted. See also **4.307**.

Provision is also made for credit against corporation tax in respect of any withholding tax charged on interest or royalties by Greece or Portugal and any withholding tax charged on royalties by Spain.

14.1002 Definitions

TCA 1997, s 267G contains a number of definitions, including the following.

Member State

Member State means a Member State of the European Communities.

Directive

Directive means Council Directive 2003/49/EC of 3 June 2003 (OJ No L 157, 26.6.2003, p 49) as amended.

Company

For the purposes of TCA 1997 Part 8 Chapter 6, *company* means a company of a Member State, and *company of a Member State* has the meaning assigned to it by Article 3(a) of the Directive. In Article 3(a), "company of a Member State" means any company—

   (i)   taking one of the forms listed in the Annex to the Directive (see below); and
  (ii)   which in accordance with the tax laws of a Member State is considered to be resident in that Member State and is not, within the meaning of a double taxation convention on income concluded with a third state, considered to be resident for tax purposes outside the Community; and
 (iii)   which is subject to one of the following taxes without being exempt, or to a tax which is identical or substantially similar and which is imposed after the date of entry into force of the Directive in addition to, or in place of, those existing taxes:

Austria	Körperschaftsteuer
Belgium	impôt des sociétés/ vennootschapsbelasting
Denmark	Selskabsskat
Finland	yhteisöjen tulovero/inkomstskatten för samfund

France	impôt sur les sociétés
Germany	Körperschaftsteuer
Greece	phoros eisodematos nomikon prosopon
Ireland	corporation tax
Italy	imposta sul reddito delle persone giuridiche
Luxembourg	impôt sur le revenue des collectivités
Netherlands	Vennootschapsbelasting
Portugal	imposto sobre o rendimento das pessoas colectivas
Spain	impuesto sobre sociedados
Sweden	statlig inkomstskatt
UK	corporation tax

The forms of company listed in the Annex to the Directive are:

Austria	Aktiengesellschaft, Gesellschaft mit beschränkter Haftung (GmbH),
Belgium	société anonyme/naamloze vennootschap, société en commandite par actions/commanditaire vennootschap op aandelen, société privé à responsabilité limitée/besloten vennootschap met beperkte aansprakelijkheid, and those public law bodies that operate under private law
Denmark	aktieselskab, anpartsselskab
Finland	osakeyhtiö/aktiebolag, osuuskunta/andelslag, säästöpankki/sparbank, vakuutusyhtiö/försäkringsbolag
France	société anonyme, société en commandite par actions, société à responsabilité limitée, and industrial and commercial public establishments and undertakings
Germany	Aktiengesellschaft, Kommanditgesellschaft auf Aktien, Gesellschaft mit beschränkter Haftung (GmbH), bergrechtliche Gewerkschaft
Greece	anonume etairia
Ireland	Public companies limited by shares or by guarantee, private companies limited by shares or by guarantee, bodies registered under the Industrial and Provident Societies Acts, building societies registered under the Building Societies Acts
Italy	società per azioni, società in accomandita per azioni, società a responsabilità limitata, and private entities carrying on industrial and commercial activities
Luxembourg	société anonyme, société en commandite par actions, société à responsabilité limitée
Netherlands	naamloze vennootschap, besloten vennootschap met beperkte aansprakelijkheid
Portugal	commercial companies or civil law companies having a commercial form, cooperatives and public undertakings incorporated in accordance with Portuguese law
Spain	sociedad anónima, sociedad comanditaria por acciones, sociedad de responsabilidad limitada, public law bodies which operate under private law
Sweden	aktiebolag, försäkringsaktiebolag
UK	companies incorporated under the law of the United Kingdom

Interest

Interest means income from debt-claims of every kind, whether or not secured by mortgage and whether or not carrying a right to participate in the debtor's profits and, in particular, income from securities and income from bonds or debentures, including premiums and prizes attaching to such securities, bonds or debentures, but does not include penalty charges for late payment.

Royalties

Royalties means payments of any kind as consideration for—

(a) the use of, or the right to use—

   (i) any copyright of literary, artistic or scientific work, including cinematograph films and software,

   (ii) any patent, trade mark, design or model, plan, secret formula or process,

(b) information concerning industrial, commercial or scientific experience;

(c) the use of, or the right to use, industrial, commercial or scientific equipment;

Tax

In relation to a Member State other than the State, *tax* means any tax imposed in that Member State which is specified in Article 3(a)(iii) of the Directive (see list under *Company* above).

14.1003 Credit relief

Where interest or royalties are received by an Irish resident company from an associated company (see below), credit will be allowed for—

(a) any withholding tax charged on the interest or royalties by Greece or Portugal; and

(b) any withholding tax charged on the royalties by Spain,

for the purposes of the derogations provided for in the Directive against corporation tax in respect of the interest or royalties to the extent that credit for such withholding tax would not otherwise be allowed (TCA 1997, s 267J(1)).

Greece and Portugal are exempted under the Directive from the obligation to exempt interest and royalties from taxation for a transitional period of five years from the date of entry into force of the Directive; during the first two years of this transitional period, the withholding rate applicable is 10% and, for the remaining three years, 5%. The transitional period may be extended.

Where credit for tax payable under the laws of a Member State other than Ireland is allowed to a company by virtue of TCA 1997, s 267J(1), TCA 1997 Schedule 24 is to apply for that purpose as if that paragraph were arrangements (ie, a tax treaty) providing that the tax so payable is to be allowed as a credit against Irish tax (TCA 1997, s 267J(2)). TCA 1997, s 267J is to apply without prejudice to a provision of a bilateral agreement (tax treaty, protocol or other agreement between Ireland and another state) (TCA 1997, s 267J(3)).

A company is treated as an *associated company* of another company during an uninterrupted period of at least 2 years throughout which—

(a)   one of them directly controls not less than 25% of the voting power of the other company; or

(b)   in respect of those companies, a third company directly controls not less than 25% of the voting power of each of them (TCA 1997, s 267G(2)).

Anti-avoidance

TCA 1997, s 267J will not apply to interest or royalties unless it can be shown that the payment of the interest or royalties was made for bona fide commercial reasons and does not form part of any arrangement or scheme of which the main purpose or one of the main purposes is avoidance of liability to income tax, corporation tax or capital gains tax (TCA 1997, s 267K(1).

14.11 CAPITAL GAINS: UNILATERAL RELIEF

14.1101 Introduction
14.1102 Credit relief

14.1101 Introduction

Unilateral credit relief may be claimed in respect of tax suffered on capital gains in certain foreign territories: Belgium, Cyprus, France, Germany, Italy, Japan, Luxembourg, the Netherlands, Pakistan and Zambia. Ireland concluded tax treaties with these countries prior to the introduction of capital gains tax. Where a person, including a company, chargeable to Irish tax on a capital gain suffers tax on that gain in the other country concerned, the foreign tax is creditable against Irish tax on the gain.

14.1102 Credit relief

Relief ("unilateral relief") from corporation tax in respect of chargeable gains accruing to a company on the disposal of an asset (a "specified asset") located in a territory other than Ireland is to be given in respect of tax payable under the law of any specified territory by allowing that tax as a credit against corporation tax in respect of chargeable gains, notwithstanding that there are not for the time being in force any arrangements (a tax treaty) providing for such relief (TCA 1997, Sch 24 paragraph 9FB(1)).

A *specified territory* is any of the following territories with the government of which arrangements have been made: the Kingdom of Belgium, Cyprus, the Republic of France, the Federal Republic of Germany, the Italian Republic, Japan, the Grand Duchy of Luxembourg, the Kingdom of the Netherlands, Pakistan or Zambia (TCA 1997, Sch 24 paragraph 9FB(7)).

Unilateral relief is such relief as would fall to be given under TCA 1997, Sch 24 if arrangements with the government of the specified territory in question contained the provisions in TCA 1997, Sch 24 paragraph 9FB(3)-(5) (see below), and a reference to that Schedule to credit under arrangements is to be construed as including a reference to unilateral relief (TCA 1997, Sch 24 paragraph 9FB(2)).

Credit for tax paid under the law of a specified territory and computed by reference to a capital gain realised by a company from its disposal of a specified asset is to be allowed against Irish corporation tax on chargeable gains computed by reference to that capital gain (TCA 1997, Sch 24 paragraph 9FB(3)). Such credit will not be allowed for tax paid under the law of a specified territory to the extent that credit may be given for that tax under—

  (i)   arrangements with the government of the territory, or
  (ii)   any other provision of TCA 1997, Sch 24 (TCA 1997, Sch 24 paragraph 9FB(4)).

Where—

  (a)   unilateral relief may be given in respect of any chargeable gain, and
  (b)   it appears that any assessment made in respect of the chargeable gain is not made in respect of the full amount thereof, or is incorrect having regard to any credit falling to be given by way of unilateral relief, such assessment may be made or amended as is necessary to ensure that the total amount of the

chargeable gain is assessed, and the proper credit, if any, is given in respect thereof (TCA 1997, Sch 24 paragraph 9FB(5)).

For the purposes of unilateral relief, references to tax payable or paid under the law of a territory outside the State include only references to taxes which are charged on capital gains and which correspond to income tax, corporation tax or capital gains tax (TCA 1997, Sch 24 paragraph 9FB(6)).

Chapter 15

Self-Assessment and Administration

15.1 SELF-ASSESSMENT

15.101   Introduction

In principle, there are two main methods of collecting taxes on the income of companies, namely:

(i)   by assessment on the company in receipt of the income; and

(ii)   by deduction at source from certain other types of payment made by certain persons (eg annual payments made by companies and other persons, interest on deposits paid by banks and building societies – see **4.3**).

Taxes Consolidation Act 1997 (TCA 1997) Part 41 (ss 950-959) contains the main rules for the collection of the taxes on income by assessment (now widely referred to as "self-assessment").

15.102   Self-assessment: main features

15.102.1   General

The self-assessment system for the collection of tax, contained in TCA 1997 Part 41, is stated to apply to *chargeable persons* in respect of *chargeable periods*. Any person who is a chargeable person in respect of any tax for a given chargeable period, including a company for an accounting period, is required to make a return to the inspector of taxes of income and other particulars for the tax concerned for that period and to pay the appropriate amount of tax in accordance with the provisions of the self-assessment legislation.

Various definitions relevant for the purposes of self-assessment are given in TCA 1997, s 950(1), and some of the more important of these are as follows.

15.102.2   Tax

Tax is defined as income tax, corporation tax or capital gains tax, whichever is relevant. Self-assessment therefore applies, inter alia, to the collection of corporation tax (and capital gains tax where appropriate) from companies.

15.102.3   Chargeable period

A *chargeable period* means a year of assessment or, in the case of a company, an accounting period (from TCA 1997, s 321(2)).

15.102.4   Chargeable person

In relation to a chargeable period, *chargeable person* means any person who is chargeable to tax for that period, whether on his own account or on account of some other person. For this purpose, "chargeable" can be taken to mean having any income or profits for the chargeable period in respect of which tax is chargeable or having any chargeable gains for the period on which corporation tax or capital gains tax, as the case may be, is chargeable. The fact that the income or chargeable gains in any chargeable period may be covered by deductions, reliefs or losses would not prevent a person being a chargeable person in relation to the tax in question for that period.

A non-resident company may be a chargeable person in relation to income tax if it has any Irish source income (apart from income arising from a trade carried on through a branch or agency in the State in which case liability to corporation tax arises – see **3.107.1**), unless such income is exempted under any provision, or is completely relieved from Irish tax, by the operation of a double tax treaty. Similarly, a non-resident company may be a chargeable person for capital gains tax if it has chargeable gains arising to it from the disposal of certain Irish based assets (see **9.102.2**).

A company (as with any other person) may be a chargeable person in more than one capacity and, if so, it is required to meet all the obligations of a chargeable person in each such capacity (TCA 1997, s 950(3)).

A person who is not a chargeable person for one chargeable period may be a chargeable person for another chargeable period. For example, a company may not be a chargeable person for a particular accounting period because it is not resident in the State for that period but may become a chargeable person for a later period on having become resident for that period.

15.102.5   Company directors

A director of a company (other than an excepted company) is always a chargeable person for the purposes of income tax (and the levies), notwithstanding that his total income may consist entirely of Schedule E emoluments subject to PAYE or may consist only of Schedule E emoluments and other income deducted in arriving at his tax-free allowances for PAYE purposes. Similarly, the spouse of a director of a company (other than an excepted company) is a chargeable person for any tax year in which both spouses are assessable jointly under TCA 1997, s 1017. However, for any tax year for which a spouse of a director is assessed as a single person, the spouse is not a chargeable person for income tax if he or she has no income other than income subject to PAYE (and is not a director).

A director of an "excepted company" (or the jointly assessable spouse of such a director) is not a chargeable person provided he or she is not a chargeable person for any other reason (for example, through having income other than Schedule E income subject to PAYE system). For this purpose, an excepted company is one in respect of which, during the three years ending on 5 April in the year of assessment for which the exception is to apply, the following three conditions are met:

(i)   the company was not entitled to any assets other than cash or money on deposit not exceeding €130 (but a company whose only assets were cash and/or deposits in excess of €130 does not meet this condition);

   (ii)   the company did not carry on a trade, business or other activity, including the making of investments; and

  (iii)   the company did not pay any charges on income within TCA 1997, s 243 (see **4.4**) (TCA 1997, s 950(1)).

In effect, the exclusion of a director as a chargeable person in the case of an "excepted company" is limited to situations in which the company is dormant. There is no exclusion for, say, a director of a charitable company or for the director of a sporting club incorporated as a company. The requirement for a director of a company to make a self-assessment tax return (and, if necessary, to pay preliminary tax) applies therefore in almost all cases, even where the director is not in receipt of any fees, emoluments or any other remuneration from the company.

The Revenue have issued a Statement of Practice, IT/1/93, stating that the surcharge (see **15.208.4**) will not be applied in the case of non-proprietary directors all of whose income is taxed directly or indirectly under PAYE, and who are not otherwise chargeable persons. A proprietary director is defined as one who (whether alone or with his/her spouse) beneficially owns, or is able either directly or indirectly to control, more than 15% of the ordinary share capital of the company concerned.

For the purposes of the foregoing rules, *director* is defined in TCA 1997, s 116 (benefit-in-kind rules) as follows:

   (a)   in relation to a body corporate the affairs whereof are managed by a board of directors or similar body, a member of that board or similar body;

   (b)   in relation to a body corporate the affairs whereof are managed by a single director or similar person, that director or person; and

   (c)   in relation to a body corporate the affairs whereof are managed by the members themselves, any member of the body corporate.

Furthermore, any person in accordance with whose directions or instructions the directors (as defined above) of a body corporate are accustomed to act is deemed to be a director, except if the directors are accustomed to act in accordance with such directions or instructions by reason only that they are taking advice given by the person concerned in a professional capacity.

15.102.6   Outline of self-assessment

Self-assessment for a company normally involves the following steps in relation to an accounting period:

  1.   the company is required to make a payment of "preliminary tax" on or before the due date for preliminary tax for the chargeable period in respect of its liability to tax for the period;

  2.   the company is required, after the end of the chargeable period and no later than the "specified return date", to complete and file with the inspector of taxes a tax return giving details of its income and/or chargeable gains and other required information in respect of the chargeable period;

  3.   following receipt of the tax return, the inspector of taxes will make an assessment on the company for the relevant tax: the assessment will detail the income and/or chargeable gains liable to tax, show the calculation of the

amount of the tax chargeable, deduct credits and reliefs against tax, and show the balance of the tax payable after deducting the preliminary tax paid;

4.   the company is required to pay the balance of tax due not later than one month from the date on which the assessment is made (unless the assessment is made before the due date for payment of preliminary tax, in which case it should be paid on or before that date);

5.   if the preliminary tax paid exceeds the net tax payable (after deducting credits and reliefs against tax), the excess is repayable to the company, with interest.

The above-described procedure involves the making of an assessment by the inspector of taxes before the liability for any chargeable period is finalised. However, the essential feature of the self-assessment system is the obligation on the taxpayer company to estimate its liability to the tax concerned and to ensure that it makes a sufficient preliminary tax payment, usually before any assessment is made by the inspector.

The legislation on self-assessment also contains rules for dealing with a chargeable person who, for any relevant chargeable period, fails to make a preliminary tax payment and/or fails to file a tax return with the inspector. In such cases, preliminary tax becomes payable on a notice served by the inspector and the inspector is empowered to make an estimated assessment for the tax the inspector considers ought to be paid. In addition, if not satisfied that a tax return made by a chargeable person is complete and correct, the inspector may make an estimated assessment.

15.102.7   Audit of tax returns

A return of income may, some time after it has been submitted, be reviewed by the inspector of taxes and subjected to an examination, usually referred to as a "desk audit". This examination may result in queries being raised by the inspector with the chargeable person or with that person's tax adviser and, if the inspector is not satisfied with the answers to those queries, the case may be subjected to a full Revenue or "field" audit, which will be carried out on the taxpayer's business premises.

Alternatively, the inspector may decide to subject a chargeable person to a full audit even where he has no immediate questions to raise. A certain number of Revenue audits are undertaken on a random basis as an "incentive" to chargeable persons to file true and correct returns in the first place. Where a full audit is undertaken, it is likely that all or a number of aspects of the chargeable person's tax and financial affairs will be examined until the inspector is satisfied that the chargeable person's tax liability is fully and correctly ascertained. In line with the Revenue Commissioners' "Charter of Rights", the taxpayer may request an internal review of a Revenue audit. Taxpayers may obtain a review either by the appropriate Regional Director or the Director of Customer Services (see *Tax Briefing* 21, which also explains the general Revenue approach to such reviews).

The Revenue booklet, IT 32 "Revenue Audit-Guide for Small Business" explains their general approach to selecting businesses for audit and to the carrying out of an audit. The booklet indicates that the vast majority of audit cases are selected through a screening process which involves reviewing:

(a)   the taxpayer's compliance history;

(b)   the figures in the taxpayer's returns and accounts, in the light of trends and patterns in that particular business sector; and

(c)   other available information.

In some cases, the Revenue select particular trades or professions as the basis for an intensive screening exercise.

15.102.8   Amendment of assessments

In practice, the initial assessment for a chargeable period is usually made by the inspector based on the income and/or chargeable gains disclosed in the return for that period without any detailed review of the return. This enables the bulk of tax returns to be processed quickly after they are filed with the inspector to the point where at least an initial assessment can be made and a demand issued to the chargeable person to pay the balance of tax (after crediting the preliminary tax paid) which the chargeable person's own return indicates is due.

If the inspector's subsequent review of the return, whether with or without a full audit, shows that the assessment based on the chargeable person's return has understated or overstated the correct liability to tax, the inspector will amend the original assessment to show the correct net tax due (or tax repayable). Any tax underpaid is then demanded from the chargeable person or, where the effect of the amendment is to reduce the net liability, the tax overpaid is refunded to that person.

15.102.9   Appeals against assessments

A chargeable person who disagrees with the amount of the tax in an assessment or amended assessment may appeal against that assessment but subject to certain conditions and limitations. The rules relating to appeals against assessments are discussed more fully in **15.209**. A chargeable person is not entitled to appeal against any assessment unless the net tax liability shown therein is greater than the net tax payable calculated on the basis of information contained in the chargeable person's own tax return.

15.102.10 Interest on tax

Interest is chargeable on any tax underpaid or on any tax paid late (ie, not paid on or before the due date for the tax in question). The question of interest on tax, including interest in cases of fraud or neglect, is discussed in more detail in **15.207**.

15.102.11 Obligations of chargeable person

Every company which is a chargeable person is required, for every chargeable period for which it is so chargeable, to do the following:

(a)   to make a payment of preliminary tax of a required minimum amount on or before the due date for preliminary tax for the chargeable period in respect of its liability for the tax concerned for that period,

(b)   to furnish a complete tax return containing the information required for the tax concerned on or before the "specified return date" for the chargeable period, and

(c)   to pay any balance of the tax concerned (in excess of the preliminary tax paid) which is shown in the inspector's assessment to be due for the chargeable period, such payment to be made by the date by which the corporation tax return for the period is due (or, exceptionally, where the assessment is made before the due date for payment of preliminary tax, on or before that date).

If a company is, at or about the same time, a chargeable person for both corporation tax and capital gains tax (as a result of a disposal of development land), it must take the appropriate action for each of the two taxes. In relation to (a) and (c) above, separate payments of both preliminary tax and any tax balance of corporation tax and capital gains tax are required and separate assessments will be made by the inspector.

As regards (b), separate tax return forms are necessary where liability to both corporation tax and capital gains tax arises at or around the same time.

An essential feature of the self-assessment system is that a chargeable company's obligations to make a preliminary tax payment and to file a tax return for each chargeable period exist whether or not the inspector of taxes has issued to it any notice to pay preliminary tax or to make a tax return. Failure by the company to meet its obligations by the required dates is likely to result in a liability for interest on the tax ultimately found to be payable and a surcharge for the late filing of the return.

15.103 Preliminary tax

15.103.1 Introduction

Every company which is a chargeable person as respects any relevant chargeable period is liable to pay the amount of preliminary tax appropriate to that period in respect of the tax concerned (TCA 1997, s 952(1)).

Preliminary tax, in relation to an accounting period of a company, means the amount of tax which in the opinion of the company is likely to become payable by that company for that period by reason of an assessment or assessments made by the inspector of taxes (or which would be made if the inspector did not elect under TCA 1997, s 954(4) (see **15.105.4**) not to make an assessment) (TCA 1997, s 952(2)).

Exceptionally, preliminary tax (as such) for a chargeable period is not payable in any case where the company has received an assessment for tax for that period before the due date for payment of preliminary tax (TCA 1997, s 952(4)). However, in such a case, the amount of the tax charged in the assessment is payable, instead of any preliminary tax, on the due date for the preliminary tax (TCA 1997, s 958(3)(a)). This will happen only where the company has filed the return for the tax concerned before its preliminary tax due date.

There are two important requirements relating to the payment of preliminary tax in the case of a company, namely:

(i)   the payment must be made by or on behalf of the company no later than the due date for payment of the preliminary tax; and

(ii)   the amount to be paid as preliminary tax must be not less than 90% of the tax payable for the chargeable period (TCA 1997, s 958(4C), (4E)).

A company which does not satisfy both of these requirements regarding the preliminary tax payment for a chargeable period will have failed its preliminary tax obligation so that, normally, it will become liable to interest on the tax assessed (after the tax return has been filed), the interest being charged from the due date for the preliminary tax to the actual date of payment.

15.103.2 Due date for preliminary tax

For preliminary tax to be paid on time, it must be paid "on or before" the relevant due date. In the event that the due date is a Saturday, Sunday or public holiday, it is advisable to make the payment on the immediately preceding working day, although in practice the Revenue Commissioners will probably accept a payment received on the first working day following such a due date as being paid on time.

Accounting periods ending on or before 31 December 2005

See the 2007 edition of this book.

Accounting periods ending on or after 1 January 2006

Preliminary tax for any accounting period ending on or after 1 January 2006 is due and payable one month before the end of the accounting period. Specifically, it is due not later than the day which is 31 days before the last day of the accounting period. Where, however, that day is later than the 21st day of the month in which the first-mentioned day occurs, the tax is due and payable not later than the 21st day of that month (TCA 1997, s 958(2B)(a)).

In the case of an accounting period which is less than one month and one day, preliminary tax is due on the last day of the accounting period. Where that day is later than the 21st day of the month in which that day occurs, the tax is due and payable not later than the 21st day of that month (TCA 1997, s 958(2B)(b)). Implicitly, the preliminary tax amount is 90% of the tax payable for the accounting period in question. If, however, a company fails to satisfy its preliminary tax obligations, as described in **15.103.3** below, the tax due and payable on the preliminary tax date becomes the full amount of the tax payable for that period (TCA 1997, s 958(4C)).

As a transitional measure, for accounting periods ending on or after 1 January 2003 and before 1 January 2006, preliminary tax was due in two instalments. (See the 2007 edition of this book regarding the preliminary tax regime for the transitional period.)

As seen in **15.103.1** above, preliminary tax for an accounting period of a company is essentially the amount of tax which in the opinion of the company will ultimately become payable by that company. Accordingly, the preliminary tax payable for any accounting period should, taken literally, be the amount of the tax which, in the opinion of the company concerned, will be the amount of the tax finally payable for that period.

What is of practical relevance is that interest on overdue tax will arise unless the amount paid by way or preliminary tax is at least 90% of the final liability or, in the case of a small company, 100% of the corresponding corporation tax for the preceding accounting period (TCA 1997, s 958(4C).

A company is a *small company* in relation to an accounting period if the corresponding corporation tax for the preceding chargeable period payable by the company does not exceed the relevant limit in relation to the accounting period (TCA 1997, s 958(1)(b)).

Corresponding corporation tax for the preceding chargeable period means an amount determined by the formula $T \times C/P$ where—

T   is the corporation tax payable by the company for the preceding chargeable period;

C   is the number of days in the chargeable period; and

P   is the number of days in the preceding chargeable period (TCA 1997, s 958(1)(a)).

The *relevant limit,* in relation to an accounting period for which preliminary tax is payable after 5 December 2007, is €200,000 (previously €150,000), but that amount is reduced proportionately where the length of the accounting period is less than 12 months (TCA 1997, s 958(1)(a)).

So, for example, if the length of the current accounting period of a company is 12 months and the corporation tax for its preceding accounting period of 10 months is €160,000, the corresponding corporation tax for the preceding period is €160,000 x 12/10 = €192,000. As this is less than the relevant limit of €200,000, the company is a small company for the current accounting period. If, in another case, the length of the current accounting period of a company is 10 months and the corporation tax for its preceding accounting period of 12 months is €216,000, the corresponding corporation tax for the preceding period is €216,000 x 10/12 = €180,000. The relevant limit in relation to the current accounting period is €200,000 x 10/12 = €166,667. As the corresponding corporation tax is not less than the relevant limit, the company is not a small company for the current accounting period.

Start-up companies

A start-up company with a tax liability not exceeding the relevant limit in its first accounting period is relieved of the obligation to pay preliminary tax for that period. Where in relation to an accounting period of a company—

(a)   the tax payable for the period does not exceed the relevant limit, and

(b)   the period commenced on the company coming within the charge to corporation tax,

the preliminary tax appropriate to the period is taken as nil and the minimum preliminary tax provisions of TCA 1997, s 958(4C) and (4E) (see **15.103.3** below) will not apply (TCA 1997, s 958(2B)(c)).

15.103.3   Minimum preliminary tax

Provisions in TCA 1997, s 958(4C) and (4E) set out the minimum amount of tax which a company must pay by the due date as preliminary tax for a chargeable period so as to ensure that the due date for all of the tax charged in the assessment is not to be backdated to the due date for preliminary tax (see **15.106.3** under *(c) Due date: assessment made after preliminary tax due date – preliminary tax requirements not met*).

The minimum preliminary tax payment required (ie, to avoid interest arising in respect of overdue tax) is 90% of the corporation tax payable for that period or, in the case of a "small company" (see **15.103.2**), the lower of that amount and the corresponding corporation tax for the preceding accounting period (TCA 1997, s 958(4C)(b)). For certain start-up companies for which the preliminary tax liability is nil, see **15.103.2**.

Where a chargeable gain arises in respect of a disposal made by a company in an accounting period but after the date on which preliminary tax is due for that period, the company is treated as having satisfied its preliminary tax obligations where—

(a) the company pays preliminary tax equal to 90% of the liability for the accounting period apart from the liability relating to the chargeable gain on that disposal, and

(b) the company makes a "top-up" payment within one month after the end of the accounting period so that the aggregate of that payment and the preliminary tax (where paid in accordance with TCA 1997, s 958(2B)(a) – see **15.103.2** above) for the period is not less than 90% of the tax payable for that period (TCA 1997, s 958(4E)).

TCA 1997, s 958(4E) includes a similar provision as respects a *relevant company*, ie a company in respect of which its profits or gains for tax purposes are computed in accordance with relevant accounting standards (RAS – see **3.305.6**) which are, or include, relevant accounting standards in relation to profits or gains or losses on financial assets or liabilities. Such a company's preliminary tax obligations are treated as having been satisfied where—

(a) the company pays preliminary tax equal to 90% of the liability for the accounting period apart from the liability relating to profits or gains or losses accruing, and not realised, in the accounting period on financial assets or financial liabilities as are attributable to changes in value of those assets or liabilities in the part of the period that is after the end of the month immediately preceding the month in which preliminary tax for the period is payable, and

(b) the company makes a "top-up" payment within one month after the end of the accounting period so that the aggregate of that payment and the preliminary tax (where paid in accordance with TCA 1997, s 958(2B)(a) – see **15.103.2** above) for the period is not less than 90% of the tax payable for that period.

There is no similar provision for the case in which a company is required to pay income tax on relevant payments (treated as corporation tax, and due at the same time as preliminary tax is due – see **3.206**), even in the case of a relevant payment made in the final month of an accounting period. The Revenue have, however, indicated that treatment similar to that provided for in relation to chargeable gains would in practice be applied in cases involving income tax on relevant payments. It is to be hoped that such treatment would also be forthcoming in other cases where clear hardship would otherwise result, for example, in relation to a balancing charge triggered by a disposal of a building in the final month of an accounting period of where the disposal takes place some time after a trade has ceased.

No specific provision is made for cases in which companies have suffered tax by deduction at source and for which a credit against corporation tax is accordingly due. Such companies will have paid tax on an accelerated basis, in some cases (for example, where professional services withholding tax has applied) to a substantial extent. This anomaly is not new but will be all the more acute under the accelerated preliminary tax regime. What has been confirmed by the Revenue in this regard is that preliminary tax may be calculated net of professional services withholding tax, relevant contracts tax (under TCA 1997, s 531 – payments to subcontractors in certain industries) and any other tax suffered by deduction at source in respect of income received.

Such tax deducted may not, however, be taken into account in arriving at the amount of a company's corresponding corporation tax for the preceding chargeable period for the purpose of determining whether or not it is a "small company". Technically this would seem to be correct since corresponding corporation tax refers to "corporation tax payable" which in turn refers to the amount of corporation tax payable by a company before any deduction for such items as DIRT, professional services withholding tax etc. (These items are income tax rather than corporation tax, and are allowed, by virtue of TCA 1997, s 24(2) or s 526(1), by way of set-off against corporation tax, but not as deductions in arriving at corporation tax.)

Should it not then be the case that preliminary tax for a current period is also an amount before any similar deduction for tax deducted at source? One possible reason why this would not necessarily follow is that preliminary tax is simply "tax payable" and not corporation tax payable (see TCA 1997, s 952(2) and also, for example, TCA 1997, s 958(4C)(b)(i)(I) which refers to 90% of "the tax payable"). The position as confirmed by the Revenue removes at least some of the hardship that would otherwise result but the outcome is nevertheless unsatisfactory in that any tax already deducted from income at the time preliminary tax becomes payable is not recognised as tax already paid by that date.

Failure to pay an adequate amount of tax as described above results in the tax which is due and payable for the period in question being deemed to have been due and payable on the due date for the payment of preliminary tax for that period (TCA 1997, s 958(4C)(b)). Thus, interest on overdue tax will become payable by reference to the preliminary tax dates.

Tax will also be deemed to have become due and payable by a company on the due date for the payment of preliminary tax if—

(a)   the company has defaulted in the payment of preliminary tax for the accounting period concerned (TCA 1997, s 958(4C)(a)); or

(b)   the preliminary tax payable by the company for that period was not paid by the date on which it was due and payable (TCA 1997, s 958(4C)(c)).

For the transitional period, accounting periods ending on or after 1 January 2002 and before 1 January 2006, see the 2007 edition of this book.

Preliminary tax pooling in a group

In respect of accounting periods ending on or after 1 February 2007, overpayments of preliminary tax by members of a group (within the meaning of TCA 1997, s 411 – see **8.103.1**) may be re-allocated against underpayments by other group members (excluding small companies) thereby limiting the amount of interest on underpayments of preliminary tax. This will be possible where—

(a)   a company (the "surrendering company") which is a member of a group pays an amount of preliminary tax for an accounting period (the "relevant period") in accordance with TCA 1997, s 958(2B) (see **15.103.2** above under *Accounting periods ending on or after 1 January 2003*), being an amount which exceeds 90% of the tax payable by that company for the relevant period,

(b)   another company (the "claimant company") which is a member of the group pays an amount of preliminary tax for an accounting period which coincides with the relevant period, in accordance with TCA 1997, s 958(2B), being an amount which is less than 90% of the tax payable by that company for the period, and

(c)   the claimant company is not a small company in relation to the relevant period (TCA 1997, s 958(11)(b)).

Where two companies, at any time on or before the specified return date (the latest date by which the a tax return is to be delivered) for the accounting period of the surrendering company, jointly give notice to the Collector-General in such form as the Revenue may require, then as regards any relevant balance—

(i)   an additional amount of preliminary tax equal to the relevant balance is treated for the purposes of TCA 1997, s 958(4C)(b)(ii) (90% rule to avoid interest charge) to have been paid by the claimant company on the due date for the payment of preliminary tax for the relevant period provided the company pays 100% of the tax payable for the period on or before the specified return date, and

(ii)   the surrendering company is treated as having surrendered the relevant balance to the claimant company and that balance will not be available for use by any other company (TCA 1997, s 958(11)(c), (d)).

A *relevant balance* is the part of a balance specified in the notice given to the Collector-General. A *balance* is the amount represented by the formula A–B where—

A   is the amount of preliminary tax paid by the surrendering company for the relevant period, and

B   is 90% of the tax payable by the surrendering company for that period.

A payment for a relevant balance (a payment by a claimant company to a surrendering company under an agreement relating to an amount of preliminary tax surrendered, being a payment not exceeding that amount) is not to be taken into account in computing profits or losses of either company for corporation tax purposes and is not to be regarded as a distribution or a charge on income for any purposes of the Corporation Tax Acts (TCA 1997, s 958(11)(e)).

The group pooling provision does not affect the liability to corporation tax of any company to which it relates. The amount on which the claimant company would otherwise be liable to pay interest in accordance with TCA 1997, s 1080 (see **15.207**) is to be reduced by any relevant balance deemed to have been paid by it in accordance with (i) above.

Revenue practice regarding loans to participators

TCA 1997, s 438 imposes a charge to income tax at the standard rate on the grossed-up equivalent of a loan or advance made by a close company to a participator or associate of a participator (see **10.204**). Income tax so deducted forms part of the company's corporation tax liability and must be included on the company's corporation tax return. Where a company has been assessed to tax under this section, provision is made for relief in respect of the tax paid in the event that the loan is repaid after the date of the assessment.

Revenue has reviewed the operation of the above provision in the context of the preliminary tax provisions. For the purposes of satisfying a company's preliminary tax obligations for an accounting period, Revenue will not require the company to take account of the provisions of TCA 1997, s 438 with regard to the imposition of the charge to income tax in circumstances where the participator or associate of the participator repays the loan or advance in question by the due date for filing of the company's corporation tax return.

This practice should be relied on only to the extent that the loan arrangements concerned are undertaken in good faith and for purposes other than tax avoidance. It will not apply in the case of "bed and breakfast" type of arrangements where a new loan/ advance is taken out on, or shortly after, repayment of an existing loan/advance. In such cases, Revenue will insist that the provisions of the section be taken into account for preliminary tax purposes. However, in circumstances where it is the practice of a director to operate a current account with the company and this account is cleared annually from the director's own resources (eg, the director's remuneration), such an arrangement will not be regarded as a "bed and breakfast" type arrangement.

In addition, and without prejudice to Revenue's entitlement to review, amend or withdraw its practices from time to time as appropriate, the practice set out above will be subject to ongoing review by the Revenue Commissioners, and Revenue reserves the right to amend or withdraw this practice on foot of such review as respects preliminary tax payments due after such amendment or withdrawal.

15.103.4   Interest on preliminary tax

TCA 1997, s 1080(2) provides that any tax charged by an assessment to income tax or corporation tax is to carry interest at the rate specified in the Table to that subsection (see **15.106.2**) from the due date for that tax until it is paid. When the inspector makes an assessment on a chargeable person (normally after the relevant tax return has been filed), interest is charged on any part of the tax in the assessment (including the preliminary tax element) which was not paid by the appropriate due date (see **15.106**).

15.103.5   Preliminary tax overpaid

The amount of tax paid as preliminary tax for any chargeable period may exceed the liability to tax of the chargeable person for that period. In that case, the amount overpaid is to be repaid to the chargeable person together with interest. The position governing interest is dealt with in TCA 1997, s 865A (see **15.212**).

In relation to interest due to a chargeable person, there is no overpayment of preliminary tax unless the amount paid exceeds the tax finally due as determined after the relevant tax return has been filed. A payment of preliminary tax which is in excess of the minimum payment required, but which is less than the final liability for the current period, does not entitle the chargeable person to any interest.

The rate of interest in respect of repayments of preliminary tax overpaid is 0.011% per day or part of a day.

No interest is payable in respect of an overpayment of preliminary tax if that interest is less than €10 (TCA 1997, s 865A(4)(a)). Interest is receivable without any deduction of tax and is not treated as income for any tax purpose.

15.103.6   Preliminary tax: two taxes on same date

The minimum amount payable as preliminary tax must be determined separately for each tax involved, even where a chargeable person is required to pay preliminary tax for two taxes on the same due date. It is not possible, for interest purposes, to offset an overpayment of preliminary tax for, say, corporation tax against an underpayment of preliminary tax for capital gains tax.

15.104 Corporation tax return

15.104.1 Latest date for return

TCA 1997, s 951(1) requires every chargeable person, as respects a chargeable period, to prepare and file a return for the tax concerned for that chargeable period "on or before the specified return date for the chargeable period". The return must be delivered to the "appropriate inspector". The return must be in a form prescribed by the Revenue Commissioners or in a form used under the authority of the Revenue Commissioners (which may include a return by any electronic, photographic or other process approved by the Commissioners) (TCA 1997, s 950(1)).

The obligation to make the tax return by the specified return date exists whether or not the chargeable person is issued with a return form to complete (TCA 1997, s 951(4)). If a notice to prepare a return is not sent to a company for a chargeable period, the company should obtain a return form, complete it and deliver it to the appropriate inspector by the specified return date. For the exception from the obligation to make the tax return provided by TCA 1997, s 951(6), see below.

The "specified return date" is the latest date by which the relevant tax return for a chargeable period must be delivered to the appropriate inspector if the return is to be treated as filed on time. Failure to file a full and true return of all the particulars required for any tax by the specified return date may make the chargeable person liable to the 5% or 10% late return surcharge based on the amount of the relevant tax (see **15.208**).

TCA 1997, s 950(1) defines *specified return date for the chargeable period*, where a chargeable period is an accounting period (ie, for corporation tax purposes), as the last day of the period of 9 months commencing on the day immediately following the end of the accounting period, but in any event not later than the 21st of the month in which that period of nine months ends. Where the chargeable period is an accounting period which ends on or before the date of commencement of the winding up of a company and the specified return date in respect of that period would otherwise fall on a date after the date of commencement of the winding up but not within a period of 3 months after that date, the date which falls 3 months after the date of commencement of the winding up, but in any event not later than the 21st of the month in which that period of three months ends (TCA 1997, s 950(1) – (c) in the meaning of "specified return date for the chargeable period").

Where the chargeable period is a year of assessment (eg, for capital gains tax purposes) the specified return date is 31 October in the year of assessment following that year (TCA 1997, s 950(1)).

15.104.2 The appropriate inspector

The "appropriate inspector", to whom the chargeable person is required to send the tax return, is normally the inspector from whom the person last received a notice in writing that he is the inspector to whom the taxpayer is required to send the return. If a company has not received any such notice from an inspector, but has previously sent tax returns to a particular inspector, it should send the tax return to that inspector. If the company has no inspector within either of the above descriptions, it should send the tax return to the "inspector of returns" (TCA 1997, s 950(1)).

The *inspector of returns* is an inspector specifically nominated as such by the Revenue Commissioners (TCA 1997, s 950(1)). The inspector of returns is required to take delivery of tax returns from any chargeable person who does not otherwise have an inspector to whom the tax return should be sent. The name and address of the inspector of returns is published annually in Iris Oifigiúil (TCA 1997, s 951(11)(c)).

15.104.3　　Exclusion from tax return obligation

TCA 1997, s 951(6) authorises an inspector, by a notice in writing to a person (who would otherwise be a chargeable person), to exclude that person from the obligation to make a tax return. The notice may state that the person to whom it is given is not required to make a return for such chargeable period or periods as may be specified in the notice or until the happening of some event specified in the notice.

This provision is intended to apply to, say, a company which satisfies the inspector that its income, allowances and other circumstances are such that it is not likely to have any liability to tax for one or more chargeable periods.

Should any company, which has been given a notice excluding it from the obligation to make a return of income, become chargeable to capital gains tax for any year of assessment, that company has an obligation to make a return of its chargeable gains for that year (TCA 1997, s 951(6)(b)).

15.104.4　　Notices to make returns

As already explained, any company which is chargeable to tax for a chargeable period is obliged to prepare and file the appropriate tax return whether or not it receives a notice from the inspector. By virtue of TCA 1997 ss 951(12), 1052 and 1054 (penalties, and increased penalties in the case of a body of persons, for failure to make certain returns etc) are applied to a company which fails to file a return by the specified due date, notwithstanding that it has not received a notice from the inspector. By virtue of TCA 1997, s 951(3), a company which has delivered a return by reason of TCA 1997, s 951(1) is deemed to have been required by a notice under TCA 1997, s 884 (see also **15.205**) to deliver the return and any provision in that section relating to the taking of any action on the failure of a company to deliver a return or statement pursuant to a notice given under the section is to apply to the company, where such a notice has not been given, as if it had been given such notice, on the specified return date for the relevant chargeable period (see **15.205** regarding penalties in TCA 1997 ss 1070 and 1071 for failure to comply with requirements of TCA 1997, s 884).

The effect of the foregoing provisions is to enable the application to self-assessment of other provisions in the Tax Acts which provide for certain actions to be taken when a person does not comply with a notice to make a tax return (in particular, TCA 1997, s 1052 – "penalties for failure to make certain returns etc").

15.104.5　　Foreign accounts/offshore funds

TCA 1997, s 895(6) provides that where, in a chargeable period, a resident person opens, either directly or indirectly, a "foreign account" (or causes to be opened a foreign account in relation to which that person is the beneficial owner of the deposit held in that account), that person is deemed for that period to be a chargeable person for the purposes of TCA 1997, s 950 or 1084 (surcharge for late returns). The return of income which the person is thereby obliged to submit must include the following details in relation to the foreign account:

(a) the name and address of the relevant person with whom the account was opened;

(b) the date on which the account was opened;

(c) the amount of the deposit made in opening the account; and

(d) the name and address of the intermediary, if any, who provided a relevant service in relation to the opening of the account.

A *foreign account* is defined as an account in which a deposit is held at a location outside the State. A *deposit* means a sum of money paid to a person on terms under which it will be repaid with or without interest and either on demand or at a time or in circumstances agreed by or on behalf of the person making the payment and the person to whom it is made.

TCA 1997, s 895(2) provides for certain returns to be made by intermediaries. An *intermed*iary for this purpose is any person carrying on in the State a trade or business in the ordinary course of the operations of which he provides a *relevant service*, ie acting in the State as an intermediary in or in connection with the opening of foreign accounts with relevant persons by or on behalf of residents. A *relevant person* means a person who in the normal course of his trade or business receives or holds deposits.

Every intermediary is obliged, as respects a relevant chargeable period, to prepare and deliver to the appropriate inspector, on or before the specified return date for the chargeable period, a return specifying, in respect of every resident in respect of whom he has acted in the chargeable period as an intermediary in the opening of a foreign account—

(i) the full name and permanent address of the resident;

(ii) the resident's tax reference number;

(iii) the full name and address of the relevant person with whom the foreign account was opened;

(iv) the date on which the account was opened; and

(v) the amount of the deposit made in opening the foreign account (TCA 1997, s 895(2)).

The *specified return date for the chargeable period*, in relation to a chargeable period, means, where the chargeable period is a year of assessment, 31 January in the year following that year, and, where it is an accounting period of a company, the last day of the period of 9 months commencing on the day immediately following the end of the period.

TCA 1997, s 895(3) requires any resident person who has requested an intermediary to provide him with a relevant service to furnish that intermediary with the details required by the intermediary for inclusion in the return to be made to the appropriate inspector. The intermediary is required to take all reasonable care (including the requesting of documentary evidence where necessary) to confirm that the details furnished are true and correct.

Where the intermediary fails—

(a)   to make the required return for any relevant chargeable period;

(b)   to include in the return details of any resident to whom he provided a relevant service in the relevant chargeable period; or

(c)   to take reasonable care to confirm the details required to be furnished to him by a resident to whom he has provided a relevant service,

he will, as respects each such failure, be liable to a penalty of €2,535.

Where a resident fails—

(a)   to furnish details of the kind referred to above to an intermediary who has provided him with a relevant service; or

(b)   knowingly or wilfully furnishes that intermediary with incorrect details of that kind,

he will be liable to a penalty of €2,535.

The *appropriate inspector*, in relation to an intermediary or a resident, is normally the inspector from whom the intermediary or resident last received a notice in writing that he is the inspector to whom the intermediary or resident is required to deliver a return or statement. If an intermediary or resident has not received any such notice from an inspector, the inspector to whom it is customary to deliver such a return or statement is the appropriate inspector. If there is no inspector within either of the above descriptions, the appropriate inspector is the inspector of returns specified in TCA 1997, s 950 (see above).

TCA 1997, s 896 applies similar provisions in relation to investments in offshore funds (as defined by TCA 1997, s 743(1) – see **3.210**) where an interest in such a fund is acquired on or after 1 June 1995.

As respects a material interest in an offshore fund, TCA 1997, s 895 is to apply, with any necessary modifications, where it would not otherwise apply to

(a)   every person carrying on in the State a trade or business in the ordinary course of the operations of which such person acts as an intermediary in, or in connection with, the acquisition of such an interest in the same manner as it applies to every intermediary within the meaning of TCA 1997, s 895(1); and

(b)   to a person resident or ordinarily resident in the State who acquires such an interest, in the same manner as it applies to a person resident in the State opening an account, in which a deposit which he beneficially owns is held, at a location outside the State,

as if in TCA 1997, s 895—

(i)   references to a deposit were references to any payment made by a person resident or ordinarily resident in the State in acquiring such an interest;

(ii)   references to a foreign account were references to such an interest;

(iii)   references, however expressed, to the opening of a foreign account were references to the acquisition of such an interest; and

(iv)   references to a relevant person were references to an offshore fund.

For the above purposes, *offshore fund* has the meaning assigned to it in TCA 1997, s 743(1), ie it may consist of:

(a)   a company resident outside the State;

(b)   a unit trust scheme the trustees of which are not resident in the State; or

(c)   any other arrangements taking effect under foreign law and under which rights in the nature of co-ownership are created,

except that a relevant UCITS within the meaning of TCA 1997, s 893(1) (see **12.809**) is not to be regarded as an offshore fund.

15.104.6   Contents of tax return

TCA 1997, s 951(1)(b) provides that, in the case of any person chargeable to corporation tax for a chargeable period which is an accounting period, the tax return for that period must be in the prescribed form and must contain all such matters and particulars in relation to the period as would be required in a return delivered pursuant to a notice given to the chargeable person by the appropriate inspector under TCA 1997, s 884.

TCA 1997, s 884(2) sets out the matters and particulars which should be included in a corporation tax return, as follows (see also **15.205**):

(a)   the profits of the company computed in accordance with the Corporation Tax Acts—

    (i)   specifying the income taken into account in computing those profits, with the amount from each source,

    (ii)   giving particulars of all disposals giving rise to chargeable gains or allowable losses under the provisions of the Capital Gains Tax Acts and the Corporation Tax Acts and particulars of those chargeable gains or allowable losses, and

    (iii)   giving particulars of all charges on income to be deducted against those profits for the purposes of the assessment to corporation tax (see **4.4**) other than those included in (d) below,

(b)   the distributions received by the company from companies resident in the State;

(c)   payments made from which income tax is deductible and to which the provisions of TCA 1997, s 238(2)-(5) (interest etc not payable out of taxed profits – see **4.303**) apply; and

(d)   all amounts which under TCA 1997, s 438 (loans to participators etc – see **10.204**) are deemed to be annual payments.

A notice under TCA 1997, s 884 may also require the inclusion in the return to be delivered by the company in question of particulars of any surplus ACT carried forward in relation to the company (TCA 1997, s 845B(4)) (see **11.203**).

Every notice under TCA 1997, s 884 may require a return of profits arising in any period during which the company was within the charge to corporation tax together with particulars of distributions received in that period from companies resident in the State.

Every return made under TCA 1997, s 884 must include a declaration to the effect that the return is correct and complete (TCA 1997, s 884(5)).

A return under TCA 1997, s 884 which includes profits which are payments on which the company has borne income tax by deduction must specify the amount of income tax so borne (TCA 1997, s 884(6)). A notice under CTA 1976 s 143 may require the inclusion in the return of particulars of management expenses, capital allowances and balancing charges which have been taken into account in arriving at the profits included in the return (TCA 1997, s 884(7)).

TCA 1997, s 951(1)(a) provides that, in the case of any person chargeable to capital gains tax for a year of assessment, the tax return for that period must be in the prescribed form and must contain all such matters and particulars in relation to the period as would be required in a return delivered pursuant to a notice given to the chargeable person by the appropriate inspector under TCA 1997, s 877.

TCA 1997, s 913 extends the application of TCA 1997, s 877 so as to require an income tax return to give particulars of any chargeable gains in the year of assessment to which the return relates, as well as details of any assets acquired which may give rise to chargeable gains if disposed of at a later date.

15.104.7 "Full and true disclosure"

An important requirement of the self-assessment regime is that the tax return to be delivered by a chargeable person for a chargeable period should contain a full and true disclosure of all material facts necessary for the making of an assessment for the tax concerned for the relevant chargeable period (TCA 1997, s 955(2)). The phrase "a full and true return" is used here, where appropriate, to refer to any tax return giving such a full and true disclosure of all the material facts for the relevant assessment.

Clearly, a tax return must, if it is to be "full and true", disclose all items of income, profits or chargeable gains, as the case may be, in respect of which the person making the return is chargeable to tax for the relevant chargeable period. In principle, the return should correctly state the amount of each item of income, profits or chargeable gains to be taxed. Furthermore, to the extent that any deductions, allowances or reliefs are claimed for the relevant chargeable period, full and correct details must be given of the facts in relation to these deductions, allowances or reliefs.

Where a full and true disclosure as described above has been made for a chargeable period, an assessment for the period may not be made on the chargeable person after the end of four years commencing at the end of the chargeable period in which the return is delivered, and

(i)   no additional tax is payable after the end of that period of four years; and

(ii)   no tax may be repaid after the end of a period of four years commencing at the end of the chargeable period for which the return is delivered,

by reason of any matter contained in the return (TCA 1997, s 955(2)(a)).

Failure to make a full and true return for any chargeable period is likely to have adverse consequences for the chargeable person making a return, for example:

(a)   unless and until a full and true return has been made by or on behalf of a chargeable person, the four year time limit to the period in which an assessment or an amended assessment can be made on that person does not commence to run (see **15.107**);

(b)   failure to file a full and true return may result in interest being charged on any additional tax becoming payable when an assessment is subsequently amended (see **15.108**);

(c)   failure to file a full and true return on or before the return filing date may result in the late return surcharge being imposed if the failure is fraudulent or negligent or the failure is realised but not rectified in good time (see **15.208**); and

(d) other penalties may be imposed if an incorrect return is made negligently or fraudulently (see **15.205**).

15.104.8 Expression of doubt

It will sometimes be the case that a company (or the company's professional adviser who is responsible for completing the person's tax return) will be uncertain as to whether or not a particular fact, circumstance or transaction is material to the making of the assessment for the relevant chargeable period in respect of the return. Alternatively, the company (or adviser) may be uncertain as to the proper law or treatment governing a particular point or matter. The company may not know, therefore, whether or not it is necessary to refer to the fact or to take the matter into account in completing the tax return. It will, as a matter of good practice, be desirable to have the matter resolved at the earliest opportunity. The Revenue Commissioners have set out guidelines for tax practitioners on making enquiries to tax offices.

Where a doubt cannot be resolved in advance, TCA 1997, s 955(4) provides that a chargeable person, say a company, should complete the return to the best of its belief as to the law applicable to, or the treatment for tax purposes of, the matter in doubt. The company is then required to draw the matter in question to the inspector's attention by specifying the doubt.

In any case in which a chargeable company makes an "expression of doubt", in relation to any matter disclosed in its tax return, it is treated as if a full and true disclosure were made regarding that matter. Consequently, the adverse consequences of failing to make a full and true return are avoided.

There is one exception to the "expression of doubt" rule. TCA 1997, s 955(4)(b) states that if the inspector is not satisfied that the chargeable person's doubt is genuine or, alternatively, if the inspector is of the opinion that the chargeable person was acting with a view either to evasion or avoidance of tax, the chargeable person is treated as not making a full and true disclosure with regard to the matter in question. If a chargeable company is not satisfied with the inspector's decision on the genuineness of the doubt or that tax evasion or avoidance is involved, it has the right to appeal to the Appeal Commissioners on this issue.

The Revenue Commissioners have indicated that it is their policy to deal with expressions of doubt as they are raised, even if the matter in doubt does not lead to immediate tax consequences (eg the amount of a loss available for carry forward).

15.104.9 Partnership returns

TCA 1997, s 880 requires a precedent acting partner of a partnership, on receipt of a notice from the inspector, to make a return of partnership income and information relating to chargeable gains (see **13.701**). TCA 1997, s 951(2) deems the precedent partner of any partnership to be a chargeable person for purposes of TCA 1997, s 951. The precedent acting partner is required to deliver the partnership return for each relevant year of assessment no later than the specified return date for that year whether or not a notice to do so has been received from the appropriate inspector.

15.104.10 Late return: surcharge and penalties

If a chargeable person fails to file a return by the specified return date for any of the taxes for any chargeable period, TCA 1997, s 1084 imposes an automatic "late return surcharge" (see also **15.208**). If an incomplete or incorrect return is filed negligently or fraudulently, this surcharge is also imposed unless the errors and/or omissions are corrected and advised to the inspector by the specified return date. The amount of the late return surcharge depends on when the return is submitted. The amount of the surcharge is:

(a)   5% of the amount of tax, subject to a maximum surcharge of €12,695, where the return of income is delivered before the expiry of two months after the specified date; or

(b)   10% of the amount of tax, subject to a maximum surcharge of €63,485, where the return of income is not delivered within two months after the specified date.

There is a relaxation of the surcharge provisions in the case of new business. In such cases delays in filing will be subject to surcharge from the second filing date only. The late return surcharge is calculated normally, without giving any allowance for any preliminary tax which may have been paid.

In addition to the late return surcharge, the Revenue Commissioners may apply to the court for penalties for failure by a chargeable person to file a tax return for any chargeable period or, if fraud or negligence is involved, for filing an incorrect return. The rules relating to the late return surcharge and to the penalties are dealt with in more detail in **15.208**.

15.105   Assessment to corporation tax

15.105.1   Introduction

TCA 1997 ss 954-956 contain rules regarding the making of assessments for tax under the self-assessment procedure and, where appropriate, for amending assessments. These rules are superimposed upon, and modify, earlier provisions for assessments and additional assessments which applied before the introduction of self-assessment.

In principle, corporation tax is charged by the making of an assessment by an inspector of taxes on the chargeable company in respect of its income for the relevant accounting period. However, as indicated in **15.103**, each chargeable company is required to self-assess and pay its preliminary tax by its due date before any assessment is made.

Assessments on income are normally made under such one or more of the Schedules and Cases under which the taxpayer is chargeable to the tax in question.

TCA 1997, s 918(1) provides that, generally, assessments to tax under Schedules D, E and F are to be made by inspectors of taxes or such other officers as the Revenue Commissioners shall appoint for the purpose. In practice, the assessments are made by inspectors of taxes. The inspector making an assessment is required to give the person assessed due notice of every assessment on him and to state the time allowed within which the person may appeal against the assessment (TCA 1997, s 918(2)).

Each assessment to tax must, normally, state the Schedule under which it is made. Where two or more assessments under different Schedules or Cases are contained in the one notice of assessment (as is now the normal practice), the tax payable may be stated in one sum, but the income/profits assessed should be shown under the different Schedules/ Cases. If two or more assessments are contained in the one notice, any notice of appeal by the chargeable person must specify the particular assessment or assessment against which the appeal is made (TCA 1997, s 921(3)).

TCA 1997, s 922(2) provides that, if an inspector does not receive a statement (ie a tax return) from a person liable to the tax, the inspector is required to make an assessment on that person for such an amount of tax which, to the best of the inspector's judgment, ought to be charged for the relevant chargeable period. The inspector is similarly required to make an estimated assessment if not satisfied with any tax return filed or if the inspector has received any information suggesting that the return made may not be a full return (TCA 1997, s 922(3)). Where the inspector or any other Revenue official acting with the knowledge of the inspector issues an assessment in the name of the inspector, that assessment will be deemed to be made by the inspector to the best of his judgment (TCA 1997, s 950(2)).

TCA 1997, s 870(1) provides that an assessment, charge, warrant or other proceeding purporting to be made in accordance with the Income Tax Acts, the Corporation Tax Acts or the Capital Gains Tax Acts is not to be quashed or deemed to be void or voidable "for want of form" nor will it be affected by reason of a "mistake, defect or omission therein" if the assessment is "in substance and in effect in conformity with or according to the intent and meaning of those Acts, and if the person or property charged or intended to be charged or affected thereby is designated therein according to common intent and understanding". TCA 1997, s 870(2) states that, in particular, an assessment will not be impeached by a mistake concerning the name or surname of the taxpayer, the description of any profits or property, or the amount of the tax charged. For cases where the UK equivalent provisions were applied, see *Fleming v London Produce* 44 TC 582; *Hoare Trustees v Gardner* [1978] STC 89, and contrast *Baylis v Gregory* [1987] STC 297.

TCA 1997, s 870 does not apply where the assessment is exactly as the Inspector intended, even if based on an erroneous view of the law or facts (*Bath & West Counties Property Trust Ltd v Thomas* [1978] STC 30). However, the discretionary power of the court under TCA 1997, s 941 extends to making an order that a corrected assessment should be raised (see *IRC v McGuckian* [1994] STC 888, where the Northern Ireland Court of Appeal held that, where an inspector had raised an assessment under the incorrect charging provisions as a result of the withholding of material information by the taxpayer, the court would make an order of this kind). TCA 1997, s 929(1) provides that any person who is assessed more than once in the same year "for the same cause" and "on the same amount" may apply to the Appeal Commissioners to have the double assessment vacated. TCA 1997, s 929(3) provides that where the Revenue Commissioners are satisfied that there has been a double assessment, they are to order the excess assessment to be vacated. TCA 1997, s 929(3) provides for repayment to be made where tax has been paid on foot of double assessments.

TCA 1997, s 929 is a mechanical provision designed to give relief for administrative errors. It is extended by TCA 1997, s 953(10) to cover notices of preliminary tax under the self-assessment procedure. In *Bye v Coren* [1986] STC 393, the Court of Appeal upheld the practice of making alternative assessments in respect of the same receipt; the court indicated that where it happened that both assessments had become final and conclusive, relief would be available under the provision equivalent to TCA 1997, s 929.

The foregoing general rules now need to be considered subject to the rules specific to self-assessment (which modify the general rules in certain respects).

15.105.2   Assessment under rules of self-assessment

The following is an outline of the more important self-assessment principles applying for a chargeable period:

1. the assessment should be made on the chargeable person by the inspector by reference to the details of income, profits, deductions, allowances, reliefs and any other relevant facts included or claimed in the return (except where 2. applies) (TCA 1997, s 954(2));

2. if no tax return is filed by the chargeable person by the relevant return filing date (see **15.104**), or if the inspector is not satisfied with any return filed, the inspector is entitled to make an assessment according to the best of the inspector's judgment (see **15.105.3** below);

3. the inspector is not entitled to make any assessment for a chargeable period before the relevant return filing date for that chargeable period, unless the chargeable person has filed the tax return for that period (TCA 1997, s 954(1));

4. the amount of tax specified as payable in the assessment (after deducting any preliminary tax already paid) should be paid on or before the due date for the tax in the assessment (see **15.106**), except to the extent that a valid appeal is made against any tax assessed which exceeds the tax payable based on the facts disclosed in the relevant tax return (see **15.209**);

5. the inspector is entitled to amend an assessment (or a previously amended assessment) if he finds that the assessment (or amended assessment) does not charge the correct amount of tax (see **15.107.5**);

6. no assessment (or amendment to an assessment) may, in principle, be made more than six years after the end of the chargeable period in which a "full and true" return was filed by the chargeable person (see **15.107.2**); but

7. an assessment may be made at any time without time limit if no return is made for that tax or if any return made is not a "full and true" one (although the six year time limit may be activated from the end of a later chargeable period in which the previous default is fully rectified).

Example 15.105.2.1

On 11 April 2004, Haxall Ltd files its corporation tax return for the year ended 31 December 2003. Tredegar Ltd files its corporation tax return for the same period on 21 September 2004. Tredegar Ltd pays the instalments on the appropriate amount of its preliminary tax for the period by the due dates, 21 November 2003 and 21 June 2004.

The inspector is entitled to make a corporation tax assessment for the year ended 31 December 2003 on Haxall Ltd at any time after 11 April 2004. The tax due on foot of this assessment is, however, not payable by Haxall Ltd until 21 November 2003 and 21 June 2004 (the due dates for payment of the two instalments of preliminary tax – see **5.106.3**).

In the case of Tredegar Ltd, TCA 1997, s 954(1) prevents the inspector making any assessment on it for the year ended 31 December 2003 before 21 September 2004 (the specified return date) since that company's return is only filed on that date.

In practice, inspectors of taxes normally make assessments within a month or two after the relevant tax returns are filed so that the six-year time limit mentioned in 6. above is not normally an issue for the original assessment. This time limit is normally more relevant to the question of an amendment of an assessment. The rules relating to the time limit for assessment are therefore discussed more fully in that context in **15.107.2**, but an example may be useful here to illustrate the time limit in a more straightforward case.

Example 15.105.2.2

The position is as in Example **15.105.2.1** in the case of Haxall Ltd, except that the following alternative situations arise:

1. the corporation tax return for the year ended 31 December 2003 filed on 11 April 2004 is accepted as a full and true return for corporation tax.

2. the company's corporation tax return understated its income for the year ended 31 December 2003 by €11,000, but it corrected this omission by making a return of that income on 10 January 2005.

The consequences of each situation are as follows:

1. The latest date by which the inspector may make the assessment for the year ended 31 December 2003 on Haxall Ltd for corporation tax is 31 December 2010, ie 6 years after the end of the accounting period in which the full and true return was made.

2. The latest date by which the inspector may make the latest assessment for corporation tax is 31 December 2011, ie 6 years after the end of the year ended 31 December 2005 (the period in which the return became a "full and true" return on the correction of the earlier omission).

TCA 1997, s 954(2) requires the inspector to make an assessment for any relevant chargeable period by reference to the particulars contained in the chargeable person's return. This is subject to TCA 1997, s 954(3) which permits the inspector to make an estimated assessment (see **15.105.3** below).

In practice, in most cases of tax returns filed by the specified return date, the inspector makes the relevant assessment on the basis of the facts as disclosed in the return, subject to a routine check to ensure that the return appears to be in order. Thus, the assessment made will be based on the return and will enable any balance of tax or any overpayment to be determined by reference to the information disclosed in the return so that that balance may be demanded, or any overpayment refunded, at an early date. If, on a closer examination of the return, the inspector later considers that the tax has been underassessed, he may make an appropriate amendment of the assessment (see **15.107.5**).

An assessment made on a company by the inspector is normally required to detail the income assessed under the various Schedules and to show the calculation of the company's tax liability for the accounting period assessed after giving allowances and reliefs and after deducting any credits against tax to which the company is entitled. The amount previously paid as preliminary tax for the year is then deducted and any balance of tax due for the period is stated at the foot of the assessment. Alternatively, if the amount of the preliminary tax paid is greater than the amount of the tax assessed for the period, the amount of the repayment due to the company will be shown.

TCA 1997, s 954(5) allows the inspector, in two situations, to state only the amount of tax charged in the assessment without detailing the income assessed. The first of these is where the assessment is made under TCA 1997, s 954(3) for tax estimated by the inspector in a case where no tax return has been filed by the chargeable person (see next paragraph). The second is where the chargeable person has submitted a "voluntary self-assessment" computation showing the amount of the relevant tax payable and where the inspector does not disagree with that computation.

15.105.3   Assessment: no return or inadequate return

TCA 1997, s 954(3) authorises an inspector to make an assessment for a chargeable period for such amount of tax as, according to the best of his judgment, he thinks ought to be assessed. TCA 1997, s 959(2) provides that where the inspector, or a Revenue official acting with the knowledge of the inspector, issues an assessment in the name of the inspector, the assessment will be deemed to have been made by the inspector to the best of his judgment. The inspector is permitted to make the assessment under TCA 1997, s 922 on his own estimate of the tax to be charged in any of the following circumstances:

(a)   the chargeable person has failed to deliver a tax return for the relevant tax on or before the specified return date for the chargeable period;

(b)   the inspector is not satisfied with any return which has been submitted; or

(c)   the inspector has received any information as to the insufficiency of the return (for example, information suggesting that income has been omitted from the return); "information" here includes information received from a member of the Garda Síochána.

The inspector is obliged by TCA 1997, s 954(2) to make the assessment on the income, deductions etc stated in the chargeable person's tax return (assuming one is made by the relevant specified return date) unless the inspector is not satisfied with the return or has any information to suggest that it is not a full and true return.

The grounds on which the inspector may be dissatisfied with a return are not stated, but it is reasonable to suppose that the inspector should have some reasonable cause before he can apply TCA 1997, s 954(3) to make an assessment based otherwise than on the information in the tax return. However, the inspector has the right to query any fact in a return or to make other enquiries to ascertain whether there is any reason to be dissatisfied with the return (TCA 1997, s 956). The inspector's right to make enquiries is discussed further in connection with the amendment of assessments (see **15.107.5**).

15.105.4   Election not to assess

TCA 1997, s 954(4) provides that no assessment is required to be made if the inspector is satisfied that the chargeable person, say a company, has paid all the relevant tax for which it is liable for the accounting period in question. This condition is met if the company has paid the full liability for the relevant tax based on the income and/or chargeable gains of the period as disclosed in the relevant tax return for that period (assuming the inspector is satisfied with that return).

If the inspector applies this provision and decides not to make an assessment for a particular accounting period, he is required to give notice of this decision to the chargeable company. In applying any relevant provision in the Tax Acts, accordingly, the tax actually paid by the chargeable company is treated as if it were paid under an assessment. If, for example, the amount of corporation tax paid as preliminary tax for the year ended 31 December 1997 proves to be greater than the final liability for the period, the company is entitled to receive interest on the tax overpaid as if it were tax paid under an assessment.

The inspector may, notwithstanding the above provision, subsequently decide to make an assessment for any chargeable period if he considers this to be necessary.

15.105.5 Right to require an assessment

TCA 1997, s 954(6) entitles a chargeable person to give a notice in writing to the inspector requiring that an assessment for tax be made, but only if the chargeable person has filed the relevant tax return for the chargeable period. On being given such notice, the inspector is required to make the assessment "forthwith", notwithstanding that the inspector may have given the chargeable person notice of an earlier election under TCA 1997, s 954(4) not to make an assessment.

15.105.6 Appeals against assessments

TCA 1997, s 957(1)(b) provides that no appeal may be made against the amount of any income, profits or gains or the amount of any allowance, deduction or relief specified in an assessment or amended assessment made on a chargeable person where the inspector has determined the amount by accepting without the alteration of, and without departing from the statement or statements or the particular or particulars regarding, income, profits or gains or, as respects capital gains tax, chargeable gains, or allowances, deductions or reliefs specified in the return delivered by the chargeable person. Accordingly, for an assessment based on a return made under TCA 1997, s 954(2), a chargeable company is precluded from denying its own figures or particulars as given in the tax return filed.

As regards an assessment to tax where the amount of any income or profits specified in the assessment differs from the income or profits as disclosed in the relevant tax return, TCA 1997, s 933(1) entitles the chargeable person to appeal to the Appeal Commissioners against the assessment (see **15.209.2**). Similarly, there is a right of appeal under TCA 1997, s 949 where an assessment does not deal properly with the allowances, deductions or reliefs specified in the tax return.

15.106 Payment of tax

15.106.1 Introduction

Normally, corporation tax to be paid is the net tax payable for the chargeable period, ie the total tax charged in the assessment reduced by any credits against that tax, but less the amount paid as preliminary tax.

Alternatively, if the preliminary tax paid exceeds the net tax payable, the amount of that excess is repayable, with interest, to the chargeable person (see **15.103.5.**). In any case in which the tax has been overpaid under the self-assessment system, the Collector-General will normally issue a cheque to the chargeable person shortly after the inspector's assessment based on the return has been issued. It should not be necessary for the chargeable person to take any further action to obtain this repayment.

15.106.2 Rates of interest and interest on tax

TCA 1997, s 1080(2) provides that the interest payable on any tax due and payable (which will include preliminary tax – see also **15.103.4**) by a chargeable person for a chargeable period (accounting period in the case of a company) is to be determined in accordance with paragraph (c) of that subsection.

For the above purposes, *tax* means income tax, corporation tax or capital gains tax, as appropriate (TCA 1997, s 1080(1)). TCA 1997, s 1080 does not accordingly apply to taxes such as PAYE, relevant contracts tax, professional services withholding tax, DIRT and other withholding taxes (such as dividend withholding tax) or exit taxes that are collected by employers and other parties in a fiduciary capacity.

TCA 1997, s 1080(2)(c) provides that the interest to be charged is–

(i) where one of the periods specified in column (1) of the Table to TCA 1997, s 1080(2) (see Table below) includes or is the same as the *period of delay* (the period during which the tax in question remains unpaid), the amount determined by the formula–

$$T \times D \times P$$

where–

T   is the tax due and payable which remains unpaid,

D   is the number of days (including part of a day) forming the period of delay, and

P   is the appropriate percentage in column (2) of the Table opposite the period specified in column (1) of the Table within which the period of delay falls or which is the same as the period of delay, and

(ii) where a continuous period formed by two or more of the periods specified in column (1) of the Table, but not (as in (i) above) only one such period, includes or is the same as the period of delay, the aggregate of the amounts due in respect of each relevant period (see below) which forms part of the period of delay, and the amount due in respect of each such relevant period is to be determined by the formula–

$$T \times D \times P$$

where–

T   is the tax due and payable which remains unpaid,

D   is the number of days (including part of a day) forming the relevant period, and

P   is the appropriate percentage in column (2) of the Table opposite the period specified in column (1) of the Table into which the relevant period falls or which is the same as the relevant period.

TABLE

Period (1)	Percentage (2)
From 6 April 1963 to 31 July 1971	0.0164%
From 1 August 1971 to 30 April 1975	0.0246%
From 1 May 1975 to 31 July 1978	0.0492%
From 1 August 1978 to 31 March 1998	0.0410%
From 1 April 1998 to 31 March 2005	0.0322%
From 1 April 2005 to the date of payment	0.0273%

In relation to a "period of delay" which falls into more than one of the periods specified in column of the above Table, *relevant period* means any part of the period of delay which falls into, or is the same as, a period specified in that column.

In respect of chargeable periods beginning on or after 1 January 2005, the above-described interest position applies as respects tax due and payable by a chargeable person for a chargeable period. This contrasts with the former position whereby the interest provisions applied to "any tax charged by any assessment to tax". The practical effect of the revised position is that when tax is being paid late it will be necessary to calculate and to include the interest arising thereon up to the day of payment; otherwise, part of the tax paid may be allocated against interest accrued leaving part of the tax still outstanding and giving rise to further interest on that part. Previously, in the absence of an assessment (for example in a case where preliminary tax was overdue), it was not necessary to pay interest until an assessment was raised and a demand for interest was received.

For the exceptional penal rate of 2% per month applicable in cases of fraud or neglect in respect of accounting periods beginning before 1 January 2005, see **15.207**.

Interest payable on tax is not allowed as a deduction in computing any income, profits or other gains which are chargeable to income tax, capital gains tax or any other tax. The person paying the interest must pay it without deducting any tax (TCA 1997, s 1080(3)).

All provisions of every enactment, and of the rules of court, so far as they relate to the collection or recovery of tax, apply equally to interest payable on tax as if the interest were a part of the tax. In particular, Bankruptcy Act 1988 s 81 and sections 98 and 285 of the Companies Act 1963 are applied in this way (TCA 1997, s 1080(4)).

15.106.3 Due date for tax charged in assessment

The rules for determining the date on which tax specified in an assessment made on a company is due and payable are contained in TCA 1997, s 958(3), (4C) and (4E). In most cases, this tax refers to the balance of the tax shown in the assessment after deducting the preliminary tax, if any, previously paid in respect of the tax concerned. Obviously, if no preliminary tax was paid, the entire amount of tax charged (after any credits) is payable and, in relation to any such case, any reference to the "balance of the tax" should be read as referring to the entire amount of tax charged (after any credits).

The due date for the balance of the tax assessed is important since it is from this due date that interest on the tax in question begins to run against the chargeable person if and to the extent that the tax is not paid by the due date. TCA 1997, s 1080(2) charges interest on any unpaid tax at the rate specified in the Table to that subsection (see **15.106.2** above) from the relevant due date to the date on which that tax is paid.

The due date for payment of tax by a company differs depending on whether it is fixed under TCA 1997, s 958(3) or 958(4C), (4E). The circumstances in which each subsection applies and the effect on the due date are now outlined. In most cases, TCA 1997, s 958(3) gives the later and therefore more favourable date.

(a) Due date: Assessment made before due date for Preliminary Tax

TCA 1997, s 958(3)(a)(i) deals with the question of the due date for the tax payable by a company for an accounting period in any case where the assessment is made before the due date for paying preliminary tax for the period in question. In any such case, the due date for payment of the tax in the assessment is the same day as the due date for the preliminary tax.

(b) Due date: Assessment made after Preliminary Tax due date – Preliminary Tax requirements met

TCA 1997, s 958(3)(a)(vi) fixes the due date for the balance of the tax payable by a company under an assessment to tax where, and only where, both of the following conditions, as set out in TCA 1997, s 958(4C) and (4E), are met:

(a) the chargeable company has made a payment of preliminary tax in respect of the tax no later than the due date for that preliminary tax; and

(b) the amount paid as preliminary tax is not less than 90% of the corporation tax payable for the accounting period or, in the case of a "small company", not less than the "corresponding corporation tax" for the preceding period.

Where those conditions are met, tax payable for the accounting period in question is due and payable on or before the specified return date (see **15.104.1**) for that period. (For the peculiar effect of this provision on companies in liquidation, see **12.901.3**.) Tax specified in any assessment subsequently made for the accounting period is deemed to have been due and payable on or before the specified return date for that period (TCA 1997, s 958(3)(d)).

Payment of capital gains tax for any year of assessment is due by 31 October in that year as respects chargeable gains arising in the period 1 January to 30 September in that year ("tax payable for the initial period") and, as respects chargeable gains arising in the period 1 October to 31 December in that year, by 31 January in the year following that year ("tax payable for the later period") (TCA 1997, s 958(3)(a)(v)). Tax specified in any assessment subsequently made for the year is deemed to have been due and payable—

(a) as respects tax payable for the initial period, on or before 31 October in the year; and

(b) as respects tax payable for the later period, on or before 31 January in the following year (TCA 1997, s 958(3)(c)(ii)).

(c) Due date: Assessment made after Preliminary Tax due date – Preliminary Tax requirements not met

The provisions of TCA 1997, s 958(4C) and (4E) apply (instead of TCA 1997, s 958(3)(a)(iv)) to determine the due date for the tax specified in an assessment (other than an assessment made before the due date for preliminary tax) in any of the following cases:

(i) the chargeable person failed to make any payment of preliminary tax for the relevant chargeable period,

(ii) the chargeable person's payment of preliminary tax was not made on or before the due date for preliminary tax, or

(iii) the preliminary tax paid proves to be less than the minimum amount required under the 90% or "corresponding corporation tax" test (see **15.103**).

In any such case, the provisions of TCA 1997, s 958(4C) and (4E) deem the tax specified in the assessment to have been due and payable on the due date for the payment of the preliminary tax. In other words, the due date for the tax charged in the assessment is backdated to the preliminary tax due date so that interest on the tax is charged from the preliminary tax date until the actual date of payment.

In any case where a chargeable company has paid preliminary tax later than the due date for that tax, or where the company believes that the preliminary tax paid may be less than the required minimum payment, it would be advisable for the company to file the relevant tax return as early as possible so that the balance due can be assessed by the inspector and paid as soon as possible to minimise the exposure to interest. Alternatively, a further payment of tax may be made without waiting for the assessment.

On the other hand, if the company is satisfied that the amount paid as preliminary tax, although paid late, will prove to be greater than its liability when the assessment is ultimately made, no action is required (other than to ensure that the relevant return is filed no later than the specified return date so as to avoid incurring the late return surcharge).

15.107 Amendment of assessments

15.107.1 Introduction

An inspector may, at any time (except where the six year time limit applies – see below), amend an assessment to tax already made on a chargeable person by making such alterations in the assessment or such additions thereto as the inspector thinks necessary (TCA 1997, s 955(1)). This position applies even if all the tax in the assessment (before the amendment) has been paid, whether any tax repayment has been made to the chargeable person, or whether or not the assessment has been previously amended on one or more occasions. The inspector is required to give the taxpayer notice of the assessment as amended.

Where an inspector discovers—

(a)   that any profits which ought to have been assessed to corporation tax have not been assessed;

(b)   that an assessment to corporation tax is or has become insufficient; or

(c)   that any relief which has been given is or has become excessive,

the inspector is to make an assessment in the amount, or the further amount, which ought in his opinion to be charged (TCA 1997, s 919(5)(b)). Consequent on the introduction of self-assessment, this provision does not apply in respect of accounting periods ending on or after 1 October 1989. All matters which would have been included in an additional first assessment made in accordance with TCA 1997, s 919(5)(b) are to be included in an amendment of the first assessment or assessments made in accordance with TCA 1997, s 955 (self-assessment: amendment of and time limit for assessments – see also **15.206**).

In short, self-assessment works on the basis that there is one assessment (referred to herein as "the original assessment") on each chargeable person for the relevant tax for each chargeable period and that, if necessary, the original assessment may be amended (and the assessment as so amended may be further amended as often as is necessary), whereas under the previous method of assessing tax there could be a first assessment and then one or more additional assessments.

The effect of an amendment to an assessment made under TCA 1997, s 955 may be to alter, or add to, the original assessment in any way which the inspector considers necessary to ensure that the correct amount of tax is charged on the person concerned. In particular, an amendment may be made to include or correct any amount of income, chargeable gains or profits omitted from or included as incorrect amounts in the original assessment, to disallow any incorrect deduction or allowance or to make any other correction necessary to arrive at the proper amount of tax chargeable. An amendment may also be made to reduce the tax chargeable if this is appropriate.

An amendment to an assessment on a company will have been made in most cases because the company has not delivered a full and proper statement (or has delivered an incorrect statement) of its income, profits or chargeable gains in the relevant tax return and the inspector has becomes aware of this fact only after the tax return has been filed. However, the inspector's right to amend the assessment is not restricted to such cases. TCA 1997, s 955(5) permits the inspector to make any amendment which he considers necessary to ensure that the tax stated in the original assessment, or in a previous amendment to the original assessment, is equal to the tax correctly payable by the chargeable person.

15.107.2 Time limit for assessment or amendment of assessment

TCA 1997, s 955(2) places a four year time limit on the right of an inspector to make an assessment or to amend an assessment on any chargeable person for any relevant chargeable period, but subject to a number of important exceptions (see **15.107.3** below).

Under the self-assessment regime, the general rule is that no assessment or amendment to an assessment to tax for any relevant chargeable period may be made any later than four years after the end of the chargeable period in which the chargeable person has filed a "full and true" tax return with the inspector. For example, if X Ltd had filed a full and true corporation tax return for the tax year ended 30 November 2003 on 16 August 2004, the latest date on which the inspector can assess the company to corporation tax for that period, or amend any assessment for that period, is 30 November 2008. The critical date appears to be the date on which the inspector makes or amends the assessment as opposed to the date on which notice of the assessment is served on the taxpayer (*Honig v Sarsfield* [1986] STC 246).

A "full and true" tax return for any chargeable period is a return that contains a full and true disclosure of all material facts necessary for the making of an assessment for the chargeable period for which the return is made.

If the taxpayer fails to file any tax return for a chargeable period for any tax, or if it transpires that the tax return submitted does not contain the required "full and true disclosure" of all the material facts, no time limit at all applies. However, where the original return has not met this condition, the chargeable person may rectify the position by submitting a revised return and, if this results in the necessary full and true disclosure, no assessment or amendment to an assessment for the relevant chargeable period can be made later than six years after the end of the chargeable period in which the revised return is filed.

The provision in TCA 1997, s 955(2) permitting an assessment or amendment of an assessment to be made at any time where there is not such a "full and true return" is of wider application than TCA 1997, s 919 where only in a case of fraud or neglect was it possible to override the [then 10 year] time limit for assessments for chargeable periods before self-assessment. Under self-assessment, even an accidental (and uncorrected) omission or incorrect statement of any material fact from or in the relevant tax return may enable an assessment to be made or amended after the end of the four-year period.

15.107.3 Amendments permitted after four years

TCA 1997, s 955(2)(b) lists five circumstances in which an amendment which may be made to an assessment at any time, whether before or after the end of the four year limit following the chargeable period in which a full and true return was given. An assessment for any relevant chargeable period may be amended at any time:

(i)   if the relevant tax return for that chargeable period does not contain a full and true disclosure of all material facts necessary for making the assessment of the tax concerned (see above);

(ii)   if an amendment is necessary to give effect to a determination of an appeal against an assessment (see **15.209.6**);

(iii)   to take account of any fact or matter arising due to an event occurring after the return is submitted;

(iv)   to correct a calculation error; or

(v)   to correct a mistake of fact whereby the assessment does not properly reflect the facts disclosed by the chargeable person.

15.107.4 Appeals regarding time limit

Where a chargeable company is aggrieved by an assessment (or an amendment to an assessment) because it considers that the inspector is prevented by the four year time limit from making that assessment or amendment, it is entitled under TCA 1997, s 955(3) to appeal to the Appeal Commissioners on that ground. This is a special form of appeal against an assessment and is to be distinguished from the type of appeal on other grounds discussed in **15.209**.

An appeal under TCA 1997, s 955(3) is likely to occur in a case where the assessment or amendment is made by the inspector after the end of the appropriate four year period because he considers that the chargeable company did not make a full and true disclosure of all the material facts relevant to the assessment in question. The company may dispute this in which event it may require the Appeal Commissioners to decide the matter.

If the Appeal Commissioners rule in favour of the chargeable company on this matter, the assessment or the assessment as amended is void and ineffective. In the case of an appeal against an amendment made after the end of the six year period to an earlier assessment, if the chargeable company's successful appeal on the time limit point is the only point in dispute, the assessment as it stood before the disputed amendment will stand (if not under appeal for other reasons). If the Appeal Commissioners decide in favour of the inspector, the assessment or the amended assessment stands good (if not under appeal for other reasons).

A chargeable person may be dissatisfied with the determination of the Appeal Commissioners in relation to an appeal made on the grounds that the assessment (or amendment of an assessment) was made after the end of the six-year period. In any such case, the chargeable person may invoke TCA 1997, s 942 (which applies to any appeal against an assessment) to require the point to be reheard by the Circuit Court judge (see **15.209.13**).

15.107.5 Inspector's right to make enquiries and amend assessments

TCA 1997, s 956(1) permits the inspector to make such enquiries or to take any other action which he thinks necessary, within the powers given to him by the Tax Acts, to examine the figures, statements and other particulars given in the chargeable person's tax return. This position applies whether or not the inspector has previously accepted all or some of the particulars stated in the return.

If as a result of these enquiries or other action, the inspector ascertains that the return is not accurate or complete in any respect, or if he is not satisfied that it is accurate or complete, he may make such amendment to a previous assessment as he considers necessary. Alternatively, if no assessment has yet been made, the inspector may make the assessment to reflect his own estimate of the correct position.

The inspector's right to make enquiries or to take any other actions to examine the particulars in a chargeable person's tax return for any relevant chargeable period is subject to the same four-year time limit as applies to the making of an assessment (see above). No enquiries or other actions may be made after the end of the four years unless the inspector has reasonable grounds for believing (at the time he makes these enquiries) that the return is inaccurate due to being completed in a fraudulent or negligent manner.

TCA 1997, s 956(2) entitles any chargeable person who believes that any enquiries or other actions taken by an inspector are debarred by the four-year time limit to appeal to the Appeal Commissioners against the inspector's action. The chargeable person, say a company, makes this appeal by giving written notice to the inspector to the effect that it considers that the four-year time limit applies. This notice must be given within 30 days from the date on which the inspector makes the enquiry or takes the action. Pending the determination of this appeal, the inspector's enquiry or action will then be suspended as is any action required of the chargeable person by the inspector.

The Appeal Commissioners' decision on this issue is directed only to the question as to whether or not the inspector has reasonable grounds for believing that any alleged inaccuracy in the chargeable person's return for the relevant chargeable period is due to fraud or negligence. The Appeal Commissioners are not required to determine whether there is actually any fraud or negligence, but only whether there are any reasonable grounds for the belief that there might be.

If the Appeal Commissioners decide the matter in favour of the chargeable person, the inspector cannot continue the enquiry or action which is the subject of the appeal. If the decision is in favour of the inspector, the enquiry or action may proceed.

15.107.6 Appeal against amended assessment

A chargeable person is entitled under TCA 1997, s 957(3) to appeal against an amended assessment (except in the case of an amendment made by the inspector to reflect the result of the determination of an appeal), but subject to the following restrictions:

(a) no appeal may be made against the amount of any item of income or profits, deduction or relief specified in the amended assessment which does not differ from the amount of the said item stated in the chargeable person's return for the relevant tax (TCA 1997, s 957(1)(b)); and

(b)   no appeal may be made against any item of income, profits, deduction or relief specified in the amended assessment which has been agreed with the inspector before the amendment to the assessment was made (TCA 1997, s 957(1)(c)).

Subject to these restrictions, a chargeable company may appeal against any additions to, deletions from, or alterations in, the assessment as a result of the amendment. For example, a right of appeal exists against any new income assessed, any deductions or reliefs disallowed or any increase in the amount of any income assessed. The chargeable company has no further right, however, to appeal against the matters other than the above mentioned additions to, deductions from, or alterations in, the assessment than it would have had if the assessment had not been amended (TCA 1997, s 957(3)).

Before any appeal may be made against any amended assessment for a relevant accounting period, a chargeable company must have filed its tax return for that period and must have paid an amount of tax at least equal to the tax which would be payable if the amended assessment were made based only on the data in the company's tax return (TCA 1997, s 957(2)).

15.108   Payment of tax in amended assessments

15.108.1   Introduction

On the amendment of an assessment, tax additional to that under the assessment before the amendment may become payable. Alternatively, there may be a reduction in the tax previously charged by the assessment so that, assuming the tax previously charged was paid, a repayment is due to the chargeable person.

TCA 1997, s 958(8) provides for the fixing of the due date of any additional tax chargeable as the result of an amendment of an assessment (other than an amendment made to reflect the result of the determination of an appeal – see **15.209.6**). The additional tax may be payable as the result of the first amendment to the original assessment or may result from a second or subsequent amendment to a previously amended assessment.

15.108.2   Additional tax on first amendment

In the case of a first amendment to an original assessment for any relevant chargeable period, TCA 1997, s 958(8) provides that the due date (for interest purposes) for the additional tax resulting from the amendment is either:

(a)   the date which is one month after the date of the amendment, but only where the chargeable person has filed a "full and true" return for the relevant tax before the date of the original assessment; or

(b)   in any other case, the same day as the due date for the tax charged by the original assessment.

In other words, the due date (from which interest on any additional tax resulting from the amendment is charged) is backdated to the due date for the tax charged by the original assessment if either no tax return was filed before the date on which the original assessment was made, or the relevant tax return filed before that date was not a "full and true" return. For the purposes of the above rules, a "full and true" return is one containing a full and true disclosure of all material facts necessary for the making of the assessment (see **15.107.2**).

The position as described in (a) above is clearly more favourable to the chargeable person. For this to apply, the full and true return may be given to the inspector at any time before the original assessment is made. It is not essential for this purpose that the return is filed before the specified return date. Even though filing the return after that date gives rise to the late return surcharge (see **15.208**), late filing does not prevent (a) applying provided that the "full and true" return is filed before the inspector makes the original assessment.

In relation to the position in (b), reference may be made to the discussion in **15.106.3**. As indicated there, the due date for the tax in the original assessment depends on whether or not a chargeable company had properly discharged its preliminary tax obligation for the relevant accounting period (ie, whether or not it had paid, on or before the due date for the preliminary tax, the required minimum amount of preliminary tax).

In summary, taking the rules of TCA 1997, s 958(8) together with the rules for the due date for the original tax assessed, the due date for any additional tax resulting from the first amendment to the original assessment made on a company, and the circumstances in which each date applies, are as set out in the following table:

Circumstances in which additional tax due date applies	Due date for additional tax
If full and true return filed before original assessment	One month after date of amendment
If full and true return not filed before original assessment, but preliminary tax requirements met	One month from the date the assessment was made
Any other case	Due date for payment of preliminary tax

The most favourable (ie, latest) due date will apply if the company had made a tax return including a full and true disclosure of all material facts necessary for the making of the original assessment and that return was filed before the original assessment was made. Where that is the case, it will not be necessary to consider the preliminary tax obligation.

Where the corporation tax return was not filed before the date of the original assessment, or where the return so filed did not contain a full and true disclosure of all material facts necessary for the making of the original assessment, it is then necessary to consider whether the company had made an adequate payment of preliminary tax and, if so, whether that payment was made no later than the preliminary tax due date. Unless the answer to both questions is in the affirmative, interest will be charged on any additional tax in the amended assessment from the due date for preliminary tax to the date on which the additional tax is paid.

As to whether or not a corporation tax return filed before the original assessment contained the required full and true disclosure, see **15.104.7**. The inspector may initially have accepted the return as satisfying that requirement but may subsequently discover that the requirement was not in fact satisfied. In that event, the due date for the additional tax is no longer one month from the date of the amendment but is, instead, backdated so that interest will run from the due date for tax charged in the original assessment. That date will be determined by reference to the preliminary tax test: if the test is satisfied, the date is one month from the date of the assessment; if not, it is the date on which preliminary tax was due.

As noted in **15.104.8**, where in delivering a return which is in all other respects a full and true return, the chargeable company expresses a genuine doubt on any matter in the return, that return is deemed by TCA 1997, s 958(8) to be a full and true return.

15.108.3 Additional tax on second and subsequent amendment

In the case of a second or subsequent amendment to an original assessment made on a company, TCA 1997, s 958(8) provides that the due date (for interest purposes) for any additional tax becoming payable as the result of the amendment is either:

(a) one month after the date of the second or subsequent amendment, but only in a case in which the chargeable company had filed a full and true return for the relevant tax before the date of the amendment immediately preceding the current amendment; or

(b) the same day as the due date for the tax charged by the assessment before the current amendment if the full and true return was not filed before the date of the preceding amendment.

In other words, the due date for any additional tax in the second or subsequent amendment is decided in a manner similar to that for a first amendment except that the most favourable due date (ie, one month after the date of the second, or subsequent, amendment) depends on whether or not a full and true return had been made before the most recent previous amendment (eg, before the second amendment where the additional tax arises from a third amendment). Otherwise, TCA 1997, s 958(8) provides that the due date for the additional tax in the second, or subsequent, amendment is the same date as the due date for the tax in the most recent previous amendment.

As with the position for tax due on a first amendment of an assessment, the position for a second amendment can also be summarised, as follows:

Circumstances in which additional tax due date applies	Due date for additional tax
If full and true return filed before first amendment	One month after date of second amendment
If full and true return not filed before first amendment, but preliminary tax requirements met	Due date for tax charged by assessment before current amendment
Any other case	Due date for payment of preliminary tax

For any additional tax as the result of a third amendment, the due date is determined under the above table by substituting "third" for "second" in the *Due date for additional tax* column and by substituting "second" for "first" in each place in the first column (and with corresponding substitutions for any further amendments).

Should a company discover that a tax return it has submitted does not contain the required full and true disclosure, it should remedy the position at the earliest opportunity by supplying the necessary correcting information in writing to the inspector. Even if the inspector has at that time made the original assessment, the submission of the correcting information before the first amendment (which will be too late to affect that amendment) will be effective to give the latest possible due date for any additional tax on a second or later amendment.

15.2 ADMINISTRATION

15.201 Introduction

15.201.1 The Revenue Commissioners

TCA 1997, s 849(2) provides that all duties of tax (meaning income tax, corporation tax and capital gains tax) are to be under the care and management of the Revenue Commissioners.

The general administration and control of taxes is vested in the Revenue Commissioners. The Board of Revenue Commissioners consists of three Commissioners appointed by the Taoiseach and subject to the control of the Minister for Finance. Part II of the Revenue Commissioners Order 1923 provides that the Revenue Commissioners are bound to obey all orders and instructions of the Minister for Finance. The powers and duties of the Revenue Commissioners are provided for in TCA 1997, s 849 as respects tax.

TCA 1997, s 849(3) provides that the Revenue Commissioners may do all such acts as may be deemed necessary and expedient for raising, collecting, receiving, and accounting for the taxes in the like and as full and ample a manner as they are authorised to do in relation to any other duties under their care and management, and, unless the Minister for Finance otherwise directs, are to appoint such officers and other persons for collecting, receiving, managing, and accounting for any duties of the taxes as are not required to be appointed by some other authority.

All such appointments are to continue in force, notwithstanding the death, or ceasing to hold office, of any Revenue Commissioner, and the holders are to have power to execute the duties of their respective offices, and to enforce, in the execution thereof, all laws and regulations relating to the taxes in every part of the State (TCA 1997, s 849(4)).

The Commissioners may suspend, reduce, discharge, or restore, as they see cause, any such officer or person (TCA 1997, s 849(5)).

Any act or thing required or permitted by TCA 1997, s 849 or any other statute to be done by the Revenue Commissioners in relation to the taxes may be done by any one Revenue Commissioner (TCA 1997, s 849(6)).

The Revenue Commissioners are required to appoint from their officers a person to act as Collector-General, to hold office at their will and pleasure (TCA 1997, s 851(1)).

The duty of the Collector-General is to collect and levy the taxes from time to time charged in all assessments to income tax (TCA 1997, s 851(2)), corporation tax (TCA 1997, s 973(1)) and capital gains tax (TCA 1997 976(1)) and of which particulars have been transmitted to him by any of the provisions of the Tax Acts.

The Commissioners may nominate persons from their officers or employees to exercise on behalf of the Collector-General and at his direction any or all of the powers and function conferred on him by any of the provisions of the Tax Acts (TCA 1997, s 851(3)(a)). The powers and functions of the Collector-General may also by exercisable on his behalf and at his direction by persons nominated by the Revenue Commissioners from their officers or employees (TCA 1997, s 851(3)(b)).

15.201.2   Inspectors of taxes

Inspectors of taxes are also appointed by the Revenue Commissioners and they and all other officers or persons employed in the execution of the Tax Acts are required to observe and follow the orders, instructions and directions of the Revenue Commissioners (TCA 1997, s 852(1)). The Revenue Commissioners may revoke an appointment made by them under TCA 1997, s 852.

15.201.3   Appeal Commissioners

Appeal Commissioners are appointed by the Minister for Finance with authority to execute such powers and to perform such duties as are assigned to them by the Income Tax Acts (TCA 1997, s 850(1)). The principal function of the Appeal Commissioners is to hear appeals by taxpayers aggrieved by tax assessments made upon them by an inspector of taxes or such other officer appointed by the Revenue Commissioners for the purpose (TCA 1997, s 933(1)(a) and TCA 1997, s 945(1)). The Appeal Commissioners are also required to hear appeals by taxpayers against decisions of inspectors of taxes and other officers of the Revenue Commissioners on other matters, such as claims for exemption from tax, reliefs and allowances under the Tax Acts and claims for repayment of tax.

15.202   Particulars to be supplied by new company

Every company which is incorporated in the State or which commences to carry on a trade, profession or business in the State is obliged under TCA 1997, s 882, within thirty days of—

(a) the date on which it commences to carry on a trade, profession or business, wherever carried on;

(b) the date at which there is a material change in information previously delivered by the company under TCA 1997, s 882; and

(c) the giving of a notice to the company by an inspector requiring a statement under TCA 1997, s 882,

to deliver to the Revenue Commissioners a statement in writing containing particulars of—

(i) in the case of every company—

(I) the name of the company,

(II)   the address of the company's registered office,

(III)   the address of its principal place of business,

(IV)   the name and address of the secretary (see below) of the company,

(V)   the date of commencement of the trade, profession or business,

(VI)   the nature of the trade, profession or business,

(VII)   the date up to which accounts relating to such trade, profession or business will be made up, and

(VIII) such other information as the Revenue Commissioners consider necessary for the purposes of the Tax Acts;

(ii)   in the case of a company which is incorporated, but not resident, in the State—

(I)   the name of the territory in which the company is, by virtue of the law of that territory, resident for tax purposes (where "tax" means tax imposed in that territory and which corresponds to income tax or corporation tax),

(II)   where TCA 1997, s 23A(2) does not apply by virtue of TCA 1997, s 23A(3) (certain "relevant companies" treated as not resident – see **3.106.2**), the name and address of the company referred to in TCA 1997, s 23A(3) which carries on a trade in the State, and

(III)   where the company is treated as not resident in the State by virtue only of TCA 1997, s 23A(4) (treated as not resident in accordance with a tax treaty – see **3.106.2**)—

(A) if the company is controlled by another company the principal class of the shares of which is substantially and regularly traded on one or more than one recognised stock exchange in a relevant territory or territories (see **3.106.2**), the name of the other company and the address of its registered office, and

(B) in any other case, the name and address of the individuals who are the ultimate beneficial owners (see below) of the company, and

(iii)   in the case of a company which is neither incorporated nor resident in the State but which carries on a trade, profession or business in the State—

(I)   the address of the company's principal place of business in the State,

(II)   the name and address of the agent, manager, factor or other representative of the company, and

(III)   the date of commencement of the company's trade, profession or business in the State (TCA 1997, s 882(2)).

Secretary includes any person mentioned in TCA 1997, s 1044(2) (the secretary of the company or other officer, by whatever name called, performing the duties of secretary) and, in the case of a company not resident in the State, the agent, manager, factor or other representative of the company.

Failure to deliver a statement under TCA 1997, s 882 renders the company in question liable to a penalty of €630 and, if the failure continues after judgment has been given by the court before which proceedings for the penalty have been commenced, to a further penalty of €60 for each day on which the failure so continues. In addition, the secretary of the company will be liable to a separate penalty of €125 (TCA 1997, s 1073

– see **15.205**). Failure to deliver a statement may also result in the Revenue Commissioners, or such officer of the Revenue Commissioners as is nominated by them for the purpose, giving a notice in writing to the registrar of companies (within the meaning of the Companies Act 1963) stating that the company has failed to deliver the statement.

In (ii)(III)(A) above, control is to be construed in accordance with TCA 1997, s 432 (see **2.401**). In (ii)(III)(B), ultimate beneficial owners in relation to a company means—

(i)   the individual or individuals who have control of the company, or

(ii)   where a person, whether alone or together with other persons, who controls the company controls it in the capacity as the trustee of a settlement (see **2.301.4**), any person who in relation to the settlement—

(I)   is the settlor (see **2.301.4**), or

(II)   is, or can under any scheme or arrangement reasonably expect to become, a beneficiary under the settlement, or

(III)   where such settlor or beneficiary is a company, the ultimate beneficial owners of that company.

The above provisions of TCA 1997, s 882 apply, in the case of companies which were incorporated on or after 11 February 1999, as on and from that day and, in the case of companies incorporated before 11 February 1999, as on and from 1 October 1999.

15.203   Notice of liability to corporation tax

Every company chargeable to corporation tax for any accounting period and which has not made a return of its profits for that period must, not later than one year after the end of that period, give notice to the inspector that it is so chargeable (TCA 1997, s 883). Failure to give such notice renders the company liable to a penalty of €630 and, if the failure continues after judgment has been given by the court before which proceedings for the penalty have been commenced, to a further penalty of €60 for each day on which the failure so continues. In addition, the secretary of the company will be liable to a separate penalty of €125 (TCA 1997, s 1074).

15.204   Application of administrative provisions

15.204.1   Introduction

The provisions specified below apply to corporation tax as well as to income tax, and, where appropriate, to capital gains tax. Prior to the enactment of TCA 1997, the equivalent provisions, which were provisions of the Income Tax Acts only, were deemed by CTA 1976 s 147(1) and (2) to apply for corporation tax purposes as they applied for income tax purposes.

15.204.2   Time limit for repayment claims

TCA 1997, s 865 *Limit of time for repayment claims*

TCA 1997, s 865 provides for a general right to repayment of tax overpaid and repayment is to be made irrespective of whether the tax was overpaid under an assessment or otherwise and irrespective of whether or not there was a mistake or otherwise on the part of the taxpayer. Repayment is conditional on a valid claim being made within four years from the end of the period to which it relates. This time limit applies to repayment claims in respect of the year 2003 and onwards. TCA 1997, s 865 applies to repayment claims made on or after 31 October 2003.

Where, in respect of an accounting period (or a year of assessment if capital gains tax is concerned), a company has paid, whether directly or by deduction, an amount of tax that is not due from it or which, but for an error or mistake in a return or statement made by it for the purposes of an assessment to tax, would not have been due from the company, it will be entitled to repayment of the tax so paid (TCA 1997, s 865(2)). This is referred to as the "general right to repayment" provision and it encompasses two broad categories of refundable tax, being:

(a)   tax "which is not due"; and

(b)   tax resulting from a return made by the taxpayer but which would not have been due if that return had not contained an error or mistake.

With regard to (a), this refers mainly to overpayments of tax arising as a result of "a mistaken assumption made by the Revenue Commissioners". Thus, a PAYE taxpayer who has been incorrectly taxed through excessive deductions for a number of years would fall into this category. Other examples would include "correlative adjustments" and overpayments of preliminary tax.

In strictness, it would seem that a correlative adjustment here would include only tax treaty cases where the associated enterprises article provides that the correlative adjustment "shall" be made (eg, Australia, Denmark, the US), or possibly might include cases where the adjustment "may" be made (eg, Czech Republic). In other cases where there is no such stipulation in the associated enterprises article (eg, Japan), the Irish Revenue may agree to make the adjustment. In these cases it must be doubtful that the tax in question "is not due" as any adjustment is made by way of concession. This will have some relevance to the question of interest on the refund: since the interest position here would be governed by TCA s 865A(2) rather than s 865A(1), it would rarely become payable in view of the 93 day provision (see **15.212**) whereby interest doesn't begin to run until 93 days after the claim is a valid claim.

In relation to correlative adjustments, the treaty-based position on time limits would take precedence over domestic law. Thus, in the case of Australia, the time limit is six years from the end of the period to which the adjustment relates. In the case of Denmark, no time limit is prescribed.

Interest on refunds arising from a mistaken assumption of the Revenue is governed by TCA s 865A(1) and runs from the date the tax in question had been paid (or from the end of the chargeable period in question).

With regard to (b) above, this essentially replaces the error or mistake provision of TCA 1997, s 930 but both provisions operate in parallel up to 31 December 2004 and a claim under either is possible during that period. The starting date for TCA 1997, s 865(2) claims is, however, 31 October 2003, the date appointed by order of the Minister.

TCA s 930 is deleted with effect from a date specified in a Ministerial order (in fact, 31 December 2004) and this relates to claims for periods ending before 2005 so that previous time limits remain in place for claims made on or before 31 December 2004 for such periods. Accordingly, for a period up to 31 December 2004, an error or mistake claim should be possible under either TCA 1997, s 865(2) or TCA 1997, s 930. There is no entitlement to interest on a refund of tax resulting from a TCA 1997, s 930 claim; refunds in these cases do not constitute repayments of preliminary tax. Under TCA 1997, s 865(2) on the other hand, a repayment resulting from an error or mistake claim, which must be made within four years from the end of the period to which the claim relates, does attract interest – in theory only, however, since the 93 day rule (see **15.212**) will mean that payments of interest will not often arise.

No repayment may be made in the absence of a valid claim made for that purpose (TCA 1997, s 865(3)). A statement or return required to be delivered by the company in accordance with any provision of the Tax Acts or the Capital Gains Tax Acts for an accounting period will be treated as a valid claim where all the information reasonably required by the Revenue Commissioners to enable them to determine if and to what extent a repayment of tax is due to the company for the period is contained in the statement or return (TCA 1997, s 865(1)(b)(i)). In the absence of such information in the statement or return, a claim to repayment will be treated as valid when that information has been furnished by the company (TCA 1997, s 865(1)(b)(ii)).

In the cases of certain tax treaties (eg, the Ireland-US treaty – see **14.111.4**), where the associated enterprises article has been invoked to adjust the profits of a company in one of the treaty countries, there is a requirement to make a compensating adjustment by way of a reduction in the tax payable by the company in the other treaty country. To the extent that a repayment claim arises from a such a *correlative adjustment* (defined as an adjustment of profits under the terms of a tax treaty), the claim will not be regarded as a valid claim until the quantum of the correlative adjustment is agreed in writing by the competent authorities of the two Contracting States (TCA 1997, s 865(1)(b)(iii)).

A claim to repayment by a company must be made—

(a)   in the case of a claim made on or before 31 December 2004 (but not in a case dealt with in TCA 1997, s 865(2) – see further below), in relation to any accounting period ending on or before 31 December 2002, within ten years;

(b)   in the case of a claim made on or after 1 January 2005 in relation to any accounting period ending on or before 31 December 2002, within four years; and

(c)   in the case of a claim made in accordance with TCA 1997, s 865(2) (see below) or in the case of any kind of claim in relation to any accounting period ending on or after 1 January 2003, within four years,

after the end of the accounting period to which the claim relates (TCA 1997, s 865(4)). Where there is an entitlement to a repayment of tax under any provision other than TCA 1997, s 865 and that provision provides for a shorter period within which the claim is to be made (eg, two-year time limit for claims in respect of trading losses – see **4.101-3**), or for a longer such period, that period is to apply in place of the relevant period mentioned in (a) to (c) above (TCA 1997, s 865(5)).

The ten-year time limit mentioned in (a) above refers to cases other than those dealt with in TCA 1997, s 865(2). Examples of cases not falling within that subsection would be TCA s 481 (relief for investment in films – see **7.3**), s 482 (relief for expenditure on significant buildings and gardens – see **3.203.6**), and s 848A (donations to approved bodies – see **3.203.8**). Relief in these cases is subject to a claim being made. Until a claim is made, the tax in question is due (and the issue is clearly not one of error or mistake) so that these kinds of cases do not fall within TCA 1997, s 865(2). Claims relating to these cases would have been subject to the former ten-year time limit and this will continue to be the position for periods ending before 2003 and provided the claim is made by 31 December 2004.

Claims referred to in (c) above relate to (i) claims made solely under the "general right to repayment" provision in s 865(2), for whatever period, and (ii) any other kind of claim relating to a period beginning on or after 1 January 2003. The time limit is four years.

15.204.3 Other administrative provisions

TCA 1997, s 207(3) *Repayment claims*

Every claim under TCA 1997, s 207 (rents of properties belonging to hospitals and other charities) is to be verified by affidavit, and proof of the claim may be given by the treasurer, trustee, or any duly authorised agent.

TCA 1997, s 207(4) *False or fraudulent claim for exemption*

Any person making a false or fraudulent claim under TCA 1997, s 207 (rents of properties belonging to hospitals and other charities) in respect of interest, annuities, dividends or shares of annuities charged or chargeable under Schedule C shall forfeit the sum of €125.

TCA 1997, s 211(5) *Repayment claims*

Every claim under TCA 1997, s 211 (friendly societies) is to be verified by affidavit, and proof of the claim may be given by the treasurer, trustee, or any duly authorised agent.

TCA 1997, s 211(6) *False or fraudulent claim for exemption*

Any person making a false or fraudulent claim under TCA 1997, s 211 (friendly societies) in respect of interest, annuities, dividends or shares of annuities charged or chargeable under Schedule C shall forfeit the sum of €125.

TCA 1997, s 213(3) *Repayment claims*

Every claim under TCA 1997, s 213 (trade unions) is to be verified by affidavit, and proof of the claim may be given by the treasurer, trustee, or any duly authorised agent.

TCA 1997, s 213(4) *False or fraudulent claim for exemption*

Any person making a false or fraudulent claim under TCA 1997, s 213 (trade unions) in respect of interest, annuities, dividends or shares of annuities charged or chargeable under Schedule C shall forfeit the sum of €125.

TCA 1997, s 483 *Relief for certain gifts*

Relief is given in respect of income tax or corporation tax for the year of assessment or accounting period in which a person makes a gift of money to the Minister for Finance for use for any purpose for or towards the cost of which public moneys are provided. For income tax purposes, the amount is to be deducted from or set off against any income of the person chargeable to tax for the year of assessment and tax is, where necessary, to be discharged or repaid accordingly.

In the case of a company, the amount of the gift is deemed to be a loss incurred by it in a separate trade in the accounting period in which the gift is made.

TCA 1997, s 860 *Administration of oaths*

A Peace Commissioner may administer an oath to be taken before a commissioner by any officer or person in any matter relating to the execution of the Tax Acts, and an Appeal Commissioner may administer an oath to be taken before the Appeal Commissioners under the Tax Acts by any officer or person in any matter touching the execution of the Tax Acts.

TCA 1997, s 861(1) *Forms*

Every assessment, duplicate, charge, bond, warrant, notice of assessment or of demand, or other document required to be used in assessing, charging, collecting and levying tax is to be in accordance with the forms prescribed from time to time in that behalf by the Revenue Commissioners, and a document in the form prescribed and supplied or approved by them is to be valid and effectual.

TCA 1997, s 862 *Exercise of powers under Tax Acts*

Anything required under the Tax Acts to be done by the Minister for Finance may be signified under the hand of the Secretary-General, a Deputy Secretary or an assistant secretary of the Department of Finance.

TCA 1997, s 863 *Loss or destruction of assessments and other documents*

In the case of any loss, destruction, defacement or damage to any assessment, duplicate of assessment or any return or other document relating to income tax, corporation tax or capital gains tax so as to be illegible or useless, the Revenue Commissioners, inspectors, the Collector-General or other officers having powers in relation to income tax, corporation tax or capital gains tax may do all such acts and things as they might have done, which will be as valid and effectual as they would have been, had the assessment or duplicate not been made or the return or other document had not been made or furnished.

TCA 1997, s 868 *Execution of warrants*

Warrants issued under the authority of the Tax Acts are to be executed by the respective persons to whom they are directed and members of the Garda Síochána are to aid in the execution of the Tax Acts.

TCA 1997, s 869 *Delivery, service and evidence of notices and forms*

Any notice, form or other document which under the Tax Acts or the Capital Gains Tax Acts is to be given, served, sent or delivered to or on a person by the Revenue Commissioners or by an inspector or other officer of the Revenue Commissioners may be either delivered to the person or left, in the case of a company, at its registered office or place of business. Such notice, form or other document may be served by post addressed, in the case of a company, to it at either its registered office or its place of business.

Any notice which under the above mentioned Acts is authorised or required to be given by the Revenue Commissioners may be signed and given by any duly authorised officer of the Revenue Commissioners and, if so signed, is to be as valid and effectual as if signed under the hands of the Revenue Commissioners and given by them.

Prima facie evidence of any notice given under the Acts by the Revenue Commissioners or an inspector or other officer of the Revenue Commissioners may be given in any proceedings by production of a document purporting to be a copy of the notice, and it will not be necessary to prove the official positions or position of the persons or person by whom the notice purports to be given or, if it is signed, the signatures or signature or that the persons or person signing and giving it were or was authorised to do so.

Notices to be given or delivered to, or served on, the Appeal Commissioners are to be valid and effectual if given or delivered to or served on their Clerk.

TCA 1997, s 870 *Effect of want of form, error etc, on assessments, charges, warrants and other proceedings*

An assessment, charge, warrant or other proceeding which purports to be made in pursuance of the Income Tax Acts, the Corporation Tax Acts or the Capital Gains Tax Acts may not be quashed or deemed to be void or voidable for want of form, or be affected by reason of mistake, defect, or omission therein, if the same is in substance and effect in conformity with or according to the intent and meaning of those Acts, and if the person or property charged or intended to be charged or affected thereby is designated therein according to common intent and understanding.

An assessment or a charge made on an assessment may not be impeached or affected by reason of a mistake therein as to the name or surname of a person liable, or the description of any profits or property, or the amount of the tax charged, or by reason of any variance between the notice and the certificate of charge or assessment. However, in cases of charge, the notice of charge is to be duly served on the person intended to be charged, and the notice and certificate are respectively to contain, in substance and effect, the particulars on which the charge is made, and every such charge is to be heard and determined on its merits by the Appeal Commissioners.

TCA 1997, s 873 *Proof that person is commissioner or officer*

In any proceedings under or arising out of the Tax Acts before a court or person empowered to take evidence, *prima facie* proof of the fact that any person was a commissioner or officer may be given by proving that, at the time when any matter in controversy in any such proceedings arose, that person was reputed to be or had acted as a commissioner or officer.

TCA 1997, s 874 *Limitation of penalties on officers employed in execution of Tax Acts and Capital Gains Tax Acts*

A commissioner, sheriff, county registrar, clerk, inspector, assessor, or Collector who acts, or is employed, in the execution of the Tax Acts or the Capital Gains Tax Acts, is not to be liable to any penalty in respect of such execution except as provided for in those Acts. Where any civil or criminal proceedings, against any officer or person employed in relation to any duty of income tax, corporation tax or capital gains tax on account of the seizure or detention of any goods, is brought to trial, and a verdict or judgment is given thereupon against the defendant, if the court or judge certifies that there was probable cause for the seizure, the plaintiff is not to be entitled to any damages besides the goods seized, or their value, nor to any costs, and the defendant is not to be liable to any punishment.

TCA 1997, s 875 *Exemption of appraisements and valuations from stamp duty*

No appraisement or valuation given or made in pursuance and for the purposes of the Tax Acts or the Capital Gains Tax Acts may be liable to any stamp duty.

TCA 1997, s 886 *Obligation to keep certain* records

Every person who on his own or on another's behalf carries on or exercises any trade, profession or other activity the profits or gains of which are chargeable under Schedule D, or who is chargeable to tax under Schedule D or Schedule F in respect of any source of income, or who is chargeable to capital gains tax in respect of chargeable gains, is obliged to keep, or cause to be kept on his behalf, such records as will enable true returns to be made, for the purposes of income tax, corporation tax and capital gains tax, of such profits or gains or chargeable gains.

The records must be kept on a continuous and consistent basis, ie the entries therein must be made in a timely manner and be consistent from one year to the next.

Where accounts are made up to show the profits or gains from any such trade, profession or activity or in relation to a source of income, of any person, that person must retain, or cause to be retained on his behalf, linking documents. For this purpose, *linking documents* means documents that are drawn up in the making up of accounts and which show details of the calculations linking the records to the accounts.

Records includes accounts, books of account, documents and any other data maintained manually or by electronic, photographic or other process, relating to—

(a) all sums of money received and expended in the course of the carrying on or exercising of a trade, profession or other activity and the matters in respect of which the receipt and expenditure take place,

(b) all sales and purchases of goods and services where the carrying on or exercising of a trade, profession or other activity involves the purchase or sale of goods or services,

(c) the assets and liabilities of the trade, profession or other activity referred to in (a) or (b), and

(d) all transactions which constitute an acquisition or disposal of an asset for capital gains tax purposes.

Records required to be kept or retained by virtue of TCA 1997, s 886 are to be kept in written form in an official language of the State, or, subject to TCA 1997, s 887(2) (use of electronic data processing – records may be stored, maintained, transmitted, reproduced or communicated by any electronic, photographic or other process approved of by the Revenue Commissioners and subject to such conditions as they may impose) by means of any electronic, photographic or other process.

Linking documents and records kept in accordance with the above described provisions must be retained by the person required to keep the records for a period of 6 years after the completion of the transactions, acts or operations to which they relate or, in the case of a person who fails to comply with TCA 1997, s 951(1) (self-assessment – obligation to made a return – see **15.104**), requiring the preparation and delivery of a return on or before the specified return date for a year of assessment, until the expiry of a period of 6 years from the end of the year of assessment in which a return has been delivered showing the profits or gains or chargeable gains derived from the said transactions, acts or operations.

The above requirement regarding linking documents will not require the retention of linking documents and records in respect of which the inspector notifies in writing the person who is required to retain them that retention is not required, or will not apply to the books and papers of a company which have been disposed of in accordance with section 305(1) of the Companies Act 1963.

Any person who fails to comply with the above provisions in respect of any records or linking documents in relation to a return for any year of assessment will be liable to a penalty of €1,520. The penalty will not be imposed, however, if it is proved that no person is chargeable to tax in respect of the profits or gains for that year of assessment.

TCA 1997, s 898 *Furnishing copies of rates and producing valuations to inspector*

For the purpose of assessing tax chargeable under Schedule D, where required by notice in writing from an inspector, the secretary or clerk to a rating authority, or the person acting as such, is obliged to transmit to the inspector true copies of the last county rate or municipal rate made by the authority for its rating area or any part thereof.

TCA 1997, s 901 *Delivery of books and papers relating to tax*

A person who has in his custody or possession any books or papers relating to income tax or corporation tax must within one month after notice in writing from the Revenue Commissioners requiring him to do so, deliver them to the person named in the notice, and if he fails to do so, he will incur a penalty of €60 for every such offence.

TCA 1997, s 928(1) *Particulars of sums to be collected*

After assessments to income tax have been made, the inspectors are to transmit particulars of the sums to be collected to the Collector-General for collection.

TCA 1997, s 929 *Double assessment*

Vacation of second assessment made by error or mistake in relation to the same year of assessment or the same accounting period for the same cause and on the same account.

TCA 1997, s 947 *Appeals against determinations under* TCA 1997 ss 98 *(treatment of premiums etc as rent),* 99 *(charge on assignment of lease granted at undervalue) and* 100 *(charge on sale of land with right to reconveyance) –* see **3.209** and **3.208**.

TCA 1997, s 998 *Recovery of moneys due*

Every sum due in respect of income tax, corporation tax and capital gains tax and every fine, penalty, or forfeiture incurred in connection with income tax is to be deemed to be a debt due to the Minister for Finance for the benefit of the Central Fund and is to be payable to the Revenue Commissioners and may (without prejudice to any other mode of recovery thereof) be sued for and recovered by action, or other appropriate proceeding, at the suit of the Attorney General in any court of competent jurisdiction.

TCA 1997, s 1004 *Unremittable income*

Where proof is given to the Revenue Commissioners which satisfies them that particular income cannot, by reason of legislation in the country in which it arises or of executive action of that country, be remitted to the State, the Revenue Commissioners may, for the purposes of collection, treat the assessment of any amount which includes that income as if it did not include that income, subject to that treatment being terminated as and when the Revenue Commissioners cease to be satisfied as described above.

TCA 1997, s 1049 *Receivers appointed by the court*

Receiver having the direction and control of any property in respect of which income tax or corporation tax is charged is assessable and chargeable to tax in like manner and to the like amount as would be assessed and charged if the property were not under the direction and control of the court.

TCA 1997, s 1055 *Penalty for assisting in making incorrect return etc*

Any person who assists in or induces the making or delivery for the purposes of income tax or corporation tax of any return, account, statement or declaration which he knows to be incorrect is to be liable to a penalty of €630.

TCA 1997, s 1056 *Penalty for false statement made to obtain allowance*

Without prejudice to any other penalty to which he may be liable, a person is to be guilty of an offence under TCA 1997, s 1056 if—

(a) in relation to his liability to tax for a year of assessment, he knowingly makes any false statement or false representation—

    (i) in any return, statement or declaration made with reference to income tax or corporation tax, or

    (ii) for the purpose of obtaining any allowance, reduction, rebate or repayment of tax, or

(b) in relation to liability to income tax or corporation tax of any other person for a year of assessment, he knowingly and wilfully aids, abets, assists, incites or induces that other person—

    (i) to make or deliver a false or fraudulent account, return, list, declaration or statement with reference to property, profits or gains or to tax, or

    (iii) unlawfully to avoid liability to tax by failing to disclose the full amount of his income from all sources (TCA 1997, s 1056(2)).

A person guilty of an offence under TCA 1997, s 1056 is to be liable:

(a) on summary conviction where the amount of the specified difference is—

    (i) less than €1,520, to a fine not exceeding 25% of the amount of the specified difference or, at the discretion of the court, to a term of imprisonment not exceeding 12 months or to both,

    (ii) equal to or greater than €1,520, to a fine not exceeding €1,520 or, at the discretion of the court, to a term of imprisonment not exceeding 12 months or to both, or

(b) on conviction on indictment where the amount of the specified difference is—

    (i) less than €6,345, to a fine not exceeding 25% of the amount of the specified difference or, at the discretion of the court, to a term of imprisonment not exceeding 2 years or to both,

(ii)   equal to or greater than €6,345 but less than €12,695, to a fine not exceeding 50% of the amount of the specified difference or, at the discretion of the court, to a term of imprisonment not exceeding 3 years or to both,

(iii) equal to or greater than €12,695 but less than €31,740, to a fine not exceeding the amount of the specified difference or, at the discretion of the court, to a term of imprisonment not exceeding 4 years or to both,

(iv)   equal to or greater than €31,740 but less than €126,970, to a fine not exceeding twice the amount of the specified difference or, at the discretion of the court, to a term of imprisonment not exceeding 8 years or to both,

(v)   equal to or greater than €126,970, to a fine not exceeding twice the amount of the specified difference and to a term of imprisonment not exceeding 8 years (TCA 1997, s 1056(3)).

The *specified difference* referred to above is the difference between—

(a)   the amount of tax payable in relation to the liability to income tax or corporation tax of a person or, as the case may be, of another person, for a year of assessment; and

(b)   the amount which would have been the amount so payable if—

(i)   any statement or representation referred to in (a) above in relation to TCA 1997, s 1056(2) had not been false,

(ii)   any account, return, list, declaration or statement referred to in (b)(i) above in relation to TCA 1997, s 1056(2) had not been false or fraudulent, or

(iii) the full amount of income referred to in (b)(ii) above in relation to TCA 1997, s 1056(2) had been disclosed.

TCA 1997, s 1078(4) and (6)-(8) (Revenue offences) are, with any necessary modifications, to apply for the purposes of TCA 1997, s 1056 as they apply for the purposes of that section. Thus, section 13 of the Criminal Procedure Act 1967 is to apply in relation to an offence under TCA 1997, s 1056 as if in lieu of the penalties specified there the penalties described above were specified. In any proceeding under TCA 1997, s 1056, a return or statement delivered to an inspector or other officer of the Revenue Commissioners under any provisions of the Tax Acts and purporting to be signed by any person is to be deemed, until the contrary is proved, to have been so delivered, and to have been signed by that person. Proceedings in respect of an offence under TCA 1997, s 1056 may be instituted within 10 years from the date of the commission of the offence or incurring of the penalty, as the case may be. Section 1 of the Probation of Offenders Act 1907 will not apply in relation to offences under TCA 1997, s 1056.

TCA 1997, s 1056 does not apply to a declaration given under section 2 or 3 of the Waiver of Certain Tax, Interest and Penalties Act 1993 by reason only of any false statement or false representation being made in relation to subsection (3)(a)(iii) of the said section 2 (waiver of certain tax and related interest and penalties) or subsection (6)(b)(III) or the said section 3 (waiver of certain interest and penalties in respect of certain tax), as the case may be.

TCA 1997, s 1057 *Fine for obstruction of officers in execution of duties*

Fine of €125 on any person or person in that person's employ who obstructs, molests or hinders an officer or any person employed in relation to any duty of income tax or corporation tax in the execution of his duty, or of any of the powers or authorities by law given to the officer or person, or any person acting in the aid of an officer or any person so employed.

TCA 1997, s 1058 *Refusal to allow deduction of tax*

A person refusing to allow a deduction of income tax or corporation tax authorised by the Tax Acts to be made out of any payment is to forfeit the sum of €60, and every agreement for payment of interest, rent, or other annual payment in full without allowing any such deduction will be void.

TCA 1997, s 1066 *False evidence: punishment as for perjury*

If any person on examination on oath or in any affidavit or deposition authorised by the Tax Acts wilfully and corruptly gives false evidence, or wilfully and corruptly swears any matter or thing which is false or untrue, he is, on conviction, to be subject and liable to such punishment to which persons convicted of perjury are subject and liable.

TCA 1997, s 1067 *Admissibility of statements and documents in criminal and tax proceedings*

Statements made or documents produced by or on behalf of a person are not inadmissible in any such proceedings mentioned below by reason only that it has been drawn to his attention that:

(a)   in relation to income tax or corporation tax the Revenue Commissioners may accept pecuniary settlements instead of instituting proceedings; and

(b)   though no undertaking can be given as to whether or not the Revenue Commissioners will accept such a settlement in the case of any particular person, it is their practice to be influenced by the fact that a person has made a full confession of any fraud or default to which he has been a party, and has given full facilities for investigation

and that he was or may have been induced thereby to make the statements or produce the documents.

The proceedings referred to above are:

(a)   any criminal proceedings against the person in question for any form of fraud or wilful default in connection with or in relation to income tax or corporation tax; and

(b)   any proceedings against him for the recovery of any sum due from him, whether by way of tax, fine, forfeiture or penalty, in connection with or in relation to income tax or corporation tax.

TCA 1997, s 1068 *Failure to act within the required time*

For the purposes of Part 47 Ch 1 (penalties, offences, interest on overdue tax etc), a person is to be deemed not to have failed to do anything required to be done within a limited time if he did it within such further time, if any, as the Commissioners or officer concerned may have allowed, and where a person had a reasonable excuse for not doing anything required to be done, he is to be deemed not to have failed to do it if he did it without unreasonable delay after the excuse had ceased.

TCA 1997, s 1069(2) *Evidence of income for purposes of* TCA 1997 Part 47 Ch 1 *(penalties, offences, interest on overdue tax etc)*

Any assessment no longer variable by the Appeal Commissioners on appeal, or by the order of any court, is to be sufficient evidence that the income in respect of which income tax or corporation tax is charged in the assessment arose or was received as stated therein.

TCA 1997, s 1070 *Saving for criminal proceedings*

The provisions of the Tax Acts may not affect any criminal proceedings for any felony or misdemeanour.

TCA 1997, s 1081 *Effect on interest of reliefs given by discharge or repayment*

Where for any year of assessment or accounting period relief from any tax referred to in TCA 1997, s 1080(2) (income tax, corporation tax or capital gains tax – see **15.106.2**) is given to any person by a discharge of any of that tax, such adjustment is to be made of the amount of interest payable under that subsection in relation to that tax, and such repayment is to be made of any amounts of interest previously paid under the subsection in relation to the tax, as are necessary to secure that the total sum, if any, paid or payable under the subsection in relation to the tax is the same as it would have been if the tax discharged had never been due and payable.

Where relief from tax paid for any year of assessment or accounting period is given to any person by repayment, that person may require that the amount repaid is to be treated, as far as possible, as if it were a discharge of the tax charged on him (whether alone or together with other persons) by any assessment for the same year. The relief may not, however, be applied to any assessment made after the relief was given and it may not be applied to more than one assessment so as to reduce, without extinguishing, the amount of tax charged thereby (TCA 1997, s 1081(1)).

No relief, whether by way of discharge or repayment may be treated as affecting tax charged by an assessment to—

(a)   income tax or any income tax due and payable unless it is a relief from income tax;

(b)   corporation tax or any corporation tax due and payable unless it is a relief from corporation tax; or

(c)   capital gains tax or capital gains tax due and payable unless it is a relief from capital gains tax (TCA 1997, s 1081(2)).

The provisions of the Tax Acts specified below apply in relation to proceedings for the recovery of penalties relating to income tax and corporation tax. The provisions are as follows:

TCA 1997, s 1052(4) *Proceedings for recovery of penalties for failure to make certain returns etc*

In proceedings for recovery of a penalty incurred in relation to a return of income—

(a) a certificate signed by an officer of the Revenue Commissioners, certifying that he has examined his relevant records and that it appears from them that a stated notice was duly given to the defendant on a stated day, is to be evidence until the contrary is proved that that person received the notice;

(b) a certificate signed by an officer of the Revenue Commissioners, certifying that he has examined his relevant records and that it appears from them that during a stated period a stated notice or precept has not been complied with by the defendant, is to be evidence until the contrary is proved that the defendant did not during that period comply with that notice or precept;

(c) in the case of proceedings relating to a return referred to in TCA 1997, s 879 (returns of income) or s 880 (partnership returns), a certificate signed by an officer of the Revenue Commissioners, certifying that he has examined his relevant records and that it appears from them that, during a stated period, a stated return was not received from the defendant, is to be evidence until the contrary is proved that the defendant did not, during that period, deliver that return;

(d) a certificate signed by an officer of the Revenue Commissioners, certifying that he has examined his relevant records and that it appears from them that during a stated period the defendant has failed to do a stated act, furnish stated particulars or deliver a stated account in accordance with any of the provisions specified in TCA 1997 Schedule 29 column 3, is to be evidence until the contrary is proved that the defendant did so fail;

(e) a certificate certifying as provided in (a), (b), (c) or (d) and purporting to be signed by an officer of the Revenue Commissioners or an inspector may be tendered in evidence without proof and is to be deemed until the contrary is proved to have been signed by such officer or inspector.

TCA 1997, s 1059

Power to add penalties to assessments – where an increased rate of income tax or corporation tax is imposed as a penalty, the penalty and increased rate of tax may be added to the assessment, and collected and levied in like manner as any tax included in such assessment may be collected and levied.

TCA 1997, s 1061

Recovery of penalties – a duly authorised officer of the Revenue Commissioners may sue in his own name by civil proceedings for the recovery of a penalty under TCA 1997, s 305, s 783, s 886 or ss 1052-1060 in the High Court as a liquidated sum and the provisions of section 94 of the Courts of Justice Act 1924 are to apply accordingly.

For the purpose of the above-mentioned proceedings, a certificate signed by a Revenue Commissioner certifying the following facts, namely, that a person is an officer of the Revenue Commissioners and that he has been authorised by them for the above mentioned purpose is to be evidence until the contrary is proved.

TCA 1997, s 1062

Proceedings for certain penalties – proceedings may be instituted for the recovery of any penalty recoverable under the Tax Acts, notwithstanding that the amount cannot be definitely ascertained because the amount of income tax or corporation tax by reference to which such penalty is to be calculated has not been finally ascertained. If, at the hearing of such proceedings the amount of the tax has not been fully ascertained, the Court may, if it is of opinion that such penalty is recoverable, adjourn such proceedings and may not give any judgment or make any order for the payment of such penalty until the amount of such tax has been finally ascertained.

TCA 1997, s 1063

Time limit for recovery of fines and penalties – proceedings for the recovery of any fine or penalty incurred under the Tax Acts in relation to or in connection with income tax may, subject to TCA 1997, s 1060 (see above), be begun at any time within 6 years after the date on which such fine or penalty was incurred.

TCA 1997, s 1065

Mitigation and application of fines and penalties – the Revenue Commissioners may, in their discretion, mitigate any fine or penalty, or stay or compound any proceedings for recovery thereof, and may also, after judgment, further mitigate the fine or penalty, and may order any person imprisoned for any offence to be discharged before the term of his imprisonment has expired. The Minister for Finance may mitigate any such fine or penalty, either before or after judgment.

Where, however, a fine or penalty is mitigated or further mitigated after judgment, the amount or amounts so mitigated may not be greater than 50% of the amount of the fine or penalty.

Moneys arising from fines, penalties and forfeitures, and all costs, charges and expenses payable in respect thereof or in relation thereto respectively, are to be accounted for and paid to the Revenue Commissioners or as they direct.

15.205 Returns

Under the self-assessment system (see **15.104**), every company chargeable to corporation tax in respect of an accounting period is obliged to prepare and deliver to the appropriate inspector on or before the specified return date a return in the prescribed form of all such matters and particulars in relation to the accounting period as would be required to be contained in a return delivered on foot of a notice given by the appropriate inspector to that company under TCA 1997, s 884. In practice, since the introduction of self-assessment, the question of the giving of a notice by an inspector under TCA 1997, s 884 is of less significance than was previously the case.

TCA 1997, s 884(2) provides that a company may be required by a notice served on it by an inspector or other officer of the Revenue Commissioners to deliver to the officer, within the time limited by the notice, a return containing certain matters and particulars. In view of the obligation, under the self-assessment regime, on every company chargeable to corporation tax to make a return without the giving of a notice, the giving of such a notice is likely to be a relatively rare occurrence. TCA 1997, s 884(2) nevertheless remains of particular importance as it sets out the matters and particulars which should be included in a corporation tax return. These are as follows:

(a)   the profits of the company computed in accordance with the Corporation Tax Acts—

(i) specifying the income taken into account in computing those profits, with the amount from each source,

(ii) giving particulars of all disposals giving rise to chargeable gains or allowable losses under the provisions of the Capital Gains Tax Acts and the Corporation Tax Acts and particulars of those chargeable gains or allowable losses, and

(iii) giving particulars of all charges on income to be deducted against those profits for the purposes of the assessment to corporation tax (relevant only in relation to distributions made before 6 April 1999 see **4.4**) other than those included in (d) below,

  (b) the distributions received by the company from companies resident in the State and (in respect of such distributions made before 6 April 1999) the tax credits to which the company is entitled in respect of those distributions;

  (c) payments made from which income tax is deductible and to which the provisions of TCA 1997, s 238(3)-(5) (interest etc not payable out of taxed profits – see **4.303**) apply; and

  (d) all amounts which under TCA 1997, s 438 (loans to participators etc – see **10.204**) are deemed to be annual payments.

Every notice under TCA 1997, s 884 may require a return of profits arising in any period during which the company was within the charge to corporation tax together with particulars of distributions received in that period from companies resident in the State and of tax credits to which the company is entitled in respect of those distributions.

Every return made under TCA 1997, s 884 must include a declaration to the effect that the return is correct and complete (TCA 1997, s 884(5)).

A return under 884 which includes profits which are payments on which the company has borne income tax by deduction must specify the amount of income tax so borne (TCA 1997, s 884(6)). A notice under TCA 1997, s 884 may require the inclusion in the return of particulars of management expenses, capital allowances and balancing charges which have been taken into account in arriving at the profits included in the return (TCA 1997, s 884(7)).

The disposals required to be included in a return in accordance with (a)(ii) above include disposals deemed under certain capital gains tax provisions not to be such. TCA 1997 ss 586 and 587 (see **9.404** – company reorganisation by exchange of shares and **9.405** – company reconstructions and amalgamations) treat disposals involved in certain reorganisations and reconstructions as not being disposals for capital gains tax purposes. Such disposals by a company must, however, be included in the corporation tax return made by the company for the accounting period in which they occur (TCA 1997, s 884(3)).

TCA 1997, s 913(3), (4) and (5)(b) (power to demand information about the acquisition of assets) deal with returns and information for the purposes of capital gain tax. A company may, by virtue of TCA 1997, s 884(8), be required by notice issued under those provisions to supply particulars of any assets acquired by it in the period specified in the notice, including particulars of the person from whom the asset was acquired and of the consideration for the acquisition, not including any assets exempted by TCA 1997, s 607 (government and other securities) or TCA 1997, s 613 (miscellaneous exemptions) (see **9.102.15**) or any assets acquired as trading stock.

Particulars of any acquisition deemed by TCA 1997, s 586 or 587 (see above) not to be an acquisition for capital gains tax purposes must be included. These provisions are to apply in relation to a notice under TCA 1997, s 884 as they apply in relation to a notice under TCA 1997, s 913.

Where a company which has been required by TCA 1997, s 884 to deliver a return fails to deliver the return, or where the inspector is not satisfied with the return delivered, an authorised officer may serve on the company a notice requiring it to do any of the following things, that is:

(a) to deliver to the inspector or authorised officer copies of such accounts, including balance sheets, of the company as may be specified or described in the notice, within such period as may be specified therein, including, where the accounts have been audited, a copy of the auditor's certificate;

(b) to make available, within such time as may be specified in the notice, for inspection by an inspector or by an authorised officer, all such books, accounts and documents in the possession or power of the company as may be specified or described in the notice, being books, accounts and documents which contain information as to profits, assets or liabilities of the company (TCA 1997, s 884(9)(b)).

The inspector or authorised officer may take copies of, or take extracts from, any books, accounts or documents made available for his inspection under TCA 1997, s 884(9). An *authorised officer* means an inspector or other officer of the Revenue Commissioners authorised by them in writing to exercise the powers conferred on them by TCA 1997, s 884(9).

If a company has been required by notice served under TCA 1997, s 884 to deliver a return and it fails to comply with that notice, it will be liable to a penalty of €630 and where the failure continues after judgment has been given by the court before which proceedings for the penalty have been commenced, to a further penalty of €60 for each day on which the failure so continues (TCA 1997, s 1071(1)(a)). In addition, the secretary of the company will be liable to a separate penalty of €125 (TCA 1997, s 1071(1)(b). Where, however, the failure continues after the expiration of one year from the date on which notice was served, the above-mentioned penalties will be €1,265 and €250 respectively (TCA 1997, s 1071(2)).

Where, at any time later than three months after the time at which a return is required to be made in accordance with TCA s 884, a company has not paid any penalty to which it is liable under TCA s 1071(1)(a) or (2) for failing to make the return, the company secretary will, in addition to any penalty to which he is liable under TCA 1997, s 1071, be liable to pay such amount of any penalty to which the company is so liable as is not paid by the company (TCA 1997, s 1071(2A)). The secretary will be entitled to recover from the company a sum equal to the amount of any penalty so paid.

Where a company fraudulently or negligently:

(a) delivers an incorrect return under the provisions of TCA 1997, s 884;

(b) makes any incorrect return, statement or declaration in connection with any claim for any allowance, deduction or relief in respect of corporation tax; or

(c) submits to an inspector, the Revenue Commissioners or the Appeal Commissioners any incorrect accounts in connection with the ascertainment of the company's liability to corporation tax,

the company will be liable to a penalty of €630 or, in the case of fraud, €1,265, and the amount, or, in the case of fraud, twice the amount, of the difference between (i) and (ii) below. The secretary will be liable to a separate penalty of €125, or, in the case of fraud, €250 (TCA 1997, s 1072(1)). The difference mentioned above is the difference between:

(i) the amount of corporation tax payable by the company for the accounting period or periods comprising the period to which the return, statement, declaration or accounts, relate; and

(ii) the amount which would have been the amount so payable if the return, statement, declaration or accounts had been correct (TCA 1997, s 1072(2)).

Where any return, statement, declaration or accounts was or were made neither fraudulently nor negligently and it comes to the notice of the company that it or they was or were incorrect, then, unless the error is remedied without unreasonable delay, the return, statement, declaration or accounts is or are to be treated as having been negligently made or submitted by it (TCA 1997, s 1072(3)).

Where a company fails to meet its obligations to furnish information as required by TCA 1997, s 882 (see **15.202**), it becomes liable to a penalty of €630 and, if the failure continues after judgment has been given by the court before which proceedings for the penalty have been commenced, to a further penalty of €60 for each day on which the failure so continues (TCA 1997, s 1073(1)(a)). The company secretary will also be liable for a separate penalty of €125 (TCA 1997, s 1073(1)(b)).

Where, at any time later than three months after the time at which a statement is required to be delivered in accordance with TCA 1997, s 882, a company has not paid any penalty to which it is liable under TCA 1997, s 1073(1)(a) for failing to deliver the statement, the company secretary will, in addition to any penalty to which he is liable under TCA 1997, s 1073(1)(b), be liable to pay such amount of any penalty to which the company is so liable as is not paid by the company (TCA 1997, s 1073(2)(a)). The secretary will be entitled to recover from the company a sum equal to the amount of any penalty so paid.

For the purposes of TCA 1997 ss 1071-1073, *secretary* includes the company secretary or other officer (by whatever name called) performing the duties of secretary and, in the case of a company which is not resident in the State, the agent, manager, factor or other representative of the company. In the case of a company the secretary of which is not an individual resident in the State, "secretary" includes an individual resident in the State who is a director of the company (TCA 1997, s 1076(1)).

TCA 1997, s 1078(5) provides that where an offence, including failure to comply with any provision requiring the furnishing of a return of income, profits or gains etc, is committed by a company and is shown to have been committed with the consent or connivance of any person who, at the time of the offence, was a director, manager, secretary or other officer of the company, or a member of the committee of management or controlling authority of the company, that person is also to be regarded as being guilty of the offence and may be proceeded against and punished accordingly.

Any return under the Corporation Tax Acts is to be in such form as the Revenue Commissioners prescribe (TCA 1997, s 861(2)(b)).

15.206 Assessments to corporation tax

Assessments to corporation tax are to be made by an inspector (TCA 1997, s 919(1)). Where a company on whose profits corporation tax is to be assessed is resident in the State, the tax is to be assessed on the company, and where the company is not so resident, the tax is to be assessed on the company in the name of any agent, manager, factor or other representative of the company (TCA 1997, s 919(2)).

The inspector is to give notice to the company assessed, or, in the case of a non-resident company, to the agent, manager, factor or other representative of the company assessed, of every assessment made by him (TCA 1997, s 919(3)).

Where a company makes default in the delivery of a statement in respect of corporation tax, or the inspector is not satisfied with a statement which has been delivered, or has received any information as to its insufficiency, the inspector is to make an assessment on the company concerned in such sum as, according to the best of the inspector's judgment, ought to be charged on that company (TCA 1997, s 919(4)).

If an inspector discovers—

(a) that any profits which ought to have been assessed to corporation tax have not been assessed;

(b) that an assessment to corporation tax is or has become insufficient; or

(c) that any relief which has been given is or has become excessive,

the inspector is to make an assessment in the amount, or the further amount, which ought in his opinion to be charged (TCA 1997, s 919(5)(b)). Consequent on the introduction of self-assessment, this provision does not apply in respect of accounting periods ending on or after 1 October 1989. All matters which would have been included in an additional first assessment made in accordance with TCA 1997, s 919(5)(b) are to be included in an amendment of the first assessment or assessments made in accordance with TCA 1997, s 955 (self-assessment: amendment of and time limit for assessments – see **15.107.1-107.2**).

Subject to any provision allowing a longer period, and with effect from 1 January 2005 (the date from which the four-year time limit came into effect), an assessment to corporation tax may not be made more than four years after the end of the accounting period to which it relates (TCA 1997, s 919(5)(c)). However, where any form of fraud or neglect has been committed by or on behalf of any company in connection with or in relation to corporation tax, an assessment may be made on that company at any time for any accounting period for which, by reason of the fraud or neglect, corporation tax would otherwise be lost to the Exchequer (TCA 1997, s 919(5)(d)). Other exceptions to the application of the four-year time limit for making an assessment on a company are as follows:

(i) where a return of income does not contain a full and true disclosure;

(ii) to give effect to the outcome of an appeal against an assessment;

(iii) to take account of a matter arising after the making of a return of income;

(iv) to correct an error in calculation;

(v)   to correct a mistake in circumstances where the correction results in aligning the assessment with the position as disclosed by the company.

An objection to the making of an assessment on the ground that the time limited for making it has expired may only be made on appeal from the assessment (TCA 1997, s 919(5)(e)).

For the foregoing purposes, *neglect* means negligence or a failure to give any notice, to make any return, statement or declaration, or to produce or furnish any list, document or other information required by or under the enactments relating to corporation tax. A company will, however, be deemed not to have failed to do anything required to be done within a limited time if it did it within such further time, if any, as the Revenue Commissioners or officer concerned may have allowed. Where a company had reasonable excuse for not doing anything required to be done, it is to be deemed not to have failed to do it if it did it without unreasonable delay after the excuse had ceased (TCA 1997, s 919(5)(a)).

15.207   Collection of corporation tax

TCA 1997, s 928(1) provides that after assessments to income tax and corporation tax have been made, the inspectors are to transmit particulars of the sums to be collected to the Collector-General for collection. In relation to corporation tax, the Collector-General is required by TCA 1997, s 973 to collect and levy the corporation tax charged from time to time on all assessment of which particulars have been transmitted to him under TCA 1997, s 928(1).

All such powers as are exercisable with respect to the collecting and levying of sums of income tax under Schedule D, of which particulars are transmitted under TCA 1997, s 928(1), are to extend with respect to sums of corporation tax of which particulars are transmitted under that section (TCA 1997, s 973(2)).

TCA 1997, s 1080 (interest on overdue tax), apart from TCA 1997, s 1080(2)(b), applies for the purposes of corporation tax as well as for income tax purposes (see **15.103.4**). (TCA 1997, s 1080(2)(b) provides that interest on unpaid tax is to run on any tax charged by an assessment to income tax notwithstanding any appeal against the assessment, from the date it would run if there had been no assessment.) TCA 1997, s 1080(2) provides that any tax charged by any assessment to income tax or corporation tax carries interest at the rate specified in the Table to TCA 1997, s 1080(2) (see **15.106.2**) for each day or part of a day from the date the tax becomes due and payable until payment.

Interest payable under TCA 1997, s 1080 is to be payable without any deduction of income tax and is not allowable as a deduction in computing any income, profits or losses for any of the purposes of the Tax Acts (TCA 1997, s 1080(3)(a)). The interest will be deemed to be a debt due to the Minister for Finance for the benefit of the Central Fund and is payable to the Revenue Commissioners (TCA 1997, s 1080(3)(b)). Subject to TCA 1997, s 1080(5) (see below), the provisions of every enactment relating to the recovery of any tax charged by an assessment and the provisions of every rule of court so relating, and the provisions of section 4 of the Preferential Payments in Bankruptcy (Ireland) Act 1889 and sections 98 and 285 of the Companies Act 1963, are to apply to the recovery of any amount of interest payable on that tax as if the amount of interest in question were a part of that tax (TCA 1997, s 1080(4)).

In proceedings instituted under TCA 1997, s 1080(4):

(a) a certificate by the Collector certifying that a stated amount of interest is due and payable by the person against whom the proceedings were instituted is to be evidence until the contrary is proved that that amount is so due and payable; and

(b) a certificate certifying as above and purporting to be signed by the Collector may be tendered in evidence without proof and is to be deemed until the contrary is proved to have been signed by the Collector (TCA 1997, s 1080(5)).

Where for any accounting period beginning before 1 January 2005 an assessment is made for the purposes of recovering an undercharge to corporation tax which is attributable to the fraud or neglect of any person, the amount of the tax undercharged is to carry interest at the rate of 2% per month or part of a month from the date or dates on which the tax undercharged for that period would have been payable, if it had been included in an assessment made on the expiration of six months from the end of that accounting period, to the date of payment of the tax undercharged (TCA 1997, s 1082(2)). *Neglect* means negligence or a failure to give any notice, to make any return, statement or declaration, or to produce or furnish any list, document or other information required by or under the enactments relating to corporation tax. TCA 1997, s 1080(3)–(5) (see above) is to apply to interest chargeable under TCA 1997, s 1082. Except in the case of a successful appeal under TCA 1997, s 1082(5) (see below), TCA 1997, s 1080(2) is not to apply to tax carrying interest under TCA 1997, s 1082.

Where an assessment to recover an undercharge to corporation tax is made—

(a) the inspector concerned is to give notice to the person assessed that the tax charged will carry interest in accordance with TCA 1997, s 1082;

(b) the person assessed may appeal against the assessment on the ground that interest should not be charged under TCA 1997, s 1082 and the provisions of the Tax Acts relating to appeals against assessments are to apply and have effect in relation to the appeal as they apply in relation to those appeals with any necessary modifications; and

(c) if, on the appeal, it is determined that the tax charged by the assessment should not carry interest under TCA 1997, s 1082, TCA 1997, s 1080(2) is to apply to that tax charged by an assessment to income tax (TCA 1997, s 1082(5)).

The priority attaching to assessed taxes under sections 98 and 285 of the Companies Act 1963 is to apply to corporation tax (TCA 1997, s 974).

15.208 Surcharge for late returns

15.208.1 Introduction

Where a company fails to deliver a return of income for any accounting period or year of assessment on or before the "specified return date for the chargeable period" (see below), it becomes liable to a surcharge equal to a percentage of the tax liability for that period (TCA 1997, s 1084). *Tax* means income tax, corporation tax or capital gains tax as may be appropriate. The surcharge is treated in all respects as part of the company's liability to tax; it is treated as an increase in the amount of tax for the accounting period or year of assessment in question (TCA 1997, s 1084(2)). For accounting periods ending before 6 April 1995, the surcharge was at the rate of 10% of the tax liability. For accounting periods ending on or after 6 April 1995, and for the year 1995-96 and later years, the surcharges applying are as follows:

(a)   where the return of income is delivered before the expiry of two months from the specified return date for the chargeable period, 5% of the amount of the tax liability, subject to a maximum amount of €12,695;

(b)   where the return of income is not delivered before the expiry of two months from the specified return date for the chargeable period, 10% of the amount of the tax liability, subject to a maximum amount of €63,485.

The *specified return date for the chargeable period* in relation to a chargeable period means:

(a)   where a chargeable period is an accounting period, the last day of the period of nine months commencing on the day immediately following the end of the accounting period but in any event not later than the 21st of the month in which that period of nine months ends;

(b)   where the chargeable period is an accounting period which ends on or before the date of commencement of the winding up of a company and the specified return date in respect of that period would otherwise fall on a date after the date of commencement of the winding up but not within a period of 3 months after that date, the date which falls 3 months after the date of commencement of the winding up but in any event not later than the 21st of the month in which that period of three months ends; and

(c)   where the chargeable period is a year of assessment (eg, for capital gains tax purposes) 31 January in the year of assessment following the year of assessment (TCA 1997, s 950(1)).

The amount of tax on which the surcharge is calculated is to be reduced by the aggregate of:

(i)   any tax deducted by virtue of any of the provisions of the Tax Acts or the Capital Gains Tax Acts from any income, profits or chargeable gains charged in the assessment to tax in so far as that tax has not been repaid or is not repayable to the chargeable person and in so far as the tax so deducted may be set against the tax contained in the assessment to tax; and

(ii)   any other amounts which are set off in the assessment to tax against the tax contained therein (TCA 1997, s 1084(2)(b)).

Chargeable person means, in relation to a year of assessment or accounting period, a person who is a chargeable person for the purposes of TCA 1997 Part 41 (self-assessment – see **15.102.4**).

The amount of tax on which the 5% or 10% surcharge is levied is the chargeable person's "net" liability to the tax concerned, ie the total amount of the tax charged in the assessment (the "gross liability") as reduced by the specific "deductions from tax" mentioned in (i), (ii) and (iii) above. In arriving at the gross liability to the relevant tax, all income, profits or chargeable gains (whichever applies) which ought to be included in the tax return, whether or not actually included in the return, must be brought into the computation of the total income, profits or chargeable gains on which the gross liability is computed (after any allowances or deductions from income).

The deductions under (i) in arriving at the net liability subject to the surcharge are limited to any Irish tax which has been deducted under any of the provisions in the Tax Acts which require or permit the person making certain payments to withhold the tax. Furthermore, only tax suffered on items of income, profits or gains which are included in income, profits or gains chargeable to tax by the assessment are deductible.

Examples of deductions under (i) are income tax deducted at source from annual payments received and Irish income tax deducted from Schedule C income or from foreign dividends paid through a bank or other paying agent in the State.

Examples of deductions under (ii) are the tax credits included in the Schedule F income of individuals or other persons chargeable to income tax and the amounts of any credits available for foreign tax for credit against Irish tax arising out of a double taxation agreement (see **14.202**).

An example of a deduction under (iii) is the actual amount of any professional services withholding tax which is set off in the tax assessment for the relevant chargeable period under TCA 1997, s 526. No deduction for this withholding tax is given to the extent that a refund is obtained under the interim refund procedure of TCA 1997, s 527.

15.208.2 Assessment of surcharge

If the tax contained in the assessment is not the amount of tax as increased by the surcharge, then all of the provisions of the Tax Acts and the Capital Gains Tax Acts (apart from TCA 1997, s 1084) including, in particular, those relating to the collection and recovery of tax and the payment of interest on unpaid tax, are to apply as if the tax contained in the assessment were the amount of the tax as so increased (TCA 1997, s 1084(2)).

In other words, the amount payable as tax for the relevant chargeable period becomes a total amount of tax equal to the aggregate of the actual tax payable and the 5% or 10% surcharge. Interest is payable on this new total tax figure from the appropriate due date for the tax charged by the assessment to the date on which the appropriate payment is made (except to the extent that tax has already been paid).

If a chargeable company had made the necessary minimum payment of preliminary tax on or before the due date for the preliminary tax, the due date for the tax, as now increased by the surcharge, is one month from the date of the corporation tax assessment (see **15.106.3**) and no interest will be chargeable if the remaining tax and the surcharge is paid by that date. In applying the 90% test in relation to the minimum preliminary tax payable, the surcharge must be included in the tax payable.

In any case where the relevant tax return was not filed on time and where additional tax becomes payable as the result of one or more amendments to the original assessment, the additional tax in each amended assessment must also be increased by 5% or 10% as a further amount of surcharge. Again, interest becomes payable on the additional tax and the surcharge thereon from the appropriate due date for the additional tax to the date of payment. For the due dates of the additional tax (and surcharge) in the amended assessment, see **15.108**.

Where a company makes a fraudulent or negligent return of income on or before the specified date in relation to the return, it is treated as having failed to make a timely return for the purposes of the surcharge unless the error in the return is remedied on or before the specified date (TCA 1997, s 1084(1)(b)(i)).

15.208.3 Returns

If a return of income is incorrect (but not fraudulently or negligently so) and it comes to the company's notice that it is incorrect, the company will be regarded as having failed to make a timely return unless the error in the return is remedied without unreasonable delay (TCA 1997, s 1084(1)(b)(ii)).

For the purposes of TCA 1997, s 1084, where a company delivers a return of income on or before the specified return date for the chargeable period but the inspector, by reason of being dissatisfied with any statement of profits or gains arising to the company from any trade or profession which is contained in the return, requires the company, by notice in writing served on it under TCA 1997, s 900 (power of an inspector or other authorised officer to require production of account and books), to do any thing, the company will be deemed not to have delivered the return on or before the specified return date for the chargeable period unless it does that thing within the time specified in the notice (TCA 1997, s 1084(1)(b)(iii)).

Also for the purposes of TCA 1997, s 1084, references to such of the specified sections (see above) as are applied in relation to capital gains tax by TCA 1997, s 913 are to be construed as including references to those sections as so applied (TCA 1997, s 1084(1)(b)(iv)).

In view of the potentially serious impact of TCA 1997, s 1084, it is important to be clear as to what precisely constitutes a return of income for the purposes of the section. TCA 1997, s 1084(1) defines *return of income* as a return, statement, declaration or list which a person is required to deliver to the inspector under any one or more of the specified provisions. It is relevant therefore to look at each of the specified provisions to ascertain what is required for the purposes of submitting a correct and complete return of income.

The *specified provisions* are as follows:

TCA 1997, s 877 *Returns by persons chargeable*

Every person chargeable under the Income Tax Acts, when required to do so by a notice given to him by an inspector, is obliged, within the time limited by such notice, to prepare and deliver to the inspector, a statement in writing as required by the Income Tax Acts, signed by him, containing the amount of the profits or gains arising to him, from each and every source chargeable according to the respective schedules, estimated for the period specified in the notice and according to the provisions of the Income Tax Acts, and with a declaration that such amounts are estimated in respect of all the sources of income mentioned in the Income Tax Acts, describing the same, after deducting only such sums as are allowed

TCA 1997, s 878 *Persons acting for incapacitated persons and* non-*residents*

Obligation to deliver such a statement as is described in TCA 1997, s 877 (see above) of the profits or gains in respect of which tax is to be charged on him on account of any incapacitated person or non-resident person who, by reason of such incapacity or non-residence, cannot by personally charged under the Income Tax Acts, together with the prescribed declaration.

TCA 1997, s 879 *Power to require return of income*

Obligation on individuals, when required to do so, to prepare and deliver a return of all the sources of his income for the year of assessment in relation to which the notice is given, the amount of income from each source and such certain further particulars as may be required.

TCA 1997, s 880 *Partnership returns*

Power to require return as to sources of partnership income and amounts derived therefrom

TCA 1997, s 881 *Returns by married persons*

TCA 1997, s 884 *Returns of profits by companies (see* **15.205** *above)*

TCA 1997, s 888 *Returns etc by lessors, lessees and agents*

Obligation on any lessor, or former lessor, of premises to give information as to the provisions of the lease and the terms subject to which the lease was granted and as to payments made to or by him in relation to the premises (TCA 1997, s 888(2)(a))

Obligation on any person who as agent manages premises or is in receipt of rent or other payments arising from premises to prepare and deliver to the inspector a return containing the full name and address of all such premises, the name and address of every person to whom such premises belong, a statement of all rents and other such payments arising from such premises, and such other particulars relating to all such premises as may be specified in the notice (TCA s 888(2)(d))

TCA 1997, s 1023 *Application for separate assessments*

Husband and wife

A return of income, for the purposes of the surcharge, is therefore confined to returns, statements, declarations or lists required under one or more of the above described provisions. For companies, the principal relevant provision will be TCA 1997, s 884 but any one or more of the other provisions may also be relevant, depending on circumstances.

It will be seen, therefore, that not all information requested on the return form (form CT1) in use for corporation tax purposes must be provided so as to result in a company making a correct and complete return of income for the purposes of the surcharge. For example, details of remuneration and expenses for directors, which are routinely required on forms CT1, are not part of a "return of income" for the purposes of TCA 1997, s 884 or for the purposes of any of the specified sections. Failure to furnish those details will not, therefore, result in the company concerned failing to furnish a return of income for the purposes of TCA 1997, s 1084.

TCA 1997, s 1084(2), which imposes the surcharge, does so only on the chargeable person required to make the specified return (for example, the precedent acting partner) and not on any other person who could be charged to tax as a result of any income or other information in the return (for example, the other partners in the firm). However, if a chargeable person becomes liable to the 5% or 10% surcharge for failure to file one of these other returns on time, the surcharge is imposed on all the chargeable person's tax (net of deductions from tax) and not just the tax affected by one of these other returns.

For example, if a company chargeable to corporation tax for a chargeable period is the precedent acting partner in a partnership, it must ensure that both its own tax return and the partnership's tax return for the chargeable period are delivered to the appropriate inspector no later than the specified return date for the chargeable period. Failure to meet the filing deadline for either return will result in the precedent acting partner being liable to the 5% or 10% surcharge on its own tax liability for the chargeable period. It does not result in any other partner being liable to the surcharge, but of course the other partners must ensure that their own tax returns are filed on time.

15.208.4   Revenue Statement of Practice

As set out in their Statement of Practice (SP-GEN/1/93) issued in April 1993, the Revenue Commissioners are prepared to relax strict enforcement of a number of provisions relating to the surcharge for the late filing of tax returns. These concessions are intended to be limited to "normally complying taxpayers" who may occasionally slip up so far as timely filing of tax returns is concerned.

SP-GEN/1/93 provides that, in order to allow for postal or other minor delays, returns received by the inspector within seven days of the proper return filing date (the specified return date for the chargeable period) will normally be accepted as being filed on time (so that no surcharge will be made). However, the Statement goes on to confirm that this is not a general extension of the return filing date as provided in TCA 1997, s 950(1), but is intended to be restricted to occasional late delivery of returns.

In particular, the Revenue Commissioners reserve the right to deny or withdraw the benefit of this seven day concession in the case of taxpayers or their advisers who abuse this procedure and regularly make tax returns within the seven days extended period.

SP-GEN/1/93 also provides that a late filing of a tax return more than seven days after the return filing date will be accepted without resulting in liability to the surcharge (or other penalty) in the case of an occasional late filing by a chargeable person, but only where all the following three requirements are met:

(a)   the return is made within four weeks from the return filing date,

(b)   the chargeable person has paid on time the "correct" amount of preliminary tax for the chargeable period (year of assessment or accounting period) to which the return relates, and

(c)   the inspector or other officer dealing with the return has reasonable grounds to believe that, having regard to the previous behaviour of the chargeable person in relation to returns, payments etc, the default results from an uncharacteristic slip by an otherwise complying taxpayer.

In order to obtain this concession, the Statement recommends that the chargeable person (or tax adviser) should attach a note to the return being filed (within the four week period) giving the reasons why it is considered that the concession should apply. If the inspector is satisfied that these conditions are all met, the return will generally be accepted as made on time without further enquiry. The inspector may not necessarily apply this procedure in the event of a subsequent default of this nature, particularly if it follows closely after a previous default.

A Statement of Practice (SP-CT/2/90) entitled "Company's Self-assessment: Return of Directors Details" issued by the Revenue Commissioners refers to the return of directors' emoluments, benefits etc which must be given on page 5 of the normal corporation tax return form (CT1). This information is now required in the form CT1 instead of in the previous forms (RR1 and RR2) used for the purpose.

SP-CT/2/90 makes it clear that an error in, or omission from, the details of directors' emoluments does not, of itself, mean that the corporation tax return is an incomplete one so as to make the company liable to the surcharge. The reason for this decision is that a return of the director's emoluments is not a return of the company's profits, but is information gathering to be used for other purposes by the Revenue. This is in line with what is stated above (see under *Returns*) to the effect that not all information requested on forms CT1 must be provided so as to result in a company making a correct and complete return of income for the purposes of the surcharge.

15.209 Appeals

15.209.1 Introduction

TCA 1997 Part 40 Ch 1 (ss 932-944) deals with the matter of appeals against income tax and corporation tax assessments. The relevant provisions are concerned with appeals against assessments, procedure on appeals, confirmation and amendment of assessments, determination of liability in cases of default, statement of case for the High Court, and appeals to the Circuit Court.

Where an Appeal Commissioner is interested in his own right or in the right of any other person in any matter under appeal, he may not take part in, or be present at, the hearing or determination of the appeal (TCA 1997, s 856(3)).

15.209.2 Appeals against assessments: general

A person aggrieved by an assessment to income tax made on him by the inspector or other authorised officer is entitled to appeal to the Appeal Commissioners on giving, within thirty days after the date of the notice of assessment, notice in writing to the inspector or other officer (TCA 1997, s 933(1)). If the inspector of other officer considers that the person is not entitled to make such an appeal, he is to refuse the application and notify the person in writing accordingly specifying the grounds for the refusal. A person whose application is refused is entitled to appeal against the refusal by notice in writing to the Appeal Commissioners within 15 days of the date of issue of the notice of refusal. On receipt of that appeal, the Appeal Commissioners will request the inspector or other officer to furnish them with a copy of the notice of refusal and on receipt thereof will, as soon as possible:

(i) refuse the application, giving notice in writing to the applicant specifying the grounds for their refusal,

(ii) allow the application and give notice in writing accordingly to both the applicant and the inspector or other officer, or

(iii) notify in writing both the applicant and the inspector or other officer that they have decided to arrange a hearing to enable them to determine whether or not to allow the application for an appeal.

An appeal against an assessment for any accounting period may only be made to the extent that the assessment is in some respect at variance with the details of income, profits or gains, deductions or any other relief, or any other relevant particulars, specified in the return made by the company for that period (TCA 1997, s 957(1)(b)).

An appeal cannot be made until a tax return has been made by the company for the period in question and it has paid the tax due in accordance with the statements and particulars included in that return (TCA 1997, s 957(2)). The notice of appeal must state each amount or matter in the assessment or amended assessment with which the company is aggrieved and the grounds in detail of its appeal as respects each such amount or matter (TCA 1997, s 957(4)).

The times and places for the hearing of appeals will be appointed from time to time by the Appeal Commissioners (TCA 1997, s 933(2)(a)). The inspector or other officer is to give notice in writing to each person who has given notice of appeal of the time and place appointed for the hearing. Such notice will not be given where the inspector or other officer and the appellant come to an agreement that the assessment is to stand good, is to be amended in a particular manner or is to be discharged or cancelled. Alternatively, such notice will not be given if the appellant gives notice to the inspector or other officer that he does not wish to proceed with the appeal. Where settlement of an appeal by agreement seems likely, the inspector or other officer may refrain from giving notice of the appeal hearing or may, with the agreement of the appellant, withdraw a notice already given (TCA 1997, s 933(2)(b)).

Where, on application in writing to the Appeal Commissioners, a person who has given notice of appeal satisfies the Appeal Commissioners that the information submitted to the inspector or other officer is such that the appeal is likely to be determined on the first occasion of its hearing, the Appeal Commissioners may direct the inspector or other officer to give the notice in writing of the time and place of the hearing so that the inspector may not refrain from giving such notice as described in TCA 1997, s 933(2)(b) (TCA 1997, s 933(2)(c)).

Where, in respect of an assessment in respect of which notice of appeal has been given (other than an assessment the appeal against which has been determined by the Appeal Commissioners or which has become final and conclusive) the inspector or other officer and the appellant come to an agreement, whether in writing or otherwise, that the assessment is to stand good, is to be amended in a particular manner or is to be discharged or cancelled, the inspector or other officer will give effect to that agreement. Accordingly, if the assessment is to stand good or is to be amended, the assessment or amended assessment is to have the same force and effect as if it were an assessment in respect of which no notice of appeal had been given (TCA 1997, s 933(3)(a), (b)).

An agreement not in writing is to be deemed not to be an agreement unless the fact that the agreement was come to, and the terms agreed upon, are confirmed by notice in writing given by the inspector or other officer to the appellant or by the appellant to the inspector or other officer, and 21 days have elapsed since the giving of that notice without the person receiving it giving notice in writing to the person by whom it was given that he desires to repudiate or withdraw from the agreement (TCA 1997, s 933(3)(c)).

Where an appellant does not with to proceed with the appeal against the assessment and gives notice in writing to the inspector or other officer to that effect, TCA 1997, s 933(3)(b) (see above) is to have effect as if the appellant and the inspector or other officer had, on the appellant's notice being received, come to an agreement in writing that the assessment should stand good (TCA 1997, s 933(3)(d)).

References above to an agreement being come to with an appellant and the giving of notice to or by an appellant include references to an agreement being come to with, and the giving of notice to or by, a person acting on behalf of the appellant in relation to the appeal (TCA 1997, s 933(3)(e)).

ITA s 432 gives a taxpayer a right of appeal to the Appeal Commissioners against any determination of the Revenue Commissioners (or any other authorised officer, including an inspector) in relation to the following matters:

(a)   all claims for exemptions or for any allowance or deduction under the Tax Acts;

(b)   all claims for repayment of tax under the Tax Acts; and

(c)   all claims to relief from tax under the Tax Acts where relief is measured in the provision under which it is given.

All appeals against assessments to income tax are to be heard and determined by the Appeal Commissioners and their determination on any such appeal is to be final and conclusive unless the person assessed requires that his appeal be reheard by the judge of the Circuit Court in accordance with TCA 1997, s 942 or unless, under the Tax Acts, a case is required to be stated for the opinion of the High Court (TCA 1997, s 933(4)).

Where a person fails to give notice of appeal against an assessment given to him, the assessment is to be final and conclusive (TCA 1997, s 933(6)(a)).

On the hearing of an appeal against an assessment, the Appeal Commissioners may make an order dismissing the appeal, and the assessment is to have the same effect and force as if it were an assessment in respect of which no notice of appeal had been given, in the following circumstances:

(a)   where no application is or has been made to the Appeal Commissioners before or during the hearing of the appeal by or on behalf of the appellant for an adjournment of the proceedings on the appeal, or such application is or has been made and is or was refused (such application not to be refused within 9 months of the end of the year of assessment to which the assessment appealed against relates, or from the date on which the notice of the assessment was given to the appellant, whichever is the earlier); and

(b)   a return of his income for the relevant year of assessment has not been made by the appellant, or such a return has been made but

   (i)   all the statements of profits and gains, schedules and other evidence relating to such return have not been furnished by or on behalf of the appellant,

   (ii)   information requested from the appellant by the Appeal Commissioners in the hearing of the appeal has not been supplied to the appellant,

   (iii)   the terms of a precept issued by the Appeal Commissioners under TCA 1997, s 935 (see below) have not been complied with by the appellant, or

   (iv)   any questions as to an assessment or assessments put by the Appeal Commissioners under TCA 1997, s 938 have not been answered to their satisfaction (TCA 1997, s 933(6)(c)).

The appeal will not be dismissed in the circumstances described above, however, if on the hearing of the appeal the Appeal Commissioners are satisfied that sufficient information has been furnished by or on behalf of the appellant to enable them to determine the appeal at that hearing.

15.209.3   Late appeal

Notice of appeal not given within the thirty days prescribed by TCA 1997, s 933(1) is to be regarded as having been so given where, on an application in writing having been made to him within 12 months after the date of the notice of assessment, the inspector or other officer being satisfied that, owing to absence, sickness or other reasonable cause, the applicant was prevented from giving notice of appeal within the time limited and that the application was then made without unreasonable delay, notifies the applicant in writing that his application has been allowed (TCA 1997, s 933(7)(a)).

If on an application for the admission of a late appeal the inspector or other officer is not satisfied that it should be admitted, he will by notice in writing inform the applicant that his application has been refused (TCA 1997, s 933(7)(b)). Within 15 days after the date of that notice, the applicant may by notice in writing require the inspector or other officer to refer his application to the Appeal Commissioners and, in relation to any application so referred, TCA 1997, s 933(7)(a) and (b) are to apply as if references to the inspector or other officer were references to the Appeal Commissioners (TCA 1997, s 933(7)(c)).

Notwithstanding TCA 1997, s 933(7)(a), an application made after the expiration of the time specified (ie, the period of 12 months beginning with the date of the notice of assessment) which, but for that expiration, would have been allowed, may be allowed if at the time of the application—

(i)   there has been made to the inspector or other officer a return of income, statements or profits and gains and such other information as in his opinion would enable the appeal to be settled by agreement under TCA 1997, s 933(3) (see above); and

(ii)   the tax charged by the assessment in respect of which the application is made has been paid together with any interest thereon chargeable under TCA 1997, s 1080 (TCA 1997, s 933(7)(d)).

Where on an application referred to in TCA 1997, s 933(7)(d), the inspector or other officer is not satisfied that the information submitted would not be sufficient to enable the appeal to be settled by agreement, or if the tax and interest have not been paid, he will by notice in writing inform the applicant that his application has been refused (TCA 1997, s 933(7)(e)).

Within 15 days after the date of the notice of refusal, the applicant may by notice in writing require the inspector or other officer to refer his application to the Appeal Commissioners and they may allow the application if—

(i)   it is one which, but for the expiration of the period specified in TCA 1997, s 933(7)(a) (the 12 month period beginning with the date of the notice of assessment), would have been allowed if the application had been referred to the Appeal Commissioners under TCA 1997, s 933(7)(c) (see above);

(ii)   at the time the application is referred to the Appeal Commissioners the tax charged by the assessment in question, with any interest thereon chargeable under TCA 1997, s 1080, has bee paid; and

(iii)   the information submitted to the inspector or other officer is such that in the opinion of the Appeal Commissioners the appeal is likely to be determined on the first occasion of its hearing (TCA 1997, s 933(7)(f)).

An overpayment of tax on the determination of an appeal carries interest at 0.0161% per day or part of a day for a period ending on the date of the repayment. That period will commence on the day following the end of the chargeable period (accounting period or, where capital gains tax is involved, year of assessment) for which the overpayment arises or, if later than that date, the date of payment of the amount or amounts giving rise to the overpayment or, depending on the circumstances, will commence on the day that is 93 days after the end of the day on which a valid repayment claim was made (TCA 1997, s 865A – see **15.212**).

15.209.4   Failure to attend appeal hearing

Where a person who has given notice of appeal against an assessment does not attend before the Appeal Commissioners at the time and place appointed for the hearing, the assessment is, subject to TCA 1997, s 933(8), to have the same force and effect as if it were an assessment in respect of which no notice of appeal had been given (TCA 1997, s 933(6)(b)).

Where a person who has given notice of appeal against an assessment does not attend before the Appeal Commissioners at the time and place appointed for the hearing of the appeal, TCA 1997, s 933(6)(b) will not have effect if:

(a)   at the said time and place another person attends on behalf of the appellant and the Appeal Commissioners consent to hear that person; or

(b)   on an application in that behalf having been made to them in writing or otherwise at or before the said time, the Appeal Commissioners postpone the hearing; or

(c)   on an application in writing having been made to them after the said time the Appeal Commissioners, being satisfied that, owing to absence, sickness or other reasonable cause, the appellant was prevented from appearing before them at the said time and place and that the application was made without unreasonable delay, direct that the appeal be treated as one the time for the hearing of which has not yet been appointed (TCA 1997, s 933(8)).

15.209.5   Action for recovery of tax in case of late appeal or failure to attend appeal hearing

Where action for the recovery of tax charged by an assessment by way of the institution of proceedings in any court, or the issue of a certificate under TCA 1997, s 962 (recovery by sheriff or county registrar), has been taken, neither TCA 1997, s 933(7) nor TCA 1997, s 933(8) is to apply in relation to that assessment until the said action has been completed (TCA 1997, s 933(9)(a)).

In any such case, where an application under TCA 1997, s 933(7)(a) is allowed or, on an application under TCA 1997, s 933(8)(c), the Appeal Commissioners direct as provided therein, the applicant will not in any case be entitled to repayment of any sum paid or borne by him in respect of the costs of any such court proceedings or, as the case may be, of any fees or expenses charged by the county registrar or sheriff executing a certificate under TCA 1997, s 962 (TCA 1997, s 933(9)(b)).

15.209.6 Procedure on appeals

The inspector or other authorised officer is entitled to attend every appeal, to be present during all the time of the hearing and at the determination of the appeal, to produce any lawful evidence in support of the assessment concerned and to give reasons in support of the assessment (TCA 1997, s 934(1)).

In the case of any appeal, the Appeal Commissioners may permit any barrister or solicitor to plead before them on behalf of the appellant or on behalf of the inspector or other officer, either *viva voce* or in writing, and may hear any accountant, being any person admitted as a member of an incorporated society of accountants, or any person who has been admitted as a member of the Irish Taxation Institute (TCA 1997, s 934(2)). The Appeal Commissioners may also permit any other person representing the appellant to plead before them where they are satisfied that such permission should be given.

Where on an appeal it appears to the Appeal Commissioners by whom the appeal is heard, or to a majority of such Commissioners, by examination of the appellant on oath or affirmation, or by other lawful evidence, that the appellant is overcharged by any assessment, they are to abate or reduce the assessment accordingly. Otherwise, the Commissioners are to determine the appeal by ordering that the assessment is to stand (TCA 1997, s 934(3)).

Where on any appeal it appears to the Appeal Commissioners that the person assessed ought to be charged in an amount exceeding the amount contained in the assessment, they are to charge him with the excess (TCA 1997, s 934(4)).

Unless the circumstances of the case otherwise require—

(a) where on an appeal against an assessment which assesses an amount which is chargeable to tax it appears to the Appeal Commissioners that the appellant is overcharged by the assessment they may, in determining the appeal, reduce only the amount which is chargeable to tax;

(b) where on such an appeal it appears to the Appeal Commissioners that the appellant is correctly charged by the assessment they may, in determining the appeal, order that the amount which is chargeable to tax is to stand good; and

(c) where on such an appeal it appears to the Appeal Commissioners that the appellant ought to be charged in an amount exceeding the amount contained in the assessment, they are to charge the excess by increasing only the amount which is chargeable to tax (TCA 1997, s 934(5)).

Where an appeal is determined by the Appeal Commissioners, the inspector or other officer is, unless either—

(i) the person assessed requires that his appeal is to be reheard under TCA 1997, s 942, or

(ii) under the Tax Acts a case is required to be stated for the opinion of the High Court,

required to give effect to the Commissioners' determination and thereupon, if the determination is that the assessment is to stand good or is to be amended, the assessment or the amended assessment is to have the same force and effect as if it were an assessment in respect of which no notice of appeal had been given (TCA 1997, s 934(6)).

Every determination of an appeal by the Appeal Commissioners is to be recorded by them in the prescribed form at the time the determination is made and the Commissioners are, within 10 days after the determination, to transmit that form to the inspector or other officer (ITA 1967 s 421(7)).

15.209.7   Power to issue precepts

After notice of appeal against an assessment has been given, the Appeal Commissioners may if considered necessary by them issue a precept to the appellant ordering him to deliver to them, within the time limited by the precept, a schedule containing such particulars for their information as they may demand as respects the property of the appellant, the trade, profession or employment carried on or exercised by him, the amount of his profits or gains, distinguishing the particular amounts derived from each separate source, or any deductions made in arriving at his profits or gains (TCA 1997, s 935).

Any inspector or other officer may at all reasonable times inspect and take copies of, or extracts from, any schedule.

15.209.8   Objection by inspector to schedules

The inspector or other officer may, within a reasonable time to be allowed by the Appeal Commissioners, after examination by him of any schedule, object to the schedule or any part of it and must then state in writing the cause of his objection according to the best of his knowledge or information. Notice of the objection must be given in writing to the person chargeable to enable that person to appeal against it. No appeal is to be confirmed or altered until any appeal against the objection has been heard and determined (TCA 1997, s 936).

15.209.9   Confirmation and amendment of assessments

If the Appeal Commissioners see cause to disallow an objection of the inspector or other officer to a schedule, or if on the hearing of an appeal they are satisfied with the assessment, or if after the delivery of a schedule they are satisfied with it and have no information as to its insufficiency, they will confirm or alter the assessment in accordance with the schedule, as the case may require (TCA 1997, s 937).

15.209.10   Questions as to assessments or schedules

Where the Appeal Commissioners are dissatisfied with a schedule or require further information in relation to it, they may by precept put questions in writing concerning the schedule or any matter which is contained or ought to be contained in it concerning any deductions made in arriving at the profits or gains and the particulars thereof. They may require true and particular answers in writing, signed by the person chargeable, to be given within seven days after the service of the precept.

The chargeable person may answer the questions in writing or tender himself to be examined orally before the Commissioners and may object to and refuse to answer any question. The substance of any answer given by him orally will be taken down in writing in his presence and be read over to him and, after he has been enabled to amend any such answer, he may be required to verify the answer on oath. The procedure described above will also apply in the case of any clerk, agent or servant of the person chargeable who tenders himself to be examined on behalf of that person (TCA 1997, s 938).

15.209.11 Summoning and examination of witnesses

The Appeal Commissioners may summon any person whom they think able to give evidence respecting an assessment made on another person to appear before them to be examined and may examine such person on oath (ITA 1967 s 426). The clerk, agent, servant or other person confidentially employed in the affairs of the chargeable person is also to be examined in the same way and subject to the same restrictions as in the case of a person chargeable who tenders himself to be examined orally. The oath will be that the evidence to be given, regarding the matter in question, by the person sworn shall be the truth, the whole truth and nothing but the truth, and the oath is to be subscribed by the person by whom it is made.

A person who after being duly summoned will be liable to a penalty of €950 if he neglects or refuses to appear before the Appeal Commissioners, appears but refuses to be sworn or to subscribe the oath, or refuses to answer any lawful question regarding the matters under consideration (TCA 1997, s 939(3)). The penalty will not apply to any clerk, agent, servant or other person as mentioned above.

15.209.12 Statement of case for High Court

Immediately after the determination of an appeal by the Appeal Commissioners, the appellant or the inspector or other officer, if dissatisfied with the determination as being erroneous in point of law, may declare his dissatisfaction to the Commissioners who heard the appeal (TCA 1997, s 941(1)). The requirement to express dissatisfaction "immediately" is directory rather than mandatory so that failure to express dissatisfaction immediately will not nullify the right of appeal (*The State (Multiprint Label Systems) v Neylon* 3 ITR 159).

The appellant or inspector of other officer, as the case may be, may then within 21 days after the determination, by notice in writing addressed to the Clerk to the Commissioners, require the Commissioners to state and sign a case for the opinion of the High Court thereon. The case is to set out the facts and the determination of the Commissioners and the party requiring it is to transmit the case, when stated and signed, to the High Court within seven days after receiving it. The requirement to transmit the case to the High Court within the time limit stated is mandatory (*Valleybright Ltd (in voluntary liquidation) v Richardson* [1985] STC 70, *Brassington v Guthrie* [1992] STC 47, *Petch v Gurney* [1994] STC 689). At or before that time, the party requiring it is to send notice in writing of the fact that the case has been stated on his application, together with a copy of the case, to the other party.

The High Court will hear and determine any question or questions of law arising on the case, and will reverse, affirm or amend the determination in respect of which the case has been stated, or will remit the matter to the Appeal Commissioners with the opinion of the Court thereon, or may make such other order in relation to the matter, and may make such order as to costs as may seem fit (TCA 1997, s 941(6)). The High Court has no jurisdiction to hear fresh evidence (*Kudehinbu v Cutts* [1994] STC 560). The High Court may cause the case to be sent back for amendment and the case will then be amended accordingly and judgment delivered after it has been amended (TCA 1997, s 941(7)).

An appeal is to lie from the decision of the High Court to the Supreme Court (TCA 1997, s 941(8)). If the amount of the assessment is altered by the order or judgment of the Supreme Court or the High Court, then—

(a) if too much tax has been paid, the amount overpaid is to be refunded with interest in accordance with TCA 1997, s 865A (see **15.212**); or

(b) if too little tax has been paid, the amount unpaid is to be deemed to be arrears of tax (except so far as any penalty is incurred on account of arrears), and is to be paid and recovered accordingly (TCA 1997, s 941(9)).

15.209.13 Appeal to Circuit Court

Any person aggrieved by the determination of the Appeal Commissioners in an appeal may, on giving notice in writing to the inspector or other officer, within ten days after the determination, require that his appeal be reheard by the appropriate judge of the Circuit Court. The Appeal Commissioners will transmit to the Circuit Court judge any statement or schedule in their possession which was delivered to them for the purposes of the appeal (TCA 1997, s 942(1)).

The appropriate judge of the Circuit Court is the judge in whose circuit is situated the place where the assessment was made in the case of a non-resident person, the estate of a deceased person, an incapacitated person, or a trust. In any other case, the place will be the place to which the notice of assessment was addressed.

At or before the time of the rehearing, the inspector or other officer is to transmit to the judge the prescribed form in which the Appeal Commissioners' determination of the appeal is recorded (TCA 1997, s 942(2)). The judge will with all convenient speed rehear and determine the appeal, and will have and exercise the same powers and authorities in relation to the assessment appealed against, the determination, and all matters consequent thereon, as the Appeal Commissioners might have and exercise, and his determination thereon is, subject to TCA 1997, s 943, to be final and conclusive (TCA 1997, s 942(3)).

The provisions of TCA 1997, s 934(2) will, with any necessary modifications, apply in relation to a rehearing of an appeal by a judge of the Circuit Court as they do in relation to the hearing of an appeal by the Appeal Commissioners. Accordingly, the judge may permit any barrister or solicitor to plead before him on behalf of the appellant or on behalf of the inspector or other officer, either *viva voce* or in writing, and may hear any accountant, being any person admitted as a member of an incorporated society of accountants, or any person who has been admitted as a member of the body incorporated under the Companies Act 1963, on 31 December 1975, as "The Institute of Taxation in Ireland".

Where an appeal is determined by the judge, the inspector or other officer will, unless a case is required to be stated for the opinion of the High Court, give effect to the judge's determination. If the determination is that the assessment is to stand or is to be amended, the assessment, or the amended assessment, will have the same force and effect as if it were an assessment in respect of which no notice of appeal had been given (TCA 1997, s 942(6)).

Where, following an application for the rehearing of an appeal by the Circuit Court judge, there is an agreement (within the meaning of TCA 1997, s 933(3)(b), (c) and (d) – see under **15.209.2**) between the appellant and the inspector or other officer in relation to the assessment, the inspector is to give effect to the agreement. If the agreement is that the assessment is to stand good or is to be amended, the assessment or the amended assessment is to have the same force and effect as if it were an assessment in respect of which no notice of appeal had been given (TCA 1997, s 942(8)).

TCA 1997, s 941 (*Statement of case for High Court* – see above) is to apply to a determination given by a judge of the Circuit Court in the same way as it applies to a determination by the Appeal Commissioners and any case stated by a judge pursuant to that section is to set out the facts, the determination of the Appeal Commissioners and the determination of the judge (TCA 1997, s 943).

15.209.14 Communication of decision of Appeal Commissioners

Where, following argument on an appeal, the Appeal Commissioners have postponed giving their determination for the purpose of considering the argument or for the purpose of affording to the appellant the opportunity of submitting in writing further evidence or argument, they may, unless they consider a further hearing necessary, cause their determination to be sent by post to the parties to the appeal (TCA 1997, s 944(1)).

Where the determination of an appeal is sent to the parties, a declaration of dissatisfaction under TCA 1997, s 941(1) or a notice requiring a rehearing under TCA 1997, s 942(1) may be made or given in writing within twelve days after the day on which the determination is sent to the person making the declaration or giving the notice (TCA 1997, s 944(2)).

15.209.15 Publication of determinations of Appeal Commissioners

The Appeal Commissioners may publish details of their decisions in such cases as they consider appropriate. The identity of the taxpayers in question may not be divulged in such publication. TCA 1997, s 944A provides that the Appeal Commissioners may make arrangements for the publication of reports of such of their determinations as they consider appropriate. In doing so, they must ensure that any such report is in a form which, in so far as possible, prevents the identification of any person whose affairs are dealt with in the determination. TCA 1997, s 944A applies to appeals determined by the Appeal Commissioners after 11 March 1998.

15.209.16 Making of claims etc and appeals and rehearings

Notwithstanding any other provisions of the Tax Acts or the Capital Gains Tax Acts—

(a) all claims to exemption or for any allowance or deduction under those Acts;

(b) all claims for repayment of income tax, corporation tax or capital gains tax under those Acts; and

(c) (i) all claims to relief under those Acts where relief is measured in the provision under which it is given, and

(ii) all matters and questions relating to any relief so measured,
in relation to which a right of appeal from a decision is, otherwise than by TCA 1997, s 949, not specifically provided,

are to be stated in such manner and form as may be prescribed by the Revenue Commissioners and are to be submitted to and determined by the Revenue Commissioners or other authorised officer (including an inspector) (TCA 1997, s 864(1)). Any person aggrieved by any determination on any such claim, matter or question may, subject to TCA 1997, s 957 (self-assessment: appeals – see **15.107.6**), and on giving notice in writing to the Revenue Commissioners or other officer within thirty days after notification to the person aggrieved of the determination, appeal to the Appeal Commissioners (TCA 1997, s 949(1)).

The Appeal Commissioners will hear and determine an appeal to them under TCA 1997, s 949(1) as if it were an appeal against an assessment to income tax (and presumably corporation tax) and all of the provisions of TCA 1997, s 933, with respect to such appeals, together with the provisions of the Tax Acts relating to the rehearing of an appeal and the statement of a case for the opinion of the High Court on a point of law, are to apply accordingly with any necessary modifications (TCA 1997, s 949(2)).

Where a right of appeal to the Appeal Commissioners is given by any provision (other than TCA 1997, s 1037 – non-residents: charge on percentage of turnover) of the Tax Acts or the Capital Gains Tax Acts and such provision, while applying the provisions of the Tax Acts relating to appeals against assessments, does not apply to the provisions of those Acts relating to the rehearing of appeals, such provision is to be deemed to apply the said provisions relating to the rehearing of appeals (TCA 1997, s 949(3)).

Where a notice of appeal is not given within the time limited by TCA 1997, s 949(1) (thirty days after the notification to the person aggrieved by the determination), or a person who has given notice of appeal does not attend before the Appeal Commissioners at the time and place appointed for the hearing of his appeal, the provisions of TCA 1997, s 933(5), (7), (8) and (9) are, with any necessary modifications, to apply (TCA 1997, s 949(4)).

15.209.17 Payment of tax on determination of appeal

Having lodged an appeal against an assessment, a company will, as a pre-condition of the appeal, have paid corporation tax for the relevant accounting period in accordance with the statements and particulars included in the return for that period (see **15.209.2**). On the determination of the appeal, whether by agreement between the company and the inspector or by the Appeal Commissioners, any additional tax resulting from the determination becomes payable.

The due date (and accordingly the date from which interest on overdue tax is to be calculated) for payment of the additional tax is fixed by TCA 1997, s 958(9). This due date may in fact fall on a date which is earlier than the date the appeal is determined. The additional tax becomes payable even where the appeal is to be reheard by the Circuit Court Judge or where the Appeal Commissioners' decision is the subject of an appeal on a point of law to the High Court or the Supreme Court.

Any additional tax becoming payable on the determination of an appeal against an assessment or amended assessment is due and payable—

(a) not later than one month from the date on which the appeal is determined – subject to conditions (see below); or

(b) where the conditions mentioned below are not met, on the same date as the tax charged by the assessment which was the subject of the appeal is due and payable.

The conditions referred to in (a) and (b) above are that:

(i)   the tax paid prior to the appeal proves to be not less than 90% of the tax found to be payable on the determination of the appeal; and

(ii)   the tax charged by the assessment was due and payable in accordance with TCA 1997, s 958(3) (and not in accordance with TCA 1997, s 958(4C) and (4E), ie, where the preliminary tax requirements were not met) (see **15.106.3**).

15.210   Penalties

Where a person has been required by notice given under or for the purposes of certain provisions relating to corporation tax (see below) to furnish any information or particulars and he fails to comply with the notice, he will be liable to a penalty of €125 and, if the failure continues after judgment has been given by the court before which proceedings for the penalty have been commenced, to a further penalty of €10 for each day on which the failure so continues (TCA 1997, s 1075(1)). Where the person is a company, however, it will be liable to a penalty of €630 and, if the failure continues after judgment has been given by the court before which proceedings for the penalty have been commenced, to a further penalty of €60 for each day on which the failure so continues. In addition, the secretary of the company will be liable to a separate penalty of €125 (TCA 1997, s 1075(3)).

The provisions in question are:

(a)   TCA 1997, s 401 (change in ownership of company: disallowance of trading losses – see **4.110**);

(b)   TCA 1997, s 427 (information as to arrangements for transferring relief – see **8.313**);

(c)   TCA 1997 Part 13 (close companies – see **10.105**).

Where the person fraudulently or negligently furnishes any incorrect information or particulars of a kind mentioned above, or in TCA 1997, s 239 (income tax on payments – see **4.306**), he will be liable to a penalty of €125 or, in the case of fraud, €315 (TCA 1997, s 1075(2)). Where the person is a company, however, it will be liable to a penalty of €630 or, in the case of fraud, €1,265. The secretary of the company will be liable to a separate penalty of €125 or, in the case of fraud, €250 (TCA 1997, s 1075(4)).

The provisions of TCA 1997, s 1053(3) will apply for the purposes of TCA 1997, s 1075 as they apply for the purposes of TCA 1997, s 1053. TCA 1997, s 1053(3) provides that where any return, statement, declaration or accounts of a kind mentioned in TCA 1997 Schedule 29 column 1 was made or submitted by a person neither fraudulently nor negligently and it comes to his notice that it was incorrect, then, unless the error is remedied without unreasonable delay, the return, statement, declaration or accounts will be treated as having been negligently made or submitted by him.

15.211   Time limits

The following table summarises the principal time limits relevant to the tax position of companies. Included also are references to claims where no time limits are provided for.

Losses and other deficiencies

Reference TCA 1997		Time limit
s 83(3)	Carry forward of excess management expenses and trade charges of investment companies	None
s 396(1)	Carry forward of trading losses	None
s 396(2)	Set off of trading loss against total profits of current or immediately preceding accounting periods	2 years
s 397	Terminal loss claim	None
s 399(1)	Set off of Case IV loss	None
s 399(2)	Set off of excess Case V deficiencies over surpluses against other Case V income – of immediately preceding accounting periods of subsequent accounting periods	2 years None
s429	Claim to group relief	2 years

Capital Allowances

Reference TCA 1997		Time limit
s 284(5)	Claim to wear and tear by lessor of machinery or plant	2 years
s 307(2)	Disclaimer of initial allowance in respect of machinery or plant, industrial buildings or dredging expenditure	2 years
s 307(4)	Set off of excess capital allowances given by way of discharge or repayment of tax or in charging income under Case V against total profits of current or immediately preceding accounting periods	2 years
s 312(5)(a)	Election for transfer of assets at tax written down value in place of market value in case of "control" sale	None

Obligations on company

Reference TCA 1997		Time limit
s 239(4)	Return of annual and other payments and related tax	9 months
s 700(3)	Return of payments of interest by Industrial and Provident Society	1 May next after end of year of assessment
s 882	Particulars to be supplied by new companies etc	30 days after commencement of trade etc
s 883	Notice of liability to corporation tax	1 year after end of accounting period

| s 884 | Returns of profits | As required by notice |
| s 1084 | Return of profits – surcharge | Specified date (see **15.208**) |

15.212 Interest on repayment of tax

If a repayment or part of a repayment to which a company is entitled for a chargeable period (accounting period or, where capital gains tax is concerned, year of assessment) arises as a result of a mistaken assumption by the Revenue Commissioners in the application of any provision of the Tax Acts or the Capital Gains Tax Acts, the repayment or part repayment carries interest for each day or part of a day for the period commencing with the day after the end of the chargeable period for which the repayment is due or, if later, the date on which the tax was paid, and ending on the day the repayment is made (TCA 1997, s 865A(1)). An exception to this provision is the case in which, in accordance with TCA 1997, s 1006A(2), (2A), an overpayment is set against any liability due under the Tax Acts or is withheld until such time as an outstanding tax return has been delivered and interest on the overpayment is accordingly not due.

A repayment or part repayment of tax due otherwise than for a reason mentioned above (ie, as a result of a mistaken assumption by the Revenue Commissioners) will, again subject to TCA 1997, s 1006A(2A) (see above), carry interest for the period beginning on the day that is 93 days after the day on which the repayment claim becomes a "valid claim" (see **15.204**) and ending on the day the repayment is made (TCA 1997, s 865A(2)). Thus, in the majority of cases in which a repayment of tax is due, interest will not begin to run for 93 days after the date on which the repayment claim becomes a valid claim. (See also **15.209.13** in relation to interest on overpaid tax on determination by the Circuit Court judge.)

Interest payable in accordance with TCA 1997, s 865A is simple interest payable at 0.011% per day or part of a day (TCA 1997, s 865A(3)) but no interest will be payable if it amounts to less than €10 (TCA 1997, s 865A(4)(a)). Income tax is not deductible on payment of interest nor will such interest be taken into account in computing income, profit or gains for the purposes of the Tax Acts ((TCA 1997, s 865A(4)(b)). The rate of interest on repayments of tax is simple interest at 0.011% per day or part of a day.

Table of Statutes

Other Legislation

Table of Cases

C

H

I

M

S

T

Y

Z

Index

The South Western Regional Fisheries Board

non-commercial state-sponsored bodies, income arising to, disregarded, 3.213.11

Spain

double tax treaty, 14.103

Special European Union Programme For Peace And Reconciliation, 3.204.1

special investment business, 12.603.2

Special Purpose Investment Companies (SPICS), 12.807

special trading houses

manufacturing relief, 7.205.7

sporting bodies

exempted income, 3.204.7

SSAP 20, 3.402

staff recruitment and training

pre-commencement expenditure

capital allowances for, 5.602

specialist palliative care units, industrial building allowances, 5.401.10

specialty debt, 4.304

stallion fee exemption, 13.107.7

stallion profits or gains

taxation of, 13.107.8

Stamp Duties Consolidation Act 1999, 2.2

stamp duty

buy-back of shares, 11.313

capital duty: charge, 9.410.1

capital duty: reconstructions and amalgamations of companies, 9.410.2

charge of, 9.409.1

exemption of appraisements and valuations, 15.204.3

intellectual property, exemption for sale or transfer of, 9.409.2

reconstructions and amalgamations of companies, 9.409.3

transfers between associated companies, 9.214

standard rate per cent

meaning of, 2.601

State, Securities Issued by the, 3.208.7

statements and documents

admissibility of, 15.204.3

state-sponsored bodies

exempt income of, 3.213.11

stock lending, sale and repo transactions, 3.212, 9.102.6, 9.102.15, 14.212

stock relief

farming companies

see **farming companies**

stocks and work in progress, valuation of

see **valuation of stocks and work in progress**

stock-in-trade, see trading stock

strip market, 3.207.3

strips of securities, 3.207.3

authority for stripping of Irish gilts, 3.207.3

creation and acquisition of, 3.207.3

definitions of terms, 3.207.3

mark to market, 3.207.3

non-resident investors, 3.207.3

reassembly into a unit, 3.207.3

stud farms, 13.107.1

see also **farming companies**

bloodstock valuations, illustrations of, 13.107.2

brood mares, 13.107.2

foals, 13.107.2

mares bought in foal, 13.107.2

racing activities, 13.107.4

stallions, stallion fees etc., 13.107.6

stallion fee exemption, 13.107.7

transfers between stud farm and racing, 13.107.4

valuation of bloodstock as trading stock, 13.107.2

valuation of broodmares: agreement with Revenue Commissioners, 13.107.3

realisable value, 13.107.3

stock records, 13.107.3

yearlings, two year olds etc, 13.107.2

student accommodation

relief for lessors of, general,6.5

guidelines, 6.503

relief, 6.504